OTHER KAPLAN BOOKS FOR COLLEGE-BOUND STUDENTS

College Admissions and Financial Aid

Unofficial, Unbiased, Insider's Guide to the 360 Most Interesting Colleges
Conquer the Cost of College
Parent's Guide to College Admissions
Yale Daily News Guide to Succeeding in College

Test Preparation

ACT
SAT & PSAT
SAT Math Workbook
SAT Verbal Workbook
SAT Math Mania
SAT Verbal Velocity
SAT II: Biology
SAT II: Chemistry
SAT II: Mathematics
SAT II: Writing
TOEFL

Scholarships

2003 EDITION

by Gail Schlachter, R. David Weber,
and the Staff of Reference Service Press

Introduction by Douglas Bucher

Simon & Schuster

NEW YORK · LONDON · SINGAPORE · SYDNEY · TORONTO

Kaplan Publishing
Published by Simon & Schuster
1230 Avenue of the Americas
New York, NY 10020

For bulk sales to schools, colleges, and universities, please contact: Order Department, Simon & Schuster, 100 Front Street, Riverside, NJ 08075. Phone: (800) 223-2336. Fax: (800) 943-9831.

Project Editor: Ruth Baygell
Contributing Editor: Trent Anderson and Seppy Basili
Editorial Coordinator: Dea Alessandro
Cover Design: Cheung Tai
Page Layout: Hugh Haggerty
Production Manager: Michael Shevlin
Executive Editor: Del Franz

Special Thanks to: Martha Arango, Jan Gladish, Sara Pearl, and Joyce Smith

The material in this book is up-to-date at the time of publication. However, the sponsoring organizations may have instituted changes in their funding program after this book was published.

Manufactured in the United States of America
Published simultaneously in Canada

August 2002

10 9 8 7 6 5 4 3 2

ISBN 0-7432-3044-2

CONTENTS

Lots of books list scholarships. What makes this book different?

1. The funding opportunities described here can be used at any number of schools. Look through other scholarship books and you'll see that most of them contain large numbers of scholarships that can be used only at a particular college or university. So, even if you're lucky, only a handful of these school-specific scholarships will be for the schools you're considering. And even this handful of scholarship listings is of little value since the schools you apply to (or are considering applying to) will gladly send you information about all their scholarship programs free of charge. *But, not one of the scholarships listed in this book is limited to only one particular school.* The result: More listings in this book have the potential to be of use to you.

2. Only the biggest and the best funding programs are covered in this book. Most of the other scholarship books are bulked up with awards that may be worth only a few hundred dollars. While any free money you can get your hands on for college is good, you will have to be careful that you don't waste your time and money chasing scholarships that will hardly put a dent in your overall college cost burden. *The scholarships in this book all offer the potential to receive at least one thousand dollars per year.* So more of the scholarships in this book will really be worth the investment of your time.

3. Not one dollar of the programs listed in this book needs to be repaid. Most scholarship books list awards that are really loans. We're not against loans, especially college loans with reduced interest rates or delayed repayment. In fact, in the appendix you'll find information about state and federal college loan programs. *But of the funding opportunities covered in this book, not one dollar has to be repaid, provided stated requirements are met.* Accepting one of these need not add to the debt burden you'll face when you finish school.

In fact, we're so convinced this book contains the most helpful and most accurate scholarship information on the market that we offer satisfaction guaranteed or your money back (details on the inside front cover).

About the Authors

PART ONE

Douglas Bucher

Douglas Bucher is Director of Financial Aid Operations at New York University, the largest private university in the United States. He formerly served as President of the Eastern Association of Student Financial Aid Administrators and is a member of the New York Association of Student Financial Aid Administrators. He teaches seminars for the U.S. Department of Education and has conducted a variety of sessions on financial aid at many professional conferences. He also teaches a graduate seminar course in New York University's School of Education and acts as a consultant for public, private, and proprietary two- and four-year colleges and universities.

PART TWO

Gail Schlachter

Dr. Gail Schlachter is President of Reference Service Press, a publishing company specializing in the development of electronic and print directories of financial aid. Dr. Schlachter has taught library-related courses on the graduate school level and has presented dozens of workshops and lectures to the field. Since 1991, she has been a visiting professor at San Jose State University. Dr. Schlachter has served on the councils of the American Library Association and the California Library Association, is a past president of the American Library Association's Reference and User Services Association, and has served as editor-in-chief of *Reference and User Services Quarterly*, the official journal of ALA's Reference and User Services Association.

In recognition of her outstanding contributions to the field of reference librarianship, Dr. Schlachter has been a recipient of both the Isadore Gilbert Mudge Award and the Louis Shores–Oryx Press Award. In addition, her financial aid print resources have won numerous awards, including the *Choice* "Outstanding Reference Book Award," *Library Journal*'s "Best Reference Book of the Year" award, the National Education and Information Center Advisory Committee "Best of the Best" award, and the Knowledge Industry Publications' "Award for Library Literature."

R. David Weber

Dr. R. David Weber has served as Reference Service Press's chief editor since 1988. In that capacity, he has been involved in building, refining, and maintaining RSP's award-winning financial aid database. In addition, Dr. Weber has taught at both East Los Angeles and Harbor Colleges, where he has been named "Teacher of the Year" every year since 1991. Besides his work in the area of financial aid, Dr. Weber has written a number of critically acclaimed reference books, including *Dissertations in Urban History* and the three-volume *Energy Information Guide*.

Reference Service Press

Reference Service Press (RSP) began in 1977 with a single financial aid publication, *Directory of Financial Aids for Women*, and now specializes in the development of financial aid resources in multiple formats, including books, large-print books, disks, CD-ROMs, print-on-demand reports, and online sources. RSP is committed to collecting, organizing, and disseminating—in both print and electronic format—the most current and accurate information available on scholarships, fellowships, loans, grants, awards, internships, and other types of funding opportunities. The company has compiled one of the largest financial aid databases currently available—with up-to-date information on more than 22,000 portable programs (not restricted to any one school) that are open to high school students, high school graduates, undergraduates, graduate students, professionals, and postdoctorates. The database identifies billions of dollars in funding opportunities that will be awarded to millions of recipients each year.

RSP publishes a number of award-winning financial aid directories aimed at specific groups. After you've mined the resources described in this book, you might be interested in continuing your funding search by looking through other RSP books. You may be able to find these titles in your local public or academic library. Or contact RSP to order your own copy:

Reference Service Press
5000 Windplay Drive, Suite 4
El Dorado Hills, CA 95762
Phone: (916) 939-9620; Fax: (916) 939-9626
E-mail: findaid@aol.com
Website: www.rspfunding.com

Specialized Financial Aid Directories from Reference Service Press

College Student's Guide to Merit and Other No-Need Funding, 2002–2004
Named "best of the best" by *Choice*. The focus here is on 1,300 merit scholarships and other no-need funding programs open specifically to students currently in or returning to college. 472 pages. ISBN 1-58841-041-2. $32, plus $5 shipping.

Directory of Financial Aids for Women, 2001–2003
Published since 1977, this is the only comprehensive and current source of information on 1,600 scholarships, fellowships, loans, grants internships, and awards designed primarily or exclusively for women. *School Library Journal* calls this "the cream of the crop." 552 pages. ISBN 1-58841-000-5. $45, plus $5 shipping.

Financial Aid for African Americans, 2001–2003
Named "Editor's Choice" by *Reference Books Bulletin*, this directory describes 1,400 scholarships, fellowships, loans, grants, awards, and internships for African Americans. 508 pages. ISBN 1-58841-001-3. $37.50, plus $5 shipping.

Financial Aid for Asian Americans, 2001–2003
Use this award-winning source to find funding for Americans of Chinese, Japanese, Korean, Vietnamese, Filipino, or other Asian origin. Nearly 1,100 opportunities described. 336 pages. ISBN 1-58841-002-1. $35, plus $5 shipping.

Financial Aid for Hispanic Americans, 2001–2003

Called a "landmark resource" by *Reference Books Bulletin*, this directory describes more than 1,300 funding programs open to Americans of Mexican, Puerto Rican, Central American, or other Latin American heritage. 472 pages. ISBN 1-58841-003-X. $37.50, plus $5 shipping.

Financial Aid for Native Americans, 2001–2003

Detailed information is provided in this award-winning directory on nearly 1,500 funding opportunities open to American Indians, Native Alaskans, and Native Pacific Islanders. 546 pages. ISBN 1-58841-004-8. $37.50, plus $5 shipping.

Financial Aid for Research and Creative Activities Abroad, 2002–2004

Nearly 1,400 funding programs (scholarships, fellowships, grants, etc.) available to support research, professional, or creative activities abroad are described here. 478 pages. ISBN 1-58841-005-6. $45, plus $5 shipping.

Financial Aid for Study and Training Abroad, 2001–2003

This directory, which *Children's Bookwatch* calls "invaluable," covers more than 1,000 financial aid opportunities available to support structured or independent study abroad. 398 pages. ISBN 1-58841-031-5. $39.50, plus $5 shipping.

Financial Aid for the Disabled and Their Families, 2002–2004

Named one of the "Best Reference Books of the Year" by *Library Journal*, this directory describes in detail more than 1,000 funding opportunities for these groups. 484 pages. ISBN 1-58841-042-0. $40, plus $5 shipping.

Financial Aid for Veterans, Military Personnel, and Their Dependents, 2002–2004

According to *Reference Book Review*, this directory (with its 1,100 entries) is "the most comprehensive guide available on the subject." 334 pages. ISBN 1-58841-043-9. $40, plus $5 shipping.

High School Senior's Guide to Merit and Other No-Need Funding, 2002–2004

Described here are 1,100 merit awards and other no-need funding programs that never look at income when awarding money to high school seniors for college. 400 pages. ISBN 1-58841-044-7. $29.50, plus $5 shipping.

Money for Graduate Students in the Biological & Health Sciences, 2001–2003

If you are looking for money to support graduate study or research in the biological or health sciences, use this directory (1,100 funding programs are described). 332 pages. ISBN 1-58841-038-2. $42.50, plus $5 shipping.

Money for Graduate Students in the Humanities, 2001–2003

This directory identifies nearly 1,000 funding opportunities available to support graduate study, training, research, and creative activities in the humanities. "Highly recommended" by *Choice*. 320 pages. ISBN 1-58841-008-0. $40, plus $5 shipping.

Money for Graduate Students in the Physical & Earth Sciences, 2001–2003

More than 800 funding opportunities for graduate study or research in the physical and earth sciences are described in detail and accessed through five indexes. 262 pages. ISBN 1-58841-039-0. $35, plus $5 shipping.

Money for Graduate Students in the Social & Behavioral Sciences, 2001–2003

1,100 funding opportunities for graduate study and research in the social sciences are covered in detail and indexed by title, sponsor, subject, geographic coverage, and deadline. 332 pages. ISBN 1-58841-010-2. $42.50, plus $5 shipping.

RSP Funding for Nursing Students, 2002–2004

More than 600 scholarships, fellowships, and loans that support study or research for nurses or nursing students (both undergraduate and graduate) are described in this directory—more than twice the number of programs listed in any other nursing-related directory. 220 pages. ISBN 1-58841-046-3. $30, plus $5 shipping.

Preface

While getting a college degree may be the best investment you will ever make, paying for it is another matter. Going to college is expensive. It can cost $100,000 or more just to complete a bachelor's degree. That's more than most students can afford to pay on their own. What can they do?

Fortunately, money is available. According to Anna and Robert Leider in their book *Don't Miss Out* (published annually by Octameron Associates), there is more than $85 billion in financial aid available each year. Of this, at least $54 billion comes from federal loans and grants, $16 billion from the colleges, $6 billion from tuition tax credits, $5 billion from the states, $3 billion from employer-paid tuition plans, and $2 billion from private sources.

How can you find out about financial aid that might be available to you? For some sources of funding, it's not difficult at all. To learn about federal resources, you can either call (800) 4-FED-AID or visit the U.S. Department of Education's Website (www.ed.gov). To find out what your state is offering, turn to the appendix in this book; you'll find contact information there. You can also write to the colleges of your choice or check with your employer to learn about funding from those sources.

But information on private sources of funding is much more elusive. That's where this book can help you. Here, in one place, you can get detailed information on more than 3,000 of the biggest and best scholarships available to fund education after high school. These programs are open to high school seniors, high school graduates, currently enrolled college students, and those returning to college after a break. They can be used to support study in any area, in junior and community colleges, vocational and technical institutes, four-year colleges, and universities. No other source can match the scope, currency, and detail provided in this book. That's why we have a satisfaction guaranteed or your money back offer (see details on the inside front cover).

What's Unique about This Book?

All scholarship directories identify funding opportunities. But, there are six important features that make this book unique.

- **The directory covers only programs open to support college studies.** Most other directories mix together programs for a number of groups—high school students, college students, and even graduate students or postdoctorates. Now, you won't have to spend your time sifting through programs that aren't aimed at you.

- **Only free money is identified.** If a program requires repayment or charges interest, it's not listed. Here's your chance to find out about more than $1 billion in aid, knowing that not one dollar of that will need to be repaid, provided stated requirements are met.

- **The funding opportunities covered in this book are not all based on need or on academics.** You'll find many sources that award money based on career plans, writing ability, research skills, religious or ethnic background, military or organizational activities, athletic success, personal characteristics, and even pure luck in random drawings.

- **You can take the money awarded by these scholarships to any number of schools.** Unlike other financial aid directories that often list large numbers of scholarships available only to students enrolled at one specific school, all of the entries in this book are "portable."

- **Only the biggest and best funding programs are covered in this book.** To be listed here, a program has to offer at least $1,000 per year. Many go way beyond that, paying $20,000 or more each year, or covering the full cost of college attendance. Other scholarship books are often bulked up with awards that may be worth only a few hundred dollars. While any free money you can get your hands on for college is good, you will have to be careful that you don't waste your time and energy chasing scholarships that will hardly put a dent in your overall college cost burden.

- **The directory has been designed to make your search as easy as possible.** You can identify funding programs by discipline, specific subject, sponsoring organization, where you live, where you want to go to school, and when you want to apply. Plus, you'll find all the information you need to decide if a program is right for you: eligibility requirements, financial data, duration, special features, limitations, number awarded, and application date. You even get fax numbers, toll-free numbers, email addresses, and website locations (when available), along with complete contact information.

What's Not Covered?

While this book is intended to be the most current and comprehensive source of free money available to college students in the United States, there are some things we've specifically excluded from the directory:

- **Funding not aimed at incoming, currently enrolled, or returning college students.** If a program is open only to a different category of student (e.g., graduate school students) or if it is not specifically for college students (e.g., a photographic competition open to adults of any age), it is not covered here.

- **Individual school-based programs.** The directory identifies "portable" programs—ones that can be used at any number of schools. Financial aid administered by individual schools solely for the benefit of their own students is not covered. Write directly to the schools you are considering to get information on their offerings.

- **Money for study outside the United States.** Only funding that supports study in the United States is covered here. For information on sources of funding to go abroad, see the titles listed in the "Reference Service Press" section in this directory.

- **Very restrictive programs.** In general, programs are excluded if they are open only to a very limited geographic area (a medium-sized city or a couple of counties), are available to a very limited membership group (e.g., a local union or a tightly targeted organization), or offer very limited financial support (under $1,000 per year).

- **Programs that did not respond to our research inquiries.** Despite our best efforts (up to four letters and three telephone follow-up calls), some organizations did not supply information and, consequently, their programs are not described in this edition of the directory.

How to Use This Book

We've divided this book into four sections: introductory materials; a detailed list of free money available for college, organized by discipline; an appendix listing federal and state sources of educational benefits; and a set of indexes to help you pinpoint appropriate funding programs.

Getting Started
The first section of the directory, written by Douglas Bucher, the Director of Financial Aid Operations at New York University, offers tips on searching for scholarships, applying for aid, and avoiding scholarship search scams.

Scholarship Listings
The main section of the directory, prepared by Gail Schlachter, R. David Weber, and the staff of Reference Service Press, describes more than 3,000 scholarships, competitions, and awards that provide free money for college. The programs listed are sponsored by federal and state government agencies, professional organizations, foundations, educational associations, and military/veterans organizations. All areas of the sciences, social sciences, and humanities are covered.

To help you tailor your search, the entries in this section are grouped into four main categories:

Unrestricted by Subject Area. Described here are 1,242 funding opportunities that can be used to support study in any subject area (although the programs may be restricted in other ways).

Humanities. Described here are 469 funding programs that 1) reward outstanding artistic and creative work by students or 2) support college studies in the humanities, including architecture, art, creative writing, design, history, journalism, languages, literature, music, and religion.

Sciences. Described here are 936 sources of free money that 1) reward student speeches, essays, inventions, organizational involvement, and other activities in the sciences or 2) support college studies in a number of scientific fields, including agricultural sciences, chemistry, computer science, engineering, environmental sciences, food science, horticulture, mathematics, marine sciences, nursing, nutrition, pharmacology, and technology.

Social Sciences. Described here are 549 sources of financial that 1) reward outstanding speeches, essays, organizational involvement, and other activities in the social sciences or 2) support college studies in various social science fields, including accounting, business administration, criminology, economics, education, geography, home economics, international relations, labor relations, political science sales and marketing, sociology, social services, sports and recreation, and tourism.

Each program entry in the first section of the guide has been prepared to give you a concise but clear picture of the available funding. Information (when available) is provided on organization address and telephone numbers (including fax and toll-free numbers), email address and website location, eligibility, money awarded, duration, special features, limitations, number of awards, and application deadline. The sample entry below illustrates a typical entry.

Appendix: Federal and State Financial Aid
In this section, sources of information on federal and state educational benefits are provided. Use this listing as the first step in your search for federal and state-based financial aid. You'll find here the name, address, telephone number, email address, and website (when available) of the agencies in your state that administer educational assistance and loan funds for college students.

Indexes
To help you find the aid you need, we have included five indexes; these will let you access the listings by specific subject, residency, sponsoring organization, and tenability (where you want to study). These indexes use a word-by-word alphabetical arrangement. Note: Numbers in the index refer to *entry* numbers, not to page numbers.

Subject Index. Use this index when you want to identify funding programs by specific subject.

Residency Index. Some programs listed in this book are restricted to residents of a particular city, county, state, or region. Others are open to students wherever they live. This index helps you identify programs available only to residents in your area as well as programs that have no residency restrictions.

Tenability Index. Some programs described in this book are restricted to persons attending schools in specific cities, countries, states, or regions. This index will help you locate funding specifically for the geographic area where you attend or plan to attend school.

Sponsoring Organization Index. This index makes it easy to identify agencies that offer free money for college. Sponsoring organizations are listed alphabetically, word by word. In addition, we've used a code to help you identify which programs sponsored by these organizations fall within your general area of interest (unrestricted by subject area, humanities, sciences, or social sciences).

Calendar Index. Since most financial aid programs have specific deadline dates, some may have already closed by the time you begin to look for funding. You can use the Calendar Index to identify which programs are still open.

SAMPLE ENTRY

① **527**
② **KAPLAN/NEWSWEEK "MY TURN" ESSAY CONTEST**

③ Kaplan, Inc.
Attn: Community Outreach Director
888 Seventh Avenue
New York, NY 10106
Phone: (800) KAP-TEST

④ **Summary:** To recognize and reward high school students who write outstanding essays on topics related to their personal development and growth.

⑤ **Eligibility:** This program is open to 1) U.S. high school students planning to attend college after graduation. Applicants must write an essay of 500 to 1,000 words that shares an opinion, experience, or personal feeling. Selection is based on: 1) effectiveness, insight, creativity, and completeness in addressing the question; 2) organization and development of the ideas expressed, with clear and appropriate examples to support them; and 3) consistency in the use of language, variety in sentence structure and range of vocabulary, and use of proper grammar, spelling, and punctuation.

⑥ **Financial data:** The first-place winner receives $5,000; the second-place winner receives $2,000; and the third place winners receive $1,000.

⑦ **Duration:** The contest is held annually.

⑧ **Additional information:** This contest is co-sponsored by Kaplan, Inc. and *Newsweek* magazine.

⑨ **Number awarded:** 10 each year: 1 first-place winner, 1 second-place winner, and 8 third-place winners.

⑩ **Deadline:** March 1 of each year.

Definitions

① **Entry number:** Consecutive number assigned to the references and used to index the entry.

② **Program title:** Title of scholarship, forgivable loan, competition, or award.

③ **Sponsoring organization:** Name, address, telephone number, toll-free number, fax number, e-mail address, and Website location (when information was supplied) for organization sponsoring the program.

④ **Summary:** Identifies the major program requirements; read the rest of the entry for additional detail.

⑤ **Eligibility:** Qualifications required of applicants.

⑥ **Financial data:** Financial details of the program, including fixed sum, average amount, or range of funds offered, expenses for which funds may and may not be applied, and cash-related benefits supplied (e.g., room and board).

⑦ **Duration:** Time period for which support is provided; renewal prospects.

⑧ **Additional information:** Any benefits, features, restrictions, or limitations associated with the program.

⑨ **Number of awards:** Total number of recipients each year or other specified period.

⑩ **Deadline:** The month by which applications must be submitted.

How to Get the Most Out of This Book

To Locate Financial Aid by Discipline. If you want to get an overall picture of the funding available for any area of college study, turn to the first category, "Unrestricted by Subject Area." You'll find nearly 1,250 general programs that support study in any area (although they may be restricted in other ways). If you've decided on your area of specialization, turn next to the appropriate chapter (Humanities, Sciences, or Social Sciences) and browse through the listings there.

To Find Information on a Particular Financial Aid Program. If you know the name and disciplinary focus of a particular financial aid program, you can go directly to the appropriate category in part two, where you'll find program profiles grouped by discipline and arranged alphabetically by title.

To Browse Quickly Through the Listings. Turn to the section in part two that interests you (unrestricted by subject area, humanities, sciences, social sciences) and read the "Summary" field in each entry. In seconds, you'll know if this is an opportunity that might apply to you. If it is, be sure to read the rest of the information in the entry, to make sure you meet all of the program requirements before writing for an application form. Remember, don't apply if you don't qualify!

To Locate Financial Aid for Studies in a Particular Subject Area. Turn to the subject index first if you are interested in identifying available funding in a specific subject area. As part of your search, be sure to check the listings in the index under the heading "General Programs"; these programs support studies in any area (although they may be restricted in other ways).

To Locate Financial Aid Based on Where You Live. Use the Residency Index to identify funding that has been set aside to support applicants from your area. To help you identify the funding that's right for you, the index has been subdivided by broad subject area. When using this index, always check the listings under the term "United States," since the programs indexed there have no geographic restrictions and can be used in any area.

To Locate Financial Aid Based on Where You Want to Study. To identify funding that's available to support study in a particular geographic location, use the Tenability Index. You'll be able to target your search, because the index has been subdivided by broad subject area. When using this index, be sure to check the listings under the term "United States," since the programs indexed there have no geographic restrictions and can be used in any area.

To Locate Financial Aid Programs Sponsored by a Particular Organization. The Sponsoring Organization Index makes it easy to determine which groups are providing free money for college and to identify specific financial aid programs offered by a particular sponsor. Each entry number in the index is coded to indicate broad subject coverage, to help you target appropriate entries.

Let Us Hear from You

We'd like to hear from you. Send your comments, suggestions, questions, problems, or success stories to: Gail Schlachter, Kaplan Scholarships 2003 Editor, 5000 Windplay Drive, Suite 4, El Dorado Hills, CA 95762, or email her at findaid@aol.com.

PART ONE

GETTING STARTED

by Douglas Bucher

Searching for Scholarships

If you are reading this book, it's a good bet that you are looking for money to help you achieve your higher-education goals. As you will see, the key to success in this area is motivated, energetic research—a process that you have already started by reading these very words. There are numerous sources of aid available; many of these are listed in this volume. In addition, this book includes other strategies for finding resources, locally and globally, using both technology, such as computers and the Internet, and old-fashioned methods, such as talking to people who may be able to help.

It is important, however, to understand that the resources available are rather scarce. You may have heard about billions and trillions of dollars in unclaimed aid each year, but this is simply not true; resources are available in limited numbers to the most talented applicants.

Does this mean that you shouldn't try? Are the chances so remote that you would be wasting your time enduring the research and application process? Quite the contrary. What it means is that you must commit yourself to being thorough and tenacious. Only by applying to as many sources as possible, as early as possible, and in an appropriate, intelligent manner, will you be able to increase your chances of receiving assistance.

This does not mean that you should pay another person or company to do this research for you. All of the information we will discuss is available to you in books or other easily obtainable sources that will cost you little or nothing to use. Any company that says you have to pay them to research the same data you could research on your own is not worthy of your dollars. Ignore all of the guarantees and promises. In most cases, the companies will provide no more information than you could have gleaned yourself.

Scholarship Scams

For years, in fact, students' desire to finance their education has been fodder for those who would take advantage of people with trusting natures. Financial aid personnel at colleges and universities have been aware of such unethical approaches for some time now, and, recently, the Federal Trade Commission (FTC) issued a warning about these "scholarship scams." Among the telltale signs you should look for—and then stay far away from—are:

"We guarantee you'll get a scholarship or your money back." In reality, almost every financial aid applicant is eligible for something. A guarantee like this is, therefore, worth nothing.

"You can't get this information anywhere else." Nonsense. We live in an information-rich society. Any legitimate source of financial aid will make information widely available through a number of means and media. Don't pay a premium for what is free or readily available in an inexpensive format—like this one!

"Credit card or bank account number required to hold scholarship." Don't even think about it. Legitimate scholarship providers do not require this information as a condition for receiving funds.

"We'll do all the work." Okay, this one is tempting. We are all very busy people with a million things to do who feel that we can't possibly find the time to do this kind of research. But there is only one person who is going to benefit from the kind of work that this entails, and that is you. A pitch like this appeals to the lazy instincts in all of us, but there is no one you can expect to be more motivated to do the research than yourself.

"The scholarship will cost you some money." This one hardly deserves comment. There is a strong preconception in this country that, as a general rule, you need to spend money to make money. While this may be true on Wall Street, it doesn't apply here. The investment you are making is in your education, and the best resource you can invest is your time.

"You are a finalist" or *"have been selected"* in a contest you never entered. The absurdity of this is clear once you think about it for a moment. It is very flattering to think that some organization pored through the records of every person in the country to find that you are the most qualified to receive its generous award—and you didn't even apply! Remember, if it seems too good to be true, it is.

In other words, *caveat emptor!*

Setting a Timetable for Your Search

If there is one piece of advice that can be a key to a successful search for scholarship funding, it is to start early. In fact, keep in mind that each step described in this book requires a good deal of time. Furthermore, many small sources of funding have deadlines some nine to twelve months before the beginning of the term for which you will be applying.

But applying is only one of the final steps in the process we are talking about. In order to find opportunities, you must be willing to spend time and effort doing research on various sources of aid. There are many sources of information, and while some of them may seem redundant, the greater the effort you make to scour all of the information available, the more likely it is that you will find sources of funding for which you are eligible.

Keeping in mind that some sources have early deadlines, when should you start? The answer depends on your personal pace. If you have the time and energy to research a subject extensively for a short period of time, you could start some 14 months before the beginning of school. If, on the other hand, you wish to make this a more leisurely process, give yourself a good 18 months.

In any case, the bottom line is that you can never begin too early. When you are done reading this, sit down with a calendar and make a plan. When can you start? How much time can you devote each week?

Here is a summary timetable to help you plan:

- *24–18 months before money is needed:* Perform the extensive searches discussed in this chapter.

- *18–12 months before money is needed:* Write for applications; follow up if necessary.

- *12–9 months before money is needed:* Mail all applications with required documentation.

- *9–6 months before money is needed:* Follow up with any organization from which you have not heard a decision (if deadline has passed).

- *Summer before school:* Notify the financial aid office of any scholarships you have been awarded. Be sure to ask what effect this will have on earlier awards and your options.

- *Late summer right before school:* Write thank-you notes to organizations.

- *Fall:* Begin the process again for renewing scholarships and finding new sources of aid.

So, now that you have a plan, get started!

Types of Scholarships

The types of scholarships you may receive for your education can be broken down into three general categories: individual scholarships, state scholarships, and loans.

Individual Scholarships

While going through your college search, be sure to ask admissions officers about scholarships. Each school has different rules for scholarship consideration. Be sure to find out about all scholarships available, what must be done to be considered, and—very important—the deadline by which to apply. More and more schools are offering scholarships for reasons other than athletic or academic achievement. Some scholarships are reserved for very specific types of students. See if any of these exist at the colleges to which you are applying. Much of this information may be on their home page, so you can research on your own.

Become familiar with your college's financial aid office, which might be able to provide additional information on scholarship sources. At some schools, the financial aid officers are more familiar with scholarship sources than the admissions officers.

Another great source of scholarship information might be the academic departments with which you are affiliated. Many of the faculty members know about scholarships specifically for your major. Some departments have their own scholarships that other offices on campus may not even know about. Professors also have many contacts outside of the college that might be sources of scholarship information.

Scholarships might be available in your own backyard. Don't assume that you must do a national search to find them. Asking the right questions and developing the right contacts are the best ways to make your search an effective one.

State Scholarship Resources

Some state education authorities and other state agencies offer assistance above and beyond the usual tuition-assistance programs. Some states offer aid for particular fields of study to residents of the state who remain in-state to complete their studies. You should contact your state's higher-education agency to investigate opportunities. See the appendix at the back of this book for the name and address of the agency to contact in your state.

Loans and "Loanships"

There is another form of aid that predominates in certain fields, particularly those with a shortage of qualified professionals. Often called *loanships,* these arrangements provide funding for school and a guaranteed job after graduation.

Sometimes offered by private employers, sometimes by government agencies, loanships work in the following way. An organization provides funding for a student's academic expenses in the form of a loan. In return, the student agrees to work for the organization (under terms usually outlined in a contract) for a given period of time. If the student keeps up his or her part of the bargain, the loan will be forgiven or reduced. If the student chooses not to work for the organization, he or she is given a repayment schedule and must pay back the entire balance with interest. Depending on the field, the jobs provided are usually competitively paid, though, more often than not, located in areas that are underserved or understaffed.

The benefits of this kind of arrangement are clear—your education is paid for and you have a job waiting for you after graduation. You need to consider, however, whether or not you really want to work under the conditions outlined or in the particular field described.

Some organizations offer regular loans as well as scholarships. Some philanthropic agencies even offer interest-free loans to students. These can be very good opportunities to save money on interest you would otherwise pay on federal or private loans. Again, consider carefully the terms of any loan agreement you sign.

Getting on with the Search

There are a number of sources of aid to consider, and several strategies for finding them. Some sources may be obscure, while others may be quite obvious to you. Who might have money to give? Unions, professional organizations, high schools, clubs, lodges, foundations, and local and state governments might have resources to share with you. At the very least, they are worth exploring.

A parent can easily check with his or her union or professional organization regarding available opportunities. A teacher, guidance counselor, or professor might know of opportunities with a variety of organizations. The key to finding aid in this way is networking.

People you know are wonderful sources of information. If you are a bright, motivated person and let people know what you want out of life, many simply will inform you whenever a possible opportunity presents itself. The key, of course, is to not be shy. Talk to people, ask advice, and let them know that you are serious about what you want to accomplish. If you approach this correctly, you may be surprised at the results you can achieve—as well as the wonderful friendships you will develop.

Many high school guidance offices have a list of scholarships that have been secured by former students. These scholarships are often provided by local agencies that lack the resources to publicize them in other ways. Contacting guidance offices at local high schools is an effective way to canvass the entire community. While the local scholarships might be small, they add up to larger sums of money. I like to tell the story of a student I met while working at Michigan State University. She applied for many scholarships in her small town. Most averaged about $200, but she won ten of them, which amounted to enough to pay half her tuition. While it is great to win the big dollars, don't forget about the smaller ones.

You might even consider contacting various civic, fraternal, religious, and business organizations in your community. Many of these organizations have scholarships that are not well publicized. These awards are also usually small, but they add up quickly. These organizations enjoy supporting the future of their community through education, and make themselves visible in the yellow pages or on lists at local Chambers of Commerce. Even if you don't know anyone at a given organization, you should still contact it about the possibility of a scholarship.

I have met students in my career who actually talked some of these organizations into creating scholarships. A few hundred dollars may not be much to an organization, but it can really help an individual recipient. Soliciting these organizations may make you that lucky recipient. They may like your tenacity and award you a scholarship for this. Don't be pushy, but do be aggressive.

Employers represent another major local source of scholarships. You may be working part time or full time for a company that offers scholarships to its employees. If it is a national chain, your boss may not even know if a scholarship exists. Ask him or her to check with the central office. If you are planning to attend school locally and keep your job, you might want to check out tuition remission scholarships from your employer.

Many parents or relatives have employers that offer scholarships to dependents. Have your parents check with their benefits/personnel office to see if any programs exist. Don't assume you have to be a high school student or live at home to qualify; you'll find out if such restrictions exist when you ask. Many of these scholarships can be awarded to dependents other than just sons or daughters. Ask all your family members to check out the possibilities.

Graduate Funding

Of course, as in any kind of research, it is important to narrow your focus. One important distinction to keep in mind is the difference between graduate and undergraduate studies. A graduate student is one who is pursuing an advanced degree beyond the bachelor's. Graduate degrees include master's and doctorates of various types. When an individual has not yet received a bachelor's degree, he or she is referred to as an undergraduate student.

While some aid resources are specifically geared towards undergraduate students, others are earmarked solely for graduate students involved in advanced study of a given field. Knowing this will help you avoid wasting your time on resources for which you are not eligible. Concentrate only on scholarships available to you.

Kaplan, Reference Service Press, and the staff of the *Yale Daily News* have put together a comprehensive guide on fellowships and grants available for graduate school. The book, called the *Yale Daily News Guide to Fellowships and Grants*, identifies the biggest and best funding programs under which free money is available for graduate work. The book is available in bookstores, or you can order directly from Kaplan; call 1-800-KAP-ITEM, or go online to kaptest.com.

Books

There are many places to search for scholarships. This book contains extensive lists of scholarships, but no book can be totally inclusive. Therefore, as with any research project, you should not depend on only one source. Multiple sources will yield the most extensive data and thus the most scholarship dollars.

There is usually a scholarship section in the reference room of any public library. Many of these books focus exclusively on particular types of scholarships for majors/grade levels, etc., saving you time you would otherwise spend reading fruitlessly. Of course, there is always the chance that human error may enter into the picture, and you may overlook a valuable source. Having family members look through the same books you're reading will allow you to compare lists and eliminate duplicates. Many people also do group searches with friends. The possibility of your friends' applying for the same scholarships should not deter you, since most scholarships offer more than one award, and having more eyes search the same books will reduce the chance of overlooking resources.

Electronic Resources

Students are increasingly turning to the Internet for scholarship searches, many of which allow you to access data free of charge. The great advantage of using the Internet is that it is less labor-intensive than using books; the computer can match details about yourself with criteria in the database faster than you can, saving valuable time. Another advantage is that most of these sites are up-to-date and have the most current information. Criteria for scholarships change, and using the Internet will allow you to search for the most current criteria. Every day new scholarships are created and these are added immediately to these databases. In addition, many schools list their own scholarships in these services, so you may discover special scholarships at schools you may attend. In some cases, you can apply online for scholarships.

There's a good deal of overlap among these databases, but you'll find exclusive listings in each one. Try, then, to search a number of databases; eliminate duplicates by checking the application information on the listings. These

databases are updated periodically but not simultaneously, so look for a record of when each scholarship was last updated. If you get duplicates, use the application information from the most recently updated scholarship listing.

One reason to avoid using only one database is that the search criteria may be coded differently. Picking as many selection criteria as reasonably possible will allow you to get the best match. Even if some of the criteria are borderline, select them anyway so that you can at least read about the scholarships available. Unlike books, with most Internet databases you see only the scholarships that are matched to your input. You never know how many scholarships you might have missed in a given search because of a mismatch between the way you answered the questions and the way the scholarships were coded in the database.

It's important to have a good basic knowledge about financial aid before searching for scholarships. The Kaplan Website at kaptest.com is a good place to begin your Internet review. There you'll find some excellent information on financial aid. Use school, federal, and state sources of aid along with private scholarships to maximize your financial options.

An excellent scholarship database can be found on the Website of the National Association of Student Financial Aid Administrators (NASFAA): www.nasfaa.org. This organization is the professional association for financial aid administrators. The site also has some other excellent information about financial aid for all levels of education. More importantly, it has links to extensive resources for financial aid.

A site that is considered one of the best is found at www.finaid.org. Called FinAid! The SmartStudent Guide to Financial Aid, this site has information and links on almost every aspect of the aid process. There are two sections of particular interest: sources of aid that provide very specific information on scholarships, fellowships, and grants; and information on study abroad and graduate fellowships.

Many colleges now have Websites that may have important information about aid. You may be able to get information about scholarships offered through the college, and how to apply. Many of these sites also have links to other financial aid information or scholarship search databases. Check the sites of all colleges you are considering.

Some other sites that may be of interest in your research are:

• U.S. Department of Education; www.ed.gov/funding.html
• U.S. Department of Education: Project EASI (Easy Access for Students and Institutions); easi.ed.gov
• FastWeb—Scholarship Search; www.fastweb.com
• Scholarship Resource Network Express; www.srnexpress.com
• Scholarships.com; www.scholarships.com
• Reference Service Funding; www.rpsfunding.com
• Sallie Mae's WiredScholar; www.wiredscholar.com

Many high schools, colleges, and libraries have purchased scholarship databases with which you can broaden your search. They may not be as up-to-date as the Internet sources, but they should not be overlooked. It can't be stressed enough that you shouldn't pay to use any of these databases. You may be contacted by companies that will search databases; be careful if you decide to deal with them. Often, all they have done is bought the same software as these schools or libraries and all you will do is pay them to input your data. Even if you don't have your own computer, you can usually get access to one at your school or public library.

The power of the Internet to help in your search cannot be ignored. Don't expect it to be your only source, though. Use it as just another tool to augment your search.

How to Apply

As previously mentioned, early planning is important to a successful scholarship search. Once you have your list of addresses of possible donors, you must contact them. Be sure to check the application deadlines for the scholarships you have discovered. Eliminate any for which the deadline has passed, or will soon pass (usually within six to eight weeks). This way you will not waste the donor's or your time. Scholarships that you eliminate now could be resources for the following years. Remember, the college experience lasts more than one year; your scholarship research should extend for the number of years you need to complete your degree.

Writing the First Letter

Your first letter to a scholarship provider should be a very simple letter of introduction. Some providers may have you do initial processing online through a scholarship database. If you must write a letter, it probably will not be read by the actual committee that will choose the scholarship recipient, so there is no need to go into great detail about yourself or why you are applying. Keep it simple so the request moves quickly. Use a regular business letter format.

Today's Date

AAA Foundation
999 7th Avenue
New York, NY 10000

Attn.: Talent Scholarship Office

Dear AAA Foundation,

I am a high school student at ABC High School and am applying to attend XYZ College for fall 2003.

I would like to receive application forms for the Talent Scholarship that I read about in Kaplan's *Scholarships 2003*.

Also, I would like to receive any other scholarship or fellowship program information that is available through your organization. Enclosed is a self-addressed, stamped envelope for your convenience. I have also provided a phone number and e-mail address if you would like to contact me.

Thank you in advance for your assistance and information.

Sincerely,

Suzy Student
123 High Street
Philadelphia, PA 19100
(555) 444-4444
suzys@xxx.com

Sample Letter of Introduction

Getting Started

If your search identified specific offices or people to contact, be sure to address the letter to them. If you have a phone number, call to make sure the letter is going directly to the right office. Some organizations are very large, and your letter may get lost or routed to the wrong office. This can delay or prevent the processing of your application. It's always helpful to get a specific name to which an introduction letter can be addressed; be sure to get this person's correct title (i.e., Dr., Ms., etc.). As with a job interview, a good first impression is important and can move your request along more quickly. If there is no phone number or specific office, you should send your letter to the attention of the scholarship's name. Someone in the organization will know which office should receive your request.

Be sure to date your letter so you remember when it was sent. Include your return address so that the organization can easily send you the application. Keep your letter brief; its purpose is simply to request an application. It will not be used to make any recipient decisions; that is the purpose of the application.

The text should mention the specific scholarships for which you are applying. Some agencies administer more than one scholarship, so you must help ensure that they send you the correct application. If an organization administers more than one scholarship and you are applying for more than one of them, you should use a separate letter for each scholarship. Mail these letters in separate envelopes.

The letter should briefly describe how you will use the scholarship money (i.e., to attend a certain college, to conduct research, etc.) and also mention how you found out about the scholarship. Many agencies like to know how their information is disseminated. They want to make sure it is going to the correct "market" and to a diverse population. They will appreciate this data as they plan future cycles. You should also tell them when you intend to use the money so that they send you information for the right year, and ask them to send any other scholarship applications that they administer that may be appropriate for you. Include a phone number and/or an e-mail address in case the organization wants to contact you.

There is no need to send the letter by certified mail, but be sure to include a self-addressed, stamped envelope with the letter. Many of these organizations are nonprofit and will appreciate the help to reduce postage costs. A self-addressed envelope will also get you an earlier response, since the organization won't have to type an envelope. Remember, time is critical!

The Follow-Up Letter

Once the initial letters have been mailed, you must carefully keep track of responses. Be sure to note the application deadline (if known) of each scholarship for your records. Obviously, those due the soonest should be watched very carefully.

If you still have not received anything after six to eight weeks, it is appropriate to send a second letter. You should send your original letter (with a new date) again as if it had never been sent to the organization. It is not wise to send a different letter that says something about the organization's not getting or answering your first request. That could be perceived as being too pushy. You don't want to turn off any possible donors.

If the organization did receive your letter, you might receive a duplicate application. By using this timetable, though, you will receive the application in time to meet the deadline, even if the original is lost. Keep in mind that many of these organizations are very large and receive many requests, and that papers have a tendency to get lost.

If you send a second letter and still receive no response, you might not want to send another letter. Even if the organization's listing contains the most up-to-date information, there's a chance the organization may no longer be offering scholarships. You might want to call to see if it has your application and will mail it soon, or if it is no longer offering the scholarship. If you don't have a contact number, use directory assistance.

When you do call, remember to be very polite. You might want to begin your conversation by asking general questions about the scholarship. This way you can discreetly find out if it is still being offered. If it isn't being offered, ask if the organization has any new scholarship programs for which you qualify. If so, have them send you an application. If the scholarship is still being offered, tell them you have sent a request and want to make sure they have received it (remember, don't be too aggressive). You may find that it is not easy to confirm that they have the request. If this is the case, ask if you can fax a copy of the letter. Some agencies will be able to tell you if they have the letter, in which case you should ask when you can expect to receive the application. Be sure to confirm the deadline for submission.

Don't get frustrated if you are not able to secure applications from all agencies; some will drop out for various reasons along the way. You want to contact as many agencies as possible at the beginning of your search to make up for this attrition.

Be sure to keep good records on the progress of each individual search. Record notes and conversations on the file copy of the letter so you can easily check the status of the search. Organizations that drop out along the way should be considered when you begin your search again the following year.

The Application

Once you have secured the applications, it's time to begin the process of completing them. You should approach this step as if you are applying for a job. Initial impressions on paper are very important, so you want your application to stand out from all the others.

Neatness is very important. You should type your application and make several photocopies so you can go through some drafts before the final edition. Use all personal resources to review your various drafts. The application should be your own, but seeking input from others can improve it.

Be sure to read the entire application and any accompanying instructions before completing it, because failing to answer as instructed might eliminate you from consideration. For most scholarships, there are many more applicants than recipients. It is easy to eliminate the applicants who did not provide all requested information. Don't lose out because of a mistake that could have been avoided with proper planning.

If you can, use a word processing program to type your answers. This will allow you to save a backup copy of each application and enable you to change answers easily after reviewing them. You can also use these backups for future applications or to reapply for scholarships that require you to submit an application each year. Remember also that if you don't get a scholarship one year, you can still use the backups to apply in subsequent years. You will also find that many applications ask the same questions; a word processing program will enable you to copy and paste various answers once they have gone through several drafts.

If you can't word process the application, use photocopies to mark up typed or handwritten drafts. Type the final draft very carefully, since correction fluid may make your application look sloppy compared to others. A correcting typewriter can be helpful. Check around; you may find such a typewriter at school, at a library, or at a friend's or parent's office.

Many applications may require supplemental information from other sources. If such information is needed, be sure to plan your time to secure what is requested. Some items, such as academic transcripts and letters of reference, may take some time to obtain. Don't wait until the last minute; it may be too late to send in a complete application. The importance of planning cannot be overemphasized.

If letters of recommendations are needed, seek people who will provide the most positive influence on your application. You might need recommendations for many of the applications. If this is the case, it is best to have these recommendations tailored to the specific application, because general recommendations do not make as much of an impact. Find out if the recommendations are to be sealed and included with the application or to be sent in separately by the recommendation writers. If the recommendations must be separate, tell the writers not to send them until the day you expect your application to reach the organization, as it is easier for the scholarship provider to match up documents if the application arrives first. If any of the documents is misplaced, you could be eliminated from consideration.

If the instructions say nothing about enclosing other documents, you might consider including a cover letter with your application. This letter should be short and precise, highlighting the reasons why you would make an excellent recipient of the scholarship. A letter with bullet points might be most effective. You might also want to include a statement of your academic and career objectives and how the donor's scholarship may influence these. A cover letter might help differentiate your application from the others, but don't overdo it. A quick summary is all that is needed.

In mailing your application, there are different techniques that can be used to ensure that it is received. A simple approach is to send the application via certified mail, so that you can be sure the envelope gets to the organization. Another approach is to send a response form for the organization with a self-addressed, stamped envelope. This could be a check-off letter to acknowledge that all necessary documents have been received. This approach may be particularly helpful if documents are being sent under separate cover. If you send the application via first-class mail, you might want to call the scholarship office (if you have the phone number) a few weeks later to make sure it was received.

There is little you can do after mailing the application except wait for a decision. Remember that the odds of getting scholarships from all the organizations to which you apply are small. If you keep good records, you can reapply for the same scholarship in subsequent years. Persistence pays off.

When You Get Your Scholarship(s)

Congratulations! You've done the hard work, and are now receiving aid from one or a number of organizations. What should you do next?

Thank-You Letters

If you are awarded a scholarship by an organization, foundation, or individual, an important final step is the thank-you letter. After all, many of these organizations award scholarships for purely philanthropic reasons, and the only immediate reward they can expect is sincere thanks. Thank-you letters are an effective method to communicate gratitude, lay groundwork for future renewal, and encourage the continuation of these programs for future recipients.

The letter itself need not be a terribly complicated affair. Short, simple, sincere, and to the point will do just fine (see the sample letter on the next page). You do not need to, nor should you, copy this version verbatim. Your thank-you letter should, like your initial letters and application, let your own personality shine through. If you have nice penmanship, a handwritten version may help achieve the desired personal effect. Remember, you are receiving an award because you deserve it and because someone is willing to grant it. Don't be afraid to let your happiness show!

Today's Date

AAA Foundation
999 7th Avenue
New York, NY 10000

To Whom It May Concern (or, if you have a contact
name, by all means use it!),

I am taking this occasion to express my deep gratitude for
the opportunity that your generous (grant, loan, etc.) has
given me. I know that it will allow me to achieve my
goals, and I hope that the results will justify your faith in
me.

Thank you for your time and attention.

Sincerely,

Your name

Sample Thank-You Letter

Notifying the School

You must tell your school about any outside scholarships you receive. Most financial aid packages need to be adjusted in order to "make room" for outside sources of aid. This is because most packages contain federal aid, and therefore have to follow federal guidelines as to how much aid a student who receives other forms of aid can receive. The internal policies of various schools might also require changes to your package. Most financial aid offices will reduce the least desirable forms of aid first (loans with higher interest rates, work-study). Your school will find out about the scholarship money anyway; it's better for you to know from the start how it affects your aid package, rather than encounter a potentially unpleasant surprise during your school year.

Notifying your school of your scholarships is important for another reason. If your school guarantees its own scholarship over your academic period and the outside award does not, or is explicitly one-time-only, it may make more financial sense to turn down the outside offer in order to keep the money your school is offering. While it is frustrating to make such a decision after winning an award, you must do what logically is best for you and your finances.

Depending on the kind of outside aid you are receiving, you might also have to make arrangements with the business, or bursar's, office of your college. Depending on the documentation you have, your school might extend credit to you based upon a certain expectation of funds.

Finally, remember that the aid you are receiving may be contingent on certain aspects of your enrollment; you may have to register for a certain number of credits or a certain major, for example. Keep any requirements for the award in mind as you enroll in school.

Renewing Scholarships for Subsequent Years

Renewal procedures vary depending on the kind of award you receive. Some groups offer one-time-only forms of aid, while others automatically renew previous recipients as long as they are enrolled in an eligible program. More commonly, scholarship programs require new applications each year from all interested parties. Remember that you've done it before; use your knowledge of the process to your advantage. Start early in gathering applications, recommendations, and other supporting materials to reapply for your hard-won award. At this time, you should also consider using the research you have already done to reapply for aid for which you may not have been eligible the previous year. There is no reason to limit your options and waste your hard work from the year before.

Once you are in school, there are usually many announcements of large-scale scholarship competitions. Most schools have specific offices that coordinate these prestigious awards. Sometimes this coordination is done at the financial aid office, but not always. Begin at the aid office; if they don't coordinate or know about these awards, check with the academic dean. Academic deans administer applications for the many awards that are associated with strong academic performance.

Summary

Hopefully, this discussion of scholarship searching has been and will be helpful to you. If you remember nothing else from this chapter, be sure to recall the following key points:

Start Early

Give yourself plenty of time to find what you are looking for and apply for it. Missed deadlines are nobody's fault but your own, and even the most benevolent organization will usually not make exceptions to its deadline rules.

Use All Resources and Strategies Available to You

Don't hobble your search by ignoring possibilities you don't know much about. Investigate everything, because you never know when an unlikely source of funding may decide to grant you a scholarship. Look everywhere you can, using every tool available to you. Be sure to use the power of the World Wide Web. Anything else would be cheating yourself.

Know What You Are Looking For

On the other hand, when it becomes clear that a particular source is not appropriate for you, move on. If you are going to be an undergraduate student and you find a listing of graduate aid, it is probably pointless to follow that path any farther.

Follow All Steps and Instructions

You would be surprised at how many people ignore this simple advice. Remember, you are asking for assistance with your education. The least you can do is follow the instructions given to you precisely. One of the qualities these organizations might be looking for is an ability to read and understand instructions and deadlines.

Be Confident and Self-Assured but Polite and Respectful

Actually, this is good advice for life in general, and is even more valuable in this context. You need to have a good self-image, a high level of confidence in your abilities, and pride in your past achievements. But remember, nobody owes you anything, and if you treat people with anything less than polite respect, you almost are automatically proving yourself to be unworthy of their assistance. Just show folks the same respect and courtesy that you expect to be shown yourself.

Remember to Thank Those Who Have Helped

Remember, the most that many of these organizations and individuals receive in return for their generosity is the occasional thank you (and maybe a tax deduction!). An expression of gratitude will confirm that they have made the right choice, and will lay the groundwork for possible renewals.

Don't Pay Anyone to Do This Work for You

No need to dwell on this any further. You have been warned, but if you want to learn more about this subject, the FTC in 1996 inaugurated "Project $cholar$cam," an educational campaign to alert students and parents about fraudulent scholarship companies. These warnings can be found on its Website (www.ftc.gov/bcp/conline/ edcams/scholarship).

With that, good luck in your search for financial aid and, more importantly, best wishes on all of your academic endeavors.

A Special Note for International Students

In our quickly shrinking world, cross-border education has become an ever more important feature of American colleges. Large and small schools alike are sending students abroad in increasing numbers and have opened at least part of their U.S. enrollment to students from around the world.

If you are a non-U.S. student who is considering coming here to study, you probably already know that while American colleges and universities are highly regarded around the world, the American custom of actually paying for an education truly is a foreign notion. Many countries provide free or heavily subsidized higher education for their citizens. Study in the United States, in contrast, requires careful financial planning—especially for international students, who are cut off from most need-based U.S. government aid programs.

While some students who come here receive funding from their college or university—or from the U.S. government—and others are supported by their home government, the vast majority are here without support other than their savings and family back home. The rules governing those residing in the United States on a student visa largely prohibit or limit the ability to work. The result is that for all but the wealthiest families, study in the United States requires a great deal of sacrifice, and for many is not even in the realm of possibility. To exacerbate matters, recent economic developments and currency movements have made the decision to come to or stay in the United States even more difficult for great numbers of individuals, particularly from parts of Asia.

Fortunately, many of the resources discussed in this book are not necessarily limited to U.S. students. Most of the advice within these pages applies to the international student just as much as to the domestic. In fact, the one piece of advice that this book hopes to drive home more than any other—start early!—applies to international students even more. Despite the Internet revolution (a technology which you should certainly take advantage of), much business continues to be transacted through the mail. As you may know, international post brings a whole new meaning to the term "snail mail."

Of course, a key part of your research should be to look for financial assistance at the school you plan to attend. The admissions and financial aid offices may have information on both institutional and external sources of assistance. Many schools also have offices that specialize in assisting international students in all facets of the enrollment process, including finding or facilitating sources of funding. Check your college's Website for a guide to services it offers.

There are other sources of information particularly designed for international students, as well:

In addition to administering the Fulbright program, the Institute of International Education (IIE) is a particularly rich source of information on all aspects of international education in the United States.

Institute of International Education
809 United Nations Plaza
New York, NY 10017-3580 USA
Phone: (212) 883-8200
Fax: (212) 984-5452
Website: www.iie.org

Another source of information for international students is NAFSA: Association of International Educators. This is the professional association of those who administer the college international student offices mentioned above.

NAFSA: Association of International Educators
1307 New York Avenue, NW
Eighth Floor
Washington, DC 20005-4701 USA
Phone: (202) 737-3699
Fax: (202) 737-3657
Website: www.nafsa.org

You may also visit the Financial Aid Information Page (FinAid) at www.edupass.org for more general information about financing a U.S. education.

Kaplan's Access America program can help prospective international students navigate through all facets of study in the United States. For more information, see the Access America page near the end of this book.

Kaplan International Programs
700 South Flower, Suite 2900
Los Angeles, CA 90017 USA
Phone (if calling from within the United States): 800-818-9128
Phone (if calling from outside the United States): 213-452-5800
Fax: 213-892-1364
Website: www.kaplaninternational.com
Email: world@kaplan.com

While financial resources for international students are by no means plentiful, opportunities do exist. As international education becomes an ever more important feature of American higher education, you can be sure that more sources of funding will become available. Some schools have begun to work with banks to develop financing tools for this key population. More developments are sure to follow.

PART TWO

SCHOLARSHIP LISTINGS

by Gail Schlachter
R. David Weber
and the staff
of Reference Service Press

Unrestricted by Subject Area

Described here are 1,242 sources of free money that can be used to support study in any subject area (although the programs may be restricted in other ways). These programs are available to high school seniors, high school graduates, currently enrolled college students, and/or returning students to fund studies on the undergraduate level in the United States. If you already know in which area you'd like to specialize in college, you should also check the listings in one of the next three chapters: Humanities, Sciences, and/or Social Sciences. Finally, be sure to use the Subject Index to locate available funding in a specific subject area.

Scholarship Listings

1
A. PATRICK CHARNON SCHOLARSHIP

Center for Education Solutions
252 15th Avenue
P.O. Box 210362
San Francisco, CA 94121-0632
Phone: (415) 668-2957
Web Site: www.cesresources.org/charnon.html
Summary: To provide financial assistance to undergraduate students who demonstrate a commitment to strengthening communities.
Eligibility: Applicants must be admitted or enrolled in a full-time undergraduate program of study at an accredited 4-year college or university. They must demonstrate "exceptional dedication and commitment to their communities." Along with their application, they must submit a 500- to 1,000-word essay explaining what they would like to do during their undergraduate program or what they would like to accomplish following completion of their college studies. The selection committee looks for candidates who value tolerance, compassion, and respect for all people in their communities and who have demonstrated their commitments to those values by their actions.
Financial data: The stipend is $1,500 per year.
Duration: 1 year; may be renewed up to 3 additional years.
Additional information: This program was established in 1995. Requests for applications must be accompanied by a self-addressed, stamped envelope.
Number awarded: 1 each year.
Deadline: April of each year.

2
ABBIE SARGENT MEMORIAL SCHOLARSHIP PROGRAM

Abbie Sargent Memorial Scholarship
295 Sheep Davis Road
Concord, NH 03301
Phone: (603) 224-1934   Fax: (603) 228-8432
Summary: To provide financial assistance to college students who graduated from a private or public high school in New Hampshire.
Eligibility: This program is open to residents of New Hampshire who have graduated from an approved public or private high school, have good grades, are able to demonstrate financial need, are dependable, and are able to show responsible behavior. Applicants must be enrolled (full or part time) at an institution of higher learning. Preference is given to students involved in agriculturally-related studies.
Financial data: A stipend is awarded (exact amount not specified).
Duration: 1 year.
Number awarded: 1 or more each year.
Deadline: March of each year.

3
ABE AND ESTHER HAGIWARA STUDENT AID AWARD

Japanese American Citizens League
Attn: National Scholarship Awards
1765 Sutter Street
San Francisco, CA 94115
Phone: (415) 921-5225   Fax: (415) 931-4671
E-mail: jacl@jacl.org
Web Site: www.jacl.org
Summary: To provide financial assistance to student members of the Japanese American Citizens League (JACL) who can demonstrate severe financial need.
Eligibility: This program is open to JACL members who are enrolled or planning to enroll in a college, university, trade school, or business college. Applicants must be undergraduate or graduate students who are able to demonstrate that, without this aid, they will have to delay or terminate their education. Selection is based on financial need, academic record, and extracurricular school or community activities.
Financial data: The stipend depends on the availability of funds but usually ranges from $1,000 to $5,000.
Duration: 1 year.
Additional information: Requests for applications must be accompanied by a self-addressed stamped envelope.
Number awarded: At least 1 each year.
Deadline: March of each year.

4
ADA MUCKLESTONE MEMORIAL SCHOLARSHIPS

American Legion Auxiliary
Attn: Department of Illinois
2720 East Lincoln Street
P.O. Box 1426
Bloomington, IL 61702-1426
Phone: (309) 663-9366
Summary: To provide financial assistance for postsecondary education to the children of Illinois veterans.
Eligibility: Eligible to apply for these scholarships are Illinois residents. Applicants must be the children of veterans who served during eligibility dates for membership in the American Legion. They must be high school seniors or high school graduates who have not yet attended an institution of higher learning. They must be sponsored by their local American Legion Auxiliary unit. Winners are selected on the basis of character, Americanism, leadership, scholarship, and need.
Financial data: The first winner receives a scholarship of $1,200, the second winner a scholarship of $1,000, and several other winners each receive $800.
Duration: 1 year.
Number awarded: Varies each year.
Deadline: March of each year.

5
ADELANTE! FUND SCHOLARSHIP PROGRAM

Adelante! U.S. Education Leadership Fund
8415 Datapoint Drive, Suite 400
San Antonio, TX 78229
Phone: (210) 692-1971   Fax: (210) 692-1951
Summary: To provide financial aid, internships, and leadership training to upper-division Hispanic students enrolled in member schools of the Hispanic Association of Colleges and Universities (HACU).
Eligibility: This program is open to Hispanic students currently enrolled in HACUs. Applicants must have at least a 3.0 grade point average, be eligible to receive financial aid, be juniors or seniors in college, agree to attend the Adelante Leadership Institute, be eligible to participate in a summer internship, exhibit leadership, and provide 2 letters of recommendation. Most recipients are the first in their families to complete a college education.
Financial data: The maximum stipend is $3,000 per year.
Duration: 1 year.
Additional information: The first scholarships from this fund were awarded in 1999. Scholarship applicants receive added value if they submit their resumes and transcripts to the Adelante Fund's student data pool, which is made available to businesses and corporations for employment opportunities. Recipients must participate in a summer internship and the Adelante Leadership Institute.
Number awarded: Varies each year; recently, 22 students received scholarships.

6
ADGA SCHOLARSHIP

American Dairy Goat Association
P.O. Box 865
Spindale, NC 28160
Phone: (828) 286-3801   Fax: (828) 287-0476
E-mail: adga@adga.org
Web Site: www.adga.org/scholar.htm
Summary: To provide financial assistance for college to members of the American Dairy Goat Association (ADGA) and their families.
Eligibility: This program is open to current regular and junior members of the association who are enrolled in an accredited college or university. Applicants may be part of a family or joint association membership. Selection is based on a statement of the goals of their dairy goat project (15 percent); a chart with an estimate of the profit and loss incurred in their project (5 percent); a list of dairy goat-related awards, demonstrations, public service, and group-related activities (15 percent); leadership experiences designed to aid others involved with dairy goats (10 percent); activities and community service experiences and awards not related to dairy goats (15 percent); an essay describing their dairy goat experience (20 percent); academic performance, as measured by high school or college ranking, grade point average in high school or college, and SAT and/or ACT scores (10 percent); and neatness and organization of application (10 percent). Financial need is not considered.
Financial data: Stipends are $1,000 or $750 per year.

Duration: 1 year; may be renewed for up to 3 additional years.
Additional information: There are 3 types of scholarships offered: the ADGA/Dean Family Scholarships at $1,000, the ADGA/Jim Morrison Scholarships at $750, and the ADGA/Dean Family Ohio Scholarships at $1,000. Recipients must enroll in an accredited college or university; they may major in any field. Only 1 association scholarship will be awarded per individual per year.
Number awarded: 30 each year: 10 of each of the 3 types.
Deadline: May of each year.

7
ADO MEMORIAL SCHOLARSHIPS

American Darts Organization
230 North Crescent Way, #K
Anaheim, CA 92801
Phone: (714) 254-0212   Fax: (714) 254-0214
Summary: To provide financial aid for college to players in the American Darts Organization (ADO) Youth Playoff Program.
Eligibility: This program is open to ADO members who are U.S. citizens, have lived in the United States for at least 2 years, are area or national winners in the ADO Youth Playoff Program, are under 21 years of age, are enrolled in (or accepted at) an accredited American college on a full-time basis, and have at least a 2.0 grade point average.
Financial data: Stipends are: $500 for quarter finalists in the National Championship; $750 for each semifinalist; $1,000 for each runner-up; and $1,500 for each National Champion. Any participant/winner who is eligible to compete in more than 1 area/national championship may repeat as a scholarship winner, up to $8,000 in prizes. Funds may be used for any legitimate college expense, including fees for parking stickers, library fees, student union fees, tuition, and books.
Duration: The funds are awarded annually.
Number awarded: 8 each year: 4 quarter finalists, 2 semifinalists, 1 runner-up, and 1 National Champion.

8
A.E. ROBERT FRIEDMAN-PDCA SCHOLARSHIP FUND

Painting and Decorating Contractors of America
3913 Old Lee Highway, Second Floor
Fairfax, VA 22030
Phone: (703) 383-0800   (877) 500-PDCA
Fax: (703) 359-2576
Web Site: www.pdca.org
Summary: To provide financial assistance for college or graduate school to students who are nominated by a member of the Painting and Decorating Contractors of America.
Eligibility: To be eligible for a scholarship, applicants must be nominated by an active member of the Painting and Decorating Contractors of America, be between 18 and 24 years of age, and be attending a postsecondary educational institution as an undergraduate or graduate student. Selection is based on character, financial need, and academic record.
Financial data: The stipend is $1,000 per year.
Duration: 1 year; may be renewed for 1 additional year.
Additional information: This program was established in 1978.
Number awarded: Varies each year; recently, 14 of these scholarships were awarded.
Deadline: November of each year.

9
AFL-CIO SKILLED TRADES EXPLORING SCHOLARSHIPS

Boy Scouts of America
Attn: Learning for Life Division, S210
1325 West Walnut Hill Lane
P.O. Box 152079
Irving, TX 75015-2079
Phone: (972) 580-2418
Web Site: www.learning-for-life.org/exploring
Summary: To provide financial assistance for trade school to graduating high school seniors who are Explorer Scouts.
Eligibility: This program is open to graduating high school seniors who are Explorers and interested in attending a public or proprietary institution or union apprentice program. Their achievements must reflect a high degree of motivation, commitment, and skills. Selection is based on academic record, recommendations, and a 500-word essay on why the applicant should be selected

for the scholarship. All completed applications must be approved by the local council scout executive.
Financial data: The stipend is $1,000.
Duration: 1 year.
Number awarded: 2 each year.
Deadline: April of each year.

10
AGENDA FOR DELAWARE WOMEN TRAILBLAZER SCHOLARSHIPS

Delaware Higher Education Commission
Carvel State Office Building
820 North French Street
Wilmington, DE 19801
Phone: (302) 577-3240   (800) 292-7935
Fax: (302) 577-6765   E-mail: dhec@state.de.us
Web Site: www.doe.state.de.us/high-ed
Summary: To provide financial assistance for undergraduate education to women in Delaware.
Eligibility: This program is open to women who are Delaware residents and will enroll in a public or private nonprofit college in Delaware as an undergraduate student in the coming year. Applicants must have a cumulative grade point average of 2.5 or higher. Selection is based on financial need, academic performance, community or school involvement, and leadership ability.
Financial data: The stipend is $2,500 per year.
Duration: 1 year; may be renewed.
Number awarded: 1 or more each year.
Deadline: April of each year.

11
AGNES JONES JACKSON SCHOLARSHIPS

National Association for the Advancement of Colored People
Attn: Education Department
4805 Mt. Hope Drive
Baltimore, MD 21215-3297
Phone: (410) 358-8900   Fax: (410) 358-9785
Web Site: www.naacp.org
Summary: To provide financial assistance to members of the National Association for the Advancement of Colored People (NAACP) who are attending or planning to attend college on a full-time basis.
Eligibility: Members of the NAACP who are full-time undergraduates or full- or part-time graduate students are eligible to apply. The minimum grade point average is 2.5 for graduating high school seniors and undergraduate students, or 3.0 for graduate students. All applicants must be able to demonstrate financial need (family income must be less than $30,000 for a family of 1, ranging up to $52,300 for a family of 8), be under 25 years of age, and be U.S. citizens. Renewal awards may be reduced or denied based on insufficient NAACP activities.
Financial data: The stipend is $1,500 for undergraduate students or $2,500 for graduate students.
Duration: 1 year; recipients may apply for renewal.
Number awarded: 1 or more each year.
Deadline: April of each year.

12
AIAC SCHOLARSHIPS

Alabama Indian Affairs Commission
770 South McDonough Street
Montgomery, AL 36104
Phone: (334) 242-2831   (800) 436-8261
Fax: (334) 240-3408   E-mail: aiac@midspring.com
Web Site: aiac.state.al.us/scholar.htm
Summary: To provide financial assistance for college to American Indians residing in Alabama.
Eligibility: This program is open to residents of Alabama who have a tribal roll card in a state- or federally-recognized Indian tribe. Applicants must attend or plan to attend an academic institution in the state, unless their chosen program of study is not offered in an Alabama school. Both merit and need-based scholarships are awarded.
Financial data: A stipend is awarded (exact amount not specified).
Duration: 1 year; recipients may reapply.
Number awarded: Varies each year.

Scholarship Listings

13
AIR FORCE ROTC GENERAL MILITARY COURSE INCENTIVE

U.S. Air Force
Attn: Headquarters AFROTC/RRUC
551 East Maxwell Boulevard
Maxwell AFB, AL 36112-6106
Phone: (334) 953-2091   (800) 522-0033, ext. 2091
Fax: (334) 953-5271
Web Site: www.afrotc.com/scholarships/icschol/gmci/gmci.htm
Summary: To provide financial assistance to college sophomores interested in serving as Air Force officers following completion of their bachelor's degree.
Eligibility: This program is open to U.S. citizens who are entering the spring semester of their sophomore year in the general military course at a college or university with an Air Force ROTC unit on campus or a college with a cross-enrollment agreement with such a school. Applicants must be full-time students, have a grade point average of 2.0 or higher both cumulatively and during the prior term, be enrolled in both the Aerospace Studies 200 class and the Leadership Laboratory, pass the Air Force Officer Qualifying Test, meet Air Force physical fitness and weight requirements, and be able to graduate before they become 27 years of age. They must agree to serve for at least 4 years as active-duty Air Force officers following graduation from college.
Financial data: Selected cadets receive up to $1,500 for tuition and a stipend of $250 per month.
Duration: 1 semester (the spring semester of junior year); nonrenewable.
Additional information: Upon successful completion of their sophomore year, recipients of these scholarships may upgrade to the Professional Officer Course Incentive. They also remain eligible to apply for other AFROTC in-college scholarship programs.

14
AIR FORCE ROTC HIGH SCHOOL SCHOLARSHIPS

U.S. Air Force
Attn: Headquarters AFROTC/RRUC
551 East Maxwell Boulevard
Maxwell AFB, AL 36112-6106
Phone: (334) 953-2091   (800) 522-0033, ext. 2091
Fax: (334) 953-5271
Web Site: www.afrotc.com
Summary: To provide financial assistance for postsecondary education to high school seniors or graduates who are willing to serve as Air Force officers following completion of their bachelor's degree.
Eligibility: Applicants must be high school seniors and U.S. citizens at least 17 years of age who have been accepted at a college or university with an Air Force ROTC unit on campus or a college with a cross-enrollment agreement with such a college. Students must 1) be in the top 40 percent of their class, 2) have a cumulative grade point average of 2.5 or higher, and 3) have an ACT composite score of 24 or higher or an SAT score of 1100 or higher. At the time of graduation with a bachelor's degree, scholarship recipients must be no more than 27 years of age. Applicants must agree to serve for at least 4 years as active-duty Air Force officers following graduation from college.
Financial data: Type 1 scholarships provide payment of full tuition and most laboratory fees, as well as $510 for books. Type 2 scholarships pay the same benefits except tuition is capped at $15,000 per year; students who attend an institution where tuition exceeds $15,000 must pay the difference. Type 7 scholarships pay full tuition and most laboratory fees, but students must attend a college or university where the tuition is less than $9,000 per year; they may not attend an institution with higher tuition and pay the difference. Approximately 7.5 percent of scholarship offers are for Type 1, approximately 17.5 percent are for Type 2, and approximately 75 percent are for type 7. All recipients are also awarded a tax-free subsistence allowance for 10 months of each year that is $250 per month during their freshman and sophomore years, $300 per month during their junior year, and $350 per month during their senior year.
Duration: 4 years.
Additional information: Recently, approximately 25 percent of these scholarships were offered to students planning to major in electrical engineering and meteorology, approximately 50 percent to majors in other technical areas (aeronautical engineering, aerospace engineering, architectural engineering, architecture, chemical engineering, civil engineering, computer engineering, computer science, environmental engineering, industrial engineering, mathematics, mechanical engineering, nuclear engineering, and physics), and 25 percent to all other majors, with preference for foreign area studies, (Caribbean, eastern Europe, Far East, Latin America, Mediterranean, Middle East, north Africa, Russia, south Asia, southeast Asia, sub-Sahara Africa, and western Europe) and foreign languages (Arabic, Chinese Mandarin, Dutch, French, German, Italian, Japanese, Korean, Persian Farsi, Polish, Port Brazilian, Russian, Spanish, Tagalog, Turkish, and Vietnamese). While scholarship recipients can major in any subject, they must enroll in 4 years of aerospace studies courses at 1 of the 143 colleges and universities that have an Air Force ROTC unit on campus; students may also attend 850 other colleges that have cross-enrollment agreements with the institutions that have an Air Force ROTC unit on campus. Recipients must attend a 4-week summer training camp at an Air Force base, usually between their sophomore and junior years. Most cadets incur a 4-year active-duty commitment. Pilots incur a 10-year active-duty service commitment after successfully completing Specialized Undergraduate Pilot Training and navigators incur a 6-year commitment after successfully completing Specialized Undergraduate Navigator Training. The minimum service obligation for intelligence and Air Battle Management career fields is 5 years.
Number awarded: Approximately 3,500 each year.
Deadline: November of each year.

15
AIR FORCE ROTC HISTORICALLY BLACK COLLEGES AND UNIVERSITIES SCHOLARSHIP PROGRAM

U.S. Air Force
Attn: Headquarters AFROTC/RRUC
551 East Maxwell Boulevard
Maxwell AFB, AL 36112-6106
Phone: (334) 953-2091   (800) 522-0033, ext. 2091
Fax: (334) 953-5271
Web Site: www.afrotc.com/scholarships/icschol/minority/index.htm
Summary: To provide financial assistance to students at Historically Black Colleges and Universities (HBCUs) who are willing to serve as Air Force officers following completion of their bachelor's degree.
Eligibility: This program is open to U.S. citizens at least 17 years of age who are currently enrolled or have been accepted at an HBCU with an Air Force ROTC unit on campus. Applicants do not need to be African American as long as they are attending an HBCU and have a cumulative grade point average of 2.5 or higher. At the time of graduation with a bachelor's degree, they may be no more than 27 years of age. They must agree to serve for at least 4 years as active-duty Air Force officers following graduation from college.
Financial data: Currently, awards are type 2 AFROTC scholarships that provide for payment of tuition and fees, to a maximum of $15,000 per year, plus an annual book allowance of $510. All recipients are also awarded a tax-free subsistence allowance for 10 months of each year that is $250 per month during the sophomore year, $300 during the junior year, and $350 during the senior year.
Duration: The regular HBCU program provides 2 to 3 years of support, the enhanced program 2 1/2 years to 3 1/2 years. Both versions allow completion of a bachelor's degree.
Additional information: While scholarship recipients can major in any subject, they must complete 4 years of aerospace studies courses at 1 of the HBCUs that have an Air Force ROTC unit on campus. Recipients must also attend a 4-week summer training camp at an Air Force base, usually between their sophomore and junior years; 2-year scholarship awardees attend in the summer after their junior year. Current military personnel are eligible for early release from active duty in order to enter the Air Force ROTC program. Following completion of their bachelor's degree, scholarship recipients earn a commission as a second lieutenant in the Air Force and serve at least 4 years.

16
AIR FORCE ROTC HOST MINORITY SCHOLARSHIP PROGRAM

U.S. Air Force
Attn: Headquarters AFROTC/RRUC
551 East Maxwell Boulevard
Maxwell AFB, AL 36112-6106
Phone: (334) 953-2091   (800) 522-0033, ext. 2091
Fax: (334) 953-5271
Web Site: www.afrotc.com/scholarships/icschol/minority/host_minority.htm
Summary: To provide financial assistance to students at designated predominantly Hispanic universities who are willing to serve as Air Force officers following completion of their bachelor's degree.

24

Eligibility: Applicants must be U.S. citizens at least 17 years of age who are currently enrolled or have been accepted as sophomores or juniors at a designated predominantly Hispanic university that has an Air Force ROTC unit on campus. They do not need to be Hispanic as long as they have completed 1 or 2 years of study at the university and have a cumulative grade point average of 2.5 or higher. At the time of graduation with a bachelor's degree, applicants may be no more than 27 years of age. They must agree to serve for at least 4 years as active-duty Air Force officers following graduation from college.

Financial data: Currently, awards are type 2 AFROTC scholarships that provide for payment of tuition and fees, to a maximum of $15,000 per year, plus an annual book allowance of $510. All recipients are also awarded a tax-free subsistence allowance for 10 months of each year that is $250 per month during the sophomore year, $300 during the junior year, and $350 during the senior year.

Duration: 2 to 3 years, until completion of a bachelor's degree.

Additional information: Currently, the designated universities are New Mexico State University, the University of New Mexico, the University of Puerto Rico at Rio Piedras, the University of Puerto Rico at Mayaguez, and the University of Texas at San Antonio. While scholarship recipients can major in any subject, they must complete 4 years of aerospace studies courses. They must also attend a 4-week summer training camp at an Air Force base, usually between their sophomore and junior years; 2-year scholarship awardees attend in the summer after their junior year. Current military personnel are eligible for early release from active duty in order to enter the Air Force ROTC program. Following completion of their bachelor's degree, scholarship recipients earn a commission as a second lieutenant in the Air Force and serve at least 4 years.

17 AIR FORCE ROTC ONE-YEAR COLLEGE PROGRAM (OYCP)

U.S. Air Force
Attn: Headquarters AFROTC/RRUC
551 East Maxwell Boulevard
Maxwell AFB, AL 36112-6106
Phone: (334) 953-2091   (800) 522-0033, ext. 2091
Fax: (334) 953-5271
Web Site: www.afrotc.com/scholarships/icschol/oneyear/index.htm

Summary: To provide financial assistance to students who already have a baccalaureate degree or can complete it in 1 year and are willing to serve as Air Force officers following completion of their studies.

Eligibility: This program is open to U.S. citizens who currently hold a baccalaureate degree or can complete it within 1 year. Applicants must meet Air Force ROTC entry standards (medical condition, drug screen, weight and fitness standards, and Air Force Officer Qualification Test minimum score). Scholarship recipients must have a cumulative college grade point average of 2.5 or higher and be under 27 years of age at the time commissioning is scheduled; applicants with prior active-duty military service may have the age limit extended for the total active-duty days served on a day-for-day basis up to a maximum of 3 years. Non-scholarship cadets must have at least a 2.0 grade point average and be younger than 35 years of age upon commissioning and entering active duty. Recently, this program was open to students pursuing any undergraduate or graduate degree.

Financial data: Scholarships are type 2 AFROTC scholarships that provide payment of tuition and fees up to $15,000, a book allowance of $510, and a stipend for 10 months of the year at $350 per month. Non-scholarship cadets receive the Professional Officer Course Incentive which provides up to $3,000 for tuition and $450 for books.

Duration: 1 year.

Additional information: Participants attend a 7-week field training encampment during the summer prior to entering the program as contract cadets. Upon completion of the program, recipients enter active duty as first lieutenants in the U.S. Air Force with an initial service period of 4 years. They are not eligible for pilot, navigator, or nonline specialties.

Number awarded: Varies each year.

Deadline: March of each year.

18 AIR FORCE ROTC PROFESSIONAL OFFICER CORPS INCENTIVE

U.S. Air Force
Attn: Headquarters AFROTC/RRUC
551 East Maxwell Boulevard
Maxwell AFB, AL 36112-6106
Phone: (334) 953-2091   (800) 522-0033, ext. 2091
Fax: (334) 953-5271
Web Site: www.afrotc.com/scholarships/icschol/gmci/poci.htm

Summary: To provide financial assistance for undergraduate and graduate education to individuals who have completed 2 years of college and who are willing to serve as Air Force officers following completion of their bachelor's degree.

Eligibility: Applicants must be U.S. citizens who have completed 2 years of the general military course at a college or university with an Air Force ROTC unit on campus or a college with a cross-enrollment agreement with such a college. They must be full-time students, have a grade point average of 2.0 or higher both cumulatively and for the prior term, be enrolled in both Aerospace Studies class and Leadership Laboratory, pass the Air Force Officer Qualifying Test, meet Air Force physical fitness and weight requirements, and be able to graduate before they become 27 years of age. They must agree to serve for at least 4 years as active-duty Air Force officers following graduation from college with either a bachelor's or graduate degree.

Financial data: This scholarship provides $3,000 per year for tuition and $450 per year for books.

Duration: Until completion of a graduate degree.

Additional information: Scholarship recipients must complete 4 years of aerospace studies courses at 1 of the 143 colleges and universities that have an Air Force ROTC unit on campus; students may also attend other colleges that have cross-enrollment agreements with the institutions that have an Air Force ROTC unit on campus. Recipients must also attend a 4-week summer training camp at an Air Force base between their junior and senior year.

Number awarded: Approximately 800 each year.

19 AIR FORCE SERGEANTS ASSOCIATION SCHOLARSHIPS

Air Force Sergeants Association
Attn: Scholarship Program
5211 Auth Road
Suitland, MD 20746
Phone: (301) 899-3500   (800) 638-0594
E-mail: staff@afsahq.org
Web Site: www.amf.org/scholarship.html

Summary: To provide financial assistance for undergraduate education to the dependent children of Air Force enlisted personnel.

Eligibility: Eligible to apply for these scholarships are the unmarried children (including stepchildren and legally adopted children) of enlisted personnel serving in the U.S. Air Force, Air National Guard, or Air Force Reserves, or in retired status. Applicants must be under the age of 23 and dependent upon the parent or guardian for more than half of their support. Selection is based on academic ability (minimum SAT score of 1100 and minimum grade point average of 3.5), character, leadership, writing ability, and potential for success. Financial need is not a consideration.

Financial data: Stipends range from $1,000 to $2,500 per year. Scholarships may be used for tuition, room and board, fees, books, supplies, and transportation.

Duration: 1 year; may be renewed if the student maintains full-time enrollment.

Additional information: This program began in 1968. Requests for applications must be accompanied by a stamped self-addressed envelope.

Number awarded: Varies each year. Recently, 17 of these scholarships were awarded, including the Frank C. Fini, the Hardy B. Abbott, and the Claude Klobus Scholarships (each at $2,500), 3 additional named grants at $2,000 each, 6 $1,500 awards, and 5 $1,000 scholarships.

Deadline: April of each year.

20 AIR FORCE SPOUSE SCHOLARSHIPS

Aerospace Education Foundation
1501 Lee Highway
Arlington, VA 22209-1198
Phone: (703) 247-5839   (800) 291-8480
Fax: (703) 247-5853   E-mail: AEFStaff@aef.org
Web Site: www.aef.org

Summary: To provide financial assistance for undergraduate or graduate study to spouses of Air Force members.

Eligibility: This program is open to spouses of Air Force active duty, Air National Guard, or Air Force Reserve members. Spouses who are themselves military members or in ROTC are not eligible. Applicants must have a minimum grade point average of 3.5 in college (or high school if entering college for the first time) and be able to provide proof of acceptance into an accredited undergraduate or graduate degree program. They must submit a 2-page essay on their academic and career goals, the motivation that led them to that decision, and how Air Force and

other local community activities in which they are involved will enhance their goals. Selection is based on the essay and 2 letters of recommendation.

Financial data: The stipend is $1,000 per year; funds are sent to the recipients' schools to be used for any reasonable cost related to pursuing a degree.

Duration: 1 year; nonrenewable.

Additional information: This program was established in 1995.

Number awarded: 30 each year.

Deadline: January of each year.

21
AIR LINE PILOTS ASSOCIATION SCHOLARSHIP PROGRAM

Air Line Pilots Association
Attn: Lee Alger
1625 Massachusetts Avenue, N.W.
Washington, DC 20036
Phone: (202) 797-4059   E-mail: AlgerL@alpa.org
Web Site: www.alpa.org

Summary: To provide financial assistance for postsecondary education to the children of disabled or deceased members of the Air Line Pilots Association.

Eligibility: Sons and daughters of medically retired, disabled, or deceased members of the Air Line Pilots Association are eligible to apply. Although the program envisions selection of students enrolling as college freshman, eligible individuals who are already enrolled in college may also apply. Selection is based on a number of factors, including academic record and financial need.

Financial data: The scholarship is $3,000 per year, up to a maximum total award of $12,000.

Duration: 1 year; may be renewed up to 3 additional years, if the student maintains adequate academic standing of a minimum 3.0 grade point average.

Number awarded: Each year the association grants 1 new award and continues 3 previously-made awards.

Deadline: March of each year.

22
AIRMEN MEMORIAL FOUNDATION SCHOLARSHIP PROGRAM

Air Force Sergeants Association
Attn: Scholarship Program
5211 Auth Road
Suitland, MD 20746
Phone: (301) 899-3500   (800) 638-0594
E-mail: staff@afsahq.org
Web Site: www.amf.org/topamf.htm

Summary: To provide financial assistance for the postsecondary education of dependent children of enlisted Air Force personnel.

Eligibility: Applicants must be the unmarried dependent children (including stepchildren and legally adopted children), under the age of 23, of enlisted personnel serving in the U.S. Air Force, Air National Guard, or Air Force Reserves, whether on active duty or retired. Selection is based on academic ability (minimum SAT score of 1100 and minimum grade point average of 3.5), character, leadership, writing ability, and potential for success; financial need is not a consideration.

Financial data: The stipend is $1,500 or $1,000; funds may be used for tuition, room and board, fees, books, supplies, and transportation.

Duration: 1 year; may be renewed if recipient maintains full-time enrollment.

Additional information: The Air Force Sergeants Association administers this program on behalf of the Airmen Memorial Foundation. The highest ranked applicant receives the Sharon L. Piccoli Memorial Scholarship. Requests for applications must be accompanied by a stamped self-addressed envelope.

Number awarded: 20 each year: the Sharon L. Piccoli Memorial Scholarship at $1,500 and 19 others at $1,000 each.

Deadline: April of each year.

23
AK-SAR-BEN COMMUNITY COLLEGE SCHOLARSHIP

Knights of Ak-Sar-Ben
Attn: Ak-Sar-Ben Scholarship Program
6800 Mercy Road, Suite 206
Omaha, NE 68106
Phone: (402) 554-9600   Fax: (402) 554-9609
Web Site: www.aksarben.org/programs/scholarship.htm

Summary: To provide financial assistance to students from Nebraska and western Iowa who plan to attend a community college within the Ak-Sar-Ben region.

Eligibility: This program is open to high school seniors, high school graduates, and currently-enrolled community college students in Nebraska and western Iowa who are interested in attending college in the Ak-Sar-Ben region. For the purposes of this program, western Iowa is defined as the following counties: Adair, Adams, Audubon, Buena Vista, Calhoun, Carroll, Cass, Cherokee, Clay, Crawford, Dickinson, Fremont, Greene, Guthrie, Harrison, Ida, Lyon, Mills, Monona, Montgomery, O'Brien, Osceola, Page, Pottawattamie, Plymouth, Ringold, Sac, Shelby, Sioux, Taylor, Union, and Woodbury. Applicants must be U.S. citizens. They must submit their application to the financial aid office at the community college they are attending or planning to attend; the college nominates 3 incoming freshmen and 3 currently-enrolled students from this group. As part of the application process, students must include a completed application form, a 300-word personal essay, 2 letters of reference, a transcript, and their federal student aid report. Selection is based on leadership potential, academic achievement, desire to earn a degree, and financial need.

Financial data: The stipend is $1,000, paid in 2 equal installments. To receive the second installment, recipients must have maintained at least a 2.5 grade point average the previous semester. Funds must be used for tuition, fees, and books.

Duration: 1 year.

Additional information: Since the sponsor's scholarship program was established in 1945, more than 13,000 scholarships have been awarded. Recipients must attend school on a full-time basis.

Number awarded: Up to 12 each year.

Deadline: March of each year.

24
AK-SAR-BEN LEADERSHIP COLLEGE SCHOLARSHIP

Knights of Ak-Sar-Ben
Attn: Ak-Sar-Ben Scholarship Program
6800 Mercy Road, Suite 206
Omaha, NE 68106
Phone: (402) 554-9600   Fax: (402) 554-9609
Web Site: www.aksarben.org/programs/scholarship.htm

Summary: To provide financial assistance to students from Nebraska and western Iowa who plan to attend a 4-year college or university within the Ak-Sar-Ben region.

Eligibility: This program is open to high school seniors in Nebraska and western Iowa who are interested in attending college in the Ak-Sar-Ben region. Applicants must be U.S. citizens and rank in the top 50 percent of their graduating class. As part of the application process, students must submit a completed application form, a 300-word personal essay, 2 letters of reference, a transcript, and the original college funding estimator form and report from the Educational Planning Center. Selection is based on leadership potential, academic achievement, desire to earn a college degree, and financial need.

Financial data: The stipend totals $10,000 ($2,500 per year). Funds must be used for tuition, fees, books, room, and board (at university-owned housing only).

Duration: 4 years, provided the recipient maintains a 3.0 grade point average in college.

Additional information: Since the sponsor's scholarship program was established in 1945, more than 13,000 scholarships have been awarded. Recipients must attend a 4-year college or university in Nebraska (any eligible school) or western Iowa (Briar Cliff College, Buena Vista College, Dordt College, Iowa State University, Morningside College, or Northwestern College).

Number awarded: 20 each year.

Deadline: February of each year.

25
AL-AMEEN SCHOLARSHIP

AL-AMEEN
10520 Wilshire Boulevard, Suite 908
Los Angeles, CA 90024
E-mail: alameenScholarship@yahoo.com
Web Site: www.al-ameen.org

Summary: To provide financial assistance to Muslim high school seniors in California who are interested in going on to college.

Eligibility: Eligible to apply for this program are Muslim high school seniors who are residents of California, have a grade point average of 3.0 or higher, and have at least 1000 on their SAT or an equivalent score on the ACT. Preference is given to students who have been accepted at a public university in southern California. There are no degree or subject restrictions. To apply, students must submit a completed application form, an application essay of up to 500 words on what

Islam has taught them in terms of ethics and the importance of education, an official high school transcript, a history of their employment, a copy of their resume, and certification of their SAT/ACT scores. Selection is based on: academic record, school activities, other activities (e.g., volunteering, work), financial need, and other factors that may help in distinguishing the applicant.
Financial data: Stipends range up to $3,000; funds are sent directly to the recipient's school.
Duration: 1 year; may be renewed for 1 additional year.
Additional information: This program was established in 2000. Recipients must send a progress summary each quarter or semester (funds will not be released unless this summary is submitted).
Number awarded: 2 or more each year: at least 1 male and 1 female.

26
ALABAMA JUNIOR AND COMMUNITY COLLEGE ATHLETIC SCHOLARSHIPS

Alabama Commission on Higher Education
Attn: Grants and Scholarships Department
100 North Union Street
P.O. Box 302000
Montgomery, AL 36130-2000
Phone: (334) 242-2274   Fax: (334) 242-0268
E-mail: wwall@ache.state.al.us
Web Site: www.ache.state.al.us
Summary: To provide financial assistance to athletes in Alabama interested in attending a junior or community college.
Eligibility: Eligible are full-time students enrolled in public junior and community colleges in Alabama. Selection is based on athletic ability as determined through try-outs.
Financial data: Awards cover the cost of tuition and books.
Duration: Scholarships are available as long as the recipient continues to participate in the designated sport or activity.
Additional information: Interested students must contact a coach, athletic director, or financial aid officer at their junior or community college.
Number awarded: Varies each year.

27
ALABAMA POLICE OFFICERS' AND FIRE FIGHTERS' SURVIVORS' EDUCATIONAL ASSISTANCE PROGRAM

Alabama Commission on Higher Education
Attn: Grants and Scholarships Department
100 North Union Street
P.O. Box 302000
Montgomery, AL 36130-2000
Phone: (334) 242-2274   Fax: (334) 242-0268
E-mail: wwall@ache.state.al.us
Web Site: www.ache.state.al.us
Summary: To provide financial assistance to the spouses and dependents of police officers and fire fighters killed in Alabama.
Eligibility: This program is open to the unremarried widows, daughters, and sons of police officers and fire fighters killed in the line of duty in Alabama. Applicants may be high school seniors or currently-enrolled undergraduates at a public institution in Alabama.
Financial data: Grants are offered to cover tuition, fees, books, and supplies. There is no limit on the amount awarded to recipients.
Duration: 1 year; may be renewed.
Additional information: Recipients must attend public institutions in Alabama.
Number awarded: Varies each year.

28
ALABAMA STUDENT ASSISTANCE PROGRAM

Alabama Commission on Higher Education
Attn: Grants and Scholarships Department
100 North Union Street
P.O. Box 302000
Montgomery, AL 36130-2000
Phone: (334) 242-2274   Fax: (334) 242-0268
E-mail: wwall@ache.state.al.us
Web Site: www.ache.state.al.us
Summary: To provide financial assistance to undergraduate students who are residents of Alabama.

Eligibility: This program is open to residents of Alabama who are attending or planning to attend eligible Alabama institutions (nearly 80 schools participate in this program). Applicants must be able to demonstrate financial need. Eligible students are required to submit the Free Application for Federal Student Aid.
Financial data: Stipends range from $300 to $2,500 per academic year.
Duration: 1 year; may be renewed.

29
ALABAMA STUDENT GRANT PROGRAM

Alabama Commission on Higher Education
Attn: Grants and Scholarships Department
100 North Union Street
P.O. Box 302000
Montgomery, AL 36130-2000
Phone: (334) 242-2274   Fax: (334) 242-0268
E-mail: wwall@ache.state.al.us
Web Site: www.ache.state.al.us
Summary: To provide financial assistance to undergraduates at private colleges or universities in Alabama.
Eligibility: Eligible are undergraduate students who are attending 1 of 14 designated private colleges or universities in Alabama on at least a half-time basis. Alabama residency is required but financial need is not considered.
Financial data: Up to $1,200 per year.
Additional information: The participating schools are Birmingham-Southern College, Concordia College, Faulkner University, Huntingdon College, Judson College, Miles College, Oakwood College, Samford University, Selma University, Southeastern Bible College, Southern Vocational College, Spring Hill College, Stillman College, and the University of Mobile.
Number awarded: Varies each year.
Deadline: Each participating institution sets its own deadline date.

30
ALABAMA 2-YEAR COLLEGE ACADEMIC SCHOLARSHIPS

Alabama Commission on Higher Education
Attn: Grants and Scholarships Department
100 North Union Street
P.O. Box 302000
Montgomery, AL 36130-2000
Phone: (334) 242-2274   Fax: (334) 242-0268
E-mail: wwall@ache.state.al.us
Web Site: www.ache.state.al.us
Summary: To provide financial assistance to junior college students in Alabama.
Eligibility: Eligible are students who have been accepted for enrollment at any Alabama public 2-year postsecondary educational institution. Selection is based on academic merit. Preference is given to Alabama residents.
Financial data: Scholarships are available to cover the cost of in-state tuition and books.
Duration: 1 year; may be renewed if the recipient maintains a high level of academic achievement.
Number awarded: Varies each year.

31
ALASKA FREE TUITION FOR SPOUSES AND DEPENDENTS OF ARMED SERVICES MEMBERS

Office of Veterans Affairs
P.O. Box 5800
Fort Richardson, AK 99505-5800
Phone: (907) 428-6068   Fax: (907) 428-6019
E-mail: laddie_shaw@ak-prepared.com
Web Site: www.ak-prepared.com/vetaffairs/state_benefits.htm
Summary: To provide financial assistance for postsecondary education to dependents and spouses in Alaska of service members who died or were declared prisoners of war or missing in action.
Eligibility: Eligible for this benefit are the spouses and dependent children of Alaska residents who died in the line of duty, died of injuries sustained in the line of duty, or were listed by the Department of Defense as a prisoner of war or missing in action. Applicants must be in good standing at a state-supported educational institution in Alaska.
Financial data: Those eligible may attend any state-supported educational institution in Alaska without payment of tuition or fees.
Duration: 1 year; may be renewed.

Additional information: Information is available from the financial aid office of state-supported universities in Alaska.
Number awarded: Varies each year.

32
ALASKA LEGION AUXILIARY SCHOLARSHIP

American Legion Auxiliary
Attn: Department of Alaska
P.O. Box 220887
Anchorage, AK 99522-0887
Phone: (907) 248-4583   Fax: (907) 248-4398
Summary: To provide financial assistance for postsecondary education to veterans' children in Alaska.
Eligibility: Eligible to apply for this scholarship are the sons and daughters of veterans who served during eligibility dates for membership in the American Legion; applicants must be between 17 and 24, be high school seniors or graduates who have not yet attended an institution of higher learning, and be residents of Alaska.
Financial data: The stipend is $1,000, half of which is payable each semester toward tuition, matriculation, laboratory, or similar fees.
Duration: 1 year.
Number awarded: 1 each year.
Deadline: March of each year.

33
ALBERT M. LAPPIN SCHOLARSHIP

American Legion
Attn: Department of Kansas
1314 S.W. Topeka Boulevard
Topeka, KS 66612-1886
Phone: (785) 232-9315   Fax: (785) 232-1399
Summary: To provide financial assistance for postsecondary education to the children of members of the Kansas American Legion or American Legion Auxiliary.
Eligibility: Applicants must be high school seniors who plan to attend an approved Kansas college, university, or trade school; freshmen or sophomores at those schools are also eligible. At least 1 of their parents must be a member of an American Legion post or Auxiliary in Kansas.
Financial data: This scholarship is $1,000.
Duration: 1 year.
Number awarded: 1 each year.
Deadline: February of each year.

34
ALBERT T. MARCOUX MEMORIAL SCHOLARSHIP

American Legion
Attn: Department of New Hampshire
State House Annex
25 Capitol Street, Room 431
Concord, NH 03301-6312
Phone: (603) 271-5338   Fax: (603) 271-5352
Summary: To provide financial assistance for postsecondary education to the children of members of the New Hampshire Department of the American Legion or American Legion Auxiliary.
Eligibility: Applicants must submit evidence of 1) a parent's current membership in a New Hampshire post of the American Legion or unit of the American Legion Auxiliary, 2) residence in New Hampshire for at least 3 years, 3) acceptance to an accredited college or university, 4) a grade point average of 3.0 or better in their junior and senior high school years, and 5) financial need.
Financial data: The scholarship is $1,000.
Duration: 1 year.
Number awarded: 1 each year.
Deadline: April of each year.

35
ALEXANDER GRAHAM BELL ASSOCIATION COLLEGE SCHOLARSHIP AWARDS

Alexander Graham Bell Association for the Deaf
Attn: Financial Aid Coordinator
3417 Volta Place, N.W.
Washington, DC 20007-2778
Phone: (202) 337-5220   Fax: (202) 337-8314
Phone: TTY: (202) 337-5221   E-mail: financialaid@agbell.org
Web Site: www.agbell.org/financialaid/agbell_programs.cfm
Summary: To provide financial assistance for postsecondary education to undergraduate and graduate students with moderate to profound hearing loss.
Eligibility: Applicants must have had a hearing loss since birth or before acquiring language with a 60 dB or greater loss in the better ear in the speech frequencies of 500, 1000, and 2000 Hz. They must use speech and residual hearing and/or speechreading (lipreading) as their preferred, customary form of communication and demonstrate a potential for leadership. In addition, applicants must be accepted by or already attending full time a college or university that primarily enrolls students with normal hearing. Preference is given to undergraduates.
Financial data: Awards range up to $1,000.
Duration: 1 year.
Additional information: In past years, individual awards have been designated as the Allie Raney Hunt Memorial Scholarship Award, the David Von Hagen Scholarship Award, the Elsie Bell Grosvenor Scholarship Awards, the Franklin and Henrietta Dickman Memorial Scholarship Awards, the Herbert P. Feibelman Jr. (PS) Scholarship Award, the Lucille A. Abt Scholarship Awards, the Maude Winkler Scholarship Awards, the Oral Hearing-Impaired Section Scholarship Award, the Robert H. Weitbrecht Scholarship Awards, the Second Century Fund Awards, and the Volta Scholarship Award. Some of those awards included additional eligibility requirements. Only the first 500 requests for applications are accepted.
Number awarded: Varies each year.
Deadline: Applications must be requested between September and December of each year and submitted by February of each year.

36
ALICE YURIKO ENDO MEMORIAL SCHOLARSHIP

Japanese American Citizens League
Attn: National Scholarship Awards
1765 Sutter Street
San Francisco, CA 94115
Phone: (415) 921-5225   Fax: (415) 931-4671
E-mail: jacl@jacl.org
Web Site: www.jacl.org
Summary: To provide financial assistance to student members of the Japanese American Citizens League (JACL) who are pursuing an undergraduate education, particularly in public or social service.
Eligibility: This program is open to JACL members who are currently enrolled or planning to reenter a college, university, trade school, business college, or other institution of higher learning. Selection is based on academic record, extracurricular activities, and community involvement. Preference is given to a student planning a future in public or social service and/or residing in the Eastern District Council area.
Financial data: The stipend depends on the availability of funds but usually ranges from $1,000 to $5,000.
Duration: 1 year.
Additional information: Requests for applications must be accompanied by a self-addressed stamped envelope.
Number awarded: 1 each year.
Deadline: March of each year.

37
ALL-AMERICAN SCHOLAR PROGRAM

United States Achievement Academy
2570 Polumbo Drive
Lexington, KY 40509
Phone: (859) 269-5674   Fax: (859) 268-9068
E-mail: aas@usaa-academy.com
Web Site: www.usaa-academy.com
Summary: To provide financial assistance for college to students who are nominated by their teachers or professors.
Eligibility: This program is open to students in grades 6 through college. Candidates must be nominated by a teacher or professor for inclusion in the *National All-American Collegiate Scholar Directory*. Once nominated, they may apply for 1 of these scholarship grants.
Financial data: Stipends are awarded.

Duration: 1 year.
Number awarded: Varies each year; since the program was established, it has granted more than $650,000 in scholarships.
Deadline: Nominations may be submitted at any time.

38
ALL-INK.COM SCHOLARSHIP

All-Ink
P.O. Box 50868
Provo, UT 84605-0868
Phone: (877) 491-4465   Fax: (413) 431-9761
E-mail: scholarship@all-ink.com
Web Site: www.all-ink.com/storeinfo/scholarship/rules/rules.html
Summary: To provide financial assistance for college to students who enter an online competition.
Eligibility: This program is open to all students who are enrolled at or planning to enroll at a college or university. Applicants must submit an online form that includes a 100-word essay on a person who has had a great impact on their lives and why, extracurricular activities in high school or college, honors received in high school or college, and a 100-word essay on what they hope to accomplish in their professional and personal lives.
Financial data: Stipends are either $1,000 or $500.
Duration: 1 year.
Additional information: Applications must be submitted on line; applications mailed through the U.S. Postal Service are neither accepted nor returned. Also, no information is available over the telephone.
Number awarded: 4 each year: 2 at $1,000 and 2 at $500.
Deadline: December or July of each year.

39
ALL-USA ACADEMIC TEAM FOR COMMUNITY COLLEGES

Phi Theta Kappa
Attn: Scholarship Department
1625 Eastover Drive
P.O. Box 13729
Jackson, MS 39236-3729
Phone: (601) 957-2241, ext. 560   (800) 946-9995, ext. 560
Fax: (601) 957-2312   E-mail: scholarship.programs@ptk.org
Web Site: www.ptk.org
Summary: To recognize and reward the outstanding achievements of community college students.
Eligibility: Community, technical, and junior colleges in the United States are eligible to nominate candidates for this award. Nominees must be attending a school that is a member of the American Association of Community Colleges (membership in Phi Theta Kappa is not required), have completed at least 12 semester hours in pursuit of an associate's degree, and have achieved a cumulative grade point average of at least 3.25. Selection is based on awards, honors, and recognition for academic achievement; grade point average; participation in honors programs; and service to the college and the community.
Financial data: The award is $2,500.
Duration: The competition is held annually.
Additional information: Funds for this program are supplied by USA Today, the American Association of Community Colleges, and Phi Theta Kappa.
Number awarded: 20 each year.
Deadline: December of each year.

40
ALL-USA COLLEGE ACADEMIC TEAM

USA Today
c/o Carol Skalski
1000 Wilson Boulevard, 10th Floor
Arlington, VA 22229
Phone: (703) 276-5890   E-mail: allstars@usatoday.com
Web Site: allstars.usatoday.com
Summary: To recognize and reward outstanding college students in the United States.
Eligibility: Full-time college or university students at accredited 4-year institutions in the United States may be nominated by college presidents or faculty members. U.S. citizenship is not required. Nominees identify their 1) honors and awards; 2) campus activities; 3) community and professional activities; and 4) internships, outside study, research, and publications. They also write a 500-

word essay on 1 of those 4 items describing what they did, why it is their most outstanding intellectual endeavor, and how it may benefit society. Applications must also include 2 letters of recommendation, an official grade transcript, and an essay by the nominating professor or president on why the endeavor described by the nominee is outstanding. Selection is based on scholarship, academic talent, creativity, and leadership.
Financial data: Winners receive $2,500 cash prizes and are guests of USA Today at a special awards luncheon.
Duration: This competition is held annually.
Additional information: Co-sponsors of this competition are the National Association of Independent Colleges and Universities, the National Association of State Universities and Land-Grant Colleges, the American Association of Colleges for Teacher Education, the Council for Advancement and Support of Education, and the American Council on Education.
Number awarded: 60 students are chosen for the All-USA Academic Team and receive recognition in USA Today; of those, 20 are named to the first team and receive cash prizes.
Deadline: November of each year.

41
ALL-USA HIGH SCHOOL ACADEMIC TEAM

USA Today
c/o Carol Skalski
1000 Wilson Boulevard, 10th Floor
Arlington, VA 22229
Phone: (703) 276-5890   E-mail: allstars@usatoday.com
Web Site: allstars.usatoday.com
Summary: To recognize and reward outstanding high school students in the United States.
Eligibility: Teachers and principals at any high school in the United States may nominate outstanding students at their school. Nominees write a 250-word essay describing their most outstanding intellectual endeavor, including its significance to them, their community, or society; the endeavor can be in art, music, literature, poetry, scientific research, history, community service, or public affairs. Applications must also include 3 letters of recommendation, an official grade transcript, and an essay by the nominating teacher that addresses the merits of the intellectual endeavor described by the nominee. Selection is based on academic record, creativity, leadership, and independent scholarly or artistic work.
Financial data: Winners receive $2,500 cash prizes and are guests of USA Today at a special awards luncheon.
Duration: This competition is held annually.
Additional information: Co-sponsors of this competition are the National Association of Secondary School Principals and the National Education Association.
Number awarded: 20 students are chosen for the All-USA High School Academic Team and receive recognition in USA Today.
Deadline: February of each year.

42
ALLIANT ENERGY COLLEGE-TO-WORK PROGRAM

Wisconsin Foundation for Independent Colleges, Inc.
735 North Water Street, Suite 800
Milwaukee, WI 53202-4100
Phone: (414) 273-5980   Fax: (414) 273-5995
E-mail: wfic@execpc.com
Web Site: www.wficweb.org
Summary: To provide financial assistance and work experience to women and minority students at private colleges in Wisconsin.
Eligibility: This program is open to women and minority students at the 21 independent colleges or universities in Wisconsin. Applicants must be interested in an internship at Alliant Energy as part of the program.
Financial data: The stipend is $3,000.
Duration: 1 year.
Additional information: The participating schools are Alverno College, Beloit College, Cardinal Stritch University, Carroll College, Carthage College, Concordia University of Wisconsin, Edgewood College, Lakeland College, Lawrence University, Marian College, Marquette University, Milwaukee Institute of Art & Design, Milwaukee School of Engineering, Mount Mary College, Northland College, Ripon College, St. Norbert College, Silver Lake College, Viterbo University, and Wisconsin Lutheran College.
Number awarded: 5 each year.

43
ALLIE MAE ODEN MEMORIAL SCHOLARSHIP

Ladies Auxiliary of the Fleet Reserve Association
Attn: Scholarship Administrator
125 North West Street
Alexandria, VA 22314-2754
Phone: (703) 683-1400   (800) 372-1924
Fax: (703) 549-6610
Web Site: www.fra.org
Summary: To provide financial assistance for the postsecondary education of children and grandchildren of the Fleet Reserve Association (FRA) or its Ladies Auxiliary.
Eligibility: Eligible to apply for these scholarships are the children and grandchildren of members of the association or its ladies auxiliary. Selection is based on financial need, academic proficiency, and character.
Financial data: This scholarship is $2,500.
Duration: 1 year; may be renewed.
Additional information: Membership in the FRA is open to active-duty, retired, and reserve members of the Navy, Marine Corps, and Coast Guard.
Number awarded: 1 each year.
Deadline: April of each year.

44
ALPHA KAPPA ALPHA ENDOWMENT SCHOLARSHIPS

Alpha Kappa Alpha
Attn: Educational Advancement Foundation
5656 South Stony Island Avenue
Chicago, IL 60637
Phone: (773) 947-0026   (800) 653-6528
Fax: (773) 947-0277   E-mail: akaeaf@aol.com
Web Site: www.akaeaf.org
Summary: To provide financial assistance for postsecondary education to students (especially Black women) who meet designated requirements.
Eligibility: This program is open to all students; the sponsor is a traditionally African American women's sorority. Each of these scholarships includes specific requirements established by the donor of the endowment that supports it; for further information, contact the sponsor.
Financial data: Award amounts are determined by the availability of funds from the endowment. Most stipends average $1,000 per year.
Duration: 1 year or longer.
Number awarded: Varies each year; recently, 16 of these scholarships were awarded.
Deadline: February of each year.

45
ALPHA KAPPA ALPHA FINANCIAL ASSISTANCE SCHOLARSHIPS

Alpha Kappa Alpha
Attn: Educational Advancement Foundation
5656 South Stony Island Avenue
Chicago, IL 60637
Phone: (773) 947-0026   (800) 653-6528
Fax: (773) 947-0277   E-mail: akaeaf@aol.com
Web Site: www.akaeaf.org
Summary: To provide financial assistance for postsecondary education to undergraduate and graduate students (especially African American women) who demonstrate financial need.
Eligibility: This program is open to undergraduate or graduate students who have completed at least 1 year in an accredited degree-granting institution or a work-in-progress program in a noninstitutional setting, are planning to continue their program of education, and can demonstrate financial need. Applicants must have a grade point average of 2.5 or higher. Men and women of all ethnic groups are eligible for these scholarships, but the sponsor is a traditionally African American women's sorority.
Financial data: Awards range from $500 to $1,500 per year.
Duration: 1 year; nonrenewable.
Number awarded: Varies each year. Recently, 38 of these scholarships were awarded: 26 to undergraduates and 12 to graduate students.
Deadline: February of each year.

46
ALPHA KAPPA ALPHA MERIT SCHOLARSHIPS

Alpha Kappa Alpha
Attn: Educational Advancement Foundation
5656 South Stony Island Avenue
Chicago, IL 60637
Phone: (773) 947-0026   (800) 653-6528
Fax: (773) 947-0277   E-mail: akaeaf@aol.com
Web Site: www.akaeaf.org
Summary: To provide financial assistance for postsecondary education to undergraduate and graduate students (especially African American women) who have excelled academically.
Eligibility: This program is open to undergraduate and graduate students who have completed at least 1 year in an accredited degree-granting institution and are planning to continue their program of education. Applicants must have demonstrated exceptional academic achievement (grade point average of 3.0 or higher) and present evidence of leadership through community service and involvement. Men and women of all ethnic groups are eligible for these scholarships, but the sponsor is a traditionally African American women's sorority.
Financial data: The stipend is $1,000 per year.
Duration: 1 year; nonrenewable.
Number awarded: Varies each year. Recently, 27 of these scholarships were awarded: 20 to undergraduates and 7 to graduate students.
Deadline: February of each year.

47
ALTERNATIVE HIGH SCHOOL STUDENT SCHOLARSHIP PROGRAM

Utah Elks Association
c/o Jim Szatkowski
2996 South Vista Circle Drive
Bountiful, UT 84010-7814
Phone: (201) 292-1570   E-mail: jamesski@inovion.com
Web Site: www.inovion.com/~jamesski/Utah_Elks
Summary: To provide financial assistance for college to seniors in alternative high schools in Utah.
Eligibility: This program is open to seniors graduating from an alternative high school in Utah. As part of the application process, students must submit an official application form, a statement (up to 300 words) on where they have been and where they want to go, a letter from a parent or another responsible adult expressing confidence in the applicant's ability, a similar letter from another responsible person (other than a relative or educator), a transcript, and other exhibits, additional letters, copies of certificates, awards, or other printed material supporting the application.
Financial data: A stipend is awarded (exact amount not specified).
Duration: 1 year.
Number awarded: Varies each year.
Deadline: March of each year.

48
AMARANTH FUND AWARDS

California Masonic Foundation
Attn: Scholarship Committee
1111 California Street
San Francisco, CA 94108-2284
Phone: (415) 292-9196   (800) 900-2727
Fax: (415) 776-7170   E-mail: foundation@mhcsf.org
Web Site: www.californiamasons.org
Summary: To provide financial assistance to women high school seniors in California who are interested in attending college.
Eligibility: This program is open to graduating women high school seniors who have been residents of California for at least 1 year and have a grade point average of 3.0 or higher. Applicants must be planning to attend a 2-year or 4-year institution of higher education as a full-time freshman in the following fall. They must be U.S. citizens or permanent residents and able to show evidence of financial need. Along with their application, they must submit a personal essay outlining their background, goals, and scholastic achievements; a copy of their latest high school transcript; 2 letters of recommendation; a copy of the last Federal 1040 income tax return filed by their parents; the FAFSA financial aid application; their SAT or ACT scores; and a copy of their college acceptance letter.

Selection is based on academic achievement, applicant essay, and financial need. Preference is given to women who have a Masonic relationship or are members of Masonic youth groups.

Financial data: The amount of the stipend varies, depending on the availability of funds.

Duration: 1 year; may be renewed for up to 3 additional years.

Additional information: Requests for applications must be accompanied by a self-addressed stamped envelope.

Number awarded: Varies each year.

Deadline: March of each year for new applicants; April of each year for renewal applicants.

49
AMBASSADOR MINERVA JEAN FALCON HAWAI'I SCHOLARSHIP

Hawai'i Community Foundation
900 Fort Street Mall, Suite 1300
Honolulu, HI 96813
Phone: (808) 566-5570   (888) 731-3863
Fax: (808) 521-6286   E-mail: scholarships@hcf-hawaii.org
Web Site: www.hcf-hawaii.org

Summary: To provide financial assistance to Hawaii residents who are interested in attending college.

Eligibility: This program is open to Hawaii residents who are enrolled in or planning to enroll in an accredited college or university. Applicants must be full-time students at the undergraduate level and able to demonstrate academic achievement (at least a 2.7 grade point average), good moral character, and financial need. In addition to filling out the standard application form, applicants must write a short statement indicating their reasons for attending college, their planned course of study, and their career goals. Preference is given to applicants of Filipino ancestry.

Financial data: The amounts of the awards depend on the availability of funds and the need of the recipient.

Duration: 1 year.

Additional information: Recipients may attend college in Hawaii or on the mainland. This scholarship was first offered in 2001.

Number awarded: Varies each year.

Deadline: February of each year.

50
AMERICAL DIVISION VETERANS ASSOCIATION SCHOLARSHIP

Americal Division Veterans Association
P.O. Box 1381
Boston, MA 02104

Summary: To provide financial assistance for college to the dependents of members of the Americal Division Veterans Association.

Eligibility: This program is open to the sons, daughters, grandsons, and granddaughters of members of the Americal Division Veterans Association or of persons who served with the Americal Division on active duty.

Financial data: The stipend is either $3,000 or $2,000 per year.

Duration: 1 year.

Additional information: Information is also available from Ronald Ward, 9619 Dana Avenue, St. Louis, MO 63123.

Number awarded: 3 each year.

51
AMERICAN ASSOCIATION OF AIRPORT EXECUTIVES SCHOLARSHIP

American Association of Airport Executives Foundation
Attn: AAAE Foundation Scholarship Program
601 Madison Street, Suite 400
Alexandria, VA 22314
Phone: (703) 824-0500   Fax: (703) 820-1395
Web Site: www.airportnet.org

Summary: To provide financial assistance to undergraduate and graduate students who are accredited airport executive (AAE) members (or the dependents of members) of the American Association of Airport Executives.

Eligibility: This program is open to accredited airport executive members of the association, along with their spouses and children. Applicants must be attending or planning to attend school (on the undergraduate or graduate school level) on a full-time basis.

Financial data: Varies; generally, the stipend is $1,000.

Duration: 1 year.

Additional information: Recipients must attend an accredited college or university.

Number awarded: Varies each year.

Deadline: May of each year.

52
AMERICAN ASSOCIATION OF JAPANESE UNIVERSITY WOMEN SCHOLARSHIP PROGRAM

American Association of Japanese University Women
c/o Mrs. Shihoko Tatsugawa, Scholarship Committee Co-Chair
1481 Sunnyhill Drive
Monterey Park, CA 91754

Summary: To provide financial assistance to female students currently enrolled in college in California.

Eligibility: This program is open to female students enrolled in accredited colleges or universities in California. They must have junior, senior, or graduate standing. Applicants must be a contributor to U.S.-Japan relations, cultural exchanges, and leadership development in the areas of their designated study. To apply, they must submit a current resume, an official transcript of the past 2 years of college work, 2 letters of recommendation, and an essay (up to 2 pages in English or 1,200 characters in Japanese) on 1 of the following topics: what I hope to accomplish in my field of study to develop leadership and role model qualities; or thoughts on how my field of study can contribute to U.S.-Japan relations and benefit international relations.

Financial data: The stipend is $1,000.

Duration: 1 year.

Additional information: The association was founded in 1970 to promote the education of women as well as to contribute to U.S.-Japan relations, cultural exchanges, and leadership development. Requests for applications must include a stamped self-addressed envelope.

Number awarded: 1 or more each year.

Deadline: September of each year.

53
AMERICAN FOREIGN SERVICE ASSOCIATION ACADEMIC MERIT AWARDS

American Foreign Service Association
2101 E Street, N.W.
Washington, DC 20037
Phone: (202) 338-4045   (800) 704-AFSA
Fax: (202) 338-6820   E-mail: scholar@afsa.org
Web Site: www.afsa.org

Summary: To provide financial assistance for college to dependents of U.S. government employees involved in foreign service activities.

Eligibility: Applicants must be graduating high school seniors who are dependents of foreign service employees in the Department of State, the Commerce Service, the Foreign Agriculture Service, or the Agency for International Development. The parent may be active, retired with pension, or deceased but must have served at least 1 year abroad and must be a member of the American Foreign Service Association (AFSA) or the Associates of the American Foreign Service Worldwide (AAFSW). Selection is based on grade point average, SAT scores, rank in class, an essay, letters of recommendation, extracurricular activities, and special circumstances.

Financial data: The stipend is $1,700 per year for winners; honorable mention is $500 per year.

Duration: 1 year; may be renewed.

Number awarded: Varies each year: recently, 16 winners and 7 honorable mentions were selected.

Deadline: February of each year.

54
AMERICAN FOREIGN SERVICE ASSOCIATION FINANCIAL AID SCHOLARSHIPS

American Foreign Service Association
2101 E Street, N.W.
Washington, DC 20037
Phone: (202) 338-4045   (800) 704-AFSA
Fax: (202) 338-6820   E-mail: scholar@afsa.org
Web Site: www.afsa.org

Summary: To provide financial assistance to undergraduate students who are dependents of U.S. government employees involved in foreign service activities.
Eligibility: Applicants must be or plan to be full-time undergraduates at an accredited college, postsecondary art school, conservatory, community college, or university in the United States and tax or legal dependent children of foreign service employees in the Department of State, the Commerce Service, the Foreign Agriculture Service, or the Agency for International Development. The parent may be active, retired with pension, or deceased but must have served at least 1 year abroad. Scholarships are established by private donors as a group or individually; each has its own particular eligibility rules, but most require financial need.
Financial data: Awards range from $1,000 to $3,000 annually.
Duration: 1 year; may be renewed if the recipient maintains satisfactory progress.
Additional information: Recipients may use these scholarships for 1 year of study abroad under the auspices of their U.S. college or university.
Number awarded: Varies each year; recently, 64 students received scholarships worth $123,490.
Deadline: February of each year.

55
AMERICAN GENERAL SCHOLARSHIPS

American General Career Distribution Group
Attn: Scholarship Program
P.O. Box 22492
Nashville, TN 37202-2492
Phone: (615) 320-3149
Summary: To provide financial assistance for college to high school seniors in selected states.
Eligibility: This program is open to high school seniors in the following states: Alabama, California, Florida, Georgia, Kentucky, Mississippi, North Carolina, Ohio, Pennsylvania, Texas, Tennessee, and Virginia. Applicants must "demonstrate the positive traits of kindness, respect, and good citizenship."
Financial data: Stipends are either $1,500 or $500.
Duration: 1 year.
Number awarded: 220 each year: 170 at $500 and 50 at $1,500.
Deadline: February of each year.

56
AMERICAN GI FORUM OF THE UNITED STATES SCHOLARSHIPS

American GI Forum of the United States
Attn: Hispanic Education Foundation
100 Decker Drive, Suite 200
Irving, TX 75062-2206
Phone: (972) 717-4575   Fax: (972) 650-0842
E-mail: agif-hef@sernational.org
Web Site: www.agifnat.org
Summary: To provide financial assistance for postsecondary education to needy and qualified students of Hispanic descent.
Eligibility: High school seniors, high school graduates, and college students are eligible to apply if they need money to attend college. Selection is based on academic achievement, financial need, general leadership qualities, and career aspirations. Each local chapter administers its own program; for the chapter chair in your area, contact the national office.
Financial data: The amount awarded varies, depending upon the availability of funds and the recipient's financial need.
Duration: 1 year; recipients may reapply.
Number awarded: Varies each year.
Deadline: Each chapter sets its own application deadline.

57
AMERICAN GOAT SOCIETY YOUTH SCHOLARSHIPS

American Goat Society
c/o Judy Ratcliff, Secretary
P.O. Box 330
Broad Run, VA 20137
Phone: (540) 349-4709   E-mail: ags_office@yahoo.com
Web Site: www.americangoatsociety.com/ags_scholarships.htm
Summary: To provide financial assistance to members or the families of members of the American Goat Society (AGS) who are interested in attending college.
Eligibility: This program is open to current junior or regular AGS members and

children of members. Applicants must be either high school seniors or currently enrolled in an accredited college, university, or trade school. No applicant may be more than 21 years of age. Selection is based on experiences in dairy goat projects and activities (35 percent), experiences in leadership (25 percent), experiences not goat related (20 percent), academic performance (10 percent), and neatness and organization of the application (10 percent).
Financial data: A stipend is awarded (exact amount not specified).
Duration: 1 year; may be renewed for up to 3 additional years, as long as the recipient maintains at least a 3.0 grade point average. An official transcript must be sent to the association each year for verification.
Additional information: This program includes the John Howland Scholarship.
Number awarded: 2 each year.
Deadline: April of each year.

58
AMERICAN LEGION AUXILIARY NATIONAL PRESIDENT'S SCHOLARSHIP

American Legion Auxiliary
777 North Meridian Street, Third Floor
Indianapolis, IN 46204
Phone: (317) 635-6291   Fax: (317) 636-5590
E-mail: alahq@legion-aux.org
Web Site: www.legion-aux.org/scholarship.htm
Summary: To provide financial assistance for the postsecondary education of children of war veterans.
Eligibility: To be eligible, applicants must be children of veterans who served in World War I, World War II, Korea, Vietnam, Grenada, Lebanon, Panama, or the Persian Gulf. They must be high school seniors who have completed at least 50 hours of volunteer service within the community. Each Department (state) organization of the American Legion Auxiliary nominates 1 candidate for the National President's Scholarship annually. Nominees must submit a 1,000-word essay on "America's Veterans Build a Better America for Me." Selection is based on character (15 percent), Americanism (15 percent), leadership (15 percent), scholarship (40 percent), and financial need (15 percent).
Financial data: Stipends are $2,500, $2,000, or $1,000.
Duration: 1 year; recipients may not reapply.
Additional information: Applications are available from the local Unit or from the Department Secretary or Department Education Chair of the state in which the applicant resides.
Number awarded: 15 each year: in each of the 5 divisions of the Auxiliary, 1 scholarship for $2,500, 1 for $2,000, and 1 for $1,000 are awarded.
Deadline: March of each year.

59
AMERICAN LEGION AUXILIARY NON-TRADITIONAL STUDENT SCHOLARSHIPS

American Legion Auxiliary
777 North Meridian Street, Third Floor
Indianapolis, IN 46204
Phone: (317) 635-6291   Fax: (317) 636-5590
E-mail: alahq@legion-aux.org
Web Site: www.legion-aux.org/scholarship.htm
Summary: To provide financial assistance for postsecondary education to nontraditional students affiliated with the American Legion.
Eligibility: This program is open to members of the American Legion, American Legion Auxiliary, or Sons of the American Legion who have paid dues for the 2 preceding years and the calendar year in which application is being made. Applicants must be 1) nontraditional students returning to school after some period of time during which their formal education was interrupted or 2) students who have had at least 1 year of college and are pursuing an undergraduate degree. Selection is based on scholastic standing and academic achievement (25 percent), character and leadership (25 percent), initiative and goals (25 percent), and financial need (25 percent).
Financial data: The scholarship is $1,000 per year, paid directly to the school.
Duration: 1 year.
Additional information: Applications are available from the president of the candidate's own unit or from the secretary or education chair of the department.
Number awarded: 5 each year: 1 in each Division of the American Legion Auxiliary.
Deadline: Applications must be submitted to the unit president by March.

60
AMERICAN MAINE-ANJOU ASSOCIATION SCHOLARSHIP

American Maine-Anjou Association
760 Livestock Exchange Building
Kansas City, MO 64102
Phone: (816) 474-9555   Fax: (816) 474-9556
E-mail: anjou@qni.com
Web Site: www.maine-anjou.org
Summary: To provide financial assistance to high school seniors and currently-enrolled college students who have been active in the American Maine-Anjou Association (AMAA).
Eligibility: Applicants must be current junior members of the association, be at least a graduating high school student (but not more than 21 years of age), and have manifested an interest in association projects. As part of the application process, students must complete an official application form, submit transcripts and 3 letters of recommendations, and provide information on their class ranking and standardized test scores.
Financial data: The stipend is $1,000. In addition, a $500 scholarship is awarded to the individual selected to serve as the association's national queen for the upcoming year.
Duration: 1 year; nonrenewable.
Additional information: The scholarship must be used within 12 months of issuance.

61
AMERICAN MORGAN HORSE INSTITUTE EDUCATIONAL SCHOLARSHIPS

American Morgan Horse Institute, Inc.
Attn: AMHI Scholarships
P.O. Box 837
Shelburne, VT 05482-0519
Phone: (802) 985-8477   Fax: (802) 985-8430
Summary: To provide financial assistance for college to high school seniors who have experience with and an interest in Morgan horses.
Eligibility: This program is open to high school seniors who have experience with and an interest in registered Morgan horses. Selection is based on ability and aptitude for serious study, community service, leadership, financial need, and achievement with Morgan horses.
Financial data: The stipend is $3,000.
Duration: Scholarships are available annually.
Additional information: Only inquiries that include a stamped self-addressed envelope will be answered.
Number awarded: 5 each year.
Deadline: February of each year.

62
AMERICAN POLICE HALL OF FAME EDUCATIONAL SCHOLARSHIP FUND

American Police Hall of Fame and Museum
Attn: Chair, Scholarship Fund
3801 Biscayne Boulevard
Miami, FL 33137
Phone: (305) 573-0070
Summary: To provide financial assistance for college to children of deceased law enforcement officers.
Eligibility: Applicants must be the son or daughter of a law enforcement officer killed in the line of duty. They must be attending or planning to attend a private or public college or a vocational program. Financial need is not considered in the selection process.
Financial data: The stipend is $1,500 per year.
Duration: 1 year; may be renewed up to 3 additional years if funds permit.
Number awarded: Varies each year, depending on the availability of funds.

63
AMERICAN POSTAL WORKERS UNION VOCATIONAL SCHOLARSHIP PROGRAM

American Postal Workers Union
Attn: Scholarship Program
1300 L Street, N.W.
Washington, DC 20005
Phone: (202) 842-4268
Web Site: www.apwu.org
Summary: To provide financial assistance for vocational education to children of members of the American Postal Workers Union (APWU).
Eligibility: Eligible are the children, stepchildren, or legally adopted children of active or deceased members of the APWU who have been in good standing for at least 1 year or were members for 1 year immediately preceding death. Applicants must be high school seniors who plan to attend an accredited trade, technical, industrial, or vocational school. Selection is based on school records, personal qualifications, evidence of a commitment to an occupation, response to contemporary questions, and an essay on the union way of life.
Financial data: The stipend is $1,000 per year.
Duration: 1 year; may be renewed up to 2 additional years or until completion of the program.
Number awarded: 1 each year.
Deadline: February of each year.

64
AMERICAN QUARTER HORSE FOUNDATION SCHOLARSHIP PROGRAM

American Quarter Horse Foundation
Attn: Scholarship Coordinator
2601 I-40 East
P.O. Box 200
Amarillo, TX 79168
Phone: (806) 376-5181   (888) 209-8322
Fax: 806) 376-5807   E-mail: aqhamail@aqha.org
Web Site: www.aqha.com/horse/foundation
Summary: To provide financial assistance for postsecondary education to members of the American Quarter Horse Association (AQHA) and the American Quarter Horse Youth Association (AQHYA).
Eligibility: All applicants must have been members in good standing of either association for the preceding 2 years and be under the age of 21. Selection is based on the most recent cumulative grade point average (at least 2.5 is required), financial need, academic and extracurricular honors and awards, and letters of recommendation. Recipients may major in any field.
Financial data: The stipend is $1,000 per year.
Duration: Up to 4 years.
Additional information: This program began in 1976. The program includes the following named awards (with the numbers of each awarded recently): the AQHF Education or Nursing Scholarship (1), the AQHF Engineering Scholarship (1), AQHF General Scholarships (25), the AQHF Journalism or Communications Scholarship (1), AQHF Racing Scholarships (5), the AQHF Telephony Scholarship for Senior Equine Veterinary Students (1), the AQHF Working Student Scholarship (1) the Dr. Gerald O'Connor Michigan Scholarship (new scholarship), the Excellence in Equine/Agricultural Involvement Scholarship (1), Farm and Ranch Heritage Scholarships (4), the Indiana Quarter Horse Youth Association Scholarship (1), the Nebraska Quarter Horse Youth Association Scholarship (1), the Swayze Woodruff Memorial Mid-South Scholarship (1), and the VQHA/Ray Melton Memorial Scholarship (new scholarship).
Number awarded: Varies each year; recently, 43 new scholarships were awarded and 77 previous awardees received renewals.
Deadline: March of each year.

65
AMERICAN WATER SKI EDUCATIONAL FOUNDATION SCHOLARSHIPS

American Water Ski Educational Foundation
Attn: Executive Director
1251 Holy Cow Road
Polk City, FL 33868-8200
Phone: (863) 324-2472   Fax: (863) 324-3996
E-mail: 102726.2751@compuserve.com
Web Site: usawaterski.org
Summary: To provide financial assistance to currently-enrolled college students who participate in water skiing.
Eligibility: Applicants must be full-time students at 2-year or 4-year accredited colleges. They must have completed at least their freshmen year and be active members of a sport division within USA Water Ski (AWSA, ABC, AKA, WSDA, NSSA, NCWSA, NWSRA, and AWA). U.S. citizenship is required. As part of the application, they must submit a 500-word essay on a topic that changes annually but relates to water skiing; recently, the topic was, "You just assumed the position of Marketing Director for USA Water Ski. What measures would you implement to increase spectator appeal for all 8 sports divisions of water skiing?" Selection is

33

based on the essay, academic record, leadership, extracurricular involvement, letters of recommendation, AWSA membership activities, and financial need.
Financial data: The stipend is $1,500 per year.
Duration: 1 year; may be renewed for up to 2 additional years.
Additional information: This program includes the following named scholarships: the Jennifer Odom Scholarship, the AWSEF Scholarship, the William D. Clifford Scholarship, the Barbara Bolding/Jim Grew Scholarship, the Elmer Stalling/Southern Region Scholarship, and the "Big" Al Wagner/Western Region Scholarship.
Number awarded: 6 each year.
Deadline: March of each year.

66
AMERICA'S JUNIOR MISS

America's Junior Miss
751 Government Street
P.O. Box 2786
Mobile, AL 36652-2786
Phone: (334) 438-3621   Fax: (334) 431-0063
E-mail: sherry@ajm.org
Web Site: www.ajm.org
Summary: To recognize, reward, and encourage excellence in young women while promoting their self esteem.
Eligibility: Any high school girl who is a U.S. citizen, has never been married, will be a senior during the school year in which the national finals are held, and is a resident of the community and state in which she enters is eligible to apply. Candidates must display a 3-minute routine of talent or give a 3-minute speech on a subject of their choice. No bathing suit competitions are held. Local Junior Miss winners advance to state competitions that determine the candidates for the national title. Selection is based on judges' interview (25 percent), talent in creative and performing arts (25 percent), scholastic achievement (20 percent), fitness (15 percent), and poise (15 percent).
Financial data: More than $5 million in college scholarships and other awards are presented to participating Junior Misses at local, state, and national levels each year. Awards vary in each community and state. Scholarships awarded at the national level include $50,000 for the girl chosen as America's Junior Miss, $25,000 for the first runner-up, $15,000 for the second runner-up, and $12,000 for each of the 5 other finalists. Other scholarships include $10,000 as the overall scholastic award, $10,000 as the overall talent award, $10,000 as the overall poise award, $10,000 as the overall fitness award, $5,000 as the overall spirit award, $2,500 for each of the 4 preliminary scholastic winners, $2,500 for each of the 4 preliminary talent winners, $2,500 for each of the 4 preliminary poise winners, $2,500 for each of the 4 preliminary fitness winners, $1,000 for each of the 3 preliminary spirit winners, the Be Your Best Self Award of $1,500, the Springdale Mall Community Service Award of $1,000, the Mobile Register Daily Journal Award of $1,000, the Calagaz Photo Scrapbook Award of $1,000, the Uppseedaisees Hostess Award of $5,000, and the Angela Moore Discover Your Own Style Award of $5,000. Many colleges also provide scholarships to local, state, and national participants.
Duration: The competition is held annually.
Additional information: Until 1989, this competition was known as America's Junior Miss Pageant. From then through 1992, the program was called America's Young Woman of the Year. In 1993, the program was renamed America's Junior Miss.
Number awarded: At the national level, a total of 38 awards were available. Because each participant may win more than 1 award, a total of 20 girls received scholarships. The number of local and state awards varies.
Deadline: Local program deadlines vary. Girls should apply during the summer between their sophomore and junior years.

67
AMERICA'S NATIONAL TEEN-AGER SCHOLARSHIP PROGRAM

National Teen-Ager Scholarship Foundation
Attn: Cheryl Snow
4708 Mill Crossing West
Colleyville, TX 76034
Phone: (817) 577-2220   Fax: (817) 428-7232
E-mail: csnow@dallas.net
Web Site: www.nationalteen.com
Summary: To recognize (locally and nationally) the scholastic and leadership achievements of America's teenage girls and to provide cash, tuition scholarships, and awards to the participants.

Eligibility: Girls who are 12 to 15 years of age are eligible to apply for the junior division and girls who are 16 to 18 may enter the senior division. Entrants must have no children and never been married. Selection is based on scholastic achievement (30 percent), leadership and community involvement (30 percent), communication skills and an interview (30 percent), and appearance (10 percent). There is no swimsuit competition. Each contestant must be able to demonstrate a talent or submit an essay on "What's Right about America."
Financial data: More than $5 million in cash, tuition scholarships, and awards are presented in the state and regional pageants. On the national level, the foundation awards a $10,000 scholarship to the winner in the senior division and a $5,000 scholarship to the winner in the junior division. In addition, a number of academic institutions offer scholarships to state or national winners.
Duration: The contest is held annually.
Additional information: The contest began in 1971, to recognize the leadership achievements of America's teenagers and to provide travel, entertainment, and scholarships for their college education.
Deadline: Deadline dates vary. Check with the sponsors of your local and state pageant. If you don't know the local address, write to the National Headquarters of America's National Teen-Ager at Box 610187, Dallas, TX 75261.

68
AMGEN SCHOLARSHIP

Patient Advocate Foundation
753 Thimble Shoals Boulevard, Suite B
Newport News, VA 23606
Phone: (800) 532-5274   Fax: (757) 873-8999
E-mail: help@patientadvocate.org
Web Site: www.patientadvocate.org
Summary: To provide financial assistance for college to individuals whose studies have been interrupted or delayed by a diagnosis of cancer or other life threatening diseases.
Eligibility: Eligible to apply for this scholarship are individuals seeking to initiate or complete a course of study that has been interrupted or delayed by a diagnosis of cancer or other critical or life threatening diseases. Applicants must be able to demonstrate financial need, have earned at least a 3.0 grade point average, be enrolled or planning to enroll as a full-time student, and write an essay on why they have chosen their particular field of study.
Financial data: The stipend is $5,000.
Duration: 1 year.
Additional information: Recipients must pursue a course of study that will make them immediately employable after graduation.
Number awarded: 1 each year.
Deadline: April of each year.

69
AMVETS NATIONAL LADIES AUXILIARY SCHOLARSHIPS

AMVETS Ladies Auxiliary
Attn: National Scholarship Officer
4647 Forbes Boulevard
Lanham, MD 20706-4380
Phone: (301) 459-6255
Summary: To provide financial assistance for college to members and certain dependents of members of AMVETS Auxiliary.
Eligibility: Applicants must belong to AMVETS Auxiliary or be the child or grandchild of a member. They must be in at least the second year of undergraduate study at an accredited college or university. Applications must include 3 letters of recommendation and an essay (from 200 to 500 words) by the applicants about their past accomplishments, career and educational goals, and objectives for the future. Selection is based on the letters of reference (15 percent), scholarship (25 percent), aim as described on the essay (25 percent), and financial need (35 percent).
Financial data: Scholarships are $1,000 or $750 each.
Duration: 1 year.
Number awarded: Up to 7 each year: 2 at $1,000 and 5 at $750.
Deadline: May of each year.

70
ANGUS FOUNDATION SCHOLARSHIPS

National Junior Angus Association
Attn: Director Junior Activities
3201 Frederick Boulevard
St. Joseph, MO 64506
Phone: (816) 383-5100   Fax: (816) 233-9703
E-mail: jfisher@angus.org
Web Site: www.angus.org/njaa
Summary: To provide financial assistance to students who have been members of the National Junior Angus Association (NJAA) and are enrolled or planning to enroll in college.
Eligibility: Applicants must have been a member of the association in the past and must presently be a junior, regular, or life member of the American Angus Association. They must be either a high school senior or already enrolled in college working full time on an undergraduate degree and younger than 25 years of age. All fields of study are eligible. Selection is based on involvement in Angus associations, other agriculture-related associations, school organizations, and church, civic, and community groups.
Financial data: The stipends are $2,500 or $1,000.
Duration: 1 year. Recipients of the $1,000 awards may reapply for 1 additional year; recipients of the $2,500 awards may not reapply.
Additional information: This program is sponsored by the Angus Foundation. It was established in 1997.
Number awarded: 17 each year: 2 at $2,500 and 15 at $1,000.
Deadline: May of each year.

71
ANNA GEAR JUNIOR SCHOLARSHIP

American Legion Auxiliary
Department of Virginia
Attn: Education Chair
1805 Chantilly Street
Richmond, VA 23230
Phone: (804) 355-6410   Fax: (804) 358-1940
Summary: To provide financial assistance for college to junior members of the American Legion Auxiliary in Virginia.
Eligibility: This program is open to seniors at accredited high schools in Virginia. Applicants must have held junior membership in the American Legion Auxiliary for the 3 previous years.
Financial data: The stipend is $1,000.
Duration: 1 year.
Number awarded: 1 each year.
Deadline: April of each year.

72
ANNE A. AGNEW SCHOLARSHIP

South Carolina State Employees Association
P.O. Box 5206
Columbia, SC 29250-5206
Phone: (803) 765-0680   Fax: (803) 779-6558
E-mail: scsea@aol.com
Summary: To provide financial assistance to members of the South Carolina State Employees Association (SCSEA) and the spouses and children of SCSEA members who are currently enrolled in college.
Eligibility: This scholarship is open to active, honorary, and associate SCSEA members as well as their spouses and children. Also eligible are deserving others who have completed at least 1 academic year and are currently enrolled at a recognized and accredited college, university, trade school, or other institution of higher learning. High school students and college freshmen with no previous college credits are not eligible, but graduate students are. As part of the application process, students must submit a completed application form, an official transcript of college work, and a 200-word statement on educational objectives. Selection is based not only on financial need and academic record, but also character, school and community activities, writing skills, personal motivations, and leadership potential.
Financial data: The amounts awarded are determined each year.
Duration: 1 year.
Additional information: This scholarship was established in 1976.
Deadline: February of each year.

73
ANNE AND MATT HARBISON AWARD

P. Buckley Moss Society
601 Shenandoah Village Drive, Box 1C
Waynesboro, VA 22980
Phone: (540) 943-5678   Fax: (540) 949-8408
E-mail: society@mosssociety.org
Web Site: www.mosssociety.org
Summary: To provide financial assistance for college to high school seniors with learning disabilities.
Eligibility: Eligible to be nominated for this scholarships are high school seniors with learning disabilities, including problems with reading comprehension, spoken language, writing, reasoning, and organization. Nominations may be submitted by society members only. The nomination packet must include a completed application form, a letter from the student's counselor or principal verifying senior status, verification of a learning disability from a school staff member, 2 letters of recommendation, a high school transcript, and a statement (up to 500 words) from the student describing how the award would be used. The following factors are considered in the selection process: the extent to which the student's disability hinders learning and overall functioning in the school environment and the process by the which the student has overcome the barriers inherent in the learning disability in order to pursue postsecondary education.
Financial data: The stipend is $1,000. Funds are paid to the recipient's college or university.
Duration: 1 year; may be renewed for up to 3 additional years.
Number awarded: 1 or more each year.
Deadline: March of each year.

74
APPALOOSA YOUTH EDUCATIONAL SCHOLARSHIP

Appaloosa Youth Foundation, Inc.
c/o Appaloosa Horse Club
Attn: Youth Coordinator
2720 West Pullman Road
Moscow, ID 83843-4024
Phone: (208) 882-5578, ext. 282   Fax: (208) 882-8150
E-mail: aphc@appaloosa.com
Web Site: www.appaloosa.com
Summary: To provide financial assistance for college to members or dependents of members of the Appaloosa Horse Club.
Eligibility: This program is open to members of the Appaloosa Youth Association or the Appaloosa Horse Club who are attending or planning to attend a college or university. Applicants must submit 3 letters of recommendation, a high school or college transcript (grade point average of 2.5 or higher), copies of SAT or ACT exam scores, and an essay in which they describe what their experience with horses has meant to them, why they desire to continue their education, the personal qualities that qualify them to receive a scholarship, any circumstances regarding financial need, and how receiving this scholarship will enhance their educational experiences. Selection is based on the essay (10 percent), involvement in the Appaloosa industry, (30 percent), grade point average (50 percent), extracurricular equine activities (5 percent), and extracurricular school and community activities (5 percent).
Financial data: The stipend is $1,000.
Duration: 1 year; may be renewed.
Number awarded: 8 each year, of which 5 are awarded in each of the 5 territories of the Appaloosa Horse Club, 2 are awarded at large, and 1 is awarded to a previous winner as a continuing scholarship.
Deadline: June of each year.

75
ARBY'S BIG BROTHERS BIG SISTERS SCHOLARSHIP AWARD

Big Brothers Big Sisters of America
Attn: Prospect Research Manager
230 North 13th Street
Philadelphia, PA 19107
Phone: (215) 665-7754   Fax: (215) 567-0394
E-mail: GJones@bbbsa.org
Web Site: www.bbbsa.org
Summary: To provide financial assistance to students from low- and middle-income families, primarily those headed by single parents, who have participated in the Big Brothers Big Sisters program as matched Little Brothers or Little Sisters.

Eligibility: Nominations for this program must be submitted by a Big Brothers Big Sisters agency. Nominees must have been matched Little Brothers or Little Sisters in an affiliated Big Brothers Big Sisters program for at least 1 year. The match need not be current. Nominees may be presently enrolled or accepted at an accredited college or university. Candidates are selected on the basis of academic achievement, volunteer work, community involvement, and financial need.
Financial data: The stipends are $5,000 or $1,000 per year.
Duration: 1 year; the $1,000 scholarships are nonrenewable; the $5,000 scholarships may be renewed for up to 3 additional years.
Number awarded: 12 each year: 2 at $5,000 and 10 at $1,000.
Deadline: March of each year.

76
ARIZONA LEVERAGING EDUCATIONAL ASSISTANCE PARTNERSHIP GRANTS

Arizona Commission for Postsecondary Education
2020 North Central Avenue, Suite 550
Phoenix, AZ 85004-4503
Phone: (602) 258-2435   Fax: (602) 258-2483
E-mail: toni@www.acpe.asu.edu
Web Site: www.acpe.asu.edu
Summary: To provide financial assistance to undergraduate and graduate students in Arizona who can demonstrate financial need.
Eligibility: This program is open to Arizona residents who are attending or planning to attend a participating eligible Arizona postsecondary educational institution as either a full-time or part-time undergraduate or graduate student. Applicants must be able to demonstrate financial need.
Financial data: Awards range from $100 to $2,500 per year.
Duration: 1 year; may be renewed.
Additional information: This program was formerly known as the Arizona State Student Incentive Grant Program.
Deadline: Each participating institution in Arizona sets its own deadline.
Number awarded: Varies each year.

77
ARIZONA PRIVATE POSTSECONDARY EDUCATION STUDENT FINANCIAL ASSISTANCE PROGRAM

Arizona Commission for Postsecondary Education
2020 North Central Avenue, Suite 550
Phoenix, AZ 85004-4503
Phone: (602) 258-2435   Fax: (602) 258-2483
E-mail: toni@www.acpe.asu.edu
Web Site: www.acpe.asu.edu
Summary: To provide financial assistance to graduates of Arizona community colleges who wish to attend a private postsecondary institution in the state.
Eligibility: This program is open to students who have graduated or are about to graduate from a public community college in Arizona with an associate degree. Applicants must be planning to attend a private baccalaureate degree-granting institution in Arizona and be enrolled in a bachelor's degree program on a full-time basis. They must be able to demonstrate financial need.
Financial data: The award is $1,500 per year. Participants must agree when they accept the award to repay the full amount if they do not graduate with their bachelor's degree within 3 years of the initial receipt of the award.
Duration: 2 years.
Additional information: This program was formerly known as the Arizona Postsecondary Education Voucher Program.
Deadline: Applications are accepted throughout the year to accommodate the various enrollment periods for the different private postsecondary institutions.
Number awarded: Varies; grants are awarded on a priority of receipt basis.

78
ARKANSAS ACADEMIC CHALLENGE SCHOLARSHIP

Arkansas Department of Higher Education
Attn: Financial Aid Division
114 East Capitol Avenue
Little Rock, AR 72201-3818
Phone: (501) 371-2050   (800) 54-STUDY
Fax: (501) 371-2001   E-mail: finaid@adhe.arknet.edu
Web Site: www.arscholarships.com/challenge.html
Summary: To provide financial assistance to undergraduate students in Arkansas.
Eligibility: This program is open to Arkansas residents who are graduating high school seniors, are planning to attend an approved Arkansas 2- or 4-year public or private college or university, and can demonstrate financial need. (The maximum family income is $50,000 for a family with 1 dependent child; it increases $5,000 for each additional dependent child and another $10,000 for each additional dependent child in college full time.) Eligibility depends on a correlation between ACT scores, grade point average, and whether the applicant wishes to attend a 2-year or a 4-year institution. Students with an ACT score of 15 to 18 must have a grade point average of 3.25 or higher if they wish to attend a 4-year school or 3.0 for a 2-year school. Students with an ACT score of 19 must have a grade point average of 3.0 or higher if they wish to attend a 4-year school or 2.75 for a 2-year school. Students with an ACT score of 20 to 25 must have a grade point average of 2.75 or higher if they wish to attend a 4-year school or 2.5 for a 2-year school. Students with an ACT score of 25 to 36 must have a grade point average of 2.5 or higher if they wish to attend a 4-year school or 2.25 for a 2-year school.
Financial data: The maximum stipend is $2,500 per year.
Duration: 1 year; may be renewed up to 3 additional years if the recipient maintains full-time enrollment and a grade point average of 2.75 or higher.
Additional information: This program was established in 1991.
Number awarded: Varies each year; recently, 8,728 of these scholarships were awarded.
Deadline: May of each year.

79
ARKANSAS GOVERNOR'S DISTINGUISHED SCHOLARS PROGRAM

Arkansas Department of Higher Education
Attn: Financial Aid Division
114 East Capitol Avenue
Little Rock, AR 72201-3818
Phone: (501) 371-2050   (800) 54-STUDY
Fax: (501) 371-2001   E-mail: finaid@adhe.arknet.edu
Web Site: www.arscholarships.com/governorscholars.html
Summary: To provide financial assistance to exceptional high school seniors in Arkansas.
Eligibility: This program is open to high school seniors who are U.S. citizens or permanent residents, are residents of Arkansas, can demonstrate leadership, and are planning to enroll in a college or university in Arkansas. Applicants must have an SAT score of 1410 or higher, have an ACT score of 32 or higher, or be a National Merit Finalist. Selection is based on high school grade point average, class rank, ACT or SAT score, school leadership, and community leadership.
Financial data: Stipends up to $10,000 per year are provided.
Duration: 1 year; may be renewed for up to 3 additional years provided the recipient maintains a 3.0 cumulative grade point average and completes at least 24 semester hours each year.
Additional information: This program was established in 1997.
Number awarded: Up to 250 each year.
Deadline: January of each year.

80
ARKANSAS GOVERNOR'S SCHOLARS PROGRAM

Arkansas Department of Higher Education
Attn: Financial Aid Division
114 East Capitol Avenue
Little Rock, AR 72201-3818
Phone: (501) 371-2050   (800) 54-STUDY
Fax: (501) 371-2001   E-mail: finaid@adhe.arknet.edu
Web Site: www.arscholarships.com/governorscholars.html
Summary: To provide financial assistance to outstanding high school seniors in Arkansas.
Eligibility: This program is open to high school seniors who are U.S. citizens or permanent residents, are residents of Arkansas, can demonstrate leadership, and are planning to enroll in a college or university in the state. Applicants must have achieved an SAT score of at least 1220, an ACT score of at least 27, or a grade point average of at least 3.5 in academic courses. Selection is based on high school grade point average, class rank, ACT or SAT score, school leadership, and community leadership.
Financial data: The stipend is $4,000 per year.
Duration: 1 year; may be renewed for up to 3 additional years provided the recipient maintains a 3.0 cumulative grade point average and completes at least 24 semester hours each year.
Additional information: This program was established in 1983.
Number awarded: Up to 75 each year.
Deadline: January of each year.

81
ARKANSAS LAW ENFORCEMENT OFFICERS' DEPENDENTS' SCHOLARSHIPS

Arkansas Department of Higher Education
Attn: Financial Aid Division
114 East Capitol Avenue
Little Rock, AR 72201-3818
Phone: (501) 371-2050   (800) 54-STUDY
Fax: (501) 371-2001   E-mail: finaid@adhe.arknet.edu
Web Site: www.arscholarships.com/lawenforcement.html
Summary: To provide financial assistance for undergraduate education to the dependents of deceased or disabled Arkansas law enforcement officers, fire fighters, or other designated public employees.
Eligibility: This program is open to the spouses and/or children (natural, adopted, or step) of Arkansas residents who were killed or permanently disabled in the line of duty as law enforcement officers, municipal police officers, sheriffs and deputy sheriffs, constables, state correction employees, game wardens, state park employees who are commissioned law enforcement officers or emergency response employees, full-time or volunteer fire fighters, state forestry employees engaged in fighting forest fires, certain Arkansas Highway and Transportation Department employees, and public school teachers. Children must be less than 23 years of age; spouses may not have remarried; all applicants must have been Arkansas residents for at least 6 months.
Financial data: The scholarship covers tuition, on-campus room charges, and fees (but not books, school supplies, food, materials, or dues for extracurricular activities) at any state-supported college or university in Arkansas.
Duration: Up to 8 semesters, as long as the student is pursuing a baccalaureate or associate degree.
Number awarded: Varies each year.
Deadline: July of each year for fall term, November of each year for spring or winter term, April of each year for first summer session, or June of each year for second summer session.

82
ARKANSAS MISSING IN ACTION/KILLED IN ACTION DEPENDENTS' SCHOLARSHIP PROGRAM

Arkansas Department of Higher Education
Attn: Financial Aid Division
114 East Capitol Avenue
Little Rock, AR 72201-3818
Phone: (501) 371-2050   (800) 54-STUDY
Fax: (501) 371-2001   E-mail: finaid@adhe.arknet.edu
Web Site: www.arscholarships.com/miakia.html
Summary: To provide financial assistance for educational purposes to dependents of Arkansas veterans who were killed in action or became POWs or MIAs after January 1, 1960.
Eligibility: This program is open to the natural children, adopted children, stepchildren, and spouses of Arkansas residents who became a prisoner of war, killed in action, missing in action, or killed on ordnance delivery after January 1, 1960. Applicants may be working or planning to work 1) on an undergraduate degree in Arkansas or 2) on a graduate or professional degree in Arkansas if their undergraduate degree was not received in Arkansas. Applicants need not be current Arkansas residents, but their parent or spouse must have been an Arkansas resident at the time of entering military service or at the time they were declared a prisoner of war, killed in action, or missing in action.
Financial data: The program pays for tuition, general registration fees, special course fees, activity fees, room and board (if provided in campus facilities), and other charges associated with earning a degree or certificate.
Duration: 1 year; undergraduates may obtain renewal as long as they make satisfactory progress toward a baccalaureate degree; graduate students may obtain renewal as long as they maintain a minimum grade point average of 2.5 and make satisfactory progress toward a degree.
Additional information: Return or reported death of the veteran will not alter benefits. Applications must be submitted to the financial aid director at an Arkansas state-supported institution of higher education or state-supported technical/vocational school.
Number awarded: Varies each year; recently, 4 of these scholarships were awarded.
Deadline: July for the fall term; November for the spring term; April for summer term I; June for summer term II.

83
ARKANSAS SECOND EFFORT SCHOLARSHIP

Arkansas Department of Higher Education
Attn: Financial Aid Division
114 East Capitol Avenue
Little Rock, AR 72201-3818
Phone: (501) 371-2050   (800) 54-STUDY
Fax: (501) 371-2001   E-mail: finaid@adhe.arknet.edu
Web Site: www.arscholarships.com/secondeffort.html
Summary: To provide financial assistance for undergraduate study to students in Arkansas who have earned a General Educational Development (GED) certificate.
Eligibility: Arkansas residents who did not graduate from high school but completed their GED certificate in the previous year are eligible to be considered for this award if they are attending or going to be attending an approved Arkansas 2- or 4-year public or private postsecondary institution. They must be at least 18 years of age or a former member of a high school class that has graduated. The students who received the highest GED scores are awarded this scholarship. Financial need is not considered. Students do not apply for this award; eligible candidates are contacted directly by the Arkansas Department of Higher Education if they achieve the highest scores.
Financial data: The stipend is $1,000 per year or the cost of tuition, whichever is less.
Duration: 1 year; may be renewed for an additional 3 years (or equivalent for part-time students) or until completion of a baccalaureate degree, provided the recipient maintains a grade point average of 2.5 or higher.
Number awarded: 10 each year.

84
ARMENIAN RELIEF SOCIETY UNDERGRADUATE SCHOLARSHIP

Armenian Relief Society of Eastern U.S.A., Inc.
Attn: Scholarship Committee
80 Bigelow Avenue, Suite 200
Watertown, MA 02472
Phone: (617) 926-3801   Fax: (617) 924-7238
Summary: To provide financial assistance for college to undergraduate students of Armenian ancestry.
Eligibility: This program is open to students of Armenian ancestry who are attending an accredited 4-year college or university in the United States. Applicants must have completed at least 1 semester of college. Selection is based on merit, financial need, and Armenian community involvement. Full-time enrollment is required.
Financial data: The amount awarded varies.
Duration: 1 year.
Additional information: Students may not receive more than 2 scholarships from the Armenian Relief Society.
Deadline: March of each year.

85
ARMENIAN STUDENTS' ASSOCIATION OF AMERICA SCHOLARSHIPS

Armenian Students' Association of America, Inc.
Attn: Nathalie Yaghoobian
333 Atlantic Avenue
Warwick, RI 02888
Phone: (401) 461-4116   Fax: (401) 461-6112
E-mail: headasa@aol.com
Web Site: www.asainc.org/scholarships.html
Summary: To provide financial assistance for undergraduate and graduate education to students of Armenian ancestry.
Eligibility: Applicants must be of Armenian descent, have completed or be in the process of completing at least the first year of college (including graduate, medical, and law school) as a full-time student at a 4-year college or university, have a strong academic record, have participated in extracurricular activities, and be able to demonstrate financial need.
Financial data: The stipends range from $500 to $2,500.
Duration: 1 year.
Additional information: There is a $15 application fee.
Number awarded: Varies each year.
Deadline: Interested students must submit a request form for an application by mid-January; they must submit a completed application package by the middle of March.

Scholarship Listings

86
ARMENIAN-AMERICAN CITIZENS' LEAGUE SCHOLARSHIP PROGRAM

Armenian-American Citizens' League Educational and Scholarship Fund, Inc.
Attn: Scholarship Awards Chairperson
P.O. Box 14
Moorpark, CA 93020-0014
Summary: To provide financial assistance to college students in California who are of Armenian descent.
Eligibility: Applicants must be full-time college students with at least a 3.0 grade point average, permanent U.S. residents and residents of California for the past 2 years, and of Armenian descent. As part of the application process, students must submit a summary statement of their educational and professional goals, a completed scholarship application form, 2 original letters of reference, a list of activities, a financial statement, and official transcripts. Selection is based on scholastic achievement, financial need, and community involvement.
Financial data: A stipend is awarded (exact amount not specified). Funds may be used for tuition, required fees, room, board, books, instructional equipment, and other similar expenses.
Duration: 1 year.
Number awarded: Several each year.
Deadline: February of each year.

87
ARMY AVIATION ASSOCIATION OF AMERICA SCHOLARSHIPS

Army Aviation Association of America Scholarship Foundation
755 Main Street, Suite 4D
Monroe, CT 06468-2830
Phone: (203) 268-2450   Fax: (203) 268-5870
E-mail: aaaa@quad-a.org
Web Site: www.quad-a.org/scholarship.htm
Summary: To provide financial aid for postsecondary education to members of the Army Aviation Association of America (AAAA) and their relatives.
Eligibility: This program is open to AAAA members and their spouses, unmarried siblings, and unmarried children. Applicants must be enrolled or accepted for enrollment as an undergraduate or graduate student at an accredited college or university. Graduate students must include a 250-word essay on their life experiences, work history, and aspirations. Some scholarships are specifically reserved for enlisted, warrant officer, company grade, and Department of the Army civilian members. Selection is based on academic merit and personal achievement.
Financial data: Stipends range from $1,000 to $15,000.
Duration: Scholarships may be for 1 year, 2 years, or 4 years.
Number awarded: Varies each year; since the program began in 1963, the foundation has awarded more than $1.5 million to nearly 900 qualified applicants.
Deadline: April of each year.

88
ARMY COLLEGE FUND

U.S. Army
TAPC-PDE-EI
Attn: Education Incentives and Counseling Branch/CDR USPERSCOM
200 Stovall Street, Suite 3N17
Alexandria, VA 22332-0472
Phone: (703) 325-0285   (800) 872-8272
Fax: (703) 325-6599   E-mail: pdeei@hoffman.army.mil
Web Site: www.armyeducation.army.mil/ACF.hmtl
Summary: To provide financial assistance for postsecondary education to Army enlistees after they have completed their service obligation.
Eligibility: Eligible for this program are high school seniors or graduates who enlist in an approved Army job specialty for at least 2 years, score 50 or above on the Armed Forces Qualification Test (AFQT), enroll in the Montgomery GI Bill, and attend a Department of Veterans Affairs-approved postsecondary educational institution on a full-time basis after completion of their service obligation.
Financial data: The ACF provides money for college in addition to that which the enlistee receives under the Montgomery GI Bill. The maximum benefit is $26,000 for a 2-year enlistment, $33,000 for a 3-year enlistment, or $40,000 for a 4-year enlistment. For military occupational specialties, the maximum benefit (including payments under the Montgomery GI Bill) is $50,000.
Duration: 36 months; funds must be utilized within 10 years of leaving the Army.

Additional information: Applications and further information are available from local Army recruiters.
Number awarded: Varies each year.
Deadline: Applications may be submitted at any time.

89
ARMY ROTC ADVANCED COURSE

U.S. Army
Attn: ROTC Cadet Command
Fort Monroe, VA 23651-5238
Phone: (757) 727-4558   (800) USA-ROTC
E-mail: atccps@monroe.army.mil
Web Site: www.rotc.monroe.army.mil
Summary: To provide financial assistance to non-scholarship participants in the Army ROTC Program who have qualified for the Advanced Course.
Eligibility: Non-scholarship cadets in the ROTC Program are eligible to apply for this program if they have qualified for the ROTC Advanced Course. The Advanced Course is usually taken during the final 2 years of college.
Financial data: Participants receive a stipend of $300 per month during their junior year and $350 per month during their senior year, as well as pay for attending the 6-week advanced camp during the summer between the junior and senior years of college.
Duration: 2 years.
Additional information: Non-scholarship graduates may serve 3 years on active duty and 5 years in the Reserve Forces, or they may select or be selected to serve all 8 years on Reserve Forces Duty (RFD). If RFD is selected, graduates attend an Officer Basic Course and spend the remainder of their 8-year obligation in the Reserve Forces.
Number awarded: Varies each year.

90
ARMY ROTC CAMPUS-BASED SCHOLARSHIP PROGRAM

U.S. Army
Attn: ROTC Cadet Command
Fort Monroe, VA 23651-5238
Phone: (757) 727-4558   (800) USA-ROTC
E-mail: atccps@monroe.army.mil
Web Site: www.rotc.monroe.army.mil
Summary: To provide financial assistance to students who are already enrolled in college and are willing to serve as Army officers following completion of that degree.
Eligibility: Applicants for these scholarships must be U.S. citizens at least 17 years of age who have already completed 1 or 2 years in a college or university with an Army ROTC unit on campus or in a college with a cross-enrollment agreement with a college with an Army ROTC unit on campus. They must have 2 or 3 years remaining for their bachelor's degree (or 4 years of a 5-year bachelor's program) and must complete that degree before the age of 27 (although veterans with prior active-duty military service are allowed 1 additional year for each year of military service, up to a maximum of 3 years or 30 years of age upon graduation). Scores of at least 920 on the SAT or 19 on the ACT are also required and applicants must have achieved at least a 2.5 grade point average in their prior college study. Following graduation, scholarship recipients must agree to serve as officers in the military.
Financial data: These scholarships provide financial assistance for college tuition and educational fees, up to an annual amount of $16,000. In addition, a flat rate of $450 is provided for the purchase of textbooks, classroom supplies, and equipment. Recipients are also awarded a stipend for up to 10 months of each year that is $250 per month during their sophomore year, $300 per month during their junior year, and $350 per month during their senior year.
Duration: 2 or 3 years, until the recipient completes the bachelor's degree.
Additional information: Applications must be made through professors of military science at 1 of the schools hosting the Army ROTC program. Preference is given to students who have already enrolled as non-scholarship students in military science classes at 1 of the 275 institutions with an Army ROTC unit on campus, at 1 of the 75 college extension centers, or at 1 of the more than 1,000 colleges with cross-enrollment or extension agreements with 1 of the colleges with an Army ROTC unit. Scholarship winners must serve in the military for 8 years. That service obligation may be fulfilled 1) by serving on active duty for 2 to 4 years followed by service in the Army National Guard (ARNG), the United States Army Reserve (USAR), or the Inactive Ready Reserve (IRR) for the remainder of the 8 years; or 2) by serving 8 years in an ARNG or USAR troop

program unit that includes a 3- to 6-month active-duty period for initial training.
Number awarded: Varies each year; a recent allocation provided for 700 4-year scholarships, 1,800 3-year scholarships, and 2,800 2-year scholarships.
Deadline: December of each year.

91
ARMY ROTC 4-YEAR SCHOLARSHIPS

U.S. Army
Attn: ROTC Cadet Command
Fort Monroe, VA 23651-5238
Phone: (757) 727-4558   (800) USA-ROTC
E-mail: atccps@monroe.army.mil
Web Site: www-rotc.monroe.army.mil
Summary: To provide financial assistance to high school seniors or graduates who are willing to serve as Army officers following completion of their bachelor's degree.
Eligibility: Applicants for this program must 1) be U.S. citizens; 2) be at least 17 years of age by October of the year in which they are seeking a scholarship; 3) be no more than 27 years of age when they graduate from college after 4 years (veterans with prior active-duty military service are allowed 1 additional year for each year of military service, up to a maximum of 3 years or 30 years of age upon graduation); 4) score at least 920 on the SAT or 19 on the ACT; 5) have a high school grade point average of 2.5 or higher; and 6) meet medical and other regulatory requirements. Current college or university students may apply if their school considers them beginning freshmen with 4 academic years remaining for a bachelor's degree. Recipients must agree to serve as Army officers following college graduation.
Financial data: This scholarship provides up to $16,000 for college tuition and educational fees. In addition, a flat rate of $450 is provided for the purchase of textbooks, classroom supplies, and equipment. Recipients are also awarded a stipend for up to 10 months of each year that is $250 per month during their freshman and sophomore years, $300 per month during their junior year, and $350 per month during their senior year.
Duration: 4 years, until completion of a baccalaureate degree.
Additional information: Scholarship recipients participate in the Army ROTC program as part of their college curriculum by enrolling in 4 years of military science classes and attending a 6-week summer camp between the junior and senior years. Following graduation, they receive a commission as either a Regular Army, Army Reserve, or Army National Guard officer. Scholarship winners must serve in the military for 8 years. That service obligation may be fulfilled 1) by serving on active duty for 2 to 4 years followed by service in the Army National Guard (ARNG), the United States Army Reserve (USAR), or the Inactive Ready Reserve (IRR) for the remainder of the 8 years; or 2) by serving 8 years in an ARNG or USAR troop program unit that includes a 3- to 6-month active-duty period for initial training.
Number awarded: Approximately 1,500 each year.
Deadline: November of each year.

92
ARNITA YOUNG-BOSWELL SCHOLARSHIP PROGRAM

National Hook-Up of Black Women, Inc.
1809 East 71st Street, Suite 205
Chicago, IL 60649
Phone: (773) 667-7061   Fax: (773) 667-7064
Summary: To provide financial assistance to African American high school and college students who are interested in earning an undergraduate degree.
Eligibility: This program is open to African American high school seniors or currently-enrolled college students. They must be attending or preparing to attend an accredited school. Applicants must have at least a 2.75 grade point average. They must demonstrate written communication skills by preparing an essay of 300 to 500 words on a topic that changes annually; recently, the topic was "Electing a U.S. President: Should the Electoral College Process Remain a Component of the Election Procedure?" Selection is based on academic record, financial need, community service, concern for the African American family, and a desire to complete a college degree.
Financial data: The stipend is $1,000. Funds are paid directly to the college or university of the recipient's choice.
Duration: 1 year.
Additional information: Information is also available from Dolores B. Sturdivant, NHBW Scholarship Committee Chair, 2480 16th Street, N.W., Suite 206, Washington, DC 20009.
Number awarded: 5 each year.
Deadline: February of each year.

93
ASHBY B. CARTER FOUNDERS AWARDS

National Alliance of Postal and Federal Employees
1628 11th Street, N.W.
Washington, DC 20001-5011
Phone: (202) 939-6325   E-mail: napfe@patriot.net
Web Site: www.napfe.com
Summary: To provide financial assistance for college to the dependents of members of the National Alliance of Postal and Federal Employees.
Eligibility: Eligible to apply for this support are the sons, daughters, and other dependents of members of the alliance who are seniors in high school. The sponsoring member must have been in good standing in the union for at least 3 years. Retirees and deceased members who at the time of death were in good standing may also serve as a sponsor. Selection is based on scholastic achievement (grade point average of 2.5 or higher), community involvement, leadership ability, and character.
Financial data: Stipends are $5,000, $4,000, and $3,500.
Duration: 1 year; nonrenewable.
Additional information: This union was organized for the immediate purpose of preventing the elimination of Blacks from the railway mail service, but it "has kept its doors open to all eligible persons regardless of race, sex, creed, or religion." This program was established in 1955.
Number awarded: 3 each year.
Deadline: March of each year.

94
ASHBY B. CARTER SCHOLASTIC ACHIEVEMENT AWARDS

National Alliance of Postal and Federal Employees
1628 11th Street, N.W.
Washington, DC 20001-5011
Phone: (202) 939-6325   E-mail: napfe@patriot.net
Web Site: www.napfe.com
Summary: To provide financial assistance for college to the dependents of members of the National Alliance of Postal and Federal Employees.
Eligibility: Eligible to apply for this support are the sons, daughters, and other dependents of members of the alliance who are seniors in high school. The sponsoring member must have been in good standing in the union for at least 3 years. Retirees and deceased members who at the time of death were in good standing may also serve as a sponsor. Selection is based on scholastic achievement, applicant's field of interest, and participation in school activities.
Financial data: Stipends are $3,200, $2,400, and $1,900.
Duration: 1 year; nonrenewable.
Additional information: This union was organized for the immediate purpose of preventing the elimination of Blacks from the railway mail service, but it "has kept its doors open to all eligible persons regardless of race, sex, creed, or religion." This program was established in 1955.
Number awarded: 3 each year.
Deadline: March of each year.

95
ASHLEY MARIE EASTERBROOK INTERNET SCHOLARSHIP

Foundation for Ashley's Dream
P.O. Box 1808
Troy, MI 48099
Phone: (800) 790-1880   E-mail: info@ashleysdream.org
Web Site: www.ashleysdream.org/html/scholarship_info.htm
Summary: To provide financial assistance to high school seniors who have been involved in community activities, especially those related to prevention of drunken driving.
Eligibility: This program is open to high school seniors whose grade point average is less than 3.74. Applicants must submit 2 letters of recommendation and an essay that describes their community involvement. The foundation is especially interested in students whose community work relates to the prevention of drunken driving, but that is not a requirement.
Financial data: The stipend is $4,000.
Duration: 1 year.
Additional information: This program was established in 1999 as a memorial to Ashley Easterbrook, who was killed by a drunken driver when she was a teenager.
Number awarded: 2 each year.
Deadline: March of each year.

Scholarship Listings

96
ASLA STUDENT ADVANTAGE SCHOLARSHIP

Arkansas Student Loan Authority
101 East Capitol Avenue, Suite 401
Little Rock, AR 72201
Phone: (800) 443-6030
Web Site: www.asla.state.ar.us/1000_scholarship/index.html
Summary: To provide assistance for college to residents of Arkansas or students attending a postsecondary institution in the state.
Eligibility: This program is open to 1) residents of Arkansas, who may be attending a postsecondary institution in or out of the state, and 2) residents of other states attending a postsecondary institution in Arkansas. Postsecondary educational institutions include 2-year colleges, 4-year colleges and universities, and technical and trade schools. Applicants may enter online or by submitting a postcard with their name, address, telephone number, and name of their educational institution. Winners are selected at random.
Financial data: The stipend is $1,000. Funds are mailed to the financial aid office at the designated school.
Duration: 1 year.
Number awarded: 5 each year.
Deadline: March of each year.

97
ASSISTANCE FOR SURVIVING CHILDREN OF NAVAL PERSONNEL DECEASED AFTER RETIREMENT (CDR)

Navy-Marine Corps Relief Society
Attn: Education Division
801 North Randolph Street, Suite 1228
Arlington, VA 22203-1978
Phone: (703) 696-4960   Fax: (703) 696-0144
E-mail: education@hq.nmcrs.org
Web Site: www.nmcrs.org
Summary: To provide financial assistance for the postsecondary education of children of Navy or Marine Corps personnel who died as a result of disabilities or length of service.
Eligibility: Eligible for this assistance are the unmarried, dependent children, stepchildren, or legally adopted children under the age of 23 of deceased members of the Navy or Marine Corps who died after retirement due to disability or length of service.
Financial data: Grants up to $2,000 per year are available.
Additional information: This program is limited to undergraduate studies and vocational training.
Number awarded: Varies each year.
Deadline: June of each year.

98
ASSISTANCE FOR SURVIVING CHILDREN OF NAVAL PERSONNEL DECEASED WHILE ON ACTIVE DUTY (CDAD)

Navy-Marine Corps Relief Society
Attn: Education Division
801 North Randolph Street, Suite 1228
Arlington, VA 22203-1978
Phone: (703) 696-4960   Fax: (703) 696-0144
E-mail: education@hq.nmcrs.org
Web Site: www.nmcrs.org
Summary: To provide financial assistance for the postsecondary education of children of deceased Navy or Marine Corps personnel.
Eligibility: Eligible for this assistance are the unmarried, dependent children, stepchildren, or legally adopted children under the age of 23 of members of the Navy or Marine Corps who died while on active duty. Applicants must possess a current valid dependents' Uniformed Services Identification and Privilege Card.
Financial data: Under this program, the Navy-Marine Corps Relief Society provides assistance through a combination of interest free loans and grants. The amount of assistance is determined by the needs and circumstances of each individual.
Additional information: This program is limited to undergraduate studies and vocational training.
Number awarded: Varies each year.
Deadline: June of each year.

99
ASSOCIATION OF BLIND CITIZENS SCHOLARSHIP

Association of Blind Citizens
P.O. Box 246
Holbrook, MA 02343
Phone: (781) 961-1023   Fax: (519) 275-6713
E-mail: president@assocofblindcitizens.org
Web Site: www.assocofblindcitizens.org
Summary: To provide financial assistance for college to individuals who are blind or visually impaired.
Eligibility: Eligible to apply for this support are high school seniors, high school graduates, and currently-enrolled college students who are blind or visually impaired. They must be interested in working on a college degree. To apply, students must submit a 500-word biography, indicating how the scholarship award would help them achieve their goal of attending college; a high school or college transcript; a certificate of legal blindness or a letter from their ophthalmologist; and 2 letters of reference.
Financial data: The stipend is $1,000. Funds may be used to pay for tuition, accommodations, or related expenses resulting from vision impairment.
Duration: 1 year.
Additional information: Recipients may attend any type of postsecondary institution, including vocational and technical schools.
Number awarded: 1 each year.
Deadline: April of each year.

100
AUDRE LORDE SCHOLARSHIP

ZAMI, Inc.
P.O. Box 2502
Decatur, GA 30031
Phone: (404) 370-0920   E-mail: zami@zami.org
Web Site: www.zami.org/scholarship.htm
Summary: To provide financial assistance to lesbians of African descent who are entering or attending a college in the southeast.
Eligibility: This program is open to "out" lesbians of African descent who are graduating high school seniors or enrolled in a technical, undergraduate, or graduate program located in 1 of the following states: Georgia, Florida, Mississippi, Louisiana, South Carolina, North Carolina, Tennessee, Alabama, Arkansas, Texas, Virginia, and Kentucky. Applicants must have at least a 2.5 grade point average. Priority is given to lesbians who are over 40 years of age.
Financial data: The stipend is $1,000.
Duration: 1 year.
Additional information: This fund was established in 1995; the first scholarships were awarded in 1997.
Number awarded: Up to 10 each year.

101
AUTOMOTIVE EDUCATIONAL FUND SCHOLARSHIP PROGRAM

Automotive Hall of Fame
Attn: Automotive Educational Fund
21400 Oakwood Boulevard
Dearborn, MI 48124
Phone: (313) 240-4000   Fax: (313) 240-8641
Web Site: www.automotivehalloffame.org
Summary: To provide funding to undergraduate and graduate students who are interested in preparing for an automotive career upon graduation from college (regardless of their major).
Eligibility: This program is open to 1) high school seniors who have been accepted to an 18-month or 2-year program, and 2) current undergraduate or graduate students who have completed at least 1 year at a 4-year institution. Applicants must have a sincere interest in pursuing an automotive career upon graduation, regardless of their major (except divinity and pre-med). Financial need is not a requirement.
Financial data: Stipends range from $250 to $2,000. Funds are sent to the recipient's institution.
Duration: 1 year; may be renewed.
Additional information: The following scholarships are part of this program: Universal Underwriters Scholarship, M.H. Yager Memorial Scholarship, J. Irving Whalley Memorial Scholarship, Walter W. Stillman Scholarship, John E. Echlin Memorial Scholarship, TRW Foundation Scholarship, Charles V. Hagler

Memorial Scholarship, John W. Koons, Sr., Memorial Scholarship, Harold D. Draper, Sr., Memorial Scholarship, Dr. Dorothy M. Ross Scholarship, Zenon C.R. Hansen Memorial Scholarship, John Goerlich Memorial Scholarship, Larry H. Averill Memorial Scholarship, Brouwer D. McIntyre Memorial Scholarship, Carlyle Fraser Fund Scholarship in Honor of Wilton D. Looney, and Ken Krum-Bud Kouts Memorial Scholarship.

Number awarded: Varies; generally, 26 to 30 each year.

Deadline: May of each year.

102
AUTOMOTIVE RECYCLERS ASSOCIATION SCHOLARSHIPS

Automotive Recyclers Association
Attn: ARA Scholarship Foundation
3975 Fair Ridge Drive, Suite 20
Terrace Level North
Fairfax, VA 22033-2924
Phone: (703) 385-1001   (888) 385-1005
Fax: (703) 385-1494   E-mail: badillo@autorecyc.org
Web Site: www.autorecyc.org

Summary: To provide financial assistance for college to children of employees of direct members of the Automotive Recyclers Association (ARA).

Eligibility: This program is open to high school seniors and college students whose parent is a current employee of a direct member of the association with a hire date at least 1 year prior to March 15 of the application year. First-time applicants must have earned at least a 3.0 grade point average in their previous educational program. Selection is based on academic achievement; financial need is not considered.

Financial data: The stipend is $1,000 per year.

Duration: 1 year; may be renewed as long as the recipient maintains at least a 2.5 grade point average.

Additional information: Information is also available from the ARA Scholarship Advisor, 1299 Caldwell Court, Sunnyvale, CA 94087.

Number awarded: 50 each year.

Deadline: March of each year.

103
AWARD OF EXCELLENCE ASTHMA SCHOLARSHIPS

American Academy of Allergy, Asthma & Immunology
611 East Wells Street
Milwaukee, WI 53202-3889
Phone: (414) 272-6071   (800) 822-2762
Fax: (414) 272-6070   E-mail: info@aaaai.org
Web Site: www.aaaai.org

Summary: To provide financial assistance for college to high school seniors with asthma.

Eligibility: This program is open to U.S. citizens who are graduating high school seniors with asthma. Applicants must submit a high school transcript, a letter of recommendation from a principal or guidance counselor, and a 1-page essay on how the student manages asthma while continuing to accomplish education and career goals. Selection is based on academic achievement, extracurricular activities, and community service.

Financial data: The stipend is $1,000 per year.

Duration: 1 year; nonrenewable.

Additional information: This program includes 1 scholarship designated as the Tanner McQuiston Scholarship.

Number awarded: 16 each year.

Deadline: January of each year.

104
AYERS/GALLATIN ENDOWMENT SCHOLARSHIP

Epsilon Sigma Alpha
Attn: ESA Foundation Assistant Scholarship Director
P.O. Box 270517
Fort Collins, CO 80527
Phone: (970) 223-2824   Fax: (970) 223-4456
Web Site: www.esaintl.com/esaf

Summary: To provide financial assistance for college to students from any state studying any major.

Eligibility: Applicants may be either 1) graduating high school seniors in the top 25 percent of their class or with minimum scores of 20 on the ACT or 950 on the SAT, or 2) students already enrolled in college with a grade point average of 3.0 or higher. Students enrolled for training in a technical school or returning to school

after an absence are also eligible. Selection is based on character, scholastic ability, leadership and ability skills, and financial need.

Financial data: The stipend is $1,000.

Duration: 1 year; may be renewed.

Additional information: Epsilon Sigma Alpha (ESA) is a women's service organization, but scholarships are available to both men and women. Information is also available from Verneene Forssberg, 403 South High, Pratt, KS 67124, (316) 672-3636, Fax: (316) 672-3688, E-mail: vernf@genmail.pcc.cc.ks.us. Completed applications must be submitted to the ESA State Counselor who verifies the information before forwarding them to the scholarship director.

Number awarded: 1 each year.

Deadline: January of each year.

105
BANK OF NEW HAMPSHIRE LEAP SCHOLARSHIPS

New Hampshire Charitable Foundation
37 Pleasant Street
Concord, NH 03301-4005
Phone: (603) 225-6641   (800) 464-6641
Fax: (603) 225-1700   E-mail: info@nhcf.org
Web Site: www.nhcf.org

Summary: To provide financial assistance for college to graduating high school seniors in New Hampshire.

Eligibility: This program is open to seniors at high schools in New Hampshire who will be enrolling full time in a postsecondary institution. Selection is based on financial need, academic achievement, involvement in school activities, community volunteer activity, and work experience.

Financial data: The stipend is $2,500 per year.

Duration: 1 year.

Additional information: This program is offered by Bank of New Hampshire as part of its Local Educational Advancement Programs (LEAP). Recipients are also offered 3-month paid internships with the bank during the summer after their first year of postsecondary education. Further information is available from the bank at (800) 922-5705.

Number awarded: 9 each year.

Deadline: March of each year.

106
BARKING FOUNDATION SCHOLARSHIPS

Barking Foundation
Attn: Executive Director
49 Florida Avenue
P.O. Box 855
Bangor, ME 04402-0885
Phone: (207) 990-2910   Fax: (207) 990-2975
E-mail: info@barkingfoundation.org
Web Site: www.barkingfoundation.org

Summary: To provide financial assistance to residents of Maine for education at the undergraduate, graduate, and postgraduate level.

Eligibility: This program is open to students who have been residents of Maine for at least 4 years and are interested in pursuing higher education anywhere in the United States. Applicants may be entering college, already enrolled in college, pursuing a graduate degree, or studying at the postgraduate level. They must submit an essay, up to 750 words, describing a challenge or adventure in their life. Selection is based on financial need; academic, community, organizational, and co-curricular accomplishments; character; demonstrated values; potential and aspirations; and references.

Financial data: The stipend is $3,000.

Duration: 1 year; may be renewed for 1 additional year.

Number awarded: Approximately 25 each year.

Deadline: February of each year.

107
BASEBALL LEADERSHIP SCHOLARSHIP

American Legion
Attn: Americanism and Children & Youth Division
P.O. Box 1055
Indianapolis, IN 46206-1055
Phone: (317) 630-1249   Fax: (317) 630-1223
E-mail: acy@legion.org
Web Site: www.legion.org

Summary: To recognize and reward outstanding participants in the American Legion baseball program.

Eligibility: Eligible are participants in the American Legion baseball program who are high school graduates or college freshmen. In each of the 50 states and Puerto Rico, the department baseball committee selects a player who demonstrates outstanding leadership, citizenship, character, scholarship, and financial need.

Financial data: The award is a $5,000 scholarship. Funds are disbursed jointly to the winner and the school.

Duration: Students have 4 years to utilize the scholarship funds from the date of the award, excluding any time spent on active military duty.

Additional information: The scholarship may be used for summer college classes or graduate work. Students may attend any college or university that is accredited, above the high school level, and within the continental limits of the United States (unless the winner is from a possession of the United States, in which case he can select a school in that possession or in the continental United States).

Number awarded: 51 each year: 1 in each state and Puerto Rico.

108
BCTGM SCHOLARSHIPS

Bakery, Confectionery, Tobacco Workers and Grain Millers International Union
Attn: Scholarship Program
10401 Connecticut Avenue, 4th Floor
Kensington, MD 20895-3961
Phone: (301) 933-8600   Fax: (301) 946-8452

Summary: To provide financial assistance for college to members and children of members of the Bakery, Confectionery, Tobacco Workers and Grain Millers (BCTGM) International Union.

Eligibility: Applicants must have an affiliation with the union: a member in good standing; the son, daughter, stepchild or legally adopted child of a union member; the child of a deceased union member who had at least 5 years of membership; a member or child of a member who retired as a union member; or an employee or child of an employee at the International Union office. They must be 1) high school students planning to enter a postsecondary institution for the first time following their graduation, 2) high school graduates who have never attended college or a recognized technical/vocational school, or 3) members who have never applied for union support and are currently enrolled in college or planning to resume their college studies. All applicants must take the SAT or a recognized equivalent. In addition, they must write an essay, from 500 to 750 words, on "Organized Labor's Contribution to the Welfare of North America" or a related topic. Scholarships are not available to applicants who do not intend to work without interruption for a bachelor's degree; to members' children who are or have already attended college; to graduate students (except members); to spouses of members; or to grandchildren of members.

Financial data: The stipend is $1,000 per year. The money is paid directly to the recipient's school.

Duration: 1 year; nonrenewable.

Number awarded: 20 each year; at least 1 of the 20 scholarships is designated for a Canadian and at least 5 are designated for members.

Deadline: January of each year.

109
BEACON BRIGHTER TOMORROWS SCHOLARSHIP

Rhode Island Foundation
Attn: Scholarship Coordinator
One Union Station
Providence, RI 02903
Phone: (401) 274-4564   Fax: (401) 331-8085
E-mail: libbym@rifoundation.org
Web Site: www.rifoundation.org

Summary: To provide financial assistance for college to spouses and dependents of workers insured by Beacon Mutual Insurance Company who were killed or permanently disabled in industrial accidents.

Eligibility: This program is open to spouses and/or legal dependents of workers insured by the company who were killed or permanently disabled in an industrial accident. Applicants must have been accepted into an accredited postsecondary institution on a full- or part-time basis. The must submit an essay (up to 300 words) on what they hope they will be doing in their professional life 10 years from now. Financial need is considered in the selection process.

Financial data: Stipends range from $1,000 to $2,000.

Number awarded: 1 to 2 each year.

Deadline: May of each year.

110
"BEEN THERE, DONE THAT" NATIONAL CONTEST

Princeton Review Management, L.L.C.
Attn: Contest Administrator
2315 Broadway
New York, NY 10024-4332
Phone: (800) 2-REVIEW   E-mail: info@review.com
Web Site: www.review.com

Summary: To recognized and reward outstanding essays by high school students on "What Every Student Should Know About Surviving High School."

Eligibility: Only high school students in North America may enter this competition. They are invited to submit an essay, poem, song, story, or comic strip (up to 1,000 words) on "What Every Student Should Know About Surviving High School." Entries must be in English and, except for comics, must be typed or computer printed. Contestants must also complete an entry form. Entries are judged on creativity, expression, and content.

Financial data: Winners receive a $1,000 college scholarship, a free Princeton Review SAT or ACT prep course, and a year's subscription to *TIME Magazine.* Each winning entry is published on Princeton Review's Internet site: www.review.com.

Duration: The competition is held annually.

Additional information: This contest is sponsored jointly by Princeton Review and TIME Magazine.

Number awarded: 3 scholarship winners each year.

Deadline: April of each year.

111
BEN BALL SCHOLARSHIP

Texas Tennis Foundation
2111 Dickson, Suite 33
Austin, TX 78704-4788
Phone: (512) 443-1334   Fax: (512) 443-4748
Web Site: www.ustatexas.org

Summary: To provide financial assistance for college to students in Texas who have an interest in tennis.

Eligibility: This program is open to students who have an interest in tennis, are U.S. citizens, and live in Texas. They must be high school students who will be entering college or college students who are in good standing at their respective colleges or universities. Financial need must be demonstrated. Qualified students must submit a completed application, federal income tax returns from the previous 2 years, an academic transcript, a copy of their SAT or ACT test results, a list of extracurricular activities (including tennis activities), a personal statement, and a letter of recommendation. Selection is based on merit and financial need.

Financial data: The stipend is $1,000.

Duration: 1 year.

Additional information: This program was established in 1983. Recipients must attend school on a full-time basis. They must send a brief written report following their first semester of the scholarship year; this report should indicate their educational achievements during the semester, tennis activities if any, and goals for the second semester.

Number awarded: 2 each year.

Deadline: April of each year.

112
BEN SELLING SCHOLARSHIP

Oregon Student Assistance Commission
Attn: Private Awards Grant Department
1500 Valley River Drive, Suite 100
Eugene, OR 97401-2146
Phone: (541) 687-7395   (800) 452-8807, ext. 7395
Fax: (541) 687-7419   E-mail: awardinfo@mercury.osac.state.or.us
Web Site: www.osac.state.or.us

Summary: To provide financial assistance for college to residents of Oregon.

Eligibility: This program is open to residents of Oregon who are entering their sophomore or higher years in college. Applicants must have a cumulative grade point average of 3.5 or higher.

Financial data: Scholarship amounts vary, depending upon the needs of the recipient.

Duration: 1 year.

Number awarded: Varies each year.

Deadline: February of each year.

113
BENJAMIN EATON SCHOLARSHIPS

National Foster Parent Association
Attn: Information and Services Office
P.O. Box 81
Alpha, OH 45301-0081
Phone: (800) 557-5238   Fax: (937) 431-9377
E-mail: nfpa@donet.com
Web Site: www.nfpainc.org/scholrsp.html
Summary: To assist students whose families are members of the National Foster Parent Association and who are interested in attending college or vocational school.
Eligibility: This program is open to students who are in foster care at the time of application; are entering the first year of college or its equivalent (including vocational school, job training, correspondence studies, or GED work); and reside with an association member family. Adopted children and birth children of foster parents are also eligible. Students entering a college or university must be high school seniors (regardless of age); students entering vocational or equivalent training must be at least 17 years of age, whether in or out of school. All applicants must submit a statement (300 to 500 words) on why they want to further their education and why they should be considered for this scholarship. Financial need is considered in the selection process.
Financial data: The amount awarded varies, depending upon the need of the recipient and the funds available each year.
Duration: 1 year.
Additional information: This scholarship is named in memory of Benjamin Eaton who, in 1636 at the age of 7, became the nation's first recorded foster child.
Number awarded: Varies each year; recently, 5 of these scholarships were awarded.
Deadline: March of each year.

114
BENJAMIN FRANKLIN/EDITH GREEN SCHOLARSHIP

Oregon Student Assistance Commission
Attn: Private Awards Grant Department
1500 Valley River Drive, Suite 100
Eugene, OR 97401-2146
Phone: (541) 687-7395   (800) 452-8807, ext. 7395
Fax: (541) 687-7419   E-mail: awardinfo@mercury.osac.state.or.us
Web Site: www.osac.state.or.us
Summary: To provide financial assistance for college to graduating high school seniors in Oregon.
Eligibility: This program is open to seniors graduating from high schools in Oregon. Applicants must be planning to attend a 4-year college or university in Oregon.
Financial data: Scholarship amounts vary, depending upon the needs of the recipient.
Duration: 1 year; nonrenewable.
Number awarded: Varies each year.
Deadline: February of each year.

115
BESSIE COLEMAN SCHOLARSHIP AWARD

The Weekly
Attn: Coleman Scholarship
P.O. Box 151789
Dallas, TX 75315
Phone: (214) 428-8958   Fax: (214) 428-2807
E-mail: theweeklysks@earthlink.net
Summary: To provide financial assistance to high school seniors planning to attend an historically African American college or university.
Eligibility: This program is open to high school seniors who are interested in attending an historically African American college or university. As part of the application process, students must write an essay (700 to 1,500 words) comparing themselves to Bessie Coleman (the first African American to receive an international pilots license) and indicating how they plan to "make a name" for themselves in their chosen profession. Neither income nor grade point average is considered in the selection process.
Financial data: The stipend is $5,000.
Duration: 1 year.
Additional information: This program is sponsored jointly by The Weekly and American Airlines.
Number awarded: 2 each year: 1 to a male and 1 to a female.
Deadline: January of each year.

116
BETTY HANSEN NATIONAL SCHOLARSHIPS

Danish Sisterhood of America
Attn: Scholarship Chair
7326 Lehigh Court
Zephryhills, FL 34540-1014
Phone: (813) 715-0642
Web Site: danishsisterhood.org/html/scholarships.html
Summary: To provide financial assistance for educational purposes to members or relatives of members of the Danish Sisterhood of America.
Eligibility: This program is open to members or the family of members of the sisterhood who are interested in attending an accredited 4-year college or university as an undergraduate or graduate student. Members must have belonged to the sisterhood for at least 1 year. Selection is based on academic excellence (at least a 2.5 grade point average). Upon written request, the scholarship may be used for study in Denmark.
Financial data: The stipend is $1,000.
Duration: 1 year; nonrenewable.
Number awarded: Up to 10 each year.
Deadline: February of each year.

117
BIA HIGHER EDUCATION GRANT PROGRAM

Bureau of Indian Affairs
Attn: Office of Indian Education Programs
1849 C Street, N.W.
MS 3512-MIB
Washington, DC 20240
Phone: (202) 219-1127
Web Site: www.doi.gov/bureau-indian-affairs.html
Summary: To provide financial assistance for postsecondary education to undergraduate and graduate students who belong to federally-recognized Indian tribes.
Eligibility: This program is open to federally-recognized Indian tribal governments and tribal organizations. Individuals who are members of federally-recognized Indian tribes may submit applications directly to the Bureau of Indian Affairs (BIA) if the agency serving their reservation provides direct services for this program. Individual applicants must be enrolled or planning to enroll in an accredited college or university and must be able to demonstrate financial need. Priority is given to students residing near or within the boundary of an Indian reservation. Graduate study is included only if money is available after all qualified undergraduate students have been funded. All students must achieve and maintain a cumulative grade point average of at least 2.0.
Financial data: Individual awards depend on the financial need of the recipient; they range from $300 to $5,000 and average $2,800 per year. Recently, a total of $20,290,000 was available for this program.
Duration: 1 year; may be renewed for up to 4 additional years.
Additional information: Funds may be used for either part-time or full-time study. This program was authorized by the Snyder Act of 1921.
Number awarded: Approximately 9,500 students receive assistance through this program annually.
Deadline: June of each year for fall term; October of each year for spring term; April of each year for summer school.

118
BIG Y 50TH ANNIVERSARY EMPLOYEE COMMEMORATIVE SCHOLARSHIPS

Big Y Foods, Inc.
Attn: Scholarship Committee
P.O. Box 7840
Springfield, MA 01102-7840
Phone: (413) 504-4062
Web Site: www.bigy.com
Summary: To provide financial assistance to outstanding undergraduate and graduate students in the Big Y Foods market area (Massachusetts and Connecticut).
Eligibility: This program is open to high school seniors, college students, and graduate students of any age who reside within western and central Massachusetts or the state of Connecticut. Big Y employees and their dependents are also eligible to apply. Applicants must submit a transcript, standardized test scores, 2 letters of recommendation, and a completed application form.

Financial data: The stipend is $1,000.
Duration: 1 year; nonrenewable.
Number awarded: 6 each year.
Deadline: January of each year.

119
BIG 33 SCHOLARSHIPS

Big 33 Scholarship Foundation
511 Bridge Street
P.O. Box 213
New Cumberland, PA 17070
Phone: (717) 774-3303   (877) PABIG-33
Fax: (717) 774-1749   E-mail: info@big33.org
Web Site: www.big33.org/scholarships.index.shtml
Summary: To provide financial assistance for college to graduating high school seniors in Ohio and Pennsylvania.
Eligibility: This program is open to seniors graduating from high schools in Ohio and Pennsylvania. Applications are available from high school guidance counselors. Selection is based on special talents, leadership, obstacles overcome, academic achievement (at least a 2.0 grade point average), community service, unique endeavors, financial need, and a 1-page essay on why the applicant deserves the scholarship.
Financial data: Stipends up to $5,000 are available, but most are $1,000.
Duration: 1 year; nonrenewable.
Additional information: Funds for this program are raised by the foundation through its sponsorship of an annual high school All-Star football game.
Number awarded: Varies each year; recently, 188 of these scholarships were awarded: 1 at $5,000, 2 at $1,600, 1 at $1,500, 134 at $1,000, 1 at $700, 1 at $650, 34 at $500, and 14 for odd amounts less than $500.
Deadline: February of each year.

120
BILL & BARBARA HOLTHAUS FAMILY 4-H SCHOLARSHIP

Colorado 4-H Youth Development Program
c/o Colorado State University Cooperative Extension
Jefferson County Extension Office
15200 West Sixth Avenue, Suite C
Golden, CO 80501-5018
Phone: (303) 271-6620
Summary: To provide financial assistance to high school seniors who are members of the Colorado 4-H and interested in attending college in the state.
Eligibility: This program is open to incoming freshmen currently enrolled as Colorado 4-H members who have completed a minimum of 3 years of 4-H work prior to the current year. Selection is based on leadership and citizenship involvement, 4-H achievements, and academic potential.
Financial data: The stipend is $1,000.
Duration: 1 year.
Additional information: Recipients must attend a 4-year college or university in Colorado.
Number awarded: 2 each year.
Deadline: May of each year.

121
BILL MCADAM SCHOLARSHIP FUND

Hemophilia Foundation of Michigan
Attn: Cathy McAdam
22226 Doxtator
Dearborn, MI 48128
Phone: (313) 563-0515   Fax: (313) 563-1412
E-mail: mmcadam@match.org
Summary: To provide financial assistance for college to students with a bleeding disorder or members of their families.
Eligibility: This program is open to 1) students with a bleeding disorder (hemophilia, von Willebrand, etc.) or 2) members of their families (spouse, partner, child, sibling). Applicants must be U.S. citizens and enrolled or planning to enroll at an accredited 2- or 4-year college.
Financial data: The stipend is $2,000.
Duration: 1 year.
Number awarded: 1 each year.
Deadline: May of each year.

122
BILL MOON SCHOLARSHIP PROGRAM

NATSO Foundation
1199 North Fairfax Street, Suite 801
Alexandria, VA 22314
Phone: (703) 549-2100   Fax: (703) 684-9667
E-mail: foundation@natso.com
Web Site: www.natsofoundation.org
Summary: To provide financial assistance for college to travel plaza and truckstop industry employees and their dependents.
Eligibility: This program is open to employees in the travel plaza and truckstop industry and their legal dependents. Selection is based on academic merit, extracurricular and community activities, and a short essay.
Financial data: The stipend is $2,500.
Duration: 1 year.
Additional information: The NATSO Foundation was established by the National Association of Truck Stop Operators in 1990. It began awarding scholarships in 1993.
Number awarded: 12 each year.
Deadline: April of each year.

123
BLACKFEET HIGHER EDUCATION PROGRAM

Blackfeet Nation
Attn: Higher Education Program
P.O. Box 850
Browning, MT 59417
Phone: (406) 338-7539   Fax: (406) 338-7530
E-mail: bhep@3rivers.net
Web Site: www.blackfeetnation.com
Summary: To provide financial assistance for undergraduate education to members of the Blackfeet Tribe.
Eligibility: Applicants must be enrolled members of the Blackfeet Tribe and be enrolled or accepted for enrollment in an academically recognized college or university pursuing an undergraduate degree. They must submit a 1-page letter describing their career goals and academic plans, high school or GED transcripts, college transcripts (if they have previously attended college), a copy of the admission letter from the college or university they plan to attend, a financial needs analysis, and a certificate of degree of Indian blood. Scholarships are awarded according to the following priorities: 1) renewal of grants to students currently funded who are in good academic and financial aid standing and submitted the application packet on time; 2) college seniors not currently funded who can graduate within the current academic year; 3) 2-year degree graduates who apply within 1 year of earning their associates degree; 4) high school seniors who apply within 1 year of earning their high school diploma; 5) applicants previously funded who are in good academic and financial aid standing and submit the application packet in a timely manner; and 6) candidates who submit late applications (supported only if funding permits).
Financial data: The amount awarded varies, depending upon the recipient's educational requirements and financial needs. The maximum for an unmarried student with no dependents is $3,200 per year or $3,800 for a student with 3 or more dependents. Funds are sent to the school's financial aid officer.
Duration: 1 year; may be renewed up to a total of 10 semesters or 15 quarters.
Additional information: Recipients must enroll as full-time students and earn no less than 12 credit hours per term with a grade point average of 2.0 or higher as freshmen, 13 credits and 2.2 as sophomores, 14 credits and 2.4 as juniors, and 15 credits and 2.6 as seniors. Students who attend private schools or institutions outside of Montana must pay the difference in tuition, unless no comparable program exists in Montana public institutions.
Number awarded: Varies each year.
Deadline: February of each year; March of each year for summer term.

124
BLACKHORSE ASSOCIATION SCHOLARSHIPS

Blackhorse Association
c/o Chairperson, Scholarship Committee
P.O. Box 10423
Fort Irwin, CA 92310
E-mail: criderjj@mindspring.com
Web Site: www.11thacr-bha.org

Summary: To provide financial assistance for college to children of former members of the 11th Armored Cavalry (Blackhorse) Regiment.

Eligibility: This program is open to children and stepchildren of former members of the regiment (including the 58th CE and 409th RR). Applicants must be enrolled or planning to enroll in an accredited college or university at the undergraduate level. Preference is given to 1) children of deceased members, 2) children of members who were wounded or otherwise incapacitated while serving the regiment, and 3) applicants who demonstrate financial need.

Financial data: The stipend is $1,500 per year.

Duration: 4 years.

Number awarded: Varies each year.

Deadline: March of each year.

125
BLANCHE NAUGHER FOWLER CHARITABLE SCHOLARSHIP

Blanche Naugher Fowler Charitable Scholarship Trust
c/o AmSouth Bank
2330 University Boulevard
P.O. Box 2028
Tuscaloosa, AL 35403

Summary: To provide financial assistance to undergraduate or graduate students attending colleges or universities in Alabama.

Eligibility: Applications may be submitted by students attending or accepted at a public or private nonprofit college or university (at least a 4-year baccalaureate-level institution) located in Alabama. Applicants must submit an application form, a transcript, a letter of admission or other evidence of acceptance to or enrollment in a school located in Alabama, SAT or ACT test scores, 2 letters of recommendation, a 1-page statement of career goals and aspirations, and a list of all honors, activities, interests, and employment experiences. Financial need is not required, but applicants who wish to be considered on the basis of financial need must also submit a completed College Scholarship Service Financial Aid Form (FAF) and current tax return.

Financial data: A stipend is awarded (exact amount not specified).

Duration: 1 year; may be renewed.

Deadline: March of each year.

126
BOETTCHER FOUNDATION SCHOLARSHIPS

Boettcher Foundation
Attn: Directory, Scholars Program
600 17th Street, Suite 2210 South
Denver, CO 80202-5422
E-mail: scholarships@boettcherfoundation.org
Web Site: www.boettcherfoundation.org

Summary: To provide merit scholarships to Colorado high school seniors who are interested in attending a college or university in the state.

Eligibility: This program is open to seniors who have attended high school in Colorado for at least the last 2 years and are in the upper 5 percent of their graduating class with scores of at least 27 on the ACT or 1200 on the SAT. U.S. citizenship is required. Selection is based on scholastic record, leadership potential, service to community and school, and character. Financial need is not considered.

Financial data: These scholarships provide full tuition and fees at a participating accredited 4-year undergraduate institution in Colorado, a stipend of $2,800 per year to help cover living expenses, and a book allowance. Funds are paid directly to the recipient's institution. Each college or university receives $1,000 per scholar per year attending that school to fund special opportunities and programs for the scholars. In addition, all scholars nominate 1 teacher who has had a special influence on their lives; nominees each receive $1,000 to be used at their home schools. Scholars may choose to exchange half of 1 year's scholarship for a $5,500 international education grant to be used for a study abroad program arranged through their college or university.

Duration: These are 4-year scholarships, but they are not renewed annually if the recipient fails to maintain a 3.0 GPA.

Additional information: The participating institutions are Adams State College, Colorado Christian University, Colorado College, Colorado School of Mines, Colorado State University, Fort Lewis College, Mesa State College, Metropolitan State University, Regis University, University of Colorado at Boulder, University of Colorado at Colorado Springs, University of Colorado at Denver, University of Denver, University of Northern Colorado, University of Southern Colorado, and Western State College. These funds may not be used for study outside Colorado. Except in unusual circumstances, the recipient is expected to carry a minimum course load of 12 credit hours.

Number awarded: 40 each year.

Deadline: November of each year.

127
BOOTSTRAP SCHOLARSHIP

Arizona Community Foundation
2122 East Highland Avenue, Suite 400
Phoenix, AZ 85016
Phone: (602) 381-1400   (800) 222-8221
Fax: (602) 381-1575
Web Site: www.azfoundation.org

Summary: To provide financial assistance to high school seniors in Arizona who are single parents and interested in attending a community college.

Eligibility: This program is open to Arizona high school seniors who are single parents, can demonstrate financial need, have a determination to succeed, have earned at least a 2.75 grade point average, and agree to a mentoring commitment. They must be interested in attending a community college in Arizona.

Financial data: The stipend is $2,000 per year.

Duration: 1 or more years.

128
BPW FOUNDATION OF MARYLAND SCHOLARSHIP

Maryland Federation of Business and Professional Women's Clubs, Inc.
c/o Donna Smith
11204 Eastwood Drive
Hagerstown, MD 21742
Phone: (410) 569-2100   (877) INFO BPW
E-mail: marynov@erols.com
Web Site: www.bpwmaryland.org/HTML/scholarships.html

Summary: To provide financial assistance for college to mature women in Maryland.

Eligibility: This program is open to women in Maryland who are at least 25 years of age and who are interested in pursuing undergraduate studies to upgrade their skills for career advancement, to train for a new career field, or to reenter the job market. Priority is given to women interested in entering such nontraditional fields as engineering, business management, and the health sciences.

Financial data: The stipend is $1,000.

Duration: 1 year.

Number awarded: 1 or more each year.

129
BRISTOL-MYERS SQUIBB ONCOLOGY/IMMUNOLOGY SCHOLARSHIP

Patient Advocate Foundation
753 Thimble Shoals Boulevard, Suite B
Newport News, VA 23606
Phone: (800) 532-5274   Fax: (757) 873-8999
E-mail: help@patientadvocate.org
Web Site: www.patientadvocate.org

Summary: To provide financial assistance for college to individuals who are cancer survivors or are living with AIDS/HIV.

Eligibility: Eligible to apply for this scholarship are individuals seeking to initiate or complete a course of study that has been interrupted or delayed because of cancer or AIDS/HIV. Applicants must be able to demonstrate financial need, have earned at least a 3.0 grade point average, be enrolled or planning to enroll as a full-time student, and write an essay on why they have chosen their particular field of study.

Financial data: The stipend is $5,000.

Duration: 1 year.

Additional information: Recipients must pursue a course of study that will make them immediately employable after graduation.

Number awarded: 1 each year.

Deadline: April of each year.

130
BROOME & ALLEN BOYS CAMP AND SCHOLARSHIP FUND

American Sephardi Federation
Attn: Scholarship and Education Committee
15 West 16th Street
New York, NY 10011
Phone: (212) 294-8350   Fax: (212) 294-8348
Web Site: www.amsephfed.org

Summary: To provide financial assistance for undergraduate and graduate studies to Sephardic Jews in America.

Eligibility: Eligible to apply for this support are high school students, currently-enrolled college students (including students enrolled in trade or business schools), college graduates, and currently-enrolled graduate students who are of Sephardic Jewish descent. Selection is based on academic achievement, extracurricular activities, school commendations, and financial need.
Financial data: Awards vary, depending upon the needs of the recipient.
Duration: 1 year; recipients may reapply.
Number awarded: Varies each year.
Deadline: May of each year.

131
BUDDY PELLETIER SURFING FOUNDATION SCHOLARSHIP

Buddy Pelletier Surfing Foundation Fund
P.O. Box 671
Morehead City, NC 28557
Phone: (252) 727-7917   Fax: (252) 727-7965
Web Site: www.buddy.pelletier.com
Summary: To provide financial assistance for college to high school senior or college surfers.
Eligibility: Applicants must be 1) a surfer, 2) a high school senior or currently enrolled in college, and 3) able to demonstrate both merit and financial need. Official transcripts, 2 letters of recommendation, and a short statement (250 to 500 words) on future goals are required.
Financial data: The stipend is $1,000.
Duration: 1 year.
Additional information: This program was started in 1995 after professional surfer Buddy Pelletier waged an unsuccessful battle with cancer.
Number awarded: 3 each year.
Deadline: April of each year.

132
BUENA M. CHESSHIR MEMORIAL WOMEN'S EDUCATIONAL SCHOLARSHIP

Virginia Business and Professional Women's Foundation
P.O. Box 4842
McLean, VA 22103-4842
E-mail: bpwva@advocate.net
Web Site: www.bpwva.advocate.net/foundation.htm
Summary: To provide financial assistance to mature women in Virginia who are interested in upgrading their skills or education at an academic institution in the state.
Eligibility: Applicants must be Virginia residents, U.S. citizens, and at least 25 years of age. They must be accepted into an accredited program or course of study at a Virginia institution and have a definite plan to use the desired training to improve their chances for upward mobility in the work force. Selection is based on demonstrated financial need and defined career goals.
Financial data: Scholarships range from $100 to $1,000 and may be used for tuition, fees, books, transportation, living expenses, and dependent care.
Duration: Recipients must complete their course of study within 2 years.
Additional information: Scholarships may not be used for study at the doctoral level except for law and medicine.
Number awarded: 1 or more each year.
Deadline: March of each year.

133
BUFFETT FOUNDATION SCHOLARSHIP PROGRAM

Buffett Foundation
Attn: Scholarship Office
P.O. Box 4508
Decatur, IL 62525
Phone: (402) 451-6011   E-mail: buffettfound@aol.com
Web Site: www.BuffettScholarships.org
Summary: To provide financial assistance to entering or currently-enrolled college students in Nebraska.
Eligibility: This program is open to U.S. citizens who are Nebraska residents. Applicants must be entering or currently enrolled in a Nebraska state school or a 2-year college or trade school in Nebraska. They must be in financial need, be the only family member presently receiving a grant from the foundation, have at least a 2.5 grade point average, and have applied for federal financial aid. Selection is based on academic performance and financial need. Preference is shown to minority students, students with disabilities, and married or unmarried students with dependents.

Financial data: Up to $2,300 per semester. Funds are sent directly to the recipient's school and must be used to pay tuition and fees; funds may not be used to pay for books or other expenses.
Duration: Up to 5 years for a 4-year college, or up to 3 years for a 2-year school. Students on scholarship may not drop out for a period of time and be reinstated as a scholarship recipient; they must reapply along with first-time students.
Additional information: Students on a 12-month program or the quarter system may use the scholarship for summer tuition; students on the semester system may not use funds for summer school. Students who are not working must enroll in at least 12 credit hours; students who are working must enroll in at least 9 credit hours.
Deadline: Generally, April of each year.

134
CAEF SCHOLARSHIPS

Chinese-American Educational Foundation
Attn: Scholarship Committee
P.O. Box 728
San Mateo, CA 94401-0728
Summary: To provide financial assistance to undergraduate (upper division) and graduate students of Chinese descent.
Eligibility: Applicants must be Chinese Americans, U.S. citizens or permanent residents, and enrolled full time as college juniors, college seniors, or graduate students at the time the award is received. They must have at least a "B" grade point average. All scholarship awards are based on merit.
Financial data: Graduate stipends are $1,500; undergraduate stipends are $1,000 per year.
Duration: 1 year.
Additional information: Applicants must include a self-addressed stamped postcard in their packet. Recipients must attend an accredited institution.
Number awarded: 9 each year: 7 undergraduate awards and 2 graduate student awards.
Deadline: March of each year.

135
CAL GRANT A

California Student Aid Commission
Attn: Grant Programs Customer Service
10811 International Drive
P.O. Box 419027
Rancho Cordova, CA 95741-9027
Phone: (916) 526-7590   (888) CA-GRANT
Fax: (916) 526-8002   E-mail: custsvcs@csac.ca.gov
Web Site: www.csac.ca.gov
Summary: To provide financial assistance to low- and middle-income students in California who need help to pay tuition/fee costs.
Eligibility: This program is open to California residents who are U.S. citizens or eligible noncitizens, have financial need, are attending a qualifying college in California at least half time, are in a program of study leading directly to an undergraduate degree or certificate, do not possess a bachelor's degree prior to receiving a Cal Grant award, and do not owe a refund on any state or federal educational grant or have defaulted on a student loan. They must complete and file both the Free Application for Federal Student Aid and grade point average verification forms. Selection is based on financial need and grade point average. The income ceiling for dependent students and independent students with dependents other than a spouse is $76,500 with 6 or more family members, $70,900 with 5 family members, $66,200 with 4 family members, $60,900 with 3 family members, or $59,400 with 2 family members. For independent students, the income ceiling is $27,800 for married students with no dependents other than a spouse or $24,300 for single students. The asset ceiling is $51,200 for dependent students or $24,400 for independent students. All graduating high school seniors in California who have a grade point average of 3.0 or higher, meet the Cal Grant financial and academic requirements, and apply on time receive a Cal Grant A Entitlement Award. Other eligible students who have a grade point average of 3.0 or higher may apply for a Cal Grant A Competitive Award; selection of those is based on family income, parents' educational level, grade point average, time out of high school, and whether or not the applicant comes from a single-parent household. The performance standards and resources available to the applicant's high school may also be taken into account.
Financial data: Grants provide full payment of tuition and fees at campuses of

the University of California ($3,429 per year) and the California State University system ($1,428). At independent colleges and universities in California, up to $9,708 for tuition and fees is available. Students who qualify for a Cal Grant A and want to attend a California community college may reserve a tuition/fee award for up to 3 years until they transfer to a tuition/fee charging college.

Duration: 1 year; may be renewed up to 3 additional years. Students in a teaching credential or mandatory 5-year program may apply for a fifth year of support.

Additional information: Students who did not receive 1 of these grants when they graduate from high school and attend a California community college may apply when they transfer to a 4-year institution. They are guaranteed an award if they have a grade point average of 2.4 or higher at the community college, meet the admissions requirements for the qualifying 4-year college or university, meet the Cal Grant eligibility and financial requirements, and are younger than 24 years of age. Students can accept only 1 type of Cal Grant.

Number awarded: Varies each year; recently, 24,300 entitlement and 11,250 competitive grants were awarded. Up to half of the competitive grants are reserved for students transferring from community colleges.

Deadline: High school seniors must apply for an entitlement grant by February of each year. Students entering a community college and applying for a competitive grant must do so by the end of August of each year.

136
CAL GRANT B

California Student Aid Commission
Attn: Grant Programs Customer Service
P.O. Box 419027
Rancho Cordova, CA 95741-9027
Phone: (916) 526-7590   (888) CA-GRANT
Fax: (916) 526-8002   E-mail: custsvcs@csac.ca.gov
Web Site: www.csac.ca.gov

Summary: To provide financial assistance to disadvantaged and low-income students in California who need help to pay tuition/fee costs.

Eligibility: This program is open to California residents who are U.S. citizens or eligible noncitizens, have financial need, are attending a qualifying college in California at least half time, are in a program of study leading to an undergraduate degree or certificate, do not possess a bachelor's degree prior to receiving a Cal Grant award, and do not owe a refund on any state or federal educational grant or have defaulted on a student loan. They must complete and file both the FAFSA and grade point average verification forms. Selection is based on financial need and grade point average. The income ceiling for dependent students and independent students with dependents other than a spouse is $42,000 with 6 or more family members, $38,900 with 5 family members, $34,800 with 4 family members, $31,300 with 3 family members, or $27,800 with 2 family members. For independent students, the income ceiling is $27,800 for married students with no dependents other than a spouse or $24,300 for single students. The asset ceiling is $51,200 for dependent students or $24,400 for independent students. All graduating high school seniors in California who have a grade point average of 2.0 or higher, meet the Cal Grant financial and academic requirements, and apply on time receive a Cal Grant B Entitlement Award. Other eligible students who have a grade point average of 2.0 or higher may apply for a Cal Grant B Competitive Award; selection of those is based on family income, parents' educational level, grade point average, time out of high school, whether or not the applicant comes from a single-parent household, and the performance standards and resources available to the applicant's high school.

Financial data: In the first year of college, these grants provide only an allowance of $1,551 for books and living expenses. When renewed or applied for after the freshman year, grants provide that living allowance plus full payment of tuition and fees at campuses of the University of California ($3,429 per year) and the California State University system ($1,428). At independent colleges and universities in California, up to $9,708 for tuition and fees is available.

Duration: 1 year; may be renewed up to 3 additional years. Students in a teaching credential or mandatory 5-year program may apply for a fifth year of support.

Additional information: Students who did not receive 1 of these grants when they graduate from high school and attend a California community college may apply when they transfer to a 4-year institution. They are guaranteed an award if they have a grade point average of 2.4 or higher at the community college, meet the admissions requirements for the qualifying 4-year college or university, meet the Cal Grant eligibility and financial requirements, and are younger than 24 years of age. Students can accept only 1 type of Cal Grant.

Number awarded: Varies each year; recently, 24,300 entitlement and 11,250 competitive grants were awarded. Up to half of the competitive grants are reserved for students transferring from community colleges.

Deadline: High school seniors must apply for an entitlement grant by February of each year. Students entering a community college and applying for a competitive grant must do so by the end of August of each year.

137
CAL GRANT C

California Student Aid Commission
Attn: Grant Programs Customer Service
P.O. Box 419027
Rancho Cordova, CA 95741-9027
Phone: (916) 526-7590   (888) CA-GRANT
Fax: (916) 526-8002   E-mail: custsvcs@csac.ca.gov
Web Site: www.csac.ca.gov

Summary: To provide financial assistance to vocational school students in California who need help with tuition and training costs.

Eligibility: This program is open to California residents who are U.S. citizens or eligible noncitizens, have financial need, have a high school GPA of 2.0 or higher, are attending a qualifying occupational or vocational training program in California at least half time, are in a program of study that is at least 4 months in length, do not possess a bachelor's degree prior to receiving a Cal Grant award, and do not owe a refund on any state or federal educational grant or have defaulted on a student loan. They must complete and file both the FAFSA and grade point average verification forms. The income ceiling for dependent students and independent students with dependents other than a spouse is $76,500 with 6 or more family members, $70,900 with 5 family members, $66,200 with 4 family members, $60,900 with 3 family members, or $59,400 with 2 family members. For independent students, the income ceiling is $27,800 for married students with no dependents other than a spouse or $24,300 for single students. The asset ceiling is $51,200 for dependent students or $24,400 for independent students.

Financial data: Grants provide $576 for books, tools, and equipment. Students who attend a school other than a California community college may also receive up to $2,596 in assistance.

Duration: 1 year; may be renewed.

Additional information: Students can accept only 1 type of Cal Grant.

Number awarded: Varies each year; recently, 7,761 of these grants were awarded.

Deadline: February of each year.

138
CALIFORNIA FEE WAIVER PROGRAM FOR CHILDREN OF VETERANS

California Department of Veterans Affairs
Attn: Division of Veterans Services
1227 O Street, Room 101
Sacramento, CA 94295-0001
Phone: (916) 503-8397   (800) 952-LOAN (within CA)
Fax: (916) 653-2563   E-mail: ruckergl@cdva.ca.gov
Web Site: www.cdva.ca.gov/service/feewaiver.asp

Summary: To provide financial assistance for postsecondary education to the children of disabled or deceased veterans in California.

Eligibility: Eligible for this program are the children of veterans who either died of a service-connected disability or have a service-connected disability of any level of severity. The applicants must plan to attend a California postsecondary school. California veteran status is not required for this program, although the applicant's income, including the value of support received from the parents, cannot exceed $8,959 annually. Dependents in college who are eligible to receive federal education benefits from the U.S. Department of Veterans Affairs are not eligible for these fee waivers.

Financial data: This program provides for waiver of registration fees to students attending any publicly-supported community or state college or university in California.

Duration: 1 year; may be renewed.

Number awarded: Varies each year.

139
CALIFORNIA FEE WAIVER PROGRAM FOR DEPENDENTS OF DECEASED OR DISABLED NATIONAL GUARD MEMBERS

California Department of Veterans Affairs
Attn: Division of Veterans Services
1227 O Street, Room 101
P.O. Box 942895
Sacramento, CA 94295-0001
Phone: (916) 503-8397   (800) 952-LOAN (within CA)
Fax: (916) 653-2563   E-mail: ruckergl@cdva.ca.gov
Web Site: www.cdva.ca.gov/service/feewaiver.asp
Summary: To provide financial assistance for postsecondary education to dependents of disabled and deceased members of the California National Guard.
Eligibility: Eligible for this program are spouses, children, and unremarried widow(er)s of members of the California National Guard who, in the line of duty and in the active service of the state, were killed, died of a disability, or became permanently disabled.
Financial data: Full-time college students receive a waiver of tuition and registration fees at any publicly-supported community or state college or university in California.
Duration: 1 year; may be renewed.
Number awarded: Varies each year.

140
CALIFORNIA FEE WAIVER PROGRAM FOR DEPENDENTS OF TOTALLY DISABLED VETERANS

California Department of Veterans Affairs
Attn: Division of Veterans Services
1227 O Street, Room 101
P.O. Box 942895
Sacramento, CA 94295-0001
Phone: (916) 503-8397   (800) 952-LOAN (within CA)
Fax: (916) 653-2563   E-mail: ruckergl@cdva.ca.gov
Web Site: www.cdva.ca.gov/service/feewaiver.asp
Summary: To provide financial assistance for the undergraduate education of dependents of disabled and other California veterans.
Eligibility: Eligible for this program are spouses, children, and unremarried widow(er)s of veterans who are currently totally service-connected disabled (or are being compensated for a service-connected disability at a rate of 100 percent) or who died of a service-connected cause or disability. The veteran parent must have served during a qualifying war period and must have been discharged or released from military service under honorable conditions. The child cannot be over 27 years of age (extended to 30 if the student was in the military); there are no age limitations for spouses or surviving spouses. This program does not have an income limit. Dependents in college are not eligible if they are qualified to receive educational benefits from the U.S. Department of Veterans Affairs.
Financial data: Full-time college students receive a waiver of tuition and registration fees at any publicly-supported community or state college or university in California.
Duration: Children of eligible veterans may receive postsecondary benefits until the needed training is completed or until the dependent reaches 27 years of age (extended to 30 if the dependent serves in the armed forces). Widow(er)s and spouses are limited to a maximum of 48 months' full-time training or the equivalent in part-time training.
Number awarded: Varies each year.

141
CALIFORNIA GOVERNOR'S SCHOLARS AWARDS

ScholarShare Investment Board
Attn: State Program Administrator
P.O. Box 942809
Sacramento, CA 94209
Phone: (916) 323-9740
Web Site: www.scholarshare.com/gsp/index.html
Summary: To provide financial assistance for college to high school students in California who achieve high scores on certain examinations in the Standardized Testing and Reporting (STAR) program.
Eligibility: This program is open to students in grades 9 through 11 at comprehensive public high schools in California. To qualify for these awards, students must have attended their school for at least 12 consecutive months and then take all of the following examinations: Stanford 9 Reading, Stanford 9 Mathematics, and California English Language Arts Standards Test. Students who achieve combined scores that rank either in the top 5 percent of all students in their grade level in the state or in the top 10 percent of students in their grade level at their school qualify for these awards. They are notified by the State of California, and they claim their award using the sponsor's web site or a printed form.
Financial data: For each year they achieve a qualifying score, students receive an award of $1,000. They may earn up to $3,000 if they qualify in each year. Funds are invested in an account in the Golden State ScholarShare College Savings Trust where they earn interest until the student enters college. Students may then withdraw the money from their account at any time in their college career. Once withdrawn, the funds must be used immediately for qualified educational expenses (tuition, fees, books, supplies, room, and board).
Duration: When the funds are withdrawn, they become a 1-time award.
Additional information: Recipients may use their award funds any time prior to their 30th birthday. Awards may be used at any postsecondary institution that is eligible to participate in the U.S. Department of Education Federal Title IV financial aid programs, including schools outside the United States. This program was established in 2000. Information is also available from the ScholarShare Program Manager, P.O. Box 60009, Los Angeles, CA 90060-0009, (877) 728-4338.
Number awarded: Varies each year.

142
CALIFORNIA LAW ENFORCEMENT PERSONNEL DEPENDENTS GRANT PROGRAM

California Student Aid Commission
Attn: Specialized Programs
10811 International Drive
P.O. Box 419029
Rancho Cordova, CA 95741-9029
Phone: (916) 526-8276   (888) CA-GRANT
Fax: (916) 526-7977   E-mail: specialized@csac.ca.gov
Web Site: www.csac.ca.gov
Summary: To provide financial assistance for postsecondary education to the dependents of California law enforcement officers who have been totally disabled or killed in the line of duty.
Eligibility: To be eligible, an applicant must be the natural child, adopted child, or spouse of a California peace officer (Highway Patrol, marshal, sheriff, police officer), employee of the Department of Corrections or Youth Authority, or fire fighter whose total disability or death was the result of an accident or injury caused by external violence or physical force incurred in the performance of duty. Applicants must be enrolled in a minimum of 6 units at a California postsecondary institution accredited by the Western Association of Schools and Colleges and be able to demonstrate financial need.
Financial data: The amount of the award depends on the need of the recipient, to a maximum of $9,708 at independent schools and colleges in California, $3,429 at branches of the University of California, or $1,428 at branches of the California State University system.
Duration: 1 academic year; may be renewed for up to 5 additional years at 4-year colleges and universities or up to 3 additional years at community colleges.
Additional information: If the student receives other scholarships or grants, the award may be adjusted or withdrawn, depending upon financial need. Acceptance of work-study, loans, or employment will generally not affect the amount of money offered through this program.
Number awarded: Varies; generally, 7 each year.
Deadline: Applications may be submitted at any time.

143
CALIFORNIA LEAGUE OF FOOD PROCESSORS SCHOLARSHIP PROGRAM

California League of Food Processors
980 Ninth Street, Suite 230
Sacramento, CA 95814
Phone: (916) 444-9260   Fax: (916) 444-2746
Summary: To provide financial assistance for college to the children of employees who work for companies affiliated with the California League of Food Processors (CLFP).
Eligibility: Applicants must be the children of employees who work for companies affiliated with CLFP. They must be accepted at or currently attending an accredited 4-year college or university in California and have earned a cumulative grade point average of 2.5 or higher. All applications must be accompanied by the following items: a transcript of the 2 most recent years of study, 2 letters of recommendation (written within the last 6 months by someone

other than a family member), and a completed application form. Selection is based on academic record (20 percent), extracurricular activities (15 percent), work experience (15 percent), professional and career goals (25 percent), and financial need (25 percent).

Financial data: The stipend is $1,000.

Duration: 1 year.

Number awarded: 7 each year. In addition, the league issues 12 $1,000 scholarships directly to California universities.

Deadline: October of each year.

144
CALIFORNIA LEGION AUXILIARY PAST DEPARTMENT PRESIDENT'S JUNIOR SCHOLARSHIP

American Legion Auxiliary
Attn: Department of California
Veterans War Memorial Building
401 Van Ness Avenue, Room 113
San Francisco, CA 94102-4586
Phone: (415) 861-5092   Fax: (415) 861-8365
E-mail: calegionaux@calegionaux.org
Web Site: www.calegionaux.org/scholarships.html

Summary: To provide financial assistance for college to the children of California veterans who are active in the American Legion Junior Auxiliary.

Eligibility: This program is open to the children, grandchildren, and great-grandchildren of veterans who served in World War I, World War II, Korea, Vietnam, Grenada/Lebanon, Panama, or Desert Shield/Desert Storm who are in their senior year at an accredited high school. Applicants must have been members of the Junior Auxiliary for at least 3 consecutive years and be residents of California (if eligibility for Junior Auxiliary membership is by a current member of the American Legion or Auxiliary in California, the applicant may reside elsewhere). Selection is based on scholastic merit (20 percent); active participation in Junior Auxiliary (15 percent); record of service or volunteerism within the applicant's community, school, and/or unit (35 percent); a brief description of the applicant's desire to pursue a higher education (15 percent); and 3 letters of reference (15 percent).

Financial data: The stipend depends on the availability of funds but ranges from $300 to $1,000.

Duration: 1 year.

Additional information: The recipient must attend college in California.

Number awarded: 1 each year.

Deadline: April of each year.

145
CALIFORNIA LEGION AUXILIARY SCHOLARSHIPS FOR CONTINUING OR REENTRY STUDENTS

American Legion Auxiliary
Attn: Department of California
Veterans War Memorial Building
401 Van Ness Avenue, Room 113
San Francisco, CA 94102-4586
Phone: (415) 861-5092   Fax: (415) 861-8365
E-mail: calegionaux@calegionaux.org
Web Site: www.calegionaux.org/scholarships.html

Summary: To provide financial assistance to California residents who are the children of veterans and require assistance to continue their education.

Eligibility: This program is open to California residents who are the children of veterans of World War I, World War II, Korea, Vietnam, Grenada/Lebanon, Panama, or Desert Shield/Desert Storm. Applicants must be continuing or reentry students at a college or university in California. Selection is based on financial need (30 percent), character (20 percent), scholastic merit (20 percent), Americanism (20 percent), and leadership (10 percent).

Financial data: The stipend is $1,000.

Duration: 1 year.

Number awarded: 2 each year.

Deadline: March of each year.

146
CALIFORNIA MASONIC FOUNDATION EDUCATIONAL SCHOLARSHIPS

California Masonic Foundation
Attn: Scholarship Committee
1111 California Street
San Francisco, CA 94108-2284
Phone: (415) 292-9196   (800) 900-2727
Fax: (415) 776-7170   E-mail: foundation@mhcsf.org
Web Site: www.californiamasons.org

Summary: To provide financial assistance to California high school seniors who are interested in attending college.

Eligibility: This program is open to graduating high school seniors who have been residents of California for at least 1 year and have a grade point average of 3.0 or higher. Applicants must be planning to attend a 2-year or 4-year institution of higher education as a full-time freshman in the following fall. They must be U.S. citizens or permanent residents and able to show evidence of financial need. Along with their application, they must submit a personal essay outlining their background, goals, and scholastic achievements; a copy of their latest high school transcript; 2 letters of recommendation; a copy of the last Federal 1040 income tax return filed by their parents; the FAFSA financial aid application; their SAT or ACT scores; and a copy of their college acceptance letter. Selection is based on academic achievement, applicant essay, and financial need. Preference is given to applicants who have a Masonic relationship or are members of Masonic youth groups.

Financial data: Stipends range from $500 to $2,500 per year.

Duration: 1 year; may be renewed for up to 3 additional years.

Additional information: Requests for applications must be accompanied by a self-addressed stamped envelope.

Number awarded: Varies each year; recently, 80 of these scholarships were awarded.

Deadline: March of each year for new applicants; April of each year for renewal applicants.

147
CALIFORNIA PEACE OFFICERS' MEMORIAL FOUNDATION SCHOLARSHIPS

California Peace Officers' Memorial Foundation
Attn: Scholarship Committee Chair
2495 Natomas Park Drive, Suite 555
Sacramento, CA 95833-2935
Phone: (916) 921-0660   (800) 937-6722
Fax: (916) 614-1875   E-mail: camemorial@prodigy.net
Web Site: www.camemorial.org/scholar.htm

Summary: To provide financial assistance for college to surviving children and spouses of law enforcement officers in California who died in the line of duty.

Eligibility: This program is open to surviving spouses and natural and adopted children of California officers who died in the line of duty, regardless of how long ago. Applicants must be enrolled or planning to enroll in a California postsecondary institution accredited by the Western Association of Schools and Colleges or an out-of-state institution with equivalent accreditation. Financial need is considered in the selection process.

Financial data: A stipend is paid (exact amount not specified).

Duration: 1 year; may be renewed.

Number awarded: 6 each year.

Deadline: March of each year.

148
CALIFORNIA SCOTTISH RITE FOUNDATION MEMORIAL SCHOLARSHIP FUND

California Scottish Rite Foundation
855 Elm Avenue
Long Beach, CA 90813-4491
Phone: (562) 436-7787

Summary: To provide financial assistance for college to California residents.

Eligibility: This program is open to California residents between 17 and 25 years of age who are attending or planning to attend an accredited college or university as a full-time student. Applicants must be able to demonstrate high ideals and ability, strong grades in school (at least a 3.0 grade point average), financial need, and part-time employment. No affiliation with a Masonic-related organization is required.

Financial data: The stipend is $1,500 per year.
Duration: 1 year; may be renewed until graduation if funds permit and the recipient maintains acceptable progress.
Additional information: This program was established in 1966. Requests for applications must be submitted in writing; telephone requests will not be honored.
Number awarded: Varies each year, depending on the availability of funds.
Deadline: March of each year.

149
CALIFORNIA STATE EMPLOYEES ASSOCIATION SCHOLARSHIP GRANT PROGRAM

California State Employees Association
Attn: Foundation
1108 O Street
Sacramento, CA 95814
Phone: (916) 444-8134
Web Site: www.calcsea.org
Summary: To provide financial assistance to the dependent children of members of the California State Employees Association (CSEA) who need education or training to improve future job opportunities.
Eligibility: Applicants must have at least a 3.0 grade point average and be at least a high school senior (although junior college, community college, and/or continuing education students are considered). Their parent or guardian must be a member of CSEA in good standing (active or retired). Financial need must be documented.
Financial data: Stipends range from $500 to $1,000 (the exact amount is determined by the selection committee).
Duration: 1 year; recipients may reapply.
Additional information: Recipients must use the funds for a scholastic or vocational course of study.
Number awarded: Several each year.
Deadline: March of each year.

150
CALIFORNIA TEACHERS ASSOCIATION SCHOLARSHIPS FOR DEPENDENT CHILDREN

California Teachers Association
Attn: Human Rights Department
P.O. Box 921
Burlingame, CA 94011-0921
Phone: (650) 697-1400   E-mail: scholarships@cta.org
Web Site: www.cta.org
Summary: To provide financial assistance for higher education to dependent children of members of the California Teachers Association (CTA).
Eligibility: This program is open to dependent children of members of the association who are active, retired, or deceased. Selection is based on academic record, extracurricular/community activities, and recommendations. For the Del A. Weber Scholarship Fund, the applicant must be attending continuation high school. The Ralph J. Flynn Memorial Fund provides the scholarship for the highest scoring applicant.
Financial data: The stipend is $2,000 per year.
Duration: 1 year; nonrenewable.
Number awarded: 25 each year.
Deadline: February of each year.

151
CALIFORNIA-HAWAII ELKS MAJOR PROJECT UNDERGRADUATE SCHOLARSHIP FOR STUDENTS WITH DISABILITIES

California-Hawaii Elks Major Project, Inc.
Attn: Scholarship Committee
5450 East Lamona Avenue
Fresno, CA 93727-2224
Phone: (559) 255-4531   Fax: (559) 456-2659
Web Site: www.cheo.org
Summary: To provide financial assistance for postsecondary education to residents of California and Hawaii with disabilities.
Eligibility: This program is open to residents of California or Hawaii who have a physical impairment, neurological impairment, visual impairment, hearing impairment, and/or speech/language disorder. Applicants must be a senior in high school, be a high school graduate, or have passed the GED test. U.S. citizenship is required. Selection is based on financial need, grade point average, severity of

disability, seriousness of purpose, and depth of character. Applications are available from an Elks Lodge in California or Hawaii; students must first request an interview with the lodge's scholarship chairman or Exalted Ruler.
Financial data: The annual stipend is $1,000 for community colleges and vocational schools or $2,000 per year for 4-year colleges or universities.
Duration: 1 year; may be renewed for up to 3 additional years.
Number awarded: 24 to 48 each year.
Deadline: March of each year.

152
CALIFORNIANS FOR DISABILITY RIGHTS SCHOLARSHIP

Californians for Disability Rights
c/o Education Committee Chair
4020 North Walnuthaven Drive
Covina, CA 91722-3928
Phone: (626) 962-7909
Summary: To provide financial assistance for college to students with disabilities in California.
Eligibility: This program is open to persons with a verified physical, mental, or learning disability that substantially limits 1 or more major life activities. Applicants must be admitted to or enrolled in an accredited state university, community college, private college, or university in California. Selection is based on academic achievement (at least a 2.0 grade point average for undergraduates or 3.0 for graduate students), financial need, and leadership in activities that have improved the lives of people with disabilities in California.
Financial data: The stipend is $1,500.
Duration: 1 year.
Additional information: Information is also available from Michael Dunn, 1712 J Street, Suite 2, Sacramento, CA 95814
Number awarded: 1 each year.
Deadline: April of each year.

153
CAMPAIGN FOR AFRICAN AMERICAN ACHIEVEMENT SCHOLARSHIP A

National Urban League
Attn: Scholarship Coordinator
120 Wall Street
New York, NY 10005
Phone: (212) 558-5373   Fax: (212) 344-8948
E-mail: info@nul.org
Web Site: www.nul.org
Summary: To provide financial assistance for college to African American high school seniors affiliated with the National Urban League.
Eligibility: This program is open to graduating high school seniors who have exemplary academic and other achievements at the highest levels. Applicants must be inducted members of the Urban League/Congress of National Black Churches (CNBC) Achievers Society or McKnight Achievers.
Financial data: The stipend is $2,500 per year.
Duration: 4 years.
Number awarded: Approximately 100 each year.
Deadline: January of each year.

154
CAMPAIGN FOR AFRICAN AMERICAN ACHIEVEMENT SCHOLARSHIP B

National Urban League
Attn: Scholarship Coordinator
120 Wall Street
New York, NY 10005
Phone: (212) 558-5373   Fax: (212) 344-8948
E-mail: info@nul.org
Web Site: www.nul.org
Summary: To provide financial assistance for college to African American and other high school seniors affiliated with the National Urban League.
Eligibility: This program is open to graduating high school seniors who demonstrate outstanding academic and personal achievement, community service, and leadership. Special consideration is given to applicants who are affiliated with 1 of the partner organizations of the Campaign for African American Achievement and with the National Urban League.
Financial data: The stipend is $2,500 per year.

Duration: 4 years.
Number awarded: Approximately 100 each year.
Deadline: January of each year.

155
CAPTAIN CALIENDO COLLEGE ASSISTANCE FUND SCHOLARSHIPS

U.S. Coast Guard Chief Petty Officers Association
Attn: CCCAF Scholarship Committee
5520-G Hempstead Way
Springfield, VA 22151-4009
Phone: (703) 941-0395   Fax: (703) 941-0397
E-mail: CGCPOA@aol.com
Summary: To provide financial assistance for postsecondary education to children of members or deceased members of the U.S. Coast Guard Chief Petty Officers Association (CPOA) or of enlisted personnel of the Coast Guard.
Eligibility: Eligible are children of members or deceased members of the CPOA and children of regular, reserve, retired, or deceased enlisted personnel of the U.S. Coast Guard. Applicants may not be older than 24 years of age (the age limit does not apply to disabled children). Selection criteria include an essay, up to 500 words, on a topic that changes annually; a recent topic was "What problems are created using biotechnology to feed the world?" Financial status of the applicant's parents is not considered.
Financial data: First place is $1,500; second place is $1,250; third place is $1,000; fourth place is $750; fifth place is $500.
Duration: 1 year; recipients may reapply.
Number awarded: 5 each year.
Deadline: February of each year.

156
CAREER AID FOR TECHNICAL STUDENTS PROGRAM

New Hampshire Charitable Foundation
37 Pleasant Street
Concord, NH 03301-4005
Phone: (603) 225-6641   (800) 464-6641
Fax: (603) 225-1700   E-mail: info@nhcf.org
Web Site: www.nhcf.org
Summary: To provide financial assistance to New Hampshire residents pursuing a vocational or technical career.
Eligibility: This program is open to residents of New Hampshire entering a 2-year or 3-year degree program or a shorter-term technical degree training program that leads to an associate degree, a trade license, or certification. Applicants must be younger than 24 years of age and planning to enroll at least half time at a community college, vocational school, trade school, or other short-term training program. They must be able to demonstrate financial need. Although academic excellence is not considered in the selection process, applicants should be able to demonstrate reasonable achievement and a commitment to their chosen field of study.
Financial data: Stipends range from $100 to $2,500, depending on the need of the recipient. A total of $200,000 is distributed annually.
Duration: 1 year.
Number awarded: Varies each year.
Deadline: June of each year.

157
CAROLINE H. NEWHOUSE SCHOLARSHIP FUND

Career Transition for Dancers
c/o The Caroline & Theodore Newhouse Center for Dancers
200 West 57th Street, Suite 808
New York, NY 10019-3211
Phone: (212) 581-7043   Fax: (212) 581-0474
E-mail: info@careertransition.org
Web Site: www.careertransition.org/progsscholarmain.html
Summary: To provide financial assistance to current and former professional dancers interested in acquiring an academic degree or a new skill.
Eligibility: This program is open to current and former professional dancers who are at least 27 years of age and can demonstrate paid employment as a dancer for at least 100 weeks over a period of 7 years or more. Applicants must have earned at least $8,000 per year from dance employment in the 7 best years of their performing career. The performing years need not be consecutive or current. Applicants must be interested in beginning an academic or retraining process to take the first step toward a required degree or acquisition of an important new skill.
Financial data: Recipients are entitled to grants totaling $2,500 over their lifetime. Funds may be used for tuition, fees, books, and materials at schools,

institutes, and specialized certificate programs.
Duration: Funding may extend over a period of years, as long as the total awarded does not exceed $2,500.
Additional information: Since this program was established in 1985, it has awarded 1,233 grants totaling $1,079,484. It is sponsored by the American Federation of Television and Radio Artists, the American Guild of Musical Artists, the Screen Actors Guild, the American Guild of Variety Artists, and other performing arts organizations. Information is also available from the Los Angeles office, 5757 Wilshire Boulevard, Suite 902, Los Angeles, CA 90036-3635, (323) 549-6660, Fax: (323) 549-6810, E-mail: info-la@careertransition.org.
Number awarded: Varies each year; recently, 219 grants worth more than $230,000 were awarded.

158
CARSON SCHOLARS

Carson Scholars Fund
305 West Chesapeake Avenue, Suite L-202
Towson, MD 21204
Fax: (410) 828-1007
Web Site: www.carsonscholars.org
Summary: To recognize and reward outstanding students in grades 4 through 12 in Maryland, Delaware, and Washington, D.C. with college scholarships.
Eligibility: Students in grades 4 through 12 in Maryland, Delaware, and Washington, D.C. are eligible to be nominated by their schools. They must have at least a 3.75 grade point average and be excellent role models. Financial need is not considered in the selection process.
Financial data: Scholarships are $1,000 and are awarded for each year the student is selected. The awards are held in a trust until the recipient attends a 4-year institution of higher learning. Each trust is invested, so that the yield at the time of issuance should be substantially larger than the original award.
Additional information: This fund was established in 1994.

159
CARVER SCHOLARS PROGRAM

Roy J. Carver Charitable Trust
202 Iowa Avenue
Muscatine, IA 52761-3733
Phone: (319) 263-4010   Fax: (319) 263-1547
E-mail: info@carvertrust.org
Web Site: www.carvertrust.org
Summary: To provide financial assistance for college to students in Iowa who have overcome significant obstacles to attend college.
Eligibility: This program is open to students attending a 4-year college in Iowa and applying during their sophomore year for support in their junior year. Applicants must present evidence of unusual social and/or other barriers to attending college full time; examples of prior recipients include single parents returning to school to improve their lives, young people with disabilities, artists who score poorly on standardized tests but show exceptional talent, and members of impoverished families. They must be full-time students, have at least a 2.8 grade point average, be U.S. citizens, and submit a financial profile indicating insufficient personal, family, and institutional resources to pay full-time college tuition. A particular goal of the program is to assist students "who fall between the cracks of other financial aid programs." Applications must be submitted to the financial aid office at the Iowa college or university the applicant attends.
Financial data: Stipends generally average $3,800 at public universities and $7,600 at private colleges in Iowa.
Duration: 1 year; may be renewed 1 additional year.
Additional information: This program was established in 1988.
Number awarded: Varies each year; since the program's establishment, it has awarded more than 850 scholarships.
Deadline: April of each year.

160
CATHOLIC ORDER OF FORESTERS FRATERNAL SCHOLARSHIP PROGRAM

Catholic Order of Foresters
Attn: Fraternal Scholarship Committee
355 Shuman Boulevard
P.O. Box 3012
Naperville, IL 60566-7012
Phone: (630) 983-4900   (800) 552-0145
Web Site: www.catholicforester.com

Summary: To provide financial assistance for college to high school seniors who are insured by Catholic Order of Foresters.

Eligibility: Applicants must be high school seniors who have been insured members for at least 2 years prior to applying for the award; students insured under the Family Plan Term Rider or Children Term Rider do not qualify. Selection is based on class rank and ACT or SAT scores; financial need is not considered.

Financial data: The stipend is $1,250 per year. Funds are sent directly to the college or university where the recipient is enrolled.

Duration: 4 years, as long as recipient maintains satisfactory progress toward a degree.

Additional information: Catholic Order of Foresters, established in 1883, is an organization of Catholics helping Catholics by offering life insurance.

Number awarded: 20 each year.

Deadline: October of each year.

161
CATHOLIC WORKMAN COLLEGE SCHOLARSHIPS

Catholic Workman
Attn: Scholarships
111 West Main
P.O. Box 47
New Prague, MN 56071
Phone: (952) 758-2229   (800) 346-6231
Fax: (952) 758-6221

Summary: To provide financial assistance for undergraduate education to Catholic Workman participants.

Eligibility: Applicants must have been insured members of the fraternal life insurance society of Catholic Workman for at least 12 months and accepted to or currently enrolled in an accredited college or university. They must submit high school or college transcripts (grade point average of 2.5 or higher), 2 letters of recommendation, a 1-page list of their volunteer experiences, and a 50-word essay describing 1 of those volunteer experiences. There is no age requirement. Selection is based on a lottery by state (smaller state memberships are lumped together).

Financial data: Scholarships for entering freshmen are $500 per year; scholarships for entering sophomores, juniors, and seniors are $1,000 per year.

Duration: 1 year; recipients may reapply.

Additional information: Recipients may attend any accredited college or university in the United States; they must be full-time students.

Number awarded: 20 each year: 8 for entering freshmen and 12 for entering sophomores, juniors, and seniors.

Deadline: June of each year.

162
CCLVI SCHOLARSHIPS FOR LOW VISION STUDENTS

Council of Citizens with Low Vision International
c/o American Council of the Blind
1155 15th Street, N.W., Suite 1004
Washington, DC 20005
Phone: (202) 467-5081   (800) 424-8666
Fax: (202) 467-5085
Web Site: www.cclvi.org/scholarship.txt

Summary: To provide financial aid for postsecondary education to persons with low vision.

Eligibility: Applicants must be certified by an ophthalmologist as having low vision (acuity of 20/70 or worse in the better seeing eye with best correction or side vision with a maximum diameter of no greater than 30 degrees). They may be part-time or full-time entering freshmen, undergraduates, or graduate students. A cumulative grade point average of at least 3.0 is required.

Financial data: Stipends range from $500 to $1,200.

Duration: 1 year.

Additional information: Information is also available from Janis Stanger, 1239 American Beauty Drive, Salt Lake City, UT 84116, E-mail: stangers3@msn.com.

Number awarded: 2 each year.

Deadline: February of each year.

163
CESAR A. BATALLA MEMORIAL SCHOLARSHIP FUND

ASPIRA of Connecticut, Inc.
1600 State Street
Bridgeport, CT 06605
Phone: (203) 336-5762   Fax: (203) 366-5803

Summary: To provide financial assistance to economically disadvantaged college students in Connecticut who have been members of ASPIRA.

Eligibility: This program is open to economically disadvantaged Connecticut students who have graduated from high school, are enrolled full time in an institution of higher learning, and have participated in ASPIRA's development programs. Selection is based on good character, community involvement, leadership, and academic achievement.

Financial data: The stipend ranges from $500 to $1,000.

Duration: 1 year.

Additional information: This scholarship, which began in 1999, honors the memory of 1 of Connecticut's most influential Latino community leaders and philanthropists.

Number awarded: 2 each year.

164
CFA SCHOLARS AWARDS

Composite Fabricators Association
1655 North Fort Meyer Drive, Suite 510
Arlington, VA 22209-2022
Phone: (703) 525-0511   Fax: (703) 525-0743
E-mail: cfa-info@cfa-hq.org
Web Site: www.cfa-hq.org

Summary: To provide financial assistance for college to high school seniors who are employed by, or whose parent or guardian is employed by, a member firm of the Composite Fabricators Association (CFA).

Eligibility: This program is open to high school seniors planning to pursue a degree at an accredited 4-year college or university. A CFA member company must employ the applicant's parent or legal guardian or the applicant. Selection is based on merit, as demonstrated by academic achievement; leadership in school, civic, and other extracurricular activities; and motivation to serve and succeed in all endeavors. Special financial circumstances may also be considered.

Financial data: The stipend is $2,000. Funds must be used for tuition and/or required books, supplies, and equipment.

Duration: 1 year; nonrenewable.

Additional information: This program is sponsored by Interplastic Corporation.

Number awarded: 5 each year.

Deadline: January of each year.

165
CHADWICK FOUNDATION SCHOLARSHIPS

Chadwick Foundation
88 West Second South
P.O. Box 486
Soda Springs, ID 83276
Phone: (208) 547-2166   Fax: (208) 547-2210

Summary: To provide financial assistance to currently-enrolled college or graduate students, particularly those from southeast Idaho.

Eligibility: This program is open to college students at the sophomore or higher level and to graduate students. Students from southeast Idaho are given priority. To apply, students must submit a completed application form, an essay describing their future plans, at least 2 letters of recommendation, and a current transcript. Financial need is not considered in the selection process.

Financial data: The amount awarded varies, depending upon the funds available and the needs of the recipient.

Duration: 1 year; recipients may reapply.

Number awarded: Varies each year.

Deadline: September of each year.

166
CHAIRSCHOLARS FOUNDATION NATIONAL SCHOLARSHIPS

ChairScholars Foundation, Inc.
16101 Carencia Lane
Odessa, FL 33556-3278
Phone: (813) 920-2737
Web Site: www.chairscholars.org

Summary: To provide financial assistance for college to physically challenged students.

Eligibility: This program is open to high school seniors and college freshmen who are physically challenged. Applicants should be chair confined, although this is not a requirement. They should be able to demonstrate financial need, have a record of satisfactory academic performance (at least a "B+" average), and show

some form of community service or social contribution in the past.

Financial data: The stipend is $5,000 per year. Funds are to be used for tuition and school expenses.

Duration: Up to 4 years for high school seniors; up to 3 years for college freshmen.

Number awarded: 8 each year.

Deadline: March of each year.

167
CHAPPIE HALL MEMORIAL SCHOLARSHIP PROGRAM

101st Airborne Division Association
2703 Michigan Avenue, P.O. Box 929
Fort Campbell, KY 42223-0929
Phone: (270) 439-0445   Fax: (270) 439-6645
E-mail: assn101abn@aol.com
Web Site: www.screamingeagle.org

Summary: To provide financial assistance for the postsecondary education of the spouses, children, or grandchildren of members of the 101st Airborne Division.

Eligibility: Eligible to apply for these scholarships are individuals who maintained a 2.0 or better grade point average during the preceding school year and whose parent, grandparent, or spouse is (or, if deceased, was) a regular (not associate) member of the 101st Airborne Division. Selection is based on career objectives, academic record, and financial need.

Financial data: The amount awarded varies, depending upon the needs of the recipient and the funds available.

Number awarded: At least 1 each year.

Deadline: May of each year.

168
CHARLES C. ELY TRUST SCHOLARSHIPS

Mellon New England
Attn: Vice President
One Boston Place, 024-0084
Boston, MA 02108
Phone: (617) 722-3891

Summary: To provide financial aid for college to male students from Massachusetts.

Eligibility: This program is open to males who have graduated from a high school in Massachusetts or have lived for more than 2 years in the state. Applicants may be applying to attend an institution of higher learning anywhere in the United States. Along with their application and transcripts, they must submit a statement regarding their plans for future study and pursuing a career after graduation from college. Selection is based on academic performance, character, abilities and talents, and financial need.

Financial data: Stipends range from $1,000 to $3,000, depending on need.

Duration: 1 year.

Number awarded: Varies each year.

Deadline: April of each year.

169
CHARLES GALLAGHER STUDENT FINANCIAL ASSISTANCE PROGRAM

Missouri Department of Higher Education
Attn: Missouri Student Assistance Resource Services (MOSTARS)
3515 Amazonas Drive
Jefferson City, MO 65109-5717
Phone: (573) 751-3940   (800) 473-6757
Fax: (573) 751-6635
Web Site: www.mocbhe.gov

Summary: To provide financial assistance to college students in Missouri who demonstrate financial need.

Eligibility: This program is open to residents of Missouri who are full-time students working on their first baccalaureate degree at a participating postsecondary school in the state. Applicants must be able to demonstrate financial need. Students pursuing a degree or certificate in theology or divinity are not eligible. U.S. citizenship or permanent resident status is required.

Financial data: The annual award is the lesser of 1) the unmet financial need (after counting any federal Pell Grant the student receives); 2) half of the school's prior year tuition and fees; or 3) $1,500.

Duration: 1 year; may be renewed.

Additional information: Currently, 84 postsecondary schools in Missouri are

approved to participate in this program; applications and further information are available at the financial aid office of those schools.

Number awarded: Varies each year.

Deadline: March of each year.

170
CHARLES W. AND ANNETTE HILL SCHOLARSHIP FUND

American Legion
Attn: Department of Kansas
1314 S.W. Topeka Boulevard
Topeka, KS 66612-1886
Phone: (785) 232-9315   Fax: (785) 232-1399

Summary: To provide financial assistance for postsecondary education (particularly in science and business) to the children of members of the Kansas American Legion.

Eligibility: This program is open to graduating seniors at high schools in Kansas who have a grade point average of 3.0 or higher. Applicants must be a descendant of a member of the American Legion. Preference is given to applicants planning to major in science, engineering, or business administration at a Kansas college, university, junior college, or trade school. Selection is based on high school transcripts, 3 letters of recommendation, an essay of 250 to 500 words on "Why I want to go to college," and financial need.

Financial data: The stipend is $1,000.

Duration: 1 year; may be renewed if the recipient maintains at least a 3.0 grade point average in college.

Number awarded: 1 each year.

Deadline: February of each year.

171
CHARLIE DECKER, JR. SCHOLARSHIP AWARD

United States Navy Radioman Association
P.O. Box 15313
Norfolk, VA 23511
Web Site: www.radioman.org

Summary: To provide financial assistance for college to members of the United States Navy Radioman Association (USNRMA) and their dependents.

Eligibility: This program is open to USNRMA members and their spouses and dependent children. Applicants must be enrolled or accepted for enrollment as an undergraduate or graduate student at an accredited college or university. They must submit an essay of at least 100 words on themselves, including a significant experience in their life; a special talent, interest, or characteristic; and ambitions for their future. Selection is based on the essay, SAT scores, and extracurricular activities. Financial need is not considered.

Financial data: A stipend is awarded (exact amount not specified).

Duration: 1 year.

Additional information: Membership in the USNRMA is open to current and former U.S. radiomen and to non-radiomen who have provided significant support to the field of naval communications. Members must have served or be serving in the U.S. Navy or Coast Guard as an active-duty radioman or in a capacity closely related to Navy or Coast Guard communication.

Number awarded: 1 or more each year.

Deadline: August of each year.

172
THE CHARTER FUND SCHOLARSHIPS

The Charter Fund
Attn: Jeanette Montoya
370 17th Street, Suite 5300
Denver, CO 80202
Phone: (303) 572-1727   Fax: (303) 628-3839

Summary: To provide financial assistance for postsecondary education to financially needy residents of Colorado.

Eligibility: These scholarships are available to residents of Colorado who can demonstrate financial need. Applicants must be entering freshmen at an accredited institution studying any field.

Financial data: Awards range from $100 to $1,500.

Duration: 1 year; nonrenewable.

Number awarded: Approximately 90 each year.

Deadline: May of each year.

173
CHARTERED STATE ASSOCIATION YOUTH SCHOLARSHIP

National Burglar & Fire Alarm Association
8300 Colesville Road, Suite 750
Silver Spring, MD 20910
Phone: (301) 907-3202   Fax: (301) 585-1866
E-mail: staff@alarm.org
Web Site: www.alarm.org/nbfaa/Scholarships/scholarships.html
Summary: To provide financial assistance for college to high school seniors whose parents are active-duty law enforcement and fire service personnel in selected states.
Eligibility: This program is open to seniors graduating from high schools in California, Connecticut, Indiana, New Jersey, Pennsylvania, Virginia, and the metropolitan New York area. Applicants must be the children of active-duty law enforcement and fire service personnel.
Financial data: Stipends are $6,500 or $3,500.
Duration: 1 year.
Additional information: This program began in 1992 in the metropolitan New York area. The sponsors plan to expand it to all states. It is sponsored by the National Burglar & Fire Alarm Association and Security Dealer magazine.
Number awarded: 2 each year: 1 at $6,500 and 1 at $3,500.

174
CHEN SCHOLARSHIP

Coors Hispanic Employee Network
P.O. Box 1454
Golden, CO 80401
E-mail: paulandchris@prodigy.net
Summary: To provide financial assistance for college to high school seniors in Colorado who are of Hispanic descent.
Eligibility: Applicants must be U.S. citizens, be Colorado residents, be of Hispanic heritage, be high school seniors, have at least a 2.5 grade point average, and be planning to attend college after graduation. Selection is based on academic record, financial need, and educational plans. To apply, students must submit a signed application, a personal statement, a transcript, and 2 letters of recommendation.
Financial data: The stipend is $1,000 per year.
Duration: 1 year.
Additional information: This program was established in 1991. Additional information is available from Grace Valdez at (303) 277-5258 or Ron Martinez at (303) 277-5037.
Number awarded: Several each year.
Deadline: February of each year.

175
CHEROKEE NATION UNDERGRADUATE SCHOLARSHIP

Cherokee Nation of Oklahoma
Attn: Office of Higher Education
P.O. Box 948
Tahlequah, OK 74465
Phone: (918) 456-0671, ext. 2208   (800) 256-0671
Fax: (918) 458-6195   E-mail: HigherEd@cherokee.org
Web Site: www.cherokee.org
Summary: To provide financial assistance for postsecondary education to undergraduate students who belong to the Cherokee Nation of Oklahoma.
Eligibility: This program is open to members of the Cherokee Nation of Oklahoma who are enrolled in or planning to enroll in an accredited college or university. All tribal members, regardless of permanent residence, who qualify for federal Pell grant funding may apply for additional assistance from the U.S. Bureau of Indian Affairs (BIA). Tribal members who are residents of Oklahoma and who do not qualify for Pell grants may apply for Cherokee Nation scholarship funding. First preference is given to students whose permanent residence is within the Cherokee nation area (defined as those counties within and contiguous to the Cherokee Nation boundaries); second preference is given to residents of other Oklahoma counties. If funding is not available to award scholarships to all the students in either of the geographic location categories, academic performance (measured by grade point average and ACT score for entering freshmen, by grade point average for current college students) is used to determine scholarship winners. In the event of an academic performance tie, financial need is used to break the tie. Additional preferences are given to applicants who can demonstrate Cherokee Nation community service, completion of the Cherokee Nation history course, Tribal Youth Council participation, tribal leadership activities, Miss Cherokee Pageant participation, and involvement in other activities offered by the tribe.

Financial data: All Cherokee Nation members, regardless of permanent residence, who qualify for federal Pell grant funding are eligible for up to $750 per semester in additional funding from the BIA. Tribal members who are residents of Oklahoma and who do not qualify for Pell grants and apply for Cherokee Nation scholarships are eligible for $500 per semester as a freshman, up to $750 per semester as a sophomore, and up to $1,000 per semester as a junior or senior.
Duration: Up to 8 semesters.
Number awarded: Approximately 450 to 500 students can be supported each year.
Deadline: May of each year.

176
CHERYL GRIMMEL AWARD

Patient Advocate Foundation
753 Thimble Shoals Boulevard, Suite B
Newport News, VA 23606
Phone: (800) 532-5274   Fax: (757) 873-8999
E-mail: help@patientadvocate.org
Web Site: www.patientadvocate.org
Summary: To provide financial assistance for college to individuals whose studies have been interrupted or delayed by a diagnosis of cancer or other life threatening diseases.
Eligibility: Eligible to apply for this scholarship are individuals seeking to initiate or complete a course of study that has been interrupted or delayed by a diagnosis of cancer or other critical or life threatening diseases. Applicants must be able to demonstrate financial need, have earned at least a 3.0 grade point average, be enrolled or planning to enroll as a full-time student, and write an essay on why they have chosen their particular field of study.
Financial data: The stipend is $5,000.
Duration: 1 year.
Additional information: Recipients must pursue a course of study that will make them immediately employable after graduation.
Number awarded: 1 each year.
Deadline: April of each year.

177
CHESTER M. VERNON MEMORIAL EAGLE SCOUT SCHOLARSHIP

Boy Scouts of America
Attn: National Jewish Committee on Scouting, S226
1325 West Walnut Hill Lane
P.O. Box 152079
Irving, TX 75015-2079
Phone: (972) 580-2000
Web Site: www.jewishscouting.org/awards/eagle.html
Summary: To provide financial assistance for college to Jewish Boy Scouts, Varsity Scouts, and Explorers.
Eligibility: This program is open to Jewish Boy Scouts, Varsity Scouts, and Explorers who have received the Eagle Scout Award and have also earned the Ner Tamid emblem. Applicants must be enrolled in an accredited high school in their final year and must be an active member of a synagogue. They must have demonstrated practical citizenship in their synagogue, school, Scouting unit, and community. Selection is based on high school record, including school activities, awards, honors, and grade point average; participation in community organizations; participation in religious youth organizations, clubs, or groups, including honors earned and offices held; involvement in Scouting; career goals; and 4 letters of recommendation, from leaders of their religious institution, school, community, and Scouting unit.
Financial data: The stipend is $1,000 per year.
Duration: 4 years.
Additional information: This scholarship was first awarded in 1993.
Number awarded: 1 every other year.
Deadline: December of the year in which the scholarship is awarded.

178
CHEYENNE AND ARAPAHO HIGHER EDUCATION GRANTS

Cheyenne and Arapaho Tribes of Oklahoma
Attn: Department of Education
P.O. Box 38
Concho, OK 73022
Phone: (405) 262-0345   (800) 247-4612, ext. 154
Fax: (405) 262-3872

Summary: To provide financial assistance to enrolled Cheyenne-Arapaho tribal members who are interested in pursuing postsecondary education.

Eligibility: To be eligible, applicants must be at least one-quarter degree of Cheyenne-Arapaho Indian, at least a high school graduate (or the equivalent), approved for admission by a college or university, and in financial need. Applicants may be either enrolled or planning to enroll in a postsecondary school. The vast majority of students assisted under this program are at the undergraduate level, although graduate and/or married students are eligible for consideration and assistance. Summer and part-time students may apply as well, as long as application is made well in advance of enrollment and is accompanied by an official need evaluation.

Financial data: The amount of the award depends on the need of the applicant.

Duration: 1 year; renewable.

Number awarded: 40 to 80 each year.

Deadline: May of each year for fall semester; October for spring semester; or March of each year for summer session.

179
CHICK EVANS CADDIE SCHOLARSHIPS

Western Golf Association
Attn: Evans Scholars Foundation
1 Briar Road
Golf, IL 60029-0301
Phone: (847) 724-4600   Fax: (847) 724-7133

Summary: To provide financial assistance for college to students who have worked as golf caddies.

Eligibility: Candidates for these scholarships must have completed their junior year in high school, rank in the upper quarter of their graduating class, have a grade point average of 3.0 or higher in college preparatory classes, have taken the ACT or SAT, and have been a full-time caddie on a regular basis for at least 2 years. Applicants from 12 states (Colorado, Illinois, Indiana, Kansas, Michigan, Minnesota, Missouri, Ohio, Oregon, Pennsylvania, Washington, and Wisconsin) must attend designated universities; applicants from other states must attend their state university, as approved by the scholarship committee. Selection is based on character, integrity, leadership, and financial need.

Financial data: The awards cover tuition and housing at universities approved by the scholarship committee.

Duration: 1 year; may be renewed for up to 3 additional years.

Additional information: Applicants from the 12 designated states must attend the following universities: Colorado: the University of Colorado at Boulder; Illinois: Northwestern University, the University of Illinois at Urbana-Champaign, Marquette University, or Northern Illinois University; Indiana: Purdue University or Indiana University; Kansas: University of Missouri at Columbia; Michigan: University of Michigan or Michigan State University; Minnesota: University of Minnesota; Missouri: University of Missouri at Columbia; Ohio: Ohio State University or Miami University; Oregon: University of Oregon or Oregon State University; Pennsylvania: Pennsylvania State University; Washington: University of Washington; Wisconsin: University of Wisconsin at Madison. At 14 of those universities (Colorado, Northwestern, Illinois, Marquette, Northern Illinois, Purdue, Indiana, Missouri, Michigan, Michigan State, Minnesota, Ohio State, Miami, and Wisconsin), Evans Scholars reside in Chapter Houses maintained by the foundation. At other universities, they reside on campus. Applications are sent only to sponsoring clubs where the candidate caddies and which documents the caddie record.

Number awarded: Varies each year.

Deadline: October of each year.

180
CHICKASAW NATION HIGHER EDUCATION FOUNDATION SCHOLARSHIP

Chickasaw Nation
Attn: Division of Education and Training
224 Rosedale Road
Ada, OK 74820
Phone: (580) 310-6620   Fax: (580) 436-3733
Web Site: www.Chickasaw.net

Summary: To provide financial assistance to members of the Chickasaw Nation who are working on an undergraduate degree.

Eligibility: This program is open to members of the Chickasaw Nation who are working full or part time on an undergraduate degree at an accredited college or university, have a grade point average of 3.0 or higher, and can exhibit strong educational and personal goals. Evidence of financial need is not required. To apply, students must submit a copy of their Chickasaw Nation citizenship card and/or Certificate of Degree of Indian Blood; documentation of any awards, honors, or achievements; proof of their ACT/SAT scores; a copy of their high school transcript; a copy of their current college transcript (if appropriate); proof of enrollment in the semester for which they will be requesting aid; and an essay on their personal interests and long-term goals, including past participation in school and tribal activities.

Financial data: A stipend is paid (exact amount not specified).

Duration: 1 year; recipients may reapply.

Number awarded: Varies each year.

Deadline: May of each year for fall semester; November of each year for spring semester; April of each year for summer term.

181
CHICKASAW NATION HIGHER EDUCATION FOUNDATION SCHOLARSHIP

Chickasaw Nation
Attn: Department of Education
P.O. Box 1548
Ada, OK 74820
Phone: (580) 310-6620
Web Site: www.Chickasaw.net

Summary: To provide financial assistance to members of the Chickasaw Nation who are working on an undergraduate degree.

Eligibility: This program is open to members of the Chickasaw Nation who are working full time on an undergraduate degree at an accredited college or university, have at least a 2.5 grade point average, can exhibit strong educational and personal goals, have applied for federal financial aid, and have "unmet need" as determined by their school of enrollment. To apply, students must submit a copy of their Chickasaw citizenship card, a copy of their high school transcript, a copy of their current college transcript (if appropriate), and a copy of their pre-enrollment (class schedule) for the semester in which they will be requesting aid.

Financial data: A stipend is paid (exact amount not specified).

Duration: 1 year; recipients may reapply.

Number awarded: Varies each year.

Deadline: May of each year.

182
CHICKASAW NATION HIGHER EDUCATION GRANT

Chickasaw Nation
Attn: Division of Education and Training
224 Rosedale Road
Ada, OK 74820
Phone: (580) 310-6620   Fax: (580) 436-3733
Web Site: www.Chickasaw.net

Summary: To provide financial assistance to members of the Chickasaw Nation who are working on an undergraduate degree.

Eligibility: This program is open to members of the Chickasaw Nation who are working full or part time on an undergraduate, graduate, or doctoral degree at an accredited college or university; have at least a 2.0 grade point average; have applied for federal financial aid; and have "unmet need" as determined by their school of enrollment. To apply, students must submit a copy of their Chickasaw Nation citizenship card and/or Certificate of Degree of Indian Blood; a copy of their high school transcript; proof of ACT/SAT score; a copy of their current college transcript (if appropriate); a copy of their pre-enrollment (class schedule) for the semester in which they will be requesting aid; and documentation of financial need.

Financial data: A stipend is paid (exact amount not specified).

Duration: 1 year; recipients may reapply.

Number awarded: Varies each year.

Deadline: May of each year for fall semester; November of each year for spring semester.

183
CHICKASAW NATION HIGHER EDUCATION GRANT

Chickasaw Nation
Attn: Department of Education
P.O. Box 1548
Ada, OK 74820
Phone: (580) 310-6620
Web Site: www.Chickasaw.net

Summary: To provide financial assistance to members of the Chickasaw Nation

who are working on an undergraduate degree.

Eligibility: This program is open to members of the Chickasaw Nation who are working full time on an undergraduate degree at an accredited college or university, have at least a 2.0 grade point average, have applied for federal financial aid, and have "unmet need" as determined by their school of enrollment. To apply, students must submit a copy of their Chickasaw citizenship card, a copy of their high school transcript, a copy of their current college transcript (if appropriate), and a copy of their pre-enrollment (class schedule) for the semester in which they will be requesting aid.

Financial data: A stipend is paid (exact amount not specified).

Duration: 1 year; recipients may reapply.

Number awarded: Varies each year.

Deadline: May of each year.

184
CHIEF MANUELITO SCHOLARSHIP PROGRAM

Navajo Nation
Attn: Office of Navajo Nation Scholarship and Financial Assistance
P.O. Box 1870
Window Rock, AZ 86515-1870
Phone: (520) 871-7640   (800) 243-2956
Fax: (520) 871-6561   E-mail: onnsfacentral@navajo.org
Web Site: www.onnsfa.navajo.org

Summary: To provide financial assistance to academically superior members of the Navajo Nation who are interested in pursuing undergraduate education.

Eligibility: This program is open to enrolled members of the Navajo Nation who are attending or planning to enroll as full-time students at an accredited college or university. Applicants who are graduating high school seniors must have the following minimum combinations of ACT score and GPA: 21 and 3.8, 22 and 3.7, 23 and 3.6, 24 and 3.5, 25 and 3.4, 26 and 3.3, 27 and 3.2, 28 and 3.1, or 29 and 3.0. They must have completed in high school at least 1 unit of Navajo language, at least half a unit of Navajo government, and (effective in 2003) at least half a unit of Navajo Studies. Applicants who are current undergraduate students must have completed at least 24 semester credit hours with an overall grade point average of 3.0 or higher.

Financial data: The stipend is $5,000 per year.

Duration: 1 year; may be renewed if the recipient maintains full-time status and a 3.0 grade point average.

Number awarded: Varies each year; recently, 59 of these scholarships were awarded.

Deadline: April of each year.

185
CHIEF MASTER SERGEANTS OF THE AIR FORCE SCHOLARSHIPS

Air Force Sergeants Association
Attn: Scholarship Program
5211 Auth Road
Suitland, MD 20746
Phone: (301) 899-3500   (800) 638-0594
E-mail: staff@afsahq.org
Web Site: www.amf.org/cmsaf.htm

Summary: To provide financial assistance for the postsecondary education of dependent children of enlisted Air Force personnel.

Eligibility: Applicants must be the unmarried dependent children (including stepchildren and legally adopted children), under the age of 23, of enlisted personnel serving in the U.S. Air Force, Air National Guard, or Air Force Reserves, whether on active duty or retired. Selection is based on academic ability (minimum SAT score of 1000 and minimum grade point average of 3.5), character, leadership, writing ability, and potential for success; financial need is not a consideration. A unique aspect of these scholarships is that applicants may supply additional information regarding circumstances that entitle them to special consideration; examples of such circumstances include student disabilities, financial hardships, parent disabled and unable to work, parent missing in action/killed in action/prisoner of war, or other unusual extenuating circumstances.

Financial data: Stipends are $3,000, $2,000, or $1,000; funds may be used for tuition, room and board, fees, books, supplies, and transportation.

Duration: 1 year; may be renewed if the recipient maintains full-time enrollment.

Additional information: The Air Force Sergeants Association administers this program on behalf of the Airmen Memorial Foundation. It was established in 1987 and named in honor of CMSAF Richard D. Kisling, the late third Chief Master

Sergeant of the Air Force. In 1997, following the deaths of CMSAF's (Retired) Andrews and Harlow, it was given its current name. Requests for applications must be accompanied by a stamped self-addressed envelope.

Number awarded: 11 each year: 1 at $3,000, 2 at $2,000, and 8 at $1,000.

Deadline: April of each year.

186
CHIEF PETTY OFFICERS SCHOLARSHIP FUND

Senior Enlisted Academy Alumni Association
Attn: CPO Scholarship Fund
1269 Elliot Avenue
Newport, RI 02841-1525
E-mail: john@seaaa.org
Web Site: www.seaaa.org/scholarship.htm

Summary: To provide financial assistance for college to the dependents of Navy Chief Petty Officers (CPOs).

Eligibility: This program is open to the spouses and children (natural born, adopted, or step) of active, reserve, retired, and deceased Navy CPOs. Applicants must be high school graduates or seniors planning to graduate and must intend to enter their first year of college or university with the goal of obtaining an associate, bachelor's, or graduate degree. Members of the armed services are not eligible. Scholarships are awarded in 5 categories: 1) active duty east coast (stationed east of or at Great Lakes, Illinois); 2) active duty west coast (stationed west of Great Lakes, Illinois); 3) active duty stationed outside the continental United States; 4) reserve; and 5) retired and deceased.

Financial data: The amount of the stipends depends on the availability of funds; awards are sent directly to the recipient's school.

Duration: 1 year.

Number awarded: 10 each year: 2 in each of the categories.

Deadline: March of each year.

187
CHILDREN, ADULT, AND FAMILY SERVICES SCHOLARSHIP

Oregon Student Assistance Commission
Attn: Private Awards Grant Department
1500 Valley River Drive, Suite 100
Eugene, OR 97401-2146
Phone: (541) 687-7395   (800) 452-8807, ext. 7395
Fax: (541) 687-7419   E-mail: awardinfo@mercury.osac.state.or.us
Web Site: www.osac.state.or.us

Summary: To provide financial assistance for college to residents of Oregon who are involved in foster care or related programs.

Eligibility: This program is open to residents of Oregon who are either 1) graduating high school seniors currently in foster care or participating in the Independent Living Program (ILP); and 2) GED recipients and continuing college students formerly in foster care. Applicants must be attending or planning to attend a public college or university in Oregon.

Financial data: Scholarship amounts vary, depending upon needs of the recipient.

Duration: 1 year.

Additional information: Information on this scholarship is also available from Children, Adult, and Family Services.

Number awarded: Varies each year.

Deadline: February of each year.

188
CHILDREN OF AIR TRAFFIC CONTROL SPECIALISTS SCHOLARSHIP PROGRAM

Air Traffic Control Association
Arlington Courthouse Plaza 11
2300 Clarendon Boulevard, Suite 711
Arlington, VA 22201
Phone: (703) 522-5717   Fax: (703) 522-7251
E-mail: atca@worldnett.att.net
Web Site: www.atca.org

Summary: To provide financial assistance for college to children of air traffic control specialists.

Eligibility: This program is open to U.S. citizens who are the children, natural or adopted, of a person currently or formerly serving as an air traffic control specialist with the U.S. government, with the U.S. military, or in a private facility in the United States. Applicants must be enrolled or planning to enroll at least half time in a baccalaureate or graduate program at an accredited college or

university. Financial need is considered in the selection process.

Financial data: The amounts of the awards depend on the availability of funds and the number, qualifications, and need of the applicants.

Duration: 1 year; may be renewed.

Number awarded: Varies each year, depending on the number, qualifications, and need of the applicants.

Deadline: April of each year.

189
"CHILI" CURRIER SCHOLARSHIP FUND

New Mexico Land Title Association
c/o James Owensby
Elliott & Waldron Title Company
1819 North Turner, Suite B
Hobbs, NM 88240
Phone: (503) 393-7706

Summary: To provide financial assistance for college to students in New Mexico.

Eligibility: This program is open to U.S. citizens who are current New Mexico residents, have graduated from a New Mexico high school (or received a GED through a New Mexico Department of Education approved program), and are attending a postsecondary institution of higher education in the state. Applicants must be enrolled for a minimum of 6 hours if they have a full-time job, for a minimum of 9 hours if they have a part-time job, or for a minimum of 12 hours (full-time student) if they are not employed. Financial need and academic achievement must be demonstrated. All applicants must be recommended by an individual within the title industry and an individual from their own community.

Financial data: Initially, each scholarship is $200 per semester for part-time students and $500 for full-time students. Recipients who reapply and have maintained at least a 3.0 grade point average are awarded an additional $100 per semester after completion of every third semester, up to a maximum of $700 per semester. Funds must be used for tuition and/or books.

Duration: 1 semester; may be renewed.

Number awarded: Varies each year.

190
CHINA TIMES GRADUATING HIGH SCHOOL SENIORS AWARD

China Times Cultural Foundation
136-39 41st Avenue, Suite 1A
Flushing, NY 11355
Phone: (718) 460-4900   Fax: (718) 460-4900
E-mail: ctcfmail@yahoo.com

Summary: To provide financial assistance for college to Chinese high school graduating seniors.

Eligibility: This program is open to graduating seniors at U.S. high schools who are Chinese but of any nationality. Applicants must submit a copy of their 11th and 12th grade report cards; a letter of acceptance from the college they are planning to attend; a copy of their SAT test score; a short essay, in either Chinese or English, describing their family, personal interests, and aspirations; and any other documents indicating extraordinary achievements in extracurricular activities. Financial need is not considered. Special consideration is given to applicants involved in the advancement of Chinese culture.

Financial data: A stipend is paid (exact amount not specified).

Duration: 1 year.

Additional information: This foundation was established in 1986. During its first 10 years, it distributed more than $1.6 million in scholarships.

Number awarded: 1 or more each year.

Deadline: June of each year.

191
CHITTENDEN BANK SCHOLARSHIP

Vermont Student Assistance Corporation
Champlain Mill
1 Main Street, Fourth Floor
P.O. Box 2000
Winooski, VT 05404-2601
Phone: (802) 655-9602   (800) 642-3177
Fax: (802) 654-3765   TDD: (802) 654-3766
Phone: TDD: (800) 281-3341 (within VT)   E-mail: info@vsac.org
Web Site: www.vsac.org

Summary: To provide financial assistance for college to high school seniors in Vermont.

Eligibility: This scholarship is available to U.S. citizens who are residents of Vermont and graduating from a high school in the state. Applicants must be able to document financial need, have applied to the Vermont Student Assistance Corporation for a Vermont Grant, and have filed a Free Application for Federal Student Aid no later than 4 weeks before the scholarship deadline. The following are required as part of the application process: a completed application form, a copy of an acceptance letter from a postsecondary institution, 3 letters of recommendation, a resume, an official transcript, and 5 required essays. Selection is based on academic record, character, leadership, and financial need.

Financial data: The stipend is $2,500.

Duration: 1 year; may be renewed up to 3 additional years if the recipient maintains at least a 3.0 grade point average.

Additional information: Recipients may attend either a 2-year or 4-year school.

Number awarded: 2 each year.

Deadline: April of each year.

192
CHITWOOD AKERS, HEMOPHILIA ACCESS, INC. SCHOLARSHIP FUND

Hemophilia Access, Inc.
P.O. Box 367
Nolensville, TN 37135
Phone: (800) 399-RELY   Fax: (888) 499-RELY
Web Site: www.hemophiliaccess.com

Summary: To provide financial assistance for college to persons with hemophilia or to members of their family.

Eligibility: Eligible to apply are persons with hemophilia or the children, spouses, or siblings of persons (alive or deceased) with hemophilia. Applicants must be attending or applying to an accredited postsecondary institution.

Financial data: Stipends are either $1,000 or $500.

Duration: 1 year.

Number awarded: Several each year.

193
CHOCTAW NATION HIGHER EDUCATION PROGRAM

Choctaw Nation
Attn: Higher Education Department
P.O. Drawer 1210
Durant, OK 74702-1210
Phone: (580) 924-8280   (800) 522-6170 (within OK)
Fax: (580) 924-4148
Web Site: www.choctawnation.com

Summary: To provide financial assistance to Choctaw Indians who are interested in pursuing postsecondary education.

Eligibility: Applicants must be at least one-quarter Choctaw or mixed with another federally-recognized tribe to equal one-quarter Indian blood. They must be high school seniors or graduates who are interested in going on to college. Graduate students may receive assistance if funds are available.

Financial data: Funds will cover the unmet need, up to $1,600 per year; for students attending a private college or university or a school outside of Oklahoma, the Choctaw Nation will fund 50 percent of the unmet need, up to the maximum of $1,600 per year.

Duration: 1 year; may be renewed for up to 4 additional years as long as the recipient enrolls in at least 12 hours per semester with a minimum grade point average of 2.0.

Additional information: Recipients must be working on a college degree.

Number awarded: Varies each year.

Deadline: March of each year.

194
CHRISTIAN MISSIONARY SCHOLARSHIP AWARD

Thomasson Foundation Inc.
11711 North Meridian Street, Suite 600
P.O. Box 80238
Indianapolis, IN 46280-0238
Phone: (317) 843-5678

Summary: To provide financial assistance for college to the children of Christian missionaries.

Eligibility: This program is open to the children of full-time Christian missionaries. An interview may be required. Selection is based on academic performance, financial need, standardized test scores, recommendations, and an

essay written by the applicants.

Financial data: A stipend is awarded (exact amount not specified). Funds are to be used for tuition, board, room, fees, and books.

Duration: 1 year; renewable as long as the recipient maintains full-time status and a 2.0 grade point average.

Additional information: Students must attend an accredited postsecondary institution in the United States on a full-time basis.

Number awarded: Varies each year.

195
CHUCK PEACOCK HONORARY SCHOLARSHIP

Aircraft Electronics Association
Attn: President
4217 South Hocker Drive
Independence, MO 64055-4723
Phone: (816) 373-6565   Fax: (816) 478-3100
E-mail: info@aea.net
Web Site: www.aea.net

Summary: To provide financial assistance for college to members of the Aircraft Electronics Association and their relatives.

Eligibility: This program is open to high school seniors, high school graduates, and currently-enrolled college students who are either members or the children, grandchildren, or other dependents of members of the association. The scholarship may be used for any field of study.

Financial data: The stipend is $1,500; funds must be used for tuition.

Duration: 1 year.

Additional information: This scholarship honors the founder of the Aircraft Electronics Association.

Number awarded: 1 each year.

Deadline: February of each year.

196
CLAIRE OLIPHANT MEMORIAL SCHOLARSHIPS

American Legion Auxiliary
Attn: Department of New Jersey
146 Route 130
Bordentown, NJ 08505-2226
Phone: (609) 291-9338   Fax: (609) 291-8175

Summary: To provide financial assistance for the postsecondary education of New Jersey residents who are the children or grandchildren of veterans.

Eligibility: This program is open to the children and grandchildren of living, deceased, or divorced veterans. Applicants must be residents of New Jersey for 2 years and members of the current graduating class of a senior high school or equivalent.

Financial data: This scholarship is $1,800.

Duration: 1 year.

Additional information: Rules and applications are distributed to all New Jersey senior high school guidance departments.

Number awarded: 1 each year.

Deadline: March of each year.

197
CLYDE RUSSELL SCHOLARSHIP

Clyde Russell Scholarship Fund
P.O. Box 2457
Augusta, ME 04338

Summary: To assist Maine residents in their educational pursuits.

Eligibility: Awards are available to applicants in 3 categories: high school seniors, full-time and part-time college and graduate students, and Maine residents interested in pursuing further educational/cultural opportunities. For high school and college students, selection is based on personal traits and qualities, extracurricular activities, community activities, academic ability and motivation, financial need, and personal goals and objectives. For other Maine residents, selection is based on the nature of the project, projected costs, personal traits and qualities, community activities, and professional/educational characteristics.

Financial data: Up to $10,000.

Duration: 1 year; nonrenewable.

Number awarded: 3 each year: 1 to a high school senior; 1 to a college student; and 1 to a citizen of Maine who is interested in pursuing further educational/cultural opportunities.

Deadline: January of each year.

198
COALITION OF HIGHER EDUCATION ASSISTANCE ORGANIZATIONS SCHOLARSHIPS

Coalition of Higher Education Assistance Organizations
1101 Vermont Avenue, N.W., Suite 400
Washington, DC 20005-3586
Phone: (202) 289-3910   Fax: (202) 371-0197
Web Site: www.coheao.org/scholarshipinfo.html

Summary: To provide financial assistance to students at colleges and universities that are members of the Coalition of Higher Education Assistance Organizations (COHEAO).

Eligibility: This program is open to students entering their sophomore, junior, or senior year at a member institution. Applicants must have a grade point average of 3.5 or higher and be a U.S. citizen.

Financial data: Stipends are normally $1,000 or $500.

Duration: 1 year.

Additional information: This program, established in 1994, includes 2 named scholarships: the Claiborne & Nuala Pell Scholarship and the Burke Tracey Scholarship. Information on these scholarships is available only through the Internet, not the mail.

Number awarded: Normally, 6 of these scholarships are awarded each year: 3 at $1,000 and 3 at $500. Recently, the sponsor was able to award 4 additional scholarships: 1 at $1,000, 1 at $500, and 2 at $250.

Deadline: February of each year.

199
COAST GUARD MUTUAL ASSISTANCE EDUCATION GRANT PROGRAM

Coast Guard Mutual Assistance
Attn: Commandant (G-ZMA)
2100 Second Street, S.W., Room 5502
Washington, DC 20593-0001
Phone: (202) 267-2557   (800) 881-2462
Fax: (202) 267-4299
Web Site: www.cgmahq.org

Summary: To provide financial assistance for undergraduate education to the children and spouses of members of Coast Guard Mutual Assistance (CGMA).

Eligibility: Eligible to apply for these grants are the children and spouses of members of the organization who are enrolled or planning to enroll as full-time undergraduate students in an accredited college, university, or vocational/trade school. Children must be under 23 years of age, unmarried, a non-service member, and dependent upon the CGMA member for more than half of their support. Financial need is considered in the selection process.

Financial data: Grants are $1,000.

Duration: 1 year; may be renewed as long as the recipient maintains at least a 2.0 grade point average.

Additional information: CGMA membership is open to active-duty and retired Coast Guard personnel.

Number awarded: At least 250 each year.

Deadline: March of each year.

200
COCA-COLA FIRST GENERATION SCHOLARSHIP PROGRAM

Oregon Independent College Foundation
121 S.W. Salmon Street, Suite 1230
Portland, OR 97204
Phone: (503) 227-7568   Fax: (503) 227-2454
E-mail: danaoicf@teleport.com

Summary: To provide financial assistance to high school seniors in Oregon who are the first in their family to go to college.

Eligibility: This program is open to Oregon high school seniors who are the first in their immediate family to go to college. Applicants must plan to enroll full time as first-year students at a college or university that is a member of the Oregon Independent College Foundation (OICF). Selection is based on financial need and involvement in school and community activities.

Financial data: The stipend is $5,000 per year.

Duration: 1 year; may be renewed if the recipient maintains at least a 3.0 grade point average and participates in campus and community life.

Additional information: The OICF member institutions are Marylhurst University, Lewis and Clark College, Pacific University, Warner Pacific College, the University of Portland, George Fox College, Linfield College, Reed College,

Concordia College, and Willamette University. Funding for this program is provided by the Coca-Cola Foundation.

Number awarded: 9 each year: 1 at each of the participating institutions.

201
COCA-COLA FIRST GENERATION SCHOLARSHIPS

Wisconsin Foundation for Independent Colleges, Inc.
735 North Water Street, Suite 800
Milwaukee, WI 53202-4100
Phone: (414) 273-5980   Fax: (414) 273-5995
E-mail: wfic@execpc.com
Web Site: www.wficweb.org

Summary: To provide financial assistance to entering freshmen at private institutions in Wisconsin who are the first in their family to attend college.

Eligibility: This program is open to entering freshmen at the 21 independent colleges or universities in Wisconsin. Applicants must be the first in their family to attend college. Selection is based on financial need and involvement and leadership in campus and community activities.

Financial data: The stipend is $5,000 per year.

Duration: 1 year; may be renewed if the recipient remains in good academic standing and enrolled full time.

Additional information: The participating schools are Alverno College, Beloit College, Cardinal Stritch University, Carroll College, Carthage College, Concordia University of Wisconsin, Edgewood College, Lakeland College, Lawrence University, Marian College, Marquette University, Milwaukee Institute of Art & Design, Milwaukee School of Engineering, Mount Mary College, Northland College, Ripon College, St. Norbert College, Silver Lake College, Viterbo University, and Wisconsin Lutheran College.

Number awarded: 21 each year: 1 at each of the participating schools.

Deadline: June of each year.

202
COCA-COLA SCHOLARSHIPS

Coca-Cola Scholars Foundation, Inc.
P.O. Box 442
Atlanta, GA 30301-0442
Phone: (404) 676-2121   (800) 306-COKE
E-mail: scholars@cocacola.com
Web Site: www.thecoca-colacompany.com/scholars

Summary: To provide financial aid for the postsecondary education of meritorious students.

Eligibility: Applicants must be high school seniors who are planning to attend an accredited U.S. college or university. Awards are based on an individual's character, personal merit (demonstrated by leadership in school, civic, and other extracurricular activities, academic achievement, and motivation to serve and succeed in all endeavors), and commitment. Selection is sensitive to the ethnic and economic backgrounds of applicants, reflecting as much as possible the demographic profiles of the various selection districts. Candidates are ineligible if they are already in college; children or grandchildren of employees, officers, or owners of Coca-Cola bottling companies, the Coca-Cola Company, or any bottler or company divisions or subsidiaries; U.S. students attending foreign schools; or international students wishing to attend U.S. postsecondary institutions.

Financial data: Awards are $5,000 or $1,000 per year.

Duration: All scholarships are for 4 years.

Additional information: This program was established by Coca-Cola bottlers to celebrate the 1986 Coca-Cola Centennial. Applications are available only from school guidance counselors.

Number awarded: 250 each year: 50 at $5,000 per year and 200 at $1,000 per year.

Deadline: October of each year; approximately 2,000 semifinalists, dispersed proportionately across the 11 selection districts, are chosen and they submit an additional application, including detailed biographical data, an essay, secondary school report, and recommendations, by the end of January.

203
COLLEGE FUND/UNCF ACADEMIC MAJOR-BASED SCHOLARSHIPS

College Fund/UNCF
Attn: Director, Educational Services
8260 Willow Oaks Corporate Drive
P.O. Box 10444
Fairfax, VA 22031-4511
Phone: (703) 205-3400
Web Site: www.uncf.org

Summary: To provide financial assistance to students who are interested in pursuing specified majors at member institutions of the United Negro College Fund (UNCF).

Eligibility: These programs are open to students planning to pursue designated majors at UNCF-member institutions. Applicants must be high school graduates with strong academic backgrounds (minimum grade point average of 2.5). Students who have completed their junior year in high school with a record of distinction may also be considered. Financial need must be demonstrated. Applications should be submitted directly to the UNCF-member institution the student plans to attend.

Financial data: The awards are intended to cover tuition and range from a minimum of $500 to a maximum of $7,500 per year.

Duration: 1 year; may be renewed.

Additional information: Examples of the scholarships that have been available include the Amway/Ebony Business Leadership Scholarship for business administration; the Avon (WISE) Women in Search of Excellence Scholarship for business or economics (for women only, half of whom must be of nontraditional college age); the GAP Foundation Scholars Program for fashion design, merchandise management, retail management, or business administration; the General Motors Engineering Excellence Awards for engineering; the Harry C. Jaecker Scholarship for pre-medical students; the John Lennon Scholarship Fund for the performing arts and communications; the Carmen Rosario Battle Scholarship for mathematics or Spanish; the Metropolitan Life Scholarship Program for teacher education and health-related fields; the Michael Jackson Scholarship for the performing arts and communications; the Morgan Stanley Scholarship for finance and banking; the PaineWebber Scholarships for business-related fields; the Quaker Oats Scholarship Program for accounting, business administration, engineering, and liberal arts; the Raymond W. Cannon Memorial Scholarship Program for pharmacy or pre-law; the Reader's Digest Scholarship for communications, English, or journalism; the William Wrigley, Jr. Scholarship for business, engineering, and chemistry; the Rhythm Nation/Janet Jackson Scholarship for communications, the fine arts, music, and the performing arts; the RMCC/UNCF Health and Medical Scholars Program for pre-medical and health professions; the Stan Scott Scholarship for journalism; the Tenneco Scholarship for business, mathematics, and science; the Texaco Scholarship Program for engineering; the Revlon Women's Health and Medical Scholarship for pre-medicine or other health care-related fields (women only); and the Wyeth-Ayerst/American Home Products Scholarship for health-based or science-based careers. Recipients must attend a UNCF-member institution of higher learning. These are: Miles College, Oakwood College, Stillman College, Talladega College, and Tuskegee University in Alabama; Philander Smith College in Arkansas; Bethune-Cookman College, Edward Waters College, and Florida Memorial College in Florida; Clark Atlanta University, Interdenominational Theological Center, Morehouse College, Morris Brown College, Paine College, and Spelman College in Georgia; Dillard University and Xavier University in Louisiana; Rust College and Tougaloo College in Mississippi; Barber-Scotia College, Bennett College, Johnson C. Smith University, Livingstone College, Saint Augustine's College, and Shaw University in North Carolina; Wilberforce University in Ohio; Benedict College, Claflin College, Morris College, and Voorhees College in South Carolina; Fisk University, Knoxville College, Lane College, and LeMoyne-Owens College in Tennessee; Huston-Tillotson College, Jarvis Christian College, Paul Quinn College, and Wiley College in Texas; and Saint Paul's College and Virginia Union University in Virginia.

Number awarded: A total of nearly 1,200 UNCF scholarships are awarded each year.

Deadline: Deadline dates vary, depending upon the individual institution's requirements.

204
COLLEGE RETENTION/GENERAL PROGRAM OF THE HISPANIC SCHOLARSHIP FUND

Hispanic Scholarship Fund
Attn: Selection Committee
One Sansome Street, Suite 1000
San Francisco, CA 94104
Phone: (415) 445-9930   (877) HSF-INFO, ext. 33
Fax: (415) 445-9942   E-mail: info@hsf.net
Web Site: www.hsf.net
Summary: To provide financial assistance to Hispanic American students who are pursuing postsecondary education on the undergraduate or graduate level.
Eligibility: This program is open to U.S. citizens or permanent residents of at least half Hispanic background who are currently enrolled full time in a community college, 4-year college or university, professional school, or graduate school. Applicants must have completed at least 15 units of college work with a grade point average of 2.7 or higher. They may be attending school in the United States or Puerto Rico. Selection is based on academic achievement, letters of recommendation, a personal statement (demonstrating writing and language skills, personal strengths and goals, professionalism, community involvement, and other qualities), and financial need.
Financial data: The stipends normally range from $1,000 to $2,500 per year.
Duration: 1 year; may reapply.
Additional information: Since this program began in 1975, more than $47 million has been awarded to more than 40,000 Hispanic students. Requests for applications must be accompanied by a self-addressed stamped envelope.
Number awarded: More than 4,000 each year.
Deadline: October of each year.

205
COLLEGE-SPONSORED ACHIEVEMENT SCHOLARSHIP AWARDS

National Merit Scholarship Corporation
Attn: National Achievement Scholarship Program
1560 Sherman Avenue, Suite 200
Evanston, IL 60201-4897
Phone: (847) 866-5100
Summary: To provide financial assistance to outstanding African American high school students interested in going to college.
Eligibility: After recipients of the National Merit Scholarship Corporation's National Achievement Scholarships and Corporate-Sponsored Achievement Scholarships have been chosen, the remaining African American National Merit finalists are contacted and asked to report their current college choice. Those who reply that a sponsor college or university is their first choice are referred to officials of that institution as candidates for the College-Sponsored Achievement Scholarship Program. College officials select the award winners.
Financial data: College officials calculate each winner's stipend (based on financial information reported directly to the college), which ranges from $250 to $2,000 per year. Some colleges use a method known as "packaging aid" to meet the financial need of their award winners; in such instances, a College-Sponsored Achievement Scholarship may be supplemented with loans, employment, and grants. However, unless all of the winner's need is met with gift aid, the stipend must represent at least half of the student's need, up to a maximum annual stipend of $2,000.
Duration: 1 year; renewable for up to 3 additional years.
Additional information: Approximately 35 colleges and universities in the United States offer scholarships as part of this program. Every scholarship offered through this program is awarded with the condition that it can be used only at the institution funding it; therefore, an offer is canceled if a winner changes college choice.
Number awarded: Varies; generally, approximately 200 each year.

206
COLLEGE-SPONSORED MERIT SCHOLARSHIP AWARDS

National Merit Scholarship Corporation
Attn: Department of Educational Services and Selection
1560 Sherman Avenue, Suite 200
Evanston, IL 60201-4897
Phone: (847) 866-5100
Summary: To identify and honor scholastically talented high school students and provide them with financial support for college.
Eligibility: After recipients of National Merit Scholarships and Corporate-

Sponsored Merit Scholarships have been chosen, the remaining National Merit finalists are contacted and asked to report their current college choice. Those who reply that a sponsor college or university is their first choice are referred to officials of that institution as candidates for the College-Sponsored Merit Scholarship Program. College officials select the award winners.
Financial data: College officials determine each winner's stipend within a range of $250 to $2,000 per year. The college may meet part of a winner's financial need with loans, employment, and grants; however, unless the student's total need (as calculated by the college) is met with gift aid, the Merit Scholarship must represent at least half the winner's need, up to an annual maximum stipend of $2,000.
Duration: 1 year; renewable for up to 3 additional years.
Additional information: Every scholarship offered through this program is awarded with the condition that it can be used only at the institution funding it; therefore, an offer is canceled if a winner changes college choice.
Number awarded: Approximately 4,000 each year, offered by approximately 200 colleges and universities.

207
COLLEGENET SCHOLARSHIP

CollegeNET
805 S.W. Broadway, Suite 1600
Portland, OR 97205-3356
Phone: (503) 973-5253   Fax: (503) 973-5252
Web Site: www.collegenet.com
Summary: To provide financial assistance to students using the CollegeNET service to apply to college.
Eligibility: This program is open to all students who use the CollegeNET online system to apply to college. Currently, more than 40 colleges and universities have contracted with CollegeNET to receive applications from prospective students. All students who submit their applications via CollegeNET and then successfully enroll as a full-time student at a CollegeNET client school in the fall are eligible for this scholarship. If they are subsequently nominated by their institution, they must submit an essay on a topic that changes annually; recently, the topic was "War of Civilizations" and its relationship to the terrorist attack of September 11, 2001. Final selection of the scholarship winners is based on the essay.
Financial data: Stipends are $10,000, $5,000, and $1,000.
Duration: 1 year.
Additional information: CollegeNET was launched in 1995 and began offering this scholarship in 1997.
Number awarded: 3 each year.
Deadline: Students must submit their college application by the end of August of each year. Each participating college then nominates its students in January and those nominees have 3 weeks to prepare their essays and submit them online.

208
COLORADO BUSINESS AND PROFESSIONAL WOMEN'S FOUNDATION SCHOLARSHIP

Colorado Business and Professional Women's Foundation, Inc.
Attn: Scholarship Committee
P.O. Box 1189
Boulder, CO 80306
Phone: (303) 595-5405, ext. 2
Web Site: ben.boulder.co.us/business/colobpwf/cbpwf_scholar_award.htm
Summary: To provide financial assistance for college to women (preferably mature women) residing in Colorado.
Eligibility: This program is open to women who have resided in Colorado for the preceding 12 months. Applicants must be U.S. citizens, must attend or plan to attend an educational institution of higher learning or vocational training located and accredited in Colorado, and must be able to demonstrate financial need, scholastic ability, leadership skills, and career goals. Priority is given to students of nontraditional age. To apply, eligible students must submit a completed application form, 3 letters of recommendation, a copy of their acceptance letter, a needs assessment, a summary of their educational and career goals, a copy of their most recent high school or college transcript, proof of U.S. citizenship, and a copy of their prior year's tax return.
Financial data: Stipends range from $500 to $1,000. Funds are to be used for tuition, fees, or books.
Duration: 1 semester; recipients may reapply.
Number awarded: Varies each year; recently, 14 of these scholarships were awarded.
Deadline: Applications may be submitted in March, June, or October.

209
COLORADO DEPENDENTS TUITION ASSISTANCE PROGRAM

Colorado Commission on Higher Education
1380 Lawrence Street, Suite 1200
Denver, CO 80204
Phone: (303) 866-2723   Fax: (303) 866-4266
E-mail: cche@state.co.us
Web Site: www.state.co.us/cche_dir/hecche.html
Summary: To provide financial assistance for postsecondary education to the dependents of disabled or deceased Colorado National Guardsmen, law enforcement officers, and fire fighters.
Eligibility: Eligible for the program are dependents of Colorado law enforcement officers, fire fighters, and National Guardsmen disabled or killed in the line of duty, as well as dependents of prisoners of war or service personnel listed as missing in action. Students must be Colorado residents enrolled at a school participating in the program. Dependents of disabled personnel must demonstrate financial need.
Financial data: Eligible students receive free tuition at Colorado public institutions of higher education. If the recipient wishes to attend a private college, university, or proprietary school, the award is limited to the amount of tuition at a comparable state-supported institution.
Duration: Up to 8 academic semesters or 12 academic quarters, provided the recipient maintains a grade point average of 2.5 or higher.
Additional information: Recipients must attend accredited postsecondary institutions in Colorado.
Number awarded: Varies each year.

210
COLORADO LEVERAGING EDUCATIONAL ASSISTANCE PARTNERSHIP (CLEAP)

Colorado Commission on Higher Education
1380 Lawrence Street, Suite 1200
Denver, CO 80204
Phone: (303) 866-2723   Fax: (303) 866-4266
E-mail: cche@state.co.us
Web Site: www.state.co.us/cche_dir/hecche.html
Summary: To provide financial assistance for undergraduate education to residents of Colorado who can demonstrate financial need.
Eligibility: Eligible for the program are residents of Colorado who are enrolled or accepted for enrollment in eligible postsecondary institutions in Colorado. Selection is based on financial need.
Financial data: The amount of assistance varies, to a maximum of $5,000 per year.
Duration: 1 year; renewable.
Additional information: Applications are available either from Colorado Commission on Higher Education or from the financial aid office of eligible Colorado institutions. This program was formerly known as the Colorado Student Incentive Grant (CSIG) Program.
Number awarded: Varies each year.
Deadline: Each participating institution sets its own deadlines.

211
COLORADO PRIVATE SCHOOL ASSOCIATION SCHOLARSHIP

Colorado Private School Association
P.O. Box 46125
Denver, CO 80201
Phone: (303) 360-0437   Fax: (303) 860-0433
E-mail: sdurham1@uswest.net
Web Site: www. olorado-psa.org
Summary: To provide financial assistance to high school seniors in Colorado interested in attending a postsecondary private technical college.
Eligibility: This program is open to high school seniors and graduates (or the equivalent) in Colorado who are planning to attend an accredited postsecondary private technical trade college that is a member of the Colorado Private School Association. Applicants must demonstrate financial need, have earned at least a 3.0 grade point average in high school, and be a Colorado resident.
Financial data: The stipend is $1,000. Funds are paid jointly to the recipient and the recipients school and may be used to pay for tuition, fees, books, or supplies.
Duration: 1 year.
Additional information: The scholarship must be used during the calendar year for which the scholarship is awarded.
Number awarded: 2 each year.
Deadline: April of each year.

212
COLORADO STATE GRANGE SCHOLARSHIPS

Colorado State Grange Leadership and Scholarship Foundation
Attn: Scholarship Foundation Secretary
3905 Independence Court
Wheat Ridge, CO 80033-4109
Phone: (303) 424-3542   E-mail: rnekipl@aol.com
Web Site: www.grange.org/Colorado/scolarships.htm
Summary: To provide financial assistance for college to Colorado Grange members or their children.
Eligibility: This program is open to initiated or associate Colorado Grange members with at least 1 year's membership and their children or grandchildren. They may be high school seniors or currently-enrolled college students. Supportive members and their relatives are not eligible. Selection is based on scholastic achievement, Grange involvement, activities, personality, character, and promise of success.
Financial data: The amount awarded is determined annually by the foundation board. Funds are paid, in 2 equal installments, to either the recipient's school or to the recipient in the name of the school.
Duration: 1 year.
Additional information: Recipients must attend a college or university in Colorado on a full-time basis.
Number awarded: Varies each year.
Deadline: March of each year.

213
COLORADO STUDENT GRANTS

Colorado Commission on Higher Education
1380 Lawrence Street, Suite 1200
Denver, CO 80204
Phone: (303) 866-2723   Fax: (303) 866-4266
E-mail: cche@state.co.us
Web Site: www.state.co.us/cche_dir/hecche.html
Summary: To provide financial assistance for undergraduate education to residents of Colorado who can demonstrate financial need.
Eligibility: Eligible for the program are residents of Colorado who are enrolled or accepted for enrollment in participating postsecondary institutions in Colorado. Selection is based on financial need, as indicated by the student's expected family contribution (EFC) and the amount required for a Federal Pell Grant. Students whose EFC is between zero and 150 percent of that required for a Pell Grant are in level 1, students whose EFC is between 150 and 200 percent of that required for the minimum Pell Grant are in level 2, and all other students who demonstrate financial need are in level 3.
Financial data: The amount of assistance varies. Students in level 1 receive at least $1,500 or the maximum amount of unmet need, whichever is less; students in level 2 receive up to $2,500 or the maximum amount of unmet need, whichever is less; students in level 3 receive up to $500.
Duration: 1 year; renewable.
Additional information: Applications are available either from Colorado Commission on Higher Education or from the financial aid office of eligible Colorado institutions.
Number awarded: Varies each year.
Deadline: Each participating institution sets its own deadlines.

214
COLORADO UNDERGRADUATE MERIT SCHOLARSHIP PROGRAM

Colorado Commission on Higher Education
1380 Lawrence Street, Suite 1200
Denver, CO 80204
Phone: (303) 866-2723   Fax: (303) 866-4266
E-mail: cche@state.co.us
Web Site: www.state.co.us/cche_dir/hecche.html
Summary: To provide financial assistance for postsecondary education to residents of Colorado with special skills.
Eligibility: Eligible for the program are residents of Colorado (as well as a limited number of non-residents) who are enrolled or accepted for enrollment at public, private, and proprietary schools of higher education in Colorado. High school seniors must demonstrate academic achievement on the basis of grade point average or class rank, standardized test scores, or a competitive process or portfolio review. Transfer students must demonstrate academic excellence by

transferring into the institution with a cumulative college grade point average of 3.0 or higher.

Financial data: The amount of assistance varies, up to actual cost of tuition and fees.

Duration: 1 year; renewable if the recipient maintains a GPA of 3.0 or higher.

Additional information: Applications are available either from Colorado Commission on Higher Education or from the financial aid office of eligible Colorado institutions.

Number awarded: Varies each year.

Deadline: Each participating institution sets its own deadlines.

215
COMMANDER WILLIAM S. STUHR SCHOLARSHIPS

Commander William S. Stuhr Scholarship Fund
c/o Joseph A. LaRivere, Executive Director
1200 Fifth Avenue, Suite 9-D
New York, NY 10029

Summary: To provide financial assistance for the postsecondary education of the dependent children of retired or active-duty military personnel.

Eligibility: This program is open to the dependent children of military personnel who are serving on active duty or retired with pay after 20 years' service (not merely separated from service). Applicants must be high school seniors who rank in the top 10 percent of their class and have scores of at least 1250 on the SAT or 27 on the ACT. They must plan to attend a 4-year accredited college. Selection is based on academic performance, extracurricular activities, demonstrated leadership potential, and financial need.

Financial data: The stipend is $1,130 per year, up to a lifetime total of $4,500.

Duration: 4 years.

Additional information: This program was established in 1965. Recipients and their families attend a scholarship awards function in late May or early June; the fund pays air transportation to the event. Applications may be obtained only by writing and enclosing a self-addressed stamped envelope. The fund does not respond to telephone, fax, or e-mail inquiries.

Number awarded: 5 each year: 1 for a child of a military servicemember from each of the 5 branches (Air Force, Army, Coast Guard, Marine Corps, and Navy).

Deadline: February of each year.

216
COMMUNITY CARING PROGRAM SCHOLARSHIP

Community Caring Program
P.O. Box 52
Royal Oak, MI 48068-0052
Phone: (248) 691-6864

Summary: To provide financial assistance for any level of education to Michigan residents.

Eligibility: Students under the age of 25 who are Michigan residents are eligible to apply for this program. They may be pre-elementary, elementary, secondary, or postsecondary students. Financial need is required. Applications may be made by the candidate, school principal, guidance counselor, or other appropriate personnel who is knowledgeable about the student's skills, abilities, and potential for success. A personal interview may be required. Selection is based on a number of factors, including community and personal activities, financial need, goals, resourcefulness, and cooperation. Applications from children facing life threatening illness are given special attention.

Financial data: The stipend is $1,000. Funds are paid to the recipient's school and may be used for books, tuition, and other educational expenses.

Duration: 1 year.

Additional information: This program was established in 1995 by a group of community leaders in the Detroit metropolitan area.

Number awarded: 45 each year.

Deadline: March of each year.

217
CONGRESSIONAL BLACK CAUCUS SPOUSES SCHOLARSHIP FUND PROGRAM

Congressional Black Caucus Foundation, Inc.
Attn: Director, Educational Programs
1004 Pennsylvania Avenue, S.E.
Washington, DC 20003
Phone: (202) 675-6739 (800) 784-2577
Fax: (202) 547-3806 E-mail: spouses@cbcfonline.org
Web Site: www.cbcfonline.org/cbcspouses/scholarship.html

Summary: To provide financial assistance to minority and other students who reside in a congressional district represented by an African American.

Eligibility: This program is open to 1) minority and other graduating high school seniors planning to attend an accredited institution of higher education and 2) currently-enrolled full-time undergraduate, graduate, and doctoral students in good academic standing with at least a 2.5 grade point average. Applicants must reside, attend school, or have attended high school in a congressional district represented by an African American member of Congress. Relatives of caucus members, spouses, and staff are not eligible.

Financial data: The program provides tuition assistance.

Duration: 1 year.

Additional information: The program was established in 1988.

Number awarded: Varies each year.

Deadline: May or September of each year.

218
CONGRESSIONAL HISPANIC CAUCUS INSTITUTE SCHOLARSHIP AWARDS

Congressional Hispanic Caucus Institute, Inc.
504 C Street, N.E.
Washington, DC 20002
Phone: (202) 543-1771 (800) 392-3532
Fax: (202) 546-2143 E-mail: chci@chci.org
Web Site: www.chci.org

Summary: To provide financial assistance for college or graduate school to students of Hispanic descent.

Eligibility: This program is open to U.S. citizens and permanent residents who are Hispanic as defined by the U.S. Census Bureau (individuals of Mexican, Puerto Rican, Cuban, Central and South American, and other Spanish and Latin American descent). Applicants must be attending or planning to attend an accredited community college, 4-year university, or professional or graduate program. They must submit evidence of financial need, consistent and active participation in public service activities, and 3 250-word essays on 1) the most important problem facing the nation today and the role they can play in solving it; 2) the field of study they plan to pursue and why; and 3) the impact of the backlash against affirmative action on Latino enrollment, the Latino community, and higher education in general.

Financial data: The stipend is $5,000 at 4-year and graduate institutions or $2,000 at 2-year community colleges.

Duration: 1 year.

Number awarded: Each year, at least 10 of these scholarships are awarded to students at 4-year and graduate institutions and 5 to students at 2-year community colleges.

Deadline: March of each year.

219
CONNECTICUT AID FOR PUBLIC COLLEGE STUDENTS

Connecticut Department of Higher Education
Attn: Office of Student Financial Aid
61 Woodland Street
Hartford, CT 06105-2326
Phone: (860) 947-1855 Fax: (860) 947-1311
Web Site: www.ctdhe.org

Summary: To provide financial assistance for undergraduate education to Connecticut residents attending public colleges in Connecticut.

Eligibility: Applicants must be residents of Connecticut who are attending a public college in Connecticut. Selection is based on financial need.

Financial data: Awards up to the amount of unmet financial need are provided.

Duration: 1 year.

Additional information: Applications are submitted through college financial aid offices.

Number awarded: Varies each year.

220
CONNECTICUT CAPITOL SCHOLARSHIPS

Connecticut Department of Higher Education
Attn: Office of Student Financial Aid
61 Woodland Street
Hartford, CT 06105-2326
Phone: (860) 947-1855 Fax: (860) 947-1311
Web Site: www.ctdhe.org

Summary: To provide financial assistance for undergraduate education to high school seniors or graduates in Connecticut.

Eligibility: Applicants must be residents of Connecticut who are U.S. citizens or nationals and high school seniors or graduates. They must be in the top 20 percent of their graduating class or have SAT scores of at least 1200, and they must be planning to attend a college in Connecticut or in a state that has a reciprocity agreement with Connecticut. Financial need must be demonstrated.

Financial data: Awards up to $2,000 are provided.

Duration: 1 year.

Additional information: These awards were formerly known as the Connecticut Scholastic Achievement Grants. Applications must be submitted through high school guidance offices.

Number awarded: Varies each year.

Deadline: February of each year.

221
CONNECTICUT INDEPENDENT COLLEGE STUDENT GRANTS

Connecticut Department of Higher Education
Attn: Office of Student Financial Aid
61 Woodland Street
Hartford, CT 06105-2326
Phone: (860) 947-1855   Fax: (860) 947-1311
Web Site: www.ctdhe.org

Summary: To provide financial assistance for undergraduate education to students attending independent colleges in Connecticut.

Eligibility: Applicants must be residents of Connecticut who are attending an independent college in the state. Selection is based on financial need.

Financial data: Awards up to $8,548 per year are provided.

Duration: 1 year.

Additional information: Applications are submitted through college financial aid offices.

Number awarded: Varies each year.

222
CONNECTICUT TUITION SET ASIDE AID

Connecticut Department of Higher Education
Attn: Office of Student Financial Aid
61 Woodland Street
Hartford, CT 06105-2326
Phone: (860) 947-1855   Fax: (860) 947-1311
Web Site: www.ctdhe.org

Summary: To provide financial assistance for undergraduate education to students from any state attending public colleges in Connecticut.

Eligibility: Applicants may be residents of any state but must be attending a public college in Connecticut. Selection is based on financial need.

Financial data: Awards up to the amount of unmet financial need are provided.

Duration: 1 year.

Additional information: Applications are submitted through college financial aid offices.

Number awarded: Varies each year.

223
CONNECTICUT TUITION WAIVER FOR VETERANS

Connecticut Department of Higher Education
Attn: Education and Employment Information Center
61 Woodland Street
Hartford, CT 06105-2326
Phone: (860) 947-1810   (800) 842-0229 (within CT)
Fax: (860) 947-1310
Web Site: www.ctdhe.org

Summary: To provide financial assistance for postsecondary education to certain Connecticut veterans.

Eligibility: Eligible are honorably discharged Connecticut veterans who served at least 90 days during World War II, the Korean hostilities, in Vietnam, or as part of Operations Desert Shield and Desert Storm, or who served in a combat or combat-support role in the peace-keeping mission in Lebanon, the Grenada invasion, Operation Earnest Will, or the Panama invasion.

Financial data: The program provides a waiver of 100 percent of tuition for general fund courses at a Connecticut public college or university, or 50 percent of tuition for extension and summer courses at Connecticut State University.

Duration: Up to 4 years.

Additional information: This is an entitlement program; applications are available at the respective college financial aid offices.

Number awarded: Varies each year.

224
CORELLA AND BERTRAM F. BONNER SCHOLARS PROGRAM

Corella and Bertram F. Bonner Foundation
10 Mercer Street
Princeton, NJ 08540
Phone: (609) 924-6663   Fax: (609) 683-4626
E-mail: info@bonner.org
Web Site: www.bonner.org

Summary: To provide scholarships to high school seniors who need help paying for college and who have a commitment to strengthening their communities through service.

Eligibility: This program is open to graduating high school seniors planning to attend a participating college throughout the southeastern and midwestern United States. Applicants must have significant financial need, a solid academic performance in high school (graduating in the top 40 percent of their class), acceptance at a participating college, and demonstrated responsibility and good citizenship at home, school, church/synagogue, or in the community. Interested students must contact the admissions office at the participating Bonner college they wish to attend.

Financial data: Scholarships receive a stipend of $2,100 as school year support, a summer earnings stipend of up to $1,500 for each of their first 2 summers, a summer living stipend (for living and travel expenses) of up to $1,000 for each of their first 2 summers and $500 for the third summer, and a grant of up to $1,600 for reducing their total educational loan indebtedness at the time of graduation.

Duration: 1 year; may be renewed up to 3 additional years.

Additional information: This program was established in 1990. Currently, there are more than 1,500 Bonner Scholars at 25 college campuses throughout the southeast and midwest. The participating colleges are: Antioch College (Yellow Springs, Ohio), Berea College (Berea, Kentucky), Berry College (Rome, Georgia), Carson-Newman College (Johnson City, Tennessee), College of the Ozarks (Point Lookout, Missouri), Concord College (Athens, West Virginia), Davidson College (Davidson, North Carolina), DePauw University (Greencastle, Indiana), Earlham College (Richmond, Indiana), Emory & Henry College (Emory, Virginia), Ferrum College (Ferrum, Virginia), Guilford College (Greensboro, North Carolina), Hood College (Frederick, Maryland), Mars Hill College (Mars Hill, North Carolina), Maryville College (Maryville, Tennessee), Morehouse College (Atlanta, Georgia), Oberlin College (Oberlin, Ohio), Rhodes College (Memphis, Tennessee), Spelman College (Atlanta, Georgia), Union College (Barbourville, Kentucky), University of Richmond (Richmond, Virginia), Warren Wilson College (Asheville, North Carolina), Waynesburg College (Waynesburg, Pennsylvania), West Virginia Wesleyan College (Buckhannon, West Virginia), and Wofford College (Spartanburg, South Carolina). This is a service-for-scholarship program. Bonner Scholars are expected to serve their communities by performing at least 10 hours of community service each week during the academic year and full-time service during the summer.

225
CORPORATE-SPONSORED ACHIEVEMENT SCHOLARSHIPS

National Merit Scholarship Corporation
Attn: National Achievement Scholarship Program
1560 Sherman Avenue, Suite 200
Evanston, IL 60201-4897
Phone: (847) 866-5100

Summary: To provide financial assistance to outstanding African American high school students planning to attend college.

Eligibility: Because winners of these scholarships must meet preferential criteria specified by sponsors, not all finalists for the National Achievement Scholarship Program are considered for this award, and the awards are not subject to regional allocation. Further, corporate sponsors frequently offer their awards to finalists who are children of their employees or residents of an area where a plant or office is located. Some companies offer scholarships for students who plan to pursue particular college majors or careers. Finalists who have qualifications that especially interest a sponsor are identified and winners are selected from among eligible candidates.

Financial data: Most of these scholarships provide stipends that are individually determined, taking into account college costs and family financial circumstances. Variable stipend awards of this type range from at least $500 to $2,000 per year,

although some have a higher annual minimum and a few range as high as $10,000 per year. Some renewable awards provide a fixed annual stipend (between $1,000 and $5,000) that is the same for every recipient of the sponsor's awards. Other corporate-sponsored scholarships are nonrenewable and provide a single payment (from $2,000 to $5,000) for the recipient's first year of college study.
Duration: 1 year; most awards are renewable up to 3 additional years.
Additional information: These awards are sponsored by approximately 80 corporations, company foundations, and professional organizations.
Number awarded: Approximately 160 each year.

226
CORPORATE-SPONSORED MERIT AND SPECIAL SCHOLARSHIPS

National Merit Scholarship Corporation
Attn: Department of Educational Services and Selection
1560 Sherman Avenue, Suite 200
Evanston, IL 60201-4897
Phone: (847) 866-5100
Summary: To honor scholastically talented high school students and provide them with financial support for college undergraduate study.
Eligibility: High school seniors who are high scorers in the National Merit Scholarship Program but who are not awarded scholarships are considered for this program. Those who are named as finalists receive these Merit Scholarships, awarded by corporate sponsors to students who fulfill preferential criteria specified by the award sponsor; usually, the criteria require that the recipient be the child of an employee of the sponsoring corporation, although some are offered to residents of a service area or community where a business has plants or offices or to students with career plans the sponsor wishes to encourage. Some corporate sponsors also offer Special Scholarships; those are offered to students who did not qualify as finalists in the National Merit Scholarship Program but may receive these awards because the corporate sponsor wishes to award scholarships to the specified groups, even though not all have achieved status as Merit Scholars. Some of the Corporate and Special Scholarships are merit-based; others consider financial need.
Financial data: Most of these scholarships provide stipends that are individually determined, taking into account college costs and family financial circumstances. Variable stipend awards of this type range from at least $500 to $2,000 per year, although some have a higher annual minimum and a few range as high as $10,000 per year. Some renewable awards provide a fixed annual stipend (between $1,000 and $5,000) that is the same for every recipient of the sponsor's awards. Other corporate-sponsored scholarships are nonrenewable and provide a single payment (from $2,000 to $5,000) for the recipient's first year of college study.
Duration: 1 year; many may be renewed up to 3 additional years.
Additional information: Each year, approximately 400 corporations, company foundations, and businesses fund these scholarships.
Number awarded: Approximately 1,200 Corporate-Sponsored Merit Scholarships and 1,400 Corporate-Sponsored Special Scholarships are awarded each year.

227
COSA YOUTH DEVELOPMENT PROGRAM SCHOLARSHIPS

Confederation of Oregon School Administrators
Attn: COSA Foundation
707 13th Street, S.E., Suite 100
Salem, OR 97301-4035
Phone: (503) 581-3141   Fax: (503) 581-9840
E-mail: nancy@oasc.org
Web Site: www.cosa.k12.or.us
Summary: To provide financial assistance to high school seniors in Oregon who are interested in attending a community college, college, or university in the state.
Eligibility: This program is open to graduating high school seniors in Oregon. Applicants should be interested in attending a community college, college, or university in the state. They must have been active in community and school affairs, have at least a 3.5 grade point average, and enroll in the fall term after graduating from high school. To apply, students must submit a completed application form, a 1-page autobiography (that states personal goals), the name of the school they plan to attend, and the endorsement of a member of the Confederation of Oregon School Administrators (COSA). Financial need is not considered in the selection process.
Financial data: The stipend is $1,000. Funds are paid directly to the recipient.

Duration: 1 year; nonrenewable.
Additional information: This program is supported by MetLife Resources. This program includes the following named awards: the Joe Benninghoff Scholarship, the George Martin Scholarship, the Wilma Wells Scholarship, and the David Putnam Scholarship.
Number awarded: 4 each year.
Deadline: February of each year.

228
CREEK NATION HIGHER EDUCATION UNDERGRADUATE GRANT PROGRAM

Creek Nation of Oklahoma
Attn: Higher Education Program
P.O. Box 580
Okmulgee, OK 74447
Phone: (918) 756-8700, ext. 615   (800) 482-1979, ext. 615
E-mail: highed@ocevnet
Web Site: www.ocevnet.org/creek/highed.html
Summary: To provide educational grants to aid Creek undergraduate students who are interested in pursuing postsecondary studies.
Eligibility: Eligible to apply are Creek students of any degree of Indian blood who are attending or planning to attend an accredited institution of higher learning. Financial need must be demonstrated.
Financial data: The amount awarded varies, up to a maximum of $2,000 per year. The exact amount depends upon the financial needs of the recipient. Full-time students may use these funds to pay for tuition and fees, books and supplies, room and board, transportation, and personal expenses (including medical and child care). Part-time students (less than 12 credits) may use their funds for tuition, fees, and books, not to exceed the in-state cost at a 2- or 4-year college or university.
Duration: 1 year; may be renewed for a maximum of 10 semesters of funding as long as the recipient enrolls in at least 15 hours per term and maintains a grade point average of 2.0 or higher.
Additional information: The Creek Nation of Oklahoma administers the Higher Education Program. This program expends funds appropriated by Congress for the education of Indian students. Recipients who withdraw from school are suspended until they have financed themselves for 1 full semester and passed 12 credit hours with a grade point average of 2.0 or higher.
Number awarded: Varies each year.
Deadline: May of each year.

229
CREEK NATION TRIBAL FUNDS GRANT PROGRAM

Creek Nation of Oklahoma
Attn: Higher Education Program
P.O. Box 580
Okmulgee, OK 74447
Phone: (918) 756-8700, ext. 615   (800) 482-1979, ext. 615
E-mail: highed@oceynet
Web Site: www.ocevnet.org/creek/highed.html
Summary: To provide financial assistance to enrolled citizens of the Muscogee (Creek) Nation attending an accredited college or university.
Eligibility: All enrolled citizens of the Muscogee (Creek) Nation are eligible to apply (with no minimum blood quantum required) if they are enrolled or planning to enroll in an accredited college or university. Financial need is not required.
Financial data: The maximum stipend is $500 per semester for full-time students (12 credit hours or more per semester) or $250 per semester for part-time students (less than 12 hours). Support may not exceed $1,000 per year. The award may be used to supplement other financial aid sources.
Duration: 1 year; may be renewed up to 3 additional years (as long as the recipient maintains at least a 2.5 grade point average).
Additional information: Recipients who withdraw from school or earn less than a 1.5 grade point average are suspended until they have financed themselves for 1 full semester and passed 12 credit hours with at least a grade point average of 2.0.
Number awarded: Varies each year.
Deadline: May of each year.

230
CREEK NATION TRIBAL INCENTIVE GRANT PROGRAM

Creek Nation of Oklahoma
Attn: Higher Education Program
P.O. Box 580
Okmulgee, OK 74447
Phone: (918) 756-8700, ext. 615   (800) 482-1979, ext. 615
E-mail: highed@ocevnet
Web Site: www.ocevnet.org/creek/highed.html
Summary: To provide financial assistance to enrolled citizens of the Muscogee (Creek) Nation attending an accredited college or university.
Eligibility: All enrolled citizens of the Muscogee (Creek) Nation are eligible to apply (with no minimum blood quantum required) if they are enrolled or planning to enroll in an accredited college or university and have earned a grade point average of 3.0 or higher.
Financial data: The maximum award is $1,000 per academic year.
Duration: 1 semester; may be renewed for up to 9 additional semesters.
Additional information: Recipients who withdraw from school are suspended until they have financed themselves for 1 full semester and passed 12 credit hours with an acceptable grade point average.
Number awarded: Varies each year.
Deadline: June of each year.

231
CUBAN AMERICAN SCHOLARSHIP PROGRAM

Cuban American Scholarship Fund
Attn: Victor Cueto
P.O. Box 6422
Santa Ana, CA 92706
Phone: (714) 835-7676
Summary: To provide financial assistance for postsecondary education to Cuban American students in California.
Eligibility: This program is open to students who are California residents, U.S. citizens or permanent residents, of Cuban descent, and enrolled or planning to enroll as a full-time student in an accredited college or university. A grade point average of 3.0 or higher is required. Selection is based on a statement describing Cuban and family background, personal and academic achievements, current educational status, career goals, community involvement, and financial need.
Financial data: The stipend depends on the need of the recipient and the availability of funds.
Duration: 1 year.
Number awarded: 1 or more each year.
Deadline: April of each year.

232
CUNAT VISIONARY SCHOLARSHIP

Key Club International
Attn: Manager of Youth Funds
3636 Woodview Trace
Indianapolis, IN 46268-3196
Phone: (317) 875-8755, ext. 244   (800) KIWANIS, ext. 244
Fax: (317) 879-0204   E-mail: youthfunds@kiwanis.org
Web Site: www.keyclub.org
Summary: To provide financial assistance for college to high school seniors who are Key Club International members.
Eligibility: Applicants must be graduating high school seniors, be bound for college, have at least a 3.0 grade point average, and have been involved in Key Club for at least 2 years. Applicants must submit a short essay (150 words or less) on the role leadership will play in their future. Selection is based on participation in school activities and organizations; participation in religious and community activities; honors, awards, and special recognition; 3 letters of recommendation; and an essay on how you have exemplified the ideals of Key Club. Financial need is not considered in the selection process.
Financial data: The stipend is $2,500.
Duration: 1 year.
Number awarded: 1 each year.
Deadline: March of each year.

233
CYSTIC FIBROSIS SCHOLARSHIPS

Cystic Fibrosis Scholarship Foundation
2814 Grant Street
Evanston, IL 60201
Phone: (847) 328-0127   E-mail: MKBCFSF@aol.com
Web Site: www.cff.org
Summary: To provide financial assistance to undergraduate or graduate students who have cystic fibrosis.
Eligibility: This program is open to students enrolled or planning to enroll in college (either a 2-year or a 4-year program), vocational school, or graduate school. Applicants must have cystic fibrosis. Selection is based on academic achievement, leadership, and financial need.
Financial data: Stipends range from $1,000 to $2,000. Funds are sent directly to the student's institution to be used for tuition, books, room, and board.
Duration: 1 year.
Additional information: These scholarships were first awarded for 2002.
Deadline: March of each year.

234
DAISY AND L.C. BATES MINORITY SCHOLARSHIP PROGRAM

Southwestern Bell Foundation
P.O. Box 165316
Little Rock, AR 72216
Summary: To provide financial assistance for college to minority high school seniors in Arkansas.
Eligibility: This program is open to minority high school seniors in Arkansas who are planning to attend a 4-year academic institution in the state. As part of the application process, they must submit a short essay on "the importance of a college education." Selection is based on academic achievement, community service, school activities, leadership qualities, financial need, and written communication skills.
Financial data: The stipend is $2,500 per year.
Duration: 1 year; nonrenewable.
Additional information: Recipients must attend a 4-year academic institution in Arkansas.
Number awarded: 10 each year.
Deadline: March of each year.

235
DALE L. MORELAND MEMORIAL SCHOLARSHIP

Chickasaw Foundation
P.O. Box 1726
Ada, OK 74821-1726
Phone: (580) 421-9030   Fax: (580) 421-9031
Web Site: www.cflink.org/scholars.htm
Summary: To provide financial assistance for college to members of the Chickasaw Nation.
Eligibility: This program is open to Chickasaw students who are currently enrolled at an accredited institution of higher education in their freshman through senior year. All academic majors are eligible. Applicants must have a grade point average of 2.5 or higher and must submit a 1-page essay on their long-term goals and plans for achieving them. Financial need is not considered in the selection process.
Financial data: A stipend is awarded (exact amount not specified).
Duration: 1 year.
Number awarded: 1 each year.
Deadline: May of each year.

236
DANIEL CARDILLO CHARITABLE FUND

Maine Community Foundation
Attn: Program Director
245 Main Street
Ellsworth, ME 04605
Phone: (207) 667-9735   (877) 700-6800
Fax: (207) 667-0447   E-mail: info@mainecf.org
Web Site: www.mainecf.org/scholar.html
Summary: To provide financial assistance to Maine residents who are interested in attending college or participating in other programs.

Eligibility: This program is open to young residents of Maine who are 1) interested in attending a college or university; 2) attending an inspirational, educational, and/or leadership program; or 3) participating in an art, music, or athletic program. It is available both to students who are and those who are not in college. Applicants must have a demonstrated need for financial assistance, a demonstrated compassion for others, and a "passion for life activity" and be seeking through the program or educational opportunity to be funded a chance to pursue that passion. They must submit an application form signed by their parent or legal guardian; an essay on how their life has exemplified the qualities, characteristics, and values demonstrated by Daniel Cardillo; a financial information form (if applying for aid to attend college); a letter of acceptance; and 2 letters of reference.

Financial data: A stipend is paid (exact amount not specified).

Duration: Recipients must use the funds within 12 months of the grant or forfeit the award.

Additional information: This program was established in 1999.

Number awarded: 1 or more each year.

Deadline: April of each year for college students; April or December for other applicants.

237
DANIEL V. MARONEY, JR. SCHOLARSHIP COMPETITION

Amalgamated Transit Union
Attn: Scholarship Program Office
5025 Wisconsin Avenue, N.W.
Washington, DC 20016-4139
Phone: (202) 537-1645   Fax: (202) 244-7824
Web Site: www.atu.org

Summary: To provide financial assistance for postsecondary education to members or children of members of the Amalgamated Transit Union (ATU).

Eligibility: This program is open to high school students or graduates who are planning to enter a college, or a technical or vocational postsecondary school, for the first time. Applicants must be a member of the union in good standing, or the child, stepchild, or legally adopted child of a union member in good standing, or the child of a deceased person who was a retired member in good standing at the time of death; spouses and grandchildren of members are not eligible. Selection is based on a biographical questionnaire and an essay of no less than 500, but no more than 750, words on "Organized Labor's Contribution to the Welfare of the People of the United States (or Canada)." Essays may be written in French, English, or Spanish.

Financial data: Annual awards are $2,000 or $1,000.

Duration: 1 year.

Number awarded: 6 each year, of which 5 are for $2,000 (of those, 1 is designated for a Canadian) and 1 is for $1,000 (for use at a trade or vocational school).

Deadline: January of each year.

238
DANIELS COLLEGE PREP AND SCHOLARSHIP PROGRAM

Daniels Fund
55 Madison Street, Suite 255
Denver, CO 80206
Phone: (303) 393-7220   Fax: (303) 393-7339
Web Site: www.danielsfund.org/programs/scholarship/scholarship_main.shtml

Summary: To provide financial assistance for college to underprivileged high school students in Colorado, Utah, Wyoming, and New Mexico.

Eligibility: Underprivileged high school students in Colorado, Utah, Wyoming, and New Mexico may apply to participate in the Daniels College Prep Program, which gives students with financial need the tools they will need to attend college. Upon completion of the program, the participants may apply for 1 of the following scholarships: 1) Level One provides 4-year scholarships to any 4-year accredited college or university in the United States; 2) Level Two provides transition scholarships to any community college, but only if the participant intends to transfer to an accredited 4-year college for the junior and senior years. Selection is based, in part, on need (family income must be no more than $40,000 per year).

Financial data: Stipends are generally $2,000 per year.

Duration: 4 years for both types of scholarships.

Additional information: This scholarship was first awarded in 2000. Daniels, who never graduated from college, made his fortune in the cable industry and was ranked the 223rd richest man in America by *Forbes* magazine.

Number awarded: Varies each year.

239
DANISH SISTERHOOD OF AMERICA PAST NATIONAL OFFICERS SCHOLARSHIP

Danish Sisterhood of America
Attn: Scholarship Chair
7326 Lehigh Court
Zephryhills, FL 34540-1014
Phone: (813) 715-0642
Web Site: danishsisterhood.org/html/scholarships.html

Summary: To provide financial assistance for educational purposes to members or relatives of members of the Danish Sisterhood of America.

Eligibility: This program is open to members or the family of members who concurrently hold a National Scholarship from the sisterhood. Applicants must have a grade point average of 3.8 or higher.

Financial data: The stipend is determined by the national board upon recommendation of the scholarship chair.

Duration: 1 year; nonrenewable.

Number awarded: 1 each year.

Deadline: February of each year.

240
DAUGHTERS OF THE CINCINNATI SCHOLARSHIP PROGRAM

Daughters of the Cincinnati
Attn: Scholarship Administrator
122 East 58th Street
New York, NY 10022
Phone: (212) 319-6915
Web Site: fdncenter.org/grantmaker/cincinnati

Summary: To provide financial assistance for the postsecondary education of daughters of active-duty, deceased, or retired military officers.

Eligibility: Applicants must be daughters of commissioned officers of the regular Army, Navy, Air Force, Coast Guard, or Marine Corps on active duty, deceased, or retired. Only seniors in high school may apply. The Scholastic Assessment Test or the College Entrance Examination Board is required. Selection is based on merit and need.

Financial data: Scholarship amounts vary but generally range from $1,000 to $3,000 per year. Funds are paid directly to the college of the student's choice.

Duration: Scholarships are awarded annually and may be renewed up to 3 additional years while recipients are studying at an accredited college and are in good standing.

Additional information: Scholarships are tenable at the college of the recipient's choice.

Number awarded: Approximately 12 each year.

Deadline: March of each year.

241
DAVID AND DOVETTA WILSON SCHOLARSHIPS

David and Dovetta Wilson Scholarship Fund, Inc.
115-67 237th Street
Elmont, NY 11003-3926
Phone: (516) 285-4573   (800) 759-7512
E-mail: info@wilsonfund.org
Web Site: www.wilsonfund.org

Summary: To provide financial assistance to high school seniors who are interested in going to college.

Eligibility: This program is open to graduating high school seniors who have actively participated in community and religious projects and can demonstrate financial need. Applicants must submit 3 letters of recommendation, high school transcripts, and an essay (up to 250 words) on "How My College Education Will Help Me Make a Positive Impact on My Community."

Financial data: Stipends up to $1,000 are awarded.

Duration: 1 year.

Additional information: Among the awards granted by this organization are the Jeffrey Whitehead Memorial Award, established in 1995, for a graduating high school senior who intends to pursue a career in social service; the Jim Dwyer Award of Excellence, established in 1996, for a recipient whose interests indicate an inclination toward journalism and communication; the Leon Eason Award of Dedication, established in 1997, for the recipient who best embodies the qualities of commitment and dedication to pursuing his or her goals; the Batya Lewton Award of Inspiration, established in 1996, for a student pursuing a career in the field of education; the Mother Dovetta Wilson Leadership Award, established in 1998, for a

recipient whose achievements and efforts exemplify our commitment to each other, our community, our nation, and the world; and the Mother Elnora Johnson Robinson Visionary Award, established in 2000, for a recipient who best displays a zeal for life and a true respect for education. Recipients must attend an accredited college or university. A processing fee of $20 must accompany each application.

Number awarded: 9 each year.

Deadline: February of each year.

242
DAVID HANCOCK MEMORIAL SCHOLARSHIP

Key Club International
Attn: Manager of Youth Funds
3636 Woodview Trace
Indianapolis, IN 46268-3196
Phone: (317) 875-8755, ext. 244   (800) KIWANIS, ext. 244
Fax: (317) 879-0204   E-mail: youthfunds@kiwanis.org
Web Site: www.keyclub.org

Summary: To provide financial assistance for college to high school seniors who are Key Club International members.

Eligibility: Applicants must be graduating high school seniors, be bound for college, have at least a 3.0 grade point average, and have been involved in Key Club for at least 2 years. Applicants must attach additional supporting documentation (up to 10 pages) to show leadership and academic achievement. Selection is based on participation in school activities and organizations; participation in religious and community activities; honors, awards, and special recognition; 3 letters of recommendation; and an essay on how they have exemplified the ideals of Key Club. Financial need is not considered in the selection process.

Financial data: The stipend is $1,000 per year.

Duration: 4 years.

Additional information: This award is funded by Kiwanis International Foundation.

Number awarded: 1 each year.

Deadline: March of each year.

243
DAVID J. FITZMAURICE SCHOLARSHIP

International Union of Electronic, Electrical, Salaried, Machine, and Furniture Workers
Attn: Department of Social Action
1275 K Street, N.W., Suite 600
Washington, DC 20005
Phone: (202) 513-6300   Fax: (202) 513-6357
E-mail: Humphrey@cwa-union.org
Web Site: www.iue-cwa.org

Summary: To provide financial assistance for the undergraduate education of children of members of the International Union of Electronic, Electrical, Salaried, Machine, and Furniture Workers (IUE).

Eligibility: This program is open to children of IUE members (including retired or deceased members). They must be accepted for admission or already enrolled as full-time students at an accredited college, university, nursing school, or technical school offering college credit courses. Families of full-time IUE officers or employees are not eligible to apply. Selection is based on academic record, leadership ability, ambition, good character, commitment to equality, service to the community, and a concern for improving the quality of life for all people.

Financial data: The stipend is $2,000 per year.

Duration: 1 year.

Additional information: Winners who are also awarded local, district, or division scholarships have the option of either accepting the David J. Fitzmaurice Scholarship or the other awards and the dollar difference (if any) between the Fitzmaurice Scholarship and the local, district, or division award.

Number awarded: 1 each year.

Deadline: April of each year.

247
DC TUITION ASSISTANCE GRANT PROGRAM

Government of the District of Columbia
Attn: Tuition Assistance Grant Office
One Judiciary Square
441 Fourth Street, N.W.
Washington, DC 20001
Phone: (202) 727-2824
Phone: TTY: (202) 727-1675
Web Site: www.tuitiongrant.w...

Summary: To provide finan...
who are interested in a...
United States or a priv...

Eligibility: This p...
are high school...
high school...
universiti...
a priv...

Davis-Putter Scholarship Fund
25 Main Street
Belleville, NJ 07109
E-mail: davisputter@hotmail.com

Summary: To provide financial assistance to undergraduate and graduate student activists.

Eligibility: This program is open to undergraduate and graduate students who are "involved in building the movement for social and economic justice." While U.S. citizenship is not required, preference is given to applicants who are involved in the progressive movement in the United States. To apply, students must submit a completed application, a personal statement, financial aid reports, recommendation letters, transcripts, and a photograph.

Financial data: Grants range up to $6,000, depending upon need.

Duration: 1 year.

Additional information: This fund was established in 1961. Early recipients fought for civil rights, against McCarthyism, and to stop the war in Vietnam. More recently, grantees have included students active in the struggle against racism, sexism, homophobia, and other forms of oppression. Applicants may not be requested prior to March 1.

Number awarded: Several each year.

Deadline: April of each year.

246
D.C. LEVERAGING EDUCATIONAL ASSISTANCE PROGRAM (LEAP)

District of Columbia Department of Human Services
Attn: LEAP Staff
2100 Martin Luther King Jr. Avenue S.E., Suite 401
Washington, DC 20020
Phone: (202) 727-3685   Fax: (202) 727-2739
Web Site: www.dhs.washington.dc.us

Summary: To provide financial assistance to Washington, D.C. residents for education or training beyond high school.

Eligibility: In order to be eligible for this money, applicants must meet all of the following criteria: be an established D.C. resident for at least 18 months prior to filing the application; be a U.S. citizen or permanent resident; be enrolled or accepted for enrollment in an undergraduate program at an eligible college or university on at least a half-time basis; have completed at least 1 full academic year; have substantial financial need; and be in good academic standing. All applicants must file a Free Application for Federal Student Aid (FAFSA) and submit a photocopy of their Student Aid Report (SAR) with their LEAP application.

Financial data: A stipend is awarded, based on need.

Duration: 1 year; recipients may reapply.

Additional information: This program is funded through matching funds by the District of Columbia and the federal government. Neither faxed nor duplicated copies of the application are accepted.

Number awarded: Varies each year.

Deadline: June of each year.

(877) 485-6751

...shingtondc.gov

...cial assistance to residents of the District of Columbia
...tending a public college or university anywhere in the
...ate institution in the Washington metropolitan area.
...ogram is open to all residents of the District of Columbia who
... seniors or recent graduates, regardless of where they attended
... Applicants must be interested in attending 1) a public college or
... anywhere in the United States (except in the District of Columbia); 2)
...te nonprofit college or university in the Washington metropolitan area
...ned as the District of Columbia, the cities of Alexandria, Falls Church, and
...airfax, and the counties of Arlington, Fairfax, Montgomery, and Prince George's);
or 3) a private Historically Black College or University (HBCU) in Maryland or
Virginia. Financial need is not required, although students who can demonstrate
need remain eligible for other need-based assistance programs.

Financial data: Awards at public institutions are equal to the difference between
the in-state and out-of-state tuition, to an annual maximum of $10,000 or lifetime
maximum of $50,000. At private institutions, the maximum award is $2,500 per
year or $12,500 over a lifetime. Funds are sent directly to the eligible school and
may be used for tuition and fees only.

Duration: 1 year; may be renewed up to 4 additional years or until completion of
a bachelor's degree.

Additional information: This program was enacted by Congress in 1999.

Number awarded: Varies each year.

Deadline: June of each year.

248
DCAT SCHOLARSHIPS

Drug, Chemical and Allied Trades Association
Attn: Scholarship Program Coordinator
510 Route 130, Suite B1
East Windsor, NJ 08520
Phone: (609) 448-1000   (800) 640-DCAT
Fax: (609-448-19441   E-mail: gdeaner@dcat.org
Web Site: www.dcat.org/scholar.htm

Summary: To provide financial assistance for the undergraduate education of
children of employees of member companies of the Drug, Chemical and Allied
Trades (DCAT) Association.

Eligibility: Eligible are high school graduating seniors who are the sons or
daughters of full-time employees of association member companies in good
standing at the time the award is granted. They must have been accepted by or
anticipating freshman entry into an accredited U.S. college or university as a full-
time student (in any field of study) for the fall semester immediately following the
date of the award. Children of scholarship awards committee members are not
eligible. Selection is based on academic achievement (as measured by SAT or ACT
scores) and leadership qualities.

Financial data: These scholarships are $1,000 per year; checks are issued to both
the student and the qualifying college or university before the beginning of each
fall semester.

Duration: 1 year; may be renewed up to 3 additional years if the recipient
maintains satisfactory progress toward a degree. Students who interrupt their
education may postpone the award for up to 1 year.

Additional information: Applications are available from the personnel
departments of DCAT Association member companies where the parents are
employed.

Number awarded: Varies each year; recently, 11 of these scholarships were
awarded.

Deadline: January of each year.

249
DEB RICHARD FOUNDATION SCHOLARSHIP

Deb Richard Foundation
125 Hidden Cove Lane
Ponte Vedra Beach, FL 32082
E-mail: debrichard@mediaone.net
Web Site: www.debrichard.org/scholarships.htm

Summary: To provide financial assistance for college to physically challenged
high school seniors.

Eligibility: Any graduating high school senior with a physical challenge is eligible
to apply for this scholarship. Applicants must have at least a 2.5 grade point
average (transcripts are required) and submit medical documentation (with a
history of the physical challenge). Financial need is not considered in the selection
process.

Financial data: The stipend is $5,000 per year.

Duration: 1 year; may be renewed up to 4 additional years, provided the student
continues to work on a degree and maintains the grades necessary to remain in
good standing.

Additional information: Recipients must enroll as a full-time student during
the following school year.

Number awarded: 2 each year: 1 to a graduating senior in northeast Florida and
1 nationally.

250
DEF COLLEGE SCHOLARSHIPS

American Wholesale Marketers Association
Attn: Distributors Education Foundation
1128 16th Street, N.W.
Washington, DC 20036-4808
Phone: (202) 463-2124   Fax: (202) 467-0559
E-mail: info@awmanet.org
Web Site: www.awmanet.org/edu/scholar.cfm

Summary: To provide financial assistance for postsecondary education to
American Wholesale Marketers Association (AWMA) member employees and
their children.

Eligibility: Eligible are employees (and their families) of member companies in
good standing with the association; officers and directors of the association cannot
apply. Applicants must have completed at least 1 year at an accredited college or
university and must be enrolled on a full-time basis in an undergraduate,
graduate, or professional program. Winners of the scholarship awards are selected
in a random drawing; only 1 per family and 1 per company (including branches)
may be awarded.

Financial data: The scholarships are $1,000 per year.

Duration: 1 year; nonrenewable.

Number awarded: Approximately 17 each year.

Additional information: The AWMA offers these scholarships through its
Distributors Education Foundation (DEF).

Deadline: June of each year.

251
DEGREE OF HONOR FRATERNAL AWARDS PROGRAM

Degree of Honor Protective Association
445 Minnesota Street
St. Paul, MN 55101-1080
Phone: (651) 228-7600   Fax: (651) 224-7446
Web Site: www.doh.org

Summary: To provide financial assistance to high school senior members of
Degree of Honor who wish to pursue a college education.

Eligibility: Eligible are graduating high school seniors who hold a Degree of
Honor certificate of insurance and have completed the Fraternal Heart 3-year
program. In order to complete that program, students must accomplish
designated assignments in 4 major areas (home, school, church, and fraternal) and
in 2 of 6 minor areas (sports, hobbies, civic, physical fitness, reading, and arts).
They begin the program when they are between 10 and 14 years of age and
complete it before their 17th birthday.

Financial data: The award is $1,500.

Additional information: This program began in 1984.

Number awarded: Up to 5 each year.

Deadline: March of each year.

252
DEGREE OF HONOR HIGH SCHOOL SCHOLARSHIPS

Degree of Honor Protective Association
445 Minnesota Street
St. Paul, MN 55101-1080
Phone: (651) 228-7600   Fax: (651) 224-7446
Web Site: www.doh.org
Summary: To provide financial assistance to high school senior members of Degree of Honor who wish to pursue a college education.
Eligibility: Eligible are graduating high school seniors who hold a Degree of Honor certificate of insurance with a minimum of 2 years' tenure.
Financial data: The award is $1,000.
Additional information: This program began in 1959.
Number awarded: 20 each year.
Deadline: March of each year.

253
DELAWARE EDUCATIONAL BENEFITS FOR CHILDREN OF DECEASED VETERANS AND OTHERS

Delaware Higher Education Commission
Carvel State Office Building
820 North French Street
Wilmington, DE 19801
Phone: (302) 577-3240   (800) 292-7935
Fax: (302) 577-6765   E-mail: dhec@state.de.us
Web Site: www.doe.state.de.us/high-ed
Summary: To provide financial assistance for undergraduate education to dependents of deceased Delaware veterans and state police officers and members of the armed forces declared prisoners of war or missing in action.
Eligibility: Applicants for this assistance must have been Delaware residents for 3 years and be the children, between 16 and 24 years of age, of members of the armed forces who were Delaware residents when they entered the services and who 1) were killed while on active duty; 2) died from disease, wounds, injuries, or disabilities suffered as a result of active service; or 3) have been declared prisoners of war or missing in action. Also eligible are children of Delaware State Police Officers who were killed in the line of duty or died as a result of disease, wounds, or disabilities incurred in the pursuit of official duties. Financial need must be demonstrated.
Financial data: Eligible students receive full tuition at any state-supported institution in Delaware or, if the desired educational program is not available at a state-supported school, at any private institution in Delaware. If the desired educational program is not offered at either a public or private institution in Delaware, this program pays the full cost of tuition at the out-of-state school the recipient attends. Students who wish to attend a private or out-of-state school even though their program is offered at a Delaware public institution receive the equivalent of the average tuition and fees at the state school, currently set at $525 per year.
Duration: 1 year; may be renewed for 3 additional years.
Number awarded: Varies each year.
Deadline: Applications may be submitted at any time but at least 3 weeks before the beginning of classes.

254
DELAWARE GOVERNOR'S WORKFORCE DEVELOPMENT GRANTS

Delaware Higher Education Commission
Carvel State Office Building
820 North French Street
Wilmington, DE 19801
Phone: (302) 577-3240   (800) 292-7935
Fax: (302) 577-6765   E-mail: dhec@state.de.us
Web Site: www.doe.state.de.us/high-ed
Summary: To provide financial assistance for part-time education to Delaware working adults with financial need.
Eligibility: This program is open to residents of Delaware and individuals employed in Delaware who are 18 years of age and older. Applicants must be 1) employed on a part-time basis only by 1 or more employers; 2) employed by a small business (with 100 or fewer employees); 3) employed temporarily or by a temporary staffing agency; or 4) self-employed. Applicants must be able to demonstrate financial need and part-time enrollment in a participating Delaware college or training program. Full-time students and students who receive any other federal or state educational grants are not eligible.
Financial data: Awards up to $1,500 per year are available.
Duration: 1 year; renewable.

Additional information: Current income limitations are $31,255 per year for a family of 1, rising to $89,190 for a family of 8.
Number awarded: Varies each year.
Deadline: Applications may be submitted at any time, but they must be received by the end of the drop/add date at the participating college.

255
DELAWARE SCHOLARSHIP INCENTIVE PROGRAM

Delaware Higher Education Commission
Carvel State Office Building
820 North French Street
Wilmington, DE 19801
Phone: (302) 577-3240   (800) 292-7935
Fax: (302) 577-6765   E-mail: dhec@state.de.us
Web Site: www.doe.state.de.us/high-ed
Summary: To provide financial assistance for postsecondary education to Delaware residents with financial need.
Eligibility: This program is open to Delaware residents who are 1) enrolled full time in an undergraduate degree program at a Delaware or Pennsylvania college or university, and 2) enrolled full time in a graduate degree program at an accredited out-of-state institution or at a private institution in Delaware if their major is not offered at the University of Delaware or Delaware State University. All applicants must be able to demonstrate financial need and have a grade point average of 2.5 or higher.
Financial data: The amount awarded depends on the need of the recipient but does not exceed the cost of tuition, fees, and books. Currently, the maximum for undergraduates ranges from $700 to $2,200 per year, depending on grade point average; the maximum for graduate students is $1,000 per year.
Duration: 1 year; renewable.
Number awarded: Approximately 1,500 each year.
Deadline: April of each year.

256
DELAWARE STATE GOLF ASSOCIATION SCHOLARSHIP

Delaware State Golf Association Scholarship Fund, Inc.
P.O. Box 101
Rehoboth Beach, DE 19971
Summary: To provide financial assistance for college to high school seniors in Delaware who are members of the Delaware State Golf Association.
Eligibility: Eligible to apply for this program are high school seniors in Delaware who belong to the Delaware State Golf Association. Selection is based on an essay on why the applicant desires this scholarship (including career plans), letters of reference, academic record, financial need, golf accomplishments, and extracurricular activities.
Financial data: A stipend is awarded (exact amount not specified).
Duration: 1 year.
Number awarded: 1 or more each year.
Deadline: March of each year.

257
DELLA VAN DEUREN MEMORIAL SCHOLARSHIPS

American Legion Auxiliary
Department of Wisconsin
Attn: Department Secretary/Treasurer
2930 American Legion Drive
P.O. Box 140
Portage, WI 53901-0140
Phone: (608) 745-0124   Fax: (608) 745-1947
E-mail: alawi@amlegionauxwi.org
Web Site: www.amlegionauxwi.org
Summary: To provide financial assistance for the postsecondary education of Wisconsin residents who are members or children of members of the American Legion Auxiliary.
Eligibility: This program is open to members and children of members of the American Legion Auxiliary. Applicants must be high school seniors or graduates with a grade point average of 3.2 and in need of financial assistance. They must be Wisconsin residents, although they are not required to attend school in Wisconsin.
Financial data: The stipend is $1,000.
Duration: 1 year; nonrenewable.
Number awarded: 2 each year.
Deadline: March of each year.

258
DEPARTMENT OF ARKANSAS ACADEMIC SCHOLARSHIP

American Legion Auxiliary
Department of Arkansas
Attn: Department Secretary
1415 West Seventh Street
Little Rock, AR 72201-2903
Phone: (501) 374-5836
Summary: To provide financial assistance for postsecondary education to children of veterans who are residents of Arkansas.
Eligibility: Eligible to apply for this scholarship are children of veterans in Arkansas who served during eligibility dates for membership in the American Legion. Both the student and the parent must be residents of Arkansas. The student must be a high school senior or graduate who has not yet attended an institution of higher learning. Selection is based on character (15 percent), Americanism (15 percent), leadership (15 percent), financial need (15 percent), and scholarship (40 percent).
Financial data: This scholarship is $1,000; funds are paid in 2 equal installments.
Duration: 1 year.
Number awarded: 1 each year.
Deadline: March of each year.

259
DEPARTMENT OF CHILDREN AND FAMILY SERVICES SCHOLARSHIP PROGRAM

Illinois Department of Children and Family Services
Attn: Scholarship Coordinator
406 East Monroe Street
Springfield, IL 62701-1498
Phone: (217) 785-2509   Fax: (217) 524-3715
E-mail: JHamm@idcfs.state.il.us
Web Site: www.state.il.us/dcfs
Summary: To provide financial support for postsecondary education to children under the care of the Illinois Department of Children and Family Services (DCFS).
Eligibility: This program is open to high school seniors and students currently enrolled in college who are under guardianship of the Illinois DCFS or have left guardianship through adoption or private guardianship arrangements. Applicants must be attending or planning to attend the following Illinois institutions: Chicago State University, Eastern Illinois University, Governors State University, Illinois State University, Northeastern Illinois University, Northern Illinois University, Southern Illinois University, University of Illinois, or Western Illinois University. Along with their application, they must submit a transcript of high school grades or a copy of their GED certificate, ACT or SAT test scores, and 3 letters of recommendation. Selection is based on scholastic record and aptitude, community and extracurricular activities, and interest in higher education. Some scholarships are reserved for the children of veterans.
Financial data: Scholarships provide waiver of all tuition and fees at designated universities plus a stipend of $444.85 per month. Funding is not provided for room, board, or dormitory fees.
Duration: Up to 4 years, provided the student maintains full-time enrollment and a grade point average of 2.0 or higher. College students who receive their first scholarship when they are 19 years of age are eligible only for 3 years of support; those who start when they are 20 may receive only 2 years of support, and those who start when they are 21 may receive only 1 year of support.
Additional information: Recipients may attend colleges or universities other than those designated and receive the stipend, but they are not eligible for any allowance for tuition and fees.
Number awarded: 48 each year; of those, 4 are awarded to children of veterans.
Deadline: March of each year.

260
DESCENDANTS OF THE SIGNERS OF THE DECLARATION OF INDEPENDENCE SCHOLARSHIP

Descendants of the Signers of the Declaration of Independence
Attn: Scholarship Chair
7 Colby Court, Unit 4-144
Bedford, NH 03110
Summary: To provide financial assistance for postsecondary education to members of the Society for Descendants of the Signers of the Declaration of Independence (DSDI).
Eligibility: Eligible are high school seniors planning to attend a 4-year college or university in the United States on a full-time basis or current full-time college students. Membership in the society is required. Applications must include high school and college transcripts, 3 letters of recommendation, a list of extracurricular activities, and proof of direct lineal descent from a signer of the Declaration of Independence. Selection is based on merit.
Financial data: Scholarships range from $1,000 to $1,200.
Number awarded: 6 to 9 each year.
Deadline: March of each year.

261
DIAMOND STATE SCHOLARSHIPS

Delaware Higher Education Commission
Carvel State Office Building
820 North French Street
Wilmington, DE 19801
Phone: (302) 577-3240   (800) 292-7935
Fax: (302) 577-6765   E-mail: dhec@state.de.us
Web Site: www.doe.state.de.us/high-ed
Summary: To provide financial assistance for postsecondary education to Delaware high school seniors with outstanding academic records.
Eligibility: Graduating high school seniors who are Delaware residents with a combined score of 1200 on the SAT or 27 on the ACT and who rank in the upper quarter of their class are eligible for these scholarships if they plan to enroll in an accredited college or university on a full-time basis. Awards may be used at any regionally accredited college or university, including study abroad programs, as long as the grant funds are paid to an American institution.
Financial data: Awards up to $1,250 per year are available.
Duration: 1 year; may be renewed up to 3 additional years.
Number awarded: Approximately 50 each year.
Deadline: March of each year.

262
DICK MITCHELL SCHOLARSHIP

Texas Farm Bureau
P.O. Box 2689
Waco, TX 76702-2689
Phone: (254) 772-3030   E-mail: rglasson@txfb.org
Web Site: www.txfb.org/educate/dicksch.htm
Summary: To provide financial assistance for college to high school students whose families are members of the Texas Farm Bureau (TFB).
Eligibility: This program is open to high school juniors and seniors who are the son or daughter of a current TFB member or employee. Applicants must have attended the Texas Farm Bureau High School Citizenship Seminar.
Financial data: The stipend is $1,000 per year.
Duration: 1 year.
Additional information: This program was established in 1991.
Number awarded: 1 each year.
Deadline: March of each year.

263
DISABLED WORKERS COMMITTEE SCHOLARSHIP

Disabled Workers Committee
Attn: Barbara Shepard
Gold Star Park
489 Gold Star Highway, Suite 110
Groton, CT 06340
Summary: To provide financial assistance for college to children of people with disabilities in Connecticut.
Eligibility: This program is open to seniors graduating from high schools in Connecticut who are the children of totally and permanently disabled persons, injured in the workplace. Selection is based on academic achievement and financial need.
Financial data: The stipend is $2,500 per year.
Duration: 1 year; may be renewed for up to 3 additional years.
Number awarded: 1 each year.
Deadline: March of each year.

264
DISCOVER CARD TRIBUTE AWARD

American Association of School Administrators
Attn: Awards and Scholarships
1801 North Moore Street
Arlington, VA 22209-1813
Phone: (703) 875-0708   Fax: (703) 807-1849
E-mail: tributeaward@aasa.org
Web Site: www.aasa.org/Discover.htm

Summary: To provide college aid to high school juniors who have demonstrated excellence in many areas of their lives, in addition to academics.

Eligibility: This program is open to high school juniors who are enrolled in public or accredited private schools in the 50 United States and the District of Columbia. Home-schooled students are also eligible, but students attending Department of Defense or other American schools overseas are not. Both U.S. citizens and non-citizens are eligible if they plan to graduate from their U.S. high school and continue their education or training at a U.S. postsecondary institution. All applicants must have earned a cumulative grade point average of 2.75 or higher. In addition to academic achievement, applicants must submit evidence of outstanding accomplishments in such areas as special talents, leadership, obstacles overcome, and community service.

Financial data: State scholarships are $2,500 each. National scholarships are $25,000 each.

Duration: 1 year.

Additional information: If winners choose to delay their education or enter military service, their scholarships are reserved for up to 2 years from the date of their high school graduation or up to 3 months following their military discharge. This program, which began in 1991, is sponsored jointly by Discover Card and by the American Association of School Administrators (AASA). Information is also available from Discover Card Tribute Award Scholarship, AASA, P.O. Box 9338, Arlington, VA 22219.

Number awarded: 468 each year: 9 scholarships in each of the 50 states and the District of Columbia and 9 national scholarships.

Deadline: January of each year.

265
DISTRICT MATCHING/KIWANIS INTERNATIONAL FOUNDATION SCHOLARSHIP

Key Club International
Attn: Manager of Youth Funds
3636 Woodview Trace
Indianapolis, IN 46268-3196
Phone: (317) 875-8755, ext. 244   (800) KIWANIS, ext. 244
Fax: (317) 879-0204   E-mail: youthfunds@kiwanis.org
Web Site: www.keyclub.org

Summary: To recognize and reward high school seniors who are members of the Key Club and best represent its basic principles: care and sharing in their homes, schools, and communities.

Eligibility: Eligible to be nominated for this award are graduating high school seniors who have been active members of the club for at least 2 years, are bound for college, have earned at least a 3.0 grade point average, and have exemplified to the highest degree the basic principles of the club: caring and sharing in their homes, schools, and communities. Financial need is not considered.

Financial data: The award is $1,000.

Duration: The award is presented annually.

Additional information: This program is available in participating Key Club districts; funding is provided by a $500 contribution on behalf of the Kiwanis International Foundation and a matching $500 contribution on behalf of the participating Key Club and/or Kiwanis district or Kiwanis district foundation. Check with the sponsor to learn if your district is participating.

Number awarded: 1 to 3 per year in each participating district.

Deadline: Each participating district sets its own deadline.

266
DIXIE BOYS BASEBALL SCHOLARSHIP

Dixie Boys Baseball
P.O. Box 877
Marshall, TX 75671
Phone: (903) 927-2255   Fax: (903) 927-1846
E-mail: boys@dixie.org
Web Site: dixie.org

Summary: To provide financial assistance for college to high school seniors who

have participated in a Dixie Boys, Dixie Pre-Majors, or Dixie Majors franchised baseball program.

Eligibility: This program is open to high school senior males who played baseball in a Dixie Boys, Dixie Pre-Majors, or Dixie Majors franchised program. To apply, students must submit a completed application form, a financial statement, a letter of recommendation from a school official, a letter of recommendation from a parent or guardian, a letter of recommendation from a person other than a relative, a statement of participation, a high school transcript, a high school photograph, and a handwritten personal essay. While it is a basic requirement that the applicants have participated in the baseball program, ability is not a factor. Selection is based on scholarship and financial need.

Financial data: The stipend is $2,000.

Duration: 1 year.

Additional information: This scholarship was created in 1984.

Deadline: March of each year.

267
THE "DOC" AND CATHY HOLSTED HONORARIUM SCHOLARSHIP

Epsilon Sigma Alpha
Attn: ESA Foundation Assistant Scholarship Director
P.O. Box 270517
Fort Collins, CO 80527
Phone: (970) 223-2824   Fax: (970) 223-4456
Web Site: www.esaintl.com/esaf

Summary: To provide financial assistance for college students from Oklahoma.

Eligibility: This program is open to residents of Oklahoma who are either 1) graduating high school seniors in the top 25 percent of their class or with minimum scores of 20 on the ACT or 950 on the SAT, or 2) students already in college with a grade point average of 3.0 or higher. Students enrolled for training in a technical school or returning to school after an absence are also eligible. Selection is based on character, scholastic ability, leadership and ability skills, and financial need.

Financial data: The stipend is $1,000.

Duration: 1 year; may be renewed.

Additional information: Epsilon Sigma Alpha (ESA) is a women's service organization, but scholarships are available to both men and women. Recipients may major in any subject. Information is also available from Verneene Forssberg, 403 South High, Pratt, KS 67124, (316) 672-3636, Fax: (316) 672-3688, E-mail: vernf@genmail.pcc.cc.ks.us. Completed applications must be submitted to the ESA State Counselor who verifies the information before forwarding them to the scholarship director.

Number awarded: 1 each year.

Deadline: January of each year.

268
DOG WRITERS' EDUCATIONAL TRUST SCHOLARSHIPS

Dog Writers' Educational Trust
P.O. Box 22322
St. Petersburg, FL 33742-2322
Phone: (727) 577-7237
Web Site: www.dwet.org

Summary: To provide financial assistance for college to students who have a dog-related background.

Eligibility: This program is open to students who are seniors in high school or are enrolled in or about to enter college or graduate school. They must be citizens of North America and be interested in dogs or have participated in junior handling classes at dog shows. Applicants whose parents or other close relatives have been active as dog breeders, exhibitors, judges, or club officers are also considered. All applicants must submit 250-word essays on : 1) their personal goals in college and in their career; and 2) why people own dogs. Preference is given to those who are active in the sport of dogs. Adults returning to school are encouraged to apply. Selection is based on involvement with dog-related activities, scholastic ability, financial need, and character.

Financial data: Stipends are $2,000 or $1,000.

Duration: 1 year; may be renewed.

Additional information: More than 250 grants totaling more than $250,000 have been awarded since 1975. There is a nonrefundable $10 application fee.

Number awarded: 6 each year.

Deadline: January of each year.

269
DOLPHIN SCHOLARSHIP

Dolphin Scholarship Foundation
5040 Virginia Beach Boulevard, Suite 104-A
Virginia Beach, VA 23462
Phone: (757) 671-3200   Fax: (757) 671-3330
E-mail: dsf@exis.net
Web Site: www.dolphinscholarship.org
Summary: To provide financial assistance for the postsecondary education of children of members or former members of the Submarine Service.
Eligibility: Eligible to apply for these scholarships are the unmarried children and stepchildren under 24 years of age of members or former members of the Submarine Service who 1) qualified in submarines and served in the submarine force for at least 8 years, 2) served in submarine support activities for at least 10 years, or 3) died on active duty in the submarine force regardless of time served. Applicants must be working or intending to work toward a bachelor's degree at an accredited 4-year college or university. Awards are based on scholastic proficiency, non-scholastic activities, and financial need.
Financial data: Scholarships are $3,000 per year.
Duration: 1 year; may be renewed for 3 additional years.
Number awarded: Approximately 25 each year.
Deadline: March of each year.

270
DONALD AND PEARL MCMURCHIE SCHOLARSHIP

Presbytery of South Dakota
406 South Second Avenue, Suite 102
Sioux Falls, SD 57104-6904
Phone: (605) 339-1912
Summary: To provide financial assistance to members of the Presbyterian Church (USA) who are interested in attending an institution of higher learning affiliated with that denomination.
Eligibility: This program is open to Presbyterians who are interested in working on an undergraduate or graduate degree at an institution of higher learning affiliated with the Presbyterian Church (USA). Preference is given to applicants who have graduated from a high school in South Dakota, who intend to enter full-time service to the church, who have financial need, and/or who can demonstrate scholastic achievement.
Financial data: The amount of each scholarship is determined on an individual basis, depending upon the availability of funds and the qualifications of the applicants.
Duration: 1 year.
Number awarded: Varies each year.
Deadline: August of each year.

271
DONNELLY AWARDS

Team Tennis Charities
Attn: Donnelly Awards
445 North Wells, Suite 404
Chicago, IL 60610
Phone: (312) 245-5300   Fax: (312) 245-5321
Web Site: www.wtt.com
Summary: To provide financial assistance to young tennis players who have diabetes.
Eligibility: This program is open to scholar/athletes between 14 and 21 years of age who play interscholastic, intercollegiate, or intramural tennis and have type I diabetes. Applicants must submit a short essay on the significance of diabetes in their lives. Selection is based on values, commitment, sportsmanship, community involvement, and financial need.
Financial data: The award is $5,000. Funds may be used for education, athletic development, and/or medical care.
Duration: 1 year.
Additional information: This program was established in 1998 by the Billie Jean King Foundation in cooperation with the American Diabetes Association.
Number awarded: 2 each year.
Deadline: May of each year.

272
DOROTHY CAMPBELL MEMORIAL SCHOLARSHIP

Oregon Student Assistance Commission
Attn: Private Awards Grant Department
1500 Valley River Drive, Suite 100
Eugene, OR 97401-2146
Phone: (541) 687-7395   (800) 452-8807, ext. 7395
Fax: (541) 687-7419   E-mail: awardinfo@mercury.osac.state.or.us
Web Site: www.osac.state.or.us
Summary: To provide financial assistance for college to women in Oregon who are interested in golf.
Eligibility: This program is open to residents of Oregon who are U.S. citizens or permanent residents. Applicants must be female high school seniors or graduates with a cumulative grade point average of 2.75 or higher and a strong continuing interest in golf. They must be or planning to become full-time students at an Oregon 4-year college. Along with their application they must submit a 1-page essay on the contribution that golf has made to their development. Financial need must be demonstrated.
Financial data: Scholarship amounts vary, depending upon the needs of the recipient.
Duration: 1 year; may be renewed up to 3 additional years.
Number awarded: Varies each year.
Deadline: February of each year.

273
DR. KATE WALLER BARRETT GRANT

American Legion Auxiliary
Department of Virginia
Attn: Education Chair
1805 Chantilly Street
Richmond, VA 23230
Phone: (804) 355-6410   Fax: (804) 358-1940
Summary: To provide financial assistance for the postsecondary education of Virginia residents who are children of veterans or of members of the American Legion Auxiliary.
Eligibility: To be eligible, applicants must be the children of veterans or of members of the American Legion Auxiliary who are high school seniors and who need financial assistance to attend an accredited educational institution in Virginia.
Financial data: The stipend is $1,000.
Duration: 1 year.
Number awarded: 1 each year.
Deadline: March of each year.

274
DR. KATHRYN WHITTEN SCHOLARSHIPS

Dr. Kathryn Whitten Trust
c/o F&M Trust
302 Pine Street
P.O. Box 891
Long Beach, CA 90801
Phone: (562) 437-0011   Fax: (562) 436-5048
Summary: To provide financial assistance for college.
Eligibility: This support is available to high school seniors and currently-enrolled college students in any state. College students must be enrolled full time (at least 12 units per semester or quarter) and have at least a 3.0 grade point average. To apply, all students must submit a completed application form, their transcripts, a budget, and an authorization letter. Selection is based on scholastic achievement, financial need, student activities, and future potential.
Financial data: Stipends range from $2,500 to $10,000 per year.
Duration: 1 year; may be renewed up to 3 additional years.
Additional information: Recipients may attend school in any state.
Number awarded: Several each year.
Deadline: August of each year.

275
DR. MAE DAVIDOW MEMORIAL SCHOLARSHIP

American Council of the Blind
Attn: Coordinator, Scholarship Program
1155 15th Street, N.W., Suite 1004
Washington, DC 20005
Phone: (202) 467-5081   (800) 424-8666
Fax: (202) 467-5085   E-mail: info@acb.org
Web Site: www.acb.org
Summary: To provide financial assistance to blind students entering their freshman year of college.
Eligibility: This program is open to entering freshmen who are legally blind. They must be U.S. citizens. In addition to letters of recommendation and academic transcripts, applications must include an autobiographical sketch. Selection is based on demonstrated academic record, involvement in extracurricular and civic activities, and academic objectives. The severity of the applicant's visual impairment and his/her study methods are also taken into account.
Financial data: The stipend is $1,500. In addition, the winner receives a $1,000 cash scholarship from the Kurzweil Foundation and, if appropriate, a Kurzweil 1000 Reading System.
Duration: 1 year.
Additional information: This scholarship is sponsored by the Pennsylvania Council of the Blind, an affiliate of the American Council of the Blind. Scholarship winners are expected to be present at the council's annual conference; the council will cover all reasonable expenses connected with convention attendance.
Number awarded: 1 each year.
Deadline: February of each year.

276
DR. NICHOLAS S. DICAPRIO SCHOLARSHIP

American Council of the Blind
Attn: Coordinator, Scholarship Program
1155 15th Street, N.W., Suite 1004
Washington, DC 20005
Phone: (202) 467-5081   (800) 424-8666
Fax: (202) 467-5085   E-mail: info@acb.org
Web Site: www.acb.org
Summary: To provide financial assistance to outstanding blind students.
Eligibility: Eligible to apply are legally blind U.S. citizens or resident aliens who are undergraduate students. In addition to letters of recommendation and academic transcripts, applications must include an autobiographical sketch. Selection is based on demonstrated academic record, involvement in extracurricular and civic activities, and academic objectives. The severity of the applicant's visual impairment and his/her study methods are also taken into account.
Financial data: The stipend is $2,500. In addition, the winner receives a $1,000 cash scholarship from the Kurzweil Foundation and, if appropriate, a Kurzweil 1000 Reading System.
Duration: 1 year.
Additional information: The scholarship winner is expected to be present at the council's annual national convention; the council will cover all reasonable costs connected with convention attendance.
Number awarded: 1 each year.
Deadline: February of each year.

277
DR. SYNGMAN RHEE SCHOLARSHIP

Dong Ji Hoi Society
c/o Dianne Lim, Scholarship Chair
91-201 Kaana Place
Kapolei, HI 96707
Summary: To provide financial assistance to Korean Americans in Hawaii who are interested in pursuing postsecondary education.
Eligibility: This program is open to graduating high school seniors in Hawaii who are Korean or at least half-Korean ancestry. U.S. citizenship is required. Preference is given to students of Christian faith. Selection is based on grade point average (3.5 or higher), class rank, SAT score, community service, and extracurricular activities; financial need may also be considered.
Financial data: The stipend is $1,250 per year.
Duration: Up to 4 years.
Additional information: Recipients may study in Hawaii or on the mainland. Requests for applications must include a self-addressed stamped envelope.

Number awarded: 10 to 16 each year.
Deadline: June of each year.

278
DR. THOMAS T. YATABE MEMORIAL SCHOLARSHIP

Japanese American Citizens League
Attn: National Scholarship Awards
1765 Sutter Street
San Francisco, CA 94115
Phone: (415) 921-5225   Fax: (415) 931-4671
E-mail: jacl@jacl.org
Web Site: www.jacl.org
Summary: To provide financial assistance to student members of the Japanese American Citizens League (JACL) who are pursuing undergraduate education.
Eligibility: This program is open to JACL members who are currently enrolled or planning to reenter a college, university, trade school, business college, or other institution of higher learning. Selection is based on academic record, extracurricular activities, and community involvement.
Financial data: The stipend depends on the availability of funds but usually ranges from $1,000 to $5,000.
Duration: 1 year.
Additional information: Requests for applications must be accompanied by a self-addressed stamped envelope.
Number awarded: At least 1 each year.
Deadline: March of each year.

279
DUMITRU GOLEA GOLDY-GEMU SCHOLARSHIPS

Romanian Orthodox Episcopate of America
Attn: Scholarship Committee
P.O. Box 309
Grass Lake, MI 49240-0309
Phone: (517) 522-3656   Fax: (517) 522-5907
E-mail: roeasolia@aol.com
Web Site: www.roea.org
Summary: To provide financial assistance for college to students of Romanian origin.
Eligibility: Eligible to apply for this support are undergraduate students of Romanian origin. Financial need is considered in the selection process.
Financial data: The stipend is $1,000.
Duration: 1 year.
Number awarded: 2 each year.
Deadline: April of each year.

280
EAGLE SCOUT OF THE YEAR

American Legion
Attn: Americanism and Children & Youth Division
P.O. Box 1055
Indianapolis, IN 46206-1055
Phone: (317) 630-1249   Fax: (317) 630-1223
E-mail: acy@legion.org
Web Site: www.legion.org
Summary: To provide financial assistance for the postsecondary education of outstanding Eagle Scouts whose parent is a member of the American Legion.
Eligibility: Applicants for this award must be either 1) a registered, active member of a Boy Scout Troop, Varsity Scout Team, or Venturing Crew sponsored by an American Legion Post or Auxiliary Unit or 2) a registered active member of a Boy Scout Troop, Varsity Scout Team, or Venturing Crew and also the son or grandson of a member of the American Legion or American Legion Auxiliary. Candidates must also 1) be active members of their religious institution and have received the appropriate religious emblem; 2) have demonstrated practical citizenship in church, school, Scouting, and community; 3) be at least 15 years of age and enrolled in high school; and 4) submit at least 4 letters of recommendation, including 1 each from leaders of their religious institution, school, community, and Scouting.
Financial data: The Scout of the Year receives $10,000; each second-place winner receives $2,500.
Duration: 4 years; recipients are eligible to receive their scholarships immediately upon graduation from an accredited high school and must utilize the award within 4 years of their graduation date.

Additional information: The recipients may use the scholarships at any school of their choice, provided it is accredited for education above the high school level and located within the United States or its possessions.

Number awarded: 1 Scout of the Year and 3 second-place winners each year.

Deadline: Nominations must be received by the respective department headquarters by the end of February of each year and by the national headquarters before the end of March.

281
EAGLES MEMORIAL FOUNDATION EDUCATIONAL GRANTS

Fraternal Order of Eagles
Attn: Memorial Foundation
4710 14th Street West
Bradenton, FL 34207
Phone: (941) 758-5456

Summary: To provide financial assistance for the postsecondary education of the children of members of the Fraternal Order of Eagles who died in action.

Eligibility: Applicants must be the minor (under age 25) unmarried children of a deceased parent who was a member of the Fraternal Order of Eagles or its Ladies Auxiliary at the time of death; the member must have died from injuries or diseases incurred or aggravated in the line of duty while serving 1) in the armed forces of the United States, Canada, Mexico, the Philippines, or the United Kingdom; 2) as law enforcement officers in the United States; 3) as full-time or volunteer fire fighters; or 4) as full-time or volunteer emergency medical service officers.

Financial data: Up to $6,000 per school year.

Duration: 1 year; may be renewed for 4 additional years.

Number awarded: Varies each year.

282
EASLEY NATIONAL SCHOLARSHIP AWARDS

National Academy of American Scholars
Attn: Merit Committee
5196 Benito Street, Suite 15, Room A
Montclair, CA 91763-4028
Phone: (909) 621-6856   E-mail: staff@naas.org
Web Site: www.naas.org/senior.htm

Summary: To recognize and reward high school seniors who have exhibited outstanding academic excellence and personal integrity.

Eligibility: This program is open to U.S. citizens or permanent residents who are enrolled in a public, private, or parochial high school as a senior or who are home-schooled seniors. Applicants must have been (or will be) accepted at an accredited 4-year institution and be planning to pursue a bachelor's degree. They must have earned at least a 2.0 grade point average and completed either the SAT or ACT. Selection is made without regard to financial need, affiliation status, or study area.

Financial data: Scholarship levels are $2,000, $3,000, $4,000, or $5,000 per year. Finalists receive $200 plus a merit certificate. The scholarships are paid to the recipient's institution of choice.

Duration: 4 years.

Additional information: Send a legal-sized self-addressed stamped envelope and $3 handling fee to the sponsor to receive an application and information packet. Walk-in, phone-in, and e-mail requests are not accepted.

Number awarded: 4 scholarships plus 10 finalists each year.

Deadline: January of each year.

283
EASTERN REGION KOREAN AMERICAN SCHOLARSHIPS

Korean American Scholarship Foundation
Eastern Region
Attn: Scholarship Committee
1952 Gallows Road, Suite 340 B
Vienna, VA 22182
Phone: (703) 748-5935   Fax: (703) 748-1874
E-mail: eastern@kasf.org
Web Site: www.kasf.org

Summary: To provide financial assistance for postsecondary education to Korean American students who attend school in the eastern states.

Eligibility: This program is open to Korean American students who are currently enrolled in a college or university in an eastern state as a full-time undergraduate or graduate student. Applicants may reside anywhere in the United States as long as they attend school in the eastern region: Connecticut, Delaware, District of Columbia, Kentucky, Maine, Maryland, Massachusetts, New Hampshire, New Jersey, New York, Pennsylvania, Rhode Island, Vermont, Virginia, and West

Virginia. Selection is based on academic achievement, activities, community service, and financial need.

Financial data: Awards are $1,000 or more.

Duration: 1 year; renewable.

Number awarded: Varies each year.

Deadline: June of each year.

284
EASTERN STAR EDUCATIONAL SCHOLARSHIPS

Eastern Star-Grand Chapter of California
16960 Bastanchury Road, Suite E
Yorba Linda, CA 92886-1711
Phone: (714) 986-2380
Web Site: www.oescal.org/scholarship/Scholarships.htm

Summary: To provide financial assistance for college to students in California.

Eligibility: Applicants must meet 1 of the following criteria: 1) members of the Order of the Eastern Star; 2) graduating high school seniors entering their first year of college or university; 3) students who have begun their higher education but need financial aid to continue; or 4) those who have not been able to go directly from high school to college. California residency and U.S. citizenship are required. Undergraduate and graduate students are eligible. Applicants must be attending or planning to attend a college, university, community college, or trade school in California, although consideration is given to students applying for out-of-state schools. Selection is based on scholastic record (minimum grade point average of 3.0), financial need, the purpose and need for higher education, and character of the applicant.

Financial data: Annual stipends vary but range from $500 to $1,000 for students in 4-year colleges and universities and from $250 to $500 for students in community colleges and trade schools.

Duration: 1 year; may be renewed.

Additional information: Information is also available from the Chair of the Scholarship Committee, May Laing, 19469 Oneida Road, Apple Valley, CA 92307-5171, (760) 242-5768.

Number awarded: Varies each year.

Deadline: March of each year.

285
E.C. HALLBECK MEMORIAL SCHOLARSHIP PROGRAM

American Postal Workers Union
Attn: Scholarship Program
1300 L Street, N.W.
Washington, DC 20005
Phone: (202) 842-4268
Web Site: www.apwu.org

Summary: To provide financial assistance for postsecondary education to children of members of the American Postal Workers Union (APWU).

Eligibility: Eligible are the children, grandchildren, stepchildren, and legally adopted children of active or deceased members of the union who have been in good standing for at least 1 year or were members for 1 year immediately preceding death. Applicants must be high school seniors who plan to attend an accredited college, university, or community college as full-time students. Selection is based on school records, personal qualifications, SAT or ACT scores, responses to questions on contemporary issues, and an essay (up to 500 words) on "What the union way of life means to me."

Financial data: The stipend is $1,000 per year.

Duration: 4 years.

Additional information: This program was established in 1969.

Number awarded: 5 each year: 1 in each of the union's 5 areas.

Deadline: February of each year.

286
EDEN SERVICES ANN M. MARTIN SCHOLARSHIP

Autism Society of America
Attn: Awards and Scholarships
7910 Woodmont Avenue, Suite 300
Bethesda, MD 20814-3015
Phone: (301) 657-0881   (800) 3AUTISM
Fax: (301) 657-0869
Web Site: www.autism-society.org

Summary: To provide financial assistance for college to high school seniors or graduates with autism.

Eligibility: This program is open to high school seniors or graduates who have

been accepted to or are already enrolled in an accredited postsecondary school (college, trade school, etc.) and who have autism. Applicants must submit 3 copies of 1) documentation of their status as an individual with autism; 2) secondary school transcripts; 3) documentation of acceptance into an accredited postsecondary educational or vocational program of study; 4) 2 letters of recommendation; and 5) a 500-word statement outlining the applicant's qualifications and proposed plan of study. As part of the application process, applicants may be required to participate in a telephone interview.
Financial data: The stipend is $1,000.
Duration: 1 year.
Number awarded: 1 each year.
Deadline: April of each year.

287
EDUCATION EXCHANGE COLLEGE GRANT PROGRAM

EDS
5400 Legacy Drive
Plano, TX 75024-3199
Phone: (972) 604-6000   E-mail: info@eds.com
Web Site: www.theexchangeintl.com/edexchange.htm
Summary: To provide financial assistance for college to needy high school seniors.
Eligibility: This program is open to all graduating college-bound high school seniors. To enter, students must pick up an application at a participating Exchange member institution (primarily banks and credit unions). For a list of financial institutions that will have applications, write to EDS or visit their web site. Selection is based on extracurricular activities, character, leadership, financial need, and a required essay.
Financial data: Stipends are either $5,000 or $1,000. A total of $100,000 is distributed annually.
Duration: 1 year.
Additional information: This program was established in 1994.
Number awarded: 84 each year: 4 at $5,000 and 80 at $1,000.
Deadline: March of each year.

288
EDWARD AND HELEN DELPOZZO FAMILY SCHOLARSHIP

American Legion
Attn: Department of Massachusetts
State House
24 Beacon Street, Suite 546-2
Boston, MA 02133-1044
Phone: (617) 727-2966   Fax: (617) 727-2969
Summary: To provide financial assistance for postsecondary education to the children and grandchildren of members of the American Legion in Massachusetts.
Eligibility: Eligible to apply are the children and grandchildren of members in good standing in the American Legion's Department of Massachusetts (or who were members in good standing at the time of death). Applicants must be entering their freshman year of college.
Financial data: The stipend is $1,000.
Duration: 1 year.
Number awarded: 1 or more each year.
Deadline: March of each year.

289
EDWARD T. CONROY MEMORIAL SCHOLARSHIP PROGRAM

Maryland Higher Education Commission
Attn: State Scholarship Administration
16 Francis Street
Annapolis, MD 21401-1781
Phone: (410) 260-4545   (800) 974-1024
Fax: (410) 974-5376   TTY: (800) 735-2258
E-mail: ssamail@mhec.state.md.us
Web Site: www.mhec.state.md.us
Summary: To provide financial assistance in Maryland for postsecondary education to specified categories of veterans, public safety employees, and their children and spouses.
Eligibility: This program is open to the following categories of people: 1) children of state or local public safety employees or volunteers killed in the line of duty; 2) children of armed forces members whose death or 100 percent disability was directly caused by military service; 3) children of armed forces members declared to be a prisoner of war or missing in action as a result of armed conflict in southeast Asia on

or after January 1, 1960; 4) veterans who suffer, as a direct result of military service, a disability of 50 percent or greater and have exhausted or are no longer eligible for federal veterans' educational benefits; and 5) state or local public safety officers or volunteers who were 100 percent disabled in the line of duty. The parent, veteran, POW, or public safety officer or volunteer must have been a resident of Maryland at the time of death or when declared disabled. Financial need is not considered.
Financial data: Funds may be used for tuition and mandatory fees at any Maryland postsecondary institution, but they may not exceed the equivalent annual tuition and mandatory fees of a resident undergraduate student at the University of Maryland at College Park (approximately, $3,800 per year).
Duration: Up to 5 years of full-time study or 8 years of part-time study.
Additional information: Recipients must enroll at a 2-year or 4-year Maryland college or university as a full-time or part-time degree-seeking undergraduate or graduate student or attend a private career school.
Number awarded: Varies each year.
Deadline: July of each year.

290
EDWARD THATCHER ASTLE MEMORIAL SCHOLARSHIP

Edward Thatcher Astle Memorial Foundation
P.O. Box 182
Annandale, NJ 08801
Summary: To provide financial assistance for college to graduating high school seniors.
Eligibility: Eligible to apply for this support are graduating high school seniors who have earned at least a 3.0 grade point average, need financial assistance to attend college or trade school, are U.S. citizens, and, if more than 18 years of age, are registered to vote in their home state. There are no restrictions on the basis of sex, race, religion, creed, or areas of study (although the chosen area of study must be important to society). A recommendation from the student's guidance department or high school teacher is required. Candidates will be interviewed. They must show that they are willing to work to help pay for their education during the summer or after school. Applicants may elect to include a short essay on their ancestors and their heritage. If candidates appear to be equally qualified academically, selection is based on the interview, area of study, and financial need.
Financial data: $6,000 is awarded each year; this amount is divided equally among the recipients (may be 1 or more). Funds must be used for first-year tuition.
Duration: 1 year; may be renewed for 1 additional year.
Additional information: Requests for applications must be accompanied by a self-addressed stamped envelope.
Number awarded: 1 or more each year.
Deadline: March of each year.

291
ELIZABETH AND WALLACE KINGSBURY SCHOLARSHIP

United Daughters of the Confederacy
Attn: Education Director
328 North Boulevard
Richmond, VA 23220-4057
Phone: (804) 355-1636   Fax: (804) 353-1396
E-mail: hqudc@aol.com
Web Site: www.hqudc.org
Summary: To provide financial assistance for postsecondary education to lineal descendants of Confederate veterans who have been members of the Children of the Confederacy for at least 3 years.
Eligibility: Eligible to apply for these scholarships are lineal descendants of worthy Confederates or collateral descendants who have been members of the Children of the Confederacy for at least 3 years. Applicants must submit a family financial report and certified proof of the Confederate record of 1 ancestor, with the company and regiment in which he served. They must have at least a 3.0 grade point average in high school.
Financial data: The amount of the scholarship depends on the availability of funds.
Duration: 1 year; may be renewed for up to 3 additional years.
Additional information: Information is also available from Dorothy S. Broom, Second Vice President General, 595 Lominack Road, Prosperity, SC 29127, (803) 364-3003. Members of the same family may not hold scholarships simultaneously, and only 1 application per family will be accepted within any 1 year. Requests for applications must be accompanied by a self-addressed stamped envelope.
Number awarded: 1 each year.
Deadline: February of each year.

292
ELKS NATIONAL FOUNDATION EAGLE SCOUT SCHOLARSHIPS

Boy Scouts of America
Attn: Eagle Scout Service, S220
P.O. Box 152079
Irving, TX 75015-2079
Phone: (972) 580-2431
Web Site: www.scouting.org/nesa/scholar/index.html
Summary: To provide financial assistance for college to Eagle Scouts.
Eligibility: Eagle Scouts who are graduating high school seniors are eligible to apply for these scholarships. They must have an SAT score of at least 1090 and/or an ACT score of 26. Selection is based on financial need, scholastic accomplishment, involvement in Scouting, and school and community activities.
Financial data: Stipends are $2,000 or $1,000 per year.
Duration: 4 years.
Additional information: These scholarships are provided by the Elks National Foundation.
Number awarded: Each year, 4 scholarships of $2,000 per year (for a total award of $8,000) and 4 scholarships of $1,000 per year (for a total award of $4,000) are presented.
Deadline: February of each year.

293
EMANUELE AND EMILIA INGLESE MEMORIAL SCHOLARSHIP

National Italian American Foundation
Attn: Education Director
1860 19th Street, N.W.
Washington, DC 20009
Phone: (202) 387-0600   Fax: (202) 387-0800
E-mail: scholarships@niaf.org
Web Site: www.niaf.org/scholarships
Summary: To provide financial assistance for college to Italian American students who are the first generation of their family to attend college.
Eligibility: This program is open to Italian American undergraduate students who trace their lineage from the Lombardy region and who are the first generation of their family to attend college. Applicants must have a grade point average of 3.0 or higher and be able to demonstrate financial need. U.S. citizenship or permanent resident status is required.
Financial data: The stipend is $2,500.
Duration: 1 year.
Additional information: Applications can only be submitted online. At the completion of the scholarship year, recipients must submit a 500-word narrative describing the benefits of the scholarship.
Number awarded: 1 each year.
Deadline: April of each year.

294
EMI/NAT KING COLE SCHOLARSHIP PROGRAM

Citizens' Scholarship Foundation of America
Attn: Scholarship Management Services
1505 Riverview Road, P.O. Box 297
St. Peter, MN 56082
Phone: (507) 931-1682   (800) 537-4180
Fax: (507) 931-9168   E-mail: info_sms@csfa.org
Summary: To assist African American students at 2-year or technical colleges who plan to continue their postsecondary education at 4-year institutions.
Eligibility: Applicants must be U.S. citizens, African Americans, enrolled as full-time sophomores at an accredited 2-year college or technical school, and planning to transfer to a 4-year college or university. They must have earned at least a 3.0 grade point average in their college classes. Selection is based on academic record, potential to succeed, leadership and participation in school and community activities, career goals, and an outside appraisal. Financial need must be demonstrated.
Financial data: The stipend is $2,500, payable in 2 equal installments. Funds are sent directly to the recipient and are made payable jointly to the recipient and the recipient's school.
Duration: 1 year; may be renewed for 1 additional year if the recipient maintains a satisfactory academic record.
Additional information: This program is administered by Scholarship Management Services, a department of Citizens' Scholarship Foundation of America, and sponsored by EMI Music Foundation. Recipients must attend school

on a full-time basis.
Number awarded: A limited number are offered each year. Half are granted to students majoring in the arts (dance, theater, music, visual, or multi-media) and half are granted to students in other majors.
Deadline: November of each year.

295
EMI/SELENA SCHOLARSHIP PROGRAM

Citizens' Scholarship Foundation of America
Attn: Scholarship Management Services
1505 Riverview Road
P.O. Box 297
St. Peter, MN 56082
Phone: (507) 931-1682   (800) 537-4180
Fax: (507) 931-9168   E-mail: info_sms@csfa.org
Summary: To assist Hispanic students at 2-year or technical colleges who plan to continue their postsecondary education at 4-year institutions.
Eligibility: Applicants must be U.S. citizens, Hispanic Americans, enrolled as full-time sophomores at an accredited 2-year college or technical school, and planning to transfer to a 4-year college or university. They must have earned at least a 3.0 grade point average in their college classes. Selection is based on academic record, potential to succeed, leadership and participation in school and community activities, career goals, and an outside appraisal. Financial need must be demonstrated.
Financial data: The stipend is $2,500, payable in 2 equal installments. Funds are sent directly to the recipient and are made payable jointly to the recipient and the recipient's school.
Duration: 1 year; may be renewed for 1 additional year if the recipient maintains a satisfactory academic record.
Additional information: This program honors Tejano/Pop music megastar Selena Quintanilla Perez who tragically died in 1995, at the age of 23. It is administered by Scholarship Management Services, a department of Citizens' Scholarship Foundation of America, and sponsored by EMI Music Foundation. Recipients must attend school on a full-time basis.
Number awarded: Up to 10 each year. Of these, 5 awards are granted to students majoring in the arts or music and 5 awards are granted to students in other majors.
Deadline: November of each year.

296
ENCOMPASS MERIT SCHOLARSHIP PROGRAM

Encompass
c/o Compaq Computer Corporation
153 Taylor Street
TAY2-2/F15
Littleton, MA 01460
Phone: (508) 467-9153   E-mail: information@decus.org
Web Site: www.decus.org/encompass/Scholarship.shtml
Summary: To provide financial assistance for college to members of Encompass and their children.
Eligibility: This program is open to high school seniors who will be entering college as a full-time student in the following fall, are U.S. citizens, and are members or children of members of Encompass. Selection is based on merit; family financial circumstances are not considered.
Financial data: The stipend is $1,000 per year.
Duration: Up to 4 years or until completion of a baccalaureate degree, whichever occurs first.
Additional information: Encompass is an association of information technology professionals interested in computer products, services, and technologies of Compaq Computer Corporation. It was established in 2001 as a replacement for a prior organization named DECUS, which began offering scholarships in 1991.
Number awarded: 1 each year.

297
ERIC DELSON MEMORIAL SCHOLARSHIP PROGRAM

Citizens' Scholarship Foundation of America
Attn: Scholarship Management Services
1505 Riverview Road
P.O. Box 297
St. Peter, MN 56082
Phone: (507) 931-1682   (800) 537-4180
Fax: (507) 931-9168   E-mail: info_sms@csfa.org

Summary: To help finance postsecondary education for students with hemophilia.

Eligibility: Students diagnosed with clinical hemophilia are eligible to apply for this program if they are 1) high school seniors, high school graduates, or currently-enrolled college students and 2) currently-enrolled or planning to enroll in an accredited 2-year or 4-year college, university, or vocational-technical school. This program is not open to students with related blood disorders (e.g., von Willebrand Disease). Selection is based on academic record, potential to succeed, leadership, participation in school and community activities, honors, work experience, statement of educational and career goals, recommendations, and unusual personal or family circumstances.

Financial data: The stipend is $2,500. Funds are paid in 2 equal installments directly to the recipient.

Duration: 1 year; may be renewed for up to 3 additional years, provided the recipient maintains a 3.0 grade point average.

Additional information: This program is funded by Caremark Therapeutic Services and administered by the Citizens' Scholarship Foundation of America.

Number awarded: Up to 3 each year.

Deadline: June of each year.

298
ERIC DOSTIE MEMORIAL COLLEGE SCHOLARSHIP

Kelley Communications
21 Sawmill Way
Georgetown, MA 01833
Phone: (978) 352-7657   (800) 249-7977
Fax: (978) 352-6254   E-mail: info@kelleycom.com
Web Site: www.kelleycom.com

Summary: To provide financial assistance for college to students with hemophilia or members of their families.

Eligibility: This program is open to 1) students with hemophilia or a related bleeding disorder or 2) members of their families. Applicants must be U.S. citizens and enrolled or planning to enroll full time in an accredited 2- or 4-year college program. They can apply directly, or they can be nominated by their families, peers, hemophilia treatment center staff, teachers, or local chapters. Applicants must write an essay describing how they plan to use their education to serve humankind and to encourage self improvement and enrichment. In addition to the essay, selection is based on scholastic achievement, community service, and financial need.

Financial data: The stipend is $1,000.

Duration: 1 year.

Number awarded: 6 each year.

Deadline: January of each year.

299
ERNESTINE MATTHEWS TRUST SCHOLARSHIP AWARD

Ernestine Matthews Trust
P.O. Box 10367
Rockville, MD 20849

Summary: To provide financial assistance for college to high school seniors in Maryland, Pennsylvania, Virginia, West Virginia, and the District of Columbia.

Eligibility: Applicants must be high school seniors in the District of Columbia, Maryland, Pennsylvania, Virginia, or West Virginia who are graduating in the top third of their high school class and are able to document financial need. Applicants must submit a completed application form, their high school transcript, verification of their class standing, 2 letters of recommendation, and a statement that they will neither smoke nor use alcoholic beverages while receiving money from the trust.

Financial data: The amount awarded varies, up to a maximum of $1,500 per year.

Duration: 1 year; may be renewed.

Deadline: March of each year.

300
ESPN SPORTSFIGURES SCHOLARSHIPS

ESPN, Inc.
Attn: SportsFigures Scholarships
P.O. Box 5439
Blair, NE 68008-5439
Web Site: sportsfigures.espn.go.com

Summary: To provide financial assistance for college to high school seniors, especially those who have participated in interscholastic sports.

Eligibility: This program is open to seniors at public and private high schools in the United States. U.S. citizenship is required. Applicants must submit a 250-word essay on how their combination of academic, extracurricular, and athletic activities has enhanced or otherwise affected their high school experience. Selection is based on academic achievement (60 percent), school and community service (20 percent), and leadership in interscholastic sports (20 percent). In case of a tie, final selection is based on the essay that is judged on the basis of adherence and relevance to the essay topic (75 percent); and grammar, sentence structure, and spelling (25 percent).

Financial data: Awards are $2,500.

Duration: The competition is held annually.

Number awarded: 12 each year: 1 female and 1 male in each of 6 regions of the United States (northeast, southeast, north central, south central, Rocky Mountain, and west).

Deadline: March of each year.

301
ETHEL AND EMERY FAST SCHOLARSHIP

Ethel and Emery Fast Scholarship Foundation, Inc.
12620 Rolling Road
Potomac, MD 20854

Summary: To provide financial assistance to qualified Native Americans enrolled as undergraduates or graduate students.

Eligibility: Applicants must 1) be Native Americans enrolled in a federally-recognized tribe, 2) have successfully completed 1 year of their undergraduate or graduate school program, 3) be enrolled in school full time, and 4) be able to demonstrate financial need. To apply, students must submit a completed application. documentation of Native American eligibility, an original transcript, a letter confirming enrollment, a federal income tax return, a statement of financial need, and a personal statement (up to 2 pages) describing educational and career goals.

Financial data: A stipend is awarded (exact amount not specified). Funds are paid directly to the recipient's college or university and can only be used to pay for tuition, room, board, and fees.

Duration: 1 year.

Number awarded: Varies each year.

Deadline: August of each year for the fall semester; December of each year for the spring semester.

302
E.U. PARKER SCHOLARSHIP

National Federation of the Blind
c/o Peggy Elliott
Chair, Scholarship Committee
805 Fifth Avenue
Grinnell, IA 50112
Phone: (641) 236-3366
Web Site: www.nfb.org

Summary: To provide financial assistance to blind students studying or planning to study at the postsecondary level.

Eligibility: This program is open to legally blind students who are pursuing or planning to pursue a full-time undergraduate or graduate course of study. Selection is based on academic excellence, service to the community, and financial need.

Financial data: The stipend is $3,000.

Duration: 1 year; recipients may resubmit applications up to 2 additional years.

Additional information: Scholarships are awarded at the federation convention in July. Recipients attend the convention at federation expense; that funding is in addition to the scholarship grant.

Number awarded: 1 each year.

Deadline: March of each year.

303
EUGENE & ELINOR KOTUR SCHOLARSHIP TRUST FUND

Ukrainian Fraternal Association
Attn: Scholarship Program
1327 Wyoming Avenue
Scranton, PA 18509-2849
Phone: (570) 342-0937

Summary: To provide financial assistance to currently-enrolled undergraduate and graduate students who are of Ukrainian heritage.

Eligibility: This program is open to students of Ukrainian ancestry who are

currently enrolled in an undergraduate (freshman year excepted) or graduate program of study at 1 of the following colleges or universities: Brown University, California Institute of Technology, Carnegie Mellon, Connecticut University, Cornell University, Dartmouth College, Duke University, George Washington University, Harvard University, Haverford University, Indiana University, John Hopkins University, Massachusetts Institute of Technology, McGill University, Michigan State University, Yale University, Notre Dame University, Oberlin College, Purdue University, Princeton University, Rochester University, Swarthmore College, Tulane University, University of California at Berkeley or Los Angeles, University of Chicago, University of Michigan, University of Pennsylvania, University of Toronto, University of Washington, University of Wisconsin, Vanderbilt University, or Williams College. As part of the application process, students must submit a short autobiography, a photograph, and a copy of their latest transcripts. Selection is based on financial need and academic record.
Financial data: The amount of the scholarship varies, depending upon need. However, each award is at least $1,000. Funds are paid directly to the recipient.
Duration: 1 year.
Additional information: The Ukrainian Fraternal Association is the first fraternal organization in the United States and Canada to grant outright student stipends.
Number awarded: Varies each year.
Deadline: May of each year.

304
EUGENE P. LINK COLLEGE SCHOLARSHIP

United University Professions
150 Wolf Road
Albany, NY 12205
Phone: (518) 458-7935   (800) 342-4206
Fax: (518) 459-3242   E-mail: csparks@uupmail.org
Web Site: www.uupinfo.org
Summary: To provide financial assistance for undergraduate students currently enrolled in the State University of New York system.
Eligibility: Applicants must be undergraduate students at 1 of the state operated campuses of SUNY who have completed at least 16 credits and who have maintained a grade point average of 3.75. These campuses include: Alfred, Canton, Cobleskill, Delhi, Farmingdale, Morrisville, Brockport, Buffalo, Cortland, Fredonia, Geneseo, New Paltz, Old Westbury, Oneonta, Oswego, Plattsburgh, Potsdam, Purchase, Albany, Binghamton, Stony Brook, Brooklyn, Syracuse, the College of Optometry at New York, the Institute of Technology at Utica/Rome, Empire State College, and the Maritime College at Fort Schuyler. Applicants must exhibit dedication to the goals of the trade and labor union movement, be enrolled in school on a full-time basis, and show good character and service to the university.
Financial data: The stipend is $650 per semester, with annual adjustments tied to tuition.
Duration: 1 semester; renewable, provided the recipients remain in active, full-time registration and attendance as an undergraduate and maintain their grade point average, good character, and record of service.
Additional information: This program was established in 1985.
Deadline: February of each year.

305
EVELYN BARTY SCHOLARSHIP AWARDS PROGRAM

Billy Barty Foundation
929 West Olive Avenue, Suite C
Burbank, CA 91506
Phone: (818) 953-5410   (800) 891-4022
Fax: (818) 953-7129
Summary: To provide financial assistance for the postsecondary education of people of short stature or members of their families.
Eligibility: This program is open to high school seniors, high school graduates, and students currently enrolled in a 4-year college or university who are less than 4 feet 10 inches tall. Their parents and siblings are also eligible. Selection is based on scholarship, leadership, and financial need.
Financial data: The amount of the scholarship varies.
Duration: 1 year; recipients may reapply.
Additional information: These scholarships were named in honor of the average-sized sister of Billy Barty after her recent death. She had devoted many hours of volunteer time to the foundation.
Number awarded: Up to 5 each year.
Deadline: October of each year.

306
EVERLY SCHOLARSHIP

Everly Scholarship Fund, Inc.
Attn: John R. Lolio, Jr.
Fairway Corporate Center
4300 Haddonfield Road, Suite 311
Pennsauken, NJ 08109
Summary: To provide college financial assistance to high school seniors in New Jersey.
Eligibility: Any student is eligible receive aid from this scholarship who meets the following requirements: 1) has scored at least 1000 on the SAT, 2) has at least a 3.0 grade point average, 3) is in the top 20 percent of their high school class, and 4) has been a resident of New Jersey for at least 12 months. Finalists are interviewed. Financial need is not considered in the selection process.
Financial data: Stipends range up to $2,500 per year. Funds are paid to the student in equal installments each semester upon receipt of the term bill and verification of payment (cancelled check or receipt).
Duration: 1 year; renewed as long as the recipient maintains at least a 2.75 grade point average the first year and at least a 3.0 average in subsequent years.
Additional information: Recipients may attend school in any state as long as it is an accredited institution. Recipients must attend school on a full-time basis.
Deadline: April of each year.

307
EXCELLENCE IN SERVICE AWARDS

Florida Office of Collegiate Volunteerism
Attn Selection Committee
345 South Magnolia Drive, Suite D-12
Tallahassee, FL 32301
Phone: (850) 922-2922   Fax: (850) 922-2928
E-mail: focv@mailer.fsu.edu
Web Site: www.fsu.edu/~focv
Summary: To recognize and reward dedicated college student volunteers in Florida.
Eligibility: Full-time undergraduate or graduate students attending a college or university in Florida are eligible. They must participate in community service activities that 1) benefit the campus and community, 2) address social, political, or economic issues, and 3) demonstrate leadership through advocacy for social change. Students must be nominated by a community agency supervisor or campus faculty or staff member. The nominees' volunteer efforts must provide service for the community at large; religious, fraternal, or professional groups providing services only to members will not be considered. All volunteer efforts must have been performed in Florida or as part of a Florida campus-sponsored activity. The recipients are selected on the basis of their contributions to their communities during their college careers.
Financial data: The award is $1,000.
Duration: The award is presented annually.
Number awarded: 3 each year.
Deadline: Nominations must be submitted in January.

308
FACT "HIGH SCHOOL SENIOR" SCHOLARSHIP

Federation of American Consumers and Travelers
Attn: Scholarship Program
318 Hillsboro Avenue
P.O. Box 104
Edwardsville, IL 62025
Phone: (800) 872-3228
Summary: To provide financial assistance to members (or children or grandchildren of members) of the Federation of American Consumers and Travelers (FACT) who are graduating high school seniors.
Eligibility: This program is open to federation members and their children and grandchildren. Applicants must be high school seniors at an accredited public, private, or parochial high school in the United States. They must be enrolling in a 2- or 4-year undergraduate degree program at an accredited college or university, or in a course of study at a trade school approved by the federation. Selection is based on personal factors, an essay on career plans, and financial need.
Financial data: Stipends are either $10,000 or $2,500. Funds are paid directly to the recipient's educational institution for tuition, books, and related educational expenses.
Duration: 1 year or longer.
Number awarded: 2 each year: 1 at $10,000 and 1 at $2,500.
Deadline: January of each year.

309
FACT "IN-SCHOOL" SCHOLARSHIP

Federation of American Consumers and Travelers
Attn: Scholarship Program
318 Hillsboro Avenue
P.O. Box 104
Edwardsville, IL 62025
Phone: (800) 872-3228
Summary: To provide financial assistance to members (or children or grandchildren of members) of the Federation of American Consumers and Travelers (FACT) who are currently enrolled in college.
Eligibility: This program is open to federation members and their children and grandchildren. Applicants must be currently enrolled, full time, at an accredited college, university, or trade school. Selection is based on personal factors, an essay on career plans, and financial need.
Financial data: Stipends are either $10,000 or $2,500. Funds are paid directly to the recipient's educational institution for tuition, books, and related educational expenses.
Duration: 1 year or longer.
Number awarded: 2 each year: 1 at $10,000 and 1 at $2,500.
Deadline: January of each year.

310
FACT "SECOND CHANCE" SCHOLARSHIP

Federation of American Consumers and Travelers
Attn: Scholarship Program
318 Hillsboro Avenue
P.O. Box 104
Edwardsville, IL 62025
Phone: (800) 872-3228
Summary: To provide financial assistance to members (or children or grandchildren of members) of the Federation of American Consumers and Travelers (FACT) who graduated from high school 4 or more years ago but missed the chance at that time to go on to college.
Eligibility: This program is open to federation members and their children and grandchildren. Applicants must have graduated from high school 4 or more years ago. They must not have attended school as a full-time student during that period, and they must now be enrolling in a 2- or 4-year undergraduate degree program at an accredited college or university, or in a course of study at a trade school approved by the federation. Selection is based on personal factors, an essay on career plans, and financial need.
Financial data: Stipends are either $10,000 or $2,500. Funds are paid directly to the recipient's educational institution for tuition, books, and related educational expenses.
Duration: 1 year or longer.
Number awarded: 2 each year: 1 at $10,000 and 1 at $2,500.
Deadline: January of each year.

311
FATHER BILL MENSTER SCHOLARSHIP

Iowa Department of AMVETS
Attn: Scholarship Selection Committee
P.O. Box 77
Des Moines, IA 50301
Phone: (515) 284-4257
Summary: To provide financial assistance to the descendants of current Iowa AMVETS.
Eligibility: This program is open to graduating high school seniors in Iowa who are the sons, daughters, or grandchildren of a current Iowa AMVET member. Stepchildren, foster children, and other children dependent upon the member for support and living with the member in a regular parent-child relationship are also eligible, as is a deceased member's child. Applications must be endorsed by an Iowa AMVET post. Financial need is considered in the selection process.
Financial data: The stipend is at least $1,500.
Duration: 1 year.
Additional information: Any honorably discharged veteran is eligible for membership in AMVETS. Recipients may attend any accredited college, university, community college, technical institute, or trade school in Iowa.
Deadline: March of each year.

312
FATHER KREWITT SCHOLARSHIP AWARD

Catholic Kolping Society of America
c/o Edward Farkas
9 East Eighth Street
Clifton, NJ 07011
Phone: (973) 478-8635   E-mail: EdFarkas@aol.com
Web Site: www.kolping.org/Scholar.htm
Summary: To provide financial assistance for college to members of the Catholic Kolping Society of America and their dependents.
Eligibility: This program is open to members, children of members, and grandchildren of members who are attending college. Applicants must submit an essay (500 to 1,000 words) on a Christian topic that changes annually.
Financial data: The award is $1,000.
Duration: The competition is held annually.
Additional information: This program was established in 1978.
Deadline: February of each year.

313
FEDERAL EMPLOYEE EDUCATION AND ASSISTANCE FUND SCHOLARSHIPS

Federal Employee Education and Assistance Fund
Attn: Educational Programs
8441 West Bowles Avenue, Suite 200
Littleton, CO 80123-3245
Phone: (303) 933-7580   (800) 323-4140
Fax: (303) 933-7587   E-mail: feeahq@aol.com
Web Site: www.feea.org/scholarships.shtml
Summary: To provide financial assistance for the postsecondary education of civilian federal and postal employees and their families.
Eligibility: Eligible are civilian federal and postal employees with at least 3 years of federal service and their dependent spouses and children; military retirees and active-duty personnel are not eligible. All applicants must have at least a 3.0 grade point average and high school seniors must provide copies of their SAT or ACT scores, although those scores for students already in college are optional. Applicants must be working or planning to work toward a degree at an accredited 2- or 4-year postsecondary, graduate, or postgraduate program; employees may be part-time students, but dependents must be full time. Selection is based on academic achievement, community service, a recommendation, and an essay on a topic selected annually.
Financial data: Stipends range from $300 to $1,500.
Duration: 1 year; recipients may reapply.
Additional information: Funding for these scholarships is provided by donations from federal and postal employees and by a contribution from the Blue Cross and Blue Shield Association. Requests for applications must be accompanied by a self-addressed stamped envelope.
Number awarded: Varies each year; recently, 424 of these scholarships, for a total of $252,350, were awarded.
Deadline: March of each year.

314
FEDERAL PELL GRANTS

Department of Education
Attn: Federal Student Aid Information Center
P.O. Box 84
Washington, DC 20044-0084
Phone: (800) 4-FED-AID
Web Site: www.ed.gov
Summary: To provide financial assistance for undergraduate education to students with financial need.
Eligibility: Students who have not earned a bachelor's or professional degree are eligible for these grants if they meet specified financial need qualifications and are U.S. citizens or eligible noncitizens working toward a degree in an eligible program. They must have a valid Social Security number and have completed registration with the Selective Service if required.
Financial data: The amount of the award is based on the cost of attendance at the recipient's college or university, minus the expected family contribution, up to a specified maximum, which depends on annual program funding. Recently, awards ranged from $400 to $3,750 and averaged $2,311 per year.
Duration: Up to 5 years of undergraduate study.
Number awarded: Varies each year; under this program, the federal government

guarantees that each participating school will receive enough money to pay the Pell grants of its eligible students. Recently, 3,969,000 new awards were anticipated for this program.

Deadline: Students may submit applications between January of the current year through June of the following year.

315
FEDERAL SUPPLEMENTAL EDUCATIONAL OPPORTUNITY GRANTS

Department of Education
Attn: Federal Student Aid Information Center
P.O. Box 84
Washington, DC 20044-0084
Phone: (800) 4-FED-AID
Web Site: www.ed.gov
Summary: To provide financial assistance for undergraduate education to students with exceptional financial need.
Eligibility: Students who have not earned a bachelor's or professional degree are eligible for these grants if they meet specified financial need qualifications and are U.S. citizens or eligible noncitizens working toward a degree in an eligible program. They must have a valid Social Security number and have completed registration with the Selective Service if required. Applicants for Federal Pell Grants who demonstrate the greatest financial need qualify for these grants.
Financial data: The amount of the award is based on the cost of attendance at the recipient's college or university, minus the expected family contribution. Awards range between $100 and $4,000 per year and recently averaged $748.
Duration: Up to 5 years of undergraduate study.
Number awarded: Varies each year, depending on the availability of funds; under this program, the federal government does not guarantee that each participating school will receive enough money to pay the FSEOG grants of all of its eligible students. Recently, 1,169,668 new awards were anticipated for this program.
Deadline: Each participating school sets its own deadline.

316
FEDERATION LIFE INSURANCE OF AMERICA SCHOLARSHIPS

Federation Life Insurance of America
Attn: President
6011 South 27th Street
Milwaukee, WI 53221-4804
Phone: (414) 281-6281
Summary: To provide financial assistance for college to members of Federation Life Insurance.
Eligibility: This program is open to members of Federation Life Insurance. They must have been members in good standing for at least 5 years and cannot be older than 25. Applicants must be enrolled or accepted for enrollment at an accredited college or university. They must be working on a bachelor's degree and enrolled full time. Freshman applicants must include a copy of their acceptance notice. As part of the application process, students must write an essay (up to 500 words) on a leader with Polish or Slavic heritage who has made a significant contribution to their community.
Financial data: A stipend is awarded (exact amount not specified).
Duration: 1 year; may be renewed up to 3 additional years.
Number awarded: Varies each year.
Deadline: June of each year.

317
FEEA/NARFE SCHOLARSHIP FUND

Federal Employee Education and Assistance Fund
Attn: Educational Programs
8441 West Bowles Avenue, Suite 200
Littleton, CO 80123-3245
Phone: (303) 933-7580   (800) 323-4140
Fax: (303) 933-7587   E-mail: feeahq@aol.com
Web Site: www.feea.org/narfe_scholarship.shtml
Summary: To provide financial assistance for the undergraduate education of children and grandchildren of members of the National Association of Retired Federal Employees (NARFE).
Eligibility: This program is open to the children and grandchildren of members of the association. Applicants must be full-time students, enrolled or planning to enroll in a 2-year or 4-year postsecondary accredited undergraduate degree program, with at least a 3.0 grade point average. Selection is based on merit only.

Financial data: The stipend is $1,000 per year.
Duration: 1 year; recipients may reapply.
Additional information: This program began in 1998. It is administered by the Federal Employee Education and Assistance Fund.
Number awarded: 50 each year: 5 in each of the 10 NARFE regions.
Deadline: April of each year.

318
FEEA/WORLD TRADE CENTER/PENTAGON FUND SCHOLARSHIPS

Federal Employee Education and Assistance Fund
Attn: Educational Programs
8441 West Bowles Avenue, Suite 200
Littleton, CO 80123-3245
Phone: (303) 933-7580   (800) 323-4140
Fax: (303) 933-7587   E-mail: feeahq@aol.com
Web Site: www.feea.org/wtc_pentagon/wtc_pentagon.shtml
Summary: To provide financial assistance for college to children and spouses of civilian federal employees killed or injured in the Pentagon on September 11, 2001.
Eligibility: This program is open to children who lost a civilian federal employee parent in the attack on the Pentagon on September 11, 2001. Children whose parent was critically injured are also eligible, as are victims' spouses who were already attending college on September 11. Spouses wishing to return to college are considered on a case-by-case basis.
Financial data: Full college scholarships are available.
Number awarded: All affected family members will be supported.

319
FIERI NATIONAL SCHOLARSHIPS

Fieri National Scholarship Fund
c/o Evelyn Rossetti
309 West 105th Street, Number 8
New York, NY 10025
Phone: (212) 921-5338   E-mail: harnickfl@aol.com
Web Site: www.fieri.org
Summary: To provide financial assistance to Italian American students working on an undergraduate or graduate degree.
Eligibility: This program is open to Italian American high school seniors, currently-enrolled college students, and graduate students. Part-time and evening students are encouraged to apply. Selection is based on academic achievement and merit, involvement in community and other activities, recommendations, financial need (most recent federal and state income tax returns required), and an essay on the significance of Italian culture and/or ethnicity to the applicant and why the applicant should be recognized as an outstanding Italian American student.
Financial data: The stipend is $1,500. Local chapters also award scholarships in various amounts.
Duration: 1 year.
Additional information: This scholarship was established in 1994.
Number awarded: 1 each year.
Deadline: September of each year.

320
FILIPINO CHAMBER OF COMMERCE OF HAWAII SCHOLARSHIPS

Filipino Chamber of Commerce of Hawaii
905 Umi Street, Room 306
Honolulu, HI 96819
Phone: (808) 843-0322   E-mail: fcch@aloha.net
Summary: To provide financial assistance for college to high school seniors in Hawaii who have been involved with Filipino culture.
Eligibility: This program is open to seniors at high schools in Hawaii who have a grade point average of 3.5 or higher and have been accepted at a postsecondary institution. Applicants must be involved with and seek to perpetuate the Filipino culture. Selection is based on academic achievement, high school activities, awards and honors, and an essay on their community service.
Financial data: Stipends range from $1,000 to $1,500.
Duration: 1 year.
Number awarded: 1 or more each year.
Deadline: February of each year.

321
FIRST CATHOLIC SLOVAK LADIES ASSOCIATION COLLEGE AND GRADUATE SCHOLARSHIPS

First Catholic Slovak Ladies Association
Attn: Director of Fraternal Scholarship Aid
24950 Chagrin Boulevard
Cleveland, OH 44122-5634
Phone: (216) 464-8015   (800) 464-4642, ext. 128
Fax: (216) 464-8717
Web Site: www.fcsla.com
Summary: To provide financial assistance to college students who are members of the First Catholic Slovak Ladies Association.
Eligibility: Applicants must be students at an accredited college or university in the United States or Canada. They must have been beneficial members of the First Catholic Slovak Ladies Association for at least 3 years on a $1,000 legal reserve certificate, a $5,000 term certificate, or an annuity certificate. An autobiographical essay of approximately 500 words, including a statement of the applicant's goals and objectives, must accompany each application.
Financial data: The stipend is $1,250 for undergrads or $1,750 for graduate students.
Duration: 1 year; recipients may receive only 1 college scholarship but they may later apply for a graduate scholarship.
Number awarded: 80 each year: 41 for freshmen, 17 for sophomores, 8 for juniors, 7 for seniors, and 7 for full-time graduate students.
Deadline: February of each year.

322
FIRST COMMAND EDUCATIONAL FOUNDATION SCHOLARSHIPS

First Command Educational Foundation
Attn: Vice President and Secretary
4100 South Hulen
P.O. Box 2387
Fort Worth, TX 76113-2387
Phone: (817) 569-2218   (800) 443-2104
Fax: (817) 569-2176   E-mail: memurray@firstcommand.com
Web Site: www.firstcommand.com/source/scholarships.htm
Summary: To provide financial assistance for college to the children of active, retired, or deceased military personnel.
Eligibility: This program is open to the sons and daughters of active, retired, or deceased military personnel (officer or enlisted). Students must be nominated by an officers' spouses' club or a noncommissioned officers' spouses' club at participating U.S. military installations worldwide. Selection is based primarily on academic achievement and financial need.
Financial data: Scholarships are available in the amounts of $3,000, $2,000, or $1,000.
Duration: 1 year.
Additional information: The sponsoring organization was formerly known as the USPA & IRA Educational Foundation, founded in 1983. Since its establishment, it has awarded more than 2,200 scholarships worth more than $2.3 million.
Number awarded: Varies each year; recently, 146 were awarded.

323
FIRST MARINE DIVISION ASSOCIATION SCHOLARSHIPS

First Marine Division Association
14325 Willard Road, Suite 107
Chantilly, VA 20151-2110
Phone: (703) 803-3195   Fax: (703) 803-7114
E-mail: oldbreed@aol.com
Summary: To provide financial assistance for the undergraduate education of dependents of veterans of the First Marine Division.
Eligibility: This program is open to dependents of veterans who are honorably discharged, totally and permanently disabled, or deceased from any cause and who served in the First Marine Division or in a unit attached to that Division. Applicants must be attending or planning to attend an accredited college, university, or trade school as a full-time undergraduate student.
Financial data: The amounts of the awards vary; payments are made directly to the educational institution.
Duration: 1 year; may be renewed up to 3 additional years.
Additional information: Award winners who marry before completing the course or who drop out for non-scholastic reasons must submit a new application before benefits can be resumed.
Number awarded: Varies each year.

324
FITZGERALD SCHOLARSHIPS

Delta Epsilon Sigma
c/o Dr. J. Patrick Lee, Secretary-Treasurer
Barry University
11300 N.E. Second Avenue
Miami, FL 33161
Phone: (305) 899-3020   E-mail: jplee@mail.barry.edu
Web Site: socrates.barry.edu/des/info1.html
Summary: To provide financial assistance for college to members of Delta Epsilon Sigma (a national scholastic honor society).
Eligibility: Eligible to be nominated for this program are members of Delta Epsilon Sigma who are in their junior year of college. Nominations must be submitted by their chapter. Nominees must have been initiated into the society.
Financial data: The stipend is $1,000. Funds must be used to pay for tuition.
Duration: 1 year (the recipient's senior year).
Additional information: These scholarships are named in honor of the founder and first secretary-treasurer of the society.
Number awarded: 12 each year.
Deadline: February of each year.

325
FLEET RESERVE ASSOCIATION SCHOLARSHIP

Fleet Reserve Association
Attn: Scholarship Administrator
125 North West Street
Alexandria, VA 22314-2754
Phone: (703) 683-1400   (800) 372-1924
Fax: (703) 549-6610
Web Site: www.fra.org
Summary: To provide financial assistance for undergraduate or graduate education to members of the Fleet Reserve Association (FRA) and to the spouses and children of naval personnel.
Eligibility: Applicants for these scholarships must be 1) dependent children or spouses of members of the U.S. Navy, Marine Corps, or Coast Guard (regular and reserve) serving on active duty, retired with pay, or deceased while on active duty or retired with pay, and 2) members of the FRA. Selection is based on financial need, scholastic standing, character, and leadership qualities.
Financial data: The amount awarded varies, depending upon the needs of the recipient and the funds available.
Duration: 1 year; may be renewed.
Additional information: Membership in the FRA is restricted to active-duty, retired, and reserve members of the Navy, Marines, and Coast Guard.
Number awarded: 1 each year.
Deadline: April of each year.

326
FLORIDA ACADEMIC SCHOLARS AWARD PROGRAM

Florida Department of Education
Attn: Office of Student Financial Assistance
1940 North Monroe Street, Suite 70
Tallahassee, FL 32303-4759
Phone: (850) 410-5185   (888) 827-2004
Fax: (850) 488-3612   E-mail: osfa@mail.doe.state.fl.us
Web Site: www.firn.edu/doe/osfa
Summary: To provide financial assistance for college to outstanding high school seniors in Florida.
Eligibility: Eligible are seniors in Florida public and private high schools who have been Florida residents for at least 1 year and will attend eligible Florida institutions of higher education. Applicants must have achieved an SAT score of 1270 or higher, an ACT score of 28 or higher, or a high school grade point average of 3.5 or higher. They must also have completed a specified curriculum while in high school. U.S. citizenship or permanent resident status is required.
Financial data: The scholarships provide 100 percent of tuition and mandatory fees at Florida public colleges and universities or an equivalent amount at private institutions (recently, $1,504 per semester at 4-year universities or $1,058 per semester at 2-year colleges). Students also receive a stipend of $300 for college-related expenses.
Duration: Recipients may use this award 1) for up to 110 percent of the number of credit hours required to complete a standard undergraduate degree at their institution; 2) 7 years from high school graduation (if initially funded within 3

years after high school graduation); or 3) until completion of their first baccalaureate degree program, whichever comes first.

Additional information: These scholarships are offered as part of the Florida Bright Futures Scholarship Program, established in 1997 with funding from the lottery.

Number awarded: Varies each year.

Deadline: March of each year.

327
FLORIDA ACADEMIC TOP SCHOLARS AWARD PROGRAM

Florida Department of Education
Attn: Office of Student Financial Assistance
1940 North Monroe Street, Suite 70
Tallahassee, FL 32303-4759
Phone: (850) 410-5185   (888) 827-2004
Fax: (850) 488-3612   E-mail: osfa@mail.doe.state.fl.us
Web Site: www.firn.edu/doe/osfa

Summary: To provide financial assistance for college to outstanding high school seniors in Florida.

Eligibility: Eligible to receive a Florida Academic Scholars Award are seniors in Florida public and private high schools who have been Florida residents for at least 1 year and will attend eligible Florida institutions of higher education. They must have completed a specified curriculum while in high school. U.S. citizenship or permanent resident status is required. The Academic Top Scholars Award is presented to the student with the highest academic ranking in each county, based on grade point average and SAT/ACT test scores.

Financial data: The Academic Top Scholars awardees receive an annual stipend of $1,500 in addition to their Academic Scholars Award.

Duration: Recipients may use this award 1) for up to 110 percent of the number of credit hours required to complete a standard undergraduate degree at their institution; 2) 7 years from high school graduation (if initially funded within 3 years after high school graduation); or 3) until completion of their first baccalaureate degree program, whichever comes first.

Additional information: These scholarships are offered as part of the Florida Bright Futures Scholarship Program, established in 1997 with funding from the lottery.

Number awarded: 67 each year: 1 in each Florida county.

Deadline: March of each year.

328
FLORIDA AMERICAN LEGION EAGLE SCOUT OF THE YEAR AWARDS

American Legion
Attn: Department of Florida
1912 Lee Road
P.O. Box 547936
Orlando, FL 32854-7936
Phone: (407) 295-2631   Fax: (407) 299-0901
E-mail: fllegion@orl.mindspring.com
Web Site: www.floridalegion.org

Summary: To recognize and reward outstanding Eagle Scouts in Florida.

Eligibility: This program is open to Florida high school students who have earned the Eagle Scout award and religious medal. Applicants must 1) belong to an Eagle Scout troop chartered to an American Legion Post, 2) be the son or grandson of an American Legion member, or 3) have a parent eligible to join the American Legion.

Financial data: The awards are $1,000 or $500.

Duration: 1 year; nonrenewable.

Number awarded: 3 each year: 1 at $1,000 and 2 at $500.

Deadline: February of each year.

329
FLORIDA AMERICAN LEGION SCHOLARSHIPS

American Legion
Attn: Department of Florida
1912 Lee Road
P.O. Box 547936
Orlando, FL 32854-7936
Phone: (407) 295-2631   Fax: (407) 299-0901
E-mail: fllegion@orl.mindspring.com
Web Site: www.floridalegion.org

Summary: To provide financial assistance for college to the descendants of American Legion members in Florida.

Eligibility: This program is open to the direct descendants (children, grandchildren, great-grandchildren, and legally adopted children) of a member of the American Legion's Department of Florida or of a deceased U.S. veteran who would have been eligible for membership in the American Legion. Applicants must be seniors attending a Florida high school.

Financial data: The scholarships are $2,500, $1,500, or $1,000.

Duration: 1 year; nonrenewable.

Number awarded: 3 each year.

Deadline: November of each year.

330
FLORIDA COLLEGE STUDENT OF THE YEAR AWARD

College Student of the Year, Inc.
412 N.W. 16th Avenue
P.O. Box 14081
Gainesville, FL 32604-2081
Phone: (352) 373-6907   (888) 547-6310
Fax: (352) 373-8120   E-mail: info@studentleader.com
Web Site: www.floridaleader.com/soty

Summary: To recognize and reward outstanding Florida college or graduate students who are involved in campus and community activities, excel academically, and exhibit financial self reliance by working and earning scholarships to pay their way through school.

Eligibility: Applicants do not need to be Florida residents, but they must be currently enrolled at least half time in a Florida-based community college, private university, state university, or accredited vocational, technical, or business school. They may be undergraduate or graduate students, must have earned at least a 3.25 grade point average, and must write an essay (up to 600 words) that addresses this topic: "What I have accomplished that makes a difference at my college and in my community." U.S. citizenship is not required and applicants may be of any age. Students do not have to be nominated by their colleges to be eligible; students are permitted and encouraged to apply on their own. There is no limit to the number of applicants who can apply from a particular institution. Ineligible to apply are current employees or relatives of employees of *Florida Leader* magazine, Oxendine Publishing, Inc., College Student of the Year, Inc., or any cosponsor. Winners are selected on the basis of 3 main criteria: academic excellence, financial self reliance, and community and campus service. Financial need is not a requirement.

Financial data: Nearly $50,000 in scholarships and prizes is available each year. The actual distribution of those funds among the various recipients depends on the support provided by the sponsors. Recently, the winner received a $3,000 scholarship from SunTrust Education Loans, a $1,000 scholarship from Publix Super Markets, and several other gifts and prizes. The first runner-up received a $2,500 scholarship from SunTrust, a $750 scholarship from Publix Super Markets, and other gifts and prizes. The other finalists each received a $2,000 scholarship from SunTrust, a $750 scholarship from Public Super Markets, and other gifts and prizes. The honorable mention winners each received a $1,000 scholarship from SunTrust, a $350 scholarship from Publix Super Markets, and other gifts and prizes.

Duration: The prizes are awarded annually.

Additional information: This competition, established in 1987, is managed by *Florida Leader* magazine; scholarships are provided by SunTrust Education Loans and Publix Super Markets; several other sponsors provide the other prizes.

Number awarded: 20 each year: 1 winner, 1 first runner-up, 5 other finalists, and 13 honorable mentions.

Deadline: January of each year.

331
FLORIDA EMPLOYMENT AND TRAINING PROGRAM

Florida Governor's Council on Indian Affairs
Attn: Employment and Training Program
1341 Cross Creek Circle
Tallahassee, FL 32301
Phone: (850) 488-0730   (800) 322-9186
E-mail: info@fgcia.com
Web Site: www.fgcia.com

Summary: To provide financial assistance to needy Native Americans in Florida or Georgia who are interested in obtaining additional education or training.

Eligibility: Unemployed, underemployed, or economically disadvantaged Native Americans (Native Hawaiians, Alaskan Natives, American Indians) are eligible to apply for this support. The Florida Governor's Council on Indian Affairs provides this service for 63 of the 67 counties in Florida and all of the state of Georgia.

Financial data: Tuition and other services are offered to recipients.
Duration: Up to 1 year.
Additional information: Funds may be used for a vocational-technical degree, an A.A. or Associate Degree, GED preparation, or adult education.
Number awarded: Varies each year.

332
FLORIDA GOLD SEAL VOCATIONAL SCHOLARS AWARD

Florida Department of Education
Attn: Office of Student Financial Assistance
1940 North Monroe Street, Suite 70
Tallahassee, FL 32303-4759
Phone: (850) 410-5185   (888) 827-2004
Fax: (850) 488-3612   E-mail: osfa@mail.doe.state.fl.us
Web Site: www.firn.edu/doe/osfa
Summary: To provide financial assistance for vocational education to outstanding high school seniors in Florida.
Eligibility: This program is open to graduating high school seniors in Florida who plan to attend a vocational, technical, trade, or business school in the state. Applicants must have achieved a grade point average of 3.0 or higher in their required academic program and 3.5 or higher in their vocational classes in high school. They must also have achieved the following minimum scores: 1) on the CPT, 83 in reading, 83 in sentence skills, and 72 in algebra; 2) on the SAT, 440 in verbal and 440 in mathematics; or 3) on the ACT, 17 in English, 18 in reading, and 19 in mathematics. U.S. citizenship or permanent resident status is required.
Financial data: The scholarships cover 75 percent of tuition and mandatory fees (including lab fees up to $300 per semester) at public vocational-technical institutions in Florida, or an equivalent amount at private schools (currently, $911 per semester at 4-year schools or $576 per semester at 2-year schools).
Duration: Recipients may use this award 1) for up to 90 semester hours; 2) 7 years from high school graduation (if initially funded within 3 years after high school graduation); or 3) until completion of their first baccalaureate degree program, whichever comes first.
Additional information: These scholarships are offered as part of the Florida Bright Futures Scholarship Program, established in 1997 with funding from the lottery.
Number awarded: Varies each year.
Deadline: March of each year.

333
FLORIDA LEGION AUXILIARY DEPARTMENT SCHOLARSHIP

Florida Legion Auxiliary Scholarship
P.O. Box 547917
Orlando, FL 32854-7917
Phone: (407) 293-7411   Fax: (407) 299-6522
E-mail: alaflorida@aol.com
Summary: To provide financial assistance for postsecondary education to the children of Florida veterans.
Eligibility: This program is open to children of honorably discharged veterans who are Florida residents. Applicants must be attending a postsecondary school in the state on a full-time basis.
Financial data: The scholarships are up to $1,000 for a 4-year university and up to $500 for a junior college or technical-vocational school. All funds are paid directly to the institution.
Duration: 1 year; may be renewed if the recipient needs further financial assistance and has maintained at least a 2.5 grade point average.
Number awarded: Depends on the availability of funds.
Deadline: February of each year.

334
FLORIDA LEGION AUXILIARY MEMORIAL SCHOLARSHIP

Florida Legion Auxiliary Scholarship
P.O. Box 547917
Orlando, FL 32854-7917
Phone: (407) 293-7411   Fax: (407) 299-6522
E-mail: alaflorida@aol.com
Summary: To provide financial assistance for educational purposes to members and female dependents of members of the Florida American Legion Auxiliary.
Eligibility: Applicants must be members of the Florida Auxiliary or daughters or granddaughters of members who have at least 3 years of continuous membership. They must be sponsored by their local units, be Florida residents, and be attending

Florida schools. Selection is based on academic record and financial need.
Financial data: The scholarships are up to $1,000 for a 4-year university and up to $500 for a junior college or technical-vocational school. All funds are paid directly to the institution.
Duration: 1 year; may be renewed if the recipient needs further financial assistance and has maintained at least a 2.5 grade point average.
Additional information: Recipients must attend a Florida college, university, or technical school. All awards are for full-time study and are to be used for 2 semesters of the school year.
Number awarded: Depends on the availability of funds.
Deadline: February of each year.

335
FLORIDA LIMITED ACCESS COMPETITIVE GRANTS

Florida Department of Education
Attn: Office of Student Financial Assistance
1940 North Monroe Street, Suite 70
Tallahassee, FL 32303-4759
Phone: (850) 410-5185   (888) 827-2004
Fax: (850) 488-3612   E-mail: osfa@mail.doe.state.fl.us
Web Site: www.firn.edu/doe/osfa
Summary: To provide financial assistance to students in Florida who wish to transfer from a community college or state university to an eligible private college or university.
Eligibility: This program is open to Florida residents who are community college graduates or transfer students from state universities and who enroll in 1 of the designated limited access programs at eligible private colleges or universities in Florida. Limited access programs are defined as high priority employment fields that require a baccalaureate degree for which state universities have insufficient capacity to serve all qualified applicants. Preference is given to Florida residents who graduated from Florida high schools or community colleges.
Financial data: The scholarships provide an amount equivalent to 50 percent of the state's cost to fund an undergraduate student at a public postsecondary institution.
Duration: Up to 4 semesters or 6 quarters, provided the recipient maintains satisfactory academic progress, full-time enrollment, and a grade point average of 2.0 or higher.
Number awarded: Varies each year; recently, this program provided 705 awards.
Deadline: Deadlines are established by each of the participating private institutions.

336
FLORIDA MERIT SCHOLARS AWARD PROGRAM

Florida Department of Education
Attn: Office of Student Financial Assistance
1940 North Monroe Street, Suite 70
Tallahassee, FL 32303-4759
Phone: (850) 410-5185   (888) 827-2004
Fax: (850) 488-3612   E-mail: osfa@mail.doe.state.fl.us
Web Site: www.firn.edu/doe/osfa
Summary: To provide financial assistance for college to outstanding high school seniors in Florida.
Eligibility: Eligible are seniors in Florida public and private high schools who have been Florida residents for at least 1 year and will attend eligible Florida institutions of higher education. Applicants must have achieved an SAT score of 970 or higher, ACT score of 20 or higher, or grade point average in a specified curriculum of 3.0 or higher. U.S. citizenship or permanent resident status is required.
Financial data: The scholarships cover 75 percent of tuition and mandatory fees (including lab fees up to $300 per semester) at public colleges and universities in Florida, or an equivalent amount at private schools (currently, $911 per semester at 4-year universities or $576 per semester at 2-year colleges).
Duration: Recipients may use this award 1) for up to 110 percent of the number of credit hours required to complete a standard undergraduate degree at their institution; 2) 7 years from high school graduation (if initially funded within 3 years after high school graduation); or 3) until completion of their first baccalaureate degree program, whichever comes first.
Additional information: These scholarships are offered as part of the Florida Bright Futures Scholarship Program, established in 1997 with funding from the lottery.
Number awarded: Varies each year.
Deadline: March of each year.

337
FLORIDA PTA SCHOLARSHIP PROGRAMS

Florida PTA
1747 Orlando Central Parkway
Orlando, FL 32809
Phone: (407) 855-7604   (800) 373-5782
Fax: (407) 240-9577   E-mail: info@floridapta.org
Web Site: www.floridapta.org/scholarships.htm
Summary: To provide financial assistance for college to high school seniors in Florida.
Eligibility: This program is open to seniors graduating from high schools in Florida. Applicants must have attended a Florida PTA/PTSA high school for at least 2 years and have a grade point average of 2.5 or higher. They must be planning to enroll as a full-time undergraduate student at a Florida postsecondary institution. U.S. citizenship is required. Financial need is considered in the selection process. The program includes 4 types of scholarships: academic, vocational-technical, community/junior college, and fine arts.
Financial data: The stipend is $1,000 per year.
Duration: 1 year. Academic scholarships may be renewed if the recipient maintains a grade point average of 2.5 or higher. The other 3 types are nonrenewable.
Number awarded: Varies each year; recently, the program awarded 2 academic scholarships, 2 vocational-technical scholarships, 2 community/junior college scholarships, and 4 fine arts scholarships.
Deadline: February of each year.

338
FLORIDA SCHOLARSHIPS FOR CHILDREN OF DECEASED OR DISABLED VETERANS

Florida Department of Education
Attn: Office of Student Financial Assistance
1940 North Monroe Street, Suite 70
Tallahassee, FL 32303-4759
Phone: (850) 410-5185   (888) 827-2004
Fax: (850) 488-3612   E-mail: osfa@mail.doe.state.fl.us
Web Site: www.firn.edu/doe/osfa
Summary: To provide financial assistance for the postsecondary education of children of Florida veterans who are disabled, deceased, or officially classified as prisoners of war or missing in action.
Eligibility: Eligible for these scholarships are residents of Florida between 16 and 22 years of age who are the dependent children of 100 percent disabled or deceased wartime veterans or of servicemen officially classified as prisoners of war or missing in action. Veteran parents who served in Vietnam, Korea, World War II, or World War I must have been residents of Florida for 5 years prior to the student's application; veteran parents who served in the Iranian Rescue Mission, the Lebanon and Grenada military arenas, the Newfoundland air tragedy, the USS Stark attack, Operation Just Cause in Panama, or the Persian Gulf War must have been residents of Florida for 1 year prior to the student's application.
Financial data: Qualified students who attend a Florida public institution of higher education receive payment of tuition and fees. Students who attend an eligible nonpublic Florida institution of higher education receive an award equal to the amount they would be required to pay for the average tuition and fees at a public institution at the comparable level.
Duration: 1 quarter or semester; may be renewed for up to 11 additional quarters or 7 additional semesters as long as the student maintains a grade point average of 2.0 or higher and full-time enrollment.
Number awarded: Varies each year; recently, this program provided 215 awards.
Deadline: March of each year.

339
FLORIDA STUDENT ASSISTANCE GRANTS

Florida Department of Education
Attn: Office of Student Financial Assistance
1940 North Monroe Street, Suite 70
Tallahassee, FL 32303-4759
Phone: (850) 410-5185   (888) 827-2004
Fax: (850) 488-3612   E-mail: osfa@mail.doe.state.fl.us
Web Site: www.firn.edu/doe/osfa
Summary: To provide financial assistance for undergraduate studies to needy Florida residents.
Eligibility: Full-time undergraduate students who are attending an eligible public or private Florida institution are invited to apply. They must be U.S. citizens or eligible noncitizens. A minimum of 1 year of Florida residency is required. Financial need must be documented; applicants must submit the Free Application for Federal Student Aid. Priority is given to students with the lowest total family resources.
Financial data: Awards at Florida public institutions range from $200 to the average prior academic year cost of matriculation and other registration fees. For students at eligible nonpublic Florida colleges and universities, awards range from $200 to the average prior academic year cost of matriculation and other fees at state universities plus $1,000. No award may exceed the student's demonstrated financial need.
Duration: Grants may be received for up to 9 semesters or 14 quarters or until receipt of a bachelor's degree, whichever comes first.
Additional information: This program receives funding from Florida general revenues and the federal Leveraging Educational Assistance Partnership program.
Number awarded: Varies each year; recently, this program provided 40,040 awards.
Deadline: May of each year.

340
FLORIDA WOMEN'S STATE GOLF ASSOCIATION SCHOLARSHIP

Florida Women's State Golf Association
Attn: Executive Director
10,000 North US History 98, Number 107
Lakeland, FL 33809
Phone: (863) 815-1646   Fax: (863) 816-9701
E-mail: fwsga@usga.org
Web Site: www.fwsga.org
Summary: To provide financial assistance for college to women in Florida who have an interest in golf.
Eligibility: This program is open to females in Florida who have an interest in golf but are not skilled enough to qualify for an athletic scholarship. Applicants must have a need for financial assistance. They must have a grade point average of 3.0 or higher and attend or be planning to attend a junior college, college, university, or technical school in Florida.
Financial data: The amount awarded varies, depending upon the needs of the recipient. Funds are paid directly to the recipient's school.
Duration: 1 year.
Number awarded: 1 or more each year.
Deadline: February of each year.

341
FLOYD BORING AWARD

Boy Scouts of America
Attn: Learning for Life Division, S210
1325 West Walnut Hill Lane
P.O. Box 152079
Irving, TX 75015-2079
Phone: (972) 580-2418
Web Site: www.learning-for-life.org/exploring
Summary: To recognize and reward Explorer Scouts who have made an exceptional contribution to law enforcement agencies.
Eligibility: This program is open to Explorer Scouts who assist law enforcement agencies with meaningful and exceptional service. Candidates must be active members of a Law Enforcement Explorer post currently registered with the Boy Scouts of America. They must submit a statement from their post advisor that describes the act for which they are being nominated, 3 letters of recommendation, and their own 1,000-word statement that describes the act for which they are being nominated.
Financial data: The award consists of a plaque and a $2,000 scholarship to the college of the awardee's choice.
Duration: 1 year; nonrenewable.
Additional information: This program was established in 1972. In 1998, it was renamed to honor the organizer of the Association of Former Agents of the U.S. Secret Service (which sponsors the program).
Number awarded: 2 each year.
Deadline: March of each year.

342
FLOYD GRAY ENDOWMENT SCHOLARSHIP

Epsilon Sigma Alpha
Attn: ESA Foundation Assistant Scholarship Director
P.O. Box 270517
Fort Collins, CO 80527
Phone: (970) 223-2824   Fax: (970) 223-4456
Web Site: www.esaintl.com/esaf
Summary: To provide financial assistance for college to students from any state studying any major.
Eligibility: This program is open to graduating high school seniors, students already enrolled in college, trainees in technical school, and students returning to school after an absence. Applicants must have a grade point average between 3.0 and 3.5. Selection is based on character, scholastic ability, leadership and ability skills, and financial need.
Financial data: The stipend is $1,000.
Duration: 1 year; may be renewed.
Additional information: Epsilon Sigma Alpha (ESA) is a women's service organization, but scholarships are available to both men and women. Information is also available from Verneene Forssberg, 403 South High, Pratt, KS 67124, (316) 672-3636, Fax: (316) 672-3688, E-mail: vernf@genmail.pcc.cc.ks.us. Completed applications must be submitted to the ESA State Counselor who verifies the information before forwarding them to the scholarship director.
Number awarded: 1 each year.
Deadline: January of each year.

343
FLOYD QUALLS MEMORIAL SCHOLARSHIPS

American Council of the Blind
Attn: Coordinator, Scholarship Program
1155 15th Street, N.W., Suite 1004
Washington, DC 20005
Phone: (202) 467-5081   (800) 424-8666
Fax: (202) 467-5085   E-mail: info@acb.org
Web Site: www.acb.org
Summary: To provide financial assistance to students who are blind.
Eligibility: Students who are legally blind may apply for these scholarships. Recipients are selected in each of 4 categories: entering freshmen in academic programs, undergraduates (sophomores, juniors, and seniors) in academic programs, graduate students in academic programs, and vocational school students or students pursuing an associate's degree from a community college. In addition to letters of recommendation and copies of academic transcripts, applications must include an autobiographical sketch. Selection is based on demonstrated academic record, involvement in extracurricular and civic activities, and academic objectives. The severity of the applicant's visual impairment and his/her study methods are also taken into account.
Financial data: The stipend is $2,500. In addition, the winners receive a $1,000 cash scholarship from the Kurzweil Foundation and, if appropriate, a Kurzweil 1000 Reading System.
Duration: 1 year.
Additional information: Scholarship winners are expected to be present at the council's annual conference; the council will cover all reasonable expenses connected with convention attendance.
Number awarded: 8 each year: 2 in each of the 4 categories.
Deadline: February of each year.

344
FORD OPPORTUNITY PROGRAM SCHOLARSHIP

Oregon Student Assistance Commission
Attn: Private Awards Grant Department
1500 Valley River Drive, Suite 100
Eugene, OR 97401-2146
Phone: (541) 687-7388   (800) 452-8807, ext. 7388
Fax: (541) 687-7424   E-mail: fordprograms@mercury.osac.state.or.us
Web Site: www.osac.state.or.us
Summary: To provide financial assistance to Oregon residents who are single parents seeking a college degree.
Eligibility: This program is open to residents of Oregon who are U.S. citizens or permanent residents. Applicants must be single heads of household with custody of a dependent child or children. They must have a cumulative high school or college grade point average of 3.0 or higher or a GED score of 260 or higher, and

they must be planning to earn a 4-year degree at an Oregon college. Selection is based on community service, work ethic, personal initiative, and financial need.
Financial data: Scholarship amounts vary, depending upon the needs of the recipient.
Duration: 1 year; may be renewed for up to 3 additional years.
Additional information: This program, funded by the Ford Family Foundation, began in 1996.
Number awarded: 30 each year.
Deadline: February of each year.

345
FORD SCHOLARS PROGRAM

Oregon Student Assistance Commission
Attn: Private Awards Grant Department
1500 Valley River Drive, Suite 100
Eugene, OR 97401-2146
Phone: (541) 687-7388   (800) 452-8807, ext. 7388
Fax: (541) 687-7424   E-mail: fordprograms@mercury.osac.state.or.us
Web Site: www.osac.state.or.us
Summary: To provide financial assistance to Oregon residents who are seeking a college degree.
Eligibility: This program is open to residents of Oregon who are U.S. citizens or permanent residents. Applicants must be 1) graduating high school seniors; 2) high school graduates who have not yet been full-time undergraduates; or 3) individuals who have completed 2 years at an Oregon community college and are entering their junior year at an Oregon 4-year college. They must have a cumulative high school or college grade point average of 3.0 or higher or a GED score of 260 or higher, and they must be planning to receive a 4-year degree at an Oregon college. Selection is based on community service, work ethic, personal initiative, and financial need.
Financial data: Scholarship amounts vary, depending upon the needs of the recipient.
Duration: 1 year; may be renewed for up to 3 additional years.
Additional information: This program, funded by the Ford Family Foundation, began in 1994.
Number awarded: 100 each year.
Deadline: February of each year.

346
FORMER FOSTER CHILDREN SCHOLARSHIP

Oregon Student Assistance Commission
Attn: Private Awards Grant Department
1500 Valley River Drive, Suite 100
Eugene, OR 97401-2146
Phone: (541) 687-7395   (800) 452-8807, ext. 7395
Fax: (541) 687-7419   E-mail: awardinfo@mercury.osac.state.or.us
Web Site: www.osac.state.or.us
Summary: To provide financial assistance for college to residents of Oregon who have been a ward of the court.
Eligibility: This program is open to residents of Oregon who have been a ward of the court and in legal custody of Children, Adult, and Family Services for at least 12 months between the ages of 16 and 21. Applicants must enroll in college within 3 years of their high school graduation or removal from the care of Children, Adult, and Family Services (whichever is sooner). They must attend or be planning to attend a college in Oregon. Awards are presented on a first-come, first-served basis depending on the date when the applicant files the Free Application for Federal Student Aid (FAFSA).
Financial data: Scholarship amount vary, depending upon needs of the recipient.
Duration: 1 year; may be renewed if requirements are met and funding is available.
Additional information: Information on this scholarship is also available from Children, Adult, and Family Services.
Number awarded: Varies each year.
Deadline: February of each year.

347
FOUR-YEAR SBAA EDUCATIONAL SCHOLARSHIP FUND

Spina Bifida Association of America
Attn: Scholarship Committee
4590 MacArthur Boulevard, N.W., Suite 250
Washington, DC 20007-4226
Phone: (202) 944-3285, ext. 19   (800) 621-3141
Fax: (202) 944-3295   E-mail: sbaa@sbaa.org
Web Site: www.sbaa.org

Summary: To provide financial assistance to members of the Spina Bifida Association of America (SPAA) who are interested in pursuing higher education or technical school training.

Eligibility: Eligible to apply for these scholarships are persons of any age born with spina bifida who are current members of the association. Applicants must be high school juniors entering their senior year at the time of application. Selection is based on academic record, other efforts shown in school, financial need, work history, community service, leadership, and commitment to personal goals.

Financial data: The stipend is $5,000 per year.

Duration: 4 years.

Additional information: This program was established in 1998.

Number awarded: Varies each year.

Deadline: August of each year.

348
FOURTH DEGREE PRO DEO AND PRO PATRIA SCHOLARSHIP PROGRAM

Knights of Columbus
Attn: Director of Scholarship Aid
P.O. Box 1670
New Haven, CT 06507-0901
Phone: (203) 772-2130, ext. 332   Fax: (203) 773-3000

Summary: To provide financial assistance to entering freshmen at Catholic colleges and universities.

Eligibility: Eligible are students entering their freshman year in a program leading to a baccalaureate degree at a Catholic college or university in the United States; applicants must be members in good standing of the Columbian Squires or Knights of Columbus, or the son or daughter of a member, or the child of a deceased member who was in good standing at the time of death. Selection is based on secondary school record, class rank, and aptitude test scores.

Financial data: The scholarships are $1,500 per year.

Duration: 1 year; may be renewed up to 3 additional years upon evidence of satisfactory academic performance.

Additional information: Of the scholarships for Catholic University of America, preference on 2 is given to Columbian Squires; of the scholarships for other Catholic colleges, preference on 2 is given to Columbian Squires.

Number awarded: 62 each year, of which 12 are to Catholic University of America and 50 are to other Catholic institutions.

Deadline: February of each year.

349
FRANCIS P. MATTHEWS AND JOHN E. SWIFT EDUCATIONAL TRUST SCHOLARSHIPS

Knights of Columbus
Attn: Director of Scholarship Aid
P.O. Box 1670
New Haven, CT 06507-0901
Phone: (203) 772-2130, ext. 332   Fax: (203) 773-3000

Summary: To provide financial assistance for postsecondary education at Catholic colleges or universities to children of disabled or deceased veterans, law enforcement officers, or firemen who are/were also Knights of Columbus members.

Eligibility: Eligible are children of members of the sponsoring organization who were either totally and permanently disabled or killed as a result of military service during World War II, the Korean conflict, the Vietnam War, or the Persian Gulf War; of full-time law enforcement officers who became disabled or lost their lives as a result of criminal violence; or of firemen who became disabled or were killed in the line of duty. For the children of veterans, the death or disability must have occurred during a period of conflict or within 10 years of its official termination. Students must be high school seniors at the time of application.

Financial data: The amounts of the awards vary but are designed to cover tuition, room and board, books, and required fees at the Catholic college or university of the recipient's choice.

Duration: 1 year; may be renewed up to 3 additional years.

Additional information: Recipients must attend Catholic colleges.

Number awarded: Varies each year.

Deadline: April of each year.

350
FRANK L. WEIL MEMORIAL EAGLE SCOUT SCHOLARSHIP

Boy Scouts of America
Attn: National Jewish Committee on Scouting, S226
1325 West Walnut Hill Lane
P.O. Box 152079
Irving, TX 75015-2079
Phone: (972) 580-2000
Web Site: www.jewishscouting.org/awards/eagle.html

Summary: To provide financial assistance for college to Jewish Boy Scouts Varsity Scouts, and Explorers.

Eligibility: This program is open to Jewish Boy Scouts, Varsity Scouts, and Explorers who have received the Eagle Scout Award and have also earned the Ner Tamid emblem. Applicants must be enrolled in an accredited high school in their final year and must be an active member of a synagogue. They must have demonstrated practical citizenship in their synagogue, school, Scouting unit, and community. Selection is based on high school record, including school activities, awards, honors, and grade point average; participation in community organizations; participation in religious youth organizations, clubs, or groups, including honors earned and offices held; involvement in Scouting; career goals; and 4 letters of recommendation, from leaders of their religious institution, school, community, and Scouting unit.

Financial data: First place is $1,000 and second place is $500.

Duration: 1 year; not renewable.

Additional information: These scholarships are awarded in memory of the former chairman of the National Jewish Committee on Scouting and president of the Jewish Welfare Board.

Number awarded: 3 each year: 1 first place and 2 second place awards.

Deadline: December of each year.

351
FRED SCHEIGERT SCHOLARSHIPS

Council of Citizens with Low Vision International
Attn: Scholarship Chair
1859 North Washington Avenue, Suite 2000
Clearwater, FL 33755-1862
Phone: (800) 733-2258   E-mail: bernice@tsoft.net
Web Site: www.cclvi.org/scholarship.txt

Summary: To provide financial aid for postsecondary education to persons with low vision.

Eligibility: Applicants must be certified by an ophthalmologist as having low vision (acuity of 20/70 or worse in the better seeing eye with best correction or side vision with a maximum diameter of no greater than 30 degrees). They may be part-time or full-time entering freshmen, undergraduates, or graduate students. A cumulative grade point average of at least 3.0 is required.

Financial data: The stipend is $1,000.

Duration: 1 year.

Additional information: Information is also available from Janis Stanger, 1239 American Beauty Drive, Salt Lake City, UT 84116.

Number awarded: 2 each year.

Deadline: April of each year.

352
FREDDIE MAC SCHOLARSHIPS

National Urban League
Attn: Scholarship Coordinator
120 Wall Street
New York, NY 10005
Phone: (212) 558-5373   Fax: (212) 344-8948
E-mail: info@nul.org
Web Site: www.nul.org

Summary: To provide financial assistance for college to African American high school seniors from low- and moderate-income families.

Eligibility: The sponsor of this program is dedicated to revitalizing urban communities and increasing home ownership opportunities among low- and moderate-income families. Graduating high school seniors are eligible if they are African Americans who come from such communities and demonstrate potential for success in a competitive academic environment.

Financial data: The stipend is $5,000 per year.

Duration: 2 years: the first 2 years of college study.

Additional information: Funding for these scholarships is provided by the

Freddie Mac Foundation.
Number awarded: 15 each year.
Deadline: January of each year.

353
FREEDOM SCIENTIFIC TECHNOLOGY SCHOLARSHIP AWARD PROGRAM

Freedom Scientific Inc.
11800 31st Court North
St. Petersburg, FL 33716
Phone: (727) 803-8000   (800) 444-4443
Web Site: www.FreedomScientific.com
Summary: To provide financial assistance to blind students in the form of vouchers for the purchase of assistive technology devices.
Eligibility: This program is open to legally blind students who are either 1) graduating high school seniors planning to pursue a full-time course of study at a college or university, or 2) college seniors planning to enter graduate school. Applicants must be residents of the United States or Canada. The program is administered through 6 partner organizations: 4 for high school seniors in the United States, 1 for high school seniors in Canada, and 1 for graduate students in the United States and Canada. Selection is based on general guidelines of academic achievement and promise, extracurricular or community service leadership and accomplishments, and demonstrated personal qualities and character. The partner organizations may supplement those general guidelines with their own specific criteria and may also select especially deserving students across all levels of higher education. Students may apply to the partner organization of their choice or, if they have no preference, to the organization assigned for the geographic region in which they live.
Financial data: The awards consist of vouchers, for $2,500 or $1,500, to be used to purchase Freedom Scientific hardware, software, accessories, training, and/or tutorials.
Duration: These are 1-time awards.
Additional information: This program, which began for the 2001-02 school year, is sponsored by Freedom Scientific, maker of technology-based products for people who are blind or vision-impaired. The partner organizations include the National Federation of the Blind, 1800 Johnson Street, Baltimore, MD 21230, (410) 659-9314, Web site: www.nfb.org, which also serves as the regional organization for Connecticut, Delaware, Maine, Maryland, Massachusetts, New Hampshire, New Jersey, New York, Pennsylvania, Puerto Rico, Rhode Island, Vermont, Virginia, West Virginia, and the District of Columbia; the American Foundation for the Blind, Attn: Scholarship Committee, 11 Penn Plaza, Suite 300, New York, NY 10001, (212) 502-7661, (800) AFB-LINE, Fax: (212) 502-7771, TDD: (212) 502-7662, E-mail: afbinfo@afb.net, Web site: www.afb.org/scholarships.asp, which also serves as the regional organization for Alabama, Arkansas, Florida, Georgia, Louisiana, Mississippi, North Carolina, South Carolina, Tennessee, and Texas; the American Council of the Blind, 1155 15th Street, N.W., Suite 1004, Washington, DC 20005, (202) 467-5081, (800) 424-8666, Fax: (202) 467-5085, E-mail: info@acb.org, Web site: www.acb.org, which also serves as the regional organization for Illinois, Indiana, Iowa, Kansas, Kentucky, Michigan, Minnesota, Missouri, Nebraska, Ohio, Oklahoma, and Wisconsin; the Braille Institute of America, 741 North Vermont Avenue, Los Angeles, CA 90029-3594, (323) 663-1111, (800) BRAILLE, Fax: (323) 663-0867, E-mail: info@brailleinstitute.org, Web site: www.brailleinstitute.org, which also serves as the regional organization for Alaska, Arizona, California, Colorado, Hawaii, Idaho, Montana, Nevada, New Mexico, North Dakota, Oregon, South Dakota, Utah, Washington, and Wyoming; the Canadian National Institute for the Blind, 1929 Bayview Avenue, Toronto, Ontario M4G 3E8, (416) 486-2500, Web site: www.cnib.ca, which accepts all applications from high school seniors in Canada; and Recording for the Blind and Dyslexic 20 Roszel Road, Princeton, NJ 08540, (609) 452-0606, (800) 221-4792, Web site: www.rfbd.org, which accepts all applications for graduate study in the United States and Canada.
Number awarded: 50 each year: 40 high school seniors in the United States (20 at $2,500 and 20 at $1,500), 5 high school seniors in Canada (3 at $2,500 and 2 at $1,500), and 5 graduate students in the United States or Canada (3 at $2,500 and 2 at $1,500). A total of $101,000 is awarded each year.
Deadline: Each partner organization sets its own deadline, but most are by March of each year.

354
FRIENDS OF BILL RUTHERFORD SCHOLARSHIP

Oregon Student Assistance Commission
Attn: Private Awards Grant Department
1500 Valley River Drive, Suite 100
Eugene, OR 97401-2146
Phone: (541) 687-7395   (800) 452-8807, ext. 7395
Fax: (541) 687-7419   E-mail: awardinfo@mercury.osac.state.or.us
Web Site: www.osac.state.or.us
Summary: To provide financial assistance for college to children of elected state officials in Oregon.
Eligibility: This program is open to graduates of Oregon high schools attending or planning to attend college. Applicants must be dependent children of individuals holding statewide elected office (Governor, Secretary of State, Treasurer, Commissioner of Labor, Superintendent of Public Instruction, and Attorney General) or currently serving in the Oregon State Legislature.
Financial data: Scholarship amounts vary, depending upon the needs of the recipient.
Duration: 1 year.
Number awarded: Varies each year.
Deadline: February of each year.

355
GALLUP ORGANIZATION/CORNHUSKER STATE GAMES SCHOLARSHIP PROGRAM

Cornhuster State Games
Trabert Hall
2202 South 11th Street
P.O. Box 82411
Lincoln, NE 68501
Phone: (402) 471-2544   (800) 30-GAMES
Fax: (402) 471-9712   E-mail: csg@cornhuskerstategames.com
Web Site: www.cornhuskerstategames.com/scholar.htm
Summary: To provide financial assistance for college to athletes who participate in the Cornhusker State Games in Nebraska.
Eligibility: This program is open to athletes who participate in the winter or summer Cornhusker State Games. All residents of Nebraska are eligible to participate in the winter and summer games; residents of Harrison, Mills, and Pottawattamie counties in Iowa are also eligible to participate in the winter games. Athletes must reside in Nebraska or 1 of the 3 Iowa counties for at least 30 days prior to the competition and must have amateur status in the sport in which they compete. High school athletes must abide by the rules of the Nebraska School Activities Association or (for the winter games) the Iowa High School Athletic Association. College athletes must abide by national collegiate rules. Participants who are high school graduates (including members of the current graduating class) are eligible for these scholarships. Selection is based on academic honors (15 points), athletic achievements (15 points), other activities (10 points), and an essay of 200 words or less in which they outline their educational objectives (20 points), career goals (20 points), and what this scholarship means to them (20 points).
Financial data: The stipend is $1,000.
Duration: 1 year.
Additional information: The winter games are held at more than 40 locations in and around Omaha and Lincoln in February. The summer games are held in Lincoln in July. The scholarships are sponsored by The Gallup Organization. Recipients must attend a postsecondary educational institution in Nebraska.
Number awarded: 5 each year.
Deadline: June of each year.

356
GATES MILLENNIUM UNDERGRADUATE SCHOLARS PROGRAM

Bill and Melinda Gates Foundation
P.O. Box 10500
Fairfax, VA 22031-8044
Phone: (877) 690-GMSP
Web Site: www.gmsp.org
Summary: To provide financial assistance for college to outstanding low-income minority students.
Eligibility: This program is open to African Americans, Alaska Natives, American Indians, Hispanic Americans, and Asian Pacific Islander Americans who are graduating high school seniors with a grade point average of 3.3 or higher.

Principals, teachers, guidance counselors, tribal higher education representatives, and other professional educators are invited to nominate students with outstanding academic qualifications, especially those likely to succeed in the fields of mathematics, science, engineering, education, or library science. Nominees should have significant financial need and demonstrated leadership abilities through participation in community service, extracurricular, or other activities. U.S. citizenship or permanent resident status is required. Nominees must be planning to enter an accredited college or university as a full-time, degree-seeking freshman in the following fall.

Financial data: The program covers the cost of tuition, fees, books, and living expenses not paid for by grants and scholarships already committed as part of the recipient's financial aid package.

Duration: 4 years or the completion of the undergraduate degree, if the recipient maintains at least a 3.0 grade point average.

Additional information: This program, established in 1999, is funded by the Bill and Melinda Gates Foundation and administered by the United Negro College Fund with support from the American Indian Graduate Center, the Hispanic Scholarship Fund, and the Organization of Chinese Americans.

Number awarded: Under the Gates Millennium Scholars Program, a total of 4,000 students receive support each year.

Deadline: January of each year.

357
GATORADE SPORTSMANSHIP AWARD

American Legion
Attn: Americanism and Children & Youth Division
P.O. Box 1055
Indianapolis, IN 46206-1055
Phone: (317) 630-1249   Fax: (317) 630-1223
E-mail: acy@legion.org
Web Site: www.legion.org

Summary: To recognize and reward outstanding participants in the American Legion baseball program.

Eligibility: This program is open to participants in the American Legion baseball regional tournaments and the American Legion World Series. Candidates must be high school seniors or graduates who will be entering college as a freshman in the fall. Selection is based on leadership, scholarship, character, citizenship, and playing ability throughout the season.

Financial data: The outstanding participants in the regional tournaments receive $1,000 scholarships; the outstanding participant in the American Legion World Series receives a $2,000 scholarship.

Duration: The awards are presented annually.

Additional information: These awards, first presented in 1986, are funded by Stokely-Van Camp, the maker of Gatorade. The player selected at the World Series is also designated as the James F. Daniel, Jr. Memorial Sportsmanship Award winner.

Number awarded: 9 each year: 8 winners in regional tournaments and 1 winner at the American Legion World Series.

358
GEAR UP CONNECTICUT COLLEGE SCHOLARSHIP PROGRAM

Connecticut Department of Higher Education
Attn: Office of Student Financial Aid
61 Woodland Street
Hartford, CT 06105-2326
Phone: (860) 947-1853   Fax: (860) 947-1311
E-mail: gearup@ctdhe.org
Web Site: www.ctdhe.org

Summary: To provide financial assistance for college to high school seniors in Connecticut who participated in specified pre-college programs.

Eligibility: This program is open to residents of Connecticut under 22 years of age who are U.S. citizens, nationals, or permanent residents and planning to enter an accredited college or university as a freshman. Applicants must have participated in 1 of the following programs: 1) ConnCAP (a pre-college program administered by the Connecticut Department of Higher Education); 2) Upward Bound, Talent Search, or Educational Opportunity Center (the TRIO programs administered by the U.S. Department of Education); 3) ConnCAB (a transition to college program administered by the Connecticut Department of Higher Education); or 4) other pre-college programs affiliated with the Connecticut Department of Higher Education. They must receive a Pell grant from the U.S. Department of Education.

Financial data: Stipends range from $200 to $4,000. These scholarships are considered "last dollar" or gap-filling grants and are awarded to students only after they have been formally accepted into the college or university of their choice and have received a financial aid package.

Duration: 1 year; may be renewed if the recipient maintains full-time enrollment, Pell eligibility, and satisfactory academic progress.

Additional information: GEAR UP stands for Gaining Early Awareness and Readiness for Undergraduate Programs. Funding for this program is provided by the Connecticut Department of Higher Education and the U.S. Department of Education.

Number awarded: Varies each year.

Deadline: May of each year.

359
GENE AND SONAM HILL COMPUTERCRAFT CORPORATION SCHOLARSHIP

Chickasaw Foundation
P.O. Box 1726
Ada, OK 74821-1726
Phone: (580) 421-9030   Fax: (580) 421-9031
Web Site: www.cflink.org/scholars.htm

Summary: To provide financial assistance to members of the Chickasaw Nation who are majoring in fields of interest to ComputerCraft Corporation.

Eligibility: This program is open to Chickasaw students who are currently enrolled at an accredited institution of higher education in their freshman through senior year. The sponsor recruits computer engineers, graphic designers, biologists, conference managers, and international trade specialists. Preference may be given to those majors, but all fields of study are eligible. Applicants must have a grade point average of 2.5 or higher and must submit a 1-page essay on their long-term goals and plans for achieving them. Financial need is not considered in the selection process.

Financial data: The stipend is $1,500 per year.

Duration: 1 year.

Number awarded: 1 each year.

Deadline: May of each year.

360
GENE BAKER MEMORIAL SCHOLARSHIP

Aircraft Electronics Association
Attn: President
4217 South Hocker Drive
Independence, MO 64055-4723
Phone: (816) 373-6565   Fax: (816) 478-3100
E-mail: info@aea.net
Web Site: www.aea.net

Summary: To provide financial assistance for college to members of the Aircraft Electronics Association and their relatives.

Eligibility: This program is open to high school seniors, high school graduates, and currently-enrolled college students who are either members or the children, grandchildren, or other dependents of members of the Aircraft Electronics Association. The scholarship may be used for any field of study.

Financial data: The stipend is $1,500; funds must be used for tuition.

Duration: 1 year.

Additional information: This scholarship is named in memory of the first executive director of the Aircraft Electronics Association.

Number awarded: 1 each year.

Deadline: February of each year.

361
GENERAL CLIFTON B. CATES MEMORIAL SCHOLARSHIP

Fourth Marine Division Association
c/o Frank L. Pokrop
2854 South 44th Street
Milwaukee, WI 53219
Phone: (414) 543-3474

Summary: To provide financial assistance for postsecondary education to the surviving children of disabled or deceased Fourth Marine Division veterans.

Eligibility: Eligible to apply are sons and daughters of World War II Fourth Marine Division veterans who are 100 percent disabled (the disability need not be service connected) or deceased. Dependents of veterans who served in units attached to the Fourth Marine Division during World War II may also apply. The applicants must be able to document financial need.

Financial data: The stipend is $2,400 per year.
Duration: 1 year; may be renewed up to 3 additional years.
Number awarded: 1 or more each year, depending upon funds available.
Deadline: March of each year.

362
GENERAL JOHN PAUL RATAY FUND

The Retired Officers Association
Attn: Educational Assistance Program
201 North Washington Street
Alexandria, VA 22314-2539
Phone: (703) 838-8816   (800) 245-8762, ext. 816
Fax: (703) 838-5819   E-mail: edassist@troa.org
Web Site: www.troa.org/Education/ScholarshipFund.asp
Summary: To provide financial support for the undergraduate education of dependent children of auxiliary members of The Retired Officers Association (TROA).
Eligibility: This program is open to never married children under age 24 who are dependents of the widows of deceased retired military officers. Selection is based on scholastic ability (minimum grade point average of 3.0), potential, character, leadership, and financial need. Eligibility ends when the student graduates or is no longer enrolled in full-time study.
Financial data: The stipend is $3,000 per year.
Duration: 1 year; may be renewed for 4 additional years.
Additional information: Applicants for the TROA Educational Assistance Program loans are automatically considered for these scholarships; no separate application is necessary. Grants are in addition to the amount of the loan. No grants are made for graduate study.
Number awarded: Varies each year.
Deadline: February of each year.

363
GEOGRAPHICALLY-BASED SCHOLARSHIPS OF THE COLLEGE FUND/UNCF

College Fund/UNCF
Attn: Director, Educational Services
8260 Willow Oaks Corporate Drive
P.O. Box 10444
Fairfax, VA 22031-4511
Phone: (703) 205-3400
Web Site: www.uncf.org
Summary: To provide financial assistance to high school juniors or seniors from designated areas who are interested in attending a member institution of the United Negro College Fund (UNCF).
Eligibility: These programs are open to students from designated geographical areas. Applicants must be high school graduates with strong academic backgrounds (minimum grade point average of 2.5). Students who have completed their junior year in high school with a record of distinction may also be considered. Financial need must be demonstrated. Applications should be submitted directly to the UNCF-member institution the student plans to attend.
Financial data: The awards are intended to cover tuition and range from a minimum of $500 to a maximum of $7,500 per year.
Duration: 1 year; may be renewed.
Additional information: Among the scholarships that have been available are the Cleveland Foundation Scholarship Program for students from Cleveland; the Ahmanson Foundation Scholarship for students from the Los Angeles area; the John W. Anderson Foundation Scholarship for students from Indiana; the Columbus Foundation Scholarship for students from Columbus, Ohio; the Atkinson Foundation Scholarship for students from the San Mateo, California area; the Hewlett Packard Scholarship Program for students from California; the James M. Johnston Foundation Scholarship for students from Washington, D.C.; the Jay Levine Scholarship for students from Detroit; the Pacific Northwest Scholarship Program for students from Oregon and Washington; the Pennsylvania State Employees Scholarship Fund for students from Pennsylvania; the Richmond College Scholarship for students from Richmond, Virginia; and the Whirlpool Foundation Scholarship for students from northwest Indiana, Benton Harbor, Michigan, and Nashville, Tennessee. Recipients must attend a UNCF-member institution of higher learning. These are: Miles College, Oakwood College, Stillman College, Talladega College, and Tuskegee University in Alabama; Philander Smith College in Arkansas; Bethune-Cookman College, Edward Waters College, and Florida Memorial College in Florida; Clark Atlanta University,

Interdenominational Theological Center, Morehouse College, Morris Brown College, Paine College, and Spelman College in Georgia; Dillard University and Xavier University in Louisiana; Rust College and Tougaloo College in Mississippi; Barber-Scotia College, Bennett College, Johnson C. Smith University, Livingstone College, Saint Augustine's College, and Shaw University in North Carolina; Wilberforce University in Ohio; Benedict College, Claflin College, Morris College, and Voorhees College in South Carolina; Fisk University, Knoxville College, Lane College, and LeMoyne-Owens College in Tennessee; Huston-Tillotson College, Jarvis Christian College, Paul Quinn College, and Wiley College in Texas; and Saint Paul's College and Virginia Union University in Virginia.
Number awarded: A total of nearly 1,200 UNCF scholarships are awarded each year.
Deadline: Deadline dates vary, depending upon the individual institution's requirements.

364
GEORGE F. WHITE SCHOLARSHIP

New England Newspaper Advertising Executives Association
Attn: Scholarship Committee Chair
70 Washington Street, Suite 214
Salem, MA 01970
Phone: (978) 744-8940   Fax: (978) 744-0333
Web Site: www.nenews.org
Summary: To provide financial assistance to students who are interested in going to college (on the undergraduate or graduate school level) and are related to an employee (or are an employee) of a newspaper affiliated with the New England Newspaper Advertising Executives Association (NENAEA).
Eligibility: This program is open to any person who has an immediate family member (mother, father, aunt, uncle, brother, sister, grandmother, grandfather, spouse) currently employed at an NENAEA-member newspaper. Current employees may also apply. Applicants may be high school seniors, college students, or graduate students. There are no restrictions on the applicant's major. Financial need is not considered in the selection process.
Financial data: The stipend is $2,000.
Duration: 1 year.
Number awarded: 1 each year.
Deadline: May of each year.

365
GEORGE WATTERS MEMORIAL SCHOLARSHIP

Lincoln Community Foundation
215 Centennial Mall South, Suite 200
Lincoln, NE 68508
Phone: (402) 474-2345   Fax: (402) 476-8532
E-mail: lcf@lcf.org
Web Site: www.lcf.org
Summary: To provide financial assistance for college to high school seniors in Nebraska who have a connection to the Nebraska Petroleum Marketer and Convenience Store Association.
Eligibility: Eligible to apply for this aid are graduating high school seniors in Nebraska who are interested in attending a 2-year or 4-year college or university in the state. Applicants must be in the upper one third of their graduating class and either the child of an association member or the child of a full- or part-time employee of a member. They must be able to demonstrate academic achievement and leadership; financial need is not considered.
Financial data: A stipend is awarded (exact amount not specified).
Duration: 1 year.
Additional information: Information is also available from Nebraska Petroleum Marketers, Attn: Tim Keigher, 1320 Lincoln Mall, Lincoln, NE 68508.
Number awarded: 1 or more each year.
Deadline: The deadline is established by Nebraska Petroleum Marketers.

366
GEORGIA GOVERNOR'S SCHOLARSHIP

Georgia Student Finance Commission
Attn: Scholarships and Grants Division
2082 East Exchange Place, Suite 200
Tucker, GA 30084-5305
Phone: (770) 724-9030   (800) 776-6878
Fax: (770) 724-9031   E-mail: info@mail.gsfc.state.ga.us
Web Site: www.gsfc.org/grants/ggov.htm

Summary: To provide financial assistance for college to outstanding high school seniors in Georgia.

Eligibility: Eligible to apply are Georgia residents planning to attend accredited institutions of higher education in the state as full-time entering freshmen. They must be graduating from a Georgia high school as a Georgia Scholar, STAR Student, valedictorian, or salutatorian and be in compliance with the Georgia Drug-Free Postsecondary Education Act. U.S. citizenship or permanent resident status is required.

Financial data: Awards up to $1,575 per year are provided.

Duration: 1 year; may be renewed for up to 3 additional years if the recipient maintains a cumulative grade point average of 3.0 or higher.

Additional information: Information about the program is also available from local high school counselors.

Number awarded: Varies each year; recently, 3,063 of these scholarships were awarded.

367
GEORGIA LAW ENFORCEMENT PERSONNEL DEPENDENTS GRANT

Georgia Student Finance Commission
Attn: Scholarships and Grants Division
2082 East Exchange Place, Suite 200
Tucker, GA 30084-5305
Phone: (770) 724-9030   (800) 776-6878
Fax: (770) 724-9031   E-mail: info@mail.gsfc.state.ga.us
Web Site: www.gsfc.org/grants/glepd.htm

Summary: To provide financial assistance for postsecondary education to children of disabled or deceased Georgia law enforcement officers, fire fighters, and prison guards.

Eligibility: Eligible to apply are dependent children of law enforcement officers, fire fighters, and prison guards in Georgia who have been permanently disabled or killed in the line of duty. Applicants must be enrolled as full-time undergraduate students in a Georgia private or public college, university, or technical institution. U.S. citizenship or permanent resident status and compliance with the Georgia Drug-Free Postsecondary Education Act are required.

Financial data: The grant is $2,000 per academic year, not to exceed $8,000 during an entire program of study.

Duration: 1 year; may be renewed (if satisfactory progress is maintained) for up to 3 additional years.

Number awarded: Varies each year; recently, 34 of these grants were awarded.

Deadline: July of each year.

368
GEORGIA LEAP GRANT PROGRAM

Georgia Student Finance Commission
Attn: Scholarships and Grants Division
2082 East Exchange Place, Suite 200
Tucker, GA 30084-5305
Phone: (770) 724-9030   (800) 776-6878
Fax: (770) 724-9031   E-mail: info@mail.gsfc.state.ga.us
Web Site: www.gsfc.org/grants/leap/htm

Summary: To provide financial assistance for postsecondary education to residents of Georgia who demonstrate financial need.

Eligibility: This program is open to Georgia residents who are enrolled as regular undergraduate students in an eligible Georgia public or private college, university, or technical college. Applicants must be able to demonstrate substantial financial need and must be eligible for a federal Pell Grant. They must be at least a half-time student maintaining satisfactory academic progress. U.S. citizenship or permanent resident status and compliance with the Georgia Drug-Free Postsecondary Education Act are required.

Financial data: The maximum grant is $2,000 per academic year.

Duration: 1 year; may be renewed (if satisfactory progress is maintained) for up to 3 additional years.

Number awarded: Varies each year.

369
GEORGIA LEGION AUXILIARY PAST DEPARTMENT PRESIDENTS SCHOLARSHIP

American Legion Auxiliary
Attn: Department of Georgia
3035 Mt. Zion Road
Stockbridge, GA 30281-4101
Phone: (678) 289-8446

Summary: To provide financial assistance for postsecondary education to the children of Georgia veterans.

Eligibility: Eligible for these scholarships are residents of Georgia who are high school seniors and children of veterans. Applicants must be sponsored by a local unit of the American Legion Auxiliary in Georgia. Selection is based on a statement explaining why they want to further their education and their need for a scholarship.

Financial data: The stipend is $1,000.

Duration: 1 year.

Number awarded: 2 each year.

Deadline: May of each year.

370
GEORGIA PUBLIC SAFETY MEMORIAL GRANT

Georgia Student Finance Commission
Attn: Scholarships and Grants Division
2082 East Exchange Place, Suite 200
Tucker, GA 30084-5305
Phone: (770) 724-9030   (800) 776-6878
Fax: (770) 724-9031   E-mail: info@mail.gsfc.state.ga.us
Web Site: www.gsfc.org/grants/gps.htm

Summary: To provide financial assistance for postsecondary education to children of Georgia public safety officers who have been permanently disabled or killed in the line of duty.

Eligibility: This program is open to dependent children of Georgia law enforcement officers, fire fighters, EMT, correction officers, or prison guards who have been permanently disabled or killed in the line of duty. Applicants must be enrolled or accepted as full-time undergraduate students in a Georgia public college, university, or technical institution and be in compliance with the Georgia Drug-Free Postsecondary Education Act. U.S. citizenship or permanent resident status is required.

Financial data: The award covers the cost of attendance at a public postsecondary school in Georgia, minus any other aid received.

Duration: 1 year; may be renewed (if satisfactory progress is maintained) for up to 3 additional years.

Number awarded: Varies each year; recently, 35 of these grants were awarded.

Deadline: July of each year.

371
GEORGIA TUITION EQUALIZATION GRANTS

Georgia Student Finance Commission
Attn: Scholarships and Grants Division
2082 East Exchange Place, Suite 200
Tucker, GA 30084-5305
Phone: (770) 724-9030   (800) 776-6878
Fax: (770) 724-9031   E-mail: info@mail.gsfc.state.ga.us
Web Site: www.gsfc.org/grants/gteg.htm

Summary: To provide financial assistance to students who wish to attend a private college or university in Georgia.

Eligibility: This program is open to Georgia residents who are attending accredited private colleges or universities in Georgia. Also eligible are juniors and seniors who are attending a college or university located within 50 miles of their home within Georgia but in a state bordering Georgia (South Carolina, Tennessee, Alabama, or Florida). Applicants must be U.S. citizens or permanent residents and in compliance with the Georgia Drug-Free Postsecondary Education Act.

Financial data: The stipend is $1,050 per year.

Duration: 1 year; may be renewed.

Additional information: The eligible out-of-state schools include Clemson University, Florida A&M University, Florida State University, Troy State University at Dothan, University of Tennessee at Chattanooga, and Jacksonville State University (Alabama). Recipients must be full-time students.

Number awarded: Varies each year; recently, 30,474 grants were awarded.

372
GERALD AND PAUL D'AMOUR FOUNDERS' SCHOLARSHIPS FOR ACADEMIC EXCELLENCE

Big Y Foods, Inc.
Attn: Scholarship Committee
P.O. Box 7840
Springfield, MA 01102-7840
Phone: (413) 504-4062
Web Site: www.bigy.com

Summary: To provide financial assistance to outstanding undergraduate and graduate students in the Big Y Foods market area (Massachusetts and Connecticut).
Eligibility: This program is open to high school seniors, college students, and graduate students of any age who reside within western and central Massachusetts or the state of Connecticut. Big Y employees and their dependents are also eligible to apply. Applicants must submit a transcript, standardized test scores, 2 letters of recommendation, and a completed application form.
Financial data: The stipend is $1,000.
Duration: 1 year; nonrenewable.
Additional information: This program was established in 1981.
Number awarded: 80 each year.
Deadline: January of each year.

373
GERALD DRAKE MEMORIAL SCHOLARSHIP

National Federation of the Blind of California
Attn: Nancy Burns
1240 North Griffith Park Drive
Burbank, CA 91506
Phone: (818) 558-6524   Fax: (818) 842-1018
E-mail: webmaster@nfbcal.org
Web Site: www.nfbcal.org
Summary: To provide financial assistance for undergraduate or graduate education to blind students in California.
Eligibility: Legally blind full-time students in California may apply for a scholarship, but they must attend the convention of the National Federation of the Blind of California. Applicants must submit an essay in which they describe their educational goals, involvement in the blindness community, and eye condition. High school seniors and college freshmen must submit their high school transcripts; other college students must submit transcripts of all undergraduate and graduate work. Selection is based on academic merit.
Financial data: The stipend is $1,500.
Duration: 1 year.
Number awarded: 1 each year.
Deadline: May of each year.

374
GERTRUDE BOTTS SAUCIER SCHOLARSHIP

United Daughters of the Confederacy
Attn: Education Director
328 North Boulevard
Richmond, VA 23220-4057
Phone: (804) 355-1636   Fax: (804) 353-1396
E-mail: hqudc@aol.com
Web Site: www.hqudc.org
Summary: To provide financial assistance for postsecondary education to lineal descendants of Confederate veterans who are residents of Texas, Mississippi, or Louisiana.
Eligibility: Eligible to apply for these scholarships are lineal descendants of worthy Confederates or collateral descendants who are members of the Children of the Confederacy or the United Daughters of the Confederacy. Applicants must reside in Texas, Mississippi, or Louisiana and must submit a family financial report and certified proof of the Confederate record of 1 ancestor, with the company and regiment in which he served. They must have at least a 3.0 grade point average in high school.
Financial data: The amount of the scholarship depends on the availability of funds.
Duration: 1 year; may be renewed for up to 3 additional years.
Additional information: Information is also available from Dorothy S. Broom, Second Vice President General, 595 Lominack Road, Prosperity, SC 29127, (803) 364-3003. Members of the same family may not hold scholarships simultaneously, and only 1 application per family will be accepted within any 1 year. Requests for applications must be accompanied by a self-addressed stamped envelope.
Number awarded: 1 each year.
Deadline: February of each year.

375
GIBRAN KAHLIL GIBRAN EDUCATIONAL FUND SCHOLARSHIPS

Gibran Kahlil Gibran Educational Fund, Inc.
Four Longfellow Place, Suite 3801
Boston, MA 02114
Phone: (617) 523-4455
Summary: To provide financial assistance for college to students of Syrian or Lebanese descent.
Eligibility: This program is open to high school seniors and college students who are of Syrian or Lebanese descent. Selection is based on work experience, extracurricular activities, and financial need.
Financial data: A stipend is awarded (exact amount not specified). Funds must be used for tuition and other college expenses.
Duration: 1 year.
Additional information: This program was established by Mary K. Gibran, in honor of her late brother, Kahlil Gibran, an artist, poet, and author of *The Prophet.*
Deadline: May of each year.

376
GILBERT GRANT PROGRAM

Massachusetts Office of Student Financial Assistance
454 Broadway, Suite 200
Revere, MA 02151
Phone: (617) 727-9420   Fax: (617) 727-0667
E-mail: osfa@osfa.mass.edu
Web Site: www.osfa.mass.edu/osfaprograms/gilbertgrant.asp
Summary: To provide financial assistance for the postsecondary education of Massachusetts residents who are attending accredited independent institutions.
Eligibility: Applicants for these scholarships must have been permanent legal residents of Massachusetts for at least 1 year and attending independent, regionally accredited colleges or universities in Massachusetts. U.S. citizenship or permanent resident status is required. Selection is based on financial need.
Financial data: Awards range from $200 to $2,500 per year, depending on the need of the recipient.
Duration: 1 year; may be renewed.
Number awarded: Varies each year.
Deadline: Deadlines are established by the school the student attends.

377
GIRL SCOUT ACHIEVEMENT AWARD

American Legion Auxiliary
777 North Meridian Street, Third Floor
Indianapolis, IN 46204
Phone: (317) 635-6291   Fax: (317) 636-5590
E-mail: alahq@legion-aux.org
Web Site: www.legion-aux.org/scholarship.htm
Summary: To provide financial assistance for college to members of the Girl Scouts.
Eligibility: Candidates must belong to the Girl Scouts; have received the Gold Award; be an active member of a religious institution (and have received the appropriate religious emblem); have demonstrated practical citizenship in religious institution, school, Scouting, and community; be in at least the ninth grade; and submit at least 4 letters of recommendation, with 1 letter required from each of the following group leaders: religious institution, school, community, and Scouting. Candidates must be nominated at the local level; those selected at the state level compete at the national level.
Financial data: The stipend is $1,000.
Duration: 1 year; the award must be utilized within 1 year of high school graduation.
Additional information: The scholarship may be used to attend any accredited school in the United States.
Number awarded: 1 each year.
Deadline: Local nominations must be submitted no later than February of each year.

378
GIRLS INCORPORATED SCHOLARS PROGRAM

Girls Incorporated
Attn: Scholarships and Awards
120 Wall Street, Third Floor
New York, NY 10005-3902
Phone: (212) 509-2000   Fax: (212) 509-8708
E-mail: girlsincorporated@girls-inc.org
Web Site: www.girls-inc.org
Summary: To provide financial assistance for the postsecondary education of Girls Incorporated members.
Eligibility: This program is open to members of Girls Incorporated affiliates who are currently in high school (in grades 10 through 12) and have been members of the association for at least 2 years. They must have at least a 2.0 grade point average. Selection is based on extracurricular activities, goals and objectives, soundness of ideas, motivation, communication skills, and presentation. Financial need is not considered. Academic record is of secondary importance.
Financial data: The scholarships are either $1,000 or $10,000. Funds are held in escrow and paid directly to the recipient's college, professional school, or technical institute.
Duration: Up to 5 years.
Additional information: This program was established in 1992 and replaces the Reader's Digest Career Key Awards. Funds may not be used for education at a vocational or technical school.
Number awarded: 10 $1,000 scholarships and 7 to 10 $10,000 scholarships are awarded each year.

379
GLADYS A. AND RUSSELL M. BIRTWISTLE AWARD

Vasa Order of America
Attn: Vice Grand Master
1926 Rancho Andrew
Alpine, CA 91901
Phone: (619) 445-9707   Fax: (619) 445-7334
E-mail: drulf@connectnet.com
Web Site: www.vasaorder.com
Summary: To provide financial assistance for postsecondary education to members of the Vasa Order of America from designated states.
Eligibility: Applicants must have been members of the organization for at least 1 year and live in districts 1 (Connecticut), 2 (Massachusetts), or 3 (Rhode Island). They must be high school seniors or college undergraduates who plan to continue their education on a full-time basis at an accredited institution. Selection is based on a grade transcript, letters of recommendation from school and local Vasa lodge officials, and an essay of up to 1,000 words on a topic related to Vasa.
Financial data: The stipend is $2,000.
Duration: 1 year.
Additional information: Vasa Order of America is a Swedish American fraternal organization incorporated in 1899.
Number awarded: 1 each year.
Deadline: February of each year.

380
GLAMOUR'S TOP TEN COLLEGE WOMEN COMPETITION

Glamour
140 East 45th Street
New York, NY 10017
Phone: (212) 880-8141   (800) 244-GLAM
Fax: (212) 880-6922   E-mail: TTCW@glamour.com
Web Site: www.glamour.com
Summary: To recognize and reward outstanding college women.
Eligibility: Any woman who is a junior and enrolled full time in courses leading to an undergraduate degree at an accredited college or university is eligible to enter this competition. Her application must be approved and signed by the appropriate members of her school's faculty and administration (i.e., her faculty advisor, the director of public relations, the director of student activities, or the dean of students). There is no limit on the number of applicants from any 1 school. Each applicant must write an essay (of 500 to 700 words) describing the most meaningful and stimulating achievements in her field of studies and relating those experiences to what she hopes to achieve in her life goals. Winners are selected from the following categories: creative arts/communications/humanities; science and technology/health; politics/international relations; business and

economics/entrepreneurship; and public service/education.
Financial data: Each winner receives national recognition for herself and her college, a $1,000 cash prize, and a trip to New York City. Along with a photograph, a synopsis of the winner's accomplishments is featured in the October issue of *Glamour* magazine.
Duration: The competition is held annually.
Additional information: The first competition was held in 1990.
Number awarded: 10 each year.
Deadline: January of each year.

381
GOLUB FOUNDATION FOUNDERS' SCHOLARSHIPS

Golub Foundation
Attn: Price Chopper Scholarship Office
501 Duanesburg Road
P.O. Box 1074
Schenectady, NY 12301
Phone: (518) 355-5000   (800) 877-0870
Summary: To provide financial assistance for college to high school seniors living in Massachusetts, Connecticut, Pennsylvania, New Hampshire, Vermont, and New York.
Eligibility: To qualify, high school seniors must live in the Price Chopper marketing areas; these include 1) Massachusetts (Berkshire, Hampden, Hampshire, Middlesex, Worcester); 2) Connecticut (Litchfield, Windham); 3) Pennsylvania (Lackawana, Luzerne, Susquehana, Wayne, Wyoming); 4) New Hampshire (Grafton, Sullivan); 5) Vermont (Bennington, Caledonia, Chittenden, Franklin, Lamoille, Orange, Orleans, Rutland, Washington, Windham, Windsor), and 6) New York (Albany, Broome, Chenango, Clinton, Columbia, Cortland, Delaware, Dutchess, Essex, Franklin, Fulton, Greene, Hamilton, Herkimer, Jefferson, Lewis, Madison, Montgomery, Oneida, Onondaga, Orange, Oswego, Otsego, Rensselaer, St. Lawrence, Saratoga, Schenectady, Schoharie, Tioga, Ulster, Warren, Washington). Applicants must plan to attend school in 1 of those 6 states, be able to demonstrate outstanding leadership and scholastic abilities, and write an essay that describes their leadership skills as they relate either to school or outside activities. Finalists must attend a personal interview.
Financial data: The stipend is $2,000 per year.
Duration: 4 years.
Number awarded: 2 each year.
Deadline: March of each year.

382
GOLUB FOUNDATION TWO YEAR SCHOLARSHIPS

Golub Foundation
Attn: Price Chopper Scholarship Office
501 Duanesburg Road
P.O. Box 1074
Schenectady, NY 12301
Phone: (518) 355-5000   (800) 877-0870
Summary: To provide financial assistance to high school seniors living in Massachusetts, Connecticut, Pennsylvania, New Hampshire, Vermont, and New York who want to attend a community or junior college in those states.
Eligibility: To qualify, high school seniors must live in the Price Chopper marketing areas; these include 1) Massachusetts (Berkshire, Hampden, Hampshire, Middlesex, Worcester); 2) Connecticut (Litchfield, Windham); 3) Pennsylvania (Lackawana, Luzerne, Susquehana, Wayne, Wyoming); 4) New Hampshire (Grafton, Sullivan); 5) Vermont (Bennington, Caledonia, Chittenden, Franklin, Lamoille, Orange, Orleans, Rutland, Washington, Windham, Windsor), and 6) New York (Albany, Broome, Chenango, Clinton, Columbia, Cortland, Delaware, Dutchess, Essex, Franklin, Fulton, Greene, Hamilton, Herkimer, Jefferson, Lewis, Madison, Montgomery, Oneida, Onondaga, Orange, Oswego, Otsego, Rensselaer, St. Lawrence, Saratoga, Schenectady, Schoharie, Tioga, Ulster, Warren, Washington). Applicants must plan to attend a community or junior college school in 1 of those 6 states, be able to demonstrate outstanding leadership and entrepreneurial ability or a commitment to humanity, and have an excellent scholastic record. They must write an essay on how their future occupation or profession will aid the community in which they live. Finalists must attend a personal interview.
Financial data: The stipend is $1,000 per year.
Duration: 2 years.
Number awarded: 1 each year.
Deadline: March of each year.

383
GONGORO NAKAMURA MEMORIAL SCHOLARSHIP

Japanese American Citizens League
Attn: National Scholarship Awards
1765 Sutter Street
San Francisco, CA 94115
Phone: (415) 921-5225   Fax: (415) 931-4671
E-mail: jacl@jacl.org
Web Site: www.jacl.org
Summary: To provide financial assistance to student members of the Japanese American Citizens League (JACL) who are high school seniors interested in pursuing undergraduate education.
Eligibility: This program is open to JACL members who are high school seniors interested in attending a college, university, trade school, business college, or other institution of higher learning. Preference is given to students with an interest in public speaking or debate. Selection is based on academic record, extracurricular activities, and community involvement.
Financial data: The stipend depends on the availability of funds but usually ranges from $1,000 to $5,000.
Duration: 1 year.
Additional information: Requests for applications must be accompanied by a self-addressed stamped envelope.
Number awarded: At least 1 each year.
Deadline: March of each year.

384
GOUGH FAMILY SCHOLARSHIP

Gough Scholarship Fund
Attn: J. David Gough, Fund Administrator
CMR 443
Box 655
APO AE 09096
Phone: 49 61 22 935424   E-mail: goughd@wiesbaden.vistec.net
Summary: To provide financial assistance to undergraduate and graduate students.
Eligibility: This program is open to students who are pursuing or planning to pursue an undergraduate, technical, or graduate degree. Selection is based on an essay, up to 3 pages in length, on why they deserve the scholarship and how they intend to use their education.
Financial data: The stipend is $1,000 per year.
Duration: 1 year; may be renewed.
Number awarded: 2 to 4 each year.
Deadline: March, June, September, or December of each year.

385
GOVERNOR GASTON CAPERTON SCHOLARSHIP

Greater Kanawha Valley Foundation
Attn: Scholarship Coordinator
One Huntington Square, 16th Floor
900 Lee Street, East
P.O. Box 3041
Charleston, WV 25331-3041
Phone: (304) 346-3620   Fax: (304) 346-3640
E-mail: tgkvf@tgkvf.com
Web Site: www.tgkvf.com/scholarship.html
Summary: To provide financial assistance for college to high school seniors in West Virginia.
Eligibility: This program is open to seniors at high schools in West Virginia who are interested in attending a college or university in the state. Applicants must have a cumulative grade point average of 3.0 or higher and an ACT score of 25 or higher and/or an SAT score of 1100 or higher. Financial need is considered in the selection process.
Financial data: Awards cover the cost of tuition, books, fees, room, and board, up to the cost of attending West Virginia University; the average is $10,000 per year. If recipients attend a college or university in the state where costs exceed those at West Virginia University, they are responsible for the additional cost.
Duration: 4 years.
Additional information: Recipients must enroll in a 4-year degree program on a full-time basis.
Number awarded: 1 each year.
Deadline: February of each year.

386
GOVERNOR JAMES G. MARTIN COLLEGE SCHOLARSHIPS

North Carolina State Education Assistance Authority
Attn: Scholarship and Grant Services
P.O. Box 14103
Research Triangle Park, NC 27709-4103
Phone: (919) 549-8614   Fax: (919) 549-8481
Web Site: www.ncseaa.edu
Summary: To provide financial assistance to entering freshmen at colleges and universities in North Carolina.
Eligibility: Each of the 51 participating 4-year institutions in North Carolina may nominate 1 entering freshman who is a North Carolina resident and U.S. citizen. Selection is based on exceptional academic merit, diverse extracurricular activities with particular emphasis on community service, and evidence of strong leadership.
Financial data: The stipend is $1,000 per year.
Duration: 1 year; may be renewed for up to 4 additional years as long as the recipient remains enrolled full time with a grade point average of at least 2.0.
Additional information: This program was established in 1993 by the Public Service Company of North Carolina, Inc. to honor former Governor James G. Martin for his service to the state of North Carolina.
Number awarded: 5 each year.
Deadline: April of each year.

387
GRAND LODGE OF IOWA MASONIC SCHOLARSHIP

Grand Lodge of Iowa, A.F. & A.M.
Attn: Scholarship Selection Committee
P.O. Box 279
Cedar Rapids, IA 52406-0279
Phone: (319) 365-1438   Fax: (319) 365-1439
E-mail: WRC@netins.net
Summary: To provide financial assistance for college to high school seniors in Iowa.
Eligibility: This program is open to high school seniors who are graduating from a public high school within the state of Iowa. Applicants need not have a Masonic connection. Finalists are interviewed. Selection is based on service to school and community (with special emphasis on leadership roles in those areas), academic record, communication skills, and financial need.
Financial data: The amount awarded varies; recently, the stipend was $1,900. Funds may be used for tuition, fees, and books.
Duration: 1 year.
Additional information: Recipients may study at a postsecondary institution in any state. Applicants must fill out an original application form, not a copy of the form.
Number awarded: Varies each year; recently, 75 were awarded.
Deadline: January of each year.

388
GRAND ROYAL ARCH CHAPTER OF MAINE SCHOLARSHIP

Maine Education Services
Attn: MES Foundation
One City Center, 11th Floor
Portland, ME 04101
Phone: (800) 922-6352   E-mail: info@mesfoundation.com
Web Site: www.mesfoundation.com/sch_applications/default.asp
Summary: To provide financial assistance for college to graduating high school seniors in Maine.
Eligibility: This program is open to seniors in Maine who are nominated by their high school; each high school in Maine may nominate 1 student. Selection is based on academic excellence, community contributions, the high school's recommendation, a commitment to remain chemical-free, and financial need.
Financial data: Stipends range from $500 to $1,500 per year; funds are paid jointly to the students and their college.
Duration: 4 years.
Number awarded: 5 each year: 1 at $1,500, 1 at $1,250, 1 at $1,000, 1 at $750, and 1 at $500.
Deadline: March of each year.

389
GRANGE INSURANCE ASSOCIATION SCHOLARSHIPS

Grange Insurance Association
Attn: Scholarship Committee
200 Cedar Street
Seattle, WA 98121
Phone: (206) 448-4911   (800) 2-GRANGE
Web Site: www.grange.com/scholarship.htm
Summary: To provide financial assistance for postsecondary education to members or children of members of the Grange in selected western states.
Eligibility: Applicants may be either high school seniors or currently-enrolled students in an academic or vocational program who are Grange members or children of Grange members in the 7 states where the Grange Insurance Association operates (California, Colorado, Idaho, Montana, Oregon, Washington, or Wyoming). Selection is based on scholastic ability, extracurricular activities, character references, aptitudes and attitudes expressed in a letter of application, and financial need.
Financial data: Scholarships are $1,000 or $750.
Duration: 1 year.
Additional information: This program includes the Paul and Ethel Holter Scholarship of $1,000.
Number awarded: Varies each year. Recently, 28 of these scholarships were awarded: 2 at $1,000 and 26 at $750. Students wishing to pursue vocational studies received 3 of the awards (1 at $1,000 and 2 at $750) and students in academic programs received 25 (1 at $1,000 and 24 at $750).
Deadline: March of each year.

390
GREAT LAKES HEMOPHILIA FOUNDATION EDUCATION AND TRAINING ASSISTANCE SCHOLARSHIPS

Great Lakes Hemophilia Foundation
638 North 18th Street, Suite 108
P.O. Box 704
Milwaukee, WI 53201-0704
Phone: (414) 257-0200   Fax: (414) 257-1225
Phone: (888) 797-GLHF   E-mail: info@glhf.org
Web Site: www.glhf.org/scholar.htm
Summary: To provide financial assistance for postsecondary education to Wisconsin residents with a bleeding disorder and their families.
Eligibility: This program is open to residents of Wisconsin who have a bleeding disorder and their parents, spouses, children, and siblings. Applicants must be attending or planning to attend college, vocational school, technical school, or certification program.
Financial data: Stipends up to $2,000 are available.
Duration: 1 year.
Number awarded: Several each year.
Deadline: April of each year.

391
GUISTWHITE SCHOLAR PROGRAM

Phi Theta Kappa
Attn: Scholarship Department
1625 Eastover Drive
P.O. Box 13729
Jackson, MS 39236-3729
Phone: (601) 957-2241, ext. 560   (800) 946-9995, ext. 560
Fax: (601) 957-2312   E-mail: scholarship.programs@ptk.org
Web Site: www.ptk.org
Summary: To provide financial assistance for college to members of Phi Theta Kappa, the international honor society for 2-year colleges.
Eligibility: This program is open to members of the society. Applicants must be completing an associate's degree at a community, technical, or junior college in the United States or Canada, be planning to transfer to an accredited senior institution, and have a cumulative grade point average of at least 3.5. Selection is based on academic achievement, participation in Phi Theta Kappa programs, and service to their colleges and communities.
Financial data: The stipend is $5,000 per year.
Duration: 1 year.
Number awarded: 10 each year.
Deadline: May of each year.

392
GUY DAVIS SCHOLARSHIPS

Oregon School Employees Association
Attn: Scholarship Committee
4735 Liberty Road South
P.O. Box 4027
Salem, OR 97302-1027
Phone: (503) 588-0121   (800) 252-6732
Web Site: www.osea.org
Summary: To provide financial assistance for college to relatives of members of the Oregon School Employees Association (OSEA).
Eligibility: Applicants must meet the following requirements: at least 1 parent, grandparent, sibling, aunt, uncle, or legal guardian must be a member in good standing of OSEA; must be a graduating high school senior; must have at least a 3.0 cumulative grade point average (an official transcript must be submitted); and must submit a double-spaced essay (between 400 and 700 words) on a topic that changes annually but relates to the role of the union in the applicant's family. Financial need is not considered in the selection process.
Financial data: The stipend is $1,250.
Duration: 1 year.
Additional information: This program began in 1978. Scholarship funds must be used by the fall of the following year.
Number awarded: 7 each year: 1 in each OSEA zone.
Deadline: February of each year.

393
HACE NATIONAL SCHOLARSHIP PROGRAM

Hispanic Alliance for Career Enhancement
Attn: Student Development Program
14 East Jackson Avenue, Suite 1310
Chicago, IL 60604
Phone: (312) 435-0498, ext. 21   Fax: (312) 435-1494
E-mail: haceorg@enteract.com
Web Site: www.hace-usa.org/programs/scholar.htm
Summary: To provide financial assistance to Hispanic students working on an undergraduate or graduate degree.
Eligibility: Applicants may be undergraduate or graduate students who are enrolled full time (undergraduates: 12+ credits; graduate students, 6+ credits) in an institution of higher education in the United States. They must be working on a bachelor's degree or higher. Undergraduates must have completed at least 12 credit hours of college course work before applying. All applicants must have at least a 2.5 grade point average. Selection is based on academic achievement, letters of recommendation, community involvement, leadership skills, and financial need.
Financial data: A stipend is awarded (exact amount not specified).
Duration: 1 year; nonrenewable.
Number awarded: Several each year.
Deadline: August of each year.

394
HAE WON PARK MEMORIAL SCHOLARSHIP

W.O.R.K.: Women's Organization Reaching Koreans
P.O. Box 125
Verdugo City, CA 91046
Phone: (213) 239-0784   E-mail: kaylorenpark@pol.net
Web Site: www.work-la.org
Summary: To provide financial assistance to undergraduate women of Korean heritage.
Eligibility: This program is open to women of Korean heritage who are enrolled at an undergraduate institution and have demonstrated a desire and commitment to serve their community. To apply, they must submit 2 letters of recommendation, attach a copy of their transcript, fill out a short application, and write short essays on the following: 1) community organization participation, 2) personal background, and 3) an issue that would be important to the sponsoring organization. Financial need is not considered in the selection process.
Financial data: The stipend is $1,000.
Duration: 1 year.
Additional information: This scholarship was established in 1992.
Number awarded: 1 each year.
Deadline: May of each year.

395
HAL CONNOLLY SCHOLAR-ATHLETE AWARD

California Governor's Committee for Employment of Disabled Persons
Employment Development Department
Attn: Scholar-Athlete Awards Program
800 Capitol Mall, MIC 41
Sacramento, CA 95814
Phone: (916) 654-8055   (800) 695-0350
Fax: (916) 654-9821   TTY: (916) 654-9820
E-mail: gcedp@edd.ca.gov
Web Site: www.gcedp.org
Summary: To provide supplemental financial assistance to potential college freshmen in California who have participated in athletics although disabled.
Eligibility: Applicants must be high school seniors with disabilities, no more than 19 years of age on January 1 of the year of application, who have competed in California high school athletics at a varsity or equivalent level and possess academic and athletic records that demonstrate qualities of leadership and accomplishment. They must have completed high school with a grade point average of 2.8 or better and plan to attend an accredited college or university in California, but they do not have to intend to participate formally in collegiate athletic activities. Selection is based on cumulative grade point average (15 percent), cumulative grade point average as it relates to the nature of the student's disability (15 percent), athletic accomplishments as they relate to the student's disability (30 percent), an essay on "How Sports Participation Has Affected My Life at School and in the Community As a Person with a Disability" (25 percent), and overall personal achievement (15 percent). The top finalists may be interviewed before selections are made. Male and female students compete separately.
Financial data: The awards are $1,000, contingent upon the winners' acceptance at an accredited California college or university. Funds may be used for tuition, books, supplies, and other educational expenses. Exceptions are granted to students who choose to attend schools out of state primarily to accommodate their disability.
Duration: Awards are granted annually.
Number awarded: Up to 6 each year: 3 to male students and 3 to female students.
Deadline: January of each year.

396
HAROLD GREEN SCHOLARSHIP

Texas Tennis Foundation
2111 Dickson, Suite 33
Austin, TX 78704-4788
Phone: (512) 443-1334   Fax: (512) 443-4748
Web Site: www.ustatexas.org
Summary: To provide financial assistance for college to students in Texas who have an interest in tennis.
Eligibility: This program is open to students who have an interest in tennis, are U.S. citizens, and live in Texas. They must be high school students who will be entering college or college students who are in good standing at their respective colleges or universities. Financial need must be demonstrated. Qualified students must submit a completed application, federal income tax returns from the previous 2 years, an academic transcript, a copy of their SAT or ACT test results, a list of extracurricular activities (including tennis activities), a personal statement, and a letter of recommendation. Selection is based on merit and financial need.
Financial data: The stipend is $1,000.
Duration: 1 year.
Additional information: This program was established in 1981. Recipients must attend school on a full-time basis. They must send a brief written report following their first semester of the scholarship year; this report should indicate their educational achievements during the semester, tennis activities if any, and goals for the second semester.
Number awarded: 2 each year.
Deadline: April of each year.

397
HAROLD HAYDEN MEMORIAL SCHOLARSHIP

National Association of Black County Officials
440 First Street, Suite 410
Washington, DC 20001
Summary: To provide financial assistance for college to high school and currently-enrolled college students nominated by members of the National Association of Black County Officials (NABCO).

Eligibility: This program is open to high school seniors and currently-enrolled college students. To apply, students must submit a completed application form, an endorsement from a NABCO member, and a brief (up to 3 pages) autobiographical essay. Selection is based on academic record, leadership record, character and personality, personal achievement, interest in government and politics, and commitment to human and civil rights. Financial need is also considered in the selection process.
Financial data: A stipend is awarded (exact amount not specified).
Duration: 1 year.
Additional information: This fund was established in 1984 to honor a co-founder of the NABCO.
Number awarded: Several each year.
Deadline: March of each year.

398
HARTFORD WHALERS BOOSTER CLUB SCHOLARSHIPS

Hartford Foundation for Public Giving
85 Gillett Street
Hartford, CT 06105
Phone: (860) 548-1888   Fax: (860) 524-8346
Web Site: www.hfpg.org
Summary: To provide financial assistance to high school seniors from Connecticut who are interested in playing hockey in college.
Eligibility: This program is open to Connecticut residents who are graduating high school seniors. Applicants must be interested in attending a 4-year college or university with a hockey program. Selection is based on academic achievement and hockey ability.
Financial data: A stipend up to $1,000 per year is provided.
Duration: 1 year.
Additional information: Funding for this program is provided by the Hartford Whalers Booster Club, Attn: Scholarship Committee, P.O. Box 273, Hartford, CT 06141.
Number awarded: 1 each year.
Deadline: March of each year.

399
HAWAII EDUCATION ASSOCIATION HIGH SCHOOL STUDENT SCHOLARSHIP

Hawaii Education Association
Attn: Scholarship Committee
1649 Kalakaua Avenue
Honolulu, HI 96826
Phone: (808) 949-6657   Fax: (808) 944-2032
Summary: To provide financial assistance for college to high school seniors whose parents belong to the Hawaii Education Association (HEA).
Eligibility: This program is open to the children of HEA members. Applicants must be graduating high school seniors and interested in attending a 2-year or 4-year accredited institution of higher learning. As part of the application process, students must submit a completed application form, an official high school transcript, a personal statement, a statement of financial need, and recommendations from at least 3 teachers. Selection is based on ability, the personal statement, financial need, and the teacher recommendations.
Financial data: The stipend is $1,000.
Duration: 1 year.
Number awarded: 5 each year.
Deadline: March of each year.

400
HAWAII EDUCATION ASSOCIATION UNDERGRADUATE COLLEGE STUDENT SCHOLARSHIP

Hawaii Education Association
Attn: Scholarship Committee
1649 Kalakaua Avenue
Honolulu, HI 96826
Phone: (808) 949-6657   Fax: (808) 944-2032
Summary: To provide financial assistance to currently-enrolled college students whose parents belong to the Hawaii Education Association (HEA).
Eligibility: This program is open to the children of HEA members. Applicants must be currently-enrolled in a 2-year or 4-year accredited institution of higher learning. As part of the application process, students must submit a completed application form, an official college transcript, a personal statement, a statement

of financial need, and a recommendation from a college faculty member. Selection is based on ability, the personal statement, financial need, and the faculty recommendation.

Financial data: The stipend is $1,000.

Duration: 1 year.

Number awarded: 4 each year.

Deadline: March of each year.

401
HAWAII ROTARY YOUTH FOUNDATION SCHOLARSHIPS

Hawaii Rotary Youth Foundation
3536 Harding Avenue, Room 600
Honolulu, HI 96816
Phone: (808) 735-1073 Fax: (808) 735-1073

Summary: To provide financial assistance for postsecondary education to high school students in Hawaii.

Eligibility: Eligible are students graduating from a public or private high school in Hawaii. U.S. citizenship is required; Rotarians or their spouses, children, grandchildren, stepchildren, brothers, or sisters are ineligible. Selection is based on academic achievements, intent to major in programs beneficial to Hawaii, financial need, personal involvement in campus and community activities, and employment experience.

Financial data: For students attending a mainland 4-year college or university, the scholarship covers tuition, fees, and books to a maximum of $3,500; for students attending a college or university in Hawaii not on their island of residency, the scholarship is $1,500; for students whose residences are on the same island as the college or university they will attend, the award is $1,000.

Duration: 1 year; may not be renewed.

Additional information: This foundation was incorporated in 1976 by Maurice J. Sullivan, who guided it until his death in 1998.

Number awarded: Varies each year; recently, 50 scholarships were awarded.

Deadline: February of each year.

402
HAWAII UNION BUILDERS FOUNDATION SCHOLARSHIPS

Hawaii Union Builders Foundation
1109 Bethel Street, Lower Level
Honolulu, HI 96813
Phone: (808) 538-1505
Web Site: www.hilocal675.com/plumbershawaii/CommSvc.htm

Summary: To provide financial assistance for college to high school seniors in Hawaii.

Eligibility: This program is open to graduating high school seniors who have lived in Hawaii for at least 5 years. Applicants must be planning to attend a 2-year or 4-year college or university. Selection is based on participation in athletics, financial need, community involvement, special awards and honors, and other evidence of personal motivation and eagerness to learn. Special consideration is given to children of union members.

Financial data: The stipend is $1,000.

Duration: 1 year.

Additional information: This program was established in 1991 when 17 member unions of the Hawaii Building and Construction Trades Council (BTC) formed the BTC Educational and Charitable Foundation. In 2000, that organization adopted its current name.

Number awarded: 10 each year.

Deadline: March of each year.

403
HAWAIIAN CIVIC CLUB OF HONOLULU SCHOLARSHIP

Hawaiian Civic Club of Honolulu
Attn: Scholarship Committee
P.O. Box 1513
Honolulu, HI 96806
E-mail: newmail@hotbot.com
Web Site: hcchscholarship.tripod.com/scholarship/index.html

Summary: To provide financial assistance for undergraduate or graduate studies to persons of Hawaiian descent.

Eligibility: Applicants must be of Hawaiian descent (descendants of the aboriginal inhabitants of the Hawaiian Islands prior to 1778), residents of Hawaii, able to demonstrate academic achievement, and enrolled or planning to enroll full time in an accredited 2-year college, 4-year college, or graduate school.

Graduating seniors and current undergraduate students must have a grade point average of 2.5 or higher; graduate students must have at least a 3.0 grade point average. As part of the selection process, applicants must submit a 3-page essay on a topic that changes annually but relates to issues of concern to the Hawaiian community; a recent topic related to the availability of "Native Hawaiian" as a choice of ethnicity in the Year 2000 Census.

Financial data: The amount of the stipend depends on the availability of funds. Scholarship checks are made payable to the recipient and the institution and are mailed to the college or university financial aid office. Funds may be used for tuition, fees, books, and other educational expenses.

Duration: 1 year.

Additional information: Recipients may attend school in Hawaii or on the mainland. Information on this program is also available from Ke Ali'i Pauahi Foundation, Attn: Financial Aid and Scholarship Services, 1887 Makuakane Street, Honolulu, HI 96817-1887, (808) 842-8216, Fax: (808) 841-0660, E-mail: finaid@ksbe.edu, Web site: www.pauahi.org.

Number awarded: Varies each year; recently, 47 of these scholarships were awarded.

Deadline: April of each year.

404
HAWAIIAN HOMES COMMISSION SCHOLARSHIPS

Ke Ali'i Pauahi Foundation
Attn: Financial Aid & Scholarship Services
1887 Makuakane Street
Honolulu, HI 96817-1887
Phone: (808) 842-8216 (800) 842-4682, ext. 8216
Fax: (808) 841-0660 E-mail: finaid@ksbe.edu
Web Site: www.pauahi.org

Summary: To provide financial assistance for undergraduate or graduate studies to persons of Hawaiian descent.

Eligibility: Applicants must be 50 percent or more of Hawaiian descent (descendants of the aboriginal inhabitants of the Hawaiian Islands prior to 1778). They must be U.S. citizens, enrolled in full-time study in an undergraduate or graduate degree program, and able to demonstrate financial need and academic excellence.

Financial data: The amount awarded depends upon the financial needs of the recipient.

Duration: This is a 1-time grant.

Additional information: Recipients may attend school either in or outside of Hawaii. This program is jointly sponsored by the Ke Ali'i Pauahi Foundation and the Department of Hawaiian Home Lands. Information is also available from the Department's offices in O'ahu at (808) 586-3836, on Kaua'i at (808) 274-3131, on Moloka'i at (808) 562-6104, in East Hawai'i at (808) 974-4250, or in West Hawai'i at (808) 887-8216.

Deadline: February of each year.

405
HEINZ UNDERGRADUATE SCHOLARSHIPS

School Food Service Foundation
Attn: Program Manager
700 South Washington Street, Suite 300
Alexandria, VA 22314-4287
Phone: (703) 739-3900, ext. 119 (800) 877-8822, ext. 119
Fax: (703) 739-3915 E-mail: sfsf@asfsa.org
Web Site: www.asfsa.org

Summary: To provide financial aid for college to school food service professionals and their children.

Eligibility: The sponsor, nominator, or applicant for these scholarships must be employed as a school food service professional or be the dependent of an employee who is so employed. Applicants or nominees must be registered to attend an accredited college, university, or vocational-technical institution and have a grade point average of 3.0 or higher from the most recently attended academic institution. Selection is based on a personal essay (on what the applicants expect to gain from continuing their education and their professional goals), high school or college transcripts, 2 letters of recommendation, and a current resume of education, work experience, community service, and extracurricular activities.

Financial data: The stipend is $2,500.

Duration: 1 year; may be renewed but only so the student receives 2 awards within a 4-year period.

Number awarded: Varies each year.

Deadline: March of each year.

406
HELEN MCSPADDEN MEMORIAL ENDOWMENT SCHOLARSHIP

Epsilon Sigma Alpha
Attn: ESA Foundation Assistant Scholarship Director
P.O. Box 270517
Fort Collins, CO 80527
Phone: (970) 223-2824   Fax: (970) 223-4456
Web Site: www.esaintl.com/esaf
Summary: To provide financial assistance for continuing education to reentry students from Colorado studying any major.
Eligibility: Colorado residents returning to school to learn new job skills or obtain a degree after an absence are eligible. Selection is based on character, scholastic ability, leadership and ability skills, and financial need.
Financial data: The stipend is $1,500.
Duration: 1 year; may be renewed.
Additional information: Epsilon Sigma Alpha (ESA) is a women's service organization, but scholarships are available to both men and women. Information is also available from Verneene Forssberg, 403 South High, Pratt, KS 67124, (316) 672-3636, Fax: (316) 672-3688, E-mail: vernf@genmail.pcc.cc.ks.us. Completed applications must be submitted to the ESA State Counselor who verifies the information before forwarding them to the scholarship director.
Number awarded: 1 each year.
Deadline: January of each year.

407
HELLENIC TIMES SCHOLARSHIPS

Hellenic Times Scholarship Fund
Attn: Nick Katsoris
823 Eleventh Avenue, Fifth Floor
New York, NY 10019-3535
Phone: (212) 986-6881   Fax: (212) 977-3662
E-mail: HTSFund@aol.com
Web Site: www.HTSFund.org
Summary: To provide financial assistance for postsecondary education to students of Greek descent.
Eligibility: Applicants must be of Greek descent, between 17 and 30 years of age, and enrolled in an accredited college or university as graduate or undergraduate students. Students who are receiving other financial aid that exceeds 75 percent of their annual tuition are ineligible. Selection is based on need and merit.
Financial data: The amount of the awards depends on the availability of funds and the number of recipients.
Additional information: This program began in 1990.
Number awarded: Varies; approximately $150,000 is available for this program each year.
Deadline: February of each year.

408
HELPING HANDS BOOK SCHOLARSHIP PROGRAM

Helping Hands
P.O. Box 590006
Fort Lauderdale, FL 33359
Fax: (954) 726-1922 E-mail: director@helpinghandsbookscholarship.com
Web Site: www.helpinghandsbookscholarship.com
Summary: To provide high school seniors and college students with funds to purchase text books and other study materials.
Eligibility: Students who are 16 years of age or older and who are planning to attend or are currently attending a 2-year or 4-year college, university, or technical/vocational institute are eligible to apply. Selection is based on academic record and career potential.
Financial data: These stipends range from $100 to $1,000. Funds are intended to be used to purchase text books and study materials. Checks are sent directly to the recipient.
Duration: 1 semester; recipients may reapply.
Additional information: There is a $5 application fee.
Number awarded: Up to 50 each year.
Deadline: July for the fall semester; December for the winter semester.

409
HEMOPHILIA FOUNDATION OF MICHIGAN ACADEMIC ASSISTANCE AWARDS

Hemophilia Foundation of Michigan
Attn: Client Services Coordinator
2301 Platt Road, Suite 100
Ann Arbor, MI 48104
Phone: (734) 975-2838   (800) 482-3041
Fax: (734) 975-2889   E-mail: hfm-colleen@ic.net
Web Site: www.hfmich.org/support_scholarships.cfm
Summary: To provide financial assistance for college to Michigan residents with hemophilia.
Eligibility: High school seniors, high school graduates, and currently-enrolled college students are eligible to apply if they are Michigan residents and have hemophilia or another bleeding disorder. Family members of people with bleeding disorders and family members of people who have died from the complications of a bleeding disorder are also eligible. Applicants are required to submit a completed application form, a transcript, and a letter of recommendation.
Financial data: Stipends range from $500 to $1,500.
Duration: 1 year.
Number awarded: Varies each year.
Deadline: February of each year.

410
HEMOPHILIA HEALTH SERVICES MEMORIAL SCHOLARSHIPS

Hemophilia Health Services
Attn: Scholarship Committee
6820 Charlotte Pike, Suite 100
Nashville, TN 37209-4234
Phone: (800) 800-6606, ext. 5177   Fax: (615) 850-5100
E-mail: Scholarship@HemophiliaHealth.com
Web Site: www.HemophiliaHealth.com
Summary: To provide financial assistance to undergraduate or graduate students with hemophilia or other bleeding disorders.
Eligibility: This program is open to individuals with hemophilia and other bleeding disorders. Applicants must be high school seniors; college freshmen, sophomores, or juniors; or college seniors planning to attend graduate school or students already enrolled in graduate school. Selection is based on academic achievement in relation to tested ability, involvement in extracurricular and community activities, and financial need.
Financial data: Stipends range from $500 to $1,000. Funds are paid directly to the recipient.
Duration: 1 year; recipients may reapply.
Additional information: This program, which started in 1995, includes the following named scholarships: the Tim Haas Scholarship, the Ricky Hobson Scholarship, and the Jim Stineback Scholarship. Recipients must enroll full time.
Number awarded: Several each year.
Deadline: April of each year.

411
HEMOPHILIA RESOURCES OF AMERICA SCHOLARSHIPS

Hemophilia Resources of America
Attn: Scholarships
45 Route 46 East, Suite 609
P.O. Box 2011
Pine Brook, NJ 07058
Phone: (973) 276-0254   (800) 549-2654
Fax: (973) 276-0998   E-mail: hra@hrahemo.com
Web Site: www.hrahemo.com
Summary: To provide financial assistance for college to 1) persons with a bleeding disorder or 2) their dependents.
Eligibility: Eligible to apply for this program are persons with hemophilia or von Willebrand disease and their children. They must be interested in working on a college degree at a 2-year or 4-year institution (including vocational-technical school). Selection is based on an essay on future goals and aspirations; school, work, community, and volunteer activities; 2 letters of recommendation; and financial need.
Financial data: Stipends range from $500 to $2,500.
Duration: 1 year.
Additional information: This program began in 1995.

Number awarded: 1 or more each year. More than $25,000 in scholarships is provided each year.
Deadline: April of each year.

412
HENRY AND CHIYO KUWAHARA MEMORIAL SCHOLARSHIPS

Japanese American Citizens League
Attn: National Scholarship Awards
1765 Sutter Street
San Francisco, CA 94115
Phone: (415) 921-5225   Fax: (415) 931-4671
E-mail: jacl@jacl.org
Web Site: www.jacl.org
Summary: To provide financial assistance to student members of the Japanese American Citizens League (JACL) who are interested in pursuing undergraduate or graduate education.
Eligibility: This program is open to JACL members who are high school seniors, undergraduates, or graduate students. Applicants must be attending or planning to attend a college, university, trade school, or business college. Selection is based on academic record, extracurricular activities, and community involvement.
Financial data: The stipend depends on the availability of funds but usually ranges from $1,000 to $5,000.
Duration: 1 year.
Additional information: Requests for applications must be accompanied by a self-addressed stamped envelope.
Number awarded: 6 each year: 2 each to entering freshmen, continuing undergraduates, and entering or currently-enrolled graduate students.
Deadline: March of each year.

413
HERB KOHL EDUCATIONAL FOUNDATION EXCELLENCE SCHOLARSHIPS

Herb Kohl Educational Foundation, Inc.
825 North Jefferson Street, Suite 250
Milwaukee, WI 53202
Phone: (414) 271-6600   (800) 603-0096
Summary: To provide financial assistance for college to Wisconsin high school seniors.
Eligibility: High school seniors in Wisconsin are eligible to apply for this support. Applications for public school students are available from the Wisconsin Department of Public Instruction (DPI) or for independent and religious schools from the Wisconsin Council of Religious and Independent Schools (WCRIS). As part of the application process, several essays, official transcripts, and 4 letters of recommendation are required. Applications are reviewed by school district officials (or equivalent individuals in a private school setting), who then select a limited number of nominees. Selection is based on academic achievement, leadership, citizenship, community service, honesty, integrity, or other special talents.
Financial data: The stipend is $1,000. Funds may be used to pay for tuition and fees during the first year of college only and are paid directly to the recipient's postsecondary institution.
Duration: 1 year (the first year of college); nonrenewable.
Additional information: This program was started in 1990 by Senator Herb Kohl. It is administered and cosponsored by the foundation, DPI, WCRIS, the Wisconsin Newspaper Association, Cooperative Educational Service Agencies, and other education-related associations.
Number awarded: 100 each year.
Deadline: January of each year.

414
HERB KOHL EDUCATIONAL FOUNDATION INITIATIVE SCHOLARSHIPS

Herb Kohl Educational Foundation, Inc.
825 North Jefferson Street, Suite 250
Milwaukee, WI 53202
Phone: (414) 271-6600   (800) 603-0096
Summary: To provide financial assistance for college to Wisconsin high school seniors who are unlikely to be eligible for other academic-based scholarships.
Eligibility: This program is open to graduating seniors at designated high schools in Wisconsin. Students should 1) be unlikely to be eligible for other academic-based scholarships; 2) have achieved an academic record that represents their maximum effort; 3) have shown strong promise of succeeding in college and beyond; 4) have demonstrated a high level of motivation to achieve; and 5) may have overcome significant personal obstacles or adversity. Recipients are selected by their teachers and school administrators.
Financial data: The stipend is $1,000. Funds may be used to pay for tuition and fees during the first year of college only and are paid directly to the recipient's postsecondary institution.
Duration: 1 year (the first year of college); nonrenewable.
Additional information: This program was started in 1990 by Senator Herb Kohl. It is administered and cosponsored by the foundation, DPI, WCRIS, the Wisconsin Newspaper Association, Cooperative Educational Service Agencies, and other education-related associations.
Number awarded: Each year, the foundation designates 100 high schools throughout Wisconsin to select a recipient.
Deadline: January of each year.

415
HERBERT LEHMAN SCHOLARSHIPS FOR AFRICAN-AMERICAN UNDERGRADUATE

NAACP Legal Defense and Educational Fund
99 Hudson Street, Suite 1600
New York, NY 10013-2897
Phone: (212) 965-2225   Fax: (212) 219-1595
E-mail: mbagley@naacpldf.org
Web Site: www.naacpldf.org
Summary: To provide financial assistance to African American undergraduate and students.
Eligibility: This program is open to African Americans who are high school seniors planning to attend 4-year colleges and universities where African Americans are significantly underrepresented. U.S. citizenship is required. Selection is based on academic potential (as evidenced by high school records, test scores, and personal essays), character, educational goals, academic abilities, and community and school involvement.
Financial data: A stipend is awarded; amount not specified
Duration: 1 year; may be renewed for up to 3 additional years if satisfactory academic performance is maintained and if funds continue to be available.
Additional information: The NAACP Legal Defense and Educational Fund established this program in 1964 so African American students in the South could attend formerly segregated schools. In recent years it has been expanded to encourage and increase student diversity at all colleges and universities where African Americans are significantly underrepresented.
Deadline: April of each year.

416
HERMIONE GRANT CALHOUN SCHOLARSHIPS

National Federation of the Blind
c/o Peggy Elliott
Chair, Scholarship Committee
805 Fifth Avenue
Grinnell, IA 50112
Phone: (641) 236-3366
Web Site: www.nfb.org
Summary: To provide financial assistance to female blind students interested in pursuing a degree at the undergraduate or graduate level.
Eligibility: This program is open to legally blind women students who are pursuing or planning to pursue a full-time undergraduate or graduate course of study. Selection is based on academic excellence, service to the community, and financial need.
Financial data: The stipend is $3,000.
Duration: 1 year; recipients may resubmit applications up to 2 additional years.
Additional information: Scholarships are awarded at the federation convention in July. Recipients attend the convention at federation expense; that funding is in addition to the scholarship grant.
Number awarded: 1 each year.
Deadline: March of each year.

417
HIAS SCHOLARSHIPS

Hebrew Immigrant Aid Society
Attn: HIAS Scholarship Awards
333 Seventh Avenue
New York, NY 10001-5004
Phone: (212) 967-4100   E-mail: info@hias.org
Web Site: www.hias.org/PAGES/scholarships/scholars.htm
Summary: To provide financial assistance for educational purposes to Jewish refugees and asylees.
Eligibility: This program is open to Jewish refugees and asylees who arrived in the United States from the former Soviet Union, Iran, Bosnia, or other countries. Applicants must have been assisted by the Hebrew Immigrant Aid Society (HIAS). They may be either high school seniors planning to pursue postsecondary education or students already enrolled in college or graduate school. Previous recipients are not eligible to apply. Selection is based on merit, financial need, and service within the Jewish community.
Financial data: The stipend is $1,500.
Duration: 1 year; nonrenewable.
Additional information: This program was established in 1974. Requests for applications must be accompanied by a self-addressed stamped envelope.
Number awarded: Varies each year; recently, 134 of these scholarships were awarded.
Deadline: March of each year.

418
HILDEGARD LASH MERIT SCHOLARSHIP

Orphan Foundation of America
Attn: Director of Student Services
Tall Oaks Village Center
12020-D North Shore Drive
Reston, VA 20190-4877
Phone: (571) 203-0270   (800) 950-4673
Fax: (571) 203-0273   E-mail: scholarships@orphan.org
Web Site: www.orphan.org
Summary: To provide financial assistance for postsecondary education to students currently or previously in foster care.
Eligibility: Applicants must currently be in foster care or have been in foster care at the time of their 18th birthday or high school graduation. Both parents must be deceased. Applicants must be enrolled full time at a 4-year college or university and entering their sophomore, junior, or senior year. Selection is based on academic record, recommendations, an essay, extracurricular involvement, and other personal achievements. Finalists are interviewed by phone.
Financial data: The stipend is $5,000. Half the funds are paid at the beginning of the first semester and the other half at the beginning of the second semester if the recipient maintains a full-time course load and a 3.2 or higher grade point average.
Duration: 1 year; nonrenewable.
Additional information: This program was established in 1997 with funds from the Hildegard Lash Foundation. Mrs. Lash had died penniless in 1987 as a victim of financial abuse by a trusted fiduciary. When the foundation recovered the embezzled funds, it established this program.
Number awarded: 1 each year.
Deadline: August of each year.

419
HISPANIC OUTLOOK SCHOLARSHIP FUND

Hispanic Outlook in Higher Education
210 Route 4 East, Suite 310
P.O. Box 68
Paramus, NJ 07652-0068
Phone: (201) 587-8800   Fax: (201) 587-9105
Web Site: www.hispanicoutlook.com/scholar.html
Summary: To provide financial assistance for college to high school seniors of Hispanic descent.
Eligibility: Applicants must be high school seniors of Hispanic descent, with at least 1 parent from a Spanish-speaking Latin American country or Spain. They must be legal residents or citizens of the United States, have earned at least a 3.5 grade point average, and be entering as a full-time student at a 2-year or 4-year accredited college recommended in the *Hispanic Outlook in Higher Education Magazine's* "Publisher's Picks List." To apply, students must submit a completed application form, a letter of acceptance from the college they will be attending, a copy of their

high school transcripts, and a letter of recommendation from their high school counselor. Scholarships are awarded on the basis of merit.
Financial data: The stipend is $1,000.
Duration: 1 year; renewable if the recipient maintains at least a 3.5 GPA.
Additional information: This scholarship is not transferable; students who change schools lose the scholarship.
Deadline: April of each year.

420
HISTORICALLY BLACK COLLEGE/UNIVERSITY SCHOLARSHIP PROGRAM

U.S. Army
Attn: ROTC Cadet Command
Fort Monroe, VA 23651-5238
Phone: (757) 727-4558   (800) USA-ROTC
E-mail: atccps@monroe.army.mil
Web Site: www-rotc.monroe.army.mil
Summary: To provide financial assistance to high school seniors or graduates who are willing to serve as Army officers following completion of their bachelor's degree and who wish to attend an Historically Black College or University (HBCU).
Eligibility: Applicants for this program must 1) be U.S. citizens; 2) be at least 17 years of age by October of the year in which they are seeking a scholarship; 3) be no more than 27 years of age when they graduate from college after 4 years (veterans are allowed 1 additional year for each year of military service, up to a maximum of 3 years or 30 years of age upon graduation); 4) score at least 920 on the SAT or 19 on the ACT; 5) have a high school grade point average of 2.5 or higher; and 6) meet medical and other regulatory requirements. Current college or university students may apply if their school considers them beginning freshmen with 4 academic years remaining for a bachelor's degree. Recipients must agree to serve as Army officers following college graduation and must also agree to attend 1 of the 20 institutions designated as HBCUs.
Financial data: This scholarship provides financial assistance for college tuition and educational fees up to an annual amount of $16,000. In addition, a flat rate of $450 per year is provided for the purchase of textbooks, classroom supplies and equipment. Recipients are also awarded a stipend for up to 10 months of each year that is $250 per month during their freshman and sophomore years, $300 per month during their junior year, and $350 per month during their senior year.
Duration: 4 years.
Additional information: Scholarship recipients participate in the Army ROTC program as part of their college curriculum by enrolling in 4 years of military science classes, pursuing an Army-approved academic discipline, and attending a 6-week summer camp between the junior and senior years. Following graduation, they receive a commission as either a Regular Army, Army Reserve, or Army National Guard officer. Scholarship winners must serve in the military for 8 years. That service obligation may be fulfilled 1) by serving on active duty for 2 to 4 years followed by service in the Army National Guard (ARNG), the United States Army Reserve (USAR), or the Inactive Ready Reserve (IRR) for the remainder of the 8 years; or 2) by serving 8 years in an ARNG or USAR troop program unit that includes a 3- to 6-month active duty period for initial training.
Number awarded: A limited number of these scholarships are offered each year.
Deadline: November of each year.

421
HOOTIE & THE BLOWFISH SPONSORED SCHOLARSHIPS

National Minority Junior Golf Scholarship Association
Attn: Scholarship Committee
1140 East Washington Street, Suite 102
Phoenix, AZ 85034-1051
Phone: (602) 258-7851   Fax: (602) 258-3412
Web Site: www.nmgf.org
Summary: To provide financial assistance for college to minority high school seniors from South Carolina who excel at golf.
Eligibility: Eligible to apply for this award are minority high school seniors from South Carolina who are interested in attending college. Applicants are asked to write a 500-word essay on this question: "One of the principal goals of education and golf is fostering ways for people to respect and get along with individuals who think, dress, look, and act differently. How might you make this goal a reality?" Selection is based on academic record, personal recommendations, participation in golf, school and community activities (including employment, extracurricular activities, and other responsibilities), and financial need.

Financial data: The stipend is $3,500 per year. Funds are paid directly to the recipient's college.

Duration: 1 year.

Additional information: This program is cosponsored by the association and the musical group Hootie & the Blowfish.

Number awarded: 2 each year.

422
HOPE GRANTS FOR DIPLOMA/CERTIFICATE-SEEKING STUDENTS ATTENDING PUBLIC INSTITUTIONS

Georgia Student Finance Commission
Attn: Scholarships and Grants Division
2082 East Exchange Place, Suite 200
Tucker, GA 30084-5305
Phone: (770) 724-9030   (800) 546-HOPE
Fax: (770) 724-9031   E-mail: hope@mail.gsfc.state.ga.us
Web Site: www.gsfc.org

Summary: To help outstanding students who are interested in earning a certificate or diploma at a public technical institute in Georgia.

Eligibility: This program is open to Georgia residents who are attending any branch of the University System of Georgia, or any branch of the Georgia Department of Technical and Adult Education, to earn a certificate or diploma. Students whose family income is less than $50,000 per year must also complete a Free Application for Federal Student Aid (FAFSA), but students whose family income is greater than $50,000 per year are not required to complete the FAFSA and are still eligible for these scholarships. U.S. citizenship or permanent resident status is required.

Financial data: These scholarships pay tuition and mandatory fees at public technical institutes in Georgia along with a book allowance of up to $100 per quarter.

Duration: This assistance may be used for a total of 2 technical programs of study leading to a certificate or diploma.

Additional information: HOPE stands for Helping Outstanding Pupils Educationally. Full-time enrollment is not required. HOPE awards may be applied only to tuition amounts not covered by Pell or other federal grants received.

Number awarded: Varies each year.

423
HOPE SCHOLARSHIPS FOR DEGREE-SEEKING STUDENTS ATTENDING PRIVATE COLLEGES AND UNIVERSITIES

Georgia Student Finance Commission
Attn: Scholarships and Grants Division
2082 East Exchange Place, Suite 200
Tucker, GA 30084-5305
Phone: (770) 724-9030   (800) 546-HOPE
Fax: (770) 724-9031   E-mail: hope@mail.gsfc.state.ga.us
Web Site: www.gsfc.org

Summary: To help outstanding students who are attending or planning to attend a private college or university in Georgia.

Eligibility: This program is open to Georgia residents who are attending or planning to attend a private college or university within the state. Students who are applying as high school seniors must have earned at least 1) a 3.0 cumulative grade point average or 80 numeric grade average if they followed the college preparatory track in high school, or 2) a 3.2 cumulative grade point average or 85 numeric grade average if they followed any other high school track. Students who are applying for the first time as college students must have earned at least a 3.0 grade point average in college regardless of their high school grade point average. Students whose family income is less than $50,000 per year must also complete a Free Application for Federal Student Aid (FAFSA), but students whose family income is greater than $50,000 per year are not required to complete the FAFSA and are still eligible for these scholarships. All applicants, however, must also apply for a Georgia Tuition Equalization Grant (TEG). U.S. citizenship or permanent resident status is required. Recipients may utilize these scholarships as part of a study abroad program as long as they remain enrolled as matriculating students at their home institution in Georgia.

Financial data: The stipend for HOPE Scholarships at private colleges and universities is up to $3,000 per year. Funds may be used only for tuition and mandatory fees; the combined TEG award and this scholarship may not exceed the actual cost of tuition and fees.

Duration: 1 year; may be renewed for up to 3 additional years if the recipient maintains a 3.0 cumulative grade point average in college.

Additional information: HOPE stands for Helping Outstanding Pupils Educationally. Full-time enrollment (at least 12 hours) is required.

Number awarded: Varies each year.

424
HOPE SCHOLARSHIPS FOR DEGREE-SEEKING STUDENTS ATTENDING PUBLIC INSTITUTIONS

Georgia Student Finance Commission
Attn: Scholarships and Grants Division
2082 East Exchange Place, Suite 200
Tucker, GA 30084-5305
Phone: (770) 724-9030   (800) 546-HOPE
Fax: (770) 724-9031   E-mail: hope@mail.gsfc.state.ga.us
Web Site: www.gsfc.org

Summary: To help outstanding students who are attending or planning to attend a public college or university in Georgia.

Eligibility: This program is open to Georgia residents who are attending or planning to attend any branch of the Georgia University System, or any branch of the Georgia Department of Technical and Adult Education, as a matriculated student seeking an undergraduate degree. Students who are applying as high school seniors must have earned at least 1) a 3.0 cumulative grade point average or 80 numeric grade average if they followed the college preparatory track in high school, or 2) a 3.2 cumulative grade point average or 85 numeric grade average if they followed any other high school track. Students who are applying for the first time as college students must have earned at least a 3.0 grade point average in college regardless of their high school grade point average. Students whose family income is less than $50,000 per year must also complete a Free Application for Federal Student Aid (FAFSA), but students whose family income is greater than $50,000 per year are not required to complete the FAFSA and are still eligible for these scholarships. U.S. citizenship or permanent resident status is required. Recipients may utilize these scholarships as part of a study abroad program as long as they remain enrolled as matriculating students at their home institution in Georgia.

Financial data: These scholarships pay tuition and mandatory fees at public colleges and universities in Georgia along with a book allowance of up to $150 per semester.

Duration: 1 year; may be renewed as long as the recipient maintains at least a 3.0 grade point average.

Additional information: HOPE stands for Helping Outstanding Pupils Educationally. Full-time enrollment is not required. HOPE awards may be applied only to tuition amounts not covered by Pell or other federal grants received.

Number awarded: Varies each year.

425
HOPI SCHOLARSHIP

Hopi Tribe
Attn: Grants and Scholarship Program
P.O. Box 123
Kykotsmovi, AZ 86039
Phone: (520) 734-3533   (800) 762-9630

Summary: To provide financial assistance to students of Hopi ancestry who are pursuing an undergraduate, graduate, or postgraduate degree.

Eligibility: This program is open to students who are pursuing an associate, baccalaureate, graduate, or postgraduate degree. Applicants must be an enrolled member of the Hopi Tribe. Entering freshmen must be in the top 10 percent of their graduating class or score at least 21 on the ACT or score at least 930 on the SAT. Undergraduate students must have at least a 3.0 grade point average. Graduate, postgraduate, and professional students must have at least a 3.2 grade point average for all graduate course work. Selection is based on academic merit.

Financial data: The stipend is $1,000 per semester.

Duration: 1 year; may be renewed.

Additional information: Recipients must attend school on a full-time basis.

Number awarded: Varies each year.

Deadline: July of each year.

426
HOPI SUPPLEMENTAL GRANT

Hopi Tribe
Attn: Grants and Scholarship Program
P.O. Box 123
Kykotsmovi, AZ 86039
Phone: (520) 734-3533   (800) 762-9630

Summary: To provide financial assistance to students of Hopi ancestry who are pursuing an undergraduate, graduate, or postgraduate degree.

Eligibility: This program is open to students who are pursuing an associate,

baccalaureate, graduate, or postgraduate degree. Applicants must be an enrolled member of the Hopi Tribe. They must be able to demonstrate financial need. Entering freshmen must have a 2.0 high school grade point average or a minimum composite score of 45 percent on the GED exam. Continuing students must have at least a 2.0 grade point average for all college work.

Financial data: Up to $4,000 per semester and up to $2,750 for the summer session, depending on the need of the recipient.

Duration: 1 year; may be renewed.

Additional information: This grant is awarded as a secondary source of financial aid to eligible students who are also receiving aid from the Bureau of Indian Affairs Higher Education program. Recipients must attend school on a full-time basis.

Number awarded: Varies each year.

Deadline: July of each year for fall semester; November for spring semester.

427
HOPI TUITION/BOOK SCHOLARSHIP

Hopi Tribe
Attn: Grants and Scholarship Program
P.O. Box 123
Kykotsmovi, AZ 86039
Phone: (520) 734-3533   (800) 762-9630
Summary: To provide financial assistance to students of Hopi ancestry who are pursuing an undergraduate, graduate, or postgraduate degree.

Eligibility: This program is open to students who are pursuing an associate, baccalaureate, graduate, or postgraduate degree. Applicants must be an enrolled member of the Hopi Tribe. They must be pursuing a postsecondary degree for at least 1 of the following reasons: personal growth, career enhancement, career change, and/or continuing education. Both full- and part-time students may apply. Financial need is not required, but students must have applied for federal aid before applying for this award.

Financial data: The scholarship covers the cost of tuition/fees and books.

Duration: 1 year; may be renewed if the recipient maintains a minimum cumulative GPA of 2.0.

Number awarded: Varies each year.

Deadline: July of each year for fall semester; November for spring semester.

428
HORACE MANN SCHOLARSHIPS

Horace Mann Companies
Attn: Scholarship Program
P.O. Box 20490
Springfield, IL 62708
Phone: (217) 788-5373
Web Site: www.horacemann.com
Summary: To provide financial assistance for college to children of teachers.

Eligibility: Applicants must be college-bound high school seniors whose parent or legal guardian is employed by a U.S. public school district or public college/university. The student must have at least a 3.0 GPA and a score of at least 23 on the ACT or 1100 on the SAT. Selection is based on an essay, grades, 2 letters of recommendation, school and community activities, and academic honors. Financial need is not considered.

Financial data: Scholarships are either $5,000 or $1,000 per year. Funds are paid directly to the student's college or university for tuition, fees, and other educational expenses.

Duration: 4 years or 1 year.

Number awarded: 31 each year: 1 at $5,000 per year for 4 years, 10 at $1,000 per year for 4 years, and 20 at $1,000 for 1 year.

Deadline: February of each year.

429
HOUSTON LIVESTOCK SHOW AND RODEO FCCLA SCHOLARSHIPS

Family, Career and Community Leaders of America-Texas Association
Attn: Scholarship Coordinator
3530 Bee Caves Road, Suite 101
Austin, TX 78746
Phone: (512) 306-0099   Fax: (512) 306-0041
E-mail: texas@texasfccla.org   Web Site: www.texasfccla.org/scholarships.htm
Summary: To provide financial assistance for college to high school seniors in Texas who have been members of Family, Career and Community Leaders of America (FCCLA).

Eligibility: This program is open to FCCLA members who are high school seniors in Texas in the upper quarter of their graduating class. Applicants must have passed the TAAS Mastery/Exit Level exam and have achieved scores of at least 900 on the SAT or 20 on the ACT. They must plan to enroll in a bachelor's degree program at a Texas college or university, although there is no restriction on the major field of study. U.S. citizenship is required. As part of the application process, applicants must submit a 2-page essay on the importance of a college education to them and their career goals. Selection is based on academic achievement; activities, honors, and awards; extracurricular activities; community activities; and financial need.

Financial data: The stipend is $1,250 per semester.

Duration: 4 years.

Number awarded: 10 each year.

Deadline: February of each year.

430
HOWARD COUGHLIN MEMORIAL SCHOLARSHIP FUND

Office and Professional Employees International Union
Attn: Scholarship Fund
1660 L Street, N.W., Suite 801
Washington, DC 20036
Phone: (202) 393-4464   Fax: (202) 347-0649
Web Site: www.opeiu.edu
Summary: To provide financial assistance for postsecondary education to members and children of members of the Office and Professional Employees International Union (OPEIU).

Eligibility: Applicants must be either 1) a member or an associate member of the union in good standing, unless the member leaves employment to study on a full-time basis, retires, becomes disabled, or is terminated by employer layoffs and plant closings; or 2) the child, stepchild, or legally adopted child of a union member in good standing or an associate member. All applicants must submit high school transcripts and SAT or ACT scores (or equivalent examination by a recognized technical or vocational school); applicants who are already enrolled in a college, university, or technical/vocational school must also submit a college transcript. Students may be enrolled on either a full-time or part-time basis. Only 1 award will be made to a family for a lifetime.

Financial data: $1,250 per year for full-time study or $500 per year for part-time study.

Duration: 5 years.

Number awarded: 18 each year: 12 full-time scholarships (at least 1 per region) and 6 part-time scholarships (at least 1 per region).

Deadline: March of each year.

431
HOWARD E. & MARJORY M. SMITH 4-H SCHOLARSHIP

Colorado 4-H Youth Development Program
c/o Colorado State University Cooperative Extension
Jefferson County Extension Office
15200 West Sixth Avenue, Suite C
Golden, CO 80501-5018
Phone: (303) 271-6620
Summary: To provide financial assistance for college to high school seniors in Colorado who have been members of 4-H.

Eligibility: This scholarship is open to 4-H members who are graduating high school seniors in Colorado, have at least a 3.0 GPA, and can demonstrate financial need. They must promote basic, traditional family values. Finalists are interviewed.

Financial data: The stipend is $1,000; funds are not awarded until the successful completion of the recipient's first semester of college.

Duration: 1 year.

Number awarded: 1 each year.

Deadline: May of each year.

432
HOWARD R. SWEARER STUDENT HUMANITARIAN AWARD

Campus Compact
c/o Brown University
188 Benefit Street
Box 1975
Providence, RI 02912
Phone: (401) 863-2842   Fax: (401) 863-3779
E-mail: campus@compact.org
Web Site: www.compact.org
Summary: To recognize and reward college students for outstanding public

service.

Eligibility: Only undergraduate students at Campus Compact-member institutions may be nominated (for a list of those colleges, write to the sponsor). Nominees should be able to demonstrate outstanding public service performed during the preceding 12 months. Of special interest to the sponsor is a student project that illustrates an innovative approach to a social, educational, environmental, health, economic, or legal issue within a community. The application should demonstrate the student's initiative and ability to translate ideas into practical results. Preference is given to nominees who have 1) connected service with academic study; 2) developed systems to ensure long-term support for the project; and 3) linked service to its larger social context through policy work and awareness raising.

Financial data: The award is $1,500. Funds are to be used to support service programs of the recipients' design or choice; they cannot be used for personal or school expenses.

Duration: The awards are granted annually.

Additional information: Support for this program, which began in 1987, is provided by Sallie Mae. Campus Compact operates at more than 750 colleges and universities.

Number awarded: 5 each year.

Deadline: February of each year.

433
HOWARD ROCK FOUNDATION UNDERGRADUATE SCHOLARSHIP PROGRAM

CIRI Foundation
2600 Cordova Street, Suite 206
Anchorage, AK 99503
Phone: (907) 263-5582   (800) 764-3382
Fax: (907) 263-5588   E-mail: tcf@ciri.com
Web Site: www.ciri.com/tcf

Summary: To provide financial assistance for undergraduate study to Alaska Natives and their lineal descendants (adopted or natural).

Eligibility: This program is open to Alaska Native enrollees under the Alaska Native Claims Settlement Act (ANCSA) of 1971: original enrollees of the ANCSA, members of a traditional IRA or tribal government, members of an Alaska Village Initiatives member organization, or lineal descendants of an original enrollee of the ANCSA regional or village corporation. Proof of eligibility is required. Applicants must have at least a 2.5 grade point average and must be able to demonstrate financial need. There is no Alaska residency requirement or age limitation. Applicants must be accepted or enrolled full time in a 4-year undergraduate program. Preference is given to third- and fourth-year students.

Financial data: The stipend is $2,500 per year. Funds are to be used for tuition, university fees, books, course-required supplies, and (for students who must live away from their permanent home in order to attend college) room and board. Checks are made payable to the student and the university and are sent directly to the student's university.

Duration: 1 year.

Additional information: This program was established in 1986. The CIRI Foundation assumed its administration in 1999. Recipients must attend school on a full-time basis.

Deadline: March of each year.

434
H.S. AND ANGELINE LEWIS SCHOLARSHIP AWARDS

American Legion Auxiliary
Department of Wisconsin
Attn: Department Secretary/Treasurer
2930 American Legion Drive
P.O. Box 140
Portage, WI 53901-0140
Phone: (608) 745-0124   Fax: (608) 745-1947
E-mail: alawi@amlegionauxwi.org
Web Site: www.amlegionauxwi.org

Summary: To provide financial assistance for postsecondary education to Wisconsin residents who are related to veterans or members of the American Legion Auxiliary.

Eligibility: This program is open to the children, wives, and widows of veterans who are high school seniors or graduates with a grade point average of 3.2 or higher. Grandchildren and great-grandchildren of veterans are eligible if they are members of the American Legion Auxiliary. Applicants must be in need of

financial assistance and residents of Wisconsin, although they do not need to attend a college in Wisconsin.

Financial data: The stipend is $1,000.

Duration: 1 year; nonrenewable.

Number awarded: 6 each year: 1 to a graduate student and 5 to undergraduates.

Deadline: March of each year.

435
IDA M. CRAWFORD SCHOLARSHIP

Oregon Student Assistance Commission
Attn: Private Awards Grant Department
1500 Valley River Drive, Suite 100
Eugene, OR 97401-2146
Phone: (541) 687-7395   (800) 452-8807, ext. 7395
Fax: (541) 687-7419   E-mail: awardinfo@mercury.osac.state.or.us
Web Site: www.osac.state.or.us

Summary: To provide financial assistance for college to graduates of Oregon high schools.

Eligibility: This program is open to graduates of accredited high schools in Oregon who are attending or planning to attend college. Applicants must have a cumulative grade point average of 3.5 or higher. Students planning to study law, medicine, music, theology, or teaching are not eligible.

Financial data: Scholarship amounts vary, depending upon the needs of the recipient.

Duration: 1 year.

Number awarded: Varies each year.

Deadline: February of each year.

436
IDAHO GOVERNOR'S CHALLENGE SCHOLARSHIP— ACADEMIC

Idaho State Board of Education
Len B. Jordan Office Building
650 West State Street, Room 307
P.O. Box 83720
Boise, ID 83720-0037
Phone: (208) 334-2270   Fax: (208) 334-2632
E-mail: board@osbe.state.id.us
Web Site: www.sde.state.id.us/osbe/Scholarships/governor.htm

Summary: To provide financial assistance to outstanding high school seniors in Idaho who wish to pursue postsecondary education.

Eligibility: This program is open to graduating high school seniors who are U.S. citizens, Idaho residents, and planning to enroll as full-time students at an eligible postsecondary educational institution in the state. Applicants must have maintained a grade point average of 2.8 or better, must take the ACT or SAT examinations, and must have demonstrated a commitment to public service.

Financial data: The stipend is $3,000 per year.

Duration: 1 year; may be renewed for up to 3 additional years.

Number awarded: 6 each year.

Deadline: December of each year.

437
IDAHO GOVERNOR'S CHALLENGE SCHOLARSHIP— PROFESSIONAL/TECHNICAL

Idaho State Board of Education
Len B. Jordan Office Building
650 West State Street, Room 307
P.O. Box 83720
Boise, ID 83720-0037
Phone: (208) 334-2270   Fax: (208) 334-2632
E-mail: board@osbe.state.id.us
Web Site: www.sde.state.id.us/osbe/Scholarships/governor.htm

Summary: To provide financial assistance to outstanding high school seniors in Idaho who wish to pursue professional-technical education.

Eligibility: This program is open to graduating high school seniors who are U.S. citizens, Idaho residents, and planning to enroll as full-time students in a professional-technical program in the state. Applicants must have maintained a grade point average of 2.8 or better and have demonstrated a commitment to public service. They must identify their proposed program; selection is based in part on their identified professional-technical program.

Financial data: The stipend is $3,000 per year.

Duration: 1 year; may be renewed for up to 2 additional years.
Number awarded: 6 each year.
Deadline: December of each year.

438
IDAHO LEGION SCHOLARSHIPS

American Legion
Attn: Department of Idaho
901 Warren Street
Boise, ID 83706-3825
Phone: (208) 342-7061   Fax: (208) 342-1964
E-mail: idlegion@micron.net
Web Site: netnow.micron.net/~idlegion
Summary: To provide financial support for the postsecondary education of children or grandchildren of members of the American Legion or American Legion Auxiliary in Idaho.
Eligibility: Eligible for these scholarships are the children or grandchildren of members of the American Legion or American Legion Auxiliary in Idaho who have been members for at least 2 consecutive years. Applicants must be Idaho residents and high school seniors who plan to attend accredited colleges, universities, or vocational-technical schools within the state.
Financial data: The amounts of the awards depend on the needs of the recipients.
Duration: 1 year.
Number awarded: Varies each year.

439
IDAHO LEVERAGING EDUCATIONAL ASSISTANCE STATE PARTNERSHIP PROGRAM

Idaho State Board of Education
Len B. Jordan Office Building
650 West State Street, Room 307
P.O. Box 83720
Boise, ID 83720-0037
Phone: (208) 334-2270   Fax: (208) 334-2632
E-mail: board@osbe.state.id.us
Web Site: www.sde.state.id.us/osbe/Scholarships/LEAP.htm
Summary: To provide financial assistance to students from any state attending college or university in Idaho.
Eligibility: This program is open to students from any state attending a public or private college or university within Idaho. Eligible students must have financial need; they may be enrolled part time.
Financial data: Awards range up to $5,000 per year for full-time students.
Additional information: For applications and information about deadlines, contact the financial aid office at the college you plan to attend. This program was formerly known as the Idaho State Student Incentive Grant.
Number awarded: Varies each year, depending upon the availability of funds.

440
IDAHO MINORITY AND "AT RISK" STUDENT SCHOLARSHIP

Idaho State Board of Education
Len B. Jordan Office Building
650 West State Street, Room 307
P.O. Box 83720
Boise, ID 83720-0037
Phone: (208) 334-2270   Fax: (208) 334-2632
E-mail: board@osbe.state.id.us
Web Site: www.sde.state.id.us/osbe/Scholarships/minority.htm
Summary: To help talented disabled and other "at risk" high school seniors in Idaho pursue a college education.
Eligibility: This program focuses on talented students who may be at risk of failing to meet their ambitions because of physical, economic, or cultural limitations. Applicants must be high school graduates, be Idaho residents, and meet at least 3 of the following 5 requirements: 1) have a disability; 2) be a member of an ethnic minority group historically underrepresented in higher education; 3) have substantial financial need; 4) be a first-generation college student; 5) be a migrant farm worker or a dependent of a farm worker.
Financial data: The stipend is up to $3,000 per year.
Duration: 1 year; may be renewed for up to 3 additional years.
Additional information: This program was established in 1991 by the Idaho state legislature. Information is also available from high school counselors and financial aid offices of colleges and universities in Idaho. Recipients must plan to attend or

be attending 1 of 8 participating postsecondary institutions in the state on a full-time basis. For a list of those schools, write to the State of Idaho Board of Education.
Number awarded: Varies each year.

441
IDAHO POW/MIA SCHOLARSHIPS

Idaho Division of Veterans Services
Attn: Office of Veterans Advocacy
805 West Franklin Street, Room 201
Boise, ID 83702-5560
Phone: (208) 334-1245   Fax: (208) 334-4753
Web Site: www.idvs.state.id.us/idvsserv.html
Summary: To support the postsecondary education of dependent children of Idaho veterans who are listed as prisoners of war or missing in action.
Eligibility: Eligible for these scholarships are dependent children of Idaho veterans who are listed as prisoners of war or missing in action in southeast Asia or Korea.
Financial data: Each scholarship provides a full waiver of tuition and fees at public institutions of higher education or public vocational schools within Idaho, as well as $100 per semester for books and equipment and $100 per month for housing and subsistence.
Duration: Benefits are available for a maximum of 36 months.
Number awarded: Varies each year.

442
IDAHO PROMISE CATEGORY A SCHOLARSHIP

Idaho State Board of Education
Len B. Jordan Office Building
650 West State Street, Room 307
P.O. Box 83720
Boise, ID 83720-0037
Phone: (208) 334-2270   Fax: (208) 334-2632
E-mail: board@osbe.state.id.us
Web Site: www.sde.state.id.us/osbe/Scholarships/cat_a_promise_scholar.htm
Summary: To provide financial assistance to outstanding high school seniors in Idaho.
Eligibility: This program is open to graduating high school seniors who are Idaho residents and planning to enroll full time in academic or professional-technical programs in public or private institutions in the state. Academic applicants must also be in the top 10 percent of their class with a cumulative grade point average of 3.5 or higher and an ACT score of 28 or higher. Professional-technical applicants must have a cumulative grade point average of 2.8 or higher and must take the COMPASS test (reading, writing, and algebra scores are required). U.S. citizenship is also required.
Financial data: The stipend is $3,000 per year.
Duration: 1 year; may be renewed for up to 3 additional years.
Additional information: This program was formerly known as the State of Idaho Scholarship Program.
Number awarded: Approximately 30 each year. Academic students receive 75 percent of the awards and professional-technical students receive 25 percent.
Deadline: December of each year.

443
I.D.E.S. FOUR YEAR COLLEGE SCHOLARSHIPS

Supreme Council of I.D.E.S.
223237 Main Street
Hayward, CA 94541
Phone: (510) 886-5555   Fax: (510) 866-6306
Web Site: www.idesofca.org
Summary: To provide financial assistance for college to high school seniors who are members of the I.D.E.S.
Eligibility: Applicants must be members of the I.D.E.S. in good standing (for at least 1 year prior to applying for the scholarship), be interested in attending a 4-year college, have maintained at least a 3.0 grade point average, be graduating from high school, and furnish 3 letters of recommendation (at least 1 of which must be from the principal or dean of the high school the applicant is attending). Financial need is considered in the selection process.
Financial data: The stipends awarded are $1,000, $900, $800, $700, and $600.
Duration: 1 year.
Additional information: The sponsor was incorporated by Portuguese immigrants in 1891 as the Irmandade do Divino Espirito Santo (Brotherhood of the Holy Spirit) de Mission San Jose California (I.D.E.S). Recipients must maintain

membership with the I.D.E.S. until the final scholarship payment is made.
Number awarded: 5 each year.
Deadline: April of each year.

444
IFPTE SCHOLARSHIPS

International Federation of Professional and Technical Engineers
8630 Fenton Street, Suite 400
Silver Spring, MD 20910
Phone: (301) 565-9016   Fax: (301) 565-0018
Web Site: www.ifpte.org/scholarship.html
Summary: To provide financial assistance for college to the children and grandchildren of members of the International Federation of Professional and Technical Engineers (IFPTE).
Eligibility: This program is open to high school seniors whose parents or grandparents belong to IFPTE. Applicants must wish to continue their education beyond high school (in accredited public or private colleges or universities, community colleges, or technical institutes). To apply, students must submit an official transcript, 3 letters of recommendation, an essay (at least 500 words) on "What Being a Member of a Union Family Has Meant to Me," and a completed application form. Evidence of standardized test scores is optional. Selection is based on the essay (40 percent), academic achievement (20 percent), and school and community activities (40 percent).
Financial data: The stipend is $1,500. Funds must be used for tuition.
Duration: 1 year.
Number awarded: 3 each year.
Deadline: March of each year.

445
I.H. MCLENDON MEMORIAL SCHOLARSHIPS

Hartford Foundation for Public Giving
85 Gillett Street
Hartford, CT 06105
Phone: (860) 548-1888   Fax: (860) 524-8346
Web Site: www.hfpg.org
Summary: To provide financial assistance for college to high school seniors in Connecticut who have sickle cell disease.
Eligibility: This program is open to Connecticut residents who have sickle cell disease. Applicants must be graduating high school seniors, have a GPA of 3.0 or higher, be in the top third of their class, and be interested in attending a 2- or 4-year college or university. As part of the application, they must submit a statement outlining personal and career goals and how the scholarship will help them achieve those goals. Selection is based on that essay, 3 letters of recommendation, and an interview.
Financial data: The stipend is $1,000.
Duration: 1 year.
Additional information: Funding for this program is provided by the Sickle Cell Disease Association of America—Connecticut Chapter, c/o Garey E. Coleman, Gengras Ambulatory Care Center, Suite 2101, 114 Woodland Street, Hartford, CT 06105-1299, (860) 714-5540, (800) 527-0119, Fax: (860) 714-8007.
Number awarded: 1 each year.
Deadline: April of each year.

446
ILLINOIS AMVETS SERVICE FOUNDATION SCHOLARSHIPS

Illinois AMVETS
2200 South Sixth Street
Springfield, IL 62703
Phone: (217) 528-4713   (800) 638-VETS (within IL)
Fax: (217) 528-9896
Web Site: www.amvets.com
Summary: To provide financial assistance for the postsecondary education in Illinois of children of veterans or current military personnel.
Eligibility: Applicants must be unmarried high school seniors in Illinois who are the children of veterans who served after September 15, 1940 and either received an honorable discharge or are presently serving in the military. Selection is based on financial need (40 percent), academic achievement (30 percent), extracurricular or community activities (20 percent), and aims (10 percent).
Financial data: The stipend is $1,000.
Duration: 1 year.
Number awarded: 30 each year.
Deadline: February of each year.

447
ILLINOIS GRANT PROGRAM FOR DEPENDENTS OF CORRECTIONAL OFFICERS

Illinois Student Assistance Commission
Attn: Scholarship and Grant Services
1755 Lake Cook Road
Deerfield, IL 60015-5209
Phone: (847) 948-8550   (800) 899-ISAC
Fax: (847) 831-8549   TDD: (847) 831-8326, ext. 2822
E-mail: cssupport@isac.org
Web Site: www.isac1.org/ilaid/depcorof.html
Summary: To provide financial assistance for postsecondary education to the children or spouses of disabled or deceased Illinois corrections workers.
Eligibility: This program is open to the spouses and children of Illinois corrections officers who were at least 90 percent disabled or killed in the line of duty. Applicants must be enrolled on at least a half-time basis in either undergraduate or graduate study at an approved Illinois public or private 2-year or 4-year college, university, or hospital school. They need not be Illinois residents at the time of application.
Financial data: The grants provide funds for tuition and mandatory fees.
Duration: Up to 8 academic semesters or 12 academic quarters of study.
Number awarded: Varies each year.

448
ILLINOIS GRANT PROGRAM FOR DEPENDENTS OF POLICE OR FIRE OFFICERS

Illinois Student Assistance Commission
Attn: Scholarship and Grant Services
1755 Lake Cook Road
Deerfield, IL 60015-5209
Phone: (847) 948-8550   (800) 899-ISAC
Fax: (847) 831-8549   TDD: (847) 831-8326, ext. 2822
E-mail: cssupport@isac.org
Web Site: www.isac1.org/ilaid/polfirgt.html
Summary: To provide financial assistance for postsecondary education to the children or spouses of disabled or deceased Illinois police or fire officers.
Eligibility: This program is open to the spouses and children of Illinois police and fire officers who were at least 90 percent disabled or killed in the line of duty. Applicants must be enrolled on at least a half-time basis in either undergraduate or graduate study at an approved Illinois public or private 2-year or 4-year college, university, or hospital school. They need not be Illinois residents at the time of application.
Financial data: The grants provide funds for tuition and mandatory fees.
Duration: Up to 8 academic semesters or 12 academic quarters of study.
Number awarded: Varies each year.

449
ILLINOIS LEGION BOY SCOUT SCHOLARSHIPS

American Legion
Attn: Department of Illinois
2720 East Lincoln Street
P.O. Box 2910
Bloomington, IL 61702-2910
Phone: (309) 663-0361   Fax: (309) 663-5783
E-mail: hdqs@illegion.org
Web Site: www.illegion.org
Summary: To provide financial assistance for postsecondary education to Boy Scouts in Illinois.
Eligibility: Applicants must be residents of Illinois, high school seniors, and qualified Boy Scouts or Explorers. Selection is based on a 500-word essay on the Americanism and Boy Scout programs of the American Legion.
Financial data: Awards are $1,000 or $200.
Duration: 1 year.
Number awarded: 5 each year: 1 at $1,000 and 4 runners-up at $200 each.
Deadline: April of each year.

450
ILLINOIS LEGION SCHOLARSHIPS

American Legion
Attn: Department of Illinois
2720 East Lincoln Street
P.O. Box 2910
Bloomington, IL 61702-2910
Phone: (309) 663-0361   Fax: (309) 663-5783
E-mail: hdqs@illegion.org
Web Site: www.illegion.org
Summary: To provide financial assistance for the postsecondary education of children of members of American Legion posts in Illinois.
Eligibility: Eligible to apply for these scholarships are students graduating from high schools in Illinois who plan to further their career education at an accredited college, university, vocational school, or trade school. They must be the children or grandchildren of members of American Legion posts in Illinois. Selection is based on academic performance and financial need.
Financial data: The stipend is $1,000.
Duration: 1 year.
Number awarded: 20 each year: 4 in each of the Illinois department's 5 divisions.
Deadline: March of each year.

451
ILLINOIS MERIT RECOGNITION SCHOLARSHIPS

Illinois Student Assistance Commission
Attn: Scholarship and Grant Services
1755 Lake Cook Road
Deerfield, IL 60015-5209
Phone: (847) 948-8550   (800) 899-ISAC
Fax: (847) 831-8549   TDD: (847) 831-8326, ext. 2822
E-mail: cssupport@isac.org
Web Site: www.isac1.org/ilaid/mrs.html
Summary: To provide financial assistance for college to outstanding students in Illinois.
Eligibility: Eligible are Illinois high school seniors who rank in the top 5 percent of their class through the end of the sixth semester of high school. U.S. citizenship or permanent resident status is required. Recipients must use the award within 1 year of high school graduation as at least a half-time student at an accredited Illinois public or private 2- or 4-year college, university, or hospital school. They may also attend 1 of the nation's 4 military service academies. Financial need is not considered in the selection process.
Financial data: The stipend is $1,000. Funds may be used for payment of tuition, fees, and other educational expenses.
Duration: 1 year; nonrenewable.
Additional information: Information on this award is also available from high school counselors. The amount of funding available each year depends on action by the state legislature.
Number awarded: Varies each year.
Deadline: June of the year following high school graduation.

452
ILLINOIS MIA/POW SCHOLARSHIP

Illinois Department of Veterans' Affairs
833 South Spring Street
P.O. Box 19432
Springfield, IL 62794-9432
Phone: (217) 782-6641   (800) 437-9824 (within IL)
Fax: (217) 524-0344   TDD: (217) 524-4645
E-mail: webmail@dva.state.il.us
Web Site: www.state.il.us/agency/dva
Summary: To provide financial assistance for the undergraduate education of Illinois dependents of disabled or deceased veterans or those listed as prisoners of war or missing in action, or for the rehabilitation or education of disabled dependents of those veterans.
Eligibility: To be eligible, applicants must be the spouses, natural children, legally adopted children, or stepchildren of a veteran or service member who 1) has been declared by the U.S. Department of Defense or the U.S. Department of Veterans Affairs to be permanently disabled from service-connected causes with 100 percent disability, deceased as the result of a service-connected disability, a prisoner of war, or missing in action, and 2) at the time of entering service was an Illinois resident or was an Illinois resident within 6 months of entering such service.

Financial data: An eligible dependent is entitled to full payment of tuition and certain fees at any Illinois state-supported college, university, or community college. In lieu of that benefit, an eligible dependent who has a physical, mental, or developmental disability is entitled to receive a grant to be used to cover the cost of treating the disability at 1 or more appropriate therapeutic, rehabilitative, or educational facilities. For disabled dependents, the total benefit cannot exceed the cost equivalent of 4 calendar years of full-time enrollment, including summer terms, at the University of Illinois.
Duration: This scholarship may be used for a period equivalent to 4 calendar years, including summer terms. Dependents have 12 years from the initial term of study to complete the equivalent of 4 calendar years. Disabled dependents who elect to use the grant for rehabilitative purposes may do so as long as the total benefit does not exceed the cost equivalent of 4 calendar years of full-time enrollment at the University of Illinois.
Additional information: An eligible child must begin using the scholarship prior to his or her 26th birthday. An eligible spouse must begin using the scholarship prior to 10 years from the effective date of eligibility (e.g., prior to August 12, 1989 or 10 years from date of disability or death).
Number awarded: Varies each year.

453
ILLINOIS MONETARY AWARD PROGRAM

Illinois Student Assistance Commission
Attn: Scholarship and Grant Services
1755 Lake Cook Road
Deerfield, IL 60015-5209
Phone: (847) 948-8550   (800) 899-ISAC
Fax: (847) 831-8549   TDD: (847) 831-8326, ext. 2822
E-mail: cssupport@isac.org
Web Site: www.isac1.org/ilaid/map.html
Summary: To provide financial assistance to undergraduate students in Illinois.
Eligibility: Applicants must be Illinois residents and U.S. citizens or eligible noncitizens. They must be able to demonstrate financial need, be enrolled at least half time as an undergraduate student at an approved Illinois institution of higher education, and not be in default on any student loan. High school grades and test scores are not considered in the selection process.
Financial data: The actual dollar amount of the award depends on financial need and the cost of the recipient's schooling; in no case does the award exceed the actual cost of tuition and fees or $4,740 per year, whichever is less. The funds may be used only for tuition and mandatory fees; funds cannot be spent on books, travel, or housing. All awards are paid directly to the recipient's school.
Duration: 1 year; may be renewed up to 4 additional years.
Number awarded: Varies each year.
Deadline: Funding for this program is limited. To increase your chances of receiving funding, apply as soon after the beginning of January as possible.

454
ILLINOIS VETERAN GRANT PROGRAM

Illinois Student Assistance Commission
Attn: Scholarship and Grant Services
1755 Lake Cook Road
Deerfield, IL 60015-5209
Phone: (847) 948-8550   (800) 899-ISAC
Fax: (847) 831-8549   TDD: (847) 831-8326, ext. 2822
E-mail: cssupport@isac.org
Web Site: www.isac1.org/ilaid/ivggp.html
Summary: To provide financial assistance for the undergraduate and graduate education of Illinois veterans.
Eligibility: Anyone from Illinois who served honorably in the U.S. armed forces is entitled to this scholarship if they served for at least 1 year on active duty (or were assigned to active duty in the Persian Gulf or to military operations in Somalia, regardless of length of service). Applicants must have been Illinois residents for at least 6 months before entering service and they must have returned to Illinois within 6 months after separation from service. They must have served in the U.S. Air Force, Army, Coast Guard, Marines, or Navy; members of the Reserve Officer Training Corps and a state's National Guard are not eligible.
Financial data: This scholarship pays all in-state and in-district tuition and fees at all state-supported colleges, universities, and community colleges.
Duration: This scholarship may be used for the equivalent of up to 4 years of full-time enrollment, provided the recipients maintain the minimum grade point average determined by their college or university.

Additional information: This is an entitlement program; once eligibility has been established, no further applications are necessary.
Number awarded: Varies each year.
Deadline: Applications may be submitted at any time.

455
IMAGINE AMERICA SCHOLARSHIPS

Career Training Foundation
Attn: Imagine America Scholarship Program
10 G Street, N.E., Suite 750
Washington, DC 20002
Phone: (202) 336-6800   Fax: (202) 408-8102
E-mail: scholarships@career.org
Web Site: www.career.org/scholarships
Summary: To provide financial assistance to high school seniors interested in attending a participating career college or school.
Eligibility: This program is open to seniors graduating from participating high schools in the United States. Each high school is allowed to nominate up to 2 students to receive a scholarship. Nominees are selected on the basis of the likelihood of their successfully completing postsecondary education, grade point average (must be 2.5 or higher), financial need, and demonstrated voluntary community service during their senior year. The students indicate which of more than 400 participating career colleges and schools they wish to attend, and that school decides how many of those nominees it wishes to accept.
Financial data: Stipends are $1,000. Scholarships are actually awarded by the participating career colleges and schools, which may prorate the award over more than 1 payment period or semester.
Duration: 1 year; nonrenewable.
Additional information: This program was established in 1998. For a list of participating high schools and career schools, check the web site at www.petersons.com/cca. Information is also available in *Guide to Career Colleges*, published jointly by Peterson's and the Career College Association (CCA) and available at all participating high schools. Recipients must enroll at the specified career school in their selected course of study prior to the end of October of the year of the award.
Number awarded: Up to 10,000 each year.

456
IMCEA MEMORIAL SCHOLARSHIP

International Military Community Executives Association
Attn: Sari Schneider
12222 Grassy Hill Court
Fairfax, VA 22033
Phone: (703) 273-0073   Fax: (703) 273-1171
E-mail: incea@imcea.com
Web Site: www.imcea.com/awards.htm
Summary: To provide financial assistance for college to the children of members of the International Military Community Executives Association.
Eligibility: This program is open to the sons and daughters of association members who are graduating high school seniors or currently enrolled in college. Applicants must submit a transcript of their recent academic work.
Financial data: The stipend is $1,000.
Duration: 1 year.
Number awarded: 1 each year.
Deadline: May of each year.

457
IMMUNE DEFICIENCY FOUNDATION SCHOLARSHIP

Immune Deficiency Foundation
40 West Chesapeake Avenue, Suite 308
Towson, MD 21204-4803
Phone: (410) 321-6647   (800) 296-4433
Fax: (410) 321-9165   E-mail: idf@primaryimmune.org
Web Site: www.primaryimmune.org
Summary: To provide financial assistance for undergraduate education to students with a primary immune deficiency disease.
Eligibility: Eligible to apply for these scholarships are students at any college, university, or community college who have a primary immune deficiency disease. Applicants must submit an autobiographical statement, 2 letters of recommendation, a family financial statement, and a letter of verification from their immunologist. Financial need is the main factor considered in selecting the

recipients and the size of the award.
Financial data: Scholarships range from $250 to $2,000, depending on the recipient's financial need, number of applicants, and availability of funds.
Duration: 1 year; may be renewed.
Additional information: This program is administered by the Immune Deficiency Foundation (IDF) with funding from the American Red Cross, Aventis Behring, Baxter Healthcare Corporation, Bayer Corporation, FFF Enterprise, Inc., and ZLB Bioplasma Inc.
Number awarded: The foundation attempts to award some aid to all qualified applicants; recently, the roster included 31 recipients.
Deadline: March of each year.

458
INA BRUDNICK SCHOLARSHIP AWARD

Crohn's and Colitis Foundation of America
Attn: Public Relations Coordinator
386 Park Avenue South, 17th Floor
New York, NY 10016-8804
Phone: (212) 685-3440   (800) 932-2423
Fax: (212) 779-4098   E-mail: info@ccfa.org
Web Site: www.ccfa.org
Summary: To provide financial assistance to college students with Crohn's disease or other related physical conditions.
Eligibility: Eligible to apply are individuals under 24 years of age who have Crohn's disease, colitis, or an ostomy. They must be able to demonstrate financial need.
Financial data: The stipend is $2,500.
Duration: 1 year.
Additional information: This scholarship is provided by ConvaTec, a Bristol-Myers Squibb Company.
Number awarded: 1 or more each year.
Deadline: October of each year.

459
INCENTIVE AWARDS OF THE SEMINOLE NATION JUDGEMENT FUND

Seminole Nation of Oklahoma
Attn: Judgement Fund
P.O. Box 1498
Wewoka, OK 74884
Phone: (405) 257-6287
Web Site: www.cowboy.net/native/seminole/judgement_fund.html
Summary: To recognize and reward undergraduate student members of the Seminole Nation of Oklahoma who achieve high grades in college.
Eligibility: This program is open to enrolled members of the Seminole Nation who are descended from a member of the Seminole Nation as it existed in Florida on September 18, 1923. Applicants must be attending a college or university as an undergraduate student and complete either 1) 12 units with a grade point average of 3.5 or higher, or 2) 15 units with a grade point average of 3.0 or higher.
Financial data: Students who complete 12 credit hours with a grade point average of 3.5 or higher receive an award of $300 per semester. Students who complete 15 credit hours with a grade point average of 3.0 or higher receive an award of $500 per semester. The total of all incentive awards to an applicant may not exceed $4,000.
Duration: 1 semester; may be renewed each semester the student completes the required number of units with the required minimum grade point average.
Additional information: The General Council of the Seminole Nation of Oklahoma approved a plan for use of the Judgement Fund Award in 1990. This aspect of the program went into effect in September of 1991.
Number awarded: Varies each year.
Deadline: Applications must be submitted within 60 days of the end of the semester.

460
INDIANA HIGHER EDUCATION GRANT PROGRAM

State Student Assistance Commission of Indiana
ISTA Center Building
150 West Market Street, Suite 500
Indianapolis, IN 46204-2811
Phone: (317) 232-2350   (888) 528-4719 (within IN)
Fax: (317) 232-3260   E-mail: grants@ssaci.state.in.us
Web Site: www.in.gov/ssaci/programs/hea.html

Summary: To provide financial assistance to Indiana residents who are pursuing full-time undergraduate study.

Eligibility: To be eligible, applicants must be Indiana residents; be high school seniors, high school graduates, or GED certificate recipients; attend or be planning to attend an eligible Indiana postsecondary institution as a full-time undergraduate student pursuing an associate or first bachelor's degree; and have demonstrated financial need for tuition assistance.

Financial data: This program offers tuition assistance from $200 to several thousand dollars per year, depending on the level of appropriations, the number of eligible students making application, the calculation of student's financial need, and the cost of tuition and fees at the schools of choice.

Duration: 1 year.

Additional information: Recipients must attend school, on a full-time basis, in Indiana.

Number awarded: Varies each year.

Deadline: February of each year.

461
INDIANA PART-TIME GRANT PROGRAM

State Student Assistance Commission of Indiana
ISTA Center Building
150 West Market Street, Suite 500
Indianapolis, IN 46204-2811
Phone: (317) 232-2350   (888) 528-4719 (within IN)
Fax: (317) 232-3260   E-mail: grants@ssaci.state.in.us
Web Site: www.in.gov/ssaci/programs/parttime.html

Summary: To provide financial assistance to Indiana residents who are pursuing part-time undergraduate study.

Eligibility: To be eligible, applicants must be Indiana residents; be high school seniors, high school graduates, or GED certificate recipients; attend or be planning to attend an eligible Indiana postsecondary institution as a part-time undergraduate student pursuing an associate or first bachelor's degree; and have demonstrated financial need for tuition assistance.

Financial data: The amount of the award depends on the need of the recipient and the number of credit hours taken.

Duration: 1 term (quarter or semester); may be renewed.

Additional information: Recipients must attend school, on part-time basis, in Indiana.

Number awarded: Varies each year.

462
INDIANA REMISSION OF FEES PROGRAM FOR CHILDREN OF DISABLED VETERANS

Indiana Department of Veterans' Affairs
302 West Washington Street, Room E-120
Indianapolis, IN 46204-2738
Phone: (317) 232-3910   (800) 400-4520
Fax: (317) 232-7721   E-mail: jkiser@dva.state.in.us
Web Site: www.state.in.us/veteran

Summary: To provide financial assistance for undergraduate or graduate education to children of disabled or deceased veterans in Indiana.

Eligibility: This program is open to Indiana residents who are the natural or adopted children of veterans who served in the active-duty U.S. armed forces during a period of wartime. The veteran parent must also 1) be rated as disabled by the U.S. Department of Veterans Affairs or the Department of Defense; 2) have received a Purple Heart Medal; or 3) have been a resident of Indiana at the time of entry into the service and was declared a POW or MIA after January 1, 1960. Students at the Indiana Soldiers' and Sailors' Children's Home are also eligible.

Financial data: Children of eligible veterans receive a 100 percent remission of tuition and all mandatory fees for undergraduate or graduate work at state-supported postsecondary schools and universities in Indiana.

Duration: Up to 124 semester hours of study.

Number awarded: Varies each year.

463
INDIANHEAD DIVISION SCHOLARSHIPS

Second (Indianhead) Division Association
Attn: Scholarship Foundation
P.O. Box 460
Buda, TX 78610-0460

Summary: To provide financial assistance for college to children and grandchildren of members of the Second (Indianhead) Division Association.

Eligibility: This program is open to 1) children and grandchildren of veterans who have been members of the association for the past 3 years and hold a current membership, and 2) children and grandchildren of men or women killed in action while serving with the Second Division. Applicants may be high school seniors or currently-enrolled college students. They must submit a personal letter giving reasons for the request and plans for the future; a high school and, if appropriate, college transcript; ACT or SAT test scores; a statement from their school principal attesting to their character and involvement in extracurricular activities; 2 letters of recommendation from current teachers or professors; a 200- to 300-word essay on such subjects as "What Being an American Means to Me," "Why I Should Receive This Scholarship," or "What Significant Part of U.S. Army History Has the Second Infantry Division Contributed;" and a statement from their parents or guardians on the financial support they will be able to provide the applicant.

Financial data: The stipend is usually $1,000 per year.

Duration: 1 year; may be renewed.

Number awarded: 1 or more each year.

Deadline: May of each year.

464
INFINITEC SCHOLARSHIP AWARDS

Council for Exceptional Children
Attn: Foundation for Exceptional Children
1110 North Glebe Road, Suite 300
Arlington, VA 22201-5704
Phone: (703) 245-0607   (888) CEC-SPED
Fax: (703) 264-9494   TTY: (703) 264-9446
E-mail: fec@cec.sped.org
Web Site: www.cec.sped.org/fd

Summary: To provide financial assistance for postsecondary education to students who use augmentative communication devices.

Eligibility: Applicants must use an augmentative communication device or other technology-based alternative to oral communication. Eligible communication devices and systems may range along a continuum from simple picture boards to highly complex computer-based systems. Applicants must be planning to enroll for the first time in full-time postsecondary education and be able to document financial need. They must submit a 250-word statement of philosophical, educational, and occupational goals as part of the application process. Selection is based on academic achievement, ability, promise, and financial need.

Financial data: The stipends are $1,000 and $500.

Duration: 1 year; may not be renewed.

Additional information: Scholarships may be used for 2- or 4-year college programs or for vocational or fine arts training programs. The sponsor of this program, Infinitec, Inc., is a joint project of United Cerebral Palsy Association of Greater Chicago and UCPA, Inc. (the national organization).

Number awarded: 2 each year: 1 at $1,000 and 1 at $500.

Deadline: January of each year.

465
INTERNATIONAL BROTHERHOOD OF BOILERMAKERS SCHOLARSHIP PROGRAM

International Brotherhood of Boilermakers, Iron Ship Builders, Blacksmiths, Forgers and Helpers
Attn: Scholarship Program
753 State Avenue, Suite 570
Kansas City, KS 66101
Phone: (913) 371-2640   Fax: (913) 281-8101
Web Site: www.boilermakers.org

Summary: To provide financial assistance for postsecondary education to the dependents of members of the International Brotherhood of Boilermakers, Iron Ship Builders, Blacksmiths, Forgers and Helpers.

Eligibility: This program is open to dependents of union members in good standing (including dependents of retired, disabled, or deceased members). Applicants must be high school seniors who will be entering their first year of a 2-year or 4-year program at a degree-granting, accredited college or university. Applications must be accompanied by ACT or SAT scores, high school transcripts, and a 300- to 500-word essay on a topic that changes annually (recently: "What should be the role of labor in local or national legislative issues that affect workers?"). Selection is based on academic achievement, performance on the essay, career goals, outside school activities, and extracurricular activities.

Financial data: The stipends range from $1,000 to $5,000; funds are paid directly to the financial aid office of the recipient's accredited college or university.

Duration: 1 year.
Number awarded: Varies each year; recently, 23 of these scholarships were awarded: 2 at $5,000, 1 at $4,000, 5 at $3,000, 2 at $2,500, 9 at $2,000, and 4 at $1,000 (including scholarships from the Canadian Federation of Labour and local lodges).
Deadline: March of each year.

466
IOWA AMVET PUBLICATIONS SCHOLARSHIP

Iowa Department of AMVETS
Attn: Scholarship Selection Committee
P.O. Box 77
Des Moines, IA 50301
Phone: (515) 284-4257
Summary: To provide financial assistance to the descendants of current Iowa AMVETS.
Eligibility: This program is open to graduating high school seniors in Iowa who are the sons, daughters, or grandchildren of a current Iowa AMVET member. Stepchildren, foster children, and other children dependent upon the member for support and living with the member in a regular parent-child relationship are also eligible, as is a deceased member's child. Applications must be endorsed by an Iowa AMVET post. Financial need is considered in the selection process.
Financial data: The stipend is at least $1,500.
Duration: 1 year.
Additional information: Any honorably discharged veteran is eligible for membership in AMVETS. Recipients may attend any accredited college, university, community college, technical institute, or trade school in Iowa.
Deadline: March of each year.

467
IOWA GRANTS

Iowa College Student Aid Commission
200 Tenth Street, Fourth Floor
Des Moines, IA 50309-3609
Phone: (515) 281-3501   Fax: (515) 242-5996
E-mail: icsac@max.state.ia.us
Web Site: www.state.ia.us/collegeaid
Summary: To provide financial assistance for undergraduate study to needy Iowa residents.
Eligibility: To be eligible to apply, a student must be a resident of Iowa; a U.S. citizen, national, or permanent resident; and currently enrolled or planning to enroll at least part time (3 hours minimum) in an undergraduate degree program at an eligible Iowa school. The grant is based on financial need, with priority given to the neediest applicants.
Financial data: Up to $1,000 per year (may be adjusted for less than full-time study).
Duration: Up to 4 years of undergraduate study.
Additional information: Each eligible campus is allotted funds to distribute to students with the greatest need at the campus. This program was established in 1990.
Number awarded: More than 1,600 each year.
Deadline: Applicants must submit a FAFSA form as early as possible after January 1. For priority consideration, the form must be completed and mailed in time to reach the processing center by the third week in April.

468
IOWA LEGION BOY SCOUT OF THE YEAR SCHOLARSHIP

American Legion
Attn: Department of Iowa
720 Lyon Street
Des Moines, IA 50309-5481
Phone: (515) 282-5068   Fax: (515) 282-7583
E-mail: iaamerleg@juno.com
Summary: To provide financial assistance for postsecondary education to outstanding Boy Scouts in Iowa.
Eligibility: Members of the Boy Scouts in Iowa who have received the Eagle Scout Award are eligible to receive this scholarship. The Boy Scout Committee of the American Legion selects the recipient on the basis of outstanding service to his religious institution, school, and community.
Financial data: The first-place winner receives a $2,000 scholarship, second place a $600 scholarship, and third place a $400 scholarship. All awards must be used for payment of tuition at the recipient's college or university.
Duration: 1 year.
Number awarded: 3 each year.

469
IOWA TUITION GRANTS

Iowa College Student Aid Commission
200 Tenth Street, Fourth Floor
Des Moines, IA 50309-3609
Phone: (515) 281-3501   Fax: (515) 242-5996
E-mail: icsac@max.state.ia.us
Web Site: www.state.ia.us/collegeaid
Summary: To provide financial assistance to Iowa residents who are interested in attending a private college or university.
Eligibility: To be eligible to apply, a student must be a resident of Iowa; a U.S. citizen, national, or permanent resident; and currently enrolled or planning to enroll at least part time (3 hours minimum) in an undergraduate degree program at an eligible private school in Iowa. Selection is based on financial need; priority is given to the neediest applicants.
Financial data: Up to $4,000 per year (may be adjusted for less than full-time study).
Duration: Up to 4 years of full-time undergraduate study.
Additional information: This program was established in 1969.
Number awarded: More than 14,000 each year.
Deadline: Applicants must submit a FAFSA form as early as possible after January 1. For priority consideration, the form must be completed and mailed in time to reach the processing center by the end of June.

470
IOWA UNCOMMON STUDENT AWARDS

Hoover Presidential Library Association, Inc.
Attn: Manager of Academic Programs
302 Parkside Drive
P.O. Box 696
West Branch, IA 52358-0696
Phone: (319) 643-5327   (800) 828-0475
Fax: (319) 643-2391   E-mail: info@hooverassoc.org
Web Site: www.hooverassoc.org
Summary: To provide financial assistance for college to high school students in Iowa who complete a project during the summer prior to their senior year.
Eligibility: Iowa residents may apply for these awards during their junior year in high school. Applicants must submit a project proposal and 2 letters of recommendation. Based on those proposals, finalists are selected to visit the Hoover Presidential Library and Museum in West Branch for a summer weekend, and then complete the project during the remainder of the summer. In the fall, they return to the Library and Museum to present their completed projects to a committee which selects the scholarship winners on the basis of that work. Grades, test scores, and financial need are not considered in the selection process.
Financial data: Each of the finalists receives a $750 award. The winners receive $5,000 scholarships, $2,500 paid to the accredited college or university of their choice for their freshman year and $2,500 for their sophomore year.
Duration: The competition is held annually. The scholarships are for 2 years.
Number awarded: 15 finalists are selected each year. Of those, 3 are chosen to receive scholarships.
Deadline: Project proposals must be submitted by March of each year.

471
IRENE CORREIA RAMOS SCHOLARSHIP

Portuguese Heritage Scholarship Foundation
Attn: Academic Secretary
P.O. Box 30246
Bethesda, MD 20824-0246
Phone: (301) 652-2775   E-mail: phsf@vivaportugal.com
Web Site: www.vivaportugal.com/phsf/apply.htm
Summary: To provide financial assistance for college to students of Portuguese American heritage.
Eligibility: Eligible to apply for this support are high school seniors or currently-enrolled college students who are of Portuguese American ancestry. Applicants must be U.S. residents and attending or planning to attend an accredited 4-year college or university. Selection is based on academic achievement and financial need.
Financial data: The stipend is $2,000 per year.
Duration: 4 years, provided the recipient maintains a GPA of 3.0 or higher.
Additional information: Recipients must attend college on a full-time basis.
Number awarded: 1 each year.
Deadline: January of each year.

472
IRMA AND KNUTE CARLSON AWARD

Vasa Order of America
Attn: Vice Grand Master
1926 Rancho Andrew
Alpine, CA 91901
Phone: (619) 445-9707   Fax: (619) 445-7334
E-mail: drulf@connectnet.com
Web Site: www.vasaorder.com
Summary: To provide financial assistance for postsecondary education to members of the Vasa Order of America.
Eligibility: Applicants must have been members of the organization for at least 1 year. They may be college juniors, seniors, or graduate students. Selection is based on a grade transcript, letters of recommendation from school and local Vasa lodge officials, and an essay of up to 1,000 words on a topic related to Vasa.
Financial data: The stipend is $1,000.
Duration: 1 year.
Additional information: Vasa Order of America is a Swedish American fraternal organization incorporated in 1899.
Number awarded: 1 each year.
Deadline: February of each year.

473
IRMA GESCHE SCHOLARSHIP

Rebekah Assembly of Texas
Attn: Scholarship Committee
16400 KC Road 4060
Scurry, TX 75158
Summary: To provide financial assistance for college to high school seniors in Texas.
Eligibility: This scholarship is available to Texas high school seniors who are interested in attending a 2-year or 4-year college or university in the state. Selection is based on academic ability, community service, personal development, and financial need. Applicants must submit a completed application along with a high school transcript, a typed letter describing their educational goals, and 3 letters of recommendation.
Financial data: The stipend is $1,000.
Duration: 1 year.
Number awarded: 1 each year.
Deadline: December of each year.

474
ISIA SCHOLARSHIP

Ice Skating Institute of America Education Foundation
17120 North Dallas Parkway, Suite 140
Dallas, TX 75248-1187
Phone: (972) 735-8800   Fax: (972) 735-8815
Web Site: www.skateisi.com/scholarapp.htm
Summary: To provide financial assistance to high school seniors and currently-enrolled undergraduates who are members of the Ice Skating Institute of America (ISIA).
Eligibility: Applicants may be graduating high school seniors or currently-enrolled college students. They must have completed at least 3 years of high school with at least a 3.0 grade point average, have been a member of ISIA for at least 4 years, have participated in group ice skating classes at an ISIA administrative member (rink or club) using the ISIA test program for at least 2 years, and have completed 240 hours of service (paid or voluntary) with an ISIA administrative member rink or skating school. As part of the application process, students must submit an official transcript, SAT/ACT scores, 2 evaluation forms, and a statement (up to 500 words) on "Why I should receive an ISIA Scholarship Award." Selection is based on community service, education awards and recognition, educational goals, and competitive ice skating experience.
Financial data: The stipend is at least $2,000 per year.
Duration: 1 year.
Additional information: Recipients must attend college on a full-time basis.
Deadline: March of each year.

475
IVAN FRANKO SCHOLARSHIP FUND

Ukrainian Fraternal Association
Attn: Scholarship Program
1327 Wyoming Avenue
Scranton, PA 18509-2849
Phone: (570) 342-0937
Summary: To provide financial assistance for college to high school seniors or currently-enrolled college students who are of Ukrainian heritage.
Eligibility: Applicants must be seniors in high school or currently enrolled in college and members in good standing (for at least 2 years) of the Ukrainian Fraternal Association. They must satisfy 1 of the following minimum insurance requirements: $2,000 Endowment (E-18; E-15; E-20); $4,000 T-20, T-65,or E-65 policy; $4,000 single premium life (SL) or single premium endowment at 65 (SE-65); or $10,000 term insurance (TM-10). AD/D policies do not qualify. As part of the application process, students must submit a short autobiography, a photograph, a copy of their latest transcripts, and recommendations from their local branch secretary or supreme council member. They must also write an essay on a topic that changes annually. Selection is based on financial need, academic record, and the written essay.
Financial data: The amount of the scholarship varies, depending upon the needs of the recipient. Funds are paid directly to the recipient.
Duration: 1 year.
Additional information: The Ukrainian Fraternal Association is the first fraternal organization in the United States and Canada to grant outright student stipends.
Number awarded: Varies each year.
Deadline: May of each year.

476
IVYANE D.F. DAVIS MEMORIAL SCHOLARSHIP

Delaware Child Placement Review Board
Attn: Ivyane D.F. Davis Memorial Scholarship
820 North French Street
Wilmington, DE 19801
Phone: (302) 577-8750   Fax: (302) 577-2605
Web Site: www.state.de.us/cprb/scholarship.htm
Summary: To provide financial assistance for college to students who have been in the foster care system in Delaware.
Eligibility: Applicants for these scholarships must 1) be residents of Delaware for at least 1 year prior to the application and 2) have been in foster care in the state on or after January 1, 1986. Selection is based on academic achievement, community service, participation in extracurricular activities, promise of success, and financial need.
Financial data: A stipend is awarded (exact amount not specified).
Duration: 1 year; may be renewed.
Additional information: This program was established in 1989. Recipients may attend an accredited postsecondary academic institution or vocational school anywhere in the country.
Number awarded: Varies each year.
Deadline: March of each year.

477
JACKIE ROBINSON SCHOLARSHIP

Jackie Robinson Foundation
Attn: Scholarship Program
3 West 35th Street, 11th Floor
New York, NY 10001-2204
Phone: (212) 290-8600   Fax: (212) 290-8081
Web Site: www.jackierobinson.org
Summary: To provide financial assistance to minority high school seniors interested in pursuing postsecondary education.
Eligibility: To apply for the scholarship, students must be members of an ethnic minority group, U.S. citizens, high school seniors, and accepted at a 4-year college or university. They must be able to demonstrate high academic achievement (SAT score of 900 or higher or ACT score of 23 or higher), financial need, and leadership potential.
Financial data: Up to $6,000 per year.
Duration: 4 years.
Additional information: The program also offers personal and career counseling on a year-round basis, a week of interaction with other scholarship

students from around the country, and assistance in obtaining summer jobs and permanent employment after graduation. It was established in 1973 by a grant from Chesebrough-Pond.

Number awarded: 100 or more each year.

Deadline: March of each year.

478
JACS SCHOLARS PROGRAM

Joint Action in Community Service, Inc.
Attn: JACS Scholarship Committee
5225 Wisconsin Avenue, N.W., Suite 404
Washington, DC 20015-2014
Phone: (202) 537-0996   Fax: (202) 363-0239

Summary: To provide college aid to former Job Corps members.

Eligibility: This program is open to former Job Corps members enrolled in colleges, universities, or trade schools. This scholarship is not available to students pursuing graduate or postgraduate degrees. Selection is based on background information, activities while in the Job Corps, activities since leaving the Job Corps, previous awards, and letters of recommendation. Financial status is not considered.

Financial data: The stipend is $1,000. Funds are paid directly to the recipient's educational institution.

Duration: 1 year.

Additional information: This program was established in 1986. Until 1993, it was named the Jerome D. Schaller Scholarship Award.

Number awarded: 1 or more each year.

Deadline: February of each year.

479
JAGANNATHAN SCHOLARSHIPS

North Carolina State Education Assistance Authority
Attn: Scholarship and Grant Services
P.O. Box 14103
Research Triangle Park, NC 27709-4103
Phone: (919) 549-8614   Fax: (919) 549-8481
Web Site: www.ncseaa.edu

Summary: To provide financial assistance to high school seniors planning to attend 1 of the branches of the University of North Carolina.

Eligibility: This program is open to high school seniors in North Carolina who are planning to attend any of the constituent institutions of the University of North Carolina as a full-time student. Special consideration is given to applicants whose parents are employees of Tolaram Polymers, Cookson Fibers, and related companies. Selection is based on academic achievement (as measured by class rank, cumulative grade point average, and SAT scores), leadership, and financial need.

Financial data: Awards cannot exceed demonstrated financial need, to a maximum of $3,500 per year.

Duration: 1 year; may be renewed up to 3 additional years if the recipient continues to demonstrate financial need and maintains satisfactory academic progress.

Additional information: This program was established by industrialist N.S. Jagannathan and began in the 1996-97 academic year.

Number awarded: Varies each year; recently, a total of 12 students received $34,380 in scholarships through this program.

Deadline: February of each year.

480
JAMES AND CHARLOTTE GIGNILLIAT SCHOLARSHIP

South Carolina Historical Society
100 Meeting Street
Charleston, SX 29401-2299
Phone: (843) 723-3225   Fax: (843) 723-8584
E-mail: info@schistory.org
Web Site: www.schistory.org

Summary: To provide financial assistance for college to students of Huguenot descent.

Eligibility: Applicants must be a descendant of a Huguenot who immigrated to the United States from Switzerland or France prior to November 18, 1787 (proof of descent is required). They may be high school seniors or currently-enrolled college students. Selection is based on academic ability, leadership, and extracurricular activities. Financial need is not considered in the selection process.

Financial data: Stipends range from $500 to $1,000 per year.

Duration: 1 year; may be renewed.

Additional information: Recipients must attend school on a full-time basis.

Deadline: February of each year.

481
JAMES B. CAREY SCHOLARSHIP

International Union of Electronic, Electrical, Salaried, Machine, and Furniture Workers
Attn: Department of Social Action
1275 K Street, N.W., Suite 600
Washington, DC 20005
Phone: (202) 513-6300   Fax: (202) 513-6357
E-mail: Humphrey@cwa-union.org
Web Site: www.iue-cwa.org

Summary: To provide financial assistance for undergraduate education to the children of members of the International Union of Electronic, Electrical, Salaried, Machine, and Furniture Workers (IUE).

Eligibility: This program is open to children of IUE members (including retired or deceased members). They must be accepted for admission or already enrolled as full-time students at an accredited college, university, nursing school, or technical school offering college credit courses. Families of full-time union officers or employees are not eligible to apply. Selection is based on academic record, leadership ability, ambition, good character, commitment to equality, service to the community, and a concern for improving the quality of life for all people.

Financial data: The stipend is $1,000 per year.

Duration: 1 year.

Additional information: Winners who are also awarded local, district, or division scholarships have the option of either accepting the James B. Carey Scholarship or the other awards and the dollar difference (if any) between the Carey Scholarship and the local, district, or division award.

Number awarded: 9 each year: 8 divided among the 6 union districts and 1 at large.

Deadline: April of each year.

482
JAMES F. BYRNES SCHOLARSHIPS

James F. Byrnes Foundation
P.O. Box 6781
Columbia, SC 29260-6781
Phone: (803) 254-9325   E-mail: info@byrnesscholars.org
Web Site: www.byrnesscholars.org

Summary: To provide financial assistance for college to South Carolina residents who have lost 1 or both parents by death.

Eligibility: Applicants must be residents of South Carolina who have lost 1 or both parents by death. They must be able to demonstrate financial need, a satisfactory scholastic record, and the characteristics of character, ability, and enterprise. Both high school seniors and currently-enrolled college students are eligible, but preference is given to high school applicants. Semifinalists are interviewed.

Financial data: Awards are in the range of $2,750 per year.

Duration: Up to 4 years.

Additional information: This program was established in 1948 with the proceeds of Byrne's first book, *Speaking Frankly*, and later augmented with revenues from his subsequent books and by friends. To date, the foundation has awarded more than 985 scholarships. Recipients may attend college in any state. The scholarship is for those planning to pursue a bachelor's degree and cannot be used at a technical college.

Number awarded: Varies; currently, approximately 70 scholars are supported at any particular time.

Deadline: February of each year.

483
JAMES L. AND LAVON MADDEN MALLORY DISABILITY SCHOLARSHIP

Easter Seals Iowa
P.O. Box 4002
Des Moines, IA 50333
Phone: (515) 289-1933, ext. 209

Summary: To provide financial assistance to disabled graduating high school seniors in Iowa who are interested in pursuing postsecondary education.

Eligibility: To be eligible, a student must have a permanent disability, plan to attend an accredited college or university, be a graduating high school senior, be a resident of Iowa, be in the upper 40 percent of his or her class or have a grade point average of at least 2.8, and be able to show financial need.

Financial data: The stipend is $1,000.

Duration: 1 year.

Number awarded: 1 each year.

Deadline: April of each year.

484
JAMES R. HOFFA MEMORIAL SCHOLARSHIPS

International Brotherhood of Teamsters
Attn: James R. Hoffa Memorial Scholarship Fund
25 Louisiana Avenue, N.W.
Washington, DC 20001
Phone: (202) 624-8735   E-mail: Scholarship@teamster.org
Web Site: www.teamster.org/scholarship/scholarship.htm

Summary: To provide financial assistance for postsecondary education to the children and grandchildren of active, retired, or deceased Teamsters.

Eligibility: This program is open to the children or grandchildren of active, retired, deceased, or laid-off members of the International Brotherhood of Teamsters with at least 12 months of consecutive membership in good standing. Applicants must be high school seniors in the top 10 percent of their graduating class who plan to attend an accredited college or university; students who have already graduated from high school are not eligible. Canadian students may apply during their junior or senior year of high school but not both. Selection is based on SAT or ACT scores, academic achievement, character, potential, and financial need.

Financial data: Scholarships are $2,500 or $1,000 per year.

Duration: The $2,500 annual awards are for 4 years and the $1,000 awards are for 1 year only.

Additional information: Recipients of the 4-year scholarships must maintain a minimum grade point average consistent with the scholarship requirements of their institution; if their institution has not established a minimum academic requirement for its scholarship recipients, the minimum grade point average for renewal of these scholarships is 3.0.

Number awarded: Each year, 25 4-year scholarships (5 per region) and 50 1-time scholarships (10 per region) are awarded.

Deadline: March of each year

485
JAMES R. LEVA SCHOLARSHIP PROGRAM

New Jersey Utilities Association
50 West State Street, Suite 1006
Trenton, NJ 08608
Phone: (609) 392-1000   Fax: (609) 396-4231
Web Site: www.njua.org

Summary: To provide financial assistance for college 1) to employees who work for New Jersey Utilities Association member companies and 2) to their families.

Eligibility: Applicants must be 1) regular, full-time employees of a member company or 2) the spouse or dependent children of member utilities' employees. Employee applicants must meet eligibility criteria for any tuition aid program the member company might have or, if none exists, must have at least 6 months of company service. All applicants must enroll or be enrolled in an approved course of study at an accredited junior college, college, or university. Selection is based on past academic performance and future potential, school and community participation, work experience, career and educational aspirations, financial need, unusual personal or family circumstances, and recommendations.

Financial data: The stipend is $2,000 per year. Funds are sent directly to the recipient's school and are intended to cover expenses not paid by an employer tuition aid/educational assistance program.

Duration: 1 year.

Deadline: April of each year.

486
JANET SHALEY JAMES MEMORIAL SCHOLARSHIP

Chickasaw Foundation
P.O. Box 1726
Ada, OK 74821-1726
Phone: (580) 421-9030   Fax: (580) 421-9031
Web Site: www.cflink.org/scholars.htm

Summary: To provide financial assistance for college to members of the Chickasaw Nation.

Eligibility: This program is open to Chickasaw students who are currently enrolled at an accredited institution of higher education in their freshman through senior year. All academic majors are eligible. Applicants must have a grade point average of 3.0 or higher and must submit a 1-page essay on their long-term goals and plans for achieving them. Financial need is not considered in the selection process.

Financial data: A stipend is awarded (exact amount not specified).

Duration: 1 year.

Number awarded: 1 each year.

Deadline: May of each year.

487
JAY RAMSDELL SCHOLARSHIPS

Jay Ramsdell Foundation
Attn: Daniel Lay
First National Bank
Trust Department
P.O. Box 258
Bar Harbor, ME 04609
E-mail: oct60@acadia.net
Web Site: www.jramsdellfoundation.org

Summary: To provide financial assistance for college to high school seniors in Maine who have been active in athletics.

Eligibility: This program is open to residents of Maine who are seniors graduating from a high school in the state. Students must be nominated by the athletic director at their high school; each director may nominate 1 student. Nominees must have been active in athletics; special attention is paid to team managers and statisticians. Financial need must be demonstrated, although need is not the primary consideration in making the award.

Financial data: The stipend is $5,000. Funds are paid to the college or university after the recipient has successfully completed the first semester and is enrolled for the second semester.

Duration: 1 year; recipients may reapply.

Additional information: These scholarships were first awarded in 1990.

Number awarded: 1 each year.

488
JAYCEE WAR MEMORIAL FUND SCHOLARSHIP PROGRAM

United States Junior Chamber of Commerce
Attn: JWMF, Department 94922
4 West 21st Street
Tulsa, OK 74114-1116
Phone: (918) 584 2481   Fax: (918) 584-4422
Web Site: www.usjaycees.org

Summary: To provide financial assistance for college to deserving students.

Eligibility: Applicants for these scholarships must be U.S. citizens, possess academic potential and leadership, and demonstrate financial need. Applications must be first submitted to the student's respective state Junior Chamber of Commerce organization.

Financial data: The stipend is $1,000 per year. Funds are sent directly to the recipient's college or university.

Duration: 1 year.

Additional information: This program was established in 1944. Requests for applications must be accompanied by a self-addressed stamped envelope and a $5 application fee.

Number awarded: 25 each year.

Deadline: Applications must be submitted to the Junior Chamber state president by February of each year.

489
JEAN AND ALBERT NERKEN SCHOLARSHIPS

Hebrew Free Loan Society
205 East 42nd Street, Suite 1318
New York, NY 10017
Phone: (212) 687-0188   Fax: (212) 682-1120
Web Site: www.ujafedny.org

Summary: To provide financial assistance to Jewish students enrolled in colleges, universities, graduate schools, and professional schools.

Eligibility: This program is open to Jewish students who can demonstrate

significant financial need. Applicants must be enrolled in colleges, universities, graduate schools, or professional schools approved by the United Jewish Appeal-Federation of Jewish Philanthropies of New York. Funding is not provided for religious studies or to students who are receiving full tuition waivers.
Financial data: Stipends up to $5,000 per year are available.
Duration: 1 year.
Additional information: This program is administered by the Hebrew Free Loan Society but funded by UJA-Federation.
Number awarded: Approximately 25 each year.
Deadline: May of each year.

490 JEAN FITZGERALD SCHOLARSHIP

Hawai'i Community Foundation
900 Fort Street Mall, Suite 1300
Honolulu, HI 96813
Phone: (808) 566-5570   (888) 731-3863
Fax: (808) 521-6286   E-mail: scholarships@hcf-hawaii.org
Web Site: www.hcf-hawaii.org
Summary: To provide financial assistance to women tennis players in Hawaii who are just beginning college.
Eligibility: This program is open to female Hawaiian residents who have been active members of the Hawai'i Pacific Tennis Association for at least 4 years and are entering their freshman year in college as full-time students. They must be able to demonstrate academic achievement (at least a 2.7 grade point average), good moral character, and financial need. In addition to filling out the standard application form, applicants must write a short statement indicating their reasons for attending college, their planned course of study, and their career goals.
Financial data: The amounts of the awards depend on the availability of funds and the need of the recipient; recently, grants averaged $6,500.
Duration: 1 year.
Additional information: Recipients may attend college in Hawaii or on the mainland.
Number awarded: Varies each year; recently, 1 scholarship was awarded.
Deadline: February of each year.

491 JEANNE E. BRAY MEMORIAL SCHOLARSHIP

National Rifle Association of America
Attn: Law Enforcement Activities Division
11250 Waples Mill Road
Fairfax, VA 22030-7400
Phone: (703) 267-1640
Web Site: www.nra.org
Summary: To provide financial assistance for college to children of law enforcement officers who are members of the National Rifle Association (NRA).
Eligibility: This program is open to NRA members who are the dependent children of 1) currently serving full-time commissioned peace officers who are also NRA members; 2) deceased full-time commissioned peace officers who lost their lives in the performance of assigned peace officer duties and were current members of NRA at the time of their death; 3) retired full-time commissioned peace officers who are also NRA members; and 4) full-time commissioned peace officers, disabled and retired as a result of a line of duty incident, who are also current NRA members. Applicants must be U.S. citizens with a grade point average of 3.0 or higher and scores of at least 750 on the SAT I or 20 on the ACT.
Financial data: The stipend is $2,000 per year.
Duration: Up to 4 years.
Number awarded: 1 or more each year.
Deadline: November of each year.

492 JENNICA FERGUSON MEMORIAL SCHOLARSHIP

National Federation of the Blind
c/o Peggy Elliott
Chair, Scholarship Committee
805 Fifth Avenue
Grinnell, IA 50112
Phone: (641) 236-3366
Web Site: www.nfb.org
Summary: To provide financial assistance to blind students studying or planning to study at the postsecondary level.

Eligibility: This program is open to legally blind students who are pursuing or planning to pursue an undergraduate or graduate course of study. Full-time enrollment is required. Selection is based on academic excellence, service to the community, and financial need.
Financial data: The stipend is $5,000.
Duration: 1 year; recipients may resubmit applications up to 2 additional years.
Additional information: Scholarships are awarded at the federation convention in July. Recipients attend the convention at federation expense; that funding is in addition to the scholarship grant.
Number awarded: 1 each year.
Deadline: March of each year.

493 JEROME B. STEINBACH SCHOLARSHIP

Oregon Student Assistance Commission
Attn: Private Awards Grant Department
1500 Valley River Drive, Suite 100
Eugene, OR 97401-2146
Phone: (541) 687-7395   (800) 452-8807, ext. 7395
Fax: (541) 687-7419   E-mail: awardinfo@mercury.osac.state.or.us
Web Site: www.osac.state.or.us
Summary: To provide financial assistance for college to residents of Oregon.
Eligibility: This program is open to residents of Oregon who are entering their sophomore or higher years in college. Applicants must have a cumulative grade point average of 3.5 or higher. U.S. citizenship is required.
Financial data: Scholarship amounts vary, depending upon the needs of the recipient.
Duration: 1 year.
Number awarded: Varies each year.
Deadline: February of each year.

494 JEROME L. HAUCK SCHOLARSHIP

Harness Horsemen International Foundation, Inc.
Bank Plaza Building
14 Main Street
Robbinsville, NJ 08691
Phone: (609) 259-3717   Fax: (609) 259-3778
Summary: To provide financial assistance to needy high school seniors or graduates who are related to a groom or a member of an affiliate of the Harness Horsemen International (HHI).
Eligibility: This program is open to the children of full-time grooms or the children of members of an HHI member association. Candidates must be either seniors at a public or private secondary school or high school graduates. Selection is based on financial need, extracurricular activities, community service, academic record, citizenship, leadership, character, and personality.
Financial data: The stipend is $1,000 per year.
Duration: 4 years (as long as the recipient remains a full-time student and maintains a cumulative grade point average of 2.0 or higher). Funds are paid directly to the recipient's college or university.
Number awarded: 1 each year.
Deadline: May of each year.

495 JERRY HARVEY ENDOWMENT SCHOLARSHIP

Epsilon Sigma Alpha
Attn: ESA Foundation Assistant Scholarship Director
P.O. Box 270517
Fort Collins, CO 80527
Phone: (970) 223-2824   Fax: (970) 223-4456
Web Site: www.esaintl.com/esaf
Summary: To provide financial assistance to students from Texas studying any major in college.
Eligibility: This program is open to residents of Texas who are either 1) graduating high school seniors in the top 25 percent of their class or with minimum scores of 20 on the ACT or 950 on the SAT, or 2) students already in college with a grade point average of 3.0 or higher. Students enrolled for training in a technical school or returning to school after an absence are also eligible. Selection is based on character, scholastic ability, leadership and ability skills, and financial need.
Financial data: The stipend is $1,500.
Duration: 1 year; may be renewed.

Additional information: Epsilon Sigma Alpha (ESA) is a women's service organization, but scholarships are available to both men and women. Information is also available from Verneene Forssberg, 403 South High, Pratt, KS 67124, (316) 672-3636, Fax: (316) 672-3688, E-mail: vernf@genmail.pcc.cc.ks.us. Completed applications must be submitted to the ESA State Counselor who verifies the information before forwarding them to the scholarship director.

Number awarded: 2 each year.

Deadline: January of each year.

496
JEWISH WAR VETERANS NATIONAL EDUCATIONAL GRANTS

Jewish War Veterans of the U.S.A.
1811 R Street, N.W.
Washington, DC 20009-1659
Phone: (202) 265-6280   Fax: (202) 234-5662
E-mail: jwv@erols.com
Web Site: www.penfed.com/jwv

Summary: To provide financial assistance for the postsecondary education of descendants of members of the Jewish War Veterans of the U.S.A.

Eligibility: Eligible to apply are children, grandchildren, and great-grandchildren of members or of deceased members of Jewish War Veterans in good standing who have been accepted by an accredited 4-year college or university or a 3-year hospital school of nursing as a freshman. Applicants must be high school seniors in the upper 25 percent of their class. The selection process emphasizes extracurricular activities at school, in the Jewish community, and in the community at large.

Financial data: First prize is the $1,000 Bernard Rotberg Memorial Scholarship; second prize is the $750 Louis S. Silvey Grant; third prize is $500.

Duration: 1 year; nonrenewable.

Number awarded: 3 each year.

Additional information: Applications must be submitted through your Jewish War Veterans' department commander.

Deadline: Applications must be submitted to the department commander by April of each year.

497
J.F. SCHIRMER SCHOLARSHIP

American Mensa Education and Research Foundation
1229 Corporate Drive West
Arlington, TX 76006-6103
Phone: (817) 607-0060   (800) 66-MENSA
Fax: (817) 649-5232   E-mail: Scholarships@merf.us.mensa.org
Web Site: merf.us.mensa.org

Summary: To provide financial assistance for postsecondary education to qualified students.

Eligibility: Any student who is enrolled or will enroll in a degree program at an accredited American institution of postsecondary education in the fall following the application deadline is eligible to apply. Membership in Mensa is not required, but applicants must be U.S. citizens or permanent residents. There are no restrictions as to age, race, gender, level of postsecondary education, or financial need. Selection is based on a 550-word essay that describes the applicant's career, vocational, or academic goals.

Financial data: The stipend is $1,000.

Duration: 1 year; may be renewed for up to 3 additional years if the recipient remains in school and achieves satisfactory grades.

Additional information: Applications are available only through participating Mensa local groups.

Number awarded: 1 each year.

Deadline: January of each year.

498
JIM COOK HONORARY SCHOLARSHIP

Aircraft Electronics Association
Attn: President
4217 South Hocker Drive
Independence, MO 64055-4723
Phone: (816) 373-6565   Fax: (816) 478-3100
E-mail: info@aea.net
Web Site: www.aea.net

Summary: To provide financial assistance for college to members of the Aircraft Electronics Association and their relatives.

Eligibility: This program is open to high school seniors, high school graduates, and currently-enrolled college students who are either members or the children, grandchildren, or other dependents of members of the Aircraft Electronics Association. The scholarship may be used for any field of study.

Financial data: The stipend is $1,500; funds must be used for tuition.

Duration: 1 year.

Additional information: This scholarship honors the first chair of the Aircraft Electronics Association Education Foundation.

Number awarded: 1 each year.

Deadline: February of each year.

499
JO ANNE J. TROW UNDERGRADUATE SCHOLARSHIPS

Alpha Lambda Delta
Attn: Executive Director
P.O. Box 4403
Macon, GA 31208-4403
Phone: (478) 301-4324   Fax: (478) 301-4387
E-mail: ald@mercer.edu
Web Site: www.mercer.edu/ald/trow_scholarship.htm

Summary: To provide financial assistance for undergraduate study to members of Alpha Lambda Delta.

Eligibility: This program is open to members who have a 3.5 cumulative grade point average or higher. Each chapter may submit 1 application (chapters initiating 150 to 299 members may submit 2 applicants and chapters initiating more than 300 members may submit 3 applicants). Each applicant must have been initiated during the previous calendar year. Selection is based on academic record, recommendations, the applicant's statements, and campus and community service activities.

Financial data: The stipend is $1,000.

Duration: 1 year; nonrenewable.

Additional information: Alpha Lambda Delta is a national society that honors academic excellence during a student's first year in college. This program began in 1988.

Number awarded: At least 26 each year.

Deadline: April of each year.

500
JOE FRANCOMANO SCHOLARSHIP

Junior Achievement
Attn: Scholarships/Education Team
One Education Way
Colorado Springs, CO 80906-4477
Phone: (719) 540-6255   Fax: (719) 540-6175
E-mail: dwatkins@ja.org
Web Site: www.ja.org

Summary: To provide financial assistance for college to high school seniors who have participated in the Junior Achievement program.

Eligibility: This program is open to graduating high school seniors with financial need who have participated in the Junior Achievement program. Their grade point average must be at least 3.0, and they must be able to demonstrate leadership and involvement in extracurricular and community activities. A personal essay (500 words) and 3 letters of recommendation are also required.

Financial data: The stipend is $5,000 per year.

Duration: 4 years.

Additional information: Recipients must attend a 4-year college or university.

Number awarded: 1 each year.

Deadline: January of each year.

501
JOE HARPER SCHOLARSHIP

California Correctional Peace Officers Association
755 Riverpoint Drive, Suite 200
West Sacramento, CA 95605-1634
Phone: (916) 372-6060
Web Site: www.ccpoa.org

Summary: To provide financial assistance to the members and the families of members of the California Correctional Peace Officers Association (CCPOA).

Eligibility: This program is open to the members, along with the sons, daughters, current spouses, mothers, fathers, brothers, and sisters of members, of the California Correctional Peace Officers Association. Both high school seniors and current college students are eligible. High school applicants must have at least a

Scholarship Listings

3.0 grade point average; college applicants must have at least a 3.5. An essay (750 words or less) is required on this topic: "My goals, present and future, and why I deserve this scholarship." Selection is based on academic record, school activities, financial need, and community service.

Financial data: Each year, the association distributes more than $100,000 in scholarship funds.

Duration: 1 year; may be renewed, if the recipient maintains at least a 3.5 grade point average in college.

Number awarded: Varies each year.

Deadline: April of each year.

502 JOE JAEGERS FAMILY ENDOWMENT SCHOLARSHIP

Epsilon Sigma Alpha
Attn: ESA Foundation Assistant Scholarship Director
P.O. Box 270517
Fort Collins, CO 80527
Phone: (970) 223-2824 Fax: (970) 223-4456
Web Site: www.esaintl.com/esaf
Summary: To provide financial assistance for college to students from any state studying any major.
Eligibility: Applicants may be either 1) graduating high school seniors in the top 25 percent of their class or with minimum scores of 20 on the ACT or 950 on the SAT, or 2) students already enrolled in college with a grade point average of 3.0 or higher. Students enrolled in a technical school or returning to school after an absence are also eligible. Selection is based on character, scholastic ability, leadership and ability skills, and financial need.
Financial data: The stipend is $1,000.
Duration: 1 year; may be renewed.
Additional information: Epsilon Sigma Alpha (ESA) is a women's service organization, but scholarships are available to both men and women. Information is also available from Verneene Forssberg, 403 South High, Pratt, KS 67124, (316) 672-3636, Fax: (316) 672-3688, E-mail: vernf@genmail.pcc.cc.ks.us. Completed applications must be submitted to the ESA State Counselor who verifies the information before forwarding them to the scholarship director.
Number awarded: 1 each year.
Deadline: January of each year.

503 JOHN B. LYNCH SCHOLARSHIP

John B. Lynch Scholarship Foundation
P.O. Box 4248
Wilmington, DE 19807-0248
Phone: (302) 654-3444
Summary: To provide financial assistance for college to students who reside or attend school in Delaware.
Eligibility: This program is open to 1) residents of Delaware, 2) students who live within 20 miles of Delaware, and 3) students who attend a high school, college, or university in Delaware. Applicants must have completed at least 1 semester of college with a grade point average of 2.75 or higher. If funding is available, graduating high school seniors may also be eligible if they have at least a 3.0 grade point average and an 1100 SAT score. All applicants must be younger than 30 years of age and attending or planning to attend college as a full-time undergraduate student.
Financial data: A stipend is awarded (exact amount not specified).
Duration: 1 year.
Number awarded: Varies each year.
Deadline: March of each year.

504 JOHN CORNELIUS/MAX ENGLISH MEMORIAL SCHOLARSHIP AWARD

Marine Corps Tankers Association
Attn: Phil Morell, Scholarship Chair
1112 Alpine Heights Road
Alpine, CA 91901-2814
Phone: (619) 445-8423 Fax: (619) 445-8423
Summary: To provide financial assistance for postsecondary education to members, survivors of members, or dependents of members of the Marine Corps Tanker Association.
Eligibility: This program is open to members, dependents of members, or survivors of members of the Marine Corps Tankers Association. Membership in the association is open to any person who is active duty, reserve, retired, or honorably discharged and was a member of, assigned to, attached to, or performed duty with any Marine Corps Tank Unit. Marine or Navy Corpsmen assigned to tank units are also eligible. Applicants must be high school seniors, high school graduates, undergraduate students, or graduate students who are enrolled or planning to enroll in any program of postsecondary education. Selection is based on academic record, school activities, leadership potential, community service, church involvement, and future plans. Financial need is also considered but is not a major factor.
Financial data: The stipend is $1,500.
Duration: 1 year; recipients may reapply.
Additional information: This program is also known as the Marine Corps Tankers Association Scholarship.
Number awarded: 8 to 12 each year.
Deadline: March of each year.

505 JOHN EDGAR THOMSON FOUNDATION AID

John Edgar Thomson Foundation
The Rittenhouse Claridge
201 South 18th Street, Suite 318
Philadelphia, PA 19103
Phone: (215) 545-6083 Fax: (215) 545-6083
Summary: To provide financial assistance to daughters of railroad employees who died while employed by a railroad in the United States.
Eligibility: This program is open to women whose parent died in the active employ of a railroad in the United States, although the cause of death need not be work related. Applicants must live in the home of the surviving parent or guardian (unless attending college full time and living on campus), be in good health, and receive satisfactory academic grades. Eligibility of the daughter is also dependent upon the parent's remaining unmarried. Consideration is given to other factors as well, including the financial status of the family.
Financial data: Payments are made on a monthly basis to assist with the education or maintenance of eligible daughters. The payment is available from infancy to age 18 or, under certain circumstances, to age 22 (for pursuit of higher education). This supplement to family income is to be used in its entirety for the benefit of the recipient. The grant may be terminated at any time if the financial need ceases or the daughter or surviving parent is either unable or fails to meet the eligibility requirements.
Duration: Monthly payments may be made up to 22 years.
Additional information: This foundation was established in 1882. Grantees are encouraged to participate in religious services of their faith.
Number awarded: Varies; generally, 100 or more each year.

506 JOHN H. LYONS, SR. SCHOLARSHIP PROGRAM

International Association of Bridge, Structural, Ornamental and Reinforcing Iron Workers
Attn: Scholarship Committee
1750 New York Avenue, N.W., Suite 400
Washington, DC 20006
Phone: (202) 383-4825
Summary: To provide financial assistance for postsecondary education to the children of members of the International Association of Bridge, Structural, Ornamental and Reinforcing Iron Workers.
Eligibility: Only sons and daughters of members of the union are eligible to apply for this program. Parents must have been members for at least 5 years or, if deceased, must have been in good standing at the time of death. The brother or sister of a recipient is not eligible to apply. Applicants must be seniors in high school and should rank in the upper half of their graduating class. Selection is based on academic standing, college entrance examination scores (SAT or ACT), extracurricular activities, leadership, character references, and citizenship.
Financial data: Up to $2,500 per year. Funds are paid directly to the recipients.
Duration: 1 year; may be renewed for up to 3 additional years.
Additional information: Winners may attend any accredited college or university in the United States or Canada. Winners must attend college on a full-time basis.
Number awarded: 2 each year.
Deadline: March of each year.

507
JOHN I. HAAS SCHOLARSHIP

John I. Haas, Inc.
1112 North 16th Avenue
P.O. Box 1441
Yakima, WA 98907
Phone: (509) 248-4187
Summary: To provide financial assistance for college to the children of farmers engaged in growing hops.
Eligibility: This program is open to graduating high school seniors who are the sons or daughters of families that operate a hop farm in any part of the United States. Applicants must submit an essay of 750 to 1,000 words on their long-term goals and what they have done and plan to do to achieve their goals. Selection is based on academic achievement (grade point average of 2.5 or higher), community and extracurricular activities, and the essay.
Financial data: The stipend is $5,000. Funds are prorated over the academic year (by quarter or semester) and paid to the winner or directly to the winner's school.
Duration: 1 year (the first year of college).
Number awarded: 1 each year.
Deadline: March of each year.

508
JOHN M. AZARIAN MEMORIAL ARMENIAN YOUTH SCHOLARSHIP

John M. Azarian Memorial Armenian Youth Scholarship Fund
c/o John M. Azarian, Jr.
Azarian Management and Development Company
6 Prospect Street, Suite 1B
Midland Park, NJ 07432
Phone: (201) 444-7111
Summary: To provide financial assistance for college to students of Armenian descent.
Eligibility: This program is open to U.S. citizens and permanent residents who are enrolled full time in an accredited college or university. Students must complete an application form and submit 2 letters of reference. Selection is based on financial need, merit, and involvement in the Armenian community.
Financial data: Stipends range from $500 to $3,000.
Duration: 1 year.
Number awarded: Varies each year; recently, 9 of these scholarships were awarded.
Deadline: April of each year.

509
JOHN W. MCDEVITT (FOURTH DEGREE) SCHOLARSHIPS

Knights of Columbus
Attn: Director of Scholarship Aid
P.O. Box 1670
New Haven, CT 06507-0901
Phone: (203) 772-2130, ext. 332   Fax: (203) 773-3000
Summary: To provide financial assistance to entering freshmen at Catholic colleges and universities.
Eligibility: Eligible are students entering their freshman year in a program leading to a baccalaureate degree at a Catholic college or university in the United States; applicants must be members in good standing of the Knights of Columbus, or the wife, widow, son, or daughter of a current member or of a deceased member who was in good standing at the time of death. Selection is based on secondary school record, class rank, and aptitude test scores.
Financial data: The scholarships are $1,500 per year.
Duration: 1 year; may be renewed up to 3 additional years upon evidence of satisfactory academic performance.
Number awarded: Approximately 36 each year.
Deadline: February of each year.

510
JORDAN SCHOLARSHIP FUND

International Council of Community Churches
21116 Washington Parkway
Frankfort, IL 60423-3112
Phone: (815) 464-5690   Fax: (815) 464-5692
E-mail: ICCC60423@aol.com

Summary: To provide financial assistance for college to members of a Community Church in good standing with the International Council of Community Churches.
Eligibility: This program is open to high school seniors and older adults seeking to further their education who are in need of financial assistance. Applicants must be active members of a Community Church in good standing with the International Council of Community Churches. They must submit an application form, proof of financial need, 2 letters of recommendation (1 must be from a pastor of a member church), grade transcripts, and a statement of education and career goals.
Financial data: The maximum stipend is $1,000.
Duration: 1 year.
Additional information: This fund was established in 1960 in memory of Helen Moucey Jordan, a major national leader in the Women's Christian Fellowship.
Number awarded: Several each year.

511
JOSE D. GARCIA MIGRANT EDUCATION PROGRAM SCHOLARSHIP

Oregon Student Assistance Commission
Attn: Private Awards Grant Department
1500 Valley River Drive, Suite 100
Eugene, OR 97401-2146
Phone: (541) 687-7395   (800) 452-8807, ext. 7395
Fax: (541) 687-7419   E-mail: awardinfo@mercury.osac.state.or.us
Web Site: www.osac.state.or.us
Summary: To provide financial assistance for college to students in Oregon who participated in a migrant education program.
Eligibility: This program is open to high school graduates and GED recipients who have participated in the Oregon Migrant Education Program and are planning to enroll at least half time in their freshman year of college. U.S. citizenship or permanent resident status is required.
Financial data: Scholarship amounts vary, depending upon need of the recipient.
Duration: 1 year; nonrenewable.
Number awarded: Varies each year.
Deadline: February of each year.

512
JOSI SCHOLARSHIP CHALLENGE GRANT FUND

Florida Department of Education
Attn: Office of Student Financial Assistance
1940 North Monroe Street, Suite 70
Tallahassee, FL 32303-4759
Phone: (850) 410-5185   (888) 827-2004
Fax: (850) 488-3612   E-mail: osfa@mail.doe.state.fl.us
Web Site: www.firn.edu/doe/osfa
Summary: To provide financial assistance to Hispanic American high school seniors and graduate students in Florida.
Eligibility: This program is open to Florida residents of Spanish culture who were born in, or whose natural parent was born in, Mexico, Spain, or a Hispanic country of the Caribbean, Central America, or South America. Applicants must be citizens or eligible noncitizens of the United States, enrolled or planning to enroll as full-time undergraduate or graduate students at an eligible postsecondary school in Florida, able to demonstrate financial need as determined by a nationally recognized needs analysis service, and have earned a cumulative grade point average of 3.0 or higher in high school or, if a graduate school applicant, in undergraduate course work.
Financial data: The grant is $2,000 per academic year. Available funds are contingent upon matching contributions from private sources.
Duration: 1 year; may be renewed if the student maintains full-time enrollment and a grade point average of 3.0 or higher and continues to demonstrate financial need.
Number awarded: Varies each year; recently, this program presented 98 awards.
Deadline: March of each year.

513
JOSEPH B. FERNANDES SCHOLARSHIP

Portuguese Heritage Scholarship Foundation
Attn: Academic Secretary
P.O. Box 30246
Bethesda, MD 20824-0246
Phone: (301) 652-2775   E-mail: phsf@vivaportugal.com
Web Site: www.vivaportugal.com/phsf/apply.htm

115

Summary: To provide financial assistance for college to students of Portuguese American heritage.

Eligibility: Eligible to apply for this support are high school seniors or currently-enrolled college students who are of Portuguese American ancestry. Applicants must be U.S. residents and attending or planning to attend an accredited 4-year college or university. Selection is based on academic achievement and financial need.

Financial data: The stipend is $2,000 per year.

Duration: 4 years, provided the recipient maintains a grade point average of 3.0 or higher.

Additional information: Recipients must attend college on a full-time basis.

Number awarded: 1 each year.

Deadline: January of each year.

514
JOSEPH K. LUMSDEN MEMORIAL SCHOLARSHIP

Sault Tribe
Attn: Higher Education Programs
531 Ashmun Street
Sault Ste. Marie, MI 49783
Phone: (906) 635-6050   Fax: (906) 635-4870
Web Site: www.saulttribe.org

Summary: To provide financial assistance to members of the Sault Tribe in Michigan who are upper-division or graduate students.

Eligibility: This program is open to members of the Sault Tribe who are college juniors or higher and are one-quarter Indian blood quantum or more. Applicants must be attending an accredited Michigan public college or university and have a cumulative grade point average of at least 3.0.

Financial data: The stipend is $1,000 per year.

Duration: 1 year; may be renewed.

Number awarded: 1 each year.

Deadline: February of each year.

515
JOSEPH P. GAVENONIS SCHOLARSHIPS

American Legion
Attn: Department of Pennsylvania
Attn: Scholarship Secretary
P.O. Box 2324
Harrisburg, PA 17105-2324
Phone: (717) 730-9100   Fax: (717) 975-2836
E-mail: hq@pa-legion.com
Web Site: www.pa-legion.com

Summary: To provide financial assistance for postsecondary education to the children of Pennsylvania Legionnaires.

Eligibility: This program is open to children of living members in good standing at an American Legion Post in Pennsylvania and to children of Pennsylvania American Legion members who are deceased, killed in action, or missing in action. Preference is given to children of members with the most continuous years of membership. Applicants must be entering a 4-year college or university in Pennsylvania; students who have already completed 1 year are not eligible.

Financial data: This scholarship is $1,000 annually.

Duration: 4 years, provided a satisfactory grade point average is maintained at the end of each semester.

Number awarded: 1 or more each year.

Deadline: May of each year.

516
JOSEPHINE DE KAN FELLOWSHIPS

Josephine De Kan Fellowship Trust
Attn: Judy McClain, Secretary
P.O. Box 3389
San Dimas, CA 91773
Phone: (909) 592-0607
Web Site: www.dekarman.org

Summary: To provide financial assistance to outstanding college seniors or students in their last year of a Ph.D. program.

Eligibility: This program is open to students in any discipline who will be entering their senior undergraduate year or their terminal year of a Ph.D. program in the fall of the next academic year. Postdoctoral students are not eligible. Foreign students may apply if they are already enrolled in a university in

the United States. Applicants must be able to demonstrate exceptional ability and seriousness of purpose. Special consideration is given to applicants in the humanities and to those who have completed their qualifying examinations for the doctoral degree.

Financial data: The stipend is $8,000 per year. Funds are paid in 2 installments to the recipient's school. No funds may be used for travel.

Duration: 1 year; may not be renewed or postponed.

Additional information: This fund was established in 1954 by Dr. Theodore von Kan, renowned aeronautics expert and director of the Guggenheim Aeronautical Laboratory at the California Institute of Technology. Study must be carried out in the United States.

Number awarded: Approximately 10 each year.

Deadline: December of each year.

517
JULIETTE M. ATHERTON SCHOLARSHIP

Hawai'i Community Foundation
900 Fort Street Mall, Suite 1300
Honolulu, HI 96813
Phone: (808) 566-5570   (888) 731-3863
Fax: (808) 521-6286   E-mail: scholarships@hcf-hawaii.org
Web Site: www.hcf-hawaii.org

Summary: To provide financial assistance for college to Protestants who are ministers, the dependents of ministers in Hawaii, or students preparing for the ministry.

Eligibility: This program is open to 1) the dependent sons or daughters of ordained and active Protestant ministers in an established denomination in Hawaii; 2) students planning to attend an accredited graduate school of theology with the goal of being ordained in an established Protestant denomination; 3) ordained Protestant ministers in an established denomination in Hawaii planning to pursue an advanced degree related to their ministerial profession; or 4) ordained Protestant ministers in an established denomination in Hawaii planning to pursue education in a field related to ministry through course work, workshops, or seminars. Applicants must be residents of the state of Hawaii, able to demonstrate financial need, interested in attending an accredited 2- or 4- year college or university as full-time students, and able to demonstrate academic achievement (2.7 grade point average or above).

Financial data: The amounts of the awards depend on the availability of funds and the need of the recipient; recently, grants averaged $2,100 per year.

Duration: 1 year.

Additional information: Recipients may attend school in Hawaii or on the mainland.

Number awarded: Varies each year; recently, 62 of these scholarships were awarded.

Deadline: February of each year.

518
JUNIOR ACHIEVEMENT OF MAINE SCHOLARSHIP

Junior Achievement of Maine, Inc.
Attn: Scholarship Committee
185 Lancaster Street, Suite 204
Portland, ME 04101
Phone: (207) 773-5200   Fax: (207) 773-4422

Summary: To provide financial assistance for college to high school seniors in Maine who have participated in Junior Achievement.

Eligibility: This program is open to high school seniors in Maine who have participated in a Junior Achievement program (including JA BASE, JA Economics, JA TITAN, JA Personal Finance) or taught a JA class in an elementary school. Applicants must also have applied to a 2-year, 4-year, or community college. Also eligible are college students currently enrolled at a 2-year, 4-year, or community college who have taught a JA program in the elementary or middle grades. Selection is based on academic accomplishments (at least a 2.5 grade point average), participation in the program, and short answers to 3 questions: what influence has Junior Achievement had on you and your future plans, why do you feel it is important to continue your education at the collegiate level, and where do you see yourself in 10 years?

Financial data: The stipend is $1,000.

Duration: 1 year.

Number awarded: 1 each year.

Deadline: March of each year.

519
JUNIOR AIR RIFLE NATIONAL CHAMPIONSHIP SCHOLARSHIPS

American Legion
Attn: Americanism and Children & Youth Division
P.O. Box 1055
Indianapolis, IN 46206-1055
Phone: (317) 630-1249   Fax: (317) 630-1223
E-mail: acy@legion.org
Web Site: www.legion.org
Summary: To provide college scholarships to the top competitors in the American Legion Junior Position Air Rifle Tournament.
Eligibility: This program is open to students between the ages of 14 and 20 who compete in air rifle tournaments sponsored by local posts of the American Legion. Based on posted scores in the precision and sporter categories, the top 30 competitors and state and regional champions compete in a qualification round, also a postal tournament. The top 15 shooters then participate in a shoulder-to-shoulder match in August at the Olympic Training Center, Colorado Springs, Colorado.
Financial data: The awards are $1,000 college scholarships.
Duration: The awards are presented annually.
Number awarded: 2 each year: 1 in the precision category and 1 in the sporter category.

520
KAE SUMNER EINFELDT SCHOLARSHIP AWARD

Tall Clubs International
1583 East Silver Star Road
P.O. Box 256
Ocoee, FL 34761
Phone: (888) I-M-TALL-2   E-mail: tci-admin@tall.org
Web Site: www.tall.org
Summary: To provide financial assistance for college to high school seniors and current college students who meet the minimum height requirements of the Tall Clubs International (TCI).
Eligibility: This program is open to 1) graduating high school seniors who will be attending a 2-year or 4-year college or university, and 2) students currently attending a 2-year or 4-year institution of higher learning who are younger than 21 years of age. Applicants must live within a geographic area served by a participating TCI and must meet the minimum TCI height requirements: 5'10" for females and 6'2" for males. Applications must be submitted to the local TCI club, which nominates the most outstanding applicant for the national competition. Selection is based on academic record and achievements, involvement in school clubs and activities, personal achievements, volunteer activities, and an essay on "What being tall means to me."
Financial data: The stipend is $1,000.
Duration: 1 year.
Additional information: Local TCI clubs may also award scholarships.
Number awarded: 2 or 3 each year.
Deadline: Local clubs must submit their nominations by May of each year.

521
KAGRO FOUNDATION SCHOLARSHIPS

Korean American Grocers Association of California
Attn: KAGRO Foundation
3727 West Sixth Street, Suite 402
Los Angeles, CA 90020
Phone: (213) 380-3771   Fax: (213) 380-3772
Summary: To provide financial assistance to students in the areas where members of the KAGRO Foundation conduct their business.
Eligibility: Applicants must be residents of California who are between their junior year in high school and their senior year in an accredited college or university. Selection is based on scholastic achievement, citizenship and community involvement, future potential, and financial need.
Financial data: The amount awarded varies, depending upon the needs of the recipient.
Duration: 1 year.
Additional information: The KAGRO Foundation was established by the Korean American Grocers Association of California. Most of its members are located in southern California.
Number awarded: 1 or more each year.
Deadline: August of each year.

522
KAMEHAMEHA SCHOOLS FINANCIAL AID

Ke Ali'i Pauahi Foundation
Attn: Financial Aid & Scholarship Services
1887 Makuakane Street
Honolulu, HI 96817-1887
Phone: (808) 842-8216   (800) 842-4682, ext. 8216
Fax: (808) 841-0660   E-mail: finaid@ksbe.edu
Web Site: www.pauahi.org
Summary: To provide financial assistance to Native Hawaiians who are interested in pursuing postsecondary education.
Eligibility: Native Hawaiians (or part Hawaiians) who have graduated from high school in Hawaii are eligible to apply if they can demonstrate academic excellence and financial need. They must be pursuing undergraduate or graduate degrees at accredited 2-year or 4-year colleges in Hawaii; graduate students may attend out-of-state schools if their major field of study is not available in Hawaii. Students who graduated from the Kamehameha Schools are not eligible to apply.
Financial data: The amount awarded varies, depending upon the financial need of the recipient; recently, the average award was $3,200.
Duration: 1 year; may be renewed.
Additional information: For the purposes of this program, "Native Hawaiian" means any descendant of the aboriginal inhabitants of the Hawaiian islands prior to 1778.
Number awarded: Varies each year; recently, 1,630 students received these scholarships.
Deadline: February of each year.

523
KANSAS COMPREHENSIVE GRANTS

Kansas Board of Regents
Attn: Student Financial Aid
1000 S.W. Jackson Street, Suite 520
Topeka, KS 66612-1368
Phone: (785) 296-3518   Fax: (785) 296-0983
E-mail: dlindeman@ksbor.org
Web Site: www.kansasregents.com/students/financial_aid/awards.html
Summary: To provide need-based grants to Kansas residents who are attending college in the state.
Eligibility: This program is open to residents of Kansas who are enrolled full time at 1) the 17 private colleges and universities located in the state, 2) the 6 public universities, or 3) Washburn University. Financial need must be demonstrated.
Financial data: Stipends range from $200 to $3,000 per year at the private institutions and from $100 to $1,100 at the public institutions.
Duration: 1 year; may be renewed as long as the recipient remains in academic "good standing" and is able to demonstrate financial need.
Additional information: There is a $10 application fee.
Number awarded: Varies; generally, 7,000 or more each year. The funding level allows about 1 in 3 eligible students to be assisted.
Deadline: March of each year.

524
KANSAS EDUCATIONAL BENEFITS FOR DEPENDENTS OF POWS/KIAS/MIAS OF THE VIETNAM WAR

Kansas Commission on Veterans' Affairs
Jayhawk Towers
700 S.W. Jackson Street, Suite 701
Topeka, KS 66603-3150
Phone: (785) 296-3976   Fax: (785) 296-1462
E-mail: KVH007@ink.org
Web Site: www.kcva.org
Summary: To provide financial assistance for postsecondary education to children of Kansas veterans who were prisoners of war or killed in Vietnam.
Eligibility: Applicants for these benefits may be residents of any state as long as their veteran parent was a legal resident of Kansas upon entering military service and, while serving in Vietnam after January 1, 1960, either died of service-connected causes or was declared by the Secretary of Defense to be a prisoner of war or missing in action.
Financial data: Eligible dependents receive free tuition and fees at any Kansas state-supported college, university, community college, or area vocational school.
Duration: Up to 12 semesters.
Number awarded: Varies each year.

525
KANSAS ETHNIC MINORITY SCHOLARSHIP PROGRAM

Kansas Board of Regents
Attn: Student Financial Aid
1000 S.W. Jackson Street, Suite 520
Topeka, KS 66612-1368
Phone: (785) 296-3518   Fax: (785) 296-0983
E-mail: dlindeman@ksbor.org
Web Site: www.kansasregents.com/students/financial_aid/minority.html
Summary: To provide financial assistance to minority students who are interested in attending college in Kansas.
Eligibility: Eligible to apply are Kansas residents who fall into 1 of these minority groups: American Indian, Alaskan Native, African American, Asian, Pacific Islander, or Hispanic. Applicants may be current college students (enrolled in community colleges, colleges, or universities in Kansas), but high school seniors graduating in the current year receive priority consideration. Minimum academic requirements include 1 of the following: 1) ACT score of 21 or higher or SAT score of 816 or higher; 2) cumulative grade point average of 3.0 or higher; 3) high school rank in upper one third; 4) completion of the Regents Scholars Curriculum (4 years of English, 3 years of mathematics, 3 years of science, 3 years of social studies, and 2 years of foreign language); 5) selection by National Merit Corporation in any category; or 6) selection by College Board as a Hispanic Scholar.
Financial data: A stipend of up to $1,850 is provided, depending on financial need and availability of state funds.
Duration: 1 year; may be renewed for up to 3 additional years (4 additional years for designated 5-year programs) if the recipient maintains a 2.0 cumulative grade point average and has financial need.
Additional information: There is a $10 application fee.
Number awarded: Approximately 200 each year.
Deadline: March of each year.

526
KANSAS STATE SCHOLARSHIP

Kansas Board of Regents
Attn: Student Financial Aid
1000 S.W. Jackson Street, Suite 520
Topeka, KS 66612-1368
Phone: (785) 296-3518   Fax: (785) 296-0983
E-mail: dlindeman@ksbor.org
Web Site: www.kansasregents.com/students/financial_aid/state.html
Summary: To provide need-based assistance to students who are in the top 20 to 40 percent of their high school class in Kansas and planning to go on to college.
Eligibility: High school seniors in Kansas are selected for this program on the basis of ACT Assessment scores, completion of the Regents Scholars Curriculum (4 years of English, 3 years of mathematics, 3 years of science, 3 years of social studies, and 2 years of foreign language), and academic record. Financial need must be documented.
Financial data: The stipend ranges up to $1,000 per year, depending upon the recipient's needs.
Duration: Up to 4 academic years (unless enrolled in a designated 5-year program) as long as the recipient maintains a 3.0 grade point average and financial need.
Additional information: The school the recipient listed first in the school section of the Free Application for Federal Student Aid will be notified by the Board of Regents that the student has been funded. The award will be listed in the financial aid letter the school sends the recipient. There is a $10 application fee. Recipients must attend school, full time, in Kansas.
Number awarded: Varies; generally, at least 1,200 each year. Usually, between 35 and 40 percent of high school seniors who complete the Regents Scholars Curriculum are designated as Kansas State Scholars.
Deadline: April of each year.

527
KAPLAN/NEWSWEEK "MY TURN" ESSAY CONTEST

Kaplan, Inc.
Attn: Community Outreach Director
888 Seventh Avenue
New York, NY 10106
Phone: (800) KAP-TEST
Summary: To recognize and reward high school students who write outstanding essays on topics related to their personal development and growth.

Eligibility: This program is open to U.S. high school students planning to attend college after graduation. Applicants must write an essay of 500 to 1,000 words that shares an opinion, experience, or personal feeling. Selection is based on 1) effectiveness, insight, creativity, and completeness; 2) organization and development of the ideas expressed, with clear and appropriate examples to support them; and 3) consistency in the use of language, variety in sentence structure and range of vocabulary, and use of proper grammar, spelling, and punctuation.
Financial data: The first-place winner receives $5,000; the second-place winner receives $2,000; and the third-place winners receive $1,000.
Duration: The contest is held annually.
Additional information: This contest is co-sponsored by Kaplan, Inc. and *Newsweek* Magazine.
Number awarded: 10 each year: 1 first-place winner, 1 second-place winner, and 8 third-place winners.
Deadline: March 1 of each year.

528
KAREN B. LEWIS CAREER EDUCATION SCHOLARSHIP

Virginia Business and Professional Women's Foundation
P.O. Box 4842
McLean, VA 22103-4842
E-mail: bpwva@advocate.net
Web Site: www.bpwva.advocate.net/foundation.htm
Summary: To provide financial assistance to girls and women pursuing postsecondary job-oriented career education (in business, trade, or industrial occupations) in Virginia.
Eligibility: This program is open to women who are at least 18 years of age, are U.S. citizens and Virginia residents, have been accepted into an accredited training program in Virginia, have a definite plan to use their education in a business, trade, or industrial occupation, and are able to demonstrate financial need.
Financial data: Scholarships range from $100 to $1,000 per year; funds may be used for tuition, fees, books, transportation, living expenses, and dependent care.
Duration: Funds must be used within 12 months. Prior recipients may reapply, but they are not given priority.
Number awarded: At least 1 is awarded each year.
Deadline: March, June, or December of each year.

529
KATHERINE VAZ SCHOLARSHIP

Luso-American Education Foundation
Attn: Administrative Director
7080 Donlon Way, Suite 202
P.O. Box 2967
Dublin, CA 94568
Phone: (925) 828-3883   Fax: (925) 828-3883
Web Site: www.luso-american.org/laefx
Summary: To provide financial assistance for undergraduate study to members of the Luso-American community who are deaf or interested in studying writing.
Eligibility: This program is open to college and high school students with a connection to the Portuguese community in America. Applicants must be either deaf or interested in studying writing.
Financial data: The stipend is $1,000.
Duration: 1 year; renewable.
Number awarded: 1 each year.
Deadline: February of each year.

530
KAY/MOORE SCHOLARSHIP FOR YOUNG ADULTS WITH CANCER

Special Love, Inc.
117 Youth Development Court
Winchester, VA 22602
Phone: (540) 667-3774   (888) 930-2707
Fax: (540) 667-8144
Web Site: www.speciallove.org
Summary: To provide financial assistance for college to students who have undergone or are undergoing cancer treatments.
Eligibility: This program is open to high school seniors and currently-enrolled college students who have undergone or are undergoing cancer treatments. Priority is given to applicants who have participated in Special Love programs

(although participation is not mandatory for consideration). Selection is based on academic potential and financial need.
Financial data: The stipend is either $2,000 or $1,000, paid in 2 equal installments. Funds are paid directly to the recipient's school.
Duration: 1 year.
Number awarded: 25 each year: 20 at $1,000 and 5 at $2,000.
Deadline: May of each year.

531
KENJI KAJIWARA MEMORIAL SCHOLARSHIP

Japanese American Citizens League
Attn: National Scholarship Awards
1765 Sutter Street
San Francisco, CA 94115
Phone: (415) 921-5225   Fax: (415) 931-4671
E-mail: jacl@jacl.org
Web Site: www.jacl.org
Summary: To provide financial assistance to student members of the Japanese American Citizens League (JACL) who are pursuing undergraduate education.
Eligibility: This program is open to JACL members who are currently enrolled or planning to reenter a college, university, trade school, business college, or other institution of higher learning. Selection is based on academic record, extracurricular activities, and community involvement.
Financial data: The stipend depends on the availability of funds but usually ranges from $1,000 to $5,000.
Duration: 1 year.
Additional information: Requests for applications must be accompanied by a self-addressed stamped envelope.
Number awarded: At least 1 each year.
Deadline: March of each year.

532
KENJI KASAI MEMORIAL SCHOLARSHIP

Japanese American Citizens League
Attn: National Scholarship Awards
1765 Sutter Street
San Francisco, CA 94115
Phone: (415) 921-5225   Fax: (415) 931-4671
E-mail: jacl@jacl.org
Web Site: www.jacl.org
Summary: To provide financial assistance to student members of the Japanese American Citizens League (JACL) who are high school seniors interested in pursuing undergraduate education.
Eligibility: This program is open to JACL members who are high school seniors interested in attending a college, university, trade school, business college, or other institution of higher learning. Selections is based on academic record, extracurricular activities, and community involvement.
Financial data: The stipend depends on the availability of funds but usually ranges from $1,000 to $5,000.
Duration: 1 year.
Additional information: Requests for applications must be accompanied by a self-addressed stamped envelope.
Number awarded: At least 1 each year.
Deadline: March of each year.

533
KENNETH JERNIGAN SCHOLARSHIP

National Federation of the Blind
c/o Peggy Elliott
Chair, Scholarship Committee
805 Fifth Avenue
Grinnell, IA 50112
Phone: (641) 236-3366
Web Site: www.nfb.org
Summary: To provide financial assistance to blind students studying or planning to study at the postsecondary level.
Eligibility: This program is open to legally blind students who are pursuing or planning to pursue a full-time undergraduate or graduate course of study. Selection is based on academic excellence, service to the community, and financial need.
Financial data: The stipend is $10,000.

Duration: 1 year; recipients may resubmit applications up to 2 additional years.
Additional information: Scholarships are awarded at the federation convention in July. Recipients attend the convention at federation expense; that funding is in addition to the scholarship grant. This scholarship is given by the American Action Fund for Blind Children and Adults, a nonprofit organization that assists blind people.
Number awarded: 1 each year.
Deadline: March of each year.

534
KENTUCKY COLLEGE ACCESS PROGRAM GRANTS

Kentucky Higher Education Assistance Authority
Attn: Student Aid Branch
West Frankfort Office Complex
1050 U.S. Highway 127 South, Suite 102
Frankfort, KY 40601-4323
Phone: (502) 696-7394   (800) 928-8926, ext. 7394
Fax: (502) 696-7373   TTY: (800) 855-2880
E-mail: mwells@kheaa.com
Web Site: www.kheaa.com/prog_cap.html
Summary: To provide financial assistance to college students in Kentucky who have financial need.
Eligibility: This program is open to Kentucky residents enrolled in 2-year or 4-year public or private nonprofit colleges, proprietary schools, or vocational-technical schools for a minimum of 6 semester hours in an academic program that takes at least 2 years to complete. Applicants must be able to demonstrate financial need (the total expected family contribution toward educational expenses cannot exceed $3,550). Students majoring in divinity, theology, or religious education are not eligible.
Financial data: The maximum stipend is $1,260 per year. Eligible part-time college students receive an award calculated at the rate of $53 per credit hour.
Duration: Students at 2-year schools may receive the equivalent of 5 semesters of grants; students at 4-year schools may receive the equivalent of 9 semesters of grants.
Number awarded: Varies each year; awards are made to eligible students until funds are depleted. Recently, approximately 45,000 students received these grants.
Deadline: Applications may be submitted at any time, but students who file by March of each year have the best chance of receiving funds.

535
KENTUCKY DECEASED OR DISABLED LAW ENFORCEMENT OFFICER AND FIRE FIGHTER DEPENDENT TUITION WAIVER

Kentucky Fire Commission
Attn: Executive Director
2750 Research Park Drive—Barn Annex
P.O. Box 14092
Lexington, KY 40512-4092
Phone: (859) 246-3483   (800) 782-6823
Fax: (859) 246-3484   E-mail: larry.collier@kctcs.net
Web Site: www.kctcs.net/firecommission/index.htm
Summary: To provide financial assistance for college to the children and spouses of Kentucky police officers or fire fighters deceased or disabled in the line of duty.
Eligibility: This program is open to spouses, widow(er)s, and children of Kentucky residents who became a law enforcement officer, fire fighter, or volunteer fire fighter and who 1) was killed while in active service or training for active service; 2) died as a result of a service-connected disability; or 3) became permanently and totally disabled as a result of active service or training for active service. Children must be younger than 23 years of age; spouses and widow(er)s may be of any age.
Financial data: Recipients are entitled to a waiver of tuition at state-supported universities, community colleges, and technical training institutions in Kentucky.
Duration: 1 year; may be renewed up to a maximum total of 36 months.
Number awarded: Varies each year; all qualified applicants are entitled to this aid.

536
KENTUCKY EDUCATIONAL EXCELLENCE SCHOLARSHIPS

Kentucky Higher Education Assistance Authority
Attn: Student Aid Branch
West Frankfort Office Complex
1050 U.S. Highway 127 South, Suite 102
Frankfort, KY 40601-4323
Phone: (502) 696-7397   (800) 928-8926, ext. 7397
Fax: (502) 696-7373   TTY: (800) 855-2880
E-mail: kees@kheaa.com

Web Site: www.kheaa.com/keeshome.html

Summary: To provide financial assistance for college to Kentucky residents who achieve high grade point averages and ACT scores in high school.

Eligibility: This program is open to Kentucky high school students who achieve at least a 2.5 grade point average each year in high school and a score of at least 15 on the ACT (or SAT equivalent). Students must graduate from a high school in Kentucky and fulfill the state's core curriculum requirements. They must attend an accredited public or private institution in Kentucky, including community and technical colleges.

Financial data: For each year in high school that students achieve at least a 2.5 grade point average, they receive at least $125 per year for college. Higher grade point averages mean larger scholarships, rising to $500 per year for a 4.0 grade point average. In addition, students receive a bonus award based on their best ACT score, starting at $36 for 15 and rising to $500 for a score of 28 or higher. The maximum potential award is $2,500 per year of college for a student who achieves a 4.0 grade point average for each of 4 years of high school (thus earning an annual college scholarship of $2,000—$500 for each of the years with a 4.0 grade point average) plus a bonus of $500 for an ACT score of 28 or higher.

Duration: Up to 4 years, provided the recipient earns at least a 2.5 grade point average during the first year of college and at least a 3.0 during each succeeding year. In those last 3 years, a student whose grade point average falls below 3.0 but remains 2.5 or higher will receive only 50 percent of their scholarship award for the next academic year; a student whose grade point average falls below 2.5 will lose the scholarship for the next award period. Eligibility is restored if the student reestablishes at least a 2.5 grade point average. Students in designated programs that require 5 years for a bachelor's degree (architecture, landscape architecture, and engineering) are entitled to 5 years of support from this program.

Additional information: This program began in the 1998-99 academic year. Grades earned prior to that year are not considered so graduates that year could use only their senior-year grades to establish a scholarship, the class of 2000 could use 2 years, and the class of 2001 3 years. The class of 2002 is the first in which students can earn the maximum award with 4 years of high school grades considered. Students who do achieve 4.0 grade averages for all 4 years of high school and an ACT score of 28 or higher are designated Jeff Green Scholars. Scholarships must be used within 5 years of high school graduation. Part-time students at Kentucky colleges and universities receive only a proportionate amount of the award they earned while in high school.

Number awarded: Varies each year; all students who qualify receive awards. In a recent year, 19,931 students qualified for scholarships.

537
KENTUCKY TUITION GRANTS

Kentucky Higher Education Assistance Authority
Attn: Student Aid Branch
West Frankfort Office Complex
1050 U.S. Highway 127 South, Suite 102
Frankfort, KY 40601-4323
Phone: (502) 696-7394   (800) 928-8926, ext. 7394
Fax: (502) 696-7373   TTY: (800) 855-2880
E-mail: mwells@kheaa.com
Web Site: www.kheaa.com/prog_ktg.html

Summary: To provide financial assistance to Kentucky residents who are attending independent colleges in the state.

Eligibility: This program is open to Kentucky residents enrolled in eligible Kentucky independent nonprofit institutions as full-time undergraduate students in eligible courses of study. They must be able to demonstrate financial need. Programs in divinity, theology, or religious education are not eligible.

Financial data: Awards range from $200 to $1,800 per academic year.

Duration: Students at 2-year schools may receive the equivalent of 5 semesters of grants; students at 4-year schools may receive the equivalent of 9 semesters of grants.

Number awarded: Varies each year; awards are made to eligible students until funds are depleted. Recently, approximately 14,600 students received these grants.

Deadline: Applications may be submitted at any time, but students who file by March of each year have the best chance of receiving funds.

538
KENTUCKY VETERANS TUITION WAIVER PROGRAM

Kentucky Department of Veterans Affairs
Attn: Division of Field Operations
545 South Third Street, Room 123
Louisville, KY 40202
Phone: (502) 595-4447   (800) 928-4012 (within KY)
Fax: (502) 595-4448

Web Site: www.kvc.state.ky.us/agencies/finance/depts/kvc/index.htm

Summary: To provide financial assistance for postsecondary education to the children, spouses, or unremarried widow(er)s of disabled or deceased Kentucky veterans.

Eligibility: This program is open to the children, stepchildren, adopted children, spouses, and unremarried widow(er)s of veterans who are residents of Kentucky (or were residents at the time of their death). The qualifying veteran must meet 1 of the following conditions: 1) died on active duty; 2) died as a direct result of a service-connected disability (as determined by the U.S. Department of Veterans Affairs); 3) has a 100 percent service-connected disability; 4) is totally disabled from a non-service connected cause but has wartime service; 5) died after service during a wartime period; or 6) was a prisoner of war or declared missing in action. The military service may have been as a member of the U.S. armed forces, the Kentucky National Guard while on state active duty, or a Reserve component on active duty. Children of veterans must be between 17 and 23 years of age; no age limit applies to spouses or unremarried widow(er)s. All applicants must be attending or planning to attend a 2-year, 4-year, or vocational-technical school operated and funded by the Kentucky Department of Education.

Financial data: Eligible dependents and survivors are exempt from tuition and matriculation fees at any state-supported institution of higher education in Kentucky.

Duration: Tuition is waived when the recipient completes 36 months of training, receives a college degree, or (in the case of children of veterans) reaches 23 years of age, whichever comes first. Spouses and unremarried widow(er)s are not subject to the age limitation.

Number awarded: Varies each year.

539
KERMIT B. NASH ACADEMIC SCHOLARSHIP

Sickle Cell Disease Association of America, Inc.
Attn: Scholarship Committee
200 Corporate Pointe, Suite 495
Culver City, CA 90230-8727
Phone: (310) 216-6363   (800) 421-8453
Fax: (310) 215-3722
Web Site: www.sicklecelldisease.org

Summary: To provide financial assistance for college to graduating high school seniors who have sickle cell disease.

Eligibility: This program is open to graduating high school seniors who have sickle cell disease (not the trait). Applicants must have a grade point average of 3.0 or higher. They must submit a personal essay, up to 1,000 words, on an aspect of the impact of the disease on their lives or on society. Selection is based on grade point average, general academic achievement and promise, SAT scores, leadership and community service, severity of academic challenges and obstacles posed by sickle cell disease, and the quality of their essay.

Financial data: The stipend is $5,000 per year.

Duration: Up to 4 years.

Additional information: The Sickle Cell Disease Association of America (SCDAA) was formerly the National Association for Sickle Cell Disease. Requests for applications must be submitted in writing; telephone requests are not honored.

Number awarded: 1 each year.

540
KEVIN CHILD SCHOLARSHIP

National Hemophilia Foundation
Attn: Administration Department
116 West 32nd Street, 11th Floor
New York, NY 10001
Phone: (212) 328-3700   (800) 42-HANDI
Fax: (212) 328-3777   E-mail: info@hemophilia.org
Web Site: www.hemophilia.org

Summary: To provide financial assistance for postsecondary education to students with hemophilia.

Eligibility: This program is open to students entering their first year of undergraduate study as well as those currently enrolled in college. Applicants must have hemophilia or another bleeding disorder.

Financial data: The stipend is $1,000 or $500.

Duration: 1 year.

Additional information: The program was established by the Child family after the death of 21-year old Kevin in 1989.

Number awarded: 2 each year: 1 at $1,000 and 1 at $500.

Deadline: June of each year.

541
KEY CLUB/SIGMA PHI EPSILON BALANCED MAN SCHOLARSHIP

Key Club International
Attn: Manager of Youth Funds
3636 Woodview Trace
Indianapolis, IN 46268-3196
Phone: (317) 875-8755, ext. 244   (800) KIWANIS, ext. 244
Fax: (317) 879-0204   E-mail: youthfunds@kiwanis.org
Web Site: www.keyclub.org
Summary: To provide financial assistance for college to high school senior men who are Key Club International members.
Eligibility: This program is open to male members of Key Club International who are college-bound graduating high school seniors with a grade point average of 3.0 or higher. Applicants must have demonstrated leadership ability, have demonstrated service to a community-service organization, have some athletic experience (varsity, intramural, or recreational), and intend to enroll in a 4-year college or university. Financial need is not considered in the selection process.
Financial data: The stipend is $2,500.
Duration: 1 year.
Additional information: This award is sponsored by Sigma Phi Epsilon but there is no expectation, written or implied, that the recipient will affiliate with that fraternity.
Number awarded: 2 each year.
Deadline: April of each year.

542
KIDS' CHANCE OF WEST VIRGINIA SCHOLARSHIPS

Greater Kanawha Valley Foundation
Attn: Scholarship Coordinator
One Huntington Square, 16th Floor
900 Lee Street, East
P.O. Box 3041
Charleston, WV 25331-3041
Phone: (304) 346-3620   Fax: (304) 346-3640
E-mail: tgkvf@tgkvf.com
Web Site: www.tgkvf.com/scholarship.html
Summary: To provide financial assistance for college to students whose parents were injured in a West Virginia work-related accident.
Eligibility: This program is open to children between the ages of 16 and 25 whose parents were seriously injured in a West Virginia work-related accident. Applicants may reside in any state and be pursuing any field of study at an accredited trade or vocational school, college, or university. They must have at least a 2.5 grade point average and demonstrate good moral character. Preference is given to applicants who can demonstrate financial need, academic excellence, leadership abilities, and contributions to school and community.
Financial data: The stipend is $1,000 per year.
Duration: 1 year; may be renewed.
Additional information: This program is sponsored by Kids' Chance of West Virginia, Inc.
Number awarded: 3 each year.
Deadline: February of each year.

543
KIMMY MEDALLION SCHOLARSHIPS

The Charter Fund
Attn: Jeanette Montoya
370 17th Street, Suite 5300
Denver, CO 80202
Phone: (303) 572-1727   Fax: (303) 628-3839
Summary: To provide financial assistance for postsecondary education to financially needy residents of Colorado.
Eligibility: These scholarships are available to residents of Colorado who can demonstrate financial need. Applicants must be entering freshmen at an accredited institution studying any field. Selection is based on academic achievement, creativity, compassion, and character.
Financial data: Awards range from $2,500 to $5,000.
Duration: 1 year; nonrenewable.
Number awarded: Several each year.
Deadline: May of each year.

544
KING OR QUEEN OF BRIDGE SCHOLARSHIP

American Contract Bridge League
Attn: Director of Junior Programs
2990 Airways Boulevard
Memphis, TN 38116-3847
Phone: (901) 332-5586   Fax: (901) 398-7754
E-mail: Harley.Bress@acbl.org
Web Site: www.acbl.org
Summary: To recognize and reward outstanding Junior Corps members of the American Contract Bridge League.
Eligibility: This program is open to Junior Corps members who are graduating high school seniors. Selection is based on outstanding tournament performance, as well as excellence in bridge-related administrative, recreational, and promotional activities.
Financial data: The award is a $1,000 scholarship.
Duration: The award is presented annually.
Additional information: Funding for this program is provided by the Homer Shoop International Palace of Sports.
Number awarded: 1 each year.

545
KITTIE M. FAIREY EDUCATIONAL FUND SCHOLARSHIP PROGRAM

The Foundation Scholarship Program
Attn: Kittie M. Fairey Educational Fund Scholarship Program
P.O. Box 1465
Taylors, SC 29687-1465
Phone: (864) 268-3363   Fax: (864) 268-7160
E-mail: fssp@infi.net
Web Site: www.scholarshipprograms.org/fsp_kittiefairey.html
Summary: To provide financial assistance to high school seniors in South Carolina who are interested in attending college in the state.
Eligibility: This program is open to seniors enrolled in a South Carolina high school. Applicants must have a grade point average of 3.0 or higher, have a combined SAT score of 900 or higher, be planning to attend an accredited college or university in the state full time, and come from a family whose adjusted gross income is not more than $40,000. Selection is based on academic achievement and financial need.
Financial data: Awards are limited to up to half of the standard fees of the institutions for room, board, and tuition for students living on campus. Students living off campus are eligible for up to half of tuition costs. Payment is made directly to the college or university.
Duration: 1 year; may be renewed up to 3 additional years.
Number awarded: 1 or more each year.
Deadline: February of each year.

546
KOLSTAD AWARD

Soaring Society of America, Inc.
P.O. Box 2100
Hobbs, NM 88241-2100
Phone: (505) 392-1177   Fax: (505) 392-8154
E-mail: info@ssa.org
Web Site: www.ssa.org
Summary: To provide financial assistance for college to members of the Soaring Society of America (SSA).
Eligibility: To be eligible for this grant for academic studies, pilots must be SSA members between the ages of 14 and 20 who have earned the FAI Silver Badge or the SSA Century I, Century II, or Century III award. Applicants must submit a completed application form, a summary of their cross-country flights, a statement of their educational plans, and complete documentation of their service to the club.
Financial data: The stipend is $1,250.
Duration: 1 year.
Additional information: The Century I award requires cross-country flight of 100 km (62.1 miles), Century II requires 200 km (124.2 miles), and Century II required 300 km (186.3 miles).
Number awarded: 2 each year.
Deadline: September of each year.

547
KOREAN UNIVERSITY CLUB SCHOLARSHIP

Korean University Club
c/o Martha C. Im
1608 Laukahi Street
Honolulu, HI 96821
Summary: To provide financial assistance to Korean Americans in Hawaii who are interested in working on a college degree.
Eligibility: Applicants must be high school seniors/graduates, U.S. citizens, residents of Hawaii, and at least part Korean. They must be able to demonstrate financial need.
Financial data: The stipend is $1,400 per year.
Duration: 4 years.
Additional information: Recipients may attend either a 2-year college (if they plan to transfer to a 4-year college/university) or a 4-year college/university in Hawaii.
Number awarded: 1 each year.
Deadline: March of each year.

548
KUCHLER-KILLIAN MEMORIAL SCHOLARSHIP

National Federation of the Blind
c/o Peggy Elliott
Chair, Scholarship Committee
805 Fifth Avenue
Grinnell, IA 50112
Phone: (641) 236-3366
Web Site: www.nfb.org
Summary: To provide financial assistance for undergraduate or graduate study to legally blind students.
Eligibility: This program is open to legally blind students who are pursuing or planning to pursue a full-time undergraduate or graduate course of study. Selection is based on academic excellence, service to the community, and financial need.
Financial data: The stipend is $3,000.
Duration: 1 year; recipients may resubmit applications up to 2 additional years.
Additional information: Scholarships are awarded at the federation convention in July. Recipients attend the convention at federation expense; that funding is in addition to the scholarship grant.
Number awarded: 1 each year.
Deadline: March of each year.

549
KUKUI, INC. SCHOLARSHIP FUND

Ke Ali'i Pauahi Foundation
Attn: Financial Aid & Scholarship Services
1887 Makuakane Street
Honolulu, HI 96817-1887
Phone: (808) 842-8216   (800) 842-4682, ext. 8216
Fax: (808) 841-0660   E-mail: finaid@ksbe.edu
Web Site: www.pauahi.org
Summary: To provide financial assistance to Native Hawaiians who are interested in pursuing postsecondary education outside of Hawaii.
Eligibility: Applicants must be of Hawaiian ancestry and have graduated from a high school in Hawaii other than Kamehameha Schools. They must be enrolled as a full-time undergraduate student an accredited postsecondary institution outside the state of Hawaii. Preference is given to applicants who demonstrate financial need, have maintained their status as a Hawaii resident, and can demonstrate evidence of voluntary service to the Hawaiian community.
Financial data: A stipend is awarded (exact amount not specified).
Duration: 1 year; may be renewed.
Additional information: For the purposes of this program, "Native Hawaiian" means any descendant of the aboriginal inhabitants of the Hawaiian islands prior to 1778. This program is sponsored by KUKUI, Inc.
Number awarded: Varies each year.
Deadline: February of each year.

550
KYUTARO AND YASUO ABIKO MEMORIAL SCHOLARSHIP

Japanese American Citizens League
Attn: National Scholarship Awards
1765 Sutter Street
San Francisco, CA 94115
Phone: (415) 921-5225   Fax: (415) 931-4671
E-mail: jacl@jacl.org
Web Site: www.jacl.org
Summary: To provide financial assistance to student members of the Japanese American Citizens League (JACL) who are pursuing undergraduate education.
Eligibility: This program is open to JACL members who are currently enrolled or planning to reenter a college, university, trade school, business college, or other institution of higher learning. Selection is based on academic record, extracurricular activities, and community involvement. Preference is given to students majoring in journalism or agriculture.
Financial data: The stipend depends on the availability of funds but usually ranges from $1,000 to $5,000.
Duration: 1 year.
Additional information: Requests for applications must be accompanied by a self-addressed stamped envelope.
Number awarded: At least 1 each year.
Deadline: March of each year.

551
L. EINAR AND EDITH L. NILSSON AWARD

Vasa Order of America
Attn: Vice Grand Master
1926 Rancho Andrew
Alpine, CA 91901
Phone: (619) 445-9707   Fax: (619) 445-7334
E-mail: drulf@connectnet.com
Web Site: www.vasaorder.com
Summary: To provide financial assistance for college to members of the Vasa Order of America from designated states.
Eligibility: Applicants must have been members of the organization for at least 1 year and live in district 1 (Connecticut), district 2 (Massachusetts), or district 3 (Rhode Island). They must be high school seniors or college undergraduates who plan to continue their education on a full-time basis at an accredited institution. Selection is based on a grade transcript, letters of recommendation from school and local Vasa lodge officials, and an essay of up to 1,000 words on a topic related to Vasa.
Financial data: The stipend is $2,000.
Duration: 1 year.
Additional information: Vasa Order of America is a Swedish American fraternal organization incorporated in 1899.
Number awarded: 1 each year.
Deadline: February of each year.

552
LA FRA NATIONAL PRESIDENT'S SCHOLARSHIP

Ladies Auxiliary of the Fleet Reserve Association
Attn: Scholarship Administrator
125 North West Street
Alexandria, VA 22314-2754
Phone: (703) 683-1400   (800) 372-1924
Fax: (703) 549-6610
Web Site: www.fra.org
Summary: To provide financial assistance for the postsecondary education of children and grandchildren of naval personnel.
Eligibility: Eligible to apply for these scholarships are the children and grandchildren of Navy, Marine, Coast Guard, active Fleet Reserve, Fleet Marine Corps Reserve, and Coast Guard Reserve personnel on active duty, retired with pay, or deceased while on active duty or retired with pay. Selection is based on financial need, academic proficiency, and character. Preference is given to dependents of members of the Fleet Reserve Association and the Ladies Auxiliary of the Fleet Reserve Association, if other factors are equal.
Financial data: The stipend is $2,500.
Duration: 1 year; may be renewed.
Number awarded: 1 each year.
Deadline: April of each year.

553
LA FRA SCHOLARSHIP

Ladies Auxiliary of the Fleet Reserve Association
Attn: Scholarship Administrator
125 North West Street
Alexandria, VA 22314-2754
Phone: (703) 683-1400   (800) 372-1924
Fax: (703) 549-6610
Web Site: www.fra.org
Summary: To provide financial assistance for the postsecondary education of daughters and granddaughters of naval personnel.
Eligibility: Eligible to apply for these scholarships are the daughters and granddaughters of Navy, Marine, Coast Guard, active Fleet Reserve, Fleet Marine Corps Reserve, and Coast Guard Reserve personnel on active duty, retired with pay, or deceased while on active duty or retired with pay. Selection is based on financial need, academic proficiency, and character. Preference is given to dependents of members of the Fleet Reserve Association and the Ladies Auxiliary of the Fleet Reserve Association, if other factors are equal.
Financial data: This scholarship is $2,500.
Duration: 1 year; may be renewed.
Number awarded: 1 each year.
Deadline: April of each year.

554
LAMEY-WELLEHAN MAINE DIFFERENCE SCHOLARSHIP

Lamey-Wellehan Shoes
Attn: President
110 Lisbon Street
P.O. Box 1317
Lewiston, ME 04243-1317
Phone: (207) 784-6941   Fax: (207) 784-9650
E-mail: jim@lwshoes.com
Summary: To provide financial assistance to residents of Maine who are attending college in the state.
Eligibility: This program is open to Maine residents attending a college in the state. Financial need is considered in the selection process, but the primary consideration is the applicant's ability to contribute to the economy and the environment of Maine.
Financial data: The stipend is $1,000.
Duration: 1 year.
Number awarded: 1 each year.
Deadline: May of each year.

555
LARRY AND MARY DAVIS SCHOLARSHIPS

Western States Roofing Contractors Association
Attn: Davis Memorial Foundation
1400 Marsten Road, Suite N
Burlingame, CA 94010
Phone: (650) 548-0114   Fax: (650) 548-0936
Web Site: wsrca.com
Summary: To provide financial assistance for college to students from western states who have a connection to the roofing industry.
Eligibility: This program is open to members of the roofing industry, their employees, and their immediate family who are attending or planning to attend a technical trade school, college, or university. Applicants must be residents of western states.
Financial data: The stipend is $2,500.
Duration: 1 year.
Additional information: This program was established in 1996.
Number awarded: 4 each year.

556
LATIN AMERICAN EDUCATIONAL FOUNDATION SCHOLARSHIPS

Latin American Educational Foundation
Attn: Scholarship Selection Committee
924 West Colfax Avenue, Suite 103
Denver, CO 80204
Phone: (303) 446-0541   Fax: (303) 446-0526
E-mail: laefaa@uswest.net
Web Site: www.laef.org
Summary: To provide financial aid to Hispanic American undergraduate students in Colorado.
Eligibility: This program is open to Colorado residents who are of Hispanic heritage and/or actively involved in the Hispanic community. Applicants must have been accepted at an accredited college, university, or vocational school and must have a cumulative grade point average of 3.0 or higher. Selection is based on community involvement, academic achievement, letters of recommendation, a personal essay, an interview, and financial need.
Financial data: The amount of the award depends on the need of the recipient, ranging from $500 to $3,000. Scholarships may be used at Colorado colleges and universities or at out-of-state institutions. Most colleges and universities within Colorado participate in the Colorado Higher Education Partnership; member institutions provide additional funds to match the award granted by this foundation.
Duration: 1 year; recipients may reapply.
Additional information: Recipients are required to perform 10 hours of community service during the academic year.
Number awarded: Varies each year; recently, 227 of these scholarships were awarded.
Deadline: February of each year.

557
LATINGIRL SCHOLARSHIP

Latingirl: The Hispanic Teen Magazine
Attn: Latingirl Scholarship
P.O. Box 625
Hoboken, NJ 07030-0625
Fax: (201) 876-9640   E-mail: editor@latingirlmag.com
Web Site: www.latingirlmag.com
Summary: To provide financial assistance for college to Hispanic women graduating from high school.
Eligibility: This program is open to women of Hispanic descent who are graduating high school seniors. Applicants must submit a 300-word essay on their background and their potential contribution to the Hispanic community. Selection is based on the essay, academic achievement, and financial need.
Financial data: The stipend is $1,000.
Duration: 1 year.
Additional information: These scholarships were first offered in 1999.
Number awarded: 10 each year.
Deadline: April of each year.

558
LAURA BLACKBURN MEMORIAL SCHOLARSHIP

American Legion Auxiliary
Attn: Department of Kentucky
105 North Public Square
P.O. Box 189
Greensburg, KY 42743-1530
Phone: (502) 932-7533
Summary: To provide financial assistance for postsecondary education to descendants of veterans in Kentucky.
Eligibility: This program is open to the children, grandchildren, and great-grandchildren of veterans who served in the armed forces during eligibility dates for membership in the American Legion. Applicants must be Kentucky residents enrolled in their senior year at an accredited high school.
Financial data: The stipend is $1,000.
Duration: 1 year.
Additional information: Further information is also available from the Education Chair, Ruth James, 7340 Lilydale Road, Byrdstown, TN 38549.
Number awarded: 1 each year.
Deadline: March of each year.

559
LAVYRL JOHNSON MEMORIAL SCHOLARSHIP

National Federation of the Blind of California
Attn: Nancy Burns
1240 North Griffith Park Drive
Burbank, CA 91506
Phone: (818) 558-6524   Fax: (818) 842-1018
E-mail: webmaster@nfbcal.org
Web Site: www.nfbcal.org
Summary: To provide financial assistance for undergraduate or graduate education to blind students in California.

Eligibility: Legally blind full-time students in California may apply for a scholarship, but they must attend the convention of the National Federation of the Blind of California. Applicants must submit an essay in which they describe their educational goals, involvement in the blindness community, and eye condition. High school seniors and college freshmen must submit their high school transcripts; other college students must submit transcripts of all undergraduate and graduate work. Selection is based on academic merit.
Financial data: The stipend is $1,500.
Duration: 1 year.
Number awarded: 1 each year.
Deadline: May of each year.

560
LAWRENCE C. YEARDLEY SCHOLARSHIPS

Greater Kanawha Valley Foundation
Attn: Scholarship Coordinator
One Huntington Square, 16th Floor
900 Lee Street, East
P.O. Box 3041
Charleston, WV 25331-3041
Phone: (304) 346-3620   Fax: (304) 346-3640
E-mail: tgkvf@tgkvf.com
Web Site: www.tgkvf.com/scholarship.html
Summary: To provide financial assistance for college to residents of West Virginia.
Eligibility: This program is open to residents of West Virginia who are attending a college or university anywhere in the country. Applicants must have at least a 2.5 grade point average and demonstrate good moral character. Selection is based on financial need and academic excellence.
Financial data: The stipend is $1,000 per year.
Duration: 1 year; may be renewed.
Number awarded: 2 each year.
Deadline: February of each year.

561
LAWRENCE E. AND THELMA J. NORRIE MEMORIAL SCHOLARSHIP

Foundation for Amateur Radio, Inc.
P.O. Box 831
Riverdale, MD 20738
E-mail: turnbull@erols.com
Web Site: www.amateurradio-far.org
Summary: To provide funding to licensed radio amateurs who are interested in pursuing postsecondary studies (particularly in the sciences).
Eligibility: Applicants must be a resident of the United States and hold an amateur radio license of technician plus class or higher. Special consideration is given to applicants who have demonstrated academic merit, financial need, and an interest in promoting the amateur radio service. Preference is given to juniors, seniors, and graduate students with a grade point average of 3.0 or higher who are pursuing a degree in science or engineering.
Financial data: The stipend is $2,500.
Duration: 1 year.
Additional information: Recipients must attend an accredited school (university, college, or technical institute) on a full-time basis.
Number awarded: 1 each year.
Deadline: May of each year.

562
LAWRENCE LUTERMAN MEMORIAL SCHOLARSHIPS

American Legion
Attn: Department of New Jersey
Attn: Scholarship Judges
135 West Hanover Street
Trenton, NJ 08618
Phone: (609) 695-5418   Fax: (609) 394-1532
E-mail: newjersey@legion.org
Web Site: www.nj.legion.org
Summary: To provide financial assistance for the postsecondary education of the descendants of members of the Department of New Jersey, American Legion.
Eligibility: In order to be eligible for these scholarships, applicants must be high school seniors and the natural or adopted descendants of members of the American Legion's New Jersey Department. Scholarships are based on character

(20 percent), Americanism (20 percent), leadership (20 percent), scholarship (20 percent), and financial need (20 percent).
Financial data: The stipend is $1,000 per year.
Duration: These scholarships are for 4 years, 2 years, or 1 year.
Number awarded: 6 each year: 2 for 4 years, 2 for 2 years, and 2 for 1 year.
Deadline: February of each year.

563
LAWRENCE MARCELINO MEMORIAL SCHOLARSHIP

National Federation of the Blind of California
Attn: Nancy Burns
1240 North Griffith Park Drive
Burbank, CA 91506
Phone: (818) 558-6524   Fax: (818) 842-1018
E-mail: webmaster@nfbcal.org
Web Site: www.nfbcal.org
Summary: To provide financial assistance for graduate or undergraduate education to blind students in California.
Eligibility: Legally blind full-time students in California may apply for a scholarship, but they must attend the convention of the National Federation of the Blind of California. Applicants must submit an essay in which they describe their educational goals, involvement in the blindness community, and eye condition. High school seniors and college freshmen must submit their high school transcripts; other college students must submit transcripts of all undergraduate and graduate work. Selection is based on academic merit.
Financial data: The stipend is $2,500.
Duration: 1 year.
Number awarded: 1 each year.
Deadline: May of each year.

564
LCDR LOREN PETER GARLINGER, USN SCHOLARSHIP

The Retired Officers Association
Attn: Educational Assistance Program
201 North Washington Street
Alexandria, VA 22314-2539
Phone: (703) 838-8816   (800) 245-8762, ext. 816
Fax: (703) 838-5819   E-mail: edassist@troa.org
Web Site: www.troa.org/Education/ScholarshipFund.asp
Summary: To provide financial support for the undergraduate education of dependent children of members of The Retired Officers Association (TROA).
Eligibility: This program is open to never married dependent children under age 24 of active, reserve, and retired uniformed service personnel (Army, Navy, Air Force, Marines, Coast Guard, Public Health Service, or National Oceanographic and Atmospheric Administration). Parents who are officers eligible for membership in the association must be members. Unmarried dependent children of enlisted personnel are also eligible to apply. Selection is based on scholastic ability (minimum grade point average of 3.0), potential, character, leadership, and financial need. Applicants must be entering their senior year of college.
Financial data: The stipend is $3,000 per year.
Duration: 1 year.
Additional information: Applicants for the TROA Educational Assistance Program loans are automatically considered for these scholarships; no separate application is necessary. Grants are in addition to the amount of the loan.
Number awarded: Varies each year.
Deadline: February of each year.

565
LEAGUE FOUNDATION ACADEMIC SCHOLARSHIPS

Lesbian, Bisexual, Gay and Transgendered United Employees (LEAGUE) at AT&T Foundation
Attn: Academic Scholarships
2020 K Street, N.W., Suite 600
P.O. Box 57237
Washington, DC 20037-7237
Phone: (703) 713-7820   TDD: (800) 855-2880
E-mail: attleague@aol.com
Web Site: www.league-att.org
Summary: To provide financial assistance for college to high school seniors who identify with the gay, lesbian, bisexual, or transgender communities.
Eligibility: To be considered for this award, applicants must meet the following

be actively involved in community service; identify as a gay, lesbian, bisexual, or transgendered person; send 3 sealed letters of recommendation from adults who know their abilities and skills; provide a copy of their high school transcripts and college or university acceptance letter; and write 250-word essays on 1) their academic, career, and personal goals and plans for service to the community, especially on how they plan to increase respect for the individual and aid inclusion of human differences; and 2) how being a lesbian, gay, bisexual, or transgendered person has affected their personal life. Selection is based on academic record, personal plans, community service, leadership, and concern for others.

Financial data: Stipends are $2,500 (for the Matthew Shepard Memorial Scholarships), $2,000 (for the Ed Chilcott Memorial Scholarship), or $1,500.

Duration: 1 year.

Additional information: This program began in 1997. The first Matthew Shepard Scholarship was offered in 1999 and the first Ed Chilcott Memorial Scholarship was offered in 2001.

Number awarded: Varies each year; recently, 8 scholarships were provided, including 1 designated at the Ed Chilcott Memorial Scholarship and 2 designated as Matthew Shepard Scholarships.

Deadline: April of each year.

566
LEE DUBIN SCHOLARSHIP FUND

Children of Lesbians and Gays Everywhere
Attn: Scholarship Committee
3543 18th Street, #1
San Francisco, CA 94110
Phone: (415) 861-5437   E-mail: jude@colage.org
Web Site: www.colage.org/kids/scholarship.html

Summary: To provide financial assistance for college to children of lesbian, gay, bisexual, and transgender (LGBT) parents.

Eligibility: This program is open to undergraduate students who have a grade point average of 2.0 or higher and 1 or more LGBT parent. Applicants must be able to demonstrate ability in and commitment to affecting change in the LGBT community. As part of the application process, they must submit a 500- to 1,000-word essay on why support from this fund is important and meaningful to them; their community service, extracurricular activities, honors, or other special events that will help the committee see their strengths; how their experience as a child of LGBT parents has impacted their sense of civic responsibility; an event that dealt with social and/or political differences and their response to that situation; and how they think their reaction was impacted by their experience with their parents. Special consideration is given to applicants with demonstrated financial need.

Financial data: Stipends range from $500 to $1,000 per year.

Duration: 1 year; may be renewed.

Additional information: This program began in 1994.

Number awarded: At least 4 each year.

Deadline: April of each year.

567
LEGACY AWARDS

Golf Course Superintendents Association of America
Attn: Scholarship Coordinator
1421 Research Park Drive
Lawrence, KS 66049-3859
Phone: (785) 832-3678   (800) 472-7878, ext. 678
E-mail: psmith@gcsaa.org
Web Site: www.gcsaa.org

Summary: To provide financial assistance for college to the offspring of members of the Golf Course Superintendents Association of America (GCSAA).

Eligibility: This program is open to the children and grandchildren of GCSAA members who have been active in the association for 5 or more consecutive years or are retired or deceased. Applicants must be studying in a field unrelated to golf course management. They must be enrolled full time at an accredited institution of higher learning or, in the case of high school seniors, be accepted at such an institution for the next academic year. Selection is based on academic achievement, extracurricular and community involvement, leadership, outside employment, and an original 100-word essay on the applicant's parent's or grandparent's involvement with GCSAA. Financial need is not considered.

Financial data: The stipend is $1,500 per year.

Duration: 1 year.

Additional information: This program is sponsored by Syngenta Professional Products.

Number awarded: Several each year.

Deadline: April of each year.

568
LEGISLATIVE INCENTIVES FOR FUTURE EXCELLENCE (LIFE) SCHOLARSHIP PROGRAM

South Carolina Commission on Higher Education
Attn: Director of Student Services
1333 Main Street, Suite 200
Columbia, SC 29201
Phone: (803) 737-2244   Fax: (803) 737-2297
E-mail: CFreeman@che400.state.sc.us
Web Site: www.che400.state.sc.us

Summary: To provide financial assistance for postsecondary education to residents of South Carolina.

Eligibility: This program is open to residents of South Carolina who graduated from high school or completed a home-school program within the past 4 years. Applicants must enroll in an eligible South Carolina public or private college or university within 2 years and 3 months of high school graduation. As an entering college freshman, they must have earned at least a 3.0 grade point average in high school, and (for students planning to attend a 4-year college or university) have a minimum score of 1100 on the SAT or 24 on the ACT. Continuing college students must have completed an average of 30 credit hours for each academic year and maintained a minimum 3.0 grade point average. Students transferring must have completed 30 credit hours for a second-year transfer, 60 for a third-year transfer, or 90 for a fourth-year transfer; their cumulative grade point average must be 3.0 or higher. U.S. citizenship or permanent resident status is required. Applicants may not have been convicted of any felonies or alcohol- or drug-related charges.

Financial data: The stipend is $3,000 per year at 4-year colleges or universities. Students at public and private 2-year colleges may receive the cost of tuition and fees. Funds may be applied only toward the cost of attendance at an eligible South Carolina institution.

Duration: 1 year; may be renewed up to a total of 10 semesters for a 5-year program, 8 semester for a 4-year program, 4 semester for a 2-year program, or 2 semesters for a 1-year certificate or diploma program.

Additional information: The South Carolina General Assembly established this program in 1998.

Number awarded: Varies each year; recently, 13,114 students received support from this program.

569
LEON M. ABBOTT SCOTTISH RITE SCHOLARSHIP PROGRAM

Ancient and Accepted Scottish Rite of Freemasonry, Northern Jurisdiction
Supreme Council, 33
Attn: Education and Charity Fund
P.O. Box 519
Lexington, MA 02420-0519
Phone: (781) 862-4410   Fax: (781) 863-1833
E-mail: whall@supremecouncil.org
Web Site: www.supremecouncil.org

Summary: To provide financial assistance to 1) the descendants of members of the Scottish Rite or 2) members of the Order of DeMolay or Job's Daughters in the states represented by the Northern Masonic Jurisdiction.

Eligibility: Eligible to apply for this program are the children and grandchildren of members of the Scottish Rite Masons. Also eligible are members of youth organizations sponsored by the Masonic fraternity (i.e., DeMolay or Job's Daughters) that are located in the Northern Masonic Jurisdiction. Applicants must be high school graduates. Financial need is considered in the selection process.

Financial data: Stipends generally range from $500 to $1,000 per year, but the actual amount depends on the funds available.

Duration: 1 year or longer.

Number awarded: Varies each year; recently, 361 of these scholarships were awarded.

Deadline: March of each year.

570
LEONETTE LEAL FELICIANO MEMORIAL AWARD

Portuguese Heritage Scholarship Foundation
Attn: Academic Secretary
P.O. Box 30246
Bethesda, MD 20824-0246
Phone: (301) 652-2775   E-mail: phsf@vivaportugal.com
Web Site: www.vivaportugal.com/phsf/apply.htm
Summary: To provide financial assistance for college to students of Portuguese American heritage.
Eligibility: Eligible to apply for this support are high school seniors or currently-enrolled college students who are of Portuguese American ancestry. Applicants must be U.S. residents and attending or planning to attend an accredited 4-year college or university. Selection is based on community involvement and academic achievement.
Financial data: The stipend is $1,000 per year.
Duration: 1 year; nonrenewable.
Additional information: Recipients must attend college on a full-time basis.
Number awarded: 1 each year.
Deadline: January of each year.

571
LEST WE FORGET POW/MIA/KIA SCHOLARSHIP FUND

Maine Community Foundation
Attn: Program Director
245 Main Street
Ellsworth, ME 04605
Phone: (207) 667-9735   (877) 700-6800
Fax: (207) 667-0447   E-mail: info@mainecf.org
Web Site: www.mainecf.org/scholar.html
Summary: To provide financial assistance for postsecondary education to Vietnam veterans or the dependents of Vietnam or other veterans in Maine.
Eligibility: This program is open to residents of Maine who are Vietnam veterans or the descendants of veterans who served in the Vietnam Theater. As a second priority, children of veterans from other time periods are also considered. Graduating high school seniors, nontraditional students, undergraduates, and graduate students are eligible to apply. Selection is based on financial need, extracurricular activities, work experience, academic achievement, and a personal statement of career goals and how the applicant's educational plans relate to them.
Financial data: The stipend is $1,000 per year.
Duration: 1 year.
Additional information: This fund was transferred to the Maine Community Foundation in 1996. There is a $3 processing fee.
Number awarded: 3 to 6 each year.
Deadline: April of each year.

572
LETENDRE EDUCATION FUND FOR HOMELESS CHILDREN SCHOLARSHIP

National Coalition for the Homeless
Attn: Director of Education
1012 14th Street, N.W., Suite 600
Washington, DC 20005-3410
Phone: (202) 737-6444, ext. 312   Fax: (202) 737-6445
Web Site: nch.ari.net/letendreindex.html
Summary: To provide financial assistance for college to high school seniors and recent graduates who are currently or formerly homeless.
Eligibility: This program is open to students who are homeless or who have been homeless during their school attendance. This includes students who live in shelters, cars, campgrounds, or other places "not meant for human habitation." Also eligible are students who are living with friends or relatives temporarily because they lack permanent housing. Applicants must be high school seniors, students enrolled in GED or other alternative education programs, or students who recently obtained their diploma or GED certificate. They must be able to demonstrate higher than average achievement. Student essays and other application materials are evaluated for statements of goals/dreams, determination to go to college, likelihood of success, use of language, creativity, and willingness to discuss the experience of homelessness.
Financial data: The stipend is $1,000. Funds must be used for tuition, application fees, books, preparation courses, visits to prospective colleges, or other educationally-related expenses.

Duration: 1 year; nonrenewable.
Additional information: This fund was established in 1998; the first 6 scholarships were awarded in 1999.
Number awarded: At least 2 each year.
Deadline: September of each year.

573
LEWIS A. KINGSLEY FOUNDATION SCHOLARSHIP FUND

United States Naval Sea Cadet Corps
Attn: Executive Director
2300 Wilson Boulevard
Arlington, VA 22201-3308
Phone: (703) 243-6910   Fax: (703) 243-3985
Summary: To provide financial assistance to Naval Sea Cadet Corps cadets and former cadets who are interested in continuing their education at an accredited 4-year college/university.
Eligibility: This program is open to cadets and former cadets who are interested in continuing their education at an accredited 4-year college or university. They must have been a member of the corps for at least 2 years, have attained a minimum rating of NSCC E-3, be recommended by their commanding officer or other official, have earned at least a 3.0 grade point average, and have been accepted by an accredited college or university. Applicants may submit financial need statements. All other factors being equal, these statements may be considered in determining award recipients. Applicants who have received full scholarships from other sources (e.g., ROTC) will be considered for this award only if there are no other qualified applicants.
Financial data: The stipend is $1,000.
Duration: 1 year.
Additional information: Cadets are also eligible to apply for scholarships sponsored by the Navy League of the United States.
Number awarded: 5 each year.
Deadline: May of each year.

574
LILLIAN AND ARTHUR DUNN SCHOLARSHIPS

National Society Daughters of the American Revolution
Attn: Scholarship Committee
1776 D Street, N.W.
Washington, DC 20006-5392
Phone: (202) 628-1776
Web Site: www.dar.org/natsociety/edout_scholar.html
Summary: To provide financial assistance for the postsecondary education of children of active members of the Daughters of the American Revolution (DAR).
Eligibility: Eligible to apply for these scholarships are children of active DAR members who are graduating seniors at accredited high schools and who plan to continue their education at a college or university in the United States. Applicants must be sponsored by a local chapter of the DAR. Selection is based on academic excellence, commitment to the field of study, and financial need. U.S. citizenship is required.
Financial data: This award is $2,000 per year.
Duration: Up to 4 years.
Additional information: Information is also available from Cindy B. Findley, DAR Scholarship Committee Chair, 4929 Warfield Drive, Greensboro, NC 27406-8338, (336) 674-5777, E-mail: cfindley@bellsouth.net. Requests for applications must be accompanied by a self-addressed stamped envelope.
Number awarded: 1 or more each year.
Deadline: February of each year.

575
LILLY SCHIZOPHRENIA REINTEGRATION SCHOLARSHIPS

Lilly Schizophrenia Reintegration Awards Office
734 North LaSalle Street
PMB 1167
Chicago, IL 60610
Phone: (800) 809-8202   Fax: (312) 664-5454
E-mail: lillyscholarships@ims-chi.com
Web Site: www.zyprexa.com/scholar.htm
Summary: To provide financial assistance for postsecondary education to students diagnosed with schizophrenia.
Eligibility: This program is open to students diagnosed with schizophrenia, schizophreniform, or schizoaffective disorder who are receiving medical

treatment for the disease and are actively involved in rehabilitative or reintegrative efforts. They must be interested in pursuing postsecondary education, including trade or vocational school programs, high school equivalency programs, associate degrees, bachelor or arts and science degrees, and graduate programs. As part of the application process, students must write an essay describing their skills, interests, and personal and professional goals.

Financial data: The amount awarded varies, depending upon the specific needs of the recipient. Funds may be used to pay for tuition and related expenses, such as textbooks and laboratory fees.

Duration: 1 year.

Additional information: This program, established in 1998, is funded by Eli Lilly and Company.

Number awarded: Varies each year; recently, more than 80 of these scholarships were awarded.

Deadline: January of each year.

576
LINDA RIDDLE/SGMA ENDOWED SCHOLARSHIP

Women's Sports Foundation
Attn: Award and Grant Programs Manager
Eisenhower Park
1899 Hempstead Turnpike, Suite 400
East Meadow, NY 11554-1000
Phone: (516) 542-4700   (800) 227-3988
Fax: (516) 542-4716   E-mail: wosport@aol.com
Web Site: www.womenssportsfoundation.org

Summary: To provide financial assistance for college to women athletes.

Eligibility: Eligible to apply for these scholarships are female high school seniors who plan to enter college in the following fall and pursue a full-time course of study at an accredited 2-year or 4-year college or university. Special consideration is given to applicants interested in pursuing a career in sports. Selection is based on academic performance (at least a 3.5 grade point average), athletic participation, and financial need.

Financial data: The stipend is at least $1,500.

Duration: 1 year.

Additional information: Funding for this program is provided by the Sporting Goods Manufacturer's Association (SGMA).

Number awarded: Up to 10 each year.

Deadline: November of each year.

577
LOLA B. CURRY SCHOLARSHIP

United Daughters of the Confederacy
Attn: Education Director
328 North Boulevard
Richmond, VA 23220-4057
Phone: (804) 355-1636   Fax: (804) 353-1396
E-mail: hqudc@aol.com
Web Site: www.hqudc.org

Summary: To provide financial assistance for postsecondary education to lineal descendants of Confederate veterans in Alabama.

Eligibility: Eligible to apply for these scholarships are Alabama residents who are lineal descendants of worthy Confederates or collateral descendants who are members of the Children of the Confederacy or the United Daughters of the Confederacy. Applicants must submit a family financial report and certified proof of the Confederate record of 1 ancestor, with the company and regiment in which he served. They must have at least a 3.0 grade point average in high school.

Financial data: The amount of the scholarship depends on the availability of funds.

Duration: 1 year; may be renewed.

Additional information: Information is also available from Dorothy S. Broom, Second Vice President General, 595 Lominack Road, Prosperity, SC 29127, (803) 364-3003. Members of the same family may not hold scholarships simultaneously, and only 1 application per family will be accepted within any 1 year. Requests for applications must be accompanied by a self-addressed stamped envelope.

Number awarded: 1 each year.

Deadline: February of each year.

578
LONG & FOSTER SCHOLARSHIP PROGRAM

Long & Foster, Realtors
Attn: Corporate Marketing Department
11351 Random Hills Road
Fairfax, VA 22030-6082
Phone: (703) 359-1500
Web Site: www.longandfoster.com/scholarship

Summary: To provide financial assistance for college to high school seniors in Long & Foster service area (Maryland, Virginia, Delaware, Pennsylvania, and Washington, D.C.).

Eligibility: This program is open to graduating high school seniors in Long & Foster service area, which includes parts of Maryland, Virginia, Delaware, Pennsylvania, and Washington, D.C. Applicants must be U.S. citizens, planning to enroll in a 4-year college or university, and able to demonstrate leadership and involvement in a variety of school activities. They must have at least a 3.0 grade point average, have held positions of responsibility and leadership in school, and write an essay on either a meaningful high school experience or their expectations for college. Selection is based on financial need, academic performance, leadership, extracurricular activities, and work experience.

Financial data: The stipend is $1,000. Funds are paid to the recipient's school.

Duration: 1 year; nonrenewable.

Additional information: Recipients may pursue any subject major.

Number awarded: 100 each year.

Deadline: February of each year.

579
LORA E. DUNETZ SCHOLARSHIP

National Federation of the Blind
c/o Peggy Elliott
Chair, Scholarship Committee
805 Fifth Avenue
Grinnell, IA 50112
Phone: (641) 236-3366
Web Site: www.nfb.org

Summary: To provide financial assistance for college to legally blind students, especially those planning to enter the medical field.

Eligibility: This program is open to legally blind students who are pursuing or planning to pursue a full-time undergraduate or graduate course of study. Preference is given to applicants planning to enter the medical field. Selection is based on academic excellence, service to the community, and financial need.

Financial data: The stipend is $3,000.

Duration: 1 year; recipients may resubmit applications up to 2 additional years.

Additional information: Scholarships are awarded at the federation convention in July. Recipients attend the convention at federation expense; that funding is in addition to the scholarship grant.

Number awarded: 1 each year.

Deadline: March of each year.

580
LORILLARD TEENH.I.P. AWARDS

Lorillard Tobacco Company
Attn: TeenH.I.P. Awards
c/o Weber Shandwick
676 North St. Clair
Chicago, IL 60611
Web Site: www.buttoutnow.com

Summary: To recognize and reward elementary and high school students who are academic stars, are active in their school and community, and don't smoke.

Eligibility: This competition is open to U.S. residents between the ages of 8 and 18. They must have at least a 2.5 grade point average and be a nonsmoker. To apply, students must submit a completed application form, a transcript, 2 letters of recommendation, and a required essay. Students who are home schooled are also eligible to compete. Applicants are evaluated on the following criteria: well-roundedness (participation and success in sports, arts, employment, and/or community service); leadership; academics; and creatively/originality in the essay.

Financial data: The awards are $10,000 each. Funds must be used for college. In addition, winners are given a trip for 2 to a "hot teen" destination, as determined by the sponsor (valued at $2,500).

Duration: The competition is held annually.

Additional information: TeenH.I.P. stands for: Teens Helping Influence People. The

competition was first held in 2000. Recipients must attend college on a full-time basis.

Number awarded: 10 each year.

Deadline: May of each year.

581
LOUISE C. NACCA MEMORIAL SCHOLARSHIP

Cerebral Palsy of Essex and West Hudson
Attn: Scholarship Committee
7 Sanford Avenue
Belleville, NJ 07109
Phone: (973) 751-0200

Summary: To provide financial assistance to students with disabilities in New Jersey who are interested in pursuing postsecondary education.

Eligibility: This program is open to high school seniors, high school graduates, and currently-enrolled college students who reside in New Jersey and have a permanent physical disability. There is no restriction on the type of disability. Applicants must be between 18 and 45 years of age and interested in pursuing education and/or training that leads to an occupation.

Financial data: Stipends range from $1,300 to $10,000 per year.

Duration: 1 year.

Additional information: Recipients may attend any type of school or educational facility beyond the secondary school level (including college, university, professional school, or trade school) in any state.

Number awarded: Varies each year; recently, 56 of these scholarships were awarded.

Deadline: January of each year.

582
LOUISIANA LEVERAGING EDUCATIONAL ASSISTANCE PARTNERSHIP

Louisiana Office of Student Financial Assistance
1885 Wooddale Boulevard
P.O. Box 91202
Baton Rouge, LA 70821-9202
Phone: (225) 922-1012   (800) 259-5626, ext. 1012
Fax: (225) 922-1089   E-mail: custserv@osfa.state.la.us
Web Site: www.osfa.state.la.us

Summary: To provide need-based funds to academically qualified high school seniors and graduates in Louisiana who are planning to attend college.

Eligibility: Applicants must be Louisiana residents, have substantial financial need, be enrolled as a full-time undergraduate student, be a U.S. citizen or eligible noncitizen, have earned at least a 2.0 grade point average in high school (or a minimum average score of 45 on the GED), have achieved a composite score of at least 20 on the ACT, have applied for federal aid, not owe a refund on federal aid, and not be in default on federal aid. The Louisiana Office of Student Financial Assistance allocates award funds to Louisiana postsecondary schools based on prior fall enrollment. Students are selected for the award by the financial aid officers at their participating schools.

Financial data: Individual grants range from $200 to $2,000 per year; the average award is $600; a total of approximately $2.0 million is distributed each year. Funds may be used for educational expenses, including tuition, fees, supplies, and living expenses (e.g., room and board, transportation).

Duration: 1 year; may be renewed.

Additional information: Schools approved for these allocations include Louisiana colleges and universities, technical institutes, and proprietary schools (such as business and cosmetology schools). This program was formerly known as Louisiana State Student Incentive Grants. Not all schools participate in this program each year; schools must submit an application and be approved for participation annually. For a list of current participants, write to the Louisiana Office of Student Financial Assistance.

Number awarded: Approximately 3,000 each year.

583
LOUISIANA TOPS—HONORS AWARD

Louisiana Office of Student Financial Assistance
1885 Wooddale Boulevard
P.O. Box 91202
Baton Rouge, LA 70821-9202
Phone: (225) 922-1012   (800) 259-5626, ext. 1012
Fax: (225) 922-1089   E-mail: custserv@osfa.state.la.us
Web Site: www.osfa.state.la.us

Summary: To provide financial assistance for college to graduating high school seniors in Louisiana with outstanding academic records.

Eligibility: All components of the Tuition Opportunity Program for Students (TOPS) are open to graduating seniors at high schools in Louisiana who have completed a core curriculum of 16.5 units and have filed a Free Application for Federal Student Aid (FAFSA). Applicants must be registered with Selective Service (if required), may have no criminal convictions, and must enter an eligible postsecondary institution as a first-time freshman by the first semester following the first anniversary of their high school graduation (unless entering into military service). Independent students or at least 1 parent or legal guardian of dependent students must have been a Louisiana resident for at least 24 months prior to the date of high school graduation. For the Honors component, students must have at least a 3.5 grade point average and a minimum score of 27 on the ACT.

Financial data: This program provides tuition reimbursement plus $800 per year to students who attend public colleges or universities in Louisiana or provides the equivalent of the average public tuition charged in Louisiana plus $800 per year to students attending independent colleges or universities in the state.

Duration: 1 year; may be renewed for up to 3 additional years if the recipient continues to attend a Louisiana public or independent college or university as a full-time undergraduate student and maintains at least a 3.0 grade point average.

Additional information: Recipients must attend a college or university in Louisiana.

Number awarded: Varies each year.

Deadline: April of each year for priority consideration; June of each year for final consideration.

584
LOUISIANA TOPS—OPPORTUNITY AWARD

Louisiana Office of Student Financial Assistance
1885 Wooddale Boulevard
P.O. Box 91202
Baton Rouge, LA 70821-9202
Phone: (225) 922-1012   (800) 259-5626, ext. 1012
Fax: (225) 922-1089   E-mail: custserv@osfa.state.la.us
Web Site: www.osfa.state.la.us

Summary: To provide financial assistance for college to graduating high school seniors in Louisiana.

Eligibility: All components of the Tuition Opportunity Program for Students (TOPS) are open to graduating seniors at high schools in Louisiana who have completed a core curriculum of 16.5 units and have filed a Free Application for Federal Student Aid (FAFSA). Applicants must be registered with Selective Service (if required), may have no criminal convictions, and must enter an eligible postsecondary institution as a first-time freshman by the first semester following the first anniversary of their high school graduation (unless entering into military service). Independent students or at least 1 parent or legal guardian of dependent students must have been a Louisiana resident for at least 24 months prior to the date of high school graduation. For the Opportunity component, students must have at least a 2.5 grade point average and a minimum score of 20 on the ACT.

Financial data: This program provides tuition reimbursement to students who attend public colleges or universities in Louisiana or provides the equivalent of the average public tuition charged in Louisiana to students attending independent colleges or universities in the state.

Duration: 1 year; may be renewed for up to 3 additional years if the recipient continues to attend a Louisiana public or independent college or university as a full-time undergraduate student and maintains at least a 2.3 grade point average at the end of the first academic year and 2.5 at the end of all other academic years.

Additional information: Recipients must attend a college or university in Louisiana.

Number awarded: Varies each year.

Deadline: April of each year for priority consideration; June of each year for final consideration.

585
LOUISIANA TOPS—PERFORMANCE AWARD

Louisiana Office of Student Financial Assistance
1885 Wooddale Boulevard
P.O. Box 91202
Baton Rouge, LA 70821-9202
Phone: (225) 922-1012   (800) 259-5626, ext. 1012
Fax: (225) 922-1089   E-mail: custserv@osfa.state.la.us
Web Site: www.osfa.state.la.us

Summary: To provide financial assistance for college to graduating high school seniors in Louisiana with outstanding academic records.

Eligibility: All components of the Tuition Opportunity Program for Students (TOPS) are open to graduating seniors at high schools in Louisiana who have completed a core curriculum of 16.5 units and have filed a Free Application for Federal Student Aid (FAFSA). Applicants must be registered with Selective Service (if required), may have no criminal convictions, and must enter an eligible postsecondary institution as a first-time freshman by the first semester following the first anniversary of their high school graduation (unless entering into military service). Independent students or at least 1 parent or legal guardian of dependent students must have been a Louisiana resident for at least 24 months prior to the date of high school graduation. For the Performance component, students must have at least a 3.5 grade point average and a minimum score of 23 on the ACT.

Financial data: This program provides tuition reimbursement plus $400 per year to students who attend public colleges or universities in Louisiana or provides the equivalent of the average public tuition charged in Louisiana plus $400 per year to students attending independent colleges or universities in the state.

Duration: 1 year; may be renewed for up to 3 additional years if the recipient continues to attend a Louisiana public or independent college or university as a full-time undergraduate student and maintains at least a 3.0 grade point average.

Additional information: Recipients must attend a college or university in Louisiana.

Number awarded: Varies each year.

Deadline: April of each year for priority consideration; June of each year for final consideration.

586
LOUISIANA TOPS—TECH AWARD

Louisiana Office of Student Financial Assistance
1885 Wooddale Boulevard
P.O. Box 91202
Baton Rouge, LA 70821-9202
Phone: (225) 922-1012   (800) 259-5626, ext. 1012
Fax: (225) 922-1089   E-mail: custserv@osfa.state.la.us
Web Site: www.osfa.state.la.us

Summary: To provide financial assistance to graduating high school seniors in Louisiana who are interested in pursuing a technical or vocational education.

Eligibility: All components of the Tuition Opportunity Program for Students (TOPS) are open to graduating seniors at high schools in Louisiana who have completed a core curriculum of 16.5 units and have filed a Free Application for Federal Student Aid (FAFSA). Applicants must be registered with Selective Service (if required), may have no criminal convictions, and must enter an eligible postsecondary institution as a first-time freshman by the first semester following the first anniversary of their high school graduation (unless entering into military service). Independent students or at least 1 parent or legal guardian of dependent students must have been a Louisiana resident for at least 24 months prior to the date of high school graduation. For the Tech component, students must have at least a 2.5 grade point average and a minimum score of 19 on the ACT. Applicants must plan to attend a public postsecondary school that provides skill or occupational training.

Financial data: This program provides payment of tuition and certain fees.

Duration: 1 year; may be renewed for 1 additional year if the recipient earns an average of 30 clock hours per week for each term and maintains at least a 2.5 grade point average.

Additional information: Recipients must attend a public technical or vocational school in Louisiana.

Number awarded: Varies each year.

Deadline: April of each year for priority consideration; June of each year for final consideration.

587
LOUISIANA VETERANS STATE AID PROGRAM

Department of Veterans Affairs
1885 Wooddale Boulevard, 10th Floor
P.O. Box 94095, Capitol Station
Baton Rouge, LA 70804-9095
Phone: (225) 922-0500   Fax: (225) 922-0511
E-mail: jstrickland@vetaffairs.com
Web Site: www.gov.state.la.us/depts/veteraaffairs.htm

Summary: To provide financial aid for postsecondary education to children and widow(er)s of certain disabled or deceased Louisiana veterans.

Eligibility: Eligible under this program are children (between the ages of 16 and 25) of veterans who served during World War I, World War II, the Korean war, or the Vietnam conflict and sustained a disability rated as 90 percent or more by the U.S. Department of Veterans Affairs as a result of wartime service or subsequent to release from such service. The disabled veteran parent must have resided in Louisiana for at least 2 years. Also eligible are children or widow(er)s (of any age) of veterans who had been residents of Louisiana for at least 1 year preceding entry into service and who died in war service in the line of duty or from an established wartime service-connected disability subsequently.

Financial data: Eligible persons accepted as full-time students at Louisiana state-supported colleges, universities, trade schools, or vocational-technical schools will be admitted free and are exempt from payment of all tuition, laboratory, athletic, medical, and other special fees. Free registration does not cover books, supplies, room and board, or fees assessed by the student body on themselves (such as yearbooks and weekly papers).

Duration: Tuition, fee exemption, and possible payment of cash subsistence allowance are provided for a maximum of 4 school years to be completed in not more than 5 years from date of original entry.

Additional information: Attendance must be on a full-time basis. Surviving spouses must remain unmarried and must take advantage of the benefit within 10 years after eligibility is established.

Number awarded: Varies each year.

Deadline: Applications must be received no later than 3 months prior to the beginning of a semester.

588
LOWRIDER MAGAZINE SCHOLARSHIP FUND

Lowrider Magazine
P.O. Box 6390
Fullerton, CA 92834-6930
Phone: (714) 213-1000

Summary: To assist Chicano/Latino students who are interested in finishing their college education.

Eligibility: Applicants must be of Latino descent, have at least a 3.0 grade point average, and be currently enrolled as college sophomores, juniors, or seniors. They must submit an official transcript, 2 letters of recommendation, a 1-page essay outlining their financial situation, and a 2-page essay on 1 of 3 topics that change annually.

Financial data: Stipends are available for tuition and books only.

Duration: 1 year.

Additional information: This program started in 1990. No phone calls are accepted. Requests for applications must be accompanied by a self-addressed stamped envelope.

Number awarded: Varies each year.

Deadline: May of each year.

589
LULAC GENERAL AWARDS

League of United Latin American Citizens
Attn: LULAC National Education Service Centers
2000 L Street, N.W., Suite 610
Washington, DC 20036
Phone: (202) 835-9646   E-mail: LNESCAward@aol.com
Web Site: www.lulac.org/Programs/Scholar.html

Summary: To provide financial assistance to Hispanic American students interested in postsecondary education.

Eligibility: Applicants must be U.S. citizens or permanent residents who are currently enrolled or planning to enroll at an accredited college or university as graduate or undergraduate students. Although grades are considered in the selection process, emphasis is placed on the applicant's motivation, sincerity, and integrity, as revealed through a personal interview and in an essay. Need, community involvement, and leadership activities are also considered. Candidates must live near a participating local council of the League of United Latin American Citizens (LULAC) and must apply directly to that council.

Financial data: The amount of the stipend varies, depending upon need, from $250 to $1,000 per year.

Duration: 1 year.

Additional information: This program represents an attempt to forge a partnership between the corporate world and the community. Under its fundsharing concept, LULAC's National Education Service Center gathers contributions nationally from corporations, while LULAC councils raise money

locally. The total corporate donations are then apportioned back to the councils according to effort. Applications must be obtained directly from participating LULAC councils; for a list, send a self-addressed stamped envelope to the sponsor.

Number awarded: Varies; approximately 500 each year.

Deadline: March of each year.

590
LULAC HONORS AWARDS

League of United Latin American Citizens
Attn: LULAC National Education Service Centers
2000 L Street, N.W., Suite 610
Washington, DC 20036
Phone: (202) 835-9646   E-mail: LNESCAward@aol.com
Web Site: www.lulac.org/Programs/Scholar.html

Summary: To provide financial assistance to Hispanic American students interested in postsecondary education.

Eligibility: This program is open to Hispanic Americans who are U.S. citizens or permanent residents currently enrolled or planning to enroll at an accredited college or university as a graduate or undergraduate student. Applicants who are already in college must have a grade point average of 3.25 or higher. Entering freshmen must have ACT scores of 20 or higher or SAT scores of 840 or higher. In addition, applicants must demonstrate motivation, sincerity, and integrity through a personal interview and in an essay. Need, community involvement, and leadership activities are also considered. Candidates must live near a participating local council of the League of United Latin American Citizens (LULAC) and must apply directly to that council.

Financial data: The amount of the stipend varies, depending upon need, from $250 to $1,000 per year.

Duration: 1 year.

Additional information: This program represents an attempt to forge a partnership between the corporate world and the community. Under its fundsharing concept, LULAC's National Education Service Center gathers contributions nationally from corporations, while LULAC councils raise money locally. The total corporate donations are then apportioned back to the councils according to effort. Applications must be obtained directly from participating LULAC councils; for a list, send a self-addressed stamped envelope to the sponsor.

Number awarded: Varies each year.

Deadline: March of each year.

591
LULAC NATIONAL SCHOLASTIC ACHIEVEMENT AWARDS

League of United Latin American Citizens
Attn: LULAC National Education Service Centers
2000 L Street, N.W., Suite 610
Washington, DC 20036
Phone: (202) 835-9646   E-mail: LNESCAward@aol.com
Web Site: www.lulac.org/Programs/Scholar.html

Summary: To provide financial assistance to Hispanic American students interested in postsecondary education.

Eligibility: This program is open to Hispanic Americans who are U.S. citizens or permanent residents currently enrolled or planning to enroll at an accredited college or university as a graduate or undergraduate student. Applicants who are already in college must have a grade point average of 3.5 or higher. Entering freshmen must have ACT scores of 23 or higher or SAT scores of 970 or higher. In addition, applicants must demonstrate motivation, sincerity, and integrity through a personal interview and in an essay. Need, community involvement, and leadership activities are also considered. Candidates must live near a participating local council of the League of United Latin American Citizens (LULAC) and must apply directly to that council.

Financial data: Stipends are at least $1,000 per year.

Duration: 1 year.

Additional information: This program represents an attempt to forge a partnership between the corporate world and the community. Under its fundsharing concept, LULAC's National Education Service Center gathers contributions nationally from corporations, while LULAC councils raise money locally. The total corporate donations are then apportioned back to the councils according to effort. Applications must be obtained directly from participating LULAC councils; for a list, send a self-addressed stamped envelope to the sponsor.

Number awarded: Varies each year.

Deadline: March of each year.

592
LUSO-AMERICAN FRATERNAL FEDERATION YOUTH COUNCIL RECOGNITION SCHOLARSHIP

Luso-American Education Foundation
Attn: Administrative Director
7080 Donlon Way, Suite 202
P.O. Box 2967
Dublin, CA 94568
Phone: (925) 828-3883   Fax: (925) 828-3883
Web Site: www.luso-american.org/laefx

Summary: To provide financial assistance for undergraduate study to members of the Luso-American Fraternal Federation.

Eligibility: This program is open to graduating high school seniors who are entering a 4-year college or university. Applicants must be current youth members, in good standing, of the federation who have not previously received a federation scholarship. Selection is based on promise of success in college, financial need, qualities of leadership, vocational promise, and sincerity of purpose.

Financial data: The award is $1,000 per year.

Duration: 4 years.

Additional information: This program is funded by the Luso-American Fraternal Federation and administered by the Luso-American Education Foundation. Membership in the Luso-American Fraternal Federation is limited to people who hold Luso-American Life Insurance policies or annuities.

Number awarded: 1 each year.

Deadline: February of each year.

593
LUTHERAN CAMPUS SCHOLARSHIP PROGRAM

Aid Association for Lutherans
Attn: Scholarships
4321 North Ballard Road
Appleton, WI 54919-0001
Phone: (920) 734-5721   (800) 225-5225
Fax: (920) 730-3757   E-mail: aalmail@aal.org
Web Site: www.aal.org

Summary: To provide financial assistance to members of the Aid Association for Lutherans who are attending a Lutheran institution.

Eligibility: Applicants must be members of the association, have an insurance policy or annuity in their name (associate members are not eligible), and be attending 1 of the 49 Lutheran campuses in an undergraduate program. Selection is based primarily on financial need, although some consideration is given to individual achievement.

Financial data: Amounts of the awards are set by the participating colleges, but they range from $200 to $1,000 per year.

Duration: 1 year; most are renewable up to 3 additional years.

Additional information: Each participating college selects the recipients of these scholarships; for further information, see the financial aid office at your college.

Number awarded: Approximately 1,600 each year.

Deadline: Each participating college determines its own deadline.

594
MABEL AND LAWRENCE S. COOKE SCHOLARSHIP

Boy Scouts of America
Attn: Eagle Scout Service, S220
1325 West Walnut Hill Lane
P.O. Box 152079
Irving, TX 75015-2079
Phone: (972) 580-2431
Web Site: www.scouting.org/nesa/scholar/index.html

Summary: To provide financial assistance for college to Eagle Scouts.

Eligibility: Eagle Scouts who are graduating high school seniors are eligible to apply for these scholarships. They must have an SAT score of at least 1090 and/or an ACT score of 26. Selection is based on financial need, scholastic accomplishment, involvement in Scouting, and school and community activities. The recipient must enroll as a full-time student at an accredited 4-year college or university.

Financial data: Stipends are either $12,000 or $5,000 per year.

Duration: 4 years, as long as the recipient remains in the upper third of his class.

Number awarded: Each year, 1 scholarship of $12,000 per year (for a total award of $48,000) and 4 scholarships of $5,000 per year (for a total award of $20,000) are presented.

Deadline: February of each year.

595
MAE LASLEY/OSAGE SCHOLARSHIPS

Mae Lasley/Osage Scholarship Fund
c/o Catholic Diocese of Tulsa
P.O. Box 690240
Tulsa, OK 74169-0240
Phone: (918) 294-1904
Web Site: www.osagetribe.com/education.htm
Summary: To provide financial assistance to Osage Indians who are attending a college or university.
Eligibility: This program is open to Osage Indians who are attending a college or university as an undergraduate or graduate student. Priority is given to applicants who are Catholics.
Financial data: Stipends range from $250 to $1,000 per year.
Duration: 1 year; recipients may reapply.
Number awarded: 1 or more each year.
Deadline: April of each year.

596
MAINE COMMUNITY FOUNDATION SECOND CHANCE FUND

Maine Community Foundation
Attn: Program Director
245 Main Street
Ellsworth, ME 04605
Phone: (207) 667-9735   (877) 700-6800
Fax: (207) 667-0447   E-mail: info@mainecf.org
Web Site: www.mainecf.org/scholar.html
Summary: To provide financial assistance for vocational or technical school to Maine residents who have been schooled in nontraditional settings.
Eligibility: This program is open to Maine residents who are high school graduates or GED certificate holders. Applicants must have been schooled in such nontraditional settings as the Juvenile Correctional Facilities Division of the Maine Department of Corrections (formerly known as the Maine Youth Center) or other components of the Maine criminal justice system. Students who have otherwise been judged "at risk" and educated in alternative or nontraditional settings are also eligible. They must be interested in pursuing a vocational or technical degree at a vocational or technical college within the Maine state system. Selection is based on demonstrated academic performance and promise, social integration, unlikelihood of recidivism, vocational prospects, and financial need.
Financial data: Stipends range from $500 to $1,000 per year. Funds may be used for tuition, room and board, books, lab fees and equipment.
Duration: 1 year; may be renewed.
Additional information: This program was established in 1999.
Number awarded: 1 or more each year.
Deadline: April of each year.

597
MAINE DIVERSITY ALLIANCE SCHOLARSHIPS

Maine Diversity Alliance
P.O. Box 1951
Portland, ME 04104
Summary: To provide financial assistance for college to Maine high school seniors of any sexual orientation.
Eligibility: This program is open to seniors at secondary schools (high school and vocational schools) in Maine. Applicants must be planning to enter a college, university, or technical school. They must submit an essay on the topic: "In a society that routinely discriminates, what can I do to protect others from discrimination?" Sexual orientation is not considered in the selection process.
Financial data: Stipends range from $500 to $1,000.
Duration: 1 year; nonrenewable.
Number awarded: 2 each year.
Deadline: March of each year.

598
MAINE INNKEEPERS ASSOCIATION AFFILIATED SCHOLARSHIPS

Maine Innkeepers Association
Attn: Executive Director
305 Commercial Street
Portland, ME 04101
Phone: (207) 773-7670

Summary: To provide financial assistance for college to Maine residents who are affiliated with the Maine Innkeepers Association (MIA).
Eligibility: This program is open to Maine residents who are seniors graduating from a high school in the state. Applicants must be 1) members of a family whose property has been affiliated with the association for at least 3 consecutive years; 2) members of a family whose business has been an allied member of the association for at least 3 consecutive years; and 3) persons who have been employed full time for at least 3 years by an active member property or allied member business. They must submit an official high school transcript, a letter of acceptance from an institution of higher education, 2 letters of reference from teachers or counselors, a third letter from their employer, and a 500-word essay describing their career goals and reasons for applying for the scholarship. Selection is based on academic record, employment history, extracurricular activities, career plans, and financial need.
Financial data: Stipends range from $500 to $1,000.
Duration: 1 year; recipients may reapply.
Number awarded: Up to 8 per year.
Deadline: April of each year.

599
MAINE MASONIC AID FOR CONTINUING EDUCATION

Maine Education Services
Attn: MES Foundation
One City Center, 11th Floor
Portland, ME 04101
Phone: (800) 922-6352   E-mail: info@mesfoundation.com
Web Site: www.mesfoundation.com/sch_applications/default.asp
Summary: To provide financial assistance for college to students in Maine who meet the federal definition of an independent student.
Eligibility: This program is open to residents of Maine who meet at least 1 of the following criteria: 1) are at least 24 years of age; 2) are married; 3) are enrolled in a graduate level or professional education program; 4) have legal dependents other than a spouse; 5) are an orphan or ward of the court (or were a ward of the court until age 18); or 6) are a veteran of the U.S. armed forces. Selection is based on seriousness of educational intent, commitment to future contribution to their community, and financial need.
Financial data: Stipends up to $1,000 are provided.
Duration: 1 year.
Number awarded: 24 each year.
Deadline: January of each year.

600
MAINE STATE CHAMBER OF COMMERCE SCHOLARSHIPS

Maine Education Services
Attn: MES Foundation
One City Center, 11th Floor
Portland, ME 04101
Phone: (800) 922-6352   E-mail: info@mesfoundation.com
Web Site: www.mesfoundation.com/sch_applications/default.asp
Summary: To provide financial assistance for a college-level technical, education, or business program to residents of Maine.
Eligibility: This program is open to residents of Maine who are 1) high school seniors planning to pursue a technical associate degree at a 2-year college; 2) high school seniors planning to pursue a business-related bachelor's degree at a 4-year college or university; and 3) adult learners planning to attend a 2-year college to pursue a degree in a business- or education-related field (those applicants must meet federal financial aid criteria for independent student status, i.e., be 24 years of age or older, or be married, or have legal dependents other than a spouse, or be an orphan or ward of the court, or be a veteran of the U.S. armed forces). Preference is given to applicants planning to attend college in Maine. Selection is based on academic achievement, employment and community activities, a letter of recommendation from a high school or community official, an essay describing challenges that businesses face in Maine, and financial need.
Financial data: The stipend is $1,500.
Duration: 1 year.
Number awarded: 3 each year: 1 to a high school senior pursuing a technical degree at a 2-year college, 1 to a high school senior pursuing a business degree at a 4-year institution, and 1 to an adult learner pursuing a 2-year degree in business or education.
Deadline: April of each year.

601
MAINE STATE GRANT PROGRAM

Finance Authority of Maine
Attn: Education Finance Programs
5 Community Drive
P.O. Box 949
Augusta, ME 04332-0949
Phone: (207) 623-3263   (800) 228-3734
Fax: (207) 623-0095   TDD: (207) 626-2717
E-mail: info@famemaine.com
Web Site: www.famemaine.com
Summary: To provide financial assistance to Maine residents for postsecondary education.
Eligibility: Eligible to apply are residents of Maine who have lived in the state for at least 1 year, have graduated from an approved secondary school, can demonstrate financial need, and are enrolled as full-time or part-time students in an approved institution for their first undergraduate degree. Approved schools include all accredited 2- and 4-year colleges, universities, and nursing programs in Maine, as well as regionally accredited 2- and 4-year colleges in states that have a reciprocity agreement with Maine (Connecticut, Massachusetts, New Hampshire, Pennsylvania, Rhode Island, Vermont, and Washington, D.C.).
Financial data: The maximum annual stipend is $1,250 at private schools in Maine, $1,000 at public schools in Maine, $500 at public schools outside of Maine, or $1,000 at private schools outside of Maine.
Duration: 1 year; may be renewed up to 4 additional years if the recipient remains a Maine resident and maintains satisfactory academic progress.
Additional information: This program was formerly known as the Maine Student Incentive Scholarship Program.
Number awarded: Scholarships are presented to students who demonstrate the greatest financial need. The award process continues until all available funds have been exhausted.
Deadline: April of each year.

602
MAINE STATE SOCIETY OF WASHINGTON, D.C. FOUNDATION SCHOLARSHIP PROGRAM

Maine State Society of Washington, D.C.
c/o Ronald Berube
6310 Pinestand Lane
Alexandria, VA 22312
Summary: To provide financial assistance to students who are currently enrolled full time at a university or 4-year degree-granting, nonprofit institution of higher learning within Maine.
Eligibility: This program is open to full-time students enrolled at a 4-year degree-granting, nonprofit institution of higher learning in Maine. High school seniors are not eligible to apply. Applicants must have been legal residents of Maine for at least 4 years (or have at least 1 parent who has been a resident of Maine for at least 4 years). They must be under 25 years of age, be enrolled in at least 14 semester hours or the equivalent, have at least a 3.0 grade point average, be working on a baccalaureate degree, and write an essay (up to 500 words) with background information on their qualifications for this scholarship.
Financial data: The stipend is $1,000.
Duration: 1 year; nonrenewable.
Number awarded: 3 each year.
Deadline: March of each year.

603
MAINE TUITION WAIVER PROGRAM FOR CHILDREN AND SPOUSES OF EMERGENCY SERVICES PERSONNEL KILLED IN THE LINE OF DUTY

Finance Authority of Maine
Attn: Education Finance Programs
5 Community Drive
P.O. Box 949
Augusta, ME 04332-0949
Phone: (207) 623-3263   (800) 228-3734
Fax: (207) 623-0095   TDD: (207) 626-2717
E-mail: info@famemaine.com
Web Site: www.famemaine.com
Summary: To provide financial assistance to children and spouses of deceased emergency services personnel in Maine.

Eligibility: This program is open to children and spouses of emergency services personnel who have been killed in the line of duty. Applicants must be enrolled in or accepted for enrollment in a branch of the University of Maine system, the Maine Technical College System, or the Maine Maritime Academy.
Financial data: Eligible students receive waivers of tuition and fees.
Duration: 1 year; may be renewed up to 3 additional years.

604
MAINE TUITION WAIVER PROGRAM FOR CHILDREN AND SPOUSES OF FIRE FIGHTERS AND LAW ENFORCEMENT OFFICERS KILLED IN THE LINE OF DUTY

Finance Authority of Maine
Attn: Education Finance Programs
5 Community Drive
P.O. Box 949
Augusta, ME 04332-0949
Phone: (207) 623-3263   (800) 228-3734
Fax: (207) 623-0095   TDD: (207) 626-2717
E-mail: info@famemaine.com
Web Site: www.famemaine.com
Summary: To provide financial assistance to children and spouses of deceased law enforcement officers and fire fighters in Maine.
Eligibility: This program is open to children and spouses of fire fighters and law enforcement officers who have been killed in the line of duty or died as a result of injuries received during the performance of their duties. Applicants must be enrolled in or accepted for enrollment in a branch of the University of Maine system, the Maine Technical College System, or the Maine Maritime Academy.
Financial data: Eligible students receive waivers of tuition and fees.
Duration: 1 year; may be renewed up to 3 additional years.

605
MAINE TUITION WAIVER PROGRAM FOR FOSTER CHILDREN UNDER THE CUSTODY OF THE DEPARTMENT OF HUMAN SERVICES

Finance Authority of Maine
Attn: Education Finance Programs
5 Community Drive
P.O. Box 949
Augusta, ME 04332-0949
Phone: (207) 623-3263   (800) 228-3734
Fax: (207) 623-0095   TDD: (207) 626-2717
E-mail: info@famemaine.com
Web Site: www.famemaine.com
Summary: To provide financial assistance to foster children in Maine.
Eligibility: Applicants must have been foster children under the custody of the Maine Department of Human Services when they graduate from high school. They must be enrolled in or accepted for enrollment in a branch of the University of Maine system, the Maine Technical College System, or the Maine Maritime Academy.
Financial data: Eligible students receive waivers of tuition and fees.
Duration: 1 year; may be renewed up to 3 additional years.

606
MAINE VETERANS DEPENDENTS EDUCATIONAL BENEFITS

Bureau of Maine Veterans' Services
117 State House Station
Augusta, ME 04333-0117
Phone: (207) 626-4464   (800) 345-0116 (within ME)
Fax: (207) 626-4471   E-mail: mvs@me.ngb.army.mil
Web Site: www.state.me.us/va/defense/vb.htm
Summary: To provide financial assistance for the undergraduate education of dependents of disabled and other Maine veterans.
Eligibility: Applicants for these benefits must be children (high school seniors or graduates under 25 years of age), non-divorced spouses, or unremarried widow(er)s of veterans who meet 1 or more of the following requirements: 1) living and determined to have a total permanent disability resulting from a service-connected disability; 2) killed in action; 3) died from a service-connected disability; 4) died while totally and permanently disabled due to a service-connected disability but whose death was not related to the service-connected disability; or 5) a member of the armed forces on active duty who has been listed for more than 90 days as missing in action, captured, forcibly detained, or interned

in the line of duty by a foreign government or power. The veteran parent must have been a resident of Maine at the time of entry into service or a resident of Maine for 5 years preceding application for these benefits. Children may be seeking no higher than a bachelor's degree. Spouses, widows, and widowers may pursue an advanced degree if they already have a bachelor's degree at the time of enrollment into this program.

Financial data: Recipients are entitled to free tuition in institutions of higher education supported by the state of Maine.

Duration: Benefits extend for a maximum of 8 semesters. Recipients have 6 consecutive academic years to complete their education.

Additional information: College preparatory schooling and correspondence courses do not qualify under this program.

Number awarded: Varies each year.

607
MAINE VIETNAM VETERANS SCHOLARSHIP FUND

Maine Community Foundation
Attn: Program Director
245 Main Street
Ellsworth, ME 04605
Phone: (207) 667-9735   (877) 700-6800
Fax: (207) 667-0447   E-mail: info@mainecf.org
Web Site: www.mainecf.org/scholar.html

Summary: To provide financial assistance for postsecondary education to Vietnam veterans or the dependents of Vietnam or other veterans in Maine.

Eligibility: This program is open to residents of Maine who are Vietnam veterans or the descendants of veterans who served in the Vietnam Theater. As a second priority, children of veterans from other time periods are also considered. Graduating high school seniors, nontraditional students, undergraduates, and graduate students are eligible to apply. Selection is based on financial need, extracurricular activities, work experience, academic achievement, and a personal statement of career goals and how the applicant's educational plans relate to them.

Financial data: The stipend is $1,000 per year.

Duration: 1 year.

Additional information: This program was established in 1985. There is a $3 processing fee.

Number awarded: 3 to 6 each year.

Deadline: April of each year.

608
MAINELY CHARACTER SCHOLARSHIP

Finance Authority of Maine
Attn: Education Finance Programs
5 Community Drive
P.O. Box 949
Augusta, ME 04332-0949
Phone: (207) 623-3263   (800) 228-3734
Fax: (207) 623-0095   TDD: (207) 626-2717
E-mail: info@famemaine.com
Web Site: www.famemaine.com

Summary: To provide financial assistance for college to Maine residents who demonstrate principles of character.

Eligibility: This program is open to residents of Maine who are high school seniors or have received a high school diploma and are entering the first year of postsecondary education. Selection is based on character through an assessment process including a written essay that demonstrates the principles of courage, integrity, responsibility, and concern. A personal interview is also required.

Financial data: The stipend is $5,000.

Duration: 1 year; nonrenewable.

Number awarded: 1 or more each year.

Deadline: February of each year.

609
MAKING COLLEGE COUNT SCHOLARSHIPS

General Motors Corporation
Chevrolet Motor Division
Attn: GM Scholarship Administration Center
702 West Fifth Avenue
Naperville, IL 60563-2948
Phone: (888) 377-5233

Web Site: www.makingitcount.com/roadtocollege/scholarship/chevy_about.asp

Summary: To provide financial assistance to outstanding high school students.

Eligibility: To be eligible for this award, students must meet the following requirements: be completing their senior year of high school; have earned at least a 3.2 grade point average; be able to demonstrate both academic excellence and outstanding community service; be a U.S. citizen or have eligibility to work in the United States; and intend to enroll in college the fall after graduation. Included in the application package must be a 500- to 750-word statement on their high school experiences, a letter of recommendation from an appropriate teacher or administrator, and an official transcript. Selection is based on strength of academic performance, leadership and participation in school and community activities, work experience, career and educational aspiration, and the strength of the personal statement.

Financial data: The stipend is $1,000.

Duration: 1 year.

Additional information: This program is sponsored by the Chevrolet Motor Division of General Motors Corporation and administered by CollegeLink.com Incorporated, 55 Hammarlund Way, Middletown, RI, (401) 845-8800, Fax: (401) 845-8821.

Number awarded: 25 each year.

Deadline: May of each year.

610
MANCHESTER REGIONAL COMMUNITY FOUNDATION MEDALLION FUND

New Hampshire Charitable Foundation
37 Pleasant Street
Concord, NH 03301-4005
Phone: (603) 225-6641   (800) 464-6641
Fax: (603) 225-1700   E-mail: info@nhcf.org
Web Site: www.nhcf.org

Summary: To provide financial assistance to New Hampshire residents pursuing a vocational or technical career.

Eligibility: This program is open to residents of New Hampshire of any age who are enrolling in an accredited vocational or technical program that does not lead to a 4-year baccalaureate degree. Applicants must be planning to attend a community college, vocational school, trade school, apprenticeship, or other short-term training program. They must be able to demonstrate financial need. Although academic excellence is not considered in the selection process, applicants should be able to demonstrate reasonable achievement and a commitment to their chosen field of study.

Financial data: Stipends are provided (exact amount not specified).

Duration: 1 year.

Number awarded: Varies each year.

Deadline: Applications may be submitted at any time.

611
MARCH OF DIMES YOUTH LEADERSHIP SCHOLARSHIPS

March of Dimes Birth Defects Foundation
Attn: Vice President for Research
1275 Mamaroneck Avenue
White Plains, NY 10605
Phone: (914) 997-4555   Fax: (914) 997-4560
E-mail: mkatz@modimes.org
Web Site: www.modimes.org

Summary: To provide financial assistance for college to high school seniors who have been involved in volunteer activities related to the health of babies.

Eligibility: This program is open to graduating high school seniors who are planning to pursue a degree at an accredited postsecondary institution. Applicants must have a grade point average of 3.0 or higher and a record of a leadership role in volunteer service that improves the health of babies. They must include with their applications 1) short essays on their community activities, school activities, a challenge that they have overcome, and their future goals, and 2) a major essay on what their volunteer work has done for them and their community. Financial need is not considered in the selection process.

Financial data: The stipend is $2,500.

Duration: 1 year.

Additional information: This program was established in 1999.

Number awarded: 10 each year.

Deadline: May of each year.

Scholarship Listings

612
MARCUS GARVEY SCHOLARSHIP

West Indian Foundation, Inc.
Attn: Scholarship Committee
1229 Albany Avenue
P.O. Box 320394
Hartford, CT 06132-0394
Phone: (860) 241-0379   Fax: (860) 241-0379
E-mail: westindian@snet.net
Web Site: www.westindianfoundation.org
Summary: To provide financial assistance for college to Connecticut high school
seniors of West Indian parentage.
Eligibility: This program is open to seniors graduating from high schools in
Connecticut who are of West Indian parentage. Selection is based on an essay on
"The Significance of the Life of Marcus Garvey," academic achievement,
community service, and financial need.
Financial data: The stipend is $1,000.
Duration: 1 year.
Number awarded: 1 each year.
Deadline: June of each year.

613
MARGARET GONZALES SCHOLARSHIP

Las Mujeres de LULAC
Attn: Scholarship Committee
P.O. Box 2203
Albuquerque, NM 87103
Summary: To provide financial assistance to nontraditional Hispana students to
continue their postsecondary education in New Mexico.
Eligibility: This program is open to Hispanic women who are residents of New
Mexico; are enrolled in an accredited college, university, community college,
vocational school, or certified career enhancement program in the state; and are
nontraditional students who are returning to school to complete a degree, for
career development, or for employment training. A personal interview may be
required. Financial need is considered in the selection process.
Financial data: A stipend is awarded (exact amount not specified).
Duration: 1 year.
Number awarded: 1 or more each year.
Deadline: May of each year.

614
MARGARET P. CROZIER MEMORIAL SCHOLARSHIP

The Retired Officers Association
Attn: Educational Assistance Program
201 North Washington Street
Alexandria, VA 22314-2539
Phone: (703) 838-8816   (800) 245-8762, ext. 816
Fax: (703) 838-5819   E-mail: edassist@troa.org
Web Site: www.troa.org/Education/ScholarshipFund.asp
Summary: To provide financial support for the undergraduate education of
dependent children of members of The Retired Officers Association (TROA).
Eligibility: This program is open to never married dependent children under age
24 of active, reserve, and retired uniformed service personnel (Army, Navy, Air
Force, Marines, Coast Guard, Public Health Service, or National Oceanographic
and Atmospheric Administration). Parents who are officers eligible for
membership in the association must be members. Unmarried dependent children
of enlisted personnel are also eligible to apply. Selection is based on scholastic
ability (minimum grade point average of 3.0), potential, character, leadership, and
financial need. Applicants must be entering their senior year of college.
Financial data: The stipend is $3,000 per year.
Duration: 1 year.
Additional information: Applicants for the TROA Educational Assistance
Program loans are automatically considered for these scholarships; no separate
application is necessary. Grants are in addition to the amount of the loan.
Number awarded: Varies each year.
Deadline: February of each year.

615
MARGUERITE ROSS BARNETT MEMORIAL SCHOLARSHIP

Missouri Department of Higher Education
Attn: Missouri Student Assistance Resource Services (MOSTARS)
3515 Amazonas Drive
Jefferson City, MO 65109-5717
Phone: (573) 751-3940   (800) 473-6757
Fax: (573) 751-6635
Web Site: www.mocbhe.gov
Summary: To provide financial assistance for college to students in Missouri who
are employed while attending school part time.
Eligibility: This program is open to residents of Missouri who are enrolled at least
half time but less than full time at participating Missouri postsecondary institutions.
Applicants must be able to demonstrate financial need and employment of 20 hours
or more per week. Students pursuing a degree or certificate in theology or divinity
are not eligible. U.S. citizenship or permanent resident status is required.
Financial data: The maximum annual award is the least of 1) the actual tuition
charged at the school the recipient is attending part time; 2) the amount of tuition
charged to a Missouri undergraduate resident enrolled part time in the same class
level at the University of Missouri; or 3) the recipient's demonstrated financial need.
Duration: 1 semester; may be renewed until the recipient has obtained a
baccalaureate degree or has completed 150 semester credit hours, whichever
comes first.
Additional information: Awards are not available for summer study.
Number awarded: Varies each year.
Deadline: March of each year.

616
MARI AND JAMES MICHENER SCHOLARSHIP

Japanese American Citizens League
Attn: National Scholarship Awards
1765 Sutter Street
San Francisco, CA 94115
Phone: (415) 921-5225   Fax: (415) 931-4671
E-mail: jacl@jacl.org
Web Site: www.jacl.org
Summary: To provide financial assistance to student members of the Japanese
American Citizens League (JACL) who are pursuing undergraduate education.
Eligibility: This program is open to JACL members who are currently enrolled or
planning to reenter a college, university, trade school, business college, or other
institution of higher learning. Selection is based on academic record,
extracurricular activities, and community involvement.
Financial data: The stipend depends on the availability of funds but usually
ranges from $1,000 to $5,000.
Duration: 1 year.
Additional information: Requests for applications must be accompanied by a
self-addressed stamped envelope.
Number awarded: 1 each year.
Deadline: March of each year.

617
MARIA & ANTONIO PEREIRA SCHOLARSHIP

Portuguese Heritage Scholarship Foundation
Attn: Academic Secretary
P.O. Box 30246
Bethesda, MD 20824-0246
Phone: (301) 652-2775   E-mail: phsf@vivaportugal.com
Web Site: www.vivaportugal.com/phsf/apply.htm
Summary: To provide financial assistance for college to students of Portuguese
American heritage.
Eligibility: Eligible to apply for this support are high school seniors or currently-
enrolled college students who are of Portuguese American ancestry. Applicants
must be U.S. residents and attending or planning to attend an accredited 4-year
college or university. Selection is based on academic achievement and financial
need.
Financial data: The stipend is $2,000 per year.
Duration: 4 years, provided the recipient maintains a grade point average of 3.0 or
higher.
Additional information: Recipients must attend college on a full-time basis.
Number awarded: 1 each year.
Deadline: January of each year.

618
MARIA C. JACKSON—GENERAL GEORGE A. WHITE STUDENT AID FUND

Oregon Student Assistance Commission
Attn: Private Awards Grant Department
1500 Valley River Drive, Suite 100
Eugene, OR 97401-2146
Phone: (541) 687-7395   (800) 452-8807, ext. 7395
Fax: (541) 687-7419   E-mail: awardinfo@mercury.osac.state.or.us
Web Site: www.osac.state.or.us
Summary: To support the postsecondary education of veterans or the children of veterans and military personnel in Oregon.
Eligibility: Applicants must be U.S. veterans or the children of veterans (or of active-duty personnel) who are high school graduates and residents of Oregon studying at institutions of higher learning in the state. The veteran or active-duty service member parent must have resided in Oregon at the time of enlistment. A minimum grade point average of 3.75, either in high school (if the student is a graduating high school senior) or in college (for graduate and continuing undergraduate students), is required. Selection is based on scholastic ability and financial need.
Financial data: Scholarship amounts vary, depending upon the needs of the recipient.
Duration: 1 year; may be renewed up to 3 additional years.
Number awarded: Varies each year.
Deadline: February of each year.

619
MARIE KIRKLAND SCHOLARSHIP

Royal Neighbors of America
Attn: National Headquarters
230 16th Street
Rock Island, IL 61201-8645
Phone: (309) 788-4561   (800) 627-4762
E-mail: contact@royalneighbors.org
Web Site: www.royalneighbors.org
Summary: To provide financial assistance for college to women members of the Royal Neighbors of America.
Eligibility: Applicants must have been members of the society for at least 2 years immediately prior to the application deadline, be high school seniors recommended by their local lodge and field representative, be in the top quarter of their graduating class, and have been admitted to an accredited 4-year college or university as a full-time student. Selection is based on character and personal goals, school and community activities, ability to meet the specific entrance requirements of the accredited college or university selected, and general aptitude for college work as indicated by aptitude tests or scholastic records. The recipient is the woman judged to be most qualified from all applicants for Royal Neighbors of America scholarships.
Financial data: The stipend is $2,500 per year.
Duration: 4 years.
Additional information: This program was established in 1998.
Number awarded: 1 each year.
Deadline: December of each year.

620
MARIE L. ROSE HUGUENOT SCHOLARSHIPS

Huguenot Society of America
Attn: Office of the Scholarship Committee
122 East 58th Street
New York, NY 10022
Phone: (212) 755-0592
Summary: To provide financial assistance for undergraduate education to the descendants of Huguenots.
Eligibility: Applicants must be able to submit proof of descent from a Huguenot who emigrated from France and either settled in what is now the United States or left France for other countries before 1787. The scholarships are available to students at 1 of 50 participating universities; for a list, contact the Huguenot Society.
Financial data: The award is $3,000 per year.
Duration: 1 year.
Additional information: Applications are available only from financial aid offices at the participating universities and must be submitted to those offices. Applications sent directly to the Huguenot Society are not accepted.
Number awarded: Varies each year.

621
MARINE CORPS INTELLIGENCE EDUCATIONAL FOUNDATION SCHOLARSHIPS

Marine Corps Intelligence Educational Foundation
Attn: Chairman, Scholarship Committee
P.O. Box 1028
Quantico, VA 22134-1028
Web Site: mcia-inc.org/mcief.htm
Summary: To provide financial assistance for college to members of the Marine Corps Intelligence Association (MCIA) and their dependent children.
Eligibility: This program is open to current MCIA members, their dependent children, and their survivors. Applicants must be attending or planning to attend an accredited 4-year college or university. They must submit an essay on their reasons for seeking the scholarship, their course of study, and their long-range goals. Selection is based on the essay, academic achievement, extracurricular activities, and work experience. Financial need is not considered.
Financial data: The stipend is $1,000.
Duration: 1 year.
Additional information: Membership in the MCIA is open to Marine Corps intelligence personnel, including active duty, reserve, and retired.
Number awarded: 1 or more each year.

622
MARINE CORPS LEAGUE SCHOLARSHIPS

Marine Corps League
Attn: National Executive Director
P.O. Box 3070
Merrifield, VA 22116-3070
Phone: (703) 207-9588   (800) MCL-1775
Fax: (703) 207-0047   E-mail: mcl@mcleague.org
Web Site: www.mcleague.org
Summary: To provide college aid to students whose parents served in the Marines and to members of the Marine Corps League or Marine Corps League Auxiliary.
Eligibility: The scholarships are awarded to qualified applicants in the following order of preference: 1) sons and daughters of Marines who lost their lives in the line of duty; 2) children and grandchildren of active Marine Corps Leaguers and/or Auxiliary members; and 3) members of the Marine Corps League and/or Marine Corps League Auxiliary who are honorably discharged and in need of rehabilitation training not provided by government programs. Applicants must be seeking further education and training as a full-time student and be recommended by the commandant of an active chartered detachment of the Marine Corps League or the president of an active chartered unit of the Auxiliary. Financial need is not considered in the selection process.
Financial data: The stipend varies. Funds are paid directly to the recipient.
Duration: 1 year; may be renewed up to 3 additional years (all renewals must complete an application and attach a transcript from the college or university).
Additional information: Information is also available from the Marine Corps League Scholarship Committee, Robert A. Creedon, Chairman, 5111 West 85th Lane, Crown Point, IN 46307-1570.
Number awarded: Varies, depending upon the amount of funds available each year.
Deadline: June of each year.

623
MARINE CORPS SCHOLARSHIPS

Marine Corps Scholarship Foundation, Inc.
P.O. Box 3008
Princeton, NJ 08543-3008
Phone: (609) 921-3534   (800) 292-7777
Fax: (609) 452-2259   E-mail: mcsf@aosi.com
Web Site: www.marine-scholars.org
Summary: To provide financial assistance for postsecondary education to the children of present or former members of the U.S. Marine Corps.
Eligibility: This program is open to the children of 1) Marines on active duty or in the Reserves; 2) former Marines and Marine Reservists who have received an honorable discharge, received a medical discharge, or were killed in the service of the country; and 3) active-duty, reserve, and former U.S. Navy Corpsmen who are serving or have served with the U.S. Marine Corps. Applicants must be high school seniors, high school graduates, or current students in an accredited college, university, or postsecondary vocational-technical school. Preference is given to sons and daughters of those Marines who were disabled, wounded, or

killed while serving in combat. In addition to student achievement and potential, citizenship, and participation in school and community activities, applicants must have a record of financial need (awards are not made to members of families with annual incomes in excess of $49,000).

Financial data: The amounts awarded vary from $500 to $2,500 per year, depending upon the recipient's financial needs and educational requirements.

Duration: 1 year; may be renewed upon reapplication.

Additional information: Recipients may pursue only undergraduate study at accredited colleges, universities, or postsecondary technical institutions.

Number awarded: Varies each year; recently, 1,080 of these scholarships, with a total value of approximately $1,500,000, were awarded.

Deadline: March of each year.

624
MARION HUBER LEARNING THROUGH LISTENING AWARDS

Recording for the Blind and Dyslexic
Attn: Public Affairs Department
Anne T. Macdonald Center
20 Roszel Road
Princeton, NJ 08540
Phone: (609) 452-0606   (800) 221-4792
Web Site: www.rfbd.org

Summary: To provide financial assistance to outstanding high school students with learning disabilities who plan to continue their education.

Eligibility: The recipients are chosen from learning disabled students who are graduating seniors in public or private high schools in the United States or its territories and planning to continue their education at a 2-year or 4-year college or vocational school. They must be registered Recording for the Blind and Dyslexic borrowers and have earned at least a 3.0 grade point average in grades 10 through 12. Selection is based on outstanding scholastic achievement, leadership, enterprise, and service to others.

Financial data: Stipends are $6,000 or $2,000.

Duration: 1 year.

Additional information: This program was established in 1992.

Number awarded: 6 each year: 3 at $6,000 and 3 at $2,000.

Deadline: February of each year.

625
MARION J. BAGLEY SCHOLARSHIP

American Legion Auxiliary
Attn: Department of New Hampshire
State House Annex
25 Capitol Street, Room 432
Concord, NH 03301-6312
Phone: (603) 271-2211

Summary: To provide financial assistance for postsecondary education to New Hampshire residents.

Eligibility: This program is open to New Hampshire residents who are high school seniors, high school graduates or equivalent, or attending a school of higher learning. Applicants must submit 3 letters of recommendation; a list of school, church, and community activities or organizations in which they have participated; transcripts; and a 1,000-word essay on "My obligations as an American." Financial need is considered in the selection process.

Financial data: The stipend is $1,000.

Duration: 1 year.

Additional information: Requests for applications must be accompanied by a self-addressed stamped envelope.

Number awarded: 1 each year.

Deadline: April of each year.

626
MARSH SCHOLARSHIP

Eastern Surfing Association
P.O. Box 582
Ocean City, MD 21843
Phone: (410) 213-0515   (800) WE-SHRED
Fax: (410) 213-0515   E-mail: centralhq@surfesa.org
Web Site: www.surfesa.org

Summary: To provide financial assistance for college to members of the Eastern Surfing Association.

Eligibility: This program is open to current members in good standing.

Applicants must submit an essay, up to 500 words, detailing their educational goals and how their choice of educational institutions will help them reach those goals. Selection is based on academic record and U.S. citizenship, not athletic ability.

Financial data: Scholarships range from $500 to $1,000.

Additional information: This scholarship was established in 1981 in honor of Mike Marsh, who earned a law degree despite his battle against cancer. Information is also available from the ESA Marsh Scholarship Program, c/o Henningsen, 25 Old Post Road, Rye, NY 10580.

Number awarded: 2 or 3 each year.

Deadline: May of each year.

627
MARTIN BARNES SCHOLARSHIPS

Martin Barnes Scholarship Fund
413 Sixth Street, S.E.
Washington, DC 20003

Summary: To provide financial assistance for college to high school seniors, undergraduates, and graduate students.

Eligibility: Applicants may be high school seniors or currently-enrolled undergraduate or graduate students. They must be U.S. citizens, have at least a 2.5 grade point average, and have performed at least 100 hours of community service within the current academic year in the field of human outreach. As part of the application, students must submit an essay on the topic: "The Contributions I Would Make to Win the War on Drugs." Also required are 3 written recommendations or character references. Selection is based on community service, leadership, and academic record.

Financial data: The stipend is $500 for high school seniors or $1,000 for undergraduate or graduate students. Funds are paid directly to the recipient's school.

Duration: 1 year.

Number awarded: 2 each year: 1 to a high school senior and 1 to an undergraduate or graduate student.

Deadline: May of each year.

628
MARTIN LUTHER KING, JR. SCHOLARSHIP

North Carolina Association of Educators.
Attn: Minority Affairs Commission
P.O. Box 27347
Raleigh, NC 27611-7347
Phone: (919) 832-3000, ext. 211   (800) 662-7924, ext. 211
Fax: (919) 839-8229
Web Site: www.ncae.org

Summary: To provide financial assistance for college to minority and other high school seniors in North Carolina.

Eligibility: Applicants must be North Carolina residents enrolled as seniors in high school. They must be planning to continue their education upon graduation. Applications are considered and judged by members of the association's Minority Affairs Commission. Selection is based on character, personality, and scholastic achievement.

Financial data: The amount of the stipend depends on the availability of funding.

Duration: 1 year.

Number awarded: 1 each year.

Deadline: January of each year.

629
MARY MACON MCGUIRE EDUCATIONAL GRANT

Virginia Federation of Women's Clubs
Attn: Scholarship/Fellowship/Grant Committee
513 Forest Avenue
P.O. Box 8750
Richmond, VA 23226
Phone: (800) 699-8392   E-mail: sadlers@mediaone.net
Web Site: www.vfwc.f2s.com

Summary: To provide financial assistance to women heads of households in Virginia who have returned to school.

Eligibility: This program is open to women residents of Virginia who are heads of households. Applicants must be currently enrolled in a course of study (vocational or academic) at an accredited Virginia school. They must have returned to school to upgrade their education and employment skills so as to

better provide for their families. Selection is based on 3 letters of recommendation (1 of a general nature, 2 from recent professors, teachers, counselors, or advisors); a resume of educational and employment history, financial circumstances, and community activities; and a essay up to 2,000 words that outlines the financial need for the grant as well as the reasons for entering the field of study selected.
Financial data: The stipend is $5,000. Funds are paid directly to the student.
Duration: 1 year.
Additional information: This program began in 1929 as a loan fund. It was converted to its current form in 2000. Information is also available from the Committee Chair, Fran Barner, P.O. Box 126, Boykins, VA 23827.
Number awarded: 1 each year.
Deadline: March of each year.

630
MARY P. OENSLAGER SCHOLASTIC ACHIEVEMENT AWARDS

Recording for the Blind and Dyslexic
Attn: Public Affairs Department
Anne T. Macdonald Center
20 Roszel Road
Princeton, NJ 08540
Phone: (609) 452-0606   (800) 221-4792
Web Site: www.rfbd.org
Summary: To recognize and reward the outstanding academic achievements of blind college seniors.
Eligibility: To be eligible for this award, candidates must 1) be legally blind; 2) have received, or will receive, a bachelor's degree from a 4-year accredited college or university in the United States or its territories during the year the award is given; 3) have an overall academic average of 3.0 or more on a 4.0 scale; and 4) be registered borrowers from Recording for the Blind and Dyslexic. Selection is based on evidence of leadership, enterprise, and service to others.
Financial data: Scholastic Achievement winners receive $6,000 each, Special Honors winners $3,000 each, and Honors winners $1,000 each.
Duration: The awards are presented annually.
Number awarded: 9 each year: 3 Scholastic Achievement winners, 3 Special Honors winners, and 3 Honors winners.
Additional information: These awards are named for the founder of the program who established it in 1959 and endowed it with a gift of $1 million in 1990.
Deadline: February of each year.

631
MARY TINKER SCHOLARSHIP FUND

Osage Tribal Education Department
Attn: Education Coordinator
1333 Grandview
Pawhuska, OK 74056
Phone: (918) 287-1038   (800) 390-6724
Fax: (918) 287-2416   E-mail: jhopper@mmind.net
Web Site: www.osagetribe.com/education.htm
Summary: To provide financial assistance for college to members of the Osage Tribe.
Eligibility: This program is open to Osage Tribal students who are enrolled or planning to enroll in a 2-year or 4-year college or university.
Financial data: The amount of the award depends on the availability of funds and the need of the recipient.
Duration: 1 semester; may be renewed.
Number awarded: Varies each year.
Deadline: July of each year for fall semester; December for spring semester.

632
MARYLAND DELEGATE SCHOLARSHIP PROGRAM

Maryland Higher Education Commission
Attn: State Scholarship Administration
16 Francis Street
Annapolis, MD 21401-1781
Phone: (410) 260-4518   (800) 974-1024
Fax: (410) 974-5376   TTY: (800) 735-2258
E-mail: ssamail@mhec.state.md.us
Web Site: www.mhec.state.md.us
Summary: To provide financial assistance for vocational, undergraduate, and graduate education in Maryland.
Eligibility: This program is open to students enrolled or planning to enroll either part time or full time in a vocational, undergraduate, or graduate program in

Maryland. Applicants must be Maryland residents. Awards are made by state delegates to students in their district. Financial need must be demonstrated if the State Scholarship Administration makes the award for the delegate.
Financial data: The amount awarded varies.
Duration: 1 year; may be renewed for up to 3 additional years if the recipient maintains satisfactory academic progress.
Additional information: Recipients may attend an out-of-state institution if their major is not available at a Maryland school and if their delegate agrees. Students should contact all 3 delegates in their state legislative district for application instructions.
Deadline: February of each year.

633
MARYLAND DISTINGUISHED SCHOLAR PROGRAM

Maryland Higher Education Commission
Attn: State Scholarship Administration
16 Francis Street
Annapolis, MD 21401-1781
Phone: (410) 260-4569   (800) 974-1024
Fax: (410) 974-5376   TTY: (800) 735-2258
E-mail: ssamail@mhec.state.md.us
Web Site: www.mhec.state.md.us
Summary: To provide financial assistance for college to outstanding high school juniors in Maryland.
Eligibility: Eligible to apply are outstanding high school juniors in Maryland who intend to pursue an undergraduate degree on a full-time basis at an accredited Maryland college or university. Students may qualify in 1 of 3 ways: 1) superior academic achievement, in which finalists are selected on the basis of GPA (minimum 3.7) and scores on PSAT, SAT, or ACT exams; 2) National Achievement Scholarship and National Merit Scholarship programs, in which finalists automatically receive these scholarships if they enroll in eligible Maryland institutions; and 3) superior talent in the arts, in which finalists are selected in statewide auditions or portfolio evaluations in visual art, music, dance, or drama. Financial need is not considered.
Financial data: The scholarship is $3,000 per year.
Duration: 1 year; may be renewed up to 3 additional years if the recipient maintains at least a 3.0 grade point average and remains enrolled at an eligible Maryland institution.
Number awarded: 350 each year.
Deadline: March of each year.

634
MARYLAND EDUCATIONAL ASSISTANCE GRANT

Maryland Higher Education Commission
Attn: State Scholarship Administration
16 Francis Street
Annapolis, MD 21401-1781
Phone: (410) 260-4518   (800) 974-1024
Fax: (410) 974-5376   TTY: (800) 735-2258
E-mail: ssamail@mhec.state.md.us
Web Site: www.mhec.state.md.us
Summary: To provide financial assistance to undergraduate students in Maryland.
Eligibility: This program is open to Maryland residents who are high school seniors or full-time students in a regular undergraduate program leading to a degree, diploma, or certificate at a Maryland degree-granting institution or hospital school of nursing. Financial need must be documented.
Financial data: Stipends range from $400 to $2,700 per year, depending on need.
Duration: 1 year; recipients may reapply for up to 3 additional years if they maintain a minimum cumulative grade point average of 2.0.
Additional information: Recipients must attend school in Maryland.
Deadline: February of each year.

635
MARYLAND GUARANTEED ACCESS GRANT

Maryland Higher Education Commission
Attn: State Scholarship Administration
16 Francis Street
Annapolis, MD 21401-1781
Phone: (410) 260-4555   (800) 974-1024
Fax: (410) 974-5376   TTY: (800) 735-2258
E-mail: ssamail@mhec.state.md.us
Web Site: www.mhec.state.md.us

Summary: To provide financial assistance to undergraduate students in Maryland.
Eligibility: This program is open to Maryland residents who are full-time undergraduate students in a program leading to a degree, diploma, or certificate at a Maryland degree-granting institution or diploma school of nursing. Applicants must have earned a GPA of 2.5 or higher in high school, be under 22 years of age, be entering college within 1 year of high school graduation, have completed a college prep or tech prep program, and have a family income that is less than 130 percent of the federal poverty level. Currently, the maximum allowable total income is $11,167 for a family of 1, rising to $38,649 for a family of 8 plus $3,926 for each additional family member.
Financial data: The amounts of the awards depend on the need of the recipient, to a maximum of $9,200 per year.
Duration: 1 year; recipients may reapply for up to 3 additional years if their family income remains below 150 percent of the federal poverty level.
Deadline: February of each year.

636
MARYLAND PART-TIME GRANT PROGRAM

Maryland Higher Education Commission
Attn: State Scholarship Administration
16 Francis Street
Annapolis, MD 21401-1781
Phone: (410) 260-4565   (800) 974-1024
Fax: (410) 974-5376   TTY: (800) 735-2258
E-mail: ssamail@mhec.state.md.us
Web Site: www.mhec.state.md.us
Summary: To provide financial assistance to students in Maryland who are attending college on a part-time basis.
Eligibility: This program is open to students at Maryland colleges who are enrolled for at least 6 but no more than 11 credits each semester. Applicants must be able to demonstrate financial need. Both they and their parents must be Maryland residents.
Financial data: Grants range from $200 to $1,000 per year.
Duration: 1 year; may be renewed for up to 7 additional years.
Additional information: Applications are available at the financial aid office of each college or university in Maryland.
Number awarded: Varies each year.
Deadline: February of each year.

637
MARYLAND SENATORIAL SCHOLARSHIPS

Maryland Higher Education Commission
Attn: State Scholarship Administration
16 Francis Street
Annapolis, MD 21401-1781
Phone: (410) 260-4518   (800) 974-1024
Fax: (410) 974-5376   TTY: (800) 735-2258
E-mail: ssamail@mhec.state.md.us
Web Site: www.mhec.state.md.us
Summary: To provide financial assistance for vocational, undergraduate, and graduate education in Maryland.
Eligibility: This program is open to students enrolled either part time or full time in a vocational, undergraduate, or graduate program in Maryland. Applicants must be Maryland residents and must be able to demonstrate financial need. Awards are made by state senators to students in their districts.
Financial data: Stipends range from $200 to $2,000 per year, depending on the need of the recipient.
Duration: 1 year; may be renewed up to 3 additional years or until a degree is earned.
Additional information: Recipients may attend an out-of-state institution if their major is not available at a Maryland school and if their senator agrees.
Deadline: February of each year.

638
MARYLAND TUITION WAIVER FOR FOSTER CARE RECIPIENTS

Maryland Higher Education Commission
Attn: State Scholarship Administration
16 Francis Street
Annapolis, MD 21401-1781
Phone: (410) 260-4565   (800) 974-1024
Fax: (410) 974-5376   TTY: (800) 735-2258
E-mail: ssamail@mhec.state.md.us
Web Site: www.mhec.state.md.us

Summary: To provide financial assistance for college to residents of Maryland who have lived in foster care.
Eligibility: This program is open to Maryland residents who either 1) resided in a foster care home on or after their 18th birthday, or 2) resided in a foster care home on their 14th birthday and were then adopted. Applicants must enroll as a degree candidate at a public 2-year or 4-year educational institution in Maryland on or before the date they become 21 years of age.
Financial data: Recipients are exempt from paying tuition and mandatory fees at public colleges and universities in Maryland.
Duration: 1 year; may be renewed for an additional 4 years or until completion of a bachelor's degree, whichever comes first, provided the recipient maintains satisfactory academic progress.
Number awarded: Varies each year.
Deadline: February of each year.

639
MAS AND MAJIU UYESUGI MEMORIAL SCHOLARSHIP

Japanese American Citizens League
Attn: National Scholarship Awards
1765 Sutter Street
San Francisco, CA 94115
Phone: (415) 921-5225   Fax: (415) 931-4671
E-mail: jacl@jacl.org
Web Site: www.jacl.org
Summary: To provide financial assistance to student members of the Japanese American Citizens League (JACL) who are high school seniors interested in pursuing undergraduate education.
Eligibility: This program is open to JACL members who are high school seniors interested in attending a college, university, trade school, business college, or other institution of higher learning. Selection is based on academic record, extracurricular activities, and community involvement.
Financial data: The stipend depends on the availability of funds but usually ranges from $1,000 to $5,000.
Duration: 1 year.
Additional information: Requests for applications must be accompanied by a self-addressed stamped envelope.
Number awarded: At least 1 each year.
Deadline: March of each year.

640
MASAO AND SUMAKO ITANO MEMORIAL SCHOLARSHIP

Japanese American Citizens League
Attn: National Scholarship Awards
1765 Sutter Street
San Francisco, CA 94115
Phone: (415) 921-5225   Fax: (415) 931-4671
E-mail: jacl@jacl.org
Web Site: www.jacl.org
Summary: To provide financial assistance to student members of the Japanese American Citizens League (JACL) who are high school seniors interested in pursuing undergraduate education.
Eligibility: This program is open to JACL members who are high school seniors interested in attending a college, university, trade school, business college, or other institution of higher learning. Selection is based on academic record, extracurricular activities, and community involvement.
Financial data: The stipend depends on the availability of funds but usually ranges from $1,000 to $5,000.
Duration: 1 year.
Additional information: Requests for applications must be accompanied by a self-addressed stamped envelope.
Number awarded: At least 1 each year.
Deadline: March of each year.

641
MASSACHUSETTS CASH GRANT PROGRAM

Massachusetts Office of Student Financial Assistance
454 Broadway, Suite 200
Revere, MA 02151
Phone: (617) 727-9420   Fax: (617) 727-0667
E-mail: osfa@osfa.mass.edu
Web Site: www.osfa.mass.edu/osfaprograms/cashgrant.asp

Summary: To provide financial assistance to Massachusetts residents who are attending state-supported colleges and universities.

Eligibility: Applicants for these scholarships must have been permanent legal residents of Massachusetts for at least 1 year and must be an undergraduate at a state-supported college or university. U.S. citizenship or permanent resident status is required. Financial need must be demonstrated.

Financial data: These awards provide assistance in meeting institutionally-held charges, such as mandatory fees and tuition. The amount of the award depends on the need of the recipient.

Duration: 1 year; may be renewed.

Additional information: This program complements the Tuition Waiver Program.

Number awarded: Varies each year.

Deadline: Deadlines are established by the financial aid office of each participating Massachusetts institution.

642
MASSACHUSETTS DSS ADOPTED CHILDREN TUITION WAIVER

Massachusetts Office of Student Financial Assistance
454 Broadway, Suite 200
Revere, MA 02151
Phone: (617) 727-9420   Fax: (617) 727-0667
E-mail: osfa@osfa.mass.edu
Web Site: www.osfa.mass.edu/osfaprograms/dsswaiver.asp

Summary: To provide financial assistance for postsecondary education to students adopted through the Massachusetts Department of Social Services (DSS).

Eligibility: This program is open to students under 24 years of age who were adopted through DSS by state employees or eligible Massachusetts residents, regardless of the date of adoption. Applicants must be U.S. citizens or permanent residents attending or planning to attend a Massachusetts public institution of higher education as an undergraduate student.

Financial data: All tuition for state-supported courses is waived.

Duration: Up to 4 academic years.

Number awarded: Varies each year.

643
MASSACHUSETTS DSS TUITION WAIVER FOR FOSTER CARE CHILDREN

Massachusetts Office of Student Financial Assistance
454 Broadway, Suite 200
Revere, MA 02151
Phone: (617) 727-9420   Fax: (617) 727-0667
E-mail: osfa@osfa.mass.edu
Web Site: www.osfa.mass.edu/osfaprograms/dssfostercare.asp

Summary: To provide financial assistance for postsecondary education to foster children in the custody of the Massachusetts Department of Social Services (DSS).

Eligibility: This program is open to students under 24 years of age who are current or former foster children placed in the custody of the state of Massachusetts through a care and protection petition. Applicants must have been in the custody of the state for at least 12 consecutive months and not have been adopted or returned home. They must be U.S. citizens or permanent residents attending or planning to attend a Massachusetts public institution of higher education as a full-time undergraduate student.

Financial data: All tuition for state-supported courses is waived.

Duration: Up to 4 academic years.

Number awarded: Varies each year.

644
MASSACHUSETTS EDUCATIONAL FINANCING AUTHORITY PREPAID TUITION PROGRAM WAIVER

Massachusetts Office of Student Financial Assistance
454 Broadway, Suite 200
Revere, MA 02151
Phone: (617) 727-9420   Fax: (617) 727-0667
E-mail: osfa@osfa.mass.edu
Web Site: www.osfa.mass.edu/osfaprograms/mefa.asp

Summary: To provide financial assistance for postsecondary education to Massachusetts residents who participate in the Massachusetts Educational Financing Authority (MEFA) Prepaid Tuition Program.

Eligibility: This program is open to students who are the owner or a qualifying beneficiary of a MEFA Prepaid Tuition Program. Applicants must be admitted to a Massachusetts public institution of higher education that participates in the MEFA Prepaid Tuition Program.

Financial data: If the tuition charged by the participating public institution exceeds the amount received as a tuition credit pursuant to the student's participation in Prepaid Tuition Program, the institution may waive the difference.

Duration: Up to 4 academic years.

Additional information: Information on the Prepaid Tuition Program is available from MEFA at (617) 261-9760.

Number awarded: Varies each year.

645
MASSACHUSETTS JOINT ADMISSIONS TUITION ADVANTAGE PROGRAM

Massachusetts Office of Student Financial Assistance
454 Broadway, Suite 200
Revere, MA 02151
Phone: (617) 727-9420   Fax: (617) 727-0667
E-mail: osfa@osfa.mass.edu
Web Site: www.osfa.mass.edu/osfaprograms/jointwaiver.asp

Summary: To provide financial assistance to Massachusetts students who transfer from a community college to a state-supported 4-year institution in the state.

Eligibility: This program is open to students who completed an associate degree at a public community college in Massachusetts within the prior calendar year as a participant in a Joint Admissions Program. Applicants must have earned a grade point average of 3.0 or higher and be transferring to a state college or participating university.

Financial data: Eligible student receive a waiver of tuition equal to 33 percent of the resident tuition rate at the college or university they attend.

Duration: Up to 2 academic years, if the recipient maintains at least a 3.0 grade point average.

Number awarded: Varies each year.

646
MASSACHUSETTS LEGION DEPARTMENT GENERAL SCHOLARSHIPS

American Legion
Attn: Department of Massachusetts
State House
24 Beacon Street, Suite 546-2
Boston, MA 02133-1044
Phone: (617) 727-2966   Fax: (617) 727-2969

Summary: To provide financial assistance for postsecondary education to the children and grandchildren of members of the American Legion in Massachusetts.

Eligibility: Eligible to apply are the children and grandchildren of members in good standing in the American Legion's Department of Massachusetts (or who were members in good standing at the time of death). Applicants must be entering their freshman year of college.

Financial data: Stipends are $1,000 or $500.

Duration: 1 year.

Number awarded: 18 each year: 8 at $1,000 and 10 at $500.

Deadline: March of each year.

647
MASSACHUSETTS NATIVE AMERICAN TUITION WAIVER PROGRAM

Massachusetts Office of Student Financial Assistance
454 Broadway, Suite 200
Revere, MA 02151
Phone: (617) 727-9420   Fax: (617) 727-0667
E-mail: osfa@osfa.mass.edu
Web Site: www.osfa.mass.edu/osfaprograms/ctuitionwav.asp

Summary: To provide financial assistance for the postsecondary education of Massachusetts residents who are Native Americans.

Eligibility: Applicants for these scholarships must have been permanent legal residents of Massachusetts for at least 1 year and certified by the Bureau of Indian Affairs as Native Americans. They may not be in default on any federal student loan.

Financial data: Eligible students are exempt from any tuition payments for an undergraduate degree or certificate program at public colleges or universities in Massachusetts.

Duration: Up to 4 academic years, for a total of 130 semester hours.

Additional information: Recipients may enroll either part or full time in a Massachusetts publicly-supported institution.
Number awarded: Varies each year.

648
MASSACHUSETTS NEED BASED TUITION WAIVER PROGRAM

Massachusetts Office of Student Financial Assistance
454 Broadway, Suite 200
Revere, MA 02151
Phone: (617) 727-9420   Fax: (617) 727-0667
E-mail: osfa@osfa.mass.edu
Web Site: www.osfa.mass.edu/osfaprograms/needtuitionwav.asp
Summary: To provide financial assistance for the postsecondary education of Massachusetts residents who demonstrate financial need.
Eligibility: Applicants for these scholarships must have been permanent legal residents of Massachusetts for at least 1 year, be U.S. citizens, be in compliance with Selective Service registration, not be in default on any federal student loan, be enrolled for at least 3 undergraduate units in an eligible program at a Massachusetts institution of higher learning, and be able to document financial need.
Financial data: Eligible students are exempt from any tuition payments for an undergraduate degree or certificate program at public colleges or universities in Massachusetts.
Duration: Up to 4 academic years, for a total of 130 semester hours.
Additional information: Recipients may enroll either part or full time in a Massachusetts publicly-supported institution.
Number awarded: Varies each year.

649
MASSACHUSETTS PART-TIME GRANT PROGRAM

Massachusetts Office of Student Financial Assistance
454 Broadway, Suite 200
Revere, MA 02151
Phone: (617) 727-9420   Fax: (617) 727-0667
E-mail: osfa@osfa.mass.edu
Web Site: www.osfa.mass.edu/osfaprograms/ptgrant.asp
Summary: To provide financial assistance to Massachusetts residents who are attending state-supported colleges and universities on a part-time basis.
Eligibility: Applicants for these scholarships must have been permanent legal residents of Massachusetts for at least 1 year and must be a part-time undergraduate at a state-supported college or university. U.S. citizenship or permanent resident status is required. Financial need must be demonstrated.
Financial data: Awards cover from $200 up to tuition cost, depending on the need of the recipient.
Duration: 1 year; may be renewed.
Number awarded: Varies each year.
Deadline: Deadlines are established by the financial aid office of each participating Massachusetts institution.

650
MASSACHUSETTS PUBLIC SERVICE GRANT PROGRAM

Massachusetts Office of Student Financial Assistance
454 Broadway, Suite 200
Revere, MA 02151
Phone: (617) 727-9420   Fax: (617) 727-0667
E-mail: osfa@osfa.mass.edu
Web Site: www.osfa.mass.edu/osfaprograms/psgrant.asp
Summary: To provide financial assistance for college to children or widow(er)s of deceased public service officers in Massachusetts.
Eligibility: Only Massachusetts residents are eligible. They must be 1) the children or spouses of fire fighters, police officers, or corrections officers who died in the line of duty; 2) children of prisoners of war or military service personnel missing in action in southeast Asia whose wartime service was credited to Massachusetts and whose service was between February 1, 1955 and the termination of the Vietnam campaign; or 3) children of veterans whose service was credited to Massachusetts and who were killed in action or died as a result of their service.
Financial data: Scholarships provide up to the cost of tuition at a state-supported college or university in Massachusetts; if the recipient attends a private college or university, the scholarship is equivalent to tuition at a public institution, up to $2,500.
Duration: 1 year; renewable.
Number awarded: Varies each year.
Deadline: April of each year.

651
MASSACHUSETTS REHABILITATION COMMISSION OR COMMISSION FOR THE BLIND TUITION WAIVER PROGRAM

Massachusetts Office of Student Financial Assistance
454 Broadway, Suite 200
Revere, MA 02151
Phone: (617) 727-9420   Fax: (617) 727-0667
E-mail: osfa@osfa.mass.edu
Web Site: www.osfa.mass.edu/osfaprograms/ctuitionwav.asp
Summary: To provide financial assistance for postsecondary education to Massachusetts residents who are clients of specified state agencies.
Eligibility: Applicants for these scholarships must be certified as clients by the Massachusetts Rehabilitation Commission or Commission for the Blind. They must have been permanent residents of Massachusetts for at least 1 year, must be U.S. citizens or permanent residents, and may not be in default on any federal student loan.
Financial data: Eligible clients are exempt from any tuition payments for an undergraduate degree or certificate program at public colleges or universities in Massachusetts.
Duration: Up to 4 academic years, for a total of 130 semester hours.
Additional information: Recipients may enroll either part or full time in a Massachusetts publicly-supported institution.
Number awarded: Varies each year.

652
MASSACHUSETTS VETERANS TUITION WAIVER PROGRAM

Massachusetts Office of Student Financial Assistance
454 Broadway, Suite 200
Revere, MA 02151
Phone: (617) 727-9420   Fax: (617) 727-0667
E-mail: osfa@osfa.mass.edu
Web Site: www.osfa.mass.edu/osfaprograms/ctuitionwav.asp
Summary: To provide financial assistance for postsecondary education to Massachusetts residents who are veterans.
Eligibility: Applicants for these scholarships must have been permanent legal residents of Massachusetts for at least 1 year and veterans who served actively during the Spanish-American War, World War I, World War II, Korea, Vietnam, the Lebanese peace keeping force, the Grenada rescue mission, the Panamanian intervention force, the Persian Gulf, or Operation Restore Hope in Somalia. They may not be in default on any federal student loan.
Financial data: Eligible veterans are exempt from any tuition payments for an undergraduate degree or certificate program at public colleges or universities in Massachusetts.
Duration: Up to 4 academic years, for a total of 130 semester hours.
Additional information: Recipients may enroll either part or full time in a Massachusetts publicly-supported institution.
Number awarded: Varies each year.

653
MASSGRANT PROGRAM

Massachusetts Office of Student Financial Assistance
454 Broadway, Suite 200
Revere, MA 02151
Phone: (617) 727-9420   Fax: (617) 727-0667
E-mail: osfa@osfa.mass.edu
Web Site: www.osfa.mass.edu/osfaprograms/massgrant.asp
Summary: To provide financial assistance for the postsecondary education of Massachusetts residents who are attending approved schools in designated states.
Eligibility: Applicants for these scholarships must have been permanent legal residents of Massachusetts for at least 1 year and attending state-approved postsecondary schools (public, private, independent, for profit, or nonprofit) as full-time undergraduate students in Connecticut, Maine, Maryland, Massachusetts, New Hampshire, Pennsylvania, Rhode Island, Vermont, or Washington, D.C. U.S. citizenship or permanent resident status is required. Selection is based on financial need, with an expected family contribution between zero and $3,550.
Financial data: Awards range from $300 to $2,900 per year.
Duration: 1 year; may be renewed for up to 4 additional years.
Number awarded: Varies each year.
Deadline: April of each year.

654
MAX AND EMMY DREYFUSS JEWISH UNDERGRADUATE SCHOLARSHIP FUND

Jewish Social Service Agency of Metropolitan Washington
6123 Montrose Road
Rockville, MD 20852
Phone: (301) 881-3700   Fax: (301) 770-8741
Phone: TTY: (301) 984-5662
Web Site: www.jssa.org/scholarship.html
Summary: To provide financial assistance for postsecondary education to Jewish students from the Washington, D.C. area.
Eligibility: This program is open to Jewish residents of the metropolitan Washington area who are younger than 30 years of age and enrolled or accepted for enrollment as full-time students in accredited 4-year undergraduate degree programs. Applicants must be U.S. citizens or working toward citizenship. Students in community colleges, Israeli schools, or year-abroad programs are not eligible. Selection is based primarily on financial need.
Financial data: Up to $3,500 per year, although most awards range from $1,500 to $2,000.
Duration: 1 year; may be renewed up to 3 additional years.
Number awarded: 8 to 10 each year.
Deadline: May of each year.

655
MAX HAYS MEMORIAL SCHOLARSHIP

Indiana Golf Course Superintendents Association
c/o Steve Christie, Scholarship Chair
Automatic Irrigation Supply Company
116 Shadowlawn Drive
Fishers, IN 46038
Phone: (317) 466-SUPT   (888) 221-SUPT
E-mail: igcsa@aol.com
Web Site: www.igcsa.com/scholarship_programs.htm
Summary: To provide financial assistance for college to children of Indiana Golf Course Superintendents Association (IGCSA) members or employees at IGCSA member clubs.
Eligibility: This program is open to children of IGCSA members or those who work at IGCSA member clubs. Applicants may be majoring in any subject. They must attend an accredited school. Selection is based on merit.
Financial data: The stipend is at least $1,000.
Duration: 1 year.
Additional information: This program was established in 1995.
Number awarded: 1 each year.
Deadline: July of each year.

656
MAY T. HENRY SCHOLARSHIP

May T. Henry Scholarship Fund
c/o Central National Bank and Trust Company
Attn: Trust Department
P.O. Box 3448
Enid, OK 73702-3448
Phone: (580) 233-3535
Summary: To provide financial assistance to high school seniors who are interested in attending a state-supported college, university, or technical school in Oklahoma.
Eligibility: Any student entering any field of study is eligible to apply if the following requirements are met: the student must plan to attend a college, university, or technical school supported by the state of Oklahoma; the student has graduated or will be graduating from an accredited high school or equivalent institution. Both financial need and scholastic performance are considered in the selection process.
Financial data: The stipend is $1,000 per year. Funds are paid directly to the recipient.
Duration: 1 year; may be renewed for up to 3 additional years.
Additional information: This fund was established in 1985.
Deadline: March of each year.

657
MEFUSA SCHOLARSHIPS FOR AFRICAN AMERICANS

Minority Educational Foundation of the United States of America
Attn: Scholarship Program
3160 Wedgewood Court
Reno, NV 89509-7103
Summary: To provide financial assistance to African American high school seniors who are interested in attending a community college.
Eligibility: This program is open to African Americans graduating from high schools anywhere in the United States. Applicants must be planning to attend a community college on a full-time basis. As part of the selection process, they must submit a 1,000-word essay on their educational and career goals, how a community college education will help them to achieve those goals, and how they plan to serve the African American community after completing their education. Selection is based on the essay, high school grade point average (2.5 or higher), SAT or ACT scores, involvement in the African American community, and financial need.
Financial data: The stipend is $5,000 per year.
Duration: 1 year; may be renewed 1 additional year if the recipient maintains full-time enrollment and a grade point average of 2.5 or higher.
Additional information: The Minority Educational Foundation of the United States of America (MEFUSA) was established in 2001 to meet the needs of minority students who "show a determination to get a college degree," but who, for financial or other personal reasons, are not able to attend a 4-year college or university. Requests for applications should be accompanied by a self-addressed stamped envelope, the student's e-mail address, and the source where they found the scholarship information.
Number awarded: Up to 100 each year.
Deadline: April of each year.

658
MEFUSA SCHOLARSHIPS FOR LATINO/AS

Minority Educational Foundation of the United States of America
Attn: Scholarship Program
3160 Wedgewood Court
Reno, NV 89509-7103
Summary: To provide financial assistance to Latino/a high school seniors who are interested in attending a community college.
Eligibility: This program is open to Latino/as graduating from high schools anywhere in the United States. Applicants must be planning to attend a community college on a full-time basis. As part of the selection process, they must submit a 1,000-word essay on their educational and career goals, how a community college education will help them to achieve those goals, and how they plan to serve the Latino community after completing their education. Selection is based on the essay, high school grade point average (2.5 or higher), SAT or ACT scores, involvement in the Latino community, and financial need.
Financial data: The stipend is $5,000 per year.
Duration: 1 year; may be renewed 1 additional year if the recipient maintains full-time enrollment and a grade point average of 2.5 or higher.
Additional information: The Minority Educational Foundation of the United States of America (MEFUSA) was established in 2001 to meet the needs of minority students who "show a determination to get a college degree," but who, for financial or other personal reasons, are not able to attend a 4-year college or university. Requests for applications should be accompanied by a self-addressed stamped envelope, the student's e-mail address, and the source where they found the scholarship information.
Number awarded: Up to 100 each year.
Deadline: April of each year.

659
MELVA T. OWEN MEMORIAL SCHOLARSHIP

National Federation of the Blind
c/o Peggy Elliott
Chair, Scholarship Committee
805 Fifth Avenue
Grinnell, IA 50112
Phone: (641) 236-3366
Web Site: www.nfb.org
Summary: To provide financial assistance to blind students studying or planning to study at the postsecondary level.
Eligibility: This program is open to legally blind students who are pursuing or

planning to pursue a full-time undergraduate or graduate course of study. Scholarships, however, will not be awarded for the study of religion or solely to further general or cultural education; the academic program should be directed towards attaining financial independence. Selection is based on academic excellence, service to the community, and financial need.

Financial data: The stipend is $7,000.

Duration: 1 year; recipients may resubmit applications up to 2 additional years.

Additional information: Scholarships are awarded at the federation convention in July. Recipients attend the convention at federation expense; that funding is in addition to the scholarship grant.

Number awarded: 1 each year.

Deadline: March of each year.

660 MENOMINEE INDIAN TRIBE ADULT VOCATIONAL TRAINING PROGRAM

Menominee Indian Tribe of Wisconsin
Attn: Tribal Education Office
P.O. Box 910
Keshena, WI 54135
Phone: (715) 799-5110   Fax: (715) 799-1364
E-mail: vnuske@itol.com

Summary: To provide financial assistance to Menominee Indians who are interested in obtaining a diploma or certificate (1-year program) or associate of arts (2-year program) at a vocational-technical/junior college.

Eligibility: Grants are available to adult students who are one-fourth or more degree Menominee, are enrolled or accepted for enrollment in an appropriate postsecondary school, and are in financial need. Individuals who do not possess at least one-fourth degree Menominee blood quantum but meet the following criteria are also eligible for this program: 1) possess a minimum of one-eighth Menominee blood and 2) possess one-quarter degree Indian blood. Preference is given to applicants in this order: those who live on or near the Menominee Reservation, those who live in Wisconsin and have been accepted for enrollment in an accredited institution in Wisconsin, and those who live in the United States and have been accepted for enrollment in an accredited institution in the United States outside of Wisconsin.

Financial data: Up to $2,200 each year.

Duration: The maximum training period for Adult Vocational Training students is 24 months. Training for nursing is 36 months. Renewal awards require the student to maintain a minimum grade point average of 2.0 and to carry at least 12 credits per term.

Additional information: Part-time study is not supported under this program.

Deadline: February of each year.

661 MENOMINEE INDIAN TRIBE HIGHER EDUCATION PROGRAM

Menominee Indian Tribe of Wisconsin
Attn: Tribal Education Office
P.O. Box 910
Keshena, WI 54135
Phone: (715) 799-5110   Fax: (715) 799-1364
E-mail: vnuske@itol.com

Summary: To provide financial assistance to Menominee Indians who are interested in pursuing postsecondary studies.

Eligibility: Funds are available to students who are at least one-quarter degree Menominee Indians and are enrolled or accepted for enrollment in accredited colleges or universities. Individuals who do not possess at least one-quarter degree Menominee blood quantum are still eligible if they meet the following criteria: 1) possess a minimum of one-eighth Menominee blood and 2) possess one-quarter degree Indian blood. Preference is given to applicants in this order: continuing undergraduate students in good standing; new undergraduates, awarded on a first-come, first-served basis; late applicants, depending on the availability of funds; and second-term applicants, only on projected availability of funds.

Financial data: Up to $2,200 per year for full-time students, for tuition, books, and fees only. Part-time students are also eligible for assistance, but the maximum funding available to students is $13,000 of combined part-time/full-time study.

Duration: Up to 10 semesters.

Number awarded: Varies each year.

Deadline: February of each year.

662 MERIT- AND NEED-BASED SCHOLARSHIPS OF THE COLLEGE FUND/UNCF

College Fund/UNCF
Attn: Director, Educational Services
8260 Willow Oaks Corporate Drive
P.O. Box 10444
Fairfax, VA 22031-4511
Phone: (703) 205-3400
Web Site: www.uncf.org

Summary: To provide financial assistance to high school juniors or seniors who are interested in attending a member institution of the United Negro College Fund (UNCF).

Eligibility: These programs are open to high school graduates with strong academic backgrounds (minimum grade point average of 2.5). Students who have completed their junior year in high school with a record of distinction may also be considered. Selection is based on merit and financial need. Applications should be submitted directly to the UNCF-member institution the student plans to attend.

Financial data: The awards are intended to cover tuition and range from a minimum of $500 to a maximum of $7,500 per year.

Duration: 1 year; may be renewed.

Additional information: Among the scholarships that have been available are the A. Montgomery Ward Foundation Scholarship, the Burton G. Bettingen Foundation Scholarship, the Bryant Gumbel/Walt Disney World Tournament Scholarship Program, the Grumman Scholarship for Peace and Justice, the Malcolm X Scholarship Program, the Principal Financial Group Scholarship Program, the Citigroup Fellows Program, and the Edwards Stephenson Scholarship. Recipients must attend a UNCF-member institution of higher learning. These are: Miles College, Oakwood College, Stillman College, Talladega College, and Tuskegee University in Alabama; Philander Smith College in Arkansas; Bethune-Cookman College, Edward Waters College, and Florida Memorial College in Florida; Clark Atlanta University, Interdenominational Theological Center, Morehouse College, Morris Brown College, Paine College, and Spelman College in Georgia; Dillard University and Xavier University in Louisiana; Rust College and Tougaloo College in Mississippi; Barber-Scotia College, Bennett College, Johnson C. Smith University, Livingstone College, Saint Augustine's College, and Shaw University in North Carolina; Wilberforce University in Ohio; Benedict College, Claflin College, Morris College, and Voorhees College in South Carolina; Fisk University, Knoxville College, Lane College, and LeMoyne-Owens College in Tennessee; Huston-Tillotson College, Jarvis Christian College, Paul Quinn College, and Wiley College in Texas; and Saint Paul's College and Virginia Union University in Virginia.

Number awarded: A total of nearly 1,200 UNCF scholarships are awarded each year.

Deadline: Deadline dates vary, depending upon the individual institution's requirements.

663 MERVYN'S CALIFORNIA/WOMEN'S SPORTS FOUNDATION COLLEGE SCHOLARSHIP

Women's Sports Foundation
Attn: Award and Grant Programs Manager
Eisenhower Park
1899 Hempstead Turnpike, Suite 400
East Meadow, NY 11554-1000
Phone: (516) 542-4700   (800) 227-3988
Fax: (516) 542-4716   E-mail: wosport@aol.com
Web Site: www.womenssportsfoundation.org

Summary: To provide financial support for college to female high school seniors who wish to continue their participation in athletics.

Eligibility: Eligible to apply for these scholarships are female high school seniors who have participated in 1 or more interscholastic sports and plan to attend college as a full-time student in the following fall. U.S. citizenship or permanent resident status is required. Selection is based on academic performance (at least a 3.0 grade point average), athletic participation, financial need, and community service. Special scholarships are given to an athlete who 1) has overcome a physical challenge, 2) coaches other youths or adults, 3) has helped promote the benefits of athletic participation and sportsmanship in her community, and 4) plans a career in athletics and has given the most to her sport and community.

Financial data: The stipends are $10,000, $5,000, or $1,000.

Duration: 1 year.

Additional information: Funding for this program is provided by Mervyn's California.

Number awarded: 286 each year: 282 at $1,000 (1 to a resident representing each Mervyn's California store in Arizona, California, Colorado, Idaho, Louisiana, Michigan, Minnesota, Nevada, New Mexico, Oklahoma, Oregon, Texas, Utah, and Washington plus 10 to residents of other states) as well as 4 special scholarships (3 at $5,000, and 1 at $10,000).

Deadline: April of each year.

664
MEXICAN FIESTA SCHOLARSHIPS

Wisconsin Hispanic Scholarship Foundation, Inc.
1220 West Windlake Avenue
Milwaukee, WI 53215
Phone: (414) 383-7066   Fax: (414) 383-6677
E-mail: mexicanf@aol.com
Web Site: www.mexicanfiesta.org

Summary: To provide financial assistance to Hispanic American students in Wisconsin who are interested in attending college.

Eligibility: Applicants must be at least 50 percent Hispanic American, be high school seniors or full-time undergraduate or graduate students, have earned at least a 2.75 grade point average, be Wisconsin residents, and be bilingual in Spanish and English.

Financial data: The amount of the stipend depends on the number of students selected.

Duration: 1 year; recipients may reapply.

Additional information: Recipients can attend college in any state. Funds for this program are raised each year at the Mexican Fiesta, held in Milwaukee for 3 days each August. Recipients must perform 20 hours of volunteer work in the Hispanic community.

Number awarded: Varies; a total of $20,000 is awarded in scholarships each year.

Deadline: May of each year.

665
MICHAEL AND MARIE MARUCCI SCHOLARSHIP

National Federation of the Blind
c/o Peggy Elliott
Chair, Scholarship Committee
805 Fifth Avenue
Grinnell, IA 50112
Phone: (641) 236-3366
Web Site: www.nfb.org

Summary: To provide financial assistance to legally blind students pursuing a degree in a field that requires study abroad.

Eligibility: This program is open to legally blind students who are pursuing or planning to pursue a full-time undergraduate or graduate course of study. Applicants must be studying 1) a foreign language or comparative literature; 2) history, geography, or political science with a concentration in international studies; or 3) any other discipline that involves study abroad. They must be able to demonstrate competence in a foreign language. Selection is based on academic excellence, service to the community, and financial need.

Financial data: The stipend is $3,000.

Duration: 1 year; recipients may resubmit applications up to 2 additional years.

Additional information: Scholarships are awarded at the federation convention in July. Recipients attend the convention at federation expense; that funding is in addition to the scholarship grant.

Number awarded: 1 each year.

Deadline: March of each year.

666
MICHAEL J. QUILL SCHOLARSHIP FUND

Transport Workers Union of America
80 West End Avenue, Fifth Floor
New York, NY 10023
Phone: (212) 873-6000   Fax: (212) 721-1431

Summary: To provide financial assistance to high school seniors who are children of disabled or other members of the Transport Workers Union of America (TWU) and need financial assistance to pursue postsecondary education.

Eligibility: Applicants must be high school seniors and either 1) a child of a former union member who was forced to stop working, short of pension age, by a disabling illness or injury and who was a union member in good standing when forced to stop work; 2) a child of a union member in good standing; 3) a child of a deceased member who was a union member in good standing at the time of death; 4) a child of a pensioner or deceased pensioner who was a union member in good standing at the time of retirement; or 5) a dependent brother or sister, under the age of 21, of a union member in good standing. Winners are selected from eligible applicants in a public drawing held in May of each year.

Financial data: The scholarship provides $1,200 per year.

Duration: 1 year; may be renewed for up to 3 additional years upon successful completion of a regular course of studies in the preceding year.

Number awarded: 15 each year.

Deadline: April of each year.

667
MICHELIN/TANA SCHOLARSHIP PROGRAM

The Foundation Scholarship Program
Attn: Michelin/TANA Scholarship Program
P.O. Box 1465
Taylors, SC 29687-1465
Phone: (864) 268-3363   Fax: (864) 268-7160
E-mail: fssp@infi.net
Web Site: www.scholarshipprograms.org/fsp_golf.html

Summary: To provide financial assistance for college to employees of members of the Tire Association of North America (TANA) and their dependents.

Eligibility: This program is open to part-time employees and dependent children of full-time employees of tire dealers who are TANA members. Employees and dependent children of Michelin North America, Inc. are not eligible. Applicants must be high school seniors who have a cumulative grade point average of 3.0 or higher. Along with their application, they must submit an essay in which they describe themselves, including the kind of person they are, their strengths, and their most important achievements in school and in their community; they may also include their hobbies, interests, sports, volunteer work, employment, future plans, or career goals. Selection is based on academic achievement, academic performance, scholastic aptitude, leadership contributions, and the essay. Financial need is not considered.

Financial data: Stipend are $2,500 or $1,250 per year. Funds are sent directly to the recipient's college or university to be used for tuition, fees, books, room, and board.

Duration: 1 year; may be renewed up to 3 additional years provided the recipient maintains a grade point average of 3.0 or higher.

Additional information: This program is administered by The Foundation Scholarship Program on behalf of TANA and Michelin North America, Inc.

Number awarded: 3 each year: 1 at $2,500 and 2 at $1,250.

Deadline: February of each year.

668
MICHELLE KWAN R.E.W.A.R.D.S. SCHOLARSHIPS

General Motors Corporation
Chevrolet Motor Division
Attn: GM Scholarship Administration Center
702 West Fifth Avenue
Naperville, IL 60563-2948
Phone: (888) 377-5233   Fax: (630) 961-1948
Web Site: www.chevrolet.com/rewards

Summary: To provide financial assistance for college to women athletes graduating from high school.

Eligibility: This program is open to women high school seniors who have been active in athletics (including school teams, intramural athletics, organized athletic clubs, or other community-based sports organizations) and plan to remain involved in athletics in college. Applicants must be U.S. citizens or permanent residents and have a grade point average of 3.2 or higher. They must be able to demonstrate financial need, leadership, community involvement, and volunteerism. As part of the application process, they must submit an essay on their athletic participation, leadership experiences, honors and awards, community activities, and career goals.

Financial data: The stipend is $2,000 for the first year and $1,000 for each of the next 3 years.

Duration: 4 years, provided the recipient maintains at least a 3.0 college grade point average, normal progress towards a degree, and active participation in athletics.

Additional information: This program was established by Chevrolet and the ice skater Michelle Kwan in 2001.

Number awarded: 10 each year.

Deadline: March of each year.

669
MICHIGAN COMPETITIVE SCHOLARSHIP PROGRAM

Michigan Higher Education Assistance Authority
Attn: Office of Scholarships and Grants
P.O. Box 30462
Lansing, MI 48909-7962
Phone: (517) 373-3394   (888) 4-GRANTS
Fax: (517) 335-5984   E-mail: treasscholgrant@michigan.gov
Web Site: www.michigan.gov/mistudentaid
Summary: To provide financial assistance for college to residents of Michigan.
Eligibility: This program is open to Michigan residents who are attending or planning to attend an eligible Michigan college at least half time. Applicants must demonstrate financial need, achieve a qualifying score on the ACT test (the qualifying score varies according to the date of the student's graduation from high school), and be a U.S. citizen or permanent resident. Students working on a degree in theology, divinity, or religious education are ineligible.
Financial data: Awards are restricted to tuition and fees, to a maximum of $1,300 per academic year.
Duration: 1 year; the award may be renewed until 1 of the following circumstances is reached: 1) 10 years following high school graduation; 2) completion of an undergraduate degree; or 3) receipt of 10 semesters or 15 quarters of undergraduate aid.
Number awarded: Varies each year; recently, 28,463 students received these scholarships.
Deadline: February of each year for high school seniors; March of each year for college students.

670
MICHIGAN EDUCATIONAL OPPORTUNITY GRANTS

Michigan Higher Education Assistance Authority
Attn: Office of Information and Resources
P.O. Box 30466
Lansing, MI 48909-7966
Phone: (517) 373-0457   (877) FA-FACTS
Fax: (517) 335-6851   E-mail: oir@michigan.gov
Web Site: www.michigan.gov/mistudentaid
Summary: To provide financial assistance to students at Michigan public community colleges and universities.
Eligibility: This program is open to Michigan residents who are enrolled at least half time at a public community college or university in the state. U.S. citizenship or permanent residence is required. Financial need must be demonstrated; if funds are insufficient to meet the needs of all eligible applicants, preference is given to students with the greatest financial need.
Financial data: The maximum award is $1,000 per academic year.
Duration: 1 year.
Additional information: Information is available at college and university financial aid offices. This program was established in 1986.
Number awarded: Varies each year; recently, 5,564 of these grants were awarded.

671
MICHIGAN ELKS ASSOCIATION CHARITABLE GRANT FUND SCHOLARSHIP

Michigan Elks Association
c/o Franz A. Brenner, Secretary-Treasurer
43904 Leeann Lane
Canton, MI 48187
Summary: To provide financial assistance for college to "special needs" students in Michigan.
Eligibility: This program is open to "special needs" students who are Michigan residents. For the purposes of this program, "special needs" students are defined as those who have physical impairments, visual impairments, hearing impairments, speech impairments, or other disabilities. Applicants must be high school seniors and planning to attend an accredited college, university, trade school, or vocational school.
Financial data: A stipend is awarded (exact amount not specified).
Duration: 1 year.
Additional information: Funds may not be used for graduate study.
Number awarded: Varies each year.

672
MICHIGAN MERIT AWARD

Michigan Department of Treasury
Attn: Michigan Merit Award
P.O. Box 30716
Lansing, MI 48909
Phone: (517) 241-4430   (888) 95-MERIT
Fax: (517) 241-4638   E-mail: MeritAward@state.mi.us
Web Site: www.meritaward.state.mi.us
Summary: To recognize and reward high school seniors in Michigan who achieve high scores on the Michigan Educational Assessment Program High School Tests.
Eligibility: Students do not apply for these awards. They are automatically granted to high school seniors who take all 4 MEAP tests and 1) score at level 1 ("exceeds State standards") or level 2 ("meets State standards") on all 4 tests, or 2) score at level 1 or level 2 on 2 of the 4 MEAP tests and pass an alternate test (SAT, ACT, or Work Keys Skills Test) with a qualifying score. Students who were juniors in high school in 1999 or later and subsequently complete a GED are also eligible if they achieve the required scores.
Financial data: Students who attend an approved institution in Michigan receive $2,500. Students who attend an approved institution outside Michigan receive $1,000. All funds are paid directly to the institution.
Duration: These are 1-time awards. Students who attend an approved institution in Michigan may elect to have the funds paid in 2 installments of $1,250 each for their freshman and sophomore years. Recipients may utilize the awards up to 7 years after they graduate from high school or complete a GED and may be utilized for graduate school.
Additional information: The Michigan legislature passed the law establishing this program in 1999.
Number awarded: Varies each year; recently, 48,760 students received these awards.

673
MICHIGAN POSTSECONDARY ACCESS STUDENT SCHOLARSHIPS

Michigan Higher Education Assistance Authority
Attn: Office of Scholarships and Grants
P.O. Box 30462
Lansing, MI 48909-7962
Phone: (517) 373-3394   (888) 4-GRANTS
Fax: (517) 335-5984   E-mail: treasscholgrant@michigan.gov
Web Site: www.michigan.gov/mistudentaid
Summary: To provide financial assistance for college to residents of Michigan.
Eligibility: This program is open to Michigan residents who are planning to enroll at least half time in a program leading to an associate degree at a Michigan community college, public university, or independent nonprofit college or university. Applicants must be eligible for a federal Pell Grant and have scored at level 1 or level 2 on the Michigan Education Assessment Program (MEAP) tests in reading, writing, mathematics, and science. Students who meet all requirements except the MEAP test level are eligible to receive assistance in their second year of college if they maintain satisfactory academic progress in their first year. Students working on a degree in theology or divinity are ineligible.
Financial data: The amount of the award is the value of allowable tuition and fees remaining after subtracting the amount of assistance the student receives from a Michigan Competitive Scholarship, Michigan Tuition Grant, federal Pell Grant, and an imputed federal Hope Scholarship Tax Credit. Students who do not qualify for support during their first year of college because they fail to meet the MEAP requirement but who maintain satisfactory academic progress during that first year are entitled to an award of up to $500, not to exceed tuition and fees, for the second year of college enrollment.
Duration: Up to 2 years of full-time college enrollment.
Additional information: This program was established in 2000.
Number awarded: Varies each year.

674
MICHIGAN TUITION GRANT PROGRAM

Michigan Higher Education Assistance Authority
Attn: Office of Scholarships and Grants
P.O. Box 30462
Lansing, MI 48909-7962
Phone: (517) 373-3394   (888) 4-GRANTS
Fax: (517) 335-5984   E-mail: treasscholgrant@michigan.gov
Web Site: www.michigan.gov/mistudentaid

Summary: To provide financial assistance for undergraduate or graduate education to residents of Michigan.

Eligibility: This program is open to Michigan residents who are attending or planning to attend an independent, private, nonprofit degree-granting Michigan college or university at least half time as an undergraduate or graduate student. Applicants must demonstrate financial need and be a U.S. citizen, permanent resident, or approved refugee. Students working on a degree in theology, divinity, or religious education are ineligible.

Financial data: Awards are limited to tuition and fees, to a maximum of $2,750 per academic year.

Duration: 1 year; the award may be renewed for a total of 10 semesters or 15 quarters of undergraduate aid, 6 semesters or 9 quarters of graduate aid, or 8 semesters or 12 quarters of graduate dental student aid.

Number awarded: Varies each year; recently, 28,441 of these grants were awarded.

Deadline: Priority is given to students who apply before the end of August of each year.

675
MICHIGAN TUITION INCENTIVE PROGRAM

Michigan Higher Education Assistance Authority
Attn: Office of Information and Resources
P.O. Box 30466
Lansing, MI 48909-7966
Phone: (517) 373-0457   (877) FA-FACTS
Fax: (517) 335-6851   E-mail: oir@michigan.gov
Web Site: www.michigan.gov/mistudentaid

Summary: To provide financial assistance for college to high school seniors in Michigan.

Eligibility: This program is open to Michigan residents who have (or have had) Medicaid coverage for 24 months within a 36 consecutive month period as identified by the Family Independence Agency (FIA). That financial eligibility can be established as early as sixth grade. Students who meet the financial eligibility guidelines are then eligible for this assistance if they graduate from high school or complete a GED prior to becoming 20 years of age. All applicants must be U.S. citizens or eligible non-citizens (including those designated as refugee, asylum granted, humanitarian parole, indefinite parole, or Cuban-Haitian entrant). Phase I is for students who enroll in a program leading to an associate degree or certificate. Phase II is for students who enroll at least half time at a Michigan degree-granting college or university in a 4-year program other than theology or divinity. Participants must have earned at least 56 transferable semester credits or an associate degree or certificate in Phase I before admission to Phase II.

Financial data: Phase I provides payment of tuition and mandatory fees. Phase II pays tuition and mandatory fees up to $500 per semester to a lifetime maximum of $2,000.

Duration: Students may participate in Phase I for up to 80 semester credits. Course work for Phase II must be completed within 30 months of completion of Phase I requirements.

Additional information: Information is available at college and university financial aid offices.

Number awarded: Varies each year.

676
MICHIGAN VETERANS TRUST FUND TUITION GRANTS

Michigan Veterans Trust Fund
611 West Ottawa Street, Third Floor
Lansing, MI 48913
Phone: (517) 373-3130   Fax: (517) 335-1631

Summary: To provide financial assistance for postsecondary education to the children of Michigan veterans who are totally disabled or deceased as a result of service-connected causes.

Eligibility: This program is open to children of Michigan veterans who are totally disabled as a result of wartime service, or died from service-connected conditions, or were killed in action, or are listed as missing in action. Applicants must be 16 to 26 years of age and must have lived in Michigan at least 12 months prior to the date of application. They must be or plan to become a full-time undergraduate student at a public institution of higher education in Michigan.

Financial data: Recipients are exempt from payment of the first $2,800 per year of tuition or any other fee that takes the place of tuition.

Duration: Benefits are limited to 36 months of full-time undergraduate education.

Number awarded: Varies each year.

677
MIDWEST REGION KOREAN AMERICAN SCHOLARSHIPS

Korean American Scholarship Foundation
Midwest Region
Attn: Scholarship Committee
6600 North Lincoln Avenue, Suite 316
Lincolnwood, IL 60712
Phone: (847) 677-1694   Fax: (847) 677-1694
E-mail: midwestern@kasf.org
Web Site: www.kasf.org

Summary: To provide financial assistance for postsecondary education to Korean American students who attend school in the midwest.

Eligibility: This program is open to Korean American students who are currently enrolled in a college or university in the midwestern states as full-time undergraduate or graduate students. Applicants may reside anywhere in the United States as long as they attend school in the midwest region: Illinois, Indiana, Iowa, Kansas, Michigan, Minnesota, Missouri, Nebraska, North Dakota, Ohio, South Dakota, and Wisconsin. Selection is based on academic achievement, activities, community service, and financial need.

Financial data: Awards are $1,000 or more.

Duration: 1 year; renewable.

Number awarded: Varies each year.

Deadline: June of each year.

678
MIDWEST STUDENT EXCHANGE PROGRAM

Midwestern Higher Education Commission
Attn: Program Officer
1300 South Second Street, Suite 130
Minneapolis, MN 55454-1015
Phone: (612) 626-1602   Fax: (612) 626-8290
E-mail: wrightjm@tc.umn.edu
Web Site: www.mhec.org/msep/index.htm

Summary: To provide a tuition discount to students from selected midwestern states who are attending schools affiliated with the Midwest Student Exchange Program.

Eligibility: The Midwest Student Exchange Program is an interstate initiative established by the commission to increase interstate educational opportunities for students in its member states. The Tuition Discount Program includes the 6 participating states of Kansas, Michigan, Minnesota, Missouri, Nebraska and North Dakota. Residents of these states may enroll in programs in the other participating states, but only at the level at which their home state admits students. All of the enrollment and eligibility decisions for the program are made by the institution.

Financial data: Participants in this program are eligible to receive reduced out-of-state tuition rates at designated community colleges, colleges, or universities participating in the program and at least 10 percent off the tuition at designated private colleges and universities participating in the program. Actual savings through the program will vary from institution to institution, depending upon the tuition rates. Participating students generally save between $500 and $3,000.

Duration: Students receive these benefits as long as they are enrolled in the program to which they were originally admitted and are making satisfactory progress towards a degree.

Additional information: Extension of the tuition privileges to students already enrolled is at the discretion of the institution.

Number awarded: Varies each year.

679
MIKE AND JANICE PARKER GENERAL EDUCATION SCHOLARSHIP

Chickasaw Foundation
P.O. Box 1726
Ada, OK 74821-1726
Phone: (580) 421-9030   Fax: (580) 421-9031
Web Site: www.cflink.org/scholars.htm

Summary: To provide financial assistance for college to members of the Chickasaw Nation.

Eligibility: This program is open to Chickasaw students who are currently enrolled at an accredited institution of higher education in their freshman through senior year. All academic majors are eligible. Applicants must have a grade point average of 2.5 or higher and must submit a 1-page essay on their long-term goals and plans for achieving them. Financial need is not considered in the

selection process.
Financial data: The stipend is $500 each semester ($1,000 per year).
Duration: 2 semesters.
Number awarded: 2 each year.
Deadline: May of each year.

680
MIKE HYLTON AND RON NIEDERMAN SCHOLARSHIP

Factor Support Network Pharmacy
c/o Sharon Hylton
900 Avenida Acaso, Suite A
Camarillo, CA 93012
Phone: (877) FSN-4-YOU   Fax: (805) 482-6324
www.factorsupport.com
Summary: To provide financial assistance to persons with hemophilia and to their immediate families.
Eligibility: Scholarships are available for persons with bleeding disorders, their spouses, and their children. Applicants must be attending or planning to attend a postsecondary institution, including trade and technical schools. To apply, they must submit a completed application form, a short essay, and a reference form.
Financial data: The stipend is $1,000. Funds are paid directly to the recipient.
Duration: 1 year.
Additional information: Information is also available from Marsha Niederman, P.O. Box 6175, Freehold, NJ 07728, (732) 780-5986, Fax (732) 780-4801, E-mail: Minatcc@aol.com.
Number awarded: 10 each year.
Deadline: April of each year.

681
MILDRED R. KNOLES OPPORTUNITY SCHOLARSHIPS

American Legion Auxiliary
Attn: Department of Illinois
2720 East Lincoln Street
P.O. Box 1426
Bloomington, IL 61702-1426
Phone: (309) 663-9366
Summary: To assist Illinois veterans or their children who have started college but need financial aid to continue their education in college or graduate school.
Eligibility: Eligible to apply for these scholarships are veterans or children and grandchildren of veterans of World War I, World War II, Korea, Vietnam, Grenada/Lebanon, Panama, or Desert Storm who have begun college but need financial assistance to complete their college or graduate education. Applicants must have resided in Illinois for at least 3 years prior to application. Selection is based on character, Americanism, leadership, financial need, and academic record.
Financial data: Stipends are $1,200 or $800.
Duration: 1 year.
Additional information: Applications may be obtained only from a local unit of the American Legion Auxiliary.
Number awarded: Varies; each year 1 scholarship of $1,200 and several of $800 are awarded.
Deadline: March of each year.

682
MILITARY ORDER OF THE PURPLE HEART SCHOLARSHIP PROGRAM

Military Order of the Purple Heart
Attn: Scholarships
5413-B Backlick Road
Springfield, VA 22151-3960
Phone: (703) 642-5360   Fax: (703) 642-2054
E-mail: info@purpleheart.org
Web Site: www.purpleheart.org
Summary: To provide financial assistance for college to spouses and children of members of the Military Order of the Purple Heart.
Eligibility: This program is open to children and grandchildren (natural or adopted) and spouses of veterans who are members in good standing of the order or who received the Purple Heart. Applicants must be U.S. citizens, graduating seniors or graduates of an accredited high school, enrolled or accepted for enrollment in a full-time program of study in a college or trade school, and carrying a grade point average of at least 3.5. Selection is based on high school and/or college transcripts, a financial statement showing need, and an essay of 150

words on why the applicant wishes to attend or continue college.
Financial data: The stipend is $1,750 per year.
Duration: 1 year; may be renewed up to 3 additional years.
Number awarded: Varies each year.
Deadline: March of each year.

683
MILLENNIUM SCHOLARSHIP PROGRAM OF THE CHICKASAW NATION

Chickasaw Nation
Attn: Division of Education and Training
224 Rosedale Road
Ada, OK 74820
Phone: (580) 310-6620   Fax: (580) 436-3733
Web Site: www.Chickasaw.net
Summary: To provide financial assistance for college to graduating high school seniors who are members of the Chickasaw Nation.
Eligibility: This program is open to members of the Chickasaw Nation who are graduating from high school with a grade point average of 2.5 or higher. Applicants must submit a copy of their Chickasaw Nation citizenship card and/or Certificate of Degree of Indian Blood, an essay of 500 to 600 words; 2 letters of recommendation, documentation of financial need, a copy of their current high school transcript, and a letter of admission as a full-time student to a college, university, vocational school, or other approved course of study or job training. First preference is given to applicants who are not eligible for federal grants.
Financial data: The stipend is $1,000.
Duration: 1 year; nonrenewable.
Number awarded: Up to 50 each year.
Deadline: April of each year.

684
MILLIE BROTHER SCHOLARSHIP

CODA International
P.O. Box 30715
Santa Barbara, CA 93130-0715
E-mail: coda@coda-international.org
Web Site: www.coda-international.org/scholarship.htm
Summary: To provide financial assistance for the postsecondary education of children of deaf parents.
Eligibility: This program is open to the hearing children of deaf parents who are high school seniors or graduates. Applicants must submit a 2-page essay on their experience as the child of deaf parents, how it has shaped them as individuals, and their future career aspirations; essays are judged on organization, content, creativity, and sense of purpose. In addition to the essay, selection is based on a high school transcript and 2 letters of recommendation.
Financial data: The stipend is $1,500.
Duration: 1 year.
Additional information: Winning essays are published in the *CODA Connection*, the newsletter of Children of Deaf Adults (CODA) International. Information is also available from Dr. Robert Hoffmeister, Chair, Scholarship Committee, Boston University, Programs in Deaf Studies, 605 Commonwealth Avenue, Boston, MA 02215, (617) 353-3205, TTY: (617) 353-3205.
Number awarded: 2 each year.
Deadline: May of each year.

685
MILTON WEINTRAUB SCHOLARSHIP FUND

Association of Theatrical Press Agents and Managers
1560 Broadway
New York, NY 10036-2501
Phone: (212) 719-3666   (800) 858-3667
Fax: (212) 302-1585   E-mail: info@atpam.com
Web Site: www.atpam.com
Summary: To provide financial assistance for postsecondary education to members and families of members of the Association of Theatrical Press Agents and Managers (ATPAM).
Eligibility: Applicants must be either association members in good standing pursuing a graduate or undergraduate degree or relatives of members (children, grandchildren, nieces, nephews, stepchildren, or spouses) interested in pursuing an undergraduate degree. First-time applicants must submit a transcript of their most recent grades and a 250-word essay on trade unionism; renewal applicants

146

must provide proof of scholastic achievement equivalent to a "B+" average; all applicants must submit a brief biography.

Financial data: Awards are $1,000, $750, or $500.

Duration: 1 year; may be renewed.

Additional information: This fund was established in 1969 in memory of Milton Weintraub, secretary-treasurer of ATPAM from 1942 to 1968.

Number awarded: Varies each year. Recently, 12 of these scholarships were awarded: 6 at $1,000, 4 at $750, and 2 at $500.

Deadline: July of each year.

686
MINNESOTA ACADEMIC EXCELLENCE SCHOLARSHIP

Minnesota Higher Education Services Office
1450 Energy Park Drive, Suite 350
St. Paul, MN 55108-5227
Phone: (651) 642-0567   (800) 657-3866
Fax: (651) 642-0675   TTY: (800) 627-3529
E-mail: info@heso.state.mn.us
Web Site: www.mheso.state.mn.us

Summary: To provide financial assistance for postsecondary education to outstanding high school seniors or graduates in Minnesota.

Eligibility: Minnesota residents who have demonstrated outstanding ability, achievement, and potential in English, creative writing, fine arts, foreign language, mathematics, science, or social science may apply for these scholarships if they have been admitted as full-time students at the University of Minnesota, a Minnesota state university, or a private, baccalaureate degree-granting college or university in Minnesota.

Financial data: Scholarships at public institutions cover the cost of full-time attendance; scholarships at private institutions cover an amount equal to the lesser of the actual tuition and fees charged by the institution or the tuition and fees in comparable public institutions.

Duration: 1 year; may be renewed up to 3 additional years.

Additional information: This program was established by the Minnesota Legislature in 1991. Funds for this program come from the sale of special collegiate license plates.

Number awarded: Varies each year.

687
MINNESOTA CHILD CARE ASSISTANCE

Minnesota Higher Education Services Office
1450 Energy Park Drive, Suite 350
St. Paul, MN 55108-5227
Phone: (651) 642-0567   (800) 657-3866
Fax: (651) 642-0675   TTY: (800) 627-3529
E-mail: info@heso.state.mn.us
Web Site: www.mheso.state.mn.us

Summary: To provide financial assistance for child care to students in Minnesota who are not receiving Minnesota Family Investment Program (MFIP) benefits.

Eligibility: Minnesota residents who are in a Minnesota school working on an undergraduate degree or vocational certificate and who have children age 12 and under (14 and under if disabled) may receive this assistance to help pay child care expenses. Recipients must demonstrate financial need but must not be receiving MFIP benefits.

Financial data: The amount of the assistance depends on the income of applicant and spouse, number in applicant's family, and number of eligible children in applicant's family. The maximum available is $2,600 per eligible child per academic year.

Duration: 1 year; may be renewed as long as the recipient remains enrolled on at least a half-time basis in an undergraduate program.

Additional information: Assistance may cover up to 40 hours per week per eligible child.

Number awarded: Varies each year. Recently, a total of $4 million was provided for this program.

688
MINNESOTA PRESIDENT'S SERVICE SCHOLARSHIP

Minnesota Higher Education Services Office
1450 Energy Park Drive, Suite 350
St. Paul, MN 55108-5227
Phone: (651) 642-0567   (800) 657-3866
Fax: (651) 642-0675   TTY: (800) 627-3529
E-mail: info@heso.state.mn.us
Web Site: www.mheso.state.mn.us

Summary: To provide supplemental financial assistance to high school seniors from Minnesota who receive President's Student Service Scholarships.

Eligibility: Each Minnesota high school may nominate 2 students (juniors or seniors) to receive President's Student Service Scholarships from the Corporation for National Service. Selection of those scholarship recipients is based on the nominees' records of volunteer service. Students who are selected to receive 1 of those scholarships are eligible to receive this additional funding.

Financial data: The grant is $500, which may be used as the local matching funds required to receive the national grant or, if other local funds are available, as a supplemental award for the student. In that case, the total scholarship to the student is $1,500, including $500 from the national program, $500 as the local matching grant, and $500 from this program.

Duration: These are 1-time grants.

Additional information: This program was established by the Minnesota Legislature in 1997.

Number awarded: Although each high school may nominate 2 students, only 1 of them can receive a grant through this program. Recently, 97 Minnesota students received these grants.

Deadline: Schools must submit nominations by June of each year.

689
MINNESOTA SAFETY OFFICERS' SURVIVOR PROGRAM

Minnesota Higher Education Services Office
1450 Energy Park Drive, Suite 350
St. Paul, MN 55108-5227
Phone: (651) 642-0567   (800) 657-3866
Fax: (651) 642-0675   TTY: (800) 627-3529
E-mail: info@heso.state.mn.us
Web Site: www.mheso.state.mn.us

Summary: To provide financial assistance for college to survivors of deceased Minnesota public safety officers.

Eligibility: Eligible for this support are dependent children (under 23 years of age) and surviving spouses of public safety officers killed in the line of duty on or after January 1, 1973. Applicants must be Minnesota residents who are enrolled at least half time in an undergraduate degree or certificate program at a Minnesota public postsecondary institution or at a private, residential, 2- or 4-year, liberal arts, degree-granting college or university in Minnesota.

Financial data: Scholarships cover tuition and fees at state-supported institutions or provide an equivalent amount at private colleges and universities.

Duration: 1 year; may be renewed for a maximum of 8 semesters or 12 quarters.

Number awarded: Varies each year. Recently, a total of $40,000 was available for this program.

690
MINNESOTA STATE GRANT PROGRAM

Minnesota Higher Education Services Office
1450 Energy Park Drive, Suite 350
St. Paul, MN 55108-5227
Phone: (651) 642-0567   (800) 657-3866
Fax: (651) 642-0675   TTY: (800) 627-3529
E-mail: info@heso.state.mn.us
Web Site: www.mheso.state.mn.us

Summary: To provide financial assistance to undergraduate students in Minnesota who demonstrate financial need.

Eligibility: Minnesota residents who are enrolled for at least 3 credits as undergraduate students at 1 of 128 eligible schools in Minnesota are eligible to apply for these grants. They must be either 1) an independent student who has resided in Minnesota for purposes other than postsecondary education for at least 12 months; 2) a dependent student whose parent or legal guardian resides in Minnesota; 3) a student who graduated from a Minnesota high school, if the student was a resident of Minnesota during high school; or 4) a student who, after residing in Minnesota for a minimum of 1 year, earned a high school equivalency certificate in Minnesota. Students in default on a student loan or more than 30 days behind for child support owed to a public agency are not eligible.

Financial data: Applicants are required to contribute at least 46 percent of their cost of attendance (tuition and fees plus allowances for room and board, books and supplies, and miscellaneous expenses) from savings, earnings, loans, or other assistance from school or private sources. The other 54 percent is to be contributed by parents (for dependent students) or by independent students, along with a federal Pell Grant and these State Grants. The average State Grant is approximately $1,770; the minimum award is $100 per year and the maximum

ranges from $4,348 at a public technical college to $7,651 at a private 4-year college.

Duration: Assistance continues until the student has completed a baccalaureate degree or full-time enrollment of 8 semesters or 12 quarters, whichever comes first.

Additional information: Students may continue to receive assistance even if they enroll for as few as 3 credits, but their cost of attendance is prorated accordingly.

Number awarded: Varies each year; recently, approximately 61,000 undergraduate students received support through this program.

Deadline: June of each year.

691
MINNIE PEARL SCHOLARSHIP PROGRAM

EAR Foundation
c/o Baptist Hospital
1817 Patterson Street
Nashville, TN 37203-2110
Phone: (615) 329-7807   (800) 545-HEAR
Fax: (615) 329-7935   TDD: (800) 545-HEAR
Web Site: www.earfoundation.org

Summary: To provide financial assistance to hearing impaired students who want to attend college.

Eligibility: Applicants must be mainstreamed high school seniors with severe to profound bilateral hearing loss who have been accepted but are not yet attending a junior college, college, university, or technical school. Their communication may be manual or oral. They must have earned at least a 3.0 grade point average, plan to attend school on a full-time basis, and be U.S. citizens.

Financial data: The stipend is $2,000.

Duration: 1 year; may be renewed.

Additional information: This program was established in 1986.

Number awarded: Varies each year; recently, 11 of these scholarships were awarded.

Deadline: February of each year.

692
MISS AMERICA COMPETITION SCHOLARSHIPS

Miss America Pageant
Attn: Scholarship Department
Two Miss America Way, Suite 1000
Atlantic City, NJ 08401
Phone: (609) 345-7571, ext. 27   (800) 282-MISS
Fax: (609) 347-6079   E-mail: doreen@missamerica.org
Web Site: www.missamerica.org

Summary: To provide educational scholarships as the ultimate reward to winners of the Miss America Pageant on local, state, and national levels.

Eligibility: To enter an Official Miss America Preliminary Pageant, candidates must meet certain basic requirements and agree to abide by all the rules of the local, state, and national Miss America Pageants. Among the qualifications required are that the applicant be female, between the ages of 17 and 26, a high school graduate, single (never have been married or had a marriage annulled), of good moral character, and a citizen of the United States. A complete list of all eligibility requirements is available from each local and state pageant.

Financial data: Approximately $29 million in educational scholarship funds is awarded annually at the local, state, and national Miss America Pageants. For example, Miss America receives $40,000 in scholarship money, the first runner-up $30,000, second runner-up $20,000, third runner-up $15,000, fourth runner-up $10,000, semifinalists $8,000 each, and each national contestant $3,000. In addition, all talent preliminary winners receive $2,000, all swimsuit preliminary winners $500, 8 non-finalist talent winners $1,000, and 1 non-finalist interview winner $1,000. Special awards include the Albert A. Marks, Jr. Non-Finalist Interview Award of $2,500, the Bernie Wayne Scholarship for the Performing Arts of $2,500, 3 Fruit of the Loom Quality of Life Awards of $13,000, the Rembrandt Award for Mentorship of $5,000, the Waterford Crystal Scholarship for Business Marketing & Management of $2,500, and the Konica Scholarship for the Visual Arts of $5,000.

Duration: The pageants are held every year.

Additional information: Scholarships are to be used for tuition, room, board, supplies, and other college expenses. Use of the scholarships must begin within 1 year from the date of the award (2 years if the recipient is Miss America) unless a reasonable extension is requested and granted. Training under the scholarship should be continuous and completed within 4 years from the date the scholarship

is activated; otherwise, the balance of the scholarship may be canceled without further notice.

Deadline: Varies, depending upon the date of local pageants leading to the state and national finals.

693
MISS AMERICAN COED PAGEANT

American Coed Pageants
4120 Piedmont Road
Pensacola, FL 32503
Phone: (850) 432-8662   Fax: (850) 469-8841
E-mail: nationals@americancoedpageants.com
Web Site: www.americancoed.com

Summary: To recognize and reward girls who could become "tomorrow's leaders."

Eligibility: In the coed division, contestants must be between 18 and 20 years of age, never have been married, had a child, or been pregnant. This is not intended to be a typical "beauty" contest; while appearance is important, it is not more important than the contestant's school activities, family relations, community and church involvement, and personality. Pageant scoring is based on poise and appearance in formal wear, personality during an interview, and presentation and appearance in the interview outfit. Girls may also enter several additional optional contests: talent, Miss Photogenic, Miss Model, and sportswear. Other optional contests (speech, academic achievement, and volunteer service) are only open to girls in the junior teen and teen divisions.

Financial data: This is a 2-tiered contest, held first on the state level. State winners receive up to $300 in travel expenses to compete in the national competition; a $500 cash award; the official state crown, banner, and trophy; and a free weekend at next year's pageant to crown their successor. Prizes in the optional contests include $250 for talent, $250 for Miss Photogenic, $100 for Miss Model, $250 for sportswear, $150 for speech, $150 for academic achievement, and $150 for volunteer service. In the national competition, more than $10,000 in cash, trophies, and prizes are awarded each year.

Duration: The competition is held annually.

Additional information: Similar competitions are held in a princess division for girls aged 3 to 6, a sweetheart division for girls aged 7 to 9, a pre-teen division for girls aged 10 to 12, a junior teen division for girls aged 13 to 15, and a teen division for girls aged 16 and 17. The total entry fee is $370 (a $20 registration fee and a $350 sponsor fee). The sponsor fees are used to pay all the contestants' prizes and cash awards, as well as trophies, flowers, entertainment, judges, chaperones, pageant staff expenses, cost of vacation for state winners, and the other costs associated with producing the state pageant.

Number awarded: Varies on the state and national level.

Deadline: State deadlines vary; check with your state pageant director to determine the deadline in your area.

694
MISS BLACK AMERICA

Miss Black America Pageant
P.O. Box 25668
Philadelphia, PA 19144
Phone: (215) 844-8872

Summary: To recognize and reward beautiful and talented Black American women.

Eligibility: All African American women, including married contestants and contestants with children, are eligible. Finalists who compete in the national pageant are selected after competitions on the local and state levels. The winner at the national pageant is chosen by a panel of judges on the basis of beauty, talent, and personality.

Financial data: Miss Black America receives cash, merchandise, and trips worth more than $15,000, as well as screen tests, performance contracts, and a variety of other prizes. Cash and merchandise prizes are also awarded to the runners-up.

Duration: The competition is held annually.

Additional information: There is a $40 application fee, a $550 sponsorship fee, and a $350 food and lodging fee. The fees can be covered by sponsors or by selling subscriptions to *Black America Magazine*.

695
MISS NEW JERSEY EDUCATIONAL SCHOLARSHIP PROGRAM

New Jersey Higher Education Student Assistance Authority
4 Quakerbridge Plaza
P.O. Box 540
Trenton, NJ 08625-0540
Phone: (609) 588-2228   (800) 792-8670
Fax: (609) 588-2390   E-mail: osacs@osa.state.nj.us
Web Site: www.hesaa.org

Summary: To provide financial assistance for postsecondary education to students in New Jersey who demonstrate community involvement.
Eligibility: This program is open to residents of New Jersey who have demonstrated involvement in civic, cultural, or charitable affairs for at least 3 years prior to applying for the scholarship. Applicants must be enrolled in or accepted to a full-time initial bachelor's or graduate degree program at an approved public institution of higher education in New Jersey. Male students must submit proof of registration with Selective Service.
Financial data: The award covers the annual cost of tuition at the public institution in New Jersey that the recipient attends.
Duration: 1 year; may be renewed.
Additional information: This program is sponsored by the Miss New Jersey Scholarship Foundation, 901 Asbury Avenue, Ocean City, NJ 08226, (609) 525-9294.
Number awarded: 1 each year.
Deadline: June of each year.

696
MISSISSIPPI EDUCATIONAL ASSISTANCE FOR MIA/POW DEPENDENTS

Mississippi State Veterans Affairs Board
3460 Highway 80 East
P.O. Box 5947
Pearl, MS 39288-5947
Phone: (601) 576-4850   Fax: (601) 576-4868
E-mail: cburnham@vab.state.ms.us
Web Site: www.vab.state.ms.us

Summary: To provide financial assistance for college to the children of Mississippi residents who are POWs or MIAs.
Eligibility: This entitlement program is open to the children of members of the armed services whose official home of record and residence is in Mississippi and who are officially reported as being either a prisoner of a foreign government or missing in action. Applicants must be attending or planning to attend a state-supported college or university in Mississippi.
Financial data: This assistance covers all costs of college attendance.
Duration: Up to 8 semesters.
Number awarded: Varies each year.

697
MISSISSIPPI EMINENT SCHOLARS GRANTS

Mississippi Office of Student Financial Aid
3825 Ridgewood Road
Jackson, MS 39211-6453
Phone: (601) 432-6997   (800) 327-2980 (within MS)
Fax: (601) 432-6527   E-mail: sfa@ihl.state.ms.us

Summary: To provide financial assistance for postsecondary education to high school seniors with exceptional academic records in Mississippi.
Eligibility: This program is open to graduating high school seniors in Mississippi who have a grade point average of 3.5 or higher and 1) score of 29 or higher on the ACT, 2) score of 1280 or higher on the SAT, or 3) are recognized as a semifinalist or finalist by the National Merit Scholarship Program or the National Achievement Scholarship Program. Applicants must have been residents of Mississippi for at least 1 year and be planning to enroll as a full-time student at a college or university in the state.
Financial data: The stipend is $2,500 per year, not to exceed tuition and required fees.
Duration: 1 year; may be renewed for up to 4 additional years or completion of an undergraduate degree, as long as the recipient maintains continuous full-time enrollment and a cumulative grade point average of 3.5 or higher.
Additional information: For further information, consult the student financial aid office on the campus of the educational institution where you plan to enroll.
Number awarded: Varies each year.
Deadline: September of each year.

698
MISSISSIPPI HIGHER EDUCATION LEGISLATIVE PLAN FOR NEEDY STUDENTS

Mississippi Office of Student Financial Aid
3825 Ridgewood Road
Jackson, MS 39211-6453
Phone: (601) 432-6997   (800) 327-2980 (within MS)
Fax: (601) 432-6527   E-mail: sfa@ihl.state.ms.us
Web Site: www.ihl.state.ms.us/financialaid/help.html

Summary: To provide financial assistance for postsecondary education to needy students in Mississippi who wish to attend public institutions in the state.
Eligibility: This program is open to residents of Mississippi who graduated from high school within the immediate past 2 years and are currently enrolled or planning to enroll full time at a college or university in the state. High school seniors entering their freshman year in college must 1) have a cumulative high school grade point average of 2.5 or higher, 2) have an ACT score of 20 or higher, and 3) meet specific high school core curriculum requirements. College freshmen entering their sophomore year must have achieved a cumulative grade point average of 2.5 or higher on all college course work previously completed. All applicants must be able to demonstrate financial need with an average family adjusted gross income of $36,500 or less over the prior 2 years.
Financial data: Students in this program receive a full waiver of tuition at any eligible Mississippi public institution of higher learning or eligible Mississippi public community/junior college. Students attending a private institution receive an award amount equal to the award of a student attending the nearest comparable public institution.
Duration: Up to 8 semesters.
Number awarded: Varies each year, depending on the availability of funds; awards are granted on a first-come, first-served basis.
Deadline: March of each year.

699
MISSISSIPPI LAW ENFORCEMENT OFFICERS AND FIREMEN SCHOLARSHIP PROGRAM

Mississippi Office of Student Financial Aid
3825 Ridgewood Road
Jackson, MS 39211-6453
Phone: (601) 432-6997   (800) 327-2980 (within MS)
Fax: (601) 432-6527   E-mail: sfa@ihl.state.ms.us

Summary: To provide financial assistance for postsecondary education to the spouses and children of disabled or deceased Mississippi law enforcement officers and fire fighters.
Eligibility: Children and spouses of full-time law enforcement officers and fire fighters who became permanently and totally disabled or who died in the line of duty are eligible to apply if they are high school seniors or graduates interested in attending a state-supported postsecondary institution in Mississippi. Children may be natural, adopted, or stepchildren up to the age of 23; spouses may be of any age.
Financial data: Students in this program receive full payment of tuition fees, the average cost of campus housing, required fees, and applicable course fees at state-supported colleges and universities in Mississippi. Funds may not be used to pay for books, food, school supplies, materials, dues, or fees for extracurricular activities.
Duration: Up to 8 semesters.
Number awarded: Varies each year.
Deadline: Applications may be submitted at any time.

700
MISSISSIPPI LEVERAGING EDUCATIONAL ASSISTANCE PARTNERSHIP PROGRAM

Mississippi Office of Student Financial Aid
3825 Ridgewood Road
Jackson, MS 39211-6453
Phone: (601) 432-6997   (800) 327-2980 (within MS)
Fax: (601) 432-6527   E-mail: sfa@ihl.state.ms.us
Web Site: www.ihl.state.ms.us/financialaid/leap.html

Summary: To provide financial assistance for postsecondary education to Mississippi residents who demonstrate significant financial need.
Eligibility: Applicants must be current legal Mississippi residents who are enrolled or accepted for enrollment as full-time undergraduate students at a nonprofit college or university in Mississippi and who demonstrate substantial financial need.

Financial data: The amount of assistance varies.

Duration: 1 year; may be renewed for up to 3 additional years.

Additional information: Participating colleges and universities in Mississippi select the recipients of these grants through their regular financial aid award process. For further information, consult the student financial aid office on the campus of the educational institution where you are or will be enrolled. This program was formerly known as the Mississippi State Student Incentive Grant Program.

Number awarded: Varies each year.

Deadline: Each participating college and university establishes its own deadline date for applications.

701
MISSISSIPPI RESIDENT TUITION ASSISTANCE GRANTS

Mississippi Office of Student Financial Aid
3825 Ridgewood Road
Jackson, MS 39211-6453
Phone: (601) 432-6997   (800) 327-2980 (within MS)
Fax: (601) 432-6527   E-mail: sfa@ihl.state.ms.us

Summary: To provide financial assistance for postsecondary education to Mississippi residents who demonstrate significant financial need.

Eligibility: Applicants must have been legal Mississippi residents for at least 4 years; be receiving less than the full federal Pell Grant; have a cumulative high school or equivalent grade point average of 2.5 or higher and an ACT score of 15 or higher; be accepted on a full-time basis at a 2-year or 4-year public or private accredited college or university in Mississippi; and not be in default on any educational loan.

Financial data: Awards depend on the availability of funds and the need of the recipient; the maximum award for a freshman or sophomore is $500 per year; the maximum award for a junior or senior is $1,000 per year.

Duration: 1 year; may be renewed for up to 4 additional years or completion of an undergraduate degree, as long as the recipient maintains continuous full-time enrollment and a 2.5 grad point average.

Additional information: For further information, consult the student financial aid office on the campus of the educational institution where you are enrolled.

Number awarded: Varies each year.

Deadline: September of each year.

702
MISSOURI COLLEGE GUARANTEE PROGRAM

Missouri Department of Higher Education
Attn: Missouri Student Assistance Resource Services (MOSTARS)
3515 Amazonas Drive
Jefferson City, MO 65109-5717
Phone: (573) 751-3940   (800) 473-6757
Fax: (573) 751-6635   Web Site: www.mocbhe.gov

Summary: To provide financial assistance for college to full-time students in Missouri who have financial need.

Eligibility: This program is open to residents of Missouri who are attending or planning to attend participating Missouri postsecondary institutions as full-time undergraduate students. Applicants must have a high school grade point average of 2.5 or higher and a score of 20 or higher on the ACT or 950 or higher on the SAT. They must be able to demonstrate financial need. Students pursuing a degree or certificate in theology or divinity are not eligible. U.S. citizenship or permanent resident status is required.

Financial data: The maximum annual award is based on the tuition cost at the University of Missouri.

Duration: 1 year; may be renewed.

Additional information: This program was established in 1999.

Number awarded: Varies each year.

Deadline: March of each year.

703
MISSOURI HIGHER EDUCATION ACADEMIC SCHOLARSHIP PROGRAM

Missouri Department of Higher Education
Attn: Missouri Student Assistance Resource Services (MOSTARS)
3515 Amazonas Drive
Jefferson City, MO 65109-5717
Phone: (573) 751-3940   (800) 473-6757
Fax: (573) 751-6635
Web Site: www.mocbhe.gov

Summary: To provide financial assistance for college to outstanding high school seniors in Missouri.

Eligibility: This program is open to high school seniors in Missouri who score in the top 3 percent of all Missouri students taking the SAT or ACT. Applicants must be planning to attend a participating college or university in Missouri full time. Students pursuing a degree or certificate in theology or divinity are not eligible. U.S. citizenship or permanent resident status is required.

Financial data: Up to $2,000 per year.

Duration: 1 year; may be renewed for up to 4 additional years or until completion of a baccalaureate degree, if the recipient maintains full-time status and satisfactory academic progress.

Additional information: This program is also known as the Missouri "Bright Flight" program. Awards are not available for summer study.

Number awarded: Approximately 6,500 each year.

Deadline: July of each year.

704
MISSOURI PUBLIC SURVIVOR GRANT PROGRAM

Missouri Department of Higher Education
Attn: Missouri Student Assistance Resource Services (MOSTARS)
3515 Amazonas Drive
Jefferson City, MO 65109-5717
Phone: (573) 751-3940   (800) 473-6757
Fax: (573) 751-6635
Web Site: www.mocbhe.gov

Summary: To provide financial assistance for college to spouses and children of disabled and deceased Missouri public employees and public safety officers.

Eligibility: This program is open to dependent children and spouses of 1) highway and transportation department employees who were killed or permanently disabled while engaged in the construction or maintenance of Missouri highways, roads, and bridges; and 2) Missouri public safety officers who were killed or permanently disabled in the line of duty. Applicants must be Missouri residents enrolled or accepted for enrollment as a full-time undergraduate student at a participating Missouri college or university; children must be younger than 24 years of age. Students pursuing a degree or certificate in theology or divinity are not eligible. U.S. citizenship or permanent resident status is required.

Financial data: The maximum annual grant is the lesser of 1) the actual tuition charged at the school where the recipient is enrolled, or 2) the amount of tuition charged to a Missouri undergraduate resident enrolled full time in the same class level and in the same academic major as an applicant at the University of Missouri at Columbia.

Duration: 1 year; may be renewed.

Number awarded: Varies each year.

Deadline: There is no application deadline, but early submission of the completed application is encouraged.

705
MISSOURI STATE COUNCIL ENDOWMENT SCHOLARSHIP

Epsilon Sigma Alpha
Attn: ESA Foundation Assistant Scholarship Director
P.O. Box 270517
Fort Collins, CO 80527
Phone: (970) 223-2824   Fax: (970) 223-4456
Web Site: www.esaintl.com/esaf

Summary: To provide financial assistance for college to students from Missouri.

Eligibility: This program is open to residents of Missouri who are either 1) graduating high school seniors in the top 25 percent of their class or with minimum scores of 20 on the ACT or 950 on the SAT, or 2) students already enrolled in college with a grade point average of 3.0 or higher. Students enrolled for training in a technical school or returning to school after an absence are also eligible. Selection is based on character, scholastic ability, leadership and ability skills, and financial need.

Financial data: The stipend is $1,000.

Duration: 1 year; may be renewed.

Additional information: Epsilon Sigma Alpha (ESA) is a women's service organization, but scholarships are available to both men and women. Information is also available from Verneene Forssberg, 403 South High, Pratt, KS 67124, (316) 672-3636, Fax: (316) 672-3688, E-mail: vernf@genmail.pcc.cc.ks.us. Completed applications must be submitted to the ESA State Counselor who verifies the information before forwarding them to the scholarship director.

Number awarded: 1 each year.

Deadline: January of each year.

706
MISSOURI VIETNAM VETERANS SURVIVOR GRANT PROGRAM

Missouri Department of Higher Education
Attn: Missouri Student Assistance Resource Services (MOSTARS)
3515 Amazonas Drive
Jefferson City, MO 65109-5717
Phone: (573) 751-3940   (800) 473-6757
Fax: (573) 751-6635
Web Site: www.mocbhe.gov
Summary: To provide financial assistance for college to survivors of certain deceased Missouri Vietnam veterans.
Eligibility: This program is open to surviving spouses and children of veterans who served in the military in Vietnam or the war zone in southeast Asia, who were residents of Missouri when first entering military service and at the time of death, whose death was attributable to illness that could possibly be a result of exposure to toxic chemicals during the Vietnam conflict, and who served in the Vietnam theater between 1961 and 1972. Applicants must be Missouri residents enrolled in a program leading to a certificate, associate degree, or baccalaureate degree at an approved postsecondary institution in the state. Students pursuing a degree or certificate in theology or divinity are not eligible. U.S. citizenship or permanent resident status is required.
Financial data: The maximum annual grant is the lesser of 1) the actual tuition charged at the school where the recipient is enrolled, or 2) the amount of tuition charged to a Missouri undergraduate resident enrolled full time in the same class level and in the same academic major as an applicant at the University of Missouri at Columbia.
Duration: 1 semester; may be renewed until the recipient has obtained a baccalaureate degree or has completed 150 semester credit hours, whichever comes first.
Additional information: Awards are not available for summer study.
Number awarded: Varies each year.

707
MISSOURI'S A+ SCHOOLS TUITION ASSISTANCE PROGRAM

Missouri Department of Elementary and Secondary Education
Attn: Director, A+ Schools/Tech Prep
1050 Jefferson Street, Fifth Floor
P.O. Box 480
Jefferson City, MO 65102-0480
Phone: (573) 751-1394   Fax: (573) 751-4261
E-mail: wworts@mail.dese.state.mo.us
Web Site: www.dese.state.mo.us
Summary: To provide financial assistance to high school seniors who graduate from a designated "A+ School" in Missouri and are interested in attending a community college or vocational institute in the state.
Eligibility: This program is open to students who graduate from a designated "A+ School" in Missouri. Applicants must meet the following requirements: have attended a designated A+ School for 3 consecutive years prior to graduation, have a grade point average of at least 2.5, have at least a 95 percent attendance record, perform at least 50 hours of unpaid tutoring or mentoring, maintain a record of good citizenship and avoid the unlawful use of drugs, and be planning to attend a community college or postsecondary vocational-technical school on a full-time basis in Missouri.
Financial data: Recipients are offered state-paid assistance (full tuition and books) to attend any public community college or technical school in the state.
Duration: 1 year; may be renewed if the recipient maintains a 2.5 grade point average.
Additional information: The A+ Schools program is a school-improvement initiative established by the Outstanding Schools Act of 1993. The program provides incentives for local high schools to reduce the dropout rate, raise academic expectations, provide better career pathways for all students, and work more closely with business and higher education leaders. Since 1994, 133 Missouri high schools representing 127 school districts have received A+ School designation.
Number awarded: Since the tuition program began in 1997, more than 6,000 students have qualified for assistance.

708
MITCHELL SCHOLARSHIPS

The Mitchell Institute
22 Monument Square, Suite 200
Portland, ME 04101
Phone: (207) 773-7700   (888) 220-7209
Fax: (207) 773-1133   E-mail: info@mitchellinstitute.org
Web Site: www.mitchellinstitute.org/scholarship/index.html
Summary: To provide financial assistance for college to graduating high school seniors in Maine.
Eligibility: Eligible to apply for these scholarships are high school seniors in Maine who plan to attend a 2-year or 4-year college or university in the state. Some scholarships are available to students planning to attend college out of state. Nontraditional students and students who earned their high school diplomas through GED or Job Corps programs are eligible. Students who attend high school in Maine but are not legal residents of Maine are not eligible. Selection is based on academic achievement and potential, financial need, and community service.
Financial data: The stipend is $1,000 per year.
Duration: 2 years or 4 years (depending on whether the recipient attends a 2-year or 4-year institution.
Additional information: This program was established in 1994.
Number awarded: 160 each year: 1 to a graduating senior from each public high school in Maine, along with 30 additional awards available to students from other backgrounds (gradating from private or parochial schools, home-schooled students, Maine residents attending high school out of state, nontraditional students).
Deadline: March of each year.

709
MITSUYUKI YONEMURA MEMORIAL SCHOLARSHIP

Japanese American Citizens League
Attn: National Scholarship Awards
1765 Sutter Street
San Francisco, CA 94115
Phone: (415) 921-5225   Fax: (415) 931-4671
E-mail: jacl@jacl.org
Web Site: www.jacl.org
Summary: To provide financial assistance to student members of the Japanese American Citizens League (JACL) who are high school seniors interested in pursuing undergraduate education.
Eligibility: This program is open to JACL members who are high school seniors interested in attending a college, university, trade school, business college, or other institution of higher learning. Selection is based on academic record, extracurricular activities, and community involvement.
Financial data: The stipend depends on the availability of funds but usually ranges from $1,000 to $5,000.
Duration: 1 year.
Additional information: Requests for applications must be accompanied by a self-addressed stamped envelope.
Number awarded: At least 1 each year.
Deadline: March of each year.

710
MODERN WOODMEN OF AMERICA FRATERNAL COLLEGE SCHOLARSHIP PROGRAM

Modern Woodmen of America
Attn: Fraternal Scholarship Administrator
1701 First Avenue
P.O. Box 2005
Rock Island, IL 61204-2005
Phone: (309) 786-6481
Web Site: www.modern-woodmen.org
Summary: To encourage members of Modern Woodmen of America to develop their talents and to continue their formal education beyond high school.
Eligibility: This program is open to high school seniors who have been beneficial members of Modern Woodmen for at least 2 years. Applicants must be in the upper half of their graduating class. They must intend to pursue a bachelor's degree on a full-time, continuous basis. Selection of regional and national winners is based on qualities of character and leadership (both in academic and extracurricular activities), scholastic records (based on standardized test scores and grade point average), and aptitude for college work. Additional awards are presented to students selected randomly.

Financial data: National scholarships are $16,000 (paid over 4 years). Regional scholarships are $12,000, $11,000, $10,000, $9,000, $8,000, or $7,000, also paid in equal installments over 4 years. Additional awards are $1,000.

Duration: National and regional scholarships are for 4 years. The additional awards are 1-time grants.

Additional information: The scholarships and awards may be used at any accredited 4-year college or university in the United States.

Number awarded: Each year, 3 national scholarships, 36 regional scholarships (6 in each of the sponsoring organization's 6 regions), and 24 additional awards are presented.

Deadline: December of each year.

711
MONTANA ATHLETIC FEE WAIVER

Montana Guaranteed Student Loan Program
2500 Broadway
P.O. Box 203101
Helena, MT 59620-3101
Phone: (406) 444-6594   (800) 537-7508
Fax: (406) 444-1869   E-mail: scholars@mgslp.state.mt.us
Web Site: www.mgslp.state.mt.us/parents/fee_waivers.html

Summary: To provide financial assistance for undergraduate education to athletes attending universities in Montana.

Eligibility: Athletes selected by the staff of branches of the Montana University System are eligible for these fee waivers.

Financial data: Students eligible for this benefit are entitled to attend any unit of the Montana University System without payment of undergraduate registration, incidental, or out-of-state fees.

Duration: Undergraduate students are eligible for continued fee waiver as long as they maintain reasonable academic progress as full-time students.

Number awarded: Varies each year, to the maximum authorized by the National Collegiate Athletic Association, National Association of Intercollegiate Athletics, or appropriate affiliated conferences for officially sanctioned or recognized intercollegiate sports.

712
MONTANA COMMUNITY COLLEGE HONOR SCHOLARSHIPS

Montana Guaranteed Student Loan Program
2500 Broadway
P.O. Box 203101
Helena, MT 59620-3101
Phone: (406) 444-6594   (800) 537-7508
Fax: (406) 444-1869   E-mail: scholars@mgslp.state.mt.us
Web Site: www.mgslp.state.mt.us/parents/cchonor.html

Summary: To provide financial assistance for undergraduate education to outstanding community college students in Montana.

Eligibility: Eligible for this benefit are residents of Montana who are graduating from a community college in the state and planning to attend a branch of the Montana University System.

Financial data: Students eligible for this benefit are entitled to attend any unit of the Montana University System without payment of undergraduate registration or incidental fees.

Duration: The waiver is valid through the completion of the first academic year.

Additional information: The scholarship must be utilized within 9 months after receiving an associate degree from the community college.

Number awarded: Varies each year; 1 scholarship is awarded to a member of a graduating class for each 25 associate degree graduates or major fraction thereof.

713
MONTANA CUSTODIAL STUDENT FEE WAIVER

Montana Guaranteed Student Loan Program
2500 Broadway
P.O. Box 203101
Helena, MT 59620-3101
Phone: (406) 444-6594   (800) 537-7508
Fax: (406) 444-1869   E-mail: scholars@mgslp.state.mt.us
Web Site: www.mgslp.state.mt.us/parents/fee_waivers.html

Summary: To provide financial assistance for undergraduate education to residents of custodial facilities in Montana.

Eligibility: Eligible for this benefit are residents of Montana who attend the Mountain View School at Helena, the Pine Hills School at Miles City, or similar

public or private institutions. Applicants must be recommended by the Department of Institutions or the administration of the private institutions. Financial need is considered.

Financial data: Students eligible for this benefit are entitled to attend any unit of the Montana University System without payment of undergraduate registration or incidental fees.

Duration: Undergraduate students are eligible for continued fee waiver as long as they maintain reasonable academic progress as full-time students.

Number awarded: Varies each year.

714
MONTANA DEPENDENTS OF PRISONERS OF WAR FEE WAIVER

Montana Guaranteed Student Loan Program
2500 Broadway
P.O. Box 203101
Helena, MT 59620-3101
Phone: (406) 444-6594   (800) 537-7508
Fax: (406) 444-1869   E-mail: scholars@mgslp.state.mt.us
Web Site: www.mgslp.state.mt.us/parents/fee_waivers.html

Summary: To provide financial assistance to dependents of veterans declared missing in action or prisoners of war in southeast Asia.

Eligibility: To be eligible for this fee waiver, students must be the spouses or children of residents of Montana who, while serving in southeast Asia after January 1, 1961 either in the armed forces or as a civilian, have been declared missing in action or prisoner of war. Financial need is considered.

Financial data: Students eligible for this benefit are entitled to attend any unit of the Montana University System without payment of undergraduate registration or incidental fees.

Duration: Undergraduate students are eligible for continued fee waivers as long as they maintain reasonable academic progress as full-time students.

Number awarded: Varies each year.

715
MONTANA GEAR UP SCHOLARSHIPS

Montana Guaranteed Student Loan Program
2500 Broadway
P.O. Box 203101
Helena, MT 59620-3101
Phone: (406) 444-6594   (800) 537-7508
Fax: (406) 444-1869   E-mail: scholars@mgslp.state.mt.us
Web Site: www.mgslp.state.mt.us/parents/gear_up.html

Summary: To provide financial assistance for college to high school seniors in Montana who have participated in designated federal programs.

Eligibility: This program is open to high seniors in Montana who are enrolled in Educational Talent Search or Upward Bound, federal TRIO programs that assist students who come from low-income families in which neither parent has a college degree. Applicants must be eligible to receive a federal Pell Grant; have a recommendation from their TRIO counselor, and intend to enroll on a full-time basis for an undergraduate degree or certificate at an institution in Montana.

Financial data: Stipends range from $100 to $3,500, depending on the need of the recipient.

Duration: 1 year; may be renewed up to 3 additional years if the recipient maintains satisfactory academic progress.

Number awarded: Approximately 60 each year.

Deadline: February of each year.

716
MONTANA HIGH SCHOOL HONOR SCHOLARSHIPS

Montana Guaranteed Student Loan Program
2500 Broadway
P.O. Box 203101
Helena, MT 59620-3101
Phone: (406) 444-6594   (800) 537-7508
Fax: (406) 444-1869   E-mail: scholars@mgslp.state.mt.us
Web Site: www.mgslp.state.mt.us/parents/hshonor.html

Summary: To provide financial assistance for undergraduate education to outstanding high school students in Montana.

Eligibility: This program is open to residents of Montana who are graduating from high school and planning to attend a branch of the Montana University System or a community college in the state. Applicants must have been enrolled

in an accredited high school for at least 3 years prior to graduation, rank in the top quarter of their class, and have a grade point average of 3.0 or higher.

Financial data: Students eligible for this benefit are entitled to attend any unit of the Montana University System or any community college in the state without payment of undergraduate registration or incidental fees.

Duration: The waiver is valid through the completion of the first academic year.

Additional information: The scholarship must be utilized within 9 months after high school graduation.

Number awarded: Varies each year; 1 scholarship is awarded to a member of any class with 25 or fewer graduates, and 1 additional scholarship is awarded for each additional 25 graduates or major fraction thereof.

717
MONTANA HONOR SCHOLARSHIPS FOR NATIONAL MERIT SCHOLARSHIP SEMIFINALISTS

Montana Guaranteed Student Loan Program
2500 Broadway
P.O. Box 203101
Helena, MT 59620-3101
Phone: (406) 444-6594   (800) 537-7508
Fax: (406) 444-1869   E-mail: scholars@mgslp.state.mt.us
Web Site: www.mgslp.state.mt.us/parents/merit.html

Summary: To provide financial assistance for undergraduate education to National Merit Scholarship semifinalists in Montana.

Eligibility: Eligible for this benefit are residents of Montana who are National Merit Scholarship semifinalists.

Financial data: Students eligible for this benefit are entitled to attend any unit of the Montana University System without payment of undergraduate registration or incidental fees.

Duration: The waiver is valid through the completion of the first academic year of enrollment.

Additional information: The scholarship must be utilized within 9 months after high school graduation.

Number awarded: Varies each year.

718
MONTANA HONORABLY DISCHARGED VETERAN FEE WAIVER

Montana Guaranteed Student Loan Program
2500 Broadway
P.O. Box 203101
Helena, MT 59620-3101
Phone: (406) 444-6594   (800) 537-7508
Fax: (406) 444-1869   E-mail: scholars@mgslp.state.mt.us
Web Site: www.mgslp.state.mt.us/parents/fee_waivers.html

Summary: To provide financial assistance for undergraduate education to selected Montana veterans.

Eligibility: This program is open to honorably discharged veterans who served with the U.S. armed forces in any war and who are residents of Montana. Only veterans who at some time qualified for U.S. Department of Veterans Affairs (VA) educational benefits, but who are no longer eligible, are entitled to this waiver. Veterans who served in the armed forces subsequent to the conflict in Vietnam and are pursuing their initial undergraduate degree are also eligible if they received an Armed Forces Expeditionary Medal for service in Lebanon, Grenada, or Panama, or served in a combat theater in the Persian Gulf between August 2, 1990 and April 11, 1991. Financial need is considered in the selection process.

Financial data: Students eligible for this benefit are entitled to attend any unit of the Montana University System without payment of undergraduate registration or incidental fees.

Duration: Undergraduate students are eligible for continued fee waiver as long as they maintain reasonable academic progress as full-time students.

Number awarded: Varies each year.

719
MONTANA INDIAN STUDENT FEE WAIVER

Montana Guaranteed Student Loan Program
2500 Broadway
P.O. Box 203101
Helena, MT 59620-3101
Phone: (406) 444-6570   (800) 537-7508
Fax: (406) 444-1869   E-mail: scholars@mgslp.state.mt.us

Web Site: www.mgslp.state.mt.us/parents/fee_waivers.html

Summary: To provide financial assistance to Montana Indian students interested in pursuing postsecondary education.

Eligibility: Eligible to apply are Native American students (one-quarter Indian blood or more) who have been residents of Montana for at least 1 year prior to application, have graduated from an accredited high school or federal Indian school, and can demonstrate financial need.

Financial data: Students eligible for this benefit are entitled to attend any unit of the Montana University System without payment of undergraduate registration or incidental fees.

Duration: Undergraduate students are eligible for continued fee waiver as long as they maintain reasonable academic progress as full-time students.

Number awarded: Up to 48 each year.

720
MONTANA SEPTEMBER 11, 2001 VICTIMS FEE WAIVER

Montana Guaranteed Student Loan Program
2500 Broadway
P.O. Box 203101
Helena, MT 59620-3101
Phone: (406) 444-6594   (800) 537-7508
Fax: (406) 444-1869   E-mail: scholars@mgslp.state.mt.us
Web Site: www.mgslp.state.mt.us/parents/fee_waivers.html

Summary: To provide financial assistance for undergraduate education in Montana to dependents of victims of the September 11, 2001 terrorist action.

Eligibility: This program is open to persons whose spouse, parent, or legal guardian was a victim of the September 11, 2001 terrorist actions at the New York World Trade Center, the Pentagon, or the Pennsylvania airplane crash. The term "victim" includes a person killed as a direct result of physical injuries suffered on or about September 11 directly related to the terrorist actions and includes rescuers, relief workers, or fire and policy personnel. It does not include any individuals identified by federal law enforcement personnel as likely perpetrators of the terrorist activities. Applicants must be enrolled in a program leading to their initial associate or baccalaureate degree at a unit of the Montana University System.

Financial data: Students eligible for this benefit are entitled to attend any unit of the Montana University System without payment of undergraduate registration, incidental fees, or out-of-state fees.

Duration: Undergraduate students are eligible for continued fee waiver as long as they maintain reasonable academic progress as full-time students.

Number awarded: Varies each year.

721
MONTANA WAR ORPHANS FEE WAIVER

Montana Guaranteed Student Loan Program
2500 Broadway
P.O. Box 203101
Helena, MT 59620-3101
Phone: (406) 444-6594   (800) 537-7508
Fax: (406) 444-1869   E-mail: scholars@mgslp.state.mt.us
Web Site: www.mgslp.state.mt.us/parents/fee_waivers.html

Summary: To provide financial assistance for undergraduate education to the children of Montana veterans who died in the line of duty or as a result of service-connected disabilities.

Eligibility: This program is open to children of members of the U.S. armed forces who served on active duty during World War II, the Korean conflict, or the conflict in Vietnam; were legal residents of Montana at the time of entry into service; and were killed in action or died as a result of injury, disease, or other disability while in the service. Applicants must be no older than 25 years of age. Financial need is considered in the selection process.

Financial data: Students eligible for this benefit are entitled to attend any unit of the Montana University System without payment of undergraduate registration or incidental fees.

Duration: Undergraduate students are eligible for continued fee waiver as long as they maintain reasonable academic progress as full-time students.

Number awarded: Varies each year.

722
MONTGOMERY GI BILL (ACTIVE DUTY)

Department of Veterans Affairs
810 Vermont Avenue, N.W.
Washington, DC 20420
Phone: (202) 418-4343   (888) GI-BILL1
Web Site: www.gibill.va.gov

Summary: To provide financial assistance for postsecondary education to new enlistees in any of the armed forces after they have completed their service obligation.
Eligibility: This program is open to veterans who received an honorable discharge and have a high school diploma, a GED, or, in some cases, up to 12 hours of college credit. Applicants must also meet the requirements of 1 of the following categories: 1) entered active duty for the first time after June 30, 1985, had military pay reduced by $100 per month for the first 12 months, and continuously served for 3 years, or 2 years if that was original enlisted, or 2 years if they entered Selected Reserve within a year of leaving active duty and served 4 years (the 2 by 4 program); 2) entered active duty before January 1, 1977, served at least 1 day between October 19, 1984 and June 30, 1985, stayed on active duty through June 30, 1988 (or June 30, 1987 if they entered Selective Reserve within 1 year of leaving active duty and served 4 years), and as of December 31, 1989 had entitlement left from the Vietnam Era GI Bill; 3) not eligible under the first 2 categories, but on active duty on September 30, 1990 and separated involuntarily after February 2, 1991, or involuntarily separated on or after November 30, 1993, or voluntarily separated under either the Voluntary Separation Incentive (VSI) or Special Separation Benefit (SSB) program, and before separation had military pay reduced by $1,200; or 4) on active duty on October 9, 1996 and had money remaining in a VEAP account on that date and elected this program by October 9, 1997, or entered full-time National Guard duty under title 32 between July 1, 1985 and November 28, 1989 and elected this program during the period October 9, 1996 through July 8, 1997, and had military pay reduced by $100 a month for 12 months or made a $1,200 lump-sum contribution. Following completion of their service obligation, participants may enroll in colleges or universities for associate, bachelor, or graduate degrees; in business, technical, or vocational schools; for apprenticeships or on-job training programs; in correspondence courses; in flight training; for tutorial assistance benefits if the individual is enrolled at least half time; or in state-approved alternative teacher certification programs.
Financial data: For recipients in categories 1, 3 and 4 whose initial active-duty obligation was 3 years or more, the current monthly stipend for college or university work is $800 for full-time study, $600 for three-quarter time study, or $400 for half-time study; for apprenticeship and on-the-job training, the monthly stipend is $600 for the first 6 months, $440 for the second 6 months, and $280 for the remainder of the program. For enlistees whose initial active-duty obligation was less than 3 years, the current monthly stipend for college or university work is $650 for full-time study, $487.50 for three-quarter time study, or $325 for half-time study; for apprenticeship and on-the-job training, the monthly stipend is $487.50 for the first 6 months, $357.50 for the second 6 months, and $227.50 for the remainder of the program. For veterans in category 2 with remaining eligibility, the current monthly stipend for institutional study full time is $988 for no dependents, $1,024 with 1 dependent, $1,055 with 2 dependents, and $16 for each additional dependent; for three-quarter time study, the monthly stipend is $741.50 for no dependents, $768 with 1 dependent, $791.50 with 2 dependents, and $12 for each additional dependent; for half-time study, the monthly stipend is $494 for no dependents, $512 with 1 dependent, $527.50 with 2 dependents, and $8.50 for each additional dependent. For those veterans pursuing basic job training, the current monthly stipend for the first 6 months is $702.75 for no dependents, $715.13 with 1 dependent, $726 with 2 dependents, and $5.25 for each additional dependent; for the second 6 months, the current monthly stipend is $496.98 for no dependents, $505.73 with 1 dependent, $513.43 with 2 dependents, and $3.85 for each additional dependent; for the third 6 months, the current monthly stipend is $303.80 for no dependents, $309.93 with 1 dependent, $314.65 with 2 dependents, and $2.45 for each additional dependent; for the remainder of the training period, the current monthly stipend is $291.90 for no dependents, $297.68 with 1 dependent, $302.93 with 2 dependents, and $2.45 for each additional dependent. Other rates apply for less than half-time study, cooperative education, correspondence courses, and flight training.
Duration: 36 months; active-duty servicemembers must utilize funds within 10 years of leaving the armed services; reservists may draw on their funds while still serving.
Additional information: Further information is available from local armed forces recruiters. This is the basic VA education program, referred to as Chapter 30.
Number awarded: Varies each year.

723
MONTGOMERY GI BILL (SELECTED RESERVE)

Department of Veterans Affairs
810 Vermont Avenue, N.W.
Washington, DC 20420
Phone: (202) 418-4343   (888) GI-BILL1
Web Site: www.gibill.va.gov

Summary: To provide financial assistance for postsecondary education to reservists in the armed services.
Eligibility: Eligible to apply are members of the Reserve elements of the Army, Navy, Air Force, Marine Corps, and Coast Guard, as well as the Army National Guard and the Air National Guard. To be eligible, a reservist must 1) have a 6-year obligation to serve in the Selected Reserves signed after June 30, 1985 (or, if an officer, to agree to serve 6 years in addition to the original obligation); 2) complete Initial Active Duty for Training (IADT); 3) meet the requirements for a high school diploma or equivalent certificate before completing IADT; and 4) remain in good standing in a drilling Selected Reserve unit. Reservists who enlisted after June 30, 1985 can receive benefits for undergraduate degrees, graduate training, or technical courses leading to certificates at colleges and universities. Reservists whose 6-year commitment began after September 30, 1990 may also use these benefits for a certificate or diploma from business, technical, or vocational schools; cooperative training; apprenticeship or on-the-job training; correspondence courses; independent study programs; tutorial assistance; remedial, deficiency, or refresher training; flight training; or state-approved alternative teacher certification programs.
Financial data: The current monthly rate is $272 for full-time study, $204 for three-quarter time study, $135 for half-time study, or $68 for less than half-time study. For apprenticeship and on-the-job training, the monthly stipend is $204 for the first 6 months, $149.60 for the second 6 months, and $95.20 for the remainder of the program. Other rates apply for cooperative education, correspondence courses, and flight training. training,
Duration: Up to 36 months for full-time study, 48 months for three-quarter study, 72 months for half-time study, or 144 months for less than half-time study.
Additional information: This program is frequently referred to as Chapter 1606 (formerly Chapter 106). Reservists who are enrolled for three-quarter or full-time study are eligible to participate in the work-study program. Benefits end 10 years from the date the reservist became eligible for the program. The Department of Veterans Affairs (VA) may extend the 10-year period if the individual could not train because of a disability caused by Selected Reserve service. Certain individuals separated from the Selected Reserve due to downsizing of the military between October 1, 1991 and September 30, 1999 will also have the full 10 years to use their benefits.
Number awarded: Varies each year.
Deadline: Applications may be submitted at any time.

724
MONTGOMERY GI BILL TUITION ASSISTANCE TOP-UP

Department of Veterans Affairs
810 Vermont Avenue, N.W.
Washington, DC 20420
Phone: (202) 418-4343   (888) GI-BILL1
Web Site: www.gibill.va.gov

Summary: To supplement the financial assistance provided by the military services to their members.
Eligibility: This program is open to military personnel who have served at least 2 full years on active duty and are approved for Tuition Assistance by their military service. Applicants must be participating in the Montgomery GI Bill (MGIB) Active Duty program and be eligible for MGIB benefits.
Financial data: This program pays the difference between what the military services pay for Tuition Assistance (normally 75% of tuition and fees) and the full amount of tuition and fees.
Duration: Up to 36 months of payments are available.
Additional information: This program was established in 2000.
Number awarded: Varies each year.

725
MORRIS SCHOLARSHIP

Morris Scholarship Fund
Attn: Scholarship Selection Committee
525 S.W. Fifth Street, Suite A
Des Moines, IA 50309-4501
Phone: (515) 282-8192   Fax: (515) 282-9117
E-mail: morris@assoc-mgmt.com

Web Site: www.assoc-mgmt.com/users/morris

Summary: To provide financial assistance to minority undergraduate and graduate students in Iowa who are interested in pursuing postsecondary education.

Eligibility: This program is open to minority students (African Americans, Asian/Pacific Islanders, Hispanics, or Native Americans) who are interested in studying at a college, graduate school, or law school. Applicants must be either Iowa residents and high school graduates who are attending a college or university anywhere in the United States or non-Iowa residents who are attending a college or university in Iowa; preference is given to native Iowans who are attending an Iowa college or university. Selection is based on academic achievement, a statement of educational and career goals, community service, and financial need.

Financial data: The stipend is $1,500 per year.

Duration: 1 year; may be renewed.

Additional information: This fund was established in 1977 in honor of the J.B. Morris family, who founded the Iowa branches of the National Association for the Advancement of Colored People and published the *Iowa Bystander* newspaper.

Number awarded: 30 each year.

Deadline: January of each year.

726
MORTON A. GIBSON MEMORIAL SCHOLARSHIP

Jewish Social Service Agency of Metropolitan Washington
6123 Montrose Road
Rockville, MD 20852
Phone: (301) 881-3700   Fax: (301) 770-8741
Phone: TTY: (301) 984-5662
Web Site: www.jssa.org/scholarship.html

Summary: To provide financial assistance for postsecondary education to Jewish students from the Washington, D.C. area.

Eligibility: This program is open to current high school seniors who have performed significant volunteer service in the Jewish community or under the auspices of Jewish organizations in the Washington, D.C. area. Applicants must have been admitted as full-time students to an accredited 4-year undergraduate program in the United States. They must be U.S. citizens or working toward citizenship. Students in community colleges, Israeli schools, or year-abroad programs are not eligible. Selection is based on volunteer service, financial need, and academic achievement.

Financial data: The stipend is $2,500.

Duration: 1 year.

Number awarded: 2 each year.

Deadline: May of each year.

727
MR. AND MRS. TAKASHI MORIUCHI SCHOLARSHIP

Japanese American Citizens League
Attn: National Scholarship Awards
1765 Sutter Street
San Francisco, CA 94115
Phone: (415) 921-5225   Fax: (415) 931-4671
E-mail: jacl@jacl.org   Web Site: www.jacl.org

Summary: To provide financial assistance to student members of the Japanese American Citizens League (JACL) who are high school seniors interested in pursuing undergraduate education.

Eligibility: This program is open to JACL members who are high school seniors interested in attending a college, university, trade school, business college, or other institution of higher learning. Selection is based on academic record, extracurricular activities, and community involvement.

Financial data: The stipend depends on the availability of funds but usually ranges from $1,000 to $5,000.

Duration: 1 year.

Additional information: Requests for applications must include a self-addressed stamped envelope.

Number awarded: At least 1 each year.

Deadline: March of each year.

728
MVSNA STUDENT SCHOLARSHIP

Missouri Vocational Special Need Association
c/o Cindy Grizzell, Awards Chair
Waynesville Technical Academy
810 Roosevelt
Waynesville, MO 65583
Phone: (573) 774-6101   E-mail: cgrizzell@waynesville.k12.mo.us

Summary: To provide financial assistance to vocational-technical students in Missouri who are members of designated special populations.

Eligibility: This program is open to Missouri vocational-technical students who are members of special populations, defined as individuals who are academically or economically disadvantaged, have limited English proficiency, or are nontraditional, disabled, pregnant teenagers, single/teen parents, or foster children. Applicants must submit brief essays on their professional or career goals; the challenges they have had to overcome to reach their educational goals; how they have received help from their school, teachers, or community; and how the award will help them in pursuing continued education. Selection is based on the students' selection of a realistic career goal, financial need, unusual circumstances, and personal references.

Financial data: A stipend is awarded (exact amount not specified).

Duration: 1 year.

Number awarded: 1 each year.

Deadline: April of each year.

729
MYRTLE BEINHAUER SCHOLARSHIP

Sons of Norway Foundation
c/o Sons of Norway
1455 West Lake Street
Minneapolis, MN 55408-2666
Phone: (612) 827-3611   (800) 945-8851
Fax: (612) 827-0658   E-mail: fraternal@sofn.com
Web Site: www.sofn.com/foundation/scholarships.html

Summary: To provide financial assistance for college education to members and descendants of members of Sons of Norway.

Eligibility: This program is open to high school graduates who are current members of Sons of Norway or the children or grandchildren of current members. Applicants must be enrolled in college, trade school, or vocational school. Selection is based on goals, grade point average, letter of recommendation, and extracurricular activities.

Financial data: The stipend is approximately $3,000; grants are made payable jointly to students and their institutions of higher learning.

Duration: Students may receive a maximum of 2 awards within a 5-year period.

Additional information: This program was established in 1998.

Number awarded: 1 each year.

Deadline: February of each year.

730
NAAS-II SCHOLARSHIP AWARDS

National Academy of American Scholars
Attn: Merit Committee
5196 Benito Street, Suite 15, Room A
Montclair, CA 91763-4028
Phone: (909) 621-6856   E-mail: staff@naas.org
Web Site: www.naas.org/college.htm

Summary: To recognize and reward college freshmen who have exhibited outstanding character and scholastic excellence.

Eligibility: Applicants must be U.S. citizens or permanent residents enrolled in an accredited 2- or 4-year institution as college freshmen or sophomores, younger than 25, and pursuing a bachelor's degree with a cumulative GPA of 2.0 or higher. Selection is made without regard to financial need, affiliation status, or study area.

Financial data: The stipend ranges from $1,000 to $3,000 per year. The scholarships are paid to the recipient's institution.

Duration: 1 year; renewable.

Additional information: Send a legal-sized self-addressed stamped envelope and $1 handling fee to the sponsor to receive an application and information packet. Walk-in, phone-in, and e-mail requests are not accepted.

Number awarded: 1 each year.

Deadline: February of each year.

731
NACA REGIONAL COUNCIL STUDENT LEADER SCHOLARSHIPS

National Association for Campus Activities
Attn: Educational Foundation
13 Harbison Way
Columbia, SC 29212-3401
Phone: (803) 732-6222   Fax: (803) 749-1047
E-mail: dionneb@naca.org
Web Site: www.naca.org
Summary: To provide financial assistance to outstanding college student leaders.
Eligibility: Eligible for this program are full-time undergraduate students who have made significant contributions to their campus communities, have played leadership roles in campus activities, and have demonstrated leadership skills and abilities. Financial need is not considered in the selection process.
Financial data: The amounts of the awards vary each year; scholarships are to be used for educational expenses, including tuition, books, fees, or other related expenses.
Additional information: This program was established in 1996.
Number awarded: Up to 11 each year: 1 in each of the association's 11 regions.
Deadline: April of each year.

732
NANNIE W. NORFLEET SCHOLARSHIP

American Legion Auxiliary
Attn: Department of North Carolina
P.O. Box 25726
Raleigh, NC 27611-5726
Phone: (919) 832-4051   E-mail: ala_nc@bellsouth.net
Summary: To provide financial assistance for college to members of the American Legion Auxiliary in North Carolina and their children and grandchildren.
Eligibility: This program is open to North Carolina residents who are members of the American Legion Auxiliary or high school seniors (with preference to the children and grandchildren of members). Applicants must be able to demonstrate financial need.
Financial data: The stipend is $2,000 per year.
Duration: 1 year.
Number awarded: 1 each year.
Deadline: March of each year.

733
NASE SCHOLARSHIP PROGRAM

National Association for the Self-Employed
P.O. Box 612067
DFW Airport
Dallas, TX 75261-2067
Phone: (800) 232-NASE   Web Site: www.nase.org
Summary: To provide financial assistance for college to dependents of members of the National Association for the Self-Employed (NASE).
Eligibility: This program is open to dependents of members of NASE who are between 16 and 24 years of age.
Financial data: The stipend is $4,000.
Duration: 1 year.
Additional information: This program was established in 1988 so NASE could provide children of the self-employed and micro-business owners with scholarship opportunities similar to those for students whose parents work in large corporations.
Number awarded: 20 each year.
Deadline: May of each year.

734
NASP TRIO SCHOLARSHIP

Pride Foundation
c/o Greater Seattle Business Association
2150 North 107th Street, Suite 205
Seattle, WA 98133-9009
Phone: (206) 363-9188   Fax: (206) 367-8777
E-mail: office@the-gsba.org
Web Site: www.the-gsba.org
Summary: To provide financial assistance to students at colleges and universities that are members of the Northwest Association of Special Programs (NASP).
Eligibility: This program is open to students at colleges and universities in Alaska, Idaho, Montana, Oregon, and Washington that belong to NASP. Applicants must be current or former participants in a federal TRIO program (Upward Bound, Talent Search, Student Support Services, etc.) that serves disadvantaged youth. They do not need to be a sexual minority, but they should have a demonstrated history of student leadership and activism furthering the causes of human rights, gender issues, and/or sexual minority rights. Selection is based on financial need, community involvement, and commitment to human rights.
Financial data: Stipends range from $1,000 to $5,000.
Duration: 1 year; recipients may reapply.
Additional information: The Pride Foundation was established in 1987 to strengthen the lesbian, gay, bisexual, and transgender community. It may be contacted directly at 1801 12th Avenue, Seattle, WA 98122, (206) 323-3318, (800) 735-7287, E-mail: giving@pridefoundation.org, Web site: www.pridefoundation.org. Its scholarship program is administered in collaboration with the Greater Seattle Business Association.
Number awarded: 1 each year. Since it began offering scholarships in 1992, the foundation has awarded a total of $204,266 to 154 recipients.
Deadline: February of each year.

735
NATIONAL ACHIEVEMENT SCHOLARSHIP PROGRAM

National Merit Scholarship Corporation
Attn: National Achievement Scholarship Program
1560 Sherman Avenue, Suite 200
Evanston, IL 60201-4897
Phone: (847) 866-5100
Summary: To provide financial assistance for college to Black American high school seniors with exceptional scores on standardized examinations.
Eligibility: To be eligible, a student must be enrolled full time in a secondary school; be progressing normally toward graduation or completion of high school requirements; spend no more than 4 years in grades 9 to 12 inclusive; be a U.S. citizen (or intend to become a citizen as soon as qualified); plan to attend a college or university in the United States that is totally accredited by its regional accrediting commission on higher education; take the PSAT/NMSQT at the proper time in high school and no later than the 11th grade; and mark section 13 on the PSAT/NMSQT answer sheet, which identifies the student as a Black American who is requesting consideration in the Achievement Program. Final selection is based on the student's academic record, a self description, PSAT/NMSQT and SAT scores, and a recommendation written by the principal or another official. Financial information is not considered, nor are college choice, course of study, or career plans.
Financial data: The award is $2,000.
Duration: 1 year.
Additional information: A sizeable group of each year's Achievement Program's nonwinners are commended to the attention of U.S. institutions of higher education for the College-Sponsored Achievement Program or for the Corporate-Sponsored Achievement Program. Each winner must enroll as a full-time day student in a course of study leading to 1 of the traditional baccalaureate degrees. Recipients must meet the standards of performance and terms set forth in their scholarship offer. Students who have completed high school, or who are now enrolled in college or have attended college in the past, are not eligible for consideration.
Number awarded: Approximately 440 each year.
Deadline: Applicants must take the PSAT/NMSQT no later than October of their junior year.

736
NATIONAL ALLIANCE FOR EXCELLENCE ACADEMIC SCHOLARSHIPS

National Alliance for Excellence
63 Riverside Avenue
Red Bank, NJ 07701
Phone: (732) 747-0028   Fax: (732) 842-2962
E-mail: info@excellence.org
Web Site: www.excellence.org
Summary: To provide financial assistance for postsecondary education in the United States or abroad.
Eligibility: Applicants must be U.S. citizens attending or planning to attend a college or university in the United States or an approved foreign study program

on a full-time basis. They may be high school seniors, college students, graduate students, or returning students. For these scholarships, applicants must have minimum SAT scores of 1300 or ACT scores of 30 as well as a 3.7 minimum grade point average for college students and completed GRE scores for graduate students. Selection is based on talent and ability without regard to financial need.
Financial data: Stipends range from $1,000 to $5,000 per year.
Duration: 1 year.
Additional information: The National Alliance for Excellence was formerly the Scholarship Foundation of America. A $5 processing fee is charged.
Deadline: Applications may be submitted at any time. Awards are given out on a continuous basis.

737
NATIONAL ALLIANCE FOR SCHOLASTIC ACHIEVEMENT SCHOLARSHIPS

National Alliance for Scholastic Achievement
Attn: #600
10820 Beverly Boulevard A5
Whittier, CA 90601-2569
Web Site: www.eee.org/bus/nasa/informtn.htm
Summary: To provide financial assistance for college to high school seniors who demonstrate outstanding academic achievement.
Eligibility: This program is open to high school seniors who have been accepted or anticipate being accepted at a 4-year academic institution. Applicants must have a grade point average of 2.75 or higher and have taken the SAT or ACT test. Financial need, race, and gender are not considered in the selection process. Generally, grade point averages are 3.9 to 4.0 for the top award, 3.7 to 4.0 for the second award, 3.5 to 3.9 for third, 3.0 to 3.8 for fourth, and 2.75 to 3.6 for fifth. U.S. citizenship or permanent resident status is required.
Financial data: The top award is $3,750 per year, second award is $2,500 per year, third award is $1,250 per year, fourth award is $750 per year, and fifth award is $500 per year.
Duration: 1 year; may be renewed up to 4 additional years.
Additional information: Requests for an application must be accompanied by a self-addressed stamped envelope.
Number awarded: 5 each year.
Deadline: March of each year

738
NATIONAL AMPUTEE GOLF ASSOCIATION SCHOLARSHIP

National Amputee Golf Association
11 Walnut Hill Road
Amherst, NH 03031
Phone: (603) 672-6444   (800) 633-NAGA
Fax: (603) 672-2987   E-mail: b1naga@aol.com
Web Site: www.nagagolf.org
Summary: To provide financial assistance for postsecondary education to members of the National Amputee Golf Association and their dependents.
Eligibility: This program is open to amputee members in good standing in the association and their dependents. Applicants must submit information on their scholastic background (grade point average in high school and college, courses of study); type of amputation and cause (if applicable), a cover letter describing their plans for the future; and documentation of financial need. They need not be competitive golfers. Selection is based on academic record, financial need, involvement in extracurricular or community activities, and area of study.
Financial data: The stipend is up to $1,000 per year, depending on need.
Duration: Up to 4 years, provided the recipient maintains at least half-time enrollment and a grade point average of 2.0 or higher and continues to demonstrate financial need.
Number awarded: 1 or more each year.
Deadline: June of each year.

739
NATIONAL ASSOCIATION OF HISPANIC FEDERAL EXECUTIVES SCHOLARSHIP

National Association of Hispanic Federal Executives Scholarship Foundation Inc.
5717 Marble Arch Way
Alexandria, VA 22315
Phone: (703) 971-3204   E-mail: BillRodriguez@compuserve.com
Web Site: www.nahfe.org/scholars.htm
Summary: To provide financial assistance for college to Hispanic American high school seniors.

Eligibility: Eligible to apply are graduating high school seniors of Hispanic American descent. Scholarships are awarded in 3 categories: 1) deserving Hispanic high school seniors on the basis of outstanding academic achievement (3.5 or greater grade point average), community service, and financial need; 2) deserving Hispanic high school seniors on the basis of satisfactory academic achievement (from 2.8 to 3.5 grade point average), community involvement, and financial need; and 3) deserving Hispanic high school seniors on the basis of academic merit only (3.5 or greater grade point average). As part of the application process, students must submit a completed application form, a copy of their high school transcript, 2 letters of recommendation, and a 300-word essay describing their professional or career goals. For scholarships in the first 2 categories listed above, students must also provide proof of financial need (e.g., a copy of the most recent income tax return).
Financial data: A stipend is awarded (exact amount not specified).
Duration: Up to 4 years.
Additional information: This program was established in 1999.
Deadline: May of each year.

740
NATIONAL ASSOCIATION OF RAILWAY BUSINESS WOMEN SCHOLARSHIPS

National Association of Railway Business Women
c/o Doris Stemmer, Publications Chair
1622 Cohasset Drive
Cincinnati, OH 45255
Web Site: www.narbw.org
Summary: To provide financial assistance for college to members of the National Association of Railway Business Women (NARBW) and their families.
Eligibility: This program is open to NARBW members, their dependents, and other family members (including grandchildren, nieces, and nephews). Applicants may be high school seniors or currently-enrolled college students. Selection is based on scholastic ability, ambition, potential, and financial need.
Financial data: Stipends are $1,500, $1,200, $1,000, or $500.
Duration: 1 year; recipients may reapply.
Additional information: This organization was formed in 1941 and today has more than 1,500 members in 35 chapters nationwide. The scholarship program was established in 1977. The program includes the following named scholarships: Orpha M. Wardle Memorial Scholarship, JoAnn Rowe Memorial Scholarship, Cora Nelson Abrahamson Memorial Scholarship, and Connie Newton Memorial Scholarship.
Number awarded: Varies each year; recently, 10 of these scholarships were awarded.

741
NATIONAL BETA CLUB SCHOLARSHIP PROGRAM

National Beta Clubs
151 West Lee Street
Spartanburg, SC 29306-3012
Phone: (864) 583-4554   (800) 845-8281
Fax: (864) 542-9300   E-mail: betaclub@betaclub.org
Web Site: www.betaclub.org
Summary: To recognize and reward outstanding senior Beta Club members.
Eligibility: This competitive program is open to Beta Club members who best exemplify the club's goals of academic excellence, leadership, and school/community service. Each Beta Club may nominate 2 high school senior members to compete. Nominees will be required to complete application and nomination forms and return them to their Beta Club sponsor. Nominees must also take the American College Test (ACT) or Scholastic Assessment Test (SAT). Advancement to the semifinalist stage is contingent upon the submission of test scores and class rank. Selection is based on academic excellence, demonstrated leadership, character, and school and community service.
Financial data: Stipends range from $1,000 to $15,000 per year.
Duration: The competition is held annually.
Additional information: The National Beta Club is an academic, leadership, and service organization for students in grades 5 to 12.
Number awarded: 209 each year: 204 at $1,000 and 5 at $15,000.
Deadline: December of each year.

742
NATIONAL BUSINESS ASSOCIATION SCHOLARSHIP PROGRAM

National Business Association
5151 Beltline Road, Suite 1150
P.O. Box 700728
Dallas, TX 75370
Phone: (972) 458-0900   (800) 456-0440
Fax: (972) 960-9149
Web Site: www.nationalbusiness.org/NBAWEB/scholarship.htm
Summary: To provide financial assistance for college to children of members of the National Business Association (NBA).
Eligibility: This program is open to the dependent children of active NBA members who are high school seniors or college freshmen, sophomores, or juniors. Applicants should be average to above average students, defined as high school seniors in the top third but not top 10 percent of their class, college students with a grade point average of 2.5 to 3.5, or students with scores on the ACT of 18 to 26 or the SAT of 850 to 1190. Financial need is not considered in the selection process.
Financial data: The stipend is $1,500. Funds are paid directly to the recipient's institution.
Duration: 1 year; may be renewed.
Additional information: Recipients must enroll full time.
Number awarded: At least 10 each year.
Deadline: March of each year.

743
NATIONAL DEAN'S LIST SCHOLARSHIPS

Educational Communications Scholarship Foundation
721 North McKinley Road
Lake Forest, IL 60045
Phone: (847) 295-6650   Fax: (847) 295-3972
E-mail: feedback@honoring.com
Web Site: www.honoring.com/deanslist/scholar
Summary: To provide financial assistance to college students who are listed in *The National Dean's List*.
Eligibility: This program is open to college students who are U.S. citizens and 1) have a grade point average of "B+" or better or 2) rank in the upper 10 percent of their class. Candidates must first be nominated by their dean, honor society advisor, or other college official to have their name appear in *The National Dean's List*. All students listed in that publication automatically receive an application for these scholarships in the mail. Selection is based on grade point average, achievement test scores, leadership qualifications, work experience, evaluation of an essay, and some consideration for financial need.
Financial data: Scholarships are $1,000; payments are issued directly to the financial aid office at the institution the student attends.
Duration: 1 year.
Number awarded: 50 each year.
Deadline: May of each year.

744
NATIONAL EAGLE SCOUT SCHOLARSHIPS

Boy Scouts of America
Attn: Eagle Scout Service, S220
1325 West Walnut Hill Lane
P.O. Box 152079
Irving, TX 75015-2079
Phone: (972) 580-2431
Web Site: www.scouting.org/nesa/scholar/index.html
Summary: To provide financial assistance for college to Eagle Scouts.
Eligibility: Eagle Scouts who are graduating high school seniors are eligible to apply for these scholarships. They must have an SAT score of at least 1090 and/or an ACT score of at least 26. Selection is based on financial need, scholastic accomplishment, involvement in Scouting, and school and community activities.
Financial data: The amount of the award depends on the availability of funds. Awards may be used only for tuition, room, board, and books by full-time students at 4-year colleges and universities.
Duration: 1 year; not renewable.
Number awarded: Varies each year, depending on the availability of funds and the number of applications; recently, 12 have been awarded each year.
Deadline: February of each year.

745
NATIONAL FEDERATION OF THE BLIND OF CALIFORNIA SCHOLARSHIPS

National Federation of the Blind of California
Attn: Nancy Burns
1240 North Griffith Park Drive
Burbank, CA 91506
Phone: (818) 558-6524   Fax: (818) 842-1018
E-mail: webmaster@nfbcal.org
Web Site: www.nfbcal.org
Summary: To provide financial assistance for graduate or undergraduate education to blind students in California.
Eligibility: Legally blind full-time students in California may apply for a scholarship, but they must attend the convention of the National Federation of the Blind of California. Applicants must submit an essay in which they describe their educational goals, involvement in the blindness community, and eye condition. High school seniors and college freshmen must submit their high school transcripts; other college students must submit transcripts of all undergraduate and graduate work. Selection is based on academic merit.
Financial data: The stipend is $1,000.
Duration: 1 year.
Number awarded: 3 each year.
Deadline: May of each year.

746
NATIONAL FEDERATION OF THE BLIND SCHOLARSHIPS

National Federation of the Blind
c/o Peggy Elliott
Chair, Scholarship Committee
805 Fifth Avenue
Grinnell, IA 50112
Phone: (641) 236-3366
Web Site: www.nfb.org
Summary: To provide financial assistance to blind students studying or planning to study at the postsecondary level.
Eligibility: This program is open to legally blind students who are pursuing or planning to pursue an undergraduate or graduate course of study. In general, full-time enrollment is required, although 1 scholarship may be awarded to a part-time student who is working full time. Selection is based on academic excellence, service to the community, and financial need.
Financial data: Stipends are $7,000, $5,000, or $3,000.
Duration: 1 year; recipients may resubmit applications up to 2 additional years.
Additional information: Scholarships are awarded at the federation convention in July. Recipients attend the convention at federation expense; that funding is in addition to the scholarship grant.
Number awarded: 18 each year: 2 at $7,000, 3 at $5,000, and 13 at $3,000.
Deadline: March of each year.

747
NATIONAL FRATERNAL SOCIETY OF THE DEAF SCHOLARSHIPS

National Fraternal Society of the Deaf
1118 South Sixth Street
Springfield, IL 62703
Phone: (217) 789-7429   Fax: (217) 789-7489
Phone: TTY: (217) 789-7438   E-mail: thefrat@nfsd.com
Web Site: www.nfsd.com
Summary: To provide financial assistance for postsecondary education to members of the National Fraternal Society of the Deaf.
Eligibility: Deaf, hard of hearing, or hearing persons who are enrolled in or accepted to a postsecondary educational institution are eligible to apply if they have been members of the society for at least 1 year prior to application.
Financial data: The stipend is $1,000.
Duration: The scholarships are awarded annually. No person may win more than 2 scholarships.
Number awarded: 10 each year.
Deadline: June of each year.

748
NATIONAL GYMNASTICS FOUNDATION AND USA GYMNASTICS SCHOLARSHIP PROGRAM

USA Gymnastics
Attn: Men's Scholarship Program
201 South Capitol Avenue, Suite 300
Indianapolis, IN 46225
Phone: (317) 237-5050, ext. 230
Web Site: www.usa-gymnastics.org/men/scholarship-guidelines.html
Summary: To provide financial assistance for college to male elite-level gymnasts.
Eligibility: This program is open to high school seniors and currently-enrolled college students who are gymnasts pursuing their college or postsecondary education. Applicants must be training at the elite level, with an emphasis on international competition, and have earned at least a 2.0 grade point average. To apply, students must submit a typed application, 3 letters of recommendation, and a college or high school transcript. Financial need is considered in the selection process (tax forms may be required).
Financial data: The size of the scholarship varies, depending upon the funds raised throughout the year in support of the program. Funds must be used for college or postsecondary educational expenses.
Duration: 1 year.
Additional information: The National Gymnastics Foundation and USA Gymnastics administer this scholarship. Acceptance of this scholarship could affect NCAA eligibility. Recipients must submit a report at the end of the year about their experiences as a scholarship recipient.
Number awarded: Varies each year.
Deadline: April of each year.

749
NATIONAL HONOR SOCIETY SCHOLARSHIPS

National Association of Secondary School Principals
Attn: Department of Student Activities
1904 Association Drive
Reston, VA 20191-1537
Phone: (703) 860-0200   (800) 253-7746
Fax: (703) 476-5432   E-mail: dsa@nassp.org
Web Site: www.nassp.org
Summary: To recognize and reward outstanding high school seniors.
Eligibility: Each public, private, and parochial high school in the United States may nominate 2 seniors who are members of their National Honor Society chapter. Nominees must be able to demonstrate on their applications that they possess outstanding character, scholarship, service, and leadership.
Financial data: Each scholarship is $1,000.
Additional information: The program is funded by the National Association of Secondary School Principals; Herff Jones, Inc. donates funds for 2 of the scholarships.
Number awarded: 200 each year.
Deadline: Nominations must be submitted by January of each year.

750
NATIONAL ITALIAN AMERICAN FOUNDATION GENERAL CATEGORY I SCHOLARSHIPS

National Italian American Foundation
Attn: Education Director
1860 19th Street, N.W.
Washington, DC 20009
Phone: (202) 387-0600   Fax: (202) 387-0800
E-mail: scholarships@niaf.org
Web Site: www.niaf.org/scholarships
Summary: To provide financial assistance to Italian American college students.
Eligibility: This program is open to Italian American students (defined as having at least 1 ancestor who has immigrated from Italy). Applicants must be currently enrolled or entering an accredited college or university in the United States with a grade point average of 3.25 or higher. Selection is based on academic performance, field of study, career objectives, and the potential, commitment, and abilities applicants have demonstrated that would enable them to make significant contributions to their chosen field of study. Some scholarships also require financial need.
Financial data: Stipends range from $2,000 to $5,000.
Duration: 1 year. Recipients are encouraged to reapply.
Additional information: Applications can only be submitted online. At the

completion of the scholarship year, recipients must submit a 500-word narrative describing the benefits of the scholarship.
Number awarded: Varies each year.
Deadline: April of each year.

751
NATIONAL KIDNEY FOUNDATION OF CONNECTICUT SCHOLARSHIP PROGRAM

National Kidney Foundation of Connecticut
920 Farmington Avenue
West Hartford, CT 06107
Phone: (860) 232-6054   (800) 441-1280
Fax: (860) 236-1367   E-mail: info@kidneyct.org
Web Site: www.kidneyct.org/services.htm
Summary: To provide financial assistance for college to residents of Connecticut who have kidney or urological problems or their dependents.
Eligibility: This program is open to dialysis and kidney transplant patients in Connecticut and their dependents, as well as people with Childhood Nephrotic Syndrome. Applicants may be entering college as freshmen, continuing students, or older students returning to school. Selection is based on academic performance, financial need, and history of community service.
Financial data: Stipends up to $2,000 per year are available.
Duration: 1 year; may be renewed.
Number awarded: Varies each year. A total of $10,000 is available for this program annually.
Deadline: May of each year.

752
NATIONAL MERIT SCHOLARSHIP PROGRAM

National Merit Scholarship Corporation
Attn: Department of Educational Services and Selection
1560 Sherman Avenue, Suite 200
Evanston, IL 60201-4897
Phone: (847) 866-5100
Summary: To identify and honor scholastically talented high school students and provide them with financial support for undergraduate study.
Eligibility: To be eligible, a student must be enrolled full time in a secondary school, progressing normally toward graduation or completion of high school, and planning to enter college in the fall following high school graduation; be a U.S. citizen or a permanent resident in the process of becoming a U.S. citizen; and be taking the PSAT/NMSQT at the proper time in the high school program and no later than the third year in grades 9 through 12, regardless of grade classification or educational pattern. On the basis of the PSAT/NMSQT results, approximately 15,000 of the highest scorers are designated as semifinalists; they are apportioned among states in proportion to the number of graduating seniors in each state, to assure equitable geographical representation. Finalists for National Merit Scholarships must be graduating seniors who are selected from among the semifinalists on the basis of SAT scores, academic performance in all of grades 9 through 12, and recommendations by high school principals.
Financial data: The award is $2,000.
Duration: 1 year.
Additional information: From the 15,500 semifinalists, approximately 14,000 finalists are named each year. Those finalists who are not selected to receive National Merit Scholarships are commended to the attention of U.S. institutions of higher education for the College-Sponsored Merit Scholarship Program or for the Corporate-Sponsored Merit and Special Scholarship Program.
Number awarded: Approximately 2,400 each year.
Deadline: Applicants must take the PSAT/NMSQT no later than October of their junior year.

753
NATIONAL MINORITY JUNIOR GOLF SCHOLARSHIP ASSOCIATION SCHOLARSHIPS

National Minority Junior Golf Scholarship Association
Attn: Scholarship Committee
1140 East Washington Street, Suite 102
Phoenix, AZ 85034-1051
Phone: (602) 258-7851   Fax: (602) 258-3412
Web Site: www.nmgf.org
Summary: To provide financial assistance for college to minority high school seniors who excel at golf.

Eligibility: Eligible to apply for this award are minority high school seniors who are interested in attending college. Applicants are asked to write a 500-word essay on this question: "One of the principal goals of education and golf is fostering ways for people to respect and get along with individuals who think, dress, look, and act differently. How might you make this goal a reality?" Selection is based on academic record, personal recommendations, participation in golf, school and community activities (including employment, extracurricular activities, and other responsibilities), and financial need.

Financial data: The stipend is at least $1,000 per year. Funds are paid directly to the recipient's college.

Duration: 1 year or longer.

Additional information: This program was established in 1984. Since then, more than $500,000 in scholarships has been awarded.

Number awarded: Varies; generally 80 or more each year.

754
NATIONAL YOUTH OF THE YEAR PROGRAM

Boys & Girls Clubs of America
Attn: Regional Service Director
3 West 35th Street, Ninth Floor
New York, NY 10001-2204
Phone: (212) 351-5478   Fax: (212) 351-5493
E-mail: jhurley@bgca.org
Web Site: www.bgca.org

Summary: To recognize and reward outstanding leadership and service by participants in the Boys & Girls Clubs.

Eligibility: Each local club selects a Youth of the Year; selection may be based on academic performance, contributions to family and spiritual life, or service to the club. Recipients must be between the ages of 14 and 18 and have a record of active and continuing service to their club for at least 1 year. Each club Youth of the Year is nominated to be the state Youth of the Year, and those enter regional competitions. The 5 regional winners are then invited to Washington, D.C. for interviews and selection of the National Youth of the Year.

Financial data: The regional winners receive $5,000 scholarships and the National Youth of the Year receives an additional scholarship of $10,000; funds are held in trust and then made available to the recipients as needed for tuition, books, school fees, and transportation.

Duration: The competition is held annually.

Additional information: This program is sponsored in part by the Reader's Digest Association, Inc.

Number awarded: 5 regional scholarships are awarded each year and 1 of the recipients receives the national scholarship.

Deadline: Local clubs must submit their nominations by May of each year.

755
NATIONAL 4TH INFANTRY (IVY) DIVISION ASSOCIATION SCHOLARSHIP

National 4th Infantry (IVY) Division Association
c/o Alexander Cooker, Scholarship Administrator
78 North Dupont Road
Carneys Point, NJ 08069
Phone: (609) 299-4406   E-mail: alexcooker@aol.com
Web Site: www.4thinfantry.org

Summary: To provide financial assistance for college to members of the National 4th Infantry (IVY) Division Association and their families.

Eligibility: This program is open to association members in good standing and all blood relatives of active association members in good standing. Recipients are chosen by lottery.

Financial data: The stipend is $1,000.

Duration: 1 year; may be renewed.

Additional information: The trust fund from which these scholarships are awarded was created by the officers and enlisted men of the 4th Infantry Division as a living memorial to the men of the division who died in Vietnam. Originally, it was only open to children of members of the division who died in the line of duty while serving in Vietnam between August 1, 1966 and December 31, 1977. When all those eligible had completed college, it adopted its current requirements.

Number awarded: 3 each year.

756
NAUW SOUTHWEST SECTION SCHOLARSHIP

National Association of University Women
Southwest Section
c/o Fannie Love, Scholarship Chairperson
27476 Eagles Nest Drive
Corona, CA 92883

Summary: To provide financial assistance for college to currently-enrolled undergraduates in selected states.

Eligibility: Eligible to apply for this scholarship are full-time undergraduates (at a 2-year or 4-year school) who have permanent residency in 1 of the following states: California, Arizona, New Mexico, Colorado, Nevada, or Hawaii. Finalists are interviewed (applicants must provide their own transportation to the interview). Selection is based on academic record (must have at least a 3.0 to apply), honors or awards, extracurricular activities, an essay on future plans, the interview, and financial need. Students who have previously received a scholarship from a branch of the National Association of University Women are not eligible to apply for this support.

Financial data: The stipend is $1,000.

Duration: 1 year; nonrenewable.

Deadline: November of each year.

757
NAVAJO NATION FINANCIAL NEED-BASED ASSISTANCE PROGRAM

Navajo Nation
Attn: Office of Navajo Nation Scholarship and Financial Assistance
P.O. Box 1870
Window Rock, AZ 86515-1870
Phone: (520) 871-7640   (800) 243-2956
Fax: (520) 871-6561   E-mail: onnsfacentral@navajo.org
Web Site: www.onnsfa.navajo.org

Summary: To provide financial assistance to members of the Navajo Nation who are interested in pursuing undergraduate education.

Eligibility: This program is open to enrolled members of the Navajo Nation who have proof of one-quarter or more Navajo Indian blood quantum on their certificate of Indian blood. Applicants must be attending or planning to attend an accredited institution of higher education to pursue an associate or baccalaureate degree. Financial need must be demonstrated.

Financial data: The amount awarded varies, depending upon the needs of the recipient.

Duration: 1 year; may be renewed (if the recipient maintains at least a 2.0 grade point average) for up to a total of 10 semesters of full-time undergraduate study, 5 academic terms or 64 semester credit hours at 2-year institutions, or 50 semester credit hours of part-time undergraduate study.

Deadline: April of each year for fall term; September of each year for winter or spring term; March of each year for summer session.

758
NAVAJO NATION TRUST FUND FOR VOCATIONAL EDUCATION

Navajo Nation
Attn: Office of Navajo Nation Scholarship and Financial Assistance
P.O. Box 1870
Window Rock, AZ 86515-1870
Phone: (520) 871-7640   (800) 243-2956
Fax: (520) 871-6561   E-mail: onnsfacentral@navajo.org
Web Site: www.onnsfa.navajo.org

Summary: To provide financial assistance for vocational education to members of the Navajo Nation.

Eligibility: This program is open to enrolled members of the Navajo Nation who are attending or planning to attend full time a postsecondary vocational education institution on the Navajo Nation or in the states of Arizona, Colorado, New Mexico, or Utah. Applicants must be registered voters in their respective chapters. Preference is given to first-time applicants who have not previously received any form of financial assistance (from the Bureau of Indian Affairs, Job Training Partnership Act, Crownpoint Institute of Technology, etc.).

Financial data: The amount of the award is determined by each local chapter, which receives funding from the Nation based on the number of registered voters.

Duration: 1 year; may be renewed.

Deadline: April of each year.

759
NAVAL HELICOPTER ASSOCIATION UNDERGRADUATE SCHOLARSHIPS

Naval Helicopter Association
Attn: Scholarship Fund
P.O. Box 180578
Coronado, CA 92178-0578
Phone: (619) 435-7139   Fax: (619) 435-7354
E-mail: nhascholars@hotmail.com
Web Site: www.nhascholars.com
Summary: To provide financial assistance for full-time undergraduate study to students in the United States.
Eligibility: This program is open to U.S. citizens, regardless of race, religion, age, or gender, who are seniors in high school or currently enrolled in or accepted at an accredited college or university in the United States for undergraduate study. Selection is based on academic proficiency, scholastic achievements and awards, extracurricular activities, employment history, letters of recommendation, and a personal statement on educational plans and future goals.
Financial data: The stipend is $1,000 per year.
Duration: 1 year; may be renewed if the recipient maintains at least a 2.75 grade point average.
Additional information: Recipients must enroll full time.
Number awarded: 5 each year.
Deadline: November of each year.

760
NAVAL RESERVE ASSOCIATION SCHOLARSHIPS

Naval Reserve Association
1619 King Street
Alexandria, VA 22314
Phone: (703) 548-5800   (866) 672-4968
Fax: (703) 683-3647   E-mail: admin@navy-reserve.org
Web Site: www.navy-reserve.org
Summary: To provide financial assistance for college to the children of members of the Naval Reserve Association.
Eligibility: This program is open to the children of association members who are enrolled or accepted for enrollment at a college or university.
Financial data: The amounts of the stipends vary but recently averaged more than $4,000 per year.
Duration: 1 year.
Number awarded: Varies each year; recently, 6 of these scholarships were awarded.

761
NAVAL SEA CADET CORPS SCHOLARSHIP FUND

United States Naval Sea Cadet Corps
Attn: Executive Director
2300 Wilson Boulevard
Arlington, VA 22201-3308
Phone: (703) 243-6910   Fax: (703) 243-3985
Summary: To provide financial assistance to Naval Sea Cadet Corps cadets and former cadets who are interested in continuing their education at an accredited 4-year college/university.
Eligibility: This program is open to cadets and former cadets who are interested in continuing their education at an accredited 4-year college or university. They must have been a member of the corps for at least 2 years, have a minimum rating of NSCC E-3, be recommended by their commanding officer or other official, have earned at least a 3.0 grade point average, and have been accepted by an accredited college or university. Applicants may submit financial need statements. All other factors being equal, these statements may be considered in determining award recipients. Applicants who have received full scholarships from other sources (e.g., ROTC) will be considered for this award only if there are no other qualified applicants.
Financial data: The stipend is $1,000.
Duration: 1 year.
Additional information: Cadets are also eligible to apply for scholarships sponsored by the Navy League of the United States.
Number awarded: 1 each year.
Deadline: May of each year.

762
NAVY COLLEGE FUND

U.S. Navy
Attn: Navy Personnel Command (PERS-602)
5720 Integrity Drive
Millington, TN 38055
Phone: (901) 874-3070   (800) USA-NAVY
Fax: (901) 874-2651   E-mail: p602e2@bupers.navy.mil
Web Site: www.bupers.navy.mil
Summary: To provide financial assistance for postsecondary education to Navy enlistees after they have completed their service obligation.
Eligibility: Eligible for this program are high school seniors and graduates between 17 and 35 years of age who enlist in the Navy for 3 to 4 years of active duty. They must score 50 or above on the AFQT and also enroll in the Montgomery GI Bill. Sailors currently on active duty in selected Navy ratings with critical personnel shortages are also eligible. Applicants must be interested in attending a Department of Veterans Affairs-approved postsecondary educational institution on a full-time basis after completion of their service obligation.
Financial data: The Navy College Fund provides, in conjunction with the Montgomery GI Bill, up to $50,000 for college tuition and expenses.
Duration: Enlistees may begin using this educational benefit on a part-time basis after 2 years of continuous active duty. Funds must be utilized within 10 years of leaving the Navy.
Additional information: Applications and further information are available from local Navy recruiters and from the Navy Recruiting Command, 801 North Randolph Street, Arlington, VA 22203-1991.
Number awarded: Varies each year.
Deadline: Applications may be submitted at any time.

763
NAVY LEAGUE SCHOLARSHIPS

Navy League of the United States
2300 Wilson Boulevard
Arlington, VA 22201-3308
Phone: (703) 528-1775   Fax: (703) 528-2333
E-mail: mail@navyleague.org
Web Site: www.navyleague.org/scholarships.htm
Summary: To provide financial assistance for postsecondary education to dependent children of naval personnel.
Eligibility: This program is open to U.S. citizens who are high school seniors or graduates with a grade point average of 3.0 or higher. Applicants must be able to demonstrate financial need; be a dependent direct descendant of a person who is or has honorably served in a U.S. sea service (including the Navy, Marine Corps, Coast Guard, or Merchant Marines) or currently be an active member of the U.S. Naval Sea Cadet Corps; and be entering their freshman year of college. As part of the selection process, they must submit a 200-word essay on their personal goals and their educational and career objectives. Native Americans are given special consideration for 1 of the scholarships.
Financial data: The stipend is $2,500 per year.
Duration: 1 year or 4 years.
Additional information: This program includes the following named awards: the Renee and Earnest G. Campbell Scholarship, the Eileen and John R. Anderson, IV Scholarship, the Stanley Levinson Scholarship, the Jewell Hilton Bonner Scholarship (special consideration given to Native Americans), the Wesley G. Cameron Scholarship, the USS Mahan Scholarship (preference to a direct descendant of a sea service person who served in the USS Mahan or to the dependent of a sea service person who is so serving), and the All Wives Welfare Council U.S. Naval Facility, Philippines Subic Bay—Cubi Point Scholarship Program (restricted to a dependent of a sea service person who was permanently homeported at the U.S. Naval Facility Philippines—Subic Bay, Cubi Point, or San Miguel—between 1980 and 1992). Requests for applications must be accompanied by a stamped self-addressed envelope.
Number awarded: Approximately 15 each year: 5 for 4 years and 10 for 1 year.
Deadline: March of each year.

Scholarship Listings

764
NAVY SUPPLY CORPS FOUNDATION SCHOLARSHIPS

Navy Supply Corps Foundation
U.S. Navy Supply Corps School
1425 Prince Avenue
Athens, GA 30606-2205
Phone: (706) 354-4111   Fax: (706) 354-0334
E-mail: evans@usnscf.com
Web Site: www.usnscf.com
Summary: To provide financial assistance for the undergraduate education of children of Navy Supply Corps personnel.
Eligibility: Eligible to apply for these scholarships are the children of Navy Supply Corps officers (including warrant) or enlisted personnel on active duty, in reserve status, retired with pay, or deceased. Enlisted ratings that apply are AK (Aviation Storekeeper), SK (Storekeeper), MS (Mess Specialist), DK (Disbursing Clerk), SH (Ship Serviceman), LI (Lithographer), and PC (Postal Clerk). Selection is based on scholastic ability, character, and leadership ability. Recipients must attend a 2-year or 4-year accredited college on a full-time basis and have at least a 3.0 grade point average in high school and/or college.
Financial data: The amount of assistance varies.
Duration: 1 year; may be renewed.
Number awarded: Varies each year.
Deadline: April of each year.

765
NAVY-MARINE CORPS ROTC 2-YEAR SCHOLARSHIPS

U.S. Navy
Attn: Chief of Naval Education and Training
Code OTE6/081
250 Dallas Street
Naval Air Station
Pensacola, FL 32508-5220
Phone: (850) 452-4941, ext. 320   (800) NAV-ROTC, ext. 320
Fax: (850) 452-2486   E-mail: nrotc.scholarship@cnet.navy.mil
Web Site: www.cnet.navy.mil/nrotc/nrotc.htm
Summary: To provide financial assistance to college students who are willing to serve as Navy or Marine Corps officers following completion of their bachelor's degree.
Eligibility: This program is open to students who have completed at least 2 years of college (or 3 years if enrolled in a 5-year program) with a grade point average of at least 2.5 overall and 2.0 in calculus and physics. Preference is given to students at colleges with a Navy ROTC unit on campus or at colleges with a cross-enrollment agreement with a college with an NROTC unit. Applicants must be U.S. citizens between the ages of 17 and 21 who plan to pursue an approved course of study in college and complete their degree before they reach the age of 27. Former and current enlisted military personnel are also eligible if they will complete the program by the age of 30.
Financial data: These scholarships provide payment of full tuition and required educational fees, as well as a specified amount for textbooks, supplies, and equipment. The program also provides a stipend for 10 months of the year that is $300 per month as a junior and $350 per month as a senior.
Duration: 2 years, until the recipient completes the bachelor's degree.
Additional information: Applications must be made through professors of naval science at 1 of the schools hosting the Navy ROTC program. Prior to final selection, applicants must attend, at Navy expense, a 6-week summer training course at the Naval Science Institute at Newport, Rhode Island. Recipients must also complete 4 years of study in naval science classes as students either at 1 of the 68 colleges with NROTC units or at 1 of the more than 100 institutions with cross-enrollment agreements (in which case they attend their home college for their regular academic courses but attend naval science classes at a nearby school with an NROTC unit). After completing the program, all participants are commissioned as ensigns in the Naval Reserve or second lieutenants in the Marine Corps Reserve with an 8-year service obligation, including 4 years of active duty. Current military personnel who are accepted into this program are released from active duty and are not eligible for active-duty pay and allowances, medical benefits, or other active-duty entitlements.
Number awarded: Approximately 800 each year.
Deadline: March of each year.

766
NAVY-MARINE CORPS ROTC 4-YEAR SCHOLARSHIPS

U.S. Navy
Attn: Chief of Naval Education and Training
Code OTE6/081
250 Dallas Street
Naval Air Station
Pensacola, FL 32508-5220
Phone: (850) 452-4941, ext. 320   (800) NAV-ROTC, ext. 320
Fax: (850) 452-2486   E-mail: nrotc.scholarship@cnet.navy.mil
Web Site: www.cnet.navy.mil/nrotc/nrotc.htm
Summary: To provide financial assistance to graduating high school seniors who are willing to serve as Navy or Marine officers following completion of their bachelor's degree.
Eligibility: Eligible to apply for these scholarships are graduating high school seniors who have been accepted at a college with a Navy ROTC unit on campus or a college with a cross-enrollment agreement with such a college. Applicants must be U.S. citizens between the ages of 17 and 23 who are willing to serve for 4 years as active-duty Navy officers following graduation from college. They must not have reached their 27th birthday by the time of college graduation and commissioning; applicants who have prior active-duty military service may be eligible for age adjustments for the amount of time equal to their prior service, up to a maximum of 36 months. The qualifying scores for the Navy option are 530 verbal and 520 mathematics on the SAT or 22 on both English and math on the ACT; for the Marine Corps option they are 1000 total on the SAT or 45 composite on the ACT. Current enlisted and former military personnel are also eligible if they will complete the program by the age of 30.
Financial data: These scholarships provide payment of full tuition and required educational fees, as well as a specified amount for textbooks, supplies, and equipment. The program also provides a stipend for 10 months of the year that is $250 per month as a freshman and sophomore, $300 per month as a junior, and $350 per month as a senior.
Duration: 4 years.
Additional information: Students may apply for either a Navy or Marine Corps option scholarship but not for both. Navy option applicants apply through Navy recruiting offices; Marine Corps applicants apply through Marine Corps recruiting offices. Recipients must also complete 4 years of study in naval science classes as students either at 1 of the 68 colleges with NROTC units or at 1 of the more than 100 institutions with cross-enrollment agreements (in which case they attend their home college for their regular academic courses but attend naval science classes at a nearby school with an NROTC unit). After completing the program, all participants are commissioned as ensigns in the Naval Reserve or second lieutenants in the Marine Corps Reserve with an 8-year service obligation, including 4 years of active duty. Current military personnel who are accepted into this program are released from active duty and are not eligible for active-duty pay and allowances, medical benefits, or other active-duty entitlements.
Number awarded: Approximately 2,200 each year.
Deadline: January of each year;

767
NCAIAW SCHOLARSHIP

North Carolina Association of Health, Physical Education, Recreation and Dance
Attn: Executive Director
Box 974
Boiling Springs, NC 28017
Phone: (888) 840-6500
Summary: To provide financial assistance to women involved in sports at an institution that is a member of the former North Carolina Association of Intercollegiate Athletics for Women (NCAIAW).
Eligibility: This program is open to women who have been a participant on 1 or more varsity athletic teams either as a player or in the support role of manager, trainer, etc. Applicants must be attending 1 of the following former NCAIAW colleges or universities in North Carolina: Appalachian, Belmont Abbey, Bennett, Campbell, Davidson, Duke, East Carolina, Gardner-Webb, High Point, Mars Hill, Meredith, North Carolina A&T, North Carolina State, Queens, Pembroke State, Salem, St. Mary's, University of North Carolina at Ashville, University of North Carolina at Chapel Hill, University of North Carolina at Charlotte, University of North Carolina at Wilmington, Wake Forest, or Western Carolina. They must be college seniors at the time of application, be able to demonstrate high standards of scholarship, and show evidence of leadership potential (as indicated by participation in school and community activities).

Financial data: The stipend is $1,000. Funds are sent to the recipient's school.

Duration: 1 year.

Additional information: This scholarship was established in 1983. Information is also available from Phyllis Pharr, Department of Physical Education, Queens College, 1900 Selwyn Avenue, Charlotte, NC 28274, (704) 337-2228, Fax: (704) 337-2237, E-mail: pharrp@queens.edu.

Number awarded: 1 each year.

Deadline: August of each year.

768
NEBRASKA ELKS ASSOCIATION VOCATIONAL SCHOLARSHIP GRANTS

Nebraska Elks Association
c/o John Lund, Scholarship Committee
319 E A Street
Ogallala, NE 69153-2608
Phone: (308) 284-2871   E-mail: lundski@megavision.com
Web Site: members.tripod.com/ne_elks/scholarship_info.htm

Summary: To provide financial assistance to high school seniors in Nebraska who plan to attend a vocational school in the state.

Eligibility: This program is open to seniors graduating from high schools in Nebraska. Applicants must be planning to attend a 2-year or less vocational-technical program for an associate degree, diploma, or certificate. Selection is based on motivation (general worthiness, desire); aptitude toward chosen vocation; grades and test scores; completeness, neatness, and accuracy in following instructions when filling out the application; and financial need. Each Nebraska Elks Lodge can submit 1 application.

Financial data: A stipend is awarded (exact amount not specified).

Duration: 1 year.

Number awarded: 6 each year.

Deadline: January of each year.

769
NEBRASKA RURAL SCHOOLS SCHOLARSHIP

Lincoln Community Foundation
215 Centennial Mall South, Suite 200
Lincoln, NE 68508
Phone: (402) 474-2345   Fax: (402) 476-8532
E-mail: lcf@lcf.org
Web Site: www.lcf.org

Summary: To provide financial assistance for college to residents of rural Nebraska.

Eligibility: Eligible to apply for this college aid are graduating seniors or former graduates of a high school in rural Nebraska (for this program, defined as a community with a population of less than 10,000). Applicants must either attend or plan to attend a 2-year or 4-year college or university in the state. They should apply through that school. Financial need must be demonstrated. High school applicants must be graduating in the top 10 percent of their class; college applicants must have earned at least a 3.5 grade point average.

Financial data: A stipend is awarded (exact amount not specified).

Duration: 1 year; may be renewed.

Number awarded: 1 or more each year.

Deadline: July of each year.

770
NEBRASKA WAIVER OF TUITION FOR VETERANS' DEPENDENTS

Department of Veterans' Affairs
State Office Building
301 Centennial Mall South, Sixth Floor
P.O. Box 95083
Lincoln, NE 68509-5083
Phone: (402) 471-2458   Fax: (402) 471-2491
E-mail: dparker@mail.state.ne.us
Web Site: www.vets.state.ne.us

Summary: To provide financial assistance for educational purposes to veterans' dependents in Nebraska.

Eligibility: Eligible are spouses, widow(er)s, and children who are residents of Nebraska and whose father or spouse was a member of the U.S. armed forces killed in action in World War I, killed in action on December 7, 1941 or subsequently, or died subsequent to discharge as a result of injury or illness sustained while a member of the armed forces. Also eligible are children, spouses, or widow(er)s whose parent or spouse is totally disabled or classified missing in action or prisoner of war after August 4, 1964.

Financial data: Tuition is waived at the University of Nebraska, any of the state colleges, or any of the technical community colleges in the state.

Additional information: Applications may be submitted through 1 of the recognized veterans' organizations or any county service officer.

Number awarded: Varies each year.

771
NED MCWHERTER SCHOLARS PROGRAM

Tennessee Student Assistance Corporation
Parkway Towers
404 James Robertson Parkway, Suite 1950
Nashville, TN 37243-0820
Phone: (615) 741-1346   (800) 342-1663
Fax: (615) 741-6101   E-mail: tsac@mail.state.tn.us
Web Site: www.state.tn.us/tsac

Summary: To recognize and reward outstanding Tennessee high school seniors and recent graduates.

Eligibility: This program is open to recent high school graduates and high school seniors in Tennessee who are residents of the state, whose parents are residents of the state, who ranked in the top 5 percent on the ACT or SAT tests (recently, 29 on the ACT or 1280 on the SAT), and who earned at least a 3.5 grade point average in high school. Selection is based on academic record, test scores, and demonstrated leadership.

Financial data: Stipends up to $6,000 per year are provided.

Duration: 1 year; may be renewed for up to 3 additional years if the recipient remains a full-time student and maintains a minimum grade point average of 3.0 per term and 3.2 per year.

Additional information: This program was established in 1986. Recipients must attend a college or university in Tennessee.

Number awarded: Varies; generally, 50 or more each year.

Deadline: February of each year.

772
NEIGHBORS OF WOODCRAFT COLLEGE SCHOLARSHIPS

Neighbors of Woodcraft
Attn: Scholarship Committee
911 Main Street
P.O. Box 1897
Oregon City, OR 97045-0897
Phone: (503) 656-8118   (800) 456-1771
E-mail: membership@nowfbs.com
Web Site: www.nowfbs.com/scholar.htm

Summary: To provide college aid to members of the Neighbors of Woodcraft.

Eligibility: Applicants must be under the age of 25, at least a high school graduate (students already enrolled in college are eligible), a member of Neighbors of Woodcraft for at least 2 years (or covered under the Family Plan Rider or Children's Rider for 2 years in Neighbors of Woodcraft), and enrolled or planning to enroll full time at a state accredited college, trade, or business school. This program is not open to graduate students. Selection is based on high school or college academic record, SAT/ACT scores, and 2 letters of recommendation. Financial need is also considered. If the applicant has been out of school for 1 year or more, a recommendation from an employer is required.

Financial data: Stipends range from $600 to $1,000 per year.

Duration: 1 year.

Additional information: This program was established in 1968. Membership in Neighbors of Woodcraft is currently available only to residents of California, Colorado, Idaho, Montana, Nevada, Oregon, Utah, Washington, and Wyoming. Recipients must remain a Benefit, Family Plan, or Children's Rider member in good standing throughout the scholarship period. They must attend school on a full-time basis.

Number awarded: Varies; generally, 30 or more each year.

Deadline: March of each year.

773
NEIGHBORS OF WOODCRAFT ORPHAN SCHOLARSHIP PROGRAM

Neighbors of Woodcraft
Attn: Scholarship Committee
911 Main Street
P.O. Box 1897
Oregon City, OR 97045-0897
Phone: (503) 656-8118   (800) 456-1771
E-mail: membership@nowfbs.com
Web Site: www.nowfbs.com/orphan.htm
Summary: To provide financial aid for college to children of members of the Neighbors of Woodcraft who become orphaned at age 18 or younger.
Eligibility: This program is open to 1) children whose parents are both deceased and who were both members in good standing at the time of their deaths and 2) to insured junior members who were in good standing at the time both parents died. Applicants must be between the ages of 18 and 24. They must have been accepted as a full-time student at an accredited college, university, or other degree-granting school.
Financial data: The stipend is $2,500 per year; funds must be used for tuition and housing.
Duration: 4 years.
Additional information: Membership in Neighbors of Woodcraft is currently available only to residents of California, Colorado, Idaho, Montana, Nevada, Oregon, Utah, Washington, and Wyoming.
Number awarded: Varies each year.

774
NELSON A. DEMERS SCHOLARSHIP

New England Newspaper Advertising Executives Association
Attn: Scholarship Committee Chair
70 Washington Street, Suite 214
Salem, MA 01970
Phone: (978) 744-8940   Fax: (978) 744-0333
Web Site: www.nenews.org
Summary: To provide financial assistance to students who are interested in going to college (on the undergraduate or graduate school level) and are related to an employee (or are an employee) of a newspaper affiliated with the New England Newspaper Advertising Executives Association (NENAEA).
Eligibility: This program is open to any person who has an immediate family member (mother, father, aunt, uncle, brother, sister, grandmother, grandfather, spouse) currently employed at a NENAEA-member newspaper. Current employees may also apply. Applicants may be high school seniors, college students, or graduate students. There are no restrictions on the applicant's major. Financial need is not considered in the selection process.
Financial data: The stipend is $2,000.
Duration: 1 year.
Number awarded: 1 each year.
Deadline: May of each year.

775
NELSON URBAN SCHOLARSHIP FUND

Morris Scholarship Fund
Attn: Scholarship Selection Committee
525 S.W. Fifth Street, Suite A
Des Moines, IA 50309-4501
Phone: (515) 282-8192   Fax: (515) 282-9117
E-mail: morris@assoc-mgmt.com
Web Site: www.assoc-mgmt.com/users/morris
Summary: To provide financial assistance to African Americans studying at the undergraduate or graduate school level in Iowa.
Eligibility: This program is open to African Americans who are Iowa residents, enrolled full or part time at the undergraduate or graduate school level, and interested in working with "at risk" minority students in the elementary or secondary schools.
Financial data: The awards generally range from $2,500 to $5,000.
Duration: 1 year.
Number awarded: At least 2 each year.
Deadline: February of each year.

776
NERA DEPENDENT SCHOLARSHIP

Naval Enlisted Reserve Association
Attn: National Headquarters
6703 Farragut Avenue
Falls Church, VA 22042-2189
Phone: (800) 776-9020   Fax: (703) 534-3617
Web Site: www.nera.org/scholar/index.html
Summary: To provide financial assistance for college to children and grandchildren of members of the Naval Enlisted Reserve Association (NERA).
Eligibility: This program is open to children and grandchildren of association members who are graduating seniors or currently enrolled in college and have a grade point average of 3.0 or higher. Applicants must submit high school and/or college transcripts, letters of recommendation, a letter from the sponsoring NERA member indicated relationship to the applicant, information on extracurricular activities, and a 2-page essay on "Taking Freedom for Granted."
Financial data: The stipend is $1,000.
Duration: 1 year.
Additional information: This program is funded in part by USAA Insurance Corporation.
Number awarded: 1 each year.
Deadline: April of each year.

777
NERA RESERVIST SCHOLARSHIP

Naval Enlisted Reserve Association
Attn: National Headquarters
6703 Farragut Avenue
Falls Church, VA 22042-2189
Phone: (800) 776-9020   Fax: (703) 534-3617
Web Site: www.nera.org/scholar/index.html
Summary: To provide financial assistance for college to active and retired sea service enlisted reservists who are also members of the Naval Enlisted Reserve Association (NERA).
Eligibility: This program is open to active drill and retired enlisted reservists of the Coast Guard, Navy, and Marines who are members of the association. Applicants must be attending an accredited college in pursuit of a bachelor's degree. They must submit 1) a brief cover letter indicating their name, address, telephone number, rate, Social Security number, rate, chapter affiliation, and course of study; 2) high school or college transcripts through the end of the previous academic term; and 3) information on extracurricular activities.
Financial data: The stipend is $1,500.
Duration: 1 year.
Additional information: This program is funded in part by USAA Insurance Corporation.
Number awarded: 1 each year.
Deadline: April of each year.

778
NEREF SCHOLARSHIP PROGRAM

North East Roofing Educational Foundation, Inc.
Attn: Scholarship Program
1400 Hancock Street, Seventh Floor
Quincy, MA 02169
Phone: (617) 472-5590   Fax: (617) 479-478
Web Site: www.nerca.org
Summary: To provide financial assistance for college to members of the North East Roofing Contractors Association (NERCA) and their families.
Eligibility: This program is open to members of NERCA, their employees, and their immediate family members (spouses, natural children, adopted children, and stepchildren). Applicants must be high school seniors or graduates who plan to enroll in a full-time undergraduate course of study at an accredited 2-year or 4-year college, university, or vocational-technical school. Selection is based on academic record, potential to succeed, leadership and participation in school and community activities, honors, work experience, a statement of educational and career goals, and an outside appraisal. Financial need is not considered.
Financial data: The stipend is $1,500.
Duration: 1 year.
Number awarded: 2 each year.
Deadline: February of each year.

779
NEVADA WOMEN'S FUND SCHOLARSHIPS

Nevada Women's Fund
770 Smithridge Drive, Suite 300
Reno, NV 89502
Phone: (775) 786-2335   Fax: (775) 786-8152
E-mail: info@nwfonline.com
Summary: To provide funding to women in Nevada who are interested in pursuing a college education.
Eligibility: This program is open to women who are pursuing or planning to pursue academic study or vocational training. Preference is given to northern Nevada residents and those attending northern Nevada institutions. Selection is based on academic achievement, financial need, and community service. Particular attention is paid to applications from reentry women, minorities, and women who are single parents. Some programs are designated for graduate study, but most are for undergraduate work.
Financial data: Stipends range from $500 to $5,000 per year. Recently, a total of $134,500 was awarded.
Duration: 1 year; may be renewed.
Additional information: This program includes the following named scholarships: the Amy Biehl Memorial Scholarship, the Betty Smith Scholarships, the Beverly Cavallo Memorial Scholarship, the Bill and Dottie Raggio Scholarship, the Bill and Moya Lear Charitable Foundation Scholarship, the Bruce and Nora James Scholarships, the Charles H. Stout Endowed Scholarship, the Charles H. Stout Foundation Scholarships, the Charlotte L. MacKenzie Scholarship, the Derrivan/Rinaldi Scholarship, the E.L. Cord Foundation Scholarships, the Elaine Joan Garcia Memorial Scholarship, the Feltner Family Scholarships, the Friends of the Fund Scholarships, the Helaine Greenburg "55 and Alive" Scholarship, the Helen Close Charitable Fund Scholarships, the Jan Evans Memorial Scholarship, the Margaret Eddelman O'Donnell Scholarship, the Martha H. Jones Scholarships, the Mary Davis Spirit of Enterprise Scholarship, the Public Resource Foundation Scholarships, the Ruth Hoover Memorial Scholarship, the Salomon Smith Barney "Women in Business" Scholarships, the Scholar to Scholar Award, the St. Thomas More Women's Guild Scholarship, the Sue Wagner Scholarship, the Timken-Sturgis Scholarship, the Walter J. Zitter Foundation Scholarship, the Webster Family Scholarship, and the Women of Achievement Alumni Scholarships.
Number awarded: Varies each year. Recently 83 of these scholarships were awarded: 13 at $500, 32 at $1,000, 2 at $1,250, 2 at $1,500, 15 at $2,000, 13 at $2,500, 1 at $3,000, and 5 at $5,000.
Deadline: February of each year.

780
NEW ENGLAND REGIONAL STUDENT PROGRAM

New England Board of Higher Education
45 Temple Place
Boston, MA 02111
Phone: (617) 357-9620   Fax: (617) 338-1577
E-mail: pubinfo@nebhe.org
Web Site: www.nebhe.org
Summary: To enable students in New England to attend colleges within the region at reduced tuition when their area of study is not offered at their own state's public institutions.
Eligibility: This program is open to residents of the 6 New England states: Connecticut, Maine, Massachusetts, New Hampshire, Rhode Island, and Vermont. Students may apply for this support when their chosen field of study is not offered at any of the public institutions within their own state. Contact the New England Board of Higher Education for a catalog of degree programs and states which qualify for this program. Undergraduate program eligibility is based on entire degree programs only, not on concentrations or options within degree programs. Some highly specialized graduate programs might be available even if they are not listed in the catalog.
Financial data: With this program, students accepted at a public college or university in New England (but outside their own state) generally pay 150 percent of the in-state tuition for residents of the state.
Duration: Up to 4 years.
Additional information: In addition to reduced tuition, participants in this program also receive admission preference among out-of-state applicants. Students must apply for this program when they apply to their chosen out-of-state public college or university.
Number awarded: Over 7,400 students take advantage of this program each year.

781
NEW HAMPSHIRE CHARITABLE FOUNDATION ADULT STUDENT AID PROGRAM

New Hampshire Charitable Foundation
37 Pleasant Street
Concord, NH 03301-4005
Phone: (603) 225-6641   (800) 464-6641
Fax: (603) 225-1700   E-mail: info@nhcf.org
Web Site: www.nhcf.org
Summary: To provide funding for postsecondary education to adults in New Hampshire who are returning to school.
Eligibility: This program is open to New Hampshire residents who are 24 years of age or older. Applicants should 1) have had little or no education beyond high school, and 2) be now returning to school to upgrade skills for employment or career advancement, to qualify for a degree program, or to make a career change. They must demonstrate that they have secured all available financial aid and still have a remaining unmet need. Preference for funding is given in the following order: 1) students who have previously received funding through this program and have successfully completed prior work; 2) students with the least amount of higher education or training; and 3) single parents. Only undergraduate students are eligible.
Financial data: The maximum award is $500 each term. Most awards are in the form of grants, although no-interest or low-interest loans are also available.
Duration: 1 academic term; may be renewed up to 2 additional terms.
Additional information: A $15 application fee is required.
Number awarded: Varies each year.
Deadline: May, August, or December of each year.

782
NEW HAMPSHIRE CHARITABLE FOUNDATION STATEWIDE STUDENT AID PROGRAM

New Hampshire Charitable Foundation
37 Pleasant Street
Concord, NH 03301-4005
Phone: (603) 225-6641   (800) 464-6641
Fax: (603) 225-1700   E-mail: info@nhcf.org
Web Site: www.nhcf.org
Summary: To provide financial assistance for postsecondary education to New Hampshire residents.
Eligibility: This program is open to New Hampshire residents who are graduating high school seniors or undergraduate students between 17 and 23 years of age or graduate students of any age. Applicants must be enrolled in or planning to enroll in an accredited 2- or 4-year college, university, or vocational school on at least a half-time basis. The school may be in New Hampshire or another state. Selection is based on financial need, academic merit, community service, school activities, and work experience. Priority is given to students with the fewest financial resources and to vocational-technical school students.
Financial data: Awards range from $500 to $2,500 and average $1,800. Most are made in the form of grants (recently, 82 percent of all awards) or no-interest or low-interest loans (recently 18 percent of all awards).
Duration: 1 year; approximately one third of the awards are renewable.
Additional information: Through this program, students submit a single application for more than 250 different scholarship and loan funds. Many of the funds have additional requirements, covering such elements as the field of study; residency in region, county, city, or town; graduation from designated high schools; and special attributes (of Belgian descent, employee of designated firms, customer of Granite State Telephone Company, disabled, suffering from a life-threatening or serious chronic illness, of Lithuanian descent, dependent of a New Hampshire police officer, dependent of a New Hampshire Episcopal minister, of Polish descent, former Sea Cadet or Naval Junior ROTC, or employed in the tourism industry). The Citizens' Scholarship Foundation of America reviews all applications; recipients are selected by the New Hampshire Charitable Foundation. A $15 application fee is required.
Number awarded: Varies each year; recently, a total of $2.3 million was awarded.
Deadline: April of each year.

783
NEW HAMPSHIRE FEDERATION OF TEACHERS SCHOLARSHIPS

New Hampshire Federation of Teachers
553 Route 3A
Ruggles IV
Bow, NH 03304-3212
Phone: (603) 223-0747   Fax: (603) 226-0331
E-mail: nhaft1@aol.com
Web Site: www.nhft.org/html/scholarship.html
Summary: To provide financial assistance for college to children of members of the New Hampshire Federation of Teachers (NHFT).
Eligibility: This program is open to children of NHFT members who are seniors in high school planning to attend college. Applicants must submit an essay, up to 5 pages in length, on the reasons John Dewey advocated that teachers need unions. Selection is based on the essay (50 percent) as well as academic achievement, curricular and community activities, honors and awards, and financial need.
Financial data: Stipends are $1,000 or $500 per year.
Duration: 1 year.
Number awarded: 3 each year: 1 at $1,000 and 2 at $500.
Deadline: April of each year.

784
NEW HAMPSHIRE INCENTIVE PROGRAM

New Hampshire Postsecondary Education Commission
2 Industrial Park Drive, Suite 7
Concord, NH 03301-8512
Phone: (603) 271-2555   Fax: (603) 271-2696
Phone: TDD: (800) 735-2964   E-mail: pedes@nhsa.state.nh.us
Web Site: webster.state.nh.us/postsecondary/fin.html
Summary: To provide financial assistance to New Hampshire residents who are interested in attending college.
Eligibility: Residents of New Hampshire are eligible to apply for this program if they are U.S. citizens or permanent residents, are accepted at or enrolled full time in an eligible postsecondary institution in 1 of the 6 New England states, and can demonstrate both academic ability and financial need. Upperclassmen must have a grade point average of 2.0 or higher.
Financial data: The stipends range between $225 and $1,000, although most are $500 per year.
Duration: 1 year.
Additional information: The only application for this program is the FAFSA.
Number awarded: Varies each year; recently, 2,586 of these awards were granted.
Deadline: April of each year.

785
NEW HAMPSHIRE LEGION DEPARTMENT SCHOLARSHIP

American Legion
Attn: Department of New Hampshire
State House Annex
25 Capitol Street, Room 431
Concord, NH 03301-6312
Phone: (603) 271-5338   Fax: (603) 271-5352
Summary: To provide financial assistance for the vocational education of students in New Hampshire.
Eligibility: Students who are or will be graduates of a New Hampshire high school and have been New Hampshire residents for at least 3 years may apply for this scholarship if they are entering their first year of college.
Financial data: The stipend is $1,000.
Duration: 1 year.
Number awarded: 2 each year.
Deadline: April of each year.

786
NEW HAMPSHIRE LEGION DEPARTMENT VOCATIONAL SCHOLARSHIP

American Legion
Attn: Department of New Hampshire
State House Annex
25 Capitol Street, Room 431
Concord, NH 03301-6312
Phone: (603) 271-5338   Fax: (603) 271-5352
Summary: To provide financial assistance for the postsecondary education of students in New Hampshire.
Eligibility: Students who are or will be graduates of a New Hampshire high school and have been New Hampshire residents for at least 3 years may apply for this scholarship if they are entering their first year of higher education in a vocational field.
Financial data: The scholarship is $1,000.
Duration: 1 year.
Number awarded: 1 each year.
Deadline: April of each year.

787
NEW HAMPSHIRE LEVERAGED INCENTIVE GRANT PROGRAM

New Hampshire Postsecondary Education Commission
2 Industrial Park Drive, Suite 7
Concord, NH 03301-8512
Phone: (603) 271-2555   Fax: (603) 271-2696
Phone: TDD: (800) 735-2964   E-mail: pedes@nhsa.state.nh.us
Web Site: webster.state.nh.us/postsecondary/fin.html
Summary: To provide financial assistance to New Hampshire residents who are attending college in the state and can demonstrate financial need.
Eligibility: This program is open to residents of New Hampshire who are currently enrolled as sophomores, juniors, or seniors at accredited colleges and universities in the state. Selection is based on financial need (as determined by federal formulas) and academic merit (as determined by the institution).
Financial data: The stipend depends on the need of the recipient, as determined by the institution.
Duration: 1 year; may be renewed.
Additional information: Information is available at the financial aid office of New Hampshire institutions.
Number awarded: Varies each year.

788
NEW HAMPSHIRE SCHOLARSHIPS FOR ORPHANS OF VETERANS

New Hampshire Postsecondary Education Commission
2 Industrial Park Drive, Suite 7
Concord, NH 03301-8512
Phone: (603) 271-2257   Fax: (603) 271-2696
Phone: TDD: (800) 735-2964   E-mail: pedes@nhsa.state.nh.us
Web Site: webster.state.nh.us/postsecondary/fin.html
Summary: To provide financial assistance for the postsecondary education of children of deceased New Hampshire veterans.
Eligibility: Applicants must be New Hampshire residents between 16 and 25 years of age whose parent(s) died as a result of a service-related disability incurred during World War I, World War II, the Korean conflict, or the southeast Asian conflict. These parents must have been residents of New Hampshire at the time of death.
Financial data: The stipend is $1,000 per year, to be used for the payment of room, board, books, and supplies.
Duration: 1 year; may be renewed for up to 3 additional years.
Number awarded: Varies each year.

789
NEW JERSEY LEGION AUXILIARY DEPARTMENT SCHOLARSHIPS

American Legion Auxiliary
Attn: Department of New Jersey
146 Route 130
Bordentown, NJ 08505-2226
Phone: (609) 291-9338   Fax: (609) 291-8175
Summary: To provide financial assistance for postsecondary education to the children or grandchildren of veterans in New Jersey.
Eligibility: Eligible for these scholarships are the children or grandchildren of honorably discharged veterans of the U.S. armed forces; applicants must have resided in New Jersey for at least 2 years and be members of a New Jersey senior high school graduating class.
Financial data: The amount awarded varies, depending upon the needs of the recipient and the money available.
Duration: 1 year.
Number awarded: Several each year.
Deadline: March of each year.

790
NEW JERSEY POW/MIA TUITION BENEFIT PROGRAM

Division of Veterans Programs
101 Eggert Crossing Road
P.O. Box 340
Trenton, NJ 08625-0340
Phone: (609) 530-7045 (800) 624-0508 (within NJ)
Fax: (609) 530-7075
Web Site: www.state.nj.us/military/veterans/programs.html
Summary: To provide financial assistance for the postsecondary education of children of New Jersey veterans reported as missing in action or prisoners of war during the southeast Asian conflict.
Eligibility: Eligible to apply for this assistance are New Jersey residents attending or accepted at a New Jersey public or independent postsecondary institution whose parents were military service personnel officially declared prisoners of war or missing in action after January 1, 1960.
Financial data: This program entitles recipients to full undergraduate tuition at any public or independent postsecondary educational institution in New Jersey.
Duration: Assistance continues until completion of a bachelor's degree.
Number awarded: Varies each year.
Deadline: February of each year for the spring term and September for the fall and spring terms.

791
NEW JERSEY STATE GOLF ASSOCIATION CADDIE SCHOLARSHIP

New Jersey State Golf Association
Attn: Education Director
1000 Broad Street
Bloomfield, NJ 07003
Phone: (973) 338-8334 Fax: (973) 338-5525
E-mail: njstategolf@aol.com
Web Site: www.njsga.org
Summary: To provide financial assistance to students who have caddied at a New Jersey State Golf Association (NJSGA) member club.
Eligibility: This program is open to students who have caddied at an association club for at least 1 year. However, if their parents are members of a private golf club, they are not eligible. Applicants must have their golf club's golf professional or caddie master attest to their eligibility as a caddie at the club, include a copy of their parent's income tax forms, and submit a copy of their transcript. Selection is based on scholastic achievement, SAT scores, qualities of character and leadership, length and quality of service as a caddie, and financial need.
Financial data: Stipends range from $1,200 to $2,500 per year.
Duration: 1 year; may be renewed up to 3 additional years if the recipient continues to meet program eligibility requirements.
Additional information: A full tuition, fee, room, board, and book allowance scholarship is offered to the most deserving applicant who plants to attend Rutgers, the State University of New Jersey. Applications for that scholarship must be submitted by February of each year. Recipients must attend school on a full-time basis.
Number awarded: Approximately 20 each year.
Deadline: April of each year.

792
NEW JERSEY SURVIVOR TUITION BENEFITS PROGRAM

New Jersey Higher Education Student Assistance Authority
4 Quakerbridge Plaza
P.O. Box 540
Trenton, NJ 08625-0540
Phone: (609) 588-2228 (800) 792-8670
Fax: (609) 588-2390 E-mail: osacs@osa.state.nj.us
Web Site: www.hesaa.org
Summary: To provide financial assistance to the spouses and children of New Jersey emergency service personnel or law enforcement officers killed in the performance of their duties.
Eligibility: Surviving spouses, daughters, and sons of either law enforcement officials or emergency service personnel killed on the job are eligible for this program. Only New Jersey residents may apply. For spouses, applications must be submitted within 8 years from the date of their husband's death; for children, applications must be submitted within 8 years following high school graduation.
Financial data: Grants pay the actual cost of tuition up to the highest tuition

charged at a New Jersey public institution of higher education.
Duration: 1 year; may be renewed for up to 7 additional years as long as the recipient attends a New Jersey institution of higher education as an undergraduate student on at least a half-time basis.
Additional information: This program was formerly called the New Jersey Public Tuition Benefits Program.
Number awarded: Varies each year.
Deadline: September of each year for fall and spring term; February of each year for spring term only.

793
NEW JERSEY TUITION AID GRANTS

New Jersey Higher Education Student Assistance Authority
4 Quakerbridge Plaza
P.O. Box 540
Trenton, NJ 08625-0540
Phone: (609) 588-2228 (800) 792-8670
Fax: (609) 588-2390 E-mail: osacs@osa.state.nj.us
Web Site: www.hesaa.org
Summary: To provide financial assistance for undergraduate education to students in New Jersey.
Eligibility: This program is open to U.S. citizens and eligible noncitizens who have been residents of New Jersey for at least 12 consecutive months before receiving the grant. Applicants must be, or planning to be, full-time undergraduates at approved New Jersey colleges, universities, and degree-granting proprietary schools. They must demonstrate financial need by completing the Free Application for Federal Student Aid (FAFSA).
Financial data: The amounts awarded vary, based on the needs of the recipient, the cost to attend the recipient's college, and the funds available for distribution that year. Currently, grants range in value from $866 to $7,074 per year.
Duration: 1 year; may be renewed if the recipient maintains satisfactory academic progress and continued eligibility.
Deadline: May of each year for renewal students; September of each year for new applicants for fall term; February of each year for new applicants for spring term only.

794
NEW JERSEY URBAN SCHOLARS PROGRAM

New Jersey Higher Education Student Assistance Authority
4 Quakerbridge Plaza
P.O. Box 540
Trenton, NJ 08625-0540
Phone: (609) 588-2228 (800) 792-8670
Fax: (609) 588-2390 E-mail: osacs@osa.state.nj.us
Web Site: www.hesaa.org
Summary: To provide financial assistance to outstanding high school seniors from urban areas in New Jersey who are interested in attending college.
Eligibility: High school staff in urban and economically distressed areas in New Jersey are invited to nominate candidates for this award. Nominees must be seniors at New Jersey high schools who rank in the top 10 percent of their class and have a minimum grade point average of 3.0. They must be planning to attend a college or university in New Jersey as a full-time undergraduate. Students may not apply directly for this program; they must be nominated by their high school.
Financial data: Scholars receive $1,000 per year, regardless of financial need.
Duration: Up to 5 semesters at a 2-year institution; up to 8 semesters at a 4-year institution; up to 10 semesters if enrolled in an official 5-year program.

795
NEW MEXICO ATHLETIC SCHOLARSHIPS

New Mexico Commission on Higher Education
Attn: Financial Aid and Student Services
1068 Cerrillos Road
P.O. Box 15910
Santa Fe, NM 87506-5910
Phone: (505) 827-7383 (800) 279-9777
Fax: (505) 827-7392 E-mail: highered@che.state.nm.us
Web Site: www.nmche.org
Summary: To provide financial assistance to student-athletes in New Mexico.
Eligibility: This program is open to both residents and non-residents of New Mexico who are accepted by the athletic department of a public postsecondary institution in New Mexico.
Financial data: Awards vary but are applied to tuition and fees.

Duration: 1 year; may be renewed.
Additional information: Information is available from the athletic department or financial aid office at the participating New Mexico public institution.
Number awarded: Varies each year.
Deadline: Deadlines are established by the participating institutions.

796
NEW MEXICO CHILDREN OF DECEASED MILITARY AND STATE POLICE PERSONNEL SCHOLARSHIPS

New Mexico Veterans' Service Commission
P.O. Box 2324
Santa Fe, NM 87504-2324
Phone: (505) 827-6300   Fax: (505) 827-6372
E-mail: nmvsc@state.nm.us
Web Site: www.state.nm.us/veterans
Summary: To provide financial assistance for the postsecondary education of the children of deceased military and state police personnel in New Mexico.
Eligibility: This program is open to the children of 1) military personnel killed in action or as a result of such action during a period of armed conflict; 2) members of the New Mexico National Guard killed while on active duty; and 3) New Mexico State Police killed on active duty. Applicants must be between the ages of 16 and 26 and enrolled in a state-supported school in New Mexico. Children of deceased veterans must be nominated by the New Mexico Veterans' Service Commission; children of National Guard members must be nominated by the adjutant general of the state; children of state police must be nominated by the New Mexico State Police Board. Selection is based on merit and financial need.
Financial data: The scholarships provide payment of matriculation fees, board, room, books, and supplies at state-supported institutions of higher education in New Mexico.
Duration: 1 year; may be renewed.

797
NEW MEXICO COMPETITIVE SCHOLARSHIPS

New Mexico Commission on Higher Education
Attn: Financial Aid and Student Services
1068 Cerrillos Road
P.O. Box 15910
Santa Fe, NM 87506-5910
Phone: (505) 827-7383   (800) 279-9777
Fax: (505) 827-7392   E-mail: highered@che.state.nm.us
Web Site: www.nmche.org
Summary: To provide financial assistance to residents of other states who wish to attend a college or university in New Mexico.
Eligibility: Students who are not residents of New Mexico but who wish to attend public institutions of higher education in New Mexico may apply for these scholarships. Selection is based on high school grade point average and ACT scores.
Financial data: For recipients, the out-of-state portion of tuition is waived and a stipend of at least $100 is paid.
Additional information: Information is available at the financial aid office of any New Mexico public postsecondary institution.

798
NEW MEXICO LEGISLATIVE ENDOWMENT SCHOLARSHIPS

New Mexico Commission on Higher Education
Attn: Financial Aid and Student Services
1068 Cerrillos Road
P.O. Box 15910
Santa Fe, NM 87506-5910
Phone: (505) 827-7383   (800) 279-9777
Fax: (505) 827-7392   E-mail: highered@che.state.nm.us
Web Site: www.nmche.org
Summary: To provide financial assistance for postsecondary education to residents of New Mexico.
Eligibility: This assistance is available to residents of New Mexico enrolled or planning to enroll at a public institution of higher education in the state. Applicants must be able to demonstrate substantial financial need. Preference is given to 1) students transferring from New Mexico 2-year public postsecondary institutions to 4-year institutions and 2) returning adult students at 2-year and 4-year public institutions. Recipients must be enrolled at least half time.
Financial data: Full-time students receive up to $2,500 per year at 4-year institutions or up to $1,000 per year at 2-year institutions. Part-time students are

eligible for prorated awards.
Duration: 1 year; may be renewed.
Additional information: Information is available at the financial aid office of any New Mexico public postsecondary institution.
Number awarded: Varies each year.

799
NEW MEXICO LOTTERY SUCCESS SCHOLARSHIPS

New Mexico Commission on Higher Education
Attn: Financial Aid and Student Services
1068 Cerrillos Road
P.O. Box 15910
Santa Fe, NM 87506-5910
Phone: (505) 827-7383   (800) 279-9777
Fax: (505) 827-7392   E-mail: highered@che.state.nm.us
Web Site: www.nmche.org
Summary: To provide financial assistance to college students in New Mexico.
Eligibility: This program is open to full-time students at New Mexico public colleges and universities who graduated from a public or private high school in New Mexico or obtained a New Mexico GED. Applicants who earn at least a 2.5 grade point average during their first college semester are eligible to begin receiving the award for their second semester of full-time enrollment.
Financial data: Scholarships are equal to 100 percent of tuition at the New Mexico public postsecondary institution where the student is enrolled.
Duration: Up to 8 consecutive semesters.
Additional information: Information is available at the financial aid office of any New Mexico public postsecondary institution. Funding for these scholarships is provided from state lottery proceeds. The program began in 1997.
Number awarded: Varies each year, depending on the availability of funds.

800
NEW MEXICO SCHOLARS PROGRAM

New Mexico Commission on Higher Education
Attn: Financial Aid and Student Services
1068 Cerrillos Road
P.O. Box 15910
Santa Fe, NM 87506-5910
Phone: (505) 827-7383   (800) 279-9777
Fax: (505) 827-7392   E-mail: highered@che.state.nm.us
Web Site: www.nmche.org
Summary: To provide financial assistance for college to graduating high school seniors in New Mexico.
Eligibility: This program is open to graduating high school seniors in New Mexico who plan to attend a public institution of higher education or selected private college in the state. Applicants must be in the top 5 percent of their high school graduating class, have an SAT score of at least 1140, or have an ACT score of at least 25. If 1 member of a family is enrolled in college, the family income may be no greater than $30,000 a year; if 2 or more members of the family are enrolled in college, the family income may be no greater than $40,000.
Financial data: This program provides recipients with tuition, fees, and books at a participating college or university in New Mexico.
Duration: 1 year; may be renewed.
Additional information: Information is available at financial aid office of participating New Mexico postsecondary institutions; the institutions participating include all public college and universities in the state and 3 private colleges: St. John's College in Santa Fe, the College of Santa Fe, and the College of the Southwest.
Number awarded: Varies each year, depending on the availability of funds.

801
NEW MEXICO STATE STUDENT INCENTIVE GRANTS

New Mexico Commission on Higher Education
Attn: Financial Aid and Student Services
1068 Cerrillos Road
P.O. Box 15910
Santa Fe, NM 87506-5910
Phone: (505) 827-7383   (800) 279-9777
Fax: (505) 827-7392   E-mail: highered@che.state.nm.us
Web Site: www.nmche.org
Summary: To provide financial assistance to residents of New Mexico attending public or private nonprofit colleges in the state.
Eligibility: This program is open to full-time and half-time undergraduate

students at public or private nonprofit colleges and universities in New Mexico who can demonstrate substantial financial need. Applicants must be U.S. citizens and New Mexico residents.

Financial data: The amount of the award is set by the participating college or university; generally, the awards range from $200 to $2,500 per year.

Duration: 1 year; may be renewed.

Additional information: Information is available at the financial aid office of the participating New Mexico private and public institutions.

Number awarded: Varies each year, depending on the availability of funds.

802
NEW MEXICO VIETNAM VETERANS SCHOLARSHIPS

New Mexico Veterans' Service Commission
P.O. Box 2324
Santa Fe, NM 87504-2324
Phone: (505) 827-6300   Fax: (505) 827-6372
E-mail: nmvsc@state.nm.us
Web Site: www.state.nm.us/veterans

Summary: To provide financial assistance for the undergraduate and graduate education of Vietnam veterans in New Mexico.

Eligibility: Applicants must be Vietnam veterans who were residents of New Mexico at the time of original entry into the armed forces and are recipients of the Vietnam Campaign Medal. Undergraduate students and students enrolled in a program leading to a master's degree are eligible.

Financial data: The scholarships pay tuition, fees, and books at any postsecondary institution in New Mexico, up to $1,520 for tuition and fees and $500 for books.

Duration: 1 year.

803
NEW MEXICO 3 PERCENT SCHOLARSHIP PROGRAM

New Mexico Commission on Higher Education
Attn: Financial Aid and Student Services
1068 Cerrillos Road
P.O. Box 15910
Santa Fe, NM 87506-5910
Phone: (505) 827-7383   (800) 279-9777
Fax: (505) 827-7392   E-mail: highered@che.state.nm.us
Web Site: www.nmche.org

Summary: To provide financial assistance for college to residents of New Mexico.

Eligibility: This assistance is available to residents of New Mexico enrolled or planning to enroll at a public institution of higher education in the state as an undergraduate or graduate student. Selection is based on moral character, satisfactory initiative, scholastic standing, personality, and additional criteria established by each participating college or university. At least one third of the scholarships are based on financial need.

Financial data: The amount of assistance varies but covers at least tuition and some fees.

Duration: 1 year; may be renewed.

Additional information: Information is available at the financial aid office of any New Mexico public postsecondary institution.

Number awarded: Varies each year.

804
NEW YORK AID FOR PART-TIME STUDY (APTS) PROGRAM

New York State Higher Education Services Corporation
Attn: Student Information
99 Washington Avenue
Albany, NY 12255
Phone: (518) 473-1574   (888) NYS-HESC
Fax: (518) 473-3749   TDD: (800) 445-5234
E-mail: webmail@hesc.com   Web Site: www.hesc.com

Summary: To provide money for students who are attending college on a part-time basis in New York.

Eligibility: To be considered for this award, students must be enrolled part time (at least 3 but less than 12 semester hours per semester) in an undergraduate degree program in New York; meet the income limits established for this program (students whose parents could not claim them as dependents may earn no more than $34,250 per year; the total family income if parents do claim the student as a dependent may not exceed $50,550 per year); be a New York resident and a U.S. citizen or permanent resident or refugee; have a tuition bill of at least $100 per year; not have used up their Tuition Assistance Program (TAP) eligibility; and not

be in default on a student loan. Interested students need to get an application from the college they are attending, complete the application, and return it to their college for processing as early as possible. Funds are distributed by the New York State Higher Education Services Corporation (NYSHESC) to participating colleges in New York. College financial aid administrators select recipients from eligible students.

Financial data: Up to $2,000 per year; awards may not exceed actual tuition charges.

Duration: 1 year; recipients may reapply for up to 8 years of part-time study if they maintain a grade point average of at least 2.0.

Number awarded: Varies each year; recently, more than 20,000 students received more than $12 million in assistance through this program.

805
NEW YORK AID TO NATIVE AMERICANS

New York State Education Department
Attn: Native American Education Unit
Education Building Annex, Room 478
Albany, NY 12234
Phone: (518) 474-0537   Web Site: www.nysed.gov

Summary: To provide financial assistance to Native Americans in New York who are interested in attending postsecondary institutions within the state.

Eligibility: Student aid is available to Native Americans who meet these qualifications: are on official tribal rolls of a New York State tribe or are the child of an enrolled member; are residents of New York State; and are or will be graduates of an accredited high school or hold a New York State General Equivalency Diploma or are enrolled in college credit programs working for the State High School Equivalency Diploma. Recipients must be accepted by an approved accredited postsecondary institution within New York State.

Financial data: The stipend is $1,750 per year for full-time study (at least 12 credit hours per semester or 24 credit hours per year); students registering for less than full-time study are funded on a prorated basis. Funding is available for summer course work on a special needs basis. Funds spent for summer school are deducted from the recipient's maximum entitlement.

Duration: 1 year; renewable for up to 3 additional years (4 additional years for specific programs requiring 5 years to complete degree requirements).

Additional information: The New York State tribes include members of the Iroquoian tribes (St. Regis, Mohawk, Oneida, Onondaga, Cayuga, Seneca Nation, Tonawanda Band of Seneca, and Tuscarora), the Shinnecock tribe, and the Poospatuck tribe. Remedial, noncredit, and college preparation courses are not fundable.

Number awarded: Varies; approximately 500 each year.

Deadline: July of each year for the fall semester; December of each year for spring semester; May of each year for summer session.

806
NEW YORK COUNCIL FOR THE HUMANITIES YOUNG SCHOLARS CONTEST

New York Council for the Humanities
Attn: Director of Education Programs
150 Broadway, Suite 1700
New York, NY 10038
Phone: (212) 233-1131, ext. 24   E-mail: pkay@nyhumanities.org
Web Site: www.nyhumanities.org

Summary: To recognize and reward outstanding essays written by New York high school students on a topic that changes annually.

Eligibility: This program is open to full-time high school students (grades 9 through 12) who are residents of New York. They are invited to write an essay on a topic that changes annually (recently, it was "Tearing Down Walls"). Contestants may write about an actual event or an event portrayed in a work of fiction. Scholars are expected to research their subjects thoroughly, using both secondary and, whenever possible, primary source materials. They must write an analytical essay (between 2,000 and 3,000 words) explaining why there is something significant to be learned from the topic they discuss. Students are strongly encouraged to develop their topics and write their essays with the guidance of a teacher/mentor. Selection is based on the essay's research, argument, structure, and originality.

Financial data: The first-prize winner receives a $5,000 college scholarship; the second-prize winner receives a $3,000 scholarship; and the third-prize winner receives a $2,000 scholarship. Funds are paid directly to the recipients once they present evidence of full-time matriculation. Honorable mentions each receive $500. Additional prizes of $250 may be awarded.

Duration: The competition is held annually.

Additional information: The first-prize essay is published in *culturefront*, the council's quarterly magazine for the humanities. This competition was first held in 1993. Essays are not returned.

Number awarded: 6 to 18 each year: 3 winners, 3 honorable mentions, and up to 12 additional prizes.

Deadline: May of each year.

807
NEW YORK LEGION AUXILIARY SCHOLARSHIP

American Legion Auxiliary
Attn: Department of New York
112 State Street, Suite 409
Albany, NY 12207
Phone: (518) 463-2215   Fax: (518) 427-8443

Summary: To provide financial assistance for postsecondary education to New York residents who are the children or grandchildren of deceased veterans.

Eligibility: Eligible to apply are the children or grandchildren of deceased veterans who are high school seniors or graduates and New York residents.

Financial data: This scholarship is $1,000.

Duration: 1 year.

Additional information: The recipient of this scholarship may also accept other scholarships.

Number awarded: 1 each year.

Deadline: March of each year.

808
NEW YORK MEMORIAL SCHOLARSHIPS FOR FAMILIES OF DECEASED POLICE OFFICERS, PEACE OFFICERS AND FIRE FIGHTERS

New York State Higher Education Services Corporation
Attn: Student Information
99 Washington Avenue
Albany, NY 12255
Phone: (518) 473-1574   (888) NYS-HESC
Fax: (518) 473-3749   TDD: (800) 445-5234
E-mail: webmail@hesc.com
Web Site: www.hesc.com

Summary: To provide financial aid to the children or spouses of police officers, peace officers, fire fighters, and volunteer fire fighters in New York State who died as the result of injuries sustained in the line of duty.

Eligibility: Applicants must be New York State residents who are attending or accepted at an approved program of study in New York and whose parent or spouse was a police officer, peace officer (including corrections officer), fire fighter, or volunteer fire fighter in New York and died as the result of injuries sustained in the line of duty. Awards are made for full-time study in 1) collegiate programs of at least 1 year's duration leading to a degree, diploma, or certificate; 2) hospital programs leading to licensure or certification in nursing or other fields of medical or health technology; and 3) 2-year programs in registered private business schools.

Financial data: This award is equal to the applicant's actual tuition costs or the undergraduate tuition charged at the State University of New York (SUNY) system, whichever is less. Students attending institutions with tuition charges higher than SUNY tuition may, if eligible, receive additional assistance through New York's Tuition Assistance Program (TAP). This award also provides funds to meet the nontuition costs of attending college, including room, board, books, supplies, and transportation.

Duration: This program is available for 4 years of full-time undergraduate study (or for 5 years in an approved 5-year bachelor's degree program).

Number awarded: Varies each year; recently, more than 60 students received $558,000 in assistance through this program.

Deadline: April of each year.

809
NEW YORK STATE LEADERS OF TOMORROW SCHOLARSHIPS

Capital Area School Development Association
University at Albany
East Campus
One University Place, A-409
Rensselaer, NY 12144-3456
Phone: (518) 525-2788   Fax: (518) 525-2797
E-mail: casdalot@uamail.albany.edu
Web Site: www.albany.edu/%7Ecasda/Leaders/leaders.htm

Summary: To provide financial assistance for college to seniors graduating from high schools in New York State.

Eligibility: The principal of every public and non-public high school in New York State is entitled to nominate 2 graduating seniors for this program. For each high school, 1 nominee is selected. Nominees must have at least a 3.0 grade point average, leadership skills, U.S. citizenship, and experience in extracurricular and community activities. They must plan to attend a New York State accredited college, university, trade school, or community college as a full-time student.

Financial data: The stipend is $1,000 per year.

Duration: Up to 4 years, provided the recipient remains enrolled full time at an accredited New York State institution with a grade point average of 3.0 or higher. The college program must be completed within 5 years of high school graduation.

Additional information: Funds are provided by the New York Lottery.

Number awarded: 1 from each high school in New York State.

Deadline: March of each year.

810
NEW YORK STATE PERSIAN GULF VETERANS TUITION AWARD PROGRAM

New York State Higher Education Services Corporation
Attn: Student Information
99 Washington Avenue
Albany, NY 12255
Phone: (518) 473-1574   (888) NYS-HESC
Fax: (518) 473-3749   TDD: (800) 445-5234
E-mail: webmail@hesc.com
Web Site: www.hesc.com

Summary: To provide tuition assistance to eligible Persian Gulf veterans enrolled in a postsecondary education program in New York.

Eligibility: To be eligible, veterans must have served in the U.S. armed forces in the hostilities that occurred in the Persian Gulf from August 2, 1990 to the end of the hostilities. Applicants must have received the Southwest Asia Service Medal between August 2, 1990 and November 30, 1995. They must have been discharged from the service under other than dishonorable conditions, must be a New York resident, must be enrolled full or part time at an undergraduate or graduate degree-granting institution in New York State or in an approved vocational training program in New York State, and must apply for a New York Tuition Assistance Program (TAP) award if a full-time student (12 or more credits) or a Pell Grant if a part-time student (at least 3 but less than 12 credits).

Financial data: Awards are $1,000 per semester for full-time study or $500 for part-time study, but in no case can the award exceed the amount charged for tuition. Total awards for undergraduate and graduate study under this program cannot exceed $10,000.

Duration: For full-time undergraduate study, up to 8 semesters, or up to 10 semesters for a program requiring 5 years for completion; for full-time graduate study, up to 6 semesters; for full-time vocational programs, up to 4 semesters; for part-time undergraduate study, up to 16 semesters, or up to 20 semesters for a 5-year program; for part-time graduate study, up to 12 semesters; for part-time vocational programs, up to 8 semesters.

Additional information: If a TAP award is also received, the combined academic year award cannot exceed tuition costs. If it does, the TAP award will be reduced accordingly.

Number awarded: Varies each year.

Deadline: April of each year.

811
NEW YORK STATE SCHOLARSHIPS FOR ACADEMIC EXCELLENCE

New York State Education Department
Office of K-16 Initiatives and Access Programs
Attn: Scholarship Unit
Education Building Addition, Room 1078
Albany, NY 12234
Phone: (518) 486-1319   E-mail: kiap@mail.nysed.gov
Web Site: www.highered.nysed.gov/kiap/scholarships/sac.htm

Summary: To provide financial assistance to graduating high school seniors in New York State who achieve high grades on the Regents exams.

Eligibility: This program is open to seniors at high schools in New York who have been accepted as a full-time student in an approved undergraduate program of study at a postsecondary institution in the state. Applicants must be U.S. citizens or qualifying non-citizens and New York State residents. Awards are based on student grades in certain Regents exams. The top graduating scholar at each registered high

school in the state automatically receives 1 of these scholarships. The remaining scholarships are awarded to other outstanding high school graduates in the same ratio of total students graduating from each high school in the state as compared to the total number of students who graduated during the prior school year.

Financial data: The annual stipends are either $1,500 or $500. Awards cannot exceed the actual cost of attendance.

Duration: Up to 4 years (or 5 years in approved 5-year baccalaureate programs). Recipients must remain enrolled full time, in good academic standing, and not in default on any guaranteed loan administered by the New York State Higher Education Services Corporation (HESC).

Additional information: Information is also available from the HESC, 99 Washington Avenue, Albany, NY 12255, (518) 473-1574, (888) NYS-HESC, Fax: (518) 473-3749, TDD: (800) 445-5234, E-mail: webmail@hesc.com. If a recipient begins study at an out-of-state institution, the scholarship is revoked and cannot be reinstated even if the student subsequently enrolls at a New York State institution.

Number awarded: 8,000 each year: 2,000 at $1,500 and 6,000 at $500.

Deadline: April of each year.

812
NEW YORK TUITION ASSISTANCE PROGRAM (TAP)

New York State Higher Education Services Corporation
Attn: Student Information
99 Washington Avenue
Albany, NY 12255
Phone: (518) 473-1574   (888) NYS-HESC
Fax: (518) 473-3749   TDD: (800) 445-5234
E-mail: webmail@hesc.com
Web Site: www.hesc.com

Summary: To help New York State residents pay undergraduate or graduate tuition at postsecondary institutions in the state.

Eligibility: To be eligible for this program, applicants must reside in New York; be a U.S. citizen, permanent resident, conditional entrant, or refugee; and not exceed the income limitations for this program: for undergraduate students who are dependents or are married or have tax dependents, the limit is $80,000 net taxable family income; for graduate students who are dependents or are married or have tax dependents, the limit is $20,000 net taxable family income; for single independent undergraduate students with no dependents, the limit is $10,000 net taxable income; for single independent graduate students with no dependents, the limit is $5,666 net taxable income. Applicants must be enrolled in school full time in New York (at least 12 credits per semester); have tuition charges of at least $200 per year; and not be in default on a federal or state loan.

Financial data: TAP awards are based on net taxable income, tuition charges, and type of institution attended. For undergraduate students at degree-granting and not-for-profit institutions, the award range is $275 to $5,000 for dependent students or independent students who are married or have tax dependents, or $425 to $3,025 for independent students who are single with no dependents. For students at proprietary registered non-degree private business schools, the award range is $100 to $800 for dependent students or independent students who are married or have tax dependents, or $100 to $640 for independent students who are single with no dependents. For all graduate students, awards range from $75 to $550.

Duration: Up to 4 years for undergraduate students (or 5 years in approved 5-year baccalaureate programs); up to 4 years for graduate or professional students. The combined undergraduate-graduate total cannot exceed 8 years.

Number awarded: Varies each year; recently, nearly 342,000 students received approximately $636 million in assistance through this program.

Deadline: April of each year.

813
NEW YORK VIETNAM VETERANS TUITION AWARD (VVTA) PROGRAM

New York State Higher Education Services Corporation
Attn: Student Information
99 Washington Avenue
Albany, NY 12255
Phone: (518) 473-1574   (888) NYS-HESC
Fax: (518) 473-3749   TDD: (800) 445-5234
E-mail: webmail@hesc.com
Web Site: www.hesc.com

Summary: To provide tuition assistance to eligible Vietnam veterans enrolled in a postsecondary education program in New York.

Eligibility: To be eligible, veterans must have served in the U.S. armed forces in Indochina between December 22, 1961 and May 7, 1975, must have been discharged

from the service under other than dishonorable conditions, must be a New York resident, must be enrolled full or part time at an undergraduate or graduate degree-granting institution in New York State or in an approved vocational training program in the state, and must apply for a New York Tuition Assistance Program (TAP) award if a full-time student (12 or more credits) or a Pell Grant if a part-time student (at least 3 but less than 12 credits).

Financial data: Awards are $1,000 per semester for full-time study or $500 for part-time study, but in no case can the award exceed the amount charged for tuition. Total awards for undergraduate and graduate study under this program cannot exceed $10,000.

Duration: For full-time undergraduate study, up to 8 semesters, or up to 10 semesters for a program requiring 5 years for completion; for full-time graduate study, up to 6 semesters; for full-time vocational programs, up to 4 semesters; for part-time undergraduate study, up to 16 semesters, or up to 20 semesters for a 5-year program; for part-time graduate study, up to 12 semesters; for part-time vocational programs, up to 8 semesters.

Additional information: If a TAP award is also received, the combined academic year award cannot exceed tuition costs. If it does, the TAP award will be reduced accordingly.

Number awarded: Varies each year.

Deadline: April of each year.

814
NFDA MEMORIAL SCHOLARSHIP

National Fastener Distributors Association
Attn: Scholarship Fund
1717 East Ninth Street, Suite 1185
Cleveland, OH 44114-2803
Phone: (216) 579-1571   Fax: (216) 579-1531
E-mail: nfda@nfda-fastener.org   Web site: www.nfda-fastener.org

Summary: To provide financial assistance for college to 1) children of employees of companies affiliated with the National Fastener Distributors Association and 2) employees of member companies.

Eligibility: Scholarship awards are given in 2 categories: 1) children of employees of member companies who are entering their freshman year of college and 2) employees of member companies who are working at least 20 hours and taking 6 or more credits per semester at an accredited college or university. Selection is based primarily on academic record, including standardized test scores. Other factors include school activities, community involvement, and work experience. Financial need, if considered at all, is a secondary factor.

Financial data: Stipends range from $500 to $2,000. A total of $20,000 to $30,000 is distributed annually. Awards are made directly to scholarship winners (rather than to their colleges).

Duration: 1 year; nonrenewable.

Additional information: Current college students are not eligible to apply, unless they are employed by a member firm.

Number awarded: Varies each year; recently, 33 of these scholarships were awarded.

Deadline: March of each year.

815
NGWA AUXILIARY SCHOLARSHIP

National Ground Water Association
Attn: Julie Bullock
601 Dempsey Road
Westerville, OH 43081-8978
Phone: (614) 898-7791   (800) 551-7379
Fax: (614) 898-7786   E-mail: ngwa@ngwa.org
Web Site: www.ngwa.org

Summary: To provide financial assistance for college to members of the National Ground Water Association (NGWA) and their families.

Eligibility: This program is open to members of the association and relatives of members who are enrolled in or accepted for enrollment in a college or university. Applicants may pursue any field of study; a major related to the industry is not required. They must have a grade point average of 2.5 or higher. Financial need is considered in the selection process.

Financial data: A stipend is awarded (exact amount not specified).

Duration: 1 year; nonrenewable.

Number awarded: Varies each year; recently, 3 of these scholarships were awarded.

Deadline: March of each year.

816
NICHOLAS C. VRATARIC SCHOLARSHIP FUND

Paper, Allied-Industrial, Chemical and Energy Workers International Union
Attn: Scholarship Awards Program
P.O. Box 1475
Nashville, TN 37202
Phone: (615) 834-8590   Fax: (615) 834-7741
Web Site: www.paceunion.org
Summary: To provide financial assistance for postsecondary education to members of the Paper, Allied-Industrial, Chemical and Energy Workers (PACE) International Union
Eligibility: This program is open to members of the union who are currently enrolled in a program to further their education. Applicants must submit a 500-word essay on the history of their local. Selection is based on a random drawing.
Financial data: The stipend is $1,000.
Duration: 1 year.
Additional information: PACE was formed in 1999 as a result of the merger of the United Paperworkers International Union and the Oil, Chemical and Atomic Workers International Union.
Number awarded: 2 each year.
Deadline: March of each year.

817
NLUS STOCKHOLM SCHOLARSHIP FUND

United States Naval Sea Cadet Corps
Attn: Executive Director
2300 Wilson Boulevard
Arlington, VA 22201-3308
Phone: (703) 243-6910   Fax: (703) 243-3985
Summary: To provide financial assistance to Naval Sea Cadet Corps cadets and former cadets who are interested in continuing their education at an accredited 4-year college/university.
Eligibility: This program is open to cadets and former cadets who are interested in continuing their education at an accredited 4-year college or university. They must have been a member of the corps for at least 2 years, have a minimum rating of NSCC E-3, be recommended by their commanding officer or other official, have earned at least a 3.0 grade point average, and have been accepted by an accredited college or university. Applicants may submit financial need statements. All other factors being equal, these statements may be considered in determining award recipients. Applicants who have received full scholarships from other sources (e.g., ROTC) will be considered for this award only if there are no other qualified applicants.
Financial data: The stipend is $2,000 per year.
Duration: Up to 4 years.
Additional information: This program was established by the Navy League of the United States (NLUS) through a bequest by Carl G. Stockholm, a past national president, to provide financial assistance to a selected cadet. This assistance is provided for up to 4 years and, during that time, no other Stockholm Scholarships are awarded; there can be only 1 designated "Stockholm Scholar" at any 1 time.
Number awarded: 1 every 4 years.
Deadline: May of the competition year.

818
NMIA SCHOLARSHIP PROGRAM

National Military Intelligence Association
Attn: Industry and Scholarship Coordinator
9200 Centerway Road
Gaithersburg, MD 20879
Phone: (301) 840-NMIA   Fax: (301) 840-8502
E-mail: kuntzmanj@hotmail.com
Web Site: www.nmia.org/Scholarship.html
Summary: To provide financial assistance for college to the children of members of the National Military Intelligence Association (NMIA).
Eligibility: This program is open to children of NMIA members who are attending, or planning to attend, an accredited college or university.
Financial data: The stipend depends on the availability of funds.
Duration: 1 year.
Additional information: Membership in the NMIA is open to military and civil service personnel; Reserve, National Guard, retired, and former service personnel; and U.S. civilians in the industrial sector supporting the U.S. intelligence system.
Number awarded: 1 or more each year.

819
NMJGSA/JACKIE ROBINSON FOUNDATION SCHOLARSHIP

National Minority Junior Golf Scholarship Association
Attn: Scholarship Committee
1140 East Washington Street, Suite 102
Phoenix, AZ 85034-1051
Phone: (602) 258-7851   Fax: (602) 258-3412
Web Site: www.nmgf.org
Summary: To provide financial assistance for college to minority high school seniors who excel at golf.
Eligibility: Eligible to apply for this award are minority high school seniors who are interested in attending college. Applicants are asked to write a 500-word essay on this question: "One of the principal goals of education and golf is fostering ways for people to respect and get along with individuals who think, dress, look, and act differently. How might you make this goal a reality?" Selection is based on academic record, personal recommendations, participation in golf, school and community activities (including employment, extracurricular activities, and other responsibilities), and financial need.
Financial data: The stipend is $6,000 per year. Funds are paid directly to the recipient's college.
Duration: 4 years.
Number awarded: 1 each year.

820
NO-ADDICTION SCHOLARSHIP ESSAY COMPETITION

NO-ADdiction Campaign
4920 N.W. 165th Street
Miami, FL 33014
Phone: (305) 621-5551, ext. 1304   (800) 662-3342
Fax: (305) 621-0536   E-mail: Noad@aol.com
Summary: To recognize and reward outstanding essays written by high school students on why they have chosen not to use drugs or alcohol and what they have done to further prevention efforts in their school or community.
Eligibility: This essay contest is open to all high school students (grades 9 through 12) in the United States who attend school full time and are legal residents. They are invited to write a 300-word essay voicing their opposition to the use of drugs and alcohol and describing the prevention efforts they have taken that go beyond just saying "no." Each school holds its own internal competition and selects 1 student's essay to be forwarded for national judging. Selection on the national level is based on the essay, extracurricular activities, and demonstrated leadership skills.
Financial data: The stipend is $1,000. Funds must be used for postsecondary education in the United States. Scholarship recipients not yet graduating will have the funds deposited in a trust account to be available upon graduation.
Duration: The competition is held annually.
Number awarded: 10 each year.
Deadline: April of each year.

821
NOBUKO R. KODAMA FONG MEMORIAL SCHOLARSHIP

Japanese American Citizens League
Attn: National Scholarship Awards
1765 Sutter Street
San Francisco, CA 94115
Phone: (415) 921-5225   Fax: (415) 931-4671
E-mail: jacl@jacl.org
Web Site: www.jacl.org
Summary: To provide financial assistance to student members of the Japanese American Citizens League (JACL) who are pursuing undergraduate education.
Eligibility: This program is open to JACL members who are currently enrolled or planning to reenter a college, university, trade school, business college, or other institution of higher learning. Selection is based on academic record, extracurricular activities, and community involvement. Preference is given to residents of the Pacific Northwest District.
Financial data: The stipend depends on the availability of funds but usually ranges from $1,000 to $5,000.
Duration: 1 year.
Additional information: Requests for applications must be accompanied by a self-addressed stamped envelope.
Number awarded: 1 each year.
Deadline: March of each year.

822
NORMAN AND RUTH GOOD SCHOLARSHIP

Lincoln Community Foundation
215 Centennial Mall South, Suite 200
Lincoln, NE 68508
Phone: (402) 474-2345   Fax: (402) 476-8532
E-mail: lcf@lcf.org
Web Site: www.lcf.org
Summary: To provide financial assistance to upper-division students attending private colleges in Nebraska.
Eligibility: Eligible to apply are juniors or seniors attending a private college in Nebraska. Applicants must have at least a 3.5 grade point average and be pursuing a degree program, not special studies. Financial need is considered.
Financial data: The amount awarded varies, up to one half of the recipient's educational expenses.
Duration: 1 year.
Number awarded: 1 or more each year.
Deadline: April of each year.

823
NORMAN M. CROOKS MEMORIAL SCHOLARSHIP

Association on American Indian Affairs, Inc.
Attn: Scholarship Coordinator
P.O. Box 268
Sisseton, SD 57262
Phone: (605) 698-3998   Fax: (605) 698-3316
E-mail: aaia_scholarships@sbtc.net
Web Site: www.indian-affairs.org/scholarships.cfm
Summary: To provide financial assistance to Native American students interested in postsecondary education.
Eligibility: Applicants must be Native American students interested in undergraduate or graduate education. Selection is based on merit and financial need. Applicants must submit an essay (1 to 2 pages) describing their educational goals, a budget of educational costs and resources, a copy of a certificate of at least one-quarter Indian blood or of registration with a federally-recognized Indian tribe, and their most recent transcript. Preference is given to students planning to return to their communities, both reservation and urban.
Financial data: The stipend is $1,000 per year. Funds are paid directly to accredited educational institutions to be used for tuition, books, and other academic-related expenses.
Duration: 1 year; renewable if academic progress is satisfactory.
Additional information: Recipients may attend any accredited college or university of their choice level.
Number awarded: 1 or more each year.
Deadline: August of each year.

824
NORTH CAROLINA APPROPRIATED GRANTS

North Carolina State Education Assistance Authority
Attn: Scholarship and Grant Services
P.O. Box 14103
Research Triangle Park, NC 27709-4103
Phone: (919) 549-8614   Fax: (919) 549-8481
Web Site: www.ncseaa.edu
Summary: To provide financial assistance to students enrolled in a branch of the University of North Carolina.
Eligibility: This program is open to North Carolina residents attending 1 of the 16 branches of the University of North Carolina as full-time or part-time undergraduate, graduate, or professional degree students. Selection is based on financial need as determined by the respective institution.
Financial data: The amount of the awards depends on the availability of funds and the need of the recipients.
Duration: 1 year; may be renewed.
Additional information: The funds available for this program are allocated each year by the North Carolina legislature.
Number awarded: Varies each year.

825
NORTH CAROLINA COMMUNITY COLLEGE GRANT PROGRAM

North Carolina Community College System
Attn: Student Support Services
200 West Jones Street
Raleigh, NC 27603-1379
Phone: (919) 733-7051   Fax: (919) 733-0680
Web Site: www.ncccs.cc.nc.us
Summary: To provide financial assistance to students attending community colleges in North Carolina.
Eligibility: This program is open to North Carolina residents enrolled at least half time at 1 of the 58 institutions in North Carolina's community college system. Applicants must be able to demonstrate financial need. Students who already hold a bachelor's degree are ineligible.
Financial data: Stipends depend on the recipient's enrollment status and financial need; they range from $200 to $1,650 for full-time students, from $150 to $1,263 for three quarter-time student, and from $100 to $825 for half-time students.
Duration: 1 year; may be renewed.
Additional information: This program was established in 1999 as a replacement for the North Carolina Community College Scholarship Program. It is jointly administered by the North Carolina State Education Assistance Authority, the North Carolina Community College System, College Foundation of North Carolina, and financial aid administrators at the community college. There are no special application forms for the scholarships. Students apply to their local community college, not to the system office. Each eligible school selects its own recipients.
Number awarded: Approximately 3,000 each year.

826
NORTH CAROLINA INCENTIVE SCHOLARSHIP AND GRANT PROGRAM FOR NATIVE AMERICANS

North Carolina State Education Assistance Authority
Attn: Scholarship and Grant Services
P.O. Box 14103
Research Triangle Park, NC 27709-4103
Phone: (919) 549-8614   Fax: (919) 549-8481
Web Site: www.ncseaa.edu
Summary: To provide financial assistance to Native American residents of North Carolina interested in pursuing an undergraduate or doctoral degree at a public institution in the state.
Eligibility: This program is open to residents of North Carolina who maintain cultural identification as a Native American through membership in an Indian tribe recognized by the United States or by the state of North Carolina, or through tribal affiliation or community recognition. Incoming freshmen must rank in the top half of their graduating class at a North Carolina high school; incoming transfers must possess an associate degree and must have earned a grade point average of 2.5 or higher at the 2-year college, or they must possess a certificate in a program that articulates directly with an academic program at a constituent university and must have earned a GPA of 2.0 or higher at the college. Applicants must be admitted or enrolled in a regular undergraduate degree-granting program at 1 of the 16 constituent institutions of the University of North Carolina or in a doctoral program at North Carolina State University, the University of North Carolina at Chapel Hill, or the University of North Carolina at Greensboro. Financial need must be demonstrated.
Financial data: The maximum stipend is $3,000 per year for undergraduate study or $5,000 per year for doctoral students.
Duration: 1 year; may be renewed if the student maintains financial need and satisfactory academic progress.
Number awarded: Varies each year; recently, a total of 363 students were receiving $1,564,848 through this program.
Deadline: Deadline dates vary; check with the participating school.

827
NORTH CAROLINA INCENTIVE SCHOLARSHIP PROGRAM

North Carolina State Education Assistance Authority
Attn: Scholarship and Grant Services
P.O. Box 14103
Research Triangle Park, NC 27709-4103
Phone: (919) 549-8614   Fax: (919) 549-8481
Web Site: www.ncseaa.edu
Summary: To provide financial assistance to graduates of North Carolina high schools or community colleges who enroll in predominately Black colleges or

173

universities in the state.

Eligibility: This program is open to students who enroll as undergraduates at 1 of the following predominately Black schools in North Carolina: Elizabeth City State University, Fayetteville State University, North Carolina A&T State University, North Carolina Central University, the University of North Carolina at Pembroke, or Winston-Salem State University. To be eligible, recipients must meet certain admissions standards, including specified grade point averages, submit to standardized assessments, and participate in required public service activities. A geographic requirement limiting participation to persons from certain northeastern counties is in effect at Elizabeth City State University.

Financial data: The value of the award varies, depending on the cost of education at the recipient's institution, other financial aid received, and the financial resources of the recipient and/or family. Annual awards do not exceed $3,000 per recipient.

Duration: 1 year; may be renewed.

Number awarded: Varies each year; recently, a total of 585 students were receiving $586,899 through this program.

Deadline: Deadline dates vary; check with the participating school.

828
NORTH CAROLINA LEGISLATIVE TUITION GRANTS

North Carolina State Education Assistance Authority
Attn: Scholarship and Grant Services
P.O. Box 14103
Research Triangle Park, NC 27709-4103
Phone: (919) 549-8614   Fax: (919) 549-8481
Web Site: www.ncseaa.edu

Summary: To provide financial assistance to students enrolled in private colleges in North Carolina.

Eligibility: This program is open to North Carolina residents attending 1 of 37 legislatively-designated private colleges in the state on a full-time basis. Financial need is not considered in the selection process. Students of theology, divinity, religious education, or any other course of study designed primarily for career preparation in a religious vocation are not eligible.

Financial data: Up to $1,800 per year. Funds are paid to the institution on behalf of the recipient.

Duration: 1 year; may be renewed.

Additional information: The funds available for this program are allocated each year by the North Carolina legislature.

Number awarded: Varies each year; recently, a total of 28,808 students were receiving $40,963,379 through this program.

829
NORTH CAROLINA PTA SCHOLARSHIPS

North Carolina PTA
3501 Glenwood Avenue
Raleigh, NC 27612-4934
Phone: (919) 787-0534   (800) 255-0417 (within NC)
Fax: (919) 787-0569   E-mail: office@ncpta.org
Web Site: www.ncpta.org/scholarship.html

Summary: To provide financial assistance for college to high school seniors who are members of the North Carolina PTA/PTSA.

Eligibility: This program is open to graduating seniors in North Carolina who are members of their high school PTA/PTSA. Applicants must submit a copy of their most recent high school transcript, 2 letters of recommendation from high school faculty, a copy of their PTA/PTSA membership card, and an essay of up to 200 words on their involvement with their PTA/PTSA. Finalists are interviewed.

Financial data: The stipend is $1,000.

Duration: 1 year.

Number awarded: 1 or more each year.

Deadline: January of each year.

830
NORTH CAROLINA SCHOLARSHIPS FOR CHILDREN OF WAR VETERANS

Division of Veterans Affairs
Albemarle Building
325 North Salisbury Street, Suite 1065
Raleigh, NC 27603-5941
Phone: (919) 733-3851   Fax: (919) 733-2834
E-mail: Charlie.Smith@ncmail.net
Web Site: www.doa.state.nc.us/doa/vets/va.htm

Summary: To provide financial assistance for postsecondary education to the children of disabled and other classes of North Carolina veterans.

Eligibility: Eligible applicants come from 5 categories. Class I-A: the veteran parent must have died in wartime service or as a result of a service-connected condition incurred in wartime service. Class I-B: the veteran parent must be rated by the U.S. Department of Veterans Affairs (VA) as 100 percent disabled as a result of wartime service and currently or at the time of death drawing compensation for such disability. Class II: the veteran parent must be rated by the VA as much as 20 but less than 100 percent disabled due to wartime service, or receiving a statutory award for arrested pulmonary tuberculosis, and currently or at the time of death drawing compensation for such disability. Class III: the veteran parent must be currently or have been at time of death receiving a VA pension for total and permanent disability, or the veteran parent must be deceased but does not qualify under any other provisions. Class IV: the veteran parent was a prisoner of war or missing in action. For all classes, the veteran parent must have been a legal resident of North Carolina at the time of entrance into the armed forces or the child must have been born in North Carolina and lived in the state continuously since birth.

Financial data: Students in Classes I-A, II, III, and IV receive $4,500 per academic year if they attend a private college or junior college; if attending a public postsecondary institution, they receive free tuition, a room allowance, a board allowance, and exemption from certain mandatory fees. Students in Class I-B receive $1,500 per academic year if they attend a private college or junior college; if attending a public postsecondary institution, they receive free tuition and exemption from certain mandatory fees.

Duration: 4 academic years.

Number awarded: An unlimited number of awards are made under Classes I-A, I-B, and IV. Classes II and III are limited to 100 awards each year in each class.

Deadline: April of each year.

831
NORTH CAROLINA STATE CONTRACTUAL SCHOLARSHIP FUND PROGRAM

North Carolina State Education Assistance Authority
Attn: Scholarship and Grant Services
P.O. Box 14103
Research Triangle Park, NC 27709-4103
Phone: (919) 549-8614   Fax: (919) 549-8481
Web Site: www.ncseaa.edu

Summary: To provide financial assistance for education at private colleges and universities to students in North Carolina with financial need.

Eligibility: Eligible for this program are North Carolina residents who are enrolled as full-time or part-time undergraduate students at 1 of 37 approved North Carolina private colleges and universities. Students enrolled in a program of study in theology, divinity, religious education, or any other program of study designed primarily for career preparation in a religious vocation are not eligible.

Financial data: Awards up to $1,100 per year available, depending on financial need.

Duration: 1 year.

Additional information: Recipients are selected by the financial aid offices of the 37 eligible private institutions in North Carolina.

Number awarded: Varies each year; recently, a total of 12,516 students received $29,485,584 through this program.

832
NORTH CAROLINA STUDENT INCENTIVE GRANT

North Carolina State Education Assistance Authority
Attn: Scholarship and Grant Services
P.O. Box 14103
Research Triangle Park, NC 27709-4103
Phone: (919) 549-8614   Fax: (919) 549-8481
Web Site: www.ncseaa.edu

Summary: To provide financial assistance for postsecondary education to students in North Carolina with substantial financial need.

Eligibility: Applicants for this program must 1) be U.S. citizens; 2) be North Carolina residents; 3) be enrolled or accepted for enrollment on a full-time basis at a North Carolina postsecondary institution; 4) not be enrolled in a program designed primarily for career preparation in a religious vocation; 5) maintain satisfactory academic promise; and 6) be able to demonstrate substantial financial need.

Financial data: Awards range from $200 to $1,500 per year, depending on financial need; the average award is approximately $700.

Duration: 1 year.

Additional information: This program is offered by the North Carolina State Education Assistance Authority through College Foundation, Inc. of Raleigh, North Carolina.

Number awarded: Varies each year; recently, a total of 3,291 students received $2,103,591 through this program.

Deadline: March of each year.

833
NORTH DAKOTA EDUCATIONAL ASSISTANCE FOR DEPENDENTS OF VETERANS

Department of Veterans Affairs
1411 32nd Street South
P.O. Box 9003
Fargo, ND 58106-9003
Phone: (701) 239-7165   Fax: (701) 239-7166

Summary: To provide financial assistance for the postsecondary education of spouses, widow(er)s, and children of disabled and other North Dakota veterans.

Eligibility: This program is open to the spouses, widow(er)s, and dependent children of veterans who are totally disabled as a result of service-connected causes, or who were killed in action, or who have died as a result of wounds or service-connected disabilities, or who were identified as prisoners of war or missing in action. Veteran parents must have been born in and lived in North Dakota until entrance into the armed forces (or must have resided in the state for at least 6 months prior to entrance into military service) and must have served during wartime.

Financial data: Eligible dependents receive free tuition and are exempt from fees at any state-supported institution of higher education, technical school, or vocational school.

Duration: Up to 36 months or 8 academic semesters.

Number awarded: Varies each year.

834
NORTH DAKOTA FEE WAIVER FOR SURVIVORS OF DECEASED FIRE FIGHTERS AND PEACE OFFICERS

North Dakota University System
Attn: Director of Financial Aid
State Capitol, Tenth Floor
600 East Boulevard Avenue, Department 215
Bismarck, ND 58505-0230
Phone: (701) 328-4114   Fax: (701) 328-2961
E-mail: peggy_wipf@ndus.nodak.edu
Web Site: www.ndus.nodak.edu

Summary: To waive tuition and fees for survivors of deceased fire fighters and peace officers at public institutions in North Dakota.

Eligibility: Eligible for this benefit are residents of North Dakota who are the survivors of fire fighters and peace officers who died as a direct result of injuries received in the performance of official duties. Applicants must be attending or planning to attend a public college or university in North Dakota.

Financial data: Qualified students are entitled to a waiver of all tuition and fees (except fees charged to retire outstanding bonds).

Duration: 1 academic year; renewable.

Number awarded: Varies each year.

835
NORTH DAKOTA INDIAN SCHOLARSHIP PROGRAM

North Dakota University System
Attn: North Dakota Indian Scholarship Program
919 South Seventh Street, Suite 603
Bismarck, ND 58504
Phone: (701) 328-9661   Fax: (701) 328-9662
E-mail: rhonda_schauer@ndus.nodak.edu
Web Site: www.ndus.nodak.edu/student_info/financial_aid

Summary: To provide financial assistance to Native American students in North Dakota colleges and universities.

Eligibility: Applicants must be at least one-quarter degree Indian blood, residents of North Dakota or enrolled members of a tribe resident in North Dakota, and accepted as full-time undergraduate students by an institution of higher learning or vocational education in North Dakota. Students must have at least a 2.0 grade point average, although priority in funding is given to those with a grade point average of 3.5 or higher. Participants in internships, student teaching, teaching assistance, or cooperative education programs are eligible only if participation in that program is

required for the degree and only if tuition must be paid for the credits earned.

Financial data: The amount of the stipend varies from $700 to $2,000 depending on scholastic ability, funds available, total number of applicants, and financial need. The award is divided into semester or quarter payments. The money is to be used to pay registration, health fees, board, room, books, and other necessary items handled by the institution. Any remaining balance may be used to cover the student's personal expenses.

Duration: 1 academic year; renewable up to 3 additional years, if the recipient maintains a 2.0 grade point average and continues to be in financial need.

Number awarded: Varies; approximately 150 each year.

Deadline: July of each year.

836
NORTH DAKOTA SCHOLARS PROGRAM

North Dakota University System
Attn: Director of Financial Aid
State Capitol, Tenth Floor
600 East Boulevard Avenue, Department 215
Bismarck, ND 58505-0230
Phone: (701) 328-4114   Fax: (701) 328-2961
E-mail: peggy_wipf@ndus.nodak.edu
Web Site: www.ndus.nodak.edu

Summary: To provide financial assistance to high school seniors in North Dakota who are interested in attending college in the state.

Eligibility: This program is open to seniors at high schools in North Dakota who are in the upper 20 percent of their graduating class at the end of their junior year and score in the upper 20th percentile of all North Dakota ACT test takers. Applicants must be interested in attending a college or university in North Dakota.

Financial data: Students who attend a public or tribal college receive full payment of tuition. Students who attend a private institution in North Dakota receive a stipend equivalent to tuition at North Dakota State University or the University of North Dakota.

Duration: 1 academic year; renewable up to 3 additional years, if the recipient maintains a cumulative grade point average of 3.5 or higher.

Number awarded: 40 to 45 each year.

837
NORTH DAKOTA VETERANS DEPENDENTS FEE WAIVER

North Dakota University System
Attn: Director of Financial Aid
State Capitol, Tenth Floor
600 East Boulevard Avenue, Department 215
Bismarck, ND 58505-0230
Phone: (701) 328-4114   Fax: (701) 328-2961
E-mail: peggy_wipf@ndus.nodak.edu
Web Site: www.ndus.nodak.edu

Summary: To waive tuition and fees for dependents of disabled or deceased veterans at public institutions in North Dakota.

Eligibility: Eligible for this benefit are the dependents of veterans who were North Dakota residents who were killed in action, died of service-related causes, were prisoners of war, or were declared missing in action. Applicants must be attending or planning to attend a public college or university in North Dakota.

Financial data: Qualified students are entitled to a waiver of all tuition and fees (except fees charged to retire outstanding bonds).

Duration: 1 academic year; renewable.

Number awarded: Varies each year.

838
NORTHERN CALIFORNIA DX FOUNDATION SCHOLARSHIP

Foundation for Amateur Radio, Inc.
P.O. Box 831
Riverdale, MD 20738
E-mail: turnbull@erols.com
Web Site: www.amateurradio-far.org

Summary: To provide funding for college to licensed radio amateurs.

Eligibility: This program is open to licensed radio amateurs who plan to seek a bachelor's degree at a college or university in the United States. There is no restriction on the field of study. Applicants must have at least a General Class license; preference is given to active HF operators indicating an interest in DXing who provide a supplementary statement describing their DX activities.

Financial data: The stipend is $1,000.
Duration: 1 year.
Additional information: Recipients must attend an accredited school (university, college, or technical institute) on a full-time basis.
Number awarded: 1 each year.
Deadline: May of each year.

839
NSCC NAMED SCHOLARSHIP PROGRAM

United States Naval Sea Cadet Corps
Attn: Executive Director
2300 Wilson Boulevard
Arlington, VA 22201-3308
Phone: (703) 243-6910   Fax: (703) 243-3985
Summary: To provide financial assistance to Naval Sea Cadet Corps cadets and former cadets who are interested in continuing their education at an accredited 4-year college/university.
Eligibility: This program is open to cadets and former cadets who are interested in continuing their education at an accredited 4-year college or university. They must have been a member of the corps for at least 2 years, have a minimum rating of NSCC E-3, be recommended by their commanding officer or other official, have earned at least a 3.0 grade point average, and have been accepted by an accredited college or university. Applicants may submit financial need statements. All other factors being equal, these statements may be considered in determining award recipients. Applicants who have received full scholarships from other sources (e.g., ROTC) will be considered for this award only if there are no other qualified applicants.
Financial data: The stipend is $1,000.
Duration: 1 year.
Additional information: Cadets are also eligible to apply for scholarships sponsored by the Navy League of the United States.
Number awarded: 5 each year.
Deadline: May of each year.

840
NYLE SCHOLARSHIP

Northeastern Young Lumber Execs
c/o Northeastern Retail Lumber Association
585 North Greenbush Road
Rensselaer, NY 12144
Phone: (518) 286-1010   (800) 292-6752
Fax: (518) 286-1755   E-mail: tjacobie@nrla.org
Web Site: www.nrla.org
Summary: To provide financial assistance to employees of member firms of Northeastern Young Lumber Execs (NYLE) and their families.
Eligibility: This program is open to employees of firms with at least 1 employee registered as an NYLE member in good standing. Spouses and children are also eligible. Applicants must be attending or interested in attending a postsecondary institution.
Financial data: The stipend is $1,000.
Duration: 1 year.
Number awarded: 1 each year.
Deadline: May of each year.

841
NYSSPE PAST OFFICERS' SCHOLARSHIP

New York State Society of Professional Engineers
c/o Kelly K. Norris
RPI Technology Park
385 Jordan Road
Troy, NY 12180-7620
Phone: (518) 283-7490   Fax: (518) 283-7495
E-mail: kknorris@nysspe.org
Web Site: www.nysspe.org/scholar.html
Summary: To provide financial assistance for college to the children of members of the New York State Society of Professional Engineers (NYSSPE).
Eligibility: Eligible to apply for this scholarship are high school seniors in New York whose parent is a member of NYSSPE. Selection is based solely on academic merit.
Financial data: The stipend is $1,000.
Duration: 1 year.
Number awarded: 1 each year.
Deadline: November of each year.

842
OCA AVON COLLEGE SCHOLARSHIP

Organization of Chinese Americans, Inc.
1001 Connecticut Avenue, N.W., Suite 601
Washington, DC 20036
Phone: (202) 223-5500   Fax: (202) 296-0540
E-mail: oca@ocanatl.org
Web Site: www.ocanatl.org
Summary: To provide financial assistance to Asian Pacific American women entering their first year at a 2-year or 4-year college.
Eligibility: This program is open to Asian Pacific American women (including east Asian Americans, Filipino Americans, Pacific Islander Americans, south Asian Americans, and southeast Asian Americans) who are entering their first year of college. Applicants must be U.S. citizens or permanent residents who have earned at a grade point average or 3.0 or higher in high school. Selection is based on academic achievement, community service, and financial need.
Financial data: The stipend is $2,000.
Duration: 1 year.
Additional information: This program is administered by the Organization of Chinese Americans (OCA), Inc. and funded by the Avon Foundation. Recipients must write a paper by the end of their freshman year describing their college experience as an Asian Pacific American woman.
Number awarded: 1 or more each year.
Deadline: April of each year.

843
OCA/UPS FOUNDATION GOLD MOUNTAIN SCHOLARSHIP

Organization of Chinese Americans, Inc.
1001 Connecticut Avenue, N.W., Suite 601
Washington, DC 20036
Phone: (202) 223-5500   Fax: (202) 296-0540
E-mail: oca@ocanatl.org
Web Site: www.ocanatl.org
Summary: To provide financial assistance for college to Asian Pacific Americans who are the first person in their family to attend an institution of higher education.
Eligibility: This program is open to Asian Pacific American students entering their first year of college in the following fall. Applicants must be the first person in their immediate family to attend college, have a cumulative grade point average of 3.0 or higher, be in financial need, and be a U.S. citizen or permanent resident.
Financial data: The stipend is $2,000.
Duration: 1 year.
Additional information: This program is funded by the UPS Foundation and administered by the Organization of Chinese Americans (OCA).
Number awarded: 4 each year.
Deadline: April of each year.

844
ODEN LUCE TRUST SCHOLARSHIPS

Oden Luce Trust
c/o Bank of America, N.A.
Attn: Private Bank Center, Seattle
WA501-22-01
P.O. Box 34474
Seattle, WA 98124-1474
Phone: (206) 358-7977   (800) 526-7307
Fax: (206) 358-1059
Summary: To provide financial assistance for college to high school seniors and graduates who are Umatilla Indians.
Eligibility: Eligible to apply for these funds are members of the Confederated Tribes of the Umatilla Indian Reservation who are graduating or have graduated from high school, need financial assistance to attend or continue attending college, and are interested in obtaining a liberal arts or professional degree.
Financial data: The amount of each scholarship is determined by the funds available and the need of the recipients.
Duration: 1 year; may be renewed.
Additional information: Funds may also be used by qualified students who have completed the tenth grade and are interested in pursuing a vocational education.
Number awarded: Varies each year.

845
OFFICE OF HAWAIIAN AFFAIRS EDUCATION FOUNDATION SCHOLARSHIPS

Ke Ali'i Pauahi Foundation
Attn: Financial Aid & Scholarship Services
1887 Makuakane Street
Honolulu, HI 96817-1887
Phone: (808) 842-8216   (800) 842-4682, ext. 8216
Fax: (808) 841-0660   E-mail: finaid@ksbe.edu
Web Site: www.pauahi.org
Summary: To provide financial assistance for undergraduate or graduate studies to persons of Hawaiian descent.
Eligibility: Applicants must be of Hawaiian descent (descendants of the aboriginal inhabitants of the Hawaiian Islands prior to 1778). They must be U.S. citizens, enrolled in full-time study at a regionally accredited 2-year, 4-year, or graduate degree program, and able to demonstrate financial need and academic excellence. Residency in Hawaii is not required.
Financial data: The amount awarded depends upon financial needs of the recipient.
Duration: This is a 1-time grant.
Additional information: This program is jointly sponsored by the Ke Ali'i Pauahi Foundation and the Office of Hawaiian Affairs.
Deadline: February of each year.

846
OHIO ACADEMIC SCHOLARSHIP PROGRAM

Ohio Board of Regents
Attn: State Grants and Scholarships
30 East Broad Street, 36th Floor
P.O. Box 182452
Columbus, OH 43218-2452
Phone: (614) 466-7420   (888) 833-1133
Fax: (614) 752-5903   E-mail: cshaid@regents.state.oh.us
Web Site: www.regents.state.oh.us/sgs
Summary: To provide financial assistance to outstanding high school seniors in Ohio.
Eligibility: Graduating high school seniors who are residents of Ohio are eligible to apply for this program if they plan to enroll for full-time undergraduate study at a college or university in Ohio. Selection is based on test scores and high school grades. Each high school in the state identifies the top 5 applicants and submits those 5 applications to the Ohio Board of Regents. The top candidate receives an award and the remaining applicants are placed in a statewide pool and chosen on a competitive basis until all the awards have been presented.
Financial data: The stipend is $2,100 per year.
Duration: Up to 8 semesters or 12 quarters.
Additional information: This program was established in 1978.
Number awarded: 1 for each public, private, or vocational high school in Ohio; additional awards are then granted until a total of 1,000 have been presented.
Deadline: February of each year.

847
OHIO ELKS ASSOCIATION EDUCATION GRANT

Ohio Elks Association
169 Grove Street
P.O. Box 304
Marysville, OH 43040-0304
Phone: (937) 642-9485   Fax: (937) 642-9486
E-mail: ohioelks@midohio.net
Web Site: web-ster.net/ohioelks
Summary: To provide financial assistance for college to Ohio residents.
Eligibility: Any prospective student (male or female) who resides within the jurisdiction of a B.P.O. Elks Lodge belonging to the Ohio Elks Association and who plans to pursue or continue pursuing postsecondary education may apply. Applicants must be U.S. citizens. An application package must include a completed application form, a statement (up to 200 words) of future goals, 3 letters of recommendation, and an official high school and (if appropriate) college transcript. Selection is based on motivation (350 points), academic record (200 points), aptitude (150 points), and financial need (300 points).
Financial data: The stipend is $1,000 per year. Funds are sent to the recipient's institution upon verification of enrollment. Funds must be used for tuition, fees, room, and board; it may not be used for general living expenses (e.g., apartment rent, mortgage payments, automobile expenses, child care).

Duration: 1 year; recipients may apply for 1 more year of support. No student will be awarded more than 2 annual grants.
Additional information: No student may receive more than 1 Ohio Elks Association or Elks National Foundation grant in the same year. Grants may not be used for correspondence courses.
Number awarded: 86 each year.
Deadline: March of each year.

848
OHIO INSTRUCTIONAL GRANT PROGRAM

Ohio Board of Regents
Attn: State Grants and Scholarships
30 East Broad Street, 36th Floor
P.O. Box 182452
Columbus, OH 43218-2452
Phone: (614) 466-7420   (888) 833-1133
Fax: (614) 752-5903   E-mail: cshaid@regents.state.oh.us
Web Site: www.regents.state.oh.us/sgs
Summary: To provide financial assistance for the undergraduate education of students in Ohio.
Eligibility: To be eligible for these scholarships, students must be Ohio residents and U.S. citizens who are attending or planning to attend eligible colleges and universities in Ohio or Pennsylvania as full-time undergraduate students. Financial need (family income of $31,000 per year or less) must be demonstrated.
Financial data: Awards range from $168 to $5,160 per year, but may not exceed tuition costs.
Duration: 1 year; may be renewed up to 3 additional years.
Additional information: This program was established in 1970.
Number awarded: Varies, depending upon the funds available. Recently, approximately 83,000 students received these grants.
Deadline: September of each year.

849
OHIO LEGION AUXILIARY DEPARTMENT PRESIDENT'S SCHOLARSHIP

American Legion Auxiliary
Attn: Department of Ohio
1100 Brandywine Boulevard, Building D
P.O. Box 2760
Zanesville, OH 43702-2760
Phone: (740) 452-8245   Fax: (740) 452-2620
E-mail: alaoh@msmip.com
Summary: To provide financial assistance for postsecondary education to the descendants of veterans in Ohio.
Eligibility: This program is open to the children, grandchildren, and great-grandchildren of living or deceased veterans of World War I, World War II, Korea, Vietnam, Lebanon/Grenada, Panama, or Desert Storm. Applicants must be residents of Ohio, a senior at an accredited high school, and sponsored by an American Legion Auxiliary Unit. Applications must include an original article (up to 500 words) written by the applicant on "What the American Flag Represents to Me." The winner is selected on the basis of character, Americanism, leadership, scholarship, and financial need.
Financial data: Awards are $1,500 or $1,000. Funds are paid to recipient's school.
Duration: 1 year.
Number awarded: 2 each year: 1 at $1,500 and 1 at $1,000.
Deadline: February of each year.

850
OHIO LEGION SCHOLARSHIPS

American Legion
Attn: Department of Ohio
P.O. Box 8007
Delaware, OH 43015
Phone: (740) 362-7478   Fax: (740) 362-1429
E-mail: ohlegion@iwaynet.net
Web Site: www.ohioamericanlegion.org
Summary: To provide financial assistance for postsecondary education to Ohio Legionnaires, their spouses, and descendants.
Eligibility: Eligible to apply for these scholarships are residents of Ohio who are Legionnaires, direct descendants of living or deceased Legionnaires, and surviving spouses or children of deceased U.S. military personnel who died on active duty or

of injuries received on active duty. All applicants must be attending or planning to attend colleges, universities, or other approved postsecondary schools in Ohio. Selection is based on academic achievement as measured by course grades, scholastic test scores, difficulty of curriculum, participation in outside activities, and the judging committee's general impression.

Financial data: Stipends are at least $2,000.

Duration: 1 year.

Number awarded: Varies each year.

Deadline: April of each year.

851
OHIO PART-TIME STUDENT INSTRUCTIONAL GRANT PROGRAM

Ohio Board of Regents
Attn: State Grants and Scholarships
30 East Broad Street, 36th Floor
P.O. Box 182452
Columbus, OH 43218-2452
Phone: (614) 466-7420   (888) 833-1133
Fax: (614) 752-5903   E-mail: cshaid@regents.state.oh.us
Web Site: www.regents.state.oh.us/sgs

Summary: To provide financial assistance for the part-time undergraduate education of students in Ohio.

Eligibility: To be eligible for these scholarships, students must be Ohio residents who are attending or planning to attend public, private, and proprietary colleges and universities in Ohio and take fewer than 12 credit hours per term. Financial need must be demonstrated. Special consideration is given to single heads of household and displaced homemakers. Participating schools select the recipients.

Financial data: Participating schools determine the amount of each award, based on guidelines set by the Board of Regents and the need of the recipient.

Duration: 1 year; may be renewed up to 3 additional years.

Additional information: This program was established in 1993.

Number awarded: Varies each year; recently, 28,349 students received these grants.

Deadline: Each participating college or university sets its own deadline.

852
OHIO SAFETY OFFICERS COLLEGE MEMORIAL FUND

Ohio Board of Regents
Attn: State Grants and Scholarships
30 East Broad Street, 36th Floor
P.O. Box 182452
Columbus, OH 43218-2452
Phone: (614) 466-7420   (888) 833-1133
Fax: (614) 752-5903   E-mail: cshaid@regents.state.oh.us
Web Site: www.regents.state.oh.us/sgs

Summary: To provide financial assistance for the undergraduate education of children of Ohio peace officers and fire fighters killed in the line of duty.

Eligibility: To be eligible for these scholarships, students must be Ohio residents under the age of 26 whose parent was an Ohio peace office or fire fighter killed in the line of duty.

Financial data: At Ohio public colleges and universities, the program provides full payment of tuition. At Ohio private colleges and universities, the stipend is equivalent to the average amounts paid to students attending public institutions, currently $3,270 per year.

Duration: 1 year; may be renewed up to 3 additional years.

Additional information: Eligible institutions are Ohio state-assisted colleges and universities and Ohio institutions approved by the Board of Regents. This program was established in 1980.

Number awarded: Varies each year; recently, 54 students received benefits.

Deadline: Application deadlines are established by each participating college and university.

853
OHIO STATE CLAIMS ASSOCIATION SCHOLARSHIPS

Griffith Foundation for Insurance Education
172 East State Street, Suite 305A
Columbus, OH 43215-4321
Phone: (614) 341-2392   Fax: (614) 442-0402
E-mail: griffithfoundation@attglobal.net
Web Site: www.griffithfoundation.org/student/OSCAann.html

Summary: To provide financial assistance for college to children of members of Ohio State Claims Association (OSCA) affiliated organizations.

Eligibility: This program in open to the children, stepchildren, and adopted children of members of an affiliated organization of OSCA. Applicants must be either high school seniors who have been accepted and intend to enroll in an accredited college or university in the United States pursuing an undergraduate degree or full-time students already enrolled. They must commit to take 1 course in risk management and insurance or submit evidence that they have already taken such a course. Selection is based on academic achievement, extracurricular activities and honors, work experience, 3 letters of recommendation, and financial need.

Financial data: Stipends up to $5,000 per year are provided.

Duration: 1 year; renewable.

Additional information: Information is also available from the OSCA Scholarship Chair, Edward A. Borocz, c/o Admiral Adjusting Company, P.O. Box 360227, Strongsville, OH 44136, (440) 572-7700, E-mail: Eborocz@aol.com.

Number awarded: 1 or more each year.

Deadline: April of each year.

854
OHIO STUDENT CHOICE GRANTS

Ohio Board of Regents
Attn: State Grants and Scholarships
30 East Broad Street, 36th Floor
P.O. Box 182452
Columbus, OH 43218-2452
Phone: (614) 466-7420   (888) 833-1133
Fax: (614) 752-5903   E-mail: cshaid@regents.state.oh.us
Web Site: www.regents.state.oh.us/sgs

Summary: To provide financial assistance for the undergraduate education of students attending private colleges in Ohio.

Eligibility: To be eligible for these scholarships, students must be Ohio residents attending or planning to attend private colleges in Ohio as full-time undergraduate students. Neither financial need nor academic merit is considered.

Financial data: Award amounts vary annually; recently, they averaged $1,062.

Duration: 1 year; may be renewed up to 3 additional years.

Additional information: This program was established in 1984.

Number awarded: Varies each year; recently, 45,742 students received these grants.

Deadline: Application deadlines established by participating colleges and universities.

855
OHIO WAR ORPHANS SCHOLARSHIP

Ohio Board of Regents
Attn: State Grants and Scholarships
30 East Broad Street, 36th Floor
P.O. Box 182452
Columbus, OH 43218-2452
Phone: (614) 466-7420   (888) 833-1133
Fax: (614) 752-5903   E-mail: cshaid@regents.state.oh.us
Web Site: www.regents.state.oh.us/sgs

Summary: To provide financial assistance for the undergraduate education of the children of deceased or disabled Ohio veterans.

Eligibility: To be eligible for these scholarships, students must be between the ages of 16 and 21 at the time of application; must have been residents of Ohio for the past year or, if the parent was not a resident of Ohio at the time of enlistment, for the year immediately preceding application and any other 4 of the last 10 years; and must be enrolled for full-time undergraduate study at an eligible Ohio college or university. At least 1 parent must have been a member of the U.S. armed forces, including the organized Reserves and Ohio National Guard for a period of 90 days or more (or discharged because of a disability incurred after less than 90 days of service) who served during World War I, World War II, the Korean conflict, the Vietnam era, or the Persian Gulf War, and who, as a result of such service, either was killed or became at least 60 percent service-connected disabled. Also eligible are children of veterans who have a permanent and total non-service connected disability and are receiving disability benefits from the U.S. Department of Veterans Affairs. Children of veteran parents who served in the organized Reserves or Ohio National Guard are also eligible if the parent was killed or became permanently and totally disabled while at a scheduled training assembly of any duration or length or active duty for training pursuant to bona fide orders issued by a competent authority.

Financial data: At Ohio public colleges and universities, the program provides full payment of tuition. At Ohio private colleges and universities, the stipend is

equivalent to the average amounts paid to students attending public institutions, currently $3,930 per year.

Duration: 1 year; may be renewed up to 4 additional years.

Additional information: Eligible institutions are Ohio state-assisted colleges and universities and Ohio institutions approved by the Board of Regents. This program was established in 1957.

Number awarded: Varies, depending upon the funds available. If sufficient funds are available, all eligible applicants are given a scholarship. Recently, 861 students received benefits from this program.

Deadline: June of each year.

856
OKLAHOMA FEE WAIVER FOR DEPENDENTS OF PEACE OFFICERS AND FIRE FIGHTERS

Oklahoma State Regents for Higher Education
Attn: Director of Scholarship and Grant Programs
500 Education Building
State Capitol Complex
Oklahoma City, OK 73105-4503
Phone: (405) 524-9239   (800) 858-1840
Fax: (405) 524-9230   E-mail: studentinfo@osrhe.edu
Web Site: www.okhighered.org

Summary: To provide financial assistance for the postsecondary education of dependents of deceased Oklahoma peace officers and fire fighters.

Eligibility: Applicants for this assistance must be dependents of Oklahoma peace officers or fire fighters who lost their lives in the line of duty.

Financial data: Eligible applicants are entitled to receive free tuition at any Oklahoma state-supported postsecondary educational, technical, or vocational school.

Duration: Assistance continues for 5 years or until receipt of a bachelor's degree, whichever occurs first.

Number awarded: Varies each year.

857
OKLAHOMA FEE WAIVER FOR PRISONERS OF WAR, PERSONS MISSING IN ACTION, AND DEPENDENTS

Oklahoma State Regents for Higher Education
Attn: Director of Scholarship and Grant Programs
500 Education Building
State Capitol Complex
Oklahoma City, OK 73105-4503
Phone: (405) 524-9239   (800) 858-1840
Fax: (405) 524-9230   E-mail: studentinfo@osrhe.edu
Web Site: www.okhighered.org

Summary: To provide financial assistance for the postsecondary education of Oklahoma veterans (or their dependents) who were declared prisoners of war or missing in action.

Eligibility: Applicants for this assistance must be veterans who were declared prisoners of war or missing in action after January 1, 1960 and were residents of Oklahoma at the time of entrance into the armed forces or when declared POW/MIA. Dependents of those veterans are also eligible as long as they are under the age of 24.

Financial data: Eligible applicants are entitled to receive free tuition at any Oklahoma state-supported postsecondary educational, technical, or vocational school.

Duration: Assistance continues for 5 years or until receipt of a bachelor's degree, whichever occurs first.

Additional information: This assistance is not available to persons eligible to receive federal benefits.

Number awarded: Varies each year.

858
OKLAHOMA HIGHER LEARNING ACCESS PROGRAM

Oklahoma State Regents for Higher Education
Attn: Director of Scholarship and Grant Programs
500 Education Building
State Capitol Complex
Oklahoma City, OK 73105-4503
Phone: (405) 524-9239   (800) 858-1840
Fax: (405) 524-9230   E-mail: studentinfo@osrhe.edu
Web Site: www.okhighered.org

Summary: To provide financial assistance to Oklahoma residents who complete a specified high school curriculum.

Eligibility: Applicants for this program sign up during their 8th, 9th, or 10th grade year at an Oklahoma high school. If they complete a specified high school curriculum and demonstrate a commitment to academic success, they receive assistance when they attend college. Applicants must 1) demonstrate financial need (currently defined as a family income less than $50,000); 2) achieve a grade point average of 2.5 or higher both cumulatively and in the required curriculum; 3) fulfill an agreement to attend school, do homework regularly, refrain from substance abuse and criminal or delinquent acts, and have school work and records reviewed by mentors; and 4) be admitted as a regular entering freshman at an Oklahoma college, university, or area vocational-technical school.

Financial data: Students enrolled at an institution in the Oklahoma State System of Higher Education receive resident tuition, paid to the institution on their behalf. Students enrolled at an accredited private institution have tuition paid at an amount equivalent to the resident tuition at a comparable institution of the state system. Students enrolled in eligible vocational-technical programs have their tuition paid. No provision is made for other educational expenses, such as books, supplies, room, board, or other special fees.

Duration: Up to 5 years or until completion of a bachelor's degree, whichever occurs first. The award must be taken up within 3 years of high school graduation.

Additional information: The required curriculum consists of 17 units: 4 of English, 2 of laboratory science, 3 of mathematics, 2 of history (including 1 of U.S. history), 1 of citizenship skills (economics, geography, government, or non-Western culture), 2 of a foreign language or computer technology, 1 of fine arts (music, art, drama) or speech, and 2 additional units from those subjects or computer science.

Number awarded: Varies each year.

Deadline: Applications must be submitted by June following completion of the student's 8th, 9th, or 10th grade year.

859
OKLAHOMA INDEPENDENT LIVING ACT TUITION WAIVERS

Oklahoma State Regents for Higher Education
Attn: Director of Scholarship and Grant Programs
500 Education Building
State Capitol Complex
Oklahoma City, OK 73105-4503
Phone: (405) 524-9239   (800) 858-1840
Fax: (405) 524-9230   E-mail: studentinfo@osrhe.edu
Web Site: www.okhighered.org

Summary: To provide financial assistance for college to residents in Oklahoma who have been in a foster care program of the Department of Human Services (DHS).

Eligibility: This program is open to residents of Oklahoma who graduated within the previous 3 years from an accredited high school in the state or from a high school bordering Oklahoma as approved by the State Board of Education, or who have completed the GED requirements. Applicants must be younger than 21 years of age and have been in DHS custody for at least 9 months between 16 and 18 years of age. They must currently be enrolled at an Oklahoma public college or university or in certain programs at technology centers.

Financial data: Under this program, all resident tuition fees are waived.

Duration: 1 year; may be renewed until the student reaches 26 years of age or completes a baccalaureate degree or program certificate, whichever comes first.

Additional information: The Oklahoma State Legislature established this program in 2000.

Number awarded: Varies each year.

860
OKLAHOMA STATE REGENTS ACADEMIC SCHOLARS PROGRAM

Oklahoma State Regents for Higher Education
Attn: Director of Scholarship and Grant Programs
500 Education Building
State Capitol Complex
Oklahoma City, OK 73105-4503
Phone: (405) 524-9239   (800) 858-1840
Fax: (405) 524-9230   E-mail: studentinfo@osrhe.edu
Web Site: www.okhighered.org

Summary: To provide financial assistance for college to outstanding high school seniors and recent graduates in Oklahoma.

Eligibility: High school seniors or graduates from any state automatically are eligible for this funding if they have been named a National Merit Scholar, a National Merit Scholar Finalist, or a Presidential Scholar. In addition, Oklahoma residents can be eligible for support under this program if they have scored within the 99.5 to 100 percentile levels on the SAT or ACT; those percentiles apply to the total student population as well as to separate subdivisions—male, female, Black Non-Hispanic, Native American, Hispanic American, Asian-Pacific Islander, and White Non-Hispanic. Applicants must apply within 27 months of their high school graduation date.

Financial data: The program provides funding for tuition, fees, room and board, and textbooks. The exact amount of funding awarded varies each year but is currently $5,500 per year for students at the University of Oklahoma, Oklahoma State University, or University of Tulsa, $4,000 per year for students at other 4-year public or private colleges or universities in Oklahoma, or $3,500 per year for students at Oklahoma 2-year colleges.

Duration: Up to 5 years of undergraduate study, as long as the recipient remains a full-time student with a minimum grade point average of 3.25.

Additional information: Recipients may enroll in either public or private schools. Recipients must attend a school in Oklahoma.

Deadline: September of each year.

Number awarded: Varies each year; recently, 1,444 scholars participated in this program.

861
OKLAHOMA TUITION AID GRANT PROGRAM

Oklahoma State Regents for Higher Education
500 Education Building
State Capitol Complex
Oklahoma City, OK 73105-4503
Phone: (405) 858-4356   (877) 662-6231
Fax: (405) 858-4576   E-mail: otaginfo@otag.org
Web Site: www.okhighered.org

Summary: To provide financial assistance for postsecondary education to Oklahoma residents who demonstrate financial need.

Eligibility: This program is open to residents of Oklahoma who are attending or planning to attend public or private institutions in Oklahoma. To apply, they must complete the Free Application for Federal Student Aid and demonstrate financial need.

Financial data: The annual stipend is $1,000 or 75 percent of enrollment costs, whichever is less.

Duration: 1 year; renewable.

Additional information: This program is supported by state funds and by federal funds from the Leveraging Educational Assistance Partnership (LEAP) Program.

Number awarded: Varies each year.

Deadline: Applications are accepted through June of each year, but students should apply as early after the beginning of January as possible and by the end of April for best consideration.

862
OKLAHOMA TUITION SCHOLARSHIP PROGRAM

Oklahoma State Regents for Higher Education
Attn: Director of Scholarship and Grant Programs
500 Education Building
State Capitol Complex
Oklahoma City, OK 73105-4503
Phone: (405) 524-9239   (800) 858-1840
Fax: (405) 524-9230   E-mail: studentinfo@osrhe.edu
Web Site: www.okhighered.org

Summary: To provide financial assistance for postsecondary education to Oklahoma residents who demonstrate financial need.

Eligibility: This program is open to residents of Oklahoma who were residents for 2 years prior to high school graduation, have graduated from an accredited Oklahoma high school, apply within 3 years of graduating from high school, have earned a score of at least 26 on the ACT, have earned a cumulative high school grade point average of 3.25 or higher, and graduate in the top 15 percent of their class. The income of the student's parents, custodial parents, or guardian for the most recent calendar year, including income from both taxable and nontaxable sources, may not exceed $70,000 per year. Students must apply during their senior year of high school and must meet the admission standards for the type of institution they seek to attend. They must apply for state and federal financial aid. Students who have been adjudicated as a delinquent or convicted as an adult for a violent offense are not eligible.

Financial data: Students enrolled in an institution in the Oklahoma State System of Higher Education receive a scholarship in an amount equivalent to resident tuition. Students enrolled in a private Oklahoma institution receive a scholarship in an amount equivalent to the average cost of resident tuition at a similar Oklahoma public college or university. Students enrolled in postsecondary programs or courses that are offered as a result of an approved cooperative agreement between area public technology centers and Oklahoma public 2-year colleges are awarded a scholarship in an amount equivalent to resident tuition, not to exceed the average cost of 2 years of full-time resident tuition at an Oklahoma public 2-year college.

Duration: 1 year; may be renewed as long as the recipient maintains a grade point average of 2.75 or higher.

Additional information: The Oklahoma State Legislature established this program in 1999, to begin with students who graduate from high school during the 2002-03 academic year. Scholarship benefits are not awarded for remedial courses.

Number awarded: Varies each year.

863
OLIN L. LIVESEY SCHOLARSHIP

Olin L. Livesey Scholarship Fund
3538 Central Avenue, Suite 2-A
Riverside, CA 92506-2700
Phone: (909) 684-6778   E-mail: ollsf@scholarshipsite.org
Web Site: www.scholarshipsite.org/ollsf

Summary: To provide financial assistance to high school seniors interested in attending college.

Eligibility: This program is open to graduating high school seniors. They are invited to submit a preliminary application; an optional 1-page resume of clubs, offices held, or any other pertinent information on their activities; and 3 letters of recommendation. Based on this information, finalists are chosen; they must submit the following additional information: income verification; transcript/report cards; letter of acceptance; processing fee of $15; and other forms as required. Selection is based on financial need, standardized test scores, and academic record.

Financial data: Awards are made in the following categories: noncitizen, from $250 to $1,000; community, from $500 to $2,000; state, from $1,000 to $5,000; regional, from $2,000 to $7,500; and national, from $2,500 to $10,000. More than $1 million is distributed each year.

Duration: Awards may be issued for 1 year or, if the recipient prefers, prorated over 4 years.

Additional information: Finalists must submit a $15 processing fee when they submit the second-level application. Only those finalists who are awarded a scholarship are notified.

Number awarded: Varies each year; recently, 174 of these awards were presented.

Deadline: Preliminary applications must be submitted by the end of May; finalists must submit the second-level applications by mid-July.

864
OLIVER AND ESTHER R. HOWARD SCHOLARSHIP

Fleet Reserve Association
Attn: Scholarship Administrator
125 North West Street
Alexandria, VA 22314-2754
Phone: (703) 683-1400   (800) 372-1924
Fax: (703) 549-6610
Web Site: www.fra.org

Summary: To provide financial assistance for undergraduate education to children of members of the Fleet Reserve Association or its Ladies Auxiliary.

Eligibility: Applicants for these scholarships must be dependent children of members of the association or its ladies auxiliary (in good standing as of April 1 of the year of the award), or of members in good standing at the time of death. They must be interested in working on an undergraduate degree. Awards alternate annually between female dependents (in even-numbered years) and male dependents (in odd-numbered years). Selection is based on financial need, scholastic standing, character, and leadership qualities.

Financial data: The amount awarded varies, depending upon the needs of the recipient and the funds available.

Duration: 1 year; may be renewed.

Additional information: Membership in the Fleet Reserve Association is restricted to active-duty, retired, and reserve members of the Navy, Marine Corps, and Coast Guard.

Number awarded: 1 each year.

Deadline: April of each year.

865
OPTIMIST INTERNATIONAL COMMUNICATION CONTEST FOR THE DEAF AND HARD OF HEARING

Optimist International
Attn: Program and Youth Clubs Department
4494 Lindell Boulevard
St. Louis, MO 63108
Phone: (314) 371-6000   (800) 500-8130, ext. 224
Fax: (314) 371-6006   E-mail: programs@optimist.org
Web Site: www.oi.org/prog-ccdhh.html
Summary: To recognize and reward outstanding presentations made by deaf high school students.
Eligibility: All students in public, private, or parochial elementary, junior high, and senior high schools in the United States, Canada, or the Caribbean who are identified by their school as having a hearing loss or impairment may enter. They are invited to make a presentation from 4 to 5 minutes on a topic that changes annually; a recent topic was "We Are the Future." Competition is first conducted at the level of individual clubs, with winners advancing to zone and then district competitions.
Financial data: Each district winner receives a $1,500 college scholarship, payable to an educational institution of the recipient's choice, subject to the approval of Optimist International.
Duration: The competition is held annually.
Additional information: Entry information is available only from local Optimist Clubs.
Number awarded: Nearly 500 Optimist International clubs and 45 districts participate in this program. Each participating district offers 1 scholarship; some districts may offer a second award with separate competitions for signing and oral competitors, or for male and female entrants.
Deadline: Each club sets its own deadline. The district deadline is the end of September of each year.

866
OPTIMIST INTERNATIONAL ESSAY CONTEST

Optimist International
Attn: Program and Youth Clubs Department
4494 Lindell Boulevard
St. Louis, MO 63108
Phone: (314) 371-6000   (800) 500-8130, ext. 224
Fax: (314) 371-6006   E-mail: programs@optimist.org
Web Site: www.oi.org/prog-essay.html
Summary: To recognize and reward outstanding essays by high school students on a topic that changes annually.
Eligibility: This competition is open to high school sophomores, juniors, and seniors in the United States, the Caribbean, or Canada who are younger than 19 years of age. They are invited to write an essay of 400 to 500 words on a topic that changes each year; a recent topic was "My Place in a Changing World." They compete on the local club, district, and national/international levels.
Financial data: The international first-place winner receives $5,000; second place, $3,000; third place, $2,000. Funds are to be used to pay college costs. District winners are awarded a $650 college scholarship.
Duration: The competition is held annually.
Additional information: This competition was first held in 1983. Nearly 1,000 Optimist International local clubs participate in the program each year. Entry information is available only from local Optimist Clubs.
Number awarded: 3 international winners each year.
Deadline: Essays must be submitted to local clubs by the end of February of each year. The district deadline is in April.

867
OPTIMIST INTERNATIONAL JUNIOR BOWLING CHAMPIONSHIP

Optimist International
Attn: Sports Programs Department
4494 Lindell Boulevard
St. Louis, MO 63108
Phone: (314) 371-6000   (800) 500-8130, ext. 235
Fax: (314) 371-6006   E-mail: bowling@optimist.org
Web Site: www.oi.org/prog-bowling.html
Summary: To recognize and reward outstanding high school bowlers.
Eligibility: This program is open to bowlers in the United States and Canada who

are 18 years of age and younger. Competitions are held in 2 divisions: boys scratch (no handicap) and girls scratch. All competitors first bowl an 8-game qualifier. The top 24 qualifiers in each division advance to the semi-final round, where they bowl a 6-game match play format, followed by a 1-game position match play format. Winners of each match play game receive a bonus of 20 pins. The top 5 semi-finalists (including cumulative scores from the qualifying and semi-final rounds along with all bonus pins awarded) advance to the final round. At that final round (held in a different city each year), the top 5 semi-finalists in each division bowl a stair-step style format to determine the top 5 positions and the eventual champion.
Financial data: A total of $10,000 in scholarships is presented to the winners in each division (boys and girls).
Duration: The competition is held annually.
Additional information: This competition was first held in 2000. The registration fee is $90. All bowlers must be sanctioned by the Young American Bowling Alliance (YABA) or pay a $3 participation fee at each level of competition. The semi-finalists are responsible for their own travel and lodging expenses to participate in the final round.
Number awarded: Each year, 5 boys and 5 girls win scholarships.

868
OPTIMIST INTERNATIONAL ORATORICAL CONTEST

Optimist International
Attn: Program and Youth Clubs Department
4494 Lindell Boulevard
St. Louis, MO 63108
Phone: (314) 371-6000   (800) 500-8130, ext. 224
Fax: (314) 371-6006   E-mail: programs@optimist.org
Web Site: www.oi.org/prog-oratoric.html
Summary: To recognize and reward outstanding orators at the high school or younger level.
Eligibility: All students in public, private, or parochial elementary, junior high, and senior high schools in the United States, Canada, or the Caribbean who are under 16 years of age may enter. All contestants prepare their own orations of 4 to 5 minutes, but they may receive advice and make minor changes or improvements in the oration at any time. Each year a different subject is selected for the orations; a recent topic was "If I Could Change the World." Orations may be delivered in a language other than English if that language is an official language of the country in which the sponsoring club is located. Selection is based on poise (20 points), content of speech (35 points), delivery and presentation (35 points), and overall effectiveness (10 points). Competition is first conducted at the level of individual clubs, with winners advancing to zone and then district competitions. At the discretion of the district, boys may compete against boys and girls against girls in separate contests.
Financial data: Each district awards either 2 scholarships of $1,500 (1 for a boy and 1 for a girl) or (if the district chooses to have a combined gender contest) a first place scholarship of $1,500, a second place scholarship of $1,000, and a third place scholarship of $500.
Duration: The competition is held annually.
Additional information: This competition was first held in 1928. Nearly 2,000 Optimist International local clubs participate in the program each year. Entry information is available only from local Optimist Clubs.
Number awarded: Each year, more than $159,000 is awarded in scholarships.
Deadline: Each local club sets its own deadline. The district deadline is the end of June.

869
OREGON ASSOCIATION OF STUDENT COUNCILS SCHOLARSHIPS

Confederation of Oregon School Administrators
Attn: COSA Foundation
707 13th Street, S.E., Suite 100
Salem, OR 97301-4035
Phone: (503) 581-3141   Fax: (503) 581-9840
E-mail: nancy@oasc.org
Web Site: www.cosa.k12.or.us
Summary: To provide financial assistance to high school seniors in Oregon who are interested in attending a community college, college, or university in the state.
Eligibility: This program is open to graduating high school seniors in Oregon. Applicants should be interested in attending a community college, college, or

university in the state. They must have been active in community and school affairs, have at least a 3.5 grade point average, and enroll in the fall term after graduating from high school. Preference is given to students who have been involved in leadership and service. To apply, students must submit a completed application form, a 1-page autobiography (that states personal goals), the name of the school they plan to attend, and the endorsement of a member of the Confederation of Oregon School Administrators (COSA). Financial need is not considered in the selection process.

Financial data: The stipend is $1,000. Funds are paid directly to the recipient.

Duration: 1 year; nonrenewable.

Additional information: This program is offered through the Oregon Association of Student Councils.

Number awarded: 2 each year.

Deadline: February of each year.

870
OREGON DECEASED OR DISABLED PUBLIC SAFETY OFFICER GRANT PROGRAM

Oregon Student Assistance Commission
1500 Valley River Drive, Suite 100
Eugene, OR 97401-2130
Phone: (541) 687-7400   (800) 452-8807
Fax: (541) 687-7419   E-mail: awardinfo@mercury.osac.state.or.us
Web Site: www.ossc.state.or.us/disabled_officers.html

Summary: To provide financial assistance for college to the children of disabled or deceased Oregon peace officers.

Eligibility: This program is open to the natural, adopted, or stepchildren of Oregon public safety officers (fire fighters, State Fire Marshal, chief deputy fire marshal, deputy state fire marshals, police chiefs, police officers, sheriffs, deputy sheriffs, county adult parole and probation officers, correction officers, and investigators of the Criminal Justice Division of the Department of Justice) who, in the line of duty, were killed or disabled. Applicants must be enrolled or planning to enroll as a full-time undergraduate student at a public or private college or university in Oregon. Financial need must be demonstrated.

Financial data: At a public 2- or 4-year college or university, the amount of the award is equal to the sum of tuition and fees. At an eligible private college, the award amount is equal to the sum of tuition and fees charged to students attending the University of Oregon.

Duration: 1 year; may be renewed for up to 3 additional years, if the student maintains satisfactory academic progress and demonstrates continued financial need.

Number awarded: Varies each year.

871
OREGON DUNGENESS CRAB COMMISSION SCHOLARSHIP

Oregon Student Assistance Commission
Attn: Private Awards Grant Department
1500 Valley River Drive, Suite 100
Eugene, OR 97401-2146
Phone: (541) 687-7395   (800) 452-8807, ext. 7395
Fax: (541) 687-7419   E-mail: awardinfo@mercury.osac.state.or.us
Web Site: www.osac.state.or.us

Summary: To provide financial assistance for college to dependents of licensed Oregon Dungeness Crab fishermen or crew.

Eligibility: This program is open to seniors graduating from high schools in Oregon who are planning to attend college. Applicants must be dependents of licensed Oregon Dungeness Crab fishermen or crew.

Financial data: Scholarship amounts vary, depending upon the needs of the recipient.

Duration: 1 year; nonrenewable.

Number awarded: Varies each year.

Deadline: February of each year.

872
OREGON LEGION AUXILIARY DEPARTMENT SCHOLARSHIPS

American Legion Auxiliary
Attn: Department of Oregon
30450 S.W. Parkway Avenue
P.O. Box 1730
Wilsonville, OR 97070-1730
Phone: (503) 682-3162   Fax: (503) 685-5008

Summary: To provide financial assistance for postsecondary education to the dependents of Oregon veterans.

Eligibility: To be eligible for these scholarships, an applicant must be the wife of a veteran with a disability, the widow of a deceased veteran, or the child of a veteran or current military service member. Oregon residency is required. Selection is based on ability, aptitude, character, seriousness of purpose, and financial need.

Financial data: The scholarship is $1,000. It must be used for education other than high school: college, university, business school, vocational school, or any other accredited postsecondary school in the state of Oregon.

Duration: The awards are offered each year. They are nonrenewable.

Number awarded: 3 each year; 1 of these is to be used for vocational or business school.

Deadline: March of each year.

873
OREGON LEGION AUXILIARY NATIONAL PRESIDENT'S SCHOLARSHIP

American Legion Auxiliary
Attn: Department of Oregon
30450 S.W. Parkway Avenue
P.O. Box 1730
Wilsonville, OR 97070-1730
Phone: (503) 682-3162   Fax: (503) 685-5008

Summary: To provide financial assistance for postsecondary education to the children of war veterans in Oregon.

Eligibility: Applicants for this scholarship must be the children of veterans who served in World War I, World War II, Korea, Vietnam, Grenada, Lebanon, Panama, or the Persian Gulf. They must be high school seniors or graduates who have not yet attended an institution of higher learning. Selection is based on character, Americanism, leadership, scholarship, and financial need. The winner then competes for the American Legion Auxiliary National President's Scholarship. If the Oregon winner is not awarded a national scholarship, then he or she receives the first-place award and the second winner receives the second-place award; if the Oregon winner is also a national winner, then the second-place winner in Oregon receives the first-place award and the alternate receives the second-place award.

Financial data: The first-place award is $1,000 and the second-place award is $500.

Duration: The awards are offered each year. They are nonrenewable.

Additional information: The awards may be used at any college of the recipient's choice.

Number awarded: 2 each year.

Deadline: March of each year.

874
OREGON OCCUPATIONAL SAFETY AND HEALTH DIVISION WORKERS MEMORIAL SCHOLARSHIPS

Oregon Student Assistance Commission
Attn: Private Awards Grant Department
1500 Valley River Drive, Suite 100
Eugene, OR 97401-2146
Phone: (541) 687-7395   (800) 452-8807, ext. 7395
Fax: (541) 687-7419   E-mail: awardinfo@mercury.osac.state.or.us
Web Site: www.osac.state.or.us

Summary: To provide financial assistance for undergraduate or graduate education to the children and spouses of disabled or deceased workers in Oregon.

Eligibility: This program is open to residents of Oregon who are U.S. citizens or permanent residents. Applicants must be high school seniors or graduates who 1) are dependents or spouses of an Oregon worker who has suffered permanent total disability on the job; or 2) are receiving, or have received, fatality benefits as dependents or spouses of a worker fatally injured in Oregon. Selection is based on financial need and an essay of up to 500 words on "How has the injury or death of your parent or spouse affected or influenced your decision to further your education."

Financial data: Scholarship amounts vary, depending upon the needs of the recipient.

Duration: 1 year.

Number awarded: Varies each year.

Deadline: February of each year.

875
OREGON OPPORTUNITY GRANTS

Oregon Student Assistance Commission
1500 Valley River Drive, Suite 100
Eugene, OR 97401-2130
Phone: (541) 687-7400   (800) 452-8807
Fax: (541) 687-7419   E-mail: awardinfo@mercury.osac.state.or.us
Web Site: www.ossc.state.or.us/ong.html
Summary: To provide financial assistance for college to residents of Oregon who have financial need.
Eligibility: This program is open to residents of Oregon who are attending or planning to attend a nonprofit college or university in Oregon as a full-time student. Applicants must have an annual family income below specified levels; for dependent students, the maximum family income ranges from $26,580 for a household size of 2 to $55,110 for a household size of 9; for independent students, the maximum family income ranges from $7,400 for a household size of 1 to $35,960 for a household size of 8. Students who are working on a degree in theology, divinity, or religious education are not eligible.
Financial data: Awards depend on the need of the recipient. At public schools, the maximum annual award was $1,044 at a community college or $1,254 at an institution within the Oregon University system. Specific award amounts are established for each eligible private college or university within Oregon, ranging from $1,930 at Mount Angel Seminary to $4,380 at Reed College. Contact the sponsor for the amount of the supplemental awards available at other private institutions.
Duration: 1 year; may be renewed for up to 3 additional years, if the student maintains satisfactory academic progress and demonstrates continued financial need.
Additional information: This program was formerly known as Oregon Need Grants.
Number awarded: Varies each year.

876
OREGON SALMON COMMISSION SCHOLARSHIP

Oregon Student Assistance Commission
Attn: Private Awards Grant Department
1500 Valley River Drive, Suite 100
Eugene, OR 97401-2146
Phone: (541) 687-7395   (800) 452-8807, ext. 7395
Fax: (541) 687-7419   E-mail: awardinfo@mercury.osac.state.or.us
Web Site: www.osac.state.or.us
Summary: To provide financial assistance for college to dependents of licensed Oregon salmon fishermen.
Eligibility: This program is open to seniors graduating from high schools in Oregon who are planning to attend college. Applicants must be dependents of licensed Oregon salmon fishermen.
Financial data: Scholarship amounts vary, depending upon the needs of the recipient.
Duration: 1 year; nonrenewable.
Number awarded: Varies each year.
Deadline: February of each year.

877
OREGON STATE COUNCIL ENDOWMENT SCHOLARSHIPS

Epsilon Sigma Alpha
Attn: ESA Foundation Assistant Scholarship Director
P.O. Box 270517
Fort Collins, CO 80527
Phone: (970) 223-2824   Fax: (970) 223-4456
Web Site: www.esaintl.com/esaf
Summary: To provide financial assistance to students from Oregon studying any major in college.
Eligibility: This program is open to residents of Oregon who are either 1) graduating high school seniors in the top 25 percent of their class or with minimum scores of 20 on the ACT or 950 on the SAT, or 2) students already in college with a grade point average of 3.0 or higher. Students enrolled for training in a technical school or returning to school after an absence are also eligible. Selection is based on character, scholastic ability, leadership and ability skills, and financial need.
Financial data: The stipend is $1,000.
Duration: 1 year; may be renewed.

Additional information: Epsilon Sigma Alpha (ESA) is a women's service organization, but scholarships are available to both men and women. Recipients may major in any subject. Information is also available from Verneene Forssberg, 403 South High, Pratt, KS 67124, (316) 672-3636, Fax: (316) 672-3688, E-mail: vernf@genmail.pcc.cc.ks.us. Completed applications must be submitted to the ESA State Counselor who verifies the information before forwarding them to the scholarship director.
Number awarded: 3 each year.
Deadline: January of each year.

878
OREGON STATE FISCAL ASSOCIATION SCHOLARSHIP

Oregon Student Assistance Commission
Attn: Private Awards Grant Department
1500 Valley River Drive, Suite 100
Eugene, OR 97401-2146
Phone: (541) 687-7395   (800) 452-8807, ext. 7395
Fax: (541) 687-7419   E-mail: awardinfo@mercury.osac.state.or.us
Web Site: www.osac.state.or.us
Summary: To provide financial assistance for college to members of the Oregon State Fiscal Association and their children.
Eligibility: This program is open to members of the association and their children who are enrolled or planning to enroll at a college or university in Oregon as an undergraduate or graduate student. Members must study public administration, finance, economics, or related fields, but they may enroll part time. Children may pursue any program of study, but they must be full-time students.
Financial data: Scholarship amounts vary, depending upon the needs of the recipient.
Duration: 1 year.
Number awarded: Varies each year.
Deadline: February of each year.

879
OREGON TRAWL COMMISSION SCHOLARSHIP

Oregon Student Assistance Commission
Attn: Private Awards Grant Department
1500 Valley River Drive, Suite 100
Eugene, OR 97401-2146
Phone: (541) 687-7395   (800) 452-8807, ext. 7395
Fax: (541) 687-7419   E-mail: awardinfo@mercury.osac.state.or.us
Web Site: www.osac.state.or.us
Summary: To provide financial assistance for college to dependents of licensed Oregon Trawl fishermen or crew.
Eligibility: This program is open to residents of Oregon who are attending or planning to attend college. Applicants must be dependents of licensed Oregon Trawl fishermen or crew.
Financial data: Scholarship amounts vary, depending upon the needs of the recipient.
Duration: 1 year; nonrenewable.
Number awarded: Varies each year.
Deadline: February of each year.

880
OREGON TRUCKING ASSOCIATION SCHOLARSHIP

Oregon Student Assistance Commission
Attn: Private Awards Grant Department
1500 Valley River Drive, Suite 100
Eugene, OR 97401-2146
Phone: (541) 687-7395   (800) 452-8807, ext. 7395
Fax: (541) 687-7419   E-mail: awardinfo@mercury.osac.state.or.us
Web Site: www.osac.state.or.us
Summary: To provide financial assistance for college to children of members of the Oregon Trucking Association and their employees.
Eligibility: This program is open to graduating seniors at high schools in Oregon planning to attend college. Applicants must be the children of association members or children of employees (for at least 1 year) of members.
Financial data: Scholarship amounts vary, depending upon the needs of the recipient.
Duration: 1 year; nonrenewable.
Number awarded: Varies each year.
Deadline: February of each year.

Scholarship Listings

881
ORPHAN FOUNDATION OF AMERICA SCHOLARSHIPS

Orphan Foundation of America
Attn: Director of Student Services
Tall Oaks Village Center
12020-D North Shore Drive
Reston, VA 20190-4877
Phone: (571) 203-0270   (800) 950-4673
Fax: (571) 203-0273   E-mail: scholarships@orphan.org
Web Site: www.orphan.org
Summary: To provide financial assistance for postsecondary education to students currently or previously in foster care.
Eligibility: Applicants must have spent at least 12 months in foster care before their 18th birthday, not have been subsequently adopted, and currently be under 25 years of age. They must have been accepted into an accredited postsecondary school or program. First time applicants must include an essay entitled "Introducing Me," in which they describe their interests, career goals, what is important to them, how they spend their time, how foster care shaped their personality, work experience, community involvement, and any major challenges they have overcome and what they learned from them. Renewal applicants must write an essay on either 1) the difficulties they have encountered in school, and work, and in personal life, how they overcame them, and what they learned; or 2) how they want their life to be a year from now, including what they will have accomplished, where they will live, how they will spend their time, with whom they will spend their time, and how they are going about creating that life. In addition to those essays, selection is based on 2 letters of recommendation, transcripts, and financial need.
Financial data: Stipends range up to $10,000 per year. Recently, the average was more than $4,000.
Duration: 1 year; may be renewed if the recipient maintains at least a 2.0 grade point average and financial need.
Additional information: As part of this program, Casey Family Programs added its support in 2001.
Number awarded: Varies each year; recently, 293 applicants received aid, including 186 through the Casey Family Programs.
Deadline: April of each year.

882
OSAGE ACADEMIC SCHOLARSHIPS

Osage Tribal Education Department
Attn: Education Coordinator
1333 Grandview
Pawhuska, OK 74056
Phone: (918) 287-1038   (800) 390-6724
Fax: (918) 287-2416   E-mail: jhopper@mmind.net
Web Site: www.osagetribe.com/education.htm
Summary: To provide financial assistance for college to members of the Osage tribe.
Eligibility: This program is open to Osage Tribal students who are enrolled in or planning to enroll in a 2-year or 4-year college or university. Applicants must have earned a grade point average of 3.25 or higher during the preceding semester.
Financial data: The amount of the award depends on the availability of funds and the need of the recipient.
Duration: 1 semester; may be renewed.
Additional information: This program is funded by the Morris E. and Ethel Carlton Wheeter Scholarship Trust.
Number awarded: Varies each year.
Deadline: July of each year for fall semester; December of each year for spring semester.

883
OSAGE HIGHER EDUCATION GRANTS

Osage Tribal Education Department
Attn: Education Coordinator
1333 Grandview
Pawhuska, OK 74056
Phone: (918) 287-1038   (800) 390-6724
Fax: (918) 287-2416   E-mail: jhopper@mmind.net
Web Site: www.osagetribe.com/education.htm
Summary: To provide financial assistance for college to members of the Osage tribe.
Eligibility: This program is open to Osage Tribal students who are enrolled or planning to enroll in a 2-year or 4-year college or university.
Financial data: The amount of the award depends on the availability of funds and the need of the recipient.
Duration: 1 semester; may be renewed.
Number awarded: Varies each year.
Deadline: July of each year for fall semester; December of each year for spring semester; April of each year for summer term.

884
OSAGE TRIBAL EDUCATION COMMITTEE PROGRAM

Osage Tribal Education Committee
c/o Oklahoma Area Education Office
4149 Highline Boulevard, Suite 380
Oklahoma City, OK 73108
Phone: (405) 605-6051, ext. 300   Fax: (405) 605-6057
Summary: To provide financial assistance for postsecondary education to undergraduate and graduate Osage students.
Eligibility: This program is open to students enrolled in accredited postsecondary educational programs at the college, university, or technical/vocational level who can prove Osage Indian blood. Applicants may be candidates for an associate, baccalaureate, or graduate degree.
Financial data: The amount of the award depends on the financial need of the recipient.
Duration: 1 year; may be renewed for up to 4 additional years.
Number awarded: Varies each year.
Deadline: June of each year for fall term; December of each year for spring term; April of each year for summer school.

885
OSCAR AND MILDRED LARSON AWARD

Vasa Order of America
Attn: Vice Grand Master
1926 Rancho Andrew
Alpine, CA 91901
Phone: (619) 445-9707   Fax: (619) 445-7334
E-mail: drulf@connectnet.com
Web Site: www.vasaorder.com
Summary: To provide financial assistance for postsecondary education to students of Swedish heritage.
Eligibility: Applicants must be Swedish born or of Swedish ancestry; residents of the United States, Canada, or Sweden; and enrolled or accepted as full-time undergraduate or graduate students in an accredited 4-year college or university in the United States. Membership in Vasa Order of America is not required. Selection is based on a grade transcript, letters of recommendation from school and local Vasa lodge officials, and an essay of up to 1,000 words on a topic related to Vasa.
Financial data: The stipend is $4,000 per year.
Duration: 1 year; may be renewed up to 3 additional years for a total award of $16,000.
Additional information: Vasa Order of America is a Swedish American fraternal organization incorporated in 1899.
Number awarded: 1 each year.
Deadline: February of each year.

886
OTIS SPUNKMEYER STUDENT SCHOLARSHIPS

DECA
1908 Association Drive
Reston, VA 20191-1594
Phone: (703) 860-5000   Fax: (703) 860-4013
E-mail: decainc@aol.com
Web Site: www.deca.org/scholarships/index.html
Summary: To provide financial assistance for college to DECA members.
Eligibility: This program is open to DECA members who can demonstrate evidence of DECA participation, grades, leadership ability, and community service involvement. Awards are made on the basis of merit, not financial need.
Financial data: The stipend is $1,000.
Duration: 1 year.
Number awarded: 15 each year.
Deadline: February of each year.

887
PACE INTERNATIONAL UNION SCHOLARSHIP AWARDS PROGRAM

Paper, Allied-Industrial, Chemical and Energy Workers International Union
Attn: Scholarship Awards Program
P.O. Box 1475
Nashville, TN 37202
Phone: (615) 834-8590   Fax: (615) 834-7741
Web Site: www.paceunion.org
Summary: To provide financial assistance for postsecondary education to children of members of the Paper, Allied-Industrial, Chemical and Energy Workers (PACE) International Union
Eligibility: Applicants must be 1) high school seniors planning to attend a college or university and 2) children of active members in good standing with the union. Selection is based on scholastic achievement, character, and financial need.
Financial data: The stipend is $1,000; funds are paid directly to the college or university designated by the recipient.
Duration: 1 year.
Additional information: PACE was formed in 1999 as a result of the merger of the United Paperworkers International Union and the Oil, Chemical and Atomic Workers International Union.
Number awarded: 20 each year: 2 in each region of the union.
Deadline: March of each year.

888
PACERS TEAMUP SCHOLARSHIPS

Pacers Foundation, Inc.
Foundation Coordinator
125 South Pennsylvania Street
Indianapolis, IN 46204
Phone: (317) 917-2864   Fax: (317) 917-2599
E-mail: Foundation@pacers.com
Web Site: www.pacers.com
Summary: To provide financial assistance for college to high school seniors in Indiana who have made significant contributions to their community.
Eligibility: This program is open to high school seniors in Indiana who will be attending college and have proven records of community service. Interested students must write a 500-word essay on the importance of their community service activity to themselves and others, the societal need that it addresses, how their neighborhood or community has benefited, what they have learned from their community service experience, and how it will impact their future. Along with the essay, they must submit their high school transcript, their class rank and grade point average, and a letter of recommendation from a community leader with whom they have done service. All enclosures must be sent together and collated per set or their application will be automatically disqualified. Applicants are evaluated on their record of service to the community, on their letter of recommendation, and on their application essay.
Financial data: The stipend is $2,000. Funds are paid directly to the recipient's school.
Duration: 1 year; nonrenewable.
Additional information: Funds may be used at any accredited 4-year college or university, community college, or junior college.
Number awarded: 5 each year.
Deadline: February of each year.

889
PADGETT BUSINESS SERVICES SCHOLARSHIP PROGRAM

Padgett Business Services
c/o Linda Whitney
P.O. Box 860022
Shawnee Mission, KS 66286-0022
Phone: (913) 583-1925   (800) 723-4388
Summary: To provide financial assistance to high school seniors whose parents own and operate a small business.
Eligibility: Applicants must be 1) the dependent of a small business owner who employs fewer than 20 individuals, owns at least 10 percent of the stock or capital in the business, and is active in the day-to-day operations; and 2) a graduating high school senior planning to attend an accredited postsecondary institution. They may reside in the United States or Canada. Applications must be obtained from a local Padgett Business Service office (the phone number and address will be in the local telephone directory). Applicants must submit a completed questionnaire

and write a 100-word essay describing their education and career plans.
Financial data: The stipend is $500, except for the International Scholarship (1 awarded annually), which is $4,000.
Duration: 1 year.
Additional information: This program began in 1990. Since then, more than $400,000 has been awarded.
Deadline: February of each year.

890
PAGE EDUCATION FOUNDATION SCHOLARSHIPS

Page Education Foundation
P.O. Box 581254
Minneapolis, MN 55458-1254
Phone:(612) 332-0406   E-mail: pagemail@mtn.org
Web Site: www.page-ed.org
Summary: To provide funding for college to students of color in Minnesota.
Eligibility: This program is open to students of color who are graduating from high school and planning to attend a postsecondary school in Minnesota. Applicants must submit an essay of 400 to 500 words on the importance of education and community service. Selection is based on the essay, 3 letters of recommendation, and financial need.
Financial data: Stipends range from $750 to $2,000 per year.
Duration: 1 year; may be renewed up to 3 additional years.
Additional information: This program was founded by Alan Page, a former football player for the Minnesota Vikings. While attending college, the Page Scholars fulfill a service-to-children contract that brings them into contact with K-8 grade school students of color.
Number awarded: Nearly 100 each year; recently, 55 percent of the scholars were African American, 39 percent Asian American, 4 percent Hispanic American, and 2 percent Native American.
Deadline: April of each year.

891
PALMETTO FELLOWS SCHOLARSHIPS

South Carolina Commission on Higher Education
Attn: Director of Student Services
1333 Main Street, Suite 200
Columbia, SC 29201
Phone: (803) 737-2244   Fax: (803) 737-2297
E-mail: CFreeman@che400.state.sc.us
Web Site: www.che400.state.sc.us
Summary: To provide financial assistance for postsecondary education to high school seniors in South Carolina who have achieved a high score on a college entrance examination.
Eligibility: This program is open to high school seniors in South Carolina who 1) scored at least 1200 on the SAT or 27 on the ACT; 2) have a GPA of at least 3.5; and 3) rank in the top 5 percent of the class at the end of their junior year. Applicants must plan to attend a 4-year postsecondary institution in South Carolina during the fall immediately following their graduation. U.S. citizenship or permanent resident status is required.
Financial data: Up to $5,000 per year, half provided by the South Carolina Commission on Higher Education and half by the institution the student attends.
Duration: 1 year; may be renewed for 3 additional years.
Additional information: Applications are forwarded to principals at high schools attended by students who attain the qualifying examination scores.
Number awarded: Varies each year; recently, 876 of these scholarships were awarded.
Deadline: December of each year.

892
PALOMINO HORSE BREEDERS OF AMERICA YOUTH SCHOLARSHIP AND EDUCATIONAL FUND

Palomino Horse Breeders of America
Attn: Youth Scholarship and Educational Fund
15253 East Skelly Drive
Tulsa, OK 74116-2637
Phone: (918) 438-1234   Fax: (918) 438-1232
E-mail: yellahrses@aol.com
Web Site: www.palominohba.com/youthguidelines.htm
Summary: To provide financial assistance for college to youth members of the Palomino Horse Breeders of America (PHBA-Y).
Eligibility: This program is open to 1) high school seniors who have been a

member in good standing of the PHBA-Y during the previous 2 years and either rank in the upper 20 percent of their high school graduating class or achieved a rank above the 80th percentile on a national college entrance examination; and 2) full-time students who have completed at least 1 semester of college and are younger than 21 years of age. Applicants must submit information on their personal achievements and contributions toward the betterment of PHBA-Y and PHBA, extracurricular activities (including, but not limited to, student government, 4-H, FFA, sports, and community service), any honors or awards received, and their need for financial aid.

Financial data: The amount of the stipend varies each year.

Duration: 1 year; may be renewed if the recipient maintains a grade point average of 2.5 or higher.

Number awarded: Varies each year.

Deadline: January of each year.

893
PAPA JOHN'S SCHOLARSHIPS

Papa John's International, Inc.
Attn: Scholarship Program
2002 Papa John's Boulevard
Louisville, KY 40299
Phone: (502) 261-7272   (800) 865-9373
E-mail: scholarmail@aol.com
Web Site: www.papajohns.com

Summary: To provide financial assistance for college to high school seniors at selected U.S. high schools.

Eligibility: This program is open to graduating seniors at approximately 3,000 high schools in the United States.

Financial data: Most scholarships are for $1,000, although some are as high as $2,500 and 1 is for $10,000.

Duration: 1 year; recipients may reapply for 1 additional year.

Additional information: Approximately half of the 2,509 Papa John's restaurants participate in this program. Each works with a local high school and all information must come from that high school.

Number awarded: Approximately 1,300 of these scholarships are awarded each year.

894
PARKING INDUSTRY INSTITUTE SCHOLARSHIPS

Parking Industry Institute
1112 16th Street, N.W., Suite 300
Washington, DC 20036
Phone: (202) 296-4336   (800) 647-PARK
Fax: (202) 331-8523

Summary: To provide financial assistance for college to employees or the dependents of employees working for a firm that is a member of the National Parking Association.

Eligibility: This program is open to 1) the children and spouses of full-time employees (employed at least 3 years) of a firm that is a member of the National Parking Association; and 2) full-time and part-time employees (employed at least 1 year) of a firm that is a member of the National Parking Association. A personal interview may be required. Selection is based on merit, scholastic and extracurricular achievements, character, and financial need.

Financial data: Stipends range from $250 to $2,500 per year. Recipients whose computed financial need is greater than the scholarship maximum are permitted to accept additional funds equal to the amount that the need exceeds $2,000. For other students, additional monetary awards accepted above $500 per year reduces the Parking Industry Institute Scholarship amount accordingly (but not below $250). Funds are sent directly to the recipient's school.

Duration: 1 year; applicants may reapply.

Additional information: The Parking Industry Institute is a foundation of the National Parking Association.

Deadline: February of each year.

895
PASF GRANTS

Portuguese-American Scholarship Foundation
Attn: Scholarship Committee Chair
88 Ferry Street
Newark, NJ 07105
E-mail: pasf@vivaportugal.com
Web Site: www.vivaportugal.com/nj/org/pasf/index.htm

Summary: To provide financial assistance for college to New Jersey residents of Portuguese ancestry.

Eligibility: This program is open to New Jersey high school seniors who are Portuguese born or whose parent or grandparent was Portuguese born (proof may be required). Applicants must be U.S. citizens or permanent residents (Alien Registration Card may be required) and have been continuous residents of New Jersey for the 12-month period immediately preceding receipt of the award. They must have at least a 3.0 grade point average and be applying for admission to a 4-year college or university. Financial need must be demonstrated.

Financial data: The stipend is at least $1,000.

Duration: 1 year; may be renewed for up to 3 additional years.

Number awarded: Varies each year; recently, 10 were awarded.

Deadline: February of each year.

896
PATRICIA AND GAIL ISHIMOTO MEMORIAL SCHOLARSHIP

Japanese American Citizens League
Attn: National Scholarship Awards
1765 Sutter Street
San Francisco, CA 94115
Phone: (415) 921-5225   Fax: (415) 931-4671
E-mail: jacl@jacl.org
Web Site: www.jacl.org

Summary: To provide financial assistance to student members of the Japanese American Citizens League (JACL) who are high school seniors interested in pursuing undergraduate education.

Eligibility: This program is open to JACL members who are high school seniors interested in attending a college, university, trade school, business college, or other institution of higher learning. Selection is based on academic record, extracurricular activities, and community involvement.

Financial data: The stipend depends on the availability of funds but usually ranges from $1,000 to $5,000.

Duration: 1 year.

Additional information: Requests for applications must be accompanied by a self-addressed stamped envelope.

Number awarded: At least 1 each year.

Deadline: March of each year.

897
PATTY & MELVIN ALPERIN FIRST GENERATION/DAVID M. GOLDEN MEMORIAL SCHOLARSHIPS

Rhode Island Foundation
Attn: Scholarship Coordinator
One Union Station
Providence, RI 02903
Phone: (401) 274-4564   Fax: (401) 331-8085
E-mail: libbym@rifoundation.org
Web Site: www.rifoundation.org

Summary: To provide financial assistance for college to students in Rhode Island whose parents did not attend college.

Eligibility: This program is open to college-bound Rhode Island high school seniors and graduates whose parents did not have the benefit of attending college. Applicants must intend to pursue either a 2-year degree at an accredited nonprofit postsecondary institution or a 4-year college degree. Along with their application, they must submit an essay (up to 300 words) on what it means to them to be of the first generation in their family to pursue a college education. Selection is based on academic excellence, character, and financial need.

Financial data: The stipend is $1,000.

Duration: 1 year; may be renewed for up to 3 additional years if the recipient maintains good academic standing.

Number awarded: 2 or 3 each year.

Deadline: May of each year.

898
PAUL H. D'AMOUR FOUNDER'S FELLOWSHIPS

Big Y Foods, Inc.
Attn: Scholarship Committee
P.O. Box 7840
Springfield, MA 01102-7840
Phone: (413) 504-4062
Web Site: www.bigy.com

Summary: To provide financial assistance to outstanding undergraduate and graduate students in the Big Y Foods market area (Massachusetts and Connecticut).

Eligibility: This program is open to high school seniors, college students, and graduate students of any age who reside within western and central Massachusetts or the state of Connecticut. Big Y employees and their dependents are also eligible to apply. Applicants must submit a transcript, standardized test scores, 2 letters of recommendation, and a completed application form.

Financial data: The stipend is $2,000.

Duration: 1 year; nonrenewable.

Additional information: This program was established in 1981.

Number awarded: 5 each year.

Deadline: January of each year.

899
PAUL JENNINGS SCHOLARSHIP

International Union of Electronic, Electrical, Salaried, Machine, and Furniture Workers
Attn: Department of Social Action
1275 K Street, N.W., Suite 600
Washington, DC 20005
Phone: (202) 513-6300   Fax: (202) 513-6357
E-mail: Humphrey@cwa-union.org
Web Site: www.iue-cwa.org

Summary: To provide financial assistance for undergraduate education to the children of officials of the International Union of Electronic, Electrical, Salaried, Machine, and Furniture Workers (IUE).

Eligibility: This program is open to children of local union elected officials. They must be accepted for admission or already enrolled as full-time students at an accredited college, university, nursing school, or technical school offering college credit courses. Families of full-time international union officers or employees are not eligible to apply. Selection is based on academic record, leadership ability, ambition, good character, commitment to equality, service to the community, and a concern for improving the quality of life for all people.

Financial data: The stipend is $3,000 per year.

Duration: 1 year.

Additional information: Winners who are also awarded local, district, or division scholarships have the option of either accepting the Paul Jennings Scholarship or the other awards and the dollar difference (if any) between the Jennings Scholarship and the local, district, or division award.

Number awarded: 1 each year.

Deadline: April of each year.

900
PAUL R. KACH, 33 DEMOLAY ESSAY COMPETITION

Ancient Accepted Scottish Rite of Freemasonry, Southern Jurisdiction
Supreme Council, 33
Attn: Director of Education
1733 16th Street, N.W.
Washington, DC 20009-3199
Phone: (202) 232-3579   Fax: (202) 387-1843
E-mail: grndexec@srmason-sj.org
Web Site: www.srmason-sj.org

Summary: To recognize and reward members of the Order of DeMolay who submit outstanding essays in a competition.

Eligibility: This program is open to active DeMolays in 2 categories: grades 11 and above and grades 10 and below. Entrants must submit an essay of 1,000 to 1,500 words on a topic that changes annually; a recent topic was "Violence in Schools." Essays are first submitted to a regional competition and regional winners are entered in the national competition. The content of the essay is the primary concern in the judging, but grammar and spelling are also considered.

Financial data: National winners receive $1,500; regional winners receive $300.

Duration: The competition is held annually.

Number awarded: In each of the 2 categories, 1 national winner and 8 regional winners are selected.

Deadline: January of each year.

901
PAUL TSONGAS SCHOLARSHIP PROGRAM

Massachusetts Office of Student Financial Assistance
454 Broadway, Suite 200
Revere, MA 02151
Phone: (617) 727-9420   Fax: (617) 727-0667
E-mail: osfa@osfa.mass.edu
Web Site: www.osfa.mass.edu/osfaprograms/paultsongas.asp

Summary: To provide financial assistance to Massachusetts students who attend 1 of the state colleges in Massachusetts.

Eligibility: This program is open to residents of Massachusetts who have graduated from high school within 3 years and are attending or planning to attend a state college in Massachusetts. Applicants must be U.S. citizens or permanent residents and have at least a 3.75 grade point average and 1200 SAT score.

Financial data: Eligible students receive a waiver of tuition and mandatory fees.

Duration: Up to 4 academic years, if the recipient maintains at least a 3.3 grade point average in college.

Number awarded: 45 each year: 5 at each state college in Massachusetts.

902
PEARL HARBOR SURVIVORS ASSOCIATION SCHOLARSHIPS

Pearl Harbor Survivors Association
c/o John E. Baskette, Chair, Scholarship Committee
559 Shelton Drive
Hollister, MO 65672
Phone: (417) 334-8506

Summary: To provide financial assistance for college to descendents of members of the Pearl Harbor Survivors Association (PHSA).

Eligibility: This program is open to the direct, adopted, and step-descendents of PHSA members or deceased members who are U.S. citizens and either high school seniors or currently enrolled in college. Along with their application, they must submit an essay of 250 words or less on their future goals and how higher education will help attain those goals, and an essay of up to 500 words on a topic that changes annually.

Financial data: The stipend is $1,500 per year for students in a college or university or $1,000 per year for students in a technical or trade school.

Duration: 1 year.

Number awarded: 4 each year: 2 to university and college students and 2 to technical and trade school students.

Deadline: July of each year.

903
PELLEGRINI SCHOLARSHIP FUND

Swiss Benevolent Society of New York
Attn: Scholarship Fund
608 Fifth Avenue, Suite 309
New York, NY 10020-2303
Phone: (212) 246-0655   Fax: (212) 246-1366
E-mail: info@swissbenevolentny.com
Web Site: www.swissbenevolentny.com/scholarships.htm

Summary: To provide financial assistance to undergraduate and graduate students of Swiss descent in the northeast.

Eligibility: Eligible to apply are undergraduate and graduate students who are residents of Connecticut, New Jersey, Pennsylvania, Delaware, or New York. Applicants must demonstrate a strong academic record (at least a 3.0 grade point average), aptitude in their chosen field of study, and financial need. Either the applicant or at least 1 parent must be a Swiss citizen.

Financial data: The stipend ranges from $500 to $4,000 per year. Funds are paid directly to the recipient's school in 2 installments (beginning of fall semester and beginning of spring semester).

Duration: 1 year; recipients may reapply.

Number awarded: Approximately 55 each year.

Deadline: March of each year.

904
PENNSYLVANIA EDUCATIONAL GRATUITY FOR VETERANS' DEPENDENTS

Bureau for Veterans Affairs
Fort Indiantown Gap
Annville, PA 17003-5002
Phone: (717) 865-8910   (800) 54 PA VET (within PA)
Fax: (717) 865-8589   E-mail: chengeveld@state.pa.us
Web Site: sites.state.pa.us/PA_Exec/Military_Affiars/va/benefits.htm
Summary: To provide financial assistance for postsecondary education to the children of disabled or deceased Pennsylvania veterans.
Eligibility: Children of honorably discharged veterans who are rated totally and permanently disabled as a result of wartime service or who have died of such a disability are eligible if they are between 16 and 23 years of age, have lived in Pennsylvania for at least 5 years immediately preceding the date of application, can demonstrate financial need, and have been accepted or are currently enrolled in a Pennsylvania state or state-aided secondary or postsecondary educational institution.
Financial data: The stipend is $500 per semester. The money is paid directly to the recipient's school and is to be applied to the costs of tuition, board, room, books, supplies, and/or matriculation fees.
Duration: The allowance is paid for up to 4 academic years or for the duration of the course of study, whichever is less.
Number awarded: Varies each year.

905
PENNSYLVANIA GRANTS FOR POW/MIA DEPENDENTS

Pennsylvania Higher Education Assistance Agency
Attn: State Grant and Special Programs Division
1200 North Seventh Street
P.O. Box 8114
Harrisburg, PA 17105-8114
Phone: (717) 720-2800   (800) 692-7392
Phone: TDD: (717) 720-2366   E-mail: info@pheaa.org
Web Site: www.pheaa.org
Summary: To provide financial assistance for the postsecondary education of the children of POWs/MIAs from Pennsylvania.
Eligibility: This program is open to dependent children of members or former members of the U.S. armed services who served on active duty after January 31, 1955, who are or have been prisoners of war or are or have been listed as missing in action, and who were residents of Pennsylvania for at least 12 months preceding service on active duty. Eligible children must be enrolled in a program of at least 1 year in duration on at least a half-time basis at an approved school and must demonstrate financial need.
Financial data: The amount of the award depends on the financial need of the recipient, up to a maximum of $3,300 at a Pennsylvania school or $800 at a school outside of Pennsylvania that is approved for participation in the program.
Duration: 1 year; may be renewed for 3 additional years.
Additional information: With certain exceptions, recipients may attend any accredited college in the United States. Excluded from coverage are 2-year public colleges located outside Pennsylvania and schools in states bordering on Pennsylvania that do not allow their state grant recipients to attend Pennsylvania schools (i.e., New York, Maryland, and New Jersey).
Number awarded: Varies each year.
Deadline: April of each year for renewal applicants and any nonrenewals who will enroll in a baccalaureate degree program; July of each year for nonrenewals who will enroll in a 2-year or 3-year terminal program.

906
PENNSYLVANIA GRANTS FOR VETERANS

Pennsylvania Higher Education Assistance Agency
Attn: State Grant and Special Programs Division
1200 North Seventh Street
P.O. Box 8114
Harrisburg, PA 17105-8114
Phone: (717) 720-2800   (800) 692-7392
Phone: TDD: (717) 720-2366   E-mail: info@pheaa.org
Web Site: www.pheaa.org
Summary: To provide financial assistance for the postsecondary education of Pennsylvania veterans.
Eligibility: This program is open to veterans who served on active duty with the U.S. armed services (or were a cadet or midshipman at a service academy), were

released or discharged under conditions other than dishonorable, have resided in Pennsylvania for at least 12 months immediately preceding the date of application, graduated from high school, and are enrolled on at least a half-time basis in an approved program of study that is at least 2 academic years in length. First priority is given to veterans who have separated from active duty after January 1 of the current year. All veterans are considered without regard to the financial status of their parents.
Financial data: The amount of the award depends on the financial need of the recipient, up to a maximum of $3,300 at a Pennsylvania school or $800 at a school outside of Pennsylvania that is approved for participation in the program.
Duration: 1 year; may be renewed for 3 additional years.
Additional information: With certain exceptions, recipients may attend any accredited college in the United States. Excluded from coverage are 2-year public colleges located outside Pennsylvania and schools in states bordering on Pennsylvania that do not allow their state grant recipients to attend Pennsylvania schools (i.e., New York, Maryland, and New Jersey).
Number awarded: Varies each year.
Deadline: April of each year for renewal applicants and any nonrenewals who will enroll in a baccalaureate degree program; July of each year for nonrenewals who will enroll in a 2-year or 3-year terminal program.

907
PENNSYLVANIA KNIGHTS TEMPLAR EDUCATIONAL FOUNDATION SCHOLARSHIPS

Pennsylvania Youth Foundation
Attn: Educational Endowment Fund
1244 Bainbridge Road
Elizabethtown, PA 17022-9423
Phone: (717) 367-1536   (800) 266-8424 (within PA)
E-mail: pyf@pagrandlodge.org
Web Site: www.pagrandlodge.org/pyf/scholar/index.html
Summary: To provide financial assistance for college to residents of Pennsylvania.
Eligibility: This program is open to residents of Pennsylvania who are pursuing a 2-year college, 4-year college, or graduate degree. Applicants are considered without regard to age, race, religion, national origin, sex, or Masonic ties or affiliations.
Financial data: The stipend varies.
Duration: 1 year.
Additional information: Further information is also available from Knights Templar Educational Foundation, Office of Walter Pearce, Eminent Grand Recorder, Masonic Temple, One North Broad Street, Philadelphia, PA 19107-2598, (215) 567-5936.
Number awarded: 1 or more each year.
Deadline: March of each year.

908
PENNSYLVANIA POSTSECONDARY EDUCATIONAL GRATUITY PROGRAM

Pennsylvania Higher Education Assistance Agency
Attn: State Grant and Special Programs Division
1200 North Seventh Street
P.O. Box 8114
Harrisburg, PA 17105-8114
Phone: (717) 720-2800   (800) 692-7392
Phone: TDD: (717) 720-2366   E-mail: info@pheaa.org
Web Site: www.pheaa.org
Summary: To provide financial assistance for postsecondary education to the children of Pennsylvania public service personnel who died in the line of service.
Eligibility: This program is open to residents of Pennsylvania who are the children of Pennsylvania police officers, fire fighters, rescue and ambulance squad members, correction employees, and National Guard members who died in the line of duty after January 1, 1976. Applicants must be 25 years of age or younger and enrolled or accepted at a Pennsylvania community college, state-owned institution, or state-related institution as a full-time student pursuing undergraduate studies that will lead to an associate or baccalaureate degree. They must have already applied for other scholarships, including state and federal grants and financial aid from the postsecondary institution to which they are applying.
Financial data: Grants provide waiver of tuition, fees, room, and board charged by the institution, less awarded scholarships and federal and state grants.
Duration: Up to 5 years.

Additional information: This program began in the 1998-99 winter/spring term.
Number awarded: Varies each year.
Deadline: March of each year.

909
PENNSYLVANIA RAINBOW SCHOLARSHIP

Pennsylvania Youth Foundation
Attn: Educational Endowment Fund
1244 Bainbridge Road
Elizabethtown, PA 17022-9423
Phone: (717) 367-1536   (800) 266-8424 (within PA)
E-mail: pyf@pagrandlodge.org
Web Site: www.pagrandlodge.org/pyf/scholar/index.html
Summary: To provide financial assistance for college to members of Rainbow Girls in Pennsylvania.
Eligibility: This program is open to active Pennsylvania Rainbow Girls in good standing. Applicants must have completed at least 1 year in an accredited college, university, or nursing school.
Financial data: The stipend depends on the availability of funds.
Duration: 1 year; may be renewed.
Additional information: Information is also available from Eva Gresko, RD #3, Box 102, Huntington, PA 16652-8703, (814) 658-3774.
Number awarded: Varies each year, depending on the availability of funds.
Deadline: Requests for applications must be submitted by January of each year. Completed applications are due by the end of February.

910
PENNSYLVANIA STATE GRANTS

Pennsylvania Higher Education Assistance Agency
Attn: State Grant and Special Programs Division
1200 North Seventh Street
P.O. Box 8114
Harrisburg, PA 17105-8114
Phone: (717) 720-2800   (800) 692-7392
Phone: TDD: (717) 720-2366   E-mail: info@pheaa.org
Web Site: www.pheaa.org
Summary: To provide financial assistance for postsecondary education to students in Pennsylvania who have financial need.
Eligibility: Seniors graduating from high schools in Pennsylvania are eligible to apply for these grants if they meet financial need requirements and plan to attend a postsecondary school in Pennsylvania on at least a half-time basis. They may also attend accredited colleges in other states, except those states that border Pennsylvania and do not allow their grant recipients to attend Pennsylvania schools (i.e., Maryland, New Jersey, and New York).
Financial data: Grants depend on financial need and the type of school attended. Recently, full-time students received up to $3,300 per year at Pennsylvania schools and up to $600 per year at schools located outside of Pennsylvania; half-time students received up to $1,650 per year at Pennsylvania schools and up to $300 per year at schools located outside of Pennsylvania.
Duration: 1 year; may be renewed for 3 additional years.
Number awarded: Varies each year.
Deadline: April of each year for renewal applicants, new applicants who plan to enroll in a baccalaureate degree program, and new applicants to college transfer programs at 2-year public or junior colleges; July of each year for first-time applicants for business, trade, or technical schools, hospital schools of nursing, or 2-year terminal programs at community, junior, or 4-year colleges.

911
PEOPLES PROMISE SCHOLARSHIP PROGRAM

Maine Education Services
Attn: MES Foundation
One City Center, 11th Floor
Portland, ME 04101
Phone: (800) 922-6352   E-mail: info@mesfoundation.com
Web Site: www.mesfoundation.com/sch_applications/default.asp
Summary: To provide financial assistance for college and work experience to high school seniors in Maine.
Eligibility: This program is open to seniors at high schools in Maine who plan to pursue a postsecondary education. Selection is based on academic achievement, involvement in school activities, community volunteer activity, work experience, and financial need.

Financial data: The stipend is $2,500.
Duration: 1 year.
Additional information: Each scholarship recipient is also offered a 3-month paid internship with Peoples Heritage Bank during the summer after their first year of college.
Number awarded: 10 each year.
Deadline: April of each year.

912
PETER CONNACHER MEMORIAL TRUST FUND

Oregon Student Assistance Commission
Attn: Private Awards Grant Department
1500 Valley River Drive, Suite 100
Eugene, OR 97401-2146
Phone: (541) 687-7395   (800) 452-8807, ext. 7395
Fax: (541) 687-7419   E-mail: awardinfo@mercury.osac.state.or.us
Web Site: www.osac.state.or.us
Summary: To provide financial assistance for college to ex-prisoners of war and their descendants.
Eligibility: Applicants must be American citizens who 1) were military or civilian prisoners of war or 2) are the descendants of ex-prisoners of war. They may be undergraduate or graduate students. A copy of the ex-prisoner of war's discharge papers from the U.S. armed forces must accompany the application. In addition, written proof of POW status must be submitted, along with a statement of the relationship between the applicant and the ex-prisoner of war (father, grandfather, etc.). Selection is based on academic record and financial need. Preference is given to Oregon residents or their dependents.
Financial data: The scholarship amount is set by the commission and cannot exceed the amount of the annual tuition, required fees, and books/supplies at an institution in the Oregon State System of Higher Education. Funds are sent directly to the recipient's school.
Duration: 1 year; may be renewed for up to 3 additional years for undergraduate students or 2 additional years for graduate students. Renewal is dependent on evidence of continued financial need and satisfactory academic progress.
Additional information: Funds for this program are provided by the Columbia River Chapter of the American Ex-prisoners of War, Inc. Recipients must attend college on a full-time basis.
Number awarded: Varies each year.
Deadline: February of each year.

913
PETER CROSSLEY MEMORIAL SCHOLARSHIP

Oregon Student Assistance Commission
Attn: Private Awards Grant Department
1500 Valley River Drive, Suite 100
Eugene, OR 97401-2146
Phone: (541) 687-7395   (800) 452-8807, ext. 7395
Fax: (541) 687-7419   E-mail: awardinfo@mercury.osac.state.or.us
Web Site: www.osac.state.or.us
Summary: To provide financial assistance for college to seniors graduating from public alternative high schools in Oregon.
Eligibility: This program is open to seniors graduating from public alternative high schools in Oregon. Applicants must submit an essay on "How I Faced Challenges and Overcame Obstacles to Graduate from High School."
Financial data: Scholarship amounts vary, depending upon the needs of the recipient.
Duration: 1 year.
Number awarded: Varies each year.
Deadline: February of each year.

914
PETER DOCTOR MEMORIAL IROQUOIS INDIAN EMLEN AWARDS

Peter Doctor Memorial Iroquois Indian Scholarship Foundation, Inc.
P.O. Box 731
Basom, NY 14013
Phone: (716) 542-2025
Summary: To provide financial assistance to undergraduate or graduate students of New York Iroquois descent.
Eligibility: This program is open to undergraduate or graduate students who are of Iroquois Indian descent (i.e., a parent or grandparent must be enrolled).

Applicants must have completed at least 1 year in a technical school, college, or university. Interviews may be required. Selection is based on need.

Financial data: Stipends range up to $2,000.

Duration: 2 years for medical students; 1 year for all other recipients.

Deadline: May of each year.

915
PETER DOCTOR MEMORIAL IROQUOIS INDIAN SCHOLARSHIP GRANTS

Peter Doctor Memorial Iroquois Indian Scholarship Foundation, Inc.
P.O. Box 731
Basom, NY 14013
Phone: (716) 542-2025

Summary: To provide financial assistance to New York Iroquois Indians currently enrolled in college on the undergraduate or graduate school level.

Eligibility: This program is open to enrolled New York Iroquois Indian students who have completed at least 1 year in a technical school, college, or university. Both undergraduate and graduate students are eligible. There is no age limit or grade point average requirement. Interviews may be required. Applicants must have tribal certification. Selection is based on need.

Financial data: Stipends range up to $1,500.

Duration: 2 years for medical students; 1 year for all other recipients.

Deadline: May of each year.

916
PFIZER EPILEPSY SCHOLARSHIP AWARD

Pfizer Inc.
c/o IntraMed Educational Group
230 Park Avenue, 10th Floor
New York, NY 10003
Phone: (800) AWARD-PF   E-mail: info@epilepsy-scholarship.org
Web Site: www.epilepsy-scholarship.org

Summary: To provide financial assistance for postsecondary education to students with epilepsy.

Eligibility: Applicants must be under a physician's care for epilepsy (and taking prescribed medication) and must submit an application with 2 letters of recommendation (1 from the physician) and verification of academic status. They must be high school seniors entering college in the fall; college freshmen, sophomores, or juniors continuing in the fall; or college seniors planning to enter graduate school in the fall. Selection is based on demonstrated achievement in academic and extracurricular activities; financial need is not considered.

Financial data: The stipend is $3,000.

Duration: 1 year; nonrenewable.

Number awarded: 16 each year.

Deadline: February of each year.

917
PGA OF AMERICA SPONSORED SCHOLARSHIPS

National Minority Junior Golf Scholarship Association
Attn: Scholarship Committee
1140 East Washington Street, Suite 102
Phoenix, AZ 85034-1051
Phone: (602) 258-7851   Fax: (602) 258-3412
Web Site: www.nmgf.org

Summary: To provide financial assistance for college to minority high school seniors who excel at golf.

Eligibility: Eligible to apply for this award are minority high school seniors who are interested in attending college. Applicants are asked to write a 500-word essay on this question: "One of the principal goals of education and golf is fostering ways for people to respect and get along with individuals who think, dress, look, and act differently. How might you make this goal a reality?" Selection is based on academic record, personal recommendations, participation in golf, school and community activities (including employment, extracurricular activities, and other responsibilities), and financial need.

Financial data: The stipend is $2,000 per year. Funds are paid directly to the recipient's college.

Duration: 4 years.

Additional information: This program is cosponsored by the association and the PGA of America.

Number awarded: 5 each year.

918
PGE—ENRON FOUNDATION SCHOLARSHIP AWARD FOR INDEPENDENT COLLEGES

Oregon Independent College Foundation
121 S.W. Salmon Street, Suite 1230
Portland, OR 97204
Phone: (503) 227-7568   Fax: (503) 227-2454
E-mail: danaoicf@teleport.com

Summary: To provide financial assistance to high school seniors planning to study at an independent college in Oregon.

Eligibility: This program is open to Oregon high school seniors who plan to enroll full time as first-year students at a college or university that is a member of the Oregon Independent College Foundation (OICF). Selection is based on academic record in high school, achievements in school or community activities, and a written statement, up to 500 words, on the meaning of good citizenship and how the fulfillment of their personal goals will help applicants live up to that definition.

Financial data: The stipend is $2,500 per year.

Duration: 4 years for entering freshmen.

Additional information: The OICF member institutions are Marylhurst University, Lewis and Clark College, Pacific University, Warner Pacific College, the University of Portland, George Fox College, Linfield College, Reed College, Concordia College, and Willamette University. Funding for this program is provided by the PGE—Enron Foundation.

Number awarded: 38 each year: 4 at 9 of the participating institutions and 2 at the tenth (Concordia).

Deadline: March of each year.

919
PHI ETA SIGMA HONOR SOCIETY DISTINGUISHED MEMBER ENDOWED SCHOLARSHIPS

Phi Eta Sigma
c/o John F. Sagabiel
Western Kentucky University
525 Grise Hall
1 Big Red Way
Bowling Green, KY 42101

Summary: To provide financial assistance for college to members of Phi Eta Sigma Honor Society.

Eligibility: Members of the honor society who are enrolled full time in an undergraduate course of study are eligible to apply for this scholarship. To apply, eligible students must submit 3 copies of the application form, 3 official current transcripts, a photograph, and 3 copies each of up to 3 letters of recommendation. Selection is based on grade point average (applicants must have at least a 3.5), participation in Phi Eta Sigma chapter activities, creative ability, participation in service and leadership groups, potential for success in their chosen field, academic recognition and awards, work experience, and letters of recommendation.

Financial data: The stipend is $5,000.

Duration: 1 year.

Additional information: Many local chapters also award scholarships. Recipients must attend school on a full-time basis.

Number awarded: 29 each year.

Deadline: February of each year.

920
PHI ETA SIGMA HONOR SOCIETY UNDERGRADUATE SCHOLARSHIPS

Phi Eta Sigma
c/o John F. Sagabiel
Western Kentucky University
525 Grise Hall
1 Big Red Way
Bowling Green, KY 42101

Summary: To provide financial assistance for college to members of Phi Eta Sigma Honor Society.

Eligibility: Members of the honor society who are enrolled full time in an undergraduate course of study are eligible to apply for this scholarship. To apply, eligible students must submit 3 copies of the application form, 3 official current transcripts, a photograph, and 3 copies each of up to 3 letters of recommendation. Selection is based on grade point average (applicants must have at least a 3.5), participation in Phi Eta Sigma chapter activities, creative ability, participation in service and leadership groups, potential for success in their chosen field, academic

recognition and awards, work experience, and letters of recommendation.
Financial data: The stipend is $1,000.
Duration: 1 year.
Additional information: Many local chapters also award scholarships. Recipients must attend school on a full-time basis.
Number awarded: 90 each year.
Deadline: February of each year.

921
PHI THETA KAPPA SCHOLARSHIP PROGRAM

Phi Theta Kappa
Attn: Scholarship Department
1625 Eastover Drive
P.O. Box 13729
Jackson, MS 39236-3729
Phone: (601) 957-2241, ext. 560   (800) 946-9995, ext. 560
Fax: (601) 957-2312   E-mail: scholarship.programs@ptk.org
Web Site: www.ptk.org
Summary: To provide financial assistance for college to members of Phi Theta Kappa.
Eligibility: Members of Phi Theta Kappa, the international honor society of 2-year colleges, may apply for these scholarships if they wish to transfer to 4-year or senior-level institutions. Scholarships are funded by participating universities, which also establish the specific requirements for their institutions.
Financial data: The amounts and terms of the awards are established by the senior institutions; more than $22 million in awards are available each year.
Duration: Varies at each institution.
Additional information: For a listing of all participating universities and information on the scholarships they offer, write to Phi Theta Kappa.
Number awarded: More than 530 institutions in 48 states, the District of Columbia, and Canada offer scholarships to Phi Theta Kappa members.
Deadline: Deadlines are established by participating institutions.

922
PINE TREE STATE 4-H FOUNDATION POSTSECONDARY EDUCATION SCHOLARSHIPS

Pine Tree State 4-H Foundation
c/o University of Maine
5741 Libby Hall
Orono, ME 04469-5741
Phone: (207) 581-3739   Fax: (207) 581-3212
E-mail: brendaz@umext.maine.edu
Web Site: www.umaine/edu.4hfoundation
Summary: To provide financial assistance to 4-H members in Maine who are interested in attending college.
Eligibility: This program is open to 1) seniors who are graduating from a Maine high school, and 2) residents of Maine who have graduated from high school but have delayed going to college for no more than 1 year. Applicants must be involved in 4-H activities. Selection is based primarily on academic achievement and 4-H activities; financial need is not considered.
Financial data: The stipend is $1,000.
Duration: 1 year; nonrenewable.
Additional information: This program includes the following named scholarships: the Parker—Lovejoy Scholarship, the Claude C. Clement Scholarship, the Verna Church Witter Scholarship, and the Evelyn L. Trotzy Scholarship.
Number awarded: 4 each year.
Deadline: March of each year.

923
POLICE CORPS

Department of Justice
Office of Justice Programs
Attn: Office of the Police Corps and Law Enforcement Education
810 Seventh Street, N.W.
Washington, DC 20531
Phone: (800) 421-6770
Web Site: www.ojp.usdoj.gov/opclee/about.htm
Summary: To provide financial assistance to undergraduate and graduate students willing to serve as police officers for at least 4 years.
Eligibility: To be eligible for this program, a student must attend (or be about to attend) a public or nonprofit 4-year college or university. Undergraduate students must attend full time. Students who attend community college are eligible once

they transfer to a 4-year institution. Participants may choose to study criminal justice and law enforcement or may pursue degrees in other fields. Men and women of all races and ethnic backgrounds are eligible, regardless of family income or resources. All participants must possess the necessary mental, physical, and moral characteristics required to be an effective police officer. They must be of good character, meet the standards of the police force with which they will serve, and demonstrate motivation and dedication to law enforcement and public service. Students interested in the Police Corps apply to the "lead agency" of the participating state in which they wish to serve (currently, 28 states and the Virgin Islands participate). Applications are then evaluated on a competitive basis.
Financial data: Students accepted into the Police Corps receive up to $7,500 a year to cover the expenses of study toward a baccalaureate or graduate degree. Allowable educational expenses for full-time students include reasonable room and board. A student may receive up to $30,000 in this program.
Duration: Up to 4 years.
Additional information: Participants become members of state and local police departments in geographic areas that have the greatest need for additional police officers. All serve on community patrol, usually in low-income, high-crime urban areas or in isolated rural areas. Participants who seek a baccalaureate degree must fulfill a 4-year service obligation as police officers upon graduation from college. Those who pursue graduate study complete their service in advance.

924
POLICE CORPS SCHOLARSHIPS FOR DEPENDENT CHILDREN OF OFFICERS KILLED IN THE LINE OF DUTY

Department of Justice
Office of Justice Programs
Attn: Office of the Police Corps and Law Enforcement Education
810 Seventh Street, N.W.
Washington, DC 20531
Phone: (800) 421-6770
Web Site: www.ojp.usdoj.gov/opclee/about.htm
Summary: To provide college scholarships to dependent children of law enforcement officers killed in the line of duty.
Eligibility: If law enforcement officers are killed in the line of duty after the state in which they served joins the Police Corps, their dependent children may be eligible for these scholarships. To be considered "dependent" at the time of the parent's death, students must be under 21 or be receiving more than one half of their financial support from their parents. This is a noncompetitive program. To be eligible for this program, a student must attend (or be about to attend) a public or nonprofit 4-year college or university on a full-time basis. Students who attend community college are eligible once they transfer to a 4-year institution.
Financial data: Eligible students receive up to $7,500 a year to cover the expenses of study toward a baccalaureate degree. Allowable educational expenses include tuition, fees, required books, and transportation between home and school. Full-time students may also claim reasonable expenses for room and board. A student may receive up to $30,000 in this program
Duration: 1 year; may be renewed up to 3 additional years.
Additional information: Students incur no service obligation. Currently, 28 states and the Virgin Islands participate in the Police Corps. For a list of those states, contact the sponsor.

925
POLISH HERITAGE ASSOCIATION OF MARYLAND SCHOLARSHIP GRANTS

Polish Heritage Association of Maryland, Inc.
c/o Scholarship Committee Chair
301 Holden Road
Towson, MD 21286
Phone: (410) 825-4870
Summary: To provide financial assistance for college to students from Maryland who are of Polish descent.
Eligibility: This program is open to students currently enrolled on a full-time basis at an accredited college or university in the United States. Applicants must be of Polish descent (i.e., have at least 2 Polish grandparents), be a resident of Maryland, and be working on a baccalaureate degree.
Financial data: The stipend is $1,000.
Duration: 1 year.
Additional information: This program was established in 1974.
Number awarded: 6 each year.
Deadline: March of each year.

926
POLISH NATIONAL ALLIANCE SCHOLARSHIPS

Polish National Alliance
Attn: Education Department
6100 North Cicero Avenue
Chicago, IL 60646-4386
Phone: (773) 286-0500   (800) 621-3723, ext. 312
Summary: To provide financial assistance for college to members of the Polish National Alliance (PNA).
Eligibility: This program is open to members (at least 5 years) of the PNA who are enrolled full time in college as sophomores, juniors, or seniors (incoming freshmen are not eligible to apply). Also eligible are qualifying students who have been members of PNA for only 2 years but whose parents have been members for at least 5 years. Applicants who joined PNA after January 1, 1992 must have a participating plan of insurance to qualify for this scholarship; this requirement excludes the Five Year Term Centennial. Selection is based on academic record, educational goals, involvement in PNA fraternal and youth activities, and extracurricular activities.
Financial data: Stipends range from $500 to $1,500. Funds are paid directly to the recipient's college.
Duration: 1 year.
Additional information: Recipients may study only at U.S. colleges or universities.
Number awarded: 200 each year.
Deadline: April of each year.

927
POLISH WOMEN'S ALLIANCE SCHOLARSHIPS

Polish Women's Alliance
Attn: Scholarship Committee
205 South Northwest Highway
Park Ridge, IL 60068
Phone: (847) 384-1208   (888) 522-1898
E-mail: vpres@pwaa.org
Summary: To provide financial assistance for the undergraduate education of members of the Polish Women's Alliance.
Eligibility: Applicants must have been a member of Polish Women's Alliance for at least 5 years, have at least $3,000 in insurance coverage, and remain members for at least 7 years after receiving the last scholarship funds. Full-time students may apply for support for their sophomore, junior, or senior year. Selection is based on an essay describing the applicant's reasons for pursuing a college degree.
Financial data: A stipend is provided (exact amount not specified).
Duration: 1 year; may be renewed through the fourth year of undergraduate study.
Number awarded: Varies each year.
Deadline: March of each year.

928
PORTLAND WOMEN'S CLUB SCHOLARSHIP

Oregon Student Assistance Commission
Attn: Private Awards Grant Department
1500 Valley River Drive, Suite 100
Eugene, OR 97401-2146
Phone: (541) 687-7395   (800) 452-8807, ext. 7395
Fax: (541) 687-7419   E-mail: awardinfo@mercury.osac.state.or.us
Web Site: www.osac.state.or.us
Summary: To provide financial assistance to college students who graduated from a high school in Oregon
Eligibility: This program is open to graduates of high schools in Oregon who had a cumulative high school grade point average of 3.0 or higher. Preference is given to women.
Financial data: Scholarship amounts vary, depending upon the needs of the recipient.
Duration: 1 year; may be renewed if the recipient shows satisfactory academic progress and continued financial need.
Number awarded: Varies each year.
Deadline: February of each year.

929
PORTUGUESE FOUNDATION SCHOLARSHIPS

Portuguese Foundation, Inc.
86 New Park Avenue
Hartford, CT 06106-2127
Phone: (860) 236-5514   Fax: (860) 236-5514
E-mail: fgrosa@snet.net
Summary: To provide financial assistance for college to students of Portuguese ancestry in Connecticut.
Eligibility: To apply for this assistance, students must be of Portuguese ancestry, U.S. citizens or permanent residents, and residents of Connecticut. They must be high school seniors, currently-enrolled college students, or students working on a master's or doctoral degree. Along with the application, qualified students must supply an essay describing financial need, an essay detailing proof of Portuguese ancestry and interest in the Portuguese language and culture, 2 letters of recommendation, their high school or college transcripts, a copy of the FAFSA form or their most recent federal income tax return, and their SAT report. Selection is based on financial need and academic record.
Financial data: Stipends are at least $1,000 each; a total of $12,000 is distributed annually.
Duration: 1 year; recipients may reapply.
Additional information: This program started in 1992. Undergraduate recipients must attend school on a full-time basis; graduate students may attend school on a part-time basis. No recipients may receive more than 4 scholarships from the foundation.
Number awarded: 9 each year.

930
PORTUGUESE HERITAGE SCHOLARSHIP FOUNDATION GENERAL SCHOLARSHIPS

Portuguese Heritage Scholarship Foundation
Attn: Academic Secretary
P.O. Box 30246
Bethesda, MD 20824-0246
Phone: (301) 652-2775   E-mail: phsf@vivaportugal.com
Web Site: www.vivaportugal.com/phsf/apply.htm
Summary: To provide financial assistance for college to students of Portuguese American heritage.
Eligibility: Eligible to apply for this support are high school seniors or currently-enrolled college students who are of Portuguese American ancestry. Applicants must be U.S. residents and attending or planning to attend an accredited 4-year college or university. Selection is based on academic achievement and financial need.
Financial data: The stipend is $2,000 per year.
Duration: 4 years, provided the recipient maintains a grade point average of 3.0 or higher.
Additional information: Recipients must attend college on a full-time basis.
Number awarded: 1 or more each year.
Deadline: January of each year.

931
POWER OF AMERICA SCHOLARSHIPS

Power of America Fund
c/o The Greater New Orleans Foundation
1055 St. Charles Avenue, Suite 100
New Orleans, LA 70130
Phone: (504) 598-4663   Fax: (504) 598-4676
Web Site: www.powerofamerica.org
Summary: To provide financial assistance for college to the surviving dependents of the victims of the September 11, 2001 terrorist attacks.
Eligibility: Eligible to receive this aid are the surviving dependents of any of the September 11, 2001 victims, including the hijacked airplane passengers and crews, those who died in the World Trade Center and the Pentagon attacks, and rescue workers who lost their lives. There will be no financial need requirements to qualify.
Financial data: The educational grant is $2,500.
Duration: This is intended as a 1-time award.
Additional information: Monies for this scholarship come from power companies in the United States. The scholarship program will be coordinated by the College Board and administered by the Educational Testing Service of Princeton, New Jersey.
Number awarded: Varies each year.
Deadline: Grants will be provided upon the dependents' initial enrollment at accredited American institutions of higher learning.

932
PRESIDENT'S STUDENT SERVICE SCHOLARSHIPS

Corporation for National Service
Attn: President's Student Service Scholarships
1201 New York Avenue, N.W.
Washington, DC 20525
Phone: (202) 606-5000   E-mail: info@studentservicescholarship.org
Web Site: www.student-service-awards.org
Summary: To provide financial assistance for college to high school students who have provided outstanding volunteer/community service.
Eligibility: Any high school principal may nominate 2 candidates to receive a matching scholarship. Eligible to be nominated are high school juniors and seniors, in public and private schools, who have performed community service for at least 100 hours within a 1-year period. The types of service that could be recognized include: volunteer work for community organizations like the Boys and Girls Club; service through churches or synagogues; involvement in service-oriented school organizations; individual efforts to help others and improve the local community; and activities connected with service-learning programs in the school district.
Financial data: The matching scholarship totals $1,000 ($500 is supplied by the Corporation for National Service and a matching amount is provided by the school district or other organizations/agencies in the recipient's community).
Duration: The competition is held annually.
Additional information: Each year, at least $3 million in matching funds is available.
Number awarded: Communities are encouraged to provide 1 or more matching scholarships for both juniors and seniors in high school. Recently, approximately 1,600 scholarships were awarded.
Deadline: Certification forms are accepted until the end of June of each year; if the number of certifications exceeds available funds, awards are made on a first-come, first-served basis.

933
PRIDE COLLEGE SCHOLARSHIP PROGRAM

Dobson Communications Corporation
Attn: PRIDE Scholarship
13439 North Broadway Extension
Oklahoma City, OK 73114
Phone: (405) 529-8382   (800) 522-9404
E-mail: cdavis@dobson.net
Web Site: www.dobson.net
Summary: To provide financial assistance for college to currently-enrolled students residing in the 18 states served by Dobson companies.
Eligibility: This program is open to full-time college students who have at least a 3.25 grade point average and live in a household for which Dobson (or any Dobson-owned company) currently provides services (a copy of the latest invoice received by the applicant from the Dobson company that provides the service must be included in the application package). In addition, applicants are required to submit a completed application form, transcripts of their most recent years of education, a wallet-sized professional photograph, and 200-word essays on each of the following topics: 1) what attributes or goals would they look for in future PRIDE recipients; develop a question and an answer that could be asked in an interview of PRIDE applicants, 3) what 1 word best describes them, 4) if they could improve 1 thing in their community, what would that be, and 5) where do they see themselves in 10 years.
Financial data: The stipend is $1,000.
Duration: The scholarships are awarded every other year, in odd-numbered years.
Additional information: This program was established in 1996. PRIDE stands for Promoting Individual Development and Education. Dobson-owned companies include: Dobson Communications Corporation, McLoud Telephone Company, Dobson Telephone Company, Dobson Cellular Systems, and Logix Communications; for a list of states served by these companies, write to the sponsor.
Number awarded: 50 every 2 years.
Deadline: October of every even-numbered year.

934
PRINCE KUHIO HAWAIIAN CIVIC CLUB SCHOLARSHIP

Prince Kuhio Hawaiian Civic Club
Attn: Scholarship Chair
P.O. Box 4728
Honolulu, HI 96812
Summary: To provide financial assistance for undergraduate or graduate studies to persons of Hawaiian descent.

Eligibility: Applicants must be of Hawaiian descent (descendants of the aboriginal inhabitants of the Hawaiian Islands prior to 1778), able to demonstrate academic and leadership potential, and enrolled or planning to enroll in an accredited degree program. Graduating seniors and current undergraduate students must have a grade point average of 2.5 or higher; graduate students must have at least a 3.3 grade point average. Priority is given to members of the Prince Kuhio Hawaiian Civic Club in good standing, including directly related family members. Special consideration is given to applicants majoring in Hawaiian studies, Hawaiian language, and journalism.
Financial data: A stipend is awarded (exact amount not specified).
Duration: 1 year.
Additional information: Information on this program is also available from the Ke Ali'i Pauahi Foundation, Attn: Financial Aid and Scholarship Services, 1887 Makuakane Street, Honolulu, HI 96817-1887, (808) 842-8216, Fax: (808) 841-0660, E-mail: finaid@ksbe.edu, Web site: www.pauahi.org.
Number awarded: Varies each year.
Deadline: April of each year.

935
PRINCIPAL'S LEADERSHIP AWARD

National Association of Secondary School Principals
Attn: Department of Student Activities
1904 Association Drive
Reston, VA 20191-1537
Phone: (703) 860-0200   (800) 253-7746
Fax: (703) 476-5432   E-mail: dsa@nassp.org
Web Site: www.nassp.org
Summary: To recognize and reward outstanding high school seniors.
Eligibility: Each principal of a public, private, or parochial high school in the United States may nominate 1 student leader from the senior class. School winners compete on the national level.
Financial data: Each scholarship is $1,000.
Duration: The competition is held annually.
Additional information: Funding for this program is provided by Herff-Jones, Inc.
Number awarded: 150 each year.
Deadline: Principals must submit the nomination from their school winner by December of each year.

936
PRISCILLA MAXWELL ENDICOTT SCHOLARSHIPS

Connecticut Women's Golf Association
Attn: Scholarship Chairwoman
22 David Drive
Simsbury, CT 06070
Summary: To provide financial assistance for college to women golfers from Connecticut.
Eligibility: This program is open to high school seniors and college students who are residents of Connecticut attending or planning to attend a 4-year college or university. Applicants must be active women golfers with a handicap. Selection is based on grades and financial need.
Financial data: Stipends up to $1,000 are provided.
Duration: 1 year.
Number awarded: 5 each year.
Deadline: April of each year.

937
PRIVATE COLLEGES & UNIVERSITIES MAGAZINE COMMUNITY SERVICE SCHOLARSHIP PROGRAM FOR MINORITY STUDENTS

Private Colleges & Universities
Attn: PC&U Scholarship Program
239 Littleton Road
P.O. Box 349
Westford, MA 01886
Phone: (978) 692-2313
Summary: To provide financial assistance to high school seniors and graduates of color who are planning to enroll as a freshman in a private college or university.
Eligibility: All students of color who are currently residents of the United States or its territories and who plan to enroll in a baccalaureate degree program at a participating private college or university (for a list, write to the sponsor) are eligible to apply. To apply, students must complete the application form, write a 1,000-word statement about their community service activities, submit a high

school transcript, and include a recommendation by someone in their community (not a family member). Selection is based on academic merit (transcripts, class rank, and grade point average) and on service to the community.

Financial data: The stipend is $1,000.

Duration: 1 year; nonrenewable.

Number awarded: Up to 20 each year.

Deadline: December of each year.

938
PRUDENTIAL SPIRIT OF COMMUNITY AWARDS

National Association of Secondary School Principals
Attn: Department of Student Activities
1904 Association Drive
Reston, VA 20191-1537
Phone: (703) 860-0200   (800) 253-7746, ext. 324
Fax: (703) 476-5432   E-mail: dsa@nassp.org
Web Site: www.nassp.org

Summary: To recognize and reward outstanding community service by middle level and high school students.

Eligibility: This program is open to students in grades 5 through 12 at public and private schools in the United States (including the District of Columbia and Puerto Rico). Each school may select 1 honoree for every 1,000 students. At the local level, honorees are chosen on the basis of their individual community service activity or significant leadership in a group activity that has taken place during the previous year. Local honorees are then certified by their school principal, Girl Scout Council executive director, or county 4-H agent to compete at the state level. As a result of that judging, 1 high school and 1 middle level student in each state, the District of Columbia, and Puerto Rico are named state honorees. The state honorees then compete for national awards.

Financial data: Each state honoree receives $1,000, a silver medallion, and an expense-paid trip to Washington, D.C. to compete at the national level. National honorees receive an additional $5,000, a gold medallion, and a crystal trophy for their school.

Duration: The competition is held annually.

Additional information: This program is sponsored by Prudential Insurance Company of America, 751 Broad Street, Newark, NJ 07102-3777, Web site: www.prudential.com/community.

Number awarded: 104 state honorees are chosen each year: 1 middle level student and 1 high school student from each state, the District of Columbia, and Puerto Rico; 10 of those (5 middle level students and 5 high school students) are named national honorees.

Deadline: Students must submit applications to their principal, Girl Scout council, or county 4-H agent by October of each year.

939
PUEBLO OF JEMEZ SCHOLARSHIP PROGRAM

Pueblo of Jemez
Attn: Department of Education
P.O. Box 60
Jemez Pueblo, NM 87024
Phone: (505) 834-9102   Fax: (505) 834-7900
E-mail: scholarships@jemezpueblo.org
Web Site: www.jemezpueblo.org

Summary: To provide financial assistance to Jemez Pueblo students who are interested in earning a college degree.

Eligibility: Applicants must be at least one quarter Jemez and recognized under the Jemez Pueblo census office (a certificate of Indian blood must be provided). They must submit 2 letters of recommendation, a copy of their letter of acceptance from the institution they are or are planning to attend, and an official transcript from the high school or college they last attended. It is required that all students fill out the Free Application for Federal Student Aid (FAFSA) and apply for aid from the college they plan to attend.

Financial data: A stipend is awarded (exact amount not specified).

Duration: 1 semester; may be renewed.

Additional information: Recipients may work on any postsecondary degree: A.A., A.S., B.A., B.S., etc. Recipients are required to maintain at least a 2.0 grade point average and enroll in at least 12 credit hours per semester.

Number awarded: Varies each year.

Deadline: For fall: applications are due in March and supporting documents are due in June; for spring: applications are due in September and supporting documents are due in October.

940
PUEBLO OF LAGUNA HIGHER EDUCATION PROGRAM

Pueblo of Laguna
Attn: Department of Education
P.O. Box 207
Laguna, NM 87026
Phone: (505) 552-7182   Fax: (505) 552-7235
E-mail: pauljo@efortress.com

Summary: To provide financial assistance for college to regular members of the Pueblo of Laguna.

Eligibility: This program is open to regular enrolled members of the Pueblo of Laguna. Applicants must have a high school diploma or GED certificate, be seeking their first degree as an undergraduate student, be accepted by an accredited college or university in the United States, be intending to enroll full time, and have applied for other financial assistance.

Financial data: Stipends are intended to cover unmet financial need, to a maximum of $7,000 per year.

Duration: 1 year; may be renewed for a maximum of 5 academic years if the recipient maintains full-time enrollment and a grade point average of 2.0 or higher.

Additional information: Recipients must have applied for other financial aid and may not pursue vocational training under this program.

Number awarded: Varies each year.

Deadline: May of each year for the fall term or academic year; September of each year for the winter/spring term; or April of each year for the summer session.

941
PUEBLO OF LAGUNA TRIBAL SCHOLARSHIP PROGRAM

Pueblo of Laguna
Attn: Department of Education
P.O. Box 207
Laguna, NM 87026
Phone: (505) 552-7182   Fax: (505) 552-7235
E-mail: pauljo@efortress.com

Summary: To provide financial assistance for college to regular members of the Pueblo of Laguna.

Eligibility: This program is open to regular enrolled members of the Pueblo of Laguna. Applicants must have a high school diploma or GED certificate, be seeking their first degree as an undergraduate student, be accepted by an accredited college or university in the United States, and be intending to enroll full time. Financial need is not required for these tribal scholarships.

Financial data: The maximum stipend is $2,000 per year.

Duration: 1 year; may be renewed for a maximum of 5 academic years if the recipient maintains full-time enrollment and a grade point average of 2.0 or higher.

Number awarded: Varies each year.

Deadline: May of each year for the fall term or academic year; September of each year for the winter/spring term; or April of each year for the summer session.

942
PUEBLO OF SAN FELIPE HIGHER EDUCATION PROGRAM

Pueblo of San Felipe
Attn: Higher Education Program
P.O. Box 4339
San Felipe, NM 87001
Phone: (505) 867-5234   Fax: (505) 867-8867
E-mail: sanfelhe@unm.edu

Summary: To provide financial assistance for college to high school seniors who are enrolled members of the Pueblo of San Felipe.

Eligibility: This program is open to recognized enrolled members of the Pueblo of San Felipe who are interested in working on an associate of arts degree or baccalaureate degree at an accredited institution of higher education. They must apply in either the second half of their junior year in high school or in the first half of their senior year. As part of the application process, students must submit a copy of their high school transcript, a copy of their letter of acceptance from a college or university, 2 letters of recommendation, a certificate of Indian blood (must be at least one quarter San Felipe and recognized under the Southern Pueblos Agency or the San Felipe Census Office), a certificate of tribal verification, and a needs analysis. Financial need is considered in the selection process.

Financial data: A stipend is awarded (exact amount not specified).

Duration: 1 semester; may be renewed for up to a total of 4 years.

Additional information: Recipients must register for at least 12 units per

semester in college. No remedial courses will be funded.

Number awarded: Varies each year.

Deadline: January of each year for the fall semester, October of each year for the spring semester, or February of each year for the summer term.

943
QUARTER CENTURY WIRELESS ASSOCIATION MEMORIAL SCHOLARSHIPS

Foundation for Amateur Radio, Inc.
P.O. Box 831
Riverdale, MD 20738
E-mail: turnbull@erols.com
Web Site: www.amateurradio-far.org

Summary: To provide funding for college to licensed radio amateurs who are recommended by members of the Quarter Century Wireless Association (QWCA).

Eligibility: This program is open to licensed radio amateurs who intend to seek at least an associate degree; graduate students may apply as well. There is no restriction on the course of study or license class. Further, there is no residence area preference. Applicants must be recommended by a member of the association. These awards are not available to 2 members from the same family in the same year or to previous winners of this scholarship.

Financial data: The stipends are $1,000 or $750.

Duration: 1 year; nonrenewable.

Additional information: Recipients must attend an accredited school (university, college, or technical institute) on a full-time basis.

Number awarded: 15 each year; 13 at $1,000 and 2 at $750.

Deadline: May of each year.

944
RACE RELATIONS MULTIRACIAL STUDENT SCHOLARSHIP

Christian Reformed Church
Attn: Ministry of Race Relations
10356 Artesia Boulevard
Bellflower, CA 90706

Summary: To provide financial assistance to undergraduate and graduate minority students interested in attending colleges related to the Christian Reformed Church in North America (CRCNA).

Eligibility: Students of various ethnicities both in the United States and Canada are eligible to apply. Normally, applicants are expected to be members of CRCNA congregations who plan to pursue their educational goals at Calvin Theological Seminary or any of the colleges affiliated with the CRCNA. Students who have no prior history with the CRCNA must attend a CRCNA-related college or seminary for a full academic year before they are eligible to apply for this program. The following minimum grades must be achieved by the applicants in the year of study prior to applying for the scholarship: freshman: minimum required to enter the college; sophomore: 2.0; junior: 2.3; senior 2.6; graduate level: entrance and sustaining grade required by the institution.

Financial data: First-year students receive $500 per semester. Other levels of students may receive up to $2,000 per academic year.

Duration: 1 year.

Additional information: This program was first established in 1971 and revised in 1991. Recipients are expected to train to engage actively in the ministry of racial reconciliation in church and in society. They must be able to work in the United States or Canada upon graduating and must consider working for 1 of the agencies of the CRCNA.

Deadline: March of each year.

945
RACIAL ETHNIC EDUCATIONAL SCHOLARSHIPS

Synod of the Trinity
Attn: Scholarships
3040 Market Street
Camp Hill, PA 17011-4599
Phone: (717) 737-0421   (800) 242-0534
Fax: (717) 737-8211   E-mail: Scholarships@syntrin.org
Web Site: www.syntrin.org/program/funding.htm

Summary: To provide financial assistance to ethnic minority students in Pennsylvania, West Virginia, and designated counties in Ohio who are in financial need.

Eligibility: Persons applying for aid must be members of a racial minority group (Asian, African American, Hispanic American, or Native Americans); residents of Pennsylvania, West Virginia, or the Ohio counties of Belmont, Harrison, Jefferson, Monroe, or Columbiana; and accepted or enrolled as a full-time student at an accredited undergraduate or vocational school. Financial aid is given only after the synod has determined that an applicant is eligible and that family resources are insufficient to meet college costs. Recipients may be of any religious persuasion.

Financial data: Awards range from $100 to $1,000 per year, depending on the need of the recipient.

Duration: 1 year; may be renewed.

Additional information: Students may not apply for this program and the Synod of the Trinity Educational Scholarship Program.

Number awarded: Varies each year.

Deadline: March of each year.

946
RALPH J. ROSSIGNUOLO SCHOLARSHIP

Iowa Department of AMVETS
Attn: Scholarship Selection Committee
P.O. Box 77
Des Moines, IA 50301
Phone: (515) 284-4257

Summary: To provide financial assistance to the descendants of current Iowa AMVETS.

Eligibility: This program is open to graduating high school seniors in Iowa who are the sons, daughters, or grandchildren of a current Iowa AMVET member. Stepchildren, foster children, and other children dependent upon the member for support and living with the member in a regular parent-child relationship are also eligible, as is a deceased member's child. Applications must be endorsed by an Iowa AMVET post. Financial need is considered in the selection process.

Financial data: The stipend is at least $1,500.

Duration: 1 year.

Additional information: Any honorably discharged veteran is eligible for membership in AMVETS. Recipients may attend any accredited college, university, community college, technical institute, or trade school in Iowa.

Deadline: March of each year.

947
RAOUL TEILHET SCHOLARSHIP

California Federation of Teachers
1200 West Magnolia Boulevard
Burbank, CA 91506
Phone: (818) 843-8226   Fax: (818) 843-4662
Web Site: www.cft.org

Summary: To provide financial assistance for undergraduate studies to high school seniors whose parents belong to the California Federation of Teachers (CFT).

Eligibility: Scholarships are available to high school seniors whose parents belong to CFT. Applicants must be planning to attend community colleges, 4-year colleges or universities, or trade, technical, or art schools. When applying, students must submit 3 sealed letters of reference, an essay (no more than 500 words) on career goals, and a union verification form that's been signed by an officer of the member's local. Selection is based on academic achievement, special talents and skills, participation in extracurricular activities, community service, the required essay, and financial circumstances.

Financial data: The stipend is $1,000 for students attending 2-year schools or $2,000 for students attending 4-year colleges or universities.

Duration: 1 year; nonrenewable.

Additional information: This program was established in 1998.

Deadline: February of each year.

948
RATH DISTINGUISHED MERIT SCHOLARSHIPS

Wisconsin Foundation for Independent Colleges, Inc.
735 North Water Street, Suite 800
Milwaukee, WI 53202-4100
Phone: (414) 273-5980   Fax: (414) 273-5995
E-mail: wfic@execpc.com
Web Site: www.wficweb.org

Summary: To provide financial assistance to students attending or interested in attending a private college or university in Wisconsin.

Eligibility: Each participating institution in Wisconsin may nominate up to 2

students for these scholarships. Nominees who are entering freshmen must have graduated in the top 25 percent of their class, have at least a 3.0 grade point average, and be able to demonstrate leadership and community service. Nominees already attending private colleges in Wisconsin must be at the sophomore, junior, or senior level; have at least a 3.0 grade point average; and be able to demonstrate campus or community leadership as well as a general interest in benefiting society.
Financial data: The stipend is $9,000.
Duration: 1 year.
Additional information: The participating schools are Alverno College, Beloit College, Cardinal Stritch University, Carroll College, Carthage College, Concordia University of Wisconsin, Edgewood College, Lakeland College, Lawrence University, Marian College, Marquette University, Milwaukee Institute of Art & Design, Milwaukee School of Engineering, Mount Mary College, Northland College, Ripon College, St. Norbert College, Silver Lake College, Viterbo University, and Wisconsin Lutheran College.
Number awarded: 17 each year.
Deadline: Nominations must be submitted no later than February.

949
RED RIVER VALLEY FIGHTER PILOTS ASSOCIATION SCHOLARSHIP GRANT PROGRAM

Red River Valley Association Foundation
P.O. Box 882
Boothbay Harbor, ME 04538
Phone: (207) 633-0333   Fax: (207) 633-0330
E-mail: afbridger@aol.com
Web Site: www.eos.net/rrva/scholarship.html
Summary: To provide financial assistance for postsecondary education to the spouses and children of selected service personnel and members of the Red River Valley Fighter Pilots Association.
Eligibility: This program is open to the spouses and children of 1) service members missing in action (MIA) or killed in action (KIA) in armed conflicts by U.S. forces from August 1964 through the present time; 2) surviving dependents of U.S. military aircrew members killed in a non-combat aircraft accident in which they were performing aircrew duties; and 3) current members of the association and deceased members who were in good standing at the time of their death. Applicants must be interested in attending an accredited college or university. Selection is based on demonstrated academic achievement, college entrance examination, financial need, and accomplishments in school, church, civic, and social activities.
Financial data: The amount awarded varies, depending upon the need of the recipient. Recently, undergraduate stipends have ranged from $500 to $3,500 and averaged $1,725; graduate stipends have ranged from $500 to $2,000 and averaged $1,670. Funds are paid directly to the recipient's institution and are to be used for tuition, fees, books, and room and board for full-time students.
Duration: 1 year.
Additional information: This program was established in 1970, out of concern for the families of aircrews (known as "River Rats") who were killed or missing in action in the Red River Valley of North Vietnam.
Number awarded: Varies each year; recently, 24 undergraduate and 14 graduate scholarships were awarded.
Deadline: March of each year.

950
REGIONAL UNIVERSITY BACCALAUREATE SCHOLARSHIP PROGRAM

Oklahoma State Regents for Higher Education
Attn: Director of Scholarship and Grant Programs
500 Education Building
State Capitol Complex
Oklahoma City, OK 73105-4503
Phone: (405) 524-9239   (800) 858-1840
Fax: (405) 524-9230   E-mail: studentinfo@osrhe.edu
Web Site: www.okhighered.org
Summary: To provide financial assistance for postsecondary education to Oklahoma residents who are attending designated publicly-supported regional universities.
Eligibility: This program is open to residents of Oklahoma who are attending 1 of 10 designated regional public institutions in the state and working on an undergraduate degree. Applicants must 1) be designated a National Merit Semifinalist or Commended Student, or 2) achieve an ACT score of at least 30 and have an exceptional grade point average and class ranking as determined by the collegiate institution. Selection is based on academic promise.
Financial data: The stipend is $3,000 per year. Awardees also receive a resident tuition waiver from the institution.
Duration: Up to 4 years if the recipient maintains a cumulative grade point average of 3.25 or higher and full-time enrollment.
Additional information: Applicants apply through the financial aid office of the university. The participating regional universities are the University of Central Oklahoma, East Central University, Northeastern State University, Northwestern Oklahoma State University, Southeastern Oklahoma State University, Southwestern Oklahoma State University, Cameron University, Langston University, Rogers State University, Oklahoma Panhandle State University, and the University of Science and Arts of Oklahoma.
Number awarded: Up to 165 each year: 15 at each of the 11 participating regional universities.

951
RETIRED ENLISTED ASSOCIATION SCHOLARSHIP PROGRAM

Retired Enlisted Association
Attn: National Scholarship Committee
1111 South Abilene Court
Aurora, CO 80012-4909
Phone: (303) 752-0660   (800) 338-9337
Fax: (303) 752-0835   E-mail: treahq@trea.org
Web Site: www.trea.org
Summary: To provide financial assistance for postsecondary education to the dependents of Retired Enlisted Association members.
Eligibility: This program is open to dependent children and grandchildren of association or auxiliary members who are high school seniors or full-time college students and interested in pursuing postsecondary education. Selection is based on a 300-word essay on "What Higher Education Means to me," 2 letters of recommendation, educational accomplishments, extracurricular activities, work experience, and financial need.
Financial data: The stipends are $1,000 per year.
Duration: 1 year; recipients may reapply.
Additional information: Recipients may attend technical schools, 4-year colleges, or universities.
Number awarded: 40 each year.
Deadline: April of each year.

952
REV. JIMMY CREECH PROFILE OF JUSTICE COLLEGE SCHOLARSHIP

Methodist Federation for Social Action-Nebraska Chapter
c/o Eric Ford
Box 130
Elmwood, NE 68349
Web Site: www.umaffirm.org/cornet/jcschol.html
Summary: To provide financial assistance to members of a United Methodist church in the Nebraska Annual Conference who are working on an undergraduate or graduate degree.
Eligibility: This program is open to currently-enrolled undergraduate and graduate students who are members of a United Methodist church in the Nebraska Annual Conference. Selection is based on the amount and length of time the applicants have participated actively in the programs (youth and other) of the United Methodist Church, the students' involvement in peace and social justice issues, and the students' personal essay (at least 1 page) on their commitment to peace and justice.
Financial data: A stipend is awarded (exact amount not specified).
Duration: 1 year.
Number awarded: 1 each year.

953
RHODE ISLAND ASSOCIATION OF FORMER LEGISLATORS SCHOLARSHIP

Rhode Island Foundation
Attn: Scholarship Coordinator
One Union Station
Providence, RI 02903
Phone: (401) 274-4564   Fax: (401) 331-8085
E-mail: libbym@rifoundation.org
Web Site: www.rifoundation.org
Summary: To provide financial assistance for college to graduating high school

seniors in Rhode Island who have been involved in public service activities.

Eligibility: This program is open to graduating high school seniors who are Rhode Island residents. Applicants must have distinguished themselves by their outstanding involvement in public service, have been accepted into an accredited postsecondary institution, and be able to demonstrate financial need. Along with their application, they must submit an essay (up to 300 words), explaining the nature of their community service participation, the work's influence on them, and how they plan to continue their public service work into the future.

Financial data: The stipend is $1,000 per year.

Duration: 1 year; nonrenewable.

Number awarded: 5 each year.

Deadline: June of each year.

954
RHODE ISLAND EDUCATIONAL BENEFITS FOR DISABLED AMERICAN VETERANS

Division of Veterans' Affairs
480 Metacom Avenue
Bristol, RI 02809-0689
Phone: (401) 253-8000   Fax: (401) 254-2320
Phone: TDD: (401) 254-1345   E-mail: dfoehr@gw.dhs.state.ri.us
Web Site: www.dhs.state.ri.us

Summary: To provide assistance to disabled veterans in Rhode Island who wish to pursue higher education at a public institution in the state.

Eligibility: This program is open to permanent residents of Rhode Island who have been verified by the Department of Veterans Affairs (DVA) as having a disability of at least 10 percent resulting from military service.

Financial data: Eligible veterans are entitled to take courses at any public institution of higher education in Rhode Island without the payment of tuition, exclusive of other fees and charges.

Number awarded: Varies each year.

955
RICHARD F. WALSH/ALFRED W. DI TOLLA/HAROLD P. SPIVAK FOUNDATION SCHOLARSHIP

Richard F. Walsh/Alfred W. Di Tolla/Harold P. Spivak Foundation
1430 Broadway, 20th Floor
New York, NY 10018
Phone: (212) 730-1770   Fax: (212) 730-7809

Summary: To provide financial assistance for college studies to the children of members of the International Alliance of Theatrical Stage Employees, Moving Picture Technicians, Artists and Allied Crafts of the United States, its Territories and Canada (IATSE).

Eligibility: This program is open to the sons or daughters of IATSE members in good standing. Applicants must be high school seniors at the time of application and have applied for admission to an accredited college or university in a baccalaureate program. Selection is based on academic record, SAT scores, and letters of recommendation.

Financial data: The stipend is $1,750 per year.

Duration: 4 years.

Number awarded: 2 each year.

Deadline: December of each year.

956
RICHARD R. TUFENKIAN MEMORIAL SCHOLARSHIP

Armenian Educational Foundation, Inc.
Attn: Scholarship Committee
600 West Broadway, Suite 130
Glendale, CA 91204
Phone: (818) 242-4154   Fax: (818) 242-4913
E-mail: aefscholar@aol.com

Summary: To provide financial assistance to undergraduate students of Armenian descent.

Eligibility: To qualify for this program, applicants must be of Armenian descent. They must be enrolled or planning to enroll full time as a junior or senior at an accredited college or university in the United States. Selection is based on financial need, academic record (at least a 3.0 grade point average), and Armenian community service and involvement.

Financial data: The stipend is $1,500; fund are sent to the recipient upon presenting proof of registration for the upcoming fall semester/quarter.

Duration: 1 year.

Number awarded: 5 each year.

Deadline: July of each year.

957
ROBERT C. BYRD HONORS SCHOLARSHIP PROGRAM

Department of Education
Office of Postsecondary Education
Attn: Institutional Development and Undergraduate Education Programs
1990 K Street, N.W.
Washington, DC 20006-8500
Phone: (202) 502-7582   Fax: (202) 502-7861
E-mail: argelia.velez-rodriguez@ed.gov
Web Site: www.ed.gov

Summary: To provide financial assistance for college to outstanding high school seniors.

Eligibility: Applicants must be U.S. citizens or eligible noncitizens who are graduating from high school and planning to attend an accredited college or university as full-time students. These awards are administered by an officially designated state educational agency (SEA) in each state that establishes the exact requirements for that state; typically, states require students to rank in the upper quarter of their high school class and have minimum scores of 1200 on the SAT or 27 on the ACT.

Financial data: The amounts of these awards depend on annual appropriations by Congress; recently, they averaged $1,500 per year.

Duration: 1 year; may be renewed up to 3 additional years.

Additional information: For the name and address of the SEA in your state, contact the Office of Postsecondary Education.

Number awarded: Varies each year; each state is allocated a number of these scholarships proportional to its population. Recently, 7,310 new scholarships were granted and 19,644 scholars received continuing awards.

Deadline: March of each year.

958
ROBERT D. BLUE SCHOLARSHIP

Treasurer of State
State Capitol Building
Des Moines, IA 50319-0005
Phone: (515) 281-6859   Fax: (515) 281-7562
E-mail: treasurer@tos.state.ia.us
Web Site: www.treasurer.state.ia.us

Summary: To provide financial assistance to Iowa residents who are currently attending a college or university in Iowa.

Eligibility: This program is open to graduating high school seniors and students currently attending a college or university as an undergraduate or graduate student. Applicants must have spent the majority of their lives in Iowa and be attending or planning to attend a college or university in the state. They must submit a completed application form, an official transcript, 3 letters of recommendation, a statement of expenses and awards from their college financial aid office, and a 500-word essay on an individual from their community who has demonstrated the responsibilities of being a citizen in that community. Selection is based on high school grade point average, financial need, references, and the essay.

Financial data: Stipends range from $500 to $1,000.

Duration: 1 year.

Additional information: This fund was established in 1949 and renamed the Robert D. Blue Scholarship in 1990.

Number awarded: Varies each year; recently, 64 of these scholarships were awarded.

Deadline: May of each year.

959
ROBERT GUTHRIE PKU SCHOLARSHIP

National PKU News
6869 Woodlawn Avenue, N.E., Suite 116
Seattle, WA 98115-5469
E-mail: schuett@pkunews.org
Web Site: www.pkunews.org

Summary: To provide financial assistance for college to students with phenylketonuria (PKU).

Eligibility: This program is open to college-age people with PKU who are on the required diet. Applicants must be accepted to an accredited college or technical

school before the scholarship is awarded, but they may apply before acceptance is confirmed. Residents of all countries are eligible to apply. Selection is based on academic achievement and financial need.

Financial data: Stipends vary but recently have been $2,000.

Duration: 1 year.

Number awarded: Varies each year; recently, 2 of these scholarships were awarded.

Deadline: October of each year.

960
ROBERT THAL SCHOLARSHIP

Key Club International
Attn: Manager of Youth Funds
3636 Woodview Trace
Indianapolis, IN 46268-3196
Phone: (317) 875-8755, ext. 244   (800) KIWANIS, ext. 244
Fax: (317) 879-0204   E-mail: youthfunds@kiwanis.org
Web Site: www.keyclub.org

Summary: To provide financial assistance for college to high school seniors who are Key Club International members.

Eligibility: Applicants must be graduating high school seniors, be bound for college, have at least a 3.0 grade point average, and be a member of a local Key Club. Selection is based on participation in school activities and organizations; participation in religious and community activities; honors, awards, and special recognition; 3 letters of recommendation; and an essay on how they have exemplified the ideals of Key Club. Financial need is not considered in the selection process.

Financial data: The stipend is $1,000.

Duration: 1 year.

Additional information: This award, established in 1994, is funded by Kiwanis International Foundation.

Number awarded: 1 each year.

Deadline: March of each year.

961
ROGER L. FOSTER SCHOLARSHIP

Virginia Police Chiefs Foundation
1606 Santa Rosa Road, Suite 134
Richmond, VA 23288
Phone: (804) 285-8227   Fax: (804) 285-3363
E-mail: lex@vachiefs.org
Web Site: www.vachiefs.org/vpcf/vpch_scholar.html

Summary: To provide financial assistance for college to children of policy officers in Virginia.

Eligibility: This program is open to dependent children of active police officers employed in Virginia who are currently enrolled or accepted at a college or university. Along with their application, they must submit an essay (up to 500 words) on their leadership style as it relates to their extracurricular school and community service activities. Selection is based on the essay, academic achievement, community and civic achievements, and financial need.

Financial data: A stipend is awarded (exact amount not specified).

Duration: 1 year.

Number awarded: 1 or more each year.

Deadline: April of each year.

962
ROGER W. EMMONS MEMORIAL SCHOLARSHIP

Oregon Student Assistance Commission
Attn: Private Awards Grant Department
1500 Valley River Drive, Suite 100
Eugene, OR 97401-2146
Phone: (541) 687-7395   (800) 452-8807, ext. 7395
Fax: (541) 687-7419   E-mail: awardinfo@mercury.osac.state.or.us
Web Site: www.osac.state.or.us

Summary: To provide financial assistance for college to children and grandchildren of solid waste company members in Oregon.

Eligibility: This program is open to seniors graduating from high schools in Oregon who are planning to attend college. Applicants must be children or grandchildren of solid waste company members, or children or grandchildren of employees (for at least 3 years) of members of Oregon Refuse and Recycling Association.

Financial data: Scholarship amounts vary, depending upon the needs of the recipient.

Duration: 1 year; may be renewed.

Number awarded: Varies each year.

Deadline: February of each year.

963
RONALD REAGAN FUTURE LEADERS PROGRAM

Phillips Foundation
7811 Montrose Road, Suite 100
Potomac, MD 20854
Phone: (301) 340-7788, ext. 6028   Fax: (301) 424-0245
E-mail: jhollingsworth@phillips.com
Web Site: www.thephillipsfoundation.org/futureleaders.htm

Summary: To provide financial assistance to college students who are "activists for the cause of freedom, American values, and constitutional principles."

Eligibility: This program is open to U.S. citizens enrolled as full-time students in accredited 4-year degree-granting institutions in the United States or its possessions who are applying during their sophomore or junior year. Applicants must submit an essay of 500 to 750 words describing their background, educational and career objectives, and scope of participation in activities that promote the cause of freedom, American values, and constitutional principles (such as leadership and achievements in responsible political organizations or clubs, community activities, newspaper columns, speeches, or debates). The award is merit-based, but evidence of financial need is welcome and will be taken into consideration.

Financial data: The stipend is $10,000 per year.

Duration: 1 year. Recipients who apply as sophomores use the scholarship during their junior year and may apply for renewal for their senior year. Recipients who apply as juniors use the scholarship during their senior year.

Additional information: These grants were first awarded in 2000 under their former name, the Phillips Foundation "Future Leaders" Program. The current name was adopted for the 2002-03 academic year.

Number awarded: At least 2 each year.

Deadline: January of each year.

964
ROOFING INDUSTRY SCHOLARSHIPS

National Roofing Foundation
10255 West Higgins Road, Suite 600
Rosemont, IL 60018-5607
Phone: (847) 299-9070   Fax: (847) 299-1183
E-mail: nrca@nrca.net
Web Site: www.nrca.net

Summary: To provide financial assistance for college to students affiliated with the National Roofing Contractors Association.

Eligibility: This program is open to the employees or immediate family members of regular contractor members of the association. They must be high school seniors or graduates who plan to enroll or students who are already enrolled in a full-time undergraduate course of study at an accredited 2-year or 4-year college, university, or vocational-technical school. Selection is based on academic record, potential to succeed, leadership and participation in school and community activities, honors, work experience, a statement of educational and career goals, and an outside appraisal; financial need is not considered.

Financial data: The stipend is $1,000 per year.

Duration: Up to 4 years of undergraduate study as long as the recipient maintains at least a grade point average of "C+" or equivalent.

Number awarded: 1 or more each year.

Deadline: January of each year.

965
ROOTHBERT FUND SCHOLARSHIPS AND GRANTS

Roothbert Fund, Inc.
475 Riverside Drive, Room 252
New York, NY 10115
Phone: (212) 870-3116

Summary: To help students who are in financial need and primarily motivated by spiritual values.

Eligibility: These scholarships are for undergraduate and graduate study at an accredited college or university (or, on occasion, for study at a secondary school). The competition is open to all qualified applicants in the United States, regardless

of sex, age, ethnicity, nationality, or religion. Financial need must be demonstrated. Preference is given to applicants with outstanding academic records who are considering teaching as a vocation. Finalists are invited to New York, New Haven, Philadelphia, or Washington, D.C. for an interview; applicants must affirm their willingness to attend the interview if invited. The fund does not pay transportation expenses for those asked to interview. Being invited for an interview does not guarantee a scholarship, but no grants are awarded without an interview.

Financial data: Grants average $2,000 per year.

Duration: 1 year; may be renewed.

Additional information: On occasion, the fund makes grants to fellows no longer on stipend (individually or in groups) to help pay the cost of retreats, conferences, community service projects, or other activities that increase the recipients' spiritual capacities. Special consideration is given to projects that involve 2 or more fellows working together. In their first year of grant support, recipients must attend a weekend meeting at Pendle Hill, a Quaker study center near Philadelphia.

Number awarded: Varies each year.

Deadline: January of each year.

966
ROSAGENE HUGGINS MEMORIAL SCHOLARSHIP

Epsilon Sigma Alpha
Attn: ESA Foundation Assistant Scholarship Director
P.O. Box 270517
Fort Collins, CO 80527
Phone: (970) 223-2824   Fax: (970) 223-4456
Web Site: www.esaintl.com/esaf

Summary: To provide financial assistance for college to students from any state studying any major.

Eligibility: Applicants may be either 1) graduating high school seniors in the top 25 percent of their class or with minimum scores of 20 on the ACT or 950 on the SAT, or 2) students already enrolled in college with a grade point average of 3.0 or higher. Students enrolled for training in a technical school or returning to school after an absence are also eligible. Selection is based on character, scholastic ability, leadership and ability skills, and financial need.

Financial data: The stipend is $1,000.

Duration: 1 year; may be renewed.

Additional information: Epsilon Sigma Alpha (ESA) is a women's service organization, but scholarships are available to both men and women. Information is also available from Verneene Forssberg, 403 South High, Pratt, KS 67124, (316) 672-3636, Fax: (316) 672-3688, E-mail: vernf@genmail.pcc.cc.ks.us. Completed applications must be submitted to the ESA State Counselor who verifies the information before forwarding them to the scholarship director.

Number awarded: 1 each year.

Deadline: January of each year.

967
ROSE ELLEN BILLS MEMORIAL SCHOLARSHIP

Foundation for Amateur Radio, Inc.
P.O. Box 831
Riverdale, MD 20738
E-mail: turnbull@erols.com
Web Site: www.amateurradio-far.org

Summary: To provide funding to licensed radio amateurs who are interested in going to college.

Eligibility: There is no restriction on the course of study. Applicants must be U.S. residents and intend to work on a bachelor's degree. The minimum license requirement is General Class.

Financial data: The stipend is $2,000.

Duration: 1 year.

Additional information: Recipients must attend an accredited school (university, college, or technical institute) on a full-time basis.

Number awarded: 2 each year.

Deadline: May of each year.

968
ROY WILKINS SCHOLARSHIP PROGRAM

National Association for the Advancement of Colored People
Attn: Education Department
4805 Mt. Hope Drive
Baltimore, MD 21215-3297
Phone: (410) 358-8900   Fax: (410) 358-9785
Web Site: www.naacp.org

Summary: To provide financial assistance to student members of the National Association for the Advancement of Colored People (NAACP) who are interested in pursuing postsecondary education.

Eligibility: Applicants must be students who are graduating high school seniors, have a grade point average of 2.5 or higher, and will be full-time students at an accredited college in the United States. Membership and participation in the association is highly desirable. U.S. citizenship and financial need are required.

Financial data: The stipend is $1,000 per year.

Duration: 1 year; nonrenewable.

Additional information: This program was established in 1963.

Number awarded: 20 each year.

Deadline: April of each year.

969
ROYAL NEIGHBORS OF AMERICA NONTRADITIONAL SCHOLARSHIPS

Royal Neighbors of America
Attn: National Headquarters
230 16th Street
Rock Island, IL 61201-8645
Phone: (309) 788-4561   (800) 627-4762
E-mail: contact@royalneighbors.org
Web Site: www.royalneighbors.org

Summary: To provide financial assistance for college to members of the Royal Neighbors of America who are nontraditional students.

Eligibility: Applicants must have been members of the society for at least 2 years immediately prior to the application deadline, be 23 years of age or older, provide (if currently an undergraduate college student) a transcript of college grades, and have been admitted to an accredited college, university, community college, or vocational school. Selection is based on character and personal goals, participation in school and community activities, ability to meet the specific entrance requirements of the accredited college or university or of the vocational school selected, and financial need.

Financial data: The stipend is $1,000 per year for full-time students or $500 per year for part-time students.

Duration: 1 year; nonrenewable.

Number awarded: 15 each year.

Deadline: December of each year.

970
ROYAL NEIGHBORS OF AMERICA STATE SCHOLARSHIPS

Royal Neighbors of America
Attn: National Headquarters
230 16th Street
Rock Island, IL 61201-8645
Phone: (309) 788-4561   (800) 627-4762
E-mail: contact@royalneighbors.org
Web Site: www.royalneighbors.org

Summary: To provide financial assistance for college to members of the Royal Neighbors of America in designated states.

Eligibility: Applicants must have been members of the society for at least 2 years immediately prior to the application deadline, be high school seniors recommended by their local lodge and field representative, be in the top third of their graduating class, and have been admitted to an accredited college, university, community college, or vocational school as a full-time student. Selection is based on character and personal goals, school and community activities, ability to meet the specific entrance requirements of the accredited college or university or of the vocational school selected, and general aptitude for college work as indicated by aptitude tests or scholastic records.

Financial data: Stipends are $1,000 or $500 per year.

Duration: 1 year; nonrenewable.

Additional information: These scholarships are currently available in the following states or territories that offer a state scholarship: California, Colorado,

Florida, CMA Illinois, Northern Illinois, Southern Illinois, Indiana, Iowa, Kansas, Michigan, Minnesota, Missouri, Montana, Nebraska, North Dakota, Oklahoma, Oregon, South Dakota, Texas, Washington, Wisconsin, and Wyoming.
Number awarded: More than 20 each year.
Deadline: December of each year.

971
ROYAL NEIGHBORS OF AMERICA TRADITIONAL SCHOLARSHIPS

Royal Neighbors of America
Attn: National Headquarters
230 16th Street
Rock Island, IL 61201-8645
Phone: (309) 788-4561　　　　　　　　　(800) 627-4762
E-mail: contact@royalneighbors.org
Web Site: www.royalneighbors.org
Summary: To provide financial assistance for college to members of the Royal Neighbors of America.
Eligibility: Applicants must have been members of the society for at least 2 years immediately prior to the application deadline, be high school seniors recommended by their local lodge and field representative, be in the top quarter of their graduating class, and have been admitted to an accredited 4-year college or university as a full-time student. Selection is based on character and personal goals, school and community activities, ability to meet the specific entrance requirements of the accredited college or university selected, and general aptitude for college work as indicated by aptitude tests or scholastic records.
Financial data: The stipend is $2,000 per year.
Duration: 4 years.
Number awarded: 10 each year.
Deadline: December of each year.

972
RURAL AMERICAN SCHOLARSHIP

Rural American Scholarship Fund
P.O. Box 2674
Oak Harbor, WA 98277-2674
Phone: (360) 679-1979　　　　　　　　　Fax: (360 679-1979
E-mail: ginnyrasf@aol.com
Summary: To provide financial assistance to older students from rural areas who are attending a college or university in the Northwest.
Eligibility: This program is open to students who currently reside in or hail from a rural community. Applicants must be at least 23 years of age, have completed at least 90 college credits or an associate degree, have a cumulative grade point average of 2.8 or higher, are currently underemployed or holding an unfulfilling position, and are attending 1 of 13 designated colleges in the Northwest. Along with their application, they must submit 2 letters of recommendation; a brief autobiography describing their academic strengths and weaknesses, work experience, career objectives, and other significant events in their life; a detailed statement of why they are applying for the scholarship, their proposed field of study, how that relates to their future plans, and where they plan to use their education; and information on financial need. As part of the selection process, an interview will be used to assess need, motivation, determination, and performance.
Financial data: A stipend is awarded (exact amount not specified).
Duration: 1 year; may be renewed.
Number awarded: Varies each year.
Deadline: March of each year.

973
RUSCH-SHEPARD EDUCATIONAL SCHOLARSHIPS

Synod of the Trinity
Attn: Scholarships
3040 Market Street
Camp Hill, PA 17011-4599
Phone: (717) 737-0421　　　　　　　　　(800) 242-0534
Fax: (717) 737-8211　　　　　E-mail: Scholarships@syntrin.org
Web Site: www.syntrin.org/program/funding.htm
Summary: To provide financial assistance for college to children of clergy in the Presbyterian Synod of the Trinity.
Eligibility: This program is open to children of clergy in the Synod of the Trinity of the Presbyterian Church (USA): Pennsylvania, West Virginia, and the Ohio

counties of Belmont, Harrison, Jefferson, Monroe, and Columbiana. Applicants must be able to demonstrate financial need.
Financial data: A stipend is awarded (exact amount not specified).
Duration: 1 year; may be renewed.
Number awarded: Varies each year.
Deadline: March of each year.

974
RUTH ANN JOHNSON SCHOLARSHIPS

Greater Kanawha Valley Foundation
Attn: Scholarship Coordinator
One Huntington Square, 16th Floor
900 Lee Street, East
P.O. Box 3041
Charleston, WV 25331-3041
Phone: (304) 346-3620　　　　　　　　　Fax: (304) 346-3640
E-mail: tgkvf@tgkvf.com
Web Site: www.tgkvf.com/scholarship.html
Summary: To provide financial assistance for college to residents of West Virginia.
Eligibility: This program is open to residents of West Virginia who are attending or planning to attend a college or university anywhere in the country. Applicants must have at least a 2.5 grade point average and demonstrate good moral character. Selection is based on financial need and academic excellence.
Financial data: The stipend is $1,000 per year.
Duration: 1 year; may be renewed.
Number awarded: 46 each year.
Deadline: February of each year.

975
RUTH E. BLACK SCHOLARSHIP FUND

American Association of University Women-Honolulu Branch
1802 Keeaumoku Street
Honolulu, HI 96822
Phone: (808) 537-4702
Summary: To provide financial assistance to women in Hawaii who wish to pursue postsecondary education.
Eligibility: Eligible to apply are undergraduate women who are residents of Hawaii and are currently enrolled in an accredited college, university, or vocational-technical institute in the state. Selection is based on academic record after at least 2 semesters of college or university study, career plans, personal involvement in school and community activities, and financial need. First-time applicants receive priority.
Financial data: The amount awarded varies, depending upon the needs of the recipient. Generally, individual awards range from $500 to $1,000.
Duration: 1 year.
Additional information: This program was established in 1969 and given its current name in 1975.
Number awarded: Varies; at least 1 each year.
Deadline: February of each year.

976
RUTH GREGG MEMORIAL ENDOWMENT SCHOLARSHIP

Epsilon Sigma Alpha
Attn: ESA Foundation Assistant Scholarship Director
P.O. Box 270517
Fort Collins, CO 80527
Phone: (970) 223-2824　　　　　　　　　Fax: (970) 223-4456
Web Site: www.esaintl.com/esaf
Summary: To provide financial assistance for college to students from any state studying any major.
Eligibility: Applicants may be either 1) graduating high school seniors in the top 25 percent of their class or with minimum scores of 20 on the ACT or 950 on the SAT, or 2) students already enrolled in college with a grade point average of 3.0 or higher. Students enrolled in a technical school or returning to school after an absence are also eligible. Selection is based on character, scholastic ability, leadership and ability skills, and financial need.
Financial data: The stipend is $1,000.
Duration: 1 year; may be renewed.
Additional information: Epsilon Sigma Alpha (ESA) is a women's service organization, but scholarships are available to both men and women. Information is also available from Verneene Forssberg, 403 South High, Pratt, KS 67124, (316)

672-3636, Fax: (316) 672-3688, E-mail: vernf@genmail.pcc.cc.ks.us. Completed applications must be submitted to the ESA State Counselor who verifies the information before forwarding them to the scholarship director.
Number awarded: 1 each year.
Deadline: January of each year.

977
SABURO KIDO MEMORIAL SCHOLARSHIP

Japanese American Citizens League
Attn: National Scholarship Awards
1765 Sutter Street
San Francisco, CA 94115
Phone: (415) 921-5225   Fax: (415) 931-4671
E-mail: jacl@jacl.org
Web Site: www.jacl.org
Summary: To provide financial assistance to student members of the Japanese American Citizens League (JACL) who are pursuing undergraduate education.
Eligibility: This program is open to JACL members who are currently enrolled or planning to reenter a college, university, trade school, business college, or other institution of higher learning. Selection is based on academic record, extracurricular activities, and community involvement.
Financial data: The stipend depends on the availability of funds but usually ranges from $1,000 to $5,000.
Duration: 1 year.
Additional information: Requests for applications must be accompanied by a self-addressed stamped envelope.
Number awarded: At least 1 each year.
Deadline: March of each year.

978
SAFE DRIVING CHALLENGE SCHOLARSHIPS

Illinois AMVETS
2200 South Sixth Street
Springfield, IL 62703
Phone: (217) 528-4713   (800) 638-VETS (within IL)
Fax: (217) 528-9896
Web Site: www.amvets.com
Summary: To recognize and reward the winners of a driving competition in Illinois.
Eligibility: This program is open to students in Illinois high schools, preferably in the 10th or 11th grade. Entrants must have completed a recognized high school or private driver training program, have been issued and currently possess a valid driver's license, have a driving record free of moving violations, and not have previously competed in this program. The competition includes 3 areas: 1) a written test covering motoring laws and driving theory; 2) road driving, in which students are scored on their ability to maneuver through traffic, drive on congested areas, make turns in intersections, and drive on a highway; and 3) off road or skills course, in which students are tested for parallel parking, emergency lane changes, stops, and maneuvering through a serpentine course both forward and reverse.
Financial data: The first-place winner receives a $1,500 scholarship, second a $1,000 scholarship, and third a $500 scholarship. Any winner who subsequently decides not to attend college receives a cash award equal to half the value of the scholarship.
Duration: The competition is held annually.
Number awarded: 3 each year.
Deadline: May of each year.

979
SAFE PASSAGE EDUCATIONAL SCHOLARSHIP FUND

USTA Tennis Foundation Inc.
70 West Red Oak Lane
White Plains, NY 10604-3602
Phone: (914) 696-7000   Fax: (914) 696-7167
Summary: To provide financial assistance for college to minority or at-risk high school seniors who participate in USTA youth tennis programs.
Eligibility: Applicants must be African Americans, other ethnic minorities, or at-risk students. They must be high school seniors and participants (for at least 2 year) in a USTA youth tennis program or independent tennis program, including USTA National Junior Tennis League, USA School Tennis, USA Team Tennis, and USTA Player Development and Independent Tennis Programs. As part of the

application process, students must submit an official high school transcript, ACT/SAT examination scores, a typed personal statement, and an official financial aid form. Selection is based on scholastic performance, extracurricular activities, course work, commitment to pursuing a career, financial need, and promise of success.
Financial data: The stipend is either $1,000 per year for 4 years or $4,000 for the freshmen year in college. Funds are paid directly to the recipient's school.
Duration: Either 1 year or 4 years.
Additional information: This program was established in 2000. Recipients must enroll in college on a full-time basis.
Number awarded: Several each year.
Deadline: May of each year.

980
SALVATORE TADDONIO FAMILY FOUNDATION SCHOLARSHIP

Salvatore Taddonio Family Foundation
Attn: Samuel David Cheris
c/o Relera, Inc.
8055 East Tufts Avenue, Suite 900
Denver, CO 80237-2842
Phone: (303) 409-1910   Fax: (303) 409-6963
E-mail: sam.cheris@relera.com
Summary: To provide financial assistance for college to residents of Colorado.
Eligibility: This program is open to Colorado residents who are enrolled or accepted for enrollment at a college in the state on a full-time basis and whose parents are Colorado residents. High school seniors must have a grade point average of 3.0 or higher. Applicants must have been born in the United States. Selection is based on merit, including extracurricular activities, community service activities, and an essay on how applicants plan to use their educational experience at college to better the community in which they live.
Financial data: The stipend is based on the in-state tuition, fees, and books at the University of Colorado at Denver.
Duration: 1 year; may be renewed if recipient maintains at least a 3.0 grade point average in college.
Additional information: This fund was established in 1990.
Number awarded: Several each year.
Deadline: July of each year.

981
SAM ROSE MEMORIAL SCHOLARSHIP

Ladies Auxiliary of the Fleet Reserve Association
Attn: Scholarship Administrator
125 North West Street
Alexandria, VA 22314-2754
Phone: (703) 683-1400   (800) 372-1924
Fax: (703) 549-6610
Web Site: www.fra.org
Summary: To provide financial assistance for the postsecondary education of children and grandchildren of deceased members of the Fleet Reserve Association (FRA) or of Navy personnel.
Eligibility: Children and grandchildren of deceased members of the association or those who were eligible to be members at the time of death are given preference for this scholarship, but children and grandchildren of active-duty and retired Navy, Marine, and Coast Guard personnel are also considered. Selection is based on financial need, academic proficiency, and character.
Financial data: This scholarship is $2,500.
Duration: 1 year.
Number awarded: 1 each year.
Deadline: April of each year.

982
SAM S. KUWAHARA MEMORIAL SCHOLARSHIP

Japanese American Citizens League
Attn: National Scholarship Awards
1765 Sutter Street
San Francisco, CA 94115
Phone: (415) 921-5225   Fax: (415) 931-4671
E-mail: jacl@jacl.org
Web Site: www.jacl.org
Summary: To provide financial assistance to student members of the Japanese

American Citizens League (JACL) who are pursuing or planning to pursue undergraduate education, particularly in agriculture.

Eligibility: This program is open to JACL members who are either high school seniors or current undergraduates. Applicants must be enrolled or planning to enter or reenter a college, university, trade school, business college, or other institution of higher learning. Selection is based on academic record, extracurricular activities, and community involvement. Preference is given to students who wish to study agriculture or a related field.

Financial data: The stipend depends on the availability of funds but usually ranges from $1,000 to $5,000.

Duration: 1 year.

Additional information: Requests for applications must be accompanied by a self-addressed stamped envelope.

Number awarded: 2 each year: 1 for a graduating high school senior and 1 for a continuing undergraduate.

Deadline: March of each year.

983
SAM WALTON COMMUNITY SCHOLARSHIPS

Wal-Mart Foundation
Attn: Scholarship Department
702 S.W. Eighth Street
Bentonville, AR 72716-8071
Phone: (501) 277-1905   (800) 530-9925
Fax: (501) 273-6850
Web Site: www.walmartfoundation.org

Summary: To provide financial assistance to high school seniors who live in communities served by Wal-Mart stores.

Eligibility: This program is open to graduating seniors at high schools designated by each Wal-Mart store and SAM'S CLUB in the community where it operates. Students interested in applying must contact their local Wal-Mart store or SAM'S CLUB; applications are not available from the foundation, high school counselors, or the Internet. Wal-Mart associates and their children are not eligible. Selection is based on academic record, ACT and/or SAT scores, work experience, community and extracurricular involvement, and financial need.

Financial data: The stipend is $1,000. Funds must be used during the recipient's first year in college.

Duration: 1 year.

Additional information: This program has awarded $29 million in 29,000 scholarships since it was established in 1981. Further information is available from Citizen's Scholarship Foundation of America, P.O. Box 297, St. Peter, MN 56082, (507) 931-1682, (800) 537-4180, Fax: (507) 931-9168; E-mail: info_sms@csfa.org.

Number awarded: More than 3,000 each year: 1 at each participating Wal-Mart store and SAM'S CLUB.

Deadline: February of each year.

984
SAMMY AWARDS

USA Today
Attn: Scholar Athlete Milk Mustache of the Year (SAMMY)
7950 Jones Branch Drive
McLean, VA 22108-0905
Phone: (800) WHY-MILK
Web Site: www.whymilk.com

Summary: To provide financial assistance for college to outstanding scholar-athletes in grades 9 through 12.

Eligibility: Eligible to apply for these awards are legal residents of the 48 contiguous United States and the District of Columbia who are currently enrolled in grade 12 and who participate in a high school or club sport. The country is divided into 25 geographic regions, and 3 finalists are selected from each region. From those, 1 winner from each region is chosen. Selection is based on academic achievement (35 percent), athletic performance (35 percent), leadership (15 percent), citizenship/community service (10 percent), and an essay on the "milk experience" (5 percent).

Financial data: College scholarships of $7,500 each are awarded. In addition, each winner, plus 2 guests, are invited to attend the winners' ceremony in Washington, D.C. The value of travel for each winner and the 2 guests is $2,936, including round-trip airfare and 2 nights' hotel accommodations.

Duration: The awards are presented annually.

Additional information: This program started in 1998. Funds for this award are provided by the National Fluid Milk Processor Promotion Board, 1250 H Street,

N.W., Suite 950, Washington, DC 20005; Dairy Management, Inc., 10255 West Higgins Road, Rosemont, IL 60018; and USA Today.

Number awarded: 25 each year (1 from each of 25 geographic districts).

Deadline: March of each year.

985
SAMSUNG AMERICAN LEGION SCHOLARSHIPS

American Legion
Attn: Americanism and Children & Youth Division
P.O. Box 1055
Indianapolis, IN 46206-1055
Phone: (317) 630-1249   Fax: (317) 630-1223
E-mail: acy@legion.org
Web Site: www.legion.org

Summary: To provide financial assistance for postsecondary education to children and grandchildren of veterans who participate in Girls State or Boys State.

Eligibility: This program is open to high school students entering their senior year who are selected to participate in Girls State or Boys State, sponsored by the American Legion Auxiliary or American Legion in their state. If they are also the child or grandchild of a veteran who saw active-duty service during World War I, World War II, Korea, Vietnam, Lebanon/Grenada, Panama, or the Persian Gulf War, they are eligible for these scholarships. Finalists are chosen at each participating Girls and Boys State, and they are then nominated for the national awards. Selection is based on academic record, community service, school involvement, and financial need; special consideration is given to the descendants of U.S. veterans of the Korean War.

Financial data: The awards are $5,000 per year.

Duration: 4 years.

Additional information: These scholarships were first presented in 1996, following a gift in July 1995 to the American Legion from Samsung Corporation of Korea, as an act of appreciation for U.S. involvement in the Korean War.

Number awarded: Varies each year; recently, 7 of these scholarships were awarded.

986
SARA E. JENNE SCHOLARSHIP

Montana State Elks Association
c/o Ted Byers
P.O. Box 1456
Great Falls, MT 59401
Phone: (406) 727-1288
Web Site: www.libby.org/mtelks

Summary: To provide financial assistance to second-year students at Montana colleges and universities.

Eligibility: This program is open to students who have completed their first year of education at a Montana university, college, vocational school, or community college with at least a 2.0 grade point average. Selection is based primarily on financial need, effort, activities, and community involvement (and less on academic achievement).

Financial data: A stipend is awarded (exact amount not specified).

Duration: 1 year.

Additional information: This program was established in 1977.

Number awarded: 1 or more each year.

987
SAULT HIGHER EDUCATION GRANT PROGRAM

Sault Tribe
Attn: Higher Education Programs
531 Ashmun Street
Sault Ste. Marie, MI 49783
Phone: (906) 635-6050   Fax: (906) 635-4870
Web Site: www.saulttribe.org

Summary: To provide financial assistance for college to members of the Sault Tribe in Michigan.

Eligibility: This program is open to members of the Sault Tribe who have been accepted into an accredited Michigan public college or university and have entered or will enter full time into a certificate- or degree-granting program. Students must apply for all institutional and governmental financial aid before tribal grant awards will be considered.

Financial data: The amounts of the awards depend on the availability of funds

and the need of the recipient. Funds must be used for tuition, fees, books, supplies, room, and board.

Duration: 1 year; may be renewed if the recipient maintains at least a 2.0 grade point average.

Number awarded: Varies each year.

Deadline: February of each year.

988 SAULT TRIBE HIGHER EDUCATION SELF-SUFFICIENCY FUND

Sault Tribe
Attn: Higher Education Programs
531 Ashmun Street
Sault Ste. Marie, MI 49783
Phone: (906) 635-6050   Fax: (906) 635-4870
Web Site: www.saulttribe.org

Summary: To recognize and reward members of the Sault Tribe in Michigan who complete college-level courses.

Eligibility: This program is open to members of the Sault Tribe who are enrolled in a certificate- or degree-granting program at a community college, 4-year college, or university in the United States, regardless of blood quantum or financial need. Applicants need to complete successfully their academic program each term.

Financial data: For full-time students (12 credits or more), the award is $500 per semester or $333 per quarter. For part-time students (11 credits or less), the award is $40 per semester credit or $26.65 per quarter credit. The maximum award is $1,000 for a calendar year.

Duration: The awards are granted each term the students complete their programs successfully.

Number awarded: Varies each year.

Deadline: October of each year.

989 SBAA EDUCATIONAL SCHOLARSHIP FUND

Spina Bifida Association of America
Attn: Scholarship Committee
4590 MacArthur Boulevard, N.W., Suite 250
Washington, DC 20007-4226
Phone: (202) 944-3285, ext. 19   (800) 621-3141
Fax: (202) 944-3295   E-mail: sbaa@sbaa.org
Web Site: www.sbaa.org

Summary: To provide financial assistance to members of the Spina Bifida Association of America (SPAA) who are interested in pursuing higher education or technical school training.

Eligibility: Eligible to apply for these scholarships are persons of any age born with spina bifida who are current members of the association. Applicants must 1) be a high school graduate or possess a GED, and 2) be enrolled in or accepted by a college, junior college, graduate program, or approved trade, vocational, or business school. Selection is based on academic record, other efforts shown in school, financial need, work history, community service, leadership, and commitment to personal goals.

Financial data: The amount of the award depends on the need of the recipient and the availability of funds.

Duration: 1 year.

Additional information: This program was established in 1988.

Number awarded: Varies each year; recently, a total of $10,000 was available for this program.

Deadline: March of each year.

990 SCHNEIDER-EMANUEL AMERICAN LEGION SCHOLARSHIPS

American Legion
Department of Wisconsin
Attn: Scholarship Chairperson
2930 American Legion Drive
P.O. Box 388
Portage, WI 53901-0388
Phone: (608) 745-1090   Fax: (608) 745-0179
E-mail: info@wilegion.org
Web Site: www.wilegion.org

Summary: To provide financial assistance for the postsecondary education of members of the American Legion in Wisconsin and their children.

Eligibility: Applicants must be 1) a child whose father or mother or legal guardian is a member of the Department of Wisconsin of the American Legion; 2) a child whose father is deceased and whose mother is a member of the Department of Wisconsin of the American Legion Auxiliary; 3) a member or the child of a member of the Sons of the American Legion, Detachment of Wisconsin; or 4) a veteran and an American Legion member in Wisconsin. All applicants must have participated in Legion and Auxiliary youth programs. Selection is based on moral character, scholastic excellence, participation in American Legion activities, and general extracurricular activities.

Financial data: The stipend is $1,000.

Duration: 1 year.

Additional information: Recipients must have graduated from an accredited Wisconsin high school but may attend a college or university anywhere in the United States.

Number awarded: 3 each year.

Deadline: February of each year.

991 SCHOLARSHIP TRUST FOR THE DEAF AND NEAR DEAF

Travelers Protective Association of America
3755 Lindell Boulevard
St. Louis, MO 63108-3476
Phone: (314) 371-0533   Fax: (314) 371-0537
E-mail: tpanathq@freewwweb.com

Summary: To provide assistance to deaf and hearing impaired persons who need funds to obtain additional education, mechanical devices, specialized medical treatment, or other treatments.

Eligibility: The only requirement for aid is that applicants must be U.S. citizens who are deaf or hearing impaired.

Financial data: Varies each year; since the fund was established, more than $800,000 has been awarded. Money may be used for mechanical devices, tuition at schools that specialize in educating the deaf (e.g., Gallaudet University, Rochester Institute of Technology, Central Institute for the Deaf), note takers and interpreters in classes in regular schools that do not provide those services to the deaf, speech and language therapy (especially for those who have had the Cochlear Implant), medical or other specialized treatments, and computer programs that assist deaf and their families learn and apply skills presented in the classroom.

Duration: 1 year; recipients may reapply.

Additional information: This fund was established in 1975. Funds have been awarded to children as young as 2 months and to adults as old as 82 years.

Number awarded: Varies each year; since the trust was established more than 1,300 awards have been made.

Deadline: Requests may be submitted at any time.

992 SCHOLARSHIPS FOR MILITARY CHILDREN

Defense Commissary Agency
1300 E Avenue
Fort Lee, VA 23801-1800
Phone: (804) 734-8134   Fax: (804) 734-8248
Web Site: www.commissaries.com

Summary: To provide financial assistance for college to the children of military personnel.

Eligibility: This program is open to sons and daughters of U.S. military ID card holders, including active duty, retirees, and Guard/Reserves, who are enrolled or accepted for enrollment at a college or university. The eligibility of applicants, including survivors of deceased members, is based on the DoD ID Card Directive, which provides for eligibility up to 21 years of age or 23 if still enrolled as a full-time student. Applicants must have a grade point average of 3.0 or higher and write a short essay on "What Being a Military Dependent Means to Me." Selection is based on merit.

Financial data: The stipend is $1,500.

Duration: 1 year.

Additional information: This program, established in 2001, is funded by manufacturers and partners of the commissary system.

Number awarded: 1 scholarship is allocated for each of the 287 commissaries worldwide operated by the Defense Commissary Agency (DeCA).

Deadline: February of each year.

993
SCHOLARSHIPS FOR WOMEN RESIDENTS OF THE STATE OF DELAWARE

American Association of University Women-Wilmington, Delaware Branch
1800 Fairfax Boulevard
Wilmington, DE 19803-3199
Phone: (302) 428-0939   Fax: (775) 890-9043
E-mail: aauwwilm@magpage.com
Web Site: www.udel.edu/educ/aauw/procedure.html
Summary: To provide financial assistance for postsecondary education to women residents of Delaware.
Eligibility: This program is open to women who are residents of Delaware and U.S. citizens pursuing a baccalaureate or graduate degree at an accredited college or university. Applicants must be either a high school graduate or a senior at a public or private high school in New Castle County. Selection is based on scholastic record, contributions to school and community, results of standardized testing, and financial need. An interview is required.
Financial data: A stipend is awarded (exact amount not specified).
Duration: 1 year.
Additional information: Information is also available from Elizabeth M. Greer, 2829 Kennedy Road, Wilmington, DE 19810-3446, (302) 479-0485, E-mail: betsygreer@aol.com
Number awarded: Varies each year.
Deadline: February of each year.

994
SCHUYLER S. PYLE SCHOLARSHIP

Fleet Reserve Association
Attn: Scholarship Administrator
125 North West Street
Alexandria, VA 22314-2754
Phone: (703) 683-1400   (800) 372-1924
Fax: (703) 549-6610   Web Site: www.fra.org
Summary: To provide financial assistance for undergraduate or graduate education to members of the Fleet Reserve Association (FRA) who are current or former naval personnel and their spouses and children.
Eligibility: Applicants for these scholarships must be dependent children or spouses of members of the association in good standing as of April 1 of the year of the award or at the time of death. FRA members are also eligible. Selection is based on financial need, academic standing, character, and leadership qualities.
Financial data: The amount awarded varies, depending upon the needs of the recipient and the funds available.
Duration: 1 year; may be renewed.
Additional information: Membership in the FRA is restricted to active-duty, retired, and reserve members of the Navy, Marine Corps, and Coast Guard.
Number awarded: 1 each year.
Deadline: April of each year.

995
SEAFARERS SCHOLARSHIP PROGRAM FOR DEPENDENTS

Seafarers International Union
Attn: Scholarship Program
5201 Auth Way
Camp Springs, MD 20746
Phone: (301) 899-0675   Fax: (301) 899-7355
Summary: To provide financial assistance for the college education of dependents of members of the Seafarers International Union (SIU).
Eligibility: Eligible are the spouses and unmarried children of members of the union. Children who are high school graduates or seniors in high school must be under the age of 19; children who are already enrolled as full-time students in a program leading to a bachelor's degree in an accredited institution must be under the age of 25. The qualifying spouse or parent must have credit for a total of 1,095 days of covered employment with an employer who is obligated to make contributions to the Seafarers Health and Benefits Plan. Selection is based on secondary school records, SAT or ACT scores, college transcripts (if any), character references, extracurricular activities, and an autobiographical essay.
Financial data: Scholarships are $5,000 per year.
Duration: 4 years.
Number awarded: 5 each year.
Deadline: April of each year.

996
SEAFARERS SCHOLARSHIP PROGRAM FOR SEAFARERS

Seafarers International Union
Attn: Scholarship Program
5201 Auth Way
Camp Springs, MD 20746
Phone: (301) 899-0675   Fax: (301) 899-7355
Summary: To provide financial assistance for the college education of members of the Seafarers International Union.
Eligibility: Applicants must be high school graduates who have credit for a total of 730 days of employment with an employer who is obligated to make contributions to the Seafarers' Welfare Plan. They must be active seamen and members of the union.
Financial data: Scholarships are either for $20,000 (paid at the rate of $5,000 per year) or for $6,000 (paid at the rate of $3,000 per year). The $20,000 scholarships are intended to cover a 4-year college-level course of study and the $6,000 scholarships are designed for 2-year courses of study at a postsecondary vocational school or community college. Selection is based on high school equivalency scores or secondary school records, SAT or ACT scores, college transcripts (if any), references on character or personality, and an autobiographical essay.
Duration: The $20,000 scholarships are for 4 years and the $6,000 scholarships are for 2 years.
Number awarded: 2 $6,000 scholarships and 1 $20,000 scholarship are awarded each year; a second $20,000 scholarship may be awarded to a qualified applicant.
Deadline: April of each year.

997
SEATTLE JUNIOR CHAMBER OF COMMERCE SCHOLARSHIP PROGRAM

Seattle Junior Chamber of Commerce
Attn: Seattle Jaycees Scholarship Committee
109 West Mercer Street
Seattle, WA 98119
Phone: (206) 286-2014
Summary: To provide financial assistance to high school seniors and currently-enrolled undergraduate and graduate students interested in going to college in Washington.
Eligibility: Applicants must be currently enrolled, accepted, or have an application pending at an institution of higher education (public or private) located in the state of Washington. Past recipients may apply again, but they may not be awarded the scholarship more than twice. Nonresidents may apply, provided they are or will be enrolled in an academic institution in the state. Selection is based on community service and/or extracurricular community involvement (80 percent), management/leadership skills, and academic record.
Financial data: The stipend is $1,000 per year. Funds are paid directly to the recipient's institution and are to be used for tuition and fees.
Duration: 1 year; recipients may reapply.
Additional information: This program was established in 1988. Since then, more than $260,000 in scholarships has been awarded. There is a $5 processing fee.
Number awarded: Varies each year; recently, 40 of these scholarships were presented: 20 to graduating high school seniors and 20 to students at other academic levels.
Deadline: March of each year.

998
SECOND CHANCE ENDOWMENT SCHOLARSHIP

Epsilon Sigma Alpha
Attn: ESA Foundation Assistant Scholarship Director
P.O. Box 270517
Fort Collins, CO 80527
Phone: (970) 223-2824   Fax: (970) 223-4456
Web Site: www.esaintl.com/esaf
Summary: To provide financial assistance for continuing education to nontraditional students from Illinois.
Eligibility: This program is open to Illinois residents who are nontraditional students. Applicants must be interested in pursuing continuing education to acquire new job skills or update present skills. Selection is based on character, scholastic ability, leadership and ability skills, and financial need.
Financial data: The stipend is $1,000.
Duration: 1 year; nonrenewable.
Additional information: Epsilon Sigma Alpha (ESA) is a women's service

organization, but scholarships are available to both men and women. Information is also available from Verneene Forssberg, 403 South High, Pratt, KS 67124, (316) 672-3636, Fax: (316) 672-3688, E-mail: vernf@genmail.pcc.cc.ks.us. Completed applications must be submitted to the ESA State Counselor who verifies the information before forwarding them to the scholarship director.
Number awarded: 1 each year.
Deadline: January of each year.

999
SECOND MARINE DIVISION ASSOCIATION MEMORIAL SCHOLARSHIP

Second Marine Division Association
Attn: Memorial Scholarship Fund
P.O. Box 8180
Camp Lejeune, NC 28547-8180
Phone: (910) 451-3167
Summary: To provide financial assistance for the postsecondary education of the children of veterans or members of the Second Marine Division.
Eligibility: This program is open to unmarried dependent children of individuals who are serving or have served in the Second Marine Division or in a unit attached to it. Applicants must be high school seniors, high school graduates, or full-time students in accredited colleges or vocational-technical schools, with family incomes of less than $42,000 and a grade point average of at least 2.5.
Financial data: The award is $1,000 per year.
Duration: 1 year; may be renewed.
Additional information: Requests for applications may be received by sending a self-addressed stamped envelope to Martin T. McNulty, Board of Trustees, SMDA Memorial Scholarship Fund, 111 Brimer Road, Newman, GA 30263, (770) 252-3330. Scholarship grants are not awarded for graduate study.
Number awarded: Varies each year.
Deadline: March of each year.

1000
SEMINOLE AND MICCOSUKEE INDIAN SCHOLARSHIP PROGRAM

Florida Department of Education
Attn: Office of Student Financial Assistance
1940 North Monroe Street, Suite 70
Tallahassee, FL 32303-4759
Phone: (850) 410-5185   (888) 827-2004
Fax: (850) 488-3612   E-mail: osfa@mail.doe.state.fl.us
Web Site: www.firn.edu/doe/osfa
Summary: To provide financial assistance to Florida's Seminole and Miccosukee Indians who wish to pursue postsecondary education.
Eligibility: Scholarships are awarded to Florida residents who hold certification of membership or eligibility of membership in the Seminole Indian Tribe of Florida or the Miccosukee Indian Tribe of Florida and who meet the following criteria: are Florida residents; have complied with registration requirements of the Selective Service System; have participated in the college-level communication and computation skills test (CLAST) program; are enrolled as either a graduate or undergraduate student at an eligible public or private college or university in Florida for at least 1 credit hour per term; can demonstrate financial need; and are not in default or owing repayment on any federal or state grant, loan, or scholarship program.
Financial data: The amount of the award depends on the recommendation by the respective tribe but may not exceed the annual cost of education for 4 years of undergraduate study or 2 years of graduate study.
Duration: 1 year; renewable, provided the recipient continues to demonstrate academic progress by meeting all academic and other requirements set by the college or university attended.
Additional information: Information is also available from the Seminole Tribe of Florida, Attn: Higher Education Coordinator, Dorothy S. Osceola Memorial Building, 3100 North 63rd Avenue, Third Floor, Hollywood, FL 33024, (954) 989-6840, or the Miccosukee Indian Tribe of Florida, Attn: Higher Education Coordinator, P.O. Box 440021, Tamiami Station, Miami, FL 33144, (305) 223-8380.
Number awarded: Varies; recently 23 awards were available through this program.
Deadline: The deadlines are established by the respective tribes.

1001
SEMINOLE HIGHER EDUCATION PROGRAM

Seminole Tribe of Florida
Attn: Department of Education
6300 Stirling Road
Hollywood, FL 33024
Phone: (954) 989-6840, ext. 1316   (800) 683-7800
Fax: (954) 893-8856   E-mail: bwilmes@semtribe.com
Web Site: www.seminoletribe.com
Summary: To provide financial assistance for college to members of the Seminole Tribe of Florida.
Eligibility: This program is open to Seminole tribal members who are applying or currently enrolled in a program of higher education.
Financial data: The amount of the award depends on the availability of funds and the need of the recipient.
Duration: 1 year; may be renewed.
Number awarded: Varies each year.

1002
SENECA NATION OF INDIANS SCHOLARSHIP FUND

Seneca Nation of Indians
Attn: Higher Education Program
8183 Center Road
P.O. Box 231
Salamanca, NY 14779
Phone: (716) 945-1790
Summary: To provide financial assistance to Seneca Nation members who are interested in pursuing postsecondary education.
Eligibility: Enrolled members of the Seneca Nation are eligible to apply if they are interested in pursuing postsecondary education and are in financial need. They must be accepted in an accredited program of study at the graduate or undergraduate level. First priority is given to students with permanent residence on the reservation, second priority to students with permanent residence within New York state, and third priority to students with permanent residence outside New York state.
Financial data: The maximum annual stipends are $8,000 for first priority students, $5,000 for second priority students, or $3,000 for third priority students. Awards provide for payment of tuition and fees, books and supplies (up to $800 per academic year), room and board (for full-time students living on campus), transportation (up to $600 per academic year for full-time commuters and students living off campus), and a personal expense allowance (up to $500 per academic year).
Duration: 1 year; may be renewed if the recipient maintains a 2.0 GPA.
Number awarded: Varies each year.
Deadline: Applications may be submitted at any time.

1003
SERTEENS SCHOLARSHIPS

Sertoma International
Attn: Sponsorships Department
1912 East Meyer Boulevard
Kansas City, MO 64132-1174
Phone: (816) 333-8300   Fax: (816) 333-4320
Phone: TTY: (816) 333-8300   E-mail: cneely@sertoma.org
Web Site: www.sertoma.org
Summary: To provide financial assistance for college to members of Serteens.
Eligibility: This program is open to members of the organization in Canada and the United States who are graduating from high school and planning to attend college in the following fall. Applicants must have maintained a grade point average of 3.0 or higher during their sophomore, junior, and senior year of high school. Selection is based on academic achievement, participation in Serteen Club activities, and participation in non-Serteen service activities.
Financial data: The stipend is $1,000 per year.
Duration: 1 year.
Additional information: Serteens is the high school affiliate of Sertoma, which stands for SERvice TO MAnkind, a volunteer service organization with 25,000 members in 800 clubs across North America.
Number awarded: 4 each year.
Deadline: March of each year.

1004
SERTOMA COLLEGIATE CLUB SCHOLARSHIPS

Sertoma International
Attn: Sponsorships Department
1912 East Meyer Boulevard
Kansas City, MO 64132-1174
Phone: (816) 333-8300   Fax: (816) 333-4320
Phone: TTY: (816) 333-8300   E-mail: cneely@sertoma.org
Web Site: www.sertoma.org
Summary: To provide financial assistance for college to members of Sertoma Collegiate Club.
Eligibility: This program is open to members of the organization in Canada and the United States. Applicants must have a cumulative grade point average of 3.0 or higher for all college-level course work. Selection is based on academic achievement and participation in both Sertoma Collegiate Club programs and non-Sertoma service activities.
Financial data: The stipend is $1,000 per year.
Duration: 1 year.
Additional information: Sertoma, which stands for SERvice TO MAnkind, is a volunteer service organization with 25,000 members in 800 clubs across North America.
Number awarded: 4 each year.
Deadline: March of each year.

1005
SERTOMA SCHOLARSHIPS FOR HEARING-IMPAIRED STUDENTS

Sertoma International
Attn: Sponsorships Department
1912 East Meyer Boulevard
Kansas City, MO 64132-1174
Phone: (816) 333-8300   Fax: (816) 333-4320
Phone: TTY: (816) 333-8300   E-mail: cneely@sertoma.org
Web Site: www.sertoma.org
Summary: To provide financial assistance for college to hearing impaired students.
Eligibility: This program is open to students who have a clinically significant bilateral hearing loss and are interested in working on a bachelor's degree at a 4-year college or university. Students working on a community college degree, associate degree, or vocational program degree are ineligible. Applicants must be able to document their hearing loss. They must be entering or continuing undergraduate studies on a full-time basis in the United States or Canada. A grade point average of at least 3.2 is required. Selection is based on past performance, goals, a statement of purpose, and overall merit. Financial need is not considered.
Financial data: The stipend is $1,000 per year.
Duration: 1 year; may be renewed up to 4 times.
Additional information: Sertoma, which stands for SERvice TO MAnkind, is a volunteer service organization with 25,000 members in 800 clubs across North America. Funding for this program is provided by Oticon, Phonic Ear, Starkey, the Lenexa Kansas Sertoma Club, and the Sertoma Foundation. To request an application, students must send a self-addressed, stamped envelope.
Number awarded: 20 each year.
Deadline: April of each year.

1006
SHEET METAL WORKERS' INTERNATIONAL SCHOLARSHIP FUND

Sheet Metal Workers' International Association
Attn: Scholarship Fund
1750 New York Avenue, N.W., Sixth Floor
Washington, DC 20006-5386
Phone: (202) 662-0858   (877) 552-4926
Fax: (202) 662-0859   E-mail: scholarship@smwia.workfam.com
Web Site: www.smwia.org
Summary: To provide financial assistance for the undergraduate education of members of the Sheet Metal Workers' International Association (SMWIA), covered employees, and their immediate families.
Eligibility: Eligible to apply for this program are association members, covered employees, and dependent spouses and children of members or covered employees. Children must be under 25 years of age. Grandchildren are not eligible. Applicants must be full-time students or accepted to be full-time students at an accredited college or university. They may be majoring in any field but must be undergraduate students. Selection is based on biographical information, academic record, extracurricular activities, national tests scores, letters of recommendation, and an essay on the importance of the association to the applicant's family.
Financial data: The stipend is $4,000 per year.
Duration: 4 years.
Additional information: Certain schools have agreed to work with SMWIA by offering supportive grants to scholarship recipients. If accepted to a participating school and approved for a scholarship under the fund, students can significantly increase the amount of financial assistance available to them for the year. Write to the association for a list of participating schools.
Number awarded: 30 each year.
Deadline: February of each year.

1007
SHEPHERD SCHOLARSHIP

Ancient Accepted Scottish Rite of Freemasonry, Southern Jurisdiction
Supreme Council, 33
Attn: Director of Education
1733 16th Street, N.W.
Washington, DC 20009-3199
Phone: (202) 232-3579   Fax: (202) 387-1843
E-mail: grndexec@srmason-sj.org
Web Site: www.srmason-sj.org
Summary: To provide financial assistance to undergraduate and graduate students who are working on degrees in areas associated with service to our country.
Eligibility: Undergraduate and graduate student applicants are expected to have taken part in social, civic, religious, or fraternal activities in their communities. Selection is based on dedication, ambition, academic record, financial need, and promise of outstanding performance.
Financial data: The stipend is $1,500 per year.
Duration: 4 years.
Number awarded: 1 or more each year.
Deadline: March of each year.

1008
SHOSHONE TRIBAL SCHOLARSHIP PROGRAM

Shoshone Higher Education Program
P.O. Box 628
Fort Washakie, WY 82514
Phone: (307) 332-3538   Fax: (307) 335-8143
Summary: To provide financial assistance to members of the Shoshone Tribe who are interested in undergraduate education.
Eligibility: Enrolled members of the Eastern Shoshone Tribe are eligible to apply. They must be able to demonstrate financial need. The tribal program provides funding for students who do not qualify for the Bureau of Indian Affairs (BIA) Higher Education Program or the BIA Adult Vocational Training Program. Aid is provided to students enrolled in 2-year or 4-year degree programs, in vocational training, or in extension type college courses.
Financial data: Up to $5,000 per year or the unmet financial need, whichever is less.
Duration: 1 year; may be renewed.
Additional information: Recipients must attend college full time.
Number awarded: Varies; generally, at least 90 each year.
Deadline: May of each year for the fall term; November of each year for the spring term; April of each year for the summer term.

1009
SIKH EDUCATION AID FUND

Association of Sikh Professionals
P.O. Box 140
Hopewell, VA 23860
Phone: (804) 541-9290
Summary: To provide financial assistance to undergraduate and graduate students who are either Sikhs or are interested in Sikh studies.
Eligibility: This program is open to high school seniors, college students, and graduate students interested in Sikh studies and/or Sikh activities. Students who are Sikhs may also apply for assistance for education in any field.
Financial data: The stipends range from $500 to $2,000.
Duration: 1 year.
Number awarded: Varies each year.
Deadline: June of each year.

1010
SMITH'S PERSONAL BEST SCHOLARSHIP

Smith's Food & Drug Stores
1550 South Redwood Road
P.O. Box 30550
Salt Lake City, UT 84104
Phone: (801) 973-1700   Fax: (801) 973-1702
E-mail: mgilford@sfdc.com
Summary: To provide financial assistance for college to high school students in Utah, Nevada, and New Mexico who have overcome personal and family challenges.
Eligibility: Eligible to apply for this support are high school sophomores, juniors, and seniors in Utah, Nevada, and New Mexico who have faced personal challenges in their lives, have shown personal courage in overcoming those challenges, and may not have the opportunity to continue their education without financial help. The application is in 2 parts; the first section is filled out by the student and the other is a nomination form to be filled out by an adult who knows the student well (a teacher, counselor, club advisor, employer, etc.). Family members may not nominate students.
Financial data: The stipend is $1,000. Funds are presented upon graduation from high school and may be used at a college, university, vocational school, or trade school.
Duration: 1 year.
Additional information: These funds are provided by Smith's Food & Drug Stores in cooperation with the Utah Education Association Foundation, the Clark County Public Education Foundation, and the New Mexico Educational Assistance Foundation.
Number awarded: 25 or more each year.
Deadline: March of each year.

1011
SOCIETY OF DAUGHTERS OF THE UNITED STATES ARMY SCHOLARSHIPS

Society of Daughters of the United States Army
c/o Janet B. Otto
7717 Rockledge Court
Springfield, VA 22152-3854
Summary: To provide financial assistance for the postsecondary education of daughters of active, retired, or deceased career Army warrant and commissioned officers.
Eligibility: This program is open to the daughters, adopted daughters, stepdaughters, or granddaughters of career commissioned officers or warrant officers of the U.S. Army (active, regular, or reserve) who are currently on active duty, retired after 20 years of active duty or for medical reasons, or deceased while on active duty or after retiring from active duty with 20 or more years of service. Applicants have at least a 3.0 grade point average and be studying or planning to study at the undergraduate level. Selection is based on depth of character, leadership, seriousness of purpose, academic achievement, and financial need.
Financial data: Scholarships amount to a maximum of $1,000, paid directly to the college or school for tuition, laboratory fees, books, or other expenses.
Duration: 1 year; may be renewed up to 4 additional years if the recipient maintains at least a 3.0 grade point average.
Additional information: Recipients may attend any accredited college, professional, or vocational school. This program includes named scholarships from the following funds: the Colonel Hayden W. Wagner Memorial Fund, the Eugenia Bradford Roberts Memorial Fund, and the Margaret M. Prickett Scholarship Fund. Requests for applications must be accompanied by a self-addressed stamped envelope.
Number awarded: Varies each year.
Deadline: February of each year.

1012
SOLVAY PHARMACEUTICALS, INC. CF FAMILY SCHOLARSHIP PROGRAM

Solvay Pharmaceuticals, Inc.
901 Sawyer Road
Marietta, GA 30062
Phone: (770) 578-5898   (800) 354-0026, ext. 5898
Fax: (770) 578-5586
Summary: To provide financial assistance for college to students with Cystic Fibrosis (CF).

Eligibility: This program is open to all high school, vocational school, college, and graduate students with CF. U.S. citizenship is required. Students must submit a completed application with a photograph, an official school transcript, all requested financial information, and a letter of reference, along with a creative representation (essay, poem, photograph, etc.) of their choice; no materials are returned. Selection is based primarily on academic achievement, the ability to serve as a role model, and financial need.
Financial data: The stipend is $2,000 per year.
Duration: Up to 4 years.
Additional information: This program started in 1992. Winners, upon mailing in a prescription from their prescribers, also receive a 1-year supply of CREON MINIMICROSPHERES (Pancrelipase Delayed-Release Capsules, USP) Brand pancreatic enzymes.
Number awarded: 20 each year.
Deadline: June of each year.

1013
SONIA STREULI MAGUIRE OUTSTANDING SCHOLASTIC ACHIEVEMENT AWARD

Swiss Benevolent Society of New York
Attn: Scholarship Fund
608 Fifth Avenue, Suite 309
New York, NY 10020-2303
Phone: (212) 246-0655   Fax: (212) 246-1366
E-mail: info@swissbenevolentny.com
Web Site: www.swissbenevolentny.com/scholarships.htm
Summary: To provide financial assistance to college seniors and graduate students of Swiss descent in the northeast.
Eligibility: Eligible to apply are college seniors and graduate students who are residents of Connecticut, New Jersey, Pennsylvania, Delaware, or New York. Applicants must be able to demonstrate sustained academic excellence (at least a 3.8 grade point average) in a demanding course of study. Either the applicant or at least 1 parent must be a Swiss citizen. Financial need is not considered in the selection process.
Financial data: The stipend ranges from $4,000 to $6,000 per year. Funds are paid directly to the recipient's school in 2 installments (beginning of fall semester and beginning of spring semester).
Duration: 1 year; nonrenewable.
Number awarded: 1 or 2 each year.
Deadline: March of each year.

1014
SOO YUEN BENEVOLENT ASSOCIATION SCHOLARSHIPS

Soo Yuen Benevolent Association
401 J Street
Sacramento, CA 95814
Phone: (916) 448-5532
Summary: To provide financial assistance for college to children of members of the Soo Yuen Benevolent Association.
Eligibility: This program is open to children of members of the association who are interested in attending college. Membership in the association is limited to members of the following clans: Louie (including Loui, Lui, Lei), Fong (including Fang), and Kwong (including Kwang, Kuang, and Kong). Applicants must be high school seniors with a grade point average of 3.0 or higher. As part of the selection process, a personal interview may be required.
Financial data: A stipend is awarded (exact amount not specified).
Duration: 1 year.
Number awarded: 1 or more each year.
Deadline: January of each year.

1015
SOOZIE COURTER SCHOLARSHIP

Genetics Institute, Inc.
555 East Lancaster Avenue
St. Davids, PA 19087
Phone: (800) 841-6871
Summary: To provide financial assistance for college to persons with hemophilia.
Eligibility: This program is open to persons with hemophilia (A or B) who are attending college or are planning to attend college. This must need financial assistance to pursue an undergraduate degree.
Financial data: The stipends are $5,000 for recipients at an academic institution

and $1,000 for recipients at a vocational school.

Duration: 1 year.

Number awarded: 20 each year: 10 to students with hemophilia A (5 at an academic institution and 5 at a vocational school) and 10 to students with hemophilia B (5 at an academic institution and 5 at a vocational school).

Deadline: March of each year.

1016
SOPHIA HAGOPIAN MEMORIAL SCHOLARSHIP

Armenian Educational Foundation, Inc.
Attn: Scholarship Committee
600 West Broadway, Suite 130
Glendale, CA 91204
Phone: (818) 242-4154   Fax: (818) 242-4913
E-mail: aefscholar@aol.com

Summary: To provide financial assistance to undergraduate students of Armenian descent.

Eligibility: To qualify for this program, applicants must be of Armenian descent. They must be enrolled or planning to be enrolled full time as a junior or senior at an accredited college or university in the United States. These are merit awards; selection is based on academic record (at least a 3.4 grade point average) and Armenian community service and involvement.

Financial data: The stipend is $1,500; funds are sent to the recipient upon presenting proof of registration for the upcoming fall semester/quarter.

Duration: 1 year.

Number awarded: 4 each year.

Deadline: July of each year.

1017
SOUTH CAROLINA EDUCATION ASSISTANCE FOR CHILDREN OF CERTAIN WAR VETERANS

South Carolina Office of Veterans Affairs
1205 Pendleton Street, Room 226
Columbia, SC 29201-3789
Phone: (803) 734-0200   Fax: (803) 734-0197
E-mail: va@govoepp.state.sc.us
Web Site: www.govoepp.state.sc.us/vetaff.htm

Summary: To provide free college tuition to the children of disabled and other South Carolina veterans.

Eligibility: Eligible for this assistance are the children of wartime veterans who were legal residents of South Carolina both at the time of entry into military or naval service and during service, or who have been residents of South Carolina for at least 1 year. Veteran parents must 1) be permanently and totally disabled from any cause, service connected or not; 2) have been a prisoner of war; 3) have been killed in action; 4) have died from other causes while in service; 5) have died of a disease or disability resulting from service; 6) be currently missing in action; 7) have received the Medal of Honor or Purple Heart Medal; or 8) be now deceased but qualified under categories 1 or 2 above. The veteran's child must be 26 years of age or younger and pursuing an undergraduate degree.

Financial data: Children who qualify are eligible for free tuition at any South Carolina state-supported college, university, medical school, or technical education institution. The waiver applies to tuition only. The costs of room and board, certain fees, and books are not covered.

Duration: Eligibility generally terminates upon the child's 26th birthday, although in some circumstances eligibility is extended to the 31st birthday.

Number awarded: Varies each year.

1018
SOUTH CAROLINA JUNIOR GOLF FOUNDATION SCHOLARSHIP PROGRAM

The Foundation Scholarship Program
Attn: South Carolina Junior Golf Foundation Scholarship Program
P.O. Box 1465
Taylors, SC 29687-1465
Phone: (864) 268-3363   Fax: (864) 268-7160
E-mail: fssp@infi.net
Web Site: www.scholarshipprograms.org/fsp_golf.html

Summary: To provide financial assistance for college to residents of South Carolina who have a competitive or recreational interest in golf.

Eligibility: This program is open to residents of South Carolina who are seniors in high school or already attending college in the state. Applicants must have a grade point average of 2.75 or higher and a competitive or recreational interest in golf. Along with their application, they must submit an essay in which they describe themselves, including the kind of person they are, their strengths, and they most important achievements in school and in their community; they may also include their hobbies, interests, sports, volunteer work, employment, future plans, or career goals; their essay should describe their golf experiences, either through competition or work. Selection is based on merit, including SAT or ACT scores, rank in class, and grade point average.

Financial data: The stipend is $2,500 per year. Funds are sent directly to the college, university, or technical college to be used for educational expenses, including tuition, fees, books, room, and board.

Duration: 1 year; may be renewed up to 3 additional years or until completion of a bachelor's degree, whichever is earlier.

Additional information: This program is administered by The Foundation Scholarship Program on behalf of the South Carolina Junior Golf Foundation.

Number awarded: 1 or more each year.

Deadline: February of each year.

1019
SOUTH CAROLINA LEGION AUXILIARY GIFT SCHOLARSHIPS

American Legion Auxiliary
Attn: Department of South Carolina
132 Pickens Street
Columbia, SC 29205-2903
Phone: (803) 799-6695   Fax: (803) 799-7907
E-mail: alauxsc@aol.com

Summary: To provide financial assistance for postsecondary education to South Carolina junior members of the American Legion Auxiliary.

Eligibility: Eligible to apply for these scholarships are South Carolina residents who have been junior members of the American Legion Auxiliary for at least 3 consecutive years.

Financial data: This scholarship is $1,000.

Duration: 1 year.

Number awarded: 2 each year.

1020
SOUTH CAROLINA NEED-BASED GRANTS PROGRAM

South Carolina Commission on Higher Education
Attn: Director of Student Services
1333 Main Street, Suite 200
Columbia, SC 29201
Phone: (803) 737-2244   Fax: (803) 737-2297
E-mail: CFreeman@che400.state.sc.us
Web Site: www.che400.state.sc.us

Summary: To provide financial assistance for postsecondary education to South Carolina residents with financial need.

Eligibility: This program is open to residents of South Carolina who meet the qualifications of financial need as established by the financial aid office at the college or university in South Carolina that they are attending or planning to attend. Assistance is provided at participating South Carolina public or private 2- or 4-year colleges and universities.

Financial data: Grants up to $2,500 per academic year are available to full-time students and up to $1,250 per academic year to part-time students.

Duration: 1 year; may be renewed for a maximum of 8 full-time equivalent terms toward the first one-year program, the first associate degree, the first 2-year program leading to a baccalaureate degree, or the first baccalaureate degree.

Additional information: Further information on this program is available from college financial aid offices in South Carolina.

Number awarded: Varies each year; recently, 10,659 students received support from this program.

1021
SOUTH CAROLINA "OTHER RACE" PROGRAM

South Carolina Commission on Higher Education
Attn: Director of Student Services
1333 Main Street, Suite 200
Columbia, SC 29201
Phone: (803) 737-2244   Fax: (803) 737-2297
E-mail: CFreeman@che400.state.sc.us   Web Site: www.che400.state.sc.us

Summary: To provide financial assistance to "other race" students at public colleges or universities in South Carolina.

Eligibility: Eligible to apply are residents of South Carolina who are members of a "minority race" at the public college or university in South Carolina they are or will be attending (African American students at traditionally White institutions and White students at traditionally Black institutions). Each eligible college selects recipients, based on academic performance and related criteria. Full-time entering freshmen must have a high school grade point average of at least 3.0; continuing full-time college students must have a cumulative grade point average of at least 2.0; part-time students must have completed at least 12 hours of college work with a grade point average of at least 2.0 and be at least 21 years old or have been out of school at least 2 years prior to reenrolling. U.S. citizenship is required.
Financial data: Up to $1,000 per year, funding permitting.
Duration: 1 year; may be renewed.
Number awarded: Varies each year, but no more than 20 percent of the grant funds at each institution may be used for entering freshmen.

1022
SOUTH CAROLINA TUITION GRANTS PROGRAM

South Carolina Higher Education Tuition Grants Commission
Attn: Executive Director
101 Business Park Boulevard, Suite 2100
Columbia, SC 29203-9498
Phone: (803) 896-1120   Fax: (803) 896-1126
E-mail: info@sctuitiongrants.org
Web Site: www.state.sc.us/tuitiongrants
Summary: To provide financial assistance to students at independent colleges and universities in South Carolina.
Eligibility: Eligible to apply are residents of South Carolina who are attending or accepted for enrollment as full-time students at eligible private institutions in the state. Applicants must graduate in the upper 75 percent of their high school class or score 900 or above on the SAT or 19 or above on the ACT. Selection is based on financial need.
Financial data: The amounts of the awards depend on the need of the recipient and the tuition and fees at the institution to be attended. Recently, the average grant was approximately $2,400. Funds may not be used for part-time enrollment, room and board charges, summer school enrollment, or graduate school enrollment.
Duration: 1 year; may be renewed.
Additional information: Further information on this program is available from college financial aid offices at the 20 participating private institutions in South Carolina.
Number awarded: Varies each year.
Deadline: June of each year.

1023
SOUTH DAKOTA BEEF BUCKS SCHOLARSHIP

South Dakota Cattlemen's Association
P.O. Box 314
Kennebec, SD 57544
Phone: (605) 869-2272   Fax: (605) 869-2279
E-mail: sdcattl@wcenet.com
Web Site: www.sdcattlemen.org/Assoc/scholarship.htm
Summary: To provide financial assistance for college to the high school seniors who are the children of members of the South Dakota Cattlemen's Association (SDCA) or the association's Auxiliary.
Eligibility: Applicants must be high school seniors and the sons or daughters (or under the legal guardianship) of a current active or associate member of SDCA or the association's auxiliary. Applicants do not have to be studying in the field of agriculture to apply for or receive the scholarship. Finalists are interviewed. Selection is based on educational goals, leadership abilities, extracurricular activities, and academic achievement. Financial need is not considered in the selection process.
Financial data: The stipend is $1,000. Funds are paid directly to the recipient's school upon proof of registration.
Duration: 1 year.
Additional information: This program is funded by the South Dakota Cattlemen's Association and the South Dakota Cattlemen's Association Auxiliary. Recipients must attend school in South Dakota.
Number awarded: At least 1 each year.

1024
SOUTH DAKOTA FREE TUITION FOR CHILDREN OF DECEASED VETERANS

South Dakota Board of Regents
Attn: Scholarship Committee
306 East Capitol Avenue, Suite 200
Pierre, SD 57501-3159
Phone: (605) 773-3455   Fax: (605) 773-5320
E-mail: info@bor.state.sd.us
Web Site: www.ris.sdbor.edu
Summary: To provide free tuition at South Dakota postsecondary institutions to children of deceased veterans.
Eligibility: This program is open to residents of South Dakota younger than 25 years of age. The applicant's parent must have been killed in action or died of other causes while on active duty and must have been a resident of South Dakota for at least 6 months immediately preceding entry into active service.
Financial data: Eligible children are entitled to attend any South Dakota state-supported institution of higher education or state-supported technical or vocational school free of tuition and mandatory fees.
Duration: 8 semesters or 12 quarters of either full- or part-time study.
Number awarded: Varies each year.

1025
SOUTH DAKOTA FREE TUITION FOR DEPENDENTS OF POWS AND MIAS

South Dakota Board of Regents
Attn: Scholarship Committee
306 East Capitol Avenue, Suite 200
Pierre, SD 57501-3159
Phone: (605) 773-3455   Fax: (605) 773-5320
E-mail: info@bor.state.sd.us
Web Site: www.ris.sdbor.edu
Summary: To provide free tuition at South Dakota postsecondary institutions to dependents of POWs and MIAs.
Eligibility: This program is open to residents of South Dakota who are the spouses or children of prisoners of war or of persons listed as missing in action. Applicants may not be eligible for equal or greater benefits from any federal financial assistance program.
Financial data: Eligible dependents are entitled to attend any South Dakota state-supported institution of higher education or state-supported technical or vocational school free of tuition and mandatory fees.
Duration: 8 semesters or 12 quarters of either full- or part-time study.
Additional information: Recipients must attend a state-supported school in South Dakota.
Number awarded: Varies each year.

1026
SOUTH DAKOTA FREE TUITION FOR SURVIVORS OF DECEASED FIREFIGHTERS, LAW ENFORCEMENT OFFICERS, AND EMERGENCY MEDICAL TECHNICIANS

South Dakota Board of Regents
Attn: Scholarship Committee
306 East Capitol Avenue, Suite 200
Pierre, SD 57501-3159
Phone: (605) 773-3455   Fax: (605) 773-5320
E-mail: info@bor.state.sd.us
Web Site: www.ris.sdbor.edu
Summary: To provide free tuition at South Dakota postsecondary institutions to children of deceased fire fighters, law enforcement officers, and emergency medical technicians.
Eligibility: This program is open to residents of South Dakota who are the survivor of a fire fighter, certified law enforcement officer, or emergency medical technician who died as a direct result of injuries received in performance of official duties. Applicants must have been accepted for enrollment at a state-supported institution of higher education or technical or vocational school.
Financial data: Eligible survivors are entitled to attend any South Dakota state-supported institution of higher education or state-supported technical or vocational school free of tuition.
Duration: Until completion of a bachelor's or vocational degree; the degree must be earned within 36 months or 8 semesters.
Number awarded: Varies each year.

1027
SOUTH DAKOTA FREE TUITION FOR VETERANS AND OTHERS WHO PERFORMED WAR SERVICE

South Dakota Board of Regents
Attn: Scholarship Committee
306 East Capitol Avenue, Suite 200
Pierre, SD 57501-3159
Phone: (605) 773-3455   Fax: (605) 773-5320
E-mail: info@bor.state.sd.us
Web Site: www.ris.sdbor.edu
Summary: To provide free tuition at South Dakota postsecondary institutions to certain veterans.
Eligibility: This program is open to current residents of South Dakota who have been discharged from the military forces of the United States under honorable conditions. Applicants must meet 1 of the following criteria: 1) served on active duty at any time between August 2, 1990 and March 3, 1991; 2) received an Armed Forces Expeditionary medal, Southwest Asia Service medal, or other U.S. campaign or service medal for participation in combat operations against hostile forces outside the boundaries of the United States; or 3) have a service-connected disability rating of at least 10 percent. Qualifying veterans must apply for this benefit within 20 years from the end of service or from their rating as disabled.
Financial data: Eligible veterans are entitled to attend any South Dakota state-supported institution of higher education or state-supported technical or vocational school free of tuition and mandatory fees.
Duration: Eligible veterans are entitled to receive 1 month of free tuition for each month of qualifying service, from a minimum of 1 year to a maximum of 4 years.
Number awarded: Varies each year.

1028
SOUTH DAKOTA NATIONAL GUARD SURVIVORS TUITION ASSISTANCE

South Dakota Board of Regents
Attn: Scholarship Committee
306 East Capitol Avenue, Suite 200
Pierre, SD 57501-3159
Phone: (605) 773-3455   Fax: (605) 773-5320
E-mail: info@bor.state.sd.us
Web Site: www.ris.sdbor.edu
Summary: To provide financial assistance for the postsecondary education of dependents of disabled and deceased members of the South Dakota National Guard.
Eligibility: This program is open to the spouses and children of members of the South Dakota Army or Air National Guard who died or sustained a total and permanent disability while on state active duty or any authorized duty training. Applicants must be younger than 25 years of age and proposing to pursue undergraduate study at a public institution of higher education in South Dakota.
Financial data: Qualifying applicants are eligible for a 100 percent reduction in tuition at any state-supported postsecondary institution in South Dakota.
Duration: 8 semesters or 12 quarters of either full- or part-time study.
Number awarded: Varies each year.

1029
SOUTH PARK JAPANESE COMMUNITY SCHOLARSHIP

Japanese American Citizens League
Attn: National Scholarship Awards
1765 Sutter Street
San Francisco, CA 94115
Phone: (415) 921-5225   Fax: (415) 931-4671
E-mail: jacl@jacl.org
Web Site: www.jacl.org
Summary: To provide financial assistance to student members of the Japanese American Citizens League (JACL) who are high school seniors interested in pursuing undergraduate education.
Eligibility: This program is open to JACL members who are high school seniors interested in attending a college, university, trade school, business college, or other institution of higher learning. Selection is based on academic record, extracurricular activities, and community involvement.
Financial data: The stipend depends on the availability of funds but usually ranges from $1,000 to $5,000.
Duration: 1 year.
Additional information: This scholarship was established by the Japanese

American Citizens League group in Seattle, Washington. Requests for applications must be accompanied by a self-addressed stamped envelope.
Number awarded: At least 1 each year.
Deadline: March of each year.

1030
SOUTHERN REGION KOREAN AMERICAN SCHOLARSHIPS

Korean American Scholarship Foundation
Southern Region
Attn: Scholarship Committee
6185 Buford Highway, Building G
Norcross, GA 30971
Phone: (770) 368-9700   Fax: (770) 446-6977
E-mail: southern@kasf.org
Web Site: www.kasf.org
Summary: To provide financial assistance for postsecondary education to Korean American students who attend school in the southern states.
Eligibility: This program is open to Korean American students who are currently enrolled in a college or university in the southern states as full-time undergraduate or graduate students. Applicants may reside anywhere in the United States as long as they attend school in the southern region: Alabama, Arkansas, Florida, Georgia, Louisiana, Mississippi, North Carolina, Oklahoma, South Carolina, Tennessee, and Texas. Selection is based on academic achievement, activities, community service, and financial need.
Financial data: Awards are $1,000 or more.
Duration: 1 year; renewable.
Number awarded: Varies each year.
Deadline: June of each year.

1031
S.P.I.N. SCHOLARSHIPS

Special People in Need
500 West Madison Street, Suite 3700
Chicago, IL 60661-2511
Phone: (312) 715-5000   E-mail: ipeter@wilvaine.com
Summary: To provide funding to individuals with disabilities who are interested in pursuing a college degree.
Eligibility: This program is open to people with disabilities who are enrolled or planning to enroll at a college or university. Applicants must submit transcripts of relevant scholastic records, a letter of recommendation from an educator, evidence of financial need, and a letter from their educational institution agreeing to serve as the administrator of the scholarship. Support is not provided to international or graduate students.
Financial data: The amount awarded varies, depending upon needs of the recipient.
Duration: These are generally 1-time awards.
Number awarded: Varies each year.
Deadline: Applications may be submitted at any time; funds are awarded twice a year.

1032
SPIRIT OF YOUTH SCHOLARSHIP FOR JUNIOR MEMBERS

American Legion Auxiliary
777 North Meridian Street, Third Floor
Indianapolis, IN 46204
Phone: (317) 635-6291   Fax: (317) 636-5590
E-mail: alahq@legion-aux.org
Web Site: www.legion-aux.org/scholarship.htm
Summary: To provide financial assistance for postsecondary education to junior members of the American Legion Auxiliary.
Eligibility: Applicants for this scholarship must have been junior members of the Auxiliary for at least the past 3 years. They must be students in the 12th grade of an accredited high school in the United States and have earned a minimum grade point average of 3.0. Each unit of the Auxiliary may select a candidate for application to the department level, and each department submits a candidate for the national award. Nominees must submit a 1,000-word essay on "The Veteran in My Life." Selection is based on character (20 percent), Americanism (20 percent), leadership (20 percent), and scholarship (40 percent).
Financial data: The scholarship is $1,000 per year, to be used at an accredited institution of higher learning or a professional or technical school that awards a certificate upon completion of an accredited course.
Duration: 4 years.

Additional information: Applications are available from the president of the candidate's own unit or from the secretary or education chair of the department. The awardees must enroll for a minimum of 12 semester hours of work or its equivalent.

Number awarded: 5 each year: 1 in each Division of the American Legion Auxiliary.

Deadline: Applications must be submitted to the unit president by March and nominations from each department must be received at national headquarters by April of each year.

1033
SPJST GENERAL SCHOLARSHIP AND LEADERSHIP GRANT

SPJST Supreme Lodge
Attn: Scholarship Department
P.O. Box 100
Temple, TX 76503
Phone: (254) 773-1575

Summary: To provide financial assistance for college to members or the children of members of the SPJST Supreme Lodge.

Eligibility: This program is open to members and the children of members who are interested in attending college on the undergraduate level. Both high school seniors and currently-enrolled college students are eligible. To apply, students must submit an official transcript, SAT or ACT scores, a personal statement explaining why they wish to go to college and how the scholarship will help them (up to 300 words), 3 references, and a photography and biography. Selection is based on academic record, references, the personal statement and SPJST involvement.

Financial data: A stipend is awarded (exact amount not specified).

Duration: 1 year.

Additional information: SPJST was founded as a fraternal benefit society in 1897 by Czech pioneers in Texas. It currently operates under Texas insurance laws.

Number awarded: Varies each year.

Deadline: January of each year.

1034
SPORTSMANSHIP RECOGNITION PROGRAM SCHOLARSHIP

Kentucky High School Athletic Association
2280 Executive Drive
Lexington, KY 40505
Phone: (859) 299-5472   Fax: (859) 293-5999

Summary: To recognize and reward outstanding student-athletes (including cheerleaders) in Kentucky high schools.

Eligibility: This program is open to high school seniors in Kentucky who have participated in athletics or cheerleading. All applicants must have at least a 2.5 grade point average, 3 letters of recommendation from coaches and administrators illustrating the student's traits of good sportsmanship, demonstrated leadership within the school and the community, and a 2-page response to a case study developed for each competition. A male and a female are recognized from each school in the state. They are chosen on the basis of these traits: playing the game by the rules; treating game officials and others with due respect, shaking hands with opponents, taking victory and defeat without undue emotionalism, controlling their tempers, being positive with officials and others who criticize them, cooperating with officials and others, being positive with opponents, letting student and adult audiences know that inappropriate behavior reflects poorly on the team, and serving as a role model for future student-athletes. These students are awarded a certificate and are entered into a regional competition. The regional winners are given a plaque and are considered for the Sportsmanship Recognition Program Scholarship. Selection is based on grade point average, recommendations, leadership roles and honors, and the case study essay.

Financial data: The scholarship is $2,500.

Duration: 1 year.

Number awarded: 2 each year: 1 female and 1 male.

Deadline: Applications must be submitted to the school's athletic director in March.

1035
ST. ANDREWS SOCIETY OF BALTIMORE PAST PRESIDENTS' HERITAGE SCHOLARSHIP

St. Andrews Society of Baltimore
2122 Carroll Mill Road
Phoenix, MD 21131
Phone: (410) 329-5085   E-mail: rebelsoldier@starpower.net

Web Site: members.tripod.com/~StAndrewsSociety/scholarship.htm

Summary: To provide financial assistance for college to high school seniors in Maryland who are of Scottish descent.

Eligibility: This program is open to Maryland residents who are graduating high school seniors and of Scottish descent. To apply, qualified students must submit a completed application form, their Financial Aid Form, their Report to Filer, a copy of their college or university acceptance letter and financial aid award letter, an essay on "Scotland's Gift to Our Nation," and a statement of genealogical data to support their claim of Scottish heritage. Finalists are interviewed.

Financial data: A stipend is awarded (exact amount not specified). The check is written jointly to the recipients and their college or university.

Duration: 4 years.

Deadline: March of each year.

1036
STANLEY A. DORAN MEMORIAL SCHOLARSHIPS

Fleet Reserve Association
Attn: Scholarship Administrator
125 North West Street
Alexandria, VA 22314-2754
Phone: (703) 683-1400   (800) 372-1924
Fax: (703) 549-6610
Web Site: www.fra.org

Summary: To provide financial assistance for undergraduate or graduate education to children of members of the Fleet Reserve Association (FRA) who are current or former naval personnel.

Eligibility: Applicants for these scholarships must be the dependent children of members of the association in good standing as of April 1 of the year of the award or at the time of death. Selection is based on financial need, scholastic standing, character, and leadership qualities.

Financial data: The amount awarded varies, depending on the needs of the recipient and the funds available.

Duration: 1 year; may be renewed.

Additional information: Membership in the FRA is restricted to active-duty, retired, and reserve members of the Navy, Marine Corps, and Coast Guard.

Number awarded: 3 each year.

Deadline: April of each year.

1037
STANLEY E. JACKSON SCHOLARSHIP AWARD FOR ETHNIC MINORITY GIFTED/TALENTED STUDENTS WITH DISABILITIES

Council for Exceptional Children
Attn: Foundation for Exceptional Children
1110 North Glebe Road, Suite 300
Arlington, VA 22201-5704
Phone: (703) 245-0607   (888) CEC-SPED
Fax: (703) 264-9494   TTY: (703) 264-9446
E-mail: fec@cec.sped.org
Web Site: www.cec.sped.org/fd

Summary: To provide financial assistance to gifted minority students with disabilities who are interested in pursuing postsecondary education or training.

Eligibility: Applicants must be gifted or talented in 1 or more of the following categories: general intellectual ability, specific academic aptitude, creativity, leadership, or visual or performing arts. They must be disabled, financially needy, ready to begin college, and a member of an ethnic minority group (e.g., Asian, African American, Hispanic American, or Native American). Candidates must submit a 250-word statement of philosophical, educational, and occupational goals as part of the application process. Selection is based on academic achievement, ability, promise, and financial need.

Financial data: Stipends range from $500 to $1,000.

Duration: 1 year; nonrenewable.

Additional information: Scholarships may be used for 2- or 4-year college programs or for vocational, technical, or fine arts training programs. This program is funded by General Motors Corporation Recipients must enroll full time.

Number awarded: 1 or more each year.

Deadline: January of each year.

1038
STANLEY E. JACKSON SCHOLARSHIP AWARD FOR ETHNIC MINORITY STUDENTS WITH DISABILITIES

Council for Exceptional Children
Attn: Foundation for Exceptional Children
1110 North Glebe Road, Suite 300
Arlington, VA 22201-5704
Phone: (703) 245-0607   (888) CEC-SPED
Fax: (703) 264-9494   TTY: (703) 264-9446
E-mail: fec@cec.sped.org
Web Site: www.cec.sped.org/fd
Summary: To provide financial assistance to minority students with disabilities who are interested in pursuing postsecondary education or training.
Eligibility: Applicants must be students with disabilities who intend to enroll for the first time on a full-time basis in a college, university, vocational-technical school, or fine arts institute and are able to document financial need. Only minority (African American, Asian, Native American, or Hispanic) students are eligible for the award. Candidates must submit a 250-word statement of philosophical, educational, and occupational goals as part of the application process. Selection is based on academic achievement, ability, promise, and financial need.
Financial data: Stipends range from $500 to $1,000.
Duration: 1 year; nonrenewable.
Additional information: Scholarships may be used for 2- or 4-year college programs or for vocational, technical, or fine arts training programs. This program is funded by General Motors Corporation Recipients must enroll full time.
Number awarded: 1 or more each year.
Deadline: January of each year.

1039
STANLEY E. JACKSON SCHOLARSHIP AWARD FOR GIFTED/TALENTED STUDENTS WITH DISABILITIES

Council for Exceptional Children
Attn: Foundation for Exceptional Children
1110 North Glebe Road, Suite 300
Arlington, VA 22201-5704
Phone: (703) 245-0607   (888) CEC-SPED
Fax: (703) 264-9494   TTY: (703) 264-9446
E-mail: fec@cec.sped.org   Web Site: www.cec.sped.org/fd
Summary: To provide financial assistance for postsecondary education to gifted students with educationally handicapping disabilities.
Eligibility: Applicants must be disabled and have also demonstrated gifted and/or talented abilities in any 1 or more of the following categories: general intellectual ability, specific academic aptitude, creativity, leadership, or visual or performing arts. They must 1) have not yet begun college and 2) be able to document financial need. Candidates must submit a 250-word statement of philosophical, educational, and occupational goals as part of the application process. Selection is based on academic achievement, ability, promise, and financial need.
Financial data: Stipends range from $500 to $1,000.
Duration: 1 year; nonrenewable.
Additional information: Scholarships may be used for 2- or 4-year college programs or for vocational, technical, or fine arts training programs. This program is funded by General Motors Corporation Recipients must enroll full time.
Number awarded: 1 or more each year.
Deadline: January of each year.

1040
STANLEY E. JACKSON SCHOLARSHIP AWARD FOR STUDENTS WITH DISABILITIES

Council for Exceptional Children
Attn: Foundation for Exceptional Children
1110 North Glebe Road, Suite 300
Arlington, VA 22201-5704
Phone: (703) 245-0607   (888) CEC-SPED
Fax: (703) 264-9494   TTY: (703) 264-9446
E-mail: fec@cec.sped.org
Web Site: www.cec.sped.org/fd
Summary: To provide financial assistance for postsecondary education to students with disabilities.

Eligibility: Applicants must be disabled, have not yet begun college, and be able to document financial need. They must submit a 250-word statement of philosophical, educational, and occupational goals as part of the application process. Selection is based on academic achievement, ability, promise, and financial need.
Financial data: Stipends range from $500 to $1,000.
Duration: 1 year; nonrenewable.
Additional information: Scholarships may be used for 2- or 4-year college programs or for vocational, technical, or fine arts training programs. This program is funded by General Motors Corporation Recipients must enroll full time.
Number awarded: 1 or more each year.
Deadline: January of each year.

1041
STANLEY Z. KOPLIK CERTIFICATE OF MASTERY TUITION WAIVER PROGRAM

Massachusetts Office of Student Financial Assistance
454 Broadway, Suite 200
Revere, MA 02151
Phone: (617) 727-9420   Fax: (617) 727-0667
E-mail: osfa@osfa.mass.edu
Web Site: www.osfa.mass.edu/osfaprograms/stanleycert.asp
Summary: To provide financial assistance for postsecondary education to Massachusetts residents who earn a Stanley Z. Koplik Certificate of Mastery while in high school.
Eligibility: This program is open to permanent Massachusetts residents who are U.S. citizens or permanent residents. In order to become a candidate for the Stanley Z. Koplik Certificate of Mastery, students must score "Advanced" on at least 1 grade 10 MCAS test subject and score "Proficient" on the remaining sections of the grade 10 MCAS. Once they become candidates, they must then fulfill additional requirements through 1 of the following combinations covering both arts/humanities and mathematics/science: 2 AP exams; 2 SAT II exams; 1 SAT II exam and 1 AP exam; 1 SAT II exam and 1 other achievement; or 1 AP exam and 1 other achievement. They must score at least 3 on any AP exam; if there are SAT II and AP exams in the same subject area, they must receive a score on the SAT II exam determined by the Department of Education to be comparable to a score of 3 on the AP exam. In subject areas where they are no corresponding AP exams, a student must achieve an SAT II score designated by the Department of Education.
Financial data: Recipients of Koplik Certificates are eligible for an award of a non-need-based tuition waiver for state-supported undergraduate courses in Massachusetts.
Duration: Up to 4 academic years, provided the student maintains a college grade point average of 3.3 or higher.
Number awarded: Varies each year.

1042
STATE VOCATIONAL REHABILITATION SERVICES PROGRAM

Department of Education
Office of Special Education and Rehabilitative Services
Attn: Rehabilitation Services Administration
400 Maryland Avenue, S.W., Room 3221, MES
Washington, DC 20202-2500
Phone: (202) 205-8719   Fax: (202) 205-9340
E-mail: roseann_ashby@ed.gov
Web Site: www.ed.gov/offices/OSERS/RSA/PGMS/bvrs.html
Summary: To provide financial assistance for postsecondary education to individuals with disabilities as part of their program of vocational rehabilitation.
Eligibility: To be eligible for vocational rehabilitation services, an individual must 1) have a physical or mental impairment that is a substantial impediment to employment; 2) be able to benefit in terms of employment from vocational rehabilitation services; and 3) require vocational rehabilitation services to prepare for, enter, engage in, or retain gainful employment. Priority is given to applicants with the most significant disabilities. Persons accepted for vocational rehabilitation develop an Individualized Written Rehabilitation Program (IWRP) in consultation with a counselor for the vocational rehabilitation agency in the state in which they live. The IWRP may include a program of postsecondary education if the disabled person and counselor agree that such a program will fulfill the goals of vocational rehabilitation. In most cases, the IWRP will provide for postsecondary education only to a level at which the disabled person will become employable, but that may include graduate education if the approved

occupation requires an advanced degree as a minimum condition of entry. Students accepted to a program of postsecondary education as part of their IWRP must apply for all available federal, state, and private financial aid.

Financial data: Funding for this program is provided by the federal government through grants to state vocational rehabilitation agencies. Grants under the basic support program currently total nearly $2.4 billion per year. States must supplement federal funding with matching funds of 21.3 percent. Persons who are accepted for vocational rehabilitation by the appropriate state agency receive financial assistance based on the cost of their education and other funds available to them, including their own or family contribution and other sources of financial aid. Allowable costs in most states include tuition, fees, books, supplies, room, board, transportation, personal expenses, child care, and expenses related to disability (special equipment, readers, attendants, interpreters, or notetakers).

Duration: Assistance is provided until the disabled person achieves an educational level necessary for employment as provided in the IWRP.

Additional information: You will need to contact your state vocational rehabilitation agency to apply for this program.

Number awarded: Varies each year. Recently, more than 1.2 million (of whom more than 80 percent have significant disabilities) were participating in this program.

1043
STEPHEN BUFTON MEMORIAL EDUCATION FUND GRANTS

American Business Women's Association
9100 Ward Parkway
P.O. Box 8728
Kansas City, MO 64114-0728
Phone: (816) 361-6621   (800) 228-0007
Fax: (816) 361-4991   E-mail: abwa@abwahq.org
Web Site: www.abwahq.org

Summary: To provide financial assistance to women undergraduate and graduate students who are members of the American Business Women's Association (ABWA) or part of a member's household.

Eligibility: ABWA members or individuals who are part of an ABWA member's household may apply for these grants if they are at least at the junior level in college and have achieved a cumulative grade point average of 2.5 or higher. They must be sponsored by an ABWA chapter that has contributed to the fund in the previous chapter year. U.S. citizenship is required.

Financial data: The maximum grant is $1,200. Funds are to be used only for tuition, books, and fees.

Duration: 1 year; grants are not automatically renewed.

Additional information: The ABWA does not provide the names and addresses of local chapters; it recommends that applicants check with their local Chamber of Commerce, library, or university to see if any chapter has registered a contact's name and number.

1044
STEPHEN SAPAUGH MEMORIAL SCHOLARSHIP

Key Club International
Attn: Manager of Youth Funds
3636 Woodview Trace
Indianapolis, IN 46268-3196
Phone: (317) 875-8755, ext. 244   (800) KIWANIS, ext. 244
Fax: (317) 879-0204   E-mail: youthfunds@kiwanis.org
Web Site: www.keyclub.org

Summary: To provide financial assistance for college to high school seniors who are Key Club International members.

Eligibility: Applicants must be graduating high school seniors, be bound for college, have at least a 3.0 grade point average, and have been involved in Key Club for at least 2 years. Selection is based on participation in school activities and organizations; participation in religious and community activities; honors, awards, and special recognition; 3 letters of recommendation; and an essay on how they have exemplified the ideals of Key Club. Financial need is not considered in the selection process.

Financial data: The stipend is $1,000 per year.

Duration: 4 years.

Additional information: This award is funded by Kiwanis International Foundation.

Number awarded: 1 each year.

Deadline: March of each year.

1045
STERLING SCHOLAR AWARDS OF UTAH

Deseret News
Attn: Marketing/Promotion Department
30 East 100 South
Salt Lake City, UT 84111
Phone: (801) 237-2900
Web Site: deseretnews.com/scholars

Summary: To provide financial assistance for college to outstanding high school seniors in Utah.

Eligibility: This program is open to graduating seniors at high schools in Utah. Candidates must be nominated by their principals in 1 of the following categories: English, mathematics, social science, science, foreign language, computer technology, trade and technical education, family and consumer sciences, business and marketing, speech and drama, visual arts, music, and dance. Nominees submit portfolios demonstrating their work; the contents of the portfolio depend on the category for which they have been nominated. Selection is based on scholarship (50 points), leadership (25 points), and citizenship (25 points). The program is conducted in 5 regions throughout Utah: Wasatch Front (Box Elder, Cache, Weber, Davis, Salt Lake, Tooele, and Utah counties), Northeast (Rich, Morgan, Summit, Wasatch, Duchesne, Dagget, and Uintah counties), Central (Juab, Sanpete, Millard, Sevier, Piute, and Wayne counties), Southwest (Beaver, Iron, Garfield, Washington, and Kane counties), and Southeast (Carbon, Emery, Grand, and San Juan counties).

Financial data: In the Wasatch Front region, a total of $21,000 is awarded, including a general scholarship award of $1,500 and category awards of $1,000 for first place and $250 for the runner-up. In the Northeast region, each category winner receives $500 plus a scholarship to a Utah college and each category runner-up receives $300 plus a scholarship to a Utah college. For information on the awards in the other regions, contact your high school principal or counselor. Many Utah colleges and universities also designate special awards exclusively for Sterling Scholars.

Duration: 1 year.

Additional information: This program was established in 1962 by the Deseret News and KSL-TV. Those firms administer the program directly in the Wasatch Front region but only establish the guidelines for the other regions.

Number awarded: In the Wasatch Front region, 39 awards are presented (a winner and 2 runners-up in each category); 1 of those recipients is selected to receive the additional general scholarship award, 1 to be designated the Douglas Bates Awardee, and 1 to be designated the Philo T. Farnsworth Awardee.

Deadline: In the Wasatch Front region, schools must submit nominations by January of each year and nominees must complete their portfolios by February.

1046
STEVE DEARDUFF SCHOLARSHIP

Community Foundation for Greater Atlanta, Inc.
50 Hurt Plaza, Suite 449
Atlanta, GA 30303
Phone: (404) 688-5525   Fax: (404) 688-3060
E-mail: bchen@atlcf.org
Web Site: www.atlcf.org/Scholar02.html

Summary: To provide financial assistance to Georgia residents who are working on an undergraduate or graduate degree, especially in medicine and social work.

Eligibility: This program is open to legal resident of Georgia who are enrolled in or accepted at an accredited institution of higher learning on the undergraduate or graduate school level. Applicants must be able to demonstrate a history of outstanding community service and potential for success in their chosen field. They must have at least a 2.0 grade point average. Preference is given to candidates entering the fields of medicine or social work.

Financial data: Stipends range up to $2,000 per year.

Duration: 1 year.

Deadline: March of each year.

1047
STEVEN KNEZEVICH TRUST SCHOLARSHIPS

Steven Knezevich Trust
9830 North Courtland Drive
Mequon, WI 53092

Summary: To provide financial assistance for postsecondary education to students of Serbian descent.

Eligibility: Applicants for assistance from this fund must submit information on

the college they are attending, a copy of their grade transcript for the past 2 semesters, documentation of their financial need, 2 stamped envelopes (1 addressed to themselves, 1 to their school's financial aid office), and a copy of a Serbian map showing the area in which their family was located. Undergraduates and graduate students are eligible.

Financial data: The amount of the award depends on the need of the recipient and the availability of funds.

Number awarded: Varies each year.

Deadline: November of each year.

1048
STUDENT AID FUND FOR NONREGISTRANTS

Mennonite Board of Education
500 South Main Street
P.O. Box 1142
Elkhart, IN 46515-1142
Phone: (217) 294-7531   Fax: (217) 294-7446
E-mail: timjb@juno.com

Summary: To provide financial assistance for postsecondary education to men who are ineligible to receive government grants and loans because they have declined to register with the U.S. Selective Service System for reasons of Christian conscience.

Eligibility: Eligible to receive assistance from this fund are students who have declined to register with the U.S. Selective Service because of their Christian conscience. They must be either 1) enrolled in a Mennonite college or seminary or 2) Mennonite students enrolled in non-Mennonite institutions.

Financial data: Aid is available in the form of both grants and loans. The amount of assistance is based on formulas that would have been used if the student were eligible for government aid. For loans, no interest is charged until 6 months following completion of undergraduate study; at that time (even if the recipient continues on to graduate school), the loan must be repaid with a fixed interest rate based upon the long-term 120 percent AFR monthly rate, set 90 days after the student graduates or discontinues school; the minimum payment is $50 per month and the total repayment period cannot exceed 10 years.

Additional information: This fund was established in 1983 by the Mennonite Board of Congregational Ministries (MBCM) but is administered by the Mennonite Board of Education (MBE). The home congregations of Mennonite nonregistrants are invited to contribute to the fund; students are expected to be an integral part of the communication process with their congregations.

Number awarded: Varies each year.

Deadline: August of each year.

1049
STUTZ MEMORIAL SCHOLARSHIP

American Legion
Attn: Department of New Jersey
Attn: Scholarship Judges
135 West Hanover Street
Trenton, NJ 08618
Phone: (609) 695-5418   Fax: (609) 394-1532
E-mail: newjersey@legion.org
Web Site: www.nj.legion.org

Summary: To provide financial assistance for the postsecondary education of children of members of the American Legion's New Jersey Department.

Eligibility: In order to be eligible for these scholarships, applicants must be natural or adopted children of members of the American Legion's New Jersey Department and high school seniors. Scholarships are based on character (20 percent), Americanism (20 percent), leadership (20 percent), scholarship (20 percent), and financial need (20 percent).

Financial data: This scholarship is $1,000 per year.

Duration: 4 years.

Number awarded: 1 each year.

Deadline: February of each year.

1050
SUNSTUDENTS SCHOLARSHIP PROGRAM

Phoenix Suns Charities
201 East Jefferson Street
P.O. Box 1369
Phoenix, AZ 85001-1369
Phone: (602) 379-7969   Fax: (602) 379-7922

Summary: To provide financial assistance for college to high school seniors in Arizona.

Eligibility: High school seniors in Arizona who have a cumulative grade point average of at least 2.5 and who have been involved in charitable activities or volunteer service (in school, church, or community) are eligible to submit an essay (300 words or less) on a topic that changes annually (recently: "Who would you consider to be the most important person of the 20th century and why?"). Applications must be accompanied by 2 letters of recommendation, 1 of which must be from a high school teacher or administrator. Selection is based on the content and overall presentation of the essay, letters of recommendation, community involvement, and academic record.

Financial data: The stipend is $1,000.

Duration: The scholarship is offered annually.

Number awarded: 10 each year.

Deadline: February of each year.

1051
SUPERCOLLEGE.COM STUDENT SCHOLARSHIPS

SuperCollege.com
Attn: Scholarship Application Request
4546 B10 El Camino Real, Number 281
Los Altos, CA 94022
Web Site: www.supercollege.com

Summary: To provide financial assistance for college to U.S. citizens and permanent residents.

Eligibility: This program is open to U.S. citizens and permanent residents who are high school students or college undergraduates. Applicants must submit an essay, up to 500 words, that they are planning to use (or have used) to apply to college or for another scholarship. They may also use an essay they have written for a class. Selection is based on the essay and academic and extracurricular achievement.

Financial data: Stipends range from $500 to $2,500 per year. Funds must be used for tuition or tuition-related fees, textbooks, or room and board for undergraduate study at an accredited college or university in the United States.

Duration: 1 year.

Additional information: SuperCollege.com funds this program from a portion of the proceeds of its books, *Get Into Any College: Secrets of Harvard Students* and *Get Free Cash for College: Scholarship Secrets of Harvard Students*.

Number awarded: 1 each year.

Deadline: May of each year.

1052
SUPREME COUNCIL OF S.E.S. SCHOLARSHIPS

Supreme Council of S.E.S.
733 Benton Street
P.O. Box 247
Santa Clara, CA 95052-0247
Phone: (408) 248-3788   (800) 248-1895
Fax: (408) 248-9671   E-mail: seslife@pacbell.net

Summary: To provide financial assistance to high school seniors who have been members of the Supreme Council of S.E.S. for the past 2 years.

Eligibility: Applicants must have been members of S.E.S. (established by Portuguese immigrants in "memory of the sons of Portugal") for at least 2 years prior to filing a scholarship application and have their premiums paid to date. They must be graduating high school seniors at the time of application or have graduated from high school during the current year. All applicants must have at least a 3.0 grade point average in their sophomore, junior, and first semester of their senior year in high school (verified by official transcript). Selection is based on academic records, other objective measures of achievement, course of study, school service, community service, extracurricular activities, and work experience.

Financial data: Stipends range from $500 to $1,400 (payable in 2 equal installments); a total of $20,000 is distributed annually.

Duration: 1 year.

Additional information: This organization is also known as Conselho Supremo da Sociedade do Espirito Santo (Society of the Holy Spirit). Recipients must attend college on a full-time basis.

Number awarded: 25 each year: 1 at $1,400; 1 at $1,200; 1 at $1,100; 2 at $1,000; 4 at $900; 5 at $800; 6 at $700; and 5 at $500.

Deadline: March of each year.

1053
SUPREME COUNCIL OF U.P.E.C. SCHOLARSHIP

Conselho Supremo da Uniao Portuguesa do Estado da California
1120 East 14th Street
San Leandro, CA 94577
Phone: (510) 483-7676   Fax: (510) 483-5015
Summary: To provide financial assistance for college to high school seniors who are members of the Conselho Supremo da Uniao Portuguesa do Estado da California (U.P.E.C.).
Eligibility: Eligible to apply for these scholarships are graduating high school seniors who have been members of the U.P.E.C. for the past 2 years, have maintained at least a 3.0 grade point average in their sophomore through senior years (official transcripts required), and have participated in at least 3 extracurricular activities in high school. Students must apply for either the Full Scholarship (applying to a 4-year school only) or the Junior Scholarship (applying to a 2-year school only). Also required in the application process are 3 letters of recommendation, a recent photograph, and an essay (up to 1,500 words) on their main academic interest and why they chose it. Applicants must intend to attend school on a full-time basis. Financial need is considered in the selection process.
Financial data: Stipends range from $500 to $2,000.
Duration: 1 year.
Additional information: This organization is also known as the Supreme Council of the U.P.E.C.
Number awarded: 20 each year.
Deadline: February of each year.

1054
SURFLANT SCHOLARSHIP FOUNDATION AWARD

SURFLANT Scholarship Foundation
9459 Selby Place
Norfolk, VA 23503
Phone: (757) 423-1772   E-mail: cnslschf@erols.com
Summary: To provide financial assistance for the postsecondary education of the children of active-duty or retired personnel serving under the administrative control of Commander, Naval Surface Force, U.S. Atlantic Fleet (SURFLANT).
Eligibility: Applicants for this scholarship must be high school seniors or graduates planning to enter college to obtain a bachelor's degree. They must be the children of active-duty or retired personnel serving under the administrative control of Commander, Naval Surface Force, U.S. Atlantic Fleet, or who served in such a SURFLANT unit for at least 3 years at any time after January, 1975. Awards are based on academic proficiency, extracurricular activities, character, all-around ability, and financial need.
Financial data: Each of these scholarships is $2,000.
Duration: 1 year; may be renewed.
Additional information: Requests for applications must be accompanied by a self-addressed stamped envelope, along with the name, rank, and social security number of the military sponsor; the name and social security number of the dependent requesting the application; and the dates and SURFLANT duty station of the military sponsor.
Number awarded: 16 each year.
Deadline: April of each year.

1055
SURVIVING DEPENDENTS OF MONTANA FIRE FIGHTERS/PEACE OFFICERS WAIVER

Montana Guaranteed Student Loan Program
2500 Broadway
P.O. Box 203101
Helena, MT 59620-3101
Phone: (406) 444-6594   (800) 537-7508
Fax: (406) 444-1869   E-mail: scholars@mgslp.state.mt.us
Web Site: www.mgslp.state.mt.us/parents/fee_waivers.html
Summary: To provide financial assistance for undergraduate education to dependents of deceased fire fighters or peace officers in Montana.
Eligibility: Eligible for this benefit are residents of Montana who are surviving spouses or children of Montana fire fighters or peace officers killed in the course and scope of employment. Financial need is considered.
Financial data: Students eligible for this benefit are entitled to attend any unit of the Montana University System without payment of undergraduate registration or incidental fees.
Duration: Undergraduate students are eligible for continued fee waiver as long as

they maintain reasonable academic progress as full-time students.
Additional information: The waiver does not apply if the recipient is eligible for educational benefits from any governmental or private program that provides comparable benefits.
Number awarded: Varies each year.

1056
SURVIVING DEPENDENTS OF MONTANA NATIONAL GUARD MEMBER WAIVER

Montana Guaranteed Student Loan Program
2500 Broadway
P.O. Box 203101
Helena, MT 59620-3101
Phone: (406) 444-6594   (800) 537-7508
Fax: (406) 444-1869   E-mail: scholars@mgslp.state.mt.us
Web Site: www.mgslp.state.mt.us/parents/fee_waivers.html
Summary: To provide financial assistance for undergraduate education to dependents of deceased National Guard members in Montana.
Eligibility: Eligible for this benefit are residents of Montana who are surviving spouses or children of Montana National Guard members killed as a result of injury, disease, or other disability incurred in the line of duty while serving on state active duty. Financial need is considered.
Financial data: Students eligible for this benefit are entitled to attend any unit of the Montana University System without payment of undergraduate registration or incidental fees.
Duration: Undergraduate students are eligible for continued fee waiver as long as they maintain reasonable academic progress as full-time students.
Additional information: The waiver does not apply if the recipient is eligible for educational benefits from any governmental or private program that provides comparable benefits.
Number awarded: Varies each year.

1057
SURVIVORS' AND DEPENDENTS' EDUCATIONAL ASSISTANCE PROGRAM

Department of Veterans Affairs
810 Vermont Avenue, N.W.
Washington, DC 20420
Phone: (202) 418-4343   (888) GI-BILL1
Web Site: www.gibill.va.gov
Summary: To provide financial assistance for postsecondary education to children and spouses of veterans whose deaths or permanent and total disabilities were service connected.
Eligibility: Eligible for this assistance are spouses and children of 1) veterans who died or are permanently and totally disabled as the result of a disability arising from active service in the armed forces; 2) veterans who died from any cause while rated permanently and totally disabled from a service-connected disability; 3) servicemembers listed for more than 90 days as currently missing in action or captured in the line of duty by a hostile force; and 4) servicemembers listed for more than 90 days as presently detained or interned by a foreign government or power. Children must be between 18 and 26 years of age, although extensions may be granted. Spouses and children over 14 years of age with physical or mental disabilities are also eligible.
Financial data: Monthly stipends from this program are $670 for full-time study at an academic institution, $503 for three-quarter time, or $335 for half-time. For farm cooperative work, the monthly stipends are $541 for full-time, $406 for three-quarter time, or $271 for half-time. For an apprenticeship or on-the-job training, the monthly stipend is $488 for the first 6 months, $365 for the second 6 months, $242 for the third 6 months, and $122 for the remainder of the program.
Duration: Up to 45 months (or the equivalent in part-time training). Spouses must complete their training within 10 years of the date they are first found eligible.
Additional information: Benefits may be used for the pursuit of associate, bachelor, or graduate degrees at colleges and universities, including independent study, cooperative training, and study abroad programs. Courses leading to a certificate or diploma from business, technical, or vocational schools may also be taken. Other eligible programs include apprenticeships, on-job training programs, farm cooperative courses, correspondence courses (for spouses only), secondary school programs (for recipients who are not high school graduates), tutorial assistance, remedial deficiency and refresher training, or work-study (for recipients who are enrolled at least three-quarter time). Eligible children who are

handicapped by a physical or mental disability that prevents pursuit of an educational program may receive special restorative training that includes language retraining, lip reading, auditory training, Braille reading and writing, and similar programs. Eligible spouses and children over 14 years of age who are handicapped by a physical or mental disability that prevents pursuit of an educational program may receive specialized vocational training that includes specialized courses, alone or in combination with other courses, leading to a vocational objective that is suitable for the person and required by reason of physical or mental handicap. Ineligible courses include bartending or personality development courses; correspondence courses by dependent or surviving children; non-accredited independent study courses; any course given by radio; vocational flight training; self-improvement courses such as reading, speaking, woodworking, basic seamanship, and English as a second language; audited courses; any course that is avocational or recreational in character; courses not leading to an educational, professional, or vocational objective; courses taken and successfully completed previously; courses taken by a federal government employee and paid for under the Government Employees' Training Act; and courses taken while in receipt of benefits for the same program from the Office of Workers' Compensation Programs.

Number awarded: Varies each year.

Deadline: Applications may be submitted at any time.

1058
SUSAN W. FREESTONE EDUCATION AWARD

New York State Grange
100 Grange Place
Cortland, NY 13045
Phone: (607) 756-7553   Fax: (607) 756-7757
Summary: To provide financial assistance for college to members of the Grange in New York.
Eligibility: This program is open to high school seniors who have been a member of a Junior Grange in New York and/or are currently a member of a Subordinate Grange. Applicants must be interested in enrolling in an approved 2-year or 4-year college or university in New York. Selection is based on high school activities and grades.
Financial data: The stipend is $1,000 per year for current Subordinate Grange members who also have been a Junior Grange member. Current Subordinate Grange members who were not Junior Grangers are eligible for a $500 grant.
Duration: 1 year (the first year of college); may be renewed for the second year of college if the recipient applies again and supplies a satisfactory transcript of work from the college.
Number awarded: Up to 10 each year.
Deadline: April of each year.

1059
SUSIE HOLMES MEMORIAL SCHOLARSHIP

International Order of Job's Daughters
Supreme Guardian Council Headquarters
Attn: Executive Manager
233 West Sixth Street
Papillion, NE 68046-2177
Phone: (402) 592-7987   Fax: (402) 592-2177
E-mail: sgc@iojd.org
Web Site: www.iojd.org
Summary: To provide financial assistance for college to members of Job's Daughters.
Eligibility: This program is open to high school graduates who are members of Job's Daughters. Applicants must be able to demonstrate dedicated, continuous, and joyful service to Job's Daughters; regular attendance at Supreme and/or Grand Sessions; participation in competitions at Supreme and/or Grand Sessions; friendship and impartiality in their Bethel; good character and integrity; and a grade point average of 2.5 or higher.
Financial data: The stipend is $1,000.
Duration: 1 year.
Additional information: Information is also available from the Education Scholarships Committee, c/o Elaine Davies, Chair, 9432 Asbury Circle, Westminster, CA 92683-6509, (714) 531-8384, E-mail: raydavies@earthlink.net.
Number awarded: 1 or more each year.
Deadline: April of each year.

1060
SYNOD OF LIVING WATERS RACIAL ETHNIC COLLEGE SCHOLARSHIP

Synod of Living Waters
318 Seaboard Lane, Suite 205
Franklin, TN 37067-8242
Phone: (615) 261-4008   Fax: (615) 261-4010
E-mail: info@synodoflivingwaters.com
Web Site: www.synodoflivingwaters.com
Summary: To provide financial assistance to minority college students who reside within the boundaries of the Presbyterian Synod of Living Waters.
Eligibility: This program is open to members of racial ethnic minorities (African American, Asian American, Hispanic American, or Native American) who reside within the Synod of Living Waters (Alabama, Kentucky, Mississippi, and Tennessee). Applicants must be full-time students attending a synod Presbyterian college with a grade point average of 3.0 or higher. They must be able to demonstrate participation in the spiritual life of their school and financial need.
Financial data: The stipend is $1,000.
Duration: 1 year.
Number awarded: 10 each year.

1061
SYNOD OF THE TRINITY EDUCATIONAL SCHOLARSHIPS

Synod of the Trinity
Attn: Scholarships
3040 Market Street
Camp Hill, PA 17011-4599
Phone: (717) 737-0421   (800) 242-0534
Fax: (717) 737-8211   E-mail: Scholarships@syntrin.org
Web Site: www.syntrin.org/program/funding.htm
Summary: To provide financial assistance for college to disadvantaged Presbyterian students in Pennsylvania, West Virginia, and designated counties in Ohio.
Eligibility: Persons applying for aid must be economically disadvantaged; members of the Presbyterian Church (USA) or attending a Presbyterian Church (USA) college within the Synod of the Trinity; residents of that synod (Pennsylvania, West Virginia, and the Ohio counties of Belmont, Harrison, Jefferson, Monroe, and Columbiana); and accepted or enrolled as a full-time student at an accredited undergraduate or vocational school. Priority is given to applicants entering or enrolled at synod-related colleges. Financial aid is given only after the synod has determined that an applicant is eligible and that family resources are insufficient to meet college costs.
Financial data: Awards range from $100 to $1,000 per year, depending on the need of the recipient.
Duration: 1 year; may be renewed.
Additional information: The synod-related institutions are Arcadia University (Glenside, Pennsylvania), Davis and Elkins College (Elkins, West Virginia), Grove City College (Grove City, Pennsylvania), Lafayette College (Easton, Pennsylvania), Waynesburg College (Waynesburg, Pennsylvania), Westminster College (New Wilmington, Pennsylvania), and Wilson College (Chambersburg, Pennsylvania). Students may not apply for this program and the Racial Ethnic Educational Scholarship Program of the Synod of the Trinity.
Number awarded: Varies each year.
Deadline: March of each year.

1062
TAILHOOK EDUCATIONAL FOUNDATION SCHOLARSHIPS

Tailhook Educational Foundation
P.O. Box 26626
San Diego, CA 92196-0626
Phone: (800) 269-8267
Web Site: www.tailhook.org
Summary: To provide financial assistance for postsecondary education to veterans or the dependents of veterans associated with naval aviation and/or aircraft carriers.
Eligibility: This program is open to veterans (and their dependent children) who served either 1) in the U.S. Navy, U.S. Marine Corps, or U.S. Coast Guard as a naval aviator, naval flight officer, or designated naval air crewman, or 2) on board a U.S. Navy aircraft carrier in any capacity as a member of ship's company or assigned airwing. Applicants may be high school seniors, high school graduates, college students, or graduate students. Selection is based on educational and

extracurricular achievements, merit, and citizenship.

Financial data: The stipend is $1,500.
Duration: 1 year.
Number awarded: 15 each year.
Deadline: March of each year.

1063
TALBOTS WOMEN'S SCHOLARSHIP FUND

Talbots
c/o Citizens' Scholarship Foundation of America
Scholarship Management Services
1505 Riverview Road
P.O. Box 297
St. Peter, MN 56082
Phone: (507) 931-1682   (800) 537-4180
Fax: (507) 931-9168   E-mail: info_sms@csfa.org
Web Site: www.talbots.com/about/scholar/scholar.asp
Summary: To provide financial assistance to women returning to college after an absence of at least 10 years.
Eligibility: This program is open to women who earned their high school diploma or GED at least 10 years ago and are now seeking a degree from an accredited 2- or 4-year college or university or vocational-technical school. Applicants must have at least 2 full-time semesters remaining to complete their undergraduate degree. As part of the selection process, they must submit an essay on their plans as they relate to their educational and career objectives and long-term goals. In addition to that essay, selection is based on academic record, leadership and participation in community activities, honors, work experience, an outside appraisal, and financial need.
Financial data: Stipends are either $10,000 or $1,000. Checks are mailed to the recipient's home address and are made payable jointly to the student and the school.
Duration: 1 year; nonrenewable.
Additional information: Applications are available at Talbots' stores in the United States. Only the first 1,000 eligible applications received are processed.
Number awarded: 55 each year: 5 at $10,000 and 50 at $1,000.
Deadline: March of each year.

1064
TARGET ALL-AROUND SCHOLARSHIPS

Target Stores
33 South Sixth Street
P.O. Box 1392
Minneapolis, MN 55440-1392
Phone: (800) 537-4180
Web Site: www.target.com/target_group/community/community_sge.jhtml
Summary: To provide financial assistance for college to high school seniors committed to helping their communities.
Eligibility: Eligible to be considered for this support are high school seniors and current college students who are younger than 24 years of age and making contributions to their community through volunteer service, education, and family involvement. Applicants must have a grade point average of 2.0 or higher and be enrolled or planning to enroll full time at an accredited 2- or 4-year college, university, or vocational-technical school in the continental United States. Selection is based on number of community volunteer service hours, the applicant's list of volunteer leadership awards and honors, an appraisal form completed by a volunteer supervisor or leader, and the applicant's short essay on volunteer service. Applications are available at any Target store.
Financial data: Each Target store awards 2 scholarships at $1,000 each. Those students are then considered for the Grand Scholarships, which are worth $10,000.
Duration: 1 year.
Additional information: This program is administered by the Citizens' Scholarship Foundation of America, P.O. Box 297, St. Peter, MN 56082, (507) 931-1682, (800) 537-4180, Fax: (507) 931-9168, E-mail: info_sms@csfa.org. This program is not currently offered in Alaska, Hawaii, Puerto Rico, or outside the United States.
Number awarded: 4 Grand Scholarship winners, plus 2 local winners chosen by each Target store (for a total of more than 2,100 scholarships).
Deadline: October of each year.

1065
TENNESSEE DEPENDENT CHILDREN SCHOLARSHIP

Tennessee Student Assistance Corporation
Parkway Towers
404 James Robertson Parkway, Suite 1950
Nashville, TN 37243-0820
Phone: (615) 741-1346   (800) 342-1663
Fax: (615) 741-6101   E-mail: tsac@mail.state.tn.us
Web Site: www.state.tn.us/tsac
Summary: To provide financial assistance for postsecondary education to the dependent children of disabled or deceased Tennessee law enforcement officers, fire fighters, or emergency medical service technicians.
Eligibility: This program is open to Tennessee residents who are the dependent children of a Tennessee law enforcement officer, fire fighter, or emergency medical service technician who was killed or totally and permanently disabled in the line of duty. Applicants must be enrolled or accepted for enrollment as a full-time undergraduate student at a college or university in Tennessee.
Financial data: The award covers tuition and fees, books, supplies, and room and board, minus any other financial aid for which the student is eligible.
Duration: 1 year; may be renewed.
Additional information: This program was established in 1990.
Deadline: July of each year.

1066
TENNESSEE EDUCATIONAL ASSISTANCE FOR CHILDREN OF VETERANS

Department of Veterans Affairs
215 Eighth Avenue North
Nashville, TN 37243-1010
Phone: (615) 741-2930   Fax: (615) 741-4785
E-mail: jhill7@mail.state.tn.us
Web Site: www.state.tn.us/veteran/benefitsstate.html
Summary: To provide financial assistance for postsecondary education to children of deceased Tennessee veterans or those declared prisoners of war or missing in action.
Eligibility: Applicants for this assistance must be the children of veterans who were killed in action or died as the result of injuries in World War II, the Korean conflict, or the Vietnam hostilities. Also eligible are minor children (under the age of 21) of veterans who were declared prisoners of war or missing in action in Vietnam. The deceased, missing, or prisoner of war parent must have been a resident of Tennessee at the time of death or at the time the parent was reported missing or a prisoner of war.
Financial data: Qualifying students are eligible to receive free tuition and exemption from certain fees at any college or university owned and operated by the state of Tennessee.
Duration: Assistance continues until 1 of the following occurs: 1) the student completes his or her education; 2) the student completes 130 semester hours; or 3) the student completes 9 semesters toward graduation.
Number awarded: Varies each year.

1067
TENNESSEE LEGION EAGLE SCOUT OF THE YEAR SCHOLARSHIP

American Legion
Attn: Department of Tennessee
215 Eighth Avenue North
Nashville, TN 37203-3583
Phone: (615) 254-0568   Fax: (615) 255-1551
E-mail: tnamerleg@datatek.com
Summary: To provide financial assistance for postsecondary education to outstanding Eagle Scouts in Tennessee.
Eligibility: The Tennessee nominee for American Legion Scout of the Year receives this scholarship. Applicants must be 1) registered, active members of a Boy Scout Troop or Varsity Scout Team sponsored by an American Legion Post in Tennessee or Auxiliary Unit in Tennessee, or 2) registered, active members of a duly chartered Boy Scout Troop or Varsity Scout Team and the sons or grandsons of American Legion or Auxiliary members.
Financial data: The award is $1,500.
Duration: 1 year.
Additional information: Funds may be used to attend any postsecondary institution in the United States.
Number awarded: 1 each year.

1068
TENNESSEE STUDENT ASSISTANCE AWARD

Tennessee Student Assistance Corporation
Parkway Towers
404 James Robertson Parkway, Suite 1950
Nashville, TN 37243-0820
Phone: (615) 741-1346   (800) 342-1663
Fax: (615) 741-6101   E-mail: tsac@mail.state.tn.us
Web Site: www.state.tn.us/tsac
Summary: To provide financial assistance to students in Tennessee who have financial need.
Eligibility: This program is open to students in Tennessee who are U.S. citizens, are Tennessee residents, are enrolled at least half time as undergraduate students, and can demonstrate financial need.
Financial data: The maximum award is $1,938 at eligible Tennessee public postsecondary institutions or up to $4,530 at eligible Tennessee independent postsecondary institutions.
Duration: 1 year; nonrenewable.
Additional information: This program was established in 1976.
Number awarded: Varies each year.
Deadline: April of each year.

1069
TERRA AVIONICS COLLEGIATE SCHOLARSHIP

Aircraft Electronics Association
Attn: President
4217 South Hocker Drive
Independence, MO 64055-4723
Phone: (816) 373-6565   Fax: (816) 478-3100
E-mail: info@aea.net
Web Site: www.aea.net
Summary: To provide financial assistance for college to members of the Aircraft Electronics Association and their children.
Eligibility: This program is open to high school seniors, high school graduates, and currently-enrolled college students who are either members or the children of members of the association. They must submit an essay (up to 2,500 words) on this topic: "How to Prosper in Today's General Aviation Market." The scholarship may be used for any field of study.
Financial data: The stipend is $2,500; funds must be used for tuition.
Duration: 1 year.
Number awarded: 1 each year.
Deadline: February of each year.

1070
TET '68 SCHOLARSHIP

TET '68, Inc.
Attn: Scholarship Competition
P.O. Box 31885
Richmond, VA 23294
Phone: (804) 550-3642   E-mail: TET68INFO@aol.com
Web Site: www.tet68.org/TET68sch.html
Summary: To provide financial assistance to high school seniors whose parent served in Vietnam.
Eligibility: This program is open to high school seniors whose parent or stepparent is a Vietnam veteran. Qualified seniors are invited to write a short essay on "What is Freedom" and submit this for judging. Each application must include the following: a copy of the parent's or stepparent's DD214 showing Vietnam service with Campaign Ribbon Award, the essay (500 word maximum), and a cover sheet that includes the applicant's full name, address and phone number; the name, address, and phone number of a contact person at the applicant's high school; and the name, address, and phone number of a contact person at the senior's chosen college.
Financial data: The scholarship is $1,000.
Duration: The competition is held annually.
Additional information: This program began in 1988. The sponsor owns the winning essays and can publish them.
Number awarded: 3 each year.
Deadline: March of each year.

1071
TEXAS CHILDREN OF DISABLED OR DECEASED FIREMEN, PEACE OFFICERS, GAME WARDENS, AND EMPLOYEES OF CORRECTIONAL INSTITUTIONS EXEMPTION PROGRAM

Texas Higher Education Coordinating Board
Attn: Grants and Special Programs
1200 East Anderson Lane
P.O. Box 12788, Capitol Station
Austin, TX 78711-2788
Phone: (512) 427-6101   (800) 242-3062
Fax: (512) 427-6127   E-mail: grantinfo@thecb.state.tx.us
Web Site: www.collegefortexans.com
Summary: To provide educational assistance to the children of disabled or deceased Texas fire fighters, peace officers, game wardens, and employees of correctional institutions.
Eligibility: Eligible are children of disabled or deceased Texas paid or volunteer fire fighters, peace officers, custodial employees of the Department of Corrections, or game wardens whose disability or death occurred in the line of duty. Applicants must be under 21 years of age.
Financial data: Eligible students are exempted from the payment of all dues, fees, and tuition charges at publicly-supported colleges and universities in Texas.
Duration: Support is provided for up to 120 semester credit hours of undergraduate study or until the recipient reaches 26 years of age.
Number awarded: Varies each year; recently, 101 students received support through this program.

1072
TEXAS CHILDREN OF U.S. MILITARY WHO ARE MISSING IN ACTION OR PRISONERS OF WAR EXEMPTION PROGRAM

Texas Higher Education Coordinating Board
Attn: Grants and Special Programs
1200 East Anderson Lane
P.O. Box 12788, Capitol Station
Austin, TX 78711-2788
Phone: (512) 427-6101   (800) 242-3062
Fax: (512) 427-6127   E-mail: grantinfo@thecb.state.tx.us
Web Site: www.collegefortexans.com
Summary: To provide educational assistance to the children of Texas military personnel declared prisoners of war or missing in action.
Eligibility: Eligible are dependent children of Texas residents who are either prisoners of war or missing in action. Applicants must be under 21 years of age, or under 25 if they receive the majority of support from their parent(s).
Financial data: Eligible students are exempted from the payment of all dues, fees, and tuition charges at publicly-supported colleges and universities in Texas.
Duration: Up to 8 semesters.
Number awarded: Varies each year; recently, 3 of these exemptions were granted.

1073
TEXAS EARLY HIGH SCHOOL GRADUATION SCHOLARSHIPS

Texas Higher Education Coordinating Board
Attn: Grants and Special Programs
1200 East Anderson Lane
P.O. Box 12788, Capitol Station
Austin, TX 78711-2788
Phone: (512) 427-6101   (800) 242-3062
Fax: (512) 427-6127   E-mail: grantinfo@thecb.state.tx.us
Web Site: www.collegefortexans.com
Summary: To provide financial assistance to students in Texas who are planning to attend college after completing high school in less than 3 years.
Eligibility: This program is open to residents of Texas who completed the requirements for graduation from a public high school, grades 9 through 12, in the state in no more than 36 consecutive months. Applicants may be planning to attend a college or university in Texas on either a part-time or full-time basis.
Financial data: The maximum award from this program is $1,000. If the award is used at a private college or university, the school must provide a matching scholarship of $1,000 to equal the award from the state.
Duration: 1 year; nonrenewable.
Additional information: Interested students should contact their high school counselor. This program was established in 1995.
Number awarded: Varies each year; recently, 3,923 of these scholarships were awarded.

1074
TEXAS EDUCATIONAL BENEFITS FOR VETERANS AND DEPENDENTS

Texas Veterans Commission
P.O. Box 12277
Austin, TX 78711-2277
Phone: (512) 463-5538   Fax: (512) 475-2395
E-mail: texas.veterans.commission@tvc.state.tx.us
Web Site: www.tvc.state.tx.us
Summary: To provide free tuition assistance to Texas veterans and to children of Texas veterans who are deceased, missing in action, or prisoners of war.
Eligibility: Eligible for this program are 1) veterans who were legal residents of Texas at the time they entered military service and who served in World War I, World War II, Korea, or for 180 days during any subsequent designated national emergency (Vietnam, Grenada and Lebanon, Panama, the Persian Gulf, or any future national emergency declared in accordance with federal law); 2) children of Texas servicemen who died or were killed in military service, are missing in action, or are prisoners of war; or 3) children of members of the Texas National Guard or Texas Air National Guard killed since January 1, 1946 while on active duty in the service of either Texas or the United States. Any person claiming this benefit must also have been a legal resident of Texas for at least 12 months at the time of application.
Financial data: Veterans or their children who are eligible for this benefit are entitled to free tuition and fees at state-supported colleges and universities in Texas.
Duration: Exemptions may be claimed up to a cumulative total of 150 credit hours.
Additional information: Another name for this program is the Hazelwood Act. Information is also available from the Texas Higher Education Coordinating Board, Division of Student Services, P.O. Box 12788, Capitol Station, Austin, TX 78711-2788, (512) 427-6101. This benefit is available only after eligible veterans have used their Montgomery GI Bill or other federal entitlements, or after the time limits for the entitlements have expired.
Number awarded: Varies each year.

1075
TEXAS EXEMPTION FOR HIGHEST RANKING HIGH SCHOOL GRADUATE PROGRAM

Texas Higher Education Coordinating Board
Attn: Grants and Special Programs
1200 East Anderson Lane
P.O. Box 12788, Capitol Station
Austin, TX 78711-2788
Phone: (512) 427-6101   (800) 242-3062
Fax: (512) 427-6127   E-mail: grantinfo@thecb.state.tx.us
Web Site: www.collegefortexans.com
Summary: To recognize and reward the top students in Texas high schools.
Eligibility: This award is presented to the highest ranking graduate (i.e., valedictorians) of accredited high schools in Texas. Applicants may be Texas residents, nonresidents, or foreign students.
Financial data: Tuition is waived for award winners at any public college or university in Texas.
Duration: 1 year; nonrenewable.
Number awarded: Varies each year; recently, 755 of these exemptions were granted.

1076
TEXAS FARM BUREAU TALENT FIND CONTEST

Texas Farm Bureau
P.O. Box 2689
Waco, TX 76702-2689
Phone: (254) 772-3030   E-mail: rglasson@txfb.org
Web Site: www.txfb.org/educate/talentsch.htm
Summary: To recognize and reward members of the Texas Farm Bureau (TFB) who present outstanding demonstrations of talent.
Eligibility: Contestants in this program must be between 16 and 19 years of age and a TFB member or a member of a TFB family. They must present an act that is confined to a normal stage setting and not deemed dangerous in nature to audience or participant. They may not have received direct remuneration for the performance of the talent or be Farm Bureau employees, dealers, and/or servicing agents' families. Selection is based on audience appeal, performance, appearance, and professionalism.

Financial data: District winners receive $1,000 scholarships. Winners at the state contest have the opportunity to receive additional funding to increase their scholarship to $1,500 as runner-up or $2,000 as state winner.
Duration: The contest is held annually.
Number awarded: 13 district winners are selected each year. Of those, 1 is designated as runner-up and 1 as the state winner.

1077
TEXAS FISH AND GAME SCHOLARSHIPS

Texas FFA Association
614 East 12th Street
Austin, TX 78701
Phone: (512) 480-8045   Fax: (512) 472-0555
E-mail: txffa@txaged.org
Web Site: www.txaged.org
Summary: To provide financial assistance for college to high school students in Texas who have sold at least 1 subscription to *Texas Fish and Game Magazine* while in high school.
Eligibility: This program is open to high school students in Texas who plan to attend a trade or technical school, 2-year college, or 4-year college or university. All applicants must have sold at least 1 subscription to *Texas Fish and Game Magazine.* Selection is based on community activities (20 points), work experience (20 points), school activities (20 points), need for the scholarship (10 points), and a 150-word paragraph explaining why awarding the scholarship to the applicant would be a wise investment (30 points).
Financial data: The stipend is $1,000.
Duration: 1 year.
Additional information: Information on these scholarships is also available from *Texas Fish and Game Magazine,* P.O. Box 148, Marble Falls, TX 78654, (830) 693-0936. If a high school freshman, sophomore, or junior receives a scholarship, the money is held in trust until the student graduates and is accepted to a school of higher education.
Number awarded: 30 each year: 3 in each area of the state.

1078
TEXAS KNIGHTS TEMPLAR GRANTS

Texas Knights Templar Educational Foundation
507 South Harwood Street
Dallas, TX 75201
Phone: (214) 651-6070   Fax: (214) 744-3622
Summary: To provide financial assistance to undergraduate and graduate students from Texas.
Eligibility: Applicants must have completed at least 30 college hours and be residents of Texas. They must be in school full time and have at least 2 years to go before graduating. Selection is based on academic ability, character, responsibility, leadership, community service, and financial need.
Financial data: Grants range up to $3,000 per year although most are for $1,000. Funds must be used for tuition and living expenses.
Duration: 1 semester or year.
Additional information: Interested students must send a stamped self-addressed 9 x 12 inch envelope.
Number awarded: Varies each year.
Deadline: May for the fall semester; September for the spring semester.

1079
TEXAS LEVERAGING EDUCATIONAL ASSISTANCE PARTNERSHIP PROGRAM

Texas Higher Education Coordinating Board
Attn: Grants and Special Programs
1200 East Anderson Lane
P.O. Box 12788, Capitol Station
Austin, TX 78711-2788
Phone: (512) 427-6101   (800) 242-3062
Fax: (512) 427-6127   E-mail: grantinfo@thecb.state.tx.us
Web Site: www.collegefortexans.com
Summary: To provide financial assistance to students at colleges and universities in Texas who are also receiving other state funds.
Eligibility: This program is open to Texas residents who are enrolled or accepted for enrollment at least half time at a college or university in Texas on the undergraduate or graduate level. Financial need must be demonstrated. Applicants must also be receiving funding from another state program (either the

Texas Public Educational Grant Program for students at public colleges and universities or the Texas Tuition Equalization Grant Program for students at private colleges and universities).

Financial data: The stipend depends on the need of the recipient, to a maximum of $1,250; recently, the average annual award was $828 for students at public colleges and universities and $832 for students at private colleges and universities.

Duration: 1 year; may be renewed.

Number awarded: Varies each year; recently, 837 of these grants were awarded to students at public colleges and universities and 1,855 to students at private colleges and universities.

1080
TEXAS NEW HORIZONS SCHOLARSHIP PROGRAM

Texas Higher Education Coordinating Board
Attn: Grants and Special Programs
1200 East Anderson Lane
P.O. Box 12788, Capitol Station
Austin, TX 78711-2788
Phone: (512) 427-6101   (800) 242-3062
Fax: (512) 427-6127   E-mail: grantinfo@thecb.state.tx.us
Web Site: www.collegefortexans.com
Summary: To provide educational assistance to students in Texas who are attending colleges and universities in the state.
Eligibility: This program is open to residents of Texas who are enrolled at least half time at public or independent colleges and universities in the state. Applicants must be able to document financial need.
Financial data: The maximum award is the lesser of the student's financial need or the amount of tuition and fees charged at a public institution.
Duration: 1 year.
Additional information: This program began in 1998. Further information is available from the financial aid office at any public or eligible independent college or university in Texas.
Number awarded: Varies each year.

1081
TEXAS STUDENTS IN FOSTER OR OTHER RESIDENTIAL CARE EXEMPTION PROGRAM

Texas Higher Education Coordinating Board
Attn: Grants and Special Programs
1200 East Anderson Lane
P.O. Box 12788, Capitol Station
Austin, TX 78711-2788
Phone: (512) 427-6101   (800) 242-3062
Fax: (512) 427-6127   E-mail: grantinfo@thecb.state.tx.us
Web Site: www.collegefortexans.com
Summary: To provide educational assistance to students in Texas who were in foster care.
Eligibility: Eligible are students who have been in foster care or other residential care under the conservatorship of the Texas Department of Protective and Regulatory Services on or after the day preceding their 18th birthday, the day of their 14th birthday (if they were also eligible for adoption on or after that day), or the day they graduated from high school or received the equivalent of a high school degree. Applicants must enroll as an undergraduate not later than the third anniversary of the date they were discharged from the foster or other residential care (but no later than their 21st birthday).
Financial data: Eligible students are exempted from the payment of all dues, fees, and tuition charges at publicly-supported colleges and universities in Texas.
Duration: 1 year.
Number awarded: Varies each year; recently, 464 students received support through this program.

1082
TEXAS TANF EXEMPTION PROGRAM

Texas Higher Education Coordinating Board
Attn: Grants and Special Programs
1200 East Anderson Lane
P.O. Box 12788, Capitol Station
Austin, TX 78711-2788
Phone: (512) 427-6101   (800) 242-3062
Fax: (512) 427-6127   E-mail: grantinfo@thecb.state.tx.us
Web Site: www.collegefortexans.com

Summary: To provide educational assistance to students in Texas who are receiving Temporary Assistance to Needy Families (TANF).
Eligibility: Eligible are students who graduated from a public high school in Texas and who, during the final year of high school, received TANF for at least 6 months. Applicants must be younger than 22 years of age at the time of enrollment in college and must enroll in college within 24 months of high school graduation.
Financial data: Eligible students are exempted from the payment of all fees (other than building use fees) and tuition charges at publicly-supported colleges and universities in Texas.
Duration: 1 year.
Number awarded: Varies each year; recently, 156 of these awards were made.

1083
TEXAS TENNIS FOUNDATION SCHOLARSHIP

Texas Tennis Foundation
2111 Dickson, Suite 33
Austin, TX 78704-4788
Phone: (512) 443-1334   Fax: (512) 443-4748
Web Site: www.ustatexas.org
Summary: To provide financial assistance for college to students in Texas who have an interest in tennis.
Eligibility: This program is open to students who have an interest in tennis, are U.S. citizens, and live in Texas. They must be high school students who will be entering college or college students who are in good standing at their respective colleges or universities. Financial need must be demonstrated. Qualified students must submit a completed application, federal income tax returns from the previous 2 years, an academic transcript, a copy of their SAT or ACT test results, a list of extracurricular activities (including tennis activities), a personal statement, and a letter of recommendation. Selection is based on merit and financial need.
Financial data: The stipend is $1,000.
Duration: 1 year.
Additional information: Recipients must attend school on a full-time basis. They must send a brief written report following their first semester of the scholarship year; this report should indicate their educational achievements during the semester, tennis activities if any, and goals for the second semester.
Number awarded: 1 or more each year.
Deadline: April of each year.

1084
TEXAS TUITION ASSISTANCE GRANT PROGRAM

Texas Higher Education Coordinating Board
Attn: Grants and Special Programs
1200 East Anderson Lane
P.O. Box 12788, Capitol Station
Austin, TX 78711-2788
Phone: (512) 427-6101   (800) 242-3062
Fax: (512) 427-6127   E-mail: grantinfo@thecb.state.tx.us
Web Site: www.collegefortexans.com
Summary: To provide financial assistance to undergraduate students attending college in Texas.
Eligibility: This program is open to residents of Texas who are undergraduates enrolled on a full-time basis at public or nonprofit independent colleges in the state. Candidates must apply within 2 years of high school graduation. For the original award, applicants must have a high school grade point average of 80 on a scale of 100; for continuation awards, students must have at least a 2.5 grade point average in college.
Financial data: Awards are made for the student's unmet financial need or the tuition charged at a public senior level institution, whichever is lesser.
Duration: 1 year; may be renewed.
Additional information: Information and application forms may be obtained from the director of financial aid at the public college or university in Texas the applicant attends. Study must be conducted in Texas; funds cannot be used to support attendance at an out-of-state institution.
Number awarded: Varies each year; recently, 264 of these awards were granted.

1085
TEXAS TUITION EQUALIZATION GRANT PROGRAM

Texas Higher Education Coordinating Board
Attn: Grants and Special Programs
1200 East Anderson Lane
P.O. Box 12788, Capitol Station
Austin, TX 78711-2788
Phone: (512) 427-6101   (800) 242-3062
Fax: (512) 427-6127   E-mail: grantinfo@thecb.state.tx.us
Web Site: www.collegefortexans.com
Summary: To provide financial assistance to undergraduate and graduate students attending private postsecondary schools in Texas.
Eligibility: This program is open to Texas residents or National Merit Scholarship finalists who are enrolled at least half time as an undergraduate or graduate student at an eligible nonprofit independent college in the state. Applicants may not be majoring in theology or religion or be on an athletic scholarship. Financial need is considered in the selection process.
Financial data: The maximum awarded is the lesser of the student's unmet need or the amount they would pay at a public institution (currently, $3,380). Recently, the average grant was $2,272.
Duration: 1 year; may be renewed.
Additional information: Information and application forms may be obtained from the director of financial aid at any participating nonprofit independent college or university in Texas. Study must be conducted in Texas; funds cannot be used to support attendance at an out-of-state institution.
Number awarded: Varies each year; recently, 27,379 of these grants were awarded.

1086
TEXAS URBAN SCHOLARSHIP PROGRAM

Texas Association of Developing Colleges
1140 Empire Central, Suite 550
Dallas, TX 75247
Phone: (214) 630-2511   Fax: (214) 631-2030
Summary: To provide financial assistance for college to high school seniors from the major urban areas throughout Texas.
Eligibility: This program is open to graduating high school seniors who are U.S. citizens, will be attending college on a full-time basis, are able to demonstrate financial need, and are graduating (or have graduated) from a high school in the following cities in Texas: Abilene, Amarillo, Arlington, Austin, Beaumont, Corpus Christi, Dallas, El Paso, Fort Worth, Garland, Houston, Irving, Laredo, Lubbock, Mesquite, Pasadena, Plano, San Antonio, and Waco.
Financial data: Annual stipends are $700 for students at technical, junior, or community colleges, $1,000 for student at public 4-year colleges and universities, or $2,000 for students at independent 4-year colleges.
Duration: 1 year.
Additional information: This scholarship was created in 1995 during the 74th Texas legislative session in cooperating with Southwestern Bell Telephone, GTE/Verizon, and Sprint/United Centel Telephone-Texas. It is administered by the Texas Association of Developing Colleges. Students from nonmetropolitan areas of the state may be covered by the Rural Scholarship Fund, which was also created at the same time.
Number awarded: Approximately 350 per year. A total of $400,000 is available for the program each year.
Deadline: June of each year.

1087
TEXAS WAIVERS OF NONRESIDENT TUITION FOR MILITARY PERSONNEL AND THEIR DEPENDENTS

Texas Veterans Commission
P.O. Box 12277
Austin, TX 78711-2277
Phone: (512) 463-5538   Fax: (512) 475-2395
E-mail: texas.veterans.commission@tvc.state.tx.us
Web Site: www.tvc.state.tx.us
Summary: To exempt military personnel stationed in Texas and their dependents from the payment of nonresident tuition at public institutions of higher education in the state.
Eligibility: Eligible for these waivers are officers or enlisted persons of the Army, Army Reserve, Army National Guard, Air National Guard, Air Force, Air Force Reserve, Navy, Navy Reserve, Marine Corps, Marine Corps Reserve, Coast Guard,

or Coast Guard Reserve who are assigned to duty in Texas, along with the spouses and children of those individuals. Spouses and children residing in Texas while the military person is assigned to duty outside of the state are also eligible, as are spouses and children of members of the armed forces who died while in military service.
Financial data: Although persons eligible under this program are classified as nonresidents, they are entitled to pay the resident tuition at Texas institutions of higher education, regardless of their length of residence in Texas.
Number awarded: Varies each year.

1088
TFB AGRICULTURE RESEARCH AND EDUCATION FOUNDATION SCHOLARSHIP

Texas Farm Bureau
P.O. Box 2689
Waco, TX 76702-2689
Phone: (254) 751-2286   E-mail: scook@txfb.org
Web Site: www.txfb.org/educate/youthsch.htm
Summary: To provide financial assistance for college to high school seniors whose families are members of the Texas Farm Bureau (TFB).
Eligibility: This program is open to Texas graduating high school seniors whose families have been TFB members for at least the prior 2 years. Selection is based on academic achievement, extracurricular activities, recommendations, and financial need.
Financial data: The stipend is $1,000 per year.
Duration: 1 year; may be renewed up to 3 additional years.
Additional information: This program was established by the Texas Farm Bureau Agriculture Research and Education Foundation in 1996.
Number awarded: Varies each year, depending on the availability of funds.
Deadline: March of each year.

1089
THEODORE R. AND VIVIAN M. JOHNSON SCHOLARSHIP PROGRAM

State University System of Florida
Attn: Office of Academic and Student Services
325 West Gaines Street, Suite 1501
Tallahassee, FL 32399-1950
Phone: (850) 201-7216   Fax: (850) 201-7185
E-mail: lpage@borfl.org
Web Site: www.borfl.org
Summary: To provide financial assistance to Florida undergraduate students with disabilities.
Eligibility: Eligible are disabled students working on a degree at a public 4-year university in Florida. Applicants must provide documentation of a disability, 3 reference letters, evidence of financial need, an official transcript, and a completed application form.
Financial data: The maximum stipend is $3,500 per year.
Duration: 1 year; may be renewed if recipient maintains at least a 2.0 grade point average and enrolls in at least 18 credits each academic year.
Additional information: This program is administered by the equal opportunity program at each of the 10 public 4-year institutions in Florida. Contact that office for further information.
Number awarded: Several each year.
Deadline: May of each year.

1090
THIRD WAVE SCHOLARSHIP PROGRAM FOR YOUNG WOMEN

Third Wave Foundation
116 East 16th Street, Seventh Floor
New York, NY 10002
Phone: (212) 388-1898   Fax: (212) 982-3321
E-mail: ThirdwaveF@aol.com
Web Site: www.thirdwavefoundation.org/scholarship.html
Summary: To provide financial assistance for college to women who have been involved in feminist activities.
Eligibility: This program is open to full-time and part-time students under 30 years of age who are enrolled in, or have been accepted to, an accredited university, college, or community college. Applicants should have been involved as activists, artists, or cultural workers on such issues as racism, homophobia,

sexism, or other forms of inequality. They must submit an essay of 500 words or less on their current social change involvement and how it relates to their educational and life goals. Selection is based primarily on financial need.

Financial data: Stipends range from $1,000 to $5,000 per year.

Duration: 1 year.

Number awarded: Varies each year.

Deadline: March or September of each year.

1091
THOMAS WOOD BALDRIDGE SCHOLARSHIP

United States Junior Chamber of Commerce
Attn: Thomas Wood Baldridge Scholarship
4 West 21st Street
Tulsa, OK 74114-1116
Phone: (918) 584-2481   Fax: (918) 584-4422
Web Site: www.usjaycees.org

Summary: To provide financial assistance for college to members of the United States Junior Chamber of Commerce (Jaycees) and their children.

Eligibility: This program is open to Jaycee members and the immediate family members of Jaycees. Applicants must be enrolled in or accepted for admission to a college or university. They must be U.S. citizens, possess academic potential and leadership qualities, and demonstrate financial need. Applications must be sent to the Jaycee state president, who then selects 1 semifinalist and forwards the application to the national office.

Financial data: The stipend is $3,000 per year. Funds are sent directly to the recipient's college or university.

Duration: 1 year; nonrenewable.

Number awarded: 1 each year.

Deadline: Applications must be submitted to the state president by February of each year.

1092
TIP

Family Independence Agency
Attn: Tuition Incentive Program
P.O. Box 30037
Lansing, MI 48909
Phone: (800) 243-2847

Summary: To help pay the college tuition and mandatory fees for students from low-income families in Michigan.

Eligibility: Applicants must be U.S. citizens, be Michigan residents, be receiving (or have received) Medicaid from the Family Independence Agency, and be under the age of 20. They must apply any time after completing the sixth grade but before graduating from high school or receiving a GED.

Financial data: In the first phase, TIP pays tuition and mandatory fees for associate degree or certificate program courses at participating colleges or universities (100 percent at community colleges and public universities; limited reimbursement at participating independent nonprofit colleges and universities); those classes must be taken within 4 years following high school graduation or GED completion. In phase 2, TIP provides up to $2,000 in tuition benefits to qualified students continuing their education beyond the associate degree or certificate program level. TIP does not provide for mileage, books, room and board, or extra tuition for out-of-district students.

Duration: College or university courses must be taken within 4 years following high school graduation or GED completion. The program pays for a maximum of 80 semester or 120 term credits.

Additional information: The following community colleges in Michigan participate in this program: Alpena, Bay De Noc, Bay Mills, Delta, Glen Oaks, Gogebic, Grand Rapids, Henry Ford, Jackson, Kalamazoo Valley, Kellogg, Kirtland, Lake Michigan, Lansing, Macomb, Mid Michigan, Monroe County, Montcalm, Mott, Muskegon, North Central Michigan, Northwestern Michigan, Oakland, St. Clair County, Schoolcraft, Southwestern Michigan, Washtenaw, Wayne County, and West Shore. The participating 4-year public universities are: Ferris State, Lake Superior State, Michigan State, Michigan Technological, and Northern Michigan. The participating independent, nonprofit colleges and universities are: Adrian College, Andrews University, Aquinas College, Baker College, Cleary College, Concordia College, Cornerstone College, Davenport College, Detroit College of Business, Focus: Hope, Grace Bible College, Great Lakes Christian College, Great Lakes College, Lawrence University, Lewis College of Business, Madonna University, Marygrove College, Northwood University, Reformed Bible College, Rochester College, Siena Heights College, Spring Arbor College, Suomi College,

University of Detroit, and Williams Tyndale College. Recipients must attend a participating college or university in Michigan.

Deadline: Applications may be submitted at any time.

1093
TORAJI AND TOKI YOSHINAGA SCHOLARSHIP

Hawai'i Community Foundation
900 Fort Street Mall, Suite 1300
Honolulu, HI 96813
Phone: (808) 566-5570   (888) 731-3863
Fax: (808) 521-6286   E-mail: scholarships@hcf-hawaii.org
Web Site: www.hcf-hawaii.org

Summary: To provide financial assistance to Hawaii residents who are attending college in the state at schools other than the University of Hawaii.

Eligibility: This program is open to Hawaii residents who are sophomores attending college at a school in the state that is not part of the University of Hawaii system. Applicants must meet at least 3 of the following criteria: 1) born in Hawaii; 2) graduate of a Hawaii high school; 3) registered to vote in Hawaii; and 4) lived in Hawaii for 4 years. They must be able to demonstrate academic achievement (at least a 2.7 grade point average), good moral character, and financial need. In addition to filling out the standard application form, applicants must write a short statement indicating their reasons for attending college, their planned course of study, and their career goals.

Financial data: The amounts of the awards depend on the availability of funds and the need of the recipient; recently, grants averaged $1,000.

Duration: 1 year.

Additional information: This program was established in 1999. Recipients must be full-time students.

Number awarded: Varies each year; recently, 2 of these scholarships were awarded.

Deadline: February of each year.

1094
TOWNSHIP OFFICIALS OF ILLINOIS SCHOLARSHIP FUND

Township Officials of Illinois
408 South Fifth Street
Springfield, IL 62701-1804

Summary: To provide financial assistance for college to high school seniors in Illinois.

Eligibility: Applicants must be high school seniors in Illinois who have maintained at least a "B" average, have demonstrated an active interest in extracurricular activities (which may include interest in local government and community service), and will be attending a postsecondary institution in Illinois (including junior colleges and 4-year colleges and universities). They must submit an essay (up to 300 words) on "the importance of township government." In addition, applicants must submit a current high school transcript, a letter of recommendation from a high school teacher or counselor, and a completed application form. Financial need is not considered in the selection process.

Financial data: The stipend is $2,000.

Duration: 1 year.

Additional information: The 6 scholarships awarded are: Troy A. Kost Scholarship, Carolyn Langan Scholarship, Delbert W. Miller Scholarship, William Z. Ahrends Scholarship, Barbara A. Behm Scholarship, and Township Officials of Illinois Memorial Scholarship.

Number awarded: 6 each year.

Deadline: February of each year.

1095
TOYOTA COMMUNITY SCHOLARS PROGRAM

Toyota USA Foundation
Attn: Foundation Administrator, A404
19001 South Western Avenue
Torrance, CA 90509
Phone: (310) 618-6766   Fax: (310) 618-7800
Web Site: www.toyota.com

Summary: To provide financial assistance to high school seniors who have outstanding records of academic performance and volunteerism.

Eligibility: Each high school in the United States may nominate 1 graduating senior for these scholarships; schools with more than 600 graduating seniors may nominate 2 of them. Nominees must be U.S. citizens, nationals, or permanent residents who plan to pursue an undergraduate degree at an accredited 4-year

college or university in the United States. Selection is based on academic record (grade point average of 3.0 or higher) and involvement in a service organization or project that has a positive impact on the school and/or community.

Financial data: The stipend is $2,500 or $5,000 per year. Winners also receive an all-expenses-paid trip to Louisville, Kentucky where they meet fellow awardees and are recognized for their achievements.

Duration: 4 years.

Additional information: This program started in 1996.

Number awarded: 12 national winners ($5,000 per year) and 88 regional winners ($2,500 per year) are selected each year.

Deadline: November of each year.

1096
TROY BARBOZA EDUCATION FUND

Hawai'i Community Foundation
900 Fort Street Mall, Suite 1300
Honolulu, HI 96813
Phone: (808) 566-5570   (888) 731-3863
Fax: (808) 521-6286   E-mail: scholarships@hcf-hawaii.org
Web Site: www.hcf-hawaii.org

Summary: To provide financial assistance for postsecondary education to disabled public employees in Hawaii or their dependents.

Eligibility: This program is open to 1) disabled public employees in Hawaii who were injured in the line of duty or 2) daughters, sons, or other immediate family members of public employees in Hawaii who were disabled or killed in the line of duty. The public employee must work or have worked in a job where lives are risked for the protection and safety of others. Also eligible are private citizens who have performed a heroic act for the protection and welfare of others.

Financial data: The amount awarded varies, depending upon the needs of the recipient and the funds available.

Duration: 1 year.

Number awarded: 1 or more each year.

Deadline: February of each year.

1097
TRUCKLOAD CARRIERS ASSOCIATION SCHOLARSHIP

Truckload Carriers Association
Attn: Director of Operations
2200 Mill Road
Alexandria, VA 22314
Phone: (703) 838-1950   Fax: (703) 836-6610
E-mail: tca@truckload.org
Web Site: www.truckload.org

Summary: To provide funding for students associated with independent contractors affiliated with the Truckload Carriers Association.

Eligibility: Eligible to apply for this funding is any college junior or senior in good standing who is the employee or the child, grandchild, or spouse of an employee of an independent contractor affiliated with a trucking company. Independent contractors affiliated with trucking companies may also apply. Applicants must be attending an accredited 4-year college or university. Selection is based on financial need, scholastic achievement, character, and integrity. Those students pursuing transportation and business degrees are given special consideration. Scholarships are awarded without regard to sex, race, color, national origin, or religion.

Financial data: Stipends are $2,000 per year.

Duration: 1 semester; may be renewed automatically for 1 additional semester.

Number awarded: Varies each year; recently, 15 of these scholarships were awarded.

Deadline: May of each year.

1098
TUITION WAIVER PROGRAM FOR DEPENDENTS OF DECEASED KENTUCKY VETERANS

Kentucky Department of Veterans Affairs
Attn: Division of Field Operations
545 South Third Street, Room 123
Louisville, KY 40202
Phone: (502) 595-4447   (800) 928-4012 (within KY)
Fax: (502) 595-4448
Web Site: www.kvc.state.ky.us/agencies/finance/depts/kvc/index.htm

Summary: To provide financial assistance for postsecondary education to the children or unremarried widow(er)s of deceased Kentucky veterans.

Eligibility: This program is open to the children, stepchildren, adopted children, and unremarried widow(er)s of veterans who were residents of Kentucky when they entered military service or joined the Kentucky National Guard. The qualifying veteran must have been killed in action during a wartime period or died as a result of a service-connected disability incurred during a wartime period. Applicants must be attending or planning to attend a state-supported college or university in Kentucky to pursue an undergraduate or graduate degree.

Financial data: Eligible dependents and survivors are exempt from tuition and matriculation fees at any state-supported institution of higher education in Kentucky.

Duration: There are no age or time limits on the waiver.

Number awarded: Varies each year.

1099
TWLE SCHOLARSHIP AWARDS

Texas Women in Law Enforcement
P.O. Box 797784
Dallas, TX 75379-7784
E-mail: KADdy@twle.com
Web Site: www.twle.com

Summary: To provide financial assistance for college to members of the Texas Women in Law Enforcement (TWLE) and their relatives.

Eligibility: Application requirements for members of TWLE: must have been an active member of TWLE for the past 2 years; must be currently enrolled in college; must submit a 1-page essay stating why they deserve the scholarship; and must be majoring in criminal justice or a related field. Requirements for relatives of TWLE members: must be the spouse, child, brother, sister, niece, nephew, or grandchild of the member; must be in the top 25 percent of their graduating class; must have a minimum 3.0 grade point average; must score at least 950 on the SAT or 21 on the ACT; must submit 2 letters of recommendation; and must submit a 1-page essay stating why they deserve the scholarship. For these relatives, the sponsor must have been an active member of TWLE for the past 2 years.

Financial data: The stipend is $1,000.

Duration: 1 year.

Number awarded: At least 4 each year.

Deadline: January of each year.

1100
TWO/TEN INTERNATIONAL FOOTWEAR FOUNDATION COLLEGE SCHOLARSHIP PROGRAM

Two/Ten International Footwear Foundation
Attn: Scholarship Coordinator
1466 Main Street
Waltham, MA 02451
Phone: (781) 736-1500   (800) FIND-210
Fax: (781) 736-1555
Web Site: www.twoten.org

Summary: To provide financial assistance to full-time undergraduate students who work, or whose parent works, in the footwear, leather, or allied industries.

Eligibility: This program is open to undergraduate students (including students enrolled in nursing programs or at vocational-technical schools). Either their parent (natural, step, or adopted) must be employed (for at least 1 year) in the footwear, leather, or allied industries or the applicants must be employed for at least 500 hours in 1 of those industries. Applicants must be within 4 years of their high school graduation. High school seniors may also apply. Selection is based on academic achievement and financial need.

Financial data: Awards range from $200 to $3,000, depending on the need of the recipient. Funds are sent directly to the recipient's school.

Duration: 1 year; may be renewed.

Additional information: Recipients must attend school on a full-time basis. Funds may be used to pay for study abroad, if the study is sanctioned by the recipient's home institution. Awards may be used only in 2- or 4-year accredited programs of study.

Number awarded: Varies; generally, more than 200 new awards and 300 renewals each year.

Deadline: Requests for applications must be submitted by December of each year; completed applications are due in January of each year.

1101
TY COBB UNDERGRADUATE SCHOLARSHIP PROGRAM

Ty Cobb Educational Foundation
P.O. Box 725
Forest Park, GA 30298
E-mail: tycobb@mindspring.com
Summary: to provide financial assistance to Georgia residents who need financial assistance to complete their college education.
Eligibility: This program is open to undergraduate students who are residents of Georgia, have demonstrated financial need, and have completed at least 45 quarter hours or 30 semester hours with a grade point average of 3.0 or better in an accredited college or university. Students with the highest academic averages and the greatest need are given priority.
Financial data: The amount awarded varies, depending upon the needs of the recipient. Funds are paid directly to the recipient's school.
Duration: 1 academic year; may be renewed.
Additional information: Recipients may attend college in any state. Recipients must attend college full time.
Number awarded: Varies each year.
Deadline: June of each year.

1102
UNDERGRADUATE AWARDS OF THE SEMINOLE NATION JUDGEMENT FUND

Seminole Nation of Oklahoma
Attn: Judgement Fund
P.O. Box 1498
Wewoka, OK 74884
Phone: (405) 257-6287
Web Site: www.cowboy.net/native/seminole/judgement_fund.html
Summary: To provide financial assistance for undergraduate study to members of the Seminole Nation of Oklahoma.
Eligibility: This program is open to enrolled members of the Seminole Nation who are descended from a member of the Seminole Nation as it existed in Florida on September 18, 1923. Applicants must be attending or planning to attend a college or university to pursue an undergraduate degree.
Financial data: The stipend for full-time students is $900 per year for freshmen, $1,100 per year for sophomores, $1,500 per year for juniors, or $1,700 for seniors. Part-time students receive the actual cost of tuition, books, and fees, to a maximum of $250 per semester. The total of all undergraduate degree awards to an applicant may not exceed $5,200.
Duration: 1 year; may be renewed as long as the recipient maintains a grade point average of 2.0 or higher.
Additional information: The General Council of the Seminole Nation of Oklahoma approved a plan for use of the Judgement Fund Award in 1990. This aspect of the program went into effect in September of 1991.
Number awarded: Varies each year.
Deadline: November of each year for fall semester; April of each year for spring semester.

1103
UNION PLUS CREDIT CARD SCHOLARSHIP

Union Privilege
1125 15th Street. N.W., Suite 300
Washington, DC 20005
Phone: (202) 293-5330   Fax: (202) 293-5311
E-mail: info-members@unionprivilege.org
Web Site: www.unionprivilege.org
Summary: To provide college aid to AFL-CIO union members, their spouses, and/or their children.
Eligibility: Eligible to apply for this support are AFL-CIO union members (at least 1 year of membership), their spouses, and their children. The union member must be participating in the Union Plus Credit Card program, but the member does not need to have a union credit card to apply. Only undergraduate study is supported; study may be at any accredited college, university, community college, technical school, or trade school. Applicants must submit a sealed letter of recommendation and an essay (up to 500 words) that, among other things, highlights their relationship with the union and labor movement. All applications must be signed by an officer of the member's local. Selection is based on academic achievement and potential, character, leadership, social awareness, career goals, and financial need.

Financial data: Stipends range from $500 to $4,000.
Duration: 1 year; nonrenewable.
Number awarded: Varies each year; recently, 126 of these scholarships were awarded. At least $200,000 in scholarships is offered each year.
Deadline: January of each year.

1104
UNITED DAUGHTERS OF THE CONFEDERACY SCHOLARSHIPS

United Daughters of the Confederacy
Attn: Education Director
328 North Boulevard
Richmond, VA 23220-4057
Phone: (804) 355-1636   Fax: (804) 353-1396
E-mail: hqudc@aol.com
Web Site: www.hqudc.org
Summary: To provide financial assistance for postsecondary education to lineal descendants of Confederate veterans.
Eligibility: Eligible to apply for these scholarships are lineal descendants of worthy Confederates or collateral descendants who are members of the Children of the Confederacy or the United Daughters of the Confederacy. Applicants must be high school seniors or college students and submit a family financial report and certified proof of the Confederate record of 1 ancestor, with the company and regiment in which he served. They must have at least a 3.0 grade point average in high school.
Financial data: The amount of the scholarships depends on the availability of funds.
Duration: 1 year; may be renewed up to 3 additional years.
Additional information: Applications must be submitted through the division or chapter of their home state. Each division or chapter may present only 1 candidate for any 1 scholarship. Unrestricted scholarships are named the Admiral Raphael Semmes Memorial Scholarship, the Janet B. Seippel Scholarship, the Cody Bachman Memorial Scholarship, the Donors Scholarship, the Cora Bell Wesley Memorial Scholarship, the Cornelia Branch Stone Scholarship, the David Stephen Wylie Scholarship, the Henry Clay Darsey Memorial Scholarship, the Hector W. Church Memorial Scholarship, the Major Madison Bell Scholarship, the Mary B. Poppenheim Memorial Scholarship, the Matthew Fontaine Maury Scholarship, the Mrs. Ella M. Franklin Memorial Scholarship, the Mrs. L.H. Raines Memorial Scholarship, the S.A. Cunningham Scholarship, the Dorothy Williams Scholarships, and the Stonewall Jackson Scholarship. The unrestricted scholarships may be used at any institution approved by the Education Committee of the United Daughters of the Confederacy. Information is also available from Dorothy S. Broom, Second Vice President General, 595 Lominack Road, Prosperity, SC 29127, (803) 364-3003. Members of the same family may not hold scholarships simultaneously, and only 1 application per family will be accepted within a current year. All requests for applications must be accompanied by a self-addressed stamped envelope.
Number awarded: 16 unrestricted scholarships are available; another 10 scholarships with varying restrictions are also offered.
Deadline: February of each year.

1105
UNITED FOOD AND COMMERCIAL WORKERS INTERNATIONAL UNION SCHOLARSHIP PROGRAM

United Food and Commercial Workers International Union
Attn: Scholarship Program
1775 K Street, N.W.
Washington, DC 20006-1598
Phone: (202) 223-3111   Fax: (202) 466-1562
Web Site: www.ufcw.org
Summary: To provide financial assistance for postsecondary education to members of the United Food and Commercial Workers International Union (UFCW) and their children.
Eligibility: This program is open to UFCW members or their unmarried children. Applicants must be under 20 years of age, be high school seniors, and have taken the SAT or the ACT examination. Selection is based on test scores, scholastic records and achievements, personal qualifications, and merit.
Financial data: The stipend is $1,000 per year.
Duration: 4 years.
Number awarded: 7 each year.
Deadline: Preliminary applications must be completed by the end of December; the additional form necessary to complete the application process must be submitted by mid-March.

1106
UNITED METHODIST FOUNDATION ANNUAL CONFERENCE SCHOLARS PROGRAM

United Methodist Foundation for Christian Higher Education
1001 19th Avenue South
P.O. Box 871
Nashville, TN 37202-0871
Phone: (615) 340-7385   Fax: (615) 340-7048
Summary: To provide financial assistance to undergraduate and seminary students attending schools affiliated with the United Methodist Church.
Eligibility: This program is open to entering freshmen at United Methodist-related colleges or universities and first-year students at United Methodist-related seminaries or theological schools. Applicants must be U.S. citizens and active members of the United Methodist Church for at least 1 year prior to application. Members of the A.M.E., A.M.E. Zion, and other "Methodist" denominations are not eligible.
Financial data: The stipend is $1,000.
Duration: 1 year.
Additional information: Students may obtain applications from their annual conference council office or the chair of their conference Board of Higher Education and Campus Ministry.
Number awarded: Varies; each annual conference Board of Higher Education and Campus Ministry is entitled to nominate 1 student.
Deadline: Nominations from the annual conference must be received in the scholarship office of the General Board of Higher Education and Ministry by May of each year.

1107
UNITED METHODIST SCHOLARSHIP PROGRAM

United Methodist Church
Attn: Office of Loans and Scholarships
1001 19th Avenue South
P.O. Box 871
Nashville, TN 37202-0871
Phone: (615) 340-7344   Fax: (615) 340-7367
E-mail: umscholar@gbhem.org
Web Site: www.gbhem.org
Summary: To provide financial assistance to students attending schools affiliated with the United Methodist Church.
Eligibility: This program is open to U.S. citizens and permanent residents who have been active, full members of a United Methodist Church for at least 1 year prior to applying; members of the A.M.E., A.M.E. Zion, and other "Methodist" denominations are not eligible. Undergraduates must have been admitted to a full-time degree program at a United Methodist-related college or university and have earned a grade point average of 2.5 or above. Most graduate scholarships are designated for persons pursuing a degree in theological studies (M.Div., D.Min., Ph.D.) or higher education administration, or for older adults changing their careers. Some scholarships are designated for racial ethnic undergraduate or graduate students. Applications are available from the financial aid office of the United Methodist school the applicant attends or from the chair of their annual conference Board of Higher Education and Campus Ministry.
Financial data: The funding is intended to supplement the students' own resources.
Duration: 1 year; renewal policies are set by participating universities.
Number awarded: Varies each year.

1108
UNITED STATES ARMY WARRANT OFFICERS ASSOCIATION FAMILY MEMBER SCHOLARSHIP PROGRAM

United States Army Warrant Officers Association
462 Herndon Parkway, Suite 207
Herndon, VA 20170-5235
Phone: (703) 742-7727   (800) 5-USAWOA
Fax: (703) 742-7728   E-mail: usawoa@erols.com
Web Site: www.penfed.org/usawoa/ScholProgFS.htm
Summary: To provide financial assistance for college to dependents of members of the United States Army Warrant Officers Association.
Eligibility: This program is open to children and dependent stepchildren, under the age of 23, of regular members of the association. Spouses of members are also eligible. Applicants must plan to attend an accredited U.S. college, university, or vocational-technical institution on a full-time basis.

Financial data: The stipend is at least $1,000.
Duration: 1 year; may be renewed.
Additional information: This program includes the Carrie A. Clayburn Memorial Scholarship, the Pentagon Federal Credit Union USAWOA Scholarship, and the St. Louis Gateway Chapter USAWOA Scholarship.
Number awarded: Varies each year; recently, 11 of these scholarships were awarded.
Deadline: April of each year.

1109
UNITED STATES CUSTOMS SERVICE LAW ENFORCEMENT EXPLORER SCHOLARSHIPS

U.S. Customs Service
Attn: Law Enforcement Liaison Office
1301 Constitution Avenue, Room 3422
Washington, DC 20229
Phone: (202) 927-2294
Summary: To provide financial assistance for college to outstanding Explorer Scouts.
Eligibility: Applicants must be registered Explorers, active in a law enforcement post with the U.S. Customs Service, and at least a high school senior. They must demonstrate a high degree of motivation, commitment, and community concern. Completed applications must be submitted first to a local council for certification. Then, applications (along with the required attachments) must be completed and sent to the U.S. Customs Service.
Financial data: The stipend is $1,000. Funds are paid directly to the recipient's school.
Duration: 1 year.
Number awarded: 1 or more each year.
Deadline: March of each year.

1110
UNITED STATES NAVAL RESERVE SCHOLARSHIP FUND

Naval Enlisted Reserve Association
Attn: National Headquarters
6703 Farragut Avenue
Falls Church, VA 22042-2189
Phone: (800) 776-9020   Fax: (703) 534-3617
Web Site: www.nera.org/scholar/index.html
Summary: To provide financial assistance for college to enlisted members of the Naval Reserve and their families.
Eligibility: This program is open to drilling Naval Reservists who are in a satisfactory participation status, including Training and Administration of Reserves (TAR) personnel, Canvasser Recruiters (CANREC), and U.S. Navy personnel assigned to a Naval Reserve Activity (NRA). Members of their families are also eligible. Applicants must be enrolled in an accredited college or university.
Financial data: The stipend is $1,000.
Duration: 1 year.
Additional information: This program, established in 2000, is funded by USAA Insurance Corporation.
Number awarded: 15 each year.
Deadline: April of each year.

1111
UNITED STATES SENATE YOUTH PROGRAM SCHOLARSHIPS

William Randolph Hearst Foundation
90 New Montgomery Street, Suite 1212
San Francisco, CA 94105-4504
Phone: (415) 543-4057   (800) 841-7048
Fax: (415) 243-0760   E-mail: ussyp@hearstfdn.org
Web Site: www.ussenateyouth.org
Summary: To recognize and reward outstanding high school student leaders.
Eligibility: This program is open to high school juniors and seniors who are currently serving in 1 of the following student government offices: student body president, student body vice president, student body secretary, student body treasurer, class president, class vice president, class secretary, class treasurer, student council representative, or student representative to a district, regional, or state-level civic or educational organization. Selection is based on quality of leadership demonstrated. Recipients must, within 2 years after high school graduation, enroll at an accredited U.S. college or university, pledging to include courses in government or related subjects in their undergraduate program.

Financial data: Winners receive an expense-paid trip to Washington, D.C. for 1 week (to be introduced to the operation of the federal government and Congress) and are presented with a $2,000 scholarship.
Duration: The competition is held annually.
Number awarded: 104 each year: 2 from each state, Washington, D.C., and the Department of Defense Dependents Schools Overseas.
Deadline: September of each year.

1112
UPS FOUNDATION SCHOLARSHIPS

Wisconsin Foundation for Independent Colleges, Inc.
735 North Water Street, Suite 800
Milwaukee, WI 53202-4100
Phone: (414) 273-5980   Fax: (414) 273-5995
E-mail: wfic@execpc.com
Web Site: www.wficweb.org
Summary: To provide financial assistance to students attending private colleges in Wisconsin.
Eligibility: This program is open to currently-enrolled students at 1 of the 21 independent colleges or universities in Wisconsin. Applicants may be majoring in any field, but they must have earned at least a 3.0 grade point average. Recipients are selected by the participating schools.
Financial data: The stipend is $3,500.
Duration: 1 year.
Additional information: The participating schools are Alverno College, Beloit College, Cardinal Stritch University, Carroll College, Carthage College, Concordia University of Wisconsin, Edgewood College, Lakeland College, Lawrence University, Marian College, Marquette University, Milwaukee Institute of Art & Design, Milwaukee School of Engineering, Mount Mary College, Northland College, Ripon College, St. Norbert College, Silver Lake College, Viterbo University, and Wisconsin Lutheran College.
Number awarded: 21 each year: 1 at each of the participating colleges and universities.
Deadline: May of each year.

1113
URBAN LEAGUE OF RHODE ISLAND SCHOLARSHIP PROGRAM

Urban League of Rhode Island, Inc.
246 Prairie Avenue
Providence, RI 02905
Phone: (401) 351-5000, ext. 110   Fax: (401) 454-1946
Web Site: www.ulri.org
Summary: To provide financial assistance for undergraduate study to minorities who are Rhode Island residents.
Eligibility: This program is open to minorities who are Rhode Island residents accepted for admission or currently enrolled in an accredited undergraduate institution. Priority is given to recent high school graduates. Applicants who have been out of high school for a number of years but never attended a postsecondary school and former college students currently attending an undergraduate institution are also eligible. Selection is based on academic achievement, financial need, a 250-word essay on why the applicant is pursuing a postsecondary education, and an interview.
Financial data: Stipends range from $500 to $1,250 per year, depending on the need of the recipient.
Duration: 1 year.
Number awarded: Varies each year.
Deadline: April of each year.

1114
U.S. BANK INTERNET SCHOLARSHIP PROGRAM

U.S. Bank
U.S. Bank Place
601 Second Avenue South
Minneapolis, MN 55402
Phone: (612) 872-2657   (800) 872-2657
Web Site: www.usbank.com/cgi/cfm/studentloans/marketing.cfm
Summary: To provide funding for college to high school seniors who apply through an online procedure.
Eligibility: This program is open to high school seniors planning to enroll full time at a 2-year or 4-year accredited college or university that participates in the Federal Family Education Loan Program (FFELP). U.S. citizenship or permanent resident status is required. Applications are available only through an online procedure. Selection is based on merit, academic standing, and community service.
Financial data: The stipend is $1,000.
Duration: 1 year; nonrenewable.
Additional information: This program began in 1997.
Number awarded: 25 each year.
Deadline: February of each year.

1115
US ONCOLOGY SCHOLARSHIP

Patient Advocate Foundation
753 Thimble Shoals Boulevard, Suite B
Newport News, VA 23606
Phone: (800) 532-5274   Fax: (757) 873-8999
E-mail: help@patientadvocate.org
Web Site: www.patientadvocate.org
Summary: To provide financial assistance for college to individuals whose studies have been interrupted or delayed by a diagnosis of cancer or other life threatening diseases.
Eligibility: Eligible to apply for this scholarship are individuals seeking to initiate or complete a course of study that has been interrupted or delayed by a diagnosis of cancer or other critical or life threatening diseases. Applicants must be able to demonstrate financial need, have earned at least a 3.0 grade point average, be enrolled or planning to enroll as a full-time student, and write an essay on why they have chosen their particular field of study.
Financial data: The stipend is $5,000.
Duration: 1 year.
Additional information: Recipients must pursue a course of study that will make them immediately employable after graduation.
Number awarded: 1 each year.
Deadline: April of each year.

1116
U.S. SKI & SNOWBOARD TEAM SCHOLARSHIP ASSISTANCE

United States Ski and Snowboard Association
Attn: U.S. Ski & Snowboard Team Foundation
1500 Kearns Boulevard
Box 100
Park City, UT 84060
Phone: (435) 649-9090   Fax: (435) 649-3613
E-mail: info@ussa.org
Web Site: www.usskiteam.com
Summary: To provide financial assistance to the U.S. Ski & Snowboard Team athletes.
Eligibility: This program is open to U.S. Ski & Snowboard Team athletes. Eligible athletes must first apply for assistance from the USOC, be in good standing, and have earned at least a 2.0 grade point average. All current athletes and retired athletes are eligible to apply for this assistance. Financial need is not considered in the selection process.
Financial data: The amount awarded varies each year, depending upon the number of eligible recipients. Funds are to be used for tuition and books.
Duration: 1 year.
Additional information: The sponsor also offers language and internship programs.
Number awarded: Varies; in recent years, up to 17 have been awarded annually.

1117
U.S. SUBMARINE VETERANS OF WORLD WAR II SCHOLARSHIPS

U.S. Submarine Veterans of World War II
Attn: Scholarship Program
5040 Virginia Beach Boulevard, Suite 104-A
Virginia Beach, VA 23462
Phone: (757) 671-3200   Fax: (757) 671-3330
Summary: To provide financial assistance for the postsecondary education of the children of members of the U.S. Submarine Veterans of World War II.
Eligibility: Eligible to apply for these scholarships are the unmarried children of officers and enlisted personnel who are (or were at time of death) paid-up regular members of the organization. Applicants must be high school seniors or have

graduated within the previous 4 years and may not have reached the age of 24. Selection is based on scholastic proficiency.

Financial data: The stipend is $3,000.

Duration: 1 year; may be renewed for up to 3 additional years.

Additional information: Some of these awards are named in honor of former officials of the organization; they include the Captain Art Rawson Award, the Rear Admiral Savvy J. Hoffman Award, and the H.T. Van de Kerkhoff Award.

Number awarded: Varies each year.

Deadline: April of each year.

1118
USA FUNDS ACCESS TO EDUCATION SCHOLARSHIPS

Citizens' Scholarship Foundation of America
Attn: Scholarship Management Services
1505 Riverview Road
P.O. Box 297
St. Peter, MN 56082
Phone: (507) 931-1682   (800) 537-4180
Fax: (507) 931-9168   E-mail: scholarship@usafunds.org
Web Site: www.usafunds.org/Borrowers/Access_to_Education_Scholarship.html

Summary: To provide financial assistance to undergraduate and graduate students, especially those who are members of ethnic minority groups or have physical disabilities.

Eligibility: This program is open to high school seniors and graduates who plan to enroll or are already enrolled in full-time undergraduate or graduate course work at an accredited 2- or 4-year college, university, or vocational-technical school. Half-time undergraduate students are also eligible. Up to 50 percent of the awards are targeted to students who have a documented physical disability or are a member of an ethnic minority group, including but not limited to Native Hawaiian, Alaskan Native, Black/African American, Asian, Pacific Islander, American Indian, or Hispanic/Latino. Residents of all 50 states, the District of Columbia, Puerto Rico, Guam, the U.S. Virgin Islands, and all U.S. territories and commonwealths are eligible. Preference is given to applicants from the following areas: Arizona, Hawaii and the Pacific Islands, Indiana, Kansas, Maryland, Mississippi, Nevada, and Wyoming. Applicants must also be U.S. citizens or eligible non-citizens and come from a family with an annual adjusted gross income of $35,000 or less. In addition to financial need, selection is based on past academic performance and future potential, leadership and participation in school and community, work experience, career and educational aspirations and goals, and references.

Financial data: The stipend is $1,500 per year for full-time undergraduate or graduate students or $750 per year for half-time undergraduate students. Funds are paid jointly to the student and the school.

Duration: 1 year; may be renewed until the student receives a final degree or certificate or until the total award to a student reaches $6,000, whichever comes first. Renewal requires the recipient to maintain a grade point average of 2.5 or higher.

Additional information: This program, established in 2000, is sponsored by USA Funds which serves as the education loan guarantor and administrator in the 8 states and the Pacific Islands where the program gives preference.

Number awarded: From 200 to 300 each year.

Deadline: April of each year.

1119
USCF NATIONAL SCHOLAR-CHESSPLAYER OUTSTANDING ACHIEVEMENT AWARD

United States Chess Federation
3054 U.S. Route 9W
New Windsor, NY 12553
Phone: (845) 562-8350, ext. 128   (800) 388-KING
Fax: (845) 561-CHES   E-mail: clubs@uschess.org
Web Site: www.uschess.org

Summary: To provide financial assistance for college to high school students who excel in academics, chess play, and sportsmanship.

Eligibility: This program is open to high school juniors and seniors who are members of the United States Chess Federation and have shown outstanding merit in academics, sportsmanship, and chess. To apply, students must submit a completed application form, a high school transcript, 2 letters of recommendation, a recent photograph, and an essay (up to 500 words) describing the positive influence that chess has had on their life. Financial need is not considered in the selection process.

Financial data: First place is $1,200; second place is $600; third place is $300; fourth place is $200; fifth and six places are $100 each.

Duration: 1 year.

Number awarded: 6 each year.

Deadline: February of each year.

1120
USSVI SCHOLARSHIPS

United States Submarine Veterans, Inc.
Attn: Paul W. Orstad, Scholarship Chairman
30 Surrey Lane
Norwich, CT 06369-6541
Phone: (860) 889-4750   E-mail: porstad@ebmail.gdeb.com
Web Site: ussvi.org/sclrship.htm

Summary: To provide financial assistance for college to the children and grandchildren of members of the United States Submarine Veterans, Inc. (USSVI).

Eligibility: This program is open to children and grandchildren of USSVI members who are high school seniors planning to attend college or already enrolled as college students. Applicants must be unmarried and under 21 years of age (or 23 if currently enrolled in a full-time course of study). Selection is based on academic proficiency, extracurricular activities, school and community awards, and financial need.

Financial data: The stipend depends on the availability of funds and the need of the recipient.

Duration: 1 year.

Number awarded: Varies each year; recently, a total of $7,700 in scholarships was awarded.

Deadline: April of each year.

1121
USTA TENNIS FOUNDATION COLLEGE EDUCATIONAL SCHOLARSHIP

USTA Tennis Foundation Inc.
70 West Red Oak Lane
White Plains, NY 10604-3602
Phone: (914) 696-7000   Fax: (914) 696-7167

Summary: To provide financial assistance for college to high school seniors who participated extensively in USTA youth tennis programs.

Eligibility: Applicants must be high school seniors who are or have been a participant in the following USTA youth tennis programs: USA School Tennis, USA Tennis—NJTL, USA Team Tennis, or USTA Player Development. As part of the application process, students must submit an official high school transcript, ACT/SAT examination scores, a typed personal statement, and an official financial aid form. Selection is based on scholastic performance, extracurricular activities, course work, commitment to pursuing a career, financial need, and promise of success. Students who are receiving full grants and scholarships in the sport of tennis from their respective schools are not eligible to apply for this scholarship.

Financial data: The stipend is $6,000, payable over a 4-year period. Funds are paid directly to the recipient's school.

Duration: 4 years.

Additional information: Recipients must enroll in college on a full-time basis.

Number awarded: Several each year.

Deadline: May of each year.

1122
UTAH CENTENNIAL OPPORTUNITY PROGRAM FOR EDUCATION

Utah Higher Education Assistance Authority
Board of Regents Building, The Gateway
60 South 400 West
Salt Lake City, UT 84101-1284
Phone: (801) 321-7200   (800) 418-8757
Fax: (801) 321-7299   TDD: (801) 321-7130
E-mail: uheaa@utahsbr.edu
Web Site: www.uheaa.org

Summary: To provide financial assistance and work study to students at designated Utah institutions.

Eligibility: Students at participating colleges in Utah may request an application directly from their college's financial aid offices. The participating institutions in Utah are: Brigham Young University, College of Eastern Utah, Dixie State College, LDS Business College, Salt Lake Community College, Snow College, Southern

Utah University, University of Utah, Utah State University, Utah Valley State College, Weber State University, and Westminster College. Applicants must meet the federal guidelines for financial need. They must also be willing to accept a work study assignment in 1) an institutional job on campus; 2) school assistant jobs, as tutors, mentors, or teacher assistants, to work with educationally disadvantaged and high risk school pupils, by contract, at individual schools or school districts; 3) community service jobs, with volunteer community service organizations; or 4) matching jobs, by contract with government agencies, private businesses, or nonprofit corporations.

Financial data: The maximum award to each eligible student is $5,000, of which no more than $2,500 may be a grant and the remainder provided in the form of a work study award. For the work study portion, students receive the current federal minimum wage.

Duration: 1 year; may be renewed.

Number awarded: Varies each year.

1123
UTAH ELKS ASSOCIATION HANDICAPPED SCHOLARSHIP AWARD

Utah Elks Association
c/o Jim Szatkowski
2996 South Vista Circle Drive
Bountiful, UT 84010-7814
Phone: (201) 292-1570   E-mail: jamesski@inovion.com
Web Site: www.inovion.com/~jamesski/Utah_Elks

Summary: To provide financial assistance for college to high school seniors in Utah who are disabled.

Eligibility: Eligible to apply for this award are high school seniors in Utah who have a physical disability that impedes or restricts normal progress. As part of the application process, the student must submit a total of 4 to 5 letters of recommendation, a support letter from a doctor stating the continuing nature of the disability, official high school transcripts, and a personal statement (300 words or less) on educational and career goals. The local Elks lodge must endorse the application. Financial need must be documented.

Financial data: A stipend is awarded (exact amount not specified).

Duration: 1 year.

Number awarded: Varies each year, depending upon the funds available.

1124
UTAH LEGION AUXILIARY NATIONAL PRESIDENT'S SCHOLARSHIP

American Legión Auxiliary
Attn: Department of Utah
B-61 State Capitol Building
Salt Lake City, UT 84114
Phone: (801) 538-1014

Summary: To provide financial assistance for postsecondary education to veterans' children in Utah.

Eligibility: Applicants for these scholarships must be the children of veterans who served in World War I, World War II, Korea, Vietnam, Grenada, Lebanon, Panama, or the Persian Gulf. They must be high school seniors or graduates who have not yet attended an institution of higher learning. Selection is based on character, Americanism, leadership, scholarship, and financial need. The winners then compete for the American Legion Auxiliary National President's Scholarship. If the Utah winners are not awarded a national scholarship, then they receive these departmental scholarships.

Financial data: Awards are $2,000 or $1,500.

Duration: 1 year.

Number awarded: 2 each year: 1 at $2,000 and 1 at $1,500.

Deadline: February of each year.

1125
UTAH LEVERAGING EDUCATIONAL ASSISTANCE PARTNERSHIP PROGRAM

Utah Higher Education Assistance Authority
Board of Regents Building, The Gateway
60 South 400 West
Salt Lake City, UT 84101-1284
Phone: (801) 321-7200   (800) 418-8757
Fax: (801) 321-7299   TDD: (801) 321-7130
E-mail: uheaa@utahsbr.edu   Web Site: www.uheaa.org

Summary: To provide financial assistance for college to students in Utah with financial need.

Eligibility: Students at participating colleges in Utah may request an application directly from their college's financial aid offices. The participating colleges in Utah are: College of Eastern Utah, Dixie State College, Salt Lake Community College, Snow College, Southern Utah University, University of Utah, Utah State University, Utah Valley State College, Weber State University, and Westminster College. Applicants must have substantial financial need. Students taking correspondence courses are not eligible.

Financial data: The maximum stipend is $2,500.

Duration: 1 year; may be renewed.

Number awarded: Varies each year.

1126
UTILITY WORKERS UNION OF AMERICA MERIT SCHOLARSHIPS

Utility Workers Union of America
Attn: Merit Scholarships Awards Program
815 16th Street, N.W., Suite 605
Washington, DC 20006
Phone: (202) 347-8105   Fax: (202) 347-4872

Summary: To provide financial assistance for the postsecondary education of children of members of the Utility Workers Union of America.

Eligibility: Eligible are children of members of the Utility Workers Union of America who plan to graduate from high school in spring following application and enter college in the following fall. Applicants must take the Preliminary Scholastic Assessment Test/National Merit Scholarship Qualifying Test in the fall, prior to their applying. Awards are based on high school academic records, test scores, quality of leadership, and significant accomplishments.

Financial data: The stipend ranges from $500 to $2,000 per year, depending on the recipient's family income and the cost of attending the chosen college.

Duration: Up to 4 years or until completion of the bachelor's degree, whichever occurs first.

Additional information: This program was established in 1961.

Number awarded: 2 each year.

Deadline: December of each year.

1127
VADM ROBERT L. WALTERS SCHOLARSHIP

Surface Navy Association
2550 Huntington Avenue, Suite 202
Alexandria, VA 22303
Phone: (703) 960-6800   (800) NAVY-SNA
Fax: (703) 960-6807   E-mail: navysna@aol.com
Web Site: www.navysna.org/awards/VADMApplication.html

Summary: To provide financial assistance for college to members of the Surface Navy Association (SNA) and their dependents.

Eligibility: This program is open to SNA members and their dependent children and spouses who are pursuing or planning to pursue their first undergraduate degree. All applicants or their sponsors must 1) be in their second or subsequent consecutive year of membership; 2) submit a 200-word essay about themselves; 3) list their extracurricular activities, community service activities, academic honors and or positions of leadership that represent their interests, with an estimate of the amount of time involved with each activity; and 4) provide 3 letters of reference. High school seniors should also include a transcript of high school grades and a copy of ACT or SAT scores. Applicants who are on active duty or drilling reservists should also include a letter from their commanding officer commenting on their military service and leadership potential, a transcript of grades from their most recent 4 semesters of school, a copy of their ACT or SAT scores if available, and an indication of whether they have applied for or are enrolled in the Enlisted Commissioning Program. Applicants who are not high school seniors, active duty, or drilling reservists should also include a transcript of the grades from their most recent 4 semesters of school and a copy of ACT or SAT test scores (unless they are currently attending a college or university). Selection is based on demonstrated leadership, community service, academic achievement, and commitment to pursuing higher educational objectives.

Financial data: The stipend is $1,000 per year.

Duration: Up to 4 years.

Number awarded: Varies each year.

Deadline: January of each year.

1128
VASA ORDER OF AMERICA COLLEGE OR VOCATIONAL SCHOOL SCHOLARSHIPS

Vasa Order of America
Attn: Vice Grand Master
1926 Rancho Andrew
Alpine, CA 91901
Phone: (619) 445-9707   Fax: (619) 445-7334
E-mail: drulf@connectnet.com
Web Site: www.vasaorder.com

Summary: To provide financial assistance for college or vocational education to members of the Vasa Order of America.

Eligibility: Applicants must have been members of the organization for at least 1 year. They must be planning to continue their academic or vocational education on a full-time basis. Selection is based on a grade transcript, letters of recommendation from school and local Vasa lodge officials, and an essay of up to 1,000 words on a topic related to Vasa.

Financial data: Stipends are $1,000.

Duration: 1 year.

Additional information: Vasa Order of America is a Swedish American fraternal organization incorporated in 1899.

Number awarded: 10 each year.

Deadline: February of each year.

1129
VENTURE STUDENT AID AWARD

Venture Clubs of the Americas
c/o Soroptimist International of the Americas
Program Department
Two Penn Center Plaza
1528 John F. Kennedy Boulevard, Suite 1000
Philadelphia, PA 19102-1883
Phone: (215) 557-9300   Fax: (215) 568-5200
E-mail: program@soroptimist.org
Web Site: www.soroptimist.org

Summary: To provide financial assistance for the education of persons with physical disabilities.

Eligibility: Physically disabled men and women between 15 and 40 years of age who are interested in pursuing higher education should apply to their local Venture Club. Each club selects 1 candidate, on the basis of financial need and the capacity to profit from further education, to compete regionally. Each of the 7 regions selects a semifinalist to compete in the final judging. Financial need and the capacity to profit from further education are the main criteria on which selection is based.

Financial data: The regional winners receive a cash award of $500. The national winner receives a $5,000 award and the national runner-up receives $2,500.

Duration: 1 year.

Number awarded: 7 regional semifinalists, 1 national winner, and 1 national runner-up each year.

Deadline: December of each year.

1130
VERIZON SCHOLARSHIP PROGRAM

Hispanic Scholarship Fund
Attn: Selection Committee
One Sansome Street, Suite 1000
San Francisco, CA 94104
Phone: (415) 445-9936   (877) HSF-INFO, ext. 33
Fax: (415) 445-9942   E-mail: info@hsf.net
Web Site: www.hsf.net

Summary: To provide financial assistance to Hispanic American high school seniors in selected states who are interested in attending college.

Eligibility: Applicants must be U.S. citizens or permanent residents of at least half Hispanic background who are seniors in public high school systems in designated northeastern states. They must have at least a 3.0 grade point average in high school and be accepted at an accredited 4-year institution for the following fall. As part of the application process, they must submit a 2-page essay on their Hispanic background and potential contribution to the Hispanic community; their current high school status, activities, and achievements; and career goals. In addition to that essay, selection is based on academic achievement, a letter of recommendation, and financial need.

Financial data: The stipend is $1,500.

Duration: 1 year.

Additional information: The participating states currently include Maine, Massachusetts, New Hampshire, New Jersey, New York, Pennsylvania, Rhode Island, and Vermont. Funding for this program is provided by Verizon. Requests for applications must be accompanied by a self-addressed stamped envelope.

Number awarded: Varies each year.

Deadline: February of each year.

1131
VERMONT AMERICAN LEGION EAGLE SCOUT OF THE YEAR SCHOLARSHIP

American Legion
Attn: Department of Vermont
P.O. Box 396
Montpelier, VT 05601-0396
Phone: (802) 223-7131   Fax: (802) 223-7131

Summary: To provide financial assistance for postsecondary education to outstanding Eagle Scouts in Vermont.

Eligibility: The Vermont nominee for American Legion Scout of the Year receives this scholarship. Applicants must be either 1) registered, active members of a Boy Scout Troop or Varsity Scout Team sponsored by an American Legion Post in Vermont or Auxiliary Unit in Vermont, or 2) registered, active members of a duly chartered Boy Scout Troop or Varsity Scout Team and the sons or grandsons of American Legion or Auxiliary members. They must be active members of their religious institution; have received the appropriate religious emblem; have demonstrated practical citizenship in church, school, Scouting, and community; have received the Eagle Scout award; be at least 15 years old; and be enrolled in high school.

Financial data: The award is $1,000.

Duration: 1 year.

Number awarded: 1 each year.

Deadline: February of each year.

1132
VERMONT INCENTIVE GRANTS

Vermont Student Assistance Corporation
Champlain Mill
1 Main Street, Fourth Floor
P.O. Box 2000
Winooski, VT 05404-2601
Phone: (802) 655-9602   (800) 642-3177
Fax: (802) 654-3765   TDD: (802) 654-3766
Phone: TDD: (800) 281-3341 (within VT)   E-mail: info@vsac.org
Web Site: www.vsac.org

Summary: To provide financial assistance for postsecondary education to needy residents of Vermont.

Eligibility: This program is open to residents of Vermont who wish to attend college, either within or outside Vermont, as a full-time undergraduate student. U.S. citizenship or permanent resident status is required. Selection is based on financial need.

Financial data: Scholarships range from $500 to $8,650 per year.

Duration: 1 year; may be renewed.

Number awarded: Varies each year.

1133
VERMONT PART-TIME GRANTS

Vermont Student Assistance Corporation
Champlain Mill
1 Main Street, Fourth Floor
P.O. Box 2000
Winooski, VT 05404-2601
Phone: (802) 655-9602   (800) 642-3177
Fax: (802) 654-3765   TDD: (802) 654-3766
Phone: TDD: (800) 281-3341 (within VT)   E-mail: info@vsac.org
Web Site: www.vsac.org

Summary: To provide financial assistance to needy residents of Vermont who wish to attend college on a part-time basis.

Eligibility: This program is open to residents of Vermont who are enrolled or accepted for enrollment in an undergraduate degree, diploma, or certificate program. Applicants must be taking fewer than 12 credits per semester and not

have received a baccalaureate degree. Financial need is considered in the selection process.

Financial data: The amounts of the awards depend on the number of credit hours and the need of the recipient.

Duration: 1 year; may be renewed.

Number awarded: Varies each year.

1134
VERMONT-NEA/MAIDA F. TOWNSEND SCHOLARSHIPS

Vermont-NEA
10 Wheelock Street
Montpelier, VT 05602-3737
Phone: (802) 223-6375   (800) 649-6375
E-mail: scholar@vtnea.org
Web Site: www.vtnea.org.scholar.htm

Summary: To provide financial assistance for undergraduate or graduate studies to the sons and daughters of Vermont-NEA members.

Eligibility: Eligible to apply are the sons and daughters of Vermont-NEA members—high school seniors, undergraduates, and graduate students. Students majoring in any discipline are eligible, but preference may be give to those majoring or planning to major in education. The application process requires the submission of transcripts and 2 letters of recommendation. Each applicant must also submit an essay (under 400 words) on a topic that changes annually; recently, the topic was: "What is public education's role in promoting responsible environmental stewardship?" Selection is based on merit, not financial need.

Financial data: The stipend is $1,000. Funds are paid directly to the recipients.

Duration: 1 year; nonrenewable.

Additional information: This scholarship was established in 1991.

Number awarded: Varies each year; recently, 5 were awarded.

Deadline: January of each year.

1135
VETERANS EDUCATIONAL ASSISTANCE PROGRAM (VEAP)

Department of Veterans Affairs
810 Vermont Avenue, N.W.
Washington, DC 20420
Phone: (202) 418-4343   (888) GI-BILL1
Web Site: www.gibill.va.gov

Summary: To permit military service personnel to participate voluntarily in a plan for future education in which the participant's savings are administered and augmented by the government.

Eligibility: Veterans who served and military service members currently serving are eligible if they 1) entered active duty after December 31, 1976 and before July 1, 1985; 2) were released under conditions other than dishonorable or continue on active duty; 3) served for a continuous period of 181 days or more (or were discharged earlier for a service-connected disability); and 4) have satisfactorily contributed to the program. No individuals on active duty could enroll in this program after March 31, 1987. Veterans who enlisted for the first time after September 7, 1980 or entered active duty as an office or enlistee after October 16, 1981 must have completed 24 continuous months of active duty.

Financial data: Participants contribute to the program, through monthly deductions from their military pay, from $25 to $100 monthly, up to a maximum of $2,700. They may also, while on active duty, make a lump sum contribution to the training fund. At the time the eligible participant elects to use the benefits to pursue an approved course of education or training, the Department of Veterans Affairs (VA) will match the contribution at the rate of $2 for every $1 made by the participant.

Duration: Participants receive monthly payments for the number of months they contributed, or for 36 months, whichever is less. The amount of the payments is determined by dividing the number of months benefits will be paid into the participant's training fund total. Participants have 10 years from the date of last discharge or release from active duty within which to use these benefits.

Additional information: A participant may leave this program at the end of any 12-consecutive-month period of participation and those who do so may have their contributions refunded. This is the basic VA educational program for veterans and military personnel who entered active duty from January 1, 1977 through June 30, 1985. Veterans and service members who began active duty prior to that period and those who have entered subsequently may qualify for the Montgomery GI Bill. An individual who contributed or could have contributed to VEAP before being involuntarily separated from active duty with an honorable discharge after December 4, 1991 may make an irrevocable election before such separation to

receive Montgomery GI Bill benefits. Benefits are available for the pursuit of an associate, bachelor, or graduate degree at a college or university; a certificate or diploma from a business, technical, or vocational school; apprenticeship or on-job training programs; cooperative courses; correspondence-school courses; tutorial assistance; remedial, refresher, and deficiency training; flight training; study abroad programs leading to a college degree; nontraditional training away from school; and work-study for students enrolled at least three-quarter time. Ineligible courses include bartending or personality development courses; farm cooperative courses; non-accredited independent study courses; any course given by radio; self-improvement courses such as reading, speaking, woodworking, basic seamanship, and English as a second language; audited courses; any course that is avocational or recreational in character; courses not leading to an educational, professional, or vocational objective; courses taken and successfully completed previously; courses taken by a federal government employee and paid for under the Government Employees' Training Act; courses paid for in whole or in part by the armed forces while on active duty; and courses taken while in receipt of benefits for the same program from the Office of Workers' Compensation Programs.

Number awarded: Varies each year.

Deadline: Applications may be submitted at any time.

1136
VETERANS OF FOREIGN WARS OF MEXICAN ANCESTRY SCHOLARSHIP PROGRAM

Veterans of Foreign Wars of the United States of Mexican Ancestry
Central California Committee
c/o Emilio Olguin
651 Harrison Road
Monterey Park, CA 91755-6732
Phone: (626) 288-0498

Summary: To provide financial assistance for postsecondary education to Mexican American students in California.

Eligibility: This program is open to high school seniors of Mexican descent who reside in California. They must have earned at least a 3.5 grade point average and need financial assistance to attend college. Preference is given to the children of veterans.

Financial data: Stipends range from $500 to $1,000.

Duration: 1 year.

Additional information: Students who live in the central portion of California (from Los Angeles to Fresno) should write to the Central California Committee to obtain an application; students who live north of there should contact Robert Gonzalez, 3210 Santa Maria Avenue, Santa Clara, CA 95051-1622, (408) 248-1677; students who live south of there should contact Gilbert Castorena, 3981 Coleman Avenue, San Diego, CA 92154-2516, (619) 690-0907.

Number awarded: Varies; a total of $9,000 is available for these scholarships each year: $3,000 in each of the 3 districts.

Deadline: March of each year.

1137
VICE ADMIRAL E.P. TRAVERS SCHOLARSHIP

Navy-Marine Corps Relief Society
Attn: Education Division
801 North Randolph Street, Suite 1228
Arlington, VA 22203-1978
Phone: (703) 696-4960   Fax: (703) 696-0144
E-mail: education@hq.nmcrs.org
Web Site: www.nmcrs.org

Summary: To provide financial assistance for postsecondary education to the spouses and children of Navy and Marine personnel.

Eligibility: This program is open to the dependent children of active-duty and retired servicemembers, as well as the spouses of active-duty servicemembers. Applicants must have a minimum cumulative grade point average of 2.0 and must demonstrate financial need.

Financial data: The stipend is $2,000 per year.

Duration: 1 year; may be renewed up to 3 additional years.

Number awarded: Up to 500 each year.

Deadline: February of each year.

1138
VICTORIA S. AND BRADLEY L. GEIST FOUNDATION SCHOLARSHIP

Hawai'i Community Foundation
900 Fort Street Mall, Suite 1300
Honolulu, HI 96813
Phone: (808) 566-5570   (888) 731-3863
Fax: (808) 521-6286   E-mail: scholarships@hcf-hawaii.org
Web Site: www.hcf-hawaii.org
Summary: To provide financial assistance to Hawaii residents who are interested in attending college and have been in the foster care (or similar) system.
Eligibility: This program is open to Hawaii residents who 1) are permanently separated from their parents and currently in (or formerly in) the foster care system; or 2) are permanently separated from their parents and currently in (or formerly in) a hanai family situation. Applicants must be or planning to become full-time students at the undergraduate or graduate school level. They must be able to demonstrate academic achievement, good moral character, and financial need. In addition to filling out the standard application form, applicants must 1) write a short statement indicating their reasons for attending college, their planned course of study, and their career goals, and 2) supply a confirmation letter from their social worker, foster parent, hanai parent, or other appropriate individual.
Financial data: The amounts of the awards depend on the availability of funds and the need of the recipient; recently, grants averaged $2,400.
Duration: 1 year.
Additional information: Recipients may attend college in Hawaii or on the mainland.
Number awarded: Varies each year; recently, 54 of these scholarships were awarded.
Deadline: February of each year.

1139
VIETNOW SCHOLARSHIPS

VietNow National Headquarters
1835 Broadway
Rockford, IL 61104-5409
Phone: (815) 227-5100   (800) 837-VNOW
Fax: (815) 227-5127   E-mail: vnnatl@inwave.com
Web Site: www.vietnow.com
Summary: To provide financial assistance for college to dependents of certain veterans.
Eligibility: Applicants must be either 1) a dependent (biological child, stepchild, adopted child, or foster child) under the age of 35 of a VietNow member in good standing, or 2) a dependent of a veteran listed as missing in action, prisoner of war, or killed in action. Selection is based on academic achievement, ability, and extracurricular activities; financial need is a minor consideration.
Financial data: The stipend is $1,000 per year.
Duration: 1 year.
Number awarded: 8 each year.
Deadline: March of each year.

1140
VII CORPS DESERT STORM VETERANS ASSOCIATION SCHOLARSHIP

VII Corps Desert Storm Veterans Association
c/o Creighton Abrams at the Army Historical Foundation, Inc.
2425 Wilson Boulevard
Arlington, VA 22201
Phone: (703) 522-7901   E-mail: info@desertstormvets.org
Web Site: www.desertstormvets.org
Summary: To provide financial assistance for college to students who served, or are the family members of individuals who served, with VII Corps in Operations Desert Shield, Desert Storm, or related activities.
Eligibility: Applicants must have served, or be a family member of those who served, with VII Corps in Operations Desert Shield/Desert Storm, Provide Comfort, or 1 of the support base activities. Scholarships are limited to students entering or enrolled in accredited technical institutions (trade or specialty), 2-year colleges, and 4-year colleges or universities. Awards will not be made to individuals receiving military academy appointments or full 4-year scholarships. Letters of recommendation and a transcript are required. Selection is not based on financial need or solely on academic standing; consideration is also given to extracurricular

activities and other self-development skills and abilities obtained through on-the-job training or correspondence courses. Priority is given to survivors of VII Corps soldiers who died during Operations Desert Shield/Desert Storm or Provide Comfort, veterans who are also members of the VII Corps Desert Storm Veterans Association, and family members of veterans who are also members of the VII Corps Desert Storm Veterans Association.
Financial data: The stipend is $5,000 per year. Funds are paid to the recipients upon proof of admission or registration at an accredited institution, college, or university.
Duration: 1 year; recipients may reapply.
Number awarded: 3 each year.
Deadline: January of each year.

1141
VIKKI CARR SCHOLARSHIP AWARDS

Vikki Carr Scholarship Foundation
P.O. Box 57756
Sherman Oaks, CA 91413
Summary: To provide financial assistance to Latino students in California and Texas who are interested in pursuing their education at the college level.
Eligibility: Students of Latino heritage who are interested in postsecondary education and are in financial need may apply if they are between the ages of 17 and 22, legal U.S. residents, and residents of California or Texas. Selection is based on scholastic ability, financial need, community service, motivation, goals, and a 200-word autobiographical essay.
Financial data: Amount of the award ranges from $250 to $1,500.
Duration: 1 year; renewable.
Additional information: Texas residents should request information and applications from P.O. Box 780968, San Antonio, TX 78278. California residents should contact the foundation in Sherman Oaks, California.
Number awarded: Number varies, from 6 to 19 each year.
Deadline: February of each year.

1142
VIRGINIA COLLEGE SCHOLARSHIP ASSISTANCE PROGRAM

State Council of Higher Education for Virginia
Attn: Financial Aid Office
James Monroe Building
101 North 14th Street, Ninth Floor
Richmond, VA 23219-3659
Phone: (804) 225-2600   (877) 515-0138
Fax: (804) 225-2604   TDD: (804) 371-8017
E-mail: fainfo@schev.edu
Web Site: www.schev.edu
Summary: To provide financial assistance for college to residents of Virginia who demonstrate extreme financial need.
Eligibility: This program is open to residents of Virginia who have been admitted into a Virginia public 2- or 4-year college or university or a participating Virginia private nonprofit 4-year college or university. Applicants must be enrolled or planning to enroll at least half time, be a U.S. citizen or eligible noncitizen, and have a computed expected family contribution that is less than half the total cost of attendance.
Financial data: The amount awarded ranges from $400 to $5,000 per year, depending on the need of the recipient.
Duration: 1 year; may be renewed for up to 3 additional years if the recipient maintains at least half-time status and satisfactory academic progress.
Additional information: Applications and further information are available at the financial aid office of colleges and universities in Virginia. This program, established in 1973, is funded in part with federal funds from the Leveraging Educational Assistance Partnership (LEAP) program.
Number awarded: Varies each year.

1143
VIRGINIA COMMONWEALTH AWARDS

State Council of Higher Education for Virginia
Attn: Financial Aid Office
James Monroe Building
101 North 14th Street, Ninth Floor
Richmond, VA 23219-3659
Phone: (804) 225-2600   (877) 515-0138
Fax: (804) 225-2604   TDD: (804) 371-8017
E-mail: fainfo@schev.edu

Web Site: www.schev.edu

Summary: To provide financial assistance to needy undergraduate students and some graduate students enrolled in Virginia colleges or universities.

Eligibility: This program is open to residents of Virginia who are undergraduate students enrolled at least half time in Virginia's public colleges and universities. Applicants must be U.S. citizens or eligible noncitizens and able to demonstrate financial need. Some full-time graduate students, regardless of need or residency, are also eligible.

Financial data: Awards may be as much as all tuition and required fees.

Duration: 1 year.

Additional information: Applications and further information are available at the financial aid office of colleges and universities in Virginia.

Number awarded: Varies each year.

Deadline: Deadline dates vary by school.

1144
VIRGINIA FOSTER CHILDREN GRANTS

State Council of Higher Education for Virginia
Attn: Financial Aid Office
James Monroe Building
101 North 14th Street, Ninth Floor
Richmond, VA 23219-3659
Phone: (804) 225-2600   (877) 515-0138
Fax: (804) 225-2604   TDD: (804) 371-8017
E-mail: fainfo@schev.edu
Web Site: www.schev.edu

Summary: To provide financial assistance to community college students in Virginia who were in foster care.

Eligibility: This program is open to residents of Virginia who were in foster care, in the custody of the Department of Social Services, or considered a special needs adoption when their high school diploma or GED was awarded. Applicants may not have been previously enrolled in a postsecondary institution as a full-time student for more than 5 years, but they must be attending a community college in Virginia full time in an eligible academic program of at least 1 academic year in length. Colleges rank eligible first-year applicants on the basis of when the college received the application for admission, federal financial aid data, and appropriate supporting documentation. Renewal applicants are given priority for selection.

Financial data: Awards up to full tuition and fees are provided to students who are not receiving other assistance.

Duration: 1 year; may be renewed.

Additional information: Applications and further information are available at the financial aid office of community colleges in Virginia. This program was established in 2000.

Number awarded: Varies each year.

1145
VIRGINIA GRADUATE AND UNDERGRADUATE ASSISTANCE PROGRAM

State Council of Higher Education for Virginia
Attn: Financial Aid Office
James Monroe Building
101 North 14th Street, Ninth Floor
Richmond, VA 23219-3659
Phone: (804) 225-2600   (877) 515-0138
Fax: (804) 225-2604   TDD: (804) 371-8017
E-mail: fainfo@schev.edu
Web Site: www.schev.edu

Summary: To provide financial assistance to full-time students attending public colleges or universities in Virginia.

Eligibility: This program is open to full-time undergraduate and graduate students who have been admitted into a participating public college or university in Virginia; both residents and non-residents of Virginia are eligible. Selection is based on academic performance.

Financial data: The amount of aid depends on the availability of funds from a combination of endowment income and state appropriations. Awards may be used to pay tuition, fees, room, board, or other educational expenses unless restricted further by the donor.

Additional information: Applications and further information are available at the financial aid office of colleges and universities in Virginia. This program was established in 1992.

Number awarded: Varies each year.

1146
VIRGINIA GUARANTEED ASSISTANCE PROGRAM

State Council of Higher Education for Virginia
Attn: Financial Aid Office
James Monroe Building
101 North 14th Street, Ninth Floor
Richmond, VA 23219-3659
Phone: (804) 225-2600   (877) 515-0138
Fax: (804) 225-2604   TDD: (804) 371-8017
E-mail: fainfo@schev.edu
Web Site: www.schev.edu

Summary: To provide financial assistance to exceptionally needy students at public colleges and universities in Virginia.

Eligibility: This program is open to residents of Virginia who are currently attending an elementary or secondary school in the state. Students are eligible to receive these awards if they graduate from a Virginia high school with a cumulative grade point average of 2.5 or higher, are classified as a dependent, are a U.S. citizen or eligible noncitizen, are able to demonstrate financial need, and are admitted to a Virginia public 2- or 4-year college or university as a full-time student.

Financial data: Awards vary by institution but range up to the full cost of tuition, required fees, and an allowance for books. Students with the greatest need receive the largest awards.

Duration: 1 year; may be renewed as long as the recipient maintains full-time enrollment with at least a 2.0 grade point average, demonstrated financial need, residency in Virginia, and satisfactory academic progress.

Additional information: Applications and further information are available at the financial aid office of colleges and universities in Virginia.

Number awarded: Varies each year.

1147
VIRGINIA PART-TIME ASSISTANCE PROGRAM

State Council of Higher Education for Virginia
Attn: Financial Aid Office
James Monroe Building
101 North 14th Street, Ninth Floor
Richmond, VA 23219-3659
Phone: (804) 225-2600   (877) 515-0138
Fax: (804) 225-2604   TDD: (804) 371-8017
E-mail: fainfo@schev.edu
Web Site: www.schev.edu

Summary: To provide financial assistance to community college students in Virginia who are attending part time.

Eligibility: This program is open to residents of Virginia who are attending a community college in the state on a part-time basis. Applicants must be able to demonstrate financial need.

Financial data: Awards up to full tuition and fees are available.

Duration: 1 year; may be renewed.

Additional information: Applications and further information are available at the financial aid office of community colleges in Virginia.

Number awarded: Varies each year.

1148
VIRGINIA TUITION ASSISTANCE GRANT PROGRAM

State Council of Higher Education for Virginia
Attn: Financial Aid Office
James Monroe Building
101 North 14th Street, Ninth Floor
Richmond, VA 23219-3659
Phone: (804) 225-2600   (877) 515-0138
Fax: (804) 225-2604   TDD: (804) 371-8017
E-mail: fainfo@schev.edu
Web Site: www.schev.edu

Summary: To provide financial assistance to undergraduate and graduate students attending private colleges or universities in Virginia.

Eligibility: Undergraduate and graduate or professional students who are Virginia residents attending private colleges or universities in the state on a full-time basis in a degree-seeking program are eligible for this program. There is no financial need requirement. Students pursuing religious training or theological education are not eligible.

Financial data: The amount awarded varies, depending on annual appropriations

and number of applicants; recently, the maximum award was $3,000.

Duration: 1 year; may be renewed.

Additional information: This program was established in 1972.

Number awarded: Varies each year.

Deadline: The deadline for priority consideration for fall semester is July of each year. Applicants submitted through the end of November are considered only if funds are available.

1149
VIRGINIA UNDERGRADUATE STUDENT FINANCIAL ASSISTANCE (LAST DOLLAR) PROGRAM

State Council of Higher Education for Virginia
Attn: Financial Aid Office
James Monroe Building
101 North 14th Street, Ninth Floor
Richmond, VA 23219-3659
Phone: (804) 225-2600   (877) 515-0138
Fax: (804) 225-2604   TDD: (804) 371-8017
E-mail: fainfo@schev.edu
Web Site: www.schev.edu

Summary: To provide financial assistance to minority undergraduate students enrolled in Virginia colleges or universities.

Eligibility: Eligible to apply for this program are minority undergraduate students who are enrolled at least half time for the first time (as freshmen) in state-supported 2-year or 4-year colleges or universities in Virginia. They must be enrolled in an eligible baccalaureate program. The program is intended to assist students who 1) receive financial aid packages that do not fully meet their need or include excessive self-help (loan or work) as determined by the institution; 2) apply and are accepted for admission after an institution has awarded all available grant resources; and 3) are accepted for admission and do not originally apply for financial aid but later determine that aid is needed to attend and apply after other financial aid resources are depleted.

Financial data: The stipends range from $200 per term to the total cost of attendance (tuition, required fees, room, board, supplies, and personal expenses).

Duration: 1 year; nonrenewable.

Additional information: Applications and further information are available at the financial aid office of colleges and universities in Virginia. This program was established in 1988.

Number awarded: Varies each year.

Deadline: Deadline dates vary by school.

1150
VIRGINIA WAR ORPHANS EDUCATION PROGRAM

Virginia Department of Veterans' Affairs
270 Franklin Road, S.W., Room 503
Roanoke, VA 24011-2215
Phone: (540) 857-7104   Fax: (540) 857-7573
Web Site: www.vdva.vipnet.org

Summary: To provide educational assistance to the children of disabled and other Virginia veterans or service personnel.

Eligibility: To be eligible, applicants must meet the following requirements: 1) be between 16 and 25 years of age; 2) be accepted at a state-supported secondary or postsecondary educational institution in Virginia; 3) have at least 1 parent who served in the U.S. armed forces and is permanently and totally disabled due to an injury or disease incurred in a time of war or other period of armed conflict, has died as a result of injury or disease incurred in a time of war or other period of armed conflict, or is listed as a prisoner of war or missing in action; 4) be the dependent of a parent who was a resident of Virginia at the time of entry into active military service or for at least 5 consecutive years immediately prior to the date of application or death.

Financial data: Eligible individuals receive free tuition and are exempted from any fees charged by state-supported schools in Virginia.

Duration: Entitlement extends to a maximum of 48 months.

Additional information: Individuals entitled to this benefit may use it to pursue any vocational, technical, undergraduate, or graduate program of instruction. Generally, programs listed in the academic catalogs of state-supported institutions are acceptable, provided they have a clearly defined educational objective (such as a certificate, diploma, or degree).

Number awarded: Varies; generally more than 150 each year.

1151
VOCATIONAL REHABILITATION FOR DISABLED VETERANS

Department of Veterans Affairs
810 Vermont Avenue, N.W.
Washington, DC 20420
Phone: (202) 418-4343   (800) 827-1000
Web Site: www.va.gov

Summary: To provide vocational rehabilitation to certain categories of veterans with disabilities.

Eligibility: This program is open to veterans who have a service-connected disability of at least 10 percent and a serious employment handicap or 20 percent and an employment handicap. They must have been discharged or released from military service under other than dishonorable conditions. The Department of Veterans Affairs (VA) must determine that they would benefit from a training program that would help them prepare for, find, and keep suitable employment. The program may be 1) institutional training at a certificate, 2-year college, 4-year college or university, or technical program; 2) unpaid on-the-job training in a federal, state, or local agency or a federally recognized Indian tribal agency, training in a home, vocational course in a rehabilitation facility or sheltered workshop, independent instruction, or institutional non-farm cooperative; or 3) paid training through a farm cooperative, apprenticeship, on-the-job training, or on-the-job non-farm cooperative.

Financial data: While in training and for 2 months after, eligible disabled veterans may receive subsistence allowances in addition to their disability compensation or retirement pay. For institutional training, the full-time monthly rate is $433.06 with no dependents, $537.19 with 1 dependent, $633.04 with 2 dependents, and $46.14 for each additional dependent; the three-quarter time monthly rate is $325.41 for no dependents, $403.49 with 1 dependent, $473.29 with 2 dependents, and $35.48 for each additional dependent; the half-time monthly rate is $217.73 for no dependents, $269.77 with 1 dependent, $317.11 with 2 dependents, and $23.67 for each additional dependent. For unpaid on-the-job training, the monthly rate is $433.06 for no dependents, $537.19 with 1 dependent, $633.04 with 2 dependents, and $46.14 for each additional dependent. For paid training, the monthly rate is based on the wage received, to a maximum of $378.65 for no dependents, $457.91 with 1 dependent, $527.72 with 2 dependents, and $34.32 for each additional dependent. The VA also pays the costs of tuition, books, fees, supplies, and equipment; it may also pay for special supportive services, such as tutorial assistance, prosthetic devices, lipreading training, and signing for the deaf. If during training or employment services the veteran's disabilities cause transportation expenses that would not be incurred by nondisabled persons, the VA will pay for at least a portion of those expenses. If the veteran encounters financial difficulty during training, the VA may provide an advance against future benefit payments.

Duration: Up to 48 months of full-time training or its equivalent in part-time training. If a veteran with a serious disability receives services under an extended evaluation to improve training potential, the total of the extended evaluation and the training phases of the rehabilitation program may exceed 48 months. Usually, the veteran must complete a rehabilitation program within 12 years from the date of notification of entitlement to compensation by the VA. Following completion of the training portion of a rehabilitation program, a veteran may receive counseling and job search and adjustment services for 18 months.

Additional information: The program may also provide employment assistance, self-employment assistance, training in a rehabilitation facility, or college and other training. Veterans who are seriously disabled may receive services and assistance to improve their ability to live more independently in their community. After completion of the training phase, the VA will assist the veteran to find and hold a suitable job.

Number awarded: Varies each year.

Deadline: Applications are accepted at any time.

1152
VOCATIONAL SCHOOL AWARDS OF THE SEMINOLE NATION JUDGEMENT FUND

Seminole Nation of Oklahoma
Attn: Judgement Fund
P.O. Box 1498
Wewoka, OK 74884
Phone: (405) 257-6287
Web Site: www.cowboy.net/native/seminole/judgement_fund.html

Summary: To provide financial assistance for vocational school to members of the Seminole Nation of Oklahoma.

Eligibility: This program is open to enrolled members of the Seminole Nation who are descended from a member of the Seminole Nation as it existed in Florida on September 18, 1923. Applicants must be attending or planning to attend a vocational school.

Financial data: The stipend for full-time students is $25 per week, to a maximum of $1,200 per year. The stipend for part-time students is $12 per week, to a maximum of $600 per year. Other benefits include a grant up to $250 to cover the actual cost of tuition, books, and fees; and a grant of $100 or the actual cost, whichever is less, of the fee to obtain a license upon completion of a vocational course. Students who take correspondence courses may receive up to $400 per year or the actual cost of tuition, books, or fees, whichever is less; no stipend is provided to those students. The total of all vocational school awards to an applicant may not exceed $2,400.

Duration: 1 year; may be renewed for 1 additional year.

Additional information: The General Council of the Seminole Nation of Oklahoma approved a plan for use of the Judgement Fund Award in 1990. This aspect of the program went into effect in September of 1991.

Number awarded: Varies each year.

Deadline: Applications must be submitted within 30 days of the completion of a vocational course.

1153
VSGA SCHOLARSHIP PROGRAM

Virginia State Golf Association
830 Southlake Boulevard, Suite A
Richmond, VA 23236
Phone: (804) 378-2300   Fax: (804) 378-2369
E-mail: info@vsga.org
Web Site: www.vsga.org

Summary: To provide money for college to young Virginians who have an interest in golf.

Eligibility: This program is open to high school seniors in Virginia who are interested in golf and wish to attend a college or university in the state. Selection is based on interest in golf (ability is not considered), academic achievement, citizenship, character, and financial need. U.S. citizenship is required.

Financial data: Stipends range from $1,000 to $5,000. The Spencer-Wilkinson Grant for the top female applicant is $2,000.

Duration: 1 year; may be renewed.

Additional information: This program was established in 1984. Since then, more than 300 students have received a total of $800,000 in scholarships. The top female applicant is awarded the Spencer-Wilkinson Grant, sponsored by the association's Women's Division. Recipients must attend a college or university in Virginia.

Number awarded: Varies each year; recently, 35 of these scholarships were awarded.

Deadline: February of each year.

1154
WALTER H. MEYER—GARRY L. WHITE MEMORIAL EDUCATIONAL FUND

College Planning Network
Attn: Vicki Breithaupt
Campion Tower
914 East Jefferson
Seattle, WA 98122-5366
Phone: (206) 323-0624   E-mail: seacpn@collegeplan.org
Web Site: www.collegeplan.org

Summary: To provide financial assistance for undergraduate or graduate study to residents of Washington state.

Eligibility: This program is open to residents of Washington who are attending or planning to attend a college or university in the United States, Canada, or Europe. Both undergraduate and graduate students are eligible. Selection is based on an essay explaining how receipt of the scholarship will help them meet their educational goals, a list of significant activities and honors, 2 letters of recommendation, academic transcripts, and financial need.

Financial data: The stipend depends on the need of the recipient but is at least $3,000 per year.

Duration: 1 year.

Number awarded: 8 each year.

Deadline: February of each year.

1155
WALTER L. MITCHELL MEMORIAL SCHOLARSHIP AWARDS

International Chemical Workers Union Council
Attn: Research and Education Department
1655 West Market Street
Akron, OH 44313
Phone: (216) 867-2444   Fax: (216) 867-0544
E-mail: icwuchq@icwuc.org
Web Site: www.icwuc.org

Summary: To provide financial assistance for postsecondary education to the children of members of the International Chemical Workers Union Council.

Eligibility: Eligible are children or stepchildren of union members who are entering college in the following fall. The qualifying parent must have been a member in good standing for at least 1 year, or have died within the past year, or be on sick leave or layoff and in good standing at the beginning of that sick leave or layoff. Selection is based on biographical information, ACT or SAT scores, and high school record.

Financial data: The stipend is $1,000.

Duration: 1 year; nonrenewable.

Additional information: The Al Barkan Memorial Award is supported by a grant from the American Income Life Insurance Company

Number awarded: 19 each year: 2 in each of the 6 regions, 6 at large, and the Al Barkan Memorial Award for the top-ranked alternate. In addition, the Jim Hull Memorial Award is presented to an applicant from Region 4.

Deadline: February of each year.

1156
WASHINGTON APPLE COMMISSION FARMWORKER EDUCATION SCHOLARSHIP FUND

Washington Apple Education Foundation
P.O. Box 3720
Wenatchee, WA 98807
Phone: (509) 663-7713   Fax: (509) 682-1293
E-mail: waef@waef.org
Web Site: www.waef.org

Summary: To provide financial assistance to students who are employed within the Washington apple industry or the children of those employees.

Eligibility: This program is open to Washington residents. Applicants must be either employed or the children of employees within the Washington apple industry. They may be high school seniors or currently-enrolled college students. Selection is based on standardized tests, academic performance, demonstrated leadership ability, industry and promise of useful citizenship, financial need, a statement of intent, and personal references. Students who are related to the staff or board or committee members of either the Washington Apple Education Foundation or the Washington Apple Commission are not eligible to receive an award.

Financial data: The amount awarded varies, depending upon the needs of the recipient and the funds available. The money may be used to pay for tuition, room, board, books, educational supplies, and miscellaneous institutional fees.

Duration: 1 year; recipients may reapply.

Additional information: This scholarship is funded by the Washington Apple Commission and administered by the Washington Apple Education Foundation.

Number awarded: Varies each year.

Deadline: March of each year.

1157
WASHINGTON APPLE EDUCATION FOUNDATION MEMORIAL COMMISSION SCHOLARSHIP FUND

Washington Apple Education Foundation
P.O. Box 3720
Wenatchee, WA 98807
Phone: (509) 663-7713   Fax: (509) 682-1293
E-mail: waef@waef.org
Web Site: www.waef.org

Summary: To provide financial assistance to students who are involved in Washington's tree fruit industry.

Eligibility: This program is open to Washington residents. Applicants must be involved in Washington's tree fruit industry, either by pursuing a career in the industry or by having been raised in a family employed within the industry. They may be high school seniors or currently-enrolled college students. Selection is based on standardized tests, academic performance, demonstrated leadership

ability, industry and promise of useful citizenship, financial need, a statement of intent, and personal references. Students who are related to the staff or board or committee members of the Washington Apple Education Foundation are not eligible to receive an award.

Financial data: The stipend is $1,250. The money may be used to pay for tuition, room, board, books, educational supplies, and miscellaneous institutional fees.

Duration: 1 year; recipients may reapply.

Number awarded: 4 each year.

Deadline: March of each year.

1158
WASHINGTON AWARD FOR VOCATIONAL EXCELLENCE

Washington State Workforce Training and Education Coordinating Board
128 Tenth Avenue, S.W.
P.O. Box 43105
Olympia, WA 98504-3105
Phone: (360) 753-5662   Fax: (360) 586-5862
E-mail: wtecb@wtb.wa.gov
Web Site: www.wa.gov/wtb/wave-abt.html

Summary: To provide financial assistance to Washington residents who are attending vocational-technical schools.

Eligibility: High schools, skills centers, and community and technical colleges nominate students who are engaged in vocational or technical training for these awards. Selection is based on occupational proficiency, vocational student leadership, community activities, work experience, character, attitude, attendance, and other qualities.

Financial data: Awards do not exceed the annual undergraduate tuition and fees at public research universities in the state (currently $3,256 per year).

Duration: Up to 6 quarters or 4 semesters, provided the student maintains at least a 3.0 grade point average.

Number awarded: 147 each year: 3 in each state legislative district.

Deadline: February of each year.

1159
WASHINGTON CORRECTIONAL ASSOCIATION SCHOLARSHIPS

Washington Correctional Association
Attn: Scholarship Program
P.O. Box 5853
Lacey, WA 98509-5853
E-mail: wca@bmi.net
Web Site: www.bmi.net/wca/scholarship.html

Summary: To provide financial assistance for college to members of the Washington Correctional Association (WCA).

Eligibility: This program is open to members of the association in good standing. Applicants must be interested in attending an accredited college, university, vocational school, or community college.

Financial data: A stipend is provided (exact amount not specified). Funds may not be used to duplicate funding from other sources but may be used to supplement them.

Duration: 1 year.

Number awarded: Varies each year.

1160
WASHINGTON LEGION CHILDREN AND YOUTH SCHOLARSHIPS

American Legion
Attn: Department of Washington
3600 Ruddell Road S.E.
P.O. Box 3917
Lacey, WA 98509-3917
Phone: (360) 491-4373   Fax: (360) 491-7442
E-mail: francesal@uswest.net
Web Site: www.walegion.org

Summary: To provide financial assistance for the postsecondary education of the children of members of the American Legion or American Legion Auxiliary in Washington.

Eligibility: Applicants must be the sons or daughters of Washington Legionnaires or Auxiliary members, living or deceased, who are high school seniors in need of financial assistance to attend an accredited institution of higher education, trade, or vocational school in the state of Washington.

Financial data: The scholarships are either $2,500 or $1,500, payable in equal amounts per semester.

Duration: 1 year.

Number awarded: 2 each year: 1 at $2,500 and 1 at $1,500.

Deadline: March of each year.

1161
WASHINGTON PROMISE SCHOLARSHIP

Washington Higher Education Coordinating Board
917 Lakeridge Way
P.O. Box 43430
Olympia, WA 98504-3430
Phone: (360) 753-7801   (888) 535-0747
Fax: (360) 753-7808   TDD: (360) 753-7809
E-mail: wapromise@hecb.wa.gov
Web Site: www.hecb.wa.gov

Summary: To provide financial assistance to graduating high school seniors in Washington who meet academic and family income requirements.

Eligibility: This program is open to Washington residents who are graduating in the top 15 percent of their high school class and whose family income is equal to or less than 135 percent of the state's median (currently, $40,400 for a family of 1, ranging to $104,700 for a family of 7, plus $2,300 for each additional family member). Applicants must plan to attend a public or private 2- or 4-year college or university in Washington.

Financial data: The stipend depends on the number of students who qualify, to a maximum of $1,641 per year.

Duration: 1 year; may be renewed 1 additional year.

Additional information: This program was created by the Washington legislature in 1999.

Number awarded: Varies each year; recently, approximately 2,250 students qualified for these scholarships.

Deadline: August of each year.

1162
WASHINGTON SCHOLARS PROGRAM

Washington Higher Education Coordinating Board
917 Lakeridge Way
P.O. Box 43430
Olympia, WA 98504-3430
Phone: (360) 753-7850   Fax: (360) 753-7808
Phone: TDD: (360) 753-7809   E-mail: finaid@hecb.wa.gov
Web Site: www.hecb.wa.gov

Summary: To provide financial assistance for education at colleges and universities in Washington to the top 1 percent of students who graduate from high schools in the state.

Eligibility: High school principals in Washington may nominate graduating seniors in the top 1 percent of their class for this program. Students are selected to receive awards based on academic accomplishments, leadership, and community service.

Financial data: Awards do not exceed the annual undergraduate tuition and fees at public research universities in the state (currently $3,256 per year).

Duration: Aid is provided for 12 quarters or 8 semesters of undergraduate study.

Additional information: Recipients may study at an independent or public college or university in Washington.

Number awarded: 147 each year: 3 in each state legislative district.

1163
WASHINGTON STATE AMERICAN INDIAN ENDOWED SCHOLARSHIP PROGRAM

Washington Higher Education Coordinating Board
917 Lakeridge Way
P.O. Box 43430
Olympia, WA 98504-3430
Phone: (360) 753-7843   Fax: (360) 753-7808
Phone: TDD: (360) 753-7809   E-mail: finaid@hecb.wa.gov
Web Site: www.hecb.wa.gov

Summary: To provide financial assistance to American Indian students in Washington.

Eligibility: American Indian students who are Washington residents are eligible for this program if they have close social and cultural ties to an American Indian tribe and/or community in the state and agree to use their education to benefit

other American Indians. They must demonstrate financial need and be enrolled, or intend to enroll, at a Washington state college or university on a full-time basis; all qualified applicants are considered, but upper-division and graduate students receive priority. Students who are working on a degree in religious, seminarian, or theological academic studies are not eligible.

Financial data: The stipend is $1,000 per year.

Duration: 1 year.

Additional information: This program was created by the Washington legislature in 1990.

Deadline: May of each year.

1164
WASHINGTON STATE ELKS ASSOCIATION VOCATIONAL GRANTS

Washington State Elks Association
4512 South Pine Street
P.O. Box 110760
Tacoma, WA 98411-0760
Phone: (253) 472-6223

Summary: To provide financial assistance to high school seniors in Washington state who are interested in pursuing vocational training or a 2-year associate degree.

Eligibility: This program is open to graduating high school students and GED students in Washington state. Applicants must be U.S. citizens and planning to work on an associate degree, diploma, certificate, or other course of vocational training that does not exceed 2 years in length. Students seeking education that requires a 4-year degree are ineligible. Selection is based on the applicant's personal statement, a letter from the parent, letters of endorsement, academic record, financial need, and achievements.

Financial data: Stipends range from $500 to $1,500.

Duration: 1 year.

Number awarded: Varies; generally, at least 40 each year.

Deadline: January of each year.

1165
WASHINGTON STATE NEED GRANT

Washington Higher Education Coordinating Board
917 Lakeridge Way
P.O. Box 43430
Olympia, WA 98504-3430
Phone: (360) 753-7850   Fax: (360) 753-7808
Phone: TDD: (360) 753-7809   E-mail: finaid@hecb.wa.gov
Web Site: www.hecb.wa.gov

Summary: To assist needy and disadvantaged Washington residents in obtaining a postsecondary education at 1 of Washington's 2-year or 4-year public or private colleges or universities, selected proprietary schools, or public vocational-technical institutions.

Eligibility: To be eligible for the award, a student must be needy or disadvantaged, a resident of Washington, enrolled or accepted for enrollment as at least a half-time undergraduate student, and a U.S. citizen or in the process of becoming one. Applicants may not be pursuing a degree in theology.

Financial data: Grants range from $1,450 to $2,400 per year. Students with dependents can receive a dependent care allowance of $545.

Duration: 1 academic year; renewal is possible for up to 3 additional years.

Additional information: Consideration is automatic with the institution's receipt of the student's completed financial aid application. This program began in 1969.

Number awarded: Varies each year; recently, approximately 47,000 students received more than $57 million in benefits from this program.

Deadline: Varies according to the participating institution; generally in October of each year.

1166
WASHINGTON STATE PTA SCHOLARSHIPS

Washington State PTA
Attn: WSPTA Scholarship Foundation
15100 S.E. 38th Street
PMB 707
Bellevue, WA 98006-1765
Phone: (253) 565-2153   (800) 562-3804
Fax: (253) 565-7753   E-mail: wapta@wastatepta.org
Web Site: www.wastatepta.org

Summary: To provide financial assistance for postsecondary education to graduates of Washington public high schools.

Eligibility: This program is open to graduates of public high schools in Washington state who are entering postsecondary institutions; applicants may be current graduating seniors or graduates from prior years entering their freshman year. Selection is based primarily on financial need; academic criteria are not considered as long as the candidates are able to meet the admission requirements of the school they wish to attend.

Financial data: Stipends are $1,000 for 4-year colleges or universities and $500 for community colleges, voc-tech schools, or other accredited institutions.

Duration: 1 year; nonrenewable.

Number awarded: Varies each year; a total of $55,000 per year is available for these scholarships.

Deadline: February of each year.

1167
WASHINGTON STATE TUITION AND FEE WAIVER PROGRAM

Washington Higher Education Coordinating Board
917 Lakeridge Way
P.O. Box 43430
Olympia, WA 98504-3430
Phone: (360) 753-7850   Fax: (360) 753-7808
Phone: TDD: (360) 753-7809   E-mail: finaid@hecb.wa.gov
Web Site: www.hecb.wa.gov

Summary: To provide financial assistance to needy or disadvantaged Washington residents who are interested in attending college in the state.

Eligibility: This program is open to Washington residents who are disadvantaged and need financial assistance to attend a public 2- or 4-year college or university in Washington. The application for this program is automatic, if the student applies for financial aid from a public Washington state institution.

Financial data: Public colleges and universities in Washington waive all or part of the tuition for students who qualify for this program. More than $13 million is distributed annually; the average fee waiver is worth approximately $1,000.

Duration: 1 year; may be renewed.

Additional information: This program was created by the Washington legislature in 1971.

Number awarded: Varies; generally, at least 7,100 per year.

1168
WASHOE TRIBE ADULT VOCATIONAL SCHOLARSHIPS

Washoe Tribe
Attn: Education Department
919 Highway 395 South
Gardnerville, NV 89410
Phone: (775) 883-1446

Summary: To provide financial assistance to members of the Washoe Tribe who are interested in obtaining a diploma or certificate at a vocational or technical junior college.

Eligibility: Eligible to apply for these scholarships are adult members of the Washoe Tribe who are pursuing (or planning to pursue) vocational education. Applicants are required to seek all other sources of funding, in addition to applying for this program. In the process, they must complete a Free Application for Federal Student Aid (FAFSA) and receive a Student Aid Report.

Financial data: A stipend is awarded (exact amount not specified).

Duration: The maximum training period is generally 24 months.

Number awarded: Varies each year.

Deadline: Applications may be submitted at any time.

1169
WASHOE TRIBE HIGHER EDUCATION SCHOLARSHIPS

Washoe Tribe
Attn: Education Department
919 Highway 395 South
Gardnerville, NV 89410
Phone: (775) 883-1446

Summary: To provide financial assistance for college to members of the Washoe Tribe.

Eligibility: Eligible to apply for these scholarships are members of the Washoe Tribe who are working on (or planning to work on) an associate or bachelor's degree. Applicants are required to seek all other sources of funding, in addition to applying for this program. In the process, they must complete a Free Application

for Federal Student Aid (FAFSA) and receive a Student Aid Report.
Financial data: A stipend is awarded (exact amount not specified).
Duration: 1 year; recipients may reapply.
Number awarded: Varies each year.
Deadline: August or December of each year.

1170
WASHOE TRIBE INCENTIVE SCHOLARSHIPS

Washoe Tribe
Attn: Education Department
919 Highway 395 South
Gardnerville, NV 89410
Phone: (775) 883-1446
Summary: To provide financial assistance for college to members of the Washoe Tribe.
Eligibility: Eligible to apply for these scholarships are members of the Washoe Tribe who are currently enrolled in college on a full-time basis and have earned at least a 3.0 grade point average. As part of the application process, students must complete a Free Application for Federal Student Aid (FAFSA) and receive a Student Aid Report.
Financial data: A stipend is awarded (exact amount not specified).
Duration: 1 year; recipients may reapply.
Number awarded: Varies each year.
Deadline: January or September of each year.

1171
WASIE FOUNDATION SCHOLARSHIP PROGRAM

Wasie Foundation
Attn: Program Officer
U.S. Bank Place, Suite 4700
601 Second Avenue South
Minneapolis, MN 55402-4319
Phone: (612) 332-3883   Fax: (612) 332-2440
Summary: To provide financial assistance to undergraduates who are attending selected academic institutions in Minnesota.
Eligibility: This program is open to U.S. citizens who have been accepted as full-time students at 1 of the participating schools in Minnesota: College of St. Benedict, College of St. Catherine, College of St. Scholastica, Dunwoody Institute, Hamline University, Mayo Medical School, St. John's University, St. Mary's University of Minnesota, University of Minnesota, University of St. Thomas, and William Mitchell College of Law. A personal statement, academic transcripts, and a photograph must be submitted with the complete application. Preference is given to individuals of Polish ancestry who are members of the Christian faith. Preference is also given to individuals from north and northeast Minneapolis and surrounding communities. Selection is based on financial need, academic ability, education and career goals, leadership qualities, and involvement in volunteer and extracurricular activities.
Financial data: A stipend is awarded (exact amount not specified).
Duration: 1 year; recipients may reapply.
Additional information: This program started in the 1960s. The Wasie Scholarship is very competitive. In the past, only 20 percent of the applicants have received scholarships. Recipients must attend school on a full-time basis.
Number awarded: Generally, 9 each year.
Deadline: March of each year.

1172
WAYNE S. RICH SCHOLARSHIP

Pine Tree State 4-H Foundation
c/o University of Maine
5741 Libby Hall
Orono, ME 04469-5741
Phone: (207) 581-3739   Fax: (207) 581-3212
E-mail: brendaz@umext.maine.edu
Web Site: www.umaine/edu.4hfoundation
Summary: To provide financial assistance to 4-H members in Maine and New Hampshire who are interested in attending college.
Eligibility: This program is open to 1) seniors who are graduating from a high school in Maine or New Hampshire, and 2) residents of Maine or New Hampshire who have graduated from high school but have delayed going to college for no more than 1 year. Applicants must be active in 4-H activities. Selection is based primarily on academic achievement and 4-H activities; financial need is not

considered.
Financial data: The stipend is $1,000.
Duration: 1 year; nonrenewable.
Number awarded: 1 each year.
Deadline: March of each year.

1173
WBOC TV 16 STUDENT SCHOLARSHIP PROGRAM

WBOC TV 16
1729 North Salisbury Boulevard
P.O. Box 2057
Salisbury, MD 21802-2057
Phone: (410) 749-1111, ext. 288   Fax: (410) 749-2361
E-mail: mollyr@dmv.com
Web Site: www.wboc.com
Summary: To provide financial assistance for college to seniors graduating from high schools in Delaware, Maryland, Virginia, and Washington, D.C.
Eligibility: This program is open to high school seniors in WBOC TV 16's viewing area (Delaware, Maryland, Virginia, and Washington, D.C.). Applicants must include a letter explaining how they achieved their accomplishments, how they are making "A Difference through Leadership" in their school or community, and what they hope to achieve for themselves and others by pursuing higher education. In addition to that letter, selection is based on leadership qualities, school and community involvement, grades, and SAT scores; financial need is not considered.
Financial data: The stipend is $1,600. Funds are paid directly to the recipient's school.
Duration: 1 year; nonrenewable.
Additional information: This program began in 1992.
Number awarded: Varies each year; recently, 8 of these scholarships were awarded.
Deadline: December of each year.

1174
WEST VIRGINIA HIGHER EDUCATION ADULT PART-TIME STUDENT GRANT PROGRAM

West Virginia Higher Education Policy Commission
Attn: Coordinator, Scholarship Programs
1018 Kanawha Boulevard, East, Suite 700
Charleston, WV 25301-2827
Phone: (304) 558-4618   (888) 825-5707
Fax: (304) 558-5719   E-mail: wicks@hepc.wvnet.edu
Web Site: www.hepc.wvnet.edu/students/heaps.html
Summary: To provide financial assistance to West Virginia residents who have been out of high school for at least 2 years and are pursuing postsecondary education in the state on a part-time basis.
Eligibility: This program is open to West Virginia residents who are U.S. citizens or permanent residents. Applicants must be enrolled or accepted for enrollment in a certificate, associate, or bachelor's degree program on a part-time basis at an eligible West Virginia institution, including a community college, a technical college, an adult technical preparatory education program or training, a state college or university, an independent college or university, or an approved distance education program (including web-based courses). They may not have been enrolled in a high school diploma program, other than a GED program, for at least 2 years. At the time of application, they must be making satisfactory academic progress as determined by the institution. In addition, they must be eligible to participate in the federal Pell Grant program, demonstrate financial need, qualify as an independent student according to federal financial aid rules, not be in default on a higher education loan, and demonstrate that they have applied for, accepted, or both, other student financial assistance in compliance with federal financial aid rules.
Financial data: For students enrolled at a public college or university, the maximum grant is based on the actual per credit tuition and fees. For students at other eligible institutions, the award is based on the average per credit tuition and fees charged by all of the public undergraduate institutions of higher education during the previous year. Total aid, including this award, may not exceed the recipient's total cost of education as defined by their institution.
Duration: 1 year; may be renewed until the program of study is completed, up to a maximum of 9 additional years.
Number awarded: Varies each year.

1175
WEST VIRGINIA HIGHER EDUCATION GRANT PROGRAM

West Virginia Higher Education Policy Commission
Attn: Coordinator, Scholarship Programs
1018 Kanawha Boulevard, East, Suite 700
Charleston, WV 25301-2827
Phone: (304) 558-4614 (888) 825-5707
Fax: (304) 558-5719 E-mail: wicks@hepc.wvnet.edu
Web Site: www.hepc.wvnet.edu/students/wvgrant.html
Summary: To provide financial assistance to West Virginia residents who wish to attend an approved institution of higher education in West Virginia or Pennsylvania.
Eligibility: This program is open to U.S. citizens who have been residents of West Virginia for at least 1 year prior to applying. Applicants must plan to enroll as full-time undergraduate students at an approved college or university in West Virginia or Pennsylvania. Selection is based on financial need and academic performance.
Financial data: Awards are limited to payment of tuition and fees, from a minimum of $350 per year to a maximum of $2,532 per year. Funds are sent directly to the institution.
Duration: 1 year; may be renewed for up to 3 additional years.
Number awarded: Varies each year; recently, approximately 12,000 students received this assistance.
Deadline: February of each year.

1176
WEST VIRGINIA PROMISE SCHOLARSHIPS

West Virginia Higher Education Policy Commission
Attn: PROMISE Scholarship Program
1018 Kanawha Boulevard, East, Suite 700
Charleston, WV 25301-2827
Phone: (304) 558-4418 (877) WV-PROMISE
Fax: (304) 558-3264 E-mail: Morgenstern@hepc.wvnet.edu
Web Site: www.promisescholarships.org
Summary: To provide financial assistance for college to high school seniors in West Virginia who have complied with core academic requirements.
Eligibility: This program is open to high school seniors in West Virginia who have earned a grade point average of 3.0 or higher in core courses (4 credits of English/language arts, 3 credits of mathematics, 3 credits of social sciences, and 3 credits of natural sciences) and overall. All applicants (including those who earn a GED or who are home schooled) must attain a composite score of 21 or higher on the ACT or a combined score of 1000 or higher on the SAT. High school graduates must apply for this program within 2 years of high school graduation if they still qualify as an entering college freshman. GED recipients must have earned the GED within 2 years of the date their high school class would normally have graduated and must apply for this program within 2 years after attaining the GED; they must have earned a score of 250 or higher on the GED examination. Home-schooled students must have attained a score of 250 or higher on the GED examination and must have earned the GED within 1 year of the time of completion of instruction, but not later than 20 years of age. All applicants must have lived in West Virginia for at least 12 months immediately preceding application for this program. Half of the credits required for high school graduation must have been completed in a public or private high school in West Virginia. Home-schooled students must have been provided instruction in West Virginia for 2 years immediately preceding application. Selection is based on merit; financial need is not considered.
Financial data: Students who attend a West Virginia state college or university receive a full tuition scholarship. Students who attend a West Virginia private college receive an equivalent dollar scholarship, recently for $2,709.
Duration: 1 year; may be renewed for 1 additional year in an associate degree program, for 3 additional years in a baccalaureate degree program, or for 4 additional years in an approved 5-year undergraduate degree program. Recipients must maintain a grade point average of 2.75 or higher during the first year of college and at least 3.0 cumulatively in successive years.
Additional information: This program was approved by the West Virginia legislature in 1999. The first scholarships were awarded to the high school class of 2002. PROMISE stands for Providing Real Opportunities for Maximizing In-state Student Excellence.
Number awarded: Varies each year; recently, a total of $10 million was appropriated for this program.
Deadline: January of each year.

1177
WEST VIRGINIA WAR ORPHANS EDUCATIONAL PROGRAM

West Virginia Division of Veterans' Affairs
Charleston Human Resource Center
1321 Plaza East, Suite 101
Charleston, WV 25301-1400
Phone: (304) 558-3661 (888) 838-2332 (within WV)
Fax: (304) 558-3662 E-mail: WVVetAff@aol.com
Summary: To provide financial assistance for postsecondary education to the children of deceased West Virginia veterans.
Eligibility: Applicants must have been residents of West Virginia for at least 1 year, be between the ages of 16 and 23, and have a veteran parent who entered service as a resident of West Virginia, served during World War I, World War II, the Korean conflict, the Vietnam conflict from August 5, 1964 to May 7, 1975, the Lebanon conflict from August 1, 1982 to February 26, 1984, Grenada from October 23, 1983 to November 21, 1983, Panama from December 20, 1989 to January 31, 1990, or Desert Storm from August 1, 1990 to April 11, 1991, and died of injuries or disease as a result of that service.
Financial data: High school students are eligible for a grant of $110 to $250 per semester. Students attending a state-supported college, university, or vocational school in West Virginia who are not receiving any aid from the U.S. Department of Veterans Affairs (VA) are entitled to a waiver of tuition and also to receive up to $500 per year for fees, board, room, books, supplies, and other expenses. Students attending a state-supported postsecondary institution who are receiving VA assistance receive waiver of tuition and registration fees only. Students attending a private postsecondary school in West Virginia are only eligible for the monetary grant of $500 per year if they are not receiving any VA assistance.
Duration: 1 year; may be renewed upon reapplication if the student maintains a cumulative grade point average of at least 2.0.
Number awarded: Varies each year.
Deadline: July for the fall semester; November for the spring semester.

1178
WESTERN CHAPTER COMPOSITE FABRICATORS ASSOCIATION SCHOLARSHIP

Composite Fabricators Association
Attn: Western Chapter Scholarship
1655 North Fort Myer Drive, Suite 510
Arlington, VA 22209-2022
Phone: (703) 525-0511 Fax: (703) 525-0743
E-mail: cfa-info@cfa-hq.org
Web Site: www.cfa-hq.org/west-chap-scholar.htm
Summary: To provide financial assistance for college to employees of member firms of the Western Chapter of Composites Fabricators Association (CFA) and their dependents.
Eligibility: Applicants must be an employee, spouse, child, or grandchild of a person who is employed by a company that is a member of the CFA Western Chapter located in Alaska, Arizona, California, Colorado, Hawaii, Idaho, Montana, New Mexico, Nevada, Oregon, Texas, Utah, Washington, or Wyoming. They may be full-time students at an accredited college or university or high school seniors planning to enroll full time. As part of the selection process, they must submit academic transcripts; a statement (from 500 to 700 words) on educational goals and career objectives; a resume of extracurricular school activities, work experience, and community involvement; a personal reference; and a reference from a professor or teacher.
Financial data: The stipend is $2,000.
Duration: 1 year.
Number awarded: 2 each year.
Deadline: May of each year.

1179
WESTERN REGION KOREAN AMERICAN SCHOLARSHIPS

Korean American Scholarship Foundation
Western Region
Attn: Scholarship Committee
3435 Wilshire Boulevard, Suite 2450B
Los Angeles, CA 90010
Phone: (213) 380-KASF Fax: (213) 380-KASF
E-mail: western@kasf.org
Web Site: www.kasf.org
Summary: To provide financial assistance for postsecondary education to Korean

American students attending college in the western states.

Eligibility: This program is open to full-time Korean American students who have completed at least 1 year of study at a 4-year college, graduate school, or professional school in the western region (Alaska, Arizona, California, Colorado, Hawaii, Idaho, Montana, Nevada, New Mexico, Oregon, Utah, Washington, or Wyoming). Selection is based on academic achievement, community service, activities, and financial need.

Financial data: Awards are $5,000, $3,000, $2,000 or $100.

Duration: 1 year; renewable.

Number awarded: Varies each year. Recently, this region of the foundation awarded 54 scholarships: 20 at $5,000, 1 at $3,000, 28 at $2,000, and 5 at $100.

Deadline: February of each year.

1180
WESTERN SUNBATHING ASSOCIATION SCHOLARSHIP PROGRAM

Western Sunbathing Association
c/o Oliver Ellsworth
850 20th, Number 302
Boulder, CO 80302-7749

Summary: To provide financial assistance for college to members or the children of members of the Western Sunbathing Association.

Eligibility: This program is open to students who have been or whose parents have been members of the association for at least 3 years. Applicants must be seniors in high school or currently enrolled in an accredited postsecondary school. They must be under 27 years of age and have at least a 2.5 grade point average. Applicants must write an essay on what nudism means to them. Selection is based on academic records, leadership, and potential for growth. No preference is given for financial need, gender, race, creed, or religion.

Financial data: The stipend is $1,000; the funds are paid directly to the recipient's school.

Duration: 1 year.

Additional information: The Western Sunbathing Association is 1 of 7 regions of the American Association for Nude Recreation. This scholarship program was established in 1990 and first awarded in 1992. No student may win this award more than twice. Recipients must attend an accredited postsecondary school.

Number awarded: 2 each year.

Deadline: March of each year.

1181
WFLA NATIONAL SCHOLARSHIP

Western Fraternal Life Association
1900 First Avenue, N.E.
Cedar Rapids, IA 52402-5472
Phone: (800) 535-5472

Summary: To provide financial assistance for college to members of the Western Fraternal Life Association (WFLA).

Eligibility: Applicants must have been WFLA members in good standing for at least 2 years prior to the application deadline. They must have been accepted as a full-time student at a college, university, or vocational-technical institute (a copy of the acceptance letter must be submitted). Selection is based on academic ability (as demonstrated by test scores and transcripts, community involvement, and extracurricular activities).

Financial data: The maximum stipend is $1,000. Funds, which must be used for tuition and books, are paid directly to the recipient's school.

Duration: 1 year; recipients may reapply (but they are eligible to win only twice).

Number awarded: 7 each year.

Deadline: February of each year.

1182
W.H. "HOWIE" MCCLENNAN SCHOLARSHIP

International Association of Fire Fighters
Attn: Office of the General President
1750 New York Avenue, N.W., Suite 300
Washington, DC 20006-5395
Phone: (202) 737-8484   Fax: (202) 737-8418
Web Site: www.iaff.org

Summary: To provide financial assistance for postsecondary education to children of deceased members of the International Association of Fire Fighters.

Eligibility: This program is open to the children (including legally adopted children) of members of the union who died in the line of duty. Applicants must

be attending or planning to attend an accredited 2-year college, 4-year college or university, or vocational training institution in the United States or Canada. Selection is based primarily on financial need, although consideration is also given to academic performance (at least a 2.0 grade point average) and a 200-word essay on the applicant's reason for wanting to continue their education.

Financial data: The stipend is $2,500 per year.

Duration: Up to 4 years.

Number awarded: Varies each year.

Deadline: January of each year.

1183
WHO'S WHO AMONG AMERICAN HIGH SCHOOL STUDENTS SCHOLARSHIPS

Educational Communications Scholarship Foundation
721 North McKinley Road
Lake Forest, IL 60045
Phone: (847) 295-6650   Fax: (847) 295-3972
E-mail: feedback@honoring.com
Web Site: www.honoring.com/highschool/scholar

Summary: To provide financial assistance to high school honor students who are listed in *Who's Who Among American High School Students*.

Eligibility: This program is open to high school students with a grade point average of 3.0 or better who are U.S. citizens and have been involved in school or community activities. Candidates must first be nominated by a school official, youth activity sponsor, or educational organization to have their name appear in *Who's Who Among American High School Students*. All students listed in that publication automatically receive an application for these scholarships in the mail. Selection is based on grade point average, achievement test scores, leadership qualifications, work experience, evaluation of an essay, and some consideration for financial need.

Financial data: Scholarships are $1,000; payments are issued directly to the financial aid office at the institution the student attends.

Duration: 1 year.

Number awarded: 200 each year.

Deadline: May of each year.

1184
WIB TECH SCHOLARSHIP

Maine Technical College System
Attn: Director of State and Federal Programs
323 State Street
Augusta, ME 04330-7131
Phone: (207) 287-1070   Fax: (207) 287-1037
E-mail: gcrocker@mtcs.net
Web Site: www.mtcs.net

Summary: To provide financial assistance to students with disabilities who are interested in attending a technical college in Maine.

Eligibility: This program is open to Maine residents who have graduated from high school (or have a GED certificate) and have a disability (physical, mental, or emotional). They must be enrolled or planning to enroll in a technical college in Maine and be a client of a partner agency. Candidates are assessed and selected by a Workforce Investment Board (WIB) local career center where they are eligible for and enrolled in the job training system. The local career center sends the student to the Maine Technical College of their choice to make application for admission. If admitted to the college, a scholarship is automatically awarded.

Financial data: Eligible students receive a full tuition scholarship. Funds are awarded on a first-come, first-served basis.

Duration: 1 semester; may be renewed.

Number awarded: Varies each year.

Deadline: Inquiries may be made at any time.

1185
WILLIAM C. CAMPBELL SCHOLARSHIPS

Greater Kanawha Valley Foundation
Attn: Scholarship Coordinator
One Huntington Square, 16th Floor
900 Lee Street, East
P.O. Box 3041
Charleston, WV 25331-3041
Phone: (304) 346-3620   Fax: (304) 346-3640
E-mail: tgkvf@tgkvf.com
Web Site: www.tgkvf.com/scholarship.html

Summary: To provide financial assistance for college to residents of West Virginia who have been involved in golf.

Eligibility: This program is open to residents of West Virginia who 1) played golf in the state as an amateur for recreation or competition, or 2) have been or are presently employed in West Virginia as a caddie, grounds keeper, bag boy, or other golf-related position. Applicants must be enrolled or planning to enroll at an accredited college or university in West Virginia as a full-time student. As part of the application process, they must include 1) a reference from a coach, golf professional, or employer, and 2) an essay explaining how the game of golf has made an impact in their life. In addition to the essay and reference, selection is based on academic accomplishments (at least a 2.5 grade point average), volunteer service, character, and level of exposure to the game of golf; skill level is not a major requirement.

Financial data: The stipend is $1,000 per year.

Duration: 1 year; nonrenewable.

Additional information: This program is sponsored by the West Virginia Golf Association, P.O. Box 850, Hurricane, WV 25526, (304) 757-3444, Fax: (304) 757-3479, E-mail: mail@wvga.org, Web site: www.wvga.org.

Number awarded: Varies each year; recently, 3 of these scholarships were awarded.

Deadline: February of each year.

1186
WILLIAM E. DOCTER SCHOLARSHIPS

William E. Docter Educational Fund
c/o St. Mary Armenian Church
P.O. Box 39224
Washington, DC 20016
Phone: (202) 364-1440   Fax: (202) 364-1441
E-mail: WEDFund@aol.com
Web Site: www.WEDFund.org

Summary: To assist undergraduate or graduate students of Armenian ancestry.

Eligibility: This program is open to U.S. citizens of Armenian ancestry; preference is given to those with 2 parents of Armenian ancestry. Applicants must be pursuing undergraduate, graduate, or vocational study or training in the United States or Canada. They must include with their application a 1-page description of their program of study or training and their career objectives, 2 letters of recommendation, and evidence of financial need.

Financial data: Awards up to $5,000, in the form of grants and/or loans, are available.

Duration: 1 year; may be renewed.

Additional information: This fund was established in 1998.

Number awarded: Varies each year; recently, 13 students received support from this fund.

Deadline: April of each year.

1187
WILLIAM J. AND A. HASKELL MCMANNIS EDUCATIONAL TRUST FUND SCHOLARSHIP

McMannis Educational Trust Fund
c/o Marine Bank Trust Division
P.O. Box 8480
Erie, PA 16553
Phone: (814) 871-9324

Summary: To provide financial assistance to students pursuing a bachelor's or master's degree.

Eligibility: This program is open to college students at the freshman, sophomore, junior, senior, or master's degree level.

Financial data: Stipends range from $200 to $5,000.

Duration: 1 year; nonrenewable.

Number awarded: Varies each year.

1188
WILLIAM L. BOYD, IV, FLORIDA RESIDENT ACCESS GRANTS

Florida Department of Education
Attn: Office of Student Financial Assistance
1940 North Monroe Street, Suite 70
Tallahassee, FL 32303-4759
Phone: (850) 410-5185   (888) 827-2004
Fax: (850) 488-3612   E-mail: osfa@mail.doe.state.fl.us
Web Site: www.firn.edu/doe/osfa

Summary: To provide financial assistance to students at private colleges and universities in Florida.

Eligibility: Applicants must be full-time undergraduate students who are attending an eligible private nonprofit Florida college or university and who have been Florida residents for at least 1 year. Selection is not based on financial need.

Financial data: The amount of the award is specified by the state legislature annually; actual amounts depend on the number of applicants and availability of funds.

Duration: Up to 9 semesters or 14 quarters, provided the student maintains full-time enrollment and a grade point average of 2.0 or higher.

Additional information: Applications are available from the financial aid office at the college you plan to attend.

Number awarded: Varies each year; recently, this program provided 23,425 awards.

1189
WILLIAM L. HAWKINSON FOUNDATION FOR PEACE & JUSTICE SCHOLARSHIP

William L. Hawkinson Foundation for Peace & Justice
c/o Grace University Lutheran Church
324 Harvard Street, S.E.
Minneapolis, MN 55414
Phone: (612) 331-8125

Summary: To provide financial assistance for college to students in selected midwestern states who are committed to peace and justice.

Eligibility: Eligible to be nominated for this scholarship are currently-enrolled college students who reside in or attend school in 1 of the following midwestern states: Iowa, Minnesota, North Dakota, South Dakota, or Wisconsin. Nominated students must submit a copy of their current academic transcript, a nomination form, and a 2-page essay on their commitment to peace and justice. Finalists are interviewed in Minneapolis.

Financial data: The stipend is $1,500.

Duration: 1 year.

Number awarded: 1 each year.

Deadline: April of each year.

1190
WILLIAM R. STANITZ SCHOLARSHIP

Romanian Orthodox Episcopate of America
Attn: Scholarship Committee
P.O. Box 309
Grass Lake, MI 49240-0309
Phone: (517) 522-3656   Fax: (517) 522-5907
E-mail: roeasolia@aol.com
Web Site: www.roea.org

Summary: To provide financial assistance for college to active members of American Romanian Orthodox Youth (AROY).

Eligibility: To qualify for this scholarship, applicants must be active AROY members, high school graduates, and currently enrolled or planning to enroll in college. The application packet submitted should include biographical history, educational background and grades, AROY and church activities, extracurricular interests and achievements, reasons why applying for the scholarship, photograph, and letter of recommendation from a parish priest or AROY advisor regarding parish/AROY activities. Recipients are selected in a random drawing.

Financial data: The stipend is $1,000.

Duration: 1 year.

Additional information: This fund was established in 1971.

Number awarded: At least 2 each year.

Deadline: June of each year.

1191
WILLIAM (WIDDY) NEALE SCHOLARSHIPS

Connecticut State Golf Association
35 Cold Spring Road, Suite 212
Rocky Hill, CT 06067
Phone: (860) 257-4171   Fax: (860) 257-8355
E-mail: ctstategolf@asga.org
Web Site: www.csgalinks.org

Summary: To assist college to high school seniors who have worked at a golf club that is a member of the Connecticut State Golf Association (CSGA).

Eligibility: This program is open to seniors graduating from high schools in

Connecticut who have worked at a CSGA member golf club for 1 full golf season in the pro shop, with the maintenance crew, or in the clubhouse, locker room, or dining room. Applicants must be recommended by the CSGA club representative, golf professional, course superintendent, or other official; each club may recommend only 1 student. Selection is based on grades, character, citizenship, community service, and financial need.

Financial data: Stipends range from $1,000 to $1,500.

Duration: 1 year; may be renewed up to 3 additional years provided the recipient maintains satisfactory academic standing and continues to demonstrate financial need.

Additional information: Information is also available from Herbert Emanuelson, Scholarship Chairman, 1575 Boston Post Road, Building B, P.O. Box 364, Guilford, CT 06437.

Number awarded: 10 to 13 each year.

Deadline: June of each year.

1192
WILLIE RUDD SCHOLARSHIP

International Union of Electronic, Electrical, Salaried, Machine, and Furniture Workers
Attn: Department of Social Action
1275 K Street, N.W., Suite 600
Washington, DC 20005
Phone: (202) 513-6300   Fax: (202) 513-6357
E-mail: Humphrey@cwa-union.org
Web Site: www.iue-cwa.org

Summary: To provide financial assistance for undergraduate education to the children of members of the International Union of Electronic, Electrical, Salaried, Machine, and Furniture Workers (IUE).

Eligibility: This program is open to children of IUE members (including retired or deceased members). They must be accepted for admission or already enrolled as full-time students at an accredited college, university, nursing school, or technical school offering college credit courses. Families of full-time union officers or employees are not eligible to apply. Selection is based on academic record, leadership ability, ambition, good character, commitment to equality, service to the community, and a concern for improving the quality of life for all people.

Financial data: The stipend is $1,000 per year.

Duration: 1 year.

Additional information: Winners who are also awarded local, district, or division scholarships have the option of either accepting the James B. Carey Scholarship or the other awards and the dollar difference (if any) between the Carey Scholarship and the local, district, or division award.

Number awarded: Varies each year.

Deadline: April of each year.

1193
WILLIS AND MILDRED PELLERIN FOUNDATION SCHOLARSHIPS

Willis and Mildred Pellerin Foundation
P.O. Box 400
Kenner, LA 70063
Phone: (504) 467-9591, ext. 201

Summary: To provide financial assistance for college to students in Louisiana.

Eligibility: This program is open to high school seniors and currently-enrolled college students (except seniors) with demonstrated financial need who plan to pursue an undergraduate degree on a full-time basis at an accredited 4-year college or university in Louisiana. In order to apply, a student must have at least a 2.5 grade point average and an ACT score of at least 20. Selection is based on scholastic record, financial need, extracurricular activities, work experience, career and educational goals, unusual personal or family circumstances, and character.

Financial data: The financial assistance offered is half scholarship, half loan (which must be repaid weekly during the course of the semester). Funds are issued directly to the recipient. The checks are made payable jointly to the student and the school and must be endorsed by both. Funds may be used to pay for tuition, required fees, books, room, board, and other related educational expenses.

Duration: 1 year; may be renewed, if the recipient maintains full-time status and at least a 2.5 grade point average.

Additional information: Recipients who maintain a grade point average of 3.5 or better may be entitled to an achievement bonus; these are paid directly to the student are separate from the scholarship check. Recipients must attend school on a full-time basis.

Deadline: February of each year.

1194
WILSON WADE MEMORIAL SCHOLARSHIPS

California Masonic Foundation
Attn: Scholarship Committee
1111 California Street
San Francisco, CA 94108-2284
Phone: (415) 292-9196   (800) 900-2727
Fax: (415) 776-7170   E-mail: foundation@mhcsf.org
Web Site: www.californiamasons.org

Summary: To provide financial assistance to women high school seniors in California who are interested in attending college in the state.

Eligibility: This program is open to graduating women high school seniors who have been residents of California for at least 1 year and have a grade point average of 3.0 or higher. Applicants must be planning to attend a 4-year institution of higher education in California as a full-time freshman in the following fall. They must be U.S. citizens or permanent residents and able to show evidence of financial need. Along with their application, they must submit a personal essay outlining their background, goals, and scholastic achievements; a copy of their latest high school transcript; 2 letters of recommendation; a copy of the last Federal 1040 income tax return filed by their parents; the FAFSA financial aid application; their SAT or ACT scores; and a copy of their college acceptance letter. Selection is based on academic achievement, applicant essay, and financial need. Preference is given to women who have a Masonic relationship or are members of Masonic youth groups.

Financial data: The amount of the stipend varies, depending on the availability of funds.

Duration: 1 year; may be renewed for up to 3 additional years.

Additional information: Requests for applications must be accompanied by a self-addressed stamped envelope.

Number awarded: Varies each year.

Deadline: March of each year for new applicants; April of each year for renewal applicants.

1195
WINCH FUND SCHOLARSHIPS

Francis A. Winch Fund
3538 Central Avenue, Suite 2-A
Riverside, CA 92506-2700
Phone: (909) 684-6778   E-mail: scholars@urs2.net
Web Site: www.scholarshipsite.org

Summary: To provide supplemental funding to undergraduate and graduate students already in college.

Eligibility: This program is open to students who have sophomore, junior, senior, or graduate standing at their college or university and have never received an Olin L. Livesey Scholarship. As part of the application process, they must submit an essay on 1 of the following topics: 1) what book have you read, since entering college, that has had the most impact on your thought and life? 2) who do you consider to be 1 of the more influential individuals of the 20th century? or 3) what is the greatest benefit a college education can offer an individual? Selection is based on achievement, need, purpose, and recommendations.

Financial data: There are 3 types of awards: book supplements, from $100 to $1,000; tuition supplements, from $250 to $5,000; and comprehensive supplements, from $500 to $7,500. Book supplements are mailed directly to the recipient, to pay for the costs of books, materials, and supplies. Tuition and comprehensive supplements are sent to the recipient's financial aid office.

Duration: 1 year; recipients may reapply.

Additional information: There is an $18 processing fee.

Number awarded: Varies each year.

Deadline: Applications may be submitted at any time.

Scholarship Listings

1196
WINNIE C. DAVIS CHILDREN OF THE CONFEDERACY SCHOLARSHIP

United Daughters of the Confederacy
Attn: Education Director
328 North Boulevard
Richmond, VA 23220-4057
Phone: (804) 355-1636   Fax: (804) 353-1396
E-mail: hqudc@aol.com
Web Site: www.hqudc.org
Summary: To provide financial assistance for postsecondary education to lineal descendants of Confederate veterans who are members of the Children of the Confederacy.
Eligibility: Eligible to apply for these scholarships are lineal descendants of worthy Confederates or collateral descendants. Applicants must submit a family financial report and certified proof of the Confederate record of 1 ancestor, with the company and regiment in which he served. In addition, applicants themselves must be, or have been until age 18, participating members of the Children of the Confederacy. They must have at least a 3.0 grade point average in high school.
Financial data: The amount of this scholarship depends on the availability of funds.
Duration: 1 year; may be renewed for up to 3 additional years.
Additional information: Information is also available from Dorothy S. Broom, Second Vice President General, 595 Lominack Road, Prosperity, SC 29127, (803) 364-3003. Members of the same family may not hold scholarships simultaneously, and only 1 application per family will be accepted within any 1 year. All requests for applications must be accompanied by a self-addressed stamped envelope.
Number awarded: 1 each year.
Deadline: February of each year.

1197
WINNING WAY SCHOLARSHIP CONTEST

American Academic Services
Attn: Scholarship
P.O. Box 208
Westminster, MD 21158
Phone: (410) 876-0793
Web Site: www.winningway.com/winninwayweb/scholarship.html
Summary: To recognize and reward high school seniors who write outstanding essays for college admission.
Eligibility: High school seniors are invited to submit a college admissions essay either prescribed by the college or created by themselves. The essay should not exceed 700 words.
Financial data: The winner receives a $1,000 scholarship to the college of their choice; the winning essay is posted on this web site.
Duration: The competition is held annually.
Additional information: Scholarship application forms are shipped with each *Winning Way Guide* purchased online. Schools and school systems that use *The Winning Way Guide* receive a scholarship application form with each book.
Number awarded: 1 each year.
Deadline: May of each year.

1198
WISCONSIN ACADEMIC EXCELLENCE SCHOLARSHIP PROGRAM

Wisconsin Higher Educational Aids Board
131 West Wilson Street, Room 902
P.O. Box 7885
Madison, WI 53707-7885
Phone: (608) 267-2213   Fax: (608) 267-2808
E-mail: alice.winters@heab.state.wi.us
Web Site: heab.state.wi.us/programs.html
Summary: To provide financial assistance for college to Wisconsin high school seniors with the highest grade point averages in their schools.
Eligibility: This program is open to seniors at each public and private high school throughout Wisconsin who have the highest grade point averages. Applicants must plan to attend a branch of the University of Wisconsin, a Wisconsin technical college, or an independent institution in the state as a full-time student in the following fall.
Financial data: The awards provide full tuition, up to $2,250 per year, during the first 3 years of undergraduate study; for subsequent years, the maximum award is

equal to full tuition and fees at a campus of the University of Wisconsin.
Duration: Up to 10 semesters.
Number awarded: The number of scholarships allotted to each high school is based on total student enrollment.

1199
WISCONSIN AMERICAN LEGION EAGLE SCOUT OF THE YEAR

American Legion
Department of Wisconsin
Attn: Scholarship Chairperson
2930 American Legion Drive
P.O. Box 388
Portage, WI 53901-0388
Phone: (608) 745-1090   Fax: (608) 745-0179
E-mail: info@wilegion.org
Web Site: www.wilegion.org
Summary: To provide financial assistance for postsecondary education to outstanding Boy Scouts in Wisconsin.
Eligibility: The Wisconsin nominee for American Legion Scout of the Year receives this scholarship. Applicants must be 1) registered, active members of a Boy Scout Troop or Varsity Scout Team sponsored by an American Legion Post in Wisconsin or Auxiliary Unit in Wisconsin, or 2) a registered, active member of a Boy Scout Troop or Varsity Scout Team and the son or grandson of an American Legion or Auxiliary member.
Financial data: The state award is a $1,000 scholarship.
Duration: 1 year.
Number awarded: 1 each year.

1200
WISCONSIN HEARING AND VISUALLY HANDICAPPED STUDENT GRANT PROGRAM

Wisconsin Higher Educational Aids Board
131 West Wilson Street, Room 902
P.O. Box 7885
Madison, WI 53707-7885
Phone: (608) 266-0888   Fax: (608) 267-2808
E-mail: sandy.thomas@heab.state.wi.us
Web Site: heab.state.wi.us/programs.html
Summary: To provide financial support for undergraduate study to Wisconsin residents who are legally deaf or blind.
Eligibility: To be eligible for a grant, the student must be a Wisconsin resident, must have financial need as determined by the institution the student attends, must submit evidence of hearing or visual loss certified by a medical examiner, and must be enrolled in a nonprofit, accredited public or private college, university, or vocational-technical school located in Wisconsin.
Financial data: Grants range from $250 to $1,800 per academic year.
Duration: 1 year; may be renewed up to 4 additional years.
Additional information: If the disability prevents the student from studying in a Wisconsin institution, he or she may attend an out-of-state institution that specializes in the training of deaf and/or blind students.
Number awarded: Varies each year.

1201
WISCONSIN HIGHER EDUCATION GRANT

Wisconsin Higher Educational Aids Board
131 West Wilson Street, Room 902
P.O. Box 7885
Madison, WI 53707-7885
Phone: (608) 266-0888   Fax: (608) 267-2808
E-mail: sandy.thomas@heab.state.wi.us
Web Site: heab.state.wi.us/programs.html
Summary: To provide financial assistance to financially needy undergraduate students attending public institutions of higher education in Wisconsin.
Eligibility: Eligible are Wisconsin residents enrolled at least half time at any branch of the University of Wisconsin or at any vocational-technical institution in the state. Selection is based on financial need.
Financial data: Awards range from $250 to $1,800 per year.
Duration: Up to 10 semesters.
Number awarded: Varies each year.

1202
WISCONSIN INDIAN STUDENT ASSISTANCE GRANTS

Wisconsin Higher Educational Aids Board
131 West Wilson Street, Room 902
P.O. Box 7885
Madison, WI 53707-7885
Phone: (608) 266-0888   Fax: (608) 267-2808
E-mail: sandy.thomas@heab.state.wi.us
Web Site: heab.state.wi.us/programs.html
Summary: To provide financial aid for higher education to Native Americans in Wisconsin.
Eligibility: Wisconsin residents who have at least 25 percent Native American blood (of a certified tribe or band) are eligible to apply if they are able to demonstrate financial need and are interested in attending college on the undergraduate or graduate school level. Applicants must attend a Wisconsin institution (public, independent, or proprietary). They may be enrolled either full or part time.
Financial data: Awards range from $250 to $1,100 per year. Additional funds are available on a matching basis from the U.S. Bureau of Indian Affairs.
Duration: Up to 5 years.
Deadline: Generally, applications can be submitted at any time.

1203
WISCONSIN LEGION AUXILIARY MERIT AND MEMORIAL SCHOLARSHIPS

American Legion Auxiliary
Department of Wisconsin
Attn: Department Secretary/Treasurer
2930 American Legion Drive
P.O. Box 140
Portage, WI 53901-0140
Phone: (608) 745-0124   Fax: (608) 745-1947
E-mail: alawi@amlegionauxwi.org
Web Site: www.amlegionauxwi.org
Summary: To provide financial assistance for postsecondary education to Wisconsin residents who are the children or spouses of veterans.
Eligibility: This program is open to the children, wives, and widows of veterans who are high school seniors or graduates with a grade point average of 3.2 or higher. Grandchildren and great-grandchildren of veterans are eligible if they are members of the American Legion Auxiliary. Applicants must be able to demonstrate financial need and be residents of Wisconsin, although they do not need to attend college in Wisconsin.
Financial data: The stipend is $1,000.
Duration: 1 year; nonrenewable.
Number awarded: 6 each year.
Deadline: March of each year.

1204
WISCONSIN LEGION AUXILIARY STATE PRESIDENT'S SCHOLARSHIP

American Legion Auxiliary
Department of Wisconsin
Attn: Department Secretary/Treasurer
2930 American Legion Drive
P.O. Box 140
Portage, WI 53901-0140
Phone: (608) 745-0124   Fax: (608) 745-1947
E-mail: alawi@amlegionauxwi.org
Web Site: www.amlegionauxwi.org
Summary: To provide financial assistance for postsecondary education to members or the children of members of the American Legion Auxiliary in Wisconsin.
Eligibility: Eligible are the members or children of members of the American Legion Auxiliary who are in need of financial aid to continue their education and high school seniors or graduates with a grade point average of at least 3.2. Applicants must be Wisconsin residents, but they are not required to attend college in Wisconsin.
Financial data: The stipend is $1,000.
Duration: 1 year.
Number awarded: 3 each year.
Deadline: March of each year.

1205
WISCONSIN MINORITY UNDERGRADUATE RETENTION GRANTS

Wisconsin Higher Educational Aids Board
131 West Wilson Street, Room 902
P.O. Box 7885
Madison, WI 53707-7885
Phone: (608) 267-2212   Fax: (608) 267-2808
E-mail: mary.kuzdas@heab.state.wi.us
Web Site: heab.state.wi.us/programs.html
Summary: To provide financial assistance to minorities in Wisconsin who are currently enrolled in college.
Eligibility: African Americans, Hispanic Americans, and American Indians in Wisconsin are eligible to apply if they are enrolled as sophomores, juniors, seniors, or fifth-year undergraduates in a 4-year nonprofit institution or as second-year students in a 2-year program at a public vocational institution in the state. The grant also includes students who were admitted to the United States after December 31, 1975 and who are a former citizen of Laos, Vietnam, or Cambodia or whose ancestor was a citizen of 1 of those countries. They must be nominated by their institution and be able to demonstrate financial need.
Financial data: Stipends range from $250 to $2,500 per year.
Duration: Up to 4 years.
Additional information: The Wisconsin Higher Educational Aids Board administers this program for students in private nonprofit institutions and public vocational institutions. The University of Wisconsin has a similar program for students attending any of the branches of that system. Eligible students should apply through their school's financial aid office.
Number awarded: Varies each year.
Deadline: Deadline dates vary by institution; check with your school's financial aid office.

1206
WISCONSIN PART-TIME STUDY GRANTS FOR VETERANS AND THEIR DEPENDENTS

Wisconsin Department of Veterans Affairs
30 West Mifflin Street
P.O. Box 7843
Madison, WI 53707-7843
Phone: (608) 266-1311   (800) WIS-VETS
Fax: (608) 267-0403   E-mail: wdvaweb@dva.state.wi.us
Web Site: dva.state.wi.us/ben_education.asp
Summary: To provide financial assistance for undergraduate or graduate education to 1) Wisconsin veterans or 2) the widow(er)s or dependent children of deceased veterans.
Eligibility: Applicants for these grants must be veterans (must have served on active duty for at least 2 consecutive years or for at least 90 days during specified wartime periods) and residents of Wisconsin at the time of making the application. They must also have been Wisconsin residents either at the time of entry into active duty or for at least 5 consecutive years after completing service on active duty. Unremarried widow(er)s and minor or dependent children of deceased veterans who would qualify if the veteran were alive today are also eligible for these grants, as long as they are Wisconsin residents. Students who have not yet completed a bachelor's degree may receive these grants even if they are also obtaining Montgomery GI Bill benefits from the federal Department of Veterans Affairs. Recipients must enroll in part-time study (11 credits or less if they do not have a bachelor's degree or 8 credits or less if they do). They may enroll at any accredited college, university, or vocational technical school in Wisconsin, whether state-supported or private; they may also attend out-of-state schools that are within 50 miles of the Wisconsin border if the course is not offered at a Wisconsin school within 50 miles of their residence. Qualifying programs include undergraduate study, graduate study if the student has only a bachelor's degree, correspondence courses, on-the-job training, apprenticeships, internships, and any other study related to the student's occupational, professional, or educational goals. Graduate students are not eligible if 1) they have already received a master's degree, doctor's degree, or equivalent; or 2) they are still entitled to federal Department of Veterans Affairs educational benefits. Students with a current gross annual income greater than $47,500 (plus $500 for each dependent in excess of 2) are not eligible.
Financial data: Eligible applicants are entitled to reimbursement of up to 85 percent of the costs of tuition and fees. Veterans with a service-connected disability that is rated 30 percent or higher may be reimbursed for up to 100 percent of

243

tuition and fees. Students must pay the costs when they register and then obtain reimbursement after completion of the course of study.

Duration: Applicants may receive no more than 4 of these grants during a 12-month period.

Number awarded: Varies each year.

Deadline: Applications may be submitted at any time, but they must be received within 60 days following completion of the course.

1207
WISCONSIN RETRAINING GRANTS

Wisconsin Department of Veterans Affairs
30 West Mifflin Street
P.O. Box 7843
Madison, WI 53707-7843
Phone: (608) 266-1311   (800) WIS-VETS
Fax: (608) 267-0403   E-mail: wdvaweb@dva.state.wi.us
Web Site: dva.state.wi.us/ben_retraininggrants.asp

Summary: To provide funds to recently unemployed Wisconsin veterans or their families who need financial assistance while being retrained for employment.

Eligibility: This program is open to Wisconsin veterans (must have served on active duty for at least 2 consecutive years or for at least 90 days during specified wartime periods) who are current residents of Wisconsin and were also residents of Wisconsin either at the time of entry into service or for 5 consecutive years after completing service on active duty. Unremarried spouses and minor or dependent children of deceased veterans who would have been eligible for the grant if they were living today are also eligible. The applicant must have become unemployed within the year prior to the date of application and not have a family income of more than $36,600 (plus $500 for each dependent in excess of 2). Applicants must be retraining at accredited schools in Wisconsin or in a structured on-the-job program. Course work toward a college degree does not qualify. Training does not have to be full time, but the program must be completed within 2 years.

Financial data: The maximum grant is $3,000 per year; the actual amount varies, depending upon the amount of the applicant's unmet need. In addition to books, fees, and tuition, the funds may be used for living expenses.

Duration: 1 year; may be renewed 1 additional year.

Number awarded: Varies each year.

Deadline: Applications may be submitted at any time.

1208
WISCONSIN TALENT INCENTIVE PROGRAM (TIP) GRANTS

Wisconsin Higher Educational Aids Board
131 West Wilson Street, Room 902
P.O. Box 7885
Madison, WI 53707-7885
Phone: (608) 266-1665   Fax: (608) 267-2808
E-mail: john.whitt@heab.state.wi.us
Web Site: heab.state.wi.us/programs.html

Summary: To provide supplemental grants to the most needy and educationally disadvantaged students in Wisconsin during their postsecondary schooling.

Eligibility: To be eligible for a grant, a student must be a Wisconsin resident, be a first-year (freshman) college student, and possess at least 2 of the following characteristics: 1) be a member of a minority group (Hispanic, Native American, Indian, Black, or Asian American); 2) be a student with a disability, be a first-generation postsecondary student, or be currently or formerly incarcerated in a correctional institution; 3) be a dependent student whose expected parents' contribution is $2,000 or less; 4) be a student who is or will be enrolled in a special academic support program due to insufficient preparation; 5) be a member of a family receiving welfare benefits; 6) be a member of a family whose parent is ineligible for unemployment compensation and has no current income from employment.

Financial data: Grants range up to $1,800 per year for first-year students and up to $1,250 per year for continuing students.

Duration: Up to 10 semesters.

Additional information: Additional information is available from the Wisconsin Educational Opportunity Program, 101 West Pleasant Street, Bottlehouse Atrium, Milwaukee, WI 53212.

Number awarded: Varies each year.

1209
WISCONSIN TUITION AND FEE REIMBURSEMENT GRANTS

Wisconsin Department of Veterans Affairs
30 West Mifflin Street
P.O. Box 7843
Madison, WI 53707-7843
Phone: (608) 266-1311   (800) WIS-VETS
Fax: (608) 267-0403   E-mail: wdvaweb@dva.state.wi.us
Web Site: dva.state.wi.us/ben_education.asp

Summary: To provide financial assistance for the undergraduate education of Wisconsin veterans.

Eligibility: This program is open to veterans (must have served on active duty for at least 2 consecutive years or for at least 90 days during specified wartime periods) who are current residents of Wisconsin and were also residents of Wisconsin either at the time of entry into service or for 5 consecutive years after completing service on active duty. Students may attend any institution, center, or school within the University of Wisconsin System or the Wisconsin Technical College System as part-time or full-time undergraduates. Any applicant with a current gross annual income greater than $47,500 (plus $500 for each dependent in excess of 2) does not qualify.

Financial data: This program provides reimbursement of up to 85 percent of the costs of tuition and fees. Veterans with a service-connected disability that is rated 30 percent or higher may be reimbursed for up to 100 percent of tuition and fees.

Duration: These grants are available for courses taken within 10 years of separation from active-duty military service. Veterans may receive reimbursement for up to 120 credits of part-time study or 8 semesters of full-time study.

Number awarded: Varies each year.

Deadline: Applications may be submitted at any time, but no later than 60 days after the ending date of the semester for which reimbursement is sought.

1210
WISCONSIN TUITION GRANT

Wisconsin Higher Educational Aids Board
131 West Wilson Street, Room 902
P.O. Box 7885
Madison, WI 53707-7885
Phone: (608) 267-2212   Fax: (608) 267-2808
E-mail: mary.kuzdas@heab.state.wi.us
Web Site: heab.state.wi.us/programs.html

Summary: To provide assistance to financially needy undergraduate students attending private institutions of higher education in Wisconsin.

Eligibility: Eligible are Wisconsin residents enrolled in independent, nonprofit colleges and universities in Wisconsin. Selection is based on financial need.

Financial data: Awards range from $250 to $2,300 per year, depending on the recipient's need and the difference between the tuition actually paid by the student and the tuition that would have been paid if the student attended the University of Wisconsin at Madison.

Duration: Up to 10 semesters.

Number awarded: Varies each year.

1211
WOMEN MARINES ASSOCIATION SCHOLARSHIP PROGRAM

Women Marines Association
P.O. Box 447
Kailua, HI 96743
E-mail: wma@womenmarines.org
Web Site: www.womenmarines.org/programs.htm

Summary: To provide financial assistance for postsecondary education to students sponsored by members of the Women Marines Association (WMA).

Eligibility: Applicants must be sponsored by a WMA member and fall into 1 of the following categories: 1) have served or are serving in the U.S. Marine Corps or Reserve; 2) are a direct descendant by blood, legal adoption, or stepchild of a Marine on active duty or who has served honorably in the U.S. Marine Corps, regular or reserve; 3) are a sibling or a descendant of a sibling by blood, legal adoption or stepchild of a Marine on active duty or who has served honorably in the U.S. Marine Corps, regular or reserve; or 4) have completed 2 years in a Marine Corps JROTC program. No WMA member is allowed to sponsor more than 1 applicant per year. High school applicants must have maintained at least a 3.5 grade point average for their sophomore, junior, and first semester of their senior year of high school and must have a minimum combined math/verbal SAT score of 1100 or a minimum combined math/verbal ACT score of 25. College

applicants must have at least a 3.0 grade point average.

Financial data: The stipend is $1,000.

Duration: 1 year.

Additional information: Applicants must know a WMA member; the WMA will not supply listings of the names or addresses of chapters or individual members.

Number awarded: Varies each year.

Deadline: March of each year.

1212
WOMEN'S ARMY CORPS VETERANS' ASSOCIATION SCHOLARSHIP

Women's Army Corps Veterans' Association
P.O. Box 5577
Fort McClellan, AL 36205-5577
E-mail: info@armywomen.org
Web Site: www.armywomen.org

Summary: To provide financial assistance for college to the relatives of Army military women.

Eligibility: Eligible to apply are high school seniors who are the relatives of current, former, or retired women who have served honorably on active duty in the Army of the United States, the Regular Army, the Army National Guard, the U.S. Army Reserve, the Women's Army Auxiliary Corps, or the Women's Army Corps in commissioned, warrant, noncommissioned, or enlisted status for 90 days or longer after May 14, 1942. Applicants must submit a 500-word statement about their future goals and how the scholarship would be used. Selection is based on academic record, class rank, standardized test scores, and extracurricular activities. Financial need is not considered in the selection process.

Financial data: A stipend is awarded (exact amount not specified).

Duration: 1 year.

Number awarded: 1 or more each year.

Deadline: April of each year.

1213
WOMEN'S BASKETBALL COACHES ASSOCIATION SCHOLARSHIP AWARD

Women's Basketball Coaches Association
Attn: Talent Coordinator/Awards Manager
4646 Lawrenceville Highway
Lilburn, GA 30247-3620
Phone: (770) 279-8027   Fax: (770) 279-8473
E-mail: krwalton@wbca.org
Web Site: www.wbca.org

Summary: To provide financial assistance for undergraduate or graduate study to women's basketball players.

Eligibility: This program is open to women's basketball players who are competing in any of the 5 intercollegiate divisions (NCAA Divisions I, II, III, NAIA, and JC/CC). Applicants must be interested in completing an undergraduate degree or beginning work on an advanced degree. They must be nominated by a member of the Women's Basketball Coaches Association (WBCA). Selection is based on sportsmanship, commitment to excellence as a student-athlete, honesty, ethical behavior, courage, and dedication to purpose.

Financial data: The stipend is $1,000 per year.

Duration: 1 year.

Number awarded: 2 each year.

1214
WOMEN'S OVERSEAS SERVICE LEAGUE SCHOLARSHIPS FOR WOMEN

Women's Overseas Service League
P.O. Box 7124
Washington, DC 20044-7124

Summary: To provide financial assistance for college to women who are committed to a military or other public service career.

Eligibility: This program is open to women who are committed to a military or other public service career. Applicants must have completed at least 12 semester or 18 quarter hours of postsecondary study with at a grade point average or 2.5 or higher. They must be working on an academic degree (the program may be professional or technical in nature) and must agree to enroll for at least 6 semester or 9 quarter hours of study each academic period. Applicants are asked to submit all of the following: an official transcript, a 1-page description of career goals, 3 current letters of reference, and a brief statement describing sources of financial

support and the need for scholarship assistance. They must also provide information on their educational background, employment experience, civic and volunteer activities, and expected degree completion date.

Financial data: Stipends range from $500 to $1,000 per year.

Duration: 1 year; may be renewed 1 additional year.

Additional information: The Women's Overseas Service League is a national organization of women who have served overseas in or with the armed forces.

Deadline: February of each year.

1215
WOMEN'S SEAMEN'S FRIEND SOCIETY OF CONNECTICUT SCHOLARSHIP

Women's Seamen's Friend Society of Connecticut, Inc.
74 Forbes Avenue
New Haven, CT 06512
Phone: (203) 467-3887

Summary: To provide financial assistance for college to selected Connecticut residents, including merchant seafarers and/or their dependents.

Eligibility: Eligible to apply for this funding are 1) Connecticut residents who are merchant seafarers and/or their dependents; they may major in any field of study; 2) Connecticut residents who are students at state maritime academies; and 3) Connecticut residents majoring in marine sciences at an out-of-state or in-state college, university, or other approved educational institution. Selection is based on academic achievement, letters of recommendation, proposed program of study, and financial need.

Financial data: These awards are supplemental and are not intended to be the primarily source of financial assistance.

Duration: 1 year.

Number awarded: Varies each year.

Deadline: March for summer session studies or research; May for the next academic year.

1216
WOMEN'S WESTERN GOLF FOUNDATION SCHOLARSHIP

Women's Western Golf Foundation
c/o Mrs. Richard Willis
393 Ramsay Road
Deerfield, IL 60015

Summary: To provide undergraduate scholarships to high school senior girls who are interested in the sport of golf.

Eligibility: Applicants must be high school senior girls who intend to graduate in the year they submit their application. They must meet entrance requirements of, and plan to enroll at, an accredited college or university. Selection is based on academic achievement, financial need, excellence of character, and involvement with the sport of golf. Skill or excellence in the game is not a criterion.

Financial data: The stipend is $2,000 per year. The funds are to be used to pay for room, board, tuition, and other university fees or charges.

Duration: 1 year; renewable up to 3 additional years if the recipient maintains a grade point average of 3.0 or higher.

Number awarded: 15 each year.

Deadline: February of each year.

1217
WOODMANSEE SCHOLARSHIP

Woodmansee Scholarship Fund
c/o Pioneer Trust Bank, N.A.
Attn: Trust Department
109 Commercial Street, N.E.
P.O. Box 2305
Salem, OR 97308-2305
Phone: (503) 363-3136, ext. 246

Summary: To provide financial assistance for college to graduating high school seniors in Oregon.

Eligibility: Any senior or graduate from a public or private high school in Oregon is eligible. Applicants must be Oregon residents and planning to attend an institution of higher education in the state. Selection is based on financial need and academic ability.

Financial data: This scholarship covers up to one half the cost of the recipient's board, room, tuition, books, and fees.

Duration: 4 years, provided the recipient maintains satisfactory academic progress.

Additional information: This trust was established in 1987. All funds from the trust will be spent by the year 2012.

Number awarded: Varies each year.
Deadline: March of each year.

1218
W.P. BLACK SCHOLARSHIPS

Greater Kanawha Valley Foundation
Attn: Scholarship Coordinator
One Huntington Square, 16th Floor
900 Lee Street, East
P.O. Box 3041
Charleston, WV 25331-3041
Phone: (304) 346-3620   Fax: (304) 346-3640
E-mail: tgkvf@tgkvf.com
Web Site: www.tgkvf.com/scholarship.html
Summary: To provide financial assistance for college to residents of West Virginia.
Eligibility: This program is open to residents of West Virginia who are attending a college or university anywhere in the country. Applicants must have at least a 2.5 grade point average and demonstrate good moral character. Selection is based on financial need and academic excellence.
Financial data: The stipend is $1,000 per year.
Duration: 1 year; may be renewed.
Number awarded: 78 each year.
Deadline: February of each year.

1219
WSTLA PRESIDENTS' SCHOLARSHIP

Washington State Trial Lawyers Association
1809 Seventh Avenue, Suite 1500
Seattle, WA 98101-1328
Phone: (206) 464-1011   Fax: (206) 464-0703
E-mail: wstla@wstla.org
Web Site: www.wstla.org
Summary: To provide financial assistance for college to Washington residents who have a disability or have been a victim of injury.
Eligibility: Applicants must be Washington residents and should be able to 1) demonstrate academic achievement and planned advancement toward a degree in an institution of higher learning, 2) document financial need, 3) illustrate a history of achievement despite having been a victim of injury or overcoming a disability, handicap, or similar challenge, and 4) show a record of commitment to helping people in need or protecting the rights of injured persons.
Financial data: Stipends average $2,500. Funds are paid directly to the recipient's chosen institution of higher learning in Washington and must be used for tuition, room, board, and fees.
Duration: 1 year.
Additional information: This fund was established in 1991.
Number awarded: 1 or more each year.
Deadline: March of each year.

1220
XX OLYMPIAD MEMORIAL AWARD

Jewish War Veterans of the U.S.A.
1811 R Street, N.W.
Washington, DC 20009-1659
Phone: (202) 265-6280   Fax: (202) 234-5662
E-mail: jwv@erols.com
Web Site: www.penfed.com/jwv
Summary: To recognize and reward outstanding high school athletes.
Eligibility: This award is presented to an outstanding senior high school athlete. Selection is based on athletic accomplishment (60 percent), academic achievement (20 percent), community service (10 percent), and leadership and citizenship (10 percent). The award is presented on a non-sectarian basis.
Financial data: The award at the national level is a $1,000 U.S. savings bond. Local awards vary.
Duration: The award is presented annually.
Number awarded: 2 each year.
Additional information: This award was established to honor the memory of the 11 members of the Israeli Olympic team who were murdered at the XX Olympiad held in Munich, Germany in September 1972. Applications must be submitted through your Jewish War Veterans' department commander.
Deadline: The names of department winners must be submitted to national headquarters by June of each year.

1221
YAKAMA ADULT VOCATIONAL TRAINING PROGRAM

Yakama Indian Nation
Department of Human Services
Attn: Adult Vocational Training Office
P.O. Box 151
Toppenish, WA 98948
Phone: (509) 865-5121, ext. 540   Fax: (509) 865-6994
Summary: To provide financial assistance to Yakama Indians who are interested in attending an accredited vocational school, college, or trade institute.
Eligibility: Yakama Indians who are at least 18 years of age, at least high school seniors, members of the Yakama Indian tribe, residents of the Yakama Indian Nation service area for the last 6 months, and unemployed or underemployed are eligible to apply for this program.
Financial data: The amount awarded depends on the recipient's need.
Duration: 1 year; may be renewed.
Additional information: In addition to financial assistance, this program provides career guidance and vocational training.
Number awarded: Varies each year.
Deadline: Applications may be submitted at any time.

1222
YAKAMA COLLEGE STUDENT ASSISTANCE PROGRAM

Yakama Indian Nation
Department of Human Services
Attn: Higher Education Programs
P.O. Box 151
Toppenish, WA 98948
Phone: (509) 865-5121, ext. 531   Fax: (509) 865-6994
Summary: To provide financial assistance to Yakama Indians who wish to pursue postsecondary education.
Eligibility: This program is open to enrolled members of U.S. Indian tribes; preference is given to enrolled Yakama members. Applicants must be high school seniors or graduates (or GED recipients), accepted to a college or university as full-time students, and in financial need.
Financial data: The amounts of the awards depend on the need of the recipient, to a maximum of $2,000 per year.
Duration: 1 year; may be renewed.
Additional information: The Yakama Nation through the Bureau of Indian Affairs provides this assistance to students to pursue a 2-year or 4-year professional degree in any field.
Number awarded: Varies each year.
Deadline: June of each year for fall quarter or semester; October of each year for winter quarter or spring semester; January of each year for spring quarter; April of each year for summer term.

1223
YAKAMA TRIBAL SCHOLARSHIP

Yakama Indian Nation
Department of Human Services
Attn: Higher Education Programs
P.O. Box 151
Toppenish, WA 98948
Phone: (509) 865-5121   (800) 543-2802
Fax: (509) 865-6994
Summary: To provide financial assistance to Yakama tribal members interested in pursuing undergraduate or graduate education.
Eligibility: Eligible to apply are Yakama students of one-quarter or more blood quantum. They must be at least high school graduates and enrolled or planning to enroll in a postsecondary institution. Applicants must have at least a 2.0 grade point average. Scholarships are awarded on the basis of academic achievement rather than financial need.
Financial data: Eligible undergraduate students receive $1,500 per year; graduate students receive $3,000 per year. Part-time students receive funding for tuition, books, and transportation; this amount may never exceed the Tribal Scholarship amount.
Duration: 1 year; may be renewed.
Additional information: Before being awarded the scholarship, recipients must attend an orientation session. Students who drop out of school after receiving scholarship awards must refund the Yakama Tribal Scholarships before being granted additional funding. Tuition amounts kept by the student's college do not count against student refunds.

Number awarded: Varies each year.
Deadline: June of each year for fall quarter or semester; October of each year for winter quarter or spring semester; January of each year for spring quarter; April of each year for summer term.

1224
YATES SCHOLARSHIPS

Georgia State Golf Association
Attn: Georgia State Golf Foundation
121 Village Parkway, Building 3
Marietta, GA 30067
Phone: (770) 955-4272   (800) 949-4742
Fax: (770) 955-1156
Web Site: www.gsga.org/foundation.htm
Summary: To provide financial assistance for college to employees of member clubs of the Georgia State Golf Association (GSGA) and their children.
Eligibility: This program is open to employees of GSGA member clubs and their children. Applicants may be majoring or planning to major in any area of study.
Financial data: Stipend amounts vary but average nearly $2,500 per year.
Duration: 1 year; may be renewed.
Number awarded: Varies each year; recently 11 of these scholarships were awarded.
Deadline: March of each year.

1225
YOF SCHOLARSHIPS

Youth Opportunities Foundation
8820 South Sepulveda Boulevard, Suite 208
P.O. Box 45762
Los Angeles, CA 90045
Phone: (310) 670-7664   Fax: (310) 670-5238
Summary: To provide financial assistance to Hispanic American students in California who are interested in pursuing postsecondary education.
Eligibility: Financial assistance is available to graduating high school seniors in California if they have at least 1 parent of Latin American origin, rank in the top 10 percent of their class, have SAT scores of at least 1100, and have a demonstrated record of leadership activities.
Financial data: Stipends range from $100 to $1,000.
Duration: These are 1-time grants.
Number awarded: Varies each year.
Deadline: March of each year.

1226
YOSHIYAMA AWARD FOR EXEMPLARY SERVICE TO THE COMMUNITY

Hitachi Foundation
1509 22nd Street, N.W.
P.O. Box 19247
Washington, DC 20036-9247
Phone: (202) 457-0588, ext. 598   Fax: (202) 296-1098
Web Site: www.hitachi.org
Summary: To recognize and reward high school seniors for outstanding community service.
Eligibility: Anyone other than a family member or relative may nominate a graduating high school senior for this award. Selection is based on the significance and extent of the candidate's community service and the relevance of those activities to solving serious community and societal problems; grade point average, SAT scores, and school club memberships are not considered.
Financial data: The award is $2,500 per year.
Duration: Funds are dispersed over a 2-year period.
Number awarded: Varies each year; recently, 11 of these awards were granted.
Deadline: March of each year.

1227
YOUNG LADIES' RADIO LEAGUE SCHOLARSHIP

Foundation for Amateur Radio, Inc.
P.O. Box 831
Riverdale, MD 20738
E-mail: turnbull@erols.com
Web Site: www.amateurradio-far.org

Summary: To provide funding to licensed radio amateurs (especially women) who are interested in earning a bachelor's or graduate degree in the United States.
Eligibility: Applicants must hold at least an FCC Technician Class or equivalent foreign authorization and intend to work on a bachelor's or graduate degree in the United States. There are no restrictions on the course of study or residency location. Preference is given to female applicants.
Financial data: The stipend is $1,500.
Duration: 1 year.
Additional information: This program is sponsored by the Young Ladies' Radio League. Recipients must attend an accredited school (university, college, or technical institute) on a full-time basis.
Number awarded: 1 each year.
Deadline: May of each year.

1228
YOUTH DEVELOPMENT FOUNDATION SCHOLARSHIPS

American Paint Horse Association
Attn: Youth Coordinator
2800 Meacham Boulevard
P.O. Box 961023
Fort Worth, TX 76161-0023
Phone: (817) 834-APHA, ext. 248   Fax: (817) 834-3152
E-mail: gtheis.apha.com
Web Site: www.apha.com
Summary: To provide financial assistance for college to members of the American Paint Horse Association (APHA).
Eligibility: Applicants must be members in good standing (regular or junior) of the association involved in horse activity using a paint horse or contributing actively to a regional club for at least a year prior to and at the time of application. They must be high school graduates who have never been married and are applying within 1 year of the date of high school graduation. A 3.0 minimum grade point average is required. Selection is based on 1) scholastic record, including a 500-word essay on educational plans and goals (15 percent); 2) APHA club activities (25 percent); 3) APHA horse activities (25 percent); 4) extracurricular activities (20 percent); and 5) 3 letters of recommendation (15 percent).
Financial data: The stipend is $1,000 per year. Funds are paid directly to the recipient's school.
Duration: 1 year; may be renewed for up to 4 additional years.
Additional information: Recipients must attend school on a full-time basis (at least 12 hours).
Number awarded: Varies each year; recently, 34 of these scholarships (12 new and 22 renewal) were awarded.
Deadline: February of each year.

1229
YOUTH EDUCATION SUMMIT GRAND SCHOLARSHIPS

National Rifle Association of America
Attn: Field Operations Division, Event Services Coordinator
11250 Waples Mill Road
Fairfax, VA 22030
Phone: (703) 267-1353   (800) 672-3888, ext. 1353
Fax: (703) 267-3939
Web Site: www.nrafoundation.org
Summary: To recognize and reward high school students who develop a communications portfolio based on their experience at the Youth Education Summit (Y.E.S.) of the National Rifle Association (NRA).
Eligibility: Applicants to the Y.E.S. program must be high school sophomores or juniors with a minimum 3.0 grade point average. Participants are chosen to visit the Washington, D.C. area in June to spend 6 days touring the city and learning about American government and history, the U.S. constitution, the Bill of Rights, and the role and mission of the association. During the following year, the participants develop a communications portfolio that relates their experience at Y.E.S. and conveys the mission and goals of the association and its many programs and services as learned during the Y.E.S. week. Portfolios may be developed for presentation on television, radio, the Internet, or in print. The project submissions selected as the best receive these awards.
Financial data: The stipends are $4,000, $2,000, $1,000, and $500. Funds are paid directly to the accredited college or technical school of the student's choice.
Duration: These scholarships are presented annually.
Number awarded: 5 each year: 1 at $10,000, 1 at $5,000, 2 at $2,000, and 1 at $1,000.
Deadline: January of each year.

1230
YOUTH EDUCATION SUMMIT SCHOLARSHIPS

National Rifle Association of America
Attn: Field Operations Division, Event Services Coordinator
11250 Waples Mill Road
Fairfax, VA 22030
Phone: (703) 267-1353   (800) 672-3888, ext. 1353
Fax: (703) 267-3939
Web Site: www.nrafoundation.org
Summary: To provide financial assistance for college to high school students who participate in the Youth Education Summit (Y.E.S.) of the National Rifle Association (NRA).
Eligibility: Applicants to the Y.E.S. program must be high school sophomores or juniors with a minimum 3.0 grade point average. They must include information on their school activities, a description of their shooting sports activities, an essay of 2 to 5 pages on the second amendment and its significance in American society, transcripts, and recommendations. Based on their applications, approximately 20 students each year are chosen to visit the Washington, D.C. area in June to spend 6 days touring the city and learning about American government and history, the U.S. constitution, the Bill of Rights, and the role and mission of the association. The participants in the program judged as most outstanding, based on their original applications and their work in Washington, are selected to receive these scholarships.
Financial data: The stipends are $1,000, $500, and $250. Funds are paid directly to the accredited college or technical school of the student's choice.
Duration: These scholarships are presented annually.
Number awarded: 8 each year: 1 at $4,000, 1 at $2,000, 2 at $1,000, 1 at $750, 2 at $500, and 1 at $250.
Deadline: March of each year.

1231
YOUTH EXCEL AWARD PROGRAM

Amateur Athletic Union
P.O. Box 22409
Lake Buena Vista, FL 32830
Phone: (407) 934-7200
Web Site: www.aausports.org
Summary: To provide financial assistance to high school senior student-athletes who have "surmounted their life circumstances and distinguished themselves both in the classroom and in athletic endeavors."
Eligibility: This program is open to high school seniors who are student-athletes and can demonstrate excellence in athletics and academics, despite adversity. Applicants must have at least a 2.5 grade point average, have participated in at least 1 sanctioned high school sport, and have been active in their community. Interested students must submit a completed application form and an essay describing their adversity and how they overcame it. Essays are judged on content, not on writing style. Financial need is not considered in the selection process.
Financial data: Stipends are $3,500, $1,000, and $500.
Duration: 1 year.
Number awarded: 3 each year.
Deadline: December of each year.

1232
YOUTH OPPORTUNITIES FUND SCHOLARSHIPS

Key Club International
Attn: Manager of Youth Funds
3636 Woodview Trace
Indianapolis, IN 46268-3196
Phone: (317) 875-8755, ext. 244   (800) KIWANIS, ext. 244
Fax: (317) 879-0204   E-mail: youthfunds@kiwanis.org
Web Site: www.keyclub.org
Summary: To provide financial assistance for college to high school seniors who are Key Club International members.
Eligibility: This program is open to graduating high school seniors who are bound for college, have at least a 3.0 grade point average, have demonstrated commitment to Key Club, and have performed significant Key Club service.

Applicants may not have served as an International Board member or governor. Selection is based on participation in school activities and organizations; participation in religious and community activities; honors, awards, and special recognition; 3 letters of recommendation; and an essay on how they have exemplified the ideals of Key Club. Financial need is not considered in the selection process.
Financial data: The stipend is $1,000 per year.
Duration: 4 years.
Number awarded: 4 each year.
Deadline: March of each year.

1233
YUTAKA NAKAZAWA MEMORIAL SCHOLARSHIP

Japanese American Citizens League
Attn: National Scholarship Awards
1765 Sutter Street
San Francisco, CA 94115
Phone: (415) 921-5225   Fax: (415) 931-4671
E-mail: jacl@jacl.org
Web Site: www.jacl.org
Summary: To provide financial assistance to student members of the Japanese American Citizens League (JACL) who are high school seniors interested in pursuing undergraduate education.
Eligibility: This program is open to JACL members who are high school seniors interested in attending a college, university, trade school, business college, or other institution of higher learning. Selection is based on academic record, extracurricular activities, and community involvement.
Financial data: The stipend depends on the availability of funds but usually ranges from $1,000 to $5,000.
Duration: 1 year.
Additional information: Requests for applications must be accompanied by a self-addressed stamped envelope.
Number awarded: 1 each year.
Deadline: March of each year.

1234
ZETA JONES HALDIN MEMORIAL ENDOWMENT SCHOLARSHIP

Epsilon Sigma Alpha
Attn: ESA Foundation Assistant Scholarship Director
P.O. Box 270517
Fort Collins, CO 80527
Phone: (970) 223-2824   Fax: (970) 223-4456
Web Site: www.esaintl.com/esaf
Summary: To provide financial assistance for postsecondary education to students from Florida studying any major.
Eligibility: This program is open to residents of Florida who are either 1) graduating high school seniors in the top 25 percent of their class or with minimum scores of 20 on the ACT or 950 on the SAT, or 2) students already in college with a grade point average of 3.0 or higher. Students enrolled for training in a technical school or returning to school after an absence are also eligible. Selection is based on character, scholastic ability, leadership and ability skills, and financial need.
Financial data: The stipend is $1,000.
Duration: 1 year; may be renewed.
Additional information: Epsilon Sigma Alpha (ESA) is a women's service organization, but scholarships are available to both men and women. Information is also available from Verneene Forssberg, 403 South High, Pratt, KS 67124, (316) 672-3636, Fax: (316) 672-3688, E-mail: vernf@genmail.pcc.cc.ks.us. Completed applications must be submitted to the ESA State Counselor who verifies the information before forwarding them to the scholarship director.
Number awarded: 1 each year.
Deadline: January of each year.

1235
ZONTA CLUBS OF LOUISIANA WOMAN'S SCHOLARSHIP

Zonta Clubs of Louisiana
c/o Sharon Ratcliffe
7521 Plum Street
New Orleans, LA 70118
E-mail: cathysimoneaux@email.com
Web Site: www.insideneworleans.com/community/groups/zonta
Summary: To provide financial assistance for college to women residents of Louisiana.
Eligibility: This program is open to women residents of Louisiana who are the major wage earner of their family. Applicants must have been accepted at a Louisiana university, college, or vocational-technical school in non-remedial courses and have satisfactory scores on the SAT, ACT, or entrance exam. U.S. citizenship and evidence of financial need are required.
Financial data: The stipend depends on the need of the recipient and the availability of funds.
Duration: 1 semester; may be renewed if the recipient enrolls in at least 6 hours per semester and maintains a grade point average of 2.5 or higher.
Number awarded: 1 or more each year.

1236
10-10 INTERNATIONAL NET, INC. SCHOLARSHIPS

Foundation for Amateur Radio, Inc.
P.O. Box 831
Riverdale, MD 20738
E-mail: turnbull@erols.com
Web Site: www.amateurradio-far.org
Summary: To provide funding to licensed radio amateurs who are interested in working on an undergraduate or graduate degree.
Eligibility: Applicants must be radio amateurs who have HF privileges and hold at least a novice class license or equivalent foreign authorization. There is no restriction on the course of study, but applicants must intend to seek at least an associate degree from a college or university in the United States; those seeking a graduate degree are also eligible. Applicants must provide a recommendation from a member of the 10-10 International Net.
Financial data: The stipend is $1,000.
Duration: 1 year.
Additional information: Recipients must attend an accredited school (university, college, or technical institute) on a full-time basis.
Number awarded: 4 each year.
Deadline: May of each year.

1237
102D INFANTRY DIVISION ASSOCIATION MEMORIAL SCHOLARSHIPS

102d Infantry Division Association
c/o James A. Alspaugh
Scholarship Committee Secretary
4311 East 55th Street
Tulsa, OK 74135-4830
Phone: (918) 492-7304   E-mail: JAASLP@aol.com
Summary: To provide financial assistance for postsecondary education to the descendants of members of the 102d Infantry Division Association.
Eligibility: Eligible to apply for these scholarships are the children, grandchildren, and great-grandchildren of dues-paying members (or if deceased a dues-paying member at the time of death) of the 102nd Infantry Division Association who served between August 1942 and March 1946. Applicants may be high school seniors or graduates or college freshmen, sophomores, or juniors. Selection is based on academic transcripts; SAT or ACT scores; high school honors, prizes, and scholarships; school and community activities; work experience; 5 letters of recommendation; and an essay on the applicant's educational plans and personal life goals.
Financial data: A stipend is awarded (exact amount not specified).
Duration: Some scholarships are for 2 years; others are for 1 year.
Additional information: Information is also available from Wilson R. Reed, 6383 Vale Street, Alexandria, VA 22312-1436, (703) 354-1917.
Number awarded: Varies each year.
Deadline: June of each year.

1238
11TH ARMORED CAVALRY VETERANS OF VIETNAM AND CAMBODIA SCHOLARSHIP

11th Armored Cavalry Veterans of Vietnam and Cambodia
c/o John Sorich
5037 France Avenue South
Minneapolis, MN 55410
Phone: (612) 929-1472   Fax: (612) 929-1472
Web Site: www.11thcavnam.com
Summary: To provide financial assistance to members of the 11th Armored Cavalry Veterans of Vietnam and Cambodia (ACVVC) and to their dependents.
Eligibility: This program is open to 11th ACVVC members and to their dependents. In addition, dependents of deceased troopers who served with the 11th Armored Cavalry in Vietnam or Cambodia may apply (a copy of the father's obituary must be supplied). Affiliation with the cavalry must be documented. Financial need is considered in the selection process.
Financial data: The total stipend is $3,000; funds are paid directly to the recipient's school, in 2 equal installments.
Duration: 1 year; nonrenewable.
Additional information: Recipients must use the awarded money within 20 months of being notified.
Number awarded: 10 to 15 each year.
Deadline: May of each year.

1239
25TH INFANTRY DIVISION ASSOCIATION EDUCATIONAL MEMORIAL SCHOLARSHIP AWARD

25th Infantry Division Association
P.O. Box 7
Flourtown, PA 19031-0007
E-mail: TropicLtn@aol.com   Web Site: www.25thida.com
Summary: To provide financial assistance for postsecondary education to the children of veterans and current members of the 25th Infantry Division Association.
Eligibility: This program is open to 1) children and grandchildren of active members of the association; 2) children of former members of the division deceased during active combat with the division or as a result of it; and 3) active members of an association chapter with the division who are scheduled for release from active service or discharge on or before December 31 of the award year. Applicants must be enrolling in the freshman year of an accredited 4-year college or university and intending to pursue work toward a baccalaureate degree by enrolling in at least 12 semester hours of study each semester. They must submit 1) a personal letter describing the reasons for their request, future plans, school interests and activities, and financial situation; 2) a transcript of high school credits; 3) most recent ACT or SAT scores; 4) 3 letters of recommendation; 5) a letter of acceptance from the institution they plan to attend; and 6) a photograph.
Financial data: Stipends up to $1,500 are available.
Duration: Each grant is a 1-time award, which may be spent over any period of time.
Additional information: Information is also available from the Scholarship Committee Chairman, 3930 South Bridlewood Drive, Bountiful, UT 84010. This program includes the George and Rosemary Murray Scholarship Award.
Number awarded: Varies each year.
Deadline: March of each year.

1240
37TH DIVISION VETERANS SCHOLARSHIP

37th Division Veterans Association
35 East Chestnut Street, Suite 425
Columbus, OH 43215
Phone: (614) 228-3788
Summary: To provide financial assistance for postsecondary education to descendants of 37th Division veterans.
Eligibility: This program is open to descendants of veterans who served honorably with a unit of the 37th Infantry Division until its deactivation in 1968. The veteran must be an active or life member of the association or, if deceased, must have been a member at the time of his death. Applicants may be seniors in high school or already enrolled in a college program. They must demonstrate financial need.
Financial data: Each award is $1,000.
Duration: 1 year.
Number awarded: Varies each year.
Deadline: March of each year.

1241
4A—AT&T NATIONAL SCHOLARSHIP PROGRAM

Asian/Pacific American Association for Advancement at AT&T
c/o June Tom, 4A National Scholarship Committee
795 Folsom Street, Room 2114A
San Francisco, CA 94107
Summary: To provide financial assistance to full-time college juniors.
Eligibility: Eligible to apply for this assistance are third-year college juniors currently enrolled full time in an accredited undergraduate program in the United States. Applicants must be U.S. citizens or permanent residents. As part of the application process, students must submit a completed application form (including a list of awards and activities), a letter of recommendation, and a 350-word essay on the following topic: "Identify a need in the Asian-American community where diversity can be improved. What contributions would you like to make or have done to accomplish this?" After the initial screening process, the remaining eligible applicants are evaluated on their scholastic discipline, personal achievement, and community involvement.
Financial data: The stipend is $2,000 per year.
Duration: 1 year.
Additional information: The address to use to request applications depends upon the state in which you reside. Students in Maine, New Jersey, and Pennsylvania should write to Bhavana Shah, AT&T, 429 Ridge Road, Room C-178, Dayton, NJ 08810. Students in Idaho, Montana, North Dakota, Oregon, South Dakota, Utah, Washington, Wyoming, Colorado, Kansas, Minnesota, Nebraska, and Wisconsin should write to Mary Monzon, AT&T, 1150 Inca Street, Number 82, Denver, CO 80204. Students in Alabama, Arkansas, Georgia, Louisiana, Mississippi, Florida, Kentucky, Missouri, Oklahoma, and Tennessee should write to Jennifer Rose, AT&T, 6021 South Rio Grand Avenue, Room 1E4-226, Orlando, FL 32809. Students in Alaska, California, Arizona, Hawaii, Nevada, New Mexico, and Texas should write to June Tom, AT&T, 795 Folsom Street, Room 2114A, San Francisco, CA 94107. Students in Washington, D.C., Delaware, Maryland, North Carolina, South Carolina, Virginia, West Virginia, and New York should write to Lida Saleh, AT&T, 3033 Chainbridge Road, Room B250, Oakton, VA 22185. Students in Connecticut, Maine, Michigan, New Hampshire, Rhode Island, Vermont, Illinois, Indiana, Iowa, and Ohio should write to Suwathin Phiansunthon, AT&T, 307 Middletown Lincroft Road, Room 1J313, Lincroft, NJ 07738.
Number awarded: 6 each year.
Deadline: April of each year.

1242
82D AIRBORNE DIVISION ASSOCIATION AWARDS

82d Airborne Division Association
Attn: President, Educational Fund
P.O. Box 65089
Fayetteville, NC 28306-5089
Phone: (919) 822-4534
Summary: To provide financial assistance for postsecondary education to members of the 82d Airborne Division Association and their dependent children.
Eligibility: Eligible to apply for this award are 1) dependent children of 82d Airborne Division Association voting members; 2) dependent children of 82d Airborne servicemen killed in combat; 3) dependent children of deceased Life or All American members of the 82d Airborne Division Association; and 4) former active-duty 82d Airborne Division troopers who are association members, are within 2 years of honorable discharge, and served no more than 2 enlistments. Applicants must be enrolled in an accredited university or college. Selection is based on academic achievement and financial need.
Financial data: The stipend is $1,500 per year. Funds are paid to the recipient's college or university.
Duration: 1 semester (the second in a school year); recipients may reapply for up to 3 additional annual awards.
Additional information: In years when a suitable candidate applies, 1 of these awards is designated the General Mathew B. Ridgeway Scholarship.
Number awarded: Varies each year.
Deadline: October of each year.

Humanities

Described here are 469 funding programs that 1) reward outstanding artistic and creative work by students or 2) support college studies in the humanities, including architecture, art, creative writing, design, history, journalism, languages, literature, music, and religion. These programs are available to high school seniors, high school graduates, currently enrolled college students, and/or returning students to fund studies on the undergraduate level in the United States. If you haven't already checked the "Unrestricted by Subject Area" chapter, be sure to do that next; identified there are 1,242 more sources of free money that can be used to support study in the humanities or any other subject area (although the programs may be restricted in other ways). Finally, be sure to consult the Subject Index to locate available funding in a specific subject area.

1243
A/E PRONET SCHOLARSHIP

Design Firm Management Education Foundation
c/o Francine Larose, SDA/C, President
Hornberger + Worstell
170 Maiden Lane, Sixth Floor
San Francisco, CA 94108
Phone: (415) 391-1080   E-mail: larose@hwiarchitect.com
Web Site: www.dfmef.org
Summary: To provide financial assistance to undergraduate and graduate students enrolled in a program that emphasizes design firm/risk management.
Eligibility: This program is open to full-time students enrolled in at least the second year of a 4- or 5-year undergraduate program, the second semester of a 2-year undergraduate program, or the first year in a graduate program. Applicants must be pursuing a course of study that includes classes related to the development of design firm management skills. They must submit an essay in which they explain how they will apply the course of study that is supported by the scholarship.
Financial data: The stipend depends on the actual cost of the course of study. A total of $1,500 is available for this program each year.
Duration: 1 year.
Additional information: The sponsor of this program is a/e ProNet, established in 1987 to bring together independent insurance professionals who provide service to architectural and engineering professionals. Currently, approximately 2,500 architecture and engineering firms are served by a/e ProNet members.
Number awarded: 1 or more each year.
Deadline: February of each year.

1244
ABE VORON SCHOLARSHIP

Broadcast Education Association
Attn: Scholarships
1771 N Street, N.W.
Washington, DC 20036-2891
Phone: (202) 429-5354   E-mail: bea@nab.org
Web Site: www.beaweb.org
Summary: To provide financial assistance to upper-division and graduate students who are interested in preparing for a career in broadcasting.
Eligibility: This program is open to juniors, seniors, and graduate students enrolled full time at a college or university where at least 1 department is an institutional member of the Broadcast Education Association. Applicants must be studying for a career in radio. Selection is based on evidence that the applicant possesses integrity, superior academic ability, potential to be an outstanding electronic media professional, and a sense of personal and professional responsibility.
Financial data: The stipend is $5,000.
Duration: 1 year; may not be renewed.
Additional information: Information is also available from Peter B. Orlik, Central Michigan University, 344 Moore Hall, Mt. Pleasant, MI 48859, (517) 774-7279.
Number awarded: 1 each year.
Deadline: September of each year.

1245
AFCEA COMPUTER GRAPHIC DESIGN SCHOLARSHIPS

Armed Forces Communications and Electronics Association
Attn: Educational Foundation
4400 Fair Lakes Court
Fairfax, VA 22033-3899
Phone: (703) 631-6149   (800) 336-4583, ext. 6149
Fax: (703) 631-4693   E-mail: scholarship@afcea.org
Web Site: www.afcea.org
Summary: To provide scholarships to deserving college students who are working on a degree in computer graphic design.
Eligibility: This program is open to full-time students entering their junior or senior year at an accredited degree-granting 4-year college or university in the United States. Applicants must be U.S. citizens working toward a degree in computer graphic design or a related field. They must submit a sample of digital graphic artwork for intranets and internets, especially web-based graphics. Along with the artwork (in .JPG or .GIF format on CD, zip disk, or diskette), they must include a textual statement of 200 to 300 words that describes the image submitted, how it was created, and what, if any, specific intent or purpose it represents. Selection is based on artistic creativity, mastery of web technology, a statement of

career goals, school and community activities, and financial need.
Financial data: The stipend is $2,000.
Duration: 1 year; may be renewed.
Additional information: Requests for applications must be accompanied by a self-addressed stamped envelope.
Number awarded: 1 or more each year.
Deadline: October of each year.

1246
AGNES MCINTOSH GARDEN CLUB OBJECTIVES SCHOLARSHIP

Florida Federation of Garden Clubs, Inc.
Attn: Scholarship Chair
6065 21st Street S.W.
Vero Beach, FL 32968-9427
Phone: (561) 778-1023
Web Site: www.ffgc.org
Summary: To provide financial aid to Florida undergraduates and graduate students majoring in designated areas.
Eligibility: This program is open to Florida residents who are enrolled as full-time juniors, seniors, or graduate students in a Florida college. They must have at least a 3.0 grade point average, be in financial need, and be majoring in ecology, horticulture, landscape design, conservation, botany, forestry, marine biology, city planning, or allied subjects. Selection is based on academic record, commitment to career, character, and financial need.
Financial data: The stipend is $1,500. The funds are sent directly to the recipient's school and distributed semiannually.
Duration: 1 year.
Additional information: If the recipient's grade point average drops below 3.0, the second installment of the scholarship is not provided.
Number awarded: 1 each year.
Deadline: April of each year.

1247
AGO REGIONAL COMPETITIONS FOR YOUNG ORGANISTS

American Guild of Organists
475 Riverside Drive, Suite 1260
New York, NY 10115
Phone: (212) 870-2310   Fax: (212) 870-2163
E-mail: info@agohq.org
Web Site: www.agohq.org
Summary: To recognize and reward outstanding student organists.
Eligibility: Eligible to compete are student organists 23 years of age or younger. Competitions are held in each of the 9 regions of the American Guild of Organists (AGO); contestants may enter the region either where they reside or where they attend school. The repertoire consists of 4 pieces: 1) a designated work by Bach; 2) a hymn chosen from a designated list; 3) a work by a living composer; and 4) an additional composition of the competitor's choice. The total performance time may not exceed 40 minutes. Students first compete in their local chapter; winners advance to the regional competitions.
Financial data: Each region awards a cash prize of $1,000 to the first-place winner and $500 to the second-place winner.
Duration: The competition is held biennially.
Additional information: Further information is available from the competition director, Charles Boyd Tompkins, Furman University, 3300 Poinsett Highway, Greenville, SC 29613-1154, (864) 294-2969, Fax: (864) 294-3035, E-mail: charles.tompkins@furman.edu. A $25 registration fee is charged.
Number awarded: First and second prizes are awarded in each region.
Deadline: Competitors must register with their chapter by mid-January of each odd-numbered year.

1248
AIA/AAF MINORITY/DISADVANTAGED SCHOLARSHIP

American Institute of Architects
Attn: American Architectural Foundation
1735 New York Avenue, N.W.
Washington, DC 20006-5292
Phone: (202) 626-7318   Fax: (202) 626-7420
E-mail: info@archfoundation.org
Web Site: www.archfoundation.org/scholarships/index.htm
Summary: To provide financial assistance to high school and college students

from minority and/or disadvantaged backgrounds who are interested in studying architecture in college.

Eligibility: This program is open to students from minority and/or disadvantaged backgrounds who are high school seniors, students in a community college or technical school transferring to an accredited architectural program, or college freshmen entering a professional degree program at an accredited program of architecture. Students who have completed 1 or more years of a 4-year college curriculum are not eligible. Initially, candidates must be nominated by 1 of the following organizations or persons: an individual architect or firm, a component of the American Institute of Architects (AIA), a community design center, a guidance counselor or teacher, the dean or professor at an accredited school of architecture, or the director of a community or civic organization. Nominees are reviewed and eligible candidates are invited to complete an application form in which they write an essay describing the reasons they are interested in becoming an architect and provide documentation of academic excellence and financial need. Selection is based primarily on financial need.

Financial data: Awards range from $500 to $2,500 per year, depending upon individual need. Students must apply for supplementary funds from other sources.

Duration: 9 months; may be renewed for up to 2 additional years.

Additional information: This program is offered jointly by the American Architectural Foundation (AAF) and the AIA.

Number awarded: 20 each year.

Deadline: Nominations are due by December of each year; final applications must be submitted in January.

1249
AIA/AAF SCHOLARSHIP FOR FIRST PROFESSIONAL DEGREE

American Institute of Architects
Attn: American Architectural Foundation
1735 New York Avenue, N.W.
Washington, DC 20006-5292
Phone: (202) 626-7318   Fax: (202) 626-7420
E-mail: info@archfoundation.org
Web Site: www.archfoundation.org/scholarships/index.htm

Summary: To provide financial assistance to students in professional degree programs in architecture.

Eligibility: This program is open to students who are in the final 2 years of a first professional degree: 1) the third or fourth year of a 5-year program for a bachelor of architecture or equivalent degree; 2) the fourth or fifth year of a 6-year program (4 + 2 or other combination) that results in a master of architecture or equivalent degree; or 3) the second or third year of a 3- to 4-year program that results in a master of architecture and whose undergraduate degree is in a discipline other than architecture. All programs must be accredited by the National Architectural Accrediting Board (NAAB) or recognized by the Royal Architectural Institute of Canada (RAIC). Selection is based on a statement of goals, academic performance, a drawing, and financial need.

Financial data: Awards range from $500 to $2,500 per year, depending upon individual need.

Additional information: This program is offered jointly by the American Architectural Foundation (AAF) and the American Institute of Architects (AIA). This program is administered in conjunction with the architectural department at NAAB and RAIC schools; application forms are available only from the dean's office when the student is in 1 of the final 2 years of the program.

Number awarded: Varies each year.

Deadline: January of each year.

1250
AIKO SUSANNA TASHIRO HIRATSUKA MEMORIAL SCHOLARSHIP

Japanese American Citizens League
Attn: National Scholarship Awards
1765 Sutter Street
San Francisco, CA 94115
Phone: (415) 921-5225   Fax: (415) 931-4671
E-mail: jacl@jacl.org
Web Site: www.jacl.org

Summary: To provide financial assistance for undergraduate education in the performing arts to student members of the Japanese American Citizens League.

Eligibility: This program is open to JACL members who are pursuing undergraduate study in the performing arts. Applicants should provide published performance reviews and/or evaluations by their instructor. Selection is based on

academic record, extracurricular activities, and community involvement. Professional artists are not eligible.

Financial data: The stipend depends on the availability of funds but usually ranges from $1,000 to $5,000.

Duration: 1 year.

Additional information: Requests for applications must be accompanied by a self-addressed stamped envelope.

Number awarded: 1 each year.

Deadline: March of each year.

1251
ALABAMA JUNIOR AND COMMUNITY COLLEGE PERFORMING ARTS SCHOLARSHIPS

Alabama Commission on Higher Education
Attn: Grants and Scholarships Department
100 North Union Street
P.O. Box 302000
Montgomery, AL 36130-2000
Phone: (334) 242-2274   Fax: (334) 242-0268
E-mail: wwall@ache.state.al.us
Web Site: www.ache.state.al.us

Summary: To provide financial assistance to performing artists interested in attending a junior or community college in Alabama.

Eligibility: Eligible are full-time students enrolled in public junior and community colleges in Alabama. Selection is based on artistic talent as determined through competitive auditions.

Financial data: Awards cover up to the cost of in-state tuition.

Additional information: Further information is available from financial aid officers at the appropriate Alabama junior or community college.

Number awarded: Varies each year.

1252
ALBERT K. MURRAY FINE ARTS EDUCATIONAL FUND SCHOLARSHIP

Albert K. Murray Fine Arts Educational Fund
Attn: Chair, Scholarship Committee
9665 Young America Road
P.O. Box 367
Adamsville, OH 43802-0367
Phone: (740) 796-4797   Fax: (740) 796-4799

Summary: To provide financial aid to students enrolled in an art program in college.

Eligibility: Applicants must be U.S. citizens and enrolled full time in an art degree program at an accredited college or university in the United States. Selection is based on academic merit and financial need.

Financial data: The amount of the stipend depends on the recipient's financial need. Funds must be used for tuition and related educational expenses (fees, books, supplies), not for room or board. Funds are paid directly to the recipient's school.

Duration: 1 quarter.

Additional information: Recipients must attend school on a full-time basis.

Deadline: July for September grants; October for December grants; January for March grants; or April for June grants.

1253
ALBERT M. BECKER MEMORIAL SCHOLARSHIP

New York State Legion Press Association
c/o Scholarship Chairman
American Legion (NYSLPA)
P.O. Box 1239
Syracuse, NY 13201-1239

Summary: To provide financial support to the children of members of the American Legion or American Legion Auxiliary in New York who are interested in careers in communications.

Eligibility: Applicants for this scholarship must be the children of members of the American Legion or American Legion Auxiliary, or members of the Sons of the American Legion, or junior members of the American Legion Auxiliary, or graduates of the New York Boys State or Girls State. They must be entering or attending an accredited 4-year college, pursuing a degree in communications (including public relations, journalism, reprographics, newspaper design or management, or other related fields acceptable to the scholarship committee). Applicants must also submit a 500-word essay on why they chose the field of communications as a future vocation.

Financial need and class standing are not considered.
Financial data: This scholarship is $1,000.
Duration: 1 year.
Number awarded: 1 each year.
Deadline: May of each year.

1254
ALEXANDER M. TANGER SCHOLARSHIPS

Broadcast Education Association
Attn: Scholarships
1771 N Street, N.W.
Washington, DC 20036-2891
Phone: (202) 429-5354   E-mail: bea@nab.org
Web Site: www.beaweb.org
Summary: To provide financial assistance to upper-division and graduate students who are interested in preparing for a career in broadcasting.
Eligibility: This program is open to juniors, seniors, and graduate students enrolled full time at a college or university where at least 1 department is an institutional member of the Broadcast Education Association. Applicants may be studying any area of broadcasting. Selection is based on evidence that the applicant possesses high integrity, superior academic ability, potential to be an outstanding electronic media professional, and a sense of personal and professional responsibility.
Financial data: The stipend is $2,500.
Duration: 1 year; may not be renewed.
Additional information: Information is also available from Peter B. Orlik, Central Michigan University, 344 Moore Hall, Mt. Pleasant, MI 48859, (517) 774-7279.
Number awarded: 2 each year.
Deadline: September of each year.

1255
ALFRED G. AND ELMA M. MILOTTE SCHOLARSHIP

Alfred G. and Elma M. Milotte Scholarship Fund
c/o Seafirst Bank
Attn: Charitable Investment Services
P.O. Box 24565
Seattle, WA 98124
Summary: To provide financial assistance to high school seniors or graduates in Washington state who are interested in "portraying wilderness areas in a manner to benefit citizens of the United States now and in the years to come."
Eligibility: This program is open to high school seniors, high school graduates, or students who hold a GED certificate in Washington state. They must have resided in the state for at least 5 years prior to application. Applicants must be able to portray, through photography or other artistic forms, their interest in natural history, environmental studies, or animal behavior. They must have earned at least a 3.0 cumulative grade point average (transcripts are required), write a statement of their educational and career goals, and submit 2 letters of reference. Financial need is not considered in the selection process.
Financial data: These are tuition scholarships.
Duration: 1 year.
Additional information: Recipients may attend any college university, trade school, or art institute.
Deadline: February of each year.

1256
ALFRED T. GRANGER STUDENT ART FUND

Vermont Student Assistance Corporation
Champlain Mill
1 Main Street, Fourth Floor
P.O. Box 2000
Winooski, VT 05404-2601
Phone: (802) 655-9602   TDD: (802) 654-3766
Fax: (802) 654-3765   TDD: (802) 654-3766
Phone: TDD: (800) 281-3341 (within VT)   E-mail: info@vsac.org
Web Site: www.vsac.org
Summary: To provide financial assistance to residents of Vermont who are interested in pursuing an undergraduate or graduate degree in a field related to design.
Eligibility: This program is open to residents of Vermont who are graduating high school seniors, high school graduates, or GED recipients. Applicants must be interested in attending an accredited postsecondary institution to pursue a degree in architecture, interior design, studio art, architectural engineering, mechanical drawing, or lighting design. Selection is based on academic achievement, a

portfolio, letters of recommendation, required essays, and financial need.
Financial data: The stipend is $5,000 per year for graduate students or $2,500 per year for undergraduates.
Duration: 1 year; recipients may reapply.
Number awarded: 2 graduate scholarships and 4 undergraduate scholarships are awarded each year.
Deadline: May of each year.

1257
ALLISON FISHER NON-SUSTAINING SCHOLARSHIP

National Association of Black Journalists
Attn: Media Institute Program Associate
8701-A Adelphi Road
Adelphi, MD 20783-1716
Phone: (301) 445-7100, ext. 108   Fax: (301) 445-7101
E-mail: warren@nabj.org
Web Site: www.nabj.org
Summary: To provide financial assistance to undergraduate or graduate student members of the National Association of Black Journalists (NABJ) who are majoring in print journalism.
Eligibility: This competition is open to African American undergraduate or graduate students who are currently attending an accredited 4-year college or university. Applicants must be majoring in print journalism and have a grade point average of 3.0 or higher. They must submit 6 samples of their published or broadcasted work, an official college transcript, 2 letters of recommendation, a resume, and a 500- to 800-word essay describing their accomplishments as a student journalist, their career goals, and their interest in the field.
Financial data: The stipend is $2,500.
Duration: 1 year.
Additional information: All scholarship winners must become members of the association before they enroll in college.
Number awarded: 1 or more each year.
Deadline: April of each year.

1258
ALPHA CORRINE MAYFIELD SCHOLARSHIP

National Federation of Music Clubs
1336 North Delaware Street
Indianapolis, IN 46202-2481
Phone: (317) 638-4003   Fax: (317) 638-0503
E-mail: info@nfmc-music.org
Web Site: www.nfmc-music.org/BienSeniorDivision.htm
Summary: To recognize and reward outstanding young opera singers who are members of the National Federation of Music Clubs (NFMC).
Eligibility: Entrants must be opera singers, senior members of the federation, U.S. citizens, and between 20 and 35 years of age.
Financial data: The award is $1,000.
Duration: The competition is held biennially, in odd-numbered years.
Additional information: Applications and further information are available from Doris Jean Cranfill, 1004 West 88th Street, Kansas City, MO 64114-2741; information on all federation awards is available from Chair, Competitions and Awards Board, Mrs. Lamoine M. Hall, Jr., 4137 Whitfield Avenue, Fort Worth, TX 76109-5432. There is a $10 entry fee.
Number awarded: 1 every other year.
Deadline: January of odd-numbered years.

1259
AMERICAN ACADEMY OF CHEFS *BALESTRERI/CUTINO* SCHOLARSHIPS

American Academy of Chefs
P.O. Box 3466
St. Augustine, FL 32085-3466
Phone: (904) 824-4468   (800) 624-9458
Fax: (904) 825-4758   E-mail: acf@acfchefs.net
Web Site: www.acfchefs.org/academy/aacschol3.html
Summary: To provide financial assistance to students enrolled in culinary programs.
Eligibility: This program is open to students who are currently enrolled in an accredited postsecondary culinary program. Applicants must have completed at least 1 grading or marking period and have a career goal of becoming (or already be) a chef or pastry chef. Selection is based on 2 letters of recommendation, 2 brief essays by the applicants (1 on why they want to become a chef/pastry chef or

continue their education in the field and 1 on what they hope to contribute to the culinary industry), and financial need.

Financial data: The stipend is $1,000.
Duration: 1 year.
Number awarded: 3 each year.
Deadline: March of each year.

1260
AMERICAN ACADEMY OF CHEFS *CHAINE DES ROTISSEURS* SCHOLARSHIPS

American Academy of Chefs
P.O. Box 3466
St. Augustine, FL 32085-3466
Phone: (904) 824-4468   (800) 624-9458
Fax: (904) 825-4758   E-mail: acf@acfchefs.net
Web Site: www.acfchefs.org/educate/eduschlr.html
Summary: To provide financial assistance to students enrolled in culinary programs.
Eligibility: This program is open to students who are currently enrolled full time in a 2-year culinary program. Applicants must have completed at least 1 grading or marking period. Selection is based on 2 letters of recommendation, 2 brief essays by the applicants (1 on their career goals and 1 on what they hope to contribute to the culinary industry), and financial need.
Financial data: The stipend is $1,000.
Duration: 1 year.
Number awarded: 20 each year.
Deadline: November of each year.

1261
AMERICAN ACADEMY OF CHEFS *CHAIR'S* SCHOLARSHIPS

American Academy of Chefs
P.O. Box 3466
St. Augustine, FL 32085-3466
Phone: (904) 824-4468   (800) 624-9458
Fax: (904) 825-4758   E-mail: acf@acfchefs.net
Web Site: www.acfchefs.org/educate/eduschlr.html
Summary: To provide financial assistance to students enrolled in culinary programs.
Eligibility: This program is open to students who are currently enrolled full time in a 2- or 4-year culinary program. Applicants must have completed at least 1 grading or marking period and have a career goal of becoming a chef or pastry chef. Selection is based on 2 letters of recommendation, 2 brief essays by the applicants (1 on why they want to become a chef/pastry chef and 1 on what they hope to contribute to the culinary industry), and financial need.
Financial data: The stipend is $1,000.
Duration: 1 year.
Number awarded: 10 each year.
Deadline: June of each year.

1262
AMERICAN BAPTIST MINORITY STUDENT SCHOLARSHIPS

American Baptist Churches USA
Attn: Educational Ministries
P.O. Box 851
Valley Forge, PA 19482-0851
Phone: (610) 768-2067   (800) ABC-3USA, ext. 2067
Fax: (610) 768-2056   E-mail: paula.weiss@abc-usa.org
Web Site: www.abc-em.org/dm/fa.cfm
Summary: To provide financial assistance to minority students at American Baptist-related colleges and universities, particularly for studies in religion and human services.
Eligibility: This program is open to minority students who are freshmen attending a college or university in the United States or Puerto Rico that is affiliated with American Baptist Churches USA. Applicants must be full-time students, U.S. citizens, and members of an American Baptist church for at least 2 year before applying. Preference is given to students preparing for careers in church leadership or human services. Students receiving assistance from other American Baptist scholarship programs are not eligible.
Financial data: The stipend is $1,000 per year. Funds are paid directly to the recipient's school and credited towards tuition.
Duration: 1 year.
Number awarded: Varies each year.
Deadline: May of each year.

1263
AMERICAN BAPTIST UNDERGRADUATE SCHOLARSHIPS

American Baptist Churches USA
Attn: Educational Ministries
P.O. Box 851
Valley Forge, PA 19482-0851
Phone: (610) 768-2067   (800) ABC-3USA, ext. 2067
Fax: (610) 768-2056   E-mail: paula.weiss@abc-usa.org
Web Site: www.abc-em.org/dm/fa.cfm
Summary: To provide financial assistance to undergraduate students at American Baptist-related colleges and universities, particularly for studies in religion and human services.
Eligibility: This program is open to undergraduate students who are attending a college or university in the United States or Puerto Rico that is affiliated with American Baptist Churches USA. Applicants must be full-time students, U.S. citizens, and members of an American Baptist church for at least 2 year before applying. Preference is given to students preparing for careers in church leadership or human services. Students receiving assistance from other American Baptist scholarship programs are not eligible.
Financial data: The stipend is $1,000 per year. Funds are paid directly to the recipient's school and credited towards tuition.
Duration: 1 year; may be renewed.
Number awarded: Varies each year.
Deadline: May of each year.

1264
AMERICAN CULINARY FEDERATION OF CENTRAL VERMONT SCHOLARSHIP

Vermont Student Assistance Corporation
Champlain Mill
P.O. Box 2000
Winooski, VT 05404-2601
Phone: (802) 655-9602   (800) 642-3177
Fax: (802) 654-3765   TDD: (802) 654-3766
Phone: TDD: (800) 281-3341 (within VT)   E-mail: info@vsac.org
Web Site: www.vsac.org
Summary: To provide financial assistance to Vermont residents who are interested in attending a culinary arts program.
Eligibility: This scholarship is available to residents of Vermont who are high school seniors, high school graduates, or the equivalent and who plan to attend a culinary arts programs (e.g., an accredited apprenticeship program, chief training program, or pastry arts program). Applicants must have at least a 3.0 grade point average, be able to document financial need, have applied to the Vermont Student Assistance Corporation for a Vermont Grant, and have filed a Free Application for Federal Student Aid no later than 4 weeks before the scholarship deadline. The following are required as part of the application process: a completed application form, a copy of an acceptance letter from the culinary arts program, a letter of recommendation, a resume, an official transcript, and 5 required essays.
Financial data: The stipend is $1,000 and must be used within 1 year after being awarded.
Duration: 1 year.
Number awarded: 1 or more each year.
Deadline: March of each year.

1265
AMERICAN FOUNDATION FOR TRANSLATION AND INTERPRETATION SCHOLARSHIP PROGRAM

American Foundation for Translation and Interpretation
c/o Western Michigan University
335 Moore Hall
Kalamazoo, MI 49008-5093
Phone: (616) 387-3212   Fax: (616) 387-3103
E-mail: peter.krawutschke@wmich.edu
Web Site: www.afti.org/AFTIawards.htm
Summary: To provide financial assistance to undergraduate and graduate students in translator or interpreter education programs.
Eligibility: This program is open to students enrolled or planning to enroll in graduate or undergraduate programs in translator or interpreter education at accredited U.S. colleges and universities. Applicants must be full-time students who have completed at least 1 year of postsecondary education and have at least 1 year of academic work remaining to complete their program of study. Preference

is given to students in B.A./B.S. or M.A. and Ph.D. granting programs. Applicants may be enrolled in programs either for literary translation or for non-literary translation and interpreter training.

Financial data: The stipend is $2,500.

Duration: 1 year; nonrenewable.

Additional information: This program, established in 2001, is funded by grants from the American Translators Association (ATA) and corporate contributions. Information is also available from the ATA, 225 Reinekers Lane, Suite 590, Alexandria, VA 22314, (703) 683-6100, Fax: (703) 683-6122, E-mail: ata@atanet.org.

Number awarded: 2 each year: 1 to a student in a literary translation program and 1 to a student in a program of non-literary translation or interpreter training.

Deadline: February of each year.

1266
AMERICAN NATIONAL CHOPIN PIANO COMPETITION

Chopin Foundation of the United States, Inc.
1440 John F. Kennedy Causeway, Suite 117
Miami, FL 33141
Phone: (305) 868-0624   Fax: (305) 865-5150
E-mail: info@chopin.org   Web Site: www.chopin.org/competition.html

Summary: To recognize and reward young American pianists for their outstanding performances of Chopin's works.

Eligibility: This competition is open to American citizens (native born or naturalized) who are between the ages of 17 and 28. Most entrants are currently enrolled in college. In the competition, they must play preselected works of Chopin.

Financial data: First prize is $15,000 and 20 concerts arranged by the foundation; second prize is $10,000; third prize is $5,000; fourth prize is $4,000; fifth prize is $3,000; and sixth prize is $2,000. Special awards in the amount of $1,000 are also awarded for best performance of a polonaise, best performance of a mazurka, and best performance of a concerto. The 4 top winners go to Warsaw, Poland (all expenses paid) to compete in the International Chopin Piano Competition.

Duration: The competition is held every 5 years (2005, 2010, etc.).

Additional information: The first competition took place in 1975. The application fee is $65.

Number awarded: 6 prizes and 3 special awards.

Deadline: November of the year prior to the competition.

1267
AMERICAN WATERCOLOR SOCIETY SCHOLARSHIP PROGRAM FOR STUDENTS

American Watercolor Society
Attn: Scholarship Chair
47 Fifth Avenue
New York, NY 10003
E-mail: AWS@watercolor-online.com
Web Site: www.watercolor-online.com/AWS/studentscholarships.html

Summary: To provide financial assistance to art students with interests in watercolor.

Eligibility: This program is open to students enrolled full time at an accredited college or university with a major in fine arts. The applicant's fine arts instructor or department head must verify that the student's primary process of painting is with the use of water based paints on paper surfaces. The application must be accompanied by 6 35mm slides of the student's work. Selection is based on the quality of the work submitted.

Financial data: The stipend is $2,000. Funds are sent directly to the student's college or university.

Duration: 1 year; may be renewed.

Additional information: Further information is available from E. Gordon West, AWS Scholarship Program Chair, 2638 Waterford, San Antonio, TX 78217, E-mail: gojowe@earthlink.net.

Number awarded: Varies each year.

1268
AMERICA'S FIRST FREEDOM STUDENT COMPETITION

Council for America's First Freedom
The Columbian Block Building
1301 East Cary Street, Suite C
Richmond, VA 23219-2111
Phone: (804) 643-1786   Fax: (804) 644-5024
E-mail: caff@erols.com
Web Site: www.firstfreedom.org

Summary: To recognize outstanding essays, posters, and speeches on religious freedom by high school students in Virginia.

Eligibility: This competition is open to high school students in Virginia (including home schoolers) who are interested in competing in poster, essay, or oratory contests dealing with religious freedom. No more than 1 finalist per category can be chosen from any 1 school and no more than 1 finalist per category from any home-schooling region.

Financial data: First-place awards in each category are $1,000; second-place awards in each category are $500.

Duration: The competition is held annually.

Additional information: This competition started in 1991.

Number awarded: 6 each year: 1 first-place winner and 1 second-place winner in each of the 3 categories (posters, essays, and oratory).

Deadline: October of each year.

1269
ANCHORAGE PRESS THEATRE FOR YOUTH PLAYWRITING AWARD

John F. Kennedy Center for the Performing Arts
Education Department
Attn: Kennedy Center American College Theater Festival
2700 F Street, N.W.
Washington, DC 20566
Phone: (202) 416-8857   Fax: (202) 416-8802
E-mail: skshaffer@kennedy-center.org
Web Site: kennedy-center.org/education/actf/actfancr.html

Summary: To reward student authors of plays on themes that appeal to young people.

Eligibility: Students at an accredited junior or senior college in the United States or in countries contiguous to the continental United States are eligible to compete, provided their college agrees to participate in the Kennedy Center American College Theater Festival (KCACTF). Undergraduate students must be carrying a minimum of 6 semester hours, graduate students must be carrying a minimum of 3 semester hours, and continuing part-time students must be enrolled in a regular degree or certificate program. These awards are presented to the best student-written plays based on a theme appealing to young people from kindergarten through grade 12.

Financial data: The prize is $1,000. The winner also receives a $1,250 fellowship to attend the Bonderman IUPUI National Youth Theatre Playwriting Development Workshop and Symposium in Indianapolis. In addition, Anchorage Press publishes the winning play.

Duration: The award is presented annually.

Additional information: This award, first presented in 1997, is supported by the Children's Theatre Foundation of America. It is part of the Michael Kanin Playwriting Awards Program. The sponsoring college or university must pay a registration fee of $250 for each production.

Number awarded: 1 each year.

Deadline: November of each year.

1270
ANDREW M. ECONOMOS SCHOLARSHIP

Broadcast Education Association
Attn: Scholarships
1771 N Street, N.W.
Washington, DC 20036-2891
Phone: (202) 429-5354   E-mail: bea@nab.org
Web Site: www.beaweb.org

Summary: To provide financial assistance to upper-division and graduate students who are interested in preparing for a career in broadcasting.

Eligibility: This program is open to juniors, seniors, and graduate students enrolled full time at a college or university where at least 1 department is an institutional member of the Broadcast Education Association (BEA). Applicants must be interested in studying for a career in radio. Selection is based on evidence that the applicant possesses high integrity, superior academic ability, potential to be an outstanding electronic media professional, and a sense of personal and professional responsibility.

Financial data: The stipend is $5,000.

Duration: 1 year; may not be renewed.

Additional information: Information is also available from Peter B. Orlik, Central Michigan University, 344 Moore Hall, Mt. Pleasant, MI 48859, (517) 774-7279. This program is sponsored by the RCS Charitable Foundation and administered by the BEA.

Number awarded: 1 each year.

Deadline: September of each year.

1271
ANGELUS AWARDS

Angelus Awards Student Film Festival
c/o Family Theater Productions
7201 Sunset Boulevard
Hollywood, CA 90046
Phone: (800) 874-0999   E-mail: info@angelus.org
Web Site: www.angelus.org
Summary: To recognize and reward outstanding student films on themes that "explore the complexity of the human condition."
Eligibility: This program is open to undergraduate and graduate film and video students. Applicants must submit films that reflect the following values: tolerance and respect for diversity in the human community, peacemaking and dialogue in lieu of gratuitous violence, respect for human life instead of its degradation or disposability, equality and dignity in relationships, and hope and the possibility of change over nihilism and despair. All genres (drama, comedy, animation, documentary, and narrative) are accepted. Entries must 1) be in English, have English subtitles, or be dubbed in English; 2) be under 90 minutes in length; 3) have been completed during the previous 2 years while the filmmaker was a student at a recognized educational institute; and 4) be submitted on 1/2 or 3/4 inch VHS (NTSC) for jury screening.
Financial data: More than $10,000 in awards is presented each year. Recent individual awards include the Patrick Peyton Excellence in Filmmaking Award at $2,500, the Mole-Richardson Award for Production Design at $1,500, the outstanding documentary/nonfiction filmmaking award at $1,500, the outstanding animation award at $1,500, and the special recognition award at $1,500.
Duration: The festival is held annually.
Additional information: A $25 fee must accompany each entry.
Number awarded: Varies each year.
Deadline: June of each year.

1272
ANNABELLA DRUMMOND MCMATH SCHOLARSHIP

United Daughters of the Confederacy
Attn: Education Director
328 North Boulevard
Richmond, VA 23220-4057
Phone: (804) 355-1636   Fax: (804) 353-1396
E-mail: hqudc@aol.com
Web Site: www.hqudc.org
Summary: To provide financial assistance for education in liberal arts fields to mature women who are lineal or collateral descendants of Confederate veterans.
Eligibility: Eligible to apply for these scholarships are women over the age of 30 who are lineal or collateral descendants of Confederate soldiers or sailors. Applicants must be enrolled or accepted for enrollment as a graduate or undergraduate student at a college or university in Alabama, Arkansas, Florida, Georgia, Kentucky, Louisiana, Maryland, Mississippi, Missouri, North Carolina, South Carolina, Tennessee, Texas, or Virginia. Their field of study must be the liberal arts, including history, literature, ancient or modern languages, philosophy, or government and political science. Selection is based more on need than academic excellence.
Financial data: Stipends may be awarded in amounts sufficient to cover tuition, books, and scholastic supplies.
Duration: 1 year; may be renewed.
Number awarded: 1 or more each year.
Deadline: May of each year.

1273
ANNE M. GANNETT AWARD FOR VETERANS

National Federation of Music Clubs
1336 North Delaware Street
Indianapolis, IN 46202-2481
Phone: (317) 638-4003   Fax: (317) 638-0503
E-mail: info@nfmc-music.org
Web Site: www.nfmc-music.org/annual_senior_div.htm
Summary: To provide financial assistance for the undergraduate education of members of the National Federation of Music Clubs (NFMC) whose careers have been delayed or interrupted as a result of their service in the U.S. armed forces.
Eligibility: Eligible to apply are undergraduate students who are majoring in music and whose musical careers were interrupted by military service. Student membership in the federation and U.S. citizenship are required.
Financial data: This award is $1,250.
Duration: 1 year.
Additional information: Applications and further information are also available from Mrs. Joe Ince, 723 St. Francis, Gonzales, TX 78629-3530, (210) 672-3757; information on all federation scholarships is available from Chair, Competitions and Awards Board, Mrs. Lamoine M. Hall, Jr., 4137 Whitfield Avenue, Fort Worth, TX 76109-5432.
Number awarded: 1 each year.
Deadline: February of each year.

1274
ANNE SEAMAN MEMORIAL SCHOLARSHIP

Professional Grounds Management Society
720 Light Street
Baltimore, MD 21230-3816
Phone: (410) 223-2861   (800) 609-PGMS
Fax: (410) 752-8295   E-mail: pgms@assnhqtrs.com
Web Site: www.pgms.org
Summary: To provide financial assistance for the postsecondary education of students in fields related to grounds management.
Eligibility: Applicants must be studying landscape and grounds management, turf management, irrigation technology, or a closely-related field. They must submit a cover letter describing educational and professional goals and intended use of the scholarship funds; a resume listing past employment, awards, and certificates; college or school transcripts; and 2 letters of recommendation. A member of the Professional Grounds Management Society must sponsor each applicant. Financial need is considered in the selection process.
Financial data: Amount of the scholarship varies each year.
Number awarded: 1 or more each year.
Deadline: June of each year.

1275
ARCHIBALD RUTLEDGE SCHOLARSHIP COMPETITION

State Department of Education
1429 Senate Street, Room 1010A
Columbia, SC 29201
Phone: (803) 734-8485   E-mail: sspade@sde.state.sc.us
Web Site: www.sde.state.sc.us/archive/students/rutledge.htm
Summary: To recognize and reward high school seniors in South Carolina who participate in a competition in art, creative writing, drama, or music.
Eligibility: This program is open to high school seniors in South Carolina public schools who are planning to attend a South Carolina college or university. Applicants compete by submitting samples of their work in 1 of 4 areas: 1) art, limited to 2-dimensional work such as drawing and painting media, printmaking, and collage; no 3-dimensional work or photographs are accepted; 2) creative writing, as a sonnet, lyric, or narrative poem, up to 1 page; 3) drama, a 1-act play with a performing time of 20 to 45 minutes; or 4) music, a composition of 3 to 5 minutes for solo or small ensemble, vocal or instrumental, any appropriate style. In addition to the work, they must submit a process folio that contains documentation of the planning and development of the project and a 1-page reflection statement addressing the intent of the work and comparing the final product with the original concept. A panel of professionals in the field selects up to 10 finalists, based on originality, creativity, and the correlation and implications of the process folio for the final composition. Finalists must attend the scholarship competition, at which they present a portfolio of a number of selected works as specified by the judges.
Financial data: The award consists of a $5,000 scholarship, to be used for tuition, room, board, and instructional resource expenses.
Duration: 1 year.
Number awarded: 4 each year: 1 in each of the 4 categories.
Deadline: January of each year.

1276
ARMED SERVICES YMCA ANNUAL ESSAY CONTEST

Armed Services YMCA
6225 Brandon Avenue, Suite 215
Springfield, VA 22150-2510
Phone: (703) 866-1260, ext. 16   E-mail: essaycontest@asymca.org
Web Site: www.asymca.org
Summary: To recognize and reward outstanding essays by children of armed service personnel.
Eligibility: This program is open to children, from pre-school through high school, of the uniformed services (active duty, Reserve, Guard, and retired) and civilian (DoD, Coast Guard, and American Mission) families. Applicants in grades 8 and below should submit entries of 300 words or less on why the library is their favorite hangout, why reading is their favorite thing to do, what's their favorite book and why, who's their favorite author and why, or a topic of their own choice. Applicants in grades 9 through 12 should submit entries, 500 words or less, that are creative essays, poetry, stories, or news articles.
Financial data: For grades through 8, first prize is a $500 savings bond and second prize is a $100 savings bond. For grades 9 through 12, first prize is a $1,000 savings bond, second prize is a $500 savings bond, and honorable mention is a $100 savings bond.
Duration: The contest is held annually.
Additional information: This program, established in 1997, is cosponsored by the Armed Services YMCA and the United States Naval Institute.
Number awarded: A total of 14 prizes are awarded each year. A first prize and a second prize are awarded for 7 categories: pre-school and kindergarten, first and second grade, third and fourth grade, fifth and sixth grade, seventh and eighth grade, and high school. An additional 4 honorable mentions are awarded at the high school level.
Deadline: April of each year.

1277
ART MERIT AWARDS

American Foreign Service Association
2101 E Street, N.W.
Washington, DC 20037
Phone: (202) 338-4045   (800) 704-AFSA
Fax: (202) 338-6820   E-mail: scholar@afsa.org
Web Site: www.afsa.org
Summary: To provide financial assistance for education in the arts to dependents of U.S. government employees involved in foreign service activities.
Eligibility: Applicants must be graduating high school seniors who are who are dependents of foreign service employees in the Department of State, the Commerce Service, the Foreign Agriculture Service, or the Agency for International Development. The parent may be active, retired with pension, or deceased but must have served at least 1 year abroad and must be a member of the American Foreign Service Association (AFSA) or the Associates of the American Foreign Service Worldwide (AAFSW). The student must demonstrate extraordinary talent in the field of visual arts, musical arts, dance, drama, or creative writing.
Financial data: Winners receive $1,700 per year and honorable mentions win $500.
Duration: 1 year; may be renewed.
Number awarded: Varies each year; recently, the program selected 1 winner and no honorable mention.
Deadline: February of each year.

1278
ARTS AND SCIENCES AWARDS

Alexander Graham Bell Association for the Deaf
Attn: Financial Aid Coordinator
3417 Volta Place, N.W.
Washington, DC 20007-2778
Phone: (202) 337-5220   Fax: (202) 337-8314
Phone: TTY: (202) 337-5221   E-mail: financialaid@agbell.org
Web Site: www.agbell.org/financialaid/agbell_programs.cfm
Summary: To provide financial aid to hearing impaired students who are participating in extracurricular activities in arts and sciences.
Eligibility: Applicants must be diagnosed as having a moderate to profound hearing loss (55 dB or greater loss in the better ear in the speech frequencies of 500, 1000, and 2000 Hz) and must use speech, residual hearing, and/or speechreading as

their primary form of communication. They must be between 6 and 19 years of age and enrolled in an art or science program as an extracurricular activity, such as those sponsored by a museum, nature center, art center, zoological park, or dance or music school. Programs that offer academic credit, travel or study abroad, recreational summer camps, sports or sport camps, figure skating, or gymnastics are not eligible.
Financial data: The amount of the award varies, depending upon the cost of the program in which the recipient is enrolled.
Duration: 1 year; may be renewed upon reapplication.
Number awarded: Varies each year.
Deadline: Applications must be requested between December and February of each year and submitted by May of each year.

1279
ARTS COMPETITION SCHOLARSHIPS

National Foundation for Advancement in the Arts
800 Brickell Avenue, Suite 500
Miami, FL 33131
Phone: (305) 377-1140   (800) 970-ARTS
Fax: (305) 377-1149   E-mail: ARTSawards@ARTSawards.org
Web Site: www.ARTSawards.org
Summary: To recognize and reward outstanding high school students in the arts.
Eligibility: Applicants must be U.S. citizens or permanent residents who are graduating high school seniors, or, if not enrolled in high school, are 17 or 18 years old. Applicants may enter competitions in dance, film and video, instrumental music, jazz, photography, theater, visual arts, voice, or writing by submitting samples of their work, as videotape, audiotape, or portfolios. On the basis of the tapes or portfolios, award winners are invited to Miami for the final competitions. Artists with physical or other disabilities are encouraged to apply; appropriate adjustments are made to accommodate the needs of the physically challenged.
Financial data: First-level awards are $3,000 each, second level $1,500, third level $1,000, fourth level $500, and fifth level $100; honorable mention recipients receive $100 awards but are not invited to Miami.
Duration: The competition is held annually.
Additional information: ARTS (Arts Recognition and Talent Search) is sponsored by the National Foundation for Advancement in the Arts which is funded by many corporations, foundations, and individuals. The names of all ARTS applicants are provided to 100 participating colleges, universities, and professional institutions, which have $3 million in scholarships available for ARTS participants. The application fee is $25 for early applications and $35 for regular applications.
Number awarded: Up to 125 award candidates compete in Miami (20 in dance, 5 in film and video, 20 in instrumental music, 5 in jazz, 5 in photography, 20 in theater, 20 in visual arts, 10 in voice, and 20 in writing); an unlimited number of honorable mention awards are made to candidates who are not invited to Miami.
Deadline: Early applications must be submitted by May of each year; regular applications are due by September of each year.

1280
ASSOCIATED LANDSCAPE CONTRACTORS OF AMERICA EDUCATIONAL FOUNDATION SCHOLARSHIP

Associated Landscape Contractors of America
Attn: Educational Foundation
150 Elden Street, Suite 270
Herndon, VA 20170
Phone: (703) 736-9666   (800) 395-ALCA
Fax: (703) 736-9668
Web Site: www.alca.org
Summary: To provide financial assistance to students at colleges and universities that have a connection to the Associated Landscape Contractors of America (ALCA).
Eligibility: This program is open to students at colleges and universities that 1) have an accredited ALCA landscape contracting curriculum, 2) have an ALCA student chapter, and/or 3) participate in ALCA student career days activities. Applicants must provide information on awards, honors, and scholarships received in high school or college; high school, college, and community activities related to horticulture; ALCA events attended; work experience; and brief essays on what they have learned about financial management as part of their education that will help them in their career, how their landscape industry related curriculum has helped them in achieving their career goals, the kind of training and work experience they will complete to attain their goals, their plan to attain more

leadership and human relations skills, their reasons for desiring the scholarship, their career objectives as they relate to the field of landscape contracting and horticulture, and where they see their career 5 years after graduation.
Financial data: A stipend is awarded (exact amount not specified).
Duration: 1 year.
Number awarded: 1 or more each year.
Deadline: January of each year.

1281
ASSOCIATION FOR WOMEN IN ARCHITECTURE SCHOLARSHIPS

Association for Women in Architecture
2550 Beverly Boulevard
Los Angeles, CA 90057
Phone: (213) 389-6490
Web Site: www.awa-la.org
Summary: To provide financial assistance to women undergraduates in California who are interested in careers in architecture.
Eligibility: Eligible to apply are women students who have completed at least 1 full year of study in any of the following fields: architecture; civil, structural, mechanical, or electrical engineering as related to architecture; landscape architecture; urban and land planning; interior design; architectural rendering and illustration; or environmental design. They must be residents of California or attending school in California. Interviews are required for semifinalists. Selection is based on grades, a personal statement, financial need, recommendations, and the quality and organization of materials submitted.
Financial data: Stipends are $2,500, $1,500, or $1,000.
Duration: 1 year.
Number awarded: 4 each year: 1 at $2,500, 1 at $1,500, and 2 at $1,000.
Deadline: April of each year.

1282
ASSOCIATION FOR WOMEN IN SPORTS MEDIA SCHOLARSHIPS

Association for Women in Sports Media
P.O. Box 726
Farmington, CT 06034-0726
Web Site: www.awsmonline.org/scholarship.htm
Summary: To provide financial assistance to women undergraduate and graduate students who are interested in pursuing a career in sportswriting.
Eligibility: This program is open to women who are enrolled in college or graduate school full time and plan to pursue a career in sportswriting, sports copy editing, sports broadcasting, or sports public relations. Entrants are required to submit a letter explaining why they are interested in a career in sports journalism, a resume highlighting their journalism experience, a letter of recommendation, up to 5 samples of their work, and a $5 application fee.
Financial data: The stipend is $1,000.
Duration: 1 year; nonrenewable.
Additional information: Information is also available from Stefanie Krasnow, Senior Editor, *Sports Illustrated*, 135 West 50th Street, Fourth Floor, New York, NY 10020-1393, (212) 522-3124, Fax: (212) 522-1001, E-mail: stefanie_krasnow@simail.com.
Number awarded: 4 each year: 1 each in writing, copy editing, public relations, and television.
Deadline: October of each year.

1283
ASSOCIATION FOR WOMEN JOURNALISTS SCHOLARSHIP FOR WOMEN

Association for Women Journalists
P.O. Box 2199
Fort Worth, TX 76113
Phone: (214) 740-9251   E-mail: ssprague@kera.org
Web Site: www.awjdfw.org/scholarships2.asp
Summary: To provide financial assistance to women studying journalism at a college or university in Texas.
Eligibility: This program is open to full-time juniors and seniors at colleges and universities in Texas. Applicants must be majoring in print or broadcast journalism and have a grade point average of 2.5 or higher in their major. They must submit 3 samples of their print or broadcast work, a letter of recommendation from an instructor or adviser, a statement of professional goals

and how the scholarship will help, and a statement of financial need (if that is to be considered).
Financial data: A stipend is awarded (exact amount not specified). Funds are paid directly to the college or university to be applied to tuition.
Duration: 1 year.
Number awarded: 1 or more each year.
Deadline: February of each year.

1284
ATLANTA PRESS CLUB JOURNALISM SCHOLARSHIP AWARD

Atlanta Press Club, Inc.
260 14th Street, N.W., Suite 300
Atlanta, GA 30318
Phone: (404) 577-7377   Fax: (404) 892-2637
Web Site: www.atlpressclub.org
Summary: To provide financial assistance to college students majoring in journalism at a Georgia college or university.
Eligibility: Students currently enrolled in journalism at a college or university in Georgia at the freshmen, sophomore, or junior level are eligible to apply for this award. Selection is based on skill, achievement, and commitment to journalism. Financial need is not considered in the selection process. A personal interview may be required.
Financial data: The stipend is $1,000; nonrenewable.
Duration: 1 year.
Additional information: The broadcast awards are sponsored by WXIA-TV, Channel 11 and WAGA-TV, Fox 5 (this 1 must go to an outstanding student from the Atlanta University complex).
Number awarded: 4 each year: 2 to print journalism students and 2 to broadcast journalism students.
Deadline: February of each year.

1285
ATLAS SHRUGGED ESSAY CONTEST

Ayn Rand Institute
Attn: Contests Manager
4640 Admiralty Way, Suite 406
Marina del Rey, CA 90292-6617
Phone: (310) 306-9232, ext. 209   Fax: (310) 306-4925
E-mail: seans@aynrand.org
Web Site: www.aynrand.org
Summary: To recognize and reward outstanding essays written by college students on Ayn Rand's novel, *Atlas Shrugged*.
Eligibility: Entrants must be enrolled full time in an undergraduate degree program. They must submit a typewritten essay on Ayn Rand's novel, *Atlas Shrugged*. The essay must be between 1,000 and 1,200 words. Selection is based on style and content. Judges look for writing that is clear, articulate, and logically organized. To win, an essay must demonstrate an outstanding grasp of the philosophical and psychological meaning of the novel.
Financial data: First prize is $5,000; second prizes are $1,000; third prizes are $400.
Duration: The competition is held annually.
Additional information: This competition began in the academic year 1998-99.
Number awarded: 9 each year: 1 first prize, 3 second prizes, and 5 third prizes.
Deadline: February of each year.

1286
A.W. PERIGARD FUND SCHOLARSHIP

Society of Satellite Professionals International
Attn: Scholarship Program
225 Reinekers Lane, Suite 600
Alexandria, VA 22314
Phone: (703) 549-8696   Fax: (703) 549-9728
E-mail: sspi@sspi.org
Web Site: www.sspi.org
Summary: To provide financial assistance to students interested in majoring in satellite-related disciplines in college.
Eligibility: This program is open to high school seniors, college undergraduates, and graduate students majoring or planning to major in fields related to satellite communications, including broadcasting, business, communications, engineering, international policy studies, journalism, law, science, space applications, or telecommunications. Applicants may be from any country. Selection is based on academic and leadership achievement, commitment to pursue education and

career opportunities in the satellite communications industry, potential for significant contribution to that industry, a personal statement of 500 to 750 words on interest in satellite communications and why the applicant deserves the award, and a creative work (such as a research report, essay, article, videotape, artwork, computer program, or scale model of an antenna or spacecraft design) that reflects the applicant's interests and talents. Financial need is also considered.

Financial data: The stipend is $2,000.
Duration: 1 year.
Number awarded: 1 each year.
Deadline: June of each year.

1287
AWARD TO HONOR EXCELLENCE IN NEWSPAPER ADVERTISING (ATHENA)

Newspaper Association of America
Attn: Manager, Public Relations
1921 Gallows Road, Suite 600
Vienna, VA 22182-3900
Phone: (703) 902-1698   Fax: (703) 902-1699
E-mail: brouz@naa.org
Web Site: www.naa.org
Summary: To recognize and reward outstanding creative advertisements in the newspaper industry.
Eligibility: Entries must be published in a newspaper for the first time during the preceding calendar year. They may be submitted by agencies, clients, printing companies, and/or newspapers. Nominations may be made in any of 10 categories: automotive, beverage, business products and services, entertainment, financial, health care products and services, leisure and travel, media, public service, and student ads.
Financial data: The grand prize is $100,000; the student ad prize is $5,000. Gold, silver, and bronze medals are also awarded.
Duration: The competition is held annually.
Additional information: This program was revived in 1997 after a prolonged hiatus. An entry fee of $65 ($20 for students) must accompany each submission.
Number awarded: Varies each year; recently, 50 prizes were awarded, including 1 grand prize, 1 student prize, 9 gold awards, 13 silver awards, and 26 bronze awards (of which 7 were in the student division).
Deadline: April of each year.

1288
BACH ORGAN AND KEYBOARD MUSIC SCHOLARSHIP

Rhode Island Foundation
Attn: Scholarship Coordinator
One Union Station
Providence, RI 02903
Phone: (401) 274-4564   Fax: (401) 331-8085
E-mail: libbym@rifoundation.org
Web Site: www.rifoundation.org
Summary: To provide financial assistance to students in Rhode Island who demonstrate ability in playing the organ or other keyboard instrument and to church organists.
Eligibility: This program is open to music majors specializing in organ or piano in pursuit of a college degree. They must be Rhode Island residents and church organists who are a member of the American Guild of Organists (AGO). They must submit a letter of reference from their organ/keyboard teacher or church official and an essay (up to 300 words) on what they hope they will be doing in their professional life 10 years from now. Financial need is considered in the selection process.
Financial data: Stipends range from $300 to $1,000.
Number awarded: 1 to 3 each year.
Deadline: June of each year.

1289
BAF SATELLITE & TECHNOLOGY SCHOLARSHIP

Society of Satellite Professionals International
Attn: Scholarship Program
225 Reinekers Lane, Suite 600
Alexandria, VA 22314
Phone: (703) 549-8696   Fax: (703) 549-9728
E-mail: sspi@sspi.org
Web Site: www.sspi.org
Summary: To provide financial assistance to students interested in majoring in satellite-related disciplines in college.

Eligibility: This program is open to high school seniors, college undergraduates, and graduate students majoring or planning to major in fields related to satellite communications, including broadcasting, business, communications, engineering, international policy studies, journalism, law, science, space applications, or telecommunications. Applicants may be from any country. Selection is based on academic and leadership achievement, commitment to pursue education and career opportunities in the satellite communications industry, potential for significant contribution to that industry, a personal statement of 500 to 750 words on interest in satellite communications and why the applicant deserves the award, and a creative work (such as a research report, essay, article, videotape, artwork, computer program, or scale model of an antenna or spacecraft design) that reflects the applicant's interests and talents. Financial need is not considered.
Financial data: The stipend is $2,500.
Duration: 1 year.
Number awarded: 1 each year.
Deadline: June of each year.

1290
BANK OF AMERICA ACHIEVEMENT AWARDS

Bank of America Foundation
Attn: Achievement Awards Program
CAS-704-08-03
314 Montgomery Street, Eighth Floor
San Francisco, CA 94104-1866
Phone: (415) 953-0927   Fax: (415) 622-3469
E-mail: judy.d.granucci-tufo@bankofamerica.com
Web Site: www.bankofamerica.com/foundation
Summary: To recognize and reward outstanding high school seniors in California.
Eligibility: Eligible are high school seniors in California who are chosen by faculty committees in their schools. The committees select students to receive certificates in specific study areas (agriculture, art, business, communications, computer studies, drama, English, English as a Second Language, foreign language, history, home economics, mathematics, music, religious studies, science, social science, and trades and industrial studies). Small high schools (those with 199 or fewer students in grades 10-12) may award a total of 7 certificates and large high schools (those with 200 or more students) present a total of 14 certificates. In addition, the faculty committees select graduating seniors to receive plaques in 4 general study areas (applied arts, fine arts, liberal arts, and science and mathematics); certificate winners may not also receive plaques; the number of plaques awarded by each high school also depends on the size of the school (2 plaques with enrollment of 1 to 199 students in grades 10 through 12, 3 plaques with 200 to 599 students, and 4 plaques for schools with more than 600 students). Winners of plaques are then eligible to enter the Achievement Awards competition. Of all plaque winners statewide, 320 finalists (8 in each of 10 regions in each of the 4 general study areas) are selected to enter competitions involving 1) an essay judged on written expression, logical progression, ability to focus on topic, and creative interpretation, and 2) a group discussion judged on cooperation, sound and logical thinking, oral communication and command of English, and originality of thought.
Financial data: The cash awards are $2,000 for first-place winners, $1,500 for second-place winners, $1,000 for third-place winners, and $500 for fourth-place winners.
Number awarded: All 320 finalists receive cash awards; the top 40 finalists (1 in each general study area in each region) receive first-place awards and other finalists receive awards depending on their scores in the competition.
Deadline: Schools must select their plaque recipients before the end of January of each year.

1291
BENJAMIN C. BLACKBURN SCHOLARSHIP

Friends of the Frelinghuysen Arboretum
Attn: Scholarship Chair
P.O. Box 1295
Morristown, NJ 07962-1295
Phone: (973) 326-7603   Fax: (973) 644-9627
Summary: To provide financial assistance to residents of New Jersey who are working on an undergraduate or graduate degree in horticulture, landscape architecture, or related fields.
Eligibility: This program is open to New Jersey residents who are working on an undergraduate or graduate degree in 1 of the following: horticulture, botany, landscape architecture, or a related field. Undergraduates must have completed at

least 24 college credits. The following are required to apply: a completed application form, transcripts from all colleges attended, 2 professors' recommendations, and 2 community recommendations. Financial need is not considered in the selection process.

Financial data: The stipend is $2,500.

Duration: 1 year.

Number awarded: 2 each year.

Deadline: April of each year.

1292
BERTHA MACDONALD SCHOLARSHIP

St. Andrew's Society of New Hampshire
c/o Karol C. Gooch
276 Haley Road
Kittery, ME 03904
E-mail: sasnh@lochdhu.com
Web Site: www.lochdhu.com/sasnh/schlrshp.htm

Summary: To provide financial assistance for study and training to students (of any age) of the Scottish performing arts.

Eligibility: Students of the Scottish performing arts (music, dancing, piping, fiddling, clarsach, drumming, and song) are eligible to apply. Preference is given to applicants from New England. All applicants must have at least 2 years of experience in their specialty. They must be seeking additional training (school, workshop, lessons). A recommendation from their current teacher is required (no application without this letter will be considered); the letter should address the applicant's skill level, progress made this year, commitment, demonstrated proficiency, and anticipated development. Selection is based on the applicant's objectives, commitment, demonstrated proficiency, anticipated development, and future goals.

Financial data: The amount of the stipend varies, depending upon the scope of training requested. Grants are sent directly to the recipient's school and must be returned if the student does not attend.

Duration: 1 year.

Additional information: Academic and arts/crafts scholarships are not provided.

Deadline: March of each year.

1293
BESS MYERSON CAMPUS JOURNALISM AWARDS

Anti-Defamation League
Attn: Department of Campus Affairs/Higher Education
823 United Nations Plaza
New York, NY 10017
Phone: (212) 885-7813   Fax: (212) 867-0779
E-mail: rossj@adl.org
Web Site: www.adl.org

Summary: To recognize and reward outstanding college newspaper articles written by undergraduate or graduate students on issues of racial, ethnic, and religious tolerance, cultural differences, or communications between peoples of diverse backgrounds.

Eligibility: This competition is open to all recognized campus newspapers at colleges and universities throughout the United States. Articles must be submitted by the newspaper (no more than 1 entry in each of the 2 categories listed below) and must have been written by enrolled undergraduate or graduate students. To be eligible, entries should address 1 of the following issues: anti-Semitism, racism, or bigotry; coverage of issues in the Middle East; countering Holocaust denial; responding to the challenge of extremist speakers; community responses to hate crimes; or intergroup relations between ethnic, racial, or religious groups. Articles may deal with issues of campus, local, national, and international concerns. There are 2 separate award categories: 1) news reporting and features; and 2) editorials and opinions (including editorial cartoons). Individual articles and editorials, as well as series of articles and/or editorials on a particular subject, will be considered. If a series of writings is submitted, the series will be evaluated in its entirety as a single entity. All entries must have been published during the preceding academic year.

Financial data: Prizes are awarded in each of the 2 categories listed above: first prize: $1,000; second prize: $750; third prize: $600. Awards are to be shared equally between the newspapers and the author(s) of the article(s).

Duration: The competition is held annually.

Additional information: This award was established by Bess Myerson, the first Jewish woman to be awarded the title of Miss America.

Number awarded: 6 each year: 3 in each of the 2 award categories.

Deadline: February of each year.

1294
BEV SELLERS MEMORIAL SCHOLARSHIP

Young Singers Foundation
P.O. Box 470168
Tulsa, OK 74147-0168
Phone: (918) 622-1444   (800) 992-7464
Fax: (918) 665-0894   E-mail: Michelle@sweetadelineintl.org

Summary: To provide financial assistance to college students majoring or minoring in vocal music.

Eligibility: This program is open to students who have completed at least 1 year of college, are enrolled full time, are working on a degree with a major or minor in vocal music (performance or education), and have at least a 3.5 grade point average in vocal music classes.

Financial data: The stipend is $1,000.

Duration: 1 year.

Number awarded: 1 or more each year.

1295
BLOSSOM KALAMA EVANS MEMORIAL SCHOLARSHIPS

Hawai'i Community Foundation
900 Fort Street Mall, Suite 1300
Honolulu, HI 96813
Phone: (808) 566-5570   (888) 731-3863
Fax: (808) 521-6286   E-mail: scholarships@hcf-hawaii.org
Web Site: www.hcf-hawaii.org

Summary: To provide financial assistance to Hawaiians who are interested in majoring in 1) Hawaiian language or 2) Hawaiian studies.

Eligibility: Eligible to apply are residents of Hawaii who are full-time juniors, seniors, or graduate students majoring in either Hawaiian studies or Hawaiian language. Applicants must demonstrate financial need and academic achievement (at least a 2.7 grade point average). Preference is given to applicants of Hawaiian ancestry. Applicants must write an essay describing their interests and goals in pursuing Hawaiian studies or language and how they plan to use their studies to contribute to the community. Members of the Hawaiian Girls Golf Association are not eligible.

Financial data: The amounts of the awards depend on the availability of funds and the need of the recipient; recently, grants averaged $1,500.

Duration: 1 year.

Number awarded: Varies each year; recently, 5 of these scholarships were awarded.

Deadline: February of each year.

1296
BLOUNT YOUNG ARTISTS CONCERTO COMPETITION

Montgomery Symphony Orchestra
Attn: Young Artists Concerto Competition Committee
P.O. Box 1864
Montgomery, AL 36102
Phone: (334) 240-4004

Summary: To recognize and reward talented young musicians from southern states.

Eligibility: This competition is open to musicians in junior and senior high school who reside in and attend school in Alabama, Florida, Georgia, Kentucky, Louisiana, Mississippi, North Carolina, South Carolina, Tennessee, and Virginia. Students of strings, winds, brass, percussion, and piano are eligible to enter. Acceptable music for the competition includes 1 movement from any work in the standard concerto repertoire. Memorization is preferred but not required.

Financial data: First prize is $2,500 in cash, a $7,500 scholarship (to pay for music education at any institution of higher learning, summer music festival, seminar, etc.), and the opportunity to perform with the Montgomery Symphony Orchestra. Second prize is $4,000; third prize is $1,000; fourth prize is $500; and merit prizes are $250. The second- through fourth-place winners perform at the Young Artists recital.

Duration: The competition is held annually.

Additional information: This program is jointly sponsored by the Montgomery Symphony Orchestra and the Blount Foundation. Arrangements for accompanists are the responsibility of each entrant. The competition is not open to the public, but the public is invited to attend an awards ceremony at the end of the day. Winners must be available for rehearsals and publicity.

Number awarded: 8 cash prizes (including 4 merit prizes) and 1 scholarship are awarded each year.

Deadline: January of each year.

1297
BOB BAXTER SCHOLARSHIP

Bob Baxter Scholarship Foundation
c/o Jean-Rae Turner
P.O. Box 241
Elizabeth, NJ 07207-0241
Phone: (973) 923-7156
Summary: To provide financial assistance to high school seniors and college students in New Jersey who are interested in preparing for a career in press photography.
Eligibility: Applicants must be residents of New Jersey and attend or plan to attend a school of photography. They may be high school seniors or college freshmen, sophomores, or juniors. Applicants must submit a portfolio showing a cross-section of their work: news, sports, feature (human interest), scenic, portraits, etc. The photographs may be in color or black-and-white. If applicants have published in school newspapers, they are encouraged to include copies.
Financial data: The stipend is either $2,000 or $1,000.
Duration: 1 year.
Additional information: This program was established in 1980 by Bob Baxter, then in the U.S. Veterans' Hospital in East Orange, New Jersey.
Number awarded: 1 each year.
Deadline: April of each year.

1298
BOB EAST SCHOLARSHIP

National Press Photographers Foundation
3200 Croasdaile Drive, Suite 306
Durham, NC 27705-2586
Phone: (919) 383-7246   (800) 289-6772
Fax: (919) 383-7261   E-mail: info@nppa.org
Web Site: www.nppa.org
Summary: To provide financial assistance to college photojournalists who are interested in continuing college or going to graduate school.
Eligibility: Applicants must be either undergraduates in the first 3 and a half years of college or planning to pursue graduate work. Eligible students must give evidence of photographic aptitude and academic ability, be able to demonstrate financial need, and submit at least 5 single images in addition to a picture story.
Financial data: The stipend is $1,000.
Duration: 1 year.
Additional information: Recipients may attend a school in the United States or Canada. Further information is available from Chuck Fadely, *The Miami Herald*, One Herald Plaza, Miami, FL 33132, (305) 376-2015. The scholarship must be used at the beginning of the next semester or it will be forfeited and given to an alternate.
Number awarded: 1 each year.
Deadline: February of each year.

1299
BOB EDDY SCHOLARSHIP PROGRAM

Connecticut Society of Professional Journalists Foundation, Inc.
Attn: Scholarship Committee
71 Kenwood Avenue
Fairfield, CT 06430
Phone: (203) 255-2127   Fax: (203) 255-2127
E-mail: DEstock963@aol.com
Web Site: www.ctspj.org
Summary: To provide financial assistance to upper-division students residing or studying in Connecticut who are interested in preparing for a career in journalism.
Eligibility: This program is open to juniors or seniors who are either Connecticut residents (may attend school in any state) or from other states enrolled in a 4-year college or university in Connecticut. All applicants must be preparing for a career in journalism, provide registrar-signed transcripts of all academic courses, fill out an application form, submit writing samples, tapes, or related work in any media that shows an interest and competency in journalism, and write a 500-word essay on why they want to become a journalist. Financial need must be demonstrated.
Financial data: Stipends are $2,500, $1,500, $1,000, or $500.
Duration: 1 year.
Number awarded: 4 each year: 1 at $2,500, 1 at $1,500, 1 at $1,000, and 1 at $500.
Deadline: April of each year.

1300
BOBBI MCCALLUM MEMORIAL SCHOLARSHIP

Seattle Post-Intelligencer
Attn: Assistant Managing Editor
101 Elliott Avenue West
Seattle, WA 98119-4220
Phone: (206) 448-8316   E-mail: janetgrimley@seattlepi.com
Web Site: www.seattlepi.com
Summary: To provide financial assistance to women college students in Washington who are interested in pursuing a career in journalism.
Eligibility: This program is open to women journalism majors entering their junior or senior year at any university in the state of Washington. Graduating community college students transferring to a 4-year school are also eligible. Attached to each application must be 5 examples of news writing (published or unpublished). Selection is based on need, talent, and motivation to pursue a career in print journalism.
Financial data: The stipend is $1,000.
Duration: The scholarship is offered annually.
Additional information: This scholarship was established in 1970 by the late Dr. Walter Scott Brown in memory of Bobbi McCallum, a prizewinning reporter and columnist for the *Seattle Post-Intelligencer* who died in 1969 at age 25 while a patient of Dr. Brown. The scholarship is administered by the newspaper and the Seattle Foundation.
Number awarded: 1 each year.
Deadline: March of each year.

1301
BOOKS CHANGE LIVES ESSAY CONTEST

North Texas Association of Phi Beta Kappa
P.O. Box 12341
Dallas, TX 75225
Phone: (972) 669-5041   E-mail: mthorn2805@aol.com
Web Site: www.geocities.com/Athens/Ithaca/3799
Summary: To recognize and reward outstanding essays written by high school juniors in Texas on their favorite books.
Eligibility: This competition is open to high school juniors in selected school districts in Texas (schools and districts change from year to year). To enter, students must choose a book that has been important to them and write an essay (up to 750 words) telling how the book affected them, gave them new insight, or otherwise changed their life.
Financial data: The winners receive a $1,000 Evelyn Oppenheimer Scholarship. Funds are paid directly to the recipient's college.
Duration: The competition is held annually.
Additional information: The scholarship lapses if the winner does not enroll in college by the fall of the academic year following high school graduation.
Number awarded: 2 or more each year.
Deadline: February of each year.

1302
BROADCAST CABLE FINANCIAL MANAGEMENT ASSOCIATION SCHOLARSHIP

Broadcast Cable Financial Management Association
701 Lee Street, Suite 640
Des Plaines, Il 60016
Phone: (847) 296-0200   Fax: (847) 296-7510
Web Site: www.bcfm.com
Summary: To provide financial assistance to members of the Broadcast Cable Financial Management Association who are interested in working on an undergraduate or graduate degree.
Eligibility: All fully-paid members in good standing are eligible to apply for the scholarship. They must be interested in working on an undergraduate or graduate degree at an accredited college or university that has some relevance to their current job and/or to the broadcast or cable industries. To apply, individuals must submit an application, attach a current resume, include 2 letters of reference, and submit a 1-page essay that addresses the following: their current job responsibilities, the courses they intend to take, and a description of their career goals.
Financial data: The stipend is generally $1,000; a total of $5,000 is distributed annually.
Duration: 1 year; may be renewed.
Number awarded: 1 or more each year.
Deadline: April of each year.

1303
BROADCAST EDUCATION ASSOCIATION 2-YEAR/COMMUNITY COLLEGE AWARD

Broadcast Education Association
Attn: Scholarships
1771 N Street, N.W.
Washington, DC 20036-2891
Phone: (202) 429-5354   E-mail: bea@nab.org
Web Site: www.beaweb.org
Summary: To provide financial assistance to community college students who are interested in preparing for a career in broadcasting.
Eligibility: This program is open to students enrolled full time at a community college where at least 1 department is an institutional member of the Broadcast Education Association. Applicants must be studying for a career in broadcasting. Selection is based on evidence that the applicant possesses high integrity, superior academic ability, potential to be an outstanding electronic media professional, and a sense of personal and professional responsibility.
Financial data: The stipend is $1,500.
Duration: 1 year; may not be renewed.
Additional information: Information is also available from Peter B. Orlik, Central Michigan University, 344 Moore Hall, Mt. Pleasant, MI 48859, (517) 774-7279.
Number awarded: 2 each year.
Deadline: September of each year.

1304
BROADCAST JOURNALISM SCHOLARSHIPS

Native American Journalists Association
Attn: College Scholarships
3359 36th Avenue South
Minneapolis, MN 55406
Phone: (612) 729-9244   Fax: (612) 729-9373
E-mail: najaeducation@aol.com
Web Site: www.naja.com
Summary: To provide financial assistance to student members of the Native American Journalists Association (NAJA) who are interested in a career in broadcast journalism.
Eligibility: This program is open to NAJA members pursuing a degree in broadcast journalism. Applications must include proof of enrollment in a federal or state recognized tribe, work samples, transcripts, a personal statement that demonstrates financial need and the student's reasons for pursuing a career in journalism, and a letter of recommendation from an academic advisor or a member of the community that attests to the applicant's ability to complete the desired education.
Financial data: The stipends are $2,500.
Duration: 1 year.
Number awarded: 2 to 4 each year.
Deadline: June of each year.

1305
BROADCAST MUSIC INC. STUDENT COMPOSER AWARDS

Broadcast Music Inc.
Attn: BMI Foundation
320 West 57th Street
New York, NY 10019-3790
Phone: (212) 830-2537   Fax: (212) 262-2824
E-mail: classical@bmi.com
Web Site: www.bmi.com
Summary: To recognize and reward outstanding student composers from the western hemisphere.
Eligibility: Applicants must be citizens or permanent residents of countries in North, Central, or South America or the Caribbean Island nations and must be enrolled in accredited public, private, or parochial secondary schools, enrolled in accredited colleges or conservatories of music, or engaged in the private study of music with recognized and established teachers (other than a relative). They must not have reached their 26th birthday by December 31 of the year of application. Any composer having won the award 3 times previously is not eligible to enter the contest again. Compositions may be for vocal, instrumental, electronic, or any combination of these. Manuscripts may be submitted either on usual score paper or reproduced by a generally accepted reproduction process. Any inaccuracies in the score will be taken adversely into account in the final judging. Electronic

music and tapes of graphic works that cannot adequately be presented in score may be submitted on cassette tapes. Selection is based on 1) formal content of the composition; 2) melodic, harmonic, and rhythmic idioms, but only in terms of their consistency and suitability for the intent of the particular composition; 3) instrumentation, orchestration, and vocal writing; and 4) age of the composer (if 2 compositions are of equal merit, preference is given to the younger contestant).
Financial data: Prizes range from $500 to $3,000.
Additional information: The score judged "most outstanding" in the competition receives the William Schuman Prize, named in honor of the chairman of this competition for 40 years. The outstanding composition scored for solo violin, violin and 1 or 2 other instruments, or violin and electronic tape receives the Boudleaux Bryant Prize, first awarded in 1994.
Number awarded: Varies each year; recently, 9 of these awards were presented. A total of $20,000 in prizes is awarded each year.
Deadline: February of each year.

1306
BRONISLAW KAPER AWARDS FOR YOUNG ARTISTS

Los Angeles Philharmonic
Attn: Education Department
135 North Grand Avenue
Los Angeles, CA 90012
Phone: (213) 972-0703
Summary: To recognize and reward outstanding high school musicians in California.
Eligibility: This program is open to current residents of California who are no older than 17 years of age or seniors in high school. Applicants must be pianists (in even-numbered years) or string players (in odd-numbered years) who wish to enter a concerto competition at the Dorothy Chandler Pavilion in Los Angeles.
Financial data: First prize is $2,500, second prize is $1,000, and third prize is $500. In addition, a special prize of $2,000 is awarded to the student judged the most promising musician. Prize-winners are also considered for solo opportunities with the Los Angeles Philharmonic.
Duration: The competition is held annually.
Additional information: First prize is made possible by the Foothill Philharmonic Committee, second prize by the Valley Juniors of the Los Angeles Philharmonic, third prize by Encore, and the most promising musician award by concertmaster emeritus David Frisina.
Number awarded: 4 each year.
Deadline: April of each year.

1307
BUSINESS WIRE SPECIAL SCHOLARSHIP FOR PRSSA MEMBERS

Business Wire
Attn: Public Relations
40 East 52nd Street, 19th Floor
New York, NY 10022
Phone: (800) 221-2462   E-mail: dans@bizwire.com
Web Site: www.bizwire.com
Summary: To provide financial assistance for college to members of the Public Relations Student Society of America (PRSSA).
Eligibility: This program is open to members of PRSSA who have at least a 3.0 grade point average, write an essay on their future goals and aspirations, and submit exhibits of writing ability, research capability, and grasp of public relations functions.
Financial data: The stipend is $1,000.
Duration: 1 year.
Additional information: This special scholarship was established in 2000 in honor of Business Wire's 40th anniversary. Stipends are awarded annually.
Deadline: August of each year.

1308
CALIFORNIA PLANNING FOUNDATION STATEWIDE SCHOLARSHIPS

California Chapter of the American Planning Association
Attn: California Planning Foundation
1333 36th Street
Sacramento, CA 95816
Phone: (916) 736-2434   Fax: (916) 456-1283
E-mail: sgassoc@msn.com
Web Site: www.calapa.org

Summary: To provide financial assistance to undergraduate students in accredited planning programs at California universities.
Eligibility: This program is open to undergraduate students enrolled in accredited planning programs at universities in California. Selection is based on academic excellence, commitment to the profession, promise of involvement in the American Planning Association (APA), and financial need.
Financial data: Stipends are $2,500 or $1,000.
Duration: 1 year.
Additional information: Information is also available from Linda C. Dalton, (805) 756-2186, Fax: (805) 756-5292, E-mail: ldalton@calpoly.edu.
Number awarded: 3 each year: 1 at $2,500 and 2 at $1,000.

1309
"CAP" LATHROP ENDOWMENT SCHOLARSHIP FUND

CIRI Foundation
2600 Cordova Street, Suite 206
Anchorage, AK 99503
Phone: (907) 263-5582   (800) 764-3382
Fax: (907) 263-5588   E-mail: tcf@ciri.com
Web Site: www.ciri.com/tcf
Summary: To provide financial assistance for undergraduate or graduate studies in telecommunications or broadcast to Alaska Natives and to their lineal descendants (natural or adopted).
Eligibility: This program is open to Alaska Native enrollees under the Alaska Native Claims Settlement Act (ANCSA) of 1971 and their lineal descendants. Proof of eligibility must be submitted. Preference is given to original enrollees/descendants of Cook Inlet Region, Inc. (CIRI) who have at least a 3.0 grade point average. There is no Alaska residency requirement or age limitation. Applicants must be accepted or enrolled full time in a 2-year undergraduate, 4-year undergraduate, or graduate degree program. They must be majoring in telecommunications or broadcast. Financial need is considered in the selection process.
Financial data: The stipend is $3,500 per year. Funds must be used for tuition, university fees, books, required class supplies, and campus housing and meal plans for students who must live away from their permanent home to attend college. Checks are sent directly to the recipient's school.
Duration: 1 year (2 semesters).
Additional information: This program was established in 1997. Recipients must attend school on a full-time basis and must plan to work in the broadcast or telecommunications industry in Alaska upon completion of their academic degree.
Deadline: May of each year.

1310
CAREER ADVANCEMENT SCHOLARSHIPS

Business and Professional Women's Foundation
Attn: Scholarships
2012 Massachusetts Avenue, N.W.
Washington, DC 20036-1070
Phone: (202) 293-1200, ext. 169   Fax: (202) 861-0298
Web Site: www.bpwusa.org
Summary: To provide financial assistance to mature women who are employed or seeking employment in the work force and to increase the pool of women qualified for positions that promise career opportunity.
Eligibility: Applicants must be women who are at least 25 years of age, citizens of the United States, within 2 years of completing their course of study, officially accepted into an accredited program or course of study at an American institution (including those in Puerto Rico and the Virgin Islands), in financial need, and planning to use the desired training to improve their chances for advancement, train for a new career field, or enter/reenter the job market. They must be in a transitional period in their lives and be interested in studying 1 of the following fields: biological sciences, business studies, computer science, engineering, humanities, mathematics, paralegal studies, physical sciences, social science, teacher education certification, or for a professional degree (J.D., D.D.S., M.D.). Study at the Ph.D. level and non-degree programs are not covered.
Financial data: Awards range from $500 to $1,000 per year.
Duration: 1 year; recipients may reapply.
Additional information: The scholarship may be used to support part-time study as well as academic or vocational/paraprofessional/office skills training. The program was established in 1969. Scholarships cannot be used to pay for classes already in progress. The program does not cover study at the doctoral level,

correspondence courses, postdoctoral studies, or studies in foreign countries. Training must be completed within 24 months.
Number awarded: Between 200 and 250 each year.
Deadline: April of each year.

1311
CAROLE SIMPSON NON-SUSTAINING SCHOLARSHIP

National Association of Black Journalists
Attn: Media Institute Program Associate
8701-A Adelphi Road
Adelphi, MD 20783-1716
Phone: (301) 445-7100, ext. 108   Fax: (301) 445-7101
E-mail: warren@nabj.org
Web Site: www.nabj.org
Summary: To provide financial assistance to undergraduate or graduate student members of the National Association of Black Journalists (NABJ) who are majoring in broadcast journalism.
Eligibility: This competition is open to African American undergraduate or graduate students who are currently attending an accredited 4-year college or university. Applicants must be majoring in broadcast journalism and have a grade point average of 2.5 or higher. They must submit 6 samples of their published or broadcasted work, an official college transcript, 2 letters of recommendation, a resume, and a 500- to 800-word essay describing their accomplishments as a student journalist, their career goals, and their interest in the field.
Financial data: The stipend is $2,500.
Duration: 1 year.
Additional information: All scholarship winners must become members of the association before they enroll in college.
Number awarded: 1 or more each year.
Deadline: April of each year.

1312
CAROLE SIMPSON SCHOLARSHIP

Radio and Television News Directors Foundation
1000 Connecticut Avenue, N.W., Suite 615
Washington, DC 20036-5302
Phone: (202) 467-5218   Fax: (202) 223-4007
E-mail: karenb@rtndf.org
Web Site: www.rtndf.org/asfi/scholarships/undergrad.shtml
Summary: To provide financial assistance to outstanding undergraduate students, especially minorities, who are interested in preparing for a career in electronic journalism.
Eligibility: Eligible are sophomore or more advanced undergraduate students enrolled in an electronic journalism sequence at an accredited or nationally recognized college or university. Applicants must submit 1 to 3 examples of reporting or producing skills on audio or video cassette tapes (no more than 15 minutes total), a description of their role on each story and a list of who worked on each story and what they did, a statement explaining why they are seeking a career in broadcast or cable journalism, and a letter of endorsement from a faculty sponsor that verifies the applicant has at least 1 year of school remaining. Preference is given to undergraduate students of color.
Financial data: The stipend is $2,000, paid in semiannual installments of $1,000 each.
Duration: 1 year.
Additional information: The Radio and Television News Directors Foundation (RTNDF) also provides an expense-paid trip to the Radio-Television News Directors Association (RTNDA) annual international conference. It defines electronic journalism to include radio, television, cable, and online news. Previous winners of any RTNDF scholarship or internship are not eligible.
Number awarded: 1 each year.
Deadline: April of each year.

1313
CENTRAL COAST SECTION SCHOLARSHIP

California Chapter of the American Planning Association
Attn: California Planning Foundation
1333 36th Street
Sacramento, CA 95816
Phone: (916) 736-2434   Fax: (916) 456-1283
E-mail: sgassoc@msn.com
Web Site: www.calapa.org

Summary: To provide financial assistance to undergraduate students in accredited planning programs at California universities.

Eligibility: This program is open to undergraduate students enrolled in accredited planning programs at universities in California. Selection is based on academic excellence, commitment to the profession, promise of involvement in the American Planning Association (APA), and financial need.

Financial data: This stipend is either $1,000 or $500.

Duration: 1 year.

Additional information: This program is sponsored by the Central Coast section of the California Chapter of the American Planning Association. Information is also available from Linda C. Dalton, (805) 756-2186, Fax: (805) 756-5292, E-mail: ldalton@calpoly.edu.

Number awarded: Each year, either 1 scholarship at $1,000 or 2 at $500 are awarded.

1314
CFJS SCHOLARSHIPS

Central Florida Jazz Society
Attn: Scholarship Chair
P.O. Box 540133
Orlando, FL 32854-0133
Phone: (407) 539-CFJS

Summary: To provide financial assistance to high school seniors and college students interested in furthering their studies in jazz music.

Eligibility: This scholarship competition is open to high school seniors and currently-enrolled college freshmen, sophomores, and juniors. There are no age restrictions. All applicants must be interested in furthering their studies in jazz music. Auditions are held. A rhythm section of professional musicians is provided. There is an initial screening of all applicants, so an audio tape must be submitted with each application. The tape should contain 1 to 2 choruses of 2 selections of different tempos. In addition to the tape, 1 reference letter from an individual familiar with the applicant's musicianship, character, and seriousness of interest in jazz studies is required. Selection is based on performance: expressiveness, artistic flair, musicianship, style, taste, tone, control, intonation, technique, rhythmic feel, improvisation, showmanship, appearance, and professionalism.

Financial data: Awards are $1,500, $1,000, or $500. Funds may be used to pay for college or to purchase musical instruments.

Duration: The scholarship competition is held annually. The winner of the top award is ineligible to compete for that award again.

Additional information: Information is also available from Moe Lowe, 40 Oakleigh Drive, Maitland, FL 32751, (407) 644-3506.

Number awarded: 4 each year: 1 at $1,500, 1 at $1,000, and 2 at $500.

Deadline: March of each year.

1315
CHALLENGERS NATIONAL MISSION SPEAK OUT CONTEST

Southern Baptist Convention
North American Mission Board
Attn: Youth Mission Education
4200 North Point Parkway
Alpharetta, GA 30022-4176
Phone: (770) 410-6000   E-mail: ahuesing@namb.net
Web Site: www.namb.net

Summary: To recognize and reward outstanding orators in the Southern Baptist Convention's Challengers Speak Out Contest.

Eligibility: Challengers is an organization of young men (sophomores, juniors, or seniors in high school) within the Southern Baptist Convention. Challengers can represent their state in this national speech competition. They must prepare a speech, from 5 to 7 minutes in length, on 1 of the following topics: my Challengers journey; me, a missionary; discovering my gifts for mission service; the cooperative program: supporting missions around the world; encountering God through Bible study; or what Challengers means to me. Selection is based on content (50 points), composition (25 points), and delivery (25 points).

Financial data: At the national level, first place is a $600 scholarship plus $400 for a mission project/trip of the winner's choice. Second place is a $300 scholarship plus $200 for a project/trip. Third place is a $200 scholarship plus $100 for a project/trip.

Duration: The competition is held annually.

Additional information: The winner also serves as a page at the Southern Baptist Convention and has the opportunity to present his speech at the Challengers Rally.

Number awarded: 3 each year.

1316
CHAPEL OF FOUR CHAPLAINS ANNUAL ESSAY CONTEST

Chapel of Four Chaplains
Naval Business Center
1201 Constitution Avenue
Philadelphia, PA 19112
Phone: (215) 218-1943   Fax: (215) 218-1949
E-mail: chapel@fourchaplains.org
Web Site: www.fourchaplains.org

Summary: To recognize and reward outstanding high school senior essays on a topic related to the work of the sponsoring organization.

Eligibility: Eligible to compete in this essay contest are public and private high school seniors. The children of members of the Chapel of Four Chaplains, youth committee, board of directors, or trustees are ineligible. The topic of the essay may change annually; recently, the topic related to the efforts of the sponsoring organization to initiate its Save-A-Life Program and Bill of Responsibilities at high schools across the country. Essays must be typed, double spaced, and no more than 450 words. Selection is based on exploration of the essay topic, incorporation of the Four Chaplains story within the essay, personal commitment, proper grammar and spelling, and clear and logical order.

Financial data: First prize is $1,000, second $750, third $500, fourth $400, and fifth $300.

Duration: The competition is held annually.

Additional information: The sponsor may publish the winning essay.

Number awarded: 5 each year.

Deadline: November of each year.

1317
CHAPEL OF FOUR CHAPLAINS NATIONAL ART CONTEST

Chapel of Four Chaplains
Naval Business Center
1201 Constitution Avenue
Philadelphia, PA 19112
Phone: (215) 218-1943   Fax: (215) 218-1949
E-mail: chapel@fourchaplains.org
Web Site: www.fourchaplains.org

Summary: To recognize and reward outstanding high school student art on a topic related to the work of the sponsoring organization.

Eligibility: Eligible to compete in this art contest are seniors at public and private high schools. Students are invited to submit any form of flat art (except photography) on a theme related to the efforts of the sponsoring organization to initiate its Save-A-Life Program and Bill of Responsibilities at high schools across the country. They are encouraged to capture the spirit of the theme in whatever manner they wish, through representational, stylized, or abstract means of expression. The medium may be watercolor, crayons, tempera, collage, pen and ink, oil crayons, linoleum block or woodcut print, or any combination of those. The maximum size is 24"x30". The artwork should not contain any wording, including slogans, descriptions, narrative, or dialogue balloons.

Financial data: First prize is $1,000, second prize is $750, and third prize is $500.

Duration: The competition is held annually.

Number awarded: 3 each year.

Deadline: November of each year.

1318
CHAPEL OF FOUR CHAPLAINS "PROJECT LIFESAVER"

Chapel of Four Chaplains
Naval Business Center
1201 Constitution Avenue
Philadelphia, PA 19112
Phone: (215) 218-1943   Fax: (215) 218-1949
E-mail: chapel@fourchaplains.org
Web Site: www.fourchaplains.org

Summary: To recognize and reward outstanding high school senior teams that develop projects related to the work of the sponsoring organization.

Eligibility: Seniors in public and private high schools are invited to form teams to participate in this program. A team consists of a team leader, 5 team members, and a teacher (with faculty approval) who acts as team advisor. The team creates a plan to initiate the sponsor's Save-A-Life program within their school. Selection is based on creativity of the project, community involvement in developing the project, organizational skills of the students, proper grammar and punctuation in the project paper, and incorporation of the Four Chaplains story within the project.

Financial data: The prizes for the winning project include $1,000 to the team leader, $1,000 to the team advisor, and $750 to each of the 5 team members.
Duration: The competition is held annually.
Number awarded: 1 project each year.
Deadline: November of each year.

1319
CHARLES AND LUCILLE KING FAMILY FOUNDATION SCHOLARSHIPS

Charles and Lucille King Family Foundation, Inc.
366 Madison Avenue, 10th Floor
New York, NY 10017
Phone: (212) 682-2913   Fax: (212) 949-0728
E-mail: info@kingfoundation.org
Web Site: www.kingfoundation.org
Summary: To provide financial assistance to undergraduate students who are majoring in television or film and to graduate students at selected universities.
Eligibility: This program is open to students who are entering their junior or senior year at a 4-year U.S. college or university and majoring in television or film. U.S. citizenship is not required. Selection is based on academic ability, professional potential, and financial need. In addition,   special grants are available to undergraduate and graduate students at New York University, the University of California at Los Angeles, and the University of Southern California.
Financial data: Stipends range up to $2,500.
Duration: 1 year; students who receive an award as a junior may renew the award in their senior year if they earn at least a 3.0 grade point average.
Additional information: The foundation was established in 1989.
Number awarded: Varies; generally, up to 20 each year.
Deadline: April of each year.

1320
CHARLES D. MAYO STUDENT SCHOLARSHIP

International Furnishings and Design Association
Attn: IFDA Educational Foundation
204 E Street, N.E.
Washington, DC 20002
Phone: (202) 547-1588   Fax: (202) 547-6348
E-mail: info@ifdaef.org
Web Site: www.ifdael.org/scholarships.html
Summary: To provide financial assistance to undergraduate students pursuing degrees in design.
Eligibility: This program is open to full-time undergraduate students in fields related to design. Applicants must submit a 200- to 300-word essay on their future plans and goals and why they believe they deserve the scholarship. Selection is based on the essay; the applicant's achievements, awards, and accomplishments; and a letter of recommendation from a design educator, a mentor, or a practitioner in the field. Financial need is not considered.
Financial data: The stipend is $1,000.
Duration: 1 year.
Additional information: This program was established in 1998.
Number awarded: 1 each year.
Deadline: September of each year.

1321
CHARLES DUBOSE SCHOLARSHIP

Connecticut Architecture Foundation
Attn: Executive Vice President
87 Willow Street
New Haven, CT 06511
Phone: (203) 865-2195
Summary: To provide financial assistance to Connecticut residents who are pursuing a bachelor's or master's degree in architecture.
Eligibility: This program is open to students who have completed at least 2 years of a bachelor of architecture program or are enrolled in a master of architecture program. Connecticut residents are encouraged to apply. Applicants may be attending any college offering a 5-year accredited degree in architecture. Preference is given to students at the University of Pennsylvania, Georgia Institute of Technology, and the Fontainebleau summer program. Selection is based on academic record and financial need.
Financial data: Stipends range from $5,000 to $10,000.
Duration: 1 year; may be renewed.

Additional information: This program was established in 1986 by DuBose Associates, Inc.
Number awarded: 1 or 2 each year.
Deadline: April of each year.

1322
CHARLES E. PETERSON PRIZE

Athenaeum of Philadelphia
Attn: Assistant Director for Programs
219 South Sixth Street
Philadelphia, PA 19106-3794
Phone: (215) 925-2688   Fax: (215) 925-3755
E-mail: magee@PhilaAthenaeum.org
Web Site: www.PhilaAthenaeum.org
Summary: To recognize and reward sets of measured drawings prepared by students or teams of students that meet Historic American Buildings Survey (HABS) standards.
Eligibility: This program is designed to increase awareness and knowledge of historic buildings throughout the United States. Students or teams of students in architecture, architectural history, interior design, and American studies who have faculty sponsorship are eligible to compete. There is no entrance fee. Participants are required to produce a set of measured drawings made to HABS standards. The drawings must be of a building that has not yet been recorded by HABS through measured drawings, or it must be an addendum to existing HABS drawings that makes a substantial contribution to the understanding of significant features of the building. Applicants should contact the HABS office to determine if a structure has already been recorded.
Financial data: First prize is $2,500, second prize is $2,000, third prize is $1,500, and fourth prize is $1,000.
Duration: The competition is held annually.
Additional information: Acceptable entries are transmitted to the permanent HABS collection in the Library of Congress. The prize honors Charles E. Peterson, founder of the HABS program. Information is also available from the National Park Service, HABS/HAER Division, 1849 C Street, N.W., NC300, Washington, DC 20240, Fax: (202) 343-9624, Web site: www.cr.nps.gov/habshaer/joco/pete.
Number awarded: 4 prizes are awarded each year.
Deadline: June of each year.

1323
CHARLES M. GETCHELL AWARD

Southeastern Theatre Conference, Inc.
Attn: New Play Project
P.O. Box 9868
Greensboro, NC 27429-0868
Phone: (336) 272-3645   Fax: (336) 272-8810
E-mail: staff@setc.org
Web Site: www.setc.org
Summary: To recognize and reward new plays written by students and playwrights from the member region of the Southeastern Theatre Conference (SETC).
Eligibility: This program is open to students and playwrights residing in the SETC region (Alabama, Florida, Georgia, Kentucky, North Carolina, South Carolina, Tennessee, Virginia, and West Virginia). Applicants must submit a full-length play or 2 related 1-act plays. Submissions must be unproduced and unpublished; readings and workshops are eligible. Musicals and children's plays are not accepted.
Financial data: The award is $1,000. The winning author attends the SETC convention at the organization's expense and the winning play is considered for publication in *Southern Theatre* magazine.
Duration: The competition is held annually.
Additional information: Information is also available from Susan Sharp, Jackson State Community College, Department of Theatre, 2046 North Parkway, Jackson, TN 38301.
Number awarded: 1 each year.
Deadline: May of each year.

1324
CHARLES M. SCHULZ AWARD FOR COLLEGE CARTOONISTS

Scripps Howard Foundation
Attn: National Journalism Awards Administrator
312 Walnut Street, 28th Floor
Cincinnati, OH 45202-4040
Phone: (513) 977-3035   (800) 888-3000
Fax: (513) 977-3800   E-mail: cottingham@scripps.com
Web Site: www.scripps.com/foundation
Summary: To recognize and reward outstanding college cartoonists.
Eligibility: Any student cartoonist at a college newspaper or magazine in the United States or its territories may enter this competition. Work must have been completed during the calendar year of the contest. Cartoons may be panels, strips, and/or editorial cartoons. Entries must include a 250-word statement by the cartoonist outlining his or her goals in cartooning.
Financial data: The prize is $2,500 and a trophy.
Duration: The competition is held annually.
Number awarded: 1 each year.
Deadline: January of each year.

1325
CHOPIN FOUNDATION OF THE UNITED STATES SCHOLARSHIP PROGRAM FOR YOUNG PIANISTS

Chopin Foundation of the United States, Inc.
1440 John F. Kennedy Causeway, Suite 117
Miami, FL 33141
Phone: (305) 868-0624   Fax: (305) 865-5150
E-mail: info@chopin.org
Web Site: www.chopin.org/scholarship.html
Summary: To recognize and reward (with scholarships) outstanding young American pianists who demonstrate "a special affinity for the interpretation of Chopin's music."
Eligibility: This program is open to any qualified American pianist (citizen or legal resident) between the ages of 14 and 17 whose field of study is music and whose major is piano. Enrollment at the secondary or undergraduate school level as a full-time student is required. Applicants must submit a formal application, along with a statement of career goals, a minimum of 2 references from piano teachers or performers, and an audio tape of 20 to 30 minutes of Chopin's works. Each piece must be an unedited performance; the audio tape must be of good quality.
Financial data: The award is $1,000.
Duration: 1 year; renewable for up to 4 years, as long as the recipient continues to study piano, maintains satisfactory academic progress, and submits an annual audiocassette of unedited performances of Chopin's works for evaluation as follows: year 1, 2 mazurkas, 2 etudes, and 2 nocturnes; year 2, 6 preludes, 2 waltzes, 1 ballad or barcarole in F sharp major Op. 60 or Fantasia in F minor Op. 49; year 3, 1 sonata and 1 of the following polonaises: Andante Spianato and Grand Polonaise in E flat major Op. 222, Polonaise in F sharp minor Op. 44, or Polonaise-Fantasie in A flat major Op. 61; year 4, at least 1 movement of the concerto.
Additional information: This program offers scholarship renewals in order to support and encourage winners throughout the 4 years of preparation necessary to qualify for the American National Chopin Piano Competition held every 5 years in Miami, Florida. There is a $25 registration fee.
Number awarded: 10 each year.
Deadline: February of each year.

1326
CHRISTOPHERS POSTER CONTEST

The Christophers
Attn: Youth Department Coordinator
12 East 48th Street
New York, NY 10017
Phone: (212) 759-4050   Fax: (212) 838-5073
E-mail: youth-coordinator@christophers.org
Web Site: www.christophers.org/poster.html
Summary: To recognize and reward posters drawn by high school students that best communicate the idea "that each one of us has an opportunity to make a very real difference, whether in our immediate communities or the world at large."
Eligibility: This competition is open to all students in grades 9 through 12 who prepare posters on the theme: "You Can Make a Difference." The posters must be 15"x20" and the original work of 1 student. Selection is based on overall impact,

effectiveness in conveying the theme, originality, and artistic merit.
Financial data: First prize is $1,000, second prize is $500, third prize is $250, and honorable mentions are $50.
Duration: The competition is held annually.
Additional information: The Christophers, a nonprofit organization, use the mass media to share 2 basic ideas: "There's nobody like you" and "you can make a difference." The competition began in 1990.
Number awarded: 8 each year: 1 each for first, second, and third place plus 5 honorable mentions.
Deadline: January of each year.

1327
CIRCLE OF LIFE ESSAY PROGRAM

American Indian Science and Engineering Society-Michigan Professional Chapter
c/o Lori Sherman
Native American Outreach
Michigan Technical University
1400 Townsend Drive
Houghton, MI 49931-1295
Phone: (906) 482-2920   E-mail: lasherma@mtu.edu
Web Site: www.ttap.mtu.edu/col/index.html
Summary: To recognize and reward American Indian high school students who write an essay on their spiritual values.
Eligibility: This program is open to American Indian students in grades 7 through 12. Applicants must write an essay about the values that guide them throughout their lives. Prizes are awarded to the authors of essays that most clearly express the moral, ethical, and spiritual responsibilities by which a person lives.
Financial data: The first-place student receives a $1,000 scholarship and a $200 personal cash award; the runner-up receives a $500 scholarship and a $200 personal cash award; other top essays receive $100 personal cash awards. All essays are published in *Winds of Change* magazine throughout the year.
Duration: This competition is held annually.
Additional information: This program, which began in 1996, is sponsored by the George Bird Grinnell American Indian Children's Education Foundation, the John Templeton Foundation, and the Honeywell Foundation.
Number awarded: 8 each year: 1 1st winner, 1 runner-up, and 6 other top essayists.
Deadline: March of each year.

1328
CLAN MACBEAN FOUNDATION GRANTS

Clan MacBean Foundation
Attn: Director
441 Wadsworth Boulevard, Suite 213
Denver, CO 80226
Phone: (303) 233-6002
Summary: To provide financial assistance to students interested in studying subjects or conducting research in college relating to 1) Scottish culture or 2) the "Human Family."
Eligibility: This program is open to students who have enrolled or are enrolling in college, pursuing a course of study that relates directly to Scottish culture. If pursuing a specific project, it must 1) reflect direct involvement in the preservation or enhancement of Scottish culture or 2) contribute directly to the improvement and benefit of the "Human Family." Trustees of the MacBean Foundation, their spouses, and their children are not eligible to apply for these funds.
Financial data: Grants up to $5,000 are available. Funds may be used for tuition, fees, books, room and board, printing and publishing costs, historical research fees, and/or initial costs in establishing a project.
Duration: 1 year.
Number awarded: 1 or more each year.
Deadline: April of each year.

1329
COATING AND GRAPHIC ARTS DIVISION SCHOLARSHIP

Technical Association of the Pulp and Paper Industry
P.O. Box 105113
Atlanta, GA 30348-5113
Phone: (770) 446-1400   (800) 332-8686
Fax: (770) 446-6947
Web Site: www.tappi.org
Summary: To provide financial assistance to student members of the Technical

Association of the Pulp and Paper Industry (TAPPI) who are interested in preparing for a career in the paper industry, with a focus on coating and graphic arts.

Eligibility: This program is open to full-time students who are interested in preparing for a career in the paper industry by majoring in a scientific or technical discipline related to the manufacture and/or graphic arts end use of coated paper and paperboard. Applicants must be juniors or higher; graduate students are also eligible if they have not advanced to doctoral candidacy. They must be student members of the association. A grade point average of 3.0 or higher is required. Financial need is not considered in the selection process.

Financial data: The stipend is $1,000.

Duration: 1 year.

Number awarded: Up to 4 each year.

Deadline: January of each year.

1330
COLBURN-PLEDGE MUSIC SCHOLARSHIP

Colburn-Pledge Music Scholarship Foundation
Attn: Secretary
101 Cardinal Avenue
San Antonio, TX 78209

Summary: To provide financial assistance to pre-college and college students who are Texas residents and interested in studying classical music.

Eligibility: Applicants must be 1) residents of Texas, 2) studying a string instrument (violin, viola, cello, bass) in classical music with the intention of becoming a professional musician, and 3) less than high school age, currently in high school, or currently in college. Financial need must be demonstrated.

Financial data: Stipends range up to $2,000.

Duration: 1 year.

Additional information: Recipients may attend college, music schools, or music camps in Texas or in any other state.

Deadline: April of each year.

1331
COLLEGE PHOTOGRAPHER OF THE YEAR

National Press Photographers Foundation
c/o University of Missouri at Columbia
Attn: CPOY Coordinator
105 Lee Hills Hall
Columbia, MO 65211
Phone: (573) 882-4442   Fax: (573) 884-4999
E-mail: info@cpoy.org
Web Site: www.cpoy.org

Summary: To recognize and reward the outstanding photographic work of college students.

Eligibility: Students currently working on an undergraduate or graduate degree are eligible to submit work completed during the previous academic year. Single picture categories are: 1) spot news; 2) general news; 3) feature; 4) sports action; 5) sports feature; 6) portrait; 7) pictorial; 8) illustration; and 9) personal vision. Multiple picture categories are: 10) picture story; 11) sports portfolio; 12) documentary; 13) portfolio; and 14) online or multimedia photo story or essay. Professional photographers who have worked 2 years or more are not eligible.

Financial data: In the portfolio competition, the first-place winner receives an expenses-paid trip to receive the award, a summer internship at 1 of a consortium of newspapers, the Colonel William J. Lookadoo Award of $1,000, a Canon camera, and 100 rolls of Fuji film; second-place winner receives the Milton Freier Award of $500 and 60 rolls of Fuji film; third-place winner receives $250 and 40 rolls of Fuji film. For each of the other individual categories, first-place winners receive small cash awards.

Duration: The competition is held annually, in the fall.

Additional information: The competition is conducted by the National Press Photographers Foundation, Kappa Alpha Mu, and the University of Missouri's School of Journalism. Contributing newspapers that sponsor the internship portion of the award include the *Detroit Free Press, Sacramento Bee, Seattle Times, Virginian-Pilot, Dallas Morning News,* and *Hartford Courant.* The entry fee is $25 per photographer.

Deadline: October of each year.

1332
COLLEGE STUDENT CORRESPONDENT SCHOLARSHIP PROGRAM

New Jersey Press Foundation
Attn: Scholarship Awards Committee
840 Bear Tavern Road, Suite 305
West Trenton, NJ 08628-1019
Phone: (609) 406-0600   E-mail:foundation@njpa.org
Web Site: www.njpa.org/foundation/index.html

Summary: To provide financial assistance to New Jersey residents who are majoring in journalism and have written for a New Jersey newspaper during an internship or as a stringer.

Eligibility: This program is open to New Jersey residents who are majoring in journalism in college. Students must be full-time students and be nominated by a newspaper editor in the state. Selection is based on the quality of their writing, editing, photography, or other journalistic work published in New Jersey Press Association-member noncampus newspapers during a 12-month period between September 1 of the past year and August 31 of the current year; the work can be done during an internship or as a stringer/correspondent. Students who have worked as full-time or permanent part-time employees for a professional newspaper are ineligible.

Financial data: The stipend is $1,000. College seniors who are not planning to return to college or go on to graduate school may use the funds to help pay off undergraduate school loans.

Duration: The scholarship is presented annually.

Number awarded: 12 each year.

Deadline: August of each year.

1333
CONNECTICUT BROADCASTER'S SCHOLARSHIPS

Connecticut Broadcaster's Association
c/o Paul Taff, President
P.O. Box 678
Glastonbury, CT 06033
Phone: (860) 633-5031

Summary: To provide financial assistance to Connecticut residents who are studying a field related to broadcasting in college.

Eligibility: This program is open to Connecticut residents who are college juniors or seniors. Applicants must be majoring in communications, marketing, or other field related to broadcasting. Selection is based on academic achievement, community service, goals in the chosen field, and financial need.

Financial data: The stipend is $5,000.

Duration: 1 year.

Number awarded: 2 each year.

Deadline: April of each year.

1334
CONNECTICUT BUILDING CONGRESS SCHOLARSHIPS

Connecticut Building Congress
Attn: Scholarship Fund
2600 Dixwell Avenue, Suite 7
Hamden, CT 06514
Phone: (203) 281-3183   Fax: (203) 248-8932
E-mail: cbc@constructioncorner.com
Web Site: www.constructioncorner.com/cbc

Summary: To provide financial assistance to high school seniors in Connecticut who are interested in studying a field related to construction in college.

Eligibility: This program is open to graduating seniors at high schools in Connecticut. Applicants must be interested in attending a 2- or 4-year college or university to major in a field related to construction, including architecture, engineering, or management. Selection is based on academic achievement, service to school and community, and financial need.

Financial data: Stipends range from $500 to $2,000 per year.

Duration: Up to 4 years.

Number awarded: 2 to 4 each year.

Deadline: February of each year.

1335
CONSTANCE EBERHART MEMORIAL AWARDS

National Opera Association
Attn: Executive Secretary
P.O. Box 60869
Canyon, TX 79016-0869
Phone: (806) 651-2857   Fax: (806) 651-2958
E-mail: rhansen@mail.wtamu.edu
Web Site: www.noa.org
Summary: To provide financial assistance for continuing education to opera students.
Eligibility: Any opera student between the ages of 18 and 24 may enter this audition and competition. Their teacher or coach must be a member of the National Opera Association. Applicants must submit a cassette tape with 2 arias, and judges select the finalists on the basis of those recordings. Finalists are then invited to auditions where they present 4 arias in contrasting styles and periods, in 3 languages, including 1 originally in English.
Financial data: Prizes range from $250 to $1,000; funds are paid directly to the winner's school, voice teacher, or vocal coach for further study. In addition, the first-place winner receives a scholarship for summer study at the American Institute of Musical Studies (AIMS) Graz Experience in Austria and a full scholarship for the summer opera program at the Banff Center School of Fine Arts.
Duration: The competition is held annually.
Additional information: Information is also available from Barbara Hill Moore, Southern Methodist University, Meadows School of the Arts, Division of Music, Dallas, TX 75275-0356, (214) 768-3580, Fax: (972) 516-9929, E-mail: bhmoore@mail.smu.edu. Contestants must pay a $30 nonrefundable entry fee.
Number awarded: 3 each year.
Deadline: October of each year.

1336
COUNTRY MUSIC BROADCASTERS SCHOLARSHIPS

Broadcast Education Association
Attn: Scholarships
1771 N Street, N.W.
Washington, DC 20036-2891
Phone: (202) 429-5354   E-mail: bea@nab.org
Web Site: www.beaweb.org
Summary: To provide financial assistance to upper-division and graduate students who are interested in preparing for a career in radio.
Eligibility: This program is open to juniors, seniors, and graduate students enrolled full time at a college or university where at least 1 department is an institutional member of the Broadcast Education Association (BEA). Applicants must be studying for a career in radio. Selection is based on evidence that the applicant possesses high integrity, superior academic ability, potential to be an outstanding electronic media professional, and a sense of personal and professional responsibility.
Financial data: The stipend is $3,000.
Duration: 1 year; may not be renewed.
Additional information: Information is also available from Peter B. Orlik, Central Michigan University, 344 Moore Hall, Mt. Pleasant, MI 48859, (517) 774-7279. This program is sponsored by Country Music Broadcasters, Inc. of Nashville, Tennessee and administered by the BEA.
Number awarded: 13 each year.
Deadline: September of each year.

1337
CRISTINA NAZARIO SCHOLARSHIP FOR THE FINE ARTS

Portuguese Heritage Scholarship Foundation
Attn: Academic Secretary
P.O. Box 30246
Bethesda, MD 20824-0246
Phone: (301) 652-2775   E-mail: phsf@vivaportugal.com
Web Site: www.vivaportugal.com/phsf/apply.htm
Summary: To provide financial assistance for college to students of Portuguese American heritage interested in studying fine arts or related fields.
Eligibility: Eligible to apply for this support are high school seniors or currently-enrolled college students who are of Portuguese American ancestry. Applicants must be U.S. residents and attending or planning to attend an accredited 4-year college or university. They must be interested in studying fine arts, architecture,

or historic preservation. Selection is based on academic achievement and artistic accomplishments. Preference is given to students from the Washington, D.C. area, but all qualified applicants are considered.
Financial data: The stipend is $2,000 per year.
Duration: 4 years, provided the recipient maintains a grade point average of 3.0 or higher.
Additional information: Recipients must attend college on a full-time basis.
Number awarded: 1 each year.
Deadline: January of each year.

1338
CRISTINA SARALEGUI SCHOLARSHIP PROGRAM

National Association of Hispanic Journalists
Attn: Scholarships
National Press Building
529 14th Street, N.W., Suite 1193
Washington, DC 20045-2100
Phone: (202) 662-7143   (888) 346-NAHJ
Fax: (202) 662-7144   E-mail: alopez@nahj.org
Web Site: www.nahj.org
Summary: To provide financial assistance and work experience to Hispanic American undergraduate students interested in preparing for careers in the media.
Eligibility: College sophomores are eligible to apply if they are of Hispanic descent, fluent in Spanish, and interested in majoring in broadcast journalism. Applications, which may be submitted in English or Spanish, must include an autobiographical essay of 500 words describing some aspect of the relationship between Hispanic Americans and the press. Selection is based on academic excellence, a demonstrated interest in journalism as a career, and financial need.
Financial data: The stipend is $5,000 per year; the program also provides funding to attend the association's convention and an internship during the summer following the junior year.
Duration: 2 years.
Additional information: This program, which began in 2000, is sponsored by the Spanish-language talk show host Cristina Saralegui and administered by the National Association of Hispanic Journalists (NAHJ) as part of its Rubui show.
Number awarded: 1 each year.
Deadline: February of each year.

1339
"CULINARY CONCERT" AWARD

International Association of Culinary Professionals Foundation
Attn: Program Coordinator
304 West Liberty Street, Suite 201
Louisville, KY 40202
Phone: (502) 581-9786, ext. 237   (800) 928-4227
Fax: (502) 589-3602   E-mail: iacp@hqtrs.com
Web Site: www.iacpfoundation.org
Summary: To offer financial assistance to students interested in pursuing a degree in the culinary arts.
Eligibility: This program is open to beginning and currently-enrolled students in a nationally accredited culinary school. Applicants must submit an essay on their culinary goals and how they plan to achieve them. Selection is based on merit (including a grade point average of 3.0 of higher), food service work experience, and financial need.
Financial data: The stipend is $12,500.
Duration: 1 year.
Additional information: There is a $25 application fee.
Number awarded: 1 each year.
Deadline: November of each year.

1340
DAR AMERICAN HISTORY SCHOLARSHIP

National Society Daughters of the American Revolution
Attn: Scholarship Committee
1776 D Street, N.W.
Washington, DC 20006-5392
Phone: (202) 628-1776
Web Site: www.dar.org/natsociety/edout_scholar.html
Summary: To provide financial assistance to high school seniors planning to major in American history in college.

Eligibility: Eligible to apply for these scholarships are graduating high school seniors who plan to major in American history. Applicants must be sponsored by a local chapter of the Daughters of the American Revolution (DAR). Judging first takes place at the state level; 2 state winners then enter the national competition. Selection is based on academic excellence, commitment to field of study, and financial need. U.S. citizenship is required.

Financial data: First-place stipends are $2,000 per year, second-place stipends are $1,000 per year, and third-place stipends are $1,000 per year.

Duration: 4 years.

Additional information: Information is also available from Cindy B. Findley, DAR Scholarship Committee Chair, 4929 Warfield Drive, Greensboro, NC 27406-8338, (336) 674-5777, E-mail: cfindley@bellsouth.net. Requests for applications must be accompanied by a self-addressed stamped envelope.

Number awarded: Up to 3 each year.

Deadline: Applications must be submitted to the state chair by January of each year.

1341
DAVID L. WOLPER STUDENT DOCUMENTARY ACHIEVEMENT AWARD

International Documentary Association
1201 West Fifth Street, Suite M320
Los Angeles, CA 90017-2029
Phone: (310) 284-8422   Fax: (310) 785-9334
E-mail: ida@artnet.net
Web Site: www.documentary.org

Summary: To recognize and reward outstanding documentaries produced by college students.

Eligibility: This program is open to full-time college students. Their non-fiction documentaries may have been produced on videotape or film (35mm or 16mm) but must be submitted on video cassette.

Financial data: The prize is a $1,000 honorarium and a $1,000 certificate toward the purchase of Eastman Kodak motion picture film.

Duration: The competition is held annually, in the fall.

Additional information: The winner and runners-up are given the opportunity to participate in the IDA/David L. Wolper Student Documentary Achievement Reel (which is made available to film schools at cost). The fee for entries submitted by the discount deadline (May of each year) is $55 for members or $75 for nonmembers. The fee for entries submitted by the final deadline (June of each year) is $75 for members or $125 for nonmembers.

Number awarded: 1 first-prize winner each year.

Deadline: June of each year.

1342
DAVID S. BARR AWARDS

Newspaper Guild-CWA
501 Third Street, N.W., Second Floor
Washington, DC 20001-2797
Phone: (202) 434-7177   Fax: (202) 434-1472
Web Site: newsguild.org

Summary: To recognize and reward student journalists whose work has helped promote justice.

Eligibility: This program is open to high school students (including those enrolled in vocational, technical, or special education programs) and college students (including those in community colleges and in graduate programs). Applicants must submit work published or broadcast during the preceding academic year; entries should help to right a wrong, correct an injustice, or promote justice and fairness.

Financial data: The award is $1,500 for college students or $500 for high school students.

Duration: The awards are presented annually.

Number awarded: 2 each year.

Deadline: May of each year.

1343
DAVID W. SELF SCHOLARSHIP

United Methodist Youth Organization
P.O. Box 340003
Nashville, TN 37203-0003
Phone: (615) 340-7184   (877) 899-2780, ext. 7184
Fax: (615) 340-1764   E-mail: umyouthorg@gbod.org
Web Site: www.umyouth.org/scholarships.html

Summary: To provide financial assistance to Methodist high school seniors or graduates who wish to prepare for a church-related career.

Eligibility: Students who are beginning college are eligible to apply if they are members of the United Methodist Church, have been active in their local church for at least 1 year, can demonstrate financial need, have maintained at least a "C" average throughout high school, and are interested in pursuing a church-related career after graduation.

Financial data: The stipend is up to $1,000.

Duration: 1 year; nonrenewable.

Additional information: Recipients must enroll full time in their first year of undergraduate study.

Deadline: May of each year.

1344
DEGENRING SCHOLARSHIP FUND

American Baptist Women of New Jersey
36-10 Garden View Terrace
East Windsor, NJ 08520

Summary: To provide financial assistance to Baptist women in New Jersey who are interested in attending college.

Eligibility: This program is open to Baptist women in New Jersey who are interested in pursuing a postsecondary degree and preparing for a career involving Christian work. They must have been members of an American Baptist church in New Jersey for at least 5 years. Selection is based on financial need and career goals.

Financial data: The amount awarded varies, depending upon the need of the recipient and her career goals in Christian work.

Duration: 1 year.

Number awarded: 1 or more each year.

Deadline: February of each year.

1345
DERIVATIVE DUO SCHOLARSHIP

Pride Foundation
c/o Greater Seattle Business Association
2150 North 107th Street, Suite 205
Seattle, WA 98133-9009
Phone: (206) 363-9188   Fax: (206) 367-8777
E-mail: office@the-gsba.org
Web Site: www.the-gsba.org

Summary: To provide financial assistance to Washington residents engaged in undergraduate study of performing arts or the health sciences.

Eligibility: This program is open to undergraduate students majoring in the performing arts or the health sciences who are Washington residents. Applicants must demonstrate a connection between their studies and involvement in the community around issues of social justice. Selection is based on financial need, community involvement, and commitment to human rights.

Financial data: Stipends range from $1,000 to $5,000.

Duration: 1 year; recipients may reapply.

Additional information: The Pride Foundation was established in 1987 to strengthen the lesbian, gay, bisexual, and transgender community. It may be consulted directly at 1801 12th Avenue, Seattle, WA 98122, (206) 323-3318, (800) 735-7287, E-mail: giving@pridefoundation.org, Web site: www.pridefoundation.org. Its scholarship program is administered in collaboration with the Greater Seattle Business Association.

Number awarded: 1 each year. Since it began offering scholarships in 1992, the foundation has awarded a total of $204,266 to 154 recipients.

Deadline: February of each year.

1346
DES MOINES SYMPHONY ALLIANCE COLLEGE DIVISION YOUNG ARTIST COMPETITION

Des Moines Symphony Alliance
221 Walnut Street
Des Moines, IA 50309
Phone: (515) 280-4000   Fax: (515) 280-4005
E-mail: info@dmsymphony.org
Web Site: www.dmsymphony.org

Summary: To recognize and reward outstanding college student musicians in Iowa.

Eligibility: Eligible to compete are currently-enrolled full-time undergraduate or graduate students under 25 years of age who are either residents of Iowa or students in an Iowa college or university. Competitions are held in 3 categories: 1) piano; 2) violin,

viola, cello, and bass; 3) brass, woodwinds, harp, and percussion. Each contestant must play an entire standard concerto accompanied by piano and a solo or concert piece in a contrasting style to the concerto; all selections must be performed from memory. Applicants must submit cassette tapes, and finalists are invited to an audition. The total performance time is 15 minutes for preliminaries and 20 minutes for finals.
Financial data: First prize in each category is $1,000 and second prize is $750. The Grand Prize winner also receives a full tuition plus room and board scholarship to the summer Aspen Music School and may be invited to perform with the Des Moines Symphony.
Duration: The competition is held annually.
Additional information: Information is also available from Judith G. Pruchnicki, 107 35th Street, Des Moines, IA 50312-4508, (515) 277-1158. A non-refundable fee of $30 must accompany the application and tape.
Number awarded: 6 each year: a first and second prize in each of the 3 categories.
Deadline: January of each year.

1347
DICK LARSEN SCHOLARSHIP

Washington News Council
P.O. Box 3672
Seattle, WA 98124-3672
Phone: (206) 464-7902
Web Site: www.wanewscouncil.org
Summary: To provide financial assistance to Washington residents who are interested in majoring in a communication-related field at an academic institution in the state.
Eligibility: This program is open to graduating high school seniors and currently-enrolled college students who have a serious interest in communications, including journalism, politics, public relations, or related fields. To be eligible, students must be a graduate of a Washington state high school and accepted or enrolled at a 4-year public or private university in the state. Financial need must be demonstrated. As part of the application process, students must submit a completed application form, 2 letters of reference, a school transcript, and 3 samples of their work. Finalists may be interviewed.
Financial data: The stipend is $2,000.
Duration: 1 year.
Additional information: This scholarship was established in 1999. It is administered by the Seattle Foundation.
Number awarded: 2 each year.
Deadline: May of each year.

1348
DIGITAL ART COMPETITION

Butler Institute of American Art
Attn: Beecher Center for Technology in the Arts
524 Wick Avenue
Youngstown, OH 44502
Phone: (330) 743-1107   Fax: (330) 743-9567
Web Site: www.butlerart.com
Summary: To recognize and reward outstanding computer-generated art.
Eligibility: Artwork submitted to this competition must be original and have been created by using a computer. Submissions may be on formatted floppy disks or zip disks (Mac or PC), low resolution (72 dpi) files and under 1 MB per image uncompressed. They can be submitted as TIFF, JPEG, EPS, or PSD of approximately 640 x 480 pixels or as traditional slides. Images of a person may appear in artwork only with the permission of the person involved.
Financial data: First prize is $1,000, second $500, and third $250.
Duration: The competition is held annually.
Additional information: Each artist may submit up to 5 images at $10 per image, or $5 per image for students.
Number awarded: 3 each year.
Deadline: January of each year.

1349
DINAH SHORE MEMORIAL SCHOLARSHIP

National Academy of Television Arts and Sciences-Nashville Chapter
Attn: Memorial Scholarship Board of Trust
27 Music Square East
Nashville, TN 37203
Phone: (615) 259-0040   Fax: (615) 226-2686
E-mail: emmynash@aol.com
Web Site: www.emmyonline.org/nashville

Summary: To provide financial assistance to students at colleges and universities in the Midsouth Region who are majoring in a field related to communications.
Eligibility: This program is open to high school seniors in the Midsouth Region (the states of Tennessee and North Carolina and the television market of Huntsville, Alabama). Applicants must have been accepted at an accredited 4-year college or university and be intending to pursue a career in broadcasting, mass communications, television, video, or a directly related field. In addition to a completed application form, candidates must submit a complete resume listing their creative work, field and work experiences, school activities, and honors and/or advanced placement courses; official transcripts; SAT or ACT scores; 2 letters of recommendation; and an essay, up to 500 words, on the problems and challenges the applicant sees in the future of the electronic media.
Financial data: The stipend is $1,000.
Duration: 1 year.
Number awarded: 2 each year.
Deadline: April of each year.

1350
DONALD AND PEARL MCMURCHIE SCHOLARSHIP

Summary: To provide financial assistance to members of the Presbyterian Church (USA) who are interested in attending an institution of higher learning affiliated with that denomination.
See Listing #270.

1351
DONNA REED PERFORMING ARTS SCHOLARSHIPS

Donna Reed Foundation for the Performing Arts
1305 Broadway
Denison, IA 51442
Phone: (712) 263-3334   (800) 336-4692
Fax: (712) 263-8026   E-mail: info@donnareed.org
Web Site: www.donnareed.org
Summary: To provide financial assistance to high school seniors interested in pursuing higher education in the performing arts.
Eligibility: This program is open to high school seniors who wish to pursue an education or a career in 1 of the following 5 performing arts: acting, dance (ballet, modern, jazz, tap), vocal (classical, jazz, popular), musical theater, and instrumental (classical, jazz, popular). Applicants must graduate or have graduated from high school during the period between September prior to applying and August after applying. They submit audio or video tapes; based on those tapes, finalists are invited to a live competition in June at the Donna Reed Festival and Workshops for the Performing Arts in Denison, Iowa. Selection is based on talent. Grades and financial need are not considered.
Financial data: National winners receive $4,000 and finalists receive $500. Funds may be used for an accredited postsecondary or approved program of study of the recipient's choice.
Duration: Scholarships are awarded annually.
Additional information: The widower and friends of the actress Donna Reed established this foundation in 1987, the year after her death. It is based in, and the workshops are held in, Denison, Iowa, Donna Reed's birthplace. A $35 application fee is required for the first discipline category the applicant enters; additional entries require an additional $25 fee. Fees may be waived in cases of financial need.
Number awarded: 15 each year: in each of the 5 divisions, 1 national winner and 2 other finalists. In addition, each of the 15 national finalists receive free tuition and all expenses to participate in the Donna Reed Festival and Workshops for the Performing Arts. Another 10 finalists (2 in each division) receive free tuition to the workshops but are responsible for their own transportation, housing, food, and miscellaneous expenses.
Deadline: March of each year.

1352
DORE SCHARY AWARDS

Anti-Defamation League
Attn: Department of Campus Affairs/Higher Education
823 United Nations Plaza
New York, NY 10017
Phone: (212) 885-7813   Fax: (212) 867-0779
E-mail: rossj@adl.org
Web Site: www.adl.org
Summary: To recognize and reward outstanding student film and video productions on human relations topics.

Eligibility: This competition is open to all students majoring in film and/or television whose productions were completed during the preceding calendar year. The productions must deal with such themes as prejudice and discrimination, interreligious understanding, cultural pluralism, safeguarding democratic ideals, ethnic and minority portraits, and problems and achievements. Selection is based on contribution to human relations understanding, freshness of approach, realization of concept, and overall technical quality. Entries may be submitted in any of 4 categories: film narrative, film documentary, video narrative, and video documentary.
Financial data: The prizes are $1,000. Winners are flown to Los Angeles for the awards ceremony.
Duration: The competition is held annually.
Additional information: This program was established in 1982.
Number awarded: 4 each year: 1 in each of the categories.
Deadline: March of each year.

1353
DOROTHY DANN BULLOCK MUSIC THERAPY AWARD

National Federation of Music Clubs
1336 North Delaware Street
Indianapolis, IN 46202-2481
Phone: (317) 638-4003   Fax: (317) 638-0503
E-mail: info@nfmc-music.org
Web Site: www.nfmc-music.org/annual_student.htm
Summary: To recognize and reward outstanding members of the National Federation of Music Clubs (NFMC) who are majoring in music therapy.
Eligibility: Eligible to enter are music therapy majors (college sophomores, juniors, and seniors) in accredited schools offering music therapy degrees approved by National Association of Music Therapists. Student membership in the federation and U.S. citizenship are required.
Financial data: This award is $1,000; funds must be used for further study.
Additional information: Information on this award is also available from Mrs. William B. Walker, 4029 Brookfield, Louisville, KY 40207; information on all federation scholarships is available from Chair, Competitions and Awards Board, Mrs. Lamoine M. Hall, Jr., 4137 Whitfield Avenue, Fort Worth, TX 76109-5432.
Number awarded: 1 each year.
Deadline: February of each year.

1354
DOUGLAS HASKELL AWARDS

American Institute of Architects-New York Chapter
Attn: New York Foundation for Architecture
200 Lexington Avenue, Sixth Floor
New York, NY 10016
Phone: (212) 683-0023, ext. 14   E-mail: pwest@aiany.org
Web Site: www.aiany.org/nyfoundation
Summary: To recognize and reward excellent college student writing on architecture and related design subjects.
Eligibility: Students must be enrolled in a professional architecture or related program (e.g., art history, interior design, urban studies, or landscape architecture). Submissions are limited to articles on architecture, urban design, or related topics published during the past 3 years, unpublished works scheduled for publication in the current year, and student-edited journals released this year or last. Entries-which may consist of a criticism, a news story, an essay or feature article, or a book review-must be accompanied by a 100-word statement describing the purpose of the piece, its intended audience, and the date and place of publication. Each entrant is limited to 2 submissions. Entrants must send 9 copies of each article and 3 copies of each journal.
Financial data: The minimum prize is $2,000.
Duration: The competition is held annually.
Additional information: The New York Foundation for Architecture is an affiliate of the American Institute of Architects, New York Chapter.
Number awarded: 1 or more each year.
Deadline: March of each year.

1355
EASTERN STAR TRAINING AWARDS FOR RELIGIOUS LEADERSHIP

Order of the Eastern Star
Attn: General Grand Chapter
1618 New Hampshire Avenue, N.W.
Washington, DC 20009-2578
Phone: (202) 667-4737   (800) 648-1182
Fax: (202) 462-5162

Summary: To provide financial assistance for college to individuals who are willing to dedicate their lives to full-time religious service.
Eligibility: In general, awards are made to applicants preparing for leadership in various fields of religious service, such as ministers, missionaries, directors of church music, directors of religious education, and counselors of youth leadership. They need not be affiliated with the Masonic Fraternity or the Order of the Eastern Star. Specific eligibility is determined by each Grand Jurisdiction (state or province) and each chapter under jurisdiction of the General Grand Chapter.
Financial data: The amounts are determined by each jurisdiction or committee on the basis of funds available, number of applicants, and needs of the individual. Funds are paid directly to the recipient's school and may be used, as needed, for books, tuition, board, or medical aid.
Duration: 1 year; may be renewed.
Additional information: This program was established in 1952.
Number awarded: Varies each year.
Deadline: Deadlines vary by jurisdiction or committee; check with the unit in your area for details.

1356
ED BRADLEY SCHOLARSHIP

Radio and Television News Directors Foundation
1000 Connecticut Avenue, N.W., Suite 615
Washington, DC 20036-5302
Phone: (202) 467-5218   Fax: (202) 223-4007
E-mail: karenb@rtndf.org
Web Site: www.rtndf.org/asfi/scholarships/undergrad.shtml
Summary: To provide financial assistance to outstanding undergraduate students, especially minorities, who are preparing for a career in electronic journalism.
Eligibility: Eligible are sophomore or more advanced undergraduate students enrolled in an electronic journalism sequence at an accredited or nationally recognized college or university. Applicants must submit 1 to 3 examples of reporting or producing skills on audio or video cassette tapes (no more than 15 minutes total), a statement explaining why they are interested in a career in broadcast or cable journalism, and a letter of endorsement from a faculty sponsor that verifies the applicant has at least 1 year of school remaining. Preference is given to undergraduate students of color.
Financial data: The stipend is $10,000, paid in semiannual installments of $5,000 each.
Duration: 1 year.
Additional information: The Radio and Television News Directors Foundation (RTNDF) also provides an expense-paid trip to the Radio-Television News Directors Association (RTNDA) annual international conference. It defines electronic journalism to include radio, television, cable, and online news. Previous winners of any RTNDF scholarship or internship are not eligible.
Number awarded: 1 each year.
Deadline: April of each year.

1357
ED E. AND GLADYS HURLEY FOUNDATION GRANTS

Ed E. and Gladys Hurley Foundation
NationsBank of Texas, N.A., Trustee
Attn: Scott Wagoner
P.O. Box 831515
Dallas, TX 75283-1515
Phone: (214) 559-6476   Fax: (214) 559-6364
Summary: To provide financial assistance to men and women in Texas who are interested in becoming Protestant ministers or who wish to pursue religious education.
Eligibility: Eligible to apply for these funds are men and women in Texas who can demonstrate financial need and who are interested in 1) studying to become ministers or 2) pursuing other phases of religious education of the Protestant faith. Applicants must be U.S. residents and willing to attend a college in Texas.
Financial data: The maximum grant is $1,000 per year.
Duration: 1 year.
Number awarded: Varies each year.
Deadline: April of each year.

1358
EDITH H. HENDERSON SCHOLARSHIP

Landscape Architecture Foundation
Attn: Scholarship Program
636 Eye Street, N.W.
Washington, DC 20001-3736
Phone: (202) 216-2356   Fax: (202) 898-1185
E-mail: msippel@asla.org
Web Site: www.laprofession.org
Summary: To provide financial assistance to undergraduate or graduate students in landscape architecture.
Eligibility: Eligible to apply are landscape architecture students in any year of graduate or undergraduate work. The prize is awarded to a student committed to the goal of developing practical communication skills as part of the role of a landscape architect. Applicants must submit a review of 200 to 400 of the book *Edith Henderson's Home Landscape Companion*. They must also participate in a class in public speaking or creative writing. Selection is based on the essay and class participation, professional experience, community involvement, extracurricular activities, and financial need.
Financial data: This scholarship is $1,000.
Additional information: This scholarship was established in honor of an Atlanta-based landscape architect who is a former vice president of both the American Society of Landscape Architects and the Garden Club of America.
Number awarded: 1 each year.
Deadline: March of each year.

1359
EDSF WORLDWIDE ELECTRONIC DOCUMENT COMMUNICATION SCHOLARSHIPS

Electronic Document Systems Foundation
24238 Hawthorne Boulevard
Torrance, CA 90505-6506
Phone: (310) 791-9521   (800) 669-7567
E-mail: info@edsf.org
Web Site: www.edsf.org
Summary: To provide financial assistance to students interested in preparing for a career in the field of electronic document technology.
Eligibility: To apply, students must be 1) full-time juniors, seniors, or advanced college students or 2) first- or second-year students attending a technical, trade, or 2-year school. All applicants must be interested in preparing for a career in the field of document/communication systems. This involves document preparation, production, and/or delivery, including marketing, graphic communications and arts, printing, web authoring, electronic publishing, computer science, and telecommunications. A minimum 3.0 grade point average is required. There is no formal application form; interested students are asked to send 7 copies of the following: a letter requesting consideration for this scholarship, a response to this question: "What do you see as the future of document management," a statement of career goals, a list of extracurricular activities, a transcript (high school or postsecondary grades for the 2-year school applicants, a college transcript for the upper-division applicants), and recommendations from 2 faculty members. Financial need is not considered in the selection process.
Financial data: The stipend is either $2,000 (David Hoods Memorial Scholarship for college juniors or seniors) or $1,000 (for college freshmen or sophomores).
Duration: 1 year.
Additional information: These scholarships were first awarded in 1999. Application packets can be sent electronically to jcmowlds@aol.com in a Word document or pdf format.
Number awarded: 7 each year.
Deadline: July of each year.

1360
EDWARD D. STONE, JR. AND ASSOCIATES MINORITY SCHOLARSHIP

Landscape Architecture Foundation
Attn: Scholarship Program
636 Eye Street, N.W.
Washington, DC 20001-3736
Phone: (202) 216-2356   Fax: (202) 898-1185
E-mail: msippel@asla.org
Web Site: www.laprofession.org
Summary: To provide financial assistance to minority college students who wish to study landscape architecture.
Eligibility: This program is open to African American, Hispanic American, Native American, and minority college students of other cultural and ethnic backgrounds, if they are entering their final 2 years of undergraduate study in landscape architecture. Applicants must submit a 500-word essay on a design or research effort they wish to pursue (explaining how it will contribute to the advancement of the profession and to their ethnic heritage), 4 to 8 35mm color slides or black-and-white photographs of their best work, and 2 letters of recommendation. Selection is based on professional experience, community involvement, extracurricular activities, and financial need.
Financial data: The stipend is $1,000.
Duration: 1 year.
Number awarded: 2 each year.
Deadline: March of each year.

1361
EDWARD PAYSON AND BERNICE PI'ILANI IRWIN SCHOLARSHIP TRUST FUND

Hawai'i Community Foundation
900 Fort Street Mall, Suite 1300
Honolulu, HI 96813
Phone: (808) 566-5570   (888) 731-3863
Fax: (808) 521-6286   E-mail: scholarships@hcf-hawaii.org
Web Site: www.hcf-hawaii.org
Summary: To provide financial assistance to Hawaii residents who are interested in preparing for a career in journalism.
Eligibility: This program is open to Hawaii residents who are studying journalism or communications as college juniors, seniors, or graduate students. They must be able to demonstrate academic achievement (at least a 2.7 grade point average), good moral character, and financial need. In addition to filling out the standard application form, applicants must write a short statement indicating their reasons for attending college, their planned course of study, their career goals, and why they have chosen to major in journalism.
Financial data: The amounts of the awards depend on the availability of funds and the need of the recipient; recently, grants averaged $1,300.
Duration: 1 year.
Additional information: Recipients may attend college in Hawaii or on the mainland.
Number awarded: Varies each year; recently, 22 of these scholarships were awarded.
Deadline: February of each year.

1362
EISENHOWER HISPANIC-SERVING INSTITUTIONS FELLOWSHIPS

Department of Transportation
Federal Highway Administration
Attn: National Highway Institute
4600 North Fairfax Drive, Suite 800
Arlington, VA 22203-1553
Phone: (703) 235-0538   Fax: (703) 235-0593
E-mail: ilene.payne@fhwa.dov.gov
Web Site: www.nhi.fhwa.dot.gov/fellowships.html
Summary: To provide financial assistance for undergraduate study in transportation-related fields to students at Hispanic Serving Institutions.
Eligibility: These fellowships are intended for students who are enrolled at federally-designated 4-year Hispanic-Serving Institutions (HSIs) and who are pursuing a degree in a transportation-related field (i.e., engineering, accounting, business, architecture, environmental sciences, etc.). Applicants must have entered their junior year, have at least a 3.0 grade point average, and have a faculty sponsor.
Financial data: The stipend covers the fellow's full cost of education, including tuition and fees.
Duration: 1 year.
Number awarded: Varies each year; recently, 18 students received support from this program.
Deadline: February of each year.

1363
EISENHOWER HISTORICALLY BLACK COLLEGES AND UNIVERSITIES FELLOWSHIPS

Department of Transportation
Federal Highway Administration
Attn: National Highway Institute
4600 North Fairfax Drive, Suite 800
Arlington, VA 22203-1553
Phone: (703) 235-0538   Fax: (703) 235-0593
E-mail: ilene.payne@fhwa.dov.gov
Web Site: www.nhi.fhwa.dot.gov/fellowships.html
Summary: To provide financial assistance for undergraduate study in transportation-related fields to students at Historically Black Colleges and Universities.
Eligibility: These fellowships are intended for students who are enrolled at federally-designated 4-year Historically Black Colleges and Universities (HBCUs) and who are pursuing a degree in a transportation-related field (i.e., engineering, accounting, business, architecture, environmental sciences, etc.). Applicants must have entered their junior year, have at least a 3.0 grade point average, and have a faculty sponsor.
Financial data: The stipend covers the fellow's full cost of education, including tuition and fees.
Duration: 1 year.
Number awarded: Varies; recently, 14 students received support from this program.
Deadline: February of each year.

1364
ELEANOR ALLWORK GRANTS

American Institute of Architects-New York Chapter
Attn: New York Foundation for Architecture
200 Lexington Avenue, Sixth Floor
New York, NY 10016
Phone: (212) 683-0023, ext. 14   E-mail: pwest@aiany.org
Web Site: www.aiany.org/nyfoundation
Summary: To provide financial assistance to students in New York who are majoring in architecture.
Eligibility: This program is open to U.S. citizens and permanent residents of New York City who are majoring in architecture. They must be enrolled in an accredited program at a college or university in the state. Only nominations are accepted; nominations must be submitted by the dean of the student's architectural school. Selection is based on academic record and financial need.
Financial data: Stipends are either $7,500 (designated as Honor Grants) or $2,500 (designated as Citation Grants).
Duration: 1 year.
Additional information: This program was established in 1977.
Number awarded: Varies each year. The sponsor intends to distribute $15,000 in some combination of Honor Grants and Citation Grants.
Deadline: March of each year.

1365
ELICE T. JOHNSTON SCHOLARSHIP FOR THE CERAMIC ARTS

Clayfolk
Attn: Scholarship Committee
P.O. Box 274
Talent, OR 97540
Summary: To provide financial assistance to ceramic art students in California and Oregon who are interested in pursuing upper-division college courses, workshops at accredited institutions, and study at foreign institutions.
Eligibility: Applicants must be residents of Oregon or northern California and have completed 2 years of college or the equivalent level of art education; this may include sculpture, drawing, design, and the study of aesthetics or technical ceramics. They must be looking for funding to further their education in upper-division college or art school courses, workshops at accredited institutions, or study abroad at accredited institutions. Applications are considered only after the following supporting documents are received: a portfolio of work (8 to 12 slides and/or photographs), a brief statement about their work and how they plan to use the award, 2 letters of recommendation, a recent academic transcript, a copy of the College Scholarship Service Financial Aid Form (FAF) or a 1040 tax form from the previous year, and a self-addressed stamped envelope to use in returning the portfolio. Financial need is considered in the selection process.
Financial data: The stipend is $1,000. Funds are provided directly to the recipient.
Duration: 1 year; may be renewed.
Deadline: June of each year.

1366
ELIE WIESEL PRIZE IN ETHICS

Elie Wiesel Foundation for Humanity
Attn: Program Coordinator
529 Fifth Avenue, Suite 1802
New York, NY 10017
Phone: (212) 490-7777   Fax: (212) 490-6006
E-mail: essaycontest@eliewieselfoundation.org
Web Site: www.eliewieselfoundation.org
Summary: To recognize and reward outstanding student essays on a topic related to ethics.
Eligibility: Eligible to compete are full-time juniors and seniors at accredited colleges and universities in the United States and Canada. Essays must be submitted by the college or university, each of which may submit only 3 student works. Essays must be between 3,000 and 4,000 words in length and on a theme of the student's choice. Readers look for adherence to design format, carefully proofread essays, well thought out essays that do not stray from the topic, depth of feeling and genuine grappling with a moral dilemma, originality and imagination, eloquence of writing style, and intensity and unity in the essay.
Financial data: First prize is $5,000, second prize is $2,500, third prize is $1,500, and each honorable mention is $500.
Duration: The competition is held annually.
Number awarded: 5 prizes each year: a first, second, and third prize as well as 2 honorable mentions.
Deadline: November of each year.

1367
ELIZABETH MCCULLAGH SCHOLARSHIP

Florida Federation of Garden Clubs, Inc.
Attn: Scholarship Chair
6065 21st Street S.W.
Vero Beach, FL 32968-9427
Phone: (561) 778-1023
Web Site: www.ffgc.org
Summary: To provide financial aid to Florida high school seniors who are interested in majoring in a field related to horticulture in college.
Eligibility: This program is open to Florida residents who are high school seniors and planning to attend a college or university in the state. They must have at least a 3.0 grade point average, be in financial need, and be interested in majoring in horticulture, botany, landscape design, conservation of natural resources, civic beautification, public sanitation, nature studies, or an allied field of study. Selection is based on academic record, commitment to career, character, and financial need.
Financial data: The stipend is $1,500. The funds are sent directly to the recipient's school and distributed semiannually.
Duration: 1 year.
Additional information: If the recipient's grade point average drops below 3.0, the second installment of the scholarship is not provided.
Number awarded: 1 each year.
Deadline: April of each year.

1368
ELLEN MASIN PERSINA SCHOLARSHIP

National Press Club
Attn: General Manager Office
529 14th Street, N.W.
Washington, DC 20045
Phone: (202) 662-7599
Web Site: www.press.org
Summary: To provide funding to minority high school seniors interested in preparing for a journalism career in college.
Eligibility: This program is open to minority high school seniors who have been accepted to college and plan to pursue a career in journalism. Applicants must 1) demonstrate an ongoing interest in journalism through work in high school and/or other media; 2) submit a 1-page essay on why they want to pursue a career in journalism; and 3) have at least a 2.75 grade point average in high school. Financial need is considered in the selection process.
Financial data: The stipend is $5,000 per year.
Duration: 4 years.
Additional information: The program began in 1991. In the past, the Press Club has drawn on the Washington Association of Black Journalists and Youth

Connections (a nationwide organization that produces free papers written by high school students).

Number awarded: 1 or more each year.

Deadline: February of each year.

1369
ELLIS VIRGINIA ALLISON ACCOMPANYING AWARD

National Federation of Music Clubs
1336 North Delaware Street
Indianapolis, IN 46202-2481
Phone: (317) 638-4003   Fax: (317) 638-0503
E-mail: info@nfmc-music.org
Web Site: www.nfmc-music.org/BienStudentSpecial.htm

Summary: To recognize and reward outstanding young musicians who are members of the National Federation of Music Clubs (NFMC).

Eligibility: Applicants must be majoring in vocal or instrumental accompanying. They must be between 18 and 25 years of age, U.S. citizens, and student members of the federation.

Financial data: This award is $2,000.

Additional information: Information on this award is also available from Marjorie S. Gloyd, 1480 West Belfry Court, Green Valley, AZ 85614; information on all federation scholarships is available from Chair, Competitions and Awards Board, Mrs. Lamoine M. Hall, Jr., 4137 Whitfield Avenue, Fort Worth, TX 76109-5432. There is a $30 entry fee.

Number awarded: 1 every other year.

Deadline: February of odd-numbered years.

1370
ERNEST HEMINGWAY WRITING AWARDS

Kansas City Star
Attn: Lisa Lopez
1729 Grand Boulevard
Kansas City, MO 64108
Phone: (816) 234-4907   E-mail: lopezl@kcstarnet.com

Summary: To recognize and reward outstanding newspaper articles written by high school students.

Eligibility: This competition is open to articles written by high school students during the previous calendar year and published in a student news publication (newspapers, news magazines, and magazine supplements published by student newspapers). Entries must be submitted by high schools, which may nominate up to 2 students in each of 4 areas: feature writing, newswriting (emphasis on breaking news or the presentation of new information), sports writing, and commentary (including editorials and signed columns). Each student must submit 2 examples of original work per category.

Financial data: The prize is a $2,500 college scholarship.

Duration: The competition is held annually.

Additional information: This competition was established in 1995. It honors Ernest Hemingway, who wrote for his high school newspaper shortly before joining the *Kansas City Star* in 1917.

Number awarded: 4 each year: 1 in each category.

Deadline: January of each year.

1371
EUGENIA VELLNER FISCHER AWARD FOR THE PERFORMING ARTS

Miss America Pageant
Attn: Scholarship Department
Two Miss America Way, Suite 1000
Atlantic City, NJ 08401
Phone: (609) 345-7571, ext. 27   (800) 282-MISS
Fax: (609) 347-6079   E-mail: doreen@missamerica.org
Web Site: www.missamerica.org

Summary: To provide financial assistance to women who are pursuing a degree in the performing arts and who, in the past, competed at some level in the Miss America competition.

Eligibility: This program is open to women who are working on an undergraduate, master's, or higher degree in the performing arts and who competed at the local, state, or national level in a Miss America competition in 1992 or later. Applicants may be studying dance, instrumental, monologue, or vocal. They must submit an essay, up to 500 words, on the factors that influenced their decision to enter the field of performing arts, what they consider to be their major strengths in the field, and how they plan to use their degree in the field.

Selection is based on grade point average, class rank, extracurricular activities, financial need, and level of participation within the system.

Financial data: Stipends range from $2,500 to $10,000.

Duration: 1 year; renewable.

Additional information: This scholarship was established in 1999.

Number awarded: 1 or more each year.

Deadline: June of each year.

1372
EVANGELICAL LUTHERAN CHURCH IN AMERICA CLINICAL EDUCATOR SCHOLARSHIPS THEOLOGICAL STUDY

Evangelical Lutheran Church in America
Division for Ministry
Attn: Specialized Pastoral Care and Clinical Education
8765 West Higgins Road
Chicago, IL 60631-4195
Phone: (773) 380-2876   (800) 638-3522, ext. 2876
Fax: (773) 380-2829   E-mail: dstiger@elca.org
Web Site: www.elca.org/dm/spcce/ces_guidelines.html

Summary: To provide financial assistance to members of the Evangelical Lutheran Church in America (ELCA) interested in preparing for certification as educators in pastoral care and counseling ministries.

Eligibility: This program is open to active members of ELCA congregations (either lay or ordained) who are preparing to become CPE supervisors, pastoral counseling educators, and other certified clinical ministry educators. Applicants must be ecclesiastically endorsed or in the process of seeking SPC endorsement, and all training positions/programs must comply with the Inter-Lutheran Coordinating Committee (ILCC) Specialized Pastoral Care, Endorsement Standards and Procedures, Call Criteria and Program Guidelines (2000 edition). They must submit 1) a statement of the nature of the training program and how it fits into both long- and short-range goals for their ministry; 2) a statement of acceptance and contract from a training supervisor; 3) a statement explaining financial need; 4) supervisory and self-evaluations from previous clinical education programs, including units of CPE and/or pastoral counseling training experiences; and 5) if presently serving in a ministry under all, a letter stating the extent to which financial support and/or compensatory time will be provided by the congregation or employing organization for this training.

Financial data: Grants up to $3,000 per year are awarded.

Duration: 1 year; may be renewed.

Number awarded: Varies each year.

Deadline: March and September of each year.

1373
FASHION GROUP INTERNATIONAL OF PORTLAND SCHOLARSHIP

Oregon Student Assistance Commission
Attn: Private Awards Grant Department
1500 Valley River Drive, Suite 100
Eugene, OR 97401-2146
Phone: (541) 687-7395   (800) 452-8807, ext. 7395
Fax: (541) 687-7419   E-mail: awardinfo@mercury.osac.state.or.us
Web Site: www.osac.state.or.us

Summary: To provide financial assistance to students in Oregon interested in pursuing a career in a fashion-related field.

Eligibility: This program is open to residents of Oregon planning to pursue a career in a fashion-related field. Applicants must be enrolled at a college or university in Oregon as sophomores or higher undergraduates or graduate students with a cumulative grade point average of 3.0 or higher. Semifinalists are interviewed by the sponsor.

Financial data: Scholarship amounts vary, depending upon the needs of the recipient.

Duration: 1 year.

Additional information: This program is sponsored by Fashion Group International of Portland.

Number awarded: Varies each year.

Deadline: February of each year.

Scholarship Listings

1374
FEDERAL JUNIOR DUCK STAMP PROGRAM AND SCHOLARSHIP COMPETITION

Fish and Wildlife Service
Federal Duck Stamp Office
Attn: Junior Duck Manager
1849 C Street, N.W., Suite 2058
Washington, DC 20240
Phone: (202) 208-4354   (877) 887-5508
Fax: (202) 208-6296   E-mail: georgia_bednar@fws.gov
Web Site: duckstamps.fws.gov
Summary: To recognize artwork submitted to the Junior Duck Stamp Program.
Eligibility: This competition is open to students in public or private kindergartens through high schools in the United States; home-schooled students are also eligible. U.S. citizenship or permanent resident status are required. Applicants submit paintings of ducks as part of the federal government's Junior Duck Stamp program that supports awards and scholarships for conservation education. They must submit their applications to a designated receiving site in their home state. Each state selects 12 first-place winners (3 in each of 4 grade level groups: K-3, 4-6, 7-9, and 10-12), and then designates 1 of those 12 as best of show to compete in the national competition.
Financial data: First prize at the national level is $2,500. The winner also receives a free trip to Washington, D.C. in the fall to attend the (adult) Federal Duck Stamp Contest, along with an art teacher, a parent, and a state coordinator.
Duration: The competition is held annually.
Additional information: This program was first authorized by Congress in 1994.
Number awarded: 1 national first prize is awarded each year.
Deadline: Applications must be submitted to the respective state receiving site by March of each year.

1375
FEDERATED GARDEN CLUBS OF CONNECTICUT SCHOLARSHIP

Federated Garden Clubs of Connecticut, Inc.
14 Business Park Drive
P.O. Box 854
Branford, CT 06405-0854   Phone: (203) 488-5528
Summary: To provide financial assistance to Connecticut residents who are interested in majoring in horticulture-related fields at a Connecticut college or university.
Eligibility: Applicants must be legal residents of Connecticut who are studying at a college or university in the state in horticulture, floriculture, landscape design, conservation, forestry, botany, agronomy, plant pathology, environmental control, city planning, land management, or related subjects. They must be entering their junior or senior year of college or be a graduate student, have at least a 3.0 grade point average, and be in financial need.
Financial data: Stipends are generally about $1,000 each. Funds are sent to the recipient's school in 2 equal installments.
Duration: 1 year.
Number awarded: Varies each year, depending upon the funds available.
Deadline: June of each year.

1376
FELIX MORLEY JOURNALISM COMPETITION

Institute for Humane Studies at George Mason University
3401 North Fairfax Drive, Suite 440
Arlington, VA 22201-4432
Phone: (703) 993-4880   (800) 697-8799
Fax: (703) 993-4890   E-mail: ihs@gmu.edu
Web Site: www.TheIHS.org/tab1/morley.html
Summary: To recognize and reward the best writing by student journalists whose work demonstrates an appreciation of classical liberal principles.
Eligibility: This competition is open to writers under 26 years of age who are full-time students at the college, university, or high school level. They should submit 3 to 5 articles, editorials, opinion pieces, essays, or reviews published in student newspapers or other periodicals during the preceding year that reflect classical liberal principles (inalienable individual rights; their protection through the institutions of private property, contract, and the rule of law; voluntarism in all human relations; and the self-ordering market, free trade, free migration, and peace). Selection is based on writing ability, potential for development as a writer, and an appreciation of classical liberal principles.
Financial data: First prize is $2,500, second prize $1,000, third prize $750, and runners up $250.
Duration: The competition is held annually.
Additional information: The competition is named for Felix Morley, editor of the *Washington Post* from 1933 to 1940 and winner of a Pulitzer Prize.
Number awarded: 3 prizes and several runners-up are awarded each year.
Deadline: November of each year.

1377
FELLOWSHIP SCHOLARSHIP

The Fellowship of United Methodists in Music & Worship Arts
Attn: Scholarship Chair
P.O. Box 24787
Nashville, TN 37202
Phone: (615) 749-6875   Fax: (615) 749-6874
E-mail: FUMMWA@aol.com
Summary: To provide financial assistance to students who are training for a ministry in the United Methodist Church in the areas of music, worship, drama, dance, visuals, and other liturgical arts.
Eligibility: Applicants must be 1) high school seniors, currently-enrolled undergraduate or graduate students, or students engaged in special education in worship or the arts related to worship at an accredited university, college, or school of theology; 2) members of the United Methodist Church for at least 1 year immediately before applying; 3) able to demonstrate participation in Christian activities at a local church or campus; and 4) able to demonstrate exceptional musical or other artistic talents, leadership abilities, and outstanding promise. Selection is based on talent, leadership ability and promise, intent to continue service in the United Methodist Church as a church professional, and financial need.
Financial data: The amount awarded varies from year to year.
Duration: 1 year.
Additional information: The Fellowship of United Methodists in Music & Worship Arts is an organization of pastors, worship leaders, church musicians, and others involved in visual arts, drama, dance, and church architecture who are "dedicated to a fellowship of service, Christian nurture of persons, and the glory of God."
Number awarded: Varies; generally, 3 each year, plus the Thom Jones Scholarship (for recipients outstanding in worship, the arts, or liturgical arts).
Deadline: February of each year.

1378
FERNANDES TRUST SCHOLARSHIP

Portuguese Foundation, Inc.
86 New Park Avenue
Hartford, CT 06106-2127
Phone: (860) 236-5514   Fax: (860) 236-5514
E-mail: fgrosa@snet.net
Summary: To provide financial assistance for college to students of Portuguese ancestry in Connecticut.
Eligibility: To apply for this assistance, students must be of Portuguese ancestry, U.S. citizens or permanent residents, residents of Connecticut, and interested in studying the Portuguese language or in disseminating Portuguese culture. They must be high school seniors, currently-enrolled college students, or students working on a master's or doctoral degree. Along with the application, qualified students must supply an essay describing financial need, an essay detailing proof of Portuguese ancestry and interest in the Portuguese language and culture, 2 letters of recommendation, their high school or college transcripts, a copy of the FAFSA form or their most recent federal income tax return, and their SAT report. Selection is based on financial need and academic record.
Financial data: Stipends are at least $1,500 each.
Duration: 1 year; recipients may reapply.
Additional information: Undergraduate recipients must attend school on a full-time basis; graduate students may attend school on a part-time basis. No recipient may be awarded more than 4 scholarships from the foundation.
Number awarded: 1 each year.

1379
FLORIDA PTA SCHOLARSHIP PROGRAMS

Summary: To provide financial assistance for college to high school seniors in Florida.
See listing #337.

276

1380
FLORIDA SOCIETY OF NEWSPAPER EDITORS MINORITY SCHOLARSHIP PROGRAM

Florida Society of Newspaper Editors
c/o Kevin Walsh, Scholarship Committee
Florida Press Association
122 South Calhoun Street
Tallahassee, FL 32301-1554
Phone: (850) 222-5790   Fax: (850) 224-6012
E-mail: info@fsne.org
Web Site: www.fsne.org/minorityscholar.html
Summary: To provide financial assistance and work experience to minority upper-division students majoring in journalism at a college or university in Florida.
Eligibility: This program is open to minority students in accredited journalism or mass communication programs at Florida 4-year colleges and universities. Applicants must be full-time students in their junior year, have at least a 3.0 grade point average, and be willing to participate in a paid summer internship at a Florida newspaper. As part of the application process, they must write a 300-word autobiographical essay explaining why they want to pursue a career in print journalism and provide a standard resume, references, and clips or examples of relevant classroom work.
Financial data: Winners are given a paid summer internship at a participating newspaper between their junior and senior year. Upon successfully completing the internship, the students are awarded a $3,600 scholarship (paid in 2 equal installments) to be used during their senior year.
Duration: 1 summer for the internship; 1 academic year for the scholarship.
Deadline: December of each year.

1381
FORT COLLINS SYMPHONY ORCHESTRA SENIOR CONCERTO COMPETITION

Fort Collins Symphony Orchestra
College at Oak Plaza
P.O. Box 1963
Fort Collins, CO 80522
Phone: (970) 482-4823   Fax: (970) 482-4858
E-mail: note@fcsymphony.org
Summary: To recognize and reward outstanding young pianists and instrumentalists.
Eligibility: Applicants must be students 25 years of age or younger and submit cassette tapes of a standard, readily available solo concerto or similar work played from memory. Based on the tapes, semifinalists are invited to Fort Collins for a second round in March. From the semifinalists, finalists are chosen for the third round of performances in April.
Financial data: The first-place winner receives the Adeline Rosenberg Memorial Prize of $5,000. Second prize is $3,000 and third prize is $2,000. The awards are cash prizes only, not scholarships.
Duration: The competition is held annually.
Additional information: The competition is for piano in even-numbered years and instruments in odd-numbered years. The entry fee is $50. Requests for applications must be accompanied by a self-addressed stamped envelope.
Number awarded: 10 semifinalists and 3 finalists are chosen each year; all 3 finalists receive a prize.
Deadline: January of each year.

1382
FOUNDATION OF THE WALL AND CEILING INDUSTRY SCHOLARSHIPS

Association of the Wall and Ceiling Industries-International
Attn: Foundation of the Wall and Ceiling Industry
803 West Broad Street, Suite 600
Falls Church, VA 22046
Phone: (703) 538-1615   Fax: (703) 534-8307
Web Site: www.awci.org/fwcischolarship.shtml
Summary: To provide financial assistance for college study in disciplines related to the wall and ceiling industry to employees of firms that are members of the Association of the Wall and Ceiling Industries-International (AWCI) and their dependents.
Eligibility: This program is open to employees of AWCI member companies and their dependents. Applicants must be pursuing or planning to pursue, as a full-time

student, postsecondary education in the field of construction management, engineering, or architecture. They must have a grade point average of 3.0 or higher during their last 2 semesters of study. Students in graduate school, technical school, associate degree programs, and 4-year colleges and universities are all eligible.
Financial data: The stipend is $2,000.
Duration: 1 year.
Number awarded: Up to 5 each year.

1383
THE FOUNTAINHEAD ESSAY CONTEST

Ayn Rand Institute
Attn: Contests Manager
4640 Admiralty Way, Suite 406
Marina del Rey, CA 90292-6617
Phone: (310) 306-9232, ext. 209   Fax: (310) 306-4925
E-mail: seans@aynrand.org
Web Site: www.aynrand.org
Summary: To recognize and reward outstanding essays written by high school students on Ayn Rand's novel, *The Fountainhead.*
Eligibility: Entrants must be juniors or seniors in high school. They must submit a typewritten essay on Ayn Rand's novel, *The Fountainhead.* The essay must be between 800 and 1,600 words. Selection is based on style and content. Judges look for writing that is clear, articulate, and logically organized. To win, an essay must demonstrate an outstanding grasp of the philosophical and psychological meaning of the novel.
Financial data: First prize is $10,000; second prizes are $2,000; third prizes are $1,000; finalist prizes are $100; and semifinalist prizes are $50.
Duration: The competition is held annually.
Additional information: The institute publishes the winning essay in its fall newsletter. This competition began in the academic year 1985-86.
Number awarded: 251 each year: 1 first prize, 5 second prizes, 10 third prizes, 35 finalist prizes, and 200 semifinalist prizes.
Deadline: April of each year.

1384
FRANCES A. MAYS SCHOLARSHIP AWARD

Virginia Association for Health, Physical Education, Recreation, and Dance
c/o Robert Davis
126 Westmoreland Street
Richmond, VA 23226-1330
Summary: To recognize and reward outstanding students majoring in health, physical education, recreation, or dance in Virginia.
Eligibility: Any college or university student working on a degree in health, physical education, recreation, or dance may be nominated for this award. Nominees must be college seniors, have been students for 3 years at a Virginia college or university, and demonstrate outstanding personal qualities, high ideals, academic achievement, and professional ethics. In addition, they must be members of the Virginia Association of Health, Physical Education, Recreation, and Dance and the American Association for Health, Physical Education, Recreation, and Dance.
Financial data: A monetary award is presented (exact amount not specified).
Duration: The award is presented annually.
Deadline: September of each year.

1385
FREEDOM FROM RELIGION FOUNDATION COLLEGE ESSAY CONTEST

Freedom from Religion Foundation
P.O. Box 750
Madison, WI 53701
Phone: (608) 256-8900   E-mail: ffrf@mailbag.com
Web Site: www.ffrf.org
Summary: To recognize and reward outstanding student essays on the separation of church and state.
Eligibility: Any currently-enrolled college student may write an essay on a topic that changes annually but involves rejecting religion; a recent topic was "Growing Up a Freethinker (Atheist/Agnostic)." Students may write about their own experiences in rejecting religion in a religious society or use a philosophical or historical approach. Essays should be 5 to 6 typed double-spaced pages, accompanied by a paragraph biography identifying the student's college or university, year in school, major, and interests.
Financial data: First prize is $1,000, second prize is $500, and third prize is $250.

Duration: The competition is held annually.

Additional information: First prize was previously designated as the Saul Jakel Memorial Award, but after 1996 it was redesignated the Phyllis Stevenson Grams Memorial Award. This contest has been held since 1979. Applicants must send a self-addressed stamped envelope to receive additional information.

Number awarded: 3 each year.

Deadline: July of each year.

1386
FREEDOM FROM RELIGION FOUNDATION HIGH SCHOOL ESSAY CONTEST

Freedom from Religion Foundation
P.O. Box 750
Madison, WI 53701
Phone: (608) 256-8900   E-mail: ffrf@mailbag.com
Web Site: www.ffrf.org

Summary: To recognize and reward outstanding essays written by high school students on free thought or state/church separation themes.

Eligibility: This program is open only to college-bound high school seniors. They are invited to write an essay on a topic that changes annually but relates to freethinking and separation of church and state; recently, the topic was "Why Religion Does NOT Belong in Public Schools." Essays should be 3 or 4 typewritten pages in length, double spaced, with standard margins. Contestants may present an anecdotal essay describing personal experiences in rejecting religion in a religious society or they may use an historical approach in dealing with the general theme. They should include a paragraph biography, their address and telephone number, the name of the college they will be attending, and their planned major.

Financial data: First prize is $1,000, second prize is $500, and third prize is $250.

Duration: The competition is held annually.

Additional information: First prize is designated as the Blanche Fearn Memorial Award.

Number awarded: 3 each year.

Deadline: July of each year.

1387
FTE UNDERGRADUATE FELLOWSHIPS

The Fund for Theological Education, Inc.
825 Houston Mill Road, Suite 250
Atlanta, GA 30329
Phone: (404) 727-1450   Fax: (404) 727-1490
E-mail: fte@thefund.org
Web Site: www.thefund.org

Summary: To provide financial assistance to undergraduate students who are considering the ministry as a career.

Eligibility: Eligible to be nominated for this financial assistance are college students with a strong academic record and a gift for the ministry. They must be considering-but not sure about-ministry as a career. Nominations may be submitted by professors, administrators, chaplains, or campus ministers. Applicants must then submit a personal application. U.S. or Canadian citizenship is required. Selection criteria include imagination, creativity, compassion, a capacity for critical thinking, leadership skills, personal integrity, spiritual depth, dedication to a faith tradition, and an ability to understand and to serve the needs of others.

Financial data: The stipend is $1,500 per year; travel expenses for participation in the summer conference are also covered.

Duration: 1 year.

Additional information: Fellows are invited to attend a summer conference that offers lectures, student panels, and an opportunity to meet with some of the leading American scholars and theological educators. This program started in 1999.

Number awarded: Up to 50 each year.

Deadline: February of each year.

1388
GARDEN STATE ASSOCIATION OF BLACK JOURNALISTS SCHOLARSHIP

Garden State Association of Black Journalists
1050 State Highway 35, Suite 250
Shrewsbury, NJ 07702

Summary: To provide financial assistance to high school and college students in New Jersey interested in preparing for a career in journalism.

Eligibility: Using the New Jersey State Department of Education Schools Directory, the sponsor annually selects 10 schools (high schools and colleges/universities) from the northern half of New Jersey and 10 from the southern half of the state; applications are sent to the guidance departments at those schools. Students at those schools are then chosen to apply. Winners are selected on the basis of grades, letters of recommendations, samples of work, community service, and an essay on their interest in journalism as a career. Financial need is not considered in the selection process.

Financial data: A stipend is awarded (exact amount not specified). After proof of enrollment has been verified, a check is sent to the recipient.

Duration: 1 year; scholarships are not renewable.

1389
GCFM HORTICULTURE SCHOLARSHIP

Garden Club Federation of Maine
c/o Pat Brandenberger
35 Naples Road
Harrison, ME 04040
Phone: (207) 532-3937

Summary: To provide financial assistance to Maine residents who are studying a garden-related field in college.

Eligibility: This program is open to college juniors, seniors, and graduate students who are residents of Maine. Applicants must be majoring in horticulture, floriculture, landscape design, conservation, forestry, botany, agronomy, plant pathology, environmental control, city planning, or another garden-related field. Selection is based on goals, activities, academic achievement, personal commitment, 3 letters of recommendation, and financial need.

Financial data: The stipend is $2,500.

Duration: 1 year.

Number awarded: 1 each year.

Deadline: February of each year.

1390
GEORGE AND LYNNA GENE COOK SCHOLARSHIP

Lincoln Community Foundation
215 Centennial Mall South, Suite 200
Lincoln, NE 68508
Phone: (402) 474-2345   Fax: (402) 476-8532
E-mail: lcf@lcf.org
Web Site: www.lcf.org

Summary: To provide financial assistance for college to Nebraska residents who are members of the First Church of God and attending a college or university affiliated with the denomination.

Eligibility: This program is open to Nebraska residents who are pursuing studies in ministry at any First Church of God college or university affiliated with the church body headquartered in Anderson, Indiana. If there are no applicants seeking a degree in ministry, the scholarship may be awarded to a candidate seeking a degree in education. All applicants must be members of First Church of God congregations in Nebraska. Preference is given to those who demonstrate financial need.

Financial data: A stipend is awarded (exact amount not specified).

Duration: 1 year.

Number awarded: 1 or more each year.

Deadline: March of each year.

1391
GEORGE CHAPLIN SPIRIT AWARD

Honolulu Advertiser
Attn: Assistant to the Editor
615 Kapiolani Boulevard
Honolulu, HI 96813
Phone: (808) 525-8081   E-mail: lesliek@aloha.net
Web Site: www.honoluluadvertiser.com

Summary: To provide financial assistance and internships to students from Hawaii who are entering college and planning to major in journalism.

Eligibility: This program is open to high school seniors in Hawaii who are residents of the state, accepted into a 4-year college or university, and planning to major in journalism. An interview and a principal's recommendation are required.

Financial data: The amount awarded varies each year.

Duration: 1 year.

Additional information: Recipients are also offered a paid internship at the *Honolulu Advertiser.*

1392
GEORGE MORRISON LANDSCAPE ARCHITECTURE SCHOLARSHIP

Florida Federation of Garden Clubs, Inc.
Attn: Scholarship Chair
6065 21st Street S.W.
Vero Beach, FL 32968-9427
Phone: (561) 778-1023
Web Site: www.ffgc.org
Summary: To provide financial aid to undergraduate or graduate students who are working on a degree in landscape architecture at southern universities.
Eligibility: This program is open to graduate students at a southern college accredited by the American Society of Landscape Architects, or to juniors and seniors majoring in landscape architecture at a Florida university. They must have at least a 3.0 grade point average and be in financial need. Selection is based on academic record, commitment to career, character, and financial need.
Financial data: The stipend is $1,500. The funds are sent directly to the recipient's school and distributed semiannually.
Duration: 1 year.
Additional information: If the recipient's grade point average drops below 3.0, the second installment of the scholarship is not provided.
Number awarded: 1 each year.
Deadline: April of each year.

1393
GEORGIA PRESS EDUCATIONAL FOUNDATION SCHOLARSHIPS

Georgia Press Educational Foundation, Inc.
Attn: Member Services
3066 Mercer University Drive, Suite 200
Atlanta, GA 30341-4137
Phone: (770) 454-6776   Fax: (770) 454-6778
E-mail: mail@gapress.org   Web Site: www.gapress.org
Summary: To provide financial assistance to high school seniors and college students in Georgia who are interested in preparing for a career in journalism.
Eligibility: This program is open to high school seniors and currently-enrolled college students in Georgia. They must be U.S. citizens or permanent residents, have been legal residents of Georgia for at least 3 years or be the children of parents who have been legal residents of Georgia for at least 2 years, have had prior newspaper experience, and be recommended by a high school counselor, college professor, or member of the Georgia Press Educational Foundation. Selection is based on academic record, standardized test scores, career plans, and financial need.
Financial data: Stipends range from $1,000 to $1,500.
Duration: 1 year.
Additional information: Among the scholarships offered through this program are the Morris Newspaper Corporation Scholarship, established in 1987 by Charles Morris of the Morris Newspaper Corporation in Savannah, and the Durwood McAlister Scholarship, established in 1992 by *The Atlanta Journal*. Recipients of scholarships of $1,000 or more are required to intern for at least 4 weeks with a Georgia newspaper.
Number awarded: Varies each year; recently, more than 20 students received more than $23,000 in support from this program.
Deadline: January of each year.

1394
GERALD BOYD/ROBIN STONE NON-SUSTAINING SCHOLARSHIP

National Association of Black Journalists
Attn: Media Institute Program Associate
8701-A Adelphi Road
Adelphi, MD 20783-1716
Phone: (301) 445-7100, ext. 108   Fax: (301) 445-7101
E-mail: warren@nabj.org   Web Site: www.nabj.org
Summary: To provide financial assistance to undergraduate or graduate student members of the National Association of Black Journalists (NABJ) who are majoring in print journalism.
Eligibility: This competition is open to African American undergraduate or graduate students who are currently attending an accredited 4-year college or university. Applicants must be majoring in print journalism and have a grade point average of 3.0 or higher. They must submit 6 samples of their published or broadcasted work, an official college transcript, 2 letters of recommendation, a resume, and a 500- to 800-word essay describing their accomplishments as a

student journalist, their career goals, and their interest in the field.
Financial data: The stipend is $2,500.
Duration: 1 year.
Additional information: All scholarship winners must become members of the association before they enroll in college.
Number awarded: 1 or more each year.
Deadline: April of each year.

1395
GIBSON-LAEMEL SCHOLARSHIP

Connecticut Association for Health, Physical Education, Recreation and Dance
c/o Jodie Hellman, Scholarship Chair
Memorial Middle School
P.O. Box 903
Middlebury, CT 06762
Phone: (203) 758-2496
Web Site: www.ctahperd.org/laemel.htm
Summary: To provide financial assistance to college juniors and seniors from Connecticut who are interested in pursuing a career in health, physical education, recreation, or dance.
Eligibility: This program is open to residents of Connecticut who are enrolled as rising college juniors or seniors preparing for a career in the professional studies of health (meaning school health teaching, not nursing, public health, or psychology), physical education, recreation, or dance. Applicants must submit 1) a 350-word statement expressing their thoughts and feelings on why they are entering the field of health, physical education, recreation, or dance; 2) transcripts (with a grade point average of 2.7 or higher); and 3) letters of recommendation from 2 professionally related sources.
Financial data: The stipend is $1,000 per year. Funds are paid to the recipient's college or university to be applied toward tuition, room, and board.
Duration: 1 year.
Number awarded: 1 each year.
Deadline: May of each year.

1396
GLADYS C. ANDERSON MEMORIAL SCHOLARSHIP

American Foundation for the Blind
Attn: Scholarship Committee
11 Penn Plaza, Suite 300
New York, NY 10001
Phone: (212) 502-7661   (800) AFB-LINE
Fax: (212) 502-7771   TDD: (212) 502-7662
E-mail: afbinfo@afb.net
Web Site: www.afb.org/scholarships.asp
Summary: To provide financial assistance to legally blind undergraduate women who are studying religious or classical music.
Eligibility: To be eligible, applicants must be legally blind women who are U.S. citizens and have been accepted in a college or university program in religious or classical music. Applications must include a typewritten statement, up to 2 pages in length, describing educational and career goals, work experience, extracurricular activities, and how scholarship funds will be used. Candidates must also submit a sample performance tape (a voice or instrumental selection).
Financial data: The stipend is $1,000.
Duration: 1 academic year.
Number awarded: 1 each year.
Deadline: March of each year.

1397
GLENN MILLER SCHOLARSHIP COMPETITION

Glenn Miller Birthplace Society
Attn: Scholarship Program
107 East Main Street
P.O. Box 61
Clarinda, IA 51632
Phone: (712) 542-4439   Fax: (712) 542-2461
E-mail: gmbs@heartland.net   Web Site: www.glennmiller.org
Summary: To provide financial assistance to present and prospective college music majors.
Eligibility: Eligible to apply are 1) graduating high school seniors planning to major in music in college and 2) freshmen music majors at an accredited college, university, or school of music. Both instrumentalists and vocalists may compete.

Those who entered as high school seniors and did not win first place are eligible to enter again as college freshmen. Each entrant must submit an audition tape, from which finalists are selected. Finalists are auditioned in person. They must perform a composition of concert quality, up to 5 to 10 minutes in length. Selection is based on talent in any field of applied music; the competition is not intended to select Glenn Miller look-alikes or sound-alikes.

Financial data: The first-place instrumentalist receives $2,200; the second-place instrumentalist receives $1,100. The first-place vocalist receives $1,800; the second-place vocalist receives $900. The funds are to be used for any school-related expense.

Duration: The competition is held annually, in June.

Additional information: Finalists compete in auditions at the Glenn Miller Festival stage show, in Clarinda, Iowa. The scholarship for the first-place vocalist is designated as the GMBS-Ralph Brewster Vocal Scholarship; the scholarship for the second-place vocalist is designated as the GMBS-Jack Pullan Memorial Vocal Scholarship. Applicants selected as finalists on the basis of their audition tapes are responsible for their own transportation expenses to go to Clarinda to perform at the auditions. A $25 application fee is required but is returned to applicants who are not selected to be finalists and to those who are selected as finalists and complete the required audition.

Number awarded: 4 each year.

Deadline: March of each year.

1398
GOLDEN KEY ART COMPETITION

Golden Key National Honor Society
1189 Ponce de Leon Avenue
Atlanta, GA 30306-4624
Phone: (404) 377-2400   (800) 377-2401
E-mail: mboone@goldenkey.gsu.edu   Web Site: goldenkey.gsu.edu

Summary: To recognize and reward members of the Golden Key National Honor Society who are studying art.

Eligibility: Eligible to apply for this program are members of the society who submit slides of their work in the following categories: 1) sculpture; 2) photography; 3) painting; 4) drawing; 5) computer-generated art, set design, graphic design and illustration; 6) printmaking; 7) applied art jewelry, textiles, and ceramics; and 8) mixed media. All entries must be original work, submitted on a slide.

Financial data: Winners receive $1,000 scholarships and other finalists receive $100.

Duration: These awards are presented annually.

Number awarded: Up to 80 each year: 1 winner chosen from up to 10 finalists in each of the 8 categories.

Deadline: March of each year.

1399
GOLDEN KEY LITERARY ACHIEVEMENT AWARDS

Golden Key National Honor Society
1189 Ponce de Leon Avenue
Atlanta, GA 30306-4624
Phone: (404) 377-2400   (800) 377-2401
E-mail: mboone@goldenkey.gsu.edu   Web Site: goldenkey.gsu.edu

Summary: To recognize and reward literary achievements by members of the Golden Key National Honor Society.

Eligibility: This contest is open to members of the Golden Key National Honor Society. Applicants must submit original compositions in the 4 categories of fiction, nonfiction, poetry, or news/feature writing. All entries must be original and only 1 composition per member is accepted. Entries may not exceed 1,000 words, excluding the title page. Selection is based on originality, creativity, and clarity.

Financial data: The winners receive $1,000 scholarships and publication of their work in CONCEPTS.

Duration: The competition is held annually.

Number awarded: 4 each year: 1 in each category.

Deadline: March of each year.

1400
GOLDEN KEY PERFORMING ARTS SHOWCASE

Golden Key National Honor Society
1189 Ponce de Leon Avenue
Atlanta, GA 30306-4624
Phone: (404) 377-2400   (800) 377-2401
E-mail: mboone@goldenkey.gsu.edu
Web Site: goldenkey.gsu.edu

Summary: To recognize and reward members of the Golden Key National Honor

Society who are studying the performing arts.

Eligibility: Eligible to apply for this program are members of the society who are studying in the following 6 categories: vocal performance, dance, drama, original musical composition, instrumental performance, or filmmaking. Selection is based on videotaped performances, up to 10 minutes in length.

Financial data: Winners receive $1,000 scholarships and the chance to perform at the society's annual convention.

Duration: These awards are presented annually.

Number awarded: 6 each year: 1 in each of the 6 categories.

Deadline: February of each year.

1401
GRADY-RAYAM PRIZE IN SACRED MUSIC

"Negro Spiritual" Scholarship Foundation
1111 North Orange Avenue
Orlando, FL 32804-6407
Phone: (407) 426-1717, ext. 105   Fax: (407) 426-1705
Web Site: www.negrospiritual.org

Summary: To recognize and reward African American high school seniors in Florida who excel at singing "Negro spirituals."

Eligibility: African American high school seniors in Florida are invited to enter a vocal competition where they perform Negro spirituals.

Financial data: Winners earn tuition assistance grants for college; other finalists receive monetary gifts and/or certificates of recognition.

Duration: The competition is held annually, in February.

Additional information: The scholarship is named for a Catholic Bishop and a world-renowned opera singer.

Deadline: November of each year.

1402
GRANDMA MOSES SCHOLARSHIP

Western Art Association
Attn: Foundation
13730 Loumont Street
Whittier, CA 90601

Summary: To provide financial assistance for art school to women high school seniors whose art demonstrates a "congruence with the art of Grandma Moses."

Eligibility: This program is open to female graduating high school seniors. Applicants must be planning to study art in a college, university, or specialized school of art. Preference is given to applicants from the western United States. Candidates must submit samples of their artwork; selection is based on the extent to which their work "manifests a congruence with the work of the famed folk artist, Grandma Moses." Financial need is not considered.

Financial data: The stipend is $3,000 per year.

Duration: 1 year; may be renewed up to 3 additional years.

Additional information: Requests for applications should be accompanied by a self-addressed stamped envelope, the student's e-mail address, and the source where they found the scholarship information.

Number awarded: 1 each year.

Deadline: March of each year.

1403
GREAT FALLS ADVERTISING FEDERATION ADVERTISING EDUCATION MEMORIAL SCHOLARSHIP

Great Falls Advertising Federation
Attn: Advertising Scholarship Committee
P.O. Box 634
Great Falls, MT 59403
Phone: (406) 761-6453   (800) 803-3351
Fax: (406) 453-1128   E-mail: gfaf@gfaf.com
Web Site: www.gfaf.com

Summary: To provide financial assistance to high school seniors in Montana interested in pursuing a career related to advertising.

Eligibility: This program is open to residents of Montana who are high school seniors planning to attend a college or university. Applicants must be interested in pursuing a career in advertising, marketing, electronic media, graphics design, or a related field. They must submit a letter listing their special interests and talents and describing how they will use the scholarship, a resume listing their educational background and awards and honors they have received, a marketing communications plan for a hypothetical client of their choice, and a marketing communications program with a budget, advertising strategy, media strategy,

sales promotion strategy, and other communications strategies.
Financial data: The stipend is $1,000.
Duration: 1 year.
Additional information: This program began in 1983.
Number awarded: 1 each year.
Deadline: February of each year.

1404
GREAT FALLS ADVERTISING FEDERATION ART EDUCATION MEMORIAL SCHOLARSHIP

Great Falls Advertising Federation
Attn: Advertising Scholarship Committee
P.O. Box 634
Great Falls, MT 59403
Phone: (406) 761-6453   (800) 803-3351
Fax: (406) 453-1128   E-mail: gfaf@gfaf.com
Web Site: www.gfaf.com
Summary: To provide financial assistance to high school seniors in Montana interested in studying art at the postsecondary level.
Eligibility: This program is open to seniors graduating from high schools in Montana. Applicants must be interested in studying art at a college, university, or seminar or with a recognized private teacher of the recipient's choice (approval by the sponsoring organization may be required). They must submit a resume, a letter describing specific plans for use of the scholarship, 10 to 20 slides or color photographs of their work, and at least 3 letters of recommendation.
Financial data: The stipend is $1,000.
Duration: 1 year.
Additional information: This program began in 1983.
Number awarded: 1 each year.
Deadline: February of each year.

1405
GRETCHEN E. VAN ROY MUSIC EDUCATION SCHOLARSHIP

National Federation of Music Clubs
1336 North Delaware Street
Indianapolis, IN 46202-2481
Phone: (317) 638-4003   Fax: (317) 638-0503
E-mail: info@nfmc-music.org
Web Site: www.nfmc-music.org/annual_student.htm
Summary: To provide financial assistance to college student members of the National Federation of Music Clubs (NFMC) who are majoring in music education.
Eligibility: Applicants must be college juniors majoring in music education at a college or university. U.S. citizenship and membership in the student division of the federation are required.
Financial data: The stipend is $1,000.
Additional information: Information on this award is also available from Mrs. Ralph Suggs, 606 East Ridge Village Drive, Miami, FL 33157; information on all federation scholarships is available from Chair, Competitions and Awards Board, Mrs. Lamoine M. Hall, Jr., 4137 Whitfield Avenue, Fort Worth, TX 76109-5432.
Number awarded: 1 each year.
Deadline: February of each year.

1406
GUIDEPOSTS YOUNG WRITERS CONTEST

Guideposts
16 East 34th Street
New York, NY 10016
Phone: (212) 251-8100   Fax: (212) 684-0679
Summary: To recognize and reward outstanding true spiritual stories written by high school students.
Eligibility: Entrants must be high school juniors or seniors. They must submit a true first-person story about a memorable or moving experience and how faith in God has made a difference in their lives. Manuscripts must be written in English, be double spaced, and be no more than 1,200 words. Children of *Guideposts* employees and staff members are not eligible.
Financial data: First prize is an $8,000 scholarship to an accredited school of the winner's choice. Second prize: $7,000 scholarship; third prize: $5,000 scholarship; fourth through eighth prizes: $1,000 scholarship; ninth through 25th prizes: portable electronic typewriter.
Duration: The competition is held annually. Scholarships must be used within 5 years of high school graduation.

Additional information: Manuscripts will not be returned unless accompanied by a self-addressed stamped envelope.
Number awarded: 25 each year.
Deadline: November of each year.

1407
HAMPTONS INTERNATIONAL FILM FESTIVAL STUDENT AWARDS

Hamptons International Film Festival
3 Newtown Mews
East Hampton, NY 11937
Phone: (631) 324-4600   Fax: (631) 324-5116
E-mail: hiff@hamptonsfest.org   Web Site: www.hamptonsfest.org
Summary: To recognize and reward outstanding student films and videos entered in the Hamptons International Film Festival.
Eligibility: This festival accepts works produced by undergraduate and graduate students that have been completed within the past year. Entries may be in 16mm, 35mm, video (Beta SP), or DVD format. Works may not have been released theatrically or shown on television prior to the festival.
Financial data: The prizes are $2,500.
Duration: The festival is held annually.
Additional information: Further information is available from Jeremiah Newton, Director of Student Showcase and Awards, New York University, Tisch School of the Arts, 721 Broadway, New York, NY 10003, (212) 998-1760, E-mail: jjn1@is4.nyu.edu.
Number awarded: 10 student works are honored each year: 5 by undergraduates and 5 by graduate students.
Deadline: June of each year.

1408
HAROLD E. FELLOWS SCHOLARSHIPS

Broadcast Education Association
Attn: Scholarships
1771 N Street, N.W.
Washington, DC 20036-2891
Phone: (202) 429-5354   E-mail: bea@nab.org
Web Site: www.beaweb.org
Summary: To provide financial assistance to upper-division and graduate students who are interested in preparing for a career in broadcasting.
Eligibility: This program is open to juniors, seniors, and graduate students enrolled full time at a college or university where at least 1 department is an institutional member of the Broadcast Education Association (BEA). Applicants may be studying in any area of broadcasting. They must have worked (or their parent must have worked) as an employee or paid intern at a station that is a member of the National Association of Broadcasters (NAB). Selection is based on evidence that the applicant possesses high integrity, superior academic ability, potential to be an outstanding electronic media professional, and a sense of personal and professional responsibility.
Financial data: The stipend is $1,250.
Duration: 1 year; may not be renewed.
Additional information: Information is also available from Peter B. Orlik, Central Michigan University, 344 Moore Hall, Mt. Pleasant, MI 48859, (517) 774-7279. This program is sponsored by the NAB and administered by the BEA.
Number awarded: 4 each year.
Deadline: September of each year.

1409
HARRIET IRSAY SCHOLARSHIP GRANT

American Institute of Polish Culture, Inc.
1440 79th Street Causeway, Suite 117
Miami, FL 33141
Phone: (305) 864-2349   Fax: (305) 865-5150
E-mail: info@ampolinstitute.org
Web Site: www.ampolinstitute.org
Summary: To provide financial assistance to Polish American and other students interested in working on an undergraduate or graduate degree in journalism or related fields.
Eligibility: These are merit scholarships. They are available to students working on an undergraduate or graduate degree in the following fields: journalism, communications, and/or public relations. Preference is given to American students of Polish heritage. Applicants must submit a completed application, a detailed resume, and 3 letters of recommendation.
Financial data: The stipend is $1,000.

Duration: 1 year.
Additional information: There is a $25 processing fee.
Number awarded: 12 to 15 each year.
Deadline: February of each year.

1410
HARRIETT BARNHART WIMMER SCHOLARSHIP

Landscape Architecture Foundation
Attn: Scholarship Program
636 Eye Street, N.W.
Washington, DC 20001-3736
Phone: (202) 216-2356   Fax: (202) 898-1185
E-mail: msippel@asla.org   Web Site: www.laprofession.org
Summary: To recognize and reward the outstanding achievements of women undergraduates majoring in landscape architecture.
Eligibility: Undergraduate women in their senior year who are majoring in landscape architecture are eligible to apply. They must be able to demonstrate excellence in design ability and sensitivity to the environment. They are required to submit a letter of recommendation from a design instructor, a 500-word autobiographical essay that addresses personal and professional goals, and a sample of design work. Selection is based on professional experience, community involvement, extracurricular activities, and financial need.
Financial data: The award is $1,000.
Duration: The award is granted annually.
Additional information: This scholarship was established by the firm of Wimmer Yamada and Associates in memory of a pioneer in the field of landscape architecture and founder of the firm. Group projects may not be submitted; all work must reflect individual projects only.
Number awarded: 1 each year.
Deadline: March of each year.

1411
HARRY BARFIELD KBA SCHOLARSHIP PROGRAM

Kentucky Broadcasters Association
101 Enterprise Drive
Frankfort, KY 40601
Phone: (502) 848-0426   Fax: (502) 848-5710
Web Site: www.kba.org
Summary: To provide financial assistance to currently-enrolled college students in Kentucky who are majoring in broadcasting.
Eligibility: Applicants must be Kentucky residents, currently enrolled in college in Kentucky (preferably but not limited to second-semester sophomore status), and majoring in broadcasting or telecommunications. To apply, students must submit a completed application form, a college transcript, a 500-word essay discussing career goals, a list of extracurricular activities and scholarships, and 1 recommendation from a faculty member. Financial need is not considered.
Financial data: The stipend is $1,000.
Duration: 1 year; may be renewed for 1 additional year if the recipient maintains a 3.0 grade point average.
Additional information: Information on this program, which began in 1993, is also available from the KBA Scholarship Chair, Carl Nathe, University of Kentucky, Mathews Building, Room 104, Lexington, KY 40506-0047, (859) 257-1754.
Number awarded: 2 each year.
Deadline: May of each year.

1412
HARRY S. TRUMAN SCHOLARSHIP PROGRAM

Harry S. Truman Scholarship Foundation
712 Jackson Place, N.W.
Washington, DC 20006
Phone: (202) 395-4831   Fax: (202) 395-6995
E-mail: office@truman.gov   Web Site: www.truman.gov
Summary: To provide financial assistance to undergraduate students who have outstanding leadership potential, plan to pursue careers in government or other public service, and wish to attend graduate school in the United States or abroad to prepare themselves for a public service career.
Eligibility: Students must be nominated to be considered for this program. Nominees must be full-time students with junior standing at a 4-year institution, committed to a career in government or public service, in the upper quarter of their class, and U.S. citizens or nationals. Each participating institution may nominate up to 4 candidates (and up to 3 additional students who completed their first 2 years at

a community college); community colleges and other 2-year institutions may nominate former students who are enrolled as full-time students with junior-level academic standing at accredited 4-year institutions. Selection is based on extent and quality of community service and government involvement, academic performance, leadership record, suitability of the nominee's proposed program of study for a career in public service, and writing and analytical skills. Priority is given to candidates who plan to enroll in a graduate program that specifically trains them for a career in public service, including government at any level, uniformed services, public interest organizations, nongovernmental research and/or educational organizations, public and private schools, and public service oriented nonprofit organizations. The fields of study may include agriculture, biology, engineering, environmental management, physical and social sciences, and technology policy, as well as such traditional fields as economics, education, government, history, international relations, law, nonprofit management, political science, public administration, public health, and public policy. Interviews are required.
Financial data: The scholarship provides up to $30,000: up to $3,000 for the senior year of undergraduate education and as much as $27,000 for graduate studies. Scholars who plan to complete a master's degree in 1 or 2 years receive $13,500 per year. Scholars whose graduate program will require 3 or more years are eligible to receive $9,000 per year for 3 years. Scholars in law programs are eligible to receive $13,500 for the second year of law school and $13,500 at the start of the third year's second semester if they provide evidence that they will enter public service upon graduation or upon completion of a judicial clerkship after graduation.
Duration: 1 year of undergraduate study and up to 3 years of graduate study, as long as the recipient maintains satisfactory academic performance.
Additional information: Recipients may attend graduate school in the United States or in foreign countries.
Number awarded: 75 to 80 each year: a) 1 "state" scholarship is available to a qualified resident nominee in each of the 50 states, the District of Columbia, Puerto Rico, and (considered as a single entity) Guam, the Virgin Islands, American Samoa, and the Commonwealth of the Northern Mariana Islands; and b) up to 30 at-large scholars.
Deadline: January of each year.

1413
HAWAII CHAPTER/DAVID T. WOOLSEY SCHOLARSHIP

Landscape Architecture Foundation
Attn: Scholarship Program
636 Eye Street, N.W.
Washington, DC 20001-3736
Phone: (202) 216-2356   Fax: (202) 898-1185
E-mail: msippel@asla.org   Web Site: www.laprofession.org
Summary: To provide financial assistance to landscape architecture students from Hawaii.
Eligibility: This program is open to third-, fourth-, or fifth-year undergraduate students and graduate students in landscape architecture from Hawaii. Applicants are required to submit 2 letters of recommendation (1 from a design instructor), a 500-word autobiographical essay that addresses personal and professional goals, and a sample of design work. Selection is based on professional experience, community involvement, extracurricular activities, and financial need.
Financial data: This scholarship is $1,000.
Additional information: This scholarship was established in memory of an alumnus of California Polytechnic University and former principal in the firm of Woolsey, Miyabara and Associates.
Number awarded: 1 each year.
Deadline: March of each year.

1414
HAZEL SIMMONS HODGES GARDEN CLUB OBJECTIVES SCHOLARSHIP

Florida Federation of Garden Clubs, Inc.
Attn: Scholarship Chair
6065 21st Street S.W.
Vero Beach, FL 32968-9427
Phone: (561) 778-1023
Web Site: www.ffgc.org
Summary: To provide financial aid to Florida undergraduate students majoring in designated areas related to gardening.
Eligibility: This program is open to Florida residents who are either high school seniors planning to enroll in a Florida college or current Florida college students entering their sophomore year. They must have at least a 3.0 grade point average,

be in financial need, and be majoring in horticulture, landscape design, conservation of natural resources, civic beautification, public sanitation, botany, or allied subjects. Selection is based on academic record, commitment to career, character, and financial need.

Financial data: The stipend is $1,500. The funds are sent directly to the recipient's school and distributed semiannually.

Duration: 1 year.

Additional information: If the recipient's grade point average drops below 3.0, the second installment of the scholarship is not provided.

Number awarded: 1 each year.

Deadline: April of each year.

1415
THE HEALTH OF THE EARTH PHOTO CONTEST

Forestry Ecology Network
Attn: Dorothy Carter
P.O. Box 2118
Augusta, ME 04338
Phone: (207) 628-6404   Fax: (207) 628-5741
E-mail: fen@powerlink.net
Web Site: www.powerlink.net/fen

Summary: To recognize and reward high school seniors in Maine who submit outstanding photographs that illustrate the misuse of the earth.

Eligibility: This competition is open to seniors at high schools in Maine. Applicants must submit 2 photographs: 1 illustrating a positive ecological relationship and the other an example of the misuse of the earth. The photographs can be of, but are not limited to, the ocean, shore, watershed, rivers, lakes, forest, land, flora, birds, animals, or atmosphere. They may be in black and white or color, and they should be submitted as prints at least 4x6 inches in size. They may be matted but should be sent unframed.

Financial data: The prize is a $2,000 college scholarship.

Duration: The competition is held annually.

Additional information: This competition was first held in 2001.

Number awarded: 1 each year.

Deadline: July of each year.

1416
HEARST JOURNALISM AWARDS PROGRAM BROADCAST NEWS COMPETITION

William Randolph Hearst Foundation
90 New Montgomery Street, Suite 1212
San Francisco, CA 94105-4504
Phone: (415) 543-6033   (800) 841-7048
Fax: (415) 243-0760
Web Site: www.hearstfdn.org

Summary: To recognize and reward outstanding college student broadcast news journalists.

Eligibility: Eligible are full-time undergraduate students majoring in journalism at 1 of the 105 accredited colleges and universities that are members of the Association of Schools of Journalism and Mass Communication (ASJMC). For each of the 2 semifinal competitions, each student submits either an audiotape or a videotape originating with and produced by the undergraduate student with primary responsibility for the entry. Entries must have been "published" in the sense of having been made available to an anonymous audience of substantial size. For the first competition of each year, entries must be soft news, non-deadline reporting of personalities, events, or issues. They may be based on, but not limited to, public affairs, business, investigations, science, sports, or weather. For the second competition of each year, entries must be hard news, including enterprise reporting. They may be based on, but not limited to, public affairs reporting, business reporting, investigative reporting, science reporting, sports reporting, or weather reporting, as long as they have a hard news focus. All entries must have been produced since September of the previous year and must consist of at least 2 reports. Broadcast news tapes are judged on the basis of writing quality, understandability, clarity, depth, focus, editing, knowledge of subject, and broadcast skills. The 10 audiotapes and 10 videotapes selected by the judges as the best in the semifinals are then entered in the finals. The finalists submit new and different tapes, up to 10 minutes in length with a minimum of 3 reports, of which only 1 may have been submitted previously. The reports must include at least 1 news story and 1 feature. Judges select the top 5 audiotapes and the top 5 videotapes, and those 10 finalists go to San Francisco for an on-the-spot news assignment to rank the winners.

Financial data: In each of the 2 semifinal competitions, the first-place winner receives a $2,000 scholarship, second place $1,500, third place $1,000, fourth place $750, fifth place $600, and sixth through tenth places $500 each; identical grants are awarded to the journalism schools attended by the winning students. For the finals competition, additional scholarships are awarded of $5,000 to the first-place winner, $4,000 for second, $3,000 for third, and $1,000 for each of the other 7 finalists; in addition, the students who make the best use of radio for news coverage and the best use of television for news coverage each receive another scholarship of $1,000. Scholarship funds are paid to the college or university and credited to the recipients' educational costs (tuition, matriculation and other fees, and room and board provided by or approved by the college or university). Schools receive points for their students who place in the top 20 places in the semifinals and in the finals; the school with the most points receives an additional cash prize of $10,000, second wins $5,000, and third wins $2,500. The total amount awarded in scholarships and grants in this and the writing and photojournalism competitions is $400,000 per year.

Duration: The competition is held annually.

Additional information: This program began in 1960. It is conducted by the William Randolph Hearst Foundation under the auspices of the ASJMC. If scholarship funds are awarded after a competing student has graduated, the college or university may credit funds retroactively.

Number awarded: 20 semifinal and 10 final winners are chosen each year, and 2 additional scholarships are awarded each year for best use of radio and best use of television.

Deadline: The deadline for the first competition is in early December of each year and for the second competition in early February of each year. Additional entries by finalists must be submitted by the end of March of each year. The competition among the top 10 finalists takes place in San Francisco in June.

1417
HEARST JOURNALISM AWARDS PROGRAM PHOTOJOURNALISM COMPETITION

William Randolph Hearst Foundation
90 New Montgomery Street, Suite 1212
San Francisco, CA 94105-4504
Phone: (415) 543-6033   Fax: (415) 243-0760
Web Site: www.hearstfdn.org

Summary: To recognize and reward outstanding college student photojournalists.

Eligibility: Eligible are full-time undergraduate students majoring in journalism at 1 of the 105 accredited colleges and universities that are members of the Association of Schools of Journalism and Mass Communication (ASJMC). For each of the 3 semifinal competitions, each student submits photographs in 35mm slide form. For the first competition of each year, the categories are portrait/personality and feature; entries consist of 2 photographs in each of those 2 categories. For the second competition of each year, the categories are sports and news; entries consist of 2 photographs in each of those 2 categories. For the third competition of each year, the category is picture story/series; each entry must include 1 picture story/series, with up to 15 images. All photographs must have been taken since September of the previous year and may be in color or black and white. Photography is judged on the basis of photographic quality, versatility, consistency, human interest, news value, and originality. The judges select the top 10 entrants in each of the 3 competitions; of those 10, the top 4 scoring entrants qualify for the photojournalism finals. Those 12 finalists must submit a portfolio consisting of prints of the slides previously judged, plus 2 additional photographs (published or unpublished) from each of the other categories in the overall contest; complete portfolios must thus consist of 2 pictures each in news, features, sports, portrait/personality, plus a picture story/series. Based on those portfolios, judges select the top 6 finalists to go to San Francisco for on-the-spot assignments to rank the winners.

Financial data: In each of the 3 semifinal competitions, the first-place winner receives a $2,000 scholarship, second place $1,500, third place $1,000, fourth place $750, fifth place $600, and sixth through tenth places $500 each; identical grants are awarded to the journalism schools attended by the winning students. For the finals competition, additional scholarships are awarded of $5,000 to the first-place winner, $4,000 for second, $3,000 for third; and $1,000 for each of the other 3 finalists. In addition, the photographers who submit the best single photo and the best picture story each receive another scholarship of $1,000. Scholarship funds are paid to the college or university and credited to the recipients' educational costs (tuition, matriculation and other fees, and room and board provided by or approved by the college or university). Schools receive points for their students who place in the top 20 places in the semifinals and in the finals; the school with

the most points receives an additional cash prize of $10,000, second wins $5,000, and third wins $2,500. The total amount awarded in scholarships and grants in this and the writing and broadcast news competitions is $400,000 per year.

Duration: The competition is held annually.

Additional information: This program began in 1960. If is conducted by the William Randolph Hearst Foundation under the auspices of the ASJMC. If scholarship funds are awarded after a competing student has graduated, the college or university may credit funds retroactively.

Number awarded: 30 semifinal and 6 final winners are chosen each year, and 2 additional scholarships are awarded each year for the best single photo and best picture story.

Deadline: The deadline for the first competition is in early November of each year, for the second competition in late January of each year, and for the third competition in mid-March of each year. Additional entries by finalists must be submitted by late May of each year. The competition among the top 6 finalists takes place in San Francisco in June.

1418
HEARST JOURNALISM AWARDS PROGRAM WRITING COMPETITION

William Randolph Hearst Foundation
90 New Montgomery Street, Suite 1212
San Francisco, CA 94105-4504
Phone: (415) 543-6033   Fax: (415) 243-0760
Web Site: www.hearstfdn.org

Summary: To recognize and reward outstanding college student journalists.

Eligibility: Eligible are full-time undergraduate students majoring in journalism at 1 of the 105 accredited colleges or universities that are members of the Association of Schools of Journalism and Mass Communication (ASJMC). Each entry consists of a single article written by the student with primary responsibility for the work and published in a campus or professional publication. Each month, a separate competition is held; October: feature writing-a background, color, or mood article as opposed to a conventional news story or personality profile; November: editorials or signed columns of opinion-must be well researched and express a clear and cogent viewpoint; December: in-depth writing-must illustrate the student's ability to handle a complex subject clearly, precisely, and with sufficient background; January: sports writing-relevant to an event or issue, not to a sports personality; February: personality profile-a personality sketch of someone; March: spot news writing-articles written about a breaking news event and against a deadline. The 6 monthly winners and the 2 finalists who place highest in their top 2 scores in the monthly competitions qualify for the national writing championship held in San Francisco in June; at that time, competition assignments consist of an on-the-spot assignment and a news story and personality profile from a press interview of a prominent individual in the San Francisco area. Writing is judged on the basis of knowledge of subject, understandability, clarity, color, reporting in depth, and construction.

Financial data: In each of the 6 competitions, the first-place winner receives a $2,000 scholarship, second place $1,500, third place $1,000, fourth place $750, fifth place $600, and sixth through tenth places $500; identical grants are awarded to the journalism schools attended by the students. For the finalists whose articles are judged best in the national writing championship, additional scholarships of $5,000 are awarded to the first-place winner, $4,000 for second place, $3,000 for third place, and $1,000 each for the other 5 finalists. Scholarship awards are paid to the college or university and credited to the recipients' educational costs (tuition, matriculation and other fees, and room and board provided by or approved by the college or university). Schools receive points for each of their students who place in the top 20 places in each monthly competition; the school with the most points receives an additional cash prize of $10,000, second wins $5,000, and third wins $2,500. The total amount awarded in scholarships and grants in this and the photojournalism and broadcast news competitions is $400,000 per year.

Duration: The competition is held annually.

Additional information: This program began in 1960. It is conducted by the William Randolph Hearst Foundation under the auspices of the ASJMC. If scholarship funds are awarded after a competing student has graduated, the college or university may credit funds retroactively.

Number awarded: Each year, 60 scholarships are awarded to the monthly winners, and an additional 8 are presented to the national finalists.

Deadline: Articles for the monthly competitions must be submitted by, respectively, October, November, December, January, February, and March of each year. The championship is held in June of each year.

1419
HEBREW LADIES SHELTERING HOME FUND

Jewish Federation of Greater Hartford, Inc.
Attn: Endowment Foundation
333 Bloomfield Avenue
West Hartford, CT 06117
Phone: (860) 523-7460   Fax: (860) 231-0576
E-mail: endowment@jewishhartford.org
Web Site: www.jewishgivinginhartford.org

Summary: To provide financial assistance for college to Jewish students in Connecticut.

Eligibility: This program is open to Jewish residents of Connecticut who are graduating from high school or already enrolled in college. Applicants must be interested in pursuing Jewish education. Selection is based on academic record and financial need.

Financial data: Stipends range from $500 to $1,000.

Duration: 1 year.

Number awarded: 2 to 3 each year.

Deadline: April of each year.

1420
HEIDA HERMANNS YOUNG ARTISTS COMPETITION

Connecticut Alliance for Music, Inc.
61 Unquowa Road
Fairfield, CT 06430-5015
Phone: (203) 319-8271

Summary: To recognize and reward outstanding young singers and instrumentalists.

Eligibility: This competition is open to instrumentalists between 19 and 30 years of age and singers between 19 and 35 years of age; neither category of contestant may be under professional management. Applicants first submit cassette tapes of 15 minutes' duration with specified categories of works. On the basis of the tapes, semifinalists are selected to compete in Southport or Danbury where they perform additional specified works. Finals are held the next day in Southport. The divisions alternate annually: voice and strings in odd-numbered years; piano and woodwinds in even-numbered years.

Financial data: In each of the 2 divisions, first prize is $3,000, second prize is $1,500, and third prize is $750.

Duration: The competition is held annually.

Additional information: Cassette tapes must be accompanied by a $40 application fee.

Number awarded: Each year, 3 prizes are awarded in each of the 2 divisions (voice and instrument).

Deadline: October of each year.

1421
HELEN J. SIOUSSAT SCHOLARSHIPS

Broadcast Education Association
Attn: Scholarships
1771 N Street, N.W.
Washington, DC 20036-2891
Phone: (202) 429-5354   E-mail: bea@nab.org
Web Site: www.beaweb.org

Summary: To provide financial assistance to upper-division and graduate students who are interested in preparing for a career in broadcasting.

Eligibility: This program is open to juniors, seniors, and graduate students enrolled full time at a college or university where at least 1 department is an institutional member of the Broadcast Education Association. Applicants may be studying in any area of broadcasting. Selection is based on evidence that the applicant possesses high integrity, superior academic ability, potential to be an outstanding electronic media professional, and a sense of personal and professional responsibility.

Financial data: The stipend is $1,250.

Duration: 1 year; may not be renewed.

Additional information: Information is also available from Peter B. Orlik, Central Michigan University, 344 Moore Hall, Mt. Pleasant, MI 48859, (517) 774-7279.

Number awarded: 2 each year.

Deadline: September of each year.

1422
HELEN JAMES BREWER SCHOLARSHIP

United Daughters of the Confederacy
Attn: Education Director
328 North Boulevard
Richmond, VA 23220-4057
Phone: (804) 355-1636　　　　　　Fax: (804) 353-1396
E-mail: hqudc@aol.com　　　　　　Web Site: www.hqudc.org
Summary: To provide financial assistance for education in southern history and literature to lineal descendants of Confederate veterans in certain southern states.
Eligibility: Eligible to apply for these scholarships are lineal descendants of worthy Confederates or collateral descendants who are current or former members of the Children of the Confederacy or current members of the United Daughters of the Confederacy. Applicants must intend to study English or southern history and literature and must submit a family financial report and certified proof of the Confederate record of 1 ancestor, with the company and regiment in which he served. They must have at least a 3.0 grade point average in high school. Residency in Alabama, Florida, Georgia, South Carolina, Tennessee, or Virginia is required.
Financial data: The amount of this scholarship depends on availability of funds.
Duration: 1 year; may be renewed.
Additional information: Information is also available from Dorothy S. Broom, Second Vice President General, 595 Lominack Road, Prosperity, SC 29127, (803) 364-3003. Members of the same family may not hold scholarships simultaneously, and only 1 application per family will be accepted within any 1 year. All requests for applications must be accompanied by a self-addressed stamped envelope.
Number awarded: 1 each year.
Deadline: February of each year.

1423
HENRY AND CHIYO KUWAHARA CREATIVE ARTS AWARD

Japanese American Citizens League
Attn: National Scholarship Awards
1765 Sutter Street
San Francisco, CA 94115
Phone: (415) 921-5225　　　　　　Fax: (415) 931-4671
E-mail: jacl@jacl.org　　　　　　Web Site: www.jacl.org
Summary: To encourage creative projects by student members of the Japanese American Citizens League (JACL).
Eligibility: This program is open to JACL members who are interested in pursuing undergraduate or graduate education in the creative arts. Professional artists may not apply. Selection is based on academic record, extracurricular activities, and community involvement. Preference is given to students who are interested in creative projects that reflect the Japanese American experience and culture.
Financial data: The stipend depends on the availability of funds but usually ranges from $1,000 to $5,000.
Duration: 1 year.
Additional information: Requests for applications must be accompanied by a self-addressed stamped envelope.
Number awarded: At least 1 each year.
Deadline: March of each year.

1424
HERBERT FERNANDES SCHOLARSHIP

Luso-American Education Foundation
Attn: Administrative Director
7080 Donlon Way, Suite 202
P.O. Box 2967
Dublin, CA 94568
Phone: (925) 828-3883　　　　　　Fax: (925) 828-3883
Web Site: www.luso-american.org/laefx
Summary: To provide financial assistance for undergraduate study in Portuguese language to students in California.
Eligibility: This program is open to students of Portuguese descent who are sophomores, juniors, or seniors at 4-year colleges or universities in California with a minimum grade point average of 3.5. Applicants must be California residents who are interested or involved in the Luso-American community and have taken or will enroll in Portuguese language classes. Selection is based on promise of success in college, financial need, qualities of leadership, vocational promise, and sincerity of purpose.
Financial data: The award is $1,000.
Duration: 1 year; renewable.
Number awarded: 1 each year.
Deadline: February of each year.

1425
HERMINE DALKOWITZ TOBOLOWSKY SCHOLARSHIP

Texas Federation of Business and Professional Women's Foundation, Inc.
1331 West Airport Freeway, Suite 303
Euless, TX 76040-4150
Phone: (817) 283-0862　　　　　　Fax: (817) 283-0862
E-mail: info@bpwtx.org
Web Site: www.bpwtx.org/foundation.htm
Summary: To provide financial assistance to women in Texas who are preparing to enter selected professions.
Eligibility: This program is open to women in Texas who are interested in attending school to prepare for a career in law, public service, government, political science, or women's history.
Financial data: A stipend is awarded (exact amount not specified).
Duration: 1 year.
Additional information: This program was established in 1995.
Number awarded: 1 or more each year.

1426
HIGH SCHOOL SENIORS ART SCHOLARSHIPS

Texas Arts and Crafts Educational Foundation, Inc.
P.O. Box 291527
Kerrville, TX 78029-1527
Phone: (830) 896-5711　　　　　　Fax: (830) 896-5569
E-mail: fair@tacef.org
Web Site: www.tacef.org
Summary: To recognize and reward outstanding 2- or 3-dimensional artwork created by high school seniors in Texas.
Eligibility: Eligible to compete are seniors (under the age of 21) attending an accredited high school in Texas who are planning to continue their education in an accredited college or specialty school. They are invited to submit color slides of their 2- or 3-dimensional art in 1 of the following categories: fiber, ceramics, glass, graphics/drawing, jewelry, leather, metal works, mixed media, painting, photography, sculpture, or wood. When submitting, they must include a descriptive summary (maximum 1 page) of the inspiration for and the method used to create their work.
Financial data: Scholarships are awarded to the winner's college or specialty school of choice. First place is $2,000; second place is $1,500; and third place is $1,000. If any of the winners choose to attend Schreiner College, the college will donate a matching dollar amount.
Duration: The competition is held annually.
Number awarded: 3 each year.
Deadline: January of each year.

1427
HISPANIC COLLEGE FUND SCHOLARSHIPS

Hispanic College Fund
Attn: National Director
One Thomas Circle, N.W., Suite 375
Washington, D.C. 20005
Phone: (800) 644-4223　　　　　　Fax: (202) 296-5400
E-mail: hispaniccollegefund@earthlink.net
Web Site: www.hispanicfund.org
Summary: To provide financial assistance to Hispanic American undergraduate students who are interested in preparing for a career in a business-related field.
Eligibility: This program is open to full-time undergraduate students of Hispanic origin who are U.S. citizens. Applicants must have a cumulative grade point average of 3.0 or better and a major in accounting, actuarial science, architecture, business administration, communications, computer science, computer engineering, economics, electrical engineering, finance, financial management, human resources, industrial engineering, information technology, international business, management, management information systems, marketing, mechanical engineering, multimedia production, or statistics. Students at community and junior colleges are eligible if they plan to pursue a bachelor's degree at a 4-year institution. The colleges or universities the applicants are attending must certify their financial need, defined as a family income at or below 60 percent of the area's median family income, based on family size. Preference is given to students who can demonstrate leadership qualities (extracurricular activities on their college campuses and/or in civic activities in their communities).
Financial data: Stipends range from $500 to $5,000 and average about $2,000.
Duration: 1 year.

Number awarded: Varies each year; recently, 206 students were supported by this program, including 79 freshmen, 46 sophomores, 51 juniors, and 30 seniors.
Deadline: April of each year.

1428
HISPANIC DESIGNERS FOUNDERS SCHOLARSHIPS

Hispanic Designers, Inc.
Attn: National Hispanic Education and Communications Projects
1101 30th Street, N.W., Suite 500
Washington, DC 20007
Phone: (202) 337-9636   Fax: (202) 337-9635
E-mail: HispDesign@aol.com   Web Site: www.hispanicdesigners.org
Summary: To provide financial assistance to Hispanic students enrolled in fashion design schools.
Eligibility: Applicants must be Hispanic or of Hispanic descent, be able to demonstrate financial need, be U.S. citizens or residents, have participated in an internship or work training program in the field of fashion, and have at least a 3.0 grade point average. They must be enrolled in an accredited postsecondary institution studying for a degree or in a certified program in fashion design or a related field. As part of the selection process, they must submit samples of design work which are judged on the basis of creativity and originality.
Financial data: The stipend is $5,000.
Duration: 1 year.
Additional information: This program was established in 1999 with a grant from Absolut Vodka. The program includes the following named scholarships: the Adolfo Founders Scholarship (for the best knitwear collection design), the Paloma Picasso Founders Scholarship (for the best accessory or jewelry collection design), the Fernando Sanchez Founders Scholarship (for the best at-home and leisure collection design), the Oscar de La Renta Founders Scholarship (for the best design of an evening wear collection following the "Oscar" style), and the Carolina Herrera Founders Scholarship (for the best design of an evening wear collection with the "CH" look). No telephone inquiries are accepted.
Number awarded: 5 each year.
Deadline: August of each year.

1429
HOLOCAUST REMEMBRANCE PROJECT

Holland & Knight Charitable Foundation, Inc.
400 North Ashley Drive, Suite 2050
P.O. Box 2877
Tampa, FL 33601
Phone: (813) 227-8500   (866) 452-2737
E-mail: tholcomb@hklaw.com   Web Site: www.holocaust.hklaw.com
Summary: To recognize and reward outstanding essays written by high school students on a topic (changes annually) related to the Holocaust.
Eligibility: High school students in the United States and Mexico are invited to enter this essay contest. They are expected to study the Holocaust and then, in a 1,000-word essay, write on a topic (which changes annually) related to the Holocaust. Recently, participants were asked to analyze and write about how the remembrance, history, and lessons of the Holocaust can ensure that modern man will "Never Again" embrace genocide or terrorism as public policy. In preparation for writing, students are encouraged to research their essay using a variety of sources, including historical and reference material, interviews, eyewitness accounts, oral testimonies, official documents and other primary sources, readings from diaries, letters, autobiographies, works of poetry, video or audio tapes, films, art, CD-ROMs, and Internet sources. Selection is based on 1) evidence of relevant reading and thoughtful use of resource materials; 2) treatment of the assigned theme; and 3) clear and effective writing, including the use of language, correct grammar, and a coherent organization.
Financial data: First-place winners receive a 5-day, all expense-paid trip to Washington, D.C. to visit the U.S. Holocaust Memorial Museum and other historic sites with teachers and Holocaust survivors (valued at over $2,000), a gold meal, and a certificate of participation. They also compete for a share of $20,000 in scholarships (scholarships range from $500 to $5,000); each first-place winner is guaranteed at least a $500 scholarship. These scholarships are paid to the recipients' colleges or universities, after they graduate from high school and upon receipt of proof of registration. Second-place winners receive $300, a silver medal, and a certificate of participation. Third-place winners receive $100, a bronze medal, and a certification of participation. Fourth-place winners receive $25 and a certificate of participation.

Duration: The competition is held annually. Former first-place winners are not eligible to enter in subsequent years.
Additional information: The project's national essay contest is intended as a living memorial to the millions of innocent victims of the Holocaust. There is no entry fee. No electronic transmissions or facsimiles will be accepted. Submissions are not returned.
Number awarded: 100 each year: 15 first-place winners, 15 second-place winners, 15 third-place winners, and 55 fourth-place winners.
Deadline: April of each year.

1430
HONORARY STATE REGENTS' AMERICAN HISTORY SCHOLARSHIP

Daughters of the American Revolution-Colorado State Society
923 Tenth Street
Golden, CO 80401
Phone: (303) 278-7151   E-mail: darcolo@aol.com
Web Site: members.aol.com/coloradodar/scholarships.htm
Summary: To provide financial assistance to high school seniors in Colorado who are interested in majoring in American history in college.
Eligibility: Eligible to apply are graduating high school seniors in Colorado who are 1) American citizens; 2) in the upper third of their graduating class; 3) accepted at an accredited college or university (in any state); and 4) planning to major in American history. Interested students are invited to submit their complete application to the state scholarship chair (c/o the sponsor's address); they must include a statement of their career interest and goals (up to 500 words), 2 character references, their college transcripts, a letter of sponsorship from the Daughters of the American Revolution's Colorado chapter, and a list of their scholastic achievements, extracurricular activities, honors, and other significant accomplishments. Selection is based on academic record and financial need.
Financial data: The stipend ranges up to $2,500, depending upon the availability of funds.
Duration: 1 year; nonrenewable.
Number awarded: 1 each year.
Deadline: January of each year.

1431
HOUSTON SYMPHONY IMA HOGG NATIONAL YOUNG ARTIST COMPETITION

Houston Symphony League
Attn: Director of Education and Community Relations
Jones Hall
615 Louisiana Street, Suite 102
Houston, TX 77002-2798
Phone: (713) 238-1449   Fax: (713) 222-7024
E-mail: e&o@houstonsymphony.org   Web Site: www.housym.org
Summary: To recognize and reward outstanding young musicians.
Eligibility: Eligible are U.S. citizens or foreign students who are enrolled in a U.S. college, university, or conservatory and are between 19 and 29 years of age. Entrants must submit a cassette recording of a required solo work for their instrument as well as additional non-concerto solo works of their choice, representing a style and period different from the required work. The competition is open to the following orchestral instruments: piano, violin, viola, cello, bass, flute, oboe, clarinet, bassoon, horn, trumpet, trombone, tuba, harp, and percussion. Semifinalists are selected on the basis of the tapes and invited to Houston for further competition, where they perform the required solo work and either a required concerto or 1 of several optional concertos. The finals consist of the concerto not performed in the semifinals.
Financial data: The first-prize winner receives the Grace Woodson Memorial Award of $5,000 and a performance with the Houston Symphony; the second-prize winner receives the Houston Symphony League Jerry Priest Award of $2,500 and a performance with the Houston Symphony; the third-prize winner receives the Selma Neumann Memorial Award with a cash prize of $1,000.
Additional information: Housing accommodations at no cost are provided for semifinalists and their accompanists. A non-refundable application fee of $25 must accompany the preliminary audition tapes.
Number awarded: 3 cash prizes are awarded each year.
Deadline: Preliminary audition tapes must be received by February of each year.

1432
HOWARD BROWN RICKARD SCHOLARSHIPS

National Federation of the Blind
c/o Peggy Elliott
Chair, Scholarship Committee
805 Fifth Avenue
Grinnell, IA 50112
Phone: (641) 236-3366
Web Site: www.nfb.org

Summary: To provide financial assistance to blind students studying or planning to study law, medicine, engineering, architecture, or the natural sciences at the postsecondary level.

Eligibility: This program is open to legally blind students who are pursuing or planning to pursue a full-time undergraduate or graduate course of study. Applicants must be studying or planning to study law, medicine, engineering, architecture, or the natural sciences. Selection is based on academic excellence, service to the community, and financial need.

Financial data: The stipend is $3,000.

Duration: 1 year; recipients may resubmit applications up to 2 additional years.

Additional information: Scholarships are awarded at the federation convention in July. Recipients attend the convention at federation expense; that funding is in addition to the scholarship grant.

Number awarded: 1 each year.

Deadline: March of each year.

1433
HUMANE STUDIES FELLOWSHIPS

Institute for Humane Studies at George Mason University
3401 North Fairfax Drive, Suite 440
Arlington, VA 22201-4432
Phone: (703) 993-4880
Fax: (703) 993-4890
(800) 697-8799
E-mail: ihs@gmu.edu
Web Site: www.TheIHS.org/tab1/hsf.html

Summary: To provide financial assistance to students in the United States or abroad who intend to pursue "intellectual careers" and have demonstrated an interest in classical liberal principles.

Eligibility: This program is open to students who will be full-time college juniors, seniors, or graduate students planning academic or other intellectual careers, including public policy and journalism. Applicants must have a clearly demonstrated interest in the classical liberal/libertarian tradition of individual rights and market economics. Applications from students outside the United States or studying abroad receive equal consideration. Selection is based on academic or professional performance, relevance of work to the advancement of a free society, and potential for success.

Financial data: Stipends up to $12,000 are available; the actual amounts awarded take into account the cost of tuition at the recipient's institution and any other funds received.

Duration: 1 year; may be renewed upon reapplication.

Additional information: As defined by the sponsor, the core principles of the classical liberal/libertarian tradition include the recognition of individual rights and the dignity and worth of each individual; protection of these rights through the institutions of private property, contract, the rule of law, and freely evolved intermediary institutions; voluntarism in all human relations, including the unhampered market mechanism in economic affairs; and the goals of free trade, free migration, and peace. This program began in 1983 as Claude R. Lambe Fellowships. The application fee is $25.

Number awarded: Approximately 90 each year.

Deadline: December of each year.

1434
HUMANIST ESSAY CONTEST

The Humanist
7 Harwood Drive
P.O. Box 1188
Amherst, NY 14226-7188
Phone: (716) 839-5080
Fax: (716) 839-5079
(800) 743-6646
E-mail: humanism@juno.com
Web Site: www.humanist.net/essaycon

Summary: To recognize and reward outstanding essays on humanity and the future written by students between 13 and 24 years of age.

Eligibility: This competition is open to students in 2 categories: from 13 through

17 years of age and from 18 through 24 years of age. Candidates are invited to prepare a manuscript (up to 2,500 words) that expresses their perception and vision of humanity and the future. The following is a sample of some of the topics entrants might consider: responding to the population crisis; the international project that will most benefit humanity; the dangers and opportunities of the information age; why the suffering of those in other countries should matter to us; alternatives to war in the 21st century. Entries must be printed and mailed; no e-mail or computer diskettes are accepted.

Financial data: First prize in each category: $1,000; second prize: $400; third prize: $100. If the winner indicates that a teacher, librarian, dean, or other educational adviser has been instrumental in the essay process, that individual is recognized with a special award of $50.

Duration: The competition is held annually.

Additional information: This competition started in the 1950s. All entries will be considered for publication in *The Humanist*. Entries are not returned.

Number awarded: 6 each year: 3 in each of 2 age categories.

Deadline: November of each year.

1435
IACP SCHOLARSHIPS

International Association of Culinary Professionals Foundation
Attn: Program Coordinator
304 West Liberty Street, Suite 201
Louisville, KY 40202
Phone: (502) 581-9786, ext. 237
Fax: (502) 589-3602
(800) 928-4227
E-mail: iacp@hqtrs.com
Web Site: www.iacpfoundation.org

Summary: To offer financial assistance to individuals interested in preparing for a career in the culinary arts.

Eligibility: This program is open to students pursuing or advancing their careers in the culinary arts by pursuing beginning, continuing, and specialty education courses in the United States and abroad. Some scholarships have restrictions on geographic region, educational institution, or culinary program. Financial need is considered in the selection process.

Financial data: Most scholarships and awards administered by the association offer partial tuition credit or cash stipends up to $5,000. Some awards consist of tuition credit at the culinary school that has donated the award. Cash awards are sent directly to the school chosen by the recipient and the scholarship committee.

Duration: Varies, from 1 week through 1 year and longer.

Additional information: The sponsors who have funded awards recently (and the names of some of their scholarships) include: L'Academie de Cuisine; the American Institute of Food and Wine chapters in Connecticut, Los Angeles (for the Lois Dwan Award), and Phoenix; Arts Institute International; the Ballymaloe Cookery School; the Boston Foundation (for the Julia Child Award); Lora Brody Products, Inc.; Calphalon Corporation; the Cambridge School of Culinary Arts; Cooking Hospitality Institute of Chicago; Le Cordon Bleu of London; the Culinary Institute of America; Les Dames d'Escoffier of Dallas and Seattle; the French Culinary Institute; the Simone Beck Award; the International School of Confectionary Arts; Johnson & Wales; the New England Culinary Institute; the New York Association of Cooking Teachers; Ritz-Escoffier of Paris; San Francisco Professional Food Society; Scottsdale Culinary Institute; Sullivan College National Center for Hospitality Studies; the Venda Ravioli/Cuisinart Venda Award for an apprenticeship in Italy; the Western Culinary Institute; the Wilton School of Cake Decorating and Confectionary Arts; and the Wine and Food Society of San Fernando Valley. There is a $25 application fee.

Number awarded: Approximately 60 each year; recently, the value of the scholarships was approximately $220,000.

Deadline: November of each year.

1436
IDDBA SCHOLARSHIP

International Dairy-Deli-Bakery Association
Attn: Scholarship Committee
313 Price Place, Suite 202
P.O. Box 5528
Madison, WI 53705-0528
Phone: (608) 238-7908
E-mail: iddba@iddba.org
Web Site: www.iddba.org
Fax: (608) 238-6330

Summary: To provide financial assistance for college to students employed in a supermarket dairy, deli, or bakery department (or related companies).

Eligibility: Scholarship applicants must be currently employed in a supermarket

dairy, deli, or bakery department or be employed by a company that services those departments (e.g., food manufacturers, brokers, or distributors). They must be majoring in a food-related field, e.g., culinary arts, baking/pastry arts, food science, or food marketing. While a 2.5 grade point average is required, this may be waived for first-time applicants.

Financial data: Stipends range up to $1,000. Funds are paid jointly to the recipient and the recipient's school. If the award exceeds tuition fees, the excess may be used for other educational expenses.

Duration: 1 year; recipients may not reapply.

Deadline: March for the fall semester; September for the spring semester.

1437
IDSA UNDERGRADUATE SCHOLARSHIPS

Industrial Designers Society of America
1142 Walker Road
Great Falls, VA 22066
Phone: (703) 759-0100   Fax: (703) 759-7679
E-mail: idsa@erols.com
Web Site: www.idsa.org

Summary: To provide financial assistance to upper-division students working on an undergraduate degree in industrial design.

Eligibility: Applicants must be enrolled as a full-time student in an industrial design program listed with the sponsor, be in their next-to-final year (juniors in a 4-year program, fourth-year students in a 5-year program), have earned at least a 3.0 grade point average since entering the industrial design program, be a member of an Industrial Designers Society of America student chapter, and be a U.S. citizen or resident. Applicants are asked to send a letter of intent that indicates their goals, 3 letters of recommendation, 20 visual examples of their work (i.e., slides, photographs, laser printouts), a completed application form, and a current transcript. Financial need is not considered in the selection process.

Financial data: The stipend is $2,500.

Duration: 1 year.

Number awarded: 2 each year.

Deadline: June of each year.

1438
IFDA STUDENT MERIT SCHOLARSHIP

International Furnishings and Design Association
Attn: IFDA Educational Foundation
204 E Street, N.E.
Washington, DC 20002
Phone: (202) 547-1588   Fax: (202) 547-6348
E-mail: info@ifdaef.org
Web Site: www.ifdael.org/scholarships.html

Summary: To provide financial assistance to undergraduate student members of the International Furnishings and Design Association (IFDA).

Eligibility: This program is open to association members who are full-time undergraduate students in fields related to design. Applicants must submit a 200- to 300-word essay on why they joined IFDA, their future plans and goals, and why they believe they deserve the scholarship. Selection is based on the essay; the applicant's achievements, awards, and accomplishments; and a letter of recommendation from a design educator, a mentor, or a practitioner in the field. Financial need is not considered.

Financial data: The stipend is $1,000.

Duration: 1 year.

Number awarded: 2 each year.

Deadline: September of each year.

1439
IFEC SCHOLARSHIPS

International Foodservice Editorial Council
P.O. Box 491
Hyde Park, NY 12538
Phone: (845) 229-6973   Fax: (845) 229-6993
E-mail: ifec@aol.com
Web Site: www.ifec-is-us.com

Summary: To provide financial assistance to undergraduate or graduate students who are interested in preparing for a career in communications in the food service industry.

Eligibility: This program is open to currently-enrolled college students who are working on an associate, bachelor's, or master's degree. They must be enrolled full time and planning on a career in editorial, public relations, or a related aspect of

communications in the food service industry. The following majors are considered appropriate for this program: culinary arts; hotel, restaurant, and institutional management; dietetics; food science and technology; and nutrition. Applicable communications areas include journalism, English, mass communications, public relations, marketing, broadcast journalism, creative writing, graphic arts, and photography. Selection is based on academic record, character references, and demonstrated financial need.

Financial data: Stipends range from $1,000 to $3,750 per year.

Duration: 1 year.

Number awarded: Varies each year; in recent years, 4 to 6 of these scholarships have been awarded.

Deadline: March of each year.

1440
IHA STUDENT DESIGN COMPETITION

International Housewares Association
Attn: Design Programs Coordinator
6400 Shafer Court, Suite 650
Rosemont, IL 60018
Phone: (847) 692-0136   Fax: (847) 292-4211
E-mail: vmatranga@nhma.com   Web Site: www.housewares.org

Summary: To recognize and reward outstanding young designers of housewares products.

Eligibility: Students participating in this competition must be juniors, seniors, or graduate students at an IDSA-affiliated school. They are invited to design a housewares product in any of the following categories: household and personal care small electric appliances; tabletop, serving products, and accessories; cook and bakeware; kitchenware; outdoor products and accessories; bath, laundry, closet; cleaning products; furniture; decorative accessories; and juvenile and pet products. Students may submit more than 1 entry, but they may not be awarded more than 1 prize. Selection is based on design research, design, ergonomics, and skills and communication.

Financial data: First place is $2,700, second place is $1,700, third place is $1,000, and honorable mention is $100. Winners also receive transportation and lodging for the International Housewares Show.

Duration: The competition is held annually.

Number awarded: 16 each year: 2 first places, 2 second places, 2 third places, and 10 honorable mentions.

Deadline: November of each year.

1441
IMAGES OF FREEDOM STUDENT PHOTOGRAPHY COMPETITION

American Bar Association
Attn: Division for Public Education
541 North Fairbanks Court, 15th Floor
Chicago, IL 60611-3314
Phone: (312) 988-5721   Fax: (312) 988-5494
E-mail: Andersel@staff.abanet.org
Web Site: www.abanet.org/publiced/imagescontest/home.html

Summary: To recognize and reward high school student photographers for work depicting images of freedom.

Eligibility: This program is open to students between the ages of 12 and 18. Applicants must submit photographs that illustrate the concept of freedom. Selection is based on effectiveness in expressing the theme of "speak up for democracy and diversity;" quality of the photo's design, including its composition, use of ambient light, and focusing; originality in approach to characterizing Americans speaking up for democracy and diversity or other depictions of democracy and diversity in action; and creativity in executing the image.

Financial data: The first-place winner receives a $1,000 savings bond, second place *The World Book Encyclopedia* with CD-ROM, and third place a $100 savings bond and student dictionary.

Duration: The competition is held annually.

Additional information: This competition began in 1997 as part of the American Bar Association's Law Day Program. It is run in cooperation with the National Newspaper Association, the Newspaper Association of American Foundation, and the Newspapers in Education programs of local newspapers throughout the country.

Number awarded: 3 each year.

Deadline: February of each year.

1442
IMATION COMPUTER ARTS SCHOLARSHIP PROGRAM

Imation Corporation
Attn: Community Relations
1 Imation Place
Oakdale, MN 55128-3414
Phone: (651) 704-3892   E-mail: communityrelations@imation.com
Web Site: www.imation.com
Summary: To recognize and reward high school artists who create original works of art on the computer.
Eligibility: This program is open to students at any grade in public and private high schools in the United States. Home-schooled students are also eligible to participate. Applicants create original works of art on a computer and submit them via the sponsor's web site. All art must be the original creation of the student, less than 1MB in size, and saved in JPEG format. Students must be nominated by their schools; each high school in the United States may nominate 1 candidate per 1,000 students enrolled to participate in the competition. National finalists are selected on the basis of the quality of art and creativity.
Financial data: Each national finalist receives a $1,000 scholarship, plus a medallion, a trophy for their school, and a trip with a parent, guardian, or school official to St. Paul, Minnesota in April.
Duration: Scholarships are awarded annually.
Additional information: This program began in the 1997-98 school year.
Number awarded: Each year, 25 students are selected as national finalists.
Deadline: December of each year.

1443
INDIANA BROADCASTERS ASSOCIATION SCHOLARSHIPS

Indiana Broadcasters Association
Attn: Scholarship Administrator
11919 Brookshire Parkway
Carmel, IN 46033
Phone: (317) 573-0119   (800) 342-6278 (within IN)
Fax: (317) 573-0895   E-mail: INDBA@aol.com
Web Site: www.indianabroadcasters.org
Summary: To provide financial assistance to students in Indiana who are interested in pursuing a career in a field related to broadcasting.
Eligibility: This program is open to graduating high school seniors planning to attend colleges that are members of the Indiana Broadcasters Association and to undergraduate students currently enrolled at those schools. Applicants must be majoring or planning to major in broadcasting, electronic media, telecommunications, or broadcast journalism. They must submit an essay on why they have chosen broadcasting as a career.
Financial data: The stipends are $500 for high school seniors or $1,500 for students already in college.
Duration: 1 year.
Number awarded: 14 each year: 7 to high school seniors and 7 to current undergraduate students.
Deadline: March of each year.

1444
INDIANA PROFESSIONAL CHAPTER OF SPJ DIVERSITY IN JOURNALISM SCHOLARSHIP

Society of Professional Journalists-Indiana Chapter
c/o Deborah K. Perkins
Assistant to the Dean and Academic Advisor
Indiana University School of Journalism
902 West New York Street, ES4104
Indianapolis, IN 46202-5154
Phone: (317) 274-2776   Fax: (317) 274-2786
E-mail: dperkins@iupui.edu
Summary: To provide financial assistance to minority college students in Indiana who are preparing for a career in journalism.
Eligibility: This program is open to minority students majoring in journalism and entering their sophomore, junior, or senior year at a college or university in Indiana. Minorities are defined as U.S. citizens who are African American, Hispanic, Asian American, Native American, or Pacific Islander. Applicants must submit an essay of 200 to 500 words on their personal background and journalistic views, an official college transcript, 3 examples of their journalistic work, a letter of recommendation from a college instructor, and (if they have had a professional internship) a letter of recommendation from their employer.

Financial data: The stipend is $1,000.
Duration: 1 year; recipients may reapply.
Number awarded: At least 2 each year.
Deadline: April of each year.

1445
INTERNATIONAL ASSOCIATION OF LIGHTING DESIGNERS SCHOLARSHIPS

International Association of Lighting Designers
Attn: Education Trust Fund
The Merchandise Mart, Suite 9-104
200 World Trade Center
Chicago, IL 60654
Phone: (312) 527-3677
Web Site: www.iald.org/programs/scholarships
Summary: To provide financial assistance to students pursuing a program in architectural lighting design.
Eligibility: This program is open to students who are pursuing architectural lighting design as a course of study. Applicants must submit 1) a cover letter that includes a description of their course of study and how it relates to lighting design, their educational history, extracurricular activities, and distinctions, honors, and awards; 2) their most recent academic transcript; 3) 2 letters of reference; 4) from 3 to 10 images of their artwork that shows their design ability; and 5) a personal statement, up to 1,000 words, describing an experience in lighting and how that experience has influenced their studies in lighting design. Selection is based on those submissions; financial need is not considered.
Financial data: Stipends are $2,000, $1,500, or $1,000.
Duration: 1 year.
Additional information: The $2,000 scholarship is sponsored by Lighting Design Alliance; 1 of the $1,000 scholarships is sponsored by Architectural Lighting Magazine.
Number awarded: Varies each year. Recently, 7 of these scholarships were awarded: 1 at $2,000, 1 at $1,500, and 5 at $1,000.
Deadline: February of each year.

1446
INTERNATIONAL SCHOLARSHIP PROGRAM FOR COMMUNITY SERVICE

Memorial Foundation for Jewish Culture
15 East 26th Street, Room 1703
New York, NY 10010
Phone: (212) 679-4074   Fax: (212) 889-9080
Web Site: www.mfjc.org
Summary: To assist well-qualified individuals to train for careers in a field related to Jewish community service.
Eligibility: The scholarship is open to any individual, regardless of country of origin, who is presently receiving or plans to undertake training in his/her chosen field at a recognized yeshiva, teacher training seminary, school of social work, university, or other educational institution. Applicants must be interested in pursuing professional training for careers in Jewish education, Jewish social service, the rabbinate, or as religious functionaries (e.g., shohatim, mohalim) in diaspora Jewish communities in need of such personnel. Students planning to serve in the United States, Canada, or Israel are not eligible.
Financial data: The amount of the grant varies, depending on the country in which the student will be trained and other considerations.
Duration: 1 year; may be renewed.
Additional information: Recipients must agree to serve for at least 2 to 3 years in a Jewish-deprived diaspora community where their skills are needed after completing their training.
Deadline: November of each year.

1447
INTERNATIONAL VIOLONCELLO COMPETITION

Walter W. Naumburg Foundation, Inc.
60 Lincoln Center Plaza
New York, NY 10023-6588
Phone: (212) 874-1150
Web Site: www.naumburg.org
Summary: To recognize and reward outstanding young musicians of all nationalities.
Eligibility: This program is open to musicians who are at least 17 but not more than 33 years of age. Applicants must submit a tape recording of no less than 30

minutes of satisfactory listenable quality. Based on those tapes, judges select contestants for live preliminary auditions, followed by semifinals and finals. Musicians may be of any nationality.

Financial data: First prize is $7,500 in cash plus 2 fully subsidized recitals in Alice Tully Hall, Lincoln Center, New York. Second prize is $3,500, and third prize is $2,500.

Duration: The competition is held annually.

Additional information: The preliminary auditions, semifinals, and finals are held in Alice Tully Hall in May.

Number awarded: 3 each year.

Deadline: February of each year.

1448
INVESTIGATIVE REPORTERS AND EDITORS STUDENT AWARDS

Investigative Reporters and Editors
c/o University of Missouri
School of Journalism
138 Neff Annex
Columbia, MO 65211
Phone: (573) 882-2042   Fax: (573) 882-5431
E-mail: info@ire.org
Web Site: www.ire.org

Summary: To recognize and reward outstanding investigative reporting by student journalists.

Eligibility: This competition is open to 2 categories of investigative reporting: 1) by a student in a college-affiliated newspaper, magazine, or specialty publication; and 2) by a college student whose broadcast submission has been publicly reviewed, screened, or aired.

Financial data: The award is a $1,000 scholarship and a certificate of recognition.

Duration: The awards are presented annually.

Additional information: Students who are members of Investigative Reporters and Editors (IRE) pay no entry fee; others must pay $25 (includes 1-year student membership).

Number awarded: 2 each year: 1 for print and 1 for broadcast.

Deadline: January of each year.

1449
IOWA SCHOLARSHIPS FOR THE ARTS

Iowa Arts Council
Attn: Arts in Education
600 East Locust
Des Moines, IA 50319-0290
Phone: (515) 281-4100   Fax: (515) 242-6498
Phone: TDD: (515) 242-5147   E-mail: kboon@max.state.ia.us
Web Site: www.state.ia.us/government/dca/iac

Summary: To provide financial assistance to Iowa high school seniors who plan to study the arts at a college or university in the state.

Eligibility: This program is open to graduating seniors at high schools in Iowa who have been accepted as full-time undergraduate students at an accredited college or university in the state. Applicants must be planning to major in music, dance, visual arts, theater, or literature. Selection is based on 1) proven artistic and academic abilities in the chosen artistic area and 2) future goals and objectives relating to the intended field of study.

Financial data: The stipends range from $1,000 to $2,000. Funds must be used for tuition at the Iowa institution where the recipient is enrolled.

Duration: 1 year.

Number awarded: Up to 5 each year.

Deadline: November of each year.

1450
IRENE RYAN ACTING SCHOLARSHIPS

John F. Kennedy Center for the Performing Arts
Education Department
Attn: Kennedy Center American College Theater Festival
2700 F Street, N.W.
Washington, DC 20566
Phone: (202) 416-8857   Fax: (202) 416-8802
E-mail: skshaffer@kennedy-center.org
Web Site: kennedy-center.org/education/actf/actfira.html

Summary: To recognize and reward outstanding college actors.

Eligibility: Eligible are students enrolled in an accredited junior or senior college

in the United States or in countries contiguous to the continental United States. Participants must appear as actors in plays produced by their college and entered in 1 of the 8 regional festivals of the Kennedy Center American College Theater Festival (KCACTF). Undergraduate students must be carrying a minimum of 6 semester hours, graduate students must be carrying a minimum of 3 semester hours, and continuing part-time students must be enrolled in a regular degree or certificate program. From each of the regional festivals, 2 winners and their acting partners are invited to the national festival at the John F. Kennedy Center for the Performing Arts in Washington, D.C. to participate in an "Evening of Scenes." Scholarships are awarded to outstanding student performers at each regional festival and from the "Evening of Scenes."

Financial data: Regional winners receive $500 scholarships and payment of expenses (transportation, lodging, and per diem) to attend the national festival. National winners receive $2,500 scholarships; the best partner receives the Kingsley Colton Award. All scholarship funds are paid directly to the institutions designated by the recipients and may be used for any field of study.

Duration: The competition is held annually.

Additional information: These awards have been presented since 1972 by the Irene Ryan Foundation of Encino, California. The national finalists are also eligible to receive 1) a fellowship (initiated in 1992) to participate in the National Stage Combat Workshop conducted by the Society of American Fight Directors; 2) a Classical Acting Award of Excellence (initiated in 1995) of $500; 3) the Mark Twain Comedy Acting Awards (initiated in 1999 and supported by Comedy Central) of $2,500 for first place and $2,000 for second place for comic acting; 4) the Dell'Arte Fellowship (initiated in 2001) to participate in the 1-month Dell'Arte Mad River Festival in northern California; 5) the Margolis Method Summer Intensive Acting Fellowship (initiated in 2001) to participate in a 7-day program at the Margolis Brown Theater Company in Minneapolis, Minnesota; and 6) the Sundance Theatre Laboratory Acting Fellowship (initiated in 2001) to participate in a 3-week workshop in Sundance, Utah. Actors of color are eligible to receive an apprenticeship to participate in an 11-week workshop at the Williamstown Theatre Festival in the Berkshire Hills of northwest Massachusetts. The sponsoring college or university must pay a registration fee of $250 for each production.

Number awarded: The number of regional winners varies each year; at the national festival "Evening of Scenes," 2 performers receive scholarships. Several other awards are also presented.

Deadline: The regional festivals are held in January and February of each year; the national festival is held in April of each year. Application deadlines are set within each region.

1451
JACK J. ISGUR SCHOLARSHIPS

Jack J. Isgur Foundation
c/o Morrison & Hecker L.L.P.
Attn: Charles F. Jensen
2600 Grand Avenue
Kansas City, MO 64108

Summary: To provide financial assistance to Missouri residents majoring in education and planning to teach humanities in elementary and middle schools in the state after graduation.

Eligibility: This program is open to residents of Missouri who are enrolled at a 4-year college or university. Applicants must be majoring in education with the goal of teaching the humanities (e.g., literature, philosophy, fine arts, music, art, and poetry) at the elementary or middle school level following graduation. Preference is given to students entering their junior year of college and planning to teach in rural school districts in Missouri, rather than metropolitan districts. The application process includes brief essays on the following topics: 1) What are your work and life experiences indicating an interest in teaching subjects in the humanities to grade school and middle school students in Missouri upon graduation? 2) What do you want to do as a career after graduation from college? 3) What individuals have most influenced your decision to attend college and have an interest in the field of education, and why? 4) Describe your other activities, organizations, volunteer work, or hobbies; 5) What 3 books have you read that have influenced your decision on a college field of study, and why? and 6) Where are you obtaining other funds to pay for your college education, including income from employment and support from your family.

Financial data: A stipend is awarded (exact amount not specified).

Duration: 1 year.

Number awarded: Varies each year.

Deadline: April of each year.

1452
JACKSON FOUNDATION JOURNALISM SCHOLARSHIP

Oregon Student Assistance Commission
Attn: Private Awards Grant Department
1500 Valley River Drive, Suite 100
Eugene, OR 97401-2146
Phone: (541) 687-7395   (800) 452-8807, ext. 7395
Fax: (541) 687-7419   E-mail: awardinfo@mercury.osac.state.or.us
Web Site: www.osac.state.or.us
Summary: To provide financial assistance to students in Oregon interested in majoring in journalism.
Eligibility: This program is open to graduates of Oregon high schools who are studying or planning to study journalism at a college or university in the state.
Financial data: Scholarship amounts vary, depending upon the needs of the recipient.
Duration: 1 year; nonrenewable.
Number awarded: Varies each year.
Deadline: February of each year.

1453
JACQUELINE DONNEE VOGT SCHOLARSHIP

Connecticut Architecture Foundation
Attn: Executive Vice President
87 Willow Street
New Haven, CT 06511
Phone: (203) 865-2195
Summary: To provide financial assistance to Connecticut residents who are pursuing a bachelor's degree in architecture.
Eligibility: This program is open to Connecticut residents who have completed at least 2 years of a bachelor of architecture program at a college offering a 5-year accredited degree in architecture. Selection is based on academic record and financial need.
Financial data: The stipend is $1,000.
Duration: 1 year.
Additional information: This program was established in 1990.
Number awarded: 1 each year.
Deadline: April of each year.

1454
JAMES J. WYCHOR SCHOLARSHIPS

Minnesota Broadcasters Association
Attn: Scholarship Program
3033 Excelsior Boulevard, Suite 301
Minneapolis, MN 55416
Phone: (612) 926-8123   (800) 245-5838
Fax: (612) 926-9761   E-mail: jdubois@minnesotabroadcasters.com
Web Site: www.minnesotabroadcasters.com
Summary: To provide financial assistance to Minnesota residents interested in studying broadcasting in college.
Eligibility: This program is open to residents of Minnesota who are accepted or enrolled at an accredited postsecondary institution offering a broadcast-related curriculum. Applicants must have a high school or college grade point average of 2.5 or higher and must submit a 200-word essay on why they wish to pursue a career in broadcasting or electronic media. Employment in the broadcasting industry is not required, but students who are employed must include a letter from their general manager describing the duties they have performed as a radio or television station employee and evaluating their potential for success in the industry. Financial need is not considered in the selection process. Some of the scholarships are available only to minority and women candidates. are eligible for some of the scholarships.
Financial data: The stipend is $1,500.
Duration: 1 year; recipients who are college seniors may reapply for an additional 1-year renewal.
Number awarded: 10 each year, distributed as follows: 3 within the 7-county metro area, 5 allocated geographically throughout the state (northeast, northwest, central, southeast, southwest), and 2 reserved specifically for women and minority applicants.
Deadline: May of each year.

1455
JANE FRYER MCCONAUGHY MEMORIAL SCHOLARSHIP PROGRAM

Jane Fryer McConaughy Memorial Scholarship Trust
c/o Nancy Young, Vice President
Key Trust Company of Indiana, N.A.
P.O. Box 460
Elkhart, IN 46515
Summary: To provide financial assistance to Indiana residents or students enrolled in Indiana colleges/universities.
Eligibility: Eligible to apply for this program are Indiana residents or students (from any state) attending college in Indiana. The focus is on students training for the ministry, missionary service, or the teaching profession. Priority is given to seminary students and students training for missionary services. Selection is based on career goals, academic record, and financial need.
Financial data: The amount awarded varies, depending upon the needs of the recipient.
Duration: 1 year.
Number awarded: 1 or more each year.
Deadline: April of each year.

1456
JAPAN STUDIES SCHOLARSHIP

Japan Studies Scholarship Foundation Committee
c/o Japan Information Service
50 Fremont Street, Suite 2200
San Francisco, CA 94105
Phone: (415) 356-2461
Summary: To provide financial assistance to college students in California and Nevada who are interested in studying Japanese-related subjects.
Eligibility: This program is open to residents of northern and central California and all of Nevada. Applicants must be currently-enrolled undergraduate sophomores, juniors, or seniors who are studying or researching Japanese language, Japanese culture, or Japan-U.S. relations.
Financial data: The stipend is $1,000.
Duration: 1 year; nonrenewable.
Additional information: This program was known formerly as the Japan Week Scholarship.
Number awarded: 2 each year.
Deadline: May of each year.

1457
JAZZ CLUB OF SARASOTA SCHOLARSHIP

Jazz Club of Sarasota
Attn: Scholarship Committee
330 South Pineapple Avenue, Suite 111
Sarasota, FL 34236
Phone: (941) 351-9688   Fax: (941) 366-1553
E-mail: Rod@jazzclubsarasota.com
Web Site: www.jazzclubsarasota.com
Summary: To recognize and reward outstanding elementary school, high school, and college jazz performers.
Eligibility: Elementary school, high school, and college students (through the age of 26) from any state are invited to submit a video (3 minutes of verbal introduction and 10 minutes of performance) demonstrating their talents in jazz. Instrumentalists must include 2 tunes of their choice (1 ballad and 1 "up" tempo) and at least 24 bars of jazz style improvisation on the blues. Vocalists must include 2 tunes (1 jazz ballad and 1 "up" tempo). In addition, applicants must submit a completed application form and 1 recent letter of recommendation.
Financial data: Generally, the award is $1,000 for those currently attending or entering college and $500 for those still in elementary or high school. Funds are sent to the recipient's school or jazz instructor.
Duration: The competition is held annually.
Additional information: Information is also available from Rob Gibson, Scholarship Committee Chair, 1705 Village Green Parkway, Bradenton, FL 34209. Telephone: (941) 794-1105. This competition started in 1982.
Number awarded: Varies; recently, 10 were awarded.
Deadline: March of each year.

1458
JDC-SMOLAR STUDENT JOURNALISM AWARD

American Jewish Joint Distribution Committee, Inc.
Attn: Coordinator, JDC-Smolar Student Journalism Award
711 Third Avenue
New York, NY 10017-4014
Phone: (212) 687-6200   Fax: (212) 370-5467
E-mail: admin@jdc.org
Web Site: www.jdc.org
Summary: To recognize and reward outstanding articles or stories written by students that promote an understanding of world Jewry.
Eligibility: Submissions are limited to published stories or articles written by undergraduate or graduate students (maximum age is 27) in English or accompanied by an English translation. The submitted piece should promote an understanding of overseas Jewish needs and/or offer insight into a particular aspect of the international Jewish community, excluding the United States. Submissions must have been published during the previous calendar year in a newspaper and/or magazine substantially involved in the coverage of Jewish affairs. Only 1 entry per student may be submitted.
Financial data: The award is $1,000.
Duration: The prize is awarded annually.
Additional information: The award was established in 1980.
Number awarded: 1 or more each year.
Deadline: March of each year.

1459
JEA NATIONAL HIGH SCHOOL JOURNALIST OF THE YEAR

Journalism Education Association
c/o Kansas State University
103 Kedzie Hall
Manhattan, KS 66506-1505
Phone: (785) 532-7822   Fax: (785) 532-5484
E-mail: jea@spub.ksu.edu
Web Site: www.jea.org
Summary: To recognize and reward the top high school journalists in the country.
Eligibility: This program is open to graduating high school seniors who are planning to study journalism in college and pursue a journalism career, have at least a 3.0 grade point average, and have participated in high school journalism for at least 2 years. Applicants must submit examples of their work that show 1 or more of the following characteristics: skilled and creative use of media content; inquiring mind and investigative persistence resulting in an in-depth study of issues important to the local high school audience, high school students in general, or society; courageous and responsible handling of controversial issues despite threat or imposition of censorship; variety of journalistic experiences, each handled in a quality manner, on a newspaper, yearbook, broadcast, or other medium; sustained and commendable work with community media. Applications are to be sent to the applicant's state contest coordinator; winners from the state Journalist of the Year competitions are sent to the national level for judging.
Financial data: The award is $2,000 for the top winner and $1,000 for second and third place. Funds are released when the recipient enrolls in a college journalism program.
Duration: The competition is held annually.
Number awarded: 3 each year.
Deadline: Applications must be submitted to state coordinators in February of each year.

1460
JEAN KENNEDY SMITH PLAYWRITING AWARD

John F. Kennedy Center for the Performing Arts
Education Department
Attn: Kennedy Center American College Theater Festival
2700 F Street, N.W.
Washington, DC 20566
Phone: (202) 416-8857   Fax: (202) 416-8802
E-mail: skshaffer@kennedy-center.org
Web Site: kennedy-center.org/education/actf/actfjks.html
Summary: To recognize and reward the student authors of plays on the theme of disability.
Eligibility: Students at any accredited junior or senior college in the United

States or in countries contiguous to the continental United States are eligible to compete, provided their college agrees to participate in the Kennedy Center American College Theater Festival (KCACTF). Undergraduate students must be carrying a minimum of 6 semester hours, graduate students must be carrying a minimum of 3 semester hours, and continuing part-time students must be enrolled in a regular degree or certificate program. This award is presented to the best student-written script that explores the human experience of living with a disability.
Financial data: The winning playwright receives a cash award of $2,500, active membership in the Dramatists Guild, Inc., and a fellowship providing transportation, housing, and per diem to attend a prestigious playwriting program.
Duration: The award is presented annually.
Additional information: This award, first presented in 1999, is part of the Michael Kanin Playwriting Awards Program. The Dramatists Guild, Inc. and Very Special Arts participate in the selection of the winning script. The sponsoring college or university must pay a registration fee of $250 for each production.
Number awarded: 1 each year.
Deadline: November of each year.

1461
JENNIFER CURTIS BYLER SCHOLARSHIP IN PUBLIC AFFAIRS

National Stone, Sand and Gravel Association
Attn: Director of Communications
2101 Wilson Boulevard, Suite 100
Arlington, VA 22201-3062
Phone: (703) 525-8788   (800) 342-1415
Fax: (703) 525-7782   E-mail: info@nssga.org
Web Site: www.nssag.org/careers/scholarships.htm
Summary: To provide financial assistance to children of aggregates company employees who are interested in studying public affairs in college.
Eligibility: This program is open to graduating high school seniors and students already enrolled in a public affairs major in college who are sons or daughters of an aggregates company employee. Applicants must demonstrate their commitment to a career in public affairs. Along with their application, they must submit a letter of recommendation and a 300- to 500-word statement describing their plans for a career in public affairs. Financial need is not considered in the selection process.
Financial data: The amount of the award depends on the availability of funds.
Duration: 1 year; nonrenewable.
Number awarded: 1 each year.
Deadline: December of each year.

1462
JIM DEVAN RADIO-TV SCHOLARSHIP

Georgia Radio-TV Foundation
c/o Georgia Association of Broadcasters, Inc.
8010 Roswell Road, Suite 260
Atlanta, GA 30350
Phone: (770) 395-7200   (877) 395-7200 (within GA)
Fax: (770) 395-7235
Web Site: www.gab.org
Summary: To provide financial assistance to students in Georgia interested in pursuing a career in broadcasting.
Eligibility: This program is open to residents of Georgia who are rising juniors or seniors studying for a career in radio or television at a college, professional school, or university in Georgia. As part of their application, students must submit brief essays on 10 questions (e.g., what specific area of broadcasting most interests you and why, what national network do you admire most and why, what role should news play in radio and television programming, what is the single most important fact that the judges should know about you). Selection is based primarily on depth of thought, clarity of expression, and maturity. Extracurricular activities, community involvement, and leadership potential are secondary considerations. Neither scholastic record nor financial need are considered.
Financial data: The stipend is $1,000.
Duration: 1 year.
Number awarded: 1 or more each year.
Deadline: January of each year.

1463
JOE FRANCIS HAIRCARE SCHOLARSHIPS

Joe Francis Haircare Scholarship Foundation
P.O. Box 50625
Minneapolis, MN 55405
Web Site: www.joefrancis.com
Summary: To provide financial assistance to students interested in a career in cosmetology.
Eligibility: This program is open to students enrolled in, or planning to enroll in, a cosmetology school. Applicants must be sponsored by 1 of the following: a fully-accredited, recognized barber or cosmetology school; a licensed salon owner or manager; a full-service distributor; or a member of the International Chain Association, Beauty and Barber Supply Institute, Cosmetology Advancement Foundation, or National Cosmetology Association. Selection is based on potential for a successful career, financial need, ability to benefit from training, and commitment to a long-term career in cosmetology.
Financial data: The stipend is $1,000.
Duration: 1 year.
Additional information: The sponsoring foundation was established in 1995.
Number awarded: 7 each year.
Deadline: May of each year.

1464
JOEL GARCIA MEMORIAL SCHOLARSHIPS

California Chicano News Media Association
c/o University of Southern California
Annenberg School for Communication
3800 South Figueroa Street
Los Ángeles, CA 90037-1206
Phone: (213) 743-4960   Fax: (213) 743-4989
E-mail: info@ccnma.org   Web Site: www.ccnma.org
Summary: To provide financial assistance for postsecondary education in journalism to deserving young Latino Americans in California.
Eligibility: The competition is open to all high school seniors and college students of Latino descent in California who are interested in pursuing journalism or communications careers. Applicants must submit 1) an essay of 300 to 500 words explaining their family background, including any hardships they have experienced, and what they believe is the role of Latino journalists in the news media; and 2) samples of their journalism-related work (e.g., news articles, news scripts, photographs, or audio and videotapes). Selection is based on academic achievement, commitment to the journalism field, awareness of the community in which they live, and financial need.
Financial data: Scholarships range from $500 to $2,000.
Duration: 1 year.
Number awarded: 20 to 30 each year.
Deadline: April of each year.

1465
JOHN BAYLISS BROADCAST FOUNDATION SCHOLARSHIPS

John Bayliss Broadcast Foundation
Attn: Executive Director
171 17th Street
P.O. Box 51126
Pacific Grove, CA 93950-2616
Phone: (831) 655-5229   Fax: (831) 655-5228
E-mail: info@baylissfoundation.org
Web Site: www.baylissfoundation.org/radio.html
Summary: To provide financial assistance to upper-division or graduate students who are preparing for a career in the radio industry.
Eligibility: This program is open to juniors, seniors, and graduate-level students who are studying for a career in the radio industry. They must have at least a 3.0 grade point average. Although financial need is a consideration, students of merit with an extensive history of radio-related activities are given preference. Applicants must supply transcripts, 3 letters of recommendation, and a descriptive page outlining their future broadcasting goals.
Financial data: The stipend is $5,000.
Duration: 1 year.
Additional information: Requests for applications must be accompanied by a self-addressed stamped envelope.
Number awarded: Up to 20 each year.
Deadline: April of each year.

1466
JOHN CAUBLE SHORT PLAY AWARD

John F. Kennedy Center for the Performing Arts
Education Department
Attn: Kennedy Center American College Theater Festival
2700 F Street, N.W.
Washington, DC 20566
Phone: (202) 416-8857   Fax: (202) 416-8802
E-mail: skshaffer@kennedy-center.org
Web Site: kennedy-center.org.education/actf/actfspa.html
Summary: To recognize and reward outstanding undergraduate and graduate student playwrights.
Eligibility: Students at any accredited junior or senior college in the United States or in countries contiguous to the continental United States are eligible to compete, provided their college agrees to participate in the Kennedy Center American College Theater Festival (KCACTF). Undergraduate students must be carrying a minimum of 6 semester hours, graduate students must be carrying a minimum of 3 semester hours, and continuing part-time students must be enrolled in a regular degree or certificate program. For the Short Play Awards Program, students must submit a play of 1 act without intermission that, within itself, does not constitute a full evening of theater. The plays selected as the best by the judges are considered for presentation at the national festival and their playwrights receive these awards.
Financial data: The prize is $1,000. Other benefits for the recipients of these awards include appropriate membership in the Dramatists Guild and publication by Samuel French, Inc.
Duration: The competition is held annually.
Additional information: This award, first presented in 1988, is part of the Michael Kanin Playwriting Awards Program. The sponsoring college or university must pay a registration fee of $250 for each production.
Number awarded: 1 or more each year.
Deadline: The final script must be submitted by November of each year.

1467
JOHN F. AND ANNA LEE STACEY SCHOLARSHIP FOR ART EDUCATION

National Cowboy and Western Heritage Museum
Attn: Art Director
1700 N.E. 63rd Street
Oklahoma City, OK 73111
Phone: (405) 478-2250
Summary: To provide financial assistance to students of conservative or classical art for further education in the United States or abroad.
Eligibility: This program is open to U.S. citizens between 18 and 35 years of age. Applicants must be artists whose works (paintings and drawings) have their roots in the classical tradition of western culture and favor realism or naturalism. Artists working in related fields (e.g., sculpture, collage, fashion design, decoration) are ineligible. Applicants must submit up to 10 35mm slides of their best work in any of the following categories: painting from life, drawing from the figure (nude), composition, or landscape. On the basis of these slides, a number of finalists will be selected; these finalists then submit original works for a second and final competition.
Financial data: Scholarships are $5,000; funds must be used to pursue art education along "conservative" lines.
Duration: 1 year.
Additional information: Recipients may study in the United States or abroad. Recipients must submit brief quarterly reports along with 35mm slides of their work. At the end of the scholarship, they must submit a more complete report.
Number awarded: 1 or more each year.
Deadline: January of each year.

1468
JOHN F. KENNEDY MEMORIAL SCHOLARSHIP FUND IN HISTORY

Hawai'i Community Foundation
900 Fort Street Mall, Suite 1300
Honolulu, HI 96813
Phone: (808) 566-5570   (888) 731-3863
Fax: (808) 521-6286   E-mail: scholarships@hcf-hawaii.org
Web Site: www.hcf-hawaii.org
Summary: To provide financial assistance to Hawaii residents who are studying history.

Eligibility: This program is open to Hawaii residents who are majoring in history (as a junior, senior, or graduate student) at a college or university in Hawaii. They must be able to demonstrate academic achievement (at least a 2.7 grade point average), good moral character, and financial need. Applications must be accompanied by a short statement indicating reasons for attending college, planned course of study, and career goals.

Financial data: The amounts of the awards depend on the availability of funds and the need of the recipient.

Duration: 1 year.

Additional information: Information is also available from David Hanlon, University of Hawai'i at Manoa, Department of History, 2530 Dole Street, Sakamaki A203, Honolulu, HI 96822, (808) 956-8356.

Number awarded: Varies each year.

Deadline: February of each year.

1469
JOHN LENNON SCHOLARSHIP

Broadcast Music Inc.
Attn: BMI Foundation
320 West 57th Street
New York, NY 10019-3790
Phone: (212) 830-2520   Fax: (212) 262-2824
Web Site: www.bmi.com

Summary: To recognize and reward outstanding student composers.

Eligibility: This program is open to student musicians at 36 selected schools and youth organizations. Candidates submit a song they have composed with original lyrics and music; the work may be in any genre from rock to jazz to opera. Each participating organization may submit the composition of only 1 student. Nominees must be between 15 and 24 years of age.

Financial data: First prize is a $10,000 scholarship, second a $5,000 scholarship, third a $2,000 scholarship, and honorable mention $1,000 scholarships.

Duration: 1 year.

Additional information: This program was established in 1998 by Yoko Ono in conjunction with Gibson Musical Instruments and the BMI Foundation. The selected organizations are Bard College, Berklee College of Music, Birmingham Southern College, Blair School of Music at Vanderbilt University, Brandeis University, California Institute of the Arts, California State University at Northridge, Cleveland School of the Arts, the Cleveland Music School Settlement/University Circle Campus, Duquesne University, Fiorello H. LaGuardia High School of Music & Art and Performing Arts, Interlochen Arts Academy, Johns Hopkins University/Peabody Conservatory of Music, the Julliard School, Levine School of Music, Longy School of Music, Los Angeles High School for the Arts, Lovewell Institute, Macphail Center for the Arts, Mills College, New England Conservatory, New York Youth Symphony, North Carolina School of the Arts, Oberlin College, Settlement Music School, Sherwood Conservatory of Music, Third Street Settlement School, University of Arizona, University of Hartford/The Hartt School, University of Michigan, University of Texas, University of Washington, Walnut Hill School, Wisconsin Conservatory of Music, Yale School of Music, and the Young Musician's Foundation.

Number awarded: Varies each year; recently, the program awarded 1 first prize, 2 second prizes, 1 third prize, and 4 honorable mentions.

Deadline: Participating organizations must submit the name of their nominee by February of each year.

1470
JOHNNY JENKINS SCHOLARSHIP

Georgia Cattlemen's Association
P.O. Box 24510
Macon, GA 31212

Summary: To provide financial assistance to students from southeastern states who are majoring in animal science or agricultural communications.

Eligibility: To be eligible, students must live in and attend school in 1 of the following 7 southeastern states: Alabama, Florida, Georgia, Kentucky, Mississippi, North Carolina, South Carolina, Tennessee, or Virginia. They must be majoring in animal science or agricultural communications.

Financial data: The stipend is $1,000.

Duration: 1 year.

Additional information: Information is also available from the Georgia Beef Board, P.O. Box 24570, Macon, GA 31212. Telephone: (912) 474-1815.

Number awarded: 1 each year.

Deadline: October of each year.

1471
JOSEPH EHRENREICH SCHOLARSHIPS

National Press Photographers Foundation
3200 Croasdaile Drive, Suite 306
Durham, NC 27705-2586
Phone: (919) 383-7246   (800) 289-6772
Fax: (919) 383-7261   E-mail: info@nppa.org
Web Site: www.nppa.org

Summary: To provide financial assistance to college students interested in pursuing a career in photojournalism.

Eligibility: Applicants must have completed at least 1 year at a recognized 4-year college or university in the United States or Canada that offers courses in photojournalism, be working on a bachelor's degree, be intending to pursue a career in journalism, and have at least half a year of undergraduate study remaining. These awards are aimed at those with journalism potential but with little opportunity and great need.

Financial data: The stipend is $1,000 per year.

Duration: 1 year; nonrenewable.

Additional information: This program, established in 1976, is named for the president of Ehrenreich Photo-Optical industries, importer of Nikon cameras and lenses. Further information is available from Mike Smith, *The New York Times,* Picture Desk, 229 West 43rd Street, New York, NY 10036, (212) 556-7742, E-mail: smithmi@nytimes.com. Recipients may attend school in the United States or Canada.

Number awarded: 5 each year.

Deadline: February of each year.

1472
JOSEPHINE DE KAN FELLOWSHIPS

Summary: To provide financial assistance to outstanding college seniors or students in their last year of a Ph.D. program.

See Listing #516.

1473
JOYCE WALSH JUNIOR AWARDS FOR THE HANDICAPPED

National Federation of Music Clubs
1336 North Delaware Street
Indianapolis, IN 46202-2481
Phone: (317) 638-4003   Fax: (317) 638-0503
E-mail: info@nfmc-music.org
Web Site: www.nfmc-music.org/annual_junior.htm

Summary: To recognize and reward outstanding young instrumentalists and vocalists with disabilities who are members of the National Federation of Music Clubs (NFMC).

Eligibility: Eligible to apply are disabled musicians (instrumentalists or vocalists) who are between 12 and 19 years of age, U.S. citizens, and junior members of the federation.

Financial data: The awards are $1,500 for first place and $1,000 for second place. In addition, 3 awards of $500 are given to the winner in each of the 4 NFMC regions.

Duration: The awards are presented annually.

Additional information: These awards are funded by the T-Shirt Project Endowment. Applications and further information are also available from Mrs. B.E. Walsh, 905 Dial Drive, Kennett, MO 63857-2015, (314) 888-3347; information on all federation scholarships and awards is also available from Chair, Competitions and Awards Board, Mrs. Lamoine M. Hall, Jr., 4137 Whitfield Avenue, Fort Worth, TX 76109-5432. There is a $2 entry fee.

Number awarded: 14 each year.

Deadline: January of each year.

1474
JUAN EUGENE RAMOS SCHOLARSHIP

Hispanic Designers, Inc.
Attn: National Hispanic Education and Communications Projects
1101 30th Street, N.W., Suite 500
Washington, DC 20007
Phone: (202) 337-9636   Fax: (202) 337-9635
E-mail: HispDesign@aol.com   Web Site: www.hispanicdesigners.org

Summary: To provide financial assistance to Hispanic students enrolled in a fashion design school.

Eligibility: Applicants must be Hispanic or of Hispanic descent, be able to

demonstrate financial need, be U.S. citizens or residents, have participated in an internship or work training program in the field of fashion, and have a grade point average of 3.0 or higher. They must be enrolled in an accredited postsecondary institution and studying for a degree or certified program that incorporates the importance of marketing and merchandising in fashion design.
Financial data: The stipend is $5,000 per year; awards are paid directly to institution.
Duration: 1 year.
Additional information: This program was established in 1995. No telephone inquiries are accepted.
Number awarded: 1 each year.
Deadline: August of each year.

1475
JULIETTE M. ATHERTON SCHOLARSHIP

Summary: To provide financial assistance for college to Protestants who are ministers, the dependents of ministers in Hawaii, or students preparing for the ministry.
See Listing #517.

1476
JUNE P. GALLOWAY SCHOLARSHIP

North Carolina Association of Health, Physical Education, Recreation and Dance
Attn: Executive Director
Box 974
Boiling Springs, NC 28017
Phone: (888) 840-6500
Summary: To provide financial assistance for college to members of the North Carolina Association of Health, Physical Education, Recreation and Dance (NCAAHPERD).
Eligibility: Eligible to apply for this scholarship are rising seniors majoring in health, physical education, recreation, and/or dance who are members of NCAAHPERD and have earned at least a 2.0 grade point average for all college work and a 3.0 average for their major. Applicants must demonstrate leadership and contributions to the profession. Financial need is not considered in the selection process.
Financial data: The stipend is $1,000 per year.
Duration: 1 year.
Additional information: Information is also available from Dawn Clark, 2304 Jefferson Drive, Greenville, NC 27858.
Number awarded: 1 each year.
Deadline: April of each year.

1477
JUNG-SOOK LEE AWARD

Association for Education in Journalism and Mass Communication
Attn: Communication Technology and Policy Division
234 Outlet Pointe Boulevard, Suite A
Columbia, SC 29210-5667
Phone: (803) 798-0271   Fax: (803) 772-3509
E-mail: aejmchq@vm.sc.edu
Web Site: www.aejmc.org
Summary: To recognize and reward outstanding college student papers on communication technology and policy.
Eligibility: Undergraduate and graduate students are invited to submit research papers or articles intended for professional publication that focus on communication technology and policy. Papers or articles are to be no more than 25 pages in length and written during the past year.
Financial data: Cash prizes are awarded.
Duration: The competition is held annually.
Additional information: Information is also available from Alice Chan, Cornell University, Department of Communication, 309 Kennedy Hall, Ithaca, NY 14853-4203, (607) 255-2111, Fax: (607) 254-1322, E-mail: apc18@cornell.edu.
Number awarded: 3 each year.
Deadline: March of each year.

1478
KAB BROADCAST SCHOLARSHIP PROGRAM

Kansas Association of Broadcasters
Attn: Scholarship Committee
1916 S.W. Sieben Court
Topeka, KS 66611-1656
Phone: (785) 235-1307   Fax: (785) 233-3052
E-mail: info@kab.net

Web Site: www.kab.net/programs/student/brdcast_scholarship.html
Summary: To provide financial assistance to college students in Kansas who are interested in pursuing a career in broadcasting.
Eligibility: This program is open to residents of Kansas who are enrolled as full-time students at a postsecondary institution in the state, either as a junior or senior at a 4-year college or university or as a sophomore at a 2-year college. Applicants must have at least a 2.5 grade point average and submit a letter from the head of the college radio/TV department certifying their eligibility. Along with their application, they must submit a 3-page essay explaining why they selected broadcasting as a career, the specific area of broadcasting that most interests them and why, their first job preference after college, their career goal for 10 years after college, their eventual career goal, the broadcast activities in which they have participated, their feeling about broadcast advertising and its importance to a station, the role they think the government should play in a broadcast station's operations, how they think broadcasting could better serve society, the radio or television station they most admire, how their college career will improve their value as a broadcaster, and their most rewarding broadcast-related experience. Selection is based on the depth of thought, clarity of expression, and legibility of the essay; commitment to broadcasting as revealed in the essay; extracurricular activities; community involvement; and financial need.
Financial data: Stipends are $1,000 per year for students at a 4-year college or university or $500 per year for students at a 2-year college. A total of $6,600 is available for this program each year.
Duration: 1 year; may be renewed.
Number awarded: Varies each year; the available funds are distributed to the most qualified applicants regardless of whether they attend 2-year or 4-year schools.
Deadline: April of each year.

1479
KANSAS AMERICAN LEGION MUSIC SCHOLARSHIP

American Legion
Attn: Department of Kansas
1314 S.W. Topeka Boulevard
Topeka, KS 66612-1886
Phone: (785) 232-9315   Fax: (785) 232-1399
Summary: To provide financial assistance for postsecondary education to music students in Kansas.
Eligibility: High school seniors and college freshmen and sophomores may apply for this scholarship if they are studying or planning to study music at an approved college or university in Kansas.
Financial data: The stipend is $1,000.
Duration: 1 year.
Number awarded: 1 each year.
Deadline: February of each year.

1480
KATHERINE VAZ SCHOLARSHIP

Summary: To provide financial assistance for undergraduate study to members of the Luso-American community who are deaf or interested in studying writing.
See Listing #529.

1481
KATU THOMAS R. DARGAN MINORITY SCHOLARSHIP

KATU Channel 2 Portland
Attn: Human Resources
P.O. Box 2
Portland, OR 97207-0002
Phone: (503) 231-4222   Web Site: www.katu.com
Summary: To provide financial assistance and work experience to minority students from Oregon and Washington who are studying broadcasting or communications in college.
Eligibility: This program is open to Native Americans, African Americans, Hispanic Americans, or Asian Americans who are U.S. citizens, currently enrolled in the first, second, or third year at a 4-year college or university or an accredited community college in Oregon or Washington, or, if a resident of Oregon or Washington, at a school in any state. Applicants must be majoring in broadcasting or communications and have a grade point average of 3.0 or higher. Community college students must be enrolled in a broadcast curriculum that is transferable to a 4-year accredited university. Finalists will be interviewed. Selection is based on financial need, academic achievement, and an essay on personal and professional goals.
Financial data: The stipend is $4,000. Funds are sent directly to the recipient's school.

Duration: 1 year; recipients may reapply if they have maintained a 3.0 grade point average.

Additional information: Winners are also eligible for a paid internship in selected departments at Fisher Broadcasting/KATU in Portland, Oregon.

Number awarded: 1 or more each year.

Deadline: April of each year.

1482
KEN KASHIWAHARA SCHOLARSHIP

Radio and Television News Directors Foundation
1000 Connecticut Avenue, N.W., Suite 615
Washington, DC 20036-5302
Phone: (202) 467-5218   Fax: (202) 223-4007
E-mail: karenb@rtndf.org
Web Site: www.rtndf.org/asfi/scholarships/undergrad.shtml

Summary: To provide financial assistance to outstanding undergraduate students, especially minorities, who are interested in preparing for a career in electronic journalism.

Eligibility: Eligible are sophomore or more advanced undergraduate students enrolled in an electronic journalism sequence at an accredited or nationally recognized college or university. Applicants must submit 1 to 3 examples of reporting or producing skills on audio or video cassette tapes (no more than 15 minutes total), a description of their role on each story and a list of who worked on each story and what they did, a statement explaining why they are seeking a career in broadcast or cable journalism, and a letter of endorsement from a faculty sponsor that verifies the applicant has at least 1 year of school remaining. Preference is given to undergraduate students of color.

Financial data: The stipend is $2,500, paid in semiannual installments of $1,250 each.

Duration: 1 year.

Additional information: The Radio and Television News Directors Foundation (RTNDF) also provides an expense-paid trip to the Radio-Television News Directors Association (RTNDA) annual international conference. It defines electronic journalism to include radio, television, cable, and online news. Previous winners of any RTNDF scholarship or internship are not eligible.

Number awarded: 1 each year.

Deadline: April of each year.

1483
KENNEDY CENTER AMERICAN COLLEGE THEATER FESTIVAL TEN-MINUTE PLAY FESTIVAL AWARD

John F. Kennedy Center for the Performing Arts
Education Department
Attn: Kennedy Center American College Theater Festival
2700 F Street, N.W.
Washington, DC 20566
Phone: (202) 416-8857   Fax: (202) 416-8802
E-mail: skshaffer@kennedy-center.org
Web Site: kennedy-center.org/education/actf/actfsitv.html

Summary: To recognize and reward outstanding 10-minute plays by student playwrights.

Eligibility: Students at any accredited junior or senior college in the United States or in a country contiguous to the continental United States are eligible to compete in a regional 10-minute play festival. Undergraduate students must be carrying a minimum of 6 semester hours, graduate students must be carrying a minimum of 3 semester hours, and continuing part-time students must be enrolled in a regular degree or certificate program. The 8 regional winners are then entered in the national competition.

Financial data: The national prize is $1,000. Dramatic Publishing Company publishes each of the 8 regional winners.

Duration: The competition is held annually.

Additional information: This award, first presented in 2000, is part of the Michael Kanin Playwriting Awards Program. Colleges and universities that have at least 1 participating or associate entry in the Kennedy Center American College Theater Festival (KCACTF) may enter this festival at no additional charge. Regional submissions from schools with no entries in the KCACTF must pay a $20 entry fee per submission to this festival.

Number awarded: 1 each year.

Deadline: November of each year.

1484
KEVIN BARRY PERDUE MEMORIAL SCHOLARSHIP

Foundation for Amateur Radio, Inc.
P.O. Box 831
Riverdale, MD 20738
E-mail: turnbull@erols.com
Web Site: www.amateurradio-far.org

Summary: To provide funding to licensed radio amateurs who are interested in studying humanities or the social sciences in college.

Eligibility: Applicants must have at least a technician class license and intend to pursue a course of study in the liberal arts, humanities, or social science fields. They must intend to earn a bachelor's degree from a U.S. college or university.

Financial data: The stipend is $2,000.

Duration: 1 year.

Additional information: Recipients must attend an accredited school (university, college, or technical institute) on a full-time basis.

Number awarded: 1 each year.

Deadline: May of each year.

1485
KING OLAV V NORWEGIAN-AMERICAN HERITAGE FUND

Sons of Norway Foundation
c/o Sons of Norway
1455 West Lake Street
Minneapolis, MN 55408-2666
Phone: (612) 827-3611   (800) 945-8851
Fax: (612) 827-0658   E-mail: fraternal@sofn.com
Web Site: www.sofn.com/foundation/scholarships.html

Summary: To provide support to college students of Norwegian heritage who are interested in pursuing further study of that heritage.

Eligibility: This program is open to North Americans of Norwegian heritage, 18 years of age or older, who have demonstrated an interest in their heritage and who desire to further the study of that heritage at a recognized educational institution in North America or Norway. The program of study may include arts, crafts, literature, history, music, or folklore. Applicants must submit a 500-word essay that describes their reasons for applying for the scholarship, the course of study to be pursued, the length of the course, the name of the institution which they plan to attend, the tuition and costs, the amount of financial aid desired, how their course of study will benefit their community, and how their study corresponds to the goals and objectives of the Sons of Norway Foundation. Selection is based on the essay, academic potential, benefit to Sons of Norway and the wider Norwegian community, involvement in school and community activities, work experience, and financial need.

Financial data: Stipends range from $250 to $3,000, depending upon the number of recipients in any given year.

Duration: 1 year; a student may be awarded 2 scholarships within a 5-year period.

Additional information: Awards are also made to Norwegians who wish to study the American heritage in North America. Applications may not be submitted by fax or e-mail. Final reports are requested (but are not required).

Number awarded: Varies each year. Since 1984, 167 of these scholarships have been awarded.

Deadline: February of each year.

1486
KNIGHT RIDDER MINORITY SCHOLARS PROGRAM

Knight Ridder, Inc.
Attn: Office of Diversity
50 West San Fernando Street, Suite 1200
San Jose, CA 95113
Phone: (408) 938-6000
Web Site: www.kri.com

Summary: To provide financial assistance and work experience to minority high school seniors who are interested in going to college to prepare for a career in journalism.

Eligibility: Graduating minority high school seniors are eligible to apply if they are attending a school in an area served by Knight Ridder and are interested in majoring in journalism in college. Candidates first apply to their local Knight Ridder newspaper and compete for local scholarships; selected winners are then nominated for this award.

Financial data: The stipend is up to $10,000 per year.

Duration: 1 year; may be renewed for up to 3 additional years, if the recipient

maintains at least a 3.0 grade point average.

Additional information: Scholarship recipients are offered an internship opportunity at a Knight Ridder newspaper during the summer. At the end of the program, recipients must work at a Knight Ridder newspaper for 1 year.

Number awarded: 4 each year.

1487
KNIGHTS OF PYTHIAS POSTER CONTEST

Knights of Pythias
Office of Supreme Lodge
59 Coddington Street, Suite 202
Quincy, MA 02169-4150
Phone: (617) 472-8800   Fax: (617) 376-0363
E-mail: kop@earthlink.net
Web Site: www.pythias.org

Summary: To recognize and reward outstanding posters by high school students on topics that change annually.

Eligibility: This contest is open to any student enrolled in high school (grades 9 through 12) in the United States or Canada. Posters must be 14 by 22 inches. No collage, paste-on, or stencil lettering is allowed. Competitions are first held by each Knights of Pythias local lodge, with winners advancing to the Grand Domain (state or province) and from there to the national level. These winning entries are then submitted to the Supreme Lodge contest. Posters are evaluated on the basis of message, originality, effective display of message, and neatness. The topic changes periodically; recently, it was "Avoid Violence in Schools."

Financial data: Supreme Lodge prizes are $1,000 for first place, $500 for second place, $250 for third place, and $100 for fourth through eighth places. Grand Lodge prizes vary.

Duration: The contest is held annually.

Number awarded: 8 each year on the national level.

Deadline: Local lodges select their winners by the end of April of each year and submit them to the Grand Lodge in their Grand Domain (state or province) by the middle of May. Grand Domain winners must be submitted to the Supreme Lodge by the middle of June.

1488
KODAK SCHOLARSHIP PROGRAM

University Film and Video Foundation
c/o Linda Alexander
SMPTE
595 West Hartsdale Avenue
White Plains, NY 10607
Web Site: www.kodak.com/US/en/motion/programs/student/scholarship.shtml

Summary: To provide tuition scholarships or production grants to film students.

Eligibility: Eligible to be nominated for this support are juniors, seniors, and graduate students enrolled in cinematography and production at U.S. and Canadian colleges and universities offering degrees in motion picture filmmaking. Each school may nominate up to 2 candidates. Finalists may be requested to submit portfolios for review by the selection committee.

Financial data: Up to $5,000 is awarded to each recipient. Funds are paid directly to the recipient's school and may be used for tuition or as a production grant.

Duration: 1 year.

Additional information: This program is administered on behalf of Kodak (as part of the Kodak Worldwide Student Program) by the University Film and Video Foundation. Applications may not be submitted directly by students. They must be nominated by their university or college.

Number awarded: Varies each year.

1489
KOSCIUSZKO FOUNDATION CHOPIN PIANO COMPETITION

Kosciuszko Foundation
Attn: Cultural Department
15 East 65th Street
New York, NY 10021-6595
Phone: (212) 734-2130   (800) 287-9956
Fax: (212) 628-4552   E-mail: thekf@aol.com
Web Site: www.kosciuszkofoundation.org/grants/chopin00.shtml

Summary: To recognize and reward outstanding pianists.

Eligibility: The competition is open to U.S. citizens, permanent residents of the United States, and international full-time students with valid student visas; all entrants must be between 16 and 22 years of age. Contestants prepare a program

of 60 to 75 minutes encompassing a selection of works by Chopin, a mazurka by Szymanowski, a major work by J.S. Bach, a complete classical (Beethoven, Haydn, Mozart or Schubert) sonata, a major 19th-century work by a composer other than Chopin, and a contemporary work by an American, Polish, or Polish American composer; jurors choose works from the program for the auditions. Preliminary competitions take place in Chicago, Houston, and New York; winners advance to the national competitions, in New York.

Financial data: The preliminary competitions provide small cash prizes and round-trip airfare to the national finals. In the national competitions, first place is $5,000, second place $2,500, and third place $1,500.

Duration: The competition is held annually; the preliminaries are held in March and the national finals in April.

Additional information: The first-prize winner also performs at concerts arranged by the Kosciuszko Foundation in the United States and Poland. Applications must be accompanied by a nonrefundable fee of $35.

Number awarded: 3 nation prizes are awarded each year.

Deadline: February of each year.

1490
KYUTARO AND YASUO ABIKO MEMORIAL SCHOLARSHIP

Summary: To provide financial assistance to student members of the Japanese American Citizens League (JACL) who are pursuing undergraduate education. *See Listing #550.*

1491
LAMBDA IOTA TAU SCHOLARSHIPS

Lambda Iota Tau, College Literature Honor Society
c/o Bruce W. Hozeski, Executive Secretary/Treasurer
Ball State University
Department of English
2000 West University Avenue
Muncie, IN 47306-0460   Phone: (765) 285-8580

Summary: To provide financial assistance for college to members of Lambda Iota Tau, the College Literature Honor Society.

Eligibility: Eligible to be nominated for this scholarship are initiated members of the society. Only society chapters may submit nominations. The nomination letter must include a sample of the student's essay/creative writing and an essay from the nominee on his/her career goals and objectives. Selection is based on the writing sample, academic record, leadership, character, and service. No consideration is given to age, race, creed, sex, or national citizenship of the nominee.

Financial data: The stipend is $1,000.

Duration: 1 year.

Number awarded: 3 each year.

Deadline: June of each year.

1492
LANDMARK SCHOLARS PROGRAM

Landmark Publishing Group
Attn: Director of Recruiting
150 West Brambleton Avenue
Norfolk, VA 23510
Phone: (757) 446-2456   (800) 446-2004, ext. 2456
Fax: (757) 446-2414   E-mail: csage@lcimedia.com
Web Site: www.landmarkcom.com/employment/scholarships.html

Summary: To provide work experience and financial aid for college to minority students who are interested in preparing for a career in journalism.

Eligibility: This program is open to minority college sophomores, preferably those with ties to the mid-Atlantic/southern region. Applicants must be interested in pursuing a career in journalism. They must also be interested in internships as reporters, photographers, graphic artists, sports writers, copy editors, or page designers.

Financial data: The stipend is $5,000 per year. During the summers between the sophomore and junior years and between the junior and seniors years, recipients are provided with paid internships. Following graduation, they are offered a 1-year internship with full benefits and the possibility of continued employment.

Duration: 2 years (the junior and senior year of college).

Additional information: The internships are offered at the *News & Record* in Greensboro, North Carolina, the *Virginian-Pilot* in Norfolk, Virginia, or the *Roanoke Times* in Roanoke, Virginia.

Number awarded: 1 or more each year.

Deadline: November of each year.

1493
LANDS' END SCHOLARSHIP PROGRAM

Wisconsin Foundation for Independent Colleges, Inc.
735 North Water Street, Suite 800
Milwaukee, WI 53202-4100
Phone: (414) 273-5980   Fax: (414) 273-5995
E-mail: wfic@execpc.com   Web Site: www.wficweb.org
Summary: To provide financial assistance to students attending private colleges in Wisconsin who are majoring in selected business-related fields.
Eligibility: This program is open to currently-enrolled full-time students at the 21 independent colleges or universities in Wisconsin. Applicants must be majoring in business, economics, communications, or computer science. They must have earned at least a 3.0 grade point average. Recipients are selected by the participating schools.
Financial data: The stipend is $1,000.
Duration: 1 year.
Additional information: The participating schools are Alverno College, Beloit College, Cardinal Stritch University, Carroll College, Carthage College, Concordia University of Wisconsin, Edgewood College, Lakeland College, Lawrence University, Marian College, Marquette University, Milwaukee Institute of Art & Design, Milwaukee School of Engineering, Mount Mary College, Northland College, Ripon College, St. Norbert College, Silver Lake College, Viterbo University, and Wisconsin Lutheran College.
Number awarded: 21 each year: 1 at each of the participating colleges and universities.

1494
LAUNCH YOUR CAREER IN EXHIBIT DESIGN COMPETITION

Exhibit Designers and Producers Association
5775 G Peachtree-Dunwoody Road
Atlanta, GA 30342
Phone: (404) 303-7310, ext. 297   Fax: (404) 252-0774
Web Site: www.launchyourcareerinexhibitdesign.com
Summary: To recognize and reward outstanding exhibit designs submitted by college students.
Eligibility: This competition is open to college sophomores and juniors. To enter, they must create a trade show exhibit for a fictional client described by the sponsors. All entries must include a written synopsis summarizing the design solution and how it meets the client's requirements and marketing goals. In addition, entries may include any or all of the following: a floor plan drawn to scale, computer or hand renderings, isometric projection and axonometric drawings, a scale model, a CAD model showing at least 2 views, and a VHS video (10 minutes maximum length). Selection is based on aesthetics, structure, integrated marking strategy and achievement of predetermined sales, and marketing goals and objectives.
Financial data: The first-place winner receives a $5,000 scholarship; second-place winner receives a $3,000 scholarship; third-place winner receives a $2,000 scholarship. Funds must be used to pay for tuition at the recipient's college. Plus, each of the 3 winners is offered a paid internship at 1 of the sponsoring companies' design studios/production facilities in North America.
Duration: The competition is held annually.
Additional information: The winning entries are showcased at the Exhibitor Show in Las Vegas. This program is cosponsored by the Exhibit Designers and Producers Association, Exhibitgroup/Giltspur, Freeman Companies, and Cort Trade Show Furnishings.
Number awarded: 3 each year.
Deadline: November of each year.

1495
LAWRENCE WADE JOURNALISM FELLOWSHIP

Heritage Foundation
Attn: Selection Committee
214 Massachusetts Avenue, N.E.
Washington, DC 20002-4999
Phone: (202) 546-4400   Fax: (202) 546-8328
E-mail: info@heritage.org   Web Site: www.heritage.org
Summary: To provide financial assistance and work experience to undergraduate or graduate students who are interested in a career in journalism.
Eligibility: This program is open to undergraduate or graduate students who are currently enrolled full time and are interested in a career as a journalist upon graduation. Applicants need not be majoring in journalism, but they must submit writing samples of published news stories, editorial commentaries, or broadcast scripts. Preference is given to candidates who are Asian Americans, African Americans, Hispanic Americans, or Native Americans.

Financial data: The winner receives a $1,000 scholarship and participates in a 10-week salaried internship at the Heritage Foundation.
Duration: 1 year.
Additional information: This program was established in 1991.
Number awarded: 1 each year.
Deadline: February of each year.

1496
LEAF SCHOLARSHIP

California Landscape Contractors Association
Attn: Landscape Educational Advancement Foundation
1491 River Park Drive, Suite 100
Sacramento, CA 95815
Phone: (916) 830-2780   Web Site: www.clca.org
Summary: To provide financial assistance to students in California who are majoring in ornamental horticulture.
Eligibility: This program is open to students attending an accredited California community college or state university and majoring in ornamental horticulture. The application asks for information on awards and honors; college and high school activities related to landscaping; community activities related to landscaping; other high school, college, and community activities and offices held; work experience; and brief essays on educational objectives, occupational goals as they relate to the landscape industry, reasons for choosing the field, and reasons for requesting financial assistance.
Financial data: A stipend is awarded (exact amount not specified).
Duration: 1 year.
Number awarded: 1 or more each year.
Deadline: February of each year.

1497
LEE A. LYMAN MEMORIAL MUSIC SCHOLARSHIP

Vermont Student Assistance Corporation
Champlain Mill
1 Main Street, Fourth Floor
P.O. Box 2000
Winooski, VT 05404-2601
Phone: (802) 655-9602   (800) 642-3177
Fax: (802) 654-3765   TDD: (802) 654-3766
Phone: TDD: (800) 281-3341 (within VT)   E-mail: info@vsac.org
Web Site: www.vsac.org
Summary: To provide financial assistance to residents of Vermont who are interested in pursuing a degree in music.
Eligibility: This scholarship is available to the residents of Vermont who are seniors in high school, high school graduates, or currently enrolled in college. Applicants must be enrolled or planning to enroll in a postsecondary degree program in music. They must be able to document financial need, have participated in music-related activities, have applied to the Vermont Student Assistance Corporation for a Vermont Grant, and have filed a Free Application for Federal Student Aid no later than 4 weeks before the scholarship deadline. The following are required as part of the application process: a completed application form, 1 letter of recommendation, 5 required essays, and an official transcript. Selection is based on financial need, academic record, quality of the required essays, recommendations, and participation in music-related activities.
Financial data: The stipend is $1,000.
Duration: 1 year; recipients may reapply.
Additional information: This program was established in 1995 in memory of the former director of the sponsor's Education Loan Finance Program.
Number awarded: 2 each year.
Deadline: May of each year.

1498
LEE AGGER MEMORIAL SCHOLARSHIP

Maine Media Women
Attn: Charlotte Nolan, Scholarship Committee
12 Howard's Hill Road
Harpswell, ME 04079
E-mail: cnolan@gwi.net
Summary: To provide financial assistance to women in Maine who are interested in preparing for a career in communications.
Eligibility: This program is open to women of any age who are residents of Maine, will be enrolled in a related college program in the fall, and are interested

in pursuing or furthering a career in mass communications. Applicants may be engaged in undergraduate or graduate study in journalism, public relations, or advertising. Selection is based on academic record, an essay on career goals, demonstrated interest in communications, and financial need.
Financial data: The stipend is $1,000.
Duration: 1 year.
Number awarded: 1 each year.
Deadline: March of each year.

1499
LEE-JACKSON FOUNDATION SCHOLARSHIP

Lee-Jackson Foundation
P.O. Box 8121
Charlottesville, VA 22906
Phone: (804) 977-1861
Web Site: www.lee-jackson.org
Summary: To recognize and reward students in Virginia who enter an historical essay contest and plan to attend a college or university in the United States.
Eligibility: High school juniors and seniors at any Virginia secondary school may compete for these scholarships by writing an essay that demonstrates an appreciation of the character and virtues of Generals Robert E. Lee and Thomas J. "Stonewall" Jackson. Selection is based on historical accuracy, quality of research, and clarity of written expression. Students first compete in the 8 high school regions in the state; winners are selected by a screening committee in their localities. In each region, a bonus scholarship is awarded to the paper judged the best; a grand prize is awarded to the author of the essay judged best of all the essays submitted.
Financial data: Total prizes are $10,000, $2,000, or $1,000. Each winner receives $1,000. The winners of bonus scholarships receive an additional $1,000 and the grand prize winner receives an additional $8,000. A $1,000 award is given to schools or home-school regions that encourage the most participation.
Duration: The competition is held annually.
Additional information: Applications are available from division superintendents and school principals. Winners may use the scholarships at any 4-year institution in the United States.
Number awarded: 27 each year: 3 winners in each of the 8 public high school regions of the state plus 3 to private and home-school students. Bonus scholarships are awarded to 8 public high school students (1 in each region) and 1 private or home-schooled student. The grand prize is awarded to the public school, private school, or home-schooled student whose essay is judged to be the best in the state. In addition, 9 schools (1 in each public school region plus 1 private/home-school region) receive the awards for encouraging the most participation.
Deadline: December of each year.

1500
LEN ALLEN AWARD FOR RADIO NEWSROOM MANAGEMENT

Radio and Television News Directors Foundation
1000 Connecticut Avenue, N.W., Suite 615
Washington, DC 20036-5302
Phone: (202) 467-5218   Fax: (202) 223-4007
E-mail: karenb@rtndf.org
Web Site: www.rtndf.org/asfi/scholarships/undergrad.shtml
Summary: To provide financial assistance to students whose career objective is radio newsroom management.
Eligibility: Eligible are sophomore or more advanced undergraduate or graduate students enrolled in an electronic journalism sequence at an accredited or nationally recognized college or university. Applicants must submit a 1-page essay on why they are seeking a career in radio newsroom management and a letter of endorsement from a faculty sponsor certifying that the applicant has at least 1 year of school remaining.
Financial data: The stipend is $2,000, paid in semiannual installments of $1,000 each.
Duration: 1 year.
Additional information: The Radio and Television News Directors Foundation (RTNDF) also provides an expense-paid trip to the Radio-Television News Directors Association (RTNDA) annual international convention. It defines electronic journalism to include radio, television, cable, and online news. Previous winners of any RTNDF scholarship or internship are not eligible.
Number awarded: 1 each year.
Deadline: April of each year.

1501
LEONARD M. PERRYMAN COMMUNICATIONS SCHOLARSHIP FOR ETHNIC MINORITY STUDENTS

United Methodist Communications
Attn: Public Media Division
810 12th Avenue South
P.O. Box 320
Nashville, TN 37202-0320
Phone: (615) 742-5766   Fax: (615) 742-5404
E-mail: Scholarships@Umcom.umc.org
Web Site: www.umcom.org/scholarships
Summary: To provide financial assistance to minority college students who are interested in careers in religious communications.
Eligibility: Applicants must be minorities who are enrolled in accredited institutions of higher education as juniors or seniors and are interested in pursuing careers in religious communications. For the purposes of this program, "communications" is meant to cover audiovisual, electronic, and print journalism. Selection is based on Christian commitment and involvement in the life of the church, academic achievement, journalistic experience, clarity of purpose, and professional potential as a religious journalist.
Financial data: The stipend is $2,500 per year.
Duration: 1 year.
Additional information: The scholarship may be used at any accredited institution of higher education.
Number awarded: 2 each year.
Deadline: March of each year.

1502
LEROY COLLINS MEMORIAL SCHOLARSHIP

Florida Association of Broadcasters
800 North Calhoun Street
Tallahassee, FL 32303
Phone: (850) 681-6444   (800) 825-5322
Fax: (850) 222-3957   Web Site: www.fab.org
Summary: To provide financial assistance to Florida college students majoring in a broadcast-related field.
Eligibility: Eligible to apply for this program are currently-enrolled college students in Florida who are preparing for a career in the broadcast field. Financial need is considered in the selection process.
Financial data: A stipend is awarded (exact amount not specified).
Duration: 1 year.
Additional information: This program is named for a former governor of Florida.
Number awarded: 3 each year.

1503
LETTERS ABOUT LITERATURE NATIONAL ESSAY CONTEST

Wilkes University
Attn: English Department
Kirby Hall
Wilkes-Barre, PA 18766   Phone: (717) 408-4520
Web Site: www.weeklyreader.com/features.readct.html
Summary: To recognize and reward outstanding essay "letters" written by students in grades 4 though 12 on a book that affected the way they view the world.
Eligibility: Eligible to compete in this contest are students in grades 4 through 12. They are invited to write a letter to an author-living or dead-explaining how the author's book "gave them wings" and changed their way of viewing the world and themselves. The letters written by students in grades 4 though 7 cannot exceed 500 words; the letters from students in grades 8 through 12 cannot exceed 1,000 words. The letters cannot summarize the plot of the book.
Financial data: National winners in each age category receive a $1,000 U.S. savings bond; winners on the state level are presented cash awards by participating state centers for the book.
Duration: The competition is held annually.
Additional information: The competition began in 1983. It is presented by the Library of Congress' Center for the Book and sponsored by Weekly Reader Corporation, King's College, and Wilkes University. Information about the competition for grades 4 through 7 is available from King's College, c/o The Graduate Reading Program, 133 North River Street, Wilkes-Barre, PA 18711; information about the competition for grades 8 through 12 is available from the sponsor.
Number awarded: 2 each year: 1 in each of the age categories.
Deadline: December of each year.

1504
LIBERTY GRAPHICS OUTDOOR ACTIVITIES ART CONTEST

Liberty Graphics, Inc.
Attn: Susannah Homer
P.O. Box 5
Liberty, ME 04949
Phone: (207) 589-4596   (800) 338-0015
Fax: (207) 589-4415   E-mail: design@libertygraphicstshirts.com
Web Site: www.libertygraphicstshirts.com
Summary: To recognize and reward outstanding art related to outdoor activities created by high school students in Maine.
Eligibility: Eligible to compete are high school juniors and seniors in Maine. Qualified students are invited to submit flat art using traditional media and no florescent pigments (maximum size: 22 by 33 inches). Subject matter should relate to outdoor activities, including paddle-sports, camping, hiking, rock climbing, and other "human powered outdoor activities."
Financial data: The award is $1,000 and must be used to further the recipient's art education.
Duration: The competition is held annually.
Number awarded: 1 each year.
Deadline: April of each year.

1505
LORAL SKYNET SCHOLARSHIP

Society of Satellite Professionals International
Attn: Scholarship Program
225 Reinekers Lane, Suite 600
Alexandria, VA 22314
Phone: (703) 549-8696   Fax: (703) 549-9728
E-mail: sspi@sspi.org   Web Site: www.sspi.org
Summary: To provide financial assistance to minorities and women interested in studying satellite-related disciplines in college or graduate school.
Eligibility: This program is open to women and minority high school seniors, college undergraduates, and graduate students majoring or planning to major in fields related to satellite communications, including broadcasting, business, communications, engineering, international policy studies, journalism, law, science, space applications, or telecommunications. Applicants may be from any country. Students engaged in distance learning applications are also eligible. Selection is based on academic and leadership achievement, commitment to pursue education and career opportunities in the satellite communications industry, potential for significant contribution to that industry, a personal statement of 500 to 750 words on interest in satellite communications and why the applicant deserves the award, and a creative work (such as a research report, essay, article, videotape, artwork, computer program, or scale model of an antenna or spacecraft design) that reflects the applicant's interests and talents. Financial need is not considered.
Financial data: The stipend is $2,000.
Duration: 1 year.
Number awarded: 1 each year.
Deadline: June of each year.

1506
LORRAINE HANSBERRY PLAYWRITING AWARD

John F. Kennedy Center for the Performing Arts
Education Department
Attn: Kennedy Center American College Theater Festival
2700 F Street, N.W.
Washington, DC 20566
Phone: (202) 416-8857   Fax: (202) 416-8802
E-mail: skshaffer@kennedy-center.org
Web Site: kennedy-center.org/education/actf/actflha.html
Summary: To recognize and reward the student authors of plays on the African American experience in America.
Eligibility: Students at any accredited junior or senior college in the United States or in countries contiguous to the continental United States are eligible to compete, provided their college agrees to participate in the Kennedy Center American College Theater Festival (KCACTF). Undergraduate students must be carrying a minimum of 6 semester hours, graduate students must be carrying a minimum of 3 semester hours, and continuing part-time students must be enrolled in a regular degree or certificate program. These awards are presented to the best student-written plays on the subject of the African American experience.
Financial data: The first-place award is $2,500 and the second-place award is

$1,000. The first-place winner also receives an internship to the National Playwrights Conference at the O'Neill Theater Center and publication of the play by Dramatic Publishing Company. In addition to the student awards, grants of $750 and $500 are made to the theater departments of the colleges or universities producing the first- and second-place plays.
Duration: The award is presented annually.
Additional information: This program is supported by the Kennedy Center and Dramatic Publishing Company. It honors the first African American playwright to win the New York Drama Critics Award but who died in 1965 at the age of 34. First presented in 1977, it is part of the Michael Kanin Playwriting Awards Program. The sponsoring college or university must pay a registration fee of $250 for each production.
Number awarded: 2 student winners and 2 sponsoring institutions each year.
Deadline: November of each year.

1507
LOTTA M. CRABTREE GRANTS FOR WOMEN IN THEATER

Lotta M. Crabtree Trusts
11 Beacon Street, Suite 1005
Boston, MA 02108
Phone: (617) 742-5920
Summary: To provide financial assistance for the education of women interested in careers in theater.
Eligibility: This fund is open to women in the theatrical profession who have shown marked dramatic talent and need financial assistance to continue their education. Preference is given to Massachusetts residents. Candidates must be recommended by members of the theatrical profession.
Financial data: The amount awarded varies, from $500 to $1,500.
Duration: 1 year; may be renewed.
Number awarded: Varies each year.
Deadline: Applications may be submitted at any time.

1508
LOU AND CAROLE PRATO SPORTS REPORTING SCHOLARSHIP

Radio and Television News Directors Foundation
1000 Connecticut Avenue, N.W., Suite 615
Washington, DC 20036-5302
Phone: (202) 467-5218   Fax: (202) 223-4007
E-mail: karenb@rtndf.org
Web Site: www.rtndf.org/asfi/scholarships/undergrad.shtml
Summary: To provide financial assistance for undergraduate education to students whose career objective is radio or television sports reporting.
Eligibility: This program is open to sophomores, juniors, and seniors who are enrolled full time in electronic journalism in a college or university where such a major is offered. Applicants must submit 1 to 3 examples of reporting or producing skills on audio or video cassette tapes (no more than 15 minutes total), a description of their role on each story and a list of who worked on each story and what they did, a statement explaining why they are seeking a career in broadcast or cable journalism, and a letter of endorsement from a faculty sponsor certifying that the candidate has at least 1 year of school remaining. They must be planning a career as a sports reporter in television or radio.
Financial data: The stipend is $1,000.
Duration: 1 year.
Additional information: The Radio and Television News Directors Foundation (RTNDF) also provides an expense-paid trip to the Radio-Television News Directors Association (RTNDA) annual international conference. This program was established in 2001. Previous winners of any RTNDF scholarship or internship are not eligible.
Number awarded: 1 each year.
Deadline: April of each year.

1509
LUCILLE PARRISH WARD VETERAN'S AWARD

National Federation of Music Clubs
1336 North Delaware Street
Indianapolis, IN 46202-2481
Phone: (317) 638-4003   Fax: (317) 638-0503
E-mail: info@nfmc-music.org
Web Site: www.nfmc-music.org/annual_senior_div.htm
Summary: To provide financial assistance for the undergraduate education of members of the National Federation of Music Clubs (NFMC) whose careers have

been delayed or interrupted as a result of their service in the U.S. armed forces.

Eligibility: Eligible to apply are undergraduate students who are majoring in music and whose musical careers were interrupted by service in the armed forces, including service in combat. Student membership in the federation and U.S. citizenship are required.

Financial data: This award is $2,000.

Duration: 1 year.

Additional information: Applications and further information are also available from Francis Christmann, 4409 14th Street, Lubbock, TX 79416-4801; information on all federation scholarships is available from Chair, Competitions and Awards Board, Mrs. Lamoine M. Hall, Jr., 4137 Whitfield Avenue, Fort Worth, TX 76109-5432.

Number awarded: 1 each year.

Deadline: February of each year.

1510
LUSO-AMERICAN EDUCATION FOUNDATION GENERAL FUND SCHOLARSHIP

Luso-American Education Foundation
Attn: Administrative Director
7080 Donlon Way, Suite 202
P.O. Box 2967
Dublin, CA 94568
Phone: (925) 828-3883   Fax: (925) 828-3883
Web Site: www.luso-american.org/laefx

Summary: To provide financial assistance for undergraduate study in Portuguese language and culture in California.

Eligibility: Applicants must meet at least 1 of the following requirements: 1) be of Portuguese descent; 2) be planning to enroll in Portuguese classes in a 4-year college or university; or 3) be a member of the Luso-American Fraternal Federation. All applicants must be California residents younger than 21 years of age, have graduated from an accredited high school by the summer of the year of the award, and have a minimum grade point average of 3.0. Selection is based on promise of success in college, financial need, qualities of leadership, vocational promise, and sincerity of purpose.

Financial data: The award is $1,000.

Duration: 1 year; nonrenewable.

Additional information: Funds may be utilized only at 4-year colleges and universities, but recipients who wish to attend a community college may request that funds be held in reserve for 2 years until they are ready to transfer to a 4-year institution.

Number awarded: 1 or more each year.

Deadline: February of each year.

1511
LYNN FREEMAN OLSON COMPOSITION AWARD

National Federation of Music Clubs
1336 North Delaware Street
Indianapolis, IN 46202-2481
Phone: (317) 638-4003   Fax: (317) 638-0503
E-mail: info@nfmc-music.org
Web Site: www.nfmc-music.org/BienStudentSpecial.htm

Summary: To recognize and reward outstanding young composers who are members of the National Federation of Music Clubs.

Eligibility: Applicants must be keyboard composers in the advanced division (high school graduate through 25 years of age), the high school division (grades 10 through 12), or the intermediate division (grades 7 through 9). They may be citizens of any country, but they must be members in either the junior or student division of the federation.

Financial data: The award is $1,500 for the advanced division, $1,000 for the high school division, or $500 for the intermediate division.

Additional information: Information on this award is also available from James Schnars, 28 Evonaire Circle, Belleair FL 33756-1602; information on all scholarships is available from Chair, Competitions and Awards Board, Mrs. Lamoine M. Hall, Jr., 4137 Whitfield Avenue, Fort Worth, TX 76109-5432.

Number awarded: 3 every other year: 1 in each of the divisions.

Deadline: February of odd-numbered years.

1512
MAINE INNKEEPERS ASSOCIATION HOSPITALITY SCHOLARSHIPS

Maine Innkeepers Association
Attn: Executive Director
305 Commercial Street
Portland, ME 04101
Phone: (207) 773-7670

Summary: To provide financial assistance to Maine residents who wish to prepare for a career in the hospitality industry.

Eligibility: This program is open to Maine residents who wish take courses related to the hospitality industry. Applicants must be interested in pursuing a career in the hotel and motel industry and accepted at an accredited school in Maine that specializes in hotel administration and culinary sciences. They may be graduating high school seniors, the children of members of the association, or employees of association properties; they must have a grade point average of at least 2.5. Selection is based on academic record, employment history, extracurricular activities, career plans, and financial need.

Financial data: Stipends range from $500 to $1,000.

Duration: 1 year; recipients may reapply.

Number awarded: Up to 8 per year.

Deadline: April of each year.

1513
MANAA MEDIA SCHOLARSHIPS

Media Action Network for Asian Americans
P.O. Box 11105
Burbank, CA 91510
Phone: (213) 486-4433   E-mail: manaaletters@hotmail.com
Web Site: nikkei.janet.org/~manaa

Summary: To provide financial assistance to Asian/Pacific Islander students interested in advancing a positive image of Asian Americans in the mainstream media.

Eligibility: This program is open to Asian/Pacific Islander college students interested in pursuing careers in filmmaking and in television production (but not in broadcast journalism). Applicants must be interested in advancing a positive and enlightened understanding of the Asian American experience in the mainstream media. As part of the application process, they must submit a 1,000-word essay that addresses the following questions: Where do you see yourself 10 years from now? What accomplishments and strides will you hope to have made in your career in the film and television industry? How will you have worked to advance more positive images of Asian Americans in the mainstream media? Selection is based on academic and personal merit, a desire to uplift the image of Asian Americans in film and television as demonstrated in the essay, potential as demonstrated in a work sample, and financial need.

Financial data: The stipend is $1,000.

Duration: 1 year.

Additional information: This program began in 2000.

Number awarded: 2 each year.

Deadline: April of each year.

1514
MANSON A. STEWART SCHOLARSHIPS

Classical Association of the Middle West and South
c/o Art Spisak
Southwest Missouri State University
Modern and Classical Languages
Craig Hall 377
901 South National Avenue
Springfield, MO 65804
Phone: (417) 836-5818   E-mail: als224f@smsu.edu
Web Site: www.rmc.edu/~gdaugher/mansonco.html

Summary: To provide financial assistance to undergraduate students majoring in classics at a college or university in the area of the Classical Association of the Middle West and South (CAMWS).

Eligibility: This program is open to undergraduate students who are majoring in classics at the sophomore or junior level at a college or university in the geographic area served by the association. Candidates must be nominated by the chair of their department or program; students then fill out an application and send it along with transcripts and letters of recommendation from 2 members of the association. Nominees are expected to take at least 2 courses in Latin or Greek

during the junior or senior year in which the scholarship is held.
Financial data: The award is $1,000.
Duration: 1 year.
Number awarded: A limited number are awarded each year.
Deadline: Nomination forms must be requested by January of each year; completed applications must be submitted by February of each year.

1515
MARC A. KLEIN PLAYWRITING AWARDS

Case Western Reserve University
Attn: Department of Theater Arts
10900 Euclid Avenue
Cleveland, OH 44106-7077
Phone: (216) 368-2858
Web Site: www.cwru.edu/artsci/thtr/website/theahome.htm
Summary: To recognize and reward outstanding college playwrights.
Eligibility: Any student currently enrolled in an advanced theater program at a U.S. college or university may submit an original, previously unpublished or unproduced full-length play to enter this competition. Musicals and children's plays are not accepted. Manuscripts must be endorsed by a teacher of drama, a member of a theater department, or a recognized critic, director, or playwright.
Financial data: The award is $1,000.
Duration: The competition is held annually.
Additional information: The award includes full mainstage production of the play while the playwright is in residence at Case Western Reserve University.
Number awarded: 1 each year.
Deadline: May of each year.

1516
MARCELLA SEMBRICH VOICE COMPETITION

Kosciuszko Foundation
Attn: Cultural Department
15 East 65th Street
New York, NY 10021-6595
Phone: (212) 734-2130   (800) 287-9956
Fax: (212) 628-4552   E-mail: Thekfschol@aol.com
Web Site: www.kosciuszkofoundation.org/grants/voice.shtml
Summary: To recognize and reward outstanding singers.
Eligibility: The competition is open to U.S. citizens, permanent residents of the United States, and international full-time students with valid student visas; all entrants must be between 18 and 35 years of age and preparing for professional singing careers. They must submit an audio cassette recording of a proposed program if they are selected for the competition; the program must include a Baroque or Classical aria, an aria by Giuseppe Verdi, a Polish song, a 19th-century Romantic opera aria, a contemporary American aria or song, and an aria by Stanislaw Moniuszko.
Financial data: The first-prize winner receives a $1,000 cash scholarship; round-trip airfare from New York City to Warsaw, accommodations, and meals in Poland to perform in the International Moniuszko Competition; a recital at the Moniuszko Festival in Poland; and an invitation to perform at the Sembrich Memorial Association in Lake George, New York. Second and third prizes are $750 and $500, respectively.
Duration: The competition is held triennially, in March.
Additional information: Applications must be accompanied by a nonrefundable fee of $35.
Number awarded: 3 prizes are awarded each year of the competition.
Deadline: December of the years prior to the competitions, which are held in 2004, 2007, etc.

1517
MARGARET SLOGGETT FISHER SCHOLARSHIP

Grove Farm Homestead
Attn: Scholarship Committee
P.O. Box 1631
Lihue, HI 96766
Phone: (808) 245-3202
Summary: To provide financial assistance to upper-division and graduate students from Hawaii who are interested in working on a degree in historical preservation, history, or related subjects.
Eligibility: This program is open to graduate students and college juniors and seniors who are residents of Hawaii and are working on a degree (in Hawaii or the mainland) in historical preservation, museum studies, history, anthropology, Hawaiian studies, ethnic studies, or American studies. Preference is given to Kauai residents. A letter of application, college transcripts, and 2 letters of recommendation are required to apply.
Financial data: The stipend is $1,000 per year.
Duration: 1 year.
Additional information: This program is cosponsored by the Grove Farm Homestead and the Waioli Mission House.
Deadline: April of each year.

1518
MARGOT SEITELMAN MEMORIAL SCHOLARSHIP

American Mensa Education and Research Foundation
1229 Corporate Drive West
Arlington, TX 76006-6103
Phone: (817) 607-0060   (800) 66-MENSA
Fax: (817) 649-5232   E-mail: Scholarships@merf.us.mensa.org
Web Site: merf.us.mensa.org
Summary: To provide financial assistance for postsecondary education to students who are planning a career in professional writing or teaching English grammar and writing.
Eligibility: Any student who is enrolled or will enroll in a degree program at an accredited American institution of higher education in the fall following the application deadline and is planning to study for a career in professional writing or teaching English grammar and writing is eligible to apply. Membership in Mensa is not required, but applicants must be U.S. citizens or permanent residents. There are no restrictions as to age, race, gender, level of postsecondary education, or financial need. Selection is based on a 550-word essay that describes the applicant's career, vocational, or academic goals.
Financial data: The stipend is $1,000.
Duration: 1 year; nonrenewable.
Additional information: Applications are only available through participating Mensa local groups.
Number awarded: 1 each year.
Deadline: January of each year.

1519
MARION MACCARRELL SCOTT SCHOLARSHIP

Hawai'i Community Foundation
900 Fort Street Mall, Suite 1300
Honolulu, HI 96813
Phone: (808) 566-5570   (888) 731-3863
Fax: (808) 521-6286   E-mail: scholarships@hcf-hawaii.org
Web Site: www.hcf-hawaii.org
Summary: To provide financial assistance to residents of Hawaii for undergraduate or graduate studies in fields related to achieving world cooperation and international understanding.
Eligibility: This program is open to graduates of public high schools in Hawaii. They must plan to attend school as full-time students (on the undergraduate or graduate level) on the mainland, majoring in history, government, political science, anthropology, economics, geography, international relations, law, psychology, philosophy, or sociology. They must be residents of the state of Hawaii; be able to demonstrate financial need; be interested in attending an accredited 2- or 4- year college or university; be able to demonstrate academic achievement (2.8 grade point average or above); and submit an essay on their commitment to world peace.
Financial data: The amounts of the awards depend on the availability of funds and the need of the recipient; recently, grants averaged $2,800.
Duration: 1 year.
Number awarded: Varies each year; recently, 168 of these scholarships were awarded.
Deadline: February of each year.

1520
MARION RICHTER AMERICAN MUSIC COMPOSITION AWARD

National Federation of Music Clubs
1336 North Delaware Street
Indianapolis, IN 46202-2481
Phone: (317) 638-4003   Fax: (317) 638-0503
E-mail: info@nfmc-music.org
Web Site: www.nfmc-music.org/annual_student.htm

Summary: To recognize and reward outstanding young composers who are members of the National Federation of Music Clubs.

Eligibility: This program is open to members of the federation who are juniors in college and U.S. citizens. Applicants must be majoring in composition with an emphasis on American music.

Financial data: The award is $1,250.

Duration: The competition is held annually.

Additional information: Applications and further information are available from Nettie F. Loflin, 44867 NC 8 Highway, New London, NC 28127-8659; information on all federation scholarships and awards is available from Chair, Competitions and Awards Board, Mrs. Lamoine M. Hall, Jr., 4137 Whitfield Avenue, Fort Worth, TX 76109-5432. The entry fee is $10.

Number awarded: 1 each year.

Deadline: February of each year.

1521
MARK HASS JOURNALISM SCHOLARSHIP

Oregon Student Assistance Commission
Attn: Private Awards Grant Department
1500 Valley River Drive, Suite 100
Eugene, OR 97401-2146
Phone: (541) 687-7395   (800) 452-8807, ext. 7395
Fax: (541) 687-7419   E-mail: awardinfo@mercury.osac.state.or.us
Web Site: www.osac.state.or.us

Summary: To provide financial assistance to students in Oregon interested in majoring in journalism.

Eligibility: This program is open to residents of Oregon who are studying or planning to study journalism in college.

Financial data: Scholarship amounts vary, depending upon the needs of the recipient.

Duration: 1 year; nonrenewable.

Number awarded: Varies each year.

Deadline: February of each year.

1522
MARK TWAIN COMEDY PLAYWRITING AWARD

John F. Kennedy Center for the Performing Arts
Education Department
Attn: Kennedy Center American College Theater Festival
2700 F Street, N.W.
Washington, DC 20566
Phone: (202) 416-8857   Fax: (202) 416-8802
E-mail: skshaffer@kennedy-center.org
Web Site: kennedy-center.org/education/actf/actftwain.html

Summary: To recognize and reward the student authors of comedy plays.

Eligibility: Students at any accredited junior or senior college in the United States or in countries contiguous to the continental United States are eligible to compete, provided their college agrees to participate in the Kennedy Center American College Theater Festival (KCACTF). Undergraduate students must be carrying a minimum of 6 semester hours, graduate students must be carrying a minimum of 3 semester hours, and continuing part-time students must be enrolled in a regular degree or certificate program. This award is presented to the best student-written full length comedy play.

Financial data: A first-place award of $2,500 and a second-place award of $1,500 are presented to student authors. Dramatic Publishing Company presents the winning playwright with an offer of a contract to publish, license, and market the winning play. The first-place winner also receives an all-expense paid fellowship to attend a 2-week residency at the Sundance Theatre Laboratory in Sundance, Utah. In addition to the student awards, grants of $750 and $500 are made to the theater departments of the colleges or universities producing the first- and second-place plays.

Duration: The award is presented annually.

Additional information: This award, first presented in 2000, is supported by Comedy Central, the cable television company. It is part of the Michael Kanin Playwriting Program. The sponsoring college or university must pay a registration fee of $250 for each production.

Number awarded: 2 student winners and 2 sponsoring institutions each year.

Deadline: November of each year.

1523
MARSHALL E. MCCULLOUGH MEMORIAL SCHOLARSHIPS

National Dairy Shrine
Attn: Office of Executive Director
1224 Alton Darby Creek Road
Columbus, OH 43228-9792
Phone: (614) 878-5333   Fax: (614) 870-2622
E-mail: ndairyshrine@hotmail.com
Web Site: www.dairyshrine.org

Summary: To provide financial assistance to graduating high school students interested in a career in dairy journalism.

Eligibility: This program is open to high school seniors planning to enter a 4-year college or university and major in 1) dairy/animal science with a communications emphasis or 2) agricultural journalism with a dairy/animal science emphasis. Applicants must submit brief essays on their dairy-related participation, communications-related experiences, and view of the future of the dairy industry (and their role in it). Based on those written applications, 5 finalists are selected; they submit an audio or video tape on which they respond to a specific question about the dairy industry.

Financial data: Scholarships are $2,500 or $1,000.

Duration: 1 year.

Number awarded: 2 each year; 1 at $2,500 and 1 at $1,000.

Deadline: March of each year.

1524
MARY AND WALTER HEMPHILL SCHOLARSHIPS

Indianapolis Press Club Foundation Inc.
Attn: Executive Director
150 West Market Street
Indianapolis, IN 46204
Phone: (317) 255-0469

Summary: To provide financial assistance to college students in Indiana who are interested in preparing for a career in journalism.

Eligibility: Applicants must be enrolled in an Indiana college or university and be interested in a career in the news business. Preference is given to students who are majoring in journalism or broadcast journalism. Along with their application, students must submit a 1-page essay in which they describe their career goals, how they plan to achieve those goals, why they are important to them, and how the scholarship will assist them in reaching their goal of a career in journalism. Financial need is considered in the selection process, but career potential is the primary factor considered in awarding the scholarships.

Financial data: The stipends are $1,000 or more each year.

Duration: 1 year.

Number awarded: 3 each year.

Deadline: April of each year.

1525
MARY BENEVENTO SCHOLARSHIP

Connecticut Association for Health, Physical Education, Recreation and Dance
c/o Jodie Hellman, Scholarship Chair
Memorial Middle School
P.O. Box 903
Middlebury, CT 06762
Phone: (203) 758-2496
Web Site: www.ctahperd.org/mary_benevento.htm

Summary: To provide financial assistance to high school seniors in Connecticut who are interested in studying health, physical education, recreation, or dance in college.

Eligibility: This program is open to U.S. citizens who are graduating seniors at high schools in Connecticut. Applicants must be interested in attending a college or university that offers a bachelor's degree in order to prepare for a career in the professional studies of health (meaning school health teaching, not nursing, public health, or psychology), physical education, recreation, or dance. They must submit a 300-word statement describing the educational objectives that qualify them for the scholarship award and summarizing their school and out-of-school activities and accomplishments. In addition to that essay, selection is based on scholarship, competence, future potential in their chosen career, and general worthiness.

Financial data: The stipend is $1,000 per year. Funds are paid to the recipient's college or university to be applied toward tuition, books, room, and board.

Duration: 1 year.

Number awarded: 1 each year.

Deadline: May of each year.

1526
MARY GRAHAM LASLEY SCHOLARSHIP COMPETITION

Symphony Orchestra League of Alexandria
P.O. Box 11835
Alexandria, VA 22312
Phone: (703) 548-0885   Fax: (703) 548-0985
E-mail: nseeger@alexsym.org   Web Site: www.alexsym.org/Schlrshp.html
Summary: To recognize and reward outstanding student musicians who study or reside in the Washington, D.C. area.
Eligibility: Eligible are 1) full-time undergraduate and graduate students currently studying music at a college, university, or conservatory in Virginia, Maryland, or the District of Columbia or 2) residents of those 3 areas who are currently studying elsewhere. Previous competitors (except past winners) are also eligible. Contestants may be no more than 26 years of age at the time of the competition. Solos must be performed from memory on strings, winds, piano, or percussion.
Financial data: First prize is $1,250, second $1,000, and third $750.
Duration: The competition is held annually.
Additional information: This competition is sponsored by the Alexandria Symphony Orchestra and the Symphony Orchestra League of Alexandria. Information is also available from Gay Lamb Pasley, Scholarship Competition Chair, 411 Jackson Place, Alexandria, VA 22302-3305, (703) 683-4346, E-mail: bgpasley@earthlink.net. Applications must be accompanied by a $20 nonrefundable entry fee.
Number awarded: 3 each year.
Deadline: February of each year.

1527
MARYLAND DISTINGUISHED SCHOLAR PROGRAM

Summary: To provide financial assistance for college to outstanding high school juniors in Maryland.
See Listing #633.

1528
MARYLAND LEGION AUXILIARY CHILDREN AND YOUTH FUND SCHOLARSHIP

American Legion Auxiliary
Attn: Department of Maryland
1589 Sulphur Spring Road, Suite 105
Baltimore, MD 21227
Phone: (410) 242-9519
Summary: To provide financial assistance for the postsecondary education of the daughters of veterans who are Maryland residents and wish to study arts, sciences, business, public administration, education, or a medical field.
Eligibility: Eligible for this scholarship are Maryland senior high girls with veteran parents who wish to study arts, sciences, business, public administration, education, or a medical field other than nursing at a college or university in Maryland. Preference is given to children of members of the American Legion or American Legion Auxiliary. Selection is based on character (30 percent), Americanism (20 percent), leadership (10 percent), scholarship (20 percent), and financial need (20 percent).
Financial data: The stipend is $2,000.
Duration: 1 year; may be renewed up to 3 additional years.
Number awarded: 1 each year.
Deadline: April of each year.

1529
MAS FAMILY SCHOLARSHIP PROGRAM

Cuban American National Foundation
P.O. Box 440069
Miami, FL 33144-9926
Phone: (305) 592-7768   E-mail: canfnet@icanect.net
Web Site: www.canfnet.org
Summary: To provide financial assistance to students of Cuban descent who are working on an undergraduate or graduate degree in selected subject areas.
Eligibility: This program is open to financially needy "top of the class" (top 10 percent and at least a 3.5 grade point average) Cuban American students who are directly descended from those who left Cuba or who were born in Cuba (proof will be required). "Needy" is defined by the federal formula that examines a family's financial situation in terms of how much a family can contribute to its child's education. Both undergraduate and graduate students may apply, provided they are majoring in 1 of the following subjects: engineering, business, international relations, economics, communications, or journalism. Selection is based on academic performance, leadership qualities, financial need, potential to contribute to the advancement of a free society, and the likelihood of succeeding in their chosen field. Finalists may be interviewed.
Financial data: The amount of the award depends on the cost of tuition at the recipient's selected institution, on the family's situation, and on the amount of funds received from other sources. The amount of the yearly award cannot exceed $10,000. Full scholarships are not awarded to students who will be receiving full tuition scholarships and/or stipendiary support from other sources.
Duration: 1 year; recipients may reapply and are given preference over other candidates.
Deadline: March of each year.

1530
MDDC HIGH SCHOOL JOURNALIST OF THE YEAR AWARD

Maryland-Delaware-District of Columbia Press Foundation
2191 Defense Highway, Suite 300
Crofton, MD 21114-2487
Phone: (410) 721-4000   Fax: (410) 721-4557
E-mail: mddcpress@aol.com   Web Site: www.mddcpress.com
Summary: To recognize and reward outstanding high school senior journalists in Maryland, Delaware, or the District of Columbia.
Eligibility: This program is open to high school seniors working on a Maryland, Delaware, or District of Columbia high school newspaper. Applicants must submit 5 to 10 samples of their work, a letter of recommendation from their advisor, and an autobiographical statement. They must be interested in majoring in journalism in college.
Financial data: The award is $1,500.
Duration: The award is presented annually.
Number awarded: 1 each year.
Deadline: November of each year.

1531
MEMORIAL CONSERVATION SCHOLARSHIP

New Jersey Association of Conservation Districts
c/o NJDA
P.O. Box 330, Room 204
Trenton, NJ 08625
Summary: To provide financial assistance to college students in New Jersey who are preparing for a career in a field related to the conservation and management of natural resources.
Eligibility: Eligible to apply for this support are New Jersey residents who are enrolled as full-time students at an accredited college or university in New Jersey. Applicants must have successfully completed (or will complete by the scholarship award date) at least 4 full semesters of study. They must be majoring in a field related to agriculture or natural resource conservation, including agronomy, soil science, plant science, forestry, geography, journalism, agricultural education, environmental science, wildlife or fisheries management, environmental engineering, or other areas related to conservation. Selection is based on academic commitment to a field of conservation, demonstrated scholastic ability, extracurricular activities, and financial need.
Financial data: The stipend is $1,000.
Duration: 1 year.
Number awarded: 2 each year.
Deadline: October of each year.

1532
MENNONITE WOMEN INTERNATIONAL WOMEN'S FUND

Mennonite Women
722 Main Street
P.O. Box 347
Newton, KS 67114
Phone: (316) 283-5100   Fax: (316) 283-0454
E-mail: mw@gcmc.org
Web Site: www2.southwind.net/~gcmc/mw.html
Summary: To provide financial support to train emerging Mennonite women church leaders around the world.
Eligibility: Funding is available to train women from any country for Mennonite church leadership. This training can include workshops for lay women who have very little education as well as course work for high school or college graduates. Preference is given to applicants from outside North American (who receive

approximately 75 percent of the funds each year). Applicants from Canada and the United States must demonstrate acute financial need.

Financial data: Grants normally range from $500 to $1,000. A total of approximately $6,000 is available each year.

Duration: Up to 1 year.

Additional information: Mennonite Women was formed in 1997, replacing the Women's Missionary and Service Commission of the Mennonite Church. Women from other countries who are studying in North America can use some of the funds for English lessons.

Number awarded: Varies each year.

Deadline: Applications may be submitted at any time.

1533
MESSENGER-ANDERSON JOURNALISM SCHOLARSHIP AND INTERNSHIP PROGRAM

National Gay and Lesbian Task Force
1700 Kalorama Road, N.W.
Washington, DC 20009-2624
Phone: (202) 332-6483   Fax: (202) 332-0207
Phone: TTY: (202) 332-6219   E-mail: delliot@ngltf.org
Web Site: www.ngltf.org/about/messenger.htm

Summary: To provide financial assistance and experience to members of the National Gay and Lesbian Task Force (NGLTF) interested in studying journalism in college.

Eligibility: This program is open to high school seniors and undergraduate college students who plan to pursue a bachelor's degree in journalism at an accredited 4-year college or university. Applicants must be self identified as lesbian, gay, bisexual, or transgender; have a grade point average of 2.5 or higher; and be a member of NGLTF. They must also be interested in a summer internship at NGLTF's headquarters in Washington, D.C. or its field office in New York City. Financial need is not considered in the selection process.

Financial data: The scholarship stipend is $5,000 per year for the first year and $2,500 per year for subsequent years. Intern stipends are $300 per week. Round-trip transportation and a monthly housing allowance of $300 for Washington or $500 for New York are also provided.

Duration: 1 year; may be renewed for up to 2 additional years.

Number awarded: Varies each year.

Deadline: February of each year.

1534
METROPOLITAN OPERA NATIONAL COUNCIL AUDITIONS

Metropolitan Opera
Attn: National Council Auditions
Lincoln Center
New York, NY 10023
Phone: (212) 870-4515   Fax: (212) 870-7680
E-mail: ncouncil@mail.metopera.org
Web Site: www.metopera.org/infodesk/council.html

Summary: To discover new talent for the Metropolitan Opera and to encourage young singers to prepare for their careers.

Eligibility: This competition is open to singers (women between 19 and 33 years of age, men between 20 and 33 years of age) who have a voice with operatic potential (exceptional quality, range, projection, charisma, communication, and natural beauty) as well as musical training and background. They must be able to sing correctly in more than 1 language and show artistic aptitude. Applicants should be citizens of the United States or Canada; foreign applicants must show proof of a 1-year residency. Singers must present 5 arias of their choice and of no more than 8 minutes' duration, in contrasting languages and styles. The competition begins at the district level, with winners advancing to regional auditions. The winners from the 16 regions represent their region at the national semifinals in New York and then 10 of those singers are selected as national finalists. At the National Grand Finals concert, which is held exactly 1 week later, the 10 National Grand Finalists perform 2 arias each on the stage of the Metropolitan Opera accompanied by the MET Orchestra in a nationally-broadcast concert. The national winners are selected at that concert.

Financial data: At the regional level, each first-place winner receives the $800 Mrs. Edgar Tobin Award, each second-place winner receives $600, and each third-place winner receives $400; some regions award additional prizes or encouragement awards. At the national level, each winner receives $15,000, each finalist receives $5,000, and each semifinalist receives $1,500. Educational grants up to $5,000 are available to national finalists and winners.

Duration: The competition is held annually.

Additional information: Applicants enter in the district in which they are

currently living, attending school, or have a professional singing contract. For further information on districts or regions nationwide, write or call the Metropolitan Opera. A nonrefundable fee of $20 must accompany each application.

Number awarded: The country is divided into 16 regions, in each of which 3 prizes are awarded. The 16 regional winners are national semifinalists, from whom 10 national finalists are selected. From those finalists, up to 5 national winners are chosen.

Deadline: Deadlines are chosen by local districts and regions; most of them are in early to late fall of each year. District auditions usually occur from October through February, with the winners advancing to the regional auditions, usually between October and February. The national competition in New York usually takes place in late March or early April.

1535
MICHAEL AND MARIE MARUCCI SCHOLARSHIP

Summary: To provide financial assistance to legally blind students pursuing a degree in a field that requires study abroad.
See Listing #665.

1536
MID-ATLANTIC CHAPTER SCHOLARSHIPS

Society of Satellite Professionals International
Attn: Scholarship Program
225 Reinekers Lane, Suite 600
Alexandria, VA 22314
Phone: (703) 549-8696   Fax: (703) 549-9728
E-mail: sspi@sspi.org   Web Site: www.sspi.org

Summary: To provide financial assistance to students attending college in designated mid-Atlantic states who are interested in majoring in satellite-related disciplines.

Eligibility: This program is open to high school seniors, college undergraduates, and graduate students majoring or planning to major in fields related to satellite communications, including broadcasting, business, communications, engineering, international policy studies, journalism, law, science, space applications, or telecommunications. Applicants must attend school in Delaware, the District of Columbia, Maryland, Virginia, or West Virginia. Selection is based on academic and leadership achievement, commitment to pursue education and career opportunities in the satellite communications industry, potential for significant contribution to that industry, a personal statement of 500 to 750 words on interest in satellite communications and why the applicant deserves the award, and a creative work (such as a research report, essay, article, videotape, artwork, computer program, or scale model of an antenna or spacecraft design) that reflects the applicant's interests and talents. Financial need is not considered.

Financial data: The stipend is $4,000.

Duration: 1 year.

Number awarded: 2 each year.

Deadline: June of each year.

1537
MIKE ALESKO DESIGN SCHOLARSHIP

Mike Alesko Design Scholarship Fund
c/o International News, Inc.
19226 70th Avenue South
Kent, WA 98032-2176
Phone: (253) 872-3542   Fax: (253) 872-3626
E-mail: madsf@meccausa.com
Web Site: www.madsf.org

Summary: To provide financial assistance for college to students majoring in apparel design or graphic design.

Eligibility: This program is open to high school seniors and university students majoring or planning to major in apparel design or graphic design at an accredited institution in the United States. Applicants must have at least a 2.5 grade point average and be able to demonstrate financial need.

Financial data: The stipend is $1,000.

Duration: 1 year.

Number awarded: 1 each year.

Deadline: April of each year.

1538
MIKE REYNOLDS JOURNALISM SCHOLARSHIP

Radio and Television News Directors Foundation
1000 Connecticut Avenue, N.W., Suite 615
Washington, DC 20036-5302
Phone: (202) 467-5218   Fax: (202) 223-4007
E-mail: karenb@rtndf.org
Web Site: www.rtndf.org/asfi/scholarships/undergrad.shtml
Summary: To provide financial assistance for undergraduate education to students whose career objective is radio or television news.
Eligibility: This program is open to sophomores, juniors, and seniors who are enrolled full time in electronic journalism in a college or university where such a major is offered. Applicants must submit 1 to 3 examples of reporting or producing skills on audio or video cassette tapes (no more than 15 minutes total), a description of their role on each story and a list of who worked on each story and what they did, a statement explaining why they are seeking a career in broadcast or cable journalism, and a letter of endorsement from a faculty sponsor certifying that the candidate has at least 1 year of school remaining. Preference is given to undergraduate students who demonstrate need for financial assistance by indicating media-related jobs held and contributions made to funding their own education.
Financial data: The stipend is $1,000.
Duration: 1 year.
Additional information: The Radio and Television News Directors Foundation (RTNDF) also provides an expense-paid trip to the Radio-Television News Directors Association (RTNDA) annual international conference. It defines electronic journalism to include radio, television, cable, and online news. Previous winners of any RTNDF scholarship or internship are not eligible.
Number awarded: 1 each year.
Deadline: April of each year.

1539
MISSOURI PRESS FOUNDATION'S COMMUNITY JOURNALISM SCHOLARSHIPS

Missouri Press Foundation, Inc.
802 Locust Street
Columbia, MO 65201
Phone: (573) 449-4167   Fax: (573) 874-5894
Summary: To provide financial assistance to undergraduate and graduate students in Missouri who are working on a journalism degree.
Eligibility: Upper-division students (juniors and seniors) and graduate students enrolled in newspaper journalism courses at any Missouri college or university are eligible to apply for this funding. Applicants must submit a completed application form, a 200-word essay on the role community newspapers play in Missouri," and 3 letters of recommendation. Verification of enrollment is required. Financial need is not considered in the selection process.
Financial data: The stipend is $2,000.
Duration: 1 year.
Number awarded: At least 3 each year.
Deadline: May of each year.

1540
MJSA EDUCATION FOUNDATION JEWELRY SCHOLARSHIP

Rhode Island Foundation
Attn: Scholarship Coordinator
One Union Station
Providence, RI 02903
Phone: (401) 274-4564   Fax: (401) 331-8085
E-mail: libbym@rifoundation.org   Web Site: www.rifoundation.org
Summary: To provide financial assistance to college students studying a field related to jewelry.
Eligibility: This program is open to students in colleges, universities, and postsecondary nonprofit technical schools in the United States. Applicants must be studying tool making, design, metals fabrication, or other field related to jewelry. Along with their application, they must submit an essay (up to 300 words), in which they describe their program of study, the length of the program, how far along they are towards completion, and their reason for choosing the program. Selection is based on course of study, career objectives, samples of work (if appropriate), jewelry industry experience, academic achievement, recommendations, and financial need.
Financial data: Stipends range from $500 to $2,000 per year.
Duration: 1 year; may be renewed for up to 3 additional years if the recipient maintains good academic standing.

Additional information: The MJSA Education Foundation is a nonprofit educational branch of the Manufacturing Jewelers and Suppliers of America, Inc. Its scholarship fund consists of 5 endowment funds that are managed by the Rhode Island Foundation, but a connection to Rhode Island is not required for eligibility for these scholarships.
Number awarded: Numerous scholarships are awarded each year.
Deadline: May of each year.

1541
MORRIS J. AND BETTY KAPLUN FOUNDATION ESSAY CONTEST

Morris J. and Betty Kaplun Foundation
Attn: Essay Contest Committee
P.O. Box 234428
Great Neck, NY 11023
E-mail: info@kaplun.org   Web Site: www.kaplun.org
Summary: To recognize and reward outstanding essays on topics related to being Jewish.
Eligibility: Contestants in grades 10 through 12 must write an essay of 250 to 1,500 words on a topic that changes annually but is related to being Jewish. A recent topic was "How Will Modern Technology Enhance or Hinder Jewish Survival and the Perpetuation of Its Traditions?" For students in junior high school (grades 7 through 9), the essay must be 250 to 1,000 words; a recent topic was "How a Jewish Upbringing Influences Attitudes Towards One's Family and Society."
Financial data: Prizes are $1,800, $750, and $18.
Duration: The competition is held annually.
Additional information: This contest began in 1992.
Number awarded: Each year, 1 prize of $1,800 and 5 prizes of $750 are awarded at both the high school and junior high levels; the first 50 essays submitted for each level receive $18 each.
Deadline: March of each year.

1542
MUSIC THERAPY SCHOLARSHIP

Sigma Alpha Iota Philanthropies, Inc.
34 Wall Street, Suite 515
Asheville, NC 28801-2710
Phone: (828) 251-0606   Fax: (828) 251-0644
Web Site: www.sai-national/org/phil/philschs.html
Summary: To provide financial assistance for education in music therapy to members of Sigma Alpha Iota (an organization of women musicians).
Eligibility: Members of the organization may apply for these scholarships if they wish to study music therapy at the undergraduate or graduate level. Applicants must have completed at least 2 years of approved training toward a degree in music therapy.
Financial data: The stipend is $1,000.
Duration: 1 year.
Additional information: There is a $20 nonrefundable application fee.
Number awarded: 2 every 3 years: 1 to an undergraduate and 1 to a graduate student.
Deadline: April of the year of the awards (2003, 2006, etc.).

1543
NABJ NON-SUSTAINING SCHOLARSHIP

National Association of Black Journalists
Attn: Media Institute Program Associate
8701-A Adelphi Road
Adelphi, MD 20783-1716
Phone: (301) 445-7100, ext. 108   Fax: (301) 445-7101
E-mail: warren@nabj.org
Web Site: www.nabj.org
Summary: To provide financial assistance to undergraduate or graduate student members of the National Association of Black Journalists (NABJ) who are majoring in a field related to journalism.
Eligibility: This competition is open to African American undergraduate or graduate students who are currently attending an accredited 4-year college or university. Applicants must be majoring in broadcast (radio or television), print, photography, or journalism and have a grade point average of 2.5 or higher. They must submit 6 samples of their published or broadcasted work, an official college transcript, 2 letters of recommendation, a resume, and a 500- to 800-word essay describing their accomplishments as a student journalist, their career goals, and their interest in the field.

Financial data: The stipend is $2,500.
Duration: 1 year.
Additional information: All scholarship winners must become members of the association before they enroll in college.
Number awarded: 1 or more each year.
Deadline: April of each year.

1544
NAOMI BERBER MEMORIAL SCHOLARSHIP

Print and Graphics Scholarship Foundation
Attn: Scholarship Competition
200 Deer Run Road
Sewickley PA 15143-2600
Phone: (412) 741-6860, ext. 309   (800) 910-GATF
Fax: (412) 741-2311   E-mail: pgsf@gatf.org
Web Site: www.gatf.org
Summary: To provide financial assistance to women who want to prepare for a career in the printing or publishing industry.
Eligibility: This program is open to high school senior women or women already in college. They must be interested in preparing for a career in publishing or printing while in college. This is a merit-based program; financial need is not considered.
Financial data: The stipend ranges from $500 to $1,000, depending upon the funds available each year.
Duration: 1 year; may be renewed for up to 3 additional years.
Additional information: This program is named for Naomi Berber, the first woman elected to the Graphic Arts Technical Foundation Society of Fellows. Recipients must attend school on a full-time basis.
Number awarded: 1 or more each year.
Deadline: February of each year for high school seniors; March of each year for students already in college.

1545
NATHAN TAYLOR DODSON SCHOLARSHIP

North Carolina Association of Health, Physical Education, Recreation and Dance
Attn: Executive Director
Box 974
Boiling Springs, NC 28017   Phone: (888) 840-6500
Summary: To provide financial assistance for college to members of the North Carolina Association of Health, Physical Education, Recreation and Dance (NCAAHPERD).
Eligibility: Eligible to apply for this scholarship are rising seniors majoring in health, physical education, recreation, and/or dance who are members of NCAAHPERD and have earned at least a 2.0 grade point average for all college work and a 3.0 average for their major. Applicants must demonstrate leadership and contributions to the profession. Financial need is not considered in the selection process.
Financial data: The stipend is $1,000 per year.
Duration: 1 year.
Additional information: Information is also available from Dawn Clark, 2304 Jefferson Drive, Greenville, NC 27858.
Number awarded: 1 each year.
Deadline: April of each year.

1546
NATIONAL ACADEMY OF TELEVISION ARTS AND SCIENCES SCHOLARSHIPS

National Academy of Television Arts and Sciences
Attn: Scholarship Committee
111 West 57th Street, Suite 1020
New York, NY 10019
Phone: (212) 586-8424   Fax: (212) 246-8129
E-mail: natashq@aol.com   Web Site: www.emmyonline.org
Summary: To provide financial assistance to prospective college students interested in a career in the television industry.
Eligibility: This program is open to high school seniors who plan to enter a 4-year college or university and major in a television or another communications-related field. A brief creative essay must be submitted as part of the application package. Finalists must submit a portfolio of their creative work. Selection is based on academic record, standardized test scores, creative accomplishments, field and work experience, a 1-page essay on their career aspirations, and a 2-page essay on which continuing television program, past or present, has most influenced their life and why.
Financial data: The stipend is $7,500 per year. Funds may be used for tuition,

books, living expenses, and other related educational expenses.
Duration: 4 years.
Additional information: This program was established in 1993.
Number awarded: 2 each year.
Deadline: December of each year.

1547
NATIONAL ALLIANCE FOR EXCELLENCE PERFORMING ARTS SCHOLARSHIPS

National Alliance for Excellence
63 Riverside Avenue
Red Bank, NJ 07701
Phone: (732) 747-0028   Fax: (732) 842-2962
E-mail: info@excellence.org   Web Site: www.excellence.org
Summary: To provide financial assistance for postsecondary education in the United States or abroad to students in the performing arts.
Eligibility: Applicants must be U.S. citizens attending or planning to attend a college or university in the United States or an approved foreign study program on a full-time basis. They may be high school seniors, college students, graduate students, or returning students. For these scholarships, applicants must submit a VHS videotape, up to 10 minutes in length, of their work as a dancer, actor, vocalist, or instrumentalist. Selection is based on talent and ability without regard to financial need.
Financial data: Stipends range from $1,000 to $5,000 per year.
Duration: 1 year.
Additional information: The National Alliance for Excellence was formerly the Scholarship Foundation of America. A $5 processing fee is charged.
Deadline: Applications may be submitted at any time. Awards are given out on a continuous basis.

1548
NATIONAL ASSOCIATION OF PASTORAL MUSICIANS SCHOLARSHIPS

National Association of Pastoral Musicians
Attn: NPM Scholarships
225 Sheridan Street, N.W.
Washington, DC 20011-1492
Phone: (202) 723-5800   Fax: (202) 723-2262
E-mail: npmsing@npm.org
Web Site: www.npm.org
Summary: To provide financial assistance to undergraduate or graduate student members of the National Association of Pastoral Musicians.
Eligibility: This program is open to members of the association who are enrolled part or full time in an undergraduate, graduate, or continuing education program. They must be studying in a field related to pastoral music, be able demonstrate financial need, and be intending to work for at least 2 years in the field of pastoral music following graduation. Applicants must submit a 5-minute performance cassette tape of themselves or the choir-ensemble they direct.
Financial data: Stipends range from $1,000 to $5,000. Funds must be used to pay for registration, fees, or books.
Duration: 1 year; recipients may reapply.
Additional information: This program includes the following named scholarships: the NPM Members' Scholarship ($5,000), the NPM Koinonia/Board of Directors Scholarship ($2,000), the MuSonics Corporation Scholarship ($2,000), the Paluch Foundation/WLP Scholarship ($2,000), the OCP Scholarship ($1,500), the GIA Pastoral Musician Scholarship $1,500), the Dosogne/Rendler-Georgetown Memorial Scholarship ($1,000), and the Funk Family Memorial Scholarship ($1,000).
Number awarded: 8 each year.
Deadline: February of each year.

1549
NATIONAL COUNCIL OF STATE GARDEN CLUBS SCHOLARSHIPS

National Council of State Garden Clubs, Inc.
4401 Magnolia Avenue
St. Louis, MO 63110-3492
Phone: (314) 776-7574   Fax: (314) 776-5108
Web Site: www.gardenclub.org
Summary: To provide financial assistance to upper-division and graduate students in horticulture and related disciplines.

Eligibility: This program is open to upper-division and graduate students who are studying horticulture, floriculture, landscape design, city planning, botany, biology, plant pathology, forestry, agronomy, environmental science, land management, and allied subjects. Applicants must have at least a 3.0 grade point average and be able to demonstrate financial need. All applications must be submitted to the state garden club affiliate and are judged there first; then 1 from each state is submitted for national competition. Final selection is based on academic record (40 percent), applicant's letter (25 percent), listing of honors, extracurricular activities, and work experience (10 percent), financial need (20 percent), and recommendations (5 percent).

Financial data: The stipend is $3,500.

Duration: 1 year.

Additional information: For the name and address of your state contact, write to the National Council. Information is also available from the Scholarship Chair, Barbara D. May, 171 South Street, Needham, MA 02492-2706, (781) 929-6504, E-mail: barbmay@concentric.net.

Number awarded: 33 each year.

Deadline: Applications must be submitted to the appropriate state organization by February of each year.

1550
NATIONAL FFA SCHOLARSHIPS FOR UNDERGRADUATES IN THE HUMANITIES

National FFA Organization
Attn: Scholarship Office
6060 FFA Drive
P.O. Box 68960
Indianapolis, IN 46268-0960
Phone: (317) 802-4321   Fax: (317) 802-5321
E-mail: aboutffa@ffa.org
Web Site: www.ffa.org

Summary: To provide financial assistance to FFA members who wish to study agricultural journalism and related fields in college.

Eligibility: This program is open to current and former members of the organization who are pursuing a degree in fields related to agricultural journalism and communications, floriculture, and landscape design. For some of the scholarships, applicants must be high school seniors; others are open to students currently enrolled in college. The program includes a large number of designated scholarships that specify the locations where the members must live, the schools they must attend, the fields of study they must pursue, or other requirements. Some consider family income in the selection process, but most do not.

Financial data: Stipends vary, but most are at least $1,000.

Duration: 1 year or more.

Additional information: Funding for these scholarships is provided by many different corporate sponsors.

Number awarded: Varies; generally, a total of approximately 1,000 scholarships are awarded annually by the association.

Deadline: February of each year.

1551
NATIONAL GEOGRAPHIC SOCIETY AWARD IN CARTOGRAPHY

National Geographic Society
Attn: National Geographic Maps
1145 17th Street, N.W.
Washington, DC 20036-4688
Phone: (202) 857-7000   Fax: (202) 429-5729
E-mail: dmiller@ngs.org   Web Site: www.nationalgeographic.com

Summary: To provide financial assistance to undergraduate and master's degree students who demonstrate excellence in the art, science, and technology of mapping.

Eligibility: This program is open to undergraduate students and master's candidates in cartography. Applicants must submit a statement of how the award would help them with their educational plans, an example and a brief description of a recent map or mapping project that they have completed, and copies of transcripts.

Financial data: The award consists of $1,200, a *National Geographic Atlas of the World*, and a certificate.

Duration: 1 year.

Number awarded: 2 each year: 1 to an undergraduate and 1 to a graduate student.

Deadline: January of each year.

1552
NATIONAL GREEK EXAMINATION SCHOLARSHIP

American Classical League
Attn: National Greek Examination
Miami University
Oxford, OH 45056
Phone: (513) 529-7741   Fax: (513) 529-7742
E-mail: info@aclclassics.org   Web Site: www.vroma.org/~nle/grkex.html

Summary: To recognize and reward students who achieve high scores on the National Greek Examination.

Eligibility: High school teachers and college instructors may order copies of the National Greek Examination for their students who are enrolled in first year (elementary), second year (intermediate), or third year (advanced) Attic or Homeric Greek. The examinations consist of 40 multiple choice questions at 5 levels: beginning Attic (high school seniors only), intermediate Attic (first-year college and advanced high school students), Attic prose, Attic poetry, and Homeric (*Odyssey*). The top scorers on each examination receive purple ribbons, followed by blue, red, and green ribbons. High school seniors who earn purple or blue ribbons are eligible to apply for this scholarship.

Financial data: The stipend is $1,000.

Duration: 1 year.

Additional information: This program is jointly sponsored by the American Classical League (ACL) and the National Junior Classical League (NJCL). Information is also available from Dr. Deb Davies, 123 Argilla Road, Andover, MA 01810, (978) 749-9446, E-mail: ddavies@brooksschool.org. The school the student attends must obtain the examinations and administer them to all students within the same class period during the second full week of March. The cost is $3 per student. Scholarship recipients must agree to earn 6 credits of Latin or classical Greek during the academic year.

Number awarded: 1 each year.

Deadline: The examinations must be ordered by January of each year.

1553
NATIONAL ITALIAN AMERICAN FOUNDATION GENERAL CATEGORY II SCHOLARSHIPS

National Italian American Foundation
Attn: Education Director
1860 19th Street, N.W.
Washington, DC 20009
Phone: (202) 387-0600   Fax: (202) 387-0800
E-mail: scholarships@niaf.org   Web Site: www.niaf.org/scholarships

Summary: To provide financial assistance for college to students interested in majoring in Italian language, Italian studies, or Italian American studies.

Eligibility: This program is open to students of any nationality who are currently enrolled or entering an accredited college or university in the United States with a grade point average of 3.25 or higher. Applicants must be majoring or planning to major in Italian language, Italian studies, Italian American studies, or a related field. Selection is based on academic performance, field of study, career objectives, and the potential, commitment, and abilities applicants have demonstrated that would enable them to make significant contributions to their chosen field of study. Some scholarships also require financial need.

Financial data: Stipends range from $2,000 to $5,000.

Duration: 1 year. Recipients are encouraged to reapply.

Additional information: Applications can only be submitted online. At the completion of the scholarship year, recipients must submit a 500-word narrative describing the benefits of the scholarship.

Number awarded: Varies each year.

Deadline: April of each year.

1554
NATIONAL LATIN EXAMINATION SCHOLARSHIPS

American Classical League
P.O. Box 95
Mount Vernon, VA 22121
Phone: (800) 459-9847   (888) 378-7721
Web Site: www.vroma.org/~nle

Summary: To recognize and reward students who achieve high scores on the National Latin Examination.

Eligibility: Any high school student who is enrolled or has completed a Latin course during the current academic year may take the National Latin Examination. The examinations consist of 40 multiple choice questions on comprehension,

grammar, historical background, classical literature, and literary devices. Different examinations are given for Introduction to Latin, Latin I, Latin II, Latin III-IV Prose, Latin III-IV Poetry, and Latin V-VI. The top scorers in each category receive gold medals; gold medal winners in Latin III-IV Prose, Latin III-IV Poetry, and Latin V-VI who are high school seniors are mailed applications for these scholarships.

Financial data: The stipend is $1,000.

Duration: 1 year; may be renewed.

Additional information: This program is jointly sponsored by the American Classical League (ACL) and the National Junior Classical League (NJCL). The school the student attends must obtain the examinations and administer them to all students within the same class period during the second full week of March. The cost is $3 per student. Scholarship recipients must agree to take at least 1 year of Latin or classical Greek in college.

Number awarded: Approximately 20 each year.

Deadline: The examinations must be ordered by January of each year.

1555
NATIONAL MAKE IT YOURSELF WITH WOOL CONTEST

American Sheep Industry Women
c/o Marie Lehfeldt
P.O. Box 175
Lavina, MT 59046
Phone: (406) 636-2036   E-mail: levi@midrivers.com

Summary: To encourage the use of wool by offering scholarship awards to students who sew, knit, or crochet fashionable wool garments.

Eligibility: The junior division is open to all persons between of 13 and 16 years of age, and the senior division is for 17 through 24 years of age; most states also have a pre-teen division for competitors 12 years of age and younger and an adult division for persons over 24 years of age. Competitors enter machine or hand-knitted, woven, or crocheted garments, or garments containing any part which has been knitted or crocheted; all entries must be made from loomed, knitted, or felted fabric or yarn of a minimum of 60 percent wool and no more than 40 percent synthetic fiber. All entrants must select, construct, and model the garment themselves. The garments in the junior, senior, and adult divisions may be 2-piece outfits (coat, jacket, blouse/shirt, vest or sweater with dress, skirt, pants, or shorts), ensembles (3 or more garments worn together at a time), or 1-piece garments (dresses, outerwear jackets, coats, capes, or jumpers). Preteens may enter a dress, jumper, skirt, pants, shorts, vest, sweater, blouse/shirt, or jacket. Selection is based on appropriateness of the garment to the contestant's lifestyle, coordination of fabric/yarn with garment style and design, contestant's presentation, and construction quality. Contestants must participate in the state where they live or attend school. State winners in the junior and senior divisions advance to the national competition. Scholarships are awarded to national junior and senior division winners. Selection is based on creativity, construction quality, contestant's presentation, coordination of fabric/yarn with garment style and design, and appropriateness to contestant's lifestyle.

Financial data: Scholarships awarded at the national level are $2,000 or $1,000, to be used for tuition, books, and fees; funds are paid directly to registrars of approved accredited colleges.

Duration: The competition is held annually.

Additional information: The $1,000 scholarships at the national level are sponsored by the Mohair Council of America, Lama Association of North America, and Pendleton Woolen Mills. The entry fee is $10 in the junior, senior, and adult divisions or $5 in the preteen division.

Number awarded: 4 national scholarships are awarded each year: 1 at $2,000 and 3 at $1,000.

Deadline: October of each year.

1556
NATIONAL SCULPTURE COMPETITION PRIZES

National Sculpture Competition
c/o Pennsylvania Academy of the Fine Arts
118 North Broad Street
Philadelphia, PA 19102
Phone: (215) 972-7625   Fax: (215) 569-0153
E-mail: pafa@pafa.org   Web Site: www.pafa.org

Summary: To recognize and reward outstanding creative work by students and other young sculptors.

Eligibility: Applicants must be emerging sculptors, at least 18 years of age. They may submit slides of at least 5 and no more than 10 pieces of sculpture. Based on the slides, up to 18 competitors are invited to Philadelphia where they have 28 hours

over a 5-day period to complete a full-length figure from life, with a 30"-36" armature. The finished sculptures are then judged on mastery of the figure in sculptural form as well as each competitor's comprehension of the action, unity, and rhythm of the pose; emphasis is placed on encouraging the analytic observation of the human figure, including proportion, stance, solidity, and continuity of line.

Financial data: The first-place winner receives the Walter and Michael Lantz Prize of $1,000; the second-place winner receives the Walker Hancock Prize of $500; and the third-place winner receives the Elizabeth Gordon Chandler Prize of $300. Special awards for young sculptors include the Dexter Jones Award of $1,000 for the best work in bas-relief by a sculptor younger than 40 years of age, the Roger T. Williams Prize of $750 for excellence in representational sculpture, and the Edward Fenno Hoffman Prize of $350 for sculpture that uplifts the human spirit.

Duration: The competition is held annually.

Additional information: This competition is co-sponsored by the Lyme Academy of Fine Arts, the National Sculpture Society, and the Pennsylvania Academy of the Fine Arts (where the competition is held). Expenses of applicants include a $25 entry fee, a lab fee of $50 for the candidates accepted into the figure modeling competition, travel to Philadelphia, and living expenses during the 5-day competition. Clay, modeling stands, and materials to build armatures are supplied, but competitors must supply personal sculpture tools, large plastic bags, wrapping cloth, and spray bottle. Travel assistance up to $1,000 is available to competitors who demonstrate merit and need.

Number awarded: 3 main prizes and 3 special prizes are awarded each year.

Deadline: April of each year.

1557
NATIONAL SCULPTURE SOCIETY SCHOLARSHIPS

National Sculpture Society
Attn: Scholarships
237 Park Avenue, Ground Floor
New York, NY 10017
Phone: (212) 764-5645   Fax: (212) 764-5651
E-mail: nss1893@aol.com
Web Site: www.nationalsculpture.org/scholarships.asp

Summary: To provide financial assistance for college to students of sculpture.

Eligibility: Students of figurative or representational sculpture may apply for these scholarships. Applications must include a brief biography, an explanation of the student's background in sculpture, 2 letters of recommendation, 8 to 10 photographs of work by the applicant, and proof of financial need.

Financial data: Awards of $1,000 each are paid directly to the academic institution through which the student applies, to be credited towards tuition.

Duration: 1 year.

Additional information: This program includes the Roger T. Williams Scholarship.

Number awarded: At least 3 each year.

Deadline: April of each year.

1558
NATIONAL SOLO COMPETITION-JUNIOR DIVISION

American String Teachers Association
National Office
1806 Robert Fulton Drive, Suite 300
Reston, VA 20191
Phone: (703) 476-1316   Fax: (703) 476-1317
E-mail: asta@erols.com   Web Site: www.astaweb.com

Summary: To reward outstanding performers on stringed instruments.

Eligibility: Eligible to compete are musicians under the age of 19. Competitions are held for violin, viola, cello, bass, guitar, and harp. Candidates first enter competitions in their state of residency. The state chairs then submit tapes of the winners in their state to the national chair. Musicians who live in states that do not have a state competition may submit tapes directly to the national chair. The repertoire must consist of a required work and a work of the competitor's choice; tapes of performances should run from 12 to 15 minutes. Based on those tapes, finalists are invited to the national competition.

Financial data: For each instrument, a first prize of $1,200 and a second prize of $500 are awarded. The 6 first-place winners compete for the grand prize of $2,500.

Duration: The competition is held biennially, in even-numbered years.

Additional information: Further information is also available from Jeffrey Solow, Chair, Temple University, Esther Boyer College of Music, Philadelphia, PA 19122, (215) 204-8025, Fax: (215) 204-5528, E-mail: solowcello@aol.com.

Number awarded: 6 first prizes, 6 second prizes, and 1 grand prize are awarded.

Deadline: Each state sets the date of its competition, but all state competitions must be completed by the end of December of odd-numbered years so the winning tapes reach the national chair by mid-January of the following even-numbered year. The national competition is in May.

1559
NATIONAL SOLO COMPETITION-SENIOR DIVISION

American String Teachers Association
National Office
1806 Robert Fulton Drive, Suite 300
Reston, VA 20191
Phone: (703) 476-1313   Fax: (703) 476-1317
E-mail: asta@erols.com   Web Site: www.astaweb.com
Summary: To reward outstanding performers on stringed instruments.
Eligibility: Eligible to compete are students between 19 and 25 years of age who have graduated from high school. Competitions are held for violin, viola, cello, bass, guitar, and harp. Candidates first enter their state competitions; they may enter either in their state of residency or the state in which they are studying. The state chairs then submit tapes of the winners in their state to the national chair. Musicians who live in states that do not have a state competition may submit tapes directly to the national chair. The repertoire must consist of a required work and a work of the competitor's choice; tapes of performances should run from 17 to 20 minutes. Based on those tapes, finalists are invited to the national competition.
Financial data: For each instrument, a first prize of $1,400 and a second prize of $600 are awarded. The 6 first-place winners compete for the grand prize of $4,500.
Duration: The competition is held biennially, in even-numbered years.
Additional information: Further information is also available from Jeffrey Solow, Chair, Temple University, Esther Boyer College of Music, Philadelphia, PA 19122, (215) 204-8025, Fax: (215) 204-5528, E-mail: solowcello@aol.com.
Number awarded: 6 first prizes, 6 second prizes, and 1 grand prize are awarded.
Deadline: Each state sets the date of its competition, but all state competitions must be completed by the end of December of odd-numbered years so the winning tapes reach the national chair by mid-January of the following even-numbered year. The national competition is in May.

1560
NATIONAL SPEAKERS ASSOCIATION SCHOLARSHIPS

National Speakers Association
Attn: Scholarship Coordinator
1500 South Priest Drive
Tempe, AZ 85281
Phone: (480) 968-2552   Fax: (480) 968-0911
E-mail: information.nsaspeaker.org
Web Site: www.nsaspeaker.org
Summary: To provide financial assistance to students interested in focusing on speech communication in college.
Eligibility: This program is open to college juniors, seniors, and graduate students majoring or minoring in speech communications. Preference is given to applicants who have the potential of making an impact using skills in oral communication. Selection is based on a 500-word essay on the applicants' career objectives and how they will use their skill in oral communication; a letter of recommendation from a speech teacher or the speech department head or dean; a list of awards, honors, extracurricular activities, and outside work interests; and an official transcript.
Financial data: The stipend is $4,000 per year.
Duration: 1 year.
Additional information: This program was established in 1989. It includes the following named scholarships: the Earl Nightingale Scholarship, the Cavett Robert Scholarship, the Bill Gove Scholarship, and the Nido Qubein Scholarship.
Number awarded: 4 each year.
Deadline: May of each year.

1561
NATIONAL STUDENT PLAYWRITING AWARD

John F. Kennedy Center for the Performing Arts
Education Department
Attn: Kennedy Center American College Theater Festival
2700 F Street, N.W.
Washington, DC 20566
Phone: (202) 416-8857   Fax: (202) 416-8802
E-mail: skshaffer@kennedy-center.org
Web Site: kennedy-center.org/education/actf/actfnsp.html

Summary: To recognize and reward outstanding undergraduate and graduate school playwrights.
Eligibility: Students at any accredited junior or senior college in the United States or in countries contiguous to the continental United States are eligible to compete, provided their college agrees to participate in the Kennedy Center American College Theater Festival (KCACTF). Undergraduate students must be carrying a minimum of 6 semester hours, graduate students must be carrying a minimum of 3 semester hours, and continuing part-time students must be enrolled in a regular degree or certificate program. For the Michael Kanin Playwriting Awards Program, students must submit either 1 major work or 2 or more shorter works based on a single theme or encompassed within a unifying framework; all entries must provide a full evening of theater. The work must be written while the student was enrolled, and the production must be presented during that period or within 2 years after enrollment ends. The play selected as the best by the judges is presented at the national festival and its playwright receives this award.
Financial data: The winning playwright receives 1) production of the play at the Kennedy Center as part of the KCATF national festival, with expenses paid for the production and the playwright; 2) the William Morris Agency Award of $2,500; 3) the Dramatists Guild Award of active membership in the Guild; 4) the Samuel French Award of publication of the play by Samuel French, Inc.; and 5) an all-expenses paid fellowship to participate in the Sundance Theater Laboratory in Sundance, Utah. The Association for Theatre in Higher Education (ATHE) presents a cash award of up to $1,000 to the theater department of the school producing the national wining script and $100 to the schools producing the winning plays at each of the 8 KCATF regional festivals.
Duration: The competition is held annually.
Additional information: This award was first presented in 1974. The sponsoring college or university must pay a registration fee of $250 for each production.
Number awarded: 1 each year.
Deadline: The final draft of the script must be submitted by November of each year.

1562
NATIONAL TRUMPET COMPETITION AWARDS

National Trumpet Competition
c/o Dr. Dennis Edelbrock
3500 North Third Street
Arlington, VA 22201
E-mail: edlbrk@aol.com
Web Site: www.nationaltrumpetcomp.org
Summary: To recognize and reward outstanding student trumpet players.
Eligibility: Eligible to compete are trumpet players who are intermediate school students between 11 and 13 years of age (grades 6 through 8), high school students between 14 and 18 years of age (grade 9 through 12), full-time undergraduate students up to 23 years of age, and master's degree students up to 28 years of age. Entrants compete in the following divisions: the Stu's Music Shop, Inc. Young Artists Trumpet Ensemble Division, for intermediate school students from 11 to 13 years of age and high school students from 14-18 years of age; the Noteworthy Tours Intermediate School Division, for students from 11 to 13 years of age; the Stephen and Bonnie Simon High School Division, for students from 14 to 18 years of age; the Southern Ohio Music Company Trumpet Ensemble Division, for students from 18 to 28 years of age; the Warburton Music Products College Jazz Division, for students from 18 to 28 years of age; the United Musical Instruments College Division, for undergraduate students younger than 23 years of age; and the Blackburn Trumpets Masters Division, for students from 24 to 28 years of age. For the solo divisions, intermediate and high school students should prepare an audio recording, up to 8 minutes, of literature from the standard repertoire; college and master's division students must select the works for their tapes from a list prepared by the sponsor. In the trumpet ensemble divisions (at least 4 players), intermediate and high school students submit a recording, up to 10 minutes of 2 contrasting pieces of their own choice. College ensembles play a chosen work plus a required work from a list. Based on those tapes, semifinalists are selected and invited to the competitions at George Mason University in March.
Financial data: In the Stu's Music Shop, Inc. Young Artists Trumpet Ensemble Division, first prizes at both the intermediate and high school levels are the Elbert Edelbrock Memorial Young Artist Awards of $250 and second prize at both levels are the DiMartino Young Artists Awards of $100. In the Noteworth Tours Intermediate School Division, first prize is a Bach Bb or C trumpet and second prize is the DiMartino Young Artists Award of $250. In the Stephen and Bonnie Simon High School Division, first prize is a full tuition scholarship to the Interlochen Arts Camp (worth $4,490), second prize is a Bach Bb or C trumpet, and third prize is the NTC Young Artists Endowment Award of $250. In the Southern Ohio Music Company

Trumpet Ensemble Division, first prize is the Southern Ohio Music Company Award for Artistry of $1,000, second prize is the Shulman System Award for Excellence of $750, and third prize is the Dr. Richard Cox Award of $500. In the Warburton Music Products College Jazz Division, first prize is an Edwards Bb or C trumpet, second prize is the NTC Young Artists Endowment Award of $750, and third prize is the Frank Scimonelli Award of $500. In the United Musical Instruments College Division, first prize is the Dillon Music Inc. Award for Artistic Excellence of $1,000, second prize is the Hazen Award for Artistry of $750, third prize is the Robinson Professors Award of $500, and fourth prize is the Tom Gause Memorial Award of $100. In the Blackburn Trumpets Masters Division, first prize is the Southern Ohio Music Company Award for Artistry of $1,000, second prize is the Dr. Joe Utley Artist Award of $750, and third prize is the Dillon Music Inc. Award for Artistry of $500.

Duration: The competition is held annually.

Additional information: This competition began in 1992, at George Mason University. It is the largest competitive event for young trumpet players in the world. Sponsors include Stu's Music Shop of Westminster, Maryland, Noteworthy Tours, Inc. of Sandusky, Ohio, Southern Ohio Music Company of Cincinnati, Ohio, Warburton Music Products of Geneva, Florida, United Musical Instruments U.S.A., Inc. of Elkhart, Indiana, and Blackburn Trumpets, Inc. of Decatur, Indiana. Entrants who need an NTC accompanist must pay a $60 fee. Application fees are $55 for the intermediate school division, $60 for the high school division, $65 for the college and master's divisions, and $35 per player in the trumpet ensemble divisions.

Number awarded: A total of $25,000 in cash awards and prizes are presented each year.

Deadline: January of each year.

1563
NATIVE SONS OF THE GOLDEN WEST HIGH SCHOOL PUBLIC SPEAKING CONTEST

Native Sons of the Golden West
Attn: Grand Parlor
414 Mason Street, Suite 300
San Francisco, CA 94102-1714
Phone: (415) 392-1223   (800) 337-1875

Summary: To recognize and reward outstanding high school orators in California.

Eligibility: Contestants must be high school students in California who prepare an original speech, 7 to 9 minutes in length, on any subject related to past or present history, geography, or cultural development of California. Current or recent sociological, political, or economic issues of a sensitive nature may not be used as contest subjects. Negative or overly dramatic theatrics to dramatize a speech are not permitted and will subject the student to disqualification at the initial level. Judges rate speakers on the basis of organization of speech (30 points), content (20 points), and style and delivery (50 points). Competitions are held in districts, with winners there advancing to the appropriate area contest; the 5 area winners then compete in the state contest.

Financial data: At the state level, the first-prize winner receives $2,000 and the runners-up each receive $600.

Number awarded: 5 prizes are awarded each year: 1 first prize and 4 runners-up.

Deadline: District contests are held in March of each year, area competitions in April, and the state finals in May.

1564
NCCA SCHOLARSHIPS

Nation's Capital Chef's Association
Attn: Scholarship Fund Committee
2020 Pennsylvania Avenue, N.W. Suite 790
Washington, DC 20006
Phone: (202) 244-9530   E-mail: nccainfo@nccachefs.org
Web Site: www.nccachefs.org/scholarships.html

Summary: To provide financial assistance to residents of the Washington (D.C.) Metropolitan area who are studying culinary arts.

Eligibility: This program is open to residents of the Washington metropolitan area who have completed at least 1 semester of an accredited postsecondary culinary arts or culinary training program. Applicants must demonstrate a desire to continue studies in the field of food service and/or hospitality with an emphasis in cookery, baking, or food and beverage. They must have a cumulative grade point average of 3.0 or higher. Selection is based on financial need, cumulative grade point average, completion of a Nation's Capital Chef's Association (NCCA) apprenticeship, a statement describing why the applicant needs and should receive this scholarship, letters of recommendation, work in the food service industry, and overall professionalism of the application.

Financial data: The amount of the award depends on the availability of funds and the need of the recipient. Scholarship checks are made payable jointly to the recipient and the educational institution and may be applied toward any school-based fees, tuition, or other expenses.

Duration: 1 year.

Additional information: The NCCA is the Washington affiliate of the American Culinary Federation (ACF).

Number awarded: 1 or more each year.

Deadline: Applications may be submitted at any time but they are reviewed by the scholarship committee in the middle of February, June, and October of each year.

1565
NEBRASKA PRESS ASSOCIATION FOUNDATION SCHOLARSHIPS

Nebraska Press Association Foundation
845 S Street
Lincoln, NE 68508
Phone: (402) 476-2851   (800) 369-2850
Fax: (402) 476-2942   E-mail: nebpress@nebpress.com
Web Site: www.nebpress.com

Summary: To provide financial assistance to high school seniors in Nebraska who are interested in preparing for a career in print journalism.

Eligibility: This program is open to high school seniors in Nebraska who are interested in attending a college or university in the state and majoring in print journalism. Preference is given to students with specific interests in news, editorial, photography, circulation, production, or advertising. To apply, students must complete an application; they are encouraged to send 2 letters of reference. Selection is based on academic record, financial need, and good citizenship in school and the community.

Financial data: The stipend is $1,000.

Duration: 1 year.

Deadline: February of each year.

1566
NELL GOFF MEMORIAL SCHOLARSHIP

Nell Goff Memorial Scholarship Fund
c/o Janet Meryweather, Scholarship Chair
P.O. Box 56
Salisbury Cove, ME 04672-0056
Phone: (207) 288-3709

Summary: To provide financial assistance to upper-division and graduate students from Maine who are majoring in a garden-related field.

Eligibility: This program is open to residents of Maine who are college juniors, seniors, or graduate students. Applicants must be majoring in horticulture, floriculture, landscape design, conservation, forestry, botany, agronomy, plant pathology, environmental control, city planning, or other garden-related field. Selection is based on aptitude in the field of horticulture, financial need, academic record, vocational interest, potential, and character. Preference is given to residents of Hancock and southern Washington counties.

Financial data: The stipend is $1,000 per year.

Duration: 1 year; may be renewed.

Additional information: Information is also available from Shari Roobenian, Scholarship Co-chair, P.O. Box 29, Salisbury Cove, ME 04672-0029, (207) 288-4580.

Number awarded: 1 or more each year.

Deadline: February of each year.

1567
NEW HAMPSHIRE ASSOCIATION OF BROADCASTERS SCHOLARSHIPS

New Hampshire Association of Broadcasters
10 Chestnut Drive
Bedford, NH 03110
Phone: (603) 472-9800   Fax: (603) 472-9803
E-mail: info@nhab.org
Web Site: www.nhab.org

Summary: To provide financial assistance to New Hampshire residents interested in preparing for a career in broadcasting.

Eligibility: Eligible to apply for this program are residents of New Hampshire

who are working on or planning to work on an undergraduate or graduate degree in broadcasting or communications.

Financial data: The stipend is $1,500.

Duration: 1 year.

Additional information: Applications are also available from the New Hampshire Charitable Foundation, 37 Pleasant Street, Concord, NH 03301-4005, (603) 225-6641, Fax: (603) 225-1700, E-mail: info@nhcf.org.

Number awarded: 3 each year.

1568
NEW JERSEY PRESS FOUNDATION INTERNSHIP/SCHOLARSHIP PROGRAM FOR COLLEGE STUDENTS

New Jersey Press Foundation
Attn: Scholarship Awards Committee
840 Bear Tavern Road, Suite 305
West Trenton, NJ 08628-1019
Phone: (609) 406-0600   E-mail:foundation@njpa.org
Web Site: www.njpa.org/foundation/index.html

Summary: To provide financial assistance and internship opportunities to journalism majors in New Jersey.

Eligibility: This program is open to college students whose permanent home addresses are in New Jersey. They must be majoring in journalism in college and interested in participating in a summer internship at a daily, weekly, or other newspaper in New Jersey. Students who have worked as full-time or permanent part-time employees for a professional newspaper are ineligible. To apply, students must submit a completed application, an autobiographical essay, an official transcript, 2 letters of recommendations, and 3 work samples or clippings. Financial need is considered in the selection process.

Financial data: This program provides a $3,000 stipend and a paid internship (at least $300 per week) to each recipient, for a total award of $6,000 per year. Approximately one half of the internship salary is subsidized by the New Jersey Press Foundation. Funds are paid directly to the recipient's school.

Duration: The scholarship covers 1 academic year; the internship lasts 10 weeks during the summer.

Additional information: Recipients may attend college in any state.

Number awarded: 6 each year.

Deadline: November of each year.

1569
NEW YORK PRESS ASSOCIATION SCHOLARSHIPS

New York Press Association
Attn: Educational Coordinator
1681 Western Avenue
Albany, NY 12203-4305
Phone: (518) 464-6483   Fax: (518) 464-6489
E-mail: kminor@nynewspapers.com   Web Site: www.nynewspapers.com

Summary: To provide financial assistance for undergraduate education to journalism students in New York.

Eligibility: This program is open to students who have been residents of New York state for at least 1 year and are enrolled or will be enrolled in a New York state school with a recognized program of undergraduate study in print journalism. Applicants must submit 3 faculty and/or work recommendations, 3 clips of published work, and a 200- to 300-word essay on the importance of print journalism in today's world. Selection is based on the essay, prior involvement and commitment to journalism, writing samples, academic record and achievement, recommendations, and completeness of the application.

Financial data: The stipend is $5,000.

Duration: 1 year.

Number awarded: 1 each year.

Deadline: January of each year.

1570
NEWHOUSE FOUNDATION SUSTAINING SCHOLARSHIP

National Association of Black Journalists
Attn: Media Institute Program Associate
8701-A Adelphi Road
Adelphi, MD 20783-1716
Phone: (301) 445-7100, ext. 108   Fax: (301) 445-7101
E-mail: warren@nabj.org
Web Site: www.nabj.org

Summary: To provide financial assistance and work experience to African American high school seniors planning to attend college and major in print journalism.

Eligibility: This program is open to African American high school seniors who plan to enroll in an accredited 4-year college or university and major in print journalism. Applicants must submit a resume, 6 samples of their published work, an official transcript, 2 letters of recommendation, and a 500- to 800-word essay describing their accomplishments as a student journalist, career goals, and interest in the field.

Financial data: The stipend is $5,000 per year.

Duration: 1 year; may be renewed for up to 3 additional years if the recipient maintains at least a 3.0 grade point average, majors in print journalism, works with the campus newspaper, works for 10 weeks as a paid intern (minimum salary of $325 per week) for 3 summers at a Newhouse Newspaper.

Additional information: All scholarship winners must become members of the association before they enroll in college.

Number awarded: 1 or more each year.

Deadline: April of each year.

1571
THE NEWSEUM COURAGE IN STUDENT JOURNALISM AWARDS

The Newseum
Attn: Education Director
1101 Wilson Boulevard
Arlington, VA 22209
Phone: (703) 284-3716   Fax: (703) 522-4831
E-mail: lhall@freedomforum.org   Web Site: www.freedomforum.org

Summary: To recognize and reward secondary school student journalists and school officials who have supported the First Amendment.

Eligibility: This program is open to deserving high school student journalists and school officials who have stood up in support of the First Amendment. Student applicants must have shown determination, despite difficulty and resistance, in exercising their First Amendment press rights. School administrator applicants must have demonstrated support, under difficult circumstances, for the First Amendment press rights of their school's student media. Entrants should submit a written description (up to 600 words) of how their case meets the entry criteria, along with 2 letters of support and supporting materials or press clippings.

Financial data: The winners in each category (student and administrator) receive a $5,000 award.

Duration: The award is presented annually.

Additional information: This program started in 1998.

Number awarded: 2 each year: 1 student and 1 school official.

Deadline: June of each year.

1572
NEWSPRINT SOUTH, INC. SCHOLARSHIPS

Mississippi Press Association Education Foundation
Attn: Scholarship Coordinator
351 Edgewood Terrace
Jackson, MS 39206
Phone: (601) 981-3060   Fax: (601) 981-3676
E-mail: foundation@mspress.org
Web Site: www.mspress.org/edufound

Summary: To provide financial assistance to high school seniors and currently-enrolled undergraduates in Mississippi who are preparing for a career in journalism.

Eligibility: Eligible to apply are incoming freshmen and currently-enrolled college students in Mississippi who are majoring in print journalism. Applicants must have at least a 3.0 grade point average. To apply, students must submit a completed application, an official transcript, a resume, 4 published writing samples or clips, and a letter of recommendation from a school faculty member. Financial need is not considered in the selection process.

Financial data: The stipend is $1,000, payable in 2 equal installments.

Duration: 1 year; may be renewed for up to 3 additional years provided the recipient maintains at least a 3.0 grade point average and participates in summer internships.

Number awarded: 2 each year.

1573
NFB HUMANITIES SCHOLARSHIP

National Federation of the Blind
c/o Peggy Elliott
Chair, Scholarship Committee
805 Fifth Avenue
Grinnell, IA 50112
Phone: (641) 236-3366
Web Site: www.nfb.org
Summary: To provide financial assistance to legally blind students pursuing a degree in the humanities.
Eligibility: This program is open to legally blind students who are pursuing or planning to pursue a full-time undergraduate or graduate course of study. Applicants must be studying the traditional humanities, such as art, English, foreign languages, history, philosophy, or religion. Selection is based on academic excellence, service to the community, and financial need.
Financial data: The stipend is $3,000.
Duration: 1 year; recipients may resubmit applications up to 2 additional years.
Additional information: Scholarships are awarded at the federation convention in July. Recipients attend the convention at federation expense; that funding is in addition to the scholarship grant.
Number awarded: 1 each year.
Deadline: March of each year.

1574
NFMC BIENNIAL STUDENT AUDITION AWARDS

National Federation of Music Clubs
1336 North Delaware Street
Indianapolis, IN 46202-2481
Phone: (317) 638-4003   Fax: (317) 638-0503
E-mail: info@nfmc-music.org
Web Site: www.nfmc-music.org/BienStudentAuditns.htm
Summary: To recognize and reward outstanding young musicians who are members of the National Federation of Music Clubs (NFMC).
Eligibility: Instrumentalists must be between 16 and 26 years of age; vocalists must be between 18 and 26. All applicants must be U.S. citizens and either student or junior division members of the federation. Competition categories include: women's voice, men's voice, piano, organ, harp/classical guitar, violin, viola, violoncello, double bass, orchestral woodwinds, orchestral brass, and percussion. Awards are presented at the national level after auditions at the state and district levels.
Financial data: The winner in each category is awarded $1,500.
Additional information: Applications and further information on these awards are available from Myrleann Newton, 488 Saddlery Drive, West, Gahanna, OH 43230-6815; information on all federation scholarships is available from Chair, Competitions and Awards Board, Mrs. Lamoine M. Hall, Jr., 4137 Whitfield Avenue, Fort Worth, TX 76109-5432. The entry fee is $30 for each category.
Deadline: November of even-numbered years for competitions in the following years.

1575
NICK ADAMS SHORT STORY COMPETITION

Associated Colleges of the Midwest
Attn: Program Officer
205 West Wacker Drive, Suite 1300
Chicago, IL 60606
Phone: (312) 263-5000   Fax: (312) 263-5879
E-mail: acm@acm.edu
Web Site: www.acm.edu/faculty/nickadams/
Summary: To recognize and reward outstanding short stories written by college students at schools belonging to the Associated Colleges of the Midwest (ACM).
Eligibility: Eligible to compete are students at colleges that belong to ACM. They may submit up to 2 stories to their campus's English department. The story need not have been written especially for the competition, but it cannot have been previously published off-campus. Each department selects the 4 best stories submitted and sends them to ACM's national office. The finalist is selected from that group.
Financial data: The prize is $1,000.
Duration: The prize is awarded annually.
Additional information: The prize is named for the young hero of many Hemingway stories and was given by an anonymous donor to encourage young writers who are students at ACM colleges (Beloit College, University of Chicago,

Carleton College, Coe College, Cornell College, Colorado College, Grinnell College, Knox College, Lake Forest College, Lawrence University, Macalester College, Monmouth College, Ripon College, and St. Olaf College).
Number awarded: 1 each year.
Deadline: March of each year.

1576
NORMA ROSS WALTER SCHOLARSHIP PROGRAM

Willa Cather Pioneer Memorial and Educational Foundation
Attn: Scholarship Program
326 North Webster
Red Cloud, NE 68970
Phone: (402) 746-2653
Web Site: www.willacather.org/Scholarship.htm
Summary: To provide financial assistance to female graduates of Nebraska high schools who are or will be majoring in English at an accredited college or university.
Eligibility: Applicants must be prospective first-year college students who have graduated or plan to graduate from a Nebraska high school. Only women may apply. They must plan to continue their education as English majors (journalism is not acceptable) at an accredited college or university. Selection is based on intellectual promise, creativity, and character.
Financial data: The stipend is $8,000, payable at the rate of $2,000 per year.
Duration: 4 years, provided the recipient maintains a satisfactory academic record (majoring in English with at least a 3.0 grade point average).
Number awarded: 1 each year.
Deadline: December of each year.

1577
NOSOTROS SCHOLARSHIP PROGRAM

Nosotros
Attn: Office of the President
650 North Bronson Avenue, Suite 102
Los Angeles, CA 90004
Phone: (323) 466-8566   Fax: (323) 466-8540
E-mail: nosotrosnews@nosotros.org
Web Site: www.nosotros.org
Summary: To help adult Hispanic students in California pursue postsecondary education in the performing arts.
Eligibility: Applicants must be pursuing a degree in film, television, theater, comedy, acting, directing, producing, script writing, stage production, film production, music choreography, or related fields. They must be at least 25 years of age, California residents, and of Latino/Hispanic descent.
Financial data: A stipend is awarded (exact amount not specified).
Duration: 1 year.
Additional information: Recipients must attend school on a full-time basis. Telephone inquiries are prohibited and may result in disqualification.
Deadline: March of each year.

1578
NPPF STILL SCHOLARSHIP

National Press Photographers Foundation
3200 Croasdaile Drive, Suite 306
Durham, NC 27705-2586
Phone: (919) 383-7246   (800) 289-6772
Fax: (919) 383-7261   E-mail: info@nppa.org
Web Site: www.nppa.org
Summary: To provide financial assistance to outstanding photojournalism students.
Eligibility: Applicants must have completed at least 1 year at a recognized 4-year college or university in the United States or Canada that offers courses in photojournalism, be working on a bachelor's degree, be intending to pursue a career in journalism, and have at least half a year of undergraduate study remaining. These awards are aimed at those with journalism potential but with little opportunity and great need.
Financial data: The award is $1,000.
Duration: 1 year.
Additional information: Further information is available from Bill Sanders, 640 N.W. 100 Way, Coral Springs, FL 33071, (954) 341-9718, E-mail: bsand@worldnet.att.net.
Number awarded: 1 each year.
Deadline: February of each year.

1579
NPPF TELEVISION NEWS SCHOLARSHIP

National Press Photographers Foundation
3200 Croasdaile Drive, Suite 306
Durham, NC 27705-2586
Phone: (919) 383-7246   (800) 289-6772
Fax: (919) 383-7261   E-mail: info@nppa.org
Web Site: www.nppa.org
Summary: To provide financial assistance to outstanding photojournalism students in television news.
Eligibility: Applicants must be enrolled at a recognized 4-year college or university in the United States or Canada that offers courses in television news photojournalism, working on a bachelor's degree as a junior or senior, and intending to pursue a career in journalism. As part of the selection process, they must submit a videotape containing examples of their work (including up to 3 complete stories with voice narration from their professor or advisor) and a 1-page biographical sketch that includes a personal statement on professional goals. Financial need and academic achievement are also considered.
Financial data: The award is $1,000.
Duration: 1 year.
Additional information: Further information is available from Dave Hamer, 3702 North 53rd Street, Omaha, NE 68104, E-mail: DaveHamer@compuserve.com.
Number awarded: 1 each year.
Deadline: February of each year.

1580
NSPA JOURNALISM HONOR ROLL AWARD

National Scholastic Press Association
2221 University Avenue, S.E., Suite 121
Minneapolis, MN 55414
Phone: (612) 625-8335   Fax: (612) 626-0720
E-mail: info@studentpress.org
Web Site: www.studentpress.org/nspa/contests.html
Summary: To recognize and reward outstanding high school journalists.
Eligibility: This program is open to high school seniors who have achieved a grade point average of 3.75 or higher and have worked in student media for 1 or more years. The publication on which the student works must have a current membership in the National Scholastic Press Association (NSPA). Candidates must be nominated by their teacher. The nominee judged most outstanding receives this award. Selection is based on cumulative grade point average, publications experience (including years on staff, positions held, and workshops/conventions attended), college plans, and an essay of 500 words or less that explains "Why I'm choosing a career in journalism."
Financial data: The award is a $1,000 scholarship.
Duration: The competition is held annually.
Number awarded: 1 each year.
Deadline: March of each year.

1581
NSPA/BRASLER PRIZE

National Scholastic Press Association
2221 University Avenue, S.E., Suite 121
Minneapolis, MN 55414
Phone: (612) 625-8335   Fax: (612) 626-0720
E-mail: info@studentpress.org
Web Site: www.studentpress.org/nspa/contests.html
Summary: To recognize and reward outstanding high school journalists.
Eligibility: This program is open to high school journalists who submit samples of stories that they have written in 5 categories: news, multicultural, features, sports, and editorials. In each category, 1 student is selected as the author of the Story of the Year. Selection of those stories is based on leadership, quality of writing, sensitivity, and fairness. The first-place winners in each category then compete for this prize.
Financial data: The prize is $1,000.
Duration: The competition is held annually.
Additional information: This competition is co-sponsored by the Los Angeles Times.
Number awarded: 1 each year.
Deadline: August of each year.

1582
NYACT NICK MALGIERI SCHOLARSHIP AWARD

International Association of Culinary Professionals Foundation
Attn: Program Coordinator
304 West Liberty Street, Suite 201
Louisville, KY 40202
Phone: (502) 581-9786, ext. 237   (800) 928-4227
Fax: (502) 589-3602   E-mail: iacp@hqtrs.com
Web Site: www.iacpfoundation.org
Summary: To offer financial assistance to students from designated states who are interested in pursuing a degree in the culinary arts.
Eligibility: This program is open to residents of Connecticut, New Jersey, and New York who are beginning students in a baking and pastry program at a nationally accredited culinary school. Applicants must submit an essay on their culinary goals and how they plan to achieve them. Selection is based on merit (including a grade point average of 3.0 of higher), food service work experience, and financial need.
Financial data: The stipend is $8,000.
Duration: 1 year.
Additional information: Funding for this program is provided by the New York Association of Cooking Teachers (NYACT). There is a $25 application fee.
Number awarded: 1 each year.
Deadline: November of each year.

1583
OHIO NEWSPAPERS FOUNDATION MINORITY SCHOLARSHIPS

Ohio Newspapers Foundation
1335 Dublin Road, Suite 216-B
Columbus, OH 43215-7038
Phone: (614) 486-6677   Fax: (614) 486-4940
E-mail: kpouliot@ohionews.org
Web Site: www.ohionews.org
Summary: To provide financial assistance for college to minority high school seniors in Ohio planning to pursue careers in journalism.
Eligibility: This program is open to high school seniors in Ohio who are members of minority groups (African American, Hispanic, Asian American, or American Indian) and planning to pursue careers in newspaper journalism. Applicants must have a high school grade point average of 2.5 or higher and demonstrate writing ability in an autobiography of 750 to 1,000 words that describes their academic and career interests, awards, extracurricular activities, and journalism-related activities.
Financial data: The award is $1,500.
Duration: 1 year.
Number awarded: 3 each year.
Deadline: March of each year.

1584
OHIO NEWSPAPERS FOUNDATION UNIVERSITY JOURNALISM SCHOLARSHIP

Ohio Newspapers Foundation
1335 Dublin Road, Suite 216-B
Columbus, OH 43215-7038
Phone: (614) 486-6677   Fax: (614) 486-4940
E-mail: kpouliot@ohionews.org   Web Site: www.ohionews.org
Summary: To provide financial assistance to students majoring in journalism at a college or university in Ohio.
Eligibility: This program is open to sophomores, juniors, and seniors at Ohio colleges and universities who have a grade point average of 2.5 or higher. Applicants must demonstrate the ability to write clearly in an autobiography of 750 to 1,000 words that describes their academic and career interests, awards, extracurricular activities, and journalism-related activities. Emphasis should be given to newspaper or print journalism.
Financial data: The award is $1,500.
Duration: 1 year.
Number awarded: 1 each year.
Deadline: March of each year.

1585
OKLAHOMA ASSOCIATION OF BROADCASTERS SCHOLARSHIP AWARDS

Oklahoma Association of Broadcasters
Attn: OAB Education Foundation
6520 North Western, Suite 104
Oklahoma City, OK 73116
Phone: (405) 848-0771   Fax: (405) 848-0772
E-mail: csoab@aol.com   Web Site: www.oabok.org
Summary: To provide financial assistance to upper-division students majoring in broadcasting in Oklahoma.
Eligibility: Applicants must be enrolled at an Oklahoma college or university and majoring in broadcasting. They must be entering their junior or senior year, have earned at least a 3.0 grade point average, be taking a full course load (at least 12 credits), and be planning to enter the broadcast industry upon graduation. Selection is based on financial need, achievements, industry goals, and extracurricular activities.
Financial data: The stipend is $1,000.
Duration: 1 year.
Additional information: This program includes the following named awards: the Sadie Adwon Scholarship, the Stan Forrer Memorial Scholarship, the Jack Morris Scholarship, the Mark Rawlings Scholarship, the Carl C. Smith Scholarship, the Harold C. & Frances Langford Stuart Scholarship, and the Bill Teegins Scholarship.
Number awarded: 7 each year.
Deadline: December of each year.

1586
OKLAHOMA CITY CHAPTER SCHOLARSHIPS

Association for Women in Communications-Oklahoma City Chapter
Attn: Brenda K. Jones, Scholarship Coordinator
2217 N.W. 44 Court
Oklahoma City, OK 73112
Summary: To provide financial assistance to women studying journalism or a related field in Oklahoma on the undergraduate or graduate level.
Eligibility: This program is open to women who are 1) juniors or seniors enrolled at a 4-year Oklahoma college or university in journalism or a related field; 2) sophomores enrolled at a 2-year Oklahoma college in journalism or a related field; or 3) graduate students in journalism or a related field at an Oklahoma university. As part of the application process, applicants must submit a statement of 300 to 500 words explaining why they are applying for the scholarship, their plan for completing their education, the number of hours they plan to take each semester, proposed date of graduation, the school they have chosen and why, long-term career goals, and how they learned about the scholarship. In addition to that essay, selection is based on aptitude, interest in pursuing a career in journalism or a related field, academic achievement, community service, and financial need. Preference is given to student or professional members of the Association of Women in Communications.
Financial data: Stipends are $1,000 or $500.
Duration: 1 year.
Additional information: Recipients must enroll full time.
Number awarded: Several each year.
Deadline: March of each year.

1587
OREGON ASSOCIATION OF BROADCASTERS COLLEGE AND UNIVERSITY SCHOLARSHIPS

Oregon Association of Broadcasters
Attn: Executive Director
P.O. Box 449
Eugene, OR 97440-0449
Phone: (541) 343-2101   Fax: (541) 343-0662
E-mail: theoab@ordata.com
Web Site: www.or-broadcasters.org/scholarship.htm
Summary: To provide financial assistance to students in Oregon who are interested in majoring in broadcast-related fields in college.
Eligibility: This program is open to Oregon residents who are either enrolled or accepted for enrollment at a 2- or 4-year public or private college or university in the state. They must be planning to enroll or be currently enrolled in a full-time undergraduate course of study, majoring in broadcast journalism, production, management, or another broadcast-related field. Applicants must be first- or second-year students in a 2-year program or sophomores, juniors, or seniors in a

4-year program. Preference is given to applicants with at least a 3.0 cumulative grade point average and demonstrated academic and/or professional experience in broadcasting or other electronic-media fields. As part of the application process, students must submit an essay that explains their reasons for choosing a broadcast major and includes any broadcast activities in which they have participated, their first job preference after college, their 10-year goals, any other scholarships they have received, and any academic honors they have received. Financial need is not considered in the selection process.
Financial data: The stipend is $1,000.
Duration: 1 year.
Additional information: Information is also available from Jim Upshaw, Scholarship Committee, University of Oregon, School of Journalism and Communication, Eugene, OR 97403-1275.
Number awarded: 4 each year.
Deadline: March of each year.

1588
OREGON ASSOCIATION OF BROADCASTERS HIGH SCHOOL SENIOR SCHOLARSHIPS

Oregon Association of Broadcasters
Attn: Executive Director
P.O. Box 449
Eugene, OR 97440-0449
Phone: (541) 343-2101   Fax: (541) 343-0662
E-mail: theoab@ordata.com
Web Site: www.or-broadcasters.org/scholarship.htm
Summary: To provide financial assistance to high school seniors in Oregon who are interested in majoring in broadcast-related fields in college.
Eligibility: This program is open to high school seniors who are Oregon residents, are accepted at a 2- or 4-year public or private college or university in the state, are planning to enroll full time, are planning to major in a broadcast-related field, and have at least a 3.0 grade point average. Preference is given to applicants with demonstrated academic and/or professional experience in broadcasting or other electronic-media fields. As part of the application process, students must submit an essay that explains their reasons for choosing a broadcast major and identifies any broadcast activities in which they have participated, their first job preference after college, their 10-year goals, any other scholarships they have received, and any academic honors they have received. Financial need is not considered in the selection process.
Financial data: The stipend is $1,000.
Duration: 1 year.
Additional information: Information is also available from Jim Upshaw, Scholarship Committee, University of Oregon, School of Journalism and Communication, Eugene, OR 97403-1275.
Number awarded: 2 each year.
Deadline: March of each year.

1589
OUTDOOR WRITING AND JOURNALISM SCHOLARSHIP

BACKPACKER
33 East Minor Street
Emmaus, PA 18098-0099
Phone: (610) 967-5171   Fax: (610) 967-8181
E-mail: scholarships@backpacker.com
Web Site: www.backpacker.com/scholarship
Summary: To provide financial assistance to college students who have encouraged others to experience wilderness through their writing.
Eligibility: This scholarship is available to students who have demonstrated a commitment and aptitude for addressing outdoor-related issues and topics through writing. Applicants must be enrolled full time in an undergraduate program at a 4-year college or university. They must have earned at least a 3.0 grade point average, be juniors or seniors in college, and submit 1) 3 writing samples (i.e., essays, newspaper clips, short stories) that best exemplify their writing skills; 2) an essay on how their current writing experience figures into their goals for the future; 3) an essay on how they would spend $10,000 on the outdoors if they were given that sum; and 4) either a 500-word column on a current wilderness or outdoor industry issue or a 500-word essay on the importance of preserving our wilderness. Financial need is not considered in the selection process.
Financial data: The stipend is $1,000.
Duration: The competition is held annually.

Additional information: This program began in 1998, as part of the magazine's 25th anniversary celebration.
Number awarded: 5 each year.
Deadline: October of each year.

1590
OVERSEAS PRESS CLUB FOUNDATION SCHOLARSHIPS

Overseas Press Club
Attn: OPC Foundation
40 West 45th Street
New York, NY 10036
Phone: (212) 626-9220   Fax: (212) 626-9210
E-mail: megatOPCF@aol.com
Web Site: www.opcofamerica.org/txtfdn.tm
Summary: To provide financial assistance to students who are preparing for a career as a foreign correspondent.
Eligibility: This program is open to undergraduate and graduate students who are studying in the United States and are interested in working as a foreign correspondent after graduation. Applicants are invited to submit an essay (up to 500 words) on an area of the world or an international topic that they believe deserves better coverage. Also, they should attach a 1-page letter about themselves: their education, relevant experience, and how they plan to use the funds if they are selected. They should not send resumes, clippings, or photographs. Selection is based on the clarity and focus of the essay along with the professional commitment of the applicant.
Financial data: The stipend is $2,000.
Duration: The competition is held annually.
Number awarded: 11 each year.
Deadline: December of each year.

1591
PACIFIC PRINTING & IMAGING ASSOCIATION SCHOLARSHIPS

Pacific Printing & Imaging Association
Attn: Scholarship Department
5319 S.W. Westgate Drive, Suite 117
Portland, OR 97221-2430
Phone: (503) 297-3328   (877) 762-7742
Fax: (503) 297-3320   E-mail: marcus@pacprinting.com
Web Site: www.ppi-assoc.org
Summary: To provide funding to students who intend to enter the printing and imaging industry.
Eligibility: This program is open to high school seniors and graduates from Alaska, Hawaii, Idaho, Montana, Oregon, and Washington. Applicants must have been accepted to either 1) a 2-year associate degree/certificate program in printing/graphic communications technology, or 2) a 4-year bachelor's degree program in printing management. Scholarships are not available for fine arts, graphic design, or graphic illustration. Funding is awarded on the basis of academic achievement.
Financial data: The annual stipend is $3,500 for a 4-year bachelor's degree program or $1,250 for an associate degree program.
Duration: 1 year.
Additional information: These scholarships are underwritten by a number of printing industry members and suppliers. In addition to receiving financial aid, scholarship recipients are linked with mentors from Pacific Printing & Imaging Association companies. Recipients must attend community and state colleges, trade schools, or California Polytechnic State University at San Luis Obispo.
Number awarded: Several every year.
Deadline: March of each year.

1592
PANASONIC YOUNG SOLOISTS AWARD

Very Special Arts
Attn: Education Office
1300 Connecticut Avenue, N.W., Suite 700
Washington, DC 20036
Phone: (202) 628-2800   (800) 933-8721
Fax: (202) 737-0725   TTY: (202) 737-0645
E-mail: soloists@vsarts.org
Web Site: www.vsarts.org/programs/ysp/index.html
Summary: To provide recognition and financial assistance to performing musicians who are physically or mentally challenged.
Eligibility: Contestants must be vocalists or instrumentalists under 25 years of age who have a disability and are interested in pursuing personal or professional studies in music. They are required to submit an audition tape and a 1-page biography that describes why they should be selected to receive this award. Tapes are evaluated on the basis of technique, tone, intonation, rhythm, and interpretation.
Financial data: The winners receive up to $2,500 for the purpose of broadening their musical experience or training and a $500 award.
Duration: The competition is held annually.
Additional information: Applications must first be submitted to the respective state organization of Very Special Arts. Funding for these awards is provided by Panasonic Consumer Electronics Company.
Number awarded: 2 each year.
Deadline: October of each year.

1593
PATRICIA V. ASIP SCHOLARSHIP

Hispanic Designers, Inc.
Attn: National Hispanic Education and Communications Projects
1101 30th Street, N.W., Suite 500
Washington, DC 20007
Phone: (202) 337-9636   Fax: (202) 337-9635
E-mail: HispDesign@aol.com   Web Site: www.hispanicdesigners.org
Summary: To provide financial assistance to Hispanic students enrolled in fashion design schools.
Eligibility: Applicants must be Hispanic or of Hispanic descent, be able to demonstrate financial need, be U.S. citizens or residents, have participated in an internship or work training program in the field of fashion, and have at least a 2.5 grade point average. They must be enrolled in an accredited postsecondary institution studying for a degree or in certified programs in fashion design or a related field. Preference is given to female applicants. Selection is based on the presentation of a merchandising strategy for a ready-to-wear collection targeting the U.S. Hispanic market; the presentation must include samples of advertising in English and Spanish, description of the target customer, price range, type of store and department in which the collection would be carried, a press kit on the designer and the collection, a design hang tag for garments in the collection, and a design label or logo for the collection.
Financial data: The stipend is $5,000 per year; awards are paid directly to the recipient's institution.
Duration: 1 year.
Additional information: This program was established in 1998 to honor Patricia V. Asip, who coordinated the Hispanic Designers Model Search for her employer, JCPenney Company, Inc. No telephone inquiries are accepted.
Number awarded: 1 each year.
Deadline: August of each year.

1594
PAULA AWARD FOR YOUNG WRITERS

el ANDAR Publications
Attn: Literary Award
P.O. Box 7745
Santa Cruz, CA 95061
Phone: (831) 457-8353   Fax: (831) 457-8354
E-mail: info@elandar.com
Web Site: www.elandar.com/award/index.html
Summary: To recognize and reward outstanding literary work on themes relevant to Latino youth.
Eligibility: Writers 18 years of age and younger are invited to submit poetry, fiction, and creative nonfiction. Entries may be in Spanish, English, or a mix of both languages and should relate to Latino life and experiences. Stories and creative nonfiction should not exceed 4,000 words. Poems may be any length. Only unpublished work is eligible.
Financial data: First prize is $1,000 and a 3-year subscription to el ANDAR. Second prize is $250 and a 2-year subscription to el ANDAR. Honorable mentions receive a 1-year subscription to el ANDAR.
Duration: The competition is held annually.
Additional information: el ANDAR is a literary magazine directed to Latino youth. It established this competition in 2000. The reading fee is $15 for each story, creative nonfiction work, or 3 poems.
Number awarded: 1 first prize, 1 second prize, and up to 10 honorable mentions are selected each year.
Deadline: September of each year.

1595
PHG FOUNDATION SCHOLARSHIP

Hawai'i Community Foundation
900 Fort Street Mall, Suite 1300
Honolulu, HI 96813
Phone: (808) 566-5570   (888) 731-3863
Fax: (808) 521-6286   E-mail: scholarships@hcf-hawaii.org
Web Site: www.hcf-hawaii.org
Summary: To provide financial assistance to Hawaii residents who are interested in preparing for a career in the arts.
Eligibility: This program is open to Hawaii residents who are interested in majoring in art or arts and crafts (not video, film, or the performing arts). They may be studying part time, on the undergraduate or graduate school level. They must be able to demonstrate academic achievement (at least a 2.7 grade point average), good moral character, and financial need. In addition to filling out the standard application form, applicants must write a short statement indicating their reasons for attending college, their planned course of study, and their career goals.
Financial data: The amounts of the awards depend on the availability of funds and the need of the recipient; recently, grants averaged $1,000.
Duration: 1 year.
Additional information: Recipients may attend college in Hawaii or on the mainland. This scholarship was established by a foundation created by the Pacific Handcrafters Guild (PHG).
Number awarded: Varies each year; recently, 5 of these scholarships were awarded.
Deadline: February of each year.

1596
PHILLIPS BUSINESS INFORMATION SCHOLARSHIP

Society of Satellite Professionals International
Attn: Scholarship Program
225 Reinekers Lane, Suite 600
Alexandria, VA 22314
Phone: (703) 549-8696   Fax: (703) 549-9728
E-mail: sspi@sspi.org   Web Site: www.sspi.org
Summary: To provide financial assistance to students interested in majoring in satellite business applications in college.
Eligibility: This program is open to high school seniors, college undergraduates, and graduate students majoring or planning to major in fields related to satellite business applications, including broadcasting, business, communications, engineering, international policy studies, journalism, law, science, space applications, or telecommunications. Applicants may be from any country. Selection is based on academic and leadership achievement, commitment to pursue education and career opportunities in the satellite communications industry, potential for significant contribution to that industry, a personal statement of 500 to 750 words on interest in satellite communications and why the applicant deserves the award, and a creative work (such as a research report, essay, article, videotape, artwork, computer program, or scale model of an antenna or spacecraft design) that reflects the applicant's interests and talents. Financial need is not considered.
Financial data: The stipend is $2,000.
Duration: 1 year.
Number awarded: 1 each year.
Deadline: June of each year.

1597
PHILO T. FARNSWORTH SCHOLARSHIP

Broadcast Education Association
Attn: Scholarships
1771 N Street, N.W.
Washington, DC 20036-2891
Phone: (202) 429-5354   E-mail: bea@nab.org
Web Site: www.beaweb.org
Summary: To provide financial assistance to upper-division and graduate students who are interested in preparing for a career in broadcasting.
Eligibility: This program is open to juniors, seniors, and graduate students enrolled full time at a college or university where at least 1 department is an institutional member of the Broadcast Education Association. Applicants may be studying in any area of broadcasting. Selection is based on evidence that the applicant possesses high integrity, superior academic ability, potential to be an outstanding electronic media professional, and a sense of personal and professional responsibility.

Financial data: The stipend is $1,500.
Duration: 1 year; may not be renewed.
Additional information: Information is also available from Peter B. Orlik, Central Michigan University, 344 Moore Hall, Mt. Pleasant, MI 48859, (517) 774-7279.
Number awarded: 1 each year.
Deadline: September of each year.

1598
PLAYBOY COLLEGE FICTION CONTEST

Playboy Magazine
680 North Lake Shore Drive
Chicago, IL 60611
Phone: (312) 261-5000   Web Site: www.playboy.com
Summary: To recognize and reward outstanding fiction written by college students.
Eligibility: College and university undergraduate and graduate students of any age may enter this contest. They are invited to submit a work of fiction no more than 25 pages in length.
Financial data: First prize is $3,000 and publication in *Playboy* magazine; second prize is $500 and a 1-year subscription to *Playboy*.
Duration: The competition is held annually.
Number awarded: 2 prizes, a first and a second, are awarded each year.
Deadline: December of each year.

1599
POLISH ARTS CLUB OF BUFFALO SCHOLARSHIP

Polish Arts Club of Buffalo Inc.
P.O. Box 1362
Williamsville, NY 14231-1362
Summary: To provide financial assistance to New York residents of Polish background who are majoring in the visual or performing arts.
Eligibility: Eligible to apply for this program are legal residents of the state of New York who are of Polish background, at the junior level or above in college, and majoring in visual or performing arts. Applicants must submit a 300-word essay on a Polish artist, composer, or musician who has contributed to their field of study. Letters of recommendation are also required. Finalists are interviewed. Financial need is not considered in the selection process.
Financial data: The stipend is $1,000.
Duration: 1 year.
Deadline: April of each year.

1600
PRINCE KUHIO HAWAIIAN CIVIC CLUB SCHOLARSHIP

Summary: To provide financial assistance for undergraduate or graduate studies to persons of Hawaiian descent.
See Listing #934.

1601
PRINT AND GRAPHICS SCHOLARSHIP FOUNDATION SCHOLARSHIPS

Print and Graphics Scholarship Foundation
Attn: Scholarship Competition
200 Deer Run Road
Sewickley PA 15143-2600
Phone: (412) 741-6860, ext. 309   (800) 910-GATF
Fax: (412) 741-2311   E-mail: pgsf@gatf.org
Web Site: www.gatf.org
Summary: To provide financial assistance to qualified and interested college students who want to prepare for careers in the graphic communications industries.
Eligibility: To be eligible to apply for an award, students must be interested in a career in graphic communications; be a high school senior, a high school graduate who has not yet started college, or a currently-enrolled college student; and be willing to attend school on a full-time basis (scholarships are not awarded for part-time study). To apply, high school students must 1) take the SAT or ACT and indicate that their test scores are to be sent to the Graphic Arts Technical Foundation and 2) fill out the foundation's application form. Current college students are requested to submit transcripts and a letter of recommendation from their major area advisor. College freshmen also need to submit a high school transcript. Semifinalists are interviewed. Selection is based on academic records and honors, extracurricular activities, and letters of recommendation.

Financial data: Stipends range from $1,000 to $1,500 per year. Funds are paid directly to the college selected by the award winner; the college will be authorized to draw upon the award to pay for tuition and other fees.
Duration: 1 year; may be renewed for up to 3 additional years if the recipient maintains a 3.0 grade point average and full-time enrollment.
Number awarded: Approximately 300 per year.
Deadline: February of each year for high school seniors; March of each year for students already in college.

1602
PRIZED PIECES AWARDS

National Black Programming Consortium
145 East 125th Street, Suite 220
New York, NY 10035
Phone: (212) 828-7588   Fax: (212) 828-7930
E-mail: nbpcinfo@blackstarcom.org
Web Site: www.blackstarcom.org/html/body_prized_pieces.html
Summary: To recognize and reward outstanding films and videos entered by African American students and professionals in the Prized Pieces competition.
Eligibility: This program is open to African Americans who submit film or video that explore the Black experience in all parts of the world. Genres include, but are not limited to, experimental, performance, youth, shorts, and feature-length narratives. Entries must be submitted on 3/4" Umatic video cassette, 1/2" video cassette, or 16mm film and must be in English or have English subtitles. Projects produced outside the United States must be no more than 2 years old and projects produced in the United States must be no more than 1 year old. Industry produced films and videos, works that have been broadcast on a major network, promotions, and ads are ineligible.
Financial data: Awards are $1,000 for the best film or video, $800 for the best director of film or video, $600 for the best new film or video, $400 for the best youth film or video, and $200 for the best short film or video.
Duration: The competition is held annually.
Additional information: Information is also available from WQED Pittsburgh, Attn: Fred Logan, 4802 Fifth Avenue, Pittsburgh, PA 15213, (412) 622-1466, Fax: (412) 622-1331, E-mail: flogan@wqed.org. Awards are presented at the Prized Pieces International Black Film and Video Festival held in Pittsburgh in September. The festival is supported by the Pennsylvania Council on the Arts and several funds of the Pittsburgh Foundation. Major funding for the National Black Programming Consortium is provided by the Corporation for Public Broadcasting. The entry fee is $60.
Number awarded: 5 cash prizes are awarded each year.
Deadline: July of each year.

1603
PSSC LEGACY FUND SCHOLARSHIP

Society of Satellite Professionals International
Attn: Scholarship Program
225 Reinekers Lane, Suite 600
Alexandria, VA 22314
Phone: (703) 549-8696   Fax: (703) 549-9728
E-mail: sspi@sspi.org   Web Site: www.sspi.org
Summary: To provide financial assistance to students interested in majoring in international satellite and/or distance education applications in college.
Eligibility: This program is open to high school seniors, college undergraduates, and graduate students majoring or planning to major in fields related to international satellite and/or distance education applications, including broadcasting, business, communications, engineering, international policy studies, journalism, law, science, space applications, or telecommunications. Applicants may be from any country. Selection is based on academic and leadership achievement, commitment to pursue education and career opportunities in the satellite communications industry, potential for significant contribution to that industry, a personal statement of 500 to 750 words on interest in satellite communications and why the applicant deserves the award, and a creative work (such as a research report, essay, article, videotape, artwork, computer program, or scale model of an antenna or spacecraft design) that reflects the applicant's interests and talents. Financial need is not considered.
Financial data: The stipend is $2,000.
Duration: 1 year.
Number awarded: 1 each year.
Deadline: June of each year.

1604
RACE RELATIONS MULTIRACIAL STUDENT SCHOLARSHIP

Summary: To provide financial assistance to undergraduate and graduate minority students interested in attending colleges related to the Christian Reformed Church in North America (CRCNA).
See Listing #944.

1605
RADIO AND TELEVISION NEWS DIRECTORS FOUNDATION UNDERGRADUATE SCHOLARSHIPS

Radio and Television News Directors Foundation
1000 Connecticut Avenue, N.W., Suite 615
Washington, DC 20036-5302
Phone: (202) 467-5218   Fax: (202) 223-4007
E-mail: karenb@rtndf.org
Web Site: www.rtndf.org/asfi/scholarships/undergrad.shtml
Summary: To provide financial assistance for the undergraduate education of students whose career objective is radio or television news.
Eligibility: This program is open to sophomores, juniors, and seniors who are enrolled full time in electronic journalism in a college or university where such a major is offered. Applicants must submit 1 to 3 examples of reporting or producing skills on audio or video cassette tapes (no more than 15 minutes total), a description of their role on each story and a list of who worked on each story and what they did, a statement explaining why they are seeking a career in broadcast or cable journalism, and a letter of endorsement from a faculty sponsor certifying that the candidate has at least 1 year of school remaining.
Financial data: This scholarship is $1,000, paid in semiannual installments.
Duration: 1 year.
Additional information: The Radio and Television News Directors Foundation (RTNDF) also provides an expense-paid trip to the Radio-Television News Directors Association (RTNDA) annual international conference. It defines electronic journalism to include radio, television, cable, and online news. Previous winners of any RTNDF scholarship or internship are not eligible.
Number awarded: 9 each year.
Deadline: April of each year.

1606
RAIN BIRD SCHOLARSHIP

Landscape Architecture Foundation
Attn: Scholarship Program
636 Eye Street, N.W.
Washington, DC 20001-3736
Phone: (202) 216-2356   Fax: (202) 898-1185
E-mail: msippel@asla.org   Web Site: www.laprofession.org
Summary: To provide financial assistance to landscape architecture students who are in need of financial assistance.
Eligibility: This program is open to landscape architecture students in the final 2 years of undergraduate study and in need of financial assistance. Applicants must submit a 300-word essay describing their career goals and explaining how they will contribute to the advancement of the profession of landscape architecture. Selection is based on demonstrated commitment to the profession, extracurricular activities, and scholastic record.
Financial data: The award is $1,000.
Additional information: Funding for this scholarship is provided by the Rain Bird Sprinkler Manufacturing Corporation.
Number awarded: 1 each year.
Deadline: March of each year.

1607
RALPH V. "ANDY" ANDERSON, K0NL, SCHOLARSHIP

Foundation for Amateur Radio, Inc.
P.O. Box 831
Riverdale, MD 20738
E-mail: turnbull@erols.com   Web Site: www.amateurradio-far.org
Summary: To provide funding to licensed radio amateurs who are interested in earning a bachelor's degree.
Eligibility: There is no restriction on the course of study, but preference is given to applicants pursuing studies leading to a degree in journalism. Applicants must intend to earn a bachelor's degree and be residents of the United States or its territories. The minimum license requirement is General Class.

Financial data: The stipend is $1,000.

Duration: 1 year.

Additional information: Recipients must attend an accredited school (university, college, or technical institute) on a full-time basis.

Number awarded: 1 each year.

Deadline: May of each year.

1608
RALPH WALDO EMERSON PRIZES

Concord Review
Attn: Editor
P.O. Box 661
Concord, MA 01742
Phone: (978) 443-0022   (800) 331-5007
E-mail: fitzhugh@tcr.org   Web Site: www.tcr.org
Summary: To recognize and reward outstanding historical essays written by high school seniors in any country.

Eligibility: High school students from any country are eligible to submit historical essays to the *Concord Review*, the first and only quarterly journal in the world that publishes essays written by high school seniors from any country.

Financial data: Each Emerson Prize winner receives a check for $3,000 and a copy of David McCullough's Pulitzer Prize-winning biography, *Truman*.

Duration: The prize is awarded annually.

Additional information: These prizes were first presented in 1994. They are awarded at the New England History Teachers Association's annual meeting.

Number awarded: 5 each year.

1609
RAY AND GERTRUDE MARSHALL SCHOLARSHIP FUND

American Culinary Federation, Inc.
Attn: Scholarship Committee
10 San Bartola Drive
P.O. Box 3466
St. Augustine, FL 32085-3466
Phone: (904) 824-4468   (800) 624-9458
Fax: (904) 825-4758   E-mail: acf@acfchefs.net
Web Site: www.acfchefs.org/educate/eduschlr.html
Summary: To provide financial assistance to junior members of the American Culinary Federation.

Eligibility: This program is open to students who are current members of the federation and are enrolled in an accredited school of culinary arts or culinary training program acceptable to the institute. They must have completed 1 or more full-term grading periods in the program prior to applying for this program. Selection is based on financial need, cumulative grade point average, strength of applicant's letter, recommendations, prior work in the food service industry, and overall professionalism.

Financial data: Awards are $500 or $1,000. Funds are paid jointly to the recipient and the educational institution and may be applied toward school-based fees, tuition, or other expenses.

Duration: 1 year.

Number awarded: 1 of $1,000 and several of $500 each year.

Deadline: February, June, or October of each year.

1610
RAYMOND DAVIS SCHOLARSHIP

Society for Imaging Science and Technology
Attn: Membership Office
7003 Kilworth Lane
Springfield, VA 22151
Phone: (703) 642-9090   Fax: (703) 642-9094
E-mail: info@imaging.org   Web Site: www.imaging.org
Summary: To provide financial assistance for students interested in continuing their studies in photographic or imaging science or technology.

Eligibility: This program is open to full-time undergraduate or graduate students who have completed or will complete 2 academic years at an accredited institution before the term of the scholarship is up. Grants are made for academic study or research in photographic or imaging science or engineering. Graduate students must provide an abstract of their plan for advanced study, research, and thesis. All applicants must outline their career objectives and indicate how the academic work they propose to undertake will further their objectives. Financial need is not considered.

Financial data: Grants are $1,000 or more.

Additional information: These scholarships are presented in honor of Raymond

Davis (1888-1974), nationally known for his contributions to the fields of photographic sensitometry, colorimetry, and microphotography.

Number awarded: 1 or more each year.

Deadline: December of each year.

1611
RAYMOND E. PAGE SCHOLARSHIP

Landscape Architecture Foundation
Attn: Scholarship Program
636 Eye Street, N.W.
Washington, DC 20001-3736
Phone: (202) 216-2356   Fax: (202) 898-1185
E-mail: msippel@asla.org   Web Site: www.laprofession.org
Summary: To provide financial assistance to needy undergraduate landscape architecture students.

Eligibility: Undergraduate students in need of financial assistance are eligible to apply if they are majoring in landscape architecture. Applicants should submit a 2-page essay describing their need for financial assistance and a letter of recommendation from a current professor who is familiar with their character and goals in pursuing an education in landscape architecture.

Financial data: The stipend is $1,000.

Duration: 1 year.

Number awarded: 1 each year.

Deadline: March of each year.

1612
RDW GROUP, INC. MINORITY SCHOLARSHIP FOR COMMUNICATIONS

Rhode Island Foundation
Attn: Scholarship Coordinator
One Union Station
Providence, RI 02903
Phone: (401) 274-4564   Fax: (401) 331-8085
E-mail: libbym@rifoundation.org   Web Site: www.rifoundation.org
Summary: To provide financial assistance to Rhode Island students of color interested in preparing for a career in communications.

Eligibility: This program is open to minority undergraduate and graduate students who are Rhode Island residents. Applicants must intend to pursue a course of study in communications. They must be able to demonstrate their commitment to a career in communications and financial need. Along with their application, they must submit an essay (up to 300 words) on the impact they would like to have on the communications field.

Financial data: The stipend is $2,000.

Duration: 1 year; nonrenewable.

Additional information: This program is sponsored by the RDW Group, Inc.

Number awarded: 1 each year.

Deadline: June of each year.

1613
REGINALD K. BRACK, JR. NULITES SCHOLARSHIP

National Urban League
Attn: Scholarship Coordinator
120 Wall Street
New York, NY 10005
Phone: (212) 558-5373   Fax: (212) 344-8948
E-mail: info@nul.org   Web Site: www.nul.org
Summary: To provide financial assistance for college education in communications to African American students who belong to NULITES chapters of the National Urban League.

Eligibility: This program is open to NULITERS graduating from high school and former members currently in their freshman or sophomore year of college. Applicants must be interested in pursuing careers in communications (including, but not limited to, broadcasting, public relations, publishing, and journalism). They must have at least a 3.0 GPA. Selection is based on need, merit, community service, and academic achievement.

Financial data: The stipend is $2,500 per year.

Duration: 4 years.

Additional information: Funding for these scholarships is provided by the National Urban League and Time Inc.

Number awarded: Varies each year.

Deadline: January of each year.

1614
REID BLACKBURN SCHOLARSHIP

National Press Photographers Foundation
3200 Croasdaile Drive, Suite 306
Durham, NC 27705-2586
Phone: (919) 383-7246   (800) 289-6772
Fax: (919) 383-7261   E-mail: info@nppa.org
Web Site: www.nppa.org
Summary: To provide financial assistance to college students who are interested in pursuing a career in photojournalism.
Eligibility: Applicants must have completed at least 1 year at a recognized 4-year college or university in the United States or Canada that offers courses in photojournalism, be working on a bachelor's degree, be intending to pursue a career in journalism, and have at least half a year of undergraduate study remaining. A statement of philosophy and goals is especially important in the selection process, although financial need and academic achievement are also considered.
Financial data: The stipend is $1,000 per year.
Duration: 1 year; nonrenewable.
Additional information: This program is named for a photographer for the Columbian newspaper of Vancouver, Washington who lost his life when Mount St. Helens erupted on May 18, 1980. Further information is available from Jeremiah Coughlan, The Columbian, 701 West Eighth Street, Vancouver, WA 98660, (360) 694-3391, E-mail: coughlan@pacifier.com. Recipients may attend school in the United States or Canada.
Number awarded: 1 each year.
Deadline: February of each year.

1615
RHODE ISLAND ADVERTISING SCHOLARSHIP

Rhode Island Foundation
Attn: Scholarship Coordinator
One Union Station
Providence, RI 02903
Phone: (401) 274-4564   Fax: (401) 331-8085
E-mail: libbym@rifoundation.org   Web Site: www.rifoundation.org
Summary: To provide financial assistance to Rhode Island college students interested in preparing for a career in advertising, television, or filmmaking.
Eligibility: This program is open to currently-enrolled college students in Rhode Island who are sophomores or juniors. Applicants must intend to pursue a career in advertising, including public relations, marketing, graphic design, film, or broadcast production. They must be able to a commitment to a career in advertising and be able to demonstrate financial need. Along with their application, they must submit an essay (up to 300 words) on the impact they would like to have on the advertising industry.
Financial data: The stipend is $1,000.
Duration: 1 year; nonrenewable.
Additional information: This program is sponsored by the Ad Club of Southeastern New England, P.O. Box 41537, Providence, RI 02940, (401) 295-1563, Fax: (401) 295-4743, E-mail: adclubsene@juno.com.
Number awarded: 1 or 2 each year.
Deadline: April of each year.

1616
RICHARD M. URAY SCHOLARSHIP

National Broadcasting Society
Attn: National Vice President for Operations
P.O. Box 915
St. Charles, MO 63302-0915
Phone: (866) 272-3746, ext. 3000   E-mail: nbsaerho@swbell.net
Web Site: www.onu.edu/org/irts-aerho
Summary: To provide financial assistance for college or graduate school to members of the National Broadcasting Society (NBS).
Eligibility: This program is open to undergraduate and graduate students who are members of the society. Selection is based on academic record, service to the society, professional broadcasting achievements, and financial need.
Financial data: The stipend is $1,000.
Duration: 1 year.
Number awarded: 1 each year.
Deadline: January of each year.

1617
RICHARD S. SMITH SCHOLARSHIP

United Methodist Youth Organization
P.O. Box 340003
Nashville, TN 37203-0003
Phone: (615) 340-7184   (877) 899-2780, ext. 7184
Fax: (615) 340-1764   E-mail: umyouthorg@gbod.org
Web Site: www.umyouth.org/scholarships.html
Summary: To provide financial assistance to minority high school seniors or graduates who wish to prepare for a Methodist church-related career.
Eligibility: Minority students who are beginning college are eligible to apply if they are members of the United Methodist Church, have been active in their local church for at least 1 year, can demonstrate financial need, have maintained a "C" average throughout high school, and are interested in pursuing a church-related career after graduation.
Financial data: The stipend is up to $1,000.
Duration: 1 year; nonrenewable.
Additional information: Recipients must enroll full time in their first year of undergraduate study.
Deadline: May of each year.

1618
R.L. GILLETTE SCHOLARSHIPS

American Foundation for the Blind
Attn: Scholarship Committee
11 Penn Plaza, Suite 300
New York, NY 10001
Phone: (212) 502-7661   (800) AFB-LINE
Fax: (212) 502-7771   TDD: (212) 502-7662
E-mail: afbinfo@afb.net
Web Site: www.afb.org/scholarships.asp
Summary: To provide financial assistance to legally blind undergraduate women who are studying literature or music.
Eligibility: Women who are legally blind, U.S. citizens, and enrolled in a 4-year baccalaureate degree program in literature or music are eligible to apply. Applications must include a typewritten statement, up to 3 pages in length, describing educational and personal goals, work experience, extracurricular activities, and how scholarship funds will be used. Candidates must also submit a sample performance tape (not to exceed 30 minutes) or a creative writing sample.
Financial data: The stipend is $1,000.
Duration: 1 academic year.
Number awarded: 2 each year.
Deadline: March of each year.

1619
ROBERT F. KENNEDY JOURNALISM AWARDS

Robert F. Kennedy Memorial
1367 Connecticut Avenue, N.W., Suite 200
Washington, DC 20036
Phone: (202) 463-7575, ext. 234   Fax: (202) 463-6606
E-mail: info@rfkmemorial.org   Web Site: www.rfkmemorial.org
Summary: To recognize and reward works of journalism and photojournalism that best reflect Robert F. Kennedy's concern for the disadvantaged.
Eligibility: To be eligible, entries must have been published or broadcast in the United States for the first time during the year preceding the award. They must address the life styles, handicaps, or potentialities of the disadvantaged in the United States; provide insights into the causes, conditions, or remedies of their plight; or present critical analyses of public policies, programs, attitudes, or private endeavors relevant to their lives. Entries may be submitted either by individuals or by appropriate media organizations. Awards are made in 5 professional categories of journalistic coverage: print (newspaper, magazine), cartoons, broadcast, photojournalism, and international; a separate student competition for college undergraduates only is open to print, broadcast, and photojournalism students.
Financial data: A cash prize of $1,000 may be awarded to the entry judged most outstanding in each category. A grand prize of $2,000 may be awarded to the most outstanding of the 6 category winners.
Duration: The awards are presented annually.
Additional information: This program was established in 1968, following the death of Robert F. Kennedy. An entry fee of $25 is required for professional categories; no entry fee for students is required.

Number awarded: Varies; up to 5 category awards and 1 grand prize each year.
Deadline: January of each year.

1620
ROBERT LEWIS BAKER SCHOLARSHIP

Federated Garden Clubs of Maryland
c/o Margaret Stansbury
413 Warren Avenue
Baltimore, MD 21230-3929
Phone: (410) 528-0561
Summary: To provide financial assistance to Maryland residents who are interested in studying ornamental horticulture or landscape design on the undergraduate or graduate school level.
Eligibility: High school seniors, currently-enrolled college students, and graduate students may apply for this funding if they are Maryland residents and interested in earning a degree in ornamental horticulture or landscape design.
Financial data: Stipends range from $2,000 to $5,000; a total of $12,000 is distributed annually.
Duration: 1 year.
Additional information: This scholarship was started in 1980.
Number awarded: Varies; generally 3 to 4 each year.

1621
ROCKY MOUNTAIN CHAPTER SCHOLARSHIPS

Society of Satellite Professionals International
Attn: Scholarship Program
225 Reinekers Lane, Suite 600
Alexandria, VA 22314
Phone: (703) 549-8696   Fax: (703) 549-9728
E-mail: sspi@sspi.org
Web Site: www.sspi.org
Summary: To provide financial assistance to students attending college in designated Rocky Mountain states who are interested in majoring in satellite-related disciplines.
Eligibility: This program is open to high school seniors, college undergraduates, and graduate students majoring or planning to major in fields related to satellite communications, including broadcasting, business, communications, engineering, international policy studies, journalism, law, science, space applications, or telecommunications. Applicants must be attending schools in Arizona, Colorado, Idaho, Montana, Nevada, New Mexico, Utah, or Wyoming. Selection is based on academic and leadership achievement, commitment to pursue education and career opportunities in the satellite communications industry, potential for significant contribution to that industry, a personal statement of 500 to 750 words on interest in satellite communications and why the applicant deserves the award, and a creative work (such as a research report, essay, article, videotape, artwork, computer program, or scale model of an antenna or spacecraft design) that reflects the applicant's interests and talents. Financial need is not considered.
Financial data: The stipend is $2,000.
Duration: 1 year.
Number awarded: 1 each year.
Deadline: June of each year.

1622
ROLLING STONE COLLEGE JOURNALISM COMPETITION

Rolling Stone
Attn: College Journalism Competition
1290 Avenue of the Americas, Second Floor
New York, NY 10104-0298
E-mail: kerry.smith@rollingstone.com
Web Site: www.rollingstone.com
Summary: To recognize and reward outstanding articles published in college newspapers or magazines on popular entertainment or other subjects.
Eligibility: Entries may be submitted in 3 categories: entertainment reporting (reporting on popular music, film, or television, including artist profiles and interviews), feature writing (stylishly-written narratives and profiles that illuminate issues and trends), and essays and criticism (commentary, including expressions of opinion and humor, on any subject). All entries must have been published in a student newspaper or magazine during the previous year; the author must have been a college student (full or part time) at the time the item was published. Students may enter in more than 1 category, but they are limited

to 1 entry per category. Tear sheets (from the original newspaper or magazine) must be provided. The submissions are judged by the editors of *Rolling Stone*.
Financial data: The prize is $2,500.
Duration: The competition is held annually.
Additional information: This competition started in 1976.
Number awarded: 3 each year: 1 in each of the categories.
Deadline: July of each year.

1623
RON AUTRY SCHOLARSHIP

Community Foundation for Greater Atlanta, Inc.
50 Hurt Plaza, Suite 449
Atlanta, GA 30303
Phone: (404) 688-5525   Fax: (404) 688-3060
E-mail: bchen@atlcf.org
Web Site: www.atlcf.org/Scholar02.html
Summary: To provide financial assistance to Georgia residents who are majoring in journalism at a 4-year college or university.
Eligibility: This program is open to legal residents of Georgia who are enrolled in a 4-year college or university and pursuing studies in journalism (news, advertising, circulation, or human resources). Applicants must be upper-division students, be enrolled full time, have at least a 2.0 grade point average, and be able to demonstrate financial need.
Financial data: The maximum stipend is $1,500.
Duration: 1 year.
Number awarded: 1 each year.
Deadline: April of each year.

1624
ROSA PONSELLE SCHOLARSHIP

Rosa Ponselle Fund
39 West Main Street
Meriden, CT 06451
Phone: (203) 639-9778   Fax: (203) 238-7025
E-mail: rosaponsellemuseum@snet.net
Summary: To recognize and reward student vocalists who are preparing for an operatic vocal career.
Eligibility: Candidates may be from any state and must be at least juniors in an undergraduate program of vocal studies or in a master's degree of vocal studies at an accredited music school, college, or conservatory. College graduates are also eligible, if they have been participating since then in vocal apprenticeship programs with recognized opera companies or other vocal apprenticeship opportunities. In addition, residents of Connecticut may apply if they have completed high school and are pursuing an operatic vocal career with private instruction in voice, drama, languages, and other areas related to operatic vocal performance and have been doing so for no less than 3 years. To apply, applicants must submit a letter of recommendation from their current or most recent vocal instructor, a resume of their current repertoire (which must include at least 10 operatic arias), the proposed program for the audition (at least 4 operatic arias), and a photograph. Candidates must present a 20-minute operatic vocal program in Meriden, Connecticut, with piano accompaniment. Besides operatic arias, the program may include some classic art and Broadway songs. Selection is based on voice classification, resonance, production and breath control, vocal range, musical interpretation, pitch, diction, and stage presence. If 2 candidates are equally qualified, preference is given to permanent residents of Connecticut.
Financial data: The winning vocalist is presented with a $1,000 scholarship, with $500 paid when the winner is chosen and $500 paid upon presentation of an operatic recital for the Meriden community.
Duration: The competition is held annually.
Additional information: The winner must prepare and present an operatic vocal recital (approximately 90 minutes) for the Meriden community in mid-November. Piano accompaniment for the recital must be provided by the recitalist.
Number awarded: 1 each year.
Deadline: March of each year.

1625
ROY HOWARD NATIONAL REPORTING COMPETITION AND SEMINAR

Scripps Howard Foundation
Attn: Vickie Martin
312 Walnut Street, 28th Floor
Cincinnati, OH 45202-4040
Phone: (513) 977-3034   Fax: (513) 977-3800
E-mail: vlmartin@scripps.com
Web Site: www.scripps.com/foundation
Summary: To recognize and reward outstanding college journalism students.
Eligibility: This program is open to undergraduate journalism students in their freshman, sophomore, or junior year. They must be nominated by their college, which must submit a story or series written by the nominee involving coverage of campus or community events, issues, trends, or personalities. Entries must have been published in a campus or professional newspaper between the first of March of the previous year and the end of February of the current year. They should reflect in-depth enterprise reporting in words or in photo essays that have an impact on the campus or community. Routine coverage of events and meetings, editorials, and commentaries are not eligible. Each college or university may nominate up to 4 students.
Financial data: First-place winners receive $3,000 scholarships, runners-up receive $2,000 scholarships, and honorable mentions receive $1,000 scholarships. All finalists also receive an expense-paid trip to Indiana University for a seminar with journalism professionals and to attend the Roy W. Howard Lecture.
Duration: The competition is held annually.
Additional information: Information is also available from the Indiana University School of Journalism, 940 East Seventh, Bloomington, IN 47405, (812) 855-9249.
Number awarded: 12 finalists are selected each year. Of those, 4 are designated as first-place winners, 4 as runners-up, and 4 as honorable mentions.
Deadline: April of each year.

1626
RTNDA PRESIDENT'S AWARD FOR TELEVISION NEWSROOM MANAGEMENT

Radio and Television News Directors Foundation
1000 Connecticut Avenue, N.W., Suite 615
Washington, DC 20036-5302
Phone: (202) 467-5218   Fax: (202) 223-4007
E-mail: karenb@rtndf.org
Web Site: www.rtndf.org/asfi/scholarships/undergrad.shtml
Summary: To provide financial assistance to students whose career objective is television newsroom management.
Eligibility: This program is open to full-time graduate and undergraduate students who are enrolled in electronic journalism in a college or university where such a major is offered. Applicants must include a 1-page essay on why they are seeking a career in television newsroom management and a letter of endorsement from a faculty sponsor certifying that the applicant has at least 1 year of school remaining.
Financial data: This scholarship is $2,000.
Duration: 1 year.
Additional information: This scholarship was established in 1996. The Radio and Television News Directors Foundation (RTNDF) also provides an expense-paid trip to the Radio-Television News Directors Association (RTNDA) annual international conference. It defines electronic journalism to include radio, television, cable, and online news. Previous winners of any RTNDF scholarship or internship are not eligible.
Number awarded: 1 each year.
Deadline: April of each year.

1627
RUTH LILLY POETRY FELLOWSHIPS

Poetry Magazine
60 West Walton Street
Chicago, IL 60610
Phone: (312) 255-3703   Web Site: www.poetrymagazine.org
Summary: To provide financial assistance to undergraduate and graduate students who are studying poetry.
Eligibility: This program is open to undergraduate and graduate students in creative writing or English who have not yet received a master's or doctoral degree. Program directors and department chairs at colleges and universities in the United States are invited to nominate 1 student-poet from their program.

Nominations must be accompanied by samples of the candidate's work.
Financial data: The stipend is $15,000 per year.
Duration: 1 year.
Additional information: This program, begun in 1989, is sponsored jointly by the Modern Poetry Association and *Poetry* Magazine.
Number awarded: 2 each year.
Deadline: April of each year.

1628
R.V. "GADABOUT" GADDIS CHARITABLE FUND

Maine Community Foundation
Attn: Program Director
245 Main Street
Ellsworth, ME 04605
Phone: (207) 667-9735   (877) 700-6800
Fax: (207) 667-0447   E-mail: info@mainecf.org
Web Site: www.mainecf.org/scholar.html
Summary: To provide financial assistance to Maine students interested in the study of outdoor/nature writing.
Eligibility: This program is open to students in Maine who are college juniors or seniors studying outdoor/nature writing.
Financial data: The stipend is $1,000 per year.
Duration: 1 year.
Additional information: This program began in 1995.
Number awarded: 2 each year.
Deadline: March of each year.

1629
SAM PINE SCHOLARSHIP

Connecticut Chapter of the American Planning Association
c/o Daniel A. Tuba
163-6 Pepperidge Road
Monroe, CT 06468
E-mail: datuba@aol.com
Web Site: www.ccapa.org
Summary: To provide financial assistance to undergraduate students in planning or architecture at schools in New England and New York.
Eligibility: This program is open to undergraduate students in planning, architecture or a related field. Applicants must be attending a college or university in New England or New York. Selection is based, first, on financial need and then on academic record.
Financial data: The stipend is $2,000.
Duration: 1 year.
Number awarded: 1 each year.

1630
SAMUEL ELIOT MORISON ESSAY CONTEST

Navy League of the United States
2300 Wilson Boulevard
Arlington, VA 22201-3308
Phone: (703) 528-1775   Fax: (703) 528-2333
E-mail: mail@navyleague.org
Web Site: www.navyleague.org
Summary: To recognize and reward high school students who write outstanding essays on naval history.
Eligibility: This program is open to all high school students in the United States. They are invited to write an essay of 1,500 to 2,500 words on a topic that changes annually but relates to U.S. naval history; a recent theme was "The Information Age and the Modern Sea Services." Selection is based on accuracy and relevance of information presented, organization of materials, clarity of expression, and grammar.
Financial data: The grand prize winner receives an award of $4,000; that winner's school receives $500 and the teacher/advisor receives $250. The first runner-up wins $2,000; that winner's school receives $300 and the teacher/advisor receives $150. The second runner-up wins $1,000; that winner's school receives $250 and the teacher/advisor receives $100. All regional winners receive $400 savings bonds.
Duration: This contest is held annually.
Number awarded: 3 national winners and 16 regional winners each year.
Deadline: February of each year.

1631
SARA STUDENT DESIGN COMPETITION

Society of American Registered Architects
Attn: Program Administrator
P.O. Box 9263
Lombard, IL 60148
Phone: (630) 738-4610   Fax: (630) 495-3054
E-mail: cathiemoscato@mediaone.net
Web Site: www.sara-national.org/competitions/student_da.html
Summary: To recognize and reward the creative architectural designs of college students.
Eligibility: This program is open to undergraduate students in a Bachelor of Arts or a Bachelor of Science in Architecture degree at an accredited school of architecture, undergraduate students in a Bachelor of Architecture program, and graduate students in a Master of Architecture program pursuing their first professional degree. Applicants must be sponsored by a faculty member. The competition requires that students present a typical architectural concept of a medium-sized project other than a single-family home or vacation residence. Selection is based on the applicant's ability to resolve problems associated with architectural concepts (such as human activity needs, climatic considerations, structural integrity, cultural influences, site planning, creative insight, and coherence of architectural vocabulary); the ability to recognize and resolve situational problems of mechanical and electrical systems, environmental context, and external support systems; and the ability to integrate functional aspects of the problem in an appropriate manner. Entries must include 5 to 10 slides of the project.
Financial data: The prize for first place is a $6,000 U.S. savings bond or $3,000 cash; for second place, a $2,000 U.S. savings bond or $1,000 cash; for third place, a $1,000 U.S. savings bond or $500 cash. Each student submitting an entry also receives a complimentary 1-year student membership in the Society of American Registered Architects (SARA).
Duration: The competition is held annually.
Additional information: A $15 fee must accompany each project entered.
Number awarded: 3 each year.
Deadline: September of each year.

1632
SCHOLARSHIPS IN TECHNICAL COMMUNICATION

Society for Technical Communication
901 North Stuart Street, Suite 904
Arlington, VA 22203-1822
Phone: (703) 522-4114   Fax: (703) 522-2075
E-mail: stc@stc.org
Web Site: www.stc.org/scholarship_info.html
Summary: To provide financial assistance to students who are preparing for a career in some area of technical communications.
Eligibility: This program is open to 1) full-time undergraduate students working toward a bachelor's degree in technical communications who have completed at least 1 year of college and 2) full-time graduate students working toward a master's or doctoral degree in technical communications. Applicants must be studying communication of information about technical subjects; other majors, such as general journalism, electronic communication engineering, computer programming, entertainment, and creative writing are not eligible. Selection is based on academic record and potential for contributing to the profession of technical communication; financial need is not considered unless applicants are judged to be equal in all other respects.
Financial data: Scholarships are $2,500; funds are paid to the school for the benefit of the recipient.
Duration: 1 year.
Additional information: Information is also available from Lenore S. Ridgway, 19 Johnston Avenue, Kingston, NY 12401, (914) 339-4927.
Number awarded: 14 each year: 7 to undergraduate students and 7 to graduate students.
Deadline: February of each year.

1633
SCHOLASTIC ART AWARDS

Scholastic, Inc.
Attn: Alliance for Young Artists & Writers, Inc.
555 Broadway
New York, NY 10012
Phone: (212) 343-6493   Fax: (212) 343-4885
E-mail: A&WGeneralInfo@scholastic.com
Web Site: www.scholastic.com
Summary: To recognize and reward outstanding high school artists and photographers.
Eligibility: Eligible to participate in this competition are all students in grades 7 through 12 who are currently enrolled in public and private schools in the United States, U.S. territories, or Canada or in U.S.-sponsored schools abroad. Categories include painting; drawing; mixed media; printmaking; sculpture; photography; computer graphics; video, film, and animation; architecture and environmental design; graphic design; product design; ceramics and glass; jewelry and metalsmithing; and textile and fiber design. Participants who are graduating seniors planning to attend college may submit an art portfolio of 8 works, including at least 3 drawings, or a photography portfolio of 8 works.
Financial data: Each portfolio gold award is a $5,000 scholarship. In addition, gold awards in each category are $100, American Visions Awards for the best work in any category in each region are $100, and the Pinnacle Awards for the most outstanding work in each category are $400. There are also 4 special awards: the Portfolio Series Award, presented by Binney & Smith to the outstanding work in the portfolio category, of $20,000; the Pentad Awards (for exceptional works in the drawing, painting, and photography categories) of $1,000; the Steuben Glass Award for the best student submission in glass design of $1,000; and the Cooper-Hewitt National Design Museum "Best of Design Award" (for the best submission in the architecture and environmental design, graphic design, or product design categories) of $1,000.
Additional information: Contestants who submit outstanding portfolios but do not win are nominated for scholarships at 50 schools of art and 4 photography schools. Teachers of the Portfolio Award winners receive the Binney & Smith Portfolio Teacher Awards of $1,000 each; the photography teacher who submits the most outstanding group of entries receives the Lois E. Vinette Photography Teacher Award of $1,000; and the teacher who submit the greatest number of winning entries in any category except photography receives the Gold Apply Teacher Award of $500.
Number awarded: Each year, this competition presents 5 portfolio awards (4 for art and 1 for photography), 155 gold awards (20 for painting, 20 for drawing, 10 for mixed media, 10 for printmaking, 10 for sculpture, 15 for photography, 10 for computer graphics, 10 for video, film, and animation, 5 for architecture and environmental design, 10 for graphic design, 5 for product design, 10 for ceramics and glass, 10 for jewelry and metalsmithing, and 10 for textile and fiber design), 36 American Vision Awards (1 in each of the regions), 16 Pinnacle Awards (1 in each of the categories), 5 PENTAD Awards, and 1 of each of the 3 other special awards.
Deadline: February of each year.

1634
SCHOLASTIC WRITING AWARDS

Scholastic, Inc.
Attn: Alliance for Young Artists & Writers, Inc.
555 Broadway
New York, NY 10012
Phone: (212) 343-6493   Fax: (212) 343-4885
E-mail: A&WGeneralInfo@scholastic.com
Web Site: www.scholastic.com
Summary: To provide monetary awards to creative high school writers.
Eligibility: All students in grades 7 through 12 who are currently enrolled in public and private schools in the United States, U.S. territories, U.S.-sponsored schools abroad, and Canada are eligible. Competitions are held in Group 1 for grades 7 through 9 and Group 2 for grades 10 through 12 and in 8 categories: short story (1,300 to 3,000 words); short short story (600 to 1,300 words); personal essay/memoir (500 to 2,000 words for group 1, 750 to 3,000 words for group 2); journalism (400 to 2,000 words for Group 1, 500 to 3,000 words for Group 2); dramatic script (up to 30 minutes); poetry (35 to 100 lines for Group 1, 50 to 200 lines for Group 2); humor (600 to 3,000 words); and science fiction/fantasy (600 to 3,000 words). A separate general portfolio competition for graduating seniors only consists of a minimum of 3 and maximum of 8 narratives, individual poems,

and/or dramatic scripts up to a total of 50 pages, and the James B. Reston Portfolio for graduating seniors only consists of a minimum of 3 and maximum of 8 essays, nonfiction, and/or opinion pieces up to a total of 50 pages. Works may not have been submitted previously in this or any other competition and must be original. Each student may enter only 1 category.

Financial data: The portfolio gold awards are $5,000 scholarships. In addition, gold awards in each category are $100, American Voices Awards for the best work in any category in each region are $100, and the Pinnacle Awards for the most outstanding work in each category are $400. The New York Times James B. Reston Portfolio Gold Award is $5,000. Other special awards include the Achievement Prize for Student Poetry (sponsored by the American Academy of Achievement for the junior or senior who submits the most outstanding entry in the poetry category) of a $5,000 scholarship; the Achievement Prize for Student Fiction (sponsored by the American Academy of Achievement for the graduating senior who submits an exceptional body of work in the portfolio category) of a $10,000 scholarship; and the Otto Friedrich Journalism Award of $1,000.

Additional information: Teachers of the 5 portfolio award winners each receive $1,000 awards. The teacher who submits the greatest number of winning entries receives the Gold Apple Teacher Award of $500. Other scholarships are also available from several writing programs at various universities.

Number awarded: Each year, this competition presents 5 portfolio awards (4 Writing Portfolio Gold Awards and 1 New York Times James B. Reston Portfolio Gold Award), 130 gold awards (10 for the dramatic script category, 20 for the humor category, 10 for the journalism category, 10 for the personal essay/memoir category, 20 for the poetry category, 20 for the science fiction/fantasy category, 20 for the short story category, and 20 for the short short story category), 7 American Voices Awards (1 in each of the regions), 8 Pinnacle Awards (1 in each of the categories), and the other 3 special awards.

Deadline: January of each year.

1635
SCRIPPS HOWARD MOST VALUABLE STAFF AWARDS

Scripps Howard Foundation
Attn: Vickie Martin
312 Walnut Street, 28th Floor
Cincinnati, OH 45202-4040
Phone: (513) 977-3034   Fax: (513) 977-3800
E-mail: vlmartin@scripps.com
Web Site: www.scripps.com/foundation

Summary: To recognize and reward outstanding college newspaper and broadcast station staff members.

Eligibility: This program is open to full-time students at colleges and universities in the United States. Nominees for the newspaper awards must be staff members of the college newspaper that publishes at least weekly during the regular school year. Nominees for the broadcast awards must work at a student-operated college radio or television station licensed for broadcast by the Federal Communications Commission or available campus- or community-wide via a closed circuit system. A major in journalism or communications is not required. Students must be nominated by their newspaper or broadcast station. The letter of nomination must indicate how the student has been "most valuable" to the newspaper or station.

Financial data: Winners receive a $5,000 scholarship and an all-expenses paid trip to the annual national convention of College Media Advisers. Their newspaper or broadcast station also receive a matching $5,000 grant.

Duration: The competition is held annually.

Additional information: These awards were first presented in 2000. The program is co-sponsored by College Media Advisers.

Number awarded: 10 each year: 5 newspaper staff members and 5 broadcast station staff members.

Deadline: November of each year.

1636
SEATTLE PROFESSIONAL CHAPTER SCHOLARSHIPS

Association for Women in Communications-Seattle Professional Professional Chapter
Attn: Scholarship Chair
1412 S.W. 102nd Street, Suite 224
Seattle, WA 98146
Phone: (206) 298-4966   Fax: (206) 285-5220
E-mail: laurelr@nwfcu.com
Web Site: www.seattleawc.org

Summary: To provide financial assistance to upper-division and graduate students in Washington who are preparing for a career in communications.

Eligibility: To be eligible, students must meet the following qualifications: be a Washington state resident; be a registered student at a Washington state 4-year college (or be a sophomore at a community or 2-year college during the application period); be an entering junior, senior, or graduate student; and be accepted in, or applying to, a communications program (print and broadcast journalism, television and radio production, film, advertising, public relations, marketing, graphic design, multimedia design, photography or technical communication). Selection is based on demonstrated excellence in communications; contributions made to communications on campus and in the community; scholastic achievement; financial need; and writing samples from journalism, advertising, public relations, or broadcasting.

Financial data: The stipend is $1,500. Funds are paid directly to the recipient's school and must be used for tuition and fees.

Duration: 1 year.

Number awarded: 2 each year.

Deadline: February of each year.

1637
SEHAR SALEHA AHMAD MEMORIAL SCHOLARSHIP

Oregon Student Assistance Commission
Attn: Private Awards Grant Department
1500 Valley River Drive, Suite 100
Eugene, OR 97401-2146
Phone: (541) 687-7395   (800) 452-8807, ext. 7395
Fax: (541) 687-7419   E-mail: awardinfo@mercury.osac.state.or.us
Web Site: www.osac.state.or.us

Summary: To provide financial assistance to high school seniors in Oregon who are interested in studying English in college.

Eligibility: This program is open to Oregon graduating high school seniors who have a grade point average of 3.5 or higher. Preference is given to women.

Financial data: Scholarship amounts vary, depending upon the needs of the recipient.

Duration: 1 year; may be renewed if the recipient shows satisfactory academic progress and continued financial need.

Number awarded: Varies each year.

Deadline: February of each year.

1638
SENIOR HIGH COMMUNICATION CONTEST

American Automobile Association
Attn: Poster Program Headquarters
1000 AAA Drive
Heathrow, FL 32746-5063
Phone: (407) 444-7916   Fax: (407) 444-7956
Web Site: www.aaa.com

Summary: To recognize and reward outstanding high school students in a highway safety competition.

Eligibility: This program is open to 1) students enrolled in a public, parochial, or private secondary school in the United States or Canada; and 2) senior high students affiliated with a national youth organization (such as the Boys and Girls Clubs of America). Entries are invited in 3 subject areas: DUI prevention, safe driving practices, and motor vehicle occupant protection. For each of those subject areas, students may enter in 1 of 3 formats: graphic arts (a poster, either hand-drawn or computer-generated, or a cartoon), written (either an editorial up to 500 words or the text of a brochure), or audiovisual (either a video cassette or audio recording, both from 30 seconds to 2 minutes in documentary, drama, music, or public service announcement format). All entries are judged on originality and the relationship of the message to traffic safety. In addition, art/design and its execution are considered for poster, brochure, and cartoon entries; visual impact is considered for poster designs and brochures; content, organization, persuasive effect, and grammar are considered for editorials and brochures; and content, organization, presentation, and use of technology are considered for video cassettes and audio recordings. All entries must be the student's exclusive work in idea, design, and execution, although they must be completed under supervision of an authorized instructor. Entries must be addressed to the local AAA club and then forwarded to the national office for the national judging.

Financial data: In each of the subject areas for each medium (graphic arts, written, and audio-visual), first-place awards are $150 U.S. savings bonds, second-place awards are $125 bonds, and third-place awards are $100 bonds. The grand award winner for each medium also receives a $5,000 scholarship or bond. In addition, each judge may

award a $50 savings bond to any non-winning entry as special recognition.

Duration: The competition is held annually.

Additional information: For more than 50 years, senior high school students participated, along with elementary and junior high school students, in the National School Traffic Safety Poster Program. Starting in the 1996-97 school year, the program for senior high school students was expanded so they could submit entries in the graphic arts, written, or audiovisual media formats. Grand award winners must start postsecondary education within 1 year of graduating from high school if they wish to receive the award as a scholarship. They may elect to receive a savings bond in lieu of the scholarship.

Number awarded: Each year, 9 first-place awards, 9 second-place awards, and 9 third-place awards are presented (1 in each of the subject areas for each medium). In addition, 3 grand awards (1 for each medium) and up to 15 special recognition awards are presented each year.

Deadline: January of each year.

1639
SENTRY INSURANCE FOUNDATION SCHOLARSHIP

Wisconsin Foundation for Independent Colleges, Inc.
735 North Water Street, Suite 800
Milwaukee, WI 53202-4100
Phone: (414) 273-5980   Fax: (414) 273-5995
E-mail: wfic@execpc.com   Web Site: www.wficweb.org

Summary: To provide financial assistance to freshmen majoring in selected fields at private colleges in Wisconsin.

Eligibility: This program is open to freshmen at the 21 independent colleges or universities in Wisconsin. Applicants must be majoring in 1 of the following fields: business, economics, mathematics, management information systems, industrial design, communication design, or interior architecture and design. They must have earned at least a 3.3 grade point average.

Financial data: The stipend is $1,000.

Duration: 1 year.

Additional information: The participating schools are Alverno College, Beloit College, Cardinal Stritch University, Carroll College, Carthage College, Concordia University of Wisconsin, Edgewood College, Lakeland College, Lawrence University, Marian College, Marquette University, Milwaukee Institute of Art & Design, Milwaukee School of Engineering, Mount Mary College, Northland College, Ripon College, St. Norbert College, Silver Lake College, Viterbo University, and Wisconsin Lutheran College.

Number awarded: 21 each year: 1 at each of the participating schools.

1640
SEVENTEEN MAGAZINE ANNUAL FICTION CONTEST

Seventeen Magazine
850 Third Avenue
New York, NY 10022-6258
Phone: (212) 407-9700   Fax: (212) 935-4237
Web Site: www.seventeen.com/other/1048.html

Summary: To recognize and reward teenagers who write fiction that would interest the readers of *Seventeen*.

Eligibility: Contestants must be between 13 and 21 years of age. Their fiction must not have been published previously in any form (except in school publications). Manuscripts must be typed and be no more than 4,000 words (16 pages). Contestants may submit as many stories as they like.

Financial data: First prize is $1,000; second prize is $500; third prize is $250; and honorable mentions are $50 each.

Duration: The competition is held annually.

Additional information: Past winners of this competition include Sylvia Plath, Joyce Carol Oates, and Lorrie Moore.

Number awarded: 8 each year: 1 first prize, 1 second prize, 1 third prize, and 5 honorable mentions.

Deadline: April of each year.

1641
SHANE MEDIA SCHOLARSHIP

Broadcast Education Association
Attn: Scholarships
1771 N Street, N.W.
Washington, DC 20036-2891
Phone: (202) 429-5354   E-mail: bea@nab.org
Web Site: www.beaweb.org

Summary: To provide financial assistance to upper-division and graduate students who are interested in preparing for a career in radio.

Eligibility: This program is open to juniors, seniors, and graduate students enrolled full time at a college or university where at least 1 department is an institutional member of the Broadcast Education Association (BEA). Applicants must be studying for a career in radio. Selection is based on evidence that the applicant possesses high integrity, superior academic ability, potential to be an outstanding electronic media professional, and a sense of personal and professional responsibility.

Financial data: The stipend is $3,000.

Duration: 1 year; may not be renewed.

Additional information: Information is also available from Peter B. Orlik, Central Michigan University, 344 Moore Hall, Mt. Pleasant, MI 48859, (517) 774-7279. This program is sponsored by Shane Media Services of Houston, Texas, and administered by the BEA.

Number awarded: 1 each year.

Deadline: September of each year.

1642
SHIRLEY A. DREYER MEMORIAL ENDOWMENT SCHOLARSHIP

Epsilon Sigma Alpha
Attn: ESA Foundation Assistant Scholarship Director
P.O. Box 270517
Fort Collins, CO 80527
Phone: (970) 223-2824   Fax: (970) 223-4456
Web Site: www.esaintl.com/esaf

Summary: To provide financial assistance to residents of North Carolina interested in studying interior design in college.

Eligibility: This program is open to residents of North Carolina who are either 1) graduating high school seniors in the top 25 percent of their class or with minimum scores of 20 on the ACT or 950 on the SAT, or 2) students already enrolled in college with a grade point average of 3.0 or higher. Students enrolled for training in a technical school or returning to school after an absence are also eligible. Applicants must be interested in majoring in interior design. Selection is based on character, scholastic ability, leadership and ability skills, and financial need.

Financial data: The stipend is $1,500.

Duration: 1 year; may be renewed.

Additional information: Epsilon Sigma Alpha (ESA) is a women's service organization, but scholarships are available to both men and women. Information is also available from Verneene Forssberg, 403 South High, Pratt, KS 67124, (316) 672-3636, Fax: (316) 672-3688, E-mail: vernf@genmail.pcc.cc.ks.us. Completed applications must be submitted to the ESA State Counselor who verifies the information before forwarding them to the scholarship director.

Number awarded: 1 each year.

Deadline: January of each year.

1643
SHORT FILM AND VIDEO COMPETITION

USA Film Festival
6116 North Central Expressway, Suite 105
Dallas, TX 75206
Phone: (214) 821-6300
Web Site: www.usafilmfestival.com

Summary: To recognize and reward outstanding short films and videos.

Eligibility: Entries may be submitted by either professional, nonprofessional, or student film/videomakers in 16mm film, 35mm film, 3/4 inch videocassettes, or conventional VHS videocassettes. The 4 categories are fiction (for narrative works, dramatized events, and adaptations of literary or dramatic works), nonfiction (for documentaries or portraits of actual persons or events), animation (of graphics or 3-dimensional objects), and experimental (for works that explore personal experience of film and video forms in innovative ways). The Charles Samu Family Award is presented to the work that best represents a standard of excellence for audiences of all ages. The G. William Jones Texas Award is presented to a work by a Texas resident. The Student Award is presented to the outstanding work by a student in any category. The Music Video/Film Award is presented to the outstanding entry in that genre. Special Jury Awards are presented to outstanding entries in any category.

Financial data: The first-prize winner in each category receives $1,000. In addition, the Charles Samu Family Award is $500, the G. William Jones Texas Award is $500, the Student Award is $500, the Music Video/Film Award is $500, and the Special Jury Awards are $500.

Duration: The competition is held annually, in April.
Additional information: There is an entry fee of $40 for early submissions prior to the end of January, or $50 for regular submissions.
Deadline: February of each year.

1644
SI TV LATINO PLAYWRITING AWARD

John F. Kennedy Center for the Performing Arts
Education Department
Attn: Kennedy Center American College Theater Festival
2700 F Street, N.W.
Washington, DC 20566
Phone: (202) 416-8857   Fax: (202) 416-8802
E-mail: skshaffer@kennedy-center.org
Web Site: kennedy-center.org/education/actf/actfsitv.html
Summary: To recognize and reward outstanding plays by Latino playwrights.
Eligibility: Latino students at any accredited junior or senior college in the United States are eligible to compete, provided their college agrees to participate in the Kennedy Center American College Theater Festival (KCACTF). Undergraduate students must be carrying a minimum of 6 semester hours, graduate students a minimum of 3 semester hours, and continuing part-time students must be enrolled in a regular degree or certificate program. This award is presented to the best student-written play by a Latino.
Financial data: The prize is $2,500. The winner also receives an internship to a prestigious playwriting retreat program. Dramatic Publishing Company presents the winning playwright with an offer of a contract to publish, license, and market the winning play. A grant of $500 is made to the theater department of the college or university producing the award-winning play.
Duration: The award is presented annually.
Additional information: This award, first presented in 2000, is supported by SNumber awarded: 1 each year.
Deadline: November of each year.

1645
SIGMA ALPHA IOTA UNDERGRADUATE PERFORMANCE SCHOLARSHIPS

Sigma Alpha Iota Philanthropies, Inc.
34 Wall Street, Suite 515
Asheville, NC 28801-2710
Phone: (828) 251-0606   Fax: (828) 251-0644
Web Site: www.sai-national.org/phil/philschs.html
Summary: To recognize and reward outstanding performances in vocal and instrumental categories by undergraduate members of Sigma Alpha Iota (an organization of women musicians).
Eligibility: Undergraduate student members of the organization may enter this competition if they are vocalists or instrumentalists. Entrants must be rising seniors.
Financial data: The awards are $1,500.
Duration: The competition is held triennially.
Additional information: This program includes the Blanche Z. Hoffman Vocal Scholarship. There is a $20 nonrefundable application fee.
Number awarded: 4 every 3 years: 2 for vocalists and 2 for instrumentalists.
Deadline: April of the year of the awards (2003, 2006, etc.).

1646
SIGNET CLASSIC SCHOLARSHIP ESSAY CONTEST

Penguin Putnam Inc.
Attn: Signet Classic
375 Hudson Street
New York, NY 10014
Phone: (212) 366-2000
Web Site: www.penguinputnam.com/scessay
Summary: To recognize and reward the best essays written by high school students on topics that relate to 1 of the books in the Signet Classic series (published by Penguin Putnam, Inc.).
Eligibility: English teachers are invited to submit essays written by high school juniors and seniors (1 each per school) on topics that change annually but relates to the books published in the Signet Classic series. Recently, the essay contest focused on *Pride and Prejudice* by Jane Austen. Essays must be between 2 and 3 pages. Submissions are judged on style, content, grammar, and originality. Judges look for clear, concise writing that is articulate, logically organized, and well supported.

Financial data: The grand-prize winners receive a $1,000 scholarship and a Signet Classic library for their school (valued at $1,700).
Duration: The competition is held annually.
Additional information: This competition started in 1996.
Number awarded: 5 grand-prize winners each year.
Deadline: April of each year.

1647
SOCIETY OF THE CINCINNATI IN THE STATE OF VIRGINIA SCHOLARSHIP

Society of the Cincinnati in the State of Virginia
P.O. Box 571
Richmond, VA 23218
Summary: To recognize and reward outstanding essays written by high school seniors in Virginia on a topic related to early American history.
Eligibility: High school seniors in public or private schools in Virginia are invited to enter this competition. They must write an essay on a given topic (changes annually) related to early American history.
Financial data: The scholarships awarded must be applied to college tuition.
Duration: These 1-time scholarships are offered annually.
Additional information: Information is also available from Jack Blackwell, 327 Albemarle Avenue, Richmond, VA 23226. Recipients must attend a college or university in Virginia.
Deadline: February of each year.

1648
SOM BACHELOR OF ARCHITECTURE TRAVELING FELLOWSHIP

Skidmore, Owings & Merrill Foundation
224 South Michigan Avenue, Suite 1000
Chicago, IL 60604
Phone: (312) 427-4202   Fax: (312) 360-4548
E-mail: somfoundation@som.com
Web Site: www.som.com/html/som_foundation.html
Summary: To provide financial assistance to architecture students who wish to travel in the United States or abroad.
Eligibility: Applicants may be citizens of any country but must be graduating with a bachelor of architecture degree from an accredited (4+2 or 5-year) undergraduate professional degree program in the United States. Candidates must be chosen by the school they attend and submit a portfolio of their work. A jury consisting of educators, professional architects, architecture critics, and other professionals selects 2 finalists and conducts interviews to choose the recipient. Selection is based on the evaluation of the portfolios and the candidates' proposed travel/study plans.
Financial data: The stipend is $10,000.
Additional information: This award is offered through the Skidmore, Owings & Merrill (SOM) Architecture Traveling Fellowship Program. Recipients may travel to any country. In the event the recipient does not complete his/her studies and degree, the fellowship is forfeited back to the SOM Foundation.
Number awarded: 1 each year.

1649
SONS OF ITALY NATIONAL LEADERSHIP GRANT COMPETITION

Order Sons of Italy in America
Attn: Sons of Italy Foundation
219 E Street, N.E.
Washington, DC 20002
Phone: (202) 547-5106   Fax: (202) 546-8168
E-mail: sif@osia.org
Web Site: www.osia.org
Summary: To provide financial assistance for postsecondary education to students who write about the Italian American experience in the United States.
Eligibility: Eligible are U.S. citizens of Italian descent who are enrolled as full-time students in an undergraduate or graduate program at an accredited 4-year college or university. Both high school seniors and students already enrolled in college are eligible for the undergraduate awards. Applications must be accompanied by essays, from 500 to 750 words in length, on the principal contribution of Italian Americans to the development of U.S. culture and society. These merit-based awards are presented to students who have demonstrated exceptional leadership qualities and distinguished scholastic abilities.
Financial data: Awards range from $1,000 to $2,000.
Duration: 1 year; may not be renewed.

Additional information: Applications must be accompanied by a $25 processing fee.

Number awarded: Varies each year.

Deadline: February of each year.

1650
STANFIELD AND D'ORLANDO ART SCHOLARSHIP

Unitarian Universalist Association
Attn: Department of Communications
25 Beacon Street
Boston, MA 02108-2800
Phone: (617) 948-6516   Fax: (617) 367-3237
E-mail: stanfield@uua.org
Web Site: www.uua.org/info/scholarships.html

Summary: To provide financial assistance for the study of art to Unitarian Universalists.

Eligibility: This program is open to Unitarian Universalist students entering or continuing undergraduate or graduate study. Applicants should be studying or planning to study painting, drawing, photography, and/or sculpture; art history, art therapy, film, and performing arts majors are not eligible. Candidates must submit 6 to 10 samples of their work on 35mm slides. Selection is based on financial need and academic performance.

Financial data: The amount of the award depends on the need of the recipient and the availability of funds.

Duration: 1 year; recipients may reapply.

Additional information: This award, established in 1979, is funded by trusts established by Mrs. Marion Barr Stanfield and Ms. Pauly D'Orlando.

Number awarded: 1 each year.

Deadline: February of each year.

1651
STILLMAN-KELLEY AWARDS

National Federation of Music Clubs
1336 North Delaware Street
Indianapolis, IN 46202-2481
Phone: (317) 638-4003   Fax: (317) 638-0503
E-mail: info@nfmc-music.org
Web Site: www.nfmc-music.org/annual_junior.htm

Summary: To recognize and reward outstanding young musicians who are members of the National Federation of Music Clubs (NFMC).

Eligibility: Eligible are instrumentalists who are younger than 17 years of age, U.S. citizens, and junior members of the federation. Awards are rotated by NFMC region, with the central in 2003, western in 2004, northwestern in 2005, and southeastern in 2006.

Financial data: Awards, to be used for further study, are $1,000 for first place and $500 for second place.

Additional information: Information on these awards is also available from Mr. Stillman Kelly, 415 Sussex Circle, Vacaville, CA 95687; information on all federation scholarships is available from Chair, Competitions and Awards Board, Mrs. Lamoine M. Hall, Jr., 4137 Whitfield Avenue, Fort Worth, TX 76109-5432.

Number awarded: 2 each year.

Deadline: January of each year.

1652
STUDENT ACADEMY AWARDS

Academy of Motion Picture Arts and Sciences
Attn: Academy Foundation
8949 Wilshire Boulevard
Beverly Hills, CA 90211-1972
Phone: (310) 247-3000, ext. 130   Fax: (310) 859-9619
E-mail: rmiller@oscars.org   Web Site: www3.oscars.org/saa

Summary: To support and encourage college filmmakers with no previous professional experience.

Eligibility: Films must have been completed within the preceding year as part of the curricular structure of an accredited U.S. college, university, film school, or art school. Award categories are alternative, animation, narrative, and documentary. Prints must be composite in 16mm gauge or larger, with optical or magnetic sound, and no longer than 60 minutes. Judging is based on resourcefulness, originality, entertainment, and production quality.

Financial data: Gold, silver, and bronze awards in each category are $5,000, $3,000, and $2,000, respectively.

Additional information: All regional finalist films in the narrative category are also automatically eligible for the Directors Guild of America Student Film Award; the winner receives a $1,000 cash prize, a directing internship of up to 13 weeks on a feature motion picture, a stipend for living expenses, and a travel allowance. All national award-winning films in the alternative, documentary, and narrative categories are also automatically eligible for the American Society of Cinematographers Student Award; the winner receives a $1,000 cash prize and is invited to Los Angeles to participate in the activities of the awards week. The academy reserves the right to disqualify from competition any film in which professional camera persons, directors, writers, or editors have exercised undue influence.

Number awarded: Up to 12 awards may be presented each year: 3 in each of the 4 categories.

Deadline: March of each year.

1653
STUDENT COMPETITION IN LANDSCAPE ARCHITECTURE FOR AGGREGATE OPERATIONS

National Stone, Sand and Gravel Association
Attn: Director of Communications
2101 Wilson Boulevard, Suite 100
Arlington, VA 22201-3062
Phone: (703) 525-8788   (800) 342-1415
Fax: (703) 525-7782   E-mail: info@nssga.org
Web Site: www.nssag.org/careers/index.html

Summary: To encourage beautification and reclamation activities at quarries by offering prizes to students in landscape architecture.

Eligibility: Eligible to enter the competition are students enrolled at universities in the United States and Canada in their first professional landscape architecture degree program or their first professional landscape architecture certificate program. Competitors must prepare plans for quarry operations based on an active or proposed commercial aggregates operation. Sites that are abandoned or where operations have been completed are not eligible as the basis for entries. Selection is based on 1) a problem statement; 2) identification of siting and design factors; 3) methodology (including site and operations analysis, improvement and beautification plan, and final use and reclamation plan); 4) a narrative description of the project; and 5) cost analysis.

Financial data: Students receive prizes of $2,000 for first place, $1,000 for second place, and $600 for third place. In addition, the departments of landscape architecture at the schools in which the students are enrolled receive $1,400, $600, and $400 for the respective prize winners.

Additional information: The National Stone, Sand and Gravel Association (NSSGA) sponsors this annual competition in cooperation with the American Society of Landscape Architects (ASLA). It began in 1975 to assist quarry owners and operators with ideas and incentives that would encourage beautification and reclamation activities.

Number awarded: 3 each year.

Deadline: Preliminary entry forms must be submitted by April of each year; final entry forms are due in May.

1654
STUDENT CORRUGATED PACKAGING DESIGN COMPETITION

Association of Independent Corrugated Converters
Attn: AICC Student Design Competition
113 South West Street, Third Floor
Alexandria, VA 22314
Phone: (703) 836-2422   (877) 836-2422
E-mail: Mhughes@aiccbox.org
Web Site: www.aiccbox.org/student/Student_info.asp

Summary: To recognize and reward college students who submit outstanding corrugated packaging designs.

Eligibility: This competition is open to undergraduate students enrolled in packaging courses at colleges, universities, and/or technical schools in Canada and the United States. Individual and team entries are accepted. Applicants construct, develop, and/or manufacture packaging designs using corrugated as the primary medium. Entries are accepted in 4 categories: design to a problem, design to an existing die, open design, and corrugated as art. In the selection process, heavy emphasis is placed on a written essay describing the project. The first- and second-place winners in the categories of design to a problem and open design compete in a "Show, Tell-and Sell" program in which they make a presentation as they would to a prospective client in the real world corrugated packaging industry.

Financial data: In each of the categories, first place is $500, second $250, and third $100. The first-place winners in each category also receive all-expenses paid trips to the sponsor's annual fall meeting and trade fair in September. In the "Show, Tell-and Sell" program, first place is $2,500, second place is $750, third place is $500, and fourth place is $250. The first-place winner's school receives a $5,000 grant.
Duration: The competition is held annually.
Additional information: The "Show, Tell-and Sell" program is produced later in the fall at television studios at Michigan State University and broadcast live to packaging schools throughout North America. The 4 participating student teams make their presentations from their home campuses. That portion of the competition is sponsored by the International Corrugated Packaging Foundation.
Number awarded: 12 winners (3 in each category) are selected in the first level of competition; 4 additional prizes are awarded for the "Show, Tell-and Sell" program.
Deadline: July of each year.

1655
STUDENT JOURNALIST IMPACT AWARD

Journalism Education Association
c/o Kansas State University
103 Kedzie Hall
Manhattan, KS 66506-1505
Phone: (785) 532-7822   Fax: (785) 532-5484
E-mail: jea@spub.ksu.edu
Web Site: www.jea.org
Summary: To recognize and reward high school students who, through the practice of journalism, have made a significant difference in the lives of others.
Eligibility: This program was established to recognize secondary school students (or teams of students who worked on the same entry) who, through the study and practice of journalism, have made a significant difference in their own life, the lives of others, or the students' school and/or community. The entry should contain: 1) the article, series of articles, or mass communication media (radio, broadcast, video, etc.) that made the impact; 2) a narrative of at least 250 words explaining why the piece was produced and how the entry impacted the individual, others, the school, and/or community; and 3) 3 letters describing the impact of the work; the impact of the work and not the author(s) should be the focus. The entry must be original student work and must have been published within 2 years preceding the deadline. The applicant's teacher/advisor must be a member of the Journalism Education Association.
Financial data: The award is $1,000.
Duration: The competition is held annually.
Additional information: This program, established in 1994, is a collaborative endeavor of the Journalism Education Association and the Kalos Kagathos Foundation. By entering this competition, students give the Journalism Education Association permission to reproduce their work.
Number awarded: 1 each year.
Deadline: February of each year.

1656
STUDENT RETAIL DESIGN COMPETITION

Institute of Store Planners
Attn: International Executive Office
25 North Broadway
Tarrytown, NY 10591
Phone: (914) 332-1806   Fax: (914) 332-1541
Web Site: www.ispo.org
Summary: To recognize and reward outstanding student store designers.
Eligibility: This competition is open to students presently enrolled in a recognized college-level architectural, interior design, or environmental design program. Each year, the sponsor defines a retail design problem, and students compete by submitting a fixture plan, storefront elevation, interior elevations, color and materials presentation, reflected ceiling plan, and perspectives.
Financial data: First prize is $1,000, second prize is $500, and third prize is $300. In addition, the school of the first-place winner receives $1,000.
Duration: The competition is held annually.
Additional information: Information is also available from Jeff Matthews, E-mail: j000jlm@fds.com, from Steven Brunner, E-mail: stevenbrunner@mindspring.com, and from Melony Babaloa, c/o Miller Zell Design Center, 4715 Frederick Drive S.W., Atlanta, GA 30336. The entry fee is $25.
Number awarded: 3 winners each year.
Deadline: April of each year.

1657
TADEUSZ SENDZIMIR FUND SCHOLARSHIPS

Waterbury Foundation
81 West Main Street, Fourth Floor
Waterbury, CT 06702-1216
Phone: (203) 753-1315   Fax: (203) 756-3054
E-mail: info@waterburyfoundation.org
Web Site: www.waterburyfoundation.org
Summary: To provide financial assistance to Connecticut residents who are interested in studying Polish language or culture in the United States or in Poland.
Eligibility: Applicants must be Connecticut residents currently enrolled or planning to enroll at a 4-year college or university. They must be planning to study Polish language or culture on the undergraduate or graduate school level in the United States or Poland. Preference is given to applicants of Polish descent. Students may also apply to attend a summer school in Poland. Scholarships are awarded on a competitive basis, with consideration given to academic record, extracurricular activities, work experience, financial need, and an essay.
Financial data: Scholarship awards are generally in the $400 to $1,000 range. Funds are paid directly to the recipient's school.
Duration: 1 year or 1 summer; recipients may reapply, provided they maintain at least a 2.5 grade point average.
Additional information: Recipients may attend an accredited college or university in the United States or in Poland.
Number awarded: Varies each year.
Deadline: April of each year.

1658
TERRY WALKER SCHOLARSHIP

Classical Association of the Empire State
P.O. Box 12722
Albany, NY 12212
Web Site: wwww.syr.edu/~dhmills/caes/grant.htm
Summary: To provide financial assistance to students from New York who are preparing to teach Latin in school.
Eligibility: Eligible to apply for this scholarship are currently-enrolled college students who graduated from a high school in New York and/or are currently attending college in New York. Applicants must have completed at least the sophomore year in college. Preference is given to students who are preparing to teach Latin on the elementary or secondary school level.
Financial data: The stipend is $2,000.
Duration: 1 year; recipients may reapply.
Number awarded: 1 each year.
Deadline: March of each year.

1659
TEXACO-SPHINX COMPETITION

Concert Competitions and Musical Development, Inc.
Attn: Artistic Director
3319 Greenfield Road, Suite 705
Dearborn, MI 48120-1212
Phone: (313) 336-9809   E-mail: info@sphinxcompetition.org
Web Site: www.sphinxcompetition.org
Summary: To recognize and reward outstanding junior high, high school, and college-age Black and Latino string instrumentalists.
Eligibility: This competition is open to Black and Latino instrumentalists in 2 divisions: junior, for participants who are younger than 18 years of age, and senior, for participants who are at least 18 but younger than 27 years of age. All entrants must be current U.S. residents who can compete in the instrumental categories of violin, viola, cello, and double bass. Along with their applications, they must submit a preliminary audition tape that includes all of the required preliminary repertoire for their instrument category. Based on those tapes, semifinalists are invited to participate in competitions held at sites in Detroit and Ann Arbor, Michigan.
Financial data: In the senior division, the first-place winner receives a $10,000 cash prize, solo appearances with major orchestras, and a performance with the Sphinx Symphony; the second-place winner receives a $5,000 cash prize and a performance with the Sphinx Symphony; the third-place winner receives a $3,500 cash prize and a performance with the Sphinx Symphony. In the junior division, the first-place winner receives a $5,000 cash prize and 2 performances with the Sphinx Symphony; the second-place winner receives a $3,500 cash prize and a performance with the Sphinx Symphony; the third-place winner receives

a $2,000 cash prize and a performance with the Sphinx Symphony. All semifinalists receive scholarships to attend a summer program at Aspen, Blossom, BU Tanglewood, DSO Summer Institute, Encore, Interlochen, Meadowmount, Musicorda, National Repertory Orchestra, National Symphony Summer Institute, National Orchestral Institute, or the Walnut Hill School.
Duration: The competition is held annually.
Additional information: The sponsoring organization was incorporated in 1996 to hold this competition, first conducted in 1998. The Sphinx Symphony is an all African American and Latino orchestra that performs at Orchestra Hall in Detroit. Applications must be accompanied by a $35 fee.
Number awarded: 18 semifinalists (from both divisions and all instrumental categories) are selected each year. Of those, 3 junior and 3 senior competitors win cash prizes.
Deadline: November of each year.

1660
TEXAS BROADCAST EDUCATION FOUNDATION SCHOLARSHIPS

Texas Broadcast Education Foundation
c/o Texas Association of Broadcasters
502 East 11th Street, Suite 200
Austin, TX 78701-2619
Phone: (512) 322-9944   Fax: (512) 322-0522
E-mail: tab@tab.org
Web Site: www.tab.org/scholarships.html
Summary: To provide financial assistance to undergraduates in Texas who are interested in pursuing a career in broadcasting.
Eligibility: This program is open to students enrolled in a fully-accredited program of instruction that emphasizes radio or television broadcasting or communications at a college that is a member of Texas Association of Broadcast Educators. Applicants must have at least a 2.5 grade point average and submit a letter from the department head certifying that they have a reasonable chance of successfully completing the course of instruction. Selection is based on depth of thought, clarity of expression, commitment to broadcasting, extracurricular activities, community involvement, and financial need. All students are encouraged to apply; special consideration is given to students from disadvantaged ethnic or economic backgrounds.
Financial data: The stipend is $2,000.
Duration: 1 year.
Additional information: Awards include the A.H. Belo Corporation Scholarship for a junior or senior at a 4-year college, the Bonner McLane Scholarship for a junior or senior at a 4-year college, the Tom Reiff Scholarship for a rising junior or senior at a 4-year college, an unnamed scholarship for a freshman or sophomore at a 4-year college, and another unnamed scholarship for a student at a 2-year college or technical school.
Number awarded: 8 each year.
Deadline: May of each year.

1661
TEXAS CHORAL DIRECTORS ASSOCIATION STUDENT SCHOLARSHIPS

Texas Choral Directors Association
404 West 30th Street
P.O. Box 6472
Austin, TX 78762
Phone: (512) 474-2801   Fax: (512) 474-7873
E-mail: tcda@ensemble.org
Web Site: www.ensemble.org/tcda/scholarship.htm
Summary: To provide financial assistance to upper-division students in Texas who are working on a degree in choral music or church music.
Eligibility: Eligible to apply for this scholarship are students enrolled full time in a Texas college or university who have completed at least 60 hours, have at least a 3.0 grade point average, and are enrolled in a program of study that will lead to a degree in elementary or secondary choral music or church music. Selection is based on musical contributions and accomplishments, potential for success in the choral music profession, and personal qualifications.
Financial data: The stipend is $1,000.
Duration: 1 year.
Additional information: This program includes the TCDA/B.R. (Bev) Henson Student Scholarship and the TCDA/Past Presidents Student Scholarship.
Number awarded: 3 each year.
Deadline: May of each year.

1662
TEXAS HISTORY ESSAY CONTEST

Sons of the Republic of Texas
Attn: Administrative Assistant
1717 Eighth Street
Bay City, TX 77414
Phone: (979) 245-6644   E-mail: srttexas@srttexas.org
Web Site: www.srttexas.org
Summary: To recognize and reward high school seniors who write outstanding essays on the history of Texas.
Eligibility: This program is open to graduating seniors in all high schools in Texas. Applicants submit an essay on a topic that changes annually but relates to the history of Texas; a recent topic was "Filibustering in Texas, 1800 to 1821." Essays must be between 1,500 and 2,000 words in length and conform to standard academic style. Only 1 essay may be submitted from each high school.
Financial data: First prize is $3,000, second $2,000, and third $1,000. Funds are paid to the colleges the winners plan to attend. If they do not plan to attend college, they receive the awards directly.
Duration: The prizes are awarded annually.
Number awarded: 3 each year.
Deadline: February of each year.

1663
THELMA A. ROBINSON AWARD IN BALLET

National Federation of Music Clubs
1336 North Delaware Street
Indianapolis, IN 46202-2481
Phone: (317) 638-4003   Fax: (317) 638-0503
E-mail: info@nfmc-music.org Web Site: www.nfmc-music.org/BienJuniorSpecial.htm
Summary: To recognize and reward outstanding young dancers who are members of the National Federation of Music Clubs.
Eligibility: Eligible are ballet dancers who are between 13 and 17 years of age, U.S. citizens, and members of the federation.
Financial data: The award is $2,000.
Additional information: Information on these awards is also available from Mrs. Lars Ekwurzel, 1648 S.E. Sixth Street, Deerfield Beach, FL 33441-4997; information on all federation scholarships is available from Chair, Competitions and Awards Board, Mrs. Lamoine M. Hall, Jr., 4137 Whitfield Avenue, Fort Worth, TX 76109-5432.
Number awarded: 1 every other year.
Deadline: September of even-numbered years for competition in the following year.

1664
THREAD COMMITTEE EXCELLENCE IN MANUFACTURING SCHOLARSHIP

American Textile Manufacturers Institute
Attn: Thread Committee
1130 Connecticut Avenue, N.W., Suite 1200
Washington, DC 20036-3954
Web Site: www.atmi.org/pubs.tcschool.asp
Summary: To provide financial assistance to high school seniors interested in majoring in a textile science-related program at selected schools.
Eligibility: Eligible to be nominated for this program are high school seniors interested in majoring in textile science-related programs at Auburn University, Clemson University, Georgia Institute of Technology, North Carolina State University, Philadelphia College of Textiles, or the University of Massachusetts. Nominees must have at least a 3.0 grade point average in high school and be accepted to 1 of the participating schools on a non-provisional basis.
Financial data: The stipend is $2,500 per year.
Duration: Up to 4 years.
Additional information: An application can also be requested using the institute's fax on demand service: (202) 862-0572 (request document number 2555).

1665
TIMOTHY BIGELOW AND PALMER W. BIGELOW, JR. SCHOLARSHIPS

Horticultural Research Institute
c/o American Nursery & Landscape Association
1250 I Street, N.W., Suite 500
Washington, DC 20005-3922
Phone: (202) 789-2900   Fax: (202) 789-1893
E-mail: hriresearch@anla.org

Web Site: www.anla.org/research/Scholarships/index.htm

Summary: To provide financial support to residents of New England for undergraduate or graduate study in landscape architecture or horticulture.

Eligibility: This program is open to full-time students enrolled in an accredited landscape or horticulture program in 1) the final year of a 2-year curriculum, 2) the third year of a 4-year curriculum, or 3) a graduate program. Applicants must have a minimum grade point average of 2.25 as undergraduates or 3.0 as graduate students. They must be a resident of 1 of the 6 New England states, although attendance at an institution within those states is not required. Preference is given to applicants who plan to work in an aspect of the nursery industry, including a business of their own, and to applicants who demonstrate financial need.

Financial data: The stipend is $2,500.

Duration: 1 year; nonrenewable.

Additional information: This program was created in 1988.

Number awarded: 3 each year.

Deadline: May of each year.

1666
TLMI SCHOLARSHIP PROGRAM

Tag and Label Manufacturer Institute, Inc.
40 Shurman Boulevard, Suite 295
Naperville, IL 60563
Phone: (630) 357-9222   (800) 533-8564
Fax: (630) 357-0192

Summary: To provide financial assistance to third- and fourth-year college students who are preparing for a career in the tag and label manufacturing industry.

Eligibility: This program is open to juniors and seniors who are attending school on a full-time basis and preparing for a career in the tag and label manufacturing industry (students should apply as sophomores). This includes students majoring in management, production, graphic arts, sales and marketing, and graphic design. Applicants must have a grade point average of 3.0 or higher. They must submit references from 3 persons who are not members of their families and a 1-page personal statement describing their financial circumstances, career and/or educational goals, employment experience, and reasons why they should be selected for the award. A personal interview may be required. Selection is based on academic achievement, a demonstrated interest in the industry, a statement of goals, and the interview.

Financial data: The stipend is $5,000. Funds are sent to the recipient's school and paid in 2 equal installments.

Duration: 1 year; may be renewed for 1 additional year, provided the recipient maintains a 3.0 grade point average.

Additional information: In addition the scholarships, internships may be offered to applicants.

Number awarded: 6 each year.

Deadline: March of each year.

1667
TOCA PUBLISHERS SCHOLARSHIP PROGRAM

Turf and Ornamental Communicators Association
120 West Main Street, Suite 200
P.O. Box 156
New Prague, MN 56071
Phone: (612) 758-6340

Summary: To provide financial assistance to undergraduate students preparing for a career in green industry communications.

Eligibility: To qualify, students must be majoring or minoring in technical communications or in a green industry-related field (e.g., horticulture, plant sciences, botany, agronomy, plant pathology). Applicants must demonstrate an interest in using this course of study in the field of communications. They must have at least a 2.5 grade point average and must be attending a 2-year or 4-year school that offers turf management curricula. As part of the application, students must submit 2 academic or professional references, a writing sample (a news article published or prepared for publication), a resume, their transcript, and an essay (500 words or less) that describes how they became interested in the turf and ornamental industry and their professional goals.

Financial data: The stipend is $1,000. Funds are paid through the bursar's office at the recipient's college or university.

Duration: 1 year.

Number awarded: Up to 2 each year.

Deadline: February of each year.

1668
UNITED METHODIST FOUNDATION ANNUAL CONFERENCE SCHOLARS PROGRAM

Summary: To provide financial assistance to undergraduate and seminary students attending schools affiliated with the United Methodist Church.

See Listing #1106.

1669
UNITED METHODIST SCHOLARSHIP PROGRAM

Summary: To provide financial assistance to students attending schools affiliated with the United Methodist Church.

See Listing #1107.

1670
UNITY: JOURNALISTS OF COLOR FOUNDERS NON-SUSTAINING SCHOLARSHIP

National Association of Black Journalists
Attn: Media Institute Program Associate
8701-A Adelphi Road
Adelphi, MD 20783-1716
Phone: (301) 445-7100, ext. 108   Fax: (301) 445-7101
E-mail: warren@nabj.org   Web Site: www.nabj.org

Summary: To provide financial assistance to undergraduate student members of the National Association of Black Journalists (NABJ) who are majoring in journalism or mass communications.

Eligibility: This competition is open to African American college juniors and seniors who are currently attending an accredited 4-year college or university. Applicants must be majoring in journalism or mass communication and have a grade point average of 3.0 or higher. They must submit 4 samples of their published or broadcasted work, an official college transcript, 3 letters of recommendation, and a resume. Selection is based on demonstrated experience, interest, or knowledge of multicultural issues in American society, as indicated by experience (clips or video or past journalistic work focused upon cultural, ethnic, or diversity issues), interest (a resume of work experience that clearly supports a commitment in the area accompanied by a statement of future work/career plans), and knowledge (an essay that clearly expresses a cognitive understanding of multicultural issues related to journalism and/or mass media).

Financial data: The stipend is $2,500.

Duration: 1 year.

Additional information: All scholarship winners must become members of the association before they enroll in college.

Number awarded: 1 or more each year.

Deadline: April of each year.

1671
USA WEEKEND STUDENT FICTION CONTEST

USA Weekend
Attn: Student Fiction Contest
535 Madison Avenue
New York, NY 10022
Web Site: www.usaweekend.com

Summary: To recognize and reward outstanding fiction written by high school students.

Eligibility: Eligible to compete are full-time students in grades 9 through 12 in accredited public, private, parochial, or home schools. They are invited to submit an original story (no more than 1,500 words). A substantial part of the action must be set in the summer and in the present. Teen writers should pay particular attention to the beginning of the story. Selection is based on originality and creativity (30 percent); writing ability (30 percent); correct use of English, spelling, and grammar (20 percent); and suitability for publication in a national magazine (20 percent).

Financial data: The Grand Prize winner receives a $2,000 award to be used for future college expenses; in addition, their story is published in a summer issue of *USA Weekend*. Finalists receive a $250 gift certificate for books or computer software; their story is posted on *USA Weekend's* web site. Each teacher/sponsor of the winner and finalists receives a $100 gift certificate for books or software.

Duration: The competition is held annually.

Additional information: This competition started in 1994. Information is also available from D.L. Blair, Inc., 1548 Front Street, P.O. Box 4087, Blair, NE 68009-4087, (402) 426-4701.

Number awarded: 6 each year: 1 Grand Prize winner and 5 finalists.
Deadline: February of each year.

1672
VELMA BERNECKER GWINN GARDEN CLUB OBJECTIVES SCHOLARSHIP

Florida Federation of Garden Clubs, Inc.
Attn: Scholarship Chair
6065 21st Street S.W.
Vero Beach, FL 32968-9427
Phone: (561) 778-1023
Web Site: www.ffgc.org
Summary: To provide financial aid to Florida undergraduates and graduate students majoring in designated areas related to gardening.
Eligibility: This program is open to Florida residents who are enrolled as full-time juniors, seniors, or graduate students in a Florida college. They must have at least a 3.0 grade point average, be in financial need, and be majoring in ecology, horticulture, landscape design, conservation, botany, forestry, marine biology, city planning, or allied subjects. Selection is based on academic record, commitment to career, character, and financial need.
Financial data: The stipend is $1,500. The funds are sent directly to the recipient's school and distributed semiannually.
Duration: 1 year.
Additional information: If the recipient's grade point average drops below 3.0, the second installment of the scholarship is not provided.
Number awarded: 1 each year.
Deadline: April of each year.

1673
VERCILLE VOSS STUDENT SCHOLARSHIP

International Furnishings and Design Association
Attn: IFDA Educational Foundation
204 E Street, N.E.
Washington, DC 20002
Phone: (202) 547-1588   Fax: (202) 547-6348
E-mail: info@ifdaef.org
Web Site: www.ifdael.org/scholarships.html
Summary: To provide financial assistance to undergraduate student members of the International Furnishings and Design Association (IFDA).
Eligibility: This program is open to association members who are full-time undergraduate students in fields related to design. Applicants must submit a 200- to 300-word essay on why they joined IFDA, their future plans and goals, and why they believe they deserve the scholarship. Selection is based on the essay; the applicant's achievements, awards, and accomplishments; and a letter of recommendation from a design educator, a mentor, or a practitioner in the field. Financial need is not considered.
Financial data: The stipend is $1,500.
Duration: 1 year.
Number awarded: 1 each year.
Deadline: September of each year.

1674
VERMONT HAND CRAFTERS, INC. ARTISANSHIP GRANTS

Vermont Student Assistance Corporation
Champlain Mill
1 Main Street, Fourth Floor
P.O. Box 2000
Winooski, VT 05404-2601
Phone: (802) 655-9602   (800) 642-3177
Fax: (802) 654-3765   TDD: (802) 654-3766
Phone: TDD: (800) 281-3341 (within VT)   E-mail: info@vsac.org
Web Site: www.vsac.org
Summary: To provide financial assistance to residents of Vermont who are interested in majoring in arts or crafts in college.
Eligibility: This scholarship is available to high school seniors, high school graduates, and currently-enrolled college students in Vermont who are enrolled or planning to enroll at least half time in a postsecondary degree program in the visual arts (particularly arts and crafts). Applicants must be residents of Vermont (for at least 2 years), be able to demonstrate financial need, apply to the Vermont Student Assistance Corporation for a Vermont Grant, and file a Free Application for Federal Student Aid no later than 4 weeks prior to the scholarship deadline.

The following are required as part of the application process: a completed application form, a copy of the college acceptance letter, 2 letters of recommendation, 5 required essays, and a portfolio (made up of slides, photographs, etc.). Selection is based on academic record, financial need, the portfolio, and a personal interview.
Financial data: Stipends range from $500 to $1,000.
Duration: 1 year.
Number awarded: Up to 6 each year.
Deadline: April of each year.

1675
VICTOR HERBERT ASCAP YOUNG COMPOSER AWARDS

National Federation of Music Clubs
1336 North Delaware Street
Indianapolis, IN 46202-2481
Phone: (317) 638-4003   Fax: (317) 638-0503
E-mail: info@nfmc-music.org
Web Site: www.nfmc-music.org/annual_student.htm
Summary: To recognize and reward outstanding young composers who are members of the National Federation of Music Clubs.
Eligibility: Entrants must be between 18 and 26 years of age, U.S. citizens, and student members of the federation. Awards are presented in 4 categories of student compositions: 1) sonata or comparable work for solo wind or string instrument with piano or for any combination of 3 to 5 instruments (including piano); 2) chorus work; 3) piano solo; and 4) vocal solo, with piano, organ, or orchestral accompaniment. All compositions must be at least 4 minutes in length.
Financial data: In each category, first prize is $1,000 and second prize is $500; special recognition awards of $50 are also presented.
Duration: The competition is held annually.
Additional information: Applications and further information are available from Nettie F. Loflin, 44867 NC 8 Highway, New London, NC 28127-8659; information on all federation scholarships and awards is available from Chair, Competitions and Awards Board, Mrs. Lamoine M. Hall, Jr., 4137 Whitfield Avenue, Fort Worth, TX 76109-5432. The entry fee is $5 per manuscript.
Number awarded: 8 prizes and 2 special recognition awards each year.
Deadline: February of each year.

1676
VIDEO CONTEST FOR COLLEGE STUDENTS

The Christophers
Attn: Youth Department Coordinator
12 East 48th Street
New York, NY 10017
Phone: (212) 759-4050   Fax: (212) 838-5073
E-mail: youth-coordinator@christophers.org
Web Site: www.christophers.org
Summary: To recognize and reward videos produced by college students that best "interpret the Christopher belief that each of us has the ability and opportunity to shape our world."
Eligibility: Currently-enrolled college students are invited to submit films or videos on the theme: "One Person Can Make a Difference." They may use any style or format to express this theme in 5 minutes or less. Entries may be created using film or video, but they must be submitted on 3/4 inch or VHS cassette. Selection is based on content (the ability to capture the theme), artistic and technical proficiency, and adherence to all contest rules.
Financial data: First prize is $3,000, second prize is $2,000, and third prize is $1,000. In addition to these monetary prizes, 5 certificates for Honorable Mention are also awarded.
Duration: The competition is held annually.
Additional information: The Christophers, a nonprofit organization, use the mass media to share 2 basic ideas: "There's nobody like you" and "you can make a difference." All entries are returned after the winners are announced. The winning entries are aired nationwide on the Christopher Closeup television series. The competition began in 1987. Winners agree to the use of their work in any Christopher production: broadcast, nonbroadcast, and/or promotional activities related to this contest.
Number awarded: 3 cash prizes are awarded each year.
Deadline: June of each year.

1677
VIRGINIA MUSEUM OF FINE ARTS UNDERGRADUATE FELLOWSHIPS

Virginia Museum of Fine Arts
Attn: Education and Outreach Division
2800 Grove Avenue
Richmond, VA 23221-2466
Phone: (804) 340-1400   Fax: (804) 340-1548
E-mail: lschultz@vmfa.state.va.us
Web Site: www.vmfa.state.va.us
Summary: To offer financial support to residents of Virginia who are interested in working on an undergraduate degree in the arts.
Eligibility: This program is open to 1) legal residents of Virginia and 2) undergraduate students who have been registered in-state students for at least 1 year before the application deadline. Applicants must be enrolled or planning to enroll full time at an accredited college, university, or school of the arts. They should submit a completed application form; 10 35mm slides representing recent works or 3 videos (VHS), research papers, or published articles; their most recent transcript, and references from 2 art professionals. Only noncommercial, noninstructional projects over which the applicant had control and primary creative responsibility will be considered. Applications are accepted for work or study in the following artistic fields: crafts, drawing, painting, filmmaking, mixed media, printmaking, photography, sculpture, or video. Applicants may apply in only 1 of these categories. Awards are not offered for commercial design, theater/performing arts, or architecture. Awards are made to those applicants with the highest artistic merit.
Financial data: The stipend is $4,000.
Duration: 1 year.
Additional information: This program was established in 1940. Some of the funds for this program come from a foundation that requires consideration of financial need for making awards; candidates who demonstrate such need qualify for those funds.
Deadline: February of each year.

1678
VISUAL ARTS SCHOLARSHIPS

National Alliance for Excellence
63 Riverside Avenue
Red Bank, NJ 07701
Phone: (732) 747-0028   Fax: (732) 842-2962
E-mail: info@excellence.org
Web Site: www.excellence.org
Summary: To provide financial assistance for postsecondary education in the United States or abroad to students in the visual arts.
Eligibility: Applicants must be U.S. citizens attending or planning to attend a college or university in the United States or an approved foreign study program on a full-time basis. They may be high school seniors, college students, graduate students, or returning students. For these scholarships, applicants must submit at least 20 slides of their work, 2 letters of recommendation from teachers, and computer disks if appropriate. Selection is based on talent and ability without regard to financial need.
Financial data: Stipends range from $1,000 to $5,000 per year.
Duration: 1 year.
Additional information: The National Alliance for Excellence was formerly the Scholarship Foundation of America. A $5 processing fee is charged.
Deadline: Applications may be submitted at any time. Awards are given out on a continuous basis.

1679
VOICE OF DEMOCRACY SCHOLARSHIP PROGRAM

Veterans of Foreign Wars of the United States
VFW Building
406 West 34th Street
Kansas City, MO 64111
Phone: (816) 756-3390   Fax: (816) 968-1157
Web Site: www.vfw.org
Summary: To recognize and reward outstanding high school students in a national broadcast scriptwriting competition that focuses on freedom and democracy.
Eligibility: Eligible to compete are high school students in grades 10 through 12. Contestants prepare a script, from 3 to 5 minutes in length, on a topic chosen annually but related to freedom and democracy; a recent theme was "America's Role for the Next Century." Students record the script themselves on magnetic tape or cassette and submit it for sponsorship by a local post or auxiliary of the Veterans of Foreign Wars (VFW). Scripts must reflect the entrant's own original thinking. Selection is based on delivery (20 percent), content (40 percent), and originality (40 percent).
Financial data: A total of $132,000 in national scholarships is awarded each year; first place is $20,000, second $15,000, third $10,000, fourth $6,000, fifth through seventh $5,000, eighth $4,000, ninth through eleventh $3,000, twelfth and thirteenth $2,500, fourteenth $2,000, fifteenth through twenty-second $1,500, and twenty-third through fifty-seventh $1,000. Winners in each state receive an all-expense paid trip to Washington, D.C. for the national competition.
Number awarded: 57 contestants in the national competition receive scholarships.
Deadline: October of each year.

1680
WALLY WIKOFF SCHOLARSHIP FOR EDITORIAL LEADERSHIP

National Scholastic Press Association
2221 University Avenue, S.E., Suite 121
Minneapolis, MN 55414
Phone: (612) 625-8335   Fax: (612) 626-0720
E-mail: info@studentpress.org
Web Site: www.studentpress.org/nspa/contests.html
Summary: To provide financial assistance for college to high school journalists.
Eligibility: This program is open to high school seniors who have worked on the staff of a student newspaper that is a member of the National Scholastic Press Association (NSPA). Applicants must have a grade point average of 3.25 or higher and must submit 3 published editorials and a brief recommendation from the program's adviser.
Financial data: The stipend is $1,000.
Duration: 1 year.
Additional information: This scholarship, first presented for the 1997-98 school year, is jointly sponsored by NSPA and the Educational Communications Scholarship Foundation.
Number awarded: 1 each year.
Deadline: February of each year.

1681
WALT DISNEY COMPANY FOUNDATION SCHOLARSHIP

Junior Achievement
Attn: Scholarships/Education Team
One Education Way
Colorado Springs, CO 80906-4477
Phone: (719) 540-6255   Fax: (719) 540-6175
E-mail: dwatkins@ja.org   Web Site: www.ja.org
Summary: To provide financial assistance to high school seniors who participated in the Junior Achievement program and are interested in majoring in business or the fine arts in college.
Eligibility: This program is open to graduating high school seniors who have participated in the Junior Achievement program. Applicants must have an exceptional record of academic achievement and extracurricular activities. They must be interested in majoring in business administration or the fine arts in college. Letters of recommendation are required.
Financial data: This is a full-tuition scholarship. Plus, recipients are also given $200 cash per year for incidental fees.
Duration: 4 years.
Additional information: Funding for this program is provided by the Walt Disney Company Foundation. Recipients must attend a 4-year college or university.
Number awarded: 1 each year.
Deadline: December of each year.

1682
WALTER F. WAGNER, JR. SCHOLARSHIP

Connecticut Architecture Foundation
Attn: Executive Vice President
87 Willow Street
New Haven, CT 06511
Phone: (203) 865-2195
Summary: To provide financial assistance to Connecticut residents who are pursuing a bachelor's degree in architecture.
Eligibility: This program is open to Connecticut residents who have completed at least 2 years of a bachelor of architecture program at a college offering a 5-year

accredited degree in architecture. Selection is based on academic record and financial need.

Financial data: The stipend is $1,000 per year.
Duration: 1 year; may be renewed.
Additional information: This program was established in 1985.
Number awarded: 1 each year.
Deadline: April of each year.

1683
WALTER S. PATTERSON SCHOLARSHIPS

Broadcast Education Association
Attn: Scholarships
1771 N Street, N.W.
Washington, DC 20036-2891
Phone: (202) 429-5354   E-mail: bea@nab.org
Web Site: www.beaweb.org
Summary: To provide financial assistance to upper-division and graduate students who are interested in preparing for a career in radio.
Eligibility: This program is open to juniors, seniors, and graduate students enrolled full time at a college or university where at least 1 department is an institutional member of the Broadcast Education Association (BEA). Applicants must be studying for a career in radio. Selection is based on evidence that the applicant possesses high integrity, superior academic ability, potential to be an outstanding electronic media professional, and a sense of personal and professional responsibility.
Financial data: The stipend is $1,250.
Duration: 1 year; may not be renewed.
Additional information: Information is also available from Peter B. Orlik, Central Michigan University, 344 Moore Hall, Mt. Pleasant, MI 48859, (517) 774-7279. This program is sponsored by the National Association of Broadcasters of Washington, D.C. and administered by the BEA.
Number awarded: 2 each year.
Deadline: September of each year.

1684
WALZ MEMORIAL SCHOLARSHIP

Walz Memorial Scholarship Trust
c/o First Presbyterian Church
710 Kansas City Street
Rapid City, SD 57701
Phone: (605) 343-6171
Summary: To provide financial assistance for religious studies to Presbyterian students residing in the Presbytery of South Dakota.
Eligibility: This program is open to high school seniors and graduates in the Presbytery of South Dakota who have been active in church school, choir, and/or other youth work and are an active member in the Presbyterian Church (U.S.A.). Applicants must be planning a career in 1 of the following areas: minister, director of Christian education, missionary, or other church vocation. Financial need is required. Applicants may be working on either an undergraduate or graduate degree, but they must have at least a 3.0 grade point average. Interested students must submit a standard application form, transcripts, letters substantiating their qualifications and financial need, standardized test scores, and a statement of goals and objectives. Selection is based on financial need (30 percent), goals statement (30 percent), evidence of activity in a Presbyterian church (20 percent), and academic record (grades, rank, test scores, 20 percent).
Financial data: The stipend is at least $1,000 per semester. Funds are paid to the recipient's institution.
Duration: 1 year; may be renewed.
Deadline: April of each year.

1685
WASHINGTON POST NON-SUSTAINING SCHOLARSHIP

National Association of Black Journalists
Attn: Media Institute Program Associate
8701-A Adelphi Road
Adelphi, MD 20783-1716
Phone: (301) 445-7100, ext. 108   Fax: (301) 445-7101
E-mail: warren@nabj.org
Web Site: www.nabj.org
Summary: To provide financial assistance to undergraduate or graduate student members of the National Association of Black Journalists (NABJ) who are majoring in print journalism.

Eligibility: This competition is open to African American undergraduate or graduate students who are currently attending an accredited 4-year college or university. Applicants must be majoring in print journalism and have a grade point average of 3.0 or higher. They must submit 6 samples of their published or broadcasted work, an official college transcript, 2 letters of recommendation, a resume, and a 500- to 800-word essay describing their accomplishments as a student journalist, their career goals, and their interest in the field.
Financial data: The stipend is $2,500.
Duration: 1 year.
Additional information: All scholarship winners must become members of the association before they enroll in college.
Number awarded: 1 or more each year.
Deadline: April of each year.

1686
WEB OFFSET ASSOCIATION SCHOLARSHIPS

Web Offset Association
Attn: Scholarship Committee
100 Daingerfield Road
Alexandria, VA 22314-2888
Phone: (703) 519-8156   Fax: (703) 519-7109
E-mail: jsass@printing.org
Web Site: www.printing.org/WOA
Summary: To provide financial assistance for college to students interested in fields related to graphic arts.
Eligibility: This program is open to graduating high school seniors and students currently enrolled in a postsecondary college, university, or other institution. Applicants must be emphasizing graphic arts in their studies. Selection is based on leadership potential, initiative, educational goals, community contributions, extracurricular activities, letters of recommendations, and (especially) financial need.
Financial data: Stipends range from $500 to $2,000.
Duration: 1 year; may be renewed.
Number awarded: Approximately 20 each year.
Deadline: April of each year.

1687
WELSH NATIONAL GYMANFA GANU ASSOCIATION SCHOLARSHIPS

Welsh National Gymanfa Ganu Association, Inc.
Gustavus Adolphus College Box B47
800 West College Avenue
St. Peter, MN 56082-1498
Phone: (507) 933-7540   (877) 831-0563
Fax: (507) 933-6284   E-mail: WNGGC_ellis@gustavus.edu
Web Site: www.wngga.org
Summary: To provide financial assistance to students of Welsh lineage who are enrolled in courses or projects related to Welsh religious and cultural heritage.
Eligibility: To be eligible for a scholarship, an applicant must be 1) of Welsh lineage, 2) a citizen of the United States or Canada, and 3) a member of the Welsh National Gymanfa Ganu Association. They must be enrolled in courses or projects that preserve, develop or promote Welsh religious and cultural heritage. Applicants may be of any age (there is no age limitation).
Financial data: The amount awarded varies each year, depending upon the needs of the recipient and the funds available.
Duration: 1 year; may be renewed.
Additional information: This program was established in 1983.
Number awarded: Varies each year.
Deadline: February of each year.

1688
WENDELL IRISH VIOLA AWARDS

National Federation of Music Clubs
1336 North Delaware Street
Indianapolis, IN 46202-2481
Phone: (317) 638-4003   Fax: (317) 638-0503
E-mail: info@nfmc-music.org
Web Site: www.nfmc-music.org/annual_junior.htm
Summary: To recognize and reward outstanding young violists who are members of the National Federation of Music Clubs (NFMC).
Eligibility: Eligible to compete are violists between 12 and 19 years of age.

Applicants must be members of the junior division of the federation and U.S. citizens.

Financial data: Each award is $1,000.

Additional information: Information on these awards is also available from Dr. George Keck, 421 Cherry Street, Arkadelphia, AR 71923; information on all NFMC scholarships is available from Chair, Competitions and Awards Board, Mrs. Lamoine M. Hall, Jr., 4137 Whitfield Avenue, Fort Worth, TX 76109-5432.

Number awarded: 4 each year: 1 in each of the NFMC regions.

Deadline: January of each year.

1689
WEST VIRGINIA BROADCASTERS SCHOLARSHIP

Greater Kanawha Valley Foundation
Attn: Scholarship Coordinator
One Huntington Square, 16th Floor
900 Lee Street, East
P.O. Box 3041
Charleston, WV 25331-3041
Phone: (304) 346-3620   Fax: (304) 346-3640
E-mail: tgkvf@tgkvf.com   Web Site: www.tgkvf.com/scholarship.html

Summary: To provide financial assistance for the study of communications in college to employees and family members of stations that are members of the West Virginia Broadcasters Association.

Eligibility: This program is open to residents of West Virginia who are students at a college or university anywhere in the country and majoring in communications, broadcasting, film, speech, broadcast journalism, advertising, broadcast electronics, or other arts and techniques of the communications field. Applicants must be employees or family members of stations that are members of the association, have at least a 2.5 grade point average, and demonstrate good moral character. Selection is based on financial need, grade point average, and any other unusual circumstances.

Financial data: The stipend is $1,000 per year.

Duration: 1 year; may be renewed.

Additional information: This program is sponsored by the West Virginia Broadcasters Association.

Number awarded: 10 each year.

Deadline: February of each year.

1690
WESTERN WASHINGTON CHAPTER JOURNALISM SCHOLARSHIP

Society of Professional Journalists-Western Washington Chapter
Attn: Scholarship Competition
3838 Stone Way North
Seattle, WA 98103
Phone: (206) 545-7918   E-mail: jeannelangjones@hotmail.com
Web Site: www.spjwash.org

Summary: To provide financial assistance to undergraduate students in Washington state who are majoring in journalism.

Eligibility: Undergraduate students in Washington who are currently majoring in journalism or communications (including community college students planning to pursue journalism careers at a Washington college or university) are eligible to apply. As part of the application process, students must submit a letter of application, including an answer to the question "Why have you chosen a journalism career and what do you hope to accomplish" (500 words), a copy of their resume, a letter of recommendation, an official transcript of all college credits, and 3 work samples.

Financial data: The stipend is $1,000.

Duration: 1 year.

Number awarded: 4 each year.

Deadline: March of each year.

1691
WILLIAM B. RUGGLES RIGHT TO WORK SCHOLARSHIP

National Institute for Labor Relations Research
Attn: Scholarship Selection Committee
5211 Port Royal Road, Suite 510
Springfield, VA 22151
Phone: (703) 321-9606   Fax: (703) 321-7342
E-mail: research@nilrr.org
Web Site: www.nilrr.org

Summary: To provide financial assistance for the undergraduate or graduate education of journalism students who are knowledgeable about the Right to Work principle.

Eligibility: Eligible are undergraduate or graduate students majoring in journalism in institutions of higher learning in the United States. Graduating high school seniors may also apply. Applicants must demonstrate potential for successful completion of educational requirements in an accredited journalism program and demonstrate an understanding of the principles voluntary unionism and the economic and social problems of compulsory unionism. Selection is based on scholastic ability and financial need.

Financial data: The award is $2,000.

Duration: 1 year.

Additional information: This scholarship was established in 1974 to honor the Texas journalist who coined the phrase "Right to Work."

Number awarded: 1 each year.

Deadline: February of each year.

1692
WILLIAM HEATH EDUCATION FUND

Bank of America Private Bank
600 Cleveland Street, Third Floor
Clearwater, FL 33755
Phone: (727) 298-5935   Fax: (727) 298-5940

Summary: To provide financial assistance to males who graduated from a high school in a southeastern state and are interested in pursuing a degree to serve in the ministry.

Eligibility: This program is open to male students who are graduating or have graduated from high schools in the southeast: Alabama, Florida, Georgia, Kentucky, Louisiana, Maryland, Mississippi, North Carolina, South Carolina, Tennessee, Virginia, or West Virginia. Applicants must be under the age of 35 and working on a degree (undergraduate or graduate) in order to serve in the ministry, as a missionary or as a social worker. Primary consideration is given to candidates who are of the Methodist or Episcopalian denominations. Interested students should submit an introductory letter expressing their educational or extracurricular interests, a copy of their high school diploma, a copy of their high school or college transcripts, a letter of recommendation from their dean or church minister, and a copy of their birth certificate.

Financial data: Stipends range from $500 to $1,000.

Duration: 1 year.

Number awarded: Several each year.

Deadline: June of each year.

1693
WILLIAM J. LOCKLIN SCHOLARSHIP

Landscape Architecture Foundation
Attn: Scholarship Program
636 Eye Street, N.W.
Washington, DC 20001-3736
Phone: (202) 216-2356   Fax: (202) 898-1185
E-mail: msippel@asla.org
Web Site: www.laprofession.org

Summary: To provide financial aid to landscape architecture students who plan to utilize lighting in their work.

Eligibility: Eligible are landscape architecture students pursuing a program in lighting design or focusing on lighting design in studio projects. Applications must be accompanied by a 300-word essay highlighting the design project, including the overall effect to be obtained, rationale for choice of lamp and placement of fixture, and anticipated results. Selection is based on professional experience, community involvement, extracurricular activities, and financial need.

Financial data: The stipend is $1,000.

Duration: 1 year.

Number awarded: 1 each year.

Deadline: March of each year.

1694
WOMEN IN FILM/DALLAS COLLEGE/UNIVERSITY STUDENT TUITION SCHOLARSHIP

Women in Film/Dallas
Attn: Topaz Award and Scholarship Office
2600 Stemmons Freeway, Suite 117
Dallas, TX 75207
Phone: (214) 954-4488   Fax: (214) 954-0004
E-mail: wifdfw@aol.com
Web Site: www.wifdallas.org
Summary: To provide financial assistance to women residents of Texas who are studying film and video in college.
Eligibility: This program is open to women residents of Texas who are enrolled at an accredited college or university and majoring in, or have a primary field of study in, film and video. Applicants must have consistently maintained a grade point average of 3.0 or higher. Along with their application, they must submit a 3-page essay on the goals they wish to attain with a film/video degree, 2 letters of recommendation, a letter from the college or university verifying their enrollment, and an official college or university transcript. Financial need is not considered in the selection process.
Financial data: The stipend is $1,500.
Duration: 1 year.
Number awarded: 1 each year.
Deadline: June of each year.

1695
WOMEN'S DIVISION GRANTS

United Methodist Church
General Board of Global Ministries
Attn: Women's Division
475 Riverside Drive, Room 1504
New York, NY 10115
Phone: (212) 870-3600
Summary: To provide financial assistance to Methodists interested in pursuing religious studies.
Eligibility: This program is open to 1) college undergraduates studying religion or related fields, 2) graduate students in accredited schools of theology or related fields, and 3) other people in the United States interested in full-time church vocations or study. Some funds require affiliation with the United Methodist Church. Financial need is considered in the selection process.
Financial data: The amount awarded varies, depending upon the availability of funds.
Duration: 1 year; nonrenewable.
Number awarded: Approximately 20 each year.
Deadline: January of each year.

1696
WOMEN'S JEWELRY ASSOCIATION SCHOLARSHIP

Women's Jewelry Association
Attn: Scholarship Committee
333B Route 46 West, Suite B-201
Fairfield, NJ 07004
Phone: (973) 575-7190   Fax: (973) 575-1445
Summary: To provide financial assistance to women who are interested in careers in jewelry.
Eligibility: Women who are enrolled in a jewelry-related curriculum (ranging from design to gemological analysis) at an institution of higher learning located anywhere in the United States are eligible to apply. Candidates are requested to submit prints or drawings of their work. Recipients are selected on the basis of academic achievement, recommendations, samples of work, jewelry industry experience, career objectives, and financial need.
Financial data: Stipends range from $2,500 to $5,000 per year.
Duration: 1 year.
Deadline: June of each year.

1697
WORLD POPULATION FILM/VIDEO FESTIVAL AWARDS

World Population Film/Video Festival
46 Fox Hill Road
Bernardston, MA 01337
Phone: (800) 638-9464   Fax: (413) 648-9204
E-mail: info@wpfvf.com
Web Site: www.wpfvf.com
Summary: To recognize and reward outstanding student films that deal with population issues.
Eligibility: This program is open to secondary and college students who produce films and videos that explore the connection between population growth, resource consumption, the environment, and the global future. Entries must be submitted in VHS (NTSC) format for preview judging, but they may be any length, originate in any format (film, video, or multimedia), and be any style (documentary, narrative, music video, animation, other). This is an international competition.
Financial data: A total of $10,000 in prizes is awarded.
Duration: The competition is held annually.
Additional information: This competition, first held in 1995, is sponsored by the Sopris Foundation, Searchlight Films, and Population Communications International.
Number awarded: Varies each year; recently, 5 high school and 9 college films received awards.
Deadline: June of each year.

1698
WORLD STUDIO FOUNDATION SCHOLARSHIPS

World Studio Foundation
225 Varick Street, 9th Floor
New York, NY 10014
Phone: (212) 366-1317   Fax: (212) 807-0024
E-mail: scholarships@worldstudio.org
Web Site: www.worldstudio.org/scholar/intro.html
Summary: To provide financial assistance and work experience to disadvantaged and ethnic minority undergraduate and graduate students who wish to study fine or commercial arts, design, or architecture.
Eligibility: This program is open to disadvantaged or minority college students who are currently enrolled (must attend an accredited school) and majoring in the 1 of the following areas: advertising, architecture, environmental graphics, fashion design, film/video, fine arts, furniture design, graphic design, illustration, industrial/product design, interior design, landscape architecture, new media, photography, surface/textile design, or urban planning. Most awards are offered for graduate work but undergraduate students are also eligible. International students may apply if they are enrolled at a U.S. college or university. Selection is based on a slide portfolio of work, a written statement of purpose, financial need, and a demonstrated commitment to giving back to the larger community.
Financial data: Basic scholarships range from $1,000 to $2,000, but awards between $3,000 and $5,000 are also presented at the discretion of the jury. Honorable mentions are $100.
Duration: 1 academic year.
Additional information: The foundation encourages the scholarship recipients to focus on ways that their work can address issues of social and environmental responsibility. This program includes the following named awards: the Gaggenau Award for Design, the New York Design Center Awards, the ALU Awards for Design, the Color Wheel Award, the Honda Award for Environmental Design, the Rado Watch Scholarship for Design, the Janou Pakter Award, the Impac Group Award, the Color Optics Award, the AIGA Award, the Lonn Beaudry Memorial Award, the Robert J. Hurst Award, and the Michael Manley Award.
Number awarded: Varies each year; recently, 20 scholarships and 10 honorable mentions were awarded.
Deadline: April of each year.

1699
WORLD WIDE BARACA PHILATHEA UNION SCHOLARSHIP

World Wide Baraca Philathea Union
610 South Harlem Avenue
Freeport, IL 61032-4833
Summary: To provide financial assistance to students preparing for Christian ministry, Christian missionary work, or Christian education.
Eligibility: Eligible to apply for this support are students enrolled in an

accredited college or seminary who are majoring in Christian ministry, Christian missionary work, or Christian education (e.g., church youth pastor, writer of Sunday school curriculum).

Financial data: Stipends are paid directly to the recipient's school upon receipt of the first semester transcript and a letter confirming attendance.

Duration: 1 year; may be renewed.

Deadline: March of each year.

1700
WORLDFEST-HOUSTON STUDENT FILM AWARD

Houston International Film and Video Festival
9494 Southwest Freeway, Fifth Floor
P.O. Box 56566
Houston, TX 77256-6566
Phone: (713) 965-9955   Fax: (713) 965-9960
E-mail: entry@worldfest.org
Web Site: www.worldfest.org

Summary: To recognize and reward outstanding independent films and videos, including those produced by students.

Eligibility: This competition is open to independent filmmakers from any country. For the student film and video category, there are 4 sub-categories: graduate level productions, college level productions, high school level and below productions, and student level screenplays. All films and videos must have been completed during the preceding 3 years. Entries must first be submitted on videotape; if a film is chosen to be screened during the festival, the entrant will be notified and a 16mm or 35mm print requested. The film chosen as the best in all of the student subcategories receives this award.

Financial data: The award includes $2,500 worth of Kodak raw film stock. The festival also sends information on all winning entries to the top 100 Hollywood studios, agencies, distributors, and development/production companies, as well as to other film festivals around the world.

Duration: The competition is held annually.

Additional information: An April festival has been held in Houston for many years. From 1992 through 1997, the November festival was held in Charleston, South Carolina; from 1998 through 2000, it was held in Flagstaff, Arizona. Effective 2001, the November festival was cancelled and the only activity is in Houston. The early entry fee for the student category is $40. The regular entry fee is $45. The late entry fee is $60.

Deadline: The early deadline is in November of each year. The regular deadline is in December of each year. The late deadline is in January of each year.

1701
XERNONA CLAYTON SCHOLARSHIP

Atlanta Association of Black Journalists
P.O. Box 54128
Atlanta, GA 30308
Phone: (770) 593-5837
Web Site: www.aabj.org/scholarships.htm

Summary: To provide financial assistance to African Americans and others majoring in communication-related fields at Georgia colleges or universities.

Eligibility: This program is open to African Americans and other qualified students enrolled in Georgia colleges and universities who are working on a degree in mass communications, journalism, English, public relations, and television, radio, or film. Applicants must have at least a 2.8 grade point average. To apply, students should complete an entry form, attach a required essay, and provide a current transcript. Judges rate essays on the basis of creativity, style, composition, persuasiveness, insight, and factual support of ideas. Media samples are judged on quality, demonstration of skill and talent, and degree of professionalism.

Financial data: The grand prize scholarship is $5,000; the first runner-up receives $3,000 and the second runner-up receives $2,000.

Duration: 1 year.

Additional information: All expenses are paid for the scholarship winners to attend the National Association of Black Journalists' annual convention. Additional information is also available from Ernie Suggs, 3304 Lakeshore Crossing, Atlanta, GA 30324.

Number awarded: 3 each year.

Deadline: March of each year.

1702
YOSHIKO TANAKA MEMORIAL SCHOLARSHIP

Japanese American Citizens League
Attn: National Scholarship Awards
1765 Sutter Street
San Francisco, CA 94115
Phone: (415) 921-5225   Fax: (415) 931-4671
E-mail: jacl@jacl.org   Web Site: www.jacl.org

Summary: To provide financial assistance to student members of the Japanese American Citizens League (JACL) who are pursuing undergraduate education.

Eligibility: This program is open to JACL members who are currently enrolled or planning to reenter a college, university, trade school, business college, or other institution of higher learning. Selection is based on academic record, extracurricular activities, and community involvement. Preference is given to applicants planning to study Japanese language, Japanese culture, and/or U.S.-Japan relations.

Financial data: The stipend depends on the availability of funds but usually ranges from $1,000 to $5,000.

Duration: 1 year.

Additional information: Requests for applications must be accompanied by a self-addressed stamped envelope.

Number awarded: 1 each year.

Deadline: March of each year.

1703
YOUNG AMERICAN CREATIVE PATRIOTIC ART AWARDS

Ladies Auxiliary to the Veterans of Foreign Wars
c/o National Headquarters
406 West 34th Street
Kansas City, MO 64111
Phone: (816) 561-8655   Fax: (816) 931-4753
E-mail: info@ladiesauxvfg.com
Web Site: www.ladiesauxvfg.com

Summary: To enable high school students to express their artistic talents, demonstrate their patriotism, and become eligible for funds to further their art education.

Eligibility: Any student who is a U.S. citizen in grades 9 through 12 may enter. Home-schooled students are eligible; foreign exchange students are not. Entrants may submit art on paper or canvas using water color, pencil, pastel, charcoal, tempera, crayon, acrylic, pen-and-ink, or oil. Competitions are held in individual Veterans of Foreign Wars (VFW) Auxiliaries, then at department and finally national levels. Entries are judged on the originality of concept and patriotism expressed; content and clarity of ideas; design, use of color, and technique; and the total impact of execution and contrast.

Financial data: National awards are $10,000 for first prize, $5,000 for second prize, and $2,500 for third prize. Funds must be used for continued art education or for art supplies.

Additional information: First prize also includes an expense-paid trip to the annual VFW Auxiliary National Community Service Conference and display of the art on the cover of the *National VFW Auxiliary Magazine*. Prior national first- and second-prize winners may not compete again; third- through fifth-prize winners and non-winners may repeat but must submit new entries.

Number awarded: 3 national winners are selected each year.

Deadline: Entries must be submitted to the Auxiliary Youth Activities chair by December of each year.

1704
YOUNG COMPOSERS AWARDS

National Guild of Community Schools of the Arts
Attn: Executive Director
40 North Van Brunt Street, Room 32
P.O. Box 8018
Englewood, NJ 07631
Phone: (201) 871-3337   Fax: (201) 871-7639
E-mail: info@natguild.org   Web Site: www.nationalguild.org

Summary: To recognize and reward outstanding high school composers.

Eligibility: Eligible to enter this competition are residents of the United States or Canada who are enrolled in a public or private secondary school, a recognized musical institution, or a private music studio with an established teacher. Students enrolled in an undergraduate program are not eligible. Competitions are held in 2 categories: senior for students 16 to 18 years of age and junior for students 13 to 15 years of age. Applicants must submit original compositions that may be in

any category of music. A separate award is presented to the best composition for chamber music (defined as a work for at least 2 instruments and intended to be performed by 1 performer per part) in either category.

Financial data: Prizes in the senior category are $1,000 for first and $500 for second. Junior category prizes are $500 for first and $250 for second. The chamber music prize is $1,000.

Duration: The competition is held annually.

Additional information: Since 1998, this program has been cosponsored by the Hartt School at the University of Hartford. Information is also available from Michael Yaffe, Director, Hartt School Community Division, University of Hartford, 200 Bloomfield Avenue, West Hartford, CT 06117, (860) 768-4451, E-mail: yaffe@mail.hartford.edu. The first prize in the senior category is designated the Herbert Zipper Prize. The application fee is $5.

Number awarded: 5 each year: 2 senior, 2 junior, and 1 for the best chamber music prize in either category.

Deadline: April of each year.

1705
YOUNG FEMINIST SCHOLARSHIP

Spinsters Ink
P.O. Box 22005
Denver, CO 80222
Phone: (303) 761-5552   Fax: (303) 761-5284
E-mail: spinster@spinsters-ink.com
Web Site: www.spinsters-ink.com

Summary: To recognize and reward feminists who are high school seniors and interested in writing.

Eligibility: This program is open to feminist students in their last year of high school. They are invited to submit an essay on feminism and what it means to them.

Financial data: The award is $1,000.

Duration: The competition is held annually.

Additional information: Spinsters Ink is a feminist publishing house. This program was established in 1998, as part of Spinsters Ink's 20th anniversary celebration. Recipients may use the award as a scholarship at any school of their choosing. The winner is also given the opportunity to attend Norcroft (a writing retreat for women) for 1 week during the summer. Norcroft, funded by Harmony Women's Fund, is situated on Minnesota's north shore of Lake Superior.

Number awarded: 1 each year.

Deadline: December of each year.

1706
YOUNG PRODUCERS CONTEST

Earth & Sky Radio Series
P.O. Box 2203
Austin, TX 78768
Phone: (512) 477-4474   E-mail: contest@earthsky.org
Web Site: www.earthsky.org

Summary: To recognize and reward outstanding short radio programs on a science topic produced by K-12 students.

Eligibility: This program is open to K-12 students in any country. They are invited to prepare a 75-second science or nature program modeled after the Earth & Sky radio program. All programs must be in English and must begin with the words: "This is (students' names) of (name of their school) in (name of their city or town)—Young Producer(s) for Earth & Sky." Programs can have up to 4 student team members, but there should be only 1 or 2 radio hosts. Each team must have an adult sponsor. Shows must be recorded on cassette tape. Entries must be accompanied by a written transcript of the show and a list of sources used to write the show. Original music or sound effects are encouraged. Entries are judged on: scientific accuracy, presentation, and production.

Financial data: The grand prize is a $1,000 savings bond; the runners-up receive $500 savings bonds.

Duration: The competition is held annually. Previous winners may not compete.

Additional information: This program is jointly funded by the Earth & Sky radio series and the National Science Foundation. The winning programs are aired as part of the Earth & Sky international broadcast in May.

Number awarded: 5 each year: 1 grand prize and 4 runners-up.

Deadline: December of each year.

1707
YOUNG SOLOISTS' COMPETITION COLLEGE DIVISION

National Symphony Orchestra
Attn: Young Soloists' Competition
2700 F Street, N.W.
Washington, DC 20566
Phone: (202) 416-8000   (800) 444-1324
Web Site: kennedy-center.org/nso/nsoed/performers.html

Summary: To provide a monetary award to top college student performers in a musical competition in the Washington, D.C. area.

Eligibility: This competition is open to high school graduates who are either 1) studying music in Delaware, the District of Columbia, Maryland, Virginia, or West Virginia, or 2) residents of metropolitan Washington (defined as the District of Columbia, the Maryland counties of Frederick, Montgomery, and Prince George's, the Virginia counties of Arlington, Fairfax, Loudoun, and Prince William, and the Virginia cities of Alexandria and Falls Church) currently studying elsewhere. Pianists and instrumentalists must be younger than 23 years of age and may not have completed an undergraduate degree. Singers must be younger than 26 years of age and may not have completed a doctorate. Former winners of this competition (either in the high school or college division) and performers under professional management are ineligible.

Financial data: The Bill Cerri Scholarship of $1,000, provided by WETA-FM90.9, is presented to 1 winner selected by the judges. All winners perform in a concert with the National Symphony Orchestra.

Duration: The competition is held annually.

Additional information: Information is also available from Sharyn L. Byer, Competition Chairperson, 115 Gresham Place, Falls Church, VA 22046, (703) 532-6565. Applications must be accompanied by a $15 entry fee and a self-addressed stamped envelope.

Number awarded: 1 each year.

Deadline: January of each year.

1708
YOUNG SOLOISTS' COMPETITION HIGH SCHOOL DIVISION

National Symphony Orchestra
Attn: Young Soloists' Competition
2700 F Street, N.W.
Washington, DC 20566
Phone: (202) 416-8000   (800) 444-1324
Web Site: kennedy-center.org/nso/nsoed/performers.html

Summary: To provide a monetary award to top high school student performers in a musical competition in the Washington, D.C. area.

Eligibility: This competition is open to students in grades 10 through 12 who are residents of metropolitan Washington or studying with an instrumental teacher in metropolitan Washington, defined as the District of Columbia, the Maryland counties of Frederick, Montgomery, and Prince George's, the Virginia counties of Arlington, Fairfax, Loudoun, and Prince William, and the Virginia cities of Alexandria and Falls Church. Former winners and performers under professional management are not eligible. Competitions are held in piano and instrumental.

Financial data: The Bill Cerri Scholarship of $1,000, provided by WETA-FM90.9, is presented to 1 winner selected by the judges. All winners perform in a concert with the National Symphony Orchestra.

Duration: The competition is held annually.

Additional information: Information is also available from Sharyn L. Byer, Competition Chairperson, 115 Gresham Place, Falls Church, VA 22046, (703) 532-6565. Applications must be accompanied by a $15 entry fee and a self-addressed stamped envelope.

Number awarded: 1 each year.

Deadline: January of each year.

Scholarship Listings

1709
YVAR MIKHASHOFF TUITION ASSISTANCE FOR STUDENTS

Yvar Mikhashoff Trust for New Music
P.O. Box 8
Forestville, NY 14062-0008
Phone: (716) 965-2128   Fax: (716) 965-9726
E-mail: YMTrust@aol.com
Web Site: www.emf.org/organizations/mikhashofftrust

Summary: To provide financial assistance to undergraduate or graduate students who are interested in studying new music in the United States or abroad.

Eligibility: Applicants for this program must be studying either at appropriate educational institutions or with individual instructors. Students at academic institutions must submit transcripts; applicants for private study must submit an acceptance letter from the proposed instructor. All applicants must include a short biography, 2 letters of recommendation, and a detailed proposal for study that includes a budget. Performers must submit a cassette tape (up to 20 minutes in length) from the representative 20th-century solo repertoire; composers must submit representative compositions. All proposals may be for study in the United States or abroad.

Financial data: Awards range from $1,000 to $5,000. Funds may be used for tuition only.

Duration: 1 year.

Number awarded: Varies each year; recently 2 graduate students and 2 undergraduates received support from this program.

Deadline: November of each year.

1710
ZORA NEALE HURSTON/RICHARD WRIGHT AWARDS

Hurston/Wright Foundation
P.O. Box 77287
Washington, DC 20013
Phone: (301) 459-0142   E-mail: hurstonwrightlit@aol.com
Web Site: www.hurston-wright/awards.html

Summary: To recognize and reward the best fiction written by college students of African descent.

Eligibility: This program is open to students of African descent who are enrolled full time as undergraduate or graduate students in a college or university in the United States. They are eligible to submit a previously unpublished short story or novel excerpt. Only 1 story may be submitted per applicant.

Financial data: First prize is $1,000; second and third prizes are $500 each.

Duration: The prizes are awarded annually.

Additional information: This is the only fiction competition aimed solely at emerging college writers of African descent. The award is cosponsored by Virginia Commonwealth University. Winners are required to provide verification of college enrollment.

Number awarded: 3 each year.

Deadline: December of each year.

Sciences

Described here are 936 funding programs that 1) reward student speeches, essays, inventions, organizational involvement, or other activities in the sciences or 2) support college studies in a number of scientific fields, including agricultural sciences, chemistry, computer science, engineering, environmental sciences, food science, horticulture, mathematics, marine sciences, nursing, nutrition, pharmacology, and technology. These programs are available to high school seniors, high school graduates, currently enrolled college students, and/or returning students to fund studies on the undergraduate level in the United States. If you haven't already checked the "Unrestricted by Subject Area" chapter, be sure to do that next; identified there are 1,242 more sources of free money that can be used to support study in the sciences or any other subject area (although the programs may be restricted in other ways). Finally, be sure to consult the Subject Index to locate available funding in a specific subject area.

1711
A/E PRONET SCHOLARSHIP

Summary: To provide financial assistance to undergraduate and graduate students enrolled in a program that emphasizes design firm/risk management. *See Listing #1243.*

1712
AAAE FOUNDATION SCHOLARSHIP

American Association of Airport Executives Foundation
Attn: AAAE Foundation Scholarship Program
601 Madison Street, Suite 400
Alexandria, VA 22314
Phone: (703) 824-0500   Fax: (703) 820-1395
Web Site: www.airportnet.org
Summary: To provide financial assistance to upper-division college students who are majoring in aviation.
Eligibility: This program is open to full-time college juniors or seniors who are enrolled in an aviation program and have earned at least a 3.0 grade point average. Selection is based on academic record, financial need, participation in school and community activities, work experience, and a personal statement.
Financial data: The stipend is $1,000.
Duration: 1 year.
Additional information: Recipients must attend an accredited college or university.
Number awarded: Several each year.
Deadline: May of each year.

1713
AABB-FENWAL SBB SCHOLARSHIP AWARDS

American Association of Blood Banks
Attn: Scholarship Award Program
8101 Glenbrook Road
Bethesda, MD 20814-2749
Phone: (301) 215-6539   Fax: (301) 907-6895
E-mail: marc_p@smtpgw.aabb.org   Web Site: www.aabb.org
Summary: To recognize and reward essays by students enrolled in programs accredited by the American Association of Blood Banks (AABB).
Eligibility: This program is open to students enrolled in an accredited program for the education of Specialists in Blood Banking (SBB). Applicants must submit 1 of the following types of entries: 1) a scientific paper reporting experimental work (the work may be an original concept, extension of a major concept, or application of a new procedure in the basic sciences, clinical or laboratory medicine, or educational sciences); 2) an analytical or interpretational review suitable for publication in a professional journal; or 3) an innovative educational syllabus using traditional or advanced technology modalities. The essays or scientific papers must be less than 3,000 words on a subject pertaining to blood banking or a related field. Scientific papers should describe materials and methods used, including experimental design, in sufficient detail to enable other scientists to evaluate or duplicate the work. Reviews should analyze or interpret the subject and not just restate the literature. Educational entries should include a brief summary reviewing the need for the program, how the program is innovative, and a list of references. A student may submit more than 1 entry; however, no student may receive more than 1 award.
Financial data: The award is $1,500.
Duration: The competition is held annually.
Additional information: This program began in 1968. Funding is provided by Baxter Healthcare Corporation, Biotech North America, Fenwal Division. Winning entries may not be published or printed elsewhere without the prior approval of the AABB.
Number awarded: Up to 5 each year.
Deadline: June of each year.

1714
AAHE UNDERGRADUATE SCHOLARSHIP

American Association for Health Education
Attn: Scholarship Committee
1900 Association Drive
Reston, VA 20191-1599
Phone: (703) 476-3437   (800) 213-7193
Fax: (703) 476-6638   E-mail: aahe@aahperd.org
Web Site: www.aahperd.org/aahe/programs-scholarship.html

Summary: To provide financial assistance to undergraduate students who are currently enrolled in a health education program.
Eligibility: Eligible to apply for this support are undergraduate students who are enrolled full time in a health education program at a 4-year college or university, have earned at least a 3.25 grade point average, and have never won an award from the association. All applications must be accompanied by a list of extracurricular service activities, an official transcript, 3 letters of recommendation, and an essay on career goals that includes what the student hopes to accomplish as a health educator (during training and in the future), and attributes and aspirations brought to the field of health education.
Financial data: The stipend is $1,000, plus a 1-year complimentary student membership in the association.
Duration: 1 year; nonrenewable.
Number awarded: 1 each year.
Deadline: November of each year.

1715
AAOHN FOUNDATION ACADEMIC SCHOLARSHIP

American Association of Occupational Health Nurses, Inc.
Attn: AAOHN Foundation
2920 Brandywine Road, Suite 100
Atlanta, GA 30341-4146
Phone: (770) 455-7757   Fax: (770) 455-7271
E-mail: foundation@aaohn.org
Web Site: www.aaohn.org
Summary: To provide financial assistance to registered nurses who are pursuing a bachelor's or graduate degree to prepare for a career in occupational and environmental health.
Eligibility: This program is open to registered nurses who are enrolled in a baccalaureate, master's, or doctoral degree program. Applicants must demonstrate an interest in, and commitment to, occupational and environmental health. Selection is based on 2 letters of recommendation and a 500-word essay on the applicant's professional goals as they relate to the academic activity and the field of occupational and environmental health.
Financial data: The stipend is $3,000.
Duration: 1 year; may be renewed up to 2 additional years.
Number awarded: 1 each year.
Deadline: November of each year.

1716
ABRAMS GRANT

Michigan Society of Professional Engineers
Attn: Scholarship Coordinator
215 North Walnut Street
P.O. Box 15276
Lansing, MI 48901-5276
Phone: (517) 487-9388   Fax: (517) 487-0635
E-mail: mspe@voyager.net
Web Site: www.voyager.net/mspe
Summary: To provide financial assistance to members of the Michigan Society of Professional Engineers (MSPE) who are majoring in civil or surveying engineering at a college or university in Michigan.
Eligibility: This program is open to student members of the society who are U.S. citizens and residents of Michigan. Applicants must be majoring in civil or surveying engineering at an ABET-accredited engineering program at a Michigan college or university and have earned at least a 3.0 grade point average. They must submit an essay (up to 500 words) that discusses their interest in engineering, the specific field of engineering that is being pursued, and the occupation they propose to follow after graduation. Selection is based on the essay, transcripts, 2 letters of recommendation, leadership, and interest in the engineering profession through involvement in school and/or outside activities. Financial need is not considered.
Financial data: The stipend is $3,000.
Duration: 1 year; nonrenewable.
Additional information: Information is also available from Roger Lamer, Scholarship Selection Committee Chair, (616) 247-2974, Fax: (616) 247-2997, E-mail: rlamer@steelcase.com.
Number awarded: 1 each year.
Deadline: March of each year.

1717
ACEC/MICHIGAN EDUCATION GRANT

ACEC/Michigan, Inc.
1407 South Harrison Road, Suite 225
East Lansing, MI 48823-5284
Phone: (517) 332-2066   Fax: (517) 332-4333
E-mail: wagner.steve@acd.net
Web Site: www.acec-m.org
Summary: To provide financial assistance to undergraduate and graduate students majoring in engineering or surveying.
Eligibility: Applicants must be enrolled full or part time as a sophomore, junior, senior, or graduate student working on a degree in engineering or surveying in an ABET-accredited engineering or surveying program. They must have worked during the past 24 months for a consulting engineering, surveying, or architectural/engineering firm. Selection is based on work experience, references, an essay on engineering consulting, extracurricular and community activities, and grade point average. Financial need is not considered in the selection process.
Financial data: A stipend is awarded (exact amount not specified); a total of $8,000 per year is awarded.
Duration: 1 year; recipients may reapply for 1 more award.
Number awarded: 1 or more each year.
Deadline: January of each year.

1718
ACMPE PRESIDENTIAL SCHOLARSHIPS

American College of Medical Practice Executives
Attn: Scholarship Program
104 Inverness Terrace East
Englewood, CO 80112-5306
Phone: (303) 643-9573   Fax: (303) 643-4427
E-mail: acmpe@mgma.com
Web Site: www.mgma.com/acmpe
Summary: To provide financial assistance to nominees, certified members, and fellows of the American College of Medical Practice Executives (ACMPE) who are pursuing professional development through undergraduate or graduate education.
Eligibility: Eligible to apply are ACMPE nominees, certified members, and fellows who wish to pursue an undergraduate or graduate degree in medical practice management at an accredited university or college. Applications should include a letter describing their career goals and objectives; a resume; 3 reference letters commenting on the individual's performance, character, potential to succeed, and need for scholarship support; documentation indicating acceptance into an undergraduate or graduate college or university; and academic transcripts for undergraduate or graduate work completed to date.
Financial data: The stipend is $1,500. Payments for undergraduate and graduate scholarships are sent to the university or college in which the recipient is or will be enrolled.
Duration: 1 year.
Deadline: May of each year.

1719
ACSM FELLOWS SCHOLARSHIP

American Congress on Surveying and Mapping
Attn: Awards Director
6 Montgomery Village Avenue, Suite 403
Gaithersburg, MD 20879
Phone: (240) 632-9716   Fax: (240) 632-1321
E-mail: tmilburn@acsm.net   Web Site: www.acsm.net
Summary: To provide financial assistance for the undergraduate study of surveying to members of the American Congress on Surveying and Mapping (ACSM).
Eligibility: This program is open to students who are enrolled in a 4-year college or university studying surveying as juniors or higher and are members of the sponsoring organization. Selection is based on previous academic record (30 percent), an applicant's statement of future plans (30 percent), letters of recommendation (20 percent), and professional activities (20 percent); if 2 or more applicants are judged equal based on those criteria, financial need may be considered.
Financial data: The stipend is $2,000.
Duration: 1 year.
Number awarded: 1 each year.
Deadline: December of each year.

1720
ADA DIETETIC TECHNICIAN PROGRAM SCHOLARSHIPS

American Dietetic Association
Attn: Accreditation, Education Programs, and Student Operations
216 West Jackson Boulevard, Suite 800
Chicago, IL 60606-6995
Phone: (312) 899-0040   (800) 877-1600, ext. 5400
Fax: (312) 899-4817   E-mail: education@eatright.org
Web Site: www.eatright.org
Summary: To provide financial assistance to students who are in the first year of a dietetic technician program.
Eligibility: Applicants must be in the first year of study in a CADE-approved or accredited dietetic technician program. All applicants must be U.S. citizens or permanent residents and show promise of being a valuable, contributing member of the profession. Some scholarships require membership in the association, specific dietetic practice group membership, residency in a specific state, or underrepresented minority group status. The same application form can be used for all categories.
Financial data: Awards range from $500 to $5,000.
Duration: 1 year.
Additional information: Funds must be used for the second year of study.
Number awarded: Varies each year, depending upon the funds available. Recently, the sponsoring organization awarded 209 scholarships for all its programs.
Deadline: February of each year.

1721
ADHA BACCALAUREATE SCHOLARSHIP PROGRAM

American Dental Hygienists' Association
Attn: Institute for Oral Health
444 North Michigan Avenue, Suite 3400
Chicago, IL 60611
Phone: (312) 440-8944   (800) 735-4916
Fax: (312) 440-8929   E-mail: institute@adha.net
Web Site: www.adha.org
Summary: To provide financial assistance to students preparing for careers in dental hygiene.
Eligibility: Applicants must have earned at least a 3.0 grade point average, be able to demonstrate financial need, and have completed a minimum of 1 year in a dental hygiene curriculum. Scholarships are available to 1) full-time students pursuing a baccalaureate degree in dental hygiene at a 4-year institution in the United States, and 2) dental hygienists pursuing a degree in dental hygiene or a related field in a degree completion program as either a full-time or a part-time student. Both categories of applicants must be eligible for licensure in the year of the award.
Financial data: The amount of the award depends on the need of the recipient, to a maximum of $1,500.
Duration: 1 year.
Number awarded: 1 or more each year.
Deadline: May of each year.

1722
ADHA CERTIFICATE/ASSOCIATE DEGREE SCHOLARSHIP PROGRAM

American Dental Hygienists' Association
Attn: Institute for Oral Health
444 North Michigan Avenue, Suite 3400
Chicago, IL 60611
Phone: (312) 440-8944   (800) 735-4916
Fax: (312) 440-8929   E-mail: institute@adha.net
Web Site: www.adha.org
Summary: To provide financial assistance to full-time students enrolled in certificate/associate programs in dental hygiene leading to licensure as dental hygienists.
Eligibility: Applicants must be American citizens, have earned at least a 3.0 grade point average, be able to demonstrate financial need, and have completed a minimum of 1 year in a dental hygiene curriculum. They must be enrolled in a certificate/associate degree curriculum leading to licensure as a dental hygienist in the year the award is being made.
Financial data: The amount of the award depends on the need of the recipient, to a maximum of $1,500.
Duration: 1 year.
Number awarded: 1 or more each year.
Deadline: May of each year.

1723
ADHA INSTITUTE MINORITY SCHOLARSHIP

American Dental Hygienists' Association
Attn: Institute for Oral Health
444 North Michigan Avenue, Suite 3400
Chicago, IL 60611
Phone: (312) 440-8944   (800) 735-4916
Fax: (312) 440-8929   E-mail: institute@adha.net
Web Site: www.adha.org
Summary: To provide financial assistance to minority students and males of any race enrolled in certificate/associate programs in dental hygiene.
Eligibility: This program is open to members of groups currently underrepresented in the dental hygiene profession: Native Americans, African Americans, Hispanics, Asians, and males. Applicants must have completed 1 year in a dental hygiene curriculum at the certificate/associate level with at least a 3.0 grade point average. They must intend to be full-time students and be able to demonstrate financial need.
Financial data: The amount of the award depends on the need of the recipient, to a maximum of $1,500.
Duration: 1 year; nonrenewable.
Number awarded: 2 each year.
Deadline: May of each year.

1724
ADHA PART-TIME SCHOLARSHIPS

American Dental Hygienists' Association
Attn: Institute for Oral Health
444 North Michigan Avenue, Suite 3400
Chicago, IL 60611
Phone: (312) 440-8944   (800) 735-4916
Fax: (312) 440-8929   E-mail: institute@adha.net
Web Site: www.adha.org
Summary: To provide financial assistance to students enrolled part time in doctoral, master's, baccalaureate, or certificate/associate programs in dental hygiene.
Eligibility: Applicants must have completed at least 1 year in a dental hygiene program with at least a 3.0 grade point average and be able to demonstrate financial need. They must meet all other general and specific requirements for scholarships of the American Dental Hygienists' Association (ADHA), except they may attend school on a part-time basis (rather than as a full-time student).
Financial data: The amount of the award depends on the need of the recipient, to a maximum of $1,500.
Duration: 1 year.
Number awarded: 1 each year.
Deadline: May of each year.

1725
ADMIRAL GRACE MURRAY HOPPER MEMORIAL SCHOLARSHIPS

Society of Women Engineers
230 East Ohio Street, Suite 400
Chicago, IL 60611-3265
Phone: (312) 596-5223   Fax: (312) 644-8557
E-mail: hq@swe.org
Web Site: www.swe.org
Summary: To provide financial assistance to outstanding freshmen women interested in studying engineering.
Eligibility: Incoming female freshmen who are interested in majoring in engineering at a 4-year school, college, or university are eligible to apply. The schools must be ABET accredited or SWE approved. Selection is based on merit.
Financial data: The scholarship is $1,000.
Duration: 1 year.
Additional information: This program is named for the "mother of computerized data automation in the naval service." It was established in 1992.
Number awarded: 5 each year.
Deadline: May of each year.

1726
ADOBE SYSTEMS COMPUTER SCIENCE SCHOLARSHIPS

Society of Women Engineers
230 East Ohio Street, Suite 400
Chicago, IL 60611-3265
Phone: (312) 596-5223   Fax: (312) 644-8557
E-mail: hq@swe.org   Web Site: www.swe.org
Summary: To provide financial assistance to undergraduate women majoring in computer science.
Eligibility: This program is open to women entering their junior or senior year at an ABET-accredited or SWE-approved college or university. Applicants must be majoring in computer science and have a grade point average of 3.0 or higher. Preference is given to students attending selected schools in the San Francisco Bay area of California. Selection is based on merit.
Financial data: Stipends are $2,000 or $1,500.
Duration: 1 year.
Additional information: This program was established in 2000.
Number awarded: 2 each year: 1 at $2,000 and 1 at $1,500.
Deadline: January of each year.

1727
AEA AVIATION MAINTENANCE SCHOLARSHIP

Women in Aviation, International
3647 S.R. 503 South
West Alexandria, OH 45381
Phone: (937) 839-4647   Fax: (937) 839-4645
E-mail: wai@infinet.com   Web Site: www.wiai.org
Summary: To provide financial assistance to members of Women in Aviation, International who are studying aircraft maintenance.
Eligibility: This program is open to women who are members of the sponsoring organization and seeking a degree in the aviation maintenance field at an accredited college or technical school. Preference is given to avionics majors. Applicants must have a grade point average of 2.75 or higher. Selection is based on achievements, attitude toward self and others, commitment to success, dedication to career, financial need, motivation, reliability, responsibility, and teamwork.
Financial data: The stipend is $1,000.
Duration: 1 year.
Additional information: Women in Aviation, International is a nonprofit professional organization dedicated to encouraging women to consider an aviation career, providing educational outreach activities, and networking resources to women active in the industry. This program is sponsored by the Aircraft Electronics Association (AEA).
Number awarded: 1 each year.
Deadline: December of each year.

1728
AESF UNDERGRADUATE SCHOLARSHIP PROGRAM

American Electroplaters and Surface Finishers Society
Attn: AESF Scholarship Committee
Central Florida Research Park
12644 Research Parkway
Orlando, FL 32826-3298
Phone: (407) 281-6441   Fax: (407) 281-6446
E-mail: janice@aesf.org   Web Site: www.aesf.org
Summary: To provide financial assistance to undergraduate students who are interested in majoring in subjects related to plating and surface finishing technologies.
Eligibility: This program is open to juniors and seniors in college who are majoring in chemistry, chemical engineering, environmental engineering, metallurgy, or materials science. Selection is based on career interest in surface finishing, scholarship, achievement, motivation, and potential. Financial need is not a factor.
Financial data: At least $1,500 per year. Funds are sent directly to the recipient's college or university. Schools are requested not to reduce federal, state, or institutional support for students who receive this scholarship.
Duration: 1 year; recipients may reapply for 1 additional year.
Additional information: Recipients are encouraged to submit a report or paper at the conclusion of the award period. They must be in school full time during the academic year the scholarship is received.
Number awarded: At least 1 each year.
Deadline: April of each year.

1729
AFCEA ROTC SCHOLARSHIPS

Armed Forces Communications and Electronics Association
Attn: Educational Foundation
4400 Fair Lakes Court
Fairfax, VA 22033-3899
Phone: (703) 631-6147   (800) 336-4583, ext. 6147
Fax: (703) 631-4693   E-mail: edfoundation@afcea.org
Web Site: www.afcea.org
Summary: To provide scholarships to deserving ROTC cadets who are majoring in fields related to communications and electronics.
Eligibility: Undergraduate ROTC cadets majoring in electrical or aerospace engineering, electronics, mathematics, physics, computer science, or computer engineering may apply for these scholarships. They must be nominated by their ROTC professor, be entering their junior or senior year, be U.S. citizens, be of good moral character, have demonstrated academic excellence, be motivated to complete a college education and serve as officers in the U.S. armed forces, and be able to demonstrate financial need.
Financial data: The stipend is $2,000.
Duration: 1 year; may be renewed.
Number awarded: 60 each year, divided equally among Army, Navy/Marine Corps, and Air Force ROTC programs; for each service, 10 are awarded to juniors, 10 to seniors.
Deadline: March of each year.

1730
AGCO STUDENT DESIGN COMPETITION

American Society of Agricultural Engineers
Attn: Awards Coordinator
2950 Niles Road
St. Joseph, MI 49085-9659
Phone: (616) 429-0300   Fax: (616) 429-3852
E-mail: hq@asae.org   Web Site: www.asae.org
Summary: To recognize and reward student members of the American Society of Agricultural Engineers (ASAE) who participate in the basic design of an engineering product useful to agriculture.
Eligibility: This program is open to biological and agricultural engineering students who are student members of the society. Applicants, operating as teams or individuals, submit an engineering design that involves devising a machine, component, system, or process to meet a desired need related to agricultural, food, or biological engineering. The project description they submit is judged on: establishment of need and benefit to agriculture (5 points); approach and originality (6 points); definition of design objectives and criteria (5 points); extent of analysis and synthesis of alternatives (10 points); evidence of sound evaluation and adherence to good engineering design and safety considerations (10 points); adequacy of drawings and specifications (7 points); appropriateness of tests and/or performance data (7 points); and achievement of objectives (10 points). They must also include a written report that is judged on: organization, clarity, and ease of reading (10 points); effective use of graphics, illustrations, video, etc. (5 points); and neatness, accuracy, and style (5 points). Based on the project description and written report, the top 3 entrants are invited to the society's annual meeting for an oral presentation; those are judged on: general effectiveness and audience appeal (8 points); organization and information flow (5 points); quality and adequacy of visuals (5 points); and compliance with 15-minute limit (2 points). The 3 finalists are then ranked on the basis of their total scores.
Financial data: First prize is $1,250, second prize is $1,000, and third prize is $750. Teams decide among themselves how to divide the money. The academic department of the first-place entry receives a $300 scholarship and a wall plaque.
Duration: The competition is held annually.
Number awarded: 3 each year.
Deadline: May of each year.

1731
AGNES MCINTOSH GARDEN CLUB OBJECTIVES SCHOLARSHIP

Summary: To provide financial aid to Florida undergraduates and graduate students majoring in designated areas.
See Listing #1246.

1732
AGRICULTURAL YOUTH SCHOLARSHIP

New York Farm Bureau
Attn: Scholarship Committee
Route 9W
P.O. Box 992
Glenmont, NY 12077-0992
Phone: (518) 436-8495   (800) 342-4143, ext. 5633
Fax: (518) 431-5656
Web Site: nyfb.org/programs/ScholarshipInfo.htm
Summary: To recognize and reward high school students in New York who submit outstanding essays on their involvement in agriculture.
Eligibility: This competition is open to high school juniors who live or work on a farm in New York or are involved with agriculture in some way. Farm Bureau membership is not required. Candidates must submit an essay, up to 2 pages in length, on "How Agriculture Affects My Life Now and Will Affect My Life in the Future." They must also provide information on the agricultural commodities on the farm where they live or work, their involvement in agricultural activities, their involvement in school and community activities, and their leadership roles and participation in any of those activities.
Financial data: First prize is $1,000, second $500, and third $250. All prizes must be used as college scholarships.
Duration: The competition is held annually.
Number awarded: 3 each year.
Deadline: June of each year.

1733
AGRICULTURE EDUCATION FUND SCHOLARSHIPS

Texas FFA Association
614 East 12th Street
Austin, TX 78701
Phone: (512) 480-8045   Fax: (512) 472-0555
E-mail: txffa@txaged.org   Web Site: www.txaged.org
Summary: To provide financial assistance for college to high school seniors in Texas who were involved in FFA and plan on majoring in an ag-related field in college.
Eligibility: This program is open to high school seniors in Texas who are FFA members and have been members at least 2 of the 3 previous years. Applicants must be planning to major in college in a field related to the agricultural sciences, life sciences, or natural resources. They must have completed at least 5 semesters of instruction in agriculture and/or agribusiness during high school and scored at least 950 on the SAT or 20 on the ACT. U.S. citizenship and ranking in the top half of their graduating class are also required. Selection is based on academic achievement (16 points); SAT or ACT scores (14 points); agricultural science and career related instruction (10 points); FFA achievement (20 points), including the supervised agricultural experience (10 points); financial need (10 points); and performance during interviews regarding academics (10 points), FFA achievement (5 points), and financial need (10 points).
Financial data: The stipend is $2,000.
Duration: 1 year.
Additional information: Students may not apply for both 4-H and FFA scholarships.
Number awarded: 2 each year.

1734
AIAA FOUNDATION UNDERGRADUATE DESIGN COMPETITIONS

American Institute of Aeronautics and Astronautics
Attn: Student Programs Director
1801 Alexander Bell Drive, Suite 500
Reston, VA 20191-4344
Phone: (703) 264-7536   (800) 639-AIAA
Fax: (703) 264-7551   E-mail: stephenb@aiaa.org
Web Site: www.aiaa.org
Summary: To recognize and reward outstanding designs prepared by undergraduate student members of the American Institute of Aeronautics and Astronautics (AIAA).
Eligibility: This program is open to undergraduate students who are AIAA branch or at-large student members. Individuals may enter in 2 competitions: the aircraft design competition and the hybrid rocket design competition. Teams of 3 to 10 students may enter in 3 competitions: the engine design competition, the aircraft design competition, and the space design competition. Design projects

that are used as part of an organized classroom requirement are eligible and encouraged. Designs that are submitted must be the work of the students, but a faculty advisor may provide guidance. Selection is based on technical content (35 points), organization and presentation (20 points), originality (20 points), and practical application and feasibility (25 points).
Financial data: For each of the 5 competitions, first place is $2,500, second place is $1,500, and third place is $1,000.
Duration: The competitions are held annually.
Number awarded: 3 cash awards are presented in each of the 5 competitions.
Deadline: Letters of intent must be submitted by March of each year; completed entries are due in early June of each year.

1735
AIAA FOUNDATION UNDERGRADUATE SCHOLARSHIP PROGRAM

American Institute of Aeronautics and Astronautics
Attn: Student Programs Director
1801 Alexander Bell Drive, Suite 500
Reston, VA 20191-4344
Phone: (703) 264-7536   (800) 639-AIAA
Fax: (703) 264-7551   E-mail: stephenb@aiaa.org
Web Site: www.aiaa.org
Summary: To provide financial assistance to student members of the American Institute of Aeronautics and Astronautics (AIAA).
Eligibility: Eligible to apply are college students who have completed at least 1 semester or quarter of full-time college work in engineering or science fields that relate to aerospace. They must be U.S. citizens or permanent residents, have an excellent academic record (at least a 3.0 grade point average), be student members or willing to become student members of the sponsoring organization, and be interested in a career in the aerospace field. Selection is based on grade point average, career goals, letters of recommendation, and extracurricular activities.
Financial data: The stipend is $2,000.
Duration: 1 year; may reapply.
Additional information: This program includes 4 named scholarships, awarded to the top senior applicants: the A. Thomas Young Scholarship, the L.S. "Skip" Fletcher Scholarship, the Liquid Propulsion Technical Committee Scholarship, and the Space Transportation Technical Committee Scholarship.
Number awarded: 30 each year.
Deadline: January of each year.

1736
AIR FORCE ROTC BIOMEDICAL SCIENCES SCHOLARSHIPS

U.S. Air Force
Attn: Headquarters AFROTC/RRUC
551 East Maxwell Boulevard
Maxwell AFB, AL 36112-6106
Phone: (334) 953-2091   (800) 522-0033, ext. 2091
Fax: (334) 953-5271
Web Site: www.afrotc.com/scholarships/icschol/professional/bsc.htm
Summary: To provide financial assistance to college students who are interested in a career as a physical therapist or pharmacist and are willing to serve as Air Force officers following completion of their bachelor's degree.
Eligibility: This program is open to U.S. citizens who are freshmen or sophomores in college and interested in a career as a physical therapist or pharmacist. Applicants must have a grade point average of 3.25 or higher and meet all other academic and physical requirements for participation in AFROTC. At the time of graduation with a bachelor's degree, they may be no more than 27 years of age. They must agree to serve for at least 4 years as nonline active-duty Air Force officers following graduation from college.
Financial data: Currently, awards are type 2 AFROTC scholarships that provide for payment of tuition and fees, to a maximum of $15,000 per year, plus an annual book allowance of $510. All recipients are also awarded a tax-free subsistence allowance for 10 months of each year that is $250 per month during their sophomore year, $300 during their junior year, and $350 during their senior year.
Duration: 2 or 3 years, provided the recipient maintains a GPA of 3.0 or higher.
Additional information: Recipients must also complete 4 years of aerospace studies courses at 1 of the 143 colleges and universities that have an Air Force ROTC unit on campus or 1 of the 850 colleges that have cross-enrollment agreements with those institutions. They must also attend a 4-week summer training camp at an Air Force base, usually between their sophomore and junior

years. Following completion of their bachelor's degree, scholarship recipients earn a commission as a second lieutenant in the Air Force and serve at least 4 years.
Deadline: June of each year.

1737
AIR FORCE ROTC EXPRESS SCHOLARSHIPS

U.S. Air Force
Attn: Headquarters AFROTC/RRUC
551 East Maxwell Boulevard
Maxwell AFB, AL 36112-6106
Phone: (334) 953-2091   (800) 522-0033, ext. 2091
Fax: (334) 953-5271
Web Site: www.afrotc.com/scholarships/icschol/express/index.htm
Summary: To provide financial assistance to college students who are majoring in critical Air Force officer fields and are willing to serve as Air Force officers following completion of their bachelor's degree.
Eligibility: This program is open to U.S. citizens who are freshmen in college and pursuing a degree in electrical engineering (approved by the Accreditation Board for Engineering and Technology) or meteorology (approved by the Air Force Institute of Technology). Applicants must have a grade point average of 2.5 or higher and meet all other academic and physical requirements for participation in AFROTC. At the time of graduation with a bachelor's degree, they may be no more than 27 years of age. They must agree to serve for at least 4 years as active-duty Air Force officers following graduation from college.
Financial data: Currently, awards are type 2 AFROTC scholarships that provide for payment of tuition and fees, to a maximum of $15,000 per year, plus an annual book allowance of $510. All recipients are also awarded a tax-free subsistence allowance for 10 months of each year that is $250 per month during the freshman and sophomore years, $300 during the junior year, and $350 during the senior year.
Duration: 3 1/2 years, until completion of a bachelor's degree.
Additional information: Recipients must also complete 4 years of aerospace studies courses at 1 of the 143 colleges and universities that have an Air Force ROTC unit on campus or 1 of the 850 colleges that have cross-enrollment agreements with those institutions. They must also attend a 4-week summer training camp at an Air Force base, usually between their sophomore and junior years. Following completion of their bachelor's degree, scholarship recipients earn a commission as a second lieutenant in the Air Force and serve at least 4 years.

1738
AIR FORCE ROTC NURSING SCHOLARSHIPS

U.S. Air Force
Attn: Headquarters AFROTC/RRUC
551 East Maxwell Boulevard
Maxwell AFB, AL 36112-6106
Phone: (334) 953-2091   (800) 522-0033, ext. 2091
Fax: (334) 953-5271
Web Site: www.afrotc.com/scholarships/icschol/professional/nursing.htm
Summary: To provide financial assistance to college students who are interested in a career as a nurse and are willing to serve as Air Force officers following completion of their bachelor's degree.
Eligibility: This program is open to U.S. citizens who are freshmen or sophomores in college and interested in a career as a nurse. Applicants must have a cumulative grade point average of 3.0 or higher at the end of their freshman year and meet all other academic and physical requirements for participation in AFROTC. At the time of graduation with a bachelor's degree, they may be no more than 27 years of age. They must agree to serve for at least 4 years as active-duty Air Force nurses following graduation from college.
Financial data: Currently, awards are type 2 AFROTC scholarships that provide for payment of tuition and fees, to a maximum of $15,000 per year, plus an annual book allowance of $510. All recipients are also awarded a tax-free subsistence allowance for 10 months of each year that is $250 per month during their sophomore year, $300 during their junior year, and $350 during their senior year.
Duration: 2 or 3 years, provided recipient maintains a GPA of 3.0 or higher.
Additional information: Recipients must also complete 4 years of aerospace studies courses at 1 of the 143 colleges and universities that have an Air Force ROTC unit on campus or 1 of the 850 colleges that have cross-enrollment agreements with those institutions. They must also attend a 4-week summer training camp at an Air Force base, usually between their sophomore and junior years. Following completion of their bachelor's degree, scholarship recipients earn a commission as a second lieutenant in the Air Force and serve at least 4 years.
Deadline: June of each year.

1739
AIR FORCE ROTC PRE-DENTAL SCHOLARSHIPS

U.S. Air Force
Attn: Headquarters AFROTC/RRUC
551 East Maxwell Boulevard
Maxwell AFB, AL 36112-6106
Phone: (334) 953-2091   (800) 522-0033, ext. 2091
Fax: (334) 953-5271
Web Site: www.afrotc.com/scholarships/icschol/professional/predental.htm
Summary: To provide financial assistance to college students who are interested in a career as a dentist and are willing to serve as Air Force officers following completion of their bachelor's degree.
Eligibility: This program is open to U.S. citizens who are full-time freshmen or sophomores in college and interested in a career as a dentist. Freshmen must have a cumulative grade point average of 3.65 or higher; sophomores must have at least a 3.5 grade point average. Applicants must meet all other academic and physical requirements for participation in AFROTC. They must have completed, or be scheduled to complete by the end of their junior year, 1 year of English, general or inorganic chemistry (with lab), organic chemistry (with lab), physics (equivalent to mechanics, heat, light, sound, and electricity), general biology, zoology (with lab), and mathematics (equivalent to analytical geometry and differential and integral calculus). At the time of graduation with a bachelor's degree, they may be no more than 27 years of age. They must agree to accept an Armed Forces Health Professions Scholarship or to attend the Uniformed Services University of the Health Sciences and then to become an Air Force dentist.
Financial data: Currently, awards are type 2 AFROTC scholarships that provide for payment of tuition and fees, to a maximum of $15,000 per year, plus an annual book allowance of $510. All recipients are also awarded a tax-free subsistence allowance for 10 months of each year that is $250 per month during their sophomore year, $300 during their junior year, and $350 during their senior year.
Duration: 2 or 3 years, provided the recipient maintains a grade point average of 3.0 or higher.
Additional information: Recipients must also complete 4 years of aerospace studies courses at 1 of the 143 colleges and universities that have an Air Force ROTC unit on campus or 1 of the 850 colleges that have cross-enrollment agreements with those institutions. They must also attend a 4-week summer training camp at an Air Force base, usually between their sophomore and junior years. Following completion of their dental degree, scholarship recipients earn a commission as a second lieutenant in the Air Force and serve at least 4 years.
Deadline: June of each year.

1740
AIR FORCE ROTC PRE-HEALTH SCHOLARSHIPS

U.S. Air Force
Attn: Headquarters AFROTC/RRUC
551 East Maxwell Boulevard
Maxwell AFB, AL 36112-6106
Phone: (334) 953-2091   (800) 522-0033, ext. 2091
Fax: (334) 953-5271
Web Site: www.afrotc.com/scholarships/icschol/professional/prehealth.htm
Summary: To provide financial assistance to college students who are interested in a career as a physician and are willing to serve as Air Force officers following completion of their bachelor's degree.
Eligibility: This program is open to U.S. citizens who are full-time freshmen or sophomores in college and interested in a medical career. Freshmen must have a cumulative grade point average of 3.65 or higher; sophomores must have at least a 3.5 grade point average. Applicants must meet all other academic and physical requirements for participation in AFROTC. They must have completed, or be scheduled to complete by the end of their junior year, 1 year of English, general or inorganic chemistry (with lab), organic chemistry (with lab), physics (equivalent to mechanics, heat, light, sound, and electricity), general biology, zoology (with lab), and mathematics (equivalent to analytical geometry and differential and integral calculus). At the time of graduation with a bachelor's degree, they may be no more than 27 years of age. They must agree to accept an Armed Forces Health Professions Scholarship or to attend the Uniformed Services University of the Health Sciences and then to become an Air Force doctor.
Financial data: Currently, awards are type 2 AFROTC scholarships that provide for payment of tuition and fees, to a maximum of $15,000 per year, plus an annual book allowance of $510. All recipients are also awarded a tax-free subsistence allowance for 10 months of each year that is $250 per month during their sophomore year, $300 during their junior year, and $350 during their senior year.
Duration: 2 or 3 years, provided the recipient maintains a grade point average of 3.0 or higher.
Additional information: Recipients must also complete 4 years of aerospace studies courses at 1 of the 143 colleges and universities that have an Air Force ROTC unit on campus or 1 of the 850 colleges that have cross-enrollment agreements with those institutions. They must also attend a 4-week summer training camp at an Air Force base, usually between their sophomore and junior years. Following completion of their medical degree, scholarship recipients earn a commission as a second lieutenant in the Air Force and serve at least 4 years.
Deadline: June of each year.

1741
AIR TRAFFIC CONTROL ASSOCIATION STUDENT SCHOLARSHIP PROGRAM

Air Traffic Control Association
Arlington Courthouse Plaza 11
2300 Clardendon Boulevard, Suite 711
Arlington, VA 22201
Phone: (703) 522-5717   Fax: (703) 522-7251
E-mail: atca@worldnett.att.net   Web Site: www.atca.org
Summary: To provide financial assistance to students working on a bachelor's degree or higher in aviation.
Eligibility: This program is open to half- or full-time students who are U.S. citizens, enrolled or accepted for enrollment in an accredited college or university, taking classes to prepare for an aviation-related career, working on a bachelor's or graduate degree, registered for at least 6 hours, and at least 30 semester or 45 quarter hours away from graduation. Applicants must submit an essay on "How My Educational Efforts Will Enhance My Potential Contribution to Aviation." Financial need is considered in the selection process.
Financial data: Stipends range from $1,500 to $2,500.
Duration: 1 year; may be renewed.
Number awarded: Varies each year, depending on the number, qualifications, and need of the applicants.
Deadline: April of each year.

1742
AIRBUS LEADERSHIP GRANT

Women in Aviation, International
3647 S.R. 503 South
West Alexandria, OH 45381
Phone: (937) 839-4647   Fax: (937) 839-4645
E-mail: wai@infinet.com   Web Site: www.wiai.org
Summary: To provide financial assistance for college to members of Women in Aviation, International.
Eligibility: This program is open to women who are members of the sponsoring organization and college sophomores or higher working on a college degree in an aviation-related field. They must have earned at least a 2.0 grade point average and be able to demonstrate leadership potential. All applicants must submit an essay addressing their career aspirations and how they have exhibited leadership skills, along with an application form, 3 letters of recommendation, a resume, copies of all aviation and medical certificates, and the last 3 pages of their pilot logbook, if applicable. Selection is based on achievements, attitude toward self and others, commitment to success, dedication to career, financial need, motivation, reliability, responsibility, and teamwork.
Financial data: The stipend is $1,000.
Duration: 1 year.
Additional information: Women in Aviation, International is a nonprofit professional organization dedicated to encouraging women to consider an aviation career, providing educational outreach activities, and networking resources to women active in the industry.
Number awarded: 1 or more each year.
Deadline: December of each year.

1743
AIRGAS-TERRY JARVIS MEMORIAL SCHOLARSHIP

American Welding Society
Attn: AWS Foundation, Inc.
550 N.W. LeJeune Road
Miami, FL 33126
Phone: (305) 443-9353, ext. 461   (800) 443-9353, ext. 461
Fax: (305) 443-7559   E-mail: vpinsky@aws.org

Web Site: www.aws.org/foundation/airgas.html

Summary: To provide financial assistance to college students majoring in welding engineering.

Eligibility: This program is open to full-time undergraduate students who are pursuing at least a 4-year bachelor's degree in welding engineering or welding engineering technology (although preference is given to welding engineering students interested in pursuing a career with an industrial gas or welding equipment distributor). Applicants must have a grade point average of 2.8 or higher overall and 3.0 or higher in engineering courses. Financial need is not considered in the selection process. Priority is given to applicants who reside or attend school in Alabama, Florida, or Georgia. U.S. or Canadian citizenship is required.

Financial data: The stipend is $2,500.

Duration: 1 year; recipients may reapply.

Additional information: This is 1 of the sponsor's Pioneers of Welding Scholarships.

Number awarded: 1 each year.

Deadline: January of each year.

1744
AIRLOG IMAGING CAREER CHANGE TO AVIATION SCHOLARSHIP

Women in Aviation, International
3647 S.R. 503 South
West Alexandria, OH 45381
Phone: (937) 839-4647   Fax: (937) 839-4645
E-mail: wai@infinet.com
Web Site: www.wiai.org

Summary: To provide financial assistance to members of Women in Aviation, International who are interested in making a career change to aviation.

Eligibility: This program is open to women older than 30 years of age who are members of the sponsoring organization and interested in making a career change to aviation. Applicants must be a full-time student working on a bachelor's or master's degree in an aviation field with a grade point average of 3.0 or higher. Selection is based on achievements, attitude toward self and others, commitment to success, dedication to career, financial need, motivation, reliability, responsibility, and teamwork.

Financial data: The stipend is $1,000.

Duration: 1 year.

Additional information: Women in Aviation, International is a nonprofit professional organization dedicated to encouraging women to consider an aviation career, providing educational outreach activities, and networking resources to women active in the industry.

Number awarded: 1 each year.

Deadline: December of each year.

1745
AIRLOG IMAGING MAINTENANCE SCHOLARSHIP

Women in Aviation, International
3647 S.R. 503 South
West Alexandria, OH 45381
Phone: (937) 839-4647   Fax: (937) 839-4645
E-mail: wai@infinet.com
Web Site: www.wiai.org

Summary: To provide financial assistance to members of Women in Aviation, International who are studying aircraft maintenance.

Eligibility: This program is open to women who are members of the sponsoring organization and have completed at least half of their aircraft maintenance training or have completed their training and are working on a bachelor's degree in a related field. Applicants must be full-time students with a grade point average of 3.0 or higher. Selection is based on achievements, attitude toward self and others, commitment to success, dedication to career, financial need, motivation, reliability, responsibility, and teamwork.

Financial data: The stipend is $1,000.

Duration: 1 year.

Additional information: Women in Aviation, International is a nonprofit professional organization dedicated to encouraging women to consider an aviation career, providing educational outreach activities, and networking resources to women active in the industry.

Number awarded: 1 each year.

Deadline: December of each year.

1746
ALABAMA GOLF COURSE SUPERINTENDENTS ASSOCIATION SCHOLARSHIP

Alabama Golf Course Superintendents Association
P.O. Box 661214
Birmingham, AL 35266-1214
Phone: (205) 979-5225

Summary: To provide financial assistance to students from Alabama who are majoring in turfgrass management in college.

Eligibility: To be eligible, students must be from the state of Alabama, be currently in the second or higher year of college, have a documented need for financial assistance, and be majoring in turfgrass management (with plans to enter the field).

Financial data: The stipend is $1,000.

Duration: 1 year.

Additional information: Information is also available from Don Dockery, North River Yacht Club, P.O. Box 48999, Tuscaloosa, AL 35404-9899.

Number awarded: 2 each year.

Deadline: October of each year.

1747
ALASKAN AVIATION SAFETY FOUNDATION MEMORIAL SCHOLARSHIP PROGRAM

Alaskan Aviation Safety Foundation
Attn: Scholarship Committee
4340 Postmark Drive
Anchorage, AK 99502-1066
Phone: (907) 243-7237   Fax: (907) 243-7237
Web Site: www.Alaska.net/~etc/aasf

Summary: To provide financial assistance to Alaska residents who are enrolled in an aviation-related program.

Eligibility: Students who meet the following requirements are eligible to apply: enrolled in an aviation-related program at an accredited college, university, trade school, or approved training center; spent at least 2 of the last 3 years in continuous official residency in Alaska; and completed at least 2 semesters or 30 percent of the work toward their professional goal (or, at least, have a private pilot certificate). Applications may be requested by phone, letter, or fax. School transcripts, letters of recommendation, and aviation certificates currently held must be submitted as part of the application package. Selection is based on academic background, aviation-related work experiences, other aviation-related activities, aviation awards, career goals, and financial need.

Financial data: A stipend is awarded (exact amount not specified).

Duration: 1 year.

Number awarded: Varies each year; recently, 2 were awarded.

Deadline: March of each year.

1748
ALBERT E. AND FLORENCE W. NEWTON NURSE SCHOLARSHIP

Rhode Island Foundation
Attn: Scholarship Coordinator
One Union Station
Providence, RI 02903
Phone: (401) 274-4564   Fax: (401) 331-8085
E-mail: libbym@rifoundation.org
Web Site: www.rifoundation.org

Summary: To provide financial assistance for further education to nurses in Rhode Island.

Eligibility: This program is open to 1) undergraduate students in their final year or semester seeking to become an R.N. licensed in Rhode Island; 2) active practicing R.N.s licensed in Rhode Island and pursuing a bachelor's degree in nursing; and 3) R.N.s licensed in Rhode Island seeking a graduate degree in nursing. Applicants must be studying at a Rhode Island nursing school on a full- or part-time basis and able to demonstrate financial need. As part of the selection process, they must submit an essay, up to 300 words, on their career goals as they relate to patient care.

Financial data: Stipends range from $500 to $2,500 per year.

Duration: 1 year; may be renewed.

Number awarded: Approximately 15 each year.

Deadline: March or September of each year.

1749
ALCOA FOUNDATION ACADEMIC SCHOLARSHIP

American Association of Occupational Health Nurses, Inc.
Attn: AAOHN Foundation
2920 Brandywine Road, Suite 100
Atlanta, GA 30341-4146
Phone: (770) 455-7757   Fax: (770) 455-7271
E-mail: foundation@aaohn.org
Web Site: www.aaohn.org
Summary: To provide financial assistance to registered nurses who are pursuing a bachelor's or graduate degree to prepare for a career in occupational and environmental health.
Eligibility: This program is open to registered nurses who are enrolled in a baccalaureate, master's, or doctoral degree program. Applicants must demonstrate an interest in, and commitment to, occupational and environmental health. Selection is based on 2 letters of recommendation and a 500-word essay on the applicant's professional goals as they relate to the academic activity and the field of occupational and environmental health.
Financial data: The stipend is $1,500.
Duration: 1 year; may be renewed up to 2 additional years.
Additional information: Funding for this program is provided by the Alcoa Foundation.
Number awarded: 1 each year.
Deadline: November of each year.

1750
ALFRED G. AND ELMA M. MILOTTE SCHOLARSHIP

Summary: To provide financial assistance to high school seniors or graduates in Washington state who are interested in "portraying wilderness areas in a manner to benefit citizens of the United States now and in the years to come."
See Listing #1255.

1751
ALFRED STEELE ENGINEERING SCHOLARSHIP

American Society of Plumbing Engineers
Attn: Scholarship Selection Committee
8614 West Catalpa Avenue, Suite 1007
Chicago, IL 60656-1116
Phone: (773) 693-ASPE   Fax: (773) 695-9007
E-mail: aspehq@aol.com
Web Site: www.aspe.org
Summary: To provide financial assistance for the study of engineering to members of the American Society of Plumbing Engineers (ASPE) and their families.
Eligibility: This program is open to members of the society, their spouses, and children. Applicants who are already in college must be full-time students enrolled in a school or program of engineering with a grade point average of 3.0 or higher. Seniors in high school who will graduate in June of the application year are also eligible if they have at least a 3.0 grade point average and have been accepted into a college, university, or technical school where they plan to enroll in a school or program of engineering as a full-time student. Selection is based on grade point average (1 to 5 points), letters of recommendation (10 to 15 points), personal activities and community involvement (10 to 15 points), a statement of personal achievement (15 to 30 points), and an essay on interest in engineering that demonstrates the imaginative and creative nature of the applicant (20 to 35 points).
Financial data: The stipend is $1,000 per year. Funds are paid directly to the recipient's tuition account at a college, university, or technical school.
Duration: 1 year.
Number awarded: Up to 5 each year.
Deadline: August of each year.

1752
ALFRED T. GRANGER STUDENT ART FUND

Summary: To provide financial assistance to residents of Vermont who are interested in pursuing an undergraduate or graduate degree in a field related to design.
See Listing #1256.

1753
ALICE T. SCHAFER PRIZE FOR EXCELLENCE IN MATHEMATICS

Association for Women in Mathematics
c/o University of Maryland
4114 Computer & Space Sciences Building
College Park, MD 20742-2461
Phone: (301) 405-7892   E-mail: awm@math.umd.edu
Web Site: www.awm-math.org
Summary: To recognize and reward undergraduate women who have demonstrated excellence in mathematics.
Eligibility: Women may not apply for this award; they must be nominated by a member of the mathematical community. The nominee may be at any level in her undergraduate career. Selection is based on the quality of the student's performance in advanced mathematics courses and special programs, evidence of a real interest in mathematics, and an ability to work independently. Performance in local and national mathematics competitions is also considered.
Financial data: The prize is $1,000.
Duration: The competition is held annually.
Additional information: This competition was established in 1990.
Number awarded: 1 each year.
Deadline: Nominations must be submitted by September of each year.

1754
ALLEGHENY MOUNTAIN SECTION SCHOLARSHIPS

Air & Waste Management Association-Allegheny Mountain Section
P.O. Box 81056
Pittsburgh, PA 15217
Phone: (412) 731-1339   Fax: (412) 242-7764
E-mail: wpawma@trfn.clpgh.org
Web Site: trfn.clpgh.org/wpawma/schol2.htm
Summary: To provide financial assistance to undergraduate students in western Pennsylvania and West Virginia who are interested in pursuing a career in a field related to air and waste management.
Eligibility: This program is open to students enrolled at designated colleges and universities in western Pennsylvania and West Virginia. Applicants must be undergraduates who are interested in pursuing a career in environmental science, engineering, or law.
Financial data: The stipend is $1,500.
Duration: 1 year.
Additional information: Information is also available from the scholarship chair, Dennis Hixenbaugh, (412) 747-4508, E-mail: dhixenbaugh@vaiipitt.vai.co.at.
Number awarded: Up to 3 each year.
Deadline: May of each year.

1755
ALLEN J. BALDWIN SCHOLARSHIP

ASME International
Attn: American Society of Mechanical Engineers Auxiliary, Inc.
Three Park Avenue
New York, NY 10016-5990
Phone: (212) 591-7733   (800) THE-ASME
Fax: (212) 591-7674   E-mail: horvathb@asme.org
Web Site: www.asme.org/auxiliary/scholarshiploans
Summary: To provide financial support for the study of mechanical engineering to students in their final year of undergraduate study.
Eligibility: Eligible are students completing the junior year of a 4-year program or the fourth year of a 5-year program in mechanical engineering. Applicants must be U.S. citizens enrolled in colleges and universities with accredited departments of mechanical engineering. If the school has a chapter of the Student Section of the American Society of Mechanical Engineers (ASME), the applicant must be a member. Selection is based on scholastic achievement, financial need, character, leadership, and participation in ASME activities.
Financial data: The stipend is $2,000.
Duration: 1 year.
Additional information: This program was first awarded for 2001. Further information and an application are available by sending a self-addressed stamped envelope to Mrs. Alverta Cover, 5425 Caldwell Mill Road, Birmingham, AL 35242, (205) 991-6109, E-mail: undergradauxsch@asme.org.
Number awarded: 1 or more each year.
Deadline: March of each year.

1756
ALLIED HEALTH TO BSN SCHOLARSHIP

Society of Otorhinolaryngology and Head-Neck Nurses, Inc.
116 Canal Street, Suite A
New Smyrna Beach, FL 32168
Phone: (386) 428-1695   Fax: (386) 423-7566
E-mail: info@sohnnurse.com   Web Site: www.sohnnurse.com
Summary: To provide financial assistance to allied health providers interested in working on a bachelor's degree in nursing.
Eligibility: This program is open to allied health providers who are practicing in otorhinolaryngology. They must be interested in working on a B.S. degree in nursing. Applicants must submit a copy of their current registration in a B.S.N. program, a copy of their latest transcript (must have at least a 3.0 grade point average), a statement of current financial assistance received and required, 3 letters of recommendation, and a narrative of 500 to 750 words describing their goals in nursing and the society.
Financial data: A stipend is awarded (exact amount not specified).
Duration: 1 year.
Number awarded: 1 each year.
Deadline: July of each year.

1757
ALWIN B. NEWTON SCHOLARSHIP

American Society of Heating, Refrigerating and Air-Conditioning Engineers, Inc.
Attn: Scholarship Administrator
1791 Tullie Circle, N.E.
Atlanta, GA 30329-2305
Phone: (404) 636-8400   Fax: (404) 321-5478
E-mail: benedict@ashrae.org
Web Site: www.ashrae.org
Summary: To provide financial assistance to engineering students interested in heating, ventilating, air conditioning, and refrigeration (HVAC&R).
Eligibility: This program is open to undergraduate engineering and engineering technology students enrolled in a school recognized as accredited by the American Society of Heating, Refrigerating and Air-Conditioning Engineers (ASHRAE). Applicants must be pursuing a course of study that has traditionally been preparatory for the profession of HVAC&R. They must have a grade point average of at least 3.0 and must be full-time students with at least 1 full year of undergraduate study remaining. Selection is based on potential service to the HVAC&R profession, financial need, leadership ability, recommendations from instructors, and character.
Financial data: The stipend is $3,000 per year.
Duration: 1 year.
Number awarded: 1 each year.
Deadline: November of each year.

1758
AMBUCS SCHOLARSHIPS FOR THERAPISTS

National AMBUCS, Inc.
Attn: Scholarship Coordinator
P.O. Box 5127
High Point, NC 27262
Phone: (336) 869-2166   Fax: (336) 887-8451
E-mail: ambucs@ambucs.com
Web Site: www.ambucs.com
Summary: To provide financial assistance to undergraduate and graduate students who are interested in preparing for a career serving disabled citizens in various fields of clinical therapy.
Eligibility: To be eligible for consideration, applicants must be U.S. citizens; be able to document financial need; have earned at least a 3.0 grade point average; be accepted at the upper-division or graduate level in an accredited program that qualifies the students for clinical practice in occupational therapy, physical therapy, speech language pathology, or hearing audiology; and express an intent to enter clinical practice in therapy in the United States upon completion of the funded studies. Programs for therapy assistants are not included. Applications for financial assistance must include the following: a completed application form, a copy of the enrollment certificate, college transcripts for the last 3 semesters, a 500-word essay on the applicant's interest in therapy as a career, and a statement of family financial circumstances. Selection is based on financial need, commitment to local community, demonstrated academic accomplishment, character for compassion and integrity, and career objectives.

Financial data: Most of these awards range from $500 to $1,500 per year; 1 scholarship of $6,000 for 2 years is also awarded. Funds are paid directly to the recipient's school.
Duration: 1 year.
Additional information: This program was established in 1955; since then, the association has awarded more than $5 million for more than 9,900 scholarships.
Number awarded: Approximately 400 each year, with a total value of $225,000.
Deadline: April of each year.

1759
AMERICAN ANGUS AUXILIARY SCHOLARSHIPS

National Junior Angus Association
Attn: Director Junior Activities
3201 Frederick Boulevard
St. Joseph, MO 64506
Phone: (816) 383-5100   Fax: (816) 233-9703
E-mail: jfisher@angus.org   Web Site: www.angus.org/njaa
Summary: To provide financial assistance for college to high school seniors who are members of the National Junior Angus Association (NJAA) and participate in state and regional activities related to Angus.
Eligibility: This program is open to members of the association who are nominated by state or regional scholarship chairs; each chair is entitled to nominate 1 boy and 1 girl who are judged in separate divisions. Candidates must be unmarried high school seniors who have participated in Angus projects and have a part in those activities at the time of application. In addition to participation in Angus projects and activities, selection is based on participation in school, church, community, and other ag-related (FFA, 4-H) activities; junior Angus show record; open show record; showmanship record and livestock judging contest; Angus herd improvement record; school transcripts; and letters of reference.
Financial data: For each division, first place is $1,800, second place is $1,600, third place is $1,500, fourth place is $1,400, and fifth place is $1,200. Funds are sent to the recipients' college or university upon proof of full-time enrollment.
Duration: 1 year.
Additional information: Further information is available from American Angus Auxiliary, Scholarship Chairperson, Jane Ebert, 4531 Arnold Road, Lexington, NC 27295, (336) 731-4974, Fax: (336) 731-0082, E-mail: eberlee@infoave.net. Recipients may pursue any field of study in college. The winners in the girl's division are invited to compete for the Miss American Angus title at the auxiliary's annual meeting in November.
Number awarded: 10 each year: 5 boys and 5 girls.
Deadline: May of each year.

1760
AMERICAN ASSOCIATION OF CEREAL CHEMISTS FOUNDATION UNDERGRADUATE SCHOLARSHIP PROGRAM

American Association of Cereal Chemists
Attn: Foundation
3340 Pilot Knob Road
St. Paul, MN 55121-2097
Phone: (651) 454-7250   Fax: (651) 454-0766
E-mail: aacc@scisoc.org
Web Site: www.scisoc.org/aacc/ABOUT/Fellowships/UndergradProgram.html
Summary: To provide financial assistance to undergraduate students preparing for a career in cereal chemistry and technology.
Eligibility: Applicants must have completed at least 1 term of college with a minimum grade point average of 3.0 both cumulatively and in science and mathematics courses. They must demonstrate an interest in and intent to pursue a career in grain-based food science and technology or in a related area in industry, academia, or government. Recipients must be pursuing an approved course of study leading to a degree from an institution that conducts fundamental investigations for the advancement of cereal science and technology, including oilseeds. Selection is based on a list of scholarships previously or currently held; a list of awards and honors received in high school and/or college; a list of extracurricular activities and hobbies; a summary of work experience, internships, and related to projects; 3 letters of recommendation; transcripts of college or university undergraduate work; and a letter that describes career plans and their relationship to pertinent courses taken or planned, especially courses related to cereal science or technology, including oilseeds. Age, sex, race, financial need, and previous receipt or non-receipt of this scholarship are not considered.
Financial data: Stipends are $2,000, $1,500, or $1,000 per year.
Duration: 1 year; may be renewed.

Additional information: Funding for this program is supported by annual contributions from various firms in the cereal industry and from divisions of the American Association of Cereal Chemists (AACC).

Number awarded: Up to 15 each year.

Deadline: March of each year.

1761
AMERICAN COUNCIL OF INDEPENDENT LABORATORIES ACADEMIC SCHOLARSHIPS

American Council of Independent Laboratories
Attn: ACIL Scholarship Alliance
1629 K Street, N.W., Suite 400
Washington, DC 20006-1633
Phone: (202) 887-5872   Fax: (202) 887-0021
E-mail: info@acil.org
Web Site: www.acil.org

Summary: To provide financial assistance to undergraduate and graduate students majoring in the natural and physical sciences.

Eligibility: Candidates must be at least juniors in a bachelor degree-granting institution or be graduate students. They must be majoring in 1 of the following sciences: physics, chemistry, engineering, geology, biology, or environmental sciences. Selection is based on academic achievement, career goals, leadership, and financial need. Scholarships are given annually to students in the association's 4 geographic regions: eastern, 2003; southern, 2004; western, 2005; and central, 2006.

Financial data: Stipends range from $1,000 to $2,000.

Duration: 1 year.

Number awarded: Varies each year.

Deadline: April of each year.

1762
AMERICAN DIETETIC ASSOCIATION BACCALAUREATE OR COORDINATED PROGRAM

American Dietetic Association
Attn: Accreditation, Education Programs, and Student Operations
216 West Jackson Boulevard, Suite 800
Chicago, IL 60606-6995
Phone: (312) 899-0040   (800) 877-1600, ext. 5400
Fax: (312) 899-4817   E-mail: education@eatright.org
Web Site: www.eatright.org

Summary: To provide financial assistance to students who will be at least juniors in a CADE-approved college or university program in dietetics.

Eligibility: Applicants must have completed the academic requirements in a CADE-accredited/approved college or university program for at least junior status in the dietetics program. All applicants must be U.S. citizens or permanent residents and show promise of being a valuable, contributing member of the profession. Some scholarships require membership in the association, specific dietetic practice group membership, residency in a specific state, or underrepresented minority group status. The same application form can be used for all categories.

Financial data: Awards range from $500 to $5,000.

Duration: 1 year.

Number awarded: Varies each year, depending upon the funds available. Recently, the sponsoring organization awarded 209 scholarships for all its programs.

Deadline: February of each year.

1763
AMERICAN FIRE SPRINKLER ASSOCIATION ANNUAL ESSAY SCHOLARSHIP CONTEST

American Fire Sprinkler Association
12959 Jupiter Road, Suite 142
Dallas, TX 75238-3200
Phone: (214) 349-5965   Fax: (214) 343-8898
E-mail: econtest@firesprinkler.org
Web Site: www.firesprinkler.org

Summary: To recognize and reward high school seniors who write outstanding essays on fire sprinklers.

Eligibility: This program is open to seniors at high schools in the United States. Applicants must submit an essay of 700 to 1,000 words on a topic that varies annually but relates to fire sprinklers. Recently, the topic was "Describe the history and impact of automatic fire sprinklers." Entries are first judged in regional competitions and then forwarded to the national level. Selection is based on creativity, use of original sources (e.g., personal interviews with fire chiefs or other fire safety professionals), content, accuracy, writing skills, and grammar.

Financial data: At the national level, the first-prize winner receives a $3,000 scholarship for college, the second-prize winner receives a $2,000 scholarship, and the third-prize winner receives a $1,000 scholarship. Regional winners receive $1,000 each. Funds are paid directly to the recipients' educational institutions. The school of each winning student receives an additional $500 for their general fund.

Duration: The competition is held annually.

Additional information: Students in the following states are eligible to receive additional scholarships in local competitions: Alabama, Connecticut, Florida, Georgia, New Mexico, North Carolina, South Carolina, Virginia, and Washington. This competition was first held in 1996.

Number awarded: 3 national winners and 7 regional winners receive scholarships each year.

Deadline: December of each year.

1764
AMERICAN GROUND WATER TRUST-AMTROL INC. SCHOLARSHIP

American Ground Water Trust
16 Centre Street
P.O. Box 1796
Concord, NH 03302
Phone: (603) 228-5444   Fax: (603) 228-6557
E-mail: info@agwt.org
Web Site: www.agwt.org/amtrol.htm

Summary: To provide financial assistance to high school seniors and current college students who are interested in preparing for a career in a ground water-related field.

Eligibility: This program is open to high school seniors and current college students who have earned a grade point average of 3.0 or higher in high school, are planning a career in a ground water-related field, and have completed a science/environmental project in high school that directly involved ground water resources or have had vacation/out-of-school work experience that is directly related to the environment and natural resources. Applicants must submit a 500-word essay on "Ground Water-An Important Environmental and Economic Resource for America" and a 300-word description of their high school ground water project and/or practical environmental work experience. Selection is based on the above criteria, and on the applicant's references and academic record. Financial need is not considered in the selection process. U.S. citizenship or permanent resident status is required.

Financial data: Stipends range from $1,000 to $2,000. Funds are paid directly to the recipient's college.

Duration: 1 year.

Additional information: At the American Ground Water Trust's expense, scholarship recipients may be invited to travel to a national or regional ground water conference or meeting. Funding for this program is provided by AMTROL Inc.

Number awarded: 2 each year.

Deadline: May of each year.

1765
AMERICAN INSTITUTE OF STEEL CONSTRUCTION UNDERGRADUATE SCHOLARSHIPS

American Institute of Steel Construction
One East Wacker Drive, Suite 3100
Chicago, IL 60601-2001
Phone: (312) 670-5408   Fax: (312) 670-5403
E-mail: rosenber@aiscmail.com
Web Site: www.aisc.org

Summary: To provide financial assistance to undergraduates majoring in structural engineering.

Eligibility: This program is open to undergraduates majoring in structural engineering. Selection is based on academic performance, faculty recommendations, career interests (as expressed in a short essay), and an original sample analysis/design problem with calculations.

Financial data: The stipend is at least $1,000.

Duration: 1 year.

Number awarded: 2 each year.

Scholarship Listings

1766
AMERICAN METEOROLOGICAL SOCIETY UNDERGRADUATE SCHOLARSHIPS

American Meteorological Society
Attn: Fellowship/Scholarship Coordinator
45 Beacon Street
Boston, MA 02108-3693
Phone: (617) 227-2426, ext. 246   Fax: (617) 742-8718
E-mail: amsinfo@ametsoc.org
Web Site: www.ametsoc.org/AMS/amsedu/scholfeldocs/index.html
Summary: To provide financial assistance to students majoring in meteorology or some aspect of atmospheric sciences.
Eligibility: This program is open to undergraduate students entering their final year of study and majoring in meteorology or some aspect of the atmospheric or related oceanic and hydrologic sciences. Applicants must intend to make atmospheric or related sciences their career. They must be U.S. citizens or permanent residents, be enrolled full time in an accredited U.S. institution, and have a cumulative grade point average of 3.0 or higher. Along with their application, they must submit a 100-word essay on their most important achievements that qualify them for this scholarship and a 500-word essay on their career goals in the atmospheric or related oceanic or hydrologic fields. Selection is based on academic excellence and achievement; financial need is not considered. The sponsor specifically encourages applications from women, minorities, and students with disabilities who are traditionally underrepresented in the atmospheric and related oceanic sciences.
Financial data: Stipends range from $700 to $5,000 per year.
Duration: 1 year.
Additional information: This program includes the following named scholarships: the Howard H. Hanks, Jr. Scholarship in Meteorology ($700), the AMS 75th Anniversary Scholarship ($2,000), the Ethan and Allan Murphy Memorial Scholarship ($2,000), the Howard T. Orville Scholarship in Meteorology ($2,000), the Dr. Pedro Grau Undergraduate Scholarship ($2,500, 2 awarded), the Guillermo Salazar Rodriguez Scholarship ($2,500, 2 awarded), the John R. Hope Scholarship ($2,500), the Richard and Helen Hagemeyer Scholarship ($3,000), and the Werner A. Baum Undergraduate Scholarship ($5,000). Requests for an application must be accompanied by a self-addressed stamped envelope.
Number awarded: 11 each year.
Deadline: February of each year.

1767
AMERICAN NUCLEAR SOCIETY UNDERGRADUATE SCHOLARSHIPS

American Nuclear Society
Attn: Scholarship Program
555 North Kensington Avenue
La Grange Park, IL 60526-5592
Phone: (708) 352-6611   Fax: (708) 352-0499
E-mail: outreach@ans.org   Web Site: www.ans.org/honors/scholarships
Summary: To provide financial assistance to undergraduate students who are interested in preparing for a career in nuclear science or nuclear engineering.
Eligibility: Eligible to apply are undergraduate students enrolled in nuclear science, nuclear engineering, or a nuclear-related field at an accredited institution in the United States. There are separate competitions for 1) students who have completed at least 1 academic year and who will be sophomores, and 2) students who have completed 2 or more years and will be entering as juniors or seniors. All applicants must be U.S. citizens or permanent residents, be able to demonstrate academic achievement, and be sponsored by an organization within the American Nuclear Society (ANS).
Financial data: The stipends are $1,000 for entering sophomores or $2,000 for entering juniors or seniors.
Duration: 1 year.
Additional information: This program includes the following individual scholarships: the Angelo S. Bisesti Scholarship, the Joseph R. Dietrich Scholarship, the Raymond DiSalvo Scholarship, the Environmental Sciences Divisions Scholarship, the Robert G. Lacy Scholarship, the John R. Lamarsh Scholarship, the Robert T. (Bob) Liner Scholarship, the Operations and Power Scholarship, and the Decommissioning, Decontamination and Reutilization Scholarship. Requests for applications must be accompanied by a self-addressed stamped envelope.
Number awarded: Up to 34 each year: 4 for students who have completed at least 1 year of study and 30 (including the 9 named scholarships and 21 others) for students who have completed at least 2 years of study.
Deadline: January of each year.

1768
AMERICAN REGENT CAREER MOBILITY SCHOLARSHIP

American Nephrology Nurses' Association
Attn: ANNA Foundation
East Holly Avenue, Box 56
Pitman, NJ 08071-0056
Phone: (856) 256-2320   (877) 527-0787
Fax: (856) 589-7463   E-mail: annafoundation@hotmail.com
Web Site: www.annanurse.org
Summary: To provide financial assistance to members of the American Nephrology Nurses' Association (ANNA) who are interested in pursuing a baccalaureate degree in nursing.
Eligibility: Applicants must be current association members, have been members for at least 2 years, be currently employed in nephrology nursing, and be accepted or enrolled in a baccalaureate degree program in nursing. In their application, they must indicate how the degree will apply to nephrology nursing and provide a time frame for completing their program.
Financial data: The stipend is $2,000.
Duration: 1 year.
Additional information: Funds for this program are supplied by American Regent Laboratories, Inc. Information is also available from Cynthia Frazier, Awards Chairperson, 7344 Pine Tree Lane, Fairfield, AL 35064, (205) 933-8101, ext. 6514, E-mail: cdf44@aol.com.
Number awarded: 1 each year.
Deadline: October of each year.

1769
AMERICAN SOCIETY OF CRIME LABORATORY DIRECTORS SCHOLARSHIP AWARDS

American Society of Crime Laboratory Directors
Education and Training Committee
c/o Linda Errichetto, Director
Las Vegas Metropolitan Police Department
6771-B West Charleston Boulevard
Las Vegas, NV 89146
Summary: To provide financial assistance to students preparing for careers in forensic science.
Eligibility: Applicants must be full-time undergraduate or graduate students in a forensic science program recognized by the American Society of Crime Laboratory Directors and planning a career in forensic science. They must maintain an overall grade point average of at least 3.0. Selection is not based on financial need but on the applicant's scholastic and forensic record, a personal statement, and faculty recommendations.
Financial data: The stipend is $2,000.
Number awarded: 2 each year.
Deadline: March of each year.

1770
AMERICAN SOCIETY OF NAVAL ENGINEERS SCHOLARSHIP PROGRAM

American Society of Naval Engineers
Attn: Scholarship Committee
1452 Duke Street
Alexandria, VA 22314-3458
Phone: (703) 836-6727   Fax: (703) 836-7491
E-mail: asnehq.asne@mci.mail.com
Web Site: www.navalengineers.org
Summary: To provide financial assistance to college and graduate students who are interested in the field of naval engineering.
Eligibility: This program is open to students entering the final year of a full-time or co-op undergraduate program or starting the first year of full-time graduate study leading to a designated engineering or physical science degree at an accredited college or university. Scholarships are not available to doctoral candidates or to persons already having an advanced degree. Candidates must be U.S. citizens. They must have demonstrated an interest in a career in naval engineering; programs of study include naval architecture; marine, mechanical, civil, aeronautical, ocean, electrical, and electronic engineering; and the physical sciences. Graduate student candidates must be members of the American Society of Naval Engineers (ASNE) or the Society of Naval Architects and Marine Engineers (SNAME). Selection is based on the candidate's academic record, work

350

history, professional promise and interest in naval engineering, extracurricular activities, and recommendations. Financial need may also be considered.

Financial data: The stipends are $2,500 per year for undergraduates or $3,500 per year for graduate students. Funds may be used for the payment of tuition, fees, and school-related expenses.

Duration: 1 year.

Additional information: This program was established in 1979.

Number awarded: Varies each year; recently, 14 undergraduate and 8 graduate students received scholarships.

Deadline: February of each year.

1771
AMERICAN WELDING SOCIETY DISTRICT SCHOLARSHIPS

American Welding Society
Attn: AWS Foundation, Inc.
550 N.W. LeJeune Road
Miami, FL 33126
Phone: (305) 443-9353, ext. 461   (800) 443-9353, ext. 461
Fax: (305) 443-7559   E-mail: vpinsky@aws.org
Web Site: www.aws.org/foundation/district_scholarships.html

Summary: To provide financial assistance to students interested in pursuing vocational training, community college, or a degree program in a welding or related field of study.

Eligibility: This program is open to students enrolled in a welding-related educational or training program. Applicants must be a high school graduate or possess a GED certificate. Selection is based on transcripts; a personal statement of ambitions, goals, background, and other factors that indicate a commitment to pursuing welding education; and financial need.

Financial data: Stipends average from $500 to $1,000. Funds, paid directly to the school, are applied to tuition, books, supplies, and related institutional costs.

Duration: 1 year; recipients may reapply.

Number awarded: Varies each year; recently, 156 of these scholarships were awarded.

Deadline: February of each year.

1772
AMGEN CAREER MOBILITY SCHOLARSHIP

American Nephrology Nurses' Association
Attn: ANNA Foundation
East Holly Avenue, Box 56
Pitman, NJ 08071-0056
Phone: (856) 256-2320   (877) 527-0787
Fax: (856) 589-7463   E-mail: annafoundation@hotmail.com
Web Site: www.annanurse.org

Summary: To provide financial assistance to members of the American Nephrology Nurses' Association (ANNA) who are interested in pursuing a baccalaureate degree in nursing.

Eligibility: Applicants must be current association members, have been members for at least 2 years, be currently employed in nephrology nursing, and be accepted or enrolled in a baccalaureate degree program in nursing. In their application, they must indicate how the degree will apply to nephrology nursing and provide a time frame for completing their program.

Financial data: The stipend is $2,000.

Duration: 1 year.

Additional information: Funds for this program are supplied by Amgen Inc. Information is also available from Cynthia Frazier, Awards Chairperson, 7344 Pine Tree Lane, Fairfield, AL 35064, (205) 933-8101, ext. 6514, E-mail: cdf44@aol.com.

Number awarded: 1 each year.

Deadline: October of each year.

1773
ANDERSEN CONSULTING SCHOLARSHIP PROGRAM FOR MINORITIES

Andersen Consulting Foundation
c/o Citizens' Scholarship Foundation of America
Attn: Scholarship Management Services
1505 Riverview Road
P.O. Box 297
St. Peter, MN 56082
Phone: (507) 931-1682   (800) 537-4180

Fax: (507) 931-9168   E-mail: info_sms@csfa.org

Summary: To provide financial assistance to underrepresented minorities who are studying engineering, computer science, information systems, or decision or management sciences in college.

Eligibility: This program is open to African Americans, Hispanic Americans, and Native Americans who are enrolled in the third year of full-time undergraduate study. Applicants must have at least a 3.0 grade point average and be studying engineering (electrical, industrial, mechanical, or systems are preferred), computer science, information systems (including accounting, business, computer, management, and related fields), or decision or management sciences. They must be proficient in quantitative skills and interested in a career in information systems consulting. U.S. citizenship is required, although asylees and refugees are also eligible to apply. Selection is based on academic achievement, leadership, participation in school and community activities, work experience, a statement of education and career goals related to information systems consulting, unusual circumstances, and recommendations.

Financial data: The stipend is $2,500 per year.

Duration: 1 year; may be renewed.

Number awarded: Varies each year.

Deadline: January of each year.

1774
ANN EUBANK HEALTH SCHOLARSHIP

Chickasaw Nation
Attn: Department of Education
P.O. Box 1548
Ada, OK 74820
Phone: (580) 310-6620
Web Site: www.Chickasaw.net

Summary: To provide financial assistance to members of the Chickasaw Nation who are majoring in a health care field.

Eligibility: This program is open to Chickasaw students who are currently enrolled at an accredited institution of higher education and majoring in a health care-related field. Applicants must have at least a 3.0 grade point average.

Financial data: A stipend is awarded (exact amount not specified).

Duration: 1 year.

Number awarded: 1 each year.

Deadline: May of each year.

1775
ANNA FOUNDATION CAREER MOBILITY SCHOLARSHIPS

American Nephrology Nurses' Association
Attn: ANNA Foundation
East Holly Avenue, Box 56
Pitman, NJ 08071-0056
Phone: (856) 256-2320   (877) 527-0787
Fax: (856) 589-7463   E-mail: annafoundation@hotmail.com
Web Site: www.annanurse.org

Summary: To support members of the American Nephrology Nurses' Association (ANNA) who are interested in pursuing a nursing degree.

Eligibility: This program is open to 1) association members in pursuit of a baccalaureate degree and 2) members in pursuit of a B.S.N. or other advanced nursing degree. Applicants must be current association members, have been members for at least 2 years, be currently employed in nephrology nursing, be accepted or enrolled in a degree program in nursing, and intend to pursue a career in nephrology nursing.

Financial data: The stipend is $2,000.

Duration: 1 year.

Additional information: 7 of these scholarships are sponsored by ANNA and the other is sponsored by Anthony J. Jannetti, Inc. Information is also available from Cynthia Frazier, Awards Chairperson, 7344 Pine Tree Lane, Fairfield, AL 35064, (205) 933-8101, ext. 6514, E-mail: cdf44@aol.com.

Number awarded: 4 for a baccalaureate degree and 4 for either a B.S.N. or other advanced nursing degree.

Deadline: October of each year.

1776
ANNE MAUREEN WHITNEY BARROW MEMORIAL SCHOLARSHIP

Society of Women Engineers
230 East Ohio Street, Suite 400
Chicago, IL 60611-3265
Phone: (312) 596-5223   Fax: (312) 644-8557
E-mail: hq@swe.org   Web Site: www.swe.org
Summary: To provide financial assistance to freshmen women interested in studying engineering or engineering technology.
Eligibility: Incoming female freshmen who are interested in majoring in engineering or engineering technology are eligible to apply. They must be planning to attend a school that is ABET accredited or SWE approved. Selection is based on merit.
Financial data: The stipend is $5,000.
Duration: 1 year; may be renewed for 3 additional years.
Additional information: This program was established in 1992.
Number awarded: 1 every 4 years.
Deadline: May of the years in which it is offered.

1777
ANNE SEAMAN MEMORIAL SCHOLARSHIP

Summary: To provide financial assistance for the postsecondary education of students in fields related to grounds management.
See Listing #1274.

1778
ANS DELAYED EDUCATION SCHOLARSHIP FOR WOMEN

American Nuclear Society
Attn: Scholarship Program
555 North Kensington Avenue
La Grange Park, IL 60526-5592
Phone: (708) 352-6611   Fax: (708) 352-0499
E-mail: outreach@ans.org
Web Site: www.ans.org/honors/scholarships
Summary: To encourage mature women whose formal studies in nuclear science, nuclear engineering, or a nuclear-related field have been delayed or interrupted.
Eligibility: Applicants must have experienced at least a 1-year delay or interruption of their undergraduate studies and must be entering a 4-year curriculum. They must be U.S. citizens or permanent residents, have proven academic ability, be able to demonstrate financial need, and be sponsored by an organization within the American Nuclear Society (ANS).
Financial data: The stipend is $3,500. Funds may be used by the student to cover any bona fide education costs, including tuition, books, room, and board.
Duration: 1 year.
Additional information: Requests for applications must be accompanied by a self-addressed stamped envelope.
Number awarded: 1 each year.
Deadline: January of each year.

1779
ANTHONY C. FORTUNSKI, P.E. MEMORIAL GRANT

Michigan Society of Professional Engineers
Attn: Scholarship Coordinator
215 North Walnut Street
P.O. Box 15276
Lansing, MI 48901-5276
Phone: (517) 487-9388   Fax: (517) 487-0635
E-mail: mspe@voyager.net
Web Site: www.voyager.net/mspe
Summary: To provide financial assistance to undergraduate students in Michigan who are members of the Michigan Society of Professional Engineers and majoring in engineering in college.
Eligibility: This program is open to student members of the society who are U.S. citizens and residents of Michigan. Applicants must be attending an ABET-accredited engineering program at a Michigan college or university and have earned at least a 3.0 grade point average. They must submit an essay (up to 500 words) that discusses their interest in engineering, the specific field of engineering that is being pursued, and the occupation they propose to follow after graduation.

Selection is based on the essay, transcripts, 2 letters of recommendation, leadership, and interest in the engineering profession through involvement in school and/or outside activities. Financial need is not considered. Preference is given to students majoring in manufacturing engineering and attending Lawrence Technological University.
Financial data: The stipend is $1,500.
Duration: 1 year; nonrenewable.
Additional information: Information is also available from Roger Lamer, Scholarship Selection Committee Chair, (616) 247-2974, Fax: (616) 247-2997, E-mail: rlamer@steelcase.com.
Number awarded: 1 each year.
Deadline: March of each year.

1780
ARC OF WASHINGTON TRUST FUND SCHOLARSHIP

ARC of Washington Trust Fund
c/o Neal Lessenger, Secretary
P.O. Box 27028
Seattle, WA 98125-1428
Phone: (206) 363-2206   E-mail: arcwatrustsec@qwest.net
Summary: To provide financial assistance to undergraduate and graduate students in northwestern states who have a career interest in work relating to mental retardation.
Eligibility: This program is open to upper-division and graduate students in schools in Washington, Oregon, Alaska, and Idaho who have a demonstrated interest in the field of mental retardation. To apply, students must submit a completed application form, a statement of interest in the field of mental retardation, and letters of endorsement from at least 2 faculty sponsors. Financial need is not considered in the selection process.
Financial data: The stipend is $5,000 per year, paid in 4 equal installments. Funds are sent to the recipient's school and must be used for tuition, books, and general living expenses.
Duration: 1 year.
Number awarded: Several each year.
Deadline: February of each year.

1781
ARC WELDING AWARDS-DIVISION I

James F. Lincoln Arc Welding Foundation
Attn: Secretary
22801 Saint Clair Avenue
P.O. Box 17188
Cleveland, OH 44117-1199
Phone: (216) 481-8100   Fax: (216) 486-1751
E-mail: innovate@lincolnelectric.com
Web Site: www.jflf.org/awards/school.asp
Summary: To recognize and reward students younger than 18 years of age who submit outstanding arc welding projects.
Eligibility: This program is open to students 18 years of age or younger enrolled in a shop course at any time of school or training program. Applicants must submit an arc welded project made by them or a problem concerned with the use and knowledge of arc welding. Entries must be submitted as a 3- to 25-page written description of the project or problem; drawings, photographs, and sketches are encouraged, but models or specimens may not be submitted. Written entries must have been completed during the previous 12-month period. Selection is based on the practicality or usefulness of the project or problem, how well the use or knowledge of arc welding was applied, the skill and ability with which the project or problem was completed, how clearly the project or problem is described, and how well the entry conforms to requirements.
Financial data: At the regional level, the best of region award is $500, gold awards are $250, silver awards are $125, bronze awards are $75, and merit awards are $50. At the national level, the grand award is $1,000, the gold award is $750, the silver award is $600, and the bronze award is $550. Additionally, awards of $200 are made to the schools the national winners attend.
Duration: The competition is held annually.
Number awarded: In each of 4 geographic regions, 1 best of region award, 2 gold awards, 3 silver awards, and 4 bronze awards are presented. A total of $7,500 are presented in merit awards regardless of region. At the national level, 4 students and their schools receive awards.
Deadline: May of each year.

1782
ARC WELDING AWARDS-DIVISION II-A

James F. Lincoln Arc Welding Foundation
Attn: Secretary
22801 Saint Clair Avenue
P.O. Box 17188
Cleveland, OH 44117-1199
Phone: (216) 481-8100   Fax: (216) 486-1751
E-mail: innovate@lincolnelectric.com
Web Site: www.jflf.org/awards/school.asp
Summary: To recognize and reward students older than 18 years of age who submit outstanding arc welding projects.
Eligibility: This program is open to students older than 18 years of age other than college students studying for a bachelor's or master's degree. Applicants may be enrolled in evening adult classes, high schools, vocational schools, private trade schools, in-plant training classes, technical institutes, junior colleges, community colleges, or other 2-year college courses. They must submit an arc welded project that is 1) home, artistic, or recreational equipment; 2) a shop tool, machine, or mechanical device; 3) a structure; 4) agricultural equipment; or 5) a repair. Entries must be submitted as a 3- to 25-page written description of the project; drawings, photographs, and sketches are encouraged, but models or specimens may not be submitted. Written entries must have been completed during the previous 12-month period. Selection is based on the practicality or usefulness of the project, how well the use or knowledge of arc welding was applied, the skill and ability with which the project was completed, how clearly the project is described, and how well the entry conforms to requirements.
Financial data: Prizes are $1,000 for best of program, $500 for the gold award, $250 for silver awards, $125 for bronze awards, and $50 for merit awards.
Duration: The competition is held annually.
Number awarded: 1 best of program, 1 gold award, 2 silver awards, 3 bronze awards, and up to $2,500 in merit awards are presented each year.
Deadline: May of each year.

1783
ARC WELDING AWARDS-DIVISION II-B

James F. Lincoln Arc Welding Foundation
Attn: Secretary
22801 Saint Clair Avenue
P.O. Box 17188
Cleveland, OH 44117-1199
Phone: (216) 481-8100   Fax: (216) 486-1751
E-mail: innovate@lincolnelectric.com
Web Site: www.jflf.org/awards/school.asp
Summary: To recognize and reward students older than 18 years of age who submit outstanding arc welding problems.
Eligibility: This program is open to students older than 18 years of age other than college students studying for a bachelor's or master's degree. Applicants may be enrolled in evening adult classes, high schools, vocational schools, private trade schools, in-plant training classes, technical institutes, junior colleges, community colleges, or other 2-year college courses. They must submit a problem concerned with the use and knowledge of arc welding. It may involve the use of a welding technique, process or material, joint design, testing, welding procedure, tooling, or fixturing. Entries must be submitted as a 3- to 25-page written description of the problem; drawings, photographs, and sketches are encouraged, but models or specimens may not be submitted. Written entries must have been completed during the previous 12-month period. Selection is based on the practicality or usefulness of the problem, how well the use or knowledge of arc welding was applied, the skill and ability with which the problem was completed, how clearly the problem is described, and how well the entry conforms to requirements.
Financial data: Prizes are $1,000 for best of program, $500 for the gold award, $250 for silver awards, $125 for bronze awards, and $50 for merit awards.
Duration: The competition is held annually.
Number awarded: 1 best of program, 1 gold award, 2 silver awards, 3 bronze awards, and up to $2,500 in merit awards are presented each year.
Deadline: May of each year.

1784
ARIZONA NURSERY ASSOCIATION FOUNDATION SCHOLARSHIPS

Arizona Nursery Association
Attn: ANA Foundation Endowment for Research and Scholarship
1430 West Broadway, Suite A-180
Tempe, AZ 85282
Phone: (602) 966-1610   Fax: (602) 966-0923
E-mail: info@azna.org
Web Site: www.azna.org/scholarships/index.html
Summary: To provide financial assistance to students from Arizona who are enrolled or planning to enroll in a horticulture-related curriculum in college.
Eligibility: This program is open to Arizona residents who are currently enrolled, or planning to enroll, in a horticulture-related curriculum at a university, community college, or continuing education program. Applicants must be currently employed in or have an interest in the nursery industry as a career. They must have an above average grade point average or at least 2 years of work experience in the nursery industry. Involvement in extracurricular activities related to the nursery industry must also be demonstrated. Financial need is not considered in the selection process.
Financial data: Stipends range from $500 to $3,000.
Duration: 1 year.
Number awarded: Varies each year.
Deadline: April of each year.

1785
ARNOLD SADLER MEMORIAL SCHOLARSHIP

American Council of the Blind
Attn: Coordinator, Scholarship Program
1155 15th Street, N.W., Suite 1004
Washington, DC 20005
Phone: (202) 467-5081   (800) 424-8666
Fax: (202) 467-5085   E-mail: info@acb.org
Web Site: www.acb.org
Summary: To provide financial assistance to students who are blind and are interested in studying in a field of service to persons with disabilities.
Eligibility: This program is open to students in rehabilitation, education, law, or other fields of service to persons with disabilities. Applicants must be legally blind and U.S. citizens. In addition to letters of recommendation and copies of academic transcripts, applications must include an autobiographical sketch. Selection is based on demonstrated academic record, involvement in extracurricular and civic activities, and academic objectives. The severity of the applicant's visual impairment and his/her study methods are also taken into account.
Financial data: The stipend is $2,000. In addition, the winner receives a $1,000 cash scholarship from the Kurzweil Foundation and, if appropriate, a Kurzweil 1000 Reading System.
Duration: 1 year.
Additional information: This scholarship is funded by the Arnold Sadler Memorial Scholarship Fund. Scholarship winners are expected to be present at the council's annual conference; the council will cover all reasonable expenses connected with convention attendance.
Number awarded: 1 each year.
Deadline: February of each year.

1786
ARTHUR AND GLADYS CERVENKA SCHOLARSHIP AWARD

Society of Manufacturing Engineers
Attn: Education Foundation
One SME Drive
P.O. Box 930
Dearborn, MI 48121-0930
Phone: (313) 271-1500, ext. 1707   Fax: (313) 240-6095
E-mail: cortjoy@sme.org
Web Site: www.sme.org
Summary: To provide financial assistance to students enrolled in a degree program in manufacturing engineering or manufacturing engineering technology in Florida.
Eligibility: This program is open to full-time undergraduate students enrolled in a manufacturing engineering or manufacturing engineering technology program. Applicants must have completed a minimum of 30 units with a minimum grade point average of 3.0. Preference is given to students attending

colleges or universities in Florida. Need is not considered in awarding scholarships (unless 2 or more applicants have equal qualifications).
Financial data: The stipend is $1,250.
Duration: 1 year; may be renewed.
Number awarded: 1 each year.
Deadline: January of each year.

1787
ARTHUR F. QUERN INFORMATION TECHNOLOGY GRANTS

Illinois Student Assistance Commission
Attn: Scholarship and Grant Services
1755 Lake Cook Road
Deerfield, IL 60015-5209
Phone: (847) 948-8550 (800) 899-ISAC
Fax: (847) 831-8549 TDD: (847) 831-8326, ext. 2822
E-mail: cssupport@isac.org Web Site: www.isac1.org/ilaid/quernit.html
Summary: To provide financial assistance to students in Illinois who are pursuing additional certification or an undergraduate degree in designated areas of information technology.
Eligibility: Applicants must be Illinois residents and U.S. citizens or eligible noncitizens. They must have a high school diploma or GED certificate and be pursuing additional certification or an undergraduate degree in an information technology field. Currently, the approved fields are business information and data processing services; computer and information sciences; computer engineering; electrical, electronics, and communications engineering; electrical and electronic engineering-related technology; electromechanical instrumentation and maintenance technology; information processing/data entry technician; and mathematics and computer science. Preference is given to renewal applicants, those who have already completed a baccalaureate degree, and those who demonstrate the greatest financial need.
Financial data: The maximum stipend is $2,500. Funds may be used for payment of tuition, fees, and other education expenses.
Duration: 1 year; may be renewed 1 additional year.
Number awarded: Varies each year.
Deadline: The priority filing date is at the end of April. Applications received after that date are processed in the order they are received, until funds are exhausted.

1788
ARTHUR L. WILLISTON AWARD

ASME International
Attn: General Awards Committee
Three Park Avenue
New York, NY 10016-5990
Phone: (212) 591-7735 (800) THE-ASME
Fax: (212) 591-7674 E-mail: infocentral@asme.org
Web Site: www.asme.org/students/Competitions/willistonaward.html
Summary: To recognize and reward student and junior members of ASME International (the professional society of mechanical engineers) who have written outstanding papers.
Eligibility: This program is open to undergraduate student members and associate members who received a bachelor's degree not more than 2 years earlier. Applicants must submit a paper on a subject that changes annually but that challenges the engineering abilities of participants; a recent topic was "Ethnical Engineering Solutions for a Global Society." Selection is based on originality (35 points), development (35 points), and presentation (30 points).
Financial data: First place consists of $1,000 and a bronze medal; second place is $500, and third place is $250.
Duration: The awards are presented annually.
Additional information: This award was established in 1954 and expanded in 1988 to include second and third places.
Number awarded: 3 each year.
Deadline: February of each year.

1789
ARTHUR T. SCHRAMM MEMORIAL SCHOLARSHIP

Institute of Food Technologists
Attn: Scholarship Department
221 North LaSalle Street, Suite 300
Chicago, IL 60601-1291
Phone: (312) 782-8424 Fax: (312) 782-8348
E-mail: info@ift.org Web Site: www.ift.org

Summary: To provide financial assistance to undergraduates interested in studying food science or food technology.
Eligibility: Applicants must be currently enrolled as sophomores or juniors in a food science or food technology program at an educational institution in the United States or Canada; they must have an outstanding scholastic record and a well-rounded personality. Financial need is not considered in the selection process.
Financial data: The stipend is $1,000.
Duration: 1 year; recipients may reapply if they are members of the Institute of Food Technologists (IFT).
Additional information: Correspondence and completed applications must be submitted to the department head of educational institution applicant is attending.
Number awarded: 1 each year.
Deadline: January of each year.

1790
ARTHUR W. PENSE SCHOLARSHIP

NYSARC, Inc.
393 Delaware Avenue
Delmar, NY 12054
Phone: (518) 439-8311 Fax: (518) 439-1893
E-mail: nysarc@nysarc.org Web Site: www.nysarc.org/scholar.htm
Summary: To provide financial assistance to currently-enrolled college students in New York majoring in occupational or physical therapy.
Eligibility: Nominations for this funding are to be submitted through the departments of physical or occupational therapy at the various colleges and universities in New York. Nominees must be working on a 4- or 5-year degree program leading to a career in physical or occupational therapy. They must be at least at the sophomore level.
Financial data: The stipend is $3,000.
Duration: 1 year.
Additional information: NYSARC, Inc. was formerly the New York State Association for Retarded Children.
Number awarded: 1 each year.
Deadline: January of each year.

1791
ARTS AND SCIENCES AWARDS

Summary: To provide financial aid to hearing impaired students who are participating in extracurricular activities in arts and sciences.
See Listing #1278.

1792
ASCE MAINE SECTION SCHOLARSHIP

American Society of Civil Engineers-Maine Section
c/o Holly Anderson, P.E.
Maine Department of Transportation
Highway Design Division
16 State House Section
Augusta, ME 04333-0016 Phone: (207) 287-2126
Summary: To provide financial assistance to high school seniors in Maine who are interested in studying civil engineering in college.
Eligibility: This program is open to graduating high school seniors who are Maine residents and who intend to study civil engineering in college. Women and minorities are especially encouraged to apply. Selection is based on academic performance, extracurricular activities, letters of recommendation, and statement of interest in civil engineering as a career.
Financial data: The stipend is $1,000.
Duration: 1 year; nonrenewable.
Number awarded: 1 each year.
Deadline: January of each year.

1793
ASCP SCHOLARSHIPS

American Society of Clinical Pathologists
Attn: Associate Member Section
2100 West Harrison Street
Chicago, IL 60612-3798
Phone: (312) 738-4890 (800) 621-4142
Fax: (312) 738-0102 E-mail: info@ascp.org
Web Site: www.ascp.org

Summary: To provide funding to students enrolled in programs related to clinical laboratory science.

Eligibility: This program is open to students enrolled in a NAACLS or CAAHEP accredited college/university program as a cytotechnologist (CT), histologic technician (HT) histotechnologist (HTL), medical laboratory technician (MLT), or medical technologist (MT). Applicants must be in the final clinical year of education and either U.S. citizens or permanent residents. HT and HTL applicants have no minimum grade point average requirement, but other applicants must have a 3.0 GPA or higher. Selection is based on academic achievement, leadership abilities, professional goals, and endorsements from faculty and community leaders.

Financial data: The stipend is $1,000.

Duration: 1 year.

Number awarded: 50 each year.

Deadline: October of each year.

1794
ASEV SCHOLARSHIPS

American Society for Enology and Viticulture
1784 Picasso Avenue, Suite D
P.O. Box 1855
Davis, CA 95617-1855
Phone: (530) 753-3142   Fax: (530) 753-3318
E-mail: society@asev.org
Web Site: www.asev.org/Scholarship/ScholarshipContent.htm

Summary: To provide financial assistance to graduate and undergraduate students interested in pursuing a degree in enology, viticulture, or another area related to the wine and grape industry.

Eligibility: This program is open to both graduate and undergraduate students interested in working on a degree in enology, viticulture, or another related field. Applicants must be enrolled or accepted in a full-time 4-year accredited college or university program with a minimum of junior status. They must reside in North America (including Canada and Mexico), be in financial need, and have earned a grade point average of 3.0 or higher for undergraduates or 3.2 for graduate students. As part of their application, students must supply a written statement of intent to pursue a career in the wine or grape industry.

Financial data: The awards are not in predetermined amounts and may vary from year to year.

Duration: Students receive quarter or semester stipends. Recipients are eligible to reapply each year in open competition with new applicants.

Additional information: Failure to give an honest or complete financial statement will automatically remove the student from consideration or result in retraction of the awarded scholarship.

Number awarded: Varies each year.

Deadline: February of each year.

1795
ASHP FOUNDATION STUDENT RESEARCH AWARD

American Society of Health-System Pharmacists
Attn: Research and Education Foundation
7272 Wisconsin Avenue
Bethesda, MD 20814-1439
Phone: (301) 657-3000, ext. 1447   Fax: (301) 657-8278
E-mail: foundation@ashp.org   Web Site: www.ashpfoundation.org

Summary: To recognize and reward outstanding papers or reports on pharmacy practice written by undergraduate or graduate pharmacy students.

Eligibility: This award is given to the student author of the best unpublished paper or report on a completed research project, prepared during the past year, that relates to pharmacy practice in a health system. When a nomination is submitted (students may nominate themselves), it should be accompanied by a letter from a faculty member certifying that the nominated paper is the student's own work. At the time the nominated paper or report was written, the student author should have been a full-time student in an entry-level (B.S. or Pharm.D.) program at an accredited college of pharmacy. The nominated paper should be in publishable format. Unabridged (full-length) theses or dissertations prepared as a part of an academic degree requirement may not be submitted (although papers derived from these documents are eligible). Selection is based on quality and importance of the papers to the practice of pharmacy in health systems.

Financial data: The award consists of a plaque, a $1,000 honorarium, and a $700 travel allowance (to cover the costs of attending the society's mid-year meeting, where the award is presented).

Duration: The award is presented annually.

Additional information: Funding for this award is provided through a grant from Wyeth-Ayerst Laboratories.

Number awarded: 1 each year.

Deadline: April of each year.

1796
ASHRAE GENERAL SCHOLARSHIPS

American Society of Heating, Refrigerating and Air-Conditioning Engineers, Inc.
Attn: Scholarship Administrator
1791 Tullie Circle, N.E.
Atlanta, GA 30329-2305
Phone: (404) 636-8400   Fax: (404) 321-5478
E-mail: benedict@ashrae.org
Web Site: www.ashrae.org

Summary: To provide financial assistance to engineering and engineering technology students interested in heating, ventilating, air conditioning, and refrigeration (HVAC&R).

Eligibility: This program is open to undergraduate engineering and engineering technology students enrolled in a school recognized as accredited by the American Society of Heating, Refrigerating and Air-Conditioning Engineers (ASHRAE). Applicants must be pursuing a course of study that traditionally has been preparatory for the profession of HVAC&R. They must have a grade point average of at least 3.0 and must be full-time students with at least 1 full year of undergraduate study remaining. Selection is based on potential service to the HVAC&R profession, financial need, leadership ability, recommendations from instructors, and character.

Financial data: The stipend is $3,000 per year.

Duration: 1 year.

Number awarded: 2 each year.

Deadline: November of each year.

1797
ASHRAE MEMORIAL SCHOLARSHIP

American Society of Heating, Refrigerating and Air-Conditioning Engineers, Inc.
Attn: Scholarship Administrator
1791 Tullie Circle, N.E.
Atlanta, GA 30329-2305
Phone: (404) 636-8400   Fax: (404) 321-5478
E-mail: benedict@ashrae.org
Web Site: www.ashrae.org

Summary: To provide financial assistance to engineering and engineering technology students interested in heating, ventilating, air conditioning, and refrigeration (HVAC&R).

Eligibility: This program is open to undergraduate engineering and engineering technology students enrolled in a school recognized as accredited by the American Society of Heating, Refrigerating and Air-Conditioning Engineers (ASHRAE). Applicants must be pursuing a course of study that traditionally has been preparatory for the profession of HVAC&R. They must have a grade point average of at least 3.0 and must be full-time students with at least 1 full year of undergraduate study remaining. Selection is based on potential service to the HVAC&R profession, financial need, leadership ability, recommendations from instructors, and character.

Financial data: The stipend is $3,000 per year.

Duration: 1 year.

Number awarded: 1 each year.

Deadline: November of each year.

1798
ASHRAE STUDENT DESIGN PROJECT COMPETITION

American Society of Heating, Refrigerating and Air-Conditioning Engineers, Inc.
Attn: Education Coordinator
1791 Tullie Circle, N.E.
Atlanta, GA 30329-2305
Phone: (404) 636-8400   Fax: (404) 321-5478
E-mail: jwaits@ashrae.org
Web Site: www.ashrae.org

Summary: To recognize and reward outstanding engineering student designs in a competition involving heating, ventilating, and air conditioning (HVAC).

Eligibility: All undergraduate engineering students are invited to submit entries in 3 categories: architectural system design, HVAC system selection, and HVAC system design. Judging criteria are, for architectural system design: creativity (35

percent), environmental impact (10 percent), practicality (25 percent), and communication of results (30 percent); for HVAC system selection: anticipated operating cost (20 percent), environmental impact (20 percent), comfort and health (15 percent), creativity (30 percent), and communication of results (15 percent); for HVAC system design: anticipated operating cost (10 percent), environmental impact (10 percent), comfort and health (20 percent), creativity (30 percent), and communication of results (30 percent). Students entering the architectural competition use site plans and criteria provided by the American Society of Heating, Refrigerating and Air-Conditioning Engineers (ASHRAE) to generate their building designs. Both the HVAC system selection groups and the HVAC system design groups must prepare their designs using CADD-generated architectural plans provided by ASHRAE.

Financial data: In each of the 3 categories, the first-place team receives $1,500 and 1 of its representatives receives free transportation, 2 nights' lodging, and up to $100 in expenses to attend the ASHRAE winter meeting where the award is presented. The second-place team in each category also is entitled to send a representative to that meeting, with ASHRAE providing transportation, 2 nights' lodging, and up to $100 in expenses.

Duration: The competition is held annually.

Number awarded: 3 teams (1 in each category) receive cash prizes; 6 individual team members (2 in each category) receive funds to attend the meeting.

Deadline: April of each year.

1799
ASHS SCHOLARS AWARD

American Society for Horticultural Science
113 South West Street, Suite 200
Alexandria, VA 22314-2851
Phone: (703) 836-4606   Fax: (703) 836-2024
E-mail: ashs@ashs.org
Web Site: www.ashs.org/membership/awards/infopages/scholars.html

Summary: To provide financial assistance to undergraduate students majoring in horticulture.

Eligibility: This program is open to full-time undergraduate students of any class standing who are actively pursuing a degree in horticulture at a 4-year college or university. Applicants must be nominated by the chair of the department in which they are majoring; each department may nominate only 1 students. They must submit transcripts, 3 letters of reference, a complete resume and/or vitae, and an essay of 250 to 500 words on their reasons for interest in horticulture and for selecting their intended field of work after graduation. Selection is based on academic excellence in the major and supporting areas of science; participation in extracurricular, leadership, and research activities relating to horticulture; participation in university and community service; demonstrated commitment to the horticultural science profession and related career fields; and related horticultural experiences. Financial need is not considered.

Financial data: The stipend is $1,500.

Duration: 1 year.

Additional information: This program was established in 2001.

Number awarded: 2 each year.

Deadline: February of each year.

1800
ASM FOUNDATION SCHOLARSHIP AWARDS

ASM International Foundation
Attn: Scholarship Program
9639 Kinsman Road
Materials Park, OH 44073-0002
Phone: (440) 338-5151   (800) 336-5152
Fax: (440) 338-4634   E-mail: crhayes@asminternational.org
Web Site: www.asminternational.org

Summary: To provide financial assistance to undergraduate students who are members of ASM International.

Eligibility: This program is open to student members of the association who have an intended or declared major in metallurgy or materials science engineering. Applicants must have completed at least 1 year of college. Students majoring in related science or engineering disciplines are considered if they demonstrate a strong academic interest in materials science. International students are also eligible. Selection is based on academic achievement; interest in the field (including knowledge of metallurgy or materials engineering, activities, jobs, and potential for a related career); and personal qualities (such as motivation, citizenship, social values, goals, and maturity). Financial need is not considered.

Financial data: The stipend is $1,000 per year.

Duration: 1 year; may be renewed for up to 1 additional year.

Additional information: The sponsor of these scholarships is the educational foundation of the American Society for Metals (ASM). They are presented through local ASM chapters.

Number awarded: 12 each year.

Deadline: April of each year.

1801
ASM OUTSTANDING SCHOLAR AWARDS

ASM International Foundation
Attn: Scholarship Program
9639 Kinsman Road
Materials Park, OH 44073-0002
Phone: (440) 338-5151   (800) 336-5152
Fax: (440) 338-4634   E-mail: crhayes@asminternational.org
Web Site: www.asminternational.org

Summary: To provide financial assistance to undergraduate students who are members of ASM International.

Eligibility: This program is open to student members of the association who have an intended or declared major in metallurgy or materials science engineering. Applicants must have completed at least 1 year of college. Students majoring in related science or engineering disciplines are considered if they demonstrate a strong academic interest in materials science. International students are also eligible. Selection is based on academic achievement; interest in the field (including knowledge of metallurgy or materials engineering, activities, jobs, and potential for a related career); and personal qualities (such as motivation, citizenship, social values, goals, and maturity). Financial need is not considered.

Financial data: The stipend is $2,000 per year.

Duration: 1 year; may be renewed for up to 1 additional year.

Additional information: The sponsor of these scholarships is the educational foundation of the American Society for Metals (ASM). They are presented through local ASM chapters.

Number awarded: 3 each year.

Deadline: April of each year.

1802
ASME FOUNDATION SCHOLARSHIPS

ASME International
Attn: Education Department
Three Park Avenue
New York, NY 10016-5990
Phone: (212) 591-8131   (800) THE-ASME
Fax: (212) 591-7143   E-mail: oluwanifiset@asme.org
Web Site: www.asme.org/educate/aid/scholar.htm

Summary: To provide financial assistance to undergraduate students who are members of the American Society of Mechanical Engineers (ASME).

Eligibility: This program is open to student members in good standing who are enrolled in an ABET-accredited mechanical engineering baccalaureate, mechanical engineering technology, or related program. They must be in their junior or senior year of study. Interested students should submit an application form, a nomination from the applicant's department head, a recommendation from a faculty member, and an official transcript. Only 1 nomination may be submitted per department. There are no geographic or citizenship limitations. Selection is based on scholastic ability and potential contribution to the mechanical engineering profession.

Financial data: The stipend is $1,500.

Duration: 1 year.

Additional information: This program was established in 1999. Requests for applications must be accompanied by a self-addressed stamped envelope.

Number awarded: 16 each year.

Deadline: March of each year.

1803
ASME STUDENT DESIGN CONTEST

ASME International
Attn: Student Section
Three Park Avenue
New York, NY 10016-5990
Phone: (212) 591-7722   (800) THE-ASME
Fax: (212) 591-7674   E-mail: students@asme.org
Web Site: www.asme.org/students

Summary: To recognize and reward outstanding designs by student members of the American Society of Mechanical Engineers (ASME).

Eligibility: This competition is open to student members of the society who have not yet received their first engineering degree. They may enter as individuals, but teams of 2 to 4 members are encouraged. Regional winners compete on the national level. Each year, a problem statement for a mechanical design is presented and students complete a design that meets the specifications of the problem. A recent problem involved a device that can position and orient a plastic bottle, fill it, and then screw on a cap.

Financial data: Within each region, the first-place winner receives $200, a trophy, and up to $1,000 travel allowance to participate in the finals; the second-place winner receives $100 and a plaque; and the third-place winner receives $50 and a plaque. The national first-place winner receives $3,000 and $1,000 for the student section at their institution; the second-place winner receives $1,000 and $500 for the student section at their institution; the third-place winner receives $500 and $250 for the student section at their institution.

Duration: The competition is held annually.

Additional information: Applications are submitted to the 12 regional student conferences; students in Region XIII (all the world except for the United States, Canada, and Mexico) submit applications to ASME International. Further information is also available from Pierre M. Larochelle, PE, Florida Institute of Technology, Mechanical and Aerospace Engineering Department, 150 West University Boulevard, Melbourne, FL 32901, Fax: (321) 674-8813, E-mail: pierrel@fit.edu.

Number awarded: 3 in the national finals and 3 in each regional student conference.

Deadline: Each region sets its own deadline; for Region XIII, the deadline is in March of each year.

1804
ASME/FIRST SCHOLARSHIP

ASME International
Attn: Education Department
Three Park Avenue
New York, NY 10016-5990
Phone: (212) 591-8131   (800) THE-ASME
Fax: (212) 591-7143   E-mail: oluwanifiset@asme.org
Web Site: www.asme.org/education/precollege/first/firstscholarship.htm

Summary: To provide financial assistance for college to high school seniors who have been active in the For Inspiration and Recognition of Science and Technology (FIRST) program.

Eligibility: This program is open to high school seniors who have been active with FIRST and are interested in studying mechanical engineering or mechanical engineering technology in college. Candidates must be nominated by ASME members or student members active with FIRST. The letter of nomination must attest to the student's technical, creative, and leadership contributions to the FIRST team. Other selection criteria include academic performance and financial need.

Financial data: The stipend is $5,000.

Duration: 1 year; nonrenewable.

Number awarded: 7 each year.

Deadline: February of each year.

1805
ASNT ENGINEERING UNDERGRADUATE AWARD

American Society for Nondestructive Testing, Inc.
Attn: Executive Assistant
1711 Arlingate Lane, P.O. Box 28518
Columbus, OH 43228-0518
Phone: (614) 274-6003   (800) 222-2768
Fax: (614) 274-6899   E-mail: sthomas@asnt.org
Web Site: www.asnt.org

Summary: To provide financial assistance to undergraduate engineering students who are interested in nondestructive testing and evaluation.

Eligibility: This program is open to undergraduate student enrolled in an engineering program at an ABET-accredited university who show an active interest in the field of nondestructive testing and evaluation. Students must be nominated. Nominations must include the official transcript of the student, 3 letters of recommendation from faculty members, and an essay by the student describing the role nondestructive testing and evaluation will play in his/her career.

Financial data: The award is $3,000.

Duration: The funds are presented annually.

Number awarded: Up to 3 each year.

Deadline: October of each year.

1806
ASPAN DEGREE SCHOLARSHIPS

American Society of PeriAnesthesia Nurses
Attn: Scholarship Program
10 Melrose Avenue, Suite 110
Cherry Hill, NJ 08003-3696
Phone: (877) 737-9696, ext. 13   Fax: (856) 616-9601
E-mail: aspan@aspan.org
Web Site: www.aspan.org/ScholarshipProgram.htm

Summary: To provide financial assistance for additional education to members of the American Society of PeriAnesthesia Nurses (ASPAN).

Eligibility: This program is open to registered nurses who have been members of the society for at least 2 years and have been employed for at least 2 years in any phase of the perianesthesia setting (preanesthesia, postanesthesia, ambulatory surgery, management, research, or education). Applicants must be seeking a bachelor of science or advanced degree in nursing. They must submit a statement of financial need, 2 letters of recommendation, and a narrative statement describing their level of activity or involvement in a phase of perianesthesia nursing, ASPAN and/or a component, or their community.

Financial data: The stipend is $1,000 per year; funds are sent directly to the recipient's university.

Duration: 1 year; recipients may not reapply for additional funding until 3 years have elapsed.

Number awarded: At least 2 each year.

Deadline: June of each year.

1807
ASSOCIATED GENERAL CONTRACTORS OF MAINE SCHOLARSHIPS

Associated General Contractors of Maine, Inc. Educational Foundation
P.O. Box 5519
Augusta, ME 04332
Phone: (207) 622-4741

Summary: To provide financial assistance to Maine residents interested in studying in a construction-related field.

Eligibility: This program is open to Maine residents who are entering their first, second, third, or fourth year at an accredited institution of higher education in Maine. Applicants must be enrolled in a field of study related to construction. Selection is based on academic record and financial need.

Financial data: Stipends are $3,000, $2,000, $1,500, or $1,000.

Duration: 1 year.

Number awarded: 8 each year: 1 at $3,000, 1 at $2,000, 1 at $1,500, and 5 at $1,000.

Deadline: March of each year.

1808
ASSOCIATED GENERAL CONTRACTORS OF VERMONT SCHOLARSHIP

Vermont Student Assistance Corporation
Champlain Mill
1 Main Street, Fourth Floor
P.O. Box 2000
Winooski, VT 05404-2601
Phone: (802) 655-9602   (800) 642-3177
Fax: (802) 654-3765   TDD: (802) 654-3766
Phone: TDD: (800) 281-3341 (within VT)   E-mail: info@vsac.org
Web Site: www.vsac.org

Summary: To provide financial assistance to Vermont residents who are interested in studying a field related to construction.

Eligibility: This scholarship is available to residents of Vermont who are high school seniors, high school graduates, or GED recipients and who are interested in pursuing an academic, vocational, technical, or advanced training program in a field related to construction. Applicants must be able to demonstrate financial need. Selection is based on a letter of recommendation, required essays, and financial need.

Financial data: The stipend is $1,000 and must be used within 1 year after being awarded.

Duration: 1 year.

Additional information: This program was established in 2002.

Number awarded: 1 each year.

Deadline: April of each year.

1809
ASSOCIATED LANDSCAPE CONTRACTORS OF AMERICA EDUCATIONAL FOUNDATION SCHOLARSHIP

Summary: To provide financial assistance to students at colleges and universities that have a connection to the Associated Landscape Contractors of America (ALCA). *See Listing #1280.*

1810
ASSOCIATED OREGON LOGGERS SCHOLARSHIP

Associated Oregon Loggers, Inc.
P.O. Box 12339
Salem, OR 97309-0339
Phone: (503) 364-1330   (800) 452-6023
Fax: (503) 364-0836   E-mail: aol@oregonloggers.org
Web Site: www.oregonloggers.org
Summary: To provide financial assistance to high school seniors in Oregon who are planning to major in a forest resource production field of study.
Eligibility: This program is open to high school seniors in Oregon who will be attending a 4-year college or university accredited by the Society of American Foresters. Applicants must be planning to major in a forest resource production field of study; this includes forest management, forest engineering, and forest products. Each candidate must submit the following: an application form, high school transcripts, SAT or ACT scores, verification of college acceptance, and an original essay (up to 3 pages) on "What challenges do you see in the field of forestry and what are your views on meeting these challenges?" Selection is based on academic record, SAT or ACT scores, relevant experiences, and thought process, grammatical usage, and expression in the required essay. Financial need is not considered in the selection process. Finalists may be interviewed.
Financial data: The stipend is $1,500 per year.
Duration: 1 year; may be renewed for 3 additional years.
Additional information: Recipients must attend a 4-year college or university.
Number awarded: 1 or more each year.
Deadline: March of each year.

1811
ASSOCIATION FOR MANUFACTURING TECHNOLOGY 2-YEAR SCHOLARSHIP PROGRAM

Association for Manufacturing Technology
Attn: Scholarship Coordinator
7901 Westpark Drive
McLean, VA 22102-4206
Phone: (703) 893-2900   Fax: (703) 893-1151
E-mail: AMT@mfgtech.org   Web Site: www.mfgtech.org
Summary: To provide financial assistance to students interested in earning a 2-year degree in a manufacturing technology-related field at a public, regionally accredited community, junior, or technical college.
Eligibility: Applicants must meet the following minimum requirements: be a high school graduate, have demonstrated or expressed a specific interest in manufacturing technology, have a desire to pursue education in the field, meet the entrance requirements of the participating college, meet the normal employment standards of the participating member company, and be able to demonstrate financial need.
Financial data: Up to $3,000 per year, to cover tuition, books, and related academic fees. Funds are paid directly to the recipient's institution.
Duration: 1 year; may be renewed for 1 additional year.
Additional information: This program operates as follows: An Association for Manufacturing Technology-member company decides to participate in the program; the company identifies and selects a junior, community, or technical college in its geographic area. The college must be a public, regionally accredited institution offering a 2-year manufacturing technology-related degree program. The member company works with the high school and college to publicize the scholarship and attract candidates. The college, working with the member company, selects the most deserving candidate. In addition to the scholarship, recipients must be willing to work at least 375 hours each year at the sponsoring company. The scholarship cannot 1) be used to reduce the amount of wages paid to the student or 2) be considered in any way as part of the student's compensation.
Number awarded: Between 10 to 20 companies sponsor scholarship students each year.

1812
ASSOCIATION FOR WOMEN IN ARCHITECTURE SCHOLARSHIPS

Summary: To provide financial assistance to women undergraduates in California who are interested in careers in architecture. *See Listing #1281.*

1813
ASSOCIATION FOR WOMEN IN SCIENCE UNDERGRADUATE AWARDS

Association for Women in Science
Attn: AWIS Educational Foundation
1200 New York Avenue, N.W., Suite 650
Washington, DC 20005
Phone: (202) 326-8940   (800) 886-AWIS
Fax: (202) 326-8960   E-mail: awis@awis.org
Web Site: www.awis.org
Summary: To provide financial assistance to women interested in studying engineering or the sciences on the undergraduate level.
Eligibility: This program is open to women who are high school seniors and U.S. citizens. Applicants must have a grade point average of 3.75 or higher and scores of at least 1200 on the SAT or 24 on the ACT. They must plan to study astronomy, biology, chemistry, computer and information science, engineering, geoscience, mathematics, physics, or psychology in college. Along with the application, they must submit an essay in which they write about the following: 1) their scientific interests and career aspirations in research and/or teaching; 2) what led to their interest in science and the role of special mentors, if relevant; 3) key lessons they have learned during any research or teaching experiences they have had; 4) any social, economic, academic, or other barriers they have faced and how they overcame them; and 5) why they undertook community service or volunteer activities and key lessons they learned. Financial need is not considered.
Financial data: The stipend for the awards is $1,000. Citations of merit are $300 and recognition awards are $100.
Duration: 1 year.
Additional information: This program, established in 1999, includes the Gail Naughton Award and the Dr. Vicki Lynn Schechtman Award. Information is also available from Barbara Filner, President, AWIS Educational Foundation Undergraduate Award, 7008 Richard Drive, Bethesda, MD 20817.
Number awarded: 2 each year. Recently, an additional 6 citations of merit and 19 recognition awards were presented.
Deadline: January of each year.

1814
ASSOCIATION OF CALIFORNIA WATER AGENCIES SCHOLARSHIPS

Association of California Water Agencies
910 K Street, Suite 100
Sacramento, CA 95814-3514
Phone: (916) 441-4545   Fax: (916) 325-4849
E-mail: lavonnew@acwanet.com
Web Site: www.acwanet.com
Summary: To provide financial assistance to upper-division students in California who are majoring in water resources-related fields of study.
Eligibility: Applicants must be California residents attending state-supported California colleges and universities. They should 1) have completed their sophomore work, 2) be full-time students in their junior or senior year at the time of the award, and 3) be majoring in a field related to or identified with water resources, including engineering, agricultural sciences, urban water supply, environmental sciences, and public administration. Selection is based on scholastic achievement, commitment to a career in the field of water resources, and financial need.
Financial data: The stipend is $1,500. Funds are paid directly to the recipient's school.
Duration: 1 year.
Additional information: Recipients must attend a college or university in California approved by the sponsor.
Number awarded: At least 6 each year.
Deadline: March of each year.

1815
ASSOCIATION OF CUBAN ENGINEERS SCHOLARSHIPS

Association of Cuban Engineers
Attn: President
P.O. Box 557575
Miami, FL 33255-7575
Phone: (305) 649-7429
Web Site: www.netside.net/~ace/ScholarshipCriteriaApplication.htm
Summary: To provide financial assistance to undergraduate and graduate students of Cuban-American heritage who are interested in preparing for a career in engineering.
Eligibility: This program is open to U.S. citizens and legal residents who have completed at least 50 units of college work in the United States and are majoring or planning to major in some aspect of engineering. Applicants must be attending an ABET-accredited college or university within the United States or Puerto Rico as a full-time student. They must be of Cuban-American heritage. If an insufficient number of qualified Cuban-American students apply, scholarships may be made available to other Hispanic American, African American, and women applicants. Selection is based on grade point average (up to 35 points, 3.0 or higher), financial need (up to 25 points for an applicant needing $5,470), participation in extracurricular activities (up to 25 points), and student class standing (3.75 points for sophomores, 7.5 points for juniors, 11.25 points for seniors, and 15 points for graduate students).
Financial data: Stipends range from $500 to $1,000 per year.
Duration: 1 year.
Additional information: This program includes the Luciano Goicochea Award (for the top-rated Cuban-American student at Florida International University) and the Noel Betancourt Award (for the top-rated Cuban-American student at the University of Miami).
Number awarded: Up to 20 each year.
Deadline: October of each year.

1816
ASSOCIATION OF ENERGY ENGINEERS SCHOLARSHIPS

Association of Energy Engineers
Attn: Foundation
4025 Pleasantdale Road, Suite 420
Atlanta, GA 30340
Phone: (770) 447-5083   Fax: (770) 446-3969
E-mail: info@aeecenter.org   Web Site: www.aeecenter.org
Summary: To encourage undergraduate and graduate students to take courses directly related to energy engineering or energy management.
Eligibility: This program is open to undergraduate and graduate students who are enrolled in engineering or management programs at accredited colleges and universities and who would be interested in taking courses directly related to energy engineering or energy management (preferably within a curriculum leading to a major or minor in energy engineering). Qualified students are invited to submit their applications to the association's local chapter, along with transcripts and letters of recommendation. Each chapter may then submit up to 6 nominees, no more than 2 of whom may be graduate students. Selection is based on scholarship, character, and need. In awarding scholarships, preference is given to candidates needing aid their final year; second, to candidates needing aid for the last 2 years; third, to candidates needing aid for 3 years; and finally, to first-year students.
Financial data: The foundation scholarship stipend is $500. In addition, the most outstanding candidate receives the $1,000 Victor Ottaviano Scholarship.
Duration: 1 year.
Additional information: Since this program was established in 1983, it has awarded $350,000 in scholarships. Information is also available from James P. Waltz, AEE Scholarship Committee Chair, c/o Energy Resource Associates, Inc., 1626 Holmes Street, Livermore, CA 94550-6010.
Number awarded: Several each year, including 1 Victor Ottaviano Scholarship.
Deadline: April of each year.

1817
ASSOCIATION OF FEDERAL COMMUNICATIONS CONSULTING ENGINEERS SCHOLARSHIPS

Association of Federal Communications Consulting Engineers
c/o John E. Dettra, Jr.
Dettra Communications, Inc.
7906 Foxhound Road
McLean, VA 22102-2403
Summary: To provide financial assistance to college students majoring in electrical engineering.
Eligibility: This program is open to currently-enrolled college students who are majoring in electrical engineering at an accredited college or university. They must be attending school on a full-time basis.
Financial data: $2,000 per semester. Funds are paid directly to the recipient.
Duration: 1 semester; nonrenewable.
Number awarded: Up to 2 each semester.

1818
ASSOCIATION OF FOOD AND DRUG OFFICIALS SCHOLARSHIP AWARDS

Association of Food and Drug Officials
2550 Kingston Road, Suite 333
York, PA 17402-3734
Phone: (717) 757-2888   Fax: (717) 755-8089
E-mail: afdo@afdo.org
Web Site: www.afdo.org/scholarship.asp
Summary: To provide financial assistance to currently-enrolled college students who are preparing for a career in some aspect of food, drug, or consumer product safety.
Eligibility: Applicants should be interested in preparing to serve in a career of research, regulatory work, quality control, or teaching in an area related to some aspect of food, drug, or consumer product safety. They must be able to demonstrate leadership abilities and should have earned at least a 2.5 grade point average in their first 2 years of college. To apply, an application must be submitted, along with an official transcript and 2 letters of recommendation from faculty members. Financial need is not considered in the selection process.
Financial data: The stipend is $1,500.
Duration: 1 year.
Additional information: This program, established in 1981, includes the following 2 named awards: the George M. Burditt Scholarship and the Betsy B. Woodward Scholarship.
Number awarded: 2 each year.
Deadline: January of each year.

1819
ASSOCIATION OF PERIOPERATIVE REGISTERED NURSES SCHOLARSHIP PROGRAM

Association of periOperative Registered Nurses
AORN Foundation
Attn: Nursing Research Grant Program
2170 South Parker Road, Suite 300
Denver, CO 80231-5711
Phone: (303) 755-6300, ext. 248   (800) 755-2676, ext. 248
E-mail: mparlapiano@aorn.org
Web Site: www.aorn.org/research/grantprgm.htm
Summary: To provide financial assistance to members of the Association of periOperative Registered Nurses (AORN) who wish to continue their education.
Eligibility: Eligible are registered nurses who are currently practicing in the perioperative environment, have been members of the association for at least 1 year, and want to return to school to further their education at the baccalaureate, master's, or doctoral level. Entry-level nursing students and non-members are not eligible. Applicants must submit evidence of acceptance or enrollment in an accredited nursing program or enrollment in a pre-nursing curriculum applicable to admission in a baccalaureate nursing program accredited by the National League for Nursing. Applicants educated outside of the United States must submit a transcript of recent course work in the United States demonstrating their capacity to maintain a 3.0 grade point average on the college level. Applications must include a personal statement describing current and past contributions to perioperative nursing practice, research, and education; a description of financial need; a description of how the applicant will apply the information gained from course work to perioperative nursing practice and the association; and professional goals related to completion of the degree.
Financial data: Scholarships provide funds for tuition, examinations for credit, and registration fees only; no funds are provided for room and board, transportation, parking, or other expenses. Payment is made directly to the educational institution.
Duration: 1 year; may be renewed if the recipient maintains at least a 3.0 grade point average.
Deadline: March or September of each year.

1820
ASSOCIATION OF PHYSICIAN ASSISTANTS IN CARDIOVASCULAR SURGERY SCHOLARSHIPS

Association of Physician Assistants in Cardiovascular Surgery
Attn: Education and Scholarship Committee
P.O. Box 4834
Englewood, CO 80155
Phone: (303) 221-5651   (877) 221-5651
Fax: (303) 771-2550   Web Site: www.apacvs.org/scholar.htm
Summary: To provide financial assistance to student members of the Association of Physician Assistants in Cardiovascular Surgery (APACVS).
Eligibility: This program is open to association members who are in the first or second year of work on a physician assistants' degree and have demonstrated a clear clinical interest in cardiovascular surgery. Along with their application, students must submit 3 essays that summarize their interest in cardiovascular surgery. Selection is based on academic record, maturity, leadership, and professional integrity. Financial need is not considered.
Financial data: The stipend is $1,000.
Duration: 1 year.
Additional information: Further information is also available from John Tejeda, Education and Scholarship Committee Chair, c/o Cardiac Surgeons for Northwest Ohio, Inc., 2109 Hughes Drive, Suite 800, Toledo, OH 43606, (419) 47-HEART.
Number awarded: Varies each year.
Deadline: July of each year.

1821
ASSOCIATION OF STATE DAM SAFETY OFFICIALS SCHOLARSHIPS

Association of State Dam Safety Officials
Attn: Scholarship Coordinator
450 Old Vine Street, Second Floor
Lexington, KY 40507
Phone: (859) 257-5140   Fax: (859) 323-1958
E-mail: info@damsafety.org   Web Site: www.damsafety.org
Summary: To provide financial assistance to undergraduate students interested in fields related to dam safety.
Eligibility: Applicants must be juniors or seniors with a grade point average of 3.0 or higher studying civil engineering or a related field. They must have a demonstrated interest in pursuing a career in hydraulics, hydrology, or geotechnical disciplines related to the design, construction, and operation of dams. U.S. citizenship is required. Selection is based on academic achievement, financial need, work experience and activities, and a 2-page essay describing goals and purpose for applying.
Financial data: The stipend is $5,000 per year.
Duration: 1 year; junior recipients may reapply for their senior year.
Additional information: This program was established in 1992.
Number awarded: 1 or 2 each year.
Deadline: February of each year.

1822
ASTRONAUT SCHOLARSHIP FOUNDATION SCHOLARSHIPS

Astronaut Scholarship Foundation
Attn: Executive Director
6225 Vectorspace Boulevard
Titusville, FL 32780
Phone: (407) 269-6119   Fax: (407) 267-3970
E-mail: MercurySvn@aol.com   Web Site: www.astronautscholarship.org
Summary: To provide financial assistance to undergraduate and graduate students in science and engineering.
Eligibility: This program is open to upper-division college students and those pursuing master's or doctoral degrees in physical science or engineering fields. Applicants must be attending 1 of 17 participating universities, each of which nominates 2 students. Students intending to practice professional medicine or engage in biomedical research are not eligible.
Financial data: The stipend is $8,500 per year.
Duration: 1 year; may be renewed for up to 2 additional years.
Additional information: The Astronaut Scholarship Foundation was founded in 1984 as the Mercury Seven Foundation by the 6 surviving members of the original Mercury Seven Astronauts and the widow of the seventh. The universities participating recently included Georgia Institute of Technology, Harvey Mudd College, Miami University, North Carolina A&T State University, North Carolina State University, North Dakota State University, Pennsylvania State University, Purdue University, Syracuse University, Texas A&M University, Tufts University, University of Central Florida, University of Colorado, University of Kentucky, University of Minnesota, University of Washington, and Washington University.
Number awarded: 17 each year: 1 at each of the participating universities.

1823
A.T. ANDERSON MEMORIAL SCHOLARSHIP PROGRAM

American Indian Science and Engineering Society
Attn: Higher Education Director
2201 Buena Vista, S.E., Suite 301
P.O. Box 9828
Albuquerque, NM 87119-9828
Phone: (505) 765-1052, ext. 15   Fax: (505) 765-5608
E-mail: teresa@aises.org
Web Site: www.aises.org/scholarships/index.htm
Summary: To provide financial assistance for college to members of the American Indian Science and Engineering Society.
Eligibility: This program is open to members of the society who can furnish proof of tribal enrollment or certificate of Indian blood. Applicants must be full-time students at the undergraduate or graduate school level attending an accredited 4-year college or university or a 2-year college leading to a 4-year degree in physical science, engineering, mathematics, medicine, natural resources, or science. They must submit a 500-word essay on why they chose their particular field of study, their career aspirations, an evaluation of past scholastic performance, obstacles faced as a student, and involvement and commitment to tribal community life. Selection is based on the essay, academic achievement (at least a 2.0 grade point average), leadership potential, and commitment to helping other American Indians. Financial need is not considered.
Financial data: The annual stipend is $1,000 for undergraduates or $2,000 for graduate students.
Duration: 1 year; renewable upon reapplication.
Additional information: This program was launched in 1983 in memory of A.T. Anderson, a Mohawk and a chemical engineer who worked with Albert Einstein. Anderson was 1 of the society's founders and was the society's first executive director. The program includes the following named awards: the Al Qoyawayma Award for an applicant who is majoring in science or engineering and is also pursuing a strong interest in the arts, the Norbert S. Hill, Jr. Leadership Award, the Polingaysi Qoyawayma Award for an applicant who is pursuing a teaching degree in order to teach mathematics or science in a Native community or an advanced degree for personal improvement or teaching at the college level, and the Robert W. Brocksbank Scholarship.
Number awarded: Varies; generally, 200 or more each year, depending upon the availability of funds from corporate and other sponsors.
Deadline: June of each year.

1824
AVIATION DISTRIBUTORS AND MANUFACTURERS ASSOCIATION SCHOLARSHIP PROGRAM

Aviation Distributors and Manufacturers Association
1900 Arch Street
Philadelphia, PA 19103-1498
Phone: (215) 564-3484   Fax: (215) 963-9784
E-mail: adma@fernley.com
Web Site: www.adma.org
Summary: To provide financial assistance to students who are preparing for a career in the aviation field.
Eligibility: This program is open to college students who are either 1) a third- or fourth-year student enrolled at an accredited institution in a bachelor's degree program preparing for a career in aviation management or as a professional pilot; or 2) a second-year student in an aircraft and powerplant (A&P) mechanic program at a 2-year accredited institution. Applicants must submit 2 letters of recommendation, a 500-word essay describing their desire to pursue a career in aviation, and verification of a grade point average of 3.0 or higher. Selection is based on academic performance, recommendations, extracurricular activities, leadership contributions, and financial need.
Financial data: The stipend is $1,000.
Duration: 1 year.
Number awarded: 2 each year.
Deadline: March of each year.

1825
AVIATION EMPLOYEE PLACEMENT SERVICES COLLEGE TUITION SCHOLARSHIP

Women in Aviation, International
3647 S.R. 503 South
West Alexandria, OH 45381
Phone: (937) 839-4647 Fax: (937) 839-4645
E-mail: wai@infinet.com
Web Site: www.wiai.org
Summary: To provide financial assistance to members of Women in Aviation, International who are interested in studying aviation in college.
Eligibility: This program is open to women who are members of the sponsoring organization and graduating high school seniors or graduates working to save money for college. Applicants must be interested in pursuing a bachelor's degree in an aviation field. Selection is based on achievements, attitude toward self and others, commitment to success, dedication to career, financial need, motivation, reliability, responsibility, and teamwork.
Financial data: Awards provide for payment of tuition, up to $15,000 per year. Funding does not include flight fees, although the recipient may be a flight major.
Duration: 4 years, if the recipient maintains a grade point average of 3.0 or higher.
Additional information: Women in Aviation, International is a nonprofit professional organization dedicated to encouraging women to consider an aviation career, providing educational outreach activities, and networking resources to women active in the industry. This program is sponsored by Aviation Employee Placement Services (AEPS).
Number awarded: 1 each year.
Deadline: December of each year.

1826
AVIATION MEMORIAL SCHOLARSHIP

Ninety-Nines, Inc.-Eastern New England Chapter
c/o Karla Carroll
14 Cooke Place
Warwick, RI 02888-4202
Summary: To provide financial assistance to residents of New England who are interested in preparing for a career in aviation.
Eligibility: Eligible to apply are high school seniors or beyond who are residents of or studying in 1 of the following states: Maine, New Hampshire, Rhode Island, Vermont, Massachusetts, or Connecticut. They must be planning a career in aviation and need financial assistance to pursue appropriate education or flight training. Criteria for selecting recipients include: aviation activities, science fair projects, aviation employment, recommendations, academic record, aviation goals, and financial need.
Financial data: The stipend is $1,000. Funds may be applied to academic tuition, technical school, or flight training.
Duration: 1 year.
Number awarded: 1 each year.
Deadline: January of each year.

1827
A.W. PERIGARD FUND SCHOLARSHIP

Society of Satellite Professionals International
Attn: Scholarship Program
225 Reinekers Lane, Suite 600
Alexandria, VA 22314
Phone: (703) 549-8696 Fax: (703) 549-9728
E-mail: sspi@sspi.org
Web Site: www.sspi.org
Summary: To provide financial assistance to students interested in majoring in satellite-related disciplines in college.
Eligibility: This program is open to high school seniors, college undergraduates, and graduate students majoring or planning to major in fields related to satellite communications, including broadcasting, business, communications, engineering, international policy studies, journalism, law, science, space applications, or telecommunications. Applicants may be from any country. Selection is based on academic and leadership achievement, commitment to pursue education and career opportunities in the satellite communications industry, potential for significant contribution to that industry, a personal statement of 500 to 750 words on interest in satellite communications and why the applicant deserves the award, and a creative work (such as a research report, essay, article, videotape, artwork, computer program, or scale model of an antenna or

spacecraft design) that reflects the applicant's interests and talents. Financial need is also considered.
Financial data: The stipend is $2,000.
Duration: 1 year.
Number awarded: 1 each year.
Deadline: June of each year.

1828
AWHONN EDUCATION SCHOLARSHIPS

Association of Women's Health, Obstetric and Neonatal Nurses
2000 L Street, N.W., Suite 740
Washington, DC 20036
Phone: (800) 673-8499 Fax: (202) 728-0575
Web Site: www.awhonn.org
Summary: To provide financial assistance for further education to members of the Association of Women's Health, Obstetric and Neonatal Nurses (AWHONN).
Eligibility: This program is open to members of the association who are interested in a program of study that may involve 1) working for a baccalaureate or master's degree in nursing, 2) working toward a doctorate in nursing or a related field, 3) postgraduate practitioner training, or 4) expanded role preparation in women's health or neonatal nursing.
Financial data: The stipend is $1,000.
Duration: 1 year.
Number awarded: 2 each year.
Deadline: March of each year.

1829
AWMA CONNECTICUT CHAPTER SCHOLARSHIP

Air & Waste Management Association-Connecticut Chapter
c/o Sci-Tech, Inc.
185 Silas Deane Highway
Wethersfield, CT 06109
Web Site: www.awma.org/section/newengland
Summary: To provide financial assistance to high school seniors in Connecticut who are interested in studying fields related to air and waste management in college.
Eligibility: This program is open to seniors graduating from high schools in Connecticut who plan to enroll full time in college. Applicants must be interested in pursuing courses of study in science or engineering leading to careers in the environmental field, especially air pollution control or waste management. Selection is based on their proposed plan of study, transcripts, work experience, and volunteer and extracurricular activities; financial need is not considered.
Financial data: The stipend is $1,000.
Duration: 1 year; recipients may reapply.
Number awarded: 1 or 2 each year.
Deadline: April of each year.

1830
AWMA EAST CENTRAL SECTION SCHOLARSHIPS

Air & Waste Management Association-East Central Section
c/o Sol P. Baltimore, Scholarship Committee Chair
28742 Blackstone Drive
Lathrup Village, MI 48076-2616
Phone: (248) 569-3633 Web Site: www.awma-ecs.org
Summary: To provide financial assistance to undergraduate and graduate students in midwestern states who are interested in pursuing a career in air and waste management.
Eligibility: Applicants must be enrolled in or entering their senior undergraduate year or any year of graduate or professional school at a college or university in Indiana, Kentucky, Michigan, or Ohio. They must be full-time students preparing for a career in air pollution control, toxic and/or hazardous waste management, or another environmental area. Preferred courses of study include engineering, physical or natural sciences, public health, law, and natural resources. Selection is based on academic achievement (at least a 3.0 grade point average), extracurricular activities, and financial need.
Financial data: The stipend is $1,000. Winners also receive a 1-year student membership in the Air & Waste Management Association (A&WMA).
Duration: 1 year; may be renewed.
Number awarded: 4 each year: 1 to a student at colleges or universities in each of the participating states.
Deadline: February of each year.

1831
AWMA EAST MICHIGAN CHAPTER SCHOLARSHIPS

Air & Waste Management Association-East Michigan Chapter
c/o Sol P. Baltimore, Scholarship Committee Chair
28742 Blackstone Drive
Lathrup Village, MI 48076-2616
Phone: (248) 569-3633
Summary: To provide financial assistance to undergraduate and graduate students in Michigan who are interested in pursuing a career in air and waste management.
Eligibility: Applicants must be enrolled in or entering their senior undergraduate year or any year of graduate or professional school at a college or university in Michigan. They must be full-time students preparing for a career in air pollution control, toxic and/or hazardous waste management, or another environmental area. Preferred courses of study include engineering, physical or natural sciences, public health, law, and natural resources. Selection is based on academic achievement (at least a 3.0 grade point average), extracurricular activities, and financial need.
Financial data: The stipend is $1,500. Winners also receive a 1-year student membership in the Air & Waste Management Association (A&WMA).
Duration: 1 year; may be renewed.
Additional information: This program includes the Paul R. Shutt Memorial Scholarship. Another scholarship is sponsored by the Great Lakes Steel Operations, National Steel Corporation
Number awarded: 6 each year.
Deadline: January of each year.

1832
B. CHARLES TINEY MEMORIAL STUDENT CHAPTER/CLUB SCHOLARSHIP

American Society of Civil Engineers
Attn: Student Services
1801 Alexander Bell Drive
Reston, VA 20191-4400
Phone: (703) 295-6120   (800) 548-ASCE
Fax: (703) 295-6132   E-mail: student@asce.org
Web Site: www.asce.org
Summary: To provide financial assistance to student members of the American Society of Civil Engineers (ASCE) for undergraduate study in civil engineering.
Eligibility: This program is open to ASCE members who are freshmen, sophomores, juniors, or first-year seniors enrolled in a program of civil engineering. Applicants must submit an essay (up to 500 words) in which they discuss why they chose to become a civil engineer, their specific ASCE student chapter involvement, any special financial needs, and long-term goals and plans. Selection is based on their justification for the award, educational plan, academic performance and standing, potential for development, leadership capacity, ASCE activities, and demonstrated financial need.
Financial data: The stipend is $2,000 per year.
Duration: 1 year; may be renewed.
Number awarded: Approximately 4 each year.
Deadline: February of each year.

1833
BAF SATELLITE & TECHNOLOGY SCHOLARSHIP

Summary: To provide financial assistance to students interested in majoring in satellite-related disciplines in college.
See Listing #1289.

1834
BANK OF AMERICA ACHIEVEMENT AWARDS

Summary: To recognize and reward outstanding high school seniors in California.
See Listing #1290.

1835
BANK OF AMERICA ADA ABILITIES SCHOLARSHIP PROGRAM

The Foundation Scholarship Program
Attn: Bank of America ADA Abilities Scholarship Program
P.O. Box 1465
Taylors, SC 29687-1465
Phone: (864) 268-3363   Fax: (864) 268-7160
E-mail: fssp@infi.net

Web Site: www.scholarshipprograms.org/fsp_bankofamerica.html
Summary: To provide financial assistance to disabled high school seniors or college students from selected states who are interested in preparing for a career with a banking institution.
Eligibility: This program is open to high school seniors, high school graduates, or currently-enrolled college students who have a disability (must have written documentation from an appropriate provider that the candidate meets the definition of disabled in the Americans with Disability Act). Applicants must be U.S. citizens and permanent residents of 1 of the following states: Arizona, Arkansas, California, Florida, Georgia, Idaho, Illinois, Iowa, Kansas, Maryland, Missouri, Nevada, New Mexico, North Carolina, Oklahoma, Oregon, South Carolina, Tennessee, Texas, Virginia, Washington, or the District of the Columbia. They must 1) have a cumulative grade point average of 3.0 or higher; 2) be majoring in finance, business, or computer systems; and 3) be planning a career with a banking institution.
Financial data: Award amounts for this program are determined by financial need, the annual cost of the recipient's institution, and any other financial aid (excluding loans) received by the student.
Duration: 1 year.
Additional information: This program is administered by The Foundation Scholarship Program on behalf of the Bank of America Foundation.
Number awarded: Varies each year.
Deadline: February of each year.

1836
BARBARA B. WATSON SCHOLARSHIP

American College of Medical Practice Executives
Attn: Scholarship Program
104 Inverness Terrace East
Englewood, CO 80112-5306
Phone: (303) 643-9573   Fax: (303) 643-4427
E-mail: acmpe@mgma.com   Web Site: www.mgma.com/acmpe
Summary: To provide financial assistance to undergraduate or graduate students who have returned to school to study health care leadership.
Eligibility: Applicants must be returning to school after a 5- to 10-year gap in their education to obtain relevant personal and professional growth in health care leadership. They must be pursuing graduate or undergraduate study in the field of ambulatory health care with either an administrative or clinical concentration. As part of the application process, they must submit a letter describing career goals and objectives relevant to medical practice management; a resume; 3 reference letters commenting on the individual's performance, character, potential to succeed, and need for scholarship support; and academic transcripts.
Financial data: The stipend is $1,000. The money is paid directly to the recipient's college.
Duration: 1 year.
Number awarded: 1 each year.
Deadline: May of each year.

1837
BARBARA MCBRIDE SCHOLARSHIP

Society of Exploration Geophysicists
Attn: SEG Foundation
P.O. Box 702740
Tulsa, OK 74170-2740
Phone: (918) 497-5530   Fax: (918) 497-5557
E-mail: slobianco@seg.org
Web Site: www.seg.org
Summary: To provide financial assistance to women undergraduate and graduate students who are interested in the field of geophysics.
Eligibility: Applicants must be women who are 1) high school students planning to enter college in the fall and to major in exploration geophysics; 2) undergraduate college students majoring in geophysics whose grades are above average; or 3) graduate students whose studies are directed toward a career in exploration geophysics in operations, teaching, or research. All applicants must have an interest in and aptitude for physics, mathematics, and geology. Financial need is considered, but the competence of the student as indicated by the application is given first consideration.
Financial data: The stipend ranges from $1,000 to $3,000 per year.
Duration: 1 academic year; may be renewable, based on scholastic standing, availability of funds, and continuance of a course of study leading to a career in exploration geophysics.
Number awarded: 1 each year.
Deadline: February of each year.

1838
BAROID SCHOLARSHIP

American Ground Water Trust
16 Centre Street
P.O. Box 1796
Concord, NH 03302
Phone: (603) 228-5444   Fax: (603) 228-6557
E-mail: info@agwt.org
Web Site: www.agwt.org/baroid.htm
Summary: To provide financial assistance to high school seniors and current college students who are interested in preparing for a career in a ground water-related field.
Eligibility: This program is open to high school seniors and current college students who have earned a grade point average of 3.0 or higher in high school, are planning a career in a ground water-related field, and have completed a science/environmental project in high school that directly involved ground water resources or have had vacation/out-of-school work experience that is directly related to the environment and natural resources. Applicants must submit a 500-word essay on "Ground Water-An Important Environmental and Economic Resource for America" and a 300-word description of their high school ground water project and/or practical environmental work experience. Selection is based on the above criteria, and on the applicant's references and academic record. Financial need is not considered in the selection process. U.S. citizenship or permanent resident status is required.
Financial data: Stipends range from $1,000 to $2,000. Funds are paid directly to the recipient's college.
Duration: 1 year.
Additional information: At the American Ground Water Trust's expense, scholarship recipients may be invited to travel to a national or regional ground water conference or meeting. Funding for this program is provided by Baroid.
Number awarded: 1 each year.
Deadline: May of each year.

1839
BARRY K. WENDT MEMORIAL SCHOLARSHIP

National Stone, Sand and Gravel Association
Attn: Director of Communications
2101 Wilson Boulevard, Suite 100
Arlington, VA 22201-3062
Phone: (703) 525-8788   (800) 342-1415
Fax: (703) 525-7782   E-mail: info@nssga.org
Web Site: www.nssag.org/careers/scholarships.htm
Summary: To provide financial assistance to engineering students intending to pursue a career in the aggregates industry.
Eligibility: Eligible are engineering students who intend to pursue a career in the crushed stone industry. Applications must be accompanied by a letter of recommendation and a 300- to 500-word statement describing those career plans. Financial need is not considered in the selection process.
Financial data: The amount of the award depends on the availability of funds.
Duration: 1 year.
Additional information: This program was established in 1999.
Number awarded: 1 each year.
Deadline: April of each year.

1840
BARRY M. GOLDWATER SCHOLARSHIP

Barry M. Goldwater Scholarship and Excellence in Education Foundation
Springfield Corporate Center
6225 Brandon Avenue, Suite 315
Springfield, VA 22150-2519
Phone: (703) 756-6012   Fax: (703) 756-6015
E-mail: goldh2o@erols.com
Web Site: www.act.org/goldwater
Summary: To provide financial assistance to outstanding college students planning careers in mathematics, engineering, or the natural sciences.
Eligibility: Eligible to be nominated are full-time students enrolled as sophomores or juniors who are in the top quarter of their class and majoring in the natural sciences, mathematics, or engineering with a grade point average of at least 3.0. Students intending to enter medical school are eligible if they plan a career in research rather than private practice. Status as a U.S. citizen, national, or resident alien is also required. Students must be nominated by their institutions;

4-year colleges and universities may nominate up to 4 current sophomores or juniors and 2-year colleges may nominate up to 2 sophomores. Applicants must submit an essay of approximately 600 words on their chosen career. Selection is based on academic performance and demonstrated potential for and commitment to a career in mathematics, engineering, or the natural sciences.
Financial data: Scholarships cover the cost of tuition, fees, books, and room and board up to a maximum of $7,500 per year.
Duration: Students who receive scholarships as juniors are eligible for 2 years of support or until they complete their baccalaureate degree; students who receive scholarships as seniors are eligible for 1 year of support or until they complete their baccalaureate degree.
Additional information: Information is also available from the Goldwater Scholarship Review Committee, 2201 North Dodge Street, P.O. Box 4030, Iowa City, IA 52243-4030.
Number awarded: Up to 300 each year.
Deadline: Institutions set their own deadlines; they must submit nominations to the foundation by January of each year.

1841
BECHTEL CORPORATION SCHOLARSHIP

Society of Women Engineers
230 East Ohio Street, Suite 400
Chicago, IL 60611-3265
Phone: (312) 596-5223   Fax: (312) 644-8557
E-mail: hq@swe.org   Web Site: www.swe.org
Summary: To provide financial assistance to undergraduate women who are members of the Society of Women Engineers and majoring in engineering.
Eligibility: This program is open to women who are rising sophomores, juniors, or seniors and are studying architectural, civil, electrical, environmental, or mechanical engineering with a minimum 3.0 grade point average in a space-related major. Only members of the society are considered for this award. Selection is based on merit.
Financial data: The stipend is $3,050.
Duration: 1 year.
Additional information: This award was established in 2000.
Number awarded: 1 each year.
Deadline: January of each year.

1842
BEGINNING FRESHMEN SCHOLARSHIP

National Association of Minority Engineering Program Administrators, Inc.
1133 West Morse Boulevard, Suite 201
Winter Park, FL 32789
Phone: (407) 647-8839   Fax: (407) 629-2502
E-mail: namepa@namepa.org
Web Site: www.namepa.org/awards.htm
Summary: To provide financial assistance to underrepresented minority high school seniors who are planning to major in engineering.
Eligibility: Candidates for this award must be African American, Hispanic American, or Native American high school seniors who have been approved for admission in an engineering program at an institution affiliated with the National Association of Minority Engineering Program Administrators (NAMEPA). For a list of affiliated schools, write to the sponsor. They must have at least a 3.0 GPA and minimum cumulative scores of 25 on the ACT or 1000 on the SAT. To apply, qualified students must submit a copy of their high school transcript, their test scores, a recommendation, and a 1-page essay on why they have chosen engineering as a profession. Financial need is not considered in the selection process.
Financial data: The stipend is $1,000, paid in 2 equal installments.
Duration: 1 year; nonrenewable.
Deadline: February of each year.

1843
BEN EVERSON SCHOLARSHIP

American Ground Water Trust
16 Centre Street
P.O. Box 1796
Concord, NH 03302
Phone: (603) 228-5444   Fax: (603) 228-6557
E-mail: info@agwt.org
Web Site: www.agwt.org/everson.htm

Scholarship Listings

Summary: To provide financial assistance for college to children of employees of the ground water industry.

Eligibility: This program is open to high school seniors and current college students who have earned a grade point average of 3.0 or higher in high school, are planning a career in a ground water-related field, and have completed a science/environmental project in high school that directly involved ground water resources or have had vacation/out-of-school work experience that directly related to the environment and natural resources. At least 1 parent must be employed in the ground water industry. Applicants must submit a 500-word essay on "Ground Water-An Important Environmental and Economic Resource for America" and a 300-word description of their high school ground water project and/or practical environmental work experience. Selection is based on the above criteria, and on the applicant's references and academic record. Financial need is not considered in the selection process. U.S. citizenship or permanent resident status is required.

Financial data: The stipend is $2,500. Funds are paid directly to the recipient's college.

Duration: 1 year.

Additional information: At the American Ground Water Trust's expense, scholarship recipients may be invited to travel to a national or regional ground water conference or meeting. Funding for this program is provided by Claude Laval Corporation.

Number awarded: 1 each year.

Deadline: May of each year.

1844
BENDIX/KING AVIONICS SCHOLARSHIP

Aircraft Electronics Association
Attn: Educational Foundation
4217 South Hocker Drive
Independence, MO 64055-4723
Phone: (816) 373-6565   Fax: (816) 478-3100
E-mail: info@aea.net
Web Site: www.aea.net

Summary: To provide financial assistance for college to students who are interested in preparing for a career in avionics or aircraft repair.

Eligibility: This program is open to high school seniors, vocational or technical school students, and college students who are attending (or planning to attend) an accredited school in an avionics or aircraft repair program.

Financial data: The stipend is $1,000.

Duration: 1 year.

Number awarded: 1 each year.

Deadline: February of each year.

1845
BENJAMIN C. BLACKBURN SCHOLARSHIP

Summary: To provide financial assistance to residents of New Jersey who are working on an undergraduate or graduate degree in horticulture, landscape architecture, or related fields.

See Listing #1291.

1846
BERNA LOU CARTWRIGHT SCHOLARSHIPS

ASME International
Attn: American Society of Mechanical Engineers Auxiliary, Inc.
Three Park Avenue
New York, NY 10016-5990
Phone: (212) 591-7733   (800) THE-ASME
Fax: (212) 591-7674   E-mail: horvathb@asme.org
Web Site: www.asme.org/auxiliary/scholarshiploans

Summary: To provide financial support for the study of mechanical engineering to students in their final year of undergraduate study.

Eligibility: Eligible are students completing the junior year of a 4-year program or the fourth year of a 5-year program in mechanical engineering. Applicants must be U.S. citizens enrolled in colleges and universities with accredited departments of mechanical engineering. If the school has a chapter of the Student Section of the American Society of Mechanical Engineers (ASME), the applicant must be a member. Selection is based on scholastic achievement, financial need, character, leadership, and participation in ASME activities.

Financial data: The stipend is $2,000.

Duration: 1 year.

Additional information: This scholarship was established in 1993 by Kenneth O. Cartwright in memory of his wife, the past chair of the Los Angeles Section of the ASME and chair of the Parsons Scholarship Committee. Further information and an application are available by sending a self-addressed stamped envelope to Mrs. Alverta Cover, 5425 Caldwell Mill Road, Birmingham, AL 35242, (205) 991-6109, E-mail: undergradauxsch@asme.org.

Number awarded: 6 to 12 each year.

Deadline: March of each year.

1847
BERNTSEN INTERNATIONAL SCHOLARSHIP IN SURVEYING

American Congress on Surveying and Mapping
Attn: Awards Director
6 Montgomery Village Avenue, Suite 403
Gaithersburg, MD 20879
Phone: (240) 632-9716   Fax: (240) 632-1321
E-mail: tmilburn@acsm.net
Web Site: www.acsm.net

Summary: To provide financial assistance for the undergraduate study of surveying to members of the American Congress on Surveying and Mapping.

Eligibility: This program is open to students enrolled in a 4-year college or university who are interested in working on a degree in surveying. They must be members of the sponsoring organization. Selection is based on previous academic record (30 percent), a statement of future plans (30 percent), letters of recommendation (20 percent), and professional activities (20 percent); if 2 or more applicants are judged equal based on those criteria, financial need may be considered.

Financial data: The stipend is $1,500.

Duration: 1 year.

Additional information: This award is made possible by Berntsen International, Inc., of Madison, Wisconsin.

Number awarded: 1 each year.

Deadline: December of each year.

1848
BERTHA P. SINGER SCHOLARSHIP

Oregon Student Assistance Commission
Attn: Private Awards Grant Department
1500 Valley River Drive, Suite 100
Eugene, OR 97401-2146
Phone: (541) 687-7395   (800) 452-8807, ext. 7395
Fax: (541) 687-7419   E-mail: awardinfo@mercury.osac.state.or.us
Web Site: www.osac.state.or.us

Summary: To provide financial assistance for the study of nursing to residents of Oregon.

Eligibility: This program is open to residents of Oregon who are studying nursing at a college in the state and have a cumulative grade point average of 3.0 or higher. Applicants must provide documentation of enrollment in the third year of a 4-year nursing degree program or the second year of a 2-year associate degree nursing program.

Financial data: Scholarship amounts vary, depending upon the needs of the recipient.

Duration: 1 year.

Number awarded: Varies each year.

Deadline: February of each year.

1849
BET/EMERGE PUBLICATIONS SCHOLARSHIP

National Black Nurses Association, Inc.
Attn: Scholarship Committee
8630 Fenton Street, Suite 330
Silver Spring, MD 20910
Phone: (301) 589-3200   Fax: (301) 589-3223
E-mail: nbna@erols.com
Web Site: www.nbna.org/memb_scholar.html

Summary: To provide financial assistance for undergraduate nursing education to members of the National Black Nurses Association.

Eligibility: This program is open to members of the association who are currently enrolled in a B.S.N., A.D., diploma, or L.P.N./L.V.N. program with at least 1 full year of school remaining. Selection is based on participation in student nurse activities, involvement in the African American community, and involvement in community health services-related activities.

Financial data: The stipend ranges from $500 to $2,000 per year.
Duration: 1 year; may be renewed.
Additional information: This program is sponsored by Black Entertainment Television (BET). Requests for applications must be accompanied by a self-addressed stamped envelope.
Number awarded: 1 or more each year.
Deadline: April of each year.

1850
BILLY BROCKMAN MEMORIAL SCHOLARSHIPS

Epsilon Sigma Alpha
Attn: ESA Foundation Assistant Scholarship Director
P.O. Box 270517
Fort Collins, CO 80527
Phone: (970) 223-2824   Fax: (970) 223-4456
Web Site: www.esaintl.com/esaf
Summary: To provide financial assistance to residents of Illinois majoring in an engineering or medical field.
Eligibility: This program is open to residents of Illinois who are either 1) graduating high school seniors in the top 25 percent of their class or with minimum scores of 20 on the ACT or 950 on the SAT, or 2) students already enrolled in college with a grade point average of 3.0 or higher. Students enrolled for training in a technical school or returning to school after an absence are also eligible. Applicants must be planning to major in a medical or engineering field. Selection is based on character, scholastic ability, leadership and ability skills, and financial need.
Financial data: The stipend is $1,000.
Duration: 1 year; may be renewed.
Additional information: Epsilon Sigma Alpha (ESA) is a women's service organization, but scholarships are available to both men and women. Information is also available from Verneene Forssberg, 403 South High, Pratt, KS 67124, (316) 672-3636, Fax: (316) 672-3688, E-mail: vernf@genmail.pcc.cc.ks.us. Completed applications must be submitted to the ESA State Counselor who verifies the information before forwarding them to the scholarship director.
Number awarded: 2 each year.
Deadline: January of each year.

1851
BIOQUIP PRODUCTS SCHOLARSHIP

Entomological Society of America
Attn: Entomological Foundation
9301 Annapolis Road
Lanham, MD 20706-3115
Phone: (301) 731-4535   Fax: (301) 731-4538
E-mail: esa@entsoc.org
Web Site: www.entsoc.org
Summary: To provide financial assistance to undergraduates interested in studying entomology.
Eligibility: This program is open to undergraduate students majoring in entomology, biology, zoology, or a related science at a recognized university or college in the United States, Canada, or Mexico. They must have accumulated a minimum of 30 semester hours at the time the award is presented. Selection is based on academic record, demonstrated enthusiasm, interest, and achievement in biology. Preference is given to students with demonstrated financial need.
Financial data: The stipend is $2,000.
Duration: 1 year.
Additional information: Funding for this scholarship is provided by BioQuip Products, a major supplier of entomology equipment.
Number awarded: 1 each year.
Deadline: May of each year.

1852
B.J. HARROD SCHOLARSHIPS

Society of Women Engineers
230 East Ohio Street, Suite 400
Chicago, IL 60611-3265
Phone: (312) 596-5223   Fax: (312) 644-8557
E-mail: hq@swe.org
Web Site: www.swe.org
Summary: To provide financial assistance to women entering their freshman year in college and interested in studying engineering.

Eligibility: Incoming female freshmen who are interested in majoring in engineering at a 4-year school, college, or university are eligible to apply. The schools must be ABET accredited or SWE approved. Selection is based on merit.
Financial data: The scholarship is $1,000.
Duration: 1 year.
Additional information: This program was established in 1999.
Number awarded: 2 each year.
Deadline: May of each year.

1853
B.K. KRENZER REENTRY SCHOLARSHIP

Society of Women Engineers
230 East Ohio Street, Suite 400
Chicago, IL 60611-3265
Phone: (312) 596-5223   Fax: (312) 644-8557
E-mail: hq@swe.org
Web Site: www.swe.org
Summary: To aid women who have been out of the engineering market a minimum of 2 years and are now interested in obtaining the credentials necessary to reenter the job market as an engineer.
Eligibility: Only women who have been out of the engineering job market for a minimum of 2 years and are going to return to school for an engineering degree may apply. Applicants may be either full- or part-time undergraduate or graduate students. Preference is given to degreed engineers desiring to return to the work force following a period of temporary retirement. Selection is based on merit.
Financial data: The stipend is $2,000.
Duration: 1 year.
Additional information: This program was established in 1996.
Number awarded: 1 each year.
Deadline: May of each year.

1854
BMW/SAE ENGINEERING SCHOLARSHIP

Society of Automotive Engineers
Attn: Educational Relations
400 Commonwealth Drive
Warrendale, PA 15096-0001
Phone: (724) 772-4047   Fax: (724) 776-0890
E-mail: connie@sae.org
Web Site: www.sae.org/students/bmwschol.htm
Summary: To provide financial support for college to high school seniors interested in studying engineering.
Eligibility: This program is open to U.S. citizens who intend to earn an ABET-accredited degree in engineering. Applicants must be high school seniors with a grade point average of 3.75 or higher who rank in the 90th percentile in both mathematics and verbal on the ACT or SAT. Selection is based on high school transcripts; SAT or ACT scores; school-related extracurricular activities; non-school related activities; academic honors, civic honors, and awards; and a 250-word essay on the single experience that most strongly convinced them or confirmed their decision to pursue a career in engineering. Financial need is not considered.
Financial data: The stipend is $6,000, paid at the rate of $1,500 per year.
Duration: 4 years, provided the recipient maintains a grade point average of 3.0 or higher.
Additional information: Funds for this scholarship are provided by BMW AG. Candidates must include a $5 processing fee with their applications.
Number awarded: 1 each year.
Deadline: November of each year.

1855
BOB PEARSON SCHOLARSHIP

American Society of Highway Engineers-Carolina Triangle Section
Attn: Scholarship Committee
5800 Faringdon Place, Suite 105
Raleigh, NC 27609
Phone: (919) 878-9560
Summary: To provide financial assistance to currently-enrolled college students from North Carolina who are majoring in a transportation-related field.
Eligibility: Applicants must be U.S. citizens and residents of North Carolina. They must be currently enrolled in a 4-year college or university in any state (must have completed at least 1 semester) and be working on a bachelor's degree in a

transportation-related field, preferably in a civil engineering curriculum. A copy of the applicant's college transcript is required; high school transcripts, SAT scores, and resumes may also be submitted but are not required. A personal interview may be requested. Selection is based on academic performance (30 points), activities, honors, work experience, and leadership (25 points), career goals (25 points), enrollment in a civil engineering curriculum (10 points), and dependent of a member of the Carolina Triangle Section (10 points). Financial need is not considered.

Financial data: The stipend is $1,500.

Duration: 1 year; nonrenewable.

Additional information: Recipients may attend school in any state.

Number awarded: 1 each year.

Deadline: March of each year.

1856
BOEING COMPANY CAREER ENHANCEMENT SCHOLARSHIP

Women in Aviation, International
3647 S.R. 503 South
West Alexandria, OH 45381
Phone: (937) 839-4647   Fax: (937) 839-4645
E-mail: wai@infinet.com
Web Site: www.wiai.org

Summary: To provide financial assistance to members of Women in Aviation, International who are active in aerospace and seeking financial support to advance their career.

Eligibility: Women who are members of the sponsoring organization and wish to advance their career in aerospace technology or a related management field are eligible to apply. They may be full-time or part-time employees working in the aerospace industry or a related field. Also eligible are students pursuing an aviation-related degree who are at least juniors and have earned at least a 2.5 grade point average. All applicants should submit an essay that addresses their career aspirations and goals, in addition to an application form, 3 letters of recommendation, a resume, copies of all aviation and medical certificates, and the last 3 pages of their pilot logbook, if applicable. Selection is based on achievements, attitude toward self and others, commitment to success, dedication to career, financial need, motivation, reliability, responsibility, and teamwork.

Financial data: The stipend is $1,000.

Duration: 1 year.

Additional information: Women in Aviation, International is a nonprofit professional organization dedicated to encouraging women to consider an aviation career, providing educational outreach activities, and networking resources to women active in the industry.

Number awarded: 1 each year.

Deadline: December of each year.

1857
BREAKTHROUGH TO NURSING SCHOLARSHIPS FOR ETHNIC PEOPLE OF COLOR

National Student Nurses' Association
Attn: NSNA Foundation
555 West 57th Street, Suite 1327
New York, NY 10019
Phone: (212) 581-2215   Fax: (212) 581-2368
E-mail: nsna@nsna.org
Web Site: www.nsna.org

Summary: To provide financial assistance to minority undergraduate and graduate students who wish to prepare for careers in nursing.

Eligibility: Minority undergraduate students (Black, Native American, Spanish surname, Asian, or Polynesian) currently enrolled in state-approved schools of nursing or pre-nursing associate degree, baccalaureate, diploma, generic doctorate, and generic master's programs are eligible to apply. Although graduate students in other disciplines are also eligible if they wish to study nursing or pre-nursing, no funds can be used for graduate education in nursing. Graduating high school seniors are not eligible. Selection is based on academic achievement, financial need, and involvement in student nursing organizations and community health activities.

Financial data: The stipend awarded ranges from $1,000 to $2,000. A total of $50,000 is awarded each year by the foundation for all its scholarship programs.

Duration: 1 year.

Additional information: Applications must be accompanied by a $10 processing fee.

Number awarded: 13 to 15 each year.

Deadline: January of each year.

1858
BUD GLOVER MEMORIAL SCHOLARSHIP

Aircraft Electronics Association
Attn: Educational Foundation
4217 South Hocker Drive
Independence, MO 64055-4723
Phone: (816) 373-6565   Fax: (816) 478-3100
E-mail: info@aea.net
Web Site: www.aea.net

Summary: To provide financial assistance to students preparing for a career in avionics or aircraft repair.

Eligibility: This program is open to high school seniors and currently-enrolled college students who are attending (or planning to attend) an accredited postsecondary institution in an avionics or aircraft repair program.

Financial data: The stipend is $1,000.

Duration: 1 year.

Number awarded: 1 each year.

Deadline: February of each year.

1859
BUD OHLMAN SCHOLARSHIP

Bedding Plants Foundation, Inc.
Attn: Scholarship Program
P.O. Box 280
East Lansing, MI 48826-0280
Phone: (517) 333-4617   Fax: (517) 333-4494
E-mail: bpfi@aol.com
Web Site: www.bpfi.org

Summary: To provide financial assistance to undergraduate and graduate students in horticulture.

Eligibility: This program is open to graduating high school seniors, undergraduate students at a 4-year college or university, and graduate students. Applicants must be horticulture majors who are interested in pursuing a career as a bedding plant grower for an established business. They must be U.S. or Canadian citizens or permanent residents with a grade point average of 3.0 or higher. Selection is based on academic record, recommendations, career goals, extracurricular activities, and financial need.

Financial data: The stipend ranges from $500 to $2,000 per year.

Duration: 1 year.

Number awarded: 1 each year.

Deadline: April of each year.

1860
BUDWEISER CONSERVATION SCHOLARSHIP

National Fish and Wildlife Foundation
1120 Connecticut Avenue, N.W., Suite 900
Washington, DC 20036
Phone: (202) 857-0166   Fax: (202) 857-0162
Web Site: www.nfwf.org/programs

Summary: To provide financial assistance to undergraduate and graduate students who are "poised to make a significant contribution to the field of conservation."

Eligibility: To be eligible, students must be U.S. citizens enrolled in an accredited institution of higher education in the United States and pursuing a graduate or undergraduate degree (sophomores and juniors in the current academic year only) in environmental science, natural resource management, biology, public policy, geography, political science, or related disciplines. To apply, students must submit an application form, transcripts, 3 letters of recommendation, and an essay (up to 1,500 words) which, at least in part, focuses on a specific issue affecting the conservation of fish, wildlife, or plant species in the United States. Awards are based on merit and take into consideration the applicants' academic achievements and their ability and commitment to develop innovative solutions that are designed to address real and pressing issues affecting fish, wildlife, and plant conservation efforts.

Financial data: The scholarships range up to $10,000. Funds must be used to cover expenses related to the recipients' studies, including tuition, fees, books, room, and board. Payments may supplement but not duplicate benefits from their educational institution or from other foundations, institutions, or organizations.

The combined benefits from all sources may not exceed the recipient's educational expenses.

Duration: 1 year.

Additional information: This scholarship is jointly sponsored by Anheuser-Busch and the National Fish and Wildlife Foundation. It was first awarded in 2001. The program also rewards students who are interested in conducting research on the National Wildlife Refuges, which form the largest system of lands in the world dedicated to fish and wildlife conservation (these students are known as National Wildlife Refuge Centennial Scholars).

Number awarded: 20 each year, 10 of whom are National Wildlife Refuge Centennial Scholars.

Deadline: January of each year.

1861
BURLINGTON NORTHERN SANTA FE FOUNDATION SCHOLARSHIP

American Indian Science and Engineering Society
Attn: Higher Education Director
2201 Buena Vista, S.E., Suite 301
P.O. Box 9828
Albuquerque, NM 87119-9828
Phone: (505) 765-1052, ext. 15   Fax: (505) 765-5608
E-mail: teresa@aises.org
Web Site: www.aises.org

Summary: To provide financial assistance for college to outstanding American Indian high school seniors from designated states who are members of American Indian Science and Engineering Society (AISES).

Eligibility: This program is open to AISES members who are high school seniors planning to attend an accredited 4-year college or university and major in physical science, engineering, mathematics, medicine, natural resources, science, or technology. Applicants must submit 1) proof of tribal enrollment or a certificate of Indian blood; 2) evidence of residence in the service area of the Burlington Northern and Santa Fe Corporation (Arizona, California, Colorado, Kansas, Minnesota, Montana, New Mexico, North Dakota, Oklahoma, Oregon, South Dakota, and Washington); 3) a statement of financial need; 4) a 500-word essay on why they chose their particular field of study, their career aspirations, an evaluation of past scholastic performance, obstacles faced as a student, and involvement and commitment to tribal community life; and 5) high school transcripts showing a grade point average of 2.0 or higher.

Financial data: The stipend is $2,500 per year.

Duration: 4 years or until completion of a baccalaureate degree, whichever occurs first.

Additional information: This program is funded by the Burlington Northern Santa Fe Foundation and administered by AISES.

Number awarded: 5 new awards are made each year.

Deadline: April of each year.

1862
CAB/NJAA SCHOLARSHIP

National Junior Angus Association
Attn: Director Junior Activities
3201 Frederick Boulevard
St. Joseph, MO 64506
Phone: (816) 383-5100   Fax: (816) 233-9703
E-mail: jfisher@angus.org   Web Site: www.angus.org/njaa

Summary: To provide financial assistance to students who have been members of the National Junior Angus Association (NJAA) and are interested in taking courses in selected beef-related topics in college.

Eligibility: Applicants must have been a member of the NJAA in the past and must presently be a junior, regular, or life member of the American Angus Association. They must be either a high school senior or already enrolled in college on the undergraduate level. The primary course work/declared major must be in animal science, meat science, food science, agricultural communications, or a related field. Selection is based on involvement in Angus associations, professional organizations, other agriculture-related groups, school organizations, and church and civic groups; experience in livestock production, marketing, and judging; experience in meats evaluation and processing; a statement of ambitions and goals; and transcripts.

Financial data: The stipend is $1,000.

Duration: 1 year; recipients may reapply.

Additional information: This program is sponsored by the Certified Angus Beef (CAB) Program and the NJAA. It was established in 1990.

Number awarded: 1 each year.

Deadline: May of each year.

1863
CADA SCHOLARSHIP

Colorado 4-H Youth Development Program
c/o Colorado State University Cooperative Extension
Jefferson County Extension Office
15200 West Sixth Avenue, Suite C
Golden, CO 80501-5018   Phone: (303) 271-6620

Summary: To provide financial assistance to Colorado 4-H members who will be majoring in agricultural at a college in the state.

Eligibility: This program is open to high school seniors in Colorado who are 4-H members and intend to major in an agricultural field in college. They must have at least a 3.0 grade point average and be able to demonstrate leadership and involvement in community services.

Financial data: The stipend is $1,000.

Duration: 1 year.

Additional information: This program is sponsored by the Colorado Agricultural Development Authority (CADA). Recipients must attend a community or 4-year college in Colorado.

Number awarded: 5 each year.

Deadline: May of each year.

1864
CADY MCDONNELL MEMORIAL SCHOLARSHIP

American Congress on Surveying and Mapping
Attn: Awards Director
6 Montgomery Village Avenue, Suite 403
Gaithersburg, MD 20879
Phone: (240) 632-9716   Fax: (240) 632-1321
E-mail: tmilburn@acsm.net   Web Site: www.acsm.net

Summary: To provide financial assistance for undergraduate study in surveying to women members of the American Congress on Surveying and Mapping from designated western states.

Eligibility: This program is open to women members of the sponsoring organization who are enrolled in a program of surveying at a 2-year or 4-year college or university. Applicants must be residents of Alaska, Arizona, California, Colorado, Hawaii, Idaho, Montana, Nevada, New Mexico, Oregon, Utah, Washington, or Wyoming. Selection is based on academic record (30 percent), a statement of future plans (30 percent), letters of recommendation (20 percent), and professional activities (20 percent); if 2 or more applicants are judged equal based on those criteria, financial need may be considered.

Financial data: The stipend is $1,000.

Duration: 1 year.

Number awarded: 1 each year.

Deadline: December of each year.

1865
CAHHS HEALTH CAREER SCHOLARSHIP

California Association of Hospitals and Health Systems
Committee on Volunteer Services
Attn: Scholarships
1215 K Street
P.O. Box 1442
Sacramento, CA 95812-1442
Phone: (916) 443-7401

Summary: To provide financial assistance to high school seniors who have volunteered in a California health care facility and are interested in preparing for a health career.

Eligibility: High school seniors in California who have volunteered in a hospital for at least 100 hours within the last 2 years are eligible to apply. They must intend to prepare for a health career at an accredited college, university, or technical school (in any state) and have at least a 3.0 grade point average. To apply, students must submit a completed application form, 2 letters of commendation, a high school transcript, and proof of acceptance or enrollment. Finalists may be interviewed. Selection is based on health care volunteer activities, school and community service, and desire to enter a health care profession. Financial need is not considered in the selection process.

Financial data: The stipend is $1,000. Funds must be used for tuition, fees, and books. Checks are sent to the recipient's school.
Duration: 1 year.
Number awarded: 5 each year.
Deadline: May of each year.

1866
CALCOT-SEITZ FOUNDATION SCHOLARSHIPS

Calcot-Seitz Foundation
P.O. Box 259
Bakersfield, CA 93302
Phone: (661) 327-5961   E-mail: staff@calcot.com
Web Site: www.calcot.com
Summary: To provide financial assistance to students in Arizona and California who are interested in majoring in an agricultural-related field.
Eligibility: This program is open to students from California and Arizona who are working on an agricultural-related degree at a 4-year college or university. Applicants may be high school seniors or currently-enrolled college students who are continuing their studies. Selection is based on scholastic aptitude and performance, leadership potential, demonstrated capability, financial need, and a personal interview.
Financial data: Stipends are generally $1,000 per year.
Duration: 3 years.
Additional information: In addition to the general scholarships, 4 special scholarships are awarded: 2 directors' scholarships (given to the top 2 applicants), the Joe and Joyce Sheeley Memorial Scholarship (for an applicant from Arizona), and the Julio M. Gallo Award (for a California applicant).
Number awarded: Several each year, including 4 special awards.

1867
CALIFORNIA CITRUS MUTUAL COLLEGE SCHOLARSHIPS

California Citrus Mutual
Attn: Scholarship Foundation
512 North Kaweah Avenue
Exeter, CA 93221
Phone: (559) 592-3790   Fax: (559) 592-3798
E-mail: citrus@cacitrusmutual.com
Web Site: www.cacitrusmutual.com
Summary: To provide financial assistance to California Citrus Mutual (CCM) grower members and their dependents and/or employees who are currently in college and preparing for a career in agriculture.
Eligibility: This program is open to CCM grower members and their dependents or employees. Applicants must be currently enrolled in college and preparing for a career in agriculture or a related field. Along with their completed application form, students must submit, in writing, evidence of their leadership skills, a list of their extracurricular activities, a work history, an indication of their agriculture-related interests, and an essay describing their future goals.
Financial data: The stipend is $2,000.
Duration: 1 year.
Number awarded: 1 each year.
Deadline: June of each year.

1868
CALIFORNIA EMERGENCY NURSES ASSOCIATION SCHOLARSHIP

California Emergency Nurses Association
2223 Coolcrest Way
Upland, CA 91784-1295
Phone: (909) 985-2811, ext. 4498   E-mail: peggyperkins@hotmail.com
Web Site: www.enw.org/CAL-ENA-Scholarship.htm
Summary: To provide financial assistance to members of the Emergency Nurses Association (ENA) from California who are interested in pursuing additional education.
Eligibility: This program is open to ENA members who hold a current California R.N. license and are either enrolled or accepted in an accredited program. Applicants must be seeking a baccalaureate or higher degree. They must submit 1) a copy of their curriculum vitae; 2) a letter of intent that includes how the profession of emergency nursing will benefit from their education and a description of their ENA involvement; and 3) proof of California R.N. licensure, ENA membership, and school acceptance or enrollment.
Financial data: Stipends are $1,000 or $500.

Duration: 1 year.
Number awarded: Either 1 scholarship at $1,000 or 2 at $500 are offered each year.
Deadline: April of each year.

1869
CALIFORNIA GOVERNOR'S DISTINGUISHED MATHEMATICS AND SCIENCE SCHOLARS AWARDS

ScholarShare Investment Board
Attn: State Program Administrator
P.O. Box 942809
Sacramento, CA 94209
Phone: (916) 323-9740
Web Site: www.scholarshare.com/gsp/index.html
Summary: To provide financial assistance for college to high school students in California who achieve high scores on specified mathematics and science examinations.
Eligibility: This program is open to students in grades 9 through 11 at comprehensive public high schools in California who have attended their school for at least 12 consecutive months. They must first qualify for a Governor's Scholars Award by taking the Stanford 9 Reading, Stanford 9 Mathematics, and California English Language Arts Standards Tests and ranking either in the top 5 percent of all students in their grade level in the state or in the top 10 percent of students in their grade level at their school. To qualify for this additional award, they must achieve a qualifying score on 1 authorized mathematics examination and on 1 authorized science examination from among the Advanced Placement (AP) examinations, the International Baccalaureate (IB) examinations, or the Golden State Exams (GSE). They may take the examinations any time they are in high school. The eligible examinations, with the required scores, are AP Calculus AB (5), AP Calculus BC (4 or 5), IB Math Methods (6 or 7), IB Higher Math (5, 6, or 7), GSE High School Math (6), AP Biology (5), AP Chemistry (5), AP Physics B (5), AP Physics C (4 or 5), IB Biology (6 or 7), IB Chemistry (6 or 7), IB Physics (6 or 7), GSE Biology (6), GSE Chemistry (6), GSE Physics (6), GSE Second Year Coordinated Science (6). If their score meets the required level, they are notified by the State of California and they claim their award using the sponsor's web site or a printed form.
Financial data: Students who achieve qualifying scores on both a mathematics examination and a science examination receive an award of $2,500 in addition to any funds they receive from the Governor's Scholars Award. If they receive 3 of those, their total award is $5,500. Funds are invested in an account in the Golden State ScholarShare College Savings Trust where they earn interest until the student enters college. Students may then withdraw the money from their account at any time in their college career. Once withdrawn, the funds must be used immediately for qualified educational expenses (tuition, fees, books, supplies, room, and board).
Duration: When the funds are withdrawn, they become a 1-time award.
Additional information: Recipients may use their award funds any time prior to their 30th birthday. Awards may be used at any postsecondary institution that is eligible to participate in the U.S. Department of Education Federal Title IV financial aid programs, including schools outside the United States. This program was established in 2000. Information is also available from the ScholarShare Program Manager, P.O. Box 60009, Los Angeles, CA 90060-0009, (877) 728-4338.
Number awarded: Varies each year.

1870
CALIFORNIA GOVERNOR'S OPPORTUNITY SCHOLARSHIPS

Office of the Governor
Attn: Crystal Clark
State Capitol, First Floor
Sacramento, CA 95814
Phone: (916) 445-2841
Summary: To provide financial assistance to California women interested in an undergraduate or graduate education in selected fields.
Eligibility: This program is open to women who are interested in preparing for a career in 1) business, 2) education, 3) public service and law enforcement, 4) health and human services, 5) nursing, and 6) science and technology. Applicants must be U.S. citizens or legal immigrants, be California residents, have completed at least 2 years of postsecondary education and/or at least 4 years of work experience, be accepted at an accredited California institution as a full- or part-time student, and have a grade point average of 3.3 or higher.
Financial data: The stipend is $5,000. Funds must be applied to a related academic or work program at an accredited California institution.

Duration: 1 year.
Number awarded: 6 each year: 1 in each of the categories.
Deadline: June of each year.

1871
CALIFORNIA LEGION AUXILIARY PAST PRESIDENTS' PARLEY NURSING SCHOLARSHIPS

American Legion Auxiliary
Attn: Department of California
Veterans War Memorial Building
401 Van Ness Avenue, Room 113
San Francisco, CA 94102-4586
Phone: (415) 861-5092   Fax: (415) 861-8365
E-mail: calegionaux@calegionaux.org
Web Site: www.calegionaux.org/scholarships.html
Summary: To provide financial assistance to California residents who are the children of veterans and interested in studying nursing.
Eligibility: This program is open to California residents who are the children of veterans of World War I, World War II, Korea, Vietnam, Grenada/Lebanon, Panama, or Desert Shield/Desert Storm. Applicants must be entering or continuing students of nursing at an accredited institution of higher learning in California. Selection is based on financial need (30 percent), character (20 percent), scholastic merit (20 percent), Americanism (20 percent), and leadership (10 percent).
Financial data: Stipends range from $500 to $1,500.
Duration: 1 year.
Number awarded: Varies each year.
Deadline: April of each year.

1872
CALVIN E. MOORE MEMORIAL SCHOLARSHIP

South Florida Manufacturers Association
1000 West McNab Road
Pompano Beach, FL 33069
Phone: (954) 941-3558   Fax: (954) 941-3559
Web Site: www.sfma.org
Summary: To provide financial assistance for college to high school seniors in Florida whose parents work for a company that belongs to the South Florida Manufacturers Association (SFMA).
Eligibility: This program is open to high school seniors in Florida whose parents work at an SFMA-member company, have earned at least a 3.0 grade point average, have been accepted at a Florida college or university, and are interested in working on a degree in engineering, management, or business administration.
Financial data: A stipend is awarded (exact amount not specified).
Duration: 1 year.
Number awarded: 1 or more each year.

1873
CANERS COLLEGE STUDENT SCHOLARSHIP

California Association of Nurserymen Endowment for Research and Scholarship
3947 Lennane Drive, Suite 150
Sacramento, CA 95834
Phone: (916) 928-3900   (800) 748-6214
Fax: (916) 567-0505   E-mail: can@earthlink.net
Web Site: www.can-online.org
Summary: To provide financial assistance to college students in California who are majoring in ornamental horticulture or related fields.
Eligibility: This program is open to college students in California who are currently enrolled in at least 6 credits and are majoring or planning to major in a field related to the nursery industry: ornamental horticulture, agribusiness, viticulture, or pomology. Applicants must be U.S. citizens. Grades are important, but a "B" student who has participated in horticulture-related activities may be selected over the "A" student who does not participate in 4-H, FFA, or similar activities. Motivation, character, work experience, community activities, and financial need are each considered. As part of the application process, an official transcript and 2 letters of reference must be submitted.
Financial data: Stipends range from $150 to $6,400.
Duration: 1 year.
Additional information: No e-mail or faxed applications are accepted.
Number awarded: The association awards more than 60 scholarships each year.
Deadline: March of each year.

1874
CANERS HIGH SCHOOL SENIORS SCHOLARSHIP

California Association of Nurserymen Endowment for Research and Scholarship
3947 Lennane Drive, Suite 150
Sacramento, CA 95834
Phone: (916) 928-3900   (800) 748-6214
Fax: (916) 567-0505   E-mail: can@earthlink.net
Web Site: www.can-online.org
Summary: To provide financial assistance to high school seniors in California who are planning to major in ornamental horticulture or related fields.
Eligibility: This program is open to graduating high school seniors in California who are planning to major in a field related to the nursery industry: ornamental horticulture, agribusiness, viticulture, or pomology. Applicants must be U.S. citizens. Grades are important, but a "B" student who has participated in horticulture-related activities may be selected over the "A" student who does not participate in 4-H, FFA, or similar activities. Motivation, character, work experience, community activities, and financial need are each considered. As part of the application process, an official transcript and 2 letters of reference must be submitted.
Financial data: Stipends range from $150 to $6,400.
Duration: 1 year.
Additional information: No e-mail or faxed applications are accepted.
Number awarded: The association awards more than 60 scholarships each year.
Deadline: March of each year.

1875
CAREER ADVANCEMENT SCHOLARSHIPS

Summary: To provide financial assistance to mature women who are employed or seeking employment in the work force and to increase the pool of women qualified for positions that promise career opportunity.
See Listing #1310.

1876
CAROL BAUHS BENSON MEMORIAL SCHOLARSHIP

American Dental Hygienists' Association
Attn: Institute for Oral Health
444 North Michigan Avenue, Suite 3400
Chicago, IL 60611
Phone: (312) 440-8944   (800) 735-4916
Fax: (312) 440-8929   E-mail: institute@adha.net
Web Site: www.adha.org
Summary: To provide financial assistance to students from selected states who are preparing for careers in dental hygiene.
Eligibility: Applicants must have earned at least a 3.0 grade point average, be able to demonstrate financial need, and have completed a minimum of 1 year in a dental hygiene curriculum. Scholarships are available to residents of Minnesota, North Dakota, South Dakota, and Wisconsin who are enrolled full time in a certificate/associate degree program leading to licensure in the year of the award.
Financial data: The amount of the award depends on the need of the recipient, to a maximum of $1,000.
Duration: 1 year.
Number awarded: 1 each year.
Deadline: May of each year.

1877
CAROLINA SECTION SAE SCHOLARSHIPS

Society of Automotive Engineers
Attn: Educational Relations
400 Commonwealth Drive
Warrendale, PA 15096-0001
Phone: (724) 772-4047   Fax: (724) 776-0890
E-mail: connie@sae.org
Web Site: www.sae.org/students/carolina.htm
Summary: To provide financial support to high school seniors interested in studying engineering in college and sponsored by a member of the Carolina Section of the Society of Automotive Engineers (SAE).
Eligibility: This program is open to high school seniors who intend to earn an ABET-accredited degree in engineering or a related science. Applicants must be sponsored by a member in good standing of the Carolina Section of SAE. U.S.

citizenship is required. Selection is based on academic achievement, leadership potential, involvement in extracurricular activities, and interest in engineering.

Financial data: The stipend is $1,000.

Duration: 1 year; nonrenewable.

Additional information: This program includes the Donald L. Willoughby Scholarship. Information is also available from Wanda Curtis, c/o Thomas Built Buses, Inc. P.O. Box 2450, High Point, NC 27261. Candidates must include a $5 processing fee with their applications.

Number awarded: 1 each year.

Deadline: January of each year.

1878
CAROLINA TRIANGLE SECTION ENGINEERING SCHOLARSHIPS

American Society of Highway Engineers-Carolina Triangle Section
Attn: Scholarship Committee
5800 Faringdon Place, Suite 105
Raleigh, NC 27609
Phone: (919) 878-9560

Summary: To provide financial assistance to currently-enrolled college students from North Carolina who are majoring in a transportation-related field.

Eligibility: Applicants must be U.S. citizens and residents of North Carolina. They must be currently enrolled in a 4-year college or university in any state (must have completed at least 1 semester) and be working on a bachelor's degree in a transportation-related field, preferably in a civil engineering curriculum. A copy of the applicant's college transcript is required; high school transcripts, SAT scores, and resumes may also be submitted but are not required. A personal interview may be requested. Selection is based on academic performance (30 points), activities, honors, work experience, and leadership (25 points), career goals (25 points), enrollment in a civil engineering curriculum (10 points), and dependent of a member of the Carolina Triangle Section (10 points). Financial need is not considered.

Financial data: The stipend is $1,000.

Duration: 1 year; nonrenewable.

Additional information: Recipients may attend school in any state.

Number awarded: 2 each year.

Deadline: March of each year.

1879
CARTOGRAPHY AND GEOGRAPHIC INFORMATION SOCIETY SCHOLARSHIP AWARD

American Congress on Surveying and Mapping
Attn: Awards Director
6 Montgomery Village Avenue, Suite 403
Gaithersburg, MD 20879
Phone: (240) 632-9716   Fax: (240) 632-1321
E-mail: tmilburn@acsm.net   Web Site: www.acsm.net

Summary: To provide financial assistance for undergraduate or graduate study in cartography or geographic information science to members of the American Congress on Surveying and Mapping (ACSM).

Eligibility: This program is open to members of the sponsoring organization who are enrolled in a 4-year or graduate degree program in cartography or geographic information science. Preference is given to undergraduates with junior or senior standing. Selection is based or previous academic record (30 percent), a statement of future plans (30 percent), letters of recommendation (20 percent), and professional activities (20 percent); if 2 or more applicants are judged equal based on those criteria, financial need may be considered.

Financial data: The stipend is $1,000.

Duration: 1 year.

Additional information: This award is funded by the Cartography and Geographic Information Society (CaGIS) and administered by ACSM.

Number awarded: 1 each year.

Deadline: December of each year.

1880
C.B. GAMBRELL UNDERGRADUATE SCHOLARSHIP

Institute of Industrial Engineers
Attn: Chapter Operations Board
25 Technology Park/Atlanta
Norcross, GA 30092-2988
Phone: (770) 449-0460   (800) 494-0460
Fax: (770) 441-3295

Web Site: www.iienet.org

Summary: To provide financial assistance to undergraduate student members of the Institute of Industrial Engineers (IIE).

Eligibility: This program is open to U.S. citizens who graduated from a high school in the United States and are currently enrolled in an ABET-accredited program above the freshman level. Applicants must be pursuing a full-time course of study in industrial engineering with a grade point average of 3.4 and at least 5 full quarters or 3 full semesters remaining until graduation. Students may not apply directly for this award; they must be nominated by the head of their industrial engineering department. Nominees must be IIE members. Selection is based on scholastic ability, character, leadership, potential service to the industrial engineering profession, and need for financial assistance.

Financial data: A stipend is awarded (exact amount not specified).

Duration: 1 year.

Additional information: This program was established in 2001.

Number awarded: 1 each year.

Deadline: November of each year.

1881
CELSOC UNDERGRADUATE SCHOLARSHIPS

Consulting Engineers and Land Surveyors of California
Attn: Communications Director
1303 J Street, Suite 450
Sacramento, CA 95814
Phone: (916) 441-7991   Fax: (916) 441-6312
E-mail: staff@celsoc.org
Web Site: www.celsoc.org

Summary: To provide financial assistance to students working on a bachelor's degree at an approved engineering program or land surveying program in California.

Eligibility: This program is open to U.S. citizens who are working full time on a bachelor's degree in an Accreditation Board for Engineering and Technology (ABET)-approved engineering program or in an accredited land surveying program in California. Applicants must be entering their junior, senior, or fifth year to qualify; students graduating this academic year are not eligible. Selection is based on cumulative grade point average-must be at least 3.2, with at least 3.5 in engineering and land surveying courses (28 points); a 500-word essay (25 points); work experience (20 points); recommendations (17 points); and college activities (10 points). Financial need is not considered in the selection process.

Financial data: The student selected as the most outstanding receives $7,500. Other awards range from $1,000 to $5,000. A total of $25,000 in scholarships is awarded each year.

Duration: 1 year; recipients may reapply for 1 additional year.

Number awarded: Several each year.

Deadline: January of each year.

1882
CESSNA/ONR STUDENT DESIGN/BUILD/FLY COMPETITION

American Institute of Aeronautics and Astronautics
Attn: Student Programs Director
1801 Alexander Bell Drive, Suite 500
Reston, VA 20191-4344
Phone: (703) 264-7536   (800) 639-AIAA
Fax: (703) 264-7551   E-mail: stephenb@aiaa.org
Web Site: www.aiaa.org

Summary: To recognize and reward outstanding aircraft that are designed, built, and flown by undergraduate and graduate student members of the American Institute of Aeronautics and Astronautics (AIAA).

Eligibility: This program is open to undergraduate and graduate students who are AIAA branch or at-large student members. Teams of 3 to 10 students (at least one-third of whom must be freshmen, sophomores, or juniors) may enter this competition to design, build, and fly an unmanned, radio-controlled, propeller-driven, electric-powered aircraft. The design must comply with precise specifications; once those specifications are met, the aircraft must be able to take off, circle the field, and land within designated areas. Design projects that are used as part of an organized classroom requirement are eligible and encouraged. Designs that are submitted must be the work of the students, but a faculty advisor may provide guidance. Flight scores are based on the demonstrated mission performance in the best 3 flights obtained during the contest.

Financial data: First place is $2,500, second place is $1,500, and third place is $1,000.

Duration: The competition is held annually.

Additional information: Information is also available from Tom Zickuhr, Cessna Aircraft Company, MS 178P, 5701 East Pawnee, Wichita, KS 67218, (316) 831-2810, Fax: (316) 831-2828, Web site: amber.aae.uiuc.edu/~aiaadbf.

Number awarded: 3 cash awards are presented each year.

Deadline: Letters of intent must be submitted by October of each year; the competition takes place in April of each year.

1883
CHARLES H. BENNETT MEMORIAL SCHOLARSHIP

Wisconsin Society of Professional Engineers
Attn: Engineers Foundation of Wisconsin
700 Rayovac Drive, Suite 207
Madison, WI 53711-2476
Phone: (608) 278-7000   Fax: (608) 278-7005
E-mail: wspe@wspe.org
Web Site: www.wspe.org/efw.htm

Summary: To provide financial assistance to high school seniors in Wisconsin who are interested in majoring in engineering in college.

Eligibility: This program is open to seniors graduating from high schools in Wisconsin who intend to enroll in an accredited engineering undergraduate program, earn a degree in engineering, and enter the practice of engineering after graduation. Applicants must have a grade point average of 3.0 or higher and an ACT composite score of 24 or higher. As part of the selection process, they must submit a 250-word essay on how they became interested in engineering, the field of engineering that is most interesting to them and why, and why they want to become a practicing engineer. U.S. citizenship is required. Selection is based on grade point average, ACT scores, class ranking, activities and honors, the essay, and supplemental credits (computer, chemistry, physics, calculus, etc.). Points are also given for honors/advanced placement courses and college-level courses completed.

Financial data: Varies each year. The sponsor awards a total of $7,500 in scholarships each year.

Duration: 1 year.

Additional information: This scholarship is supported by the Fox River Valley Chapter of the Wisconsin Society of Professional Engineers.

Number awarded: 1 or more each year.

Deadline: December of each year.

1884
CHARLES S. GARDNER MEMORIAL SCHOLARSHIP IN FOREST RESOURCES

Technical Association of the Pulp and Paper Industry
P.O. Box 105113
Atlanta, GA 30348-5113
Phone: (770) 446-1400   (800) 332-8686
Fax: (770) 446-6947
Web Site: www.tappi.org

Summary: To provide financial assistance to college students enrolled in a school of forest resources in the south.

Eligibility: This program is open to rising sophomores who are enrolled in a school of forest resources located in 1 of the southern states. Financial need is considered in the selection process.

Financial data: The stipend is $2,000.

Duration: 1 year.

Additional information: This scholarship is sponsored by MOTAG-South (the Millyard Operations Technical Advancement Group-South), a subcommittee of the Fiber Raw Material Supply Committee of the TAPPI Pulp Manufacture Division.

Number awarded: 1 each year.

Deadline: May of each year.

1885
CHARLES W. AND ANNETTE HILL SCHOLARSHIP FUND

Summary: To provide financial assistance for postsecondary education (particularly in science and business) to the children of members of the Kansas American Legion.

See Listing #170.

1886
CHARLIE WELLS MEMORIAL AVIATION SCHOLARSHIPS

Charlie Wells Memorial Scholarship Fund
1835 South Fourth Street
Springfield, IL 62703
E-mail: roger@wellsscholarship.com
Web Site: www.wellsscholarship.com

Summary: To provide financial assistance to students pursuing an aviation-related program in college.

Eligibility: This program is open to students who are currently majoring full time in an aviation-oriented curriculum at a college or university in the United States. Applicants must submit information on their career interests, 2 letters of reference, an essay on why they deserve the scholarship (including their past accomplishments, future goals, and financial need), and a list of their extracurricular activities.

Financial data: Stipends vary, depending on the availability of funds. Recently, they were $1,150. Funds are sent directly to the recipient's school to help pay the costs of tuition.

Duration: 1 year.

Additional information: Requests for applications must be accompanied by a self-addressed stamped envelope.

Number awarded: Varies each year; recently, 2 of these scholarships were awarded.

Deadline: March of each year.

1887
CHARLOTTE MCGUIRE SCHOLARSHIP PROGRAM

American Holistic Nurses' Association
2733 East Lakin Drive
P.O. Box 2130
Flagstaff, AZ 86003-2130
Phone: (520) 526-2196   (800) 278-AHNA
Fax: (520) 526-2752   E-mail: AHNA-Flag@flaglink.com
Web Site: ahna.org/f_assistance.htm

Summary: To provide financial assistance for undergraduate or graduate studies or research in holistic nursing.

Eligibility: This program is open to any licensed nurse or nursing student who is pursuing holistic education for personal and professional growth. Experience in holistic health care or alternative health practices is preferred. Membership in the American Holistic Nurses' Association is required (at least 6 months for the undergraduate scholarship and 1 year for the graduate award). If applying for the A.D.N./B.S.N. scholarship, nursing prerequisites should have been completed with at least a 3.0 grade point average. Selection is based on personal data, educational background, employment history, personal interests, financial need, plans for integrating holistic nursing practice into professional and personal life, and letters of reference.

Financial data: The amount awarded varies, depending upon the funds available. Funds may be used to pay for college tuition/expenses for an accredited nursing program (A.D.N., B.S.N., M.S.N., or Ph.D.), tuition/expenses for accredited programs in holistic health or alternative modalities (these programs must be approved by the association's education committee), tuition/expenses for association certificate programs, and expenses for research related to holistic health.

Duration: 1 year.

Additional information: These scholarships were first offered in 1987.

Number awarded: 2 each year: 1 for an A.D.N. or B.S.N. program and 1 for graduate study/research.

Deadline: March of each year.

1888
CHARLOTTE WOODS MEMORIAL SCHOLARSHIP

Transportation Clubs International
Attn: Gay Fielding
P.O. Box 52
Arabi, LA 70032
Phone: (504) 278-1107
Web Site: www.transportationclubsinternational.com

Summary: To provide financial assistance to college students interested in preparing for a career in a field related to transportation.

Eligibility: This program is open to students enrolled in an academic institution (vocational or degree program) that offers courses in transportation, logistics,

traffic management, or related fields. Applicants must be a member of Transportation Clubs International (or the dependent of a member) planning a career in those fields. Selection is based on scholastic ability, potential, professional interest, character, and financial need.

Financial data: The stipend is $1,000.

Duration: 1 year.

Additional information: Requests for applications must be accompanied by a stamped self-addressed envelope.

Number awarded: 1 each year.

Deadline: April of each year.

1889
CHEM-E-CAR COMPETITION

American Institute of Chemical Engineers
Attn: Awards Administrator
Three Park Avenue
New York, NY 10016-5991
Phone: (212) 591-7478   Fax: (212) 591-8882
E-mail: awards@aiche.org
Web Site: www.aiche.org/awards

Summary: To recognize and reward student members of the American Institute of Chemical Engineers (AIChE) who design a chemically powered vehicle.

Eligibility: This program is open to student members of the institute who design and construct a chemically powered vehicle within certain size constraints that is designed to carry a specified cargo a given distance and stop. Entries must be submitted by teams of undergraduate students that have at least 5 participants, including students from at least 2 chemical engineering classes. The percentage of students from each class must not be greater than 80 percent of the total number of students on the team. Faculty and graduate students may only act as sounding boards for team members and may not be idea generators for the project. Teams are told at the time of the competition the distance that the car must travel and the cargo it will carry. Winners are determined by a combined score, for traveling the correct distance and for creativity. Competitions are first held at the regional level, from which top entries proceed to the national competition.

Financial data: At the regional level, first prize is $200 and second prize is $100. At the national level, first prize is $2,000, second prize is $1,000, and third prize is $500.

Duration: The competition is held annually.

Additional information: This competition, first held in 1999, is sponsored by AIChE and General Mills, Inc. Information is also available from David Dixon, South Dakota School of Mines and Technology, Department of Chemistry and Chemical Engineering, 501 East St. Joseph Street, Rapid City, SD 57701, (605) 394-1235, Fax: (605) 394-1232, E-mail: ddixon@silver.sdsmt.edu.

Number awarded: 3 national winners are selected each year.

Deadline: Regional competitions are held in spring of each year. Eligible winners must submit applications to participate in the national competition, held in November, by May of each year.

1890
CHEVRON CORPORATION SCHOLARSHIPS

Society of Women Engineers
230 East Ohio Street, Suite 400
Chicago, IL 60611-3265
Phone: (312) 596-5223   Fax: (312) 644-8557
E-mail: hq@swe.org
Web Site: www.swe.org

Summary: To provide financial assistance to undergraduate women majoring in designated engineering specialties.

Eligibility: Women who are entering their sophomore or junior year and majoring in chemical, civil, mechanical, or petroleum engineering at an ABET-accredited school, college, or university are eligible to apply if they are U.S. citizens and have a grade point average of at least 3.5. Selection is based on merit. Membership in the sponsoring organization is required.

Financial data: The stipend is $2,000.

Duration: 1 year.

Additional information: This program was established in 1992.

Number awarded: 2 each year: 1 to an entering sophomore and 1 to an entering junior.

Deadline: January of each year.

1891
CHI EPSILON DISTRICT SCHOLARSHIPS

Chi Epsilon
c/o Dr. Robert L. Henry
University of Texas at Arlington
Box 19316
Arlington, TX 76019-0316
Phone: (817) 272-2752   Fax: (817) 272-2826
E-mail: rhenry@uta.edu
Web Site: www.chi-epsilon.org

Summary: To provide financial assistance for college to members of Chi Epsilon, the national civil engineering honor society.

Eligibility: Members of Chi Epsilon may apply at the chapter level. The faculty advisor selects the chapter's nominee and forwards the nomination to the district councilor, who chooses the district winner. Selection is based on the 4 qualities of Chi Epsilon membership: character, scholarship, sociability, and practicality.

Financial data: The stipend is $1,000.

Duration: 1 year.

Additional information: Chi Epsilon, the national civil engineering honor society, began in 1922 at the University of Illinois.

Number awarded: 10 each year: 1 in each of the organization's districts.

Deadline: November of each year.

1892
CHICAGO MERCANTILE EXCHANGE BEEF INDUSTRY SCHOLARSHIP PROGRAM

National Cattlemen's Beef Association
Attn: National Cattlemen's Foundation
9110 East Nichols Avenue, Suite 300
Centennial, CO 80112
Phone: (303) 694-0305   Fax: (303) 694-2851
E-mail: apotts@beef.org
Web Site: www.beef.org

Summary: To recognize and reward college students who write an outstanding essay on issues related to the beef industry.

Eligibility: To be eligible, students must be enrolled or planning to enroll as an undergraduate in an agriculture program at a 4-year academic institution. Interested students should write a brief letter, indicating what role they see themselves playing in the beef industry after graduation; write an essay (up to 750 words) on an issue confronting the beef industry today or in the future; and submit 2 letters of recommendation. A career in the beef industry may include: education, communications, production, research, or other related areas. Essays are judged on the basis of clarity of expression, persuasiveness, originality, accuracy, relevance, and solutions offered.

Financial data: The award is a $1,250 scholarship.

Duration: The competition is held annually.

Additional information: This program was started in 1989. It is cosponsored by the Chicago Mercantile Exchange (CME) and the National Cattlemen's Foundation.

Number awarded: 16 each year.

Deadline: November of each year.

1893
CHICAGO MERCANTILE EXCHANGE PORK INDUSTRY SCHOLARSHIP PROGRAM

National Pork Producers Council
P.O. Box 10383
Des Moines, IA 50306
Phone: (515) 223-2600   E-mail: pork@nppc.org
Web Site: www.nppc.org

Summary: To provide financial assistance to college students interested in preparing for a career in the pork industry.

Eligibility: This program is open to students who are currently enrolled in a 2-year or 4-year college agricultural program. Applicants must submit a 750-word essay on an issue confronting the U.S. pork industry today. A letter describing their future aspirations in the pork industry upon graduation along with 2 letters of reference are also required.

Financial data: The stipend is $2,500.

Duration: 1 year.

Additional information: Winners are given an all-expense paid trip to attend the next National Pork Industry Forum. This program is jointly sponsored by the Chicago Mercantile Exchange and the National Pork Producers Council.
Number awarded: 4 each year.
Deadline: December of each year.

1894
CIND M. TRESER MEMORIAL SCHOLARSHIP

Washington State Environmental Health Association
c/o Chuck Treser, Student Scholarship Committee Chair
3045 N.W. 57th Street
Seattle, WA 98107-2552
Summary: To provide financial assistance to undergraduate students (particularly minorities and students with disabilities) who are majoring in environmental health or other life sciences and are interested in pursuing a career in environmental health in the state of Washington.
Eligibility: In order to be eligible for the scholarship, undergraduates must 1) intend to become employed in the field of environmental health in Washington following graduation and 2) be enrolled in a program either accredited by the National Accreditation Council for Environmental Health Curricula or with a curriculum comparable to the model curriculum recommended by the National Accreditation Council (i.e., the program must include substantial course work in biology and microbiology, general and organic chemistry, epidemiology, biostatistics, and environmental health sciences). Applicants do not need to be members of the sponsoring organization, but they must become members if they receive the scholarship. Students of color and specially challenged students are particularly encouraged to apply.
Financial data: The stipend is $1,000. Funds are sent directly to the recipient.
Duration: 1 year.
Additional information: This program was formerly known as the Ed Pickett Memorial Student Scholarship. Recipients must attend the association's annual education conference to accept the scholarship award.
Number awarded: 1 each year.
Deadline: March of each year.

1895
C.J. "RED" DAVIDSON MEMORIAL SCHOLARSHIPS

Texas FFA Association
614 East 12th Street
Austin, TX 78701
Phone: (512) 480-8045   Fax: (512) 472-0555
E-mail: txffa@txaged.org   Web Site: www.txaged.org
Summary: To provide finanial assistance for college to high school seniors in Texas who demonstrate outstanding personal qualities and involvement in FFA.
Eligibility: This program is open to high school seniors in Texas who are FFA members and have been members at least 2 of the 3 previous years. Applicants must be planning to major in college in a field related to the agricultural sciences, life sciences, or natural resources. They must have completed at least 5 semesters of instruction in agriculture and/or agribusiness during high school and scored at least 950 on the SAT or 20 on the ACT. U.S. citizenship and ranking in the top half of their graduating class are also required. Selection is based on academic achievement (16 points); SAT or ACT scores (14 points); agricultural science and career related instruction (10 points); FFA achievement (20 points), including the supervised agricultural experience (10 points); financial need (10 points); and performance during interviews regarding academics (10 points), FFA achievement (5 points), and financial need (10 points).
Financial data: The stipend is $5,000.
Duration: 1 year.
Additional information: Students may not apply for both 4-H and FFA scholarships.
Number awarded: 6 each year.

1896
CLARE BOOTHE LUCE SCHOLARSHIPS IN SCIENCE AND ENGINEERING

Clare Boothe Luce Fund
c/o Henry Luce Foundation, Inc.
111 West 50th Street, Suite 4601
New York, NY 10020
Phone: (212) 489-7700   Fax: (212) 581-9541
E-mail: jdaniels@hluce.org
Web Site: www.hluce.org
Summary: To provide funding to women interested in studying science or engineering at the undergraduate level at designated universities.
Eligibility: This program is open to female undergraduate students (particularly juniors and seniors) majoring in biology, chemistry, computer science, engineering (aeronautical, civil, electrical, mechanical, nuclear, and others), mathematics, meteorology, and physics. Applicants must be U.S. citizens attending 1 of the 12 designated colleges and universities affiliated with this program; periodically, other institutions are invited to participate. Premedical science majors are ineligible for this competition. The participating institutions select the recipients without regard to race, age, religion, ethnic background, or need. All awards are made on the basis of merit.
Financial data: The amount awarded is established individually by each of the participating institutions. The stipends are intended to augment rather than replace any existing institutional support in these fields. Each stipend is calculated to include the cost of room and board as well as tuition and other fees or expenses.
Duration: 2 years; in certain special circumstances, awards for the full 4 years of undergraduate study may be offered.
Additional information: The participating institutions are Boston University, Colby College, Creighton University, Fordham University, Georgetown University, Marymount University, Mount Holyoke College, St. John's University, Santa Clara University, Seton Hall University, Trinity College, and University of Notre Dame.
Deadline: Varies; check with the participating institutions for their current schedule.

1897
CNA NURSING EDUCATION SCHOLARSHIP FUND

California Nurses Association
Attn: Scholarship Fund
2000 Franklin Street, Suite 300
Oakland, CA 94612
Phone: (510) 273-2200   Fax: (510) 663-1625
E-mail: execoffice@calnurses.org
Web Site: www.califnurses.org
Summary: To provide financial assistance for undergraduate or graduate education to registered nurses in California.
Eligibility: Applicants must be licensed registered nurses in California who have been accepted for admission to an accredited B.S.N. or graduate degree program. They must plan to enroll on at least a half-time basis and complete the degree within 5 years. Selection is based on letters of reference, commitment and active participation in nursing and health-related organizations, professional vision and direction, and financial need.
Financial data: The stipend is $1,000 per year.
Duration: Up to 2 years.
Additional information: Recipients who fail to complete the degree within 5 years are expected to repay the award in full.
Number awarded: 5 each year.
Deadline: June of each year.

1898
COAL DIVISION SCHOLARSHIPS

Society for Mining, Metallurgy, and Exploration, Inc.
Attn: Member Services
8307 Shaffer Parkway
P.O. Box 277002
Littleton, CO 80127-7002
Phone: (303) 973-9550   (800) 763-3132
Fax: (303) 973-3845   E-mail: sensenig@smenet.org
Web Site: www.smenet.org/education/students/sme_scholarships.cfm
Summary: To provide financial assistance to student members of the Society for Mining, Metallurgy, and Exploration (SME) who are majoring in mining engineering with an emphasis on coal.
Eligibility: This program is open to student members who have completed their sophomore year in college and are majoring in mining or mineral engineering at an ABET-accredited college. Applicants must be engaged in coal-related activities. Financial need is considered in the selection process.
Financial data: The stipends are approximately $1,500 per year.
Duration: 1 year.
Number awarded: Approximately 15 each year.
Deadline: October of each year.

1899
COATES, WOLFF, RUSSELL MEMORIAL MINING INDUSTRY SCHOLARSHIPS

Society for Mining, Metallurgy and Exploration-Wyoming Section
c/o Rob L. Thurman, Scholarship Committee
1323 Hornchurch Avenue
Casper, WY 82609
Phone: (307) 265-5596   Fax: (307) 234-2147
Summary: To provide financial assistance to Wyoming residents who are majoring in subjects related to mining, metallurgy, and exploration.
Eligibility: Applicants must be Wyoming residents currently enrolled in college as a sophomore, junior, or senior and majoring in engineering, environmental sciences, or other mineral extractive disciplines. They must have earned at least a 2.25 grade point average. An essay is required on "The Importance of Mineral Extraction to the State of Wyoming." Financial need is not considered in the selection process.
Financial data: The stipend is $1,000.
Duration: 1 year.
Number awarded: 3 each year.
Deadline: November of each year.

1900
COATING AND GRAPHIC ARTS DIVISION SCHOLARSHIP

Summary: To provide financial assistance to student members of the Technical Association of the Pulp and Paper Industry (TAPPI) who are interested in preparing for a career in the paper industry, with a focus on coating and graphic arts.
See Listing #1329.

1901
COCA-COLA FOUNDATION SCHOLARSHIPS

Institute of Food Technologists
Attn: Scholarship Department
221 North LaSalle Street, Suite 300
Chicago, IL 60601-1291
Phone: (312) 782-8424   Fax: (312) 782-8348
E-mail: info@ift.org   Web Site: www.ift.org
Summary: To provide financial assistance to undergraduates interested in studying food science or food technology.
Eligibility: Applicants must be currently enrolled as sophomores or juniors in a food science or food technology program at an educational institution in the United States or Canada. They must have an outstanding scholastic record and a well-rounded personality. Financial need is not considered in the selection process.
Financial data: The stipend is $2,000.
Duration: 1 year; recipients may reapply if they are members of the Institute of Food Technologists (IFT).
Additional information: Funds for these scholarships are provided by the Coca-Cola Foundation. Correspondence and completed applications must be submitted to the department head of the educational institution the applicant is attending.
Number awarded: 5 each year.
Deadline: January of each year.

1902
COLGATE "BRIGHT SMILES, BRIGHT FUTURES" MINORITY SCHOLARSHIPS

American Dental Hygienists' Association
Attn: Institute for Oral Health
444 North Michigan Avenue, Suite 3400
Chicago, IL 60611
Phone: (312) 440-8944   (800) 735-4916
Fax: (312) 440-8929   E-mail: institute@adha.net
Web Site: www.adha.org
Summary: To provide financial assistance to minority group students enrolled in certificate/associate programs in dental hygiene.
Eligibility: This program is open to members of groups currently underrepresented in the dental hygiene profession: Native Americans, African Americans, Hispanics, Asians, and males. Applicants must have completed at least 1 year in a dental hygiene curriculum at the certificate/associate level, have earned at least a 3.0 grade point average, and be able to demonstrate financial need. They must intend to be full-time students in the academic year for which they are applying.
Financial data: The amount of the award depends on the need of the recipient, to a maximum of $1,250.
Duration: 1 year.

Additional information: These scholarships are sponsored by the Colgate-Palmolive Company.
Number awarded: 2 each year.
Deadline: May of each year.

1903
COLLEGIATE INVENTORS COMPETITION

National Inventors Hall of Fame
Attn: Collegiate Inventors Competition
221 South Broadway Street
Akron, OH 44308-1505
Phone: (330) 849-6887   E-mail: rdepuy@invent.org
Web Site: www.invent.org/collegiate
Summary: To recognize and reward outstanding inventions by college or university students in the fields of science, engineering, and technology.
Eligibility: This competition is open to undergraduate and graduate students who are (or have been) enrolled full time at least part of the 12-month period prior to entry in a college or university in the United States. Entries may also be submitted by teams, up to 4 members, of whom at least 1 must meet the full-time requirement and all others must have been enrolled at least half time sometime during the preceding 24-month period. Applicants must submit a description of their invention, including a patent search and summary of current literature that describes the state of the art and distinguishes the originality of the invention; test data demonstrating that the idea, invention, or design is workable; the societal, economic, and environmental benefits of the invention; and supplemental material that may include photos, slides, disks, videotapes, and even samples. Entries must be original ideas and the work of a student or team and a university advisor; the invention should be reproducible and may not have been 1) made available to the public as a commercial product or process, or 2) patented or published more than 1 year prior to the date of submission for this competition. Entries are first reviewed by a program panel that selects the semifinalists. Semifinalist entries are judged on the basis of originality, inventiveness, potential value to society (socially, environmentally, and economically), and range or scope of use.
Financial data: Each winning student (or student team) receives a $20,000 cash prize and a $2,000 gift certificate to www.hpshopping.com. Advisors each receive a $10,000 cash prize. Awards are unrestricted cash gifts, not scholarships or grants.
Duration: The competition is held annually.
Additional information: This program is co-sponsored by the Hewlett-Packard Company, Corning Incorporated, the Goodyear Tire and Rubber Company, and the United States Patent and Trademark Office. It was established in 1990 as the BFGoodrich Collegiate Inventors Program.
Number awarded: Up to 6 each year.
Deadline: May of each year.

1904
COLORADO LEGION AUXILIARY PAST PRESIDENT'S PARLEY NURSE'S SCHOLARSHIP

American Legion Auxiliary
Attn: Department of Colorado
7465 East First Avenue, Suite D
Denver, CO 80230
Phone: (303) 367-5388   E-mail: ala@coloradolegion.org
Summary: To provide financial assistance to wartime veterans and their descendants in Colorado who are interested in preparing for a career in nursing.
Eligibility: This program is open to 1) daughters, sons, spouses, granddaughters, and great-granddaughters of veterans, and 2) veterans who served in the armed forces during eligibility dates for membership in the American Legion. Applicants must be Colorado residents who have been accepted by an accredited school of nursing in Colorado. As part of the application process, they must submit a 500-word essay on the topic, "Americanism." Selection is based on scholastic ability (25 percent), financial need (25 percent), references (13 percent), a 500-word essay on Americanism (25 percent), and dedication to chosen field (12 percent).
Financial data: The amount of the award depends on the availability of funds.
Duration: 1 year; nonrenewable.
Number awarded: Varies each year, depending on the availability of funds.
Deadline: April of each year.

1905
COMMITMENT TO AGRICULTURE SCHOLARSHIPS

American Farm Bureau Foundation for Agriculture
225 West Touhy Avenue
Park Ridge, IL 60068-5874
Phone: (847) 685-8764   Fax: (847) 685-8969
E-mail: agfoundation@fb.com   Web Site: www.agfoundation.org
Summary: To provide financial assistance to high school students from designated states who plan to study agriculture in college.
Eligibility: This program is open to high school seniors whose families are actively engaged in production agriculture. Applicants must be planning to study an agricultural field in college and pursue a career in agriculture. They must have an ACT composite score of 18 or higher or an SAT combined verbal and math score of 850 or higher. Financial need is not considered in the selection process.
Financial data: The stipend is $1,500.
Duration: 1 year; nonrenewable.
Additional information: This program, established in 1999, is funded by Monsanto Company with royalty payments received from its patented seed technology. Applications are available from the foundation, from state and county Farm Bureau offices, and at agricultural chemical retailer locations.
Number awarded: 100 each year.
Deadline: March of each year.

1906
COMMUNITY PHARMACY ESSAY CONTEST

National Association of Chain Drug Stores
NACDS Educational Foundation
Attn: Secretary
413 North Lee Street
Alexandria, VA 22314
Phone: (703) 549-3001, ext. 195   Fax: (703) 836-4869
E-mail: sjung@nacds.org   Web Site: www.nacds.org
Summary: To recognize and reward pharmacy students who submit essays on a theme related to the profession.
Eligibility: Applicants must be enrolled full time at an accredited U.S. college or school of pharmacy and be in good academic standing. They must submit an essay, up to 6 pages in length, on a theme that changes annually; recently, the theme was "Community Pharmacy's Unique Contribution in Safeguarding America's Health." Papers must be written under the supervision of a faculty mentor who reviews and critiques the essay while in progress. Selection is based on creativity, applicability to community retail pharmacy practice, relevance to theme, and overall presentation.
Financial data: First place is $1,500, second $1,000, and third $500. The faculty members of each of the winners receive a $500 prize.
Duration: The contest is held annually.
Number awarded: 3 each year.
Deadline: January of each year.

1907
CONGRESSIONAL BLACK CAUCUS SPOUSES CHEERIOS BRAND HEALTH INITIATIVE SCHOLARSHIP

Congressional Black Caucus Foundation, Inc.
Attn: Director, Educational Programs
1004 Pennsylvania Avenue, S.E.
Washington, DC 20003
Phone: (202) 675-6739   (800) 784-2577
Fax: (202) 547-3806   E-mail: spouses@cbcfonline.org
Web Site: www.cbcfonline.org/cbcspouses/scholarship.html
Summary: To provide financial assistance to minority and other students who reside in a congressional district represented by an African American and are interested in pursuing a health-related career.
Eligibility: This program is open to 1) minority and other graduating high school seniors planning to attend an accredited institution of higher education and 2) currently-enrolled full-time undergraduate, graduate, and doctoral students in good academic standing with at least a 2.5 GPA. Applicants must reside, attend school, or have attended high school in a congressional district represented by an African American member of Congress. They must be interested in pursuing a career in a health-related field. As part of the application process, they must include a 250-word personal statement describing how this scholarship will assist them in their educational career.
Financial data: The program provides tuition assistance.
Duration: 1 year.

Additional information: The program was established in 1998 with support from General Mills, Inc.
Number awarded: Varies each year.
Deadline: May or September of each year.

1908
CONNECTICUT ASSOCIATION OF APTOMETRISTS SCHOLARSHIP FUND

Connecticut Association of Optometrists
342 North Main Street
West Hartford, CT 06117
Phone: (860) 586-7508   Fax: (860) 586-7550
E-mail: info@cao.org
Web Site: www.cao.org
Summary: To provide financial assistance to undergraduate students from Connecticut who are enrolled in accredited colleges of optometry.
Eligibility: Applicants must be Connecticut residents enrolled in accredited colleges of optometry in the United States. Selection is based on scholarship, character, and financial need.
Financial data: The stipend depends on availability of funds and the need of the recipient.
Duration: 1 year; may be renewed.
Additional information: This program was established in 1998. Information is also available from Robert L. Ross, O.D., 500 Post Road East, Suite 280, Westport, CT 06880, (203) 226-9426, Fax (203) 226-6230, E-mail: eyedoc@erols.com.
Number awarded: Varies each year.
Deadline: June of each year.

1909
CONNECTICUT BUILDING CONGRESS SCHOLARSHIPS

Summary: To provide financial assistance to high school seniors in Connecticut who are interested in studying a field related to construction in college.
See Listing #1334.

1910
CONNECTICUT SOCIETY OF PROFESSIONAL ENGINEERS SCHOLARSHIP

Connecticut Society of Professional Engineers
2600 Dixwell Avenue, Suite 7
Hamden, CT 06514-1800
Phone: (203) 281-4322   Fax: (203) 248-8932
E-mail: info@ctengineers.org   Web Site: www.cspe.org
Summary: To provide financial assistance to high school seniors in Connecticut who are interested in preparing for a career in engineering.
Eligibility: This program is open to Connecticut residents who are attending or planning to attend an ABET-accredited engineering program at a college or university anywhere in the United States. Applicants must submit a 500-word essay on their interest in engineering, their major area of study and area of specialization, and the occupation they plan to pursue after graduation. Selection is based on the essay, academic merit, extracurricular activities, potential, and financial need.
Financial data: A stipend is awarded (exact amount not specified).
Duration: 1 year.
Number awarded: 1 to 5 each year.
Deadline: October of each year.

1911
CONSTANCE L. LLOYD SCHOLARSHIP

American College of Medical Practice Executives
Attn: Scholarship Program
104 Inverness Terrace East
Englewood, CO 80112-5306
Phone: (303) 643-9573   Fax: (303) 643-4427
E-mail: acmpe@mgma.com   Web Site: www.mgma.com/acmpe
Summary: To provide financial assistance to undergraduate or graduate women in Georgia who are pursuing a degree in health care or health care administration.
Eligibility: This program is open to women enrolled at the undergraduate or graduate level at an accredited college or university in Georgia who are pursuing either an administrative or clinically-related degree in the health care field. Applications must include a letter describing career goals and objectives relevant to medical practice management; a resume; 3 reference letters commenting on the individual's performance, character, potential to succeed, and need for

scholarship support; documentation indicating acceptance into an undergraduate or graduate college or university; and academic transcripts indicating undergraduate or graduate work completed to date.

Financial data: The stipend is $2,000.

Duration: 1 year.

Additional information: This program was established in 1993.

Number awarded: 1 each year.

Deadline: May of each year.

1912
CONSULTING ENGINEERS OF INDIANA SCHOLARSHIP

Consulting Engineers of Indiana, Inc.
One Virginia Avenue, Suite 250
Indianapolis, IN 46204-3616
Phone: (317) 637-3563   Fax: (317) 637-9968
E-mail: cei@ai.org   Web Site: www.ai.org/cei

Summary: To provide financial assistance to upper-division students in Indiana who are majoring in engineering or land surveying.

Eligibility: Applicants must be U.S. citizens pursuing a bachelor's degree at an ABET-approved engineering program or in an accredited land surveying program. They must be Indiana residents, attending an Indiana school, and entering their junior, senior, or fifth year. Selection is based on grade point average (28 points); an essay on "What is a consulting engineer and why should you consider it as a career?" (25 points); work experience (20 points); recommendations (17 points); and college activities (10 points). Financial need is not considered in the selection process.

Financial data: Stipends are either $5,000 or $3,000.

Duration: 1 year.

Number awarded: Up to 3 each year: 2 at $5,000 and 1 at $3,000.

Deadline: January of each year.

1913
CORPORATE-SPONSORED SCHOLARSHIPS FOR MINORITY UNDERGRADUATE STUDENTS WHO MAJOR IN PHYSICS

American Physical Society
Attn: Minorities Scholarship Program
One Physics Ellipse
College Park, MD 20740-3844
Phone: (301) 209-3200   Fax: (301) 209-0865
Web Site: www.aps.org/educ/com/index.html

Summary: To provide financial assistance to underrepresented minority students interested in studying physics on the undergraduate level.

Eligibility: Any African American, Hispanic American, or Native American who plans to major in physics and who is a high school senior or college freshman or sophomore may apply. U.S. citizenship is required. The selection committee especially encourages applications from students who are attending or planning to attend institutions with historically or predominantly Black, Hispanic American, or Native American enrollment. Selection is based on commitment to the study of physics and plans to pursue a physics baccalaureate degree.

Financial data: Stipends are $2,000 per year in the first year or $3,000 in the second year; funds must be used for tuition, room, and board. In addition, $500 is awarded to the host department.

Duration: 1 year; renewable for 1 additional year with the approval of the APS selection committee.

Additional information: APS conducts the scholarship program in conjunction with the Corporate Associates of the American Institute of Physics. Each scholarship is sponsored by a corporation, which is normally designated as the sponsor. A corporation generally sponsors from 1 to 10 scholarships, depending upon its size and utilization of physics in the business.

Number awarded: Varies; generally, 6 new and 11 renewed scholarships each year.

Deadline: February of each year.

1914
CORRUGATED CONTAINERS DIVISION SCHOLARSHIPS

Technical Association of the Pulp and Paper Industry
P.O. Box 105113
Atlanta, GA 30348-5113
Phone: (770) 446-1400   (800) 332-8686
Fax: (770) 446-6947
Web Site: www.tappi.org

Summary: To provide financial assistance to students who are interested in preparing for a career in the paper industry, with a focus on the manufacture and use of corrugated, solid fiber, and associated packaging materials and products.

Eligibility: This program is open to students who are attending college full time, are rising juniors or rising seniors, have earned a grade point average of 3.0 or higher, are able to demonstrate a significant interest in the corrugated container, pulp, and paper industry, and are recommended and endorsed by an instructor or faculty member. Selection is based on the candidates' potential career and contributions in the corrugated container industry. Financial need is not considered in the selection process.

Financial data: The stipend is either $2,000 or $1,000.

Duration: 1 year.

Additional information: The Bobst Group sponsors 1 of these scholarships, MHI Corrugating Machinery Company sponsors 1, and the Corrugated Containers Division of the Technical Association of the Pulp and Paper Industry sponsors 2.

Number awarded: 4 each year: 2 at $2,000 and 2 at $1,000.

Deadline: January of each year.

1915
CORTLAND COUNTY TRAPPERS ASSOCIATION SCHOLARSHIPS

Cortland County Trappers Association
c/o Ron Shippey
1817 Slocum Road
Marathon, NY 13803
E-mail: klager@odyssey.net

Summary: To provide financial assistance to high school seniors in New York who are interested in majoring in fields related to environmental conservation in college.

Eligibility: This program is open to seniors graduating from high schools in New York state who have a grade point average of "C+" or higher. Applicants must be interested in studying wildlife biology, environmental conservation, or a similar field in college. They must submit 2 letters of recommendation and a letter of intent that describes their goals in college and the future as related to their proposed major.

Financial data: The amount of the award depends on the availability of funds and the number of recipients. Funds must be used to help pay the costs of tuition and room and board during the second semester of the first year of college.

Duration: 1 semester.

Number awarded: 1 or more each year.

Deadline: May of each year.

1916
CSHEMA SCHOLARSHIP AWARD PROGRAM

National Safety Council
Attn: Campus Safety Health & Environmental Management Association
1121 Spring Lake Drive
Itasca, IL 60143-3201
Phone: (630) 775-2360   Fax: (630) 775-2185
E-mail: merrittj@nsc.org   Web Site: www.cshema.org

Summary: To provide financial assistance to undergraduate students working on a degree in a field related to the concerns of the Campus Safety Health & Environmental Management Association (CSHEMA).

Eligibility: This program is open to full-time undergraduate students who are majoring in any field but are interested in the study of safety. Applicants must write an essay on a safety-related topic that changes annually; recently, the topic was "Describe a health, safety or an environmental issue relevant to your university or college. Examine and discuss what actions and/or programs are needed to solve this issue. Financial need is not considered. Undergraduates can apply up to and including their third year of study.

Financial data: The stipend is $2,000.

Duration: 1 year.

Additional information: This program was established in 1977.

Number awarded: 1 each year.

Deadline: March of each year.

1917
D. ANITA SMALL SCIENCE & BUSINESS SCHOLARSHIP

Maryland Federation of Business and Professional Women's Clubs, Inc.
c/o Donna Smith
11204 Eastwood Drive
Hagerstown, MD 21742
Phone: (410) 569-2100   (877) INFO BPW

E-mail: marynov@erols.com
Web Site: www.bpwmaryland.org/HTML/scholarships.html
Summary: To provide financial assistance to women in Maryland who are interested in working on an undergraduate or graduate degree in a science or business-related field.
Eligibility: This program is open to women in Maryland who are at least 21 years of age and are interested in pursuing undergraduate or graduate studies in mathematics, engineering, physical sciences, computer sciences, medical sciences, or a business-related field.
Financial data: The stipend is $1,500.
Duration: 1 year.
Number awarded: 1 or more each year.

1918
DAEDALIAN FOUNDATION DESCENDANTS' SCHOLARSHIP PROGRAM

Daedalian Foundation
Attn: Scholarship Committee
55 Main Circle (Building 676)
P.O. Box 249
Randolph AFB, TX 78148-0249
Phone: (210) 945-2113   Fax: (210) 945-2112
E-mail: daedalus@daedalians.org
Web Site: www.daedalians.org
Summary: To provide financial assistance to descendants of members of the Order of Daedalians who wish to study aerospace engineering or flight.
Eligibility: This program is open to descendants of members of the order who wish to attend flight school or study aerospace engineering in college. Candidates must be nominated by a local chapter (Flight) of Daedalian. They must be attending or planning to attend an accredited college or university and enroll in an academic program that leads to a baccalaureate or higher degree. Selection is based on academic achievement and recognition, extracurricular activities, honors, and employment experience. Financial need may also be considered, but only if all other factors are equal.
Financial data: The stipend is $2,000.
Additional information: The Order of Daedalians was founded in 1934 as an organization of the nearly 14,000 aviators who served as military pilots during World War I. In the 1950s, the organization expanded eligibility to include Named Memberships for active or retired commissioned officers in the military services and their reserve components who are rated as military pilots of heavier-than-air powered aircraft.
Number awarded: Up to 3 each year.
Deadline: June of each year.

1919
DAEDALIAN MATCHING SCHOLARSHIP PROGRAM

Daedalian Foundation
Attn: Scholarship Committee
55 Main Circle (Building 676)
P.O. Box 249
Randolph AFB, TX 78148-0249
Phone: (210) 945-2113   Fax: (210) 945-2112
E-mail: daedalus@daedalians.org
Web Site: www.daedalians.org
Summary: To provide cash awards to deserving students who wish to become military pilots.
Eligibility: Eligible are students who are attending an accredited 4-year college or university and who have demonstrated the desire and potential to become a commissioned military pilot, flight crew member, astronaut, or career officer in disciplines supporting aeronautics or astronautics. Usually, students in ROTC units of all services apply to local chapters (Flights) of Daedalian; if the Flight awards a scholarship, the application is forwarded to the Daedalian Foundation for 1 of these matching scholarships. Selection is based on intention to pursue a career as a military pilot, demonstrated moral character and patriotism, scholastic and military standing and aptitude, and physical condition and aptitude for flight and space. Additional eligibility criteria may be set by a Flight Scholarship Selection Board.
Financial data: The amount awarded varies but is intended to serve as matching funds for the Flight scholarship. Generally, the maximum awarded is $2,000.
Number awarded: Up to 99 each year.
Deadline: Applications may be submitted at any time.

1920
DAIMLERCHRYSLER CORPORATION FUND SCHOLARSHIP

Society of Women Engineers
230 East Ohio Street, Suite 400
Chicago, IL 60611-3265
Phone: (312) 596-5223   Fax: (312) 644-8557
E-mail: hq@swe.org
Web Site: www.swe.org
Summary: To provide financial assistance to undergraduate women majoring in designated engineering specialties.
Eligibility: This program is open to sophomore women pursuing a degree in electrical or mechanical engineering at an ABET-accredited or SWE-approved college or university who have earned at least a 3.0 grade point average. Selection is based on merit.
Financial data: The stipend is $2,000.
Duration: 1 year; may be renewed for up to 2 additional years.
Additional information: This program was established in 1997.
Number awarded: 1 each year.
Deadline: January of each year.

1921
DAVID ALAN QUICK SCHOLARSHIP

EAA Aviation Foundation Inc.
Attn: Scholarship Office
EAA Aviation Center
3000 Poberezny Road
P.O. Box 3065
Oshkosh, WI 54903-3065
Phone: (920) 426-6884   (888) 322-3229
Fax: (920) 426-6865   E-mail: scholarships@eaa.org
Web Site: www.eaa.org/education/scholarships/index.html
Summary: To provide financial assistance to college juniors and seniors who are majoring in aerospace or aeronautical engineering.
Eligibility: This program is open to juniors and seniors enrolled at an accredited college or university and working on a degree in aerospace or aeronautical engineering. Applicants must submit a short essay on their life goals and how receiving this scholarship would help them realize those goals. Selection is based on academic record, participation in school and community activities, and career potential.
Financial data: The stipend is $1,000.
Duration: 1 year; may be renewed.
Additional information: There is a $5 application fee.
Number awarded: 1 each year.
Deadline: April of each year.

1922
DAVID ARVER MEMORIAL SCHOLARSHIP

Aircraft Electronics Association
Attn: Educational Foundation
4217 South Hocker Drive
Independence, MO 64055-4723
Phone: (816) 373-6565   Fax: (816) 478-3100
E-mail: info@aea.net   Web Site: www.aea.net
Summary: To provide financial assistance to students in selected states who are interested in studying avionics or aircraft repair in college.
Eligibility: This program is open to high school seniors and college students who plan to attend an accredited vocational or technical school in the Aircraft Electronics Association Region III; this includes the states of Illinois, Indiana, Iowa, Kansas, Michigan, Minnesota, Missouri, Nebraska, North Dakota, South Dakota, and Wisconsin. Applicants must plan to enroll in an avionics or aircraft repair academic program.
Financial data: The stipend is $1,000.
Duration: 1 year.
Number awarded: 1 each year.
Deadline: February of each year.

Scholarship Listings

1923
DAVID HOODS MEMORIAL SCHOLARSHIP

Electronic Document Systems Foundation
Attn: EDSF Scholarship Awards
24238 Hawthorne Boulevard
Torrance, CA 90505-6505
Phone: (310) 541-1481   Fax: (310) 541-4803
Web Site: www.edsf.org
Summary: To provide financial assistance to college juniors and seniors interested in working with electronic documents as a career.
Eligibility: This program is open to full-time junior and senior college students who demonstrate a strong interest in working with electronic documents as a career. Applicants may be majoring in graphic communications, computer science, telecommunications, or related fields. They must submit a statement of their career goals in the field of document/communication systems, an essay on a topic related to their view of the future of the document management and production industry, a list of current professional and college extracurricular activities and achievements, college transcripts (grade point average of 3.0 or higher), and 2 letters of recommendation. Financial need is not considered.
Financial data: The stipend is $2,000.
Duration: 1 year.
Number awarded: 1 each year.
Deadline: June of each year.

1924
DAVID SARNOFF RESEARCH CENTER SCHOLARSHIP

Society of Women Engineers
230 East Ohio Street, Suite 400
Chicago, IL 60611-3265
Phone: (312) 596-5223   Fax: (312) 644-8557
E-mail: hq@swe.org
Web Site: www.swe.org
Summary: To provide financial assistance to undergraduate women majoring in engineering or computer science.
Eligibility: This program is open to women who are entering their junior year and majoring in engineering or computer science. Applicants must be attending an accredited university and have at least a 3.5 grade point average. Selection is based on merit.
Financial data: The stipend is $1,500.
Duration: 1 year.
Additional information: This program was established in 1988.
Number awarded: 1 each year.
Deadline: January of each year.

1925
DELAWARE SOLID WASTE AUTHORITY SCHOLARSHIP

Delaware Solid Waste Authority
1128 South Bradford Street
P.O. Box 455
Dover, DE 19903-0455
Phone: (302) 739-5361   Fax: (302) 739-4287
Summary: To provide financial assistance to high school seniors and college students in Delaware who are interested in majoring in engineering or environmental sciences at a college in the state.
Eligibility: This program is open to high school seniors and full-time college students in their freshman or sophomore years who are Delaware residents and majoring in either engineering or environmental sciences at a Delaware college. Applicants must file the Free Application for Federal Students Aid (FAFSA). They must write a 500-word essay on "What would you do to protect the environment?" Selection is based on financial need, academic performance, community or school involvement, and leadership ability.
Financial data: The stipend is $2,000.
Duration: 1 year; automatically renewed for 3 additional years if a grade point average of 3.0 or higher is maintained.
Deadline: March of each year.

1926
DELL COMPUTER CORPORATION SCHOLARSHIPS

Society of Women Engineers
230 East Ohio Street, Suite 400
Chicago, IL 60611-3265
Phone: (312) 596-5223   Fax: (312) 644-8557
E-mail: hq@swe.org
Web Site: www.swe.org
Summary: To provide financial assistance to undergraduate women majoring in computer science or designated engineering specialties.
Eligibility: This program is open to women entering their junior or senior year at an ABET-accredited or SWE-approved college or university. Applicants must be majoring in computer science or computer, electrical, or mechanical engineering and have a grade point average of 3.0 or higher. Selection is based on merit and financial need.
Financial data: The stipend is $2,000.
Duration: 1 year.
Additional information: This program was established in 1999.
Number awarded: 17 each year.
Deadline: January of each year.

1927
DELTA AIR LINES SCHOLARSHIP

National Society of Black Engineers
Attn: Programs Manager
1454 Duke Street
Alexandria, VA 22314
Phone: (703) 549-2207, ext. 204   Fax: (703) 683-5312
E-mail: scholarships@nsbe.org   Web Site: www.nsbe.org
Summary: To provide financial assistance to members of the National Society of Black Engineers (NSBE) who are majoring in designated science and engineering fields.
Eligibility: This program is open to members of the society who are college juniors or seniors majoring in the following fields of study: applied or engineering physics, chemical engineering, chemistry, civil engineering, computer engineering, computer science, electrical engineering, materials science or engineering, mathematics, mechanical engineering, or physics. Applicants must have a grade point average of 3.0 or higher and a demonstrated interest in employment with Delta Air Lines. They must submit a 250-word essay describing how they will use their education to make a positive impact on the African American community and how the scholarship will advance their career goals and benefit Delta Air Lines.
Financial data: The stipend is $3,000.
Duration: 1 year.
Number awarded: 1 each year.
Deadline: November of each year.

1928
DELTA AIRLINES ENGINEERING SCHOLARSHIPS

Women in Aviation, International
3647 S.R. 503 South
West Alexandria, OH 45381
Phone: (937) 839-4647   Fax: (937) 839-4645
E-mail: wai@infinet.com   Web Site: www.wiai.org
Summary: To provide financial assistance to members of Women in Aviation, International who are studying engineering in college.
Eligibility: This program is open to women who are members of the sponsoring organization and full-time juniors or seniors with at least 2 semesters of study remaining. Applicants must be pursuing a baccalaureate degree in aerospace, aeronautical, electrical, or mechanical engineering with a grade point average of 3.0 or higher. U.S. citizenship is required. As part of the selection process, applicants must submit a design essay of 500 to 1,000 words. In addition to the essay, selection is based on achievements, attitude toward self and others, commitment to success, dedication to career, financial need, motivation, reliability, responsibility, and teamwork.
Financial data: The stipend is $5,000.
Duration: 1 year.
Additional information: Women in Aviation, International is a nonprofit professional organization dedicated to encouraging women to consider an aviation career, providing educational outreach activities, and networking resources to women active in the industry. This program is sponsored by Delta Air Lines. In addition to the scholarship, recipients are reimbursed for up to $1,000 in

travel and accommodations expenses to attend the organization's annual conference.

Number awarded: 3 each year.

Deadline: December of each year.

1929
DELTA FAUCET COMPANY SCHOLARSHIPS

Plumbing-Heating-Cooling Contractors-National Association
Attn: PHCC Educational Foundation
180 South Washington Street
P.O. Box 6808
Falls Church, VA 22040
Phone: (703) 237-8100   (800) 533-7694
Fax: (703) 237-7442   E-mail: naphcc@naphcc.org
Web Site: www.phccweb.org/foundation/delta.cfm

Summary: To provide financial assistance to undergraduate students interested in the plumbing, heating, and cooling industry.

Eligibility: This program is open to high school seniors and college freshmen who are planning to major in a field related to plumbing, heating, and cooling at a 4-year college or university or at a 2-year technical college, community college, or trade school. Applicants must be planning to pursue a career in the plumbing, heating, and cooling industry. They must be sponsored by a member with 2 years' good standing in the Plumbing-Heating-Cooling Contractors-National Association (PHCC). Selection is based on high school or college transcripts, extracurricular activities, experience in the industry, career goals, and reasons for applying.

Financial data: The stipend is $2,500 per year.

Duration: 1 year; nonrenewable.

Additional information: This program is sponsored by the Delta Faucet Company.

Number awarded: 6 each year: 4 to students at 4-year institutions and 2 to students at 2-year institutions.

Deadline: May of each year.

1930
DENISE SCHOLARSHIP FUND

New York State Grange
100 Grange Place
Cortland, NY 13045
Phone: (607) 756-7553   Fax: (607) 756-7757
E-mail: nysgrange@clarityconnect.com

Summary: To provide financial assistance to undergraduate students in New York interested in majoring in agriculture.

Eligibility: Scholarship assistance is available to undergraduate students at a 2-year or 4-year college or university anywhere in the country. Applicants must be residents of New York and interested in majoring in the field of agriculture. Financial need must be demonstrated.

Financial data: The amount awarded varies, depending upon the needs of the recipient.

Duration: 1 year.

Additional information: This program was established in 1983.

Number awarded: 1 or more each year.

Deadline: April of each year.

1931
DENVER GEOPHYSICAL SOCIETY SCHOLARSHIP

Society of Exploration Geophysicists
Attn: SEG Foundation
P.O. Box 702740
Tulsa, OK 74170-2740
Phone: (918) 497-5530   Fax: (918) 497-5557
E-mail: slobianco@seg.org
Web Site: www.seg.org

Summary: To provide financial assistance to undergraduate and graduate students who are interested in studying geophysics in Colorado.

Eligibility: Applicants must be 1) high school students planning to enter college in the fall and to major in geophysics; 2) undergraduate college students majoring in geophysics whose grades are above average; or 3) graduate students whose studies are directed toward a career in exploration geophysics in operations, teaching, or research. All applicants must have an interest in and aptitude for physics, mathematics, and geology. Financial need is considered, but the competence of the student as indicated by the application is given first

consideration. Applicants must be studying or planning to study at a college or university in Colorado.

Financial data: The stipend ranges from $1,000 to $3,000 per year.

Duration: 1 academic year; may be renewable, based on scholastic standing, availability of funds, and continuance of a course of study leading to a career in exploration geophysics.

Number awarded: 1 each year.

Deadline: February of each year.

1932
DERIVATIVE DUO SCHOLARSHIP

Summary: To provide financial assistance to Washington residents engaged in undergraduate study of performing arts or the health sciences.
See Listing #1345.

1933
DESK AND DERRICK EDUCATIONAL TRUST SCHOLARSHIP

Desk and Derrick Educational Trust
5153 East 51st Street, Suite 107
Tulsa, OK 74135
Phone: (918) 622-1675   Fax: (918) 622-1675

Summary: To provide financial assistance to currently-enrolled college students who are planning a career in the petroleum or an allied industry.

Eligibility: To be eligible, students must meet the following requirements: have completed at least 2 years of college or are currently enrolled in the second year of undergraduate study; have earned at least a 3.0 grade point average; are able to demonstrate a need for financial assistance; are a citizen of Canada or the United States; and are planning a career in the petroleum or an allied industry. Students pursuing degrees in research and development of alternate energy sources (coal, solar, wind, hydroelectric, nuclear, etc.) are also eligible. Some scholarships are set aside specifically for women.

Financial data: The amount awarded is $1,500 for full-time students or $600 for part-time students.

Duration: 1 year.

Additional information: Recipients are asked to return to the trust one half of the grant received, if possible, within 10 years of graduation.

Number awarded: Several each year; of these, 5 are set aside specifically for women.

Deadline: March of each year.

1934
THE DEVELOPMENT FUND FOR BLACK STUDENTS IN SCIENCE AND TECHNOLOGY SCHOLARSHIPS

The Development Fund for Black Students in Science and Technology
2705 Bladensburg Road, N.E.
Washington, DC 20018
Phone: (202) 635-3604   E-mail: hattie.carwell@oak.doe.gov
Web Site: ourworld.compuserve.com/homepages/dlhinson/dfb_sch.htm

Summary: To provide scholarships to African American students who enroll in scientific or technical fields of study at Historically Black Colleges and Universities (HBCUs).

Eligibility: Deans and faculty members of the various engineering and science departments at predominantly Black colleges and universities are invited to identify students to be considered for these scholarships. To be eligible, nominated students must intend to enroll at a predominantly Black college or university or already be enrolled at such a college or university. They must intend to major in a technical field and be U.S. citizens or permanent residents who intend to remain in the United States after graduation. Selection is based on academic achievement (grades and SAT scores, especially in science/math), a personal essay describing career goals and relevant extracurricular activities, recommendations, and financial need.

Financial data: The amount of the scholarship is based on merit and financial need. Awards up to $2,000 per year are available.

Duration: 1 year; may be renewed for up to 4 years, as long as the recipient remains in good academic standing and enrolled full time in a science or engineering curriculum.

Additional information: Prior to 1995, these scholarships were awarded solely or primarily through the National Merit Scholarship Corporation's National Achievement Scholarship Program. Scholarship applications are available only through the financial aid offices of prequalified schools. Currently, these are: Bennett College, Elizabeth City State University, Fisk University, Florida A&M University, Fort Valley State College, Hampton University, Howard University, Morehouse University, Morgan State University, North Carolina A&T State University, Prairie View A&M

University, Southern University and A&M College, Tennessee State University, Tuskegee University, Wilberforce University, and Xavier University of Louisiana.
Number awarded: Several each year.
Deadline: June of each year.

1935
D.J. MCDONALD MEMORIAL SCHOLARSHIPS

The National Board of Boiler and Pressure Vessel Inspectors
Attn: Director of Communications
1055 Crupper Avenue
Columbus, OH 43229-1183
Phone: (614) 888-8320   Fax: (614) 888-0750
E-mail: pbrennan@nationalboard.org
Web Site: www.nationalboard.org/Scholarships/scholar.html
Summary: To provide financial assistance to upper-division college students majoring in selected engineering fields.
Eligibility: To qualify, students must be nominated by a faculty member. These nominees must be either college juniors or seniors and majoring in mechanical, metallurgical, nuclear, or welding engineering. Nominations must be accompanied by college transcripts and a statement detailing course of study, accomplishments, professional affiliations and goals, and financial need. There is no formal application form.
Financial data: The stipend is $5,000.
Duration: 1 year.
Number awarded: 2 each year.
Deadline: Nominations must be submitted by the end of January.

1936
DON WALLER SCHOLARSHIP

Mississippi Farm Bureau
6310 I-55 North
P.O. Box 1972
Jackson, MS 39215-1972
Phone: (601) 977-4277   (800) 227-8244
E-mail: gshows@msfb.com
Web Site: www.msfb.com/programs/scholarships.html
Summary: To provide financial assistance to members of the Mississippi Farm Bureau who are majoring in agriculture at a college or university in Mississippi.
Eligibility: This program is open to members of the Farm Bureau who have already completed their freshman year in an agriculture major at a university or community college in Mississippi. Selection is based on financial need, academic ability, and leadership qualities. Applications must be submitted through the Young Farmers & Ranchers Scholarship Foundation.
Financial data: The stipend is $1,000 per year.
Duration: 1 year.
Number awarded: 1 each year.

1937
DONALD BURNSIDE MEMORIAL SCHOLARSHIPS

Aircraft Owners and Pilots Association
Attn: AOPA Air Safety Foundation
421 Aviation Way
Frederick, MD 21701-4798
Phone: (301) 695-2000   (800) 638-3101
Web Site: www.aopa.org/asf/scholarship/burnside.html
Summary: To provide funding to students who need financial assistance to continue their studies in the field of aviation.
Eligibility: This program is open to U.S. citizens who are interested in working on a degree in the field of non-engineering aviation, are juniors or seniors in college, have earned at least a 3.25 grade point average, and are able to demonstrate financial need. They must submit a 250-word essay on a topic that changes annually; recently, the topic was "Choose one recent high-profile aircraft accident in which poor pilot judgment caused an unsafe and dangerous situation. What could have been done differently?" Previous recipients are not eligible to reapply.
Financial data: The stipend is $1,000.
Duration: 1 year; recipients may not reapply.
Additional information: This program is jointly sponsored by the Air Safety Foundation of the Aircraft Owners and Pilots Association (AOPA) and the University Aviation Association. Information is also available from David A. NewMyer, Southern Illinois University at Carbondale, College of Applied Sciences

and Arts, Aviation Management and Flight, Carbondale, IL 62901-6623. Requests for applications must be accompanied by a self-addressed stamped envelope.
Number awarded: 1 each year.
Deadline: March of each year.

1938
DONALD F. HASTINGS SCHOLARSHIP

American Welding Society
Attn: AWS Foundation, Inc.
550 N.W. LeJeune Road
Miami, FL 33126
Phone: (305) 443-9353, ext. 461   (800) 443-9353, ext. 461
Fax: (305) 443-7559   E-mail: vpinsky@aws.org
Web Site: www.aws.org/foundation/hastings.html
Summary: To provide financial assistance to college students majoring in welding engineering.
Eligibility: This program is open to undergraduate students who are pursuing at least a 4-year bachelor's degree in welding engineering or welding engineering technology (although preference is given to welding engineering students). Applicants must have a minimum overall grade point average of 2.5 and be able to demonstrate financial need. Priority is given to applicants residing or attending school in Ohio or California. U.S. citizenship is required.
Financial data: The stipend is $2,500.
Duration: 1 year; recipients may reapply.
Number awarded: 1 each year.
Deadline: January of each year.

1939
DONALD F. & MILDRED TOPP OTHMER NATIONAL SCHOLARSHIP AWARDS

American Institute of Chemical Engineers
Attn: Awards Administrator
Three Park Avenue
New York, NY 10016-5991
Phone: (212) 591-7478   Fax: (212) 591-8882
E-mail: awards@aiche.org   Web Site: www.aiche.org/awards
Summary: To provide financial assistance to student members of the American Institute of Chemical Engineers (AIChE).
Eligibility: This program is open to AIChE student members who are undergraduates in chemical engineering. Each student chapter advisor may nominate 1 student member. Nominees must have completed approximately half of their degree requirements at the start of the academic year (i.e., junior standing in a 4-year program or equivalent for a 5-year co-op program). Selection is based on academic record, the support of the nominee by the student chapter advisor, involvement in student chapter and other professional activities, and the nominee's career objectives and plans as outlined in a letter.
Financial data: The stipend is $1,000.
Duration: 1 year.
Additional information: This program is sponsored by the Donald F. & Mildred Topp Othmer Foundation. Information is also available from Walter P. Walawender, Kansas State University, Chemical Engineering Department, Durland Hall, Manhattan, KS 66506-5102, (785) 532-4318, Fax; (785) 532-7372, E-mail: walawen@earth.cheme.ksu.edu.
Number awarded: 15 each year.
Deadline: April of each year.

1940
DOROTHY DANN BULLOCK MUSIC THERAPY AWARD

Summary: To recognize and reward outstanding members of the National Federation of Music Clubs (NFMC) who are majoring in music therapy.
See Listing #1353.

1941
DOROTHY LEMKE HOWARTH SCHOLARSHIPS

Society of Women Engineers
230 East Ohio Street, Suite 400
Chicago, IL 60611-3265
Phone: (312) 596-5223   Fax: (312) 644-8557
E-mail: hq@swe.org   Web Site: www.swe.org

Summary: To provide financial assistance to undergraduate women majoring in engineering.

Eligibility: This program is open to women who are entering their sophomore year and majoring in engineering at an ABET-accredited school, college, or university. Applicants must be U.S. citizens and have a grade point average of at least 3.0. Selection is based on merit.

Financial data: The stipend is $2,000.

Duration: 1 year.

Additional information: This program was established in 1991.

Number awarded: 5 each year.

Deadline: January of each year.

1942
DOROTHY M. & EARL S. HOFFMAN SCHOLARSHIPS

Society of Women Engineers
230 East Ohio Street, Suite 400
Chicago, IL 60611-3265
Phone: (312) 596-5223   Fax: (312) 644-8557
E-mail: hq@swe.org
Web Site: www.swe.org

Summary: To provide financial assistance to women interested in studying engineering in college.

Eligibility: Incoming female freshmen who are interested in majoring in engineering at a 4-year school, college, or university are eligible to apply. The schools must be ABET accredited or SWE approved. Preference is given to students at Bucknell University and Rensselaer Polytechnic Institute. Selection is based on merit.

Financial data: The stipend is $3,000 per year.

Duration: 1 year; may be renewed for up to 3 additional years.

Additional information: This program was established in 1999.

Number awarded: 3 each year.

Deadline: May of each year.

1943
DOWNEAST MAINE ISA SCHOLARSHIPS

Instrumentation, Systems and Automation Society-Downeast Maine Section
c/o Herb Short
Enterprise Engineering, Inc.
172 Main Street
Yarmouth, ME 04096
Phone: (207) 846-8453

Summary: To provide financial assistance to students from Maine who are interested in studying engineering in college in that state or in New Hampshire.

Eligibility: This program is open to 1) graduating seniors at high schools in Maine planning to pursue a career in engineering, and 2) college students who graduated from a high school in Maine and are currently enrolled in an engineering-related 2- or 4-year program at a college or university in Maine or New Hampshire. Selection is based on financial need, academic achievement, letters of recommendation, a resume, and desire to pursue a career in engineering.

Financial data: Stipends are $500 for high school seniors or $1,000 for college undergraduates.

Duration: 1 year; nonrenewable.

Number awarded: 12 each year: 8 to high school seniors and 4 to current college students.

Deadline: March of each year.

1944
DR. ALFRED C. FONES SCHOLARSHIP

American Dental Hygienists' Association
Attn: Institute for Oral Health
444 North Michigan Avenue, Suite 3400
Chicago, IL 60611
Phone: (312) 440-8944   (800) 735-4916
Fax: (312) 440-8929   E-mail: institute@adha.net
Web Site: www.adha.org

Summary: To provide financial assistance to dental hygiene students who are in a bachelor's or graduate degree program and intend to become teachers or educators.

Eligibility: This program is open to dental hygiene students at the baccalaureate, master's, and doctoral level who have completed at least 1 year of study with a grade point average of at least 3.0. Applicants must intend to pursue a career as a dental hygiene teacher or educator. Financial need and full-time enrollment must be demonstrated.

Financial data: The amount of the award depends on the need of the recipient, to a maximum of $1,500.

Duration: 1 year.

Number awarded: 1 each year.

Deadline: May of each year.

1945
DR. H. HAROLD HUME HORTICULTURE SCHOLARSHIP

Florida Federation of Garden Clubs, Inc.
Attn: Scholarship Chair
6065 21st Street S.W.
Vero Beach, FL 32968-9427
Phone: (561) 778-1023
Web Site: www.ffgc.org

Summary: To provide financial aid to Florida college seniors and graduate students majoring in horticulture.

Eligibility: This program is open to Florida residents who are enrolled as full-time seniors or graduate students in a Florida college. They must have at least a 3.0 grade point average, be in financial need, and be majoring in horticulture. Selection is based on academic record, commitment to career, character, and financial need.

Financial data: Up to $3,000. The funds are sent directly to the recipient's school and distributed semiannually.

Duration: 1 year.

Additional information: If the recipient's grade point average drops below 3.0, the second installment of the scholarship is not provided.

Number awarded: 1 or more each year.

Deadline: April of each year.

1946
DR. HANS AND CLARA ZIMMERMAN FOUNDATION HEALTH SCHOLARSHIPS

Hawai'i Community Foundation
900 Fort Street Mall, Suite 1300
Honolulu, HI 96813
Phone: (808) 566-5570   (888) 731-3863
Fax: (808) 521-6286   E-mail: scholarships@hcf-hawaii.org
Web Site: www.hcf-hawaii.org

Summary: To provide financial assistance to Hawaii residents who are interested in preparing for a career in the health field.

Eligibility: This program is open to Hawaii residents who are interested in majoring in a health-related field as full-time students at a college or university in the United States (as juniors, seniors or graduate students). They must be able to demonstrate academic achievement (grade point average of 3.0 or higher), good moral character, and financial need. In addition to filling out the standard application form, they must write a short statement indicating their reasons for attending college, their planned course of study, and their career goals.

Financial data: The amounts of the awards depend on the availability of funds and the need of the recipients; recently, scholarships averaged $2,700.

Duration: 1 year.

Additional information: This is 1 of the largest scholarship funds in Hawaii.

Number awarded: Varies each year; recently, 241 of these scholarships were awarded.

Deadline: February of each year.

1947
DR. HAROLD HILLENBRAND SCHOLARSHIP

American Dental Hygienists' Association
Attn: Institute for Oral Health
444 North Michigan Avenue, Suite 3400
Chicago, IL 60611
Phone: (312) 440-8944   (800) 735-4916
Fax: (312) 440-8929   E-mail: institute@adha.net
Web Site: www.adha.org

Summary: To provide assistance to students enrolled in a baccalaureate dental hygiene program who can demonstrate exceptional academic and clinical performance.

Eligibility: Applicants must have completed at least 1 year in a baccalaureate dental hygiene program with at least a 3.5 grade point average. They must be able to demonstrate financial need and full-time enrollment. Selection is based on academic record and clinical performance.

Financial data: The amount of the award depends on the need of the recipient, to a maximum of $1,500.
Duration: 1 year.
Number awarded: 1 each year.
Deadline: May of each year.

1948
DR. HAROLD S. WOOD AWARD FOR EXCELLENCE

General Aviation Manufacturers Association
Attn: Manager, Communications and Aviation Education
1400 K Street, N.W., Suite 801
Washington, DC 20005-2485
Phone: (202) 393-1500   Fax: (202) 842-4063
E-mail: mcurry@generalaviation.org
Web Site: www.generalaviation.org
Summary: To provide financial assistance to students in schools belonging to the National Intercollegiate Flying Association (NIFA).
Eligibility: Nominations are solicited from NIFA-member schools in each of the 11 NIFA regions. There is no limit to the number of applications submitted by each school. Eligible to be nominated by these schools are currently-enrolled students who have at least a 3.0 grade point average. Each NIFA region chooses 1 winning finalist from the entries. A national winner is then chosen from the 11 finalists. Selection, on both levels, is based on academic record (30 percent), aviation-related extracurricular activities (50 percent), and service and contributions to school and community (20 percent).
Financial data: The national winner is presented with an engraved propeller trophy and a $1,000 cash award.
Duration: 1 year; nonrenewable.
Number awarded: 11 district winners and 1 national winner.
Deadline: Nominations must be submitted in February of each year.

1949
DR. HILDA RICHARDS SCHOLARSHIP

National Black Nurses Association, Inc.
Attn: Scholarship Committee
8630 Fenton Street, Suite 330
Silver Spring, MD 20910
Phone: (301) 589-3200   Fax: (301) 589-3223
Summary: To provide financial assistance for nursing education to members of the National Black Nurses Association (NBNA).
Eligibility: This program is open to members of the association who hold a diploma or associate degree and are pursuing a B.S.N. degree with at least 1 full year of school remaining. Selection is based on participation in student nurse activities, involvement in the African American community, and involvement in community health services activities.
Financial data: The award ranges from $500 to $2,000 per year.
Duration: 1 year; may be renewed.
Additional information: Requests for applications must be accompanied by a self-addressed stamped envelope.
Number awarded: 1 or more each year.
Deadline: April of each year.

1950
DR. JUAN D. VILLARREAL—HDA FOUNDATION SCHOLARSHIPS

Hispanic Dental Association
Attn: HDA Foundation
188 West Randolph Street, Suite 1811
Chicago, IL 60601-3001
Phone: (312) 577-4013   (800) 852-7921
Fax: (312) 577-0052   E-mail: hdassoc@aol.com
Web Site: www.hdassoc.org/scholarship.html
Summary: To provide financial assistance to Hispanic dental hygiene and dental students at institutions in Texas.
Eligibility: This program is open to Hispanic dental hygiene and dental students. Applicants must have been accepted or be currently enrolled at an accredited dental school in Texas.
Financial data: Stipends are $1,000 or $500.
Duration: 1 year.
Number awarded: 1 or more each year.

1951
DR. LAURANNE SAMS SCHOLARSHIP

National Black Nurses Association, Inc.
Attn: Scholarship Committee
8630 Fenton Street, Suite 330
Silver Spring, MD 20910
Phone: (301) 589-3200   Fax: (301) 589-3223
E-mail: nbna@erols.com
Web Site: www.nbna.org/memb_scholar.html
Summary: To provide financial assistance for undergraduate nursing education to members of the National Black Nurses Association.
Eligibility: This program is open to members of the association who are currently enrolled in a B.S.N., A.D., diploma, or L.P.N./L.V.N. program with at least 1 full year of school remaining. Selection is based on participation in student nurse activities, involvement in the African American community, and involvement in community health services-related activities.
Financial data: The stipend ranges from $500 to $2,000 per year.
Duration: 1 year; may be renewed.
Additional information: Requests for applications must be accompanied by a self-addressed stamped envelope.
Number awarded: 1 or more each year.
Deadline: April of each year.

1952
DR. ROBERT H. GODDARD SCHOLARSHIP

National Space Club
2000 L Street, N.W., Suite 710
Washington, DC 20036-4907
Phone: (202) 973-8661
Summary: To provide financial assistance to undergraduate and graduate students interested in preparing for a career in space research or exploration.
Eligibility: Applicants must be U.S. citizens, at least a junior in college, and intending to pursue undergraduate or graduate studies in science or engineering. Selection is based on: official college transcript, letters of recommendation from faculty, accomplishments demonstrating creativity and leadership, plans to pursue a career in aerospace sciences or technology, and past research and participation in space-related science and engineering; financial need is considered but is not a primary factor.
Financial data: The stipend is $10,000. The winner's way is paid to the Goddard Memorial Dinner (usually held in March), where the winner is introduced to the nation's leaders in science, government, and industry.
Duration: 1 year.
Additional information: Upon completion of the scholarship, the winner may be asked to prepare and deliver a brief report to the National Space Club.
Number awarded: 1 each year.
Deadline: January of each year.

1953
DR. S. BRADLEY BURSON MEMORIAL SCHOLARSHIP

American Council of the Blind
Attn: Coordinator, Scholarship Program
1155 15th Street, N.W., Suite 1004
Washington, DC 20005
Phone: (202) 467-5081   (800) 424-8666
Fax: (202) 467-5085   E-mail: info@acb.org
Web Site: www.acb.org
Summary: To provide financial assistance to blind students who are undergraduate or graduate students studying science at an accredited college or university.
Eligibility: This program is open to legally blind undergraduate or graduate students majoring in the "hard" sciences (i.e., biology, chemistry, physics, and engineering, but not computer science) in college. They must be U.S. citizens. In addition to letters of recommendation and copies of academic transcripts, applications must include an autobiographical sketch. Selection is based on demonstrated academic record, involvement in extracurricular and civic activities, and academic objectives. The severity of the applicant's visual impairment and his/her study methods are also taken into account.
Financial data: The stipend is $1,000. In addition, the winner receives a $1,000 cash scholarship from the Kurzweil Foundation and, if appropriate, a Kurzweil 1000 Reading System.
Duration: 1 year.

Additional information: Scholarship winners are expected to be present at the council's annual conference; the council will cover all reasonable expenses connected with convention attendance.

Number awarded: 1 each year.

Deadline: February of each year.

1954
DR. TAYLOR ALEXANDER ECOLOGY SCHOLARSHIP

Florida Federation of Garden Clubs, Inc.
Attn: Scholarship Chair
6065 21st Street S.W.
Vero Beach, FL 32968-9427
Phone: (561) 778-1023
Web Site: www.ffgc.org

Summary: To provide financial aid to Florida undergraduates and graduate students majoring in ecology.

Eligibility: This program is open to Florida residents who are enrolled as full-time juniors, seniors, or graduate students in a Florida college. They must have at least a 3.0 grade point average, be in financial need, and be majoring in ecology. Selection is based on academic record, commitment to career, character, and financial need.

Financial data: The stipend is $1,500. The funds are sent directly to the recipient's school and distributed semiannually.

Duration: 1 year.

Additional information: If the recipient's grade point average drops below 3.0, the second installment of the scholarship is not provided.

Number awarded: 1 each year.

Deadline: April of each year.

1955
DR. WILLIAM S. BOYD SCHOLARSHIP

Chiropractic Association of Louisiana
c/o Scholarship Committee
3070 Teddy Drive, Suite A
Baton Rouge, LA 70809
Phone: (225) 924-6978   Fax: (225) 925-3139
E-mail: lachiro@premier.net

Summary: To provide financial assistance to students enrolled in chiropractic colleges in Louisiana.

Eligibility: Eligible to apply for this scholarship are Louisiana residents who are currently enrolled (as a junior or senior) in a CCE-accredited chiropractic college in Louisiana. Applicants must have earned at least a 2.75 grade point average, be recommended by an active member of the Chiropractic Association of Louisiana, and intend to practice in Louisiana upon graduation. Also required are 3 letters of recommendation. Financial need is not considered in the selection process.

Financial data: The amount awarded varies each year. Funds are sent directly to the recipient.

Duration: 1 year.

Additional information: Winners are invited to attend the association's annual convention; lodging and registration are paid by the association.

Number awarded: 1 or more each year.

1956
DUANE HANSON SCHOLARSHIP

American Society of Heating, Refrigerating and Air-Conditioning Engineers, Inc.
Attn: Scholarship Administrator
1791 Tullie Circle, N.E.
Atlanta, GA 30329-2305
Phone: (404) 636-8400   Fax: (404) 321-5478
E-mail: benedict@ashrae.org
Web Site: www.ashrae.org

Summary: To provide financial assistance to engineering and engineering technology students interested in heating, ventilating, air conditioning, and refrigeration (HVAC&R).

Eligibility: This program is open to undergraduate engineering and engineering technology students enrolled in a school recognized as accredited by the American Society of Heating, Refrigerating and Air-Conditioning Engineers (ASHRAE). Applicants must be pursuing a course of study that traditionally has been preparatory for the profession of HVAC&R. They must have a grade point average of at least 3.0 and must be full-time students with at least 1 full year of undergraduate

study remaining. Selection is based on potential service to the HVAC&R profession, financial need, leadership ability, recommendations from instructors, and character.

Financial data: The stipend is $3,000 per year.

Duration: 1 year.

Number awarded: 1 each year.

Deadline: November of each year.

1957
DUPONT CHALLENGE

General Learning Communications
Attn: Science Essay Awards Program
900 Skokie Boulevard, Suite 200
Northbrook, IL 60062-4028
Phone: (847) 205-3000   Fax: (847) 564-8197
Web Site: www.glcomm.com/dupont

Summary: To recognize and reward outstanding essays written by high school students on scientific subjects.

Eligibility: Students currently enrolled in grades 7 through 12 at a public or nonpublic school in the United States and its territories, a U.S.-sponsored school abroad, or any school in Canada may submit entries. Essays should be between 700 and 1,000 words and deal with any field of science. Students compete in 2 divisions: senior, for grades 10 through 12; junior, for grades 7 through 9.

Financial data: In each division, the first-place winner receives $1,500, the second-place winner receives $750, the third-place winner receives $500, and each honorable mention awardee receives $50.

Additional information: This contest is sponsored by DuPont in cooperation with General Learning Communications and the National Science Teachers Association.

Number awarded: In each division, there are 3 winners and 48 honorable mentions.

Deadline: January of each year.

1958
DUPONT COMPANY SCHOLARSHIPS

Society of Women Engineers
230 East Ohio Street, Suite 400
Chicago, IL 60611-3265
Phone: (312) 596-5223   Fax: (312) 644-8557
E-mail: hq@swe.org
Web Site: www.swe.org

Summary: To provide financial assistance to women interested in studying designated engineering specialties at schools in the eastern United States.

Eligibility: This program is open to women who are high school seniors or current college students interested in majoring in chemical or mechanical engineering at a 4-year institution in the eastern United States. Applicants already in college must have a grade point average of 3.0 or higher. The schools must be ABET accredited or SWE approved. Selection is based on merit.

Financial data: The stipend is $2,000 per year.

Duration: 1 year.

Additional information: This program was established in 2000.

Number awarded: 4 each year: 2 to women entering college for the first time and 2 to women already enrolled in college.

Deadline: May of each year for incoming freshmen; January of each year for students already in college.

1959
DUTCH AND GINGER ARVER SCHOLARSHIP

Aircraft Electronics Association
Attn: Educational Foundation
4217 South Hocker Drive
Independence, MO 64055-4723
Phone: (816) 373-6565   Fax: (816) 478-3100
E-mail: info@aea.net
Web Site: www.aea.net

Summary: To assist students preparing for a career in avionics or aircraft repair.

Eligibility: This program is open to high school seniors and currently-enrolled college students who are attending (or planning to attend) an accredited postsecondary institution in an avionics or aircraft repair program.

Financial data: The stipend is $1,000.

Duration: 1 year.

Number awarded: 1 each year.

Deadline: February of each year.

1960
DWIGHT D. GARDNER SCHOLARSHIP

Institute of Industrial Engineers
Attn: Chapter Operations Board
25 Technology Park/Atlanta
Norcross, GA 30092-2988
Phone: (770) 449-0460   (800) 494-0460
Fax: (770) 441-3295   Web Site: www.iienet.org
Summary: To provide financial assistance to undergraduate members of the Institute of Industrial Engineers (IIE) who are studying at a school in the United States, Canada, or Mexico.
Eligibility: Eligible are undergraduate students enrolled in any school in the United States and its territories, Canada, or Mexico, provided the school's engineering program is accredited by an agency recognized by the IIE and the student is pursuing a full-time course of study in industrial engineering with a grade point average of 3.4 and at least 5 full quarters or 3 full semesters remaining until graduation. Students may not apply directly for these awards; they must be nominated by the head of their industrial engineering department. Nominees must be IIE members. Selection is based on scholastic ability, character, leadership, potential service to the industrial engineering profession, and need for financial assistance.
Financial data: The stipend is $2,500.
Duration: 1 year.
Additional information: The Dwight D. Gardner Scholarship Fund, named for the IIE's first elected president, was established in 1958.
Number awarded: 4 each year.
Deadline: November of each year.

1961
E. TED SIMS, JR. MEMORIAL SCHOLARSHIP

American Society for Horticultural Science
113 South West Street, Suite 200
Alexandria, VA 22314-2851
Phone: (703) 836-4606   Fax: (703) 836-2024
E-mail: ashs@ashs.org
Web Site: www.ashs.org/membership/awards/infopages/sims.html
Summary: To provide financial assistance to undergraduate students majoring in horticulture.
Eligibility: This program is open to undergraduate students majoring in horticulture at a 4-year institution of higher education who meet these criteria: junior or senior class standing; full-time student; excellent academic performance in the major; participation in extracurricular activities related to horticulture; and commitment to the horticulture profession. Students must be nominated by the chair or head of their department; only 1 applicant may be nominated per department. Nominees must complete an application form, write a 250-word essay giving their reasons for interest in horticulture and for selecting their intended field of work after graduating from college, and provide 3 letters of reference. Financial need is not considered in the selection process.
Financial data: The stipend is $1,000.
Duration: 1 year.
Additional information: This scholarship was established in 1991.
Number awarded: 1 each year.
Deadline: February of each year.

1962
EASTER SEALS IOWA SCHOLARSHIPS

Easter Seals Iowa
P.O. Box 4002
Des Moines, IA 50333
Phone: (515) 289-1933, ext. 209
Summary: To provide scholarships to needy college sophomores, juniors, seniors, and graduate students in Iowa who are preparing for a career in a profession concerned with physical and/or psychological rehabilitation.
Eligibility: To be eligible, applicants must be residents of Iowa, attending an accredited college or university, in the upper 40 percent of their class (or have earned at least a 2.8 grade point average), attending school on a full-time basis, in financial need, and planning a career in the broad field of rehabilitation. In the medical or dentistry fields of study, the student's curriculum must be rehabilitation oriented. A student from the nursing field must be in a 4-year program.
Financial data: The stipend is $1,000.
Duration: 1 year; recipients may reapply.

Additional information: These scholarships are designated as the E.L. Peterson Scholarship, the Lynn Marie Vogel Scholarship, and the Rolfe B. Karlsson Scholarship.
Number awarded: 3 each year.
Deadline: February of each year.

1963
EASTERN IRON AND STEEL SECTION SCHOLARSHIP

Iron and Steel Society
Attn: Eastern Section
c/o Jason Bender, Student Affairs Chair
CitiSteel USA, Inc.
4001 Philadelphia Pike
Claymont, DE 19703
Phone: (302) 791-6634   Fax: (302) 791-6629
E-mail: bend1@citisteel.com
Web Site: www.iss.org/membership/localsections/eastern/studentses.html
Summary: To provide financial assistance for college to the immediate family of members of the Eastern Section of the Iron and Steel Society (ISS) and other students in eastern states.
Eligibility: This program is open to 1) immediate family of section members in good standing; 2) co-op students working within the section's geographical boundaries; and 3) students attending a college or university within those boundaries. Applicants must be entering their junior or senior year and majoring in metallurgical engineering, material science, or another technical field closely related to steelmaking. Selection is based on demonstrated qualities of leadership, need, and interest in the iron and steel industry.
Financial data: The stipend is $1,000.
Duration: 1 year.
Additional information: The boundaries of the Eastern Section include the entire states of Virginia, Delaware, Maryland, New Jersey, Massachusetts, Connecticut, Rhode Island, Vermont, New Hampshire, and Maine; the eastern portion of Pennsylvania (all counties east of and including Potter, Clinton, Centre, Mifflin, Juniata, Perry, Cumberland, and Adams); the eastern portion of New York (all counties east of and including Oswego, Onondaga, Cortland, and Tioga); and the District of Columbia.
Number awarded: 1 each year.
Deadline: September of each year.

1964
EATON MINORITY ENGINEERING SCHOLARS PROGRAM

Eaton Corporation
c/o INROADS
The Lorenzo Carter Building
1360 West Ninth Street, Suite 260
Cleveland, OH 44113   Web Site: www.eaton.com
Summary: To provide financial assistance and work experience to minority college students interested in a career as an engineer.
Eligibility: This program is open to full-time minority engineering students who are U.S. citizens or permanent residents. Applicants must have completed 1 year in an accredited engineering program and have 3 remaining years of course work before completing a bachelor's degree. They must have a GPA of 2.8 or higher and an expressed interest in at least 1 of the following areas of engineering as a major: computer, electrical, electronic, industrial, manufacturing, materials, mechanical, or software. Selection is based on academic performance, the student's school recommendation, and an expressed interest in pursuing challenging and rewarding internship assignments.
Financial data: Stipends up to $2,500 per year are provided. Funds are paid directly to the recipient's university to cover the cost of tuition, books, and fees.
Duration: 3 years.
Additional information: In addition to the scholarships, recipients are offered paid summer internships at company headquarters in Cleveland. The target schools participating in this program are Cornell, Detroit-Mercy, Florida A&M, Georgia Tech, Illinois at Chicago, Illinois at Urbana-Champaign, Lawrence Technological, Marquette, Massachusetts Institute of Technology, Michigan at Ann Arbor, Michigan at Dearborn, Michigan State, Milwaukee School of Engineering, Minnesota, Morehouse College, North Carolina A&T State, North Carolina State, Northwestern, Notre Dame, Ohio State, Purdue, Southern, Tennessee, Western Michigan, and Wisconsin at Madison.
Number awarded: Varies each year.
Deadline: January of each year.

1965
EDGAR J. SAUX SCHOLARSHIP

American College of Medical Practice Executives
Attn: Scholarship Program
104 Inverness Terrace East
Englewood, CO 80112-5306
Phone: (303) 643-9573   Fax: (303) 643-4427
E-mail: acmpe@mgma.com
Web Site: www.mgma.com/acmpe
Summary: To provide financial assistance to individuals currently employed in medical practice management who are interested in pursuing professional development through undergraduate or graduate education.
Eligibility: Eligible to apply are individuals in the early stage of a career in medical practice management who wish to pursue an undergraduate or graduate degree relevant to medical practice management at an accredited university or college. Applications must include a letter describing career goals and objectives related to medical practice management; a resume; 3 reference letters commenting on the individual's performance, character, potential to succeed, and need for scholarship support; and academic transcripts.
Financial data: The stipend is $1,000. Payments for undergraduate and graduate scholarships are sent to the university or college in which the recipient is or will be enrolled.
Duration: 1 year.
Deadline: May of each year.

1966
EDMO DISTRIBUTORS SCHOLARSHIP

Aircraft Electronics Association
Attn: President
4217 South Hocker Drive
Independence, MO 64055-4723
Phone: (816) 373-6565   Fax: (816) 478-3100
E-mail: info@aea.net
Web Site: www.aea.net
Summary: To provide financial assistance to students preparing for a career in aviation.
Eligibility: This program is open to individuals who hold at least a private pilot certificate. They must be interested in attending a technical school or college and majoring in avionics.
Financial data: The stipend is $1,000.
Duration: 1 year.
Number awarded: 1 each year.
Deadline: February of each year.

1967
EDNA AND JAMES CROWL BOTANY SCHOLARSHIP

Florida Federation of Garden Clubs, Inc.
Attn: Scholarship Chair
6065 21st Street S.W.
Vero Beach, FL 32968-9427
Phone: (561) 778-1023
Web Site: www.ffgc.org
Summary: To provide financial aid to Florida undergraduates and graduate students majoring in botany.
Eligibility: This program is open to Florida residents who are enrolled as full-time juniors, seniors, or graduate students in a Florida college. They must have at least a 3.0 grade point average, be in financial need, and be majoring in botany, with an emphasis on research in and study of wildflowers and native plants. Selection is based on academic record, commitment to career, character, and financial need.
Financial data: The stipend is $1,500. The funds are sent directly to the recipient's school and distributed semiannually.
Duration: 1 year.
Additional information: If the recipient's grade point average drops below 3.0, the second installment of the scholarship is not provided.
Number awarded: 1 each year.
Deadline: April of each year.

1968
EDSF BOARD OF DIRECTORS DOCUMENT COMMUNICATION SCHOLARSHIP

Electronic Document Systems Foundation
Attn: EDSF Scholarship Awards
24238 Hawthorne Boulevard
Torrance, CA 90505-6505
Phone: (310) 541-1481   Fax: (310) 541-4803
Web Site: www.edsf.org
Summary: To provide financial assistance to college juniors, seniors, and graduate students interested in working with electronic documents as a career.
Eligibility: This program is open to juniors, seniors, and graduate students who are pursuing a degree in the field of document communication. Applicants must submit a statement of their career goals in the field of document/communication systems, an essay on a topic related to their view of the future of the document management and production industry, a list of current professional and college extracurricular activities and achievements, college transcripts (grade point average of 3.0 or higher), and 2 letters of recommendation. Financial need is not considered.
Financial data: The stipend is $2,000.
Duration: 1 year.
Number awarded: 1 each year.

1969
EDSF BOARD OF DIRECTORS TECHNICAL SCHOOL SCHOLARSHIP

Electronic Document Systems Foundation
Attn: EDSF Scholarship Awards
24238 Hawthorne Boulevard
Torrance, CA 90505-6505
Phone: (310) 541-1481   Fax: (310) 541-4803
Web Site: www.edsf.org
Summary: To provide financial assistance to students in technical or trade schools interested in working with electronic documents as a career.
Eligibility: This program is open to first- and second-year students at technical, trade, and community schools who are pursuing a degree in the field of document communication. Applicants must submit a statement of their career goals in the field of document/communication systems, an essay on a topic related to their view of the future of the document management and production industry, a list of current professional and high school extracurricular activities and achievements, high school transcripts (grade point average of 3.0 or higher), and 2 letters of recommendation. Financial need is not considered.
Financial data: The stipend is $1,000.
Duration: 1 year.
Number awarded: 1 each year.

1970
EDSF WORLDWIDE ELECTRONIC DOCUMENT COMMUNICATION SCHOLARSHIPS

Summary: To provide financial assistance to students interested in preparing for a career in the field of electronic document technology.
See Listing #1359.

1971
EDWARD D. HENDRICKSON/SAE ENGINEERING SCHOLARSHIP

Society of Automotive Engineers
Attn: Educational Relations
400 Commonwealth Drive
Warrendale, PA 15096-0001
Phone: (724) 772-4047   Fax: (724) 776-0890
E-mail: connie@sae.org
Web Site: www.sae.org/students/hendrick.htm
Summary: To provide financial support for college to high school seniors interested in studying engineering.
Eligibility: This program is open to U.S. citizens who intend to earn an ABET-accredited degree in engineering. Applicants must be high school seniors with a GPA of 3.75 or higher who rank in the 90th percentile in both mathematics and verbal on the ACT or SAT. Selection is based on high school transcripts; SAT or ACT scores; school-related extracurricular activities; non-school related activities;

academic honors, civic honors, and awards; and a 250-word essay on the single experience that most strongly convinced them or confirmed their decision to pursue a career in engineering. Financial need is not considered.

Financial data: The stipend is $4,000, paid at the rate of $1,000 per year.

Duration: 4 years, provided the recipient maintains a grade point average of 3.0 or higher.

Additional information: Hendrickson International, a Boler Company, established an endowment to underwrite this scholarship in memory of the late Edward D. Hendrickson. Candidates must include a $5 processing fee with their applications.

Number awarded: 1 each year.

Deadline: November of each year.

1972
EDWARD DAVIS SCHOLARSHIP FUND

Auto Industry Diversity Efforts
65 Cadillac Square, Suite 2815
Detroit, MI 48226
Phone: (313) 963-2209   (877) 847-9060
Web Site: www.automag.com

Summary: To provide financial assistance to minority students interested in pursuing a career in an automotive-related profession.

Eligibility: Applicants must be minority high school seniors or currently-enrolled college students who are interested in preparing for a career in the automotive industry. High school students must have at least a 3.0 grade point average; college students must have at least a 2.5. To apply, students must complete an application; provide proof of acceptance or enrollment in an accredited college, university, vocational institute, or technical school; and submit an essay (up to 200 words) on "The Importance of Diversity in the Automobile Industry."

Financial data: A stipend is awarded (exact amount not specified).

Duration: 1 year.

Additional information: This scholarship, established in 1999, honors the first African American to own a new car dealership.

1973
EDWARD J. BRADY SCHOLARSHIP

American Welding Society
Attn: AWS Foundation, Inc.
550 N.W. LeJeune Road
Miami, FL 33126
Phone: (305) 443-9353, ext. 461   (800) 443-9353, ext. 461
Fax: (305) 443-7559   E-mail: vpinsky@aws.org
Web Site: www.aws.org/foundation/brady.html

Summary: To provide financial assistance to college students majoring in welding engineering or welding engineering technology.

Eligibility: This program is open to undergraduate students who are pursuing at least a 4-year bachelor's degree in welding engineering or welding engineering technology (although preference is given to students in welding engineering). Applicants must have a minimum grade point average of 2.5, provide a letter of reference indicating previous hands-on welding experience, be U.S. citizens, submit an essay on "Why I Want to Pursue a Career in Welding," and be able to demonstrate financial need.

Financial data: The stipend is $2,500.

Duration: 1 year; recipients may reapply.

Number awarded: 1 each year.

Deadline: January of each year.

1974
EISENHOWER HISPANIC-SERVING INSTITUTIONS FELLOWSHIPS

Summary: To provide financial assistance for undergraduate study in transportation-related fields to students at Hispanic Serving Institutions.
See Listing #1362.

1975
EISENHOWER HISTORICALLY BLACK COLLEGES AND UNIVERSITIES FELLOWSHIPS

Summary: To provide financial assistance for undergraduate study in transportation-related fields to students at Historically Black Colleges and Universities.
See Listing #1363.

1976
ELIZABETH AND STEPHEN D. BECHTEL JR. FOUNDATION FELLOWS

National Action Council for Minorities in Engineering
350 Fifth Avenue, Suite 2212
New York, NY 10118-2299
Phone: (212) 279-2626   Fax: (212) 629-5178
E-mail: awalter@nacme.org   Web Site: www.nacme.org/fellowships.html

Summary: To provide financial assistance for an undergraduate education in engineering to underrepresented minority students.

Eligibility: This program is open to African American, Latino, and American Indian engineering students. Applicants must be U.S. citizens or permanent residents applying during the second semester of their sophomore year. Selection is based on academic record and leadership skills.

Financial data: The stipend is $5,000 per year. The award must be supplemented by work-study or other student contributions.

Duration: 2 years.

Additional information: Funding for this award is provided by the Elizabeth and Stephen D. Bechtel Jr. Foundation.

Number awarded: 1 each year.

1977
ELIZABETH MCCULLAGH SCHOLARSHIP

Summary: To provide financial aid to Florida high school seniors who are interested in majoring in a field related to horticulture in college.
See Listing #1367.

1978
ELLIS F. HILLNER AWARD

Vasa Order of America
Attn: Vice Grand Master
1926 Rancho Andrew
Alpine, CA 91901
Phone: (619) 445-9707   Fax: (619) 445-7334
E-mail: drulf@connectnet.com   Web Site: www.vasaorder.com

Summary: To provide financial assistance for education in a medical field to members of the Vasa Order of America.

Eligibility: Applicants must have belonged to the organization for at least 1 year and be attending or planning to attend an accredited institution on a full-time basis for studies in the medical field. Selection is based on a transcript, letters of recommendation from school and local Vasa lodge officials, and an essay of up to 1,000 words on a topic related to Vasa.

Financial data: The stipend is $2,000.

Duration: 1 year.

Additional information: Vasa Order of America is a Swedish American fraternal organization incorporated in 1899.

Number awarded: 1 each year.

Deadline: February of each year.

1979
ELLISON ONIZUKA MEMORIAL SCHOLARSHIP

Hawai'i Community Foundation
900 Fort Street Mall, Suite 1300
Honolulu, HI 96813
Phone: (808) 566-5570   (888) 731-3863
Fax: (808) 521-6286   E-mail: scholarships@hcf-hawaii.org
Web Site: www.hcf-hawaii.org

Summary: To provide financial assistance to Hawaii residents who are interested in preparing for a career in aerospace.

Eligibility: This program is open to high school seniors in Hawaii who are interested in preparing for an aerospace career. No direct applications are accepted; candidates must be nominated by their high school principal. Nominees must be residents of the state of Hawaii; able to demonstrate financial need; interested in attending an accredited 2- or 4- year college or university; and able to demonstrate academic achievement (2.7 grade point average or above).

Financial data: The amount awarded varies.

Duration: 1 year.

Additional information: Recipients may attend school in Hawaii or on the mainland.

Number awarded: Varies each year.

Deadline: April of each year.

1980
EMPMD GILBERT CHIN SCHOLARSHIP

The Minerals, Metals & Materials Society
Attn: TMS Student Awards Program
184 Thorn Hill Road
Warrendale, PA 15086-7528
Phone: (724) 776-9000, ext. 213   Fax: (724) 776-3770
E-mail: luther@tms.org
Web Site: www.tms.org/Students/AwardsPrograms/Scholarships.html
Summary: To provide financial assistance for college to student members of The Minerals, Metals & Materials Society (TMS).
Eligibility: This program is open to undergraduate members of the society who are full-time students in a field related to electronic, magnetic, photonic, and superconducting materials. Applicants may be from any country. Selection is based on academic achievement, school and community activities, work experience, leadership, a personal profile statement, and letters of recommendation. Preference is given to students in their junior or senior year who are enrolled full time in a program that includes the study of electronic materials.
Financial data: The stipend is $2,000, plus a travel stipend of $500 (so the recipient can attend the annual meeting of the society to accept the award).
Duration: 1 year.
Additional information: Funding for this program is provided by the Electronic, Magnetic and Photonic Materials Division (EMPMD) of TMS.
Number awarded: 1 each year.
Deadline: April of each year.

1981
ENA FOUNDATION UNDERGRADUATE SCHOLARSHIP

Emergency Nurses Association Foundation
915 Lee Street
Des Plaines, IL 60016-6569
Phone: (847) 460-4100   (800) 900-9659, ext. 4101
Fax: (847) 460-4005   E-mail: foundation@ena.org
Web Site: www.ena.org/foundation
Summary: To provide financial assistance for baccalaureate study to nurses who are members of the Emergency Nurses Association (ENA).
Eligibility: This program is open to nurses (R.N., L.P.N., L.V.N.) who are pursuing a bachelor's degree. Applicants must have been members of the association for at least 12 months. They must submit a 1-page statement on their professional and educational goals and how this scholarship will help them attain those goals. Selection is based on content and clarity of the goal statement (45 percent), professional involvement (45 percent), and grade point average (10 percent).
Financial data: The stipend is $2,000.
Duration: 1 year; nonrenewable.
Additional information: Funding for this scholarship is provided by various contributions to the ENA Foundation. Each year, it is named in honor of the state whose members contributed the largest sum in donations to the foundation during the previous year, but it is open to all ENA members. Recently, it was named the Illinois ENA State Council Undergraduate Scholarship in honor of the Illinois ENA State Council.
Number awarded: Varies each year.
Deadline: September of each year.

1982
ENGINEERING DIVISION SCHOLARSHIPS

Technical Association of the Pulp and Paper Industry
P.O. Box 105113
Atlanta, GA 30348-5113
Phone: (770) 446-1400   (800) 332-8686
Fax: (770) 446-6947
Web Site: www.tappi.org
Summary: To provide financial assistance to students who are interested in preparing for a career in the paper industry, with a focus on the application of engineering principles to the design, construction, operation, and maintenance of facilities for the manufacture of pulp, paper, and related products.
Eligibility: This program is open to students who are attending college full time, are rising juniors or rising seniors, are enrolled in an engineering or science program, are members of the sponsoring organization's student chapter, have earned a grade point average of 3.0 or higher, and are able to demonstrate a significant interest in the pulp and paper industry. Selection is based on the

candidates' potential career and contributions to engineering in the pulp and paper industry. Financial need is not considered in the selection process.
Financial data: The stipend is $3,000.
Duration: 1 year.
Additional information: In addition to the financial award, scholarship recipients are encouraged to take summer employment in the pulp and paper industry. The scholarship committee will contact companies related to the pulp and paper industry on behalf of the scholarship recipients, to help them find summer employment with appropriate companies.
Number awarded: 2 each year: normally 1 to a junior and 1 to a senior.
Deadline: January of each year.

1983
ENGINEERING STUDENT DESIGN COMPETITION FOR UNDERGRADUATE STUDENTS

James F. Lincoln Arc Welding Foundation
Attn: Secretary
22801 Saint Clair Avenue
P.O. Box 17188
Cleveland, OH 44117-1199
Phone: (216) 481-8100   Fax: (216) 486-1751
E-mail: innovate@lincolnelectric.com
Web Site: www.jflf.org/awards/college.asp
Summary: To recognize and reward engineering and technology undergraduate students who solve design, engineering, or fabricating problems involving the knowledge or application of arc welding.
Eligibility: Any undergraduate student enrolled in a 4-year or longer curriculum leading to a baccalaureate degree in engineering or technology at an accredited college or university in the United States may participate. Students may submit papers representing their work on design, engineering, or fabrication problems relating to any type of building, bridge, or other generally stationary structure; any type of machine, project, or mechanical apparatus; or arc welding research, testing, procedure, or process development. Applicants may participate as individuals or in groups of up to 10 students. If both graduate and undergraduate students participate together as a group, their paper is entered in the graduate competition. Any number of entries may be submitted from 1 school, but no student may participate in more than 1 entry. Selection is based on originality or ingenuity, feasibility, results achieved or expected, engineering competence, and clarity of the presentation.
Financial data: Awards range from $250 to $2,000. Additionally, awards of $250 are made to the schools the winners attend.
Duration: The competition is held annually.
Additional information: This program began in 1936.
Number awarded: 23 each year: 1 Best of Program ($2,000), 1 Gold Award ($1,000), 2 Silver Awards ($750 each), 3 Bronze Awards ($500 each), and 16 merit awards ($250 each). The school awards are presented to the 7 schools attended by the Best of Program, Gold, Silver, and Bronze award winners.
Deadline: June of each year.

1984
ENGINEERING TECHNOLOGY SCHOLARSHIP

American Society of Heating, Refrigerating and Air-Conditioning Engineers, Inc.
Attn: Scholarship Administrator
1791 Tullie Circle, N.E.
Atlanta, GA 30329-2305
Phone: (404) 636-8400   Fax: (404) 321-5478
E-mail: benedict@ashrae.org
Web Site: www.ashrae.org
Summary: To provide financial assistance to engineering technology students interested in heating, ventilating, air conditioning, and refrigeration (HVAC&R).
Eligibility: This program is open to undergraduate engineering technology students enrolled in a school recognized as accredited by the American Society of Heating, Refrigerating and Air-Conditioning Engineers (ASHRAE). Applicants must be pursuing a course of study that traditionally has been preparatory for the profession of HVAC&R. They must have a grade point average of at least 3.0 and must be full-time students with at least 1 full year of undergraduate study remaining. Selection is based on potential service to the HVAC&R profession, financial need, leadership ability, recommendations from instructors, and character.
Financial data: The stipend is $3,000 per year.
Duration: 1 year.

Number awarded: 2 each year: 1 to a student in a program leading to a bachelor's degree in engineering technology and 1 to a student in an engineering technology program leading to an associate degree.
Deadline: April of each year.

1985
ENGINEERS FOUNDATION OF OHIO GENERAL FUND SCHOLARSHIP

Ohio Society of Professional Engineers
Attn: Engineers Foundation of Ohio
4795 Evanswood Drive, Suite 201
Columbus, OH 43229-7216
Phone: (614) 846-1144   (800) 654-9481
Fax: (614) 846-1131   E-mail: ospe@iwaynet.net
Web Site: www.ohioengineer.com/programs/Scholarships.htm
Summary: To provide financial assistance to engineering students entering their junior or senior year at a college or university in Ohio.
Eligibility: This program is open to entering juniors and seniors at ABET-accredited colleges and universities in Ohio who are majoring in engineering. Applicants must have a grade point average of 3.0 or higher, be U.S. citizens, and be Ohio residents. Along with their application, they must submit a 350-word essay on their interest in engineering, including why they became interested in the field, what specialty interests them most, and why they want to become a practicing engineer. Financial need is also considered in the selection process.
Financial data: The stipend is $1,000 per year.
Duration: 1 year; nonrenewable.
Number awarded: 1 each year.
Deadline: December of each year.

1986
ENGINEERS FOUNDATION OF WISCONSIN SCHOLARSHIP

Wisconsin Society of Professional Engineers
Attn: Engineers Foundation of Wisconsin
700 Rayovac Drive, Suite 207
Madison, WI 53711-2476
Phone: (608) 278-7000   Fax: (608) 278-7005
E-mail: wspe@wspe.org
Web Site: www.wspe.org/efw.htm
Summary: To provide financial assistance to seniors at designated universities in Wisconsin who are majoring in engineering.
Eligibility: This program is open to Wisconsin residents who are seniors at designated universities in the state and majoring in engineering. Applicants must have a grade point average of 3.0 or higher. As part of the selection process, they must submit a 250-word essay on how they became interested in engineering, the field of engineering that is most interesting to them and why, and why they want to become a practicing engineer. U.S. citizenship is required. Selection is based on grade point average, class ranking, activities and honors, the essay, and supplemental credits (computer, chemistry, physics, calculus, etc.).
Financial data: Varies each year. The sponsor awards a total of $7,500 in scholarships each year.
Duration: 1 year.
Additional information: The award rotates annually to a senior at the University of Wisconsin at Madison, University of Wisconsin at Milwaukee, MSOE, Marquette University, and University of Wisconsin at Platteville.
Number awarded: 1 or more each year.
Deadline: December of each year.

1987
ENGINEER'S FOUNDATION OF WISCONSIN-BEHLING COLLEGE FRESHMAN SCHOLARSHIP

Wisconsin Society of Professional Engineers
Attn: Engineers Foundation of Wisconsin
700 Rayovac Drive, Suite 207
Madison, WI 53711-2476
Phone: (608) 278-7000   Fax: (608) 278-7005
E-mail: wspe@wspe.org
Web Site: www.wspe.org/efw.htm
Summary: To provide financial assistance to high school seniors in Wisconsin who are interested in majoring in engineering in college.
Eligibility: This program is open to seniors graduating from high schools in Wisconsin who intend to enroll in an accredited engineering undergraduate

program, earn a degree in engineering, and enter the practice of engineering after graduation. Applicants must have a grade point average of 3.0 or higher and an ACT composite score of 24 or higher. As part of the selection process, they must submit a 250-word essay on how they became interested in engineering, the field of engineering that is most interesting to them and why, and why they want to become a practicing engineer. U.S. citizenship is required. Selection is based on grade point average, ACT scores, class ranking, activities and honors, the essay, and supplemental credits (computer, chemistry, physics, calculus, etc.). Points are also given for honors/advanced placement courses and college-level courses completed.
Financial data: The stipend is $1,000.
Duration: 1 year.
Number awarded: 1 each year.
Deadline: December of each year.

1988
ENTOMOLOGICAL FOUNDATION SCHOLARSHIPS

Entomological Society of America
Attn: Entomological Foundation
9301 Annapolis Road
Lanham, MD 20706-3115
Phone: (301) 731-4535   Fax: (301) 731-4538
E-mail: esa@entsoc.org
Web Site: www.entsoc.org
Summary: To provide financial assistance to undergraduates interested in studying entomology.
Eligibility: This program is open to undergraduate students majoring in entomology, biology, zoology, or a related science at a recognized university or college in the United States, Canada, or Mexico. They must have accumulated a minimum of 30 semester hours at the time the award is presented. Selection is based on academic record, demonstrated enthusiasm, interest, and achievement in biology. Preference is given to students with demonstrated financial need.
Financial data: The stipend is $1,500.
Duration: 1 year.
Additional information: Funding for this program is provided by the Entomological Foundation.
Number awarded: Several each year.
Deadline: May of each year.

1989
ENVIRONMENTAL DIVISION SCHOLARSHIPS

Technical Association of the Pulp and Paper Industry
P.O. Box 105113
Atlanta, GA 30348-5113
Phone: (770) 446-1400   (800) 332-8686
Fax: (770) 446-6947
Web Site: www.tappi.org
Summary: To provide financial assistance to students who are interested in preparing for a career in the paper industry, with a focus on environmental control as it relates to the pulp, paper, and allied industries.
Eligibility: This program is open to students who are attending college full time, are at least sophomores, are enrolled at an ABET-accredited or equivalent college, have earned at least a 3.0 grade point average, are able to demonstrate a significant interest in environmental control as it relates to the pulp and paper industries, and are prepared to be interviewed by a designate of the Environmental Division Scholarship Committee. Selection is based on the candidates' potential career and contributions in environmental control in the pulp and paper industry. Financial need may be considered in the selection process (candidates are given the option of discussing their need for financial assistance).
Financial data: The stipend is $2,500.
Duration: 1 year.
Number awarded: At least 1 each year.
Deadline: January of each year.

1990
ENVIRONMENTAL EDUCATIONAL SCHOLARSHIP PROGRAM

Missouri Department of Natural Resources
P.O. Box 176
Jefferson City, MO 65102
Phone: (800) 334-6946   TDD: (800) 379-2419
Web Site: dnr.state.mo.us/eesp

Summary: To provide financial assistance to underrepresented and minority students from Missouri who are studying an environmental field in college.

Eligibility: This program is open to residents of Missouri who have graduated from an accredited high school with a grade point average of 2.5 or higher. Applicants must be minority or underrepresented students who are pursuing a bachelor's or master's degree in 1 of the following fields: engineering (civil, chemical, mechanical, or agricultural), environmental sciences (including geology, biology, wildlife management, planning, natural resources, or closely-related field), environmental chemistry, or environmental law enforcement. Selection is based on grade point average and test scores, school and community activities, leadership and character, and a 1-page essay.

Financial data: A stipend is awarded (exact amount not specified).

Duration: 1 year; may be renewed if the recipient maintains at least a 2.5 grade point average and full-time enrollment.

Number awarded: Varies each year.

Deadline: November of each year.

1991
EPA TRIBAL LANDS ENVIRONMENTAL SCIENCE SCHOLARSHIP

American Indian Science and Engineering Society
Attn: Higher Education Director
2201 Buena Vista, S.E., Suite 301
P.O. Box 9828
Albuquerque, NM 87119-9828
Phone: (505) 765-1052, ext. 15   Fax: (505) 765-5608
E-mail: teresa@aises.org
Web Site: www.aises.org

Summary: To provide financial assistance to members of the American Indian Science and Engineering Society (AISES) interested in studying environmental or related sciences at the undergraduate or graduate level.

Eligibility: This program is open to AISES members who are full-time college juniors, seniors, or graduate students majoring in environmental, science, or engineering fields leading to an environmental-related career. Applicants must have a grade point average of 2.7 or higher. Non-Indians may apply, but all applicants must submit an essay on their knowledge and living experience with American Indian tribal culture, their interest in environmental studies, how that interest relates to environmental issues and needs on tribal lands, and how they will contribute their professional knowledge to a Native community.

Financial data: The stipend is $4,000 per year.

Duration: 1 year; renewable upon reapplication.

Additional information: This program is funded by the Environmental Protection Agency (EPA) and administered by AISES. Students agree to work during the summer at the EPA, a tribal location, or an environmental facility, if a position is offered.

Deadline: June of each year.

1992
ERNESTINE LOWRIE MEMORIAL FELLOWSHIP

American Nephrology Nurses' Association
Attn: ANNA Foundation
East Holly Avenue, Box 56
Pitman, NJ 08071-0056
Phone: (856) 256-2320   (877) 527-0787
Fax: (856) 589-7463   E-mail: annafoundation@hotmail.com
Web Site: www.annanurse.org

Summary: To provide financial assistance to students pursuing undergraduate or graduate education in nephrology nursing.

Eligibility: This program is open to nurses who have at least 2 years of clinical practice experience in nephrology settings. Applicants must have been accepted into full-time or part-time undergraduate or graduate study at an accredited educational institution. They must submit academic transcripts; a letter from the supervisor, dean, or department chair outlining academic plans and possible research or project plans; and 2 letters of recommendation.

Financial data: The stipend is $25,000 per year. An additional $1,000 per year may be available for travel for scientific purposes or for research/project expenses.

Duration: 1 year; may be renewed 1 additional year.

Additional information: Information is also available from Cynthia Frazier, Awards Chairperson, 7344 Pine Tree Lane, Fairfield, AL 35064, (205) 933-8101, ext. 6514, E-mail: cdf44@aol.com.

Number awarded: 1 each year.

Deadline: October of each year.

1993
ERNIE MENDES SCHOLARSHIP

Supreme Council of I.D.E.S.
223237 Main Street
Hayward, CA 94541
Phone: (510) 886-5555   Fax: (510) 866-6306
Web Site: www.idesofca.org

Summary: To provide financial assistance to high school seniors who are members of the I.D.E.S. and interested in majoring in agricultural sciences in college.

Eligibility: Applicants must be members of the I.D.E.S. in good standing (for at least 1 year prior to applying for the scholarship), be interested in majoring in agricultural sciences in college, have maintained at least a 3.0 grade point average, be graduating from high school, and furnish 3 letters of recommendation (at least 1 of which must be from the principal or dean of the high school the applicant is attending). Financial need is considered in the selection process.

Financial data: The amount awarded is determined annually.

Duration: 1 year.

Additional information: The sponsor was incorporated by Portuguese immigrants in 1891 as the Irmandade do Divino Espirito Santo (Brotherhood of the Holy Spirit) de Mission San Jose California (I.D.E.S). Recipients must maintain membership with the I.D.E.S. until the final scholarship payment is made.

Number awarded: 2 each year.

Deadline: April of each year.

1994
ERNST & YOUNG BETF COMPUTER COMPETITION PARTICIPANT SCHOLARSHIP

Black Data Processing Associates
Attn: Education and Technology Foundation
8401 Corporate Drive, Suite 405
Lanham, MD 20785
Phone: (301) 429-5169   Fax: (301) 429-5170
E-mail: betfscholarship@aol.com   Web Site: www.betf.org

Summary: To provide financial assistance for college to high school students who participate in the annual national computer competition of the Black Data Processing Associates (BDPA).

Eligibility: This program is open to high school students who participate in the annual national BDPA computer competition. Applicants must reside in the United States, have a grade point average of 2.5 or higher, and take the SAT exam. They must submit an essay on why they believe that education and a career in the field of information technology are important. Selection in based on academic aptitude, academic achievement, community involvement, involvement with the sponsoring organization, and financial need.

Financial data: The stipend is $5,000.

Duration: 1 year; may be renewed.

Additional information: The BDPA established its Education and Technology Foundation (BETF) in 1992 to advance the skill sets needed by African American and other minority adults and young people to compete in the information technology industry.

Number awarded: 1 or more each year.

Deadline: February of each year.

1995
ERNST & YOUNG BETF CONTINUING EDUCATION SCHOLARSHIP

Black Data Processing Associates
Attn: Education and Technology Foundation
8401 Corporate Drive, Suite 405
Lanham, MD 20785
Phone: (301) 429-5169   Fax: (301) 429-5170
E-mail: betfscholarship@aol.com   Web Site: www.betf.org

Summary: To provide financial assistance to college students currently enrolled in a field related to information technology.

Eligibility: This program is open to undergraduate students enrolled in a field related to information technology. Applicants must reside in the United States and have a grade point average of 3.0 or higher. They must submit an essay on why they believe that education and a career in the field of information technology are important. Selection in based on academic aptitude, academic achievement, community involvement, BDPA involvement, and financial need.

Financial data: The stipend is $10,000.

Duration: 1 year; may be renewed.

Scholarship Listings

Additional information: The Black Data Processing Associates established its Education and Technology Foundation (BETF) in 1992 to advance the skill sets needed by African American and other minority adults and young people to compete in the information technology industry.

Number awarded: 1 or more each year.

Deadline: February of each year.

1996
ERNST & YOUNG SCHOLARSHIP PROGRAM

National Society of Black Engineers
Attn: Programs Manager
1454 Duke Street
Alexandria, VA 22314
Phone: (703) 549-2207, ext. 204   Fax: (703) 683-5312
E-mail: scholarships@nsbe.org   Web Site: www.nsbe.org

Summary: To provide financial assistance to members of the National Society of Black Engineers (NSBE) who are majoring in engineering or a technical field at a designated university.

Eligibility: This program is open to members of the society who are freshmen, sophomores, or juniors majoring in engineering or computer science. Applicants must have at least a 3.0 grade point average, demonstrated leadership involvement on campus and/or in the community, and a demonstrated interest in the consulting industry. They must submit a 500-word essay describing how they will use their leadership skills and a position in the consulting industry to make an impact on the African American community.

Financial data: The stipend is $2,000.

Duration: 1 year.

Additional information: This program is supported by Ernst & Young LLP. Scholarships may be used only at 1 of the following 14 universities: Carnegie Mellon University, Cornell University, Duke University, Georgia Institute of Technology, Indiana University, North Carolina A&T University, Northwestern University, University of California at Berkeley, University of Michigan, University of Notre Dame, University of Pennsylvania, University of Texas at Austin, University of Virginia, and Washington University.

Number awarded: 1 or more each year.

Deadline: December of each year; freshmen have until January to apply.

1997
ESTHER MAYO SHERARD SCHOLARSHIP

American Health Information Management Association
Attn: Foundation of Research and Education
233 North Michigan Avenue, Suite 2150
Chicago, IL 60601-5519
Phone: (312) 233-1168   Fax: (312) 233-1090
E-mail: fore@ahima.org   Web Site: www.ahima.org/fore/programs.html

Summary: To provide financial assistance to African American members of the American Health Information Management Association (AHIMA) who are interested in pursuing an undergraduate degree in health information administration or technology.

Eligibility: This program is open to AHIMA members who are African Americans enrolled in a health information administration or health information technology program accredited by the Commission on Accreditation of Allied Health Education Programs. Applicants must be pursuing a degree on at least a half-time basis and have a grade point average of 3.0 or higher. U.S. citizenship is required. Selection is based on grade point average and academic achievement, volunteer and work experience, commitment to the health information management profession, suitability to the health information management profession, quality and suitability of references provided, and clarity of application.

Financial data: The stipend ranges from $1,000 to $5,000.

Duration: 1 year; nonrenewable.

Number awarded: 1 each year.

Deadline: May of each year.

1998
ETHNIC MINORITY BACHELOR'S SCHOLARSHIPS IN ONCOLOGY NURSING

Oncology Nursing Society
Attn: ONS Foundation
501 Holiday Drive
Pittsburgh, PA 15220-2749
Phone: (412) 921-7373, ext. 231   Fax: (412) 921-6565
E-mail: foundation@ons.org   Web Site: www.ons.org

Summary: To provide financial assistance to ethnic minorities interested in pursuing undergraduate studies in oncology nursing.

Eligibility: The candidate must 1) demonstrate an interest in and commitment to cancer nursing; 2) be enrolled in an undergraduate nursing degree program at an NLN- or CCNE-accredited school of nursing (the program must have application to oncology nursing); 3) have a current license to practice as a registered nurse or a practical (vocational) nurse; 4) not have previously received a bachelor's scholarship from this sponsor; and 5) be a member of an ethnic minority group (Native American, African American, Asian American, Pacific Islander, Hispanic/Latino, or other ethnic minority background). Applicants must submit an essay of 250 words or less on their role in caring for persons with cancer and a statement of their professional goals and their relationship to the advancement of oncology nursing. Financial need is not considered in the selection process.

Financial data: The stipend is $2,000.

Duration: 1 year.

Additional information: This program includes a mentoring component with an individual in the applicant's area of clinical interest. When appropriate, efforts are made to match the applicant and mentor by ethnicity. At the end of each year of scholarship participation, recipients must submit a summary describing their educational activities. Applications must be accompanied by a $5 fee.

Number awarded: 3 each year.

Deadline: January of each year.

1999
EUGENE P. PFLEIDER MEMORIAL SCHOLARSHIP

Society for Mining, Metallurgy, and Exploration, Inc.
Attn: Member Services
8307 Shaffer Parkway
P.O. Box 277002
Littleton, CO 80127-7002
Phone: (303) 973-9550   (800) 763-3132
Fax: (303) 973-3845   E-mail: sensenig@smenet.org
Web Site: www.smenet.org/education/students/sme_scholarships.cfm

Summary: To provide financial assistance to student members of the Society for Mining, Metallurgy, and Exploration (SME) who are majoring in mining engineering.

Eligibility: This program is open to student members who have completed their sophomore year in college and are majoring in mining engineering. Applicants must be U.S. citizens, be able to demonstrate financial need, have a strong academic record, and be committed to a career in mining engineering. Only 1 candidate from each eligible department may be nominated each academic year.

Financial data: The stipend is $1,000.

Duration: 1 year.

Number awarded: 1 each year.

Deadline: November of each year.

2000
EUGENE S. KROPF SCHOLARSHIP

University Aviation Association
c/o Bernard W. Wulle
Aviation Technology Department
1 Purdue Airport
West Lafayette, IN 47906-3398
Phone: (765) 494-9973   E-mail: bwulle@purdue.tech.edu

Summary: To provide financial assistance for college to students enrolled in an aviation-related curriculum at a college or university affiliated with the University Aviation Association (UAA).

Eligibility: Applicants must be U.S. citizens, be enrolled in a 2-year or 4-year degree in the field of aviation at a UAA-member college or university, and have earned at least a 3.0 grade point average. They must submit a 250-word essay on "How Can I Improve Aviation Education."

Financial data: The stipend is $1,000.

Duration: 1 year.

Number awarded: 1 each year.

Deadline: April of each year.

2001
EXTRACTION AND PROCESSING DIVISION SCHOLARSHIPS

The Minerals, Metals & Materials Society
Attn: TMS Student Awards Program
184 Thorn Hill Road
Warrendale, PA 15086-7528
Phone: (724) 776-9000, ext. 213   Fax: (724) 776-3770
E-mail: luther@tms.org
Web Site: www.tms.org/Students/AwardsPrograms/Scholarships.html
Summary: To provide financial assistance for college to student members of The Minerals, Metals & Materials Society (TMS).
Eligibility: This program is open to undergraduate members of the society, preferably seniors, who are full-time students majoring in the extraction and processing of minerals, metals, and materials. Applicants may be from any country. Selection is based on academic achievement, school and community activities, work experience, leadership, a personal profile statement, and letters of recommendation.
Financial data: The stipend is $2,000, plus a travel stipend of $500 (so the recipient can attend the annual meeting of the society to accept the award).
Duration: 1 year.
Additional information: Funding for this program is provided by the Extraction and Processing Division of TMS.
Number awarded: 4 each year.
Deadline: April of each year.

2002
FALÚ FOUNDATION SCHOLARSHIP

Falú Universal Business and Media School
220 East 106th Street
New York, NY 10029
Phone: (212) 360-1210   Fax: (212) 360-1231
E-mail: falu@ubms.edu
Web Site: www.ubms.edu/FaluFoundation.html
Summary: To provide funding to Hispanic students interested in pursuing a career in technology.
Eligibility: This program is open to Hispanic students who are interested in pursuing a career in computer technology or information technology. Applicants must be enrolled in or admitted to an accredited business school, college, or university.
Financial data: The stipend is $1,000.
Number awarded: 1 or more each year.

2003
FARM CREDIT ASSOCIATIONS OF TEXAS SCHOLARSHIPS

Texas FFA Association
614 East 12th Street
Austin, TX 78701
Phone: (512) 480-8045   Fax: (512) 472-0555
E-mail: txffa@txaged.org
Web Site: www.txaged.org
Summary: To provide financial assistance for college to high school seniors in Texas who demonstrate outstanding personal qualities and involvement in FFA.
Eligibility: This program is open to high school seniors in Texas who are FFA members and have been members at least 2 of the 3 previous years. Applicants must be planning to major in college in a field related to the agricultural sciences, life sciences, or natural resources. They must have completed at least 5 semesters of instruction in agriculture and/or agribusiness during high school and scored at least 950 on the SAT or 20 on the ACT. U.S. citizenship and ranking in the top half of their graduating class are also required. Selection is based on academic achievement (16 points); SAT or ACT scores (14 points); agricultural science and career related instruction (10 points); FFA achievement (20 points), including the supervised agricultural experience (10 points); financial need (10 points); and performance during interviews regarding academics (10 points), FFA achievement (5 points), and financial need (10 points).
Financial data: The stipend is $1,000.
Duration: 1 year.
Additional information: Students may not apply for both 4-H and FFA scholarships.
Number awarded: 3 each year.

2004
FARM CREDIT OF MAINE SCHOLARSHIP

Pine Tree State 4-H Foundation
c/o University of Maine
5741 Libby Hall
Orono, ME 04469-5741
Phone: (207) 581-3739   Fax: (207) 581-3212
E-mail: brendaz@umext.maine.edu   Web Site: www.umaine/edu.4hfoundation
Summary: To provide financial assistance to 4-H members in Maine who are interested in studying fields related to commercial farming, fishing, or forest products in college.
Eligibility: This program is open to 1) seniors who are graduating from a Maine high school, and 2) residents of Maine who have graduated from high school but have delayed going to college for no more than 1 year. Applicants must be interested in majoring in a field related to commercial farming, fishing, or forest products, or in another field with the intent to work in businesses related to those industries. The must be involved in 4-H activities. Selection is based primarily on academic achievement and 4-H activities; financial need is not considered.
Financial data: The stipend is $1,000.
Duration: 1 year; nonrenewable.
Number awarded: 1 each year.
Deadline: March of each year.

2005
FEDERATED GARDEN CLUBS OF CONNECTICUT SCHOLARSHIP

Summary: To provide financial assistance to Connecticut residents who are interested in majoring in horticulture-related fields at a Connecticut college or university.
See Listing #1375.

2006
FEMME VITALE SCHOLARSHIP AWARD

Odwalla, Inc.
120 Stone Pine Road
Half Moon Bay, CA 94019
Phone: (650) 726-1888, ext 4410   Fax: (650) 712-4441
E-mail: femme@odwalla.com   Web Site: www.odwalla.com
Summary: To provide financial assistance to women who are interested in working on a degree in health and nutrition.
Eligibility: This program is open to women in college who are pursuing undergraduate or graduate degrees in health and nutrition, with preference given to those interested in focusing on women's health and nutrition. Applicants must reside in a state where the sponsor's products are sold: Alaska, Arizona, California, Colorado, District of Columbia, Florida, Georgia, Idaho, Illinois, Louisiana, Massachusetts, Maryland, Michigan, Nevada, New Mexico, Oregon, Texas, Utah, Virginia, Washington, or Wisconsin. Selection is based on academic performance, commitment to community, leadership qualities, an essay on their personal vision, and financial need.
Financial data: Awards range up to $4,000.
Duration: 1 year; may be renewed for a second year and, in exceptional cases, for a third year.
Additional information: Odwalla is a California-based fresh juice company. It established this program in 1995. Send a self-addressed stamped envelope for program details and application deadline.
Number awarded: 4 each year.
Deadline: February of each year.

2007
FIS SCHOLARSHIPS

Institute of Food Technologists
Attn: Scholarship Department
221 North LaSalle Street, Suite 300
Chicago, IL 60601-1291
Phone: (312) 782-8424   Fax: (312) 782-8348
E-mail: info@ift.org
Web Site: www.ift.org
Summary: To provide financial assistance to undergraduates interested in studying food science or food technology.
Eligibility: Applicants must be currently enrolled as sophomores or juniors in a food science or food technology program at an educational institution in the

United States or Canada; they must have an outstanding scholastic record and a well-rounded personality. Financial need is not considered in the selection process.

Financial data: The stipend is $1,000.

Duration: 1 year; recipients may reapply if they are members of the Institute of Food Technologists (IFT).

Additional information: Funding for these scholarships is provided by the FIDCO Industrial Division of Food Ingredient Specialties (FIS), Inc. Correspondence and completed applications must be submitted to the department head of the educational institution the applicant is attending.

Number awarded: 5 each year.

Deadline: January of each year.

2008
FLEMING/BLASZCAK SCHOLARSHIP

Society of Plastics Engineers
Attn: SPE Foundation
14 Fairfield Drive
Brookfield, CT 06804
Phone: (203) 740-5434   Fax: (203) 775-8490
E-mail: foundation@4spe.org   Web Site: www.4spe.org

Summary: To provide college scholarships to Mexican American undergraduate and graduate students who have a career interest in the plastics industry.

Eligibility: This program is open to full-time undergraduate and graduate students of Mexican descent who are enrolled in a 4-year college or university. Applicants must be U.S. citizens or legal residents. They must have a demonstrated or expressed interest in the plastics industry and should be taking classes that would be beneficial to a career in the plastics industry (e.g., plastics engineering, polymer sciences, chemistry, physics, chemical engineering, mechanical engineering, industrial engineering, and business administration). Financial need must be documented. Along with their application, students must submit 3 letters of recommendation; a high school and/or college transcript; a 1- to 2-page statement telling why they are interested in the scholarship, their qualifications, and their career goals in the plastics industry; and documentation of their Mexican heritage.

Financial data: The stipend is $2,000 per year.

Duration: 1 year.

Additional information: This program is sponsored by Cal Mold Inc. and Formula Plastics.

Number awarded: 1 each year.

Deadline: December of each year.

2009
FLORENCE MARGARET HARVEY MEMORIAL SCHOLARSHIP

American Foundation for the Blind
Attn: Scholarship Committee
11 Penn Plaza, Suite 300
New York, NY 10001
Phone: (212) 502-7661   (800) AFB-LINE
Fax: (212) 502-7771   TDD: (212) 502-7662
E-mail: afbinfo@afb.net   Web Site: www.afb.org/scholarships.asp

Summary: To provide financial assistance to blind students who wish to study in the field of rehabilitation and/or education of the blind.

Eligibility: Applicants must be legally blind juniors, seniors, or graduate students. U.S. citizenship is required. Applicants must be studying in the field of rehabilitation and/or education of visually impaired and blind persons. Applications must include a typewritten statement, up to 3 pages in length, describing educational and personal goals, work experience, extracurricular activities, and how scholarship funds will be used. Selection includes consideration of good character and academic excellence.

Financial data: The stipend is $1,000.

Duration: 1 year.

Additional information: This scholarship is supported by the Delta Gamma Foundation and administered by the American Foundation for the Blind.

Number awarded: 1 each year.

Deadline: March of each year.

2010
FLORIDA NURSES FOUNDATION SCHOLARSHIP

Florida Nurses Foundation
P.O. Box 536985
Orlando, FL 32853-6985
Phone: (407) 896-3261   Fax: (407) 896-9042
E-mail: info@floridanurse.org

Web Site: www.floridanurse.org/grants.asp

Summary: To provide financial assistance to Florida residents who are interested in working on an undergraduate or graduate degree in nursing.

Eligibility: Applicants must have been Florida residents for at least 1 year and be currently enrolled in an accredited nursing program in Florida. They may be working on an associate, baccalaureate, master's, or doctoral degree. A student who is pursuing initial nursing education (associate or baccalaureate degree and not yet licensed as an R.N.) must have completed at least 1 semester of the nursing program in order to be eligible for the scholarship. Selection is based on academic record (at least a 2.5 grade point average for undergraduates and a 3.0 grade point average for graduate students), financial need, and potential for contribution to the nursing profession and society.

Financial data: A stipend is awarded (exact amount not specified).

Duration: 1 semester or year.

Additional information: This program was established in 1986. Recipients who withdraw from their nursing program before completing the semester or year for which this scholarship applies must repay the sponsor the entire amount advanced.

Deadline: May of each year.

2011
FNGA ACTION CHAPTER SCHOLARSHIP

Florida Nurserymen and Growers Association-Action Chapter
Attn: Regina Thomas, Scholarship Committee Chair
Farm Credit of Central Florida
57 East Third Street
Apopka, FL 32703
Phone: (407) 880-7883   Fax: (407) 880-7980

Summary: To provide financial assistance to students in Florida interested in preparing for a career in horticulture.

Eligibility: Applicants must have been accepted by or be currently enrolled in a Florida junior college, college, or university. They may be attending school full or part time, but they must be majoring in 1 of the following subjects: environmental horticulture, landscaping, landscape architecture, turf management, or a related field. All applicants must have at least a 2.75 grade point average. Selection is based on academic record, work experience, awards received, letters of recommendation, and an essay (300 words) on the applicant's career plans.

Financial data: A stipend is awarded (exact amount not specified). A total of $4,000 is available through this program each year.

Duration: 1 year.

Number awarded: 1 or more each year.

Deadline: June of each year.

2012
FOOD ENGINEERING SCHOLARSHIP PROGRAM

International Association of Food Industry Suppliers
Attn: IAFIS Foundation
1451 Dolley Madison Boulevard
McLean, VA 22101-3850
Phone: (703) 761-2600   Fax: (703) 761-4334
E-mail: info@iafis.org
Web Site: www.iafis.org/foundation.htm

Summary: To provide financial assistance to outstanding undergraduate students who are interested in working on a degree in food engineering.

Eligibility: Sophomores and juniors in food engineering are eligible to apply if they are U.S. or Canadian citizens, are majoring in food engineering at an accredited institution in the United States or Canada, have an outstanding academic record, and can demonstrate leadership potential through extracurricular activities. Age, sex, race, and financial need are not considered in the selection process. Interested students must submit their application to a designated person at their school; only 1 application will be selected for submission from any campus in any 1 year.

Financial data: The stipend of $2,500 is paid to the student in equal installments throughout the junior or senior academic year. In addition, a $500 travel grant is given to each recipient to attend Worldwide Food EXPO.

Duration: 1 year; nonrenewable.

Additional information: Information and applications are not available from the Foundation of the International Association of Food Industry Suppliers; students must contact the head of their department or other appropriate person at their school.

Number awarded: 2 each year.

Deadline: Student applications must be submitted to their department heads by the end of January; the application selected by the school to be considered in the national competition must be received at the association's office by mid-February.

2013
FOOTSTEPS ON THE GREEN AWARDS

Golf Course Superintendents Association of America
Attn: Scholarship Coordinator
1421 Research Park Drive
Lawrence, KS 66049-3859
Phone: (785) 832-3678   (800) 472-7878, ext. 678
E-mail: psmith@gcsaa.org
Web Site: www.gcsaa.org
Summary: To provide financial assistance to the offspring of members of the Golf Course Superintendents Association of America (GCSAA) who are interested in a career in golf course management.
Eligibility: This program is open to the children and grandchildren of GCSAA members who have been active members of the association for 5 or more consecutive years or are retired or deceased. Applicants must be enrolled in an undergraduate program with a major field related to golf course management. Students at a 4-year institution must have completed 12 credit hours in their major. Students at a 2-year institution must be enrolled full time and have completed at least 12 credit hours, including at least 9 hours in golf course management-related courses. All applicants must be GCSAA members. Selection is based on academic achievement, extracurricular activities, community involvement, and a 100-word essay on why they have chosen a career in golf course management along with their observations, insights, and expectations about the profession and their career goals. Financial need is not considered.
Financial data: The stipend is $3,500 per year for first place, $2,500 per year for second place, $1,500 per year for third place, and $500 per year for fourth place.
Duration: 1 year. Winners may reapply after a 1-year hiatus.
Additional information: This program is sponsored by the Trans Mississippi Golf Association.
Number awarded: 4 each year.
Deadline: April of each year.

2014
FORD MOTOR COMPANY UNDERGRADUATE SCHOLARSHIPS

American Society of Safety Engineers
Attn: ASSE Foundation
1800 East Oakton Street
Des Plaines, IL 60018
Phone: (847) 768-3441   Fax: (847) 296-9220
E-mail: mrosario@asse.org
Web Site: www.asse.org
Summary: To provide financial assistance to undergraduate women members of the American Society of Safety Engineers (ASSE).
Eligibility: This program is open to women ASSE student members who are majoring in occupational safety and health. Applicants must be full-time students who have completed at least 60 semester hours with a grade point average of 3.25 or higher. As part of the selection process, they must submit 2 essays of 300 words or less: 1) why they are seeking a degree in safety, a brief description of their current activities, and how those relate to their career goals and objectives; and 2) why they should be awarded this scholarship (including career goals and financial need).
Financial data: The stipend is $3,375 per year.
Duration: 1 year; nonrenewable.
Additional information: Funding for this program is provided by Ford Motor Company.
Number awarded: 3 each year.
Deadline: November of each year.

2015
FORE DIVERSITY SCHOLARSHIPS

American Health Information Management Association
Attn: Foundation of Research and Education
233 North Michigan Avenue, Suite 2150
Chicago, IL 60601-5519
Phone: (312) 233-1168   Fax: (312) 233-1090
E-mail: fore@ahima.org
Web Site: www.ahima.org/fore/programs.html

Summary: To provide financial assistance to minority members of the American Health Information Management Association (AHIMA) who are interested in pursuing an undergraduate degree in health information administration or technology.
Eligibility: This program is open to AHIMA members who are members of ethnic minority groups enrolled in a health information administration or health information technology program accredited by the Commission on Accreditation of Allied Health Education Programs. Applicants must be pursuing a degree on at least a half-time basis and have a grade point average of 3.0 or higher. U.S. citizenship is required. Selection is based on grade point average and academic achievement, volunteer and work experience, commitment to the health information management profession, suitability to the health information management profession, quality and suitability of references provided, and clarity of application.
Financial data: Stipends range from $1,000 to $5,000.
Duration: 1 year; nonrenewable.
Number awarded: Varies each year; recently, 2 of these scholarships were awarded.
Deadline: May of each year.

2016
FORE UNDERGRADUATE MERIT SCHOLARSHIPS

American Health Information Management Association
Attn: Foundation of Research and Education
233 North Michigan Avenue, Suite 2150
Chicago, IL 60601-5519
Phone: (312) 233-1168   Fax: (312) 233-1090
E-mail: fore@ahima.org
Web Site: www.ahima.org/fore/programs.html
Summary: To provide financial assistance to members of the American Health Information Management Association (AHIMA) who are interested in pursuing an undergraduate degree in health information administration or technology.
Eligibility: This program is open to AHIMA members who are enrolled in a health information administration or health information technology program accredited by the Commission on Accreditation of Allied Health Education Programs. Applicants must be pursuing a degree on at least a half-time basis and have a grade point average of 3.0 or higher. U.S. citizenship is required. Selection is based on grade point average and academic achievement, volunteer and work experience, commitment to the health information management profession, suitability to the health information management profession, quality and suitability of references provided, and clarity of application.
Financial data: Stipends range from $1,000 to $5,000.
Duration: 1 year; nonrenewable.
Additional information: This program includes the following named scholarships: the MedQuist-DVI-SpeechMachines Undergraduate Scholarships, the Julia LeBlond Memorial Undergraduate Scholarships, the Rita Finnegan Memorial Scholarship, the Annie Blaylock Memorial Scholarship, the MC Strategies, Inc. Scholarship, the Aspen Systems Corporation Scholarship, the Care Communications, Inc. Scholarship, and the Lucretia Spears Scholarship. Sponsors include MedQuist-DVI-SpeechMachines, St. Anthony Publishing/Medicode, Ingenix Companies (for the Julia LeBlond Memorial Scholarships), MC Strategies, Inc. (for the Rita Finnegan Memorial Scholarship), Aspen Systems Corporation, Care Communications, Inc., and the Ruth Wyeth Spears Trust (for the Lucretia Spears Scholarship).
Number awarded: Varies each year; recently, 30 of these scholarships were awarded.
Deadline: May of each year.

2017
FOUNDATION FOR NEONATAL RESEARCH AND EDUCATION SCHOLARSHIPS

Foundation for Neonatal Research and Education
East Holly Avenue, Box 56
Pitman, NJ 08071-0056
Phone: (856) 256-2343   Fax: (856) 589-7463
Summary: To provide financial assistance to neonatal nurses interested in pursuing additional education.
Eligibility: Applicants must be a professionally active neonatal nurse, engaged in a service, research, or educational role that contributes directly to the health care of neonates or to the neonatal nursing profession. They must be 1) an active

member of a professional association dedicated to enhancing neonatal nursing and the care of neonates, and 2) pursuing an advanced or an R.N. to B.S.N. degree.
Financial data: The stipends are $1,500 or $1,000.
Duration: 1 year.
Additional information: This program includes the Matthew Hester Scholarship.
Number awarded: The Matthew Hester Scholarship of $1,500 and several scholarships at $1,000 (the exact number depending on the availability of funds) are awarded each year.
Deadline: April of each year.

2018
FOUNDATION OF THE WALL AND CEILING INDUSTRY SCHOLARSHIPS

Summary: To provide financial assistance for college study in disciplines related to the wall and ceiling industry to employees of firms that are members of the Association of the Wall and Ceiling Industries-International (AWCI) and their dependents.
See Listing #1382.

2019
FRANCES A. MAYS SCHOLARSHIP AWARD

Summary: To recognize and reward outstanding students majoring in health, physical education, recreation, or dance in Virginia.
See Listing #1384.

2020
FRANCES SYLVIA ZVERINA SCHOLARSHIPS

Herb Society of America-Western Reserve Unit
c/o Priscilla Jones, Committee Chair
2640 Exeter Road
Cleveland Heights, OH 44118
Phone: (216) 932-6090   E-mail: cillers@hotmail.com
Web Site: www.herbsociety.org/scholar.htm
Summary: To provide financial assistance to college students interested in pursuing a career in a field related to horticulture.
Eligibility: This program is open to students who have completed their sophomore or junior year of college (or the senior year of a 5-year undergraduate program). Applicants may be residents of any state attending an accredited college or university anywhere in the United States. They must be planning a career in horticulture or a related field, including horticultural therapy. U.S. citizenship is required. Preference is given to applicants whose horticultural career goals involve teaching or research or work in the public or nonprofit sector (such as public gardens, botanical gardens, parks, arboreta, city planning, or public education and awareness). Selection is based on an essay that includes a description of their interests, activities, and achievements; an account of their employment record on or off campus; a description of their career goals; and a discussion of their need for financial aid.
Financial data: The stipend is $5,000.
Duration: 1 year.
Number awarded: 3 each year.
Deadline: March of each year.

2021
FRANK D. VISCEGLIA MEMORIAL SCHOLARSHIP

Boy Scouts of America
Patriots' Path Council #358
Attn: Dennis Kohl, Scout Executive
12 Mount Pleasant Turnpike
Denville, NJ 07834
Phone: (973) 361-1800   Fax: (973) 361-1954
Summary: To provide financial assistance to Eagle Scouts in New Jersey who have the potential to directly impact the delicate balance between the economy and the environment.
Eligibility: This program is open to Eagle Scouts in New Jersey. Preference is given to Scouts 1) whose Eagle service projects are related to the environment and/or the economy and 2) whose career goals are in development-related fields and/or who intend to major in related fields. Applicants must have been accepted to, have applied for, or plan to attend an accredited 4-year college. Selection is based on Scouting record, other Scout activities, a description of the Eagle Scout project, and an essay of 250 words or less on the applicant's philosophy on the future of the world's environment.

Financial data: The stipend is $1,000.
Duration: 1 year.
Additional information: This program is underwritten by the Association for Commercial Real Estate, formerly the National Association of Industrial and Office Parks.
Number awarded: 1 each year.
Deadline: May of each year.

2022
FRANK WILLIAM AND DOROTHY GIVEN MILLER ASME AUXILIARY SCHOLARSHIPS

ASME International
Attn: Education Department
Three Park Avenue
New York, NY 10016-5990
Phone: (212) 591-8131   (800) THE-ASME
Fax: (212) 591-7143   E-mail: oluwanifiset@asme.org
Web Site: www.asme.org/educate/aid/scholar.htm
Summary: To provide financial assistance to undergraduate students who are members of the American Society of Mechanical Engineers (ASME).
Eligibility: This program is open to student members in good standing who are enrolled in an ABET-accredited mechanical engineering baccalaureate program. They must be U.S. citizens and at least sophomores when they apply. Interested students should submit an application form, a nomination from the applicant's department head, a recommendation from a faculty member, and an official transcript. Only 1 nomination may be submitted per department. Selection is based on character, integrity, leadership, scholastic ability, and potential contribution to the mechanical engineering profession.
Financial data: The stipend is $2,000.
Duration: 1 year.
Additional information: This program was established in 1993. Only study in the junior or senior year is supported. Requests for applications must be accompanied by a self-addressed stamped envelope.
Number awarded: 2 each year.
Deadline: March of each year.

2023
FRED M. YOUNG SR./SAE ENGINEERING SCHOLARSHIP

Society of Automotive Engineers
Attn: Educational Relations
400 Commonwealth Drive
Warrendale, PA 15096-0001
Phone: (724) 772-4047   Fax: (724) 776-0890
E-mail: connie@sae.org
Web Site: www.sae.org/students/youngsc.htm
Summary: To provide financial support for college to high school seniors interested in studying engineering.
Eligibility: This program is open to U.S. citizens who intend to earn an ABET-accredited degree in engineering. Applicants must be high school seniors with a grade point average of 3.75 or higher who rank in the 90th percentile in both mathematics and verbal on the ACT or SAT. Selection is based on high school transcripts; SAT or ACT scores; school-related extracurricular activities; non-school related activities; academic honors, civic honors, and awards; and a 250-word essay on the single experience that most strongly convinced them or confirmed their decision to pursue a career in engineering. Financial need is not considered.
Financial data: The stipend is $4,000, paid at the rate of $1,000 per year.
Duration: 4 years, provided the recipient maintains a GPA of 3.0 or higher.
Additional information: The Young Radiator Company established this scholarship in memory of the company's founder. Candidates must include a $5 processing fee with their applications.
Number awarded: 1 each year.
Deadline: November of each year.

2024
FRESH COUNTRY FUND RAISING SCHOLARSHIP

Texas FFA Association
614 East 12th Street
Austin, TX 78701
Phone: (512) 480-8045   Fax: (512) 472-0555
E-mail: txffa@txaged.org   Web Site: www.txaged.org

Summary: To provide financial assistance for college to high school seniors in Texas who demonstrate outstanding personal qualities and involvement in FFA.

Eligibility: This program is open to high school seniors in Texas who are FFA members and have been members at least 2 of the 3 previous years. Applicants must be planning to major in college in a field related to the agricultural sciences, life sciences, or natural resources. They must have completed at least 5 semesters of instruction in agriculture and/or agribusiness during high school and scored at least 950 on the SAT or 20 on the ACT. U.S. citizenship and ranking in the top half of their graduating class are also required. Selection is based on academic achievement (16 points); SAT or ACT scores (14 points); agricultural science and career related instruction (10 points); FFA achievement (20 points), including the supervised agricultural experience (10 points); financial need (10 points); and performance during interviews regarding academics (10 points), FFA achievement (5 points), and financial need (10 points).

Financial data: The stipend is $1,000.

Duration: 1 year.

Additional information: Students may not apply for both 4-H and FFA scholarships.

Number awarded: 1 each year.

2025
FRIENDS OF OREGON STUDENTS PROGRAM

Oregon Student Assistance Commission
Attn: Private Awards Grant Department
1500 Valley River Drive, Suite 100
Eugene, OR 97401-2146
Phone: (541) 687-7395   (800) 452-8807, ext. 7395
Fax: (541) 687-7419   E-mail: awardinfo@mercury.osac.state.or.us
Web Site: www.osac.state.or.us

Summary: To provide financial assistance for undergraduate or graduate work to nontraditional students in Oregon.

Eligibility: This program is open to nontraditional (e.g., older, returning, single-parent) students in Oregon who are working and will continue to work at least 20 hours per week while attending college at least three-quarter time. Applicants must be interested in pursuing careers in the "helping professions" (e.g., health, education, social work, environmental, or public service areas). Preference is given to applicants who 1) can demonstrate a record of volunteer or work experience relevant to the chosen profession; 2) are a graduate of a public alternative Oregon high school, or a GED recipient, or transferring from an Oregon community college to a 4-year college or university; and 3) have a cumulative grade point average of 2.5 or higher during the past 3 quarters of study. As part of the selection process, applicants must provide essays and letters of reference on how they balance school, work, and personal life as well as their experiences in overcoming obstacles.

Financial data: Stipends range from $500 to $2,500 per year.

Duration: 1 year; may be renewed.

Additional information: Funding for this program is provided by the HF Fund, P.O. Box 55187, Portland, OR 97238, (503) 234-0259, E-mail: foosf@hffund.org.

Number awarded: Varies each year.

Deadline: February of each year.

2026
FRSA SCHOLARSHIP PROGRAM

Florida Roofing, Sheet Metal and Air Conditioning Contractors Association
Attn: FRSA Educational and Research Foundation
P.O. Box 4850
Winter Park, FL 32793
Phone: (407) 671-3772, ext. 123   Fax: (407) 679-0010
E-mail: frsa@floridaroof.com
Web Site: www.floridaroof.com

Summary: To provide financial assistance for college to students in Florida interested in pursuing construction-related careers.

Eligibility: This program is open to residents of Florida who are attending or planning to attend a college or university. Selection is based on academic and personal achievements with priority given to applicants pursuing construction-related careers.

Financial data: Stipends are awarded.

Duration: 1 year.

Additional information: The Florida Roofing, Sheet Metal and Air Conditioning Contractors Association (FRSA) established the FRSA Foundation in 1982.

Number awarded: 1 or more each year.

Deadline: March of each year.

2027
FSFSA UPPER DIVISION SCHOLARSHIP

Florida School Food Service Association
Attn: Administrative Assistant
124 Salem Court
Tallahassee, FL 32301
Phone: (850) 878-1832   Fax: (850) 656-0149
E-mail: admin@fsfsa.org
Web Site: www.fsfsa.org

Summary: To enable members of the Florida School Food Service Association (FSFSA) who have completed their sophomore year in college to major in food and nutrition or a related field.

Eligibility: Applicants must be current FSFSA members as well as members of the American School Food Service Association; have worked for at least the past 2 years as a permanent school food service employee in Florida; have received an associate degree or completed their sophomore year in college; be majoring in food, nutrition, or a related subject; and have a grade point average of 2.0 or higher. They must submit at least 4 letters of recommendation and a 1-page letter explaining why they have selected school food service as a profession, their professional goals, and why they feel they deserve the scholarship. Financial need is not considered in the selection process.

Financial data: The stipend is $1,000.

Duration: 1 semester; recipients may reapply.

Additional information: No student can receive more than 2 of these scholarships.

Number awarded: Several each year.

2028
FTE UNDERGRADUATE SCHOLARSHIP

Foundation for Technology Education
1914 Association Drive, Suite 201
Reston, VA 20191-1539
Phone: (703) 860-2100   Fax: (703) 860-0353
E-mail: iteaordr@iris.org
Web Site: www.iteawww.org

Summary: To provide financial support to undergraduate members of the International Technology Education Association (ITEA) who are majoring in technology education teacher preparation.

Eligibility: Applicants must be members of the association (membership may be enclosed with the scholarship application), in college but not yet seniors, majoring in technology education teacher preparation with a grade point average of 2.5 or more, and enrolled full time. Selection is based on interest in teaching, academic ability, and faculty recommendations.

Financial data: The scholarship is $1,000. Funds are provided directly to the recipient.

Duration: The scholarship is awarded annually.

Additional information: The Foundation for Technology Education (FTE) is affiliated with the ITEA.

Number awarded: 1 or more each year.

Deadline: November of each year.

2029
FUELS AND COMBUSTION TECHNOLOGIES DIVISION STUDENT BEST PAPER AWARD

ASME International
Attn: Fuels and Combustion Technologies Division
Three Park Avenue
New York, NY 10016-5990
Phone: (212) 591-7722   (800) THE-ASME
Fax: (212) 591-7674   E-mail: infocentral@asme.org
Web Site: www.asme.org/divisions/fact/Student_Papers.htm

Summary: To recognize and reward outstanding student papers on fuel technology.

Eligibility: This competition is open to both undergraduate and graduate students; graduate students may not have completed their thesis. Applicants must prepare a paper on an aspect of fuel, combustion, and combustion technology. Examples of acceptable topics include, but are not limited to, furnaces, combustors, pollution control, experimental research, mathematical modeling, combustion of fuels, waste and/or alternative fuels, and development of new diagnostics for conducting fuel and combustion experiments. Review and survey papers and papers in the area of internal combustion engines are not acceptable. Applicants first submit a 200-word abstract; based on those abstracts, finalists are

invited to submit full papers. Selection of the best paper is based on originality of the technical work described, significance of the technical work and paper, thoroughness of approach and presentation, organization of the paper, logic of approach, clarity of expression, and other pertinent factors.

Financial data: The author of the best paper receives a $1,000 honorarium, a certificate of merit, and a 1-year membership in ASME International.

Duration: The competition is held annually.

Additional information: Further information is also available from David G. Lilley, Route 1, Box 151, Stillwater, OK 74074, (405) 744-5897, Fax: (405) 744-7873, E-mail: lilley@ceat.okstate.edu.

Number awarded: 1 each year.

Deadline: Abstracts must be submitted by mid-October of each year. Full papers are due in early January.

2030
FULFILLING THE LEGACY SCHOLARSHIPS

National Society of Black Engineers
Attn: Programs Manager
1454 Duke Street
Alexandria, VA 22314
Phone: (703) 549-2207, ext. 204   Fax: (703) 683-5312
E-mail: scholarships@nsbe.org
Web Site: www.nsbe.org

Summary: To provide financial assistance to members of the National Society of Black Engineers (NSBE) who are majoring in science or engineering.

Eligibility: This program is open to members of the society who are undergraduate or graduate students majoring in science or engineering. Selection is based on an essay; academic achievement; service to the society at the local, regional, and/or national level; and other professional, campus, and community activities.

Financial data: The stipend depends on the availability of funds.

Duration: 1 year; may be renewed.

Number awarded: Varies each year, depending on the availability of funds.

Deadline: November of each year; freshmen and first-year graduate students have until January to apply.

2031
THE FUTURE OF MAINE'S ENVIRONMENT ESSAY CONTEST

Forestry Ecology Network
Attn: Dorothy Carter
P.O. Box 2118
Augusta, ME 04338
Phone: (207) 628-6404   Fax: (207) 628-5741
E-mail: fen@powerlink.net
Web Site: www.powerlink.net/fen

Summary: To recognize and reward high school seniors in Maine who write outstanding essays on Maine's environment.

Eligibility: This competition is open to seniors at high schools in Maine. Applicants must submit essays of 1,000 to 2,000 words on a topic relating to the future of Maine's environment. Essays are judged on their understanding of ecological interrelationships and originality in analysis, or in providing novel solutions to environmental problems or conceptions of the future for the Maine environment.

Financial data: The prize is a $2,000 college scholarship.

Duration: The competition is held annually.

Additional information: This competition was first held in 2001.

Number awarded: 1 each year.

Deadline: July of each year.

2032
F.W. "BEICH" BEICHLEY SCHOLARSHIP

ASME International
Attn: Education Department
Three Park Avenue
New York, NY 10016-5990
Phone: (212) 591-8131   (800) THE-ASME
Fax: (212) 591-7143   E-mail: oluwanifiset@asme.org
Web Site: www.asme.org/educate/aid/scholar.htm

Summary: To provide financial assistance to undergraduate students who are members of the American Society of Mechanical Engineers (ASME).

Eligibility: This program is open to student members in good standing who are enrolled in an ABET-accredited mechanical engineering or mechanical engineering technology baccalaureate program. They must be at least sophomores when they apply. Interested students should submit an application form, a nomination from the applicant's department head, a recommendation from a faculty member, and an official transcript. Only 1 nomination may be submitted per department. Selection is based on leadership, scholastic ability, potential contribution to the mechanical engineering profession, and financial need.

Financial data: The stipend is $2,000.

Duration: 1 year.

Additional information: This program was established in 1996. Only study in the junior or senior year is supported. Requests for applications must be accompanied by a self-addressed stamped envelope.

Number awarded: 1 each year.

Deadline: March of each year.

2033
GABRIEL E. TORRE MEMORIAL SCHOLARSHIPS FOR NON-R.N.S

American Nephrology Nurses' Association
Attn: ANNA Foundation
East Holly Avenue, Box 56
Pitman, NJ 08071-0056
Phone: (856) 256-2320   (877) 527-0787
Fax: (856) 589-7463   E-mail: annafoundation@hotmail.com
Web Site: www.annanurse.org

Summary: To provide financial assistance to members of the American Nephrology Nurses' Association (ANNA) who are interested in pursuing a baccalaureate degree.

Eligibility: Applicants must be associate members of the association, have been members for at least 2 years, and provide written documentation of their career and educational goals that includes 1) the name of the institution, 2) how the baccalaureate degree will apply to nephrology nursing practice, and 3) the projected date of graduation.

Financial data: The stipend is $1,000 per year.

Duration: 1 year.

Additional information: Information is also available from Cynthia Frazier, Awards Chairperson, 7344 Pine Tree Lane, Fairfield, AL 35064, (205) 933-8101, ext. 6514, E-mail: cdf44@aol.com.

Number awarded: 3 each year.

Deadline: October of each year.

2034
GAIL RICHARDSON SCHOLARSHIP

Vermont Student Assistance Corporation
Champlain Mill
P.O. Box 2000
Winooski, VT 05404-2601
Phone: (802) 655-9602   (800) 642-3177
Fax: (802) 654-3765   TDD: (802) 654-3766
Phone: TDD: (800) 281-3341 (within VT)   E-mail: info@vsac.org
Web Site: www.vsac.org

Summary: To provide financial assistance to residents of Vermont who are interested in majoring in a veterinary field in college.

Eligibility: This program is open to residents of Vermont who are graduating high school seniors, high school graduates, or GED recipients. Applicants must be interested in attending an accredited postsecondary institution to pursue a degree in veterinary medicine, veterinary technology, animal science, or a related field. Selection is based on academic achievement (grade point average of 2.5 or higher), required essays, letters of recommendation, and financial need.

Financial data: The stipend is $1,000 per year.

Duration: 1 year; may be renewed up to 3 additional years.

Additional information: The Vermont Student Assistance Corporation Board of Directors established this scholarship in 2001 to honor a former member.

Number awarded: 1 each year.

Deadline: April of each year.

2035
GARDEN CLUB OF OHIO SCHOLARSHIP

Garden Club of Ohio
c/o Ree Ponstingl, Scholarship Committee Chair
3349 Fairhill Drive
Rocky River, OH 44116-4212
Phone: (440) 333-5252
Summary: To provide financial assistance to Ohio residents who are majoring in horticulture or related fields in college.
Eligibility: This program is open to residents of Ohio who are 1) first-year students at a 2-year institution or 2) college juniors, college seniors, or graduate students. Applicants must have at least a 3.0 grade point average and be majoring in 1 of the following; horticulture, floriculture, landscape architecture, botany, agronomy, forestry, conservation, plant pathology, environmental control, city planning, or an allied subject. To apply, students must submit a completed application form, a transcript, a completed financial aid form, a personal statement of financial need and career goals, a list of extracurricular activities, 3 letters of recommendation, and a recent photograph.
Financial data: Stipends are generally $1,000 or more per year. Recently, a total of $34,000 was distributed.
Duration: 1 year.
Additional information: Recipients may attend school in any state.
Number awarded: Varies each year; recently, 24 were awarded.
Deadline: January of each year.

2036
GARLAND DUNCAN SCHOLARSHIPS

ASME International
Attn: Education Department
Three Park Avenue
New York, NY 10016-5990
Phone: (212) 591-8131   (800) THE-ASME
Fax: (212) 591-7143   E-mail: oluwanifiset@asme.org
Web Site: www.asme.org/educate/aid/scholar.htm
Summary: To provide financial assistance to undergraduate students who are members of the American Society of Mechanical Engineers (ASME).
Eligibility: This program is open to student members in good standing who are enrolled in an ABET-accredited mechanical engineering baccalaureate program. They must be at least sophomores when they apply. Interested students should submit an application form, a nomination from the applicant's department head, a recommendation from a faculty member, and an official transcript. Only 1 nomination may be submitted per department. Selection is based on character, integrity, leadership, scholastic ability, potential contribution to the mechanical engineering profession, and financial need.
Financial data: The stipend is $3,000.
Duration: 1 year.
Additional information: This program was established in 1993. Only study in the junior or senior year is supported. Requests for applications must be accompanied by a self-addressed stamped envelope.
Number awarded: 3 each year.
Deadline: March of each year.

2037
GARMIN SCHOLARSHIP

Aircraft Electronics Association
Attn: Educational Foundation
4217 South Hocker Drive
Independence, MO 64055-4723
Phone: (816) 373-6565   Fax: (816) 478-3100
E-mail: info@aea.net
Web Site: www.aea.net
Summary: To provide financial assistance to students preparing for a career in avionics or aircraft repair.
Eligibility: This program is open to high school seniors and currently-enrolled college students who are attending (or planning to attend) an accredited postsecondary institution in an avionics or aircraft repair program.
Financial data: The stipend is $2,000.
Duration: 1 year.
Number awarded: 1 each year.
Deadline: February of each year.

2038
GCFM HORTICULTURE SCHOLARSHIP

Summary: To provide financial assistance to Maine residents who are studying a garden-related field in college.
See Listing #1389.

2039
GCSAA ESSAY CONTEST

Golf Course Superintendents Association of America
Attn: Scholarship Coordinator
1421 Research Park Drive
Lawrence, KS 66049-3859
Phone: (785) 832-3678   (800) 472-7878, ext. 678
E-mail: psmith@gcsaa.org   Web Site: www.gcsaa.org
Summary: To recognize and reward outstanding undergraduate and graduate essays written on golf course management by members of the Golf Course Superintendents Association of America (GCSAA).
Eligibility: This contest is open to undergraduate and graduate students working on a degree in turfgrass science, agronomy, or another field related to golf course management. The essay should focus on golf course management and be from 7 to 12 pages in length. References and/or a bibliography must be included. Essays should be original, compelling, well organized, readable, persuasive, and creative. Technical accuracy, composition skills (spelling, grammar, etc.), and the student's adherence to the contest rules are considered in the selection process. Participants must be members of the association.
Financial data: First prize is $2,000, second prize is $1,500, and third prize is $1,000.
Duration: The competition is held annually.
Additional information: Winning entries may be published or excerpted in 1 of the magazines published by the sponsoring organization.
Number awarded: 3 each year.
Deadline: March of each year.

2040
GCSAA SCHOLARS PROGRAM

Golf Course Superintendents Association of America
Attn: Scholarship Coordinator
1421 Research Park Drive
Lawrence, KS 66049-3859
Phone: (785) 832-3678   (800) 472-7878, ext. 678
E-mail: psmith@gcsaa.org
Web Site: www.gcsaa.org
Summary: To provide financial assistance to student members of the Golf Course Superintendents Association of America (GCSAA) who are preparing for a career in golf management.
Eligibility: Eligible to apply for this program are members of the association who are planning careers as golf course superintendents. Applicants must have completed at least 1 year of full-time study in a recognized undergraduate program with a major related to golf/turf management. Selection is based on academic skill, potential to become a leading professional, employment history, extracurricular activities, and letters of recommendation. Financial need is not considered.
Financial data: Stipends range from $500 to $3,500. The highest ranking recipient is designated the Mendenhall Award Winner and receives a $3,500 scholarship; the second and third highest ranking recipients are designated as recipients of the Allan MacCurrach Scholarships and receive $2,500 scholarships. Other GCSAA Scholars receive awards that range from $1,500 to $2,500, and GCSAA Merit Awards are $500.
Duration: 1 year.
Number awarded: Up to 20 each year, including 1 Mendenhall Award Winner, 2 Allan MacCurrach Scholarships, up to 7 other GCSAA Scholars, and up to 10 GCSAA Merit Award winners.
Deadline: May of each year.

2041
GENERAL ELECTRIC AFRICAN AMERICAN FORUM SCHOLARSHIP

National Society of Black Engineers
Attn: Programs Manager
1454 Duke Street
Alexandria, VA 22314
Phone: (703) 549-2207, ext. 204   Fax: (703) 683-5312
E-mail: scholarships@nsbe.org   Web Site: www.nsbe.org

Summary: To provide financial assistance to members of the National Society of Black Engineers (NSBE) who are majoring in business or engineering.

Eligibility: This program is open to members of the society who are undergraduate students majoring in a program offered by a school of business or engineering. Applicants must have completed at least 12 credit hours in their major or school of concentration by their sophomore year and have a grade point average of 3.2 or higher. As part of the application process, they must answer a questionnaire on why they should be selected to receive this scholarship, how they plan to contribute to the mission of NSBE, what NSBE means to them, and their goals for the future and how NSBE membership will help them achieve their goals. Selection is based on that questionnaire, academic achievement, service to NSBE, and other professional, campus, and community activities.

Financial data: The stipend is $2,500. Travel, hotel accommodations, and registration to the national convention are also provided.

Duration: 1 year.

Additional information: This program is supported by General Electric employees with matching contributions from the GE Foundation.

Number awarded: 1 or more each year.

Deadline: November of each year.

2042
GENERAL ELECTRIC FUND SCHOLARSHIPS

Society of Women Engineers
230 East Ohio Street, Suite 400
Chicago, IL 60611-3265
Phone: (312) 596-5223   Fax: (312) 644-8557
E-mail: hq@swe.org
Web Site: www.swe.org

Summary: To provide financial assistance to outstanding freshmen women majoring in engineering.

Eligibility: Incoming female freshmen who are interested in majoring in engineering at an accredited school, college, or university are eligible to apply. U.S. citizenship is required. Selection is based on merit.

Financial data: The scholarship is $1,000 per year. Also provided is $500 for each recipient to attend the annual convention and/or to support her local section.

Duration: 1 year; renewable for 3 additional years with continued academic achievement.

Additional information: This program was established in 1975.

Number awarded: 3 each year.

Deadline: May of each year.

2043
GENERAL ELECTRIC FUND/LEAGUE OF UNITED LATIN AMERICAN CITIZENS SCHOLARSHIPS

League of United Latin American Citizens
Attn: LULAC National Education Service Centers
2000 L Street, N.W., Suite 610
Washington, DC 20036
Phone: (202) 835-9646   E-mail: LNESCAward@aol.com
Web Site: www.lulac.org/Programs/Scholar.html

Summary: To provide financial assistance to Latino students who are studying engineering or business in college.

Eligibility: Eligible to apply are Latino students who will be enrolled as college sophomores pursuing full-time studies in a program leading to a baccalaureate degree in engineering or business at colleges or universities in the United States approved by the League of United Latin American Citizens (LULAC) and General Electric. They must have a grade point average of 3.25 or better and be U.S. citizens or legal residents. Selection is based on academic performance, likelihood of pursuing a career in business or engineering, performance in business or engineering subjects, writing ability, extracurricular activities, and community involvement.

Financial data: The stipends are $5,000 per year. The funds are to be used to pay for tuition, required fees, room and board, and required educational materials and books. The funds are sent directly to the college or university and deposited in the scholarship recipient's name.

Duration: 1 year; may be renewed if the recipient maintains at least a 3.0 grade point average.

Additional information: Funding for this program is provided by the General Electric Fund. All requests for applications or information must include a self-addressed stamped envelope.

Number awarded: 2 each year.

Deadline: June of each year.

2044
GENERAL EMMETT PAIGE SCHOLARSHIPS

Armed Forces Communications and Electronics Association
Attn: Educational Foundation
4400 Fair Lakes Court
Fairfax, VA 22033-3899
Phone: (703) 631-6147   (800) 336-4583, ext. 6147
Fax: (703) 631-4693   E-mail: edfoundation@afcea.org
Web Site: www.afcea.org

Summary: To provide funding to veterans and military personnel or their family members who are majoring in science in college.

Eligibility: This program is open to veterans or persons on active duty in the uniformed military services and to their spouses or dependents who are currently enrolled in an accredited 4-year degree-granting institution in the United States. Graduating high school seniors are not eligible, but veterans entering college as freshmen may apply. Spouses or dependents must be sophomores or juniors. Applicants must be U.S. citizens, be of good moral character, have demonstrated academic excellence, be motivated to complete a college education, and be working toward a degree in aerospace engineering, electrical engineering, electronics, mathematics, physics, computer science, or computer engineering with a grade point average of 3.4 or higher. They must provide a copy of Discharge Form DD214, Certificate of Service, or facsimile of their current Department of Defense or Coast Guard Identification Card.

Financial data: The stipend is $2,000.

Duration: 1 year; may be renewed.

Additional information: Requests for applications must be accompanied by a self-addressed stamped envelope.

Number awarded: 1 or more each year.

Deadline: February of each year.

2045
GENERAL JOHN A. WICKHAM SCHOLARSHIPS

Armed Forces Communications and Electronics Association
Attn: Educational Foundation
4400 Fair Lakes Court
Fairfax, VA 22033-3899
Phone: (703) 631-6149   (800) 336-4583, ext. 6149
Fax: (703) 631-4693   E-mail: scholarship@afcea.org
Web Site: www.afcea.org

Summary: To provide scholarships to deserving college students who are working on a degree in engineering or the sciences.

Eligibility: This program is open to full-time students entering their junior or senior year at an accredited degree-granting 4-year college or university in the United States. Applicants must be U.S. citizens working toward a degree in engineering (aerospace, computer, or electrical), electronics, mathematics, physics, or computer science with a grade point average of 3.5 or higher. They must be able to demonstrate academic achievement, patriotism, and potential to contribute to the American work force.

Financial data: The stipend is $2,000.

Duration: 1 year; may be renewed.

Additional information: Requests for applications must be accompanied by a self-addressed stamped envelope.

Number awarded: 1 or more each year.

Deadline: April of each year.

2046
GENERAL MOTORS FOUNDATION UNDERGRADUATE SCHOLARSHIPS

Society of Women Engineers
230 East Ohio Street, Suite 400
Chicago, IL 60611-3265
Phone: (312) 596-5223   Fax: (312) 644-8557
E-mail: hq@swe.org
Web Site: www.swe.org

Summary: To provide financial assistance to undergraduate women majoring in engineering.

Eligibility: This program is open to women who are entering their junior year and are majoring in 1 of the following engineering disciplines: mechanical, electrical, chemical, industrial, materials, automotive, or manufacturing. They must have at least a 3.5 grade point average and hold a position of responsibility in a student organization. Selection is based on merit.

Financial data: The stipend is $1,000. Also provided is a $500 travel grant for the recipient to attend the society's national convention and student conference.
Duration: 1 year; may be renewed for 1 additional year.
Additional information: This program was established in 1991.
Number awarded: 2 each year.
Deadline: January of each year.

2047
GENERAL MOTORS/LEAGUE OF UNITED LATIN AMERICAN CITIZENS SCHOLARSHIPS

League of United Latin American Citizens
Attn: LULAC National Education Service Centers
2000 L Street, N.W., Suite 610
Washington, DC 20036
Phone: (202) 835-9646   E-mail: LNESCAward@aol.com
Web Site: www.lulac.org/Programs/Scholar.html
Summary: To encourage outstanding Latino students to complete their college education in engineering.
Eligibility: Eligible to apply are Latino students who are enrolled or planning to enroll as full-time students in a program leading to a baccalaureate degree in engineering at colleges or universities in the United States approved by the League of United Latin American Citizens (LULAC) and General Motors. Continuing college students must have a grade point average of 3.25 or better; entering college freshmen must have a high school grade point average of at least 3.5 and either an ACT composite score of at least 23 or an SAT combined score of at least 970. Selection is based on academic performance, likelihood of pursuing a career in engineering, performance in engineering-related subjects, writing ability, extracurricular activities, and community involvement.
Financial data: The stipends are $2,000 per year. The funds are to be used to pay for tuition, required fees, room and board, and required educational materials and books. The funds are sent directly to the college or university and deposited in the scholarship recipient's name.
Duration: 1 year.
Additional information: All requests for applications or information must include a self-addressed stamped envelope.
Number awarded: 20 each year.
Deadline: June of each year.

2048
GENEVIEVE CHRISTEN DISTINGUISHED UNDERGRADUATE STUDENT AWARD

American Dairy Science Association
Attn: Award Coordinator
1111 North Dunlap Avenue
Savoy, IL 61874
Phone: (217) 356-3192   Fax: (217) 398-4119
E-mail: adsa@assochq.org
Web Site: www.adsa.org/awards
Summary: To recognize and reward undergraduate students who have participated in dairy science activities.
Eligibility: This program is open to undergraduate students nominated by a faculty member at their institution; only 1 student may be nominated by a college or university each year. The nominator must be a member of the American Dairy Science Association (ADSA). Nominees must be residents of Canada, Mexico, or the United States. Selection is based on demonstrated leadership ability, academic achievement, involvement in the dairy industry, and participation in ADSA Student Affiliate Division and local club activities.
Financial data: The award consists of a plaque and a $1,000 honorarium.
Duration: The award is presented annually.
Number awarded: 1 each year.
Deadline: Nominations must be submitted by December of each year.

2049
GEOPHYSICAL SOCIETY OF ALASKA SCHOLARSHIP

Society of Exploration Geophysicists
Attn: SEG Foundation
P.O. Box 702740
Tulsa, OK 74170-2740
Phone: (918) 497-5530   Fax: (918) 497-5557
E-mail: slobianco@seg.org
Web Site: www.seg.org

Summary: To provide financial assistance to undergraduate and graduate students who are interested in studying geophysics and are residents of or students in Alaska.
Eligibility: Applicants must be 1) high school students planning to enter college in the fall and to major in geophysics; 2) undergraduate college students majoring in geophysics whose grades are above average; or 3) graduate students whose studies are directed toward a career in exploration geophysics in operations, teaching, or research. All applicants must have an interest in and aptitude for physics, mathematics, and geology. Financial need is considered, but the competence of the student as indicated by the application is given first consideration. Applicants must be residents of Alaska or studying at a college or university in the state.
Financial data: The stipend ranges from $1,000 to $3,000 per year.
Duration: 1 academic year; may be renewable, based on scholastic standing, availability of funds, and continuance of a course of study leading to a career in exploration geophysics.
Number awarded: 1 each year.
Deadline: February of each year.

2050
GEOPHYSICAL SOCIETY OF HOUSTON SCHOLARSHIP

Society of Exploration Geophysicists
Attn: SEG Foundation
P.O. Box 702740
Tulsa, OK 74170-2740
Phone: (918) 497-5530   Fax: (918) 497-5557
E-mail: slobianco@seg.org   Web Site: www.seg.org
Summary: To provide financial assistance to undergraduate and graduate students who are interested in studying geophysics in Texas.
Eligibility: Applicants must be 1) high school students planning to enter college in the fall and to major in geophysics; 2) undergraduate college students majoring in geophysics whose grades are above average; or 3) graduate students whose studies are directed toward a career in exploration geophysics in operations, teaching, or research. All applicants must have an interest in and aptitude for physics, mathematics, and geology. Financial need is considered, but the competence of the student as indicated by the application is given first consideration. Applicants must be studying or planning to study at a college or university in Houston or elsewhere in Texas.
Financial data: The stipend ranges from $1,000 to $3,000 per year.
Duration: 1 academic year; may be renewable, based on scholastic standing, availability of funds, and continuance of a course of study leading to a career in exploration geophysics.
Number awarded: 1 each year.
Deadline: February of each year.

2051
GEOPHYSICAL SOCIETY OF HOUSTON/CARLTON-FARREN SCHOLARSHIP

Society of Exploration Geophysicists
Attn: SEG Foundation
P.O. Box 702740
Tulsa, OK 74170-2740
Phone: (918) 497-5530   Fax: (918) 497-5557
E-mail: slobianco@seg.org   Web Site: www.seg.org
Summary: To provide financial assistance to undergraduate and graduate students who are interested in studying geophysics in Texas.
Eligibility: Applicants must be 1) high school students planning to enter college in the fall and to major in geophysics; 2) undergraduate college students majoring in geophysics whose grades are above average; or 3) graduate students whose studies are directed toward a career in exploration geophysics in operations, teaching, or research. All applicants must have an interest in and aptitude for physics, mathematics, and geology. Financial need is considered, but the competence of the student as indicated by the application is given first consideration. Applicants must be studying or planning to study at a college or university in Houston or elsewhere in Texas.
Financial data: The stipend ranges from $5,000 to $6,000 per year.
Duration: 1 academic year; may be renewable, based on scholastic standing, availability of funds, and continuance of a course of study leading to a career in exploration geophysics.
Number awarded: 1 each year.
Deadline: February of each year.

2052
GEOPHYSICAL SOCIETY OF OKLAHOMA CITY SCHOLARSHIP

Society of Exploration Geophysicists
Attn: SEG Foundation
P.O. Box 702740
Tulsa, OK 74170-2740
Phone: (918) 497-5530   Fax: (918) 497-5557
E-mail: slobianco@seg.org
Web Site: www.seg.org
Summary: To provide financial assistance to undergraduate and graduate students who are interested in studying geophysics in Oklahoma.
Eligibility: Applicants must be 1) high school students planning to enter college in the fall and to major in geophysics; 2) undergraduate college students majoring in geophysics whose grades are above average; or 3) graduate students whose studies are directed toward a career in exploration geophysics in operations, teaching, or research. All applicants must have an interest in and aptitude for physics, mathematics, and geology. Financial need is considered, but the competence of the student as indicated by the application is given first consideration. Applicants must be studying or planning to study at a college or university in Oklahoma.
Financial data: Stipends range from $1,000 to $3,000 per year.
Duration: 1 academic year; may be renewable, based on scholastic standing, availability of funds, and continuance of a course of study leading to a career in exploration geophysics.
Number awarded: 1 each year.
Deadline: February of each year.

2053
GEOPHYSICAL SOCIETY OF TULSA SCHOLARSHIP

Society of Exploration Geophysicists
Attn: SEG Foundation
P.O. Box 702740
Tulsa, OK 74170-2740
Phone: (918) 497-5530   Fax: (918) 497-5557
E-mail: slobianco@seg.org
Web Site: www.seg.org
Summary: To provide financial assistance to undergraduate and graduate students who are interested in studying geophysics in Oklahoma.
Eligibility: Applicants must be 1) high school students planning to enter college in the fall and to major in geophysics; 2) undergraduate college students majoring in geophysics whose grades are above average; or 3) graduate students whose studies are directed toward a career in exploration geophysics in operations, teaching, or research. All applicants must have an interest in and aptitude for physics, mathematics, and geology. Financial need is considered, but the competence of the student as indicated by the application is given first consideration. Applicants must be Oklahoma residents or students at an Oklahoma college or university.
Financial data: Stipends range from $1,000 to $3,000 per year.
Duration: 1 academic year; may be renewable, based on scholastic standing, availability of funds, and continuance of a course of study leading to a career in exploration geophysics.
Number awarded: 1 each year.
Deadline: February of each year.

2054
GEORGE A. ROBERTS SCHOLARSHIPS

ASM International Foundation
Attn: Scholarship Program
9639 Kinsman Road
Materials Park, OH 44073-0002
Phone: (440) 338-5151   (800) 336-5152
Fax: (440) 338-4634   E-mail: crhayes@asminternational.org
Web Site: www.asminternational.org
Summary: To provide financial assistance to members of the American Society for Metals (ASM) who are interested in majoring in metallurgy and materials.
Eligibility: Applicants must be citizens of the United States, Canada, or Mexico; be enrolled at a college or university in those countries; be members of the society; have an intended or declared major in metallurgy or materials science and engineering (related science or engineering majors may be considered if the applicant demonstrates a strong academic emphasis and interest in materials science and engineering); and be entering their junior or senior year in college.

Selection is based on academic achievement; interest in metallurgy/materials (including knowledge of the field, activities, jobs, and potential for a related career); personal qualities (such as social values, maturity, motivation, goals, and citizenship); and financial need.
Financial data: The stipend is $6,000.
Duration: 1 year; recipients may reapply for 1 additional year.
Additional information: This scholarship was established in 1995 by Dr. George A. Roberts, past president of ASM and retired CEO of Teledyne.
Number awarded: 7 each year.
Deadline: April of each year.

2055
GEORGE COMSTOCK SCHOLARSHIP FUND

Connecticut Association of Optometrists
342 North Main Street
West Hartford, CT 06117
Phone: (860) 586-7508   Fax: (860) 586-7550
E-mail: info@cao.org
Web Site: www.cao.org
Summary: To provide financial assistance to undergraduate students from Connecticut who are enrolled in accredited colleges of optometry.
Eligibility: Applicants must be Connecticut residents enrolled in accredited colleges of optometry in the United States. Selection is based on scholarship, character, and financial need.
Financial data: The stipend ranges from $400 to $1,000 per year. The exact amount depends upon the recipient's scholastic performance and financial need.
Duration: 1 year; may be renewed.
Additional information: Information is also available from Robert L. Ross, O.D., 500 Post Road East, Suite 280, Westport, CT 06880, (203) 226-9426, Fax (203) 226-6230, E-mail: eyedoc@erols.com.
Number awarded: 6 to 8 each year.
Deadline: June of each year.

2056
GEORGE EAGLE MEMORIAL UNDERGRADUATE SCHOLARSHIP

Ohio Environmental Health Association
P.O. Box 234
Columbus, OH 43216-0234
Web Site: oeha.tripod.com/awards.htm
Summary: To provide financial assistance to Ohio residents who are in college and preparing for a career in environmental health in the state.
Eligibility: This program is open to undergraduate students who are interested in preparing for a career in environmental health in Ohio. They must be Ohio residents, enrolled in a program leading to an undergraduate degree in environmental health or a related field, have at least sophomore standing, and intend to become employed in environmental health in Ohio following graduation.
Financial data: The stipend is $2,000.
Duration: 1 year.
Additional information: Information is also available from Joe Ebel, Licking County Health Department, 675 Price Road, Newark, OH 43055, (740) 349-6535, Fax: (740) 349-6510, E-mail: jebel@lcounty.com.
Number awarded: 1 each year.
Deadline: February of each year.

2057
GEORGIA CATTLEMEN'S ASSOCIATION/WAX COMPANY SCHOLARSHIPS

Georgia Cattlemen's Association
P.O. Box 24510
Macon, GA 31212
Summary: To provide financial assistance to college students whose parents belong to the Georgia Cattlemen's Association and who are majoring in agriculture.
Eligibility: This program is open to students whose parents are members the Georgia Cattlemen's Association. They must be currently enrolled in a college of agriculture in Georgia. Selection is based on financial need, extracurricular activities, career goals, livestock background, other awards received, and work history.
Financial data: The stipend is $1,000.
Duration: 1 year.

Additional information: This program is funded by the Wax Company, LLC. Information is also available from the Georgia Beef Board, P.O. Box 24570, Macon, GA 31212. Telephone: (912) 474-1815.
Number awarded: 1 each year.
Deadline: October of each year.

2058
GEORGIA ENGINEERING FOUNDATION SCHOLARSHIPS

Georgia Engineering Foundation, Inc.
c/o INFORUM
250 Williams Street, Suite 2112
Atlanta, GA 30303
Phone: (404) 521-2324   Fax: (404) 521-0283
E-mail: gef@mindspring.com
Web Site: www.georgiaengineeringfnd.org
Summary: To provide financial assistance undergraduate and graduate students from Georgia who are entering an approved engineering program.
Eligibility: This program is open to residents of Georgia who are attending or accepted at an ABET-accredited engineering or engineering technology program in any state. Applications from incoming freshmen must include a high school transcript with final senior grades, SAT scores, 2 letters of recommendation, and a small photograph. Applications from college and graduate students must include a transcript of all college grades, 2 letters of recommendation, and a small photograph. U.S. citizenship is required. Selection is based on demonstrated competence in mathematics, science, and communications skills; interest in a career in engineering or engineering technology; and financial need.
Financial data: Stipends range from $500 to $5,000 per year.
Duration: 1 year.
Number awarded: Approximately 45 each year.
Deadline: August of each year.

2059
GEORGIA LEGION AUXILIARY PAST PRESIDENT PARLEY NURSING SCHOLARSHIP

American Legion Auxiliary
Attn: Department of Georgia
3035 Mt. Zion Road
Stockbridge, GA 30281-4101
Phone: (678) 289-8446
Summary: To provide financial assistance to descendants of veterans in Georgia who are interested in pursuing a career in nursing.
Eligibility: This program is open to George residents who are 1) interested in nursing education and 2) the descendants of veterans. Applicants must be sponsored by a local unit of the American Legion Auxiliary. Selection is based on a statement explaining why they want to become a nurse and why they need a scholarship, a transcript of all high school or college grades, and 4 letters of recommendation (1 from a high school principal or superintendent, 1 from the sponsoring American Legion Auxiliary local unit, and 2 from other responsible people).
Financial data: The amount of the award depends on the availability of funds.
Number awarded: Varies, depending upon funds available.
Deadline: May of each year.

2060
GERALD V. HENDERSON INDUSTRIAL MINERALS MEMORIAL SCHOLARSHIP

Society for Mining, Metallurgy, and Exploration, Inc.
Attn: Member Services
8307 Shaffer Parkway
P.O. Box 277002
Littleton, CO 80127-7002
Phone: (303) 973-9550   (800) 763-3132
Fax: (303) 973-3845   E-mail: sensenig@smenet.org
Web Site: www.smenet.org/education/students/sme_scholarships.cfm
Summary: To provide financial assistance to upper-division and graduate student members of the Society for Mining, Metallurgy, and Exploration (SME) who are majoring in fields that will prepare them for a career in industrial minerals.
Eligibility: Applicants must 1) be majoring in geology, minerals engineering, mining engineering, or mineral economics at a 4-year college or university, 2) have completed at least their sophomore year in college, and 3) be a student member of the society. They must be of good character, be of sound health, have demonstrated scholastic aptitude (a grade point average of 3.0 or higher), and be

able to demonstrate financial need. Candidates for these scholarships may be proposed by any of the following: mining and minerals companies; local sections of the society; state mining institutes; high school principals; industrial minerals associations; manufacturers of mining and processing equipment; minerals research organizations; or geology and mining engineering departments at colleges or universities. An interview may be required.
Financial data: A total of $2,000 is awarded each year.
Duration: 1 year.
Number awarded: 1 or 2 each year.
Deadline: October of each year.

2061
GIBSON-LAEMEL SCHOLARSHIP

Summary: To provide financial assistance to college juniors and seniors from Connecticut who are interested in pursuing a career in health, physical education, recreation, or dance.
See Listing #1395.

2062
GILLETTE-NATIONAL URBAN LEAGUE SCHOLARSHIP AND INTERN PROGRAM

National Urban League
Attn: Scholarship Coordinator
120 Wall Street
New York, NY 10005
Phone: (212) 558-5373   (888) 839-0467
Fax: (212) 344-8948   E-mail: info@nul.org
Web Site: www.nul.org
Summary: To provide financial assistance and summer internships to minority students who are interested in completing their college education in designated areas of business and engineering.
Eligibility: Eligible to apply are minority students who are pursuing full-time studies leading to a bachelor's degree at an accredited institution of higher learning. They must be juniors or third-year students at the time the scholarship award begins, rank within the top 25 percent of their class when the application is submitted, and be majoring in the areas of engineering, marketing, manufacturing operations, finance, human resource management, business administration, or related fields. Applicants must also demonstrate work experience in related fields, extracurricular activities, leadership skills, and volunteer work. Applications must be submitted to a local Urban League office. These applications are screened and sent to the appropriate National Urban League regional office. Each regional office may nominate up to 4 potential scholarship recipients who meet the competition criteria.
Financial data: The stipend is $5,000 per year. Funds are sent directly to the recipient's college or university; the school is custodian of the funds and disburses the money consistent with the purposes of the program.
Duration: 2 years.
Additional information: During the summer between the junior and senior years, scholarship recipients work as interns at 1 of the Gillette companies.
Number awarded: 5 each year.
Deadline: Applications must be submitted to local Urban League offices by January of each year.

2063
GIVAUDAN-ROURE CORPORATION SCHOLARSHIP

Institute of Food Technologists
Attn: Scholarship Department
221 North LaSalle Street, Suite 300
Chicago, IL 60601-1291
Phone: (312) 782-8424   Fax: (312) 782-8348
E-mail: info@ift.org   Web Site: www.ift.org
Summary: To provide financial assistance to undergraduates interested in studying food science or food technology.
Eligibility: Applicants must be currently enrolled as sophomores or juniors in a food science or food technology program at an educational institution in the United States or Canada; they must have an outstanding scholastic record and a well-rounded personality. Financial need is not considered in the selection process.
Financial data: The stipend is $1,000.
Duration: 1 year; recipients may reapply if they are members of the Institute of Food Technologists.

Additional information: Funding for this scholarship is provided by Givaudan-Roure Corporation. Correspondence and completed applications must be submitted to the department head of the educational institution the applicant is attending.

Number awarded: 1 each year.

Deadline: January of each year.

2064
GOLDEN KEY ENGINEERING ACHIEVEMENT AWARDS

Golden Key National Honor Society
1189 Ponce de Leon Avenue
Atlanta, GA 30306-4624
Phone: (404) 377-2400   (800) 377-2401
E-mail: mboone@goldenkey.gsu.edu   Web Site: goldenkey.gsu.edu

Summary: To recognize and reward undergraduate members of the Golden Key National Honor Society who submit outstanding essays, diagrams, or flow charts on a problem in the field of engineering.

Eligibility: Members of the society are invited to respond to a problem posed by an honorary member within the discipline of engineering. The response may be in the form of an essay, a diagram, a flow chart, or a combination of those. Recently, entrants were asked to explain how they could provide exact time positions for each car in a stock car race. Selection is based on the creativity and viability of the response.

Financial data: The winner receives $1,000, second place $750, and third place $500.

Duration: These awards are presented annually.

Additional information: This program began in 2001.

Number awarded: 3 each year.

Deadline: February of each year.

2065
GOLDEN KEY INFORMATION SYSTEMS ACHIEVEMENT AWARDS

Golden Key National Honor Society
1189 Ponce de Leon Avenue
Atlanta, GA 30306-4624
Phone: (404) 377-2400   (800) 377-2401
E-mail: mboone@goldenkey.gsu.edu   Web Site: goldenkey.gsu.edu

Summary: To recognize and reward undergraduate members of the Golden Key National Honor Society who submit outstanding essays or designs on a problem in the field of information systems.

Eligibility: Members of the society are invited to respond to a problem posed by an honorary member within the discipline of information systems. The response may be in the form of an essay or a design. Recently, entrants were asked to identify and describe the next steps of the computer evolution and the technological steps needed to achieve it successfully. Selection is based on the creativity and viability of the response.

Financial data: The winner receives $1,000, second place $750, and third place $500.

Duration: These awards are presented annually.

Additional information: This program began in 2001.

Number awarded: 3 each year.

Deadline: February of each year.

2066
GOODRICH AEROSPACE SCHOLARSHIP

Aircraft Electronics Association
Attn: Educational Foundation
4217 South Hocker Drive
Independence, MO 64055-4723
Phone: (816) 373-6565   Fax: (816) 478-3100
E-mail: info@aea.net   Web Site: www.aea.net

Summary: To provide financial assistance to students preparing for a career in avionics or aircraft repair.

Eligibility: This program is open to high school seniors and currently-enrolled college students who are attending (or planning to attend) an accredited postsecondary institution in an avionics or aircraft repair program.

Financial data: The stipend is $2,500.

Duration: 1 year.

Number awarded: 1 each year.

Deadline: February of each year.

2067
GRACE MURRAY HOPPER "TECHNOLOGY LEADERS OF TOMORROW" SCHOLARSHIP

Cobol Alliance
8515 Miralani Drive
San Diego, CA 92126
Phone: (858) 689-4434   Fax: (858) 689-4550
E-mail:mkring@acucorp.com
Web Site: www.cobolalliance.com

Summary: To provide financial assistance to female undergraduates working on a degree in computer science.

Eligibility: This program is open to women who are currently enrolled in college and working on a degree in computer science. Selection is based on an essay, the applicant's current grade point average, and 2 letters of recommendation.

Financial data: The stipend is $5,000. Funds are paid directly to the recipient's school.

Duration: 1 year.

Additional information: This program started in 2000. Each year, the funding comes from a different organization; in 2000, the funder was Acucorp, Inc.

Number awarded: 1 each year.

Deadline: May of each year.

2068
THE GREAT 100 SCHOLARSHIP PROGRAM

The Great 100, Inc.
P.O. Box 4875
Greensboro, NC 27404-4875
Phone: (800) 729-1975   E-mail: pfarrell@netpath-rc.net
Web Site: www.great100.org/Scholarship/scholarship.htm

Summary: To provide financial assistance to undergraduate and graduate students in North Carolina who are interested in working on a degree in nursing.

Eligibility: This program is open to students working on a nursing degree, licensed practical nurses who wish to pursue education to become registered nurses, and registered nurses who wish to pursue further education in nursing. Funds are available to support study for an associate degree in nursing, a diploma in nursing, a bachelor's degree in nursing, or a master's degree in nursing. Applicants must meet the following criteria: reside in North Carolina, attend a school full time in North Carolina, major in nursing, have earned at least a 3.0 grade point average, rank in the top 10 percent of their high school graduating class, and agree to work full time as a nurse in North Carolina for 2 years following graduation. Nontraditional applicants are encouraged. As part of the application process, students must complete the official application form, write a statement (300 words or less) about the activities and accomplishments that qualify them for the scholarship, provide 2 letters of recommendation, and submit a transcript for the past 2 academic years. Selection is based on scholastic achievement, potential for contributing to the nursing profession, participation in student and community activities, character, and geographic location.

Financial data: The stipend is $1,000.

Duration: 1 year.

Additional information: This program was established in 1989. Each year, the sponsor selects at random 4 or 5 institutions in North Carolina: 2 or 3 community colleges offering an associate degree in nursing and/or a diploma, 1 college offering a bachelor's degree, and 1 university offering a master's degree. The institutions select the scholarship recipients.

Number awarded: 4 or 5 each year: 1 at each of the participating institutions.

Deadline: May of each year.

2069
GREATER KANAWHA VALLEY MATH AND SCIENCE SCHOLARSHIP

Greater Kanawha Valley Foundation
Attn: Scholarship Coordinator
One Huntington Square, 16th Floor
900 Lee Street, East
P.O. Box 3041
Charleston, WV 25331-3041
Phone: (304) 346-3620   Fax: (304) 346-3640
E-mail: tgkvf@tgkvf.com
Web Site: www.tgkvf.com/scholarship.html

Summary: To provide financial assistance to residents of West Virginia who are pursuing a degree in a mathematics or science field.

Eligibility: This program is open to residents of West Virginia who are pursuing a full-time degree in mathematics, science (chemistry, physics, or biology), or engineering at a college or university anywhere in the country. Applicants must have at least a 2.5 grade point average and demonstrate good moral character. Financial need is considered in the selection process.

Financial data: The stipend is $1,000 per year.

Duration: 1 year; may be renewed.

Number awarded: 1 each year.

Deadline: February of each year.

2070
GROTTO/JOB'S DAUGHTERS SCHOLARSHIP

International Order of Job's Daughters
Supreme Guardian Council Headquarters
Attn: Executive Manager
233 West Sixth Street
Papillion, NE 68046-2177
Phone: (402) 592-7987   Fax: (402) 592-2177
E-mail: sgc@iojd.org
Web Site: www.iojd.org

Summary: To provide financial assistance for college to members of Job's Daughters who are pursuing a degree in dentistry.

Eligibility: This program is open to high school seniors and graduates; junior college, technical, and vocational students; college and university students; and graduate students. Applicants must be Job's Daughters in good standing in their Bethels; unmarried Majority Members under 30 years of age are also eligible. They must be pursuing a degree in dentistry, preferably with some training in the field of disabilities. Selection is based on scholastic standing, Job's Daughters activities, the applicant's self-help plan, recommendation by the Executive Bethel Guardian Council, faculty recommendations, achievements outside Job's Daughters, and financial need.

Financial data: The stipend is $1,500.

Duration: 1 year.

Additional information: Information is also available from the Education Scholarships Committee, c/o Elaine Davies, Chair, 9432 Asbury Circle, Westminster, CA 92683-6509, (714) 531-8384, E-mail: raydavies@earthlink.net.

Number awarded: 1 or more each year.

Deadline: April of each year.

2071
GROUND TEST TECHNICAL COMMITTEE STUDENT ENGINEERING CONTEST

American Institute of Aeronautics and Astronautics
Attn: Student Programs Director
1801 Alexander Bell Drive, Suite 500
Reston, VA 20191-4344
Phone: (703) 264-7536   (800) 639-AIAA
Fax: (703) 264-7551   E-mail: stephenb@aiaa.org
Web Site: www.aiaa.org

Summary: To recognize and reward outstanding designs prepared by undergraduate and graduate student members of the American Institute of Aeronautics and Astronautics (AIAA).

Eligibility: This program is open to junior and senior undergraduate and graduate students who are majoring in aerospace, aeronautical, and related engineering programs. Teams of 1 to 6 students may submit designs on topics of their own choosing as long as they contain a ground test theme and are approved by the evaluation committee. Entries can be an extramural project, part of a design or special projects course, or part or all of a graduate student thesis. Abstracts, up to 500 words, must describe the problem, relevance of the project, research approach, and potential outcome. The work must be primarily that of the students; contributions of others outside the team must be clearly indicated.

Financial data: First place is $1,000 and second place is $500. The members of the first-place team also receive up to $1,000 for travel to the AIAA Ground Test Conference.

Duration: The competition is held annually.

Additional information: Information is also available from Bonnie Johnson, Director of Aerodynamic Labs, Wichita State University/National Institute for Aviation Research, 1845 North Fairmount, Wichita, KS 67260-0093, (316) 978-3569, Fax: (316) 978-3521, E-mail: bonnie.johnson@wichita.edu.

Number awarded: 2 cash awards are presented each year.

Deadline: Letters of intent must be submitted by March of each year; final reports are due in May of each year.

2072
GTE FOUNDATION SCHOLARSHIPS

Society of Women Engineers
230 East Ohio Street, Suite 400
Chicago, IL 60611-3265
Phone: (312) 596-5223   Fax: (312) 644-8557
E-mail: hq@swe.org   Web Site: www.swe.org

Summary: To provide financial assistance to undergraduate women majoring in electrical engineering or computer science.

Eligibility: This program is open to entering sophomore or junior women who are majoring in electrical engineering, computer engineering, or computer science. Applicants must be attending an accredited school and have a grade point average of 3.5 or higher. Selection is based on merit.

Financial data: The scholarship is $1,000 per year.

Duration: 1 year.

Number awarded: 9 each year.

Deadline: January of each year.

2073
GUAM SOCIETY OF PROFESSIONAL ENGINEERS SCHOLARSHIP

Guam Society of Professional Engineers
c/o Julianne T. Duwel
P.O. Box 5419
Agana, Guam 96932
Phone: (671) 734-1435   Fax: (671) 734-1437
E-mail: jtd@kuentos.guam.net

Summary: To provide financial assistance to undergraduate students from Guam who are interested in majoring in engineering.

Eligibility: Eligible to apply for this support are 1) high school seniors in Guam who have been accepted into an engineering program at an accredited college or university and 2) college students from Guam already enrolled in a college engineering course. High school applicants must have at least a 3.5 grade point average; college applicants must have a 3.0 or higher grade point average.

Financial data: The stipend depends on the availability of funds.

Duration: 1 year.

Number awarded: 1 each year.

2074
GUILIANO MAZZETTI SCHOLARSHIP AWARDS

Society of Manufacturing Engineers
Attn: Education Foundation
One SME Drive
P.O. Box 930
Dearborn, MI 48121-0930
Phone: (313) 271-1500, ext. 1707   Fax: (313) 240-6095
E-mail: cortjoy@sme.org   Web Site: www.sme.org

Summary: To provide financial assistance to undergraduate students enrolled in a degree program in manufacturing engineering or manufacturing engineering technology.

Eligibility: This program is open to full-time undergraduate students enrolled in a manufacturing engineering or technology degree program at a college or university in North America. Applicants must have completed a minimum of 30 units in a manufacturing engineering or manufacturing engineering technology curriculum with a minimum grade point average of 3.0. Need is not considered in awarding scholarships (unless 2 or more applicants have equal qualifications).

Financial data: The stipend is $1,500.

Duration: 1 year.

Number awarded: 2 each year.

Deadline: January of each year.

2075
GUS ARCHIE MEMORIAL SCHOLARSHIPS

Society of Petroleum Engineers
Attn: Professional Development Manager
222 Palisades Creek Drive
P.O. Box 833836
Richardson, TX 75083-3836
Phone: (972) 952-9452   Fax: (972) 952-9435
E-mail: twhipple@spelink.spe.org   Web Site: www.spe.org

Summary: To provide financial assistance to high school seniors interested in preparing for a career in petroleum engineering.

Eligibility: This program is open to graduating high school seniors who have a score of at least 1200 on the SAT or 27 on the ACT and are planning to enroll in a petroleum engineering program at an accredited college or university. Selection is based on academic record, career plans, and financial need.

Financial data: The stipend is $5,000 per year.

Duration: 1 year; may be renewed for up to 3 additional years, provided the recipient maintains full-time enrollment and a grade point average of 3.0 or higher both cumulatively and for the current semester.

Number awarded: 1 or more each year.

Deadline: April of each year.

2076
GUY SHULL MEMORIAL SCHOLARSHIP

Oklahoma Cattlemen's Association
Attn: Kami Krebs
P.O. Box 82395
Oklahoma City, OK 73148
Phone: (405) 235-4391   Fax: (405) 235-3608

Summary: To provide financial assistance to high school seniors in Oklahoma who are affiliated with the Oklahoma Cattlemen's Association.

Eligibility: Applicants must be high school seniors who are 1) the children or grandchildren of Oklahoma Cattlemen's Association members or 2) current members of the Oklahoma Junior Cattlemen's Association. Students must submit a completed application form, a list of the highlights of their high school leadership activities, a list of some of the awards they won during high school, a description of their career plans, and a 500-word essay on "How young people can become involved and stay involved in the cattle industry."

Financial data: The stipend is $1,000.

Duration: 1 year.

Additional information: The winner must attend the Oklahoma Cattlemen's Association convention to receive this award.

Deadline: June of each year.

2077
G.W. HOHMANN SCHOLARSHIPS

Society of Exploration Geophysicists
Attn: SEG Foundation
P.O. Box 702740
Tulsa, OK 74170-2740
Phone: (918) 497-5530   Fax: (918) 497-5557
E-mail: slobianco@seg.org
Web Site: www.seg.org

Summary: To provide financial assistance to undergraduate and graduate students who are interested in the field of geophysics.

Eligibility: Applicants must be 1) high school students planning to enter college in the fall and to major in geophysics; 2) undergraduate college students majoring in geophysics whose grades are above average; or 3) graduate students whose studies are directed toward a career in exploration geophysics in operations, teaching, or research. All applicants must have an interest in and aptitude for physics, mathematics, and geology with an emphasis on mining or electrical methods. Financial need is considered, but the competence of the student as indicated by the application is given first consideration.

Financial data: The stipend is $3,000 per year for graduate students or $1,000 per year for undergraduates.

Duration: 1 academic year; may be renewable, based on scholastic standing, availability of funds, and continuance of a course of study leading to a career in exploration geophysics.

Number awarded: 2 each year: 1 undergraduate and 1 graduate student.

Deadline: February of each year.

2078
H. FLETCHER BROWN SCHOLARSHIP

H. Fletcher Brown Trust
PNC Bank Delaware
Attn: Donald W. Davis
222 Delaware Avenue, 16th Floor
Wilmington, DE 19899
Phone: (302) 429-1338

Summary: To provide financial assistance to residents of Delaware who are interested in studying engineering, chemistry, medicine, dentistry, or law.

Eligibility: This program is open to Delaware residents who were born in Delaware, are either high school seniors entering the first year of college or college seniors entering the first year of graduate school, are of good moral character, and need financial assistance from sources outside their family. Applicants must have SAT scores of 1000 or higher, rank in the upper 20 percent of their class, and come from a family whose income is less than $75,000. The proposed fields of study must be engineering, chemistry, medicine (for an M.D. or D.O. degree only), dentistry, or law. Finalists are interviewed.

Financial data: The amount of the scholarship is determined by the scholarship committee and is awarded in installments over the length of study.

Duration: 1 year; may be renewed if the recipient maintains at least a 2.5 grade point average and continues to be worthy of and eligible for the award.

Deadline: March of each year.

2079
HARRY J. HARWICK SCHOLARSHIPS

American College of Medical Practice Executives
Attn: Scholarship Program
104 Inverness Terrace East
Englewood, CO 80112-5306
Phone: (303) 643-9573   Fax: (303) 643-4427
E-mail: acmpe@mgma.com
Web Site: www.mgma.com/acmpe

Summary: To provide financial assistance to undergraduate or graduate students who are interested in preparing for a career in medical group management.

Eligibility: Eligible are 1) graduate students enrolled in a program accredited by the Accrediting Commission on Education for Health Services Administration and 2) undergraduate students enrolled in a program that is a member of the Association of University Programs in Health Administration. Applications must include a letter describing career goals and objectives relevant to medical practice management; a resume; 3 reference letters commenting on the individual's performance, character, potential to succeed, and need for scholarship support; documentation indicating acceptance into an undergraduate or graduate college or university; and academic transcripts.

Financial data: The stipend is $2,500. The money is sent to the university where the recipient is enrolled.

Duration: 1 year.

Number awarded: 1 each year.

Deadline: May of each year.

2080
HARRY R. BALL, P.E. GRANT

Michigan Society of Professional Engineers
Attn: Scholarship Coordinator
P.O. Box 15276
Lansing, MI 48901-5276
Phone: (517) 487-9388   Fax: (517) 487-0635
E-mail: mspe@voyager.net   Web Site: www.voyager.net/mspe

Summary: To provide financial assistance to high school seniors in Michigan who are interested in pursuing a college degree in engineering.

Eligibility: This program is open to graduating seniors at high schools in Michigan who have a grade point average of 3.0 or higher and a composite ACT score of 26 or higher. U.S. citizenship is required. Applicants must have been accepted at a Michigan college or university accredited by ABET. They must be planning to enroll in an engineering program and enter the practice of engineering after graduation, and they must submit a 250-word essay on "How I Was Influenced to Pursue an Engineering Career." Selection is based on the essay; high school academic record; participation in extracurricular activities; evidence of leadership, character, and self reliance; and comments from teachers and administrators. Financial need is not considered. Semifinalists are interviewed.

Financial data: The stipend is $1,500.

Duration: 1 year; nonrenewable.

Additional information: Information is also available from Roger Lamer, Scholarship Selection Committee Chair, (616) 247-2974, Fax: (616) 247-2997, E-mail: rlamer@steelcase.com. Applications must be submitted to the local chapter scholarship representative. Contact the Michigan Society of Professional Engineers (MSPE) for their addresses and phone numbers.

Number awarded: 1 each year.

Deadline: January of each year.

2081
HARRY S. TRUMAN SCHOLARSHIP PROGRAM

Summary: To provide financial assistance to undergraduate students who have outstanding leadership potential, plan to pursue careers in government or other public service, and wish to attend graduate school in the United States or abroad to prepare themselves for a public service career.
See Listing #1412.

2082
HARTFORD CHAPTER AWARD OF EXCELLENCE

ASM International-Hartford Chapter
c/o Arnie Grot
Grot Enterprises
87 Chapman Drive
Glastonbury, CT 06033
E-mail: vice@asm-hartford.org   Web Site: www.asm-hartford.org/sch_app.htm
Summary: To provide financial aid to engineering and science students who live or go to school in Connecticut.
Eligibility: Applicants for this scholarship must be: 1) registered full time or accepted for full-time enrollment at a college or university; 2) pursuing a career in a field of engineering or science that may contribute to the future development of metallurgy and materials; 3) residents of Connecticut or attending a college or university in the state; and 4) able to demonstrate an effort to maintain their grade point average. Selection is based on educational background, employment experience, honors and recognition, a 250-word essay on how their chosen major can directly or indirectly contribute to the field of metallurgy and material science, and 2 letters of recommendation; financial need is not considered.
Financial data: The stipend is $1,000.
Duration: 1 year.
Number awarded: 1 or more each year.
Deadline: March of each year.

2083
HAWAII CHAPTER SOCIETY OF FIRE PROTECTION ENGINEERS ACADEMIC SCHOLARSHIP

Society of Fire Protection Engineers-Hawaii Chapter
Attn: Scholarship Committee
720 Iwilei Road, Suite 412
Honolulu, HI 96817
Phone: (808) 526-9019   Fax: (808) 537-5385
E-mail: scholarship@sfpehawaii.org
Web Site: www.sfpehawaii.org/scholarship_fund.htm
Summary: To provide financial assistance to members of the Society of Fire Protection Engineers (SFPE) in Hawaii.
Eligibility: This program is open to residents of Hawaii who are enrolled in a fire protection engineering undergraduate or graduate degree program at a college or university in Hawaii or a fire science curriculum in the state. Applicants must submit 1) a letter of introduction that explains when they first became interested in pursuing a career in the field of fire protection and why, their short-term and long-term career goals, and any past experience and/or accomplishments in the field of fire protection engineering; 2) transcripts of all undergraduate and graduate programs; 3) proof of permanent residence in Hawaii; 4) proof of membership in the local SFPE chapter; and 5) a 50-word statement on why they believe they should receive this scholarship. Financial need is not considered in the selection process.
Financial data: The stipend is $1,000.
Duration: 1 year.
Number awarded: 1 each year.
Deadline: October of each year.

2084
HAZEL SIMMONS HODGES GARDEN CLUB OBJECTIVES SCHOLARSHIP

Summary: To provide financial aid to Florida undergraduate students majoring in designated areas related to gardening.
See Listing #1414.

2085
THE HEALTH OF THE EARTH PHOTO CONTEST

Summary: To recognize and reward high school seniors in Maine who submit outstanding photographs that illustrate the misuse of the earth.
See Listing #1415.

2086
HEALTH PROFESSIONS PREGRADUATE SCHOLARSHIP PROGRAM

Indian Health Service
Attn: Scholarship Program
Twinbrook Metro Plaza, Suite 100
12300 Twinbrook Parkway
Rockville, MD 20852
Phone: (301) 443-6197   Fax: (301) 443-6048
Web Site: www.ihs.gov
Summary: To provide financial support to American Indian students interested in pursuing postsecondary education in pre-medicine or pre-dentistry.
Eligibility: Applicants must be American Indians or Alaska Natives; be high school graduates or the equivalent; have the capacity to complete a health professions course of study; and be enrolled or accepted for enrollment in a baccalaureate degree program for pre-medicine or pre-dentistry. Selection is based on academic performance, work experience and community background, faculty/employer recommendations, and applicant's reasons for seeking the scholarship. Recipients must intend to serve Indian people upon completion of their professional health care education.
Financial data: Awards provide for payment of a monthly stipend to cover living expenses, including room and board, tuition and required fees, and all other reasonable educational expenses; the total award is approximately $15,000 per year. Recent annual funding available for this and the Health Professions Preparatory Scholarship Program was approximately $3,750,000.
Duration: 1 year; may be renewed for up to 3 additional years.
Number awarded: Varies each year; recently, 238 awards (of which 92 were continuing) were made under this and the Health Professions Preparatory Scholarship Program.
Deadline: March of each year.

2087
HEALTH PROFESSIONS PREPARATORY SCHOLARSHIP PROGRAM

Indian Health Service
Attn: Scholarship Program
Twinbrook Metro Plaza, Suite 100
12300 Twinbrook Parkway
Rockville, MD 20852
Phone: (301) 443-6197   Fax: (301) 443-6048
Web Site: www.ihs.gov
Summary: To provide financial assistance to Native American students who need compensatory or preprofessional education to qualify for enrollment in a health professions school.
Eligibility: Applicants must be American Indians or Alaska Natives; be high school graduates or the equivalent; have the capacity to complete a health professions course of study; and be enrolled or accepted for enrollment in a compensatory or preprofessional general education course or curriculum. The qualifying fields of study include pre-medical technology, pre-dietetics, pre-nursing, pre-pharmacy, pre-physical therapy, and pre-social work. Recipients must intend to serve Indian people upon completion of professional health care education as a health care provider in the discipline for which they are enrolled at the pregraduate level.
Financial data: Awards provide a monthly stipend to cover living expenses, including room and board, tuition and required fees, and other reasonable educational expenses; the total award is approximately $15,000 per year. Recent annual funding available for this and the Health Professions Pregraduate Scholarship Program was approximately $3,750,000.
Duration: 1 year; renewable.
Number awarded: Varies each year; recently, 238 awards (of which 92 were continuing) were made under this and the Health Professions Pregraduate Scholarship Program.
Deadline: March of each year.

2088
HEINZ U.S.A. SCHOLARSHIP

Institute of Food Technologists
Attn: Scholarship Department
221 North LaSalle Street, Suite 300
Chicago, IL 60601-1291
Phone: (312) 782-8424   Fax: (312) 782-8348
E-mail: info@ift.org
Web Site: www.ift.org
Summary: To provide financial assistance to undergraduates interested in studying food science or food technology.
Eligibility: Applicants must be currently enrolled as sophomores or juniors in a food science or food technology program at an educational institution in the United States or Canada; they must have an outstanding scholastic record and a well-rounded personality. Financial need is not considered in the selection process.
Financial data: The stipend is $1,000.
Duration: 1 year; recipients may reapply if they are members of the Institute of Food Technologists.
Additional information: Funding for this scholarship is provided by Heinz U.S.A. Correspondence and completed applications must be submitted to the department head of the educational institution the applicant is attending.
Number awarded: 1 each year.
Deadline: January of each year.

2089
HELEN N. & HAROLD B. SHAPIRA UNDERGRADUATE SCHOLARSHIP

American Heart Association-Northland Affiliate
Attn: Administrative Assistant
4701 West 77th Street
Minneapolis, MN 55435
Phone: (952) 835-3300   (800) 331-6889 (within MN)
Fax: (952) 835-5828   E-mail: northland@heart.org
Web Site: www.americanheart.org
Summary: To provide financial assistance to undergraduate students in Minnesota interested in the study of heart and blood vessel diseases.
Eligibility: Undergraduate students currently enrolled in a 4-year college or university in Minnesota and working in a medically-related curriculum with potential application to patients with diseases of the heart and blood vessel system are eligible. Selection is based on merit.
Financial data: The stipend is $1,000.
Duration: 1 year; may be renewed for 1 additional year.
Number awarded: 1 each year.
Deadline: March of each year.

2090
HENRY ADAMS SCHOLARSHIP

American Society of Heating, Refrigerating and Air-Conditioning Engineers, Inc.
Attn: Scholarship Administrator
1791 Tullie Circle, N.E.
Atlanta, GA 30329-2305
Phone: (404) 636-8400   Fax: (404) 321-5478
E-mail: benedict@ashrae.org
Web Site: www.ashrae.org
Summary: To provide financial assistance to engineering and engineering technology students interested in heating, ventilating, air conditioning, and refrigeration (HVAC&R).
Eligibility: This program is open to undergraduate engineering and engineering technology students enrolled in a school recognized as accredited by the American Society of Heating, Refrigerating and Air-Conditioning Engineers (ASHRAE). Applicants must be pursuing a course of study that traditionally has been preparatory for the profession of HVAC&R. They must have a grade point average of at least 3.0 and must be full-time students with at least 1 full year of undergraduate study remaining. Selection is based on potential service to the HVAC&R profession, financial need, leadership ability, recommendations from instructors, and character.
Financial data: The stipend is $3,000 per year.
Duration: 1 year.
Number awarded: 1 each year.
Deadline: November of each year.

2091
HERBERT LEVY MEMORIAL SCHOLARSHIP

Society of Physics Students
c/o American Institute of Physics
One Physics Ellipse
College Park, MD 20740-3843
Phone: (301) 209-3007   Fax: (301) 209-0839
E-mail: sps@aip.org
Web Site: www.aip.org/education/sps/radio/programs.htm
Summary: To provide financial assistance to members of the Society of Physics Students (SPS) in their final year of undergraduate study.
Eligibility: This program is open to undergraduate students in any year of college who are active members of the society. Selection is based on 1) high scholarship performance both in physics and overall studies, 2) potential and intention for continued scholastic development in physics, 3) active participation in society programs, and 4) financial need.
Financial data: The stipend is $2,000.
Duration: 1 year.
Number awarded: 1 each year.
Deadline: February of each year.

2092
H.H. HARRIS FOUNDATION SCHOLARSHIPS

H.H. Harris Foundation
Attn: Trustee
181 West Madison Street, Suite 4800
Chicago, IL 60602
Phone: (312) 346-7900   Fax: (312) 346-0904
E-mail: JohnHH@aol.com
Web Site: www.afsinc.org
Summary: To provide financial assistance to students and professionals in the metallurgical and casting of metals field.
Eligibility: Applicants must be U.S. citizens and have at least a 2.6 grade point average. Both undergraduate and graduate students in the metallurgical and casting of metals field may apply, but undergraduates are the primary recipients. As part of the application process, 2 letters of recommendation must be submitted. Unsigned applications will not be considered. Selection is based on merit and financial need.
Financial data: The scholarship is worth at least $450 per school year; the average award is $1,000, and there is no ceiling.
Duration: 1 year.
Number awarded: Varies each year.
Deadline: June of each year.

2093
HIMSS FOUNDATION SCHOLARSHIPS

Healthcare Information and Management Systems Society
Attn: HIMSS Foundation Scholarship Program Coordinator
230 East Ohio Street, Suite 600
Chicago, IL 60611
Phone: (312) 664-4467   Fax: (312) 664-6143
Summary: To provide financial assistance to student members of the Healthcare Information and Management Systems Society (HIMSS) who are interested in the field of health care information and management systems.
Eligibility: This program is open to student members of the society, although an application for membership, including dues, may accompany the scholarship application. Applicants must be upper-division or graduate students when the scholarship is awarded; they must be enrolled in an accredited program designed to prepare them for a career in health care information or management systems, which may include industrial engineering, management engineering, operations research, computer science and information systems, mathematics, and quantitative programs in business administration and hospital administration. Selection is based on official transcripts and academic achievement, letters of recommendation, career goals and objectives, professional achievement, and society activity.
Financial data: The stipend is $5,000. The award includes an all-expense paid trip to the annual HIMSS conference and exhibition.
Duration: 1 year.
Number awarded: 3 each year: 1 to an undergraduate student, 1 to a graduate student, and 1 to a Ph.D. candidate.
Deadline: September of each year.

2094
HISPANIC COLLEGE FUND SCHOLARSHIPS

Summary: To provide financial assistance to Hispanic American undergraduate students who are interested in preparing for a career in a business-related field. *See Listing #1427.*

2095
HOLLIS HANINGTON SCHOLARSHIP

Professional Logging Contractors of Maine
P.O. Box 400
Fort Kent, ME 04743
Phone: (207) 834-3835   (888) 300-6614
Fax: (207) 834-3845   E-mail: brawders@aol.com
Web Site: www.maineloggers.com
Summary: To provide financial assistance to high school seniors in Maine who are interested in preparing for a career in the forest products industry.
Eligibility: This program is open to seniors in high school (and home schooled students) who are residents of Maine. Applicants must be planning to enter college to prepare for a career in the forest products industry.
Financial data: The stipend is $1,000. Funds are paid after successful completion of the first semester of college.
Duration: 1 year; nonrenewable.
Number awarded: 1 each year.
Deadline: March of each year.

2096
HOMER T. BORTON, P.E., MEMORIAL SCHOLARSHIP

Ohio Society of Professional Engineers
Attn: Engineers Foundation of Ohio
4795 Evanswood Drive, Suite 201
Columbus, OH 43229-7216
Phone: (614) 846-1144   (800) 654-9481
Fax: (614) 846-1131   E-mail: ospe@iwaynet.net
Web Site: www.ohioengineer.com/programs/Scholarships.htm
Summary: To provide financial assistance to high school seniors in Ohio who are interested in majoring in engineering in college.
Eligibility: This program is open to high school seniors in Ohio who will be attending a college or university in the state that is approved by the Accreditation Board of Engineering and Technology (ABET) and who plan to major in engineering. Applicants must have a grade point average of 3.0 or higher, be U.S. citizens, and have SAT scores of at least 600 in mathematics and 500 in verbal or ACT scores of at least 29 in mathematics and 25 in English. Along with their application, they must submit a 350-word essay on their interest in engineering, including why they became interested in the field, what specialty interests them most, and why they want to become a practicing engineer. Financial need is also considered in the selection process.
Financial data: The stipend is $1,000 per year.
Duration: 1 year; may be renewed up to 3 additional years.
Number awarded: 1 every 4 years (2005, 2009, etc.).
Deadline: December of the year of the award.

2097
HOOPER MEMORIAL SCHOLARSHIP

Transportation Clubs International
Attn: Gay Fielding
P.O. Box 52
Arabi, LA 70032
Phone: (504) 278-1107   Web Site: www.transportationclubsinternational.com
Summary: To provide financial assistance to college students interested in preparing for a career in fields related to transportation.
Eligibility: This program is open to students enrolled in an academic institution that offers courses in transportation, logistics, traffic management, or related fields. Applicants must intend to prepare for a career in those fields. Selection is based on scholastic ability, character, potential, professional interest, and financial need.
Financial data: The stipend is $1,500.
Duration: 1 year.
Additional information: Requests for applications must be accompanied by a stamped self-addressed envelope.
Number awarded: 1 or more each year.
Deadline: April of each year.

2098
HOPI TRIBAL PRIORITY SCHOLARSHIP

Hopi Tribe
Attn: Grants and Scholarship Program
P.O. Box 123
Kykotsmovi, AZ 86039
Phone: (520) 734-3533   (800) 762-9630
Summary: To encourage Hopi students to get a degree in an area of interest to the Hopi Tribe.
Eligibility: This program is open to enrolled members of the Hopi Tribe. They must be college juniors or seniors or graduate students. Their degree must be in a subject area that is of priority interest to the Hopi Tribe. These areas include: law, natural resources, education, medicine, health, engineering, or business. This is a highly competitive scholarship. Selection is based on academic merit and the likelihood that the applicants will use their training and expertise for tribal goals and objectives.
Financial data: The amount awarded varies, depending upon the needs of the recipient.
Duration: 1 year; may be renewed.
Additional information: Recipients must attend school on a full-time basis.
Number awarded: Varies each year.
Deadline: July of each year.

2099
HOPPERS SCHOLARSHIP

Microsoft Corporation
Attn: Radmila Sarac
Building 32/2351
One Microsoft Way
Redmond, WA 98052-6399
Summary: To provide financial assistance to women who are interested in studying computer science at a college or university in Washington.
Eligibility: This program is open to women who are accepted or enrolled in a college or university in the state of Washington. Applicants must be undergraduates with a declared major of either computer science or a related computer science intensive discipline and a grade point average of 3.0 or higher. Along with their application, they must submit essays, up to 500 words each, on 2 of the following topics: "1) What do you see as the computer industry's primary shortcomings? If you were a leader in the technical world today, in what direction would you guide technology and why? 2) Why have you chosen a degree in the discipline you are currently pursuing? 3) Describe a coding, class, or work project related to your field of study that you significantly contributed towards. Describe your contribution and what impact this project had on you or others." Along with the essays, selection is based on extracurricular activities, awards and honors, community service, work experience, letters of recommendation, and transcripts.
Financial data: The stipend is $2,500.
Duration: 1 year.
Additional information: This program was established in 1990 as part of an effort to make Microsoft a great place for women. In addition to scholarships, other Hoppers committees deal with outreach, technical women, mentoring, program, career development, and diversity. The program is named for Grace Hopper, a computer science pioneer.
Number awarded: 2 each year.
Deadline: March of each year.

2100
HORIZONS FOUNDATION SCHOLARSHIP PROGRAM

Women in Defense
c/o National Defense Industrial Association
2111 Wilson Boulevard, Suite 400
Arlington, VA 22201-3061
Phone: (703) 247-2552   Fax: (703) 522-1885
E-mail: jcasey@ndia.org
Web Site: www.wid.ndia.org
Summary: To provide financial assistance for postsecondary education to women engaged in or planning careers related to the national security interests of the United States.
Eligibility: This program is open to women who are already working in national security fields as well as women planning such careers. Applicants must 1) be currently enrolled at an accredited college or university, either full time or part time, as graduate students or upper-division undergraduates; 2) demonstrate financial need; 3) be U.S. citizens; 4) have a grade point average of 3.25 or higher; and

5) demonstrate interest in pursuing a career related to national security. The preferred fields of study include business, computer science, economics, engineering, international relations, law, mathematics, operations research, political science, and physics; others are considered if the applicant can demonstrate relevance to a career in national security or defense. Selection is based on academic achievement, participation in defense and national security activities, field of study, work experience, statements of objectives, recommendations, and financial need.

Financial data: Stipends range from $500 to $2,000.

Duration: 1 year; renewable.

Number awarded: Varies each year.

Deadline: June of each year for fall semester; October of each year for spring semester.

2101
HOWARD BROWN RICKARD SCHOLARSHIPS

National Federation of the Blind
c/o Peggy Elliott
Chair, Scholarship Committee
805 Fifth Avenue
Grinnell, IA 50112
Phone: (641) 236-3366
Web Site: www.nfb.org

Summary: To provide financial assistance to blind students studying or planning to study law, medicine, engineering, architecture, or the natural sciences at the postsecondary level.

Eligibility: This program is open to legally blind students who are pursuing or planning to pursue a full-time undergraduate or graduate course of study. Applicants must be studying or planning to study law, medicine, engineering, architecture, or the natural sciences. Selection is based on academic excellence, service to the community, and financial need.

Financial data: The stipend is $3,000.

Duration: 1 year; recipients may resubmit applications up to 2 additional years.

Additional information: Scholarships are awarded at the federation convention in July. Recipients attend the convention at federation expense; that funding is in addition to the scholarship grant.

Number awarded: 1 each year.

Deadline: March of each year.

2102
HOWARD E. ADKINS MEMORIAL SCHOLARSHIP

American Welding Society
Attn: AWS Foundation, Inc.
550 N.W. LeJeune Road
Miami, FL 33126
Phone: (305) 443-9353, ext. 461   (800) 443-9353, ext. 461
Fax: (305) 443-7559   E-mail: vpinsky@aws.org
Web Site: www.aws.org/foundation/adkins.html

Summary: To provide financial assistance to college students interested in pursuing a career related to welding.

Eligibility: This program is open to full-time college juniors and seniors who are pursuing at least a 4-year bachelor's degree in welding engineering or welding engineering technology (although preference is given to students in welding engineering). Applicants must have a grade point average of 3.2 or higher in engineering, science, and technical subjects and 2.8 overall. Financial need is not considered in the selection process. Priority is given to applicants residing or attending school in Wisconsin or Kentucky.

Financial data: The stipend is $2,500.

Duration: 1 year; recipients may reapply.

Additional information: This program was established in 1994.

Number awarded: 1 each year.

Deadline: January of each year.

2103
HP DEI SCHOLARSHIP/INTERNSHIP PROGRAM

Hewlett-Packard Company
Attn: Diversity in Education Initiative
3000 Hanover Street
Palo Alto, CA 94304-1185
Phone: (650) 857-3495   Fax: (650) 857-7594
E-mail: cathy_lipe@hp.com   Web Site: www.hp.com/go/hpscholars

Summary: To provide financial assistance and work experience to underrepresented minority high school seniors from designated communities who are interested in studying engineering or computer science in college.

Eligibility: This program is open to graduating high school seniors in Boston, El Paso, Los Angeles, or San Jose who will be enrolling as a full-time student at an accredited 4-year college or university. Applicants must be an underrepresented minority (African American, Hispanic American, or American Indian) planning to major in electrical engineering, computer engineering, or computer science. They must be interested in a summer internship at a major Hewlett-Packard (HP) location in California, Colorado, Idaho, Oregon, or Washington. Selection is based on academic achievement, letters of recommendation, an autobiographical statement, financial need, and demonstrated interest in math, science, and engineering.

Financial data: The stipend is $3,000 per year. In addition, students receive a salary when they work at HP facilities during the summer. The total value of the award exceeds $35,000 per student.

Duration: 4 years of university study plus 3 summers of internships.

Additional information: This program is offered by HP as part of its Diversity in Education Initiative (DEI). For the Boston program, further information is available from Caren Walker, Boston Public Schools, Cluster 7 Office, 77 Lawrence Avenue, Dorchester, MA 02121, (617) 635-6670, E-mail: cluster7@boston.k12.ma.us; preference is given to graduates of Boston Latin, Burke, or Boston Public Schools who plan to attend Northeastern University. For the El Paso program (named the Agilent Scholars Program and supported by the Agilent Technologies division of HP), further information is available from Elsa, E-mail: elsa@eng.utep.edu; preference is given to students who plan to attend the University of Texas at El Paso. For the Los Angeles program, further information is available from Rick Ainsworth, UCLA School of Engineering and Applied Science, 3137 Engineering 1, 405 Hilgard Avenue, Los Angeles, CA 90095-1600, (310) 206-6493, E-mail: rique@ea.ucla.edu; preference is given to graduates of high schools in the Los Angeles Unified School District who plan to attend UCLA. For the San Jose program, further information is available from Janet Yates, San Jose State University, College of Engineering, One Washington Square, San Jose, CA 95192-0083, (408) 924-3853, E-mail: dryates@pacbell.net; preference is given to graduates of schools in the East Side High School District who plan to attend San Jose State University.

Number awarded: 40 each year: 10 from each of the participating programs.

Deadline: April of each year for the Los Angeles program; March of each year for the other programs.

2104
HUBERTUS W.V. WILLEMS SCHOLARSHIP FOR MALE STUDENTS

National Association for the Advancement of Colored People
Attn: Education Department
4805 Mt. Hope Drive
Baltimore, MD 21215-3297
Phone: (410) 358-8900   Fax: (410) 358-9785
Web Site: www.naacp.org

Summary: To provide funding to male members of the National Association for the Advancement of Colored People (NAACP) interested in undergraduate or graduate education in selected scientific fields.

Eligibility: This program is open to males who are high school seniors, college students, or graduate students. Applicants must be majoring (or preparing to major) in 1 of the following fields: engineering, chemistry, physics, or mathematics. Membership and participation in the NAACP is highly desirable. The required minimum grade point average is 2.5 for graduating high school seniors and undergraduate students or 3.0 for graduate students. Applicants must be able to demonstrate financial need, defined as a family income of less than $30,000 for a family of 1 ranging to less than $52,300 for a family of 8. Full-time enrollment is required for undergraduate students, although graduate students may be enrolled full or part time. U.S. citizenship is required.

Financial data: Undergraduates receive a maximum award of $8,000, paid in annual installments of $2,000. Graduate students receive $3,000 per year.

Duration: 1 year; renewable (full-time status and a 3.0 grade point average must be maintained).

Number awarded: 1 or more each year.

Deadline: April of each year.

2105
HYDRO POWER CONTEST

HANDS-ON! Projects
9 Mayflower Road
Northborough, MA 01532
Phone: (508) 351-6023   Fax: (508) 351-6023
E-mail: hands-on@ma.ultranet.com
Web Site: www.ultranet.com/~hands-on/hydo/contest/mainpage.html
Summary: To recognize and reward students and other interested people who have ideas for turning water into power.
Eligibility: To compete, each individual or team is required to construct a device that converts the gravity potential of water into mechanical power and then to submit the device for testing under competition conditions. During the contest, the mechanical power produced by each device and its efficiency is measured. The devices in each of the 5 classes of competition that lift a weight through a fixed distance in the shortest period of time or with the least amount of water win the competition. The 5 competition classes are: student division, power class; student division, efficiency class; open division, power class; open division, efficiency class; and pro division, power class.
Financial data: In each of the 5 classes, the following awards are presented: first prize, from $300 to $900; second prize, up to $600; third prize, up to $300; and fourth prize, up to $200. In addition to these prizes, the judges at their discretion may make additional awards for the "most innovative" entry and for the entry showing the "best workmanship." If awarded, these cash prizes are $250 each. Students who participate may also be awarded scholarships. For example, the Canada Centre for Mines and Energy Technology/Natural Resources Canada (CANMET) awards a $C1,500 scholarship to a Canadian student or student team that wins 1 of the student division competition classes. The U.S. Department of Energy (DOE) awards 2 scholarships, of $1,500 each, to U.S. students or teams that win the student division competition classes. Hydro Rinehart offers 2 $500 scholarships to students or teams that place second in the student division competition classes. Aquadyne, Inc. offers 2 $300 scholarships to students or teams that place third in the student division competition classes. The American Society of Mechanical Engineers (ASME) Power Division Hydropower Committee offers a $1,000 scholarship to a mechanical engineering student winner.
Duration: The competition is held annually.
Additional information: In some years, student winners are also presented with software packages for their schools. First-place winners in each competition category receive a copy of *Guide to Hydropower Mechanical Design* by the American Society of Mechanical Engineers Hydro Power Technical Committee, and all competitors receive a complimentary 1-year subscription to *Hydro Review* magazine and a Hydro Power Contest tee shirt.
Number awarded: Up to 4 winners in each of the 5 competition classes.

2106
IAA FOUNDATION SCHOLARSHIPS

Illinois Farm Bureau
Attn: Illinois Agricultural Association Foundation
1701 North Towanda Avenue
P.O. Box 2901
Bloomington, IL 61702-2901
Phone: (309) 557-2230   Fax: (309) 557-2559
Web Site: www.ilfb.org
Summary: To provide financial assistance for college to Illinois Farm Bureau members, spouses, and children.
Eligibility: This program is open to Illinois Farm Bureau members, as well as their spouses and children. Applicants must be at least high school graduates and be majoring (or planning to major) in agriculture, agribusiness, or another ag-related course of study. They must be Illinois residents. Selection is based on scholastic ability, financial need, or both.
Financial data: Stipends range from $400 to $1,750 per year. Funds are sent directly to the recipient's college or university. The money must be used for tuition and/or room and board.
Duration: 1 year; recipients may reapply.
Number awarded: 10 each year: 1 for a student at Southern Illinois University, 1 for a student at an Illinois postsecondary institution, and 8 for students at any accredited university, college, or community college in the nation.
Deadline: February of each year.

2107
IBM RESEARCH INTERNSHIP FOR UNDERGRADUATE WOMEN

American Physical Society
Attn: Education Programs Administrator
One Physics Ellipse, Fourth Floor
College Park, MD 20740-3844
Phone: (301) 209-3231   Fax: (301) 209-0865
E-mail: otwell@aps.org
Web Site: www.aps.org/educ/cswp/index.html
Summary: To provide financial assistance and work experience to women undergraduates majoring in designated science and engineering fields.
Eligibility: This program is open to women who are college sophomores and juniors majoring in chemical engineering, chemistry, computer science or engineering, electrical engineering, materials science or engineering, mechanical engineering, or physics. Applicants must have a grade point average of 3.0 or higher and a willingness to accept a summer internship at IBM's Almaden Research Center in San Jose, California. They must submit a 250-word essay describing their interest in research and how this opportunity will advance their career goals.
Financial data: The stipend is $2,500 per year. The internship is salaried.
Duration: 2 years.
Additional information: This program was established in 1999 and originally called the IBM Research Division Student Research Scholarship for Women.
Number awarded: 1 or more each year.
Deadline: February of each year.

2108
IBM STUDENT RESEARCH SCHOLARSHIP

National Society of Black Engineers
Attn: Programs Manager
1454 Duke Street
Alexandria, VA 22314
Phone: (703) 549-2207, ext. 204   Fax: (703) 683-5312
E-mail: scholarships@nsbe.org
Web Site: www.nsbe.org
Summary: To provide financial assistance and work experience to members of the National Society of Black Engineers (NSBE) who are majoring in designated science and engineering fields.
Eligibility: This program is open to members of the society who are college sophomores or juniors majoring in the following fields of study: applied or engineering physics, chemical engineering, chemistry, computer engineering, computer science, electrical engineering, materials science or engineering, mathematics, mechanical engineering, optical engineering, or physics. Applicants must have a grade point average of 3.0 or higher and a willingness to accept a summer internship at IBM's Almaden Research Center in San Jose, California. They must submit a 250-word essay describing their interest in research and how the scholarship will advance their career goals and benefit the IBM Corporation.
Financial data: The stipend is $2,500 per year.
Duration: 2 years.
Number awarded: 1 each year.
Deadline: November of each year.

2109
IDDBA SCHOLARSHIP

Summary: To provide financial assistance for college to students employed in a supermarket dairy, deli, or bakery department (or related companies).
See Listing #1436.

2110
IDSA UNDERGRADUATE SCHOLARSHIPS

Summary: To provide financial assistance to upper-division students working on an undergraduate degree in industrial design.
See Listing #1437.

2111
IFEC SCHOLARSHIPS

Summary: To provide financial assistance to undergraduate or graduate students who are interested in preparing for a career in communications in the food service industry.
See Listing #1439.

Scholarship Listings

2112
IFFAA SCHOLARSHIPS

Iowa Foundation for Agricultural Advancement
c/o Harold Hodson
Swine Genetics International, Ltd.
30805 595th Avenue
Cambridge, IA 50046
Phone: (515) 383-4386   (800) 247-3958
Fax: (515) 383-2257   E-mail: info@iowastatefair.org
Web Site: www.iowastatefair.org
Summary: To provide financial assistance for college to Iowa high school seniors interested in majoring in animal science or livestock-related fields.
Eligibility: This program is open to students who will be entering an Iowa 2- or 4-year postsecondary institution in the following fall. Applicants must be residents of Iowa, active in 4-H or FFA livestock projects, and planning to major in animal science or a field related to livestock. Selection is based on level of 4-H or FFA involvement in livestock project work, livestock exhibition, and/or judging; scholarship; leadership; and career plans. The program also includes 1) Performance and Carcass Awards in which animals are selected on the basis of visual appraisal and then evaluated in a carcass contest for economically important traits, such as loin eye or rib eye area, tenth rib fat, and average daily gain; 2) Breeding Beef and Swine Scholarships, in which female animals in each breed are evaluated for breeding traits; and 3) Premier Exhibitor Scholarships, for 4-H members who can communicate their understanding of the future of the livestock industry and their knowledge of animal production.
Financial data: Stipends range from $250 to $2,500.
Duration: 1 year; nonrenewable.
Additional information: Information is also available from county 4-H offices in Iowa and local FFA advisors. Winners are announced at the Iowa State Fair's annual 4-H/FFA "Sale of Champions" in August, sponsored by the Iowa Foundation for Agricultural Advancement (IFFAA). The IFFAA was established in 1988 and began offering scholarships in 1990.
Number awarded: Varies each year; recently, 82 scholarships worth $89,200 were awarded.
Deadline: June of each year.

2113
IFT CHEF AMERICA SCHOLARSHIP

Institute of Food Technologists
Attn: Scholarship Department
221 North LaSalle Street, Suite 300
Chicago, IL 60601-1291
Phone: (312) 782-8424   Fax: (312) 782-8348
E-mail: info@ift.org   Web Site: www.ift.org
Summary: To provide financial assistance to undergraduates interested in studying food science or food technology.
Eligibility: Applicants must be currently enrolled as sophomores or juniors in a food science or food technology program at an educational institution in the United States or Canada; they must have an outstanding scholastic record and a well-rounded personality. Financial need is not considered in the selection process.
Financial data: The stipend is $1,000.
Duration: 1 year; recipients may reapply if they are members of the Institute of Food Technologists (IFT).
Additional information: Funding for this scholarship is provided by Chef America, Inc. Correspondence and completed applications must be submitted to the department head of the educational institution the applicant is attending.
Number awarded: 1 each year.
Deadline: January of each year.

2114
IFT 50TH ANNIVERSARY-INSPIRATION FOR TOMORROW SCHOLARSHIP

Institute of Food Technologists
Attn: Scholarship Department
221 North LaSalle Street, Suite 300
Chicago, IL 60601-1291
Phone: (312) 782-8424   Fax: (312) 782-8348
E-mail: info@ift.org   Web Site: www.ift.org
Summary: To provide financial assistance to undergraduates interested in studying food science or food technology.
Eligibility: Applicants must be currently enrolled as sophomores or juniors in a food science or food technology program at an educational institution in the

United States or Canada. They must have an outstanding scholastic record and a well-rounded personality. Financial need is not considered in the selection process.
Financial data: The stipend is $2,000.
Duration: 1 year; recipients may reapply if they are members of the Institute of Food Technologists.
Additional information: Correspondence and completed applications must be submitted to the department head of the educational institution the applicant is attending.
Number awarded: 1 each year.
Deadline: January of each year.

2115
IHC FOUNDATION SCHOLARSHIP

Indiana Health Care Foundation, Inc.
Attn: Scholarship Committee
One North Capitol, Suite 1115
Indianapolis, IN 46204
Phone: (317) 636-6406   (800) 466-4422
Fax: (317) 638-3749   Web Site: www.ihea.org
Summary: To provide financial assistance to students in Indiana who are interested in working on a nursing degree.
Eligibility: Eligible to apply for this support are residents of Indiana who have at least a high school degree or GED, have been accepted by a nursing degree program (R.N. or L.P.N.) in the state, and have a grade point average of at least 2.75. In addition to a completed application, school transcripts and 3 letters of recommendation are required. Applicants are interviewed. Special consideration is given to individuals who are interested in working with the elderly in a long-term care environment. Financial need is not considered in the selection process.
Financial data: Stipends range from $750 to $1,500 per year. Funds are paid directly to the recipient's school and must be used for tuition, fees, or campus housing.
Duration: 1 year; recipients may reapply.
Additional information: This program was established in 1997.
Deadline: February of each year.

2116
ILLINOIS COUNCIL OF TEACHERS OF MATHEMATICS SCHOLARSHIP AWARD

Illinois Council of Teachers of Mathematics
c/o Larry D. Stonecipher, ICTM Scholarship
University of Illinois
P.O. Box 19243
Springfield, IL 62794-9243
Web Site: www.ictm.org/scholarship.html
Summary: To provide financial assistance to undergraduate students in Illinois who are interested in pursuing a career as a mathematics teacher.
Eligibility: This program is open to juniors and seniors at accredited colleges and universities in Illinois. Applicants must have a grade point average of 3.0 or higher and a mathematics education major, a mathematics major with an education minor, or an education major with an official mathematics concentration. Selection is based on transcripts from all colleges attended, letters of recommendation from 2 mathematics teachers (high school or college), and a 200- to 300-word essay on why the students wish to teach mathematics and what they see as their contribution to the profession.
Financial data: The stipend is $1,500.
Duration: 1 year.
Additional information: This program began in 1989. Requests for applications must be accompanied by a self-addressed stamped envelope.
Number awarded: 2 to 5 each year.
Deadline: March of each year.

2117
ILLINOIS HOSPITAL & HEALTHSYSTEMS ASSOCIATION SCHOLARSHIP

Illinois Hospital & HealthSystems Association
1151 East Warrenville Road
P.O. Box 3015
Naperville, IL 60566
Phone: (630) 505-7777   Web Site: www.ihha.org

410

Summary: To provide financial assistance to Illinois residents accepted into or enrolled in a hospital-related health care professional curriculum.
Eligibility: Applicants must be accepted into or currently enrolled in a hospital-related health care professional curriculum. Applicants enrolled in an associate degree or hospital-based program will be considered in their first year only. Students must have been accepted in a health care professional sequence; that is, when courses are open only to student candidates for the degree or certification; pre-nursing, pre-medicine, and pre-pharmacy applicants are not eligible until they are accepted into nursing clinicals, medical school, etc. Applicants who have less than 1 academic year remaining until graduation are not eligible for consideration. Selection is based on academic record (at least a 3.5 grade point average is required) and financial need.
Financial data: The stipend is $1,000. Funds must be used for tuition, fees, or books.
Duration: 1 year.
Additional information: The school attended need not be in Illinois, but it must be accredited or recognized as an approved program by the appropriate agencies.
Deadline: April of each year.

2118
ILLINOIS LEGION AUXILIARY STUDENT NURSE SCHOLARSHIPS

American Legion Auxiliary
Attn: Department of Illinois
2720 East Lincoln Street
P.O. Box 1426
Bloomington, IL 61702-1426   Phone: (309) 663-9366
Summary: To provide financial assistance to residents of Illinois who wish to pursue a college degree in nursing.
Eligibility: Eligible to apply for these scholarships are Illinois residents who wish to pursue training in nursing. Applicants must be sponsored by a local unit of the American Legion Auxiliary in Illinois.
Financial data: These scholarships are $1,000.
Duration: 1 year.
Additional information: Applications may be obtained only from a local unit of the American Legion Auxiliary.
Number awarded: Several each year.
Deadline: March of each year.

2119
INDIAN NURSE SCHOLARSHIP AWARDS

National Society of the Colonial Dames of America
National Patriotic Service Committee
c/o Mrs. Joseph H. Calvin
9 Cross Creek Park
Birmingham, AL 35213
Summary: To provide financial assistance to American Indians interested in preparing for a career in nursing.
Eligibility: To be eligible for this scholarship, candidates must be American Indians, be high school graduates (or the equivalent), be enrolled full time in an accredited school, be in a nursing program, be within 2 years of completing the course for which the scholarship is being given, have maintained the scholastic average required by their school, be recommended by their counselor or school officer, not be receiving an Indian Health Service Scholarship, have a career goal directly related to the needs of the Indian people, and be in financial need.
Financial data: The stipends are $1,000, $750, or $500 per year. Funds are to be used for tuition or fees. The money is sent directly to the recipient's school.
Duration: 1 year; those students who continue to meet the eligibility requirements and have been recommended for continuation are given priority consideration for additional periods of support.
Additional information: This program was established in 1928. Mrs. Calvin may be reached at the above address from November through June of each year. During other times of the year, her address is Box 825, Cashiers, NC 28717.
Number awarded: A small number each year.

2120
INDIANA BUSINESS AIRCRAFT ASSOCIATION PDP SCHOLARSHIP

National Business Aviation Association, Inc.
Attn: Senior Manager, Airmen & Commercial Services
1200 18th Street, N.W., Suite 400
Washington, DC 20036-2527
Phone: (202) 783-9353   Fax: (202) 331-8364

E-mail: jevans@nbaa.org
Web Site: www.nbaa.org/scholarships/index.htm
Summary: To provide financial assistance to students enrolled at a college or university offering the Professional Development Program (PDP).
Eligibility: This program is open to full-time students at an institution that offers PDP and belongs to the National Business Aviation Association (NBAA) and the University Aviation Association (UAA). Applicants must be U.S. citizens; be enrolled in an aviation-related program; be at the sophomore, junior, or senior level (proof of enrollment must be provided); have at least a 3.0 grade point average (official transcript required); write a 250-word essay describing their goals for a career in the business aviation flight department; submit a letter of recommendation from a member of the aviation department faculty; and submit a resume.
Financial data: The stipend is $1,150. Checks are made payable to the recipient's school.
Duration: 1 year.
Additional information: The participating institutions are Central Missouri State University, Eastern Michigan University, Embry-Riddle Aeronautical University, Mercer County Community College, Purdue University, University of North Dakota, and University of Oklahoma. This program is sponsored by the Indiana Business Aviation Association.
Number awarded: 4 each year.
Deadline: August of each year.

2121
INDUSTRY MINORITY SCHOLARSHIPS

American Meteorological Society
Attn: Fellowship/Scholarship Coordinator
45 Beacon Street
Boston, MA 02108-3693
Phone: (617) 227-2426, ext. 246   Fax: (617) 742-8718
E-mail: amsinfo@ametsoc.org
Web Site: www.ametsoc.org/AMS/amsedu/scholfeldocs/index.html
Summary: To provide financial assistance to underrepresented minority students entering college and planning to major in meteorology or some aspect of atmospheric sciences.
Eligibility: Candidates must be entering their freshman year at a 4-year college or university and planning to pursue careers in the atmospheric or related oceanic and hydrologic sciences. They must be minority students traditionally underrepresented in the sciences (Hispanic American, Native American, and Black/African American students). Applicants must submit an official high school transcript showing grades from the past 3 years, a letter of recommendation from a high school teacher or guidance counselor, a copy of scores from an SAT or similar national entrance exam, and a 500-word essay on how they would use their college education in atmospheric sciences (or a closely-related field) to make their community a better place in which to live. Half of the application evaluation is based on the essay.
Financial data: The stipend is $3,000 per year.
Duration: 1 year; may be renewed for the second year of college study.
Additional information: This program is funded by grants from industry and by donations from members of the Programs in Support of Science and Education of the American Meteorological Society (AMS). Requests for an application must be accompanied by a self-addressed stamped envelope.
Number awarded: Varies each year; recently, 12 of these scholarships were awarded.
Deadline: February of each year.

2122
INDUSTRY UNDERGRADUATE SCHOLARSHIPS

American Meteorological Society
Attn: Fellowship/Scholarship Coordinator
45 Beacon Street
Boston, MA 02108-3693
Phone: (617) 227-2426, ext. 246   Fax: (617) 742-8718
E-mail: amsinfo@ametsoc.org
Web Site: www.ametsoc.org/AMS/amsedu/scholfeldocs/index.html
Summary: To encourage outstanding undergraduate students to pursue careers in the atmospheric and related oceanic and hydrologic sciences.
Eligibility: This program is open to full-time students entering their junior year who are either 1) enrolled or planning to enroll in a course of study leading to a bachelor's degree in the atmospheric or related oceanic or hydrologic sciences, or 2) enrolled in a program leading to a bachelor's degree in science or engineering who have demonstrated a clear intent to pursue a career in the atmospheric or related oceanic or hydrologic sciences following completion of appropriate

specialized education at the graduate level. Applicants must have a grade point average of 3.0 or higher and be U.S. citizens or permanent residents. Along with their application, they must submit 2 essays of 100 words or less: 1 on their career goals in the atmospheric or related oceanographic or hydrologic fields and 1 on their most important achievements that qualify them for this scholarship. The sponsor specifically encourages applications from women, minorities, and students with disabilities who are traditionally underrepresented in the atmospheric and related oceanic sciences. Selection is based on merit and potential for accomplishment in the field.

Financial data: The stipend is $2,000 per academic year.

Duration: 1 year; may be renewed for the final year of college study.

Additional information: Requests for an application must be accompanied by a self-addressed stamped envelope.

Number awarded: Varies each year; recently, 9 of these scholarships were awarded.

Deadline: February of each year.

2123
INSTITUTE OF FOOD TECHNOLOGISTS COLLEGE SCHOLARSHIPS

Institute of Food Technologists
Attn: Scholarship Department
221 North LaSalle Street, Suite 300
Chicago, IL 60601-1291
Phone: (312) 782-8424   Fax: (312) 782-8348
E-mail: info@ift.org
Web Site: www.ift.org

Summary: To provide financial assistance to undergraduates interested in studying food science or food technology.

Eligibility: Applicants must be enrolled as freshmen, sophomores, or juniors in a food science or food technology program at an educational institution in the United States or Canada. They must have an outstanding scholastic record and a well-rounded personality. Students applying as freshmen must have maintained at least a 2.5 grade point average during their first term of study. Financial need is not considered in the selection process.

Financial data: Stipends are either $1,500 or $1,000.

Duration: 1 year; recipients may reapply if they are members of the Institute of Food Technologists.

Additional information: Correspondence and completed applications must be submitted to the department head at the educational institution the applicant is attending.

Number awarded: Varies each year; recently, 59 of these scholarships were awarded: 2 at $1,500 to current sophomores and juniors, 35 at $1,000 to current sophomores and juniors, and 22 at $1,000 to current freshmen.

Deadline: January of each year for current sophomore and juniors; February of each year for current freshmen.

2124
INSTITUTE OF FOOD TECHNOLOGISTS HIGH SCHOOL SCHOLARSHIPS

Institute of Food Technologists
Attn: Scholarship Department
221 North LaSalle Street, Suite 300
Chicago, IL 60601-1291
Phone: (312) 782-8424   Fax: (312) 782-8348
E-mail: info@ift.org
Web Site: www.ift.org

Summary: To provide financial assistance to high school seniors interested in studying food science or food technology in college.

Eligibility: Applicants must be high school seniors planning to enroll in a food science or food technology program at an educational institution in the United States or Canada. They must have an outstanding scholastic record and a well-rounded personality. Financial need is not considered in the selection process.

Financial data: Stipends are either $1,500 or $1,000.

Duration: 1 year; recipients may reapply if they are members of the Institute of Food Technologists.

Additional information: Correspondence and completed applications must be submitted to the department head of the educational institution the applicant plans to attend.

Number awarded: Varies each year; recently, 23 of these scholarships were awarded: 1 at $1,500 and 22 at $1,000.

Deadline: February of each year.

2125
INSURANCE TRUST GRANTS

Michigan Society of Professional Engineers
Attn: Scholarship Coordinator
215 North Walnut Street
P.O. Box 15276
Lansing, MI 48901-5276
Phone: (517) 487-9388   Fax: (517) 487-0635
E-mail: mspe@voyager.net   Web Site: www.voyager.net/mspe

Summary: To provide financial assistance to high school seniors in Michigan who are interested in pursuing a college degree in engineering.

Eligibility: This program is open to graduating seniors at high schools in Michigan who have a grade point average of 3.0 or higher and a composite ACT score of 26 or higher. U.S. citizenship is required. Applicants must have been accepted at a Michigan college or university accredited by ABET. They must be planning to enroll in an engineering program and enter the practice of engineering after graduation. They must submit a 250-word essay on "How I Was Influenced to Pursue an Engineering Career." Selection is based on the essay; high school academic record; participation in extracurricular activities; evidence of leadership, character, and self reliance; and comments from teachers and administrators. Financial need is not considered. Semifinalists are interviewed.

Financial data: The stipend is $2,000.

Duration: 1 year; nonrenewable.

Additional information: Information is also available from Roger Lamer, Scholarship Selection Committee Chair, (616) 247-2974, Fax: (616) 247-2997, E-mail: rlamer@steelcase.com. Applications must be submitted to the local chapter scholarship representative. Contact the Michigan Society of Professional Engineers (MSPE) for their addresses and phone numbers.

Number awarded: 2 each year.

Deadline: January of each year.

2126
INTEL INTERNATIONAL SCIENCE AND ENGINEERING FAIR

Science Service
Attn: Director of Youth Programs
1719 N Street, N.W.
Washington, DC 20036
Phone: (202) 785-2255   Fax: (202) 785-1243
E-mail: sciedu@sciserv.org Web Site: www.sciserv.org

Summary: To recognize and reward outstanding high school students interested in engineering or the sciences.

Eligibility: The International Science and Engineering Fair (ISEF), known as the "World Series" of science fairs, involves students from the 9th through 12th grades who first compete in approximately 500 affiliated fairs around the world. Each fair then sends 2 individuals and 1 team (up to 3 members) to compete in the ISEF in 1 of 15 categories: behavioral and social sciences, biochemistry, botany, chemistry, computer science, earth and space sciences, engineering, environmental science, gerontology, mathematics, medicine and health, microbiology, physics, team projects, and zoology. Each entry consists of a science project and a 250-word abstract that summarizes the project. Judging of individual projects is based on creative ability (30 percent), scientific thought and engineering goals (30 percent), thoroughness (15 percent), skill (15 percent), and clarity (10 percent).

Financial data: The Intel Young Scientist Scholarships, granted to the presenters of the most outstanding research, are $50,000. In each of the categories, the first-place winner receives a $3,000 scholarship, second place $1,500, third place $1,000, and fourth place $500. Winners also quality for all-expense paid trips to attend the Nobel Prize Ceremony in Stockholm, Sweden (the Glenn T. Seaborg Nobel Prize Visit Award) and the European Union Contest for Young Scientists. The Intel Best of Category Awards, for the project that exemplifies the best in each scientific category that has also won a first-place in the category, are $5,000 to the students, $1,000 to their schools, and $1,000 to their science fair. The Intel Achievement Awards are $5,000 each for outstanding work in any field. The Intel Excellence in Teaching Awards are $10,000 and $5,000. Other prizes, worth more than $1.5 million, include scholarships from individual colleges and universities, expense-paid trips to scientific and engineering installations or national conventions, summer jobs at research institutes, and laboratory equipment provided by Intel.

Duration: The fair is held annually. The Intel Young Scientist Scholarships are paid in 8 equal installments. Most other awards are for 1 year.

Additional information: Costs for the entry fee, as well as those for transportation, meals, and housing of the finalists, are borne by the affiliated fairs. The ISEF, currently sponsored by Intel and other major corporations, was first held in 1950.

Number awarded: 3 Pinnacle Awards are presented each year. In addition, 60 other scholarships are awarded: 4 in each of the 15 categories. Other awards include 8 Intel Achievement Awards and 7 Intel Excellence in Teaching Awards (1 at $10,000 and 6 at $5,000). Many other special awards, regional awards, and scholarships from individual colleges are also presented.
Deadline: The fair is always held in May.

2127
INTEL SCIENCE TALENT SEARCH SCHOLARSHIPS

Science Service
Attn: Director of Youth Programs
1719 N Street, N.W.
Washington, DC 20036
Phone: (202) 785-2255   Fax: (202) 785-1243
E-mail: sciedu@sciserv.org   Web Site: www.sciserv.org
Summary: To recognize and reward outstanding high school seniors who are interested in attending college to prepare for a career in mathematics, engineering, or the sciences.
Eligibility: This program is open to high school seniors in the United States. Applicants must complete an independent research project and submit a written report of up to 20 pages; the project may be in the fields of biology, chemistry, engineering, mathematics, medicine, physics, psychology, or social science. Based on those reports, 300 students are designated as semifinalists, and from those 40 are chosen as finalists.
Financial data: First place: $100,000; second place: $75,000; third place: $50,000; fourth through sixth place: $25,000; seventh through tenth place: $20,000; 30 other finalists: $5,000. The first 10 awards are paid in 8 equal installments; if a student completes college in 3 years, the remaining funds may be used for the first year of graduate school.
Duration: The competition is held annually. Scholarships are for 4 years.
Additional information: The names and addresses of all semifinalists are published in a booklet that is distributed to the admissions office of every college and university in the United States. Finalists are given a 6-day all-expense paid trip to the Science Talent Institute in Washington, D.C. This program began in 1942. Through 1997, it was sponsored by the Westinghouse Foundation and administered by Science Service. Starting in 1998, Intel became the sponsor. Winners must attend college within 1 year in a program in science, mathematics, or engineering.
Number awarded: 40 each year: 1 at $100,000, 1 at $75,000, 1 at $50,000, 3 at $25,000, 4 at $20,000, and 30 at $5,000.
Deadline: November of each year.

2128
INTERNATIONAL ASSOCIATION OF FIRE CHIEFS FOUNDATION SCHOLARSHIPS

International Association of Fire Chiefs Foundation
1257 Wiltshire Road
York, PA 17403
Phone: (717) 854-9083
Summary: To provide financial assistance to fire fighters who wish to further their academic education.
Eligibility: Eligible to apply are active members of state, county, provincial, municipal, community, industrial, or federal fire departments who have demonstrated proficiency as members and at least 2 years of paid or 3 years of volunteer service. Dependents of members are not eligible. Applicants must plan to take college-level courses in the fire sciences or related academic programs. Selection is based on grade point average, number of years of service (paid or volunteer), commitment to a course of study, and financial need.
Financial data: Awards range from $250 to $4,000.
Additional information: Requests for applications must be accompanied by a self-addressed stamped envelope.
Number awarded: Varies each year; recently, 34 scholarships were awarded.
Deadline: July of each year.

2129
INTERNATIONAL COMPETITIVE SCHOLARSHIPS

Association for the Advancement of Cost Engineering
209 Prairie Avenue, Suite 100
Morgantown, WV 26505
Phone: (304) 296-8444   (800) 858-COST
Fax: (304) 291-5728   E-mail: info@aacei.org
Web Site: www.aacei.org

Summary: To provide financial assistance to undergraduate and graduate students interested in majoring in programs related to total cost management (the effective application of professional and technical expertise to plan and control resources, costs, profitability, and risk).
Eligibility: Applicants may be undergraduate students (second year standing or higher) or graduate students. They must be enrolled full time in a degree program in the United States or Canada that is related to the field of cost management/cost engineering, including engineering, construction, manufacturing, technology, business, and computer science. Selection is based on academic record (35 percent), extracurricular activities (35 percent), and an essay (30 percent) on why the study of the elements of total cost management is important.
Financial data: Individual stipends range from $750 to $3,000 per year. A total of $50,000 is awarded annually.
Duration: 1 year.
Number awarded: Several each year.
Deadline: November of each year.

2130
INTERNATIONAL SYMPOSIUM ON SUPERALLOYS SCHOLARSHIPS

The Minerals, Metals & Materials Society
Attn: TMS Student Awards Program
184 Thorn Hill Road
Warrendale, PA 15086-7528
Phone: (724) 776-9000, ext. 213   Fax: (724) 776-3770
E-mail: luther@tms.org
Web Site: www.tms.org/Students/AwardsPrograms/Scholarships.html
Summary: To provide financial assistance for college to student members of The Minerals, Metals & Materials Society (TMS).
Eligibility: This program is open to undergraduate and graduate members of the society who are full-time students majoring in metallurgical and/or materials science and engineering with an emphasis on aspects of the high-temperature, high-performance materials used in the gas turbine industry. Applicants may be from any country. Selection is based on academic achievement, school and community activities, work experience, leadership, a personal profile statement, and letters of recommendation.
Financial data: The stipend is $2,000.
Duration: 1 year.
Additional information: Funding for this program is provided by the Organizing Committee of the International Symposium on Superalloys.
Number awarded: 2 each year.
Deadline: April of each year.

2131
IOWA LEGION AUXILIARY PAST PRESIDENTS SCHOLARSHIP

American Legion Auxiliary
Attn: Department of Iowa
Attn: Education Committee
720 Lyon Street
Des Moines, IA 50309-5457
Phone: (515) 282-7987   Fax: (515) 282-7583
E-mail: info@iaamerlegaux.bestofiowa.com
Summary: To provide financial support for nursing education to dependents of Iowa veterans and to veterans who are members of the American Legion.
Eligibility: To be eligible for this scholarship, applicants must be members of the American Legion or the American Legion Auxiliary or be the children or grandchildren of veterans of World War I, World War II, Korea, Vietnam, Grenada, Lebanon, Panama, or the Persian Gulf. Applicants must reside in Iowa and be enrolled or planning to enroll in a nursing program in that state. Selection is based on character, Americanism, activities, and financial need.
Financial data: The amount of this scholarship depends on the contributions received from past unit, county, district, department, or national presidents.
Duration: 1 year.
Number awarded: 1 each year.
Deadline: May of each year.

2132
IRENE E. NEWMAN SCHOLARSHIP

American Dental Hygienists' Association
Attn: Institute for Oral Health
444 North Michigan Avenue, Suite 3400
Chicago, IL 60611
Phone: (312) 440-8944   (800) 735-4916
Fax: (312) 440-8929   E-mail: institute@adha.net
Web Site: www.adha.org
Summary: To provide financial assistance to students in a baccalaureate or graduate degree program in dental hygiene who demonstrate strong potential in public health or community dental health.
Eligibility: This program is open to students who have completed at least 1 year in a dental hygiene program at the baccalaureate, master's, or doctoral level with a grade point average of at least 3.0. Applicants must be able to demonstrate financial need and full-time enrollment. Selection is based on their potential in public health or community dental health.
Financial data: The amount of the award depends on the need of the recipient, to a maximum of $1,500.
Duration: 1 year.
Number awarded: 1 each year.
Deadline: May of each year.

2133
IRMA F. RUBE SCHOLARSHIP

Southern Association of Cytotechnologists, Inc.
Attn: Chair, Education Committee
822 Beale Street, Room 321
Memphis, TN 38163   Phone: (901) 448-6304
Summary: To provide financial assistance to students accepted into or currently enrolled in an approved cytotechnology program.
Eligibility: This program is open to students who are accepted into or are currently enrolled in an approved cytotechnology program. To be considered for this scholarship, students must have at least a 2.75 overall grade point average. They must complete an application and submit official transcripts of all college course work, proof of acceptance into an approved cytotechnology program, and 1 letter of recommendation. Selection is based on academic achievement.
Financial data: The stipend is $1,000.
Duration: 1 year.
Additional information: Funding for this program comes from Cytyc Corporation.
Number awarded: 1 each year.
Deadline: May of each year.

2134
IRON AND STEEL SOCIETY SCHOLARSHIPS

Iron and Steel Society
Attn: ISS Foundation
186 Thorn Hill Road
Warrendale, PA 15086-7528
Phone: (724) 776-1535, ext. 635   Fax: (724) 776-0430
E-mail: jannau@iss.org   Web Site: www.iss.org/foundation.htm
Summary: To provide financial assistance for college to students interested in preparing for a career in the iron and steel or steel-related industries.
Eligibility: This program is open to full-time students majoring in metallurgy, materials science, or metallurgical engineering as preparation for a career in the iron and steel or steel-related industries. Other majors are considered if the application is accompanied by a letter from an academic advisor, on official letterhead, regarding the program's preparation for advancement of steel product production, steel application, or the use of steel in material design. Interest in a career in ferrous-related industries should be demonstrated by internship, co-op, or related experiences and/or demonstrable plans to pursue such experience during college. Applicants must be a student member of the Iron and Steel Society (ISS). They may apply as early as their freshman year in college. Juniors and seniors should have a cumulative grade point average of 3.0 or higher in their major; undeclared students should have a cumulative grade point average of 3.25 or higher. Applicants must submit 1) a current resume; 2) a statement of their personal and professional goals; 3) a 300-word essay on why they are interested in working in the steel industry and what they will contribute to enhancing the well-being of the industry; and 4) letters of recommendation. Financial need is not considered in the selection process.
Financial data: The stipend is $2,000.

Duration: 1 year.
Number awarded: 8 each year, including 3 Willy Korf Memorial Fund Scholarships, 2 Ronald E. Lincoln Memorial Scholarships, 2 Benjamin F. Fairless Scholarship Awards, and 1 Charles E. Slater Scholarship. Another 8 scholarships are awarded by the ISS Foundation.
Deadline: April of each year.

2135
ISA CHEMICAL AND PETROLEUM INDUSTRIES DIVISION SCHOLARSHIP

Instrumentation, Systems, and Automation Society
Attn: ISA Educational Foundation
67 Alexander Drive
Research Triangle Park, NC 27709
Phone: (919) 549-8411   Fax: (919) 549-8288
E-mail: info@isa.org
Web Site: www.isa.org
Summary: To provide financial assistance to undergraduate and graduate students majoring in fields related to instrumentation, systems, and automation.
Eligibility: This program is open to full-time undergraduate and graduate students enrolled in a program in instrumentation, systems, automation, or a closely-related field. Applicants must have a grade point average of 3.0 or higher. They may be from any country but must be attending an institution in their own country. Applicants in a 2-year program must have completed at least 1 academic semester of 12 hours or its equivalent. Applicants in a 4-year program must be in their sophomore year or higher. Along with their application, they must submit an essay (up to 400 words) on their ambitions and qualifications as an innovator or future leader in a career in instrumentation, systems, or automation; they should describe their career objectives, how the award of this scholarship will help them attain their objectives, why they want to enter this particular field of engineering, what they have achieved and learned through their studies and activities, and what this indicates about their character and determination. Preference is given to applicants studying technology related to chemical and petroleum industries. Financial need is not considered in the selection process.
Financial data: The stipend is $2,000.
Duration: 1 year; may be renewed.
Additional information: This program was established in 2001.
Number awarded: 1 each year.
Deadline: January of each year.

2136
ISA EDUCATIONAL FOUNDATION SCHOLARSHIPS

Instrumentation, Systems, and Automation Society
Attn: ISA Educational Foundation
67 Alexander Drive
Research Triangle Park, NC 27709
Phone: (919) 549-8411   Fax: (919) 549-8288
E-mail: info@isa.org
Web Site: www.isa.org
Summary: To provide financial assistance to undergraduate and graduate students majoring in fields related to instrumentation, systems, and automation.
Eligibility: This program is open to full-time undergraduate and graduate students enrolled in a program in instrumentation, systems, automation, or a closely-related field. Applicants must have a grade point average of 3.0 or higher. They may be from any country but must be attending an institution in their own country. Applicants in a 2-year program must have completed at least 1 academic semester of 12 hours or its equivalent. Applicants in a 4-year program must be in their sophomore year or higher. Along with their application, they must submit an essay (up to 400 words) on their ambitions and qualifications as an innovator or future leader in a career in instrumentation, systems, or automation; they should describe their career objectives, how the award of this scholarship will help them attain their objectives, why they want to enter this particular field of engineering, what they have achieved and learned through their studies and activities, and what this indicates about their character and determination. Financial need is not considered in the selection process.
Financial data: A stipend is awarded (exact amount not specified).
Duration: 1 year; may be renewed.
Additional information: This program was established in 2001.
Number awarded: Varies each year; recently, 16 of these scholarships were awarded.
Deadline: January of each year.

2137
ISPE ADVANTAGE AWARD

Illinois Society of Professional Engineers
Attn: ISPE Foundation, Inc.
1304 South Lowell Avenue
Springfield, IL 62704
Phone: (217) 544-7424   Fax: (217) 544-3349
E-mail: ispe@springnet1.com
Web Site: www.springnet1.com/ispe
Summary: To provide financial assistance to college juniors and seniors in Illinois who are working on an engineering degree.
Eligibility: Applicants must be Illinois residents who are juniors or seniors in college in the state, enrolled in an engineering program (not engineering technology) accredited by the Accreditation Board of Engineering and Technology (ABET). They must have at least a 3.0 grade point average in those courses that count toward their engineering degree. Selection is based on financial need, scholastic achievement, activities, interest in engineering, and a 200-word essay on "Why I would like to become a professional engineer." This scholarship is reserved for the son or daughter of a member of the Illinois Society of Professional Engineers (ISPE), but if no applications are received from children of members, the scholarship is awarded to the most qualified applicant.
Financial data: The stipend is $1,000 per year.
Duration: 1 year.
Number awarded: 1 each year.
Deadline: January of each year.

2138
ISPE FOUNDATION SCHOLARSHIP

Illinois Society of Professional Engineers
Attn: ISPE Foundation, Inc.
1304 South Lowell Avenue
Springfield, IL 62704
Phone: (217) 544-7424   Fax: (217) 544-3349
E-mail: ispe@springnet1.com
Web Site: www.springnet1.com/ispe
Summary: To provide financial assistance to college juniors and seniors in Illinois who are working on an engineering degree.
Eligibility: Applicants must be Illinois residents who are juniors or seniors in college in the state, enrolled in an engineering program (not engineering technology) accredited by the Accreditation Board of Engineering and Technology (ABET). They must have at least a 3.0 grade point average in those courses that count toward their engineering degree. Selection is based on financial need, scholastic achievement, activities, interest in engineering, and a 200-word essay on "Why I would like to become a professional engineer."
Financial data: The stipend is $1,000 per year.
Duration: 1 year.
Number awarded: 1 each year.
Deadline: January of each year.

2139
IVOMEC SCHOLARSHIP

Mississippi Cattlemen's Association
Attn: Scholarship Applications
680 Monroe Street, Suite A
Jackson, MS 39202
Phone: (601) 354-8951   Fax: (601) 355-7128
Summary: To provide financial assistance to students from Mississippi who are enrolled in a college of agriculture at a 4-year academic institution.
Eligibility: Applicants must be enrolled at a 4-year college or university and be majoring in agriculture. To apply, students must submit a brief letter indicating the role they see themselves playing in the beef industry after graduation, write a brief essay (750 words) on an issue confronting the beef industry today, include 2 letters of reference, and complete an application form. Selection is based on academic record, extracurricular activities, honors and awards, and financial need.
Financial data: The stipend is $1,000.
Duration: 1 year.
Number awarded: 1 each year.

2140
IVY PARKER MEMORIAL SCHOLARSHIP

Society of Women Engineers
230 East Ohio Street, Suite 400
Chicago, IL 60611-3265
Phone: (312) 596-5223   Fax: (312) 644-8557
E-mail: hq@swe.org
Web Site: www.swe.org
Summary: To provide financial assistance to undergraduate women majoring in engineering.
Eligibility: This program is open to women entering their junior or senior year majoring in engineering at an ABET-accredited or SWE-approved college or university. Applicants must have a grade point average of 3.0 or higher. Selection is based on merit and financial need.
Financial data: The stipend is $2,500.
Duration: 1 year.
Additional information: This program was established in 1986.
Number awarded: 1 each year.
Deadline: January of each year.

2141
J. FIELDING REED SCHOLARSHIP

American Society of Agronomy
Attn: Scholarship Committee
677 South Segoe Road
Madison, WI 53711
Phone: (608) 273-8008   Fax: (608) 273-2021
Web Site: www.agronomy.org
Summary: To provide financial assistance to outstanding undergraduate seniors preparing for a career in soil or plant sciences.
Eligibility: This program is open to undergraduate seniors who are pursuing a career in the plant or soil sciences. Applicants must be graduating in the year in which the scholarship is presented. They must have earned at least a 3.0 cumulative grade point average and be able to document a history of community and campus leadership activities, particularly in agriculture.
Financial data: The stipend is $2,000.
Duration: 1 year.
Additional information: Funds for this program are administered by the Agronomic Science Foundation and the selection process is administered by the American Society of Agronomy.
Number awarded: 1 each year.
Deadline: February of each year.

2142
J. KEITH BRIMACOMBE PRESIDENTIAL SCHOLARSHIP

The Minerals, Metals & Materials Society
Attn: TMS Student Awards Program
184 Thorn Hill Road
Warrendale, PA 15086-7528
Phone: (724) 776-9000, ext. 213   Fax: (724) 776-3770
E-mail: luther@tms.org
Web Site: www.tms.org/Students/AwardsPrograms/Scholarships.html
Summary: To provide financial assistance to student members of The Minerals, Metals & Materials Society (TMS).
Eligibility: This program is open to undergraduate members of the society who are full-time students majoring in metallurgical engineering, materials science and engineering, or minerals processing and extraction. Applicants may be from any country. Selection is based on academic achievement, school and community activities, work experience, leadership, a personal profile statement, and letters of recommendation.
Financial data: The stipend is $5,000, plus a travel stipend of $1,000 (so the recipient can attend the annual meeting of the society to accept the award).
Duration: 1 year.
Additional information: Funding for this program is provided by the TMS Foundation.
Number awarded: 1 each year.
Deadline: April of each year.

2143
JAMES A. HOLEKAMP MEMORIAL SCHOLARSHIP IN FOREST RESOURCES

Technical Association of the Pulp and Paper Industry
P.O. Box 105113
Atlanta, GA 30348-5113
Phone: (770) 446-1400   (800) 332-8686
Fax: (770) 446-6947   Web Site: www.tappi.org
Summary: To provide financial assistance to college students enrolled in a school of forest resources in the south.
Eligibility: This program is open to rising sophomores who are enrolled in a school of forest resources located in 1 of the southern states. Financial need is considered in the selection process.
Financial data: The stipend is $2,000.
Duration: 1 year.
Additional information: This scholarship is sponsored by MOTAG-South (the Millyard Operations Technical Advancement Group-South), a subcommittee of the Fiber Raw Material Supply Committee of the TAPPI Pulp Manufacture Division.
Number awarded: 1 each year.
Deadline: May of each year.

2144
JAMES F. REVILLE SCHOLARSHIP

NYSARC, Inc.
393 Delaware Avenue
Delmar, NY 12054
Phone: (518) 439-8311   Fax: (518) 439-1893
E-mail: nysarc@nysarc.org
Web Site: www.nysarc.org/scholar.htm
Summary: To provide financial assistance to currently-enrolled college students in New York majoring in a field related to mental retardation.
Eligibility: This program is open to high school graduates enrolled full time in any year of college training in a field related to mental retardation. Applications are available through local chapters of NYSARC.
Financial data: The stipend is $3,000.
Duration: 1 year.
Additional information: NYSARC, Inc. was formerly the New York State Association for Retarded Children.
Number awarded: 2 each year.
Deadline: February of each year.

2145
JAMES I. FITZGIBBON SCHOLARSHIP AWARD

Professional Lawn Care Association of America
1000 Johnson Ferry Road, N.E., Suite C-135
Marietta, GA 30068-2112
Phone: (800) 458-3466   Fax: (770) 578-6071
Web Site: www.plcaa.org/FitzgibbonScholarshipAward.htm
Summary: To provide financial assistance to college students who are interested in preparing for a career in the lawn/landscape industry.
Eligibility: Eligible to apply are full-time college students whose parents own or are employed by a company affiliated with the Professional Lawn Care Association of America (PLCAA). Students who work at a PLCAA member company are also eligible to apply. Applicants must be interested in pursuing a career in the lawn/landscape industry. To apply, they must submit a completed application form, a recent photograph, and a current official transcript. Selection is based on scholastic achievement and financial need.
Financial data: The stipend is at least $2,500.
Duration: 1 year.
Number awarded: 1 or more each year.
Deadline: September of each year.

2146
JAMES I. MACKENZIE/THERMOSET DIVISION SCHOLARSHIP

Society of Plastics Engineers
Attn: SPE Foundation
14 Fairfield Drive
Brookfield, CT 06804
Phone: (203) 740-5447   Fax: (203) 775-8490
E-mail: foundation@4spe.org   Web Site: www.4spe.org

Summary: To provide college scholarships to students who have a career interest in the plastics industry and experience in the thermoset industry.
Eligibility: Applicants must be full-time students at either a 4-year college or in a 2-year technical program. They must have a demonstrated or expressed interest in the plastics industry; must have experience in the thermoset industry, such as courses taken, research conducted, or jobs held; and should be taking classes that would be beneficial to a career in the plastics industry (e.g., plastics engineering, polymer sciences, chemistry, physics, chemical engineering, mechanical engineering, industrial engineering, and business administration). Financial need must be documented. Along with their application, students must submit 3 letters of recommendation; a high school and/or college transcript; a 1- to 2-page statement telling why they are interested in the scholarship, their qualifications, and their career goals in the plastics industry; and a statement detailing their exposure to the thermoset industry.
Financial data: The stipend is $2,000 per year.
Duration: 1 year.
Number awarded: 1 each year.
Deadline: December of each year.

2147
JAMES "JIM BOB" NORMAN MEMORIAL SCHOLARSHIP

Texas FFA Association
614 East 12th Street
Austin, TX 78701
Phone: (512) 480-8045   Fax: (512) 472-0555
E-mail: txffa@txaged.org   Web Site: www.txaged.org
Summary: To provide financial assistance for college to high school seniors in Texas who demonstrate outstanding personal qualities and involvement in FFA.
Eligibility: This program is open to high school seniors in Texas who are FFA members and have been members at least 2 of the 3 previous years. Applicants must be planning to major in college in a field related to the agricultural sciences, life sciences, or natural resources. They must have completed at least 5 semesters of instruction in agriculture and/or agribusiness during high school and scored at least 950 on the SAT or 20 on the ACT. U.S. citizenship and ranking in the top half of their graduating class are also required. Selection is based on academic achievement (16 points); SAT or ACT scores (14 points); agricultural science and career related instruction (10 points); FFA achievement (20 points), including the supervised agricultural experience (10 points); financial need (10 points); and performance during interviews regarding academics (10 points), FFA achievement (5 points), and financial need (10 points).
Financial data: The stipend is $2,000 per year.
Duration: 4 years.
Additional information: Students may not apply for both 4-H and FFA scholarships.
Number awarded: 1 each year.

2148
JAMES L. GOODWIN MEMORIAL SCHOLARSHIPS

Connecticut Forest and Park Association
16 Meriden Road
Rockfall, CT 06481-2961
Phone: (860) 346-2372   Fax: (860) 347-7463
E-mail: conn.forest.assoc@snet.net   Web Site: www.ctwoodlands.org
Summary: To provide financial assistance to residents of Connecticut interested in studying forestry or forest management at the undergraduate or graduate level.
Eligibility: This program is open to Connecticut residents who are graduating high school seniors, currently enrolled in college, or graduate students. Applicants must be attending or planning to attend the University of Connecticut or another school accredited in forest management. Selection is based on financial need, academic record, and a personal statement on why the applicant in interested in forest management.
Financial data: Stipends range from $1,000 to $3,000 per year. Funds may be used for tuition or living costs. Payment is made only to the institution.
Duration: 1 year; may be renewed.
Additional information: This program began in 1992. Recipients are expected to communicate in writing at least twice a year with the association, to provide an informal account of their progress and any special circumstances bearing on financial need. They must also arrange with their college for a copy of their semester grades to be forwarded to the association.
Number awarded: 5 to 10 each year.
Deadline: March of each year.

2149
JAMES R. VOGT SCHOLARSHIP

American Nuclear Society
Attn: Scholarship Program
555 North Kensington Avenue
La Grange Park, IL 60526-5592
Phone: (708) 352-6611   Fax: (708) 352-0499
E-mail: outreach@ans.org
Web Site: www.ans.org/honors/scholarships
Summary: To provide financial assistance to students who are interested in preparing for a career in nuclear science.
Eligibility: This program is open to undergraduate students and first-year graduate students who are enrolled in or proposing to undertake research in radio-analytical chemistry, analytical chemistry, or analytical applications of nuclear science. Applicants must be juniors, seniors, or first-year graduate students, be U.S. citizens or permanent residents, be able to demonstrate academic achievement, and be sponsored by an organization within the American Nuclear Society (ANS).
Financial data: The award is $3,000.
Duration: 1 year.
Additional information: Requests for an application must be accompanied by a self-addressed stamped envelope.
Number awarded: 2 each year: 1 for an undergraduate and 1 for a graduate student.
Deadline: January of each year.

2150
J.C. AND RHEBA COBB MEMORIAL SCHOLARSHIP

National Community Pharmacists Association
Attn: NCPA Foundation
205 Daingerfield Road
Alexandria, VA 22314-2885
Phone: (703) 683-8200   (800) 544-7447
Fax: (703) 683-3619   E-mail: info@ncpanet.org
Web Site: www.ncpanet.org.org/students/cobbscholar.html
Summary: To provide financial assistance for full-time education in pharmacy to student members of the National Community Pharmacists Association (NCPA).
Eligibility: All pharmacy students who are student members of the association and enrolled in an accredited U.S. school or college of pharmacy on a full-time basis are eligible. Applicants must submit a copy of the most recent transcript of their college grades, 2 letters of recommendation, a resume or curriculum vitae, and a statement outlining their scholastic achievement, leadership activities, objectives for the future, and interest in civic and government affairs. Selection is based on leadership qualities, demonstrated interest in civic and government affairs, and academic achievement.
Financial data: The stipend is $2,000, paid directly to the recipient's school or college of pharmacy.
Duration: 1 year.
Additional information: Until October 1996, the NCPA, the national association representing independent retail pharmacy, was known as NARD (the National Association of Retail Druggists).
Number awarded: 1 each year.
Deadline: March of each year.

2151
JENNET COLLIFLOWER KEYS NURSING SCHOLARSHIP

Dade Community Foundation
Attn: Director of Development
200 South Biscayne Boulevard, Suite 2780
Miami, FL 33131-2343
Phone: (305) 371-2711   Fax: (305) 371-5342
E-mail: Dadecomfnd@aol.com
Summary: To provide financial assistance to upper-division students in Florida who are working on a degree in nursing.
Eligibility: This program is open to students in their junior or senior year of an undergraduate nursing degree who are Florida residents and enrolled full time in a Florida public or private university.
Financial data: The stipend is $1,000.
Duration: 1 year.
Number awarded: 2 each year.
Deadline: May of each year.

2152
JERRY ROBINSON-INWELD CORPORATION SCHOLARSHIP

American Welding Society
Attn: AWS Foundation, Inc.
550 N.W. LeJeune Road
Miami, FL 33126
Phone: (305) 443-9353, ext. 461   (800) 443-9353, ext. 461
Fax: (305) 443-7559   E-mail: vpinsky@aws.org
Web Site: www.aws.org/foundation/robinson.html
Summary: To provide financial assistance to high school seniors and graduates interested in pursuing a career in welding.
Eligibility: This program is open to students with significant financial need interested in pursuing a career in welding. By the beginning of the academic year the scholarship is awarded, applicants must 1) be at least 18 years of age, 2) have a high school diploma or GED, 3) have a grade point average of 2.5 or higher, 4) have been accepted at a college or university, and 5) plan to attend full time. They must submit an essay on why the funds are needed, how the scholarship would change their life, and how it would allow them to further the joining sciences. U.S. citizenship is required.
Financial data: The stipend is $2,500.
Duration: Up to 4 years, provided the recipient maintains full-time status, an acceptable grade point average, and enrollment in a welding program.
Additional information: This program is supported by Inweld Corporation.
Number awarded: 1 each year.
Deadline: January of each year.

2153
JIMMY A. YOUNG MEMORIAL EDUCATION RECOGNITION AWARD

American Respiratory Care Foundation
Attn: Administrative Coordinator
11030 Ables Lane
Dallas, TX 75229-4593
Phone: (972) 243-2272   Fax: (972) 484-2720
E-mail: info@aarc.org
Web Site: www.aarc.org/awards
Summary: To provide financial assistance to college students, especially minorities, interested in becoming respiratory therapists.
Eligibility: Candidates must be enrolled in an accredited respiratory therapy program, have completed at least 1 semester/quarter of the program, and have earned a grade point average of 3.0 or higher. Preference is given to nominees of minority origin. Applications must include 6 copies of an original referenced paper on some aspect of respiratory care and letters of recommendation. The foundation prefers that the candidates be nominated by a school or program, but any student may initiate a request for sponsorship by a school (in order that a deserving candidate is not denied the opportunity to compete simply because the school does not initiate the application).
Financial data: The stipend is $1,000. The award also provides airfare, 1 night's lodging, and registration for the association's international congress.
Duration: 1 year.
Number awarded: 1 each year.
Deadline: May of each year.

2154
J.O. POLLACK/NATIONAL LEAGUE FOR NURSING STUDENT ACHIEVEMENT SCHOLARSHIP

J.O. Pollack L.L.C.
1700 Irving Park Road
Chicago, IL 60613
Phone: (773) 4772100   Fax: (773) 477-2521
E-mail: jopollack5@aol.com   Web Site: www.jopollack.com
Summary: To provide financial assistance to students currently enrolled in a state-approved nursing program.
Eligibility: All applicants must be students currently enrolled in state-approved nursing programs. These programs may be on any level: baccalaureate, master's, associate, diploma, or practical nursing. Applicants must have at least a 3.0 grade point average, have performed 25 hours or more of volunteer community service (excluding clinical curriculum) related to the health care profession within the past 12 months, and write an essay (up to 500 words) on "Why I Chose the Nursing Profession as a Career." Selection is based on academic record, community service, and the essay.

Financial data: The stipend is $1,000.
Duration: 1 year.
Number awarded: 2 each year.
Deadline: March of each year.

2155
JOE CRAVENS MEMORIAL SCHOLARSHIP

Indiana Golf Course Superintendents Association
c/o Steve Christie, Scholarship Chair
Automatic Irrigation Supply Company
116 Shadowlawn Drive
Fishers, IN 46038
Phone: (317) 466-SUPT   (888) 221-SUPT
E-mail: igcsa@aol.com   Web Site: www.igcsa.com/scholarship_programs.htm
Summary: To provide financial assistance to children of Indiana Golf Course
Superintendents Association (IGCSA) members or to employees at IGCSA
member clubs who are majoring in turfgrass in college.
Eligibility: This program is open to children of IGCSA members or those who
work at IGCSA member clubs. The career goal of the applicants must be to work
in an area of turfgrass management (e.g., lawn care, sports field, golf courses,
ornamental horticulture). They must be entering the last 2 years of their
academic program at an accredited institution. Selection is based on merit.
Financial data: The stipend is at least $1,000.
Duration: 1 year.
Additional information: This program was established in 1992.
Number awarded: 1 each year.
Deadline: March of each year.

2156
JOE RODRIGUEZ JR. SCHOLARSHIP

Portuguese Heritage Scholarship Foundation
Attn: Academic Secretary
P.O. Box 30246
Bethesda, MD 20824-0246
Phone: (301) 652-2775   E-mail: phsf@vivaportugal.com
Web Site: www.vivaportugal.com/phsf/apply.htm
Summary: To provide financial assistance for college to students of Portuguese
American heritage interested in studying health sciences.
Eligibility: Eligible to apply for this support are high school seniors or currently-
enrolled college students who are of Portuguese American ancestry. Applicants
must be U.S. residents and attending or planning to attend an accredited 4-year
college or university. They must have a demonstrated interest in the study of
health sciences.
Financial data: The stipend is $2,000 per year.
Duration: 4 years, provided the recipient maintains a grade point average of 3.0 or
higher.
Additional information: Recipients must attend college on a full-time basis.
Number awarded: 1 each year.
Deadline: January of each year.

2157
JOHN A. FOCHT NATIONAL CHI EPSILON SCHOLARSHIPS

Chi Epsilon
c/o Dr. Robert L. Henry
University of Texas at Arlington
Box 19316
Arlington, TX 76019-0316
Phone: (817) 272-2752   Fax: (817) 272-2826
E-mail: rhenry@uta.edu   Web Site: www.chi-epsilon.org
Summary: To provide financial assistance for college to members of Chi Epsilon,
the national civil engineering honor society.
Eligibility: Members of Chi Epsilon may apply at the chapter level. The faculty
advisor selects the chapter's nominee and forwards the nomination to the district
councilor, who chooses the district winner. Selection is based on the 4 qualities of
Chi Epsilon membership: character, scholarship, sociability, and practicality.
Financial data: The stipend is $2,500.
Duration: 1 year.
Additional information: Chi Epsilon, the national civil engineering honor
society, began in 1922 at the University of Illinois.
Number awarded: 2 each year.
Deadline: November of each year.

2158
JOHN AND ELSA GRACIK SCHOLARSHIPS

ASME International
Attn: Education Department
Three Park Avenue
New York, NY 10016-5990
Phone: (212) 591-8131   (800) THE-ASME
Fax: (212) 591-7143   E-mail: oluwanifiset@asme.org
Web Site: www.asme.org/educate/aid/scholar.htm
Summary: To provide financial assistance to undergraduate students who are
members of the American Society of Mechanical Engineers (ASME).
Eligibility: This program is open to student members in good standing who are
enrolled in an ABET-accredited mechanical engineering baccalaureate,
mechanical engineering technology, or related program, and to high school
students accepted for enrollment in a mechanical engineering or related
program. U.S. citizenship is required. Selection is based on character, integrity,
leadership, scholastic ability, potential contribution to the mechanical
engineering profession, and financial need.
Financial data: The stipend is $1,500.
Duration: 1 year.
Additional information: This program was established in 1992. Requests for
applications must be accompanied by a self-addressed stamped envelope.
Number awarded: 16 each year.
Deadline: March of each year.

2159
JOHN AND MURIEL LANDIS SCHOLARSHIPS

American Nuclear Society
Attn: Scholarship Program
555 North Kensington Avenue
La Grange Park, IL 60526-5592
Phone: (708) 352-6611   Fax: (708) 352-0499
E-mail: outreach@ans.org
Web Site: www.ans.org/honors/scholarships
Summary: To provide financial assistance to undergraduate or graduate students
who are interested in pursuing a career in nuclear-related fields.
Eligibility: This program is open to undergraduate and graduate students at
colleges or universities located in the United States who are pursuing, or planning
to pursue, a career in nuclear science, nuclear engineering, or a nuclear-related
field. Qualified high school seniors are also eligible. Applicants must have greater
than average financial need and have experienced circumstances that render them
disadvantaged. U.S. citizenship is not required. Selection is primarily based on
financial need and potential for academic and professional success. Applicants
must be sponsored by an organization within the American Nuclear Society
(ANS). If the student does not know of a sponsoring organization, the society will
help to establish contact. Augmentation of this scholarship program with
matching or supplemental funds by the sponsoring organization is encouraged
(though not required).
Financial data: The stipend is $3,000, to be used to cover tuition, books, fees,
room, and board.
Duration: 1 year.
Additional information: Requests for an application must be accompanied by a
self-addressed stamped envelope.
Number awarded: Up to 8 each year.
Deadline: January of each year.

2160
JOHN C. LINCOLN MEMORIAL SCHOLARSHIP

American Welding Society
Attn: AWS Foundation, Inc.
550 N.W. LeJeune Road
Miami, FL 33126
Phone: (305) 443-9353, ext. 461   (800) 443-9353, ext. 461
Fax: (305) 443-7559   E-mail: vpinsky@aws.org
Web Site: www.aws.org/foundation/lincoln.html
Summary: To provide financial assistance to college students majoring in welding
engineering.
Eligibility: This program is open to undergraduate students who are pursuing at
least a 4-year bachelor's degree in welding engineering or welding engineering
technology (although preference is given to welding engineering students).
Applicants must have a minimum overall grade point average of 2.5 and be able to

demonstrate financial need. U.S. citizenship is required. Priority is given to applicants who reside or attend school in Arizona or Ohio.

Financial data: The stipend is $2,500.

Duration: 1 year; recipients may reapply.

Number awarded: 1 each year.

Deadline: January of each year.

2161
JOHN D. ISAACS SCHOLARSHIP

California Sea Grant College Program
c/o University of California at San Diego
9500 Gilman Drive, Department 0232
La Jolla, CA 92093-0232
Phone: (858) 534-4442   Fax: (858) 534-2231
Web Site: www-csgc.ucsd.edu

Summary: To recognize and reward outstanding science fair entries by California high school seniors who are interested in majoring in marine science at a California college.

Eligibility: This program is open to high school juniors and seniors in California. To be eligible, students must first have entered a regional or county science fair with a project related to marine technology or to any of the marine sciences: geology, biology, meteorology, chemistry, etc. In addition, students in their senior year must have applied to (and must by the following fall have enrolled in) a 4-year college or university in California. Selection is based on 1) the creativity, uniqueness, and superiority of the science fair project, and 2) the student's originality, curiosity, intelligence, and enthusiasm for science.

Financial data: The stipend is $3,000 per year. In addition, a grant of $500 is given to the junior or senior high school teacher identified by the recipient as having been especially supportive of his or her interest in marine science or in the development of the science fair project; this award is called the Isaacs Teacher Recognition Award.

Duration: 4 years.

Additional information: California Sea Grant College System is a statewide program of marine research, extension services, and educational activities that seek to promote wise use of marine resources for the public benefit. These awards are named in honor of John D. Isaacs, a professor of oceanography at Scripps Institution of Oceanography and Director of the University of California Institute of Marine Resources.

Number awarded: 1 each year.

Deadline: April of each year.

2162
JOHN DAWE DENTAL EDUCATION SCHOLARSHIP

Hawai'i Community Foundation
900 Fort Street Mall, Suite 1300
Honolulu, HI 96813
Phone: (808) 566-5570   (888) 731-3863
Fax: (808) 521-6286   E-mail: scholarships@hcf-hawaii.org
Web Site: www.hcf-hawaii.org

Summary: To provide financial assistance to Hawaii residents who are interested in preparing for a career in the dental field.

Eligibility: This program is open to Hawaii residents who are interested in full-time study in dentistry, dental hygiene, or dental assisting. They must be able to demonstrate academic achievement (at least a 2.7 grade point average), good moral character, and financial need. In addition to filling out the standard application form, applicants must write a short statement indicating their reasons for attending college, their planned course of study, and their career goals.

Financial data: The amounts of the awards depend on the availability of funds and the need of the recipient; recently, grants averaged $1,050.

Duration: 1 year.

Additional information: Recipients may attend college in Hawaii or on the mainland.

Number awarded: Varies each year; recently, 10 of these scholarships were awarded.

Deadline: February of each year.

2163
JOHN J. AND IRENE T. POWERS SCHOLARSHIP

Institute of Food Technologists
Attn: Scholarship Department
221 North LaSalle Street, Suite 300
Chicago, IL 60601-1291
Phone: (312) 782-8424   Fax: (312) 782-8348
E-mail: info@ift.org   Web Site: www.ift.org

Summary: To provide financial assistance to undergraduates interested in studying food science or food technology.

Eligibility: Applicants must be currently enrolled as sophomores or juniors in a food science or food technology program at an educational institution in the United States or Canada. They must have an outstanding scholastic record and a well-rounded personality. Financial need is not considered in the selection process.

Financial data: The stipend is $1,000.

Duration: 1 year; recipients may reapply if they are members of the Institute of Food Technologists (IFT).

Additional information: Correspondence and completed applications must be submitted to the department head of the educational institution the applicant is attending.

Number awarded: 1 each year.

Deadline: January of each year.

2164
JOHN L. TOMASOVIC SCHOLARSHIP

Bedding Plants Foundation, Inc.
Attn: Scholarship Program
P.O. Box 280
East Lansing, MI 48826-0280
Phone: (517) 333-4617   Fax: (517) 333-4494
E-mail: bpfi@aol.com
Web Site: www.bpfi.org

Summary: To provide financial assistance to undergraduate and graduate students in horticulture.

Eligibility: This program is open to undergraduate students at a 4-year college or university and to graduate students. Applicants must be horticulture majors who are U.S. or Canadian citizens or permanent residents with a grade point average between 3.0 and 3.5. Selection is based on academic record, recommendations, career goals, extracurricular activities, and (especially) financial need.

Financial data: The stipend ranges from $500 to $2,000 per year.

Duration: 1 year.

Number awarded: 1 each year.

Deadline: April of each year.

2165
JOHN MABRY FORESTRY SCHOLARSHIP

Railway Tie Association
Attn: Education and Information Committee
115 Commerce Drive, Suite C
Fayetteville, GA 30214
Phone: (770) 460-5553   Fax: (770) 460-5573
E-mail: ties@rta.org
Web Site: www.rta.org

Summary: To provide financial aid to upper-division college students who are enrolled in accredited forestry schools.

Eligibility: This program is open to juniors and seniors at accredited forestry schools. Selection is based on leadership qualities, career objectives, scholastic achievement, and financial need.

Financial data: The stipend is $1,250 per year.

Duration: 1 year.

Number awarded: 2 each year.

Deadline: June of each year.

2166
JOHNNY DAVIS MEMORIAL SCHOLARSHIP

Aircraft Electronics Association
Attn: Educational Foundation
4217 South Hocker Drive
Independence, MO 64055-4723
Phone: (816) 373-6565   Fax: (816) 478-3100
E-mail: info@aea.net
Web Site: www.aea.net

Summary: To provide financial assistance to students preparing for a career in avionics or aircraft repair.

Eligibility: This program is open to high school seniors and currently-enrolled college students who are attending (or planning to attend) an accredited postsecondary institution in an avionics or aircraft repair program.

Financial data: The stipend is $1,000.

Duration: 1 year.
Number awarded: 1 each year.
Deadline: February of each year.

2167
JOHNNY JENKINS SCHOLARSHIP

Summary: To provide financial assistance to students from southeastern states who are majoring in animal science or agricultural communications.
See Listing #1470.

2168
JOSEPH A. LEVENDUSKY MEMORIAL SCHOLARSHIP

Engineers' Society of Western Pennsylvania
Attn: International Water Conference
Pittsburgh Engineers' Building
337 Fourth Avenue
Pittsburgh, PA 15222
Phone: (412) 261-0710   E-mail: eswp@eswp.com
Web Site: www.eswp.com
Summary: To provide financial assistance to undergraduate students majoring in chemical engineering and committed to a career in the field of water technology.
Eligibility: Eligible to apply for this program are undergraduate students majoring in chemical engineering who are preparing for a career in water technology. They must have been employed in the field of water technology (excluding environmental wastewater, water pollution control, and water resources management) for at least 1 year. Along with their application, they must submit a 250-word essay on the occupation they want to prepare for by attending college and the reasons they have decided on the field of water technology. Financial need is considered in the selection process.
Financial data: Up to $7,000 per year.
Duration: 1 year.
Number awarded: 1 each year.
Deadline: April of each year.

2169
JOSEPH F. DRACUP SCHOLARSHIP AWARD

American Congress on Surveying and Mapping
Attn: Awards Director
6 Montgomery Village Avenue, Suite 403
Gaithersburg, MD 20879
Phone: (240) 632-9716   Fax: (240) 632-1321
E-mail: tmilburn@acsm.net
Web Site: www.acsm.net
Summary: To recognize and reward outstanding college students who are members of the American Congress on Surveying and Mapping and interested in preparing for a career in geodetic surveying.
Eligibility: Members of the sponsoring organization may apply for this scholarship if they are undergraduate students in a 4-year degree program committed to a career in geodetic surveying. Selection is based on the applicant's previous academic record (30 percent), a statement on future plans (30 percent), letters of recommendation (20 percent), and professional activities (20 percent); if 2 or more applicants are judged equal based on those criteria, financial need may be considered.
Financial data: The stipend is $2,000.
Duration: The competition is held annually.
Additional information: Funds for this award are provided by the American Association for Geodetic Surveying.
Number awarded: 1 each year.
Deadline: December of each year.

2170
JOSEPH FRASCA EXCELLENCE IN AVIATION SCHOLARSHIP

University Aviation Association
Attn: Frasca Scholarship
c/o Southern Illinois University at Carbondale
College of Applied Sciences and Arts
Carbondale, IL 62901-6623
Phone: (618) 453-8898
Summary: To provide financial assistance to upper-division college students majoring in aviation.

Eligibility: This program is open to juniors or seniors who are currently enrolled in a school affiliated with the University Aviation Association. Applicants must have earned at least a 3.0 in their college courses; have Federal Aviation Administration certification/qualifications in either aviation maintenance or flight; be a member of at least 1 aviation organization (e.g., Alpha Eta Rho, National Intercollegiate Flying Association's Flying Team, Experimental Aircraft Association, Warbirds of America); and have a record of aviation activities, projects, or events that demonstrates an interest and an enthusiasm for aviation. Preference is given to applicants who can document interest or experience in aviation simulation, work experience in aviation, interest or experience in aircraft restoration, work experience while in school, interest or experience in aerobatics, or financial need.
Financial data: The stipend is $1,000.
Duration: 1 year.
Additional information: The scholarships are awarded at the University Aviation Association banquet each year.
Number awarded: 2 each year.
Deadline: May of each year.

2171
JOSH GOTTHEIL MEMORIAL BONE MARROW TRANSPLANT CAREER DEVELOPMENT AWARDS

Oncology Nursing Society
Attn: ONS Foundation
501 Holiday Drive
Pittsburgh, PA 15220-2749
Phone: (412) 921-7373, ext. 231   Fax: (412) 921-6565
E-mail: foundation@ons.org
Web Site: www.ons.org
Summary: To provide funding for further education to professional registered nurses who can demonstrate meritorious practice in bone marrow transplant (BMT) nursing.
Eligibility: This program is open to professional registered nurses who are interested in pursuing additional education at the bachelor's or master's degree level. Applicants must be currently employed as a registered nurse working in BMT (at least 75 percent of time must be devoted to patient care) or in the position of nurse manager, nurse practitioner, clinical nurse specialist, BMT coordinator, or equivalent position. They must have at least 2 years in BMT nursing practice. Candidates are evaluated on the following criteria: 1) clarity of professional goal statement; 2) demonstrated commitment to professional development (e.g., continuing education attendance, inservices given); 3) potential for continuing professional practice in BMT nursing; 4) recommendations; 5) examples of professional expertise and/or contributions in BMT nursing; 6) demonstrated commitment to BMT nursing practice; 7) examples of compassion for the BMT patient and family; and 8) quality of the application. Applicants must not have previously received this career development award from the foundation.
Financial data: The stipend is $2,000. Funds may be used to support a continuing education program or to supplement tuition in a bachelor's or master's program.
Number awarded: 4 each year.
Deadline: November of each year.

2172
JSHS SCHOLARSHIPS

Academy of Applied Science
Attn: JSHS National Office
24 Warren Street
P.O. Box 2934
Concord, NH 03302-2934
Phone: (603) 228-4520   Fax: (603) 228-4730
E-mail: trojano@jshs.org
Web Site: www.jshs.org
Summary: To recognize and reward outstanding participants in the Army, Navy, and Air Force Junior Science and Humanities Symposia (JSHS).
Eligibility: JSHS regional sponsors invite local high schools to nominate students in grades 9 through 12 who display an interest or aptitude in science. The sponsors, 47 academic institutions in various regions of the country, select students to present papers at the regional symposia. At each regional symposium, selected paper presenters are chosen to receive scholarships. From each of the 48 regional symposia, 5 students are selected to attend the national JSHS, where 1 of them presents his or her research paper in competition for further awards.

Financial data: At each regional symposium, 1 winner receives a $4,000 scholarship and an expense-paid trip to the national symposium; 4 other students receive expense-paid trips to the national symposium. In the national competition, first-place finalists receive $16,000 scholarships, second-place finalists receive $6,000 scholarships, and third-place finalists receive $2,000 scholarships (all national scholarships are in addition to the regional scholarships). Top finalists are also awarded an expense-paid trip to the International Youth Science Forum, held in London.
Duration: This competition is held annually. National scholarships are paid over a period of 4 years for first-place winners ($5,000 per year), 3 years for second-place winners ($4,000 in each of the first 2 years and $2,000 in the third year), and 2 years for third-place winners ($4,000 the first year and $2,000 the second year).
Additional information: The JSHS program was established by the Army in 1958 and since 1963 has been administered by the Academy of Applied Science. Since 1995, funding has also been provided by the Office of Naval Research and the Air Force Office of Scientific Research.
Number awarded: Scholarships are awarded to regional winners in each of the 48 regional symposia, to 8 first-place finalists in the national symposium, to 8 second-place national finalists, and to 8 third-place national finalists.

2173
JUDITH RESNIK MEMORIAL SCHOLARSHIP

Society of Women Engineers
230 East Ohio Street, Suite 400
Chicago, IL 60611-3265
Phone: (312) 596-5223   Fax: (312) 644-8557
E-mail: hq@swe.org
Web Site: www.swe.org
Summary: To provide financial assistance to undergraduate women who are members of the Society of Women Engineers and majoring in engineering.
Eligibility: This program is open to women who are rising sophomores, juniors, or seniors and are studying aerospace, aeronautical, or astronautical engineering with a minimum 3.0 grade point average in a space-related major. They must be interested in pursuing a career in the space industry. Only members of the society are considered for this award. Selection is based on merit.
Financial data: The stipend is $2,500.
Duration: 1 year.
Additional information: This award was established in 1988 to honor society member Judith Resnik, who was killed aboard the Challenger space shuttle.
Number awarded: 1 each year.
Deadline: January of each year.

2174
JULIE VANDE VELDE LEADERSHIP SCHOLARSHIP

Institute of Food Technologists
Attn: Scholarship Department
221 North LaSalle Street, Suite 300
Chicago, IL 60601-1291
Phone: (312) 782-8424   Fax: (312) 782-8348
E-mail: info@ift.org   Web Site: www.ift.org
Summary: To provide financial assistance to undergraduates interested in studying food science or food technology.
Eligibility: Applicants must be currently enrolled as sophomores or juniors in a food science or food technology program at an educational institution in the United States or Canada. They must have an outstanding scholastic record and a well-rounded personality. Financial need is not considered in the selection process.
Financial data: The stipend is $1,000.
Duration: 1 year; recipients may reapply if they are members of the Institute of Food Technologists.
Additional information: Correspondence and completed applications must be submitted to the department head of educational institution applicant is attending.
Number awarded: 1 each year.
Deadline: January of each year.

2175
JULIETTE A. SOUTHARD/ORAL-B LABORATORIES SCHOLARSHIPS

American Dental Assistants Association
203 North LaSalle Street, Suite 1320
Chicago, IL 60601-1225
Phone: (312) 541-1550   (800) 733-2322

Summary: To provide financial assistance to members of the American Dental Assistants Association (ADAA).
Eligibility: Applicants must be American citizens, high school graduates, either student or active members of the association, and either accepted into or currently enrolled in a dental assisting education program. A letter of intent to pursue a long-range career in dental assisting must accompany the application. Selection is based on academic achievement, ability, interest in the career of dental assisting, and personal attributes.
Financial data: The amount of the award depends on the need of the recipient.
Duration: 1 year.
Additional information: This fund, named in honor of the founder of the ADAA, was established in 1929. Current sponsorship is provided by Oral-B Laboratories.
Number awarded: Varies each year.
Deadline: January of each year.

2176
JUNE P. GALLOWAY SCHOLARSHIP

Summary: To provide financial assistance for college to members of the North Carolina Association of Health, Physical Education, Recreation and Dance (NCAAHPERD).
See Listing #1476.

2177
JUSTINE E. GRANNER MEMORIAL SCHOLARSHIP

Iowa United Methodist Foundation
500 East Court Avenue, Suite C
Des Moines, IA 50309
Phone: (515) 283-1991
Summary: To provide financial assistance for college to ethnic minorities in Iowa.
Eligibility: Eligible to apply for this support are American Indian and other ethnic minority students preparing for a career in nursing, public health, or a related field at a college or school of nursing within Iowa. Applicants must have at least a 3.0 grade point average. Preference is given to graduates from Iowa high schools. Financial need is considered in the selection process.
Financial data: The stipend is $1,000.
Duration: 1 year.
Number awarded: 1 each year.
Deadline: February of each year.

2178
KANSAS JUNIOR LIVESTOCK ASSOCIATION SCHOLARSHIPS

Kansas Livestock Foundation
Attn: Scholarship
6031 S.W. 37th Street
Topeka, KS 66614-5129
Phone: (785) 273-5115   Fax: (785) 273-3399
E-mail: kla@kla.org   Web Site: kla.beef.org/youth/scholarshipapp.htm
Summary: To provide financial assistance to members of the Kansas Junior Livestock Association (KJLA) who are or will be majoring in a field related to agriculture.
Eligibility: Eligible to apply for this program are KJLA members who are entering or returning to a junior or senior college. Applicants must be majoring or planning to major in a field related to agriculture (e.g., agricultural economics, agronomy, animal science). Selection is based on academic achievement (20 points), personal livestock enterprises (25 points), 4H/FFA/KJLA activities and leadership (30 points), school activities and honors (30 points), other activities and leadership (25 points), work experience (25 points), significant honors or recognition (25 points), and career plans (20 points).
Financial data: The stipend is $1,000. Funds are paid directly to the recipient in 2 equal installments at the beginning of each semester, upon proof of enrollment.
Duration: 1 year.
Additional information: This program is offered by the Kansas Junior Livestock Association in conjunction with the Kansas Livestock Foundation.
Number awarded: 2 each year.
Deadline: April of each year.

2179
KANSAS NUTRITION COUNCIL SCHOLARSHIP

Kansas Nutrition Council
c/o Kathy Walsten, Scholarship Committee Chair
Kansas State University

255 Justin Hall
Manhattan, KS 66506 Phone: (785) 532-1676
Summary: To provide financial assistance to undergraduates or graduate students working on a degree in nutrition or dietetics at a Kansas college or university.
Eligibility: Eligible to apply for this scholarship are Kansas residents who are currently enrolled as college juniors, seniors, or graduate students at a Kansas college or university. They must be majoring in dietetics or nutrition.
Financial data: The amount of the award is $1,000, paid in 2 equal installments.
Duration: 1 year.
Number awarded: 1 each year.

2180
KAPPA DELTA PHI UNDERGRADUATE SCHOLARSHIPS

American Occupational Therapy Foundation
Attn: Scholarship Coordinator
4720 Montgomery Lane
P.O. Box 31220
Bethesda, MD 20824-1220
Phone: (301) 652-2682 Fax: (301) 656-3620
Phone: TDD: (800) 377-8555 E-mail: aotf@aotf.org
Web Site: www.aotf.org
Summary: To provide financial assistance to full-time upper-division students who are members of the American Occupational Therapy Association (AOTA) and working on a baccalaureate degree or post-baccalaureate certificate in occupational therapy.
Eligibility: Applicants must be juniors or seniors in college who are working full time on a baccalaureate degree or post-baccalaureate certification in an accredited or developing occupational therapy educational program. In addition, applicants must be members of the association, demonstrate a need for financial assistance, and have a sustained record of outstanding scholastic performance. As part of the application process, they must submit transcripts, 2 personal references, and a statement from their curriculum director.
Financial data: The stipend is $1,000 per year.
Duration: 1 year; recipients may reapply.
Additional information: Application forms are available at no cost at the association's web site; a $5 fee is charged for printed copies sent from the association's headquarters.
Number awarded: 2 each year.
Deadline: January of each year.

2181
KARL "PETE" FUHRMANN IV MEMORIAL SCHOLARSHIP

Fuhrmann Orchards
Attn: Paul Fuhrmann
510 Hansgen-Morgan Road
Wheelersburg, OH 45694
Phone: (740) 776-6406 E-mail: fuhrmann@zoomnet.net
Summary: To provide financial assistance to students from Ohio who are interested in working on a degree in horticulture in college.
Eligibility: To be eligible to apply for financial assistance from the scholarship fund, each applicant must be a graduate of an Ohio high school, a resident of Ohio, and currently enrolled or accepted in a 2-year or 4-year accredited school (in any state) with a program leading to an associate or bachelor's of science degree in horticulture. Preference is given to applicants who come from a horticultural background or who are emphasizing fruit and vegetable horticulture rather than landscape horticulture. Eligible applicants must submit a copy of their high school or college transcript and a statement (up to 200 words) on why they should be considered for the scholarship (e.g., abilities, future plans, awards, activities, interests, financial need).
Financial data: A stipend is awarded (exact amount not specified). Funds are paid to the recipient's school.
Duration: 1 year; recipients may reapply if they have maintained a full course load and a 2.5 grade point average.
Number awarded: 1 each year.
Deadline: April of each year.

2182
KATHRYN D. SULLIVAN SCIENCE AND ENGINEERING FELLOWSHIP

South Carolina Space Grant Consortium
c/o College of Charleston
Department of Geology

58 Coming Street
Charleston, SC 29424
Phone: (843) 953-5463 Fax: (843) 953-5446
E-mail: mcolgan@loki.cofc.edu Web Site: www.cofc.edu/~scsgrant
Summary: To provide financial assistance to outstanding science students in South Carolina.
Eligibility: Eligible for this award are students entering their senior year at a college or university in South Carolina or at the University of the Virgin Islands. Applicants must be studying natural science or engineering. Selection is based on academic qualifications of the applicant; 2 letters of recommendation; a description of past activities, current interests, and future plans concerning natural science-related and engineering-related studies; and faculty sponsorship. U.S. citizenship is required.
Financial data: The stipend is $7,000 per year.
Duration: 1 year.
Additional information: This program is funded by the National Aeronautics and Space Administration (NASA) through its Space Grant program and the National Oceanic and Atmospheric Administration (NOAA) through its Sea Grant program.
Number awarded: 1 each year.
Deadline: February of each year.

2183
KAWASAKI-MCGAHA SCHOLARSHIP FUND

Hawai'i Community Foundation
900 Fort Street Mall, Suite 1300
Honolulu, HI 96813
Phone: (808) 566-5570 (888) 731-3863
Fax: (808) 521-6286 E-mail: scholarships@hcf-hawaii.org
Web Site: www.hcf-hawaii.org
Summary: To provide financial assistance to residents of Hawaii who are interested in preparing for a career in computer science or international studies.
Eligibility: This program is open to residents of Hawaii who are planning to study computer science or international studies as full-time students on the undergraduate (preferably) or graduate level. Preference is given to students at Hawai'i Pacific University. Applicants must be able to demonstrate academic achievement (at least a 2.7 grade point average), good moral character, and financial need. In addition to filling out the standard application form, they must write a short statement indicating their reasons for attending college, their planned course of study, and their career goals.
Financial data: The amount of the award depends on the availability of funds and the need of the recipient; recently, grants averaged $1,000.
Duration: 1 year.
Additional information: Recipients may attend college in Hawaii or on the mainland. This program was established in 1996.
Number awarded: Varies each year; recently, 6 of these scholarships were awarded.
Deadline: February of each year.

2184
KELLIE CANNON MEMORIAL SCHOLARSHIP

American Council of the Blind
Attn: Coordinator, Scholarship Program
1155 15th Street, N.W., Suite 1004
Washington, DC 20005
Phone: (202) 467-5081 (800) 424-8666
Fax: (202) 467-5085 E-mail: info@acb.org
Web Site: www.acb.org
Summary: To provide financial assistance to students who are blind and interested in preparing for a career in the computer field.
Eligibility: Eligible to apply are high school seniors, high school graduates, and college students who are blind and are interested in majoring in college in computer information systems or data processing. In addition to letters of recommendation and copies of academic transcripts, applications must include an autobiographical sketch. Selection is based on demonstrated academic record, involvement in extracurricular and civic activities, and academic objectives. The severity of the applicant's visual impairment and his/her study methods are also taken into account.
Financial data: The stipend is $2,000. In addition, the winner receives a $1,000 cash scholarship from the Kurzweil Foundation and, if appropriate, a Kurzweil 1000 Reading System.

Duration: 1 year.

Additional information: This program is sponsored by Visually Impaired Data Processors International, an affiliate of the American Council of the Blind. The scholarship winner is expected to be present at the council's annual national convention; the council will cover all reasonable costs connected with convention attendance.

Number awarded: 1 each year.

Deadline: February of each year.

2185
KENNETH ANDREW ROE SCHOLARSHIP

ASME International
Attn: Education Department
Three Park Avenue
New York, NY 10016-5990
Phone: (212) 591-8131   (800) THE-ASME
Fax: (212) 591-7143   E-mail: oluwanifiset@asme.org
Web Site: www.asme.org/educate/aid/scholar.htm

Summary: To provide financial assistance to undergraduate students who are members of the American Society of Mechanical Engineers (ASME).

Eligibility: This program is open to student members in good standing who are enrolled in an ABET-accredited mechanical engineering baccalaureate program. They must be U.S. citizens and at least sophomores when they apply. Interested students should submit an application form, a nomination from the applicant's department head, a recommendation from a faculty member, and an official transcript. Only 1 nomination may be submitted per department. Selection is based on character, integrity, leadership, scholastic ability, potential contribution to the mechanical engineering profession, and financial need.

Financial data: The stipend is $9,000.

Duration: 1 year.

Additional information: This program was established in 1991. Only study in the junior or senior year is supported. Requests for applications must be accompanied by a self-addressed stamped envelope.

Number awarded: 1 each year.

Deadline: March of each year.

2186
KENNETH B. FISHBECK, P.E. MEMORIAL GRANT

Michigan Society of Professional Engineers
Attn: Scholarship Coordinator
215 North Walnut Street
P.O. Box 15276
Lansing, MI 48901-5276
Phone: (517) 487-9388   Fax: (517) 487-0635
E-mail: mspe@voyager.net
Web Site: www.voyager.net/mspe

Summary: To provide financial assistance to high school seniors in Michigan who are interested in pursuing a college degree in engineering.

Eligibility: This program is open to graduating seniors at high schools in Michigan who have a grade point average of 3.0 or higher and a composite ACT score of 26 or higher. U.S. citizenship and a demonstration of professional ethics are required. Applicants must have been accepted at a Michigan college or university accredited by ABET. They must be planning to enroll in an engineering program and enter the practice of engineering after graduation. They must submit a 250-word essay on "How I Was Influenced to Pursue an Engineering Career." Selection is based on the essay; high school academic record; participation in extracurricular activities; evidence of leadership, character, and self reliance; and comments from teachers and administrators. Financial need is not considered. Semifinalists are interviewed.

Financial data: The stipend is $1,000.

Duration: 1 year; nonrenewable.

Additional information: Information is also available from Roger Lamer, Scholarship Selection Committee Chair, (616) 247-2974, Fax: (616) 247-2997, E-mail: rlamer@steelcase.com. Applications must be submitted to the local chapter scholarship representative. Contact the Michigan Society of Professional Engineers (MSPE) for their addresses and phone numbers.

Number awarded: 1 each year.

Deadline: January of each year.

2187
KEY CLUB INTERNATIONAL AG-BAG SCHOLARSHIP

Key Club International
Attn: Manager of Youth Funds
3636 Woodview Trace
Indianapolis, IN 46268-3196
Phone: (317) 875-8755, ext. 244   (800) KIWANIS, ext. 244
Fax: (317) 879-0204   E-mail: youthfunds@kiwanis.org
Web Site: www.keyclub.org

Summary: To provide financial assistance for college to high school seniors who are Key Club International members and have been involved in agriculture.

Eligibility: This program is open to graduating high school seniors who are bound for college, have at least a 3.0 grade point average, have been involved in agriculture (such as 4-H or FFA), and are a member of a local Key Club. Applicants must include a chronological list of the titles, dates, positions, and organization name of memberships held within an agricultural-related group. Selection is based on participation in school activities and organizations; participation in religious and community activities; honors, awards, and special recognition; 3 letters of recommendation; and an essay on how they have exemplified the ideals of Key Club. Financial need is not considered in the selection process.

Financial data: The stipend is $1,000.

Duration: 1 year.

Additional information: This award, established in 1997, is funded by Ag-Bag International Limited. Information is also available from Mike Wallis, 2320 S.E. Ag-Bag Lane, Warrenton, OR 97146.

Number awarded: 1 each year.

Deadline: March of each year.

2188
KILBOURN-SAWYER MEMORIAL SCHOLARSHIP

Vermont Student Assistance Corporation
Champlain Mill
1 Main Street, Fourth Floor
P.O. Box 2000
Winooski, VT 05404-2601
Phone: (802) 655-9602   (800) 642-3177
Fax: (802) 654-3765   TDD: (802) 654-3766
Phone: TDD: (800) 281-3341 (within VT)   E-mail: info@vsac.org
Web Site: www.vsac.org

Summary: To provide financial assistance to high school seniors in Vermont who are interested in pursuing a degree in construction or engineering.

Eligibility: This scholarship is available to the residents of Vermont who are seniors in high school. Applicants must be planning to enroll in a 2-year or 4-year postsecondary degree program in engineering or construction. They must be able to document financial need, have applied to the Vermont Student Assistance Corporation for a Vermont Grant, and have filed a Free Application for Federal Student Aid no later than 4 weeks before the scholarship deadline. The following are required as part of the application process: a completed application form, 1 letter of recommendation, 4 required essays, and an official transcript. Selection is based on financial need and academic record.

Financial data: The stipend is $1,000.

Duration: 1 year; nonrenewable.

Additional information: This program is funded by Pizzagalli Construction Company.

Number awarded: 1 each year.

Deadline: April of each year.

2189
KILDEE SCHOLARSHIP FOR UNDERGRADUATE STUDY

National Dairy Shrine
Attn: Office of Executive Director
1224 Alton Darby Creek Road
Columbus, OH 43228-9792
Phone: (614) 878-5333   Fax: (614) 870-2622
E-mail: ndairyshrine@hotmail.com
Web Site: www.dairyshrine.org

Summary: To provide financial assistance to college students interested in pursuing undergraduate study in the dairy field.

Eligibility: This program is open to the top 25 participants in National 4-H Dairy Judging Contest and the top 25 participants in the National FFA Dairy Cattle Evaluation Contest. Applicants must be college juniors or seniors working on a

bachelor's degree in dairy or animal science or having an emphasis on dairy through another major. Selection is based on high school academic standing (5 points), college academic standing (10 points), dairy cattle judging activities (20 points), high school leadership and activities (20 points), college leadership and activities (20 points), interest, background, and experience with dairy cattle (10 points), and a 300-word essay on their plans for the future and how the scholarship would assist them in meeting their goals (15 points).
Financial data: The stipend is $2,000.
Duration: 1 year.
Number awarded: 1 each year.
Deadline: March of each year.

2190
KOCH CORPORATION SCHOLARSHIP

Aircraft Owners and Pilots Association
Attn: AOPA Air Safety Foundation
421 Aviation Way
Frederick, MD 21701-4798
Phone: (301) 695-2000   (800) 638-3101
Web Site: www.aopa.org/asf/scholarship/koch.html
Summary: To provide funding to residents of Kentucky interested in continuing their studies in the field of aviation.
Eligibility: This program is open to U.S. citizens who are residents of Kentucky enrolled in an accredited college or university pursuing a course of study focusing on aviation. Applicants must have a grade point average of 3.25 or higher. Selection is based on grade point average and a 500-word essay on a topic that changes annually; recently, the topic was "How can Kentucky flight instructors and students together improve their procedures and practices to reduce, even eliminate, the possibility of midair collisions?"
Financial data: The stipend is $1,500.
Duration: 1 year.
Additional information: This program, established in 2000, is funded by the Koch Corporation and jointly administered by the Air Safety Foundation of the Aircraft Owners and Pilots Association (AOPA) and the University Aviation Association.
Number awarded: 1 each year.
Deadline: July of each year.

2191
KSEA SCHOLARSHIPS

Korean-American Scientists and Engineers Association
1952 Gallows Drive, Suite 300
Vienna, VA 22182
Phone: (703) 748-1221   Fax: (703) 748-1331
E-mail: admin@ksea.org
Web Site: www.ksea.org/activity/scholarships.html
Summary: To provide financial assistance to upper-division and graduate student members of the Korean-American Scientists and Engineers Association (KSEA).
Eligibility: This program is open to Korean American juniors, seniors, and graduate students who graduated from a high school in the United States, are KSEA members, and are majoring in science, engineering, or a related field. As part of the application process, they must submit a 500-word essay on either of the following topics: 1) their career goals and intended contributions to society, or 2) the meaning of Korean heritage in their life. Selection is based on the essay (20 percent), experience and extracurricular activities (20 percent), recommendation letters (30 percent), and academic performance (30 percent).
Financial data: The stipend is $1,000.
Duration: 1 year.
Additional information: This program includes the following named scholarships: the Inyong Ham Scholarship and the Hyundai Scholarship.
Number awarded: About 10 each year, including 1 Inyong Ham Scholarship and 2 Hyundai Scholarships.
Deadline: January of each year.

2192
KYUTARO AND YASUO ABIKO MEMORIAL SCHOLARSHIP

Summary: To provide financial assistance to student members of the Japanese American Citizens League (JACL) who are pursuing undergraduate education.
See Listing #550.

2193
LANDS' END SCHOLARSHIP PROGRAM

Summary: To provide financial assistance to students attending private colleges in Wisconsin who are majoring in selected business-related fields.
See Listing #1493.

2194
LASERS AND ELECTRO-OPTICS SOCIETY STUDENT PROJECTS PROGRAM

Institute of Electrical and Electronics Engineers
Lasers and Electro-Optics Society
c/o Jim Moharam
University of Central Florida
Center for Research and Education in Optics and Lasers
P.O. Box 162700
Orlando, FL 32816-2700
Phone: (407) 823-6833   Fax: (407) 823-6810
Web Site: www.ieee.org/membership/students/awards/sc_lasers.html
Summary: To recognize and reward outstanding student photonics systems projects.
Eligibility: This program is open to teams of full-time degree-seeking science and engineering students, sponsored by a faculty advisor who is a member of the Lasers and Electro-Optics Society (LEOS) of the Institute of Electrical and Electronics Engineers (IEEE). The teams conceptualize, plan, and implement a photonics systems project. Selection is based on merit and significance of the proposed project, thoroughness of the plan, number of students involved, and the feasibility of completing the project with available resources. Proposals, up to 5 pages in length, should specifically address those selection criteria and list other resources available for the project. Preference is given to projects involving LEOS student members.
Financial data: The award is a $1,500 scholarship.
Duration: The awards are presented annually.
Number awarded: 3 each year.
Deadline: May of each year.

2195
LAWRENCE E. AND THELMA J. NORRIE MEMORIAL SCHOLARSHIP

Summary: To provide funding to licensed radio amateurs who are interested in pursuing postsecondary studies (particularly in the sciences).
See Listing #561.

2196
LAWRENCE "LARRY" FRAZIER MEMORIAL SCHOLARSHIP

Lincoln Community Foundation
215 Centennial Mall South, Suite 200
Lincoln, NE 68508
Phone: (402) 474-2345   Fax: (402) 476-8532
E-mail: lcf@lcf.org   Web Site: www.lcf.org
Summary: To provide financial assistance to residents of Nebraska who are interested in studying designated fields in college.
Eligibility: This program is open to residents of Nebraska who are graduating or have graduated from a high school in the state. Preference is given to applicants who intend to pursue a career in the field of aviation, insurance, or law. They must attend a 2- or 4-year college or university in Nebraska. Preference is also given to applicants who have experience in debate and who participated in Boy Scouts or Girl Scouts as youth. Selection is based on academic achievement in high school, potential to excel in college, and financial need.
Financial data: A stipend is awarded (exact amount not specified).
Duration: 1 year.
Additional information: This program is supported by the Nebraska Chapter of Chartered Property Casualty Underwriters, P.O. Box 22505, Lincoln, NE 68542.
Number awarded: 1 or more each year.
Deadline: April of each year.

2197
LAWRENCE R. FOSTER MEMORIAL SCHOLARSHIP

Oregon Student Assistance Commission
Attn: Private Awards Grant Department
1500 Valley River Drive, Suite 100
Eugene, OR 97401-2146
Phone: (541) 687-7395   (800) 452-8807, ext. 7395
Fax: (541) 687-7419   E-mail: awardinfo@mercury.osac.state.or.us
Web Site: www.osac.state.or.us
Summary: To provide financial assistance for college to residents of Oregon who are interested in preparing for a public health career.
Eligibility: This program is open to residents of Oregon who are interested in preparing for a career in public health (not private practice). First preference is given to applicants currently working and graduate students majoring in public health. Second preference is given to undergraduates entering the junior or senior year of a health program, including nursing, medical technology, and physician assistant. As part of the application process, they must submit an essay (at least 1 page in length) on their interest and experience (if any) in a public health career, migrant clinics, or community primary care clinics.
Financial data: Scholarship amounts vary, depending upon the needs of the recipient.
Duration: 1 year.
Number awarded: Varies each year.
Deadline: February of each year.

2198
LEAF SCHOLARSHIP

Summary: To provide financial assistance to students in California who are majoring in ornamental horticulture.
See Listing #1496.

2199
LEE TARBOX MEMORIAL SCHOLARSHIP

Aircraft Electronics Association
Attn: Educational Foundation
4217 South Hocker Drive
Independence, MO 64055-4723
Phone: (816) 373-6565   Fax: (816) 478-3100
E-mail: info@aea.net
Web Site: www.aea.net
Summary: To provide financial assistance to students who are interested in studying avionics or aircraft repair in college.
Eligibility: This program is open to high school seniors and currently-enrolled college students who are attending (or planning to attend) an accredited school in an avionics or aircraft repair program.
Financial data: The stipend is $2,500.
Duration: 1 year.
Additional information: Funding for this program is provided by Pacific Southwest Instruments.
Number awarded: 1 each year.
Deadline: February of each year.

2200
LEROY APKER AWARD

American Physical Society
Attn: Apker Award Committee
One Physics Ellipse
College Park, MD 20740-3844
Phone: (301) 209-3233   Fax: (301) 209-0865
E-mail: chodos@aps.org
Web Site: www.aps.org
Summary: To recognize and reward undergraduate students for outstanding work in physics.
Eligibility: This program is open to undergraduate students at colleges and universities in the United States. Nominees should have completed or be completing the requirements for an undergraduate degree with an excellent academic record and should have demonstrated exceptional potential for scientific research by an original contribution to physics. Each department of physics in the United States may nominate only 1 student. Each nomination packet should include the student's academic transcript, a description of the

original contribution written by the student (such as a manuscript or reprint of a research publication or senior thesis), a 1,000-word summary, and 2 letters of recommendation.
Financial data: The award consists of a $5,000 stipend for the student, a certificate citing the work and school of the recipient, and an allowance for travel expenses to the meeting of the American Physical Society (APS) at which the prize is presented. Each of the finalists receives an honorarium of $1,000 and a certificate. Each of the physics departments whose nominees are selected as recipients and finalists receives a certificate and an award; the departmental award is $5,000 for recipients and $500 for finalists.
Duration: The award is presented annually.
Additional information: This award was established in 1978.
Number awarded: 2 recipients each year: 1 to a student at a Ph.D. granting institution and 1 at a non-Ph.D. granting institution.
Deadline: June of each year.

2201
LEWIS J. MINOR SCHOLARSHIP

Institute of Food Technologists
Attn: Scholarship Department
221 North LaSalle Street, Suite 300
Chicago, IL 60601-1291
Phone: (312) 782-8424   Fax: (312) 782-8348
E-mail: info@ift.org
Web Site: www.ift.org
Summary: To provide financial assistance to undergraduates interested in studying food science or food technology.
Eligibility: Applicants must be currently enrolled as sophomores or juniors in a food science or food technology program at an educational institution in the United States or Canada; they must have an outstanding scholastic record and a well-rounded personality. Financial need is not considered in the selection process.
Financial data: The stipend is $1,000.
Duration: 1 year; recipients may reapply if they are members of the Institute of Food Technologists (IFT).
Additional information: Funding for these scholarships is provided by the FIDCO Industrial Division of Food Ingredient Specialties (FIS), Inc. Correspondence and completed applications must be submitted to the department head of the educational institution the applicant is attending.
Number awarded: 1 each year.
Deadline: January of each year.

2202
L.G. WELLS SCHOLARSHIPS

Confederation of Oregon School Administrators
Attn: COSA Foundation
707 13th Street, S.E., Suite 100
Salem, OR 97301-4035
Phone: (503) 581-3141   Fax: (503) 581-9840
E-mail: nancy@oasc.org
Web Site: www.cosa.k12.or.us
Summary: To provide financial assistance to high school seniors in Oregon who are interested in studying education or engineering at a community college, college, or university in the state.
Eligibility: This program is open to graduating high school seniors in Oregon. Applicants should be interested in attending a community college, college, or university in Oregon to study education or engineering. They must have been active in community and school affairs, have at least a 3.5 grade point average, and enroll in the fall term after graduating from high school. To apply, students must submit a completed application form, a 1-page autobiography (that states personal goals), the name of the school they plan to attend, and the endorsement of a member of the Confederation of Oregon School Administrators (COSA). Financial need is considered in the selection process.
Financial data: The stipend is $1,000. Funds are paid directly to the recipient.
Duration: 1 year; nonrenewable.
Additional information: At least 1 of these scholarships is reserved for a student from Baker County.
Number awarded: 3 each year.
Deadline: February of each year.

2203
LIGHT METALS DIVISION SCHOLARSHIP

The Minerals, Metals & Materials Society
Attn: TMS Student Awards Program
184 Thorn Hill Road
Warrendale, PA 15086-7528
Phone: (724) 776-9000, ext. 213   Fax: (724) 776-3770
E-mail: luther@tms.org
Web Site: www.tms.org/Students/AwardsPrograms/Scholarships.html
Summary: To provide financial assistance to student members of The Minerals, Metals & Materials Society (TMS).
Eligibility: This program is open to undergraduate members of the society who are full-time students majoring in metallurgical and/or materials science and engineering with an emphasis on both traditional and emerging light metals. Applicants may be from any country. Selection is based on academic achievement, school and community activities, work experience, leadership, a personal profile statement, and letters of recommendation.
Financial data: The stipend is $4,000, plus a travel stipend of up to $600 (so the recipient can attend the annual meeting of the society to accept the award). In addition, recipients are given the opportunity of selecting up to $300 in LMD-sponsored conference proceedings or textbooks to be donated to their college or university library in their name and up to $400 in books for themselves.
Duration: 1 year.
Additional information: Funding for this program is provided by the Light Metals Division (LMD) of TMS.
Number awarded: 3 each year.
Deadline: April of each year.

2204
LILLIAN MOLLER GILBRETH SCHOLARSHIP

Society of Women Engineers
230 East Ohio Street, Suite 400
Chicago, IL 60611-3265
Phone: (312) 596-5223   Fax: (312) 644-8557
E-mail: hq@swe.org
Web Site: www.swe.org
Summary: To provide financial assistance to undergraduate women majoring in engineering.
Eligibility: This program is open to women entering their junior or senior year who demonstrate outstanding potential and achievement. Applicants must be majoring in engineering at an accredited school, college, or university. They must have earned at least a 3.0 grade point average. Selection is based on merit.
Financial data: The scholarship is $6,000 per year.
Duration: 1 year.
Additional information: This program was established in 1958.
Number awarded: 1 each year.
Deadline: January of each year.

2205
LINDA CRAIG MEMORIAL SCHOLARSHIP

Pacers Foundation, Inc.
Foundation Coordinator
125 South Pennsylvania Street
Indianapolis, IN 46204
Phone: (317) 917-2864   Fax: (317) 917-2599
E-mail: Foundation@pacers.com
Web Site: www.pacers.com
Summary: To provide financial assistance to undergraduates currently majoring in medicine or sports medicine at an Indiana college or university.
Eligibility: This program is open to U.S. citizens who are currently enrolled at a 2-year or 4-year college or university in Indiana. Applicants must have completed at least 1 grading period (semester, quarter) and have declared a major in medicine, sports medicine, and/or physical therapy. A grade point average of 3.0 or higher is required. Selection criteria include character, integrity, and leadership.
Financial data: The stipend is $1,000. Funds are paid directly to the recipient's school.
Duration: 1 year; recipients may reapply.
Number awarded: 1 each year.
Deadline: February of each year.

2206
LITHERLAND/FTE SCHOLARSHIP

Foundation for Technology Education
1914 Association Drive, Suite 201
Reston, VA 20191-1539
Phone: (703) 860-2100   Fax: (703) 860-0353
E-mail: ideaordr@iris.org   Web Site: www.iteawww.org
Summary: To provide financial support to undergraduate members of the International Technology Education Association (ITEA) who are majoring in technology education teacher preparation.
Eligibility: Applicants must be members of the association (membership may be enclosed with the scholarship application), in college but not yet seniors, majoring in technology education teacher preparation with a grade point average of 2.5 or more, and enrolled full time. Selection is based on interest in teaching, academic ability, financial need, and faculty recommendations.
Financial data: The scholarship is $1,000. Funds are provided directly to recipient.
Duration: The scholarship is awarded annually.
Additional information: The Foundation for Technology Education (FTE) is affiliated with the ITEA.
Number awarded: 1 or more each year.
Deadline: November of each year.

2207
L.L. WATERS SCHOLARSHIP PROGRAM

American Society of Transportation and Logistics, Inc.
Attn: Scholarship Judging Panel
229 Peachtree Street, Suite 401
Atlanta, GA 30303
Phone: (404) 524-3555   Fax: (404) 524-7776
E-mail: info@astl.org
Web Site: www.astl.org/Scholar.html
Summary: To encourage advanced undergraduate and graduate study in the field of transportation.
Eligibility: This program is open to undergraduate students in their junior year at fully-accredited 4-year colleges or universities who are majoring in transportation, logistics, or physical distribution. Students in graduate school in the same areas are also eligible to apply. Recipients are selected without regard to race, color, religion, sex, or national origin. Selection is based on scholastic performance and potential as well as commitment to the pursuit of a professional career in the field. Financial need is not considered.
Financial data: The stipend is $1,000.
Duration: 1 year; recipients may apply again but not in the consecutive year.
Number awarded: 1 or more each year.
Deadline: May of each year.

2208
LLOYD A. CHACEY, P.E. MEMORIAL SCHOLARSHIP

Ohio Society of Professional Engineers
Attn: Engineers Foundation of Ohio
4795 Evanswood Drive, Suite 201
Columbus, OH 43229-7216
Phone: (614) 846-1144   (800) 654-9481
Fax: (614) 846-1131   E-mail: ospe@iwaynet.net
Web Site: www.ohioengineer.com/programs/Scholarships.htm
Summary: To provide financial assistance to students in Ohio who have been admitted to an engineering program approved by the Accreditation Board of Engineering and Technology (ABET).
Eligibility: This program is open to full-time students entering their junior or senior year in an ABET-approved engineering program at a college or university in Ohio with a grade point average of 3.0 or higher. Applicants must be U.S. citizens, residents of Ohio, and the sons, daughters, brothers, sisters, nieces, nephews, spouses, or grandchildren of current members of the Ohio Society of Professional Engineers (or related to a deceased member who was in good standing at the time of death). Selection is based on activities, leadership or work experience, membership and activity in professional and technical societies, honors won, and recommendations. Financial need is considered only as a deciding factor in case of a tie.
Financial data: The stipend is $2,000 per year. Funds may be used to pay for the recipient's tuition, fees, or other educational expenses.
Duration: 1 year; may be renewed 1 additional year.
Number awarded: 1 each year.
Deadline: December of each year.

2209
LOCKHEED AERONAUTICS COMPANY SCHOLARSHIPS

Society of Women Engineers
230 East Ohio Street, Suite 400
Chicago, IL 60611-3265
Phone: (312) 596-5223   Fax: (312) 644-8557
E-mail: hq@swe.org
Web Site: www.swe.org
Summary: To provide financial assistance to undergraduate women majoring in engineering.
Eligibility: This program is open to women who are entering their junior year and majoring in electrical or mechanical engineering. Applicants must be attending an accredited university and have a grade point average of 3.5 or higher. Selection is based on merit.
Financial data: The stipend is $1,000.
Duration: 1 year.
Additional information: This program was established in 1996.
Number awarded: 2 each year: 1 to a student in electrical engineering and 1 to a student in mechanical engineering.
Deadline: January of each year.

2210
LOCKHEED MARTIN CORPORATION SCHOLARSHIPS

Society of Women Engineers
230 East Ohio Street, Suite 400
Chicago, IL 60611-3265
Phone: (312) 596-5223   Fax: (312) 644-8557
E-mail: hq@swe.org   Web Site: www.swe.org
Summary: To provide financial assistance to freshmen women who wish to major in engineering.
Eligibility: Entering freshman women interested in majoring in engineering at an accredited school, college, or university are eligible to apply. Selection is based on merit.
Financial data: The stipend is $3,000.
Duration: 1 year.
Additional information: This program was established in 1996.
Number awarded: 2 each year.
Deadline: May of each year.

2211
LORA E. DUNETZ SCHOLARSHIP

Summary: To provide financial assistance for college to legally blind students, especially those planning to enter the medical field.
See Listing #579.

2212
LORAL SKYNET SCHOLARSHIP

Summary: To provide financial assistance to minorities and women interested in studying satellite-related disciplines in college or graduate school.
See Listing #1505.

2213
LOUIS GOLDBERG SCHOLARSHIP

Consulting Engineers Council of New Jersey
Attn: Executive Director
66 Morris Avenue, Suite 1A
Springfield, NJ 07081-1409
Phone: (973) 564-5848   Fax: (973) 564-7480
E-mail: peterallen@monmouth.com
Summary: To provide financial assistance to engineering students in New Jersey.
Eligibility: Eligible are students in their third, fourth, or fifth year of undergraduate study at an ABET-approved engineering or land surveying program in New Jersey. U.S. citizenship is required. Awards are based on grade point average (28 points), essay (25 points), work experience (20 points), recommendation (17 points), and college activities (10 points).
Financial data: The award is $1,000, of which $500 is payable upon receipt of the award and $500 upon graduation.

Additional information: The recipient is also entered in the American Consulting Engineers Council's national competition, which provides awards up to $5,000 per year.
Number awarded: 1 or more each year.
Deadline: January of each year.

2214
LOUIS STOKES SCIENCE AND TECHNOLOGY AWARD

National Association for the Advancement of Colored People
Attn: Education Department
4805 Mt. Hope Drive
Baltimore, MD 21215-3297
Phone: (410) 358-8900   Fax: (410) 358-9785
Web Site: www.naacp.org
Summary: To provide financial assistance to incoming freshmen at Historically Black Colleges and Universities (HBCUs) interested in majoring in selected scientific fields.
Eligibility: This program is open to students entering an HBCU and planning to be full-time students with a major in 1 of the following fields: computer science, engineering, biology, chemistry, or physics. Membership and participation in the NAACP is highly desirable. The required minimum grade point average is 2.5. Applicants must be able to demonstrate financial need, defined as a family income of less than $30,000 for a family of 1 ranging to $52,300 for a family of 8. U.S. citizenship is required.
Financial data: The stipend is $2,000.
Duration: 1 year; nonrenewable.
Number awarded: 1 or more each year.
Deadline: April of each year.

2215
LOWELL GAYLOR MEMORIAL SCHOLARSHIP

Aircraft Electronics Association
Attn: Educational Foundation
4217 South Hocker Drive
Independence, MO 64055-4723
Phone: (816) 373-6565   Fax: (816) 478-3100
E-mail: info@aea.net
Web Site: www.aea.net
Summary: To provide financial assistance to students who are interested in studying avionics or aircraft repair in college.
Eligibility: This program is open to high school seniors and currently-enrolled college students who are attending (or planning to attend) an accredited school in an avionics or aircraft repair program.
Financial data: The stipend is $1,000.
Duration: 1 year.
Number awarded: 1 each year.
Deadline: February of each year.

2216
LUCENT GLOBAL SCIENCE SCHOLARS PROGRAM

National Alliance for Excellence
63 Riverside Avenue
Red Bank, NJ 07701
Phone: (732) 747-0028   Fax: (732) 842-2962
E-mail: info@excellence.org
Web Site: www.excellence.org
Summary: To provide financial assistance for college to high school students in the United States and university students in other designated countries who are interested in pursuing careers in information technology.
Eligibility: This program is open to high school seniors in the United States and first-year university students in Brazil, Canada, China, Germany, Japan, Mexico, the Netherlands, Thailand, and the United Kingdom. Selection is based on a demonstrated record of distinction in science and mathematics and a desire to pursue information technology careers.
Financial data: The stipend is $5,000 per year.
Duration: 1 year; nonrenewable.
Additional information: This program is funded by Lucent Technologies. In the United States, it is administered by the National Alliance for Excellence, formerly the Scholarship Foundation of America. For the other 9 countries, students should contact the Institute of International Education, 809 United Nations Plaza,

New York, NY 10017-3580, E-mail: smartin@iie.org. Students are offered internships at Lucent's research and development and manufacturing facilities in their own countries during the summer following their freshman year in the United States or the sophomore year in other countries.
Number awarded: A total of 100 students, including 50 from the United States, receive these scholarships each year.

2217
MADA FOUNDATION SCHOLARSHIPS

Minnesota Automobile Dealers Association
Attn: MADA Foundation
277 University Avenue
St. Paul, MN 55103
Phone: (651) 291-2400 (800) 652-9029
Fax: (651) 291-2894 E-mail: lambert@mada.org
Web Site: www.mada.org/scholarships.htm
Summary: To provide financial assistance to students at Minnesota technical colleges interested in pursuing a career as an automobile service professional.
Eligibility: This program is open to students who have completed at least 2 quarters at an accredited Minnesota technical college and have an above average grade point average. Applicants must be majoring in 1 of the following fields of study: automotive mechanics, automotive body repair, parts and service management, automotive machinist, or automotive diagnostic technician. They must be nominated by an instructor or class advisor at their technical college.
Financial data: Scholarships provide for reimbursement of tuition. No cash payment is made.
Duration: 1 quarter.
Number awarded: Varies each year.

2218
MAINE ANTIQUE TRACTOR CLUB SCHOLARSHIP

Maine Antique Tractor Club
c/o Harriet Spencer, Secretary
35 North Shore Drive
Smithfield, ME 04978
Web Site: www.maineantiquetractorclub.com
Summary: To provide financial assistance to high school seniors in Maine interested in studying agriculture in college.
Eligibility: This program is open to graduating seniors at high schools in Maine who are interested in majoring in a field related to agriculture in college.
Financial data: The stipend is $1,000.
Duration: 1 year.
Additional information: Information is also available from the Scholarship Committee, c/o Bob Davids, 370 Square Road, St. Albans, ME 04971.
Number awarded: 1 or more each year.
Deadline: April of each year.

2219
MAINE CHAPTER 276 SCHOLARSHIPS

National Association of Women in Construction-Maine Chapter 276
3 Hillcrest Street
Hallowell, ME 04347
Summary: To provide financial assistance to Maine residents who are pursuing postsecondary education in a field related to construction.
Eligibility: This program is open to residents of Maine who are enrolled in a postsecondary educational program. Applicants must be pursuing a course of study that is specifically designed for construction, including carpentry, civil engineering, architecture, welding, electrical, plumbing, or construction management.
Financial data: Stipends range from $500 to $1,000.
Duration: 1 year.
Number awarded: 1 or more each year.
Deadline: April of each year

2220
MAINE METAL PRODUCTS ASSOCIATION SCHOLARSHIP

Maine Metal Products Association
Attn: Executive Director
87 Winthrop Street, Suite 400
Augusta, ME 04330
Phone: (207) 629-5220 Fax: (207) 629-5219

E-mail: mmpa@ime.net
Web Site: www.maine-metals.org/scholarship.html
Summary: To provide financial assistance to students in Maine who are interested in furthering their education in the machine or related metal working trades.
Eligibility: This program is open to students who have been accepted into a metal trades program at a college in Maine. The field of specialization may be mechanical engineering, machine tool technician, sheet metal fabrication, welding, or CADCAM for metals industry. Applicants must be sponsored by a Maine Metal Products Association member firm. They must write an essay on why and how they decided on a career in metal working. They will be interviewed by a member of the association. Selection is based on aptitude or demonstrated ability in the metal working trades, scholastic and extracurricular records, and personal qualifications of attitude, initiative, seriousness of intent, and overall impression.
Financial data: The stipend varies; funds may be applied toward the costs of tuition and textbooks.
Duration: 1 year.
Additional information: Information is also available from Maine Education Services, Attn: MES Foundation, One City Center, 11th Floor, Portland, ME 04101, (800) 922-6352.
Number awarded: Varies each year; recently, 9 of these scholarships were awarded.
Deadline: April of each year.

2221
MAINE RURAL REHABILITATION FUND SCHOLARSHIP

Maine Department of Agriculture, Food and Rural Resources
Attn: Rural Rehabilitation Fund Scholarship Committee
28 State House Station
Augusta, ME 04333-0028
Phone: (207) 287-7628 Fax: (207) 287-7548
E-mail: Rod.McCormick@state.me.us
Web Site: www.state.me.us/agriculture
Summary: To provide financial assistance to Maine residents interested in majoring in a field related to agriculture in college.
Eligibility: This program is open to residents of Maine who are enrolled or accepted for enrollment at a college or university that offers an agricultural program. Applicants must enroll full time in a program leading to a 2-year, 4-year, or advanced degree in agriculture, including agricultural business, sustainable agriculture, agricultural engineering, animal science, plant science, or soil science. They must have earned a cumulative grade point average of 2.7 or higher or a grade point average for the most recent semester of 3.0 or higher. They must also be able to demonstrate an unmet financial need.
Financial data: Awards are either $1,000 or $800 per year.
Duration: 1 year; may be renewed up to 3 additional years.
Number awarded: Varies each year; recently, 24 of these scholarships were awarded.
Deadline: June of each year.

2222
MAINE SOCIETY OF PROFESSIONAL ENGINEERS SCHOLARSHIPS

Maine Society of Professional Engineers
Attn: Secretary
142 Mills Road
Kennebunkport, ME 04046-5705
Phone: (207) 967-3741 Fax: (207) 967-3741
E-mail: kencam@cybertours.com
Summary: To provide financial assistance to high school seniors in Maine who are interested in majoring in engineering in college.
Eligibility: This program is open to high school seniors in Maine. They must be interested in preparing for a career in engineering. Selection is based on grade point average, test scores, letters of recommendation, honor awards, an essay, activities, and presentation.
Financial data: The stipend is $1,500 per year.
Duration: 1 year.
Additional information: This program includes the following named scholarships: the Vernon T. Swain, P.E., Scholarship and the Robert E. Chute, P.E., Scholarship.
Number awarded: 2 each year.
Deadline: March of each year.

2223
MALCOLM BALDRIGE SCHOLARSHIPS

Malcolm Baldrige Scholarship Fund
c/o Waterbury Foundation
81 West Main Street
Waterbury, CT 06702
Phone: (203) 753-1315   Fax: (203) 756-3054
E-mail: info@waterburyfoundation.org
Web Site: www.waterburyfoundation.org
Summary: To provide financial assistance to college students interested in a career in foreign trade or manufacturing.
Eligibility: This program is open to college sophomores and juniors who are studying foreign trade or manufacturing at a 4-year college or university. Preference is given to students attending an institution in Connecticut. Selection is based on academic achievement and accomplishment in foreign language study.
Financial data: Stipends up to $2,000 are available.
Duration: 1 year; renewable.
Number awarded: 1 to 3 each year.
Deadline: April of each year.

2224
MARGARET E. SWANSON SCHOLARSHIP

American Dental Hygienists' Association
Attn: Institute for Oral Health
444 North Michigan Avenue, Suite 3400
Chicago, IL 60611
Phone: (312) 440-8944   (800) 735-4916
Fax: (312) 440-8929   E-mail: institute@adha.net
Web Site: www.adha.org
Summary: To provide financial assistance to students enrolled in a dental hygiene program who demonstrate exceptional organizational leadership potential.
Eligibility: This program is open to students who have completed at least 1 year in a certificate/associate, baccalaureate, master's, or doctoral program in dental hygiene with at least a 3.0 grade point average. Applicants must be able to demonstrate financial need and full-time enrollment. Selection is based on organizational leadership potential.
Financial data: The amount of the scholarship depends on the need of the recipient, to a maximum of $1,500.
Duration: 1 year.
Number awarded: 1 each year.
Deadline: May of each year.

2225
MARGARET L. HAGEMAN SCHOLARSHIP

Wyoming Nurses Association
Attn: Finance Committee
Majestic Building, Suite 305
1603 Capitol Avenue
Cheyenne, WY 82001
Phone: (307) 635-3955   Fax: (307) 635-2173
Summary: To provide financial assistance to students in Wyoming who are pursuing a degree in nursing.
Eligibility: This program is open to Wyoming residents who are preparing for a career as a registered nurse or registered nurses who are pursuing advanced education in nursing. Applicants must have completed at least 1 semester in a Wyoming accredited nursing program. An interview may be required. Financial need is considered in the selection process. Preference is given to "nontraditional" students.
Financial data: The stipend is $1,200, paid in 2 equal installments.
Duration: 1 year.
Number awarded: 1 each year.
Deadline: July of each year.

2226
MARK J. SCHROEDER SCHOLARSHIP IN METEOROLOGY

American Meteorological Society
Attn: Fellowship/Scholarship Coordinator
45 Beacon Street
Boston, MA 02108-3693
Phone: (617) 227-2426, ext. 246   Fax: (617) 742-8718
E-mail: amsinfo@ametsoc.org

Web Site: www.ametsoc.org/AMS/amsedu/scholfeldocs/index.html
Summary: To provide financial assistance to students majoring in meteorology or some aspect of atmospheric sciences and who demonstrate financial need.
Eligibility: This program is open to undergraduate students entering their final year of study and majoring in meteorology or some aspect of the atmospheric or related oceanic and hydrologic sciences. Applicants must intend to make atmospheric or related sciences their career. They must be U.S. citizens or permanent residents, be enrolled full time in an accredited U.S. institution, and have a cumulative grade point average of 3.0 or higher. Along with their application, they must submit a 100-word essay on their most important achievements that qualify them for this scholarship and a 500-word essay on their career goals in the atmospheric or related oceanic or hydrologic fields. Selection is based on academic achievement and financial need. The sponsor specifically encourages applications from women, minorities, and students with disabilities who are traditionally underrepresented in the atmospheric and related oceanic sciences.
Financial data: The stipend is $5,000.
Duration: 1 year.
Additional information: This scholarship was established in 1995. Requests for an application must be accompanied by a self-addressed stamped envelope.
Number awarded: 1 each year.
Deadline: February of each year.

2227
MARSH RISK CONSULTING SCHOLARSHIPS

American Society of Safety Engineers
Attn: ASSE Foundation
1800 East Oakton Street
Des Plaines, IL 60018
Phone: (847) 768-3441   Fax: (847) 296-9220
E-mail: mrosario@asse.org   Web Site: www.asse.org
Summary: To provide financial assistance to undergraduate student members of the American Society of Safety Engineers (ASSE).
Eligibility: This program is open to ASSE student members who are majoring in occupational safety. Applicants must be full-time students who have completed at least 60 semester hours with a grade point average of 3.25 or higher. As part of the selection process, they must submit 2 essays of 300 words or less: 1) why they are seeking a degree in safety, a brief description of their current activities, and how those relate to their career goals and objectives; and 2) why they should be awarded this scholarship (including career goals and financial need).
Financial data: The stipend is $1,000 per year.
Duration: 1 year; nonrenewable.
Additional information: Funding for this program is provided by Marsh Risk Consulting.
Number awarded: 2 each year.
Deadline: November of each year.

2228
MARSHALL E. MCCULLOUGH MEMORIAL SCHOLARSHIPS

Summary: To provide financial assistance to graduating high school students interested in a career in dairy journalism.
See Listing #1523.

2229
MARY AND ORLIN TRAPP SCIENCE SCHOLARSHIP

Iowa United Methodist Foundation
500 East Court Avenue, Suite C
Des Moines, IA 50309
Phone: (515) 283-1991
Summary: To provide financial assistance to Catholic, Protestant, or other students majoring in science or mathematics at a United Methodist college in Iowa.
Eligibility: Eligible to apply for this support are students who have completed at least 1 year at a United Methodist college in Iowa. They must be majoring in science (including chemistry, physics, biology, botany, and zoology) or mathematics. First consideration is given to members of the Protestant or Catholic church. Selection is based on academic record and a broad range of other attributes, including honesty, high moral character, ethics, integrity, initiative, and leadership ability. Financial need is not considered in the selection process.
Financial data: The stipend is $2,000.
Duration: 1 year.
Number awarded: 2 each year.
Deadline: February of each year.

2230
MARY BENEVENTO SCHOLARSHIP

Summary: To provide financial assistance to high school seniors in Connecticut who are interested in studying health, physical education, recreation, or dance in college. *See Listing #1525.*

2231
MARY EILEEN DIXEY SCHOLARSHIP

American Occupational Therapy Foundation
Attn: Scholarship Coordinator
4720 Montgomery Lane
P.O. Box 31220
Bethesda, MD 20824-1220
Phone: (301) 652-2682   Fax: (301) 656-3620
Phone: TDD: (800) 377-8555   E-mail: aotf@aotf.org
Web Site: www.aotf.org

Summary: To provide financial assistance to students in New Hampshire who are working on an associate or master's degree in occupational therapy.

Eligibility: This program is open to New Hampshire residents who are enrolled in an accredited occupational therapy educational program in any state at the associate or master's degree level. Applicants must demonstrate a need for financial assistance and have a sustained record of outstanding scholastic performance. As part of the application process, they must submit transcripts, 2 personal references, and a statement from their curriculum director.

Financial data: The stipend is $1,000.

Duration: 1 year.

Additional information: Application forms are available at no cost at the association's web site; a $5 fee is charged for printed copies sent from the association's headquarters.

Number awarded: 1 each year.

Deadline: January of each year.

2232
MARY FEINDT FORUM FOR EQUAL OPPORTUNITY SCHOLARSHIP

American Congress on Surveying and Mapping
Attn: Awards Director
6 Montgomery Village Avenue, Suite 403
Gaithersburg, MD 20879
Phone: (240) 632-9716   Fax: (240) 632-1321
E-mail: tmilburn@acsm.net   Web Site: www.acsm.net

Summary: To provide financial assistance to women members of the American Congress on Surveying and Mapping who are working on an undergraduate degree in surveying.

Eligibility: This program is open to women students who are members of the sponsoring organization and enrolled in a 4-year degree program in a surveying and mapping curriculum in the United States. Selection is based on previous academic record (30 percent), future plans (30 percent), letters of recommendation (20 percent), and professional activities (20 percent); if 2 or more applicants are judged equal based on those criteria, financial need may be considered.

Financial data: The stipend is $1,000.

Duration: 1 year.

Additional information: Funding for these scholarships is provided by Forum for Equal Opportunity of the National Society of Professional Surveyors (NSPS).

Number awarded: 1 each year.

Deadline: December of each year.

2233
MARY JO CLAYTON SANDERS ENVIRONMENTAL ISSUES SCHOLARSHIP

Florida Federation of Garden Clubs, Inc.
Attn: Scholarship Chair
6065 21st Street S.W.
Vero Beach, FL 32968-9427
Phone: (561) 778-1023   Web Site: www.ffgc.org

Summary: To provide financial aid to Florida undergraduates and graduate students majoring in environmental issues.

Eligibility: This program is open to Florida residents who are enrolled as full-time juniors, seniors, or graduate students in a Florida college. They must have at least a 3.0 grade point average, be in financial need, and be majoring in environmental issues (including city planning, land management, environmental control, and allied subjects). Selection is based on academic record, commitment to career, character, and financial need.

Financial data: The stipend is $3,500. The funds are sent directly to the recipient's school and distributed semiannually.

Duration: 1 year.

Additional information: If the recipient's grade point average drops below 3.0, the second installment of the scholarship is not provided.

Number awarded: 1 each year.

Deadline: April of each year.

2234
MARY OPAL WOLANIN UNDERGRADUATE SCHOLARSHIP

National Gerontological Nurses Association
7794 Grow Drive
Pensacola, FL 32514-7072
Phone: (850) 473-1174   (800) 723-0560
Fax: (850) 484-8762

Summary: To provide financial assistance for undergraduate education to members of the National Gerontological Nurses Association (NGNA).

Eligibility: This program is open to members of the association who are full- or part-time nursing students in the junior year of a baccalaureate program or sophomore year of an associate program at a school accredited by the NLN. Applicants must submit 3 letters of recommendation, a current school catalog describing courses with gerontological nursing content, all academic transcripts (at least a 3.0 grade point average is required), a statement of purpose for requesting the scholarship, a statement of future professional and educational goals, and a statement of financial need. They must intend to work in a gerontology/geriatric setting after graduation. U.S. citizenship is required.

Financial data: The stipend is $1,500.

Duration: 1 year.

Additional information: Recipients must be willing to serve on the honors and awards committee for a minimum of 1 year and must agree to attend the association's annual conference.

Number awarded: 1 or more each year.

Deadline: July of each year.

2235
MARYLAND FIRE FIGHTER, AMBULANCE, AND RESCUE SQUAD MEMBER TUITION REIMBURSEMENT PROGRAM

Maryland Higher Education Commission
Attn: State Scholarship Administration
16 Francis Street
Annapolis, MD 21401-1781
Phone: (410) 260-4568   (800) 974-1024
Fax: (410) 974-5376   TTY: (800) 735-2258
E-mail: ssamail@mhec.state.md.us   Web Site: www.mhec.state.md.us

Summary: To provide financial assistance for postsecondary education to fire fighters, ambulance, or rescue squad members in Maryland.

Eligibility: Eligible for this support are fire fighters, ambulance, and rescue squad members who are enrolled as either full-time or part-time undergraduate or graduate students at an accredited institution of higher education in Maryland in a degree or certificate program for fire service technology or emergency medical technology.

Financial data: Awards may be used for tuition only and do not exceed the equivalent tuition of a resident undergraduate student at the University of Maryland College Park (currently, $3,480 per year).

Duration: 1 year; renewable.

Additional information: Recipients must be an active career or volunteer fire fighter, ambulance, or rescue squad member serving a Maryland community while taking courses and must continue to serve for an additional year following completion of the courses.

Number awarded: Varies each year.

Deadline: June of each year.

2236
MARYLAND LEGION AUXILIARY CHILDREN AND YOUTH FUND SCHOLARSHIP

Summary: To provide financial assistance for the postsecondary education of the daughters of veterans who are Maryland residents and wish to study arts, sciences, business, public administration, education, or a medical field. *See Listing # 1528.*

2237
MARYLAND LEGION AUXILIARY PAST PRESIDENTS' PARLEY NURSING SCHOLARSHIP

American Legion Auxiliary
Attn: Department of Maryland
1589 Sulphur Spring Road, Suite 105
Baltimore, MD 21227   Phone: (410) 242-9519
Summary: To provide financial assistance for nursing education to the daughters of Maryland veterans.
Eligibility: Eligible to apply for these scholarships are the daughters of ex-servicewomen who wish to become a registered nurse, who can show financial need, and who are residents of Maryland. Applicants must be between the ages of 16 and 22. If there are no applications from daughters of ex-servicewomen, the award may be given to the daughter of an ex-serviceman. Selection is based on academic record, potential for the nursing profession, and financial need. Applicants must submit a 300-word essay on the topic "What a Nursing Career Means to Me."
Financial data: The stipend is $1,000.
Duration: 1 year; may be renewed for up to 3 additional years.
Number awarded: 1 each year.
Deadline: April of each year.

2238
MARYLAND TUITION REDUCTION FOR NONRESIDENT NURSING STUDENTS

Maryland Higher Education Commission
Attn: State Scholarship Administration
16 Francis Street
Annapolis, MD 21401-1781
Phone: (410) 260-4546   (800) 974-1024
Fax: (410) 974-5376   TTY: (800) 735-2258
E-mail: ssamail@mhec.state.md.us
Web Site: www.mhec.state.md.us
Summary: To enable residents of states other than Maryland to attend Maryland nursing schools at reduced tuition rates.
Eligibility: This program is open to nursing students at Maryland public colleges who are residents of states other than Maryland. Applicants must enroll for at least 6 credits per semester.
Financial data: Recipients are entitled to pay the same tuition as if they were Maryland residents. They must agree to work as a full-time nurse in Maryland in an eligible institution or in a home that provides domiciliary, personal, or nursing care for 2 or more unrelated individuals. They must work for 2 years if they attended a 2-year school, for 4 years if they attended a 4-year school, or repay the scholarship with interested. The service obligation must begin within 6 months of graduation.
Duration: 1 year; may be renewed for 1 additional year at a 2-year public institution or 3 additional years at a 4-year public institution.
Deadline: February of each year.

2239
MAS FAMILY SCHOLARSHIP PROGRAM

Summary: To provide financial assistance to students of Cuban descent who are working on an undergraduate or graduate degree in selected subject areas.
See Listing #1529.

2240
MASSACHUSETTS HIGH TECHNOLOGY SCHOLAR/INTERN TUITION WAIVER PROGRAM

Massachusetts Office of Student Financial Assistance
454 Broadway, Suite 200
Revere, MA 02151
Phone: (617) 727-9420   Fax: (617) 727-0667
E-mail: osfa@osfa.mass.edu
Web Site: www.osfa.mass.edu/osfaprograms/hightechpro.asp
Summary: To provide financial assistance for postsecondary education to students at Massachusetts public institutions of higher education who are participating in a high technology scholar/intern program.
Eligibility: This program is open to students at Massachusetts public institutions who are participating as interns in a computer information science/technology and engineering program approved by the Massachusetts Board of Higher

Education. Applicants must be U.S. citizens or permanent residents who are residents of Massachusetts.
Financial data: All undergraduate tuition at state-supported institutions is waived.
Duration: Up to 4 academic years.
Number awarded: Varies each year.

2241
MASSACHUSETTS LEGION NURSING SCHOLARSHIP

American Legion
Attn: Department of Massachusetts
State House
24 Beacon Street, Suite 546-2
Boston, MA 02133-1044
Phone: (617) 727-2966   Fax: (617) 727-2969
Summary: To provide financial assistance for nursing education to the children of members of the American Legion in Massachusetts.
Eligibility: Eligible to apply are the children and grandchildren of current members in good standing in the American Legion's Department of Massachusetts (or members in good standing at the time of death). Applicants must be under the age of 22, entering their freshman year of college, in financial need, and preparing for a career as a nurse.
Financial data: The stipend is $1,000. Funds are paid directly to the recipient's school.
Duration: 1 year.
Number awarded: 1 each year.
Deadline: March of each year.

2242
MASSAGE MAGAZINE'S SCHOLARSHIP PROGRAM

Massage Magazine
1636 West First Avenue, Suite 100
Spokane, WA 99204
Phone: (509) 324-8117   (800) 872-1282
Fax: (509) 324-8606   E-mail: cindyf@massagemag.com
Web Site: www.massagemag.com/scholarship.htm
Summary: To provide financial assistance to students enrolled in massage therapy programs.
Eligibility: This program is open to students currently enrolled in schools of massage that participate in the *Massage Magazine* student program. Applicants must have completed at least 90 hours of training with a grade point average of 3.0 or higher, have a documented financial need, be able to provide a professional appraisal of their massage technique from a reputable massage therapist, and demonstrate a sincere interest in the massage therapy profession and in promoting the benefits of healing touch within their community.
Financial data: The stipend is $1,000.
Duration: 1 year.
Additional information: These scholarships were first offered in 2000.
Number awarded: 10 each year.
Deadline: December of each year.

2243
MASTER BREWERS ASSOCIATION OF THE AMERICAS ACADEMIC SCHOLARSHIP FUND

Master Brewers Association of the Americas
Attn: Chair, Scholarship Committee
2421 North Mayfair Road, Suite 310
Wauwatosa, WI 53226
Phone: (414) 774-8558   Fax: (414) 774-8556
Web Site: www.mbaa.com/scholarship/scholartx.html
Summary: To provide financial assistance for college to 1) children of members of the Master Brewers Association of the Americas or 2) persons employed for at least 5 years in the brewing industry.
Eligibility: Eligible to apply are children of members of the association or individuals who have been employed for at least 5 years in the brewing industry (which is defined to include malt houses, consulting laboratories, or similar services specializing in technical assistance to the brewing industry). Applicants must be entering their third year of full-time study in college. They must be majoring in an area related to malting or brewing, including production, research, quality assurance, engineering, and beer packaging. Preference is given to students in food science programs, particularly in which fermentation science courses are offered. Permissible majors or fields of study include (but are not

limited to): engineering (chemical, electrical, mechanical, industrial, agricultural, packaging, biochemical), biochemistry, biology, microbiology, chemistry, and agriculture. Every application should be endorsed by 2 members of the association. Financial need is not considered in the selection process.

Financial data: The annual stipend is $4,000.

Duration: 2 years (4 semesters).

Additional information: Scholarships cannot be awarded to a second person from the same family.

Number awarded: Several each year.

Deadline: February of each year.

2244
MASWE SCHOLARSHIP

Society of Women Engineers
230 East Ohio Street, Suite 400
Chicago, IL 60611-3265
Phone: (312) 596-5223   Fax: (312) 644-8557
E-mail: hq@swe.org   Web Site: www.swe.org

Summary: To provide financial assistance to college women majoring in engineering or computer science.

Eligibility: Women students entering their sophomore, junior, or senior year at an accredited school, college, or university are eligible to apply. They must be studying engineering and have a grade point average of 3.0 or higher. Selection is based on scholarship and financial need.

Financial data: The stipend is $2,000.

Duration: 1 year.

Additional information: These scholarships were established by the Men's Auxiliary of the Society of Women Engineers (MASWE) in 1971 and are continued through a fund established by the organization when it disbanded in 1976 (effective with the opening of Society of Women Engineer's membership to men).

Number awarded: 4 each year.

Deadline: January of each year.

2245
MATHEMATICS CONTEST PRIZE

American Mathematical Association of Two Year Colleges
c/o Southwest Tennessee Community College
5983 Macon Cove
Memphis, TN 38134
Phone: (901) 333-4643   Fax: (901) 333-4651
E-mail: amatyc@stcc.cc.tn.us   Web Site: www.amatyc.org

Summary: To recognize and reward students at 2-year colleges who excel in a mathematics contest.

Eligibility: Any 2-year college in the United States or Canada may enter a team of 5 or more students, or individual students if fewer than 5 students wish to compete. Students must have successfully completed at least 12 semester hours of community college course work but may not have earned a 2-year college or higher degree. Participants answer questions from a standard syllabus in college algebra and trigonometry that may involve precalculus algebra, trigonometry, synthetic and analytic geometry, and probability. All questions are short-answer or multiple choice. Students take 3 tests (in October/November, February, and March/April) of 1 hour each. The prize is awarded to the individual with the highest total score on all 3 exams.

Financial data: The prize is $3,000. Recipients must use the prize as a scholarship to continue their education at an accredited 4-year institution.

Duration: The prize is awarded annually.

Additional information: Further information is also available from Susan McLoughlin, Union County College, 1033 Springfield Avenue, Cranford, NJ 07016, E-mail: mcloughlin@hawk.ucc.edu. All colleges must pay $25 as annual dues for membership in the American Mathematical Association of Two Year Colleges (AMATYC) or $5 per individual student if fewer than 5 students compete for the year.

Number awarded: 1 each year.

Deadline: September of each year.

2246
MAXINE WILLIAMS SCHOLARSHIP PROGRAM

American Association of Medical Assistants
Attn: AAMA Endowment
20 North Wacker Street, Suite 1575
Chicago, IL 60606-2903
Phone: (312) 899-1500   (800) 228-2262
Web Site: www.aama-ntl.org

Summary: To provide financial assistance to high school graduates who are interested in becoming medical assistants.

Eligibility: This program is open to students enrolled in a postsecondary medical assisting program accredited by the Commission on Accreditation of Allied Health Education Programs (CAAHEP). Applications are only available from the directors of CAAHEP-accredited medical assisting program directors. Selection is based on academic ability (a grade point average of 3.0 or higher) and financial need.

Financial data: The stipend is $1,000 per year.

Duration: 1 year; may be renewed for 1 additional year.

Additional information: This program was established in 1959.

Number awarded: 6 each year.

Deadline: February of each year.

2247
MAYO FOUNDATION SCHOLARSHIP

National Black Nurses Association, Inc.
Attn: Scholarship Committee
8630 Fenton Street, Suite 330
Silver Spring, MD 20910
Phone: (301) 589-3200   Fax: (301) 589-3223
E-mail: nbna@erols.com   Web Site: www.nbna.org/memb_scholar.html

Summary: To provide financial assistance for undergraduate nursing education to members of the National Black Nurses Association.

Eligibility: This program is open to members of the association who are currently enrolled in a B.S.N., A.D., diploma, or L.P.N./L.V.N. program with at least 1 full year of school remaining. Selection is based on participation in student nurse activities, involvement in the African American community, and involvement in community health services-related activities.

Financial data: The award ranges from $500 to $2,000 per year.

Duration: 1 year; may be renewed.

Additional information: Requests for applications must be accompanied by a self-addressed stamped envelope.

Number awarded: 1 or more each year.

Deadline: April of each year.

2248
MCALLISTER MEMORIAL SCHOLARSHIPS

Aircraft Owners and Pilots Association
Attn: AOPA Air Safety Foundation
421 Aviation Way
Frederick, MD 21701-4798
Phone: (301) 695-2000   (800) 638-3101
Web Site: www.aopa.org/asf/scholarship/mcallister.html

Summary: To provide funding to students who need financial assistance to continue their studies in the field of aviation.

Eligibility: This program is open to U.S. citizens who are interested in working on a degree in the field of non-engineering aviation, are juniors or seniors in college, have earned at least a 3.25 grade point average, and are able to demonstrate financial need. They must submit a 250-word essay on a topic that changes annually; recently, the topic was "Which existing technology has the greatest potential for reducing general aviation accidents and how would you train pilots in its use to achieve maximum benefit?" Previous recipients are not eligible to reapply.

Financial data: The stipend is $1,000.

Duration: 1 year; recipients may not reapply.

Additional information: This program is jointly sponsored by the Air Safety Foundation of the Aircraft Owners and Pilots Association (AOPA) and the University Aviation Association. Information is also available from David A. NewMyer, Southern Illinois University at Carbondale, College of Applied Sciences and Arts, Aviation Management and Flight, Carbondale, IL 62901-6623. Requests for applications must be accompanied by a self-addressed stamped envelope.

Number awarded: 1 each year.

Deadline: March of each year.

2249
M.E. AMSTUTZ MEMORIAL AWARD

Illinois Society of Professional Engineers
Attn: ISPE Foundation, Inc.
1304 South Lowell Avenue
Springfield, IL 62704
Phone: (217) 544-7424   Fax: (217) 544-3349
E-mail: ispe@springnet1.com   Web Site: www.springnet1.com/ispe

Summary: To provide financial assistance to college juniors and seniors in Illinois who are working on an engineering degree.

Eligibility: Applicants must be Illinois residents who are juniors or seniors in college in the state, enrolled in an engineering program (not engineering technology) accredited by the Accreditation Board of Engineering and Technology (ABET). They must have at least a 3.0 grade point average in those courses that count toward their engineering degree. Selection is based on financial need, scholastic achievement, activities, interest in engineering, and a 200-word essay on "Why I would like to become a professional engineer."

Financial data: The stipend is $1,500 per year.

Duration: 1 year.

Number awarded: 1 each year.

Deadline: January of each year.

2250
M.E. FRANKS SCHOLARSHIP PROGRAM

International Association of Food Industry Suppliers
Attn: IAFIS Foundation
1451 Dolley Madison Boulevard
McLean, VA 22101-3850
Phone: (703) 761-2600   Fax: (703) 761-4334
E-mail: info@iafis.org
Web Site: www.iafis.org/foundation.htm

Summary: To provide financial assistance to outstanding undergraduate and graduate students who are interested in working on a degree in a field related to food science.

Eligibility: This program is open to students working on a degree in dairy foods, food science, food technology, food marketing, agricultural economics, or agricultural business management on the undergraduate or graduate school level. Undergraduate students must be entering their junior or senior year. Graduate students must be working on a master's or Ph.D. degree. U.S. or Canadian citizenship is required. Completed applications should be submitted to the applicant's department head/chairperson, who then forwards them on to the foundation office. Selection is based on academic performance, leadership ability, character and integrity, and career commitment. Graduate students are also evaluated on their statement of purpose for their master's or Ph.D. thesis proposal.

Financial data: The stipend is $3,000 per year. Funds are paid directly to the recipient.

Duration: 1 year; nonrenewable.

Additional information: This program is administered by the International Association of Food Industry Suppliers on behalf of the Dairy Recognition and Education Foundation, which provides the funding. Recipients must enroll in school full time.

Number awarded: 10 each year.

Deadline: October of each year.

2251
MEDTRONIC PHYSIO-CONTROL ACADEMIC SCHOLARSHIP

American Association of Occupational Health Nurses, Inc.
Attn: AAOHN Foundation
2920 Brandywine Road, Suite 100
Atlanta, GA 30341-4146
Phone: (770) 455-7757   Fax: (770) 455-7271
E-mail: foundation@aaohn.org
Web Site: www.aaohn.org

Summary: To provide financial assistance to registered nurses who are pursuing a bachelor's or graduate degree to prepare for a career in occupational and environmental health.

Eligibility: This program is open to registered nurses who are enrolled in a baccalaureate, master's, or doctoral degree program. Applicants must demonstrate an interest in, and commitment to, occupational and environmental health. Selection is based on 2 letters of recommendation and a 500-word essay on the applicant's professional goals as they relate to the academic activity and the field of occupational and environmental health.

Financial data: The stipend is $3,000.

Duration: 1 year; may be renewed up to 2 additional years.

Additional information: Funding for this program is provided by Medtronic Physio-Control Corporation.

Number awarded: 1 each year.

Deadline: November of each year.

2252
MELVILLE H. COHEE STUDENT LEADER CONSERVATION SCHOLARSHIPS

Soil and Water Conservation Society
7515 N.E. Ankeny Road
Ankeny, IA 50021-9764
Phone: (515) 289-2331   (800) THE SOIL
Fax: (515) 289-1227   E-mail: swcs@swcs.org
Web Site: www.swcs.org

Summary: To provide financial assistance to student officers of the Soil and Water Conservation Society (SWCS) who are interested in pursuing undergraduate or graduate studies with a focus on natural resource conservation.

Eligibility: Applicants must have been members of the society for more than 1 year, have served for 1 academic year or longer as a student chapter officer for a chapter with at least 15 members, have earned a grade point average of 3.0 or higher, be in school at least half time, not be an employee or immediate family member of the scholarship selection committee, and be in the junior or senior year of undergraduate study or the first or second year of graduate study in conservation or resource-related fields (such as agricultural economics, soils, planned land use management, forestry, wildlife biology, agricultural engineering, hydrology, rural sociology, agronomy, or water management) or related environmental protection or resource management fields at an accredited college or university. Financial need is not considered in the selection process.

Financial data: The stipend is $1,000.

Duration: 1 year.

Additional information: This scholarship may not be combined with other SWCS scholarships or internships.

Number awarded: 2 each year.

Deadline: February of each year.

2253
MELVIN R. GREEN SCHOLARSHIPS

ASME International
Attn: Education Department
Three Park Avenue
New York, NY 10016-5990
Phone: (212) 591-8131   (800) THE-ASME
Fax: (212) 591-7143   E-mail: oluwanifiset@asme.org
Web Site: www.asme.org/educate/aid/scholar.htm

Summary: To provide financial assistance to undergraduate students who are members of the American Society of Mechanical Engineers (ASME).

Eligibility: This program is open to student members in good standing who are enrolled in an ABET-accredited mechanical engineering baccalaureate program. They must be at least sophomores when they apply. Interested students should submit an application form, a nomination from the applicant's department head, a recommendation from a faculty member, and an official transcript. Only 1 nomination may be submitted per department. Selection is based on academic performance.

Financial data: The stipend is $3,500.

Duration: 1 year.

Additional information: This program was established in 1996. Only study in the junior or senior year is supported. Requests for applications must be accompanied by a self-addressed stamped envelope.

Number awarded: 2 each year.

Deadline: March of each year.

2254
MEMORIAL CONSERVATION SCHOLARSHIP

Summary: To provide financial assistance to college students in New Jersey who are preparing for a career in a field related to the conservation and management of natural resources.
See Listing #1531.

2255
MENLO LOGISTICS SCHOLARSHIP

Menlo Logistics, Inc.
One Lagoon Drive, Suite 300
Redwood City, CA 94065-1564
Phone: (650) 596-4000   Fax: (650) 596-4150
E-mail: headquarters@menlolog.com   Web Site: www.menlolog.com

Summary: To provide financial assistance to upper-division and graduate students who are preparing for a career in logistics or transportation.

Eligibility: Eligible to apply are full-time undergraduates who are entering their junior or senior year in college and have declared logistics/transportation as their major at an accredited 4-year college or university. Full-time graduate students who are pursuing a master's degree in a similar course of study may also apply.

Financial data: The stipend is $1,000.

Duration: 1 year; may be renewed once.

Additional information: This program is managed by the Citizens' Scholarship Foundation of America, P.O. Box 297, St. Peter, MN 56082, (507) 931-1682, (800) 537-4180, Fax: (507) 931-9168, E-mail: info_sms@csfa.org. Recipients must attend a 4-year college or university on a full-time basis.

Number awarded: 5 each year.

2256
MENTOR GRAPHICS SCHOLARSHIPS

Oregon Student Assistance Commission
Attn: Private Awards Grant Department
1500 Valley River Drive, Suite 100
Eugene, OR 97401-2146
Phone: (541) 687-7395   (800) 452-8807, ext. 7395
Fax: (541) 687-7419   E-mail: awardinfo@mercury.osac.state.or.us
Web Site: www.osac.state.or.us

Summary: To provide financial assistance to Oregon residents who are seeking a college degree in computer science or engineering.

Eligibility: This program is open to residents of Oregon who are U.S. citizens or permanent residents. Applicants must be full-time students in their junior or senior year of college and majoring in electrical engineering or computer science/engineering. Preference is given to female, African American, Native American, or Hispanic applicants. Financial need must be demonstrated.

Financial data: Scholarship amounts vary, depending upon the needs of the recipient.

Duration: 1 year.

Number awarded: Varies each year.

Deadline: February of each year.

2257
MERCEDES-BENZ U.S. INTERNATIONAL/SAE SCHOLARSHIP

Society of Automotive Engineers
Attn: Educational Relations
400 Commonwealth Drive
Warrendale, PA 15096-0001
Phone: (724) 772-4047   Fax: (724) 776-0890
E-mail: connie@sae.org
Web Site: www.sae.org/students/mercedes.htm

Summary: To provide financial support to residents of Alabama who are studying engineering at a university in the state.

Eligibility: This program is open to residents of Alabama who are juniors entering their senior year at a university in the state. Applicants must be majoring in manufacturing engineering or a mobility-related engineering discipline. U.S. citizenship is required. Selection is based on academic and leadership achievement, a declared intent to pursue a career in manufacturing engineering following graduation, and a 300-word essay on the single experience that most strongly convinced them or confirmed their decision to pursue a career in engineering. Financial need is not considered.

Financial data: The stipend is $2,500.

Duration: 1 year.

Additional information: This program is sponsored by Mercedes-Benz U.S. International. Candidates must include a $5 processing fee with their applications.

Number awarded: 1 each year.

Deadline: March of each year.

2258
MERIAL LIMITED IVOMEC GENERATIONS OF EXCELLENCE/KLF SCHOLARSHIPS

Kansas Livestock Foundation
Attn: Scholarship
6031 S.W. 37th Street
Topeka, KS 66614-5129
Phone: (785) 273-5115   Fax: (785) 273-3399
E-mail: kla@kla.org   Web Site: kla.beef.org/youth/scholarshipapp.htm

Summary: To provide financial assistance to Kansas residents who are or will be majoring in a field related to agriculture.

Eligibility: Eligible to apply for this program are Kansas residents who are entering or returning to a junior or senior college. Applicants must be majoring or planning to major in a field related to agriculture (e.g., agricultural economics, agronomy, animal science). Selection is based on academic achievement (20 points), personal livestock enterprises (25 points), 4H/FFA/KJLA activities and leadership (30 points), school activities and honors (30 points), other activities and leadership (25 points), work experience (25 points), significant honors or recognition (25 points), and career plans (20 points).

Financial data: The stipend is $1,000. Funds are paid directly to the recipient in 2 equal installments at the beginning of each semester, upon proof of enrollment.

Duration: 1 year.

Number awarded: 2 each year.

Deadline: April of each year.

2259
MERIDITH THOMS MEMORIAL SCHOLARSHIPS

Society of Women Engineers
230 East Ohio Street, Suite 400
Chicago, IL 60611-3265
Phone: (312) 596-5223   Fax: (312) 644-8557
E-mail: hq@swe.org   Web Site: www.swe.org

Summary: To provide financial assistance to women enrolled in or planning to enroll in college and major in engineering.

Eligibility: This program is open to women who are high school seniors or current college students interested in majoring in engineering at a 4-year institution in the United States. Applicants already in college must have a grade point average of 3.0 or higher. The schools must be ABET accredited or SWE approved. Selection is based on merit.

Financial data: The stipend is $2,000 per year.

Duration: 1 year.

Additional information: This program was established in 2001.

Number awarded: 2 each year.

Deadline: May of each year for incoming freshmen; January of each year for students already in college.

2260
MGMA MIDWEST SECTION SCHOLARSHIPS

American College of Medical Practice Executives
Attn: Scholarship Program
104 Inverness Terrace East
Englewood, CO 80112-5306
Phone: (303) 643-9573   Fax: (303) 643-4427
E-mail: acmpe@mgma.com
Web Site: www.mgma.com/acmpe

Summary: To provide financial assistance to members of the Medical Group Management Association (MGMA) Midwest Section who are interested in pursuing professional development through undergraduate or graduate education.

Eligibility: Eligible to apply are individuals resident in the MGMA Midwest Section (Illinois, Indiana, Iowa, Michigan, Minnesota, Nebraska, North Dakota, Ohio, South Dakota, and Wisconsin) who wish to pursue an undergraduate or graduate degree in medical practice management at an accredited university or college. Applications must include a letter describing career goals and objectives; a resume; 3 reference letters commenting on the individual's performance, character, potential to succeed, and need for scholarship support; and academic transcripts.

Financial data: The stipend is $2,000. Payments for undergraduate and graduate scholarships are sent to the school where the recipient is or will be enrolled.

Duration: 1 year.

Deadline: May of each year.

2261
MGMA WESTERN SECTION SCHOLARSHIPS

American College of Medical Practice Executives
Attn: Scholarship Program
104 Inverness Terrace East
Englewood, CO 80112-5306
Phone: (303) 643-9573   Fax: (303) 643-4427
E-mail: acmpe@mgma.com   Web Site: www.mgma.com/acmpe

Summary: To provide financial assistance to members of the Medical Group Management Association (MGMA) Western Section who are interested in pursuing professional development through undergraduate or graduate education.
Eligibility: Eligible to apply are individuals who reside in and have been members of the MGMA Western Section (Alaska, Arizona, California, Colorado, Hawaii, Idaho, Montana, Nevada, New Mexico, Oregon, Utah, Washington, and Wyoming) for at least 2 years. Applicants must wish to pursue an undergraduate or graduate degree in medical practice management at an accredited university or college. Applications must include a letter describing career goals and objectives; a resume; 3 reference letters commenting on the individual's performance, character, potential to succeed, and need for scholarship support; and academic transcripts.
Financial data: The stipend is $2,000. Payments for undergraduate and graduate scholarships are sent to the university or college in which the recipient is or will be enrolled.
Duration: 1 year.
Deadline: May of each year.

2262
MGMA/AAA SCHOLARSHIPS

American College of Medical Practice Executives
Attn: Scholarship Program
104 Inverness Terrace East
Englewood, CO 80112-5306
Phone: (303) 643-9573   Fax: (303) 643-4427
E-mail: acmpe@mgma.com   Web Site: www.mgma.com/acmpe
Summary: To provide financial assistance to members and dependents of members of the Anesthesia Administration Assembly (AAA) of the Medical Group Management Association (MGMA) who are undertaking a course of study or project to accomplish set goals for self advancement.
Eligibility: Eligible to apply are 1) members of the AAA and 2) dependents of AAA members who have been members for at least 3 years and are currently members. Applicants must be interested in pursuing an undergraduate or graduate degree relevant to medical practice management at accredited universities and colleges. They must submit a letter describing career goals and objectives; a resume; 3 reference letters commenting on the individual's performance, character, potential to succeed, and need for scholarship support; documentation indicating acceptance into an undergraduate or graduate college or university; and academic transcripts listing undergraduate or graduate work completed to date.
Financial data: The stipend is $1,500. Payments for undergraduate and graduate scholarships are sent to the university or college in which the recipient is or will be enrolled.
Duration: 1 year.
Deadline: May of each year.

2263
MGMA/APA SCHOLARSHIPS

American College of Medical Practice Executives
Attn: Scholarship Program
104 Inverness Terrace East
Englewood, CO 80112-5306
Phone: (303) 643-9573   Fax: (303) 643-4427
E-mail: acmpe@mgma.com   Web Site: www.mgma.com/acmpe
Summary: To provide financial assistance to members of the Academic Practice Assembly (APA) of the Medical Group Management Association (MGMA) who are pursuing professional development through undergraduate or graduate study.
Eligibility: Eligible to apply are members of the APA who wish to pursue an undergraduate or graduate degree relevant to medical practice management at accredited universities and colleges. Applications should include a letter describing career goals and objectives; a resume; 3 reference letters commenting on the individual's performance, character, potential to succeed, and need for scholarship support; documentation indicating acceptance into an undergraduate or graduate college or university; and academic transcripts listing undergraduate or graduate work completed to date.
Financial data: The stipend is $1,000. Payments for undergraduate and graduate scholarships are sent to the school where the recipient is or will be enrolled.
Duration: 1 year.
Deadline: September of each year.

2264
MGMA/IHPS SCHOLARSHIPS

American College of Medical Practice Executives
Attn: Scholarship Program
104 Inverness Terrace East
Englewood, CO 80112-5306
Phone: (303) 643-9573   Fax: (303) 643-4427
E-mail: acmpe@mgma.com   Web Site: www.mgma.com/acmpe
Summary: To provide financial assistance to students in fields of interest to the Integrated Healthcare Practices Society (IHPS) of the Medical Group Management Association (MGMA).
Eligibility: This program is open to current undergraduate and graduate students whose past experience, current position, and/or future plans demonstrate their potential for contributing to health care management. Applicants must submit a letter describing career goals and objectives; a resume; 3 reference letters commenting on the individual's performance, character, potential to succeed, and need for scholarship support; documentation indicating acceptance into an undergraduate or graduate college or university; and academic transcripts listing undergraduate or graduate work completed to date.
Financial data: The stipend is $1,000. Payments for undergraduate and graduate scholarships are sent to the school where the recipient is or will be enrolled.
Duration: 1 year; may be renewed.
Deadline: May of each year.

2265
MICHAEL KIDGER MEMORIAL SCHOLARSHIP

SPIE-The International Society for Optical Engineering
Attn: Michael Kidger Memorial Scholarship
1000 20th Street
P.O. Box 10
Bellingham, WA 98227-0010
Phone: (360) 676-3290   Fax: (360) 647-1445
E-mail: education@spie.org   Web Site: www.spie.org
Summary: To provide financial assistance to undergraduate and graduate students who are preparing for a career in optical design.
Eligibility: This program is open to students of optical design from any country at the undergraduate and graduate level. Applicants must have at least 1 more year, after the award, to complete their current course of study. They must submit 2 letters of recommendation and a 5-page essay explaining how the scholarship will help them contribute to long-term development in the field of optical design. Financial need is not considered in the selection process.
Financial data: A stipend is awarded (exact amount not specified).
Duration: 1 year.
Additional information: The International Society for Optical Engineering was founded in 1955 as the Society of Photo-Optical Instrumentation Engineers (SPIE). This scholarship was established in 1998 by Kidger Optics Ltd. of East Sussex, United Kingdom.
Number awarded: 1 or more each year.
Deadline: March of each year.

2266
MICRON SCIENCE AND TECHNOLOGY SCHOLARS

Micron Technology Foundation, Inc.
8000 South Federal Way
Boise, ID 83716
Phone: (208) 368-4400   E-mail: gcjones@micron.com
Web Site: www.micron.com/scholars
Summary: To provide financial assistance to high school seniors in selected states who are interested in majoring in the physical sciences.
Eligibility: This program is open to high school seniors who reside in and attend public or private schools in Idaho, Utah, Texas, and Colorado. Applicants must have a combined SAT score of at least 1350 or a composite ACT score of at least 30, have at least a 3.5 grade point average, have demonstrated leadership in school and extracurricular activities, and plan to major in engineering (electronic, computer, chemical, or mechanical), computer science, chemistry, or material sciences. Selection is based on merit (in academics and leadership).
Financial data: Stipends are either $50,000 or $15,000.
Additional information: This program began in 2000. Information about this scholarship is also available from Micron's fax-on-demand service: (800) 239-0337.

Number awarded: 11 each year: 1 at $50,000 and 10 at $15,000; 2 are awarded to students from each of 4 participating states, plus 3 floating scholarships are awarded within those states.

Deadline: December of each year.

2267
MICROSOFT CORPORATION COMPUTER SCIENCE SCHOLARSHIP

National Society of Black Engineers
Attn: Programs Manager
1454 Duke Street
Alexandria, VA 22314
Phone: (703) 549-2207, ext. 204   Fax: (703) 683-5312
E-mail: scholarships@nsbe.org
Web Site: www.nsbe.org

Summary: To provide financial assistance to members of the National Society of Black Engineers (NSBE) who are majoring in computer science or engineering.

Eligibility: This program is open to members of the society who are undergraduate students majoring in computer engineering or computer science. Applicants must have at least a 3.0 grade point average and submit a 250-word essay describing their career goals and how the scholarship will advance those goals.

Financial data: The stipend is $2,500.

Duration: 1 year.

Additional information: This program is supported by Microsoft Corporation.

Number awarded: 1 or more each year.

Deadline: November of each year.

2268
MICROSOFT CORPORATION SCHOLARSHIPS

Society of Women Engineers
230 East Ohio Street, Suite 400
Chicago, IL 60611-3265
Phone: (312) 596-5223   Fax: (312) 644-8557
E-mail: hq@swe.org
Web Site: www.swe.org

Summary: To provide financial assistance to women for the undergraduate or graduate study of computer engineering or science.

Eligibility: This program is open to women students entering their sophomore, junior, or senior years in college, as well as to first-year graduate students. Applicants must be pursuing a degree in computer science or computer engineering and have a grade point average of 3.5 or higher. They must have a career interest in the field of microcomputer software. Selection is based on merit.

Financial data: The stipend is $1,000.

Duration: 1 year.

Additional information: This program was established in 1994.

Number awarded: 9 each year.

Deadline: January of each year.

2269
MICROSOFT NATIONAL MINORITY TECHNICAL SCHOLARSHIP

Microsoft Corporation
Attn: National Minority Technical Scholarship
One Microsoft Way
Redmond, WA 98052-8303
Phone: (425) 882-8080   TTY: (800) 892-9811
Web Site: www.microsoft.com/college/scholarship.htm

Summary: To encourage undergraduate students of color to pursue careers in computer science and other related technical fields.

Eligibility: This program is open to African American, Hispanic American, and Native American students who are enrolled full time in an undergraduate program and majoring in computer science, computer engineering, or a related technical discipline (such as math or physics) with a demonstrated interest in computer science. Applicants must be enrolled in their sophomore or junior year and have earned at least a 3.0 grade point average. The application package must include a letter of referral (from a faculty member in the computer science department or department of a related discipline), a 300- to 500-word essay on career preparation in the software industry, a resume, and an official transcript. Selection is based on quality of the application, interest in the PC/software

industry (including a passion for technology), and potential to make a difference in the software industry.

Financial data: The stipend is $1,000. Funds are to be used for tuition only and may not be used for other fees.

Duration: 1 year.

Additional information: Selected recipients are offered a paid summer internship where they will have a chance to develop Microsoft products. Scholarships are made through designated schools and are not transferable to other academic institutions.

Number awarded: 5 each year.

Deadline: February of each year.

2270
MICROSOFT NATIONAL WOMEN'S TECHNICAL SCHOLARSHIP

Microsoft Corporation
Attn: National Women's Technical Scholarship
One Microsoft Way
Redmond, WA 98052-8303
Phone: (425) 882-8080   TTY: (800) 892-9811
Web Site: www.microsoft.com/college/scholarship.htm

Summary: To encourage women undergraduate students to pursue careers in computer science and other related technical fields.

Eligibility: This program is open to female students who are enrolled full time in an undergraduate program and majoring in computer science, computer engineering, or a related technical discipline (such as math or physics) with a demonstrated interest in computer science. Applicants must be enrolled in their sophomore or junior year and have earned at least a 3.0 grade point average. The application package must include a letter of referral (from a faculty member in the computer science department or department of a related discipline), a 300- to 500-word essay on career preparation in the software industry, a resume, and an official transcript. Selection is based on quality of the application, interest in the PC/software industry (including a passion for technology), and the potential to make a difference in the software industry.

Financial data: The stipend is $1,000. Funds are to be used for tuition only and may not be used for other fees.

Duration: 1 year.

Additional information: Selected recipients are offered a paid summer internship where they will have a chance to develop Microsoft products. Scholarships are made through designated schools and are not transferable to other academic institutions.

Number awarded: 5 each year.

Deadline: February of each year.

2271
MICROSOFT SCHOLARSHIP PROGRAM OF THE HISPANIC SCHOLARSHIP FUND

Hispanic Scholarship Fund
Attn: Selection Committee
One Sansome Street, Suite 1000
San Francisco, CA 94104
Phone: (415) 445-9936   (877) HSF-INFO, ext. 33
Fax: (415) 445-9942   E-mail: info@hsf.net
Web Site: www.hsf.net

Summary: To provide financial assistance to Hispanic American high school seniors who are interested in majoring in computer science, engineering, or mathematics in college.

Eligibility: This program is open to U.S. citizens or permanent residents of at least half Hispanic background who are high school seniors. Applicants must be planning to major in computer science, engineering, or mathematics as a full-time 4-year college student. They must have at least a 3.0 grade point average in high school and be accepted at an accredited 4-year institution for the following fall. As part of the application process, they must submit a 2-page essay on their Hispanic background and potential contribution to the Hispanic community; their current high school status, activities, and achievements; and career goals. In addition to that essay, selection is based on academic achievement, a letter of recommendation, and financial need.

Financial data: The stipend is $2,500.

Duration: 1 year.

Additional information: Funding for this program is provided by Microsoft Corporation. Requests for applications must be accompanied by a self-addressed stamped envelope.

Number awarded: Varies each year.
Deadline: February of each year.

2272
MID-ATLANTIC CHAPTER SCHOLARSHIPS

Summary: To provide financial assistance to students attending college in designated mid-Atlantic states who are interested in majoring in satellite-related disciplines. *See Listing #1536.*

2273
MID-CAREER SCHOLARSHIP PROGRAM

American Traffic Safety Services Foundation
Attn: Director of Development
15 Riverside Parkway, Suite 100
Fredericksburg, VA 22406-1022
Phone: (540) 368-1701   (800) 272-8772
Fax: (540) 368-1717   E-mail: foundation@atssa.com
Web Site: www.atssa.com
Summary: To provide financial assistance to federal, state, or local highway department employees who are interested in continuing their education in traffic or transportation engineering or a related field.
Eligibility: To be eligible to receive the scholarship funding, the candidate must be a U.S. citizen, be currently employed by a government agency, and have a desire to pursue continuing education in traffic or transportation engineering or a related field on the undergraduate or graduate level. Candidates are evaluated on the basis of their past academic and career performance, their proposed program of study, an essay discussing educational goals and outlining their career objectives, a personal interview, and recommendations.
Financial data: The scholarship provides up to 100 percent of the recipient's tuition costs. Funds are paid directly to the recipient's educational institution in installments, based upon the amount of tuition and other expenses approved by the sponsor.
Duration: 1 year; may be renewed.
Additional information: This program was started in 1991. Recipients are required to attend safety training courses sponsored by the foundation at some point during the fellowship period.
Number awarded: Varies each year.

2274
MID-CONTINENT INSTRUMENT SCHOLARSHIP

Aircraft Electronics Association
Attn: Educational Foundation
4217 South Hocker Drive
Independence, MO 64055-4723
Phone: (816) 373-6565   Fax: (816) 478-3100
E-mail: info@aea.net
Web Site: www.aea.net
Summary: To provide financial assistance to students who are interested in studying avionics or aircraft repair in college.
Eligibility: This program is open to high school seniors and currently-enrolled college students who are attending (or planning to attend) an accredited school in an avionics or aircraft repair program.
Financial data: The stipend is $1,000.
Duration: 1 year.
Number awarded: 1 each year.
Deadline: February of each year.

2275
MIDWEST CONCRETE INDUSTRY BOARD EDUCATIONAL FUND

Greater Kansas City Community Foundation
Attn: Scholarship Coordinator
1055 Broadway, Suite 130
Kansas City, MO 64105-1595
Phone: (816) 842-0944   Fax: (816) 842-8079
E-mail: scholars@gkccf.org
Web Site: www.gkccf.org
Summary: To provide financial assistance to undergraduate and graduate engineering students from Missouri and Kansas interested in concrete and concrete design courses.
Eligibility: This program is open to undergraduate and graduate engineering students at accredited colleges and universities who are Missouri or Kansas

residents. Applicants must be interested in pursuing a bachelor's or higher degree that includes concrete and concrete design courses.
Financial data: The amounts of the awards vary.
Duration: 1 year.
Additional information: Funding for this program is provided by the Midwest Concrete Industry Board; further information is available from Ken Jorgensen at (913) 681-2219.
Number awarded: 1 or more each year.
Deadline: April of each year.

2276
MILLER ELECTRIC INTERNATIONAL YOUTH SKILLS COMPETITION SCHOLARSHIP

American Welding Society
Attn: AWS Foundation, Inc.
550 N.W. LeJeune Road
Miami, FL 33126
Phone: (305) 443-9353, ext. 461   (800) 443-9353, ext. 461
Fax: (305) 443-7559   E-mail: vpinsky@aws.org
Web Site: www.aws.org
Summary: To recognize and reward winning students who compete in the VICA USA skills competition for welding.
Eligibility: This program is open to high school seniors who compete in the national VICA USA skills competition for welding and advance to the American Welding Society (AWS) Weld Trials at the biennial AWS International Welding and Fabricating Exposition and Convention. Applicants must be interested in pursuing a postsecondary educational activity related to the field of welding or similar joining technologies, including certificate programs, 2-year programs, 4-year programs, seminars, workshops, or certification courses.
Financial data: The winner receives a scholarship of up to $10,000 per year, up to $1,000 in AWS publications, a 4-year complimentary full AWS membership, and an AWS certification. Runners-up receive a $1,000 scholarship, a 1-year complimentary full AWS membership, and an AWS certification.
Duration: The winner's scholarship is for 4 years. Runners-up scholarships are for 1 year, to be used within 2 years of the Weld Trial Competition.
Number awarded: 1 winner and several runners-up every other year.

2277
MINERAL AND METALLURGICAL PROCESSING DIVISION SCHOLARSHIP

Society for Mining, Metallurgy, and Exploration, Inc.
Attn: Member Services
8307 Shaffer Parkway
P.O. Box 277002
Littleton, CO 80127-7002
Phone: (303) 973-9550   (800) 763-3132
Fax: (303) 973-3845   E-mail: sensenig@smenet.org
Web Site: www.smenet.org/education/students/sme_scholarships.cfm
Summary: To provide financial assistance to student members of the Society for Mining, Metallurgy, and Exploration (SME) who are preparing for a career in minerals processing.
Eligibility: This program is open to student members of the society who have completed their sophomore year in college, are majoring in metallurgy or metallurgical engineering, are U.S. citizens, are enrolled full time in an undergraduate program, and have a grade point average of 2.5 or higher. Only 1 candidate from each eligible department may be nominated each academic year. Applicants must demonstrate an interest in pursuing a career in mineral processing.
Financial data: The first-place recipient is given $2,000 (plus travel to the society's annual meeting). The other winners each receive a $1,000 scholarship.
Duration: 1 year.
Number awarded: Up to 6 each year.
Deadline: October of each year.

2278
MINING & EXPLORATION DIVISION SCHOLARSHIP

Society for Mining, Metallurgy, and Exploration, Inc.
Attn: Member Services
8307 Shaffer Parkway
P.O. Box 277002
Littleton, CO 80127-7002

Phone: (303) 973-9550   (800) 763-3132
Fax: (303) 973-3845   E-mail: sensenig@smenet.org
Web Site: www.smenet.org/education/students/sme_scholarships.cfm
Summary: To provide financial assistance to student members of the Society for Mining, Metallurgy, and Exploration (SME) who are preparing for a career in the minerals industry.
Eligibility: Applicants must have completed their sophomore year in college and be majoring in mining, geology, or a related field of specialization at an ABET-accredited college or university. They must be U.S. citizens or permanent residents, be able to demonstrate financial need, have a strong academic record, and be a student member of the society. Only 1 candidate from each eligible department may be nominated each academic year.
Financial data: A total of $3,000 is awarded each year.
Duration: 1 year.
Number awarded: 1 or more each year.
Deadline: November of each year.

2279
MINNESOTA NURSE LOAN FORGIVENESS PROGRAM

Minnesota Department of Health
Office of Rural Health and Primary Care
Attn: Loan Forgiveness Program Officer
121 East Seventh Place, Suite 460
P.O. Box 64975
St. Paul, MN 55164-0975
Phone: (651) 282-6302   (800) 366-5424 (within MN)
Fax: (651) 297-5808   E-mail: karen.welter@health.state.mn.us
Web Site: www.health.state.mn.us
Summary: To repay the loans of students who plan to become registered or licensed practical nurses and who are willing to work in a nursing home or Intermediate Care Facility for Persons with Mental Retardation or Related Conditions (ICFMR) in Minnesota after they graduate.
Eligibility: This program is open to individuals who plan to enroll or are currently enrolled in a program of study that will prepare them to be either a registered nurse or licensed practical nurse. Applicants must plan to practice in a nursing home or ICFMR in Minnesota. Applications must be submitted while the students are still in school for their training.
Financial data: For each year that a participant serves as a registered nurse or licensed practical nurse in a nursing home or ICFMR in Minnesota for a minimum of 30 hours per week, the sponsor will repay up to $3,000 on their educational loans, directly to the loan servicer.
Duration: Participants are eligible for 1 or 2 years of loan repayment, depending on the length of their nursing educational program. Participants who complete a 1-year program are eligible for 1 year of loan repayment; those who complete a 2-year program are eligible for 2 years of loan repayment.
Additional information: Applicants are responsible for securing their own loans. Eligible loans include government, commercial, and foundation loans for actual costs paid for tuition, reasonable education expenses, and reasonable living expenses related to the graduate or undergraduate education of a health professional. To remain eligible for this program, participants must complete at least 1 year of service in a designated rural area in the first 2 years following completion of their nursing educational program.
Number awarded: Up to 10 each year.
Deadline: November of each year.

2280
MINNESOTA RURAL MIDLEVEL PRACTITIONER LOAN FORGIVENESS PROGRAM

Minnesota Department of Health
Office of Rural Health and Primary Care
Attn: Loan Forgiveness Program Officer
121 East Seventh Place, Suite 460
P.O. Box 64975
St. Paul, MN 55164-0975
Phone: (651) 282-6302   (800) 366-5424 (within MN)
Fax: (651) 297-5808   E-mail: karen.welter@health.state.mn.us
Web Site: www.health.state.mn.us
Summary: To repay the loans of students who plan to become midlevel health practitioners and work in rural Minnesota.
Eligibility: This program is open to individuals who plan to enroll or are currently enrolled in a program of study that will prepare them for service as midlevel practitioners; these include nurse practitioners, nurse midwives, nurse anesthetists, advanced clinical nurse specialists, and physician assistants. They must plan to practice in a designated rural area in Minnesota after completion of their educational program (i.e., areas in Minnesota outside the cities of Duluth, Mankato, Moorhead, Rochester, and St. Cloud and outside the counties of Anoka, Carver, Dakota, Hennepin, Ramsey, Scott, and Washington). Applications must be submitted while the students are still in school for their midlevel practitioner training.
Financial data: For each year that participants serve as a midlevel practitioner in a designated rural area for a minimum of 30 hours per week, the sponsor will repay up to $3,500 on their educational loans, directly to the loan servicer.
Duration: Participants are eligible for 2 or 4 years of loan repayment, depending on the length of their midlevel educational program. Participants who complete a 1-year program are eligible for 2 years of loan repayment; those who complete a 2-year program are eligible for 4 years of loan repayment.
Additional information: Applicants are responsible for securing their own loans. Eligible loans include government, commercial, and foundation loans for actual costs paid for tuition, reasonable education expenses, and reasonable living expenses related to the graduate or undergraduate education of a health professional. To remain eligible for this program, the participant must complete at least 2 years of service in a designated rural area in the first 4 years following completion of their midlevel educational program.
Number awarded: Up to 8 each year.
Deadline: November of each year.

2281
MINNESOTA YOUTH SOYBEAN SCHOLARSHIPS

Minnesota Soybean Research and Promotion Council
Attn: Scholarship Program
360 Pierce Avenue, Suite 110
North Mankato, MN 56003-2208
Phone: (507) 388-1635   (888) 896-9678
Fax: (507) 388-6751   E-mail: sherry@soybean.Mankato.mn.us
Web Site: www.mnsoybean.org
Summary: To provide financial assistance to high school seniors or beginning college freshmen in Minnesota who have been active in the areas of soybean production or soybean nutrition.
Eligibility: This program is open to Minnesota residents who are the children of a family active in agriculture and planning to enroll in a postsecondary school (technical college, junior or community college, 4-year college, or university). Their field of study must relate to agriculture (including agribusiness, agricultural education nutrition, and production agriculture). Applicants must 1) provide a summary of their career plans and how they relate to agriculture; 2) summarize their activities and involvement in both agriculture and community, especially their involvement in their county soybean association; and 3) supply a letter of recommendation. Financial need is not considered in the selection process.
Financial data: The stipend is $1,900. Funds are disbursed only after the recipient has successfully completed the first quarter or semester of college and provided proof of enrollment.
Duration: 1 year; nonrenewable.
Number awarded: 4 each year.
Deadline: October of each year.

2282
MINORITY ACADEMIC INSTITUTIONS UNDERGRADUATE STUDENT FELLOWSHIPS

Environmental Protection Agency
Attn: National Center for Environmental Research and Quality Assurance
401 M Street, S.W.
Washington, DC 20460
Phone: (800) 490-9194
Web Site: www.epa.gov/ncerqa
Summary: To provide financial assistance and summer internships to undergraduates at minority academic institutions (MAIs) who are interested in majoring in fields related to the environment.
Eligibility: Applicants for this program must be U.S. citizens or permanent residents who are enrolled full time with a minimum grade point average of 3.0 in an accredited 4-year institution that meets the definition of the Environmental Protection Agency (EPA) as an MAI: Historically Black Colleges and Universities (HBCUs), Hispanic Serving Institutions (HSIs), and Tribal Colleges (TCs). Students must be majoring in environmental science, physical sciences, biological

sciences, chemistry, computer science, environmental health, social sciences, mathematics, or engineering. They must be available to work as interns at an EPA facility during the summer between their junior and senior years.

Financial data: The fellowship provides up to $15,200 per year, including up to $10,000 for tuition and academic fees, a stipend of $2,700 ($300 per month for 9 months), and an expense allowance of up to $2,500 for items and activities for the direct benefit of the student's education, such as books, supplies, and travel to professional conferences and workshops.

Duration: The final 2 years of baccalaureate study, including 12 weeks during the summer between those years.

Additional information: This program began in 1982. It was formerly known as Culturally Diverse Academic Institutions Undergraduate Student Fellowships program.

Number awarded: Approximately 25 each year.

Deadline: November of each year.

2283
MINORITY AFFAIRS COMMITTEE AWARD FOR OUTSTANDING SCHOLASTIC ACHIEVEMENT

American Institute of Chemical Engineers
Attn: Awards Administrator
Three Park Avenue
New York, NY 10016-5991
Phone: (212) 591-7478   Fax: (212) 591-8882
E-mail: awards@aiche.org
Web Site: www.aiche.org/awards

Summary: To recognize and reward chemical engineering students who serve as role models for minority students.

Eligibility: Members of the American Institute of Chemical Engineers (AIChE) may nominate any chemical engineering student who serves as a role model for minority students in that field. Nominees must be members of a minority group that is underrepresented in chemical engineering (i.e., African American, Hispanic American, Native American, Alaskan Native). Selection is based on the nominee's academic and scholarship achievements, including a grade point average of 3.0 or higher, scholastic awards, research contributions, and technical presentations; the nominee's exemplary outreach activities that directly benefit or encourage minority youth in their academic pursuits; a letter from the nominee describing his or her outreach activities; and extraordinary circumstances, such as job or family matters, that impose additional responsibility.

Financial data: The award consists of a plaque and a $1,500 honorarium.

Duration: The award is presented annually.

Additional information: This award was first presented in 1996.

Number awarded: 1 each year.

Deadline: Nominations must be submitted by April of each year.

2284
MINORITY GEOSCIENCE UNDERGRADUATE SCHOLARSHIPS

American Geological Institute
Attn: Minority Participation Program
4220 King Street
Alexandria, VA 22302-1502
Phone: (703) 379-2480   Fax: (703) 379-7563
Web Site: www.agiweb.org/education/mpp/ugradmpp.html

Summary: To provide financial assistance to underrepresented minority undergraduate students interested in pursuing a degree in the geosciences.

Eligibility: This program is open to members of ethnic minority groups underrepresented in the geosciences (Blacks, Hispanics, American Indians, Eskimos, Hawaiians, and Samoans). U.S. citizenship is required. Applicants must be full-time undergraduate students enrolled in an accredited institution with a major in the geosciences, including geology, geophysics, hydrology, meteorology, physical oceanography, planetary geology, and earth science education; students in other natural sciences, mathematics, or engineering are not eligible. Selection is based on a 250-word essay on career goals and why the applicant has chosen a geoscience as a major, work experience, recommendations, honors and awards, extracurricular activities, and financial need.

Financial data: Up to $10,000 per year.

Duration: 1 academic year; renewable if the recipient maintains satisfactory performance.

Additional information: Funding for this program is provided by a grant from the National Science Foundation.

Number awarded: Varies each year; recently, 11 of these scholarships were awarded.

Deadline: February of each year.

2285
MINORITY NURSE MAGAZINE SCHOLARSHIP PROGRAM

Minority Nurse
Attn: CASS Recruitment Media
1800 Sherman Avenue, Suite 404
Evanston, IL 60201
Phone: (847) 448-1011   E-mail: pam.chwedyk@careermedia.com
Web Site: www.minoritynurse.com

Summary: To provide financial assistance to members of minority groups who are pursuing a bachelor's degree in nursing.

Eligibility: This program is open to third- and fourth-year minority nursing students currently enrolled in an accredited B.S.N. program. Selection is based on academic excellence (grade point average of 3.0 or higher), demonstrated commitment of service to the student's minority community, and financial need.

Financial data: The stipends are $1,000 or $500.

Duration: 1 year.

Additional information: These scholarships were first offered in 2000. Winners are announced in the fall issue of *Minority Nurse*.

Number awarded: 4 each year: 2 at $1,000 and 2 at $500.

Deadline: June of each year.

2286
MINORITY SCHOLARSHIP AWARD IN PHYSICAL THERAPY

American Physical Therapy Association
Attn: Department of Minority/International Affairs
1111 North Fairfax Street
Alexandria, VA 22314-1488
Phone: (703) 706-3144   Fax: (703) 838-8910
E-mail: min-intl@apta.org
Web Site: www.apta.org/min-intl

Summary: To provide financial assistance to minority students who are interested in becoming a physical therapist or physical therapy assistant.

Eligibility: This program is open to minority students who will graduate from professional physical therapy education and physical therapy assistant education programs at any time during the year following the submission of an application. Selection is based on academic excellence, professional and leadership potential, and commitment to minority issues.

Financial data: The minimum award is $1,500 for physical therapy students or $750 for physical therapy assistant students.

Additional information: Applications are distributed to all physical therapy programs; they are not accepted directly from students.

Number awarded: 10 each year: 6 for physical therapy students and 4 for physical therapy assistant students.

Deadline: Nominations must be submitted by the end of November of each year.

2287
MINORITY SCHOLARSHIP AWARDS FOR COLLEGE STUDENTS IN CHEMICAL ENGINEERING

American Institute of Chemical Engineers
Attn: Awards Administrator
Three Park Avenue
New York, NY 10016-5991
Phone: (212) 591-7478   Fax: (212) 591-8882
E-mail: awards@aiche.org
Web Site: www.aiche.org/awards

Summary: To provide financial assistance for study in chemical engineering to underrepresented minority college students.

Eligibility: Eligible are undergraduate student members of the American Institute of Chemical Engineers (AIChE) who are also members of a disadvantaged minority group that is underrepresented in chemical engineering (African Americans, Hispanics, Native Americans, and Alaskan Natives). Each AIChE chapter may nominate 1 member. Selection is based on academic record (including a grade point average of 3.0 or higher), participation in AIChE student and professional activities, a 300-word letter on career objectives and plans, and financial need.

Financial data: Each scholarship is $1,000.

Duration: 1 year; nonrenewable.

Number awarded: Varies each year; recently, 16 of these scholarships were awarded.

Deadline: Nominations must be submitted by April of each year.

2288
MINORITY SCHOLARSHIP AWARDS FOR INCOMING COLLEGE FRESHMEN IN CHEMICAL ENGINEERING

American Institute of Chemical Engineers
Attn: Awards Administrator
Three Park Avenue
New York, NY 10016-5991
Phone: (212) 591-7478   Fax: (212) 591-8882
E-mail: awards@aiche.org
Web Site: www.aiche.org/awards
Summary: To provide financial assistance for study in chemical engineering to incoming college minority freshmen.
Eligibility: Eligible are members of a disadvantaged minority group that is underrepresented in chemical engineering (African Americans, Hispanics, Native Americans, and Alaskan Natives). Applicants must be graduating high school seniors planning to enroll in a 4-year university with a major in chemical engineering. They must be nominated by an American Institute of Chemical Engineers (AIChE) local section. Selection is based on academic record (including a grade point average of 3.0 or higher), participation in school and/or necessary work activities, a 300-word letter outlining the reasons for choosing chemical engineering, and financial need.
Financial data: Each scholarship is $1,000.
Duration: 1 year; nonrenewable.
Number awarded: Varies each year; recently, 14 of these scholarships were awarded.
Deadline: Nominations must be submitted by April of each year.

2289
MIRIAM SCHAEFER SCHOLARSHIP

Michigan Council of Teachers of Mathematics
Attn: Scholarship Committee
3300 Washtenaw Avenue, Suite 220
Ann Arbor, MI 48104
Phone: (734) 477-0421
Web Site: www.mictm.org/awards.html
Summary: To provide financial assistance to students who are enrolled in a teacher education program in Michigan with a mathematics specialty.
Eligibility: This program is open to Michigan residents who are currently enrolled as a junior or senior in a Michigan college or university. Applicants must be majoring in education with a mathematics specialty. They must have at least a 3.0 grade point average. To apply, they must submit an application, a short essay on their personal goals related to the teaching of mathematics, a list of extracurricular and/or community activities and interests, transcripts, evidence of junior or senior standing, and 3 letters of recommendation.
Financial data: The stipend of $1,500 is paid to the recipients, with their school as the second payee. The award is to be used for tuition, books, and fees.
Duration: 1 year; nonrenewable.
Number awarded: 4 each year.
Deadline: June of each year.

2290
MISSISSIPPI CATTLEMEN'S ASSOCIATION/WAX COMPANY SCHOLARSHIP

Mississippi Cattlemen's Association
Attn: Scholarship Applications
680 Monroe Street, Suite A
Jackson, MS 39202
Phone: (601) 354-8951   Fax: (601) 355-7128
Summary: To provide financial assistance to students majoring in agriculture who are affiliated with the Mississippi Cattlemen's Association.
Eligibility: Applicants must 1) be currently enrolled in college (in any state) as undergraduates or graduate students and 2) be majoring in agriculture. They, or their parents, must be members of the Mississippi Cattlemen's Association. To apply, students submit 3 letters of reference and complete an application form. Selection is based on academic record, extracurricular activities, honors and awards, and financial need.
Financial data: The stipend is generally around $1,000.

Duration: 1 year.
Number awarded: Several each year.
Deadline: September of each year.

2291
MISSISSIPPI CATTLEMEN'S FOUNDATION SCHOLARSHIP

Mississippi Cattlemen's Association
Attn: Scholarship Applications
680 Monroe Street, Suite A
Jackson, MS 39202
Phone: (601) 354-8951   Fax: (601) 355-7128
Summary: To provide financial assistance for college to students whose family is involved in the Mississippi cattle industry.
Eligibility: Applicants must be enrolled at a college or university in Mississippi. Their family must be involved in the Mississippi cattle industry. To apply, students must submit a brief letter indicating the role they see themselves playing in the beef industry after graduation, write a brief essay (750 words) discussing the future of the cattle industry, include 2 letters of reference, and complete an application form. Selection is based on academic record, extracurricular activities, honors and awards, and financial need.
Financial data: The stipend is $1,000.
Duration: 1 year.
Number awarded: 2 each year.

2292
MISSISSIPPI YOUNG FARMER SCHOLARSHIPS

Mississippi Farm Bureau
6310 I-55 North
P.O. Box 1972
Jackson, MS 39215-1972
Phone: (601) 977-4277   (800) 227-8244
E-mail: gshows@msfb.com
Web Site: www.msfb.com/programs/scholarships.html
Summary: To provide financial assistance to members of the Mississippi Farm Bureau who are majoring in agriculture at a college or university in Mississippi.
Eligibility: This program is open to members of the Farm Bureau who have already completed their freshman year in an agriculture major at a university or community college in Mississippi. Selection is based on financial need, academic ability, and leadership qualities.
Financial data: The stipend is $2,000 per year.
Duration: 1 year.
Number awarded: 4 each year.

2293
MISSOURI LEGION AUXILIARY PAST PRESIDENTS PARLEY SCHOLARSHIPS

American Legion Auxiliary
Attn: Department of Missouri
600 Ellis Boulevard
Jefferson City, MO 65101-2204
Phone: (573) 636-9133
Summary: To provide financial assistance for postsecondary education to Missouri residents who are members of a veteran's family and wish to study nursing.
Eligibility: Applicants for these scholarships must be residents of Missouri, the dependent children or grandchildren of a veteran, and interested in nursing as a vocation. Applicants must be a senior in an accredited high school and cannot have attended an institution of higher learning.
Financial data: This scholarship is $1,000.
Duration: 1 year.
Number awarded: 1 each year.
Deadline: March of each year.

2294
MLN SCHOLARSHIPS

Missouri League for Nursing, Inc.
Attn: Executive Director
604 Dix Road
P.O. Box 104476
Jefferson City, MO 65110-4476

Phone: (573) 635-5355   Fax: (573) 635-7908
E-mail: mln@sockets.net
Web Site: www.moleaguenursing.org
Summary: To provide financial assistance to students in Missouri who are enrolled in an accredited school of nursing.
Eligibility: This program is open to students enrolled in an accredited school of nursing in Missouri. Applicants must be Missouri residents, have completed their freshman year, and be nominated by the dean of their school.
Financial data: These scholarships cover the recipient's tuition. Funds are paid directly to the school in the student's name.
Duration: 1 year.
Additional information: Application forms are available from the dean or director of accredited nursing schools in Missouri rather than from the Missouri League for Nursing.
Number awarded: 3 each year.
Deadline: Nominations must be submitted in September of each year.

2295
MMTA SCHOLARSHIP FOUNDATION SCHOLARSHIPS

Maine Motor Transport Association
Attn: Chief Financial Officer
142 Whitten Road
Augusta, ME 04332-0857
Phone: (207) 623-4128   Fax: (207) 629-5184
E-mail: jmorgan@mmta.com   Web Site: www.mmta.com
Summary: To provide financial assistance for college to high school seniors in Maine who are interested in pursuing a career in the trucking industry.
Eligibility: This program is open to seniors graduating from high schools in Maine who are planning to attend a college, university, or technical college. Applicants must be interested in studying an area that could later be beneficial to the trucking industry.
Financial data: The stipend is $1,000.
Duration: 1 year; nonrenewable.
Number awarded: 10 each year.
Deadline: April of each year.

2296
MONCRIEF SCHOLARSHIPS

Georgia State Golf Association
Attn: Georgia State Golf Foundation
121 Village Parkway, Building 3
Marietta, GA 30067
Phone: (770) 955-4272   (800) 949-4742
Fax: (770) 955-1156   Web Site: www.gsga.org/foundation.htm
Summary: To provide financial assistance to undergraduates studying fields related to turfgrass at colleges and universities in Georgia.
Eligibility: This program is open to students at colleges and universities in Georgia. Applicants must be majoring in a field related to turfgrass management.
Financial data: Stipend amounts vary but average nearly $2,500 per year.
Duration: 1 year; may be renewed.
Number awarded: Varies each year; recently 10 of these scholarships were awarded.
Deadline: March of each year.

2297
MONTANA FEDERATION OF GARDEN CLUBS SCHOLARSHIP

Montana Federation of Garden Clubs
c/o Elizabeth Kenmeier
214 Wyant Lane
Hamilton, MT 59840
Phone: (406) 363-5693
Summary: To provide financial assistance to college students in Montana majoring in conservation and related subjects.
Eligibility: This program is open to students enrolled in Montana colleges and universities at the level of sophomore or above. Applicants must be able to document financial need, be U.S. citizens and Montana residents, have at least a 2.7 grade point average, have the potential for career success, and be majoring in conservation, horticulture, park or forestry management, floriculture, greenhouse management, land management, or related subjects. There is no application form; interested students submit a letter of application, a college transcript, a photograph, and letters of reference from instructors.

Financial data: The stipend is $1,000.
Duration: 1 year.
Number awarded: 1 or more each year.
Deadline: April of each year.

2298
MORRIS K. UDALL SCHOLARSHIPS

Morris K. Udall Scholarship and Excellence in National Environmental Policy Foundation
110 South Church Avenue, Suite 3350
Tucson, AZ 85701
Phone: (520) 670-5529   Fax: (520) 670-5530
Web Site: www.udall.gov
Summary: To provide financial assistance to 1) college sophomores and juniors who intend to pursue careers in environmental public policy and 2) Native American and Alaska Native students who intend to pursue careers in health care or tribal public policy.
Eligibility: Each 2-year and 4-year college and university in the United States and its possessions may nominate up to 3 sophomores or juniors for each of the 2 categories of this program: 1) students who intend to pursue careers in environmental public policy, and 2) Native American and Alaska Native students who intend to pursue careers in health care or tribal public policy. In the first category, majors normally include environmental engineering, agriculture, the biological and other natural sciences, natural resource management, political science, sociology, anthropology, geography, cultural studies, history, public policy, and pre-law; in the second category, typical majors or areas of study include American Indian studies, political science, sociology, geography, anthropology, tribal policy, economic development, government, health sciences, health care, and health sciences. All nominees should have plans of study that include course work in ethics and public policy and/or public or community service experience in the area of their fields. They must be U.S. citizens, nationals, or permanent residents with a grade point average of at least 3.0. Applications must include an essay of 600 words or less citing a significant public speech, legislative act, or public policy statement by former Congressman Morris K. Udall and its impact on the nominee's field of interest.
Financial data: The stipend is up to $5,000 per year. Funds are to be used for tuition, fees, books, and room and board.
Duration: 1 year; recipients nominated as sophomores may be renominated in their junior year.
Additional information: Information is also available from the Morris K. Udall Scholarship Program, 2201 North Dodge Street, P.O. Box 4030, Iowa City, IA 52243-4030, (319) 341-2332, Fax: (319) 337-1204, E-mail: udall@act.org.
Number awarded: Approximately 75 each year.
Deadline: Faculty representatives must submit their nominations by mid-February of each year.

2299
MORTAR AND PESTLE PROFESSIONALISM AWARD

American Pharmaceutical Association
Attn: Awards and Honors Program
2215 Constitution Avenue, N.W.
Washington, DC 20037-2985
Phone: (202) 429-7507   Fax: (202) 628-0443
E-mail: mka@mail.aphanet.org   Web Site: www.aphanet.org
Summary: To recognize and reward pharmacy students who demonstrate outstanding performance in pharmacy administration and who submit outstanding essays.
Eligibility: This program is open to pharmacy students in their senior year of an entry-level degree program who are nominated by the dean of their school or college. Nominees must have demonstrated exceptional service and commitment to the profession of pharmacy through involvement in professional organizations and other extracurricular learning opportunities. The students selected by their schools are then eligible to compete in an essay contest judged by the editors of leading pharmacy journals.
Financial data: The winner of the essay contest receives a laminated plaque and a $2,000 scholarship to be applied toward continuing education in pharmacy.
Duration: The awards are presented annually.
Additional information: This program is currently sponsored by McNeil Consumer Health Care.
Number awarded: 1 scholarship winner is selected each year.
Deadline: Nominees must submit their essay by November of each year.

2300
MORTON B. DUGGAN, JR. MEMORIAL EDUCATION RECOGNITION AWARD

American Respiratory Care Foundation
Attn: Administrative Coordinator
11030 Ables Lane
Dallas, TX 75229-4593
Phone: (972) 243-2272   Fax: (972) 484-2720
E-mail: info@aarc.org
Web Site: www.aarc.org/awards
Summary: To provide financial assistance to college students interested in becoming respiratory therapists.
Eligibility: Students who have completed at least 1 semester in an accredited respiratory care program are eligible, if they have earned at least a 3.0 grade point average, are U.S. citizens or applicants for U.S. citizenship, and have potential for an outstanding career in the profession of respiratory care. Candidates must submit an original referenced paper on an aspect of respiratory care. Nominations are accepted from all states, but preference is given to applicants from Georgia and South Carolina.
Financial data: The stipend is $1,000. The award also provides airfare, 1 night's lodging, and registration for the international congress of the association.
Duration: 1 year.
Number awarded: 1 each year.
Deadline: May of each year.

2301
MRCA FOUNDATION SCHOLARSHIP AWARD

Midwest Roofing Contractors Association
Attn: MRCA Foundation
4840 West 15th Street, Suite 1000
Lawrence, KS 66049-3876
Phone: (785) 843-4888   (800) 497-6722
Fax: (785) 843-7555   E-mail: mrca@mrca.org
Web Site: www.mrca.org
Summary: To provide financial assistance to students from midwestern states who are interested in pursuing a career in the construction industry.
Eligibility: This program is open to students who are enrolled or planning to enroll at an accredited college, community college, vocational school, or trade school that offers a program of preparation for a career in the construction industry. Selection is based on the applicant's academic performance, employment experience, financial need, and demonstrated intent to pursue a career in the construction industry.
Financial data: Stipends are awarded (exact amount not specified).
Duration: 1 year.
Additional information: The Midwest Roofing Contractors Association (MRCA) established the MRCA Foundation in 1987.
Number awarded: 1 or more each year.
Deadline: May of each year.

2302
MSPE AUXILIARY COLLEGE GRANT

Michigan Society of Professional Engineers
Attn: Scholarship Coordinator
215 North Walnut Street
P.O. Box 15276
Lansing, MI 48901-5276
Phone: (517) 487-9388   Fax: (517) 487-0635
E-mail: mspe@voyager.net
Web Site: www.voyager.net/mspe
Summary: To provide financial assistance to undergraduate students in Michigan who are members of the Michigan Society of Professional Engineers and majoring in engineering in college.
Eligibility: This program is open to student members of the society who are U.S. citizens and residents of Michigan. Applicants must be attending an ABET-accredited engineering program at a Michigan college or university and have earned at least a 3.0 grade point average. They must submit an essay (up to 500 words) that discusses their interest in engineering, the specific field of engineering that is being pursued, and the occupation they propose to follow after graduation. Selection is based on the essay, transcripts, 2 letters of recommendation, leadership, and interest in the engineering profession through involvement in school and/or outside activities. Financial need is not considered.

Financial data: The stipend is $1,500.
Duration: 1 year.
Additional information: Information is also available from Roger Lamer, Scholarship Selection Committee Chair, (616) 247-2974, Fax: (616) 247-2997, E-mail: rlamer@steelcase.com.
Number awarded: 1 each year.
Deadline: March of each year.

2303
MSPE AUXILIARY HIGH SCHOOL GRANTS

Michigan Society of Professional Engineers
Attn: Scholarship Coordinator
215 North Walnut Street
P.O. Box 15276
Lansing, MI 48901-5276
Phone: (517) 487-9388   Fax: (517) 487-0635
E-mail: mspe@voyager.net
Web Site: www.voyager.net/mspe
Summary: To provide financial assistance to high school seniors in Michigan who are interested in pursuing a college degree in engineering.
Eligibility: This program is open to graduating seniors at high schools in Michigan who have a grade point average of 3.0 or higher and a composite ACT score of 26 or higher. U.S. citizenship is required. Applicants must have been accepted at a Michigan college or university accredited by ABET. They must be planning to enroll in an engineering program and enter the practice of engineering after graduation. They must submit a 250-word essay on "How I Was Influenced to Pursue an Engineering Career." Selection is based on the essay; high school academic record; participation in extracurricular activities; evidence of leadership, character, and self reliance; and comments from teachers and administrators. Financial need is not considered. Preference is given to children of members of the Michigan Society of Professional Engineers (MSPE). Semifinalists are interviewed.
Financial data: The stipend is $1,500.
Duration: 1 year; nonrenewable.
Additional information: Information is also available from Roger Lamer, Scholarship Selection Committee Chair, (616) 247-2974, Fax: (616) 247-2997, E-mail: rlamer@steelcase.com. Applications must be submitted to the local chapter scholarship representative. Contact MSPE for their addresses and phone numbers.
Number awarded: 2 each year.
Deadline: January of each year.

2304
MSPE UNDESIGNATED GRANT

Michigan Society of Professional Engineers
Attn: Scholarship Coordinator
215 North Walnut Street
P.O. Box 15276
Lansing, MI 48901-5276
Phone: (517) 487-9388   Fax: (517) 487-0635
E-mail: mspe@voyager.net
Web Site: www.voyager.net/mspe
Summary: To provide financial assistance to undergraduate students in Michigan who are members of the Michigan Society of Professional Engineers and majoring in engineering in college.
Eligibility: This program is open to student members of the society who are U.S. citizens and residents of Michigan. Applicants must be attending an ABET-accredited engineering program at a Michigan college or university and have earned at least a 3.0 grade point average. They must submit an essay (up to 500 words) that discusses their interest in engineering, the specific field of engineering that is being pursued, and the occupation they propose to follow after graduation. Selection is based on the essay, transcripts, 2 letters of recommendation, leadership, and interest in the engineering profession. Financial need is not considered.
Financial data: The stipend is $2,000.
Duration: 1 year; may be renewed for 1 additional year.
Additional information: Information is also available from Roger Lamer, Scholarship Selection Committee Chair, (616) 247-2974, Fax: (616) 247-2997, E-mail: rlamer@steelcase.com.
Number awarded: 1 each year.
Deadline: March of each year.

2305
NABISCO COLLEGE SCHOLARSHIP

Institute of Food Technologists
Attn: Scholarship Department
221 North LaSalle Street, Suite 300
Chicago, IL 60601-1291
Phone: (312) 782-8424   Fax: (312) 782-8348
E-mail: info@ift.org   Web Site: www.ift.org
Summary: To provide financial assistance to college freshmen interested in studying food science or food technology.
Eligibility: Applicants must be enrolled as freshmen in a food science or food technology program at a college or university in the United States or Canada. They must have an outstanding scholastic record (at least a 2.5 grade point average) and a well-rounded personality. Financial need is not considered in the selection process.
Financial data: The stipend is $1,000.
Duration: 1 year; recipients may reapply if they are members of the Institute of Food Technologists.
Additional information: Funds for this scholarship are provided by Nabisco Inc. Correspondence and completed applications must be submitted to the department head of the educational institution the applicant is attending.
Number awarded: 1 each year.
Deadline: February of each year.

2306
NABISCO HIGH SCHOOL SCHOLARSHIP

Institute of Food Technologists
Attn: Scholarship Department
221 North LaSalle Street, Suite 300
Chicago, IL 60601-1291
Phone: (312) 782-8424   Fax: (312) 782-8348
E-mail: info@ift.org   Web Site: www.ift.org
Summary: To provide financial assistance to high school seniors interested in pursuing the study of food science or food technology.
Eligibility: Applicants must be high school seniors planning to enroll in an approved program in food science or food technology at an educational institution in the United States or Canada. They must have an outstanding scholastic record and a well-rounded personality. Financial need is not considered in the selection process.
Financial data: The stipend is $1,000.
Duration: 1 year; recipients may reapply if they are members of the Institute of Food Technologists.
Additional information: Funds for this scholarship are provided by Nabisco Inc. Correspondence and completed applications must be submitted to the department head of the educational institution the applicant is planning to attend.
Number awarded: 1 each year.
Deadline: February of each year.

2307
NACME CORPORATE SCHOLARS PROGRAM

National Action Council for Minorities in Engineering
350 Fifth Avenue, Suite 2212
New York, NY 10118-2299
Phone: (212) 279-2626   Fax: (212) 629-5178
E-mail: awalter@nacme.org   Web Site: www.nacme.org/csp.html
Summary: To support exceptional underrepresented minority undergraduates who are preparing for careers at the frontier of engineering technology.
Eligibility: This program is open to African Americans, Latinos, and American Indians who are currently enrolled full time in an undergraduate engineering program, are U.S. citizens or permanent residents, have at least a 2.75 grade point average, and have demonstrated engineering leadership potential.
Financial data: This program provides students with scholarships of up to $5,000 per year, depending on their financial need, and paid internships.
Duration: 1 year; may be renewed if recipients maintain at least a 2.75 GPA.
Additional information: This program also offers R&D work experience, academic and career mentoring, summer internships, and professional development opportunities. The National Action Council for Minorities in Engineering (NACME) supports corporate mentors with a broad range of appropriate training. Recipients attend a leadership development seminar, the cost of which is underwritten by sponsoring companies. The program was started in 1991.
Number awarded: Varies; generally, more than 60 each year.
Deadline: February of each year.

2308
NACME SUSTAINING FELLOWS AWARDS

National Action Council for Minorities in Engineering
350 Fifth Avenue, Suite 2212
New York, NY 10118-2299
Phone: (212) 279-2626   Fax: (212) 629-5178
E-mail: awalter@nacme.org
Web Site: www.nacme.org/fellowships.html
Summary: To provide financial assistance to members of underrepresented minority groups who are studying engineering in college.
Eligibility: This program is open to African Americans, Latinos, and American Indians who have completed 1 semester of college in engineering. Applicants must be U.S. citizens or permanent residents and have at least a 3.0 grade point average.
Financial data: Scholarships up to $5,000 per year are available.
Duration: 4 years.
Additional information: Funding for this program is provided by individual donors to the National Action Council for Minorities in Education (NACME).
Number awarded: Varies each year.

2309
NACME/BECHTEL UNDERGRADUATE FELLOWSHIP AWARD

National Action Council for Minorities in Engineering
350 Fifth Avenue, Suite 2212
New York, NY 10118-2299
Phone: (212) 279-2626   Fax: (212) 629-5178
E-mail: awalter@nacme.org
Web Site: www.nacme.org/fellowships.html
Summary: To provide financial assistance for education and work experience in construction engineering to underrepresented minority students.
Eligibility: This program is open to African Americans, Latinos, and American Indians who are interested in pursuing a corporate career in a construction-related engineering discipline. Applicants must be U.S. citizens or permanent residents in the second semester of their sophomore year.
Financial data: The stipend is $5,000 per year.
Duration: 2 years.
Additional information: Funding for this program is provided by The Bechtel Group. Fellows also receive an internship and a mentor.
Number awarded: 1 each year.

2310
NADONA/LTC CARING SCHOLARSHIP

National Association of Directors of Nursing Administration in Long Term Care
Attn: Education/Scholarship Committee
10999 Reed Hartman Highway, Suite 233
Cincinnati, OH 45242-8301
Phone: (513) 791-3679   (800) 222-0539
Fax: (513) 791-3699   E-mail: info@nadona.org
Web Site: www.nadona.org
Summary: To provide financial assistance to students who are working on a nursing degree and who are members of the National Association of Directors of Nursing Administration in Long Term Care (NADONA/LTC).
Eligibility: To be eligible, the candidate must be a member of the association, be currently employed in long-term care (for at least 1 year), plan to remain employed in long-term care for at least 2 years after graduation, be currently accepted or enrolled in a National League for Nursing (NLN) accredited B.S.N., master's, or higher degree program (proof of acceptance and NLN accreditation must accompany the application), and write an essay (up to 250 words) that describes why the candidate is seeking this degree and how the education will be used in the future. Students who received funds/awards from a NADONA/LTC scholarship within the last 4 years are ineligible to apply for this award.
Financial data: The amount awarded varies each year.
Duration: 1 year.
Additional information: Funds for this scholarship are provided by Professional Medical Products, Inc.
Number awarded: At least 1 each year.
Deadline: February of each year.

2311
NADONA/LTC UPWARD BOUND! SCHOLARSHIP

National Association of Directors of Nursing Administration in Long Term Care
Attn: Education/Scholarship Committee
10999 Reed Hartman Highway, Suite 233
Cincinnati, OH 45242-8301
Phone: (513) 791-3679 (800) 222-0539
Fax: (513) 791-3699 E-mail: info@nadona.org
Web Site: www.nadona.org
Summary: To provide financial assistance to nurses who are currently employed in long-term care and are interested in pursuing higher education, with a career focus on long-term care.
Eligibility: To be eligible, the candidate must be a registered nurse, a licensed practical nurse, or a certified nursing assistant (evidence of licensure or certification must accompany the application) and be currently accepted or enrolled in 1 of the following programs: 1) an L.P.N. or R.N. program; 2) an accredited R.N. program or undergraduate health care management program; 3) a baccalaureate or master's degree program in nursing or gerontology; 4) an undergraduate or graduate program in health care management. Candidates must be currently employed in long-term care (for at least 1 year) and plan to remain employed in that field for at least 2 years after graduation. They must be members of the National Association of Directors of Nursing Administration in Long Term Care or sponsored by a member.
Financial data: The amount awarded varies each year.
Duration: 1 year.
Additional information: Funds for this scholarship are provided by Whitestone.
Number awarded: At least 1 each year.
Deadline: February of each year.

2312
NANCY LORRAINE JENSEN MEMORIAL SCHOLARSHIP FUND

Sons of Norway Foundation
c/o Sons of Norway
1455 West Lake Street
Minneapolis, MN 55408-2666
Phone: (612) 827-3611 (800) 945-8851
Fax: (612) 827-0658 E-mail: fraternal@sofn.com
Web Site: www.sofn.com/foundation/scholarships.html
Summary: To provide financial assistance to women who have a connection to the Sons of Norway and are interested in studying chemistry, physics, or engineering in college.
Eligibility: This program is open to women who are U.S. citizens between 17 and 35 years of age and members (or daughters or granddaughters of members) of Sons of Norway; they must have been a member for at least 3 years. Female employees of the NASA Goddard Space Flight Center in Greenbelt, Maryland and the daughters and granddaughters of employees are also eligible. Students must have an SAT score of 1200 or higher or ACT score of 26 or higher. They must be full-time undergraduate students and have completed at least 1 quarter or semester of study in chemistry, physics, or chemical, electrical, or mechanical engineering. Selection is based on long-term career goals, clarity of study plan, academic potential, evidence of ability to succeed, and letters of recommendation attesting to good character, eagerness, earnestness, and ambition in the field of science or engineering.
Financial data: Stipends range from 50 percent of tuition for 1 quarter or semester to 100 percent for 1 year. Grants are issued jointly to the recipient and her institution.
Duration: Awards are made for either 1 term (quarter or semester) or 1 year; a student may receive up to 3 awards as an undergraduate.
Additional information: This fund was established in 1995 by Dr. and Mrs. Arthur S. Jensen in memory of their daughter, a chemical engineer whose work resulted in advances in the field of weather satellite photography but who died at the age of 35.
Number awarded: 1 each year.
Deadline: February of each year.

2313
NATA UNDERGRADUATE SCHOLARSHIPS

National Athletic Trainers' Association
Attn: Research and Education Foundation
2952 Stemmons Freeway, Suite 200
Dallas, TX 75247-6103
Phone: (214) 637-6282 (800) TRY-NATA, ext. 121
Fax: (214) 637-2206 E-mail: briana@nata.org
Web Site: www.nata.org
Summary: To provide financial aid to undergraduate student members of the National Athletic Trainers' Association (NATA).
Eligibility: Applicants must be members of the association who are recommended by an NATA certified athletic trainer, have at least a 3.2 grade point average, and intend to pursue athletic training as a profession. Students enrolled in baccalaureate programs requiring 4 years may apply after their sophomore year; students enrolled in baccalaureate programs requiring more than 4 years may apply after the third year. Ethnic minority students (African Americans, Asians, Hispanics, and Native Americans) are eligible for 1 or more designated scholarships. The main criteria in selection are service in the applicant's student athletic trainer program and (considered equally) academic achievement; a secondary consideration is participation in campus activities other than academic and athletic training. Financial need is not considered.
Financial data: The stipend is $2,000 per year.
Number awarded: At least 50 each year.
Deadline: January of each year.

2314
NATHAN TAYLOR DODSON SCHOLARSHIP

Summary: To provide financial assistance for college to members of the North Carolina Association of Health, Physical Education, Recreation and Dance (NCAAHPERD).
See Listing #1545.

2315
NATIONAL ACADEMY FOR NUCLEAR TRAINING SCHOLARSHIP PROGRAM

National Academy for Nuclear Training
Attn: Educational Assistance Program
700 Galleria Parkway, S.E., Suite 100
Atlanta, GA 30339-5957
Phone: (770) 644-8543 (800) 828-5489
Fax: (770) 644-8549 E-mail: nanteap@inpo.org
Web Site: www.nei.org
Summary: To provide financial assistance for college to students interested in careers in the nuclear power industry.
Eligibility: This program is open to U.S. citizens who are full-time students at accredited 4-year institutions and majoring in nuclear-fission or electric power-related fields, including 1) nuclear engineering, 2) power generation health physics, and 3) mechanical, electrical, or chemical engineering with a nuclear or power option. Applicants must have at least a 3.0 grade point average and between 1 and 3 years remaining before graduation. Preference is given to applicants who indicate specific interest in and preparation for careers in the U.S. nuclear power industry. Students with commitments that preclude availability for nuclear utility industry employment immediately after graduation (such as military service) are not eligible. Selection is based on academic record, activities and work experience, a statement of planned future interactions with nuclear utilities or industry organizations, a statement of career goals, and an essay or a nuclear power topic.
Financial data: The stipend is $2,500 per year. Funds are paid directly to the college or university.
Duration: 1 year; may be renewed for up to 2 additional years.
Additional information: The Institute of Nuclear Power Operations, formed in 1979 by all U.S. utilities that operate nuclear power plants, funds this program on behalf of the National Academy for Nuclear Training.
Number awarded: Approximately 150 each year.
Deadline: January of each year.

2316
NATIONAL ASSOCIATION OF HEALTH SERVICES EXECUTIVES SCHOLARSHIP PROGRAM

National Association of Health Services Executives
Attn: Educational Assistance Program
8630 Fenton Street, Suite 126
Silver Spring, MD 20910
Phone: (202) 628-3953 E-mail: nahse_hq@compuserve.com
Web Site: www.nahse.org
Summary: To provide financial assistance to African Americans who are members of the National Association of Health Services Executives (NAHSE) and interested in preparing for a career in health care administration.
Eligibility: This program is open to African Americans who are either enrolled or accepted in an accredited college or university program, pursuing a

bachelor's, master's, or doctoral degree in health care administration. Applicants must have at least a 2.5 grade point average (3.0 if graduate students), be members of NAHSE, and be able to demonstrate financial need. To apply, students must submit a completed application, 3 letters of recommendation, a recent resume, a 3-page essay on "the impact of the team concept approach to organizational improvement when restructuring into an urban integrated healthcare network," a copy of their most recent federal income tax return, transcripts from all colleges attended, and 2 photographs.

Financial data: The stipends are $2,500 per year. Funds are sent to the recipient's institution.

Duration: 1 year.

Deadline: January of each year.

2317
NATIONAL ASSOCIATION OF HISPANIC NURSES SCHOLARSHIPS

National Association of Hispanic Nurses
Attn: National Awards and Scholarship Committee Chair
1501 16th Street, N.W.
Washington, DC 20036
Phone: (202) 387-2477   Fax: (202) 483-7183
E-mail: thehispanicnurses@earthlink.net
Web Site: www.thehispanicnurses.org

Summary: To provide financial assistance for nursing education to members of the National Association of Hispanic Nurses (NAHN).

Eligibility: Eligible are members of the association enrolled in associate, diploma, baccalaureate, graduate, or practical/vocational nursing programs at NLN-accredited schools of nursing. Applicants must submit a 1-page essay that reflects their qualifications and potential for leadership in nursing for the Hispanic community. Selection is based on academic excellence (preferably a grade point average of 3.0 or higher), potential for leadership in nursing, and financial need.

Financial data: The stipend is $1,000.

Duration: 1 year.

Number awarded: Varies each year, depending on the availability of funds.

Deadline: April of each year.

2318
NATIONAL ASSOCIATION OF WOMEN IN CONSTRUCTION UNDERGRADUATE SCHOLARSHIPS

National Association of Women in Construction
Attn: Founders' Scholarship Foundation
327 South Adams
Fort Worth, TX 76104-1081
Phone: (817) 877-5551   (800) 552-3506
Fax: (817) 877-0324   E-mail: nawic@nawic.org
Web Site: www.nawic.org

Summary: To provide financial assistance to students pursuing study in a construction-related degree program.

Eligibility: This program is open to full-time students with a minimum of 1 year remaining in a course of study leading to a baccalaureate or associate degree in a construction-related degree program and a career in construction. Applicants must have a cumulative grade point average of 3.0 or higher. Selection is based on grade point average, interest in construction, extracurricular activities, employment experience, academic advisor evaluation, and financial need.

Financial data: Stipends range from $500 to $2,000 per year.

Duration: 1 year; may reapply.

Number awarded: Varies each year.

Deadline: January of each year.

2319
NATIONAL BEEF AMBASSADOR PROGRAM

American National CattleWomen, Inc.
Attn: National Beef Ambassador Coordinator
9110 East Nichols Avenue, Suite 302
P.O. Box 3881
Centennial, CO 80112
Phone: (303) 694-0313   Fax: (303) 694-2390
E-mail: ancw@beef.org   Web Site: www.ancw.org/National_Ambassador.htm

Summary: To recognize and reward young people who can serve as spokespersons for the beef industry.

Eligibility: This competition is open to students between 15 and 19 years of age who are able to serve as spokespersons for the beef industry within their schools and their communities. Students first compete on the state level. Each state sends 1 winner to the national competition. At the national competition, students make a 5- to 8-minute oral presentation on the beef industry and then spend 2 to 3 minutes answering questions about the industry posed by the judges. Their speech must be illustrated with posters that they prepared. They must have made the presentation at least 7 times prior to the competition. At least 5 of the 7 presentations must have been to non-agricultural groups.

Financial data: Awards are $2,500 for first place, $1,200 for second place, and $800 for third place. Other cash awards may also be available.

Duration: The competition is held annually.

Additional information: This program is sponsored by American National CattleWomen, Inc. in cooperation with the National Cattlemen's Beef Association, the Cattlemen's Beef Board, and the Cooperative Extension Service.

Number awarded: At least 3 each year.

Deadline: September of each year.

2320
NATIONAL COUNCIL OF STATE GARDEN CLUBS SCHOLARSHIPS

Summary: To provide financial assistance to upper-division and graduate students in horticulture and related disciplines.
See Listing #1549.

2321
NATIONAL DAIRY SHRINE/DMI MILK MARKETING SCHOLARSHIPS

National Dairy Shrine
Attn: Office of Executive Director
1224 Alton Darby Creek Road
Columbus, OH 43228-9792
Phone: (614) 878-5333   Fax: (614) 870-2622
E-mail: ndairyshrine@hotmail.com
Web Site: www.dairyshrine.org

Summary: To provide financial assistance to college students enrolled in a dairy science program and to encourage them to pursue careers in the marketing of dairy products.

Eligibility: Applicants must be college sophomores, juniors, or seniors who have a cumulative grade point average of 2.5 or higher. They must be majoring in dairy science, animal science, agricultural economics, agricultural communications, agricultural education, general agriculture, or food and nutrition. Selection is based on student organizational activities (15 percent), other organizations and activities (10 percent), academic standing and course work associated with marketing (25 percent), honors and awards (10 percent), marketing experiences (10 percent), and reasons for interest in dairy product marketing, including plans for the future (30 percent).

Financial data: Scholarships are $1,500 or $1,000.

Duration: The competition is held annually.

Additional information: This program is jointly sponsored by the National Dairy Shrine and Dairy Management Inc. (DMI).

Number awarded: 7 each year; 1 at $1,500 and 6 at $1,000 each.

Deadline: March of each year.

2322
NATIONAL FFA SCHOLARSHIPS FOR UNDERGRADUATES IN THE SCIENCES

National FFA Organization
Attn: Scholarship Office
6060 FFA Drive
P.O. Box 68960
Indianapolis, IN 46268-0960
Phone: (317) 802-4321   Fax: (317) 802-5321
E-mail: aboutffa@ffa.org   Web Site: www.ffa.org

Summary: To provide financial assistance to FFA members who wish to study agriculture and related fields in college.

Eligibility: This program is open to current and former members of the organization who are pursuing a degree in fields related to agriculture; this includes: agricultural mechanics and engineering, agricultural technology, animal science, conservation, dairy science, equine science, floriculture, food science, horticulture, irrigation, lawn and landscaping, and natural resources. For some of the

scholarships, applicants must be high school seniors; others are open to students currently enrolled in college. The program includes a large number of designated scholarships that specify the locations where the members must live, the schools they must attend, the fields of study they must pursue, or other requirements. Some consider family income in the selection process, but most do not.

Financial data: Stipends vary, but most are at least $1,000.

Duration: 1 year or more.

Additional information: Funding for these scholarships is provided by many different corporate sponsors.

Number awarded: Varies; generally, a total of approximately 1,000 scholarships are awarded annually by the association.

Deadline: February of each year.

2323
NATIONAL GEOGRAPHIC SOCIETY AWARD IN CARTOGRAPHY

Summary: To provide financial assistance to undergraduate and master's degree students who demonstrate excellence in the art, science, and technology of mapping. *See Listing #1551.*

2324
NATIONAL JUNIOR MERIT AWARDS

American Hereford Association
Attn: Department of Youth Activities
P.O. Box 014059
Kansas City, MO 64101
Phone: (816) 842-3757 Fax: (816) 842-6931
E-mail: aha@hereford.org Web Site: www.hereford.org

Summary: To recognize and reward members of the National Junior Hereford Association (NJHA) who demonstrate outstanding enthusiasm, leadership, and achievement in the Hereford industry.

Eligibility: This program is open to NJHA members who are high school seniors or already in college and under 22 years of age. Before they can receive an award, they must have completed at least 1 semester of college with a grade point average of 2.0 or higher. Selection is based on Hereford activities (15 percent), agriculture-related activities (10 percent), community and civic activities (10 percent), employment experience (5 percent), management practices (10 percent), goals (15 percent), productivity and management measures (5 percent), marketing (10 percent), summary comments (10 percent), and overall application presentation and letters of recommendation (10 percent).

Financial data: The top national winner is awarded a $1,000 scholarship and a trip to any polled Hereford ranch in the continental United States. Second- and third-place winners receive $750 and $500, respectively.

Duration: The competition is held annually.

Number awarded: 3 each year.

2325
NATIONAL JUNIOR RED ANGUS ASSOCIATION ESSAY CONTEST

Red Angus Association of America
4201 North Interstate 35
Denton, TX 76207-3415
Phone: (940) 387-3502 Fax: (940) 383-4036
Web Site: www.redangus1.org

Summary: To recognize and reward outstanding essays on the beef industry written by members of the National Junior Red Angus Association (NJRAA).

Eligibility: Students may enter 1 of the following divisions: junior division, sixth grade and under; intermediate division, seventh through ninth grades; senior division, tenth through twelfth grades; and college division, high school graduates through 21 year olds. Participants in the junior division must write a 250-word essay on "Why I Like Red Angus" and cite at least 1 reference; intermediate division participants must write a 500-word essay on "Advantages of Using Red Angus" and cite at least 2 references; senior division participants must write a 750-word essay on "A Challenge That Confronts the Beef Industry with Solutions to the Problem" and cite at least 4 references; college division participants must write a 750-word essay on "An Issue Confronting the Beef Industry Today or in the Future and the Solution" and cite at least 5 references. All participants must be current, active members of NJRAA. Selection is based on clarity of expression, spelling, and grammar (10 percent); persuasiveness (10 percent); originality of thought and topic (40 percent); accuracy of information (35 percent); and references cited (5 percent).

Financial data: Savings bonds and/or cash prizes are awarded in each of the 4 age divisions.

Duration: The competition is held annually.

Additional information: This program began in 2000. Information is also available from Dawn Bernhard, 2003 190th Street, Algona, IA 50511. Students who submit essays in the college division are encouraged to send them also to the NCBA/CME Beef Industry Scholarship Program.

Deadline: April of each year.

2326
NATIONAL PATHFINDER SCHOLARSHIP

National Federation of Republican Women
Attn: Scholarship Coordinator
124 North Alfred Street
Alexandria, VA 22314
Phone: (703) 548-9688

Summary: To provide financial assistance to college women who are currently studying in fields related to substance abuse prevention.

Eligibility: This program is open to college women currently studying in various fields related to substance abuse prevention. These programs of study include chemistry, sociology, psychology, and pharmacology (as they relate to substance abuse). Recent high school graduates and first-year college women are not eligible to apply. Applicants must be college sophomores, juniors, seniors, or master's degree students. A complete application must include the following: the application form, 3 letters of recommendation, an official transcript, a 1-page essay on why the applicant should be considered for the scholarship, and a 1-page essay on career goals. Optionally, a photograph may be supplied. Applications must be submitted to the federation president in the applicant's state. Each president chooses 1 application from her state to submit for scholarship consideration. Financial need is a factor in the selection process.

Financial data: The stipend is $2,000.

Duration: 1 year; nonrenewable.

Additional information: This program was established in 1985 in honor of First Lady Nancy Reagan.

Number awarded: 2 each year.

Deadline: January of each year.

2327
NATIONAL SOCIETY OF BLACK ENGINEERS FELLOWS SCHOLARSHIP PROGRAM

National Society of Black Engineers
Attn: Programs Manager
1454 Duke Street
Alexandria, VA 22314
Phone: (703) 549-2207, ext. 249 Fax: (703) 683-5312
E-mail: scholarships@nsbe.org
Web Site: www.nsbe.org

Summary: To provide financial assistance to members of the National Society of Black Engineers (NSBE) who are majoring in science or engineering.

Eligibility: This program is open to members of the society who are undergraduate or graduate students majoring in science or engineering. Selection is based on an essay; academic achievement; service to the society at the local, regional, and/or national level; and other professional, campus, and community activities.

Financial data: The stipend is $1,500. Travel, hotel accommodations, and registration to the national convention are also provided.

Duration: 1 year; may be renewed.

Number awarded: Approximately 120 each year.

Deadline: December of each year; freshmen have until January to apply.

2328
NATIONAL SOCIETY OF PROFESSIONAL SURVEYORS SCHOLARSHIPS

American Congress on Surveying and Mapping
Attn: Awards Director
6 Montgomery Village Avenue, Suite 403
Gaithersburg, MD 20879
Phone: (240) 632-9716 Fax: (240) 632-1321
E-mail: tmilburn@acsm.net
Web Site: www.acsm.net

Summary: To provide financial assistance for the undergraduate study of surveying to members of the American Congress on Surveying and Mapping.
Eligibility: This program is open to full-time students enrolled in a 4-year college or university who are pursuing a degree in surveying and are members of the sponsoring organization. Selection is based on previous academic record (30 percent), future plans (30 percent), letters of recommendation (20 percent), and professional activities (20 percent); if 2 or more applicants are judged equal based on those criteria, financial need may be considered.
Financial data: The stipend is $1,000.
Duration: 1 year.
Additional information: Funding for these scholarships is provided by the National Society of Professional Surveyors (NSPS).
Number awarded: 2 each year.
Deadline: December of each year.

2329
NATIONAL STUDENT NURSES' ASSOCIATION CAREER MOBILITY SCHOLARSHIPS

National Student Nurses' Association
Attn: NSNA Foundation
555 West 57th Street, Suite 1327
New York, NY 10019
Phone: (212) 581-2215   Fax: (212) 581-2368
E-mail: nsna@nsna.org
Web Site: www.nsna.org
Summary: To provide financial assistance to nurses interested in pursuing additional education.
Eligibility: This program is open to 1) registered nurses enrolled in programs leading to a baccalaureate degree with a major in nursing or 2) licensed practical/vocational nurses enrolled in programs leading to licensure as a registered nurse. Graduating high school seniors are not eligible. Selection is based on academic achievement, financial need, and involvement in student nursing organizations and community activities related to health care.
Financial data: The stipend awarded ranges from $1,000 to $2,000. A total of $50,000 is awarded each year by the foundation for all its scholarship programs.
Duration: 1 year.
Additional information: Applications must be accompanied by a $10 processing fee.
Number awarded: Varies each year.
Deadline: January of each year.

2330
NATIONAL STUDENT NURSES' ASSOCIATION GENERAL SCHOLARSHIPS

National Student Nurses' Association
Attn: NSNA Foundation
555 West 57th Street, Suite 1327
New York, NY 10019
Phone: (212) 581-2215   Fax: (212) 581-2368
E-mail: nsna@nsna.org
Web Site: www.nsna.org
Summary: To provide financial assistance to nursing or pre-nursing students.
Eligibility: Students currently enrolled in state-approved schools of nursing or pre-nursing associate degree, diploma, baccalaureate, generic master's, and generic doctoral programs are eligible to apply. Although graduate students in other disciplines are eligible if they wish to study nursing or pre-nursing, no funds can be used for graduate education in nursing. Graduating high school seniors are not eligible. Selection is based on academic achievement, financial need, and involvement in student nursing organizations and community activities related to health care.
Financial data: The stipend awarded ranges from $1,000 to $2,000. A total of $50,000 is awarded each year by the foundation for all its scholarship programs.
Duration: 1 year.
Additional information: This program includes the following named scholarships: the Alice Robinson Memorial Scholarship, the Jeannette Collins Memorial Scholarship, the Cleo Doster Memorial Scholarship, and the Mary Ann Tuft Scholarships. Applications must be accompanied by a $10 processing fee.
Number awarded: Varies each year.
Deadline: January of each year.

2331
NATIONAL STUDENT NURSES' ASSOCIATION SPECIALTY SCHOLARSHIPS

National Student Nurses' Association
Attn: NSNA Foundation
555 West 57th Street, Suite 1327
New York, NY 10019
Phone: (212) 581-2215   Fax: (212) 581-2368
E-mail: nsna@nsna.org
Web Site: www.nsna.org
Summary: To provide financial assistance to nursing students in designated specialties.
Eligibility: Students currently enrolled in state-approved schools of nursing or pre-nursing associate degree, diploma, baccalaureate, generic master's, and generic doctoral programs are eligible to apply. Although graduate students in other disciplines are eligible if they wish to study nursing or pre-nursing, no funds can be used for graduate education in nursing. Graduating high school seniors are not eligible. For this program, applicants designate their intended specialty, which may be anesthesia nursing, critical care, emergency, oncology, operating room, orthopedic, or nephrology. Selection is based on academic achievement, financial need, and involvement in student nursing organizations and community activities related to health care.
Financial data: The stipend awarded ranges from $1,000 to $2,000. A total of $50,000 is awarded each year by the foundation for all its scholarship programs.
Duration: 1 year.
Additional information: Funding for this program is provided by sponsors from industry who are interested in promoting specialties related to their products. Applications must be accompanied by a $10 processing fee.
Number awarded: Varies each year.
Deadline: January of each year.

2332
NAVAL WEATHER SERVICE ASSOCIATION SCHOLARSHIP

Naval Weather Service Association
c/o Jim Stone
428 Robin Road
Waverly, OH 45690
E-mail: jstone@navalweather.org
Web Site: www.navalweather.org
Summary: To provide financial assistance to high school seniors and currently-enrolled undergraduates who plan to work on a college degree in science or engineering.
Eligibility: This program is open to high school seniors and college undergraduates who are enrolled or planning to enroll in an undergraduate program in either 1) the physical sciences, limited to geophysics, mathematics, meteorology, oceanography, or physics; or 2) technology, limited to aerospace engineering or computer science. All applicants must be U.S. citizens and sponsored by a member of the association. Selection is based on academic record, leadership skills, character, all-around ability, and financial need.
Financial data: Stipends range from $500 to $1,500. Funds may be used to pay for tuition, fees, books, supplies, equipment, or any other educational expenses.
Duration: 1 year; recipients may reapply.
Additional information: The Naval Weather Service Association is a nonprofit organization open to retired and active-duty meteorological and oceanographic personnel of the Navy and Marine Corps.
Number awarded: 1 or more each year.
Deadline: April of each year.

2333
NAVY COLLEGE ASSISTANCE/STUDENT HEADSTART (NAVY-CASH) PROGRAM

U.S. Navy
Attn: Navy Personnel Command
5722 Integrity Drive
Millington, TN 38054-5057
Phone: (901) 874-3070   (888) 633-9674
Fax: (901) 874-2651   E-mail: nukeprograms@cnrc.navy.mil
Web Site: www.cnrc.navy.mil/nucfield
Summary: To provide financial assistance to high school seniors and current college students interested in attending college for a year and then entering the nuclear field of the Navy.

Eligibility: Applicants must be able to meet the specific requirements of the Navy's Enlisted Nuclear Field Program. They must be enrolled or accepted for enrollment at an accredited 2-year community or junior college or 4-year college or university.

Financial data: While they attend school, participants are paid a regular Navy salary at a pay grade up to E-3 (starting at $1,303.50 per month). They are also eligible for all of the Navy's enlistment incentives, including the Navy College Fund, the Loan Repayment Program, and an enlistment bonus up to $12,000.

Duration: 12 months.

Additional information: After 1 year of college, participants report for enlisted recruit training in the Navy's nuclear field. Further information on this program is available from a local Navy recruiter or the Navy Recruiting Command, 801 North Randolph Street, Arlington, VA 22203-1991.

Number awarded: Varies each year.

2334
NAVY NURSE CANDIDATE PROGRAM

U.S. Navy
Attn: Naval School of Health Sciences
Code OS1
8901 Wisconsin Avenue
Bethesda, MD 20889-5612
Phone: (301) 295-6865   (800) USA-NAVY
Fax: (301) 295-6014   E-mail: scarlstrom@nsh10.med.navy.mil
Web Site: nshs.med.navy.mil/hpsp/ncp.htm

Summary: To provide financial assistance for nursing education to students interested in serving in the Navy.

Eligibility: This program is open to full-time students in a Bachelor of Science in Nursing program. Prior to or during their junior year of college, applicants must enlist in the U.S. Navy Nurse Corps Reserve. Following receipt of their degree, they must be willing to serve as a nurse in the Navy.

Financial data: This program pays a $5,000 accession bonus upon enlistment and a stipend of $500 per month. Students are responsible for paying all school expenses.

Duration: Up to 24 months.

Number awarded: Varies each year.

2335
NAVY NURSE CORPS NROTC SCHOLARSHIP PROGRAM

U.S. Navy
Attn: Chief of Naval Education and Training
Code OTE6/081
250 Dallas Street
Naval Air Station
Pensacola, FL 32508-5220
Phone: (850) 452-4941, ext. 325   (800) NAV-ROTC, ext. 325
Fax: (850) 452-2486   E-mail: nrotc.scholarship@cnet.navy.mil
Web Site: www.cnet.navy.mil/nrotc/nrotc.htm

Summary: To provide financial assistance to graduating high school seniors who are interested in pursuing a bachelor of science degree in nursing and then serving in the Navy.

Eligibility: Eligible to apply for these scholarships are graduating high school seniors who have been accepted at a college with a Navy ROTC unit on campus or a college with a cross-enrollment agreement with such a college. Applicants must be U.S. citizens between the ages of 17 and 23 who plan to study nursing in college and are willing to serve for 4 years as active-duty Navy officers in the Navy Nurse Corps following graduation from college. They must not have reached their 27th birthday by the time of college graduation and commissioning; applicants who have prior active-duty military service may be eligible for age adjustments for the amount of time equal to their prior service, up to a maximum of 36 months. They must have achieved minimum SAT scores of 530 verbal and 520 mathematics or minimum ACT scores of 22 in both English and mathematics.

Financial data: This scholarship provides payment of full tuition and required educational fees, as well as a specified amount for textbooks, supplies, and equipment. The program also provides a stipend for 10 months of the year that is $250 per month as a freshman and sophomore, $300 per month as a junior, and $350 per month as a senior.

Duration: 4 years.

Number awarded: Varies each year.

Deadline: January of each year;

2336
NAVY-MARINE CORPS ROTC 2-YEAR COLLEGE PROGRAM

U.S. Navy
Attn: Chief of Naval Education and Training
Code OTE6/081
250 Dallas Street
Naval Air Station
Pensacola, FL 32508-5220
Phone: (850) 452-4941, ext. 320   (800) NAV-ROTC, ext. 320
Fax: (850) 452-2486   E-mail: nrotc.scholarship@cnet.navy.mil
Web Site: www.cnet.navy.mil/nrotc/nrotc.htm

Summary: To provide financial assistance for college to students who are willing to serve as Navy or Marine Corps officers following completion of their bachelor's degrees.

Eligibility: Applicants must be U.S. citizens between the ages of 17 and 21 who are already enrolled as non-scholarship students in naval science courses at a college or university with a Navy ROTC program on campus. They must apply before the spring of their sophomore year. All applications must be submitted through the professors of naval science at the college or university attended.

Financial data: Participants in this program receive free naval science textbooks, all required uniforms, and a stipend for 10 months of the year that is $300 per month as a junior and $350 per month as a senior.

Duration: 2 years.

Additional information: Following acceptance into the program, participants attend the 6-week Naval Science Institute in Newport, Rhode Island (or in Quantico, Virginia for Marine-option students). After graduation from college, they are commissioned ensigns in the Naval Reserve or second lieutenants in the Marine Corps Reserve with an 8-year service obligation, including 3 years of active duty.

Deadline: March of each year.

2337
NAWIC CHAPTER #96 SCHOLARSHIP

National Association of Women in Construction-Chapter 96
c/o Faye Hoffman
P.O. Box 19736
Yorklyn, DE 19736
Phone: (302) 452-9413   Fax: (302) 452-9005

Summary: To provide financial assistance to students in Delaware who are interested in preparing for a career in construction.

Eligibility: This program is open to Delaware residents (both male and female) who are interested in working full time on an associate or bachelor's degree in a construction-related program, including engineering. Applicants may be high school seniors, high school graduates, or currently-enrolled college students. Selection is based on grade point average, interest in construction, extracurricular activities, employment experience, academic advisor evaluation, and financial need.

Financial data: Stipends range from $500 to $1,000.

Duration: 1 year.

Number awarded: 1 or more each year.

Deadline: March of each year.

2338
NBAA AVIATION SCHOLARSHIPS

National Business Aviation Association, Inc.
Attn: Senior Manager, Airmen & Commercial Services
1200 18th Street, N.W., Suite 400
Washington, DC 20036-2527
Phone: (202) 783-9353   Fax: (202) 331-8364
E-mail: jevans@nbaa.org
Web Site: www.nbaa.org/scholarships/index.htm

Summary: To provide financial assistance to undergraduates majoring in aviation.

Eligibility: To be eligible for this scholarship, students must be U.S. citizens; be at the sophomore, junior, or senior level in college (proof of enrollment is required); and be in an aviation-related program of study at an institution belonging to the National Business Aviation Association (NBAA) and the University Aviation Association (UAA). Applicants must have at least a 3.0 grade point average. To apply, students must submit a completed application form, an official transcript, a 250-word essay on their interest in and goals for a career in the business aviation industry, a letter of recommendation from a member of the aviation department faculty, and a resume.

Financial data: The stipend is $1,000. Checks are made payable to the recipient's institution.

Duration: 1 year.

Additional information: Additional information is also available from Dr. RoyceAnn Martin, Bowling Green State University, Aerotechnology Annex, East Poe Road, Bowling Green, OH 43403. Participating UAA members institutions are Arizona State University, Auburn University, Averett College, Bowling Green State University, Central Missouri State University, Daniel Webster College, Dowling College, Eastern Michigan University, Embry-Riddle Aeronautical University, Florida Institute of Technology, Lewis University, Middle Tennessee State University, Ohio State University, Parks College, Purdue University, St. Cloud State University, Southeastern Oklahoma State University, Southern Illinois University, Texas State Community College, University of Illinois, University of Nebraska at Kearney, University of Nebraska at Omaha, University of North Dakota, Utah Valley State College, and Western Michigan University.

Number awarded: 5 each year.

Deadline: October of each year.

2339
NBNA BOARD OF DIRECTORS SCHOLARSHIP

National Black Nurses Association, Inc.
Attn: Scholarship Committee
8630 Fenton Street, Suite 330
Silver Spring, MD 20910
Phone: (301) 589-3200   Fax: (301) 589-3223

Summary: To provide financial assistance for nursing education to members of the National Black Nurses Association (NBNA).

Eligibility: This program is open to members of the association who hold a nursing license. Applicants must be currently enrolled in a B.S.N. or advanced degree program with at least 1 full year of school remaining. Selection is based on participation in student nurse activities, involvement in the African American community, and involvement in community health services activities.

Financial data: The award ranges from $500 to $2,000 per year.

Duration: 1 year; may be renewed.

Additional information: Requests for applications must be accompanied by a self-addressed stamped envelope.

Number awarded: 1 or more each year.

Deadline: April of each year.

2340
NCFC EDUCATION FOUNDATION UNDERGRADUATE SCHOLARSHIPS

National Council of Farmer Cooperatives
Attn: NCFC Education Foundation
50 F Street, N.W., Suite 900
Washington, DC 20001
Phone: (202) 626-8700   Fax: (202) 626-8722
E-mail: info@ncfc.org
Web Site: www.ncfc.org

Summary: To provide financial assistance to college students who have expressed an interest in agricultural cooperatives.

Eligibility: Students may not apply directly for these scholarships; they must be nominated by an agricultural cooperative or a state council of cooperatives. Each cooperative organization may nominate no more than 3 students. Only faculty members may request that a cooperative nominate a student. Nominees must be enrolled in an accredited 4-year college or university in the United States, have completed at least 1 full academic year of course work, have at least half an academic year remaining for completion of a degree, and either rank in the upper quarter of their class or have at least a 3.0 grade point average. They must submit an application that includes a 4- to 6-page essay on their interest in cooperatives as well as their personal goals and career aspirations, a college transcript, and a letter of recommendation.

Financial data: The awards are $1,000.

Duration: 1 year.

Additional information: This program includes the W. Malcolm Harding Scholarship, the Owen Hallberg Scholarship, and the Philip F. French Scholarship

Number awarded: 3 each year.

Deadline: Nominations must be submitted by the end of March of each year.

2341
NCPA FOUNDATION PRESIDENTIAL SCHOLARSHIPS

National Community Pharmacists Association
Attn: NCPA Foundation
205 Daingerfield Road
Alexandria, VA 22314-2885
Phone: (703) 683-8200   (800) 544-7447
Fax: (703) 683-3619   E-mail: info@ncpanet.org
Web Site: www.ncpanet.org.org/students/presscholar.html

Summary: To provide financial assistance for full-time education in pharmacy to student members of the National Community Pharmacists Association (NCPA).

Eligibility: All pharmacy students who are student members of the association and enrolled in an accredited U.S. school or college of pharmacy on a full-time basis are eligible. Applicants must submit a copy of the most recent transcript of their college grades, 2 letters of recommendation, a resume or curriculum vitae, and a statement outlining their school and citizenship accomplishments and objectives for the future. Selection is based on leadership qualities, involvement in extracurricular activities, and academic achievement.

Financial data: The stipend is $2,000, paid directly to the recipient's school or college of pharmacy.

Duration: 1 year.

Additional information: Until October 1996, the NCPA, the national association representing independent retail pharmacy, was known as NARD (the National Association of Retail Druggists).

Number awarded: 15 each year.

Deadline: March of each year.

2342
NDPRB UNDERGRADUATE SCHOLARSHIP PROGRAM

Dairy Management Inc.
O'Hare International Center
10255 West Higgins Road, Suite 900
Rosemont, IL 60018-5616
Phone: (847) 803-2000   Fax: (847) 803-2077
E-mail: marykateg@rosedmi.com
Web Site: www.dairyinfo.com

Summary: To provide financial assistance to undergraduate students in fields related to dairy science.

Eligibility: This program is open to junior and/or senior undergraduate students enrolled in college and university programs that emphasize dairy food science, technology, or marketing. Applicants in non-dairy science departments must provide evidence that they have enrolled or will enroll in at least 1 regularly offered course that specializes in the processing, chemistry, microbiology, or marketing of milk or dairy products. Students in dairy science departments must provide evidence of enrollment in a dairy foods/marketing option or specialization. Selection is based on academic performance; apparent commitment to a career in dairy science/technology, dairy marketing, or a food-related science with an emphasis on dairy products; involvement in extracurricular activities, especially those relating to dairy/food science; and evidence of leadership ability, initiative, character, and integrity. The applicant who is judged most outstanding is awarded the James H. Loper Memorial Scholarship.

Financial data: Stipends are $2,500 or $1,500.

Duration: 1 year; students who receive scholarships during their junior year may apply for a renewal for their senior year.

Additional information: Dairy Management Inc. manages this program on behalf of the National Dairy Promotion and Research Board (NDPRB).

Number awarded: 20 each year: the James H. Loper Memorial Scholarship at $2,500 and 19 other scholarships at $1,500.

Deadline: March of each year.

2343
NDTA MERIT SCHOLARSHIP PROGRAM A

National Defense Transportation Association
Attn: Forum, Education and Professional Development Committee
50 South Pickett Street, Suite 220
Alexandria, VA 22304-7296
Phone: (703) 751-5011   Fax: (703) 823-8761
Web Site: www.ndtahq.com/program_a.htm

Summary: To provide financial assistance to college students who are members or dependents of members of the National Defense Transportation Association (NDTA).

Eligibility: This program is open to NDTA members and dependents of members who have satisfactorily completed 45 semester hours of work at a regionally accredited college or university. The institution must offer at least 15 semester hours in transportation, physical distribution, logistics, or some combination of the above. Applicants must 1) include college transcripts; 2) attach a listing of academic and other honors and awards received, extracurricular activities, and work experiences; 3) identify the courses in transportation, physical distribution, or logistics that they plan to incorporate into their degree program; and 4) submit a 300- to 500-word statement outlining their career goals and methods of attaining those goals, indicating why they should be awarded the scholarship. Financial need is not considered in the selection process.

Financial data: A stipend is awarded (exact amount not specified).

Duration: 1 year; may be renewed.

Number awarded: 1 or more each year.

Deadline: April of each year.

2344
NDTA SCOTT-ST. LOUIS SCHOLASTIC AWARDS

National Defense Transportation Association-Scott-St. Louis Chapter
Attn: Scholarship Committee Chairman
P.O. Box 25486
Scott Air Force Base, IL 62225-0486

Summary: To provide financial assistance for college to students from designated midwestern states interested in pursuing a career in business, transportation, logistics, or physical distribution.

Eligibility: This program is open to students interested in pursuing a career in business, transportation, logistics, or physical distribution. High school applicants must be residents of Missouri or Illinois. College students must be enrolled full time at an accredited institution in Colorado, Iowa, Illinois, Indiana, Kansas, Michigan, Minnesota, Missouri, Montana, Nebraska, North Dakota, South Dakota, Wisconsin, or Wyoming. Applicants who are the immediate family of members of the Scott-St. Louis chapter of the National Defense Transportation Association (NDTA) may reside in any state. The field of study must be business, logistics, physical distribution, or transportation (including aeronautical engineering, automotive engineering, aviation management, business, civil engineering, finance, hotel management, logistics management, naval architecture/structural engineering, professional pilot/navigator, transportation management, transportation distribution, transportation-related data and information systems, and travel and tourism).

Financial data: The stipend is $3,000.

Duration: 1 year.

Additional information: Information is also available from Michael A. Carnes, 926 Thornbury Place, O'Fallon, IL 62269-6810, (618) 628-1417, E-mail: mcarnes@apci.net, or from John O'Hara, 1146 Great Falls Court, Manchester, MO 63021, (636) 225-9424, E-mail: john.ohara@trw.com.

Number awarded: 5 each year, of which 1 is reserved for an immediate relative of an active member of the Scott-St. Louis NDTA chapter.

Deadline: February of each year.

2345
NEHA/AAS SCHOLARSHIPS

National Environmental Health Association
Attn: NEHA Member Liaison
720 South Colorado Boulevard, Suite 970-S
Denver, CO 80246-1925
Phone: (303) 756-9090, ext. 300   Fax: (303) 691-9490
E-mail: mthomsen@neha.org
Web Site: www.neha.org

Summary: To provide financial assistance to students interested in preparing for a career in environmental health.

Eligibility: Eligible to apply for this program are students planning a career in environmental health. Undergraduates must be enrolled in an institution accredited by the National Accreditation Council on Environmental Health, have completed their first 2 years of college, and be majoring in environmental health. Graduate applicants may be enrolled in any college or university with a program of studies in environmental health sciences and/or public health. Selection for both levels is based on academic record and letters of recommendation; at least 1 letter of recommendation must be from an active member of the National Environmental Health Association (NEHA).

Financial data: Stipends range from $400 to $1,000.

Duration: 1 year; may be renewed.

Additional information: The NEHA began this scholarship program in 1984; the American Academy of Sanitarians (AAS) joined it in 1989. Information is also available from the AAS, Executive Secretary/Treasurer, 3815 Stonbriar Court, Duluth, GA 30097-2240, (770) 488-7279, Fax: (770) 488-7335.

Number awarded: Up to 3 each year.

Deadline: April of each year.

2346
NELL BRYANT ROBINSON SCHOLARSHIP

Phi Upsilon Omicron
Attn: Educational Foundation
P.O. Box 329
Fairmont, WV 26555-0329
Phone: (304) 368-0612   E-mail: rickards@access.mountain.net
Web Site: ianrwww.unl.edu/phiu

Summary: To provide financial assistance to undergraduate student members of Phi Upsilon Omicron, a national honor society in family and consumer sciences.

Eligibility: This program is open to members of the society who are working on a bachelor's degree in family and consumer sciences or a related area. Preference is given to majors in dietetics or food and nutrition. Selection is based on scholastic record, participation in society and other collegiate activities, a statement of professional aims and goals, professional and/or work experience, and recommendations.

Financial data: The stipend is $1,000.

Duration: 1 year.

Number awarded: 1 each year.

Deadline: January of each year.

2347
NELL GOFF MEMORIAL SCHOLARSHIP

Summary: To provide financial assistance to upper-division and graduate students from Maine who are majoring in a garden-related field.
See Listing #1566.

2348
NETTIE DRACUP MEMORIAL SCHOLARSHIP

American Congress on Surveying and Mapping
Attn: Awards Director
6 Montgomery Village Avenue, Suite 403
Gaithersburg, MD 20879
Phone: (240) 632-9716   Fax: (240) 632-1321
E-mail: tmilburn@acsm.net
Web Site: www.acsm.net

Summary: To provide financial assistance for the undergraduate study of surveying to members of the American Congress on Surveying and Mapping.

Eligibility: This program is open to U.S. citizens who are enrolled in a 2-year or 4-year college or university studying surveying and are members of the sponsoring organization. Selection is based on previous academic record (30 percent), an applicant's statement of future plans (30 percent), letters of recommendation (20 percent), and professional activities (20 percent); if 2 or more applicants are judged equal based on those criteria, financial need may be considered.

Financial data: The stipend is $2,000.

Duration: 1 year.

Number awarded: 1 each year.

Deadline: December of each year.

2349
NEUROSCIENCE NURSING FOUNDATION REGULAR SCHOLARSHIPS

American Association of Neuroscience Nurses
Attn: Neuroscience Nursing Foundation
4700 West Lake Avenue
Glenview, IL 60025-1485
Phone: (847) 375-4733   (888) 557-2266
Fax: (847) 375-6333   E-mail: aann@aann.org
Web Site: www.aann.org

Summary: To provide financial assistance to nurses interested in pursuing further study in neuroscience nursing.

Eligibility: This program is open to nurses who are seeking a bachelor's, master's, or doctoral degree in neuroscience nursing. Selection is based on involvement in

neuroscience nursing during the past 10 years, involvement in professional nursing other than neuroscience nursing during the past 10 years, and a personal statement on the applicant's anticipated contribution to neuroscience nursing practice, research, and/or education.

Financial data: The amount of the award depends on the availability of funds but averages approximately $1,600.

Duration: 1 year.

Additional information: This program was established in 1994.

Number awarded: The award is presented when a suitable candidate applies. Since 1994, 8 of these scholarships have been awarded.

Deadline: February of each year.

2350
NEUROSCIENCE RESEARCH PRIZE FOR HIGH SCHOOL STUDENTS

American Academy of Neurology
Attn: Neuroscience Prize Office
1080 Montreal Avenue
St. Paul, MN 55116-2325
Phone: (651) 695-1940   (800) 879-1960
Fax: (651) 695-2791   E-mail: hlewis@aan.com
Web Site: www.aan.com

Summary: To recognize and reward high school students for outstanding laboratory reports in neuroscience.

Eligibility: This program is open to students enrolled in grades 9-12 in the United States. Applicants submit an original laboratory research report, up to 10 pages in length, that represents their own written work. The report should be written in the style of a scientific paper, describing actual laboratory or field research experiments or observations performed, the results obtained, and the interpretation of those results. Selection criteria include the paper's relevance to neuroscience, creativity, scientific method, and interpretation of data.

Financial data: Winners receive a $1,000 prize and an all-expense paid trip to a professional neuroscience conference where they present their projects. Teachers are also invited to the conferences, with all their expenses paid.

Duration: The prizes are awarded annually.

Additional information: The trips are to the annual meetings of the sponsors of this program: the American Academy of Neurology (AAN) and the Child Neurology Society (CNS). Funding is provided by Novartis Pharmaceuticals Corporation.

Number awarded: 4 each year; 3 winners receive trips to the AAN meeting and 1 to the CNS meeting.

Deadline: December of each year.

2351
NEW ENGLAND WATER WORKS ASSOCIATION SCHOLARSHIP

New England Water Works Association
64 Dilla Street
Milford, MA 01757
Phone: (508) 478-6996   Fax: (508) 634-8643

Summary: To provide financial assistance to undergraduate or graduate students from New England, particularly those who are working on a degree in an area of benefit to water works practice in New England.

Eligibility: All applicants must be members or students members of either the New England section of the American Water Works Association or of the New England Water Works Association. They must be high school seniors, currently-enrolled college students, or graduate students. Selection is based on merit, character, and financial need, with preference given to applicants whose academic programs are considered to be beneficial to the water works practice in New England.

Financial data: A stipend is awarded (exact amount not specified).

Duration: 1 year.

Additional information: Information is also available from Kenneth E. Johnson, c/o Natgun Corporation, 11 Teal Road, Wakefield, MA 01880, (781) 246-1133.

Deadline: July of each year.

2352
NEW HAMPSHIRE MGMA SCHOLARSHIPS

American College of Medical Practice Executives
Attn: Scholarship Program
104 Inverness Terrace East
Englewood, CO 80112-5306
Phone: (303) 643-9573   Fax: (303) 643-4427

E-mail: acmpe@mgma.com   Web Site: www.mgma.com/acmpe

Summary: To provide financial assistance to members of the Medical Group Management Association (MGMA) in New Hampshire who are interested in pursuing undergraduate or graduate education, continuing education, or applied research.

Eligibility: Eligible to apply are individuals who reside in New Hampshire and have been members of either the MGMA or New Hampshire MGMA for 2 years. Applicants must wish to 1) pursue an undergraduate or graduate degree in medical practice management at an accredited university or college; 2) attend conferences, workshops, and seminars sponsored by either nationally recognized professional associations or accredited universities and colleges; or 3) investigate a subject related to medical practice management that could result in potentially publishable work. Applications must include a letter describing their career goals and objectives; a resume; 3 reference letters commenting on their performance, character, potential to succeed, and need for scholarship support; academic transcripts; explanation of individual need for professional development and the specific continuing education activity planned to meet this need (if relevant); and/or description of the research project (study design, time frame, and amount and use of money).

Financial data: The stipend is $1,000. Payments for undergraduate and graduate scholarships are sent to the university or college in which the recipient is or will be enrolled. Payments for continuing education or applied research are made upon receipt of documentation for expenses incurred.

Duration: 1 year.

Deadline: May of each year.

2353
NEW JERSEY LEGION AUXILIARY PAST PRESIDENTS' PARLEY NURSES SCHOLARSHIPS

American Legion Auxiliary
Attn: Department of New Jersey
146 Route 130
Bordentown, NJ 08505-2226
Phone: (609) 291-9338   Fax: (609) 291-8175

Summary: To provide financial assistance for the nursing education of New Jersey residents who are the children or grandchildren of veterans.

Eligibility: Eligible to apply for these scholarships are the children and grandchildren of living, deceased, or divorced veterans. Applicants must have been residents of New Jersey for at least 2 years and be graduating high school seniors or the equivalent who plan to study nursing.

Financial data: The amount awarded varies, depending upon the needs of the recipient and the money available.

Duration: 1 year.

Number awarded: Varies each year.

Deadline: March of each year.

2354
NEW JERSEY UTILITIES ASSOCIATION SCHOLARSHIPS

New Jersey Utilities Association
50 West State Street, Suite 1006
Trenton, NJ 08608
Phone: (609) 392-1000   Fax: (609) 396-4231
Web Site: www.njua.org

Summary: To provide financial assistance to minority, female, and disabled high school seniors in New Jersey interested in majoring in selected subjects in college.

Eligibility: Eligible to apply for this scholarship are women, minorities (Black, Hispanic American, American Indian/Alaska Native, or Asian American/Pacific Islander), and persons with disabilities who are high school seniors in New Jersey. They must be able to demonstrate financial need, be planning to enroll on a full-time basis at an institute of higher education, and be planning to work on a bachelor's degree in engineering, environmental science, chemistry, biology, business administration, or accounting. Children of employees of any New Jersey Utilities Association-member company are ineligible. Selection is based on overall academic excellence and demonstrated financial need.

Financial data: The stipend is $1,500 per year.

Duration: 4 years.

Number awarded: 2 each year.

2355
NEW YORK LEGION AUXILIARY MEDICAL AND TEACHING SCHOLARSHIPS

American Legion Auxiliary
Attn: Department of New York
112 State Street, Suite 409
Albany, NY 12207
Phone: (518) 463-2215 Fax: (518) 427-8443
Summary: To provide financial assistance to children or grandchildren of veterans who are interested in pursuing a career in the medical or teaching field in New York.
Eligibility: To be eligible for these scholarships, applicants must be New York residents who are the children or grandchildren of veterans, high school seniors or graduates, younger than 20 years of age, and interested in working in the medical or teaching field.
Financial data: The stipend is $1,000.
Duration: 1 year.
Number awarded: 10 each year: 1 in each of the 10 judicial districts in New York state.
Deadline: March of each year.

2356
NEW YORK LEGION AUXILIARY PAST PRESIDENTS PARLEY STUDENT NURSES SCHOLARSHIP

American Legion Auxiliary
Attn: Department of New York
112 State Street, Suite 409
Albany, NY 12207
Phone: (518) 463-2215 Fax: (518) 427-8443
Summary: To provide financial assistance for nursing education to the children or grandchildren of wartime veterans in New York.
Eligibility: To be eligible for these scholarships, applicants must be the children or grandchildren of veterans who served in World War I, World War II, Korea, or Vietnam; be residents of New York State; be high school seniors or graduates; and not be more than 20 years of age. Applicants must demonstrate financial need and plan to enter nursing as a career. Each American Legion Auxiliary Unit in New York may nominate 1 candidate.
Financial data: The stipend is $1,000.
Duration: 1 year.
Number awarded: 1 each year.
Deadline: March of each year.

2357
NEW YORK OCCUPATIONAL THERAPY ASSOCIATION SCHOLARSHIP

American Occupational Therapy Foundation
Attn: Scholarship Coordinator
4720 Montgomery Lane
P.O. Box 31220
Bethesda, MD 20824-1220
Phone: (301) 652-2682 Fax: (301) 656-3620
Phone: TDD: (800) 377-8555 E-mail: aotf@aotf.org
Web Site: www.aotf.org
Summary: To provide financial assistance to students who are members of the New York Occupational Therapy Association and working on a degree in occupational therapy.
Eligibility: This program is open to New York residents who are enrolled in an accredited occupational therapy educational program (associate or professional) in the state. Applicants must demonstrate a need for financial assistance, have a sustained record of outstanding scholastic performance, and be members of the New York Occupational Therapy Association. As part of the application process, they must submit transcripts, 2 personal references, and a statement from their curriculum director.
Financial data: The stipend is $150 for associate degree students or $1,000 for professional degree students.
Duration: 1 year.
Additional information: Application forms are available at no cost at the association's web site; a $5 fee is charged for printed copies sent from the association's headquarters.
Number awarded: 4 each year: 3 to professional degree students and 1 to an associate degree student.
Deadline: January of each year.

2358
NEW YORK SECTION SCHOLARSHIPS

Institute of Food Technologists
Attn: Scholarship Department
221 North LaSalle Street, Suite 300
Chicago, IL 60601-1291
Phone: (312) 782-8424 Fax: (312) 782-8348
E-mail: info@ift.org Web Site: www.ift.org
Summary: To provide financial assistance to undergraduates interested in studying food science or food technology.
Eligibility: Applicants must be currently enrolled as sophomores or juniors in a food science or food technology program at an educational institution in the United States or Canada. They must have an outstanding scholastic record and a well-rounded personality. Financial need is not considered in the selection process.
Financial data: The stipend is $1,000.
Duration: 1 year; recipients may reapply if they are members of the Institute of Food Technologists.
Additional information: Correspondence and completed applications must be submitted to the department head of the educational institution the applicant is attending.
Number awarded: 2 each year.
Deadline: January of each year.

2359
NEW YORK STATE ASSOCIATION OF AGRICULTURAL FAIRS ANNUAL SCHOLARSHIP PROGRAM

New York State Association of Agricultural Fairs
Attn: Scholarship Committee
67 Verbeck Avenue
Schaghticoke, NY 12154 Web Site: www.nyfairs.org/scholarship.htm
Summary: To provide financial assistance to residents of New York interested in pursuing higher education in agriculture or an agricultural-related field.
Eligibility: This program is open to New York state high school seniors and New York state residents currently attending college who are planning to pursue or already pursuing a degree in agriculture or an agricultural-related field. Students must first apply through a member fair of the New York State Association of Agricultural Fairs. The district director and/or a district committee selects the 3 best applications received within the district, and those are forwarded to the state organization for final determination of awardees. Selection is based on scholastic standing (25 percent), citizenship and leadership (25 percent), fair participation (20 percent), field of study (15 percent), financial need (10 percent), and presentation of application (5 percent).
Financial data: The stipend is $1,000.
Duration: 1 year.
Additional information: This program is jointly sponsored by the New York State Association of Agricultural Fairs and the New York State Showpeople's Association.
Number awarded: 5 each year.
Deadline: Students must submit their applications to the member fair by April of each year.

2360
NEW YORK STATE CHAPTER UNDERGRADUATE SCHOLARSHIP PROGRAM

Associated General Contractors of America
New York State Chapter, Inc.
Attn: AGC Scholarship Fund
1900 Western Avenue
Albany, NY 12203-5097
Phone: (518) 456-1134 Fax: (518) 456-1198
Summary: To provide financial assistance to students in New York who are majoring in construction or civil engineering.
Eligibility: Applicants must be entering the second, third, or fourth year in a 2-year or 4-year school, be intent on a career in construction, be working on a bachelor or associate degree in construction or civil engineering, be enrolled full time, be a U.S. citizen or documented permanent resident, be a New York resident attending a school in New York, and have at least a 2.75 grade point average in college. Selection is based, in part, on interest in construction, grades, extracurricular activities, employment experience, and adult evaluations.
Financial data: The stipend is $2,500 per year, payable in 2 equal installments.
Duration: Both 1-year and renewable scholarships are awarded.
Additional information: Recipients are required to seek summer employment in construction.

Number awarded: At least 12 each year. Since the program began 10 years ago, more than 180 students have received scholarships.
Deadline: May of each year.

2361
NEW YORK STATE ENA SEPTEMBER 11 SCHOLARSHIP FUND

Emergency Nurses Association Foundation
915 Lee Street
Des Plaines, IL 60016-6569
Phone: (847) 460-4100   (800) 900-9659, ext. 4101
Fax: (847) 460-4005   E-mail: foundation@ena.org
Web Site: www.ena.org/foundation
Summary: To provide financial assistance to rescue workers pursuing an undergraduate degree in nursing.
Eligibility: This program is open to pre-hospital care providers, firemen, and policemen who are going to school to obtain an undergraduate nursing degree. Rescue workers from all states are eligible.
Financial data: The stipend is $2,000.
Duration: 1 year.
Additional information: Scholarship winners are also awarded a complimentary 1-year members in the Emergency Nurses Association (ENA).
Number awarded: 1 or more each year.
Deadline: September of each year.

2362
NFB COMPUTER SCIENCE SCHOLARSHIP

National Federation of the Blind
c/o Peggy Elliott
Chair, Scholarship Committee
805 Fifth Avenue
Grinnell, IA 50112
Phone: (641) 236-3366
Web Site: www.nfb.org
Summary: To provide financial assistance to legally blind students pursuing a degree in computer science.
Eligibility: This program is open to legally blind students who are pursuing or planning to pursue a full-time undergraduate or graduate course of study in computer science. Selection is based on academic excellence, service to the community, and financial need.
Financial data: The stipend is $3,000.
Duration: 1 year; recipients may resubmit applications up to 2 additional years.
Additional information: Scholarships are awarded at the federation convention in July. Recipients attend the convention at federation expense; that funding is in addition to the scholarship grant.
Number awarded: 1 each year.
Deadline: March of each year.

2363
NICE STUDENT SCHOLARSHIP COMPETITION

American Ceramic Society
Attn: National Institute of Ceramic Engineers
P.O. Box 6136
Westerville, OH 43086-6136
Phone: (614) 890-4700   Fax: (614) 899-6109
E-mail: info@acers.org
Summary: To recognize and reward outstanding essays written by students majoring in ceramics or materials in college.
Eligibility: Entrants must be U.S. citizens enrolled in an ABET-accredited program in ceramics or materials. The students must be continuing in school in the following year as undergraduates. They are invited to submit an essay (up to 5 pages, including text, figures, tables, and references). The essay topic changes annually but relates to ceramics or materials. In addition, entrants must submit at least 2 letters of recommendation. The competition is based primarily on the essay and not on financial need, grade point average, or the recommendations; however, these components may be taken into consideration in the case of a tie.
Financial data: The winning student essayist receives $4,500; $500 is also awarded to the student branch.
Duration: The competition is held annually.
Number awarded: 2 each year.
Deadline: March of each year.

2364
NICHOLAS AND MARY TRIVILLIAN MEMORIAL SCHOLARSHIP

Greater Kanawha Valley Foundation
Attn: Scholarship Coordinator
One Huntington Square, 16th Floor
900 Lee Street, East
P.O. Box 3041
Charleston, WV 25331-3041
Phone: (304) 346-3620   Fax: (304) 346-3640
E-mail: tgkvf@tgkvf.com   Web Site: www.tgkvf.com/scholarship.html
Summary: To provide financial assistance to residents of West Virginia who are pursuing a degree in medicine or pharmacy.
Eligibility: This program is open to residents of West Virginia who are pursuing a full-time degree in the field of medicine or pharmacy at a college or university in the state. Applicants must have at least a 2.5 grade point average and demonstrate good moral character. Financial need is considered in the selection process.
Financial data: The stipend is $1,000 per year.
Duration: 1 year; may be renewed.
Number awarded: 31 each year.
Deadline: February of each year.

2365
NICHOLAS J. GRANT SCHOLARSHIP

ASM International Foundation
Attn: Scholarship Program
9639 Kinsman Road
Materials Park, OH 44073-0002
Phone: (440) 338-5151   (800) 336-5152
Fax: (440) 338-4634   E-mail: crhayes@asminternational.org
Web Site: www.asminternational.org
Summary: To provide financial assistance to members of the American Society for Metals who are interested in majoring in metallurgy and materials.
Eligibility: Applicants must be citizens of the United States, Canada, or Mexico; be enrolled at a college or university in those countries; be members of the society; have an intended or declared major in metallurgy or materials science and engineering (related science or engineering majors may be considered if the applicant demonstrates a strong academic emphasis and interest in materials science and engineering); and be entering their junior or senior year in college. Selection is based on academic achievement; interest in metallurgy/materials (including knowledge of the field, activities, jobs, and potential for a related career); personal qualities (such as social values, maturity, motivation, goals, and citizenship); and financial need.
Financial data: The scholarship provides payment of full tuition.
Duration: 1 year; recipients may reapply for 1 additional year.
Additional information: This scholarship was established in 1990 by 1 of Dr. Grant's former students.
Number awarded: 1 each year.
Deadline: April of each year.

2366
NNCC CAREER MOBILITY SCHOLARSHIP

American Nephrology Nurses' Association
Attn: ANNA Foundation
East Holly Avenue, Box 56
Pitman, NJ 08071-0056
Phone: (609) 256-2320   (877) 527-0787
Fax: (856) 589-7463   E-mail: annafoundation@hotmail.com
Web Site: www.annanurse.org
Summary: To provide financial assistance to members of the American Nephrology Nurses' Association (ANNA) who are Certified Nephrology Nurses and are interested in pursuing a baccalaureate degree in nursing to enhance their nephrology nursing practice.
Eligibility: Applicants must hold a current credential as a Certified Nephrology Nurse (CNN) by the Nephrology Nursing Certification Commission (NNCC), be a current full member of the association, have been a member for at least 2 years, be currently employed in nephrology nursing, and be accepted or enrolled in a baccalaureate degree program in nursing. In their application, they must indicate how the degree will apply to nephrology nursing.
Financial data: The stipend is $2,000.
Duration: 1 year.

Additional information: Funds for this program are supplied by the NNCC. Information is also available from Cynthia Frazier, Awards Chairperson, 7344 Pine Tree Lane, Fairfield, AL 35064, (205) 933-8101, ext. 6514, E-mail: cdf44@aol.com.
Number awarded: 5 each year.
Deadline: October of each year.

2367
NONWOVENS DIVISION SCHOLARSHIP

Technical Association of the Pulp and Paper Industry
P.O. Box 105113
Atlanta, GA 30348-5113
Phone: (770) 446-1400   (800) 332-8686
Fax: (770) 446-6947   Web Site: www.tappi.org
Summary: To provide financial assistance to undergraduate students who are interested in preparing for a career in the paper industry, with a focus on the materials, equipment, and processes for the manufacture and use of nonwovens.
Eligibility: This program is open to students who are attending a state-accredited college full time, have earned a grade point average of 3.0 or higher, are enrolled in a program preparatory to a career in the nonwovens industry or can demonstrate an interest in the areas covered by the Nonwovens Division of the Technical Association of the Pulp and Paper Industry, and are recommended and endorsed by an instructor or faculty member. Selection is based on the candidates' potential career and contributions in the pulp and paper industry as it relates to nonwovens. Financial need is not considered in the selection process.
Financial data: The stipend is $1,000.
Duration: 1 year.
Number awarded: 1 each year.
Deadline: January of each year.

2368
NORMA WELLS LOYALTY GRANT

Lambda Kappa Sigma Pharmacy Fraternity
Attn: Educational Grant Program
20110 Glenoaks Drive
Brookfield, WI 53045
Phone: (800) LKS-1913   Fax: (414) 784-8406
E-mail: lks@lks.org   Web Site: www.lks.org/educational_grants.htm
Summary: To provide financial assistance to members of Lambda Kappa Sigma for pharmaceutical education.
Eligibility: Eligible are members in good standing with Lambda Kappa Sigma who are enrolled in B.S. in pharmacy or Pharm.D. programs. Applicants must rank in the upper half of their class and present evidence of financial need. Selection is based on leadership, scholarship, dedication to the profession of pharmacy, and financial need.
Financial data: The stipend is $1,000.
Duration: 1 year.
Number awarded: 1 each year.
Deadline: October of each year.

2369
NORMAN E. HUSTON SCHOLARSHIP

Instrumentation, Systems, and Automation Society
Attn: ISA Educational Foundation
67 Alexander Drive
Research Triangle Park, NC 27709
Phone: (919) 549-8411   Fax: (919) 549-8288
E-mail: info@isa.org   Web Site: www.isa.org
Summary: To provide financial assistance to undergraduate and graduate students majoring in fields related to instrumentation, systems, and automation.
Eligibility: This program is open to full-time undergraduate and graduate students enrolled in a program in instrumentation, systems, automation, or a closely-related field. Applicants must have a grade point average of 3.0 or higher. They may be from any country but must be attending an institution in their own country. Applicants in a 2-year program must have completed at least 1 academic semester of 12 hours or its equivalent. Applicants in a 4-year program must be in their sophomore year or higher. Along with their application, they must submit an essay (up to 400 words) on their ambitions and qualifications as an innovator or future leader in a career in instrumentation, systems, or automation; they should describe their career objectives, how the award of this scholarship will help them attain their objectives, why they want to enter this particular field of engineering, what they have achieved and learned through their studies and activities, and

what this indicates about their character and determination. Financial need is not considered in the selection process.
Financial data: The stipend is $3,600.
Duration: 1 year; may be renewed.
Additional information: This program was established in 2001.
Number awarded: 1 each year.
Deadline: January of each year.

2370
NORTH CAROLINA WILDLIFE FEDERATION SCHOLARSHIP GRANTS

North Carolina Wildlife Federation Endowment and Education Fund
1024 Washington Street
P.O. Box 10626
Raleigh, NC 27605
Phone: (919) 833-1923   Fax: (919) 829-1192
E-mail: ncwflisac@aol.com
Summary: To provide financial assistance to full-time undergraduate or graduate students in North Carolina majoring in wildlife, the environment, or related areas.
Eligibility: Eligible to apply for these funds are students enrolled and attending an accredited college or university in North Carolina on a full-time basis at the undergraduate or graduate school level. They must be working on a degree in the areas of wildlife, fisheries, forestry, conservation, or the environment. Financial need is considered in the selection process, along with academic record and extracurricular activities.
Financial data: The stipend is $1,000.
Duration: 1 year.
Number awarded: 4 to 7 each year, 1 of which is restricted to individuals concentrating in eastern turkey conservation and 1 restricted to residents of Forsyth County, North Carolina.
Deadline: November of each year.

2371
NORTH POLE CHAPTER SCHOLARSHIPS

National Defense Transportation Association-North Pole Chapter
Attn: Scholarship Committee Chairman
P.O. Box 243392
Anchorage, AK 99524-3392
Phone: (907) 552-2563
Web Site: www.ndta-anchorage.org/scholarships.htm
Summary: To provide financial assistance to residents of Alaska interested in a career in transportation.
Eligibility: This program is open to residents of Alaska who are currently working in the transportation industry or have career goals for the industry. Applicants must have a grade point average in high school or college of 3.0 or higher. As part of the selection process, they must submit a 200-word essay that explains their interest in the transportation field. Financial need is not considered.
Financial data: The stipend is $1,000.
Duration: 1 year; nonrenewable.
Additional information: Information is also available from MSCREP (NDTA), 31-270 Acacia Drive, Elmendorf AFB, AK 99506-3575.
Number awarded: Varies each year; recently, 4 of these scholarships were awarded.
Deadline: June of each year.

2372
NORTHROP-GRUMMAN SCHOLARSHIP

Society of Women Engineers
230 East Ohio Street, Suite 400
Chicago, IL 60611-3265
Phone: (312) 596-5223   Fax: (312) 644-8557
E-mail: hq@swe.org   Web Site: www.swe.org
Summary: To provide financial assistance to women undergraduates who are majoring in engineering.
Eligibility: This program is open to women undergraduates who are majoring in engineering at an ABET-accredited school, college, or university in the United States. Selection is based on merit.
Financial data: The amount of the award varies each year.
Duration: 1 year.
Additional information: This program was established in 1983.
Number awarded: 1 or more each year.
Deadline: January of each year.

2373
NPFDA SCHOLARSHIPS

National Poultry and Food Distributors Association
Attn: NPFDA Scholarship Foundation
958 McEver Road Extension, Unit B-5
Gainesville, GA 30504
Phone: (770) 535-9901   Fax: (770) 535-7385
E-mail: info@npfda.org
Web Site: www.npfda.org
Summary: To provide financial assistance to students enrolled in fields related to the poultry and food industries.
Eligibility: Applications for these scholarships are available at all land grant colleges and universities in the country, along with other qualified schools. Eligible students must be enrolled full time and pursuing an agriculture or food science degree of interest to the poultry industry. Along with their applications, they must submit a 1-page narrative on their goals and ambitions and their transcripts. Selection is based on those documents, extracurricular activities, and industry-related activities.
Financial data: Stipends range from $1,500 to $2,000.
Duration: 1 year.
Additional information: The National Poultry and Food Distributors Association (NPFDA) established its Scholarship Foundation in 1979. The following named scholarships are included in the program: the Albin S. Johnson Memorial Scholarship, the William Manson Family Memorial Scholarship, and the Alfred Schwartz Memorial Scholarship.
Number awarded: 4 each year.
Deadline: May of each year.

2374
NSBP UNDERGRADUATE SCHOLARSHIP AWARD

National Society of Black Physicists
c/o North Carolina A&T State University
Department of Physics
Greensboro, NC 27411-1086
Phone: (336) 334-7646   Fax: (336) 334-7283
E-mail: president@nsbp.org
Web Site: www.nsbp.org
Summary: To provide financial assistance and work experience to African Americans interested in majoring in physics in college.
Eligibility: This program is open to African American students who are graduating high school seniors or currently enrolled as an undergraduate in an accredited 4-year institution. Applicants must be majoring or planning to major in physics and have a grade point average of 3.0 or higher. U.S. citizenship is required. As part of the selection process, applicants must submit a statement of their academic and career objectives, information on their participation in extracurricular activities, a description of any awards and honors they have received, and 3 letters of recommendation. Financial need is not considered.
Financial data: The stipend is $5,000.
Duration: Up to 4 years, provided the recipient remains an undergraduate physics major with a grade point average of 3.0 or higher.
Additional information: This program was initiated in 1992. Information is also available from Ellen Hill, Lawrence Livermore National Laboratory, P.O. Box 808, L-716, Livermore, CA 94550, (925) 422-0894, Fax: (925) 422-9537, E-mail: hill10@llnl.gov. Recipients are required to accept a summer internship at Lawrence Livermore National Laboratory (which sponsors this program) for at least 1 of the 4 summers during their undergraduate education.
Number awarded: 1 each year.
Deadline: February of each year.

2375
NSCA CHALLENGE SCHOLARSHIP

National Strength and Conditioning Association
Attn: Foundation
1955 North Union Boulevard
P.O. Box 9908
Colorado Springs, CO 80932-0908
Phone: (719) 632-6722   (800) 815-6826
Fax: (719) 632-6367   E-mail: nsca@nsca-lift.org
Web Site: www.nsca-lift.org/foundation/challenge.shtml

Summary: To provide financial assistance for postsecondary education in strength training and conditioning to members of the National Strength and Conditioning Association (NSCA).
Eligibility: Candidates must have been members of the association for at least 1 year prior to the application deadline. They must be seeking either an undergraduate or graduate degree in a strength and conditioning-related field. In addition to transcripts and letters of recommendation, applicants must submit an essay of no more than 500 words explaining their need for the scholarship, proposed course of study, and professional goals. Selection is based on scholarship (25 points), strength and conditioning experience (15 points), the essay (15 points), recommendations (5 points), honors and awards (10 points), community involvement (10 points), and NSCA involvement (20 points).
Financial data: Awards are $1,000, to be applied toward tuition.
Duration: 1 year.
Additional information: The NSCA is a nonprofit organization of strength and conditioning professionals, including coaches, athletic trainers, physical therapists, educators, researchers, and physicians. This program is funded in part by the Bob Hoffman Foundation.
Number awarded: 12 each year.
Deadline: February of each year.

2376
NSCA HIGH SCHOOL SCHOLARSHIP

National Strength and Conditioning Association
Attn: Foundation
1955 North Union Boulevard
P.O. Box 9908
Colorado Springs, CO 80932-0908
Phone: (719) 632-6722   (800) 815-6826
Fax: (719) 632-6367   E-mail: nsca@nsca-lift.org
Web Site: www.nsca-lift.org/foundation
Summary: To provide financial assistance for postsecondary education in strength training and conditioning to graduating high school seniors.
Eligibility: This program is open to high school students preparing to enter college. Applicants must demonstrate they have been accepted into an accredited postsecondary institution, their intention to graduate with a degree in the strength and conditioning field, their goals beyond college, and their record of community service.
Financial data: A stipend is awarded (exact amount not specified).
Duration: 1 year; nonrenewable.
Additional information: The NSCA is a nonprofit organization of strength and conditioning professionals, including coaches, athletic trainers, physical therapists, educators, researchers, and physicians. This program was first offered in 2003.
Number awarded: 1 or more each year.

2377
NSCA WOMEN AND MINORITY SCHOLARSHIP

National Strength and Conditioning Association
Attn: Foundation
1955 North Union Boulevard
P.O. Box 9908
Colorado Springs, CO 80932-0908
Phone: (719) 632-6722   (800) 815-6826
Fax: (719) 632-6367   E-mail: nsca@nsca-lift.org
Web Site: www.nsca-lift.org/foundation
Summary: To provide financial assistance for postsecondary education in strength training and conditioning to women and minorities.
Eligibility: This program is open to women and minorities who are 17 years of age and older. Applicants must demonstrate they have been accepted into an accredited postsecondary institution, their intention to graduate with a degree in the strength and conditioning field, their goals beyond college, and their record of community service.
Financial data: A stipend is awarded (exact amount not specified).
Duration: 1 year; nonrenewable.
Additional information: The NSCA is a nonprofit organization of strength and conditioning professionals, including coaches, athletic trainers, physical therapists, educators, researchers, and physicians. This program was first offered in 2003.
Number awarded: 1 or more each year.

2378
NSPE-AUXILIARY SCHOLARSHIP

National Society of Professional Engineers
Attn: Education Services
1420 King Street
Alexandria, VA 22314-2794
Phone: (703) 684-2833   Fax: (703) 836-4875
E-mail: jiglesias@nspe.org
Web Site: www.nspe.org/scholarships/sc1-hs.asp
Summary: To provide financial assistance for college to women interested in preparing for a career in engineering.
Eligibility: This program is open to women who are high school seniors planning to study engineering in a college program accredited by the Engineering Accreditation Commission of the Accreditation Board for Engineering and Technology (EAC-ABET). Applicants must have earned at least a 3.0 grade point average, 500 on the verbal SAT, and 600 on the math SAT (or 25 on the English ACT and 29 on the math ACT). They must submit an essay (up to 500 words) on their interest in engineering, their major area of study and area of specialization, and the occupation they propose to pursue after graduation. Selection is based on grade point average (20 points), the essay (20 points), extracurricular activities (including work experience and volunteer activities) (25 points), financial need (5 points), SAT/ACT scores (20 points), and the composite application (10 points). U.S. citizenship is required.
Financial data: The award is $1,000 per year; funds are paid directly to the institution.
Duration: 2 years.
Additional information: Recipients may attend any college or university, as long as the engineering curriculum is accredited by EAC-ABET.
Number awarded: 1 each year.
Deadline: November of each year.

2379
NSPS BOARD OF GOVERNORS SCHOLARSHIP

American Congress on Surveying and Mapping
Attn: Awards Director
6 Montgomery Village Avenue, Suite 403
Gaithersburg, MD 20879
Phone: (240) 632-9716   Fax: (240) 632-1321
E-mail: tmilburn@acsm.net
Web Site: www.acsm.net
Summary: To provide financial assistance for the undergraduate study of surveying to members of the American Congress on Surveying and Mapping.
Eligibility: This program is open to members of the sponsoring organization who are entering their junior year of a 4-year degree program in surveying. Applicants must have maintained at least a 3.0 grade point average. Selection is based on previous academic record (30 percent), future plans (30 percent), letters of recommendation (20 percent), and professional activities (20 percent); if 2 or more applicants are judged equal based on those criteria, financial need may be considered.
Financial data: The stipend is $1,000.
Duration: 1 year.
Additional information: Funding for these scholarships is provided by the National Society of Professional Surveyors (NSPS).
Number awarded: 1 each year.
Deadline: December of each year.

2380
NSSGA ENGINEERING SCHOLARSHIPS

National Stone, Sand and Gravel Association
Attn: Director of Communications
2101 Wilson Boulevard, Suite 100
Arlington, VA 22201-3062
Phone: (703) 525-8788   (800) 342-1415
Fax: (703) 525-7782   E-mail: info@nssga.org
Web Site: www.nssag.org/careers/scholarships.htm
Summary: To provide financial assistance to university students intending to pursue a career in the aggregates industry.
Eligibility: Eligible are university students who intend to pursue a career in the crushed stone industry. Applications must be accompanied by a letter of recommendation and a 300- to 500-word statement describing those career plans. Financial need is not considered in the selection process.

Financial data: Each scholarship is $2,500.
Duration: 1 year.
Number awarded: 10 each year.
Deadline: April of each year.

2381
NUCLEAR PROPULSION OFFICER CANDIDATE (NUPOC) PROGRAM

U.S. Navy
Attn: Navy Personnel Command
5722 Integrity Drive
Millington, TN 38054-5057
Phone: (901) 874-3070   (888) 633-9674
Fax: (901) 874-2651 E-mail: nukeprograms@cnrc.navy.mil
Web Site: www.cnrc.navy.mil/nucfield
Summary: To provide financial assistance to college juniors and seniors who wish to serve in the Navy's nuclear propulsion training program following graduation.
Eligibility: This program is open to U.S. citizens who are entering their junior or senior year of college as a full-time student. Strong technical majors (mathematics, physics, chemistry, or an engineering field) are encouraged but not required. Applicants must have completed at least 1 year of calculus and 1 year of physics and must have earned a grade of "C" or better in all mathematics, science, and technical courses. Normally, they must be 26 years of age or younger at the expected date of commissioning, although applicants for the design and research specialty may be 29 years old.
Financial data: Participants become active reserve enlisted Navy personnel and receive a salary of up to $2,500 per month; the exact amount depends on the local cost of living and other factors. A bonus of $10,000 is also paid at the time of enlistment and another $2,000 upon completion of nuclear power training.
Duration: Up to 30 months, until completion of a bachelor's degree.
Additional information: Following graduation, participants attend Officer Candidate School in Pensacola, Florida for 4 months and receive their commissions. They have a service obligation of 8 years (of which at least 5 years must be on active duty), beginning with 6 months at the Navy Nuclear Power Training Command in Charleston, South Carolina and 6 more months of hands-on training at a nuclear reactor facility. Further information on this program is available from a local Navy recruiter or the Navy Recruiting Command, 801 North Randolph Street, Arlington, VA 22203-1991.
Number awarded: Varies each year.

2382
NURSES FOUNDATION OF WISCONSIN SCHOLARSHIP

Nurses Foundation of Wisconsin, Inc.
6117 Monona Drive
Madison, WI 53716
Phone: (608) 221-0383
Summary: To provide financial assistance to registered nurses in Wisconsin who are interested in continuing their education.
Eligibility: This program is open to registered nurses in Wisconsin who are interested in working on a bachelor's or advanced degree in nursing. Applicants must be members of the Wisconsin Nurses Association. They must submit a copy of their Wisconsin Certificate of Registration, a copy of their association membership card, a letter that identifies their professional goals, a summary of their financial need, and 2 letters of support. The nurses who demonstrate the potential of making the greatest contributions to nursing in Wisconsin are selected.
Financial data: Up to $1,000 per year.
Duration: 1 year.
Number awarded: 1 or more each year.
Deadline: April of each year.

2383
NUTRINOVA SCHOLARSHIP

Institute of Food Technologists
Attn: Scholarship Department
221 North LaSalle Street, Suite 300
Chicago, IL 60601-1291
Phone: (312) 782-8424   Fax: (312) 782-8348
E-mail: info@ift.org   Web Site: www.ift.org
Summary: To provide financial assistance to undergraduates interested in studying food science or food technology.

Eligibility: Applicants must be currently enrolled as sophomores or juniors in a food science or food technology program at an educational institution in the United States or Canada. They must have an outstanding scholastic record and a well-rounded personality. Financial need is not considered in the selection process.
Financial data: The stipend is $1,000.
Duration: 1 year; recipients may reapply if they are members of the Institute of Food Technologists (IFT).
Additional information: Funds for this scholarship are provided by Nutrinova, Inc. Correspondence and completed applications must be submitted to the department head of the educational institution the applicant is attending.
Number awarded: 1 each year.
Deadline: January of each year.

2384
OKLAHOMA CATTLEMEN'S RANGE ROUND-UP SCHOLARSHIP

Oklahoma Cattlemen's Association
Attn: Kami Krebs
P.O. Box 82395
Oklahoma City, OK 73148
Phone: (405) 235-4391   Fax: (405) 235-3608
Summary: To provide financial assistance to high school seniors in Oklahoma who are affiliated with the Oklahoma Cattlemen's Association.
Eligibility: Applicants must be high school seniors who are 1) the children or grandchildren of Oklahoma Cattlemen's Association members or 2) current members of the Oklahoma Junior Cattlemen's Association. Students must submit a completed application form, a list of the highlights of their high school leadership activities, a list of some of the awards they won during high school, a description of their career plans, and a short essay on the most critical issue facing cattlemen in the next 10 to 20 years.
Financial data: A stipend is awarded (exact amount not specified).
Duration: 1 year.
Deadline: April of each year.

2385
OKLAHOMA ENGINEERING FOUNDATION SCHOLARSHIP

Oklahoma Engineering Foundation, Inc.
Attn: Executive Director
201 N.E. 27th Street, Room 125
Oklahoma City, OK 73105-2789
Phone: (405) 528-1435   (800) 337-OSPE (within OK)
Fax: (405) 557-1820   E-mail: okspe@aol.com
Summary: To provide financial assistance to high school seniors in Oklahoma who are interested in majoring in engineering at selected colleges.
Eligibility: This program is open to high school seniors in Oklahoma who are U.S. citizens and interested in majoring in engineering at the following schools: Oklahoma State University, University of Oklahoma, University of Tulsa, Oklahoma Christian University, Oral Roberts University, Kansas State University, or Iowa State University. Since this scholarship is aimed at students who have great potential but slightly lower admissions factors, applicants may not have qualified for a National Merit or Oklahoma Regents Scholarship. They must have at least a 3.0 grade point average, but they must have scored between 23 and 32 on the ACT composite. Selection is based on grade point average, standardized test scores, extracurricular activities, awards, volunteer activities, employment, potential to complete an engineering major, and an interview.
Financial data: Stipends range from $500 to $1,000. Funds are paid directly to the recipient's school, in 2 equal installments; recipients must maintain a 3.0 grade point average to receive the second payment.
Duration: 1 year.
Number awarded: Approximately 11 each year.
Deadline: Pre-application forms must be submitted by December of each year. Completed applications are due the following January.

2386
OLD GUARD ORAL PRESENTATION COMPETITION

ASME International
Attn: Student Section
Three Park Avenue
New York, NY 10016-5990
Phone: (212) 591-7722   (800) THE-ASME
Fax: (212) 591-7674   E-mail: students@asme.org
Web Site: www.asme.org/cma/og/oralprescontest.html
Summary: To recognize and reward student members of ASME International (the professional society of mechanical engineers) who deliver outstanding oral presentations on engineering subjects.
Eligibility: This program is open to student members who make 15-minute oral presentations, followed by 5-minute question and answer sessions, on subjects related to mechanical engineering. Entrants must be dues-paid student members who have not received an engineering degree, have been selected by their student sections to participate, and have been certified by their regional office as a student member in good standing. Selection is based on content, organization, delivery, effectiveness, and discussion. Students first compete on the regional level, from which the winners advance to the national competition.
Financial data: At the regional level, the first-place winner receives $300 plus reimbursement of expenses to participate in the national competition, second place $150, third place $100, fourth place $50, and fifth place $25. At the national level, first prize is $2,000, second $1,500, third $1,000, and fourth $500.
Duration: The prizes are presented annually.
Additional information: This program was established in 1956, expanded in 1981 to include second and third prizes, and expanded in 1992 to include fourth prize. The "Old Guard" consists of ASME dues exempt members who are over the age of 65 and have retired.
Number awarded: Each year, there are 5 winners in each region and 4 in the national competition.

2387
OLEY AND GRACE KOHLMAN SCHOLARSHIP

Junior Colorado Cattlemen's Association
8833 Ralston Road
Arvada, CO 80002
Phone: (303) 431-6422   Fax: (303) 431-6446
E-mail: cocattlemens@uswest.net
Summary: To provide financial assistance to members of the Junior Colorado Cattlemen's Association (JCCA) who are majoring in agriculture at a college in the state.
Eligibility: This program is open to JCCA members who are attending a college or university in Colorado and majoring in a field that will impact the agriculture industry. Financial need is a factor in the selection process.
Financial data: A stipend is awarded (exact amount not specified).
Duration: 1 year.
Number awarded: 1 each year.

2388
OLIVE LYNN SALEMBIER SCHOLARSHIP

Society of Women Engineers
230 East Ohio Street, Suite 400
Chicago, IL 60611-3265
Phone: (312) 596-5223   Fax: (312) 644-8557
E-mail: hq@swe.org
Web Site: www.swe.org
Summary: To aid women who have been out of the engineering market a minimum of 2 years and are now interested in obtaining the credentials necessary to reenter the job market as an engineer.
Eligibility: Only women who have been out of the engineering job market for a minimum of 2 years and are going to return to school for an engineering degree may apply. Applicants may be either full-time or part-time undergraduate or graduate students. Selection is based on merit.
Financial data: The award is $2,000.
Duration: 1 year.
Additional information: This program was established in 1979.
Number awarded: 1 each year.
Deadline: May of each year.

2389
ONA-SMITH EDUCATION SCHOLARSHIP

Oregon Nurses Foundation
9600 S.W. Oak Street, Suite 550
Portland, OR 97223
Phone: (503) 293-0011   Fax: (503) 293-0013
Web Site: www.oregonrn.org
Summary: To provide financial assistance to students in Oregon who are working on an undergraduate or graduate degree in nursing.

Eligibility: Applicants must be accepted for or enrolled full time in a bachelor's or graduate program in nursing in Oregon. Personal interviews may be required. Selection is based on leadership abilities, career plans, and scholastic record. Financial need is not considered.

Financial data: The stipend is $1,000. Funds are paid directly to the recipient's school.

Duration: 1 year.

Additional information: R.N. recipients must be current members of the Oregon Nurses Association (ONA). Non-R.N. recipients of the undergraduate baccalaureate scholarship must, upon graduation, join ONA or the constituent nurses association in their state of residence.

Number awarded: 1 or more each year.

Deadline: March of each year.

2390
ONCOLOGY NURSING CERTIFICATION CORPORATION BACHELOR'S SCHOLARSHIPS

Oncology Nursing Society
Attn: ONS Foundation
501 Holiday Drive
Pittsburgh, PA 15220-2749
Phone: (412) 921-7373, ext. 231   Fax: (412) 921-6565
E-mail: foundation@ons.org
Web Site: www.ons.org

Summary: To provide financial assistance to nurses who are interested in pursuing a bachelor's degree in oncology nursing.

Eligibility: This program is open to registered nurses and licensed practical (vocational) nurses with a demonstrated interest in and commitment to oncology nursing. They must be currently enrolled in an undergraduate degree program at an NLN- or CCNE-accredited school of nursing. They may not have previously received a bachelor's scholarship from this sponsor. Applicants must submit an essay of 250 words or less on their role in caring for persons with cancer and a statement of their professional goals and their relationship to the advancement of onology nursing. Financial need is not considered in the selection process.

Financial data: The stipend is $2,000.

Duration: 1 year.

Additional information: This program is supported by the Oncology Nursing Certification Corporation. At the end of each year of scholarship participation, recipients must submit a summary describing their educational activities. Applications must be accompanied by a $5 fee.

Number awarded: 10 each year, including 1 for an LPN/LVN.

Deadline: January of each year.

2391
ORAL-B LABORATORIES DENTAL HYGIENE SCHOLARSHIPS

American Dental Hygienists' Association
Attn: Institute for Oral Health
444 North Michigan Avenue, Suite 3400
Chicago, IL 60611
Phone: (312) 440-8944   (800) 735-4916
Fax: (312) 440-8929   E-mail: institute@adha.net
Web Site: www.adha.org

Summary: To provide financial assistance to baccalaureate students in dental hygiene.

Eligibility: This program is open to 1) full-time students pursuing a baccalaureate degree in dental hygiene at a 4-year institution in the United States, and 2) dental hygienists who are pursuing a degree completion program as either full-time or part-time students. All applicants must be able to demonstrate financial need and an intent to encourage professional excellence and scholarship, quality research, and dental hygiene through public and private education. They must have completed at least 1 year of study with a minimum grade point average of 3.5 and be eligible for licensure in the current year.

Financial data: Awards are $1,000 or $1,500 per year.

Duration: 1 year.

Additional information: Funds for these scholarships are provided by Oral-B Laboratories.

Number awarded: 2 each year: 1 at $1,000 and 1 at $1,500.

Deadline: May of each year.

2392
OREGON FOUNDATION FOR BLACKTAIL DEER OUTDOOR AND WILDLIFE SCHOLARSHIP

Oregon Student Assistance Commission
Attn: Private Awards Grant Department
1500 Valley River Drive, Suite 100
Eugene, OR 97401-2146
Phone: (541) 687-7395   (800) 452-8807, ext. 7395
Fax: (541) 687-7419   E-mail: awardinfo@mercury.osac.state.or.us
Web Site: www.osac.state.or.us

Summary: To provide financial assistance for college to students in Oregon interested in studying fields related to wildlife management.

Eligibility: This program is open to graduates of Oregon high schools attending or planning to attend college in the state. Applicants must be interested in majoring in forestry, biology, wildlife science, wildlife management, or a related field. As part of the application process, they must submit a 250-word essay on "Challenges of Wildlife Management in the Coming 10 Years" and a copy of their previous year's hunting license.

Financial data: Scholarship amounts vary, depending upon the needs of the recipient.

Duration: 1 year.

Number awarded: Varies each year.

Deadline: February of each year.

2393
OREGON LEGION AUXILIARY DEPARTMENT NURSES SCHOLARSHIP

American Legion Auxiliary
Attn: Department of Oregon
30450 S.W. Parkway Avenue
P.O. Box 1730
Wilsonville, OR 97070-1730
Phone: (503) 682-3162   Fax: (503) 685-5008

Summary: To provide financial assistance for nursing education to the wives, widows, and children of Oregon veterans.

Eligibility: Eligible for these scholarships are the wives of veterans with disabilities, the widows of deceased veterans, and the sons and daughters of veterans who are Oregon residents. Applicants must have been accepted by an accredited hospital or university school of nursing in Oregon. Selection is based on ability, aptitude, character, determination, seriousness of purpose, and financial need.

Financial data: The stipend is $1,500.

Duration: 1 year; may be renewed.

Number awarded: 1 each year.

Deadline: May of each year.

2394
OREGON SHEEP GROWERS ASSOCIATION SCHOLARSHIP

Oregon Sheep Growers Association, Inc.
1270 Chemeketa Street, N.E.
Salem, OR 97301
Phone: (503) 364-5462   Fax: (503) 585-1921

Summary: To provide financial assistance to Oregon residents who are preparing for a career in the sheep industry.

Eligibility: Applicants must be Oregon residents, currently-enrolled in college (in any state), at the sophomore level or beyond (including graduate students), majoring in an agricultural science or veterinary medicine, and interested in a career in the sheep industry.

Financial data: Stipends range up to $1,000 per year. Funds are to be used to pay for tuition, books, or related fees. Checks are made payable jointly to the recipient and the recipient's institution.

Duration: 1 year.

Additional information: Recipients may attend school in any state.

Number awarded: Up to 2 each year.

Deadline: June of each year.

2395
ORTHOPAEDIC INDUSTRY SCHOLARSHIPS

National Association of Orthopaedic Nurses
Attn: NAON Foundation
East Holly Avenue, Box 56
Pitman, NJ 08071-0056
Phone: (856) 256-2310   Fax: (856) 589-7463
E-mail: naonfnd@.ajj.com
Web Site: naon.inurse.com
Summary: To provide financial assistance to members of the National Association of Orthopaedic Nurses (NAON) who are interested in continuing their education.
Eligibility: Members who have demonstrated their commitment, success, and potential for ongoing leadership in the practice of orthopedic nursing are candidates for this award. Applicants must submit a detailed letter outlining the proposed course of study, professional goals and objectives, relevance of the program to orthopedic nursing practice, and potential areas of contributions to the association. Current members of the executive board, staff, and foundation trustees are not eligible for this scholarship.
Financial data: The foundation determines the monetary award for the scholarship.
Duration: 1 year.
Additional information: Funding for these scholarships is provided by contributions from orthopedic industry firms, including Johnson & Johnson, DePuy, and Huntleigh Healthcare. Recipients must complete a research project or provide a manuscript acceptable for publication in 1 of the association's publications by the completion of their course of study.
Deadline: October of each year.

2396
OUTDOOR AND ENVIRONMENTAL LEADERSHIP SCHOLARSHIP

BACKPACKER
33 East Minor Street
Emmaus, PA 18098-0099
Phone: (610) 967-5171   Fax: (610) 967-8181
E-mail: scholarships@backpacker.com
Web Site: www.backpacker.com/scholarship
Summary: To provide financial assistance to college students who have displayed initiative in improving the outdoors and encouraging others to do the same.
Eligibility: This scholarship is available to students who have made an effort to bring others into the outdoors through a variety of leadership initiatives and/or for students who have actively participated in efforts to improve the environment and access to wilderness activities. Applicants must be enrolled full time in an undergraduate program at a 4-year college or university. They must have earned at least a 3.0 grade point average, be juniors or seniors in college, and submit 4 essays on 1) their outdoor and environmental work and volunteer experiences and accomplishments and how they qualify the applicant for this scholarship; 2) how their current outdoor experiences figure into their goals for the future; 3) how they would spend $10,000 on the outdoors if they were given that sum; and 4) the importance or role of outdoor leaders in encouraging others to experience wilderness. Financial need is not considered in the selection process.
Financial data: The stipend is $1,000.
Duration: The competition is held annually.
Additional information: This program began in 1998, as part of the magazine's 25th anniversary celebration.
Number awarded: 5 each year.
Deadline: October of each year.

2397
OUTDOOR WRITING AND JOURNALISM SCHOLARSHIP

Summary: To provide financial assistance to college students who have encouraged others to experience wilderness through their writing.
See Listing #1589.

2398
OUTSTANDING PULSED POWER STUDENT AWARD

Institute of Electrical and Electronics Engineers
Nuclear and Plasma Sciences Society
c/o Peter J. Turchi, Chair, Pulsed Power Committee
Los Alamos National Laboratory, P-22
MS D410: Hydrodynamics and X-Ray Physics
Los Alamos, NM 87545

Phone: (505) 665-0906   Fax: (505) 667-7684
E-mail: turchi@lanl.gov
Web Site: www.eece.unm.edu/ppst/ppst/index.htm
Summary: To recognize and reward outstanding student contributions to pulsed power engineering, science, and technology.
Eligibility: This program is open to full-time undergraduate and graduate students in pulsed power engineering or science. Nominees must be a student when nominated. Selection is based on quality of research contributions (40 points), quality of educational accomplishments (30 points), and quality and significance of publications and patents (20 points).
Financial data: The award consists of $1,000 and a certificate.
Duration: The award is presented biennially.
Additional information: This award was established in 1997.
Number awarded: 1 each odd-numbered year.

2399
PACIFIC PRINTING & IMAGING ASSOCIATION SCHOLARSHIPS

Summary: To provide funding to students who intend to enter the printing and imaging industry.
See Listing #1591.

2400
PACKAGING EDUCATION FORUM FINANCIAL AID PROGRAM

Packaging Education Forum
4350 North Fairfax Drive, Suite 600
Arlington, VA 22203-1632
Phone: (703) 243-5717   Fax: (703) 524-8691
E-mail: pef@pmmi.org
Web Site: www.packingingeducation.org/info/sections/guidelines.html
Summary: To provide financial assistance to college students who are interested in preparing for a career in packaging.
Eligibility: Eligible to apply for this support are students who are currently enrolled at 1 of the participating institutions as an incoming sophomore, junior, senior, or graduate student and are following a course of education that will prepare them for a career in packaging. Applicants should be able to demonstrate participation in student chapters of 1 or more professional organizations and should have above average potential to develop professionally in packaging. U.S. citizenship or permanent resident status is required.
Financial data: Stipends generally range from $500 to $1,000.
Duration: 1 year.
Additional information: The universities currently participating are Clemson University, Rochester Institute of Technology, Rutgers University, California Polytechnic State University at San Luis Obispo, Indiana State University, Michigan State University, University of Wisconsin at Stout, University of Missouri at Rolla, University of Massachusetts at Lowell, University of Florida, and San Jose State University. Sponsors of this program include Sealed Air, Packaging Machine Manufacturers Institute, the Institute of Packaging Professionals, and DuPont.
Number awarded: Approximately 35 each year.

2401
PACKARD FOUNDATION TRIBAL SCHOLARS PROGRAM

David and Lucile Packard Foundation
Attn: Program Associate
300 Second Street, Suite 200
Los Altos, CA 94022
Phone: (650) 917-7245   Fax: (650) 941-7320
E-mail: g.nauman@packfound.org   Web Site: www.packfound.org
Summary: To provide financial assistance for undergraduate education in the sciences to American Indian students who are graduating from 1 of the 29 tribal colleges in the United States.
Eligibility: This program is open to U.S. citizens who have received a 2-year degree (or an equivalent amount of college credits) from a tribal college with an overall grade point average of 3.0 or higher. Candidates must be planning to pursue a degree in the sciences at a 4-year college or university; they must be nominated by the tribal college they have been attending.
Financial data: The stipend is $10,000 per year. Funds are paid directly to the recipient's college or university to cover the costs of tuition and fees, room and board, books, research equipment and supplies, and research-related travel.
Duration: 2 years, provided the recipient makes reasonable progress in academic work.
Additional information: This program was established in 1996.

Number awarded: Up to 15 each year.
Deadline: Nominations must be submitted by November of each year.

2402
PAMELA BALZER CAREER MOBILITY SCHOLARSHIP

American Nephrology Nurses' Association
Attn: ANNA Foundation
East Holly Avenue, Box 56
Pitman, NJ 08071-0056
Phone: (856) 256-2320   (877) 527-0787
Fax: (856) 589-7463   E-mail: annafoundation@hotmail.com
Web Site: www.annanurse.org
Summary: To provide financial assistance to members of the American Nephrology Nurses' Association (ANNA) who are interested in pursuing a baccalaureate degree in nursing.
Eligibility: Applicants must be current association members, have been members for at least 2 years, be currently employed in nephrology nursing, and be accepted or enrolled in a baccalaureate degree program in nursing. In their application, they must indicate how the degree will apply to nephrology nursing and provide a time frame for completing their program.
Financial data: The stipend is $2,500.
Duration: 1 year.
Additional information: Funds for this program are supplied by Abbott Renal Care. Information is also available from Cynthia Frazier, Awards Chairperson, 7344 Pine Tree Lane, Fairfield, AL 35064, (205) 933-8101, ext. 6514, E-mail: cdf44@aol.com.
Number awarded: 1 each year.
Deadline: October of each year.

2403
PAPER AND BOARD DIVISION SCHOLARSHIPS

Technical Association of the Pulp and Paper Industry
P.O. Box 105113
Atlanta, GA 30348-5113
Phone: (770) 446-1400   (800) 332-8686
Fax: (770) 446-6947
Web Site: www.tappi.org
Summary: To provide financial assistance to student members of the Technical Association of the Pulp and Paper Industry (TAPPI) who are majoring in a scientific or technical discipline related to the manufacture of paper and paperboard.
Eligibility: This program is open to students who are members of the association, are attending college full time or participating full time in a cooperative work-study program recognized and supported by their college, are at least sophomores on the undergraduate level, are enrolled in an engineering or science program, and are able to demonstrate a significant interest in the paper industry. Selection is based on the candidates' seriousness of purpose in pursuing a course of study related to the science and technology of the paper industry and an intent to make a career in the industry. Financial need is not considered in the selection process.
Financial data: The stipends are $1,500 or $1,000.
Duration: 1 year.
Additional information: This program was established in 1990.
Number awarded: At least 5 each year: 1 at $1,500 and at least 4 at $1,000.
Deadline: January of each year.

2404
PARTNERSHIP IN NURSING EDUCATION PROGRAM

U.S. Army
Attn: ROTC Cadet Command
Fort Monroe, VA 23651-5238
Phone: (757) 727-4558   (800) USA-ROTC
E-mail: atccps@monroe.army.mil
Web Site: www-rotc.monroe.army.mil
Summary: To provide financial assistance to high school seniors or graduates who are willing to serve as Army nurses following completion of their bachelor's degree.
Eligibility: Applicants for the Army Reserve Officers' Training Corps (ROTC) program must 1) be U.S. citizens; 2) be at least 17 years of age by October of the year in which they are seeking a scholarship; 3) be no more than 27 years of age when they graduate from college after 4 years; 4) score at least 920 on the SAT or 19 on the ACT; 5) have a high school grade point average of 2.4 or higher; and 6)

meet medical and other regulatory requirements. This program is open to ROTC scholarship applicants who wish to pursue a nursing program at 1 of 68 designated partner colleges and universities and become Army nurses after graduation.
Financial data: This scholarship provides financial assistance toward college tuition and educational fees up to an annual amount of $16,000. In addition, a flat rate of $450 is provided for the purchase of textbooks, classroom supplies and equipment. Recipients are also awarded a stipend for up to 10 months of each year that is $250 per month during their freshman and sophomore years, $300 per month during their junior year, and $350 per month during their senior year.
Duration: 4 years, until completion of a baccalaureate degree. A limited number of 2-year and 3-year scholarship programs are also available to students who are already attending an accredited B.S.N. program on a campus affiliated with ROTC.
Additional information: This program was established in 1996 to ensure that ROTC cadets seeking nursing careers would be admitted to the upper-level division of a baccalaureate program. The 68 partnership nursing schools affiliated with Army ROTC have agreed to guarantee upper-level admission to students who maintain an established grade point average during their first 2 years. During the summer, participants have the opportunity to participate in the Nurse Summer Training Program, a paid 3- to 4-week clinical elective at an Army hospital in the United States, Germany, or Korea. Following completion of their baccalaureate degree, participants become commissioned officers in the Army Nurse Corps. Scholarship winners must serve in the military for 8 years. That service obligation may be fulfilled 1) by serving on active duty for 2 to 4 years followed by service in the Army National Guard (ARNG), the United States Army Reserve (USAR), or the Inactive Ready Reserve (IRR) for the remainder of the 8 years; or 2) by serving 8 years in an ARNG or USAR troop program unit that includes a 3- to 6-month active-duty period for initial training.
Number awarded: A limited number each year.
Deadline: November of each year.

2405
PAST NATIONAL PRESIDENT FRANCES BOOTH MEDICAL SCHOLARSHIP

Veterans of Foreign Wars of Maine
c/o Donna Gallant
3 Morning Street
Scarborough, ME 04074
Phone: (207) 883-0550
Summary: To provide financial assistance to children and grandchildren of members of the Veterans of Foreign Wars (VFW) and its Ladies Auxiliary in Maine who are studying a medical field in college.
Eligibility: This program is open to Maine residents who are the children, grandchildren, stepchildren, and foster children of current or immediate past year members of the VFW or its Ladies Auxiliary in Maine. Applicants must be enrolled at a 2-year or 4-year college, university, or vocational school and majoring in a field related to medicine.
Financial data: The stipend is $1,000 per year. Funds are paid to the school of the recipient's choice.
Duration: 1 year; may be renewed.
Number awarded: 1 or more each year.
Deadline: March of each year.

2406
PAST PRESIDENTS SCHOLARSHIP

Institute of Food Technologists
Attn: Scholarship Department
221 North LaSalle Street, Suite 300
Chicago, IL 60601-1291
Phone: (312) 782-8424   Fax: (312) 782-8348
E-mail: info@ift.org
Web Site: www.ift.org
Summary: To provide financial assistance to undergraduates interested in studying food science or food technology.
Eligibility: Applicants must be currently enrolled as sophomores or juniors in a food science or food technology program at an educational institution in the United States or Canada. They must have an outstanding scholastic record and a well-rounded personality. Financial need is not considered in the selection process.
Financial data: The stipend is $1,000.
Duration: 1 year; recipients may reapply if they are members of the Institute of Food Technologists.

Additional information: Correspondence and completed applications must be submitted to the department head of the educational institution the applicant is attending.

Number awarded: 1 each year.

Deadline: January of each year.

2407
PAUL H. ROBBINS SCHOLARSHIP

National Society of Professional Engineers
Attn: Education Services
1420 King Street
Alexandria, VA 22314-2794
Phone: (703) 684-2833   Fax: (703) 836-4875
E-mail: jiglesias@nspe.org
Web Site: www.nspe.org/scholarships/sc1-hs.asp

Summary: To provide financial assistance for college to high school seniors interested in preparing for a career in engineering.

Eligibility: This program is open to high school seniors planning to study engineering in a college program accredited by the Engineering Accreditation Commission of the Accreditation Board for Engineering and Technology (EAC-ABET). Applicants must have earned at least a 3.0 grade point average, 500 on the verbal SAT, and 600 on the math SAT (or 25 on the English ACT and 29 on the math ACT). They must submit an essay (up to 500 words) on their interest in engineering, their major area of study and area of specialization, and the occupation they propose to pursue after graduation. Selection is based on grade point average (20 points), the essay (20 points), extracurricular activities (including work experience and volunteer activities) (25 points), financial need (5 points), SAT/ACT scores (20 points), and the composite application (10 points). U.S. citizenship is required.

Financial data: The stipend is $1,000 per year; funds are paid directly to the institution.

Duration: 2 years.

Additional information: Recipients may attend any college or university, as long as the engineering curriculum is accredited by EAC-ABET.

Number awarded: 1 each year.

Deadline: November of each year.

2408
PAUL IRVIN MEMORIAL MAINTENANCE SCHOLARSHIP

Women in Aviation, International
3647 S.R. 503 South
West Alexandria, OH 45381
Phone: (937) 839-4647   Fax: (937) 839-4645
E-mail: wai@infinet.com
Web Site: www.wiai.org

Summary: To provide financial assistance to members of Women in Aviation, International who are attending college full time and majoring in aircraft maintenance or a related field.

Eligibility: This program is open to women who are members of the sponsoring organization, are attending college full time, have junior or senior status, have earned at least a 3.0 grade point average, and are either majoring in aircraft maintenance (A&P) or have an A&P and are working on a bachelor's degree in a related field. Interested applicants must submit an application form, 3 letters of recommendation, a 350-word essay, a resume, copies of all aviation and medical certificates, and the last 3 pages of their pilot logbook, if applicable. The descriptive essay must cover their aviation history and goals and how the scholarship will help them achieve those goals. Selection is based on achievements, attitude toward self and others, commitment to success, dedication to career, financial need, motivation, reliability, responsibility, and teamwork.

Financial data: The stipend is $1,000.

Duration: 1 year.

Additional information: Women in Aviation, International is a nonprofit professional organization dedicated to encouraging women to consider an aviation career, providing educational outreach activities, and networking resources to women active in the industry.

Number awarded: 1 each year.

Deadline: December of each year.

2409
PAUL SMITH SCHOLARSHIP AWARD

Technical Association of the Pulp and Paper Industry
P.O. Box 105113
Atlanta, GA 30348-5113
Phone: (770) 446-1400   (800) 332-8686
Fax: (770) 446-6947
Web Site: www.tappi.org

Summary: To provide financial assistance to undergraduate or graduate students who are interested in preparing for a career in the paper industry, with a focus on science and engineering as it relates to the pulp, paper, and allied industries.

Eligibility: This program is open to students who are attending college full time, are at least sophomores on the undergraduate level or are graduate students, have earned a grade point average of 2.5 or higher, and are enrolled in a program preparatory to a career in the pulp and paper industry. Applicants must include letters of recommendation from persons familiar with their character, interest in the pulp and paper industry, educational accomplishments, school activities, and leadership roles. Selection is based on the candidates' potential career and contributions in the pulp and paper industry. Financial need is not considered in the selection process.

Financial data: The stipend is $1,000.

Duration: 1 year; nonrenewable.

Additional information: This scholarship is provided by the Finishing and Converting Division of the Technical Association of the Pulp and Paper Industry (TAPPI).

Number awarded: 1 each year.

Deadline: January of each year.

2410
PAUL W. RODGERS SCHOLARSHIP

International Association for Great Lakes Research
Attn: Business Office
2205 Commonwealth Boulevard
Ann Arbor, MI 48105
Phone: (734) 665-5303   Fax: (734) 741-2055
E-mail: officeiaglr.org
Web Site: www.iaglr.org/as/rodgersapp.html

Summary: To provide financial assistance to college seniors and graduate students interested in pursuing a course of study related to the Great Lakes aquatic ecosystem health and management.

Eligibility: This program is open to any college senior, master's degree student, or doctoral student who wishes to prepare for a future in research, conservation, education, communication, management, or other knowledge-based activity pertaining to the Great Lakes. To apply, students must submit 1) official transcripts, 2) 2 letters of reference, 3) a letter of application that includes a summary of past and prevent involvement with Great Lakes concerns, a brief description of their proposed program or thesis research topic, and relevance of the proposed program of study to Great Lakes concerns; and 4) a statement explaining how further academic training and personal goals will help the student to fulfill their personal goals as they relate to the purpose of the scholarship. Selection is based on academic record, letters of support, involvement in activities related to Great Lakes issues, and the candidate's statement. Financial need is not considered.

Financial data: The stipend is $2,000.

Duration: 1 year; nonrenewable.

Additional information: Recipients are also given a 1-year membership in the sponsoring organization and a subscription to the *Journal of Great Lakes Research*. This program was established in 1999. Recipients may not keep the scholarship if they are awarded more than $5,000 from other scholarship sources (excluding graduate assistantships). They must submit a summary of their accomplishments relevant to Great Lakes issues upon completion of their program.

Number awarded: 1 each year.

Deadline: February of each year.

2411
PAUL W. RUCKES SCHOLARSHIP

American Foundation for the Blind
Attn: Scholarship Committee
11 Penn Plaza, Suite 300
New York, NY 10001
Phone: (212) 502-7661   (800) AFB-LINE
Fax: (212) 502-7771   TDD: (212) 502-7662
E-mail: afbinfo@afb.net

Web Site: www.afb.org/scholarships.asp

Summary: To provide financial assistance to visually impaired students who wish to pursue a graduate or undergraduate degree in engineering or computer, physical, or life sciences.

Eligibility: This program is open to visually impaired undergraduate or graduate students who are U.S. citizens pursuing a degree in engineering or the computer, physical, or life sciences. Legal blindness is not required. Applicants must submit a typewritten statement, up to 3 pages in length, describing educational and personal goals, work experience, extracurricular activities, and how scholarship funds will be used.

Financial data: The stipend is $2,500.

Duration: 1 year.

Number awarded: 1 each year.

Deadline: March of each year.

2412
PAYZER SCHOLARSHIP

EAA Aviation Foundation Inc.
Attn: Scholarship Office
EAA Aviation Center
3000 Poberezny Road
P.O. Box 3065
Oshkosh, WI 54903-3065
Phone: (920) 426-6884   (888) 322-3229
Fax: (920) 426-6865   E-mail: scholarships@eaa.org
Web Site: www.eaa.org/education/scholarships/index.html

Summary: To provide financial assistance to college students who are studying or planning to study an area that emphasizes technical information.

Eligibility: This program is open to students accepted or enrolled at an accredited college, university, or other postsecondary school with an emphasis on technical information. Applicants must be interested in majoring in (and pursuing a professional career in) engineering, mathematics, or the physical or biological sciences. Selection is based on academic record, participation in school and community activities, and career potential; financial need is not considered.

Financial data: The stipend is $5,000.

Duration: 1 year.

Additional information: There is a $5 application fee.

Number awarded: 1 each year.

Deadline: April of each year.

2413
PEF GRANTS

Pennsylvania Society of Professional Engineers
Attn: Pennsylvania Engineering Foundation
908 North Second Street
Harrisburg, PA 17102
Phone: (717) 236-1844   Fax: (717) 236-2046
E-mail: info@pspe.org
Web Site: www.pspe.org

Summary: To provide financial assistance to Pennsylvania high school seniors who are interested in studying engineering at a college or university in the state.

Eligibility: This program is open to graduating seniors at high schools in Pennsylvania. Applicants must be planning to enroll in an engineering program at an ABET-accredited college or university in the state. They must have at least a 3.6 grade point average and an SAT score of 1300. Interviews are included in the selection process.

Financial data: The stipend is $1,000.

Duration: 1 year; nonrenewable.

Additional information: Scholarships are awarded by 23 local chapters of the Pennsylvania Engineering Foundation (PEF) in the state. Applications are available from the foundation, but they must be submitted to the local chapter where the student lives.

Number awarded: Varies each year.

2414
PEI SCHOLARSHIP

National Society of Professional Engineers
Attn: Practice Division Manager
1420 King Street
Alexandria, VA 22314-2794
Phone: (703) 684-2884   Fax: (703) 836-4875
E-mail: egarcia@nspe.org   Web Site: www.nspe.org/scholarships/sc1-pei.asp

Summary: To provide financial assistance to engineering students sponsored by a member of the Professional Engineers in Industry (PEI) division of the National Society of Professional Engineers (NSPE).

Eligibility: This program is open to students who 1) have completed at least 2 semesters or 3 quarters of undergraduate engineering studies, or 2) are enrolled in graduate engineering study. Applicants must be sponsored by a PEI member. Their program must be accredited by the Accreditation Board for Engineering and Technology (ABET). Preference is given to the children, dependents, and relatives of NSPE members. Students attending a community or junior college must have applied as an undergraduate engineering student at an ABET-accredited program. As part of the application process, students must submit a 500-word essay discussing their interest in engineering, the specific field of engineering that is being pursued, and the occupation they propose to follow after graduation. Selection is based on grade point average (30 points), work experience (20 points), professional and technical society membership and activities (20 points), the essay (15 points), and activities and honors (15 points).

Financial data: The stipend is $2,500.

Duration: 1 year.

Additional information: Information is also available from Neal J. Illenberg, 35 Garden Lane, Rochester, NY 14626.

Number awarded: 1 or more each year.

Deadline: May of each year.

2415
PENNSYLVANIA LEAGUE FOR NURSING L.P.N. SCHOLARSHIP

Pennsylvania League for Nursing
Attn: Awards and Scholarship Committee
1770 East Lancaster Avenue, Suite 1B
Paoli, PA 19301-1575
Phone: (610) 640-5755   Fax: (610) 640-3863
E-mail: bcmanage1b@aol.com
Web Site: www.paleaguefornursing.org/awards

Summary: To provide financial assistance to students in Pennsylvania who are studying to become an L.P.N. at a school in the state.

Eligibility: This program is open to Pennsylvania residents who are currently enrolled (full or part time) in an accredited practical nursing program in the state. As part of the selection process, applicants must submit a short statement about their career goals in nursing; a list of their school, community, and professional activities; a list of honors and awards they have received; letters of recommendation; an official transcript; and a current resume.

Financial data: A stipend is awarded (exact amount not specified).

Duration: 1 year.

Number awarded: 1 each year.

Deadline: December of each year.

2416
PENNSYLVANIA LEAGUE FOR NURSING UNDERGRADUATE SCHOLARSHIP

Pennsylvania League for Nursing
Attn: Awards and Scholarship Committee
1770 East Lancaster Avenue, Suite 1B
Paoli, PA 19301-1575
Phone: (610) 640-5755   Fax: (610) 640-3863
E-mail: bcmanage1b@aol.com
Web Site: www.paleaguefornursing.org/awards

Summary: To provide financial assistance to students in Pennsylvania who are enrolled in an undergraduate nursing program at a school in the state.

Eligibility: This program is open to Pennsylvania residents who are currently enrolled (full or part time) in an accredited nursing program in the state, including a diploma, associate nursing degree, baccalaureate degree, or R.N./B.S.N. completion program. As part of the selection process, applicants must submit a short statement about their career goals in nursing; a list of their school, community, and professional activities; a list of honors and awards they have received; letters of recommendation; an official transcript; and a current resume.

Financial data: A stipend is awarded (exact amount not specified).

Duration: 1 year.

Number awarded: 1 each year.

Deadline: December of each year.

2417
PENNSYLVANIA RAINBOW NURSING SCHOLARSHIP

Pennsylvania Youth Foundation
Attn: Educational Endowment Fund
1244 Bainbridge Road
Elizabethtown, PA 17022-9423
Phone: (717) 367-1536   (800) 266-8424 (within PA)
E-mail: pyf@pagrandlodge.org
Web Site: www.pagrandlodge.org/pyf/scholar/index.html
Summary: To provide financial assistance for nursing school to members of Rainbow Girls in Pennsylvania.
Eligibility: This program is open to active Pennsylvania Rainbow Girls in good standing. Applicants must have completed at least 1 year in an accredited nursing school.
Financial data: The stipend depends on the availability of funds.
Duration: 1 year; may be renewed.
Additional information: Information is also available from Eva Gresko, RD #3, Box 102, Huntington, PA 16652-8703, (814) 658-3774.
Number awarded: Varies each year, depending on the availability of funds.
Deadline: Requests for applications must be submitted by January of each year. Completed applications are due by the end of February.

2418
PENNSYLVANIA RAINBOW SCHOLARSHIP

Summary: To provide financial assistance for college to members of Rainbow Girls in Pennsylvania.
See Listing #909.

2419
PETER K. NEW STUDENT PRIZE COMPETITION

Society for Applied Anthropology
P.O. Box 2436
Oklahoma City, OK 73101-2436
Phone: (405) 843-5113   Fax: (405) 843-8553
E-mail: info@sfaa.net
Web Site: www.sfaa.net/pknew/pknew.html
Summary: To recognize and reward the best student research papers in applied social, health, or behavioral sciences.
Eligibility: This competition is open to currently-enrolled undergraduate or graduate students. Applicants must not have already earned a doctoral degree (e.g., a person with an M.D. degree who is now registered as a student in a Ph.D. program is not eligible). Eligible students are invited to submit a manuscript that reports on research which, in large measure, has not been previously published. Research should be in the domain of health care or human services (broadly defined). The competition is limited to manuscripts that have a single author; multiple-authored papers are not eligible. The paper should be double spaced and must be less than 45 pages in length, including footnotes, tables, and appendices. Selection is based on originality, research design/method, clarity of analysis and presentation, and contribution to the social/behavioral sciences.
Financial data: The winner receives $1,000 plus a $350 travel allowance to partially offset the cost of transportation and lodging at the society's annual meeting.
Duration: The competition is held annually.
Additional information: The winning paper is published in the society's journal, *Human Organization.* Applicants who transmit their manuscripts by facsimile must pay a fee for duplication. Manuscripts may not be submitted electronically. The winner must attend the society's annual meeting to present the paper.
Number awarded: 1 each year.
Deadline: December of each year.

2420
PETROLEUM DIVISION STUDENT PAPER COMPETITION

ASME International
Attn: Petroleum Division
11757 Katy Freeway, Suite 865
Houston, TX 77079
Phone: (281) 493-3491   Fax: (281) 493-3493
E-mail: petroleum@asme.org   Web Site: www.asmepd.org
Summary: To recognize and reward student members of ASME (the professional organization of mechanical engineering) who prepare technical papers on the petroleum industry.

Eligibility: This program is open to student members of the society who are invited to submit technical papers on the petroleum industry, including drilling, completions, facilities, pipe lines, rigs, operations, materials, equipment manufacturing, plant design and operation, maintenance, environmental protection, and innovations. Applicants must be attending an ABET-accredited (or international equivalent) college or university and have completed the majority of the work for the paper before receiving their bachelor's degree.
Financial data: First prize includes a $1,000 cash award and a certificate. Second prize includes a $500 cash award and a certificate.
Duration: The competition is held annually.
Number awarded: 2 each year.
Deadline: August of each year.

2421
PHCC EDUCATIONAL FOUNDATION NEED-BASED SCHOLARSHIP

Plumbing-Heating-Cooling Contractors-National Association
Attn: PHCC Educational Foundation
180 South Washington Street
P.O. Box 6808
Falls Church, VA 22040
Phone: (703) 237-8100   (800) 533-7694
Fax: (703) 237-7442   E-mail: naphcc@naphcc.org
Web Site: www.naphcc.org
Summary: To provide financial assistance to undergraduate students interested in the plumbing, heating, and cooling industry.
Eligibility: This program is open to high school seniors and college freshmen who are planning to major in a field related to plumbing, heating, and cooling at a 4-year college or university or a 2-year community college, technical college, or trade school. Applicants must be planning to pursue a career in the plumbing, heating, and cooling industry. They must submit a letter of recommendation from a member with 2 years' good standing in the Plumbing-Heating-Cooling Contractors-National Association (PHCC); a copy of school transcripts; a letter of recommendation from a school principal, counselor, or dean; and a demonstration of financial need.
Financial data: The stipend is $2,500 per year.
Duration: 1 year.
Number awarded: 1 each year.
Deadline: April of each year.

2422
PHCC EDUCATIONAL FOUNDATION SCHOLARSHIP PROGRAM

Plumbing-Heating-Cooling Contractors-National Association
Attn: PHCC Educational Foundation
180 South Washington Street
P.O. Box 6808
Falls Church, VA 22040
Phone: (703) 237-8100   (800) 533-7694
Fax: (703) 237-7442   E-mail: naphcc@naphcc.org
Web Site: www.phccweb.org/foundation/schapp.cfm
Summary: To provide financial assistance to undergraduate students interested in the plumbing, heating, and cooling industry.
Eligibility: This program is open to high school seniors and college freshmen who are planning to major in a field related to plumbing, heating, and cooling at a 4-year college or university or a 2-year technical college, community college, or trade school. Applicants must be planning to pursue a career in the plumbing, heating, and cooling industry. They must be sponsored by a member with 2 years' good standing in the Plumbing-Heating-Cooling Contractors-National Association (PHCC). Selection is based on high school or college transcripts, extracurricular activities, experience in the industry, career goals, and reasons for applying.
Financial data: The stipend is $3,000 per year for students at a 4-year institution or $1,500 per year for students at a 2-year institution.
Duration: Up to 4 years for students at a 4-year college or university or 2 years for students at a 2-year technical college, community college, or trade school.
Number awarded: 5 each year: 3 to students at 4-year institutions and 2 to students at 2-year institutions.
Deadline: April of each year.

Scholarship Listings

2423
PHILIP D. REED UNDERGRADUATE AWARD IN ENVIRONMENTAL ENGINEERING

National Action Council for Minorities in Engineering
350 Fifth Avenue, Suite 2212
New York, NY 10118-2299
Phone: (212) 279-2626　　　　Fax: (212) 629-5178
E-mail: awalter@nacme.org　Web Site: www.nacme.org/fellowships.html
Summary: To provide financial assistance for education and work experience in environmental engineering to underrepresented minority undergraduates.
Eligibility: College sophomores who are African American, Latino, or American Indian are eligible to be nominated by their deans for this award if they are majoring in engineering. Candidates must have at least a 3.0 grade point average and a demonstrated interest in environmental engineering. U.S. citizenship or permanent resident status is required.
Financial data: The stipend is $5,000 per year.
Duration: 2 years (the recipients' junior and senior years).
Additional information: Funding for this program, which began in 1996, is provided by the Philip D. Reed Foundation. The program may also provide internships, mentors, and support for undergraduate research.
Number awarded: 1 or 2 each year.

2424
PHILLIPS BUSINESS INFORMATION SCHOLARSHIP

Summary: To provide financial assistance to students interested in majoring in satellite business applications in college.
See Listing #1596.

2425
PHOEBE PEMBER MEMORIAL SCHOLARSHIP

United Daughters of the Confederacy
Attn: Education Director
328 North Boulevard
Richmond, VA 23220-4057
Phone: (804) 355-1636　　　　Fax: (804) 353-1396
E-mail: hqudc@aol.com　　　　Web Site: www.hqudc.org
Summary: To provide financial assistance for nursing education to lineal descendants of Confederate veterans.
Eligibility: Eligible to apply for these scholarships are lineal descendants of worthy Confederates or collateral descendants who are members of the Children of the Confederacy or the United Daughters of the Confederacy. Applicants must intend to study nursing and must submit a family financial report and certified proof of the Confederate record of 1 ancestor, with the company and regiment in which he served. They must have at least a 3.0 grade point average in high school.
Financial data: The amount of this scholarship depends on the availability of funds.
Duration: 1 year; may be renewed for up to 3 additional years.
Additional information: Information is also available from Dorothy S. Broom, Second Vice President General, 595 Lominack Road, Prosperity, SC 29127, (803) 364-3003. Members of the same family may not hold scholarships simultaneously, and only 1 application per family will be accepted within any 1 year. All requests for applications must include a self-addressed stamped envelope.
Number awarded: 1 each year.
Deadline: February of each year.

2426
PHYSICIAN ASSISTANT FOUNDATION SCHOLARSHIPS

American Academy of Physician Assistants
Attn: Physician Assistant Foundation
950 North Washington Street
Alexandria, VA 22314-1552
Phone: (703) 519-5686　　　　Fax: (703) 684-1924
E-mail: aapa@aapa.org
Web Site: www.aapa.org
Summary: To provide financial assistance to student members of the American Academy of Physician Assistants (AAPA).
Eligibility: This program is open to AAPA student members attending a physician assistant program accredited by the Commission on Accreditation of Allied Health Education Programs. Applicants must have entered the professional phase of the program. Selection is based on financial need, academic record, extracurricular activities, and future goals.
Financial data: Stipends are $5,000, $3,000, or $2,000.

Duration: 1 year; nonrenewable.
Additional information: This program was established in 1989.
Number awarded: Varies each year; recently, 57 of these scholarships were awarded.
Deadline: January of each year.

2427
PIERRE H. GUILLEMETTE SCHOLARSHIP AWARD

Rhode Island Society of Professional Land Surveyors
Attn: Scholarship Committee
P.O. Box 544
East Greenwich, RI 02818
E-mail: tdrury@rispls.org
Web Site: www.rispls.org
Summary: To provide financial assistance to Rhode Island residents studying surveying.
Eligibility: This program is open to residents of Rhode Island who are enrolled in a course of study leading to a certificate program or degree in land surveying offered by a qualified institution of higher learning. Selection is based on a statement outlining qualifications and future career goals, educational transcripts, and a resume.
Financial data: The amount of the award depends on the availability of funds.
Duration: 1 year.
Number awarded: 1 each year.
Deadline: October of each year.

2428
PIF/LIFELINE SCHOLARSHIP PROGRAM

Pilot International Foundation
244 College Street
P.O. Box 4844
Macon, GA 31208-4844
Phone: (912) 743-7403　　　　Fax: (912) 743-2173
E-mail: belinda@pilotclubs.org　Web Site: www.pilotinternational.org
Summary: To provide financial assistance to adult students who are interested in working with people with disabilities or brain disorders.
Eligibility: This program is open to adult students who are reentering the job market, preparing for a second career, or improving their professional skills for an established career. They must be preparing for or already involved in careers working with people who have disabilities/brain disorders. They should have at least a 3.5 grade point average. All applicants must be sponsored by a Pilot Club in their home town or in the city in which their college or university is located. Local Pilot Clubs are allowed to sponsor only 1 applicant per program.
Financial data: The stipend is at least $1,000.
Duration: 1 year.
Additional information: Funding for this program is provided by Lifeline Systems, Inc.
Number awarded: 1 each year.
Deadline: February of each year.

2429
PILOT INTERNATIONAL FOUNDATION SCHOLARSHIP PROGRAM

Pilot International Foundation
244 College Street
P.O. Box 4844
Macon, GA 31208-4844
Phone: (912) 743-7403　　　　Fax: (912) 743-2173
E-mail: belinda@pilotclubs.org
Web Site: www.pilotinternational.org
Summary: To provide financial assistance to undergraduate students who are interested in working with people who have disabilities or brain disorders.
Eligibility: This program is open to undergraduate students who are preparing for careers working with people who have disabilities/brain disorders or training those who will be working with them. They should have at least a 3.5 grade point average. All applicants must be sponsored by a Pilot Club in their home town or in the city in which their college or university is located. Local Pilot Clubs are allowed to sponsor only 1 applicant per program.
Financial data: The stipend is at least $1,000.
Duration: 1 year.
Number awarded: 1 each year.
Deadline: February of each year.

2430
PIONEERS OF FLIGHT SCHOLARSHIP PROGRAM

National Air Transportation Foundation
Attn: Manager, Education and Training
4226 King Street
Alexandria, VA 22302
Phone: (703) 845-9000, ext. 125   (800) 808-6282
Fax: (703) 845-8176   E-mail: info@nata-online.org
Web Site: www.nata-online.org
Summary: To provide financial assistance for college to students planning careers in general aviation.
Eligibility: Applicants must be college students intending to pursue full-time study at an accredited 4-year college or university as juniors or seniors. Students must demonstrate an interest in a career in general aviation (not the major commercial airlines) and have a grade point average of 3.0 or higher. Selection is based on academic record, a letter of recommendation, and a 250-word essay on the applicant's educational and career goals as related to general aviation.
Financial data: The stipend is $1,000.
Duration: 1 year; may be renewed 1 additional year if the recipient maintains a 3.0 grade point average and full-time enrollment.
Additional information: This program, established in 1989, is administered by the University Aviation Association (UAA), which selects the semifinalists. The National Air Transportation Foundation selects the final winners. Further information is available from the UAA, c/o John Dennison, Central Missouri State University, TR Gaines 210, Warrensburg, MO 64093, (660) 543-4975, E-mail: Dennison@cmsu1.cmsu.edu. A $5 application fee is required.
Number awarded: 2 or 3 each year.
Deadline: December of each year.

2431
PLANE AND PILOT MAGAZINE/GARMIN SCHOLARSHIP

Aircraft Electronics Association
Attn: Educational Foundation
4217 South Hocker Drive
Independence, MO 64055-4723
Phone: (816) 373-6565   Fax: (816) 478-3100
E-mail: info@aea.net
Web Site: www.aea.net
Summary: To provide financial assistance for college to students who are interested in preparing for a career in aviation.
Eligibility: This program is open to high school seniors, vocational or technical school students, and college students who are attending (or planning to attend) an accredited vocational-technical school in an avionics or aircraft repair program.
Financial data: The stipend is $2,000.
Duration: 1 year.
Number awarded: 1 each year.
Deadline: February of each year.

2432
PLANNING & THE BLACK COMMUNITY DIVISION SCHOLARSHIP

American Planning Association
Attn: Member Services Department
122 South Michigan Avenue, Suite 1600
Chicago, IL 60603-6107
Phone: (312) 431-9100   Fax: (312) 431-9985
E-mail: Fellowships@planning.org
Web Site: www.planning.org
Summary: To provide financial assistance to underrepresented minority undergraduate students interested in majoring in planning or a related field.
Eligibility: This program is open to African American, Hispanic American, and Native American undergraduate students in their second, third, or fourth year of study. Applicants must be majoring in planning or a related field (e.g., community development, environmental sciences, public administration, transportation, or urban studies). U.S. citizenship is required.
Financial data: The stipend is $2,500.
Duration: 1 year.
Number awarded: 1 each year.
Deadline: May of each year.

2433
POST SCHOLARSHIP

American Association of Airport Executives-Northeast Chapter
c/o Richard J. Williams, Executive Secretary
P.O. Box 8
West Milford, NJ 07480-0008
Web Site: www.necaaae.org
Summary: To provide financial assistance to upper-division students majoring in aviation management.
Eligibility: This program is open to juniors and seniors in colleges and universities who are majoring in aviation management. Preference is given to those with a permanent residence in the northeast region. Student preparing for a career as commercial pilots are not eligible. Transcripts, letters of recommendation, and proof of enrollment must accompany the completed application form.
Financial data: The stipend is $1,000.
Duration: 1 year.
Number awarded: 4 each year.
Deadline: February of each year.

2434
POWER ENGINEERING SOCIETY STUDENT PRIZE PAPER AWARD IN HONOR OF T. BURKE HAYES

Institute of Electrical and Electronics Engineers
Attn: Power Engineering Society
445 Hoes Lane
P.O. Box 1331
Piscataway, NJ 08855-1331
Phone: (732) 562-3864   Fax: (732) 562-3881
E-mail: pes@ieee.org
Web Site: www.ieee.org/organizations/society/power
Summary: To recognize and reward outstanding papers on power engineering by student members of the Institute of Electrical and Electronics Engineers (IEEE).
Eligibility: Individual students or teams (up to 3 in number) working in the United States or its territories or any other geographic area in which the institute has a section, branch, or chapter are eligible to submit a paper of approximately 5,000 words on the electrical power industry.
Eligibility: This program is open to regular students in a program leading to a bachelor's or master's degree in electrical engineering, or the equivalent if the student is from an institution outside the United States. Applicants must submit a paper of approximately 5,000 words on a topic related to the electric power industry. Faculty sponsorship is encouraged but papers co-authored by faculty are not eligible. Along with the paper, students must submit a supporting letter from their faculty sponsor, a short autobiographical sketch, and a permanent address and telephone number.
Financial data: The award is $1,500, a plaque, and a travel subsidy up to $1,000 for the recipient to attend the winter meeting of the Power Engineering Society.
Duration: The competition is held annually.
Additional information: This award is funded by CH2M Hill. Information is also available from Dr. Howard A. Smolleck, New Mexico State University, Klipsch School of Electrical and Computer Engineering, Box 30001/Department 3-0, Las Cruces, NM 88003-8001, (505) 646-3834, Fax: (505) 646-1435, E-mail: hsmollec@nmsu.edu.
Number awarded: 1 each year.
Deadline: September of each year.

2435
POWER SYSTEMS PROFESSIONAL SCHOLARSHIP

National Strength and Conditioning Association
Attn: Foundation
1955 North Union Boulevard
P.O. Box 9908
Colorado Springs, CO 80932-0908
Phone: (719) 632-6722   (800) 815-6826
Fax: (719) 632-6367   E-mail: nsca@nsca-lift.org
Web Site: www.nsca-lift.org/foundation/prof.shtml
Summary: To provide financial assistance for postsecondary education in strength training and conditioning to members of the National Strength and Conditioning Association (NSCA).
Eligibility: Candidates must have been members of the association for at least 1 year prior to the application deadline. They must be undergraduate or graduate students working as a strength and conditioning coach (student assistant,

volunteer, or graduate assistant) in their school's athletic department, and they must be nominated by the head strength coach at their school. In addition to transcripts and a resume, nominees must submit an essay of no more than 500 words explaining their career goals and objectives. Selection is based on scholarship (25 points), strength and conditioning experience (15 points), the essay (15 points), recommendations (5 points), honors and awards (10 points), community involvement (10 points), and NSCA involvement (20 points).

Financial data: Awards are $1,000, to be applied toward tuition.

Additional information: The NSCA is a nonprofit organization of strength and conditioning professionals, including coaches, athletic trainers, physical therapists, educators, researchers, and physicians. This program is funded in part by Power Systems, Inc.

Number awarded: 1 each year.

Deadline: April of each year.

2436
PPQ WILLIAM F. HELMS STUDENT SCHOLARSHIP PROGRAM

Department of Agriculture
Animal and Plant Health Inspection Service
Attn: Marketing and Regulatory Programs Business Services
4700 River Road, Unit 21
Riverdale, MD 20737-1230
Phone: (800) 762-2738
Web Site: www.aphis.usda.gov/ppq

Summary: To provide financial assistance and work experience to college students majoring in the agricultural or biological sciences.

Eligibility: This program is open to college sophomores and juniors who are attending an accredited college or university, are majoring in an agricultural or biological science (such as biology, plant pathology, entomology, virology, bacteriology, mycology, and ecology), are interested in a career in plant protection and quarantine, and are U.S. citizens. To apply, interested students must submit a completed application form, a personal letter describing their career goals and interest in plant protection and quarantine), transcripts, and 3 letters of recommendation.

Financial data: The stipend is $5,000 per year.

Duration: 1 year; may be renewed if the recipient maintains at least a 2.5 grade point average.

Additional information: The U.S. Department of Agriculture's (USDA) Animal and Plant Health Inspection Service (APHIS) is the agency responsible for protecting America's agriculture base; Plant Protection and Quarantine (PPQ) is the program within APHIS that deals with plant health issues. In addition to financial assistance, the Helms Scholarship Program also offers tutoring assistance, mentoring, paid work experience during vacation periods, career exploration, and possible employment upon graduation.

Number awarded: Several each year.

Deadline: February of each year.

2437
PRAXAIR INTERNATIONAL SCHOLARSHIP

American Welding Society
Attn: AWS Foundation, Inc.
550 N.W. LeJeune Road
Miami, FL 33126
Phone: (305) 443-9353, ext. 461   (800) 443-9353, ext. 461
Fax: (305) 443-7559   E-mail: vpinsky@aws.org
Web Site: www.aws.org/foundation/praxair.html

Summary: To provide financial assistance to college students majoring in welding engineering.

Eligibility: This program is open to undergraduate students who are pursuing at least a 4-year bachelor's degree in welding engineering or welding engineering technology (although preference is given to welding engineering students). Applicants must be full-time students with an overall grade point average of 2.5 or higher. They must be U.S. or Canadian citizens attending an academic institution within the United States or Canada. Selection is based on demonstrated leadership abilities in clubs and organizations, extracurricular and academic activities, and community involvement; financial need is not required.

Financial data: The stipend is $2,500.

Duration: 1 year; recipients may reapply.

Additional information: This program is supported by Praxair, Inc.

Number awarded: 1 each year.

Deadline: January of each year.

2438
PRE-VETERINARY STUDENT SCHOLARSHIP

Albuquerque Veterinary Association, Inc.
Attn: Mary H. Hume, D.V.M.
3601 Eubank N.E.
Albuquerque, NM 87111

Summary: To provide financial assistance to students in New Mexico who are interested in preparing for a career in veterinary science.

Eligibility: This program is open to residents of New Mexico who are currently enrolled in college, in a pre-veterinary program. Selection is based on academic achievement, letters of recommendation, and professional activities. Financial need is not considered in the selection process.

Financial data: A stipend is awarded (exact amount not specified).

Duration: 1 year.

Number awarded: 1 or more each year.

Deadline: April of each year.

2439
PRESSURE VESSEL AND PIPING DIVISION STUDENT PAPER COMPETITION

ASME International
Attn: Pressure Vessel and Piping Division
Three Park Avenue
New York, NY 10016-5990
Phone: (212) 591-7722   (800) THE-ASME
Fax: (212) 591-7674   E-mail: infocentral@asme.org
Web Site: www.asme.org

Summary: To recognize and reward outstanding student papers on pressure vessels and piping.

Eligibility: This competition is open to senior undergraduate and graduate students in an engineering or scientific curriculum. Applicants submit previously unpublished papers that present new knowledge or experience in a field related to pressure vessels and piping. The paper must be technically correct and should be of interest to a reasonable number of people working in the field. It may be theoretical or may present the results of laboratory studies, and it may state or analyze a problem. The paper may also be a review-type paper, but it must be of significant value to the technical field. Applicants first submit abstracts; based on those abstracts, finalists are invited to present papers at the annual Pressure Vessels and Piping Conference, where the winning paper is selected.

Financial data: Each finalist receives $500 and a certificate. The author of the winning paper receives an additional $500.

Duration: The competition is held annually.

Additional information: Further information is also available from William E. Short, II, Pressure Systems Engineering Inc., 1201A Kirkwood Highway, Wilmington, DE 19805, (302) 683-0490, Fax: (302) 683-0493, E-mail: ShortWE@aol.com.

Number awarded: 10 finalists are selected each year. Of those, 1 is chosen as the winner.

Deadline: Abstracts must be submitted by the end of September of each year. Full papers are due in mid-October.

2440
PRO PUBS CORPORATE AVIATION SCHOLARSHIP

Women in Aviation, International
3647 S.R. 503 South
West Alexandria, OH 45381
Phone: (937) 839-4647   Fax: (937) 839-4645
E-mail: wai@infinet.com   Web Site: www.wiai.org

Summary: To provide financial assistance to members of Women in Aviation, International who are interested in studying corporate aviation in college.

Eligibility: This program is open to women who are members of the sponsoring organization and graduating high school seniors, high school graduates, or current college students. Applicants must be interested in pursuing a career in the following areas of corporate or business aviation: piloting, dispatching, corporate aviation department management, or FBO management. They must have a grade point average of 2.0 or higher and be able to demonstrate financial need. Selection is based on the applicant's ability to set and achieve goals, past achievements, impressions and relationships to others important in their lives and education, and their qualities of personal integrity, responsibility, reliability, dedication, and motivation.

Financial data: The stipend is $1,000.

Duration: 1 year.

Additional information: Women in Aviation, International is a nonprofit professional organization dedicated to encouraging women to consider an aviation career, providing educational outreach activities, and networking resources to women active in the industry. This program is sponsored by Professional Publications Services, Inc.
Number awarded: 1 each year.
Deadline: December of each year.

2441
PROCTER & GAMBLE ORAL CARE-HDA FOUNDATION SCHOLARSHIPS

Hispanic Dental Association
Attn: HDA Foundation
188 West Randolph Street, Suite 1811
Chicago, IL 60601-3001
Phone: (312) 577-4013   (800) 852-7921
Fax: (312) 577-0052   E-mail: hdassoc@aol.com
Web Site: www.hdassoc.org/scholarship.html
Summary: To provide financial assistance to Hispanic students interested in pursuing a career in a dental profession.
Eligibility: This program is open to Hispanics who have been accepted into an accredited dental, dental hygiene, dental assisting, or dental technician program. Selection is based on scholastic achievement, community service, leadership skill, and commitment to improving health in the Hispanic community.
Financial data: Stipends are $1,000 or $500.
Duration: 1 year.
Additional information: This program is sponsored by Procter & Gamble Company.
Number awarded: Numerous scholarships are awarded each year.

2442
PROFESSIONAL LAND SURVEYORS OF OREGON SCHOLARSHIP

Oregon Student Assistance Commission
Attn: Private Awards Grant Department
1500 Valley River Drive, Suite 100
Eugene, OR 97401-2146
Phone: (541) 687-7395   (800) 452-8807, ext. 7395
Fax: (541) 687-7419   E-mail: awardinfo@mercury.osac.state.or.us
Web Site: www.osac.state.or.us
Summary: To provide financial assistance to students in Oregon interested in a career in land surveying.
Eligibility: This program is open to students at colleges and universities in Oregon. Applicants must be either 1) students enrolled as sophomores or above in a program leading to a career in land surveying, or 2) community college students planning to transfer to eligible 4-year institutions. Applicants from 4-year schools must intend to take the Fundamentals of Land Surveying (FLS) examination. As part of the application process, all applicants must include a brief statement of their educational and career goals related to land surveying.
Financial data: Scholarship amounts vary, depending upon the needs of the recipient.
Duration: 1 year.
Number awarded: Varies each year.
Deadline: February of each year.

2443
PSSC LEGACY FUND SCHOLARSHIP

Summary: To provide financial assistance to students interested in majoring in international satellite and/or distance education applications in college.
See Listing #1603.

2444
QUALITY ASSURANCE DIVISION SCHOLARSHIPS

Institute of Food Technologists
Attn: Scholarship Department
221 North LaSalle Street, Suite 300
Chicago, IL 60601-1291
Phone: (312) 782-8424   Fax: (312) 782-8348
E-mail: info@ift.org   Web Site: www.ift.org
Summary: To provide financial assistance to undergraduates interested in studying food science or food technology.

Eligibility: Applicants must be currently enrolled as sophomores or juniors in a food science or food technology program at an educational institution in the United States or Canada; they must have an outstanding scholastic record and a well-rounded personality. Preference is given to students who are taking or have taken at least 1 course in quality assurance and who demonstrate a definite interest in the quality assurance area. Financial need is not considered in the selection process.
Financial data: The stipend is $2,000.
Duration: 1 year; recipients may reapply if they are members of the Institute of Food Technologists (IFT).
Additional information: These scholarships are designated as the Abe Mittler Memorial Scholarship and the Louis J. Bianco Memorial Scholarship. Correspondence and completed applications must be submitted to the department head of the educational institution the applicant is attending.
Number awarded: 2 each year.
Deadline: January of each year.

2445
R. FLAKE SHAW SCHOLARSHIP PROGRAM

North Carolina Farm Bureau
5301 Glenwood Avenue
P.O. Box 27766
Raleigh, NC 27611
Phone: (919) 782-1705   Fax: (919) 783-3593
E-mail: ncfbfed@ncfb.com   Web Site: www.ncfb.com
Summary: To provide financial assistance to North Carolina high school seniors interested in studying agriculture or home economics in college.
Eligibility: This program is open to seniors at high schools in North Carolina who are interested in pursuing a career in agriculture, home economics, or an agriculturally-related field. Applicants must demonstrate satisfactory grades, good character, leadership potential, and financial need. They must obtain an application from their county Farm Bureau office, which conducts an initial screening and submits 1 application per county to the state office. Preference is given to North Carolina Farm Bureau members.
Financial data: The stipend is $2,000 per year.
Duration: 4 years, provided the recipient maintains a GPA of 2.0 or higher.
Number awarded: 6 each year.

2446
RACING SCHOLARSHIP PROGRAM

American Quarter Horse Association
Attn: Director, Racing Department
1600 Quarter Horse Drive
P.O. Box 200
Amarillo, TX 79168
Phone: (806) 376-4888   E-mail: aqhamail@aqha.org
Web Site: www.aqha.org
Summary: To provide financial assistance to students with a background in the racing industry.
Eligibility: This program is open to older students returning to school after working in the racing industry. Preference is given to applicants majoring in equine science, racetrack management, pre-veterinary, or other courses of study directly related to the racing industry. Selection is based on the most recent cumulative grade point average, financial need, academic and extracurricular honors and awards, and letters of recommendation.
Financial data: The maximum stipend is $2,500 per year.
Duration: Up to 4 years.
Number awarded: Varies each year.
Deadline: July of each year.

2447
RADIO CLUB OF AMERICA SCHOLARSHIPS

Foundation for Amateur Radio, Inc.
P.O. Box 831
Riverdale, MD 20738
E-mail: turnbull@erols.com
Web Site: www.amateurradio-far.org
Summary: To provide funding to licensed radio amateurs who are interested in studying electronic engineering or technology in college.
Eligibility: This program is open to students who have a General Class license and are enrolled or have been accepted for enrollment at a community college, college, or university. They must intend to study electronic engineering or technology and

earn an associate or bachelor's degree. Only U.S. citizens may apply.
Financial data: The stipend is $1,000.
Duration: 1 year.
Additional information: Recipients must attend an accredited school (university, college, or technical institute) on a full-time basis.
Number awarded: 5 each year.
Deadline: May of each year.

2448
RAIL TRANSPORTATION DIVISION UNDERGRADUATE SCHOLARSHIP PROGRAM

ASME International
Attn: Rail Transportation Division
Three Park Avenue
New York, NY 10016-5990
Phone: (212) 591-7797   (800) THE-ASME
Fax: (212) 591-7671   E-mail: manese@asme.org
Web Site: www.asme.org
Summary: To provide financial assistance to undergraduate students who intend to enter the railway industry.
Eligibility: This program is open to undergraduate students in mechanical engineering who are interested in a career in the railway industry and have a family connection to the industry. Applicants must submit 1) a statement of intent to pursue mechanical engineering in the railway industry as a career; 2) statement of perception of the importance of rail transportation in the overall field of transporting freight and passengers; 3) information on experiences in the railroad realm (i.e., work, model railroading, photography); 4) abstract of any papers written related to the railroad industry; 5) list of courses proposed for the upcoming term; 6) transcript of previous college years; and 7) letter of recommendation from a faculty advisor or department head. They must plan to attend a college or university in North America (including Alaska, Canada, Hawaii, Mexico, and Puerto Rico). Financial need is not considered.
Financial data: The award is $2,000 per year.
Duration: 1 year.
Additional information: Further information is also available from Grant H. Arrasmith, Manager of Division Affairs, 4012 S.E. 19th Avenue, Apartment C-203, Cape Coral, FL 33904-8063, (941) 945-0466.
Number awarded: 1 or more each year.
Deadline: September of each year.

2449
RALPH A. KLUCKEN SCHOLARSHIP

Technical Association of the Pulp and Paper Industry
P.O. Box 105113
Atlanta, GA 30348-5113
Phone: (770) 446-1400   (800) 332-8686
Fax: (770) 446-6947   Web Site: www.tappi.org
Summary: To provide financial assistance to selected high school seniors and college students who are interested in preparing for a career in the pulp and paper industry, with a focus on the use and application of polymers in paper, foil, and plastic converting.
Eligibility: This program is open to high school seniors and college students (freshmen, sophomores, or juniors) who are or will be attending college full time, have a grade point average of 2.5 or higher, can demonstrate a history of part-time and summer employment, and are able to demonstrate a significant interest in polymers, lamination, and coatings as they relate to the pulp and paper industries. Selection is based on the candidates' potential career and contributions in the pulp and paper industry. Financial need is not considered in the selection process.
Financial data: The stipend is $1,000.
Duration: 1 year.
Additional information: This program, established in 1987, is sponsored by the Polymers, Laminations and Coatings Division of the Technical Association of the Pulp and Paper Industry (TAPPI). A student may apply for the scholarship each year, but the award will not be given to the same person twice consecutively.
Number awarded: 1 each year.
Deadline: January of each year.

2450
RAYMOND DAVIS SCHOLARSHIP

Summary: To provide financial assistance for students interested in continuing their studies in photographic or imaging science or technology.
See Listing #1610.

2451
RAYMOND H. FULLER, P.E., MEMORIAL SCHOLARSHIPS

Ohio Society of Professional Engineers
Attn: Engineers Foundation of Ohio
4795 Evanswood Drive, Suite 201
Columbus, OH 43229-7216
Phone: (614) 846-1144   (800) 654-9481
Fax: (614) 846-1131   E-mail: ospe@iwaynet.net
Web Site: www.ohioengineer.com/programs/Scholarships.htm
Summary: To provide financial assistance to high school seniors in Ohio who are interested in majoring in engineering in college.
Eligibility: This program is open to high school seniors in Ohio who will be attending a college or university in the state that is approved by the Accreditation Board of Engineering and Technology (ABET) and who plan to major in engineering. Applicants must have a GPA of 3.0 or higher, be U.S. citizens, and have SAT scores of at least 600 in mathematics and 500 in verbal or ACT scores of at least 29 in mathematics and 25 in English. Along with their application, they must submit a 350-word essay on their interest in engineering, including why they became interested in the field, what specialty interests them most, and why they want to become a practicing engineer. Financial need is also considered in the selection process.
Financial data: The stipend is $1,000 per year.
Duration: 1 year; nonrenewable.
Number awarded: 2 each year.
Deadline: December of each year.

2452
REBECCA FISK SCHOLARSHIP

American Dental Hygienists' Association
Attn: Institute for Oral Health
444 North Michigan Avenue, Suite 3400
Chicago, IL 60611
Phone: (312) 440-8944   (800) 735-4916
Fax: (312) 440-8929   E-mail: institute@adha.net
Web Site: www.adha.org
Summary: To provide financial assistance to students preparing for careers in dental hygiene.
Eligibility: Applicants must have earned at least a 3.0 grade point average, be able to demonstrate financial need, and have completed a minimum of 1 year in a dental hygiene curriculum. They must be enrolled full time in a certificate/associate degree program leading to licensure in the year of the award.
Financial data: The amount of the award depends on the need of the recipient, to a maximum of $1,000.
Duration: 1 year.
Number awarded: 1 each year.
Deadline: May of each year.

2453
REDI-TAG CORPORATION SCHOLARSHIP

American Health Information Management Association
Attn: Foundation of Research and Education
233 North Michigan Avenue, Suite 2150
Chicago, IL 60601-5519
Phone: (312) 233-1168   Fax: (312) 233-1090
E-mail: fore@ahima.org
Web Site: www.ahima.org/fore/programs.html
Summary: To provide financial assistance to members of the American Health Information Management Association (AHIMA) who are single parents interested in pursuing an undergraduate degree in health information administration or technology.
Eligibility: This program is open to AHIMA members who are single parents enrolled in a health information administration or health information technology program accredited by the Commission on Accreditation of Allied Health Education Programs. Applicants must be pursuing a degree on at least a half-time basis and have a grade point average of 3.0 or higher. U.S. citizenship is required. Selection is based on grade point average and academic achievement, volunteer and work experience, commitment to the health information management profession, suitability to the health information management profession, quality and suitability of references provided, and clarity of application.
Financial data: The stipend ranges from $1,000 to $5,000.
Duration: 1 year; nonrenewable.

Additional information: Funding for this program is provided by the Redi-Tag Corporation.

Number awarded: 1 each year.

Deadline: May of each year.

2454
REGION IV BENNY BOOTLE SCHOLARSHIP

American Society of Heating, Refrigerating and Air-Conditioning Engineers, Inc.
Attn: Scholarship Administrator
1791 Tullie Circle, N.E.
Atlanta, GA 30329-2305

Phone: (404) 636-8400   Fax: (404) 321-5478
E-mail: benedict@ashrae.org   Web Site: www.ashrae.org

Summary: To provide financial assistance to engineering and engineering technology students in designated states who are interested in heating, ventilating, air conditioning, and refrigeration (HVAC&R).

Eligibility: This program is open to undergraduate engineering and engineering technology students enrolled in a school in Georgia, North Carolina, or South Carolina that is recognized as accredited by the American Society of Heating, Refrigerating and Air-Conditioning Engineers (ASHRAE). Applicants must be pursuing a course of study that traditionally has been preparatory for the profession of HVAC&R. They must have a grade point average of at least 3.0 and must be full-time students with at least 1 full year of undergraduate study remaining. Selection is based on potential service to the HVAC&R profession, financial need, leadership ability, recommendations from instructors, and character.

Financial data: The stipend is $3,000 per year.

Duration: 1 year.

Number awarded: 1 each year.

Deadline: November of each year.

2455
REGION VIII SCHOLARSHIP

American Society of Heating, Refrigerating and Air-Conditioning Engineers, Inc.
Attn: Scholarship Administrator
1791 Tullie Circle, N.E.
Atlanta, GA 30329-2305

Phone: (404) 636-8400   Fax: (404) 321-5478
E-mail: benedict@ashrae.org   Web Site: www.ashrae.org

Summary: To provide financial assistance to engineering and engineering technology students in designated states who are interested in heating, ventilating, air conditioning, and refrigeration (HVAC&R).

Eligibility: This program is open to undergraduate engineering and engineering technology students enrolled in a school in Arkansas, Louisiana, Mexico, Oklahoma, or Texas that is recognized as accredited by the American Society of Heating, Refrigerating and Air-Conditioning Engineers (ASHRAE). Applicants must be pursuing a course of study that traditionally has been preparatory for the profession of HVAC&R. They must have a grade point average of at least 3.0 and must be full-time students with at least 1 full year of undergraduate study remaining. Selection is based on potential service to the HVAC&R profession, financial need, leadership ability, recommendations from instructors, and character.

Financial data: The stipend is $3,000 per year.

Duration: 1 year.

Number awarded: 1 each year.

Deadline: November of each year.

2456
REUBEN TRANE SCHOLARSHIPS

American Society of Heating, Refrigerating and Air-Conditioning Engineers, Inc.
Attn: Scholarship Administrator
1791 Tullie Circle, N.E.
Atlanta, GA 30329-2305

Phone: (404) 636-8400   Fax: (404) 321-5478
E-mail: benedict@ashrae.org   Web Site: www.ashrae.org

Summary: To provide financial assistance to engineering and engineering technology students interested in heating, ventilating, air conditioning, and refrigeration (HVAC&R).

Eligibility: This program is open to undergraduate engineering and engineering technology students enrolled in a school recognized as accredited by the American Society of Heating, Refrigerating and Air-Conditioning Engineers (ASHRAE). Applicants must be pursuing a course of study that traditionally has been preparatory for the profession of HVAC&R. They must have a grade point

average of at least 3.0 and must be full-time students with at least 2 full years of undergraduate study remaining. Selection is based on potential service to the HVAC&R profession, financial need, leadership ability, recommendations from instructors, and character.

Financial data: The stipend is $5,000 per year.

Duration: 2 years, provided the recipient maintains full-time status and satisfactory academic standing.

Number awarded: 4 each year.

Deadline: November of each year.

2457
RHODE ISLAND OCCUPATIONAL THERAPY SCHOLARSHIP

American Occupational Therapy Foundation
Attn: Scholarship Coordinator
4720 Montgomery Lane
P.O. Box 31220
Bethesda, MD 20824-1220

Phone: (301) 652-2682   Fax: (301) 656-3620
Phone: TDD: (800) 377-8555   E-mail: aotf@aotf.org
Web Site: www.aotf.org

Summary: To provide financial assistance to residents of Rhode Island who are working on an associate or baccalaureate degree in occupational therapy.

Eligibility: This program is open to Rhode Island residents who are enrolled in an accredited occupational therapy educational program in any state at the associate degree or baccalaureate degree level. Applicants must demonstrate a need for financial assistance and have a sustained record of outstanding scholastic performance. As part of the application process, they must submit transcripts, 2 personal references, and a statement from their curriculum director.

Financial data: The stipend is $1,000.

Duration: 1 year.

Additional information: Application forms are available at no cost at the association's web site; a $5 fee is charged for printed copies sent from the association's headquarters.

Number awarded: 1 each year.

Deadline: January of each year.

2458
RICHARD A. HERBERT MEMORIAL UNDERGRADUATE SCHOLARSHIP

American Water Resources Association
Attn: Scholarship Coordinator
4 West Federal Street
P.O. Box 1626
Middleburg, VA 20118-1626

Phone: (540) 687-8390   Fax: (540) 687-8395
E-mail: info@awra.org
Web Site: www.awra.org/student/herbert.html

Summary: To provide financial assistance to undergraduate students enrolled in a program related to water resources.

Eligibility: This program is open to full-time undergraduate students enrolled in a program related to water resources. Applicants must submit a 2-page summary of their academic interests and achievements, extracurricular activities, and career goals. In addition to that statement, selection is based on cumulative grade point average, relevance of the student's curriculum to water resources, and leadership in extracurricular activities related to water resources.

Financial data: The stipend is $1,000.

Duration: 1 year.

Additional information: This program was established in 1980.

Number awarded: 1 each year.

Deadline: April of each year.

2459
RICHARD DANIEL MEMORIAL SCHOLARSHIP

Illinois Trappers Association
c/o Paul Kelley
412 North Broadway
Box 75
Hudson, IL 61748

Phone: (309) 726-1443
Web Site: home.gallatinriver.net/~willemspd/RichardDaniel.htm

Summary: To provide financial assistance for college to Illinois residents interested in majoring in fields related to natural resources.

Eligibility: This program is open to Illinois residents who are outdoorsmen: fishermen, hunters, trappers, and conservationists. Applicants must be attending or planning to attend a college or university. They must submit a transcript of all high school and college grades, a list of their leadership and community service activities, 2 letters of recommendation, and a personal letter stating their reasons for seeking the scholarship.

Financial data: A stipend is paid (exact amount not specified).

Duration: 1 year.

Number awarded: 1 or more each year.

Deadline: May of each year.

2460
RICHARD E. BARRETT SCHOLARSHIP

Bedding Plants Foundation, Inc.
Attn: Scholarship Program
P.O. Box 280
East Lansing, MI 48826-0280
Phone: (517) 333-4617   Fax: (517) 333-4494
E-mail: bpfi@aol.com   Web Site: www.bpfi.org

Summary: To provide financial assistance to undergraduate and graduate students in horticulture.

Eligibility: This program is open to undergraduate students at a 4-year college or university and to graduate students. Applicants must be horticulture majors who are interested in pursuing a career in research and/or education. They must be U.S. or Canadian citizens or permanent residents with a grade point average of 3.0 or higher. Selection is based on academic record, recommendations, career goals, extracurricular activities, and financial need.

Financial data: The stipend ranges from $500 to $2,000 per year.

Duration: 1 year.

Number awarded: 1 each year.

Deadline: April of each year.

2461
RICHARD E. MERWIN STUDENT SCHOLARSHIP

IEEE Computer Society
Attn: Student Scholarships
1730 Massachusetts Avenue, N.W.
Washington, DC 20036-1992
Phone: (202) 371-0101   Fax: (202) 728-9614
E-mail: hqofc@computer.org
Web Site: www.computer.org/students/schlrshp.htm

Summary: To recognize and reward students who are active leaders in the IEEE Computer Society student branch chapters.

Eligibility: Juniors, seniors, and graduate students in electrical engineering, computer engineering, computer science, or a well-defined computer-related field of engineering (e.g., biomedical computer engineering, design automation) are eligible to apply if they are full-time students and active members of the society's student branch chapter at their institution. Their minimum overall grade point average should be 2.5 for all undergraduate course work. Selection is based on involvement in chapter activities (40 percent), academic achievement (30 percent), other extracurricular activities in college (10 percent), and a letter of evaluation by the branch chapter advisor (20 percent).

Financial data: The stipend is $3,000, paid in 3 equal installments (August, December, and the next April).

Duration: 1 academic year.

Additional information: This program is named in honor of a past president of the society. A brief statement outlining accomplishments must be submitted by each recipient at the end of the academic year.

Number awarded: Up to 4 each year.

Deadline: May of each year.

2462
RICHARD F. HEANEY MEMORIAL SCHOLARSHIP

National Beverage Packaging Association
200 Dangerfield Road
Alexandria, VA 22314
Phone: (703) 684-1080   (800) 331-8816
Fax: (703) 548-6563   E-mail: info@processfood.com

Summary: To provide financial assistance to undergraduate and graduate students working on a degree in packaging.

Eligibility: Eligible to apply for these awards are currently-enrolled undergraduate (2-year or 4-year programs) and graduate students who are U.S. or Canadian citizens and are working on a degree in packaging. Selection is based on academic record, financial need, extracurricular activities, and a statement on why the applicant deserves the scholarship.

Financial data: Stipends are either $2,000 (for bachelor's and graduate degree students) or $1,000 (for 2-year college students).

Duration: 1 year.

Number awarded: Several each year.

2463
RICHARD L. DAVIS MANAGERS SCHOLARSHIP

American College of Medical Practice Executives
Attn: Scholarship Program
104 Inverness Terrace East
Englewood, CO 80112-5306
Phone: (303) 643-9573   Fax: (303) 643-4427
E-mail: acmpe@mgma.com
Web Site: www.mgma.com/acmpe

Summary: To provide financial assistance to individuals currently employed in medical group management who wish to pursue professional development through undergraduate or graduate education.

Eligibility: This program is open to medical group management professionals who want to pursue an undergraduate or graduate degree. Applications must include a letter describing career goals and objectives; a resume; 3 reference letters commenting on the individual's performance, character, potential to succeed, and need for scholarship support; and academic transcripts.

Financial data: Stipends up to $1,500 are available. Funds for undergraduate or graduate study are paid directly to the recipient's college.

Duration: 1 year.

Number awarded: 1 each year.

Deadline: May of each year.

2464
RICHARD L. DAVIS NATIONAL SCHOLARSHIP

American College of Medical Practice Executives
Attn: Scholarship Program
104 Inverness Terrace East
Englewood, CO 80112-5306
Phone: (303) 643-9573   Fax: (303) 643-4427
E-mail: acmpe@mgma.com
Web Site: www.mgma.com/acmpe

Summary: To provide financial assistance to undergraduate or graduate students who are interested in preparing for a career in medical group management.

Eligibility: Any undergraduate or graduate student pursuing a full-time course of study that leads to a degree in medical group management is eligible. Applications must include a letter describing career goals and objectives related to medical practice management; a resume; 3 reference letters commenting on the individual's performance, character, potential to succeed, and need for scholarship support; and academic transcripts for undergraduate or graduate work completed to date.

Financial data: The stipend is $1,500. The money is paid directly to the recipient's college.

Duration: 1 year.

Number awarded: 1 each year.

Deadline: May of each year.

2465
ROBERT B. OLIVER ASNT SCHOLARSHIP

American Society for Nondestructive Testing, Inc.
Attn: Executive Assistant
1711 Arlingate Lane
P.O. Box 28518
Columbus, OH 43228-0518
Phone: (614) 274-6003   (800) 222-2768
Fax: (614) 274-6899   E-mail: sthomas@asnt.org
Web Site: www.asnt.org

Summary: To recognize and reward outstanding undergraduate student papers in the field of nondestructive testing.

Eligibility: This program is open to undergraduate students who are enrolled in course work related to nondestructive testing. The award is offered to students submitting the best original manuscript (up to 5,000 words) on the topic. The manuscript should develop an original concept and may be based on practical experience, laboratory work, or library research. Papers may be classroom assignments in courses outside the area of nondestructive testing, such as an English class. To apply, students must be currently enrolled in school and should submit 4 copies of their paper, their curriculum, a transcript of grades, and a letter from a school official verifying the student's enrollment. Selection is based on creativity (10 points), content (50 points), format and readability (25 points), and the student's hands-on involvement in the project (15 points).

Financial data: The award is $2,500.

Duration: The award is presented annually.

Additional information: Because the award may be made after the completion of studies, there is no requirement that the recipient use the funds for school expenses. Winning manuscripts may be published in the society's journal, *Materials Evaluation.*

Number awarded: Up to 3 each year.

Deadline: February of each year.

2466
ROBERT BRADLEY DISTINGUISHED CIVIL RIGHTS LEADERSHIP AWARD

American Association of State Highway and Transportation Officials
c/o Delano R. Rackard
1511 Mail Service Center
Raleigh, NC 27699-1511
Phone: (919) 733-2300   (800) 522-0453
Fax: (919) 733-8649   E-mail: drackard@dot.state.nc.us

Summary: To recognize and reward students majoring in transportation who write outstanding essays on civil rights.

Eligibility: This program is open to students enrolled in a college, university, or technical school pursuing a career in the transportation industry. Applicants must submit an essay, up to 150 words, on the theme, "Civil Rights: Mission Possible." They must be in good academic standing and have demonstrated leadership through significant contributions and participation in school, civic, and/or community activities. Along with the essay, they must submit an official transcript, 2 recommendations from college faculty members or community leaders, a list of awards and honors received, and information on their organizational memberships and offices held.

Financial data: The award is a $1,000 scholarship.

Duration: The award is presented annually.

Number awarded: 1 each year.

Deadline: January of each year.

2467
ROBERT E. ALTENHOFEN MEMORIAL SCHOLARSHIP

American Society for Photogrammetry and Remote Sensing
Attn: ASPRS Awards Program
5410 Grosvenor Lane, Suite 210
Bethesda, MD 20814-2160
Phone: (301) 493-0290, ext. 101   Fax: (301) 493-0208
E-mail: scholarships@asprs.org
Web Site: www.asprs.org

Summary: To provide financial assistance for undergraduate or graduate education to members of the American Society for Photogrammetry and Remote Sensing (ASPRS).

Eligibility: This program is open to both undergraduate and graduate students enrolled in accredited colleges or universities in the United States or elsewhere. Applicants must be either a student member or active member of the society. Selection is based on academic record, letters of recommendation, samples of the applicant's papers or research reports, and a 2-page statement about the applicant's plans for continuing studies in theoretical photogrammetry.

Financial data: The award is $2,000 and a certificate.

Duration: The award is presented annually.

Additional information: This award is named for a past president of the ASPRS. It is administered by the International Geographic Information Foundation with funds provided by the estate of his widow.

Deadline: November of each year.

2468
ROBERT E. FOLMSBEE, P.E. MEMORIAL GRANT

Michigan Society of Professional Engineers
Attn: Scholarship Coordinator
215 North Walnut Street
P.O. Box 15276
Lansing, MI 48901-5276
Phone: (517) 487-9388   Fax: (517) 487-0635
E-mail: mspe@voyager.net
Web Site: www.voyager.net/mspe

Summary: To provide financial assistance to undergraduate students in Michigan who are members of the Michigan Society of Professional Engineers and majoring in engineering in college.

Eligibility: This program is open to student members of the society who are U.S. citizens and residents of Michigan. Applicants must be attending an ABET-accredited engineering program at a Michigan college or university and have earned at least a 3.0 grade point average. They must submit an essay (up to 500 words) that discusses their interest in engineering, the specific field of engineering that is being pursued, and the occupation they propose to follow after graduation. Selection is based on the essay, transcripts, 2 letters of recommendation, leadership, and interest in the engineering profession through involvement in school and/or outside activities. Financial need is not considered. Preference is given to construction engineering students interested in general fields of construction engineering.

Financial data: The stipend is $1,500.

Duration: 1 year.

Additional information: Information is also available from Roger Lamer, Scholarship Selection Committee Chair, (616) 247-2974, Fax: (616) 247-2997, E-mail: rlamer@steelcase.com.

Number awarded: 1 each year.

Deadline: March of each year.

2469
ROBERT F. SAMMATARO PVP DIVISION MEMORIAL SCHOLARSHIP

ASME International
Attn: Education Department
Three Park Avenue
New York, NY 10016-5990
Phone: (212) 591-8131   (800) THE-ASME
Fax: (212) 591-7143   E-mail: oluwanifiset@asme.org
Web Site: www.asme.org/educate/aid/scholar.htm

Summary: To provide financial assistance to undergraduate students who are members of the American Society of Mechanical Engineers (ASME).

Eligibility: This program is open to student members in good standing who are enrolled in an ABET-accredited mechanical engineering baccalaureate, mechanical engineering technology, or related program. Interested students should submit an application form, a nomination from the applicant's department head, a recommendation from a faculty member, and an official transcript. Only 1 nomination may be submitted per department. Applicants must demonstrate a special interest in pressure vessels and piping. Selection is based on scholastic ability and potential contribution to the mechanical engineering profession.

Financial data: The stipend is $1,000.

Duration: 1 year.

Additional information: This program was established in 2001. Requests for applications must be accompanied by a self-addressed stamped envelope.

Number awarded: 1 each year.

Deadline: March of each year.

2470
ROBERT G. PORTER SCHOLARS PROGRAM FOR UNIVERSITY STUDENTS

American Federation of Teachers
Attn: Scholars Program
555 New Jersey Avenue, N.W.
Washington, DC 20001-2079
Phone: (202) 879-4400   (800) 238-1133, ext. 4481
E-mail: porterscholars@aft.org
Web Site: www.aft.org/scholarships

Summary: To provide financial assistance to children of members of the American Federation of Teachers (AFT) who wish to pursue postsecondary education at a 4-year college or university.

Eligibility: Applicants must be the dependent of an AFT member. They must be graduating high school seniors planning to attend a 4-year college or university to prepare for a career in labor, education, health care, or government service. Selection is based on educational background, future education plans, school-related activities, community activities, honors and awards, work experience, 2 letters of recommendation, and a 350-word essay on "The Influence of the AFT in My Life."

Financial data: The stipend is $2,000 per year.

Duration: 4 years.

Number awarded: 4 each year.

Deadline: March of each year.

2471
ROBERT KIMMERLY MEMORIAL SCHOLARSHIP

Aircraft Electronics Association
Attn: President
4217 South Hocker Drive
Independence, MO 64055-4723
Phone: (816) 373-6565   Fax: (816) 478-3100
E-mail: info@aea.net
Web Site: www.aea.net

Summary: To provide financial assistance to students preparing for a career in aviation.

Eligibility: This program is open to individuals who hold at least a private pilot certificate. They must be interested in attending a technical school or college and majoring in avionics.

Financial data: The stipend is $1,000.

Duration: 1 year.

Number awarded: 1 each year.

Deadline: February of each year.

2472
ROBERT LEWIS BAKER SCHOLARSHIP

Summary: To provide financial assistance to Maryland residents who are interested in studying ornamental horticulture or landscape design on the undergraduate or graduate school level.

See Listing #1620.

2473
ROBERT M. LAWRENCE, MD EDUCATION RECOGNITION AWARD

American Respiratory Care Foundation
Attn: Administrative Coordinator
11030 Ables Lane
Dallas, TX 75229-4593
Phone: (972) 243-2272   Fax: (972) 484-2720
E-mail: info@aarc.org
Web Site: www.aarc.org/awards

Summary: To provide financial assistance to third- or fourth-year college students interested in becoming respiratory therapists.

Eligibility: College students who have completed at least 2 years in an accredited respiratory care bachelor's degree program are eligible, if they have earned at least a 3.0 grade point average, are U.S. citizens or applicants for U.S. citizenship, and have potential for an outstanding career in the profession of respiratory care. Candidates must submit an original referenced paper on an aspect of respiratory care and a paper of at least 1,200 words describing how the award will assist them in reaching their objective of a baccalaureate degree and their ultimate goal of leadership in health care. Selection is based on academic performance.

Financial data: The stipend is $2,500. The award also provides airfare, 1 night's lodging, and registration for the international congress of the association.

Duration: 1 year.

Additional information: This program is sponsored by the National Board for Respiratory Care (NBRC) and its wholly owned subsidiary, Applied Measurement Professionals, Inc. (AMP).

Number awarded: 1 each year.

Deadline: May of each year.

2474
ROBERTA PIERCE SCOFIELD BACHELOR'S SCHOLARSHIPS

Oncology Nursing Society
Attn: ONS Foundation
501 Holiday Drive
Pittsburgh, PA 15220-2749
Phone: (412) 921-7373, ext. 231   Fax: (412) 921-6565
E-mail: foundation@ons.org   Web Site: www.ons.org

Summary: To provide financial assistance to registered nurses who are interested in pursuing a bachelor's degree in oncology nursing.

Eligibility: This program is open to registered nurses with a demonstrated interest in and commitment to oncology nursing. Applicants must be currently enrolled in an undergraduate degree program at an NLN- or CCNE-accredited school of nursing. They may not have previously received a bachelor's scholarship from this sponsor. Applicants must submit an essay of 250 words or less on their role in caring for persons with cancer and a statement of their professional goals and their relationship to the advancement of onology nursing. Financial need is not considered in the selection process.

Financial data: The stipend is $2,000.

Duration: 1 year.

Additional information: This program is supported by the Oncology Nursing Certification Corporation and named in honor of its first president. At the end of each year of scholarship participation, recipients must submit a summary describing their educational activities. Applications must be accompanied by a $5 fee.

Number awarded: 3 each year.

Deadline: January of each year.

2475
ROC I SCHOLARSHIP

Region I ASSE
c/o John G. Spicher
2442 N.W. Market Street, Suite 227
Seattle, WA 98107
Phone: (206) 829-2000   Fax: (206) 829-2900
E-mail: jspicher@qvlinc.com   Web Site: roc-1asse.org/scholars.htm

Summary: To provide financial assistance to residents of designated western states who are interested in majoring in a safety or health program.

Eligibility: This program is open to residents of Alaska, California, Hawaii, Oregon, and Washington. Applicants must be high school seniors or current full-time college students enrolled or planning to enroll in an academic program related to safety. They must submit a resume, transcript, letter of recommendation from either their high school counselor or college department chair, and a 300-word letter indicating their career objectives in safety and an explanation of how the scholarship will help them achieve those goals. Other supplemental information may include participation in the student section and/or chapter leadership activities of the American Society of Safety Engineers, campus extracurricular activities (especially those that are safety related), and community or personal activities and accomplishments related to safety.

Financial data: The stipend is $2,500.

Number awarded: 1 each year.

Deadline: May of each year.

2476
ROCKEFELLER STATE WILDLIFE SCHOLARSHIP

Louisiana Office of Student Financial Assistance
1885 Wooddale Boulevard
P.O. Box 91202
Baton Rouge, LA 70821-9202
Phone: (225) 922-3258   (800) 259-5626, ext. 1012
Fax: (225) 922-1089   E-mail: custserv@osfa.state.la.us
Web Site: www.osfa.state.la.us

Summary: To offer competitive scholarships to high school seniors, college undergraduates, and graduate students in Louisiana who are interested in majoring in forestry, wildlife, or marine science.

Eligibility: This program is open to residents of Louisiana who are U.S. citizens or eligible noncitizens, are not in default on an educational loan, have applied for state student aid, are or will enroll as a full-time student in a course of study leading to an undergraduate or graduate degree in forestry, wildlife, or marine science from a Louisiana public college or university, and have earned at least a 2.5 grade point average in high school or college (if appropriate). This is a merit-based award; financial need is not considered.

Financial data: The award is $1,000 per year.
Duration: Up to 5 years of undergraduate and 2 years of graduate study.
Additional information: The recipient agrees to complete a degree in 1 of the 3 eligible fields at a Louisiana public college or university offering these degrees or repay all scholarship funds received plus interest.
Number awarded: Varies; generally, 60 students (30 new and 30 continuing) receive awards each year.
Deadline: July of each year.

2477
ROCKWELL CORPORATION SCHOLARSHIPS

Society of Women Engineers
230 East Ohio Street, Suite 400
Chicago, IL 60611-3265
Phone: (312) 596-5223   Fax: (312) 644-8557
E-mail: hq@swe.org
Web Site: www.swe.org
Summary: To provide financial assistance to undergraduate women majoring in engineering, especially those underrepresented in the field.
Eligibility: Applicants must be women majoring in engineering and entering their junior year in college at an ABET-accredited or SWE-approved college or university. Applicants must have a grade point average of 3.5 or higher and have demonstrated leadership ability. Preference is given to members of groups underrepresented in the field. Selection is based on merit.
Financial data: The stipend is $3,000.
Duration: 1 year.
Additional information: This program was established in 1991.
Number awarded: 2 each year.
Deadline: January of each year.

2478
ROCKY MOUNTAIN CHAPTER SCHOLARSHIPS

Summary: To provide financial assistance to students attending college in designated Rocky Mountain states who are interested in majoring in satellite-related disciplines.
See Listing #1621.

2479
ROCKY MOUNTAIN COAL MINING INSTITUTE SCHOLARSHIPS

Rocky Mountain Coal Mining Institute
Attn: Executive Director
8057 South Yukon Way
Littleton, CO 80128-5510
Phone: (303) 948-3300   Fax: (303) 948-1132
E-mail: RMCMI@qwest.net
Summary: To recognize and reward outstanding college students preparing for a career in the mining industry.
Eligibility: Eligible to be nominated for this program are juniors or seniors in college who are attending school full time, are U.S. citizens, and are residents or attending school in 1 of the following states: Arizona, Colorado, Montana, New Mexico, North Dakota, Texas, Utah, or Wyoming. Nominees must be pursuing a degree in engineering (e.g., civil, electrical, environmental, geological, mechanical, metallurgical, mining) or in a mining-related field (e.g., geology, mineral processing, metallurgy). Preference is given to nominees who are particularly interested in western coal. Interviews are required.
Financial data: A $2,000 tuition credit is awarded. Funds are to be used during the junior and (if renewed) senior year.
Duration: 1 year; renewable, if the recipient continues in school as a full-time student.
Number awarded: Varies; generally, 8 or more each year (1 from each of the participating states).
Deadline: January of each year.

2480
ROCKY MOUNTAIN SECTION COLLEGE SCHOLARSHIP

Society of Women Engineers-Rocky Mountain Section
Attn: Scholarship Committee Chair
P.O. Box 260692
Lakewood, CO 80226-0692
Phone: (303) 893-0822
Summary: To provide financial assistance to women who are majoring in engineering at colleges and universities in Colorado and Wyoming.
Eligibility: This program is open to women who are enrolled as an undergraduate or graduate engineering student in an ABET-accredited engineering or computer science program in Colorado or Wyoming. Applicants must have completed at least 3 semesters or 4 quarters of study. They must include with their application an essay on why they have chosen an engineering major, what they will accomplish or how they believe they will make a difference as an engineer, and who or what influenced them to study engineering. Selection is based on merit; optional financial information may be used as a determining factor only in the case of a tie. Reentry students are encouraged to apply.
Financial data: Stipends depend on the availability of funds.
Duration: 1 year.
Additional information: Information is also available from Barbara Kontogiannis, 8646 South Cresthill Lane, Highlands Ranch, CO 80126, (303) 971-5213, E-mail; barbekon@alumni.stanford.org.
Number awarded: Varies each year, depending on the availability of funds.
Deadline: March of each year.

2481
ROCKY MOUNTAIN SECTION ENTERING FRESHMAN SCHOLARSHIP

Society of Women Engineers-Rocky Mountain Section
Attn: Scholarship Committee Chair
P.O. Box 260692
Lakewood, CO 80226-0692
Phone: (303) 893-0822
Summary: To provide financial assistance to women high school seniors in Colorado or Wyoming who are interested in majoring in engineering in college.
Eligibility: Women who are high school seniors in Colorado and Wyoming may apply for this program if they are in the top 25 percent of their graduating class and are interested in majoring in engineering or computer science in college. Selection is based on academic record, extracurricular activities, an essay, and recommendations. Financial need is considered only in case of a tie.
Financial data: Stipends are $1,000 or $500.
Duration: 1 year; nonrenewable.
Additional information: Recipients may attend school in any state. Information is also available from Barbara Kontogiannis, 8646 South Cresthill Lane, Highlands Ranch, CO 80126, (303) 971-5213, E-mail; barbekon@alumni.stanford.org.
Number awarded: Varies each year. Recently, 3 of these scholarships were awarded: 1 at $1,000 and 2 at $500.
Deadline: March of each year.

2482
ROCKY MOUNTAIN-FIRST SCHOLARSHIP

Pernicka Corporation
Attn: Frona Wilson
112 Racquette Drive
Fort Collins, CO 80524
Phone: (970) 224-0220   Fax: (970) 224-3617
E-mail: rga@pernicka.com
Web Site: www.pernicka.com
Summary: To recognize and reward high school students from designated states who participate in the FIRST (For Inspiration and Recognition of Science and Technology) Robotics competition.
Eligibility: The FIRST Robotics competition involves high school students who participate on teams that include the students supported by engineers, technicians, teachers, parents, industry representatives, and (occasionally) college students and faculty. Although the composition of teams varies, most are industry-high school partnerships, university-high school partnerships, industry-university-high school partnerships, or coalitions that involve multiple companies, universities, and/or high schools competing as a single team. Each team starts with the same standard kit of parts and uses their creativity to design and build a robotic vehicle capable of performing a demanding task better than 2 opponents. Teams may enter regional competitions or go directly to the national competition. High school seniors from Colorado, Montana, New Mexico, and Wyoming who participate in the competition are eligible to apply for this scholarship. Applicants must have been admitted to an accredited college or university to pursue a career in engineering, science, or math. Along with their application, they must submit a letter of recommendation from a high school teacher or administrator, a letter of recommendation from an engineer/advisor of

Scholarship Listings

their FIRST team, a resume with their grade point average (must be 3.5 or higher) and high school transcript, and an essay on the impact FIRST has had on their life.
Financial data: The stipend is $5,000.
Duration: 1 year; nonrenewable.
Additional information: The entry fee for each competition is $4,000. Other expenses, including travel by team members to a kick-off workshop and the competition, building materials, administrative costs, shipping, and uniforms, bring the total cost for each team to approximately $15,000. Teams must secure financing from local business sponsors and other fund-raising activities.
Number awarded: 1 each year.
Deadline: March of each year.

2483
ROMAN F. AND LILLIAN E. ARNOLDY SCHOLARSHIP

American Welding Society
Attn: AWS Foundation, Inc.
550 N.W. LeJeune Road
Miami, FL 33126
Phone: (305) 443-9353, ext. 461   (800) 443-9353, ext. 461
Fax: (305) 443-7559   E-mail: vpinsky@aws.org
Web Site: www.aws.org/foundation/arnoldy.html
Summary: To provide financial assistance to college students pursuing a degree in welding.
Eligibility: This program is open to full-time undergraduate students who are pursuing a 4-year bachelor's degree in a welding program at an accredited university. Applicants must 1) provide proof of employment for at least 8 hours per week, and/or 2) participate in a university work/study program. They must have an overall grade point average of 2.0 or higher. U.S. citizenship is required.
Financial data: The stipend is $2,500.
Duration: 1 year; recipients may reapply.
Number awarded: 1 each year.
Deadline: January of each year.

2484
RUBBER DIVISION UNDERGRADUATE SCHOLARSHIP PROGRAM

American Chemical Society
Rubber Division
Attn: Chair, Scholarship Committee
P.O. Box 499
Akron, OH 44309-0499
Phone: (330) 972-6938   Fax: (330) 972-5269
E-mail: rubberdivision@uakron.edu
Web Site: www.rubber.org/_public/awards/ugscholar.htm
Summary: To provide financial assistance to undergraduate students in fields of interest to the rubber industry.
Eligibility: This program is open to incoming college juniors and seniors who have a grade point average of 3.0 or higher for all of their undergraduate work. Applicants must be enrolled in a country where the Rubber Division has a resident subdivision. Their major must be chemistry, physics, chemical engineering, mechanical engineering, polymer science, or any other technical discipline of relevance to the rubber industry. They must have a serious interest in full-time professional employment in the rubber industry.
Financial data: The stipend is $5,000 per year. Funds may be used to help cover the costs of tuition, fees, and other expenses billed by the college or university.
Duration: 1 year.
Number awarded: 1 or more each year.
Deadline: March of each year.

2485
RUDOLPH DILLMAN MEMORIAL SCHOLARSHIP

American Foundation for the Blind
Attn: Scholarship Committee
11 Penn Plaza, Suite 300
New York, NY 10001
Phone: (212) 502-7661   (800) AFB-LINE
Fax: (212) 502-7771   TDD: (212) 502-7662
E-mail: afbinfo@afb.net
Web Site: www.afb.org/scholarships.asp

Summary: To provide financial assistance to legally blind undergraduate or graduate students studying in the field of rehabilitation and/or education of visually impaired and blind persons.
Eligibility: To be eligible, applicants must be able to submit evidence of legal blindness, U.S. citizenship, and acceptance in an accredited undergraduate or graduate training program within the broad field of rehabilitation and/or education of blind and visually impaired persons. Applications must include a typewritten statement, up to 3 pages in length, describing educational and personal goals, work experience, extracurricular activities, and how scholarship funds will be used.
Financial data: The stipend is $2,500 per year.
Duration: 1 academic year; previous recipients may not reapply.
Number awarded: 4 each year: 3 without consideration of financial need and 1 to an applicant who can submit evidence of financial need.
Deadline: March of each year.

2486
R.V. "GADABOUT" GADDIS CHARITABLE FUND

Summary: To provide financial assistance to Maine students interested in the study of outdoor/nature writing.
See Listing #1628.

2487
RYAN MOTT MEMORIAL SCHOLARSHIP

Texas FFA Association
614 East 12th Street
Austin, TX 78701
Phone: (512) 480-8045   Fax: (512) 472-0555
E-mail: txffa@txaged.org   Web Site: www.txaged.org
Summary: To provide financial assistance for college to high school seniors in Texas who demonstrate outstanding personal qualities and involvement in FFA.
Eligibility: This program is open to high school seniors in Texas who are FFA members and have been members at least 2 of the 3 previous years. Applicants must demonstrate personal qualities of kindness, courtesy, hard work, and dedication to FFA. They should also possess strong leadership and communication skills that they use on an individual basis as well as in team situations. Their proposed major in college should be in the agricultural sciences, life sciences, or natural resources. Scores on ACT or SAT tests are not considered; selection is based on FFA activities (15 points); FFA awards (5 points); FFA offices (5 points); school activities, awards, and/or offices (10 points); community activities, awards, and/or offices (10 points); work experience (5 points); need for the scholarship (15 points); and a 150-word paragraph explaining why awarding the applicant would be a wise investment (15 points).
Financial data: The stipend is $1,000.
Duration: 1 year.
Additional information: This program was established in 1998 to honor Ryan Mott, an FFA student leader who died of cancer that year. Students may not apply for both 4-H and FFA scholarships.
Number awarded: 1 each year.

2488
S-B POWER TOOL SCHOLARSHIP AWARD

Society of Manufacturing Engineers
Attn: Education Foundation
One SME Drive
P.O. Box 930
Dearborn, MI 48121-0930
Phone: (313) 271-1500, ext. 1707   Fax: (313) 240-6095
E-mail: cortjoy@sme.org
Web Site: www.sme.org
Summary: To provide financial assistance to students from Arkansas, Illinois, and North Carolina who are pursuing a degree in manufacturing engineering or technology.
Eligibility: This program is open to full-time undergraduate students enrolled in a degree program in manufacturing engineering or technology in Arkansas, Illinois, or North Carolina. Applicants must have completed at least 30 units with a grade point average of 3.5 or higher and be interested in pursuing a career in manufacturing engineering or technology. Need is not considered in awarding scholarships (unless 2 or more applicants have equal qualifications).
Financial data: The stipend is $1,500 per year. Funds are paid to the recipient's institution.
Duration: 1 year; may be renewed.

Additional information: Funding for this program is provided by the S-B Power Tool Company.
Number awarded: 1 each year.
Deadline: January of each year.

2489
SAE LONG TERM MEMBER SPONSORED SCHOLARSHIPS

Society of Automotive Engineers
Attn: Educational Relations
400 Commonwealth Drive
Warrendale, PA 15096-0001
Phone: (724) 772-4047   Fax: (724) 776-0890
E-mail: connie@sae.org
Web Site: www.sae.org/students/schlrshp.htm
Summary: To provide financial support to engineering majors who are student members of the Society of Automotive Engineers (SAE).
Eligibility: This program is open to student members entering their senior year between August and February of the academic year following the award. Candidates must be nominated by the faculty advisor, the section chair, or the vice chair for student activities. Selection is based on the nominee's involvement in the society, the collegiate chapter, or the local section and its programs. Grade point average and financial need are not considered.
Financial data: The stipend is $1,000.
Duration: 1 year; nonrenewable.
Additional information: Funding for this program is provided by long-term (25, 35, and 50 year) members of the society, many of whom have chosen to fund this scholarship program in lieu of receiving a Long Term Recognition Award. The program began with the 1994/95 academic year.
Number awarded: Several each year.
Deadline: March of each year.

2490
SAE WOMEN ENGINEERS COMMITTEE SCHOLARSHIP

Society of Automotive Engineers
Attn: Educational Relations
400 Commonwealth Drive
Warrendale, PA 15096-0001
Phone: (724) 772-4047   Fax: (724) 776-0890
E-mail: connie@sae.org   Web Site: www.sae.org/students/ihscholr.htm
Summary: To provide financial support to women high school seniors interested in majoring in engineering in college.
Eligibility: This program is open to women who are high school seniors with a grade point average of 3.0 or higher. Applicants must have been accepted into an ABET-accredited engineering program. U.S. citizenship is required. Selection is based on school transcripts; SAT or ACT scores; school-related extracurricular activities; non-school related activities; academic honors, civic honors, and awards; and a 250-word essay on the single experience that most strongly convinced them or confirmed their decision to pursue a career in engineering. Financial need is not considered.
Financial data: The stipend is $1,500.
Duration: 1 year; nonrenewable.
Additional information: Candidates must include a $5 processing fee with their applications.
Number awarded: 1 each year.
Deadline: November of each year.

2491
SAGEBRUSH CIRCUIT-LEW AND JOANN EKLUND EDUCATIONAL SCHOLARSHIP

Appaloosa Youth Foundation, Inc.
c/o Appaloosa Horse Club
Attn: Youth Coordinator
2720 West Pullman Road
Moscow, ID 83843-4024
Phone: (208) 882-5578, ext. 282   Fax: (208) 882-8150
E-mail: aphc@appaloosa.com
Web Site: www.appaloosa.com
Summary: To provide financial assistance for undergraduate or graduate study to members or dependents of members of the Appaloosa Horse Club.
Eligibility: This program is open to members and children of members of the Appaloosa Horse Club who are college juniors, seniors, or graduate students.

Applicants must be majoring in a field closely related to the equine industry and have a grade point average of 3.5 or higher. Selection is based on an essay, leadership potential, sportsmanship, involvement in the Appaloosa and equine industries, grade point average, extracurricular equine activities, extracurricular school and school and community activities, and general knowledge and accomplishments in horsemanship.
Financial data: The stipend is $2,000.
Duration: 1 year.
Number awarded: 1 each year.
Deadline: June of each year.

2492
SAM S. KUWAHARA MEMORIAL SCHOLARSHIP

Summary: To provide financial assistance to student members of the Japanese American Citizens League (JACL) who are pursuing or planning to pursue undergraduate education, particularly in agriculture.
See Listing #982.

2493
SAMA/SEC-AAAE SCHOLARSHIP PROGRAM

Scholarship Managers
P.O. Box 2810
Cherry Hill, NJ 08034
Phone: (856) 573-9400   Fax: (856) 573-9799
E-mail: scholarshipmanagers@erols.com
Summary: To provide financial assistance to full-time students majoring in aviation at selected schools in the south.
Eligibility: Applicants must be enrolled full time at 1 of the following 9 participating schools: Auburn University in Alabama, Delta State University in Mississippi, Eastern Kentucky University, Fairmont State College in West Virginia, Florida Institute of Technology, Georgia State University, Hampton University in Virginia, Louisiana Tech University, or Middle Tennessee State University. They must be classified as a junior or above, have a strong interest in aviation (preferably airport management), have at least a 3.0 GPA in their major, and be able to demonstrate financial need. Selection is based on academic record, participation in school and community activities, work experience, a statement of goals and aspirations, financial need, and a recommendation.
Financial data: The stipend is $1,500. Funds are paid jointly to the student and the school and must be used for tuition, books, lab fees, or other related educational expenses. The scholarship may not be used to pay for room or board.
Duration: 1 year; nonrenewable.
Additional information: Recipients must attend school on a full-time basis, continue to major in aviation, and maintain an overall cumulative GPA of 3.0.
Number awarded: 3 each year.
Deadline: May of each year.

2494
SAMUEL FLETCHER TAPMAN STUDENT CHAPTER/CLUB SCHOLARSHIPS

American Society of Civil Engineers
Attn: Student Services
1801 Alexander Bell Drive
Reston, VA 20191-4400
Phone: (703) 295-6120   (800) 548-ASCE
Fax: (703) 295-6132   E-mail: student@asce.org
Web Site: www.asce.org
Summary: To provide financial assistance to members of the American Society of Civil Engineers (ASCE) for undergraduate study in civil engineering.
Eligibility: This program is open to ASCE members who are freshmen, sophomores, juniors, or first-year seniors enrolled in a program of civil engineering. Applicants must submit an essay (up to 500 words) in which they discuss why they chose to become a civil engineer, their specific ASCE student chapter involvement, any special financial needs, and long-term goals and plans. Selection is based on their justification for the award, educational plan, academic performance and standing, potential for development, leadership capacity, ASCE activities, and demonstrated financial need.
Financial data: The stipend is $2,000 per year.
Duration: 1 year; may be renewed.
Number awarded: Approximately 12 each year.
Deadline: February of each year.

Scholarship Listings

2495
SARAH LEE GERRISH COMMUNICATIONS AWARDS

Packaging Education Forum
4350 North Fairfax Drive, Suite 600
Arlington, VA 22203-1632
Phone: (703) 243-5717   Fax: (703) 524-8691
E-mail: pef@pmmi.org
Web Site: www.packingingeducation.org/info/sections/assistance.html
Summary: To recognize and reward college students who submit outstanding essays on a topic related to packaging.
Eligibility: This program is open to students enrolled in at least 1 packaging course at a college or university supported by the sponsoring organization. Applicants must submit an essay of 750 to 1,000 words on a topic that changes annually but relates to packaging; recently, the topic was "How is the Internet likely to change packaging development, production, distribution, and marketing practices in the next 5–10 years?"
Financial data: First place is a $1,000 scholarship, second place a $500 scholarship, and third place a $300 scholarship.
Duration: The competition is held annually.
Additional information: This competition was first held in 1996. Participating schools are Clemson University, Rochester Institute of Technology, Rutgers University, California Polytechnic State University at San Luis Obispo, Indiana State University, Michigan State University, University of Wisconsin at Stout, University of Missouri at Rolla, University of Massachusetts at Lowell, University of Florida, and San Jose State University.
Number awarded: 3 each year.
Deadline: September of each year.

2496
SCHERING PLOUGH ANIMAL HEALTH SCHOLARSHIP

South Dakota Cattlemen's Association
P.O. Box 314
Kennebec, SD 57544
Phone: (605) 869-2272   Fax: (605) 869-2279
E-mail: sdcattl@wcenet.com
Web Site: www.sdcattlemen.org/Assoc/scholarship.htm
Summary: To provide financial assistance to members of the South Dakota Cattlemen's Association (SDCA) or their children who are working on an undergraduate or graduate degree in agriculture.
Eligibility: Applicants must be members of SDCA or the children of members. They must be currently enrolled as college juniors, college seniors, or graduate students and must be working on a degree in agriculture. Selection is based on high school and college/VoTech record (25 percent), current involvement in the beef industry (25 percent), future plans (25 percent), scholarship use (15 percent), and neatness, grammar, and clarity of thought in the application.
Financial data: A stipend is paid (exact amount not specified).
Duration: 1 year.
Number awarded: 1 each year.
Deadline: October of each year.

2497
SCHOLARSHIP FOR LUTHERAN NURSING STUDENTS

Bethesda Lutheran Homes and Services, Inc.
Attn: Coordinator of Outreach Programs and Services
700 Hoffmann Drive
Watertown, WI 53094
Phone: (920) 261-3050   (800) 369-4636, ext. 416
Fax: (920) 262-6513   E-mail: theuer@blhs.org
Web Site: www.blhs.org
Summary: To provide financial assistance to nursing students who are Lutherans and interested in preparing for a career in the field of mental retardation.
Eligibility: Applicants must be active communicant members of a Lutheran congregation; have at least sophomore status at a college or university or have completed 1-year of a 2-year A.D.N. program; have earned a grade point average of 3.0 or higher; and be interested in preparing for a career as a nurse in the field of developmental disabilities. They must submit a 500-word essay on the type of career they are planning, and they must be able to document that they have completed 100 hours of volunteer and/or paid work to benefit people who are developmentally disabled. Financial need is not considered in the selection process.
Financial data: The stipend is $1,000.
Duration: 1 year.
Number awarded: 1 or more each year.
Deadline: March of each year.

2498
SCHOLARSHIP FOR LUTHERAN STUDENTS ENTERING THE FIELD OF DEVELOPMENTAL DISABILITIES

Bethesda Lutheran Homes and Services, Inc.
Attn: Coordinator of Outreach Programs and Services
700 Hoffmann Drive
Watertown, WI 53094
Phone: (920) 261-3050   (800) 369-4636, ext. 416
Fax: (920) 262-6513   E-mail: theuer@blhs.org
Web Site: www.blhs.org
Summary: To provide financial assistance to college students who are Lutherans and interested in preparing for a career in the field of mental retardation.
Eligibility: Applicants must be active communicant members of a Lutheran congregation; have at least sophomore status at a college or university (not necessarily a Lutheran institution); have earned a grade point average of 3.0 or higher; and be interested in preparing for a career in the field of developmental disabilities. They must submit a 500-word essay on the type of career they are planning, and they must be able to document that they have completed 100 hours of volunteer and/or paid work to benefit people who are developmentally disabled. Financial need is not considered in the selection process.
Financial data: The stipend is $1,000.
Duration: 1 year.
Number awarded: 1 or more each year.
Deadline: March of each year.

2499
SCHOLARSHIP FOR MEDICAL AND OTHER PROFESSIONS

American Legion Auxiliary
Attn: Department of California
Veterans War Memorial Building
401 Van Ness Avenue, Room 113
San Francisco, CA 94102-4586
Phone: (415) 861-5092   Fax: (415) 861-8365
E-mail: calegionaux@calegionaux.org
Web Site: www.calegionaux.org/scholarships.html
Summary: To provide financial assistance to California residents who are the children of veterans and interested in preparing for careers in medical and other professions.
Eligibility: Eligible for these scholarships are high school seniors or graduates who have not yet entered college because of financial or medical circumstances and who are the children of veterans of World War I, World War II, Korea, Vietnam, Grenada, Lebanon, Panama, or Desert Storm. They must plan to become a therapist, nurse, other medical professional, engineer, lawyer, law enforcement officer, or business professional. At least 5 years of California residency is required, unless the veteran parent has been hospitalized within the state or has been declared missing in action by the government. Awards are based on character (20 percent), Americanism (20 percent), leadership (10 percent), need (30 percent), and scholastic merit (20 percent).
Financial data: The stipend is $1,000 per year.
Duration: 2 years.
Number awarded: 1 each year.
Deadline: March of each year.

2500
SCHOLARSHIP TRUST GRANT

Michigan Society of Professional Engineers
Attn: Scholarship Coordinator
215 North Walnut Street
P.O. Box 15276
Lansing, MI 48901-5276
Phone: (517) 487-9388   Fax: (517) 487-0635
E-mail: mspe@voyager.net   Web Site: www.voyager.net/mspe
Summary: To provide financial assistance to high school seniors in Michigan who are interested in pursuing a college degree in engineering.
Eligibility: This program is open to graduating seniors at high schools in Michigan who have a grade point average of 3.0 or higher and a composite ACT score of 26 or higher. U.S. citizenship is required. Applicants must have been accepted at a Michigan college or university accredited by ABET. They must be planning to enroll in an engineering program and enter the practice of engineering after graduation. They must submit a 250-word essay on "How I Was Influenced to Pursue an Engineering Career." Selection is based on the essay; high school academic record; participation in extracurricular activities; evidence of

leadership, character, and self reliance; and comments from teachers and administrators. Financial need is not considered. Semifinalists are interviewed.
Financial data: The stipend is $2,000.
Duration: 1 year; nonrenewable.
Additional information: Information is also available from Roger Lamer, Scholarship Selection Committee Chair, (616) 247-2974, Fax: (616) 247-2997, E-mail: rlamer@steelcase.com. Applications must be submitted to the local chapter scholarship representative. Contact the Michigan Society of Professional Engineers (MSPE) for their addresses and phone numbers.
Number awarded: 1 each year.
Deadline: January of each year.

2501
SCHOLARSHIPS FOR TEACHERS AND OTHER PROFESSIONALS

American Legion Auxiliary
Attn: Department of California
Veterans War Memorial Building
401 Van Ness Avenue, Room 113
San Francisco, CA 94102-4586
Phone: (415) 861-5092   Fax: (415) 861-8365
E-mail: calegionaux@calegionaux.org
Web Site: www.calegionaux.org/scholarships.html
Summary: To provide financial assistance to California residents who are the children of veterans and interested in preparing for a career in teaching and other professions.
Eligibility: Eligible to apply are the children of veterans of World War I, World War II, Korea, Vietnam, Grenada/Lebanon, Panama, or Desert Storm who are high school seniors and who intend to work for a 4-year degree as a teacher, engineer, lawyer, law enforcement officer, or business professional. California residency is required, unless the veteran parent has been hospitalized within the state or has been reported as missing in action by the government. Awards are based on character (20 percent), Americanism (20 percent), leadership (10 percent), financial need (30 percent), and scholastic merit (20 percent).
Financial data: The stipend is $1,000.
Duration: 1 year.
Number awarded: 5 each year.
Deadline: March of each year.

2502
SCHOLARSHIPS IN TECHNICAL COMMUNICATION

Summary: To provide financial assistance to students who are preparing for a career in some area of technical communications.
See Listing #1632.

2503
SCHONSTEDT SCHOLARSHIP IN SURVEYING

American Congress on Surveying and Mapping
Attn: Awards Director
6 Montgomery Village Avenue, Suite 403
Gaithersburg, MD 20879
Phone: (240) 632-9716   Fax: (240) 632-1321
E-mail: tmilburn@acsm.net   Web Site: www.acsm.net
Summary: To provide financial assistance for the undergraduate study of surveying to members of the American Congress on Surveying and Mapping.
Eligibility: This program is open to students who have completed at least 2 years of a 4-year curriculum leading to a degree in surveying and are members of the sponsoring organization. Selection is based on previous academic record (30 percent), an applicant's statement of future plans (30 percent), letters of recommendation (20 percent), and professional activities (20 percent); if 2 or more applicants are judged equal based on those criteria, financial need may be considered.
Financial data: The stipend is $1,500. In addition, the surveying programs at the recipients' schools are awarded a magnetic locator.
Duration: 1 year.
Additional information: Funds for this scholarship are provided by the Schonstedt Instrument Company of Reston, Virginia.
Number awarded: 2 each year.
Deadline: December of each year.

2504
SCIENCE OLYMPIAD SCHOLARSHIPS

Science Olympiad
Attn: Executive Administrator
5955 Little Pine Lane
Rochester, MI 48306
Phone: (248) 651-4013   Fax: (248) 651-7835
Summary: To recognize and reward outstanding participants in the national Science Olympiad.
Eligibility: Students in grades 9-12, 6-9, and K-5 compete in state Science Olympiads, with 32 individual and team events in 3 broad areas: science concepts and knowledge, science processes and thinking skills, and science applications and technology. State winners at the grades 9-12 and 6-9 levels advance to the National Tournament, in which Gold Medal winners are eligible for these scholarships, awarded in a drawing and offered by the host university.
Financial data: The amounts of the scholarships vary.
Duration: The competition is held annually.
Additional information: Students may not apply for these scholarships; they are only available if the host university chooses to offer them.
Number awarded: Varies each year, depending on the number that the host university chooses to award.
Deadline: Each state organization sets a deadline for the competition in that state.

2505
SCOTTS COMPANY SCHOLARS PROGRAM

Golf Course Superintendents Association of America
Attn: Scholarship Coordinator
1421 Research Park Drive
Lawrence, KS 66049-3859
Phone: (785) 832-3678   (800) 472-7878, ext. 678
E-mail: psmith@gcsaa.org   Web Site: www.gcsaa.org
Summary: To provide assistance and work experience to students, particularly from diverse backgrounds, who are preparing for a career in golf management.
Eligibility: This program is open to high school seniors and college students (freshmen, sophomores, and juniors) who are interested in preparing for a career in golf management (the "green industry"). Women and candidates from diverse ethnic, cultural, and socio-economic backgrounds are considered. Selection is based on cultural diversity, academic achievement, extracurricular activities, leadership, employment potential, essay responses, and letters of recommendation. Financial need is not considered. Finalists are selected for summer internships and then compete for scholarships.
Financial data: Each intern receives a $500 award. Scholarship stipends are $2,500.
Duration: 1 year.
Additional information: The program is funded by a permanent endowment established by Scotts Company. Finalists are responsible for securing their own internships.
Number awarded: 5 interns and 2 scholarship winners are selected each year.
Deadline: February of each year.

2506
SDCA/MERIAL IVOMEC GENERATION OF EXCELLENCE SCHOLARSHIPS (AGRICULTURE)

South Dakota Cattlemen's Association
P.O. Box 314
Kennebec, SD 57544
Phone: (605) 869-2272   Fax: (605) 869-2279
E-mail: sdcattl@wcenet.com   Web Site: www.sdcattlemen.org/Assoc/scholarship.htm
Summary: To provide financial assistance to members of the South Dakota Cattlemen's Association (SDCA) or their children who are majoring in an agricultural field in college.
Eligibility: Applicants must be members of SDCA or the children of members. They must be currently enrolled in an accredited 2-year or 4-year college, university, or vocational-technical school. They must have completed at least 1 quarter or semester of school and must be majoring in agriculture with an emphasis in beef cattle production. Selection is based on high school and college/VoTech record (25 percent), current involvement in the beef industry (25 percent), future plans (25 percent), scholarship use (15 percent), and neatness, grammar, and clarity of thought in the application.
Financial data: A stipend is paid (exact amount not specified).
Duration: 1 year.
Number awarded: 1 each year.
Deadline: October of each year.

2507
SDCA/MERIAL IVOMEC GENERATION OF EXCELLENCE SCHOLARSHIPS (NON-AGRICULTURE)

South Dakota Cattlemen's Association
P.O. Box 314
Kennebec, SD 57544
Phone: (605) 869-2272   Fax: (605) 869-2279
E-mail: sdcattl@wcenet.com
Web Site: www.sdcattlemen.org/Assoc/scholarship.htm
Summary: To provide financial assistance to members of the South Dakota Cattlemen's Association (SDCA) or their children who are interested in promoting beef to a nonagricultural sector.
Eligibility: Applicants must be members of SDCA or the children of members. They must be currently enrolled in an accredited 2-year or 4-year college, university, or vocational-technical school. They must have completed at least 1 quarter or semester of school, must be majoring in agriculture with an emphasis in beef cattle production, and must be interested in promoting beef to a nonagriculture sector. Selection is based on high school and college/VoTech record (25 percent), current involvement in the beef industry (25 percent), future plans (25 percent), scholarship use (15 percent), and neatness, grammar, and clarity of thought in the application.
Financial data: A stipend is paid (exact amount not specified).
Duration: 1 year.
Number awarded: 1 each year.
Deadline: October of each year.

2508
SEAGATE SCHOLARSHIP PROGRAM

National Society of Black Engineers
Attn: Programs Manager
1454 Duke Street
Alexandria, VA 22314
Phone: (703) 549-2207, ext. 204   Fax: (703) 683-5312
E-mail: scholarships@nsbe.org   Web Site: www.nsbe.org
Summary: To provide financial assistance to members of the National Society of Black Engineers (NSBE) who are majoring in designated science and engineering fields.
Eligibility: This program is open to members of the society who are undergraduate or graduate students majoring in the following fields of study: chemical engineering, computer science, electrical engineering, information technology, material science, mechanical engineering, or physics. Selection is based on grade point average (at least 3.0), financial need, leadership abilities through campus activities, and a 500-word essay on how the applicant will use the scholarship to make a positive impact on the African American community.
Financial data: The stipend is $2,000.
Duration: 1 year.
Number awarded: 1 or more each year.
Deadline: November of each year; freshmen and first-year graduate students have until January to apply.

2509
SEARS CRAFTSMAN SCHOLARSHIP

National Hot Rod Association
Attn: Youth and Education Services
2035 Financial Way
P.O. Box 5555
Glendora, CA 91740-9555
Phone: (626) 914-4761, ext. 427   Fax: (626) 963-5360
Web Site: www.nhra.com/aboutnhr/youth.htm
Summary: To provide financial assistance to high school seniors, especially those interested in a career in the automotive technological or marketing fields.
Eligibility: This program is open to seniors graduating from a public, private, or parochial high school or education center. Applicants must have a grade point average of 2.0 or higher, have engaged in extracurricular activities in their school and community, be of good character, show evidence of leadership ability, and be planning to attend an accredited 2-year or 4-year college, university, or technical/vocational program. Preference is given to students planning to enter a career in the fields of automotive technology, industrial/technical manufacturing, or marketing. Selection is based on scholastic record, school activities, community involvement, a personal essay on career goals and future plans, 2 letters of recommendation, and financial need.
Financial data: The stipend is $1,000. Funds are sent directly to the recipient's school.
Duration: 1 year.

Additional information: The scholarship is funded by Sears, Roebuck and Company and administered by the National Hot Rod Association.
Number awarded: 21 each year: 3 in each of the association's 7 divisions (covering all fifty states, Canada, Mexico, and Puerto Rico).
Deadline: April of each year.

2510
SEASPACE SCHOLARSHIP PROGRAM

Seaspace, Inc.
Attn: Scholarship Committee
c/o Houston Underwater Club, Inc.
P.O. Box 3753
Houston, TX 77253-3753
Phone: (713) 467-6675   E-mail: captx@iname.com
Web Site: www.seaspace.org
Summary: To provide financial assistance to undergraduate and graduate students interested in preparing for a marine-related career.
Eligibility: This program is open to junior, senior, and graduate students who are interested in preparing for a marine-related career. They should be majoring in marine science, marine biology, wildlife and fisheries, environmental toxicology, biological oceanography, genetics, ocean engineering, aquaculture, or zoology with marine mammal applications. Preference is given to graduate students. Selection is based on academic excellence (minimum grade point average of 3.3), demonstrated course direction, and financial need.
Financial data: The amount awarded varies each year; recently, awards averaged approximately $1,750.
Duration: 1 year.
Number awarded: Varies each year; recently, 15 students received scholarships, including 4 undergraduates and 11 graduate students. To date, financial assistance has been provided to more than 150 students.
Deadline: January of each year.

2511
SEG SCHOLARSHIP PROGRAM

Society of Exploration Geophysicists
Attn: SEG Foundation
P.O. Box 702740
Tulsa, OK 74170-2740
Phone: (918) 497-5530   Fax: (918) 497-5557
E-mail: slobianco@seg.org   Web Site: www.seg.org
Summary: To provide financial assistance to undergraduate and graduate students who are interested in the field of geophysics.
Eligibility: Applicants must be 1) high school students planning to enter college in the fall and to major in geophysics; 2) undergraduate college students majoring in geophysics whose grades are above average; or 3) graduate students whose studies are directed toward a career in exploration geophysics in operations, teaching, or research. All applicants must have an interest in and aptitude for physics, mathematics, and geology. Financial need is considered, but the competence of the student as indicated by the application is given first consideration. Some of the scholarships are set aside for students at recognized colleges or universities in countries outside of the United States.
Financial data: The stipends generally range from $500 to $2,000 per year.
Duration: 1 academic year; may be renewable, based on scholastic standing, availability of funds, and continuance of a course of study leading to a career in exploration geophysics.
Number awarded: Varies each year; recently, 49 renewals and 54 new scholarships were awarded. The total value of the scholarships was $105,700.
Deadline: February of each year.

2512
SEITZ FRUIT/GOLDEN VALLEY DISTRIBUTORS SCHOLARSHIP

Texas FFA Association
614 East 12th Street
Austin, TX 78701
Phone: (512) 480-8045   Fax: (512) 472-0555
E-mail: txffa@txaged.org   Web Site: www.txaged.org
Summary: To provide financial assistance for college to high school seniors in Texas who demonstrate outstanding personal qualities and involvement in FFA.
Eligibility: This program is open to high school seniors in Texas who are FFA members and have been members at least 2 of the 3 previous years. Applicants must be planning to major in college in a field related to the agricultural sciences, life sciences,

or natural resources. They must have completed at least 5 semesters of instruction in agriculture and/or agribusiness during high school and scored at least 950 on the SAT or 20 on the ACT. U.S. citizenship and ranking in the top half of their graduating class are also required. Selection is based on academic achievement (16 points); SAT or ACT scores (14 points); agricultural science and career related instruction (10 points); FFA achievement (20 points), including the supervised agricultural experience (10 points); financial need (10 points); and performance during interviews regarding academics (10 points), FFA achievement (5 points), and financial need (10 points).

Financial data: The stipend is $1,000.

Duration: 1 year.

Additional information: Students may not apply for both 4-H and FFA scholarships.

Number awarded: 1 each year.

2513
SENTRY INSURANCE FOUNDATION SCHOLARSHIP

Summary: To provide financial assistance to freshmen majoring in selected fields at private colleges in Wisconsin.
See Listing #1639.

2514
SHARON D. BANKS UNDERGRADUATE SCHOLARSHIP

Women's Transportation Seminar
Attn: National Headquarters
1666 K Street, N.W., Suite 1100
Washington, DC 20006
Phone: (202) 496-4340   Fax: (202) 496-4349
E-mail: wts@wtsnational.org
Web Site: www.wtsnational.org/scholarship_undergrad.asp
Summary: To provide financial assistance for undergraduate education to women interested in a career in transportation.
Eligibility: This program is open to women who are pursuing an undergraduate degree in transportation or a transportation-related field (e.g., transportation engineering, planning, finance, or logistics). Applicants must have at least a 3.0 grade point average and be interested in a career in transportation. They must submit a 500-word statement about their career goals after graduation and why they think they should receive the scholarship award. Applications must be submitted first to a local chapter; the chapters forward selected applications for consideration on the national level. Minority candidates are encouraged to apply. Selection is based on transportation involvement and goals, job skills and academic record; financial need is not considered.
Financial data: The stipend is $2,000.
Duration: 1 year.
Additional information: The Women's Transportation Seminar (WTS) was founded in 1977 and now has more than 3,000 members, both female and male, in chapters throughout the United States. This scholarship program was established in 1992.
Number awarded: 1 each year.
Deadline: Applications must be submitted by October 31 to a local WTS chapter.

2515
SHAW-WORTH SCHOLARSHIP AWARD

Humane Society of the United States
Attn: New England Regional Office
P.O. Box 619
Jacksonville, VT 05342   Phone: (802) 368-2790
Summary: To provide financial assistance for college to New England high school seniors who have contributed to animal protection.
Eligibility: This program is open to seniors graduating from public, parochial, and independent high schools in New England. Applicants must have made a meaningful contribution to animal protection over a significant period of time. The contribution may have taken the form of long-term direct work on behalf of animals; inspiring leadership in animal protection organizations; papers, speeches, or presentations on humane topics; or heroic rescues of animals in danger. A humane attitude, understanding of humane ethics, and past performance on behalf of animals are essential. A passive liking for animals or a desire to enter an animal care field is not adequate justification for the award. High scholastic standing is not required and financial need is not considered.
Financial data: The stipend is $1,000. Funds are paid directly to the college of the recipient's choice.
Duration: 1 year.
Number awarded: 1 each year.
Deadline: March of each year.

2516
SHERI MCHANN MEMORIAL SCHOLARSHIP

Mississippi Cattlewomen's Association
c/o Nancy Strickland
497 Parks Road
Jackson, MS 30212
Phone: (601) 857-2284
Summary: To provide financial assistance to students in Mississippi majoring in a field related to agriculture.
Eligibility: This program is open to high school seniors or students currently enrolled in a Mississippi college or community college. Applicants must be majoring or planning to major in a field related to agriculture. They must be the child, grandchild, or legal ward of an individual producer who is currently a member of the Mississippi Cattlewomen's Association or the Mississippi Cattlemen's Association, or be a member of the Mississippi Junior Cattlemen. To apply, students must submit a 200-word essay on the contribution they will make to the Mississippi cattle industry or how they could be a spokesperson for the Mississippi cattle industry, a copy of their high school or college transcript, 2 letters of recommendation, and a completed application form. Selection is based on financial need (10 points), potential impact on the cattle industry (30 points), academic record (5 points), appearance of the application (5 points), and community activity (5 points).
Financial data: A stipend is awarded (exact amount not specified).
Duration: 1 year.
Additional information: Recipients must attend a postsecondary school in Mississippi.
Number awarded: 1 or more each year.
Deadline: September of each year.

2517
SHUICHI, KATSU AND ITSUYO SUGA SCHOLARSHIP

Hawai'i Community Foundation
900 Fort Street Mall, Suite 1300
Honolulu, HI 96813
Phone: (808) 566-5570   (888) 731-3863
Fax: (808) 521-6286   E-mail: scholarships@hcf-hawaii.org
Web Site: www.hcf-hawaii.org
Summary: To provide financial assistance for college to Hawaii residents who are interested in studying a scientific field.
Eligibility: This program is open to Hawaii residents who plan to attend an accredited 2- or 4-year college or university as a full-time undergraduate or graduate student. Applicants must be planning to study mathematics, physics, science, or technology. They must be able to demonstrate academic achievement (at least a 3.0 grade point average), good moral character, and financial need. Applications must be accompanied by a short statement indicating reasons for attending college, planned course of study, and career goals.
Financial data: The amounts of the awards depend on the availability of funds and the need of the recipient; recently, grants averaged $1,000.
Duration: 1 year.
Additional information: Recipients may attend college in Hawaii or on the mainland.
Number awarded: Varies each year; recently, 6 of these scholarships were awarded.
Deadline: February of each year.

2518
SIDNEY B. MEADOWS SCHOLARSHIPS

Southern Nursery Association
Attn: Sidney B. Meadows Scholarship Endowment Fund
1827 Powers Ferry Road, Building 4, Suite 100
Atlanta, GA 30339
Phone: (770) 953-3311   Fax: (770) 953-4411
E-mail: mail@mail.sna.org
Web Site: www.sna.org/education/sbmsef-info.shtml
Summary: To provide financial assistance to undergraduate and graduate students from designated southeastern states who are interested in pursuing a career in horticulture.
Eligibility: This program is open to residents of Alabama, Arkansas, Florida, Georgia, Kentucky, Louisiana, Maryland, Mississippi, Missouri, North Carolina, Oklahoma, South Carolina, Tennessee, Texas, Virginia, and West Virginia. Applicants must be college juniors, seniors, or graduate students enrolled full time in an accredited horticulture program or related discipline and have a grade point average of 2.25 or

higher (for undergraduates) or 3.0 or higher (for graduate students). Preference is given to applicants who plan to work in an aspect of the industry (including owning their own business) and those in financial need. U.S. citizenship is required.

Financial data: The stipend is $2,500 per year.

Duration: 1 year; may be renewed up to 1 additional year.

Additional information: This fund was established in 1989.

Number awarded: 14 each year.

Deadline: May of each year.

2519
SIGMA PHI ALPHA UNDERGRADUATE SCHOLARSHIP PROGRAM

American Dental Hygienists' Association
Attn: Institute for Oral Health
444 North Michigan Avenue, Suite 3400
Chicago, IL 60611
Phone: (312) 440-8944   (800) 735-4916
Fax: (312) 440-8929   E-mail: institute@adha.net
Web Site: www.adha.org

Summary: To provide financial assistance to full-time students enrolled in undergraduate programs in dental hygiene.

Eligibility: Applicants must be American citizens, have earned at least a 3.0 grade point average, be able to demonstrate financial need of at least $1,500, and have completed a minimum of 1 year in a dental hygiene curriculum. They must be pursuing a certificate/associate or baccalaureate degree at an accredited dental hygiene school with an active chapter of the Sigma Phi Alpha Dental Hygiene Honor Society.

Financial data: The amount of the award depends on the need of the recipient, to a maximum of $1,000.

Duration: 1 year.

Number awarded: 1 each year.

Deadline: May of each year.

2520
SILVER WINGS FRATERNITY AVIATION EXPLORER SCHOLARSHIPS

Boy Scouts of America
Attn: Learning for Life Division, S210
1325 West Walnut Hill Lane
P.O. Box 152079
Irving, TX 75015-2079
Phone: (972) 580-2418   Web Site: www.learning-for-life.org/exploring

Summary: To provide financial assistance to Explorer Scouts who are interested in pursuing flight training or an aviation curriculum.

Eligibility: This program is open to aviation Explorer Scouts who are interested in studying aviation either in a college or flight school. Applicants must submit at least 3 letters of recommendation and a 500-word essay detailing their plans for a career in aviation.

Financial data: The stipend is $1,000.

Duration: 1 year; nonrenewable.

Number awarded: 2 each year.

Deadline: March of each year.

2521
SOCIETY OF HISPANIC PROFESSIONAL ENGINEERS SCHOLARSHIPS

Society of Hispanic Professional Engineers Foundation
Attn: Kathy Borunda
5400 East Olympic Boulevard, Suite 210
Los Angeles, CA 90022
Phone: (323) 888-2080   E-mail: shpef@aol.com
Web Site: www.shpefoundation.org

Summary: To provide undergraduate or graduate scholarships to deserving Hispanic American students preparing for a career in engineering or science.

Eligibility: Applicants must be enrolled or planning to enroll in an undergraduate or graduate engineering/science program in a college or university. They must be planning to pursue a career in 1 of those areas. Selection is based on an essay on long-range goals (25 points), membership in the Society of Hispanic Professional Engineers (15 points), grade point average (15 points), counselor's comments (10 points), school and community activities (10 points), financial need (10 points), educational desire (5 points), and a resume (5 points).

Financial data: The stipends range from $500 to $7,000 per year.

Duration: 1 academic year; renewal is possible.

Number awarded: Varies each year. Since its establishment in 1976, the foundation has awarded more than 3,700 scholarships.

Deadline: April of each year.

2522
SOCIETY OF MANUFACTURING ENGINEERS COMMUNITY COLLEGE SCHOLARSHIP AWARDS

Society of Manufacturing Engineers
Attn: Education Foundation
One SME Drive
P.O. Box 930
Dearborn, MI 48121-0930
Phone: (313) 271-1500, ext. 1707   Fax: (313) 240-6095
E-mail: cortjoy@sme.org
Web Site: www.sme.org

Summary: To provide financial assistance to students enrolled or planning to enroll in a community college program in manufacturing engineering or manufacturing engineering technology.

Eligibility: This program is open to entering freshmen and sophomores with less than 60 college credit hours at a 2-year community college or trade school in the United States or Canada. Applicants must be full-time students seeking a career in manufacturing engineering or technology with a grade point average of 3.5 or higher. Need is not considered in awarding scholarships (unless 2 or more applicants have equal qualifications).

Financial data: The stipend is $1,000.

Duration: 1 year.

Number awarded: At least 3 each year.

Deadline: January of each year.

2523
SOCIETY OF MANUFACTURING ENGINEERS DIRECTORS' SCHOLARSHIP AWARD

Society of Manufacturing Engineers
Attn: Education Foundation
One SME Drive
P.O. Box 930
Dearborn, MI 48121-0930
Phone: (313) 271-1500, ext. 1707   Fax: (313) 240-6095
E-mail: cortjoy@sme.org   Web Site: www.sme.org

Summary: To provide financial assistance to undergraduate students enrolled in a degree program in manufacturing.

Eligibility: This program is open to full-time undergraduate students enrolled in a manufacturing degree program at a college or university in North America. Applicants must have completed a minimum of 30 units with a grade point average of 3.5 or higher and be interested in pursuing a career in manufacturing. Preference is given to students who demonstrate leadership skills in a community, academic, or professional environment. Need is not considered in awarding scholarships (unless 2 or more applicants have equal qualifications).

Financial data: The stipend is $5,000.

Duration: 1 year; may be renewed.

Number awarded: 1 each year.

Deadline: January of each year.

2524
SOCIETY OF NAVAL ARCHITECTS AND MARINE ENGINEERS UNDERGRADUATE SCHOLARSHIPS

Society of Naval Architects and Marine Engineers
601 Pavonia Avenue, Suite 400
Jersey City, NJ 07306
Phone: (201) 798-4800, ext. 3029   (800) 798-2188
Fax: (201) 798-4975   E-mail: efaustino@sname.org
Web Site: www.sname.org

Summary: To provide financial assistance for undergraduate study to members of the Society of Naval Architects and Marine Engineers.

Eligibility: Applicants for these scholarships must have been accepted to study naval architecture, marine engineering, or ocean engineering at a participating university. They must be members of the society entering their junior or senior year.

Financial data: Scholarships up to $2,000 per year are available.

Duration: 1 year; may be renewed 1 additional year.

Additional information: Applications for these scholarships should be submitted directly to the participating universities: Massachusetts Institute of Technology, University of Michigan, University of California at Berkeley, State University of New York Maritime College, University of New Orleans, Memorial University of Newfoundland, University of British Columbia, Texas A&M University, Virginia Polytechnic Institute, Maine Maritime Academy, Webb Institute, or Florida Atlantic University.

Number awarded: Varies each year; recently, 24 of these scholarships were awarded.

Deadline: Participating universities must submit their nominations to the society by the end of April of each year.

2525
SOCIETY OF PLASTICS ENGINEERS SCHOLARSHIPS

Society of Plastics Engineers
Attn: SPE Foundation
14 Fairfield Drive
Brookfield, CT 06804
Phone: (203) 740-5434   Fax: (203) 775-8490
E-mail: foundation@4spe.org   Web Site: www.4spe.org

Summary: To provide college scholarships to students who have a career interest in the plastics industry.

Eligibility: Applicants must be full-time students at either a 4-year college or in a 2-year technical program. They must have a demonstrated or expressed interest in the plastics industry and should be taking classes that would be beneficial to a career in the plastics industry (e.g., plastics engineering, polymer sciences, chemistry, physics, chemical engineering, mechanical engineering, industrial engineering, and business administration). Financial need must be documented. Along with their application, students must submit 3 letters of recommendation; a high school and/or college transcript; and a 1- to 2-page statement telling why they are interested in the scholarship, their qualifications, and their career goals in the plastics industry.

Financial data: General scholarships are up to $4,000 per year. Named scholarships range from $1,000 to $5,000 per year. Funds are paid directly to the recipient's school.

Duration: 1 year; may be renewed for up to 3 additional years.

Additional information: This program includes the following named scholarships: the Robert G. Dailey/Detroit Section Scholarship (1 at $4,000); the Robert E. Cramer/Product Design & Development Division/Mid-Michigan Section Scholarship (1 at $1,000); the Polymer Modifiers & Additives Division Scholarships (2 at $4,000); and the American Plastics Council (APC)/Plastics Recycling Division Scholarship (1 at $5,000).

Number awarded: 10 to 12 general scholarships are awarded each year. In addition, 5 named scholarships are also awarded.

Deadline: December of each year.

2526
SOLE SCHOLARSHIP

SOLE-The International Society of Logistics
Attn: Chair, Scholarship Committee
8100 Professional Place, Suite 211
New Carrollton, MD 20785
Phone: (301) 459-8446   Fax: (301) 459-1522
E-mail: solehq@sole.org
Web Site: www.sole.org

Summary: To provide financial assistance to students pursuing an undergraduate or graduate degree in logistics engineering.

Eligibility: Applicants may be studying on the undergraduate or graduate school level. They must be enrolled full time and majoring in logistics engineering. Selection is based on career interests, extracurricular activities, and the proposed topic of the paper required of all recipients.

Financial data: The stipend is $1,000.

Duration: 1 year.

Additional information: This program is sponsored by SOLE and the Logistics Education Foundation. All students selected to receive a scholarship are required to submit a student paper to SOLE's journal, *Logistics Spectrum.*

Number awarded: 1 or more each year.

Deadline: April of each year.

2527
SOLID WASTE PROGRAM MANAGEMENT UNDERGRADUATE SCHOLARSHIP PROGRAM

ASME International
Attn: Solid Waste Processing Division
Three Park Avenue
New York, NY 10016-5990
Phone: (212) 591-7797   (800) THE-ASME
Fax: (212) 591-7674   E-mail: manese@asme.org
Web Site: www.asme.org/divisions/swpd/studentprograms/index.html

Summary: To provide financial assistance for undergraduate studies in solid waste management.

Eligibility: Applicants must be undergraduate students in any branch of engineering who are currently enrolled in a solid waste management program. They must attend or plan to attend a college or university in North America (including Alaska, Canada, Hawaii, Mexico, and Puerto Rico). Applications must be submitted jointly by an appropriate faculty member and the student applicant. Required from the faculty member are a description of the school's solid waste management program, identification of undergraduate and graduate courses offered in the program, an indication of the number of students in the program, a summary of future plans for the solid waste management program, and a proposal for use of the school's portion of the award money. Students must submit a statement of intent to pursue a branch of engineering as a career, a statement of interest in solid waste management, information on any prior experience in the solid waste management field, copies of any papers the applicant has written on solid waste management, information on proposed studies, a list of current courses, transcripts for previous college years, and a letter of recommendation from the faculty advisor or department head. Financial need is not considered.

Financial data: The award is $3,000 per year. One half is given to the student and the other half is given to the recipient's school for support of its solid waste management program.

Duration: 1 year.

Number awarded: 1 each year.

Deadline: June of each year.

2528
SONNE SCHOLARSHIP

Illinois Nurses Association
Attn: Scholarship Committee
300 South Wacker Drive, Suite 2200
Chicago, IL 60606
Phone: (312) 360-2300   Fax: (312) 360-9380

Summary: To provide financial assistance to members of the Student Nurse Association of Illinois who are preparing for a career as a registered professional nurse.

Eligibility: Members in good standing are eligible to apply if they are enrolled in a Illinois-approved nursing program that leads to eligibility to sit for licensure examination as a registered professional nurse. Selection is based on academic record (at least a 2.5 grade point average), financial need, and an essay on "How will membership in my state nurses association enhance my nursing career?"

Financial data: Stipends are either $1,500 or $1,000. Funds are to be used to cover tuition, fees, and other educational expenses.

Duration: 1 year.

Additional information: Recipients are given a year's free membership in the Illinois Nurses Association upon graduation. Although part-time students can apply, all recipients must attend school on a full-time basis.

Number awarded: 2 to 4 each year.

Deadline: May of each year.

2529
SOUTH TEXAS UNIT SCHOLARSHIPS

Herb Society of America-South Texas Unit
Attn: Education Committee Chair
P.O. Box 6515
Houston, TX 77265-6515
Phone: (713) 513-7808
Web Site: www.herbsociety-stu.org/Scholarship.htm

Summary: To provide financial assistance to Texas students majoring in agronomy, horticulture, botany, or a related field.

Eligibility: This program is open to students who are studying agronomy, horticulture, botany, or a closely-related discipline at an accredited 4-year college

or university. Applicants must be either a permanent resident of Texas or attending an accredited college or university in Texas. They must have completed at least 2 full years of college and be entering the junior or senior year. Selection is based on academic achievement, letters of recommendation, and a 2- to 3-paragraph statement on their short- and long-term career goals, including examples of special interests or projects in plants, herbs, gardening, etc.
Financial data: The stipend is $1,000.
Duration: 1 year.
Number awarded: 2 each year.
Deadline: April of each year.

2530
SOUTHWEST CHAPTER STUDENT SCHOLARSHIPS

American Association of Airport Executives-Southwest Chapter
c/o Charles Mangum, Scholarship Committee
Falcon Field Airport
4800 Falcon Drive
Mesa, AZ 85215
Phone: (480) 644-4230   E-mail: charles_magnum@ci.mesa.az.us
Web Site: www.swaaae.org/scholarship.html
Summary: To provide financial assistance to college students pursuing a degree in airport management.
Eligibility: Students majoring in airport management in college are eligible to apply. They must submit a completed application, an autobiography (not to exceed 1 page), and a statement of their interest in aviation and airport management (not to exceed 1 page). Selection is based on academic record, extracurricular activities, and financial need.
Financial data: The stipend is $1,000, plus a $500 travel allowance for recipients to attend the award ceremony.
Duration: 1 year.
Number awarded: 2 each year.
Deadline: December of each year.

2531
SPIE SCHOLARSHIP PROGRAM

SPIE-The International Society for Optical Engineering
Attn: Scholarship Committee
1000 20th Street
P.O. Box 10
Bellingham, WA 98227-0010
Phone: (360) 676-3290   Fax: (360) 647-1445
E-mail: scholarships@spie.org   Web Site: www.spie.org
Summary: To provide financial assistance to undergraduate and graduate students who are preparing for a career in optical science or engineering.
Eligibility: This program is open to high school seniors planning to attend college, current undergraduate students, and current graduate students. Applicants must be majoring or planning to major in optical engineering, optical science, or optics at a college or university anywhere in the world. They must submit 1) a list of awards, honors, scholarships, publications, presentations, related course(s), projects, and activities with dates and grades; and 2) a description of how the award will contribute to the long-term development of optics, optical science, and engineering. Financial need is not considered in the selection process.
Financial data: Stipends typically provide support for tuition and related expenses, travel to meetings, and supplemental funding to research and teaching assistantships.
Duration: 1 year.
Additional information: The International Society for Optical Engineering was founded in 1955 as the Society of Photo-Optical Instrumentation Engineers (SPIE). This program includes the following special named scholarships: the D.J. Lovell Scholarship, sponsored by SPIE with contributions from Labsphere, Inc. and Laser Focus World; the Nakajima Scholarship, sponsored by NAC, Inc.; the William H. Price Scholarship in Optical Engineering, established in 1985 for a full-time graduate or undergraduate student in the field of optical design and engineering; the F-MADE Scholarship, sponsored by the Forum for Military Applications of Directed Energy (F-MADE) in recognition of a student's scholarly achievement in laser technology, engineering, or applications; and the BACUS Scholarship, awarded to a full-time undergraduate or graduate student in the field of microlithography with an emphasis on optical tooling and/or semiconductor manufacturing technologies, sponsored by BACUS (SPIE's photomask international technical group).
Number awarded: Varies each year.
Deadline: January of each year.

2532
SPORTY'S PILOT SHOP AVIATION EXPLORER SCHOLARSHIPS

Boy Scouts of America
Attn: Learning for Life Division, S210
1325 West Walnut Hill Lane
P.O. Box 152079
Irving, TX 75015-2079
Phone: (972) 580-2418
Web Site: www.learning-for-life.org/exploring
Summary: To provide financial assistance to Explorer Scouts who are interested in pursuing flight training or an aviation curriculum.
Eligibility: This program is open to Explorer Scouts who are interested in studying aviation either in a college or flight school. Applicants must submit at least 3 letters of recommendation and a 500-word essay detailing their plans for a career in aviation.
Financial data: The stipend is $1,000.
Duration: 1 year; nonrenewable.
Number awarded: 2 each year.
Deadline: March of each year.

2533
SPS LEADERSHIP SCHOLARSHIPS

Society of Physics Students
c/o American Institute of Physics
One Physics Ellipse
College Park, MD 20740-3843
Phone: (301) 209-3007   Fax: (301) 209-0839
E-mail: sps@aip.org
Web Site: www.aip.org/education/sps/radio/programs.htm
Summary: To provide financial assistance to members of the Society of Physics Students (SPS) in their final year of undergraduate study.
Eligibility: Eligible are full-time college juniors majoring in physics who are active members of the society. Selection is based on 1) high scholarship performance both in physics and overall studies, 2) potential for continued scholastic development in physics, and 3) active participation in society programs; those 3 criteria are given equal weight.
Financial data: First-place scholarship is $4,000, second place is $2,000, and others are $1,000.
Duration: 1 year.
Additional information: This program is sponsored by the Sigma Pi Sigma Trust Fund and the American Institute of Physics
Number awarded: 14 each year (1 first place, 1 second place, 12 others).
Deadline: February of each year.

2534
STAN BECK FELLOWSHIP

Entomological Society of America
Attn: Entomological Foundation
9301 Annapolis Road
Lanham, MD 20706-3115
Phone: (301) 731-4535   Fax: (301) 731-4538
E-mail: esa@entsoc.org
Web Site: www.entsoc.org
Summary: To assist "needy" students pursuing a degree in science who are nominated by members of the Entomological Society of America (ESA).
Eligibility: Candidates for this fellowship must be nominated by members of the society. Nominees may be studying science on any level. However, they must be "needy" students. For the purposes of this program, need may be based on physical limitations, or economic, minority, or environmental conditions.
Financial data: The fellowship is $4,000 per year.
Duration: The award is presented annually.
Additional information: Recipients are expected to be present at the society's annual meeting, where the award will be presented.
Number awarded: 1 or more each year.
Deadline: August of each year.

2535
STATE COUNCIL OF LADIES AUXILIARIES SCHOLARSHIPS

Pennsylvania Society of Professional Engineers
Attn: Pennsylvania Engineering Foundation
908 North Second Street
Harrisburg, PA 17102
Phone: (717) 236-1844   Fax: (717) 236-2046
E-mail: info@pspe.org
Web Site: www.pspe.org
Summary: To provide financial assistance to female Pennsylvania high school seniors who are interested in studying engineering at a college or university in the state.
Eligibility: This program is open to female graduating seniors at high schools in Pennsylvania. Applicants must be planning to enroll in an engineering program at an ABET-accredited college or university in the state. They must have at least a 3.6 grade point average and an SAT score of 1300. Interviews are included in the selection process.
Financial data: The stipend is $1,000.
Duration: 1 year; nonrenewable.
Additional information: Scholarships are awarded by 23 local chapters of the Pennsylvania Engineering Foundation (PEF) in the state. Applications are available from the sponsor, but they must be submitted to the local chapter where the student lives.
Number awarded: Varies each year.

2536
STATE OF ALABAMA CHIROPRACTIC SCHOLARSHIP

State of Alabama Chiropractic Scholarship Program
c/o Sam Peavy
1201 Ann Street
Montgomery, Al 36012
Phone: (334) 265-7123
Summary: To provide financial assistance to Alabama residents interested in working on a chiropractic degree.
Eligibility: This program is open to residents of Alabama who are U.S. citizens, full-time students in a chiropractic college approved by the Alabama Commission on Higher Education, and able to demonstrate financial need. Applicants must be willing to agree to return to Alabama after graduation and seek licensure as a Doctor of Chiropractic.
Financial data: The stipend is at least $1,000.
Duration: 1 year.
Additional information: This program was established in 1985 by the Alabama state legislature. Information is also available from Sandra Traylor, 201 20th Street, North, Pell City, AL 35125, (205) 884-3585.
Number awarded: Varies each year.

2537
STEPHEN S. CHANG MEMORIAL SCHOLARSHIP

Institute of Food Technologists
Attn: Scholarship Department
221 North LaSalle Street, Suite 300
Chicago, IL 60601-1291
Phone: (312) 782-8424   Fax: (312) 782-8348
E-mail: info@ift.org
Web Site: www.ift.org
Summary: To provide financial assistance to undergraduates interested in studying food science or food technology.
Eligibility: Applicants must be currently enrolled as sophomores or juniors majoring in food science or food technology at an educational institution in the United States or Canada. They must have an outstanding scholastic record and a well-rounded personality. Financial need is not considered in the selection process.
Financial data: The stipend is $1,000.
Duration: 1 year; recipients may reapply if they are members of the Institute of Food Technologists.
Additional information: Funds for this scholarship are provided by Kalsec, Inc. Correspondence and completed applications must be submitted to the department head of the educational institution the applicant is attending.
Number awarded: 1 each year.
Deadline: January of each year.

2538
STEVE DEARDUFF SCHOLARSHIP

Summary: To provide financial assistance to Georgia residents who are working on an undergraduate or graduate degree, especially in medicine and social work.
See Listing #1046.

2539
STRUCTURAL METALS DIVISION SCHOLARSHIP

The Minerals, Metals & Materials Society
Attn: TMS Student Awards Program
184 Thorn Hill Road
Warrendale, PA 15086-7528
Phone: (724) 776-9000, ext. 213   Fax: (724) 776-3770
E-mail: luther@tms.org
Web Site: www.tms.org/Students/AwardsPrograms/Scholarships.html
Summary: To provide financial assistance to student members of The Minerals, Metals & Materials Society (TMS).
Eligibility: This program is open to undergraduate members of the society who are full-time students majoring in metallurgical and/or materials science and engineering with an emphasis on the society and engineering of load-bearing materials. Applicants may be from any country. Selection is based on academic achievement, school and community activities, work experience, leadership, a personal profile statement, and letters of recommendation.
Financial data: The stipend is $2,500, plus a travel stipend of $500 (so the recipient can attend the annual meeting of the society to accept the award).
Duration: 1 year.
Additional information: Funding for this program is provided by the Structural Materials Division of TMS.
Number awarded: 2 each year.
Deadline: April of each year.

2540
STUDENT ASSOCIATION GEORGE R. FOSTER MEMORIAL SCHOLARSHIP

Institute of Food Technologists
Attn: Scholarship Department
221 North LaSalle Street, Suite 300
Chicago, IL 60601-1291
Phone: (312) 782-8424   Fax: (312) 782-8348
E-mail: info@ift.org
Web Site: www.ift.org
Summary: To provide financial assistance to high school seniors interested in pursuing the study of food science or food technology.
Eligibility: Applicants must be high school seniors planning to major in food science or food technology at an educational institution in the United States or Canada; they must have an outstanding scholastic record and a well-rounded personality. Financial need is not considered in the selection process.
Financial data: The stipend is $1,000.
Duration: 1 year; recipients may reapply if they are members of the Institute of Food Technologists.
Additional information: Correspondence and completed applications must be submitted to the department head of the educational institution the applicant plans to attend.
Number awarded: 1 each year.
Deadline: February of each year.

2541
STUDENT COMPETITION IN LANDSCAPE ARCHITECTURE FOR AGGREGATE OPERATIONS

Summary: To encourage beautification and reclamation activities at quarries by offering prizes to students in landscape architecture.
See Listing #1653.

2542
STUDENT CORRUGATED PACKAGING DESIGN COMPETITION

Summary: To recognize and reward college students who submit outstanding corrugated packaging designs.
See Listing #1654.

2543
STUDENT ENGINEER OF THE YEAR SCHOLARSHIP

American Society of Agricultural Engineers
Attn: ASAE Foundation
2950 Niles Road
St. Joseph, MI 49085-9659
Phone: (616) 429-0300   Fax: (616) 429-3852
E-mail: hq@asae.org
Web Site: www.asae.org
Summary: To recognize and reward student members of the American Society of Agricultural Engineers (ASAE) who participate in a competition to select the best student of the year.
Eligibility: This program is open to biological and agricultural engineering students who have completed at least 1 year of undergraduate study with at least a 3.0 grade point average and are members of the society. Selection is based on: scholarship, with special consideration given to students who demonstrate improvement in academic work from freshman to sophomore to junior years (20 points); character and personal development, including participation in non-university activities and service to others (10 points); student membership in the society and active participation in a student branch organization (25 points); participation in other school activities (15 points); leadership qualities, creativity, initiative, and responsibility (25 points); and level of financial self support provided by the student (5 points). In addition, the judges consider the candidate's paper, up to 500 words, on "My Goals in the Engineering Profession."
Financial data: The award is a $1,000 scholarship.
Duration: The competition is held annually.
Number awarded: 1 each year.
Deadline: January of each year.

2544
STUDENT MANUFACTURING ENGINEERING DESIGN COMPETITION

ASME International
Attn: Manufacturing Engineering Division
Three Park Avenue
New York, NY 10016-5990
Phone: (212) 591-7722   (800) THE-ASME
Fax: (212) 591-7674   E-mail: students@asme.org
Web Site: www.asme.org/divisions/med/competitions.html
Summary: To recognize and reward outstanding manufacturing engineering designs by student members of the American Society of Mechanical Engineers (ASME).
Eligibility: This competition is open to undergraduate and graduate student members of the society who submit projects that promote the art, science, and practice of manufacturing engineering. Technical areas include, but are not limited to, computer integrated manufacturing and robotics; machine tools, sensors, and controllers; manufacturing systems management and optimization; materials processing; new areas of manufacturing engineering; evolution of new materials and processes; and software and hardware contributing to improvements in manufacturing productivity.
Financial data: First prize is $1,000, second prize is $750, and third prize is $500.
Number awarded: 3 each year.
Deadline: May of each year.

2545
STUDENT SAFETY ENGINEERING DESIGN CONTEST

ASME International
Attn: Safety Engineering and Risk Analysis Division
Three Park Avenue
New York, NY 10016-5990
Phone: (212) 591-7722   (800) THE-ASME
Fax: (212) 591-7674   E-mail: students@asme.org
Web Site: www.asme.org/divisions/serad/comp.html
Summary: To recognize and reward outstanding safety engineering design papers by undergraduate and graduate students.
Eligibility: This competition is open to undergraduate and graduate students enrolled in an ABET-accredited mechanical engineering curriculum. Applicants must submit a senior design or other in-class project that describes an analysis, design, or engineering study that will prevent occupational injuries, illnesses, and deaths. Selection is based on background (20 percent), methodology (30 percent), feasibility (30 percent), and system safety (20 percent).

Financial data: First prize is $2,000 plus a travel allowance of $400 to present the winning paper; the faculty advisor receives $500. Second prize is $500; the faculty advisor receives $200.
Additional information: Applications and further information are also available from Brian C. Brady, c/o Roger Harvey, 25 Kinkel Street, Westbury, NY 11590, (516) 333-2520, E-mail: bgbrady@compuserve.com. This program is jointly sponsored by the Safety Engineering and Risk Analysis Division of ASME (the professional organization for mechanical engineering) and the National Institute for Occupational Safety and Health (NIOSH). Additional funding is provided by Bridgestone/Firestone Trust Fund, Factory Mutual Research, and several individuals.
Number awarded: 2 each year.
Deadline: May of each year.

2546
SWE BALTIMORE-WASHINGTON SECTION SCHOLARSHIPS

Society of Women Engineers-Baltimore-Washington Section
c/o N.H. Morgan, Scholarship Chair
1025 North George Mason Drive
Arlington, VA 22205
Web Site: www.swe-bws.org
Summary: To provide financial assistance to women who reside or attend school in the Washington, D.C. area and are interested in studying engineering in college.
Eligibility: This program is open to women who reside in northern Virginia, Washington, D.C., or Maryland or who are or will be students at universities or colleges in that area. Student members of the Society of Women Engineers (SWE) are given preference. Applicants must be enrolled or accepted for enrollment in an ABET-accredited or SWE-approved engineering degree program. They may be entering freshmen, current college students, reentry women, or graduate students, but they must have a grade point average of 3.0 or higher. U.S. citizenship is required. Students who receive tuition reimbursement from an employer are not eligible. Selection is based on merit and an essay on what influenced the applicant to select her current course of study, why she would like to be an engineer, and/or how she believes she will make a difference as an engineer.
Financial data: Stipends are $1,000 or $500.
Duration: 1 year.
Number awarded: Varies each year; recently, 7 of these scholarships (3 at $1,000 and 4 at $500) were awarded.
Deadline: February of each year.

2547
SWE NEW JERSEY SCHOLARSHIP

Society of Women Engineers
230 East Ohio Street, Suite 400
Chicago, IL 60611-3265
Phone: (312) 596-5223   Fax: (312) 644-8557
E-mail: hq@swe.org
Web Site: www.swe.org
Summary: To provide financial assistance to women from New Jersey interested in studying engineering in college.
Eligibility: This program is open to incoming female freshmen who are residents of New Jersey and interested in majoring in engineering at a 4-year school, college, or university. The schools must be ABET accredited or SWE approved. Selection is based on merit.
Financial data: The scholarship is $1,000.
Duration: 1 year.
Additional information: This program was established in 1998.
Number awarded: 1 each year.
Deadline: May of each year.

2548
SWE PAST PRESIDENTS SCHOLARSHIPS

Society of Women Engineers
230 East Ohio Street, Suite 400
Chicago, IL 60611-3265
Phone: (312) 596-5223   Fax: (312) 644-8557
E-mail: hq@swe.org
Web Site: www.swe.org
Summary: To provide financial assistance to women enrolled in or planning to enroll in college and major in engineering.

Eligibility: This program is open to women who are high school seniors or current undergraduate or graduate students majoring or planning to major in engineering at a 4-year institution in the United States. Applicants already in college must have a grade point average of 3.0 or higher. U.S. citizenship is required. The schools must be ABET accredited or SWE approved. Selection is based on merit.

Financial data: The stipend is $1,500 per year.

Duration: 1 year.

Additional information: This program was established in 1999.

Number awarded: 2 each year.

Deadline: May of each year for incoming freshmen; January of each year for students already in college.

2549
SYLVIA W. FARNY SCHOLARSHIP

ASME International
Attn: American Society of Mechanical Engineers Auxiliary, Inc.
Three Park Avenue
New York, NY 10016-5990
Phone: (212) 591-7733   (800) THE-ASME
Fax: (212) 591-7674   E-mail: horvathb@asme.org
Web Site: www.asme.org/auxiliary/scholarshiploans

Summary: To provide financial support for the study of mechanical engineering to students in their final year of undergraduate study.

Eligibility: Eligible are students completing the junior year of a 4-year program or the fourth year of a 5-year program in mechanical engineering. Applicants must be U.S. citizens enrolled in colleges and universities with accredited departments of mechanical engineering. If the school has a chapter of the Student Section of the American Society of Mechanical Engineers (ASME), the applicant must be a member. Selection is based on scholastic achievement, financial need, character, leadership, and participation in ASME activities.

Financial data: The grant is $2,000.

Duration: 1 year.

Additional information: This scholarship was established in 1952 to honor the 11th president and honorary member of the ASME auxiliary. Further information and an application are available by sending a self-addressed stamped envelope to Mrs. Alverta Cover, 5425 Caldwell Mill Road, Birmingham, AL 35242, (205) 991-6109, E-mail: undergradauxsch@asme.org.

Number awarded: 6 to 12 each year.

Deadline: March of each year.

2550
SYMBOL TECHNOLOGIES SCHOLARSHIP

Society of Women Engineers
230 East Ohio Street, Suite 400
Chicago, IL 60611-3265
Phone: (312) 596-5223   Fax: (312) 644-8557
E-mail: hq@swe.org
Web Site: www.swe.org

Summary: To provide financial assistance to undergraduate women majoring in engineering or computer science.

Eligibility: This program is open to women who are entering their junior year and majoring in computer science, electrical engineering, or mechanical engineering. Applicants must be attending an accredited university and have at least a 3.2 grade point average. Selection is based on merit.

Financial data: The stipend is $2,500.

Duration: 1 year.

Additional information: This program was established in 2000.

Number awarded: 1 each year.

Deadline: January of each year.

2551
TAPPI CORRUGATED CONTAINERS DIVISION SUPPLIER COMMITTEE SCHOLARSHIPS

Technical Association of the Pulp and Paper Industry
P.O. Box 105113
Atlanta, GA 30348-5113
Phone: (770) 446-1400   (800) 332-8686
Fax: (770) 446-6947
Web Site: www.tappi.org

Summary: To provide financial assistance to students who are interested in preparing for a career in the paper industry, with a focus on the manufacture and use of corrugated, solid fiber, and associated packaging materials and products.

Eligibility: This program is open to full- and part-time students who are currently enrolled and will be enrolled during the coming school year at a 4-year college or university, 2-year college, or technical trade school; have earned a grade point average of 3.0 or higher; are able to demonstrate a significant interest in the pulp and paper industry with a strong preference for the corrugated container segment of the industry; and are recommended and endorsed by an instructor or faculty member. Selection is based on the candidates' potential career and contributions in the corrugated container industry. Financial need is not considered in the selection process.

Financial data: The stipend is $2,000.

Duration: 1 year.

Additional information: These scholarships are sponsored by the Corrugated Containers Division Supplier Advisory Committee of the Technical Association of the Pulp and Paper Industry (TAPPI).

Number awarded: 2 each year.

Deadline: January of each year.

2552
TAU BETA PI/SAE ENGINEERING SCHOLARSHIP

Society of Automotive Engineers
Attn: Educational Relations
400 Commonwealth Drive
Warrendale, PA 15096-0001
Phone: (724) 772-4047   Fax: (724) 776-0890
E-mail: connie@sae.org
Web Site: www.sae.org/students/tauschol.htm

Summary: To provide financial support for college to high school seniors interested in studying engineering.

Eligibility: This program is open to U.S. citizens who intend to earn an ABET-accredited degree in engineering. Applicants must be high school seniors with a grade point average of 3.75 or higher who rank in the 90th percentile in both mathematics and verbal on the ACT or SAT. Selection is based on high school transcripts; SAT or ACT scores; school-related extracurricular activities; non-school related activities; academic honors, civic honors, and awards; and a 250-word essay on the single experience that most strongly convinced them or confirmed their decision to pursue a career in engineering. Financial need is not considered.

Financial data: The stipend is $1,000.

Duration: 1 year; nonrenewable.

Additional information: Funding for this program is provided by Tau Beta Pi, the national engineering society. Candidates must include a $5 processing fee with their applications.

Number awarded: 6 each year.

Deadline: November of each year.

2553
TECHFORCE PREENGINEERING PRIZE

National Action Council for Minorities in Engineering
350 Fifth Avenue, Suite 2212
New York, NY 10118-2299
Phone: (212) 279-2626   Fax: (212) 629-5178
E-mail: awalter@nacme.org
Web Site: www.nacme.org

Summary: To recognize and reward outstanding underrepresented minority high school seniors who are planning to pursue a career in engineering.

Eligibility: This program is open to African American, Latino, and American Indian high school seniors who have demonstrated outstanding academic achievement (including class rank in the top 10 percent, a grade point average of "B+" or better, and scores on the SAT of 1100 or better or the ACT of 24 or better), community involvement, and participation in precollege math and science programs. Students must be nominated by directors of university-based programs or those recognized by the National Association of Precollege Directors.

Financial data: Those selected are awarded a paid trip to attend the annual National Action Council for Minorities in Engineering Forum (where they make formal presentations and are recognized at a dinner attended by many of the nation's corporate, government, and academic leaders), a certificate of recognition, and a $1,000 award to be used for the cost of attending engineering school.

Duration: The prizes are awarded annually.

Number awarded: 10 each year.

Deadline: January of each year.

Scholarship Listings

2554
TECHNOLOGICAL INNOVATION SCHOLARSHIPS

National Alliance for Excellence
63 Riverside Avenue
Red Bank, NJ 07701
Phone: (732) 747-0028   Fax: (732) 842-2962
E-mail: info@excellence.org
Web Site: www.excellence.org
Summary: To provide financial assistance for postsecondary education in the United States or abroad to students interested in technological innovation.
Eligibility: Applicants must be U.S. citizens attending or planning to attend a college or university in the United States or an approved foreign study program on a full-time basis. They may be high school seniors, college students, graduate students, or returning students. For these scholarships, applicants must submit architectural plans, designs for inventions, or other mechanisms or structures, along with documentation and evaluation of design solutions. Selection is based on talent and ability without regard to financial need.
Financial data: Stipends range from $1,000 to $5,000 per year.
Duration: 1 year.
Additional information: The National Alliance for Excellence was formerly the Scholarship Foundation of America. A $5 processing fee is charged.
Deadline: Applications may be submitted at any time. Awards are given out on a continuous basis.

2555
TED PETERSON STUDENT PAPER AWARD

American Institute of Chemical Engineers
Attn: Awards Administrator
Three Park Avenue
New York, NY 10016-5991
Phone: (212) 591-7478   Fax: (212) 591-8882
E-mail: awards@aiche.org
Web Site: www.aiche.org/awards
Summary: To recognize and reward outstanding student papers in chemical engineering.
Eligibility: Published works on the application of computing and systems technology to chemical engineering that were completed while the author was pursuing graduate or undergraduate studies in chemical engineering may be submitted.
Financial data: The award consists of a plaque and $1,500.
Duration: This award is presented annually.
Additional information: This award, first presented in 1995, is sponsored by Hyprotech, Ltd. Information is also available from Mark A. Stadtherr, University of Notre Dame, Department of Chemical Engineering, 182 Fitzpatrick Hall, Notre Dame, IN 46556, (219) 631-9318, Fax: (219) 631-8366, E-mail: markst@nd.edu.
Number awarded: 1 each year.
Deadline: April of each year.

2556
TEF/FLUOR CORPORATION SCHOLARSHIPS

Texas Engineering Foundation
Attn: Programs Director
3501 Manor Road
P.O. Box 2145
Austin, TX 78768
Phone: (512) 472-9286   (800) 580-8973 (within TX)
Fax: (512) 472-2934   E-mail: scholarships@tspe.org
Web Site: www.tspe.org
Summary: To provide financial assistance to high school seniors in Texas who are interested in majoring in engineering in college.
Eligibility: This program is open to high school seniors in Texas who have a grade point average of 3.0 or higher, have minimum scores of 600 in math and 550 in verbal on the SAT or 29 in math and 25 in English on the ACT, are U.S. citizens, are planning to major in engineering in college, and are planning to attend a Texas college or university with an ABET-accredited engineering program. Applicants must submit an essay of up to 750 words on the people and/or events in their lives that led them to choose to study engineering, accomplishments that illustrate their aptitude for and interest in engineering, and the aspects of engineering that influenced their decision to select it as a profession. Applications must be submitted first to a local chapter of the Texas Society of Professional Engineers (TSPE). The finalists are selected by each local chapter and sent to the

TSPE higher education committee. The committee selects 1 applicant to receive the scholarship from each of the 5 regions in the state. Selection is based on academic record, achievement, leadership, and career goals. Financial need is not considered in the selection process.
Financial data: The stipend is $1,000.
Duration: 1 year.
Additional information: These scholarships, funded by Fluor Corporation, are sponsored by TSPE and the Texas Engineering Foundation.
Number awarded: 5 each year.
Deadline: January of each year.

2557
TEXACO SCHOLARSHIPS

Society of Women Engineers
230 East Ohio Street, Suite 400
Chicago, IL 60611-3265
Phone: (312) 596-5223   Fax: (312) 644-8557
E-mail: hq@swe.org
Web Site: www.swe.org
Summary: To provide financial assistance to undergraduate women majoring in designated engineering specialties.
Eligibility: This program is open to women entering their junior year in college and majoring in chemical, civil, computer, electrical, mechanical, or petroleum engineering. Applications must be U.S. citizens with a grade point average of 3.0 or higher. Selection is based on merit.
Financial data: The stipend is $2,000. A $1,000 travel grant is also provided for the recipient to attend the annual SWE national convention/student conference.
Duration: 1 year.
Additional information: This program was established in 1991.
Number awarded: 6 each year.
Deadline: January of each year.

2558
TEXAS CATTLEWOMEN SCHOLARSHIP

Texas CattleWomen, Inc.
Attn: Lisa Fuqua, Scholarship Chairperson
413 Lazy U Ranch Road
Quanah, TX 79252
Phone: (940) 674-2493   E-mail: lazyu@worldnet.att.net
Web Site: www.texascattlewomen.org/TCWscholarships.htm
Summary: To provide financial assistance to residents of Texas who are majoring in foods and nutrition, agricultural communications, or hotel and restaurant management in college.
Eligibility: Applicants must be graduates of a Texas high school who are currently enrolled at the sophomore through senior level in a 4-year college or university in Texas. They must have a grade point average of 3.0 or higher and be majoring in foods and nutrition, agricultural communications, or hotel and restaurant management. Selection is based on evidence of potential for continuing education, participation in student activities, evidence of leadership qualities, ability to relate well with others, financial need, and interest in and willingness to support the production and consumption of beef.
Financial data: The stipend is $1,000 per year. Funds may be used for any educational expense.
Duration: 1 year; recipients may reapply.
Number awarded: 3 each year.

2559
TEXAS FARM BUREAU YOUNG FARMER & RANCHER SCHOLARSHIP PROGRAM

Texas Farm Bureau
P.O. Box 2689
Waco, TX 76702-2689
Phone: (254) 751-2286   E-mail: scook@txfb.org
Web Site: www.txfb.org/educate/yf&rscholarships2.htm
Summary: To provide financial assistance to high school seniors whose families are members of the Texas Farm Bureau (TFB) and who wish to major in agriculture in college.
Eligibility: This program is open to Texas graduating high school seniors who are planning to pursue a college degree in agriculture and whose families are TFB members (father, mother, or legal guardian memberships qualify; grandparent,

sibling, or other relative memberships may not be used). Selection is based on academic achievement, extracurricular activities, recommendations, and financial need.

Financial data: The stipend is $1,000 per year.

Duration: 1 year; may be renewed up to 3 additional years, as long as the Farm Bureau membership remains in good standing.

Number awarded: 4 each year.

Deadline: May of each year.

2560
TEXAS OCCUPATIONAL THERAPY ASSOCIATION SCHOLARSHIP

American Occupational Therapy Foundation
Attn: Scholarship Coordinator
4720 Montgomery Lane
P.O. Box 31220
Bethesda, MD 20824-1220
Phone: (301) 652-2682.   Fax: (301) 656-3620
Phone: TDD: (800) 377-8555   E-mail: aotf@aotf.org
Web Site: www.aotf.org

Summary: To provide financial assistance to students who are members of the Texas Occupational Therapy Association and working on a degree in occupational therapy.

Eligibility: This program is open to Texas residents who are enrolled in an accredited occupational therapy educational program (associate or professional) in the state. Applicants must demonstrate a need for financial assistance, have a sustained record of outstanding scholastic performance, and be members of the Texas Occupational Therapy Association. As part of the application process, they must submit transcripts, 2 personal references, and a statement from their curriculum director.

Financial data: The stipend is $1,000.

Duration: 1 year.

Additional information: Application forms are available at no cost at the association's web site; a $5 fee is charged for printed copies sent from the association's headquarters.

Number awarded: 4 each year: 2 at the professional degree level and 2 at the associate degree level.

Deadline: January of each year.

2561
TEXAS PROFESSIONAL NURSING SCHOLARSHIPS

Texas Higher Education Coordinating Board
Attn: Grants and Special Programs
1200 East Anderson Lane
P.O. Box 12788, Capitol Station
Austin, TX 78711-2788
Phone: (512) 427-6101   (800) 242-3062
Fax: (512) 427-6127   E-mail: grantinfo@thecb.state.tx.us
Web Site: www.collegefortexans.com

Summary: To provide financial assistance for Texas students who are interested in preparing for a career as a professional nurse.

Eligibility: This program is open to undergraduate or graduate students who are residents of Texas and enrolled at least half time in a program leading to licensure as a professional nurse at a college or university in the state. Applicants must be able to demonstrate financial need.

Financial data: The stipend depends on the need of the recipient, to a maximum of $3,000. Recently, the average award was $1,974 for students at public universities, $1,012 for students at public community colleges, and $1,996 for students at private, nonprofit colleges.

Duration: 1 academic year.

Additional information: Some of these funds are targeted to students from rural communities and some to graduate students.

Number awarded: Varies each year; recently, 44 of these scholarships were awarded to students at public universities, 181 to students at public community colleges, and 31 to students at private, nonprofit colleges.

Deadline: Applicants should contact the financial aid director at the professional nursing school in which they plan to enroll for appropriate deadline dates.

2562
TEXAS TRANSPORTATION SCHOLARSHIP

Transportation Clubs International
Attn: Gay Fielding
P.O. Box 52
Arabi, LA 70032
Phone: (504) 278-1107
Web Site: www.transportationclubsinternational.com

Summary: To provide financial assistance to college students interested in preparing for a career in fields related to transportation.

Eligibility: This program is open to students enrolled in an academic institution that offers courses in transportation, logistics, traffic management, or related fields. Applicants must intend to prepare for a career in those fields. They must have been enrolled in a school in Texas during some phase of their education (elementary or secondary). Selection is based on scholastic ability, potential, character, professional interest, and financial need.

Financial data: The stipend is $1,000.

Duration: 1 year.

Additional information: Requests for applications must be accompanied by a stamped self-addressed envelope.

Number awarded: 1 each year.

Deadline: April of each year.

2563
TEXAS VOCATIONAL NURSING SCHOLARSHIPS

Texas Higher Education Coordinating Board
Attn: Grants and Special Programs
1200 East Anderson Lane
P.O. Box 12788, Capitol Station
Austin, TX 78711-2788
Phone: (512) 427-6101   (800) 242-3062
Fax: (512) 427-6127   E-mail: grantinfo@thecb.state.tx.us
Web Site: www.collegefortexans.com

Summary: To provide financial assistance for Texas students who are interested in preparing for a career as a vocational nurse.

Eligibility: This program is open to undergraduate or graduate students who are residents of Texas and enrolled at least half time in a program leading to licensure as a vocational nurse at a college or university in the state. Applicants must be able to demonstrate financial need.

Financial data: The stipend depends on the need of the recipient, to a maximum of $1,500. Recently, the average award was $583 for students at public community colleges and $1,175 for students at independent colleges.

Duration: 1 academic year.

Additional information: Some of these funds are targeted to students from rural communities.

Number awarded: Varies each year; recently, 84 of these scholarships were awarded to students at public community colleges and 4 to students at independent colleges.

Deadline: Applicants should contact the financial aid director at the vocational nursing school in which they plan to enroll for appropriate deadline dates.

2564
TEXAS YES! SCHOLARSHIPS

Texas Engineering Foundation
Attn: Programs Director
3501 Manor Road
P.O. Box 2145
Austin, TX 78768
Phone: (512) 472-9286   (800) 580-8973 (within TX)
Fax: (512) 472-2934   E-mail: scholarships@tspe.org
Web Site: www.tspe.org

Summary: To provide financial assistance for college study of engineering to high school seniors in Texas who are women or minorities or have participated in designated educational programs.

Eligibility: This program is open to high school seniors in Texas who have a grade point average of 3.0 or higher, have minimum scores of 600 in math and 550 in verbal on the SAT or 29 in math and 25 in English on the ACT, are planning to major in engineering in college, are U.S. citizens, and are planning to attend a Texas college or university with an ABET-accredited engineering program. Applicants must be women or minorities or have participated in 1 or more of the following educational programs offered by the Texas Society of Professional Engineers (TSPE): JETS or

Texas YES! chapters in junior or senior high school; MATHCOUNTS for students in the seventh and eighth grades; National Engineering Design Challenge or the Texas Engineering Challenge for high school students; TEAMS competitions for high school students; or the Texas Engineering Skills Competitions for high school students. They must submit an essay of up to 750 words on the people and/or events in their lives that led them to choose to study engineering, accomplishments that illustrate their aptitude for and interest in engineering, and the aspects of engineering that influenced their decision to select it as a profession. Selection is based on academic record, achievement, leadership, and career goals. Financial need is not considered in the selection process.

Financial data: The stipend is $1,000.

Duration: 1 year.

Additional information: These scholarships are sponsored by TSPE and the Texas Engineering Foundation.

Number awarded: 3 each year.

Deadline: January of each year.

2565
TEXAS YOUNG FARMERS SCHOLARSHIP

Texas FFA Association
614 East 12th Street
Austin, TX 78701
Phone: (512) 480-8045   Fax: (512) 472-0555
E-mail: txffa@txaged.org
Web Site: www.txaged.org

Summary: To provide financial assistance for college to high school seniors in Texas who demonstrate outstanding personal qualities and involvement in FFA.

Eligibility: This program is open to high school seniors in Texas who are FFA members and have been members at least 2 of the 3 previous years. Applicants must be planning to major in college in a field related to the agricultural sciences, life sciences, or natural resources. They must have completed at least 5 semesters of instruction in agriculture and/or agribusiness during high school and scored at least 950 on the SAT or 20 on the ACT. U.S. citizenship and ranking in the top half of their graduating class are also required. Selection is based on academic achievement (16 points); SAT or ACT scores (14 points); agricultural science and career-related instruction (10 points); FFA achievement (20 points), including the supervised agricultural experience (10 points); financial need (10 points); and performance during interviews regarding academics (10 points), FFA achievement (5 points), and financial need (10 points).

Financial data: The stipend is $2,000.

Duration: 1 year.

Additional information: Students may not apply for both 4-H and FFA scholarships.

Number awarded: 1 each year.

2566
THERMOFORMING DIVISION MEMORIAL SCHOLARSHIPS

Society of Plastics Engineers
Attn: SPE Foundation
14 Fairfield Drive
Brookfield, CT 06804
Phone: (203) 740-5434   Fax: (203) 775-8490
E-mail: foundation@4spe.org
Web Site: www.4spe.org

Summary: To provide college scholarships to students who have a career interest in the plastics industry and experience in the thermoforming industry.

Eligibility: Applicants must be full-time undergraduate or graduate students. They must have a demonstrated or expressed interest in the plastics industry; must have experience in the thermoforming industry, such as courses taken, research conducted, or jobs held; and should be taking classes that would be beneficial to a career in the plastics industry (e.g., plastics engineering, polymer sciences, chemistry, physics, chemical engineering, mechanical engineering, industrial engineering, and business administration). Financial need must be documented. Along with their application, students must submit 3 letters of recommendation; a high school and/or college transcript; a 1- to 2-page statement telling why they are interested in the scholarship, their qualifications, and their career goals in the plastics industry; and a statement detailing their exposure to the thermoforming industry.

Financial data: The stipend is $5,000 per year.

Duration: 1 year.

Number awarded: 2 each year.

Deadline: December of each year.

2567
THOMAS F. BRESNAHAN DISTINGUISHED SERVICE AWARD SCHOLARSHIP

American Society of Safety Engineers
Attn: ASSE Foundation
1800 East Oakton Street
Des Plaines, IL 60018
Phone: (847) 768-3441   Fax: (847) 296-9220
E-mail: mrosario@asse.org
Web Site: www.asse.org

Summary: To provide financial assistance to undergraduate student members of the American Society of Safety Engineers (ASSE).

Eligibility: This program is open to ASSE student members who are majoring in occupational safety. Applicants must be full-time students who have completed at least 60 semester hours with a grade point average of 3.25 or higher. As part of the selection process, they must submit 2 essays of 300 words or less: 1) why they are seeking a degree in safety, a brief description of their current activities, and how those relate to their career goals and objectives; and 2) why they should be awarded this scholarship (including career goals and financial need).

Financial data: The stipend is $2,000 per year.

Duration: 1 year; nonrenewable.

Number awarded: 1 each year.

Deadline: November of each year.

2568
THREAD COMMITTEE EXCELLENCE IN MANUFACTURING SCHOLARSHIP

Summary: To provide financial assistance to high school seniors interested in majoring in a textile science-related program at selected schools.
See Listing #1664.

2569
TIMOTHY BIGELOW AND PALMER W. BIGELOW, JR. SCHOLARSHIPS

Summary: To provide financial support to residents of New England for undergraduate or graduate study in landscape architecture or horticulture.
See Listing #1665.

2570
TISCOR/HERB GARDNER FOUNDATION AWARD

Association for the Advancement of Medical Instrumentation
Attn: AAMI Foundation Awards
1110 North Glebe Road, Suite 220
Arlington, VA 22201-4795
Phone: (703) 525-4890, ext. 226   (800) 332-2264, ext. 226
Fax: (703) 525-1424   E-mail: nwells@aami.org
Web Site: www.aami.org/membership/awards/index.html

Summary: To provide financial assistance to mid-career biomedical professionals who wish to pursue an undergraduate or advanced degree.

Eligibility: Applicants for this program must have been employed as a biomedical equipment technician or in a related technical service position for at least 3 years and show by their accomplishments, training, and employment that they are committed to the technical service field. They must be interested in advancing their career by pursuing an undergraduate or advanced degree or completing training at an appropriate technical school.

Financial data: The stipend is $1,000.

Duration: 1 year.

Additional information: Support for this program is provided by TISCOR.

Number awarded: 1 each year.

Deadline: March of each year.

2571
TMC/SAE DONALD D. DAWSON TECHNICAL SCHOLARSHIP

Society of Automotive Engineers
Attn: Educational Relations
400 Commonwealth Drive
Warrendale, PA 15096-0001
Phone: (724) 772-4047   Fax: (724) 776-0890
E-mail: connie@sae.org
Web Site: www.sae.org/students/dawsonsc.htm

Summary: To provide financial support to students pursing a college degree in engineering.

Eligibility: This program is open to U.S. citizens who intend to earn an ABET-accredited degree in engineering. Applicants must be 1) high school seniors with a grade point average of 3.25 or higher and minimum SAT scores of 600 in mathematics and 550 in verbal or ACT score of 27 or higher; 2) transfer students from 4-year colleges or universities with a grade point average of 3.0 or higher; or 3) transfer students from postsecondary technical or vocational schools with a grade point average of 3.5 or higher. Selection is based on school transcripts; evidence of some type of hands-on technical experience or activity (e.g., rebuilding engines, working on cars or trucks); SAT or ACT scores; school-related extracurricular activities; non-school related activities; academic honors, civic honors, and awards; and a 250-word essay on the single experience that most strongly convinced them or confirmed their decision to pursue a career in engineering. Financial need is not considered.

Financial data: The stipend is $1,500 per year.

Duration: 1 year; may be renewed up to 3 additional years if the recipient maintains a grade point average of 3.0 or higher.

Additional information: The Society of Automotive Engineers (SAE) and The Maintenance Council (TMC) of American Trucking Associations established this scholarship to honor the leadership of Donald D. Dawson. Candidates must include a $5 processing fee with their applications.

Number awarded: 1 each year.

Deadline: November of each year.

2572
TNLA SCHOLARSHIP PROGRAM

Texas Nursery and Landscape Association
Attn: Education and Research Foundation
7730 South IH-35
Austin, TX 78745-6698
Phone: (512) 280-5182   (800) 880-0343
Fax: (512) 280-3012   E-mail: info@txnla.org

Summary: To provide financial assistance to high school seniors and returning college students in Texas who are majoring in horticulture.

Eligibility: Eligible to apply are Texas residents. They may be either high school seniors or returning college students, but they must be majoring or planning to major in horticulture at an approved college in Texas; currently, these include: Collin County Community College, Houston Community College, Richland College, Sam Houston State, Southwest Texas State University, Stephen F. Austin State University, Tarleton University, Tarrant County Junior College, Texas A&M University, Texas State Technical College, Texas Tech University, Trinity Valley College, and Tyler Junior College. To apply, qualified students must complete an application form and submit an official transcript, 2 letters of recommendation, and a recent photograph.

Financial data: Stipends are either $500 or $1,000 per year.

Duration: From 1 to 4 years.

Number awarded: Varies each year.

Deadline: May of each year.

2573
TOBIN SORENSON SCHOLARSHIPS

Pi Lambda Theta
Attn: Scholarships Committee
4101 East Third Street
P.O. Box 6626
Bloomington, IN 47407-6626
Phone: (812) 339-3411   (800) 487-3411
Fax: (812) 339-3462   E-mail: pam@pilambda.org
Web Site: www.pilambda.org

Summary: To provide financial assistance to students preparing for careers as a teacher of physical education or a related field.

Eligibility: This program is open to students preparing for careers at the K-12 level. Applicants must be interested in becoming a physical education teacher, adaptive physical education teacher, coach, recreational therapist, dance therapist, or similar professional teaching the knowledge and use of the human body. They must be sophomores or above and have a grade point average of 3.5 or higher. Selection is based on academic achievement, potential for leadership, and extracurricular involvement in physical/sports education, recreation therapy, or similar activities (e.g., coaching, tutoring, volunteer work for appropriate organizations on or off campus).

Financial data: The stipend is $1,000.

Duration: 1 year.

Additional information: This program was established in 1999.

Number awarded: 1 every other year.

Deadline: February of each odd-numbered year.

2574
TOCA PUBLISHERS SCHOLARSHIP PROGRAM

Summary: To provide financial assistance to undergraduate students preparing for a career in green industry communications.
See Listing #1667.

2575
TOWER HILL BOTANIC GARDEN SCHOLARSHIP

Worcester County Horticultural Society
Attn: Education Secretary
Tower Hill Botanic Garden
11 French Drive
P.O. Box 598
Boylston, MA 01505-0598
Phone: (508) 869-6111, ext. 24   Fax: (508) 869-0314
E-mail: thbg@towerhillbg.org
Web Site: www.towerhillbg.org

Summary: To provide financial assistance to undergraduate or graduate students in New England who are majoring in horticulture.

Eligibility: Applicants must be entering their junior or senior year of college or be in a graduate degree program. They must be 1) either a resident of New England or attending a New England college or university and 2) majoring in horticulture or a horticulture-related field. Selection is based on interest in horticulture, sincerity of purpose, academic performance, and financial need.

Financial data: Stipends range from $1,000 to $3,000.

Duration: 1 year.

Deadline: April of each year.

2576
TRANSFER ENGINEERING STUDENT SCHOLARSHIP

National Association of Minority Engineering Program Administrators, Inc.
1133 West Morse Boulevard, Suite 201
Winter Park, FL 32789
Phone: (407) 647-8839   Fax: (407) 629-2502
E-mail: namepa@namepa.org
Web Site: www.namepa.org/awards.htm

Summary: To provide financial assistance to underrepresented minority college transfer students who are planning to major in engineering.

Eligibility: Candidates for this award must be African American, Hispanic American, or Native American college transfer students who are coming from either a junior/community college or a 3/2 dual-degree program. They must be transferring to an engineering program at an institution affiliated with the National Association of Minority Engineering Program Administrators (NAMEPA). For a list of affiliated schools, write to the sponsor. They must have at least a 3.0 grade point average. To apply, qualified students must submit a copy of their college transcript, a recommendation, and a 1-page essay on why they have chosen engineering as a profession. Financial need is not considered in the selection process.

Financial data: The stipend is $1,000, paid in 2 equal installments.

Duration: 1 year; nonrenewable.

Deadline: February of each year.

2577
TRANSIT HALL OF FAME SCHOLARSHIP AWARDS

American Public Transportation Foundation
1666 K Street, N.W., Suite 1100
Washington, DC 20006
Phone: (202) 496-4852   Fax: (202) 496-4324
E-mail: kpopkin@apta.com
Web Site: www.apta.com/services/hrtraining/scholguide.htm

Summary: to provide financial assistance to upper-division and graduate students who are preparing for a career in transportation.

Eligibility: This program is open to college sophomores, juniors, seniors, and graduate students who are preparing for a career in the transit industry. Any member organization can nominate and sponsor candidates for this scholarship.

Nominees must be enrolled in a fully-accredited institution, have and maintain at least a 3.0 grade point average, and be either employed by or demonstrate a strong interest in entering the public transportation industry. They must submit a 1,000-word essay on "What segment of the public transportation industry interests you and why?" Selection is based on demonstrated interest in the transit field as a career, need for financial assistance, academic achievement, the essay content and quality, and involvement in extracurricular citizenship and leadership activities.
Financial data: The stipend is at least $2,500. The winner of the Donald C. Hyde Memorial Essay Award receives an additional $500.
Duration: 1 year; may be renewed.
Additional information: This program was established in 1987. There is an internship component, which is designed to provide substantive training and professional development opportunities. Each year, there are 4 named scholarships offered: the Jack R. Gilstrap Scholarship for the applicant who receives the highest overall score; the Parsons Brickerhoff-Jim Lammie Scholarship for an applicant dedicated to a public transportation engineering career; the Louis T. Klauder Scholarship for an applicant dedicated to a career in the rail transit industry as an electrical or mechanical engineer; and the Dan M. Reichard, Jr. Scholarship for an applicant dedicated to a career in the business administration/management area of the transit industry. In addition, the Donald C. Hyde Memorial Essay Award is presented to the applicant who submits the best response to the required essay component of the program.
Number awarded: At least 6 each year.
Deadline: May of each year.

2578
TRUMAN D. PICARD SCHOLARSHIP PROGRAM

Intertribal Timber Council
Attn: Education Committee
1112 N.E. 21st Avenue
Portland, OR 97232
Phone: (503) 282-4296   Fax: (503) 282-1274
E-mail: itc1@teleport.com   Web Site: www.itcnet.org/picard.html
Summary: To provide financial assistance to American Indians or Alaskan Natives who are interested in studying natural resources in college.
Eligibility: Eligible to apply are 1) graduating high school seniors or 2) currently-enrolled college students. They must be enrolled in a federally-recognized tribe or Native Alaska corporation. All applicants must be either majoring or planning to major in natural resources. They must provide documentation of their interest in natural resources; commitment to education, community, and culture; academic merit; and financial need.
Financial data: The stipend is $1,200 for high school seniors entering college or $1,800 for students already enrolled in college.
Duration: 1 year.
Number awarded: 14 each year: 4 for high school seniors and 10 for college students.
Deadline: January of each year.

2579
TRW FOUNDATION SCHOLARSHIPS

Society of Women Engineers
230 East Ohio Street, Suite 400
Chicago, IL 60611-3265
Phone: (312) 596-5223   Fax: (312) 644-8557
E-mail: hq@swe.org   Web Site: www.swe.org
Summary: To provide financial assistance to women entering their sophomore year in college and majoring in engineering.
Eligibility: This program is open to entering sophomore women majoring in engineering at an accredited school, college, or university. Applicants must have a grade point average of 3.0 or higher. Selection is based on merit.
Financial data: The stipend is $2,125.
Duration: 1 year.
Additional information: This program was established in 1974.
Number awarded: 1 each year.
Deadline: January of each year.

2580
TWEET COLEMAN AVIATION SCHOLARSHIP

American Association of University Women-Honolulu Branch
1802 Keeaumoku Street
Honolulu, HI 96822
Phone: (808) 537-4702
Summary: To provide financial assistance to women in Hawaii who are interested in a career in aviation.
Eligibility: This program is open to women who are residents of Hawaii and either college graduates or attending an accredited college in the state. Applicants must be able to pass a First Class FAA medical examination. As part of their application, they must include a 2-page statement on "Why I Want to be a Pilot." Selection is based on the merit of the applicant and a personal interview.
Financial data: The amount awarded varies.
Duration: 1 year.
Additional information: This scholarship was first awarded in 1990.
Number awarded: Varies; at least 1 each year.
Deadline: September of each year.

2581
TYLENOL SCHOLARSHIPS

McNeil Consumer & Specialty Pharmaceuticals
c/o Citizens' Scholarship Foundation of America
Attn: Scholarship Management Services
1505 Riverview Road
P.O. Box 297
St. Peter, MN 56082
Phone: (507) 931-1682   (800) 537-4180
Fax: (507) 931-9168   Web Site: scholarship.tylenol.com/index.asp
Summary: To provide financial assistance for college to students intending to pursue a career in a health-related field.
Eligibility: This program is open to students who will be enrolled in an undergraduate or graduate course of study at an accredited 2-year or 4-year college, university, or vocational-technical school who have 1 or more years of school remaining. Applicants must intend to major in an area that will lead to a career in a health-related field. Selection is based on the number, length of commitment, and quality of leadership responsibilities in community activities and school activities, awards, and honors (40 percent), a clear statement of education and career goals (10 percent), and academic record (50 percent).
Financial data: Stipends are $10,000 or $1,000.
Duration: 1 year.
Additional information: This program is sponsored by McNeil Consumer & Specialty Pharmaceuticals, maker of Tylenol products, and administered by the Citizens' Scholarship Foundation of America.
Number awarded: 160 each year: 10 at $10,000 and 150 at $1,000.
Deadline: April of each year.

2582
TYSON FOUNDATION SCHOLARSHIP PROGRAM

Tyson Foundation, Inc.
2210 West Oaklawn Drive
Springdale, AR 72762-6999
Phone: (501) 290-4955   (800) 643-3410, ext. 4955
Fax: (501) 290-7984   E-mail: comments@tysonfoundation.org
Web Site: www.tysonfoundation.org
Summary: To provide financial assistance to undergraduate students in selected disciplines who reside near a plant of Tyson Foods, Inc.
Eligibility: Applicants must be undergraduate students who are enrolled full time and majoring in agriculture, biology, business administration, chemistry, computer science, engineering, microbiology, or nursing. They must be U.S. citizens or permanent residents and reside in the vicinity of a Tyson operating facility. Selection is based on academic record, recommendations, and financial need.
Financial data: The stipends depend on the need of the recipient.
Duration: 1 year; may be renewed for a total of 8 semesters (or 10 semesters for specialized degrees that require additional study).
Additional information: Tyson operating facilities are located in specified communities in Alabama, Arkansas, Florida, Georgia, Illinois, Indiana, Kentucky, Maryland, Mississippi, Missouri, North Carolina, Oklahoma, Pennsylvania, Tennessee, Texas, and Virginia. For a complete list, contact the foundation.
Number awarded: Varies; generally, 100 or more each year.
Deadline: April of each year.

2583
UABT SCHOLARSHIP PROGRAM

United Agribusiness League
Attn: Member Services
54 Corporate Park
Irvine, CA 92606-5105
Phone: (949) 975-1424   (800) 223-4590
Fax: (949) 975-1671   E-mail: csteele@ual.org
Web Site: www.ual.org
Summary: To provide financial assistance to students pursuing an undergraduate degree in agriculture or agribusiness.
Eligibility: This program is open to students presently enrolled or accepted for enrollment at an accredited college or university offering a degree in agriculture. Applicants must submit an essay on "My Future in Agribusiness," 2 letters of recommendation (may be from anyone), and their SAT scores. Their family must be participating in the United Agricultural Benefit Trust (UABT) health care program. Financial need is considered only if the applicant requests it.
Financial data: Stipends range from $1,000 to $4,000.
Duration: 1 year; may be renewed.
Number awarded: Varies each year; recently, a total of $25,000 was available for this program.
Deadline: March of each year.

2584
UNCF/MERCK UNDERGRADUATE SCIENCE RESEARCH SCHOLARSHIPS

United Negro College Fund
Attn: Merck Science Initiative
8260 Willow Oaks Corporate Drive
P.O. Box 10444
Fairfax, VA 22031-4511
Phone: (703) 205-3538   Fax: (703) 205-3574
E-mail: uncfmerck@uncf.org
Web Site: www.uncf.org/merck
Summary: To provide financial assistance and summer work experience to African American undergraduates who are interested in pursuing biomedical research.
Eligibility: This program is open to African American students currently enrolled as full-time juniors and planning to graduate in the coming year. Applicants must be majoring in a life or physical science, have completed 2 semesters of organic chemistry, be interested in biomedical research, and have a grade point average of 3.3 or higher. They must be interested in working at Merck as a summer intern. Candidates for professional (Pharm.D., D.V.M., D.D.S., etc.) and engineering degrees are ineligible. U.S. citizenship or permanent resident status is required. Selection is based on grade point average, demonstrated interest in a scientific education and a career in scientific research, and ability to perform in a laboratory environment.
Financial data: The total award is $35,000, including up to $25,000 for tuition, fees, room, and board, and at least $10,000 for 2 summer internship stipends. In addition, the department of the award recipient may receive a grant of up to $10,000.
Duration: 1 academic year plus 10 to 12 weeks during the preceding and following summers.
Additional information: This program is funded by the Merck Company Foundation. Internships are performed at a Merck research facility in Rahway, New Jersey or West Point, Pennsylvania.
Number awarded: At least 15 each year.
Deadline: December of each year.

2585
UNDERGRADUATE STUDENT AWARDS FOR RESEARCH

National Aeronautics and Space Administration
Office of Equal Opportunity Programs
Attn: Minority University Research and Education Division
Code EU
Washington, DC 20546-0001
Phone: (202) 358-0970   Fax: (202) 358-3745
E-mail: muredsupport@nasaprs.com
Web Site: mured.nasaprs.com/muredhomepage/undergra.asp
Summary: To provide financial assistance to students who are socially and economically disadvantaged or have disabilities and wish to study areas related to space.

Eligibility: This program is open to students at designated Historically Black Colleges and Universities (HBCUs) and Other Minority Universities (OMUs), including tribal colleges and universities, designated Hispanic-Serving Institutions, and other accredited colleges or universities with enrollment of a single underrepresented minority group or combination of underrepresented minority groups that exceeds 50 percent of the total student enrollment. The program targets socially and economically disadvantaged students, especially those historically underrepresented in programs of the National Aeronautics and Space Administration (NASA), and/or students with disabilities. Applicants must 1) be high school seniors or undergraduates with no more than 32 credit hours of college work; 2) have completed 4 years of mathematics and 3 years of science in high school; 3) have attained a combined SAT score of at least 1000; 4) have a minimum grade point average of 3.2 in high school and/or 3.0 in college; 5) be U.S. citizens; and 6) be able to demonstrate financial need. Students should be pursuing degrees (as full-time students) in the areas of science, mathematics, and engineering compatible with NASA's programs in space science and aerospace technology.
Financial data: Awards provide up to 50 percent of educational costs (or 75 percent for students eligible for a federal Pell Grant), to a maximum of $7,000. In addition, the award provides $4,000 for a summer research experience for students who are selected.
Duration: Up to 4 years.
Additional information: Students submit applications through participating universities; currently, those are California State University at Los Angeles, D-Q University (Davis, California), Gallaudet University (Washington, D.C.), Florida A&M University (Tallahassee, Florida), Morehouse College (Atlanta, Georgia), Spelman College (Atlanta, Georgia), Southern University and A&M College (Baton Rouge, Louisiana), Morgan State University (Baltimore, Maryland), University of Maryland, Eastern Shore (Princess Anne, Maryland), Fayetteville State University (Fayetteville, North Carolina), North Carolina A&T University (Greensboro, North Carolina), University of North Carolina at Pembroke, Shaw University (Raleigh, North Carolina), Winston-Salem State University (Winston-Salem, North Carolina), New Mexico Highlands University (Las Vegas, New Mexico), New Mexico State University (Las Cruces, New Mexico), University of New Mexico (Albuquerque, New Mexico), City College of New York, Fiorella H. LaGuardia Community College (Long Island City, New York), Tennessee State University (Nashville, Tennessee), University of Texas, Pan American (Edinburg, Texas), University of Texas at El Paso, and University of Texas at San Antonio.
Number awarded: Varies each year.
Deadline: Universities must forward applications to NASA Headquarters by April of each year.

2586
UNDERGRADUATE STUDIES IN TECHNICAL RESEARCH PROGRAM

National Society of Black Engineers
Attn: Programs Manager
1454 Duke Street
Alexandria, VA 22314
Phone: (703) 549-2207, ext. 208   Fax: (703) 683-5312
E-mail: programs@nsbe.org
Web Site: www.nsbe.org
Summary: To recognize and reward undergraduate members of the National Society of Black Engineers (NSBE) who participate in a research competition.
Eligibility: This program is open to undergraduate students who are current, paid members of the society. Competitors display their research via a poster presentation, using a variety of graphical wall displays (maps, charts, photographs, computer outputs), working models, and/or material samples that are prepared by the authors. The research projects may be senior projects, company-sponsored research programs, independent study courses, or other research activities conducted by the students. Selection is based on the content of displays and a 10-minute question-and-answer session. Students first compete at the regional level; the top 3 winners from each of the 6 regions then compete at the society's national conference.
Financial data: At the regional level, first prize is $200, second $100, and third $50. At the national level, first prize is $1,000, second $500, and third $250.
Duration: The competition is held annually.
Additional information: This program was initiated through a grant from the Alfred P. Sloan Foundation and is currently sponsored by duPont Corporation.
Number awarded: At the regional level, 18 prizes (3 in each region) are awarded; at the national level, 3 prizes are awarded.
Deadline: November of each year.

2587
UNDERGRADUATE TRAINING ASSISTANCE PROGRAM

Defense Intelligence Agency
Attn: DAH-2
Bolling Air Force Base
200 MacDill Boulevard
Washington, DC 20340-5100
Phone: (202) 231-4713   Fax: (202) 231-4889
Phone: TTY: (202) 231-5002
Web Site: www.dia.mil/Careers/Programs/utap.html
Summary: To provide full tuition and internships to high school seniors interested in majoring in specified fields and working for the U.S. Defense Intelligence Agency (DIA).
Eligibility: This competitive program is open to graduating high school seniors who are interested in majoring in 1 of the following fields in college: computer science, geography, foreign area studies, international relations, or political science. Applicants must have a high school grade point average of 3.0 or higher, have an SAT score of 1000 or higher or an ACT score of 21 or higher, be able to demonstrate financial need (household income ceiling of $60,000 for a family of 4 or $75,000 for a family of 5 or more), be U.S. citizens and from a family of U.S. citizens, and demonstrate leadership abilities through extracurricular activities, civic involvement, volunteer work, or part-time employment. Minorities, women, and people with disabilities are strongly encouraged to apply.
Financial data: Students accepted into this program receive tuition (up to $17,000 per year) at an accredited college or university selected by the student and endorsed by the sponsor; an annual salary for summer employment; and a position at the sponsoring agency after graduation.
Duration: 4 years.
Additional information: Recipients are provided challenging summer work and guaranteed a job at the agency in their field of study upon graduation. Recipients must attend school on a full-time basis. They must also work for DIA after college graduation for at least 1 and a half times the length of study. For participants who leave DIA earlier than scheduled, the agency arranges for payments to reimburse DIA for the total cost of education (including the employee's pay and allowances).
Number awarded: Only a few are awarded each year.
Deadline: November of each year.

2588
UNITED AGRIBUSINESS LEAGUE SCHOLARSHIP PROGRAM

United Agribusiness League
Attn: Member Services
54 Corporate Park
Irvine, CA 92606-5105
Phone: (949) 975-1424   (800) 223-4590
Fax: (949) 975-1671   E-mail: csteele@ual.org
Web Site: www.ual.org
Summary: To provide financial assistance to students pursuing an undergraduate degree in agriculture or agribusiness.
Eligibility: This program is open to students presently enrolled or accepted for enrollment at an accredited college or university offering a degree in agriculture. Applicants must submit a 2-page essay on "My Future in Agribusiness" and 3 letters of recommendation (1 each from a teacher, an employer, and a volunteer organization with which they have been associated). A minimum 2.5 grade point average is required. Financial need is considered only if the applicant requests it.
Financial data: Stipends range from $1,000 to $4,000.
Duration: 1 year; may be renewed.
Number awarded: Varies each year; recently, a total of $10,000 was available for this program.
Deadline: March of each year.

2589
UNITED PARCEL SERVICE SCHOLARSHIP FOR FEMALE STUDENTS

Institute of Industrial Engineers
Attn: Chapter Operations Board
25 Technology Park/Atlanta
Norcross, GA 30092-2988
Phone: (770) 449-0460   (800) 494-0460
Fax: (770) 441-3295
Web Site: www.iienet.org
Summary: To provide financial assistance to female undergraduate students who are studying industrial engineering at a school in the United States, Canada, or Mexico.
Eligibility: Eligible to be nominated are female undergraduate students enrolled in any school in the United States and its territories, Canada, or Mexico, provided the school's engineering program is accredited by an agency recognized by the Institute of Industrial Engineers (IIE) and the student is pursuing a full-time course of study in industrial engineering with a grade point average of at least 3.4. They must have at least 5 full quarters or 3 full semesters remaining until graduation. Students may not apply directly for these awards; they must be nominated by the head of their industrial engineering department. Nominees must be IIE members. Selection is based on scholastic ability, character, leadership, potential service to the industrial engineering profession, and need for financial assistance.
Financial data: The stipend is $4,000.
Duration: 1 year.
Additional information: Funding for this program is provided by the UPS Foundation.
Number awarded: 1 each year.
Deadline: November of each year.

2590
UNITED PARCEL SERVICE SCHOLARSHIP FOR MINORITY STUDENTS

Institute of Industrial Engineers
Attn: Chapter Operations Board
25 Technology Park/Atlanta
Norcross, GA 30092-2988
Phone: (770) 449-0460   (800) 494-0460
Fax: (770) 441-3295   Web Site: www.iienet.org
Summary: To provide financial assistance to minority undergraduate students who are studying industrial engineering at a school in the United States, Canada, or Mexico.
Eligibility: Eligible to be nominated are minority undergraduate students enrolled in any school in the United States and its territories, Canada, or Mexico, provided the school's engineering program is accredited by an agency recognized by the Institute of Industrial Engineers (IIE) and the student is pursuing a full-time course of study in industrial engineering with a grade point average of at least 3.4. They must have at least 5 full quarters or 3 full semesters remaining until graduation. Students may not apply directly for these awards; they must be nominated by the head of their industrial engineering department. Nominees must be IIE members. Selection is based on scholastic ability, character, leadership, potential service to the industrial engineering profession, and need for financial assistance.
Financial data: The stipend is $4,000.
Duration: 1 year.
Additional information: Funding for this program is provided by the UPS Foundation.
Number awarded: 1 each year.
Deadline: November of each year.

2591
UPS SCHOLARSHIPS

American Society of Safety Engineers
Attn: ASSE Foundation
1800 East Oakton Street
Des Plaines, IL 60018
Phone: (847) 768-3441   Fax: (847) 296-9220
E-mail: mrosario@asse.org   Web Site: www.asse.org
Summary: To provide financial assistance to undergraduate student members of the American Society of Safety Engineers (ASSE).
Eligibility: This program is open to ASSE student members who are enrolled in a 4-year degree program in occupational safety and health or a related field (e.g., safety engineering, safety management, systems safety, environmental science, industrial hygiene, ergonomics, fire science). Applicants must be full-time students who have completed at least 60 semester hours with a grade point average of 3.25 or higher. As part of the selection process, they must submit 2 essays of 300 words or less: 1) why they are seeking a degree in safety, a brief description of their current activities, and how those relate to their career goals and objectives; and 2) why they should be awarded this scholarship (including career goals and financial need).
Financial data: Stipends range from $3,000 to $6,000 per year.
Duration: 1 year; nonrenewable.
Additional information: Funding for this program is provided by the UPS Foundation.
Number awarded: Varies each year.
Deadline: November of each year.

2592
U.S. AIRCRAFT INSURANCE GROUP PDP SCHOLARSHIP

National Business Aviation Association, Inc.
Attn: Senior Manager, Airmen & Commercial Services
1200 18th Street, N.W., Suite 400
Washington, DC 20036-2527
Phone: (202) 783-9353   Fax: (202) 331-8364
E-mail: jevans@nbaa.org
Web Site: www.nbaa.org/scholarships/index.htm
Summary: To provide financial assistance to students enrolled at a college or university offering the Professional Development Program (PDP).
Eligibility: This program is open to full-time students at an institution that offers PDP and belongs to the National Business Aviation Association (NBAA) and the University Aviation Association (UAA). Applicants must be U.S. citizens; be enrolled in an aviation-related program; be at the sophomore, junior, or senior level (proof of enrollment must be provided); have at least a 3.0 grade point average (official transcript required); write a 250-word essay describing their goals for a career in the business aviation flight department; submit a letter of recommendation from a member of the aviation department faculty; and submit a resume.
Financial data: The stipend is $1,000. Checks are made payable to the recipient's school.
Duration: 1 year.
Additional information: The participating institutions are Central Missouri State University, Eastern Michigan University, Embry-Riddle Aeronautical University, Mercer County Community College, Purdue University, University of North Dakota, and University of Oklahoma. This program is sponsored by the U.S. Aircraft Insurance Group.
Number awarded: 3 each year.
Deadline: August of each year.

2593
USDA/1890 NATIONAL SCHOLARS PROGRAM

Department of Agriculture
Recruitment and Employment Division
Attn: 1890 National Scholars Program Manager
Jamie L. Whitten Federal Building, Room 301-W
14th and Independence Avenue, S.W.
Washington, DC 20250-9600
Phone: (202) 720-6905
Web Site: www.usda.gov
Summary: To provide financial assistance to high school seniors and graduates interested in majoring in a field related to agriculture or agribusiness at 1 of the 17 Historically Black 1890 Land Grant Institutions.
Eligibility: This program is open to U.S. citizens who hold a high school diploma or GED certificate with a high school grade point average of 3.0 or better and a combined verbal/math score of 1000 or more on the SAT or a composite score of 21 or more on the ACT. They must be planning to attend 1 of the 17 Historically Black 1890 Land Grant Institutions and study such fields as agriculture, agricultural business/management, agricultural economics, agricultural engineering/mechanics, agricultural production and technology, agronomy or crop science, animal sciences, botany, farm and range management, fish and game management, food sciences/technology, forestry and related services, home economics, horticulture, natural resources management, nutrition, soil conservation/soil science, wildlife management, or other related disciplines. Currently-enrolled bachelor's-level students attending an 1890 institution are not eligible.
Financial data: Each award provides annual tuition, employment, employee benefits, use of a personal computer and software while receiving the scholarship, fees, books, and room and board.
Duration: 4 years.
Additional information: The Historically Black Land Grant institutions are: Alabama A&M University, Alcorn State University, University of Arkansas at Pine Bluff, Delaware State University, Florida A&M University, Fort Valley State University, Kentucky State University, Lincoln University of Missouri, Langston University, University of Maryland-Eastern Shore, North Carolina A&T State University, Prairie View A&M University, South Carolina State University, Southern University and A&M College, Tennessee State University, Tuskegee University, and Virginia State University. Applications must be submitted to the Liaison Officer of the U.S. Department of Agriculture at a participating 1890 institution.

Number awarded: 34 or more each year: 2 at each of the participating universities.
Deadline: January of each year.

2594
USENIX STUDENT SCHOLARS PROGRAM

USENIX Association
2560 Ninth Street, Suite 215
Berkeley, CA 94710
Phone: (510) 528-8649   Fax: (510) 528-5738
E-mail: gale@usenix.org
Web Site: www.usenix.org/students/scholar.html
Summary: To provide financial assistance to undergraduate or graduate students majoring in subjects that would be of interest to the USENIX community.
Eligibility: Computer science students may not apply for this support directly. They must be nominated by a faculty member. To nominate a student, faculty members must submit a statement describing the outstanding qualities of the nominee, why this nominee is deserving of the scholarship, and how the nominee might contribute to the USENIX community in the long term.
Financial data: Stipends typically cover some or all of a student's expenses, including tuition, fees, and a stipend.
Duration: Grants are awarded annually.
Number awarded: Varies each year; recently, 4 of these scholarships were awarded.
Deadline: April, July, or November of each year.

2595
UTAH NURSES FOUNDATION GRANT-IN-AID SCHOLARSHIPS

Utah Nurses Foundation
c/o Utah Nurses Association
3761 South 700 East, Suite 201
Salt Lake City, UT 84106
Phone: (801) 293-8351   (800) 236-1617
E-mail: una@xmission.com
Web Site: www.utahnurses.org/unfapp.cfm
Summary: To provide financial assistance to Utah residents who are interested in earning a nursing degree.
Eligibility: This program is open to Utah residents (must be U.S. citizens) who have been accepted into an accredited registered nursing program (undergraduate or graduate). Applicants must submit 3 letters of recommendation, demonstration of their financial need, current official transcripts (with a grade point average of 3.0 or higher), a letter from the school verifying their acceptance in the nursing program, and a narrative statement describing their anticipated role in nursing in Utah upon completion of the nursing program. Preference is given to applicants engaged in full-time study. Selection is based on the following priorities: 1) R.N.s pursuing a B.S.N.; 2) graduate and postgraduate nursing students; 3) students in formal nursing programs (advanced practice nurses); and 4) undergraduate nursing students.
Financial data: A stipend is awarded (exact amount not specified). Funds may be used only for tuition and books.
Duration: 1 year; recipients may reapply.
Additional information: Recipients must agree to work for a Utah health care facility or Utah educational institution as a full-time employee for at least 1 year (2 years if part time). They must also agree to join the Utah Nurses Association within 6 months of graduation.
Deadline: March of each year.

2596
UTAH SOCIETY OF PROFESSIONAL ENGINEERS SCHOLARSHIP

Utah Society of Professional Engineers
c/o Owen Mills, Vice-President
488 East Winchester Street, Suite 400
Murray, UT 84107
E-mail: omills@wilso.com
Web Site: www.inovion.com/~jamesski/USPE
Summary: To provide financial assistance to high school seniors in Utah interested in studying engineering at a college or university in the state.
Eligibility: This program is open to seniors at high schools in Utah who have a cumulative grade point average of 3.0 or higher. Applicants must be interested in attending a college or university in Utah that has been accredited by the Engineering Accreditation Commission of the Accreditation Board for

Engineering and Technology (ABET-EAC). U.S. citizenship is required. Selection is based on grade point average (20 points), recommendations from at least 2 teachers (15 points), a required 500-word essay on career plans (20 points), activities and work experience during school and summer break (15 points), composite application (10 points), and SAT/ACT scores (20 points).
Financial data: A stipend is paid (exact amount not specified).
Duration: 1 year.
Number awarded: 1 or more each year.

2597
VELMA BERNECKER GWINN GARDEN CLUB OBJECTIVES SCHOLARSHIP

Summary: To provide financial aid to Florida undergraduates and graduate students majoring in designated areas related to gardening.
See Listing #1672.

2598
VERITAS DGC SCHOLARSHIP

Society of Exploration Geophysicists
Attn: SEG Foundation
P.O. Box 702740
Tulsa, OK 74170-2740
Phone: (918) 497-5530   Fax: (918) 497-5557
E-mail: slobianco@seg.org   Web Site: www.seg.org
Summary: To provide financial assistance to undergraduate and graduate students who are interested in the field of geophysics.
Eligibility: Applicants must be 1) high school students planning to enter college in the fall and to major in exploration geophysics; 2) undergraduate college students majoring in geophysics whose grades are above average; or 3) graduate students whose studies are directed toward a career in exploration geophysics in operations, teaching, or research. All applicants must have an interest in and aptitude for physics, mathematics, and geology. Financial need is considered, but the competence of the student as indicated by the application is given first consideration.
Financial data: The stipend ranges from $1,000 to $3,000 per year.
Duration: 1 academic year; may be renewable, based on scholastic standing, availability of funds, and continuance of a course of study leading to a career in exploration geophysics.
Number awarded: 1 each year.
Deadline: February of each year.

2599
VERMONT FEED DEALERS AND MANUFACTURERS ASSOCIATION SCHOLARSHIP

Vermont Student Assistance Corporation
Champlain Mill
1 Main Street, Fourth Floor
P.O. Box 2000
Winooski, VT 05404-2601
Phone: (802) 655-9602   (800) 642-3177
Fax: (802) 654-3765   TDD: (802) 654-3766
Phone: TDD: (800) 281-3341 (within VT)   E-mail: info@vsac.org
Web Site: www.vsac.org
Summary: To provide financial assistance to residents of Vermont who are interested in majoring in an agriculture or agribusiness in college.
Eligibility: This scholarship is available to high school seniors, high school graduates, and currently-enrolled college students in Vermont who are enrolled or planning to enroll in a postsecondary degree program in agriculture, including but not limited to animal sciences, equine studies, agribusiness, plant and soil science, forestry, horticulture, and veterinary medicine or technology. The following are required as part of the application process: a completed application form, a copy of the college acceptance letter, 2 letters of recommendation, and 4 required essays. Selection is based on the quality of the essays and the recommendations.
Financial data: The maximum stipend is $2,000.
Duration: 1 year; nonrenewable.
Number awarded: 1 or more each year.
Deadline: June of each year.

2600
VERMONT HOSPITAL PERSONNEL ASSOCIATION SCHOLARSHIP

Vermont Student Assistance Corporation
Champlain Mill
1 Main Street, Fourth Floor
P.O. Box 2000
Winooski, VT 05404-2601
Phone: (802) 655-9602   (800) 642-3177
Fax: (802) 654-3765   TDD: (802) 654-3766
Phone: TDD: (800) 281-3341 (within VT)   E-mail: info@vsac.org
Web Site: www.vsac.org
Summary: To provide financial assistance to adults in Vermont who are interested in majoring in a health-related field in college.
Eligibility: This scholarship is available to nontraditional-aged students who reside in Vermont, have at least a high school degree or GED, and are planning to upgrade their employment skills. Applicants must be enrolled or planning to enroll in a postsecondary degree program in a health-related field. They must be able to demonstrate financial need, apply to the Vermont Student Assistance Corporation for a Vermont Grant, and file a Free Application for Federal Student Aid no later than 4 weeks prior to the scholarship deadline. The following are required as part of the application process: a completed application form, 3 letters of recommendation, 5 required essays, a federal income tax return, and a resume. Selection is based on financial need and commitment to a career in the health care field.
Financial data: The maximum stipend is $1,000.
Duration: 1 year.
Additional information: Applications are reviewed and selection is made by the Vermont Hospital Personnel Association in association with the Vermont Student Assistance Corporation.
Number awarded: 1 or more each year.
Deadline: April of each year.

2601
VERMONT SUBCONTRACTORS ASSOCIATION SCHOLARSHIP

Vermont Student Assistance Corporation
Champlain Mill
1 Main Street, Fourth Floor
P.O. Box 2000
Winooski, VT 05404-2601
Phone: (802) 655-9602   (800) 642-3177
Fax: (802) 654-3765   TDD: (802) 654-3766
Phone: TDD: (800) 281-3341 (within VT)   E-mail: info@vsac.org
Web Site: www.vsac.org
Summary: To provide financial assistance to high school seniors in Vermont who are interested in preparing for a career in the construction industry.
Eligibility: This scholarship is available to high school seniors in Vermont who are enrolled or planning to enroll in a postsecondary degree program in business or other fields related to the construction industry. Applicants must be Vermont residents, be able to demonstrate financial need, apply to the Vermont Student Assistance Corporation for a Vermont Grant, and file a Free Application for Federal Student Aid no later than 4 weeks prior to the scholarship deadline. They must be able to demonstrate leadership abilities through their extracurricular activities. The following are required as part of the application process: a completed application form, a copy of their college acceptance letter, 2 letters of recommendation, 4 required essays, and an official transcript. Selection is based on academic record, financial need, and career plans.
Financial data: The stipend is either $1,000 or $500.
Duration: 1 year.
Number awarded: Either 1 scholarship at $1,000 or 2 scholarships at $500 each year.
Deadline: March of each year.

2602
VERTICAL FLIGHT FOUNDATION ENGINEERING SCHOLARSHIPS

Vertical Flight Foundation
Attn: Scholarship Committee
217 North Washington Street
Alexandria, VA 22314-2538
Phone: (703) 684-6777

Summary: To provide financial assistance to undergraduate and graduate students interested in preparing for an engineering career in the helicopter or vertical flight industry.

Eligibility: Applicants must be full-time students in the final 2 years of undergraduate study or the first year of graduate study at an accredited school of engineering. They need not be a member or relative of a member of the American Helicopter Society. Selection is based on academic record, letters of recommendation, and career plans.

Financial data: Awards range from $2,000 to $4,000 per year, depending on the availability of funds.

Duration: 1 year; may be renewed once as an undergraduate senior, once as a master's student, and once as a doctoral student.

Additional information: The Vertical Flight Foundation was founded in 1967 as the philanthropic arm of the American Helicopter Society.

Number awarded: 1 or more each year.

Deadline: January of each year.

2603
VETERAN'S CAUCUS SCHOLARSHIPS

American Academy of Physician Assistants-Veterans Caucus
c/o Captain Michael R. Milner
National Health Service Corps
HRSA/Boston Field Office
JFK Federal Building, Room 1826
Boston, MA 02203
Phone: (617) 565-1463   Fax: (617) 565-3027
E-mail: mmilner@hrsa.gov
Web Site: www.medvets-aapa.org/medvets/ssinstru.html

Summary: To provide financial assistance to veterans who are studying to become physician assistants.

Eligibility: This program is open to U.S. citizens who are currently enrolled in a physician assistant program. The program must be approved by the Commission on Accreditation of Allied Health Education. Applicants must be in good academic standing. Selection is based on military honors and awards received, civic and college honors and awards received, school activities, professional memberships and activities, and community involvement. An electronic copy of the applicant's DD Form 214 must accompany the application.

Financial data: Stipends range up to $1,250.

Duration: 1 year.

Additional information: This program includes the following named scholarships: the Donna Jones Moritsugu Memorial Awards, the Society of Army Physician Assistants Scholarship, the Order of St. Lazarus/Green Cross Project Award, the Society of Air Force PAs Scholarship, the Naval Association of Physician Assistants Scholarship, and the Andrea Long Memorial Scholarships.

Number awarded: Varies each year; recently, 9 of these scholarships were awarded.

Deadline: February of each year.

2604
VIRGINIA AIRPORT OPERATORS COUNCIL AVIATION SCHOLARSHIP AWARD

Virginia Airport Operators Council
c/o Betty Wilson
Virginia Aviation and Space Education Forum
5702 Gulfstream Road
Richmond, VA 23250-2422   Phone: (800) 292-1034 (within VA)

Summary: To provide financial assistance to high school seniors in Virginia who are interested in preparing for a career in aviation.

Eligibility: This program is open to high school seniors who have earned at least a 3.75 grade point average and are planning a career in the field of aviation. Applicants must have been accepted to an aviation-related program at an accredited college. Virginia residency is required. Selection is based on scholarship (35 percent), a 350- to 500-word essay on why the applicant wishes to pursue a career in aviation (35 percent), and accomplishment and leadership (30 percent).

Financial data: The stipend is $2,000.

Duration: 1 year.

Number awarded: 1 each year.

Deadline: February of each year.

2605
VIRGINIA D. HENRY SCHOLARSHIP

National Society of Professional Engineers
Attn: Education Services
1420 King Street
Alexandria, VA 22314-2794
Phone: (703) 684-2833   Fax: (703) 836-4875
E-mail: jiglesias@nspe.org   Web Site: www.nspe.org/scholarships/sc1-hs.asp

Summary: To provide financial assistance for college to women interested in preparing for a career in engineering.

Eligibility: This program is open to women who are high school seniors planning to study engineering in a college program accredited by the Engineering Accreditation Commission of the Accreditation Board for Engineering and Technology (EAC-ABET). Applicants must have earned at least a 3.0 grade point average, 500 on the verbal SAT, and 600 on the math SAT (or 25 on the English ACT and 29 on the math ACT). They must submit an essay (up to 500 words) on their interest in engineering, their major area of study and area of specialization, and the occupation they propose to pursue after graduation. Selection is based on grade point average (20 points), the essay (20 points), extracurricular activities (including work experience and volunteer activities, 25 points), financial need (5 points), SAT/ACT scores (20 points), and the composite application (10 points). U.S. citizenship is required.

Financial data: The stipend is $1,000 per year; funds are paid directly to institution.

Duration: 1 year.

Additional information: Recipients may attend any college or university, as long as the engineering curriculum is accredited by EAC-ABET.

Number awarded: 1 each year.

Deadline: November of each year.

2606
VIRGINIA LEYDA ROBERTS NURSING SCHOLARSHIP

Daughters of the American Revolution-Colorado State Society
923 Tenth Street
Golden, CO 80401
Phone: (303) 278-7151   E-mail: darcolo@aol.com
Web Site: members.aol.com/coloradodar/scholarships.htm

Summary: To provide financial assistance to high school seniors in Colorado who are interested in studying nursing in the state.

Eligibility: Eligible to apply are graduating high school seniors in Colorado who are 1) American citizens, 2) in the top third of their graduating class, and 3) accepted at 1 of the Colorado colleges offering a B.S.N.: Beth-El College of Nursing, Regis University, Colorado University at Denver, Colorado Health Sciences Center, Metro State University, University of Phoenix, University of Northern Colorado, University of Southern Colorado, or Mesa State College. Applications must include a statement of career interest and goals (up to 500 words), 2 character references, college transcripts, a letter of sponsorship from the Daughters of the American Revolution's Colorado chapter, and a list of scholastic achievements, extracurricular activities, honors, and other significant accomplishments. Selection is based on financial need and academic record.

Financial data: The stipend is $1,000.

Duration: 1 year; nonrenewable.

Number awarded: 1 each year.

Deadline: January of each year.

2607
VONA J. WAGNER MEMORIAL SCHOLARSHIP

National Association of Women in Construction-Denver Chapter 112
Attn: Gina M. Conforti, President
P.O. Box 40208
Denver, CO 80204-0204
Phone: (303) 205-5565   Fax: (303) 232-4080
E-mail: ginac@dyna-denver.com

Summary: To provide financial assistance to high school seniors in Colorado who are interested in preparing for a career in construction.

Eligibility: This program is open to high school seniors who have applied to or been admitted to a college, university, or trade school in Colorado. Applicants must be interested in studying a construction-related field in college and planning to work on a bachelor's degree or certificate of completion. They must have a grade point average of 2.5 or higher. Financial need is considered but it not an absolute requirement.

Financial data: The stipend depends on the availability of funds. Money is not paid at the time of the award but only on a reimbursement basis after the recipient submits

proof of enrollment at a Colorado institution and receipts for tuition, books, laboratory fees, and other school expenses; living expenses are not reimbursable.
Duration: 1 year; nonrenewable.
Number awarded: Varies; generally, 3 to 4 each year.
Deadline: March of each year.

2608
VSCLS SCHOLARSHIPS

Virginia Society for Clinical Laboratory Science
c/o Frankie Harris-Lyne, Scholarship Sub-Committee
Northern Virginia Community College
Medical Laboratory Technology Program
CN Building Room 222
8333 Little River Turnpike
Annandale, VA 22003
Phone: (703) 323-3415   Fax: (703) 323-4576
E-mail: nvharrf@nv.cc.va.us
Web Site: vscls.vavalleyweb.com/scholarship.html
Summary: To provide financial assistance to students in Virginia who are participating in the final year of their clinical laboratory education.
Eligibility: Applicants must be entering the final year of their clinical laboratory education in an accredited program in the Commonwealth of Virginia. This includes: CLS/MT, CLT/MLT, cytology, and histology. Applicants must be in good standing in their program both academically (must have at least a 2.0 grade point average) and professionally. They must not have received any previous financial assistance from the sponsor. Selection is based on financial need, academic record, references, and completeness of the application.
Financial data: The amount of the stipend varies annually, depending upon the amount of funds available.
Duration: 1 year.
Number awarded: Several each year.
Deadline: December of each year.

2609
W. REESE HARRIS AGRICULTURAL SCHOLARSHIP

Florida Federation of Garden Clubs, Inc.
Attn: Scholarship Chair
6065 21st Street S.W.
Vero Beach, FL 32968-9427
Phone: (561) 778-1023
Web Site: www.ffgc.org
Summary: To provide financial aid to Florida undergraduates and graduate students majoring in agriculture.
Eligibility: This program is open to Florida residents who are enrolled as full-time juniors, seniors, or graduate students in a Florida college. They must have at least a 3.0 grade point average, be in financial need, and be majoring in agriculture. Selection is based on academic record, commitment to career, character, and financial need.
Financial data: The stipend is $1,500. The funds are sent directly to the recipient's school and distributed semiannually.
Duration: 1 year.
Additional information: If the recipient's grade point average drops below 3.0, the second installment of the scholarship is not provided.
Number awarded: 1 each year.
Deadline: April of each year.

2610
WAFLORA SCHOLARSHIP

Washington Floricultural Association
Attn: WaFlorA Scholarship and Research Charitable Fund
3021 Niagara Street
Bellingham, WA 98226
Phone: (360) 738-9850   Fax: (360) 738-0343
E-mail: WaFlorA@hotmail.com
Web Site: www.WaFlorA.com
Summary: To provide financial assistance for college to students in Washington who are interested in preparing for a career in floriculture and related fields.
Eligibility: Students in Washington who are interested in preparing for a career in floriculture or horticulture are eligible to apply. They can be high school seniors, currently-enrolled college students, or professionals interested in continuing their education. Selection is based on academic record, letters of

reference, employment history, extracurricular activities related to floriculture and/or horticulture, and a statement of career goals.
Financial data: Stipends range from $500 to $2,000 each. Funds are sent directly to the recipient's school.
Duration: 1 year.
Additional information: This fund was established in 1985 with the Henry Mollgaard Memorial Scholarship. The Elaine McConkey Memorial Scholarship was added in 1992 and the Dr. Bernie Wesenberg Memorial Scholarship in 1993.
Number awarded: Normally 3 each year.
Deadline: May of each year.

2611
WALTER AND MARIE SCHMIDT SCHOLARSHIP

Oregon Student Assistance Commission
Attn: Private Awards Grant Department
1500 Valley River Drive, Suite 100
Eugene, OR 97401-2146
Phone: (541) 687-7395   (800) 452-8807, ext. 7395
Fax: (541) 687-7419   E-mail: awardinfo@mercury.osac.state.or.us
Web Site: www.osac.state.or.us
Summary: To provide financial assistance for the study of nursing to residents of Oregon.
Eligibility: This program is open to residents of Oregon who are enrolled at least half time in a program to become a registered nurse. As part of the application process, they must submit an essay on their desire to pursue a nursing career in geriatric health care. Preference is given to students from Lane County.
Financial data: Scholarship amounts vary, depending upon the needs of the recipient.
Duration: 1 year.
Number awarded: Varies each year.
Deadline: February of each year.

2612
WALTER BEALE SCHOLARSHIP

Fleet Reserve Association
Past Regional Presidents Club
c/o W. Ralph Holcombe, Secretary/Treasurer
4911 Fennell Court
Suffolk, VA 23435
Phone: (757) 484-7403   Fax: (757) 686-5952
E-mail: info@fraprpscholarships.org
Web Site: www.fraprpscholarships.org
Summary: To provide financial assistance to relatives of members of the Fleet Reserve Association (FRA) interested in studying aeronautical engineering or aviation in college.
Additional information: This program is open to spouses, children, and grandchildren of active-duty, reserve, and retired personnel of the Navy, Marine Corps, or Coast Guard who are relatives of FRA members in good standing (or who were in good standing at the time of their death). Students in a reserve officer candidate program receiving aid are not eligible. Applicants must be enrolled at an accredited college, university, or technical institution in the United States in a program related to engineering, aviation, or aeronautical engineering. Selection is based on grade point average, scholastic aptitude test scores, curriculum goals, interests, community activities, awards, and financial need.
Financial data: The amounts of the awards depend on the availability of funds and the need of the recipients; they range from $2,000 to $5,000.
Duration: 1 year; renewable.
Number awarded: 1 or more each year.
Deadline: April of each year.

2613
WALTER G. THORSELL MEMORIAL SCHOLARSHIP

American Society of Safety Engineers-Columbia-Willamette Chapter
c/o Mark Hopkins, Scholarship Committee Chair
267 South Craven Street
Monmouth, OR 97361
Phone: (503) 220-5321   E-mail: markh@e-c-co.com
Web Site: www.assecwc.org/pages/scholarships.html
Summary: To provide financial assistance for college to members of the American Society of Safety Engineers (ASSE) from Washington and Oregon.
Eligibility: This program is open to residents of Washington and Oregon who have completed at least 1 term of study toward a bachelor's degree in

occupational safety, health, or environmental studies. Applicants must be ASSE student members who are able to demonstrate interest and participation in ASSE and other safety activities. U.S. citizenship and a grade point average of at least 2.75 are required. Financial need is considered only if all other factors are equal.

Financial data: The stipend is $1,500.

Duration: 1 year.

Number awarded: 1 each year.

Deadline: April of each year.

2614
WALTER REED SMITH SCHOLARSHIP PROGRAM

United Daughters of the Confederacy
Attn: Education Director
328 North Boulevard
Richmond, VA 23220-4057
Phone: (804) 355-1636   Fax: (804) 353-1396
E-mail: hqudc@aol.com   Web Site: www.hqudc.org

Summary: To provide financial assistance for education in designated fields to mature women who are lineal descendants of Confederate veterans.

Eligibility: Eligible to apply for these scholarships are women over the age of 30 who are lineal descendants of worthy Confederates or collateral descendants and members of the Children of the Confederacy or the United Daughters of the Confederacy. Applicants must intend to study business administration, computer science, home economics, nutrition, or nursing. They must submit certified proof of the Confederate record of 1 ancestor, with the company and regiment in which he served, and must have had at least a 3.0 grade point average in high school.

Financial data: The amount of this scholarship depends on the availability of funds.

Duration: 1 year; may be renewed.

Additional information: Information is also available from Dorothy S. Broom, Second Vice President General, 595 Lominack Road, Prosperity, SC 29127, (803) 364-3003. Members of the same family may not hold scholarships simultaneously, and only 1 application per family will be accepted within any 1 year. All requests for applications must be accompanied by a self-addressed stamped envelope.

Number awarded: 1 each year.

Deadline: February of each year.

2615
WARNER LAMBERT JOINT ORAL HYGIENE GROUP SCHOLARSHIPS

American Dental Hygienists' Association
Attn: Institute for Oral Health
444 North Michigan Avenue, Suite 3400
Chicago, IL 60611
Phone: (312) 440-8944   (800) 735-4916
Fax: (312) 440-8929   E-mail: institute@adha.net
Web Site: www.adha.org

Summary: To provide financial assistance to students preparing for careers in dental hygiene.

Eligibility: Applicants must have earned at least a 3.0 grade point average, be able to demonstrate financial need, and have completed a minimum of 1 year in a dental hygiene curriculum. Scholarships are available to 1) full-time students pursuing a baccalaureate degree in dental hygiene at a 4-year institution in the United States, and 2) dental hygienists pursuing a degree in dental hygiene or a related field in a degree completion program as either a full-time or a part-time student. Both categories of applicants must be eligible for licensure in the year of the award.

Financial data: The amount of the award depends on the need of the recipient, to a maximum of $1,000.

Duration: 1 year.

Additional information: This program is sponsored by Warner Lambert Company.

Number awarded: 5 each year.

Deadline: May of each year.

2616
WASHINGTON APPLE COMMISSION SCHOLARSHIP FUND

Washington Apple Education Foundation
P.O. Box 3720
Wenatchee, WA 98807
Phone: (509) 663-7713   Fax: (509) 682-1293
E-mail: waef@waef.org
Web Site: www.waef.org

Summary: To provide financial assistance for a commodity-related degree in college to children whose parents or guardians are commercial growers or the employees of commercial growers of Washington apples.

Eligibility: This program is open to Washington residents. Applicants must be the children of parents or guardians who are 1) commercial growers or 2) the employees of commercial growers of Washington apples. They may be high school seniors or currently-enrolled college students, and they must be interested in pursuing a 2-year or 4-year undergraduate degree at an accredited college or university in a commodity-related field, including the basic sciences, nutrition, education, some areas of business and international studies, as well as horticulture and agriculture as those subjects relate to the apple industry. Selection is based on standardized tests, academic performance, demonstrated leadership ability, industry and promise of useful citizenship, financial need, a statement of intent, and personal references. Students who are related to the staff or board or committee members of either the Washington Apple Education Foundation or the Washington Apple Commission are not eligible to receive an award.

Financial data: The stipend is $2,000. Funds may be used to pay for tuition, room, board, books, educational supplies, and miscellaneous institutional fees.

Duration: 1 year; recipients may reapply.

Additional information: This scholarship was established in 1986. It is funded by the Washington Apple Commission and administered by the Washington Apple Education Foundation.

Number awarded: 3 each year.

Deadline: March of each year.

2617
WASHINGTON APPLE EDUCATION FOUNDATION MEMORIAL COMMISSION SCHOLARSHIP FUND

Summary: To provide financial assistance to students who are involved in Washington's tree fruit industry.

See Listing #1157.

2618
WASHINGTON OCCUPATIONAL THERAPY ASSOCIATION SCHOLARSHIP

American Occupational Therapy Foundation
Attn: Scholarship Coordinator
4720 Montgomery Lane
P.O. Box 31220
Bethesda, MD 20824-1220
Phone: (301) 652-2682   Fax: (301) 656-3620
Phone: TDD: (800) 377-8555   E-mail: aotf@aotf.org
Web Site: www.aotf.org

Summary: To provide financial assistance to students who are members of the Washington Occupational Therapy Association and working on a degree in occupational therapy.

Eligibility: This program is open to Washington residents who are enrolled in an accredited occupational therapy educational program (associate or professional) in the state. Applicants must demonstrate a need for financial assistance, have a sustained record of outstanding scholastic performance, and be members of the Washington Occupational Therapy Association. As part of the application process, they must submit transcripts, 2 personal references, and a statement from their curriculum director.

Financial data: The stipend is $500 for students at the associate degree level or $1,000 for students at the professional degree level.

Duration: 1 year.

Additional information: Application forms are available at no cost at the association's web site; a $5 fee is charged for printed copies sent from the association's headquarters.

Number awarded: 2 each year: 1 for students at the professional degree level and 1 for students at the associate degree level.

Deadline: January of each year.

2619
WEST VIRGINIA GOLF COURSE SUPERINTENDENTS ASSOCIATION SCHOLARSHIP PROGRAM

West Virginia Golf Course Superintendents Association, Inc.
c/o Virgil Smith
P.O. Box 5147
Vienna, WV 26003
Phone: (304) 295-5227   Fax: (304) 295-7336
Summary: To provide financial assistance to members of the West Virginia Golf Course Superintendents Association (WVGCSA) who are majoring in turf-related studies in college.
Eligibility: Eligible to apply for this program are student members of WVGCSA who are enrolled in a turf-related program at a 2-year or 4-year college or university.
Financial data: The stipend is $500 per year for recipients at 2-year colleges and $1,000 per year for recipients at 4-year colleges or universities.
Duration: 1 year; recipients may reapply, as long as they have maintained a 2.0 grade point average.

2620
WESTERN RESERVE HERB SOCIETY SCHOLARSHIPS

Herb Society of America-Western Reserve Unit
c/o Priscilla Jones, Committee Chair
2640 Exeter Road
Cleveland Heights, OH 44118
Phone: (216) 932-6090   E-mail: cillers@hotmail.com
Web Site: www.herbsociety.org/scholar.htm
Summary: To provide financial assistance to college students from Ohio interested in pursuing a career in a field related to horticulture.
Eligibility: This program is open to residents of Ohio who have completed at least 1 year of college. Applicants may be attending an accredited college or university anywhere in the United States. They must be planning a career in horticulture or a related field, including horticultural therapy. U.S. citizenship is required. Preference is given to applicants whose horticultural career goals involve teaching or research or work in the public or nonprofit sector (such as public gardens, botanical gardens, parks, arboreta, city planning, or public education and awareness). Selection is based on an essay that includes a description of their interests, activities, and achievements; an account of their employment record on or off campus; a description of their career goals; and a discussion of their need for financial aid.
Financial data: The stipend is $2,000.
Duration: 1 year.
Number awarded: 2 each year.
Deadline: March of each year.

2621
WILDLIFE LEADERSHIP AWARDS

Rocky Mountain Elk Foundation
Attn: Jason Hobson
2291 West Broadway
P.O. Box 8249
Missoula, MT 59807-8249
Phone: (406) 523-4500   (800) CALL ELK, ext. 496
Fax: (406) 523-4550   E-mail: jhobson@rmef.org
Web Site: www.rmef.org
Summary: To provide financial assistance to undergraduate students who are majoring in wildlife studies.
Eligibility: This program is open to undergraduate students enrolled in a recognized wildlife program at a 4-year college or university in the United States or Canada. They must have at least junior class standing (completed at least 72 semester hours or 108 quarter hours), have at least 1 semester or 2 quarters remaining in their degree program, and be scheduled to enroll as full-time students the following fall semester/quarter. Previous recipients of this award are ineligible. Selection is based on extracurricular activities, leadership activities, previous employment, philosophy of wildlife management, views on critical conservation issues, and career goals. Financial need is not considered in the selection process.
Financial data: The stipend is $2,000. In addition, recipients are given an engraved plaque and a 1-year membership in the foundation.
Duration: 1 year; nonrenewable.
Additional information: This program was established in 1990.
Number awarded: 10 each year.
Deadline: February of each year.

2622
WILLIAM B. HOWELL MEMORIAL SCHOLARSHIP

American Welding Society
Attn: AWS Foundation, Inc.
550 N.W. LeJeune Road
Miami, FL 33126
Phone: (305) 443-9353, ext. 461   (800) 443-9353, ext. 461
Fax: (305) 443-7559   E-mail: vpinsky@aws.org
Web Site: www.aws.org/foundation/howell.html
Summary: To provide financial assistance to college students majoring in welding engineering.
Eligibility: This program is open to full-time undergraduate students who are pursuing at least a 4-year bachelor's degree in a welding program at an accredited university. Applicants must have a minimum overall grade point average of 2.5 and be able to demonstrate financial need. U.S. citizenship is required. Priority is given to applicants residing or attending school in Florida, Michigan, or Ohio.
Financial data: The stipend is $2,500.
Duration: 1 year; recipients may reapply.
Number awarded: 1 each year.
Deadline: January of each year.

2623
WILLIAM J. AND MARIJANE E. ADAMS, JR. AGRICULTURAL ENGINEERING SCHOLARSHIP

American Society of Agricultural Engineers
Attn: ASAE Foundation
2950 Niles Road
St. Joseph, MI 49085-9659
Phone: (616) 429-0300   Fax: (616) 429-3852
E-mail: hq@asae.org
Web Site: www.asae.org
Summary: To provide financial assistance to student members of the American Society of Agricultural Engineers (ASAE).
Eligibility: This program is open to undergraduate students who have a declared major in biological or agricultural engineering (must be accredited by ABET or CEAB), are student members of the society, are in at least the second year of college, have at least a 2.5 grade point average, can demonstrate financial need, and have a special interest in agricultural machinery product design and development. Interested applicants should submit a personal letter (up to 2 pages long), stating how the money will be used, outlining their financial need, and describing their interest in the design and development of new agricultural machinery products.
Financial data: The stipend is $1,000. Funds must be used for tuition, fees, books, and on-campus room and board.
Duration: 1 year.
Number awarded: 1 each year.
Deadline: April of each year.

2624
WILLIAM J. AND MARIJANE E. ADAMS, JR. MECHANICAL ENGINEERING SCHOLARSHIP

ASME International
Attn: Education Department
Three Park Avenue
New York, NY 10016-5990
Phone: (212) 591-8131   (800) THE-ASME
Fax: (212) 591-7143   E-mail: oluwanifiset@asme.org
Web Site: www.asme.org/educate/aid/scholar.htm
Summary: To provide financial support for college to student members of the American Society of Mechanical Engineers (ASME) in California, Hawaii, or Nevada.
Eligibility: This program is open to student members of the society in Region IX (California, Hawaii, and Nevada) who have a declared major in mechanical engineering with a special interest in product development and design. Applicants must be in at least the second year of study at an ABET-accredited college or university with a minimum grade point average of 2.5. Financial need must be demonstrated.
Financial data: This scholarship is $2,000.
Additional information: Requests for applications must be accompanied by a self-addressed stamped envelope.
Number awarded: 1 each year.
Deadline: March of each year.

2625
WILLIAM JAMES LANQUIST AND DOROTHY BADING LANQUIST FUND SCHOLARSHIPS

Hawai'i Community Foundation
900 Fort Street Mall, Suite 1300
Honolulu, HI 96813
Phone: (808) 566-5570   (888) 731-3863
Fax: (808) 521-6286   E-mail: scholarships@hcf-hawaii.org
Web Site: www.hcf-hawaii.org

Summary: To provide financial assistance to Hawaii residents who are interested in preparing for a career in the physical sciences.
Eligibility: This program is open to Hawaii residents who are interested in majoring in the physical sciences or related fields (but not the biological or social sciences) on the undergraduate or graduate school level. They must be able to demonstrate academic achievement (at least a 2.7 grade point average), good moral character, and financial need. In addition to filling out the standard application form, applicants must write a short statement indicating their reasons for attending college, their planned course of study, and their career goals.
Financial data: The amounts of the awards depend on the availability of funds and the need of the recipient; recently, grants averaged $1,450.
Duration: 1 year.
Additional information: Recipients may attend college in Hawaii or on the mainland. Recipients must be full-time students.
Number awarded: Varies each year; recently, 11 of these scholarships were awarded.
Deadline: February of each year.

2626
WILLIAM L. CULLISON SCHOLARSHIP

Technical Association of the Pulp and Paper Industry
Attn: TAPPI Foundation
P.O. Box 105113
Atlanta, GA 30348-5113
Phone: (770) 446-1400   (800) 332-8686
Fax: (770) 446-6947   E-mail: foundation@tappi.org
Web Site: www.tappi.org

Summary: To provide financial assistance to college students who are interested in preparing for a career in the pulp and paper industry.
Eligibility: This program is open to full-time students who have completed the first 2 years at a university with a pulp and paper program and have earned a grade point average of 3.5 or better. Applicants must demonstrate outstanding leadership abilities and significant interest in the pulp and paper industry. Financial need is not considered in the selection process.
Financial data: The stipend is $5,000 per year.
Duration: 1 year (the junior year); may be renewed for the senior year if the recipient maintains at least a 3.0 GPA and pursues courses in the pulp and paper curriculum.
Additional information: This program was established in 1999.
Number awarded: 1 each year.
Deadline: April of each year.

2627
WILLIAM M. FANNING MAINTENANCE SCHOLARSHIP

National Business Aviation Association, Inc.
Attn: Senior Manager, Airmen & Commercial Services
1200 18th Street, N.W., Suite 400
Washington, DC 20036-2527
Phone: (202) 783-9353   Fax: (202) 331-8364
E-mail: jevans@nbaa.org
Web Site: www.nbaa.org/scholarships/index.htm

Summary: To provide financial assistance to students who are preparing for a career as an aviation maintenance technician.
Eligibility: Applicants must be either 1) a student who is currently enrolled in an accredited airframe and powerplant (A&P) program at an approved FAR Part 147 school or 2) an individual who is not currently enrolled but who has been accepted for enrollment in an A&P program. All applicants must be U.S. citizens. Application forms must be accompanied by 1) an official transcript from the applicant's program or school or a letter of acceptance, 2) a 250-word typed essay about the applicant's career goals, 3) a letter of recommendation from either a faculty member or other individual familiar with the applicant's abilities, and 4) a resume.
Financial data: The stipend is $2,500.
Duration: 1 year.
Number awarded: 2 each year.
Deadline: August of each year.

2628
WILLIAM P. MURPHY-VISION SCHOLARSHIP

Small Parts, Inc.
Attn: James Edgar
13980 N.W. 58th Court
P.O. Box 4650
Miami Lakes, FL 33014-0650
Phone: (305) 558-1038   Fax: (305) 558-0509
E-mail: parts@smallparts.com   Web Site: www.smallparts.com

Summary: To recognize and reward high school students who participate in the FIRST (For Inspiration and Recognition of Science and Technology) Robotics competition.
Eligibility: The FIRST Robotics competition involves high school students who participate on teams that include the students supported by engineers, technicians, teachers, parents, industry representatives, and (occasionally) college students and faculty. Although the composition of teams varies, most are industry-high school partnerships, university-high school partnerships, industry-university-high school partnerships, or coalitions that involve multiple companies, universities, and/or high schools competing as a single team. Each team starts with the same standard kit of parts and uses their creativity to design and build a robotic vehicle capable of performing a demanding task better than 2 opponents. Teams may enter regional competitions or go directly to the national competition. High school seniors who participate in the competition are eligible to apply for this scholarship. Along with their application, they must submit a letter of recommendation from a high school teacher or administrator, a letter of recommendation from an engineer/advisor of their FIRST team, a resume with their grade point average (must be 3.5 or higher) and high school transcript, and an essay explaining how they hope to impact the world through their studies in the field of science and/or technology.
Financial data: The stipend is $1,500 per year.
Duration: Up to 4 years.
Additional information: The entry fee for each competition is $4,000. Other expenses, including travel by team members to a kick-off workshop and the competition, building materials, administrative costs, shipping, and uniforms, bring the total cost for each team to approximately $15,000. Teams must secure financing from local business sponsors and other fund-raising activities.
Number awarded: 1 each year.
Deadline: February of each year.

2629
WILLIAM PARK WOODSIDE FOUNDER'S SCHOLARSHIP

ASM International Foundation
Attn: Scholarship Program
9639 Kinsman Road
Materials Park, OH 44073-0002
Phone: (440) 338-5151   (800) 336-5152
Fax: (440) 338-4634   E-mail: crhayes@asminternational.org
Web Site: www.asminternational.org

Summary: To provide financial assistance to members of the American Society for Metals who are interested in majoring in metallurgy and materials.
Eligibility: Applicants must be citizens of the United States, Canada, or Mexico; be enrolled at a college or university in those countries; be members of the society; have an intended or declared major in metallurgy or materials science and engineering (related science or engineering majors may be considered if the applicant demonstrates a strong academic emphasis and interest in materials science and engineering); and be entering their junior or senior year in college. Selection is based on academic achievement; interest in metallurgy/materials (including knowledge of the field, activities, jobs, and potential for a related career); personal qualities (such as social values, maturity, motivation, goals, and citizenship); and financial need.
Financial data: The scholarship provides payment of full tuition, up to $10,000 per year.
Duration: 1 year; recipients may reapply for 1 additional year.
Additional information: This scholarship was established in 1996 by Mrs. Sue Shulec Woodside in honor of her grandfather, a founding member of ASM International.
Number awarded: 1 each year.
Deadline: April of each year.

2630
WILLIAM W. BURGIN, JR. MD EDUCATION RECOGNITION AWARD

American Respiratory Care Foundation
Attn: Administrative Coordinator
11030 Ables Lane
Dallas, TX 75229-4593
Phone: (972) 243-2272   Fax: (972) 484-2720
E-mail: info@aarc.org
Web Site: www.aarc.org/awards
Summary: To provide financial assistance to second-year college students interested in becoming respiratory therapists.
Eligibility: College students who have completed at least 2 semesters at an accredited respiratory care program leading to an associate degree are eligible, if they have earned at least a 3.0 grade point average, are U.S. citizens or applicants for U.S. citizenship, and have potential for an outstanding career in the profession of respiratory care. Candidates must submit an original referenced paper on an aspect of respiratory care and a paper of at least 1,200 words describing how the award will assist them in reaching their objective of an associate degree and their ultimate goals of leadership in health care. Selection is based on academic performance.
Financial data: The stipend is $2,500. The award also provides 1 night's lodging and registration for the international congress of the association.
Duration: 1 year.
Additional information: This program is sponsored by the National Board for Respiratory Care (NBRC) and its wholly owned subsidary, Applied Measurement Professionals, Inc. (AMP).
Number awarded: 1 each year.
Deadline: May of each year.

2631
WILMA E. MOTLEY SCHOLARSHIP

American Dental Hygienists' Association
Attn: Institute for Oral Health
444 North Michigan Avenue, Suite 3400
Chicago, IL 60611
Phone: (312) 440-8944   (800) 735-4916
Fax: (312) 440-8929   E-mail: institute@adha.net
Web Site: www.adha.org
Summary: To provide financial assistance to students preparing for careers in dental hygiene.
Eligibility: Applicants must have earned a 4.0 grade point average in dental hygiene courses, be able to demonstrate financial need, and have completed a minimum of 1 year in a dental hygiene curriculum. Scholarships are available to 1) full-time students pursuing a baccalaureate degree in dental hygiene at a 4-year institution in the United States, and 2) dental hygienists pursuing a degree in dental hygiene or a related field in a degree completion program as either a full-time or a part-time student. Both categories of applicants must be eligible for licensure in the year of the award.
Financial data: The amount of the award depends on the need of the recipient, to a maximum of $1,000.
Duration: 1 year.
Number awarded: 1 each year.
Deadline: May of each year.

2632
WISCONSIN DENTAL FOUNDATION SCHOLARSHIPS

Wisconsin Dental Foundation
Attn: Selection Committee
111 East Wisconsin Avenue, Suite 1300
Milwaukee, WI 53202
Phone: (414) 276-4520   Fax: (414) 276-8431
Summary: To provide financial assistance to Wisconsin residents who are studying dental hygiene.
Eligibility: This program is open to Wisconsin residents who are enrolled in a dental hygiene program at Marquette University or a technical school in Wisconsin. Students must be applying for either 1) second-semester freshman study or 2) junior or senior study. Selection is based on depth of character, leadership, seriousness of purpose, service orientation, academic achievement, and financial need.
Financial data: Awards range from $500 to $1,000.
Duration: 1 year.
Number awarded: 20 each year.

2633
WISCONSIN SCHOLARSHIPS OF THE AMERICAN OCCUPATIONAL THERAPY FOUNDATION

American Occupational Therapy Foundation
Attn: Scholarship Coordinator
4720 Montgomery Lane
P.O. Box 31220
Bethesda, MD 20824-1220
Phone: (301) 652-2682   Fax: (301) 656-3620
Phone: TDD: (800) 377-8555   E-mail: aotf@aotf.org
Web Site: www.aotf.org
Summary: To provide financial assistance to students in Wisconsin who are working on an associate or professional degree in occupational therapy.
Eligibility: This program is open to Wisconsin residents who are enrolled in an accredited occupational therapy educational program in the state at the associate degree or professional degree level. Applicants must demonstrate a need for financial assistance and have a sustained record of outstanding scholastic performance. As part of the application process, they must submit transcripts, 2 personal references, and a statement from their curriculum director.
Financial data: The stipend is $1,000.
Duration: 1 year.
Additional information: Application forms are available at no cost at the association's web site; a $5 fee is charged for printed copies sent from the association's headquarters.
Number awarded: 2 each year: 1 at the associate degree level and 1 at the professional degree level.
Deadline: January of each year.

2634
WOCN SOCIETY ACCREDITED NURSING EDUCATION SCHOLARSHIP PROGRAM

Wound, Ostomy and Continence Nurses Society
Attn: Chair, WOCN Scholarship Committee
4700 West Lake Avenue
Glenview, IL 60025
Phone: (866) 615-8560   (888) 224-WOCN
Fax: (866) 615-8560
Web Site: www.wocn.org/education/scholarship
Summary: To provide financial assistance to individuals interested in preparing for a career in enterostomal therapy (ET) nursing (including wound, ostomy, and continence).
Eligibility: Applicants must provide evidence of 1 of the following: 1) acceptance in a wound, ostomy, and continence education program accredited by the Wound, Ostomy and Continence Nurses (WOCN) Society; 2) current enrollment in a WOCN-accredited wound, ostomy, and continence education program; or 3) certificate of completion from a WOCN-accredited wound, ostomy, and continence education program within 3 months of completion. Selection is based on motivation to be an ET nurse and financial need.
Financial data: A stipend is awarded (exact amount not specified).
Number awarded: Varies each year.
Deadline: April or October of each year.

2635
WOCN SOCIETY ADVANCED EDUCATION SCHOLARSHIP PROGRAM

Wound, Ostomy and Continence Nurses Society
Attn: Chair, WOCN Scholarship Committee
4700 West Lake Avenue
Glenview, IL 60025
Phone: (866) 615-8560   (888) 224-WOCN
Fax: (866) 615-8560
Web Site: www.wocn.org/education/scholarship
Summary: To provide financial assistance to members of the Would, Ostomy and Continence Nurses (WOCN) Society interested in pursuing an undergraduate or graduate degree.
Eligibility: This program is open to active members of the society who hold a current, unrestricted R.N. license and are seeking a baccalaureate, master's, or doctoral degree or N.P. certificate. Applicants must provide evidence of current or previous employment as a wound, ostomy, and/or continence nurse during the last 3 years, proof of WOCNCB certification, and proof of current enrollment or acceptance into an accredited nursing program or other accredited college or

university program for non-nursing degrees. Selection is based on merit, compliance with the eligibility requirements, and financial need.

Financial data: A stipend is awarded (exact amount not specified).
Duration: 1 year.
Number awarded: 1 or more each year.
Deadline: April or October of each year.

2636
WOMEN IN SCIENCE AND TECHNOLOGY SCHOLARSHIP

Virginia Business and Professional Women's Foundation
P.O. Box 4842
McLean, VA 22103-4842
E-mail: bpwva@advocate.net
Web Site: www.bpwva.advocate.net/foundation.htm
Summary: To provide financial assistance to women in Virginia who are working on a bachelor's or advanced degree in science or technology.
Eligibility: This program is open to women who are at least 18 years of age, are U.S. citizens, are Virginia residents, are accepted at or currently studying at a Virginia college or university, and are working on a bachelor's, master's, or doctoral degree in 1 of the following fields: actuarial science, biology, bioengineering, chemistry, computer science, dentistry, engineering, mathematics, medicine, physics, or a similar scientific or technical field. Applicants must have a definite plan to use their education in a scientific or technical profession. Financial need must be demonstrated.
Financial data: These scholarships range from $500 to $1,000 per year and may be used for tuition, books, transportation, living expenses, and dependent care.
Duration: 1 year; recipients may reapply (but prior recipients are not given priority).
Additional information: Recipients must complete their studies within 2 years.
Number awarded: At least 1 each year.
Deadline: March of each year.

2637
WOMEN'S NATIONAL AGRICULTURAL AVIATION ASSOCIATION SCHOLARSHIP ESSAY CONTEST

National Agricultural Aviation Association
Attn: Membership, Marketing, and Convention
1005 E Street, S.E.
Washington, DC 20003
Phone: (202) 546-5722   Fax: (202) 546-5726
E-mail: information@agaviation.org
Web Site: www.agaviation.org
Summary: To recognize and reward outstanding student essays on agricultural aviation.
Eligibility: This competition is open to the children, grandchildren, sons-in-law, daughters-in-law, or spouses of any National Agricultural Aviation Association operator, pilot member, retired operator, or pilot who maintains an active membership in the association. The contest is also open to the children, grandchildren, sons-in-law, daughters-in-law, or spouses of an allied industry member. Entrants must be high school seniors, high school graduates, or college students. They may be of any age pursuing any area of education beyond high school. They are invited to submit an essay, up to 1,500 words, on a theme related to agricultural aviation that changes annually; recently, the topic was "PAASS into the Future with Ag Aviation.com." A photograph of the entrant and a short biography should accompany the submission. Essays are judged on theme, development, clarity, and originality.
Financial data: First prize is $2,000; second prize is $1,000.
Duration: The competition is held annually.
Number awarded: 2 each year.
Deadline: August of each year.

2638
WOMEN'S SEAMEN'S FRIEND SOCIETY OF CONNECTICUT SCHOLARSHIP

Summary: To provide financial assistance for college to selected Connecticut residents, including merchant seafarers and/or their dependents.
See Listing #1215.

2639
WSPE PAST PRESIDENTS' SCHOLARSHIP

Wisconsin Society of Professional Engineers
Attn: Engineers Foundation of Wisconsin
700 Rayovac Drive, Suite 207
Madison, WI 53711-2476
Phone: (608) 278-7000   Fax: (608) 278-7005
E-mail: wspe@wspe.org
Web Site: www.wspe.org/efw.htm
Summary: To provide financial assistance to seniors at designated universities in Wisconsin who are majoring in engineering.
Eligibility: This program is open to Wisconsin residents who are seniors at designated universities in the state and majoring in engineering. Applicants must have a grade point average of 3.0 or higher. As part of the selection process, they must submit a 250-word essay on how they became interested in engineering, the field of engineering that is most interesting to them and why, and why they want to become a practicing engineer. U.S. citizenship is required. Selection is based on grade point average, class ranking, activities and honors, the essay, and supplemental credits (computer, chemistry, physics, calculus, etc.).
Financial data: Varies each year. The sponsor awards a total of $7,500 in scholarships each year.
Duration: 1 year.
Additional information: The award rotates annually to a senior at the University of Wisconsin at Madison, University of Wisconsin at Milwaukee, MSOE, Marquette University, and University of Wisconsin at Platteville.
Number awarded: 1 or more each year.
Deadline: December of each year.

2640
XEROX TECHNICAL MINORITY SCHOLARSHIP PROGRAM

Xerox Corporation
Attn: Technical Minority Scholarship Program
907 Culver Road
Rochester, NY 14609-7192
Phone: (716) 422-7689   E-mail: xtmsp@imcouncil.com
Web Site: www.xerox.com
Summary: To provide financial assistance to minorities interested in undergraduate or graduate education in the sciences and/or engineering.
Eligibility: This program is open to minorities (people of African American, Asian, Pacific Islander, American Indian, Native Alaskan, or Hispanic descent) enrolled full time in the following science and engineering degree programs at the baccalaureate level or above: chemistry, engineering (chemical, computer, electrical, imaging, mechanical, optical, software), information management, material science, or physics. Applicants must be U.S. citizens or permanent residents with a grade point average of 3.0 or higher.
Financial data: The maximum stipend is $1,000 per year.
Duration: 1 year.
Deadline: September of each year.

2641
YALE NEW HAVEN HOSPITAL MINORITY NURSING AND ALLIED HEALTH SCHOLARSHIPS

Yale New Haven Hospital
Attn: Human Resources
20 York Street
New Haven, CT 06504
Phone: (203) 688-2414   E-mail: lacamera@ynhh.org
Web Site: www.ynhh.org
Summary: To provide financial assistance to minority high school seniors in Connecticut interested in studying nursing or allied health fields in college.
Eligibility: This program is open to graduating seniors at high schools in Connecticut who are members of minority groups. Applicants must be interested in attending a 4-year college or university with an accredited program in nursing, respiratory therapy, medical technology, pharmacy, or radiation therapy. Selection is based on academic record, teacher evaluations, a personal essay, and extracurricular activities.
Financial data: The stipend is $1,500 per year.
Duration: 1 year.
Number awarded: 4 each year.
Deadline: February of each year.

2642
YANMAR/SAE SCHOLARSHIP

Society of Automotive Engineers
Attn: Educational Relations
400 Commonwealth Drive
Warrendale, PA 15096-0001
Phone: (724) 772-4047 Fax: (724) 776-0890
E-mail: connie@sae.org
Web Site: www.sae.org/students/yanmar.htm
Summary: To provide financial support to college seniors and graduate students majoring in engineering.
Eligibility: Applicants must be entering their senior year of an undergraduate engineering program or enrolled in a graduate engineering or related science program at a college or university in Canada, Mexico, or the United States. They must be pursuing a course of study or research related to the conservation of energy in transportation, agriculture, construction, and power generation. Emphasis is placed on research or study related to the internal combustion engine. Canadian, Mexican, or U.S. citizenship is required. Selection is based on academic and leadership achievement related to engineering or science, scholastic performance and special study or honors in the field of the award, and a 1-page essay on their study or research related to the field of their award. Financial need is not considered.
Financial data: The stipend is $1,000 per year.
Duration: 2 years.
Additional information: Funding for this program is provided by Yanmar Diesel American Corporation. Candidates must include a $5 processing fee with their application.
Number awarded: 1 each year.
Deadline: March of each year.

2643
YOUNG PRODUCERS CONTEST

Summary: To recognize and reward outstanding short radio programs on a science topic produced by K–12 students.
See Listing #1706.

2644
1980 NSPE ANNUAL MEETING COMMITTEE GRANT

Michigan Society of Professional Engineers
Attn: Scholarship Coordinator
215 North Walnut Street
P.O. Box 15276
Lansing, MI 48901-5276
Phone: (517) 487-9388 Fax: (517) 487-0635
E-mail: mspe@voyager.net
Web Site: www.voyager.net/mspe
Summary: To provide financial assistance to high school seniors in Michigan who are interested in pursuing a college degree in engineering.
Eligibility: This program is open to graduating seniors at high schools in Michigan who have a grade point average of 3.0 or higher and a composite ACT score of 26 or higher. U.S. citizenship is required. Applicants must have been accepted at a Michigan college or university accredited by ABET. They must be planning to enroll in an engineering program and enter the practice of engineering after graduation. They must submit a 250-word essay on "How I Was Influenced to Pursue an Engineering Career." Selection is based on the essay; high school academic record; participation in extracurricular activities; evidence of leadership, character, and self reliance; and comments from teachers and administrators. Financial need is not considered. Semifinalists are interviewed.
Financial data: The stipend is $2,000.
Duration: 1 year; nonrenewable.
Additional information: Information is also available from Roger Lamer, Scholarship Selection Committee Chair, (616) 247-2974, Fax: (616) 247-2997, E-mail: rlamer@steelcase.com. This program was established in 1980 with proceeds from the annual meeting of the National Society of Professional Engineers (NSPE) held in Detroit. Applications must be submitted to the local chapter scholarship representative. Contact the Michigan Society of Professional Engineers (MSPE) for their addresses and phone numbers.
Number awarded: 1 each year.
Deadline: January of each year.

2645
3M ACADEMIC SCHOLARSHIP

American Association of Occupational Health Nurses, Inc.
Attn: AAOHN Foundation
2920 Brandywine Road, Suite 100
Atlanta, GA 30341-4146
Phone: (770) 455-7757 Fax: (770) 455-7271
E-mail: foundation@aaohn.org
Web Site: www.aaohn.org
Summary: To provide financial assistance to registered nurses who are pursuing a bachelor's or graduate degree to prepare for a career in occupational and environmental health.
Eligibility: This program is open to registered nurses who are enrolled in a baccalaureate, master's, or doctoral degree program. Applicants must demonstrate an interest in, and commitment to, occupational and environmental health. Selection is based on 2 letters of recommendation and a 500-word essay on the applicant's professional goals as they relate to the academic activity and the field of occupational and environmental health.
Financial data: The stipend is $1,500.
Duration: 1 year; may be renewed up to 2 additional years.
Number awarded: 1 each year.
Deadline: November of each year.

2646
3M ENGINEERING AWARDS

National Action Council for Minorities in Engineering
350 Fifth Avenue, Suite 2212
New York, NY 10118-2299
Phone: (212) 279-2626 Fax: (212) 629-5178
E-mail: awalter@nacme.org
Web Site: www.nacme.org
Summary: To provide financial assistance to underrepresented minority high school seniors who are planning to pursue a career in engineering.
Eligibility: This program is open to African American, Latino, and American Indian high school seniors who have demonstrated outstanding academic achievement, community involvement, and participation in precollege math and science programs. Students must be nominated for the TechForce Preengineering Prizes by directors of university-based programs or those recognized by the National Association of Precollege Directors. The most outstanding nominees for those prizes receive these awards.
Financial data: The stipend is $2,500 per year.
Duration: 4 years, if the recipient maintains a minimum grade point average of 3.0 in college.
Number awarded: 2 each year.
Deadline: January of each year.

Social Sciences

Described here are 549 funding programs that 1) reward outstanding speeches, essays, organizational involvement, and other activities in the social sciences or 2) support college studies in various social science fields, including accounting, business administration, criminology, economics, education, geography, home economics, international relations, labor relations, political science, sales and marketing, sociology, social services, sports and recreation, and tourism. These programs are available to high school seniors, high school graduates, currently enrolled college students, and/or returning students to fund studies on the undergraduate level in the United States. If you haven't already checked the "Unrestricted by Subject Area" chapter, be sure to do that next; identified there are 1,242 more sources for free money that can be used to support study in the social sciences or any other subject area (although the programs may be restricted in other ways). Finally, be sure to consult the Subject Index to locate available funding in a specific subject area.

2647
AAHE UNDERGRADUATE SCHOLARSHIP

Summary: To provide financial assistance to undergraduate students who are currently enrolled in a health education program.
See Listing #1714.

2648
ACCOUNT FOR YOUR FUTURE SCHOLARSHIP PROGRAM

Pro2Net Corporation
1730 Minor Avenue, Suite 1900
Seattle, WA 98101
Phone: (206) 664-9000   Fax: (206) 664-6330
Phone: (888) 522-PRO2   E-mail: niquettek@pro2net.com
Web Site: accounting.pro2net.com
Summary: To provide financial assistance to undergraduate and graduate accounting students.
Eligibility: This program is open to full-time students who have completed at least 24 semester hours or 45 quarter hours at an accredited college or university with a declared major in accounting. Full-time graduate students are also eligible if they have an undergraduate degree in accounting and are pursuing a master's or doctoral degree in accounting or taxation. Applicants must have an interest in the relationship between accounting and technology and an understanding of the importance of technology to the future of the accounting industry. U.S. citizenship is not required; international students are eligible to apply. Selection is based on academic record, career goals, demonstrated understanding and interest in the accounting-technology relationship, and communication skills.
Financial data: The stipend is $1,000.
Duration: 1 year; nonrenewable.
Additional information: This program is sponsored by KPMG and John Wiley & Sons. Applications must be submitted online; Pro2Net does not accept applications sent via fax or mail. As part of the online application process, students must sign up for membership in Pro2Net.
Number awarded: 5 each year.
Deadline: May or November of each year.

2649
ACCOUNTANCY BOARD OF OHIO EDUCATIONAL ASSISTANCE PROGRAM

Accountancy Board of Ohio
77 South High Street, 18th Floor
Columbus, OH 43266-0301
Phone: (614) 466-4135   Fax: (614) 466-2628
Web Site: www.state.oh.us./acc/educasst.html
Summary: To provide scholarships to minority students enrolled in an accounting education program at Ohio academic institutions approved by the Accountancy Board of Ohio.
Eligibility: Minority students in Ohio may apply if they are beginning their sophomore year. Students who remain in good standing at their institutions and who enter a qualified fifth year program may receive a scholarship award. The criteria that must be met for a student to qualify for the scholarship are: enrolled full time in an accredited Ohio college or university, submit the initial application when a sophomore or junior, be majoring in accounting or a comparable program leading to a CPA certificate, and be in good standing academically.
Financial data: The amount of the stipend is determined annually but is intended to provide substantive relief from the cost of study.
Duration: 1 year.
Number awarded: Several each year.
Deadline: May or November of each year.

2650
ACCOUNTEMPS/AICPA STUDENT SCHOLARSHIP

American Institute of Certified Public Accountants
Attn: Academic and Career Development Division
1211 Avenue of the Americas
New York, NY 10036-8775
Phone: (212) 596-6223   Fax: (212) 596-6292
E-mail: educat@aicpa.org   Web Site: www.aicpa.org
Summary: To provide financial assistance to student affiliate members of the American Institute of Certified Public Accountants (AICPA) who are majoring in accounting, finance, or information systems.

Eligibility: Applicants must meet all of the following criteria: be AICPA student affiliate members; have a declared major in accounting, finance, or information systems; have a grade point average of 3.0 or higher; have completed at least 30 semester hours, including at least 6 semesters in accounting; be enrolled full time as an undergraduate student at a 4-year college or university; and be a U.S. citizen. Students who will be transferring to a 4-year school must include an acceptance letter from that school. Selection is based on outstanding academic achievement, leadership, and future career interests.
Financial data: The stipend is $2,500.
Duration: 1 year.
Additional information: No application materials should be sent to Accountemps.
Number awarded: 2 each year.
Deadline: March of each year.

2651
ACMPE PRESIDENTIAL SCHOLARSHIPS

Summary: To provide financial assistance to nominees, certified members, and fellows of the American College of Medical Practice Executives (ACMPE) who are pursuing professional development through undergraduate or graduate education.
See Listing #1718.

2652
ACTUARIAL SCHOLARSHIPS FOR MINORITY STUDENTS

Society of Actuaries
Attn: Minority Scholarship Coordinator
475 North Martingale Road, Suite 800
Schaumburg, IL 60173-2226
Phone: (847) 706-3509   Fax: (847) 706-3599
E-mail: snelson@soa.org
Web Site: www.beanactuary.org/minority/scholarships.htm
Summary: To provide financial assistance to minority undergraduate students who are interested in pursuing actuarial careers.
Eligibility: This program is open to African Americans, Hispanics, and Native North Americans who are U.S. citizens or have a permanent resident visa. Before applying for this program, students should have taken either the SAT or the ACT. Applicants must be admitted to a college or university offering either a program in actuarial science or courses that will prepare them for an actuarial career. Scholarships are awarded on the basis of individual merit and financial need.
Financial data: The amount of the award depends on the need and merit of the recipient. There is no limit to the size of the scholarship.
Duration: 1 year; may be renewed.
Additional information: This program is jointly sponsored by the Society of Actuaries and the Casualty Actuarial Society.
Number awarded: There is no limit to the number of scholarships awarded.
Deadline: April of each year.

2653
AER TELESENSORY SCHOLARSHIP

Association for Education and Rehabilitation of the Blind and Visually Impaired
4600 Duke Street, Suite 430
P.O. Box 22397
Alexandria, VA 22304
Phone: (703) 823-9690   Fax: (703) 823-9695
E-mail: aer@aerbvi.org
Web Site: www.aerbvi.org/general/benefits/scholarships.htm
Summary: To provide financial assistance for postsecondary education to members of the Association for Education and Rehabilitation of the Blind and Visually Impaired (AER) who wish to study for a career in service to blind and visually impaired people.
Eligibility: This program is open to current members of the association who are interested in preparing for a career in service to blind and visually impaired people (special education, orientation and mobility, rehabilitation training, etc.). Applicants must be enrolled or accepted for enrollment in an appropriate program of study.
Financial data: The stipend is $1,000.
Additional information: Funding for this scholarship is provided by TeleSensory Corporation of Mountain View, California.
Number awarded: 1 every other year.
Deadline: April of even-numbered years.

2654
AH SCHOLARSHIPS

American Humanics, Inc.
Attn: Scholarship Committee
4601 Madison Avenue, Suite B
Kansas City, MO 64112-3011
Phone: (816) 561-6415   Fax: (816) 531-3527
Web Site: www.humanics.org

Summary: To provide financial assistance to student members of American Humanics (AH) who are seeking a career as a professional with nonprofit human services or youth agencies.

Eligibility: This program is open to students who are enrolled full time at 1 of 78 designated colleges and universities that have an AH program to prepare undergraduates for careers with youth and human service agencies. Applicants must be juniors or seniors with a grade point average of 3.0 or higher. They must be active AH student members and involved in the AH student association on their campus. As part of the application process, they must list their personal activities and achievements of the past 2 years that demonstrate their interests, leadership capabilities, and commitment to the nonprofit sector. Selection is also based on essays on why they are seeking a career in the nonprofit sector and why AH should invest in them and their career preparation. Financial need is not considered.

Financial data: The stipend is $1,000.

Duration: 1 year; recipients may reapply.

Additional information: For a list of the participating colleges and universities, contact the sponsor.

Number awarded: 30 each year.

Deadline: April of each year.

2655
ALABAMA FUNERAL DIRECTORS ASSOCIATION SCHOLARSHIP

Alabama Funeral Directors Association
Attn: Executive Director
P.O. Box 241281
Montgomery, AL 36124-1281
Phone: (334) 277-9565   Fax: (334) 277-8028

Summary: To provide financial assistance to residents of Alabama who are attending an accredited mortuary science school.

Eligibility: This program is open to residents of Alabama who have completed at least 30 credit hours in an accredited mortuary science school with a grade of at least "C" in all required mortuary science classes and have an overall grade point average of 2.5 or higher. Applicants must be sponsored by an active member of the Alabama Funeral Directors Association (AFDA) and must submit a 500-word essay on "A Career in Funeral Service." They must be planning to return to Alabama to serve the public in their chosen profession. Selection is based on academic record and evaluation of the required essay; financial need is not considered.

Financial data: The stipend is $1,000. Funds are directly to the school the recipient attends.

Duration: 1 year.

Number awarded: 2 each year.

Deadline: April of each year.

2656
ALABAMA/BIRMINGHAM LEGACY SCHOLARSHIP

National Tourism Foundation
Attn: Scholarships
546 East Main Street
Lexington, KY 40508-2342
Phone: (859) 226-4444   (800) 682-8886
Fax: (859) 226-4437   E-mail: ntf@ntastaff.com
Web Site: www.ntfonline.org

Summary: To provide financial assistance to college students in Alabama who are majoring in tourism.

Eligibility: This program is open to full-time students enrolled in a 2-year or 4-year college or university in Alabama. Applicants must be Alabama residents, have at least a 3.0 grade point average, and be majoring in a travel or tourism-related field (e.g., hotel management, restaurant management, tourism).

Financial data: The stipend is $1,000.

Duration: 1 year.

Additional information: Award winners also receive complimentary registration and an all-expense paid trip (valued at more than $3,000) to the association's annual convention, as well as a 1-year subscription to *Courier* magazine, *Tuesday* newsletter, and *NTF Headlines* newsletter. In any 1 year, applicants may receive only 1 award from the association.

Number awarded: 1 each year.

Deadline: April of each year.

2657
ALBERT A. MARK SCHOLARSHIP FOR TEACHER EDUCATION

Miss America Pageant
Attn: Scholarship Department
Two Miss America Way, Suite 1000
Atlantic City, NJ 08401
Phone: (609) 345-7571, ext. 27   (800) 282-MISS
Fax: (609) 347-6079   E-mail: doreen@missamerica.org
Web Site: www.missamerica.org

Summary: To provide financial assistance to women who are pursuing a degree in education and who, in the past, competed at some level in the Miss America competition.

Eligibility: This program is open to women who are working on an undergraduate, master's, or higher degree in education and who competed at the local, state, or national level in a Miss America competition in 1992 or later. Applicants must be pursuing a career as a classroom teacher, special area teacher (i.e., art, physical education, music), school counselor, school psychologist, school nurse, or school administrator. They must submit an essay, up to 500 words, on the factors that influenced them to enter the field of education, what they consider to be the major issues facing education today, and what they would do to strengthen and improve our educational system. Selection is based on grade point average, class rank, extracurricular activities, financial need, and level of participation within the system.

Financial data: Stipends range from $2,500 to $10,000.

Duration: 1 year; renewable.

Additional information: This scholarship was established in 1997.

Number awarded: 1 or more each year.

Deadline: June of each year.

2658
ALICE YURIKO ENDO MEMORIAL SCHOLARSHIP

Summary: To provide financial assistance to student members of the Japanese American Citizens League (JACL) who are pursuing an undergraduate education, particularly in public or social service.
See Listing #36.

2659
ALLEGHENY MOUNTAIN SECTION SCHOLARSHIPS

Summary: To provide financial assistance to undergraduate students in western Pennsylvania and West Virginia who are interested in pursuing a career in a field related to air and waste management.
See Listing #1754.

2660
ALMA WHITE-DELTA KAPPA GAMMA SCHOLARSHIP

Hawai'i Community Foundation
900 Fort Street Mall, Suite 1300
Honolulu, HI 96813
Phone: (808) 566-5570   (888) 731-3863
Fax: (808) 521-6286   E-mail: scholarships@hcf-hawaii.org
Web Site: www.hcf-hawaii.org

Summary: To provide financial assistance to Hawaii residents who are majoring in education.

Eligibility: This program is open to Hawaii residents who are enrolled in an education program (as a junior, senior, or graduate student). They must be able to demonstrate academic achievement (at least a 2.7 grade point average), good moral character, and financial need. Applications must be accompanied by a short statement indicating reasons for attending college, planned course of study, and career goals. Recipients must attend college on a full-time basis.

Financial data: The amounts of the awards depend on the availability of funds and the need of the recipient; recently, awards averaged $1,000.

Duration: 1 year.

Additional information: This program was established in 1998.

Number awarded: Varies each year; recently, 12 of these scholarships were awarded.

Deadline: February of each year.

2661
AMERICAN BAPTIST MINORITY STUDENT SCHOLARSHIPS

Summary: To provide financial assistance to minority students at American Baptist-related colleges and universities, particularly for studies in religion and human services.
See Listing #1262.

2662
AMERICAN BAPTIST UNDERGRADUATE SCHOLARSHIPS

Summary: To provide financial assistance to undergraduate students at American Baptist-related colleges and universities, particularly for studies in religion and human services.
See Listing #1263.

2663
AMERICAN ENTERPRISE SPEECH CONTEST

National Management Association
2210 Arbor Boulevard
Dayton, OH 45439-1580
Phone: (937) 294-0421   Fax: (937) 294-2374
E-mail: nma@nma1.org
Web Site: nma1.org/aespeech/index.htm
Summary: To recognize and reward outstanding high school speeches on the American competitive enterprise system.
Eligibility: Eligible to compete are students in grades 9 through 12 in a high school within an area of a sponsoring chapter of the National Management Association (NMA). Contestants prepare speeches of 4 to 6 minutes on a topic related to the economic system of the United States. Non-economic issues (social, medical, environmental, political, etc.) may be utilized, but only if focused on business/entrepreneurial issues or approaches. No audio/visual aids are allowed with the presentations, and speeches may not be read verbatim, although notes are allowed. Winners of the chapter contests advance to council competition, from which winners proceed to compete in 1 of the 6 areas of the NMA. The 6 area winners then compete in the national contest. Speeches are judged on the basis of content (50 percent), delivery (30 percent), and language (20 percent).
Financial data: Chapter awards are determined by each chapter, up to a maximum of $500 for the first-place winner; each council also determines its own awards, to a maximum of $750 for the first-place winner. In each of the area contests, first prize is $2,000, second prize $1,500, and third prize $1,000. In the national contest, first prize is $10,000, second prize $5,000, third prize $3,000, and fourth through sixth prizes $500. All prizes are in the form of savings bonds.
Additional information: All costs for prizes and transportation at chapter and council levels are paid by the individual chapters and councils. The national level of NMA supplies the area prizes, national prizes, and transportation expenses for area winners to compete in the national contest.
Number awarded: 18 area and 6 national winners are selected each year; the number of chapter and council prizes awarded varies.
Deadline: Chapter contests are held in January or early February of each year, council contests in February or March, area contests in April and May, and the national contest in September or October.

2664
AMERICAN EXPRESS ACADEMIC SCHOLARSHIPS

American Hotel Foundation
Attn: Manager of Foundation Programs
1201 New York Avenue, N.W., Suite 600
Washington, DC 20005-3931
Phone: (202) 289-3180   Fax: (202) 289-3199
E-mail: ahf@ahma.com
Web Site: www.ei-ahma.org/ahf/ahf.htm
Summary: To provide financial assistance to undergraduate students interested in majoring in hospitality management in college.
Eligibility: Applicants must 1) be actively employed (at least 20 hours per week) at a hotel or motel that is a member of the American Hotel & Motel Association (AH&MA) and have been employed at least 12 months by a hotel or 2) be the dependent of an employee who meets the requirements above and has been employed in the hospitality industry in some capacity in the past. In addition, applicants must be enrolled or planning to enroll as an undergraduate student in a hospitality management program offered by a university or college. Selection is based on financial need, industry-related work experience, academic record,

extracurricular activities, career goals, response to a required essay, and neatness and completeness of the application.
Financial data: Full-time students at a 4-year institution receive $2,000; part-time students at a 4-year institution receive $1,000; full- or part-time students at a 2-year institution receive $500. Full time is defined as carrying 12 or more credit hours. Funds are paid in 2 equal installments. Checks are made out jointly to the recipient and the academic institution and must be endorsed by both. Funds may be used only for tuition, fees, and books.
Duration: 1 year.
Additional information: The Educational Institute (EI) of AH&MA offers a parallel program, the American Express EI Professional Development Scholarship, which provides funding for EI distance learning courses and professional certification programs.
Number awarded: Varies each year.
Deadline: April of each year.

2665
AMERICAN FOREIGN SERVICE ASSOCIATION NATIONAL HIGH SCHOOL ESSAY CONTEST

American Foreign Service Association
2101 E Street, N.W.
Washington, DC 20037
Phone: (202) 338-4045   (800) 704-AFSA
Fax: (202) 338-6820   E-mail: scholar@afsa.org
Web Site: www.afsa.org
Summary: To recognize and reward high school students who submit essays on a topic related to U.S. foreign relations.
Eligibility: This program is open to students in grades 9 through 12 attending a public, private, or parochial school or participating in a high school correspondence program in any of the 50 states, the District of Columbia, or the U.S. territories. U.S. students attending schools overseas are also eligible. Students whose parents are members of the U.S. Foreign Service or have served on the Advisory Committees are not eligible. Applicants must submit an essay of 750 to 1,000 words on a topic that changes annually. Recently, participants were invited to select an issue that is important in U.S. foreign policy today, explain the issue, and describe and analyze the role of members of the U.S. Foreign Service in conducting diplomacy to resolve a specific issue and its immediate consequences. Essays are judged primarily on the basis of originality of analysis and quality of research. They should demonstrate thorough understanding of the major issue of foreign affairs selected and knowledge of the role of members of the Foreign Service in conducting the foreign relations of the United States.
Financial data: The first-place winner receives $2,500 and an all-expenses paid trip to Washington, D.C. for the awards ceremony. The winners school or sponsoring organization receives $500. Second place is $1,250 and third place is $750.
Duration: The competition is held annually.
Number awarded: 3 each year.
Deadline: February of each year.

2666
AMERICAN HOTEL FOUNDATION SCHOLARSHIP PROGRAM

American Hotel Foundation
Attn: Manager of Foundation Programs
1201 New York Avenue, N.W., Suite 600
Washington, DC 20005-3931
Phone: (202) 289-3180   Fax: (202) 289-3199
E-mail: ahf@ahma.com
Web Site: www.ei-ahma.org/ahf/ahf.htm
Summary: To provide financial assistance to students working on an undergraduate degree in hospitality management at participating schools.
Eligibility: Applicants must be attending a 2-year or 4-year college in the United States or Canada that is preapproved and participating in the foundation's scholarship program (for a list of schools, write to the foundation). They must be majoring in hospitality management (including hotel and restaurant management) as full-time students with at least a 3.0 grade point average. Individual schools select the final recipients.
Financial data: The amount awarded varies by school.
Duration: 1 year.
Additional information: Approximately 65 schools are preapproved to participate in this program.
Number awarded: Varies each year; recently, nearly 250 students received

support from this program.

Deadline: Schools must submit their nominations by April of each year.

2667
AMERICAN INDIAN FELLOWSHIP IN BUSINESS SCHOLARSHIP

National Center for American Indian Enterprise Development
Attn: Scholarship Committee
953 East Juanita Avenue
Mesa, AZ 85204
Phone: (800) 4NCAIED   Fax: (602) 545-4208
E-mail: events@ncaied.org
Web Site: www.ncaied.org/fundraising/scholar.html
Summary: To provide financial assistance to American Indian undergraduates or graduate students working on a business degree.
Eligibility: To be eligible, students must be American Indians, currently-enrolled full time in college at the upper-division or graduate school level, and working on a business degree. Applicants must submit a completed application form, an essay describing their reasons for pursuing higher education, their career plans, and their community and extracurricular activities. Transcripts and documentation of tribal enrollment should accompany the application. Selection is based primarily on achievement and commitment to the community.
Financial data: A stipend is awarded (exact amount not specified).
Duration: 1 year.
Number awarded: 5 each year.
Deadline: August of each year.

2668
AMERICAN LEGION NATIONAL HIGH SCHOOL ORATORICAL CONTEST

American Legion
Attn: Americanism and Children & Youth Division
P.O. Box 1055
Indianapolis, IN 46206-1055
Phone: (317) 630-1249   Fax: (317) 630-1223
E-mail: acy@legion.org
Web Site: www.legion.org
Summary: To recognize and reward high school students who participate in an oratorical contest on a theme related to the U.S. constitution.
Eligibility: This program is open to U.S. citizens under the age of 20 who are currently enrolled in junior high or high school (grades 9 through 12). Students enter the contest through their Department (state) American Legion. Each department chooses 1 contestant to enter the regional contest. Regional winners compete in sectional contests; sectional winners compete on the national level. In all competitions, participants are evaluated on both the content and presentation of their prepared and extemporaneous speeches, which must deal with some aspect of the American Constitution or principles of government under the Constitution.
Financial data: Scholarship awards are presented to the 3 finalists in the national contest: $18,000 to the first-place winner; $16,000 to the second-place winner; and $14,000 to the third-place winner. Each Department (state) winner who participates in the first round of the national contest receives a $1,500 scholarship; each first-round winner who advances to and participates in the second round, but does not advance to the final round, receives an additional $1,500 scholarship.
Duration: The competition is held annually.
Additional information: The National Organization of the American Legion pays the travel costs of Department winners and their chaperones as they progress in national competition. Scholarships may be used to attend any accredited college or university in the United States. All contestants must be accompanied by a chaperone.
Number awarded: 3 national winners; hundreds of sectional, regional, and departmental winners.
Deadline: The dates of departmental competitions vary; check with your local American Legion post. The national competition is generally held in April.

2669
AMERICAN SOCIETY OF MILITARY COMPTROLLERS NATIONAL SCHOLARSHIP PROGRAM

American Society of Military Comptrollers
Attn: National Scholarship Program
2034 Eisenhower Avenue, Suite 145
Alexandria, VA 22314-4650
Phone: (703) 549-0360   (800) 462-5637
E-mail: asmchq@aol.com

Web Site: www.asmconline.org/national/nationalawards.shtml
Summary: To provide financial assistance to high school seniors and recent graduates interested in pursuing a career in financial management.
Eligibility: This program is open to high school seniors and to people who graduated from high school during the preceding 6 months. Applicants must be planning to enter college in a field of study directly related to financial resource management, including business administration, economics, public administration, computer science, operations research related to financial management, accounting, and finance. They must be endorsed by a chapter of the American Society of Military Comptrollers (ASMC). Selection is based on scholastic achievement, leadership ability, extracurricular activities, career and academic goals, and financial need.
Financial data: Stipends are $2,000 or $1,000 per year.
Duration: 1 year.
Additional information: The ASMC is open to all financial management professionals employed by the U.S. Department of Defense and Coast Guard, both civilian and military.
Number awarded: 10 each year: 5 at $2,000 and 5 at $1,000.
Deadline: March of each year.

2670
ANDERSEN CONSULTING SCHOLARSHIP PROGRAM FOR MINORITIES

Summary: To provide financial assistance to underrepresented minorities who are studying engineering, computer science, information systems, or decision or management sciences in college.
See Listing #1773.

2671
ANDERSEN FOUNDATION SCHOLARSHIP PROGRAM FOR MINORITIES

Arthur Andersen LLP Foundation
33 West Monroe Street
Mail stop 13-14
Chicago, IL 60603-5385
Phone: (312) 507-3402   Fax: (312) 507-4059
E-mail: aa.foundation@arthurandersen.com
Web Site: www.arthurandersen.com
Summary: To provide financial assistance to underrepresented minorities pursuing a bachelor's or master's degree in a field related to accounting.
Eligibility: This program is open to African American, Hispanic American, and Native American students beginning their third year of college course work. Applicants may be enrolled in 1) an undergraduate or integrated 5-year program in accounting, accounting information systems, taxation, or related business education program, or 2) a master's program in accounting or taxation. Selection is based on merit.
Financial data: The stipend is $2,500 per year.
Duration: 1 year.
Additional information: This program is targeted at schools that have a history of producing students who have been successful in business-related professions.
Number awarded: Varies each year; recently, 33 of these scholarships were awarded.

2672
ANNA E. HALL AND HELEN D. SNOW SCHOLARSHIPS

Phi Chi Theta Educational Foundation
Attn: Scholarship Committee
1704 Hanks Street
Lufkin, TX 75904
E-mail: phichi@lcc.net
Web Site: www.phichitheta.org/member-benefits.htm
Summary: To provide financial assistance to members of Phi Chi Theta working on a degree in business administration or economics.
Eligibility: Members who have completed at least 1 semester or 2 quarters of full-time study in business administration or economics are eligible to apply. They must be enrolled at an approved college or university in the United States in a bachelor's, master's, or doctoral degree program. Selection is based on Phi Chi Theta achievements, contributions, and awards; scholastic achievement; school and community achievements, activities, and awards; a faculty letter of recommendation; and a Phi Chi Theta member letter of recommendation.
Financial data: The stipend is $1,000.

Duration: 1 year.
Additional information: Phi Chi Theta is a national honorary society for women in business administration and economics. Information is also available from Carla D. Bjork, 5015 Penbrook Drive, Franklin, TN 37069.
Number awarded: 4 each year.
Deadline: March of each year.

2673
ANNA HARVEY TEKULSKY TRUST SCHOLARSHIPS

Mellon New England
Attn: Vice President
One Boston Place, 024-0084
Boston, MA 02108
Phone: (617) 722-3891
Summary: To provide financial aid to residents of Massachusetts interested in studying education in college.
Eligibility: Applicants must have graduated from a high school in Massachusetts or have lived for more than 2 years in the state. They may be applying to attend an institution of higher learning anywhere in the United States to major in education. Along with their application and transcripts, they must submit a statement regarding their plans for future study and pursuing a career in education after graduation from college. Selection is based on academic performance, character, abilities and talents, and financial need.
Financial data: Stipends range from $1,000 to $3,000, depending on the need of the recipient.
Duration: 1 year.
Number awarded: Varies each year.
Deadline: April of each year.

2674
ANNABELLA DRUMMOND MCMATH SCHOLARSHIP

Summary: To provide financial assistance for education in liberal arts fields to mature women who are lineal or collateral descendants of Confederate veterans.
See Listing #1272.

2675
APPLEGATE/JACKSON/PARKS FUTURE TEACHER SCHOLARSHIP

National Institute for Labor Relations Research
Attn: Future Teacher Scholarships
5211 Port Royal Road, Suite 510
Springfield, VA 22151
Phone: (703) 321-9606   Fax: (703) 321-7342
E-mail: research@nilrr.org
Web Site: www.nilrr.org
Summary: To provide financial assistance to students majoring in education who oppose compulsory unionism in the education community.
Eligibility: Applicants must be undergraduate students majoring in education in institutions of higher learning in the United States. They must write an essay of approximately 500 words demonstrating an interest in and a knowledge of the right to work principle as it applies to educators. Selection is based on scholastic ability and financial need. Applicants must also demonstrate 1) the potential to complete a degree program in education and receive a teaching license, and 2) an understanding of the principles of voluntary unionism and the problems of compulsory unionism in relation to education.
Financial data: The stipend is $1,000.
Duration: 1 year.
Additional information: This program was established in 1989 to honor Carol Applegate, Kay Jackson, and Dr. Anne Parks, 3 Michigan public school teachers who lost their jobs because they refused to pay union dues.
Number awarded: 1 each year.
Deadline: February of each year.

2676
APPRAISAL INSTITUTE EDUCATION TRUST SCHOLARSHIP

Appraisal Institute
Attn: Appraisal Institute Education Trust
875 North Michigan Avenue, Suite 2400
Chicago, IL 60611-1980
Phone: (312) 335-4129   Fax: (312) 335-4400

E-mail: ocarreon@appraisalinstitute.org
Web Site: www.appraisalinstitute.org
Summary: To provide financial assistance to graduate and undergraduate students majoring in real estate or allied fields.
Eligibility: This program is open to U.S. citizens who are graduate or undergraduate students majoring in real estate appraisal, land economics, real estate, or related fields. Applicants must submit a statement regarding their general activities and intellectual interests in college; college training; activities and employment outside of college; contemplated line of study for a degree; and career they expect to follow after graduation. Selection is based on academic excellence.
Financial data: The stipend is $3,000 for graduate students or $2,000 for undergraduate students.
Duration: 1 year.
Number awarded: At least 1 each year.
Deadline: March of each year.

2677
APPRAISAL INSTITUTE MINORITIES AND WOMEN EDUCATIONAL SCHOLARSHIP PROGRAM

Appraisal Institute
Attn: Minorities and Women Scholarship Fund
875 North Michigan Avenue, Suite 2400
Chicago, IL 60611-1980
Phone: (312) 335-4121   Fax: (312) 335-4200
E-mail: sbarnes@appraisalinstitute.org
Web Site: www.appraisalinstitute.org
Summary: To provide financial assistance to women and minority undergraduate students majoring in real estate or allied fields.
Eligibility: This program is open to members of ethnic, racial, and gender minority groups underrepresented in the real estate appraisal profession. Those groups include women, American Indians, Alaska Natives, Asians, Black or African Americans, Hispanics or Latinos, and Native Hawaiians or other Pacific Islanders. Applicants must be full- or part-time students enrolled in real estate courses within a degree-granting college, university, or junior college. They must submit evidence of demonstrated financial need and a grade point average of 2.5 or higher.
Financial data: The stipend is $1,000 per year. Funds are paid directly to the recipient's institution to be used for tuition and fees.
Duration: 1 year.
Number awarded: At least 1 each year.
Deadline: April of each year.

2678
ARC OF WASHINGTON TRUST FUND SCHOLARSHIP

Summary: To provide financial assistance to undergraduate and graduate students in northwestern states who have a career interest in work relating to mental retardation.
See Listing #1780.

2679
ARKANSAS FRESHMAN/SOPHOMORE MINORITY GRANT PROGRAM

Arkansas Department of Higher Education
Attn: Financial Aid Division
114 East Capitol Avenue
Little Rock, AR 72201-3818
Phone: (501) 371-2050   (800) 54-STUDY
Fax: (501) 371-2001   E-mail: finaid@adhe.arknet.edu
Web Site: www.arscholarships.com/minoritygrant.html
Summary: To provide financial assistance to minorities in Arkansas who want to become teachers.
Eligibility: This program is open to minority (African American, Hispanic American, or Asian American) residents of Arkansas who are full-time freshmen and sophomores in college and interested in teacher education programs. Applicants must be attending an approved Arkansas public or private college or university. They must sign a statement of interest in teaching and participate in pre-service internships in public school settings.
Financial data: The stipend is $1,000 per year.
Duration: 1 year; may be renewed for 1 additional year.
Additional information: Information is available from the teacher certifying

official at 4-year institutions or the vice president for academic affairs, academic dean, or dean of instruction at 2-year institutions.

Number awarded: Varies each year; recently, 250 of these scholarships were awarded.

2680
ARNOLD SADLER MEMORIAL SCHOLARSHIP

Summary: To provide financial assistance to students who are blind and are interested in studying in a field of service to persons with disabilities.
See Listing #1785.

2681
ARTHUR J. PACKARD MEMORIAL SCHOLARSHIP COMPETITION

American Hotel Foundation
Attn: Manager of Foundation Programs
1201 New York Avenue, N.W., Suite 600
Washington, DC 20005-3931
Phone: (202) 289-3180   Fax: (202) 289-3199
E-mail: ahf@ahma.com   Web Site: www.ei-ahma.org/ahf/ahf.htm
Summary: To recognize and reward outstanding students working on an undergraduate degree in lodging management at participating universities.
Eligibility: Applicants must be attending a 4-year college or university that is preapproved and participating in the foundation's scholarship program (for a list of schools, write to the foundation). They must be enrolled full time in a hospitality-related degree-granting program, be a sophomore or junior at the time of application, have at least a 3.5 grade point average, be a U.S. citizen or permanent resident, and be nominated by their school. Selection is based on academic performance, hospitality work experience, financial need, extracurricular involvement (activities and honors), and personal attributes.
Financial data: The national winner receives $5,000, the second-place runner-up receives $3,000, and the third-place runner-up receives $2,000.
Duration: The competition is held annually.
Additional information: Nearly 65 schools are preapproved to participate in this program.
Number awarded: 1 winner and 2 runners-up each year.
Deadline: March of each year.

2682
ASPARAGUS CLUB SCHOLARSHIPS

National Grocers Association
1005 North Glebe Road, Suite 250
Arlington, VA 22201
Phone: (703) 516-0700   Fax: (703) 516-0115
E-mail: pslaughter@nationalgrocers.org
Web Site: www.nationalgrocers.org
Summary: To provide financial assistance to family and members of the National Grocers Association (NGA) who are interested in pursuing a career related to the grocery industry.
Eligibility: This program is open to NGA members, along with their employees, children, nieces, nephews, and grandchildren. Applicants must be entering college sophomores or continuing students at a 2-year associate degree-granting institution or a 4-year bachelor's degree-granting institution. Full-time enrollment is required. Selection is based on academic accomplishment, financial need, and interest in a career in the food industry.
Financial data: Stipends range from $500 to $1,500 per year.
Duration: 1 year.
Additional information: Information is also available from Scholarship Program Administrators, Inc., 201 22nd Avenue, Suite B, P.O. Box 23737, Nashville, TN 27202-3737.
Number awarded: Varies each year.

2683
ASSOCIATED GENERAL CONTRACTORS OF VERMONT SCHOLARSHIP

Summary: To provide financial assistance to Vermont residents who are interested in studying a field related to construction.
See Listing #1808.

2684
ASSOCIATED OREGON LOGGERS SCHOLARSHIP

Summary: To provide financial assistance to high school seniors in Oregon who are planning to major in a forest resource production field of study.
See Listing #1810.

2685
ASSOCIATION OF CALIFORNIA WATER AGENCIES SCHOLARSHIPS

Summary: To provide financial assistance to upper-division students in California who are majoring in water resources-related fields of study.
See Listing #1814.

2686
ASSOCIATION OF ENERGY ENGINEERS SCHOLARSHIPS

Summary: To encourage undergraduate and graduate students to take courses directly related to energy engineering or energy management.
See Listing #1816.

2687
ASSOCIATION OF FOOD AND DRUG OFFICIALS SCHOLARSHIP AWARDS

Summary: To provide financial assistance to currently-enrolled college students who are preparing for a career in some aspect of food, drug, or consumer product safety.
See Listing #1818.

2688
ASWA SCHOLARSHIPS

American Society of Women Accountants
Attn: Administrative Director
1595 Spring Hill Road, Suite 330
Vienna, VA 22182
Phone: (703) 506-3265   (800) 326-2163
Fax: (703) 506-3266   E-mail: aswa@aswa.org
Web Site: www.aswa.org
Summary: To provide financial assistance to women interested in preparing for a career in accounting.
Eligibility: This program is open to women who are enrolled in a college, university, or professional school as either part-time or full-time students pursuing a bachelor's or master's degree in accounting. Applicants must have completed a minimum of 60 semester hours with a declared accounting major. Selection is based on career goals, communication skills, grade point average, personal circumstances, and financial need. Membership in the American Society of Women Accountants (ASWA) is not required. Applications must be submitted to a local ASWA chapter.
Financial data: The stipends range from $1,500 to $4,500 each.
Duration: 1 year; recipients may reapply.
Additional information: Founded in 1938 to assist women C.P.A.s, the organization has nearly 5,000 members in 30 chapters. Some chapters offer scholarships on the local/regional level. Funding for this program is provided by the Educational Foundation for Women in Accounting and by Robert Half International Inc.
Number awarded: Varies each year: recently, 8 of these scholarships were available, including 1 at $4,500, 1 at $3,500, 5 at $2,000, and 1 at $1,500.
Deadline: February of each year.

2689
ATTORNEY-CPA FOUNDATION UNDERGRADUATE ESSAY CONTEST

American Association of Attorney-Certified Public Accountants Foundation
Attn: Executive Director
24196 Alicia Parkway, Suite K
Mission Viejo, CA 92691
Phone: (949) 768-0336   (800) CPA-ATTY
Fax: (949) 768-7062   E-mail: aaacpa@attorney-cpa.com
Web Site: www.attorney-cpa.com
Summary: To recognize and reward outstanding undergraduate student essays on a topic related to accounting.
Eligibility: Undergraduate accounting students are invited to enter this essay

contest. The topic of the essay changes annually but always deals with the law and accounting; recently, the topic was "What is the relationship between factors that investors perceive to impair auditor independence and factors that auditors believe actually impair auditor independence?" The submitted essay should be no more than 20 pages, including footnotes and endnotes.

Financial data: The grand prize is $1,500; the runner-up receives $1,000; and regional prizes are $250.

Duration: The competition is held annually.

Number awarded: 7 each year: 1 grand prize, 1 runner-up, and 5 regional prizes.

Deadline: May of each year.

2690
AVIATION DISTRIBUTORS AND MANUFACTURERS ASSOCIATION SCHOLARSHIP PROGRAM

Summary: To provide financial assistance to students who are preparing for a career in the aviation field.

See Listing #1824.

2691
A.W. PERIGARD FUND SCHOLARSHIP

Summary: To provide financial assistance to students interested in majoring in satellite-related disciplines in college.

See Listing #1283.

2692
AWMA EAST CENTRAL SECTION SCHOLARSHIPS

Summary: To provide financial assistance to undergraduate and graduate students in midwestern states who are interested in pursuing a career in air and waste management.

See Listing #1830.

2693
AWMA EAST MICHIGAN CHAPTER SCHOLARSHIPS

Summary: To provide financial assistance to undergraduate and graduate students in Michigan who are interested in pursuing a career in air and waste management.

See Listing #1831.

2694
BAF SATELLITE & TECHNOLOGY SCHOLARSHIP

Summary: To provide financial assistance to students interested in majoring in satellite-related disciplines in college.

See Listing #1289.

2695
BANK OF AMERICA ACHIEVEMENT AWARDS

Summary: To recognize and reward outstanding high school seniors in California.

See Listing #1290.

2696
BANK OF AMERICA ADA ABILITIES SCHOLARSHIP PROGRAM

Summary: To provide financial assistance to disabled high school seniors or college students from selected states who are interested in preparing for a career with a banking institution.

See Listing #1835.

2697
BARBARA ALICE MOWER MEMORIAL SCHOLARSHIP

Barbara Alice Mower Memorial Scholarship Committee
c/o Nancy A. Mower
1536 Kamole Street
Honolulu, HI 96821
Phone: (808) 373-2901

Summary: To provide financial assistance to female residents of Hawaii who are interested in women's studies and are attending college on the undergraduate or graduate level in the United States or abroad.

Eligibility: This program is open to female residents of Hawaii who are at least

juniors in college, are interested in and committed to women's studies, and have worked or studied in the field. Selection is based on interest in studying about and commitment to helping women, previous work and/or study in that area, previous academic performance, character, personality, and future plans to help women (particularly women in Hawaii). If there are several applicants who meet all these criteria, then financial need may be taken into consideration.

Financial data: The stipend ranges from $1,000 to $3,500.

Duration: 1 year; may be renewed.

Additional information: Recipients may use the scholarship at universities in Hawaii, on the mainland, or in foreign countries. They must focus on women's studies or topics that relate to women in school.

Number awarded: 1 or more each year.

Deadline: April of each year.

2698
BARBARA B. WATSON SCHOLARSHIP

Summary: To provide financial assistance to undergraduate or graduate students who have returned to school to study health care leadership.

See Listing #1836.

2699
BETA GAMMA SIGMA SCHOLARSHIPS

Beta Gamma Sigma
Attn: Central Office
11701 Borman Drive, Suite 295
St. Louis, MO 63146-4199
Phone: (314) 432-8785 (800) 337-HNRS
Fax: (314) 432-7083 E-mail: bgshonors@betagammasigma.org
Web Site: www.betagammasigma.org

Summary: To provide financial assistance to members of Beta Gamma Sigma who are working on an undergraduate degree in business.

Eligibility: This program is open to outstanding student members of the society enrolled in an AACSB-accredited business school. Each chapter is eligible to participate in this program.

Financial data: The stipend is $1,000.

Duration: 1 year.

Additional information: Beta Gamma Sigma is a national honor society in business and management.

Number awarded: Varies each year; recently, 65 of these scholarships were awarded.

2700
BETTY STEVENS-FRECKNALL SCHOLARSHIPS

Association of Information Technology Professionals
Attn: Foundation for Information Technology Education
33405 Treasury Center
Chicago, Il 60694-3400
Phone: (847) 825-6528 (800) 244-9371
Fax: (847) 825-1693 E-mail: reithel@bus.olemiss.edu
Web Site: www.edfoundation.org

Summary: To provide financial assistance to students working on a degree (at any level) in information technology.

Eligibility: Eligible to apply are full-time students who are working on an associate, bachelor's, master's, or doctoral degree in information technology in the United States. Applicants must be members of the Association of Information Technology Professionals. Selection is based on scholastic ability, leadership potential, and financial need.

Financial data: The stipend is $2,000.

Duration: 1 year.

Number awarded: Varies each year; recently, 4 of these scholarships were awarded.

Deadline: May of each year.

2701
BEV AND WES STOCK SCHOLARSHIP

Seattle Mariners Women's Club
P.O. Box 4100
Seattle, WA 98104
Phone: (206) 628-3555

Summary: To provide financial assistance to high school athletes in Washington

state who are interested in preparing for an athletic-related career.

Eligibility: This program is open to athletes who display good character both on and off the playing field. They must be graduating high school seniors in Washington state who are planning to prepare for an athletic-related career and will be attending a college or university in the coming academic year. There is no application form. Applicants must submit a typewritten essay outlining why they are applying for the scholarship, their extracurricular activities, their goals, and how receiving the scholarship will be an advantage to them. Also required are a transcript and 3 letters of recommendation. Selection is based on merit.

Financial data: The stipend is $1,000.

Duration: 1 year; nonrenewable.

Additional information: No telephone inquiries are permitted.

Number awarded: 1 each year.

Deadline: May of each year.

2702
BI-LO MINORITY SCHOLARSHIP PROGRAM

The Foundation Scholarship Program
Attn: BI-LO Minority Scholarship Program
P.O. Box 1465
Taylors, SC 29687-1465
Phone: (864) 268-3363   Fax: (864) 268-7160
E-mail: fssp@infi.net
Web Site: www.scholarshipprograms.org/fsp_bilominority.html

Summary: To provide financial assistance to high school seniors who are interested in attending a designated Historically Black College and University (HBCU) to prepare for a career in the food retail industry.

Eligibility: This program is open to high school seniors of color who have applied for full-time enrollment in at least 1 of the following institutions: Benedict College (Columbia, South Carolina), Claflin University (Orangeburg, South Carolina), Morris College (Sumter, South Carolina), North Carolina A&T State University (Greensboro, North Carolina), or South Carolina State University (Orangeburg, South Carolina). Applicants must have a cumulative grade point average of 3.0 or higher and an SAT score of 900 or higher. They must be interested in pursuing a course of study and career in the food retail industry (e.g., accounting, business management, marketing, distribution management, communications, pharmacy, human resources, information systems, advertising, finance). Along with their application, they must submit an essay in which they describe themselves, including the kind of person they are, their strengths, and their most important achievements in school and in their community; they may also include their hobbies, interests, sports, volunteer work, employment, future plans, or career goals. In addition to the essay, academic honors, leadership activities, extracurricular activities, and financial need are considered in the selection process.

Financial data: The stipend is $1,250 per year. Funds are sent directly to the college or university.

Duration: 2 years (the freshman and sophomore year of college), provided that the recipient maintains full-time enrollment at 1 of the designated institutions and a grade point average of 3.0 or higher.

Additional information: This program is administered by The Foundation Scholarship Program on behalf of BI-LO Incorporated. Recipients must be willing to commit to 1 semester of participation in BI-LO's cooperative education program.

Number awarded: 5 each year.

Deadline: February of each year.

2703
BICK BICKSON SCHOLARSHIP FUND

Hawai'i Community Foundation
900 Fort Street Mall, Suite 1300
Honolulu, HI 96813
Phone: (808) 566-5570   (888) 731-3863
Fax: (808) 521-6286   E-mail: scholarships@hcf-hawaii.org
Web Site: www.hcf-hawaii.org

Summary: To provide financial assistance to Hawaii residents who are interested in studying marketing, law, or travel industry management in college.

Eligibility: This program is open to Hawaii residents who are interested in majoring in marketing, law, or travel industry management on the undergraduate or graduate school level. They must be able to demonstrate academic achievement (at least a 2.7 grade point average), good moral character, and financial need. In addition to filling out the standard application form, applicants must write a short statement indicating their reasons for attending

college, their planned course of study, and their career goals.

Financial data: The amounts of the awards depend on the availability of funds and the need of the recipient; recently, grants averaged $1,250.

Duration: 1 year.

Additional information: Recipients may attend college in Hawaii or on the mainland. Recipients must be full-time students.

Number awarded: Varies each year; recently, 2 of these scholarships were awarded.

Deadline: February of each year.

2704
BLUE CROSS AND BLUE SHIELD/UNITED WISCONSIN SERVICES COLLEGE-TO-WORK PROGRAM

Wisconsin Foundation for Independent Colleges, Inc.
735 North Water Street, Suite 800
Milwaukee, WI 53202-4100
Phone: (414) 273-5980   Fax: (414) 273-5995
E-mail: wfic@execpc.com
Web Site: www.wficweb.org

Summary: To provide financial assistance and work experience to students majoring in fields related to business at private colleges in Wisconsin.

Eligibility: This program is open to juniors and seniors at the 21 independent colleges or universities in Wisconsin. Applicants must be majoring in accounting, sales, marketing, or computer sciences and have a grade point average of 3.2 or higher. They must also be interested in an internship at Blue Cross and Blue Shield/United Wisconsin Services some time during the year.

Financial data: The stipend is $3,500.

Duration: 1 year for the scholarship; 10 weeks for the internship.

Additional information: The participating schools are Alverno College, Beloit College, Cardinal Stritch University, Carroll College, Carthage College, Concordia University of Wisconsin, Edgewood College, Lakeland College, Lawrence University, Marian College, Marquette University, Milwaukee Institute of Art & Design, Milwaukee School of Engineering, Mount Mary College, Northland College, Ripon College, St. Norbert College, Silver Lake College, Viterbo University, and Wisconsin Lutheran College.

Number awarded: 7 each year.

Deadline: June of each year.

2705
BOATING INDUSTRIES SCHOLARSHIPS

Recreational Boating Industries Educational Foundation
c/o Michigan Boating Industries Association
32398 Five Mile Road
Livonia, MI 48154-6109
Phone: (734) 261-0123

Summary: To provide financial assistance for college to students who are interested in preparing for a career in the boating industry.

Eligibility: Eligible to apply are high school seniors and currently-enrolled college students who are interested in preparing for a career in the boating industry (marketing, service, facilities, or management). To apply, students must submit a copy of their high school and/or college transcript, 2 current letters of reference, and an essay (200 to 300 words) on their career goals and why they feel they are deserving of a scholarship. Financial need is considered in the selection process.

Financial data: The amount awarded varies, depending upon the recipient's needs and qualifications.

Duration: 1 year; recipients may reapply.

Additional information: The sponsor will assist recipients in finding summer work at marine businesses in Michigan. Recipients may attend school in any state.

Deadline: March of each year.

2706
BOEING COMPANY CAREER ENHANCEMENT SCHOLARSHIP

Summary: To provide financial assistance to members of Women in Aviation, International who are active in aerospace and seeking financial support to advance their career.

See Listing #1856.

Scholarship Listings

2707
BROWN FOUNDATION COLLEGE SCHOLARSHIPS

Brown Foundation for Educational Equity, Excellence and Research
P.O. Box 4862
Topeka, KS 66604
Phone: (785) 235-3939   Fax: (785) 235-1001
E-mail: brownfound@juno.com
Web Site: brownvboard.org
Summary: To provide financial assistance to currently-enrolled college juniors of color who are interested in preparing for a teaching career.
Eligibility: To be eligible for this scholarship, applicants must meet the following requirements: be a minority; be a college junior; be admitted to a teacher education program; be enrolled in an institution of higher education with an accredited program in education; have at least a 3.0 grade point average; be enrolled at least half time; and submit 2 recommendations (from a teacher, counselor, or other school official and from a person familiar with the applicant). Selection is based on grade point average, extracurricular activities, career plans, essays, and recommendations.
Financial data: The stipend is $1,000 per year.
Duration: 2 years (junior and senior years).
Additional information: The first Brown Foundation Scholarships were awarded in 1989.
Number awarded: 2 each year.
Deadline: April of each year.

2708
BUDWEISER CONSERVATION SCHOLARSHIP

Summary: To provide financial assistance to undergraduate and graduate students who are "poised to make a significant contribution to the field of conservation."
See Listing #1860.

2709
BUREAU OF ALCOHOL, TOBACCO, AND FIREAMS SPECIAL AGENTS' SCHOLARSHIP

Boy Scouts of America
Attn: Learning for Life Division, S210
1325 West Walnut Hill Lane
P.O. Box 152079
Irving, TX 75015-2079
Phone: (972) 580-2418
Web Site: www.learning-for-life.org/exploring
Summary: To provide financial assistance for postsecondary education to Explorer Scouts who plan a career as law enforcement executives.
Eligibility: This program is open to Explorer Scouts who are at least seniors in high school. Selection is based on academic record, letters of recommendation, and a personal essay describing at least 3 personal attributes or skills that they believe are the most important for a law enforcement professional to develop and how their undergraduate studies will help them develop those attributes and skills. Applicants must be active members of a Law Enforcement Explorer post registered with Boy Scouts of America.
Financial data: The stipend is $1,000.
Duration: 1 year; nonrenewable.
Number awarded: 1 or more every other year, depending on availability of funds.
Deadline: March of even-numbered years.

2710
BUSINESS WIRE SPECIAL SCHOLARSHIP FOR PRSSA MEMBERS

Summary: To provide financial assistance for college to members of the Public Relations Student Society of America (PRSSA).
See Listing #1307.

2711
CALIFORNIA ASSOCIATION OF REALTORS SCHOLARSHIPS

California Association of Realtors
Attn: Scholarship Foundation
525 South Virgil Avenue
Los Angeles, CA 90020
Phone: (213) 739-8243   Fax: (213) 739-7202
E-mail: mary_martinez@car.org
Web Site: www.car.org/aboutus/scholarships/index.html

Summary: To provide financial assistance to students in California who are interested in a career in real estate.
Eligibility: This program is open to undergraduate and graduate students enrolled at California colleges and universities who are interested in studying such fields as real estate brokerage, real estate finance, real estate management, real estate development, real estate appraisal, real estate planning, real estate law, or other related areas of study. Applicants must have completed at least 12 units prior to applying, be currently enrolled for at least 6 units per semester or term, have a cumulative grade point average of at least 2.6, and have been legal residents of California for at least 1 year. Real estate licensees who wish to pursue advanced real estate designations, degrees, or credentials are also eligible.
Financial data: The stipend is $2,000 for students at 4-year colleges or universities or $1,000 for students at 2-year colleges.
Duration: 1 year.
Number awarded: Varies each year.
Deadline: September of each year.

2712
CALIFORNIA GOVERNOR'S OPPORTUNITY SCHOLARSHIPS

Summary: To provide financial assistance to California women interested in an undergraduate or graduate education in selected fields.
See Listing #1870.

2713
CALIFORNIA LABOR FEDERATION SCHOLARSHIPS

California Labor Federation, AFL-CIO
Attn: Education Committee
600 Grand Avenue, Suite 410
Oakland, CA 94610-3561
Phone: (510) 663-4000, ext. 4024   Fax: (510) 3663-4099
E-mail: ahobson@calaborfed.org   Web Site: www.calaborfed.org
Summary: To recognize and reward outstanding labor-related essays written by high school students in California.
Eligibility: All graduating high school students in public, private, or parochial schools in California are eligible to compete in this statewide competition. Applicants write an essay of up to 1,000 words on topics that change annually; recently, students could write on why labor unions are important to working people in California. Essays are submitted to high school principals who forward them for judging.
Financial data: The award is a $2,000 scholarship.
Duration: The competition is held annually.
Additional information: This program is administered by the University of California's Center for Labor Research and Education, 2521 Channing Way, Berkeley, CA 94720-5555, (510) 642-0323, Fax: (510) 642-6432, E-mail: osmer@uclink4.berkeley.edu.
Number awarded: 32 each year.
Deadline: February of each year.

2714
CALIFORNIA PLANNING FOUNDATION STATEWIDE SCHOLARSHIPS

Summary: To provide financial assistance to undergraduate students in accredited planning programs at California universities.
See Listing #1308.

2715
CALIFORNIA TOURISM SCHOLARSHIP

National Tourism Foundation
Attn: Scholarships
546 East Main Street
Lexington, KY 40508-2342
Phone: (859) 226-4444   (800) 682-8886
Fax: (859) 226-4437   E-mail: ntf@ntastaff.com
Web Site: www.ntfonline.org
Summary: To provide financial assistance to college students in California who are majoring in tourism.
Eligibility: This program is open to full-time students enrolled in a 2-year or 4-year college or university in California. Applicants must be California residents, have at least a 3.0 grade point average, and be majoring in a travel or tourism-related field (e.g., hotel management, restaurant management, tourism).

Financial data: The stipend is $1,000.
Duration: 1 year.
Additional information: Award winners also receive complimentary registration and an all-expense paid trip (valued at more than $3,000) to the association's annual convention, as well as a 1-year subscription to *Courier* magazine, *Tuesday* newsletter, and *NTF Headlines* newsletter. In any 1 year, applicants may receive only 1 award from the association.
Number awarded: 1 each year.
Deadline: April of each year.

2716
CALVIN E. MOORE MEMORIAL SCHOLARSHIP

Summary: To provide financial assistance for college to high school seniors in Florida whose parents work for a company that belongs to the South Florida Manufacturers Association (SFMA).
See Listing #1872.

2717
CAREER ADVANCEMENT SCHOLARSHIPS

Summary: To provide financial assistance to mature women who are employed or seeking employment in the work force and to increase the pool of women qualified for positions that promise career opportunity.
See Listing #1310.

2718
CARTOGRAPHY AND GEOGRAPHIC INFORMATION SOCIETY SCHOLARSHIP AWARD

Summary: To provide financial assistance for undergraduate or graduate study in cartography or geographic information science to members of the American Congress on Surveying and Mapping (ACSM).
See Listing #1879.

2719
CASE SCHOLARSHIPS

National Court Reporters Association
Attn: Council on Approved Student Education
8224 Old Courthouse Road
Vienna, VA 22182-3808
Phone: (703) 556-6272   (800) 272-6272
Fax: (703) 556-6291   TDD: (703) 556-6289
E-mail: dgaede@ncrahq.org
Summary: To provide financial assistance to student members of the National Court Reporters Association (NCRA).
Eligibility: Students must be nominated by their court reporting school (each school may nominate 2 students). Nominees must be writing 140 to 180 words per minute at the time of application, have attained an exemplary academic record, hold student membership in the association, have a proven interest in the field of verbatim reporting of proceedings, and submit an essay of up to 2 pages (a recent topic was "A Marketing Strategy for Recruiting Students into the Reporting Profession"). Selection is based on the essay and academic record.
Financial data: The first-place winner receives $1,500, second place $1,000, and third place $500. Scholarships are given directly to the students.
Duration: These are 1-time awards.
Additional information: This scholarship is offered by the Council on Approved Student Education (CASE) of the NCRA.
Number awarded: 3 each year.
Deadline: March of each year.

2720
CENIE "JOMO" WILLIAMS TUITION SCHOLARSHIPS

National Association of Black Social Workers
Attn: Chair, Scholarship Committee
8436 West McNichols
Detroit, MI 48221
Phone: (313) 862-6700   Fax: (313) 862-6998
Web Site: www.nabsw.org
Summary: To provide financial assistance for college to members of the National Association of Black Social Workers.
Eligibility: To apply, students must be African Americans, be able to demonstrate community service, have research interests related to African Americans and

African American heritage, and be enrolled full time at an accredited U.S. social work or social welfare program. They must be members of the association, have earned at least a 2.5 grade point average in college, and write a 2-page essay on their background and future plans. Recommendations are required. Financial need is considered in the selection process.
Financial data: The stipend is $2,000. Funds are sent directly to the recipient's school.
Duration: 1 year.
Number awarded: 1 or more each year.
Deadline: December of each year.

2721
CENTRAL COAST SECTION SCHOLARSHIP

Summary: To provide financial assistance to undergraduate students in accredited planning programs at California universities.
See Listing #1313.

2722
CENTRAL OHIO INSURANCE EDUCATION DAY SCHOLARSHIPS

Griffith Foundation for Insurance Education
172 East State Street, Suite 305A
Columbus, OH 43215-4321
Phone: (614) 341-2392   Fax: (614) 442-0402
E-mail: griffithfoundation@attglobal.net
Web Site: www.griffithfoundation.org/student/COIEDann.html
Summary: To provide financial assistance to undergraduate students from Ohio who are preparing for a career in a field related to insurance.
Eligibility: This program in open to U.S. citizens from Ohio who are attending a college or university anywhere in the United States. Applicants for the large scholarships must be studying insurance, risk management, or other insurance-related area and be planning to enter an insurance-related field upon graduation. Applicants for the small scholarships must be majoring in business with a grade point average of 3.5 or higher and must agree to take and complete at least 1 college insurance and risk management course. Selection is based on academic achievement, extracurricular activities and honors, work experience, 3 letters of recommendation, and financial need.
Financial data: The stipend for the large scholarships is $1,000 and $500 for the small scholarship.
Duration: 1 year.
Additional information: This program is sponsored by Insurance Women of Columbus, the Midwest Forum Chapter of the Association of Insurance Compliance Professionals, the Columbus Chapter of the Chartered Property Casualty Underwriters Society, the Columbus Association of Insurance & Financial Advisors, the Ohio Insurance Institute, the Central Ohio Chapter of the Risk & Insurance Management Society, the Columbus Chapter of the Society of Financial Service Professionals, and the Griffith Foundation for Insurance Education.
Number awarded: 5 each year: 2 large scholarships at $1,000 and 3 small scholarships at $500.
Deadline: February of each year.

2723
"CHAPPIE" JAMES MOST PROMISING TEACHER SCHOLARSHIP

Florida Department of Education
Attn: Office of Student Financial Assistance
1940 North Monroe Street, Suite 70
Tallahassee, FL 32303-4759
Phone: (850) 410-5185   (888) 827-2004
Fax: (850) 488-3612   E-mail: osfa@mail.doe.state.fl.us
Web Site: www.firn.edu/doe/osfa
Summary: To provide financial assistance to high school seniors in Florida who are interested in pursuing a teaching career.
Eligibility: All public high schools in Florida, and a proportional number of private high schools, are each eligible to nominate 1 high school senior for this program. The nominated applicant must be in the top 25 percent of the high school senior class, have a cumulative grade point average of 3.0 or higher, have been an active member of a future teacher organization (if available at the high school), and express an intent to teach in Florida public and developmental research schools.

Financial data: The stipend is $1,500 per year.
Duration: 1 year; may be renewed for 1 additional year if the recipient maintains at least a 2.5 grade point average during the first year of college.
Number awarded: Varies each year; recently, this program provided 480 awards.
Deadline: Students must submit applications to their high school principals by the end of February. Principals must submit nominations to the above address by the end of March.

2724
CHARLES MCDANIEL TEACHER SCHOLARSHIPS

Georgia Student Finance Commission
Attn: Scholarships and Grants Division
2082 East Exchange Place, Suite 200
Tucker, GA 30084-5305
Phone: (770) 724-9030   (800) 776-6878
Fax: (770) 724-9031   E-mail: info@mail.gsfc.state.ga.us
Web Site: www.gsfc.org/grants/gemts.htm
Summary: To provide financial assistance to Georgia residents who wish to pursue a career as a teacher.
Eligibility: This program is open to residents of Georgia who graduated from a public Georgia high school and are currently enrolled as full-time juniors or seniors in a college or department of education within an approved Georgia public institution. Each of the public colleges in Georgia that offers a teaching degree may nominate 1 student for these scholarships. Nominees must be working toward an initial baccalaureate degree, have a grade point average of 3.25 or higher, and indicate a strong desire to pursue a career as an elementary or secondary school teacher.
Financial data: The stipend is $1,000 per year.
Duration: 1 year.
Number awarded: Varies each year; recently, 3 of these scholarships were awarded.

2725
CHARLES W. AND ANNETTE HILL SCHOLARSHIP FUND

Summary: To provide financial assistance for postsecondary education (particularly in science and business) to the children of members of the Kansas American Legion.
See Listing #170.

2726
CHARLOTTE WOODS MEMORIAL SCHOLARSHIP

Summary: To provide financial assistance to college students interested in preparing for a career in a field related to transportation.
See Listing #1888.

2727
CHRISTA MCAULIFFE MEMORIAL SCHOLARSHIP

American Legion
Attn: Department of New Hampshire
State House Annex
25 Capitol Street, Room 431
Concord, NH 03301-6312
Phone: (603) 271-5338   Fax: (603) 271-5352
Summary: To provide financial assistance to students in New Hampshire who are interested in becoming a teacher.
Eligibility: Students who are or will be graduates of a New Hampshire high school and have been New Hampshire residents for at least 3 years may apply for this scholarship if they are entering their first year of college to study education.
Financial data: The scholarship is $1,000.
Duration: 1 year.
Number awarded: 1 each year.
Deadline: April of each year.

2728
CHRISTA MCAULIFFE SCHOLARSHIP PROGRAM

Tennessee Student Assistance Corporation
Parkway Towers
404 James Robertson Parkway, Suite 1950
Nashville, TN 37243-0820
Phone: (615) 741-1346   (800) 342-1663
Fax: (615) 741-6101   E-mail: tsac@mail.state.tn.us
Web Site: www.state.tn.us/tsac
Summary: To provide financial assistance to students in Tennessee who are interested in preparing for a teaching career.
Eligibility: This program is open to full-time college seniors in approved teacher education programs in Tennessee who have a cumulative grade point average of 3.5 or higher. They must be U.S. citizens, Tennessee residents, and interested in pursuing a teaching career in the state.
Financial data: The amount of the award depends on the availability of funding, to a maximum of $1,000.
Duration: 1 year; nonrenewable.
Additional information: This program was established in 1986.
Number awarded: Varies each year.
Deadline: March of each year.

2729
CHRISTOPHER "KIT" SMITH SCHOLARSHIP

Society of Louisiana Certified Public Accountants
2400 Veterans Boulevard, Suite 500
Kenner, LA 70062-4739
Phone: (504) 464-1040   (800) 288-5272
Fax: (504) 469-7930
Summary: To provide financial assistance to currently-enrolled college students in Louisiana who are interested in becoming certified public accountants.
Eligibility: Eligible to apply are Louisiana residents who are currently enrolled full time in an accounting program at a 4-year college or university in Louisiana. They must have completed at least 4 semesters by the fall of the academic year in which the application is filed. Selection is based on academic merit (at least a 3.0 grade point average), achievement, and an essay (up to 2 double-spaced typed pages) on the CPA's role on the job and in the community.
Financial data: The stipend ranges from $3,000 to $5,000.
Duration: 1 year.
Additional information: This program was established in 1996. Recipients must be enrolled in an accounting course at the time the scholarship is awarded.
Number awarded: 1 or 2 each year.

2730
C.J. DAVIDSON SCHOLARSHIPS

Family, Career and Community Leaders of America-Texas Association
Attn: Scholarship Coordinator
3530 Bee Caves Road, Suite 101
Austin, TX 78746
Phone: (512) 306-0099   Fax: (512) 306-0041
E-mail: texas@texasfccla.org
Web Site: www.texasfccla.org/scholarships.htm
Summary: To provide financial assistance to high school seniors in Texas who are interested in studying family and consumer sciences in college.
Eligibility: This program is open to high school seniors in Texas who have been members of Family, Career and Community Leaders (FCCLA) of America for at least 2 years and have completed at least 1 year of family and consumer sciences in high school. Applicants must have been accepted at an accredited Texas college or university where they plan to major in an area of family and consumer sciences and receive a teaching certificate. They must submit a 200-word essay on a topic of their choice related to family and consumer sciences. Their overall high school grade average must be 85 or higher. Selection is based on participation in FCCLA, school organizations and activities, and community and church organizations and activities. Financial need is also considered.
Financial data: The stipend is paid at the rate of $900 per semester.
Duration: 8 semesters.
Number awarded: 10 each year: 2 in each Texas FCCLA region.
Deadline: February of each year.

2731
CLAN MACBEAN FOUNDATION GRANTS

Summary: To provide financial assistance to students interested in studying subjects or conducting research in college relating to 1) Scottish culture or 2) the "Human Family."
See Listing #1328.

2732
CLARK E. DEHAVEN SCHOLARSHIP

National Association of Colleges & University Food Services
c/o Michigan State University
Manly Miles Building
1405 South Harrison Road, Suite 305
East Lansing, MI 48824-5242
Phone: (517) 332-2494   Web Site: www.nacufs.org
Summary: To provide financial assistance to students majoring in food service or a related field in college.
Eligibility: Applicants must be U.S. or Canadian citizens and currently enrolled full time as sophomores, juniors, or seniors in an accredited program that will lead to an undergraduate degree in food service or a related field. Awards are made only to applicants enrolled at institutions that are members of the National Association of Colleges & University Food Services. At least a 2.75 grade point average is required. To apply, students must submit a completed application form, an official transcript, 2 letters of recommendation, a letter of personal evaluation, and a resume. Selection is based on academic record, financial need, commitment to the academic program, character, and campus involvement.
Financial data: A stipend is awarded (exact amount not specified). Funds must be used for tuition, fees, room, board, and/or books.
Duration: 1 year.
Deadline: March of each year.

2733
CLOSS/PARNITZKE/CLARKE SCHOLARSHIP

Phi Upsilon Omicron
Attn: Educational Foundation
P.O. Box 329
Fairmont, WV 26555-0329
Phone: (304) 368-0612   E-mail: rickards@access.mountain.net
Web Site: ianrwww.unl.edu/phiu
Summary: To provide financial assistance to undergraduate student members of Phi Upsilon Omicron, a national honor society in family and consumer sciences.
Eligibility: This program is open to members of the society who are working on a bachelor's degree in family and consumer sciences or a related area. Selection is based on scholastic record, participation in society and other collegiate activities, a statement of professional aims and goals, professional and/or work experience, and recommendations.
Financial data: The stipend is $1,500.
Duration: 1 year.
Number awarded: 1 each year.
Deadline: January of each year.

2734
CLUB FOUNDATION SCHOLARSHIPS

Club Foundation
Attn: Scholarship Coordinator
1733 King Street
Alexandria, VA 22314-2720
Phone: (703) 739-9500   Fax: (703) 739-0124
E-mail: justicec@cmaa.org   Web Site: www.clubfoundation.org
Summary: To provide financial assistance for college education to students planning a career in private club management.
Eligibility: This program is open to students who are currently attending an accredited 4-year college or university and are actively preparing for a managerial career in the private club industry. Applicants must have completed their freshman year, must have earned at least a 2.5 grade point average, and must submit a 500- to 1,000-word essay on their career goals and interest in the private club management field. Selection is based on academic record, their essay, letters of recommendation (1 from a professor and 1 from a private club industry professional), and completion of an internship at a private club. Applications may be submitted either directly to the foundation or through association student chapters, which receive grants from the foundation for funding scholarships.
Financial data: Scholarships range up to $2,500 per year.
Duration: 1 year.
Additional information: The Club Foundation was formerly the Club Management Institute Foundation. It is the nonprofit foundation affiliated with the Club Management Association of America.
Number awarded: Up to 2 each year.
Deadline: April of each year.

2735
COMMERCIAL INVESTMENT REAL ESTATE INSTITUTE EDUCATION FOUNDATION UNIVERSITY SCHOLARSHIP PROGRAM

Commercial Investment Real Estate Institute Education Foundation
430 North Michigan, Suite 800
Chicago, IL 60611
Phone: (312) 321-4474   Fax: (312) 321-4530
E-mail: kharrelson@cirei.com
Web Site: www.cirei.com
Summary: To provide financial assistance to upper-division or graduate students working on a degree in real estate.
Eligibility: This program is open to college juniors, college seniors, and graduate students attending participating schools (write to the sponsor for a list). Applicants must be nominated by their university. They must be preparing for a career in commercial investment real estate or an allied industry. Selection is based on academic record, commitment to real estate or allied industry career, communication skills, extracurricular activities, history of employment, and personal and professional references.
Financial data: The stipend is $1,000. Recipients are also given complimentary enrollment in the sponsor's CI 101 course, "Financial Analysis for Commercial Real Estate" (tuition value is approximately $945).
Duration: 1 year.
Additional information: This program started in 1998.

2736
COMMUNITY SPIRIT AWARDS

American Humanics, Inc.
Attn: Scholarship Committee
4601 Madison Avenue, Suite B
Kansas City, MO 64112-3011
Phone: (816) 561-6415   Fax: (816) 531-3527
Web Site: www.humanics.org
Summary: To provide financial assistance to student members of American Humanics (AH) who are seeking a career as a professional with nonprofit human services or youth agencies.
Eligibility: This program is open to students who are enrolled full time at 1 of 78 designated colleges and universities that have an AH program to prepare undergraduates for careers with youth and human service agencies. Applicants must be juniors or seniors with a grade point average of 2.5 or higher. They must be active AH student members and involved in the AH student association on their campus. As part of the application process, they must list their personal activities and achievements of the past 2 years that demonstrate their interests, leadership capabilities, and commitment to the nonprofit sector. Selection is also based on essays on why they are seeking a career in the nonprofit sector and why AH should invest in them and their career preparation. Financial need is not considered.
Financial data: The stipend is $1,000.
Duration: 1 year; recipients may reapply.
Additional information: For a list of the participating colleges and universities, contact the sponsor.
Number awarded: 20 each year.
Deadline: April of each year.

2737
CONNECTICUT ASSOCIATION OF WOMEN POLICE SCHOLARSHIPS

Connecticut Association of Women Police
P.O. Box 1653
Hartford, CT 06144-1653
E-mail: admin@cawp.net   Web Site: www.cawp.net
Summary: To provide financial assistance to high school seniors in Connecticut who are interested in studying criminal justice in college.
Eligibility: This program is open to seniors graduating from high schools in Connecticut who are interested in attending a 4-year college or university to prepare for a career in criminal justice. Selection is based on financial need and an essay of 200 to 250 words on why the applicant should be selected for the scholarship, including both accomplishments and personal hardships.
Financial data: The amount of the award depends on the availability of funds and the need of the recipient.
Duration: 1 year.

Additional information: Information is also available from Officer Elizabeth Maziarz, State Library, Supreme Court Police, 231 Capitol Avenue, Hartford, CT 06106, (860) 566-4452, E-mail: sc.police@jud.state.ct.com.
Number awarded: 1 to 3 each year.
Deadline: April of each year.

2738
CONNECTICUT BROADCASTER'S SCHOLARSHIPS

Summary: To provide financial assistance to Connecticut residents who are studying a field related to broadcasting in college.
See Listing #1333.

2739
CONNECTICUT BUILDING CONGRESS SCHOLARSHIPS

Summary: To provide financial assistance to high school seniors in Connecticut who are interested in studying a field related to construction in college.
See Listing #1334.

2740
CONNECTICUT LAW ENFORCEMENT MEMORIAL SCHOLARSHIPS

Hartford Foundation for Public Giving
85 Gillett Street
Hartford, CT 06105
Phone: (860) 548-1888   Fax: (860) 524-8346
Web Site: www.hfpg.org
Summary: To provide financial assistance to residents of Connecticut who are interested in studying criminal justice in college.
Eligibility: This program is open to graduating high school seniors and current college students who are residents of Connecticut. Applicants must be attending or planning to attend a 2- or 4-year college or university to pursue a career in criminal justice. As part of the application process, they must submit a short essay explaining their motivation for working in the fields of criminal justice and the law. Selection is based on the essay, grades, community service, and outside activities.
Financial data: The stipend is either $2,000 or $1,000.
Duration: 1 year.
Additional information: Funding for this program is provided by the Connecticut Law Enforcement Memorial Scholarship Fund. Information is also available from the Scholarship Chairman, P.O. Box 2428, Waterbury, CT 06722.
Number awarded: Either 1 scholarship at $2,000 or 2 at $1,000 are awarded each year.
Deadline: May of each year.

2741
CONNECTICUT MINORITY TEACHER INCENTIVE PROGRAM

Connecticut Department of Higher Education
Attn: Office of Student Financial Aid
61 Woodland Street
Hartford, CT 06105-2326
Phone: (860) 947-1855   Fax: (860) 947-1838
E-mail: mtip@ctdhe.org
Web Site: www.ctdhe.org
Summary: To provide financial assistance and loan repayment to minority college students in Connecticut who are interested in teaching at public schools in the state.
Eligibility: This program is open to minority juniors and seniors enrolled full time in Connecticut college and university teacher preparation programs. Applicants must be nominated by the education dean at their institution.
Financial data: The maximum stipend is $5,000 per year. If recipients complete a credential and teach at a public school in Connecticut, they may receive up to $2,500 per year, for up to 4 years, to help pay off college loans.
Duration: Up to 2 years.
Number awarded: Varies each year.
Deadline: October of each year.

2742
CONNECTICUT TOURISM SCHOLARSHIP

National Tourism Foundation
Attn: Scholarships
546 East Main Street
Lexington, KY 40508-2342
Phone: (859) 226-4444   (800) 682-8886
Fax: (859) 226-4437   E-mail: ntf@ntastaff.com
Web Site: www.ntfonline.org
Summary: To provide financial assistance to college students in Connecticut who are majoring in tourism.
Eligibility: This program is open to full-time students enrolled in a 4-year college or university in Connecticut. Applicants must be Connecticut residents, be in their junior or senior year, have at least a 3.0 grade point average, and be majoring in a travel or tourism-related field (e.g., hotel management, restaurant management, tourism).
Financial data: The stipend is $1,000.
Duration: 1 year.
Additional information: Award winners also receive complimentary registration and an all-expense paid trip (valued at more than $3,000) to the association's annual convention, as well as a 1-year subscription to *Courier* magazine, *Tuesday* newsletter, and *NTF Headlines* newsletter. In any 1 year, applicants may receive only 1 award from the association.
Number awarded: 1 each year.
Deadline: April of each year.

2743
CONSTANCE L. LLOYD SCHOLARSHIP

Summary: To provide financial assistance to undergraduate or graduate women in Georgia who are pursuing a degree in health care or health care administration.
See Listing #1911.

2744
CONTINENTAL SOCIETY, DAUGHTERS OF INDIAN WARS SCHOLARSHIP

Continental Society, Daughters of Indian Wars
Attn: Scholarship Chair
201 N.W. Sixth Street
Marietta, OK 73448
Summary: To provide financial assistance to Native American college students who are interested in preparing for a career in education.
Eligibility: Applicants must be certified tribal members of a federally-recognized tribe, plan to prepare for a career in education or social service, plan to work on a reservation, be a junior at an accredited college, have earned at least a 3.0 grade point average, and carry at least 10 quarter hours or 8 semester hours. Selection is based primarily on academic achievement and commitment to the field of study; financial need is not necessary but is considered.
Financial data: The stipend is $1,000.
Duration: 1 year; may be renewed.
Number awarded: 1 each year.
Deadline: June of each year.

2745
CONTRACT MANAGEMENT INSTITUTE SCHOLARSHIP PROGRAM

National Contract Management Association
Attn: Contract Management Institute
1912 Woodford Road
Vienna, VA 22182
Phone: (703) 448-9231   (800) 344-8096
Web Site: www.ncmahq.org/cmi/scholar.html
Summary: To provide financial assistance to members of the National Contract Management Association (NCMA) and their children who are undergraduate or graduate students in areas related to acquisition management.
Eligibility: This program is open to members and their dependent children who are enrolled at an accredited academic institution in a program leading to a bachelor's or advanced degree. Applicants must be pursuing a degree or courses consistent with academic disciplines generally deemed relevant to professional acquisition management activities or duties. Undergraduate students must have a grade point average of 3.0 or higher; graduate students must have had an undergraduate grade point average of at least that level. Dependent children must have completed at least half of the academic courses or requirements for a degree from the academic institution in which they are enrolled. Selection is based on overall grade point average, a statement of the rationale for the need for the scholarship, and a description of professional objectives. Graduate and professional students are given preference over undergraduates, and NCMA members are given preference over dependent children. The highest ranked applicant is awarded the Martin L. Kaufman Memorial Scholarship.

Financial data: Regional scholarships are $2,500 per year; the Martin L. Kaufman Memorial Scholarship is $5,000 per year.
Duration: 1 year.
Additional information: Information is also available from the CMI Scholarship Committee, c/o Aviation & Missile Solutions, LLC, 620 Discovery Drive, Building 1, Suite 125, Huntsville, AL 35806-2816. Recipients must agree to remain NCMA members for at least 1 year following the academic year for which the scholarship was awarded.
Number awarded: 9 each year: 1 in each of the 8 NCMA regions plus the Martin L. Kaufman Memorial Scholarship.
Deadline: February of each year.

2746
D. ANITA SMALL SCIENCE & BUSINESS SCHOLARSHIP

Summary: To provide financial assistance to women in Maryland who are interested in working on an undergraduate or graduate degree in a science or business-related field.
See Listing #1917.

2747
DALE E. SIEFKES SCHOLARSHIP

Lincoln Community Foundation
215 Centennial Mall South, Suite 200
Lincoln, NE 68508
Phone: (402) 474-2345   Fax: (402) 476-8532
E-mail: lcf@lcf.org   Web Site: www.lcf.org
Summary: To provide financial assistance to upper-division students majoring in education in Nebraska.
Eligibility: Eligible to apply are juniors or seniors attending a college or university in Nebraska and majoring in education. They must have at least a 3.8 grade point average. Financial need is considered.
Financial data: A stipend is awarded (exact amount not specified).
Duration: 1 year.
Number awarded: 1 or more each year.
Deadline: April of each year.

2748
DANIEL T. MULHERAN MEMORIAL SCHOLARSHIP

Maryland State Funeral Directors Association
7347 Old Alexandria Ferry Road
Clinton, MD 20735
Phone: (301) 877-4003   Fax: (301) 877-4029
E-mail: msfda@aol.com   Web Site: www.msfda.net
Summary: To provide financial assistance to Maryland residents who are interested in preparing for a career in funeral service.
Eligibility: This program is open to Maryland residents who have completed at least two-thirds of their educational requirements in an accredited mortuary science program or have graduated within the past 6 months. Applicants must have an overall grade point average of 2.5 or higher and may not have earned a grade of "D" in any mortuary science class. Along with their application, they must submit 2 essays of approximately 500 words: 1) describing the process they used and the experiences they underwent to enter the funeral service profession, their perception of the value of the funeral, and how their views or perceptions of the profession have changed since they have been in funeral service; and 2) telling about themselves, such as books of interest to them, experiences that have had a significant impact on them, what they do with their own time, civic or church activities, and anything else they feel may be of interest. Selection is based on academic record and the essays; financial need is not considered.
Financial data: The stipend is $1,000.
Duration: 1 year.
Number awarded: 1 each year.
Deadline: September of each year.

2749
DASA SCHOLARSHIP ESSAY CONTEST

Delaware Association of School Administrators
Treadway Towers, Suite 312
9 East Loockerman Street
Dover, DE 19901
Phone: (302) 674-0630   Fax: (302) 674-8305
Web Site: www.state.de.us/dasa

Summary: To recognize and reward high school seniors in Delaware who write an essay on their interest in preparing for a career in education.
Eligibility: This program is open to seniors who are at high schools in Delaware where at least 1 administrator is a member of the Delaware Association of School Administrators. Applicants must be accepted as an education major in college. They are invited to submit an essay (from 300 to 500 words) on "Why I Chose Education as My Career Field." Selection is based on the essay's realistic understanding of the challenges of working in education, originality, clarity and force of expression, overall effect, and reflection of the author's commitment to the field.
Financial data: A cash prize of at least $1,000 is awarded; funds are paid directly to the college that the winner attends.
Duration: The competition is held annually.
Number awarded: 1 or more each year.
Deadline: March of each year.

2750
DAVID HOODS MEMORIAL SCHOLARSHIP

Summary: To provide financial assistance to college juniors and seniors interested in working with electronic documents as a career.
See Listing #1923.

2751
DELAWARE STATE CAP COUNCIL LABOR ESSAY CONTEST

United Automobile, Aerospace and Agricultural Implement Workers of America
Delaware State Community Action Program Council and Region 8
Attn: President
2300 West Newport Pike
Wilmington, DE 19804-3847   Phone: (302) 999-0591
Summary: To recognize and reward outstanding essays written on labor-related topics by high school seniors in Delaware.
Eligibility: This program is open to graduating high school seniors in Delaware. They are invited to write an essay (up to 4 pages) on 1 of the following labor-related topics: a great labor leader of the past, history of a specific international union (e.g., United Auto Workers, Steel Workers), women's role in labor's past, labor history of a specific era, history of labor's role in education, or history of labor's role in politics. Applicants must be planning to attend an accredited college or university as a full-time student.
Financial data: First place is $1,200, second $1,000, third $600, and fourth $400.
Duration: The competition is held annually.
Number awarded: 4 each year.
Deadline: February of each year.

2752
DELAWARE STATE SCHOLARSHIP

Alpha Delta Kappa-Delaware
c/o Cindy Gilfillan
247 Benjamin Boulevard
Bear, DE 19701
Summary: To provide financial assistance to high school seniors in Delaware who are interested in preparing for a career as a teacher.
Eligibility: Applicants must be U.S. citizens, graduating from a Delaware high school, and interested in preparing for a teaching career. They must submit a 1-page essay on "The value of an education." At least 2 letters of recommendation are required, along with an official transcript. Candidates should be in the upper third of their class. Selection is based on academic record and leadership ability.
Financial data: The stipend is $1,000.
Duration: 1 year.
Number awarded: 1 each year.
Deadline: January of each year.

2753
DELTA MU DELTA SCHOLARSHIP AWARDS

Delta Mu Delta
Attn: Scholarship Chair
P.O. Box 46935
St. Louis, MO 63146-6935
Phone: (314) 432-8785   Fax: (314) 432-7083
E-mail: deltamudelta@deltamudelta.org   Web Site: www.deltamudelta.org

Summary: To provide financial assistance to undergraduate or graduate school students majoring in business administration.

Eligibility: This program is open to undergraduate and graduate students who have completed at least half the requirements for their respective degree in business administration. Applicants must be in the top 20 percent of their class. They must have a cumulative grade point average of 3.2 or better if an undergraduate or 3.25 or better if a graduate student. Although membership in Delta Mu Delta (a national honor society in business administration) is not required, applicants must be attending a school with a chapter of the society. Selection is based on scholarship, leadership, character, motivation, potential, and need.

Financial data: Stipends are $2,000, $1,500, $1,000, $750, or $500.

Duration: 1 year.

Number awarded: Varies each year; recently, 39 of these scholarship were awarded: 1 at $2,000 (the Mildred R. Marion Award), 2 at $1,500 (the Albert J. Escher Award and the A.J. Foranoce Award), 4 at $1,000, 11 at $750 (including the Helen D. Snow Award) and 21 at $500 (including the Eta Chapter Award).

Deadline: February of each year.

2754
DELTA SIGMA PI LEADERSHIP FOUNDATION UNDERGRADUATE SCHOLARSHIPS

Delta Sigma Pi
Attn: Leadership Foundation
330 South Campus Avenue
P.O. Box 230
Oxford, OH 45056-0230
Phone: (513) 523-1907, ext. 230   Fax: (513) 523-7292
E-mail: foundation@dspnet.org
Web Site: www.dspnet.org

Summary: To provide financial assistance for college to undergraduate brothers of Delta Sigma Pi, a business education honor society.

Eligibility: This program is open to currently-enrolled undergraduate students who are majoring in business and are members in good standing of the fraternity. Applicants must have at least 1 full semester or quarter of undergraduate studies remaining. Selection is based on academic achievement, financial need, fraternal service, letters of recommendation, service activities, and the overall presentation of the required materials.

Financial data: The stipend is either $1,250 or $500.

Duration: 1 year; recipients may reapply.

Number awarded: 12 each year: 2 at $1,250 and 10 at $500.

Deadline: June of each year.

2755
DICK LARSEN SCHOLARSHIP

Summary: To provide financial assistance to Washington residents who are interested in majoring in a communication-related field at an academic institution in the state.

See Listing #1347.

2756
DON SAHLI-KATHY WOODALL FUTURE TEACHERS OF AMERICA SCHOLARSHIPS

Tennessee Education Association
801 Second Avenue North
Nashville, TN 37201-1099
Phone: (615) 242-8392   (800) 342-8262
Fax: (615) 259-4581
Web Site: www.tnea.org

Summary: To provide financial assistance to high school seniors in Tennessee who are interested in majoring in education.

Eligibility: This program is open to high school seniors in Tennessee who are planning to major in education. Application must be made by a Future Teachers of America chapter affiliated with the Tennessee Education Association.

Financial data: The stipend is $1,000.

Duration: 1 year.

Number awarded: 1 each year.

2757
DON SAHLI-KATHY WOODALL MINORITY STUDENT SCHOLARSHIPS

Tennessee Education Association
801 Second Avenue North
Nashville, TN 37201-1099
Phone: (615) 242-8392   (800) 342-8262
Fax: (615) 259-4581
Web Site: www.tnea.org

Summary: To provide financial assistance to minority high school seniors in Tennessee who are interested in majoring in education.

Eligibility: This program is open to minority high school seniors in Tennessee who are planning to major in education. Application must be made by either a Future Teachers of America chapter affiliated with the Tennessee Education Association (TEA) or by the student with the recommendation of an active TEA member. Selection is based on academic record, leadership ability, economic need, and demonstrated interest in becoming a teacher.

Financial data: The stipend is $1,000.

Duration: 1 year.

Number awarded: 1 each year.

2758
DONALD W. FOGARTY INTERNATIONAL STUDENT PAPER COMPETITION

American Production & Inventory Control Society
Attn: Educational & Research Foundation
5301 Shawnee Road
Alexandria, VA 22312-2317
Phone: (703) 354-8851, ext. 2202   (800) 444-2742, ext. 2202
Fax: (703) 354-8794   E-mail: foundation@apicshq.org
Web Site: www.apics.org

Summary: To recognize and reward outstanding student papers on resource management.

Eligibility: Entries are accepted in 4 categories: full-time graduate student, part-time graduate student, full-time undergraduate, and part-time undergraduate. Papers must be the original work of 1 or more authors and normally between 10 and 20 pages; they may have been developed as part of a regular class assignments, but theses and dissertations are not acceptable. Papers may deal with any topic related to resource management, including inventory management, logistics, manufacturing processes, master planning, just-in-time, material and capacity requirements planning, production activity control, systems and technologies, and supply chain management. Papers are first submitted to local chapters, then forwarded to regional competitions, from which the winning entries are submitted to an international level. Selection is based on relevance of the topic to resource management, timeliness, understanding of topic and depth of coverage, accuracy of material, organization and clarity of the presentation, and originality of treatment.

Financial data: First-, second-, and third-place prizes in each category at the regional level are $250, $200, and $100, respectively; at the international level they are $1,500, $1,000, and $750, respectively.

Number awarded: 12 prizes are awarded at the international level each year.

Deadline: May for the chapter competitions, June for the regional level, and July for the international contest.

2759
DR. FELIX H. REYLER MEMORIAL SCHOLARSHIP

Dade Community Foundation
Attn: Director of Development
200 South Biscayne Boulevard, Suite 2780
Miami, FL 33131-2343
Phone: (305) 371-2711   Fax: (305) 371-5342
E-mail: Dadecomfnd@aol.com

Summary: To provide financial assistance to upper-division students who are Florida residents and working on a degree in international business.

Eligibility: This program is open to juniors and seniors who are enrolled full time in a 4-year public college or university in Florida, have at least a 3.0 grade point average, are Florida residents (this does not include individuals who have resided in Florida only long enough to be granted resident status in the state university system), are U.S. citizens or permanent residents, and are working on an undergraduate degree in international business or finance. Selection is based on financial need, academic achievement, personal goals, work experience, and

extracurricular activities.
Financial data: The stipend is $2,500.
Duration: 1 year; juniors may reapply.
Number awarded: At least 2 each year.
Deadline: May of each year.

2760
DR. HANS AND CLARA ZIMMERMAN FOUNDATION EDUCATION SCHOLARSHIPS

Hawai'i Community Foundation
900 Fort Street Mall, Suite 1300
Honolulu, HI 96813
Phone: (808) 566-5570   (888) 731-3863
Fax: (808) 521-6286   E-mail: scholarships@hcf-hawaii.org
Web Site: www.hcf-hawaii.org
Summary: To provide financial assistance to Hawaii residents who are nontraditional students planning to major in education.
Eligibility: This program is open to Hawaii residents who have worked for at least 2 years and are returning to school as full-time students majoring in education. Applicants must be able to demonstrate academic achievement (at least a 2.7 grade point average), good moral character, and financial need. In addition to filling out the standard application form, they must write a short statement describing their work experience, their reasons for attending college, their planned course of study, and their career goals. Preference is given to students of Hawaiian ancestry, students from the neighbor islands who plan to teach in Hawaii, and students with some teaching experience.
Financial data: The amount of the award depends on the availability of funds and the need of the recipient; recently, grants averaged $1,650.
Duration: 1 year.
Additional information: This scholarship was established in 1997.
Number awarded: Varies each year; recently, 43 of these scholarships were awarded.
Deadline: February of each year.

2761
DR. JOSEPH C. BASILE, II MEMORIAL SCHOLARSHIP

Greater Kanawha Valley Foundation
Attn: Scholarship Coordinator
One Huntington Square, 16th Floor
900 Lee Street, East
P.O. Box 3041
Charleston, WV 25331-3041
Phone: (304) 346-3620   Fax: (304) 346-3640
E-mail: tgkvf@tgkvf.com   Web Site: www.tgkvf.com/scholarship.html
Summary: To provide financial assistance to residents of West Virginia who are pursuing a degree in education.
Eligibility: This program is open to residents of West Virginia who are pursuing or planning to pursue a full-time degree in the field of education at a college or university in the state. Applicants must have at least a 2.5 grade point average and demonstrate good moral character. Selection is based on financial need; superior academic achievement is not required.
Financial data: The stipend is $1,000 per year.
Duration: 1 year; nonrenewable.
Number awarded: 1 each year.
Deadline: February of each year.

2762
DR. TOM ANDERSON MEMORIAL SCHOLARSHIPS

National Tourism Foundation
Attn: Scholarships
546 East Main Street
Lexington, KY 40508-2342
Phone: (859) 226-4444   (800) 682-8886
Fax: (859) 226-4437   E-mail: ntf@ntastaff.com
Web Site: www.ntfonline.org
Summary: To provide financial assistance to college students majoring in tourism.
Eligibility: This program is open to full-time students enrolled in a 2- year or 4-year college or university in North America. Applicants must have at least a 3.0 grade point average and be majoring in a travel or tourism-related field (e.g., hotel management, restaurant management, tourism).
Financial data: The stipend is $2,000.
Duration: 1 year.

Additional information: Award winners also receive complimentary registration and an all-expense paid trip (valued at more than $3,000) to the association's annual convention, as well as a 1-year subscription to *Courier* magazine, *Tuesday* newsletter, and *NTF Headlines* newsletter. This program was established in 1991. In any 1 year, applicants may receive only 1 award from the association.
Number awarded: 1 each year.
Deadline: April of each year.

2763
D.W. SIMPSON & COMPANY ACTUARIAL SCIENCE SCHOLARSHIP

D.W. Simpson & Company
1800 West Larchmont Avenue
Chicago, IL 60613
Phone: (312) 867-2300   (800) 837-8338
Fax: (312) 951-8386   E-mail: actuaries@dwsimpson.com
Web Site: www.actuaryjobs.com/scholar.html
Summary: To provide financial assistance to college seniors majoring in actuarial science.
Eligibility: To be eligible, students must match the following criteria: entering their senior year of undergraduate study in actuarial science, have at least a 3.2 grade point average, have passed at least 1 actuarial examination, and be eligible to work in the United States.
Financial data: The stipend is $1,000 per semester.
Duration: 1 semester; nonrenewable.
Number awarded: 2 each year (1 per semester).
Deadline: April for the fall scholarship; October for the spring scholarship.

2764
DWIGHT P. JACOBUS SCHOLARSHIPS

Association of School Business Officials of Maryland and the District of Columbia
Attn: Executive Director
P.O. Box 419
St. Michael's, MD 21663-0419
Summary: To provide financial assistance to the residents of Maryland and the District of Columbia who are interested in majoring in business or education in Maryland or in the District.
Eligibility: This program is open to students who have been residents of Maryland or the District of Columbia for at least 1 year, have been accepted as a full-time student at an accredited institution of higher education within Maryland or the District, are able to demonstrate financial need, and have a minimum 3.0 grade point average. Both high school seniors and currently-enrolled college students may apply. They must be preparing for a career in business or in education. Selection is based on scholastic achievement, financial need, and extracurricular activities.
Financial data: The stipend is $1,000. Funds are paid directly to the recipient's school.
Duration: 1 year; recipients may reapply for continued support.
Number awarded: 6 each year; at least 1 of these will go to a student enrolled in an approved program leading to teacher certification.
Deadline: March of each year.

2765
E. URNER GOODMAN SCHOLARSHIP FUND

Boy Scouts of America
Attn: Order of the Arrow, S214
1325 West Walnut Hill Lane
P.O. Box 152079
Irving, TX 75015-2079
Phone: (972) 580-2000
Web Site: www.scouting.org
Summary: To assist members of the Boy Scouts of America's Order of the Arrow who are interested in preparing for a professional Scouting career.
Eligibility: Members of the Order of the Arrow are eligible to apply if they are planning a Scouting career. Applicants must submit a 250- to 500-word essay expressing their reasons for pursuing a professional career with the Boy Scouts of America, results of all aptitude and placement tests taken in high school and college, a high school and (if applicable) college transcript, a copy of their college or university acceptance, an employment record, and letters of recommendations.

This information provides the data used in selection. Applicants with at least 1 year of college experience receive preference over high school seniors.

Financial data: Stipends vary each year.

Duration: 1 year.

Number awarded: Varies each year; a total of $20,000 is available for these awards each year.

Deadline: January of each year.

2766
EARL G. GRAVES NAACP SCHOLARSHIP

National Association for the Advancement of Colored People
Attn: Education Department
4805 Mt. Hope Drive
Baltimore, MD 21215-3297
Phone: (410) 358-8900   Fax: (410) 358-9785
Web Site: www.naacp.org

Summary: To provide financial assistance to upper-division and graduate students majoring in business.

Eligibility: This program is open to full-time juniors, seniors, and graduate students majoring in business. Applicants must be currently in good academic standing, making satisfactory progress toward an undergraduate or graduate degree, and in the top 20 percent of their class. Financial need is not considered in the selection process.

Financial data: The stipend is $5,000 per year.

Duration: 1 year.

Number awarded: 1 or more each year.

Deadline: April of each year.

2767
EARL PHILLIPS SCHOLARSHIP

YMCA of Greater Seattle
Human Resources Department
Attn: Scholarship Committee
909 Fourth Avenue
Seattle, WA 98104
Phone: (206) 382-5003

Summary: To provide financial assistance for college to Christian minority students in Washington state who are preparing for a career with the YMCA.

Eligibility: This program is open to minority students in Washington state who are Christians and preparing for employment with the YMCA or a related organization. Appropriate courses of study in college include: human services, child development, physical education, health/fitness, psychology, education, recreation, sociology, business administration, and related fields. Applicants must be able to demonstrate leadership in the YMCA, school, or other organizations. They may be high school seniors, high school/GED program graduates, or currently-enrolled college undergraduates. Selection is based on leadership and participation in school, YMCA, and community activities; academic achievement and honors; financial need; work experience; statement of career and educational goals; and recommendations. Finalists may be interviewed.

Financial data: Up to $1,000 per year.

Duration: Up to a maximum of 4 years.

Number awarded: The number of scholarships awarded varies each year; not all applicants receive awards.

Deadline: Students must request application materials in January or February. The completed application must be returned by the end of March.

2768
EASTER SEALS IOWA SCHOLARSHIPS

Summary: To provide scholarships to needy college sophomores, juniors, seniors, and graduate students in Iowa who are preparing for a career in a profession concerned with physical and/or psychological rehabilitation.
See Listing #1962.

2769
ECOLAB ACADEMIC SCHOLARSHIP PROGRAM

American Hotel Foundation
Attn: Manager of Foundation Programs
1201 New York Avenue, N.W., Suite 600
Washington, DC 20005-3931
Phone: (202) 289-3180   Fax: (202) 289-3199
E-mail: ahf@ahma.com   Web Site: www.ei-ahma.org/ahf/ahf.htm

Summary: To provide financial assistance to students working on a college degree in hospitality management.

Eligibility: This program is open to students working on an associate or baccalaureate degree in hospitality management. They must be enrolled or intend to enroll full time (at least 12 credit hours). Applications are evaluated on the following: industry-related work experience, financial need, academic record and educational qualifications, professional and other extracurricular activities, personal attributes (including career goals), responses to a required essay, and appearance of the completed application.

Financial data: The stipend is $1,000. Funds are distributed in 2 equal installments (in August and December). Checks are made out jointly to the recipient and the recipient's academic institution. Funds may be used only for tuition, books, and fees.

Duration: 1 year.

Additional information: In addition to these academic scholarships, the program also provides support to hospital professionals seeking certification in the following operational areas: certified hotel administrator, certified lodging manager, certified engineering operations executive, and certified hospitality housekeeping executive. This program is known as EI Certification Scholarship Program. Funds are available to cover the cost of the certification study guide, examination fee, and certification fee. Both academic and certification programs are supported by Ecolab.

Number awarded: 12 each year.

Deadline: May of each year.

2770
EDGAR J. SAUX SCHOLARSHIP

Summary: To provide financial assistance to individuals currently employed in medical practice management who are interested in pursuing professional development through undergraduate or graduate education.
See Listing #1965.

2771
EDSF BOARD OF DIRECTORS DOCUMENT COMMUNICATION SCHOLARSHIP

Summary: To provide financial assistance to college juniors, seniors, and graduate students interested in working with electronic documents as a career.
See Listing #1968.

2772
EDSF BOARD OF DIRECTORS TECHNICAL SCHOOL SCHOLARSHIP

Summary: To provide financial assistance to students in technical or trade schools interested in working with electronic documents as a career.
See Listing #1969.

2773
EDSF WORLDWIDE ELECTRONIC DOCUMENT COMMUNICATION SCHOLARSHIPS

Summary: To provide financial assistance to students interested in preparing for a career in the field of electronic document technology.
See Listing #1359.

2774
EDUCATIONAL FOUNDATION COLLEGE/UNIVERSITY SCHOLARSHIPS

Colorado Society of Certified Public Accountants
Attn: Educational Foundation
7979 East Tufts Avenue, Suite 500
Denver, CO 80237-2843
Phone: (303) 741-8613   (800) 523-9082 (within CO)
Fax: (303) 773-6344   E-mail: cpa-staff@cscpa.denver.co.us
Web Site: www.cocpa.org

Summary: To provide financial assistance to college students in Colorado who are studying accounting.

Eligibility: This program is open to undergraduate and graduate students at colleges and universities in Colorado who have completed at least 8 semester hours of accounting courses (including at least 1 intermediate accounting class) and have a grade point average, both overall and in accounting, of at least 3.0. Selection is based first on scholastic achievement and second on financial need.

Financial data: Awards up to $1,000 are available.
Duration: 1 year; recipients may reapply.
Number awarded: 15 to 20 each year.
Deadline: June of each year for fall semester or quarter; November of each year for winter quarter or spring semester.

2775
EDUCATIONAL FOUNDATION HIGH SCHOOL SCHOLARSHIPS

Colorado Society of Certified Public Accountants
Attn: Educational Foundation
7979 East Tufts Avenue, Suite 500
Denver, CO 80237-2843
Phone: (303) 741-8613   (800) 523-9082 (within CO)
Fax: (303) 773-6344   E-mail: cpa-staff@cscpa.denver.co.us
Web Site: www.cocpa.org
Summary: To provide financial assistance to high school seniors in Colorado who plan to study accounting in college.
Eligibility: This program is open to seniors graduating from Colorado high schools who have a grade point average of at least 3.75. Applicants must be planning to attend a college in Colorado with an accredited program in accounting. Selection is based on scholastic achievement.
Financial data: The stipend is $1,000.
Duration: 1 year; nonrenewable.
Number awarded: 8 to 10 each year.
Deadline: February of each year.

2776
EDUCATOR OF TOMORROW AWARD

National Federation of the Blind
c/o Peggy Elliott
Chair, Scholarship Committee
805 Fifth Avenue
Grinnell, IA 50112
Phone: (641) 236-3366
Web Site: www.nfb.org
Summary: To provide financial assistance to blind students who wish to pursue a career as a teacher.
Eligibility: This program is open to legally blind students who are pursuing or planning to pursue a full-time undergraduate or graduate course of study. Applicants must be preparing for a career in elementary, secondary, or postsecondary teaching. Selection is based on academic excellence, service to the community, and financial need.
Financial data: The stipend is $3,000.
Duration: 1 year; recipients may resubmit applications up to 2 additional years.
Additional information: Scholarships are awarded at the federation convention in July. Recipients attend the convention at federation expense; that funding is in addition to the scholarship grant.
Number awarded: 1 each year.
Deadline: March of each year.

2777
EDWARD DAVIS SCHOLARSHIP FUND

Summary: To provide financial assistance to minority students interested in pursuing a career in an automotive-related profession.
See Listing #1972.

2778
EDWARD S. GOLDMACHER EDUCATIONAL FUND

International Association for Human Resource Information Management
401 North Michigan Avenue
Chicago, IL 60611
Phone: (312) 321-5141   Fax: (312) 527-6636
E-mail: goldmacher@ihrim.org
Web Site: www.ihrim.org/edcenter/grants/goldmacher/index.cfm
Summary: To provide financial assistance to undergraduate and graduate students in human resource fields.
Eligibility: This program is open to undergraduate and graduate students in the field of human resource information management, human resource management, human resource systems, or other closely-related fields.

Nominations may be submitted by instructors at accredited institutions in those fields and by members of the International Association for Human Resource Information Management (IHRIM).
Financial data: Stipends generally range from $3,500 to $5,000.
Duration: 1 year; nonrenewable.
Additional information: This program was established in 1994. Recipients must commit to provide a manuscript for publication in the IHRIM.*link* or the *IHRIM Journal* within 12 months after receipt of the award.
Number awarded: 1 or more each year.
Deadline: February of each year.

2779
EDWIN F. BLACK SCHOLARSHIP

Pacific and Asian Affairs Council
Attn: High School Program Coordinator
1601 East-West Road, Fourth Floor
Honolulu, HI 96848-1691
Phone: (808) 944-7783   Fax: (808) 944-7785
E-mail: hspaac@aloha.net
Web Site: www.aloha.net/~paac/hs/hsschinfo.htm
Summary: To provide financial assistance to students in Hawaii who have been active in the programs of the Pacific and Asian Affairs Council (PAAC).
Eligibility: This program is open to graduating seniors from a public or private high school in Hawaii who have been active student members of the council. Applicants must have applied to a 4-year college intending to major in a field related to international affairs. They must demonstrate substantial interest in and commitment to international affairs, as well as outstanding academic achievement, leadership qualities, and commitment to community service. As part of the selection process, they must submit 1) high school transcripts, 2) 2 letters of recommendation, and 3) a 700-word essay describing their academic and career goals.
Financial data: The stipend is $1,000.
Duration: 1 year.
Number awarded: 1 each year.
Deadline: April of each year.

2780
EF GLOBAL CITIZEN AWARDS

EF Educational Tours
EF Center Boston
One Education Street
Boston, MA 02141-1883
Phone: (617) 619-1300   (800) 665-5364
Fax: (617) 619-1001   Fax: (800) 775-4040
E-mail: eftours@ef.com
Web Site: www.eftours.com/public/earn/global_citizen.asp
Summary: To recognize and reward (with a trip to London and Paris and a college scholarship) high school seniors who submit essays on a topic related to global citizenship.
Eligibility: Each high school in the United States and Canada is invited to nominate 1 college-bound graduating senior who is a citizen or permanent resident. Nominees submit an essay, up to 1,500 words, on a topic that changes annually, but relates to global citizenship. Recently, the topic was "Since the events of September 11th, how has your perspective as a global citizen changed? Moving forward, what can you do to make sure that the international community remains open and accessible for people of all nations and cultures?" Selection is based on the sincerity, maturity, clarity, and overall quality of thought demonstrated in the essay.
Financial data: Winners receive an expenses-paid educational tour of London and Paris plus a scholarship of $1,000 (for U.S. recipients) or $C1,500 (for Canadian recipients). Scholarship funds are for use towards college or university tuition and are released after the sponsor receives proof of acceptance to a college or university.
Duration: The tour lasts 10 days, in July. The scholarships are for the first year of college.
Number awarded: 12 each year: 10 from the United States and 2 from Canada.
Deadline: February of each year.

2781
EILEEN J. GARRETT SCHOLARSHIP FOR PARAPSYCHOLOGICAL RESEARCH

Parapsychology Foundation, Inc.
Attn: Executive Director
228 East 71st Street
New York, NY 10021
Phone: (212) 628-1550   Fax: (212) 628-1559
E-mail: info@parapsychology.org
Web Site: www.parapsychology.org
Summary: To provide financial assistance to undergraduate or graduate students interested in studying or conducting research in parapsychology.
Eligibility: Any student attending an accredited college or university in or outside the United States who plans to pursue parapsychological studies or research is eligible to apply for support. Funding is restricted to study, research, and experimentation in the field of parapsychology; it is not for general study nor is it for those with merely a general interest in the subject matter. Applicants must demonstrate a previous academic interest in parapsychology by including, with the application form, a sample of writings on the subject. Letters of reference are also required from 3 individuals who are familiar with the applicant's work and/or studies in parapsychology.
Financial data: The stipend is $3,000.
Duration: 1 year.
Additional information: This scholarship was first awarded in 1984.
Number awarded: 1 each year.
Deadline: July of each year.

2782
EISENHOWER HISPANIC-SERVING INSTITUTIONS FELLOWSHIPS

Summary: To provide financial assistance for undergraduate study in transportation-related fields to students at Hispanic Serving Institutions.
See Listing #1362.

2783
EISENHOWER HISTORICALLY BLACK COLLEGES AND UNIVERSITIES FELLOWSHIPS

Summary: To provide financial assistance for undergraduate study in transportation-related fields to students at Historically Black Colleges and Universities.
See Listing #1363.

2784
EMMA AND MELOID ALGOOD MEMORIAL SCHOLARSHIP FUND

National Association of Black Social Workers
Attn: Chair, Scholarship Committee
8436 West McNichols
Detroit, MI 48221
Phone: (313) 862-6700   Fax: (313) 862-6998
Web Site: www.nabsw.org
Summary: To provide financial assistance for college to members of the National Association of Black Social Workers.
Eligibility: To apply, students must be African Americans, be able to demonstrate community service, have research interests related to African Americans and African American heritage, and be enrolled full time at an accredited U.S. social work or social welfare program. They must be members of the association, have earned at least a 3.0 grade point average in college, and write a 2-page essay on their background and future plans. Recommendations are required. Financial need is considered in the selection process.
Financial data: The stipend is $1,000. Funds are sent directly to the recipient's school.
Duration: 1 year.
Number awarded: 1 each year.
Deadline: December of each year.

2785
ENID HALL GRISWOLD MEMORIAL SCHOLARSHIP

National Society Daughters of the American Revolution
Attn: Scholarship Committee
1776 D Street, N.W.
Washington, DC 20006-5392
Phone: (202) 628-1776
Web Site: www.dar.org/natsociety/edout_scholar.html
Summary: To provide financial assistance for education in the social sciences.
Eligibility: Eligible to apply for these scholarships are undergraduate students entering their junior or senior year with a major in political science, history, government, or economics. Applicants must be sponsored by a local chapter of the Daughters of the American Revolution (DAR). Selection is based on academic excellence, commitment to the field of study, and financial need. U.S. citizenship is required.
Financial data: The stipend is $1,000.
Duration: 1 year; nonrenewable.
Additional information: Information is also available from Cindy B. Findley, DAR Scholarship Committee Chair, 4929 Warfield Drive, Greensboro, NC 27406-8338, (336) 674-5777, E-mail: cfindley@bellsouth.net. Requests for applications must be accompanied by a self-addressed stamped envelope.
Number awarded: Varies each year.
Deadline: February of each year.

2786
ENVIRONMENTAL DIVISION SCHOLARSHIPS

Summary: To provide financial assistance to students who are interested in preparing for a career in the paper industry, with a focus on environmental control as it relates to the pulp, paper, and allied industries.
See Listing #1989.

2787
ENVIRONMENTAL EDUCATIONAL SCHOLARSHIP PROGRAM

Summary: To provide financial assistance to underrepresented and minority students from Missouri who are studying an environmental field in college.
See Listing #1990.

2788
ESTHER MAYO SHERARD SCHOLARSHIP

Summary: To provide financial assistance to African American members of the American Health Information Management Association (AHIMA) who are interested in pursuing an undergraduate degree in health information administration or technology.
See Listing #1997.

2789
ETHNIC DIVERSITY SCHOLARSHIPS FOR COLLEGE STUDENTS

Colorado Society of Certified Public Accountants
Attn: Educational Foundation
7979 East Tufts Avenue, Suite 500
Denver, CO 80237-2843
Phone: (303) 741-8613   (800) 523-9082 (within CO)
Fax: (303) 773-6344   E-mail: cpa-staff@cscpa.denver.co.us
Web Site: www.cocpa.org
Summary: To provide financial assistance to minority college students in Colorado who are studying accounting.
Eligibility: This program is open to African American, Hispanic American, Asian American, American Indian, and Pacific Islander students studying at a college or university in Colorado at the associate, baccalaureate, or graduate level. Applicants must have completed at least 1 intermediate accounting class, be declared accounting majors, have completed at least 8 semester hours of accounting classes, and have a grade point average of at least 3.0. Selection is based first on scholastic achievement and second on financial need.
Financial data: The stipend is $1,000.
Duration: 1 year; recipients may reapply.
Number awarded: 2 each year.
Deadline: November of each year.

2790
ETHNIC DIVERSITY SCHOLARSHIPS FOR HIGH SCHOOL STUDENTS

Colorado Society of Certified Public Accountants
Attn: Educational Foundation
7979 East Tufts Avenue, Suite 500
Denver, CO 80237-2843
Phone: (303) 741-8613   (800) 523-9082 (within CO)
Fax: (303) 773-6344   E-mail: cpa-staff@cscpa.denver.co.us
Web Site: www.cocpa.org
Summary: To provide financial assistance to minority high school seniors in Colorado who plan to study accounting in college.
Eligibility: This program is open to African American, Hispanic American, Asian American, American Indian, and Pacific Islander high school seniors planning to major in accounting at a college or university in Colorado. Applicants must have a grade point average of at least 3.0. Selection is based primarily on scholastic achievement.
Financial data: The stipend is $1,000.
Duration: 1 year; nonrenewable.
Number awarded: 3 each year.
Deadline: February of each year.

2791
EUGENE C. FISH-WILMOT E. FLEMING SCHOLARSHIP

Washington Crossing Foundation
Attn: Vice Chairman
P.O. Box 503
Levittown, PA 19058-0503
Phone: (215) 949-8841
Web Site: www.gwcf.org
Summary: To provide financial assistance for undergraduate education to students from Pennsylvania planning careers in government service.
Eligibility: Eligible are high school seniors in Pennsylvania who are U.S. citizens and are planning careers of service in local, state, or federal government. Applications must be accompanied by a 1-page essay describing why the student plans a career in government service, including any inspiration derived from the leadership of George Washington in his famous crossing of the Delaware. Selection is based on understanding of career requirements, purpose in choice of a career, preparation for their career, qualities of leadership exhibited, sincerity, and historical perspective.
Financial data: The stipend is $5,000, paid at the rate of $2,000 for the first year of college study and $1,000 per year for the following 3 years.
Duration: 4 years, provided the recipient maintains a suitable scholastic level and continues his or her career objective.
Number awarded: 1 each year.
Deadline: January of each year.

2792
EVANGELICAL LUTHERAN CHURCH IN AMERICA CLINICAL EDUCATOR SCHOLARSHIPS THEOLOGICAL STUDY

Summary: To provide financial assistance to members of the Evangelical Lutheran Church in America (ELCA) interested in preparing for certification as educators in pastoral care and counseling ministries.
See Listing #1372.

2793
EXCELLENCE IN STUDENT TEACHING AWARDS

Phi Delta Kappa International
Attn: Director of Chapter Programs
408 North Union
P.O. Box 789
Bloomington, IN 47402-0789
Phone: (812) 339-1156   (800) 766-1156
Fax: (812) 339-0018   E-mail: headquarters@pdkintl.org
Web Site: www.pdkintl.org/studser/sschol.htm
Summary: To recognize and reward student members of Phi Delta Kappa who are engaged in student teaching.
Eligibility: This program is open to members of the organization who are undergraduate or graduate students engaged in student teaching.
Financial data: Winners receive $1,000 in cash, a certificate, a collection of the

organization's current publications, a second year of paid membership in the organization, and funding to attend an organizational professional development institute.
Duration: The awards are presented annually.
Additional information: Applications for this program are distributed by Phi Delta Kappa International chapters in the United States, U.S. Territories, Canadian provinces, and the foreign countries where the organization has chapters. If you cannot locate a chapter in your area, send a self-addressed stamped envelope to the headquarters office to receive a list of the chapters in your area.
Number awarded: Varies each year.
Deadline: June of each year.

2794
FAITH C. AI LAI HEA SCHOLARSHIP FOR STUDENT TEACHERS

Hawaii Education Association
Attn: Scholarship Committee
1649 Kalakaua Avenue
Honolulu, HI 96826
Phone: (808) 949-6657   Fax: (808) 944-2032
Summary: To provide financial assistance to currently-enrolled college students, particularly from the state of Hawaii, who are entering their student teaching semester.
Eligibility: This program is open to students who are enrolled in a full-time undergraduate or post-baccalaureate program at any state-approved or nationally accredited institution of higher learning. Preference is given to students in or from the state of Hawaii. Applicants must have at least a 3.5 grade point average and be entering their student teaching semester. Selection is based on ability, a personal statement, financial need, and recommendations.
Financial data: The stipend is $5,000.
Duration: 1 semester (the student teaching semester).
Additional information: The intent of this scholarship is to prevent the need for employment during the student teaching semester.
Number awarded: 2 each year.
Deadline: March of each year.

2795
FAITH C. AI LAI HEA SCHOLARSHIP FOR UNDERGRADUATE COLLEGE STUDENTS

Hawaii Education Association
Attn: Scholarship Committee
1649 Kalakaua Avenue
Honolulu, HI 96826
Phone: (808) 949-6657   Fax: (808) 944-2032
Summary: To provide financial assistance to currently-enrolled college students, particularly from the state of Hawaii, who are majoring in education.
Eligibility: This program is open to currently-enrolled college students. They must be enrolled full time and majoring in education. Preference is given to students in or from the state of Hawaii. Applicants must have at least a 3.3 grade point average. To apply, students must submit an official college transcript, a personal statement, a statement of financial need, and a recommendation from a college faculty member. Selection is based on ability, financial need, the personal statement, and the faculty recommendation.
Financial data: The stipend is $2,000, paid in 2 equal installments.
Duration: 1 year.
Number awarded: 1 each year.
Deadline: April of each year.

2796
FAMILY, CAREER AND COMMUNITY LEADERS OF AMERICA-TEXAS ASSOCIATION REGIONAL SCHOLARSHIPS

Family, Career and Community Leaders of America-Texas Association
Attn: Scholarship Coordinator
3530 Bee Caves Road, Suite 101
Austin, TX 78746
Phone: (512) 306-0099   Fax: (512) 306-0041
E-mail: texas@texasfccla.org
Web Site: www.texasfccla.org/scholarships.htm
Summary: To provide financial assistance to high school seniors in Texas who are interested in studying family and consumer sciences in college.
Eligibility: This program is open to high school seniors in Texas who have been

members of Family, Career and Community Leaders (FCCLA) of America and are interested in majoring in family and consumer sciences in college. Applicants must submit a 500-word essay on how involvement in FCCLA has prepared them for their future. Selection is based on participation in FCCLA, school organizations and activities, and community and church organizations and activities. Financial need is also considered.

Financial data: The stipend is $1,000.

Duration: 1 year; nonrenewable.

Number awarded: 5 each year: 1 in each Texas FCCLA region.

Deadline: February of each year.

2797
FARM CREDIT OF MAINE SCHOLARSHIP

Summary: To provide financial assistance to 4-H members in Maine who are interested in studying fields related to commercial farming, fishing, or forest products in college.

See Listing #2004.

2798
FEA TRUST SCHOLARSHIP AWARD CONTEST

Florida Education Association
213 South Adams Street
Tallahassee, FL 32301
Phone: (850) 201-2800
Web Site: www.floridaea.org

Summary: To provide financial assistance to the children of Florida Education Association (FEA) members who are graduating from public high schools in Florida and are interested in majoring in education in college.

Eligibility: This program is open to public high school seniors whose parents or guardians are members of FEA. Applicants must have at least a 3.0 grade point average and plan on majoring in a field related to education in college. As part of the application process, they must submit proof of achievement in extracurricular activities, up to 2 letters of recommendation, and an original essay (no more than 5 pages) on future plans. Financial need is not considered in the selection process.

Financial data: The stipend is $2,000. Funds must be used for the purchase of books or payment of tuition and fees at the recipient's college.

Duration: 1 year.

Additional information: Recipients may attend a college, university, or vocational-technical institute.

Number awarded: 3 each year.

Deadline: July of each year.

2799
FLORENCE MARGARET HARVEY MEMORIAL SCHOLARSHIP

Summary: To provide financial assistance to blind students who wish to study in the field of rehabilitation and/or education of the blind.

See Listing #2009.

2800
FLORIDA EDUCATIONAL FACILITIES PLANNERS' ASSOCIATION ASSISTANCESHIP

Florida Educational Facilities Planners' Association, Inc.
c/o James R. Reinschmidt, Selection Committee
Valencia Community College
P.O. Box 3028
Orlando, FL 3208
Web Site: www.fefpa.org

Summary: To provide financial assistance to upper-division and graduate students in Florida who are preparing for a career in educational facilities management.

Eligibility: This program is open to full-time juniors, seniors, and graduate students who are enrolled in a degree program at an accredited 4-year public university in Florida. Applicants must be Florida residents and majoring in facilities planning or in a field related to facilities planning. Part-time students with full employment will also be considered if they are working on a degree in a field related to facilities planning. Applications must be accompanied by transcripts, SAT scores, a 1-page essay on why the applicant deserves this scholarship, and a completed appraisal form from the applicant's issuing professor, supervisor, or department head. Selection is based on financial need, academic record (at least a 3.0 grade point average), community involvement, employment, the appraisal form, and the essay.

Financial data: The stipend is $3,000 per year, paid in 2 equal installments ($1,500 per semester). Funds are sent directly to the recipients.

Additional information: The sponsor is a statewide organization of facilities planners and associate members involved in the planning of public educational facilities in K-12, community colleges, and universities.

Duration: 1 year.

Additional information: Faxed applications will not be accepted. Recipients must attend a public university in Florida.

Number awarded: 2 each year.

Deadline: March of each year.

2801
FLORIDA FUNERAL DIRECTORS ASSOCIATION SCHOLARSHIPS

Florida Funeral Directors Association
P.O. Box 6009
Tallahassee, FL 32314
Phone: (904) 224-1969

Summary: To provide financial assistance to residents of Florida who are currently enrolled in a mortuary science school.

Eligibility: This program is open to Florida residents who are student members of the sponsoring organization, are currently enrolled in a school of mortuary science, have completed at least 30 credit hours in the program (with no grade lower than "C" in any required mortuary science class), and have an overall grade point average of at least 2.5.

Financial data: Stipends are $1,000, $750, or $500.

Duration: 1 semester.

Number awarded: Up to 6 each year.

2802
FLORIDA INSTRUCTIONAL AIDE SCHOLARSHIP PROGRAM

Florida Department of Education
Attn: Office of Student Financial Assistance
1940 North Monroe Street, Suite 70
Tallahassee, FL 32303-4759
Phone: (850) 410-5185   (888) 827-2004
Fax: (850) 488-3612   E-mail: osfa@mail.doe.state.fl.us
Web Site: www.firn.edu/doe/osfa

Summary: To provide tuition reimbursement to instructional aides in Florida public schools who complete undergraduate or graduate courses in a program leading to certification in an area of critical state concern.

Eligibility: Applicants must have been employed as a instructional aide in a publicly-funded Florida school system for at least 1 year and have completed 1 or more undergraduate courses as part of enrollment in a program leading to certification in specified areas with a grade point average of 2.0 or higher.

Financial data: Tuition reimbursement of up to $3,000 per year may be provided.

Additional information: The Florida legislature created this program in 2000. The designated subject areas include exceptional student education (emotionally handicapped, hearing impaired, mentally handicapped, physically handicapped, specific learning disability, speech and language impaired, varying exceptionalities, and visually impaired), computer science, foreign languages, mathematics, and science.

Number awarded: Varies each year.

Deadline: For fall classes, applications must be submitted by January of each year. For winter and/or spring classes, applications must be submitted by May of each year.

2803
FOOD MARKETING INSTITUTE SCHOLARSHIPS

DECA
1908 Association Drive
Reston, VA 20191-1594
Phone: (703) 860-5000   Fax: (703) 860-4013
E-mail: decainc@aol.com
Web Site: www.deca.org/scholarships/index.html

Summary: To provide financial assistance to DECA members who are women or minorities and interested in preparing for a marketing career.

Eligibility: This program is open to DECA members who are minorities and/or women intending to pursue a career in marketing, business, or marketing education. Applicants must be able to demonstrate supermarket industry experience, DECA activities, grades, and leadership ability. Awards are made on

the basis of merit, not financial need.
Financial data: The stipend is $1,000.
Duration: 1 year.
Additional information: This program is sponsored by the Food Marketing Institute.
Number awarded: 5 each year.
Deadline: February of each year.

2804
FORE DIVERSITY SCHOLARSHIPS

Summary: To provide financial assistance to minority members of the American Health Information Management Association (AHIMA) who are interested in pursuing an undergraduate degree in health information administration or technology.
See Listing #2015.

2805
FORE UNDERGRADUATE MERIT SCHOLARSHIPS

Summary: To provide financial assistance to members of the American Health Information Management Association (AHIMA) who are interested in pursuing an undergraduate degree in health information administration or technology.
See Listing #2016.

2806
FOUNDATION OF THE WALL AND CEILING INDUSTRY SCHOLARSHIPS

Summary: To provide financial assistance for college study in disciplines related to the wall and ceiling industry to employees of firms that are members of the Association of the Wall and Ceiling Industries-International (AWCI) and their dependents.
See Listing #1382.

2807
FRANCES A. MAYS SCHOLARSHIP AWARD

Summary: To recognize and reward outstanding students majoring in health, physical education, recreation, or dance in Virginia.
See Listing #1384.

2808
FRANK D. VISCEGLIA MEMORIAL SCHOLARSHIP

Summary: To provide financial assistance to Eagle Scouts in New Jersey who have the potential to directly impact the delicate balance between the economy and the environment.
See Listing #2021.

2809
FRANK L. GREATHOUSE GOVERNMENT ACCOUNTING SCHOLARSHIP

Government Finance Officers Association
Attn: Scholarship Committee
180 North Michigan Avenue, Suite 800
Chicago, IL 60601-7476
Phone: (312) 977-9700   Fax: (312) 977-4806
Web Site: www.gfoa.org
Summary: To recognize and reward the outstanding performance of undergraduate students who are preparing for a career in public accounting.
Eligibility: This program is open to full-time seniors in college who are enrolled in an accounting program and preparing for a career in state and local government finance. Applicants must be citizens or permanent residents of the United States or Canada and able to provide a letter of recommendation from the dean of their graduate program. Selection is based on career plans, academic record, plan of study, letters of recommendation, and grade point average. Financial need is not considered.
Financial data: The stipend is $2,000.
Duration: 1 year.
Number awarded: 1 or more each year.
Deadline: February of each year.

2810
FRIENDS OF OREGON STUDENTS PROGRAM

Summary: To provide financial assistance for undergraduate or graduate work to nontraditional students in Oregon.
See Listing #2025.

2811
FRSA SCHOLARSHIP PROGRAM

Summary: To provide financial assistance for college to students in Florida interested in pursuing construction-related careers.
See Listing #2026.

2812
FTE UNDERGRADUATE SCHOLARSHIP

Summary: To provide financial support to undergraduate members of the International Technology Education Association (ITEA) who are majoring in technology education teacher preparation.
See Listing #2028.

2813
FUKUNAGA SCHOLARSHIP

Fukunaga Scholarship Foundation
Attn: Scholarship Selection Committee
900 Fort Street Mall, Suite 600
P.O. Box 2788
Honolulu, HI 96803-2788
Phone: (808) 521-6511, ext. 227   Fax: (808) 523-3937
E-mail: eviek@servco.com   Web Site: www.servco.com/scholarship
Summary: To provide financial assistance to Hawaii residents who are interested in majoring in business in college.
Eligibility: This program is open to Hawaii residents who are graduating from high school or already enrolled in a 4-year college or university. Applicants must be majoring or planning to major in business administration. They should have at least a 3.0 grade point average and plan to return to or remain in Hawaii or the Pacific Islands region. Selection is based on academic achievement; interest in business; participation, leadership, and responsibility in school activities and community service; and financial need.
Financial data: The stipend is $2,500 per year.
Duration: Up to 4 years for high school seniors; up to the remainder of the approved undergraduate program for recipients currently in college.
Additional information: To maintain eligibility, recipients must enroll in school full time and maintain at least a 3.0 grade point average.
Number awarded: 12 to 16 each year.
Deadline: February of each year.

2814
FUTURE ENTREPRENEUR OF THE YEAR AWARD

National Association for the Self-Employed
P.O. Box 612067
DFW Airport
Dallas, TX 75261-2067
Phone: (800) 232-NASE   Web Site: www.nase.org
Summary: To provide financial assistance to high school seniors interested in studying entrepreneurship in college.
Eligibility: This program is open to high school seniors who demonstrate leadership, academic excellence, ingenuity, and entrepreneurial spirit. Applicants must be interested in a college program that stresses the philosophy of entrepreneurship rather than a specific profession.
Financial data: The maximum stipend is $24,000.
Duration: 1 year.
Number awarded: 1 each year.
Deadline: April of each year.

2815
G.A. MAVON MEMORIAL SCHOLARSHIP

Professional Independent Insurance Agents of Illinois
4360 Wabash Avenue
Springfield, IL 62707
Phone: (217) 793-6660   (800) 628-6436

Fax: (217) 793-6744   E-mail: admin@piiai.org
Web Site: www.piiai.org/youngagents/scholarship.htm
Summary: To provide financial assistance to upper-division students who are majoring in business and have an interest in insurance.
Eligibility: To be eligible for this scholarship, students must meet the following criteria: have junior or senior status in college, be in a business degree program with an interest in insurance, be a full-time student, and have a letter of recommendation from a current or retired member of the Professional Independent Insurance Agents of Illinois. To apply, students must complete an application form and submit an essay (500 words or less) on the contribution the insurance industry provides to society. Financial need is not considered in the selection process.
Financial data: The stipend is $2,000, payable in 2 equal installments. Funds are paid directly to the recipient's school.
Duration: 1 year.
Number awarded: 1 each year.
Deadline: June of each year.

2816
GAE/GFIE SCHOLARSHIPS FOR ASPIRING TEACHERS

Georgia Association of Educators
Attn: Georgia Foundation for the Improvement of Education
Professional Development Services
100 Crescent Centre Parkway, Suite 500
Tucker, GA 30084-7049
Phone: (678) 837-1100   (800) 282-7142
Web Site: www.gae.org
Summary: To provide financial assistance for college to residents of Georgia who are interested in pursuing a career as a teacher.
Eligibility: This program is open to 1) seniors graduating from a high school in Georgia who plan to attend an accredited college or university in Georgia within the next 12 months, and 2) student members of the Georgia Association of Educators (GAE) who have been admitted to a teacher education program at an accredited Georgia college or university. Scholarships are presented to the students who show the greatest potential as teachers, based on depth of thought, clarity of expression, leadership potential, extracurricular activities, community involvement, and grade point average (3.0 or higher). Financial need is also considered in the selection process.
Financial data: The stipend is $1,000. Funds are paid directly to the recipient's college or university.
Duration: 1 year.
Additional information: The GAE established the Georgia Foundation for the Improvement of Education (GFIE) to administer this program.
Number awarded: 20 each year: 10 graduating high school seniors and 10 GAE members already enrolled in college.
Deadline: March of each year.

2817
GARY MERRILL MEMORIAL FUND

Maine Community Foundation
Attn: Program Director
245 Main Street
Ellsworth, ME 04605
Phone: (207) 667-9735   (877) 700-6800
Fax: (207) 667-0447   E-mail: info@mainecf.org
Web Site: www.mainecf.org/scholar.html
Summary: To provide financial assistance for postsecondary education to students in Maine who are majoring in political science.
Eligibility: Eligible to apply for these scholarships are Maine residents who are enrolled in a Maine college or university entering their sophomore, junior, or senior year with a major in political science or government studies.
Financial data: Awards range from $500 to $1,500 per year.
Duration: 1 year.
Additional information: This program was established in 1992.
Number awarded: 1 each year.
Deadline: March of each year.

2818
GENERAL ELECTRIC AFRICAN AMERICAN FORUM SCHOLARSHIP

Summary: To provide financial assistance to members of the National Society of Black Engineers (NSBE) who are majoring in business or engineering.
employees with matching contributions from the GE Foundation.
See Listing #2041.

2819
GENERAL ELECTRIC FUND/LEAGUE OF UNITED LATIN AMERICAN CITIZENS SCHOLARSHIPS

Summary: To provide financial assistance to Latino students who are studying engineering or business in college.
See Listing #2043.

2820
GENERATIONS FOR PEACE ESSAY CONTEST

Generations for Peace
c/o St. James Lutheran Church
1315 S.W. Park Avenue
Portland, OR 97201
Phone: (503) 222-2194
Summary: To recognize and reward outstanding essays on the general subject of peace written by high school students.
Eligibility: This competition is open to all 11th and 12th grade students who are citizens and residents of the United States. Each year, the exact subject of the essay changes, but it always deals with the theme of peace. Essays may not be more than 750 words.
Financial data: The first-place essay receives $1,500; the second-place essay receives $750. Funds are paid directly to the winner's school.
Duration: The competition is held annually.
Additional information: There is a $1 handling charge.
Number awarded: 2 each year.
Deadline: April of each year.

2821
GEORGE AND DONNA NIGH PUBLIC SERVICE SCHOLARSHIP

Oklahoma State Regents for Higher Education
Attn: Director of Scholarship and Grant Programs
500 Education Building
State Capitol Complex
Oklahoma City, OK 73105-4503
Phone: (405) 524-9239   (800) 858-1840
Fax: (405) 524-9230   E-mail: studentinfo@osrhe.edu
Web Site: www.okhighered.org
Summary: To provide financial assistance for college to residents in Oklahoma who are interested in a career in public service.
Eligibility: This program is open to residents of Oklahoma who are enrolled full time in an undergraduate program at a public or private college or university in the state. Applicants must be enrolled in a degree program leading to a career in public service (as determined by the institution). Selection is based on academic achievement, including grade point average, class rank, national awards, scholastic achievement, honors, teachers' recommendations, and participation in extracurricular activities. Each participating college or university may nominate 1 recipient each year.
Financial data: The stipend is $1,000 per year.
Duration: 1 year; nonrenewable.
Additional information: This program operates in conjunction with the George and Donna Nigh Institute, Downtown College Consortium, 120 North Robinson, Suite 500 C, Oklahoma City, OK 73102, (405) 319-3085, E-mail: mbigger@okc.cc.ok.us.
Number awarded: Varies each year.

2822
GEORGE AND LYNNA GENE COOK SCHOLARSHIP

Summary: To provide financial assistance for college to Nebraska residents who are members of the First Church of God and attending a college or university affiliated with the denomination.
See Listing #1390.

2823
GEORGE M. BROOKER COLLEGIATE SCHOLARSHIP FOR MINORITIES

Institute of Real Estate Management Foundation
Attn: Foundation Coordinator
430 North Michigan Avenue
Chicago, IL 60611-4090
Phone: (312) 329-6008   Fax: (312) 410-7908
E-mail: kholmes@irem.org   Web Site: www.irem.org

Summary: To provide financial assistance to minorities interested in preparing (on the undergraduate or graduate level) for a career in the real estate management industry.
Eligibility: This program is open to junior, senior, and graduate minority (non-Caucasian) students majoring in real estate, preferably with an emphasis on management, asset management, or related fields. Applicants must be interested in entering a career in real estate management upon graduation. They must have earned a grade point average of 3.0 or higher in their major, have completed at least 2 college courses in real estate, and write an essay (up to 500 words) on why they want to follow a career in real estate management. U.S. citizenship is required. Selection is based on academic success and a demonstrated commitment to a career in real estate management.
Financial data: The stipend for undergraduates is $1,000; the stipend for graduate students is $2,500. Funds are disbursed to the institution the student attends to be used only for tuition expenses.
Duration: 1 year; nonrenewable.
Number awarded: 3 each year: 2 undergraduate awards and 1 graduate award.
Deadline: February of each year.

2824
GEORGIA GOVERNMENT FINANCE OFFICERS ASSOCIATION SCHOLARSHIP

Georgia Government Finance Officers Association
Attn: Scholarship Selection Committee
P.O. Box 6473
Athens, GA 30604-6473
E-mail: charlotte.blanton@americus-online.com
Web Site: www.ggfoa.org/Scholarships/scholarships.htm
Summary: To provide financial assistance to undergraduate or graduate students in Georgia who are preparing for a career in public finance.
Eligibility: This program is open to undergraduate or graduate students who are preparing for a career in public finance and are currently enrolled or accepted (for graduate school) as full-time students at a college or university in Georgia. Nominations must be submitted by the head of the applicable program (e.g., public administration, accounting, finance, business). Preference is given to Georgia residents who are eligible for in-state tuition.
Financial data: The stipend is $3,000.
Duration: 1 year.
Number awarded: 2 each year.
Deadline: June of each year.

2825
GERALDINE CLEWELL SCHOLARSHIP

Phi Upsilon Omicron
Attn: Educational Foundation
P.O. Box 329
Fairmont, WV 26555-0329
Phone: (304) 368-0612   E-mail: rickards@access.mountain.net
Web Site: ianrwww.unl.edu/phiu
Summary: To provide financial assistance to undergraduate student members of Phi Upsilon Omicron, a national honor society in family and consumer sciences.
Eligibility: This program is open to members of the society who are working on a bachelor's degree in family and consumer sciences or a related area. Selection is based on scholastic record, participation in the society, professional aims and goals, and recommendations.
Financial data: The stipend is $1,500.
Duration: 1 year.
Number awarded: 1 each year.
Deadline: January of each year.

2826
GIBSON-LAEMEL SCHOLARSHIP

Summary: To provide financial assistance to college juniors and seniors from Connecticut who are interested in pursuing a career in health, physical education, recreation, or dance.
See Listing #1395.

2827
GILLETTE-NATIONAL URBAN LEAGUE SCHOLARSHIP AND INTERN PROGRAM

Summary: To provide financial assistance and summer internships to minority students who are interested in completing their college education in designated areas of business and engineering.
See Listing #2062.

2828
GLOBAL AUTOMOTIVE AFTERMARKET SYMPOSIUM SCHOLARSHIPS

Global Automotive Aftermarket Symposium
Attn: Education Committee
9237 Ward Parkway, Suite 106
Kansas City, MO 64114
Phone: (816) 523-8118   Fax: (816) 523-8252
E-mail: reg@univaftmkt.org
Web Site: www.automotivescholarships.com
Summary: To provide financial assistance for college to students interested in pursuing a career in the automotive aftermarket.
Eligibility: This program is open to graduating high school seniors and to students who graduated from high school within the past 3 years. Applicants must be enrolled full time in a college-level program or an automotive technician program in the United States or Canada accredited by the National Automotive Technician Education Foundation (NATEF). They must submit school transcripts, a letter of recommendation, and a 250-word essay on why they deserve to be a scholarship recipient. Preference is given to applicants pursuing a career in the automotive aftermarket. Financial need is not considered in the selection process.
Financial data: Stipends range from $1,000 to $2,000 per year. Recipients who graduate from their program and show proof of employment in the automotive aftermarket for at least 12 months are awarded a further matching grant.
Duration: 1 year.
Additional information: Funding for this program is provided by 6 automotive aftermarket associations that donate the proceeds from the annual Global Automotive Aftermarket Symposium (GAAS). The sponsoring associations are the Automotive Parts and Accessories Association, the Automotive Service Industry Association, the Automotive Warehouse Distributors Association, the Motor & Equipment Manufacturers Association, the Specialty Equipment Market Association, and the Tire Association of North America. The first GAAS was held in 1996.
Number awarded: Varies each year.
Deadline: March of each year.

2829
GOLDEN KEY BUSINESS ACHIEVEMENT AWARDS

Golden Key National Honor Society
1189 Ponce de Leon Avenue
Atlanta, GA 30306-4624
Phone: (404) 377-2400   (800) 377-2401
E-mail: mboone@goldenkey.gsu.edu   Web Site: goldenkey.gsu.edu
Summary: To recognize and reward undergraduate members of the Golden Key National Honor Society who submit outstanding work on a problem in the field of business.
Eligibility: Members of the society are invited to respond to a problem posed by an honorary member within the discipline of business. The response must be in the form of a new business plan. Recently, entrants were asked to develop a business plan, up to 3 pages in length, for a new high technology venture that would meet a current need in society but that is not currently being met. Selection is based on the creativity and viability of the response.
Financial data: The winner receives $1,000, second place $750, and third place $500.
Duration: These awards are presented annually.
Additional information: This program began in 2001.
Number awarded: 3 each year.
Deadline: February of each year.

2830
GOLDEN KEY EDUCATION ACHIEVEMENT AWARDS

Golden Key National Honor Society
1189 Ponce de Leon Avenue
Atlanta, GA 30306-4624
Phone: (404) 377-2400   (800) 377-2401
E-mail: mboone@goldenkey.gsu.edu
Web Site: goldenkey.gsu.edu
Summary: To recognize and reward undergraduate members of the Golden Key National Honor Society who submit outstanding work on a problem in the field of education.
Eligibility: Members of the society are invited to respond to a problem posed by an honorary member within the discipline of education. The response must be in the form of an original lesson plan. Recently, entrants were asked to develop a thematic unit to develop leadership skills at the age/grade level of the children they plan to teach.
Financial data: The winner receives $1,000, second place $750, and third place $500.
Duration: These awards are presented annually.
Additional information: This program began in 2001.
Number awarded: 3 each year.
Deadline: February of each year.

2831
GOLDEN KEY INFORMATION SYSTEMS ACHIEVEMENT AWARDS

Summary: To recognize and reward undergraduate members of the Golden Key National Honor Society who submit outstanding essays or designs on a problem in the field of information systems.
See Listing #2065.

2832
GORDON SCHEER SCHOLARSHIP

Colorado Society of Certified Public Accountants
Attn: Educational Foundation
7979 East Tufts Avenue, Suite 500
Denver, CO 80237-2843
Phone: (303) 741-8613   (800) 523-9082 (within CO)
Fax: (303) 773-6344   E-mail: cpa-staff@cscpa.denver.co.us
Web Site: www.cocpa.org
Summary: To provide financial assistance to college students in Colorado who are studying accounting.
Eligibility: This program is open to undergraduate and graduate students at colleges and universities in Colorado who have completed at least 1 intermediate accounting class and have a grade point average, both overall and in accounting, of at least 3.5. Selection is based on scholastic achievement.
Financial data: The stipend is $1,250, paid in 2 installments. Funds are to be used for books, tuition, room and board, and fees and expenses.
Duration: 1 year; recipients may reapply.
Number awarded: 1 each year.
Deadline: June of each year.

2833
GREAT FALLS ADVERTISING FEDERATION ADVERTISING EDUCATION MEMORIAL SCHOLARSHIP

Summary: To provide financial assistance to high school seniors in Montana interested in pursuing a career related to advertising.
See Listing #1403.

2834
GRETCHEN E. VAN ROY MUSIC EDUCATION SCHOLARSHIP

Summary: To provide financial assistance to college student members of the National Federation of Music Clubs (NFMC) who are majoring in music education.
See Listing #1405.

2835
H. FLETCHER BROWN SCHOLARSHIP

Summary: To provide financial assistance to residents of Delaware who are interested in studying engineering, chemistry, medicine, dentistry, or law.
See Listing #2078.

2836
HAROLD D. DRUMMOND SCHOLARSHIPS IN ELEMENTARY EDUCATION

Kappa Delta Pi
Attn: Educational Foundation
3707 Woodview Trace
Indianapolis, IN 46268-1158
Phone: (317) 871-4900   (800) 284-3167
Fax: (317) 704-2323   E-mail: margo@kdp.org
Web Site: www.kdp.org
Summary: To provide financial assistance for undergraduate or graduate studies in elementary education to members of Kappa Delta Pi (an international honor society in education).
Eligibility: Applicants must be members of the society, be currently enrolled in college, and write an original essay (up to 250 words) on this topic: "Why I Want to be an Elementary School Teacher in the New Millennium." The essay must be signed by the applicant and the chapter counselor. The application form must be signed by the chapter counselor and the chapter president; each form must include the applicant's society membership number and the reasons for the needed financial support. No more than 1 application may be submitted per chapter.
Financial data: Stipends range from $500 to $1,000.
Duration: 1 year.
Number awarded: 4 each year.
Deadline: May of each year.

2837
HAROLD HAYDEN MEMORIAL SCHOLARSHIP

Summary: To provide financial assistance for college to high school and currently-enrolled college students nominated by members of the National Association of Black County Officials (NABCO).
See Listing #397.

2838
HARRIET SIMMONS SCHOLARSHIP

Oregon Student Assistance Commission
Attn: Private Awards Grant Department
1500 Valley River Drive, Suite 100
Eugene, OR 97401-2146
Phone: (541) 687-7395   (800) 452-8807, ext. 7395
Fax: (541) 687-7419   E-mail: awardinfo@mercury.osac.state.or.us
Web Site: www.osac.state.or.us
Summary: To provide financial assistance to Oregon residents majoring in education on the undergraduate or graduate level.
Eligibility: This program is open to residents of Oregon who are U.S. citizens or permanent residents. Applicants must be college seniors or fifth-year students majoring in elementary or secondary education, or graduate students in their fifth year working on an elementary or secondary certificate. Full-time enrollment and financial need are required.
Financial data: Scholarship amounts vary, depending upon the needs of the recipient.
Duration: 1 year.
Number awarded: Varies each year.
Deadline: February of each year.

2839
HARRY A. APPLEGATE SCHOLARSHIP AWARD

DECA
1908 Association Drive
Reston, VA 20191-1594
Phone: (703) 860-5000   Fax: (703) 860-4013
E-mail: decainc@aol.com
Web Site: www.deca.org/scholarships/index.html
Summary: To give DECA members an opportunity to further their education in marketing, merchandising, or management (or to prepare them for a career in the teaching of marketing education).

Eligibility: Any high school senior or graduate who is an active member of DECA and intends to pursue a full-time 2- or 4-year course of study in marketing, management, or merchandising is eligible to apply. Complete applications are to be submitted to the state advisor. Each state advisor may submit no more than 2 applications to National DECA. All awards are made on the basis of merit, not financial need.
Financial data: Stipends range from $500 to $1,500. Awards are paid directly to the recipient's college or university.
Duration: 1 year.
Deadline: State deadlines vary. The national deadline is in March.

2840
HARRY J. HARWICK SCHOLARSHIPS

Summary: To provide financial assistance to undergraduate or graduate students who are interested in preparing for a career in medical group management.
See Listing #2079.

2841
HARRY S. TRUMAN SCHOLARSHIP PROGRAM

Summary: To provide financial assistance to undergraduate students who have outstanding leadership potential, plan to pursue careers in government or other public service, and wish to attend graduate school in the United States or abroad to prepare themselves for a public service career.
See Listing #1412.

2842
HAWAII EDUCATION ASSOCIATION STUDENT TEACHER SCHOLARSHIP

Hawaii Education Association
Attn: Scholarship Committee
1649 Kalakaua Avenue
Honolulu, HI 96826
Phone: (808) 949-6657   Fax: (808) 944-2032
Summary: To provide financial assistance to members of the Hawaii Education Association (HEA) and their children during their student teaching semester.
Eligibility: This program is open to HEA members or children of members who are enrolled in a full-time undergraduate or post-baccalaureate program at any state-approved or nationally accredited institution of higher learning. Applicants must be entering their student teaching semester. Selection is based on ability, a personal statement, financial need, and recommendations.
Financial data: The stipend is $3,000.
Duration: 1 semester (the student teaching semester).
Additional information: The intent of this scholarship is to prevent the need for employment during the student teaching semester.
Number awarded: 2 each year.
Deadline: March of each year.

2843
HENRY AND DOROTHY CASTLE MEMORIAL FUND SCHOLARSHIP

Hawai'i Community Foundation
900 Fort Street Mall, Suite 1300
Honolulu, HI 96813
Phone: (808) 566-5570   (888) 731-3863
Fax: (808) 521-6286   E-mail: scholarships@hcf-hawaii.org
Web Site: www.hcf-hawaii.org
Summary: To provide financial assistance to Hawaii residents who are interested in pursuing a career in early childhood education.
Eligibility: This program is open to Hawaii residents who are interested in pursuing full-time undergraduate or graduate studies in the field of early childhood education (birth through third grade), including child care and preschool. They must be able to demonstrate academic achievement (at least a 2.7 grade point average), good moral character, and financial need. In addition to filling out the standard application form, applicants must 1) write a short statement indicating their reasons for attending college, their planned course of study, and their career goals, and 2) write an essay that states their interests and goals in studying early childhood education and how they plan to contribute to the field.

Financial data: The amounts of the awards depend on the availability of funds and the need of the recipient; recently, grants averaged $1,300.
Duration: 1 year.
Additional information: Recipients may attend college in Hawaii or on the mainland. This scholarship is funded by the Samuel N. and Mary Castle Foundation.
Number awarded: Varies each year; recently, 15 of these scholarships were awarded.
Deadline: February of each year.

2844
HENRY B. GONZALEZ AWARD

Financial Markets Center
P.O. Box 334
Philomont, VA 20131
Phone: (540) 338-7754   Fax: (540) 338-7757
Web Site: www.fmcenter.org
Summary: To recognize and reward outstanding essays, written by students and others, on central bank reform.
Eligibility: This annual contest is open to all entrants, including students enrolled in graduate and undergraduate programs, who submit a paper (up to 15,000 words) on the subject of central bank reform. Entries may be sweeping in scope or focused on a specific aspect of the Federal Reserve's structure, governance, operations, staffing, culture, or statutory authority. Preference is given to clearly-written entries accessible to a broad audience.
Financial data: The winning entry receives a cash award of $2,500 and is published by the sponsor.
Duration: The competition is held annually.
Number awarded: 1 each year.

2845
HENRY SALVATORI SCHOLARSHIP

Order Sons of Italy in America
Attn: Sons of Italy Foundation
219 E Street, N.E.
Washington, DC 20002
Phone: (202) 547-5106   Fax: (202) 546-8168
E-mail: sif@osia.org   Web Site: www.osia.org
Summary: To provide financial assistance for college to high school seniors of Italian descent who write about the principles of liberty, freedom, and equality in the United States.
Eligibility: Eligible are U.S. citizens of Italian descent who are high school seniors planning to enroll as full-time students in an undergraduate program at an accredited 4-year college or university. Applications must be accompanied by essays, from 750 to 1,000 words, on the relevance to the United States today of the Declaration of Independence, the Constitution, or the Bill of Rights and the meaning of those documents to the principles of liberty, freedom, and equality in the 21st century. The scholarship is presented to a student who has demonstrated exceptional leadership, distinguished scholarship, and an understanding of the principles for which the country was founded.
Financial data: The stipend is $5,000.
Duration: 1 year; may not be renewed.
Additional information: Applications must be accompanied by a $25 processing fee.
Number awarded: 1 each year.
Deadline: February of each year.

2846
HERMINE DALKOWITZ TOBOLOWSKY SCHOLARSHIP

Summary: To provide financial assistance to women in Texas who are preparing to enter selected professions.
See Listing #1425.

2847
HIMSS FOUNDATION SCHOLARSHIPS

Summary: To provide financial assistance to student members of the Healthcare Information and Management Systems Society (HIMSS) who are interested in the field of health care information and management systems.
See Listing #2093.

2848
HISPANIC COLLEGE FUND SCHOLARSHIPS

Hispanic College Fund
Attn: National Director
One Thomas Circle, N.W., Suite 375
Washington, D.C. 20005
Phone: (800) 644-4223   Fax: (202) 296-5400
E-mail: hispaniccollegefund@earthlink.net
Web Site: www.hispanicfund.org
Summary: To provide financial assistance to Hispanic American undergraduate students who are interested in preparing for a career in a business-related field.
Eligibility: This program is open to full-time undergraduate students of Hispanic origin who are U.S. citizens. Applicants must have a cumulative grade point average of 3.0 or better and a major in accounting, actuarial science, architecture, business administration, communications, computer science, computer engineering, economics, electrical engineering, finance, financial management, human resources, industrial engineering, information technology, international business, management, management information systems, marketing, mechanical engineering, multimedia production, or statistics. Students at community and junior colleges are eligible if they plan to pursue a bachelor's degree at a 4-year institution. The colleges or universities the applicants are attending must certify their financial need, defined as a family income at or below 60 percent of the area's median family income, based on family size. Preference is given to students who can demonstrate leadership qualities (extracurricular activities on their college campuses and/or in civic activities in their communities).
Financial data: Stipends range from $500 to $5,000 and average about $2,000.
Duration: 1 year.
Number awarded: Varies each year; recently, 206 students were supported by this program, including 79 freshmen, 46 sophomores, 51 juniors, and 30 seniors.
Deadline: April of each year.

2849
HOLOCAUST REMEMBRANCE PROJECT

Summary: To recognize and reward outstanding essays written by high school students on a topic (changes annually) related to the Holocaust.
See Listing #1429.

2850
HOOPER MEMORIAL SCHOLARSHIP

Summary: To provide financial assistance to college students interested in preparing for a career in fields related to transportation.
See Listing #2097.

2851
HOPI TRIBAL PRIORITY SCHOLARSHIP

Summary: To encourage Hopi students to get a degree in an area of interest to the Hopi Tribe.
See Listing #2098.

2852
HORIZONS FOUNDATION SCHOLARSHIP PROGRAM

Summary: To provide financial assistance for postsecondary education to women engaged in or planning careers related to the national security interests of the United States.
See Listing #2100.

2853
HOWARD BROWN RICKARD SCHOLARSHIPS

Summary: To provide financial assistance to blind students studying or planning to study law, medicine, engineering, architecture, or the natural sciences at the postsecondary level.
See Listing #2101.

2854
HOWARD F. GREENE MEMORIAL SCHOLARSHIP

Maine Society of CPAs
153 U.S. Route 1, Suite 8
Scarborough, ME 04074-9053
Summary: To provide financial assistance to students in Maine majoring in accounting.
Eligibility: This program is open to college students majoring in accounting in Maine. They must have at least a 3.0 grade point average, be able to demonstrate writing skills, and have participated in community activities. Selection is based on academic achievement, writing skills, extracurricular activities, work experience, career goals, and financial need.
Financial data: The stipend is $1,000.
Duration: 1 year.
Number awarded: 1 each year.

2855
HSMAI SCHOLARSHIPS

Hospitality Sales & Marketing Association International
1300 L Street, N.W., Suite 1020
Washington, DC 20005
Phone: (202) 789-0089   Fax: (202) 789-1725
Web Site: www.hsmai.org/events/scholarship.cfm
Summary: To provide financial assistance to students in accredited schools of hospitality management.
Eligibility: This program is open to full-time students who are currently enrolled in hospitality management or a related field, have demonstrated hospitality work experience, are interested in a career in hospitality sales and marketing, and have good academic standing. Applications are accepted from 2 categories of students: 1) baccalaureate and graduate degree candidates, and 2) associate degree candidates. Selection is based on industry-related work experience, grade point average, extracurricular involvement, 2 letters of recommendation, responses to essay questions, and presentation of the application.
Financial data: The stipend is $2,000 for baccalaureate/graduate degree recipients or $500 for associate degree recipients.
Duration: 1 year.
Number awarded: 4 each year: 2 at $2,000 and 2 at $500.
Deadline: March of each year.

2856
HUMAN RESOURCES ASSOCIATION OF THE MIDLANDS STUDENT SCHOLARSHIP

Human Resources Association of the Midlands
Chapter 019
c/o Melissa Lovitt, Awards Committee Co-Chair
Woodmen of the World
1700 Farnam Street
Omaha, NE 68102
Phone: (402) 449-7749   Fax: (402) 271-7883
E-mail: mlovitt@woodmen.com
Web Site: www.hram.org
Summary: To provide financial assistance to members of the Human Resources Association of the Midlands (HRAM) who are interested in preparing for a career in human resources.
Eligibility: This program is open to HRAM members and student members. Applicants must be upper-division college students preparing for a career in human resources. They must have a strong record of extracurricular and community activities, have at least a 3.0 grade point average, and be able to demonstrate financial need. As part of the application process, they must submit 2 letters of reference, a current resume, and a completed application form.
Financial data: The stipend is $1,000 (or less, if more than 1 recipient is chosen). Funds must be used to purchase text books.
Duration: 1 year.
Number awarded: 1 or more each year.
Deadline: June of each year.

2857
HUMANE STUDIES FELLOWSHIPS

Summary: To provide financial assistance to students in the United States or abroad who intend to pursue "intellectual careers" and have demonstrated an interest in classical liberal principles.
See Listing #1433.

2858
HYATT HOTEL FUND FOR MINORITY LODGING MANAGEMENT STUDENTS

American Hotel Foundation
Attn: Manager of Foundation Programs
1201 New York Avenue, N.W., Suite 600
Washington, DC 20005-3931
Phone: (202) 289-3180 Fax: (202) 289-3199
E-mail: ahf@ahma.com
Web Site: www.ei-ahma.org/ahf/ahf.htm
Summary: To provide financial assistance to minority college students working on a degree in hotel management.
Eligibility: Applicants must be attending a 4-year college or university that is a member of the Council on Hotel, Restaurant and Institutional Education. They must be minorities and majoring in hotel management. Each member university may nominate 1 student. The most outstanding students receive this scholarship.
Financial data: The stipend is $2,000.
Duration: 1 year.
Additional information: Funding for this program is provided by Hyatt Hotels & Resorts.
Number awarded: Varies each year; recently, 14 of these scholarships were awarded.

2859
IAA FOUNDATION SCHOLARSHIPS

Summary: To provide financial assistance for college to Illinois Farm Bureau members, spouses, and children.
See Listing #2106.

2860
IAN M. ROLLAND SCHOLARSHIP

Lincoln Financial Group
Attn: Director of Actuarial Development
1300 South Clinton Street, 1H25
Fort Wayne, IN 46801
Phone: (219) 455-2390 (800) 2-LINCOLN, ext. 2390
Fax: (219) 455-9974 E-mail: ljjackson@lnc.com
Web Site: www.lfg.com
Summary: To provide financial assistance to minority high school seniors who are interested in pursuing a career as an actuary.
Eligibility: This program is open to high school seniors who are members of minority groups underrepresented in the actuarial field. Applicants must rank in the top 10 percent of their class, have a combined verbal and math SAT score of at least 1200, and have a math SAT score of at least 650. Preference is given to applicants who choose a university with an actuarial program and major in actuarial science.
Financial data: The stipend is $5,000 per year, paid to the university that the student attends.
Duration: 1 year; may be renewed if the recipient maintains a cumulative grade point average of 3.5 or higher while in college, passes course 1 of the actuarial exams by the beginning of the junior year, and passes course 2 of the actuarial exams by January of the senior year.
Additional information: This program was established in 1999. Recipients who attend a university with an actuarial science program are expected to major in that field. Recipients who attend a university that does not have an actuarial science program are expected to major in a field consistent with a career in actuarial science; generally, that means a mathematics major with supporting course work in business, computer science, and economics.
Number awarded: 1 each year.
Deadline: January of each year.

2861
IDAHO STATE LIBRARY INDIVIDUAL CONTINUING EDUCATION GRANTS FOR LIBRARY SCIENCE CLASSES

Idaho State Library
325 West State Street
Boise, ID 83702
Phone: (208) 334-2150 (800) 458-3271
Fax: (208) 334-4016 E-mail: ghanks@isl.state.id.us
Web Site: www.lili.org.isl/cepage/cegrants.htm
Summary: To support employees of Idaho public libraries who are interested in pursuing additional training in librarianship.
Eligibility: Library staff members in Idaho may not apply directly for this support; their library director must request funds for them. The course(s) for which the grant is applied must enable the staff member to meet formal educational guidelines set by the Idaho State Library. Candidates must be planning to take either in-state undergraduate library science courses or ALA-accredited master's degree courses.
Financial data: Grants provide full tuition for undergraduate library courses or up to $500 per semester for tuition for master's degree courses.
Duration: 1 semester; may be renewed if the recipient earns a grade of "C" or better for undergraduate courses or "B" or better for graduate courses.
Deadline: Participants must submit a letter at least 30 days before the end of the semester or summer session for which they are seeking reimbursement.

2862
IDDBA SCHOLARSHIP

Summary: To provide financial assistance for college to students employed in a supermarket dairy, deli, or bakery department (or related companies).
See Listing #1436.

2863
IEHA EDUCATION FOUNDATION SCHOLARSHIP AWARD

International Executive Housekeepers Association
Attn: Education Foundation, Inc.
1001 Eastwind Drive, Suite 301
Westerville, OH 43081-3361
Phone: (614) 895-7166 (800) 200-6342
Fax: (614) 895-1248 E-mail: excel@ieha.org
Web Site: www.ieha.org
Summary: To provide financial assistance to members of the International Executive Housekeepers Association (IEHA) who are working on a degree in the field of facilities management.
Eligibility: This program is open to members of the association who are enrolled in an undergraduate, graduate, or non-degree program at an accredited postsecondary institution. Applicants must have an academic major and career interest in facilities management. Selection is based on transcripts and an original essay on housekeeping within any industry segment (e.g., hospitality, health care, education, rehabilitation centers, government buildings). The manuscripts must not exceed 2,000 words, must be typed and double spaced, must be in English, and should have been reviewed by a school representative.
Financial data: Stipends range from $200 to $1,000.
Duration: 1 year.
Number awarded: 1 or more each year.
Deadline: January of each year.

2864
IFEC SCHOLARSHIPS

Summary: To provide financial assistance to undergraduate or graduate students who are interested in preparing for a career in communications in the food service industry.
See Listing #1439.

2865
IFSEA WORTHY GOAL SCHOLARSHIP FUND

International Food Service Executives Association
Attn: President and Chief Operating Officer
2609 Surfwood Drive
Las Vegas, NV 89128
Phone: (702) 838-8821 Fax: (702) 838-8853
E-mail: hq@ifsea.org Web Site: www.ifsea.org

Summary: To provide financial aid to students interested in majoring in college in a field related to food service.

Eligibility: This program is open to full-time students in a food service-related major at a 2-year or 4-year college or university. Applicants must submit a personal financial statement, a 500-word statement on their personal background, a description of their work experience, a listing of their memberships in professional student organizations, a 250-word statement on how the scholarship will help them in achieving their goals, a transcript of grades from high school or college, and 3 letters of recommendation. Selection is based on food service work experience, membership in professional organizations, financial need, interest in food service as a career, contribution of this scholarship to personal goals, academic ability, and letters of recommendation.

Financial data: Stipends are $1,000, $700, or $500 per year.

Additional information: Information is also available from Matt Trupiano, 15724 Edgewood Street, Livonia, MI 48154-2312, (734) 542-9412, (888) 234-3732, Fax: (734) 542-9306.

Number awarded: Varies each year. Recently, 22 of these scholarships were awarded: 6 at $1,000, 5 at $700, and 11 at $500.

Deadline: January of each year.

2866
ILLINOIS COUNCIL OF TEACHERS OF MATHEMATICS SCHOLARSHIP AWARD

Summary: To provide financial assistance to undergraduate students in Illinois who are interested in pursuing a career as a mathematics teacher.
See Listing #2116.

2867
ILLINOIS CPA SOCIETY ACCOUNTING SCHOLARSHIP PROGRAM

Illinois CPA Society
222 South Riverside Plaza, Suite 1600
Chicago, Il 60606-6099
Phone: (312) 993-0407   (800) 993-0407
Fax: (312) 993-9954
Web Site: www.icpas.org/icpas/student/scholarship.htm

Summary: To provide financial assistance to Illinois students undertaking their fifth year of course work to complete the educational requirements to sit for the CPA examination in Illinois.

Eligibility: To be eligible, students must be residents of Illinois, attending a college or university in the state, and planning to sit for the CPA examination in Illinois within 3 years of the application date. Applicants must have at least a 3.0 grade point average and be able to demonstrate financial need or special circumstances; the society is especially interested in assisting students who, because of limited options or opportunities, may not have alternative means of support. Selection is based on both academic achievement and financial need.

Financial data: The maximum scholarship is $4,000.

Duration: 1 year (fifth year for accounting students planning to become a CPA).

Additional information: This scholarship was established in 1998. The scholarship does not cover the cost of CPA examination review courses. Recipients may not receive a full graduate assistantship, fellowship, or scholarship from a college or university, participate in a full-tuition reimbursement cooperative education or internship program, or participate in an employee full-tuition reimbursement program during the scholarship period.

Number awarded: Several each year.

Deadline: May of each year.

2868
ILLINOIS LEGION AUXILIARY SPECIAL EDUCATION TEACHING SCHOLARSHIPS

American Legion Auxiliary
Attn: Department of Illinois
2720 East Lincoln Street
P.O. Box 1426
Bloomington, IL 61702-1426
Phone: (309) 663-9366

Summary: To provide financial assistance to residents of Illinois who wish to study special education at the college level.

Eligibility: Eligible to apply for these scholarships are Illinois residents in the second or third year of a college degree program in the field of teaching retarded or handicapped children. Applicants must be sponsored by a local unit of the American Legion Auxiliary in Illinois.

Financial data: These scholarships are $1,000.

Duration: 1 year.

Additional information: Applications may be obtained only from a local unit of the American Legion Auxiliary.

Number awarded: Several each year.

Deadline: March of each year.

2869
ILLINOIS PTA SCHOLARSHIPS

Illinois PTA
901 South Spring Street
Springfield, IL 62704
Phone: (217) 528-9617   (800) 877-9617
Fax: (217) 528-9490   E-mail: il_office@pta.org
Web Site: www.prairienet.org/cpta/Illinois

Summary: To provide financial assistance to graduating high school seniors in Illinois who are planning to major in education in college.

Eligibility: Eligible to apply for this support are public high school seniors in Illinois who are graduating in the top 25 percent of their class. They must be interested in preparing for a career in education or in an educationally-related field. Financial need is not considered in the selection process.

Financial data: The stipend is $1,000 for the first year and $500 for subsequent years.

Duration: 1 year; renewable.

Additional information: Previous scholarship recipients are eligible to apply (for their junior or senior year in college) for continuing education scholarships.

Number awarded: 44 new scholarships (2 in each PTA district) and 12 continuing education scholarships are awarded each year.

Deadline: February of each year.

2870
ILLINOIS REAL ESTATE EDUCATIONAL FOUNDATION ACADEMIC SCHOLARSHIPS

Illinois Association of Realtors
Attn: Illinois Real Estate Educational Foundation
3180 Adloff Lane, Suite 400
P.O. Box 19451
Springfield, IL 62794-9451
Phone: (217) 529-2600   E-mail: IARaccess@iar.org
Web Site: www.illinoisrelator.org/iar/about/scholarships.htm

Summary: To provide financial assistance to Illinois residents who are preparing for a career in real estate.

Eligibility: All applicants must be U.S. citizens and Illinois residents who are attending a college or university in the state on a full-time basis and pursuing a degree with an emphasis in real estate. They must have completed at least 30 credits. As part of the application process, students must submit copies of their transcripts and letters of recommendation and reference. Selection is based on academic record, economic need, references and recommendations, and career plans in the field of real estate or an allied field (e.g., construction, land use planning, mortgage banking, property management, real estate appraising, real estate assessing, real estate brokerage, real estate development, real estate investment counseling, real estate law, and real estate syndication). Finalists are interviewed.

Financial data: The stipend is $1,000.

Duration: 1 year.

Deadline: March of each year.

2871
IMA DIVERSITY SCHOLARSHIP PROGRAM

Institute of Management Accountants
Attn: Committee on Students
10 Paragon Drive
Montvale, NJ 07645-1760
Phone: (201) 573-9000   (800) 638-4427, ext. 294
Fax: (201) 573-8438   E-mail: students@imanet.org
Web Site: www.imanet.org

Summary: To provide financial assistance to minority and disabled student members of the Institute of Management Accountants (IMA) who are interested in pursuing a career in management accounting or financial management.

Eligibility: This program is open to undergraduate and graduate students of

American Indian/Alaska Native, Asian/Pacific Islander, Black, or Hispanic heritage and students with physical disabilities (defined as hearing impairment, vision impairment, missing extremities, partial paralysis, complete paralysis, or severe distortion of limbs and/or spine). Applicants must be in their sophomore, junior, or senior year or in a graduate program with a major in management accounting, financial management, or information technology. Selection is based on 1) academic merit; 2) quality of their presentation; 3) demonstrated community leadership; 4) potential for success in a financial management position; 5) a written statement from applicants expressing how they would promote awareness of IMA membership benefits and the Certified Management Accountant (CMA) and/or Certified in Financial Management (CF)) certifications among their peers and on their campus; and 6) letters of recommendation.
Financial data: Stipends are $3,000 per year.
Duration: 1 year.
Additional information: Up to 15 finalists in each category (including the scholarship winners) receive a scholarship to take 5 parts of the CMA and/or CFM examination within a year of graduation.
Number awarded: At least 6 each year.
Deadline: February of each year.

2872
IMA MEMORIAL EDUCATION FUND SCHOLARSHIPS

Institute of Management Accountants
Attn: Committee on Students
10 Paragon Drive
Montvale, NJ 07645-1760
Phone: (201) 573-9000   (800) 638-4427, ext. 294
Fax: (201) 573-8438   E-mail: students@imanet.org
Web Site: www.imanet.org
Summary: To provide financial assistance to student members of the Institute of Management Accountants (IMA) who are interested in pursuing a career in management accounting or financial management.
Eligibility: Each institute chapter and each institute student chapter is eligible to submit 1 application for each of the 4 categories of scholarships: 1) students graduating from a 2-year college and continuing their education in a 4- or 5-year management accounting, financial management, or information technology program; 2) entering college juniors majoring in management accounting, financial management, or information technology; 3) entering college seniors majoring in management accounting, financial management, or information technology; and 4) students enrolled or planning to enroll in a graduate management accounting, financial management, or information technology program. Both part-time and full-time students are eligible to apply. They must be student members of the sponsoring organization. Selection is based on academic merit, participation in the organization, quality of their presentation, demonstrated community leadership, potential for success in a financial management position, and letters of recommendation.
Financial data: Stipends are $3,000 per year.
Duration: 1 year.
Additional information: Up to 30 finalists in each category (including the scholarship winners) receive a scholarship to take 5 parts of the Certified Management Accountant (CMA) and/or Certified in Financial Management (CFM) examination within a year of graduation.
Number awarded: At least 19 each year: 2 to graduating 2-year college students, 6 to entering juniors, 6 to entering seniors, and 5 to graduate students.
Deadline: February of each year.

2873
INDEPENDENCE ESSAY COMPETITION

Cascade Policy Institute
Attn: Program Director
813 S.W. Alder, Suite 450
Portland, OR 97205
Phone: (503) 242-0900   E-mail: essay@cascadepolicy.org
Web Site: www.cascadepolicy.org/essay.asp
Summary: To recognize and reward high school students in Oregon who write essays on liberty.
Eligibility: This program is open to private, public, and home-schooled students of high school age in Oregon. Applicants must submit an essay of up to 2,000 words on a topic that changes annually but relates to the meaning of liberty and the proper role of government in a free society. A recent topic was "Exploring the foundations of freedom."
Financial data: Awards are $1,000.

Duration: The competition is held annually.
Additional information: This competition began in 1995.
Number awarded: Up to 5 each year.
Deadline: March of each year.

2874
INDEPENDENT INSURANCE AGENTS OF UTAH SCHOLARSHIP

Independent Insurance Agents of Utah
4885 South 900 East, Suite 302
Salt Lake City, UT 84117
Phone: (801) 269-1200   Fax: (801) 269-1265
Summary: To provide financial assistance to Utah high school seniors interested in majoring in business or insurance in college.
Eligibility: This program is open to Utah high school seniors who have maintained at least a 3.0 grade point average and are active in extracurricular activities through their school, church, community, or work. Financial need is considered in the selection process. Applicants must submit an official transcript of their grades and a recent photograph. Scholarships are awarded to students who will be preparing for a career in business or in insurance.
Financial data: The stipend is $1,000.
Duration: 1 year.
Additional information: This program is jointly sponsored by the Independent Insurance Agents of Utah and the Utah Chapter of the Chartered Property Casualty Underwriters Society.
Number awarded: 2 each year: 1 to a student preparing for a business career and 1 to a student preparing for an insurance career.

2875
INDIANA SHERIFFS' ASSOCIATION SCHOLARSHIP FUND

Indiana Sheriffs' Association
P.O. Box 19127
Indianapolis, IN 46219
Phone: (317) 356-3633   (800) 622-4779 (within IN)
Fax: (317) 356-3996
Summary: To provide financial assistance to members of the Indiana Sheriffs' Association and members of their families who are preparing for a career in the law enforcement field.
Eligibility: Eligible to apply for this support are affiliate or associate members of the association or the dependent child of an active affiliate or associate member of the association. Applicants must be between 17 and 23 years of age, attending or planning to attend an Indiana college or university, and majoring or planning to major in law enforcement.
Financial data: A stipend is awarded (exact amount not specified).
Duration: 1 year; may be renewed for up to 3 additional years.

2876
INTEL INTERNATIONAL SCIENCE AND ENGINEERING FAIR

Summary: To recognize and reward outstanding high school students interested in engineering or the sciences.
See Listing #2126.

2877
INTEL SCIENCE TALENT SEARCH SCHOLARSHIPS

Summary: To recognize and reward outstanding high school seniors who are interested in attending college to prepare for a career in mathematics, engineering, or the sciences.
See Listing #2127.

2878
INTERNATIONAL COMPETITIVE SCHOLARSHIPS

Summary: To provide financial assistance to undergraduate and graduate students interested in majoring in programs related to total cost management (the effective application of professional and technical expertise to plan and control resources, costs, profitability, and risk).
See Listing #2129.

2879
INTERNATIONAL SCHOLARSHIP PROGRAM FOR COMMUNITY SERVICE

Summary: To assist well-qualified individuals to train for careers in a field related to Jewish community service.
See Listing #1446.

2880
IOWA FEDERATION OF LABOR SCHOLARSHIPS

Iowa Federation of Labor, AFL-CIO
Attn: Scholarship Program
2000 Walker Street, Suite A
Des Moines, IA 50317-5290
Phone: (515) 262-9571   (800) 372-4817
Fax: (515) 262-9573   Web Site: www.iowaaflcio.org
Summary: To recognize and reward outstanding essays on a labor-related topic written by high school seniors in Iowa.
Eligibility: This competition is open to all seniors in accredited high schools in Iowa (public, private, and parochial). Students must write an essay (from 500 to 750 words) on the history of the labor movement in the United States. It is recommended that competitors read *A History of the Labor Movement in the United States* before writing the essay.
Financial data: First prize is $1,500, second prize is $1,000, and third prize if $500. Funds may be used as a scholarship at the college or university of the recipient's choice.
Duration: The competition is held annually.
Number awarded: 3 each year.
Deadline: March of each year.

2881
IRENE W. HART MEMORIAL SCHOLARSHIP

New Hampshire Retired Educators Associations
c/o Roland R. Boucher
331 Mountain Road
Jaffrey, NH 03452
Summary: To provide financial assistance to upper-division students in New Hampshire who are majoring in the field of education.
Eligibility: Applicants must be in their junior year at an accredited college or university in New Hampshire, majoring in the field of education. They must have graduated from a New Hampshire high school. An academic transcript must be submitted, as well as an essay that describes the applicant's educational goals. Financial need is considered in the selection process.
Financial data: The stipend is $1,000. Checks are made out jointly to the recipient and the recipient's school.
Duration: 1 year.
Deadline: March of each year.

2882
J. PAUL NORWOOD MEMORIAL SCHOLARSHIP PROGRAM

Oklahoma Funeral Directors Association
6801 North Broadway, No. 106
Oklahoma City, OK 73116
Phone: (405) 843-0730   Fax: (405) 843-5404
Summary: To provide financial assistance to Oklahoma residents who are interested in attending a mortuary college.
Eligibility: Applicants for this scholarship must meet the following requirements: be supported by a member of the sponsoring organization, meet the educational requirements of the Oklahoma State Board of Embalmers and Funeral Directors, be a legal resident of Oklahoma for at least 2 years, have earned at least a 2.0 grade point average in high school, and possess the following personal characteristics: an acute mind, a pleasing personality, good character, ambition, and leadership abilities. All applicants must "have abstained from participation in activities which create behavior incidents." To apply, students must submit a completed application, a transcript, 3 letters of recommendation, demonstration of financial need, and a recent photograph.
Financial data: The maximum stipend is $1,500. Funds are sent to the recipient's school and must be used only for tuition and books.
Duration: 1 year.

2883
JACK J. ISGUR SCHOLARSHIPS

Summary: To provide financial assistance to Missouri residents majoring in education and planning to teach humanities in elementary and middle schools in the state after graduation.
See Listing #1451.

2884
JAMES A. TURNER, JR. MEMORIAL SCHOLARSHIP

American Welding Society
Attn: AWS Foundation, Inc.
550 N.W. LeJeune Road
Miami, FL 33126
Phone: (305) 443-9353, ext. 461   (800) 443-9353, ext. 461
Fax: (305) 443-7559   E-mail: vpinsky@aws.org
Web Site: www.aws.org/foundation/turner.html
Summary: To provide financial assistance to college students interested in a management career related to welding.
Eligibility: This program is open to full-time undergraduate students who are pursuing at least a 4-year bachelor's degree in business that will lead to a management career in welding store operations or a welding distributorship. Applicants must be U.S. citizens who are currently employed for at least 10 hours a week in a welding store operation or at a welding distributorship. Financial need is not required.
Financial data: The stipend is $3,000.
Duration: 1 year; recipients may reapply.
Number awarded: 1 each year.
Deadline: January of each year.

2885
JAMES CARLSON MEMORIAL SCHOLARSHIP

Oregon Student Assistance Commission
Attn: Private Awards Grant Department
1500 Valley River Drive, Suite 100
Eugene, OR 97401-2146
Phone: (541) 687-7395   (800) 452-8807, ext. 7395
Fax: (541) 687-7419   E-mail: awardinfo@mercury.osac.state.or.us
Web Site: www.osac.state.or.us
Summary: To provide financial assistance to Oregon residents majoring in education on the undergraduate or graduate school level.
Eligibility: This program is open to residents of Oregon who are U.S. citizens or permanent residents. Applicants must be college seniors or fifth-year students majoring in elementary or secondary education, or graduate students pursuing an elementary or secondary certificate. Full-time enrollment and financial need are required. Priority is given to 1) members of African American, Asian, Hispanic American, or Native American ethnic groups; 2) dependents of members of the Oregon Education Association; and 3) applicants committed to teaching autistic children.
Financial data: Scholarship amounts vary, depending upon needs of the recipient.
Duration: 1 year.
Number awarded: Varies each year.
Deadline: February of each year.

2886
JAMES F. REVILLE SCHOLARSHIP

Summary: To provide financial assistance to currently-enrolled college students in New York majoring in a field related to mental retardation.
See Listing #2144.

2887
JAMES I. FITZGIBBON SCHOLARSHIP AWARD

Summary: To provide financial assistance to college students who are interested in preparing for a career in the lawn/landscape industry.
See Listing #2145.

2888
JANE FRYER MCCONAUGHY MEMORIAL SCHOLARSHIP PROGRAM

Summary: To provide financial assistance to Indiana residents or students enrolled in Indiana colleges/universities.
See Listing #1455.

2889
JANE M. KLAUSMAN WOMEN IN BUSINESS SCHOLARSHIPS

Zonta International
557 West Randolph Street
Chicago, IL 60661-2206
Phone: (312) 930-5848   Fax: (312) 930-0951
E-mail: ZontaFdtn@aol.com   Web Site: www.zonta.org
Summary: To provide financial assistance to women pursuing an undergraduate degree in business.
Eligibility: This program is open to women who are currently enrolled in the second or third year of a business-related undergraduate degree program at a college or university anywhere in the world. Applicants first enter at the club level, and then advance to district and international levels.
Financial data: Each winner at the U.S. district level receives a $400 scholarship; the international winners receive a $4,000 scholarship.
Duration: 1 year.
Additional information: This program began in the 1998-2000 biennium.
Number awarded: Several U.S. district winner and 5 international winners each year.
Deadline: Clubs set their own deadlines but must submit their winners to the district governor by May of each year.

2890
JAPAN STUDIES SCHOLARSHIP

Summary: To provide financial assistance to college students in California and Nevada who are interested in studying Japanese-related subjects.
See Listing #1456.

2891
JEAN KERSHAW SCHOLARSHIP

Ohio Education Association
225 East Broad Street
P.O. Box 2550
Columbus, OH 43216
Phone: (614) 228-4526
Web Site: www.ohea.org/profdev/awards.htm
Summary: To provide financial assistance for college or graduate school to student members of the Ohio Education Association (OEA).
Eligibility: Eligible to apply for this fellowship are OEA student members who are enrolled in a teacher education program in Ohio or are graduating from college and have been accepted for graduate study at an Ohio college or university. Applicants must be able to provide evidence of success in their teacher education program as well as financial need.
Financial data: The stipend is $1,000.
Duration: 1 year.
Additional information: This scholarship was established in 1985.
Number awarded: 1 each year.

2892
JEDIDIAH ZABROSKY SCHOLARSHIP

Vermont Student Assistance Corporation
Champlain Mill
1 Main Street, Fourth Floor
P.O. Box 2000
Winooski, VT 05404-2601
Phone: (802) 655-9602   (800) 642-3177
Fax: (802) 654-3765   TDD: (802) 654-3766
Phone: TDD: (800) 281-3341 (within VT)   E-mail: info@vsac.org
Web Site: www.vsac.org
Summary: To provide financial assistance to Vermont residents who are studying business or education at a college in the state.
Eligibility: This scholarship is available to residents of Vermont who currently attend a public college in the state. Applicants must be pursuing a 2-year or 4-year degree in business or education and be employed at least 10 hours per week. Selection is based on academic achievement (grade point average of 2.5 or higher, school and community involvement, letters of recommendation, required essays, and financial need.
Financial data: The stipend is $2,000 and must be used within 1 year after being awarded.
Duration: 1 year.
Additional information: This program was established in 2002.
Number awarded: 1 each year.
Deadline: April of each year.

2893
JENNIFER CURTIS BYLER SCHOLARSHIP IN PUBLIC AFFAIRS

Summary: To provide financial assistance to children of aggregates company employees who are interested in studying public affairs in college.
See Listing #1461.

2894
JEWISH FUNERAL DIRECTORS OF AMERICA ESSAY CONTEST

Jewish Funeral Directors of America
Attn: Executive Director
150 Lynnway, Suite 506
Lynn, MA 01902
Phone: (781) 477-9300   Fax: (781) 477-9393
E-mail: jfdamer@aol.com   Web Site: www.jfda.org
Summary: To recognize and reward outstanding essays written by mortuary students.
Eligibility: Each year, mortuary college students are invited to enter this competition; they must write an essay of 2,000 words on a topic that changes annually but always relates to mortuary science.
Financial data: First prize is $1,500; second prize is $1,000; third prize is $500.
Duration: The competition is held annually.
Number awarded: 3 each year.

2895
JOHN BLANCHARD MEMORIAL SCHOLARSHIP

California School Library Association
717 K Street, Suite 515
Sacramento, CA 95814-3477
Phone: (916) 447-2684   Fax: (916) 447-2695
E-mail: csla@pacbell.net   Web Site: www.schoollibrary.org
Summary: To provide financial assistance to members of the California School Library Association (CSLA) who are library paraprofessionals interested in preparing for a career as a school library media teacher.
Eligibility: This program is open to members of the association who are working or have worked within the last 3 years in a classified position in the library media field either in a school or at a district or county office. Applicants must be enrolled in a college or university working on a bachelor's or advanced degree in preparation to become a school library media teacher. They must be California residents planning to work as a library media teacher in the state upon completion of their credential program.
Financial data: The stipend is $1,000 per year, paid in 2 annual installments upon submission by the recipient of documentation showing proof of continuous enrollment at a California college or university in classes leading to an appropriate degree.
Duration: 2 years.
Number awarded: This award is presented as often as funding is available.
Deadline: June of each year.

2896
JOHN C. STANINGER MEMORIAL FOUNDATION REAL ESTATE SCHOLARSHIP

John C. Staninger Memorial Foundation
c/o Northeast Florida Association of Realtors, Inc.
7801 Deercreek Club Road
Jacksonville, FL 32256
Phone: (904) 394-9494   Fax: (904) 398-8025
Summary: To provide financial assistance to students in Florida who are interested in preparing for a career in real estate.
Eligibility: Applicants must be Florida residents and currently enrolled in college. Selection is based on academic achievement, participation in school and

community activities, work experience, statement of plans and goals, and recommendations. Financial need is also considered in the selection process.

Financial data: The amount awarded varies, depending upon the needs of the recipient and the funds available.

Duration: 1 year.

Additional information: This program was established in 1978.

Number awarded: 1 or more each year.

Deadline: June of each year.

2897
JOHN CULVER WOODDY SCHOLARSHIPS

Actuarial Education and Research Fund
c/o Society of Actuaries
475 North Martingale Road, Suite 800
Schaumburg, IL 60173-2226
Phone: (847) 706-3573   Fax: (847) 706-3599
E-mail: jyore@soa.org
Web Site: www.aerf.org/grants&competitions.html

Summary: To provide financial assistance to undergraduate students who are pursuing careers in actuarial science.

Eligibility: Eligible to be nominated are undergraduate students who will have senior standing in the semester after receiving the scholarship. Applicants must rank in the top quartile of their class and have successfully completed 1 actuarial examination. Each university may nominate only 1 student. Preference is given to candidates who have demonstrated leadership potential by participating in extracurricular activities. Financial need is not considered in the selection process.

Financial data: The stipend is $2,000 per academic year.

Duration: 1 year.

Additional information: This program was established in 1996.

Number awarded: 4 each year.

Deadline: June of each year.

2898
JOHN F. GAINES SCHOLARSHIPS

Florida Association of District School Superintendents
208 South Monroe Street
P.O. Box 1108
Tallahassee, FL 32302-1108
Phone: (850) 488-5099   Fax: (850) 921-5273
E-mail: freeland_a@popmail.firm.edu
Web Site: www.fadss.org

Summary: To provide financial assistance for college to students in Florida who are interested in a career in education.

Eligibility: This program is open to seniors who are graduating from public high schools in Florida. Applicants must be planning to attend a Florida public community college or university in order to prepare for a career in pre-K through grade 12 education. Along with their application, they must submit 3 reference letters; transcripts for grades 9-11 (grade point average of 3.25 or higher); 1-page statements on their achievements in 2 of the following areas: leadership, obstacles overcome, and community service; a 1-page statement on their goals; and a 1-page statement on their commitment to and potential contribution to education.

Financial data: The stipend is $1,000.

Duration: 1 year.

Additional information: This program is jointly sponsored by Mass Mutual Insurance, the Florida School Boards Association, and the Florida Association of District School Superintendents.

Number awarded: 6 each year: 4 to students planning to attend Florida public community colleges or universities and 2 to students planning to attend Florida public universities.

Deadline: November of each year.

2899
JOHN F. KENNEDY SCHOLARS AWARD

Massachusetts Democratic Party
Attn: Executive Director
10 Granite Street
Quincy, MA 02169
Phone: (617) 472-0637   Fax: (617) 472-4391
Web Site: www.massdems.org

Summary: To provide financial assistance for college to Massachusetts residents, with preference given to registered Democrats.

Eligibility: Eligible to apply are Massachusetts residents who are currently enrolled in a college or university (anywhere in the United States), are entering their third or fourth year of study, can demonstrate a serious commitment to the study of American politics, and are qualified to receive financial aid (as certified by their financial aid officer). Preference is given to registered Democrats who have at least a 3.0 grade point average. Finalists may be interviewed in Boston.

Financial data: The stipend is $1,500.

Duration: 1 year.

Number awarded: 2 each year: 1 to a male and 1 to a female.

Deadline: April of each year.

2900
JOHN KELLY LABOR STUDIES SCHOLARSHIP FUND

Office and Professional Employees International Union
Attn: Scholarship Fund
1660 L Street, N.W., Suite 801
Washington, DC 20036
Phone: (202) 393-4464   Fax: (202) 347-0649
Web Site: www.opeiu.edu

Summary: To provide financial assistance to members of the Office and Professional Employees International Union (OPEIU) who wish to study labor relations on the undergraduate or graduate level.

Eligibility: Applicants must be a member or an associate member of the union in good standing, unless a member leaves employment to study on a full-time basis, retires, becomes disabled, or is terminated by employer layoffs and plant closings. They must be enrolled in or accepted for enrollment in a program of graduate or undergraduate study in labor studies, industrial relations, social science, or a related field. All applicants must submit high school transcripts, college transcripts (if appropriate), an essay of 300 to 500 words on occupational goals, and a statement of intent to remain within the union for a period of 2 years. Only 1 award will be made to a family for a lifetime.

Financial data: The total maximum value of the award is $2,000.

Duration: Up to 4 years.

Number awarded: 10 each year (at least 1 per region).

Deadline: March of each year.

2901
JOSEPH T. WEINGOLD SCHOLARSHIP

NYSARC, Inc.
393 Delaware Avenue
Delmar, NY 12054
Phone: (518) 439-8311   Fax: (518) 439-1893
E-mail: nysarc@nysarc.org
Web Site: www.nysarc.org/scholar.htm

Summary: To provide financial assistance to currently-enrolled college students in New York majoring in special education.

Eligibility: Nominations for this funding are to be submitted through the special education divisions of the departments of education at the various colleges and universities in New York. Nominees must be working on a degree program leading to a special education certification. They must be at least at the sophomore level.

Financial data: The stipend is $3,000.

Duration: 1 year.

Additional information: NYSARC, Inc. was formerly the New York State Association for Retarded Children.

Number awarded: 2 each year.

Deadline: January of each year.

2902
J.P. GUILFORD UNDERGRADUATE RESEARCH AWARDS

Psi Chi
825 Vine Street
P.O. Box 709
Chattanooga, TN 37401-0709
Phone: (423) 756-2044   Fax: (423) 265-1529
E-mail: psichi@psichi.org
Web Site: www.psichi.org

Summary: To recognize and reward outstanding research conducted by undergraduate members of Psi Chi (an honor society in psychology).

Eligibility: All society undergraduate students are eligible to submit completed research papers (up to 12 pages long). For the purpose of this award, "research" is broadly defined to be based on any methodology relevant to psychology,

including experiments, correlational studies, historical studies, case histories, and evaluation studies.
Financial data: First place is $1,000; second place is $650; and third place is $250.
Duration: The prizes are awarded annually.
Number awarded: 3 each year.
Deadline: April of each year.

2903
JUAN EUGENE RAMOS SCHOLARSHIP

Summary: To provide financial assistance to Hispanic students enrolled in a fashion design school.
See Listing #1474.

2904
JUNE P. GALLOWAY SCHOLARSHIP

Summary: To provide financial assistance for college to members of the North Carolina Association of Health, Physical Education, Recreation and Dance (NCAAHPERD).
See Listing #1476.

2905
KANSAS FUNERAL DIRECTORS ASSOCIATION FOUNDATION SCHOLARSHIP

Kansas Funeral Directors Association Foundation
1200 Kansas Avenue
Topeka, KS 66612
Phone: (913) 232-7789
Summary: To provide financial assistance to Kansas residents who are currently enrolled in a school of mortuary science.
Eligibility: This program is open to Kansas residents who are currently attending a mortuary school. They must have at least 1 but not more than 2 semesters of schooling left.
Financial data: Stipends range from $250 to $1,500.
Duration: 1 year.
Number awarded: 2 to 4 each year.
Deadline: September of each year.

2906
KARLA SCHERER FOUNDATION SCHOLARSHIP

Karla Scherer Foundation
737 North Michigan Avenue, Suite 2330
Chicago, IL 60611
Phone: (312) 943-9191   Fax: (312) 943-9271
Web Site: www.comnet.org/kschererf
Summary: To provide financial assistance to women who want to prepare for careers in business.
Eligibility: This program is open to women students at any level, from high school senior to doctoral candidate. Applicants must be interested in studying finance and/or economics with plans for a corporate business career in a manufacturing industry. There are no age limitations. Academic majors such as accounting, law, information management systems, marketing, and hotel management do not qualify, nor do careers in the public or service sectors (e.g., health care, banking, financial services, and consulting). Both U.S. citizens and international students may apply. Applicants must write a statement about the courses they plan to take, the college they plan to attend, and how they plan to use their education in their chosen career. Awards are not limited to a particular academic institution, a geographic location, academic achievers, or those in financial need; drive, desire, and determination to succeed are important in the selection process.
Financial data: The amount awarded varies, depending upon needs of the recipient.
Duration: 1 year; may be renewed.
Additional information: This program was established in 1989. Requests for applications must include a self-addressed stamped envelope.
Number awarded: Approximately 25 each year.
Deadline: Requests for applications must be submitted by February of each year; completed applications are due by the end of April.

2907
KAWASAKI-MCGAHA SCHOLARSHIP FUND

Summary: To provide financial assistance to residents of Hawaii who are interested in preparing for a career in computer science or international studies.
See Listing #2183.

2908
KEITH PAYNE MEMORIAL SCHOLARSHIP

Professional Independent Insurance Agents of Illinois
4360 Wabash Avenue
Springfield, IL 62707
Phone: (217) 793-6660   (800) 628-6436
Fax: (217) 793-6744   E-mail: admin@piiai.org
Web Site: www.piiai.org/youngagents/scholarship.htm
Summary: To provide financial assistance to upper-division students who are majoring in business and have an interest in insurance.
Eligibility: To be eligible for this scholarship, students must meet the following criteria: have junior or senior status in college, be in a business degree program with an interest in insurance, be a full-time student, and have a letter of recommendation from a current or retired member of the Professional Independent Insurance Agents of Illinois. To apply, students must complete an application form and submit an essay (500 words or less) on the contribution the insurance industry provides to society. Financial need is not considered in the selection process.
Financial data: The stipend is $1,000, payable in 2 equal installments. Funds are paid directly to the recipient's school.
Duration: 1 year.
Number awarded: 1 each year.
Deadline: June of each year.

2909
KEMPER SCHOLARS GRANT PROGRAM

James S. Kemper Foundation
One Kemper Drive
Long Grove, IL 60049-0001
Phone: (847) 320-2000
Summary: To provide financial assistance to freshmen at selected colleges and universities who are interested in preparing for a career in business.
Eligibility: This program is open to students enrolled as freshmen at 1 of 17 participating colleges and universities. Applicants must be interested in pursuing a career in business and must demonstrate enough "maturity, imagination, and astuteness" to learn from the program, which includes participation in a full-time summer work program with Kemper Insurance Companies.
Financial data: All scholars receive a stipend of at least $1,500 per year (regardless of financial need). Scholars who demonstrate financial need may receive up to $8,000 per year. During the summer work experience, scholars receive standard compensation.
Duration: 3 years, as long as the scholar maintains a minimum grade point average of 3.0 each academic term.
Additional information: The 17 participating schools are Beloit College (Beloit, Wisconsin), Brigham Young University (Provo, Utah), Drake University (Des Moines, Iowa), Howard University (Washington, D.C.), Illinois State University (Normal, Illinois), Lake Forest College (Lake Forest, Illinois), LaSalle University (Philadelphia, Pennsylvania), Loyola University (Chicago, Illinois), Millikin University (Decatur, Illinois), Northern Illinois University (DeKalb, Illinois), Rochester Institute of Technology (Rochester, New York), University of the Pacific (Stockton, California), University of Wisconsin at Whitewater, Valparaiso University (Valparaiso, Indiana), Washington University (St. Louis, Missouri), Washington and Lee University (Lexington, Virginia), and Wake Forest University (Winston-Salem, North Carolina). Summer assignments are within Kemper companies throughout the United States. For at least 1 of the summers, usually after the junior year, the assignment is at the home office in Long Grove, Illinois.
Number awarded: 60 to 70 each year.
Deadline: Deadlines vary at each institution.

2910
KENTUCKY EARLY CHILDHOOD DEVELOPMENT SCHOLARSHIPS

Kentucky Higher Education Assistance Authority
Attn: Student Aid Branch
West Frankfort Office Complex
1050 U.S. Highway 127 South, Suite 102
Frankfort, KY 40601-4323
Phone: (502) 696-7383   (800) 928-8926, ext. 7383
Fax: (502) 696-7373   TTY: (800) 855-2880
E-mail: dlawhorn@kheaa.com
Web Site: www.kheaa.com/prog_ecds.hmtl
Summary: To provide financial assistance to Kentucky residents who are pursuing a degree or certificate in early childhood education on a part-time basis while they work in the field.
Eligibility: This program is open to Kentucky residents who are U.S. citizens, nationals, or permanent residents enrolled at a participating institution in the state in less than 9 credit hours per academic term. Applicants must be pursuing 1) an associate of arts, associate of applied science, or bachelor of science degree in interdisciplinary early childhood education, early childhood special education, early childhood development, or a related course; 2) a Kentucky Early Childhood Development Director's Certificate; or 3) a child development associate credential. They must be employed at least 20 hours per week in a participating early childhood facility or provide training in early childhood development for an approved organization. They may have no unpaid financial obligation and may not be eligible to receive state or federal training funds through Head Start, a public preschool program, or First Steps.
Financial data: Stipends are the lesser of the tuition actually charged by the institution or $1,400 per year. Funds are either credited to the student's account or, if the student has already paid the tuition, disbursed to the student at the beginning of each school term by the institution.
Duration: 1 year; may be renewed if funds permit.
Number awarded: Varies each year.

2911
KENTUCKY SOCIETY OF CERTIFIED PUBLIC ACCOUNTANTS COLLEGE SCHOLARSHIPS

Kentucky Society of Certified Public Accountants
Attn: Educational Foundation
1735 Alliant Avenue
Louisville, KY 40299-6326
Phone: (502) 266-5272   (800) 292-1754 (within KY)
Fax: (502) 261-9512   E-mail: kycpa@kycpa.org
Web Site: www.kycpa.org
Summary: To provide financial assistance to students in Kentucky who are interested in majoring in accounting in college.
Eligibility: Eligible to apply are students who are currently enrolled as a sophomore or above in a Kentucky college or university. Applicants must have an overall grade point average of at least 2.75 and an accounting grade point average of at least 3.0. They must have completed the "principles of accounting" course and must be currently enrolled in or have completed intermediate accounting. Interested students must submit a completed application form, their college transcripts, an essay (up to 500 words) stating career goals, and 2 letters of recommendation (1 must come from an accounting professor). Selection is based on scholastic achievement and leadership potential.
Financial data: The stipend is $1,000.
Duration: 1 year.
Additional information: This program was established in 1988. Winners are presented at the society's spring awards banquet.
Number awarded: 2 each year.
Deadline: January of each year.

2912
KEVIN BARRY PERDUE MEMORIAL SCHOLARSHIP

Summary: To provide funding to licensed radio amateurs who are interested in studying humanities or the social sciences in college.
See Listing #1484.

2913
KFDA FOUNDATION SCHOLARSHIP

KFDA Foundation, Inc.
1200 South Kansas Avenue
P.O. Box 1904
Topeka, KS 66601-1904
Summary: To provide financial assistance to students from Kansas who are in their last year at a mortuary science school.
Eligibility: This program is open to students registered with the Kansas State Board of Mortuary Arts who have at least 1 but no more than 2 semesters of mortuary science school remaining. Applicants must submit a copy of their college transcript and their previous year's tax return. Selection is based on academic achievement, leadership, financial need, and special abilities.
Financial data: A stipend is awarded (exact amount not specified).
Number awarded: 1 each year.
Deadline: September of each year.

2914
KSCPA COLLEGE SCHOLARSHIPS

Kansas Society of Certified Public Accountants
Attn: Educational Foundation
1080 S.W. Wanamaker Road, Suite 200
P.O. Box 4291
Topeka, KS 66604-0291
Phone: (785) 272-4366   (800) 222-0452 (within KS)
Fax: (785) 262-4468   E-mail: connie@kscpa.org
Web Site: www.kscpa.org
Summary: To provide financial assistance to college students in Kansas who are majoring in accounting.
Eligibility: This program is open to upper-division students at each of the 6 regent institutions in Kansas and at Washburn University. Applicants must be studying accounting.
Financial data: The stipend is $1,250.
Duration: 1 year.
Number awarded: 7 each year: 1 at each of the participating institutions.
Deadline: June of each year.

2915
KSCPA HIGH SCHOOL SCHOLARSHIPS

Kansas Society of Certified Public Accountants
Attn: Educational Foundation
1080 S.W. Wanamaker Road, Suite 200
P.O. Box 4291
Topeka, KS 66604-0291
Phone: (785) 272-4366   (800) 222-0452 (within KS)
Fax: (785) 262-4468   E-mail: connie@kscpa.org
Web Site: www.kscpa.org
Summary: To provide financial assistance for college to high school seniors in Kansas who plan to major in accounting.
Eligibility: This program is open to high school seniors who will be entering a Kansas college or university the following academic year. Applicants must be planning to study accounting. Selection is based on ACT or SAT scores.
Financial data: Stipends are $1,000, $600, $500, $400, or $200.
Duration: 1 year.
Number awarded: 9 each year: 1 each at $1,000, $600, $500; and $400, plus 5 at $200.
Deadline: Test scores must be submitted by March of each year; applications are due in April.

2916
KSCPA INDEPENDENT COLLEGE SCHOLARSHIP

Kansas Society of Certified Public Accountants
Attn: Educational Foundation
1080 S.W. Wanamaker Road, Suite 200
P.O. Box 4291
Topeka, KS 66604-0291
Phone: (785) 272-4366   (800) 222-0452 (within KS)
Fax: (785) 262-4468   E-mail: connie@kscpa.org
Web Site: www.kscpa.org
Summary: To provide financial assistance to students in Kansas who are majoring in accounting at independent colleges.

Eligibility: This program is open to juniors who are majoring in accounting at independent colleges in Kansas. Each college may nominate 1 candidate.
Financial data: The stipend is $1,250.
Duration: 1 year.
Number awarded: 1 each year.
Deadline: April of each year.

2917
LAMBDA ALPHA NATIONAL DEAN'S LIST SCHOLARSHIP

Lambda Alpha
c/o National Executive Secretary
Ball State University
Department of Anthropology
Muncie, IN 47306-1099
Phone: (765) 285-1577   E-mail: 01bkswartz@bsuvc.bsu.edu
Summary: To provide financial assistance for further education to members of Lambda Alpha, the national anthropology honor society.
Eligibility: This program is open to anthropology majors with junior standing at a college or university with a chapter of the society. Candidates must be nominated by their chapters (each chapter may nominate only 1 candidate). Selection is based on undergraduate grades and letters of recommendation.
Financial data: The award is $1,000.
Duration: The award is presented annually.
Additional information: This award was first presented in 1993.
Number awarded: 1 each year.
Deadline: February of each year.

2918
LANCE HERNDON SCHOLARSHIP

Community Foundation for Greater Atlanta, Inc.
50 Hurt Plaza, Suite 449
Atlanta, GA 30303
Phone: (404) 688-5525   Fax: (404) 688-3060
E-mail: bchen@atlcf.org
Web Site: www.atlcf.org/Scholar02.html
Summary: To provide financial support to African American college students in Georgia who demonstrate entrepreneurial spirit and interest in small business development.
Eligibility: This program is open to African Americans who are legal residents of Georgia, are enrolled in college and pursuing studies in a field related to small business development, are at the upper-division level, are able to demonstrate financial need, and have at least a 2.0 grade point average (although preference is given to candidates with a cumulative average in the range of 2.0 to 2.9).
Financial data: The stipend is $1,000.
Duration: 1 year.
Deadline: 1 each year.

2919
LANDS' END SCHOLARSHIP PROGRAM

Summary: To provide financial assistance to students attending private colleges in Wisconsin who are majoring in selected business-related fields.
See Listing #1493.

2920
LARS NAERLAND SCHOLARSHIP

Nordmanns-Forbundet
Pacific Northwest Chapter
Attn: Scholarship Committee
c/o Western Viking
P.O. Box 70408
Seattle, WA 98107
Summary: To provide financial assistance to college students in the Pacific Northwest who are interested in studying about Norway or in Norway.
Eligibility: This program is open to part-time and full-time college students who have demonstrated an interest in studying subjects that would strengthen the ties between the people of Norway and the people of the United States. Applicants should be members of the Nordmanns-Forbundet or be of Norwegian descent. Special attention is paid to applicants whose project or course of study will take them to Norway or will help to foster the social, cultural, and economic ties between the Pacific Northwest and Norway. Applicants must submit 3 letters of recommendation, a copy of their high school or college transcript, and an essay explaining why they are applying for the scholarship. Financial need is not considered in the selection process.
Financial data: The stipend is generally $1,500.
Duration: 1 year.
Number awarded: At least 1 each year.
Deadline: March of each year.

2921
LAURA E. SETTLE SCHOLARSHIPS

California Retired Teachers Association
Attn: Executive Director
800 Howe Avenue, Suite 370
Sacramento, CA 95825
Phone: (916) 923-2200   Fax: (916) 923-1910
E-mail: admin@calrta.org   Web Site: www.calrta.org/scholar.htm
Summary: To provide financial assistance to undergraduate and graduate students majoring in education in California.
Eligibility: This program is open to senior undergraduates and graduate students majoring in education at a campus of the University of California (UC) or the California State University (CSU) system. Students interested in applying must contact the department of teacher education at their campus.
Financial data: The stipend is $2,000.
Duration: 1 year.
Number awarded: 1 scholarship is offered at each UC and CSU campus.

2922
LAW ENFORCEMENT CAREER SCHOLARSHIP PROGRAM

Association of Former Agents of the U.S. Secret Service, Inc.
P.O. Box 848
Annandale, VA 22003-0848   Phone: (703) 256-0188
Summary: To provide financial assistance to college students who are working toward a degree in law enforcement or police science.
Eligibility: This program is open to undergraduate students who have completed at least 1 year of study in law enforcement or police administration. Students working toward an advanced degree are also eligible if their graduate study is in law enforcement or police administration. Applications may be submitted by more than 1 member of the same family, but no more than 1 scholarship will be granted to any 1 family. Past recipients are not eligible for a second award. Financial need is not considered in the selection process.
Financial data: A stipend is awarded (exact amount not specified).
Duration: 1 year; may not reapply.
Additional information: This program includes the following named scholarships: the J. Clifford Dietrich Scholarship, the John Hays Hanly Memorial Scholarship, and the Julie Y. Cross Scholarship.
Number awarded: At least 3 each year.
Deadline: April of each year.

2923
LAW IN SOCIETY AWARD COMPETITION

Virginia State Bar
Attn: Law in Society Award Competition
707 East Main Street, Suite 1500
Richmond, VA 23219-2800
Phone: (804) 775-0500   Fax: (804) 775-0583
E-mail: lawinsociety@vsb.org   Web Site: www.vsb.org
Summary: To recognize and reward high school students in Virginia who submit outstanding essays on the role of law in society.
Eligibility: This program is open to students enrolled at a Virginia high school in grades 9 through 12 who are 19 years of age or younger. Home-schooled students at equivalent grade and age levels are also eligible. Applicants must submit an essay, up to 1,500 words in length, on a topic that changes annually but relates to a hypothetical situation on the role of law in society.
Financial data: First prize is a $1,000 U.S. savings bond or $500 in cash, second prize is a $750 U.S. savings bond or $375 in cash, third prize is a $500 U.S. savings bond or $250 cash, and honorable mention is a $100 U.S. savings bond or $50 cash.
Duration: The competition is held annually.
Number awarded: 10 each year: 1 first prize, 1 second prize, 1 third prize, and 7 honorable mentions.
Deadline: March of each year.

Scholarship Listings

2924
LAWRENCE "LARRY" FRAZIER MEMORIAL SCHOLARSHIP

Summary: To provide financial assistance to residents of Nebraska who are interested in studying designated fields in college.
See Listing #2196.

2925
LEADERSHIP FOR DIVERSITY SCHOLARSHIP

California School Library Association
717 K Street, Suite 515
Sacramento, CA 95814-3477
Phone: (916) 447-2684   Fax: (916) 447-2695
E-mail: csla@pacbell.net
Web Site: www.schoollibrary.org
Summary: To encourage minority students to get a credential as a library media teacher in California.
Eligibility: This program is open to students who are members of a traditionally underrepresented group enrolled in a college or university library media teacher credential program in California. Applicants must intend to work as a library media teacher in a California school library media center for a minimum of 3 years. Financial need is considered in awarding the scholarship.
Financial data: The stipend is $1,000.
Duration: 1 year.
Number awarded: 1 each year.
Deadline: May of each year.

2926
LESTER B. KESTERSON SCHOLARSHIP

Missouri Association of DECA
c/o Dr. Warren "Gene" Reed
Missouri Department of Elementary and Secondary Education
Division of Vocational and Adult Education-Marketing and Cooperative Education
P.O. Box 480
Jefferson City, MO 65102-0480
Phone: (573) 751-4367   E-mail: greed@mail.dese.state.mo.us
Web Site: www.dese.state.mo.us/divvoced/mce/index.html
Summary: To provide financial assistance to high school seniors who are members of the Missouri Association of DECA interested in studying marketing or management in college.
Eligibility: This program is open to high school seniors who are members of the Missouri Association of DECA enrolled in a marketing education or cooperative occupational education program. Applicants must be interested in attending an accredited 2- or 4-year postsecondary institution to continue their study of marketing and/or management. Selection is based on high school transcripts, DECA involvement, school and community activities, volunteer services, educational plans, career plans, benefits derived through DECA participation, letters of recommendation, and SAT or ACT scores.
Financial data: The stipend is $1,000.
Duration: 1 year; nonrenewable.
Number awarded: Up to 3 each year.
Deadline: February of each year.

2927
L.G. WELLS SCHOLARSHIPS

Summary: To provide financial assistance to high school seniors in Oregon who are interested in studying education or engineering at a community college, college, or university in the state.
See Listing #2202.

2928
LILLIAN P. SCHOEPHOERSTER SCHOLARSHIP

Phi Upsilon Omicron
Attn: Educational Foundation
P.O. Box 329
Fairmont, WV 26555-0329
Phone: (304) 368-0612   E-mail: rickards@access.mountain.net
Web Site: ianrwww.unl.edu/phiu
Summary: To provide financial assistance to nontraditional student members of Phi Upsilon Omicron, a national honor society in family and consumer sciences.

Eligibility: This program is open to nontraditional students who are members of the society working toward a baccalaureate degree in family and consumer sciences or a related subject. Selection is based on scholastic record, participation in society and other collegiate activities, a statement of professional aims and goals, professional and/or work experience, and recommendations.
Financial data: The stipend is $1,500.
Duration: 1 year.
Number awarded: 1 each year.
Deadline: January of each year.

2929
LITHERLAND/FTE SCHOLARSHIP

Summary: To provide financial support to undergraduate members of the International Technology Education Association (ITEA) who are majoring in technology education teacher preparation.
See Listing #2206.

2930
LORAL SKYNET SCHOLARSHIP

Summary: To provide financial assistance to minorities and women interested in studying satellite-related disciplines in college or graduate school.
See Listing #1505.

2931
LOTTE MEERS MEMORIAL SCHOLARSHIP FOR EDUCATORS

Golub Foundation
Attn: Price Chopper Scholarship Office
501 Duanesburg Road
P.O. Box 1074
Schenectady, NY 12301
Phone: (518) 355-5000   (800) 877-0870
Summary: To provide financial assistance to high school seniors who wish to become teachers and are living in Massachusetts, Connecticut, Pennsylvania, New Hampshire, Vermont, and New York.
Eligibility: To qualify, high school seniors must live in the Price Chopper marketing areas; these include 1) Massachusetts (Berkshire, Hampden, Hampshire, Middlesex, Worcester); 2) Connecticut (Litchfield, Windham); 3) Pennsylvania (Lackawana, Luzerne, Susquehana, Wayne, Wyoming); 4) New Hampshire (Grafton, Sullivan); 5) Vermont (Bennington, Caledonia, Chittenden, Franklin, Lamoille, Orange, Orleans, Rutland, Washington, Windham, Windsor), and 6) New York (Albany, Broome, Chenango, Clinton, Columbia, Cortland, Delaware, Dutchess, Essex, Franklin, Fulton, Greene, Hamilton, Herkimer, Jefferson, Lewis, Madison, Montgomery, Oneida, Onondaga, Orange, Oswego, Otsego, Rensselaer, St. Lawrence, Saratoga, Schenectady, Schoharie, Tioga, Ulster, Warren, Washington). Applicants must plan to attend school in 1 of those 6 states, be interested in majoring in education, and be able to demonstrate scholastic ability. They must write an essay that describes why they have chosen to enter the field of education and how they feel they will have an impact in this area. Finalists must attend a personal interview.
Financial data: The stipend is $2,000 per year.
Duration: 4 years.
Number awarded: 1 each year.
Deadline: March of each year.

2932
LOUIS AND FANNIE SAGER MEMORIAL SCHOLARSHIP

National Society of Accountants
Attn: NSA Scholarship Foundation
1010 North Fairfax Street
Alexandria, VA 22314-1574
Phone: (703) 549-6400, ext. 1312   (800) 966-6679
Fax: (703) 549-2512   E-mail: dgriffin@nsacct.org
Web Site: www.nsacct.org
Summary: To provide financial assistance to Virginians who are studying accounting.
Eligibility: This program is open to graduates of Virginia public high schools who are enrolled as an undergraduate at a Virginia college or university. Applicants must be majoring in accounting and have earned a grade point average of 3.0 or higher. They must submit a letter of intent outlining their reasons for seeking the award, their intended career objective, how how this scholarship award would be

used to accomplish that objective. Selection is based on academic attainment, demonstrated leadership ability, and financial need.

Financial data: The stipend ranges from $500 to $1,000 per year.
Duration: 1 year.
Number awarded: 1 each year.
Deadline: March of each year.

2933
LUCILE RUST SCHOLARSHIP

Phi Upsilon Omicron
Attn: Educational Foundation
P.O. Box 329
Fairmont, WV 26555-0329
Phone: (304) 368-0612   E-mail: rickards@access.mountain.net
Web Site: ianrwww.unl.edu/phiu
Summary: To provide financial assistance for undergraduate education to members of Phi Upsilon Omicron, a national honor society in family and consumer sciences.
Eligibility: Applicants must be members of the society studying family and consumer sciences on the undergraduate level. Selection is based on scholastic record, participation in society and other collegiate activities, a statement of professional aims and goals, professional and/or work experience, and recommendations.
Financial data: The stipend is $1,000.
Duration: 1 year.
Number awarded: 1 each year.
Deadline: January of each year.

2934
MACDONALD SCHOLARSHIP

Maine Society of CPAs
153 U.S. Route 1, Suite 8
Scarborough, ME 04074-9053
Summary: To provide financial assistance to students in Maine majoring in accounting.
Eligibility: This program is open to college accounting majors in Maine. They must have at least a 3.0 grade point average, be able to demonstrate writing skills, and have participated in community activities. Selection is based on academic achievement, writing skills, extracurricular activities, work experience, career goals, and financial need.
Financial data: The stipend is $1,000.
Duration: 1 year.
Number awarded: 1 each year.

2935
MAINE INNKEEPERS ASSOCIATION HOSPITALITY SCHOLARSHIPS

Summary: To provide financial assistance to Maine residents who wish to prepare for a career in the hospitality industry.
See Listing #1512.

2936
MAINE QUALITY CHILD CARE EDUCATION SCHOLARSHIP PROGRAM

Finance Authority of Maine
Attn: Education Finance Programs
5 Community Drive
P.O. Box 949
Augusta, ME 04332-0949
Phone: (207) 623-3263   (800) 228-3734
Fax: (207) 623-0095   TDD: (207) 626-2717
E-mail: info@famemaine.com   Web Site: www.famemaine.com
Summary: To provide financial assistance to Maine residents interested in improving their skills in the child development field.
Eligibility: This program is open to residents of Maine who are taking 1 or more childhood education courses or pursuing a child development associate (CDA) certificate, associate degree, baccalaureate degree, or post-baccalaureate teacher certification in child care related fields. Applicants must be able to demonstrate financial need.
Financial data: The stipend is $500 per course or $2,000 per year.
Duration: 1 semester or 1 year.
Number awarded: Varies each year.

2937
MAINE STATE CHAMBER OF COMMERCE SCHOLARSHIPS

Summary: To provide financial assistance for a college-level technical, education, or business program to residents of Maine.
See Listing #600.

2938
MALCOLM BALDRIGE SCHOLARSHIPS

Summary: To provide financial assistance to college students interested in a career in foreign trade or manufacturing.
See Listing #2223.

2939
MARGARET JEROME SAMPSON SCHOLARSHIPS

Phi Upsilon Omicron
Attn: Educational Foundation
P.O. Box 329
Fairmont, WV 26555-0329
Phone: (304) 368-0612   E-mail: rickards@access.mountain.net
Web Site: ianrwww.unl.edu/phiu
Summary: To provide financial assistance to undergraduate student members of Phi Upsilon Omicron, a national honor society in family and consumer sciences.
Eligibility: This program is open to members of the society who are working on a bachelor's degree in family and consumer sciences. Preference is given to majors in dietetics or food and nutrition. Selection is based on scholastic record, participation in the society, and a statement of professional aims and goals.
Financial data: The stipend is $3,000.
Duration: 1 year.
Number awarded: 4 each year.
Deadline: January of each year.

2940
MARGOT SEITELMAN MEMORIAL SCHOLARSHIP

Summary: To provide financial assistance for postsecondary education to students who are planning a career in professional writing or teaching English grammar and writing.
See Listing #1518.

2941
MARION MACCARRELL SCOTT SCHOLARSHIP

Summary: To provide financial assistance to residents of Hawaii for undergraduate or graduate studies in fields related to achieving world cooperation and international understanding.
See Listing #1519.

2942
MARION T. BURR SCHOLARSHIP

American Baptist Churches USA
Attn: Educational Ministries
P.O. Box 851
Valley Forge, PA 19482-0851
Phone: (610) 768-2067   (800) ABC-3USA, ext. 2067
Fax: (610) 768-2056   E-mail: paula.weiss@abc-usa.org
Web Site: www.abc-em.org
Summary: To provide financial assistance to Native American Baptists who are interested in preparing for a career in human services.
Eligibility: This program is open to Native Americans who are American Baptists and interested in preparing for a career in human services. Applicants must be enrolled full time in a college or seminary. U.S. citizenship is required.
Financial data: Partial tuition scholarships are offered.
Duration: 1 year.
Number awarded: Varies each year.
Deadline: May of each year.

2943
MARK MILLER AWARD

National Association of Black Accountants
Attn: Director, Center for Advancement of Minority Accountants
7249-A Hanover Parkway
Greenbelt, MD 20770
Phone: (301) 474-NABA, ext. 114   Fax: (301) 474-3114
E-mail: cquinn@nabainc.org   Web Site: www.nabainc.org
Summary: To provide financial assistance for undergraduate or graduate education in accounting-related fields to members of the National Association of Black Accountants (NABA).
Eligibility: Applicants must be paid members of the association who are full-time students pursuing a bachelor's or master's degree in accounting, finance, business administration, or taxation. Applicants must have a grade point average of at least 2.0 in their major and 2.5 overall. Selection is based on grades, financial need, and a 500-word autobiography that discusses career objectives, leadership abilities, community activities, and involvement in the association.
Financial data: The stipend is $1,000 per year.
Duration: 1 year.
Number awarded: 1 each year.
Deadline: December of each year.

2944
MARRIOTT INTERNATIONAL SCHOLARSHIPS

DECA
1908 Association Drive
Reston, VA 20191-1594
Phone: (703) 860-5000   Fax: (703) 860-4013
E-mail: decainc@aol.com
Web Site: www.deca.org/scholarships/index.html
Summary: To provide financial assistance for college to DECA members interested in the hospitality industry.
Eligibility: This program is open to DECA members who can demonstrate evidence of DECA activities, grades, leadership ability, and interest or experience in the hospitality industry. Awards are made on the basis of merit, not financial need.
Financial data: The stipend is $1,000.
Duration: 1 year.
Number awarded: 4 each year.
Deadline: February of each year.

2945
MARY BENEVENTO SCHOLARSHIP

Summary: To provide financial assistance to high school seniors in Connecticut who are interested in studying health, physical education, recreation, or dance in college.
See Listing #1525.

2946
MARY CRAIG SCHOLARSHIP FUND

American Society of Women Accountants-Billings Big Sky Chapter
c/o Cathy B. Allen
P.O. Box 23398
Billings, MT 59104-3398
Phone: (406) 245-6933   Fax: (406) 245-6922
E-mail: Cathya@mcn.net
Web Site: www.imt.net/~aswa/index.html
Summary: To provide financial assistance to students pursuing a bachelor's or master's degree in accounting at a college or university in Montana.
Eligibility: This program is open to students pursuing a bachelor's or master's degree in accounting at an accredited Montana college or university. Applicants must have completed at least 60 semester hours. Selection is based on career goals, communication skills, grade point average, personal circumstances, and financial need. Membership in the American Society of Women Accountants is not required.
Financial data: The stipend is $1,500.
Duration: 1 year.
Additional information: Information is also available from Nancy Gililland, (406) 656-9300, E-mail: mtnancy@juno.com.
Number awarded: 1 each year.
Deadline: March of each year.

2947
MARY JO CLAYTON SANDERS ENVIRONMENTAL ISSUES SCHOLARSHIP

Summary: To provide financial aid to Florida undergraduates and graduate students majoring in environmental issues.
See Listing #2233.

2948
MARY MACEY SCHOLARSHIP

Women Grocers of America
1005 North Glebe Road, Suite 250
Arlington, VA 22201
Phone: (703) 516-0700   Fax: (703) 516-0115
E-mail: wga@nationalgrocers.org   Web Site: www.nationalgrocers.org
Summary: To provide financial assistance to family and members of the Women Grocers of America (WGA) and the National Grocers Association (NGA) who are interested in pursuing a career related to the grocery industry.
Eligibility: This program is open to WGA and NGA members, along with their employees, children, nieces, nephews, and grandchildren. Applicants must be entering college sophomores or continuing students at a 2-year associate degree-granting institution, a 4-year bachelor's degree-granting institution, or a graduate program; have earned at least a 2.0 grade point average; and be majoring (or planning to major) in such areas as food marking management, food service technology, communications, or business management/administration. Excluded are students majoring in public health or hotel/restaurant fields. Scholarship recipients are chosen in a lottery from the pool of qualified candidates. Financial need is not considered.
Financial data: At least $1,000 per year.
Duration: 1 year.
Number awarded: At least 2 each year.
Deadline: May of each year.

2949
MARY MOORHEAD MARTIN FUTURE TEACHER SCHOLARSHIP

National Institute for Labor Relations Research
Attn: Future Teacher Scholarships
5211 Port Royal Road, Suite 510
Springfield, VA 22151
Phone: (703) 321-9606   Fax: (703) 321-7342
E-mail: research@nilrr.org   Web Site: www.nilrr.org
Summary: To provide financial assistance to students majoring in education who oppose compulsory unionism in the education community.
Eligibility: Applicants must be undergraduate students majoring in education in institutions of higher learning in the United States. They must write an essay of approximately 500 words demonstrating an interest in and a knowledge of the right to work principle as it applies to educators. Selection is based on scholastic ability and financial need. Applicants must also demonstrate 1) the potential to complete a degree program in education and receive a teaching license, and 2) an understanding of the principles of voluntary unionism and the problems of compulsory unionism in relation to education.
Financial data: The stipend is $1,000.
Duration: 1 year.
Additional information: This program was established in 1993.
Number awarded: 1 each year.
Deadline: February of each year.

2950
MARY MORROW-EDNA RICHARDS SCHOLARSHIP

North Carolina Association of Educators
700 South Salisbury Street
P.O. Box 27347
Raleigh, NC 27611-7347
Phone: (919) 832-3000, ext. 216   (800) 662-7924, ext. 216
Fax: (919) 839-8229   E-mail: JVaughn@nea.org
Web Site: www.ncae.org
Summary: To provide financial assistance to upper-division college students in North Carolina who are enrolled in a teacher-education program.
Eligibility: Applicants must be North Carolina residents enrolled in a teacher-education program. They must be in their junior year in college and willing to teach in North Carolina public schools for at least 2 years following graduation.

All applications should be made through a college or university. Accompanying the completed application form must be a wallet-size glossy photograph of the applicant and an official college transcript. Also, recommendations are requested from at least 3 persons. Preference is given to children of members of the North Carolina Association of Educators (NCAE) and to members of Student NCAE. Other selection criteria include: character, personality, scholastic achievement, promise as a teacher, and financial need.

Financial data: A stipend is awarded (exact amount not specified).
Duration: 1 year (the senior year of college).
Number awarded: 1 or more each year.
Deadline: January of each year.

2951
MARYLAND ASSOCIATION OF CERTIFIED PUBLIC ACCOUNTANTS SCHOLARSHIP PROGRAM

Maryland Association of Certified Public Accountants
Attn: Educational Foundation
1300 York Road, Building C
P.O. Box 4417
Lutherville, MD 21094-4417
Phone: (410) 296-6250   (800) 782-2036
Fax: (410) 296-8713   E-mail: info@macpa.org
Web Site: www.macpa.org
Summary: To provide financial assistance to accounting majors at colleges and universities in Maryland.
Eligibility: This program is open to Maryland residents attending a college or university in the state and taking enough undergraduate or graduate courses to qualify as a full-time student at their school. Applicants must have completed at least 60 total credit hours at the time of the award, including at least 6 hours in accounting courses. They must have a grade point average of 3.0 or higher and be able to demonstrate financial need. U.S. citizenship is required.
Financial data: Stipends are at least $1,000. The exact amount of the award depends upon the recipient's financial need.
Duration: 1 year; may be renewed until completion of the 150-hour requirement and eligibility for sitting for the CPA examination in Maryland. Renewal requires continued full-time enrollment and a grade point average of 3.0 or higher.
Number awarded: Several each year.
Deadline: April of each year.

2952
MARYLAND LEGION AUXILIARY CHILDREN AND YOUTH FUND SCHOLARSHIP

Summary: To provide financial assistance for the postsecondary education of the daughters of veterans who are Maryland residents and wish to study arts, sciences, business, public administration, education, or a medical field.
See Listing #1528.

2953
MAS FAMILY SCHOLARSHIP PROGRAM

Summary: To provide financial assistance to students of Cuban descent who are working on an undergraduate or graduate degree in selected subject areas.
See Listing #1529.

2954
MASSACHUSETTS AFL-CIO SCHOLARSHIP AWARDS

Massachusetts AFL-CIO
8 Beacon Street, Third Floor
Boston, MA 02108
Phone: (617) 227-8260   Fax: (617) 227-2010
Web Site: www.massaflcio.org
Summary: To recognize and reward the high school seniors in Massachusetts receiving the highest scores on a statewide labor history written examination.
Eligibility: High school seniors in Massachusetts may apply to their guidance office, social studies teacher, or principal to take a competitive examination dealing with the history and structure of the labor movement in America, legislation affecting American workers, child labor laws, minimum wages, civil rights, safety in the workplace, old age and health insurance, unemployment compensation, workers' compensation, and current labor events. The students with the highest scores on the examination receive these scholarships.
Financial data: First prize is $3,000, second prize is $2,000, and third through tenth prizes are $1,000. An additional prize of $1,000 is awarded to the vocational education student who achieves the high score among all vocational education students. In addition, prizes are awarded to students who are children of members of many central labor councils or locals throughout the state and score highest from among the children of members of that council or local who take the examination; these additional awards range in value from $100 to $3,000; the total value of scholarships provided by the Massachusetts AFL-CIO, its locals, central labor councils, and other affiliates exceeds $630,000 each year.
Duration: Most scholarships are for 1 year.
Additional information: At the state level, the first prize is designated the John F. Kennedy Memorial Scholarship, second prize the Francis E. Lavigne Memorial Award, third the Arthur R. Osborn Scholarship Award, fourth the Joseph C. Faherty Scholarship Award, fifth the Massachusetts AFL-CIO Scholarship Award, sixth the Union City Press Scholarship Award (2 awarded-1 to a male and 1 to a female), seventh the Salvatore Camelio Memorial Award, eighth the James W. DeBow Memorial Award, and ninth the American Income Life Insurance Company Award.
Number awarded: More than 300 scholarships are awarded each year, of which 9 are awarded to the students with the highest scores in the state regardless of union affiliation and most of the others to children of various councils or locals.
Deadline: Applications to take the examination must be submitted by January of each year.

2955
MAUD BERGGREN SCHOLARSHIP

Nordmanns-Forbundet
Pacific Northwest Chapter
Attn: Scholarship Committee
c/o Western Viking
P.O. Box 70408
Seattle, WA 98107
Summary: To provide financial assistance to college students in the Pacific Northwest who are interested in studying about Norway or in Norway.
Eligibility: This program is open to part-time and full-time college students who have demonstrated an interest in studying subjects that would strengthen the ties between the people of Norway and the people of the United States. Applicants should be members of the Nordmanns-Forbundet or be of Norwegian descent. Special attention is paid to applicants whose project or course of study will take them to Norway or will help to foster the social, cultural, and economic ties between the Pacific Northwest and Norway. Applicants must submit 3 letters of recommendation, a copy of their high school or college transcript, and an essay explaining why they are applying for the scholarship. Financial need is not considered in the selection process.
Financial data: The stipend is generally $1,500.
Duration: 1 year.
Number awarded: At least 1 each year.
Deadline: March of each year.

2956
MAY AND HUBERT EVERLY HEA SCHOLARSHIP

Hawaii Education Association
Attn: Scholarship Committee
1649 Kalakaua Avenue
Honolulu, HI 96826
Phone: (808) 949-6657   Fax: (808) 944-2032
Summary: To provide financial assistance to education majors in Hawaii who plan to teach in the state.
Eligibility: Eligible to apply for this scholarship are currently-enrolled college students who are attending an accredited institution of higher learning in Hawaii, are majoring in education, and are planning to teach in the state. Selection is based on financial need, a personal statement, recommendations, and academic record.
Financial data: The stipend is $1,000, paid in 2 equal installments. Funds are sent directly to the recipient's institution.
Duration: 1 year.
Number awarded: 1 each year.
Deadline: April of each year.

2957
M.E. FRANKS SCHOLARSHIP PROGRAM

Summary: To provide financial assistance to outstanding undergraduate and graduate students who are interested in working on a degree in a field related to food science.
See Listing #2250.

2958
MELVILLE H. COHEE STUDENT LEADER CONSERVATION SCHOLARSHIPS

Summary: To provide financial assistance to student officers of the Soil and Water Conservation Society (SWCS) who are interested in pursuing undergraduate or graduate studies with a focus on natural resource conservation.
See Listing #2252.

2959
MEMORIAL CONSERVATION SCHOLARSHIP

Summary: To provide financial assistance to college students in New Jersey who are preparing for a career in a field related to the conservation and management of natural resources.
See Listing #1531.

2960
MENLO LOGISTICS SCHOLARSHIP

Summary: To provide financial assistance to upper-division and graduate students who are preparing for a career in logistics or transportation.
See Listing #2255.

2961
MERLE E. FRAMPTON SCHOLARSHIP

Washington State School for the Blind
2214 East 13th Street
Vancouver, WA 98661
Phone: (360) 696-6321   E-mail: jbckford@wssb.org
Summary: To provide financial assistance to college students training to become teachers of the blind and visually impaired.
Eligibility: This program is open to students in the United States or Canada who have been accepted into a university program recognized by AERBVI as meeting the standards for training teachers of the blind and visually impaired. Applicants must be formally accepted into a program and intend to become a teacher of the blind and visually impaired. The scholarship will not fund rehabilitation teachers or orientation and mobility specialists as stand-alone certifications, although if a dual program is being pursued (vision teacher plus), the scholarship will fund those programs.
Financial data: A stipend is awarded (exact amount not specified). Funds may be used only for payment of tuition and are sent directly to the recipient's university.
Duration: 1 year.
Deadline: July of each year.

2962
MEXICAN AMERICAN GROCERS ASSOCIATION SCHOLARSHIP PROGRAM

Mexican American Grocers Association
405 North San Fernando Road
Los Angeles, CA 90031
Phone: (323) 227-1565   Fax: (323) 227-6935
Web Site: www.maga.org
Summary: To provide financial assistance to Latino/Hispanic students interested in preparing for a business career.
Eligibility: Eligible to apply are Latino/Hispanic full-time undergraduate students who are at least sophomores attending a community college or a 4-year accredited college or university with at least a 2.5 grade point average and a major in business administration or a business-related field. Applicants must demonstrate genuine financial need.
Financial data: The amount awarded varies, depending upon the financial needs of the recipient, but it generally does not exceed $2,000.
Duration: 1 year; may be renewed for up to 2 additional years.
Additional information: To date, up to $500,000 has been distributed through this program. Requests for applications must be accompanied by a self-addressed stamped envelope. Recipients from southern California must attend the scholarship awards banquet in September.
Number awarded: Varies; generally more than 50 each year.
Deadline: July of each year.

2963
MGMA MIDWEST SECTION SCHOLARSHIPS

Summary: To provide financial assistance to members of the Medical Group Management Association (MGMA) Midwest Section who are interested in pursuing professional development through undergraduate or graduate education.
See Listing #2260.

2964
MGMA WESTERN SECTION SCHOLARSHIPS

Summary: To provide financial assistance to members of the Medical Group Management Association (MGMA) Western Section who are interested in pursuing professional development through undergraduate or graduate education.
See Listing #2261.

2965
MGMA/AAA SCHOLARSHIPS

Summary: To provide financial assistance to members and dependents of members of the Anesthesia Administration Assembly (AAA) of the Medical Group Management Association (MGMA) who are undertaking a course of study or project to accomplish set goals for self advancement.
See Listing #2262.

2966
MGMA/APA SCHOLARSHIPS

Summary: To provide financial assistance to members of the Academic Practice Assembly (APA) of the Medical Group Management Association (MGMA) who are pursuing professional development through undergraduate or graduate study.
See Listing #2263.

2967
MGMA/IHPS SCHOLARSHIPS

Summary: To provide financial assistance to students in fields of interest to the Integrated Healthcare Practices Society (IHPS) of the Medical Group Management Association (MGMA).
See Listing #2264.

2968
MICHAEL AND MARIE MARUCCI SCHOLARSHIP

Summary: To provide financial assistance to legally blind students pursuing a degree in a field that requires study abroad.
See Listing #665.

2969
MICHIGAN MORTUARY SCIENCE FOUNDATION SCHOLARSHIP

Michigan Mortuary Science Foundation
c/o Michigan Funeral Directors Association
P.O. Box 27158
Lansing, MI 48909
Phone: (517) 349-9565   Fax: (517) 349-9819
E-mail: SWest@mfda.org
Web Site: www.mfda.org
Summary: To provide financial assistance to Michigan residents who are interested in preparing for a career in mortuary science.
Eligibility: Applicants must be either a resident of Michigan or a full-time mortuary science student at Wayne State University (in Detroit, Michigan). They must be attending school on a full-time basis and must submit the following material as part of the application process: a cover letter, an essay (between 1,000 and 2,500 words) on a topic that changes annually, and a letter of recommendation from the mortuary science school the applicant is attending. Selection is based on the essay, the recommendation of the mortuary college, and financial need.
Financial data: The stipends are $2,500, $1,500, or $750. Funds may be used to pay for tuition, books, supplies, room and board, and other educational expenses.
Duration: 1 year.
Number awarded: 3 each year.

2970
MICHIGAN TOURISM SCHOLARSHIP

National Tourism Foundation
Attn: Scholarships
546 East Main Street
Lexington, KY 40508-2342
Phone: (859) 226-4444   (800) 682-8886
Fax: (859) 226-4437   E-mail: ntf@ntastaff.com
Web Site: www.ntfonline.org
Summary: To provide financial assistance to college students in Michigan who are majoring in tourism.
Eligibility: This program is open to full-time students enrolled in a 4-year college or university in Michigan. Applicants must be Michigan residents, be in their junior or senior year, have at least a 3.0 grade point average, and be majoring in a travel or tourism-related field (e.g., hotel management, restaurant management, tourism).
Financial data: The stipend is $1,000.
Duration: 1 year.
Additional information: Award winners also receive complimentary registration and an all-expense paid trip (valued at more than $3,000) to the association's annual convention, as well as a 1-year subscription to *Courier* magazine, *Tuesday* newsletter, and *NTF Headlines* newsletter. In any 1 year, applicants may receive only 1 award from the association.
Number awarded: 1 each year.
Deadline: April of each year.

2971
MID-ATLANTIC CHAPTER SCHOLARSHIPS

Summary: To provide financial assistance to students attending college in designated mid-Atlantic states who are interested in majoring in satellite-related disciplines.
See Listing #1536.

2972
MINNESOTA LEGACY TOURISM SCHOLARSHIP

National Tourism Foundation
Attn: Scholarships
546 East Main Street
Lexington, KY 40508-2342
Phone: (859) 226-4444   (800) 682-8886
Fax: (859) 226-4437   E-mail: ntf@ntastaff.com
Web Site: www.ntfonline.org
Summary: To provide financial assistance to college students in Minnesota who are majoring in tourism.
Eligibility: This program is open to full-time students enrolled in a 2-year or 4-year college or university in Minnesota. Applicants must be Minnesota residents, have at least a 3.0 grade point average, and be majoring in a travel or tourism-related field (e.g., hotel management, restaurant management, tourism).
Financial data: The stipend is $1,000.
Duration: 1 year.
Additional information: Award winners also receive complimentary registration and an all-expense paid trip (valued at more than $3,000) to the association's annual convention, as well as a 1-year subscription to *Courier* magazine, *Tuesday* newsletter, and *NTF Headlines* newsletter. In any 1 year, applicants may receive only 1 award from the association.
Number awarded: 1 each year.
Deadline: April of each year.

2973
MINNESOTA YOUTH SOYBEAN SCHOLARSHIPS

Summary: To provide financial assistance to high school seniors or beginning college freshmen in Minnesota who have been active in the areas of soybean production or soybean nutrition.
See Listing #2281.

2974
MINORITIES IN GOVERNMENT FINANCE SCHOLARSHIP

Government Finance Officers Association
Attn: Scholarship Committee
180 North Michigan Avenue, Suite 800
Chicago, IL 60601-7476
Phone: (312) 977-9700   Fax: (312) 977-4806
Web Site: www.gfoa.org
Summary: To provide financial assistance to minority undergraduate and graduate students who are preparing for a career in state and local government finance.
Eligibility: This program is open to upper-division undergraduate and graduate students who are enrolled in a full-time program and preparing for a career in public finance. Applicants must be members of a minority group, citizens or permanent residents of the United States or Canada, and able to provide a letter of recommendation from the dean of their school. Selection is based on career plans, academic record, plan of study, letters of recommendation, and grade point average. Financial need is not considered.
Financial data: The stipend is $5,000.
Duration: 1 year.
Additional information: Funding for this program is provided by Fidelity Investments Tax-Exempt Services Company.
Number awarded: 1 or more each year.
Deadline: February of each year.

2975
MINORITY ACADEMIC INSTITUTIONS UNDERGRADUATE STUDENT FELLOWSHIPS

Summary: To provide financial assistance and summer internships to undergraduates at minority academic institutions (MAIs) who are interested in majoring in fields related to the environment.
See Listing #2282.

2976
MIRIAM SCHAEFER SCHOLARSHIP

Summary: To provide financial assistance to students who are enrolled in a teacher education program in Michigan with a mathematics specialty.
See Listing #2289.

2977
MISSISSIPPI SOCIETY OF CERTIFIED PUBLIC ACCOUNTANTS SCHOLARSHIP

Mississippi Society of Certified Public Accountants
Highland Village, Suite 246
Jackson, MS 39236
Phone: (601) 366-3473
Summary: To provide financial assistance to upper-division students majoring in accounting at 4-year institutions in Mississippi.
Eligibility: This program is open to residents of Mississippi who have completed their junior year of college, are majoring in accounting, have completed at least 6 hours of accounting courses above the principles or introductory level, and are attending 1 of the following schools in Mississippi: Alcorn State University, Belhaven College, Delta State University, Jackson State University, Millsaps College, Mississippi College, Mississippi State University, Mississippi University for Women, Mississippi Valley State University, University of Mississippi, University of Southern Mississippi, or William Carey College. They must be nominated by their academic institution. Nominees must submit a completed application form, verification of Mississippi residency, a written 1-page statement explaining why they plan a career in public accounting, a recent photograph, and a copy of their GMAT scores. Nominators must submit a transcript of the student's grades and letters of recommendations. Selection is based on academic excellence, recommendations, financial need, and campus involvement.
Financial data: The stipend is $1,000, paid in 2 equal installments. Checks are made payable jointly to the recipient and the recipient's school.
Duration: 1 year.
Number awarded: 1 each year.
Deadline: June of each year.

2978
MISSOURI AGENTS EDUCATION FOUNDATION SCHOLARSHIP

Missouri Agents Education Foundation
Attn: Scholarship Program
P.O. Box 1785
Jefferson City, MO 65102-1785
Phone: (573) 893-4301   (800) 617-3658
Fax: (573) 893-3708
Summary: To provide financial assistance to students, particularly in Missouri, who are preparing for a career in the insurance industry.
Eligibility: Applicants must be sponsored by a member of the Missouri Association of Insurance Agents. They must be majoring in a discipline that could lead to a career in the insurance industry. Preference is given to applicants who are 1) attending or planning to attend a college or university in Missouri and 2) entering their junior or senior year in college. To apply, they must submit a completed application form, an application essay, and an official transcript.
Financial data: The stipend is $1,000.
Duration: 1 year.
Number awarded: 1 or more each year.
Deadline: May of each year.

2979
MISSOURI TRAVEL COUNCIL SCHOLARSHIP

Missouri Travel Council
204 East High Street
Jefferson City, MO 65101-3287   Phone: (573) 636-2814
Summary: To provide financial assistance to Missouri residents pursuing a hospitality-related major at a college or university in the state.
Eligibility: This program is open to residents of Missouri currently enrolled as a sophomore or junior at an accredited college or university in the state. Applicants must be pursuing a major related to hospitality, including hotel and restaurant management, parks and recreation, etc. They must have a grade point average of 3.0 or higher and submit an essay of up to 500 words on the value of Missouri's tourism industry. The essay is judged on originality, clarity, style, and proper English usage. Scholarship winners are selected on the basis of the essay (50 percent), grade point average (20 percent), community involvement (10 percent), academic activities and achievement (10 percent), and hospitality-related experience (10 percent).
Financial data: The stipend is $1,000. Funds are paid directly to recipient's institution.
Duration: 1 year.
Number awarded: 2 each year.
Deadline: September of each year.

2980
MISSOURI TRAVEL COUNCIL SCHOLARSHIP

Missouri Travel Council
204 East High Street
Jefferson City, MO 65101
Phone: (573) 636-2814
Summary: To provide financial assistance to college students in Missouri who are majoring in a hospitality-related field.
Eligibility: This program is open to students currently enrolled as sophomores or juniors at an accredited college or university in Missouri. Applicants must be majoring in a hospitality-related field, such as hotel/restaurant management or parks and recreation. They must be Missouri residents, have at least a 3.0 grade point average, and write an essay (up to 500 words) on a topic related to Missouri's tourism industry.
Financial data: The stipend is $1,000. Funds are paid directly to recipient's school.
Duration: 1 year.
Number awarded: 2 each year.
Deadline: May of each year.

2981
MMTA SCHOLARSHIP FOUNDATION SCHOLARSHIPS

Summary: To provide financial assistance for college to high school seniors in Maine who are interested in pursuing a career in the trucking industry.
See Listing #2295.

2982
MONTANA FUNERAL DIRECTORS ASSOCIATION SCHOLARSHIPS

Montana Funeral Directors Association
P.O. Box 4267
Helena, MT 59604
Phone: (406) 449-7244   Fax: (406) 443-0979
Summary: To provide financial assistance to Montana residents who are interested in studying mortuary science.
Eligibility: This program is open to Montana residents who are beginning or working on a degree in mortuary science. The sole requirement is that the applicant be willing to return to Montana and work in the funeral service profession. In addition, the following information will strengthen an application (but is not required): at least a 3.0 grade point average, support of a funeral home that belongs to the sponsoring association, submission of a transcript of mortuary school grades, and 2 letters of recommendation. Financial need is not considered in the selection process.
Financial data: The stipend is $1,000.
Duration: 1 year.
Number awarded: Up to 2 each year.
Deadline: May of each year.

2983
MONTANA WOMEN IN TRANSITION SCHOLARSHIP

American Society of Women Accountants-Billings Big Sky Chapter
c/o Cathy B. Allen
P.O. Box 23398
Billings, MT 59104-3398
Phone: (406) 245-6933   Fax: (406) 245-6922
E-mail: Cathya@mcn.net
Web Site: www.imt.net/~aswa/index.html
Summary: To provide financial assistance to women in Montana who are single parents pursuing a degree in accounting.
Eligibility: This program is open to women in Montana who are incoming freshmen, currently enrolled, or returning to school with sufficient credits to qualify for freshman status. Applicants must be women who, either through divorce or death of a spouse, have become the sole source of support for themselves and their family and wish to pursue a degree in accounting as a means to gainful employment. Selection is based on commitment to the goal of pursuing a degree in accounting, including evidence of continued commitment after receiving this award; aptitude for accounting and business; clear evidence that the candidate has established goals and a plan for achieving those goals, both personal and professional; and financial need.
Financial data: The stipend is $1,000.
Duration: 1 year.
Additional information: Information is also available from Nancy Gililland, (406) 656-9300, E-mail: mtnancy@juno.com.
Number awarded: 1 each year.
Deadline: March of each year.

2984
MORRIS K. UDALL SCHOLARSHIPS

Summary: To provide financial assistance to 1) college sophomores and juniors who intend to pursue careers in environmental public policy and 2) Native American and Alaska Native students who intend to pursue careers in health care or tribal public policy.
See Listing #2298.

2985
MRCA FOUNDATION SCHOLARSHIP AWARD

Summary: To provide financial assistance to students from midwestern states who are interested in pursuing a career in the construction industry.
See Listing #2301.

2986
MSCPA COLLEGE SCHOLARSHIPS

Missouri Society of Certified Public Accountants
Attn: Educational Foundation
275 North Lindbergh Boulevard, Suite 10
St. Louis, MO 63141-7809
Phone: (314) 997-7966   (800) 264-7966 (within MO)
Fax: (314) 997-2592   E-mail: member@mocpa.org
Web Site: www.mocpa.org/scholarships.html
Summary: To provide financial assistance to accounting majors at colleges and universities in Missouri.
Eligibility: This program is open to residents of Missouri who are studying accounting at colleges and universities in the state. Selection is based on academic achievement, demonstrated leadership potential, and financial need.
Financial data: Stipends range from $500 to $2,000 per year.
Duration: 1 year.
Additional information: Scholarships are offered through the 6 chapters in the state; for a list of the names and addresses of the chapter presidents, contact the sponsor.
Number awarded: Varies each year. Recently, 39 of these scholarships were awarded: 2 at $2,000, 1 at $1,500, 14 at $1,000, and 22 at $500.
Deadline: February of each year.

2987
NAAPAE SCHOLARSHIPS

National Association for Asian and Pacific American Education
P.O. Box 3366
Daley City, CA 94015-3366   E-mail: jlu69@jps.net
Summary: To provide financial assistance to college students who are interested in pursuing a career in Asian and Pacific American (APA) education.
Eligibility: This program is open to high school seniors and college juniors/seniors who 1) are interested in pursuing a career in APA education; 2) have demonstrated concern and commitment to APA communities; 3) have outstanding academic records; and 4) are actively involved in school and/or community activities. Applicants must be U.S. or Canadian citizens or resident aliens. To apply, students must send a letter that contains: a list of high schools and/or colleges attended, expected date of graduation, current citizenship status, contact information for 2 referees, a statement of career goals (up to 50 words), a list of school and/or community activities, and a statement that describes their concern for the APA communities (up to 200 words). Financial need is not considered in the selection process.
Financial data: For high school seniors, the stipend is $500; for college juniors/seniors, the stipend is $1,000.
Duration: 1 year.
Number awarded: 4 awards each year: 2 to high school seniors and 2 to college juniors/seniors.
Deadline: February of each year.

2988
NABA CORPORATE SCHOLARSHIPS

National Association of Black Accountants
Attn: Director, Center for Advancement of Minority Accountants
7249-A Hanover Parkway
Greenbelt, MD 20770
Phone: (301) 474-NABA, ext. 114   Fax: (301) 474-3114
E-mail: cquinn@nabainc.org   Web Site: www.nabainc.org
Summary: To provide financial assistance for undergraduate or graduate studies to members of the National Association of Black Accountants (NABA).
Eligibility: Applicants must be paid members of the association who are full-time students pursuing a bachelor's or master's degree in accounting, finance, business administration, or taxation. Applicants must have a grade point average of at least 3.5 in their major and 3.3 overall. Selection is based on grades, financial need, and a 500-word autobiography that discusses career objectives, leadership abilities, community activities, and involvement in the association.
Financial data: Stipends range from $1,000 to $5,000 per year.
Duration: 1 year.
Number awarded: Varies each year.
Deadline: December of each year.

2989
NABA NATIONAL SCHOLARSHIP

National Association of Black Accountants
Attn: Director, Center for Advancement of Minority Accountants
7249-A Hanover Parkway
Greenbelt, MD 20770
Phone: (301) 474-NABA, ext. 114   Fax: (301) 474-3114
E-mail: cquinn@nabainc.org
Web Site: www.nabainc.org
Summary: To provide financial assistance for undergraduate or graduate education in accounting to members of the National Association of Black Accountants (NABA).
Eligibility: Applicants must be paid members of the association who are full-time students pursuing a bachelor's or master's degree in accounting, finance, business administration, or taxation. Applicants must have a grade point average of at least 3.5 in their major and 3.3 overall. Selection is based on grades, financial need, and a 500-word autobiography that discusses career objectives, leadership abilities, community activities, and involvement in the association.
Financial data: The stipend is $6,000 per year.
Duration: 1 year.
Number awarded: 1 each year.
Deadline: December of each year.

2990
NAIW EDUCATION FOUNDATION COLLEGE SCHOLARSHIPS

National Association of Insurance Women
Attn: NAIW Education Foundation
1847 East 15th Street
P.O. Box 4410
Tulsa, OK 74159-0410
Phone: (918) 744-5195   Fax: (918) 743-1968
E-mail: WebMaster@NAIWFoundation.org
Web Site: www.NAIWFoundation.org
Summary: To provide financial assistance to college students majoring in insurance and risk management.
Eligibility: This program is open to candidates for a bachelor's degree or higher in insurance, risk management, and/or actuarial science. Applicants must 1) be completing or have completed their second year of college; 2) have achieved at least a 3.0 overall grade point average; 3) have successfully completed at least 2 insurance or risk management-related courses; and 4) not be receiving full reimbursement for the cost of tuition, books, or other educational expenses from their employer or any other outside source. Selection is based on academic record and honors, extracurricular and personal activities, work experience, 3 letters of recommendation, and a 500-word essay on career path and goals.
Financial data: Stipends range from $1,000 to $4,000 per year; funds are paid jointly to the institution and to the student.
Duration: 1 year.
Additional information: The National Association of Insurance Women established the NAIW Educational Foundation in 1993. It provides financial assistance to both men and women interested in careers in the insurance industry.
Number awarded: Varies each year; recently, the foundation awarded 9 of these scholarships with a total value of more than $12,000.
Deadline: April of each year.

2991
NATA UNDERGRADUATE SCHOLARSHIPS

Summary: To provide financial aid to undergraduate student members of the National Athletic Trainers' Association (NATA).
See Listing #2313.

2992
NATHAN TAYLOR DODSON SCHOLARSHIP

Summary: To provide financial assistance for college to members of the North Carolina Association of Health, Physical Education, Recreation and Dance (NCAAHPERD).
See Listing #1545.

Scholarship Listings

2993
NATIONAL AMERICANISM ESSAY CONTEST

AMVETS National Headquarters
Attn: Programs Department
4647 Forbes Boulevard
Lanham, MD 20706-4380
Phone: (301) 459-9600   Fax: (301) 459-7924
E-mail: amvets@amvets.org
Web Site: www.amvets.org
Summary: To recognize and reward the best patriotic essays written by high school students.
Eligibility: This program is open to students in grades 6, 9, 11, and 12 at public or private (including parochial) high schools in the United States. Applicants are required to write an essay on a topic that changes annually (recently: "Why is it important to vote?"). Essays by students in grade 6 should be less than 250 words, in grade 9 less than 350 words, and in grades 11 and 12 less than 500 words. The best entries are submitted by the applicants' teachers to department (state) competitions; first-place winners from each department are entered in the national competition.
Financial data: For students in grades 6, 11, and 12, first place is a $1,000 savings bond, second place a $750 savings bond, and third place a $500 savings bond. All winners from grade 9 receive an all-expense paid trip to the Freedoms Foundation at Valley Forge, Pennsylvania for a weekend of youth-oriented activities.
Duration: The competition is held annually.
Number awarded: Prizes are awarded to 9 students: 3 each in grades 6, 11, and 12.
Deadline: June of each year.

2994
NATIONAL ASSOCIATION OF HEALTH SERVICES EXECUTIVES SCHOLARSHIP PROGRAM

Summary: To provide financial assistance to African Americans who are members of the National Association of Health Services Executives (NAHSE) and interested in preparing for a career in health care administration.
See Listing #2316.

2995
NATIONAL ASSOCIATION OF WOMEN IN CONSTRUCTION UNDERGRADUATE SCHOLARSHIPS

Summary: To provide financial assistance to students pursuing study in a construction-related degree program.
See Listing #2318.

2996
NATIONAL BLACK MBA ASSOCIATION UNDERGRADUATE SCHOLARSHIP PROGRAM

National Black MBA Association
180 North Michigan Avenue, Suite 1400
Chicago, IL 60601
Phone: (312) 236-2622, ext. 6-8086   Fax: (312) 236-4131
E-mail: lori@nbmbaa.org
Web Site: www.nbmbaa.org
Summary: To provide financial assistance to African American students interested in pursuing an undergraduate business degree.
Eligibility: This program is open to African American students who wish to pursue an undergraduate degree in a field related to business. Applicants must submit a completed application, high school or undergraduate transcripts, and an essay on a topic that changes annually. Selection is based on grade point average, extracurricular activities, and quality of the essay.
Financial data: The stipend is $1,000.
Duration: 1 year.
Additional information: This program is funded by the national office of the National Black MBA Association (NBMBAA), which develops the application and selects the essay topics. It is administered by local chapters, which select the winners. Applications must be submitted to local chapters; for the name and address of a contact person at each chapter, write to the association. Recipients must attend college on a full-time basis.
Number awarded: Each year, each NBMBAA chapter selects 1 recipient. Currently, there are 31 chapters in the United States.
Deadline: Each chapter determines its deadline date; most are in the spring.

2997
NATIONAL DAIRY SHRINE/DMI MILK MARKETING SCHOLARSHIPS

Summary: To provide financial assistance to college students enrolled in a dairy science program and to encourage them to pursue careers in the marketing of dairy products.
See Listing #2321.

2998
NATIONAL ESSAY CONTEST ON KOREA

Korean Cultural Service
c/o Embassy of Korea
2370 Massachusetts Avenue, N.W.
Washington, DC 20008
Phone: (202) 797-6343   Fax: (202) 387-0413
E-mail: essay@koreaemb.org   Web Site: www.essayonkorea.org
Summary: To recognize and reward outstanding essays by high school students on a topic related to Korea.
Eligibility: All high school students (grades 9 through 12) in the United States may enter this competition. They are invited to write an essay, 3 to 6 pages, on topics that change annually but relate to Korea; recently, students were invited to write on their choice of 4 topics on the theme of U.S.-Korea Relations in the New Millenium. Essays must be written in English; they may be fiction or nonfiction but must be original. Selection is based on originality, creativity, clarity, style, and evidence of a serious research effort.
Financial data: The grand prize is a 1-week all-expense paid trip to Korea for 2 (the student and a parent) and a $2,500 cash award; first prize is a 1-week all-expense paid trip to Korea for 2 (the student and a parent) and a $1,500 cash award; second prize is a $1,000 cash award; third prize is a $750 cash award. Each of the winner's schools receives a $1,000 contribution to a project of the principal.
Duration: The competition is held annually.
Additional information: This competition began in 1991.
Number awarded: 8 each year: 1 grand prize, 1 first prize, 3 second prizes, 3 third prizes.
Deadline: February of each year.

2999
NATIONAL FFA SCHOLARSHIPS FOR UNDERGRADUATES IN THE SOCIAL SCIENCES

National FFA Organization
Attn: Scholarship Office
6060 FFA Drive
P.O. Box 68960
Indianapolis, IN 46268-0960
Phone: (317) 802-4321   Fax: (317) 802-5321
E-mail: aboutffa@ffa.org   Web Site: www.ffa.org
Summary: To provide financial assistance to FFA members who wish to study agribusiness and related fields in college.
Eligibility: This program is open to current and former members of the organization who are pursuing a degree in fields related to business and the social sciences; this includes: agribusiness, agricultural economics, agricultural education, agricultural finance, and agricultural marketing. For some of the scholarships, applicants must be high school seniors; others are open to students currently enrolled in college. The program includes a large number of designated scholarships that specify the locations where the members must live, the schools they must attend, the fields of study they must pursue, or other requirements. Some consider family income in the selection process, but most do not.
Financial data: Stipends vary, but most are at least $1,000.
Duration: 1 year or more.
Additional information: Funding for these scholarships is provided by many different corporate sponsors.
Number awarded: Varies; generally, a total of approximately 1,000 scholarships are awarded annually by the association.
Deadline: February of each year.

3000
NATIONAL FUNERAL DIRECTORS & MORTICIANS ASSOCIATION SCHOLARSHIPS

National Funeral Directors & Morticians Association
3951 Snapfinger Parkway, Suite 570
Decatur, GA 30035
Phone: (404) 286-6680   Fax: (404) 286-6573
E-mail: nfdma@mindspring.com   Web Site: www.nfdma.com
Summary: To provide financial assistance to high school graduates interested in preparing for a career in mortuary science.
Eligibility: Eligible to apply for this program are high school graduates who, preferably, have worked in or had 1 year of apprenticeship. They may have completed some college courses (basic courses in chemistry and biology are helpful) and must be interested in preparing for a career in mortuary science. As part of the application, they must submit a completed application form, 2 letters of recommendation, a resume, a personal statement of why they are applying for the scholarship, and a copy of their high school and/or college transcripts. Selection is based on academic record, character, leadership ability, and financial need.
Financial data: The amount awarded varies.
Duration: 1 year.
Deadline: February of each year.

3001
NATIONAL ITALIAN AMERICAN FOUNDATION GENERAL CATEGORY II SCHOLARSHIPS

Summary: To provide financial assistance for college to students interested in majoring in Italian language, Italian studies, or Italian American studies.
See Listing #1553.

3002
NATIONAL PATHFINDER SCHOLARSHIP

Summary: To provide financial assistance to college women who are currently studying in fields related to substance abuse prevention.
See Listing #2326.

3003
NATIONAL PEACE ESSAY CONTEST

United States Institute of Peace
Attn: National Peace Essay Contest Project Officer
1200 17th Street, N.W., Suite 200
Washington, DC 20036-3011
Phone: (202) 429-3854   Fax: (202) 429-6063
Phone: TDD: (202) 457-1719   E-mail: essay_contest@usip.org
Web Site: www.usip.org/ed.html
Summary: To recognize and reward winners of the National Peace Essay Contest.
Eligibility: Eligible are students working toward a high school degree in a public, private, or parochial high school in grades 9 through 12 in the United States or its territories. U.S. citizens studying in other countries are also eligible. Contestants prepare a 1,500-word essay on topics that change each year; a recent topic related to the U.S. military's role in international peacekeeping. Judging of essays is based on quality of the research (one third), quality of the analysis (one third), and style and mechanics (one third).
Financial data: Each state-level winner receives a $1,000 scholarship. National-level scholarships are $10,000 for first place, $5,000 for second place, and $2,500 for third place.
Duration: The competition is held annually.
Additional information: First-place winners in each state advance to the national competition and also receive an all-expense paid trip to Washington, D.C. that includes visits with various government officials.
Number awarded: Each year, 1 winner in each state and 3 national winners receive scholarships.
Deadline: January of each year.

3004
NATIONAL RESTAURANT ASSOCIATION ACADEMIC SCHOLARSHIPS FOR UNDERGRADUATE COLLEGE STUDENTS

National Restaurant Association Educational Foundation
Attn: Scholarship Department
250 South Wacker Drive, Suite 1400
Chicago, IL 60606-5834
Phone: (312) 715-1010, ext. 733   (800) 765-2122, ext. 733
Fax: (312) 715-0807   E-mail: scholars@foodtrain.org
Web Site: www.edfound.org
Summary: To provide financial assistance to undergraduate students who are interested in preparing for a career in the hospitality industry.
Eligibility: This program is open to full-time college students who have completed the first semester of a certificate, associate, or bachelor's degree program in food service or hospitality with a grade point average of 2.75 or higher. Applicants must have 750 hours of work experience in the restaurant and hospitality industry.
Financial data: The stipend is $2,000 per year.
Duration: 1 year.
Number awarded: Approximately 200 each year.
Deadline: May or November of each year.

3005
NATIONAL RESTAURANT ASSOCIATION UNDERGRADUATE ACADEMIC SCHOLARSHIPS FOR HIGH SCHOOL STUDENTS

National Restaurant Association Educational Foundation
Attn: Scholarship Department
250 South Wacker Drive, Suite 1400
Chicago, IL 60606-5834
Phone: (312) 715-1010, ext. 733   (800) 765-2122, ext. 733
Fax: (312) 715-0807   E-mail: scholars@foodtrain.org
Web Site: www.edfound.org
Summary: To provide financial assistance to high school seniors who are interested in preparing for a career in the hospitality industry.
Eligibility: This program is open to high school seniors who have been accepted to a hospitality-related postsecondary program, either full time or substantial part time. Applicants must have a grade point average of 2.75 or better in high school and at least 250 hours of restaurant and hospitality work experience.
Financial data: The stipend is $2,000 per year.
Duration: 1 year.
Number awarded: Approximately 150 each year.
Deadline: April of each year.

3006
NATIONAL SHERIFFS' ASSOCIATION SCHOLARSHIP

National Sheriffs' Association
Attn: Scholarship Application
1450 Duke Street
Alexandria, VA 22314-3490
Phone: (703) 836-7827   Fax: (703) 683-6541
E-mail: nsamail@sheriffs.org   Web Site: www.sheriffs.org
Summary: To provide financial assistance to sheriff office employees (or the dependents of those employees) who are interested in majoring in criminal justice in college.
Eligibility: Eligible to apply for these scholarships are undergraduate students who are currently enrolled in a 2- or 4-year college and majoring in criminal justice. They must be either 1) an employee of a sheriff's office or 2) the son or daughter of an individual employed by a sheriff's office. Previous scholarship winners are not eligible to reapply. Applicants should submit an official application form, a transcript, 2 letters of recommendation, an endorsement statement from a sheriff in their county, and an essay (at least 150 words) on why they intend to pursue a career in law enforcement. Financial need is considered in the selection process.
Financial data: The stipend is $1,000.
Duration: 1 year; nonrenewable.
Number awarded: Varies; generally, at least 6 each year.
Deadline: February of each year.

3007
NATIONAL TOUR ASSOCIATION AWARD

National Tourism Foundation
Attn: Scholarships
546 East Main Street
Lexington, KY 40508-2342
Phone: (859) 226-4444   (800) 682-8886
Fax: (859) 226-4437   E-mail: ntf@ntastaff.com
Web Site: www.ntfonline.org
Summary: To provide financial assistance to travel and tourism professionals interested in continuing their education.
Eligibility: This program is open to working travel and tourism professionals in

the process of continuing their education at a college, university, or certification program. Applicants must submit 2 letters of recommendation, a resume, college transcript, a 500-word essay explaining why they want to continue their education in the travel and tourism industry, and documentation of out-of-pocket expenses incurred to pursue continuing education.
Financial data: The stipend is $1,000.
Duration: 1 year.
Additional information: Award winners also receive complimentary registration and an all-expense paid trip (valued at more than $3,000) to the association's annual convention, as well as a 1-year subscription to *Courier* magazine, *Tuesday* newsletter, and *NTF Headlines* newsletter. This program was first offered in 2000. In any 1 year, applicants may receive only 1 award from the association.
Number awarded: 1 each year.
Deadline: April of each year.

3008
NATIVE SONS OF THE GOLDEN WEST HIGH SCHOOL PUBLIC SPEAKING CONTEST

Summary: To recognize and reward outstanding high school orators in California.
See Listing #1563.

3009
NAVAJO NATION TEACHER EDUCATION PROGRAM

Navajo Nation
Office of Navajo Nation Scholarship and Financial Assistance
Attn: Navajo Nation Teacher Education Program
P.O. Box 4380
Window Rock, AZ 86515-4380
Phone: (520) 871-7453   (800) 243-2956
Fax: (520) 871-6443   E-mail: onnsfacentral@navajo.org
Web Site: www.onnsfa.navajo.org
Summary: To provide financial assistance to members of the Navajo Nation who wish to pursue a career as a bilingual or bicultural teacher.
Eligibility: This program is open to enrolled members of the Navajo Nation who are enrolled in or planning to enroll in an undergraduate teacher education program, a post-baccalaureate program for teacher licensure, or a master's degree program in education. Applicants must complete an emphasis in either Navajo Language or Navajo Culture, taken concurrently each semester with teacher education courses. Students pursuing a second master's degree are not eligible.
Financial data: Recipients are reimbursed for each course they complete at the rate of $250 per course for lower-division undergraduate courses or $500 for upper-division undergraduate and graduate courses.
Duration: 1 semester; may be renewed for undergraduate courses completed with a grade of "C" or better and for graduate courses completed with a grade of "B" or better.
Number awarded: Varies each year; recently, 250 undergraduates and 225 graduate students were participating in the program.

3010
NCCA SCHOLARSHIPS

Summary: To provide financial assistance to residents of the Washington (D.C.) Metropolitan area who are studying culinary arts.
See Listing #1564.

3011
NCFC EDUCATION FOUNDATION UNDERGRADUATE SCHOLARSHIPS

Summary: To provide financial assistance to college students who have expressed an interest in agricultural cooperatives.
See Listing #2340.

3012
NDTA MERIT SCHOLARSHIP PROGRAM B

National Defense Transportation Association
Attn: Forum, Education and Professional Development Committee
50 South Pickett Street, Suite 220
Alexandria, VA 22304-7296
Phone: (703) 751-5011   Fax: (703) 823-8761
Web Site: www.ndtahq.com/program_b.htm
Summary: To provide financial assistance to high school seniors who are members or dependents of members of the National Defense Transportation Association (NDTA) and planning to study business in college.
Eligibility: This program is open to NDTA members and dependents of members who have satisfactorily completed 3 1/2 years of academic work at an accredited high school. Community colleges which applicants plan to attend must offer a 4-year college transfer program. For applicants who plan to attend a 4-year college or university, the institution must offer courses that lead to a baccalaureate degree in business. Applicants must 1) include high school transcripts; 2) attach a listing of academic and other honors and awards received, extracurricular activities, and work experiences; and 3) submit a 300- to 500-word statement outlining their career goals and methods of attaining those goals, indicating why they should be awarded the scholarship. Financial need is not considered in the selection process.
Financial data: A stipend is awarded (exact amount not specified).
Duration: 1 year; may be renewed.
Number awarded: 1 or more each year.
Deadline: April of each year.

3013
NDTA SCOTT-ST. LOUIS SCHOLASTIC AWARDS

Summary: To provide financial assistance for college to students from designated midwestern states interested in pursuing a career in business, transportation, logistics, or physical distribution.
See Listing #2344.

3014
NEBRASKA EDUCATIONAL OFFICE PROFESSIONALS ASSOCIATION STUDENT SCHOLARSHIP

Nebraska Educational Office Professionals Association
c/o Dianne Dickey, Scholarship Director
Lincoln Public Schools District Offices, Box 59
5901 "O" Street
Lincoln, NE 68510   Web Site: neopa.unl.edu
Summary: To provide financial assistance to residents of Nebraska who are interested in preparing for an office-related career.
Eligibility: This program is open to residents of Nebraska who are graduating high school seniors or students currently enrolled in a postsecondary educational institution. Applicants must have completed 2 or more business education courses from among the following: computer classes, keyboarding, typing, shorthand, accounting, office practices and procedures, and/or bookkeeping. They must submit a 1-page essay on why they are choosing an office-related career or vocation, 3 letters of recommendation, and high school or college transcripts. Selection is based on academic achievement, initiative of the student, and financial need.
Financial data: The stipend is $1,000.
Duration: 1 year.
Number awarded: 1 each year.
Deadline: December of each year.

3015
NEBRASKA FUNERAL DIRECTORS ASSOCIATION SCHOLARSHIP

Nebraska Funeral Directors Association
P.O. Box 2118
Hastings, NE 68902-2118   Phone: (402) 462-8900
Summary: To provide financial assistance to residents of Nebraska who are interested in preparing for a career in funeral service.
Eligibility: Eligible to apply for this support are graduates of Nebraska high schools who meet all of the state's premortuary school educational requirements. Applicants must be recommended by a member of the Nebraska Funeral Directors Association.
Financial data: The stipend is at least $1,000.
Duration: 1 year.
Number awarded: 1 or more each year.

3016

NEBRASKA RURAL COMMUNITY SCHOOLS ASSOCIATION SCHOLARSHIP

Lincoln Community Foundation
215 Centennial Mall South, Suite 200
Lincoln, NE 68508
Phone: (402) 474-2345   Fax: (402) 476-8532
E-mail: lcf@lcf.org   Web Site: www.lcf.org
Summary: To provide financial assistance for college study of education to students at high schools that are members of the Nebraska Rural Community Schools Association (NRCSA).
Eligibility: Eligible to apply for this college aid are graduating seniors at schools holding current membership in NRCSA. Applicants must be interested in majoring in education in college. Selection is based on academic achievement, leadership, character and initiative, involvement in extracurricular activities, and financial need.
Financial data: A stipend is awarded (exact amount not specified).
Duration: 1 year; may be renewed.
Additional information: Information is also available from the NRCSA Scholarship Selection Committee, Broken Bow Schools, 323 North Seventh Avenue, Broken Bow, NE 68822.
Number awarded: 1 or more each year.
Deadline: February of each year.

3017

NELL BRYANT ROBINSON SCHOLARSHIP

Summary: To provide financial assistance to undergraduate student members of Phi Upsilon Omicron, a national honor society in family and consumer sciences.
See Listing #2346.

3018

NEW ENGLAND EMPLOYEE BENEFITS COUNCIL SCHOLARSHIP

New England Employee Benefits Council
440 Totten Pond Road
Waltham, MA 02451
Phone: (781) 684-8700   Fax: (781) 684-9200
Summary: To provide financial assistance to undergraduate or graduate students from or in New England who are interested in a career in the employee benefits field.
Eligibility: Eligible to apply for this assistance are either 1) New England residents attending school in any state or 2) students from any state attending school in New England. Applicants may be either undergraduate or graduate students, but they must be attending school on a full-time basis. They must intend to pursue a career in the employee benefits field. Active board members of the council, along with their children and spouses, are not eligible for this scholarship. Selection is based on academic performance, future potential, work experience, school and community activities, and specific benefit-related study, activities, and goals.
Financial data: Up to $5,000 each year.
Duration: 1 year; may be renewed until completion of a degree, up to a maximum of 4 years.
Number awarded: 2 each year.
Deadline: March of each year.

3019

NEW ENGLAND WATER WORKS ASSOCIATION SCHOLARSHIP

Summary: To provide financial assistance to undergraduate or graduate students from New England, particularly those who are working on a degree in an area of benefit to water works practice in New England.
See Listing #2351.

3020

NEW HAMPSHIRE MGMA SCHOLARSHIPS

Summary: To provide financial assistance to members of the Medical Group Management Association (MGMA) in New Hampshire who are interested in pursuing undergraduate or graduate education, continuing education, or applied research.
See Listing #2352.

3021

NEW HAMPSHIRE SOCIETY OF CERTIFIED PUBLIC ACCOUNTANTS SCHOLARSHIP PROGRAM

New Hampshire Society of Certified Public Accountants
Attn: Financial Careers Committee
1750 Elm Street, Suite 403
Manchester, NH 03104
Phone: (603) 622-1999   Fax: (603) 626-0204
E-mail: info@nhscpa.org   Web Site: www.nhscpa.org
Summary: To provide financial assistance to undergraduate and graduate students in New Hampshire who are preparing for a career as a certified public accountant.
Eligibility: Applicants must be 1) full-time students entering their junior or senior year in an accounting or business program at an accredited 4-year college or university or 2) full-time graduate students in an accredited master's degree program in accounting. New Hampshire residency is required. A recommendation or appraisal from the person in charge of the applicant's accounting program must be included in the application package. Selection is based on academic record, not financial need, although if academic measures between 2 or more students are the same, financial need may be considered secondarily.
Financial data: A stipend is awarded (exact amount not specified).
Duration: 1 year.
Number awarded: 2 or more each year.
Deadline: October of each year.

3022

NEW JERSEY FUNERAL DIRECTORS ASSOCIATION SCHOLARSHIP

New Jersey Funeral Directors Association
P.O. Box L
Manasquan, NJ 08736
Summary: To provide financial assistance to New Jersey residents who are currently enrolled in a mortuary science program.
Eligibility: This program is open to New Jersey residents who are currently enrolled in a mortuary science program. To apply, students must submit a completed application, an official transcript, letters of recommendation, and a written essay. A personal interview may be required. Selection is based on academic record, commitment to funeral service as a career, and (to a lesser extent) financial need.
Financial data: The stipend is $1,000.
Duration: 1 year.
Number awarded: 2 each year.
Deadline: June of each year.

3023

NEW JERSEY FUNERAL SERVICE EDUCATION CORPORATION SCHOLARSHIP

New Jersey Funeral Service Education Corporation
Attn: Scholarship Program
P.O. Box L
Manasquan, NJ 08736   Phone: (732) 974-9444
Summary: To provide financial assistance to New Jersey residents who are preparing for a career in mortuary science.
Eligibility: Applicants must be New Jersey residents who are planning to enter the field of funeral service in New Jersey upon completion of their professional education. They must be registered in or currently attending a mortuary science program (preparatory programs are not eligible) and have at least a 2.5 grade point average. An interview is required. Selection is based on academic performance and a commitment to funeral service rather than financial need.
Financial data: The stipend is $2,000 per year.
Duration: 1 year.
Number awarded: 4 each year.
Deadline: June of each year.

3024

NEW JERSEY SOCIETY OF CERTIFIED PUBLIC ACCOUNTANTS ACCOUNTING MANUSCRIPT CONTEST

New Jersey Society of Certified Public Accountants
Attn: Student Affairs Coordinator
425 Eagle Rock Avenue
Roseland, NJ 07068-1723
Phone: (973) 226-4494, ext. 209   Fax: (973) 226-7425

E-mail: njscpa@njscpa.org   Web Site: www.njscpa.org

Summary: To recognize and reward outstanding manuscripts on accounting written by college students in New Jersey.

Eligibility: The contest is open to sophomores, juniors, and seniors who are attending 2-year or 4-year colleges or universities in New Jersey and majoring in accounting. They are invited to submit a manuscript on accounting (up to 1,000 words). All submissions must be original work that has not been previously published. Students must select a faculty member to serve as a mentor in the development of the article. No co-authored manuscripts are accepted. Manuscripts are judged on the basis of content, creativity, clarity, ability to communicate effectively the relevance of accounting principles or practices, and ability to communicate information that is relevant to New Jersey businesses.

Financial data: First place is a $3,000 scholarship; honorable mentions are $1,000.

Duration: The competition is held annually.

Additional information: The winning manuscript is published in *New Jersey Business* magazine, which is also the co-sponsor of this award. The topic changes annually; recently it was "The Effect of Technology and its Impact on the CPA Profession."

Number awarded: Up to 4 each year: 1 first prize and up to 3 honorable mentions.

Deadline: January of each year.

3025
NEW JERSEY SOCIETY OF CERTIFIED PUBLIC ACCOUNTANTS COLLEGE SCHOLARSHIP PROGRAM

New Jersey Society of Certified Public Accountants
Attn: Student Affairs Coordinator
425 Eagle Rock Avenue
Roseland, NJ 07068-1723
Phone: (973) 226-4494, ext. 209   Fax: (973) 226-7425
E-mail: njscpa@njscpa.org   Web Site: www.njscpa.org

Summary: To provide financial assistance to college students in New Jersey who are preparing for a career as a certified public accountant.

Eligibility: This program is open to juniors at 4-year colleges in New Jersey who are entering their senior year and majoring in accounting. Students may not apply directly; they must be nominated by the accounting department chair at their college. Nominees must be New Jersey residents. Selection is based on academic achievement.

Financial data: A stipend is provided (exact amount not specified).

Duration: 1 year.

Additional information: Interested students should check with their accounting department chair to learn if their school participates.

Number awarded: Several each year.

Deadline: October of each year.

3026
NEW JERSEY SOCIETY OF CERTIFIED PUBLIC ACCOUNTANTS HIGH SCHOOL SCHOLARSHIP PROGRAM

New Jersey Society of Certified Public Accountants
Attn: Student Affairs Coordinator
425 Eagle Rock Avenue
Roseland, NJ 07068-1723
Phone: (973) 226-4494, ext. 209   Fax: (973) 226-7425
E-mail: njscpa@njscpa.org   Web Site: www.njscpa.org

Summary: To provide financial assistance to seniors in New Jersey high schools who are interested in preparing for a career as a certified public accountant.

Eligibility: This program is open to all New Jersey high school seniors who are planning to major in accounting in college. Applications for a 1-hour accounting aptitude exam are mailed to New Jersey high school guidance and business departments each September. The exam is given in November and the highest scorers receive accounting scholarships to the college of their choice.

Financial data: The stipends for 5 years range from $3,000 to $5,000.

Duration: Up to 5 years.

Additional information: This program has been offered since 1960.

Number awarded: Several each year.

Deadline: October of each year.

3027
NEW JERSEY TOURISM I SCHOLARSHIP

National Tourism Foundation
Attn: Scholarships
546 East Main Street
Lexington, KY 40508-2342
Phone: (859) 226-4444   (800) 682-8886

Fax: (859) 226-4437   E-mail: ntf@ntastaff.com
Web Site: www.ntfonline.org

Summary: To provide financial assistance to college students in New Jersey who are majoring in tourism.

Eligibility: This program is open to full-time students enrolled in a 4-year college or university in New Jersey. Applicants must be New Jersey residents, be in their junior or senior year, have at least a 3.0 grade point average, and be majoring in a travel or tourism-related field (e.g., hotel management, restaurant management, tourism).

Financial data: The stipend is $1,000.

Duration: 1 year.

Additional information: Award winners also receive complimentary registration and an all-expense paid trip (valued at more than $3,000) to the association's annual convention, as well as a 1-year subscription to *Courier* magazine, *Tuesday* newsletter, and *NTF Headlines* newsletter. In any 1 year, applicants may receive only 1 award from the association.

Number awarded: 1 each year.

Deadline: April of each year.

3028
NEW JERSEY TOURISM II SCHOLARSHIP

National Tourism Foundation
Attn: Scholarships
546 East Main Street
Lexington, KY 40508-2342
Phone: (859) 226-4444   (800) 682-8886
Fax: (859) 226-4437   E-mail: ntf@ntastaff.com
Web Site: www.ntfonline.org

Summary: To provide financial assistance to college students in New Jersey who are majoring in tourism.

Eligibility: This program is open to full-time students enrolled in a 2-year college in New Jersey. Applicants must be New Jersey residents, have at least a 3.0 grade point average, and be majoring in a travel or tourism-related field (e.g., hotel management, restaurant management, tourism).

Financial data: The stipend is $1,000.

Duration: 1 year.

Additional information: Award winners also receive complimentary registration and an all-expense paid trip (valued at more than $3,000) to the association's annual convention, as well as a 1-year subscription to *Courier* magazine, *Tuesday* newsletter, and *NTF Headlines* newsletter. In any 1 year, applicants may receive only 1 award from the association.

Number awarded: 1 each year.

Deadline: April of each year.

3029
NEW JERSEY UTILITIES ASSOCIATION SCHOLARSHIPS

Summary: To provide financial assistance to minority, female, and disabled high school seniors in New Jersey interested in majoring in selected subjects in college. *See Listing #2354.*

3030
NEW MEXICO LIBRARY ASSOCIATION COLLEGE SCHOLARSHIP FUND

New Mexico Library Association
P.O. Box 26074
Albuquerque, NM 87125
Web Site: lib.nmsu.edu/nmla/scholarships.html

Summary: To provide financial assistance to students in New Mexico who are interested in working on an undergraduate or graduate degree in library science.

Eligibility: Applicants must be New Mexico residents, interested in preparing for a career in librarianship, and accepted or currently enrolled in either 1) an undergraduate college program culminating in an associate's degree in library science or 2) an undergraduate or graduate program leading to school librarian certification. Selection is based on academic record and potential contribution to librarianship, particularly in New Mexico. Preference is given to those currently employed in a New Mexico library and to members of the New Mexico Library Association.

Financial data: The stipend is $500 per semester.

Duration: 1 semester. Candidates may reapply once, for a total of $1,000 in scholarship funds.

Additional information: Information is also available from the Education Committee Co-Chair, Cindy Watkins, New Mexico State University, University

Library, MSC 3475, P.O. Box 30006, Las Cruces, NM 88003-8006, (505) 646-7676, Fax: (505) 646-2288, E-mail: cwatkins@lib.nmsu.edu.
Number awarded: 1 each semester
Deadline: January of each year for the summer and fall terms; September of each year for the spring term.

3031
NEW YORK LEGION AUXILIARY MEDICAL AND TEACHING SCHOLARSHIPS

Summary: To provide financial assistance to children or grandchildren of veterans who are interested in pursuing a career in the medical or teaching field in New York.
See Listing #2355.

3032
NIB GRANT M. MACK MEMORIAL SCHOLARSHIP

American Council of the Blind
Attn: Coordinator, Scholarship Program
1155 15th Street, N.W., Suite 1004
Washington, DC 20005
Phone: (202) 467-5081　　　　　　　　(800) 424-8666
Fax: (202) 467-5085　　　　　　　　E-mail: info@acb.org
Web Site: www.acb.org
Summary: To provide financial assistance to students who are blind and majoring in business or management.
Eligibility: All legally blind persons who are majoring in business or management (undergraduate or graduate) and are U.S. citizens or resident aliens are eligible to apply. In addition to letters of recommendation and copies of academic transcripts, applications must include an autobiographical sketch. Selection is based on demonstrated academic record, involvement in extracurricular and civic activities, and academic objectives. The severity of the applicant's visual impairment and his/her study methods are also taken into account.
Financial data: The stipend is $2,000. In addition, the winner receives a $1,000 cash scholarship from the Kurzweil Foundation and, if appropriate, a Kurzweil 1000 Reading System.
Duration: 1 year.
Additional information: This scholarship is sponsored by National Industries for the Blind (NIB) in honor of a dedicated leader of the American Council of the Blind. Scholarship winners are expected to be present at the council's annual conference; the council will cover all reasonable expenses connected with convention attendance.
Number awarded: 1 each year.
Deadline: February of each year.

3033
NORTH AMERICAN COLLEGIATE ENTREPRENEUR AWARDS

St. Louis University
Attn: Jefferson Smurfit Center for Entrepreneurial Studies
3674 Lindell Boulevard
St. Louis, MO 63108
Phone: (314) 977-3850　　　　　　　　Fax: (314) 977-3627
E-mail: jsces@slu.edu　　　　　　　　Web Site: nace.slu.edu
Summary: To recognize and reward undergraduate students at North American universities who demonstrate exceptional entrepreneurial skill and creativity while enrolled in college.
Eligibility: This program is open to undergraduate students at universities in Canada, Mexico, and the United States who completed at least 12 credit hours during the previous year. Candidates must be nominated by a member of the faculty or staff. Nominees must have carried on business activity simultaneously with school enrollment. They must 1) describe their current and projected strategies to reach their target markets; 2) comment on their company's current and future impact on local employment opportunities and economic growth, innovations, and charitable outreach; 3) review business operations based on obstacles overcome, concern for customer service, and concern for quality of product or service; and 4) predict where their company should be in 2 to 3 years.
Financial data: First prize for the North American winner is $10,000. The faculty nominator receives $1,000. Additional cash prizes are awarded for exceptional innovation and social impact.
Duration: The prizes are awarded annually.
Additional information: This program began in 1988.
Number awarded: 1 each year.
Deadline: March of each year.

3034
NORTH CAROLINA SHERIFFS' ASSOCIATION UNDERGRADUATE CRIMINAL JUSTICE SCHOLARSHIPS

North Carolina State Education Assistance Authority
Attn: Scholarship and Grant Services
P.O. Box 14103
Research Triangle Park, NC 27709-4103
Phone: (919) 549-8614　　　　　　　　Fax: (919) 549-8481
Web Site: www.ncseaa.edu
Summary: To provide financial assistance for college to children of deceased or disabled North Carolina law enforcement officers who are pursuing careers in criminal justice.
Eligibility: Eligible for this program are North Carolina residents studying criminal justice at any of the 10 state institutions offering that major: Appalachian State University, East Carolina University, Elizabeth City State University, Fayetteville State University, North Carolina Central University, North Carolina State University, the University of North Carolina at Pembroke, the University of North Carolina at Charlotte, the University of North Carolina at Wilmington, and Western Carolina University. First priority in selection is given to children of law enforcement officers killed in the line of duty; second priority is given to children of sheriffs or deputy sheriffs who are deceased, retired (regular or disability), or currently active in law enforcement in North Carolina; third priority is given to other resident criminal justice students meeting their institution's academic and financial need criteria.
Financial data: The stipend is $2,000 per year.
Duration: 1 year; nonrenewable.
Additional information: Funding for this program is provided by the North Carolina Sheriffs' Association. Recipients are selected by the financial aid office at the university they plan to attend or are currently attending; after selection, students obtain a letter of endorsement from the sheriff of the county in North Carolina where they reside.
Number awarded: Varies each year: recently, 8 of these scholarships were awarded.

3035
NORTH DAKOTA TEACHER RETRAINING SCHOLARSHIPS

North Dakota University System
Attn: Director of Financial Aid
State Capitol, Tenth Floor
600 East Boulevard Avenue, Department 215
Bismarck, ND 58505-0230
Phone: (701) 328-4114　　　　　　　　Fax: (701) 328-2961
E-mail: peggy_wipf@ndus.nodak.edu
Web Site: www.ndus.nodak.edu
Summary: To provide financial assistance to teachers in North Dakota who hold an interim emergency license but are interested in pursuing additional training in order to qualify for full teaching licensure.
Eligibility: This program is open to elementary and secondary interim emergency license holders in North Dakota who wish to complete an approved Education Standards and Practices Board (ESPB) plan of study to qualify for full teaching licensure. Applicants must be taking course work at a public college or university in North Dakota. If funding is inadequate to support all qualified applicants, awards are granted in chronological order by the date the application is received.
Financial data: Recipients are eligible to receive reimbursement of tuition and mandatory fees. If they enroll full time (12 or more undergraduate credits per term or 9 or more graduate credits per term), they may also receive an additional stipend of $2,000 per term.
Duration: Participants must apply or reapply every term for new or continued funding. The additional stipend for full-time students is available only for 2 terms.
Additional information: This program began operating in 2002.
Number awarded: Varies each year.
Deadline: September of each year for fall term; January of each year for spring term; June of each year for summer term.

3036
NORTH POLE CHAPTER SCHOLARSHIPS

Summary: To provide financial assistance to residents of Alaska interested in a career in transportation.
See Listing #2371.

3037
NORTHWEST CHAPTER ACCOUNTING SCHOLARSHIP

Washington Society of Certified Public Accountants
Attn: Scholarship Committee
902 140th Avenue N.E.
Bellevue, WA 98005-3480
Phone: (425) 644-4800   (800) 272-8273 (within WA)
Fax: (425) 562-8853   E-mail: memberservices@wscpa.org
Web Site: www.wscpa.org
Summary: To provide financial assistance to students in Washington who are majoring in accounting.
Eligibility: This program is open to accounting students who have completed at least 2 quarters of accounting at the time of application and who plan to complete an accounting degree program in Washington with the intention of becoming a CPA. They must plan to attend an accredited 2-year or 4-year institution in Washington state. U.S. citizenship is required. Selection is based on academic achievement, campus or other activities, preparation for an accounting career as a CPA, work history, and professional potential.
Financial data: The amount of the award depends on the size of the qualified applicant pool.
Duration: 1 year.
Additional information: This program is sponsored by the Northwest Chapter of the Washington Society of CPAs. Information is also available from Sue Waltner, Fiducial Fohn Spink, 1016 South Third Street, Mount Vernon, WA 98273.
Number awarded: 1 or more each year.
Deadline: April of each year.

3038
NORTHWEST WOMEN IN EDUCATIONAL ADMINISTRATION SCHOLARSHIP

Confederation of Oregon School Administrators
Attn: COSA Foundation
707 13th Street, S.E., Suite 100
Salem, OR 97301-4035
Phone: (503) 581-3141   Fax: (503) 581-9840
E-mail: nancy@oasc.org
Web Site: www.cosa.k12.or.us
Summary: To provide financial assistance to women who are high school seniors in Oregon and interested in studying education at a community college, college, or university in the state.
Eligibility: This program is open to women who are graduating from high school in Oregon. Applicants should be interested in attending a community college, college, or university in Oregon to study education. They must have been active in community and school affairs, have at least a 3.5 grade point average, and enroll in the fall term after graduating from high school. To apply, students must submit a completed application form, a 1-page autobiography (that states personal goals), the name of the school they plan to attend, and the endorsement of a member of the Confederation of Oregon School Administrators (COSA). Financial need is not considered in the selection process.
Financial data: The stipend is $1,000. Funds are paid directly to the recipient.
Duration: 1 year; nonrenewable.
Additional information: This program is offered through Northwest Women in Educational Administration.
Number awarded: 1 each year.
Deadline: February of each year.

3039
NRA CIVIL RIGHTS DEFENSE FUND ESSAY CONTEST

National Rifle Association of America
Attn: NRA Civil Rights Defense Fund
11250 Waples Road
Fairfax, VA 22030-7400
Phone: (703) 267-1250   Fax: (703) 267-3985
Summary: To recognize and reward outstanding papers written by elementary and secondary school students on the constitutional right to keep and bear arms.
Eligibility: This program is open to students in elementary, junior high, and high school. Students must submit an essay, about 1,000 words in length, on "The Second Amendment to the Constitution: Why It Is Important to Our Nation." Essays are judged in 2 categories: senior, for grades 10 through 12, and junior, for grades 9 and below. Selection is based on originality, scholarship, and presentation.
Financial data: In each division, first prize is $1,000, second prize is $600, third

prize is $200, and honorable mention is $100. All prizes are in the form of U.S. savings bonds.
Duration: The program is held annually.
Number awarded: 8 each year: 4 in each of the 2 grade-level categories.
Deadline: October of each year.

3040
NSA ANNUAL SCHOLARSHIP AWARDS

National Society of Accountants
Attn: NSA Scholarship Foundation
1010 North Fairfax Street
Alexandria, VA 22314-1574
Phone: (703) 549-6400, ext. 1312   (800) 966-6679
Fax: (703) 549-2512   E-mail: dgriffin@nsacct.org
Web Site: www.nsacct.org
Summary: To provide financial assistance to undergraduate students majoring in accounting.
Eligibility: This program is open to undergraduate students enrolled on a full-time basis in an accounting degree program at an accredited 2-year or 4-year college or university with a grade point average of 3.0 or better. Students in 2-year colleges may apply during their first year or during their second year if transferring to a 4-year institution, provided they have committed themselves to a major in accounting throughout the remainder of their college career; students in 4-year colleges may apply for a scholarship for their second, third, or fourth year of studies, provided they have committed themselves to a major in accounting through the remainder of their college career. Evening program students are considered full time if they are pursuing an accounting degree. Only U.S. or Canadian citizens attending a U.S. accredited business school, college, or university may apply. Selection is based on academic attainment, demonstrated leadership ability, and financial need.
Financial data: The stipend is approximately $500 per year for students entering their second year of studies or approximately $1,000 per year for students entering the third or fourth year.
Duration: 1 year.
Additional information: The outstanding student in this competition, designated the Charles H. Earp Memorial Scholar, receives an additional stipend of $200 and an appropriate plaque.
Number awarded: Approximately 40 each year.
Deadline: March of each year.

3041
NSCA CHALLENGE SCHOLARSHIP

Summary: To provide financial assistance for postsecondary education in strength training and conditioning to members of the National Strength and Conditioning Association (NSCA).
See Listing #2375.

3042
NSCA HIGH SCHOOL SCHOLARSHIP

Summary: To provide financial assistance for postsecondary education in strength training and conditioning to graduating high school seniors.
See Listing #2376.

3043
NSCA WOMEN AND MINORITY SCHOLARSHIP

Summary: To provide financial assistance for postsecondary education in strength training and conditioning to women and minorities.
See Listing #2377.

3044
OHIO TOURISM SCHOLARSHIP

National Tourism Foundation
Attn: Scholarships
546 East Main Street
Lexington, KY 40508-2342
Phone: (859) 226-4444   (800) 682-8886
Fax: (859) 226-4437   E-mail: ntf@ntastaff.com
Web Site: www.ntfonline.org
Summary: To provide financial assistance to college students in Ohio who are majoring in tourism.

Eligibility: This program is open to full-time students enrolled in a 2-year or 4-year college or university in Ohio. Applicants must be Ohio residents, have at least a 3.0 grade point average, and be majoring in a travel or tourism-related field (e.g., hotel management, restaurant management, tourism).

Financial data: The stipend is $1,000.

Duration: 1 year.

Additional information: Award winners also receive complimentary registration and an all-expense paid trip (valued at more than $3,000) to the association's annual convention, as well as a 1-year subscription to *Courier* magazine, *Tuesday* newsletter, and *NTF Headlines* newsletter. In any 1 year, applicants may receive only 1 award from the association.

Number awarded: 1 each year.

Deadline: April of each year.

3045
OREGON AFL-CIO SCHOLARSHIPS

Oregon Student Assistance Commission
Attn: Private Awards Grant Department
1500 Valley River Drive, Suite 100
Eugene, OR 97401-2146
Phone: (541) 687-7395   (800) 452-8807, ext. 7395
Fax: (541) 687-7419   E-mail: awardinfo@mercury.osac.state.or.us
Web Site: www.osac.state.or.us

Summary: To provide financial assistance for college to graduating high school seniors in Oregon who submit an essay on a labor-related topic.

Eligibility: This program is open to seniors graduating from high schools in Oregon who submit an essay of 500 words or less on either why free trade is good for working people or why U.S. trade policy needs to change. Selection is based on the essay, financial need, grade point average, and an interview by a panel of individuals with expertise in labor history and labor affairs. Preference may be given to applicants from union families.

Financial data: The stipends are $3,000, $1,200, $1,000, or $850.

Duration: 1 year; nonrenewable.

Additional information: The award can be used at an accredited college or university in the United States, at any public community college in Oregon, or at any established trade school. The $3,000 and $1,000 scholarships are designated the May Darling Scholarships, the $1,200 scholarship is designated the Asa T. Williams Scholarship, and the $850 scholarship is designated the Northwest Labor Press Scholarship. This program is sponsored by the Oregon AFL-CIO, 2210 State Street, Salem, OR 97301, (503) 585-6320.

Number awarded: 4 each year.

Deadline: February of each year.

3046
OREGON ASSOCIATION OF PUBLIC ACCOUNTANTS SCHOLARSHIP FOUNDATION SCHOLARSHIP

Oregon Association of Public Accountants Scholarship Foundation
1804 N.E. 43rd Avenue
Portland, OR 97213

Summary: To provide financial assistance to Oregon residents interested in majoring in accounting in college.

Eligibility: This program is open to Oregon residents who are enrolled in or accepted by an accredited school in Oregon for the study of accounting. Applicants must intend to carry a minimum of 12 credit hours. Selection is based on financial need, scholastic achievement, personal qualifications, and professional promise.

Financial data: Historically, scholarships have ranged from $1,000 to $2,000 and totaled about $9,000 annually. Checks are made payable to the recipient and the recipient's college. Funds may be used for tuition, fees, books, or other academic expenses during the year.

Duration: 1 year; renewable.

Additional information: The Scholarship Foundation is sponsored by the Oregon Association of Independent Accountants (formerly the Oregon Association of Public Accountants). Recipients may attend a college, university, or community college. They are given an honorary 1-year student membership in the Oregon Association of Independent Accountants.

Deadline: March of each year.

3047
OREGON COLLECTORS ASSOCIATION BOB HASSON MEMORIAL AWARD

Oregon Student Assistance Commission
Attn: Private Awards Grant Department
1500 Valley River Drive, Suite 100
Eugene, OR 97401-2146
Phone: (541) 687-7395   (800) 452-8807, ext. 7395
Fax: (541) 687-7419   E-mail: awardinfo@mercury.osac.state.or.us
Web Site: www.osac.state.or.us

Summary: To recognize and reward high school seniors in Oregon who submit essays on the proper use of credit.

Eligibility: This program is open to seniors graduating from high schools in Oregon who submit a 3- to 4-page essay entitled "The Proper Use of Credit." Children and grandchildren of owners and officers of collection agencies registered in Oregon are not eligible.

Financial data: Awards are $3,000 for first place, $2,500 for second place, and $1,500 for third place. Funds must be used for tuition and other educational expenses at a college or vocational school in Oregon.

Duration: The award, presented annually, may not be renewed.

Number awarded: 3 each year.

Deadline: February of each year.

3048
OREGON STATE FISCAL ASSOCIATION SCHOLARSHIP

Summary: To provide financial assistance for college to members of the Oregon State Fiscal Association and their children.

See Listing #878.

3049
OREGON STATE PERSONNEL MANAGERS ASSOCIATION SCHOLARSHIP

Oregon Student Assistance Commission
Attn: Private Awards Grant Department
1500 Valley River Drive, Suite 100
Eugene, OR 97401-2146
Phone: (541) 687-7395   (800) 452-8807, ext. 7395
Fax: (541) 687-7419   E-mail: awardinfo@mercury.osac.state.or.us
Web Site: www.osac.state.or.us

Summary: To provide financial assistance for college to members of the Oregon State Personnel Managers Association.

Eligibility: This program is open to members of the association who are working at least part-time on an academic degree or a professional certificate in personnel management, personnel administration, human resources management, safety management, labor relations, industrial relations, industrial engineering, business administration, public relations, or a closely-related field. Applicants may be undergraduate or graduate students.

Financial data: Scholarship amounts vary, depending upon the needs of the recipient.

Duration: 1 year.

Number awarded: Varies each year.

Deadline: February of each year.

3050
OUTDOOR AND ENVIRONMENTAL LEADERSHIP SCHOLARSHIP

Summary: To provide financial assistance to college students who have displayed initiative in improving the outdoors and encouraging others to do the same.

See Listing #2396.

3051
PACKAGING EDUCATION FORUM FINANCIAL AID PROGRAM

Summary: To provide financial assistance to college students who are interested in preparing for a career in packaging.

See Listing #2400.

3052
PAFCS UNDERGRADUATE SCHOLARSHIP

Pennsylvania Association of Family and Consumer Sciences
c/o Beth Krier, President-Elect
258 East Main Street
Bath, PA 18014
Phone: (610) 837-1453   E-mail: pafcs@aol.com
Web Site: www.pafcs.org/pafcsawards.htm
Summary: To provide financial assistance to undergraduate student members of the Pennsylvania Association of Family and Consumer Sciences (PAFCS).
Eligibility: This program is open to student members of the association entering their junior or senior year of college. Applicants must be enrolled in an aspect of family and consumer sciences education.
Financial data: A stipend is provided (exact amount not specified).
Duration: 1 year.
Number awarded: 1 each year.

3053
PAT AND JIM HOST SCHOLARSHIP

National Tourism Foundation
Attn: Scholarships
546 East Main Street
Lexington, KY 40508-2342
Phone: (859) 226-4444   (800) 682-8886
Fax: (859) 226-4437   E-mail: ntf@ntastaff.com
Web Site: www.ntfonline.org
Summary: To provide financial assistance to high school seniors planning to major in tourism in college.
Eligibility: This program is open to high school seniors interested in majoring in a travel or tourism-related field (e.g., hotel management, restaurant management, tourism) in college.
Financial data: The stipend is $2,000 per year.
Duration: 4 years, provided the recipient maintains full-time enrollment and a grade point average of 3.0 or higher.
Additional information: Award winners also receive complimentary registration and an all-expense paid trip (valued at more than $3,000) to the association's annual convention, as well as a 1-year subscription to *Courier* magazine, *Tuesday* newsletter, and *NTF Headlines* newsletter.
Number awarded: 1 every 4 years (2003, 2007, etc.).
Deadline: April of the year of the award.

3054
PATRICIA V. ASIP SCHOLARSHIP

Summary: To provide financial assistance to Hispanic students enrolled in fashion design schools.
See Listing #1593.

3055
PAUL HONDA SCHOLARSHIPS

Pacific and Asian Affairs Council
Attn: High School Program Coordinator
1601 East-West Road, Fourth Floor
Honolulu, HI 96848-1691
Phone: (808) 944-7783   Fax: (808) 944-7785
E-mail: hspaac@aloha.net
Web Site: www.aloha.net/~paac/hs/hsschinfo.htm
Summary: To provide financial assistance to students in Hawaii who have been active in the programs of the Pacific and Asian Affairs Council (PAAC).
Eligibility: This program is open to graduating seniors from a public or private high school in Hawaii who have been active student members of the council. Applicants must have applied to a 4-year college intending to major in a field related to international affairs. They must demonstrate substantial interest in and commitment to international affairs, as well as outstanding academic achievement, leadership qualities, and commitment to community service. As part of the selection process, they must submit 1) high school transcripts, 2) 2 letters of recommendation, and 3) a 700-word essay describing their academic and career goals.
Financial data: The stipend is $1,000.
Duration: 1 year.
Number awarded: 4 each year.
Deadline: April of each year.

3056
PAWNBROKERS ASSOCIATION OF NORTH CAROLINA SCHOLARSHIP

North Carolina Community College System
Attn: Student Support Services
200 West Jones Street
Raleigh, NC 27603-1379
Phone: (919) 733-7051   Fax: (919) 733-0680
Web Site: www.ncccs.cc.nc.us
Summary: To provide financial assistance to North Carolina residents studying criminal justice at community colleges in the state.
Eligibility: Applicants must be North Carolina residents enrolled in a basic law enforcement training program at 1 of the 58 colleges in the North Carolina Community College System. Selection is based on financial need and academic excellence. Each year, 3 community colleges are selected to present an award to 1 of their students.
Financial data: The scholarship provides full payment of tuition.
Duration: 1 year; nonrenewable.
Additional information: There are no special application forms for the scholarship. Students apply to their local community college, not to the system office. Each eligible school selects its own recipients from applicants meeting the above criteria.
Number awarded: 3 each year.

3057
PENNSYLVANIA AFL-CIO SCHOLARSHIP ESSAY CONTEST

Pennsylvania AFL-CIO
Attn: Director of Education
231 State Street, Eighth Floor
Harrisburg, PA 17101-1110
Phone: (717) 231-2843   Fax: (717) 238-8541
Web Site: www.paaflcio.org
Summary: To recognize and reward high school and college students in Pennsylvania who have written outstanding essays on a labor topic.
Eligibility: This program is open to 1) graduating high school seniors at high schools in Pennsylvania; 2) students currently enrolled in accredited postsecondary school programs in the state; and 3) affiliated union members attending an accredited institution. Applicants must submit essays on topics that change annually but always relate to labor unions. Recently, high school students were to write a descriptive essay on the life of a union member (parent, sibling, grandparent, etc.) and why union membership is important to them. College students were to write on the effects of the global economy of working families. Union members were to write on the recent presidential election and its import on working families." All essays must be 1,500 words in length and include 3 references, of which at least 1 must be a labor organization.
Financial data: First prize is $2,000, second prize is $1,000, and third prize is $500.
Duration: The competition is held annually.
Number awarded: 9 each year: 3 in each of the 3 categories.
Deadline: January of each year.

3058
PENNSYLVANIA SOCIETY OF PUBLIC ACCOUNTANTS SCHOLARSHIPS

Pennsylvania Society of Public Accountants
900 North Second Street
Harrisburg, PA 17102
Phone: (717) 234-4129   (800) 270-3352
Fax: (717) 234-9556
Web Site: www.pspa-state.org
Summary: To provide financial assistance to accounting majors in Pennsylvania.
Eligibility: Applicants must be accounting majors, have completed at least 3 semesters in college, have at least a 3.0 grade point average, be a Pennsylvania resident, and be attending a college or university in the state. Selection is based primarily on academic merit. Student activities, leadership positions, and financial need may also be considered in the selection process.
Financial data: The stipend is $1,000 per year.
Duration: 1 year.
Number awarded: 3 each year.
Deadline: May of each year.

3059
PERCY E. SUTTON EDUCATION SCHOLARSHIP

National Association for the Advancement of Colored People
Attn: Education Department
4805 Mt. Hope Drive
Baltimore, MD 21215-3297
Phone: (410) 358-8900   Fax: (410) 358-9785
Web Site: www.naacp.org
Summary: To provide financial assistance to members of the National Association for the Advancement of Colored People (NAACP) and others who are majoring in education on the undergraduate or graduate level.
Eligibility: This program is open to full-time undergraduates and full- and part-time graduate students majoring in the field of education. The required minimum grade point average is 2.5 for graduating high school seniors and current undergraduates or 3.0 for graduate students. Membership and participation in the association is highly desirable. All applicants must be able to demonstrate financial need and be U.S. citizens.
Financial data: The stipend is $1,000 per year for undergraduate students or $2,000 per year for graduate students.
Duration: 1 year; may be renewed as long as the recipient maintains a grade point average of 2.5 or higher as an undergraduate or 3.0 or higher as a graduate student.
Number awarded: 1 or more each year.
Deadline: April of each year.

3060
PETER K. NEW STUDENT PRIZE COMPETITION

Summary: To recognize and reward the best student research papers in applied social, health, or behavioral sciences.
See Listing #2419.

3061
PHCC EDUCATIONAL FOUNDATION NEED-BASED SCHOLARSHIP

Summary: To provide financial assistance to undergraduate students interested in the plumbing, heating, and cooling industry.
See Listing #2421.

3062
PHCC EDUCATIONAL FOUNDATION SCHOLARSHIP PROGRAM

Summary: To provide financial assistance to undergraduate students interested in the plumbing, heating, and cooling industry.
See Listing #2422.

3063
PHI DELTA KAPPA INTERNATIONAL SCHOLARSHIP GRANTS FOR PROSPECTIVE EDUCATORS

Phi Delta Kappa International
Attn: Director of Chapter Programs
408 North Union
P.O. Box 789
Bloomington, IN 47402-0789
Phone: (812) 339-1156   (800) 766-1156
Fax: (812) 339-0018   E-mail: headquarters@pdkintl.org
Web Site: www.pdkintl.org/studser/sschol.htm
Summary: To provide financial assistance to students who are interested in becoming teachers.
Eligibility: Eligible to apply are high school seniors who are in the upper third of their class and interested in attending college to prepare for a teaching career. Selection is based on academic achievement, letters of recommendation, school activities, community activities, and a 750-word essay on a topic that changes annually but relates to teaching as a profession. Some scholarships are set aside specifically for dependents of Phi Delta Kappa members.
Financial data: Stipends are $1,000, $2,000, $4,000, or $5,000.
Duration: 1 year.
Number awarded: 33 each year: 30 at $1,000, 1 at $2,000, 1 at $4,000 and 1 at $5,000. At least 2 scholarships each year are set aside specifically for dependents of Phi Delta Kappa members.
Deadline: January of each year.

3064
PHI UPSILON OMICRON PAST PRESIDENT SCHOLARSHIP

Phi Upsilon Omicron
Attn: Educational Foundation
P.O. Box 329
Fairmont, WV 26555-0329
Phone: (304) 368-0612   E-mail: rickards@access.mountain.net
Web Site: ianrwww.unl.edu/phiu
Summary: To provide financial assistance to undergraduate student members of Phi Upsilon Omicron, a national honor society in family and consumer sciences.
Eligibility: Applicants must be members of the society who are studying family and consumer sciences on the undergraduate level. Selection is based on scholastic record, participation in society and other collegiate activities, a statement of professional aims and goals, professional and/or work experience, and recommendations.
Financial data: The stipend is $1,000.
Duration: 1 year.
Number awarded: 1 each year.
Deadline: January of each year.

3065
PHILLIPS BUSINESS INFORMATION SCHOLARSHIP

Summary: To provide financial assistance to students interested in majoring in satellite business applications in college.
See Listing #1596.

3066
PICPA SOPHOMORE SCHOLARSHIPS

Pennsylvania Institute of Certified Public Accountants
1650 Arch Street, 17th Floor
Philadelphia, PA 19103-2099
Phone: (215) 496-9272   (888) CPA-2001 (within PA)
Fax: (215) 496-9212   E-mail: info@picpa.org
Web Site: www.picpa.org/student/programs_and_awards.htm
Summary: To provide financial assistance to Pennsylvania sophomores majoring in accounting.
Eligibility: To qualify for this scholarship, an applicant must be a full-time sophomore at a 4-year college or university in Pennsylvania and be nominated by the accounting department chair at that school. Nominees are evaluated on the basis of academic record, SAT scores, intent to become a CPA and practice in Pennsylvania, need, faculty recommendation, work ethic, reasons for career choice, qualities of leadership, and the student's resume.
Financial data: Stipends are either $3,000, $1,500, or $1,000.
Duration: 1 year.
Number awarded: 18 each year: 5 at $3,000, 12 at $1,500, and 1 at $1,000.
Deadline: February of each year.

3067
PICPA STUDENT WRITING COMPETITION

Pennsylvania Institute of Certified Public Accountants
1650 Arch Street, 17th Floor
Philadelphia, PA 19103-2099
Phone: (215) 496-9272   (888) CPA-2001 (within PA)
Fax: (215) 496-9212   E-mail: info@picpa.org
Web Site: www.picpa.org/student/programs_and_awards.htm
Summary: To recognize and reward outstanding essays written by students in Pennsylvania on an accounting topic that changes annually.
Eligibility: This competition is open to 1) accounting and business majors at Pennsylvania colleges and universities, and 2) Pennsylvania residents who attend college out-of-state. Candidates are invited to submit an essay on an issue (changes annually) that affects the accounting profession. Recently, the topic was: "The role of accounting in the creative destruction process." Essays should be approximately 1,500 words and include a 50- to 75-word abstract. Selection is based on content, method of presentation, and writing style.
Financial data: First place is $2,000, second $1,200, and third $800. The top 3 schools receive, respectively, $1,000, $600, and $400.
Duration: The competition is held annually.
Additional information: The first-place manuscript is published in the fall issue of the *Pennsylvania CPA Journal.*
Number awarded: 3 each year.
Deadline: April of each year.

3068
PIF/LIFELINE SCHOLARSHIP PROGRAM

Summary: To provide financial assistance to adult students who are interested in working with people with disabilities or brain disorders.
See Listing #2428.

3069
PILOT INTERNATIONAL FOUNDATION SCHOLARSHIP PROGRAM

Summary: To provide financial assistance to undergraduate students who are interested in working with people who have disabilities or brain disorders.
See Listing #2429.

3070
PLANNING & THE BLACK COMMUNITY DIVISION SCHOLARSHIP

Summary: To provide financial assistance to underrepresented minority undergraduate students interested in majoring in planning or a related field.
See Listing #2432.

3071
POLICE CORPS

Summary: To provide financial assistance to undergraduate and graduate students willing to serve as police officers for at least 4 years.
See Listing #923.

3072
POST SCHOLARSHIP

Summary: To provide financial assistance to upper-division students majoring in aviation management.
See Listing #2433.

3073
POWER SYSTEMS PROFESSIONAL SCHOLARSHIP

Summary: To provide financial assistance for postsecondary education in strength training and conditioning to members of the National Strength and Conditioning Association (NSCA).
See Listing #2435.

3074
PREZELL R. ROBINSON SCHOLARS PROGRAM

North Carolina Department of Public Instruction
Attn: School Personnel Support Section
301 North Wilmington Street
Raleigh, NC 27601-2825
Phone: (919) 807-3300   E-mail: mcash@dpi.state.nc.us
Web Site: www.ncpublicschools.org/scholarships/robinson.htm
Summary: To provide an incentive to high school students in "low-wealth" school systems to choose teaching as a career objective.
Eligibility: Eligible to be considered for this award are students in grades 9 through 11 attending schools in "low-wealth" school systems or systems documenting extreme difficulty in recruiting qualified teachers. Each participating local educational agency (LEA) is invited to nominate 1 candidate per year from the designated grade levels. Each nominee must have at least a 3.0 cumulative grade point average, a desire to pursue teaching as a career objective, and a willingness to participate in programs designed to prepare them for college and a career in teaching. Robinson Scholars are eligible to receive a college scholarship if they 1) maintain a grade point average of 3.0 or higher throughout their remaining high school years; 2) pursue a program of study throughout high school to prepare them for admission to an institution of higher education; 3) achieve a score of at least 900 on the SAT; and 4) pursue a course of study for licensure to teach in the public schools of North Carolina.
Financial data: Each Robinson Scholar receives a scholarship to be used to pursue teacher licensure; the amount of the scholarship is the same as awarded to recipients of North Carolina's Prospective Teacher Scholarship Loan (currently up to $2,500 per year).
Duration: Up to 4 years (or the minimum number of years required to earn licensure based on the entry-level degree).

Additional information: This program was formerly known as the Challenge Scholars Program.
Number awarded: 50 each year.
Deadline: Nominations are due in February of each year.

3075
PRINCE KUHIO HAWAIIAN CIVIC CLUB SCHOLARSHIP

Summary: To provide financial assistance for undergraduate or graduate studies to persons of Hawaiian descent.
See Listing #934.

3076
PRO PUBS CORPORATE AVIATION SCHOLARSHIP

Summary: To provide financial assistance to members of Women in Aviation, International who are interested in studying corporate aviation in college.
See Listing #2440.

3077
PROFILE IN COURAGE ESSAY CONTEST

John F. Kennedy Library Foundation
Attn: Profile in Courage Essay Contest
Columbia Point
Boston, MA 02125-3313
Phone: (617) 929-1265   Fax: (617) 436-3395
E-mail: kennedy.foundation@nara.gov
Web Site: www.jfklibrary.org/fn_pica.htm
Summary: To recognize and reward high school authors of essays on public officials who have demonstrated political courage.
Eligibility: This contest is open to U.S. students in grades 9 through 12 attending public, private, parochial, or home schools; U.S. students enrolled in a high school correspondence course in any of the 50 states, the District of Columbia, or the U.S. territories; and U.S. citizens attending schools overseas. Applicants must submit an essay, up to 1,000 words, that identifies a current elected public official in the United States who is acting courageously to address a political issue at the local, state, national, or international level.
Financial data: The first-place winner receives $3,000, the second-place winner receives $1,000, and the other finalists receive $500.
Duration: The awards are presented annually.
Number awarded: 7 each year: 1 first place, 1 second place, and 5 other finalists.
Deadline: January of each year.

3078
PSSC LEGACY FUND SCHOLARSHIP

Summary: To provide financial assistance to students interested in majoring in international satellite and/or distance education applications in college.
See Listing #1603.

3079
PUBLIC SERVICE SCHOLARSHIP

Public Employees Roundtable
Attn: Scholarship Committee
500 North Capitol Street, Room 1204
P.O. Box 75248
Washington, DC 20013-5248
Phone: (202) 927-4923   Fax: (202) 927-4920
E-mail: mcconnell@theroundtable.org
Web Site: www.theroundtable.org
Summary: To provide financial assistance to undergraduate or graduate students who are interested in preparing for a career in public service.
Eligibility: Applicants must have completed or show they will complete at least 1 year of college by the beginning of the fall term. High school seniors are ineligible; community college students and anyone not currently enrolled must have been accepted to a 4-year degree program. College seniors accepted to a graduate school and current graduate students are also eligible. All applicants must have earned at least a 3.5 grade point average, must submit an essay on how their prospective career may help change the poor image of public service held by the American people, and must intend to pursue a government career at the local, state, or federal level. Preference is given to applicants who have prior public sector work experience. Selection is based on the quality of the essay, commitment to public service, and GPA.

Financial data: The stipend is $1,000 for full-time students or $500 for part-time graduate students.
Duration: 1 year; nonrenewable.
Additional information: This program began in 1985.
Number awarded: Varies each year; recently, 11 of these scholarships were awarded.
Deadline: May of each year.

3080
R. FLAKE SHAW SCHOLARSHIP PROGRAM

Summary: To provide financial assistance to North Carolina high school seniors interested in studying agriculture or home economics in college.
See Listing #2445.

3081
RALPH AND VALERIE THOMAS SCHOLARSHIP

National Association of Black Accountants
Attn: Director, Center for Advancement of Minority Accountants
7249-A Hanover Parkway
Greenbelt, MD 20770
Phone: (301) 474-NABA, ext. 114   Fax: (301) 474-3114
E-mail: cquinn@nabainc.org
Web Site: www.nabainc.org
Summary: To provide financial assistance for undergraduate or graduate education to members of the National Association of Black Accountants (NABA).
Eligibility: Applicants must be paid members of the association who are full-time students pursuing a bachelor's or master's degree in accounting, finance, business administration, or taxation. Applicants must have a grade point average of at least 3.5 in their major and 3.3 overall. Selection is based on grades, financial need, and a 500-word autobiography that discusses career objectives, leadership abilities, community activities, and involvement in the association.
Financial data: The stipend is $1,000 per year.
Duration: 1 year.
Number awarded: 1 each year.
Deadline: December of each year.

3082
RAMA SCHOLARSHIP FOR THE AMERICAN DREAM

American Hotel Foundation
Attn: Manager of Foundation Programs
1201 New York Avenue, N.W., Suite 600
Washington, DC 20005-3931
Phone: (202) 289-3180   Fax: (202) 289-3199
E-mail: ahf@ahma.com
Web Site: www.ei-ahma.org/ahf/ahf.htm
Summary: To provide financial assistance to minority college students working on a degree in hotel management at designated schools.
Eligibility: Applicants must be attending 1 of 14 designated hospitality management schools, which select the recipients. Preference is given to students of Asian-Indian descent and other minority groups and to JHM Hotel employees.
Financial data: The stipend varies at each of the participating schools.
Duration: 1 year.
Additional information: The participating institutions are Bethune-Cookman College, California State Polytechnic University at Pomona, Cornell University, Florida International University, Georgia State University, Greenville Technical College, Howard University, Johnson & Wales University, Michigan State University, New York University, University of Central Florida, University of Houston, University of South Carolina, and Virginia Polytechnic Institute and State University. This program is funded by JHM Hotels, Inc.
Number awarded: 14 or more each year.

3083
RAY FOLEY MEMORIAL SCHOLARSHIP PROGRAM

American Wholesale Marketers Association
Attn: Distributors Education Foundation
1128 16th Street, N.W.
Washington, DC 20036-4808
Phone: (202) 463-2124   Fax: (202) 467-0559
E-mail: info@awmanet.org
Web Site: www.awmanet.org/edu/scholar.cfm
Summary: To provide financial assistance for postsecondary education to students involved in the convenience wholesale distribution industry.

Eligibility: Applicants must be enrolled full time in an undergraduate or graduate program at an accredited college or university pursuing a business course of study (accounting or business administration). They must be able to demonstrate interest in a career in distribution of candy, tobacco, and convenience products. Selection is based on academic merit and career interest.
Financial data: The scholarships are $5,000 per year. Funds are paid directly to the college or university to cover tuition, on-campus room and board, and other direct costs; any remaining funds are paid to the student for reimbursement of school-related expenses with appropriate receipts.
Duration: 1 year; nonrenewable.
Additional information: The American Wholesale Marketers Association (AWMA) resulted from the 1991 merger of the National Association of Tobacco Distributors (NATD) and the National Candy Wholesalers Association (NCWA). This scholarship was established in memory of Ray Foley, the late executive vice-president of the NCWA.
Number awarded: 2 each year.
Deadline: May of each year.

3084
RAYMOND H. TROTT SCHOLARSHIP FOR BANKING

Rhode Island Foundation
Attn: Scholarship Coordinator
One Union Station
Providence, RI 02903
Phone: (401) 274-4564   Fax: (401) 331-8085
E-mail: libbym@rifoundation.org
Web Site: www.rifoundation.org
Summary: To provide financial assistance to Rhode Island students of color interested in preparing for a career in banking.
Eligibility: This program is open to minority residents of Rhode Island who are entering their senior year in college. Applicants must plan to pursue a career in banking and be able to demonstrate financial need. Along with their application, they must submit an essay (up to 300 words) on the impact they would like to have on the banking industry.
Financial data: The stipend is $1,000.
Duration: 1 year; nonrenewable.
Number awarded: 1 each year.
Deadline: June of each year.

3085
REDI-TAG CORPORATION SCHOLARSHIP

Summary: To provide financial assistance to members of the American Health Information Management Association (AHIMA) who are single parents interested in pursuing an undergraduate degree in health information administration or technology.
See Listing #2435.

3086
RICHARD L. DAVIS MANAGERS SCHOLARSHIP

Summary: To provide financial assistance to individuals currently employed in medical group management who wish to pursue professional development through undergraduate or graduate education.
See Listing #2463.

3087
RICHARD L. DAVIS NATIONAL SCHOLARSHIP

Summary: To provide financial assistance to undergraduate or graduate students who are interested in preparing for a career in medical group management.
See Listing #2464.

3088
RITCHIE-JENNINGS MEMORIAL SCHOLARSHIPS PROGRAM

Association of Certified Fraud Examiners
Attn: Scholarship Program
The Gregor Building
716 West Avenue
Austin, TX 78701
Phone: (512) 478-9070   (800) 245-3321
Fax: (512) 478-9297   E-mail: scholarships@cfenet.com
Web Site: www.cfenet.com/services/scholarships/index.shtml

Summary: To provide financial assistance to undergraduate and graduate students working on an accounting or criminal justice degree.
Eligibility: Eligible to apply for this support are full-time students working on an undergraduate or graduate degree in accounting or criminal justice. Selection is based on academic achievement, letters of recommendation (including at least 1 from a certified fraud examiner), and an original essay (at least 250 words) on why the applicant deserves the scholarship and how the awareness of fraud will affect his or her professional career development.
Financial data: The stipend is $1,000.
Duration: 1 year.
Number awarded: 15 each year.
Deadline: May of each year.

3089
ROBERT BRADLEY DISTINGUISHED CIVIL RIGHTS LEADERSHIP AWARD

Summary: To recognize and reward students majoring in transportation who write outstanding essays on civil rights.
See Listing #2466.

3090
ROBERT G. PORTER SCHOLARS PROGRAM FOR UNIVERSITY STUDENTS

Summary: To provide financial assistance to children of members of the American Federation of Teachers (AFT) who wish to pursue postsecondary education at a 4-year college or university.
See Listing #2470.

3091
ROBERT KAUFMAN MEMORIAL SCHOLARSHIPS

IA International Educational Foundation
9200 South Dadeland Boulevard, Suite 510
Miami, FL 33156
Phone: (305) 670-0580   Fax: (305) 670-3818
Web Site: www.iai.org/education/intro.asp
Summary: To provide financial assistance to undergraduate and graduate students interested in preparing for a career in accounting.
Eligibility: Eligible are students who are pursuing, or planning to pursue, an undergraduate or graduate degree in accounting at colleges or universities in selected countries. Applicants must be in at least their third year of college with a grade point average in accounting of 3.5 or higher. Applications must be endorsed by a member firm of IA International (formerly Independent Accountants International). Selection is based on academic achievement, standardized test scores, extracurricular activities, work experience, an essay on interest and future goals in the accounting profession, and an essay on why the applicants believe they should be awarded the scholarship. Financial need is considered only if applicants wish to compete for a full scholarship.
Financial data: Scholarships up to $5,000 are awarded to full-time students who demonstrate financial need. Awards of recognition of up to $250 to assist with the purchase of textbooks are given to full-time students without demonstration of financial need. Awards are paid directly to the student; checks are given to the sponsoring IA International member firms, which present them to the recipients after receiving proof of enrollment.
Duration: These are 1-time awards intended primarily for the purchase of textbooks.
Additional information: Each year, different countries from around the world are selected to award students scholarships. Recently, those were Australia, Canada, China, Indonesia, Mexico, the United States, and selected European countries. Applications must be submitted to an IA member firm, which will forward them to IA International headquarters.
Number awarded: Up to 20 each year.
Deadline: February of each year.

3092
ROCKY MOUNTAIN CHAPTER SCHOLARSHIPS

Summary: To provide financial assistance to students attending college in designated Rocky Mountain states who are interested in majoring in satellite-related disciplines.
See Listing #1621.

3093
ROY & HARRIET ROBINSON SCHOLARSHIP

Professional Independent Insurance Agents of Illinois
4360 Wabash Avenue
Springfield, IL 62707
Phone: (217) 793-6660   (800) 628-6436
Fax: (217) 793-6744   E-mail: admin@piiai.org
Web Site: www.piiai.org/youngagents/scholarship.htm
Summary: To provide financial assistance to upper-division students who are majoring in business and have an interest in insurance.
Eligibility: Students must meet the following criteria: have junior or senior status in college, be in a business degree program with an interest in insurance, be a full-time student, and have a letter of recommendation from a current or retired member of the Professional Independent Insurance Agents of Illinois. Students must complete an application form and submit an essay (500 words or less) on the contribution the insurance industry provides to society. Financial need is not considered.
Financial data: The stipend is $1,000, payable in 2 equal installments. Funds are paid directly to the recipient's school.
Duration: 1 year.
Number awarded: 1 each year.
Deadline: June of each year.

3094
RUDOLPH DILLMAN MEMORIAL SCHOLARSHIP

Summary: To provide financial assistance to legally blind undergraduate or graduate students studying in the field of rehabilitation and/or education of visually impaired and blind persons.
See Listing #2485.

3095
RUSS CASEY SCHOLARSHIP

Maine Restaurant Association
Attn: Chair, Scholarship Committee
5 Wade Street
P.O. Box 5060
Augusta, ME 04332-5060   Phone: (207) 623-2178
Summary: To provide financial assistance to students in Maine who are interested in preparing for a career in the food service industry.
Eligibility: This program is open to students attending a Maine institution of higher education and entering the food service industry. Applicants must submit a letter of recommendation from a restaurant where they have worked and/or a guidance counselor. Selection is based on academic achievement and interest in pursuing a career in the food service industry.
Financial data: The stipend is $1,000.
Duration: 1 year; nonrenewable.
Number awarded: 3 each year.
Deadline: March of each year.

3096
R.W. BOB HOLDEN SCHOLARSHIP

Hawaii Hotel Association
Attn: Director of Membership Services
2250 Kalakaua Avenue, Suite 404-4
Honolulu, HI 96815
Phone: (808) 924-0407   Fax: (808) 924-3843
E-mail: hha@panworld.net
Summary: To provide financial assistance to undergraduate and graduate students from Hawaii who are interested in working on a degree in hotel management.
Eligibility: Applicants must be Hawaii residents, attending or planning to attend an accredited college or university (in any state) on the undergraduate or graduate school level, majoring or planning to major in hotel management, and excellent students (at least a 3.0 GPA). Students must submit a completed application, proof of Hawaii residency, their most recent transcript, an autobiography, an essay on career goals, recommendations, and (optional) a photograph.
Financial data: A stipend is awarded (exact amount not specified).
Duration: 1 year.
Additional information: This scholarship is offered by the Hawaii Hotel Association and administered by the Hawaii Hotel Industry Foundation.
Number awarded: 1 or more each year.
Deadline: June of each year.

3097
SALES PROFESSIONALS-USA SCHOLARSHIPS

Sales Professionals-USA
P.O. Box 149
Arvada, CO 80001
Phone: (888) 763-PROS   E-mail: info@salespros-usa.com
Web Site: www.salespros-usa.com
Summary: To provide financial assistance to college students in selected states who are interested in majoring in sales.
Eligibility: Sales Professionals-USA (formerly SWAP Club International) has clubs in Colorado, Missouri, and Kansas. Each club has its own scholarship program. Students in the those states apply to the local club (for the addresses of those clubs, write to the address above). All applicants must be currently enrolled in college and majoring in business or marketing with an emphasis on sales. Scholarships are awarded in the areas where the clubs meet.
Financial data: The amounts awarded varies; each club has its own scholarship program. Generally, the stipends range from $250 to $1,000 each.
Duration: 1 year; may be renewable.
Number awarded: Varies each year.

3098
SAM PINE SCHOLARSHIP

Summary: To provide financial assistance to undergraduate students in planning or architecture at schools in New England and New York.
See Listing #1629.

3099
SARAH LEE GERRISH COMMUNICATIONS AWARDS

Summary: To recognize and reward college students who submit outstanding essays on a topic related to packaging.
See Listing #2495.

3100
SCHOLARSHIP FOR LUTHERAN STUDENTS ENTERING THE FIELD OF DEVELOPMENTAL DISABILITIES

Summary: To provide financial assistance to college students who are Lutherans and interested in preparing for a career in the field of mental retardation.
See Listing #2498.

3101
SCHOLARSHIP FOR MEDICAL AND OTHER PROFESSIONS

Summary: To provide financial assistance to California residents who are the children of veterans and interested in preparing for careers in medical and other professions.
See Listing #2499.

3102
SCHOLARSHIPS FOR MINORITY ACCOUNTING STUDENTS

American Institute of Certified Public Accountants
Attn: Academic and Career Development Division
1211 Avenue of the Americas
New York, NY 10036-8775
Phone: (212) 596-6223   Fax: (212) 596-6292
E-mail: educat@aicpa.org
Web Site: www.aicpa.org/members/div/career/mini/smas.htm
Summary: To provide financial assistance to underrepresented minority students interested in studying accounting at the undergraduate or graduate school level.
Eligibility: Undergraduate applicants must be minority students who are enrolled full time, have completed at least 30 semester hours of college work (including at least 6 semester hours in accounting), are majoring in accounting with an overall grade point average of 3.3 or higher, and are U.S. citizens or permanent residents. Minority students who are interested in a graduate degree must be 1) in the final year of a 5-year accounting program; 2) an undergraduate accounting major currently accepted or enrolled in a master's-level accounting, business administration, finance, or taxation program; or 3) any undergraduate major currently accepted in a master's-level accounting program. Selection is based primarily on merit (academic achievement); financial need is evaluated as a secondary criteria. For purposes of this program, the American Institute of Certified Public Accountants (AICPA) considers minority students to be those of Black, Native American/Alaskan Native, or Pacific Island races, or of Hispanic ethnic origin.
Financial data: Up to $5,000 per year.
Duration: 1 year; may be renewed, if recipients are making satisfactory progress toward graduation.
Additional information: These scholarships are granted by the institute's Minority Educational Initiatives Committee.
Number awarded: Varies each year; recently, 187 students received funding through this program.
Deadline: June of each year.

3103
SCHOLARSHIPS FOR TEACHERS AND OTHER PROFESSIONALS

Summary: To provide financial assistance to California residents who are the children of veterans and interested in preparing for a career in teaching and other professions.
See Listing #2501.

3104
SCHWAN'S FOOD SERVICE SCHOLARSHIP

School Food Service Foundation
Attn: Program Manager
700 South Washington Street, Suite 300
Alexandria, VA 22314-4287
Phone: (703) 739-3900, ext. 119   (800) 877-8822, ext. 119
Fax: (703) 739-3915   E-mail: sfsf@asfsa.org
Web Site: www.asfsa.org
Summary: To provide aid to members (or children of members) of the American School Food Service Association (ASFSA) who are interested in studying food service management on the undergraduate or graduate school level.
Eligibility: To apply for this program, students must meet all 4 of the following criteria: 1) plan to attend a college or vocational-technical institution that has a program designed to improve school food service; 2) be an active ASFSA member or the child of an active ASFSA member planning to study in a school food service-related field; 3) have a satisfactory academic record; and 4) express a desire to make food service a career. Applicants must submit a personal essay (up to 500 words) stating the reason for selecting food service as a profession; what they expect to gain from continuing their education; and their professional goals/plans. Support for either undergraduate or graduate education may be requested.
Financial data: The stipend is $1,000.
Duration: 1 year; may be renewed up to 3 additional years.
Additional information: Recipients must send a course completion report (grades) to the School Food Service Foundation upon completion of their courses. Recipients who fail to do this will not be eligible for future scholarship consideration.
Number awarded: Several each year.
Deadline: April of each year.

3105
SCLEOF SCHOLARSHIP AWARDS

South Carolina Law Enforcement Officers' Association
7339 Broad River Road
P.O. Box 210709
Columbia, SC 29221-0709
Phone: (803) 781-5913   (800) 922-0038
Fax: (803) 781-9208   E-mail: scleoaagm@aol.com
Web Site: www.scleoa.org/scholarships.htm
Summary: To provide financial assistance for college to high school seniors in South Carolina who submit essays on a topic related to law enforcement.
Eligibility: This program is open to seniors graduating from high schools in South Carolina whose parents or legal guardians have been South Carolina residents for at least 1 year. Applicants must submit a recommendation from their principal, headmaster, or guidance counselor; high school or preparatory school transcript; a list of honors and accomplishments; the occupation or profession the applicant is planning to pursue; a list of community activities and clubs; job history; information on financial need; and an essay up to 1,000 words on a topic that changes annually but relates to law enforcement. Recently, the topic was, "If you were writing the lottery administration legislation, what would it entail?" Applicants must be planning to attend an accredited college, university, or technical school in South Carolina. The program includes 1 award reserved for the child of a member of the South Carolina Law Enforcement Officers' Association (SCLEOA). Semifinalists are interviewed.
Financial data: Awards are $5,000, $2,000, or $1,000.
Duration: 1 year.

Number awarded: 4 each year: 1 at $5,000, 2 at $2,000 (including 1 reserved for the child of an SCLEOA member), and 1 at $1,000.
Deadline: February of each year.

3106
SEARS CRAFTSMAN SCHOLARSHIP

Summary: To provide financial assistance to high school seniors, especially those interested in a career in the automotive technological or marketing fields.
See Listing #2509.

3107
SEATTLE CHAPTER SCHOLARSHIPS

American Society of Women Accountants-Seattle Chapter
c/o Karen Gray
2450 72nd Avenue S.E.
Mercer Island, WA 98040
Web Site: www.aswaseattle.com/scholarships.htm
Summary: To provide financial assistance to students pursuing a bachelor's or master's degree in accounting at a college or university in Washington.
Eligibility: This program is open to part-time and full-time students pursuing a bachelor's or master's degree in accounting at a college or university in Washington. Applicants must have completed at least 60 semester hours and have maintained a grade point average of at least 2.5 overall and 3.0 in accounting. Membership in the American Society of Women Accountants is not required. Selection is based on career goals, communication skills, grade point average, personal circumstances, and financial need.
Financial data: The amounts of the awards vary. A total of $8,000 is available for this program each year. Funds are paid directly to the recipient's school.
Duration: 1 year.
Number awarded: May of each year.
Deadline: Varies each year.

3108
SECRETARIAL STUDIES SCHOLARSHIP

Grand Rapids Community Foundation
Attn: Education Program Associate
209-C Waters Building
161 Ottawa Avenue N.W.
Grand Rapids, MI 49503-2757
Phone: (616) 454-1751, ext. 103   Fax: (616) 454-6455
E-mail: rbishop@grfoundation.org
Web Site: www.grfoundation.org
Summary: To provide financial assistance to minority residents of Michigan who are interested in studying in a legal assistant/secretarial program at an institution in the state.
Eligibility: This program is open to minority students currently residing in Michigan. Applicants must be accepted at or enrolled in an accredited public or private 2- or 4-year college, university, vocational school, or business school with a declared major in legal assistant/legal secretarial studies. The institution must also be in Michigan.
Financial data: The stipend is $1,000.
Duration: 1 year.
Additional information: Funding for this program is provided by the law firm Warner Norcross & Judd LLP.
Number awarded: 1 each year.
Deadline: April of each year.

3109
SENTRY INSURANCE FOUNDATION SCHOLARSHIP

Summary: To provide financial assistance to freshmen majoring in selected fields at private colleges in Wisconsin.
See Listing #1639.

3110
SHARON D. BANKS UNDERGRADUATE SCHOLARSHIP

Summary: To provide financial assistance for undergraduate education to women interested in a career in transportation.
See Listing #2514.

3111
SHERYL A. HORAK LAW ENFORCEMENT EXPLORER MEMORIAL SCHOLARSHIP

Boy Scouts of America
Attn: Learning for Life Division, S210
1325 West Walnut Hill Lane
P.O. Box 152079
Irving, TX 75015-2079
Phone: (972) 580-2418   Web Site: www.learning-for-life.org/exploring
Summary: To provide financial assistance for postsecondary education to Explorer Scouts who plan a career as law enforcement executives.
Eligibility: This program is open to Explorer Scouts who are at least seniors in high school. Selection is based on academic record, leadership ability, extracurricular activities, and a personal statement on "Why I want to pursue a career in law enforcement." Applicants must be active members of a Law Enforcement Explorer post registered with Boy Scouts of America.
Financial data: The stipend is $1,000.
Duration: 1 year; nonrenewable.
Additional information: This program was established in 1987.
Number awarded: Varies each year, depending on the availability of funds.
Deadline: March of each year.

3112
SHRM FOUNDATION UNDERGRADUATE SCHOLARSHIPS

Society for Human Resource Management
Attn: Foundation Administrator
1800 Duke Street
Alexandria, VA 22314-3499
Phone: (703) 535-6020   Fax: (703) 535-6490
E-mail: speyton@shrm.org   Web Site: www.shrm.org
Summary: To provide financial assistance for college to undergraduate student members of the Society for Human Resource Management (SHRM).
Eligibility: This program is open to national undergraduate student members of the society. Applicants must have completed at least 55 semester hours of course work in a human relations major or human relations emphasis area (including at least 1 human relations management course) and have an overall GPA of 3.0 or higher.
Financial data: The stipend is $2,500.
Duration: 1 year.
Number awarded: 2 each year.
Deadline: October of each year.

3113
SIGNATURE TOURS SCHOLARSHIP

National Tourism Foundation
Attn: Scholarships
546 East Main Street
Lexington, KY 40508-2342
Phone: (859) 226-4444   (800) 682-8886
Fax: (859) 226-4437   E-mail: ntf@ntastaff.com
Web Site: www.ntfonline.org
Summary: To provide financial assistance to college students majoring in tourism.
Eligibility: This program is open to full-time students enrolled in a 2-year or 4-year college or university in North America. Applicants must have at least a 3.0 grade point average and be majoring in a travel or tourism-related field (e.g., hotel management, restaurant management, tourism).
Financial data: The stipend is $1,000.
Duration: 1 year.
Additional information: Award winners also receive complimentary registration and an all-expense paid trip (valued at more than $3,000) to the association's annual convention, as well as a 1-year subscription to *Courier* magazine, *Tuesday* newsletter, and *NTF Headlines* newsletter. Funds for this program are provided by Signature Tours. In any 1 year, applicants may receive only 1 award from the association.
Number awarded: 1 each year.
Deadline: April of each year.

3114
SIKH EDUCATION AID FUND

Summary: To provide financial assistance to undergraduate and graduate students who are either Sikhs or are interested in Sikh studies.
See Listing #1009.

3115
SOCIETY OF AUTOMOTIVE ANALYSTS SCHOLARSHIP

Society of Automotive Analysts
Attn: Scholarship
4700 West Lake Avenue
Glenview, IL 60025-1485
Phone: (847) 375-4722
Web Site: www.autoanalyst.org/scholarship/scholar.html
Summary: To provide financial assistance to undergraduate students preparing for a career in the automotive industry.
Eligibility: Eligible to apply for this scholarship are full-time undergraduate students who are majoring in business, economics, finance, marketing, or management. Applicants must have at least a 3.0 grade point average and demonstrate interest in automotive analysis. To apply, students must submit a completed application form, a typed essay (1 page) explaining their interest in the automotive industry, and 1 letter of reference.
Financial data: The stipend is $1,500. Funds are paid to the recipient's school.
Duration: 1 year; nonrenewable.
Number awarded: 3 each year.
Deadline: May of each year.

3116
SONS OF ITALY NATIONAL LEADERSHIP GRANT COMPETITION

Summary: To provide financial assistance for postsecondary education to students who write about the Italian American experience in the United States.
See Listing #1649.

3117
SOUTH CAROLINA ASSOCIATION OF CPA'S SCHOLARSHIP PROGRAM

South Carolina Association of Certified Public Accountants
Attn: Communications Director
570 Chris Drive
West Columbia, SC 29169
Phone: (803) 791-4181, ext. 1006   E-mail: kmowery@scacpa.org
Web Site: www.scacpa.org
Summary: To provide financial assistance to upper-division and graduate students majoring in accounting in South Carolina.
Eligibility: This program is open to South Carolina residents who are upper-division (rising juniors or seniors) or master's degree students majoring in accounting at a South Carolina college or university. Applicants must have at least a 3.25 overall grade point average and at least a 3.5 grade point average in accounting. Interested students must submit their college transcripts, a listing of awards and other scholarships, 2 letters of reference, a resume, a 250-word essay on their personal career goals, and certification of their accounting major. Financial need is not considered in the selection process.
Financial data: Stipends range from $500 to $1,500. Funds are paid to the recipient's school.
Duration: 1 year.
Number awarded: Varies each year.
Deadline: June of each year.

3118
SOUTH DAKOTA CPA SOCIETY SCHOLARSHIPS

South Dakota CPA Society
1000 West Avenue N, Suite 100
Sioux Falls, SD 57101-1798
Phone: (605) 334-3848   Fax: (605) 334-8595
Web Site: www.sdcpa.org/students/scholar.htm
Summary: To provide financial assistance to upper-division students in South Dakota who are majoring in accounting.
Eligibility: This program is open to accounting majors in South Dakota; they must be in their senior year. Applicants must have an excellent academic record, leadership potential, an interest in the profession of public accountancy, and a record of extracurricular activities. To apply, students must submit a completed application form, an official transcript, a brief statement of career goals, a list of awards and extracurricular activities, and a photograph. Financial need is not considered in the selection process.
Financial data: The amount of the awards depends on the availability of funds and the number of qualified applicants.
Duration: 1 year; recipients may reapply.
Number awarded: Varies each year; recently, 9 accounting students received $6,250 in these scholarships.
Deadline: April of each year.

3119
SOUTH DAKOTA RETAILERS ASSOCIATION SCHOLARSHIPS

South Dakota Retailers Association
P.O. Box 638
Pierre, SD 57501
Phone: (605) 224-5050   (800) 658-5545
E-mail: johnsonk@sdra.org   Web Site: www.sdra.org
Summary: To provide financial assistance to South Dakota residents who are interested in pursuing a career in retailing.
Eligibility: This program is open to residents of South Dakota who are interested in a career in a retail field. Applicants must have completed at least 1 quarter of study at a South Dakota vocational school or 1 year of study at a college or university in the state. Full-time enrollment is required. Selection is not based solely on financial need or on outstanding scholarship.
Financial data: The amounts of the stipends vary. A total of at least $3,000 is available for this program each year.
Duration: 1 year.
Additional information: Examples of eligible fields include, but are not limited to, agribusiness, apparel merchandising, auto mechanics, automotive technology, business administration, computer science, culinary arts, commercial baking, electrical maintenance, heating and ventilation, hotel and restaurant management, landscape design, pharmacy, printing industries, sales and marketing management, and tourism industry management.
Number awarded: Varies each year.
Deadline: May of each year.

3120
SOUTH DAKOTA TUITION REDUCTION FOR CERTAIN TEACHERS

South Dakota Board of Regents
Attn: Scholarship Committee
306 East Capitol Avenue, Suite 200
Pierre, SD 57501-3159
Phone: (605) 773-3455   Fax: (605) 773-5320
E-mail: info@bor.state.sd.us   Web Site: www.ris.sdbor.edu
Summary: To provide assistance for additional training to certain elementary and secondary school teachers and vocational instructors in South Dakota.
Eligibility: This program is open to teachers and vocational instructors who are residents of South Dakota and employed by an accredited elementary or secondary school as a teacher or vocational instructor. Applicants must be required by state law, administrative rules, or an employment contract to pursue additional undergraduate or graduate education as a condition of employment or to maintain a certificate to teach.
Financial data: Qualified teachers and instructors are entitled to pay only 50 percent of tuition (but 100 percent of required fees) at a South Dakota state-supported institution of higher education.
Duration: Recipients are entitled to the tuition reduction as long as they meet the eligibility requirements and maintain a grade point average of 3.0 or higher.
Additional information: The tuition reduction can by used for a maximum of 6 credit hours per academic year.
Number awarded: Varies each year.

3121
SOUTHWEST CHAPTER STUDENT SCHOLARSHIPS

Summary: To provide financial assistance to college students pursuing a degree in airport management.
See Listing #2530.

3122
STANLEY H. STEARMAN SCHOLARSHIP AWARD

National Society of Accountants
Attn: NSA Scholarship Foundation
1010 North Fairfax Street
Alexandria, VA 22314-1574
Phone: (703) 549-6400, ext. 1312   (800) 966-6679
Fax: (703) 549-2512   E-mail: dgriffin@nsacct.org
Web Site: www.nsacct.org
Summary: To provide funding for the undergraduate and graduate study of accounting to relatives of active or deceased members of the National Society of Accountants.
Eligibility: Both undergraduate and graduate students may apply for this award. They must be majoring in accounting, have earned at least a 3.0 grade point average, be enrolled full time at an accredited college or university (evening program students are considered full time if they are pursuing an accounting degree), and be the relative (spouse, son, daughter, grandchild, niece, nephew, or son- or daughter-in-law) of an active National Society of Accountants' member or deceased member. Applicants must submit a letter of intent outlining their reasons for seeking the award, their intended career objective, and how this scholarship award would be used to accomplish that objective. Selection is based on academic attainment, demonstrated leadership ability, and financial need.
Financial data: The stipend is $2,000 per year.
Duration: Up to 3 years.
Number awarded: 1 each year.
Deadline: March of each year.

3123
STATE FARM COMPANIES FOUNDATION EXCEPTIONAL STUDENT FELLOWSHIPS

State Farm Companies Foundation
One State Farm Plaza, B-4
Bloomington, IL 61710-0001
Phone: (309) 766-2161   Fax: (309) 766-3700
E-mail: beth.leuck.gan1@statefarm.com
Web Site: www.statefarm.com/foundati/awards.htm
Summary: To provide financial assistance to students who are majoring in business-related subjects in college.
Eligibility: Eligible are U.S. citizens attending an accredited college or university in the United States as full-time juniors or seniors with a grade point average of 3.6 or higher. They must be majoring in such areas as accounting, actuarial science, business administration, computer science, economics, finance, insurance, investments, management, marketing, mathematics, risk management, or statistics. Candidates must be nominated by an academic officer, preferably someone who is personally familiar with the student. Selection is based on academic achievement, leadership in extracurricular activities, character, potential business administrative capacity, and the nomination and recommendations of professors, advisors, and other academic officers or professional contacts.
Financial data: Each award is $3,000. The nominating institution of each recipient also receives a grant of $250 (or $500 if it is a private school).
Duration: 1 year; nonrenewable.
Number awarded: 50 each year.
Deadline: February of each year.

3124
STATLER SCHOLARSHIP OF EXCELLENCE

Community Foundation for the Capital Region
Executive Park Drive
Albany, NY 12203
Phone: (518) 446-9638   Fax: (518) 446-9708
E-mail: info@cfcr.org
Web Site: www.cfcr.org
Summary: To provide financial assistance to students working on an undergraduate or graduate degree in hotel management.
Eligibility: This program is open to students at selected schools; these schools may submit applications from 2 students. Nominated students must be undergraduates (at least sophomores) or graduate students in the hotel management field. Selection is based on academic excellence, character, and commitment to the industry.
Financial data: Each scholarship is worth up to $20,000 for the academic year, to

be used for tuition, fees, books, food, and living expenses.
Duration: 1 year.
Additional information: This program was established in 1997.
Number awarded: Varies each year; recently, 17 were selected.

3125
STEIN ROE YOUNG INVESTOR NATIONAL ESSAY CONTEST

Stein Roe Mutual Funds
Attn: Young Investor Essay Contest
One South Wacker Drive
Chicago, IL 60606
Phone: (800) 403-KIDS
Web Site: www.steinroe.com
Summary: To recognize and reward outstanding essays written by students in grades 5 through 12 on a topic (changes annually) related to money and investing.
Eligibility: This contest is open to students in grades 5 through 12 in the United States. They are invited to submit an essay on a topic related to money and investing. The topic changes annually. Recently, the question 1) for students in grades 5 though 8 was: "What are the most important lessons you have learned about money and investing? How do you think this knowledge will help you in the future?" and 2) for students in grades 9 through 12 was: "Tell us about someone who you consider a successful investor. Please include three rules you believe every investor should follow." Entries must be approximately 250 words in length. Selection is based on content, writing style, and writing mechanics (grammar, spelling, punctuation, and neatness).
Financial data: First place is $5,000; second place is $2,500; and third place is $1,000.
Duration: The competition is held annually.
Additional information: No entries may be submitted on computer disk, by fax, or via the Internet.
Number awarded: 12 each year: 3 prizes for students in each of 4 categories (grades 5 and 6, grades 7 and 8, grades 9 and 10, and grades 11 and 12).
Deadline: December of each year.

3126
STEVE DEARDUFF SCHOLARSHIP

Summary: To provide financial assistance to Georgia residents who are working on an undergraduate or graduate degree, especially in medicine and social work.
See Listing #1046.

3127
STUART CAMERON AND MARGARET MCLEOD MEMORIAL SCHOLARSHIP

Institute of Management Accountants
Attn: Committee on Students
10 Paragon Drive
Montvale, NJ 07645-1760
Phone: (201) 573-9000   (800) 638-4427, ext. 294
Fax: (201) 573-8438   E-mail: students@imanet.org
Web Site: www.imanet.org
Summary: To provide financial assistance to undergraduate or graduate student members of the Institute of Management Accountants (IMA) who are interested in pursuing a career in management accounting or financial management.
Eligibility: Each institute chapter and each institute student chapter is eligible to submit 1 application for each of the 4 categories of scholarships: 1) students graduating from a 2-year college and continuing their education in a 4- or 5-year management accounting, financial management, or information technology program; 2) entering college juniors majoring in management accounting, financial management, or information technology; 3) entering college seniors majoring in management accounting, financial management, or information technology; and 4) students enrolled or planning to enroll in a graduate management accounting, financial management, or information technology program. Both part-time and full-time students are eligible to apply. They must be student members of the sponsoring organization. Selection is based on academic merit, participation in the organization, quality of their presentation, demonstrated community leadership, potential for success in a financial management position, and letters of recommendation. The most outstanding applicant from all categories receives this scholarship.
Financial data: The stipend is $5,000.
Duration: 1 year.
Number awarded: 1 each year.
Deadline: February of each year.

3128
SWACKHAMER PEACE ESSAY CONTEST

Nuclear Age Peace Foundation
1187 Coast Village Road, Suite 123
P.M.B. 121
Santa Barbara, CA 93108-2794
Phone: (805) 965-3443   Fax: (805) 568-0466
E-mail: wagingpeace@napf.org
Web Site: www.wagingpeace.org
Summary: To recognize and reward outstanding essays by high school students on a topic related to war and peace.
Eligibility: Any high school student may enter this contest by writing an essay, up to 1,500 words, on a topic that changes annually but calls for constructive approaches to the problems of war and peace. Essays are judged on the basis of knowledge of subject matter, originality of ideas, development of point of view, insight, clarity of expression, organization, and grammar.
Financial data: First prize is $1,500, second prize is $1,000, and third prize is $500.
Duration: The competition is held annually.
Additional information: Essays become the property of the Nuclear Age Peace Foundation. The prizewinning essay is published by the foundation and sent to the Secretary-General of the United Nations, the President of the United States, and other world and national leaders.
Number awarded: 3 prizes are awarded each year.
Deadline: May of each year.

3129
TAMPA/HILLSBOROUGH LEGACY AWARD

National Tourism Foundation
Attn: Scholarships
546 East Main Street
Lexington, KY 40508-2342
Phone: (859) 226-4444   (800) 682-8886
Fax: (859) 226-4437   E-mail: ntf@ntastaff.com
Web Site: www.ntfonline.org
Summary: To provide financial assistance to college students in Florida who are majoring in tourism.
Eligibility: This program is open to full-time students enrolled in a college or university in Florida. Applicants must be Florida residents, be in their junior or senior year, have at least a 3.0 grade point average, and be majoring in a hospitality or related field (e.g., hotel management, restaurant management, tourism).
Financial data: The stipend is $1,000.
Duration: 1 year.
Additional information: Award winners also receive complimentary registration and an all-expense paid trip (valued at more than $3,000) to the association's annual convention, as well as a 1-year subscription to *Courier* magazine, *Tuesday* newsletter, and *NTF Headlines* newsletter. In any 1 year, applicants may receive only 1 award from the association.
Number awarded: 1 each year.
Deadline: April of each year.

3130
TAPPI CORRUGATED CONTAINERS DIVISION SUPPLIER COMMITTEE SCHOLARSHIPS

Summary: To provide financial assistance to students who are interested in preparing for a career in the paper industry, with a focus on the manufacture and use of corrugated, solid fiber, and associated packaging materials and products.
See Listing #2551.

3131
TDC SCHOLARSHIP

National Association of Black Accountants
Attn: Director, Center for Advancement of Minority Accountants
7249-A Hanover Parkway
Greenbelt, MD 20770
Phone: (301) 474-NABA, ext. 114   Fax: (301) 474-3114
E-mail: cquinn@nabainc.org   Web Site: www.nabainc.org
Summary: To provide financial assistance for undergraduate or graduate education to members of the National Association of Black Accountants (NABA).
Eligibility: This program is open to paid members of the association who are full-time students pursuing a bachelor's or master's degree in accounting, finance,

business administration, or taxation. Applicants must have a grade point average of at least 2.0 in their major and 2.5 overall. Selection is based on grades, financial need, and a 500-word autobiography that discusses career objectives, leadership abilities, community activities, and involvement in the association.
Financial data: The stipend is $1,000 per year.
Duration: 1 year.
Number awarded: 1 each year.
Deadline: December of each year.

3132
TENNESSEE FUNERAL DIRECTORS ASSOCIATION MEMORIAL SCHOLARSHIP PROGRAM

Tennessee Funeral Directors Association
Attn: Scholarship Committee
1616 Church Street
Nashville, TN 37203
Phone: (615) 321-8792   (800) 537-1599 (within TN)
Fax: (615) 321-8794   E-mail: TNfda@aol.com
Summary: To provide financial assistance to Tennessee residents who are preparing for a career in funeral service.
Eligibility: Applicants must be U.S. citizens and Tennessee residents who are enrolled in school on a full-time basis and have completed 2 semesters or one half of their course of study at a college accredited by the American Board of Funeral Service Education. They must have expressed the intent to enter funeral service upon graduation. As part of the application process, students must submit a completed application form, the latest family federal income tax return, college transcripts, 2 letters of recommendation, and a 2-page handwritten essay about themselves. Selection is based on financial need, academic record, recommendations, extracurricular and community activities, and the required essay.
Financial data: A stipend is awarded (exact amount not specified).
Duration: 1 year.
Additional information: This scholarship was established in 1997.

3133
TERRY WALKER SCHOLARSHIP

Summary: To provide financial assistance to students from New York who are preparing to teach Latin in school.
See Listing #1658.

3134
TEXAS CATTLEWOMEN SCHOLARSHIP

Summary: To provide financial assistance to residents of Texas who are majoring in foods and nutrition, agricultural communications, or hotel and restaurant management in college.
See Listing #2558.

3135
TEXAS CERTIFIED EDUCATIONAL AIDE EXEMPTION PROGRAM

Texas Higher Education Coordinating Board
Attn: Grants and Special Programs
1200 East Anderson Lane
P.O. Box 12788, Capitol Station
Austin, TX 78711-2788
Phone: (512) 427-6357   (800) 242-3062, ext. 6357
Fax: (512) 427-6127   E-mail: grantinfo@thecb.state.tx.us
Web Site: www.collegefortexans.com
Summary: To provide financial assistance to educational aides in Texas who wish to attend college to complete full teacher certification.
Eligibility: Applicants for this program must be Texas residents who are currently employed by a Texas public school in any capacity and have worked as an educational aide in a Texas public school for at least 1 year during the preceding 5 years. They must be enrolled at a public institution of higher education in Texas in a program leading to teacher certification. Financial need is considered in the selection process.
Financial data: Eligible students are exempted from the payment of all fees (other than class or laboratory fees) and tuition charges in publicly-supported colleges and universities in Texas. Recently, the average award was $501.
Duration: 1 year.
Number awarded: Varies each year; recently, 3,217 students received support through this program.

3136
TEXAS FIFTH-YEAR ACCOUNTING STUDENT SCHOLARSHIP PROGRAM

Texas Higher Education Coordinating Board
Attn: Grants and Special Programs
1200 East Anderson Lane
P.O. Box 12788, Capitol Station
Austin, TX 78711-2788
Phone: (512) 427-6101   (800) 242-3062
Fax: (512) 427-6127   E-mail: grantinfo@thecb.state.tx.us
Web Site: www.collegefortexans.com
Summary: To provide financial assistance to accounting students attending college in Texas.
Eligibility: This program is open to both residents and nonresidents of Texas. Applicants must be enrolled at least half time and have completed at least 120 hours of college course work, including at least 15 semester credit hours of accounting. They may not have already taken the CPA exam, but they must plan to take it in Texas and be willing to sign a written statement confirming their intent to take the written examination conducted by the Texas State Board of Public Accountancy to become certified public accountants. Selection is based on financial need and scholastic ability and performance.
Financial data: The maximum stipend is $3,000.
Duration: 1 year.
Additional information: Information and application forms may be obtained from the director of financial aid at the public college or university in Texas the applicant attends. This program began in 1996. Study must be conducted in Texas; funds cannot be used to support attendance at an out-of-state institution.
Number awarded: Varies each year; recently, 375 of these awards were granted.

3137
TEXAS TRANSPORTATION SCHOLARSHIP

Summary: To provide financial assistance to college students interested in preparing for a career in fields related to transportation.
See Listing #2562.

3138
TFB FREE ENTERPRISE SPEECH CONTEST

Texas Farm Bureau
P.O. Box 2689
Waco, TX 76702-2689
Phone: (254) 772-3030   E-mail: rglasson@txfb.org
Web Site: www.txfb.org/educate/speechsch.htm
Summary: To recognize and reward members of the Texas Farm Bureau (TFB) who present speeches on free enterprise.
Eligibility: Contestants in this program must have completed the Texas Farm Bureau High School Citizenship Seminar, be a TFB member or a member of a TFB family, and have presented at least 5 speeches concerning free enterprise.
Financial data: District winners receive $1,000 scholarships. Winners at the state contest have the opportunity to receive additional funding to increase their scholarship to $1,500 as finalists, $2,500 as runner-up, or $4,000 as state winner.
Duration: The contest is held annually.
Number awarded: 13 district winners are selected each year. Of those, 4 are designated as finalists, 1 as runner-up, and 1 as the state winner.

3139
THOMAS F. SEAY SCHOLARSHIP

Illinois Association of Realtors
Attn: Illinois Real Estate Educational Foundation
3180 Adloff Lane, Suite 400
P.O. Box 19451
Springfield, IL 62794-9451
Phone: (217) 529-2600   E-mail: IARaccess@iar.org
Web Site: www.illinoisrelator.org/iar/about/scholarships.htm
Summary: To provide financial assistance to Illinois residents who are preparing for a career in real estate.
Eligibility: All applicants must be U.S. citizens and Illinois residents who are attending a college or university in any state on a full-time basis and pursuing a degree with an emphasis in real estate. They must have completed at least 30 credits

with a GPA of at least 3.5 on a 5.0 scale. As part of the application process, students must submit copies of their transcripts and letters of recommendation and reference. Selection is based on academic record, economic need, references and recommendations, and career plans in the field of real estate or an allied field (e.g., construction, land use planning, mortgage banking, property management, real estate appraising, real estate assessing, real estate brokerage, real estate development, real estate investment counseling, real estate law, and real estate syndication). Finalists are interviewed.
Financial data: The stipend is $2,000.
Duration: 1 year.
Deadline: March of each year.

3140
THURGOOD MARSHALL SCHOLARSHIP AWARD

National Association of Blacks in Criminal Justice
c/o North Carolina Central University
106 Criminal Justice Building
P.O. Box 19788
Durham, NC 27707
Phone: (919) 683-1801   Fax: (919) 683-1903
E-mail: office@nabcj.org   Web Site: www.nabcj.org
Summary: To provide financial assistance to undergraduate students who are majoring in criminal justice or a closely-related field.
Eligibility: Eligible to apply for this program are students who are accepted or currently enrolled in a degree program in criminal justice. Applicants must be U.S. citizens, have at least a 3.0 grade point average, and write a 1,000-word essay on why they have chosen a criminal justice career. Selection is based on academic excellence and financial need (supporting documentation is required).
Financial data: The stipend is $2,000.
Duration: 1 year.
Number awarded: 1 each year.
Deadline: March of each year.

3141
THZ FO FARM FUND

Hawai'i Community Foundation
900 Fort Street Mall, Suite 1300
Honolulu, HI 96813
Phone: (808) 566-5570   (888) 731-3863
Fax: (808) 521-6286   E-mail: scholarships@hcf-hawaii.org
Web Site: www.hcf-hawaii.org
Summary: To provide financial assistance to Hawaii residents of Chinese descent who are interested in studying gerontology on the undergraduate or graduate school level.
Eligibility: This program is open to high school seniors, high school graduates, and college students in Hawaii who are of Chinese ancestry and are interested in studying gerontology as full-time undergraduate or graduate students. They must be able to demonstrate academic achievement (at least a 2.7 grade point average), good moral character, and financial need. In addition to filling out the standard application form, applicants must write a short statement indicating their reasons for attending college, their planned course of study, and their career goals.
Financial data: The amounts of the awards depend on the availability of funds and the need of the recipient; recently, grants averaged $1,000.
Duration: 1 year.
Additional information: Recipients may attend college in Hawaii or on the mainland.
Number awarded: Varies each year; recently, 7 of these scholarships were awarded.
Deadline: February of each year.

3142
TLMI SCHOLARSHIP PROGRAM

Summary: To provide financial assistance to third- and fourth-year college students who are preparing for a career in the tag and label manufacturing industry.
See Listing #1666.

3143
TOBIN SORENSON SCHOLARSHIPS

Summary: To provide financial assistance to students preparing for careers as a teacher of physical education or a related field.
See Listing #2573.

3144
TRANSIT HALL OF FAME SCHOLARSHIP AWARDS

Summary: to provide financial assistance to upper-division and graduate students who are preparing for a career in transportation.
See Listing #2577.

3145
TRAVIS C. TOMLIN SCHOLARSHIP

National Association of Black Accountants
Attn: Director, Center for Advancement of Minority Accountants
7249-A Hanover Parkway
Greenbelt, MD 20770
Phone: (301) 474-NABA, ext. 114   Fax: (301) 474-3114
E-mail: cquinn@nabainc.org   Web Site: www.nabainc.org
Summary: To provide financial assistance for undergraduate or graduate education to members of the National Association of Black Accountants (NABA).
Eligibility: Applicants must be paid members of the association who are full-time students pursuing a bachelor's or master's degree in accounting, finance, business administration, or taxation. Applicants must have a GPA of at least 3.5 in their major and 3.3 overall. Selection is based on grades, financial need, and a 500-word autobiography that discusses career objectives, leadership abilities, community activities, and involvement in the association.
Financial data: The stipend is $1,000 per year.
Duration: 1 year.
Number awarded: 1 each year.
Deadline: December of each year.

3146
TREVA C. KINTNER SCHOLARSHIPS

Phi Upsilon Omicron
Attn: Educational Foundation
P.O. Box 329
Fairmont, WV 26555-0329
Phone: (304) 368-0612   E-mail: rickards@access.mountain.net
Web Site: ianrwww.unl.edu/phiu
Summary: To provide financial assistance to older undergraduate student members of Phi Upsilon Omicron, a national honor society in family and consumer sciences.
Eligibility: Undergraduates who are members of the society, are over 30 years of age, and have completed at least half of their academic work toward a bachelor's degree in family and consumer sciences are eligible to apply. Selection is based on scholastic record, participation in the society, participation in other collegiate activities, professional goals, and personal qualifications.
Financial data: The stipend is $1,000.
Duration: 1 year.
Number awarded: 2 each year.
Deadline: January of each year.

3147
TROOPER JEFFREY S. PAROLA SCHOLARSHIP FOUNDATION AWARDS

Trooper Jeffrey S. Parola Scholarship Foundation
c/o Judy Raymond, Secretary
33 Shore Road South
Dover Foxcroft, ME 04426   Phone: (207) 564-2246
Summary: To provide financial assistance to Maine high school seniors interested in studying law enforcement or criminal justice in college.
Eligibility: This program is open to seniors graduating from high schools in Maine who are interested in entering the fields of law enforcement or criminal justice. Applicants must have a grade point average of 2.0 or higher. Selection is based on grade point average, participation in sports, and an essay.
Financial data: The stipend ranges from $200 to $1,000.
Duration: 1 year.
Additional information: Information is also available from the foundation's vice-president, John Parola, 61 Deerfield Road, Ripley, ME 04930, (207) 924-6401.
Number awarded: Varies each year. At least 1 award is presented to a graduate of Dexter High School.
Deadline: March of each year.

3148
TWLE SCHOLARSHIP AWARDS

Summary: To provide financial assistance for college to members of the Texas Women in Law Enforcement (TWLE) and their relatives.
See Listing #1099.

3149
TYSON FOUNDATION SCHOLARSHIP PROGRAM

Summary: To provide financial assistance to undergraduate students in selected disciplines who reside near a plant of Tyson Foods, Inc.
See Listing #2582.

3150
UABT SCHOLARSHIP PROGRAM

Summary: To provide financial assistance to students pursuing an undergraduate degree in agriculture or agribusiness.
See Listing #2583.

3151
UNDERGRADUATE TRAINING ASSISTANCE PROGRAM

Summary: To provide full tuition and internships to high school seniors interested in majoring in specified fields and working for the U.S. Defense Intelligence Agency (DIA).
See Listing #2587.

3152
UNITED AGRIBUSINESS LEAGUE SCHOLARSHIP PROGRAM

Summary: To provide financial assistance to students pursuing an undergraduate degree in agriculture or agribusiness.
See Listing #2588.

3153
UNITED NATIONS ASSOCIATION OF THE UNITED STATES HIGH SCHOOL ESSAY CONTEST

United Nations Association of the United States
801 Second Avenue
New York, NY 10007
Phone: (212) 907-1326   Fax: (212) 682-9187
E-mail: jgagain@unausa.org
Web Site: www.unausa.org
Summary: To recognize and reward outstanding high school student essays on a topic of international importance that changes annually.
Eligibility: This essay contest is open to students in grades 9 through 12. Students are invited to write an essay on a topic of international importance; the topic changes annually. Recently, the topic involved the steps international agencies can take to control infectious diseases in developing countries. Essays must be 1,500 words or less and must include endnotes and a bibliography of all sources. Judging takes place first on a local area; finalists then compete nationally. Selection is based on an understanding of the issues, an ability to grasp the wider implication of the issue on a global level, clarity and effectiveness of style and organization, originality in approach and treatment of the topic, evidence of research and use of bibliography, and adherence to the format and length rules.
Financial data: First prize is $1,000, second $750, and third $500.
Duration: The competition is held annually.
Number awarded: 3 each year.
Deadline: April of each year.

3154
UNITED STATES SENATE YOUTH PROGRAM SCHOLARSHIPS

Summary: To recognize and reward outstanding high school student leaders.
See Listing #1111.

3155
URBAN BANKERS OF DELAWARE SCHOLARSHIP

Urban Bankers of Delaware
P.O. Box 580
Wilmington, DE 19899-0580
Phone: (302) 451-6811   Web Site: www.ubod.org/Scholarship.htm
Summary: To provide financial assistance to needy high school seniors in Delaware interested in majoring in business in college.
Eligibility: This program is open to high school seniors who reside in Delaware, are able to demonstrate financial need, and plan to major in business at an accredited college or university. Applicants must have at least a 2.0 GPA. Finalists are interviewed.
Financial data: The stipend is $1,000.
Duration: 1 year.
Additional information: These scholarships have been awarded annually since 1993.
Deadline: March of each year.

3156
USDA/1890 NATIONAL SCHOLARS PROGRAM

Summary: To provide financial assistance to high school seniors and graduates interested in majoring in a field related to agriculture or agribusiness at 1 of the 17 Historically Black 1890 Land Grant Institutions.
See Listing #2593.

3157
UTAH CREDIT UNION SCHOLARSHIP CONTEST

Utah League of Credit Unions
Attn: Scholarship Contest
P.O. Box 84127
Salt Lake City, UT 84127
Summary: To recognize and reward outstanding essays written by high school juniors or seniors in Utah on a topic that relates to banking but changes annually.
Eligibility: Any Utah high school junior or senior who is a credit union member or whose parents are credit union members is eligible. There is no limit on the number of students who may enter from any school. Students are invited to write a 1,000-word essay on a topic (changes annually) that relates to banking or credit unions; recently, the topic was "Bankruptcy—what is the impact on consumers and our society?" Essays are evaluated on the following: content (100 points), organization (50 points), research (50 points), grammar (25 points), and presentation (25 points).
Financial data: First prize is $1,500; second prize is $1,000; and third prize is $500.
Duration: The competition is held annually.
Number awarded: 3 each year.
Deadline: September of each year.

3158
UTAH JAZZ "TEACHERS FOR ALL" SCHOLARSHIP

Utah Education Association
Attn: Children at Risk Foundation
875 East 5180 South
Murray, UT 84107
Phone: (801) 266-4461, ext. 154   (800) 594-8996
Fax: (801) 265-2249   Web Site: www.utea.org
Summary: To provide financial assistance to residents of Utah who wish to become teachers in minority communities.
Eligibility: There is no age requirement to apply. Applicants may be high school seniors, current college students, or adults not in college but who have completed a high school diploma. All applicants must be Utah residents interested in becoming teachers in minority communities. Applicants who are not minorities themselves must have experience, skills, and demonstrated commitment to working with minority communities. Foreign language ability is helpful but not required. Recipients are selected on the basis of academic achievement, participation in minority communities (e.g., civic, church, educational, or club activities), public service to minority communities, and recommendations by those familiar with their work.
Financial data: The stipend is $1,000. Upon attainment of their teaching certificate, recipients are awarded an additional $500 stipend.
Duration: 1 year.
Number awarded: 10 each year.
Deadline: February of each year.

3159
VERMONT FEED DEALERS AND MANUFACTURERS ASSOCIATION SCHOLARSHIP

Summary: To provide financial assistance to residents of Vermont who are interested in majoring in an agriculture or agribusiness in college.
See Listing #2599.

3160
VERMONT SHERIFFS' ASSOCIATION SCHOLARSHIP

Vermont Student Assistance Corporation
Champlain Mill
1 Main Street, Fourth Floor
P.O. Box 2000
Winooski, VT 05404-2601
Phone: (802) 655-9602   (800) 642-3177
Fax: (802) 654-3765   TDD: (802) 654-3766
Phone: TDD: (800) 281-3341 (within VT)   E-mail: info@vsac.org
Web Site: www.vsac.org
Summary: To provide financial assistance to residents of Vermont who are interested in majoring in law enforcement in college.
Eligibility: This program is open to residents of Vermont who are graduating high school seniors, high school graduates, or GED recipients. Applicants must be interested in attending an accredited postsecondary institution to pursue a degree in law enforcement. Selection is based on academic achievement, required essays, and financial need.
Financial data: The stipend is $1,000.
Duration: 1 year.
Number awarded: 2 each year.
Deadline: June of each year.

3161
VERMONT SUBCONTRACTORS ASSOCIATION SCHOLARSHIP

Summary: To provide financial assistance to high school seniors in Vermont who are interested in preparing for a career in the construction industry.
See Listing #2601.

3162
VIRGINIA HIGHER EDUCATION TEACHER ASSISTANCE PROGRAM

State Council of Higher Education for Virginia
Attn: Financial Aid Office
James Monroe Building
101 North 14th Street, Ninth Floor
Richmond, VA 23219-3659
Phone: (804) 225-2600   (877) 515-0138
Fax: (804) 225-2604   TDD: (804) 371-8017
E-mail: fainfo@schev.edu   Web Site: www.schev.edu
Summary: To provide financial assistance to residents of Virginia who are interested in pursuing a K-12 teacher preparation program in college.
Eligibility: This program is open to residents of Virginia who are enrolled, or intend to enroll, full time in an eligible K-12 teacher preparation program at a public or private Virginia college or university. Applicants must 1) be U.S. citizens or eligible noncitizens; 2) demonstrate financial need; 3) have a cumulative college grade point average of 2.5 or higher; and 4) be nominated by a faculty member. Preference is given to applicants enrolled in a teacher shortage content area.
Financial data: Stipends are $2,000 per year for students at 4-year institutions or $1,000 per year for students at 2-year institutions.
Duration: 1 year; may be renewed if funds are available and the recipient maintains satisfactory academic progress.
Additional information: Applications and further information are available at the financial aid office of colleges and universities in Virginia. This program, established in 2000, is funded in part with federal funds from the Special Leveraging Educational Assistance Partnership (SLEAP) program. Recently, the teacher shortage areas included special education, mathematics, chemistry, physics, earth and space science, foreign languages, technology education, minority students enrolled in any content area for teacher preparation, and male students enrolled in any approved elementary or middle-school teacher preparation program.
Number awarded: Varies each year.

3163
VIRGINIA PTA ANNUAL CITIZENSHIP ESSAY PROJECT

Virginia Congress of Parents and Teachers
1027 Wilmer Avenue
Richmond, VA 23227-2419
Phone: (804) 264-1234   Fax: (804) 264-4014
E-mail: info@vapta.org
Web Site: www.vapta.org
Summary: To recognize and reward outstanding essays on patriotic themes written by high school students in Virginia.
Eligibility: This competition is open to high school students in Virginia. They are invited to write an essay (up to 500 words) on a topic that changes annually but always relates to patriotism; recently, the topic was: "If I Were to Choose a Symbol for America, It Would Be."
Financial data: First place: $1,000 savings bond; second place: $500 savings bond; third place: $500 savings bond.
Duration: The competition is held annually.
Additional information: This annual competition began in 1999.
Number awarded: 3 prizes each year.
Deadline: February of each year.

3164
VIRGINIA PTA SCHOLARSHIPS

Virginia Congress of Parents and Teachers
1027 Wilmer Avenue
Richmond, VA 23227-2419
Phone: (804) 264-1234   Fax: (804) 264-4014
E-mail: info@vapta.org   Web Site: www.vapta.org
Summary: To provide financial assistance to high school seniors in Virginia who are interested in preparing for a teaching or related career.
Eligibility: This program is open to graduating high school students in Virginia who are planning to enter teaching or other youth-serving professions in Virginia. Applicants must have at least a 2.5 grade point average.
Financial data: The stipend is either $1,000 or $1,200 (for the 2 named scholarships) per year.
Duration: 1 year.
Additional information: This program includes 2 named scholarships: M. Frieda Koontz Scholarship ($1,200) and S. John Davis Scholarship ($1,200). Recipients must attend college in Virginia.
Number awarded: Varies each year; recently, 13 were awarded.
Deadline: February of each year.

3165
VIRGINIA SOCIETY FOR HEALTHCARE HUMAN RESOURCES ADMINISTRATION SCHOLARSHIP

Virginia Society for Healthcare Human Resources Administration
c/o Janice Gibbs
Obici Hospital HR Department
1900 North Main Street
Suffolk, VA 23434
Phone: (757) 934-4602   E-mail: jgibbs.obici.com
Summary: To provide financial assistance for college to undergraduate and graduate students in Virginia pursuing a degree in human relations and interested in working in a health care setting.
Eligibility: This program is open to residents of Virginia currently enrolled in an accredited college or university in the state and pursuing a declared major in human resources administration or a related field. Applicants must be at least a second-semester sophomore when the application is submitted and have a demonstrated interest in working in a health care setting. Selection is based on a 1-page statement outlining the applicant's life and work experiences that support an interest in human relations, specifically in a health care setting; official transcripts; and 2 letters of recommendation from faculty members.
Financial data: The stipend is $1,000.
Duration: 1 year.
Number awarded: 1 each year.
Deadline: August of each year.

3166
VIRGINIA SOCIETY OF CERTIFIED PUBLIC ACCOUNTANTS UNDERGRADUATE ACCOUNTING SCHOLARSHIP

Virginia Society of Certified Public Accountants Education Foundation
P.O. Box 4620
Glen Allen, VA 23058-4620
Phone: (804) 270-5344   Fax: (804) 273-1741
E-mail: vscpa@vscpa.com
Web Site: www.vscpa.com
Summary: To provide financial assistance to students enrolled in a Virginia college or university undergraduate accounting program.
Eligibility: Applicants must be currently enrolled in a Virginia college or university undergraduate accounting program. They must be U.S. citizens, be majoring in accounting, have completed at least 12 hours of accounting, and have at least a 3.0 grade point average. As part of the application process, students must submit their most recent official transcript, a current resume, a faculty letter of recommendation, and an essay on how they plan to finance their education.
Financial data: A stipend is awarded (exact amount not specified).
Duration: 1 year.
Deadline: July of each year.

3167
VIRGINIA TOURISM SCHOLARSHIP

National Tourism Foundation
Attn: Scholarships
546 East Main Street
Lexington, KY 40508-2342
Phone: (859) 226-4444   (800) 682-8886
Fax: (859) 226-4437   E-mail: ntf@ntastaff.com
Web Site: www.ntfonline.org
Summary: To provide financial assistance to college students in Virginia who are majoring in tourism.
Eligibility: This program is open to full-time students enrolled in a 2-year or 4-year college or university in Virginia. Applicants must be Virginia residents, have at least a 3.0 grade point average, and be majoring in a travel or tourism-related field (e.g., hotel management, restaurant management, tourism).
Financial data: The stipend is $1,000.
Duration: 1 year.
Additional information: Award winners also receive complimentary registration and an all-expense paid trip (valued at more than $3,000) to the association's annual convention, as well as a 1-year subscription to *Courier* magazine, *Tuesday* newsletter, and *NTF Headlines* newsletter. In any 1 year, applicants may receive only 1 award from the association.
Number awarded: 1 each year.
Deadline: April of each year.

3168
VOICE OF DEMOCRACY SCHOLARSHIP PROGRAM

Summary: To recognize and reward outstanding high school students in a national broadcast scriptwriting competition that focuses on freedom and democracy.
See Listing #1679.

3169
VONA J. WAGNER MEMORIAL SCHOLARSHIP

Summary: To provide financial assistance to high school seniors in Colorado who are interested in preparing for a career in construction.
See Listing #2607.

3170
WALLACE S. & WILMA K. LAUGHLIN FOUNDATION TRUST SCHOLARSHIP FUND

Wallace S. & Wilma K. Laughlin Foundation Trust
c/o Nebraska Funeral Directors Association
Attn: Laughlin Trust Committee
2727 West Second Street
P.O. Box 2118
Hastings, NE 68902-2118
Phone: (402) 462-8900   Fax: (402) 463-5683

Summary: To provide financial assistance to residents of Nebraska who are interested in preparing for a career in mortuary science.
Eligibility: This program is open to residents of Nebraska who are graduates of a Nebraska high school and have met the pre-mortuary academic requirements set by the state prior to entering a mortuary science college. Students planning to attend a 1-year course of study must apply prior to entering an accredited mortuary school. Students planning a 4-year course of study must apply prior to entering the third year of study. All applicants are interviewed. Financial need is considered in the selection process.
Financial data: Stipends are at least $1,000 per year. Funds are paid directly to the recipient's school.
Duration: 1 year.
Additional information: This scholarship is administered by the Nebraska Funeral Directors Association.
Number awarded: Varies, depending upon the funds available.

3171
WALT DISNEY COMPANY FOUNDATION SCHOLARSHIP

Summary: To provide financial assistance to high school seniors who participated in the Junior Achievement program and are interested in majoring in business or the fine arts in college.
See Listing #1681.

3172
WALTER REED SMITH SCHOLARSHIP PROGRAM

Summary: To provide financial assistance for education in designated fields to mature women who are lineal descendants of Confederate veterans.
See Listing #2614.

3173
WARNER NORCROSS & JUDD PARALEGAL ASSISTANT STUDIES SCHOLARSHIP

Grand Rapids Community Foundation
Attn: Education Program Associate
209-C Waters Building
161 Ottawa Avenue N.W.
Grand Rapids, MI 49503-2757
Phone: (616) 454-1751, ext. 103   Fax: (616) 454-6455
E-mail: rbishop@grfoundation.org   Web Site: www.grfoundation.org
Summary: To provide financial assistance to minority residents of Michigan who are interested in studying in a paralegal studies program at an institution in the state.
Eligibility: This program is open to minority students currently residing in Michigan. Applicants must be accepted at or enrolled in an accredited public or private 2- or 4-year college or university with a declared major in paralegal/legal assistant studies. The institution must also be in Michigan.
Financial data: The stipend is $2,000.
Duration: 1 year.
Additional information: Funding for this program is provided by the law firm Warner Norcross & Judd LLP.
Number awarded: 1 each year.
Deadline: April of each year.

3174
WASA/PEMCO 21ST CENTURY EDUCATOR SCHOLARSHIP

Washington Association of School Administrators
825 Fifth Avenue, S.E.
Olympia, WA 98501
Phone: (360) 943-5717
Summary: To provide financial assistance to minority and other high school seniors in the state of Washington who are interested in majoring in education in college.
Eligibility: This program is open to high school seniors who are enrolled in a Washington public or accredited private school, have at least a 3.0 grade point average, and intend to major and pursue a career in K-12 education. To apply, students must submit a completed application form, a criteria essay, a goals essay, 3 reference letters, and an official grades transcript. Selection is based on leadership, community service, honors and awards, student activities, and educational goals. Each year, 1 of the scholarships is awarded to a minority applicant.
Financial data: The stipend is $1,000 per year.
Duration: 4 years.

Additional information: This program is sponsored jointly by the Washington Association of School Administrators (WASA) and PEMCO Financial Services. Faxed applications will not be accepted.
Number awarded: 3 each year: 1 to a minority student, 1 to a student from eastern Washington, and 1 to a student from western Washington.
Deadline: March of each year.

3175
WASHINGTON APPLE COMMISSION SCHOLARSHIP FUND

Summary: To provide financial assistance for a commodity-related degree in college to children whose parents or guardians are commercial growers or the employees of commercial growers of Washington apples.
See Listing #2616.

3176
WASHINGTON CROSSING FOUNDATION SCHOLARSHIPS

Washington Crossing Foundation
Attn: Vice Chairman
P.O. Box 503
Levittown, PA 19058-0503
Phone: (215) 949-8841
Web Site: www.gwcf.org
Summary: To provide financial assistance for undergraduate education to students planning careers in government service.
Eligibility: Eligible are high school seniors who are U.S. citizens and are planning careers of service in local, state, or federal government. Applications must be accompanied by a 1-page essay describing why the student plans a career in government service, including any inspiration derived from the leadership of George Washington in his famous crossing of the Delaware. Selection is based on understanding of career requirements, purpose in choice of a career, preparation for their career, qualities of leadership exhibited, sincerity, and historical perspective.
Financial data: First place, designated the Ann Hawkes Hutton Scholarship, is $10,000 ($2,500 per year); second place, designated the I. Jerome and Harriet R. Scheckter Scholarship, is $7,500 ($1,875 per year); third place, designated the Frank and Katharine Davis Scholarship, is $5,000 ($1,250 per year); other awards include the W. James MacIntosh Scholarship for $2,500 ($625 per year) and the Theodore Clattenburg Scholarship for $1,500 ($375 per year).
Duration: 4 years, provided the recipient maintains a suitable scholastic level and continues his or her career objective.
Number awarded: 5 each year.
Deadline: January of each year.

3177
WASHINGTON SOCIETY OF CPAS FIFTH-YEAR ACCOUNTING SCHOLARSHIPS

Washington Society of Certified Public Accountants
Attn: Educational Assistance Advisory Committee
902 140th Avenue N.E.
Bellevue, WA 98005-3480
Phone: (425) 644-4800   (800) 272-8273 (within WA)
Fax: (425) 562-8853   E-mail: memberservices@wscpa.org
Web Site: www.wscpa.org
Summary: To provide financial assistance to economically disadvantaged accounting students in Washington who are pursuing the additional training required to sit for the CPA examination.
Eligibility: This program is open to accounting students at accredited colleges and universities in Washington who have completed at least 120 semester hours of academic credit and are enrolled in a program that will qualify them to sit for the CPA examination. Applicants must qualify as economically disadvantaged. Preference is given to residents of Washington state. U.S. citizenship is required. Selection is based on their intent to take the CPA examination, financial need, probability of success, underrepresentation in the profession, and accounting-related work experience.
Financial data: The stipend is $2,750. Funds may be used for tuition, fees, books, and living expenses.
Duration: 1 year; may be renewed until the recipient completes the additional 30-hour requirement.
Number awarded: 1 or more each year.
Deadline: April of each year.

3178
WASHINGTON SOCIETY OF CPAS SCHOLARSHIP FOR MINORITY ACCOUNTING MAJORS

Washington Society of Certified Public Accountants
Attn: Scholarship Committee
902 140th Avenue N.E.
Bellevue, WA 98005-3480
Phone: (425) 644-4800   (800) 272-8273 (within WA)
Fax: (425) 562-8853   E-mail: memberservices@wscpa.org
Web Site: www.wscpa.org
Summary: To provide financial assistance to minority students in Washington who are majoring in accounting.
Eligibility: This program is open to accounting majors who have completed their sophomore year at an accredited 4-year institution in Washington by fall of the year they are applying. Applicants must be members of a minority group (African American, Asian American, Hispanic American, or Native American). U.S. citizenship is required. Selection is based on academic achievement (grade point average of 3.0 or higher), campus and/or community activities, work history, a personal statement that includes their career goals and interests and how they anticipate that the accounting curriculum will enhance their career objectives, and 2 letters of recommendation.
Financial data: The stipend is $3,500 per year. Funds may be used to pay for tuition only.
Duration: 1 year; nonrenewable.
Number awarded: 1 each year.
Deadline: March of each year.

3179
WASHINGTON SOCIETY OF CPAS SCHOLARSHIPS FOR ACCOUNTING MAJORS

Washington Society of Certified Public Accountants
Attn: Scholarship Committee
902 140th Avenue N.E.
Bellevue, WA 98005-3480
Phone: (425) 644-4800   (800) 272-8273 (within WA)
Fax: (425) 562-8853   E-mail: memberservices@wscpa.org
Web Site: www.wscpa.org
Summary: To provide financial assistance to students in Washington who are majoring in accounting.
Eligibility: This program is open to accounting majors who have completed their sophomore year at an accredited 4-year institution in Washington by fall of the year they are applying. Applicants must submit a personal statement that includes their career goals and interests and how they anticipate that the accounting curriculum will enhance their career objectives. Selection is based on that statement, academic achievement (grade point average of 3.0 or higher), campus and/or community activities, work history, and 2 letters of recommendation.
Financial data: The stipend is $3,500 per year. Funds may be used to pay for tuition only.
Duration: 1 year; nonrenewable.
Number awarded: 4 each year.
Deadline: March of each year.

3180
WEETA F. COLEBANK SCHOLARSHIP

National Tourism Foundation
Attn: Scholarships
546 East Main Street
Lexington, KY 40508-2342
Phone: (859) 226-4444   (800) 682-8886
Fax: (859) 226-4437   E-mail: ntf@ntastaff.com
Web Site: www.ntfonline.org
Summary: To provide financial assistance to college students in Mississippi who are majoring in tourism.
Eligibility: This program is open to full-time students enrolled in a 4-year college or university in Mississippi. Applicants must be in their junior or senior year of study, be residents of Mississippi, have at least a 3.0 grade point average, and be majoring in a travel or tourism-related field (e.g., hotel management, restaurant management, tourism).
Financial data: The stipend is $1,000.
Duration: 1 year.
Additional information: Award winners also receive complimentary

registration and an all-expense paid trip (valued at more than $3,000) to the association's annual convention, as well as a 1-year subscription to *Courier* magazine, *Tuesday* newsletter, and *NTF Headlines* newsletter. In any 1 year, applicants may receive only 1 award from the association.
Number awarded: 1 each year.
Deadline: April of each year.

3181
WEST VIRGINIA FUNERAL DIRECTORS ASSOCIATION SCHOLARSHIPS

West Virginia Funeral Directors Association
815 Quarrier Street, Suite 215
Charles, WV 25301-2641
Phone: (304) 345-4711
Summary: To provide financial assistance to residents of West Virginia who are currently enrolled in a mortuary school.
Eligibility: Eligible to apply for this support are students currently enrolled in a mortuary school. They must be residents of West Virginia (for at least 2 years), have completed at least 1 semester or quarter of their mortuary science program, have earned at least a 2.5 grade point average in the program, and be able to demonstrate financial need.
Financial data: The stipend is $1,000.
Duration: 1 year.
Number awarded: 1 to 2 each year.

3182
WILLIAM H. ERWIN, JR. SCHOLARSHIP

Greater Kanawha Valley Foundation
Attn: Scholarship Coordinator
One Huntington Square, 16th Floor
900 Lee Street, East
P.O. Box 3041
Charleston, WV 25331-3041
Phone: (304) 346-3620   Fax: (304) 346-3640
E-mail: tgkvf@tgkvf.com
Web Site: www.tgkvf.com/scholarship.html
Summary: To provide financial assistance to students in West Virginia who are pursuing a degree in a field related to health care finance.
Eligibility: This program is open to residents of West Virginia who are entering their junior, senior, or graduate year of study at a state-operated college or university in the state. Applicants must have at least a 2.5 grade point average and demonstrate good moral character. Preference is given to students pursuing a degree in business or some phase of health care finance. Selection is based on financial need and scholastic ability.
Financial data: The stipend is $1,000 per year.
Duration: Normally, 2 years.
Additional information: Funding for this program is provided by the West Virginia Healthcare Financial Management Association.
Number awarded: 1 each year.
Deadline: February of each year.

3183
WILLIAM L. CULLISON SCHOLARSHIP

Summary: To provide financial assistance to college students who are interested in preparing for a career in the pulp and paper industry.
See Listing #2626.

3184
WISCONSIN FUNERAL DIRECTORS FOUNDATION SCHOLARSHIP PROGRAM

Wisconsin Funeral Directors Foundation, Ltd.
c/o Steil Camacho Funeral Home
206 East Harriett Street
Darlington, WI 53530
Phone: (608) 776-2461
Summary: To provide financial assistance to funeral service students in Wisconsin.
Eligibility: To apply, students must be legal residents of Wisconsin who have completed 1 year of mortuary college with at least a 3.0 grade point average (for at least 30 semester or 45 quarter credits). As part of the application, the students

must submit a statement (up to 500 words) on their goals in funeral service and how they plan to accomplish these goals.

Financial data: The stipend is $1,000.

Duration: 1 year.

Number awarded: 1 each year.

Deadline: May of each year.

3185
WISCONSIN RESTAURANT ASSOCIATION EDUCATION FOUNDATION SCHOLARSHIP IN FOODSERVICE

Wisconsin Restaurant Association
Attn: Education Foundation
2801 Fish Hatchery Road
Madison, WI 53713
Phone: (608) 270-9950   (800) 589-3211
Fax: (608) 270-9960
Web Site: www.wirestaurant.org/edfound/car_scholar_info.htm

Summary: To provide financial assistance to Wisconsin residents interested in preparing for a career in the food service industry.

Eligibility: This program is open to residents of Wisconsin who are currently working for a food service employer in the state. Applicants must be either 1) enrolled or planning to enroll in a food service program or a culinary apprenticeship program at a technical college in Wisconsin as a full-time student, or 2) enrolled or planning to enroll in a food service program at a 4-year college or university anywhere in the United States as a full-time student. Students who are already in a technical college or a 4-year institution must submit a current transcript of grades. New students and entering freshmen must provide an acceptance letter from the college or university that includes the intended program. All applicants must submit high school transcripts, a letter of nomination from their employer, and a letter of nomination from an instructor. Financial need is not considered in the selection process.

Financial data: Stipends are either $1,500 or $750.

Duration: 1 year.

Number awarded: Varies each year.

Deadline: April of each year.

3186
WLMA STUDENT GRANT-IN-AID

Washington Library Media Association
P.O. Box 50194
Bellevue, WA 98015-0194
E-mail: wlma@wlma.org   Web Site: www.wlma.org

Summary: To provide financial assistance to college students in Washington who are interested in library media training.

Eligibility: This program is open to undergraduates in Washington who are enrolled in a degree program and are interested in library media training. Selection is based on academic record, work experience, financial need, and recommendations.

Financial data: The stipend is $1,000.

Duration: 1 year.

Additional information: Information is also available from the WLMA Scholarship Chair, Camille Hefty, (253) 589-3223, E-mail: Camille_Hefty@fp.k12.wa.us.

Number awarded: 1 each year.

Deadline: April of each year.

3187
WOMEN AT RISK ACCOUNTING SCHOLARSHIPS

Educational Foundation for Women in Accounting
Attn: Administrative Office
P.O. Box 1925
Southeastern, PA 19399-1925
Phone: (610) 407-9229   Fax: (610) 407-0286
E-mail: info@efwa.org   Web Site: www.efwa.org

Summary: To provide financial support to women accounting students who are the sole source of support for themselves and their families.

Eligibility: This program is open to women who, either through divorce or death of a spouse, have become the sole source of support for themselves and their family. They must wish to pursue a degree in accounting as a means to gainful employment. Women who are single parents as a result of other circumstances are also considered. Applicants should be in their third, fourth, or fifth year of study. Selection is based on aptitude for accounting, commitment to the goal of

pursuing a degree in accounting (including evidence of continued commitment after receiving this award), clear evidence that the candidate has established goals and a plan for achieving those goals, and financial need.

Financial data: The stipend is $2,000 per year.

Duration: 1 year; may be renewed 1 additional year if the recipient completes at least 12 hours each semester.

Number awarded: 1 each year.

Deadline: April of each year.

3188
WOMEN IN TRANSITION ACCOUNTING SCHOLARSHIP

Educational Foundation for Women in Accounting
Attn: Administrative Office
P.O. Box 1925
Southeastern, PA 19399-1925
Phone: (610) 407-9229   Fax: (610) 407-0286
E-mail: info@efwa.org   Web Site: www.efwa.org

Summary: To provide financial support to women who have become the sole support of their family and wish to work on an accounting degree.

Eligibility: This program is open to women who, either through divorce of death of a spouse, have become the sole source of support for themselves and their family. They must wish to pursue a degree in accounting as a means to gainful employment. Women who are single parents as a result of other circumstances are also considered. Applicants should be incoming or current freshmen, or they may be returning to school with sufficient credits to qualify for freshman status. Selection is based on aptitude for accounting, commitment to the goal of pursuing a degree in accounting (including evidence of continued commitment after receiving this award), clear evidence that the candidate has established goals and a plan for achieving those goals, and financial need.

Financial data: The stipend is $4,000 per year.

Duration: 1 year; may be renewed 3 additional years if the recipient completes at least 12 hours each semester.

Additional information: This program, established in 1990, was formerly called the Displaced Homemaker's Scholarship.

Number awarded: 1 each year.

Deadline: April of each year.

3189
WORDA RUSSELL MEMORIAL ENDOWMENT SCHOLARSHIP

Epsilon Sigma Alpha
Attn: ESA Foundation Assistant Scholarship Director
P.O. Box 270517
Fort Collins, CO 80527
Phone: (970) 223-2824   Fax: (970) 223-4456
Web Site: www.esaintl.com/esaf

Summary: To provide financial assistance to students interested in preparing for a teaching career.

Eligibility: Applicants may be either 1) graduating high school seniors in the top 25 percent of their class or with minimum scores of 20 on the ACT or 950 on the SAT, or 2) students already enrolled in college with a grade point average of 3.0 or higher. Students enrolled in a technical school or returning to school after an absence are also eligible. Applicants must be studying or planning to study education. Selection is based on character, scholastic ability, leadership and ability skills, and financial need.

Financial data: The stipend is $1,500.

Duration: 1 year; may be renewed.

Additional information: Epsilon Sigma Alpha (ESA) is a women's service organization, but scholarships are available to both men and women. Information is also available from Verneene Forssberg, 403 South High, Pratt, KS 67124, (316) 672-3636, Fax: (316) 672-3688, E-mail: vernf@genmail.pcc.cc.ks.us. Completed applications must be submitted to the ESA State Counselor who verifies the information before forwarding them to the scholarship director.

Number awarded: 2 each year.

Deadline: January of each year.

3190
WSTLA AMERICAN JUSTICE ESSAY SCHOLARSHIP CONTEST

Washington State Trial Lawyers Association
1809 Seventh Avenue, Suite 1500
Seattle, WA 98101-1328
Phone: (206) 464-1011   Fax: (206) 464-0703
E-mail: wstla@wstla.org   Web Site: www.wstla.org

Summary: To recognize and reward students at the high school, college, and law school level in Washington who submit an essay on advocacy in the American justice system.

Eligibility: This program is open to 1) students attending a law school in the state of Washington; 2) freshmen, sophomores, and juniors at 2-year and 4-year accredited institutions of higher education in the state of Washington, as well as seniors planning to attend graduate school in the state the following year; and 3) high school students who are residents of the state of Washington planning to attend college (although it does not need to be in Washington). Applicants must submit an essay on a subject within the general topic of whether jury trials are free from corruption or distortion due to political influences or economic pressures.

Financial data: Awards are $3,000 for law students, $2,000 for college students, and $1,000 for high school students. All awards are paid directly to the recipient's institution of higher education, to be used for tuition, room, board, or fees.

Duration: The competition is held annually.

Additional information: This competition was first held in 2001.

Number awarded: 3 each year: 1 at each level of the competition.

Deadline: February of each year.

3191
WYOMING SUPERIOR STUDENT IN EDUCATION SCHOLARSHIP

University of Wyoming
College of Education
Attn: Undergraduate Studies
P.O. Box 3374
Laramie, WY 82071
Phone: (307) 766-2230

Summary: To provide financial assistance to residents of Wyoming who are interested in preparing for a career in teaching.

Eligibility: This program is open to graduates of Wyoming high schools who are currently enrolled at the University of Wyoming or a community college in the state. Applicants or their parent or legal guardian must currently be and have been a resident of Wyoming for at least 5 years. Students transferring to the university from a community college are eligible to apply for the scholarship if they enter into a teacher preparation program at their college and successfully complete the College Screening Test and Practicum Experience; students already enrolled at the university are eligible if they enroll in a teacher preparation program and successfully complete the College Screening Test and Practicum Experience. Selection is based on standardized test scores (must be in at least the 75th percentile), courses completed, extracurricular activities, and the student's responses to prepared questions.

Financial data: Tuition is waived at the University of Wyoming or any of the community colleges in the state.

Duration: 1 year; may be renewed of the recipient maintains full-time enrollment and a grade point average of 2.5 or higher. Support may be provided for up to 10 semesters, of which no more than 5 semesters may be at a community college.

Number awarded: 16 each year.

Deadline: October of each year.

3192
YELLOW RIBBON SCHOLARSHIP

National Tourism Foundation
Attn: Scholarships
546 East Main Street
Lexington, KY 40508-2342
Phone: (859) 226-4444   (800) 682-8886
Fax: (859) 226-4437   E-mail: ntf@ntastaff.com
Web Site: www.ntfonline.org

Summary: To provide financial assistance for college to students with disabilities who are planning a career in the travel and tourism industry.

Eligibility: This program is open to students with a physical or sensory disability (verified by an accredited physician) who are seeking an education at any level beyond high school. Both high school seniors and currently-enrolled college students may apply; high school applicants must have at least a 3.0 grade point average and college applicants must have at least a 2.5 grade point average. Applicants must be residents of and studying in North America, be planning a career of any capacity in the travel or tourism industry (e.g., hotel management, restaurant management, tourism), and submit an essay on how they intend to use their education in the field. They must also submit 2 letters of recommendation, 1 from a faculty member and 1 from a professional in the travel industry.

Financial data: The stipend is $5,000.

Duration: 1 year.

Additional information: Award winners also receive complimentary registration and an all-expense paid trip (valued at more than $3,000) to the association's annual convention, as well as a 1-year subscription to *Courier* magazine, *Tuesday* newsletter, and *NTF Headlines* newsletter. In any 1 year, applicants may receive only 1 award from the association.

Number awarded: 1 each year.

Deadline: April of each year.

3193
YOSHIKO TANAKA MEMORIAL SCHOLARSHIP

Summary: To provide financial assistance to student members of the Japanese American Citizens League (JACL) who are pursuing undergraduate education.
See Listing #1702.

3194
YOUNG FEMINIST SCHOLARSHIP

Summary: To recognize and reward feminists who are high school seniors and interested in writing.
See Listing #1705.

3195
YOUNG MORTGAGE BANKERS SCHOLARSHIPS

Hartford Foundation for Public Giving
85 Gillett Street
Hartford, CT 06105
Phone: (860) 548-1888   Fax: (860) 524-8346
Web Site: www.hfpg.org

Summary: To provide financial assistance for college to high school seniors in Connecticut who are interested in attending college to study a field related to banking in college.

Eligibility: This program is open to graduating seniors at Connecticut high schools who are interested in attending a 2- or 4-year college or university to study banking, finance, real estate, business, or a related field. Applicants must be in the upper third of their graduating class. As part of the application process, they must submit a personal statement outlining the reasons they wish to pursue a career in business, mortgage banking, or real estate (including a statement concerning their goals and abilities) and 3 letters of recommendation. Other selection criteria include academic achievement, community service, and financial need.

Financial data: Stipends range from $500 to $1,500 per year.

Duration: 1 year; may be renewed.

Additional information: Funding for this program is provided by the Interracial Scholarship Fund of Greater Hartford, P.O. Box 370455, West Hartford, CT 06137-0455.

Number awarded: Varies each year.

Deadline: February of each year.

3196
ZONTA INTERNATIONAL YOUNG WOMEN IN PUBLIC AFFAIRS AWARDS

Zonta International
557 West Randolph Street
Chicago, IL 60661-2206
Phone: (312) 930-5848   Fax: (312) 930-0951
E-mail: ZontaFdtn@aol.com
Web Site: www.zonta.org

Summary: To recognize and reward women in secondary school who are interested in a career in public policy, government, or volunteer organizations.

Eligibility: This program is open to young women 21 years of age or younger who are currently enrolled in a secondary school anywhere in the world. Applicants must 1) provide information on their student activities (10 points), community service activities (10 points), and international awareness (10 points); and 2) write essays on personal role models (15 points), historical role models (15 points), and world vision of steps necessary for women to achieve equality (30 points). Based on those statements and essays, winners are selected at the club level and forwarded for a district competition; district winners are entered in the international competition.

Financial data: Each winner at the U.S. district level receives a $500 prize; the international winner receives a $1,000 prize.

Duration: The competition is held annually.

Additional information: This program was established in 1990.

Number awarded: Several U.S. district winners and 1 international winner (may be the same person) each year.

Deadline: Applications must be submitted to clubs by October of each year.

APPENDIX

Federal and State Financial Aid

Of the nearly $86 billion in student aid currently available, more than one half of it (almost $54 billion) is supplied by the federal government. And, most of the federal funds are channeled through a handful of programs: the student-based Pell Grants (recently, more than $9 billion was dispensed to 4 million students); Subsidized and Unsubsidized Stafford Loans (formerly called Guaranteed Student Loans), PLUS Loans (for creditworthy parents to borrow up to the student's total cost of attendance less any aid received); Supplemental Educational Opportunity Grants (close to $700 million distributed each year), work-study (more than $1 billion distributed each year), and Perkins Loans ($1 billion in "revolving fund" capital now available). For more information on the Pell Grants and Supplemental Educational Opportunity Grants, check the listings in the "Unrestricted by Subject Area" section of this directory. To learn more about the federal loan programs, get a free copy of *The Student Guide: Financial Aid from the U.S. Department of Education* by calling (800) 4-FED-AID or visiting the Department of Education's Website: www.ed.gov.

Most states, as well as the District of Columbia, have statutes authorizing educational assistance and loan funds for students. Each year, nearly 2 million students receive close to $5 billion in state aid. Use the listing below as the first step in your search for state-based financial aid. You'll find here the name, address, telephone number, e-mail address, and Website (when available) for the agencies in your state that administer educational assistance and loan funds for students.

Alabama

State Aid
Alabama Commission on Higher Education
Grants and Scholarships Department
100 North Union Street, P.O. Box 302000
Montgomery, AL 36130-2000
(334) 242-1998
Fax: (334) 242-0268
Email: wwall@ache.state.al.us
Website: www.ache.state.al.us

Federal Aid
Kentucky Higher Education Assistance Authority
West Frankfort Office Complex
1050 U.S. 127 South, Suite 102
Frankfort, KY 40601-4323
(502) 696-7200; (800) 928-8926
Fax: (502) 696-7496
Email: webmaster@kheaa.com
Website: www.kheaa.com

Alaska

State Aid
Alaska Commission on Postsecondary Education
3030 Vintage Boulevard
Juneau, AK 99801-7109
(907) 465-2962; (800) 441-2962
Fax: (907) 465-5316
TDD: (907) 465-3143
Email: custsvc@acpe.state.ak.us
Website: www.state.ak.us/acpe

Federal Aid
USA Funds, Inc.
P.O. Box 6028
Indianapolis, IN 46206-6028
(317) 849-6510; (800) 872-4768
Fax: (317) 578-6875
Email: usafunds@usagroup.com
Website: www.usafunds.org

American Samoa

State Aid
American Samoa Community College
Board of Higher Education
P.O. Box 2609
Pago Pago, American Samoa 96799-2609
(684) 699-1141

Federal Aid
USA Funds, Inc.
P.O. Box 6028
Indianapolis, IN 46206-6028
(317) 849-6510; (800) 872-4768
Fax: (317) 578-6875
Email: usafunds@usagroup.com
Website: www.usafunds.org

Arizona

State Aid
Arizona Commission for Postsecondary Education
2020 North Central Avenue, Suite 550
Phoenix, AZ 85004-4503
(602) 258-2435
Fax: (602) 258-2483
Email: toni@www.acpe.asu.edu
Website: www.acpe.asu.edu

Federal Aid
USA Funds, Inc.
P.O. Box 6028
Indianapolis, IN 46206-6028
(317) 849-6510; (800) 872-4768
Fax: (317) 578-6875
Email: usafunds@usagroup.com
Website: www.usafunds.org

Arkansas

State Aid
Arkansas Department of Higher Education
Financial Aid Division
114 East Capitol Avenue
Little Rock, AR 72201-3818
(501) 371-2050; (800) 54-STUDY
Fax: (501) 371-2001
Email: finaid@adhe.arknet.edu
Website: www.arscholarships.com

Federal Aid
Student Loan Guarantee Foundation of Arkansas
219 South Victory Street
Little Rock, AR 72201-1884
(501) 372-1491; (800) 622-3446
Email: slgfcorporate@slgfa.org
Website: www.slgfa.org

California
State and Federal Aid
California Student Aid Commission
10811 International Drive
P.O. Box 419026
Rancho Cordova, CA 95741-9026
(916) 526-7590; (888) CA-GRANT
Fax: (916) 526-8002 (state only)
Fax: (916) 526-7937 (federal only)
Email: custsvcs@csac.ca.gov
Website: www.csac.ca.gov

Colorado
State Aid
Colorado Commission on Higher Education
1380 Lawrence Street, Suite 1200
Denver, CO 80204
(303) 866-2723
Fax: (303) 866-4266
Email: cche@state.co.us
Website: www.state.co.us/cche_dir/hecche.html

Federal Aid
Colorado Student Loan Program
999 18th Street, Suite 425
Denver, CO 80202
(303) 305-3000; (800) 727-9834
Fax: (303) 294-5076
TTY: (800) 727-5343
Email: kbreuer@cslp.org
Website: www.cslp.org

Connecticut
State Aid
Connecticut Department of Higher Education
Office of Student Financial Aid
61 Woodland Street
Hartford, CT 06105-2326
(860) 974-1855
Fax: (860) 974-1310
Website: www.ctdhe.org

Federal Aid
Connecticut Student Loan Foundation
525 Brook Street, P.O. Box 1009
Rocky Hill, CT 06067
(860) 257-4001; (800) 237-9721, ext. 259
Fax: (860) 257-1743
Email: cslfqa@mail.cslf.org
Website: www.cslf.com

Delaware
State Aid
Delaware Higher Education Commission
820 North French Street
Wilmington, DE 19802
(302) 577-3240; (800) 292-7935
Fax: (302) 577-6765
Email: dhec@state.de.us
Website: www.doe.state.de.us/high-ed

Federal Aid
Pennsylvania Higher Education Assistance Agency
1200 North Seventh Street
Harrisburg, PA 17102-1444
(717) 720-2860; (800) 692-7392
Fax: (717) 720-3907
TTY: (800) 654-5988
Website: www.pheaa.org

Florida
State and Federal Aid
Florida Department of Education
Office of Student Financial Assistance
1940 North Monroe Street
Tallahassee, FL 32303-4759
(850) 410-5185; (888) 827-2004 (state only)
(850) 410-5200; (800) 366-3475 (federal only)
Fax: (850) 488-3612
Email: osfa@mail.doe.state.fl.us
Website: www.firn.edu/doe

Georgia
State and Federal Aid
Georgia Student Finance Commission
2082 East Exchange Place
Tucker, GA 30084-5305
(770) 724-9130; (800) 776-6878
Fax: (770) 724-9004
Email: info@mail.gsfc.state.ga.us
Website: www.gsfc.org

Guam

State Aid
University of Guam
303 University Drive
Mangilao, Guam 96923
(671) 734-4469

Federal Aid
USA Funds, Inc.
P.O. Box 6028
Indianapolis, IN 46206-6028
(317) 849-6510; (800) 872-4768
Fax: (317) 578-6875
Email: usafunds@usagroup.com
Website: www.usafunds.org

Hawaii

State Aid
Hawaii State Postsecondary Education Commission
University of Hawaii
Bachman Hall, Room 209
2444 Dole Street
Honolulu, HI 96822-2302
(808) 956-8213
Fax: (808) 956-5156
Email: iha@hawaii.edu

Federal Aid
USA Funds, Inc.
P.O. Box 6028
Indianapolis, IN 46206-6028
(317) 849-6510; (800) 872-4768
Fax: (317) 578-6875
Email: usafunds@usagroup.com
Website: www.usafunds.org

Idaho

State Aid
Idaho State Board of Education
650 West State Street, Room 307
P.O. Box 83720
Boise, ID 83720-0037
(208) 334-2270
Fax: (208) 334-2632
Email: board@osbe.state.id.us
Website: www.sde.state.id.us/osbe/board.htm

Federal Aid
Northwest Education Loan Association
Processing Center, 500 Colman Building
811 First Avenue
Seattle, WA 98104
(206) 461-5300; (800) 562-3001
Fax: (206) 461-5449
Email: cheryll@nela.net
Website: www.nela.net

Illinois

State and Federal Aid
Illinois Student Assistance Commission
1755 Lake Cook Road
Deerfield, IL 60015-5209
(847) 948-8500; (800) 899-ISAC
Fax: (847) 831-8549
Email: isac@wwa.com
Website: www.isac-online.org

Indiana

State Aid
State Student Assistance Commission of Indiana
ISTA Center Building
150 West Market Street, Suite 500
Indianapolis, IN 46204-2811
(317) 232-2350; (888) 528-4719
Fax: (317) 232-3260
Email: grants@ssaci.state.in.us
Website: www.in.gov/ssaci

Federal Aid
USA Funds, Inc.
P.O. Box 6028
Indianapolis, IN 46206-6028
(317) 849-6510; (800) 872-4768
Fax: (317) 578-6875
Email: usafunds@usagroup.com
Website: www.usafunds.org

Iowa

State and Federal Aid
Iowa College Student Aid Commission
200 Tenth Street, Fourth Floor
Des Moines, IA 50309-3609
(515) 281-3501; (800) 383-4222
Fax: (515) 242-3389
Email: icsac@max.state.ia.us
Website: www.state.ia.us/collegeaid

Kansas

State Aid
Kansas Board of Regents
Student Financial Aid
1000 S.W. Jackson Street, Suite 520
Topeka, KS 66612-1368
(785) 296-3518
Fax: (785) 296-0983
Email: dlindeman@ksbor.org
Website: www.kansasregents.com

Federal Aid
USA Funds, Inc.
P.O. Box 6028
Indianapolis, IN 46206-6028
(317) 849-6510; (800) 872-4768
Fax: (317) 578-6875
Email: usafunds@usagroup.com
Website: www.usafunds.org

Kentucky

State and Federal Aid
Kentucky Higher Education Assistance Authority
1050 U.S. Hwy 127 South, Suite 102
Frankfort, KY 40601-4323
(502) 696-7200; (800) 928-8926
Fax: (502) 696-7496
Email: lrenshler@kheaa.com
Website: www.kheaa.com

Louisiana

State and Federal Aid
Office of Student Financial Assistance
1885 Wooddale Boulevard, P.O. Box 91202
Baton Rouge, LA 70821-9202
(225) 922-1011; (800) 259-LOAN
Fax: (225) 922-1089
Email: custserv@osfa.state.la.us
Website: www.osfa.state.la.us

Maine

State and Federal Aid
Finance Authority of Maine
Education Assistance Division
5 Community Drive
Augusta, ME 04332-0949
(207) 623-3263; (800) 228-3734
Fax: (207) 623-0095
TTY: (207) 626-2717
Email: info@famemaine.com
Website: www.famemaine.com

Maryland

State Aid
Maryland Higher Education Commission
State Scholarship Administration
16 Francis Street
Annapolis, MD 21401-1781
(410) 260-4565; (800) 974-1024
Fax: (410) 974-5376
TTY: (800) 735-2258
Email: ssamail@mhec.state.md.us
Website: www.mhec.state.md.us

Federal Aid
USA Funds, Inc.
P.O. Box 6028
Indianapolis, IN 46206-6028
(317) 849-6510; (800) 872-4768
Fax: (317) 578-6875
Email: usafunds@usagroup.com
Website: www.usafunds.org

Massachusetts

State Aid
Office of Student Financial Assistance
454 Broadway, Suite 200
Revere, MA 02151
(617) 727-9420
Fax: (617) 727-0667
Email: osfa@osfa.mass.edu
Website: www.osfa.mass.edu

Federal Aid
American Student Assistance
330 Stuart Street
Boston, MA 02116-5292
(617) 426-9434; (800) 999-9080
Fax: (617) 521-6249
TTY: (800) 999-0923
Email: stearns@amsa.com
Website: www.amsa.com

Michigan

State Aid
Michigan Higher Education Assistance Authority
Office of Scholarships and Grants
P.O. Box 30462
Lansing, MI 48909-7962
(517) 373-3394; (888) 4-GRANTS
Fax: (517) 335-5984
Email: treasscholgrant@michigan.gov
Website: www.michigan.gov/mistudentaid

Federal Aid
Michigan Guarantee Agency
608 West Allegan Street
P.O. Box 30047
Lansing, MI 48909-7547
(517) 373-0760; (800) 642-5626
Fax: (517) 335-6703
Email: mga@state.mi.us
Website: www.mi-studentaid.org

Minnesota
State Aid
Minnesota Higher Education Services Office
1450 Energy Park Drive, Suite 350
St. Paul, MN 55108-5227
(651) 642-0567; (800) 657-3866
Fax: (651) 642-0675
TTY: (800) 627-3529
Email: info@heso.state.mn.us
Website: www.mheso.state.mn.us

Federal Aid
Great Lakes Higher Education Corporation
2401 International Lane, P.O. Box 7658
Madison, WI 53704-3192
(608) 246-1800; (800) 236-5900
Email: service@glhec.org
Website: www.glhec.org

Mississippi
State Aid
Office of Student Financial Aid
3825 Ridgewood Road
Jackson, MS 39211-6453
(601) 432-6997; (800) 327-2980
Fax: (601) 432-6527
Email: sfa@ihl.state.ms.us
Website: www.ihl.state.ms.us

Federal Aid
USA Funds, Inc.
P.O. Box 6028
Indianapolis, IN 46206-6028
(317) 849-6510; (800) 872-4768
Fax: (317) 578-6875
Email: usafunds@usagroup.com
Website: www.usafunds.org

Missouri
State and Federal Aid
Missouri Student Assistance Resource Services (MOSTARS)
3515 Amazonas Drive
Jefferson City, MO 65109
(573) 751-2361; (800) 473-6757
Fax: (573) 751-6635
TTY: (800) 735-2966
Email: icweb@mocbhe.gov
Website: www.mocbhe.gov

Montana
State and Federal Aid
Montana Guaranteed Student Loan Program
2500 Broadway , P.O. Box 203101
Helena, MT 59620-3101
(406) 444-6594; (800) 537-7508
Fax: (406) 444-1869
Email: custserv@mgslp.state.mt.us
Website: www.mgslp.state.mt.us

Nebraska
State Aid
Coordinating Commission for Postsecondary Education
P.O. Box 95005
Lincoln, NE 68509-5005
(402) 471-2847
Fax: (402) 471-2886
Email: staff@ccpe.state.ne.us
Website: www.ccpe.state.ne.us

Federal Aid
Nebraska Student Loan Program, Inc.
P.O. Box 82507
Lincoln, NE 68501-2507
(402) 475-8686; (800) 735-8778
Fax: (402) 479-6658
Website: www.nslp.com

Nevada
State Aid
Nevada State Department of Education
700 East Fifth Street
Carson City, NV 89701
(702) 687-9200
Website: www.nde.state.nv.us

Federal Aid
USA Funds, Inc.
P.O. Box 6028
Indianapolis, IN 46206-6028
(317) 849-6510; (800) 872-4768
Fax: (317) 578-6875
Email: usafunds@usagroup.com
Website: www.usafunds.org

New Hampshire
State Aid
New Hampshire Postsecondary Education Commission
2 Industrial Park Drive, Suite 7
Concord, NH 03301-8512
(603) 271-2555
Fax: (603) 271-2696
TDD: (800) 735-2964
Email: pedes@nhsa.state.nh.us
Website: webster.state.nh.us/postsecondary

Federal Aid
New Hampshire Higher Education Assistance Foundation
4 Barrell Court, P.O. Box 877
Concord, NH 03302-0877
(603) 225-6612; (800) 525-2577
Fax: (603) 224-2581
Email: resourcectr@gsmr.org
Website: www.nhheaf.org

New Jersey
State and Federal Aid
Higher Education Student Assistance Authority
P.O. Box 540
Trenton, NJ 08625-0540
(609) 588-3226; (800) 792-8670
Fax: (609) 588-7389
TTY: (609) 588-2526
Email: osacs@hesaa.org
Website: www.hesaa.org

New Mexico
State Aid
New Mexico Commission on Higher Education
Financial Aid and Student Services
1068 Cerrillos Road, P.O. Box 15910
Santa Fe, NM 87506-5910
(505) 827-7383; (800) 279-9777
Fax: (505) 827-7392
Email: highered@che.state.nm.us
Website: www.nmche.org

Federal Aid
New Mexico Student Loan Guarantee Corporation
3900 Osuna Road, N.E., P.O. Box 92230
Albuquerque, NM 87199-2230
(505) 345-8821; (800) 279-3070
Fax: (505) 344-3631
Email: guarantee@nmslgc.org
Website: www.nmslgc.org

New York
State and Federal Aid
New York State Higher Education Services Corporation
99 Washington Avenue
Albany, NY 12255
(518) 473-1574; (888) 697-4372
Fax: (518) 474-2839
TDD: (800) 445-5234
Email: webmail@hesc.com
Website: www.hesc.com

North Carolina
State and Federal Aid
North Carolina State Education Assistance Authority
P.O. Box 14103
Research Triangle Park, NC 27709
(919) 549-8614; (800) 700-1775
Fax: (919) 549-8481
Email: information@ncseaa.edu
Website: www.ncseaa.edu

North Dakota
State Aid
North Dakota University System
Student Financial Assistance Program
State Capitol, Tenth Floor
600 East Boulevard Avenue, Department 215
Bismarck, ND 58505-0230
(701) 328-4114
Fax: (701) 328-2961
Email: ndus_office@ndus.nodak.edu
Website: www.ndus.edu

Federal Aid
Student Loans of North Dakota
P.O. Box 5524
Bismarck, ND 58506-5524
(701) 328-5754; (800) 472-2166
Fax: (701) 328-5716
TDD: (800) 643-3916
Email: bndsl@state.nd.us
Website: mystudentloanonline.com/index.jsp

Northern Marianas

State Aid
Northern Marianas College
P.O. Box 501250
Saipan, MP 96950-1250
(670) 234-3690
Fax: (670) 234-0759
Website: www.nmcnet.edu

Federal Aid
USA Funds, Inc.
P.O. Box 6028
Indianapolis, IN 46206-6028
(317) 849-6510; (800) 872-4768
Fax: (317) 578-6875
Email: usafunds@usagroup.com
Website: www.usafunds.org

Ohio

State Aid
State Grants and Scholarships
P.O. Box 182452
Columbus, OH 43218-2452
(614) 466-7420; (888) 833-1133
Fax: (614) 752-5903
Email: cshaid@regents.state.oh.us
Website: www.regents.state.oh.us/sgs

Federal Aid
Great Lakes Higher Education Corporation
2401 International Lane, P.O. Box 7658
Madison, WI 53704-3192
(608) 246-1800; (800) 236-5900
Email: service@glhec.org
Website: www.glhec.org

Oklahoma

State Aid
Oklahoma State Regents for Higher Education
Scholarship and Grant Programs
655 Research Parkway, Suite 200
Oklahoma City, OK 73104
(405) 225.9100; (800) 858-1840
Fax: (405) 225.9230
Email: tsimonton@osrhe.edu
Website: www.okhighered.org

Federal Aid
Oklahoma Guaranteed Student Loan Program
P.O. Box 3000
Oklahoma City, OK 73101-3000
(405) 234-4300; (800) 442-8642
Fax: (405) 234-4390
TTY: (405) 234-4511
Email: infobox@ogslp.org
Website: www.ogslp.org

Oregon

State and Federal Aid
Oregon Student Assistance Commission
1500 Valley River Drive, Suite 100
Eugene, OR 97401
(541) 687-7400; (800) 452-8807
Fax: (541) 687-7426
TTY: (541) 687-7357
Email: public_information@mercury.osac.state.or.us
Website: www.osac.state.or.us

Pennsylvania

State and Federal Aid
Pennsylvania Higher Education Assistance Agency
1200 North Seventh Street
Harrisburg, PA 17102
(717) 720-2860; (800) 692-7392
Fax: (717) 720-3907
TTY: (800) 654-5988
Email: info@pheaa.org
Website: www.pheaa.org

Puerto Rico

State Aid
Puerto Rico Council on Higher Education
P.O. Box 19900
San Juan, PR 00910-1900
(787) 724-7100
Fax: (787) 725-1275
Email: sa_espada@ces.prstar.net

Federal Aid
Great Lakes Higher Education Corporation
2401 International Lane, P.O. Box 7658
Madison, WI 53704-3192
(608) 246-1800; (800) 236-5900
Email: service@glhec.org
Website: www.glhec.org

Rhode Island

State and Federal Aid
Rhode Island Higher Education Assistance Authority
560 Jefferson Boulevard
Warwick, RI 02886
(401) 736-1100; (800) 922-9855
Fax: (401) 732-3541
TTY: (401) 222-6195
Email: gjsilva@riheaa.org
Website: www.riheaa.org

South Carolina

State Aid
South Carolina Commission on Higher Education
1333 Main Street, Suite 200
Columbia, SC 29201
(803) 737-2260; (877) 349-7183
Fax: (803) 737-2297
Email: shubbard@che400.state.sc.us
Website: www.che400.state.sc.us

Federal Aid
South Carolina Student Loan Corporation
P.O. Box 210219
Columbia, SC 29221
(803) 798-0916; (800) 347-2752
Fax: (803) 772-9410
Email: mfox@slc.sc.edu
Website: www.slc.sc.edu

South Dakota

State Aid
South Dakota Board of Regents
Scholarship Committee
306 East Capitol Avenue, Suite 200
Pierre, SD 57501-3159
(605) 773-3455
Fax: (605) 773-5320
Email: info@ris.sdbor.edu
Website: www.ris.sdbor.edu

Federal Aid
Education Assistance Corporation
115 First Avenue, S.W.
Aberdeen, SD 57401
(605) 225-6423; (800) 592-1802
Fax: (605) 225-5722
TTY: (800) 752-3949
Email: eac@eac-easci.org
Website: www.eac-easci.org

Tennessee

State and Federal Aid
Tennessee Student Assistance Corporation
Parkway Towers
404 James Robertson Parkway, Suite 1950
Nashville, TN 37243-0820
(615) 741-1346; (800) 342-1663
Fax: (615) 741-6101
Email: TSAC@mail.state.tn.us
Website: www.state.tn.us/tsac

Texas

State Aid
Texas Higher Education Coordinating Board
Grants and Special Programs
1200 East Anderson Lane
P.O. Box 12788, Capitol Station
Austin, TX 78711-2788
(512) 427-6101; (800) 242-3062
Fax: (512) 427-6127
Email: grantinfo@thecb.state.tx.us
Website: www.collegefortexans.com

Federal Aid
Texas Guaranteed Student Loan Corporation
P.O. Box 201725
Austin, TX 78720-1725
(512) 219-5700; (800) 845-6267
Fax: (512) 219-4633
TTY: (512) 219-4560
Email: cust.assist@tgslc.org
Website: www.tgslc.org

Utah

State and Federal Aid
Utah Higher Education Assistance Authority
60 South 400 West
Salt Lake City, UT 84101-1284
(801) 321-7200; (800) 418-8757
Fax: (801) 321-7299
Email: uheaa@utahsbr.edu
Website: www.uheaa.org

Vermont
State and Federal Aid
Vermont Student Assistance Corporation
Champlain Mill, P.O. Box 2000
Winooski, VT 05404-2601
(802) 655-9602; (800) 642-3177
Fax: (802) 654-3765
Email: info@vsac.org
Website: www.vsac.org

Virgin Islands
State Aid
Virgin Islands Joint Boards of Education
Charlotte Amalie, P.O. Box 11900
St. Thomas, VI 00801
(340) 774-4546
Fax: (340) 774-3384

Federal Aid
Great Lakes Higher Education Corporation
2401 International Lane, P.O. Box 7658
Madison, WI 53704-3192
(608) 246-1800; (800) 236-5900
Email: service@glhec.org
Website: www.glhec.org

Virginia
State Aid
State Council of Higher Education for Virginia
Financial Aid Manager
101 North 14th Street, Ninth Floor
Richmond, VA 23219-3659
(804) 225-2600; (877) 516-0138
Fax: (804) 225-2604
Email: fainfo@schev.edu
Website: www.schev.edu

Federal Aid
Educational Credit Management Corporation
7325 Boufant Springs Drive, Suite 200
Richmond, VA 23225
(804) 267-7100; (888) 775-3262
Fax: (804) 267-7159
TTY: (804) 267-7104
Website: www.ecmc.org

Washington
State Aid
Washington Higher Education Coordinating Board
917 Lakeridge Way, P.O. Box 43430
Olympia, WA 98504-3430
(360) 753-7800
Fax: (360) 753-7808
Email: info@hecb.wa.gov
Website: www.hecb.wa.gov

Federal Aid
Northwest Education Loan Association
Processing Center
500 Colman Building, 811 First Avenue
Seattle, WA 98104
(206) 461-5300; (800) 562-3001
Fax: (206) 461-5449
Email: cheryll@nela.net
Website: www.nela.net

Washington, D.C.
State Aid
Department of Human Services
Office of Postsecondary Education, Research, and Assistance
2100 Martin Luther King Jr. Avenue, S.E., Suite 401
Washington, DC 20020-5732
(202) 727-3688
Fax: (202) 727-2739
Website: dhs.washington.dc.us

Federal Aid
American Student Assistance
330 Stuart Street
Boston, MA 02116-5292
(627) 426-9434; (800) 999-9080
Fax: (617) 521-6249
TTY: (800) 999-0923
Email: stearns@amsa.com
Website: www.amsa.com

West Virginia
State Aid
West Virginia Higher Education Policy Commission
Coordinator, Scholarship Programs
1018 Kanawha Boulevard, East, Suite 700
Charleston, WV 25301-2827
(304) 558-2101; (888) 825-5707
Fax: (304) 558-5719
Email: wicks@hepc.wvnet.edu
Website: www.hepc.wvnet.edu

Federal Aid

Pennsylvania Higher Education Assistance Agency
1200 North Seventh Street
Harrisburg, PA 17102-1444
(717) 720-2860; (800) 692-7392
Fax: (717) 720-3907
Website: www.pheaa.org

Wisconsin

State Aid

Higher Educational Aids Board
P.O. Box 7885
Madison, WI 53707-7885
(608) 267-2206
Fax: (608) 267-2808
Email: HEABmail@heab.state.wi.us
Website: heab.state.wi.us

Federal Aid

Great Lakes Higher Education Corporation
2401 International Lane, P.O. Box 7658
Madison, WI 53704-3192
(608) 246-1800; (800) 236-5900
Email: service@glhec.org
Website: www.glhec.org

Wyoming

State Aid

Wyoming Department of Education
2300 Capitol Avenue, Second Floor
Cheyenne, WY 82002-0050
(307) 777-7675
Fax: (307) 777-6234
Website: www.k12.wy.us

Federal Aid

USA Funds, Inc.
P.O. Box 6028
Indianapolis, IN 46206-6028
(317) 849-6510; (800) 872-4768
Fax: (317) 578-6875
Email: usafunds@usagroup.com
Website: www.usafunds.org

INDEXES

INDEXES

Subject Index

Use this index when you want to identify funding programs by subject. To help you pinpoint your search, we've also included hundreds of "see" and "see also" references. In addition to looking for terms that represent your specific subject interests, be sure to check the "General programs" entry; hundred of programs are listed there that can be used to support study in any subject area (although the programs may be restricted in other ways). Remember: the numbers cited in this index refer to book entry numbers, not page numbers in the book.

Translators and translations: 1265. *See also* General programs; Language and linguistics; Writers and writing

Transportation: 1097, 1362–1363, 1855, 1878, 1888, 1974–1975, 2097, 2207, 2255, 2295, 2343–2344, 2371, 2432, 2466, 2514, 2562, 2577, 2642, 2726, 2782–2783, 2850, 2960, 2981, 3013, 3036, 3070, 3089, 3110, 3137, 3144. *See also* Automobile industry; Aviation; Engineering, transportation; General programs; Space sciences

Transportation engineering. *See* Engineering, transportation

Travel and tourism. *See* Tourism

Turfgrass science: 1274, 1746, 1777, 2011, 2013, 2039–2040, 2155, 2296, 2505, 2619. *See also* Biological sciences; General programs

Turkish language. *See* Language, Turkish

TV. *See* Television

Typing. *See* Secretarial sciences

Unions and unionization. *See* Industrial relations; Labor unions and members

Universities. *See* Education, higher

Unrestricted programs. *See* General programs

Urban affairs: 2432, 3070. *See also* City and regional planning; General programs

Urban development. *See* Community development

Urban planning. *See* City and regional planning

Urban studies: 1354. *See also* General programs; Urban affairs

Veterans. *See* Military affairs

Veterinary sciences: 2034, 2394, 2438, 2446, 2599, 3159. *See also* Animal science; General programs; Sciences

Video. *See* Filmmaking; Television

Vietnamese language. *See* Language, Vietnamese

Virology: 2436. *See also* General programs; Medical sciences

Visual arts. *See* Art

Visual impairments: 416, 2009, 2485, 2653, 2799, 2802, 3094. *See also* Disabilities; General programs; Health and health care

Viticulture. *See* Enology and viticulture

Vocational education. *See* Education, vocational

Voice: 1258, 1279, 1294, 1335, 1351, 1369, 1400, 1420, 1457, 1473, 1516, 1534, 1547, 1574, 1592, 1624, 1645, 1661, 1707. *See also* General programs; Music; Performing arts

Water resources: 1764, 1814, 1838, 1843, 2168, 2252, 2351, 2458, 2685, 2958, 3019. *See also* Environmental sciences; General programs; Natural resources

Web design. *See* Internet design and development

Welding: 1771, 1781–1783, 1973, 1983, 2102, 2152, 2219–2220, 2276, 2483, 2622, 2884. *See also* Building trades; General programs

Welding engineering. *See* Engineering, welding

Welfare. *See* Social services

Welsh studies: 1687. *See also* General programs

Western European studies. *See* European studies

Wildlife management: 1531, 1860, 1915, 1990, 2252, 2254, 2370, 2392, 2476, 2510, 2593, 2621, 2708, 2787, 2958–2959, 3156. *See also* Environmental sciences; General programs

Wine industry. *See* Beer and wine industries

Wine making. *See* Enology and viticulture

Women's studies and programs: 1425, 1705, 2697, 2846, 3194. *See also* General programs

Wood carving: 1426. *See also* Arts and crafts; General programs

Wood industry: 2004, 2095, 2797. *See also* Forestry management; General programs

Work. *See* Employment

World literature. *See* Literature

Wound, ostomy and continence nurses and nursing. *See* Nurses and nursing, wound, ostomy and continence

Writers and writing: 110, 527, 529, 686, 806, 820, 866, 900, 1012, 1050, 1070, 1197, 1268–1269, 1275–1277, 1279, 1282, 1285, 1293, 1301, 1316, 1323, 1327, 1351, 1354, 1366, 1370, 1376, 1383, 1385–1386, 1399, 1406, 1429, 1434, 1439, 1449, 1458, 1460, 1466, 1477, 1480, 1483, 1499, 1503, 1506, 1515, 1518, 1522, 1541, 1561, 1575, 1589, 1594, 1598, 1608, 1619, 1622, 1627–1628, 1630, 1632, 1634, 1638, 1640, 1644, 1646–1647, 1662, 1671, 1679, 1705, 1710, 1713, 1732, 1763, 1781–1783, 1788, 1795, 1892, 1906, 1957, 1983, 2029, 2031, 2064–2065, 2111, 2172, 2299, 2325, 2350, 2397, 2419, 2434, 2439, 2465, 2486, 2495, 2502, 2555, 2637, 2665, 2689, 2713, 2749, 2751, 2758, 2820, 2831, 2844–2845, 2849, 2864, 2873, 2880, 2894, 2902, 2923, 2940, 2993, 2998, 3003, 3024, 3039, 3047, 3057, 3060, 3067, 3077, 3099, 3125, 3128, 3153, 3157, 3163, 3168, 3190, 3194. *See also* General programs; Literature; specific types of writing

Youth. *See* Adolescents; Child development

Zoology: 2126, 2229, 2510, 2876. *See also* General programs; Sciences; names of specific zoological subfields

Residency Index

Some programs listed in this book are restricted to residents of a particular city, county, state, or region. Others are open to students wherever they live. The Residency Index will help you pinpoint programs available only to residents in your area as well as programs that have no residency restrictions (these are listed under the term "United States"). To use this index, look up the geographic areas that apply to you (always check the listings under "United States"), jot down the entry numbers listed after the subject areas that interest you, and use those numbers to find the program descriptions in the directory. To help you in your search, we've provided some "see also" references in each index entry. Remember: the numbers cited here refer to program entry numbers, not to page numbers in the book.

Tenability Index

Some programs listed in this book can be used only in specific cities, counties, states, or regions. Others may be used anywhere in the United States (or even abroad). The Tenability Index will help you locate funding that is restricted to a specific area as well as funding that has no tenability restrictions (these are listed under the term "United States"). To use this index, look up the geographic areas where you'd like to go (always check the listings under "United States"), jot down the entry numbers listed under the subject areas that interest you, and use those numbers to find the program descriptions in the directory. To help you in your search, we've provided some "see also" references in each index entry. Remember: the numbers cited here refer to program entry numbers, not to page numbers in the book.

Indexes

States; names of specific cities and counties

Missouri: **Unrestricted by Subject Area,** 169, 615, 677–678, 702–704, 706–707, 728, **Humanities,** 1272, 1451, 1539, **Sciences,** 1922, 2293–2294, 2344, **Social Sciences,** 2674, 2883, 2978–2980, 2986, 3013, 3097. *See also* Midwestern states; United States; names of specific cities and counties

Monona County, Iowa: **Unrestricted by Subject Area,** 23. *See also* Iowa

Montana: **Unrestricted by Subject Area,** 123, 711–721, 734, 986, 1055–1056, 1179, **Humanities,** 1591, 1621, **Sciences,** 2261, 2297, 2344, 2399, 2478–2479, **Social Sciences,** 2946, 2964, 2983, 3013, 3092. *See also* United States; names of specific cities and counties

Montgomery County, Iowa: **Unrestricted by Subject Area,** 23. *See also* Iowa

Montgomery County, Maryland: **Unrestricted by Subject Area,** 247, **Humanities,** 1708. *See also* Maryland

Nashville, Tennessee: **Sciences,** 1934, 2585, 2593, **Social Sciences,** 3156. *See also* Tennessee

Nebraska: **Unrestricted by Subject Area,** 23–24, 133, 355, 365, 677–678, 768–770, 822, 952, **Humanities,** 1565, **Sciences,** 1922, 2196, 2260, 2344, **Social Sciences,** 2747, 2924, 2963, 3013, 3170. *See also* United States; Midwestern states; names of specific cities and counties

Netherlands: **Sciences,** 2216. *See also* Europe; Foreign countries

Nevada: **Unrestricted by Subject Area,** 779, 1179, **Humanities,** 1456, 1621, **Sciences,** 2261, 2478, 2624, **Social Sciences,** 2890, 2964, 3092. *See also* Southwestern states; United States; names of specific cities

New England states: **Unrestricted by Subject Area,** 780, 784, **Humanities,** 1292, 1629, **Sciences,** 2351, 2575, **Social Sciences,** 3018–3019, 3098. *See also* Northeastern states; United States; names of specific states

New Hampshire: **Unrestricted by Subject Area,** 2, 34, 156, 283, 381–382, 601, 610, 625, 653, 781–782, 785–788, **Sciences,** 1826, 1943, 1963, 2352, **Social Sciences,** 2727, 2881, 2931, 3020. *See also* New England states; Northeastern states; United States; names of specific cities and counties

New Jersey: **Unrestricted by Subject Area,** 196, 283, 562, 695, 789–790, 792–794, 1049, **Humanities,** 1291, 1297, 1332, 1531, 1568, **Sciences,** 1845, 1963, 2213, 2254, 2353, **Social Sciences,** 2959, 3024–3028. *See also* Northeastern states; United States; names of specific cities and counties

New Mexico: **Unrestricted by Subject Area,** 189, 613, 758, 795–803, 1179, **Humanities,** 1621, **Sciences,** 2261, 2478–2479, **Social Sciences,** 2964, 3092. *See also* Southwestern states; United States; names of specific cities and counties

New Orleans, Louisiana: **Sciences,** 1934, 2524. *See also* Louisiana

New Wilmington, Pennsylvania: **Unrestricted by Subject Area,** 1061. *See also* Pennsylvania

New York: **Unrestricted by Subject Area,** 283, 304, 381–382, 804–805, 807–813, 1058, **Humanities,** 1253, 1364, 1569, 1629, 1658, **Sciences,** 1790, 1963, 2144, 2355–2357, 2360, **Social Sciences,** 2886, 2901, 2931, 3031, 3098, 3133. *See also* Northeastern states; United States; names of specific cities and counties

New York County, New York: *See* New York, New York

New York, New York: **Humanities,** 1319, 1533–1534, **Sciences,** 1896, 2585, **Social Sciences,** 3082. *See also* New York

Norfolk, Virginia: **Humanities,** 1492. *See also* Virginia

Normal, Alabama: **Sciences,** 2593, **Social Sciences,** 3156. *See also* Alabama

Normal, Illinois: **Social Sciences,** 2909. *See also* Illinois

Norman, Oklahoma: **Sciences,** 2120, 2592. *See also* Oklahoma

North Carolina: **Unrestricted by Subject Area,** 100, 203, 363, 386, 479, 662, 732, 767, 824–828, 830–832, 1030, **Humanities,** 1272, 1296, 1470, 1476, 1545, **Sciences,** 2068, 2167, 2176, 2314, 2370, 2454, 2488, **Social Sciences,** 2674, 2904, 2950, 2992, 3034, 3056, 3074. *See also* Southeastern states; Southern states; United States; names of specific cities and counties

North Dakota: **Unrestricted by Subject Area,** 677–678, 833–837, 1189, **Sciences,** 1922, 2260, 2344, 2479, **Social Sciences,** 2963, 3013, 3035. *See also* Midwestern states; United States; names of specific cities

North Miami, Florida: **Social Sciences,** 3082. *See also* Florida

Northeastern states: **Sciences,** 1958. *See also* United States; names of specific states

Northwestern states: **Unrestricted by Subject Area,** 972, **Social Sciences,** 2920, 2955. *See also* United States; names of specific states

Norway: **Humanities,** 1485, **Social Sciences,** 2920, 2955. *See also* Europe; Foreign countries

Notre Dame, Indiana: **Sciences,** 1896, 1964, 1996. *See also* Indiana

Oberlin, Ohio: **Unrestricted by Subject Area,** 224. *See also* Ohio

O'Brien County, Iowa: **Unrestricted by Subject Area,** 23. *See also* Iowa

Ohio: **Unrestricted by Subject Area,** 203, 363, 662, 677, 846, 848, 850–852, 854–855, 973, **Humanities,** 1584, **Sciences,** 1830, 1938, 1985, 2056, 2096, 2160, 2208, 2260, 2451, 2622, **Social Sciences,** 2649, 2692, 2891, 2963, 3044. *See also* Midwestern states; United States; names of specific cities and counties

Oklahoma: **Unrestricted by Subject Area,** 459, 595, 631, 656, 856–862, 882–883, 950, 1030, 1102, 1152, **Humanities,** 1585–1586, **Sciences,** 2052–2053, 2385, 2455, **Social Sciences,** 2821. *See also* Southern states; Southwestern states; United States; names of specific cities and counties

Omaha, Nebraska: **Sciences,** 1896. *See also* Nebraska

Orangeburg, South Carolina: **Sciences,** 2593, **Social Sciences,** 2702, 3156. *See also* South Carolina

Oregon: **Unrestricted by Subject Area,** 112, 114, 187, 200, 227, 272, 344–346, 354, 435, 493, 511, 618, 734, 869–872, 874–876, 878–880, 918, 962, 1179, 1217, **Humanities,** 1365, 1373, 1452, 1481, 1521, 1587–1588, 1591, **Sciences,** 1780, 1848, 2025, 2103, 2197, 2202, 2256, 2261, 2389, 2392–2393, 2399, 2442, 2475, 2611, **Social Sciences,** 2678, 2810, 2838, 2873, 2885, 2927, 2964, 3038, 3046–3049. *See also* Northwestern states; United States; names of specific cities and counties

Orlando, Florida: **Sciences,** 1822, **Social Sciences,** 3082. *See also* Florida

Osceola County, Iowa: **Unrestricted by Subject Area,** 23. *See also* Iowa

Oxford, Ohio: **Sciences,** 1822. *See also* Ohio

Pacific Northwest: *See* Northwestern states

Page County, Iowa: **Unrestricted by Subject Area,** 23. *See also* Iowa

Pembroke, North Carolina: **Sciences,** 2585. *See also* North Carolina

Pennsylvania: **Unrestricted by Subject Area,** 255, 283, 381–382, 515, 601, 653, 848, 904–906, 908, 910, 973, 1175, **Sciences,** 1754, 1963, 2413, 2415–2416, 2535, **Social Sciences,** 2659, 2931, 3052, 3058, 3066–3067. *See also* Northeastern states; United States; names of specific cities and counties

People's Republic of China: **Sciences,** 2216. *See also* Foreign countries

Petersburg, Virginia: **Sciences,** 2593, **Social Sciences,** 3156. *See also* Virginia

Philadelphia, Pennsylvania **Humanities,** 1321, 1556, **Sciences,** 1996, **Social Sciences,** 2909. *See also* Pennsylvania

Philippines: **Unrestricted by Subject Area,** 281. *See also* Foreign countries

Pine Bluff, Arkansas: **Sciences,** 2593, **Social Sciences,** 3156. *See also* Arkansas

Piscataway, New Jersey: **Sciences,** 2400, 2495, **Social Sciences,** 3051, 3099. *See also* New Jersey

Pittsburgh, Pennsylvania: **Sciences,** 1996. *See also* Pennsylvania

Plymouth County, Iowa: **Unrestricted by Subject Area,** 23. *See also* Iowa

Point Lookout, Missouri: **Unrestricted by Subject Area,** 224. *See also* Missouri

Poland: **Humanities,** 1266, 1489, 1516, 1657. *See also* Europe; Foreign countries

Pomona, California: **Social Sciences,** 3082. *See also* California

Port Gibson, Mississippi: **Sciences,** 2593, **Social Sciences,** 3156. *See also* Mississippi

Portland, Oregon: **Humanities,** 1481. *See also* Oregon

Pottawattamie County, Iowa: **Unrestricted by Subject Area,** 23. *See also* Iowa

Prairie View, Texas: **Sciences,** 1934, 2593, **Social Sciences,** 3156. *See also* Texas

Prince George's County, Maryland: **Unrestricted by Subject Area,** 247, **Humanities,** 1708. *See also* Maryland

Prince William County, Virginia: **Humanities,** 1708. *See also* Virginia

Princess Anne, Maryland: **Sciences,** 2585, 2593, **Social Sciences,** 3156. *See also* Maryland

Provo, Utah: **Social Sciences,** 2909. *See also* Utah

Sponsoring Organization Index

The Sponsoring Organization Index makes it easy to identify agencies that offer college funding. In this index, sponsoring organizations are listed alphabetically, word by word. In addition, we've used a code (within parentheses) to help you identify which programs sponsored by these organizations fall within your scope of interest: U = Unrestricted by Subject Area; H = Humanities; S = Sciences; SS = Social Sciences. Here's how the codes work: if an organization's name is followed by (U) 41, the program sponsored by that organization is described in entry 41, in the Unrestricted by Subject Area section. If that sponsoring organization's name is followed by another entry number—for example, (SS) 2649—the same or a different program is described in entry 2649, in the Social Sciences section. Remember: the numbers cited here refer to program entry numbers, not to page numbers in the book.

American Legion. Georgia Auxiliary, (U) 369, (S) 2059

American Legion. Idaho Department, (U) 438

American Legion. Illinois Auxiliary, (U) 4, 681, (S) 2118, (SS) 2868

American Legion. Illinois Department, (U) 449–450

American Legion. Iowa Auxiliary, (S) 2131

American Legion. Iowa Department, (U) 468

American Legion. Kansas Department, (U) 33, 170, (H) 1479, (S) 1885, (SS) 2725

American Legion. Kentucky Auxiliary, (U) 558

American Legion. Maryland Auxiliary, (H) 1528, (S) 2236–2237, (SS) 2952

American Legion. Massachusetts Department, (U) 288, 646, (S) 2241

American Legion. Missouri Auxiliary, (S) 2293

American Legion. New Hampshire Auxiliary, (U) 625

American Legion. New Hampshire Department, (U) 34, 785–786, (SS) 2727

American Legion. New Jersey Auxiliary, (U) 196, 789, (S) 2353

American Legion. New Jersey Department, (U) 562, 1049

American Legion. New York Auxiliary, (U) 807, (S) 2355–2356, (SS) 3031

American Legion. North Carolina Auxiliary, (U) 732

American Legion. Ohio Auxiliary, (U) 849

American Legion. Ohio Department, (U) 850

American Legion. Oregon Auxiliary, (U) 872–873, (S) 2393

American Legion. Pennsylvania Department, (U) 515

American Legion. South Carolina Auxiliary, (U) 1019

American Legion. Tennessee Department, (U) 1067

American Legion. Utah Auxiliary, (U) 1124

American Legion. Vermont Department, (U) 1131

American Legion. Virginia Auxiliary, (U) 71, 273

American Legion. Washington Department, (U) 1160

American Legion. Wisconsin Auxiliary, (U) 257, 434, 1203–1204

American Legion. Wisconsin Department, (U) 990, 1199

American Maine–Anjou Association, (U) 60

American Mathematical Association of Two Year Colleges, (S) 2245

American Mensa Education and Research Foundation, (U) 497, (H) 1518, (SS) 2940

American Meteorological Society, (S) 1766, 2121–2122, 2226

American Morgan Horse Institute, Inc., (U) 61

American National CattleWomen, Inc., (S) 2319

American Nephrology Nurses' Association, (S) 1768, 1772, 1775, 1992, 2033, 2366, 2402

American Nuclear Society, (S) 1767, 1778, 2149, 2159

American Occupational Therapy Foundation, (S) 2180, 2231, 2357, 2457, 2560, 2618, 2633

American Paint Horse Association, (U) 1228

American Pharmaceutical Association, (S) 2299

American Physical Society, (S) 1913, 2107, 2200

American Physical Therapy Association, (S) 2286

American Planning Association, (S) 2432, (SS) 3070

American Police Hall of Fame and Museum, (U) 62

American Postal Workers Union, (U) 63, 285

American Production & Inventory Control Society, (SS) 2758

American Public Transportation Foundation, (S) 2577, (SS) 3144

American Quarter Horse Association, (S) 2446

American Quarter Horse Foundation, (U) 64

American Red Cross, (U) 457

American Regent Laboratories, Inc., (S) 1768

American Respiratory Care Foundation, (S) 2153, 2300, 2473, 2630

American Sephardi Federation, (U) 130

American Sheep Industry Women, (H) 1555

American Society for Enology and Viticulture, (S) 1794

American Society for Horticultural Science, (S) 1799, 1961

American Society for Nondestructive Testing, Inc., (S) 1805, 2465

American Society for Photogrammetry and Remote Sensing, (S) 2467

American Society of Agricultural Engineers, (S) 1730, 2543, 2623

American Society of Agronomy, (S) 2141

American Society of Cinematographers, (H) 1652

American Society of Civil Engineers, (S) 1832, 2494

American Society of Civil Engineers. Maine Section, (S) 1792

American Society of Clinical Pathologists, (S) 1793

American Society of Crime Laboratory Directors, (S) 1769

American Society of Health–System Pharmacists, (S) 1795

American Society of Heating, Refrigerating and Air–Conditioning Engineers, Inc., (S) 1757, 1796–1798, 1956, 1984, 2090, 2454–2456

American Society of Highway Engineers. Carolina Triangle Section, (S) 1855, 1878

American Society of Landscape Architecture, (H) 1653, (S) 2541

American Society of Mechanical Engineers, (S) 2105

American Society of Military Comptrollers, (SS) 2669

American Society of Naval Engineers, (S) 1770

American Society of PeriAnesthesia Nurses, (S) 1806

American Society of Plumbing Engineers, (S) 1751

American Society of Safety Engineers, (S) 2014, 2227, 2475, 2567, 2591

American Society of Safety Engineers. Columbia–Willamette Chapter, (S) 2613

American Society of Transportation and Logistics, Inc., (S) 2207

American Society of Women Accountants, (SS) 2688

American Society of Women Accountants. Billings Big Sky Chapter, (SS) 2946, 2983

American Society of Women Accountants. Seattle Chapter, (SS) 3107

American String Teachers Association, (H) 1558–1559

American Textile Manufacturers Institute. Thread Committee, (H) 1664, (S) 2568

American Traffic Safety Services Foundation, (S) 2273

American Translators Association, (H) 1265

American Water Resources Association, (S) 2458

American Water Ski Educational Foundation, (U) 65

American Watercolor Society, (H) 1267

American Welding Society, (S) 1743, 1771, 1938, 1973, 2102, 2152, 2160, 2276, 2437, 2483, 2622, (SS) 2884

American Wholesale Marketers Association, (U) 250, (SS) 3083

America's Junior Miss, (U) 66

Amgen Inc., (S) 1772

AMTROL Inc., (S) 1764

AMVETS Ladies Auxiliary, (U) 69

AMVETS National Headquarters, (SS) 2993

Ancient and Accepted Scottish Rite of Freemasonry, Northern Jurisdiction, (U)

Indexes

Connecticut Association of Optometrists, (S) 1908, 2055

Connecticut Association of Women Police, (SS) 2737

Connecticut Broadcaster's Association, (H) 1333, (SS) 2738

Connecticut Building Congress, (H) 1334, (S) 1909, (SS) 2739

Connecticut Chapter of the American Planning Association, (H) 1629, (SS) 3098

Connecticut Department of Higher Education, (U) 219–223, 358, (SS) 2741

Connecticut Forest and Park Association, Inc., (S) 2148

Connecticut Law Enforcement Memorial Scholarship Fund, (SS) 2740

Connecticut Society of Professional Engineers, (S) 1910

Connecticut Society of Professional Journalists Foundation, Inc., (H) 1299

Connecticut State Golf Association, (U) 1191

Connecticut Women's Golf Association, (U) 936

Conselho Supremo da Uniñao Portuguesa do Estado da California, (U) 1053

Consulting Engineers and Land Surveyors of California, (S) 1881

Consulting Engineers Council of New Jersey, (S) 2213

Consulting Engineers of Indiana, Inc., (S) 1912

Continental Society, Daughters of Indian Wars, (SS) 2744

ConvaTec, (U) 458

Cooking Hospitality Institute of Chicago, (H) 1435

Coors Hispanic Employee Network, (U) 174

Corella and Bertram F. Bonner Foundation, (U) 224

Cornhusker State Games, (U) 355

Corning Incorporated, (S) 1903

Corporation for Public Broadcasting, (H) 1602

Cort Trade Show Furnishings, (H) 1494

Cortland County Trappers Association, (S) 1915

Council for Advancement and Support of Education, (U) 40

Council for America's First Freedom, (H) 1268

Council for Exceptional Children, (U) 464, 1037–1040

Council of Citizens with Low Vision International, (U) 162, 351

Country Music Broadcasters, Inc., (H) 1336

Creek Nation of Oklahoma, (U) 228–230

Crohn's and Colitis Foundation of America, (U) 458

Cuban American National Foundation, (H) 1529, (S) 2239, (SS) 2953

Cuban American Scholarship Fund, (U) 231

Culinary Institute of America, (H) 1435

Cystic Fibrosis Scholarship Foundation, (U) 233

Cytyc Corporation, (S) 2133

Dade Community Foundation, (S) 2151, (SS) 2759

Daedalian Foundation, (S) 1918–1919

Dairy Management, Inc., (U) 984, (S) 2321, 2342, (SS) 2997

Dairy Recognition and Education Foundation, (S) 2250, (SS) 2957

Daniels Fund, (U) 238

Danish Sisterhood of America, (U) 116, 239

Daughters of the American Revolution. Colorado State Society, (H) 1430, (S) 2606

Daughters of the Cincinnati, (U) 240

David and Dovetta Wilson Scholarship Fund, Inc., (U) 241

David and Lucile Packard Foundation, (S) 2401

Davis–Putter Scholarship Fund, (U) 245

Deb Richard Foundation, (U) 249

DECA, (U) 886, (SS) 2803, 2839, 2944

Degree of Honor Protective Association, (U) 251–252

Delaware Association of School Administrators, (SS) 2749

Delaware Child Placement Review Board, (U) 476

Delaware Higher Education Commission, (U) 10, 253–255, 261

Delaware Solid Waste Authority, (S) 1925

Delaware State Golf Association Scholarship Fund, Inc., (U) 256

Dell'Arte Mad River Festival, (H) 1450

Delta Air Lines, (S) 1927–1928

Delta Epsilon Sigma, (U) 324

Delta Faucet Company, (S) 1929

Delta Gamma Foundation, (S) 2009, (SS) 2799

Delta Mu Delta, (SS) 2753

Delta Sigma Pi, (SS) 2754

DePuy, (S) 2395

Des Moines Symphony Alliance, (H) 1346

Descendants of the Signers of the Declaration of Independence, (U) 260

Deseret News, (U) 1045

Design Firm Management Education Foundation, (H) 1243, (S) 1711

Desk and Derrick Educational Trust, (S) 1933

The Development Fund for Black Students in Science and Technology, (S) 1934

Directors Guild of America, (H) 1652

Disabled Workers Committee, (U) 263

Discover Card, (U) 264

Dixie Boys Baseball, (U) 266

Dobson Communications Corporation, (U) 933

Dog Writers' Educational Trust, (U) 268

Dolphin Scholarship Foundation, (U) 269

Donald F. & Mildred Topp Othmer Foundation, (S) 1939

Dong Ji Hoi Society, (U) 277

Donna Reed Foundation for the Performing Arts, (H) 1351

Dr. Kathryn Whitten Trust, (U) 274

Dramatic Publishing Company, (H) 1506

Dramatists Guild, Inc., (H) 1460, 1561

Drug, Chemical and Allied Trades Association, (U) 248

DuBose Associates, Inc., (H) 1321

D.W. Simpson & Company, (SS) 2763

EAA Aviation Foundation Inc., (S) 1921, 2412

EAR Foundation, (U) 691

Earth & Sky Radio Series, (H) 1706, (S) 2643

Easter Seals Iowa, (U) 483, (S) 1962, (SS) 2768

Eastern Star. Grand Chapter of California, (U) 284

Eastern Surfing Association, (U) 626

Eastman Kodak Company, (H) 1488

Eaton Corporation, (S) 1964

Ecolab, (SS) 2769

Ed E. and Gladys Hurley Foundation, (H) 1357

EDS, (U) 287

Educational Communications Scholarship Foundation, (U) 743, 1183, (H) 1680

Educational Foundation for Women in Accounting, (SS) 2688, 3187–3188

Iowa Department of AMVETS, (U) 311, 466, 946

Iowa Federation of Labor, AFL–CIO, (SS) 2880

Iowa Foundation for Agricultural Advancement, (S) 2112

Iowa. Treasurer of State, (U) 958

Iowa United Methodist Foundation, (S) 2177, 2229

Irene Ryan Foundation, (H) 1450

Iron and Steel Society, (S) 1963, 2134

Jack J. Isgur Foundation, (H) 1451, (SS) 2883

Jackie Robinson Foundation, (U) 477, 819

James F. Byrnes Foundation, (U) 482

James F. Lincoln Arc Welding Foundation, (S) 1781–1783, 1983

James S. Kemper Foundation, (SS) 2909

Jane Fryer McConaughy Memorial Scholarship Trust, (H) 1455, (SS) 2888

Japan Studies Scholarship Foundation Committee, (H) 1456, (SS) 2890

Japanese American Citizens League, (U) 3, 36, 278, 383, 412, 531–532, 550, 616, 639–640, 709, 727, 821, 896, 977, 982, 1029, 1233, (H) 1250, 1423, 1490, 1702, (S) 2192, 2492, (SS) 2658, 3193

Jay Ramsdell Foundation, (U) 487

Jazz Club of Sarasota, (H) 1457

Jewish Federation of Greater Hartford, Inc., (H) 1419

Jewish Funeral Directors of America, (SS) 2894

Jewish Social Service Agency of Metropolitan Washington, (U) 244, 654, 726

Jewish War Veterans of the U.S.A., (U) 496, 1220

JHM Hotels, Inc., (SS) 3082

J.O. Pollack L.L.C., (S) 2154

Joe Francis Haircare Scholarship Foundation, (H) 1463

John B. Lynch Scholarship Foundation, (U) 503

John Bayliss Broadcast Foundation, (H) 1465

John C. Staninger Memorial Foundation, (SS) 2896

John Edgar Thomson Foundation, (U) 505

John F. Kennedy Center for the Performing Arts. American College Theater Festival, (H) 1269, 1450, 1460, 1466, 1483, 1506, 1522, 1561, 1644

John F. Kennedy Library Foundation, (SS) 3077

John I. Haas, Inc., (U) 507

John M. Azarian Memorial Armenian Youth Scholarship Fund, (U) 508

John Templeton Foundation, (H) 1327

John Wiley & Sons, (SS) 2648

Johnson & Johnson Medical, Inc., (S) 2395

Johnson & Wales, (H) 1435

Joint Action in Community Service, Inc., (U) 478

Josephine De Kéarméan Fellowship Trust, (U) 516, (H) 1472

Journalism Education Association, (H) 1459, 1655

Junior Achievement, (U) 500, (H) 1681, (SS) 3171

Junior Achievement of Maine, Inc., (U) 518

Junior Colorado Cattlemen's Association, (S) 2387

Kalos Kagathos Foundation, (H) 1655

Kalsec, Inc., (S) 2537

Kamehameha Schools Bishop Estate, (U) 934, (H) 1600, (SS) 3075

Kansas Association of Broadcasters, (H) 1478

Kansas Board of Regents, (U) 523, 525–526

Kansas City Star, (H) 1370

Kansas Commission on Veterans' Affairs, (U) 524

Kansas Funeral Directors Association Foundation, (SS) 2905

Kansas Junior Livestock Association, (S) 2178

Kansas Livestock Foundation, (S) 2178, 2258

Kansas Nutrition Council, (S) 2179

Kansas Society of Certified Public Accountants, (SS) 2914–2916

Kaplan Educational Centers, (U) 527

Kappa Alpha Mu, (H) 1331

Kappa Delta Pi, (SS) 2836

Karla Scherer Foundation, (SS) 2906

KATU Channel 2 Portland, (H) 1481

Ke Ali'i Pauahi Foundation, (U) 403–404, 522, 549, 845

Kelley Communications, (U) 298

Kentucky Broadcasters Association, (H) 1411

Kentucky Department of Veterans Affairs, (U) 538, 1098

Kentucky Fire Commission, (U) 535

Kentucky High School Athletic Association, (U) 1034

Kentucky Higher Education Assistance Authority, (U) 534, 536–537, (SS) 2910

Kentucky Society of Certified Public Accountants, (SS) 2911

Key Club International, (U) 232, 242, 265, 541, 960, 1044, 1232, (S) 2187

KFDA Foundation, Inc., (SS) 2913

Kidger Optics Ltd., (S) 2265

Kids' Chance of West Virginia, Inc., (U) 542

King's College, (H) 1503

Kittie M. Fairey Educational Fund, (U) 545

Kiwanis International Foundation, (U) 242, 265, 960, 1044

Knight Ridder, Inc., (H) 1486

Knights of Ak–Sar–Ben, (U) 23–24

Knights of Columbus, (U) 348–349, 509

Knights of Pythias, (H) 1487

Koch Corporation, (S) 2190

Korea Society, (SS) 2998

Korean American Grocers Association of California, (U) 521

Korean American Scholarship Foundation. Eastern Region, (U) 283

Korean American Scholarship Foundation. Midwest Region, (U) 677

Korean American Scholarship Foundation. Southern Region, (U) 1030

Korean American Scholarship Foundation. Western Region, (U) 1179

Korean Cultural Service, (SS) 2998

Korean University Club, (U) 547

Korean–American Scientists and Engineers Association, (S) 2191

Kosciuszko Foundation, (H) 1489, 1516

KPMG, (SS) 2648

KSL–TV, (U) 1045

KUKUI, Inc., (U) 549

Kurzweil Foundation, (U) 275–276, 343, (S) 1785, 1953, 2184, (SS) 2680, 3032

Labsphere, Inc., (S) 2531

L'Academie de Cuisine, (H) 1435

Ladies Auxiliary of the Fleet Reserve Association, (U) 43, 552–553, 981

Lama Association of North America, (H) 1555

Lambda Alpha, (SS) 2917

National Space Club, (S) 1952

National Speakers Association, (H) 1560

National Steel Corporation. Great Lakes Steel Operations, (S) 1831, (SS) 2693

National Stone, Sand and Gravel Association, (H) 1461, 1653, (S) 1839, 2380, 2541, (SS) 2893

National Strength and Conditioning Association, (S) 2375–2377, 2435, (SS) 3041–3043, 3073

National Student Nurses' Association, (S) 1857, 2329–2331

National Symphony Orchestra, (H) 1707–1708

National Teen–Ager Scholarship Foundation, (U) 67

National Tourism Foundation, (SS) 2656, 2715, 2742, 2762, 2970, 2972, 3007, 3027–3028, 3044, 3053, 3113, 3129, 3167, 3180, 3192

National Urban League, (U) 153–154, 352, (H) 1613, (S) 2062, (SS) 2827

National 4th Infantry (IVY) Division Association, (U) 755

Nation's Capital Chef's Association, (H) 1564, (SS) 3010

Native American Journalists Association, (H) 1304

Native Sons of the Golden West, (H) 1563, (SS) 3008

NATSO Foundation, (U) 122

Navajo Nation, (U) 184, 757–758, (SS) 3009

Naval Enlisted Reserve Association, (U) 776–777, 1110

Naval Helicopter Association, (U) 759

Naval Reserve Association, (U) 760

Naval Weather Service Association, (S) 2332

Navy League of the United States, (U) 763, 817, (H) 1630

Navy Supply Corps Foundation, (U) 764

Navy–Marine Corps Relief Society, (U) 97–98, 1137

Nebraska. Department of Veterans' Affairs, (U) 770

Nebraska Educational Office Professionals Association, (SS) 3014

Nebraska Elks Association, (U) 768

Nebraska Funeral Directors Association, (SS) 3015, 3170

Nebraska Petroleum Marketer and Convenience Store Association, (U) 365

Nebraska Press Association Foundation, (H) 1565

"Negro Spiritual" Scholarship Foundation, (H) 1401

Neighbors of Woodcraft, (U) 772–773

Nell Goff Memorial Scholarship Fund, (H) 1566, (S) 2347

Nephrology Nursing Certification Commission, (S) 2366

Nevada Women's Fund, (U) 779

New England Board of Higher Education, (U) 780

New England Culinary Institute, (H) 1435

New England Employee Benefits Council, (SS) 3018

New England Newspaper Advertising Executives Association, (U) 364, 774

New England Water Works Association, (S) 2351, (SS) 3019

New Hampshire Association of Broadcasters, (H) 1567

New Hampshire Charitable Foundation, (U) 105, 156, 610, 781–782

New Hampshire Federation of Teachers, (U) 783

New Hampshire Postsecondary Education Commission, (U) 784, 787–788

New Hampshire Retired Educators Associations, (SS) 2881

New Hampshire Society of Certified Public Accountants, (SS) 3021

New Jersey Association of Conservation Districts, (H) 1531, (S) 2254, (SS) 2959

New Jersey Business Magazine, (SS) 3024

New Jersey. Division of Veterans Programs, (U) 790

New Jersey Funeral Directors Association, (SS) 3022

New Jersey Funeral Service Education Corporation, (SS) 3023

New Jersey Higher Education Student Assistance Authority, (U) 695, 792–794

New Jersey Press Foundation, (H) 1332, 1568

New Jersey Society of Certified Public Accountants, (SS) 3024–3026

New Jersey State Golf Association, (U) 791

New Jersey Utilities Association, (U) 485, (S) 2354, (SS) 3029

New Mexico Commission on Higher Education, (U) 795, 797–801, 803

New Mexico Educational Assistance Foundation, (U) 1010

New Mexico Land Title Association, (U) 189

New Mexico Library Association, (SS) 3030

New Mexico Veterans' Service Commission, (U) 796, 802

New York Association of Cooking Teachers, (H) 1435, 1582

New York Council for the Humanities, (U) 806

New York Farm Bureau, (S) 1732

New York Lottery, (U) 809

New York Press Association, (H) 1569

New York State Association of Agricultural Fairs, (S) 2359

New York State Education Department, (U) 805, 811

New York State Grange, (U) 1058, (S) 1930

New York State Higher Education Services Corporation, (U) 804, 808, 810, 812–813

New York State Legion Press Association, (H) 1253

New York State Showpeople's Association, (S) 2359

New York State Society of Professional Engineers, (U) 841

The Newseum, (H) 1571

Newspaper Association of America, (H) 1287

Newspaper Association of America Foundation, (H) 1441

Newspaper Guild–CWA, (H) 1342

Newsweek Magazine, (U) 527

Ninety–Nines, Inc. Eastern New England Chapter, (S) 1826

NO–ADdiction Campaign, (U) 820

Nordmanns–Forbundet. Pacific Northwest Chapter, (SS) 2920, 2955

North Carolina Association of Educators,, (U) 628, (SS) 2950

North Carolina Association of Health, Physical Education, Recreation and Dance, (U) 767, (H) 1476, 1545, (S) 2176, 2314, (SS) 2904, 2992

North Carolina Community College System, (U) 825, (SS) 3056

North Carolina Department of Public Instruction, (SS) 3074

North Carolina. Division of Veterans Affairs, (U) 830

North Carolina Farm Bureau, (S) 2445, (SS) 3080

North Carolina PTA, (U) 829

North Carolina Sheriffs' Association, (SS) 3034

North Carolina State Education Assistance Authority, (U) 386, 479, 824–828, 831–832, (SS) 3034

North Carolina Wildlife Federation Endowment and Education Fund, (S) 2370

North Dakota. Department of Veterans Affairs, (U) 833

North Dakota University System, (U) 834–837, (SS) 3035

North East Roofing Educational Foundation, Inc., (U) 778

Northeastern Young Lumber Execs, (U) 840

Northwest Women in Educational Administration, (SS) 3038

Nosotros, (H) 1577

3033

Starkey, (U) 1005

State Farm Companies Foundation, (SS) 3123

State of Alabama Chiropractic Scholarship Program, (S) 2536

State Student Assistance Commission of Indiana, (U) 460–461

State University System of Florida, (U) 1089

Stein Roe Mutual Funds, (SS) 3125

Steven Knezevich Trust, (U) 1047

Stokely–Van Camp, (U) 357

Stu's Music Shop, (H) 1562

Sullivan College National Center for Hospitality Studies, (H) 1435

SunTrust Education Loans, (U) 330

SuperCollege.com, (U) 1051

Supreme Council of I.D.E.S., (U) 443, (S) 1993

Supreme Council of S.E.S., (U) 1052

Surface Navy Association, (U) 1127

SURFLANT Scholarship Foundation, (U) 1054

Swiss Benevolent Society of New York, (U) 903, 1013

Symphony Orchestra League of Alexandria, (H) 1526

Syngenta Professional Products, (U) 567

Tag and Label Manufacturer Institute, Inc., (H) 1666, (SS) 3142

Tailhook Educational Foundation, (U) 1062

Talbots, (U) 1063

Tall Clubs International, (U) 520

Target Stores, (U) 1064

Tau Beta Pi, (S) 2552

Team Tennis Charities, (U) 271

Technical Association of the Pulp and Paper Industry, (H) 1329, (S) 1884, 1900, 1914, 1982, 1989, 2143, 2367, 2403, 2409, 2449, 2551, 2626, (SS) 2786, 3130, 3183

TeleSensory Corporation, (SS) 2653

Tennessee. Department of Veterans Affairs, (U) 1066

Tennessee Education Association, (SS) 2756–2757

Tennessee Funeral Directors Association, (SS) 3132

Tennessee Student Assistance Corporation, (U) 771, 1065, 1068, (SS) 2728

TET '68, Inc., (U) 1070

Texas Arts and Crafts Educational Foundation, Inc., (H) 1426

Texas Association of Developing Colleges, (U) 1086

Texas Broadcast Education Foundation, (H) 1660

Texas CattleWomen, Inc., (S) 2558, (SS) 3134

Texas Choral Directors Association, (H) 1661

Texas Engineering Foundation, (S) 2556, 2564

Texas Farm Bureau, (U) 262, 1076, 1088, (S) 2559, (SS) 3138

Texas Federation of Business and Professional Women's Foundation, Inc., (H) 1425, (SS) 2846

Texas FFA Association, (U) 1077, (S) 1733, 1895, 2003, 2024, 2147, 2487, 2512, 2565

Texas Fish and Game Magazine, (U) 1077

Texas Higher Education Coordinating Board, (U) 1071–1075, 1079–1082, 1084–1085, (S) 2561, 2563, (SS) 3135–3136

Texas Knights Templar Educational Foundation, (U) 1078

Texas Nursery and Landscape Association, (S) 2572

Texas Society of Professional Engineers, (S) 2556, 2564

Texas Tennis Foundation, (U) 111, 396, 1083

Texas Veterans Commission, (U) 1074, 1087

Texas Women in Law Enforcement, (U) 1099, (SS) 3148

Third Wave Foundation, (U) 1090

Thomasson Foundation Inc., (U) 194

TIME Magazine, (U) 110

Tire Association of North America, (U) 667, (SS) 2828

TISCOR, (S) 2570

Township Officials of Illinois, (U) 1094

Toyota USA Foundation, (U) 1095

Trans Mississippi Golf Association, (S) 2013

Transport Workers Union of America, (U) 666

Transportation Clubs International, (S) 1888, 2097, 2562, (SS) 2726, 2850, 3137

Travelers Protective Association of America, (U) 991

Trooper Jeffrey S. Parola Scholarship Foundation, (SS) 3147

Truckload Carriers Association, (U) 1097

Turf and Ornamental Communicators Association, (H) 1667, (S) 2574

Two/Ten International Footwear Foundation, (U) 1100

Ty Cobb Educational Foundation, (U) 1101

Tyson Foundation, Inc., (S) 2582, (SS) 3149

UCPA, Inc., (U) 464

Ukrainian Fraternal Association, (U) 303, 475

Union Privilege, (U) 1103

Unitarian Universalist Association, (H) 1650

United Agribusiness League, (S) 2583, 2588, (SS) 3150, 3152

United Automobile, Aerospace and Agricultural Implement Workers of America. Delaware State Community Action Program Council and Region 8, (SS) 2751

United Cerebral Palsy Association of Greater Chicago, (U) 464

United Daughters of the Confederacy, (U) 291, 374, 577, 1104, 1196, (H) 1272, 1422, (S) 2425, 2614, (SS) 2674, 3172

United Food and Commercial Workers International Union, (U) 1105

United Jewish Appeal–Federation of Jewish Philanthropies of New York, (U) 489

United Methodist Church, (U) 1107, (H) 1669, 1695

United Methodist Communications, (H) 1501

United Methodist Foundation for Christian Higher Education, (U) 1106, (H) 1668

United Methodist Youth Organization, (H) 1343, 1617

United Musical Instruments U.S.A., Inc., (H) 1562

United Nations Association of the United States, (SS) 3153

United Negro College Fund, (U) 356, (S) 2584

United States Achievement Academy, (U) 37

United States Army Warrant Officers Association, (U) 1108

United States Chess Federation, (U) 1119

United States Institute of Peace, (SS) 3003

United States Junior Chamber of Commerce, (U) 488, 1091

United States Naval Institute, (H) 1276

United States Naval Sea Cadet Corps, (U) 573, 761, 817, 839

United States Navy Radioman Association, (U) 171

United States Patent and Trademark Office, (S) 1903

United States Ski and Snowboard Association, (U) 1116

United States Submarine Veterans, Inc., (U) 1120

Wallace S. & Wilma K. Laughlin Foundation Trust, (SS) 3170

Walt Disney Company Foundation, (H) 1681, (SS) 3171

Walter W. Naumburg Foundation, Inc., (H) 1447

Walz Memorial Scholarship Trust, (H) 1684

Warburton Music Products, (H) 1562

Warner Lambert Company, (S) 2615

Warner Norcross & Judd LLP, (SS) 3108, 3173

Washington Apple Commission, (U) 1156, (S) 2616, (SS) 3175

Washington Apple Education Foundation, (U) 1156–1157, (S) 2616–2617, (SS) 3175

Washington Association of School Administrators, (SS) 3174

Washington Correctional Association, (U) 1159

Washington Crossing Foundation, (SS) 2791, 3176

Washington, D.C. Department of Human Services, (U) 246

Washington Floricultural Association, (S) 2610

Washington Higher Education Coordinating Board, (U) 1161–1163, 1165, 1167

Washington Library Media Association, (SS) 3186

Washington News Council, (H) 1347, (SS) 2755

Washington Society of Certified Public Accountants, (SS) 3177–3179

Washington Society of Certified Public Accountants. Northwest Chapter, (SS) 3037

Washington State Elks Association, (U) 1164

Washington State Environmental Health Association, (S) 1894

Washington State PTA, (U) 1166

Washington State School for the Blind, (SS) 2961

Washington State Trial Lawyers Association, (U) 1219, (SS) 3190

Washington State Workforce Training and Education Coordinating Board, (U) 1158

Washoe Tribe, (U) 1168–1170

Wasie Foundation, (U) 1171

Waterbury Foundation, (H) 1657

Wax Company, LLC, (S) 2057

WBOC TV 16, (U) 1173

Web Offset Association, (H) 1686

The Weekly, (U) 115

Weekly Reader Corporation, (H) 1503

Welsh National Gymanfa Ganu Association, Inc., (H) 1687

West Indian Foundation, Inc., (U) 612

West Virginia Broadcasters Association, (H) 1689

West Virginia Division of Veterans' Affairs, (U) 1177

West Virginia Funeral Directors Association, (SS) 3181

West Virginia Golf Association, (U) 1185

West Virginia Golf Course Superintendents Association, Inc., (S) 2619

West Virginia Healthcare Financial Management Association, (SS) 3182

West Virginia Higher Education Policy Commission, (U) 1174–1176

Western Art Association, (H) 1402

Western Culinary Institute, (H) 1435

Western Fraternal Life Association, (U) 1181

Western Golf Association, (U) 179

Western States Roofing Contractors Association, (U) 555

Western Sunbathing Association, (U) 1180

WETA–FM90.9, (H) 1707–1708

Whitestone, (S) 2311

Wilkes University, (H) 1503

Willa Cather Pioneer Memorial and Educational Foundation, (H) 1576

William E. Docter Educational Fund, (U) 1186

William L. Hawkinson Foundation for Peace & Justice, (U) 1189

William Morris Agency, (H) 1561

William Randolph Hearst Foundation, (U) 1111, (H) 1416–1418, (SS) 3154

Willis and Mildred Pellerin Foundation, (U) 1193

Wilton School of Cake Decorating and Confectionary Arts, (H) 1435

Wine and Food Society of San Fernando Valley, (H) 1435

Wisconsin Council of Religious and Independent Schools, (U) 413–414

Wisconsin Dental Foundation, (S) 2632

Wisconsin Department of Public Instruction, (U) 413–414

Wisconsin Department of Veterans Affairs, (U) 1206–1207, 1209

Wisconsin Foundation for Independent Colleges, Inc., (U) 42, 201, 948, 1112, (H) 1493, 1639, (S) 2193, 2513, (SS) 2704, 2919, 3109

Wisconsin Funeral Directors Foundation, Ltd., (SS) 3184

Wisconsin Higher Educational Aids Board, (U) 1198, 1200–1202, 1205, 1208, 1210

Wisconsin Hispanic Scholarship Foundation, Inc., (U) 664

Wisconsin Newspaper Association, (U) 413–414

Wisconsin Restaurant Association, (SS) 3185

Wisconsin Society of Professional Engineers, (S) 1883, 1986–1987, 2639

Women Grocers of America, (SS) 2948

Women in Aviation, International, (S) 1727, 1742, 1744–1745, 1825, 1856, 1928, 2408, 2440, (SS) 2706, 3076

Women in Defense, (S) 2100, (SS) 2852

Women in Film/Dallas, (H) 1694

Women Marines Association, (U) 1211

Women's Army Corps Veterans' Association, (U) 1212

Women's Basketball Coaches Association, (U) 1213

Women's Jewelry Association, (H) 1696

Women's Overseas Service League, (U) 1214

Women's Seamen's Friend Society of Connecticut, Inc., (U) 1215, (S) 2638

Women's Sports Foundation, (U) 576, 663

Women's Transportation Seminar, (S) 2514, (SS) 3110

Women's Western Golf Foundation, (U) 1216

Woodmansee Scholarship Fund, (U) 1217

Worcester County Horticultural Society, (S) 2575

W.O.R.K.: Women's Organization Reaching Koreans, (U) 394

World Population Film/Video Festival, (H) 1697

World Studio Foundation, (H) 1698

World Wide Baraca Philathea Union, (H) 1699

Wound, Ostomy and Continence Nurses Society, (S) 2634–2635

Wyeth–Ayerst Laboratories, (S) 1795

Wyoming Nurses Association, (S) 2225

Xerox Corporation, (S) 2640

Yakama Indian Nation, (U) 1221–1223

Yale New Haven Hospital, (S) 2641

Yanmar Diesel America Corporation, (S) 2642

YMCA of Greater Seattle, (SS) 2767

Calendar Index

Since most financial aid programs have specific deadline dates, some may have already closed by the time you begin to look for funding. You can use the Calendar Index to identify which programs are still open. To do that, look at the subject categories that interest you, think about when you'll be able to complete your application forms, go to the appropriate months, jot down the entry numbers listed there, and use those numbers to find the program descriptions in the directory. Keep in mind that the numbers cited here refer to program entry numbers, not to page numbers in the book. Note: not all sponsoring organizations supplied deadline information to us, so not all programs are listed in this index.

Unrestricted by Subject Area

January: 20, 79–80, 85, 103–104, 108, 115, 118, 153–154, 164, 197, 237, 248, 264, 267–268, 282, 298, 307–310, 330, 342, 352, 356, 372, 380, 387, 395, 406, 413–414, 464, 471, 495, 497, 500, 502, 513, 570, 575, 581, 599, 617, 628, 705, 725, 749, 766, 768, 829, 877, 892, 898, 900, 909, 930, 942, 963–966, 976, 998, 1014, 1033, 1037–1040, 1045, 1099, 1103, 1127, 1134, 1140, 1164, 1170, 1176, 1182, 1222–1223, 1229, 1234

February: 24, 33, 41, 44–46, 49, 53–55, 61, 63, 72, 86, 92, 106, 112, 114, 116, 119, 123, 135–137, 150, 155, 162, 170, 174, 187, 195, 198, 215, 220, 227, 239, 241, 272, 275–276, 280, 285, 291–292, 304, 312, 320–321, 324, 328, 333–334, 337, 340, 343–346, 348, 354, 360, 362, 374, 377, 379, 385, 392, 401, 404, 407, 409, 428–429, 432, 435, 446, 460, 472, 478–480, 482, 488, 490, 493, 498, 509, 511, 514, 517, 522, 529, 542, 545, 549, 551, 556, 560, 562, 564, 574, 577–578, 592, 594, 608, 614, 618, 624, 630, 632, 634–638, 660–661, 667, 669, 691, 715, 729–730, 734, 744, 771, 775, 778–779, 790–793, 845–846, 849, 866, 869, 871, 874, 876, 878–880, 885–886, 888–889, 894–895, 912–913, 916, 919–920, 928, 942, 947–948, 962, 974–975, 983, 987, 990, 992–993, 1006, 1011, 1018, 1049–1050, 1053, 1069, 1091, 1093–1094, 1096, 1104, 1114, 1119, 1124, 1128, 1130–1131, 1137–1138, 1141, 1153–1155, 1158, 1166, 1175, 1179, 1181, 1185, 1193, 1196, 1214, 1216, 1218, 1228

March: 2–4, 17, 21, 23, 32, 36, 47–48, 58–59, 64–65, 73, 75, 84, 93–96, 102, 105, 113, 123–125, 132, 134, 145–149, 151, 166, 169, 178, 186, 193, 196, 199, 208, 212, 216, 218, 232–234, 240, 242, 251–252, 256–263, 266, 269, 273, 278, 284, 287–288, 290, 299–300, 302, 311, 313, 326–327, 332, 335–336, 338, 341, 353, 361, 381–384, 388–389, 397–400, 402, 405, 412, 416–417, 430, 433–434, 444, 450, 457, 465–466, 470, 474, 476–477, 484, 492, 503–504, 506–507, 512, 518, 523, 525, 527–528, 531–534, 537, 547–548, 550, 558, 569, 579, 589–591, 597, 602, 615–616, 623, 629, 633, 639–640, 646, 656, 659, 665, 668–669, 681–682, 698, 702, 708–709, 727, 732, 737, 742, 746, 757, 763, 765, 772, 789, 807, 809, 814–816, 821, 832, 847, 872–873, 887, 896, 903, 907–908, 918, 922, 925, 927, 939, 944–946, 949, 957, 960, 972–973, 977, 982, 984, 989, 997, 999, 1003–1004, 1007, 1010, 1013, 1015, 1029, 1032, 1034–1035, 1044, 1046, 1052, 1061–1063, 1070, 1088, 1090, 1109, 1136, 1139, 1156–1157, 1160, 1171–1172, 1180, 1194, 1203–1204, 1211, 1215, 1217, 1219, 1224–1226, 1230, 1232–1233, 1239–1240

April: 1, 9–11, 19, 22, 34, 43, 48, 57, 68, 71, 81–82, 87, 99, 110–111, 117, 122, 129, 131, 133, 144, 146, 152, 159, 168, 176, 180, 184–185, 188, 191, 211, 231, 236, 243, 245, 255, 279, 286, 293, 306, 317, 325, 349, 351, 386, 390, 396, 403, 410–411, 415, 419, 443, 445, 449, 467, 481, 483, 485, 496, 499, 501, 508, 526, 541, 552–553, 557, 565–567, 571, 583–586, 595–596, 598, 600–601, 607, 625, 650, 653, 657–658, 663, 666, 680, 683, 728, 731, 748, 750, 757–758, 764, 776–777, 782–786, 791, 808, 810–813, 820, 822, 830, 842–843, 850, 853, 864, 881, 883–884, 890, 899, 905–906, 910–911, 926, 934, 936, 940–941, 951, 961, 968, 981, 994–996, 1005, 1008, 1036, 1054, 1058–1059, 1068, 1083, 1102, 1108, 1110, 1113, 1115, 1117–1118, 1120, 1186, 1189, 1192, 1194, 1212, 1222–1223, 1241

May: 6, 51, 69–70, 78, 101, 109, 120–121, 130, 167, 172, 175, 178, 180–183, 217, 228–229, 235, 244, 271, 303, 339, 358–359, 364, 369, 373, 375, 391, 394, 431, 456, 463, 475, 486, 489, 494, 515, 520, 530, 543, 554, 559, 561, 563, 573, 580, 588, 609, 611, 613, 626–627, 654, 664, 679, 684, 726, 733, 739, 743, 745, 751, 754, 761, 774, 781, 793, 805–806, 817, 838–840, 863, 897, 914–915, 940–941, 943, 958, 967, 978–979, 1008, 1051, 1078, 1089, 1097, 1106, 1112, 1121, 1163, 1178, 1183, 1197, 1215, 1227, 1236, 1238

June: 74, 81–82, 97–98, 117, 156, 161, 190, 201, 208, 230, 246–247, 250, 277, 283, 297, 314, 316, 355, 384, 451, 469, 528, 540, 583–586, 612, 622, 677, 688, 690, 695, 738, 747, 855, 858, 861, 868, 884, 932, 953, 1009, 1012, 1022, 1030, 1086, 1101, 1190–1191, 1220, 1222–1223, 1237

July: 38, 81–82, 289, 367, 370, 408, 425–427, 631, 655, 685, 703, 769, 805, 835, 882–883, 902, 905–906, 910, 956, 980, 1016, 1065, 1148, 1177

August: 135–136, 171, 207, 270, 274, 301, 347, 393, 418, 521, 674, 767, 781, 823, 1048, 1161, 1169

September: 52, 165, 217, 319, 384, 546, 572, 697, 701, 757, 790, 792–793, 848, 860, 865, 939–941, 1078, 1090, 1111, 1170

October: 117, 143, 160, 178–179, 202, 204, 208, 305, 458, 735, 752, 933, 938, 942, 959, 988, 1064, 1165, 1222–1223, 1242

November: 8, 14, 40, 81–82, 91, 126, 180, 182, 294–295, 329, 420, 426–427, 491, 576, 756, 759, 841, 1008, 1047, 1095, 1102, 1148, 1177

December: 35, 38–39, 90, 177, 236, 301, 350, 384, 408, 436–437, 442, 473, 516, 528, 619, 631, 710, 741, 781, 805, 882–884, 891, 935, 937, 955, 969–971, 1100, 1105, 1126, 1129, 1169, 1173, 1231

Any time: 37, 76–77, 88, 142, 253–254, 454, 610, 699, 704, 723, 736, 762, 931, 991, 1002, 1031, 1057, 1092, 1135, 1151, 1168, 1184, 1195, 1202, 1206–1207, 1209, 1221

Humanities

January: 1247, 1249, 1252, 1258, 1275, 1280, 1290, 1296, 1324, 1326, 1329, 1337, 1340, 1346, 1348, 1370, 1381, 1393, 1412, 1417–1418, 1426, 1430, 1448, 1462, 1467, 1473, 1514, 1518, 1551–1552, 1554, 1562, 1569, 1613, 1616, 1619, 1634, 1638, 1642, 1651, 1688, 1695, 1700, 1707–1708

February: 1243, 1255, 1265, 1273, 1277–1278, 1283–1285, 1293, 1295, 1298, 1301, 1305, 1325, 1334, 1338, 1344–1345, 1352–1353, 1361–1363, 1368–1369, 1373, 1377, 1379, 1387, 1389, 1400, 1403–1405, 1409, 1416, 1418, 1422, 1424, 1431, 1441, 1445, 1447, 1452, 1459, 1468–1469, 1471, 1475, 1479–1480, 1485, 1489, 1495–1496, 1509–1511, 1519–1521, 1526, 1533, 1544, 1548–1550, 1564–1566, 1578–1579, 1595, 1601, 1609, 1614, 1630, 1632–1633, 1636–1637, 1643, 1647, 1649–1650, 1655, 1662, 1667, 1671, 1675, 1677, 1680, 1687, 1689, 1691

March: 1250, 1259, 1264, 1292, 1300, 1314, 1327, 1351, 1354, 1358, 1360, 1364, 1372, 1374, 1390, 1396–1399, 1402, 1410, 1413, 1418, 1423, 1432, 1436, 1439, 1443, 1457–1458, 1477, 1490, 1498, 1501, 1523, 1527, 1529, 1535, 1541, 1544, 1563, 1573, 1575, 1577, 1580, 1583–1584, 1586–1588, 1591, 1601, 1604, 1606, 1611, 1618, 1624, 1628, 1652, 1658, 1666, 1690, 1693, 1699, 1701–1702

April: 1246, 1252, 1257, 1276, 1281, 1287, 1291, 1297, 1299, 1302, 1306, 1310–1312, 1319,

Indexes

638